WESTERN LITERATURE IN A WORLD CONTEXT

Volume One

The Ancient World through the Renaissance

WESTERN LITERATURE IN A WORLD CONTEXT

Volume One

The Ancient World through the Renaissance

Paul Davis
Gary Harrison
David M. Johnson
Patricia Clark Smith
John F. Crawford
THE UNIVERSITY OF NEW MEXICO

BEDFORD/ST. MARTIN'S
BOSTON ♦ NEW YORK

Editor: Nancy Lyman
Development editor: Sylvia L. Weber
Manager, publishing services: Emily Berleth
Publishing services associate: Kalea Chapman
Project management: Publication Services
(*Copy editor*, Carol Anne Peschke;
Production supervisor, Heather Raak TenHuisen;
Production coordinators, Rick Dudley and Jeff Topham)
Production manager: Patricia Ollague
Text design: Anna George
Cover design: Carolyn Joseph

Library of Congress Catalog Card Number: 92-62768

Copyright ©1995 by St. Martin's Press, Inc.

All rights reserved. No part of this book may be reproduced, stored in a retrieval system, or transmitted by any form or by any means, electronic, mechanical, photocopying, recording, or otherwise, except as may be expressly permitted by the applicable copyright statutes or in writing by the Publisher.

Manufactured in the United States of America.

hg

For information, write:
Bedford/St. Martin's
75 Arlington St.
Boston, MA 02116
(617-426-7440)

ISBN: 0-312-08124-3

ACKNOWLEDGMENTS

Homer, "The Iliad" from THE ILIAD, translated by Robert Fitzgerald. Copyright © 1974 by Robert Fitzgerald. Reprinted with the permission of Doubleday, a division of Bantam Doubleday Dell Publishing Group, Inc.

Acknowledgments and copyrights are continued at the back of the book on pages 2225–2229, which constitute an extension of the copyright page.

It is a violation of the law to reproduce these selections by any means whatsoever without the written permission of the copyright holder.

PREFACE

Placing Western Literature in a World Context

As our title suggests, this anthology places the great works of Western literature into the broader context of world literature. We group key works of Western and world literature around a set of core stories in order to allow teachers and students to compare how different cultures treat similar themes and issues. In our experience, this thematic approach to the literature of Western and non-Western traditions helps students to synthesize an otherwise unwieldy array of diverse texts and traditions in the two-semester or three-quarter sequence of most Western literature, world literature, or humanities courses.

For the past five years, we have been developing and team-teaching a new humanities course at the University of New Mexico, and it is from this experience that *Western Literature in a World Context* has come. We set out to develop a world literature course reflecting recent reevaluations of the Western tradition and its literary canon. We wanted a reading list that included works from all parts of the world—from Asia, the Middle East, Africa, Latin America, and native America, as well as the areas usually represented in world literature courses. We also wanted to study these works as more than aesthetic masterpieces; we hoped to investigate the ways in which literary works contributed to our tradition, our values, and our place in history. As we articulated these goals into a course syllabus, the great works of the Western tradition continued to hold their central place in our canon, but they entered into a dialogue with works from outside the West and with each other.

This ongoing dialogue made clear that great writings do not speak with a single voice and that the Western tradition is pluralistic and has been enriched throughout its history by its encounters with the literature and cultures of the world. By representing the diversity of our contemporary cultural situation, *Western Literature in a World Context* invites students and teachers to take part in the conversation about the formation of value and meaning in a global community. We think that our thematic and historical approach helps students appreciate the multitude of forms, styles, and themes in world literature, and enables them to draw from their readings the important features of European and non-European literary history.

Organization

Our anthology is divided into the six periods usually studied in Western and world literature courses. The subtitle of each part indicates an important motif that is examined in the Western literature of the period:

- The Ancient World: The Heroic Ideal and the Rise of Patriarchy
- The Middle Ages: The Pilgrimage of Life
- The Renaissance: Power and Discovery
- The Enlightenment: Reason and Sensibility
- The Nineteenth Century: The Romantic Self and Social Reality
- The Twentieth Century: The Modern Age and the Emerging World Culture

The works from each period are grouped into four chronologically arranged sections:

- **Representative Texts** begin each part with a sampling of Western works that explore an issue of prevailing interest during the period.
- **Western Texts**, the largest section within the chronological structure, includes works from the Euro-American tradition. Many of these selections are familiar classics, but we also include a number of newcomers to the canon, many by women and minority writers.
- **The World Context** section that follows includes texts from outside the Western tradition—from Asia, the Middle East, Latin America, Africa, and native America. These are grouped chronologically by nationality.
- **Background Texts**, the final section, features philosophical and social commentaries and other historical documents that exemplify the intellectual milieu of the period.

In two periods, this organization varies. The representative and Western texts for The Ancient World include two forebears of European literature, Graeco-Roman and Judeo-Christian, or biblical, writings. For The Twentieth Century, when many writers see themselves as addressing a global rather than a regional or national audience, we have removed the distinction between Western literature and the world context in order to suggest the emergence of a literature that transcends such a division. Instead, we present chronological sections, Modernist Texts from the earlier half of the century and Contemporary Texts of the post–World War II era.

Representative Texts

The representative texts for each part introduce important stories or themes that characterize the period and that have ongoing significance in our cultural history. Our introductions to each period and our headnotes to the representative texts emphasize what we believe to be the predominant stories or themes, but they also suggest other ways to approach these multifaceted works.

In Volume One, the classical part emphasizes the rise of the heroic ideal and the early formation of patriarchy with Homer's *Iliad* and *Odyssey* and with Genesis. Beginning with St. Augustine's *Confessions* and Dante's *The Divine Comedy,* the medieval part emphasizes the spiritual and literary motif of the pilgrimage of life. Petrarch's "Ascent of Mount Ventoux" and selections from the *Canzoniere* and Marlowe's *Doctor Faustus* present different perspectives on the Renaissance celebration of human power and the mastery of nature. In Volume Two, Voltaire's *Candide* and Rousseau's *Confessions* set up an Enlightenment dialogue about reason and sensibility. For the nineteenth century, Goethe's *Faust* and Brontë's *Wuthering Heights* introduce the entangled impulses of romanticism and realism. Finally, in the twentieth century, with Conrad's *Heart of Darkness* and Achebe's *Things Fall Apart,* we take up the importance of storytelling as a way to construct meaning, discover purpose, and define identity. As is obvious from the canonical nature of the texts we have chosen, instructors and students have much leeway here and may choose to treat these representative texts chronologically or use them to evince themes other than those we emphasize.

Western Texts

The other works of Western literature for each period, ordered chronologically by the author's birthdate (or presumed date of composition), further develop, challenge, and elaborate on the themes and stories in the representative texts. Many of these works are established classics, such as Sophocles' *Antigone,* Chaucer's *The Canterbury Tales,* Machiavelli's *The Prince,* Molière's *Tartuffe,* Ibsen's *A Doll's House,* and Kafka's *The Metamorphosis.* We also include many works that expand the traditional Western canon and show the rich diversity of literary and cultural traditions within the West, such as Christine de Pizan's *Book of the City of Ladies,* Marguerite de Navarre's *Heptameron,* Mary Rowlandson's *Narrative of the Captivity and Restoration of Mrs. Mary Rowlandson,* Harriet Jacobs's *Incidents in the Life of a Slave Girl,* and the poems of Anna Akhmatova. We have chosen these works for their literary merit and their commentary on ideas and historical developments within Western culture. In Volume Two, we include some major texts by African-American, Hispanic, and native American writers that offer opportunities to rethink the traditional boundaries of Western culture.

The World Context

The selections in The World Context sections are historically contemporary with the Western texts and often represent masterworks of the literary traditions from which they come. Whenever possible, we have included non-Western texts that raise issues and themes relevant to those raised by the Western texts. Setting up a dialogue between the Western and non-Western worlds, these works sometimes complement and sometimes challenge the assumptions of the Western texts, thereby allowing us to reconsider the meaning and values of our tradition. We match the classical texts of Greece and Rome, for example, with texts from the ancient wisdom traditions of China and India. Lao Tzu's poems in the *Tao Te Ching* and the parables of Chuang Tzu and the Buddha represent ways of being in the world that are very different from the heroic model found in Homer and the Greek tragedians; similarly, Tagore's Srivilas and Goethe's Faust gain wisdom through suffering, but the nature of their suffering is very different.

Background Texts

The philosophical, historical, and cultural documents in the background texts make it easier to place the literary works into their broader historical and cultural environments. In the background texts for the Middle Ages, for example, we include a selection from Capellanus's *Art of Courtly Love* to provide a context for the love poetry included among Western texts. In the nineteenth century, we include Madame de Staël on Napoleon, Marx and Engels on the class struggle, Darwin on the struggle for existence, and Nietzsche on the superman, all of which reflect on the transformation of ideas about the self and its place in society.

PEDAGOGY

Our **introductions to each period** and our **headnotes to the selections** set the works in their literary, historical, and cultural contexts. The part introductions begin with **time lines** that show concurrent events in history and politics; science, culture, and technology; and literature. The narrative elaborates on these events and discusses the major theme that appears in works throughout the period. We have included **maps** and time lines to assist the reader in placing the selections in their geographical and chronological context. The headnotes describe the lives and works of the authors; we also include lists of additional readings about the period and individual authors to provide guides for further study.

We have prepared an **instructor's manual** entitled *Teaching Western Literature in a World Context.* This manual provides information to supplement the headnotes in the text and includes questions for discussion and writing for each author in the Western Texts and World Context sections. Many of these questions involve comparisons of readings, often readings from different periods. We have also developed projects designed to elicit the reader's creative response to the selections.

Although we have emphasized certain stories and themes in our anthology, instructors and students using this book will inevitably take other approaches to the literature, discuss other themes, see other connections between the Western and non-Western texts, and perhaps even find other unifying stories within each period. Moreover, the users of this anthology may identify other works in world literature that they can use to supplement or replace some of our selections. We welcome your comments and suggestions.

A Note on Translations

We have set clarity and accessibility as the two key principles guiding our selection of translations. In many cases, our aim to use texts that are both precise and teachable led us to what have become standards in the canon of translations, such as Robert Fitzgerald's *Iliad,* Theodore Morrison's *Canterbury Tales,* Edward Seidensticker's *Tale of Genji,* and Earl Miner's *Narrow Road through the Provinces.* We have also used such outstanding recent works as Allen Mandelbaum's *Odyssey,* Stephen Mitchell's poems of Rilke, and Miguel León-Portilla's translations of Nahuatl poetry. In some cases, our translators are themselves distinguished poets whose treatment of their originals captures their poetic quality; among these we include John Ciardi's *Divine Comedy,* Thomas Kinsella's *Exile of the Sons of Uisliu,* Richard Wilbur's *Tartuffe,* and Judith Hemschemeyer's poems of Anna Akhmatova. On occasion, as in the King James version of the Bible, we have chosen older translations of high literary quality that have influenced later writers so that students can hear or identify literary allusions in later works.

ACKNOWLEDGMENTS

This project began in a team-taught, multicultural "great books" course at the University of New Mexico in the mid-1980s. That course, developed initially with a grant from the National Endowment for the Humanities, sought to broaden the traditional canon of Western literature and incorporate works from outside the Western tradition. The grant gave us time to develop the course and supported the luxury of team-teaching, which enabled us to discuss daily the course syllabus and our teaching strategies. Joseph B. Zavadil was a member of that committee, a member of the teaching team in its first years, and one of the editors who began to design this anthology. He died in May 1992, before we had gotten very far into the making of the book. We hope that Joe's spirit—his courage, wit, scholarship, and humanity, and his zest for living and for teaching, especially undergraduate teaching—lives on in this book.

An anthology of world literature from ancient times to the present is necessarily selective. Our selection attempts to provide our readers with a collection of writings that both epitomize the time and place of their origin and stand out as works of literary value. To help us meet these goals, we consulted colleagues who teach Western and world literature courses and specialists in the periods and places represented. We would like to express our appreciation to the following reviewers for their advice:

Ruth Albrecht, Lane Community College; Barbara Apstein, Bridgewater State College; Lillian Baggett, Union University; Michael Bright, Eastern Kentucky University; Gary Brodsky, Northeastern Illinois University; Jewel Spears Brooker, Eckerd College; Joe R. Christopher, Tarleton State University; William Combs, Western Michigan University; William Crisman, Pennsylvania State University at Altoona; Frances Ferguson, Johns Hopkins University; David Ferris, Yale University; Raymond-Jean Frontain, University of Central Arkansas; Sarah Webster Goodwin, Skidmore College; Robert H. Grimes, California University of Pennsylvania; John Hagge, Iowa State University; Spencer Hall, Rhode Island College; Jim Hauser, William Paterson College; Ann Rosalind Jones, Smith College; James P. Kain, Neumann College; Marianne E. Kalinke, University of Illinois at Urbana–Champaign; Diane M. Kammeyer, Anoka–Ramsey Community College; Carol Owens Lewis, Trident Technical College; Herbert Lindenberger, Stanford University; Jack Miller, Normandale Community College; Kostas Myrsiades, West Chester University of Pennsylvania; William F. Naufftus, Winthrop University; Elizabeth Otten, Northeast Missouri State University; Ernest R. Pinson, Union University; William Bowman Piper, Rice University; Victoria Price, Lamar University; Julie Rodakowski, Rochester Community College; Shirley Samuels, Cornell University; Carole Slade, Columbia University; David Spurr, University of Illinois at Chicago; Johnny E. Tolliver, Delaware State University; Faye P. Whitaker, Iowa State University; and Katherine H. Wilson, University of Georgia.

No book of this size happens without critical and supportive friends and advisors. We want foremost to thank our families for their patience and support over the past four years or more, during which this book occupied so much of our and their time: Mary, Kate, Ben, and Josh Davis; Marlys, Miranda, and Jeremy Harrison; Mona, Peter, Sarah, and Maia Johnson; Caleb and Josh Smith; and Patricia Zavadil. Thanks also to the support we have had from the Department of English at the University of New Mexico and to our colleagues at UNM and its branches, especially

Patricia and Rudolfo Anaya, Gail Baker, Lee Bartlett, Helen Damico, Michael Fischer, Cheryl Fresch, Gene Frumkin, Barry Gaines, Janet Gaines, Patrick Gallacher, Erlinda Gonzales-Berry, Minrose Gwin, Elizabeth Hadas, Harmony Hammond, Joy Harjo, Michael Hogan, Ted Jojola, David Jones, Enrique Lamadrid, Tony and Teresa Marquez, Wanda Martin, David McPherson, Vera Norwood, Louis Owens, Mary Power, V. B. Price, Diana Rebolledo, Patricia Risso, Diana Robin, Ruth Salvaggio, Paul Schmidt, Warren Smith, Hector Torres, Howard Tuttle, Marta Weigle, Mary Bess Whidden, Peter White, Barbara and Hugh Witemeyer, and Carolyn Woodward.

Among our UNM graduate students, Anna Carew-Miller, Janice Gould, Jefferson Voorhees, John Martinez Weston, Nora Yazzie-Hunter, and especially Anne Grigsby, who served one year as our graduate research assistant, have helped us with their suggestions and interest. Colleagues and supporters at UNM–Valencia Campus include Rigo Chavez, Michelle LeBeau, Richard Melzer, Kaye Reeves, Nancee Ryan, and Debra Venable. Thanks especially to Pat Lockhart, Margaret Shinn, and the support staff in the English Department at UNM for their administrative and technical assistance.

People at other institutions have generously shared with us their ideas: Janet Adelman, University of California at Berkeley; Paula Gunn Allen, UCLA; John Bale, Carol and Mark Gilbertson-Muggli, and Harland Nelson, all at Luther College; Reed Dasenbrock and Kevin McIlvoy, New Mexico State University; Frances Gillmor, the University of Arizona; Robert Hanning, Columbia University; Linda Hogan, the University of Colorado; Judith Kroll, the University of Texas; E. A. Mares, the University of North Texas; Bob Martin, Haskell Indian Junior College; William McGlothing, West Texas State College; Janice Monk, Southwest Institute for Research on Women at the University of Arizona; Thomas Richards, Harvard University; and Luci Tapahonso, University of Kansas. William Woods of Wichita State University and the late Dennis Jones of Luther College both were perceptive NEH evaluators of the course from which the anthology grew.

For particular advice and encouragement, thanks to Nancy Abbey, Barbara Beyers, John Bierhorst, Richard Bodner, Rita Clark, Meinrad Craighead, Thomas Cummings, Bernadette Devine, Norah Flatley, Nancy Gage, Rose Hansen, Martha Heard, Jay Koch, Lucy Lippard, Robert Lloyd, Carolyn Meyer, Patricia Nelson, Janice Northerns, Jonathan Price, John Randall, Margaret Randall, Susan Rennie, Clayton Rich, June and Michael Romero, Mimi Wheatwind, Jill T. Williams, James Wimsatt, Margaret Wimsatt, Lenore Wolfe, and Diane Wolkstein.

A profound thanks also to our undergraduate students in the Western literature course we have been teaching since 1985 in all its incarnations at UNM and UNM–Valencia. Their questions and insights have helped round out the perspectives on literature and the world context presented in this book.

For her keen interest in our project, her helpful suggestions about the tables of contents and selection of maps, and her overall guidance over the course of preparing this first edition, we want to thank especially our development editor at St. Martin's Press, Sylvia Weber. Nancy Lyman, our acquisitions editor, has been gracious with her advice, encouragement, and support. We are particularly indebted to Emily Berleth, manager of publishing services at St. Martin's, who, with publishing services associate Kalea Chapman, painstakingly saw the book through press with careful attention and patience. Others at St. Martin's who have contributed to our book include Steven Kutz, who edited the instructor's manual, and Cheryl Friedman, Mark Gallaher, Joyce Hinnefeld, and Cathy Pusateri, who first supported our project. We thank Anna George for the attractive design that effectively reinforces the organization of the text. We appreciate the editorial and technical assistance of Rick Dudley and Jeff Topham, the production coordinators at Publication Services; Heather Raak TenHuisen, production supervisor; Carol Anne Peschke, copy editor; Dan Niles and Buddy Ritchie, technical typesetters; and Richard Bunk, artist, who handled the many problems that inevitably arise in preparing a first edition of this proportion. A special thanks to Frederick T. Courtright, who coordinated the permissions contracts for us, and without whose assistance we would not have been able to include some of the outstanding editions we have here. Finally, we also appreciate the assistance of the many people—editorial assistants and copy editors—who worked behind the scenes at St. Martin's and at Publication Services for their hand in bringing this work to light.

CONTENTS

THE ANCIENT WORLD
The Heroic Ideal and the Rise of Patriarchy
1

THE RENAISSANCE
Power and Discovery
1521

WESTERN LITERATURE IN A WORLD CONTEXT

Volume One

The Ancient World through the Renaissance

THE ANCIENT WORLD

The Heroic Ideal and the Rise of Patriarchy

TIME LINE FOR THE ANCIENT WORLD

Date	*History and Politics*
B.C.E.	
7000–2000	7000–1500 Neolithic, agricultural communities; mother goddesses; weaving; metallurgy.
	3500–3000 Beginning of cities along rivers in Mesopotamia and Egypt; the development of irrigation, mathematics, calendars, bureaucracies, patriarchal institutions.
	c. 3000 The beginning of the Minoan civilization on Crete.
	2700–2200 Egypt: Old Kingdom.
	c. 2300 Akkadian Dynasty: Sargon I.
2000–1200	2000–1778 Egypt: Middle Kingdom.
	c. 2000 Greek-speaking Achaeans enter Greece.
	2000–1400 Age of Hebrew Patriarchs: Abraham, Isaac, Jacob, Joseph; sojourn in Egypt.
	1800 First Dynasty of Babylon.
	c. 1766–1122 Shang dynasty in China.
	1700 Minoan sea-empire at its height.
	c. 1500–1100 The Mycenaean Age on Greek mainland.
	1546–1200 Egypt: New Kingdom.
	1400 Downfall of Minoans on Crete.
	13th century Hebrew exodus from Egypt: Moses and the Ten Commandments.
	1250 Hebrew conquest of Canaan.
1200–900	c. 1200 Trojan War; fall of Troy.
	1200–1000 Iron Age invasions; further conquest of India by Aryans, who spread the Vedic religion.
	1200–1030 Israel: period of Judges.
	1100 Dorian invasion of Greece; destruction of Mycenaean fortresses; migration of Greeks to Asia Minor; Dark Age.
	1027–256 Chou dynasty in China.
	1000–922 Reigns of David and Solomon in Israel.
	922 Israel divided into two kingdoms.
900–600	826 Founding of Carthage.

Science, Culture, and Technology

c. 3000 Cuneiform writing and hieroglyphic writing.

2800 Egyptians begin to build the Great Pyramids; the ziggurat at Ur.

1700 Code of Hammurabi.

1600–1300 The development of alphabetic writing.

1546–1200 Worship of Osiris in Egypt.

1370–1353 Egypt: Amenhotep IV (Akhnaton) promotes monotheism.

Literature

c. 2000 *Descent of Inanna.*

1900–1600 *The Epic of Gilgamesh.* (Standard Version, 7th century B.C.E)

950–850 First Hebrew writing: J(Yahwist) Genesis 2:4bff.

850–800 Hebrew writing: E(Elohist).

(*Continued on next page*)

TIME LINE FOR THE ANCIENT WORLD (Continued)

Date	*History and Politics*
B.C.E.	
	753 Romulus founds Rome.
	721 Northern Kingdom of Israel is conquered by Assyria (Shalmaneser V) and disappears.
600–500	605–562 Babylonia: Nebuchadnezzar's reign.
	594 Solon's reforms in Athens.
	586 Jerusalem destroyed by Nebuchadnezzar; Babylonian captivity of Jews.
	560–527 Peisistratus, tyrant in Athens.
	546 Fall of Ionia (Western Turkey) to Persia.
	539 Fall of Babylon to Cyrus (Persia).
	538 Jewish remnant returns to Jerusalem.
	520–515 Palestine: second temple is built.
	509 Brutus establishes Roman Republic.
	507 Cleisthenes' democratic reforms in Athens.
500–400	
	490 Athenians defeat Persians at the Battle of Marathon.
	461–429 Athens: Age of Pericles.
	431–404 Peloponnesian War.
400–300	359–336 Philip, king of Macedonia.

Science, Culture, and Technology	*Literature*
776 First Olympic Games.	8th century Hesiod, *Theogony* and *Works and Days*.
	c. 700 Homer, *The Iliad* and *The Odyssey*.
7th–6th centuries Zoroaster in Persia; Hebrew prophets in Israel.	7th century *Epic of Gilgamesh* (Standard Version)
621 The book of Deuteronomy is "discovered" by Josiah—religious reforms.	7th–6th centuries Greek poets: Archilochus, Alcman; Alcaeus
	c. 600 Birth of Sappho.
6th century Rise of Doric and Ionic architecture.	c. 564 Aesop, writer of fables.
544 Beginnings of Attic tragedy.	550–400 Hebrew writing: P(Priestly) Genesis 1:1–2:4a.
	518 Birth of Pindar, Greek poet.
c. 500 Buddha.	
5th century Phidias sculpts Athena Parthenos and Zeus.	5th century Confucius, *The Analects*.
486 Athens: Contests for best comedy.	
485 Birth of Protagoras.	458 Aeschylus, *The Oresteia*.
479 Confucius dies.	c. 450 Lao Tzu, *Tao Te Ching*.
	c. 441 Sophocles, *Antigone*.
	444–429 Herodotus, *History of the Persian Wars*.
432 The Parthenon in Athens completed.	431 Euripides, *Medea*.
	420 Thucydides, *History of the Peloponnesian War*.
c. 400 Rise of Taoism in China.	411 Aristophanes, *Lysistrata*.
	c. 400–c. 400 C.E. *Mahabharata* in India.
399 Execution of Socrates.	4th century Chuang Tzu's writings.
c. 387 Plato founds the *Academy*.	4th century Plato, *Apology* and *Republic*.
372–298 Mencius, Chinese philosopher.	4th century Aristotle, *Poetics*.
c. 370 Hippocrates, the Greek Father of Medicine, dies.	

(*Continued on next page*)

TIME LINE FOR THE ANCIENT WORLD (Continued)

Date	*History and Politics*
B.C.E.	
	323 Death of Alexander the Great.
	321–183 India: Mauryan dynasty.
300–200	270 Rome rules all of Italy.
	264–146 Punic Wars: Rome versus Carthage.
	221–206 The first Chinese Empire: Ch'in dynasty.
200–100	200 Roman conquest of Greece begins.
	146 Fall of Corinth to Rome.
100–1	63 Rome seizes control of Palestine.
	60 First Triumvirate in Rome (Julius Caesar, Pompey, Crassus).
	44 Assassination of Caesar.
	43 Second Triumvirate (Antony, Octavian, Lepidus).
	27 Establishment of Empire by Augustus Caesar.
	5–3 Birth of Jesus of Nazareth.
C.E.	
1–300	25–220 Later Han dynasty in China.
	c. 30 Death of Jesus.
	47 Paul's missionary journeys begin.
	61–113 Pliny, the great Roman naturalist.
	70 Titus destroys the Temple in Jerusalem and exiles Jews.
	100–240 Kushan Empire in India.
300–400	320–550 Gupta Empire in India.
	306–337 Emperor Constantine.
400–500	410 The Visigoth Alaric sacks Rome.
	476 The barbarian Odoacer replaces the last emperor and ends the Roman Empire.

Science, Culture, and Technology	***Literature***
c. 336 Aristotle founds *Lyceum*.	
334 Founding of library at Alexandria.	
250–100 Hebrew scriptures translated into Greek (Septuagint).	2nd century B.C.E.–1st century C.E. *Dead Sea Scrolls*.
	70 Birth of Virgil.
	c. 54 Death of Catullus.
	c. 19 Virgil, *The Aeneid*.
	1st century *Bhagavad Gita*.
	c. 8 Ovid, *Metamorphoses*.
	c. 50 Paul's letters to Christian churches.
	66 Petronius dies.
70 Colosseum begun at Rome.	65–70 Gospel of Mark.
90 Council of Jamnia; rabbis settle canon of Hebrew Bible.	late 80s Gospel of Matthew.
c. 100 Buddhism enters China.	c. 96 The Revelation of St. John the Divine.
105 Paper invented in China.	
118–126 Construction of the Pantheon at Rome.	2nd century *The Gospel of Mary*.
	413–426 St. Augustine, *The City of God*.

INTRODUCTION

BEFORE THE DEVELOPMENT of urban civilizations about 5,000 years ago, most of the world's population lived on farms or in small villages. Village life was often organized around the worship of goddesses who ensured the health and fertility of crops, herds, and people. Many anthropologists believe that women were central to this life, as the childbearers, nurturers, and principal tenders of crops; men tended to be the herders of domestic animals and the hunters of wild ones.

Eventually, as farming populations increased along the rich alluvial plains of major rivers, like the Nile in Egypt, the Indus in Pakistan, and the Tigris and Euphrates in Mesopotamia, people began to produce a surplus of food, and their small trading centers gradually grew into cities. The urban dwellers who built irrigation systems along the Tigris and Euphrates about 3500 B.C.E. developed systems of mathematics and bookkeeping; in every city, bureaucracies evolved to coordinate the work of building palaces, temples, pyramids, and statues. As labor became more specialized and more workers were drawn away from the cyclical, seasonal, agricultural communities where women were important, power seems to have shifted more and more to men.

The discovery by Mesopotamian mathematicians and astronomers of the movement of planets through constellations of fixed stars led to a systematic cosmology involving basic celestial relationships and cyclical patterns, which were then used to justify a hierarchical earthly system of kings, priests, and underlings. This correlation between cosmic patterns and social structure, sky and earth, was institutionalized in an astronomically based religious calendar describing the major festivals for the year. From then on, priests and rulers throughout the ancient Near East would validate their programs and creeds with celestial authority, as if to say, "This is the way that god intended it!"

The temple, or ziggurat, the earthly residence of the god (or gods), took its place in the center of the city-state, where rulers—reflecting a divine pantheon of deities—regulated the course of civic and social life and influenced the fertility cycles of nature. The development of phonetic writing about 3000 B.C.E. gave rise to an extensive religious literature, depicting the roles of the gods and reinforcing human responsibilities. In the early literature of Mesopotamia (see below under World Context), one can witness the transition from a time when goddesses enjoyed as much power and respect as gods to a male-dominated society in which male deities were supreme and the role of the goddess was restricted to sex, love, and fertility. The spread of patriarchal culture characterized the third millennium B.C.E. in both Mesopotamia and Egypt. Both peoples devoted their resources to empire building and waging war with neighboring city-states. The ruling bureaucracies became more and more complex, while religion and law became increasingly codified.

These early civilizations form the historical background for the emergence of those Mediterranean nations—Greece, Rome, and Israel—that, with their ideals of heroism, law, and righteousness, have had the most direct and continuous influence on the course of Western history and thought. The literature of classical Greece promoted the values of the warrior—honor and courage; philosophy and art celebrated the intelligence and beauty of the individual. Greece's early gods and goddesses became, in the hands of its poets, not so much objects of worship as idealized models of human behavior. Greek deities extended the boundaries of human potential. The Romans reshaped the warrior model into the creation and administration of an empire, the heart of which was the Roman genius for civil law—a tradition in the ancient world stretching back to the legal codes of the Babylonian king Hammurabi (eighteenth century B.C.E.).

If the heroic outlook of the Greeks and Romans focused on the role of the individual in the here and now, the great poets and prophets of Israel continually recast the material world in terms of a transcendent authority and its spiritual destiny, the human capacity for righteousness and blessings. From the nation of Israel came a consciousness of personal morality, a code of ethics for framing human behavior derived from an awareness of divine purpose in history and an allegiance to a single deity. Focusing on obedience to God, the Hebrews developed a religious earnestness and a conscience. As the Hebrews debated about what it meant to be the "chosen people of God," the Greeks conceived of their cities as places where individuals might grow into their full potential as human beings. The counterpart to Moses high on Mt. Sinai transcribing God's laws is Socrates in the marketplace talking endlessly to his students about self-knowledge.

GREECE

The Greeks, like other heroic societies, had an ongoing disposition for war; it was a continuous theme in their society, dating back to the invasion of the Greek peninsula in the second millennium B.C.E. by nomadic warriors called Achæans, who brought with them male gods of war and a culture of domination. A different kind of influence on Greek culture came from the island of Crete, where, protected by the sea from the early invasions of the Indo-Europeans, a prosperous goddess culture developed from c. 3000–1500 B.C.E., with labyrinthine palaces, bull rituals, and powerful priestesses. The demise of what has been called the Minoan Civilization around 1400 B.C.E. was probably caused by a combination of natural disasters—volcanic eruptions, earthquakes, and floods—and invasions from the mainland by a feudal, warrior society called the Mycenaeans, named after the most famous citadel at Mycenae, ruled by the legendary Agamemnon sometime during the Mycenaean Age (c. 1500–1100 B.C.E.).

The Mycenaeans were a blend of non-Hellenic, black-haired Cretans and Hellenic peoples from the North, Homer's "brown-haired Achaeans." They used a written language scholars call Linear B, an early form of Greek. Their religion blended deities from Crete with northern Indo-European figures, resulting in a fusion of goddess and god myths. The Mycenaeans lived in a series of fortress-cities, largely in the Peloponnesus, the southern portion of Greece. The Mycenaean Age is also called the Heroic Age in Greek history because of the legendary reputations of several warrior heroes. One of the most famous heroic expeditions resulted in the destruction of Troy in northwestern Asia Minor about 1200 B.C.E., and became the source of Homer's great epics.

Shortly after the destruction of Troy, another wave of Indo-Europeans, the Dorians, who had iron implements, apparently conquered the Mycenaean fortresses (c. 1100 B.C.E.), and the Mycenaean Age came to an end. A number of uprooted Greeks moved to the coast of Asia Minor, into regions that came to be known as Ionia and Aeolia, where the seeds were planted for one of Greece's most influential creations—the Greek city-state, or *polis*. During the eighth and seventh centuries B.C.E., Greeks colonized numerous parts of the Mediterranean. The production of wine and olive oil stimulated the growth of shipping and trade among the colonies, and a merchant class was created. To allay the threat of strife between nobles and peasants over the ownership of land, the institution of the tyrant arose in city-states such as Athens and Corinth—the tyrant seized and held power without constitutional authority.

Athens was fortunate with its rulers. Toward the end of the seventh century B.C.E., Draco reformed the criminal justice system by instituting public trials to replace blood feuds. In 594 B.C.E., threatened by worsening economics and a possible rebellion, Athens elected an extraordinary leader as archon, the philosopher–poet Solon. With his goals of allowing all citizens to participate in government and of legally protecting the weaker majority from the wealthy minority, Solon moved Athens in the direction of a community of free men. He then withdrew to Cyprus and Egypt to test his reforms. When disorder broke out, Peisistratus, who traced his ancestry to Nestor—the Homeric king of Pylos—

seized power as a tyrant and used force to protect Solon's reforms. He built temples and founded the great Dionysiac festivals, which probably led to the invention of drama. A popular uprising brought Cleisthenes to power in 510 B.C.E., and the Athenian city-state became a democracy. It was every citizen's duty to participate in the *polis*, but, typically, citizenship was limited to men and to those born from citizen stock. Every "citizen," by definition, was thought to be qualified for public office. Slavery allowed wealthy citizens the time for public service. Under this kind of democracy, which promoted a balance between communal commitment and personal freedom, Athens prospered like no other Greek state.

After repulsing invasions by the Persians (499–479 B.C.E.), the Athenians grew confident in their military might and organized a naval confederacy, the Delian League, dreaming of empire. Supported by imperialism and tribute money from allies, the Golden Age of Athens was born, an age characterized by an incredible flowering of thought and culture. This Classical Age, with its sense of excellence and form, set standards of art and literature for later generations. Pericles, who came to power in 461 B.C.E., began a building program to make Athens worthy of international renown. A new Parthenon with the gigantic statue of Athena by Phidias crowned the Acropolis, the central citadel in the city. Other buildings and art works enhanced the beauty of schools and marketplaces. In his famous funeral oration, Pericles describes the qualities of judgment, harmony, and industry that characterize the Athenian ideal.

Rivalry between Athens and the city-state of Sparta finally led to war. Following the direction of its legendary law-giver Lycurgus, Sparta had developed in the sixth century B.C.E. a military state with a highly disciplined, mercenary army supported by a serf class, and had become increasingly isolated from other city-states. The Peloponnesian War between Athens and Sparta lasted for twenty-seven years, from 431 to 404 B.C.E. Pericles' death, bad judgments, a disastrous invasion of Sicily, internal rebellions, and the desertion of allies all led to Athens' defeat in 404 B.C.E. The ideals of the *polis* began to decline with the continuous intra-Hellenic warfare fueled by thousands of Greek mercenaries. Despite its victory, Sparta also faded, finally being defeated by Thebes in 371 B.C.E.

To the north, Philip seized the royal reins of Macedonia in 359 B.C.E. and ruled until he was murdered in 336 B.C.E. Philip's plans were adopted by his twenty-year-old son, Alexander, who led an army of 4,000 men eastward, liberating the Greek cities of Asia Minor and defeating Darius and the Persian army at Issus in 333 B.C.E. Although Alexander, whose favorite book was *The Iliad*, died of a fever at age thirty-two in Babylon, he did far more than simply reincarnate Achilles through his military triumphs in the ancient Near East. His remarkable career transformed ancient history by opening the wealth of Persia to Western trade and by spreading the Greek language and the ideals of Greek education and culture.

Rome

According to legend, Romulus founded Rome in 753 B.C.E., but the Romans ultimately traced their ancestry to a survivor of the Trojan War, Aeneas, who wandered the Mediterranean Sea and eventually arrived on Italy's shores, a journey recounted in Virgil's great epic, *The Aeneid*. From the eighth to the third centuries B.C.E., Rome's history was characterized by rivalries between various factions and the conquest of neighboring armies. By using alliances and military might, Rome gained control of the entire Italian peninsula by 270 B.C.E. Moving beyond its borders, Rome became involved in a protracted hundred-year war (264–146 B.C.E.) with the North African city of Carthage—the Punic Wars. Victory made Rome the undisputed ruler of the western Mediterranean. Rome then began to look eastward.

From 509 B.C.E. to 27 B.C.E., Rome was a republic ruled by twin consuls, a Senate and a popular Assembly, but the uneven distribution of wealth and power led to civil wars and slave revolts that threatened the growing empire from within. Finally, in the first century B.C.E., a civil war resulted in a division of power between Pompey, whose power lay in the east, and Julius Caesar, who had spread Roman rule to the west with his Gallic wars. These two leaders were temporarily joined by Crassus to make up the First Triumvirate in 60 B.C.E. A war between Pompey, favored by the senatorial party, and Caesar, leader of the popular party, ended with Caesar's victory at Pharsala in 48 B.C.E. The Roman historian Suetonius (75–160 C.E.) credited Julius Caesar with correcting the calendar—the Julian calendar—and with numerous public projects, but praised him above all for his brilliance as a military commander: "He was perfect in the use of arms, an accomplished rider, and able to endure fatigue beyond all belief."

Short-sighted conspirators, upset by Caesar's aggregation of power and dreaming of the return of the old Republic, arranged for Caesar's assassination in 44 B.C.E., which plunged Rome into another thirteen years of civil war. Caesar's nephew and adopted son, Gaius Julius Caesar Octavianus, joined forces with Mark Antony and Lepidus to form the Second Triumvirate in 43 B.C.E. Together they ventured into Greece to defeat Caesar's murderers, Brutus and Cassius, at Philippi in 42 B.C.E., resulting in a division of the Roman world east and west. Mixing love and politics, Antony joined forces with Cleopatra, Queen of Egypt, while Octavian eliminated his rivals and consolidated his forces in the west. The inevitable battle between them occurred at Actium in 31 B.C.E.; defeated, Antony and Cleopatra escaped to Egypt, where they committed suicide. Uniting an empire that stretched from the Straits of Gibraltar to Palestine, Octavian took the name of Augustus, established a constitutional monarchy, and inaugurated a golden age of art and literature.

The term *Pax Romana* describes the unprecedented 200 years of relative peace that began with Augustus and ended with Marcus Aurelius. It was a time when resources could be devoted to peaceful projects, rather than squandered in armaments and war. The Romans built roads, bridges, aqueducts, baths, sewers, and public buildings. Undergirding their bureaucratic system was a concept of universal law rooted in nature that declared the equality of all men and protected the individual against the state. This law, which embraced the ideal of a free society, was Rome's greatest contribution to Western civilization. The Romans systematized education, which inculcated the Latin virtues of *pietas* (duty), *gravitas* (seriousness), and *amor imperii* (love of empire). Their religion of patriotism produced the man of letters, the man of politics, the man of the world—embodied in figures such as Cicero, Horace, and Pliny the Younger.

Romans appeared to be as organized at home as in the public arena. They highly valued family life and made the eldest male in every household—the *paterfamilias*—the authority over all important matters, including marriage, religion, infidelity, dowries—even life and death. As in Greece, it was a civic duty to have children. Although upper-class women played subordinate roles to men, they were not sequestered in their homes as Athenian women seem to have been. Through birth control and abortion, they freed themselves from the lifelong burden of bearing children and developed lives outside the home. They shopped in markets and attended festivals and dinner parties with their husbands. Women were allowed to attend elementary school; some were educated by private tutors and became musicians, poets, and artists. Although they were given no true political positions and only honorary titles, they could be highly influential behind the scenes. By the second century C.E., women were involved in business, sports, and concerts; they even chose their own marriage partners.

Under the later rulers—Tiberius, Caligula, and Claudius I—the empire stretched from Britain to Mesopotamia, the largest in the history of the West. Nevertheless, the period between 14 C.E. and 96 C.E. also saw the insanity of Emperors Nero and Caligula, the burning of Rome, the defeat of a Jewish uprising, the destruction of Jerusalem, and the ongoing persecution of a new religious sect calling themselves Christians. The period from 96 C.E. to 180 C.E.—under the reigns of Nerva, Trajan, Hadrian, Antoninus Pius, and Marcus Aurelius—was a peaceful period, but something was missing in the personal lives of the people. Many seemed to lack a sense of spiritual purpose and direction, and they increasingly turned to imported mystery religions.

In the third century, the empire was weakened by a division into eastern and western halves. Constantine, who granted official tolerance to the new Christian sect in 313 C.E. and later converted to Christianity himself, moved his capital to Constantinople. Invaders from the north increasingly penetrated the frontiers of the empire, until finally Rome was sacked by Alaric and his Visigoths in 410 C.E. The Roman Empire in the West formally came to an end when the barbarian Odoacer replaced the last emperor, Romulus Augustulus, in 476 C.E.

Greek Literature

In Greece, as in all other civilizations to this day, the foundation of culture was laid by mythology and folklore, a repository of oral stories that became the cultural heritage of poets and artists. Even though the Greek historian Herodotus (fifth century B.C.E.) called Homer and Hesiod the fathers of Greek mythology, these two poets inherited from earlier periods a tradition of heroic lays, or short narrative poems that evolved into epics. Typically, epics are long narrative poems that present the history of a people or nation as a series of grand episodes involving the extraordinary actions of gods and heroes. Epics that appear to be the culmination of an extended oral or folk tradition are called folk epics, and include, besides the Greek *Iliad* and *Odyssey,* the Babylonian *Gilgamesh,* the East Indian *Mahabharata,* and the Old English *Beowulf.* The second kind of epic, the art or literary epic, is the result of a written, literary tradition and has as much concern for artistry as for history. Examples of this kind are Virgil's *Aeneid,* Dante's *Divine Comedy,* and John Milton's *Paradise Lost.* Taking myth and folklore in a different direction were the storytellers who passed along short prose anecdotes, or fables, used for teaching moral lessons; the almost legendary founder of this literary type was Aesop.

Greek poets also achieved excellence in the lyric, a term applied to poems that were accompanied by a lyre, used a variety of meters, and expressed personal feelings about topics such as love and death. The lyric, sung by a single performer, was distinguished from choral poetry, which was sung by a chorus and danced. The earliest lyric poets—Sappho, Terpander, and Alcaeus—lived on the island of Lesbos in the seventh century B.C.E. Sappho's genius was recognized by the ancients, who regarded her as the Tenth Muse; unfortunately, like the work of other lyric poets, most of her poems are lost. By the time Roman poets inherited the genre, the lyre had been left behind; there is a larger sampling of extant poems by poets such as Catullus, Horace, and Propertius.

Although the exact origins of Greek drama are still debated, Aristotle maintained that it began with the dithyramb, or choral ode, used in religious ceremonies around the figure of Dionysus. Greek comedy (from *komos,* "revel") probably originated with phallic ceremonies and fertility rites, whereas tragedy (meaning "goat-song") involved the themes of Dionysian death and resurrection. The rudiments of drama evolved from a dialogue between a leader and the chorus to the gradual introduction of additional speakers and the eventual disappearance of the chorus. Tradition holds that Aeschylus (525–456 B.C.E.) added a second actor for genuine dialogue; he also used costumes, masks, and thick-soled boots to elevate the action.

An early form of philosophical writing is found in the works of Hesiod, who mixed folklore and philosophy in order to systematize the earliest stories about deities. His *Theogony,* of which we include an excerpt, describes how creation emerged from chaos and earth, or Gaia. His portrayal of the generational conflict between the gods reflected shadowy issues within the Greek family structure. Hesiod's stories about the goddesses Styx and Hecate illustrate how a number of Greek deities had their roots in a much earlier age. Zeus himself evolved through several stages until he assumed the rather stable throne on Mt. Olympus. If Hesiod was primarily concerned with the generations of gods and goddesses in the *Theogony*, Homer's attention was on the glories of a heroic society. Homer used one of the most important cycles of stories to be passed down from the oral tradition, the stories of the Trojan War, to create his warriors.

The heroes of the Trojan War, and all that they symbolized, provided important themes for the military, intellectual, and artistic adventures of the classical age in Greece and Rome. Homer's *Iliad* (eighth century B.C.E.), the most famous account of the war and the literary standard for epics ever since, focuses on the exploits of Achilles. With a kind of nostalgia, Homer depicts a heroic age some 400–500 years in the past and celebrates the patriarchal, feudal life-styles of the Achaean warlords. Although savage at times, Achilles represents the epitome of the Greek hero and the heroic view of life: A warrior is someone with superior mental and physical abilities who uses conquest and adventure to achieve honor and glory—the ultimate goals of his life. Throughout *The Iliad*, the reader is aware that groups of men or whole armies are fighting over Helen and Troy, but the real measure of heroism rests with individual warriors.

In *The Odyssey*, Homer extends the heroic model to include Odysseus' wily intelligence and imagination. Homer weaves Odysseus' return from the war to Ithaca into a series of adventures that test him both physically and mentally. Odysseus' affairs with Círcë and Calypso reveal both strengths and frailties in a man whose desires sometimes conflict with his ideals, but throughout his voyage he excels in survival skills. Homer's Ionian audience was a feudal aristocracy who must have identified with Odysseus, Achilles, and the warrior culture of the Mycenaeans. Questions involving fertility, sexuality, planting, and life after death, traditionally associated with goddesses and *chthonic*, or underworld, rituals, were largely neglected by Homer; absent too were most of the goddesses who earlier were so prominent on Crete.

For centuries afterwards, Homer's heroic models were the inspiration to Greeks who strove for excellence and fame in the *polis* as well as on the battlefield. The heroic code of honor was initially linked to war, but its essence was in seeing life as a series of challenges that one must courageously face and overcome. That kind of psychological strategy can equally apply to peacetime, when honor becomes an incentive to meet each day forthrightly, whether the challenge is intellectual, material, or political. As Pericles stated in his famous oration, we "place the real disgrace of poverty not in owning to the fact but in declining the struggle against it." In the fifth century B.C.E., artists and writers from outside Attica were drawn to the intellectual and creative ferment of Athens, setting standards for literary forms by inventing them. Herodotus and Thucydides, for example, invented the writing of history. Plato and Aristotle broadened the tradition of philosophical and scientific writing begun by earlier thinkers like Heraclitus, Empedocles, and Pythagoras.

In the fifth century B.C.E., the development of Attic tragedy, with its roots in religious ritual, was central to the festival life of the city. On the stages of Athens, the heroic legacy of Homer was adjusted to urban responsibilities, questioned, and revised. The plays were performed at the two major Athenian festivals in honor of Dionysus: the Lenaea during January and February, and the Great Dionysia during March and April. Contests were held and dramatists were awarded prizes by an Athenian jury. Most Greek cities, even some of the smaller ones, had outdoor theaters and valued the psychological and social roles of drama in civic life.

Aeschylus, the first great tragedian, explored human suffering and the complexities of human relationships. He used materials from the legacy of family violence and rebellion embedded in the House of Atreus and its curse, the underlying family saga for the Trojan War. In *The Oresteia,* Aeschylus recalls the aftermath of the Trojan War to prepare his audience for civic duty. He ends the cyclic pattern of blood revenge in the House of Atreus by submitting Orestes' murder of his mother to a newly created court system. *The Oresteia* ends with a hymn to the newly constituted political and judicial system, a patriarchal system that has muffled the powers and voices of the feminine by transforming the powerful Furies into the Eumenides—the "gracious ones." Sophocles used a different cycle of stories to create a new kind of strong, proud heroine in his play *Antigone,* which explores the conflicting demands between loyalty to family and obedience to ruler. Ever since Homer, who had depicted the suffering as well as the glory of combat, there had been an ambivalence about the personal and social consequences of war among Greece's artists and thinkers. With the character of Antigone, Sophocles shows how militarism can lead to personal tragedy.

Two playwrights in particular attacked the political weaknesses that encouraged the Athenians to drift into the disastrous war with Sparta. Disillusioned by the wars of his own period and the heroic posturing of leaders, Euripides (c. 480–406 B.C.E.) exposed the dark and painful side of the Trojan story in the *Trojan Women* (415 B.C.E.) by showing the pettiness and cruelty of the Greek warriors, along with the extreme suffering and courage of the Trojan women. The heroine of his *Medea* (431 B.C.E.) expresses outrage at being betrayed by her man. She challenges the patriarchal pattern of family relationships and commits outrageous acts toward her children as a way of asserting her power as a woman and as a means of punishing Jason, who tarnishes the heroic tradition with his vacillation and cowardice. Of the same period, Aristophanes (c. 450–386 B.C.E.), although a devoted citizen of Athens, used his comedies to castigate certain politicians and criticize the ethos of war that was undermining the whole fabric of civic life. It is a remarkable measure of Athenian freedom that Aristophanes' plays were performed during wartime. *Lysistrata* exposed the folly of men at war by depicting a conspiracy by a council of women to deny men sexual favors until they made peace with Sparta. The women of Sparta carried out the same plan, and peace was finally arranged.

Athens' artists and writers raised disturbing questions about sexual stereotypes and the potential for limited women's roles in a heroic society. Certainly Sophocles' Antigone rivals any man with her courage and heroism in the face of death, and the women in Aristophanes' *Lysistrata* use their powers to affect policy, but generally men and women lived in two different worlds, with Athenian women living secluded lives as housewives. The acceptance of homosexuality among Greek men, often an older man with a younger, further indicated a lower status for women. After all, women and slaves made it possible for Greek citizens (all male) to spend their time debating the great issues of the day, as well as developing the deep and lasting male friendships that were praised in poems and essays.

The Peloponnesian War caused important changes in Athenian society, upsetting the balance between the individual and the state. Professional teachers, known as Sophists, taught methods of argumentation that were seen as undermining traditional civic values and promoting individual cleverness and skepticism. The most famous teacher of the time, however, was Socrates, whose teachings about personal knowledge and the inner voice further weakened the appeal of civic responsibility, even though Socrates himself had served in the army as a hoplite (an infantry soldier) and was elected to the Council. In *The Apology,* Socrates questions whether personal honesty is compatible with public service. In the instability of the war's aftermath and the decline of Athens, charges were brought against Socrates. He was convicted and condemned to death in 399 B.C.E. In 387 B.C.E., Socrates' most famous pupil, Plato (c. 427–347 B.C.E.), founded the Academy. Plato's star intellect was Aristotle, the philosopher who invented logic and then used it to codify human knowledge.

Roman Literature

From the time of his *Eclogues* (37 B.C.E.), Virgil, the most famous poet of the Roman Empire, was well known at Augustus' court and was probably beginning to plan the epic poem that would do for Rome what the earlier epics by Homer had provided Greece—the creation of mythic-historic roots. In *The Aeneid,* Virgil sought to create a founding myth of Rome's origins that would celebrate Augustus' accomplishments and support a vision of Rome's world mission in the future. The travails of Aeneas' own journey through the Mediterranean reflected in miniature the labors undertaken by Roman senators, legions, and slaves to create the empire. Understanding the anxiety that Roman intellectuals had about the impending end of an age, Virgil attempted to allay the fears of his Roman audience with the voice of Jupiter: "I set no limits to their fortunes and / no time; I give them empire without end." Later in Book IV, Virgil creates his own version of the hero by portraying Aeneas with psychological depth and complexity in his relationship with Dido, the queen of Carthage. After the publication of *The Aeneid,* Augustus was designated the second founder of Rome, a place that for a time would be called the *urbs aeterna* (the eternal city). The Greek vision of the *polis* had been extended by Rome into a grand *cosmopolis*.

Both Catullus (84–54 B.C.E.) and Ovid (43 B.C.E.–18 C.E.) wrote personal poems as well as poems on mythical subjects. Catullus, in particular, is remembered for his love poems, with their expression of sensitive feelings and portrayal of the pangs of rejection and despair. Ovid, the first-century poet laureate of love under Augustus, is most famous for his *Metamorphoses*, a compendium of Greek and Roman myths. The old stories of gods and goddesses that had once been used to illustrate the spiritual mysteries of life became, in Ovid's skillful hands, the marvelously entertaining materials of literature. He concluded the *Metamorphoses* with the prediction, "My fame shall live to all eternity," and so far it has, through his influence on poets such as Chaucer, Shakespeare, Alexander Pope, and T. S. Eliot.

Ancient Israel

The history of ancient Israel combines the Hebrews' search for the blessings of God with their transformation from a nomadic, tribal people into a settled kingdom in Palestine. For hundreds of years, Egypt and Mesopotamia struggled for control of Palestine, with Israel caught in between; consequently, the Hebrew political record was a mixture of victories and defeats, and eventually exile. In the meantime, Israel's poets, priests, and prophets assembled the Hebrew Bible, or the Old Testament, a remarkable collection of history, religion, and literature. While the heroic quest of the Greeks led to a literary and artistic celebration of individuals—the human potential—in their grandiose, often tragic, confrontation with destiny, the Hebrews participated in their own spiritual odyssey, which focused on God as well as humans, and developed the ethical guidelines for a righteous life. Both the Greeks and the Hebrews saw a world made up of conflict, adventure, and war.

Early in the second millennium B.C.E., nomadic tribes of Hebrews followed the Fertile Crescent southward through Palestine to Egypt, where they were enslaved by the Egyptians (c. 1300 B.C.E.). Following a religious prophet named Moses, the Hebrews escaped from Egyptian bondage about 1250 B.C.E. and wandered through the Sinai desert to Mt. Sinai, where they received the spiritual and legal foundation of their religion in the form of the Ten Commandments. Prepared for conquest, they journeyed to Canaan, invaded existing towns and villages, and eventually settled down. The Hebrew God, Yahweh, proved to be a fierce partisan, whether he was dealing with Sodom and Gomorrah, Hebrew backsliders at Mt. Sinai, or the Canaanite enemy. For the next 500 years or so—until the time of the exile in 586 B.C.E.—there was an extended struggle within the Israelite community between the religion of Mt. Sinai and the polytheistic practices of the indigenous religion, the Canaanite worship of Baal and Ashtorath. The Bible records a number of times when the religion of Yahweh had to be purged of Canaanite elements.

The twelfth and eleventh centuries introduced a period of warfare, when Hebrew military leaders, called judges, arose to defend various groups against invasion and then exercise a unifying political role in the region. Real progress toward national unity was made by Saul when the people banded together in the face of a common enemy, the Philistines. Credit for finally creating a united kingdom, however, is given to David, who reigned 1000–960 B.C.E. David consolidated his rule by establishing Jerusalem as the national capital, but like Saul's, his life was tragically divided by rebellion and conflict—a pattern stretching back to Genesis. Solomon's reign, 960–922 B.C.E., was the Golden Age of Israel, characterized by prosperity and peace. The Israelites fortified their cities and built a magnificent temple in Jerusalem, where the worship of Yahweh was centered.

When Solomon died, the kingdom was divided into a large northern state of Israel, with its capital at Shechem, and a small southern state of Judah. Caught up in the rivalry between Egypt and Assyria, the Northern Kingdom disappeared in 721 B.C.E. and became the "Ten Lost Tribes" of Israel. In 640 B.C.E., Josiah became king of Judah, and, discovering the book of Deuteronomy during a temple renovation, instituted broad religious reforms in accordance with the instructions of this book. In 587 B.C.E., Nebuchadnezzar of Babylon pursued a quarrel with Egypt and defeated Jerusalem, burning buildings and leveling the temple. Jewish survivors were deported to Babylon, beginning a pattern of Jewish settlements outside of Palestine that is called by the Greek word *diaspora,* or dispersion. The Jews were allowed to return to Jerusalem and rebuild the temple, but a series of outside empires, such as the Persians, the Greeks, and the Ptolemies, ruled the region. When the Syrian king Antiochus IV (175–163 B.C.E.) attempted to force the Hellenization of the Jews, the Maccabeean Revolt took place (167–160 B.C.E.). Consequently, the Jews enjoyed some independence during the next hundred years, until 64 B.C.E., when Pompey annexed Syria and Palestine came under the control of the Romans. Octavius Caesar made Herod the Great the king of Judea in 37 B.C.E.; he was a builder who renovated the temple in Jerusalem. When Herod died in 4 B.C.E., his kingdom was divided into three portions. Judea was made a province governed by procurators responsible directly to the emperor. Pontius Pilate was the procurator from 26 to 36 C.E.; he condemned the Jewish rabbi, Jesus of Nazareth, to death.

Although the Romans granted a great deal of self-government to the Jews and to their council of elders, called the Sanhedrin, Roman tolerance ended with the accession of Caligula in 37 C.E. Allowing the persecution of the Jews, he ordered his own image to be hung in the temple in Jerusalem. Unrest eventually led to a Jewish revolt in 66 C.E. In response, Rome under Vespasian and Titus destroyed Jerusalem in 70 C.E., ending that city's role as a religious center. After the Council at Jamnia in 90 C.E., where Jewish rabbis decided on the canon of the Old Testament, one further revolt against Rome under the leadership of Simon bar Kochba took place in 135 C.E. The defeated Jews were forbidden to set foot in Jerusalem, and the province of Judea was renamed Palestine.

The messianic tradition of the Jews provided a context for the emergence of Jesus of Nazareth, whose life and teachings led to the creation of a new world religion, Christianity. Under pressure from Jewish zealots to lead a political rebellion against Roman occupation, Jesus instead redefined and exemplified a new kind of spiritual warrior whose ultimate weapons were love and forgiveness, in contrast to the portions of Mosaic law that emphasize judgment and punishment. Jesus' message combined a revitalized ethic involving communal values with an apocalyptic vision of a messianic kingdom whose gates would welcome the downtrodden and the disenfranchised.

Although Jesus' early followers were fellow Jews, his message ultimately found a home in colonies of Gentiles throughout Asia Minor, as interpreted by a brilliant teacher and missionary, Paul of Tarsus. Christianity gained world recognition when the Roman emperor Constantine granted tolerance and clemency to Christians in 313 C.E. and equal status with all other religions a year later. Constantine was baptized on his deathbed in 337 C.E.

Literature of the Bible

The writers of the Old Testament drew upon various kinds of literature to portray the heroic history of the Hebrew people. In the book of Genesis, which provides a foundation for the rest of the Bible, myth, folklore, and legend describe the creation of the world, the adventures of the first humans, and the nomadic wanderings of the Hebrew patriarchs. In the book of Exodus, poetry and history portray the struggles of the Hebrews to survive in the desert and to reach the Promised Land. The book of Joshua documents the invasion of the new land and the conquering of Canaanite settlements. The entire journey from Eden to Egypt, and from Egypt to Palestine, has the quality of an epic and, indeed, some have called these books the Yahwist epic, named after an anonymous tenth-century B.C.E. writer whose narrative was later blended with those of other writers in Genesis and Exodus.

In the study of Western literature, we are accustomed to thinking of individual authors of particular works of literature, but the Hebrew Bible often yields the sense of a collective voice, a community's songs and stories that tell about its sufferings, dreams, and joys. It is not a single hero who escapes the clutches of Egyptian slave masters, but a whole people who assume a heroic stature in their journey to the Promised Land. Lyric poetry appears throughout the Bible, celebrating victories and lamenting sorrows. The Psalms remain the primary collection of lyric poetry. Even when an individual such as Job is identified, we hear behind his ideas the forceful debate of an entire intellectual community that had wrestled with the issues of God's justice for hundreds of years. Religious ceremony pervades the Old Testament, but the book of Job is the one work that approaches the kind of drama developed by the Greeks.

There are fewer kinds of literature in the New Testament, where the writers used biography, history, and letters to tell the story of Jesus' life and the early history of Christianity. The book of Revelations is an example of Apocalyptic writing.

World Context

About 2300 B.C.E., a Semitic people from the interior of the Arabian peninsula called the Akkadians conquered the non-Semitic Sumerians, and under Sargon I (2340–2284 B.C.E.) established the first known empire in history—from the Persian Gulf to the Mediterranean Sea. The Akkadians replaced the Sumerian goddesses' powers with those of the gods, and reinforced the patriarchy with private property, class distinctions, the dominance of sky gods, and the centralization of authority. Sumerian scribes created a written literature on clay tablets in cuneiform script by 1750 B.C.E., perhaps earlier. The tablets then were lost for over 2,000 years, buried under sand when Babylon was defeated by the Persian Cyrus the Great and Nineveh, the capital of Assyria, was leveled.

In the mid-nineteenth century, archaeologists discovered these clay tablets at Ninevah and at other Mesopotamian sites along the Tigris and Euphrates Rivers, and ancient history was rewritten as a result. Along with administrative records, a vast literature of Sumer and Babylon was discovered, which predated the Hebrew and Greek literature by about a thousand years.

Only when scholars translated Mesopotamian tablets and deciphered Egyptian hieroglyphs could an assessment be made of the effect of these early civilizations on Greece, Rome, and Israel. We now can conclude that the myths and epics written in Akkadian, the dialects of Babylonia and Assyria, were widely known throughout the Ancient Near East—the similarity of the Hebrew and Mesopotamian flood stories is decisive evidence. We do not fully understand, however, how and when these early materials became available to the writers of the Bible. It is not known whether Homer ever heard about the great Babylonian hero Gilgamesh, even though his Achilles and Odysseus duplicate some of Gilgamesh's exploits.

The oldest extant goddess stories in the Western world come from Sumer and center around Inanna, who was the Queen of Heaven and Earth, the morning and evening star, and the goddess of love and agriculture. Her stories date from 3500 B.C.E. to 1900 B.C.E., perhaps even earlier. The myth of Inanna's descent into the underworld probably portrays the symbolic death of nature during winter and her rebirth in the spring. The importance of Inanna in Sumerian religion is related to the important roles women played in Sumerian culture; they were involved in temple business, owned real estate, and negotiated money transactions, but gradually with the entrenchment of patriarchal institutions and religion, they lost their rights and powers. The renowned hero story about Gilgamesh is essentially the maturation journey of a young king. After battling a giant and mourning the death of his friend Enkidu, Gilgamesh goes on an extended personal journey, searching for the answers to human mortality and the ultimate meaning of life. As part of his journey, he is told a flood story that, as mentioned earlier, is similar to the one in Genesis.

In order to illustrate the wide variety of perspectives from this period in history, we also include texts from the ancient wisdom traditions of China and India. Very little is known about the earliest civilizations in these countries. Aryan-speaking tribes from the north invaded India in the third millennium B.C.E. and replaced indigenous settlements with patriarchal institutions such as the hierarchical caste system. A similar pattern of development occurred in China during the Shang dynasty (1766–1122 B.C.E.). Nomadic Eurasian peoples brought a militaristic culture to the mainland, introducing horses, the chariot, metallurgy, and class-society.

The dominant Chinese philosophy of Confucius promotes social hierarchies and patterns of obedience between groups, but Lao Tzu's poems in the *Tao Te Ching* and Chuang Tzu's collection of Taoist parables represent a different way of being in the world, quite unlike the heroic model of the Greeks and the Hebrews. Rather than conflict and domination, which are characteristic of the Western hero, the follower of Taoism seeks harmony with the Tao, or the Way, by participating in the flow of life, much as a swimmer learns to merge with various currents in a river.

The *Bhagavad Gita,* which literally means the "song of the glorious one," is a section from the grand Hindu epic *Mahabharata* and is an extended dialogue in Sanskrit between Lord Krishna and Arjuna, the chief hero of the epic, about the nature of reality and the right perspective on the upcoming battle. Out of compassion, Arjuna wants to refrain from killing his enemies; Krishna explains that the nature of karma and the multiple selves of individuals make the confrontation much more complex than Arjuna's analysis would have it. The *Bhagavad Gita* is at least 400 years later than Homer's *Iliad* and represents a spiritual complexity totally missing from the traditional depictions of warriors and their psyches in Homer's epics.

SUGGESTED READINGS

The historical background of Mesopotamian myths can be found in A. L. Oppenheim's *Ancient Mesopotamia* (1977). A recent translation of the myth texts is Stephanie Dalley's *Myths from Mesopotamia* (1989). Texts from a variety of ancient cultures appear in James B. Pritchard, ed., *Ancient Near Eastern Texts: Relating to the Old Testament* (1955). An excellent cultural history dealing with the transition from agricultural and goddess cultures to urban civilizations and patriarchal religion is William Irwin Thompson, *The Time Falling Bodies Take to Light: Mythology, Sexuality & the Origins of Culture* (1981). A stimulating treatment of the basic perspectives of ancient cultures is H. and H. A. Frankfort, John A. Wilson, and Thorkild Jacobsen, *Before Philosophy: The Intellectual Adventure of Ancient Man* (1946). A broad survey of classical culture, from history to literature, is provided by John Boardman, Jasper Griffin, and Oswyn Murray, eds., *The Oxford History of the Classical World* (1986). Individual histories of the three major cultures of this period are J. B. Bury's *A History of Greece* (1975), Michael Grant's *History of Rome* (1978), and John Bright's *A History of Israel* (1972). Excellent overviews of Greek literature are in two of C. M. Bowra's books, *The Greek Experience* (1957) and *Ancient Greek Literature* (1933). Michael Grant's *Roman Literature* (1954) is a good introduction. For the history and roles of women and the transition to patriarchy, see Gerda Lerner's *The Creation of Patriarchy* (1986), Eva Cantarella's *Pandora's Daughters*, trans. by Maureen B. Fant (1987), Merlin Stone's *When God Was a Woman* (1976), Riane Eisler's *The Chalice and the Blade: Our History, Our Future* (1987), Sarah B. Pomeroy's *Goddesses, Whores, Wives and Slaves: Women in Classical Antiquity* (1975), and Rosemary Radford Ruether, ed., *Religion and Sexism: Images of Women in the Jewish and Christian Traditions* (1974). A general introduction to the literature of the Bible is Stephen L. Harris's *Understanding the Bible* (1992).

REPRESENTATIVE TEXTS OF GREECE AND ROME

HOMER

[C. 700 B.C.E.]

Homer's great epic poems, *The Iliad* and *The Odyssey*, tell different parts of a single epic cycle about a Greek military expedition to the distant city of Troy, the war with the Trojans, and the return of the heroes to their cities and kingdoms. Various stories about the Trojan War were passed down in oral form from the time of the war until the eighth century B.C.E., when Homer created his own versions of the events. The materials surrounding the Trojan War, the heroic ideals that arose from the battlefield at Troy, constituted one of the most important legacies from the Greek Heroic Age (c. 1500–1100 B.C.E.), which was known for its sea voyages and military adventures.

The mythical cause of the war, known as the Judgment of Paris, involved the wedding between Peleus and Thetis. During the wedding, Eris, the goddess of discord, took a golden apple inscribed with the words *For the Fairest* and rolled it across the floor. The goddesses Hera, Athena, and Aphrodite all claimed the apple. Zeus chose Paris, the handsome prince of Troy, to be the judge and decide which of the three goddesses deserved the apple. The goddesses bribed him and Paris picked Aphrodite, who promised him the most beautiful woman in the world: Helen, wife of Meneláus. While on a mission to Sparta, Paris fell in love with Helen and took her and Spartan treasure back to Troy. Seeking revenge, Greek kings under the leadership of Agamemnon, Meneláus' brother, banded together in ships at Aulis, but an absence of wind prevented them from sailing to Troy. Agamemnon was persuaded by a seer to sacrifice his youngest daughter, Iphigenia, as a means of restoring the winds, an important event in Aeschylus' trilogy, *The Oresteia.* When at Troy a Greek embassy failed to secure the return of Helen and the treasure, the war settled down to a ten-year siege. In the tenth year, the point where Homer's *Iliad* begins, the action came to a climax with a quarrel between Agamemnon and Achilles, the death of Achilles' close friend, and the death of Hector, the Trojans' greatest warrior. Achilles himself was killed by Paris. The end of the war came about when the Trojans were tricked into hauling a large wooden horse filled with Achæans into the city, precipitating Troy's destruction.

Later Greeks believed that the Trojan stories constituted history and not legend, and that Homer was writing about a period of history some 400 to 500 years older than himself that was described as an Age of Heroes, an age just before the last destructive wave of northern tribes in the twelfth century B.C.E., the Dorians. We know very few heroes from either ancient Mesopotamia or Egypt, but Homer, at the end of a long oral tradition, created a grand catalogue of Greek heroes that bridged history and mythology and was a source of traditional knowledge and morality for several hundred years.

LIFE

We do not know who Homer was, where he came from in Greece, or exactly when he wrote. Not all scholars are even convinced that the same poet wrote both *The Iliad* and *The Odyssey.* As many as seven cities in Ionia, the region of Asia Minor on the east coast of the Aegean, have claimed to be his birthplace.

Because there are elements of the Ionian dialect in the poems, it is probable that Homer was a descendant of the early Greeks who migrated to Ionia after the breakup of the Mycenaean city-states. Before the rise of Athens, Ionia was the intellectual and cultural center of the Greek world. Tradition suggests that Homer was blind. There is the blind bard, Demódocus, in *The Odyssey* (Book 8) and an interesting reference at the conclusion of the *Homeric Hymn to Delian Apollo,* a poem probably not written by Homer but dated at the seventh century B.C.E. The poet says to the maidens of Delos that a blind man from Chios is the sweetest singer:

> "O maidens, what man to you is the sweetest of singers
> Who frequent this place, and whose songs give you greatest delight?"
> Then all of you answer in unison, choosing felicitous words:
> "A blind man who lives on the rugged island of Chios,
> All of whose songs in aftertime will be known as the best."

During the sixth century there was a professional group of poets on the island of Chios who recited Homeric poetry and called themselves *Homeridai* (Sons of Homer). So Homer might have been a single poet who composed the epics, or "Homer" might represent a series of poets who recited and modified oral epics until *The Iliad* and *The Odyssey* reached their final form sometime in the sixth century. A combination of these two possibilities probably approaches the truth.

It was once believed that long epic poems such as Homer's could not be memorized and must therefore be in written form, which meant that *The Iliad* and *The Odyssey* were composed and written down between 750 and 650 B.C.E., about the time when

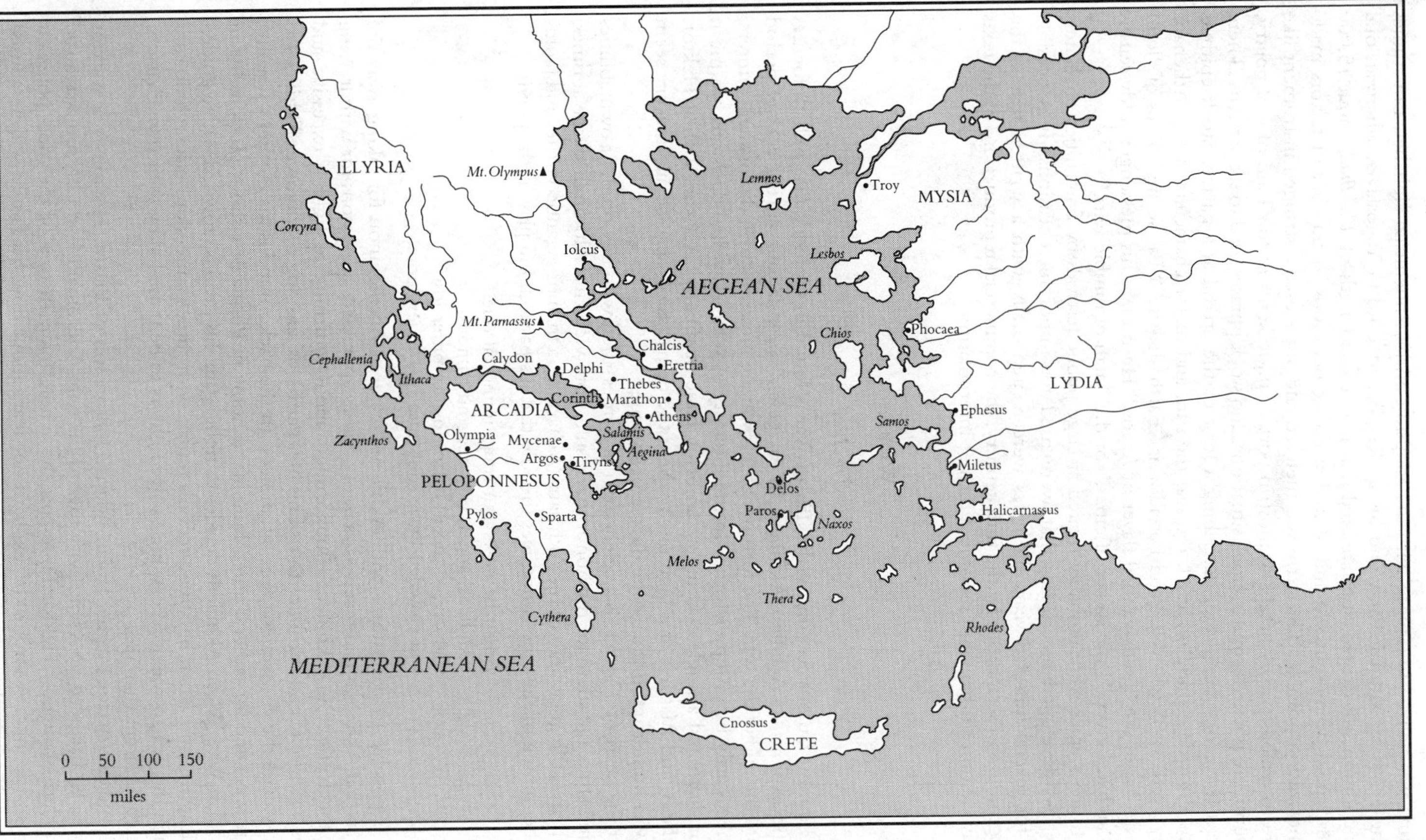

THE WORLD OF HOMER

writing was revived in Greece with the adoption of the Phoenician alphabet. But studies in the 1930s by Milman Parry and his student Albert Lord in Yugoslavia, where an oral epic tradition still existed, substantiated that poems the length of *The Iliad*, about 15,000 verses, could be memorized and recited at public occasions. A number of factors made memorization possible: The verse was metered and poets used a stringed instrument like a lyre to establish a rhythm. The most important ingredients of this kind of oral poetry, however, are poetic formulas, stock situations, and stock phrases used to set patterns. There is a set way, for example, of describing a feast or the arrival at a palace. Stock epithets are used for describing nightfall, the sea, the sun, and major characters. Thus, Athena is "grey-eyed" or "owl-eyed," and Poseidon is "Earth-shaker." "Far-seeing" Zeus of "loud thunder" uses the "gold-wanded slayer of Argos," Hermes, as his messenger. Odysseus is the "arch-deceiver," "the sacker of cities," or the "man of nimble wits."

Homer's epics were probably recited at large public festivals by fraternities of reciters who had developed repertories that were used for important occasions. It is possible that for several hundred years the epics were recited orally with a written text in the background as a script. But by the fifth century, the commercial reproductions of the texts finally canonized them and prevented further interpolation.

WORK

The Iliad

The most famous account of the Trojan War is found in Homer's *Iliad,* which focuses on the exploits of Achilles (Akhilleus in Fitzgerald's translation) during a brief period toward the end of the war. The fortunes of this war are measured by individual encounters, not necessarily by group victories. In the intensity of war, individual decisions can mean life or death and a single encounter can bring fame or infamy. Warriors such as Hektor, Akhilleus, and Aías live at a high pitch where the demands of sacrifice and bravery seem to dwarf humdrum, ordinary life during peacetime.

At the heart of *The Iliad* is a celebration of heroes, men who rely on their own abilities to win battles and strive for the honor that results from victories. Although savage at times, Akhilleus is the great hero of the Akhaians (Achaeans), a man of gigantic virtues and faults. The beginning of the epic announces the role that his passion will play in the poem:

> Anger be now your song, immortal one,
> Akhilleus' anger, doomed and ruinous,
> that caused the Akhaians loss on bitter loss
> and crowded brave souls into the undergloom.

It is possible to sympathize with Akhilleus' anger at Agamemnon for taking away the woman that Akhilleus had received as booty and to appreciate his reasons for withdrawing from the battle. But Akhilleus' stubbornness about returning to fight is excessive and causes his close friend Patróklos to risk his life. Patróklos' ensuing death forces Akhilleus to acknowledge the consequences of his choices. In the background is his mother's warning that he was fated for either a quiet, long life at home in Phthia or a short, glorious life in the Trojan War. When Akhilleus decides to fight again, his head is crowned with a golden cloud of fire, and when he announces his return with three tremendous cries, panic runs through the Trojan warriors, causing twelve fighters to be trampled by their own chariots. Akhilleus is larger than life.

The ideal warrior on the Trojan side is Hektor, son of Priam. His role as a warrior seems to be balanced by a sensitivity toward his wife Andrómakhê and his son Astýanax. By modern standards, Hektor represents the whole man. In one of the most poignant scenes in the epic, Andrómakhê explains her fears about how his family will be abused should Hektor be killed in battle. In response, Hektor explains his duty as a warrior, then turns to his son:

> As he said this, Hektor held out his arms
> to take his baby. But the child squirmed round
> on the nurse's bosom and began to wail,
> terrified by his father's great war helm—
> the flashing bronze, the crest with horsehair plume
> tossed like a living thing at every nod.

In this brief scene, Homer deftly portrays the two sides of warfare: Hektor's sentiments about defending his city are admirable, but the ugly consequences for the defeated, the surviving women and children, are terrifying. All of this is captured in Astýanax's fear of his father's military outfit. The settings of the two sides further the contrast: The stark masculine world of the Akhaian warriors on the plains in front of Troy is contrasted to the beautiful, cultured city, which shelters men, women, and children. It is a tribute to Homer's breadth as an artist that he sympathizes with both worlds and both sides of the conflict, just as he apparently admires both Akhilleus and Hektor.

After Hektor is killed and Akhilleus desecrates his body, Hektor's father risks his life by personally asking Akhilleus for his son's body. A more sympathetic side of Akhilleus is revealed during their meeting when the two of them reminisce and weep about past sorrows. Hektor's burial at the end of *The Iliad* again provides a mixed message about the nature of war and the price men and women pay for heroism.

The Odyssey

In his *Poetics,* the Greek philosopher Aristotle (384–322 B.C.E.) describes the essential plot of *The Odyssey,* and except for the mention of Poseidon, it sounds very much like a modern novel:

> A certain man is absent from home for many years; he is jealously watched by Poseidon, and left desolate. Meanwhile his home is in a wretched plight—suitors are wasting his substance and plotting against his son. At length, tempest-tost, he himself arrives . . . he attacks the suitors with his own hand and is himself preserved while he destroys them.

The Odyssey divides into three parts or songs. The first section deals with Telémachus, Odysseus' son, who has grown old enough since his father's absence to become involved in the succession to the throne. The middle portion describes Odysseus' adventures on his return journey to Ithaca. The final section handles the reunion of Odysseus and Penelope and the disposal of the suitors. Homer's imagination brought these three parts together into a single epic.

One way to read Odysseus' journey and his adventures is that Odysseus himself is gaining the necessary experience and self-knowledge to confront and finally defeat the hundred suitors who threaten his household and kingdom back in Ithaca. The stories about the return of other chieftains to their kingdoms, especially Agamemnon's reception by his wife and her lover, serve as object lessons for Odysseus' own return. Quite another perspective on Odysseus' journey is that Homer has created the quintessential world traveler and that his adventures in various locales enable the poet to paint exotic pictures of the distant frontiers of the world. He tells travel stories about lotus eating, the Cyclops, island temptresses, rock-throwing giants, and water monsters. In these terms, Troy then symbolizes that exotic, seductive city on the threshold of consciousness, compelling the wanderer in each of us to give up the security of the hearth and set out for distant lands. It is probable that Odysseus has mixed feelings about returning home and having to admit to himself that the grand adventure of his life is over, that he now should be sensible and retire, leaving challenge and risk to the next generation, his son Telémachus.

The Odyssey is unique for its fascinating, strong women. Penelope, the weaving wife, keeps her hand on Ithaca's throne while holding off the hoard of suitors for years on end. A brief glimpse of Helen confirms her reputation for beauty and power; she still exercises her charms over the opposite sex. Both Calypso and Círcë arise out of a male fantasy about spending an eternity with a beautiful woman on a desert island. Although some of Homer's best writing celebrates the attributes of warriors, his portrayal of the lovely princess Nausícaa, Odysseus' final temptation before home, is tender and sympathetic, as are his treatments of the soldier Elpénor, the nurse Eurycleia, and the loyal swineherd.

A comparison between the two principal heroes of Homer's epics is inevitable. When Odysseus visits Hades and meets the shade of Achilles, Odysseus speaks about the honor and fame equal to the gods associated with Achilles' deeds and his rank in the underworld; Achilles responds:

> Odysseus, don't embellish death for me.
> I'd rather be another's hired hand,
> working for some poor man who owns no land
> but pays his rent from what scant gains he gets,
> than to rule over all whom death has crushed.

This speech somewhat undercuts the earlier, youthful Achilles who chose glory, regardless of the fatal consequence. Odysseus represents a more complicated, thoughtful warrior who will be honored later by cultures that value mental as well as physical prowess. Although *The Iliad* was at one time considered by some scholars to be the superior poem, the complex character of Odysseus, his series of marvelous adventures, and the strong, interesting women are likely to make *The Odyssey* the favorite with many modern readers.

CONCLUSION

The modern study of Homer's epics was transformed by German archaeologist Heinrich Schliemann, who, in the 1870s–1890s, discovered the remains of the legendary city of Troy—actually several Troys one on top of the other—on the northwest coast of Turkey. He then uncovered Mycenae, the palace of the legendary King Agamemnon. Schliemann uncovered a historical world to which one could attach Homer's texts. As modern readers we can now better appreciate how the defeat of Troy provided Greece a legacy for hundreds of years. Important families traced their descent from Achaean warriors. Greek cities claimed they had been founded by returning warriors from Troy. Other peoples found their ancestors in the Trojans. In the great Roman epic *The Aeneid,* Virgil made use of the tradition that a Trojan warrior, Aeneas, survived the defeat of Troy and eventually led a small band to the shores of Italy, where he established an ancestral line that led to Julius Caesar and the Roman Empire.

As H. D. F. Kitto puts it, "The *Iliad* and the *Odyssey* have been called the Bible of the Greeks. For centuries these two poems were the basis of Greek education, both of formal school education and of the cultural life of the ordinary citizen." Homer's genius had an influence on the other arts as well. Both poems are so wonderfully visual, so filled with brilliant imagery, that whole scenes come to life. In addition, the visualization of Greek deities made them accessible and models for human behavior, not mysterious and inscrutable like the Hebrew Yahweh, a deity who was heard and not seen. Homer's visual interest was later translated into the glories of Greek drama, sculpture, and vase paintings; scenes and allusions from classical art and literature were used again and again from the Renaissance down to our own time.

Suggested Readings

Historical background for Homer's poems can be found in John Forsdyke's *Greece before Homer: Ancient Chronology and Mythology* (1964) and Martin P. Nilsson's *A History of Greek Religion* (1964). A good introduction to Homer and the issues surrounding the oral tradition is in G. S. Kirk's *Homer and the Oral Tradition* (1976). Martin Mueller's *The Iliad* (1984) and Jasper Griffin's *The Odyssey* (1987) provide excellent introductions to the individual poems. A good collection of essays on the poems is an edition by George Steiner and Robert Fagles, *Homer: A Collection of Critical Essays* (1962).

The Iliad

Translated by Robert Fitzgerald[1]

BOOK 1
Quarrel, Oath, and Promise

Anger be now your song, immortal one,[2]
Akhilleus' anger, doomed and ruinous,
that caused the Akhaians[3] loss on bitter loss
and crowded brave souls into the undergloom,
leaving so many dead men—carrion
for dogs and birds; and the will of Zeus was done.
Begin it when the two men first contending
broke with one another—
the Lord Marshal
Agamémnon, Atreus' son, and Prince Akhilleus.

Among the gods, who brought this quarrel on? 10
The son of Zeus by Lêto.[4] Agamémnon
angered him, so he made a burning wind
of plague rise in the army: rank and file
sickened and died for the ill their chief had done
in despising a man of prayer.
This priest, Khrysês,[5] had come down to the ships
with gifts, no end of ransom for his daughter;
on a golden staff he carried the god's white bands
and sued for grace from the men of all Akhaia,
the two Atreidai[6] most of all:
"O captains 20
Meneláos and Agamémnon, and you other

[1]This translator does not use the more common Latinized spelling of names, such as Achilles and Achaeans, but versions closer to Greek spelling and pronunciation.
[2]The Muse, spirit of inspiration.
[3]The Greek forces; also called Danaans and Argives.
[4]Apollo.
[5]His daughter is Khrysêis and his town is Khrysê.
[6]That is, sons of Atreus: Agamémnon and Meneláos.

Akhaians under arms!
The gods who hold Olympos, may they grant you
plunder of Priam's town and a fair wind home,
but let me have my daughter back for ransom
as you revere Apollo, son of Zeus!"

Then all the soldiers murmured their assent:
"Behave well to the priest. And take the ransom!"

But Agamémnon would not. It went against his desire,
and brutally he ordered the man away: 30
"Let me not find you here by the long ships
loitering this time or returning later,
old man; if I do,
the staff and ribbons of the god will fail you.
Give up the girl? I swear she will grow old
at home in Argos,[7] far from her own country,
working my loom and visiting my bed.
Leave me in peace and go, while you can, in safety."

So harsh he was, the old man feared and obeyed him,
in silence trailing away 40
by the shore of the tumbling clamorous whispering sea,
and he prayed and prayed again, as he withdrew,
to the god whom silken-braided Lêto bore:
"O hear me, master of the silver bow,
protector of Ténedos[8] and the holy towns,
Apollo, Sminthian,[9] if to your liking
ever in any grove I roofed a shrine
or burnt thighbones in fat upon your altar—
bullock or goat flesh—let my wish come true:
your arrows on the Danáäns for my tears!" 50

Now when he heard this prayer, Phoibos Apollo
walked with storm in his heart from Olympos' crest,
quiver and bow at his back, and the bundled arrows
clanged on the sky behind as he rocked in his anger,
descending like night itself. Apart from the ships
he halted and let fly, and the bowstring slammed
as the silver bow sprang, rolling in thunder away.
Pack animals were his target first, and dogs,
but soldiers, too, soon felt transfixing pain
from his hard shots, and pyres burned night and day. 60
Nine days the arrows of the god came down
broadside upon the army. On the tenth,
Akhilleus called all ranks to assembly. Hêra,[10]
whose arms are white as ivory, moved him to it,

---

[7] A region of southern Greece.
[8] An island off the coast.
[9] A name for Apollo meaning "mouse god."
[10] Wife of Zeus; she supports the Greeks.

as she took pity on Danáäns dying.
All being mustered, all in place and quiet,
Akhilleus, fast in battle as a lion,
rose and said:
"Agamémnon, now, I take it,
the siege is broken, we are going to sail,
and even so may not leave death behind: 70
if war spares anyone, disease will take him...
We might, though, ask some priest or some diviner,
even some fellow good at dreams—for dreams
come down from Zeus as well—
why all this anger of the god Apollo?

Has he some quarrel with us for a failure
in vows or hekatombs?[11] Would mutton burned
or smoking goat flesh make him lift the plague?"

Putting the question, down he sat. And Kalkhas,
Kalkhas Thestórides, came forward, wisest 80
by far of all who scanned the flight of birds.[12]
He knew what was, what had been, what would be,
Kalkhas, who brought Akhaia's ships to Ilion[13]
by the diviner's gift Apollo gave him.
Now for their benefit he said:
"Akhilleus,
dear to Zeus, it is on me you call
to tell you why the Archer God is angry.
Well, I can tell you. Are you listening? Swear
by heaven that you will back me and defend me,
because I fear my answer will enrage 90
a man with power in Argos, one whose word
Akhaian troops obey.
A great man in his rage is formidable
for underlings: though he may keep it down,
he cherishes the burning in his belly
until a reckoning day. Think well
if you will save me."

Said Akhilleus:
"Courage.
Tell what you know, what you have light to know.
I swear by Apollo, the lord god to whom
you pray when you uncover truth, 100
never while I draw breath, while I have eyes to see,
shall any man upon this beachhead dare
lay hands on you—not one of all the army,
not Agamémnon, if it is he you mean,
though he is first in rank of all Akhaians."

---

[11]Sacrifices to the gods.
[12]Seers used the flights of birds as oracles.
[13]Troy.

The diviner then took heart and said:

"No failure
in hekatombs or vows is held against us.
It is the man of prayer whom Agamémnon
treated with contempt: he kept his daughter,
spurned his gifts: for that man's sake the Archer 110
visited grief upon us and will again.
Relieve the Danáäns of this plague he will not
until the girl who turns the eyes of men
shall be restored to her own father—freely,
with no demand for ransom—and until
we offer up a hekatomb at Khrysê.
Then only can we calm him and persuade him."

He finished and sat down. The son of Atreus,
ruler of the great plain, Agamémnon,
rose, furious. Round his heart resentment 120
welled, and his eyes shone out like licking fire.
Then, with a long and boding look at Kalkhas,
he growled at him:

"You visionary of hell,
never have I had fair play in your forecasts.
Calamity is all you care about, or see,
no happy portents; and you bring to pass
nothing agreeable. Here you stand again
before the army, giving it out as oracle
the Archer made them suffer because of me,
because I would not take the gifts 130
and let the girl Khrysêis go; I'd have her
mine, at home. Yes, if you like, I rate her
higher than Klytaimnestra, my own wife!
She loses nothing by comparison
in beauty or womanhood, in mind or skill.

For all of that, I am willing now to yield her
if it is best; I want the army saved
and not destroyed. You must prepare, however,
a prize of honor for me, and at once,
that I may not be left without my portion— 140
I, of all Argives. It is not fitting so.
While every man of you looks on, my girl
goes elsewhere."

Prince Akhilleus answered him:

"Lord Marshal, most insatiate of men,
how can the army make you a new gift?
Where is our store of booty? Can you see it?
Everything plundered from the towns has been
distributed; should troops turn all that in?
Just let the girl go, in the god's name, now; 150
we'll make it up to you, twice over, three

times over, on that day Zeus gives us leave
to plunder Troy behind her rings of stone."

Agamémnon answered:

"Not that way
will I be gulled, brave as you are, Akhilleus.
Take me in, would you? Try to get around me?
What do you really ask? That you may keep
your own winnings, I am to give up mine
and sit here wanting her? Oh, no:
the army will award a prize to me 160
and make sure that it measures up, or if
they do not, I will take a girl myself,
your own, or Aías', or Odysseus'[14] prize!
Take her, yes, to keep. The man I visit
may choke with rage; well, let him.
But this, I say, we can decide on later.

Look to it now, we launch on the great sea
a well-found ship, and get her manned with oarsmen,
load her with sacrificial beasts and put aboard
Khrysêis in her loveliness. My deputy, 170
Aías, Idómeneus,[15] or Prince Odysseus,
or you, Akhilleus, fearsome as you are,
will make the hekatomb and quiet the Archer."

Akhilleus frowned and looked at him, then said:

"You thick-skinned, shameless, greedy fool!
Can any Akhaian care for you, or obey you,
after this on marches or in battle?
As for myself, when I came here to fight,
I had no quarrel with Troy or Trojan spearmen:
they never stole my cattle or my horses, 180
never in the black farmland of Phthía[16]
ravaged my crops. How many miles there are
of shadowy mountains, foaming seas, between!
No, no, we joined for you, you insolent boor,
to please you, fighting for your brother's sake
and yours, to get revenge upon the Trojans.
You overlook this, dogface, or don't care,
and now in the end you threaten to take my girl,
a prize I sweated for, and soldiers gave me!

Never have I had plunder like your own 190
from any Trojan stronghold battered down
by the Akhaians. I have seen more action
hand to hand in those assaults than you have,

[14] Two famous Greek warriors: Aías is known for bravery; Odysseus, hero of *The Odyssey*, is exceedingly clever.

[15] Ruler of Krete.

[16] Akhilleus' home in northern Greece.

but when the time for sharing comes, the greater
share is always yours. Worn out with battle
I carry off some trifle to my ships.
Well, this time I make sail for home.
Better to take now to my ships. Why linger,
cheated of winnings, to make wealth for you?"

To this the high commander made reply: 200
"Desért, if that's the way the wind blows. Will I
beg you to stay on my account? I will not.
Others will honor me, and Zeus who views
the wide world most of all.
No officer
is hateful to my sight as you are, none
given like you to faction, as to battle—
rugged you are, I grant, by some god's favor.
Sail, then, in your ships, and lord it over
your own battalion of Myrmidons.[17] I do not
give a curse for you, or for your anger. 210
But here is warning for you:
Khrysêis
being required of me by Phoibos Apollo,
she will be sent back in a ship of mine,
manned by my people. That done, I myself
will call for Brisêis at your hut, and take her,
flower of young girls that she is, your prize,
to show you here and now who is stronger
and make the next man sick at heart—if any
think of claiming equal place with me."

A pain like grief weighed on the son of Pêleus,[18] 220
and in his shaggy chest this way and that
the passion of his heart ran: should he draw
longsword from hip, stand off the rest, and kill
in single combat the great son of Atreus,
or hold his rage in check and give it time?
And as this tumult swayed him, as he slid
the big blade slowly from the sheath, Athêna[19]
came to him from the sky. The white-armed goddess,
Hêra, sent her, being fond of both,
concerned for both men. And Athêna, stepping 230
up behind him, visible to no one
except Akhilleus, gripped his red-gold hair.

Startled, he made a half turn, and he knew her
upon the instant for Athêna: terribly

---

[17]Akhilleus' followers.

[18]Akhilleus' father.

[19]Virgin goddess, daughter of Zeus, patron of Athens, associated with crafts and wisdom; she strongly favors the Greeks.

her grey eyes blazed at him. And speaking softly
but rapidly aside to her he said:

"What now, O daughter of the god of heaven
who bears the stormcloud, why are you here? To see
the wolfishness of Agamémnon?
Well, I give you my word: this time, and soon, 240
he pays for his behavior with his blood."

The grey-eyed goddess Athêna said to him:

"It was to check this killing rage I came
from heaven, if you will listen. Hêra sent me,
being fond of both of you, concerned for both.
Enough: break off this combat, stay your hand
upon the sword hilt. Let him have a lashing
with words, instead: tell him how things will be.
Here is my promise, and it will be kept:
winnings three times as rich, in due season, 250
you shall have in requital for his arrogance.
But hold your hand. Obey."

The great runner,
Akhilleus, answered:

"Nothing for it, goddess,
but when you two immortals speak, a man
complies, though his heart burst. Just as well.
Honor the gods' will, they may honor ours."

On this he stayed his massive hand
upon the silver pommel, and the blade
of his great weapon slid back in the scabbard.
The man had done her bidding. Off to Olympos, 260
gaining the air, she went to join the rest,
the powers of heaven in the home of Zeus.

But now the son of Pêleus turned on Agamémnon
and lashed out at him, letting his anger ride
in execration:

"Sack of wine,
you with your cur's eyes and your antelope heart!
You've never had the kidney to buckle on
armor among the troops, or make a sortie
with picked men—oh, no; that way death might lie.
Safer, by god, in the middle of the army— 270
is it not?—to commandeer the prize
of any man who stands up to you! Leech!
Commander of trash! If not, I swear,
you never could abuse one soldier more!

But here is what I say: my oath upon it
by this great staff: look: leaf or shoot
it cannot sprout again, once lopped away

from the log it left behind in the timbered hills;
it cannot flower, peeled of bark and leaves;
instead, Akhaian officers in council 280
take it in hand by turns, when they observe
by the will of Zeus due order in debate:
let this be what I swear by then: I swear
a day will come when every Akhaian soldier
will groan to have Akhilleus back. That day
you shall no more prevail on me than this
dry wood shall flourish—driven though you are,
and though a thousand men perish before
the killer, Hektor.[20] You will eat your heart out,
raging with remorse for this dishonor 290
done by you to the bravest of Akhaians."

He hurled the staff, studded with golden nails,
before him on the ground. Then down he sat,
and fury filled Agamémnon, looking across at him.
But for the sake of both men Nestor arose,
the Pylians' orator, eloquent and clear;
argument sweeter than honey rolled from his tongue.
By now he had outlived two generations
of mortal men, his own and the one after,
in Pylos[21] land, and still ruled in the third. 300
In kind reproof he said:

"A black day, this.
Bitter distress comes this way to Akhaia.
How happy Priam and Priam's sons would be,
and all the Trojans—wild with joy—if they
got wind of all these fighting words between you,
foremost in council as you are, foremost
in battle. Give me your attention. Both
are younger men than I, and in my time
men who were even greater have I known
and none of them disdained me. Men like those 310
I have not seen again, nor shall: Peiríthoös,
the Lord Marshal Dryas, Kaineus, Exádios,
Polyphêmos, Theseus—Aigeus' son,
a man like the immortal gods. I speak
of champions among men of earth, who fought
with champions, with wild things of the mountains,
great centaurs whom they broke and overpowered.
Among these men I say I had my place
when I sailed out of Pylos, my far country,
because they called for me. I fought 320
for my own hand among them. Not one man
alive now upon earth could stand against them.
And I repeat: they listened to my reasoning,

[20] Son of Priam, the best of Trojan warriors.
[21] On the western edge of the Peloponnese.

took my advice. Well, then, you take it too.
It is far better so.

Lord Agamémnon,
do not deprive him of the girl, renounce her.
The army had allotted her to him.
Akhilleus, for your part, do not defy
your King and Captain. No one vies in honor
with him who holds authority from Zeus. 330
You have more prowess, for a goddess bore you;[22]
his power over men surpasses yours.

But, Agamémnon, let your anger cool.
I beg you to relent, knowing Akhilleus
a sea wall for Akhaians in the black waves of war."

Lord Agamémnon answered:

"All you say
is fairly said, sir, but this man's ambition,
remember, is to lead, to lord it over
everyone, hold power over everyone,
give orders to the rest of us! Well, one 340
will never take his orders! If the gods
who live forever made a spearman of him,
have they put insults on his lips as well?"

Akhilleus interrupted:

"What a poltroon,[23]
how lily-livered I should be called, if I
knuckled under to all you do or say!
Give your commands to someone else, not me!
And one more thing I have to tell you: think it
over: this time, for the girl, I will not
wrangle in arms with you or anyone, 350
though I am robbed of what was given me;
but as for any other thing I have
alongside my black ship, you shall not take it
against my will. Try it. Hear this, everyone:
that instant your hot blood blackens my spear!"

They quarreled in this way, face to face, and then
broke off the assembly by the ships. Akhilleus
made his way to his squadron and his quarters,
Patróklos[24] by his side, with his companions.

Agamémnon proceeded to launch a ship, 360
assigned her twenty oarsmen, loaded beasts

[22] Thetis, a nymph, was for a time a companion of Pêleus.
[23] Coward.
[24] Akhilleus' closest friend.

for sacrifice to the god, then set aboard
Khrysêis in her loveliness. The versatile
Odysseus took the deck, and, all oars manned,
they pulled out on the drenching ways of sea.
The troops meanwhile were ordered to police camp
and did so, throwing refuse in the water;
then to Apollo by the barren surf
they carried out full-tally hekatombs,
and the savor curled in crooked smoke toward heaven. 370

That was the day's work in the army.
Agamémnon
had kept his threat in mind, and now he acted,
calling Eurýbatês and Talthýbios,
his aides and criers:
"Go along," he said,
"both of you, to the quarters of Akhilleus
and take his charming Brisêis by the hand
to bring to me. And if he balks at giving her
I shall be there myself with men-at-arms
in force to take her—all the more gall for him."
So, ominously, he sent them on their way, 380
and they who had no stomach for it went
along the waste sea shingle toward the ships
and shelters of the Myrmidons. Not far
from his black ship and hut they found the prince
in the open, seated. And seeing these two come
was cheerless to Akhilleus. Shamefast, pale
with fear of him, they stood without a word;
but he knew what they felt and called out:
"Peace to you,
criers and couriers of Zeus and men!
Come forward. Not one thing have I against you: 390
Agamémnon is the man who sent you
for Brisêis. Here then, my lord Patróklos,
bring out the girl and give her to these men.
And let them both bear witness before the gods
who live in bliss, as before men who die,
including this harsh king, if ever hereafter
a need for me arises to keep the rest
from black defeat and ruin.
Lost in folly,
the man cannot think back or think ahead
how to come through a battle by the ships." 400
Patróklos did the bidding of his friend,
led from the hut Brisêis in her beauty
and gave her to them. Back along the ships
they took their way, and the girl went, loath to go.

Leaving his friends in haste, Akhilleus wept,
and sat apart by the grey wave, scanning the endless sea.
Often he spread his hands in prayer to his mother:

"As my life came from you, though it is brief,
honor at least from Zeus who storms in heaven
I call my due. He gives me precious little. 410
See how the lord of the great plains, Agamémnon,
humiliated me! He has my prize,
by his own whim, for himself."

Eyes wet with tears,
he spoke, and her ladyship his mother heard him
in green deeps where she lolled near her old father.[25]
Gliding she rose and broke like mist from the inshore
grey sea face, to sit down softly before him,
her son in tears; and fondling him she said:
"Child, why do you weep? What grief is this?
Out with it, tell me, both of us should know." 420
Akhilleus, fast in battle as a lion,
groaned and said:

"Why tell you what you know?
We sailed out raiding, and we took by storm
that ancient town of Eëtiôn called Thêbê,
plundered the place, brought slaves and spoils away.
At the division, later,
they chose a young girl, Khrysêis, for the king.
Then Khrysês, priest of the Archer God, Apollo,
came to the beachhead we Akhaians hold,
bringing no end of ransom for his daughter; 430
he had the god's white bands on a golden staff
and sued for grace from the army of Akhaia,
mostly the two Atreidai, corps commanders.
All of our soldiers murmured in assent:
'Behave well to the priest. And take the ransom!'
But Agamémnon would not. It went against his desire,
and brutally he ordered the man away.
So the old man withdrew in grief and anger.
Apollo cared for him: he heard his prayer
and let black bolts of plague fly on the Argives. 440

One by one our men came down with it
and died hard as the god's shots raked the army
broadside. But our priest divined the cause
and told us what the god meant by plague.

I said, 'Appease the god!' but Agamémnon
could not contain his rage; he threatened me,
and what he threatened is now done—
one girl the Akhaians are embarking now
for Khrysê beach with gifts for Lord Apollo;
the other, just now, from my hut—the criers 450
came and took her, Briseus' girl, my prize,
given by the army.

[25]Nereus, father of the sea-nymphs.

If you can, stand by me:
go to Olympos, pray to Zeus, if ever
by word or deed you served him—
and so you did, I often heard you tell it
in Father's house: that time when you alone
of all the gods shielded the son of Krónos[26]
from peril and disgrace—when other gods,
Pallas Athêna, Hêra, and Poseidon,[27]
wished him in irons, wished to keep him bound, 460
you had the will to free him of that bondage,
and called up to Olympos in all haste
Aigaion, whom the gods call Briareus,[28]
the giant with a hundred arms, more powerful
than the sea-god, his father. Down he sat
by the son of Krónos, glorying in that place.
For fear of him the blissful gods forbore
to manacle Zeus.
Remind him of these things,
cling to his knees and tell him your good pleasure
if he will take the Trojan side 470
and roll the Akhaians back to the water's edge,
back on the ships with slaughter! All the troops
may savor what their king has won for them,
and he may know his madness, what he lost
when he dishonored me, peerless among Akhaians."

Her eyes filled, and a tear fell as she answered:
"Alas, my child, why did I rear you, doomed
the day I bore you?[29] Ah, could you only be
serene upon this beachhead through the siege,
your life runs out so soon. 480
Oh early death! Oh broken heart! No destiny
so cruel! And I bore you to this evil!

But what you wish I will propose
To Zeus, lord of the lightning, going up
myself into the snow-glare of Olympos
with hope for his consent.
Be quiet now
beside the long ships, keep your anger bright
against the army, quit the war.
Last night
Zeus made a journey to the shore of Ocean
to feast among the Sunburned,[30] and the gods 490
accompanied him. In twelve days he will come
back to Olympos. Then I shall be there

[26]Father of Zeus and previous ruler of the universe.
[27]God of the ocean, Zeus' brother.
[28]A giant, son of Poseidon.
[29]Akhilleus is fated to die at an early age.
[30]The Ethiopians, who lived at the edge of the world, which was surrounded by Ocean.

to cross his bronze doorsill and take his knees.
I trust I'll move him."

Thetis left her son
still burning for the softly belted girl
whom they had wrested from him.

Meanwhile Odysseus
with his shipload of offerings came to Khrysê.
Entering the deep harbor there
they furled the sails and stowed them, and unbent
forestays to ease the mast down quickly aft 500
into its rest; then rowed her to a mooring.
Bow-stones were dropped, and they tied up astern,
and all stepped out into the wash and ebb,
then disembarked their cattle for the Archer,
and Khrysêis, from the deepsea ship. Odysseus,
the great tactician, led her to the altar,
putting her in her father's hands, and said:

"Khrysês, as Agamémnon's emissary
I bring your child to you, and for Apollo
a hekatomb in the Danáäns' name. 510
We trust in this way to appease your lord,
who sent down pain and sorrow on the Argives."

So he delivered her, and the priest received her,
the child so dear to him, in joy. Then hastening
to give the god his hekatomb, they led
bullocks to crowd around the compact altar,
rinsed their hands and delved in barley baskets,
as open-armed to heaven Khrysês prayed:

"Oh hear me, master of the silver bow,
protector of Ténedos and the holy towns, 520
if while I prayed you listened once before
and honored me, and punished the Akhaians,
now let my wish come true again. But turn
your plague away this time from the Danáäns."

And this petition, too, Apollo heard.
When prayers were said and grains of barley strewn,
they held the bullocks for the knife, and flayed them,
cutting out joints and wrapping these in fat,
two layers, folded, with raw strips of flesh,
for the old man to burn on cloven faggots, 530
wetting it all with wine.

Around him stood
young men with five-tined forks in hand, and when
the vitals had been tasted, joints consumed,
they sliced the chines and quarters for the spits,
roasted them evenly and drew them off.
Their meal being now prepared and all work done,
they feasted to their hearts' content and made
desire for meat and drink recede again,

then young men filled their winebowls to the brim,
ladling drops for the god in every cup. 540
Propitiatory songs rose clear and strong
until day's end, to praise the god, Apollo,
as One Who Keeps the Plague Afar; and listening
the god took joy.
After the sun went down
and darkness came, at last Odysseus' men
lay down to rest under the stern hawsers.

When Dawn spread out her finger tips of rose
they put to sea for the main camp of Akhaians,
and the Archer God sent them a following wind.
Stepping the mast they shook their canvas out, 550
and wind caught, bellying the sail. A foaming
dark blue wave sang backward from the bow
as the running ship made way against the sea,
until they came offshore of the encampment.
Here they put in and hauled the black ship high,
far up the sand, braced her with shoring timbers,
and then disbanded, each to his own hut.

Meanwhile unstirring and with smoldering heart,
the godlike athlete, son of Pêleus, Prince
Akhilleus waited by his racing ships. 560
He would not enter the assembly
of emulous men, nor ever go to war,
but felt his valor staling in his breast
with idleness, and missed the cries of battle.

Now when in fact twelve days had passed, the gods
who live forever turned back to Olympos,
with Zeus in power supreme among them.
Thetis
had kept in mind her mission for her son,
and rising like a dawn mist from the sea
into a cloud she soared aloft in heaven 570
to high Olympos. Zeus with massive brows
she found apart, on the chief crest enthroned,
and slipping down before him, her left hand
placed on his knees and her right hand held up
to cup his chin, she made her plea to him:[31]
"O Father Zeus, if ever amid immortals
by word or deed I served you, grant my wish
and see to my son's honor! Doom for him
of all men came on quickest.
Now Lord Marshal
Agamémnon has been highhanded with him, 580
has commandeered and holds his prize of war.

[31] The posture of a supplicant.

But you can make him pay for this, profound
mind of Olympos!
Lend the Trojans power,
until the Akhaians recompense my son
and heap new honor upon him!"

When she finished,
the gatherer of cloud said never a word
but sat unmoving for a long time, silent.
Thetis clung to his knees, then spoke again:
"Give your infallible word, and bow your head,
or else reject me. Can you be afraid 590
to let me see how low in your esteem
I am of all the gods?"

Greatly perturbed,
Lord Zeus who masses cloud said:

"Here is trouble.
You drive me into open war with Hêra
sooner or later:
she will be at me, scolding all day long.
Even as matters stand she never rests
from badgering me before the gods: I take
the Trojan side in battle, so she says.

Go home before you are seen. But you can trust me 600
to put my mind on this; I shall arrange it.
Here let me bow my head, then be content
to see me bound by that most solemn act
before the gods. My word is not revocable
nor ineffectual, once I nod upon it."

He bent his ponderous black brows down, and locks
ambrosial of his immortal head
swung over them, as all Olympos trembled.
After this pact they parted: misty Thetis
from glittering Olympos leapt away 610
into the deep sea; Zeus to his hall retired.
There all the gods rose from their seats in deference
before their father; not one dared
face him unmoved, but all stood up before him,
and thus he took his throne.

But Hêra knew
he had new interests; she had seen
the goddess Thetis, silvery-footed daughter
of the Old One of the sea, conferring with him,
and, nagging, she inquired of Zeus Kroníon:

"Who is it this time, schemer? Who has your ear? 620
How fond you are of secret plans, of taking
decisions privately! You could not bring yourself,

could you, to favor me with any word
of your new plot?"

The father of gods and men
said in reply:

"Hêra, all my provisions
you must not itch to know.
You'll find them rigorous, consort though you are.
In all appropriate matters no one else,
no god or man, shall be advised before you.
But when I choose to think alone, 630
don't harry me about it with your questions."
The Lady Hêra answered, with wide eyes:

"Majesty, what a thing to say. I have not
'harried' you before with questions, surely;
you are quite free to tell what you will tell.
This time I dreadfully fear—I have a feeling—
Thetis, the silvery-footed daughter
of the Old One of the Sea, led you astray.
Just now at daybreak, anyway, she came
to sit with you and take your knees; my guess is 640
you bowed your head for her in solemn pact
that you will see to the honor of Akhilleus—
that is, to Akhaian carnage near the ships."

Now Zeus the gatherer of cloud said:

"Marvelous,
you and your guesses; you are near it, too.
But there is not one thing that you can do about it,
only estrange yourself still more from me—
all the more gall for you. If what you say
is true, you may be sure it pleases me.
And now you just sit down, be still, obey me, 650
or else not all the gods upon Olympos
can help in the least when I approach your chair
to lay my inexorable hands upon you."
At this the wide-eyed Lady Hêra feared him,
and sat quite still, and bent her will to his.
Up through the hall of Zeus now all the lords
of heaven were sullen and looked askance. Hêphaistos,[32]
master artificer, broke the silence,
doing a kindness to the snowy-armed
lady, his mother Hêra.

He began: 660
"Ah, what a miserable day, if you two
raise your voices over mortal creatures!

[32] God of fire and metallurgy.

More than enough already! Must you bring
your noisy bickering among the gods?
What pleasure can we take in a fine dinner
when baser matters gain the upper hand?
To Mother my advice is—what she knows—
better make up to Father, or he'll start
his thundering and shake our feast to bits.
You know how he can shock us if he cares to— 670
out of our seats with lightning bolts!
Supreme power is his. Oh, soothe him, please,
take a soft tone, get back in his good graces.
Then he'll be benign to us again."
He lurched up as he spoke, and held a winecup
out to her, a double-handed one,
and said:

"Dear Mother, patience, hold your tongue,
no matter how upset you are. I would not
see you battered, dearest.

It would hurt me,
and yet I could not help you, not a bit. 680
The Olympian is difficult to oppose.
One other time I took your part he caught me
around one foot and flung me
into the sky from our tremendous terrace.
I soared all day! Just as the sun dropped down
I dropped down, too, on Lemnos—nearly dead.
The island people nursed a fallen god."

He made her smile—and the goddess, white-armed Hêra,
smiling took the winecup from his hand.
Then, dipping from the winebowl, round he went 690
from left to right, serving the other gods
nectar of sweet delight.

And quenchless laughter
broke out among the blissful gods
to see Hêphaistos wheezing down the hall.
So all day long until the sun went down
they spent in feasting, and the measured feast
matched well their hearts' desire.
So did the flawless harp held by Apollo
and heavenly songs in choiring antiphon
that all the Muses sang.

And when the shining 700
sun of day sank in the west, they turned
homeward each one to rest, each to that home
the bandy-legged wondrous artisan
Hêphaistos fashioned for them with his craft.
The lord of storm and lightning, Zeus, retired
and shut his eyes where sweet sleep ever came to him,
and at his side lay Hêra, Goddess of the Golden Chair.

FROM BOOK 6

INTERLUDES IN FIELD AND CITY

[In Book 2, a council of Greek leaders decides to test the troops. Agamémnon suggests that they all go home and the men begin to leave. Inspired by Athêna, Odysseus convinces everyone to stay by reminding them of Kalkhas' prophecy of victory in the tenth year. In Book 3, both sides agree to a single combat between Meneláos and Paris to settle the war. Meneláos wins the duel, but Paris is saved from certain death by the goddess Aphrodite. In Book 4, Hêra wants to see Troy destroyed and Zeus agrees to let the war continue. In Book 5, Diomêdês performs heroic feats by slaying many Trojans and wounding others. Aeneas is wounded, but then rescued by Apollo and Aphrodite. Diomêdês finally wounds Arês, the god of war, who has been assisting the Trojans, and is now forced to withdraw, along with Hêra and Athêna. At the beginning of Book 6, the Trojans begin to retreat and Hektor is summoned back to Troy to tell the women to provide offerings to Athêna so that they might restrain Diomêdês, who is about to fight Glaukos. The two of them make an interesting discovery.–ED.]

. . . Meanwhile, driving into an open space
between the armies, Hippólokhos' son, Glaukos,
and Diomêdês advanced upon each other,
hot for combat. When the range was short,
Diomêdês, face to face with him, spoke up:

"Young gallant stranger, who are you?
I have not noticed you before in battle—
never before, in the test that brings men honor—
but here you come now, far in front of everyone,
with heart enough to risk my beam of spear. 10
A sorrowing old age they have whose children
face me in war! If you are a god from heaven,
I would not fight with any out of heaven.
No long life remained—far from it—for
Lykourgos,[33] Dryas' rugged son,
when he in his day strove with gods—that time
he chased the maenads on the sacred ridge
of manic Dionysos, on Mount Nysa.
Belabored by the ox-goad of Lykourgos,
killer that he was, they all flung down 20
their ivy-staves, while terrified Dionysos
plunged under a sea-surge. In her arms
Thetis received him, shaking from head to foot,
after that yelling man's pursuit.
And now the gods whose life is ease
turned on Lykourgos; Zeus put out his eyes;
his days were numbered, hated by them all.
I would not fight, not I, with gods in bliss,
but you, if you are man and mortal, one
who feeds on harvest of the grainland, take 30
one step nearer! and before you know it
you will come up against the edge of death."

[33]Lykourgos, king of the Edonians, used an ox-goad to drive away the wine-god Dionysos and his followers. Descriptions of Lykourgos' punishments vary.

Hippólokhos' distinguished son replied:

"Why ask my birth, Diomêdês? Very like leaves
upon this earth are the generations of men—
old leaves, cast on the ground by wind, young leaves
the greening forest bears when spring comes in.
So mortals pass; one generation flowers
even as another dies away.
My lineage?
If you are really bent on knowing all— 40
and many others know my story—listen.
Ephýra is a city on the gulf
of Argos: in Ephýra Sísyphos
Aiólidês, the craftiest of men,
lived once upon a time and fathered Glaukos,
father in turn of Prince Bellérophontês,
one to whom the gods had given beauty
with charm and bravery. But there came a day
when Proitos wished him ill—and Zeus had put him
under the power of Proitos. That strong king 50
now drove Bellérophontês out of Argos:
this because Ánteia, the queen,
lusted to couple with him secretly,
but he was honorable, she could not lure him,
and in the king's ear hissed a lie:
'Oh, Proitos,
I wish that you may die unless you kill
Bellérophontês: he desired to take me
in lust against my will.'
Rage filled the king
over her slander, but being scrupulous
he shrank from killing him. So into Lykia 60
he sent him, charged to bear a deadly cipher,
magical marks Proitos engraved and hid
in folded tablets. He commanded him
to show these to his father-in-law,
thinking in this way he should meet his end.
Guided by gods he sailed, and came to Lykia,
high country, crossed by Xánthos' running stream;
and Lykia's lord received him well.
Nine days he honored him, nine revels led
with consecrated beasts. When Dawn with rosy 70
fingers eastward made the tenth day bright,
he questioned him, and asked at length to see
what sign he brought him from his son-in-law.
When he had read the deadly cipher, changing,
he gave his first command: his guest should fight
and quell a foaming monster, the Khimaira,
of ghastly and inhuman origin,
her forepart lionish, her tail a snake's,
a she-goat in between. This thing exhaled
in jets a rolling fire.

Well, he killed her, 80
by taking heed of omens from the gods.
His second test was battle with Solýmoi,
formidable aborigines. He thought
this fight the worst he ever had with men.
A third mission was to slaughter Amazons,
women virile in war. On his return,
the king devised yet one more trap for him,
laying an ambush, with picked men of Lykia.
But not a single one went home again:
Bellérophontês killed them all.
His eyes 90
opened at last to the young man's power, godly
from godly lineage, the king detained him,
offered him his daughter, gave him, too,
a moiety of royal privileges,
and Lykians for their part set aside
their finest land for him, vineyard and plowland,
fertile for wheatfields. The king's daughter bore
three children to Bellérophontês: Ísandros,
Hippólokhos, and Laodámeia.
Zeus the Profound lay with Laodámeia, 100
who bore Sarpêdôn, one of our great soldiers.
By now one day Bellérophontês too
incurred the gods' wrath—and alone he moped
on Alêïon plain, eating his heart out,
shunning the beaten track of men. His son
Ísandros in a skirmish with Solýmoi
met his death at insatiable Arês'[34] hands,
and angry Artemis[35] killed Laodámeia.
Hippólokhos it was who fathered me,
I am proud to say. He sent me here to Troy 110
commanding me to act always with valor,
always to be most noble, never to shame
the line of my progenitors, great men
first in Ephýra, then in Lykia.
That is the blood and birth I claim."

At this,
joy came to Diomêdês, loud in battle.
With one thrust in the field where herds had cropped
he fixed his long spear like a pole, and smiled
at the young captain, saying gently:
"Why,
you are my friend! My grandfather, Oineus, 120
made friends of us long years ago. He welcomed
Prince Bellérophontês in his hall,
his guest for twenty days. They gave each other

[34] God of war.
[35] Goddess of the hunt.

beautiful tokens of amity: Grandfather's
offering was a lion-guard sewn in purple,
Bellérophontês gave a cup of gold
two-handled; it is in my house; I left it there,
coming away to Troy. I cannot remember
Tydeus, my father—I was still too young
when he departed, when the Akhaian army 130
came to grief at Thebes.
I am your friend,
sworn friend, in central Argos. You are mine
in Lykia, whenever I may come.
So let us keep away from one another's
weapons in the spear-fights of this war.
Trojans a-plenty will be left for me,
and allies, as god puts them in my path;
many Akhaians will be left for you
to bring down if you can.
Each take the other's
battle-gear; let those around us know 140
we have this bond of friendship from our fathers."

Both men jumped down then to confirm the pact,
taking each other's hands. But Zeus
had stolen Glaukos' wits away—
the young man gave up golden gear for bronze,
took nine bulls' worth for armor worth a hundred!

Now, when Hektor reached the Skaian Gates[36]
daughters and wives of Trojans rushed to greet him
with questions about friends, sons, husbands, brothers.
"Pray to the gods!" he said to each in turn, 150
as grief awaited many. He walked on
and into Priam's palace, fair and still,
made all of ashlar,[37] with bright colonnades.
Inside were fifty rooms of polished stone
one by another, where the sons of Priam
slept beside their wives; apart from these
across an inner court were twelve rooms more
all in one line, of polished stone, where slept
the sons-in-law of Priam and their wives.
Approaching these, he met his gentle mother[38] 160
going in with Laódikê, most beautiful
of all her daughters. Both hands clasping his,
she looked at him and said:
"Why have you come
from battle, child? Those fiends, the Akhaians, fighting
around the town, have worn you out; you come

[36]The main entrance to Troy.
[37]Square stones used in building.
[38]Hékabê.

to climb our Rock[39] and lift your palms to Zeus!
Wait, and I'll serve you honeyed wine.
First you may offer up a drop to Zeus,
to the immortal gods, then slake your thirst.
Wine will restore a man when he is weary 170
as you are, fighting to defend your own."

Hektor answered her, his helmet flashing:
"No, my dear mother, ladle me no wine;
You'd make my nerve go slack: I'd lose my edge.
May I tip wine to Zeus with hands unwashed?
I fear to—a bespattered man, and bloody,
may not address the lord of gloomy cloud.
No, it is you I wish would bring together
our older women, with offerings, and go visit
the temple of Athêna, Hope of Soldiers. 180
Pick out a robe, most lovely and luxurious,
most to your liking in the women's hall;
place it upon Athêna's knees; assure her
a sacrifice of heifers, twelve young ones
ungoaded ever in their lives, if in her mercy
relenting toward our town, our wives and children,
she keeps Diomêdês out of holy Troy.
He is a wild beast now in combat and pursuit.
Make your way to her shrine, visit Athêna,
Hope of Soldiers.
As for me, I go 190
for Paris, to arouse him, if he listens.
If only earth would swallow him here and now!
What an affliction the Olympian
brought up for us in him—a curse for Priam
and Priam's children! Could I see that man
dwindle into Death's night, I'd feel my soul
relieved of its distress!"

So Hektor spoke, and she walked slowly on
into the mégaron.[40] She called her maids,
who then assembled women from the city. 200
But Hékabê went down to the low chamber
fragrant with cedar, where the robes were kept,
embroidered work by women of Sidonia
Aléxandros[41] had brought, that time he sailed
and ravished Helen, princess, pearl of kings.
Hékabê lifted out her loveliest robe,
most ample, most luxurious in brocade,
and glittering like starlight under all.
This offering she carried to Athêna
with a long line of women in her train. 210

[39]The hill on which the city rests.
[40]The great hall.
[41]Paris.

On the Akrópolis, Athêna's shrine
was opened for them by Theanô, stately
daughter of Kisseus, wife to Antênor,[42]
and chosen priestess of Athêna. Now
all crying loud stretched out their arms in prayer,
while Theanô with grace took up the robe
to place it on fair-haired Athêna's knees.
She made petition then to Zeus's daughter:

"Lady,

excellent goddess, towering friend of Troy,
smash Diomêdês' lance-haft! Throw him hard 220
below the Skaian Gates, before our eyes!
Upon this altar we'll make offering
of twelve young heifers never scarred!
Only show mercy to our town,
mercy to Trojan men, their wives and children."

These were Theanô's prayers, her vain prayers.
Pallas Athêna turned away her head.

During the supplication at the shrine,
Hektor approached the beautiful house Aléxandros
himself had made, with men who in that time 230
were master-builders in the land of Troy.
Bedchamber, hall, and court, in the upper town,
they built for him near Priam's hall and Hektor's.
Now Hektor dear to Zeus went in, his hand
gripping a spear eleven forearms long,
whose bronze head shone before him in the air
as shone, around the neck, a golden ring.
He found his brother in the bedchamber
handling a magnificent cuirass[43] and shield
and pulling at his bent-horn bow, while Helen 240
among her household women sat nearby,
directing needlecraft and splendid weaving.
At sight of him, to shame him, Hektor said:

"Unquiet soul, why be aggrieved in private?
Our troops are dying out there where they fight
around our city, under our high walls.
The hue and cry of war, because of you,
comes in like surf upon this town.
You'd be at odds with any other man
you might see quitting your accursèd war. 250
Up; into action, before torches thrown
make the town flare!"

And shining like a god

Aléxandros replied:

---

[42] A Trojan lord.
[43] Armor for breast and back.

"Ah, Hektor,
this call to order is no more than just.
So let me tell you something: hear me out.
No pettishness, resentment toward the Trojans,
kept me in this bedchamber so long,
but rather my desire, on being routed,
to taste grief to the full.
In her sweet way
my lady rouses me to fight again— 260
and I myself consider it better so.
Victory falls to one man, then another.
Wait, while I put on the wargod's gear,
or else go back; I'll follow, sure to find you."

For answer, Hektor in his shining helm
said not a word, but in low tones
enticing Helen murmured:
"Brother dear—
dear to a whore, a nightmare of a woman!
That day my mother gave me to the world
I wish a hurricane blast had torn me away 270
to wild mountains, or into tumbling sea
to be washed under by a breaking wave,
before these evil days could come!—or, granted
terrible years were in the gods' design,
I wish I had had a good man for a lover
who knew the sharp tongues and just rage of men.
This one—his heart's unsound, and always will be,
and he will win what he deserves. Come here
and rest upon this couch with me, dear brother.
You are the one afflicted most 280
by harlotry in me and by his madness,
our portion, all of misery, given by Zeus
that we may live in song for men to come."

Great Hektor shook his head, his helmet flashing,
and said:
"No, Helen, offer me no rest;
I know you are fond of me. I cannot rest.
Time presses, and I grow impatient now
to lend a hand to Trojans in the field
who feel a gap when I am gone. Your part
can be to urge him—let him feel the urgency 290
to join me in the city. He has time:
I must go home to visit my own people,
my own dear wife and my small son. Who knows
if I shall be reprieved again to see them,
or beaten down under Akhaian blows
as the immortals will."

He turned away
and quickly entered his own hall, but found

Princess Andrómakhê was not at home.
With one nursemaid and her small child, she stood
upon the tower of Ilion, in tears, 300
bemoaning what she saw.
Now Hektor halted
upon his threshold, calling to the maids:
"Tell me at once, and clearly, please,
my lady Andrómakhê, where has she gone?
To see my sisters, or my brothers' wives?
Or to Athêna's temple? Ladies of Troy
are there to make petition to the goddess."

The busy mistress of the larder answered:
"Hektor, to put it clearly as you ask,
she did not go to see your sisters, nor 310
your brothers' wives, nor to Athêna's shrine
where others are petitioning the goddess.
Up to the great square tower of Ilion
she took her way, because she heard our men
were spent in battle by Akhaian power.
In haste, like a madwoman, to the wall
she went, and Nurse went too, carrying the child."

At this word Hektor whirled and left his hall,
taking the same path he had come by,
along byways, walled lanes, all through the town 320
until he reached the Skaian Gates, whereby
before long he would issue on the field.
There his warmhearted lady
came to meet him, running: Andrómakhê,
whose father, Eëtíôn, once had ruled
the land under Mount Plakos, dark with forest,
at Thêbê under Plakos—lord and king
of the Kilikians. Hektor was her lord now,
head to foot in bronze; and now she joined him.
Behind her came her maid, who held the child 330
against her breast, a rosy baby still,
Hektoridês,[44] the world's delight, as fresh
as a pure shining star. Skamándrios
his father named him; other men would say
Astýanax, "Lord of the Lower Town,"
as Hektor singlehanded guarded Troy.
How brilliantly the warrior smiled, in silence,
his eyes upon the child! Andrómakhê
rested against him, shook away a tear,
and pressed his hand in both her own, to say: 340
"Oh, my wild one, your bravery will be
your own undoing! No pity for our child,
poor little one, or me in my sad lot—

[44] The suffix *-ides* means "son of."

soon to be deprived of you! soon, soon
Akhaians as one man will set upon you
and cut you down! Better for me, without you,
to take cold earth for mantle. No more comfort,
no other warmth, after you meet your doom,
but heartbreak only. Father is dead, and Mother.
My father great Akhilleus killed when he 350
besieged and plundered Thêbê, our high town,
citadel of Kilikians. He killed him,
but, reverent at last in this, did not
despoil him. Body, gear, and weapons forged
so handsomely, he burned, and heaped a barrow
over the ashes. Elms were planted round
by mountain-nymphs of him who bears the stormcloud.[45]
Then seven brothers that I had at home
in one day entered Death's dark place. Akhilleus,
prince and powerful runner, killed all seven 360
amid their shambling cattle and silvery sheep.
Mother, who had been queen of wooded Plakos,
he brought with other winnings home, and freed her,
taking no end of ransom. Artemis
the Huntress shot her in her father's house.
Father and mother—I have none but you,
nor brother, Hektor; lover none but you!
Be merciful! Stay here upon the tower!
Do not bereave your child and widow me!
Draw up your troops by the wild figtree; that way 370
the city lies most open, men most easily
could swarm the wall where it is low:
three times, at least, their best men tried it there
in company of the two called Aías, with
Idómeneus, the Atreidai, Diomêdês—
whether someone who had it from the oracles
had told them, or their own hearts urged them on."

Great Hektor in his shimmering helmet answered:
"Lady, these many things beset my mind
no less than yours. But I should die of shame 380
before our Trojan men and noblewomen
if like a coward I avoided battle,
nor am I moved to. Long ago I learned
how to be brave, how to go forward always
and to contend for honor, Father's and mine.
Honor—for in my heart and soul I know
a day will come when ancient Ilion falls,
when Priam and the folk of Priam perish.
Not by the Trojans' anguish on that day
am I so overborne in mind—the pain 390
of Hékabê herself, or Priam king,

[45] Zeus.

or of my brothers, many and valorous,
who will have fallen in dust before our enemies—
as by your own grief, when some armed Akhaian
takes you in tears, your free life stripped away.
Before another woman's loom in Argos
it may be you will pass, or at Messêis
or Hypereiê fountain, carrying water,
against your will—iron constraint upon you.
And seeing you in tears, a man may say: 400
'There is the wife of Hektor, who fought best
of Trojan horsemen when they fought at Troy.'
So he may say—and you will ache again
for one man who could keep you out of bondage.
Let me be hidden dark down in my grave
before I hear your cry or know you captive!"

As he said this, Hektor held out his arms
to take his baby. But the child squirmed round
on the nurse's bosom and began to wail,
terrified by his father's great war helm— 410
the flashing bronze, the crest with horsehair plume
tossed like a living thing at every nod.
His father began laughing, and his mother
laughed as well. Then from his handsome head
Hektor lifted off his helm and bent
to place it, bright with sunlight, on the ground.
When he had kissed his child and swung him high
to dandle him, he said this prayer:

"O Zeus
and all immortals, may this child, my son,
become like me a prince among the Trojans. 420
Let him be strong and brave and rule in power
at Ilion; then someday men will say
'This fellow is far better than his father!'
seeing him home from war, and in his arms
the bloodstained gear of some tall warrior slain—
making his mother proud."

After this prayer,
into his dear wife's arms he gave his baby,
whom on her fragrant breast
she held and cherished, laughing through her tears.
Hektor pitied her now. Caressing her, 430
he said:

"Unquiet soul, do not be too distressed
by thoughts of me. You know no man dispatches me
into the undergloom against my fate;
no mortal, either, can escape his fate,
coward or brave man, once he comes to be.
Go home, attend to your own handiwork
at loom and spindle, and command the maids
to busy themselves, too. As for the war,

that is for men, all who were born at Ilion,
to put their minds on—most of all for me." 440

He stooped now to recover his plumed helm
as she, his dear wife, drew away, her head
turned and her eyes upon him, brimming tears.
She made her way in haste then to the ordered
house of Hektor and rejoined her maids,
moving them all to weep at sight of her.
In Hektor's home they mourned him, living still
but not, they feared, again to leave the war
or be delivered from Akhaian fury.

Paris in the meantime had not lingered: 450
after he buckled his bright war-gear on
he ran through Troy, sure-footed with long strides.
Think how a stallion fed on clover and barley,
mettlesome, thundering in a stall, may snap
his picket rope and canter down a field
to bathe as he would daily in the river—
glorying in freedom! Head held high
with mane over his shoulders flying,
his dazzling work of finely jointed knees
takes him around the pasture haunts of horses. 460
That was the way the son of Priam, Paris,
ran from the height of Pergamos;[46] his gear
ablaze like the great sun,
and laughed aloud. He sprinted on, and quickly
met his brother, who was slow to leave
the place where he had discoursed with his lady.
Aléxandros was first to speak:

"Dear fellow,"
he said, "have I delayed you, kept you waiting?
Have I not come at the right time, as you asked?"

And Hektor in his shimmering helm replied: 470
"My strange brother! No man with justice in him
would underrate your handiwork in battle;
you have a powerful arm. But you give way
too easily, and lose interest, lose your will.
My heart aches in me when I hear our men,
who have such toil of battle on your account,
talk of you with contempt. Well, come along.
Someday we'll make amends for that, if ever
we drive the Akhaians from the land of Troy—
if ever Zeus permit us, in our hall, 480
to set before the gods of heaven, undying
and ever young, our winebowl of deliverance."

[46] The citadel of Troy.

FROM BOOK 8
THE BATTLE SWAYED BY ZEUS

[In Book 7, Hektor and Aías battle to a standstill. The Trojans offer to return Helen's wealth to Meneláos, but the offer is rejected. The dead are buried during a truce. In Book 8, the battle resumes and by the end of the day the Trojans have driven the Akhaians back to their fortifications around their boats.–ED.]

...Now in the western Ocean
the shining sun dipped, drawing dark night on
over the kind grainbearing earth—a sundown
far from desired by Trojans; but the night
came thrice besought and blest by the Akhaians.
Hektor at once called Trojans to assembly,
leading the way by night back from the ships
to an empty field beside the eddying river—
a space that seemed free of the dead. The living
halted and dismounted there to listen 10
to a speech by Hektor, dear to Zeus. He held
his lance erect—eleven forearms long
with bronze point shining in the air before him
as shone, around the shank, a golden ring.
Leaning on this, he spoke amid the Trojans:

"Hear me, Trojans, Dardans, and allies!
By this time I had thought we might retire
to windy Ilion, after we had destroyed
Akhaians and their ships; but the night's gloom
came before we finished. That has saved them, 20
Argives and ships, at the sea's edge near the surf.
All right, then, let us bow to the black night,
and make an evening feast! From the chariot poles
unyoke the teams, toss fodder out before them;
bring down beeves and fat sheep from the city,
and lose no time about it—amber wine
and wheaten bread, too, from our halls. Go, gather
piles of firewood, so that all night long,
until the first-born dawn, our many fires
shall burn and send to heaven their leaping light, 30
that not by night shall the unshorn Akhaians
get away on the broad back of the sea.
Not by night—and not without combat, either,
taking ship easily, but let there be
those who take homeward missiles to digest,
hit hard by arrows or by spears as they
shove off and leap aboard. And let the next man
hate the thought of waging painful war
on Trojan master-horsemen.

Honored criers
throughout our town shall publish this command: 40
old men with hoary brows, and striplings, all
camp out tonight upon the ancient towers;

women in every mégaron kindle fires,
and every sentry keep a steady watch
against a night raid on the city, while
my troops are in the field. These dispositions,
Trojans, are to be taken as I command. And may
what I have said tonight be salutary;
likewise what I shall say at Dawn. I hope
with prayer to Zeus and other immortal gods 50
we shall repulse the dogs of war and death
brought on us in the black ships. Aye, this night
we'll guard ourselves, toward morning arm again
and whet against the ships the edge of war!
I'll see if Diomêdês has the power
to force me from the ships, back on the rampart,
or if I kill him and take home his gear,
wet with his blood. He will show bravery
tomorrow if he face my spear advancing!
In the first rank, I think, wounded he'll lie 60
with plenty of his friends lying around him
at sunup in the morning.
Would I were sure
of being immortal, ageless all my days,
and reverenced like Athêna and Apollo,
as it is sure this day will bring defeat
on those of Argos!"

This was the speech of Hektor,
and cheers rang out from the Trojans after it.
They led from under the yokes their sweating teams,
tethering each beside his chariot,
then brought down from the city beeves and sheep 70
in all haste—brought down wine and bread as well
out of their halls. They piled up firewood
and carried out full-tally hekatombs
to the immortals. Off the plain, the wind
bore smoke and savor of roasts into the sky.
Then on the perilous open ground of war,
in brave expectancy, they lay all night
while many campfires burned. As when in heaven
principal stars shine out around the moon
when the night sky is limpid, with no wind, 80
and all the lookout points, headlands, and mountain
clearings are distinctly seen, as though
pure space had broken through, downward from heaven,
and all the stars are out, and in his heart
the shepherd sings: just so from ships to river
shone before Ilion the Trojan fires.
There were a thousand burning in the plain,
and round each one lay fifty men in firelight.
Horses champed white barley, near the chariots,
waiting for Dawn to mount her lovely chair. 90

BOOK 9
A Visit of Emissaries

So Trojans kept their watch that night.
To seaward
Panic that attends blood-chilling Rout
now ruled the Akhaians. All their finest men
were shaken by this fear, in bitter throes,
as when a shifting gale
blows up over the cold fish-breeding sea,
north wind and west wind wailing out of Thrace
in squall on squall, and dark waves crest, and shoreward
masses of weed are cast up by the surf:
so were Akhaian hearts torn in their breasts. 10

By that great gloom hard hit, the son of Atreus
made his way amid his criers and told them
to bid each man in person to assembly
but not to raise a general cry. He led them,
making the rounds himself, and soon the soldiers
grimly took their places. Then he rose,
with slow tears trickling, as from a hidden spring
dark water runs down, staining a rock wall;
and groaning heavily he addressed the Argives:
"Friends, leaders of Argives, all my captains, 20
Zeus Kronidês entangled me in folly
to my undoing. Wayward god, he promised
solemnly that I should not sail away
before I stormed the inner town of Troy.
Crookedness and duplicity, I see now!
He calls me to return to Argos beaten
after these many losses. That must be
his will and his good pleasure, who knows why?
Many a great town's height has he destroyed
and will destroy, being supreme in power. 30
Enough. Now let us act on what I say:
Board ship for our own fatherland! Retreat!
We cannot hope any longer to take Troy!"

At this a stillness overcame them all,
the Akhaian soldiers. Long they sat in silence,
hearing their own hearts beat. Then Diomêdês
rose at last to speak. He said:
"My lord,
I must contend with you for letting go,
for losing balance. I may do so here
in assembly lawfully. Spare me your anger. 40
Before this you have held me up to scorn
for lack of fighting spirit; old and young,
everyone knows the truth of that. In your case,
the son of crooked-minded Krónos gave you

one gift and not both: a staff of kingship
honored by all men, but no staying power—
the greatest gift of all.
What has come over you, to make you think
the Akhaians weak and craven as you say?
If you are in a passion to sail home, 50
sail on: the way is clear, the many ships
that made the voyage from Mykênê[47] with you
stand near the sea's edge. Others here will stay
until we plunder Troy! Or if they, too,
would like to, let them sail for their own country!
Sthénelos[48] and I will fight alone
until we see the destined end of Ilion.
We came here under god."

When Diomêdês
finished, a cry went up from all the Akhaians
in wonder at his words. Then Nestor stood 60
and spoke among them:

"Son of Tydeus, formidable
above the rest in war, in council, too,
you have more weight than others of your age.
No one will cry down what you say, no true
Akhaian will, or contradict you. Still,
you did not push on to the end.
I know you are young; in years you might well be
my last-born son, and yet for all of that
you kept your head and said what needed saying
before the Argive captains. My own part, 70
as I am older, is to drive it home.
No one will show contempt for what I say,
surely not Agamémnon, our commander.
Alien to clan and custom and hearth fire
is he who longs for war—heartbreaking war—
with his own people.

Let us yield to darkness
and make our evening meal. But let the sentries
take their rest on watch outside the rampart
near the moat; those are my orders for them.
Afterward, you direct us, Agamémnon, 80
by right of royal power. Provide a feast
for older men, your counselors. That is duty
and no difficulty: your huts are full of wine
brought over daily in our ships from Thrace
across the wide sea, and all provender
for guests is yours, as you are high commander.
Your counselors being met, pay heed to him
who counsels best. The army of Akhaia
bitterly needs a well-found plan of action.

[47] Mycenae, Agamémnon's fortress city.
[48] Diomêdês' charioteer.

The enemy is upon us, near the ships, 90
burning his thousand fires. What Akhaian
could be highhearted in that glare? This night
will see the army saved or brought to ruin."

They heeded him and did his will. Well-armed,
the sentries left to take their posts, one company
formed around Thrasymêdês, Nestor's son,
another mustered by Askálaphos
and Iálmenos, others commanded by
Meríonês, Aphareus, Dêípyros,
and Kreion's son, the princely Lykomêdês. 100
Seven lieutenants, each with a hundred men,
carrying long spears, issued from the camp
for outposts chosen between ditch and rampart.
Campfires were kindled, and they took their meal.

The son of Atreus led the elder men
together to his hut, where he served dinner,
and each man's hand went out upon the meal.
When they had driven hunger and thirst away,
Old Nestor opened their deliberations—
Nestor, whose counsel had seemed best before, 110
point by point weaving his argument:
"Lord Marshal of the army, Agamémnon,
as I shall end with you, so I begin,
since you hold power over a great army
and are responsible for it: the Lord Zeus
put in your keeping staff and precedent
that you might gather counsel for your men.
You should be first in discourse, but attentive
to what another may propose, to act on it
if he speak out for the good of all. Whatever 120
he may initiate, action is yours.
On this rule, let me speak as I think best.
A better view than mine no man can have,
the same view that I've held these many days
since that occasion when, my lord, for all
Akhilleus' rage, you took the girl Brisêis
out of his lodge—but not with our consent.
Far from it; I for one had begged you not to.
Just the same, you gave way to your pride,
and you dishonored a great prince, 130
a hero to whom the gods themselves do honor.
Taking his prize, you kept her and still do.
But even so, and even now, we may
contrive some way of making peace with him
by friendly gifts, and by affectionate words."

Then Agamémnon, the Lord Marshal, answered:
"Sir, there is nothing false in your account
of my blind errors. I committed them;

I will not now deny it. Troops of soldiers
are worth no more than one man cherished by Zeus 140
as he has cherished this man and avenged him,
overpowering the army of Akhaians.
I lost my head, I yielded to black anger,
but now I would retract it and appease him
with all munificence. Here before everyone
I may enumerate the gifts I'll give.
Seven new tripods and ten bars of gold,
then twenty shining caldrons, and twelve horses,
thoroughbreds, who by their wind and legs
have won me prizes: any man who owned 150
what these have brought me could not lack resources,
could not be pinched for precious gold—so many
prizes have these horses carried home.
Then I shall give him seven women, deft
in household handicraft—women of Lesbos
I chose when he himself took Lesbos town,
as they outshone all womankind in beauty.
These I shall give him, and one more, whom I
took away from him then: Briseus' daughter.
Concerning her, I add my solemn oath 160
I never went to bed or coupled with her,
as custom is with men and women.
These will be his at once. If the immortals
grant us the plundering of Priam's town,
let him come forward when the spoils are shared
and load his ship with bars of gold and bronze.
Then he may choose among the Trojan women
twenty that are most lovely, after Helen.
If we return to Argos of Akhaia,
flowing with good things of the earth, he'll be 170
my own adopted son, dear as Orestês,
born long ago and reared in bounteous peace.
I have three daughters now at home, Khrysóthemis,
Laódikê, and Iphiánassa.
He may take whom he will to be his bride
and pay no bridal gift, leading her home
to Pêleus' hall. But I shall add a dowry
such as no man has given to his daughter.
Seven flourishing strongholds I'll give him:
Kardamylê and Enopê and Hirê 180
in the wild grassland; holy Phêrai too,
and the deep meadowland of Ántheia,
Aipeia and the vineyard slope of Pêdasos,
all lying near the sea in the far west
of sandy Pylos. In these lands are men
who own great flocks and herds; now as his liegemen,
they will pay tithes and sumptuous honor to him,
prospering as they carry out his plans.
These are the gifts I shall arrange if he
desists from anger. Let him be subdued! 190

Lord Death indeed is deaf to appeal, implacable;
of all gods therefore he is most abhorrent
to mortal men. So let Akhilleus bow to me,
considering that I hold higher rank
and claim the precedence of age."

To this
Lord Nestor of Gerênia replied:

"Lord Marshal of the army, Agamémnon,
this time the gifts you offer Lord Akhilleus
are not to be despised. Come, we'll dispatch
our chosen emissaries to his quarters 200
as quickly as possible. Those men whom I
may designate, let them perform the mission.
Phoinix,[49] dear to Zeus, may lead the way.
Let Aías follow him, and Prince Odysseus.
The criers, Hódios and Eurýbatês,
may go as escorts. Bowls for their hands here!
Tell them to keep silence, while we pray
that Zeus the son of Krónos will be merciful."

Nestor's proposal fell on willing ears,
and criers came at once to tip out water 210
over their hands, while young men filled the winebowls
and dipped a measure into every cup.
They spilt their offerings and drank their fill,
then briskly left the hut of Agamémnon.
Nestor accompanied them with final words
and sage looks, especially for Odysseus,
as to the effort they should make to bring
the son of Pêleus round.

Following Phoinix,
Aías and Odysseus walked together
beside the tumbling clamorous whispering sea, 220
praying hard to the girdler of the islands[50]
that they might easily sway their great friend's heart.
Amid the ships and huts of the Myrmidons
they found him, taking joy in a sweet harp
of rich and delicate make—the crossbar set
to hold the strings being silver. He had won it
when he destroyed the city of Eëtíôn,
and plucking it he took his joy: he sang
old tales of heroes, while across the room
alone and silent sat Patróklos, waiting 230
until Akhilleus should be done with song.
Phoinix had come in unremarked, but when
the two new visitors, Odysseus leading,
entered and stood before him, then Akhilleus
rose in wonderment, and left his chair,

[49] Akhilleus' tutor.
[50] Poseidon.

his harp still in his hand. So did Patróklos
rise at sight of the two men. Akhilleus
made both welcome with a gesture, saying:

"Peace! My two great friends, I greet your coming.
How I have needed it! Even in my anger, 240
of all Akhaians, you are closest to me."
And Prince Akhilleus led them in. He seated them
on easy chairs with purple coverlets,
and to Patróklos who stood near he said:

"Put out an ampler winebowl, use more wine
for stronger drink,[51] and place a cup for each.
Here are my dearest friends beneath my roof."

Patróklos did as his companion bade him.
Meanwhile the host set down a carving block
within the fire's rays; a chine of mutton 250
and a fat chine of goat he placed upon it,
as well as savory pork chine. Automédôn
steadied the meat for him, Akhilleus carved,
then sliced it well and forked it on the spits.
Meanwhile Patróklos, like a god in firelight,
made the hearth blaze up. When the leaping flame
had ebbed and died away, he raked the coals
and in the glow extended spits of meat,
lifting these at times from the firestones
to season with pure salt. When all was done 260
and the roast meat apportioned into platters,
loaves of bread were passed round by Patróklos
in fine baskets. Akhilleus served the meat.
He took his place then opposite Odysseus,
back to the other wall, and told
Patróklos to make offering to the gods.
This he did with meat tossed in the fire,
then each man's hand went out upon the meal.
When they had put their hunger and thirst away,
Aías nodded silently to Phoinix, 270
but Prince Odysseus caught the nod. He filled
a cup of wine and lifted it to Akhilleus,
saying:

"Health, Akhilleus. We've no lack
of generous feasts this evening—in the lodge
of Agamémnon first, and now with you,
good fare and plentiful each time.
It is not feasting that concerns us now,
however, but a ruinous defeat.
Before our very eyes we see it coming
and are afraid. By a blade's turn, our good ships 280
are saved or lost, unless you arm your valor.
Trojans and allies are encamped tonight

[51] Wine was usually mixed with water.

in pride before our ramparts, at our sterns,
and through their army burn a thousand fires.
These men are sure they cannot now be stopped
but will get through to our good ships. Lord Zeus
flashes and thunders for them on the right,[52]
and Hektor in his ecstasy of power
is mad for battle, confident in Zeus,
deferring to neither men nor gods. Pure frenzy 290
fills him, and he prays for the bright dawn
when he will shear our stern-post beaks away
and fire all our ships, while in the shipways
amid that holocaust he carries death
among our men, driven out by smoke. All this
I gravely fear; I fear the gods will make
good his threatenings, and our fate will be
to die here, far from the pastureland of Argos.
Rouse yourself, if even at this hour
you'll pitch in for the Akhaians and deliver them 300
from Trojan havoc. In the years to come
this day will be remembered pain for you
if you do not. No remedy, no remedy
will come to hand, once the great ill is done.
While there is time, think how to keep this evil
day from the Danäāns!

My dear lad,
how rightly in your case your father, Pêleus,
put it in his farewell, sending you out
from Phthía to take ship with Agamémnon!
'Now as to fighting power, child,' he said, 310
'if Hêra and Athêna wish, they'll give it.
Control your passion, though, and your proud heart,
for gentle courtesy is a better thing.
Break off insidious quarrels, and young and old,
the Argives will respect you for it more.'
That was your old father's admonition:
you have forgotten. Still, even now, abandon
heart-wounding anger. If you will relent,
Agamémnon will match this change of heart
with gifts. Now listen and let me list for you 320
what just now in his quarters he proposed:
seven new tripods, and ten bars of gold,
then twenty shining caldrons, and twelve horses,
thoroughbreds, that by their wind and legs
have won him prizes: any man who owned
what these have brought him would not lack resources,
could not be pinched for precious gold—so many
prizes have these horses carried home.
Then he will give you seven women, deft
in household handicraft: women of Lesbos 330
chosen when you yourself took Lesbos town,

---

[52]A favorable omen.

as they outshone all womankind in beauty.
These he will give you, and one more, whom he
took away from you then: Briseus' daughter,
concerning whom he adds a solemn oath
never to have gone to bed or coupled with her,
as custom is, my lord, with men and women.
These are all yours at once. If the immortals
grant us the pillaging of Priam's town,
you may come forward when the spoils are shared 340
and load your ship with bars of gold and bronze.
Then you may choose among the Trojan women
twenty that are most lovely, after Helen.
And then, if we reach Argos of Akhaia,
flowing with good things of the earth, you'll be
his own adopted son, dear as Orestês,
born long ago and reared in bounteous peace.
He has three daughters now at home, Khrysóthemis,
Laódikê, and Iphiánassa.
You may take whom you will to be your bride 350
and pay no gift when you conduct her home
to your ancestral hall. He'll add a dowry
such as no man has given to his daughter.
Seven flourishing strongholds he'll give to you:
Kardamylê and Enopê and Hirê
in the wild grassland; holy Phêrai too,
and the deep meadowland of Ántheia,
Aipeia and the vineyard slope of Pêdasos,
all lying near the sea in the far west
of sandy Pylos. In these lands are men 360
who own great flocks and herds; now as your liegemen,
they will pay tithes and sumptuous honor to you,
prospering as they carry out your plans.
These are the gifts he will arrange if you
desist from anger.

Even if you abhor
the son of Atreus all the more bitterly,
with all his gifts, take pity on the rest,
all the old army, worn to rags in battle.
These will honor you as gods are honored!
And ah, for these, what glory you may win! 370
Think: Hektor is your man this time: being crazed
with ruinous pride, believing there's no fighter
equal to him among those that our ships
brought here by sea, he'll put himself in range!"

Akhilleus the great runner answered him:

"Son of Laërtês and the gods of old,
Odysseus, master soldier and mariner,
I owe you a straight answer, as to how
I see this thing, and how it is to end.
No need to sit with me like mourning doves 380

making your gentle noise by turns. I hate
as I hate Hell's own gate that man who hides
one thought within him while he speaks another.
What I shall say is what I see and think.
Give in to Agamémnon? I think not,
neither to him nor to the rest. I had
small thanks for fighting, fighting without truce
against hard enemies here. The portion's equal
whether a man hangs back or fights his best;
the same respect, or lack of it, is given 390
brave man and coward. One who's active dies
like the do-nothing. What least thing have I
to show for it, for harsh days undergone
and my life gambled, all these years of war?
A bird will give her fledglings every scrap
she comes by, and go hungry, foraging.
That is the case with me.
Many a sleepless night I've spent afield
and many a day in bloodshed, hand to hand
in battle for the wives of other men. 400
In sea raids I plundered a dozen towns,
eleven in expeditions overland
through Trojan country, and the treasure taken
out of them all, great heaps of handsome things,
I carried back each time to Agamémnon.
He sat tight on the beachhead, and shared out
a little treasure; most of it he kept.
He gave prizes of war to his officers;
the rest have theirs, not I; from me alone
of all Akhaians, he pre-empted her. 410
He holds my bride, dear to my heart. Aye, let him
sleep with her and enjoy her!
Why must Argives
fight the Trojans? Why did he raise an army
and lead it here? For Helen, was it not?
Are the Atreidai of all mortal men
the only ones who love their wives? I think not.
Every sane decent fellow loves his own
and cares for her, as in my heart I loved
Brisêis, though I won her by the spear.
Now, as he took my prize out of my hands, 420
tricked and defrauded me, he need not tempt me;
I know him, and he cannot change my mind.
Let him take thought, Odysseus, with you
and others how the ships may be defended
against incendiary attack. By god,
he has achieved imposing work without me,
a rampart piled up overnight, a ditch
running beyond it, broad and deep,
with stakes implanted in it! All no use!
He cannot hold against the killer's charge. 430
As long as I was in the battle, Hektor

never cared for a fight far from the walls;
his limit was the oak tree by the gate.
When I was alone one day he waited there,
but barely got away when I went after him.
Now it is I who do not care to fight.
Tomorrow at dawn when I have made offering
to Zeus and all the gods, and hauled my ships
for loading in the shallows, if you like
and if it interests you, look out and see 440
my ships on Hellê's waters in the offing,[53]
oarsmen in line making the sea-foam scud!
And if the great Earthshaker[54] gives a breeze,
the third day out I'll make it home to Phthía.
Rich possessions are there I left behind
when I was mad enough to come here; now
I take home gold and ruddy bronze, and women
belted luxuriously, and hoary iron,
all that came to me here. As for my prize,
he who gave her took her outrageously back. 450
Well, you can tell him all this to his face,
and let the other Akhaians burn
if he in his thick hide of shamelessness
picks out another man to cheat. He would not
look me in the eye, dog that he is!
I will not share one word of counsel with him,
nor will I act with him; he robbed me blind,
broke faith with me: he gets no second chance
to play me for a fool. Once is enough.
To hell with him, Zeus took his brains away! 460
His gifts I abominate, and I would give
not one dry shuck for him. I would not change,
not if he multiplied his gifts by ten,
by twenty times what he has now, and more,
no matter where they came from: if he gave
what enters through Orkhómenos'[55] town gate
or Thebes of Egypt, where the treasures lie—
that city where through each of a hundred gates
two hundred men drive out in chariots.
Not if his gifts outnumbered the sea sands 470
or all the dust grains in the world could Agamémnon
ever appease me—not till he pays me back
full measure, pain for pain, dishonor for dishonor.
The daughter of Agamémnon, son of Atreus,
I will not take in marriage. Let her be
as beautiful as pale-gold Aphrodítê,
skilled as Athêna of the sea-grey eyes,
I will not have her, at any price. No, let him
find someone else, an eligible Akhaian,
kinglier than I.

[53]Hellespont (or Dardanelles).
[54]Poseidon.
[55]City north of Athens.

Now if the gods 480
preserve me and I make it home, my father
Pêleus will select a bride for me.
In Hellas[56] and in Phthía there are many
daughters of strong men who defend the towns.
I'll take the one I wish to be my wife.
There in my manhood I have longed, indeed,
to marry someone of congenial mind
and take my ease, enjoying the great estate
my father had acquired.

Now I think
no riches can compare with being alive, 490
not even those they say this well-built Ilion
stored up in peace before the Akhaians came.
Neither could all the Archer's shrine contains
at rocky Pytho,[57] in the crypt of stone.
A man may come by cattle and sheep in raids;
tripods he buys, and tawny-headed horses;
but his life's breath cannot be hunted back
or be recaptured once it pass his lips.
My mother, Thetis of the silvery feet,
tells me of two possible destinies 500
carrying me toward death: two ways:
if on the one hand I remain to fight
around Troy town, I lose all hope of home
but gain unfading glory; on the other,
if I sail back to my own land my glory
fails—but a long life lies ahead for me.
To all the rest of you I say: 'Sail home:
you will not now see Ilion's last hour,'
for Zeus who views the wide world held his sheltering
hand over that city, and her troops 510
have taken heart.

Return, then, emissaries,
deliver my answer to the Akhaian peers—
it is the senior officer's privilege—
and let them plan some other way, and better,
to save their ships and save the Akhaian army.
This one cannot be put into effect—
their scheme this evening—while my anger holds.
Phoinix may stay and lodge the night with us,
then take ship and sail homeward at my side
tomorrow, if he wills. I'll not constrain him." 520

After Akhilleus finished, all were silent,
awed, for he spoke with power.
Then the old master-charioteer, Lord Phoinix,

---

[56] A region in northern Greece; later it means Greece itself.
[57] Apollo's sanctuary at Delphi.

answered at last, and let his tears come shining,
fearing for the Akhaian ships:

"Akhilleus,
if it is true you set your heart on home
and will not stir a finger to save the ships
from being engulfed by fire—all for this rage
that has swept over you—how, child, could I
be sundered from you, left behind alone? 530
For your sake the old master-charioteer,
Pêleus, made provision that I should come,
that day he gave you godspeed out of Phthía
to go with Agamémnon. Still a boy,
you knew nothing of war that levels men
to the same testing, nothing of assembly
where men become illustrious. That is why
he sent me, to instruct you in these matters,
to be a man of eloquence and action.
After all that, dear child, I should not wish 540
to be left here apart from you—not even
if god himself should undertake to smooth
my wrinkled age and make me fresh and young,
as when for the first time I left the land
of lovely women, Hellas. I went north
to avoid a feud with Father, Amyntor
Orménidês. His anger against me rose
over a fair-haired slave girl whom he fancied,
without respect for his own wife, my mother.
Mother embraced my knees and begged that I 550
make love to this girl, so that afterward
she might be cold to the aging man. I did it.
My father guessed the truth at once, and cursed me,
praying the ghostly Furies[58] that no son
of mine should ever rest upon his knees:
a curse fulfilled by the immortals—Lord
Zeus of undergloom and cold Perséphonê.[59]
I planned to put a sword in him, and would have,
had not some god unstrung my rage, reminding me
of country gossip and the frowns of men; 560
I shrank from being called a parricide
among the Akhaians. But from that time on
I felt no tie with home, no love for lingering
under the rooftree of a raging father.
Our household and our neighbors, it is true,
urged me to stay. They made a handsome feast
of shambling cattle butchered, and fat sheep;
young porkers by the litter, crisp with fat,
were singed and spitted in Hêphaistos' fire,
rivers of wine drunk from the old man's store. 570

---

[58]Feminine spirits of revenge, especially for blood crimes.
[59]Queen of the underworld, wife of Hades.

Nine times they spent the night and slept beside me,
taking the watch by turns, leaving a fire
to flicker under the entrance colonnade,
and one more in the court outside my room.
But when the tenth night came, starless and black,
I cracked the tight bolt on my chamber door,
pushed out, and scaled the courtyard wall, unseen
by household men on watch or women slaves.
Then I escaped from that place, made my way
through Hellas where the dancing floors are wide, 580
until I came to Phthía's fertile plain,
mother of flocks, and Pêleus the king.
He gave me welcome, treated me with love,
as a father would an only son, his heir
to rich possessions. And he made me rich,
appointing me great numbers of retainers
on the frontier of Phthía, where I lived
as lord of Dolopês. Now, it was I
who formed your manhood, handsome as a god's,
Akhilleus: I who loved you from the heart; 590
for never in another's company
would you attend a feast or dine in hall—
never, unless I took you on my knees
and cut your meat, and held your cup of wine.
Many a time you wet my shirt, hiccuping
wine-bubbles in distress, when you were small.
Patient and laborious as a nurse
I had to be for you, bearing in mind
that never would the gods bring into being
any son of mine. Godlike Akhilleus, 600
you were the manchild that I made my own
to save me someday, so I thought, from misery.
Quell your anger, Akhilleus! You must not
be pitiless! The gods themselves relent,
and are they not still greater in bravery,
in honor and in strength? Burnt offerings,
courteous prayer, libation, smoke of sacrifice,
with all of these, men can placate the gods
when someone oversteps and errs. The truth is,
prayers are daughters of almighty Zeus— 610
one may imagine them lame, wrinkled things
with eyes cast down, that toil to follow after
passionate Folly. Folly is strong and swift,
outrunning all the prayers, and everywhere
arriving first to injure mortal men;
still they come healing after. If a man
reveres the daughters of Zeus when they come near,
he is rewarded, and his prayers are heard;
but if he spurns them and dismisses them,
they make their way to Zeus again and ask 620
that Folly dog that man till suffering
has taken arrogance out of him.

Relent,
be courteous to the daughters of Zeus, you too,
as courtesy sways others, and the best.
If Agamémnon had no gifts for you,
named none to follow, but inveighed against you
still in fury, then I could never say,
'Discard your anger and defend the Argives—'
never, no matter how they craved your help.
But this is not so: he will give many things 630
at once; he promised others; he has sent
his noblest men to intercede with you,
the flower of the army, and your friends,
dearest among the Argives. Will you turn
their words, their coming, into humiliation?
Until this moment, no one took it ill
that you should suffer anger; we learned this
from the old stories of how towering wrath
could overcome great men; but they were still
amenable to gifts and to persuasion. 640
Here is an instance I myself remember
not from our own time but in ancient days:
I'll tell it to you all, for all are friends.
The Kourêtês were fighting a warlike race,[60]
Aitolians, around the walls of Kálydôn,
with slaughter on both sides: Aitolians
defending their beloved Kálydôn
while the Kourêtês longed to sack the town.
The truth is, Artemis of the Golden Chair
had brought the scourge of war on the Aitolians; 650
she had been angered because Oineus[61] made
no harvest offering from his vineyard slope.
While other gods enjoyed his hekatombs
he made her none, either forgetful of it
or careless—a great error, either way.
In her anger, the Mistress of Long Arrows
roused against him a boar with gleaming tusks
out of his wild grass bed, a monstrous thing
that ravaged the man's vineyard many times
and felled entire orchards, roots, 660
blooms, apples and all. Now this great boar
Meléagros, the son of Oineus, killed
by gathering men and hounds from far and near.
So huge the boar was, no small band could master him,
and he brought many to the dolorous pyre.
Around the dead beast Artemis set on
a clash with battlecries between Kourêtês
and proud Aitolians over the boar's head

[60] The Kourêtês and the Aitolians were once friends, but now are enemies.
[61] King of Kálydôn.

and shaggy hide. As long, then, as Meléagros,
backed by the wargod, fought, the Kourêtês 670
had the worst of it for all their numbers
and could not hold a line outside the walls.
But then a day came when Meléagros
was stung by venomous anger that infects
the coolest thinker's heart: swollen with rage
at his own mother, Althaiê, he languished
in idleness at home beside his lady,
Kleopátrê.

This lovely girl was born
to Marpessê of ravishing pale ankles,[62]
Euênos' child, and Idês, who had been 680
most powerful of men on earth. He drew
the bow against the Lord Phoibos Apollo
over his love, Marpessê, whom her father
and gentle mother called Alkýonê,
since for her sake her mother gave that seabird's
forlorn cry when Apollo ravished her.
With Kleopátrê lay Meléagros,
nursing the bitterness his mother stirred,
when in her anguish over a brother slain[63]
she cursed her son. She called upon the gods, 690
beating the grassy earth with both her hands
as she pitched forward on her knees, with cries
to the Lord of Undergloom and cold Perséphonê,
while tears wetted her veils—in her entreaty
that death come to her son. Inexorable
in Érebos[64] a vampire Fury listened.
Soon, then, about the gates of the Aitolians
tumult and din of war grew loud; their towers
rang with blows. And now the elder men
implored Meléagros to leave his room, 700
and sent the high priests of the gods, imploring him
to help defend the town. They promised him
a large reward: in the green countryside
of Kálydôn, wherever it was richest,
there he might choose a beautiful garden plot
of fifty acres, half in vineyard, half
in virgin prairie for the plow to cut.
Oineus, master of horsemen, came with prayers
upon the doorsill of the chamber, often
rattling the locked doors, pleading with his son. 710
His sisters, too, and then his gentle mother
pleaded with him. Only the more fiercely

---

[62] A daughter of Euênos, Marpessê was wooed by Apollo, but a mortal, Idês, carried her off; when Apollo caught them, Idês and Apollo were about to fight, when Marpessê was allowed to choose between them and she chose Idês. They gave their daughter Kleopátrê a second name, Alkýonê, meaning a sea-bird that mourns for its mate.

[63] Meléagros had killed one of his mother's brothers.

[64] A region in the underworld.

he turned away. His oldest friends, his dearest,
not even they could move him—not until
his room was shaken by a hail of stones
as Kourêtês began to scale the walls
and fire the city.

Then at last his lady
in her soft-belted gown besought him weeping,
speaking of all the ills that come to men
whose town is taken: soldiers put to the sword; 720
the city razed by fire; alien hands
carrying off the children and the women.
Hearing these fearful things, his heart was stirred
to action: he put on his shining gear
and fought off ruin from the Aitolians.
Mercy prevailed in him. His folk no longer
cared to award him gifts and luxuries,
yet even so he saved that terrible day.
Oh, do not let your mind go so astray!
Let no malignant spirit
turn you that way, dear son! It will be worse 730
to fight for ships already set afire!
Value the gifts; rejoin the war; Akhaians
afterward will give you a god's honor.
If you reject the gifts and then, later,
enter the deadly fight, you will not be
accorded the same honor, even though
you turn the tide of war!"

But the great runner
Akhilleus answered:

"Old uncle Phoinix, bless you,
that is an honor I can live without. 740
Honored I think I am by Zeus's justice,
justice that will sustain me by the ships
as long as breath is in me and I can stand.
Here is another point: ponder it well:
best not confuse my heart with lamentation
for Agamémnon, whom you must not honor;
you would be hateful to me, dear as you are.
Loyalty should array you at my side
in giving pain to him who gives me pain.
Rule with me equally, share half my honor, 750
but do not ask my help for Agamémnon.
My answer will be reported by these two.
Lodge here in a soft bed, and at first light
we can decide whether to sail or stay."

He knit his brows and nodded to Patróklos
to pile up rugs for Phoinix' bed—a sign
for the others to be quick about departing.
Aías, however, noble son of Télamôn
made the last appeal. He said:

"Odysseus,
master soldier and mariner, let us go. 760
I do not see the end of this affair
achieved by this night's visit. Nothing for it
but to report our talk for what it's worth
to the Danáäns, who sit waiting there.
Akhilleus hardened his great heart against us,
wayward and savage as he is, unmoved
by the affections of his friends who made him
honored above all others on the beachhead.
There is no pity in him. A normal man
will take the penalty for a brother slain 770
or a dead son. By paying much, the one
who did the deed may stay unharmed at home.
Fury and pride in the bereaved are curbed
when he accepts the penalty. Not you.
Cruel and unappeasable rage the gods
put in you for one girl alone. We offer
seven beauties, and much more besides!
Be gentler, and respect your own rooftree
whereunder we are guests who speak for all
Danáäns as a body. Our desire 780
is to be closest to you of them all."

Akhilleus the great runner answered him:
"Scion[65] of Télamôn and gods of old,
Aías, lord of fighting men, you seemed
to echo my own mind in what you said!
And yet my heart grows large and hot with fury
remembering that affair: as though I were
some riffraff or camp follower, he taunted me
before them all!
Go back, report the news:
I will not think of carnage or of war 790
until Prince Hektor, son of Priam, reaches
Myrmidon huts and ships in his attack,
slashing through Argives, burning down their ships.
Around my hut, my black ship, I foresee
for all his fury, Hektor will break off combat."
That was his answer. Each of the emissaries
took up a double-handed cup and poured
libation by the shipways. Then Odysseus
led the way on their return. Patróklos
commanded his retainers and the maids 800
to make at once a deep-piled bed for Phoinix.
Obediently they did so, spreading out
fleeces and coverlet and a linen sheet,
and down the old man lay, awaiting Dawn.

---

[65] Offspring.

Akhilleus slept in the well-built hut's recess,
and with him lay a woman he had brought
from Lesbos, Phorbas' daughter, Diomêdê.
Patróklos went to bed at the other end,
and with him, too, a woman lay—soft-belted
Iphis, who had been given to him by Akhilleus 810
when he took Skyros, ringed by cliff, the mountain
fastness of Enyéus.

Now the emissaries
arrived at Agamémnon's lodge. With cups
of gold held up, and rising to their feet
on every side, the Akhaians greeted them,
curious for the news. Lord Agamémnon
put the question first:

"Come, tell me, sir,
Odysseus, glory of Akhaia—will Akhilleus
fight off ravenous fire from the ships
or does he still refuse, does anger still 820
hold sway in his great heart?"

That patient man,
the Prince Odysseus, made reply:

"Excellency,
Lord Marshal of the army, son of Atreus,
the man has no desire to quench his rage.
On the contrary, he is more than ever
full of anger, spurns you and your gifts,
calls on you to work out your own defense
to save the ships and the Akhaian army.
As for himself, he threatens at daybreak
to drag his well-found ships into the surf, 830
and says he would advise the rest as well
to sail for home. 'You shall not see,' he says,
'the last hour that awaits tall Ilion,
for Zeus who views the wide world held his sheltering
hand over the city, and her troops
have taken heart.' That was Akhilleus' answer.
Those who were with me can confirm all this,
Aías can, and the two clearheaded criers.
As to old Phoinix, he is sleeping there
by invitation, so that he may sail 840
to his own country, homeward with Akhilleus,
tomorrow, if he wills, without constraint."

When he had finished everyone was still,
sitting in silence and in perturbation
for a long time. At last brave Diomêdês,
lord of the warcry, said:

"Excellency,
Lord Marshal of the army, Agamémnon,
you never should have pled with him, or given

so many gifts to him. At the best of times
he is a proud man; now you have pushed him far 850
deeper into his vanity and pride.
By god, let us have done with him—
whether he goes or stays! He'll fight again
when the time comes, whenever his blood is up
or the god rouses him. As for ourselves,
let everyone now do as I advise
and go to rest. Your hearts have been refreshed
with bread and wine, the pith and nerve of men.
When the fair Dawn with finger tips of rose
makes heaven bright, deploy your men and horses 860
before the ships at once, and cheer them on,
and take your place, yourself, in the front line
to join the battle."

All gave their assent
in admiration of Diomêdês,
breaker of horses. When they had spilt their wine
they all dispersed, each man to his own hut,
and lying down they took the gift of sleep.

BOOK 16
A SHIP FIRED, A TIDE TURNED

[In Book 10, Diomêdês and Odysseus volunteer to spy behind enemy lines, where they kill Rhesos, the Thracian king, and steal his horses. In Book 11, the Akhaians prevail the next day and drive the Trojans back to Troy's walls, then again lose ground. Nestor urges Patróklos to disguise himself in Akhilleus' armor and lead the Myrmidons into battle. In Book 12, Hektor breaks through the wall defending the Akhaian ships and the Trojans charge through the breach. In Book 13, Idomeneus and Aías heroically hold off the Trojans. In Book 14, Agamémnon recommends abandoning the war, but then the Akhaians force the Trojans to retreat. In Book 15, the Trojans regain their lost ground and are on the verge of burning the Akhaian ships and ending the war.–ED.]

That was the way the fighting went
for one seagoing ship. Meanwhile Patróklos
approached Akhilleus his commander, streaming
warm tears—like a shaded mountain spring
that makes a rockledge run with dusky water.
Akhilleus watched him come, and felt a pang for him.
Then the great prince and runner said:

"Patróklos,
why all the weeping? Like a small girlchild
who runs beside her mother and cries and cries
to be taken up, and catches at her gown, 10
and will not let her go, looking up in tears
until she has her wish: that's how you seem,
Patróklos, winking out your glimmering tears.
Have you something to tell the Myrmidons
or me? Some message you alone have heard

from Phthía? But they say that Aktor's son,
Menoitios,[66] is living still, and Pêleus,
the son of Aíakos, lives on
amid his Myrmidons. If one of these
were dead, we should be grieved.
Or is this weeping 20
over the Argives, seeing how they perish
at the long ships by their own bloody fault!
Speak out now, don't conceal it, let us share it."

And groaning, Patróklos, you replied:
"Akhilleus, prince and greatest of Akhaians,
be forbearing. They are badly hurt.
All who were the best fighters are now lying
among the ships with spear or arrow wounds.
Diomêdês, Tydeus' rugged son, was shot;
Odysseus and Agamémnon, the great spearman, 30
have spear wounds; Eurýpylos
took an arrow shot deep in his thigh.
Surgeons with medicines are attending them
to ease their wounds.
But you are a hard case,
Akhilleus! God forbid this rage you nurse
should master me. You and your fearsome pride!
What good will come of it to anyone, later,
unless you keep disaster from the Argives?
Have you no pity?
Pêleus, master of horse, was not your father, 40
Thetis was not your mother! Cold grey sea
and sea-cliffs bore you, making a mind so harsh.
If in your heart you fear some oracle,
some word of Zeus, told by your gentle mother,
then send me out at least, and send me quickly,
give me a company of Myrmidons,
and I may be a beacon to Danáäns!
Lend me your gear to strap over my shoulders;
Trojans then may take me for yourself
and break off battle, giving our worn-out men 50
a chance to breathe. Respites are brief in war.
We fresh troops with one battlecry might easily
push their tired men back on the town,
away from ships and huts."

So he petitioned,
witless as a child that what he begged for
was his own death, hard death and doom.
Akhilleus
out of his deep anger made reply:

---

[66]Patróklos' father.

"Hard words, dear prince. There is no oracle
I know of that I must respect, no word
from Zeus reported by my gentle mother. 60
Only this bitterness eats at my heart
when one man would deprive and shame his equal,
taking back his prize by abuse of power.
The girl whom the Akhaians chose for me
I won by my own spear. A town with walls
I stormed and sacked for her. Then Agamémnon
stole her back, out of my hands, as though
I were some vagabond held cheap.
All that
we can let pass as being over and done with;
I could not rage forever. And yet, by heaven, I swore 70
I would not rest from anger till the cries
and clangor of battle reached my very ships!
But you, now, you can strap my famous gear
on your own shoulders, and then take command
of Myrmidons on edge and ripe for combat,
now that like a dark stormcloud the Trojans
have poured round the first ships, and Argive troops
have almost no room for maneuver left,
with nothing to their rear but sea. The whole
townful of Trojans joins in, sure of winning, 80
because they cannot see my helmet's brow
aflash in range of them. They'd fill the gullies
with dead men soon, in flight up through the plain,
if Agamémnon were on good terms with me.
As things are, they've outflanked the camp. A mercy
for them that in the hands of Diomêdês
no great spear goes berserk, warding death
from the Danáäns! Not yet have I heard
the voice of Agamémnon, either, shouting
out of his hateful skull. The shout of Hektor, 90
the killer, calling Trojans, makes a roar
like breaking surf, and with long answering cries
they hold the whole plain where they drove the Akhaians.
Even so, defend the ships, Patróklos.
Attack the enemy in force, or they
will set the ships ablaze with whirling fire
and rob Akhaians of their dear return.
Now carry out the purpose I confide,
so that you'll win great honor for me, and glory
among Danáäns; then they'll send me back 100
my lovely girl, with bright new gifts as well.
Once you expel the enemy from the ships,
rejoin me here. If Hêra's lord,
the lord of thunder, grants you the day's honor,
covet no further combat far from me
with Trojan soldiers. That way you'd deny me
recompense of honor. You must not,

for joy of battle, joy of killing Trojans,
carry the fight to Ilion! Some power
out of Olympos, one of the immortal gods, 110
might intervene for them. The Lord Apollo
loves the Trojans. Turn back, then, as soon
as you restore the safety of the ships,
and let the rest contend, out on the plain.
Ah, Father Zeus, Athêna, and Apollo!
If not one Trojan of them all
should get away from death, and not one Argive
save ourselves were spared, we two alone
could pull down Troy's old coronet of towers!"

These were the speeches they exchanged. Now Aías 120
could no longer hold: he was dislodged
by spear-throws, beaten by the mind of Zeus
and Trojan shots. His shining helm rang out
around his temples dangerously with hits
as his helmplates were struck and struck again;
he felt his shoulder galled on the left side
hugging the glittering shield—and yet they could not
shake it, putting all their weight in throws.
In painful gasps his breath came, sweat ran down
in rivers off his body everywhere; 130
no rest for him, but trouble upon trouble.

Now tell me, Muses, dwellers on Olympos,
how fire first fell on the Akhaian ships!
Hektor moved in to slash with his long blade
at Aías' ashwood shaft, and near the spearhead
lopped it off. Then Telamônian Aías
wielded a pointless shaft, while far away
the flying bronze head rang upon the ground,
and Aías shivered knowing in his heart
the work of gods: how Zeus, the lord of thunder, 140
cut off his war-craft in that fight, and willed
victory to the Trojans. He gave way
before their missiles as they rushed in throwing
untiring fire into the ship. It caught
at once, a-gush with flame, and fire lapped
about the stern.
Akhilleus smote his thighs
and said to Patróklos:
"Now go into action,
prince and horseman! I see roaring fire
burst at the ships. Action, or they'll destroy them,
leaving no means of getting home. Be quick, 150
strap on my gear, while I alert the troops!"

Patróklos now put on the flashing bronze.
Greaves were the first thing, beautifully fitted

to calf and shin with silver ankle chains;
and next he buckled round his ribs the cuirass,
blazoned with stars, of swift Aiákidês;[67]
then slung the silver-studded blade of bronze
about his shoulders, and the vast solid shield;
then on his noble head he placed the helm,
its plume of terror nodding high above, 160
and took two burly spears with his own handgrip.
He did not take the great spear of Akhilleus,
weighty, long, and tough. No other Akhaian
had the strength to wield it, only Akhilleus.
It was a Pêlian ash, cut on the crest
of Pêlion, given to Akhilleus' father
by Kheirôn[68] to deal death to soldiery.
He then ordered his war-team put in harness
by Automédôn, whom he most admired
after Prince Akhilleus, breaker of men, 170
for waiting steadfast at his call in battle.
Automédôn yoked the fast horses for him—
Xánthos and Balíos, racers of wind.
The stormgust Podargê, who once had grazed
green meadowland by the Ocean stream, conceived
and bore them to the west wind, Zephyros.
In the side-traces Pêdasos, a thoroughbred,
was added to the team; Akhilleus took him
when he destroyed the city of Eëtiôn.
Mortal, he ran beside immortal horses. 180
Akhilleus put the Myrmidons in arms,
the whole detachment near the huts. Like wolves,
carnivorous and fierce and tireless,
who rend a great stag on a mountainside
and feed on him, their jaws reddened with blood,
loping in a pack to drink springwater,
lapping the dark rim up with slender tongues,
their chops a-drip with fresh blood, their hearts
unshaken ever, and their bellies glutted:
such were the Myrmidons and their officers, 190
running to form up round Akhilleus' brave
companion-in-arms.

And like the god of war
among them was Akhilleus: he stood tall
and sped the chariots and shieldmen onward.

Fifty ships there were that Lord Akhilleus,
favored of heaven, led to Troy. In each
were fifty soldiers, shipmates at the rowlocks.
Five he entrusted with command and made
lieutenants, while he ruled them all as king.

[67] Pêleus, son of Aiakos.

[68] A centaur who had tutored Akhilleus; also Chiron.

One company was headed by Menésthios 200
in his glittering breastplate, son of Spérkheios,
a river fed by heaven. Pêleus' daughter,
beautiful Polydôrê, had conceived him
lying with Spérkheios, untiring stream,
a woman with a god; but the world thought
she bore her child to Periêrês' son,
Bôros, who married her in the eyes of men
and offered countless bridal gifts. A second
company was commanded by Eudôros,
whose mother was unmarried: Polymêlê, 210
Phylas' daughter, a beautiful dancer
with whom the strong god Hermês fell in love,
seeing her among singing girls who moved
in measure for the lady of belling hounds,
Artemis of the golden shaft. And Hermês,
pure Deliverer, ascending soon
to an upper room, lay secretly with her
who was to bear his brilliant son, Eudôros,
a first-rate man at running and in war.
When Eileithyía,[69] sending pangs of labor, 220
brought him forth to see the sun-rays, then
strong-minded Ekheklêos, Aktor's son,
led the girl home with countless bridal gifts;
but Phylas in his age brought up the boy
with all kind care, as though he were a son.
Company three was led by Peísandros
Maimálidês, the best man with a spear
of all Myrmidons after Patróklos.
Company four the old man, master of horse,
Phoinix, commanded. Alkimédôn, son 230
of Laërkês, commanded company five.
When all were mustered under their officers,
Akhilleus had strict orders to impart:

"Myrmidons, let not one man forget
how menacing you were against the Trojans
during my anger and seclusion: how
each one reproached me, saying, 'Ironhearted
son of Pêleus, now we see: your mother
brought you up on rage, merciless man,
the way you keep your men confined to camp 240
against their will! We might as well sail home
in our seagoing ships, now this infernal
anger has come over you!' That way
you often talked, in groups around our fires.
Now the great task of battle is at hand
that you were longing for! Now every soldier
keep a fighting heart and face the Trojans!"

---

[69] Goddess of childbirth.

He stirred and braced their spirit; every rank
fell in more sharply when it heard its king.
As when a builder fitting stone on stone 250
lays well a high house wall to buffet back
the might of winds, just so
they fitted helms and studded shields together:
shield-rim on shield-rim, helmet on helmet, men
all pressed on one another, horsehair plumes
brushed on the bright crests as the soldiers nodded,
densely packed as they were.
Before them all
two captains stood in gear of war: Patróklos
and Automédôn, of one mind, resolved
to open combat in the lead.
Akhilleus 260
went to his hut. He lifted up the lid
of a seachest, all intricately wrought,
that Thetis of the silver feet had stowed
aboard his ship for him to take to Ilion,
filled to the brim with shirts, wind-breaking cloaks,
and fleecy rugs. His hammered cup was there,
from which no other man drank the bright wine,
and he made offering to no god but Zeus.
Lifting it from the chest, he purified it
first with brimstone, washed it with clear water, 270
and washed his hands, then dipped it full of wine.
Now standing in the forecourt, looking up
toward heaven, he prayed and poured his offering out,
and Zeus who plays in thunder heard his prayer:
"Zeus of Dôdôna,[70] god of Pelasgians,
O god whose home lies far! Ruler of wintry
harsh Dôdôna! Your interpreters,
the Selloi, live with feet like roots, unwashed,
and sleep on the hard ground. My lord, you heard me
praying before this, and honored me 280
by punishing the Akhaian army. Now,
again, accomplish what I most desire.
I shall stay on the beach, behind the ships,
but send my dear friend with a mass of soldiers,
Myrmidons, into combat. Let your glory,
Zeus who view the wide world, go beside him.
Sir, exalt his heart,
so Hektor too may see whether my friend
can only fight when I am in the field,
or whether singlehanded he can scatter them 290
before his fury! When he has thrown back
their shouting onslaught from the ships, then let him
return unhurt to the shipways and to me,
his gear intact, with all his fighting men."

[70] Zeus' principal shrine is at Dôdôna.

That was his prayer, and Zeus who views the wide world
heard him. Part he granted, part denied:
he let Patróklos push the heavy fighting
back from the ships, but would not let him come
unscathed from battle.

Now, after Akhilleus
had made his prayer and offering to Zeus, 300
he entered his hut again, restored the cup
to his seachest, and took his place outside—
desiring still to watch the savage combat
of Trojans and Akhaians. Brave Patróklos'
men moved forward with high hearts until
they charged the Trojans—Myrmidons in waves,
like hornets that small boys, as boys will do,
the idiots, poke up with constant teasing
in their daub chambers on the road,
to give everyone trouble. If some traveler 310
who passes unaware should then excite them,
all the swarm comes raging out
to defend their young. So hot, so angrily
the Myrmidons came pouring from the ships
in a quenchless din of shouting. And Patróklos
cried above them all:

"O Myrmidons,
brothers-in-arms of Pêleus' son, Akhilleus,
fight like men, dear friends, remember courage,
let us win honor for the son of Pêleus!
He is the greatest captain on the beach, 320
his officers and soldiers are the bravest!
Let King Agamémnon learn his folly
in holding cheap the best of the Akhaians!"

Shouting so, he stirred their hearts. They fell
as one man on the Trojans, and the ships
around them echoed the onrush and the cries.
On seeing Menoitios' powerful son, and with him
Automédôn, aflash with brazen gear,
the Trojan ranks broke, and they caught their breath,
imagining that Akhilleus the swift fighter 330
had put aside his wrath for friendship's sake.
Now each man kept an eye out for retreat
from sudden death. Patróklos drove ahead
against their center with his shining spear,
into the huddling mass, around the stern
of Prôtesílaos' burning ship. He hit
Pyraikhmês, who had led the Paiônês
from Amydôn, from Áxios' wide river—
hit him in the right shoulder. Backward in dust
he tumbled groaning, and his men-at-arms, 340
the Paiônês, fell back around him. Dealing
death to a chief and champion, Patróklos
drove them in confusion from the ship,

and doused the tigerish fire. The hull half-burnt
lay smoking on the shipway. Now the Trojans
with a great outcry streamed away; Danáäns
poured along the curved ships, and the din
of war kept on. As when the lightning master,
Zeus, removes a dense cloud from the peak
of some great mountain, and the lookout points 350
and spurs and clearings are distinctly seen
as though pure space had broken through from heaven:
so when the dangerous fire had been repelled
Danáäns took breath for a space. The battle
had not ended, though; not yet were Trojans
put to rout by the Akhaian charge
or out of range of the black ships. They withdrew
but by regrouping tried to make a stand.

In broken
ranks the captains sought and killed each other,
Menoitios' son making the first kill. 360
As Arêilykos wheeled around to fight,
he caught him with his spearhead in the hip,
and drove the bronze through, shattering the bone.
He sprawled face downward on the ground.

Now veteran
Meneláos thrusting past the shield
of Thoas to the bare chest brought him down.
Rushed by Ámphiklos, the alert Mégês
got his thrust in first, hitting his thigh
where a man's muscles bunch. Around the spearhead
tendons were split, and darkness veiled his eyes. 370
Nestor's sons were in action: Antílokhos
with his good spear brought down Atýmnios,
laying open his flank; he fell headfirst.
Now Maris moved in, raging for his brother,
lunging over the dead man with his spear,
but Thrasymêdês had already lunged
and did not miss, but smashed his shoulder squarely,
tearing his upper arm out of the socket,
severing muscles, breaking through the bone.
He thudded down and darkness veiled his eyes. 380
So these two, overcome by the two brothers,
dropped to the underworld of Érebos.
They were Sarpêdôn's true brothers-in-arms
and sons of Amisôdaros, who reared
the fierce Khimaira,[71] nightmare to many men.
Aías,[72] Oïleus' son, drove at Kleóboulos
and took him alive, encumbered in the press,
but killed him on the spot with a sword stroke

[71] Also Chimera: a being with a lion's head, a goat's body, and a serpent's tail.
[72] A different Aías from the earlier warrior.

across his nape—the whole blade running hot
with blood, as welling death and his harsh destiny 390
possessed him. Now Pênéleos
and Lykón clashed; as both had cast and missed
and lunged and missed with spears,
they fought again with swords. The stroke of Lykôn
came down on the other's helmet ridge
but his blade broke at the hilt. Pênéleos
thrust at his neck below the ear and drove
the blade clear in and through; his head toppled,
held only by skin, and his knees gave way.
Meríonês on the run overtook Akámas 400
mounting behind his horses and hit his shoulder,
knocking him from the car. Mist swathed his eyes.
Idómeneus thrust hard at Erýmas' mouth
with his hard bronze. The spearhead passed on through
beneath his brain and split the white brain-pan.
His teeth were dashed out, blood filled both his eyes,
and from his mouth and nostrils as he gaped
he spurted blood. Death's cloud enveloped him.
There each Danáän captain killed his man.
As ravenous wolves come down on lambs and kids 410
astray from some flock that in hilly country
splits in two by a shepherd's negligence,
and quickly wolves bear off the defenseless things,
so when Danáäns fell on Trojans, shrieking
flight was all they thought of, not of combat.
Aías the Tall[73] kept after bronze-helmed Hektor,
casting his lance, but Hektor, skilled in war,
would fit his shoulders under the bull's-hide shield,
and watch for whizzing arrows, thudding spears.
Aye, though he knew the tide of battle turned, 420
he kept his discipline and saved his friends.
As when Lord Zeus would hang the sky with storm,
a cloud may enter heaven from Olympos
out of crystalline space, so terror and cries
increased about the shipways. In disorder
men withdrew. Then Hektor's chariot team
cantering bore him off with all his gear,
leaving the Trojans whom the moat confined;
and many chariot horses in that ditch,
breaking their poles off at the tip, abandoned 430
war-cars and masters. Hard on their heels
Patróklos kept on calling all Danáäns
onward with slaughter in his heart. The Trojans,
yelling and clattering, filled all the ways,
their companies cut in pieces. High in air

[73]The famous warrior from the earlier books.

a blast of wind swept on, under the clouds,
as chariot horses raced back toward the town
away from the encampment. And Patróklos
rode shouting where he saw the enemy mass
in uproar: men fell from their chariots 440
under the wheels and cars jounced over them,
and running horses leapt over the ditch—
immortal horses, whom the gods gave Pêleus,
galloping as their mettle called them onward
after Hektor, target of Patróklos.
But Hektor's battle-team bore him away.

As under a great storm black earth is drenched
on an autumn day, when Zeus pours down the rain
in scudding gusts to punish men, annoyed
because they will enforce their crooked judgments 450
and banish justice from the market place,
thoughtless of the gods' vengeance; all their streams
run high and full, and torrents cut their way
down dry declivities into the swollen sea
with a hoarse clamor, headlong out of hills,
while cultivated fields erode away—
such was the gasping flight of the Trojan horses.

When he had cut their first wave off, Patróklos
forced it back again upon the ships
as the men fought toward the city. In between 460
the ships and river and the parapet
he swept among them killing, taking toll
for many dead Akhaians. First,
thrusting past Prónoös' shield, he hit him
on the bare chest, and made him crumple: down
he tumbled with a crash. Then he rushed Thestôr,
Enop's son, who sat all doubled up
in a polished war-car, shocked out of his wits,
the reins flown from his hands—and the Akhaian
got home his thrust on the right jawbone, driving 470
through his teeth. He hooked him by the spearhead
over the chariot rail, as a fisherman
on a point of rock will hook a splendid fish
with line and dazzling bronze out of the ocean:
so from his chariot on the shining spear
he hooked him gaping and face downward threw him,
life going out of him as he fell.

Patróklos
now met Erýlaos' rush and hit him square
mid-skull with a big stone. Within his helm
the skull was cleft asunder, and down he went 480
headfirst to earth; heartbreaking death engulfed him.
Next Erýmas, Amphóteros, Epaltês,

Tlêpolemos Damastoridês, Ekhíos,
Pyris, Ipheus, Euíppos, Polymêlos,
all in quick succession he brought down
to the once peaceful pastureland.

Sarpêdôn,
seeing his brothers-in-arms in their unbelted
battle jackets downed at Patróklos' hands,
called in bitterness to the Lykians:

"Shame, O Lykians, where are you running? 490
Now you show your speed!

I'll take on this one,
and learn what man he is that has the power
to do such havoc as he has done among us,
cutting down so many, and such good men."

He vaulted from his car with all his gear,
and on his side Patróklos, when he saw him,
leapt from his car. Like two great birds of prey
with hooked talons and angled beaks, who screech
and clash on a high ridge of rock, these two
rushed one another with hoarse cries. But Zeus, 500
the son of crooked-minded Krónos, watched,
and pitied them. He said to Hêra:

"Ai!
Sorrow for me, that in the scheme of things
the dearest of men to me must lie in dust
before the son of Menoitios, Patróklos.
My heart goes two ways as I ponder this:
shall I catch up Sarpêdôn
out of the mortal fight with all its woe
and put him down alive in Lykia,[74]
in that rich land? Or shall I make him fall 510
beneath Patróklos' hard-thrown spear?"

Then Hêra
of the wide eyes answered him:

"O fearsome power,
my Lord Zeus, what a curious thing to say.
A man who is born to die, long destined for it,
would you set free from that unspeakable end?
Do so; but not all of us will praise you.
And this, too, I may tell you: ponder this:
should you dispatch Sarpêdôn home alive,
anticipate some other god's desire
to pluck a man he loves out of the battle. 520

---

[74]Lykia, south of Troy, ruled by Sarpêdôn.

Many who fight around the town of Priam
sprang from immortals; you'll infuriate these.
No, dear to you though he is, and though you mourn him,
let him fall, even so, in the rough battle,
killed by the son of Menoitios, Patróklos.
Afterward, when his soul is gone, his lifetime
ended, Death and sweetest Sleep can bear him
homeward to the broad domain of Lykia.
There friends and kin may give him funeral
with tomb and stone, the trophies of the dead." 530

To this the father of gods and men agreed,
but showered bloody drops upon the earth
for the dear son Patróklos would destroy
in fertile Ilion, far from his home.
When the two men had come in range, Patróklos
turned like lightning against Thrasydêmos,
a tough man ever at Sarpêdôn's side,
and gave him a death-wound in the underbelly.
Sarpêdôn's counterthrust went wide, but hit
the trace horse, Pêdasos, in the right shoulder. 540
Screaming harshly, panting his life away,
he crashed and whinnied in the dust; the spirit
left him with a wingbeat. The team shied
and strained apart with a great creak of the yoke
as reins were tangled over the dead weight
of their outrider fallen. Automédôn,
the good soldier, found a way to end it:
pulling his long blade from his hip
he jumped in fast and cut the trace horse free.
The team then ranged themselves beside the pole, 550
drawing the reins taut, and once more,
devoured by fighting madness, the two men clashed.
Sarpêdôn missed again. He drove his spearhead
over the left shoulder of Patróklos,
not even grazing him. Patróklos then
made his last throw, and the weapon left his hand
with flawless aim. He hit his enemy
just where the muscles of the diaphragm
encased his throbbing heart. Sarpêdôn fell
the way an oak or poplar or tall pine 560
goes down, when shipwrights in the wooded hills
with whetted axes chop it down for timber.
So, full length, before his war-car lay
Sarpêdôn raging, clutching the bloody dust.
Imagine a greathearted sultry bull
a lion kills amid a shambling herd:
with choking groans he dies under the claws.
So, mortally wounded by Patróklos
the chief of Lykian shieldsmen lay in agony
and called his friend by name:

"Glaukos, old man, 570
old war-dog, now's the time to be a spearman!
Put your heart in combat! Let grim war
be all your longing! Quickly, if you can,
arouse the Lykian captains, round them up
to fight over Sarpêdôn. You, too, fight
to keep my body, else in later days
this day will be your shame. You'll hang your head
all your life long, if these Akhaians take
my armor here, where I have gone down fighting
before the ships. Hold hard; cheer on the troops!" 580

The end of life came on him as he spoke,
closing his eyes and nostrils. And Patróklos
with one foot on his chest drew from his belly
spearhead and spear; the diaphragm came out,
so he extracted life and blade together.
Myrmidons clung to the panting Lykian horses,
rearing to turn the car left by their lords.

But bitter anguish at Sarpêdôn's voice
had come to Glaukos, and his heart despaired
because he had not helped his friend. He gripped 590
his own right arm and squeezed it, being numb
where Teukros with a bowshot from the rampart
had hit him while he fought for his own men,[75]
and he spoke out in prayer to Lord Apollo:

"Hear me, O lord, somewhere in Lykian farmland
or else in Troy: for you have power to listen
the whole world round to a man hard pressed as I!
I have my sore wound, all my length of arm
a-throb with lancing pain; the flow of blood
cannot be stanched; my shoulder's heavy with it. 600
I cannot hold my spear right or do battle,
cannot attack them. Here's a great man destroyed,
Sarpêdôn, son of Zeus. Zeus let his own son
die undefended. O my lord, heal this wound,
lull me my pains, put vigor in me! Let me
shout to my Lykians, move them into combat!
Let me give battle for the dead man here!"

This way he prayed, and Phoibos Apollo heard him,
cutting his pain and making the dark blood dry
on his deep wound, then filled his heart with valor. 610
Glaukos felt the change, and knew with joy
how swiftly the great god had heard his prayer.
First he appealed to the Lykian captains, going
right and left, to defend Sarpêdôn's body,
then on the run he followed other Trojans,

---

[75] A reference to events in Book 12.

Poulýdamas, Pánthoös' son, Agênor,
and caught up with Aineías and with Hektor,
shoulder to shoulder, urgently appealing:

"Hektor, you've put your allies out of mind,
those men who give their lives here for your sake 620
so distant from their friends and lands: you will not
come to their aid! Sarpêdôn lies there dead,
commander of the Lykians, who kept
his country safe by his firm hand, in justice!
Arês in bronze has brought him down: the spear
belonged to Patróklos. Come, stand with me, friends,
and count it shame if they strip off his gear
or bring dishonor on his body—these
fresh Myrmidons enraged for the Danáäns
cut down at the shipways by our spears!" 630

At this, grief and remorse possessed the Trojans,
grief not to be borne, because Sarpêdôn
had been a bastion of the town of Troy,
foreigner though he was. A host came with him,
but he had fought most gallantly of all.
They made straight for the Danáäns, and Hektor
led them, hot with anger for Sarpêdôn.
Patróklos in his savagery cheered on
the Akhaians, first the two named Aías, both
already aflame for war:

"Aías and Aías, 640
let it be sweet to you to stand and fight!
You always do; be lionhearted, now.
The man who crossed the rampart of Akhaians
first of all lies dead: Sarpêdôn.[76] May we
take him, dishonor him, and strip his arms,
and hurl any friend who would defend him
into the dust with our hard bronze!"

At this they burned to throw the Trojans back.
And both sides reinforced their battle lines,
Trojans and Lykians, Myrmidons and Akhaians, 650
moving up to fight around the dead
with fierce cries and clanging of men's armor.
Zeus unfurled a deathly gloom of night
over the combat, making battle toil
about his dear son's body a fearsome thing.
At first, the Trojans drove back the Akhaians,
fiery-eyed as they were; one Myrmidon,
and not the least, was killed: noble Epeigeus,
a son of Agaklês. In Boudeion,
a flourishing town, he ruled before the war, 660
but slew a kinsman. So he came as suppliant

[76]In Book 12, it says that Hektor broke through the rampart first.

to Pêleus and to Thetis, who enlisted him
along with Lord Akhilleus, breaker of men,
to make war in the wild-horse country of Ilion
against the Trojans. Even as he touched the dead man,
Hektor hit him square upon the crest
with a great stone: his skull split in the helmet,
and he fell prone upon the corpse. Death's cloud
poured round him, heart-corroding. Grief and pain
for this friend dying came to Lord Patróklos, 670
who pounced through spear-play like a diving hawk
that puts jackdaws and starlings wildly to flight:
straight through Lykians, through Trojans, too,
you drove, Patróklos, master of horse,
in fury for your friend. Sthenélaos
the son of Ithaiménês was the victim:
Patróklos with a great stone broke his nape-cord.

Backward the line bent, Hektor too gave way,
as far as a hunting spear may hurtle, thrown
by a man in practice or in competition 680
or matched with deadly foes in war. So far
the Trojans ebbed, as the Akhaians drove them.
Glaukos, commander of Lykians, turned first,
to bring down valorous Báthyklês, the son
of Khalkôn, one who had his home in Hellas,
fortunate and rich among the Myrmidons.
Whirling as this man caught him, Glaukos hit him
full in the breastbone with his spear, and down
he thudded on his face. The Akhaians grieved
to see their champion fallen, but great joy 690
came to the Trojans, and they thronged about him.
Not that Akhaians now forgot their courage,
no, for their momentum carried them on.
Meríonês brought down a Trojan soldier,
Laógonos, Onêtor's rugged son,
a priest of Zeus on Ida, honored there
as gods are. Gashed now under jaw and ear
his life ran out, and hateful darkness took him.
Then at Meríonês Aineías cast
his bronze-shod spear, thinking to reach his body 700
under the shield as he came on. But he
looked out for it and swerved, slipping the spear-throw,
bowing forward, so the long shaft stuck
in earth behind him and the butt quivered;
the god Arês deprived it of its power.
Aineías raged and sneered:

"Meríonês,
fast dodger that you are, if I had hit you
my spearhead would have stopped your dance for good!"
Meríonês, good spearman, answered him:

"For all your power, Aineías, you could hardly 710
quench the fighting spirit of every man

defending himself against you. You are made
of mortal stuff like me. I, too, can say,
if I could hit you square, then tough and sure
as you may be, you would concede the game
and give your soul to the lord of nightmare, Death."

Patróklos said to him sharply:
"Meríonês,
you have your skill, why make a speech about it?
No, old friend, rough words will make no Trojans
back away from the body. Many a one 720
will be embraced by earth before they do.
War is the use of arms, words are for council.
More talk's pointless now; we need more fighting!"

He pushed on, and godlike Meríonês
fought at his side. Think of the sound of strokes
woodcutters make in mountain glens, the echoes
ringing for listeners far away: just so
the battering din of these in combat rose
from earth where the living go their ways—the clang
of bronze, hard blows on leather, on bull's hide, 730
as longsword blades and spearheads met their marks.
And an observer could not by now have seen
the Prince Sarpêdôn, since from head to foot
he lay enwrapped in weapons, dust, and blood.
Men kept crowding around the corpse. Like flies
that swarm and drone in farmyards round the milkpails
on spring days, when the pails are splashed with milk:
just so they thronged around the corpse. And Zeus
would never turn his shining eyes away
from this mêlée, but watched them all and pondered 740
long over the slaughter of Patróklos—
whether in that place, on Sarpêdôn's body,
Hektor should kill the man and take his gear,
or whether he, Zeus, should augment the moil[77]
of battle for still other men. He weighed it
and thought this best: that for a while Akhilleus'
shining brother-in-arms should drive his foes
and Hektor in the bronze helm toward the city,
taking the lives of many. First of all
he weakened Hektor, made him mount his car 750
and turn away, retreating, crying out
to others to retreat: for he perceived
the dipping scales of Zeus.[78] At this the Lykians
themselves could not stand fast, but all turned back,
once they had seen their king struck to the heart,

[77]Turmoil.

[78]Zeus' scales for measuring the progress of the war.

lying amid swales of dead—for many
fell to earth beside him when Lord Zeus
had drawn the savage battle line. So now
Akhaians lifted from Sarpêdôn's shoulders
gleaming arms of bronze, and these Patróklos 760
gave to his soldiers to be carried back
to the decked ships. At this point, to Apollo
Zeus who gathers cloud said:

"Wipe away the blood mantling Sarpêdôn;
take him up, out of the play of spears,
a long way off, and wash him in the river,
anoint him with ambrosia, put ambrosial
clothing on him. Then have him conveyed
by those escorting spirits quick as wind,
sweet Sleep and Death, who are twin brothers. These 770
will set him down in the rich broad land of Lykia,
and there his kin and friends may bury him
with tomb and stone, the trophies of the dead."

Attentive to his father, Lord Apollo
went down the foothills of Ida[79] to the field
and lifted Prince Sarpêdôn clear of it.
He bore him far and bathed him in the river,
scented him with ambrosia, put ambrosial
clothing on him, then had him conveyed
by those escorting spirits quick as wind, 780
sweet Sleep and Death, who are twin brothers. These
returned him to the rich broad land of Lykia.

Patróklos, calling to his team, commanding
Automédôn, rode on after the Trojans
and Lykians—all this to his undoing,
the blunderer. By keeping Akhilleus' mandate,
he might have fled black fate and cruel death.
But overpowering is the mind of Zeus
forever, matched with man's. He turns in fright
the powerful man and robs him of his victory 790
easily, though he drove him on himself.
So now he stirred Patróklos' heart to fury.

Whom first, whom later did you kill in battle,
Patróklos, when the gods were calling deathward?
First it was Adrêstos, Autônoös,
and Ekheklos; then Périmos Megadês,
Eristôr, Melánippos; afterward,
Elasos, Moulios, Pylartês. These
he cut down, while the rest looked to their flight.
Troy of the towering gates was on the verge 800

---

[79]Mountain near Troy.

of being taken by the Akhaians, under
Patróklos' drive: he raced with blooded spear
ahead and around it. On the massive tower
Phoibos Apollo stood as Troy's defender,
deadly toward him. Now three times Patróklos
assaulted the high wall at the tower joint,
and three times Lord Apollo threw him back
with counterblows of his immortal hands
against the resplendent shield. The Akhaian then
a fourth time flung himself against the wall, 810
more than human in fury. But Apollo
thundered:

"Back, Patróklos, lordly man!
Destiny will not let this fortress town
of Trojans fall to you! Not to Akhilleus,
either, greater far though he is in war!"

Patróklos now retired, a long way off
and out of range of Lord Apollo's anger.
Hektor had held his team at the Skaian Gates,
being of two minds: should he re-engage,
or call his troops to shelter behind the wall? 820
While he debated this, Phoibos Apollo
stood at his shoulder in a strong man's guise:
Ásïos, his maternal uncle, brother
of Hékabê and son of Dymas, dweller
in Phrygia on Sangaríos river.
Taking his semblance now, Apollo said:

"Why break off battle, Hektor? You need not.
Were I superior to you in the measure
that I am now inferior, you'd suffer
from turning back so wretchedly from battle. 830
Action! Lash your team against Patróklos,
and see if you can take him. May Apollo
grant you the glory!"

And at this, once more
he joined the mêlée, entering it as a god.
Hektor in splendor called Kebríonês
to whip the horses toward the fight. Apollo,
disappearing into the ranks, aroused
confusion in the Argives, but on Hektor
and on the Trojans he conferred his glory.
Letting the rest go, Hektor drove his team 840
straight at Patróklos; and Patróklos faced him
vaulting from his war-car, with his spear
gripped in his left hand; in his right
he held enfolded a sparkling jagged stone.
Not for long in awe of the other man,
he aimed and braced himself and threw the stone
and scored a direct hit on Hektor's driver,

Kebríonês, a bastard son of Priam,
smashing his forehead with the jagged stone.
Both brows were hit at once, the frontal bone 850
gave way, and both his eyes burst from their sockets
dropping into the dust before his feet,
as like a diver from the handsome car
he plummeted, and life ebbed from his bones.
You jeered at him then, master of horse, Patróklos:

"God, what a nimble fellow, somersaulting!
If he were out at sea in the fishing grounds
this man could feed a crew, diving for oysters,
going overboard even in rough water,
the way he took that earth-dive from his car. 860
The Trojans have their acrobats, I see."

With this, he went for the dead man with a spring
like a lion, one that has taken a chest wound
while ravaging a cattle pen—his valor
his undoing. So you sprang, Patróklos,
on Kebríonês. Then Hektor, too, leapt down
out of his chariot, and the two men fought
over the body like two mountain lions
over the carcass of a buck, both famished,
both in pride of combat. So these two
fought now for Kebríonês, two champions, 870
Patróklos, son of Menoitios, and Hektor,
hurling their bronze to tear each other's flesh.
Hektor caught hold of the dead man's head and held,
while his antagonist clung to a single foot,
as Trojans and Danáäns pressed the fight.
As south wind and the southeast wind, contending
in mountain groves, make all the forest thrash,
beech trees and ash trees and the slender cornel
swaying their pointed boughs toward one another
in roaring wind, and snapping branches crack: 880
so Trojans and Akhaians made a din
as lunging they destroyed each other. Neither
considered ruinous flight. Many sharp spears
and arrows trued by feathers from the strings
were fixed in flesh around Kebríonês,
and boulders crashed on shields, as they fought on
around him. And a dustcloud wrought
by a whirlwind hid the greatness of him slain,
minding no more the mastery of horses.
Until the sun stood at high noon in heaven, 890
spears bit on both sides, and the soldiers fell;
but when the sun passed toward unyoking time,
the Akhaians outfought destiny to prevail.
Now they dragged off gallant Kebríonês
out of range, away from the shouting Trojans,
to strip his shoulders of his gear. And fierce

Patróklos hurled himself upon the Trojans,
in onslaughts fast as Arês, three times, wild
yells in his throat. Each time he killed nine men. 900
But on the fourth demonic foray, then
the end of life loomed up for you, Patróklos.
Into the combat dangerous Phoibos came
against him, but Patróklos could not see
the god, enwrapped in cloud as he came near.
He stood behind and struck with open hand
the man's back and broad shoulders, and the eyes
of the fighting man were dizzied by the blow.
Then Phoibos sent the captain's helmet rolling
under the horses' hooves, making the ridge 910
ring out, and dirtying all the horsehair plume
with blood and dust. Never in time before
had this plumed helmet been befouled with dust,
the helmet that had kept a hero's brow
unmarred, shielding Akhilleus' head. Now Zeus
bestowed it upon Hektor, let him wear it,
though his destruction waited. For Patróklos
felt his great spearshaft shattered in his hands,
long, tough, well-shod, and seasoned though it was;
his shield and strap fell to the ground; the Lord 920
Apollo, son of Zeus, broke off his cuirass.
Shock ran through him, and his good legs failed,
so that he stood agape. Then from behind
at close quarters, between the shoulder blades,
a Dardan fighter speared him: Pánthoös' son,
Euphórbos, the best Trojan of his age
at handling spears, in horsemanship and running:
he had brought twenty chariot fighters down
since entering combat in his chariot,
already skilled in the craft of war. This man 930
was first to wound you with a spear, Patróklos,
but did not bring you down. Instead, he ran back
into the mêlée, pulling from the flesh
his ashen spear, and would not face his enemy,
even disarmed, in battle. Then Patróklos,
disabled by the god's blow and the spear wound,
moved back to save himself amid his men.
But Hektor, seeing that his brave adversary
tried to retire, hurt by the spear wound, charged
straight at him through the ranks and lunged for him 940
low in the flank, driving the spearhead through.
He crashed, and all Akhaian troops turned pale.
Think how a lion in his pride brings down
a tireless boar; magnificently they fight
on a mountain crest for a small gushing spring—
both in desire to drink—and by sheer power
the lion conquers the great panting boar:
that was the way the son of Priam, Hektor,
closed with Patróklos, son of Menoitios,

killer of many, and took his life away. 950
Then glorying above him he addressed him:

"Easy to guess, Patróklos, how you swore
to ravage Troy, to take the sweet daylight
of liberty from our women, and to drag them
off in ships to your own land—you fool!
Between you and those women there is Hektor's
war-team, thundering out to fight! My spear
has pride of place among the Trojan warriors,
keeping their evil hour at bay.
The kites[80] will feed on you, here on this field. 960
Poor devil, what has that great prince, Akhilleus,
done for you? He must have told you often
as you were leaving and he stayed behind,
'Never come back to me, to the deepsea ships,
Patróklos, till you cut to rags
the bloody tunic on the chest of Hektor!'
That must have been the way he talked, and won
your mind to mindlessness."

In a low faint voice,
Patróklos, master of horse, you answered him:
"This is your hour to glory over me, 970
Hektor. The Lord Zeus and Apollo gave you
the upper hand and put me down with ease.
They stripped me of my arms. No one else did.
Say twenty men like you had come against me,
all would have died before my spear.
No, Lêto's son and fatal destiny
have killed me; if we speak of men, Euphórbos.
You were in third place, only in at the death.
I'll tell you one thing more; take it to heart.
No long life is ahead for you. This day 980
your death stands near, and your immutable end,
at Prince Akhilleus' hands."

His own death
came on him as he spoke, and soul from body,
bemoaning severance from youth and manhood,
slipped to be wafted to the underworld.
Even in death Prince Hektor still addressed him:

"Why prophesy my sudden death, Patróklos?
Who knows, Akhilleus, son of bright-haired Thetis,
might be hit first; he might be killed by me."

At this he pulled his spearhead from the wound, 990
setting his heel upon him; then he pushed him
over on his back clear of the spear,
and lifting it at once sought Automédôn,

---

[80]Birds of the hawk family.

companion of the great runner, Akhilleus,
longing to strike him. But the immortal horses,
gift of the gods to Pêleus, bore him away.

BOOK 18
THE IMMORTAL SHIELD

[In Book 17, Hektor claims Patróklos' armor, but the Akhaians succeed in bringing his body back to their camp.–ED.]

While they were still in combat, fighting seaward
raggedly as fire, Antílokhos[81]
ran far ahead with tidings for Akhilleus.
In shelter of the curled, high prows he found him
envisioning what had come to pass,
in gloom and anger saying to himself:

"Ai! why are they turning tail once more,
unmanned, outfought, and driven from the field
back on the beach and ships? I pray the gods
this may not be the last twist of the knife! 10
My mother warned me once that, while I lived,
the most admirable of Myrmidons
would quit the sunlight under Trojan blows.
It could indeed be so. He has gone down,
my dear and wayward friend!
Push their deadly fire away, I told him,
then return! You must not fight with Hektor!"

And while he called it all to mind,
the son of gallant Nestor came up weeping
to give his cruel news:
"Here's desolation, 20
son of Pêleus, the worst for you—
would god it had not happened!—Lord Patróklos
fell, and they are fighting over his body,
stripped of armor. Hektor has your gear."

A black stormcloud of pain shrouded Akhilleus.
On his bowed head he scattered dust and ash
in handfuls and befouled his beautiful face,
letting black ash sift on his fragrant khiton.[82]
Then in the dust he stretched his giant length
and tore his hair with both hands.
From the hut 30
the women who had been spoils of war to him
and to Patróklos flocked in haste around him,

[81] Nestor's son.
[82] A loose garment, like a tunic.

crying loud in grief. All beat their breasts,
and trembling came upon their knees.
Antílokhos
wept where he stood, bending to hold the hero's
hands when groaning shook his heart: he feared
the man might use sharp iron to slash his throat.
And now Akhilleus gave a dreadful cry.
Her ladyship
his mother heard him, in the depths offshore
lolling near her ancient father. Nymphs 40
were gathered round her: all Nêrëidês
who haunted the green chambers of the sea.
Glaukê, Thaleia, and Kymodokê,
Nesaiê, Speiô, Thoê, Haliê
with her wide eyes; Kymothoê, Aktaiê,
Limnôreia, Melitê, and Iaira,
Amphitoê, Agauê, Dôtô, Prôtô,
Pherousa, Dynaménê, Dexaménê,
Amphinomê, Kallianeira, Dôris,
Panopê, and storied Galateia, 50
Nêmertês and Apseudês, Kallianassa,
Klyméne, Ianeira, Ianassa,
Maira, Oreithyia, Amathyia,
and other Nêrëidês of the deep sea,
filling her glimmering silvery cave. All these
now beat their breasts as Thetis cried in sorrow:

"Sisters, daughters of Nêreus, hear and know
how sore my heart is! Now my life is pain
for my great son's dark destiny! I bore
a child flawless and strong beyond all men. 60
He flourished like a green shoot, and I brought him
to manhood like a blossoming orchard tree,
only to send him in the ships to Ilion
to war with the Trojans. Now I shall never see him
entering Pêleus' hall, his home, again.
But even while he lives, beholding sunlight,
suffering is his lot. I have no power
to help him, though I go to him. Even so,
I'll visit my dear child and learn what sorrow
came to him while he held aloof from war." 70

On this she left the cave, and all in tears
her company swam aloft with her. Around them
a billow broke and foamed on the open sea.
As they made land at the fertile plain of Troy,
they went up one by one in line to where,
in close order, Myrmidon ships were beached
to right and left of Akhilleus. Bending near
her groaning son, the gentle goddess wailed
and took his head between her hands in pity,
saying softly:

"Child, why are you weeping? 80
What great sorrow came to you? Speak out,
do not conceal it. Zeus
did all you asked: Akhaian troops,
for want of you, were all forced back again
upon the ship sterns, taking heavy losses
none of them could wish."

The great runner
groaned and answered:

"Mother, yes, the master
of high Olympos brought it all about,
but how have I benefited? My greatest friend
is gone: Patróklos, comrade in arms, whom I 90
held dear above all others—dear as myself—
now gone, lost; Hektor cut him down, despoiled him
of my own arms, massive and fine, a wonder
in all men's eyes. The gods gave them to Pêleus
that day they put you in a mortal's bed—
how I wish the immortals of the sea
had been your only consorts! How I wish
Pêleus had taken a mortal queen! Sorrow
immeasurable is in store for you as well,
when your own child is lost: never again 100
on his homecoming day will you embrace him!
I must reject this life, my heart tells me,
reject the world of men,
if Hektor does not feel my battering spear
tear the life out of him, making him pay
in his own blood for the slaughter of Patróklos!"

Letting a tear fall, Thetis said:

"You'll be
swift to meet your end, child, as you say:
your doom comes close on the heels of Hektor's own."

Akhilleus the great runner ground his teeth 110
and said:

"May it come quickly. As things were,
I could not help my friend in his extremity.
Far from his home he died; he needed me
to shield him or to parry the death stroke.
For me there's no return to my own country.
Not the slightest gleam of hope did I
afford Patróklos or the other men
whom Hektor overpowered. Here I sat,
my weight a useless burden to the earth,
and I am one who has no peer in war 120
among Akhaian captains—

though in council
there are wiser. Ai! let strife and rancor

perish from the lives of gods and men,
with anger that envenoms even the wise
and is sweeter than slow-dripping honey,
clouding the hearts of men like smoke: just so
the marshal of the army, Agamémnon,
moved me to anger. But we'll let that go,
though I'm still sore at heart; it is all past,
and I have quelled my passion as I must. 130

Now I must go to look for the destroyer
of my great friend. I shall confront the dark
drear spirit of death at any hour Zeus
and the other gods may wish to make an end.
Not even Hêraklês escaped that terror
though cherished by the Lord Zeus. Destiny
and Hêra's bitter anger mastered him.
Likewise with me, if destiny like his
awaits me, I shall rest when I have fallen!
Now, though, may I win my perfect glory 140
and make some wife of Troy break down,
or some deep-breasted Dardan[83] woman sob
and wipe tears from her soft cheeks. They'll know then
how long they had been spared the deaths of men,
while I abstained from war!
Do not attempt to keep me from the fight,
though you love me; you cannot make me listen."

Thetis, goddess of the silvery feet,
answered:

"Yes, of course, child: very true.
You do no wrong to fight for tired soldiers 150
and keep them from defeat. But still, your gear,
all shining bronze, remains in Trojan hands.
Hektor himself is armed with it in pride!—
Not that he'll glory in it long, I know,
for violent death is near him.

Patience, then.
Better not plunge into the moil of Arês
until you see me here once more. At dawn,
at sunrise, I shall come
with splendid arms for you from Lord Hêphaistos."

She rose at this and, turning from her son, 160
told her sister Nêrêïdês:

"Go down
into the cool broad body of the sea
to the sea's Ancient; visit Father's hall,
and make all known to him. Meanwhile, I'll visit
Olympos' great height and the lord of crafts,

[83] Allied with Troy.

Hêphaistos, hoping he will give me
new and shining armor for my son."

At this they vanished in the offshore swell,
and to Olympos Thetis the silvery-footed
went once more, to fetch for her dear son 170
new-forged and finer arms.

Meanwhile, Akhaians,
wildly crying, pressed by deadly Hektor,
reached the ships, beached above Hellê's water.
None had been able to pull Patróklos clear
of spear- and swordplay: troops and chariots
and Hektor, son of Priam, strong as fire,
once more gained upon the body. Hektor
three times had the feet within his grasp
and strove to wrest Patróklos backward, shouting
to all the Trojans—but three times the pair 180
named Aías in their valor shook him off.
Still he pushed on, sure of his own power,
sometimes lunging through the battle-din,
or holding fast with a great shout: not one step
would he give way. As from a fresh carcass
herdsmen in the wilds cannot dislodge
a tawny lion, famished: so those two
with fearsome crests could not affright the son
of Priam or repel him from the body.
He might have won it, might have won unending 190
glory, but Iris[84] running on the wind
came from Olympos to the son of Pêleus,
bidding him gird for battle. All unknown
to Zeus and the other gods she came, for Hêra
sent her down. And at his side she said:

"Up with you, Pêleidês, who strike cold fear
into men's blood! Protect your friend Patróklos,
for whom, beyond the ships, desperate combat
rages now. They are killing one another
on both sides: the Akhaians to defend him, 200
Trojans fighting for that prize
to drag to windy Ilion. And Hektor
burns to take it more than anyone—
to sever and impale Patróklos' head
on Trojan battlements. Lie here no longer.
It would be shameful if wild dogs of Troy
made him their plaything! If that body suffers
mutilation, you will be infamous!"

Prince Akhilleus answered:

"Iris of heaven,
what immortal sent you to tell me this?" 210

---

[84]Messenger of the gods.

And she who runs upon the wind replied:
"Hêra, illustrious wife of Zeus,
but he on his high throne knows nothing of it.
Neither does any one of the gods undying
who haunt Olympos of eternal snows."

Akhilleus asked:

"And now how shall I go
into the fighting? Those men have my gear.
My dear mother allows me no rearming
until I see her again here.
She promises fine arms from Lord Hêphaistos. 220
I don't know whose armor I can wear,
unless I take Aías' big shield.
But I feel sure he's in the thick of it,
contending with his spear over Patróklos."

Then she who runs upon the wind replied:
"We know they have your arms, and know it well.
Just as you are, then, stand at the moat; let Trojans
take that in; they will be so dismayed
they may break off the battle, and Akhaians
in their fatigue may win a breathing spell, 230
however brief, a respite from the war."

At this,
Iris left him, running downwind. Akhilleus,
whom Zeus loved, now rose. Around his shoulders
Athêna hung her shield[85] like a thunderhead
with trailing fringe. Goddess of goddesses,
she bound his head with golden cloud, and made
his very body blaze with fiery light.
Imagine how the pyre of a burning town
will tower to heaven and be seen for miles
from the island under attack, while all day long 240
outside their town, in brutal combat, pikemen
suffer the wargod's winnowing; at sundown
flare on flare is lit, the signal fires
shoot up for other islanders to see,
that some relieving force in ships may come:
just so the baleful radiance from Akhilleus
lit the sky. Moving from parapet
to moat, without a nod for the Akhaians,
keeping clear, in deference to his mother,
he halted and gave tongue. Not far from him 250
Athêna shrieked. The great sound shocked the Trojans
into tumult, as a trumpet blown
by a savage foe shocks an encircled town,
so harsh and clarion was Akhilleus' cry.

[85] The famous aegis with the image of Medusa on it.

The hearts of men quailed, hearing that brazen voice.
Teams, foreknowing danger, turned their cars
and charioteers blanched, seeing unearthly fire,
kindled by the grey-eyed goddess Athêna,
brilliant over Akhilleus. Three great cries
he gave above the moat. Three times they shuddered, 260
whirling backward, Trojans and allies,
and twelve good men took mortal hurt
from cars and weapons in the rank behind.
Now the Akhaians leapt at the chance
to bear Patróklos' body out of range.
They placed it on his bed,
and old companions there with brimming eyes
surrounded him. Into their midst Akhilleus
came then, and he wept hot tears to see
his faithful friend, torn by the sharp spearhead, 270
lying cold upon his cot. Alas,
the man he sent to war with team and chariot
he could not welcome back alive.

Her majesty,
wide-eyed Hêra, made the reluctant sun,
unwearied still, sink in the streams of Ocean.
Down he dropped, and the Akhaian soldiers
broke off combat, resting from the war.
The Trojans, too, retired. Unharnessing
teams from war-cars, before making supper,
they came together on the assembly ground, 280
every man on his feet; not one could sit,
each being still in a tremor—for Akhilleus,
absent so long, had once again appeared.
Clearheaded Poulýdamas, son of Pánthoös,
spoke up first, as he alone could see
what lay ahead and all that lay behind.
He and Hektor were companions-in-arms,
born, as it happened, on the same night; but one
excelled in handling weapons, one with words.
Now for the good of all he spoke among them: 290

"Think well of our alternatives, my friends.
What I say is, retire upon the town,
instead of camping on the field till dawn
here by ships. We are a long way
from our stone wall. As long as that man raged
at royal Agamémnon, we could fight
the Akhaians with advantage. I was happy
to spend last night so near the beach and think
of capturing ships today. Now, though, I fear
the son of Pêleus to my very marrow! 300
There are no bounds to the passion of that man.
He will not be contained by the flat ground
where Trojans and Akhaians share between them
raging war: he will strive on to fight
to win our town, our women. Back to Troy!

Believe me, this is what we face!
Now, starry night has made Akhilleus pause,
but when day comes, when he sorties in arms
to find us lingering here, there will be men
who learn too well what he is made of. Aye, 310
I daresay those who get away will reach
walled Ilion thankfully, but dogs and kites
of Troy will feed on many. May that story
never reach my ears! If we can follow
my battle plan, though galled by it, tonight
we'll husband strength, at rest in the market place.
Towers, high gates, great doors of fitted planking,
bolted tight, will keep the town secure.
Early tomorrow we shall arm ourselves
and man the walls. Worse luck then for Akhilleus, 320
if he comes looking for a head-on fight
on the field around the wall! He can do nothing
but trot back, after all, to the encampment,
his proud team in a lather from their run,
from scouring every quarter below the town.
Rage as he will, he cannot force an entrance,
cannot take all Troy by storm. Wild dogs
will eat him first!"

Under his shimmering helmet
Hektor glared at the speaker. Then he said:
"Poulýdamas, what you propose no longer 330
serves my turn. To go on the defensive
inside the town again? Is anyone
not sick of being huddled in those towers?
In past days men told tales of Priam's city,
rich in gold and rich in bronze, but now
those beautiful treasures of our home are lost.
Many have gone for sale to Phrygia
and fair Mêïoniê, since Lord Zeus
grew hostile toward us.

Now when the son of Krónos
Crooked Wit has given me a chance 340
of winning glory, pinning the Akhaians
back on the sea—now is no time to publish
notions like these to troops, you fool! No Trojan
goes along with you, I will not have it!
Come, let each man act as I propose.
Take your evening meal by companies;
remember sentries; keep good watch; and any
Trojan tired of his wealth, who wants
to lose everything, let him turn it over
to the army stores to be consumed in common! 350
Better our men enjoy it than Akhaians.
At first light we shall buckle armor on
and bring the ships under attack. Suppose

the man who stood astern there was indeed
Akhilleus, then worse luck for him,
if he will have it so. Shall I retreat
from him, from clash of combat? No, I will not.
Here I'll stand, though he should win; I might
just win, myself: the battle-god's impartial,
dealing death to the death-dealing man." 360

This was Hektor's speech. The Trojans roared
approval of it—fools, for Pallas Athêna
took away their wits. They all applauded
Hektor's poor tactics, but Poulýdamas
with his good judgment got not one assent.
They took their evening meal now, through the army,
while all night long Akhaians mourned Patróklos.

Akhilleus led them in their lamentation,
laying those hands deadly to enemies
upon the breast of his old friend, with groans 370
at every breath, bereft as a lioness
whose whelps a hunter seized out of a thicket;
late in returning, she will grieve, and roam
through many meandering valleys on his track
in hope of finding him; heart-stinging anger
carries her away. Now with a groan
he cried out to the Myrmidons:

"Ah, god,
what empty prophecy I made that day
to cheer Menoitios in his mégaron!
I promised him his honored son, brought back 380
to Opoeis,[86] as pillager of Ilion
bearing his share of spoils.
But Zeus will not fulfill what men design,
not all of it. Both he and I were destined
to stain the same earth dark red here at Troy.
No going home for me; no welcome there
from Pêleus, master of horse, or from my mother,
Thetis. Here the earth will hold me under.
Therefore, as I must follow you into the grave,
I will not give you burial, Patróklos, 390
until I carry back the gear and head
of him who killed you, noble friend.
Before your funeral pyre I'll cut the throats
of twelve resplendent children of the Trojans—
that is my murdering fury at your death.
But while you lie here by the swanlike ships,
night and day, close by, deep-breasted women
of Troy, and Dardan women, must lament

[86] A city in Greece, home of Menoitios, father of Patróklos.

and weep hot tears, all those whom we acquired
by labor in assault, by the long spear,
pillaging the fat market towns of men." 400

With this Akhilleus called the company
to place over the campfire a big tripod
and bathe Patróklos of his clotted blood.
Setting tripod and caldron on the blaze
they poured it full, and fed the fire beneath,
and flames licked round the belly of the vessel
until the water warmed and bubbled up
in the bright bronze. They bathed him then, and took
sweet oil for his anointing, laying nard[87]
in the open wounds; and on his bed they placed him, 410
covering him with fine linen, head to foot,
and a white shroud over it.

So all that night
beside Akhilleus the great runner,
the Myrmidons held mourning for Patróklos.
Now Zeus observed to Hêra, wife and sister:
"You had your way, my lady, after all,
my wide-eyed one! You brought him to his feet,
the great runner! One would say the Akhaian
gentlemen were progeny of yours." 420

And Hêra with wide eyes replied:

"Dread majesty,
Lord Zeus, why do you take this tone? May not
an ordinary mortal have his way,
though death awaits him, and his mind is dim?
Would anyone suppose that I, who rank
in two respects highest of goddesses—
by birth and by my station, queen to thee,
lord of all gods—that I should not devise
ill fortune for the Trojans whom I loathe?"

So ran their brief exchange. Meanwhile 430
the silvery-footed Thetis reached Hêphaistos'
lodging, indestructible and starry,
framed in bronze by the bandy-legged god.
She found him sweating, as from side to side
he plied his bellows; on his forge were twenty
tripods to be finished, then to stand
around his mégaron. And he wrought wheels
of gold for the base of each, that each might roll
as of itself into the gods' assembly,
then roll home, a marvel to the eyes. 440
The caldrons were all shaped but had no handles.
These he applied now, hammering rivets in;

[87]Spikenard, from which ointment was made.

and as he toiled surehandedly at this,
Thetis arrived.

Grace in her shining veil
just going out encountered her—that Grace
the bowlegged god had taken to wife.[88] She greeted
Thetis with a warm handclasp and said:

"My lady Thetis, gracious goddess, what
has brought you here? You almost never honor us!
Please come in, and let me give you welcome." 450

Loveliest of goddesses, she led the way,
to seat her guest on a silver-studded chair,
elaborately fashioned, with a footrest.
Then she called to Hêphaistos:

"Come and see!
Thetis is here, in need of something from you!"

To this the Great Gamelegs replied:

"Ah, then we have a visitor I honor.
She was my savior, after the long fall
and fractures that I had to bear, when Mother,[89]
bitch that she is, wanted to hide her cripple. 460
That would have been a dangerous time, had not
Thetis and Eurýnomê[90] taken me in—
Eurýnomê, daughter of the tidal Ocean.
Nine years I stayed, and fashioned works of art,
brooches and spiral bracelets, necklaces,
in their smooth cave, round which the stream of Ocean
flows with a foaming roar: and no one else
knew of it, gods or mortals. Only Thetis
knew, and Eurýnomê, the two who saved me.
Now she has come to us. Well, what I owe 470
for life to her ladyship in her soft braids
I must repay. Serve her our choicest fare
while I put up my bellows and my tools."

At this he left the anvil block, and hobbled
with monstrous bulk on skinny legs to take
his bellows from the fire. Then all the tools
he had been toiling with he stowed
in a silver chest.

That done, he sponged himself,
his face, both arms, bull-neck and hairy chest,
put on a tunic, took a weighty staff, 480
and limped out of his workshop. Round their lord
came fluttering maids of gold, like living girls:

---

[88] Hêphaistos was lame; usually his wife is Aphrodite.
[89] Hêra.
[90] Thetis' aunt.

intelligences, voices, power of motion
these maids have, and skills learnt from immortals.
Now they came rustling to support their lord,
and he moved on toward Thetis, where she sat
upon the silvery chair. He took her hand
and warmly said:

"My Lady Thetis, gracious
goddess, why have you come? You almost never honor us.
Tell me the favor that you have in mind, 490
for I desire to do it if I can,
and if it is a thing that one may do."

Thetis answered, tear on cheek:

"Hêphaistos,
who among all Olympian goddesses
endured anxiety and pain like mine?
Zeus chose me, from all of them, for this!
Of sea-nymphs I alone was given in thrall
to a mortal warrior, Pêleus Aiákidês,
and I endured a mortal warrior's bed
many a time, without desire. Now Pêleus 500
lies far gone in age in his great hall,
and I have other pain. Our son, bestowed
on me and nursed by me, became a hero
unsurpassed. He grew like a green shoot;
I cherished him like a flowering orchard tree,
only to send him in the ships to Ilion
to war with Trojans. Now I shall never see him
entering Pêleus' hall, his home, again.
But even while he lives, beholding sunlight,
suffering is his lot. I have no power 510
to help him, though I go to him. A girl,
his prize from the Akhaians, Agamémnon
took out of his hands to make his own,
and ah, he pined with burning heart! The Trojans
rolled the Akhaians back on the ship sterns,
and left them no escape. Then Argive officers
begged my son's help, offering every gift,
but he would not defend them from disaster.
Arming Patróklos in his own war-gear,
he sent him with his people into battle. 520
All day long, around the Skaian Gates,
they fought, and would have won the city, too,
had not Apollo, seeing the brave son
of Menoitios wreaking havoc on the Trojans,
killed him in action, and then given Hektor
the honor of that deed.

On this account
I am here to beg you: if you will, provide
for my doomed son a shield and crested helm,
good legging-greaves, fitted with ankle clasps,
a cuirass, too. His own armor was lost 530

when his great friend went down before the Trojans.
Now my son lies prone on the hard ground in grief."

The illustrious lame god replied:
"Take heart.
No trouble about the arms. I only wish
that I could hide him from the power of death
in his black hour—wish I were sure of that
as of the splendid gear he'll get, a wonder
to any one of the many men there are!"

He left her there, returning to his bellows,
training them on the fire, crying, "To work!" 540
In crucibles the twenty bellows breathed
every degree of fiery air: to serve him
a great blast when he labored might and main,
or a faint puff, according to his wish
and what the work demanded.
Durable
fine bronze and tin he threw into the blaze
with silver and with honorable gold,
then mounted a big anvil in his block
and in his right hand took a powerful hammer,
managing with his tongs in his left hand. 550

His first job was a shield, a broad one, thick,
well-fashioned everywhere. A shining rim
he gave it, triple-ply, and hung from this
a silver shoulder strap. Five welded layers
composed the body of the shield. The maker
used all his art adorning this expanse.
He pictured on it earth, heaven, and sea,
unwearied sun, moon waxing, all the stars
that heaven bears for garland: Plêïadês,
Hyadês, Oríôn in his might, 560
the Great Bear, too, that some have called the Wain,
pivoting there, attentive to Oríôn,
and unbathed ever in the Ocean stream.[91]

He pictured, then, two cities, noble scenes:
weddings in one, and wedding feasts, and brides
led out through town by torchlight from their chambers
amid chorales, amid the young men turning
round and round in dances: flutes and harps
among them, keeping up a tune, and women
coming outdoors to stare as they went by. 570
A crowd, then, in a market place, and there
two men at odds over satisfaction owed
for a murder done: one claimed that all was paid,

[91] The Great Bear (Ursa Major) is the Big Dipper, which never descends below the horizon.

and publicly declared it; his opponent
turned the reparation down, and both
demanded a verdict from an arbiter,
as people clamored in support of each,
and criers restrained the crowd. The town elders
sat in a ring, on chairs of polished stone,
the staves of clarion criers in their hands, 580
with which they sprang up, each to speak in turn,
and in the middle were two golden measures
to be awarded him whose argument
would be the most straightforward.

Wartime then;
around the other city were emplaced
two columns of besiegers, bright in arms,
as yet divided on which plan they liked:
whether to sack the town, or treat for half
of all the treasure stored in the citadel.
The townsmen would not bow either: secretly 590
they armed to break the siege-line. Women and children
stationed on the walls kept watch, with men
whom age disabled. All the rest filed out,
as Arês led the way, and Pallas Athêna,
figured in gold, with golden trappings, both
magnificent in arms, as the gods are,
in high relief, while men were small beside them.
When these had come to a likely place for ambush,
a river with a watering place for flocks,
they there disposed themselves, compact in bronze. 600
Two lookouts at a distance from the troops
took their posts, awaiting sight of sheep
and shambling cattle. Both now came in view,
trailed by two herdsmen playing pipes, no hidden
danger in their minds. The ambush party
took them by surprise in a sudden rush;
swiftly they cut off herds and beautiful flocks
of silvery grey sheep, then killed the herdsmen.
When the besiegers from their parleying ground
heard sounds of cattle in stampede, they mounted 610
behind mettlesome teams, following the sound,
and came up quickly. Battle lines were drawn,
and on the riverbanks the fight began
as each side rifled javelins at the other.
Here then Strife and Uproar joined the fray,
and ghastly Fate, that kept a man with wounds
alive, and one unwounded, and another
dragged by the heels through battle-din in death.
This figure wore a mantle dyed with blood,
and all the figures clashed and fought 620
like living men, and pulled their dead away.

Upon the shield, soft terrain, freshly plowed,
he pictured: a broad field, and many plowmen

here and there upon it. Some were turning
ox teams at the plowland's edge, and there
as one arrived and turned, a man came forward
putting a cup of sweet wine in his hands.
They made their turns-around, then up the furrows
drove again, eager to reach the deep field's
limit; and the earth looked black behind them, 630
as though turned up by plows. But it was gold,
all gold—a wonder of the artist's craft.

He put there, too, a king's field. Harvest hands
were swinging whetted scythes to mow the grain,
and stalks were falling along the swath
while binders girded others up in sheaves
with bands of straw—three binders, and behind them
children came as gleaners, proffering
their eager armfuls. And amid them all
the king stood quietly with staff in hand, 640
happy at heart, upon a new-mown swath.
To one side, under an oak tree his attendants
worked at a harvest banquet. They had killed
a great ox, and were dressing it; their wives
made supper for the hands, with barley strewn.

A vineyard then he pictured, weighted down
with grapes: this all in gold; and yet the clusters
hung dark purple, while the spreading vines
were propped on silver vine-poles. Blue enamel
he made the enclosing ditch, and tin the fence, 650
and one path only led into the vineyard
on which the loaded vintagers took their way
at vintage time. Lighthearted boys and girls
were harvesting the grapes in woven baskets,
while on a resonant harp a boy among them
played a tune of longing, singing low
with delicate voice a summer dirge. The others,
breaking out in song for the joy of it,
kept time together as they skipped along.

The artisan made next a herd of longhorns, 660
fashioned in gold and tin: away they shambled,
lowing, from byre to pasture by a stream
that sang in ripples, and by reeds a-sway.
Four cowherds all of gold were plodding after
with nine lithe dogs beside them.
On the assault,
in two tremendous bounds, a pair of lions
caught in the van a bellowing bull, and off
they dragged him, followed by the dogs and men.
Rending the belly of the bull, the two
gulped down his blood and guts, even as the herdsmen 670
tried to set on their hunting dogs, but failed:

no trading bites with lions for those dogs,
who halted close up, barking, then ran back.

And on the shield the great bowlegged god
designed a pasture in a lovely valley,
wide, with silvery sheep, and huts and sheds
and sheepfolds there.

A dancing floor as well
he fashioned, like that one in royal Knossos
Daidalos made for the Princess Ariadnê.[92]
Here young men and the most desired young girls 680
were dancing, linked, touching each other's wrists,
the girls in linen, in soft gowns, the men
in well-knit khitons given a gloss with oil;
the girls wore garlands, and the men had daggers
golden-hilted, hung on silver lanyards.
Trained and adept, they circled there with ease
the way a potter sitting at his wheel
will give it a practice twirl between his palms
to see it run; or else, again, in lines
as though in ranks, they moved on one another: 690
magical dancing! All around, a crowd
stood spellbound as two tumblers led the beat
with spins and handsprings through the company.

Then, running round the shield-rim, triple-ply,
he pictured all the might of the Ocean stream.

Besides the densely plated shield, he made
a cuirass, brighter far than fire light,
a massive helmet, measured for his temples,
handsomely figured, with a crest of gold;
then greaves[93] of pliant tin.

Now when the crippled god 700
had done his work, he picked up all the arms
and laid them down before Akhilleus' mother,
and swift as a hawk from snowy Olympos' height
she bore the brilliant gear made by Hêphaistos.

BOOK 19
THE AVENGER FASTS AND ARMS

Dawn in her yellow robe rose in the east
out of the flowing Ocean, bearing light
for deathless gods and mortal men. And Thetis
brought to the beach her gifts from the god of fire.

[92] Ariadnê, the daughter of King Minos, who hired Daidalos to construct his great palace and a labyrinth at Knossos on Krete.
[93] Armor for legs.

She found her dear son lying beside Patróklos,
wailing, while his men stood by
in tears around him. Now amid that throng
the lovely goddess bent to touch his shoulder
and said to him:

"Ah, child, let him lie dead,
for all our grief and pain, we must allow it; 10
he fell by the gods' will.
But you, now—take the war-gear from Hêphaistos.
No man ever bore upon his shoulders
gear so magnificent."

And she laid the armor
down before Akhilleus, clanging loud
in all its various glory. Myrmidons
began to tremble at the sound, and dared not
look straight at the armor; their knees shook.
But anger entered Akhilleus as he gazed,
his eyes grown wide and bright as blazing fire, 20
with fierce joy as he handled the god's gifts.
After appraising them in his delight
he spoke out to his mother swiftly:

"Mother,
these the god gave are miraculous arms,
handiwork of immortals, plainly—far
beyond the craft of men. By heaven, I'll wear them!
Only, I feel the dread that while I fight
black carrion flies may settle on Patróklos'
wounds, where the spearheads marked him, and I fear
they may breed maggots to defile the corpse, 30
now life is torn from it. His flesh may rot."

But silvery-footed Thetis answered:

"Child,
you must not let that prey on you. I'll find
a way to shield him from the black fly hordes
that eat the bodies of men killed in battle.
Though he should lie unburied a long year,
his flesh will be intact and firm. Now, though,
for your part, call the Akhaians to assembly.
Tell them your anger against Agamémnon
is over and done with! 40
After that, at once
put on your gear, prepare your heart, for war!"

Her promise gave her son wholehearted valor.
Then, turning, to Patróklos, she instilled
red nectar and ambrosia[94] in his nostrils
to keep his body whole.

[94]Drink and food of the gods.

And Prince Akhilleus
passed along the surf-line with a shout
that split the air and roused men of Akhaia,
even those who, up to now, had stayed
amid the massed ships—navigators, helmsmen, 50
men in charge of rations and ship stores.
Aye, even these now headed for assembly,
since he who for so long had shunned the battle,
Akhilleus, now appeared upon the field.
Resolute Diomêdês and Odysseus,
familiars of the wargod, limped along,
leaning on spears, for both had painful wounds.
They made their way to the forefront and sat down,
and last behind them entered the Lord Marshal
Agamémnon, favoring his wound: he too 60
had taken a slash, from Antênor's son, Koôn.
When everyone had crowded in, Akhilleus,
the great battlefield runner, rose and said:

"Agamémnon, was it better for us
in any way, when we were sore at heart,
to waste ourselves in strife over a girl?
If only Artemis had shot her down
among the ships on the day I made her mine,
after I took Lyrnessos!
Fewer Akhaians would have died hard 70
at enemy hands, while I abstained in anger—
Hektor's gain, the Trojans' gain. Akhaians
years hence will remember our high words,
mine and yours. But now we can forget them,
and, as we must, forego our passion. Aye,
by heaven, I drop my anger now!
No need to smolder in my heart forever! Come,
send your long-haired Akhaians into combat,
and let me see how Trojans will hold out,
if camping near the beachhead's their desire! 80
I rather think some will be glad to rest,
provided they get home, away from danger,
out of my spear's range!"

These were his words,
and all the Akhaians gave a roar of joy
to hear the prince abjure his rage.
Lord Marshal Agamémnon then addressed them,
standing up, not in the midst of them,
but where he had been sitting:

"Friends, fighters,
Danáäns, companions of Arês: it is fair
to listen to a man when he has risen 90
and not to interrupt him. That's vexation
to any speaker, able though he may be.
In a great hubbub how can any man
attend or speak? A fine voice will be muffled.

While I open my mind to the son of Pêleus,
Argives, attention! Each man weigh my words!
The Akhaians often brought this up against me,
and chided me. But I am not to blame.
Zeus and Fate and a nightmare Fury are,
for putting savage Folly in my mind 100
in the assembly that day, when I wrested
Akhilleus' prize of war from him. In truth,
what could I do? Divine will shapes these things.
Ruinous Folly, eldest daughter of Zeus,
beguiles us all. Her feet are soft, from walking
not on earth but over the heads of men
to do them hurt. She traps one man or another.
Once indeed she deluded Zeus, most noble
of gods and men, they say. But feminine
Hêra with her underhanded ways 110
tricked him, the day Alkmênê,[95] in high Thebes,
was to have given birth to Hêraklês.
Then glorying Zeus remarked to all the gods:
'Hear me, all gods and goddesses, I'll tell you
of something my heart dwells upon. This day
the childbirth goddess, Eileithyía, brings
into the light a man who will command
all those around him, being of the race of men
who come of my own blood!' But in her guile
the Lady Hêra said: 'You may be wrong, 120
unable to seal your word with truth hereafter.
Come, Olympian, swear me a great oath
he will indeed be lord of all his neighbors,
the child of your own stock in the race of men
who drops between a woman's legs today!'
Zeus failed to see her crookedness: he swore
a mighty oath, and mightily went astray,
for flashing downward from Olympos crest
Hêra visited Argos of Akhaia,
aware that the strong wife of Perseus' son, 130
Sthénelos, was big with child,
just entering her seventh month. But Hêra
brought this child into the world's daylight
beforehand by two months, and checked Alkmênê's
labor, to delay the birth of hers.
To Zeus the son of Krónos then she said:
'Zeus of the bright bolt, father, let me add
a new event to your deliberations.
Even now a superior man is born
to be a lord of Argives: Eurýstheus,[96] 140
a son of Sthénelos, the son of Perseus,
of your own stock. And it is not unfitting

[95] Alkmênê was a mortal married to the King of Thebes; she was seduced by Zeus.
[96] He became king of Argos; at one point Hêraklês performed twelve labors under his direction.

for him to rule the Argives.' This report
sharply wounded the deep heart of Zeus.
He picked up Folly by her shining braids
in sudden anger—swearing a great oath
that never to starred heaven or Olympos
Folly, who tricks us all, should come again.
With this he whirled her with one hand and flung her
out of the sky. So to men's earth she came, 150
but ever thereafter made Zeus groan to see
his dear son toil at labors for Eurýstheus.

So, too, with me: when in his shimmering helm
great Hektor slaughtered Argives near the ships,
could I ignore my folly, my delusion?
Zeus had stolen my wits, my act was blind.
But now I wish to make amends, to give
all possible satisfaction. Rouse for war,
send in your troops! I here repeat my offer
of all that Odysseus promised yesterday! 160
Stay if you will, though the wargod presses you.
Men in my service will unload the gifts
from my own ship, that you may see how richly
I reward you!"

Akhilleus answered:

"Excellency,
Lord Marshal Agamémnon, make the gifts
if you are keen to—gifts are due; or keep them.
It is for you to say. Let us recover
joy of battle soon, that's all!
No need to dither here and lose our time,
our great work still undone. When each man sees 170
Akhilleus in a charge, crumpling the ranks
of Trojans with his bronze-shod spear, let each
remember that is the way to fight his man!"

Replied Odysseus, the shrewd field commander:
"Brave as you are, and like a god in looks,
Akhilleus, do not send Akhaian soldiers
into the fight unfed! Today's mêlée
will not be brief, when rank meets rank, and heaven
breathes fighting spirit into both contenders.
No, tell all troops who are near the ships to take 180
roast meat and wine, for heart and staying power.
No soldier can fight hand to hand, in hunger,
all day long until the sun goes down!
Though in his heart he yearns for war, his legs
go slack before he knows it: thirst and famine
search him out, and his knees fail as he moves.
But that man stayed with victualing and wine
can fight his enemies all day: his heart
is bold and happy in his chest, his legs

hold out until both sides break off the battle! 190
Come, then, dismiss the rank to make their breakfast.
Let the Lord Marshal Agamémnon
bring his gifts to the assembly ground
where all may see them; may your heart be warmed.
Then let him swear to you, before the Argives,
never to have made love to her, my lord,
as men and women by their nature do.
So may your heart be peaceable toward him!
And let him sate your hunger with rich fare
in his own shelter, that you may lack nothing 200
due you in justice. Afterward, Agamémnon,
you'll be more just to others, too. There is
no fault in a king's wish to conciliate
a man with whom he has been quick to anger!"

And the Lord Marshal Agamémnon answered:

"Glad I am to hear you, son of Laërtês,
finding the right word at the right time
for all these matters. And the oath you speak of
I'll take willingly, with all my heart,
and will not, before heaven, be forsworn. 210
Now let Akhilleus wait here, though the wargod
tug his arm; and all the rest of you
wait here assembled till the gifts have come
down from our quarters, and our peace is made.
For you, Odysseus, here is my command:
choose the finest young peers of all Akhaia
to fetch out of my ship those gifts we pledged
Akhilleus yesterday; and bring the women.
Let Talthýbios[97] prepare for sacrifice,
in the army's name, a boar to Zeus and Hêlios."[98] 220

Replied Akhilleus:

"Excellency, Lord Marshal,
another time were better for these ceremonies,
some interval in the war, and when I feel
less passion in me. Look, those men lie dead
whom Hektor killed when Zeus allowed him glory,
and yet you two propose a meal! By god,
I'd send our soldiers into action now
unfed and hungry. Have a feast, I'd say,
at sundown, when our shame has been avenged!
Before that, for my part, I will not swallow 230
food or drink—my dear friend being dead,
lying before my eyes, bled white by spear-cuts,
feet turned to his hut's door, his friends in mourning

[97] Agamémnon's herald.
[98] Sun.

around him. Your concerns are none of mine.
Slaughter and blood are what I crave, and groans
of anguished men!"

But the shrewd field commander
Odysseus answered:

"Akhilleus, flower and pride
of the Akhaians, you are more powerful
than I am—and a better spearman, too—
only in sizing matters up I'd say 240
I'm just as far beyond you, being older,
knowing more of the world. So bear with me.
Men quickly reach satiety with battle
in which the reaping bronze will bring to earth
big harvests, but a scanty yield, when Zeus,
war's overseer for mankind, tips the scales.
How can a fasting belly mourn our dead?
So many die, so often, every day,
when would soldiers come to an end of fasting?
No, we must dispose of him who dies 250
and keep hard hearts, and weep that day alone.
And those whom the foul war has left unhurt
will do well to remember food and drink,
so that we may again close with our enemies,
our dangerous enemies, and be tough soldiers,
hardened in mail of bronze. Let no one, now,
be held back waiting for another summons:
here is your summons! Woe to the man who lingers
beside the Argive ships! No, all together,
let us take up the fight against the Trojans!" 260

He took as escort sons of illustrious Nestor:
Phyleus' son Mégês, Thoas, and Meríonês,
and the son of Kreion, Lykomêdês, and
Melánippos, to Agamémnon's quarters.
No sooner was the work assigned than done:
they brought the seven tripods Agamémnon
promised Akhilleus, and the twenty caldrons
shining, and the horses, a full dozen;
then they conducted seven women, skilled
in housecraft, with Brisêis in her beauty. 270
Odysseus weighed ten bars of purest gold
and turned back, followed by his young Akhaians,
bearing the gifts to place in mid-assembly.
Now Agamémnon rose. Talthýbios
the crier, with his wondrous voice, stood near him,
holding the boar. The son of Atreus drew
the sheath knife that he carried, hung
beside the big sheath of his sword, and cut
first bristles from the boar. Arms wide to heaven
he prayed to Zeus, as all the troops kept still, 280
all sitting in due order in their places,

hearing their king. In prayer he raised his eyes
to the broad sky and said:

"May Zeus, all-highest
and first of gods, be witness first, then Earth
and Hêlios and the Furies underground
who punish men for having broken oaths,
I never laid a hand on your Brisêis,
proposing bed or any other pleasure;
in my quarters the girl has been untouched.
If one word that I swear is false, 290
may the gods plague me for a perjured liar!"

He slit the boar's throat with his blade of bronze.
Then Talthýbios, wheeling, flung the victim
into the offshore water, bait for fish.
Akhilleus rose amid the Argive warriors,
saying:

"Father Zeus, you send mankind
prodigious follies. Never otherwise
had Agamémnon stung me through and through;
never would he have been so empty-headed
as to defy my will and take the girl! 300
No, for some reason Zeus had death at heart
for the Akhaians, and for many.

Well:
go to your meat, then we'll resume the fighting."

Thus he dismissed the assembly. All the men
were quick to scatter, each to his own ship.
As for the gifts, the Myrmidons took over
and bore them all to Akhilleus' ship, to stow
within his shelter. There they left the women
and drove the horses to the herd.

The girl
Brisêis, in her grace like Aphrodítê, 310
on entering saw Patróklos lying dead
of spear wounds, and she sank down to embrace him
with a sharp sobbing cry, lifting her hands
to tear her breast, soft throat, and lovely face,
this girl, shaped like the goddesses of heaven.
Weeping, she said:

"Patróklos, very dear,
most dear to me, cursed as I am, you were
alive still when I left you, left this place!
Now I come back to find you dead, my captain!
Evil follows evil so, for me. 320
The husband to whom father and mother gave me
I saw brought down by spears before our town,
with my three brothers, whom my mother bore.
Dear brothers, all three met their day of wrath.
But when Akhilleus killed my lord, and sacked

the city of royal Mynês, not a tear
would you permit me: no, you undertook
to see me married to the Prince Akhilleus,
conveyed by ship to Phthía, given a wedding
among the Myrmidons. Now must I mourn 330
your death forever, who were ever gentle."

She wailed again, and women sobbed about her,
first for Patróklos, then for each one's grief.
Meanwhile Akhaian counselors were gathered
begging Akhilleus to take food. He spurned it,
groaning:

"No, I pray you, my dear friends,
if anyone will listen!—do not nag me
to glut and dull my heart with food and drink!
A burning pain is in me. I'll hold out
till sundown without food. I say I'll bear it." 340

With this he sent the peers away, except
the two Atreidai[99] and the great Odysseus,
Nestor, Idómeneus, and old Lord Phoinix.
These would have comforted him, but none
could quiet or comfort him until he entered
the bloody jaws of war. Now pierced by memory,
he sighed and sighed again, and said:

"Ah, once
you, too, poor fated friend, and best of friends,
would set a savory meal deftly before us
in our field shelter, when the Akhaians wished 350
no time lost between onsets against Trojans.
Now there you lie, broken in battle. Ah,
lacking you, my heart will fast this day
from meat and drink as well. No greater ill
could come to me, not news of Father's death—
my father, weeping soft tears now in Phthía
for want of that son in a distant land
who wars on Troy for Helen's sake—that woman
who makes the blood run cold. No greater ill,
even should my son die, who is being reared 360
on Skyros, Neoptólemos,[100] if indeed
he's living still. My heart's desire has been
that I alone should perish far from Argos
here at Troy; that you should sail to Phthía,
taking my son aboard your swift black ship
at Skyros, to introduce him to his heritage,
my wide lands, my servants, my great hall.

[99] Sons of Atreus: Agamémnon and Meneláos.

[100] Skyros is an island in the Aegean Sea; after Akhilleus' death, his son, Neoptólemos, joined the war and killed Priam.

In this late year Pêleus may well be dead
and buried, or have few days yet to live,
beset by racking age, always awaiting 370
dire news of me, of my own death."

As he said this he wept. The counselors groaned,
remembering each what he had left at home;
and seeing them sorrow, Zeus took pity on them,
saying quickly to Athêna:

"Daughter,
you seem to have left your fighting man alone.
Should one suppose you care no more for Akhilleus?
There he sits, before the curving prows,
and grieves for his dear friend. The other soldiers
flock to meat; he thirsts and hungers. Come, 380
infuse in him sweet nectar and ambrosia,
that an empty belly may not weaken him."

He urged Athêna to her own desire,
and like a gliding sea hawk, shrilling high,
she soared from heaven through the upper air,
while the Akhaians armed throughout the ranks.
Nectar and ambrosia she instilled
within Akhilleus, that his knees be not
assailed by hollow famine; then she withdrew
to her mighty father's house. Meanwhile the troops 390
were pouring from the shipways to the field.
As when cold snowflakes fly from Zeus in heaven,
thick and fast under the blowing north wind,
just so, that multitude of gleaming helms
and bossed shields issued from the ship, with plated
cuirasses and ashwood spears. Reflected
glintings flashed to heaven, as the plain
in all directions shown with glare of bronze
and shook with trampling feet of men. Among them
Prince Akhilleus armed. One heard his teeth 400
grind hard together, and his eyes blazed out
like licking fire, for unbearable pain
had fixed upon his heart. Raging at Trojans,
he buckled on the arms Hêphaistos forged.
The beautiful greaves, fitted with silver anklets,
first he put upon his legs, and next
the cuirass on his ribs; then over his shoulder
he slung the sword of bronze with silver scabbard;
finally he took up the massive shield
whence came a radiance like the round full moon. 410
As when at sea to men on shipboard comes
the shining of a campfire on a mountain
in a lone sheepfold, while the gusts of nightwind
take them, loath to go, far from their friends
over the teeming sea; just so
Akhilleus' finely modeled shield sent light

into the heavens. Lifting his great helm
he placed it on his brows, and like a star
the helm shone with its horsetail blowing free,
all golden, that Hêphaistos had set in 420
upon the crest. Akhilleus tried his armor,
shrugging and flexing, making sure it fitted,
sure that his gleaming legs had play. Indeed
the gear sat on him light as wings: it buoyed him!
Now from a spear-case he withdrew a spear—
his father's—weighty, long, and tough. No other
Akhaian had the strength to handle it,
this great Pêlian shaft
of ashwood, given his father by the centaur
Kheirôn from the crest of Pêlion 430
to be the death of heroes.

Automédôn
and Álkimos with swift hands yoked his team,
making firm the collars on the horses,
placing the bits between their teeth, and pulling
reins to the war-car. Automédôn then
took in hand the shining whip and mounted
the chariot, and at his back Akhilleus
mounted in full armor, shining bright
as the blinding Lord of Noon.[101] In a clarion voice
he shouted to the horses of his father: 440

"Xánthos and Balíos! Known to the world
as foals of great Podargê! In this charge
care for your driver in another way!
Pull him back, I mean, to the Danáäns,
back to the main body of the army,
once we are through with battle; this time,
no leaving him there dead, like Lord Patróklos!"

To this, from under the yoke, the nimble Xánthos
answered, and hung his head, so that his mane
dropped forward from the yokepad to the ground— 450
Hêra whose arms are white as ivory
gave him a voice to say:

"Yes, we shall save you,
this time, too, Akhilleus in your strength!
And yet the day of your destruction comes,
and it is nearer. We are not the cause,
but rather a great god is, and mighty Fate.
Nor was it by our sloth or sluggishness
the Trojans stripped Patróklos of his armor.
No, the magnificent god[102] that Lêto bore
killed him in action and gave Hektor glory. 460
We might run swiftly as the west wind blows,

[101] Sun. [102] Apollo.

most rapid of all winds, they say; but still
it is your destiny to be brought low
by force, a god's force and a man's!"[103]

On this,
the Furies put a stop to Xánthos' voice.[104]
In anger and gloom Akhilleus said to him:

"Xánthos, why prophesy my death? No need.
What is in store for me I know, know well:
to die here, far away from my dear father,
my mother, too. No matter. All that matters 470
is that I shall not call a halt today
till I have made the Trojans sick of war!"

And with a shout he drove his team
of trim-hooved horses into the front line.

BOOK 22
DESOLATION BEFORE TROY

[In Book 20, the gods actively take sides. Poseidon rescues Aineías from Akhilleus because Aineías is fated to survive the war. Akhilleus, however, kills many Trojans. In Book 21, the god of the River Xánthos is angered by the numerous corpses Akhilleus dumped in the river, and turns on Akhilleus. Akhilleus is saved by gods and goddesses, who then in the excitement of warfare begin to fight each other. The remaining Trojans retreat to the city.–ED.]

Once in the town, those who had fled like deer
wiped off their sweat and drank their thirst away,
leaning against the cool stone of the ramparts.
Meanwhile Akhaians with bright shields aslant
came up the plain and nearer. As for Hektor,
fatal destiny pinned him where he stood
before the Skaian Gates, outside the city.

Now Akhilleus heard Apollo calling
back to him:

"Why run so hard, Akhilleus,
mortal as you are, after a god? 10
Can you not comprehend it? I am immortal.
You are so hot to catch me, you no longer
think of finishing off the men you routed.
They are all in the town by now, packed in
while you were being diverted here. And yet
you cannot kill me; I am no man's quarry."

---

[103] Akhilleus will be killed by Paris, aided by Apollo.

[104] Although the horse Xánthos has been given the power of speech by Hêra, it is contrary to the order of nature and the Furies silence him.

Akhilleus bit his lip and said:

"Archer of heaven, deadliest
of immortal gods, you put me off the track,
turning me from the wall this way. A hundred 20
might have sunk their teeth into the dust
before one man took cover in Ilion!
You saved my enemies with ease and stole
my glory, having no punishment to fear.
I'd take it out of you, if I had the power."

Then toward the town with might and main he ran,
magnificent, like a racing chariot horse
that holds its form at full stretch on the plain.
So light-footed Akhilleus held the pace.
And aging Priam was the first to see him 30
sparkling on the plain, bright as that star
in autumn rising, whose unclouded rays
shine out amid a throng of stars at dusk—
the one they call Oríôn's dog,[105] most brilliant,
yes, but baleful as a sign: it brings
great fever to frail men. So pure and bright
the bronze gear blazed upon him as he ran.
The old man gave a cry. With both his hands
thrown up on high he struck his head, then shouted,
groaning, appealing to his dear son. Unmoved, 40
Lord Hektor stood in the gateway, resolute
to fight Akhilleus.

Stretching out his hands,
old Priam said, imploring him:

"No, Hektor!
Cut off as you are, alone, dear son,
don't try to hold your ground against this man,
or soon you'll meet the shock of doom, borne down
by the son of Pêleus. He is more powerful
by far than you, and pitiless. Ah, were he
but dear to the gods as he is dear to me!
Wild dogs and kites would eat him where he lay 50
within the hour, and ease me of my torment.
Many tall sons he killed, bereaving me,
or sold them to far islands. Even now
I cannot see two sons of mine, Lykáôn
and Polydôros, among the Trojans massed
inside the town. A queen, Laóthoê,[106]
conceived and bore them. If they are alive
amid the Akhaian host, I'll ransom them
with bronze and gold: both I have, piled at home,
rich treasures that old Altês, the renowned, 60

[105] Sirius, the "dog star."
[106] One of Priam's concubines.

gave for his daughter's dowry. If they died,
if they went under to the homes of Death,
sorrow has come to me and to their mother.
But to our townsmen all this pain is brief,
unless you too go down before Akhilleus.
Come inside the wall, child; here you may
fight on to save our Trojan men and women.
Do not resign the glory to Akhilleus,
losing your own dear life! Take pity, too,
on me and my hard fate, while I live still. 70
Upon the threshold of my age, in misery,
the son of Krónos will destroy my life
after the evil days I shall have seen—
my sons brought down, my daughters dragged away,
bedchambers ravaged, and small children hurled
to earth in the atrocity of war,
as my sons' wives are taken by Akhaians'
ruinous hands. And at the end, I too—
when someone with a sword-cut or a spear
has had my life—I shall be torn apart 80
on my own doorstep by the hounds
I trained as watchdogs, fed from my own table.
These will lap my blood with ravenous hearts
and lie in the entranceway.
Everything done
to a young man killed in war becomes his glory,
once he is riven by the whetted bronze:
dead though he be, it is all fair, whatever
happens then. But when an old man falls,
and dogs disfigure his grey head and cheek
and genitals, that is most harrowing 90
of all that men in their hard lives endure."

The old man wrenched at his grey hair and pulled out
hanks of it in both his hands, but moved
Lord Hektor not at all. The young man's mother
wailed from the tower across, above the portal,
streaming tears, and loosening her robe
with one hand, held her breast out in the other,
saying:

"Hektor, my child, be moved by this,
and pity me, if ever I unbound
a quieting breast for you. Think of these things, 100
dear child; defend yourself against the killer
this side of the wall, not hand to hand.
He has no pity. If he brings you down,
I shall no longer be allowed to mourn you
laid out on your bed, dear branch in flower,
born of me! And neither will your lady,
so endowed with gifts. Far from us both,
dogs will devour you by the Argive ships."

With tears and cries the two implored their son,
and made their prayers again, but could not shake him. 110
Hektor stood firm, as huge Akhilleus neared.
The way a serpent, fed on poisonous herbs,
coiled at his lair upon a mountainside,
with all his length of hate awaits a man
and eyes him evilly: so Hektor, grim
and narrow-eyed, refused to yield. He leaned
his brilliant shield against a spur of wall
and in his brave heart bitterly reflected:

"Here I am badly caught. If I take cover,
slipping inside the gate and wall, the first 120
to accuse me for it will be Poulýdamas,
he who told me I should lead the Trojans
back to the city on that cursed night
Akhilleus joined the battle. No, I would not,
would not, wiser though it would have been.
Now troops have perished for my foolish pride,
I am ashamed to face townsmen and women.
Someone inferior to me may say:
'He kept his pride and lost his men, this Hektor!'
So it will go. Better, when that time comes, 130
that I appear as he who killed Akhilleus
man to man, or else that I went down
before him honorably for the city's sake.
Suppose, though, that I lay my shield and helm
aside, and prop my spear against the wall,
and go to meet the noble Prince Akhilleus,
promising Helen, promising with her
all treasures that Aléxandros brought home
by ship to Troy—the first cause of our quarrel—
that he may give these things to the Atreidai? 140
Then I might add, apart from these, a portion
of all the secret wealth the city owns.
Yes, later I might take our counselors' oath
to hide no stores, but share and share alike
to halve all wealth our lovely city holds,
all that is here within the walls. Ah, no,
why even put the question to myself?
I must not go before him and receive
no quarter, no respect! Aye, then and there
he'll kill me, unprotected as I am, 150
my gear laid by, defenseless as a woman.
No chance, now, for charms from oak or stone
in parley with him—charms a girl and boy
might use when they enchant each other talking!
Better we duel, now at once, and see
to whom the Olympian awards the glory."
These were his shifts of mood. Now close at hand
Akhilleus like the implacable god of war
came on with blowing crest, hefting the dreaded

beam of Pêlian ash on his right shoulder. 160
Bronze light played around him, like the glare
of a great fire or the great sun rising,
and Hektor, as he watched, began to tremble.
Then he could hold his ground no more. He ran,
leaving the gate behind him, with Akhilleus
hard on his heels, sure of his own speed.
When that most lightning-like of birds, a hawk
bred on a mountain, swoops upon a dove,
the quarry dips in terror, but the hunter,
screaming, dips behind and gains upon it, 170
passionate for prey. Just so, Akhilleus
murderously cleft the air, as Hektor
ran with flashing knees along the wall.
They passed the lookout point, the wild figtree
with wind in all its leaves, then veered away
along the curving wagon road, and came
to where the double fountains well, the source
of eddying Skamánder. One hot spring
flows out, and from the water fumes arise
as though from fire burning; but the other 180
even in summer gushes chill as hail
or snow or crystal ice frozen on water.
Near these fountains are wide washing pools
of smooth-laid stone, where Trojan wives and daughters
laundered their smooth linen in the days
of peace before the Akhaians came. Past these
the two men ran, pursuer and pursued,
and he who fled was noble, he behind
a greater man by far. They ran full speed,
and not for bull's hide or a ritual beast 190
or any prize that men compete for: no,
but for the life of Hektor, tamer of horses.
Just as when chariot-teams around a course
go wheeling swiftly, for the prize is great,
a tripod or a woman, in the games
held for a dead man, so three times these two
at full speed made their course round Priam's town,
as all the gods looked on. And now the father
of gods and men turned to the rest and said:

"How sad that this beloved man is hunted 200
around the wall before my eyes! My heart
is touched for Hektor; he has burned thigh flesh
of oxen for me often, high on Ida,
at other times on the high point of Troy.
Now Prince Akhilleus with devouring stride
is pressing him around the town of Priam.
Come, gods, put your minds on it, consider
whether we may deliver him from death
or see him, noble as he is, brought down
by Pêleus' son, Akhilleus."

Grey-eyed Athêna 210
said to him:

"Father of the blinding bolt,
the dark stormcloud, what words are these? The man
is mortal, and his doom fixed, long ago.
Would you release him from his painful death?
Then do so, but not all of us will praise you."

Zeus who gathers cloud replied:

"Take heart,
my dear and honored child. I am not bent
on my suggestion, and I would indulge you.
Act as your thought inclines, refrain no longer."

So he encouraged her in her desire, 220
and down she swept from ridges of Olympos.
Great Akhilleus, hard on Hektor's heels,
kept after him, the way a hound will harry
a deer's fawn he has startled from its bed
to chase through gorge and open glade, and when
the quarry goes to earth under a bush
he holds the scent and quarters till he finds it;
so with Hektor: he could not shake off
the great runner, Akhilleus. Every time
he tried to sprint hard for the Dardan gates 230
under the towers, hoping men would help him,
sending missiles down, Akhilleus loomed
to cut him off and turn him toward the plain,
as he himself ran always near the city.
As in a dream a man chasing another
cannot catch him, nor can he in flight
escape from his pursuer, so Akhilleus
could not by swiftness overtake him,
nor could Hektor pull away. How could he
run so long from death, had not Apollo 240
for the last time, the very last, come near
to give him stamina and speed?

Akhilleus
shook his head at the rest of the Akhaians,
allowing none to shoot or cast at Hektor—
none to forestall him, and to win the honor.
But when, for the fourth time, they reached the springs,
the Father poised his golden scales.

He placed
two shapes of death, death prone and cold, upon them,
one of Akhilleus, one of the horseman, Hektor,
and held the midpoint, pulling upward. Down 250
sank Hektor's fatal day, the pan went down
toward undergloom, and Phoibos Apollo left him.
Then came Athêna, grey-eyed, to the son

of Pêleus, falling in with him, and near him,
saying swiftly:
"Now at last I think
the two of us, Akhilleus loved by Zeus,
shall bring Akhaians triumph at the ships
by killing Hektor—unappeased
though he was ever in his thirst for war.
There is no way he may escape us now, 260
not though Apollo, lord of distances,
should suffer all indignity for him
before his father Zeus who bears the stormcloud,
rolling back and forth and begging for him.
Now you can halt and take your breath, while I
persuade him into combat face to face."

These were Athêna's orders. He complied,
relieved, and leaning hard upon the spearshaft
armed with its head of bronze. She left him there
and overtook Lord Hektor—but she seemed 270
Dêíphobos in form and resonant voice,
appearing at his shoulder, saying swiftly:

"Ai! Dear brother, how he runs, Akhilleus,
harrying you around the town of Priam!
Come, we'll stand and take him on."

To this,
great Hektor in his shimmering helm replied:
"Dêíphobos, you were the closest to me
in the old days, of all my brothers, sons
of Hékabê and Priam. Now I can say
I honor you still more 280
because you dared this foray for my sake,
seeing me run. The rest stay under cover."

Again the grey-eyed goddess Athêna spoke:
"Dear brother, how your father and gentle mother
begged and begged me to remain! So did
the soldiers round me, all undone by fear.
But in my heart I ached for you.
Now let us fight him, and fight hard.
No holding back. We'll see if this Akhilleus
conquers both, to take our armor seaward, 290
or if he can be brought down by your spear."

This way, by guile, Athêna led him on.
And when at last the two men faced each other,
Hektor was the first to speak. He said:

"I will no longer fear you as before,
son of Pêleus, though I ran from you
round Priam's town three times and could not face you.
Now my soul would have me stand and fight,

whether I kill you or am killed. So come,
we'll summon gods here as our witnesses, 300
none higher, arbiters of a pact: I swear
that, terrible as you are,
I'll not insult your corpse should Zeus allow me
victory in the end, your life as prize.
Once I have your gear, I'll give your body
back to Akhaians. Grant me, too, this grace."

But swift Akhilleus frowned at him and said:

"Hektor, I'll have no talk of pacts with you,
forever unforgiven as you are.
As between men and lions there are none, 310
no concord between wolves and sheep, but all
hold one another hateful through and through,
so there can be no courtesy between us,
no sworn truce, till one of us is down
and glutting with his blood the wargod Arês.
Summon up what skills you have. By god,
you'd better be a spearman and a fighter!
Now there is no way out. Pallas Athêna
will have the upper hand of you. The weapon
belongs to me. You'll pay the reckoning 320
in full for all the pain my men have borne,
who met death by your spear."

He twirled and cast
his shaft with its long shadow. Splendid Hektor,
keeping his eye upon the point, eluded it
by ducking at the instant of the cast,
so shaft and bronze shank passed him overhead
and punched into the earth. But unperceived
by Hektor, Pallas Athêna plucked it out
and gave it back to Akhilleus. Hektor said:

"A clean miss. Godlike as you are, 330
you have not yet known doom for me from Zeus.
You thought you had, by heaven. Then you turned
into a word-thrower, hoping to make me lose
my fighting heart and head in fear of you.
You cannot plant your spear between my shoulders
while I am running. If you have the gift,
just put it through my chest as I come forward.
Now it's for you to dodge my own. Would god
you'd give the whole shaft lodging in your body!
War for the Trojans would be eased 340
if you were blotted out, bane that you are."

With this he twirled his long spearshaft and cast it,
hitting his enemy mid-shield, but off
and away the spear rebounded. Furious
that he had lost it, made his throw for nothing,

Hektor stood bemused. He had no other.
Then he gave a great shout to Dêíphobos
to ask for a long spear. But there was no one
near him, not a soul. Now in his heart
the Trojan realized the truth and said: 350

"This is the end. The gods are calling deathward.
I had thought
a good soldier, Dêíphobos, was with me.
He is inside the walls. Athêna tricked me.
Death is near, and black, not at a distance,
not to be evaded. Long ago
this hour must have been to Zeus's liking
and to the liking of his archer son.
They have been well disposed before, but now
the appointed time's upon me. Still, I would not 360
die without delivering a stroke,
or die ingloriously, but in some action
memorable to men in days to come."

With this he drew the whetted blade that hung
upon his left flank, ponderous and long,
collecting all his might the way an eagle
narrows himself to dive through shady cloud
and strike a lamb or cowering hare: so Hektor
lanced ahead and swung his whetted blade.
Akhilleus with wild fury in his heart 370
pulled in upon his chest his beautiful shield—
his helmet with four burnished metal ridges
nodding above it, and the golden crest
Hêphaistos locked there tossing in the wind.
Conspicuous as the evening star that comes,
amid the first in heaven, at fall of night,
and stands most lovely in the west, so shone
in sunlight the fine-pointed spear
Akhilleus poised in his right hand, with deadly
aim at Hektor, at the skin where most 380
it lay exposed. But nearly all was covered
by the bronze gear he took from slain Patróklos,
showing only, where his collarbones
divided neck and shoulders, the bare throat
where the destruction of a life is quickest.
Here, then, as the Trojan charged, Akhilleus
drove his point straight through the tender neck,
but did not cut the windpipe, leaving Hektor
able to speak and to respond. He fell
aside into the dust. And Prince Akhilleus 390
now exulted:

"Hektor, had you thought
that you could kill Patróklos and be safe?
Nothing to dread from me; I was not there.
All childishness. Though distant then, Patróklos'
comrade in arms was greater far than he—

and it is I who had been left behind
that day beside the deepsea ships who now
have made your knees give way. The dogs and kites
will rip your body. His will lie in honor
when the Akhaians give him funeral." 400

Hektor, barely whispering, replied:

"I beg you by your soul and by your parents,
do not let the dogs feed on me
in your encampment by the ships. Accept
the bronze and gold my father will provide
as gifts, my father and her ladyship
my mother. Let them have my body back,
so that our men and women may accord me
decency of fire when I am dead."

Akhilleus the great runner scowled and said: 410

"Beg me no beggary by soul or parents,
whining dog! Would god my passion drove me
to slaughter you and eat you raw, you've caused
such agony to me! No man exists
who could defend you from the carrion pack—
not if they spread for me ten times your ransom,
twenty times, and promise more as well;
aye, not if Priam, son of Dárdanos,
tells them to buy you for your weight in gold!
You'll have no bed of death, nor will you be 420
laid out and mourned by her who gave you birth.
Dogs and birds will have you, every scrap."

Then at the point of death Lord Hektor said:
"I see you now for what you are. No chance
to win you over. Iron in your breast
your heart is. Think a bit, though: this may be
a thing the gods in anger hold against you
on that day when Paris and Apollo
destroy you at the Gates, great as you are."

Even as he spoke, the end came, and death hid him; 430
spirit from body fluttered to undergloom,
bewailing fate that made him leave his youth
and manhood in the world. And as he died
Akhilleus spoke again. He said:

"Die, make an end. I shall accept my own
whenever Zeus and the other gods desire."

At this he pulled his spearhead from the body,
laying it aside, and stripped
the bloodstained shield and cuirass from his shoulders.
Other Akhaians hastened round to see 440
Hektor's fine body and his comely face,
and no one came who did not stab the body.
Glancing at one another they would say:

"Now Hektor has turned vulnerable, softer
than when he put the torches to the ships!"

And he who said this would inflict a wound.
When the great master of pursuit, Akhilleus,
had the body stripped, he stood among them,
saying swiftly:

"Friends, my lords and captains
of Argives, now that the gods at last have let me 450
bring to earth this man who wrought
havoc among us—more than all the rest—
come, we'll offer battle around the city,
to learn the intentions of the Trojans now.
Will they give up their strongpoint at this loss?
Can they fight on, though Hektor's dead?

But wait:
why do I ponder, why take up these questions?
Down by the ships Patróklos' body lies
unwept, unburied. I shall not forget him
while I can keep my feet among the living. 460
If in the dead world they forget the dead,
I say there, too, I shall remember him,
my friend. Men of Akhaia, lift a song!
Down to the ships we go, and take this body,
our glory. We have beaten Hektor down,
to whom as to a god the Trojans prayed."

Indeed, he had in mind for Hektor's body
outrage and shame. Behind both feet he pierced
the tendons, heel to ankle. Rawhide cords
he drew through both and lashed them to his chariot, 470
letting the man's head trail. Stepping aboard,
bearing the great trophy of the arms,
he shook the reins, and whipped the team ahead
into a willing run. A dustcloud rose
above the furrowing body; the dark tresses
flowed behind, and the head so princely once
lay back in dust. Zeus gave him to his enemies
to be defiled in his own fatherland.
So his whole head was blackened. Looking down,
his mother tore her braids, threw off her veil, 480
and wailed, heartbroken to behold her son.
Piteously his father groaned, and round him
lamentation spread throughout the town,
most like the clamor to be heard if Ilion's
towers, top to bottom, seethed in flames.
They barely stayed the old man, mad with grief,
from passing through the gates. Then in the mire
he rolled, and begged them all, each man by name:

"Relent, friends. It is hard; but let me go
out of the city to the Akhaian ships. 490
I'll make my plea to that demonic heart.

He may feel shame before his peers, or pity
my old age. His father, too, is old,
Pêleus, who brought him up to be a scourge
to Trojans, cruel to all, but most to me,
so many of my sons in flower of youth
he cut away. And, though I grieve, I cannot
mourn them all as much as I do one,
for whom my grief will take me to the grave—
and that is Hektor. Why could he not have died 500
where I might hold him? In our weeping, then,
his mother, now so destitute, and I
might have had surfeit and relief of tears."

These were the words of Priam as he wept,
and all his people groaned. Then in her turn
Hékabê led the women in lamentation:

"Child, I am lost now. Can I bear my life
after the death of suffering your death?
You were my pride in all my nights and days,
pride of the city, pillar of the Trojans 510
and Trojan women. Everyone looked to you
as though you were a god, and rightly so.
You were their greatest glory while you lived.
Now your doom and death have come upon you."

These were her mournful words. But Hektor's lady
still knew nothing; no one came to tell her
of Hektor's stand outside the gates. She wove
upon her loom, deep in the lofty house,
a double purple web with rose design.
Calling her maids in waiting, 520
she ordered a big caldron on a tripod
set on the hearthfire, to provide a bath
for Hektor when he came home from the fight.
Poor wife, how far removed from baths he was
she could not know, as at Akhilleus' hands
Athêna brought him down.

Then from the tower
she heard a wailing and a distant moan.
Her knees shook, and she let her shuttle fall,
and called out to her maids again:

"Come here.
Two must follow me, to see this action. 530
I heard my husband's queenly mother cry.
I feel my heart rise, throbbing in my throat.
My knees are like stone under me. Some blow
is coming home to Priam's sons and daughters.
Ah, could it never reach my ears! I die
of dread that Akhilleus may have cut off Hektor,
blocked my bold husband from the city wall,
to drive him down the plain alone! By now
he may have ended Hektor's deathly pride.

He never kept his place amid the chariots 540
but drove ahead. He would not be outdone
by anyone in courage."

Saying this, she ran
like a madwoman through the mégaron,
her heart convulsed. Her maids kept at her side.
On reaching the great tower and the soldiers,
Andrómakhê stood gazing from the wall
and saw him being dragged before the city.
Chariot horses at a brutal gallop
pulled the torn body toward the decked ships.
Blackness of night covered her eyes; she fell 550
backward swooning, sighing out her life,
and let her shining headdress fall, her hood
and diadem, her plaited band and veil
that Aphrodítê once had given her,
on that day when, from Eëtíôn's house,
for a thousand bridal gifts, Lord Hektor led her.
Now, at her side, kinswomen of her lord
supported her among them, dazed and faint
to the point of death. But when she breathed again
and her stunned heart recovered, in a burst 560
of sobbing she called out among the women:

"Hektor! Here is my desolation. Both
had this in store from birth—from yours in Troy
in Priam's palace, mine by wooded Plakos
at Thêbê in the home of Eëtíôn,
my father, who took care of me in childhood,
a man cursed by fate, a fated daughter.
How I could wish I never had been born!
Now under earth's roof to the house of Death
you go your way and leave me here, bereft, 570
lonely, in anguish without end. The child
we wretches had is still in infancy;
you cannot be a pillar to him, Hektor,
now you are dead, nor he to you. And should
this boy escape the misery of the war,
there will be toil and sorrow for him later,
as when strangers move his boundary stones.[107]
The day that orphans him will leave him lonely,
downcast in everything, cheeks wet with tears,
in hunger going to his father's friends 580
to tug at one man's cloak, another's khiton.
Some will be kindly: one may lift a cup
to wet his lips at least, though not his throat;
but from the board some child with living parents
gives him a push, a slap, with biting words:
'Outside, you there! Your father is not with us
here at our feast!' And the boy Astýanax

[107] Steal his land.

will run to his forlorn mother. Once he fed
on marrow only and the fat of lamb,
high on his father's knees. And when sleep came 590
to end his play, he slept in a nurse's arms,
brimful of happiness, in a soft bed.
But now he'll know sad days and many of them,
missing his father. 'Lord of the lower town'[108]
the Trojans call him. They know, you alone,
Lord Hektor, kept their gates and their long walls.
Beside the beaked ships now, far from your kin,
the blowflies' maggots in a swarm will eat you
naked, after the dogs have had their fill.
Ah, there are folded garments in your chambers, 600
delicate and fine, of women's weaving.
These, by heaven, I'll burn to the last thread
in blazing fire! They are no good to you,
they cannot cover you in death. So let them
go, let them be burnt as an offering
from Trojans and their women in your honor."

Thus she mourned, and the women wailed in answer.

BOOK 24
A Grace Given in Sorrow

[In Book 23, Akhilleus and his followers participate in elaborate ceremonies for Patróklos, including a large funeral pyre, which is lit the next day. Funeral games are then held in his honor. The body of Hektor lies untended, but protected by Apollo and Aphrodite.–ED.]

The funeral games were over. Men dispersed
and turned their thoughts to supper in their quarters,
then to the boon of slumber. But Akhilleus
thought of his friend, and sleep that quiets all things
would not take hold of him. He tossed and turned
remembering with pain Patróklos' courage,
his buoyant heart; how in his company
he fought out many a rough day full of danger,
cutting through ranks in war and the bitter sea.
With memory his eyes grew wet. He lay 10
on his right side, then on his back, and then
face downward—but at last he rose, to wander
distractedly along the line of surf.
This for eleven nights. The first dawn, brightening
sea and shore, became familiar to him,
as at that hour he yoked his team, with Hektor
tied behind, to drag him out, three times
around Patróklos' tomb. By day he rested

[108] The meaning of "Astýanax."

in his own hut, abandoning Hektor's body
to lie full-length in dust—though Lord Apollo, 20
pitying the man, even in death,
kept his flesh free of disfigurement.
He wrapped him in his great shield's flap of gold
to save him from laceration. But Akhilleus
in rage visited indignity on Hektor
day after day, and, looking on,
the blessed gods were moved. Day after day
they urged the Wayfinder[109] to steal the body—
a thought agreeable to all but Hêra,
Poseidon, and the grey-eyed one, Athêna. 30
These opposed it, and held out, since Ilion
and Priam and his people had incurred
their hatred first, the day Aléxandros
made his mad choice and piqued two goddesses,
visitors in his sheepfold: he praised
a third, who offered ruinous lust.[110]
Now when Dawn grew bright for the twelfth day,
Phoibos Apollo spoke among the gods:

"How heartless and how malevolent you are!
Did Hektor never make burnt offering 40
of bulls' thighbones to you, and unflawed goats?
Even in death you would not stir to save him
for his dear wife to see, and for his mother,
his child, his father, Priam, and his men:
they'd burn the corpse at once and give him burial.
Murderous Akhilleus has your willing help—
a man who shows no decency, implacable,
barbarous in his ways as a wild lion
whose power and intrepid heart
sway him to raid the flocks of men for meat. 50
The man has lost all mercy;
he has no shame—that gift that hinders mortals
but helps them, too. A sane one may endure
an even dearer loss: a blood brother,
a son; and yet, by heaven, having grieved
and passed through mourning, he will let it go.
The fates have given patient hearts to men.
Not this one: first he took Prince Hektor's life
and now he drags the body, lashed to his car,
around the barrow[111] of his friend, performing 60
something neither nobler in report
nor better in itself. Let him take care,
or, brave as he is, we gods will turn against him,
seeing him outrage the insensate earth!"

---

[109]Hermês, messenger god and trickster.
[110]See the commentary on the Judgment of Paris in the headnote to Homer.
[111]A grave mound.

Hêra whose arms are white as ivory
grew angry at Apollo. She retorted:
"Lord of the silver bow, your words would be
acceptable if one had a mind to honor
Hektor and Akhilleus equally.
But Hektor suckled at a woman's breast, 70
Akhilleus is the first-born of a goddess—
one I nursed myself. I reared her, gave her
to Pêleus, a strong man whom the gods loved.
All of you were present at their wedding—
you too—friend of the base, forever slippery!—
came with your harp and dined there!"

Zeus the stormking
answered her:

"Hêra, don't lose your temper
altogether. Clearly the same high honor
cannot be due both men. And yet Lord Hektor,
of all the mortal men in Ilion, 80
was dearest to the gods, or was to me.
He never failed in the right gift; my altar
never lacked a feast
of wine poured out and smoke of sacrifice—
the share assigned as ours. We shall renounce
the theft of Hektor's body; there is no way;
there would be no eluding Akhilleus' eye,
as night and day his mother comes to him.
Will one of you now call her to my presence?
I have a solemn message to impart: 90
Akhilleus is to take fine gifts from Priam,
and in return give back Prince Hektor's body."

At this, Iris who runs on the rainy wind
with word from Zeus departed. Midway between
Samos and rocky Imbros,[112] down she plunged
into the dark grey sea, and the brimming tide
roared over her as she sank into the depth—
as rapidly as a leaden sinker, fixed
on a lure of wild bull's horn, that glimmers down
with a fatal hook among the ravening fish. 100
Soon Iris came on Thetis in a cave,
surrounded by a company of Nereids
lolling there, while she bewailed the fate
of her magnificent son, now soon to perish
on Troy's rich earth, far from his fatherland.
Halting before her, Iris said:

"Come, Thetis,
Zeus of eternal forethought summons you."

---

[112] Islands in the north Aegean.

Silvery-footed Thetis answered:
"Why?
Why does the great one call me to him now,
when I am shy of mingling with immortals, 110
being so heavyhearted? But I'll go.
Whatever he may say will have its weight."

That loveliest of goddesses now put on
a veil so black no garment could be blacker,
and swam where windswift Iris led. Before them
on either hand the ground swell fell away.
They rose to a beach, then soared into the sky
and found the viewer of the wide world, Zeus,
with all the blissful gods who live forever
around him seated. Athêna yielded place, 120
and Thetis sat down by her father, Zeus,
while Hêra handed her a cup of gold
and spoke a comforting word. When she had drunk,
Thetis held out the cup again to Hêra.
The father of gods and men began:
"You've come
to Olympos, Thetis, though your mind is troubled
and insatiable pain preys on your heart.
I know, I too. But let me, even so,
explain why I have called you here. Nine days
of quarreling we've had among the gods 130
concerning Hektor's body and Akhilleus.
They wish the Wayfinder to make off with it.
I, however, accord Akhilleus honor
as I now tell you—in respect for you
whose love I hope to keep hereafter. Go, now,
down to the army, tell this to your son:
the gods are sullen toward him, and I, too,
more than the rest, am angered at his madness,
holding the body by the beaked ships
and not releasing it. In fear of me 140
let him relent and give back Hektor's body!
At the same time I'll send Iris to Priam,
directing him to go down to the beachhead
and ransom his dear son. He must bring gifts
to melt Akhilleus' rage."

Thetis obeyed,
leaving Olympos' ridge and flashing down
to her son's hut. She found him groaning there,
inconsolable, while men-at-arms
went to and fro, making their breakfast ready—
having just put to the knife a fleecy sheep. 150
His gentle mother sat down at his side,
caressed him, and said tenderly:
"My child,
will you forever feed on your own heart

in grief and pain, and take no thought of sleep
or sustenance? It would be comforting
to make love with a woman. No long time
will you live on for me: Death even now
stands near you, appointed and all-powerful.
But be alert and listen: I am a messenger
from Zeus, who tells me the gods are sullen toward you 160
and he himself most angered at your madness,
holding the body by the beaked ships
and not releasing it. Give Hektor back.
Take ransom for the body."

Said Akhilleus:
"Let it be so. Let someone bring the ransom
and take the dead away, if the Olympian
commands this in his wisdom."

So, that morning,
in camp, amid the ships, mother and son
conversed together, and their talk was long.
Lord Zeus meanwhile sent Iris to Ilion. 170

"Off with you, lightfoot, leave Olympos, take
my message to the majesty of Priam
at Ilion. He is to journey down
and ransom his dear son upon the beachhead.
He shall take gifts to melt Akhilleus' rage,
and let him go alone, no soldier with him,
only some crier, some old man, to drive
his wagon team and guide the nimble wagon,
and afterward to carry home the body
of him that Prince Akhilleus overcame. 180
Let him not think of death, or suffer dread,
as I'll provide him with a wondrous guide,
the Wayfinder, to bring him across the lines
into the very presence of Akhilleus.
And he, when he sees Priam within his hut,
will neither take his life nor let another
enemy come near. He is no madman,
no blind brute, nor one to flout the gods,
but dutiful toward men who beg his mercy."

Then Iris at his bidding ran 190
on the rainy winds to bear the word of Zeus,
until she came to Priam's house and heard
voices in lamentation. In the court
she found the princes huddled around their father,
faces and clothing wet with tears. The old man,
fiercely wrapped and hooded in his mantle,
sat like a figure graven—caked in filth
his own hands had swept over head and neck
when he lay rolling on the ground. Indoors

his daughters and his sons' wives were weeping, 200
remembering how many and how brave
the young men were who had gone down to death
before the Argive spearmen.
Zeus's courier,
appearing now to Priam's eyes alone,
alighted whispering, so the old man trembled:

"Priam, heir of Dárdanos, take heart,
and have no fear of me; I bode no evil,
but bring you friendly word from Zeus,
who is distressed for you and pities you
though distant far upon Olympos. He 210
commands that you shall ransom the Prince Hektor,
taking fine gifts to melt Akhilleus' rage.
And go alone: no soldier may go with you,
only some crier, some old man, to drive
your wagon team and guide the nimble wagon,
and afterward to carry home the body
of him that Prince Akhilleus overcame.
Put away thoughts of death, shake off your dread,
for you shall have a wondrous guide,
the Wayfinder, to bring you across the lines 220
into the very presence of Akhilleus.
He, for his part, seeing you in his quarters,
will neither take your life nor let another
enemy come near. He is no madman,
no blind brute, nor one to flout the gods,
but dutiful toward men who beg his mercy."

Iris left him, swift as a veering wind.
Then Priam spoke, telling the men to rig
a four-wheeled wagon with a wicker box,
while he withdrew to his chamber roofed in cedar, 230
high and fragrant, rich in precious things.
He called to Hékabê, his lady:
"Princess,
word from Olympian Zeus has come to me
to go down to the ships of the Akhaians
and ransom our dead son. I am to take
gifts that will melt Akhilleus' anger. Tell me
how this appears to you, tell me your mind,
for I am torn with longing, now, to pass
inside the great encampment by the ships."

The woman's voice broke as she answered:
"Sorrow, 240
sorrow. Where is the wisdom now that made you
famous in the old days, near and far?
How can you ever face the Akhaian ships
or wish to go alone before those eyes,
the eyes of one who stripped your sons in battle,

how many, and how brave? Iron must be
the heart within you. If he sees you, takes you,
savage and wayward as the man is,
he'll have no mercy and no shame. Better
that we should mourn together in our hall. 250
Almighty fate spun this thing for our son
the day I bore him: destined him to feed
the wild dogs after death, being far from us
when he went down before the stronger man.
I could devour the vitals of that man,
leeching into his living flesh! He'd know
pain then—pain like mine for my dead son.
It was no coward the Akhaian killed;
he stood and fought for the sweet wives of Troy,
with no more thought of flight or taking cover." 260

In majesty old Priam said:

"My heart
is fixed on going. Do not hold me back,
and do not make yourself a raven crying
calamity at home. You will not move me.
If any man on earth had urged this on me—
reader of altar smoke, prophet or priest—
we'd say it was a lie, and hold aloof.
But no: with my own ears I heard the voice,
I saw the god before me. Go I shall,
and no more words. If I must die alongside 270
the ships of the Akhaians in their bronze,
I die gladly. May I but hold my son
and spend my grief; then let Akhilleus kill me."

Throwing open the lids of treasure boxes
he picked out twelve great robes of state, and twelve
light cloaks for men, and rugs, an equal number,
and just as many capes of snowy linen,
adding a dozen khitons to the lot;
then set in order ten pure bars of gold,
a pair of shining tripods, four great caldrons, 280
and finally one splendid cup, a gift
Thracians had made him on an embassy.
He would not keep this, either—as he cared
for nothing now but ransoming his son.

And now, from the colonnade,
he made his Trojan people keep their distance,
berating and abusing them:

"Away,
you craven fools and rubbish! In your own homes
have you no one to mourn, that you crowd here,
to make more trouble for me? Is this a show, 290

that Zeus has crushed me, that he took the life
of my most noble son? You'll soon know what it means,
as you become child's play for the Akhaians
to kill in battle, now that Hektor's gone.
As for myself, before I see my city
taken and ravaged, let me go down blind
to Death's cold kingdom!"

Staff in hand,
he herded them, until they turned away
and left the furious old man. He lashed out
now at his sons, at Hélenos and Paris, 300
Agathôn, Pammôn, Antíphonos,
Polítês, Dêíphobos, Hippóthoös,
and Dios—to these nine the old man cried:

"Bestir yourselves, you misbegotten whelps,
shame of my house! Would god you had been killed
instead of Hektor at the line of ships.
How curst I am in everything! I fathered
first-rate men, in our great Troy; but now
I swear not one is left: Mêstôr, Trôïlos,
laughing amid the war-cars; and then Hektor— 310
a god to soldiers, and a god among them,
seeming not a man's child, but a god's.
Arês killed them. These poltroons are left,
hollow men, dancers, heroes of the dance,
light-fingered pillagers of lambs and kids
from the town pens!
Now will you get a wagon
ready for me, and quickly? Load these gifts
aboard it, so that we can take the road."

Dreading the rough edge of their father's tongue,
they lifted out a cart, a cargo wagon, 320
neat and maneuverable, and newly made,
and fixed upon it a wicker box; then took
a mule yoke from a peg, a yoke of boxwood
knobbed in front, with rings to hold the reins.
They brought out, too, the band nine forearms long
called the yoke-fastener, and placed the yoke
forward at the shank of the polished pole,
shoving the yoke-pin firmly in. They looped
three turns of the yoke-fastener round the knob
and wound it over and over down the pole, 330
tucking the tab end under. Next, the ransom:
bearing the weight of gifts for Hektor's person
out of the inner room, they piled them up
on the polished wagon. It was time to yoke
the mule-team, strong in harness, with hard hooves,
a team the Mysians had given Priam.
Then for the king's own chariot they harnessed

a team of horses of the line of Trôs,[113]
reared by the old king in his royal stable.
So the impatient king and his sage crier 340
had their animals yoked in the palace yard
when Hékabê in her agitation joined them,
carrying in her right hand a golden cup
of honeyed wine, with which, before they left,
they might make offering. At the horses' heads
she stood to tell them:

"Here, tip wine to Zeus,
the father of gods. Pray for a safe return
from the enemy army, seeing your heart is set
on venturing to the camp against my will.
Pray in the second place to Zeus the stormking, 350
gloomy over Ida, who looks down
on all Troy country. Beg for an omen-bird,
the courier dearest of all birds to Zeus
and sovereign in power of flight,[114]
that he appear upon our right in heaven.
When you have seen him with your own eyes, then,
under that sign, you may approach the ships.
If Zeus who views the wide world will not give you
vision of his bird, then I at least
cannot bid godspeed to your journey, 360
bent on it though you are."

In majesty
Priam replied:

"My lady, in this matter
I am disposed to trust you and agree.
It is an excellent thing and salutary
to lift our hands to Zeus, invoking mercy."

The old king motioned to his housekeeper,
who stood nearby with a basin and a jug,
to pour clear water on his hands. He washed them,
took the cup his lady held, and prayed
while standing there, midway in the walled court. 370
Then he tipped out the wine, looking toward heaven,
saying:

"Zeus, our Father, reigning from Ida,
god of glory and power, grant I come
to Akhilleus' door as one to be received
with kindliness and mercy. And dispatch
your courier bird, the nearest to your heart
of all birds, and the first in power of flight.

[113] Great-grandfather of Priam.
[114] Eagle.

Let him appear upon our right in heaven
that I may see him with my own eyes
and under that sign journey to the ships." 380

Zeus all-foreseeing listened to this prayer
and put an eagle, king
of winged creatures, instantly in flight:
a swamp eagle, a hunter, one they call
the duskwing. Wide as a doorway in a chamber
spacious and high, built for a man of wealth,
a door with long bars fitted well, so wide
spread out each pinion. The great bird appeared
winging through the town on their right hand,
and all their hearts lifted with joy to see him. 390
In haste the old king boarded his bright car
and clattered out of the echoing colonnade.
Ahead, the mule-team drew the four-wheeled wagon,
driven by Idaíos,[115] and behind
the chariot rolled, with horses that the old man
whipped into a fast trot through the town.
Family and friends all followed weeping
as though for Priam's last and deathward ride.
Into the lower town they passed, and reached
the plain of Troy. Here those who followed after 400
turned back, sons and sons-in-law. And Zeus
who views the wide world saw the car and wagon
brave the plain. He felt a pang for Priam
and quickly said to Hermês, his own son:

"Hermês, as you go most happily
of all the gods with mortals, and give heed
to whom you will, be on your way this time
as guide for Priam to the deepsea ships.
Guide him so that not one of the Danáäns
may know or see him till he reach Akhilleus." 410

Argeiphontês[116] the Wayfinder obeyed.
He bent to tie his beautiful sandals on,
ambrosial, golden, that carry him over water
and over endless land on a puff of wind,
and took the wand with which he charms asleep—
or, when he wills, awake—the eyes of men.
So, wand in hand, the strong god glittering
paced into the air. Quick as a thought
he came to Hellê's waters and to Troy,
appearing as a boy whose lip was downy 420
in the first bloom of manhood, a young prince,
all graciousness.

[115]Priam's herald.
[116]One of Hermês' names.

After the travelers
drove past the mound of Ilos,[117] at the ford
they let the mules and horses pause to drink
the running stream. Now darkness had come on
when, looking round, the crier
saw Hermês near at hand. He said to Priam:

"You must think hard and fast, your grace;
there is new danger; we need care and prudence.
I see a man-at-arms there—ready, I think, 430
to prey on us. Come, shall we whip the team
and make a run for it? Or take his knees
and beg for mercy?"

Now the old man's mind
gave way to confusion and to terror.
On his gnarled arms and legs the hair stood up,
and he stared, breathless. But the affable god
came over and took his hand and asked:

"Old father,
where do you journey, with your cart and car,
while others rest, below the evening star?
Do you not fear the Akhaians where they lie 440
encamped, hard, hostile outlanders, nearby?
Should someone see you, bearing stores like these
by night, how would you deal with enemies?
You are not young, your escort's ancient, too.
Could you beat off an attacker, either of you?
I'll do no hurt to you but defend you here.
You remind me of my father, whom I hold dear."

Old Priam answered him:

"Indeed, dear boy,
the case is as you say. And yet some god
stretched out his hand above me, he who sent 450
before me here—and just at the right time—
a traveler like yourself, well-made, well-spoken,
clearheaded, too. You come of some good family."

The Wayfinder rejoined:

"You speak with courtesy,
dear sir. But on this point enlighten me:
are you removing treasure here amassed
for safety abroad, until the war is past?
Or can you be abandoning Ilion
in fear, after he perished, that great one
who never shirked a battle, your own princely son?" 460

Old Priam replied:

[117] Founder of Iliom, or Ilium (Troy), grandfather of Priam.

"My brave young friend, who are you?
Born of whom? How nobly you acknowledge
the dreadful end of my unfortunate son."

To this the Wayfinder replied:
"Dear sir,
you question me about him? Never surmise
I have not seen him with my very eyes,
and often, on the field. I saw him chase
Argives with carnage to their own shipways,
while we stood wondering, forbidden war
by the great anger that Akhilleus bore 470
Lord Agamémnon. I am of that company
Akhilleus led. His own ship carried me
as one of the Myrmidons. My father is old,
as you are, and his name's Polyktôr; gold
and other wealth he owns;
and I am seventh and last of all his sons.
When I cast lots among them, my lot fell
to join the siege against Troy citadel.
Tonight I've left the camp to scout this way
where, circling Troy, we'll fight at break of day; 480
our men are tired of waiting and will not stand
for any postponement by the high command."

Responded royal Priam:
"If you belong
to the company of Akhilleus, son of Pêleus,
tell me this, and tell me the whole truth:
is my son even now beside the ships?
Or has Akhilleus by this time dismembered him
and thrown him to the wild dogs?"

The Wayfinder
made reply again:
"Dear sir,
no dogs or birds have yet devoured your son. 490
Beside Akhilleus' ship, out of the sun,
he lies in a place of shelter. Now twelve days
the man has lain there, yet no part decays,
nor have the blowfly's maggots, that devour
dead men in war, fed on him to this hour.
True that around his dear friend's barrow tomb
Akhilleus drags him when dawn-shadows come,
driving pitilessly; but he mars him not.
You might yourself be witness, on the spot,
how fresh with dew he lies, washed of his gore, 500
unstained, for the deep gashes that he bore
have all closed up—and many thrust their bronze
into his body. The blest immortal ones
favor your prince, and care for every limb
even in death, as they so cherished him."

The old king's heart exulted, and he said:
"Child, it was well to honor the immortals.
He never forgot, at home in Ilion—
ah, did my son exist? was he a dream?—
the gods who own Olympos. They in turn 510
were mindful of him when he met his end.
Here is a goblet as a gift from me.
Protect me, give me escort, if the gods
attend us, till I reach Akhilleus' hut."

And in response Hermês the Wayfinder
said:

"You are putting a young man to test,
dear sir, but I may not, as you request,
accept a gift behind Akhilleus' back.
Fearing, honoring him, I could not lack
discretion to that point. The consequence, too, 520
could be unwelcome. As for escorting you,
even to Argos' famous land I'd ride
a deck with you, or journey at your side.
No cutthroat ever will disdain your guide."

With this, Hermês who lights the way for mortals
leapt into the driver's place. He caught up
reins and whip, and breathed a second wind
into the mule-team and the team of horses.
Onward they ran toward parapet and ships,
and pulled up to the moat.

Now night had fallen, 530
bringing the sentries to their supper fire,
but the glimmering god Hermês, the Wayfinder,
showered a mist of slumber on them all.
As quick as thought, he had the gates unbarred
and open to let the wagon enter, bearing
the old king and the ransom.

Going seaward
they came to the lofty quarters of Akhilleus,
a lodge the Myrmidons built for their lord
of pine trees cut and trimmed, and shaggy thatch
from mowings in deep meadows. Posts were driven 540
round the wide courtyard in a palisade,
whose gate one crossbar held, one beam of pine.
It took three men to slam this home, and three
to draw the bolt again—but great Akhilleus
worked his entryway alone with ease.
And now Hermês, who lights the way for mortals,
opened for Priam, took him safely in
with all his rich gifts for the son of Pêleus.
Then the god dropped the reins, and stepping down
he said:

"I am no mortal wagoner, 550
but Hermês, sir. My father sent me here

to be your guide amid the Akhaian men.
Now that is done, I'm off to heaven again
and will not visit Akhilleus. That would be
to compromise an immortal's dignity—
to be received with guests of mortal station.
Go take his knees, and make your supplication:
invoke his father, his mother, and his child;
pray that his heart be touched, that he be reconciled."

Now Hermês turned, departing for Olympos, 560
and Priam vaulted down. He left Idaíos
to hold the teams in check, while he went forward
into the lodge. He found Akhilleus, dear
to Zeus, there in his chair, with officers
at ease across the room. Only Automédôn
and Álkimos were busy near Akhilleus,
for he had just now made an end of dinner,
eating and drinking, and the laden boards
lay near him still upon the trestles.
Priam,
the great king of Troy, passed by the others, 570
knelt down, took in his arms Akhilleus' knees,
and kissed the hands of wrath that killed his sons.

When, taken with mad Folly in his own land,
a man does murder and in exile finds
refuge in some rich house, then all who see him
stand in awe.
So these men stood.
Akhilleus
gazed in wonder at the splendid king,
and his companions marveled too, all silent,
with glances to and fro. Now Priam prayed 580
to the man before him:

"Remember your own father,
Akhilleus, in your godlike youth: his years
like mine are many, and he stands upon
the fearful doorstep of old age. He, too,
is hard pressed, it may be, by those around him,
there being no one able to defend him
from bane of war and ruin. Ah, but he
may nonetheless hear news of you alive,
and so with glad heart hope through all his days
for sight of his dear son, come back from Troy, 590
while I have deathly fortune.
Noble sons
I fathered here, but scarce one man is left me.
Fifty I had when the Akhaians came,
nineteen out of a single belly, others
born of attendant women. Most are gone.
Raging Arês cut their knees from under them.

And he who stood alone among them all,
their champion, and Troy's, ten days ago
you killed him, fighting for his land, my prince,
Hektor.
It is for him that I have come 600
among these ships, to beg him back from you,
and I bring ransom without stint.
Akhilleus,
be reverent toward the great gods! And take
pity on me, remember your own father.
Think me more pitiful by far, since I
have brought myself to do what no man else
has done before—to lift to my lips the hand
of one who killed my son."

Now in Akhilleus
the evocation of his father stirred
new longing, and an ache of grief. He lifted 610
the old man's hand and gently put him by.
Then both were overborne as they remembered:
the old king huddled at Akhilleus' feet
wept, and wept for Hektor, killer of men,
while great Akhilleus wept for his own father
as for Patróklos once again; and sobbing
filled the room.
But when Akhilleus' heart
had known the luxury of tears, and pain
within his breast and bones had passed away,
he stood then, raised the old king up, in pity 620
for his grey head and greybeard cheek, and spoke
in a warm rush of words:

"Ah, sad and old!
Trouble and pain you've borne, and bear, aplenty.
Only a great will could have brought you here
among the Akhaian ships, and here alone
before the eyes of one who stripped your sons,
your many sons, in battle. Iron must be
the heart within you. Come, then, and sit down.
We'll probe our wounds no more but let them rest,
though grief lies heavy on us. Tears heal nothing, 630
drying so stiff and cold. This is the way
the gods ordained the destiny of men,
to bear such burdens in our lives, while they
feel no affliction. At the door of Zeus
are those two urns of good and evil gifts
that he may choose for us; and one for whom
the lightning's joyous king dips in both urns
will have by turns bad luck and good. But one
to whom he sends all evil—that man goes
contemptible by the will of Zeus; ravenous 640
hunger drives him over the wondrous earth,
unresting, without honor from gods or men.

Mixed fortune came to Pêleus. Shining gifts
at the gods' hands he had from birth: felicity,
wealth overflowing, rule of the Myrmidons,
a bride immortal at his mortal side.
But then Zeus gave afflictions too—no family
of powerful sons grew up for him at home,
but one child, of all seasons and of none.
Can I stand by him in his age? Far from my country 650
I sit at Troy to grieve you and your children.
You, too, sir, in time past were fortunate,
we hear men say. From Makar's isle of Lesbos
northward, and south of Phrygia and the Straits,
no one had wealth like yours, or sons like yours.
Then gods out of the sky sent you this bitterness:
the years of siege, the battles and the losses.
Endure it, then. And do not mourn forever
for your dead son. There is no remedy.
You will not make him stand again. Rather 660
await some new misfortune to be suffered."

The old king in his majesty replied:

"Never give me a chair, my lord, while Hektor
lies in your camp uncared for. Yield him to me
now. Allow me sight of him. Accept
the many gifts I bring. May they reward you,
and may you see your home again.
You spared my life at once and let me live."

Akhilleus, the great runner, frowned and eyed him
under his brows:

"Do not vex me, sir," he said. 670
"I have intended, in my own good time,
to yield up Hektor to you. She who bore me,
the daughter of the Ancient of the sea,
has come with word to me from Zeus. I know
in your case, too—though you say nothing, Priam—
that some god guided you to the shipways here.
No strong man in his best days could make entry
into this camp. How could he pass the guard,
or force our gateway?

Therefore, *let me be.*
Sting my sore heart again, and even here, 680
under my own roof, suppliant though you are,
I may not spare you, sir, but trample on
the express command of Zeus!"

When he heard this,
the old man feared him and obeyed with silence.
Now like a lion at one bound Akhilleus
left the room. Close at his back the officers
Automédôn and Álkimos went out—
comrades in arms whom he esteemed the most

after the dead Patróklos. They unharnessed
mules and horses, led the old king's crier 690
to a low bench and sat him down.
Then from the polished wagon
they took the piled-up price of Hektor's body.
One khiton and two capes they left aside
as dress and shrouding for the homeward journey.
Then, calling to the women slaves, Akhilleus
ordered the body bathed and rubbed with oil—
but lifted, too, and placed apart, where Priam
could not see his son—for seeing Hektor
he might in his great pain give way to rage, 700
and fury then might rise up in Akhilleus
to slay the old king, flouting Zeus's word.
So after bathing and anointing Hektor
they drew the shirt and beautiful shrouding over him.
Then with his own hands lifting him, Akhilleus
laid him upon a couch, and with his two
companions aiding, placed him in the wagon.
Now a bitter groan burst from Akhilleus,
who stood and prayed to his own dead friend:

"Patróklos,
do not be angry with me, if somehow 710
even in the world of Death you learn of this—
that I released Prince Hektor to his father.
The gifts he gave were not unworthy. Aye,
and you shall have your share, this time as well."

The Prince Akhilleus turned back to his quarters.
He took again the splendid chair that stood
against the farther wall, then looked at Priam
and made his declaration:

"As you wished, sir,
the body of your son is now set free.
He lies in state. At the first sight of Dawn 720
you shall take charge of him yourself and see him.
Now let us think of supper. We are told
that even Niobê in her extremity
took thought for bread—though all her brood had perished,
her six young girls and six tall sons. Apollo,
making his silver longbow whip and sing,
shot the lads down, and Artemis with raining
arrows killed the daughters—all this after
Niobê had compared herself with Lêto,[118]
the smooth-cheeked goddess.

She has borne two children, 730
Niobê said, How many have I borne!
But soon those two destroyed the twelve.

[118]Mother of Apollo and Artemis.

Besides,
nine days the dead lay stark, no one could bury them,
for Zeus had turned all folk of theirs to stone.
The gods made graves for them on the tenth day,
and then at last, being weak and spent with weeping,
Niobê thought of food. Among the rocks
of Sipylos'[119] lonely mountainside, where nymphs
who race Akhelôïos river go to rest,
she, too, long turned to stone, somewhere broods on 740
the gall immortal gods gave her to drink.

Like her we'll think of supper, noble sir.
Weep for your son again when you have borne him
back to Troy; there he'll be mourned indeed."

In one swift movement now Akhilleus caught
and slaughtered a white lamb. His officers
flayed it, skillful in their butchering
to dress the flesh; they cut bits for the skewers,
roasted, and drew them off, done to a turn.
Automédôn dealt loaves into the baskets 750
on the great board; Akhilleus served the meat.
Then all their hands went out upon the supper.
When thirst and appetite were turned away,
Priam, the heir of Dárdanos, gazed long
in wonder at Akhilleus' form and scale—
so like the gods in aspect. And Akhilleus
in his turn gazed in wonder upon Priam,
royal in visage as in speech. Both men
in contemplation found rest for their eyes,
till the old hero, Priam, broke the silence: 760

"Make a bed ready for me, son of Thetis,
and let us know the luxury of sleep.
From that hour when my son died at your hands
till now, my eyelids have not closed in slumber
over my eyes, but groaning where I sat
I tasted pain and grief a thousandfold,
or lay down rolling in my courtyard mire.
Here for the first time I have swallowed bread
and made myself drink wine.
Before, I could not."

Akhilleus ordered men and servingwomen 770
to make a bed outside, in the covered forecourt,
with purple rugs piled up and sheets outspread
and coverings of fleeces laid on top.
The girls went out with torches in their hands
and soon deftly made up a double bed.

[119]A mountain with a legendary woman's face that is weeping.

Then Akhilleus, defiant of Agamémnon,
told his guest:

"Dear venerable sir,
you'll sleep outside tonight, in case an Akhaian
officer turns up, one of those men
who are forever taking counsel with me— 780
as well they may. If one should see you here
as the dark night runs on, he would report it
to the Lord Marshal Agamémnon. Then
return of the body would only be delayed.
Now tell me this, and give me a straight answer:
How many days do you require
for the funeral of Prince Hektor?—I should know
how long to wait, and hold the Akhaian army."

Old Priam in his majesty replied:
"If you would have me carry out the burial, 790
Akhilleus, here is the way to do me grace.
As we are penned in the town, but must bring wood
from the distant hills, the Trojans are afraid.
We should have mourning for nine days in hall,
then on the tenth conduct his funeral
and feast the troops and commons;
on the eleventh we should make his tomb,
and on the twelfth give battle, if we must."

Akhilleus said:

"As you command, old Priam,
the thing is done. I shall suspend the war 800
for those eleven days that you require."

He took the old man's right hand by the wrist
and held it, to allay his fear.

Now crier
and king with hearts brimful retired to rest
in the sheltered forecourt, while Akhilleus slept
deep in his palisaded lodge. Beside him,
lovely in her youth, Brisêis lay.
And other gods and soldiers all night long,
by slumber quieted, slept on. But slumber
would not come to Hermês the Good Companion, 810
as he considered how to ease the way
for Priam from the camp, to send him through
unseen by the formidable gatekeepers.
Then Hermês came to Priam's pillow, saying:
"Sir, no thought of danger shakes your rest,
as you sleep on, being great Akhilleus' guest,
amid men fierce as hunters in a ring.
You triumphed in a costly ransoming,
but three times costlier your own would be

to your surviving sons—a monarch's fee— 820
if this should come to Agamémnon's ear
and all the Akhaian host should learn that you are here."

The old king started up in fright, and woke
his herald. Hermês yoked the mules and horses,
took the reins, then inland like the wind
he drove through all the encampment, seen by no one.
When they reached Xánthos, eddying and running
god-begotten river, at the ford,
Hermês departed for Olympos. Dawn
spread out her yellow robe on all the earth, 830
as they drove on toward Troy, with groans and sighs,
and the mule-team pulled the wagon and the body.
And no one saw them, not a man or woman,
before Kassandra.[120] Tall as the pale-gold
goddess Aphrodítê, she had climbed
the citadel of Pergamos at dawn.
Now looking down she saw her father come
in his war-car, and saw the crier there,
and saw Lord Hektor on his bed of death
upon the mulecart. The girl wailed and cried 840
to all the city:

"Oh, look down, look down,
go to your windows, men of Troy, and women,
see Lord Hektor now! Remember joy
at seeing him return alive from battle,
exalting all our city and our land!"

Now, at the sight of Hektor, all gave way
to loss and longing, and all crowded down
to meet the escort and body near the gates,
till no one in the town was left at home.
There Hektor's lady and his gentle mother 850
tore their hair for him, flinging themselves
upon the wagon to embrace his person
while the crowd groaned. All that long day
until the sun went down they might have mourned
in tears before the gateway. But old Priam
spoke to them from his chariot:

"Make way,
let the mules pass. You'll have your fill of weeping
later, when I've brought the body home."

They parted then, and made way for the wagon,
allowing Priam to reach the famous hall. 860
They laid the body of Hektor in his bed,
and brought in minstrels, men to lead the dirge.

---

[120] A seer who is not believed; the daughter of Priam and Hékabê.

While these wailed out, the women answered, moaning.
Andrómakhê of the ivory-white arms
held in her lap between her hands
the head of Hektor who had killed so many.
Now she lamented:

"You've been torn from life,
my husband, in young manhood, and you leave me
empty in our hall. The boy's a child
whom you and I, poor souls, conceived; I doubt 870
he'll come to manhood. Long before, great Troy
will go down plundered, citadel and all,
now that you are lost, who guarded it
and kept it, and preserved its wives and children.
They will be shipped off in the murmuring hulls
one day, and I along with all the rest.

You, my little one, either you come with me
to do some grinding labor, some base toil
for a harsh master, or an Akhaian soldier
will grip you by the arm and hurl you down 880
from a tower here to a miserable death—
out of his anger for a brother, a father,
or even a son that Hektor killed. Akhaians
in hundreds mouthed black dust under his blows.
He was no moderate man in war, your father,
and that is why they mourn him through the city.
Hektor, you gave your parents grief and pain
but left me loneliest, and heartbroken.
You could not open your strong arms to me
from your deathbed, or say a thoughtful word, 890
for me to cherish all my life long
as I weep for you night and day."

Her voice broke,
and a wail came from the women. Hékabê
lifted her lamenting voice among them:
"Hektor, dearest of sons to me, in life
you had the favor of the immortal gods,
and they have cared for you in death as well.
Akhilleus captured other sons of mine
in other years, and sold them overseas
to Samos, Imbros, and the smoky island, 900
Lemnos. That was not his way with you.
After he took your life, cutting you down
with his sharp-bladed spear, he trussed and dragged you
many times round the barrow of his friend,
Patróklos, whom you killed—though not by this
could that friend live again. But now I find you
fresh as pale dew, seeming newly dead,
like one to whom Apollo of the silver bow
had given easy death with his mild arrows."

Hékabê sobbed again, and the wails redoubled. 910
Then it was Helen's turn to make lament:

"Dear Hektor, dearest brother to me by far!
My husband is Aléxandros,
who brought me here to Troy—God, that I might
have died sooner! This is the twentieth year
since I left home, and left my fatherland.
But never did I have an evil word
or gesture from you. No—and when some other
brother-in-law or sister would revile me,
or if my mother-in-law spoke to me bitterly— 920
but Priam never did, being as mild
as my own father—you would bring her round
with your kind heart and gentle speech. Therefore
I weep for you and for myself as well,
given this fate, this grief. In all wide Troy
no one is left who will befriend me, none;
they all shudder at me."

Helen wept,
and a moan came from the people, hearing her.
Then Priam, the old king, commanded them:

"Trojans, bring firewood to the edge of town. 930
No need to fear an ambush of the Argives.
When he dismissed me from the camp, Akhilleus
told me clearly they will not harass us,
not until dawn comes for the twelfth day."

Then yoking mules and oxen to their wagons
the people thronged before the city gates.
Nine days they labored, bringing countless loads
of firewood to the town. When Dawn that lights
the world of mortals came for the tenth day,
they carried greathearted Hektor out at last, 940
and all in tears placed his dead body high
upon its pyre, then cast a torch below.
When the young Dawn with finger tips of rose
made heaven bright, the Trojan people massed
about Prince Hektor's ritual fire.
All being gathered and assembled, first
they quenched the smoking pyre with tawny wine
wherever flames had licked their way, then friends
and brothers picked his white bones from the char
in sorrow, while the tears rolled down their cheeks. 950

In a golden urn they put the bones,
shrouding the urn with veiling of soft purple.
Then in a grave dug deep they placed it
and heaped it with great stones. The men were quick
to raise the death-mound, while in every quarter
lookouts were posted to ensure against

an Akhaian surprise attack. When they had finished
raising the barrow, they returned to Ilion,
where all sat down to banquet in his honor
in the hall of Priam king. So they performed 960
the funeral rites of Hektor, tamer of horses.

The Odyssey

Translated by Allen Mandelbaum

BOOK 1
[ATHENA VISITS TELÉMACHUS][1]

Muse, tell me of the man of many wiles,
the man who wandered many paths of exile
after he sacked Troy's sacred citadel.
He saw the cities—mapped the minds—of many:
and on the sea, his spirit suffered every
adversity—to keep his life intact,
to bring his comrades back. In that last task,
his will was firm and fast, and yet he failed:
he could not save his comrades. Fools, they foiled
themselves: they ate the oxen of the Sun, 10
the herd of Hélios Hypérion;[2]
the lord of light requited their transgression—
he took away the day of their return.

Muse, tell us of these matters. Daughter of Zeus,
my starting point is any point you choose.

All other Greeks who had been spared the steep
descent to death had reached their homes—released
from war and waves.[3] One man alone was left,
still longing for his home, his wife, his rest.
For the commanding nymph, the brightest goddess, 20
Calypso, held him in her hollow grottoes:
she wanted him as husband. Even when
the wheel of years drew near his destined time—
the time the gods designed for his return
to Ithaca[4]—he still could not depend
upon fair fortune or unfailing friends.
While other gods took pity on him, one—
Poseidon[5]—still pursued: he preyed upon
divine Odysseus until the end,
until the exile found his own dear land. 30

---

[1]Book titles and summaries added.
[2]This incident is found in Book 12.
[3]Returning from Troy.
[4]Odysseus' island home off the western coast of Greece.
[5]God of the ocean.

But now Poseidon was away—his hosts,
the Ethiopians, the most remote
of men (they live in two divided parts—
half, where the sun-god sets; half, where he starts).
Poseidon, visiting the east, received
the roasted thighs of bulls and sheep. The feast
delighted him. And there he sat. But all
his fellow gods were gathered in the halls
of Zeus upon Olympus; there the father
of men and gods spoke first. His mind upon 40
the versatile Aegísthus—whom the son
of Agamemnon, famed Oréstes, killed—
he shared this musing with the deathless ones:

"Men are so quick to blame the gods: they say
that we devise their misery. But they
themselves—in their depravity—design
grief greater than the griefs that fate assigns.
So did Aegísthus[6] act when he transgressed
the boundaries that fate and reason set.
He took the lawful wife of Agamemnon; 50
and when the son of Átreus had come back,
Aegísthus murdered him—although he knew
how steep was that descent. For we'd sent Hermes,[7]
our swiftest, our most keen-eyed emissary,
to warn against that murder and adultery:
'Oréstes will avenge his father when,
his manhood come, he claims his rightful land.'
Hermes had warned him as one warns a friend.
And yet Aegísthus' will could not be swayed.
Now, in one stroke, all that he owes is paid." 60

Athena, gray-eyed goddess, answered Zeus:
"Our father, Cronos' son, you, lord of lords,
Aegísthus died the death that he deserved.
May death like his strike all who ape his sins.
But brave Odysseus' fate does break my heart:
long since, in misery he suffers, far
from friends, upon an island in the deep—
a site just at the navel of the sea.
And there, upon that island rich in trees,
a goddess has her home: the fair-haired daughter 70
of Atlas[8] the malevolent (who knows
the depths of every sea, for he controls
the giant column holding earth and sky

[6]Aegísthus conspired with Clytemnéstra to kill Agamemnon when he returned from Troy; see Book 11 of *The Odyssey*.
[7]Hermes, son of Zeus and Maia, is a messenger god and a guide to Hades for dead souls.
[8]A Titan, who supports the world on his shoulders; father of Calypso.

apart). Calypso, Atlas' daughter, keeps
the sad Odysseus there—although he weeps.
Her words are fond and fragrant, sweet and soft—
so she would honey him to cast far off
his Ithaca; but he would rather die
than live the life of one denied the sight
of smoke that rises from his homeland's hearths. 80
Are you, Olympus' lord, not moved by this?
Was not Odysseus your favorite
when, on the spacious plain of Troy, beside
the Argive [9] ships, he sacrificed to you?
What turned your fondness into malice, Zeus?"

Zeus, shepherd of the clouds, replied: "My daughter,
how can the barrier of your teeth permit
such speech to cross your lips? Can I forget
godlike Odysseus, most astute of men,
whose offerings were so unstinting when 90
he sacrificed to the undying gods,
the masters of vast heaven? Rest assured.
Only Poseidon, lord whose chariot runs
beneath the earth, is furious—it was
Odysseus who deprived the grandest Cyclops,
the godlike Polyphémus,[10] of his eye.
(Thöósa—nymph whose father, Phórcys, keeps
a close watch on the never-resting deep—
gave birth to that huge Cyclops after she
had lain in her deep sea-cave with Poseidon.) 100
And ever since his son was gouged, the god
who makes earth tremble, though he does not kill
Odysseus, will not let him end his exile.
But now we all must think of his return—
of how to bring him home again. Poseidon
will set aside his anger; certainly
he cannot have his way, for he is only
one god against us all, and we are many."

Athena, gray-eyed goddess, answered him:
"Our father, Cronos' son,[11] you, lord of lords, 110
if now the blessed gods indeed would end
the wanderings of Odysseus, let us send
the keen-eyed Hermes to Calypso's isle,
Ogýgia. Let him there at once declare
to her, the goddess with the lovely hair,

[9] A collective name for Greeks fighting at Troy.
[10] The encounter with Polyphémus, a Cyclops, is told in Book 9.
[11] The Greeks believed in three generations of Sky Gods: Uranus (Greek for "heavens") was succeeded by Cronos, who was succeeded by his son Zeus, who consolidated power and reigned over a pantheon of deities on Mt. Olympus.

our undeniable decree: Steadfast
Odysseus is to find his homeward path.
But I shall make my way to Ithaca
at once, to give his son the strength to summon
the long-haired Ithacans; when they assemble 120
he can denounce—and scatter—all the suitors:
they are forever slaughtering his sheep,
his shambling oxen with their curving horns.
Then off to sandy Pylos[12] and to Sparta
I'll send him to seek tidings of his father's
return; he may yet hear some hopeful word—
and men will then commend him for his search."

That said, Athena fastened on fine sandals:
these—golden, everlasting—carried her
with swift winds over seas and endless lands. 130
The goddess took her bronze-tipped battle lance,
heavy and huge and solid; with this shaft,
she—daughter of so great a force—can smash
the ranks of warriors who've earned her wrath.
One leap—and from Olympus' peaks she reached
the land of Ithaca. She stood before
Odysseus' door, the threshold of his court.
She gripped the bronze-tipped shaft, and taking on
the likeness of a stranger, she became
lord Méntës, chieftain of the Táphians. 140
She found the braggart suitors at the gate.
Delighting in their dicing, they reclined
on hides of oxen they themselves had skinned—
with pages and attendants serving them,
some mixing wine and water in wide bowls,
while others washed the tables down with sponges
and readied them for food, and others still
stacked meat in heaps on platters—high and full.

The very first to notice Méntës' presence
was young Telémachus. He—sad, morose— 150
sat with the suitors. In his reverie,
he saw his sturdy father—would that he,
returning suddenly, might banish these
intruders from his palace and restore
the rights and rule that had been his before.
Such was the sadness of Telémachus,
alone among the suitors, till he saw
Athena; he rushed toward the outer door,
ashamed that none had gone to greet the stranger.
He drew near, clasped her right hand, even as 160
his left relieved her of the heavy lance.

[12] A city in southern Greece ruled by Nestor.

And when he spoke, his words were like winged shafts:
"My greetings, stranger. Welcome to our feast.
Eat first—and then do tell us what you seek."

He led the way; Athena followed him.
Once they were in the high-roofed hall, he placed
her lance against a column at whose base
a polished rack, with slots for spears, was set;
within that rack there stood still other shafts,
the many spears that brave Odysseus left. 170
He led the stranger to a tall chair, wrought
with care; across its frame he spread rich cloth.
There he invited her to sit and rest
her feet upon a stool; and he himself
sat nearby, on another well-carved chair,
set far off from the suitors, lest his guest,
in all that brouhaha,[13] might look askance
at feasting with such overbearing men—
and, too, because he wanted so to gather
what news he could about his distant father. 180
That they might wash their hands, a servant poured
fresh water from a lovely golden jug
into a silver basin; at their side
she placed a polished table. The old housewife
was generous: she drew on lavish stores;
to each of them she offered much and more.
The carver offered meats of every sort,
and for their wine he set out golden cups;
and these—again, again—a page filled up.

But then the suitors swaggered in; they sat, 190
in order, on low seats and high-backed chairs.
The pages poured fresh water for their hands,
and servants brought them baskets heaped with bread.
The suitors' hands reached out. The feast was theirs.

When they had had their fill of food and drink,
the feasters felt the need for chant and dance—
at banquets, these are pleasing ornaments.
A steward now consigned a handsome harp
into the hands of Phémius,[14] who was forced,
from time to time, to entertain those lords. 200
He struck the strings, and music graced his words.

Then, as Telémachus turned toward his guest,
lest he be overheard, he held his head
close to the gray-eyed goddess—and he said:

[13]Uproar or commotion.
[14]The household bard.

"Dear guest, will you be vexed at what I say?
This harping and this chant delight these men,
for all these goods come easily to them:
they feed—but never need to recompense.
They feast at the expense of one whose white
bones, surely, either rot beneath the rain, 210
unburied and abandoned on the land,
or else are preyed upon by churning waves.
Yet, were Odysseus to return, were they
to see him here again, they would not pray
for gold or richer clothes—just faster feet.
But he has died by now, died wretchedly;
and nothing can console us now, not even
if some man on this earth should say my father
will yet return. The day of his homecoming
is lost: it is a day we'll never see. 220
But tell me one thing—tell me honestly:
Who are you? Of what father were you born?
Where is your city, where your family?
On what ship did you sail? Why did that crew
bring you to Ithaca? And who were they?
For surely you did not come here on foot!
And also tell me truthfully—is this
the first time you have come to Ithaca,
or have you been my father's guest before?
For many other foreigners have come 230
to visit us—like you, my father knew
the ways of many men and many lands."

Athena, gray-eyed goddess, answered him:
"My words to you are true: I'm Méntës, son
of wise Anchíalus; the Táphians,
tenacious oarsmen, are the men I rule.
Now I have landed here with ship and crew;
we cross the winedark sea toward Témesë—
all this in search of copper. What we stow
is gleaming iron, which we're set to barter. 240
Outside the city, moored in Rhēīthron's harbor,
close to the fields, beneath Mount Néion's forest,
my ship is waiting. Years ago, your father
and mine were guests and friends. (Just ask the brave
Laértës[15]—though they say he shuns the city;
it seems that now he much prefers to grieve
far off, alone, except for one old servant.
She, when his body aches from the hard climb
he makes, from slope to slope, to tend his vines,
still carries food and drink right to his side.) 250

"Now I have come—for I had heard indeed
that he, your father, had returned. Surely

[15] Father of Odysseus.

it is the gods who now obstruct his journey.
For bright Odysseus has not died upon
this earth: he is alive somewhere, delayed
upon an island set among vast waves,
held by harsh savages, against his will.
I am no augur or interpreter
of flights of birds, but now shall I foretell—
even as the immortals prompt my soul— 260
events my mind can see: Your father will
not be kept back from his dear land much longer,
though they may bind him fast in iron chains;
he is a man of many wiles, who can
contrive the way to reach his home again.
But you—do tell me now with honesty:
Are you, so tall, indeed Odysseus' son?
Your head and handsome eyes resemble his
extraordinarily; we two had met
quite often in the days before he left 270
for Troy, where others, too—the Argives' best—
sailed in their hollow ships. But since then I
have not seen him, and he has not seen me."

Telémachus' reply was keen and wise:
"Dear friend, I cannot be more frank than this.
My mother says I am his son, but none
can know for sure the seed from which he's sprung.
In any case, would I had been the son
of one so blessed that he grew old among
his own belongings. I, instead, am born— 280
or so they say—of one who surely was
the most forsaken man, the most forlorn.
Now you have had and heard my full response."

Athena, gray-eyed goddess, answered him:
"Despite misfortune now, your family
can count on future fame: Penelope
is mother of a son who is most worthy.
But tell me truthfully: What sort of feast
is this? A banquet? Or a wedding party?
This surely is no meal where each has brought 290
his share. Why did this crowd seek out your house?
These guzzlers seem to me no better than
a pack of swaggerers—too rude, too coarse.
Seeing their shameful doings, any man
of sense would feel both anger and contempt."

Telémachus' response was wise, precise:
"Dear guest, to all you ask, I now reply.
I tell you that as long as he, my father,
was in his native land, this house was rich
and great. But then the gods willed otherwise— 300
they made my father vanish: they devised
oblivion for him—much deeper than

oblivion known by any other man.
And though he's dead, my grief would be less deep
if he had fallen in the land of Troy,
among his fellow warriors, or else—
once he had wound up all the threads of war—
had died at home, among his very own.
Then all of the Achǽans would have built
a tomb for him; and, too, he would have won 310
much glory for his son in days to come.
Instead, the spirit-winds—the stormy Harpies—
snatched him away ingloriously: he
was banished into black obscurity.
And I am left with grief and misery.
I sigh not only over him: the gods
have given me still more calamities.
All lords with power in these isles—who rule
Dulíchium and Samos and Zacýnthus,
the wooded isle, and those who now presume 320
to rule in rocky Ithaca—continue
to woo my mother and consume my goods.
She'll not reject the hateful wedding or
accept it. Meanwhile all their gluttony
lays waste my house; they soon will ruin me."

Pallas Athena, now incensed, replied:
"The absent one, Odysseus, is indeed
the man whom you, unhappy son, could use:
he'd break the back of this marauding band.
Would he—returned—were now to take his stand 330
upon the threshold with his helmet, shield,
and pair of spears—the mighty man that I
first saw on his way back from Éphyrë,
the land of Ílus, son of Mérmerus;
along his homeward way, he stayed with us—
I saw him drinking, feasting, in our house.
(He'd sailed in his fast ship to visit Ílus,
to seek a fatal venom he could smear
on his bronze arrow-tips; but in his fear
of the undying gods' displeasure, Ílus 340
refused to give Odysseus that dread drug.
My father gave it to him, for he loved
your father so extraordinarily.)
For if Odysseus were to show himself
among this pack of suitors with the same
strength he showed them, they all would meet quick death
and bitter wooing. But of things like these—
whether or not your father, on returning,
will take revenge within his palace—we
know nothing; such things lie upon the knees 350
of gods. But for yourself, you must consider
the way in which to rid your house of suitors.
Now hear my words and think on them with care.
Tomorrow ask the lords of Ithaca

to gather here; then speak to all, and let
the gods be witnesses. Command the suitors
to scatter, each on his own way; and order
your mother, should she be inclined to wed,
to go back to her mighty father's house.
Let him prepare his daughter's wedding and 360
the gifts—appropriately rich—she merits.
As for yourself, the path I urge is this,
if you would listen: Find the fittest ship
and, with a crew of twenty oarsmen, seek
some word of your long-absent father—for
a mortal may have heard about him, or
your ears may chance to hear the voice that Zeus
so often uses when he brings men news.
Sail first to Pylos: question noble Nestor.
Then visit Sparta's king, blond Meneláus:[16] 370
of all Achǽans clad in bronze, he was
the last to reach his home. If you should hear
word that your father is still alive and steers
a homeward path, then—though you are much tried—
you surely can hold out for one more year.
But if you learn that he has died, return
to your dear land and raise a mound for him;
complete a just, unstinting funeral,
then marry off your mother to some man:
you will have done all that you should—and can. 380
But then weigh carefully in mind and soul
how best to kill the suitors in your halls—
by way of open combat or of guile.
Forget the pastimes of a child: you are
a boy no longer. Or have you not heard
what fame Oréstes gained when he avenged
the murder of his father? Everyone
knows how he killed that master of deceptions,
Aegísthus, slayer of great Agamemnon.
You, too, my friend—I see you tall, robust— 390
must never flinch or falter if you want
to win the praise of men in time to come.
But now I must return to my swift ship;
this long delay may make my comrades fret.
Consider carefully—heed what I've said."

Telémachus' reply was keen and wise:
"My guest, your words come from a friendly mind—
words like a father's to a son—and I
shall not forget them. But why not extend
your stay? Although your voyage presses, bathe— 400
refresh your spirit; then, fine gift in hand,

---

[16] Brother of Agamemnon and husband of Helen of Troy.

you can with satisfaction sail away.
That gift will be a precious, handsome thing,
a keepsake such as dear friends give to friends."

Athena, gray-eyed goddess, answered him:
"Do not delay me now. I truly wish
to leave; whatever gift your heart would give—
you'll choose a handsome one, I'm sure—can be
consigned when I stop here again, on my
return, that I may bear it home. And it 410
will earn for you a gift of equal merit."

When that was said, gray-eyed Athena left,
quick as a bird. Within his heart she'd set
resolve and strength and memories more intense—
more bent upon his father—than before.
And he was pensive, marveling, aware
that he had had some god as visitor.

At once he went among the suitors—he,
a mortal like a god. The flawless bard
was chanting still; the suitors sat in silent 420
astonishment. He sang of the Achǽans:
their sad return from Troy, the penalty
Athena made them pay. Penelope,
within her rooms above, hung on his words;
she grasped the wondrous sense of every verse.
The pensive daughter of Icárius
descended the steep stairs, escorted by
two of her maids: she did not come alone.
And when that lovely woman reached the hall,
beside a pillar that sustained the roof, 430
she stopped—a glowing shawl before her face,
and, to each side, there stood a faithful maid.
In tears, Penelope implored the singer:

"You, Phémius, know many other deeds
of men and gods—exploits that bring delight
to mortals, acts that singers celebrate.
Then, seated here among these suitors sing
of such things—while they drink their wine in silence.
But stop this dismal chant, for it consumes
the heart within my breast, since I have been 440
struck by a loss that cannot be forgotten.
Indeed, such was the man for whom I grieve
with endless memory, a man whose glory
is known through Hellas,[17] Argos—all of Greece."

This was Telémachus' astute reply:
"My mother, why not let the faithful singer

[17] Greece.

delight us as his heart impels? The singer
is not to blame; this grief was brought by Zeus,
he who assigns to those who feed on bread
the good or evil he alone decrees. 450
Do not fault Phémius if he would sing
the Dánaans'[18] sorry doom: men hold most dear
whatever song is newest to their ears.
Allow your heart and soul to listen, for
Odysseus was not the only one
to lose in Troy the day of his return:
there many other warriors met their death.
But go now to your room; tend to your tasks,
the distaff and the loom; your women can
complete the work that they began. Leave speech 460
to men: to all those here and—most—to me;
within this house, I have authority."

Amazed, while going to her room, she laid
to heart her son's wise words. Then, with her maids,
she reached the upper floor, and wept and wept
for her dear husband, her Odysseus,
until Athena, gray-eyed goddess, shed
sweet sleep upon her eyelids.

But the suitors
began to clamor in the shadowed hall:
each hoped that he might lie in bed with her. 470
For them Telémachus had these sharp words:

"How arrogant you are—beyond all measure—
you who would win my mother. Feast with pleasure
for now, but let there be no brouhaha:
to hear the song of one whose voice is like
the gods'—that is most fine. There will be time
tomorrow to assemble, one and all;
within that council I shall frankly call
on every one of you to quit my halls.
Just hold your future revels someplace else; 480
consume your own fine goods; let each for each
prepare, in turn—in his own house—a feast.
Or if you think it easier—or better—
to eat your unpaid way through one man's wealth,
feast here indeed. But I shall then implore
the gods, who live forever, asking Zeus
to grant me my requital: all of you
would then die unavenged within these halls."

The angry suitors bit their lips, amazed
to hear Telémachus speak words so brave. 490
Antínoüs, Eupēithes' son, replied:

---

[18] Another name for the Greeks at Troy.

"Telémachus, the gods indeed may teach
brash blustering to you and braggart speech.
But let us hope that they'll not intervene,
that Cronos' son will not make you the king
of seagirt Ithaca, whatever claim
your birth might bring."

To this, Telémachus'
reply was keen and wise: "Antínoüs,
though what I say may well incite your wrath,
I would be king were Zeus to grant me that. 500
I want that honor: do you really think
that kingship is a sorry destiny?
To be a king does not mean misery:
a ruler's house grows rich at once; his name
gains glory everywhere. In any case,
our seagirt Ithaca has many lords—
other Achǽan chiefs both young and old;
and since the firm Odysseus now is dead,
one of these princes may succeed him. Yet
I still shall rule in my own hall and keep 510
the servants that Odysseus won for me."

Eurýmachus, the son of Pólybus,
replied: "This matter rests on the gods' knees—
which lord of the Achǽans will be king
in seagirt Ithaca. But do be sure,
your house has you as lord, your goods are yours.
As long as there are men in Ithaca,
no one—whoever he may be—can come
and seize your wealth by force, against your will.
But, dear friend, tell me now about the stranger: 520
Where does he come from? Did he say what country
he can call home? Where is his family?
Where are his native fields? Did he bring word
about Odysseus' coming home? Or was
he traveling on his own affairs? He left
so quickly, suddenly; he did not wait
to meet us—but his aspect was not base."

Telémachus' reply was careful, weighed:
"Eurýmachus, that day is lost—the day
on which my father would return. And thus, 530
no news that men may bring can win my trust:
I pay no heed to any prophecy,
to any seer my mother may have called
into this hall. That stranger is a friend
whom I inherited. He comes from Taphos:
Méntës, the son of wise Anchíalus—
so he announced himself. And he commands
those men who love to row, the Táphians."

Though he said this, his heart knew he had met
the deathless goddess: she had been his guest. 540

The suitors, charmed by dance, entranced by song,
rejoicing, waited for the night to come.
And then dark evening fell as they caroused,
and each—to sleep—went back to his own house.
Telémachus walked toward the fair courtyard:
there stood the high-walled room, set well apart,
where he would spend the night. But as he walked,
not sleep but hope and worry filled his thoughts.
Beside him, blazing torches in her hands
to light his way, went careful Euryclēia, 550
daughter of Ops, who was Peisénor's son.
(Long years ago, when she had just been touched
by loveliness, Laértës purchased her:
he paid as much as twenty oxen cost.
And even as he honored his dear wife,
so had he honored her. But he had never
brought her to bed with him: he took much care
never to wound his wife or stir her anger.)
And it was she who led him to his door,
who bore bright torches as they crossed the court, 560
for none among the handmaids loved him more—
she was the one who'd nursed Telémachus.

Once he'd unlatched the door of his fine room,
he sat down on the bed, shed his soft tunic,
and handed it to the astute old woman.
She smoothed and folded it, then hung it on
a peg beside the bedstead. When she left,
she shut the door, drew to the silver knob,
then pulled the drop-strap fast. Telémachus—
night long, and covered by a wool-fleece wrap— 570
thought on the trip his goddess-guest had mapped.

BOOK 3
[Telémachus Visits Nestor]

[In Book 2, Telémachus calls an assembly, where the suitors are criticized for their behavior in Odysseus' palace. The suitors blame Penelope for taking too much time in choosing a new husband to replace Odysseus. In disguise, Athena assists Telémachus to prepare a ship for his journey; he leaves during the night. –ED.]

The sun had left the splendid sea: it climbed
into the bronze of heaven, bringing light
to the immortals and to those who die
on earth, the giver of the gift of grain.
The Ithacans had reached the coast of Pylos,
the sturdy fortress-city built by Néleus.[19]
Along the shore, the men of Pylos stood,

[19]Son of Poseidon and father of Nestor.

offering sacrifices—jet black bulls—
to please the dark-haired god who shakes the land:[20]
Poseidon, lord of quakes and shifting sands. 10
Nine sectors had been traced along the beach;
five hundred men had been assigned to each,
and every sector sacrificed nine bulls.
Now, after tasting of the inner parts,
the men of Pylos, with their feast in course,
were offering burnt thighbones to the god,
when, heading straight for shore, the visitors
hauled in and furled the sail of their lithe ship.
They moored. They disembarked. Athena stepped
onto the shore; Telémachus came next. 20
Then, turning first to him, the goddess said:

"There is no need to be at all ashamed,
for you have crossed this sea with but one aim:
to find what fate your father suffered—where
the earth has hidden him. But now it's Nestor,
the master horseman, whom you must seek out;
let him reveal the riches of his mind.
Nestor knows much—and he will not tell lies."

Telémachus' reply was careful, wise:
"Mentor, how shall I meet, how shall I greet him? 30
I'm still unskilled at subtle turns of speech.
When one is young, he may indeed be blamed
for questioning his elder. I'm ashamed."

This was the gray-eyed goddess's reply:
"Telémachus, your mind will prompt some words;
others will come to you—a god will urge.
I do not think that you were born and raised
without the gods' attentive tutelage."

That said, Pallas Athena moved ahead;
he followed where her rapid footsteps led. 40
They reached the center of the sacred feast.
There Nestor sat together with his sons,
surrounded by his people; some were roasting
already-skewered meats and some preparing
still other slabs on spits. But when they saw
the strangers, all the men of Pylos rushed
to welcome them with hands outstretched; they asked
the visitors to join the celebrants.
First, Nestor's son, Peisístratus, drew near.
He took them by the hand. He had them sit, 50
as members of the feast, upon soft fleece
spread on the sands, beside his father and

[20]Poseidon.

his brother, Thrasymédēs. And he fetched
choice shares of vitals for the newfound guests.
Then he poured wine into a golden cup;
and with the words that welcomed them, he pledged
Athena, daughter of aegis-bearing Zeus:

"Pray now to lord Poseidon, stranger: we
would honor him with this festivity.
And after you have poured libations and 60
offered your prayer—just as the gods command—
pass on this cup of sweet wine to your friend,
that he may pour his proper share. I'm sure
he, too, would pray to the immortals: all
men need the gods. But since your friend is young—
no older than I am—indeed you must
be first to take from me this golden cup."

When that was said, he set the cup of honey-
sweet wine into her hand. And she was pleased—
delighted with his tact and courtesy, 70
content that she was chosen to receive
the gold cup first. At once—and fervently—
the gray-eyed goddess prayed to lord Poseidon:

"Listen, Poseidon, lord who holds earth fast;
do not prevent completion of the tasks
that we have undertaken—we who pray
to you. Above all, grant to Nestor glory,
and to his sons; and to the others—all
the men of Pylos—grant a just requital,
a recompense for their fine hecatomb.[21] 80
And let Telémachus and me sail home
in safety, once we've reached our visit's goal."

So did she pray—her task well under way.
Then to Telémachus she gave the handsome
two-handled cup; and just as she had done,
Odysseus' dear son prayed to lord Poseidon.
The backs and flanks were roasted now; with this,
the men of Pylos slid them off the spits.
Each took his share of that abundant feast.
Now, with their need for food and drink appeased, 90
the horseman Nestor was the first to speak:

"It surely is more proper to inquire—
to ask our guests to tell us who they are—
after and not before we've shared this feast.
Who are you, strangers? And what is the land

[21] Literally, the word indicates a sacrifice to the gods of one hundred animals, but may indicate simply a large, public sacrifice.

from which you sailed the seaways to these sands?
Are you just traders? Or a prowling crew
that preys at random, pirates on the loose,
who risk their lives, but plunder others' goods?"

Telémachus' reply was keen and wise; 100
he did not cloak his goal in weak disguise;
Athena had endowed his heart with force,
that he might ask about his far-off father:

"O Nestor, Néleus' son, the Greeks' great pride,
you ask what is our home—I'll tell no lies.
We come from Ithaca, the sunlit city
beneath Mount Néion; but what brings me here
is nothing public—this is my affair.
I've come in search of word about my father—
the famous, the unfaltering, Odysseus. 110
They say that he, while fighting at your side,
destroyed the citadel of Troy, its might.
We have been told how other chiefs who went
to war against the Trojans met sad death.
But of his death nothing is known—such is
the will of Cronos' son; and now no one
can say if he was killed by enemies
upon dry land, or lost upon the seas
when storm winds struck the waves of Amphitrítë.
Thus, I am at your knees. I must beseech: 120
Tell me of his sad death. Were you at hand
or have you heard some word of that doomed man?
She who gave birth to him gave birth to grief.
You need not sweeten anything for me.
Forget discretion; set aside your pity:
tell me completely—all you chanced to see.
I plead with you: Recall the words and deeds
with which the firm Odysseus faithfully
fulfilled his promises to you in Troy,
the land of the Achǽans' misery. 130
With that in mind, speak truthfully to me."

The horseman, Nestor of Gerénia, answered:
"O friend, you have recalled to me the griefs
we sons of the Achǽans had to meet
when, there in Troy, we fought unstintingly.
I can recall our many miseries
as in our ships we roamed the misty sea
in search of booty, following Achilles,
and our long struggle for the citadel
of Priam—there our best, our bravest, fell.[22] 140

[22]Great heroes of the Trojan War at Priam's city of Troy are listed here: the mighty Ajax; Achilles, the central hero of *The Iliad,* who withdrew from battle, then returned to avenge the death of his friend Patróclus; and the clever Odysseus.

There lies the warlike Ajax, there Achilles,
and there Patróclus, he whose counsel matched
the gods'; and there, Antílochus, my own
dear son, unflinching, strong—a man so fast
of foot and bold in battle. And these deaths
were not the only sorrows that we met.
What mortal man could tell our trials in full?
And even if you asked to hear them all—
and stayed some five or six years here with me
to listen to that dark and dreary story— 150
before the tale was done, you would grow weary
and make your way back to your own dear country.
For nine years—unrelentingly—we tried
with wile on wile, device upon device,
to ruin Troy—until, at last, the son
of Cronos crowned our plotting with that prize.
Astute Odysseus had no equal there;
no one can vie with what is past compare—
your father so outstripped us all in guile.
(Your father—if you are indeed his child. 160
Yet as I watch your ways I am amazed:
your words are so like his; no man would think
that one so young could mime Odysseus' speech.)
And there, in all that time, I and divine
Odysseus never differed: of one mind,
whether in council or assemblies, his
and my good sense and shrewdness would advise
the best course for the Greeks. But after high
Troy[23] had been sacked, the heart of Zeus devised
a dismal homeward journey for the Argives. 170
Not all the Greeks had been both just and wise;
thus, many met a sorry death; the gray-
eyed goddess' fatal anger doomed their way.[24]
She—daughter of so powerful a father—
incited Átreus' two sons[25] to quarrel.
These two had asked the Argives to assemble
at sunset (so, when answering that call—
a summons without sanction, sense, or rule—
the sons of the Achǽans were all dull
with wine). But when they tried to justify 180
their calling for this meeting, there was strife.
For Meneláus urged them all to think
of their return across the sea's broad back.
But Agamemnon was not pleased by that.
Instead, he felt the Argives must not leave:
it surely was more urgent to appease

[23]Troy, a city of towers, was strategically located on a hill overlooking the Aegean Sea and the Hellespont.

[24]Athena was angry with the Greeks because her shrine had been violated when Cassandra had tried to take refuge in it, but was raped.

[25]Agamemnon and Meneláus.

the goddess and her terrifying wrath
by offering holy hecatombs to her.
That fool ignored this truth: that he could never
reverse Athena's anger—for the minds 190
of gods, who live forever, don't incline
to sudden shifts. And so, with words of spite,
two brothers stood and clashed; the armored Argives
rose up and, brawling bitterly, took sides.
And all night long, each side conspired against
the other: they had violence in mind—
while dark calamity was Zeus' design.
But some of us at daybreak launched our ships
across the glowing sea; on board we stored
our goods and the low-girdled Trojan women. 200
One half of the Achǽans stayed behind
with Agamemnon, shepherd of his people;
the other half embarked and left. Their ships
moved swiftly on the waters' vast abyss:
a clement god had smoothed the sea's rough surface.
When we touched Ténedos,[26] the gods received
our sacrifices: we were keen to reach
our homes. But cruel Zeus refused to heed
our longing. He—again—incited strife.
Some, shifting back to Agamemnon's plan, 210
now turned their ships around: they headed back.
Odysseus, wise and crafty lord, did that.
But I, together with the fleet I led,
fled straight ahead. I knew that Zeus was bent
upon disaster. Diomédës went
my way; he spurred his men. Blond Meneláus
sailed later, overtaking us at Lesbos.
There we were studying which route was best,
whether to keep steep Chios to our left,
heading toward Psýria, or else—as we 220
debated our long journey—to proceed
landward of Chios, past the windswept cliffs
of Mímas. Then we asked the god to send
an omen; he showed us a sign—commanded
our ships to cleave the sea directly, head
straight for Eubœa—if we wished to flee
most quickly from the threat of tragedy.
A shrill wind started up, the ships ran swiftly
across the seaways rich with fish; that night
we landed at Geræstus. There we honored 230
Poseidon, offering upon his altar
the roast thighbones of many bulls, for we
had crossed the open sea.

[26] An island off the Trojan coast. The question that troubled the various leaders was whether to hug the shoreline on the way home or to take the more direct but dangerous route across the open water.

"On the fourth day,
Diomédës and his comrades chose to stay
their ships in Argos. I sailed straight to Pylos.
The wind that favored me maintained its course:
the god who sent it never sapped its force.

"So, my dear child, I came back knowing nothing—
and still know little—of the others who
stayed on at Troy or went back with Odysseus— 240
who of those Argives has been saved, who lost.
But I shall share with you all I have heard
since my returning home—for it is just
that nothing be concealed from friends. They say
that safe return has blessed the Mýrmidons,
consummate spearmen, whom the famous son
of generous Achilles guided home.
And Philoctétës,[27] son of noble Pōias,
made safe return; so did Idómeneus
bring all his men who had survived the war 250
to their own Cretan shores—the sea stole none.
As for the son of Átreus, though your home
is far from his, you've surely heard how he
returned and met a wretched fate—the death
he met, the trap Aegísthus had devised.
But then the killer paid a horrid price.
How good a thing it is for one who dies
to leave a son behind: it was Oréstes
who took revenge upon the murderer
Aegísthus, master of deceptions. Friend, 260
may you, too (I can see that you are handsome
and sturdy), be courageous, that your name
among men still unborn may merit fame."

Telémachus' reply was keen and wise:
"O Nestor, Néleus' son, the Greeks' great glory,
Oréstes was indeed a fine avenger:
the Greeks will surely grant him ample fame,
and song, in time to come, will sing his name.
Would that the gods gave me Oréstes' force,
that I might crush the suitors' insolence. 270
Yet, for my father and for me, the gods
have not spun much good fortune. But I must—
for now—submit and suffer: I've no choice."

The horseman, Nestor of Gerénia, answered:
"O friend, you speak of this and I remember:

[27] The Mýrmidons were Achilles' warriors; his son, Neoptólemus, went to Troy to avenge his father's death; Philoctétës had been left behind on an island because of sickness, but arrived at Troy for the conclusion of the war; Idómeneus was king of Crete.

they say that many suitors of your mother,
in your own halls, are bent on treachery.
Or have you given way to them most freely?
Or did your fellow Ithacans—spurred on
by some god's voice—become your enemies? 280
Perhaps on your return you may strike down
the sinful suitors—either on your own
or even with the help of all the Argives.
For if Athena, gray-eyed goddess, chose
to love you with the care that she bestowed
on excellent Odysseus in the land
of Troy, the site of the Achǽans' sorrows
(for I have never seen the gods declare
a love as open as the love she shared—
Pallas Athena at your father's side), 290
were you to be a man Athena prized
and favored as she did your father, then
the suitors would forget all marriage plans."

Telémachus' reply was cautious, wise:
"I do not think that this will come to pass,
dear lord; what you have said is too immense—
I am amazed! Although I hope for this,
I know it's not to be, not even if
the gods should will it so."

The gray-eyed goddess
replied to him: "Telémachus, what speech 300
dares to escape the barrier of your teeth!
A god, if he is pleased to bring a man
home safely—even from a distant land—
can do that easily. Were I that man,
I'd rather face the harshest trials along
my way before the day of my return,
than to have easy passage back but find
death right at my hearthside—like Agamemnon,
trapped by Aegísthus and by his own wife.
And yet we must admit, the gods have limits: 310
not even they can free a man most dear
from death's hard clasp—the doom that all men share."

Telémachus' reply was wise, discreet:
"Mentor, despite our grief let us not speak
of these things any longer. For my father,
there will be no return. The deathless gods
already have decided on his lot:
death and dark desolation. Now, instead,
I would ask Nestor something else, for he
surpasses all men in sagacity. 320
O Nestor, Néleus' son, tell me the truth:
How was the ruler of such spacious lands,
the son of Átreus, Agamemnon, killed?

Where then was Meneláus? And what plan
allowed Aegísthus' wiles to strike a man
more mighty than himself? Was Meneláus
elsewhere, far-off from his Achǽan Argos?[28]
And did his absence, even as he wandered,
permit Aegísthus to transgress—to murder?"

The horseman Nestor then replied: "My son, 330
I'll tell you everything. This—on your own—
you've seen: you know just how things would have been
if, on return from Troy, blond Meneláus
had found Aegísthus living in that palace.
Even in death they'd never have heaped up
a burial mound: they would have let the dogs
and birds tear him apart—Aegísthus, cast
along the plain outside the city. None
of the Achǽan women would have mourned
for one who had contrived so much corruption. 340
We were at Troy—at work, at war—while he,
at ease in Argos, land where horses pasture,
connived with his beguiling words to capture
the wife of Agamemnon. And at first
bright Clytemnéstra scorned indecency:
her sentiments were just. Moreover, she
was in the company of an attendant,
a poet whom the son of Átreus,
when he set out for Troy, had strictly charged
to serve as Clytemnéstra's watchful guard. 350
But when the gods' design had so enmeshed
her will that she was ready to submit,
Aegísthus tricked her guardian: he led
that poet to a barren isle and there
left him to rot—a prey and prize for birds.
His will was now at one with hers: Aegísthus
took Clytemnéstra into his own house.
Then, on the holy altars of the gods,
he roasted many thighs, and he hung high
both woven cloths and gold: beyond all hopes 360
his heart had harbored, he had gained his goal.

"On my return from Troy, I sailed together
with Meneláus—we were friends. But when
we neared the cape of Athens, Súnium,[29]
the sacred headland, with his gentle shafts
Phoebus Apollo struck and killed the helmsman
of Meneláus while his hand held fast
the steering rudder: he, son of Onétor,

---

[28] A region in the Peloponnese, ruled by Agamemnon.

[29] The southern tip of Attica, near Athens; their route lies westward around this point toward the Peloponnese.

was Phróntis, whom no man has yet surpassed
in piloting a ship when storm winds blast. 370
So Meneláus, although he was keen
to journey on, stopped then at Súnium
to bury and to honor his companion.

"But then, while voyaging the winedark sea
in hollow ships, on rapid course he reached—
now, in his turn—steep Cape Maléa's[30] peak.
There the commanding voice of Zeus decreed
a wretched path for him: he poured shrill blasts
and swollen combers, mountainous and vast.
Lord Zeus split Meneláus' fleet in two. 380
Half of the ships were thrust to Crete. And there,
where the Cydónians have their home, along
the Iárdanus, a smooth cliff plunges, sheer,
down to the fogbound sea, beside the boundary
of Gortyn. And against that headland, west
of Phǽstus, the libeccio drives a mass
of breakers; but that sharp rock holds them back.
Just at that point, five ships struck. Though the men
were able—barely—to escape life's end,
all of those boats were battered on the reefs. 390
Meanwhile five other ships in that same fleet—
dark-prowed—were thrust by wind and wave to Egypt.
There, as he wandered—harbor after harbor—
among strange peoples, Meneláus gathered
abundant gold and many other treasures.

"Meanwhile, at home, the web Aegísthus wove
had won the woman. After that he killed
the son of Átreus and forced his will
upon the people. Seven years he ruled
Mycénae[31] rich with gold; but in the eighth, 400
he was undone: from Athens bright Oréstes
returned: he killed his father's murderer.
That done, Oréstes offered to the Argives
a funeral feast for both his hated mother
and cowardly Aegísthus. That same day
the lord of the great war-cry, Meneláus,
returned to Argos, bearing his rich trove,
all of the goods and gold his ships could stow.

"So do not wander long, far from your house—
my friend—if you have left behind your wealth, 410
with men so arrogant within your gates.
Should they divide and then devour your goods,

[30]The southern cape of the Greek mainland; further south is the island of Crete.

[31]Agamemnon's capital city, often used interchangeably by Homer with Argos.

your journey would have been of little use.
Yet you must go to see lord Meneláus.
His safe return is recent: he's come back
from lands that lie beyond a sea so vast
that any man who, driven off his course
by storm winds, reached those coasts would have small hope
of sailing home again: even the birds
can cross such waters only once a year— 420
that unremitting stretch of sea and fear.
So go now with your comrades and your ship.
Or if you want to go by land, there are
horses and chariot at hand: my sons
will guide you into sunlit Lacedǽmon,[32]
blond Meneláus' home. There, face-to-face,
you can implore, insist—and he will state
the truth. He is too wise to tell you lies."

His words were done. The sun sank. Darkness won.
Among the guests, the gray-eyed goddess said: 430
"Old man, your words have urged the wisest course.
But now cut out bulls' tongues and mix the wine.
Once we complete the offerings we owe
Poseidon and the other deathless gods,
we can give thought to sleep. For it is time.
The light has left; beneath the dark it hides.
It is not right to linger overlong
where gods are feasting. We had best be gone."

These were Athena's words. They heeded her.
Each guest refreshed his hands with water poured 440
by pages; and young servants brimmed the bowls
with wine and poured the portion of the gods—
the first drops—into every feaster's cup.
Bulls' tongues were cast upon the flames; then each
guest stood and doused them, sizzling, with his share
of wine. That done, each feaster drank his fill.
And now Athena and Telémachus
were ready to return to their quick ship.
But Nestor held them back—he would insist:

"Not Zeus nor any other deathless god 450
would ever let you take your leave like this:
as if, when you sailed off in your lithe ship,
you left a man in rags, a pauper—one
who had no cloaks or blankets in his house,
that he and those who are his guests might sleep
in peace. I do have handsome blankets, cloaks.
The son of such a man—Odysseus' own—

[32]Sparta.

will never lie down on a ship's bare deck
as long as I'm alive or am survived
by sons who, after me, within my halls 460
will welcome any guest who seeks my house."

Athena, gray-eyed goddess, answered him:
"Old friend, your words make sense. Telémachus
does well if he obeys your better way.
He, then, will go with you, sleep in your halls—
while I return to our black ship to bring
courage to all and news of everything.
I am the only older man among them:
the others are the friends who followed us—
all the same age as strong Telémachus. 470
Tonight, beside the hollow black ship, I
shall lie along the sands. But at firstlight,
I'll make my way to the Caucónians,[33]
greathearted men, who owe a debt to me—
a debt that's neither new nor small. But send
this man (since he has come to be your guest)
along his way to Sparta with a chariot
and one of your dear sons; and see that he
has horses fast and strong, untiring."

When that was said, gray-eyed Athena sped 480
away, as swift as a sea eagle: wonder
gripped everyone who saw her swift departure.
The sight astonished Nestor. The old man
held fast Telémachus as they clasped hands.
These were the words he offered then:

"O friend,

I do not think that you will prove to be
a coward or a clod, if you—so young—
can count upon the gods as your companions.
Of those who claim Olympus as their home,
your comrade is not any other than 490
Zeus' daughter, rich with spoils, Tritogenía.
And it was your brave father whom she honored
among the Argives. Favor us, Athena:
grant bright renown to me and to my sons
and to my honored wife. I'll sacrifice
to you a broad-browed heifer, one year old,
unbroken, not yet subject to the yoke,
and I shall overlay her horns with gold."

This was his prayer. Athena heard his words.
Then Nestor of Gerénia led them all, 500

[33] A tribe southwest of Pylos.

his sons and sons-in-law, to his bright halls.
Once they had reached his handsome palace, all
sat down in rows on chairs and high-backed thrones.
Then, for his guests, the old man mixed a bowl
of sweet wine that was more than ten years old—
wine from a jar whose leather lid had been
loosened by the housekeeper. From that jar
he also drew the bowl of the libation
he poured as he prayed long and fervently
to Athena, daughter of aegis-bearing Zeus. 510
Libations had been poured and, bowl on bowl,
each guest had drunk as much as pleased his soul.
Then for the night, each went to his own home.
But Nestor had Telémachus, the dear
son of divine Odysseus, sleep there,
upon a corded bedstead set beneath
the echoing arcade. Next to him slept
Peisístratus, fine spearman, sturdy captain,
the youngest—still unmarried—son of Nestor.
But Nestor slept within the high-roofed house. 520
The queen, his wife, prepared and shared his couch.

As soon as Dawn's rose fingers touched the sky
with her first light, the horseman Nestor woke,
went out, and sat on the smooth seats of stone
that—white and gleaming, oil-anointed—stood
at his high doors. These were the seats where Néleus,
whose counsel matched the gods', once sat; but he,
defeated by his fate, had gone to Hades.
The one who sat there now, scepter in hand,
was Nestor, the Achæans' guardian. 530
Now, come from their own rooms, the old man's sons
assembled: Pérseus, Strátius, and Echéphron,
Arétus, and the godlike Thrasymédës.
And when the sixth, Peisístratus, arrived,
they had Telémachus sit at his side.
The horseman Nestor was the first to speak:

"May what I will, my sons, be briskly done;
for at this rich feast for a deity,
Athena showed herself to me so plainly
that in my offerings to the gods, it's she— 540
above all—whom I'd ask to favor me.

"Come now; let one of you select a heifer
along the plain, and have a herdsman drive her,
so that we don't lose time. And let another
go back to brave Telémachus' black ship
and fetch his crew; leave only two as watchmen.
Let someone else among you find Laércës,
the goldsmith, for we need him urgently:
he has to coat the heifer's horns with gold.

The rest of you must stay together here 550
and see the servants work: they must prepare
a feast in our great halls and, round the altar,
set seats and logs as well as limpid water."

So Nestor spoke. His sons set right to work.
The herdsman brought the heifer from the plain.
And brave Telémachus' companions came
from their brisk, shapely ship. The smith was here
with hammer, anvil, tough tongs: with his gear,
his tools of bronze, he gave to gold his forms.
Unseen, the gray-eyed goddess watched the rite. 560

Old Nestor, master charioteer, brought gold.
The smith so thinned it down that it might coat
the heifer's horns—and fill with deep delight
Athena when she saw the sacrifice.
Then Strátius and Echéphron gripped the heifer;
they tugged her to the altar by the horns.
And, from within the house, Arétus brought
a basin that was bossed with floral forms—
a basin filled with lustral water—while
the basket in his other hand held barley. 570
And Thrasymédës, stubborn warrior,
stood by, with his sharp ax, ready to strike,
while Pérseus held a bowl to catch the blood.
Then Nestor, master charioteer, began
the rite: he washed his hands and sprinkled barley,
prayed to Athena fervently and cast
hairs from the heifer's head into the flames.

When they had prayed and sprinkled barley grains,
stout Thrasymédës, Nestor's son, who stood
beside the heifer, struck: the ax blade cut 580
the sinews of the neck; the heifer lost
her force. The women raised the sacred shout:
his daughters and the wives of Nestor's sons
and his dear wife, Eurýdicë, the eldest
daughter of Clýmenus. At that, the men
hauled up the forepart of the heifer's body;
they lifted her and pulled her head back tight;
Peisístratus, commanding captain, sliced
her throat. When the black blood had flowed and life
had left the bones, they quickly cut the carcass, 590
hacked out the thighs and, as is proper, wrapped
those portions in a double layer of fat;
and then they set raw meat on top of that.
Old Nestor seared these parts on burning logs.
But then, to coat the chunks, he splashed dark wine.
The young stood by with spits—forks with five tines.
And when the roasted thighs, Athena's share,
had been consigned and all the celebrants

had tasted of the heifer's vital parts,
they sliced the rest and skewered it on spits; 600
their pointed forks in hand, they roasted it.

Meanwhile the youngest daughter of Néleus' son,
Nestor, the lovely Polycástë, bathed
Telémachus. And after she had washed
and—with unstinting oil—anointed him,
she wrapped him in a tunic and rich cloak.
Fresh from the bath, the dear son of Odysseus
was handsome as a god. The seat he took
was next to Nestor, shepherd of his people.

And when the outer meats were done and drawn 610
off from the spits, then, served by noble men,
who poured wine into golden cups, they feasted.
And with their need for food and drink appeased,
the horseman Nestor was the first to speak:

"Now yoke the horses with the handsome manes
beneath the chariot of Telémachus.
My sons, the time for journeying has come."

This, Nestor said. They listened. They obeyed.
They quickly yoked brisk horses to the staves.
Within the chariot box, the housewife set 620
bread, wine, and dishes held to be the best
for kings whom Zeus has nurtured. Then they stepped
onto the chariot: Telémachus
was first, then Nestor's son, Peisístratus—
captain of men—and it was he who took
the reins and cracked the whip. The horses raced
across the fields; the towering fort of Pylos
was soon behind them. All day long the horses
shook hard the yoke they carried on their necks.
The sun sank; all the roads were dark with shadows. 630
They came to Phérae.[34] There they spent the night
as guests of Díoclës, whose father was
Ortílochus, Alphéus' son. And he
received his guests with every courtesy.

As soon as Dawn's rose fingers touched the sky,
they yoked their team of horses. Quick to mount
their many-colored chariot, they rode out,
the son of Nestor starting up the swift
horses. They reached the fertile fields of grain.
Their journey soon would end, beyond that plain— 640

[34]Uncertain location; perhaps the modern Calamata.

so quickly had their horses carried them.
The sun sank; all the roads were dark with shadows.

BOOK 4
[MENELÁUS AND HELEN]

A land of valleys ringed by deep ravines—
such was that part of Sparta they had reached.
They drove to Meneláus' house, where he
was offering his many kin a feast
to celebrate a double wedding: both
his son and flawless daughter were betrothed.
Long since—in Troy—he'd pledged Hermíonë
to Neoptólemus, son of Achilles,
the man who breaks the ranks of enemies.
The gods had brought to pass that marriage vow; 10
and so, with horses, chariots, he now
was sending to the Mýrmidons' bright city—
where Neoptólemus, her lord, was king—
his dear Hermíonë. And he had brought
Aléctor's daughter as the bride he'd sought—
a Spartan girl—for his beloved son,
strong Megapénthës, born of a slave woman.
(The gods had granted Helen no more children
after the birth of her Hermíonë,
a girl as fair as golden Aphrodítë.) 20
So, in the high-roofed hall of Sparta's king,
his family and friends were reveling
in joy. A godlike singer graced his chant
with notes upon the harp. Two acrobats—
among them all—began their whirling dance.

The travelers brought their horses to a halt
before the palace walls. Telémachus
and Nestor's son, the bright Peisístratus,
now waited at the gate. There Etëóneus,
the busy chamberlain of Meneláus, 30
was going out—but he turned back at once
to tell the people's shepherd what he'd seen.
With these winged words, he drew close to the king:

"O Meneláus, visitors have come—
two strangers—men like those descended from
the seed of mighty Zeus, who nurtured you.
Shall we unhitch their horses here or send
these visitors to one who is more free
to offer them his hospitality?"

Blond Meneláus answered with contempt: 40
"Before this I had never known that you,

Boéthus' son, could be a babbling fool.
We two, on our way home from Troy, have surely—
hoping that Zeus would end our misery—
shared to the full the hospitality
of others. Now unhitch their horses: lead
our guests into the house, to share our feast."

Then Etëóneus hurried through the hall:
in need of help, he called on other lords.
They tied the sweating horses to the stalls, 50
once they'd unhitched the yokes; they poured out wheat
together with white barley; then they propped
the chariot against the polished wall
and led the guests into the gleaming halls.
The young men were astonished when they saw
the radiance inside those high-roofed rooms,
a brightness like the light of sun or moon.
But when their eyes had feasted to the full,
the guests went to the polished baths, where they
were washed by handmaids and smoothed down with oil, 60
then clothed in tunics and soft cloaks. That done,
they took their places next to Átreus' son.
That they might wash their hands, a servant poured
fresh water from a lovely golden jug
into a silver basin; at their side
she placed a polished table. The old housewife
was generous: she drew on lavish stores;
the visitors were offered much and more.

Blond Meneláus spoke these words of welcome:
"Eat of this feast; enjoy it; when you're done, 70
we'll ask you who you are. Your fathers' stock
has not been lost, for you are surely born
of sceptered kings whom Zeus had bred; no one
who is a common man can claim such sons."

That said, he offered them the fat ox-flanks—
the choicest parts, for men of highest rank.
Their fare was ready now; their hands reached out.
Then, with their need for food and drink appeased,
Telémachus—his head held close, that none
might overhear—said this to Nestor's son: 80

"Now, Nestor's son, dear to my heart, look hard:
in these resounding halls, there's gleaming bronze
and gold, electrum, silver, ivory.
Inside, the court of Zeus on high Olympus
must look like this: these riches are prodigious.
I gaze upon such wealth—and am amazed."

He spoke, but Meneláus overheard;
and when he answered, these were his winged words:

"Dear sons, no mortal man can vie with Zeus:
his halls are everlasting—and his goods. 90
As for my wealth, there may be other men
to match me, or there may, by chance, be none.
But it has cost me many wanderings
and many griefs to bring these treasures here,
stowed in my ships; for more than seven years
I traveled till at last I reached my home.
Through Cyprus and Phoenicia I have roamed,
through Egypt. I have seen Sidónians,
Erémbians, and Ethiopians;
I saw the land of Libya, where the lambs 100
grow horns as soon as they are born, and dams
give birth three times a year; no shepherd there,
no master, can complain—they never lack
sweet milk or meat or cheese. Their year is one
long milking-time. But even as I roamed,
amassing treasures there, a traitor killed
my brother, stealthily surprising him—
with the connivance of a faithless wife.
For me, in all this wealth, there's no delight.
Whoever they may be, your fathers must 110
have told you of the trials that I endured
and how, while I was gone, my precious goods
and handsome house fell into ruin. Would
that I still had that house with but a third
part of my riches, and the gods had saved
the lives of those who died on Troy's wide plains,
so far from Argos, land where horses graze!
Indeed, I often weep for all the Greeks;
for seated in my hall, at times I ease
my heart with tears, but then again, I stop— 120
the chill of endless sadness is too much.
Yet, though I grieve for all of them, there's none
of the Achæans whom I mourn as much
as I lament Odysseus: the mere thought
of him can make me shun both food and drink;
there's none of us who did or suffered more
than lord Odysseus. Sorrow was his lot,
and I am fated never to forget
his trials: he has been gone so long, and we
know nothing—whether he's alive or dead. 130
I'm sure that he is mourned by old Laértēs
and wise Penelope and by the son
he left behind—just born—within his house,
Telémachus."

These were his words. They stirred
Telémachus to weep. And so he let
a tear fall from his eyelids to the ground
on hearing of his father; but his hands
held up his purple cloak before his eyes.

Aware of what had happened, Meneláus
debated in his heart and mind: Should he 140
await some word Telémachus might speak
or should he take the lead and test the son.

He pondered long, but he was still uncertain
when from her fragrant, high-roofed room came Helen—
like Ártemis,[35] whose bow and shafts are golden.
Her handmaids, too, were there; Adrástë placed
a well-wrought chair for her; Alcíppë brought
a soft wool rug; and Phylo carried out
a silver basket, gift to Helen from
Alcándrë, wife of Pólybus, who lived 150
in Egypt, where the opulence of Thebes
filled homes with treasures rich beyond belief.
There, Pólybus had given Meneláus
a pair of silver bathing tubs, two tripods,
and ten gold talents. And Alcándrë added
these other gracious gifts: a golden distaff
for Helen, and a basket set on wheels—
a silver basket trimmed with golden rims.
Now, next to Helen, Phylo set this gift,
the basket filled with lovely yarn; across it 160
there lay the distaff wound with violet wool.
So Helen sat, feet resting on a stool,
and asked—for she was eager to hear all:

"Zeus-nurtured Meneláus, do we know
the names of these men visiting our home?
Shall I disguise my thoughts or speak the truth?
But guile is not the course to choose. I swear
I've never seen two women or two men
as similar as are the brave Odysseus
and this young visitor who stands before us. 170
He has to be Telémachus, the son
Odysseus left behind—the boy just born—
when for my shameless sake you all sailed off—
Achæans set to wage a savage war."

The fair-haired Meneláus then replied:
"Wife, I can see what you describe: you're right.
Such were his feet, his hands, such was his gaze,
his head, his hair. And just before, when I
recalled Odysseus, telling of his pain
and of the trials he suffered for my sake, 180
this young one here held up his purple cloak
to shield his eyes as he shed tears: he cried."

[35] Virgin goddess of the hunt and childbirth.

Peisístratus, the son of Nestor, spoke:
"O Meneláus, son of Átreus,
Zeus-nurtured chief of men, just as you say,
this is indeed Odysseus' son. But he
is too discreet and shy of heart to speak
on his first visit here, that openly
before a man whose voice brings both of us
the joy we'd take in hearing from a god. 190
The horseman Nestor of Gerénia
has sent me here with him—I am his guide.
He wants to seek your counsel now, to find
what word or act could serve as his best course.
Yes, when a father leaves, the son will meet
much grief if others do not offer help;
just so, Telémachus—his father's left;
there's no one now to keep distress in check."

The fair-haired Meneláus answered him:
"Ah, now into my house has come the son 200
of one whom I loved much, who suffered pain
to serve my cause; if he returned, I planned
to favor him beyond all other Dánaans.
Would Zeus the thunderer had only let
the two of us return in our swift ships,
for then I would have handed him a town
in Argos—I'd have built a house for him
and led him here from his dear Ithaca
with all his goods, his son, and all his people;
I would have cleared out an entire town 210
and given it to him and his—a town
among those round about, where I am lord.
Then, here in Argos, we'd have often met
in love and gladness, two as friends and guests,
with nothing that could ever part our paths
till, wrapped in blackest clouds, we met our death.
A god must have been envious of that,
for he has destined him—a fate not known
by any other—never to come home."

Such were his words; they all were stirred to tears. 220
The Argive Helen, Zeus's daughter,[36] wept;
Telémachus and Meneláus wept;
and Nestor's son could not hold back his tears—
his heart recalled the great Antílochus,
his brother, killed by bright Dawn's splendid son.
Remembering him, he called upon winged words:

"Old Nestor always used to say that you,
the son of Átreus, were the most astute

[36] Helen's mother was the mortal, Leda, who was raped by Zeus in the form of a swan.

of men: he told us this whenever we
would ask about you in our house. And now, 230
if you can only do so, hear me out.
I don't delight in weeping at a feast;
there will be time for tears at Dawn's first light—
I'm sure there's nothing wrong in mourning one
who's met his fate: the only honor we
bestow on mortals in their misery
is this: we crop our hair and we shed tears.
My brother, too, has died. He hardly was
the least of Argives; you yourself may well
have known Antílochus. I never met 240
or saw him, but they say that few could match
his speed as runner and his stout warcraft."

The fair-haired Meneláus answered him:
"Dear friend, you've spoken with as much good sense
as older men's wise words and acts reflect:
you are indeed your father's son—you speak
with wisdom. One can tell quite easily
that you're the seed of one whom Cronos' son
blessed twice—when he was born and when he wed.
Zeus gave and gives these gifts throughout each day 250
to Nestor, that he may grow old at ease
within his halls, and that his sons may be
wise counselors and never-flinching spearmen.
But now, enough lament; let's feast again;
let them pour water, and we'll wash our hands.
When morning comes, Telémachus and I
will have much time to question and reply."

When that was said, Asphálion, the zealous
attendant lord of noble Meneláus,
poured water, and the feasters washed their hands. 260
Their fare was ready now; their hands reached out.

Then Zeus-born Helen hit upon this plan:
Into the wine that they were drinking, she
now cast a drug that undid every grief
and rage, obliterating any memory
of misery. Whoever drinks of this,
once it is mixed within his bowl, forgets.
On that day he will never let a tear
fall down his cheek, not even if his mother
and father die, not even if his brother 270
or son is killed by bronze before his eyes.
For Zeus's daughter had such cunning potions,
the healing drugs that she'd received in Egypt,
the gifts of Polydámna, wife of Thon.
(The soil of Egypt, giver of much grain,
provides a wealth of drugs; some, when concocted,
are helpful, some are harmful. There each man

is an expert physician. None can match
Egyptians; they belong to Pǽon's[37] clan.)
Now, when she'd spiced the wine bowls with this drug, 280
she had that brew poured out into the cups,
then spoke again:

"God-nurtured Meneláus,
you, son of Átreus, and all other sons
of worthy warriors gathered here, remember:
The god who portions good, who portions evil,
to this man, then to that, is Zeus; in truth
his power rules all things. Yet here and now,
while seated in this hall, come feast, delight
in talk. I have a tale that suits this hour.
I cannot list—much less recount in full— 290
the labors of the stout Odysseus, but
I'll tell you something he was staunch enough
to dare and do in Troy, that land where you
Achǽans suffered much. As his disguise,
he first impaired his body with harsh blows,
and then across his shoulders drew a cloak
in tatters; hidden in a beggar's guise—
so different from the man who stood beside
Achǽan ships—Odysseus made his way
up from the plain into the town of Troy. 300
The Trojans took no notice; all his foes
were calm. I was the only one to know
that it was he, however much disguised.
I questioned him; he gave some shrewd replies.
But when I bathed him, rubbed him down with oil,
gave him fresh clothes, and swore a sacred oath
not to reveal his visit to the Trojans
before he'd reached his own swift ships and tents,
he told me the Achǽan stratagem.
And after he had slaughtered many Trojans 310
with his sharp bronze, he went back to the Dánaans
with much that he had learned in Troy. The women
of Troy were wailing loud, but I was glad;
by now my heart was longing to return;
and, too, I mourned the folly Aphrodítë
inflicted on me, when she led me there
from my beloved land—when I deserted
my daughter, bridal chamber, and my husband—
a match for any man in mind and form."

The fair-haired Meneláus then replied: 320
"Indeed, dear wife, all you have said is right.
I've come to know the stratagems and minds
of many warriors; I've traveled far;

[37]Pǽon means "healer"; Egyptians were famous for their knowledge of herbs and drugs.

but I have never seen a man to match
Odysseus' never-flinching heart. How much
he did and suffered in the well-carved horse![38]
There all we Argive chieftains sat, intent
on death and doom for Troy. There, too, you came—
you must have been incited by some god
who wanted to give glory to the Trojans. 330
Handsome Dëíphobus[39] had followed you.
Three times you circled round that hollow trap;
you touched the wood, you felt it out; you called
upon the Dánaan chieftains, naming each;
you mimed in turn the voice of all the wives
of Argives in that horse. And Týdeus' son
and I and good Odysseus heard you cry
our names aloud. Both I and Diomédës
were eager to leap up and hurry out
or, still inside, to answer you at once. 340
Odysseus held us back; he blocked that course,
however keen we were. By now the rest
of the Achæans' sons kept still, except
for Ánticlus, who longed to answer you.
But stout of hand, Odysseus closed his mouth
until Athena led you off; his grip
was firm. He never flinched. He saved us all."

Telémachus' reply was thoughtful, wise:
"Zeus-nurtured Meneláus, son of Átreus,
there's little comfort in what you have said; 350
all that Odysseus did within the horse
did not prevent his sorry death; not even
a heart of iron could have saved his life.
But send us off to bed; once we are wrapped
in sleep, we might find sweet forgetfulness."

That said, the Argive Helen told her maids
to set out beds beneath the portico,
to cover them with handsome crimson rugs,
and top these, too, with blankets and soft fleece.
The maids, each with a torch in hand, went off; 360
and they prepared the beds. A herald led
the guests out to the portico. They slept
within the outer court—while Meneláus
found rest apart, inside; beside him lay
the loveliest of women, long-robed Helen.

Firstlight. As Dawn's rose fingers touched the sky,
lord Meneláus of the loud war-cry

[38]Appearing to have abandoned the fight against Troy, a group of warriors hid inside a wooden horse, which the Trojans dragged inside the walls of their city, precipitating its downfall.
[39]A Trojan prince married to Helen after Paris' death.

awoke. He dressed, set in his shoulder strap
his sharp blade. To his feet—anointed, sleek—
he tied fine sandals. As he crossed the threshold, 370
he seemed a god. Then he sat down beside
Telémachus and asked:

"What brought you here,
Telémachus, across the sea's broad back
to lovely Lacedæmon? Public matters
or something else? But do tell me the truth."

Telémachus' reply was wise, astute:
"Zeus-nurtured Meneláus, son of Átreus,
it's tidings of my father that I seek.
My home is close to ruin, my rich lands
laid waste; my house is full of enemies; 380
they're always butchering my crowds of sheep,
my herds of shambling oxen with curved horns—
my mother's suitors, men who know no bounds.
Thus, I am at your knees, I now implore:
Tell me of his sad death. Did you yourself
see how he died, or was it someone else
who brought you word of his sad wanderings?
She who gave birth to him gave birth to grief.
You need not sweeten anything for me
by way of your discretion or your pity: 390
tell me completely—all you chanced to see.
I plead with you—recall the words and deeds
with which the firm Odysseus faithfully
fulfilled his promises to you in Troy,
the land of the Achæans' misery.
With that in mind, do speak the truth to me."

Then Meneláus said: "How cowardly
they are! So keen to occupy the bed
of such a stalwart man. As when a hind
has laid her pair of newborn, suckling fawns 400
to sleep within a mighty lion's lair
and gone to roam and graze the mountain spurs
and grassy hollows, and the lion returns
to find that pair of fawns within his den
and slaughters them ferociously, so will
Odysseus kill the suitors savagely.
O father Zeus, Athena, and Apollo,
would that Odysseus might assault the suitors
with that same strength he showed when, long ago
in well-built Lesbos, in a wrestling match, 410
he faced Philomelēides, throwing him
with force: how all Achæans then rejoiced!
Could he regain that strength, his foes would meet
swift death and bitter wooing. What you need
to know, I'll tell you now; I won't deceive—

I won't use shifty or evasive speech.
I heard about your father from the Old
Man of the Sea, who speaks unerringly.
I'll tell you now all that he told to me.

"Though I was eager to go home, the gods 420
still held me there in Egypt: I had not
fulfilled their will, not offered what they want,
not sacrificed unblemished hecatombs.
Now, in the surging sea that fronts the coast
of Egypt, lies an island known as Pharos.
If favored by shrill winds, a hollow ship
has need of but one day to make that trip.
And Pharos offers timely anchorage;
there, men can draw deep water from the wells,
and launch their shapely ships across the swell. 430
The gods becalmed me there for twenty days;
none of those kindly winds that can conduct
a crew across the sea's broad back sprang up.
My stores and my men's strength all would have been
consumed if one among the gods had not
been merciful to me: Eidóthëa,[40]
the daughter of the Old Man of the Sea,
the mighty Próteus. I touched her heart
as I had touched no other's; she met me
while I was wandering alone, apart 440
from my whole crew; as always, they had gone
with their bent hooks to fish around the shore,
for hunger gnawed their bellies. She drew near:
'Stranger, are you so much the fool, so stripped
of wits, or is it that you relish this
distress—are you a man who thrives on trials?
You have been stalled so long upon this isle;
you can't find home; your comrades' will is sapped.'

"These were her words, and this was my reply:
'Whatever goddess you may be, I'll speak 450
with honesty: it's not my will that keeps
me here; I must have sinned against the gods,
the rulers of vast heaven. Tell me now—
since gods know all—which one of the immortals
impedes my journey home; and tell me how
I can sail out across the fish-rich sea.'

"These were my words. The lovely goddess answered:
'Stranger, I tell you truly—hiding nothing.
This island's often visited by one
who never errs—the Old Man of the Sea, 460
the deathless Próteus of Egypt; he

[40]Sea-goddess or sea nymph.

knows each and every secret of the deep;
he is Poseidon's servant. And they say
it's he who fathered me. If you can lie
in wait and catch that Old Man by surprise,
he'll tell you of the passage you must take,
and just how long, across the fish-rich sea,
your journey home will be. And if you wish,
he'll tell you, whom Zeus nurtured, every good
and evil that's been done within your halls 470
while you were gone upon your long, hard way.'

"These were her words, and this was my reply:
'Then tell me *how* I am to lay my snare,
lest that divine Old Man detect my plan
and so escape. It's hard for those-who-die
to get the better of a deity.'

"These were my words. The lovely goddess answered:
'The never-erring Old Man of the Sea
comes from the depths just when the sun has reached
the sky's midpoint—the time when Zephyr breathes 480
and screens him with the dark and ruffled waves.
He sleeps encircled by the sleeping herds
of seals, whom lovely Amphitrítë raised;
up from the bitter brine, the same gray swell,
these seals emerge; they bear a bitter smell.
At break of day I'll lead you to those caves
and have you lie in wait; and you must take
three of your crew along with you—but choose
the best of those who man your stalwart ships.
I'll tell you all that Old Man's traps and tricks. 490
First, one by one, he'll count those seals—and when
he's finished tallying and scanning them,
he'll lie among them as a shepherd would
among his flocks. When he lies down to rest,
be quick: attack with daring, spare no strength.
Grab him and hold him fast, however hard
he strives and writhes. He'll try to take the shape
of every animal upon this earth,
as well as water forms and dazzling shapes
that blazing fire takes. Don't let your grasp 500
fall slack; just grip him harder still—hold fast.
But when, as his own self—the very shape
he had when he laid down to rest—he pleads
to have you speak, then, warrior, do not press;
release your grip on the Old Man and ask
what god it was who blocked your homeward path
and how you are to cross the fish-rich sea.'

"That said, she plunged into the surging deep,
and I went back to where my ships were beached
along the sands. I walked; the many thoughts 510
within my heart were dark. But when I reached

the ship and shore, we had our supper, saw
night—gift of gods—descend, and then we went
to sleep beside the sea. As soon as Dawn's
rose fingers touched the sky, I went to pray
with fervor to the gods. I took with me
three men I trusted most in any test.
Meanwhile Eidóthëa had left the shore
and, after plunging down, came back with four
sealskins; she drew them up out of the sea, 520
four skins from the broad bosom of the deep,
all freshly flayed—prepared—to snare her father.
She scooped out hiding places in the sand;
there she awaited us. We drew up close;
she had us lie down in a row, then cast
a sealskin over each of us—perhaps
no hiding place can be more foul than that:
around those seals who had been bred in brine,
the stench was deadly. Who could lie beside
those monsters of the sea? But she devised 530
a way to save us: she'd brought sweet ambrosia—
its fragrance was delicious. Placing it
where each of us might smell it, she undid
the stench of seals. Through all that morning, we
just waited patiently—until that crowd
of beasts came from the waves; and then they lay
along the shoreline in a row. At midday
the Old Man rose out from the sea; he found
his plump seals, and he scanned them, took his count.
We were the first among his tallied beasts; 540
yet having caught no sign of our deceit,
he, too, lay down. Then we assaulted him;
we shouted, held him fast. But that Old Man
did not forget his guiles and wiles. At first
he turned into a thick-maned lion, then
into a snake, a leopard, a huge boar;
then he was flowing water, then a tree
that towered with its leaves. We did not let
our grasp fall slack. But when he tired at last,
that connoisseur of craft and cunning asked: 550
'O Átreus' son, tell me what god it was
who planned this trap with you? What do you want?'

"These were his words, and this was my reply:
'Old Man, why do you question me? Why try
to put me off? You must know well enough
just what I want. For so long I've been blocked,
held on this isle; I can't go home; my heart
lacks strength. But tell me—since the gods know all—
which one among the deathless ones has stalled
my trip. How can I cross the fish-rich sea?' 560

"These were my words, and his reply was quick:
'You should have brought unblemished hecatombs

to Zeus and to the other gods before
you had embarked; then you'd have sailed across
the winedark sea and reached your native shores.
It's not your fate to see your friends again,
to reach your sturdy home in your own land,
before you've reached the river Nile once more,
the sacred stream of Zeus; there you must offer
your holy hecatombs to the immortals, 570
the rulers of vast heaven. Only then
will they restore your longed-for homeward path.'

"These were his words. My heart was broken: he
would have me face a long and weary trial,
across the misty sea to reach the Nile.
Yet I replied: 'Old Man, just as you bid,
so shall I do. But come now, tell me this—
and tell me truthfully: Of the Achǽans,
did all return intact within their ships—
all those whom I and Nestor left behind 580
when we sailed out from Troy? Did any die
a harsh death on his ship or in the arms
of friends, when threads of war had reached their end?'

"These were my words. His answer came at once:
'Why ask me this, o son of Átreus?
Why do you probe my mind? Why try to find
all I might know? For when you make me speak
such truth, what you will learn will bring you grief.
So many died and many are alive.
There is no need for me to list the chiefs 590
who fell at Troy, for you were there. But two
among the captains of the bronze-clad Greeks
met death along their homeward path. A third
still lives, pent somewhere on the spacious sea.

" 'One, Ajax,[41] with his long-oared fleet, was wrecked.
Poseidon first had dashed his ships against
the giant rocks of Gýrae, but he let
Ajax escape the sea; and he indeed
would have evaded fate (despite the hate
Athena had for him), had he not bragged 600
with blinded heart. He said that he'd escaped
the sea's abyss despite the gods: Poseidon
heard Ajax rave; at once he gripped his trident
in giant hands; he struck the rock of Gýrae
and cracked it. One half stayed in place, but one
split off, plunged down into the sea; that part
was where the maddened, blustering Ajax sat;

[41] The Lesser Ajax, leader of the Locrians in the Trojan War; he raped Cassandra in Athena's temple and was punished.

it bore him down into the boundless tide.
And there, when he had drunk much brine, he died.

"'The second was your brother.[42] He indeed
escaped the fates and, unlike Ajax, saved
his hollow ships—he had great Hera's[43] aid.
But when he neared Maléa's promontory,
a storm wind drove him over fish-rich seas;
and groaning heavily, off course, he reached
the coast of what was once Thyéstës' land,
where now Thyéstës' son, Aegísthus, lived.
Yet here, too, he could hope for safe return:
the gods made that wind change; it now blew fair;
and glad, he disembarked on his own shore.
He touched the soil; he kissed it; many tears
were his—warm tears he shed upon the ground;
at long last he could see the land he'd left.
But from a lookout point, he had been seen.
Aegísthus, master of deceit, had set
a sentry; two gold talents were his prize.
For one whole year he'd watched and waited there,
lest Agamemnon might slip by unseen
and summon all the fighting strength he'd need.
That sentry hurried to Aegísthus' house
to tell of what he'd witnessed from his perch.
Aegísthus hit upon this cunning plot
at once: He posted twenty chosen men—
the city's best—at one side of the hall
to lie in wait. Along the other side,
he had a feast prepared. Then he rode out
with chariot and horses to invite
the shepherd of the people, Agamemnon—
a guest suspecting nothing of his fate—
to feast. And thus he slaughtered Átreus' son
just as one kills an ox within its stall.
Of Agamemnon's followers, not one
was left: they all died in Aegísthus' halls.'

"His words were done. My spirit now was broken.
Seated upon the sands, I cried: my soul
had lost its will to live beneath the sun.
But when my need to weep and writhe was done,
the never-erring Old Man of the Sea
said this to me: 'Enough. These endless tears
can't help us, son of Átreus. It is time
to reach your land as quickly as you can.
Either you'll find Aegísthus still alive,
or else—anticipating you—Oréstes

[42] Agamemnon.
[43] Wife and sister of Zeus.

already will have killed that pest; perhaps
the funeral feast will have you, too, as guest.'

"He said no more. My heart and mind again,
despite my grief, were comforted. Winged words
were mine as I replied: 'Now I have heard
about these two; but tell me of the third,
the one who lives—a prisoner somewhere 660
on the vast sea—unless he, too, is dead.'

"These were my words and his reply was quick:
'It is Laértës' son, the one who lived
in Ithaca. I saw him as he wept
so many tears. Against his will, he's kept
a captive in the grottoes of Calypso—
her island home, where he can only sorrow.
And he cannot return to his own land:
he has no ships at hand, no oars, no friends
to carry him across the sea's broad back. 670
And as for you, Zeus-nurtured Meneláus,
your destiny is not to die in Argos,
the land where horses pasture. The immortals
will send you to the farthest edge of earth,
to the Elysian Fields,[44] where Rhadamánthus,
the fair-haired, has his home. That land provides
the easiest of lives: it never rains
or storms, it never snows along that plain;
the Ocean always sends the West Wind's breath,
the singing breeze that brings fresh life to men. 680
The gods will give you this for Helen's sake;
you are the man Zeus' daughter chose as mate.'

"That said, he plunged into the surging sea.
And I, together with my godlike men,
went to my ships. I walked; the many thoughts
within my heart were dark. But when we reached
the ships and shore, we took our supper, saw
night—gift of gods—descend, and then we went
to sleep beside the sea. As soon as Dawn's
rose fingers touched the sky, we first drew down 690
our ships onto the glowing sea, then stepped
our masts and set our sails. My crews embarked;
each took his proper place along the thwarts,
and then they beat the gray sea with their oars.

"We sailed back to the sacred stream of Zeus,
the Nile;[45] we moored within the river mouth
and offered up unblemished hecatombs.

[44] A portion of the afterworld located on the western edge of the world and reserved for heroes; ruled by a son of Zeus, Rhadamánthus.

[45] The Nile was believed to have its source in the heavens; it was therefore sacred and related to Zeus.

When I'd appeased the anger of the gods,
the everliving ones, I raised a mound
for Agamemnon—so that his renown 700
might never die. That done, I sailed back home;
the deathless ones sent out a kindly wind
and brought me back with speed to my dear land.

"But now, don't leave just yet, stay here as guests
till the eleventh or the twelfth day comes.
When you go off, I'll give you handsome gifts,
three horses and a gleaming chariot;
and, too, a lovely cup, that you may pour
libations to the never-dying gods
and so remember me through all your days." 710

Telémachus' reply was tactful, wise:
"O son of Átreus, do not keep me here
too long. I'd gladly stay for one whole year
within your house—and with no longing for
my mother and my home. I'm pleased indeed
to hear your tales, to listen as you speak.
But I have been your guest for some time now;
and there, in sacred Pylos, all my friends
wait anxiously for me. Whatever gift
you choose to offer, let it be a treasure 720
that's suited to me. Ithaca's not right
for horses—keep them for your own delight.
Your land has ample plains; it's rich in clover
and galingale, wheat, spelt, broad-eared white barley.
But Ithaca has neither racing space
nor meadows: it is good for grazing goats.
No isle that rests upon the sea is fit
for driving chariots along, or rich
in meadows—least of all, my Ithaca,
yet it's more dear than land where horses pasture." 730

His words were done. And Meneláus smiled.
He stroked him with his hand, and then replied:
"Dear child, the way you speak is a sure sign
that you're the scion of a noble line.
I'll change my gift—indeed I can. Instead
I'll give the fairest, richest thing I have:
a mixing bowl designed with care and craft;
it is of silver, and its rim, of gold—
Hephæstus'[46] work. This bowl was given me
by gallant Phædimus, Sidónian king, 740
when, on my homeward way, he welcomed me.
And now I mean for you to take this gift."

[46] The god of fire and metallurgy.

Such were the words they shared with one another.

Meanwhile, before the palace of Odysseus,
the suitors sported on the leveled field—
as in the past—with all their arrogance:
they threw the discus, tossed the javelin.
There sat Antínoüs and, at his side,
godlike Eurýmachus, the two who led
the suitors; of that crowd, they were the best. 750
Noémon, son of Phrónius, drew close;
and turning to Antínoüs, he probed:

"Antínoüs, do we or don't we know
when we shall see Telémachus return
from sandy Pylos? When he sailed, he took
a ship of mine. And now I need it back:
I have to cross to spacious Elis—there
I have twelve mares with stout mules at the teat,
not broken in as yet. I want to lead
some suckling off and break him in."

That stunned 760
the suitors: they were sure he'd never gone
to Pylos, but was still at home, among
the flocks or with the swineherd on his own
farmlands in Ithaca. Antínoüs,
Eupēithes' son, said:

"Tell me honestly:
When did he leave? What young men followed him?
Were they the sons of chiefs or were they just
his hired men or slaves? He has enough
of these to man a ship. And tell me, too,
in truth—I want to know it well, in full: 770
Did you give him that ship against your will?
Or did you give it freely, when his plea
persuaded you?"

Noémon answered: "Freely.
Could anyone do otherwise when he
hears such a man—in deep distress—entreat?
To hold back such a gift is hard indeed.
His crew has those who are the best young men
in all of Ithaca—except for us.
Their captain, whom I saw when they embarked,
was either Mentor or, if not, a god 780
who seemed the very image of that lord.
Yet something puzzles me: Just yesterday,
at early dawn I saw good Mentor here;
yet he, some days before, embarked for Pylos!"

That said, he went back to his father's house.
His words had troubled those two lords; at once

they made their fellow suitors stop their sports
and had them sit. Enraged, Antínoüs—
with fury filling his black heart—spoke out:

"Ah yes, Telémachus indeed has won: 790
where we were sure he'd fail, he's dared and done.
Despite us all, a young man hauls a ship
down to the sea. He sets out on a trip—
his crew, a company of men most fit.
The worst is yet to come; may Zeus cut down
his stamina before his youth is done.
But come, give me a swift ship and a score
of comrades; as he sails back to these shores,
I'll wait along the straits that separate
this isle and rocky Samos. Yes, he went 800
to find his father—but he will find death."

That said, they all were stirred and urged him on.
They rose and went into Odysseus' home.

Penelope was not to waste much time
before she learned that crime was on their minds.
The herald Medon was to tell her all,
for even as he stood outside the yard,
he'd overheard their scheme. He hurried through
the hall to bring Penelope the news.
He stepped across the threshold, and she asked: 810

"Why did the noble suitors send you here?
Is it to have divine Odysseus' maids
set their own tasks aside and tend instead
to readying a banquet for that band?
Would they might end their wooing and their feasts—
were this the final meal they'd ever see!
You who, forever banqueting, exhaust
the wealth and goods of my Telémachus!
When you were boys, you surely paid no heed:
long since, you could have heard your fathers speak 820
about Odysseus, how his words and deeds
had never wronged a man within this land;
divine kings often treat one man with hate
and one with love—but that was not his way;
his rule brought harm to none. But your vile thoughts
are plain enough to see: there's nothing just
within your minds and acts. Men never do
remember one's good deeds with gratitude."

This was the prudent Medon's wise reply:
"I wish that this were their worst enterprise. 830
There's something still more vicious on their minds;
I pray that Zeus not let it come to pass.
For they intend to kill Telémachus

with their sharp bronze along his homeward path;
to seek news of his father, he has gone
to holy Pylos and fair Lacedæmon."

His words were done. Her knees, her heart, went weak.
In tears, she lost the flow and force of speech.
But then, at last, her voice returned. She said:

"Why has my son sailed off? He had no need 840
to board swift ships, those horses of the sea
that carry men across the waves. Did he
want to erase his name from memory?"

This was the prudent Medon's wise reply:
"I do not know if he was driven by
some god, or if his own heart urged him on
to Pylos—in hope that he might learn
about his father's coming back or else
about the fate that checked his homeward course."

That said, he went back through Odysseus' house. 850
But she was wrapped in devastating grief;
she could not bear to sit on any seat,
though there were many in her room; she slumped
down on the threshold, moaning wretchedly;
around her all the handmaids in her halls
were sobbing quietly—the young, the old.
These were the words of sad Penelope:

"Hear me, dear friends; for the Olympian
has burdened me with greater misery
than any woman born and bred with me. 860
Long since I lost a lionhearted husband,
unmatched among the Dánaans, one whose fame
has spread through Hellas, Argos—all of Greece.
And storm winds now have carried from this house
my own dear son; and he has left without
one word to me. Not even you gave thought—
my cruel friends—to wake me from my sleep,
though you knew well enough that he'd gone off
to board his black and hollow ship. Had I
but known that he was planning to depart, 870
then he, however anxious to embark,
would have stayed here or, if he sailed away,
left me, his mother, dead within these halls.
But now let one of you be quick to call
the servant whom my father gave to me
when I came here as bride: old Dólius,
the man who tends my orchard's many trees.
I'll have him go and sit beside Laértēs
at once, to tell him all that's happened here;
perhaps his mind can then devise a plan— 880

he might yet plead before the Ithacans,
denouncing their desire to destroy
both his and the divine Odysseus' line."

Her dear nurse, Eurycleīa, then replied:
"Whatever you may choose to do, dear bride—
to kill me with cruel bronze or let me live
within your house—there is no word I'll hide.
I knew his plans; I gave him his supplies,
all that he'd asked of me: bread and sweet wine.
And then he had me swear a solemn oath 890
that I'd not let you learn of this before
the twelfth day came—unless you missed your son
and heard that he had gone: he did not want
to have you mar your lovely face with tears.
But now, once you have bathed, put on fresh clothes,
do go upstairs with your own maids and pray
to Zeus's gray-eyed daughter: she can save
your son from death. Don't trouble old Laértēs;
he has enough distress. The blessed gods
do not—I think—detest Arcēisius'[47] race; 900
these high-roofed halls, these fields that stretch so far
will be your son's; he will survive this trial."

Her words had lulled Penelope's laments,
had checked her tears. And now her mistress went
to bathe; then she put on fresh clothes and climbed
upstairs together with her maids. She placed
some barley for Athena in a tray
and to the gray-eyed goddess prayed:

"May you,
untiring daughter of aegis-bearing Zeus,
hear what I now beseech: If the astute 910
Odysseus in his halls has ever burned
fat thighs of oxen or of sheep for you,
remember now those sacrifices: save
my son; be shield and shelter; keep him from
the suitors' savagery and insolence."

That said, she cried aloud—the sacred shout;
the goddess heard her prayers. The suitors now
began to clamor in the shadowed hall.
And one of those young braggarts then cried out:

"The queen whom we all courted surely means 920
to marry one of us: she cannot guess
that for her son we've schemed a rapid death."

---

[47]Father of Laértēs, who was Odysseus' father.

These were his words, but none among that crowd
knew what would come to pass. Antínoüs
turned to that band of suitors, saying this:

"Be still, you fools; don't bray and boast aloud,
lest someone carry word of what we plot
to those inside the house. Come, let's get up
in silence and complete the plan that pleased
the hearts of all of us; we are agreed." 930

That said, he chose their finest men—a score.
They rushed to their swift ship along the shore.
They drew their black boat to a deeper spot,
then stepped the mast and set the sail and strapped
the oars in leather thongs. Their sturdy squires
brought them their fighting gear. They moored their ship
well out, where it might ride, then disembarked.
They had their meal while waiting for the dark.

Meanwhile, within her upper room, astute
Penelope, not touching drink or food, 940
lay wondering: Would her blameless son elude
his death or would the suitors cut him down?
Just as a lion is beset by doubt
and fear when he's surrounded by a crowd
of hunters closing in—a cunning ring—
so was Penelope, while pondering,
beset, until sweet sleep came suddenly.
Then she lay back, at rest; her limbs fell slack.

And now Athena thought of something else.
She made a phantom in a woman's shape: 950
Iphthímë, daughter of Icárius
the brave. That sister of Penelope
had wed Eumélus; now she lived in Phérae.
Athena sent that phantom to the house
of the divine Odysseus; it would tell
Penelope to end her tears, to wail
no more. It glided through the bolted door
by way of the latch-thong.[48] Beside the bed
the phantom stood and said:

"Penelope,
the sleep you sleep is sad—the sleep of grief. 960
But listen: Now the gods who live at ease
would have you weep no more; you need not be

---

[48]By using a strap passed through a slit in the door, a person from the outside could bolt the door on the inside.

distressed; your son is coming back—in him
the gods have not found any fault or sin."

This was the wise Penelope's reply
as she slept sweetly at the gate of dreams:
"Why, sister, are you here? Your home is far;
you've never come to visit me before.
And you would have me set my pain apart,
the many griefs that grip my mind and heart. 970
Long since, I lost a lionhearted husband,
unmatched among the Dánaans, one whose fame
has spread through Hellas, Argos—all of Greece.
And now my own dear son, embarked upon
a hollow ship, has sailed away—so young,
he does not know what trials he'll meet; his speech
cannot keep pace when older men debate.
I mourn his father with a grief so great,
yet I weep more for him; I am afraid
that men within the land to which he's gone 980
may strike him down—or he may die at sea.
So many plot against him; they are keen
to kill him; they don't want him here back home."

To this, the shadowed phantom then replied:
"Take heart; don't fear too much. He has a guide
to whom so many men have prayed for aid:
Pallas Athena—one whose force is great.
And she takes pity on your wretchedness.
It's she who sent me here to tell you this."

Again the wise Penelope replied: 990
"If you're a god yourself or if you come
commanded by a god, I beg of you:
Tell me the fate of that unhappy one.
Is he alive somewhere beneath the sun
or is he dead by now in Hades' halls?"

To this, the shadowed phantom then replied:
"I will not tell the truth to you in full,
not let you know if he's alive or dead.
Words empty as the wind are best unsaid."

That said, the phantom glided through the door, 1000
along the latch-thong path it used before;
it joined the breath of winds. Penelope
leaped up from sleep. Her heart was warmed—she'd seen,
within the dark of night, so clear a dream.

The crew of suitors soon embarked, set sail
across the watery paths; their minds were set
on murder—on Telémachus' quick death.

There is a stony isle that looms mid-sea
between the shores of Ithaca and Samos:
its name is Ásteris. It is not wide, 1010
and yet it has twin bays where ships can lie.
There the Achǽans lay in wait for him.

BOOK 5
[CALYPSO]

Now Dawn had left her lord Tithónus'[49] side:
she rose from their shared couch, bringing her light
to the immortals and to those who die.
The gods, convened in council, sat with Zeus,
the thunder lord, whose force is absolute.
To them, Athena, as she called to mind
Odysseus' many miseries, defined
the threats that lay in wait, the troubling fate
he faced as captive in Calypso's cave:

"You, father Zeus, and all of this assembly 10
of blessed, never-dying gods, hear me:
From this time on, no sceptered king need be
benign and kind, a man of righteous mind:
let kings be cruel and corrupt, malign—
for none among his people now recall
divine Odysseus, though his rule was gentle
and fatherly. And now, against his will,
Calypso keeps him captive in her grotto,
her island home, where he can only sorrow.
And he cannot return to his own land: 20
he has no ships at hand, no oars, no friends
to carry him across the sea's broad back.
Now, too, they mean to ambush his dear son,
to murder him along his homeward run;
for news of his dear father, he has gone
to sacred Pylos and bright Lacedǽmon."

Zeus, shepherd of the clouds, replied: "My daughter,
how can the barrier of your teeth permit
such words to cross your lips? For surely this
delay—to keep Odysseus far away 30
until on his return he takes revenge
against the suitors—is the scheme you planned.
As for Telémachus, your cunning can
return him to his land on safe sea paths,
and you can thwart the suitors' plot, so that
those baffled men retreat with empty hands."

[49]The lover of Eos, the dawn goddess.

That said, he turned to Hermes, his dear son:
"Yes, you have served us well on many missions.
Go now, and tell the nymph with lovely hair
that this is our infallible decree: 40
Odysseus is to reach his home, though he
must sail alone, without the company
of gods or men. His craft will be makeshift,
planks bound by many thongs; in such a ship,
his crossing will be trying, tiring, yet
when twenty days have passed, that man of wiles
will reach Schería's[50] fertile soil, the isle
of the Phaeácians, men the gods befriend.
There they will honor him with willing hearts,
as if he were a god. They will escort 50
Odysseus to his homeland in their ship,
with bronze and gold and clothes—so many gifts:
after the sack of Troy, had he sailed back
directly, with his share of spoils intact,
not even then would he have been that rich.
Such is the destined way in which he'll come
to his own land, his friends, his high-roofed home."

That said, the keen-eyed messenger was quick.
First, to his feet he fastened handsome sandals:
these, golden, everlasting, carried him 60
with swift winds over seas and endless land.
He took the wand that charms the eyes of men:
some, he enchants with sleep, just as he can,
at will, awaken others. Wand in hand,
Hermes took flight. He passed Piéria's[51] peaks
and, from the upper air, swooped toward the waves;
then, like a bird, he skimmed—a tern that bathes
its thick wings in the brine as it hunts fish
in surge that never rests—the dread abyss.
So Hermes rode the countless troughs and crests. 70

At last he reached landfall, the distant isle.
He quit the violet waves. He made his way
on land and found the fair-haired nymph's deep cave.
She was at home. A splendid fire blazed
upon her hearth; its fragrance wafted far
across the isle—the scent of burning logs
of juniper and tender thuja boughs.
Inside that grotto, with her golden shuttle,
the nymph was weaving; moving back and forth
before her loom, she sang—her voice was graceful. 80
The grotto was surrounded by rich forests:
alder and poplar trees and pungent cypress.

---

[50]Probably the island of Corfu, off the west coast of Greece.
[51]Near Mt. Olympus.

There broad-winged birds built nests: owls, cormorants,
and chattering sea crows, who ply their tasks
among the waves. The grotto's entranceway
was ringed by robust vines with clustered grapes.
Pure water rose from four springs in a row,
but then, meandering, the four streams flowed
through gentle fields of violets and parsley.

Even a god who chanced to see that site 90
would feel the force of wonder and delight.
But when his mind had marveled at it all,
he went at once into the spacious cave.
Calypso, brightest goddess, seeing Hermes,
did not have any doubts: the deathless gods
can recognize each other, even when
their dwelling places lie so far apart.
Yet generous Odysseus was not there,
but where he always sat, along the shore,
sighing and weeping, grieving as he tore 100
his heart and watched the restless sea. Calypso
sat Hermes on a gleaming chair, then asked:

"Hermes, my honored guest—a welcome one—
what matter brings you here with your gold wand?
You've hardly been a frequent visitor.
Tell me the thoughts you want to share. If I
can answer your request, and my heart finds
it seemly, I shall help you willingly.
But first—a time for friendship, courtesy."

That said, the goddess showed him to a table 110
heaped with ambrosia, and she poured red nectar.
So Hermes ate and drank, and when his soul
had been refreshed with food, this was his answer:

"You ask—as goddess to a god—why I
am here, and you do not want me to lie.
Zeus ordered me to come, against my will:
who'd want to cross an endless stretch of brine?
Who'd want to find no mortals' town nearby
where men, to please a god, may sacrifice
choice hecatombs, roast thighs that so delight? 120
And yet there is no god that can elude
or slight the will of aegis-bearing Zeus.
He says there is a man with you, a man
most miserable, one of those who fought
nine years for Priam's citadel, then sacked
that stronghold in the tenth year and sailed back.
But since his men had sinned against Athena,
she sent harsh winds, harsh seas, as punishment.
Then all of his brave comrades died, but he,
impelled by wind and wave, has reached your realm. 130

Now Zeus would have you send him home at once:
his fate is not to die here, far from friends—
he is to see his dear ones, find again
his high-roofed house, return to his own land."

These were his words. The lovely goddess shuddered,
then answered Hermes with her own winged words:
"You gods are cruel and more jealous than
all others: if a goddess beds a man
and wants him—openly—as her dear husband,
then you begrudge her that. Your envy punished 140
rose-fingered Dawn when she embraced Oríon:
you gods, at ease, your least desire appeased,
sent down chaste Ártemis of the gold throne,
and she, in Delos, killed him with her shafts.
And when fair-haired Deméter dared to clasp
Iásion (they mingled, breast to breast,
upon a field where plows had worked three furrows),[52]
Zeus did not wait too long to find that out,
to kill him with a blazing thunderbolt.
So now, you gods resent my having chosen 150
a mortal. But when flashing lightning sent
by Zeus had smashed his ship and sunk his men,
and there, alone along the winedark sea,
he clutched the keel until the waves and wind
had cast him on my coast, I welcomed him:
it's I who fed him, I who took him in—
I hoped to give him immortality,
an endless life and yet without old age.
But since there is no god who can elude
or slight the will of aegis-bearing Zeus, 160
let this man meet his fate on restless seas.
But there's no way that I can help him leave:
I have no ships at hand, no oars, no crew
to carry him across the sea's broad back.
Yet I am fully ready to advise him,
keep nothing hidden from him, so that he
may make his way back to his own land—safely."

Stout Hermes said: "However this may be,
take care to send him off at once. Beware
of Zeus's wrath, lest in the future he 170
become your unforgiving enemy."

Then sturdy Hermes left. And having heard
the message sent by Zeus, the bright nymph went
to generous Odysseus. He was seated
along the shore; his eyes were never dry,
and his sweet life was squandered as he wept

[52]Perhaps symbolic of an agricultural ritual; Deméter is goddess of grain.

for his dear home; he now took no delight
in her: the nymph no longer pleased his sight.
By night, indeed, within Calypso's cave,
he slept with her: so side by side they lay, 180
the willing and unwilling. But by day,
his heart was rent by torment as he sat
along the sands or on the rocks; he watched
the never-resting sea and, watching, wept.
Standing beside him there, the fair nymph said:

"Unhappy man, don't stay—in tears—with me:
do not destroy your life. Most willingly
I set you free. Come now, with your bronze ax
chop down stout trunks and build a broad-beamed craft.
Let cross-planks serve as sides for those base beams, 190
to carry you across the fog-dark sea.
Within that hull I'll stow much bread and water
and red wine—you'll not suffer thirst or hunger—
and I shall clothe you and provide fair winds
to carry you unharmed to your own land,
if that is what wide heaven's gods demand—
I must give way before their powers and plans."

The patient, bright Odysseus, shuddering,
replied to what he'd heard with these winged words:
"Goddess, I know you've something else in mind— 200
something beyond my being free to leave—
in urging me to cross the dreadful deep,
the dismal, dour abyss, aboard a craft
so makeshift: even quick and agile ships,
blessed with the favoring wind of Zeus, would fail.
I shall not board these fragile planks unless
you, goddess, swear to set aside all thought
of harming me with new, pernicious plots."

He spoke. Calypso, lovely goddess, smiled.
Her hand caressed him. Her reply was this: 210
"You are indeed astute, not short on wits:
what cunning urged you on to this request?
I call as witnesses the spacious sky
and earth and waves of Styx[53] that flow below—
the most exacting, the most awesome oath
the blessed gods can swear—that I forgo
all thought of any future harm to you.
My thoughts, my plans for you, are only such
as I myself might seek were I to be
in your own place: within my breast I keep 220
no heart of iron—I feel for you, your needs."

[53] A river in Hades, the underworld.

That said, the lovely goddess led. He followed
her quick footsteps. Together, man and goddess,
they reached the hollow grotto. There he sat
on the same chair that Hermes had just left.
Calypso set before him food and drink
of every sort that suits a mortal's needs.
Then she sat opposite the bright Odysseus.
Her handmaids offered her ambrosia and nectar.
Their fare was ready now. Their hands reached out. 230
And when their thirst and hunger were appeased,
the lovely goddess was the first to speak:

"Are you, Odysseus, man of many wiles,
Laértës' godly son, still keen to leave
straightway? Is it your native land you need,
your dear home? Though you go, I wish you well.
But if your mind were to divine the trials
that fate will have you meet before you reach
your country, you would choose to stay, to keep
this house with me—and live immortally. 240
This you would do despite your longing for
your wife, for whom you yearn each day. And yet
I'm sure that I am not inferior
to her in form or stature: it's not right
for mortal women to contend or vie
with goddesses in loveliness or height."

Odysseus, man of many wiles, replied:
"Great goddess, don't be angered over this.
I'm well aware that you are right: I, too,
know that Penelope, however wise, 250
cannot compete with you in grace or stature:
she is not more than mortal, whereas you
are deathless, ageless. Even so, each day
I hope and hunger for my house: I long
to see the day of my returning home.
If once again, upon the winedark sea,
a god attacks, I shall survive that loss:
the heart within my chest is used to patience.
I've suffered much and labored much in many
ordeals among the waves and in the wars; 260
to those afflictions I can add one more."

These were his words. The sun sank. Darkness came.
And they, within the hollow of the cave,
taking delight in love, together lay.

Firstlight: when Dawn's rose fingers touched the sky,
Odysseus readied for his enterprise.
He put on cloak and tunic, while the nymph
put on a long and gleaming, gracious robe
woven of subtle threads, then bound a belt

of gold around her waist and veiled her head. 270
Now she began to plan for his departure.
She gave him a stout ax, the kind one grasps
with two hands: its bronze head had both blades honed;
its haft of olive-wood was tight and fast.
And then she handed him a polished adze.
She led him toward the island's rim—a stand
of tall trees: alder, poplar, and the high,
sky-seeking fir: well-seasoned timber, dry,
aged wood that would float lightly on the sea.
When she had shown him where those tall trees rose, 280
the fair Calypso turned back to her home.
He started cutting trunks. He worked with speed.
He chopped down all of twenty. With the bronze
axhead, he trimmed them; then, with skill, he smoothed
the timbers and aligned them, straight and sure.
Meanwhile the fairest goddess fetched the augers.
With these he bored each plank. With bolts and pins
he fitted piece to piece, and then he hammered
his hull together. As a carpenter
employs his skill—whenever he must build 290
freight ships—to trace a spacious hull, so did
the stout Odysseus give his boat due width.
He set deck beams in place and bolted them
with close-set ribs, then added long gunwales.
He hewed a mast and then attached a yard
and shaped a steering oar, to keep on course.
To fend the waves, he fenced his craft from stem
to stern with willow withes; along the deck
he strewed brushwood. Meanwhile the fairest nymph,
Calypso, brought him cloth from which to trim 300
a sail; and he was also skilled at that.
Sheets, braces, halyards—all were soon made fast.
On rollers, to the sea, he hauled his craft.
The fourth day now was come. His work was done.

The next day, fair Calypso let him go—
but only after she had bathed Odysseus
and seen that he had fresh and fragrant clothes.
On deck she placed a skin of deep-red wine
together with a giant skin of water
and then a haversack of food—with many 310
succulent provisions. As his guide,
she sent a clement, tutelary wind.
The good Odysseus gladly spread his sail:
seated, he steered—a man most versatile.
Sleep did not overtake his lids: he watched
the Pleiades, the Plowman,[54] slow to set,

[54]The constellation Boötes means "plowman."

and the Great Bear—known also as the Wain[55]—
which circles round one point and spies Oríon
and is the only set of stars that never
bathes in the Ocean's waves. The gracious goddess, 320
Calypso, had instructed him to keep
the Great Bear on his left along the deep.
Seventeen days he sailed across the sea;
on the eighteenth he saw that he'd drawn close
to shadowed peaks: he now was near the coast
of the Phaeácians' island; in the mist
that land took on the likeness of a shield.

But now Poseidon, lord of quakes and tremors,
returning from the Ethiopians,
could see—down from the Sólymi's steep peaks— 330
Odysseus sailing on the sea. Incensed,
he shook his head in this soliloquy:

"Skulduggery! While I was visiting
my Ethiopians, the gods gave way:
they turned; they mean to help the Ithacan.
And now he nears the land of the Phaeácians,
where he is fated to escape the trap
of trials that held him fast. This is my task:
to drive him back into his misery."

That said, he massed the clouds and, as he gripped 340
his trident, whipped the surge and urged all winds
to whirl at will. He hid the land, the sea.
Night scudded from the sky down to the deep.
Eurus and Notus and voracious Zephyr
and Bórëas, who's born in the bright ether,
attacked together; a prodigious breaker
rolled up along their path. The wanderer
felt weak; his knees and heart gone slack, he cried
in anguish to his unrelenting mind:

"Poor man, what end awaits me? I'm afraid 350
Calypso's words were true: she said I'd face
my worst ordeal before I ever reached
my homeland: on the sea I was to meet
disaster. Everything is now complete.
How many clouds Zeus gathers now to crowd
the vast sky to its limits! He provokes
the sea; the force of all winds crushes me.
The steep descent to death cannot be checked.
Three and four times more blessed were all the Greeks

[55] The Great Bear or Wain refers to the Big Dipper, which in northern latitudes never sets.

who died in the vast land of Troy to please 360
the sons of Átreus. Would that I had met
a death like theirs, had shared their destiny
upon the day when crowds of Trojans cast
bronze shafts at me, while battling round the body
of Péleus' slaughtered son. I would have gained
funeral rites; I would have earned much fame
from the Achæans. Now instead I find
myself a prey: I face a squalid death."

As he said this, a giant comber crashed
down on Odysseus with force so fierce 370
it whirled his craft around. He lost his grip:
the steering oar fell slack. Far from the deck
he plunged; rapacious gusts had rushed a vortex
that sheared the mast in half; into the sea
the sail yard and the sail fell—distantly;
that comber held him fast within the deep;
he could not surface quickly in the rage
of that great wave; his clothes—Calypso's gifts—
were hampering and heavy. But at last
he surfaced. It was bitter brine he spat— 380
the brine that streamed and splattered from his head.

Yet even then, half drowned, Odysseus
did not forget his battered craft: he thrust
across the waves until he gripped the planks.
He huddled in the center to escape
his fate, his death. A great wave took his craft
along its course, this way and that—just as,
across the plains in autumn, Bóréas
drives thistle-tufts that hold each other fast.
Now Notus cast the craft toward Bóréas, 390
who drove it on; and Eurus now again
gave it to Zephyr—he became its master.

But Ino, Cadmus' daughter, saw that scene—
she, nymph with lovely ankles, once had been
a mortal, one who spoke with human speech;
but, honored by the gods, she then became
Leucóthëa, a goddess of white waves.
She now took pity on the suffering
of wandering Odysseus. From the sea,
she rose up like a gull upon the wing 400
and sat down on his battered craft, saying:

"Poor man, why does such spite still drive Poseidon?
Why does he hate you with such bitter passion,
inflicting trial on trial? Yet surely he
can never ruin you, however deep
his need to see you grieve. But you do this—
you seem to be no fool: Strip off your clothes;

abandon to the winds your craft and try
to swim with your own arms and reach the land
of the Phaeácians: there you'll find escape 410
at last—such is your fate. Come, spread this shawl—
it is immortal—underneath your chest;
and have no fear of suffering or death.
But just as soon as you have touched that shore,
release the shawl; be sure to fling it far
into the winedark sea; then head for land."

That said, the goddess handed him a shawl
and then plunged back at once—much like a gull—
into the billow. That dark wave hid Ino.
But he was hesitant. The patient, bright 420
Odysseus, troubled, spoke to his own mind:

"Ah me! Let it not be that, once again,
someone immortal has devised a plan
to trap me, urging me to leave this craft.
But I shall set aside the nymph's advice;
my eyes have seen how far away it lies—
the land that, so she says, will set me free.
The better course is this: As long as these
planks are not loosened from their fastenings,
I shall stay here, and although suffering, 430
I shall resist. But if the combers wreck
my boat completely, I shall swim—for then
I cannot call on any other plan."

But while Odysseus' mind and spirit pondered,
Poseidon, lord of quakes and tremors, stirred
a giant surge, an awesome arch, a curve
the god drove hard against the wanderer;
as gusts grown fierce, impetuous, will toss
a heap of dry straw, scattering some here,
some there, so that wave tossed the boards about. 440
Odysseus gripped a floating plank; as if
to ride astride a horse, he straddled it;
then he stripped off his clothes—Calypso's gift—
and wrapped the shawl around his waist. Headlong,
he dived into the sea; his hands outstretched,
he swam like one possessed. Just then, Poseidon
saw him; he shook his head and, turning toward
his spirit, murmured this soliloquy:

"Then, after undergoing many griefs,
wander across this sea until you reach 450
the people Zeus has nurtured;[56] but I think

[56]The Phaeácians, a people loved by the gods.

that even then your present suffering
will not appear to you as some slight thing."

That said, he lashed his fair-maned horses, sped
to Ægae,[57] where he has his palaces.

But now Athena had her counterplan.
She curbed the course of all the other winds;
the goddess ordered them to cease, to rest,
except for Bóreäs—impetuous—
whom she incited now to clear the path 460
of waves that lay along Odysseus' way,
that he, escaping death and fate, might reach
the land of eager oarsmen, the Phaeácians.
Two nights, two days, delivered to the waves,
the Ithacan was driven; many times
his heart foresaw his death. But when the skies
revealed the third day born of fair-haired Dawn,
at last the wind fell still; the air was calm;
the wanderer caught sight of land nearby
as, lifted on the surge, he strained his eyes. 470
And like the joy of children when they see
new life within a father who lay ill,
bearing atrocious pain, wasting away
(invaded by a demon's curse), until
the gods had healed his horrid misery,
bringing rejoicing—such was the delight
Odysseus felt with land and trees in sight.

But when the wanderer had come in close
to shore, he heard the surge; against the shoals
it hammered hard; the wailing combers rolled 480
and thundered all along the dry land's coast.
Sea-spume enveloped every thing in sight.
There were no harbors where a ship might ride,
no havens and no coves, just jagged reefs
and jutting crags. Odysseus' knees went weak;
his heart was hesitant; he had to speak
these troubled words to his tenacious soul:

"When Zeus at last has let me see the land
that lay beyond my hopes, when I have cleared
a path across this deep abyss, nowhere 490
is there an exit place, the least escape
from this gray sea. Just jagged crags—that's all
that waits for me: the rocks are sheer; waves wail;
the water close to shore is deep; my feet
can find no footing; there is no way out.
Were I to seek the land, I might be caught,

[57] An island off the east coast of Greece.

be dashed against the rocks—have tried, but lost.
And were I to swim on and try to reach
some harbor of the sea, or sheltered beach,
I fear that once again the tempest might 500
drive me far off, across the fish-rich seas,
even as I moan deeply—or some god
may send some giant monster of the deep
against me (many such are known to be
nurtured and raised among the waves, the breed
of famous Amphitrítë[58]). I indeed
know how much hate Poseidon has for me."

But while Odysseus' mind and spirit pondered,
a comber hurled him toward the stony shore.
His skin would have been flayed, his bones been smashed, 510
had not Athena spurred his wits to act:
he rushed to seize a rock with both his hands
and, groaning, gripped it till the surge had passed.
So he escaped the wave; but its backwash
caught him; it pounded hard; it hurled him far
into the open sea. And even as
the suckers of an octopus that's dragged
out from its hole show pebbles clinging fast
and thick; so did that rock display the skin
stripped from his hands—from his tenacious grip. 520

And trapped within that backwash of the brine,
Odysseus would have died before his time
had not gray-eyed Athena counseled him.
Emerging from the surge that now rolled shoreward,
he swam, his eyes upon the land, to see
if he could find a sheltered bay or beach
that met the sea aslant. But when he reached
a river mouth, a friendly estuary,
he chose that as his landing: it was free
of reefs and offered shelter from the wind. 530
He knew that there must be a tutelary
river-god, and in his heart he prayed:

"Whoever you may be, o lord, hear me!
In my escape from pitiless Poseidon,
I've now reached you, whom many call upon.
Deserving mercy even in the eyes
of deathless gods is any man who comes—
even as I have come—a wanderer:
after long suffering, at last I reach
your current and your knees. I now beseech 540
your pity, lord; I am your suppliant."

[58] Sea nymph or goddess.

These were his words. The river-god straightway
restrained his current, curbed his waves, and gave
the gift of calm. He brought the wanderer safe
into the river mouth. The sea's attack
had overcome Odysseus; he collapsed;
his knees went weak; his sturdy hands fell slack.
All of his flesh was swollen; from his mouth
and nose, the bitter brine gushed down in spurts.
Deprived of breath and speech and strength, he lay— 550
the prey of an atrocious weariness.
When he'd found breath again and in his chest
his heart had found fresh force, Odysseus tossed
away the shawl the nymph had given him:
into the stream that mingled with the sea,
he threw it. When the river current reached
great waves, a billow brought it back to Ino;
the course was quick—straightway her hands received it.
Odysseus, as he clambered from the stream,
sank down among the reeds and kissed the earth, 560
giver of grain. And in his grief these were
the words he spoke to his tenacious soul:

"What misery is mine? What lies in wait?
If, through the sorry night, I stay awake
here on this riverside, I am afraid
that, breathless, weak, my spirit will fall prey
to bitter frost, chill dew; at break of day
a biting wind will strike. But if I try
to climb the slope and, where the undergrowth
is thick, lie down in the dark wood, I fear 570
that once fatigue and cold have disappeared
and I am gathered in by gentle sleep
I will become a prize for some wild beast."

But as he pondered, this plan seemed the best:
He headed for the woods and reached the trees
that flanked a clearing not far from the stream.
Between two bushes born in one same spot,
one bush of olives, one of thorns, he crept.
Those bushes grew so twined together that
no harsh, damp winds could penetrate their dense 580
branches, nor could the scorching sunrays strike,
and even downpours found it hard to pass.
It was beneath these branches that he crept;
and with his hands he gathered a broad bed
at once, for fallen leaves lay there in heaps,
enough to shelter two men—even three—
in wintertime, however cold it be.

The man of many trials was glad indeed
to see this shelter. In the middle, he
lay down. Over his body he heaped leaves. 590

Just as a man will hide a brand beneath
dark ashes on a lonely farm—to keep
the seed of flame alive and not have need
to trudge far off for fire to feed his hearth—
so did Odysseus wrap himself in leaves.
And on his eyes Athena poured sweet sleep:
she freed the man of trials from harsh fatigue.
The goddess closed the eyelids she held dear.

BOOK 9
[THE CYCLOPS]

[In Book 6, the princess Nausícaa and her maids are washing their clothes when they discover Odysseus. Admiring him, Nausícaa explains how he should enter the palace in order to gain assistance from Nausícaa's mother, Queen Arétë. In Book 7, Odysseus is led to the palace by Athena in disguise. He appeals to Queen Arétë for assistance on his journey. Odysseus explains to Queen Arétë and King Alcínoüs how he left Calypso's island and arrived on their island. During the contests in Book 8, a youth insults Odysseus, who then challenges the young heroes to a match. Alcínoüs steers the proceedings toward dancing and feasting. As the blind bard Demódocus sings about the wooden horse and the sacking of Troy, Odysseus weeps. He is then asked to tell his story. –ED.]

Odysseus, man of many wiles, replied:
"Alcínoüs, the king all men revere,
it surely is a pleasant thing to hear
a singer like Demódocus, a man
whose voice is like the gods'. I say we reach
the deepest of delights when, at a feast,
beside the tables heaped with bread and meat,
men, seated in due order, fill the hall
and listen to a harper: joy takes all,
and the cupbearer draws wine from the bowl 10
and brings it round and brims the cups: my soul
finds nothing on this earth more beautiful.

"But now your heart is set: you want to have
the tale of all my trials—and I must add
more tears to those I have already shed.
What should I tell you first? What should be last?
I've had so many griefs at heaven's hands.
Let me begin by telling you my name,
so that you, too, may know it; for I may—
when I've escaped from fate's most cruel day— 20
receive you, though my home is far away.

"I am Odysseus, Laértës' son.
Men know me for my many stratagems.
My fame has reached the heavens. And my home
is Ithaca, an island bright with sun.
My homeland has a steep peak, Nériton,

whose woods are rich with rustling leaves. Around
my island many other islands crowd:
Dulíchium and Samos and Zacýnthus,
so thick with woods. But Ithaca itself 30
lies low along the sea, and farther west
than any other island there; the rest
lie in a separate cluster, facing east.
My home is rough and rocky, but it breeds
robust young men. I know no thing more sweet,
more fair for any man than his own land.
Indeed, Calypso, fairest goddess, tried
to keep me in her cavern, at her side;
she wanted me as husband. So did Círcë,
Aeǽa's cunning woman: she, too, held me 40
within her halls—she wanted me to be
her mate. Both failed. They never could persuade
the soul within my breast; for if a man
is far from his own home and parents, then
even if he is housed in opulence
within that foreign land, no thing he finds
can be more sweet than what he left behind.

"Enough. My tale would tell you now instead
the trials that, when I sailed from Troy, beset
my journey homeward: sorrows that Zeus sent. 50

"The wind that carried me from Ílion
brought me to Ísmarus, the Cíconës.[59]
I sacked their city, massacred their men.
We took much treasure and we took their wives—
and shared it all, that none might be deprived
of what was his by right. I urged us then
to hurry back to shore, just as I'd planned.
But no one cared to follow my command:
stupid, they took their time; they guzzled wine
and butchered many sheep along the shore, 60
and shambling oxen with their curving horns.
Meanwhile the Cíconës who had escaped
called on their fellows, those who lived inland,
neighbors more numerous and strong, adept
at fighting from their chariots or else
on foot, if any skirmish called for that.
They came—as thick as leaves and flowers in spring—
at sunrise. And we faced the punishment
that Zeus had sent: the fate of luckless men.
Arrayed in battle order, they attacked 70
alongside our swift ships; with bronze-tipped shafts,
both we and they struck hard. All morning long,

[59] Allies of Troy, the Cíconës lived on the northern coast of the Aegean Sea.

while sacred day was still in its ascent,
we stood our ground although we were outmanned.
But once the sun had reached the hour when oxen
must be unyoked, the Cíconës broke through
and we Achæans fled. In each ship's crew,
six of my well-greaved comrades died. The rest
of us escaped that fate, that bitter death.

"Heartsick, we sailed away: we were content 80
to be alive, but we had lost dear friends;
nor did I let our lithe ships sail ahead
until we'd called three times on each of those
unfortunates the Cíconës had killed
upon the battlefield. But Bóreäs—
provoked by Zeus, who summons clouds—now swept
against us: a ferocious tempest wrapped
both land and sea; night scudded down from heaven.
Wind struck our ships aslant; the sails were ripped
and tattered—three and then four strips. In fear 90
of death, we stowed our sails within the hold,
then rowed and reached the coast. There we remained
two days, two nights—fatigued and tried, afraid.
But when, with fair-haired Dawn, the third day came,
we stepped our masts and set white sails, then sat:
the wind and helmsmen kept us on our path.
I would have reached my Ithaca intact,
if, as I rounded Cape Maléa, combers
and currents had not joined with Bóreäs
and driven me off course, beyond Cythéra.[60] 100

"For nine days I was thrust by savage winds
across the fish-rich sea. And on the tenth
we reached the Lotus-Eaters' land,[61] those men
who feed upon a flower. We went ashore,
drew water, and straightway my crewmen ate
their meal beside our ships. But once that need
for food and drink was set to rest, I sent
two crewmen and a third, who served as herald,
to see what sort of mortals held this land.
Those three were quick to find the Lotus-Eaters, 110
who did not think of slaughtering my men:
in fact, they shared their lotus food with them.
Those three who feasted on the honey-sweet,
enticing lotus fruit had not the least
desire to bring back word or soon return
at all: they wanted only to stay there,
to feed upon that food and disremember

[60] Maléa is at the southernmost tip of Greece; Cythéra is an island further south.

[61] Usually identified with North Africa; a wide range of interpretations has been used to explain the attraction of the lotus, from a mild narcotic to an aphrodisiac.

their homeward path. I had to force them back,
in tears, to their own ships; there, they were dragged
beneath the rowing benches and bound fast. 120
And I had all my other firm companions
embark with speed upon our rapid ships,
that no one—tasting lotus—might forget
his homeward way. They came on board at once;
each took his proper place along the thwarts;
and then they struck the gray sea with their oars.

"From there we sailed away with troubled hearts.
At last our ships approached the Cyclops' coast.[62]
That race is arrogant: they have no laws;
and trusting in the never-dying gods, 130
their hands plant nothing and they ply no plows.
The Cyclops do not need to sow their seeds;
for them all things, untouched, spring up: from wheat
to barley and to vines that yield fine wine.
The rain Zeus sends attends to all their crops.
Nor do they meet in council, those Cyclops,
nor hand down laws; they live on mountaintops,
in deep caves; each one rules his wife and children,
and every family ignores its neighbors.

"Outside the harbor, off the Cyclops' coast, 140
an island lies—not far, yet not too close.
And on that flat and wooded isle, wild goats
form countless herds; for here no men disturb,
no one will scare them off. Elsewhere, across
hilltops and woods, the hunters toil; but here
they do not come. Nor are there sheep or cows;
and that land always stays unsown, unplowed—
it knows no men, just flocks of bleating goats.
The Cyclops have no ships with crimson bows,
no shipwrights who might fashion sturdy hulls 150
that answer to the call, that sail across
to other peoples' towns that men might want
to visit. And such artisans might well
have built a proper place for men to settle.
In fact, the land's not poor; it could yield fruit
in season; soft, well-watered meadows lie
along the gray sea's shores; unfailing vines
could flourish; it has level land for plowing,
and every season would provide fat harvests
because the undersoil is black indeed. 160
The harbor has safe landings: there's no need
for mooring-tackle or for anchoring
or tying cables hard and fast to shore;
once he has beached, a sailor stays until

[62] Ancient tradition located the Cyclops in Sicily.

his heart decides it's time to go, to follow
fair winds offshore. At harbor head there flows
clear water from a spring within a grotto;
around it poplars grow. Through foggy night,
some god—though he himself stayed out of sight—
had been our guide: we sailed into that harbor. 170
There was no light; the ships were wrapped in mist;
cloud banks closed off the moon; the sky was black.
We did not see that isle, nor even see
the long waves rolling shoreward, till we beached
our sturdy ships. We lowered all the sails,
and then we disembarked along the sands.
We waited for bright Dawn: sleep held us fast.

"As soon as Dawn's rose fingers touched the sky,
astonished, we explored the island. Nymphs,
daughters of aegis-bearing Zeus, stirred up 180
the mountain goats so that my men might hunt
and make a meal. We hurried to our ships
to fetch curved bows and lances with long tips.
We formed three bands, and each group cast its shafts;
the god soon gave us all that we could ask.

"I had twelve ships; and each crew caught nine goats;
a tenth was given to my crew alone.
So, through that day we sat until sunset;
we had much meat; our wine was honey-sweet,
red wine my men had taken when we sacked 190
the sacred high-point of the Cíconës—
the jars we'd stowed away were not yet empty.
Our eyes turned toward the Cyclops' nearby coast:
toward smoke, the sounds of men—and sheep and goats.
But when the sun had gone and darkness won,
we stretched out on the shore. But at firstlight,
when Dawn's rose fingers touched the sky, I called
my men together and informed them all:

" 'My faithful comrades, wait for me: I'll take
my ship and crew to see who these may be— 200
are they unfeeling people, wild, unjust,
or do they welcome strangers, does their thought
include fear of the gods?'

"When that was said,
I boarded first; and then I told my comrades
to board and loose the hawsers at the stern.
And they were quick to board. They manned the thwarts,
and then they struck the gray sea with their oars.
When we had reached the nearby shore, we saw—
along the sea—a high cave roofed with laurels:
there many flocks, both sheep and goats, would sleep 210
by night; the wall that ringed that cave was steep,

a ring of rocks, set deep into the ground,
with tall pine trunks and oaks with towering boughs.
A massive man slept there; alone, far-off,
he shepherded his flocks. One set apart
from other men, he had a lawless heart.
That monster was unlike a man who feeds
on bread: in size, he seemed a wooded peak,
a summit that, apart from all the rest,
is seen alone, a solitary crest. 220

"I told my other faithful men to stay,
to keep watch on our ship, as I went off
with twelve of my best men. With me I brought
a goatskin, full of honey-sweet dark wine,
a gift that had been given me by Maron,
Evánthës' son, the priest who served Apollo,
the tutelary god of Ísmarus.
For when we sacked that site, our reverence
spared Maron and his wife and son: his home
was in Apollo's shadowed sacred grove. 230
And he rewarded me with splendid gifts:
he gave me seven talents of wrought gold,
a mixing bowl, all silver, and a wine
that he poured into jars—twelve jars in all—
wine honey-sweet, unmixed, fit for the gods.
No servant—man or woman—shared this secret:
just Maron and his wife and one housekeeper
knew of this wine. And when they drank that red,
sweet, honeyed brew, he'd pour no more than one
cup into twenty measures of pure water; 240
and from the mixing bowl a fragrance rose
so sweet and so enticing that in truth
no one would stand aside from such a brew.
I filled, then brought, one great skin of this wine,
and food within a basket; my proud soul
foresaw that I was soon to meet a man
most wild and powerful—and ignorant
of righteous thoughts and reverence for laws.
We quickly reached the cavern; he had gone
to pasture his plump flocks. And when we turned 250
into the cave, the sight left us amazed;
the crates were stuffed with cheeses, and the pens
with sheep and goats: these were in separate folds—
the firstlings, then the yearlings, then the just-born.
And all the well-wrought bowls and pails that served
for milking swam with whey. My comrades urged
our quick departure—though they wanted me
to take the cheeses, above all, and then
drive from the fold those sheep and goats and stow
those stores on our swift ship. That done—they said— 260
we should be off, to sail across the sea.
But I ignored their counsel, though that course

would have avoided many griefs for us.
Instead I had to wait to see that man,
to find out if he'd welcome me. But then
the courtesy he showed my friends was scant.

"We lit a fire, then burned a sacrifice,
and, taking cheeses, fed ourselves: we sat
and waited in the cave. Then he came back
with all his flocks. He bore a massive pack 270
of dry wood he would use at suppertime.
That pack—he threw it to the ground—crashed loud.
Afraid, we scrambled, huddling in the back.
Then he spurred on the plump herds that he milked
into the massive cave; he left the males,
the rams and he-goats, in the outer pens.
He lifted high a rock, then set it down
in place: that heavy doorstone closed his cave.
And two-and-twenty sturdy four-wheeled carts
could not have budged that boulder from the ground— 280
the towering mass that barred the entranceway.
He sat and milked his ewes and bleating goats
in turn; beneath each dam he placed her young.
At once he curdled half of the white milk,
then set the gathered curd in plaited bins.
The other half he set aside in bowls,
to have it ready to be drunk for supper.
Now that his tasks were quickly done, he lit
the fire, noticed us at last, and said:

" 'Who are you, strangers? And what was the land 290
you left when you sailed out on water paths?
Are you just traders? Or a prowling crew
that preys at random, pirates on the loose,
who risk their lives, but plunder others' goods?'

"His voice was thunder, and his form a monster's.
We shuddered. Yet I found the words to answer:
'We are Achǽans homeward bound from Troy.
Across the sea's great gulf we have been thrust
off course. Winds battered us. On our way home,
strange paths and places are what we have known; 300
but it is surely Zeus who willed it so.
We're proud to be the men of Agamemnon;
beneath the heavens, he, a son of Átreus,
is now most famous: he has sacked so great
a city, slain so many men indeed.
We hope you'll welcome us; we hope to get
some gift, as custom bids host give to guest.[63]

[63]The laws of hospitality, protected by Zeus, included gifts.

May you, o mighty one, revere the gods:
we're at your mercy now. The god of guests
is Zeus; for he protects the suppliant— 310
he watches over honored visitors.'

"That said, his ruthless heart replied at once:
'You are a fool—or just a foreigner
from very far—if you would have me fear
the gods or warn me to beware. The Cyclops
do not pay heed to aegis-bearing Zeus
or other blessed gods, weaker than us.
Be sure, I'd never spare your friends or you
in order to avoid the wrath of Zeus:
my soul alone will bid me what to do. 320
But tell me where you moored your sturdy ship
when you came here. Is it far off? Or near?
That's something I should like to have made clear.'

"He meant to snare me. But my craft matched his.
My strategy was still evasiveness:
'Poseidon, the earth-shaker, smashed my ship;
he cast her on the rocks that line your shores,
against a promontory—for the winds
had driven her toward land. But I and these,
my men, escaped the steep descent to death.' 330

"These were my words, but no words answered mine:
his heart was pitiless. And springing up,
he stretched his hands and snatched two of my men
at once and smashed them to the ground like pups:
their brains gushed out and wet the earth. He cut
those comrades limb from limb, and then he supped—
and like a mountain lion, left no shred:
he ate the flesh and innards, chewed the bones
down to the marrow. Lifting hands to Zeus,
we wept at this obscenity—helpless. 340
But when his maw was stuffed with human flesh,
as well as pure milk he then gulped, the Cyclops
stretched out within the cave, among his flocks.
My firm will planned a close approach, that I
might draw out the sharp sword that flanked my thigh
and strike his chest and midriff, holding fast
his liver—with my hand I'd grope for that.
But then I stopped, held back by second thoughts.
His death, in fact, would doom us all: our hands
would never have been able to shove back 350
the massive stone he'd set in the high entrance.
So, as we sighed, we waited for bright Dawn.

"As soon as Dawn's rose fingers touched the sky,
again he lit the fire and milked his flocks
in turn; beneath each dam, he placed her young.

That work was quickly done. Then he snatched up
two more of mine and dined on them. And when
his meal was done, he drove out his plump flocks:
to leave the cave, he thrust aside the rock.
But then, with ease, he slipped it back in place, 360
as one might close a quiver with its top.
Next, whistling loud, the Cyclops turned those flocks
up toward the mountains. I was left to plot,
devising ways to foil him; for my heart
wanted to punish him—for this I'd win
much glory from Athena. As I thought,
this plan seemed best. Beside a pen there stood
a cutoff trunk of still-green olive-wood:
once seasoned, that would be the Cyclops' staff.
And it was huge enough to serve as mast 370
for a black ship of twenty oars—a ship
that carries freight across the deep abyss;
it was that long and thick. Approaching it,
I cut off two arm's-lengths of wood and asked
my men to pare it down. They planed it smooth.
Then I, standing nearby, sharpened its point
and hardened it at once in the fierce fire.
And for that stake I found a hiding place
beneath the dung—for great heaps filled that cave.
I asked my comrades to cast lots to see 380
which men would dare to lift that stake with me
and grind it into the great Cyclops' eye
when sweet sleep overtook him. And the lots
chose those I would have chosen: they were four;
I was the fifth. When night fell, he returned—
his woolly flocks behind him. Straight away
he drove all his plump beasts into the cave:
not one was left within the outdoor pens.
All this, because he felt some slight suspicion—
or else some god inclined to favor us. 390
He lifted up and set in place the great
doorstone. And then he sat and milked his ewes
and bleating goats in turn; beneath each dam
he set her young. His work was quickly done.
Again he snatched two men and supped on them.
Then I, a bowl of our dark wine in hand,
drew near the Cyclops. And I spoke to him:

" 'Cyclops, after your feast of human flesh,
do take and drain this bowl, that you may know
what kind of wine our ship had stowed. For I 400
was bringing this to you as a libation,
hoping that, moved by mercy, you might help
to send me home. But you are furious—
intolerably mad. And after this,
who'd visit anyone so pitiless?
Why take the way that has no law, no justice?'

"These were my words. He took the bowl. He drained it.
The drink delighted him. He asked for more:
'Come now, good fellow, fill it up again.
And do tell me straightway what your name is: 410
I'll give you, as my guest, a pleasing gift.
Surely the earth, giver of grain, provides
the Cyclops with fine wine, and rain from Zeus
does swell our clustered vines. But this is better—
a wine as fragrant as ambrosia and nectar.'

"These were his words. Again I poured dark wine.
Three times I offered it and—stupidly—
three times he drank it down. But when it wound
its way around his wits, I said most gently:

" 'Cyclops, you ask me for my noted name; 420
I'll tell it to you if in recompense
you keep your promise and I get that present.
My name is No-one; No-one—so I'm called
by both my mother and my father, and all
my comrades.'

"This I said. And he replied:
'No-one, your friends come first; I'll eat you last.
This is the gift I give to you, my guest.'

"That said, the Cyclops reeled, his hulk collapsed;
he fell upon his back, with his thick neck
aslant; sleep, lord of all, now held him fast. 430
Up from his gullet, bits of human flesh
and wine were gushing: in his drunken sleep,
he'd vomited. Now it was time to thrust
the stake into heaped cinders: it grew hot.
I spurred on all my men with words of hope,
that none might flinch with fear. And when that stake
of olive-wood, though green, was glowing, just
about to blaze, I drew it from the flames.
My men stood round me; into us a god
breathed daring. And they clasped that pointed stake, 440
then drove the olive-wood into his eye.
I, reaching high, my weight thrown from above,
now whirled that stake around, as one whose bore
drills deep into the timber of a ship,
while those below him twirl it with a thong
they grasp at either end; the drill whirls round
and never rests. So did we twirl that hot
point in his eye; around the glowing wood,
blood flowed. And both his eyelids and his brow
were singed by fire as his eyeball burned; 450
his eye-roots hissed. Even as, when a smith
plunges an ax or adze into cold water,
the metal hisses as he quenches it

to give that iron strength, so did that eye
hiss round the olive stake's sharp tip. His howl
was terrifying; all the rocks rang out.
Fear drove us back. The stake, which he tugged out,
was fouled with blood. And—crazed—he threw it far;
and then he shouted to the other Cyclops,
who lived in nearby caves on windswept hilltops. 460
They heard his call and, coming from all sides,
stood near his cave and asked what was awry:

" 'What struck you, Polyphémus? Why do you
disturb the godlike night and spoil our sleep?
What mortal can, against your will, drive off
your flocks or try with treachery or force
to kill you?'

"Polyphémus, from the cave,
replied: 'My friends, no force can damage me;
No-one, No-one is using treachery.'

"They answered: 'If no one is harming you, 470
and you are all alone, it surely is
some sickness sent by Zeus; you can't elude
that kind of malady. Pray to Poseidon,
your father: he's the one to call upon.'

"That said, they left. And my heart laughed: my name,
a perfect snare, had trapped him. Racked by pain,
the Cyclops moaned and groped for that great stone,
then shoved it from the entranceway and sat
with hands outstretched in hope that he might catch
the men who, with the sheep, came from the cave— 480
he must have thought my wits were dim and slack.
But I was seeking a decisive plan,
a scheme to save both me and all my men:
I wove a web of every guile and wile,
as one will do when life's at stake—so great
a menace threatened us. This plot seemed best.
That cave held well-fed rams; and heavy fleece,
dark wool, enfolded those fine, robust beasts.
Now silently I took the twisted withes
of willow, those on which the Cyclops—he 490
whose heart was set on evil—liked to sleep.
With these I bound the sheep together, three
by three. I tied one comrade fast beneath
the belly of each middle sheep, while two
sheep—one to each side—served to guard my friend.
Three sheep for each of them, but I instead
picked out the largest ram. I grabbed his back
and curled beneath his belly. There I grasped
his splendid fleece; faceup, I held it tight.
So, anxiously we waited for firstlight. 500

"As soon as Dawn's rose fingers touched the sky,
he drove the he-goats and the rams outside
to pasture. In the fold, the unmilked dams,
their udders bursting, bleated. Although racked
by pain, their master now felt out the backs
of all the beasts that stood before him, but
that fool did not suspect that all my men
were hid beneath the bellies of the rams.
The last to leave the cave was my great ram,
bearing the weight of his own fleece and me— 510
with my thick plots. Huge Polyphémus probed
and felt about his back. And then he asked:

" 'Dear ram, why are you last to leave this cave?
You never lagged behind the other sheep;
you always were the very first to leave,
always the first to hurry out to feed,
to pasture on the tender grass, to leap
with long strides toward the riverside, to seek
the fold with longing when the sun had set.
But now you are the last to go. I'm sure 520
that you are grieving for your master's eye;
a coward and his crew first dimmed my mind
with their damned wine. That done, they left me blind.
I don't think death has caught that No-one yet.
Would you could think and speak and tell me where
he's hiding from my fury! I would dash
his brains across this cave: to smash him so
would free me from this No-one pest, these woes.'

"That said, he sent the ram out. When we'd gone
a brief way past the cave and outer pens, 530
I left the belly of the ram to set
my comrades free. That done, we quickly drove
the fat sheep with long shanks until we reached
our ship; and we turned round again, again,
to see if he was after us. And though
our comrades welcomed our escape from death,
they wept for those of us who now were lost.
But I restrained their tears; my frown forbade
such open grief. For now we had to speed—
to board the many sheep with their rich fleece, 540
then sail the salty sea. They rushed aboard;
each rower manned his place along the thwarts,
and then they struck the gray sea with their oars.
But when we'd gone as far as shouting distance,
I bellowed these sharp words to Polyphémus:

" 'Cyclops, the men you snatched with brutal force
and ate within your cave were surely not
the comrades of a coward. You have caused
much grief; and it returns to haunt you now:
you did not hesitate; hard heart, you ate 550

your guests within your house; therefore lord Zeus
has joined with other gods to batter you.'

"My words incensed him more. He ripped the top
of a huge peak, then hurled a chunk at us;
that mass fell just beyond our ship's dark prow.
The sea surged as the mass dropped; and the wash
thrust our ship backward, closer to the coast.
But grabbing a long pole, I pushed us off
and signaled with my head: I spurred my men
to fall hard on the oars, to fend against 560
shipwreck; and they rowed hard—they strained, they bent.
When we were twice as distant as we'd been,
I shouted to the Cyclops, though my men
on all sides curbed me with these cautious words:

" 'Why must you goad that savage so? Just now,
the mass that monster cast into the sea
drove back our ship to shore: we thought we'd reached
our end. And if he'd heard us breathe or speak
even the slightest word, he would have hurled
one more rough rock and smashed our heads and hull. 570
That brute has force to spare: he can throw far.'

"These were their words. But my firm heart was not
convinced. Again my anger had to taunt:
'Cyclops, if any mortal man should ask
about the shameful blinding of your eye,
then tell him that the man who gouged you was
Odysseus, ravager of cities: one
who lives in Ithaca—Laértës' son.'

"I spoke. As he replied, he groaned and sighed:
'I hear again an ancient prophecy. 580
An augur[64] once lived here, a man most worthy,
excelling all in seeing what would come,
a seer grown old among us: Télemus,
great son of Eurymus. What he foretold
is now fulfilled. He said that I would be
a victim of Odysseus: he would blind me.
But I was always watching out for one
handsome and grand, a formidable man;
instead, one small and insignificant,
a weakling, now has gouged my eye—he won 590
his way by overcoming me with wine.
But come, Odysseus, you'll receive the gift
I owe to you, my guest; and I'll convince
the great earth-shaker to escort your ship;
I am his son—he says he is my father.

[64] A soothsayer or prophet.

He is the one to heal me, if he would:
no other can—no blessed god, no man.'

"These were his words. And I replied: 'Would I
might just as surely rob you of your life
and breath and hurl you down to Hades'[65] house, 600
as I am sure that even great Poseidon
will never give you back the eye you lost.'

"These were my words. He prayed to lord Poseidon,
lifting his hands up to the starry heaven:
'Listen, Poseidon, dark-haired lord who clasps
the earth hard fast, if I'm indeed your son
and you declare yourself my father, then
don't let this ravager of towns, Odysseus,
Laértës' son, who lives in Ithaca,
return to his own land. But if his fate 610
must have him see his dear ones once again
and reach his sturdy home, his native land,
then let him struggle back—a battered man,
with all his comrades lost, and on a ship
of strangers. In his house, let him meet grief.'

"His prayer was done. The dark-haired god took heed.
Again the Cyclops lifted up a stone,
even more staggering than the one he'd thrown
before. He whirled it round; and when he hurled,
fierce force was in that toss. The stone fell just 620
behind our dark-prowed ship: it barely missed
the steering oar. And as that rough rock fell,
the sea surged high astern—but that wave helped:
its thrust drove our ship toward the island's shore.

"There, on that isle, our other sturdy ships
awaited us; our sighing shipmates sat,
in fear. We beached our boat along the sands,
then disembarked. Out of the hollow hull
we took the Cyclops' flocks, dividing all
in equal shares: what each received was just. 630
One sheep alone—my ram—was set apart;
my well-greaved crew assigned that gift to me.
Along the sands I sacrificed that ram
to Cronos' son, who gathers thunderclouds,
Zeus, lord of all; for him I roasted thighs.
But he did not accept that sacrifice:
instead his mind was set—he meant to wreck
all of my sturdy ships and faithful friends.

"All through that day we sat, until sunset:
we had much meat; our wine was honey-sweet. 640

[65]Son of Cronos, Hades was ruler of the underworld, which itself was named Hades.

But once the sun had gone and darkness won,
we stretched out on the shore. Then, at firstlight,
when Dawn's rose fingers touched the sky, I called
upon my shipmates to embark, to loose
the hawsers at the stern. They rushed aboard;
each rower manned his place along the thwarts,
and then they struck the gray sea with their oars.

"Heartsick, we sailed away: we were content
to be alive, but we had lost dear friends."

BOOK 10
[CÍRCË]

"Aeólia, the home of Ǽolus,[66]
the son of Híppotas, was our landfall.
He, cherished by the deathless ones, held all
that isle, which—floating on a sheer rock base—
is ringed by walls of bronze, unbreakable.
He has a dozen children in his halls:
six daughters and six sturdy sons—and each
is wed, for every brother has received
a sister as his wife. They always feast
together in the house of their fine father 10
and stately mother: there the food is endless.
By day the smoke of fragrant fat pours out
into the courtyard; and by night each son
sleeps richly swaddled with his trusted wife
upon a corded couch. We reached that isle:
we saw that city, saw the handsome halls.
For one full month we were his guests; he asked
to hear so much—of Troy, the Argive ships,
and the return of the Achǽans; I
withheld no thing; my telling was complete. 20
And when, in turn, I asked to leave and spoke
of help that we might need to see us home,
he did not stint; he offered me a sack
of hide he'd flayed from a nine-year-old ox.
Into that sack he stuffed the howling winds
of every sort or course: for Ǽolus—
so Zeus had said—was warden of the winds,
to spur or curb just as he willed. He stowed
that sack within my hollow ship and tied
its neck hard fast with shining silver cord, 30
lest any breeze, however slight, slip out.
He left just one wind—Zephyr—free, to speed

[66] God of the winds, he inhabited a floating island off Sicily.

my fleet, my men. And yet his careful plan
failed, for our folly had the upper hand.

"Nine days we sailed, by night and day alike,
and on the tenth our homeland came in sight,
so near that we could see men tending fires.
But sweet sleep overtook me—I was tired:
I'd held the steering oar without a let;
I'd not entrusted it to any comrade; 40
I wanted our return home to be quick.
Meanwhile my crewmen had begun to speak,
telling each other that I'd had as gifts
from Æolus, fine son of Híppotas,
silver and gold that I was bringing home.
So, turning to his shipmate, someone spoke:

" 'Just see what love, what honor he commands
from any man he meets in any land
or town! Just see what booty, splendid spoils,
he carries back from Troy, while we, who toiled 50
beside him, must return with empty hands.
To this, he now can add the friendly gift
of Æolus. Let's see what's in that sack—
see how much gold and silver he has packed.'

"That's what they urged—and their disastrous plan
prevailed. They opened up the sack. The band
of winds leaped out. The hurricane was quick
to whirl my men away from their own land:
thrust back to sea, they wept. When I awoke,
my staunch soul hesitated: should I leap 60
off from the deck and die, or should I keep
silent and stay among the living? But
I did not yield: I stayed, covered my face
and lay along the deck. The fierce gale swept
our ships back to Aeólia. My men wept.
We went ashore, drew water, and straightway
my crewmen ate their meal beside our ships.
But when we'd had our fill of food and drink,
together with two comrades I had picked—
one spearman, and another who could serve 70
as herald—I went back to Æolus.
I found him feasting with his wife and children.
We entered, sitting down along the sill,
close to the posts that flanked the door. They all,
astonished, asked:

" 'Odysseus, why have you
come back? Are you in some dark demon's grip?
We took such care in giving you a gift
to bring you to your homeland and your house
or any other place that you hold dear.'

"These were their words. Dejected, I replied: 80
'My coward comrades did me in—and, too,
that traitor, sleep. But help me, friends: you can.'

"So did I speak—my words beguiling, sweet.
They stared in silence—till their father said:
'Be quick to leave this isle. No living thing
can match your villainy. It's surely wrong
to welcome or to escort anyone
the blessed gods abhor. Now quit our shores:
you came as one who carries heaven's scorn.'

"That said, despite my tears, he drove me out. 90
From there we sailed away with bitter hearts.
Our folly, which had lost us the support
and favor of the winds, made rowing hard;
it sapped our force. And yet, without a stop,
for six days and six nights we kept on course.

"Then, on the seventh day, we saw the fort
that crowns the high point of Telépylus,
the city of the Laestrygónians,
founded by Lamus.[67] In that land, the shepherd
returning in the evening with his flock 100
can greet the herdsman who is going out.
A sleepless man could earn a double wage:
one wage for herding cattle, one for sheep
he led to grazing land: there, two times meet;
the paths of light traverse both day and night.

"We'd reached the famous harbor. On two sides,
we saw the steep rock walls with their sheer rise;
the narrow entranceway was flanked by two
long juts of land. Within that curving cove,
my comrades moored their shapely ships close by 110
each other: there no wave is ever vexed,
not surging or receding—a bright calm.

"But I held back and moored outside. I tied
my cable to a rock; my black ship stood
beyond one headland's edge. And then I climbed
a rugged slope; I stood at that lookout;
I saw no oxen's furrows and no men—
just puffs of smoke that rose up from the land.
I chose two comrades and a third as herald,
and then I sent those shipmates out to see 120
what sort of men—bread eaters—held this land.
They disembarked and took a well-tried way
that wagons used for bringing wood to town

[67]King of the Laestrygónians; their location is uncertain. The next lines seem to refer to the long summer days of northern latitudes.

down from the mountains. Just outside the town,
they met a stalwart girl beside a spring:
she was the daughter of Antíphatës
the Laestrygónian. The spring where she
was drawing limpid water was Artácia—
a well that served the Laestrygónians.
My men drew near; they asked what king ruled here 130
and who were those he ruled. She pointed out
her father's high-roofed house. When they went in,
they found his wife; but she stood mountain-high,
and they were horrified. At once she called
for firm Antíphatës; she brought him back
from the assembly place. But all he planned
was sad death for my men. He did not wait:
he grabbed one of my crew and swallowed him;
the other two were able to escape—
they reached our ships. But now it was too late: 140
the loud alarm had sounded; from all sides
stout Laestrygónians, a countless crowd,
rushed out—and they were not like men but Giants.
The boulders that they hurled down from the cliffs
were huge—the size a man could scarcely lift.
The clamor from the ships was sinister,
the sound of dying men and shattered decks;
they speared my comrades, carried them like fish—
an obscene meal.

"While they were slaughtering
my crews in the deep harbor, I drew out 150
the sharp blade from beside my thigh: I cut
the cables of my dark-prowed ship. I spurred
my men to hurry to their oars: their heart
and haste were needed to escape this trap;
the fear of death pressed all to row as one.
With luck I reached the open sea, far from
the sheer cliffs. But the other ships were lost.

"We sailed away—hearts sick and sad—set free
at last, but with our dear companions dead.
We reached Aeæa, isle of fair-haired Círcë, 160
the awesome goddess with a human voice,
twin sister of the sinister Aeétës:
they both were born of Hélios—who brought
his light to men—and Pérsë, Ocean's daughter.
In silence we put in to shore; the harbor
seemed safe; some gracious god had been our guide.
We stayed two days, two nights—fatigued and tried.

"But when, with fair-haired Dawn, the third day came,
with spear and sharpened sword in hand I climbed
up from the ship. I reached a rise from which 170
I hoped to see the signs of human work

and hear the sounds of men. And as I stood
upon that lookout point, up from wide fields
and through the forest and the underbrush,
smoke rose: it came from Círcë's house. The sight
of that black smoke inclined my heart and mind
to seek the source. But as I thought again,
another plan seemed best: I'd first go back
to my swift ship along the shore, find food
to feed my men, and then have them explore. 180

"But when I had already neared my ship,
some god took pity on my loneliness:
across my path he sent a tall-horned stag.
Down from his pasture in the forest, he—
responding to the sun's oppressive fury—
was heading to the riverbank to drink.
When he had quit the stream, I struck his back;
and right through his mid-spine, my bronze shaft passed.
He moaned; he fell into the dust; his life
took flight. I straddled him and tugged the shaft 190
out from the wound, then left it on the ground
and gathered lengths of brush and willow withes
to weave a rope two arm's-lengths long, twisted
from end to end. I tied that huge beast's feet
and slung him round my neck, then, trudging, leaned
my weight upon the spear that I'd retrieved.
That way I brought him back to the black ship:
one hand across one shoulder never could
have carried him—that stag was so immense.
I threw him down in front of our lithe ship 200
and gently urged my comrades, one by one:

" 'O friends, however sad, let's not descend
to Hades' halls before our destined day.
No, just as long as there is food and drink
in our swift ship, forget your fears of starving.'

"These were my words. My men did not delay.
They'd hid their heads with cloaks in their despair,
but now they threw those wrappings off and stared:
they saw the stag along the shore: indeed
that beast was huge. And with their eyes appeased, 210
they washed their hands and readied the fine feast.
All through that day we sat, until sunset:
we had much meat; the wine was honey-sweet.
But when the sun sank and the dark arrived,
we all stretched out and slept on the seaside.

"As soon as Dawn's rose fingers touched the sky,
I called my crew together, and I said:
'Despite your long ordeal, do hear me out:
my friends, we've lost all sense of where we are;
this island may lie east, it may lie west— 220

where sun, which brings men light, sinks to its rest
or where it's born again. Let's try at once
to see if we can find some better course.
I doubt it, for I climbed a rugged lookout:
we're on an island that is ringed about
by endless seas; so crowned, the isle lies low,
and at its center I saw curling smoke
that rose up through the forest and thick brush.'

"My words were done. And their dear hearts were torn,
recalling the fierce Laestrygónian, 230
Antíphatës, and the man-eating Cyclops.
Their groans were loud, their tears were many—yet
nothing was gained by weeping. So I split
my well-greaved men into two squads: each band
had its own chief. I headed one; the second
was led by the godlike Eurýlochus.
Within a casque of bronze we mixed our lots
to see who would go off and spy the land.
The choice fell on the firm Eurýlochus.
And he went off with two-and-twenty men; 240
both they who left and we who stayed then wept.

"Within a forest glen, they found the home
of Círcë: it was built of polished stone
and lay within a clearing. Round it roamed
the mountain wolves and lions she'd bewitched
with evil drugs. But they did not attack
my men; they circled them; their long tails wagged.
And just as dogs will fawn about their master
when he returns from feasts—they know that he
will offer them choice bits—just so, did these 250
lions and sharp-clawed wolves fawn on my men.
And yet those tough beasts terrified my friends.
They halted at the fair-haired Círcë's door;
within they heard the goddess' sweet voice sing
as she moved back and forth before her web—
imperishable, flawless, subtly-woven—
such work as only goddesses can fashion.

"Polítës, sturdy captain, the most dear
and trusted of my men, now told his friends:
'Someone inside is singing gracefully 260
as she weaves her great web. And what she sings
echoes throughout the house. Let's call to her.'

"These were his words. They did what he had asked.
She came at once. She opened her bright doors,
inviting them within; and—fools—they followed.
Eurýlochus alone did not go in;
he had foreseen some snare. She led the way
and seated them on chairs and high-backed thrones.
She mixed cheese, barley meal, and yellow honey

with wine from Prámnos; and she then combined 270
malign drugs in that dish so they'd forget
all thoughts of their own homes. When they had drunk,
she struck them with her wand, then drove them off
to pen them in her sties. They'd taken on
the bodies—bristles, snouts—and grunts of hogs,
yet kept the human minds they had before.
So they were penned, in tears; and Círcë cast
before them acorns, dogwood berries, mast—
food fit for swine who wallow on the ground.

"Meanwhile Eurýlochus rushed back to us 280
to let us know our comrades' shameful fate.
But he was speechless; though he longed for words,
his heart was struck with pain, tears filled his eyes;
nothing but lamentation filled his mind.
But when we—baffled—questioned him, at last
he told us what had happened to our friends:

" 'Odysseus, we did follow your commands:
we crossed the underbrush and reached the glen.
We found a sheltered house with smooth stone walls.
And there, intent on her great web, a goddess 290
or woman could be heard distinctly singing.
My comrades called to her; she opened wide
the gleaming doors, inviting them to enter.
They, unsuspecting, trailed along. But I
held back; I felt this was a trap. They dropped
from sight together. Though I kept close watch—
I waited long—no comrade reappeared.'

"These were his words. Across my back I cast
my massive sword of bronze with silver studs,
and then I slung my bow; I ordered him 300
to lead me back along the path he'd taken.
But he, his arms about my knees, implored:

" 'May you, whom Zeus has nurtured, leave me here;
don't force me to retrace my path. I know
that you will not return and not bring back
our men. With those we have let's sail away,
for we may still escape the evil day.'

"These were his words. I was compelled to say:
'Eurýlochus, you can stay here and eat
and drink beside the hollow black ship; I 310
must go, however; I cannot forgo
a task so necessary—this I owe.'

"That said, I left the sea and ship behind.
But after I had crossed the sacred glades
and was about to reach the halls of Círcë,
the connoisseur of potions, I saw Hermes,

who bears the golden wand, approaching me.
He'd taken on the likeness of a youth
just come of age, blessed with a young man's grace.
He clasped my hands. These were his words to me: 320

" 'Where are you wandering still, unlucky man,
alone along these slopes and ignorant
of this strange land? Círcë[68] has locked your friends
like swine behind the tight fence of her pens.
And have you come to free them? On your own,
be sure, you never will return; you'll stay
together with the others in her sties.
But come, I'll save you from her snares, I'll thwart
her plans. Now, when you enter Círcë's halls,
don't leave behind this tutelary herb. 330
I'll tell you all her fatal stratagems:
She'll mix a potion for you; she'll add drugs
into that drink; but even with their force,
she can't bewitch you; for the noble herb
I'll give you now will baffle all her plots.
When Círcë touches you with her long wand,
draw out the sharp sword at your thigh, and head
for her as if you meant to strike her dead.
Shrinking, she'll ask you then to share her bed.
And do not, then or later, turn her down, 340
for she will free your friends and be of help
to you, her guest. But first force her to swear
the blessed gods' great, massive oath: She must
forgo all thought of any other plots—
when you are stripped and naked, she must not
deceive you, leave you feeble, impotent.'

"When that was said, he gave his herb to me;
he plucked it from the ground and showed what sort
of plant it was. Its root was black; its flower
was white as milk. It's *moly* for the gods; 350
for mortal men, the mandrake[69]—very hard
to pluck; but nothing holds against the gods.

"Then Hermes crossed the wooded isle and left
for steep Olympus. And I took the path
to Círcë's house—most anxious as I went.
I stopped before the fair-haired goddess' door;
I halted, called aloud; she heard my voice.
At once she opened her bright doors and then
invited me to follow her. I went
with troubled heart. She led me to a chair, 360
robust and handsome, graced with silver studs;

---

[68] An enchantress who understands the uses of drugs and herbs.

[69] The exact identity of the magical *moly* is not known. The mandrake plant belongs to the nightshade family; because of the human shape of its root, it was thought to be magical.

a footrest stood below. And she poured out
an ample drink into a golden bowl.
With her conniving mind, she mixed her drugs
within that bowl, then offered it to me.
I drank it down. But I was not bewitched.
She struck me with her long wand. Then she said:
'Now to the sty, to wallow with your friends!'

"At that, out from its sheath along my thigh,
I drew my sword as if to have her die. 370
She howled. She clasped my knees and, as she wept,
with these winged words, made her appeal to me:

" 'Who are you? From what family? What city?
You drank my drugs, but you were not entranced.
No other man has ever passed that test;
for once that potion's passed their teeth, the rest
have fallen prey: you have within your chest
a heart that can defeat my sorcery.
You surely are the man of many wiles,
Odysseus, he whom I was warned against 380
by Hermes of the golden wand: he said
that you would come from Troy in a black ship.
But now put back your blade within that sheath
and let us lie together on my bed:
in loving, we'll learn trust and confidence.'

"These were her words. And this was my reply:
'Círcë, how can you ask for tenderness,
you who have turned my comrades into swine
and now, insidiously, try to bind
me, too—for once I'm naked on your bed, 390
you'll snare me, leave me weak and impotent?
I will not share your bed unless you swear
the mighty oath, o goddess—to insure
that you'll forgo all thoughts of further plots.'

"These were my words. As I had asked, she swore
at once. And after that great oath was pledged,
I then climbed onto Círcë's lovely bed.

"Meanwhile four girls were busy in the halls;
these maids were once dear daughters of the woods
and springs and seaward-flowing sacred streams. 400
Across the high-backed chairs, one handmaid first
draped linen cloth and then threw purple rugs.
The second drew up silver tables set
with golden baskets, while the third maid mixed
smooth honeyed wine in silver bowls and brought
fair golden cups. The fourth maid filled a tripod
with water and, beneath it, lit a fire;
and when it bubbled in the glowing bronze
caldron, she set me down inside a tub.

Over my head and shoulders she poured water— 410
gradually tempering its heat—
to free my limbs and soul from long fatigue.
And when that maid had bathed and, with rich oil,
had smoothed my body and about me cast
a tunic and a handsome cloak, she led
the way and sat me on a high-backed chair,
robust and handsome, graced with silver studs;
a footrest stood below. A servant brought
a lovely golden jug from which she poured
fresh water out into a silver bowl, 420
so I might wash my hands; then at my side
she placed a polished table. The old housewife
was generous; she drew on lavish stores,
inviting me to eat. But I was not
inclined to feed my frame: I sat and thought
of other things; my soul foresaw the worst.
Círcë, who saw me seated there denying
all food and filled with dark despair, drew near.
And, at my side, she called on these winged words:

" 'Odysseus, do not sit there like some mute, 430
with tattered heart, not touching drink or food.
Do you suspect another trap? Forget
your fears. I swore the strongest oath there is.'

"These were her words. And this was my reply:
'Círcë, what man with justice in his mind
would think of food and drink before he freed
his comrades and could see them with his eyes?
If you indeed would have me drink and eat,
release my men: bring back my faithful friends.'

"These were my words. And Círcë—wand in hand— 440
now left the hall and, opening the pens,
drove out my men; they had the shape of fat
nine-year-old hogs. They faced her. She drew close.
Upon the flesh of each of them, she spread
another herb. At that, their bodies shed
the bristles that had grown when they'd gulped down
the deadly brew she'd offered them at first.
Now they were men again—and younger than
they were before, more handsome and more grand.
They knew me quickly; each man clasped my hand. 450
Their cries of joy were long and loud; throughout
the house a clamor rose. And Círcë, too,
was moved. Then she—the lovely goddess—urged:

" 'Odysseus, man of many wiles, divine
son of Laértës, go to your swift ship
along the shore and beach it on dry land.
First store your goods and all your gear in caves,
but then return with all your faithful friends.'

"These were her words. My proud soul was convinced:
I hurried to the shore and my swift ship. 460
And there I found my faithful crew in tears.
Even as calves upon a farm are glad
when cows return from pasture, having had
their fill of grass, and come back to their stalls;
and all the calves frisk round unchecked; no pen
can hold them as they race around their dams,
lowing again, again—so did my men,
when they caught sight of me, weep tears of joy:
they felt as if they'd touched their native land,
their rugged Ithaca, where they were bred 470
and born. In tears, they uttered these winged words:

" 'You, whom Zeus nurtured, have come back; for us
this joy is like the joy that would erupt
on our return to Ithaca, our home.
But tell us now the fate of all the rest.'

"These were their words. I quietly replied:
'Come, let us beach our ship along dry land
and stow our goods and all our gear in caves.
Then, all of you be quick to follow me;
in Círcë's sacred halls you soon will see 480
your comrades eating, drinking; they can count
on never-ending stores.'

"My words were done.
At once they answered my commands. But one—
Eurýlochus[70]—did try to check their course:

" 'My sorry friends, where are we heading now?
Why court catastrophe in Círcë's house?
She'll turn us into lions, wolves, or hogs—
and we'll be forced to guard her massive halls.
So did the Cyclops catch and trap our friends—
then, too, the rash Odysseus was with them. 490
They, too, died through the madness of this man.'

"I heard his words. I had a mind to draw
the sharp blade sheathed beside my sturdy thigh.
I'd have sliced off his head and flung it down
upon the ground—although Eurýlochus
was kin of mine by marriage. But my men
drew near and checked me with these gentle words:

" 'If you—one sprung from Zeus—prefer it so,
he can stay here and watch the ship. We'll go
with you: lead us to Círcë's sacred house.' 500

[70]Related to Odysseus by marriage.

"That said, they left the ship and shore behind.
Eurýlochus came, too. He did not stay:
my rage was ominous—he was afraid.

"Meanwhile, with kindness, Círcë, in her halls,
cared for my other men: she bathed them all,
and then she smoothed their skins with gleaming oil
and wrapped them in fine tunics and soft cloaks.
We found them feasting on abundant stores.
But when they all had recognized each other,
their tears and wails were loud throughout the halls. 510
Bright Círcë, standing at my side, advised:

" 'Odysseus, man of many wiles, divine
son of Laértës, do not urge more tears.
I know indeed the many miseries
you have endured upon the fish-rich sea
and how, on land, you faced fierce enemies.
But eat this food and drink this wine—and find
the force you had when you first left behind
your homeland, rugged Ithaca. Your minds
can only think of bitter wanderings; 520
you're worn and weary, without joy or ease;
you've lived too long—too much—with grinding griefs.'

"These were her words. And our proud hearts agreed.
Day after day we stayed for one whole year:
we ate much meat; the wine was honey-sweet.

"But when the months that fill a year had passed,
and seasons had revolved, and once again
the long days reached their end, my comrades said:

" 'Wake from your trance, remember your own land,
if fate is yet to save you, if you can 530
still reach your high-walled house, your native isle.'

"These were their words. And my proud heart agreed.
Through all that day we sat, until sunset:
the meat was fine; the wine was honey-sweet.
But once the sun had gone and darkness won,
within the shadowed halls, my comrades slept.

"And I went off to Círcë's splendid bed.
I clasped her knees. She heard as I beseeched:
'Círcë, fulfill the promise made to me:
do let me leave for home. My men entreat, 540
and my own heart wants that. Whenever you
are out of hearing, all my men implore
again, again: they long to leave these shores.'

"The lovely goddess gave this quick reply:
'Odysseus, man of many wiles, divine

son of Laértës, do not spend more time
within my house if you will otherwise.
But you cannot reach home till you complete
another journey—to the house of Hades
and fierce Perséphonë.[71] There you must seek 550
the soul of that blind seer, Tirésias
the Theban:[72] he alone among the dead
preserves his wits and sober sense: this gift
Perséphonë has granted just to him,
for all the other dead are wandering shades.'

"My heart was broken as I heard her words.
Seated upon that bed, I cried: my soul
had lost its will to live, to see the light.
But when my need to weep and writhe was done,
these were the words with which I answered her: 560

" 'Círcë, who'll serve as pilot on that way?
No man has ever sailed in his black ship
to Hades' halls.'

"And her reply was quick:
'Odysseus, man of many wiles, divine
son of Laértës, there's no need to fret
about a helmsman. After you have stepped
the mast and spread your white sail, you can sit:
the breath of Bóreas will guide your ship.
But when you've crossed the Ocean, you will see
the shore and forests of Perséphonë— 570
the towering poplars and the willow trees
whose fruits fall prematurely.[73] Beach your ship
on that flat shore which lies on the abyss
of Ocean. Make your way on foot to Hades.
In those dank halls, the Pýriphlégethon
together with a branch of Styx, Cocýtus—
two roaring rivers—form one course and join
the Ácheron.[74] Just there you'll find a rock.
Draw near that spot and, as I tell you, dig
a squared-off ditch—along each side, one cubit. 580
Three times pour offerings around that pit
for all the dead: pour milk and honey first,
then pour sweet wine; let water be the third.
And scatter over these white barley meal.
Then give the helpless dead your fervent pledge

[71] Queen of the underworld.

[72] A famous, blind soothsayer in the legends of Thebes who plays important roles in Sophocles' Oedipus plays.

[73] Homer locates Hades on the western frontier of the Greek world; after Homer, Hades was ordinarily located down below the earth, similar to the Christian Hell.

[74] The rivers of Hades are the Ácheron, the Cocytus (Styx), and Pýriphlégethon.

that, when you come to Ithaca, you'll offer
as sacrifice your finest barren heifer
and heap her pyre high with handsome gifts.
But to Tirésias alone pledge this:
the finest jet black ram that you possess. 590
And after you have called upon the famed
tribes of the dead, do sacrifice a ram
and black ewe: bend their heads toward Érebus,[75]
but you must turn toward Ocean's streams. That done,
so many souls of men now dead will come.
For them, command your crew to flay and burn
the slaughtered sheep, throats slit by ruthless bronze;
and pray unto the gods, to mighty Hades
and fierce Perséphonë. Draw your sharp sword
out from the sheath that lies along your thigh: 600
keep close watch on the blood of sacrifice,
lest any of the helpless dead draw near
that pit before you meet Tirésias.
Soon he, the seer, leader of men, will come
to tell you what will be your path, how long
your homeward journey is to take, and how
you'll make your way across the fish-rich sea.'

"So Círcë said. Upon the throne of gold,
Dawn came straightway. The goddess Círcë clothed
my frame in cloak and tunic; she herself 610
put on a long and gleaming, gracious robe
of subtly-woven threads. She bound a belt
of gold around her waist; she veiled her head.
And I went through the house; with gentle words
I spurred my comrades, one by one. I urged:
'You've had enough sweet sleep. It's time to go.
Great Círcë told me all that we must know.'

"These were my words. And their proud hearts agreed.
But I was not to lead all of my men
away from Círcë's isle. One of my band, 620
our youngest man, Elpénor—not too brave
nor too alert—had lain alone, stretched out
along the roof of Círcë's house to find
some cooler air: he'd taken too much wine.
Then, when he heard the noise of our departure,
he jumped up suddenly, and so—forgetting
the long way down by ladder—off the roof
headfirst he fell. And from his spine, his neck
was broken off; his spirit went to Hades.

"But I, to those who followed me, now said: 630
'Though you may think that you are going home,

[75] The darkest region of Hades.

back to your own dear land, another road
is ours, for Círcë said we first must see
the halls of Hades and Perséphonë;
there we must meet Tirésias of Thebes.'

"My words broke their dear hearts. They sat and wept;
they tore their hair; but all of that lament
gained nothing for us. Still in tears, we went
back to the shore; alongside our black ship,
Círcë had tied a ram and jet black ewe, 640
but none of us had seen her go or come;
she passed us by so easily. How can
a man detect a god who comes and goes
if gods refuse to have their movements known?"

BOOK 11
[THE VISIT TO HADES]

"We reached the shore and ship. We drew our craft
down to the gleaming sea. We stepped the mast
and set our sail, embarked our sheep; downcast,
in tears, we went aboard. Then fair-haired Círcë,
the awesome goddess with a human voice,
sent forth a friend who favored us, a wind
that swelled our sail and spurred our ship's dark prow.
Once we'd secured our gear, we settled down;
the wind and helmsman kept us on our course.
The sail held taut; all day we sped along. 10
The sun sank; all sea roads were darkened now.

"We sailed by night to find deep Ocean's end;
we sailed until we reached the limit-land,
the shadowed home of the Cimmérians.[76]
Their city wears a shroud of mist and clouds;
the lord of light can never gaze at them—
not when he climbs the starry sky nor when
he wheels and then descends to earth again:
drear night enfolds those melancholy men.

"We landed, beached our ship, and drove ashore 20
our sheep, then made our way at Ocean's side;
we reached the place that Círcë had described.
Here Perimédës and Eurýlochus
held fast the ram and ewe we'd sacrifice.
I drew the sharp blade from beside my thigh
and dug a ditch one cubit on each side;
around that pit, for all the dead, I poured

[76] A legendary people living near the entrance to Hades.

libations: offering milk and honey first,
then sweet wine, then pure water. Over these
I scattered—properly—white barley meal. 30
Then to the lifeless, listless dead I pledged
that when I had returned to Ithaca
I'd sacrifice a splendid barren heifer
and heap her pyre high with precious gifts;
and for Tirésias I pledged the best
black ram in all the flocks that I possess.
And after I'd implored with vows and prayers
the tribes of those dead souls, I seized the sheep
and slit their throats above the pit; cloud-dark
blood ran. From Érebus there came a crowd 40
of dead souls: girls, young bachelors, and old men
much tried by grief, and tender brides still new
to sorrow. Many fighting-men came, too;
they'd died in battle, pierced by bronze-tipped spears;
and they still wore their bloodstained battle gear.
These crowded round the pit upon all sides;
they uttered strange outcries. I paled with fear.
At that, I spurred my men to flay and roast
the sheep we'd sacrificed, whose throats I'd cut
with ruthless bronze; and we prayed to the gods, 50
to Hades' force and fierce Perséphonë.
With my sharp sword again unsheathed, I watched
over the pit of sacrificial blood,
lest any of the fragile dead draw near
that blood before I met Tirésias.

"The first dead soul to come was young Elpénor,
my comrade: one who'd yet to find a grave
beneath the earth's wide ways; we'd left his corpse
unwept, unburied, there in Círcë's house;
we had another task—and hurried off. 60
The sight of him provoked my tears and pity;
and when I spoke to him, my words were winged:
'Elpénor, you on foot were faster than
my ship. How did you reach this shadowed land?'

"These were my words; this was his sad reply:
'Odysseus, man of many wiles, divine
son of Laértës, my undoing lay
in some god sending down my dismal fate
and in too much sweet wine. I lay stretched out
on Círcë's roof; too stupefied to think 70
of taking the long ladder down, I fell
headfirst, down to the ground. My neck was cracked,
split from my spine; my spirit went to Hades.
Now I beseech you in the name of those
you left behind, the absent ones: your wife
and he who reared you when you were a child,
your father, and Telémachus, the son

you left alone at home. I know that you,
on leaving Hades' halls, will find landfall
with your stout ship at the Aeǽan isle. 80
There, lord, I ask you to remember me.
Do not abandon me, unwept, unburied,
lest you provoke the anger of the gods.
Burn me and any armor that is mine,
and on the shore of the gray sea, heap high
a mound for this unhappy man. Do this
for me, and set upon that mound the oar
I used when I, alive, rowed with my friends.'

"And then the shade of my dead mother came:
she, Anticlēīa, child of generous 90
Autólycus, had been alive when I
had left for holy Ílion. I wept—
that sight had touched my soul with pity—yet,
even within my grief, I did not let
my mother's spirit near the blood before
Tirésias had heard all I would ask.

"Theban Tirésias came next. He grasped
his golden staff. He knew me, and he said:
'Odysseus, man of many wiles, divine
son of Laértēs, why have you, sad man, 100
abandoning the sunlight, cared to come
to see the dead and this dejected realm?
But now it's time to stand aside: leave free
the pit and sheathe your sharpened blade, that I
may taste this blood and tell you words of truth.'

"He spoke. I sheathed my silver-studded sword.
As soon as he had tasted that dark blood,
the prince of prophets offered me these words:

" 'You, bright Odysseus, seek a honey-sweet
homecoming, but a god will make it harsh. 110
I do not think you can elude the lord
who makes earth tremble, for his heart has stored
much fury since you blinded his dear son.
But even so—though sadly tried—you can
return to your own home if you would check
your will and your dear comrades' once you've left
behind the violet sea and your stout ship
has touched Thrinácia, the island where
you'll find the grazing cattle, splendid flocks
of Hélios, who sees and hears all things. 120
If you leave his rich herds untouched and turn
your mind to going home, then you can still
reach Ithaca, though after grim ordeals.
And even if your solitary self

escapes, your coming home will be delayed
and sad: with all your comrades lost, you'll make
that journey on a ship that's not your own;
and in your house you will meet griefs, a pack
of overbearing men, who would devour
your goods; they woo your godlike wife with gifts. 130
But you, returned, will crush their impudence;
and when, within your halls, you've killed them all
either through guile or else in open war
with your sharp bronze, then take a shapely oar
and visit many cities till you reach
a land where men know nothing of the sea
and don't use salt to season what they eat;
they're ignorant of boats with purple cheeks
and shapely oars that are the wings of ships.
I give you this clear sign—it can't be missed. 140
When, on the road, you come upon a man
who calls the oar you carry on your back
a fan for winnowing, you can be sure:
that place is where you are to plant your oar.
That done, present Poseidon with fine gifts:
a ram, a bull, a boar that mates with sows.
Then, once you have returned to Ithaca,
take care to offer holy hecatombs
to the undying gods, wide heaven's lords—
to each in turn. You will not die at sea: 150
the death that reaches you will be serene.
You will grow old—a man of wealth and ease—
surrounded by a people rich, at peace.
All I have said will surely come to be.'

"These were his words, and this was my reply:
'Tirésias, gods wove this destiny.
But tell me one thing—tell me honestly.
I see the soul of my dear mother; she
sits near the pit of blood, but does not speak
to her own son, nor does she look at me. 160
How can I let her know that I am he?'

"These were my words; this was his quick reply:
'The answer's easy; set it in your mind.
Those whom you let approach the pit of blood
will speak the truth to you, and those dead souls
whom you refuse will surely move away.'

"That said, the soul of lord Tirésias,
now he had given me his prophecy,
went back to Hades' halls. But I sat still
until my mother came to drink the blood 170
dark as a cloud. And she knew who I was
at once; I saw her tears, heard her winged words:

" 'Son, how have you, despite the mist and fog,
come here alive? The living find it hard
to reach this realm: it lies so far beyond
great rivers and dread deeps and, most of all,
the Ocean none can cross on foot; it takes
stout ships to face that journey. Have you come
with ship and comrades, after wandering long,
from Troy? Have you been back to Ithaca? 180
And have you seen your wife within your halls?'

"These were her words, and this was my reply:
'Mother, it is necessity that brought me
to Hades' house, to hear the prophecy
the spirit of Tirésias the Theban
would offer me. I've yet to near the shore
of dear Achǽa; I've not touched our isle.
I've wandered without joy, in deep dejection,
from that day when, behind bright Agamemnon,
I left for Ílion, where fine foals graze, 190
to fight against the Trojans. But I need
to hear one thing—and tell me honestly:
How did fierce death defeat you? With long sickness?
Or did the archer-goddess Ártemis,
whose arrows are more gentle, find the mark?
Tell me about my father and the son
I left in Ithaca. Are they still seen
as kin of one who's king? Or does another
possess my scepter now, since many say
that I will not return? Reveal to me 200
the mind and intent of the wife I wed.
Does she stand by my son and keep all things
just as they've always been? Or was she taken
as wife by some illustrious Achǽan?'

"My honored mother answered me at once:
'Indeed steadfast, within your house she stays.
Her dreary nights and days are wept away.
No one's usurped your kingship; and your lands
are held in peace by your Telémachus.
As suits a guardian of justice, he 210
shares in his people's festive gatherings:
men want his counsel; he's a precious guest.
Your father keeps to his own farm; he never
comes down into the town. To ease his rest
he has no bed, no cloak, and no bright blankets;
he sleeps, in winter, where the servants sleep,
in ashes by the fire; his clothes are ragged.
But when the summer and rich autumn come,
then all about the slopes of his vineyards
lie heaps of scattered fallen leaves; and there 220
he lies in sorrow, tending his great grief;

over your fate he weeps. A harsh old age
has overtaken him. So, too, my fate
was sadness, and my last years bore that weight.
The expert archer-goddess'[77] gentle shafts
did not strike me within my house; no sickness
mined me, the sort that often saps life's force,
that wears away the body hatefully;
it was lament for you—your gentleness
and wisdom—o my radiant Odysseus— 230
that robbed me of the honey-sweet of life.'

"She'd spoken. And despite my doubts, I longed
to clasp my mother's shade within my arms.
Three times—my heart kept urging me—I tried;
and three times she escaped my hands, much like
a shadow or a dream. The pain grew sharp
and sharper in my heart. My winged words said:

" 'Dear mother, why do you shrink back when I
want so to hold you fast? Can't we embrace
and, with our arms around each other, take 240
our fill of this chill grief in Hades' house?
Or are you just a phantom sent to me
by great Perséphonë, that she might add
still other tears to those that I have shed?'

"That said, my honored mother answered quickly:
'Poor child, most tried of men, Perséphonë,
daughter of Zeus, is not deceiving you
in any way: this is the law that rules
all mortals at their death. For just as soon
as life has left the white bones, and the sinews 250
no longer hold together bones and flesh,
when the erupting force of blazing fire
undoes the body, then the spirit wanders:
much like a dream, it flits away and hovers,
now here, now there. But hurry back to light;
and may your mind remember my reply,
so that you can reveal it to your wife.'

"Such were the words we shared. Then all the wives
and daughters of great lords came forward, sent
by famed Perséphonë. Those women thronged 260
around the pit of blood; and since I longed
to question each of them, I weighed the ways
in which that might be done. This plan seemed best.
Unsheathing the sharp sword along my thigh,

[77] Ártemis.

I did not let them all draw near at once.
But one by one they came; and each described
her lineage and, when I asked, replied.

"The first I saw was Tyro:[78] she declared
herself to be the daughter of Salmóneus
and wife of Crétheus, son of Æolus. 270
When she was still a girl, her heart was set
on the divine Enípeus, handsomest
of all earth's rivers. Wild with love, she watched
his lovely current. But the god who shakes
and clasps the earth took on Enípeus' shape;
and at the churning river mouth, he lay
with her. Above them rose a huge dark wave;
arching, it hid them: god and mortal girl.
Poseidon loosened Tyro's virgin girdle;
then, shedding sleep on her, he did love's work. 280
At that, he clasped her hand and spoke soft words:

" 'You can be happy, woman, in our love:
even as this year turns, you will give birth
to splendid children: matings of the gods
are never barren. Care for—tend—your sons.
Go home, keep silent, tell no one; but know—
your lover was Poseidon, god of tremors.'

"That said, Poseidon plunged beneath sea-surge.
Conceiving, she bore Pélias and Néleus;
and both became firm servants of great Zeus. 290
And Pélias, lord of great herds, lived in spacious
Iólcus; Néleus' home was sandy Pylos.
The queenly woman's other sons were born
of Crétheus: Æson, Phérës, Amytháon,
adept at fighting from his chariot.

"And after her I saw Antíopë,
Asópus' daughter, she who claimed the glory
of having slept within the arms of Zeus,
to whom she bore two sons: Amphíon, Zéthus,
the pair who founded seven-gated Thebes 300
and walled it round with towers; without these,
despite that city's strength, it would have been
too hard to keep a place so spacious safe
from enemies.

"And then I saw Alcménë,
wife of Amphítryon. After she lay

[78] A queen of Thessaly who fell in love with a river god, who was Poseidon in disguise; she bore him two sons: Pélias and Néleus, the father of Nestor.

in mighty Zeus's arms, she bore a son:
the dauntless, lionhearted Héraclës.

"And I saw Mégara, bold Creon's daughter,
wife of Alcménë's never-yielding son.

"I also saw the lovely Epicástë,[79] 310
mother of Oedipus; unknowingly,
she'd shared in a monstrosity: she married
her own son. And she wed him after he
had killed his father. But the gods did not
wait long to let men know what had been wrought.
Yet since they had devised dark misery,
the gods let him remain in handsome Thebes;
and there, despite his dismal sufferings,
he stayed with the Cadméans as their king.
But she went down into the house where Hades 320
is sturdy guardian of the gates; for she,
gripped by her grief, had tied to a high beam
her noose. But when she died, she left behind
calamities for Oedipus—as many
as the Avengers of a mother carry.

"And I saw fairest Chlóris, she whose beauty
caught Néleus; with his countless gifts, he won
as wife the youngest daughter of Amphíon,
the son of Íasus, whose power had once
possessed the Mínyae's town, Orchómenus. 330
And to her husband, Chlóris, queen of Pylos,
bore splendid sons: Nestor and Chrómius
and Periclýmenus. Then she gave birth
to Pero, gifted with amazing beauty.
All of the nearby chieftains sought her hand,
but Néleus had decreed that any man
who wanted her as wife must first bring back
the cattle with broad brows and curving horns
that Íphiclës of Phýlacë had stolen
from Tyro, Néleus' mother. Íphiclës 340
was powerful; the trial was hard; and only
the seer, Melámpus—acting on behalf
of his dear brother—dared to face that task.
But he was blocked when Zeus devised a plot:
the herdsmen caught him, bound him fast in chains.
But when the old year's months and days were done,
and seasons started their new rounds, the force
of Íphiclës relented: after he
had heard Mélampus' many prophecies,
he set him free. Zeus' will was now complete. 350

[79]Jocasta, mother and wife of Oedipus.

"And I saw Leda,[80] she who bore her husband,
Tyndáreüs, two stalwart sons: Castor,
horse-tamer, and the boxer Polydeūces.
The earth, giver of grain, now covers both.
But Zeus gave them a special dignity;
for each of them, though under earth, is dead
one day but lives the next, in turn.[81] Those brothers
were gifted by their fate with godlike honor.

"And after them I saw Iphimedēia,
Alœus' wife, who claimed that she had lain 360
with lord Poseidon. Famous Ephiáltës
and godlike Otus were the sons she bore,
but both were fated to a life cut short.
Grain-giving earth had made those two more handsome
and tall than any other man except Oríon.
Even at nine, they were nine cubits wide;
as for their height, it matched nine stretched arm's-lengths.
They even threatened the undying gods'
Olympus with confusion and assault;
upon its peak they planned to heap Mount Ossa 370
and then, on top of that, Mount Pélion,[82]
whose woods are loud with leaves; from there they'd climb
to heaven. They'd have done what they designed
if they had reached their manhood. But the son
of Zeus,[83] whom fair-haired Leto bore, killed both
before the hair beneath their temples showed
enough to beard their chins with ample growth.

"And I saw Phædra, Procris, and Ariádnë—
malicious Minos' lovely daughter[84]—she
whom Théseus tried to carry off from Crete 380
to holy Athens' hill. But their escape
brought no delight to him: along the way,
in seagirt Día, Ártemis was swayed
by Dionysus; she killed Ariádnë.

"Then I saw Clýmenë and Mæra and
the obscene Eriphýlë,[85] she who sold
her husband's life: she bartered him for gold.

"But I cannot recount or name them all:
the many wives and daughters of the brave.

---

[80]By Zeus, Leda was the mother of Helen; by Tyndáreüs, Leda was the mother of Castor, Polydeūces, and Clytemnéstra.

[81]They shared one immortality between them.

[82]Ossa and Pélion are mountains near Olympus.

[83]Apollo.

[84]Minos, king of Crete, was the father of Phædra and Ariádnë. After Theseus, king of Athens, killed the Minotaur he took Ariádnë with him to Día (Naxos). It is not clear why Dionysus wanted her killed.

[85]Polynices, Oedipus' son, bribed Eriphýlë with a golden necklace; she persuaded her husband, Amphiaráus, to join the attack on Thebes, where he was killed.

Immortal night would end before I did. 390
But now the time for sleep has come, and I
must either meet the crew on your swift ship
or else rest here. Should I begin my trip?
You and the gods must now decide on this."

These were his words. And all were silent, still—
held in the shadowed hall by some deep spell.
White-armed Arétë was the first to speak:

"Phaeácians, how does he persuade you now—
his face and frame and his astute good sense?
He is my honored guest, though all of you 400
received him, too. Then do not send him off
in haste and do not grudge the many gifts
he needs; for each of you, within his house,
has ample wealth—just as the gods have willed."

Then Echenéus, the old warrior, spoke:
"Dear friends, the words of our wise queen seem just.
Do as she says—though on Alcínoüs
our final words and actions must depend."

This was Alcínoüs' reply: "Her plan
has my consent as surely as I am 410
alive—and king of the Phaeácians.
And though he longs to see his home, our guest
can wait until tomorrow dawns; by then
I shall have gathered all the gifts at last.
While all of us must plan his trip, that task
is mainly mine: it's I who rule this land."

Odysseus, man of many wiles, replied:
"Alcínoüs, all peoples know your fame;
and even if you spoke for a delay
of one full year, while you prepared my way 420
with shipmates and fine gifts, I'd gladly wait.
Indeed, if I returned to my own land
with riches in my hands, I'd surely win
much more respect, a warmer welcoming
by all who saw me back in Ithaca."

This was the answer of Alcínoüs:
"Odysseus, you don't seem to be a cheat
or liar—though we know that dark earth breeds
so many who, in every land, deceive
with tales of things that no man's ever seen. 430
But you have grace and wisdom in your speech.
You've told with skill—as would a poet sing—
your own and all the Argives' sufferings.
But tell me this—and tell me honestly:
Did you lay eyes on any of the men

who went with you to Ílion and met
their fate along that plain? The night is long—
a length beyond foretelling. It is not
yet time to sleep within this hall. I want
more things of wonder and astonishment. 440
I could stay here until divine Dawn wakes
if you'd resume your tale of trials and pains."

Odysseus, man of many wiles, replied:
"Alcínoüs, most notable of men,
it's true that there's still time for tales and talk,
yet there is, too, a time for sleep. But if
you want to hear still more, I should not wish
to keep from you the tale of other griefs
more bitter still, the sad ordeals of friends
who had escaped the Trojans' ominous 450
war-cries but then, returning home, were killed—
the victims of an evil woman's will.

"As soon as pure Perséphonë had scattered
the women—weaker spirits—here and there,
the saddened soul of Agamemnon, son
of Átreus, came forward. And a crowd
surrounded him: within Aegísthus' halls
these men had died alongside Agamemnon.
As soon as he caught sight of me, he knew
just who I was. His moan was loud, his tears 460
were many; he stretched out his arms; he longed
to hold me fast, but all his force was gone;
the power of his agile limbs was lost.
I looked, I wept, and pity filled my heart.
And when I spoke, I offered these winged words:

"'O Agamemnon, Átreus' famed son,
how did dour death defeat so great a captain?
Was it Poseidon, hurling his harsh storms
against your ships, who finally won out?
Or did you die on land, when fighting-men 470
destroyed you as you raided herds and flocks
or tried to win their women and their town?'

"These were my words. This was his quick reply:
'Odysseus, man of many wiles, divine
son of Laértës, I was not undone
by lord Poseidon: none of his harsh storms
attacked my ships. Nor did I meet my end
on land, struck down by fighting-men. My fate
was readied by Aegísthus with the aid
of my conniving wife: inviting me 480
to feast within his halls, he butchered me
just as one kills an ox within a stall.
And so the death I died was mean and small:

around me, without let, they killed us all
as, in the house of one with power and wealth,
for wedding feasts or banquets jointly set
or revels, servants slaughter white-tusked hogs.
You surely have set eyes on many men
destroyed in single combat or the clash
of frenzied ranks, but you'd have been still more 490
distraught if you had seen, in that great hall,
our bodies round the wine bowl and the food
heaped high; our warm blood streamed across the floor.
I heard Cassandra,[86] Priam's daughter, wail
even as—clinging to me—she was killed
by Clytemnéstra, mistress of dark guile.
Face down, along the ground, my chest pierced through,
lifting my fists, dying, I beat the earth,
and my bitch-wife moved off. She had no heart:
I left for Hades, but she did not shut 500
my eyes nor did she move to close my mouth.[87]
Nothing is more obscene, more bestial, than
a woman's mind when it is all intent
on dregs—the filth my wife concocted when
she killed her own true husband. Coming home,
it was my children's and my servants' welcome
I'd hoped for; but that artist of corruption
heaped shame upon herself and on all women
in time to come, even the upright ones.'

"These were his words, and this was my reply: 510
'Long since, the bitter hate of thundering Zeus
against the sons of Átreus has used
conniving women as its instruments:
how many of us died through Helen's fault;
and Clytemnéstra, while you were far off,
devised her plot.'

"These were my words—and he
was quick to answer: 'Therefore do not be
too open with your wife: do not disclose
all that you know; tell her one thing and keep
another hidden—though you'll never meet 520
death at the hands of your Penelope,
a prudent wife, whose heart has understanding.
When we set off for war, Penelope
was still a young bride: at her breast she held
an infant son, who now must sit among
the ranks of men—a happy son, for he
will see the father whom he loves come home;

---

[86] She was brought back from Troy by Agamemnon as part of his booty.
[87] Perform the proper burial rites.

and as is right, he'll hold his father close.
But I was not allowed to sate my eyes,
to see my own beloved son: my wife 530
denied that sight to me—she killed me first.
And I should add this warning: Don't forget
to moor in secret when you bring your ship
to your dear shores: no woman merits trust.
But tell me one thing—tell me honestly:
Have you heard word of where my son now lives?
Has sandy Pylos or Orchómenus
or Meneláus' Spartan plain become
my son's new home? For certainly the bright
Oréstes has not died upon the earth.' 540

"These were his words, and this was my reply:
'Why, Agamemnon, do you ask me that?
I do not know if he's alive or dead.
Words empty as the wind are best unsaid.'

"So did we two shed tears and share sad talk.
And then Achilles, Péleus' son, approached;
and with the son of Péleus came Patróclus,
flawless Antílochus, and Ajax—he
whose form and stature outdid all the Dánaans'
except for the incomparable Achilles. 550
The shade of Æacus' swift-footed grandson
knew me. In tears he offered these winged words:

" 'Odysseus, man of many wiles, divine
son of Laértës, will your spirit find
new tasks still more audacious than this quest?
How did you dare to come to Hades, home
of shades of faded men, the helpless dead?'

"These were his words, and this was my reply:
'Achilles, Péleus' son, the bravest Dánaan,
I've come to seek Tirésias, to listen 560
to any counsel he might have: a plan
to help me reach my rocky Ithaca.
I've not yet neared the coasts of the Achæans;
I have not touched our soil. I've met sad trials.
Achilles, neither past nor future holds
a man more blessed than you. In life indeed
we Argives honored you as deity;
and now, among the dead, you are supreme.
In death you have no need to grieve, Achilles.'

"These were my words. He did not wait to answer: 570
'Odysseus, don't embellish death for me.
I'd rather be another's hired hand,
working for some poor man who owns no land

but pays his rent from what scant gains he gets,
than to rule over all whom death has crushed.
But tell me something of my worthy son:[88]
Has he, a lord of men, gone off to war,
become a chieftain? And what have you heard
of stalwart Péleus? Does he still preserve
his place of honor with the Mýrmidons, 580
or is he scorned in Hellas and in Phthía[89]
because old age has slowed his hands and feet?
I do not rise beneath the rays of sun
to take the form I had in Troy's broad land
when, to defend the Argives, my attacks
killed stalwart men: if I could only stand
beside my father for the briefest hour,
I'd make my force and formidable hands
the hated scourge of those whose savage acts
deprive him of due honor and respect.' 590

"These were his words, and this was my reply:
'Of your fine father, Péleus, I've heard nothing;
but of your dear son, Neoptólemus,
just as you wish, I'll tell you everything.
For I myself brought him in my lithe ship
to Scyros, where he joined the well-greaved Greeks.
And when our council met to plan attacks
against the Trojans, he was always first
to speak; in what he said, he never erred.
The only ones more subtle than your son 600
were godlike Nestor and myself. And when
Achæans fought along the plain of Troy,
your son did not draw back into the ranks
and ruck; he thrust ahead. No one could stand
against his fury: fierce, he killed and maimed
so many—I can't tell or list the names
of every warrior that he, defending
the Argives, killed. But I will tell you this:
Your son's bronze shaft struck down Eurýpylus,[90]
the son of Télephus—the handsomest 610
man I had ever seen except for Memnon,
who was the son of gods. And the Cetēians
who crowded round Eurýpylus were slaughtered—
all died because a woman had been bribed.
And, too, when we, the finest of the Argives,
were entering the horse Epēus built,
and it was I who led, who would decide
to shut our ambush or to open wide,
then all the other Dánaan lords and chiefs

[88]Neoptólemus.
[89]Péleus' kingdom.
[90]Leader of a group of warriors who fought on the side of the Trojans.

wiped tears away, their every limb was weak; 620
but not once did I see your son's fair face
grow pale or see him dry his cheek. Again,
again, he asked to leave the horse; he gripped
his sword-hilt and his massive bronze-tipped shaft,
longing to smash the Trojans. Once we'd sacked
the towering town of Priam, he went back—
bearing his share of spoils and one fine prize—
to board his ship; he was unscathed, intact;
no sharp speartip had struck him; no close fight
had left the wounds that war so often brings— 630
for Árës' fury strikes haphazardly.'

"That said, across the Field of Asphodels,
with long strides swift Achilles' spirit left;
my tale of his son's fame had made him glad.

"The other dead souls stood in sadness, each
shade speaking to me of his griefs. Just Ajax,
the son of Télamon, stood off, apart,
still angry with me for my victory
when I, not he, beside our ships, received
the prize Achilles' mother had adjudged: 640
the arms and armor of her son.[91] Would I
had never won that prize, for Ajax died
at his own hands because of that: earth closed
above a flawless man, one who surpassed
in feats and features all the Greeks except
for Péleus' son. I spoke with gentleness:

" 'Ajax, son of great Télamon, even
in death can't you forget your bitterness
against me for the fatal arms I won?
Those arms allowed the gods to heap disaster 650
upon the Argives: when you fell we lost
a bulwark. We Achǽans always mourn
your death as we do that of Péleus' son.
And Zeus alone must bear the blame: his venom,
his hatred for the ranks of Dánaan spearmen,
decreed your doom. My lord, dismiss your wrath;
come, hear my words; do not be obstinate.'

"So did I plead. He did not answer me.
He went back into Érebus; he joined
the other dead souls. Even in his wrath, 660
he might have spoken to me then, or I
to him. But now the heart within my chest
wanted to see the shades of the other dead.

[91] After Achilles was killed, his armor was offered as a prize to Odysseus rather than to Ajax, who then committed suicide.

"There I saw Minos—famous son of Zeus—
who, seated, holding fast his golden scepter,
delivered judgments on the dead; they gathered,
seated or standing, at the spacious gates
of Hades; they beseeched, and he passed sentence.

"And then I saw immense Oríon, driving
across the Field of Asphodels a throng 670
of savage beasts, those he had killed upon
the lonely mountain slopes. Within his hands
he gripped a club of bronze that cannot crack.

"I saw the son of splendid Gǽa, Títyus,
stretched on the ground for some six hundred cubits.
Two vultures sat, one to each side, and tore
his liver; their beaks plunged into his bowels,
he could not ward them off; for Títyus
had violated Leto, splendid mistress
of Zeus, as she was walking through the fields 680
of lovely Pánopeus, heading toward Pytho.

"And I saw Tántalus[92] in deep torment;
he stood upright within a pool, his chin
just touched by water. But despite his thirst,
he could not drink: as soon as that old man
bent over, seeking water, all that pool—
dried by a demon—shrank; and Tántalus
saw black earth at his feet. Above his head,
trees—leafy, high—bore fruit: from pomegranates
to pears, sweet figs, bright apples, and plump olives. 690
But just as soon as he reached out to touch,
winds blew that fruit up toward the shadowed clouds.

"And I saw Sísyphus'[93] atrocious pain:
he tried to push a huge stone with his hands.
He'd brace his hands and feet and thrust it up
a slope, but just when he had neared the top,
its weight reversed its course; and once again
that bestial stone rolled back onto the plain.
Sweat drenched his straining limbs: again he thrust,
and dust rose from the head of Sísyphus. 700

"And I caught sight of mighty Héraclës[94]
(that is to say, his shade; for he himself

[92]The nature of Tántalus' crime is uncertain: He might have revealed the secrets of the gods; he might have served his son's flesh to the gods.

[93]A king of Corinth known for his treachery.

[94]Under the rough master Eurystheus, Héraclës was made to perform his famous twelve labors, one of which was to fetch the dog Cerberus from Hades.

rejoices in the feats of deathless gods
and has as wife the lovely-ankled Hébë,
daughter of Zeus and golden-sandaled Hera).
Around him rose the tumult of the dead,
like birds that scatter everywhere in terror;
and he, like dark night, gripping his bare bow
and with an arrow on his bowstring, glared
menacingly, like one about to shoot. 710
Around his chest he had a giant belt
of gold embossed with horrifying things:
lions with massive manes, wild boars, and bears;
duels and battles, massacres and murders.
May he whose craft conceived that baldric never
devise a second one. As soon as he
returned my gaze, he knew just who I was.
And as he wept he offered these winged words:

"'Odysseus, man of many wiles, divine
son of Laértës, you are saddened by 720
the fate you bear, a destiny like mine
when underneath the sun I lived my life.
I was the son of Zeus, the son of Cronos,
and yet the trials that I endured were countless;
for I was made to serve a man by far
inferior to me: he set hard tests.
He even sent me here to fetch the hound
of Hades—he was sure there was no task
more dangerous. And yet I brought it back
from Hades' house, because I had the help 730
of Hermes and Athena, gray-eyed goddess.'

"His words were done. But when he had gone back,
I, lest still others come, stood there steadfast,
waiting for more dead heroes of the past.
And I'd have seen those warriors as I wished,
had crowds of dead souls not assembled then
with such a strange outcry that, terrified
and pale, I feared that fierce Perséphonë
might, from the halls of Hades, menace me
with Gorgon's head,[95] that grim monstrosity. 740

"At that, I hurried to my ship and ordered
my comrades to embark and loose the hawsers.
They came on board at once and manned the thwarts.
The current took our ship on Ocean's course.
At first we rowed, but then a fair wind rose."

[95] A powerful goddess with serpents for hair; her look could turn people to stone.

BOOK 12
[SCYLLA AND CHARÝBDIS]

"After our ship had slipped the Ocean's stream,
we coursed along the sea's broad surge and reached
the island of Aeǽa, home of Dawn's
firstlight, her space for dancing, and the site
of sunrise. There, along the sands, we beached
our sturdy ship, and then we disembarked.
We waited for bright Dawn; sleep held us fast.

"As soon as Dawn's rose fingers touched the sky,
I sent my comrades off to Círcë's house
to carry back the dead Elpénor's corpse. 10
Then we cut firewood; and as we stood
beside his pyre along a promontory,
the tears we shed were many. When his body
and armor had burned down, we heaped a mound,
and at the top we placed his shapely oar.

"We spoke of all we'd done, each thing in turn.
Círcë—not unaware that we'd come back
from Hades' house—had soon dressed handsomely.
She hurried to our side; her handmaids bore
abundant bread and meat and dark red wine. 20
She, brightest goddess, stood among us, saying:

" 'Undaunted, you have gone—alive—to see
the house of Hades; you are twice-made men—
all other mortals die but once. Yet come,
devote this day to food and drink; and when
Dawn rises, set your sail. And I'll describe
the sea paths you must take; I shall not hide
a single thing—so that you meet no snares
at sea and no misfortunes on the land.'

"These were her words, and our proud hearts agreed. 30
All through that day we sat, until sunset:
we had much meat; the wine was honey-sweet.
But once the sun had gone and darkness won,
my men lay near the cables at the stern;
then Círcë took my hand—she led me far
from my dear comrades. And she sat me down
beside her, asking me to tell her all.
I told her what we'd done, each thing in turn.
Then mighty Círcë spoke these things to me:

" 'Now all has been fulfilled. But you must hear 40
and do all that I say. A god will, too,
remind you. It will be the Sirens[96] you

[96]Known for their sweet song, the Sirens are not described physically.

meet first—and they entrance all visitors.
Whoever, unaware, comes close and hears
the Sirens' voice will nevermore draw near
his wife, his home, his infants: he'll not share
such joys again: the Sirens' lucid song
will so enchant him as they lie along
their meadow. Round about them lie heaped bones
and shriveled skin of putrefying men. 50
But row beyond the Sirens. Knead sweet wax
and stop your shipmates' ears so none of them
will hear the Sirens sing. But if you wish
to listen to their song, just stand erect
before the mast and have your men tie fast
your hands and feet, and wind the ends around
the mast itself; then with your back against
the mast, you can delight in that sweet chant.
But don't forget to tell your crew that if
you plead with them to loose those bonds, they must 60
add still more ropes and knots. When they have rowed
beyond the Sirens, you will have to choose
between two sea roads. But I'll not advise
which way you are to take; I'll just describe
what each is like, and you must then decide.

" 'One sea road runs among steep crags; the waves
of azure Amphitrítë[97] pound their base:
the blessed gods call these the Wandering Rocks.[98]
Even the birds can't make their way above
such cliffs—and they repel the trembling doves 70
that bring ambrosia to our father Zeus:
at times the sheer cliff snatches one of these,
and Zeus sends down another to complete
their ranks. And past those cliffs no mortals' ship
has ever sailed intact. There vicious blasts
of fire join the sea-surge in attack:
the sailors' bodies and the vessels' planks—
one vortex churns them all. And just one craft
alone—as all men know—has ever passed
those crags: the *Argo,* Jason's ship, when he 80
sailed homeward from Aeétës' coast. She, too,
would have been smashed against the rocks had not
Hera, for love of Jason, steered her through.

" 'The other sea road runs along two cliffs.
The first crag has a heaven-high sharp peak:
a never-fading cloud envelops it—
so dark that, round it, air is never limpid,
neither in summer nor in fall. No man
could ever scale that cliff or stand upon

[97]A sea nymph, wife of Poseidon.
[98]Possibly the straits between Sicily and Italy.

its top, though he had twenty feet and hands; 90
it is as sheer as if it had been burnished.
Midway on that cliffside, a dark cave lies.
It faces west, toward Érebus. Famous
Odysseus, you will head your ship toward that.
The cave is set so high on that cliffside
that even the most stalwart man who shot
an arrow upward from his ship could not
strike such a target. Scylla lives inside.
There she barks fearfully. Her voice is like
a newborn whelp, but she is murderous— 100
a monster who can only bring despair—
even a god would shun the sight of her.
She has twelve feet—and all of them deformed—
and six long necks: on each a vicious head
with three rows of abundant, close-set teeth,
replete with black death. Half her body's kept
deep in that cavern, but she thrusts her heads
out of her horrid home. She searches round
the rocks; she looks for dolphins and sea dogs
and any larger creatures she may chance 110
to catch, for wailing Amphitrítë breeds
a multitude of such enormous beasts.
No sailor yet can boast of sailing past
her cliff with ship intact: each of her mouths
snatches a man from every passing prow.
The second of the twin cliffs—so you'll see—
is near the first, but it is not as steep;
even an arrow can outreach that peak.
Upon that cliff there grows with ample leaves
a great fig tree. Beneath its boughs Charýbdis 120
sucks up black water. And three times a day
she vomits out the brine, and then three times
she sucks it back ferociously. Don't let
your ship draw near when she is gulping brine;
no one—not even he who makes earth tremble—
could save you then. Hold closer to the cliff
of Scylla: better far to mourn six men
than to lament the loss of all of them.'

"These were her words, and this was my reply:
'Come, tell me: Is there any stratagem, 130
goddess, through which I can escape the grim
Charýbdis, yet ward off the other when
she preys upon my men?'

"These were my words.
The goddess answered quickly: 'Can't you curb
your zeal for torments, war, ordeals—and yield
even to the immortal gods? This Scylla
is not a mortal, but a deathless horror:
atrocious, savage, and invincible.

The one defense against her is retreat.
For if you were to stop at her cliffside 140
to arm yourself, I fear that she would strike
again; again she'd stretch six heads and snatch
another six. Instead, sail straight ahead:
at full speed pass her and beseech Cratǽis,
her mother—she who, giving birth to Scylla,
brought men calamity. Cratǽis will
prevent her reaching out to prey again.
And then you'll reach the island of Thrinácia:[99]
there, Hélios' many cows and plump flocks graze;
for he has seven herds of cattle, seven 150
fair flocks of sheep—and each has fifty beasts.
They never do give birth and never die.
Their guards are Phaëthúsa and Lampétië,
the fair-haired nymphs whom bright Neǽra bore
to Hélios Hypérion. And after
she'd given birth and reared them both, their mother
sent them to the fair island of Thrinácia,
to watch their father's sheep and curved-horn cows.
If you leave his rich herds untouched and turn
your mind to going home, then you can still 160
reach Ithaca, though after dour ordeals.
And even if your solitary self
escapes, your coming home will be delayed
and sad: you will have lost all your shipmates.'

"So Círcë spoke. Upon the throne of gold,
Dawn came straightway. Then Círcë left the beach.
At that, I hurried to my ship and ordered
my comrades to embark and loose the hawsers.
They came aboard at once. The fair-haired Círcë,
the awesome goddess with a human voice, 170
sent forth a friend who favored us, a wind
that swelled our sail and spurred our ship's dark prow.
Once we'd secured our gear, we settled down;
the wind and helmsman kept us on our course.
With an uneasy heart, I told my men:

" 'The prophecies of Círcë are not meant
for one or two of us; they must be shared,
my friends: beforehand, know we may meet death
or may, escaping destiny, be spared.
Above all, Círcë urges us to flee 180
the song of the beguiling Sirens and
their flowered meadow. I alone—she says—
may hear their voices. Tie me then hard fast—
use knots I can't undo. I'll stand erect,
feet on the socket of the mast; and let

[99] Sicily.

the rope ends coil around the shaft itself;
and if I plead with you to set me free,
add still more ropes and knots most carefully.'

"So did I tell my crew all we might meet.
Meanwhile the stout ship, stirred by a fair breeze, 190
had reached the Sirens' island. Then the wind
fell off: a god had lulled the waves to sleep.
The calm was now complete. My crew stood up
and furled the sail and stowed it in the hold.
That done, they sat along the thwarts and beat
the water white with polished oars of fir.
But I, with my sharp blade, cut into bits
a great round cake of wax; I kneaded these
with my stout hands. The wax grew soft, gave way
before my force and Hélios' warm rays. 200
I sealed the ears of all my crew in turn.
That done, they bound my hands and feet, as I
stood upright on the mast box; and they tied
the ropes hard fast around the mast. They sat
and beat the gray sea with their oars. But once
we'd come in hailing distance of the Sirens,
though we were moving rapidly, they noticed
our swift ship and intoned their lucid song:

" 'Remarkable Odysseus, halt and hear
the song we two sing out: Achæan chief, 210
the gift our voices give is honey-sweet.
No man has passed our isle in his black ship
until he's heard the sweet song from our lips;
and when he leaves, the listener has received
delight and knowledge of so many things.
We know the Argives' and the Trojans' griefs:
their tribulations on the plain of Troy
because the gods had willed it so. We know
all things that come to pass on fruitful earth.'

"So did they chant with their entrancing voice. 220
My heart longed so to listen, and I asked
my men to set me free—it was my eyes
that signaled. But intent upon their oars,
they rowed ahead. Yet two of them were quick
to stand: Eurýlochus and Perimédës
bound me with more—and even tighter—bonds.
But when we'd passed beyond the Sirens' isle
and could no longer hear their voices chant,
my faithful men at once removed the wax
that shut their ears. They freed me from the mast. 230

"When we had left behind that isle, straightway
I sighted smoke and a disastrous wave
and heard a roar. My shipmates cringed; the oars
flew from their grip and dangled in the surge;

my mates had empty hands; the ship was stalled.
I went about the deck and spurred them all
with gentle words, approaching each in turn:

" 'Dear friends, we've had our share of trials and tests;
and what has happened now is hardly worse
than when the Cyclops, with his brutal force, 240
imprisoned us in his deep cave; and just
as then my courage, stratagems, good sense
allowed us to escape, I know that we
will now survive and store in memory
these dangers, too. Come, follow what I say.
Retrieve your oars; despite the seething surge,
stay at the thwarts and strike the sea, for Zeus
may set us free, may let us flee this curse.
And you, the helmsman—since our hollow ship
depends upon your grip—remember this: 250
Steer clear of smoke and fire; hug the cliff
that looms along this side, lest she swerve off
and crash, full force, against the facing rocks.'

"These were my words. My men did not delay.
Of Scylla I said nothing—after all,
we had no chance against her—lest my friends,
held fast by fear, desert their oars and cringe
down in the hold. At that point I forgot
the stern command of Círcë: I was not—
so she had said—to arm myself. Instead, 260
I put on my famed armor and advanced,
a long lance in each hand, to the foredeck:
from there I thought I'd first catch sight of Scylla
among the rocks, intent on killing us.
But though I peered and pored, my face bent toward
the misty cliff, my eyes grew weary—I
could not catch sight of her. We rowed, we wailed,
we sailed on up the strait. Along one side
lay Scylla; on the other side, divine
Charýbdis now was swallowing the brine. 270
And when she spewed it out again, she seethed
and swirled—a whirlpool—like a caldron set
above some holocaust; on high the spray
rained down upon the summits of the cliffs.
But when Charýbdis gulped the salty sea,
one saw her at the whirlpool's base, in frenzy;
her cliff roared terrifyingly; beneath
the sea, the earth's black sand lay bare; pale fear
held fast my crew; we feared the end and glued
our eyes upon Charýbdis. But just then, 280
Scylla seized six—the strongest—of my men;
she snatched them from the hollow ship; and when
I turned my eyes aside to seek my friends,
all I could see were feet and hands on high.
They called my name aloud for the last time

and shrieked in anguish. As a fisherman
who, from a jutting rock, has cast his bits
of food as bait to snare small fish, lets down
into the sea his long rod tipped with horn,
and when he's made a catch will whip it back— 290
writhing; so were my men whirled through the air,
writhing, against the rocks. There, at the door
to her deep cavern, Scylla swallowed them
as, in their horrid struggle, my dear friends
stretched out to me their hands—the saddest sight
my eyes have ever seen in all that I
have suffered in my journeys on the sea.

"Once we'd escaped the cliffs of fierce Charýbdis
and Scylla, we sped on. Soon we had reached
the sun-god's lovely island: there he kept 300
his broad-browed cows and well-fed flocks of sheep.
Still out at sea, I heard those bleating sheep
and heard the cattle lowing as they reached
their stalls. And I recalled to mind the words
of that blind seer, Tirésias of Thebes,
and of Aeǽan Círcë, who had warned me
again, again, to shun the isle of him
who brings delight to mortals, Hélios.
With an uneasy heart, I told my men:

" 'Friends, though your trials are harsh, hear what I say. 310
I must tell you Tirésias' prophecies
and those of the Aeǽan Círcë: they
warned me repeatedly to shun the land
of Hélios, who brings delight to men.
She said that here disaster waits for us.
No, row our black ship back; don't near this coast.'

"They heard what I had urged. Their dear hearts broke.
Eurýlochus replied with hateful words:
'Odysseus, your demands are merciless;
no man can match your courage, and your strength 320
will not relent. You surely must be made
of iron if you do not let your friends—
worn-out, in need of sleep—set foot ashore,
where, on this seagirt land, we might once more
prepare a proper meal. You'd have us row
to nowhere through the swift night, men astray,
far from this island, on the shadowed sea.
At night malicious winds will rise—the kind
that batter ships. How can we flee the steep
descent to death if frenzied winds attack: 330
Notus or raging Zephyr—which, despite
the will of sovereign gods, can wreck a ship?
The night is far too dark: let us submit,
prepare our meal, and rest along the beach.

As soon as Dawn has come, we'll board again
and then row out and toward the open sea.'

"These were his words, and all the rest agreed.
Then I was sure that some dark god had schemed
disaster. And I countered with winged words:

" 'Eurýlochus, I'm one against too many: 340
I am outmanned. But all of you must swear
a binding oath: If we should chance to see
a herd of cattle or a flock of sheep,
no one—through wanton arrogance—must kill
a single beast: you are to eat in peace
the food that we received from deathless Círcë.'

"These were my words. As I had urged, they vowed
at once; that done, we anchored our staunch ship
within a sheltered bay, close to a spring
that had fresh water for us. Once ashore, 350
my men had soon prepared a skillful supper.
Then, with our need for food and drink appeased,
my friends began to weep, remembering
their dear companions Scylla had devoured.
And sweet sleep came upon them as they wept.
We reached the night's last watch, when stars turn course;
then Zeus, the gatherer of clouds, provoked
a terrifying tempest: storm clouds wrapped
both sea and land; night hurtled down from heaven.

"As soon as Dawn's rose fingers touched the sky, 360
we drew our ship into a sheltered place,
a grotto at the harbor's base—a cave
with seats for nymphs and ample dancing-space.
My shipmates gathered round me, and I said:

" 'Friends, we have food and drink in our swift ship;
then, lest we meet disaster, do not touch
the cattle. They belong to a dread god,
to Hélios, who sees and hears all things.'

"These were my words. And their proud hearts agreed.
But then winds raged—they swept from south and east. 370
First, Notus, for a full month, without let;
then Eurus, too, attacked. Throughout that stretch,
with food and wine still theirs, my comrades left
the herds untouched; they did not wish for death.
But when we'd reached the end of all our stores,
my men were forced to prey along the shores.
Yet while they sought with curving hooks to snare
fish, birds, and anything that chance might bring—
such hunger gnawed their bellies—I instead

went inland; for I wanted most to pray 380
unto the gods, in hope that one of them
might offer me some stratagem. And when,
deeper inland, I'd left behind my friends
and found a place well shielded from the wind,
I washed my hands and called on all the gods
who hold Olympus as their home. But I
heard no reply. They cast sleep on my eyes.

"Meanwhile Eurýlochus provoked my men,
and what he offered was a fatal plan:

'Friends, though your trials are harsh, hear what I say. 390
All deaths are dour; the fate of men is sad;
but there's no death more miserable than
the doom starvation sends. Come, let us take
Hypérion's best cows and sacrifice
to the undying gods, who rule the skies.
If we reach Ithaca, our fathers' land,
there we—at once—shall build for Hélios
an altar heaped with many glowing gifts.
And if our taking of his tall-horned cows
enrages Hélios, and he would wreck 400
our ship and has the other gods' consent,
I'd rather have my mouth drink brine and let
the waves kill me at once than meet slow death
by lingering on an island wilderness.'

"So did he speak, and all the rest agreed.
At once they chose the sun-god's finest cattle:
just then, those broad-browed cows with curving horns
were grazing near the dark-prowed ship; my men
surrounded them and prayed unto the gods;
since we, on board our ship, had no white barley, 410
they plucked the green leaves of a tall oak tree—
over their offering, they'd scatter these.
After they'd prayed and cut the throats and flayed
the cows, they sliced the thighs in chunks and laid
a double layer of fat across those chunks,
then spread raw flesh on top. They had no wine
to splash across the blazing sacrifice
but, using water for libations, roasted
all of the vitals on the fire. And when
the thighs were scorched and they had tasted all 420
the inner parts, they set the rest on spits.

"But now sweet sleep had left my eyes, and I
walked back to the swift ship at the seaside;
and when my steps drew close to our trim craft,
I smelled the pungent fragrance of hot fat.
I groaned, then called upon the deathless gods:

"'You, father Zeus, and all the other blessed,
undying gods, you sent this wretchedness;
it's you who left me prey to senseless sleep;
you gulled me; I am ruined; now my men, 430
awaiting me, contrived this horrid plan.'

"Meanwhile Lampétiē, the long-robed nymph,
had hurried off to tell lord Hélios
that we had killed his cows. Without delay,
before his fellow gods, he cried, enraged:

"'You, father Zeus, and all the other blessed
and deathless gods—you now must take revenge:
destroy the comrades of Laértēs' son,
Odysseus; in their insolence they killed
the herds that I beheld with such delight 440
both when I climbed the starry sky and when
I wheeled and then returned to earth again.
If they're not made to pay a penalty
to match their sin, I shall descend to Hades
and shine among the dead.'

"In turn, Zeus said:
'Shine, Hélios, with light for the immortals;
and lighten, too, the lives of those who die
on earth, the giver of the gift of grain.
As for those sinners, I'll soon strike their ship
with blazing lightning—tearing her to bits 450
upon the winedark sea.'

"I heard all this
from the fair-haired Calypso after she
had heard it from the messenger Hermes.

"I reached the ship and shore and—one by one—
denounced my men. But nothing could be done—
the herds lay dead. And soon the gods sent portents:
the flayed hides crawled along the ground; the flesh
upon the spits, both roast and raw, began
to bellow; we heard sounds of lowing cows.

"My faithful comrades feasted for six days 460
upon the finest beasts of Hélios.
But when Zeus, son of Cronos, brought to us
the seventh day, no longer fury-fed,
the wind died down. We boarded quickly, stepped
our mast and spread our sail, then drove ahead—
out toward the open sea.

"When we had left
that isle behind and saw no other land,

only the sky and sea, the son of Cronos
set a black cloud above our hollow ship;
below us waves grew dark. By now our run 470
was doomed; the howling Zephyr fell upon
our course; a wind amok, its fury cracked
the forestays of the mast. The mast fell back;
the sail and all the rigging crashed, collapsed
into the bilge. And at the stern, the mast
hit hard the helmsman's head; it crushed his skull;
and like a diver, from the deck he plunged
headlong; his sturdy spirit left his bones.
Zeus thundered as he hurled a lightning bolt.
He hit the hull: it filled with sulfurous smoke; 480
our ship whirled round full circle. All my men
pitched overboard; like sea crows they were borne
by waves around our black-bowed craft. A god
deprived them of the day of their return.

"I paced the ship until a comber ripped
the keel and hull apart. The naked keel
was carried by the surge, which also snapped
the mast off from the hulk—but it still had
a backstay made of oxhide. This I grabbed.
That rope in hand, I lashed the keel and mast 490
together; hugging them, I then was driven
by the malicious winds. And after Zephyr
had slacked his storm's wild force, Notus at once
brought back the fear that I had known; for now
I'd have to cross Charýbdis once again.

"All through the night that wind did not relent.
The sun was rising when I spied the cliffs
of Scylla and the murderous Charýbdis,
who sucked in the salt waters of the sea;
she drew my mast and keel into her deeps. 500
But reaching up and toward the great fig tree,
I gripped it, clinging to it like a bat.
Yet I could find no foothold, could not climb
that tree, because its roots stretched far below;
nor could I ever reach its long, broad boughs—
so high, they wrapped Charýbdis in their shade.
I gripped that trunk; I would not yield until
she vomited again the mast and keel.
I waited long; at last they came. Just when
an elder who is called upon to judge 510
between the claims of young contenders, stands
and says the time for judgment's at an end
and leaves the marketplace to dine, so then—
such was the hour—Charýbdis spewed the mast
and keel. My hands and feet let go the trunk;
I fell into the water with a splash
next to the keel and mast; I mounted them;

and, with that vantage, soon my arms began
to row. The father of both gods and men
did not let Scylla's eyes spy me again. 520

"For nine days I was dragged; and on the tenth
the gods cast me upon Ogýgia's coast,
the island home of lovely-haired Calypso,
the awesome goddess with a human voice,
who took me in and tended me. But why
do I retell this now? Just yesterday,
within this hall, I told that tale to you
and to your noble wife. I do not hold
with telling over what has been well told."

BOOK 19
[Preparations and Eurycleia's Discovery]

[In Book 13, the Phaeácians transport Odysseus with many gifts to Ithaca. After Athena, in disguise, tells Odysseus that he is in Ithaca, he makes up a story about his identity. Athena disguises Odysseus as a vagabond, who then sets out to test the loyalties of his friends before confronting the suitors. In Book 14, Odysseus visits first Eumaéus the loyal swineherd, who believes that Odysseus is dead. Odysseus creates stories for Eumaéus and tests his hospitality. In Book 15, Athena summons Telémachus from Sparta, warning him about a potential ambush. Eumaéus provides Odysseus with information about Laértës, his father, and Anticleia, his dead mother. Eumaéus tells his life story. In Book 16, Telémachus arrives at Eumaéus' hut. After a first meeting between father and son, Athena tells Odysseus it is time to introduce himself to his son. After convincing Telémachus of his identity, Odysseus begins to make plans for confronting the suitors. In Book 17, Telémachus visits his mother in the palace. The seer Theoclýmenus declares that Odysseus is in Ithaca. Disguised, Odysseus walks to town and is insulted by Melánthius the goatherd. At the palace Odysseus' old dog, Argus, recognizes him and then dies. Antínoüs, one of the suitors, throws a stool at Odysseus. Penelope sends a message through Eumaéus requesting a conversation with the stranger. In Book 18, a fight is provoked between Odysseus and the beggar Irus, whose jaw is broken by Odysseus. The suitors now welcome Odysseus, still disguised. Athena makes Penelope very beautiful for a visit with the suitors. Odysseus is taunted by Eurýmachus, one of the suitors, who throws a stool at Odysseus; Odysseus responds to Eurýmachus by saying he would like Odysseus to return home. Telémachus tells the suitors to go home. –ED.]

Odysseus stayed behind within the hall,
devising—with Athena—ways to kill
the suitors. Soon his winged words spurred his son:

"Telémachus, it's time to take all arms
of war out of this hall: store them inside.
And if the suitors miss those arms and ask
why they were taken, use this soft reply:
'I've had to place them out of reach of smoke;
the breath of fire has fouled with soot and grime
the look they had when they were left behind— 10
when, long ago, Odysseus left for Troy.
And, too, I had this greater fear (a god
had warned me): Wine incites. If brawls break out

when you are drunk, you might draw blood—and thus
drag feasts and courting rites into the dust.
For iron of itself can tempt a man.' "

He heard what his dear father urged; at once
Telémachus obeyed: he called his nurse;
when Eurycleīa came, these were his words:

"Nurse, come now, keep the women in their rooms 20
until I've laid away my father's arms
within the storeroom, out of reach of soot.
For many years these weapons were neglected:
he left when I was still a child; his arms
have lost their luster in the grime and fumes
of hearth fires in this hall."

The dear nurse answered:
"My child, would that your mind were set at last
on caring for this house and all it has!
But come, someone must light the way for you—
a thing you'll hardly ask the maids to do." 30

Telémachus' reply was tactful, wise:
"This stranger here can serve for that: a man
who gets his daily quart of grain from me
must earn it, though he comes from far-off lands."

These were his words, but hers were left unwinged.
The two—Odysseus and his noble son—
sprang up to gather helmets, shields embossed,
and spears with beech-wood shafts. Then they went off;
Athena lit the way. She held up high
a golden lamp: she shed entrancing light. 40

At that, Telémachus cried suddenly:
"My eyes, dear father, see a prodigy:
the walls, the handsome panels, fir crossbeams,
the towering pillars are so bright—they seem
as if they had been lit by blazing flames.
Some god—of those who rule high heaven—must
have come to us."

Odysseus stopped his son:
"Be silent; curb your thoughts; do not ask questions.
This is the work of the Olympians.
Go, take your rest; I'll stay behind to find 50
just what your mother and her women think:
in tears, she'll have me tell her everything."

These were his words. As blazing torches lit
his way across the hall, Telémachus
went to the room where he had often found

the solace of sweet sleep. There he lay down,
awaiting Dawn's firstlight. But bright Odysseus
stayed in the hall, where, with Athena's help,
he schemed the suitors' day of reckoning.

Down from her room came wise Penelope— 60
like Ártemis or golden Aphrodítë.
Her women set her customary chair—
inlaid with silvered loops of ivory—
beside the fire. Icmálius' skill and craft
long years ago had built it and attached—
to form one piece—a footrest underneath;
and over this they threw an ample fleece.
That chair now served Penelope as seat.
Her white-armed women cleared away the feast,
the rich leftovers and the stained wine cups 70
from which the overbearing lords had drunk.
They cleared the braziers, raking dying coals
onto the floor, and now, for light and warmth,
piled high fresh wood. But once again Odysseus
had to endure Melántho's coarse abuse:

"Stranger, night through, must we still suffer you?
Will you roam through this house and ogle women?
Be off, you oaf; be glad you've grabbed a meal—
or else we'll fling a torch to clear you out."

Odysseus, man of many wiles, just scowled: 80
"Poor thing, why are you sick with scorn and spite?
Because I'm filthy or am dressed in rags
and beg throughout the town? This is the fate
that vagabonds and beggars can't escape.
I, too, once lived—a rich man—in my house
of wealth, where wanderers received my help
for any need, whoever they might be.
My slaves could not be counted; and I had
all other things with which a man is blessed
and said to be most prosperous. But Zeus, 90
the son of Cronos, ended all of that:
such was his wish. Thus, woman, do beware,
lest you in turn lose all the pride of place
that lets you lord it over other slaves.
Your mistress might yet turn and spurn you, or
Odysseus might return—there's hope of that.
And even if he's dead and won't come back,
by now his son is like Odysseus' self:
Telémachus, Apollo's favorite.
If any of the women in this house 100
gives way to wantonness, he'll notice it:
he's not the child he was."

These were his words—
and wise Penelope rebuked her maid:

"Arrogant slut, I am not ignorant
of your indecency—for which you'll pay.[100]
You knew what I desired; you'd heard me say
that I was always anxious, much in need
of talking to this foreigner, to glean
some word about my husband."

So she spoke,

then told the old housewife, Eurýnomë: 110
"Set out a chair and cover it with fleece
so that this stranger, seated here, can speak
and hear me out: I need to question him."

That said, Eurýnomë was quick to bring
a polished chair and cover it with fleece:
it served as patient, bright Odysseus' seat.
The first to speak was wise Penelope:
"Stranger, I must begin by asking this:
Who are you? What's your family, your city?"

Odysseus, man of many wiles, replied: 120
"Woman, no mortal on the boundless earth
could find a fault or flaw in you; your fame
ascends to heaven's heights, as does the name
a blameless king can claim: a righteous lord
who governs mighty men, who fears the gods;
he's bent on justice, and his land's black soil
is rich with wheat and barley; all the trees
are fruitful, flocks are always fertile, seas
bring fish as bounty—such prosperity
blesses his people, since he governs well. 130
So ask me—in your halls—about all else,
but not about my land and family;
recalling them my heart would fill with grief:
I've suffered many trials. It is not just
to moan and weep within another's house;
unending talk of sorrow only brings
more pain; I'd not have you or your handmaids
so vexed that you would scorn me as a man
awash with tears—his mind weighed down by wine."

This was the wise Penelope's reply: 140
"Stranger, my form and grace are gone—undone
by the immortals on the day my husband,
Odysseus, and the Argives sailed to Troy.
But were he to return, to watch with care
my life, my fame would surely be more fair
and more widespread; instead I live in grief—

[100]Melántho's affair with Eurýmachus put her in league with the suitors.

in sorrow that some god inflicts on me.
For all the lords who rule these isles—from Samos,
Dulíchium, and forest-clad Zacýnthus,
and even sunlit Ithaca itself— 150
want me, against my will, as wife: these men
lay waste my house. So I distrust all strangers
and suppliants and even hold at bay
all heralds, men who ply a public trade:
my heart is sunk in sorrow as I think
of my Odysseus. While the suitors seek
a wedding, I weave schemes. At the beginning,
within my room I set a spacious loom.
The web was wide, the threads were fine, and I
assured them all–unhesitatingly: 160
'Young men, since bright Odysseus now is dead,
be patient; though you're keen to marry me,
wait till this cloth is done, so that no thread
unravels. This is lord Laértës' shroud—
the robe he'll wear when dark death strikes him down.
I weave it now, lest some Achæan women
condemn me for neglect, for having let
a man who'd won such wealth lie at his death
without a shroud.' These were my words; and they,
with manly hearts, agreed. So I would weave 170
that mighty web by day; but then by night,
by torchlight, I undid what I had done.
I hoodwinked all of them for three long years;
but when, as spring returned, the fourth was here,
some of my shameless bitches, well aware
of all my stratagems, revealed the plot.
The suitors caught me in the act, just as
I was unraveling my lovely cloth.
I had no choice but to complete my work.
Now I cannot escape my wedding: I 180
can call upon no other stratagem.
My parents pressure me to take a husband:
my son despairs as men devour his goods;
he understands—by now he is a man
most fit to guard his house, a man to whom
Zeus gives much wealth. But though my state is sad,
tell me what is your land, your family:
you surely were not born of stone or trees—
the sort of thing of which old fables sing."

This was the man-of-many-wiles' reply: 190
"O woman cherished by Laértës' son,
Odysseus, you keep after me with questions
about my family. Well then, I'll answer—
though you will only make my sorrows harsher:
such is the rule of grief for men kept far
from their own land for many years, who are
like me—the prey of long adversity,

a wanderer through many mortals' cities.
So be it. I shall set your mind at rest.

"Along the winedark sea, by water ringed, 200
there lies a land both fair and fertile: Crete,
the home of countless men, of ninety cities.
Some speak in one, some in another fashion—
an isle of mingled tongues. There are Achæans
and—men most generous—the native Cretans,
Cydónians, three tribes of Dórians,
and fine Pelásgians.[101] Their greatest city
is Cnóssus;[102] there for nine years Minos ruled:
he had the confidence of mighty Zeus
and was the father of my father, good 210
Deucálion, who had as sons both me
and Prince Idómeneus. In his curved ship,
together with the sons of Átreus,
Idómeneus sailed off to Ílion.
My famous name is Æthon. I'm the younger;
my brother was the elder and the stronger.
I saw Odysseus there; he was my guest;
for as he made for Troy a great wind forced
your husband off his course, beyond Maléa;
and he, too, came to Crete. His fleet laid anchor 220
in the rough waters of Amnísus' harbor,
where Ēilēīthȳía's cavern stands;[103] at last—
but barely—he'd escaped a tempest's path.
He went up to the city and at once
sought out Idómeneus; he said that they
were friends, that he had been my brother's host.
But since the day my older brother left
for Troy, he had already seen his tenth
or his eleventh dawn. So it was I
who led Odysseus to my house, a guest 230
to whom I offered every care and kindness.
And to his followers, from public stores
I offered barley and dark wine and bulls
for sacrifice—to satisfy them all.
The good Achæans stayed twelve days in Crete,
penned in by mighty Bóreäs: his gusts
must have been stirred by some ferocious god—
even on land, no man could stand their force.
But on the thirteenth day, he stopped. They left."

So, telling many lies, he mimed the truth. 240
She, hearing him, shed tears that bathed her cheeks.
Just as snows melt upon the steepest peaks—

[101] Cydónians, Dórians, and Pelásgians represent the migrations of various peoples into the Greek peninsula.

[102] Cnóssus was the great palace of King Minos and the cultural center of the Minoan civilization.

[103] The goddess of childbirth had a shrine at Amnísus, on the coast near Cnóssus.

the snows the west wind heaped and south wind frees—
and with the melting snows, the rivers swell;
so did her lovely cheeks melt as she wept,
lamenting for her husband—he who sat
beside her. Though his heart felt pity for
his grieving wife, Odysseus' eyes held fast,
like horn or iron, staring, motionless,
beneath his brows; astute—he did not weep. 250

Then, with her need to moan and weep appeased,
again she spoke: "Consider carefully,
stranger; I mean to test you now, to see
if what you tell is true, if you indeed
welcomed my husband and his men to Crete
in your own house: tell me what clothes he wore
and how he seemed and who his comrades were."

Odysseus, man of many wiles, replied:
"Lady, how hard it is to speak when I
have been so distant for so long a time; 260
for this year is the twentieth since I
sailed off and left my native land behind.
But I shall tell you what my heart recalls.
The bright Odysseus wore a purple cloak
of wool with double folds; its brooch was gold
and had two clasps. The brooch displayed a hound
that held a speckled stag in his forepaws
and watched his writhing prey. All were amazed
to see how, though in gold, the hound that choked
the stag stared hard and how his victim pawed 270
the air in vain, to flee. I also saw
his tunic, which around his body glowed
like some dry onion skin; it was so thin,
so fragile—like the sun itself it shone.
And many women marveled at his clothes.
Yet you had better keep this, too, in mind:
I do not know if when he left your home
Odysseus was already dressed like this
or if he got these clothes much later, gifts
from one of the companions on his ship 280
or from some gracious guest, for he was friend
to many; the Achæans had few men
to match Odysseus. I myself gave him
a sword of bronze, a handsome purple cloak
with double folds, a tunic that was fringed,
and, to his ship, with every honor, then
escorted your Odysseus. There, behind him,
a herald followed, somewhat older than
your husband. And I can describe him, too.
He had hunched shoulders, curly hair, dark skin. 290
His name: Eurýbatës. Odysseus showed
respect for him beyond the measure known

by any other of his men, because
this herald's thoughts were like Odysseus' own."

These were the words she heard; her tears were stirred;
the signs Odysseus had revealed were sure.
But with her need to weep and grieve appeased,
Penelope again began to speak:

"Now, stranger, you who've been so wretched here
will be an honored presence, one held dear 300
within my house. The clothes of which you speak
are things that I myself had given him,
folded and taken from the room we share;
to these I'd added on the glowing brooch—
a fond adornment for him. But I can
not hope to see him in these halls again,
returned to his own house and dearest land.
So, on his hollow ship, black destiny
sent my Odysseus off, that he might see
the land of malediction, Troy-the-ugly." 310

Odysseus, man of many wiles, replied:
"O woman whom Laértēs' son, Odysseus,
has honored, do not mar your loveliness
or sap your spirit with unending sadness,
with tears for your dear husband. I indeed
don't blame you: anyone who's lost a man
with whom, at one in love, she had a child,
would mourn him, even if he could not match
Odysseus, who—they say—was like the gods.
But stop your tears and hear what I now say. 320
Without deceit, concealing nothing, I
must tell you that I have already heard
about Odysseus coming home; I learned
in the Thesprótians' rich land—so close
to Ithaca—that he is still alive
and that he'll bring back many precious things
he's gathered in that land. His faithful men
and hollow ship, upon the winedark sea,
while crossing from Thrinácia, were lost—
he'd roused the wrath of Zeus and Hélios, 330
whose herds his men had slaughtered. They all died
along rough seas. And he alone survived,
left clinging to the keel of his wrecked ship;
a comber cast him on the coast of men
who claim the gods as kin: Phaeácians.
They honored him as if he were a god;
they gave him many gifts and would have brought
your brave Odysseus home as his escort.
Indeed he'd have been back by now, but he
decided he'd gain more by gathering 340
much wealth while wandering through many lands.

Odysseus knows so many stratagems:
no other man can match his cunning plans.
Now Phēidon, king of the Thesprótians,
told me and—as he poured libations—swore
that ship and crew stood ready to escort
Odysseus home; but I left first—by chance
a ship was sailing to Dulíchium,
land rich in wheat. Before I went aboard,
King Phēidon showed me all the precious hoard 350
Odysseus had amassed: indeed your lord
had stored enough rich goods in the king's hold
to serve ten generations of his line.
The king said that Odysseus now had gone
to hear Dodóna's oracle, the tall
and sacred oak that speaks the will of Zeus;
and after he came back, Odysseus meant
to sail to Ithaca, his own dear land,
returning in the open or by stealth.
Thus he is safe, and he is soon to come: 360
he'll not delay return to his dear ones,
his fathers' land: for you, I'll swear to this.
May Zeus, the greatest god, be my first witness,
just as I call upon the cordial hearth
of good Odysseus as my witness now:
all is to happen just as I avow;
Odysseus will return within the year—
just when, at old moon's end, the new begins."

This was the wise Penelope's reply:
"I would your words might be fulfilled. My guest, 370
you'd see my kindness then—so many gifts
that any man you met would say you're blessed.
Yet this is what my soul foresees—and this
is what shall be: Odysseus won't return,
and you will get no ship to see you home;
for in this house there are no masters now
to match Odysseus—most hospitable
of men, whose cordial welcomes and farewells,
as surely as he lived, graced honored guests.
But now, my women, wash this stranger's feet; 380
prepare his bed with blankets of bright fleece
and cloaks to keep him warm until he meets
Dawn on her throne of gold. Then early on
tomorrow bathe him and anoint him, so
that he can sit beside Telémachus
in the great hall and think of banqueting.
And any of those men who would oppress
the soul of this man act in vain: their wrath
and blustering are empty things. Dear guest,
how can you judge my keenness and good sense 390
and see how I indeed surpass the rest
of womankind if you are dressed in rags
when you sit down to meals within these halls?

The days of men are brief. For one who is
malign, whose mind is harsh, all mortals wish
that he be cursed with sorrow while he lives;
and once he's died, all men despise his name.
But he whose heart and acts are kind finds fame
among all men, a name borne far and wide
by strangers—many call him excellent." 400

Odysseus, man of many wiles, replied:
"O woman honored by Laértēs' son,
Odysseus, I've indeed disliked bright fleece
and blankets since I left the snowcapped peaks
of Crete and made my way across the seas
in long-oared boats. No, I prefer to lie
as I have often lain through sleepless nights.
For I, on many nights, have rested on
a battered bed, awaiting Dawn's bright throne.
So, too, there is no need to bathe my feet: 410
my heart would not be pleased if that were done
by any servingwoman in these halls—
unless there is an old and faithful one
whose soul has suffered sorrows like my own;
I would let such a woman touch my feet."

This was the wise Penelope's reply:
"Dear guest, among the foreigners who've come
into this house no one has been as welcome
as you are now: your words show such good sense.
Among my women, one is old and wise: 420
fond nurse of the unfortunate Odysseus,
just after he was born, she took him from
his mother's arms. Though age has left her weak,
it's she who'll bathe your feet. Wise Euryclēia,
come now and wash the feet of one as old
as your own master is: by now perhaps
Odysseus' hands and feet are like our guest's,
for men much tried grow old before their time."

These were her words. At this, the old nurse hid
her face within her hands and shed hot tears, 430
while uttering these words of deep despair:

"I weep for you, my child, but can do nothing;
Zeus hated you above all other men,
although your spirit always feared the gods—
no man has roasted more fat thighs or more
choice hecatombs for Zeus the thunder lord
than you have offered him while praying for
serene old age and time to see your son
grow into glory. But to you alone
has Zeus denied the day of coming home. 440
Stranger, I think that even as you are
derided by these shameless bitches here,

so he, within a distant land, was mocked
by women when he reached some splendid house.
Now you, in order to avoid their taunts
and insults, shun their touch; you do not want
these sluts to bathe you. Wise Penelope,
the daughter of Icárius, has thus
asked me—and I respond most willingly.
I'll wash your feet to please Penelope 450
and you; my soul is stirred by grief and pity.
But hear what I declare: Though many strangers,
sore-tried, have landed here, I say that I
have never seen a man so like Odysseus
as you are—in your form, your voice, your feet."

Odysseus, man of many wiles, replied:
"Old woman, all who've seen the two of us
find we're alike—just as your keen sense must."

That said, the old nurse brought the burnished tub
she'd need to wash his feet; in this she poured 460
cold water first, and then she added warm.
But at his seat, set well back from the hearth,
Odysseus quickly turned; he faced the dark;
he had the sudden fear within his heart
that, touching him, his nurse would note his scar
and so discover who this stranger was.

This was the wound dealt by a boar's white tusk.
Long years ago he'd visited Parnassus.[104]
Autólycus, his mother's noble father,
lived there together with his sons—a man 470
whose cunning oaths and thefts no mortal matched.
It was a god who'd given him such craft—
Hermes himself,[105] for whom Autólycus
would often roast the thighs of kids and lambs;
so he could count on Hermes as a friend.
Now, when he came to Ithaca's rich land,
Autólycus had found a newborn babe,
his daughter's son. And Eurycleīa placed
that child upon his lap; and when the meal
was done, she turned to him:

"Autólycus, 480
do find a name to suit your child's dear child,
the dear grandson for whom you've always longed."

To this Autólycus replied: "The name
I now declare must be the name that you,

---

[104] The mountains rising above Apollo's famous shrine at Delphi.
[105] In addition to performing tasks as messenger god, Hermes was also patron of thieves and trickery.

my son-in-law and daughter, are to use:
Because I come as one who, on his ways
across the fertile earth, has been enraged
by many men and women, let his name
now be Odysseus, 'son of wrath and pain.'[106]
And for my part, I shall not stint when he 490
becomes a man and visits our great house,
the palace of his mother's family,
where I store all my riches, there beneath
Parnassus' peak. I'll see that he receives
fine gifts: he will return to you, content."

And so, to gain such glowing gifts, Odysseus
came to Parnassus and received the warm
words and embraces of Autólycus
and all his sons. Odysseus' mother's mother,
Amphíthëa, hugged him, and she kissed his head 500
and handsome eyes. Autólycus urged on
his noble sons: the time to feast had come.
At once they brought and butchered there a stout
five-year-old ox; they flayed and dressed it, cut
its limbs with skill and skewered it; with care
they roasted it, then gave each man his share.
They feasted till the day was done—and none
was slighted; shares were fair. Then, when the sun
sank down and darkness won, they took their rest;
the gift of sleep was welcome. But as soon 510
as Dawn's rose fingers touched the sky, they left
to hunt: the hounds and all Autólycus'
dear sons and good Odysseus. On the steeps
and slopes of Mount Parnassus, they soon reached
windswept ravines. There, risen from the deep
of Ocean's gliding flow, the sun now beat
upon the fields; the forward trackers reached
a forest glen; along the trail of scent
the hounds advanced; behind the trackers went
Autólycus' fine sons and good Odysseus, 520
who brandished his long lance. Deep in the copse,
a great boar lay—his den so densely hid
that it was proof against the strong, wet wind,
and sun could never pierce it with bright rays;
rain never poured or seeped into that den:
around it, fallen leaves lay high and thick.
Then, as the hunters pressed ahead, the boar
made out the tread of men and dogs; he burst—
his back erect and bristling—from his den;
his eyes ablaze, he stopped at bay before them. 530
Odysseus was the first to make his rush;

[106]By referring to himself as *odyssamenos,* Autólycus is playing with the name *Odysseus,* meaning someone who is angry or wrathful.

eager to kill, he lifted his long lance
with sturdy hands. The boar, too quick, attacked;
he charged aslant; his tusk tore one long gash
above the knee, but left the bone intact.
Odysseus hit; the point of his bright shaft
drove through the boar's right shoulder. With a shriek,
the beast fell back into the dust; his breath
took flight. Autólycus' dear sons bound up
Odysseus' wound with skill; then they intoned 540
a spell to check the flow of his dark blood
and hurried back to their dear father's house.
And there Autólycus and all his sons,
once they had healed Odysseus, gave him such
impressive gifts that, when they saw him off
to his own Ithaca, he went in joy.

At his return, his father and good mother
rejoiced and asked to hear in full the tale
of how he got his wound. He told them all
the truth, how he had joined Autólycus' 550
fine sons on Mount Parnassus; in that hunt,
he had been wounded by a boar's white tusk.

The old nurse[107] held his leg within her palms;
she felt the scar. Touch was enough; she let
his foot fall. When it dropped, the basin's bronze
rang out; the basin tilted; water spilled
upon the ground. Both joy and sorrow filled
her heart; tears filled her eyes; her firm voice choked.
She reached up, touched Odysseus' chin, and sobbed:

"Dear child, you surely are Odysseus, yet 560
I did not recognize you till my hands
had touched the very flesh of my dear lord."

These were her words, and then her eyes turned toward
Penelope; she wanted her to know
that this was her dear husband—here, come home.
That look was lost upon Penelope:
her mistress noticed nothing—she had been
distracted by Athena. And Odysseus
reached for his nurse's throat; with his right hand
he clutched it; with his left he pulled her close, 570
and said:

"Nurse, do you mean to ruin me?
You nursed me at your breast; now after trials
and sorrows, after more than nineteen years,

[107]Nurse Eurycleia ("wide-fame"), daughter of Ops, was bought by Laértës to be Odysseus' nurse, and later became Telémachus' nurse.

I've come back to my land. You've found me out;
a god let you discover me; but keep
this secret to yourself—you must not speak
of this to anyone within these halls,
for if you babble and I then subdue,
with some god's help, these noble suitors, you
can count on this: Though you're my nurse, I shall 580
not spare you when, within this house, I kill
the other servingwomen."

Eurycleīa,
wise nurse, replied: "My child, what words escape
the barrier of your teeth! You know my will—
its strength and stubbornness: I shall be still
as solid stone or iron. But I'll tell
another thing to you—and note it well:
If you, with some god's help, subdue that band,
I'll tell you who among these women here
dishonored you, and who were faultless, true." 590

Odysseus, man of many wiles, replied:
"Nurse, there's no need for you to speak of them;
I'll note and know how each maidservant acts.
Keep silent; let the gods command events."

These were his words. The old nurse left the room
to fetch fresh water for his feet, for all
had spilled. She bathed and then, with ample oil,
she smoothed him down; that done, Odysseus moved
his seat back toward the fire—he wanted warmth;
and with his rags he covered up the scar. 600

Then wise Penelope was first to speak:
"Stranger, there's one slight thing I've still to ask—
a question to be answered briefly, for
the hour of gentle rest will soon be here,
at least for those who can, despite their cares,
receive sweet sleep. But, given by a god,
my sorrow has no bounds: by day I find
release in grief and mourning as I tend
to household tasks, my women's work, my own;
but when night falls and sleep takes all, I lie 610
upon my bed with my afflicted heart,
besieged by tears so stubborn and so sharp
that, even as I mourn, tear me apart.
Just as the daughter of Pandáreüs,[108]

[108] The daughter of Pandáreüs, who was married to Zéthus, intended to kill one of Niobe's sons but killed her own son, Ítylus, by mistake. Turned into a nightingale by Zeus, she mourned this deed through the nightingale's song.

the nightingale of the greenwood, while perched
among the clustered leaves when spring returns,
sings sweetly, often varying her song
with shifting accents as she mourns her son,
her Ítylus, lord Zéthus' child, whom she
in madness—long ago—had killed with bronze; 620
so does my soul shift, thrust, now here, now there,
not knowing whether I should stay beside
my son and keep all things intact—my goods,
my servingwomen, and this high-roofed house—
and so respect both my dear husband's bed
and what our people want, or if I should
not wed that man who proves to be the best
of the Achǽans, one who, wooing me
within this house, would offer countless gifts.
My son, as long as he was still a child— 630
too young to judge with sense—held that I must
not marry, not desert my husband's house.
But now that he is grown, a man in full,
appalled as the Achǽans waste his wealth,
he even prays that I may leave these halls.

"But come now, hear the dream that I have dreamt
and tell me what it means. We always keep
some twenty geese: I love to watch them feed—
here, at our water trough, they peck at wheat.
But in my dream, down from the mountain peak 640
a giant eagle swooped with crooked beak;
he broke the necks of all; I saw them heaped
within this hall. My twenty geese had died—
and he flew off into the glowing sky.
Still in my dream, I wept and wailed. Meanwhile
Achǽan women, all with lovely hair,
surrounded me as I mourned bitterly
the eagle's slaughtering my geese. But he
flew back and perched upon the jutting eaves;
from there, with mortal voice, he checked my grief: 650
'Daughter of great Icárius, take heart;
this is no dream but something you have seen
with eyes awake—foretelling what will be.
The geese are those who woo you; just as I,
who was the eagle, am your husband now,
come home again, about to strike the crowd
of suitors with dark death.' These were his words.
Freed from sweet sleep, I looked about and saw
my geese within the halls, still feeding from
their trough—just as those geese have always done." 660

Odysseus, man of many wiles, replied:
"Lady, you cannot thrust this dream aside:
Odysseus' very self made plain its sense,
disclosing what, in truth, will come to pass.

The suitors' doom is plain—for all to see;
none can escape that death, that destiny."

This was the wise Penelope's reply:
"Dear guest, dreams are ambiguous and sly—
not all that men may see in them will be.
There are two gates of disembodied dreams: 670
the gate of horn and gate of ivory.
Those dreams that reach us through carved ivory
bring words that damage us, for they delude;
they promise, but they never will fulfill.
But dreams that take the gate of polished horn,
when they are seen by mortals, do foretell
what is in truth to come. Yet my strange dream
did not—I think—come through the gate of horn;
for if it had, it would have made my son
and me rejoice. But there is something else 680
which I must tell you now—and mark it well.
I hate the day that soon will dawn—the day
that will divide me from Odysseus' house.
For I today will call a test to try
the prowess of the suitors: I'll align
the axheads that Odysseus used to set—
all twelve of them—like wedges for a ship;
then, from far off, with just one shaft, he'd shoot
through all the socket hollows. And this test
will try the suitors' craft: the man most deft, 690
whose hands can string the bow, then shoot through all
those axheads with one arrow[109]—he will be
the one with whom I'll go, abandoning
the house in which I led my wedded life—
these halls so fair, so filled with treasures, halls
that I'll remember, even in my dreams."

Odysseus, man of many wiles, replied:
"O lady honored by Laértës' son,
Odysseus, don't delay this competition
within these halls. The man of many wiles 700
will have returned before these men have strung
the polished bow and shot a shaft through iron."

This was the wise Penelope's reply:
"Stranger, would you, consoling me, might sit
beside me in these halls—were that your wish,
sleep never would descend upon my lids.
Yet mortals cannot be forever sleepless;
upon all things, the deathless ones set limits
for those who dwell on earth, giver of grain.

[109]Depending on the design of the axes, a number of theories have arisen to explain how this archery contest was performed. This translation suggests that the ax handles are missing and that the empty sockets of axheads are lined up.

So now I want to go back to my rooms, 710
to lie upon my bed of sorrow, stained
with tears since dear Odysseus left to see
Ill-Ílion, abominable country,
best left unnamed. I'll lie within my room;
you rest within this hall—upon the floor,
where you can lay your bedding out, or else
upon a bed my maids will quickly fetch."

That said, she made her way to her fine rooms,
but not alone: her women went along.
There she began to weep for her dear husband; 720
she wept for her Odysseus till gray-eyed
Athena shed sweet sleep upon her lids.

BOOK 21
[The Contest with the Bow]

[In Book 20, Odysseus plans his attack on the suitors and hears the laughter of the suitors' mistresses. In the morning, the cattleman Philoétius sympathizes with Odysseus' appearance. At a feast, Telémachus stands up to the suitors, who grow frightened at the sight of blood on the food. Theoclýmenus sees this as a bad omen for the suitors.–ED.]

Athena, gray-eyed goddess, set this scheme
into the heart of wise Penelope,
the daughter of Icárius: to bring
before the suitors in Odysseus' house
his bow and gray axheads—and once the test
was done, that bow would be the tool of death.
She climbed the high stairs to her room and took
within her steady hand the curving key
of bronze—its handle was of ivory.
Then she, together with her women, reached 10
the far-off room that stored her lord's rich trove:
his battle gear in iron, bronze, and gold,
all worked with care. There lay the pliant bow,
and there, within their quiver, many shafts,
the messengers of death.

These friendly gifts
Odysseus had received from Íphitus[110]—
the son of Eurytus[111]—a godlike man.
They'd met as guests of wise Ortílochus
near Sparta, in Messénë.[112] What had led
Odysseus to that city was a debt 20
he'd come to claim for all the Ithacans:

[110]Íphitus gave Odysseus the bow that was used in the contest.
[111]A famous archer, who had challenged Apollo to an archery contest and was killed for his presumption.
[112]The coastal region of the western Peloponnesian peninsula.

for in their well-oared ships, Messénë's men
had sailed away from Ithaca with some
three hundred sheep—and shepherds, too. Though young,
Odysseus had been chosen for that mission
by both his father and the other chieftains;
to press that claim he'd had to journey long.
And, on his part, the son of Eurytus
had come in search of twelve brood mares he'd lost—
all twelve were nursing sturdy mules. (These mares 30
soon brought poor Íphitus to doom and death,
when he met Héraclës—the dauntless son
of Zeus—who perpetrated monstrous wrongs:
though Héraclës had welcomed him as guest,
in his own house he murdered Íphitus,
a ruthless killing—he had no regard
for gods or for the table he had set
before his guest. And Héraclës then kept
for his own self—now Íphitus was dead—
the stout-hoofed mares that he had coveted.) 40
While searching for his brood mares, Íphitus
had met Odysseus, and to him he gave
this gift: the bow that mighty Eurytus
of old had borne and at his death had left
to his dear son in their tall house. Odysseus,
as token of a friendship he held dear,
in turn gave Íphitus a sturdy spear
and sharp-edged sword. And yet they never had
a chance to share a meal as host and guest;
for Héraclës—before that came to pass— 50
had murdered Íphitus, the godlike man,
from whom Odysseus had that bow as gift.
This bow Odysseus never took with him
when he sailed off to wars in his black ship;
he kept that bow at home as a memento
of his beloved friend; in Ithaca
alone, Odysseus used to bear that bow.

And now the fair Penelope had reached
the storeroom, stepping on the oaken sill
the carpenter—long since—had planed with skill 60
and laid true to the line, before he shaped
and planted posts and placed the gleaming doors.
She quickly freed the handle from its thong,
thrust in the key, then aiming straight, she shot
the bolts back. As a bull will bellow when
he grazes in a meadow, even so
the fair doors, as the key struck, bellowed now.
And they were quick to open. She stepped up
and gained the platform where the storage chests
for scented clothes were kept. From there she stretched 70
her hand out, and she took down from a peg
the handsome case that held the bow. She sat
and laid the case upon her lap; she wept

and then took out the bow of her dear lord.
But when her need for tears had been appeased,
she started toward the hall, to face the suitors.
She brought the pliant bow, the many shafts
within their quiver—messengers of death.
Her maids, beside her, carried out a chest
with bronze and iron gear her lord had left— 80
and with the axheads needed for the test.
And when that lovely woman reached the hall,
beside a pillar that sustained the roof,
she stood—a glowing shawl before her face;
and to each side, there stood a faithful maid.
These were her words:

"Proud suitors, hear: I say
that you, to eat and drink without an end
or pause, harass the house of one long gone.
And you give only this as your pretext:
to take me as a wife, to see me wed. 90
Come, suitors, stand—for you can win your prize.
You see divine Odysseus' mighty bow;
whoever strings this bow with greatest ease
will be the man I follow. I shall leave
this house where I was bride and wife—so rich,
so fair a house: I shall remember it
even in dreams."

These were her words, and now
she asked Eumæus to set out before
the suitors both the axheads and the bow.
In tears, the faithful swineherd took them out 100
and set them down. And where he stood, the cowherd
sobbed when he saw the bow of his dear lord.
Antínoüs, rebuking both, spat out:

"You oafs, you only know what plows can furrow!
Why do you boors shed tears and vex the heart
within a woman's breast? She's had enough
of pain, in any case: her husband's lost.
No, sit and eat in silence, or go out
and whine elsewhere. Just leave behind the bow;
this suitors' test is crucial—and I feel 110
that stringing this smooth bow is not that simple.
There's no man here who is Odysseus' equal—
for I myself saw him; I can recall."

These were his words, but in his heart he hoped
to string the bow and shoot the iron through.
Instead he was to be the first to taste
an arrow from the hands of great Odysseus,
within whose house he had trespassed, just as
he had incited others' wantonness.

To them the strong Telémachus said this: 120
"Zeus must have muddled me: I've lost my wits.
My dear, dear mother, one with much good sense,
informs me that she'll join another man
and leave this house—and I, like some poor lout,
laugh and am glad. Then stand, you suitors; now
your prize is close at hand: you will not find
her like in all of the Achǽan lands—
in Pylos, holy Argos, or Mycénë,
in our own Ithaca or on the dark
mainland. But you know well that she is priceless; 130
there is no need for me to sing her praises.
Don't use excuses to delay; don't wait
too long before you show us how you shoot.
I, too, shall try this feat. If I succeed,
why then, I should not grieve were she to leave
this house and wed another: I'd be left
behind, but then at least I would have tried
my strength at arms my father laid aside."

At this, he threw away his crimson cloak
and stood erect, and from his shoulders took 140
and put aside his sharpened sword. He dug
for all the axheads one long trench and set
the blades in one true row; he fixed them fast
by heaping dirt around them, which he stamped.
All were amazed to see how he had traced
so straight a line on which to place twelve blades,
though he had never seen that done before.
Then, crossing to the threshold, standing there,
he tried to draw the bow. Three times it quivered—
he was that eager; each time he fell slack, 150
though in his heart he hoped to draw it taut.
He would have strung it at his fourth attempt,
had not Odysseus signaled him to stop;
though keen to show his force, he had to halt.
To them the strong Telémachus then said:

"Even in days to come—what misery!—
I'm doomed to be inept and weak. Or else
I'm still too young and cannot trust my strength
to ward off anyone who gives offense.
But come, you men with power I can't match: 160
try out the bow; let's finish with this test."

That said, he set the bow upon the ground,
leaned it against the smooth and sturdy door,
and, on the handsome bow tip, propped the shaft,
then sat again upon the chair he'd left.

Eupēithes' son Antínoüs, spoke next:
"Rise up, my friends, one at a time, from left

to right, beginning with the one most close
to where the wine is poured."

His words pleased all.

The first to rise was Œnops' son, the augur 170
Lēiódēs. There he always set his chair
well back, beside the handsome mixing bowl,
for he alone among the suitors scorned
depravity—they all had felt his wrath.
The first to face that task, he took his stand
upon the threshold. There he tried to bend
and string the bow. He failed. Too delicate
and too unused to work like that, his hands
fell slack. He told the suitors:

"Friends—I can't.

Let someone else attempt. This bow will sap 180
the zeal and strength of many stalwart men;
it is indeed far better to be dead
than to live on and never reach the goal
for which we gather here day after day
expectantly. Now, many in their hearts
have hoped and longed to wed Odysseus' wife.
But once one feels what this bow's like, he'll try
with gifts to woo and win another bride
among the long-robed women of the Argives.
As for Penelope, just have her wed 190
the man whom fate has blessed—the wealthiest."

That said, he set the bow far off, against
the smooth and sturdy doors, and propped the shaft
upon the handsome bow tip; then he sat
again upon the chair that he had left.
And now he heard Antínoüs' rebuke:

"Lēiódēs, can you let such words pass through
the barrier of your teeth—words of defeat!
I am incensed to hear you prate of how
men will be stripped of spirit by this bow— 200
and just because your own self was too weak.
Your honored mother failed to give her son
the force for bow and arrow at your birth.
But other suitors—men who can command—
will soon succeed."

When that was said, he called

the goatherd: "Light a fire in this hall,
Melánthius; beside that fire set
a bench with fleeces on it; then go fetch—
out from the stores—an ample cake of fat,
so we young men can heat and grease the bow, 210
and try again—and end this test at last."

These were his words. Melánthius was quick
to kindle the unweary fire; he fetched
an ample cake of fat out from the stores;
it melted, and the young men greased the bow.
Then they all tried to string it, but their force
fell short; just two—godlike Eurýmachus
together with Antínoüs—persisted.

But both Odysseus' swineherd and his cowherd
had gone outside the hall. Odysseus followed. 220
And when they'd left behind the gates and court,
he turned to them and spoke these gentle words:

"Cowherd and swineherd, shall I speak, or keep
my question to myself? No—my heart tells
my tongue to ask. How would you act if he—
Odysseus—needed help, if suddenly
some god had brought him back from some far land?
Would you be on the suitors' side or his?"

The cowherd answered him: "Grant us this wish,
o father Zeus! Allow him to return 230
with some god as his guide. Then you would learn
what strength I have, how much my hands can do."

And then, in that same way, Eumæus prayed
to all the gods for his wise lord's return.
But once he knew these two were loyal men,
Odysseus answered, speaking out again:

"I am at home. It's I. My trials were long,
but in the twentieth year at last I've come
to my own land. But of my servants none
has yearned for my return, except for you; 240
among the rest I've heard no others ask
to have me back. So I tell you this truth—
just as it is to be: If I subdue
the suitors through the help a god provides,
I promise each of you a wife and goods,
together with a house close to my own;
and in the future, you—for me—will be
the friends and brothers of Telémachus.
But now I also want to show you this:
a sign so clear that you will be convinced— 250
the wound inflicted by the boar's white tusk
when I, together with Autólycus'
stout sons, went out to hunt on Mount Parnassus."

As he said that, he drew aside his rags
and showed them his great scar. When they saw that
and looked at it with care, the two men wept.
They threw their arms around the wise Odysseus;

in loving welcome they embraced his head
and shoulders; and in turn he kissed their hands
and heads. And now the sun might well have set 260
with them still weeping, if Odysseus' words
had not restrained their tears. For now he urged:

"Enough of tears and moans, lest anyone—
come from the hall—might see and then report
to those inside. Let's go back one by one,
not all together; I'll be first, then you.
And let this be the signal: All that crowd
will be at one in their denying me
the bow and shaft. But, good Eumǽus, as
you bear the bow across the halls, just hand 270
that bow to me; and have the women lock
the fitted doors; if, in their rooms, they hear
men's groans and cries that echo from in here,
they're not to hurry out, but stay inside
in silence, at their work. This is your charge,
Philœ́tius: First bar the courtyard gate,
and round that bolt be quick to knot a cord."

That said, he went into the shapely house
and took his place upon the stool he'd left.
Then his two herdsmen entered in their turn. 280

By now Eurýmachus had bow in hand:
by firelight, on this side and on that,
he warmed it; even so, he could not bend
the bow; he groaned within his sturdy heart;
then, vexed, incensed, he turned and cried aloud:

"What drear defeat for me—for all of us!
It's not that I have lost a bride—though I
do grieve for that—for after all there are
so many other women in Achǽa,
some here in seagirt Ithaca itself, 290
and some in other cities; but I mourn
our falling so far short of what he was:
we cannot match that man so like the gods,
Odysseus; we're too weak to string his bow.
In time to come, who hears our name will know
our shame."

Eupēithes' son, Antínoüs,
replied: "That won't be so, Eurýmachus!
And you yourself are well aware of that.
This day is dedicated to Apollo—
a sacred day. Who then may bend a bow? 300
Delay this test; be calm. Don't touch the axheads;
just leave them here; I'm sure no one will come
into the great hall of Laértēs' son,

Odysseus, to disturb them. Now let's call
upon the bearers to prepare our cups,
for only after we have poured libations
are we to set aside the bow. Tomorrow
at dawn Melánthius must bring the best
she-goats in all his herds; when we have offered
roast thighs to the great archer-god, Apollo, 310
we'll try the bow again and end this test."

So said Antínoüs; they all were pleased.
They washed their hands with water pages poured;
boys brimmed the mixing bowls, then served the wine;
and each man's cup received libation portions.
But when those lords had poured the offerings
and drunk as much as one might wish, Odysseus,
the man of many wiles, spoke cunningly:

"Hear me, contenders for the splendid queen;
I speak just as my spirit urges me. 320
Above all I beseech Eurýmachus
and, too, godlike Antínoüs, for he
spoke justly when he asked you to delay
your archery today—instead to leave
the verdict with the gods; the victory
will be assigned by them to whom they please—
tomorrow. Let me simply try it now—
the polished bow—that I, before you, show
what strength my hands still have. Do I possess
the force that once informed my supple limbs, 330
or am I weak from wandering and neglect?"

His words aroused their fear that he might string
the polished bow—and fear can lead to wrath.
Antínoüs assaulted him; he spat:

"You, wretched wanderer, have lost your wits.
Do you need more than this? You share the feasts
of men most eminent; you hear our speech
and words—no other scrounging stranger can
lay claim to things so fine. It must be wine
that wounds your mind—wine, honey-sweet, when swigged 340
in endless gulps, indeed infects a man.
Even Eurýtion[113]—that far-famed centaur—
when he was visiting Peiríthoüs,
the Lapiths' lord, a king most generous,
was driven wild by wine; it dazed his mind;
depraved, he raped within that royal realm.
Incensed, the Lapiths then attacked; they dragged

[113]Centaurs were a race of creatures, half-man and half-horse. At a wedding among the human Lapithai, they got drunk and caused a fight when they tried to rape the women. This story is about the centaur Eurýtion, who attempts to carry off the bride.

the centaur through the gate, hacked off his ears
and nose with ruthless bronze. In frenzy he
went on his way, his heart astray, his mind 350
still blinded by the price of pain he'd paid.
So did the war between mankind and centaurs
begin; yet he himself had been the first
who—spurred by wine—had suffered such a hurt.
And I predict that you would be hurt, too,
were you to string this bow; indeed you'd get
no sympathy from any of our men;
we'd send you off straightway on our black ship
to one who slaughters men: King Échethus,
from whom you'd not escape. Why risk that fate? 360
Drink quietly, don't challenge younger men."

This was the wise Penelope's reply:
"It's neither right nor seemly to offend
a guest invited by Telémachus.
And even if that stranger, summoning
whatever force he has, at last should string
the great bow of Odysseus, do you think
he'd lead me to his house, make me his wife?
That's surely not his hope. It hardly suits
to spoil your feast with fears so far from truth." 370

Eurýmachus replied: "Penelope,
wise daughter of Icárius, indeed
it's not that we believe he'd lead you off—
that would be too improper; it's the talk
of men and women that we fear; in days
to come, some spiteful tongues—much to our shame—
might scorn us, saying: 'See how lesser men
would woo the wife of one most excellent—
and they can't even string his polished bow.
Meanwhile a beggar, one who wandered here, 380
has strung the bow with ease, and shot the shaft
through iron.' Men will surely babble that—
and we would be disgraced."

Penelope
replied with words most wise: "Eurýmachus,
there surely cannot be much good repute
within this land for you who have consumed
with scorn a noble's livelihood. Are you
to chide or to rebuke? This stranger's tall
and sturdy, and he says that he was born
of one who was a lord. Come, let us see: 390
give him the polished bow. This I affirm,
and this will surely be: If with the gift
Apollo grants, this man can string the bow,
I'll give him cloak and tunic, handsome clothes,
and, too, a pointed pike to fend off dogs
and men, a two-edged sword, and sandals for

his feet, and help him sail to any shore
his heart and mind desire."

Telémachus'
reply was keen and wise: "Dear mother, I
alone among Achæans can deny 400
or give this bow to any man I will.
Of those who rule in rugged Ithaca
or in the isles that face the grazing land
where horses pasture, Elis,[114] no one can
obstruct my will by force, not even if
I wished to give the stranger as my gift
this bow—to carry off, forever his.
But go now to your room; tend to your tasks,
the distaff and the loom; your women can
complete the work that they began. Leave speech 410
to men: to all those here and—most—to me;
within this house I have authority."

Amazed, while going to her room, she laid
to heart her son's wise words. Then, with her maids,
she reached the upper floor and wept and wept
for her dear husband, her Odysseus,
until Athena, gray-eyed goddess, shed
sweet sleep upon her lids.

The good swineherd
had in the meantime lifted up the bow
and carried it. The suitors' shouts were loud; 420
one, young and strutting, bawled:

"You swineherd wretch,
have you gone mad? Where are you taking that?
For if Apollo and the other gods
should favor us, you'll soon be food for dogs:
alone, far off from men, far from your swine,
it's you on whom the hounds you reared will dine."

Such words, the clamor in the hall, the crowd
of suitors' brouhaha dismayed the swineherd;
dead in his tracks he stopped, set down the bow.
But on the other side Telémachus 430
cried out by way of menace:

"Do not stop,
my friend, unless you want to feel regret
at having heeded all this crowd: unless
you lift that bow again, I'll pelt you out

[114]Elis is a region in the Peloponnese where the Olympic games were held.

with stones across the fields. I may be young,
but I've more force than you—would that I had
the same odds when my sinews and my strength
are matched against the suitors. Were that so,
that plotting pack would have to scurry out,
a sorry lot evicted from this house." 440

These were his words. The suitors were amused;
they set aside the spleen and spite they'd stored
against Telémachus. The swineherd walked
across the hall with bow in hand; he brought
the bow to wise Odysseus. Then he called
the old nurse to his side:

"Wise Euryclēīa,
Telémachus commands you now to shut
the doors between the women's rooms and us;
and should your women, in their chambers, hear
men's groans and outcries echo from this hall, 450
they're not to hurry out but stay inside
in silence, at their work."

These were his words.
Meanwhile Philœtius slipped out; he barred
the well-fenced courtyard's gate. That done, he found
a rope twined from papyrus strands; once meant
to serve a stately ship, that rope now lay
beneath the portico. With this he tied
the gate tight, fast. Then he went back and sat
again upon the stool he had just left.
His eyes upon Odysseus, he could see 460
his lord, bow now in hand, intent upon
its sides, its every part: he turned it round
and round, again, again—afraid that when
he, master of the bow, was far from home,
worms might have worked their mischief on the horns.
One suitor, glancing at his neighbor, mused:

"This fellow's shrewd—a connoisseur of bows.
Perhaps he has one like it stored at home,
or else that vagabond, that lord of nuisance,
intends to carve one for himself—and thus, 470
he turns it in his hands, this way and that."

And still another suitor added this:
"I hope this beggar has as little luck
in life as in the stringing of this bow."

So did the suitors babble. But the man
of many wiles, Odysseus, now had scanned
the bow on every side; and just as one
expert in song and harping works with ease

when he is called upon to stretch a string
around new pegs and so at either end 480
makes fast the twisted gut—just so, Odysseus'
stringing of that great bow was effortless.
Then he took up the bow; with his right hand,
he tried the string; it sang as clearly as
a swallow's note. The suitors were dismayed;
they all turned pale. Zeus sent a thunderclap
as omen; and it gladdened patient, bright
Odysseus—he was waiting for some sign
from cunning Cronos' son. At that, he snatched—
it lay upon his table—one lone shaft 490
(the rest, which the Achǽans soon would taste,
within their hollow quiver lay in wait).
Then, even as he sat upon the stool,
he laid that arrow on the bridge, then drew
the bowstring and notched shaft. His aim was true:
he shot clean through each axhead in that row;
not one was missed; through every socket hollow
the shaft had passed—the heavy, bronze-tipped arrow.
Then to his son he said:

"You see this guest
has not dishonored you, Telémachus: 500
I did not miss the mark nor did I strain.
Although the taunting suitors said my strength
was gone, I have it yet. And now it's time—
there's still daylight—to see that all is ready
for the Achǽans' feast; and then to add
still other pleasures, those of harp and chant—
at banquets these are pleasing ornaments."

That said, he gave the signal with his brows.
Telémachus, dear son of bright Odysseus,
strapped on his sharp sword, clasped his spear, and stood 510
beside his father, armed with gleaming bronze.

BOOK 22
[BATTLE IN THE GREAT HALL]

Astute Odysseus now threw off his rags.
He leaped onto the great threshold; he grasped
the bow; he grasped the quiver full of shafts.
He cried out to the suitors:

"Now at last
the crucial test is at an end, and yet
there is another mark, one that no man
has ever struck before. But I've a chance
to reach it—if Apollo is my friend."

That said, he shot a bitter shaft straight at
Antínoüs, who then was lifting up 10
a handsome, double-handled, golden cup;
he'd tipped it to his lips that he might drink
the wine; no thought of death had crossed his mind.
And who among the feasters could have guessed
that one, however strong, who faced a crowd
would dare an act so sure to bring revenge—
dark death and destiny—upon himself?
But taking aim, Odysseus hit his mark;
the point passed through and out the tender neck.
He sank back as the shaft struck; from his hand 20
the cup fell; mortal blood gushed from his nostrils—
a thick stream; and his feet, in frenzy, kicked
aside the table; remnants of the feast
spilled on the floor; the bread and roasted meats
were fouled with blood. The suitors saw him fall;
dismayed, they shouted, leaped up; through the halls
they rushed; their eyes were searching all around
the sturdy walls for weapons, but they found
no shield, no stalwart spear—no arms to grip.
Their anger and abuse assailed Odysseus: 30

"Stranger, if it is men your arrows seek,
this is your final test: you're sure to meet
the steep descent to death. The one you killed
was Ithaca's most noble youth: you will
be food for vultures."

So they cried; all thought
that he had hit that man by chance; those fools
were not aware that now they all were snared,
that death cords lashed them fast. Odysseus scowled:

"You thought I never would return from Troy;
and so—you dogs—you sacked my house, you forced 40
my women servants to your will and wooed
my wife in secret while I was alive.
You had no fear of the undying gods,
whose home is spacious heaven, and no fear
of men's revenge, your fate in days to come.
Now all of you are trapped in death's tight thongs."

Pale fear clutched all of them; their eyes sought out
some place of refuge from death's steep abyss.
The only one to speak—Eurýmachus:

"If now indeed you have come back, Odysseus 50
of Ithaca, then all that you ascribe
to the Achǽans is most justified:
their many acts of outrage in your house

and many in your fields. But he who now
lies dead—he caused it all: Antínoüs.
And in inciting us, he was not bent
so much on marriage as on other plans
that Cronos' son did not fulfill for him:
He wanted to be king in this rich land
of Ithaca; he laid the snare to catch 60
and kill your son. That schemer now has come
to his just end, and you can pardon us—
your people. Then we'll gather through the land
your recompense for all that we have drunk
and eaten in your halls; to that we'll add—
from each of us—a grant of gold and bronze
worth twenty oxen, to appease your heart.
Until now, who could fault the rage you felt?"

The man of wiles and cunning scowled and said:
"Eurýmachus, were you to shower me 70
with all the riches you inherited—
and add whatever other goods you can—
not even then would I restrain my hands
from slaughter till you've paid the price in full
for all your arrogance. The choice is yours:
to fight me face-to-face, or else to flee—
though I do not believe that any can
escape that steep descent."

His words were done.
Their knees, their hearts, went weak. Eurýmachus
again spoke up:

"My friends, he will not stop; 80
within his overpowering hands he holds
the quiver and the polished bow; he'll shoot
from that smooth threshold till he kills us all.
We have to think of battle. Draw your swords;
let's wield these tables as a shield against
the arrows of swift death; let's all, compact,
press on, dislodge him from the door, rush out
and hurry through the city, shout alarm;
with that, he'd soon have shot his final shaft."

That said, he drew his sharp bronze blade, two-edged, 90
and with a savage roar, rushed on against
the bowman. But the bright Odysseus shot
a bitter shaft that struck him in the chest,
below the nipple; and its sharp tip pierced
straight to his liver. Now the suitor's sword
fell clattering to the ground; he shuddered, slumped,
then crashed across the table, body bent,
and spilled his food and his two-handled cup

across the floor. His forehead struck the ground
in agony; his two legs kicked the chair; 100
it teetered; darkness fell across his eyes.

Amphínomus, with sharp drawn sword, then rushed
against Odysseus, hoping he could thrust
that bowman from the door. Telémachus
was quick; he cast his bronze-tipped spear and caught
the suitor from behind, right at the spine;
and then he drove the spearhead through his chest.
His body thudded down; his forehead struck
the ground full flush. At that, Telémachus
recoiled, with his long-shadowed spear still fixed 110
within the corpse that was Amphínomus—
afraid that if he tried to tug it out,
some one of the Achæans might well rush
at him as he bent down beside the corpse.
Instead he ran to reach his father's side;
and standing there, he spoke these winged words:

"Father,
a shield, two spears, a tight bronze helmet—these
are what you need: I'll fetch them now with speed;
and I'll return with armor for myself
and weapons for Eumæus and the cowherd— 120
we're better off with battle gear."

To this,
the man of many wiles replied: "Be quick.
The shafts I have to fend them off will finish.
I don't want them to thrust me from this door
because I'm left alone."

Telémachus
had heard Odysseus' words; and at once he left
to reach the room where splendid arms were kept.
From there he carried out four shields, eight spears,
and four bronze helmets plumed with thick horsehair.
He quickly brought them back to his dear father. 130
Then first he girt himself in bronze; and when
the herdsmen, too, put on their handsome arms,
three stood beside the dexterous, wise Odysseus.
But he, as long as he had shafts to spend,
kept aiming: every shot brought down a man
within his house; there, one by one, they fell.
But when that lord had no more shafts, he leaned
his bow against the doorpost of the hall;
it stood upright against the gleaming wall.
He strapped his shoulders with a four-ply shield, 140
and on his sturdy head he set a casque
with horsehair plumage, waving, ominous;
he gripped two stalwart spears, both tipped with bronze.

Inside the walls there stood a postern door
raised somewhat from the floor; a passageway
led from the far end of the great hall's gate,
right to that private door. That way was shut
by outer panels fitted tight. Odysseus
had told the good swineherd to watch with care
the entrance to that corridor, to stand 150
close by the only way to that far door.

Then Ageláus spoke to all the suitors:
"Friends, can't we send one man to reach that door,
alert the people, sound the loud alarm;
then we could see the last of these attacks."

Melánthius the goatherd answered him:
"Zeus-nurtured Ageláus, that can't be:
the entrance to that corridor is much
too near the handsome door; it's hard to pass
that narrow entranceway; one man's enough 160
to keep us all in check—if he is tough.
Instead, I'll fetch you weapons from the stores;
for it is there, I think, and nowhere else
that arms were hidden by Odysseus
and his famed son."

That said, Melánthius
the goatherd sought Odysseus' inner rooms.
He took twelve helmets with their horsehair plumes,
twelve shields, as many spears; these he brought back
to serve as suitors' gear when they attacked.
And when Odysseus saw them gird their arms 170
and brandish long spears with their hands, his heart
and knees went weak: he faced a monstrous task.
Now with winged words he spurred Telémachus:
"Telémachus, some woman in this house
has hatched this plot—or else Melánthius."

Telémachus' reply was wise, astute:
"Father, it's I myself who am at fault:
no other bears the blame; it's I who left
the storeroom door ajar; it seems their guard
was more alert than I. My good Eumæus, 180
rush now to seal that door, and do find out
who's opened it: one of the women or—
as I suspect—the son of Dólius,
Melánthius."

So son and father spoke.
Meanwhile Melánthius the goatherd went
off to the storeroom once again, to fetch
more weapons—but he caught Eumæus' eye.
The swineheard asked Odysseus at his side:

"Astute Odysseus, son of Zeus, that man
whom we suspect has left the hall again: 190
another storeroom-raid. But if I prove
the stronger of the two, what should I do:
am I to kill him there or haul him here
to pay for all his fetid plots and snares?"

Odysseus, man of many wiles, replied:
"Telémachus and I will stay the rush
of suitors in this hall, however harsh
their fury; meanwhile—with Philœtius
to help you—twist that traitor's feet and arms
back to his spine; and once he's trapped inside 200
the storeroom, bind him to a board and take
a length of twisted rope and tug that thing
along a towering pillar to the rafters,
that he may live—and suffer—somewhat longer."

Those two were quick to do what he had urged.
They reached the storeroom door; each took his place:
unseen, they flanked the entrance, lay in wait.
Melánthius, to gather arms, had gone
into the farthest corner of the room.
And then the goatherd came out carrying 210
a handsome helmet in one hand; the other
held fast a rust-flecked shield that had been borne
by brave Laértës when he was a boy—
the stitching on its strap was long since torn.
Those two were quick to grab him; by his hair
they dragged him back inside the room and threw
that quaking felon on the floor; they used
a ruthless rope to tie his hands and feet,
to twist them back, bound fast, to meet his spine—
as patient, bright Odysseus had asked. 220
Then with a plaited cord, which they attached,
they hoisted him along a towering pillar
up to the rafters. You, Eumæus, said—
to mock the goatherd, hanging overhead:

"Now you, Melánthius, can watch night through
on your soft bed, the sort that's rightly yours;
you won't miss Dawn's firstlight, her golden throne;
you'll see her rising from the Ocean's flow—
just when you used to drive your plump she-goats
to serve the suitors' revels in these halls." 230

They left him there, well stretched by their fierce ropes,
put on their armor, shut the polished door,
and then rejoined their wise and cunning lord.
But now the rival ranks stood face-to-face,
arrayed in rage: upon the threshold, four;
and stalwart, in the hall, so many more.

But now, beside those four, Athena stood:
Zeus' daughter, in her voice and aspect, took
the guise of Mentor. At the sight of her,
Odysseus' heart was glad. He pleaded:

"Mentor, 240
I am your friend: we shared fond years together.
I favored you. Now help me foil disaster."

Despite his words, he recognized Athena,
who rouses warriors. But facing them,
the suitors' shouts were loud. First, Ageláus,
Damástor's son, rebuked Odysseus' friend:

"Don't let his honeyed words persuade you, Mentor,
to join his side, to fight against these men.
For this is how our plan will come to pass:
Once we have killed the father and the son, 250
then we shall kill you, too; for all you want
to do within these halls, your head will pay.
And when our bronze has stripped you of your force,
we'll add those goods that you possess—your house
and land—to everything Odysseus owns
and take it all; and we'll forbid your sons
to live within your halls, and not allow
your daughters and dear wife to move about
this city, Ithaca."

On hearing that,
Athena, now incensed, with words of wrath, 260
stormed at Odysseus:

"You have surely lost
the fury and tenacious force that once
were yours when, for those nine long years, you fought
for white-armed Helen; in those wild assaults,
you killed so many; and it was your plot
that brought the city of wide roads, the Troy
of Priam, to its end. Why is it, then,
that, with your house and goods again at hand,
you weep and wail? And all of this just when
your force should crush those men. Instead, my friend, 270
come closer, at my side take up your stand;
just see what I can do when I contend
with enemies. The son of Álcimus—
I, Mentor—can repay your kindnesses."

These were Athena's words, but she did not
give him the strength he'd need to win at once;
the goddess still was bent on trying out
the power to resist and to assault

of both Odysseus and his sturdy son.
Then she herself flew upward, taking on 280
the likeness of a swallow as she perched
upon a rafter in the murky hall.

These men now led the suitors: Ageláus,
Damástor's son; Amphímedon; Peisánder,
Polýctor's son; and Demoptólemus,
Eurýnomus, and cunning Pólybus—
by far the best of all the suitors left
alive and fighting to avoid their death;
the bow, the flow of shafts, had felled the rest.
And Ageláus urged on all his comrades: 290

"Friends, this resistless man has tired at last.
Mentor—whose braggart words you heard—ran off;
they are alone now at the outer doors.
So do not cast your long spears all at once.
You six throw first, in hope that Zeus allows
Odysseus to be struck—a prize for us.
And once he's fallen, do not fear the rest."

These were his words. Then those six suitors cast
their shafts with eager force, as he had asked.
But each shot missed its mark—Athena's work. 300
One hit the sturdy doorpost of the hall;
and one, the tightly fitted door itself.
The other ash-wood shafts just struck the wall.
So did all four escape the suitors' spears;
and seeing that, Odysseus spurred his men:

"The time has come for us in turn to cast
our shafts against their ranks; my friends, don't let
that crew, to all their wrongs, now add our death."

That said, with deadly aim all hurled their shafts.
Odysseus' spear downed Demoptólemus; 310
Telémachus struck down Eurýadës;
the swineherd's shaft caught Élatus; the cowherd's,
Peisánder. Those four bit the spacious floor.
The other suitors fell back in the hall;
at that, Odysseus and his men moved up
and stripped the dead men's bodies of their bronze.

Again six suitors cast their shafts with force;
but each shot missed its mark—Athena's work.
One spearhead struck the sturdy hall's doorpost,
and one, the tightly fitted door itself; 320
two other ash-wood shafts, tipped with stout bronze,
just struck the wall. And though two shafts drew close,
they leveled nothing more than glancing blows;
Amphímedon's spear reached Telémachus,

but its bronze spearhead only grazed his wrist.
Ctesíppus' crossed above Eumæus' shield
but only scratched his shoulder, then flew on
and thudded to the ground. Now, once again,
the stout, astute Odysseus and his band
heaved hard their shafts against the suitors' ranks. 330
Odysseus, ravager of cities, struck
Eurýdamas; it was Telémachus
who downed Amphímedon; the swineherd's shaft
felled Polýbus. The cowherd heaved his spear
into Ctesíppus' chest, and then he jeered:

"You, taunting, fleering son of Polythérsës,
forget your folly and fanfaronades
forever; it's for gods alone to speak
the final word: their will exceeds our reach.
This spearhead is the gift that will requite 340
the ox-hoof gift you gave to the godlike
Odysseus when he begged within this house."

But now Odysseus and his men attacked
close in; Odysseus' massive spear struck down
Damástor's son; and once Telémachus
had wounded in the waist Leócritus,
Evénor's son, he drove his spear clean through;
the suitor crashed headlong, face to the ground.
Then from above, close to the roof, Athena
held high her aegis,[115] sign of death for mortals. 350
And terror took the suitors; through the hall
they fled like cattle when the gadfly darts
to sting the herd, in spring, when days grow long.
And just as vultures with their crooked beaks
and talons, swooping from the mountains, seek
to snatch the smaller birds (in panic, these
fly toward the plain, beneath the clouds, and yet
the vultures pounce upon and kill them—no
device and no defense can help—and men
enjoy that chase), so did Odysseus' band 360
hunt down the suitors to this side and that,
through the vast hall. As heads were struck the groans
were horrid; all the pavement streamed with blood.
But rushing out to clasp Odysseus' knees,
Lēiódës, with winged words, now made this plea:

"Odysseus, as your suppliant I ask
for your regard and mercy. This I can

[115]The breastplate or shield with Medusa's head on it, used by Athena and Zeus; it caused panic among their enemies.

assure you: Nothing I have said or done
has ever wronged the women of your house;
indeed, I tried to curb the wanton course 370
of others—they ignored what I had urged.
A squalid fate repays their unjust ways.
Yet I, an augur, one who did no wrong,
will die as they have died. Can this be true:
Those who do good will gain no gratitude?"

Odysseus, man of many wiles, just scowled:
"If you indeed declare yourself to be
their augur, then you often made this plea
within my halls: that I might be denied
a sweet return. You would have had my wife 380
choose you and bear your brats. And that is why
you won't escape a death that terrifies."

That said, his sturdy hand picked up the sword
that Ageláus, as he died, let fall
upon the ground. He struck Lēiódēs' neck—
a clean slice. As the augur tried to speak,
his head fell in the dust.

But Phémius
the singer, son of Térpius, still sought
escape from darkest fate; he had been forced
to sing at suitors' feasts. With harp in hand, 390
close to the postern door, he stood; two thoughts
debated in his mind: Was he to leave
the spacious hall and sit beside the altar
of Zeus, the god of courts and yards, for whom
Laértēs and Odysseus sacrificed
their oxen, burning many fatted thighs;
or must he rush to clasp Odysseus' knees
and make his plea? This plan seemed best: He set
his hollow harp between the mixing bowl
and silver-studded chair, then rushed ahead 400
to clasp Odysseus' knees as he beseeched
with these winged words:

"I am a suppliant,
Odysseus; I implore—grant me regard
and pity. If you were to kill a bard,
a man like me who sings to men and gods,
you'd feel remorse. My chanting is self-taught;
it is the gods who planted every sort
of song within my heart. I am as fit
to sing to you as to a deity.
Then do not be so keen to cut my throat. 410
My witness is Telémachus, your son:
I did not come through my own will or zeal
to sing at suitors' feasts within your halls.
Their force was far too much: I was compelled."

These were his words. Telémachus the strong
had heard and, turning to his father, urged:
"Stop. Do not kill a man who has no guilt.
And let us save the life of Medon, too:
that herald always cared for me when I
was still a boy, within our house—unless 420
by now the swineherd or Philœtius
has done him in, or he's met death beneath
your sword as you raced raging through the house."

These were his words, and prudent Medon heard:
he'd crouched beneath a chair; there—to escape
his fate—he wore an oxhide newly-flayed.
But he was quick to rush out. Throwing off
the oxhide, straight away he hurried toward
Telémachus to clasp his knees. And now
the herald made his plea with these winged words: 430

"Friend, here I am. Do stay your hand and ask
your father to relent: my fear is that
his sovereign force might kill me in his wrath
against the suitors, who consumed his goods
and did not honor you—for they were fools."

Astute Odysseus, as he answered, smiled:
"Take heart. My son has won: he saved your life
that you may know and tell to others, too,
that goodness gains far more than malice can.
But now, do leave these halls and sit outside; 440
stay in the courtyard, far from blood and strife—
you and the singer of such varied songs—
but I'll stay here—to finish up my work."

These were his words; the two men left the hall.
Beside the altar of great Zeus, they sat,
looking from side to side, still fearing death.

Odysseus' eyes searched round his house, to see
if any, to escape dark destiny,
were still alive and hiding. But he saw
that all were fallen in the blood and dust— 450
so many, like the fish that fishermen
draw from the gray sea in their fine-meshed nets
onto the curving beach: they lie in heaps
along the sands—the fish that long to reach
the waves, but stay beneath the bright sun's rays
and die. So did the suitors now lie heaped
one on another. Then astute Odysseus
said to his son:

"Go now, Telémachus,
and call your old nurse, Eurycleīa: I
must tell her what I have in mind."

That said, 460
Telémachus obeyed. He shook the door
and called to his old nurse:

"Come, Euryclēia,
be quick: my father wants to speak to you,
the guardian of all our women servants."

These were his words, but hers remained unwinged;
she simply came in silence, opening
the door, and stepped into the handsome hall,
led by Telémachus. She found Odysseus
standing among the bodies of the dead.
There he, befouled with blood and filth, was like 470
a lion who has torn apart an ox
along the plain and, having gorged, moves off,
blood staining all his chest and both his jaws—
the sight of him strikes fear; just so, blood smeared
Odysseus' feet and hands. And when she saw
the corpses and the countless streams of blood,
she felt the need to shout with joy—so great
a task was now complete. But she was checked:
with these winged words, Odysseus held her back:

"Old woman, check yourself; you must restrain 480
your joy—don't shout aloud. It is profane
to let your voice exult when men are slain.
These men were struck down by a god-sent fate
and by their wanton acts; for they, in truth,
had no respect for any man on earth—
not only evil men, but even those
we deem most good and fair, whoever was
unfortunate enough to cross their path.
Their insolence has earned this squalid end.
But come now, tally for me all the women 490
within these halls: which ones dishonored me
and which deserve no blame."

Then Euryclēia,
his dear nurse, answered him: "I shall indeed
tell you, my son, the truth. Within this house
you have some fifty women servants: these
we've trained to do their work—to card the wool
and to be chaste in every way. In all,
just twelve have given way to wantonness,
with no respect for me or even for
Penelope. As for Telémachus, 500
he's only reached his manhood recently:
his mother's given him no right to rule
the women of the house. But it is time
for me to climb up to her lovely rooms
and tell your wife all that has happened here;
she's steeped in the deep sleep some god has sent."

Odysseus, man of many wiles, replied:
"This is no time to wake her; go instead
to fetch the faithless women—bring them here."

That said, the old nurse left, her task was clear. 510
Meanwhile, with these winged words, Odysseus urged
Telémachus, the cowherd, and the swineherd:

"Start hauling off the dead, and have the women
assist you. Then wash down and sponge with water
the handsome seats and tables. Once you've set
the house in order, lead the women out.
Place them between the round tower and the court's
stout wall; then, with the suitors' long sharp swords,
strike—strike until those sluts have lost their lives
and can't remember how their loving plied 520
the suitors, when they dallied at their sides."

These were his words. With terrifying cries
and many tears, the crowd of women came.
First, then, they carried off the dead. They placed
each corpse beneath the courtyard's colonnade,
each body propped against another—and
Odysseus urged them on with his commands;
they had no choice—they did all that he asked.
When that was done, the women washed and sponged
the handsome chairs and tables, while with hoes, 530
Telémachus, the cowherd, and the swineherd
went through the sturdy house and scraped the floors.
The women took those scrapings out of doors.

The hall was now in order. And they led
the women out into the court—like cows—
between the round tower and the sturdy wall—
into a narrow space, with no escape.
The first to speak was wise Telémachus:

"I would not strip these women of their lives
by way of some clean death; they have defied 540
my mother and her son; they've slept beside
the suitors."[116]

That was said, and then he bound
the cable of a dark-prowed ship around
a sturdy pillar of the portico,
then ran it to the round tower, stretched it high,
so that no woman's feet might reach the ground.
Just as when doves or thrushes, wings outstretched,
head for their nests but fall into a net

---

[116]Because of the women's harlotry, Telémachus refused to use a sword for a clean death, and chose instead the dishonorable death by hanging.

that's set within a thicket, finding death
and not the place where they had hoped to rest, 550
so were those women's heads, aligned, caught tight
within a noose, that each of them might die
a dismal death. Their feet twitched for a while—
but not for long.

That done, Melánthius
was led outside the door into the court;
with savage bronze they hacked off both his ears
and nose, cut off his genitals—a raw
meal for the dogs—and then, with frenzied hearts,
hacked off his hands and feet. Their work complete,
as soon as they had washed their hands and feet, 560
again they joined Odysseus in the house.
But he urged Euryclēia, the dear nurse:

"Old nurse, bring sulfur now and cleansing fire
to purify these rooms. Then go and fetch
Penelope with all her maids at hand,
and ask the other servingwomen, too,
to gather here."

Old Euryclēia answered:
"Your words, my child, were all indeed well said.
But come now, let me fetch more seemly clothes,
a cloak and tunic, so that you'll not stand 570
here in your hall, your broad back wrapped in rags—
such tatters hardly suit."

And the astute
Odysseus answered her: "But first of all,
let fire be readied for me in this hall."

These were his words. She did not disobey.
She fetched the sulfur and the fire; with these
Odysseus cleansed the hall, the house, the court.
Meanwhile the old nurse hurried to alert
the loyal servingwomen. Crowding round
Odysseus, they embraced him: faithful, fond, 580
they kissed his head and shoulders and his hands.
Sweet need to weep and wail seized him within
his heart, for he had recognized them all.

BOOK 23
[ODYSSEUS AND PENELOPE]

The old nurse, jubilant, went up the stairs
to reach her mistress' rooms, to let her know
that her dear husband had indeed come home.
Her knees were agile and her feet were quick.
She stood beside her mistress' bed—said this:

"Penelope, dear child, awake; you may
see what your eyes have longed for every day.
Odysseus now is here; he has returned;
his absence has been long, but he has killed
the bragging suitors who have sacked his wealth, 10
defied Telémachus, and plagued this house."

This was the wise Penelope's reply:
"Dear nurse, your words are wild; the gods can drive
the wisest mortal mad, or even guide
a fool to wisdom. Yes, you once were wise,
but now the gods have led your wits astray.
Why do you mock me so when my heart grieves?
Why speak wild words that wake me from a sleep
that held my eyes in sweet embrace, more deep
than any sleep that I have known since he— 20
my dear Odysseus—sailed to Troy-the-ugly.
Now go away—back to the women's hall.
Had any of my other women dared
to wake me with such tidings, I'd have sent
her off straightway; she would have felt my wrath;
but you are old—you benefit from that."

The faithful Euryclēia did not budge:
"I am not mocking you, dear child: in truth
Odysseus—as I said—is here; he's home;
he is the stranger whom they all reviled 30
in your great hall. For some time now your son
has known that he was here, but wisely kept
secret his father's plans, until revenge
could end the outrage of those bragging men."

She said no more. With joy, Penelope
leaped from her bed, hugged the old nurse, and said—
even as tears fell from her lids—winged words:

"Come now, dear nurse, do tell me all the truth:
how did he—he was one alone—attack
those braggarts—many men, a crowded pack?" 40

The dear nurse answered her: "I did not see;
I only heard the groans of those who died.
Behind tight doors we women, terrified,
crouched at the farthest corner of our room.
I did not budge until I heard your son,
Telémachus, call me into the hall,
just as his father ordered him to do.
You'd have rejoiced to see Odysseus like
a lion, blood-flecked, fouled. The dead were piled
before the doorway to the portico 50
as he, once he had kindled mighty fires,
purged his fair hall with sulfur, while he called

on me to fetch you. Come—I'll lead you both
to joy that follows many trials. You've yearned
so long; at last he's home; he's reached his hearth
alive; he has found you and found his son;
against the suitors' malice, he has won
revenge within this house."

This was the wise
Penelope's reply: "Do not delight
as yet. You know how welcome he would be 60
to all within these halls, especially
to me and to our son, Telémachus.
Yet in your news I place but little trust.
One of the gods struck down that lordly band,
a god whom their foul crimes and arrogance
incensed; for they, in fact, had no respect
for any man on earth—whether he was
evil or excellent. Their insolence
has earned this squalid end. As for Odysseus,
far from Achæa he has lost the path 70
of his return, and he himself is gone."

Then Euryclēia answered: "My dear child,
how can the barrier of your teeth permit
such speech to cross your lips? How can you say
that your Odysseus never will return
when he is in this house, at his own hearth?
You've always had an unbelieving heart.
But there's another certain sign that I
must share with you: the wound that long ago
the white-tusked boar inflicted on Odysseus. 80
I saw this when I washed his feet; I should
have told you this, but it was he himself
who laid his hand upon my mouth; he would
not let me speak—yes, he is keen, astute.
But follow me; I stake my life—if I
have tricked you, I am forfeit, I must die."

Then wise Penelope replied: "Dear nurse,
however wise one is, it still is hard
to read the counsels of the deathless gods.
But let us hurry to my son, that I 90
may see the slaughtered and their slaughterer."

That said, she left behind her upper rooms.
Her heart was still unsure: Was she to probe
her husband from afar or, drawing close,
to kiss his head and hands? She crossed the sill
of stone and took a seat within the hall,
facing Odysseus as he sat beside
the far wall in the firelight. His eyes
cast down, he leaned against a pillar, waiting

to see if, when she saw him there, his wife 100
would speak to him. But she sat long in silence,
her heart assailed by wonder; now her eyes
stared full upon his face, and once again
she failed to recognize him—he was dressed
so miserably. But Telémachus
rebuked her:

"Mother, you are hard of heart:
why do you stay so far away from my
dear father? Were you at his side, you might
ask question after question. Yes, your heart
is stubborn—surely there's no other woman 110
who'd keep her distance from her own dear husband
who, after he has suffered many trials
in more than nineteen years away, returns
to her, in his dear land. Not even stone
is harder than the hardness your heart shows."

This was the wise Penelope's reply:
"My son, the soul within my breast is struck
with wonder; I've no words; I cannot ask;
I cannot even look him in the face.
If what I see in truth is my Odysseus 120
come home to me, we two shall certainly
know one another without questioning:
we've secret signs, unknown to all but us."

That said, the patient, bright Odysseus smiled.
He turned to his dear son with these winged words:
"Telémachus, be patient: let your mother
test me within these halls; she soon will find
the way in which I can be recognized.
Now, since I'm dressed in tattered rags and filth,
she scorns me—won't admit that I am he. 130
Meanwhile the two of us can make our plans.
Even if a slain man has left few friends
who'd seek revenge, the killer flees that land—
he's exiled from his city and his clan.
But we have killed the pillars of this town,
the noblest youths of Ithaca: I ask
that you reflect most carefully on that."

Telémachus' reply was keen and wise:
"Dear father, you yourself can see to this.
They say that you're the most astute of men— 140
no mortal can contrive more cunning plans.
We three will follow where you choose to lead;
whatever strength we have is yours to spend."

Odysseus, man of many wiles, replied:
"Then I shall tell you what seems best to me.

Once you have bathed yourselves, I'd have you dress
in tunics; let the women wear their best.
The godly singer is to take his harp
and lead us in a glad and varied dance,
so those who live nearby or those who chance 150
to pass along the road will say that we
are in the middle of a wedding feast.
Then rumors will not spread throughout the town:
no one will hear about the suitors' deaths
until we've left for our well-wooded farm.
Once we are there, we can devise a scheme—
whatever plan Olympus will concede."

His words were done. They heard, and they obeyed.
They bathed, and then they dressed; in fine array
the women gathered; and the godly singer 160
took up his hollow harp and spurred them on:
they longed for seemly dance and gracious song.
Out from the great house echoed loud the tread
of men who danced and women finely dressed.
And those who heard those sounds outside now said:

"Someone has surely wed the queen at last—
the woman whom they wanted so. That bitch
no longer guards the great house of her own
true husband, waiting—firm—for his return."

So some did say, but none knew what had passed. 170
Meanwhile Eurýnomë, the housewife, bathed
in his own halls the resolute Odysseus,
then smoothed his body down with oil and cast
a tunic round his back. That done, Athena,
the gray-eyed goddess, made him more robust
and taller, and she gave him thicker hair,
which flowed down from his head in curls and clusters
that seemed much like the hyacinth in flower.
Just as a craftsman who has learned his secrets
from both the gray-eyed goddess and Hephæstus 180
frames silver with fine gold and thus creates
a work with greater plenitude and grace,
so did the goddess now enhance the face
and head and shoulders of Odysseus.
When he came from the bath and reached the hall,
his form was like the form of the immortals.
Again he took the chair from which he'd risen,
facing his wife. He said:

"Perplexing woman!
To you the gods who hold Olympus gave
a heart more obdurate than any they 190
have ever given other—weaker—women.
What other woman has a heart so stubborn
as to deny herself her own dear husband,

who's suffered trial on trial and, after more
than nineteen years, returns to his own shores!
Come, nurse, I need to rest; prepare a couch,
that I, though all alone, may lay me down:
within her breast she has a heart of iron."

This was the wise Penelope's reply:
"Wild man! I am not proud, I do not taunt, 200
nor am I stupefied—I know full well
how you appeared when, in your long-oared ship,
you left your Ithaca. Yes, Euryclēia,
prepare the sturdy bedstead for him now
outside the solid bridal room that he
himself constructed; carry out the bed,
and over it throw cloaks, bright blankets, fleece."

These words of hers were meant to test Odysseus.
Incensed, her husband cried to his keen wife:
"Woman, your words have wounded me. Who tore 210
my bedstead from its base? For it would take
a god—if he so pleased—to shift its place.
No man alive, however young and strong,
with mortal force alone could hope to budge
that bed without great strain, for it contains
a secret in its making. No one else
contrived that bed: I fashioned it myself.
Within our court a long-leaved olive trunk
stood stout and vigorous, just like a pillar.
Around that trunk I built our bridal room. 220
I finished it with close-set stones and laid
a sturdy roof above; I added doors
that fitted faultlessly. Then I lopped off
the olive's long-leaved limbs; and so I thinned
the trunk, up from its base; with my bronze adze,
I smoothed it down with craft and care; I made
that wood run true and straight, and it became
my bedpost. Once I'd bored it with an auger,
I, starting with that part, began to shape
my frame and, with that job well done, inlaid 230
my work with silver, ivory, and gold.
Inside the frame I stretched taut oxhide thongs;
their crimson shone. My secret sign is told.
Woman, I do not know if my bed stands
where it once stood or if by now some man
has sawed the bedstead from the trunk and set
my bed elsewhere."

These were his words; her knees
and heart went weak; the secret signs that he
revealed were certain proof. She ran to greet
Odysseus, threw her arms around his neck, 240
and kissed his head and said:

"Dear heart, don't rage:
Odysseus, let the wisdom you've displayed
in all else show here now. It is the gods
who destined us to sorrow; they begrudged
our staying side by side—the two of us—
enjoying youth and coming to the start
of our old age together. Do not be
indignant if at first I did not greet
or welcome you as I do now: the heart
within my breast has always been afraid 250
that there might be some stranger who would come
to trick me with his blabber; many plot
with cunning malice. Even Argive Helen,
Zeus' daughter, never would have lain in love
beside a stranger had she known that sons
of the Achǽans were to wage a war
to bring her back again to her own land.
It surely was a god who spurred her act
of wantonness, who blinded her so that
she could not see what fate had brought to pass; 260
our sorrows, too, were born of her blindness.
But now you've listed clear, unerring signs
of our dear bed; no mortal's ever seen
that bed except for you and me and one
lone servant, Actor's child, the girl my father
had given me when I first journeyed here
to Ithaca—the maid who kept the doors
of our stout bridal chamber; and with this,
my heart, which was so stubborn, is convinced."

These were her words; they spurred his need to cry; 270
in tears Odysseus clasped his dear, wise wife.
And as the sight of land is welcomed by
the only shipwrecked sailors to survive
when whiplash winds and crashing combers sent
by lord Poseidon have destroyed their ship;
in flight from the gray sea, they swim toward shore,
their bodies caked with brine, and now at last
set foot upon the beach; their grief is past:
so at the sight of him, there was delight
in her; she twined her white arms round his neck. 280

And Dawn with her rose fingers would have found
those two still tearful had the gray-eyed goddess,
Athena, not devised this stratagem:
She slowed the night, delayed its journey's end;
and then she held back Dawn, whose throne is gold;
she did not let her yoke the racing foals
that carry light to men—the colts of Dawn,
Lampus and Pháethon. Odysseus said:

"Dear wife, we've not yet reached the end of all
our toils; in days to come, I'll face a test 290

so long and hard—so measureless—and yet
there is no part of it I can neglect.
So did the spirit of Tirésias
foresee; of this he told me on that day
when I went down to Hades' house to ask
about my comrades' and my journey back.
But come, wife, it is time for us to see
our bed, our joys, our rest, wrapped in sweet sleep."

This was the wise Penelope's reply:
"Now that the gods have brought you back again 300
to your own house and native land, your bed
stands fully ready any time you wish.
But since you called to mind that trial—it is
some god who made you think of that—speak out:
I'll have to hear of it at some time soon,
and now is just as good a time as then."

Odysseus, man of many wiles, replied:
"Strange woman! Why do you incite me so
to speak? And yet I'll tell you all I know
without disguise, though there is no delight 310
for you—and none for me—in hearing this
just as I heard it from Tirésias.
He said that I, with shapely oar in hand,
must visit many cities till I reach
a land where men know nothing of the sea
and don't use salt to season what they eat;
they're ignorant of boats with purple cheeks
and shapely oars that are the wings of ships.
He told me this clear sign, which I won't keep
from you: When on the road a man meets me 320
and says that what I'm carrying must be
a fan for winnowing, I can be sure:
that is the place where I must plant my oar
and offer lord Poseidon handsome gifts—
a ram, a bull, a boar that mates with sows.
Then, once I have returned to Ithaca,
I am to offer holy hecatombs
to the undying gods, wide heaven's lords—
to each in turn. I shall not die at sea:
the death that reaches me will be serene. 330
I shall grow old—a man of wealth and ease—
surrounded by a people rich, at peace.
All this, he said, will surely come to be."

The wise Penelope had this to say:
"Yet if the gods, at least in your old age,
allow you better days, you may escape
at last from trials and wars. So we can hope."

Such were the things they shared with one another.
Meanwhile, by bright torchlight, old Euryclēia

had joined Eurýnomë, and both were busy 340
wrapping the sturdy bedstead in soft blankets.
The old nurse then went back to her own room.
Eurýnomë, the keeper of their chamber,
led them across the court by firelight
and then went back again. And he and she
delighted in the sight of their old couch.

Telémachus, the cowherd, and the swineherd
meanwhile had stayed their feet; they danced no more;
and once they'd stopped the women, they themselves
lay down to sleep within the shadowed halls. 350

But when Odysseus and Penelope
had had their fill of love's delights, the joys
of talk were theirs, the telling one another
of all their trials. She told him of her grief
as she—fair woman—watched the vicious suitors,
that crowd who, in their wooing her, had butchered
so many beasts—both cattle and plump sheep—
as well as drawing wine beyond all measure.
Odysseus, born of Zeus, in turn rehearsed
the sorrows he'd inflicted and endured; 360
he spared her nothing. His dear wife felt deep
delight in listening, and no sweet sleep
touched her until his telling was complete.

His story started with his victory
against the Cíconës, and how he reached
the fertile land of men who feed on lotus.
He touched on all the malice of the Cyclops,
and how he'd made that monster pay his due
for having mercilessly eaten some
of his stout crew. King Ǽolus came next, 370
the lord who welcomed him, then sent him off,
though fate denied him passage to his home:
a storm wind snatched him up, thrust him across
the fish-rich sea as he groaned heavily.
And then his tale took in Telépylus,
the city of the Laestrygónians,
who wrecked his ship and killed his well-greaved men.
He also told of Círcë's wiles and craft
and how, upon a ship with many oars,
he came to Hades' somber house to meet 380
the spirit of Tirésias of Thebes;
there he saw all his comrades and his mother,
she who had borne and reared him. Then he told
how he had heard the never-ending song
the Sirens sing; and how he reached the rocks
they call the Wanderers, and grim Charýbdis,
and Scylla, she from whom no man has yet
escaped intact; and how his comrades killed
the herds of Hélios—and Zeus, the lord

of thunder, struck his swift ship with a bolt 390
of smoking lightning; all his comrades died,
and he alone escaped death's heartless Fates.
His coming to Calypso's isle, Ogýgia,
was next: that nymph had kept him in her caves;
she wanted him as husband; tending him,
she thought to make him deathless, ever young;
but she could not convince the heart within
his breast. So after many trials, he came
to the Phaeácians, who, most eagerly,
paid him the honors men bestow on gods 400
and, after they had given him much gold
and bronze and many clothes, escorted him
back to his own dear land on their swift ship.
This was the end of what he had to tell;
now sleep assaulted him, sweet sleep that can
loosen the limbs and soothe the griefs of men.

And now Athena had another scheme.
When she was sure his heart had filled its need
for love and bed and sleep, at once she roused,
from Ocean's flow, Dawn on her throne of gold 410
to carry light to men. From his soft bed
Odysseus rose; and to his wife, he said:

"By now we both have had our fill of trials.
You here, dear wife, were mourning over my
harassed and slow return; while on my part,
Zeus and the other gods combined to thwart
my longing for my native land. But now
that we have found the bed for which we yearned,
stay here, watch over all that I still own;
I shall replace the herds the braggart dead 420
consumed; I'll take much booty—do be sure—
and what I still may miss, Achǽans must
give me, until my every stall is full.
But now I leave the city; I must see
my father on our wooded farm—he grieves
for me. May you, dear wife—so wise—do this:
At sunrise, word of what I've done will spread;
men soon will know about the suitors' deaths;
so, with your women, go and stay inside
your room upstairs. See no one; ask no questions." 430

That said, he shouldered his fine armor, woke
Telémachus, the cowherd, and the swineherd,
and asked all three to wear their weaponry.
They did as he had asked: they took their arms
of bronze and, opening the doors, went out.
Odysseus led the way. Though light had touched
the earth by now, Athena cloaked those four
in night; she led them quickly from the city.

FROM BOOK 24
[The End of the Feud]

[In Book 24, Hermes leads the souls of the suitors into Hades, where Agamemnon and Achilles are discussing honorable and dishonorable deaths. Odysseus goes to find his father, Laértës, for a happy reunion. Reacting to the death of the suitors, many Ithacans take arms against Telémachus and Odysseus, who are assisted by Athena. Laértës bravely joins in the battle. At a signal from Zeus the fight is stopped; Athena asks Zeus whether there will be further war or reconciliation. Zeus explains his plan to Athena.–ED.]

. . . Zeus, summoner of clouds, replied: "My child,
why ask me this? Odysseus' taking vengeance
upon the suitors once he had returned—
was this not something you yourself had urged?
Do as you will, but this way is the best:
The suitors have been punished; bright Odysseus
has his revenge; and now let both the factions
conclude a solemn treaty; let Odysseus
rule over Ithaca for all his days,
and we'll persuade them to forget the slaughter 10
of sons and brothers. Let them live as once
they did: as friends, men blessed with peace and wealth."

Athena was already keen, but now
his words stirred her still more: she darted down
from high Olympus.

In Laértës' house
the meal, meanwhile, was done. They'd had their fill
of sweet food. Patient, bright Odysseus spoke:
"Let someone go to see if they've drawn close."

That said, the son of Dólius did as told
but, seeing enemies, stopped on the threshold. 20
At once he warned Odysseus with winged words:
"They're near already: let's be quick to gird."

That said, they rushed to put their armor on:
Odysseus' band of four—three and himself—
and all of Dólius' six sons. Laértës
and Dólius, though both were old and gray,
dressed, too, in armor—for in such a fray
they would be needed. With their bodies clothed
in gleaming bronze, they opened wide the doors;
Odysseus led the way as they rushed out. 30

Then, taking on the form and voice of Mentor,
Athena, Zeus's daughter, drew still closer.
The patient, bright Odysseus, seeing her,
was glad. He did not wait to tell his son:

"Telémachus, you'll learn this soon enough
when, in the thick of battle, you confront
the test that tries the bravest: Bring no shame
upon your father's house, for we are famed
on all this earth as men both strong and brave."

Telémachus' reply was keen and wise: 40
"If you so please, dear father, you will see
my courage: I shall not disgrace your house."

When he heard that, Laértës cried with joy:
"Dear gods, how great a day you've given me!
Indeed I'm happy now: a man who sees
his son and grandson vie in bravery!"

Gray-eyed Athena, at his side, then said:
"Arcēisius' son, most dear of all my friends,
first call upon the gray-eyed virgin and
our father Zeus, then do not wait to cast— 50
once you have balanced it—your long lance shaft."

She spoke—and gifted him with stalwart force.
He called upon the daughter of great Zeus,
then, quick to brandish his long shaft, he cast
his lance; he struck Eupēithes in his casque's
bronze cheeks. That spearhead did not stop; it pierced
straight through. He thudded down, his armor clanged.
Odysseus and his stout son fell upon
the forward ranks; with swords and two-edged spears,
they thrust and would have killed them all, cut off 60
all chance of their returning home, had not
Athena, daughter of aegis-bearing Zeus,
cried out. She checked the crowd of warriors:

"This gruesome war has lasted long enough.
Stop now, shed no more blood, and stand apart."

These were Athena's words. The townsmen heard;
and pale with fear, they lost their weapons: spears
and swords flew from their hands, dropped to the ground—
the goddess' voice had terrifying force.
They wheeled back, toward the city, keen to live. 70

Then patient, bright Odysseus' battle cry
was savage; like an eagle from on high,
he gathered force and swooped in fierce pursuit.
But now the son of Cronos cast a bolt
of blazing thunder, and it fell before
the daughter of the mighty lord of lords.
At that, Athena, gray-eyed goddess, warned:

"Laértēs' son, Odysseus, sprung from Zeus,
o man of many wiles, this is too much.
Halt now; have done with this relentless war, 80
lest you provoke the wrath of Zeus, the lord
of thunder, he whose voice is carried far."

He heard Athena's words and, glad at heart,
obeyed. A pact was sworn between the parts,
a treaty for all time: Athena's work
when she, the daughter of aegis-bearing Zeus,
had taken on lord Mentor's form and voice.

WESTERN TEXTS OF GREECE AND ROME

SAPPHO

[C. 600 B.C.E.]

Sappho, the female poet of sixth-century B.C.E. Greece whom Plato called "the tenth Muse," and upon whose work many poets of both sexes in ancient Greece and Rome modeled themselves, was honored in ancient times as the foremost writer of the Greek lyric. That reputation holds, even though we now possess very little of her work. Lyric poetry like Sappho's is invaluable because it gives us a glimpse of private emotions and everyday experience in a way Greek epic and drama seldom do. Epic writers and tragedians keep a certain distance from their great subjects, but the personal voice is central to the Greek lyric, whose practitioners write mostly in the first person about romantic love and lust, about celebrations and partings, about jealousy, betrayal, friendship, loss, death, and survival, all in the context of everyday life.

LIFE

A great body of legend and conjecture surrounds Sappho, but we know very little for certain. She was born to a well-to-do family sometime in the late seventh century B.C.E. on the Aegean island of Lesbos, off the coast of present-day Turkey, probably at Mytelene. Her mother was named Cleis; Sappho probably had two or three brothers. She is said to have been a small and dark-complected woman. Socrates calls her beautiful, but others say he must have been thinking about her poetry, not her person, and an anonymous commentator wrote that she was "like a nightingale with ill-shapen wings enfolding a tiny body." By a merchant husband or consort named Cercolis, Sappho apparently gave birth to a fair-haired daughter whom she named Cleis after her mother; she addresses her child tenderly in a number of poems.

There is a popular image of Sappho as a woman born before her time, a lonely poet dwelling with a few sympathetic women companions on a remote island outpost of Greek civilization. But in truth during Sappho's lifetime the Greek settlements on the Dodecanese Islands were lively trading centers, ports where people of Eastern and Western cultures might freely meet, small enclaves of art and learning where women were accorded high status. Sixth-century Lesbos was probably a far better place for independent and creative women to live than "Golden Age" fifth-century Athens. By all evidence, Sappho for most of her life lived and wrote within an emotionally close community of women friends and companions. The exact nature of that community is uncertain; the *moisopolon domos* or "house of the muses" Sappho refers to may have been anything ranging from an informal association of women friends gathered around her to a quite formal religious and educational order devoted to Aphrodite, with Sappho as head priestess in charge of both religious rites and the training of young novices. There is a tradition that Sappho died a suicide, throwing herself off a cliff into the sea when her love for a ferryman named Phaon was not returned, but this sounds like the folkloric sort of lover's-leap story that gets told about high places and famous people everywhere in the world. There is one fragment, in which she reminds her daughter that grief is not becoming to a poet's household, that sounds as though it might be a death-bed poem, spoken by a woman dying at home attended by her loving daughter and her friends.

WORK

Sappho is one of the great writers whose words have been deliberately and successfully banned. Except for one complete poem and four stanzas of another, all we possess of Sappho's writings are scattered lines and partial stanzas. Sappho's work disappeared not only because of the general neglect of ancient manuscripts during the Middle Ages, but also because of special acts of censorship. Owing to the lesbian themes of some of her poetry (the current word *lesbian* derives from Sappho's Lesbos), and perhaps because she was an honored female writer who depicted women as lively, intelligent, and goddess-worshipping, Sappho incurred the all-out animosity of the Christian Church patriarchy during the Middle Ages in a more thoroughgoing way than any Greek or Roman male writer did. Her poems were twice singled out for destruction by Church authorities; in the fourth century C.E., the Bishop of Constantinople decreed that her work should be destroyed, and again, in the eleventh century C.E., Pope Gregory VII ordered manuscripts of her poems to be thrown into public bonfires in Rome and Constantinople. Fragments of her work survive only because excerpts from her poems were quoted by other poets, by praiseful critics such as Longinus, and by Greek grammarians who wished to cite examples of the Aeolic dialect in which she wrote. Like a number of ancient writings, Sappho's work was restored to us in bits and pieces by nineteenth-century Egyptologists, who discovered that strips of papyrus torn from manuscripts of her poems had been used to stuff the mouths of mummified crocodiles. It is a measure of the astonishing personal intensity and music of her voice that even those fragments we possess have had the power to move readers deeply, century after century, leaving us longing to possess more of the nine books of odes, elegies, wedding songs, and hymns she is said to have written.

What has made Sappho's readers throughout time connect so strongly with her is her ability to sketch in a few words what passion and jealousy and lust and tenderness feel like, both physically and spiritually. Sometimes these emotions so transcend Sappho's gender, time, and circumstances that certain of her love poems have been translated or adapted again and again, assigned to male and female speakers alike, as in the poem beginning, "He is more than a hero," where she describes the physiological sensations of love-sickness. But she is also the first European woman writer to give us lyrical and intimate accounts of experience that is particularly female—the terrifying loss of virginity; the young woman's fear and anticipation of marriage, when it is the only way open to her; the way women talk among themselves when they are at ease with one another; the volatile friendships and rivalries among women poets; the choice of an especially finely made pair of sandals; the young girl in love putting her weaving aside impatiently, unable to concentrate on the household task her mother has set her. Sappho's poetry hymns not only the formal rites of Aphrodite, but the informal rituals that mark continuities between generations of women, as when she dresses her little daughter's fair hair, and remembers what her own mother used to tell her about fashions in headbands.

Sappho is probably best known for poems such as "He is more than a hero" that chronicle intense, aching passion, but it is fitting that the West's earliest lyric poet should also be a celebrant of the ordinary, of the way golden broom blossoms on the Greek coastline, of the pleasure of setting out fresh pillows for a welcome guest, of the shrilling of crickets and the smell of crushed grass.

Suggested Readings

Willis Barnstone's *Sappho; Lyrics in the Original Greek with Translations* (1965) contains a good introduction to Sappho's life and work. *Reflections of Women in Antiquity,* edited by Helene P. Foley (1981), contains feminist analyses of Sappho. A good introduction to the Greek lyric poets is featured in Diane Raynor's *Sappho's Lyre; Archaic Lyric and Women Poets of Ancient Greece* (1991).

"Standing by my bed"

Translated by Mary Barnard

Standing by my bed

In gold sandals
Dawn that very
moment awoke me

"At noontime"

Translated by Mary Barnard

At noontime

When the earth is
bright with flaming
heat falling straight down

the cricket sets
up a high-pitched
singing in his wings

"It's no use"

Translated by Mary Barnard

It's no use

Mother dear, I
can't finish my
weaving
You may
blame Aphrodite

soft as she is

she has almost
killed me with
love for that boy

"People do gossip"

Translated by Mary Barnard

People do gossip

And they say about
Leda,[1] that she

once found an egg
hidden under

wild hyacinths

"Sleep, darling"

Translated by Mary Barnard

Sleep, darling

I have a small
daughter called
Cleis, who is

[1] Zeus raped the Spartan queen Leda while he assumed the form of a swan. In time she gave birth to two eggs, and hatched the hero-twins Castor and Polydeuces (the Gemini of the zodiac), and Helen of Troy.

like a golden
flower
I wouldn't
take all Croesus'[1]
kingdom with love
thrown in, for her

"Don't ask me what to wear"

Translated by Mary Barnard

Don't ask me what to wear

I have no embroidered
headband from Sardis to
give you, Cleis, such as
I wore
and my mother
always said that in her
day a purple ribbon
looped in the hair was thought
to be high style indeed

but we were dark:
a girl
whose hair is yellower than
torchlight should wear no
headdress but fresh flowers

Hymen Hymenaon![1]

Translated by Mary Barnard

FIRST VOICE
Raise the rafters! Hoist
them higher! Here comes
a bridegroom taller
than Ares!

SECOND VOICE
Hymen
Hymenaon!

[1] Croesus: Lydian king (560–546 B.C.E.) proverbial for his wealth.

HYMEN HYMENAON!

[1] Hymen was the Greek god of marriage.

FIRST VOICE
He towers
above tall men as
poets of Lesbos
over all others!

SECOND VOICE
Sing Hymen
O Hymenaon

Lament for a Maidenhead

Translated by Mary Barnard

FIRST VOICE
Like a quince-apple
ripening on a top
branch in a tree top

not once noticed by
harvesters or if
not unnoticed, not reached

SECOND VOICE
Like a hyacinth in
the mountains, trampled
by shepherds until
only a purple stain
remains on the ground

"He is more than a hero"

Translated by Mary Barnard

He is more than a hero

He is a god in my eyes—
the man who is allowed
to sit beside you—he

who listens intimately
to the sweet murmur of
your voice, the enticing

laughter that makes my own
heart beat fast. If I meet
you suddenly, I can't

speak—my tongue is broken;
a thin flame runs under
my skin; seeing nothing,

hearing only my own ears
drumming, I drip with sweat;
trembling shakes my body

and I turn paler than
dry grass. At such times
death isn't far from me

"You know the place: then"

Translated by Mary Barnard

You know the place: then

Leave Crete and come to us
waiting where the grove is
pleasantest, by precincts

sacred to you; incense
smokes on the altar, cold
streams murmur through the

apple branches, a young
rose thicket shades the ground
and quivering leaves pour

down deep sleep; in meadows
where horses have grown sleek
among spring flowers, dill

scents the air. Queen! Cyprian![1]
Fill our gold cups with love
stirred into clear nectar

"I have had not one word from her"

Translated by Mary Barnard

I have had not one word from her

Frankly I wish I were dead.
When she left, she wept

[1]This poem is addressed to Aphrodite, who was conceived when Zeus ejaculated into the sea-foam off the coast of Cyprus.

a great deal; she said to
me, "This parting must be
endured, Sappho. I go unwillingly."

I said, "Go, and be happy
but remember (you know
well) whom you leave shackled by love

"If you forget me, think
of our gifts to Aphrodite
and all the loveliness that we shared

"all the violet tiaras,
braided rosebuds, dill and
crocus twined around your young neck

"myrrh poured on your head
and on soft mats girls with
all that they most wished for beside them

"while no voices chanted
choruses without ours,
no woodlot bloomed in spring without song..."

"Do you remember"

Translated by Mary Barnard

Do you remember

How a golden
broom grows on
the sea beaches

"If you will come"

Translated by Mary Barnard

If you will come

I shall put out
new pillows for
you to rest on

"Must I remind you, Cleis"

Translated by Mary Barnard

Must I remind you, Cleis,

That sounds of grief
are unbecoming in
a poet's household?

and that they are not
suitable in ours?

AESOP

[DIED 564 B.C.E.?]

The animal fable in Western literature is traditionally traced back to Aesop, a Greek slave on the Aegean island of Samos in the sixth century B.C.E. Little is known about Aesop, although he is thought to have come originally from Thrace, an area including parts of modern Macedonia, Bulgaria, and western Turkey. Legend has it that he was freed by his master and that he became a diplomat for King Croesus. Legend has also ascribed nearly all Greek animal fables to Aesop, even though many later writers contributed to the collection of stories that have become known as Aesop's Fables.

The simple format and the colloquial tone of the fables suggest their origin in oral storytelling. Indeed, in early classical times the fables seem to have been collected for use by orators as amusing illustrations or instructive examples in speeches. Aesop's animals, thinly disguising familiar human characteristics and emotions and faced with typical human dilemmas, appealed to both the young and old, the educated and uneducated. Later classical collections of Aesop were more literary, often being versified and presented for a more literate reading audience, as in the versions of Phaedrus in the first century C.E. and Avianus in the fourth century.

Aesopian fable has reappeared in nearly every age of Western literature, but it has been most significant in the Middle Ages and in the eighteenth century. William Caxton's 1484 edition of Aesop signals a medieval fascination with the beast fable that appears in the work of such writers as John Lydgate and Robert Henryson, and in works such as *Piers Plowman* or the famous "Nun's Priest's Tale" in Chaucer's *Canterbury Tales*. In the eighteenth century, Aesop's influence can be seen in such works as Jonathan Swift's *A Tale of a Tub* (1704), Bernard Mandeville's *Fable of the Bees* (1714), or Gotthold Lessing's *Fabeln* (1759). Perhaps Aesop's most famous successor is Jean de La Fontaine, the seventeenth-century French writer who devoted his literary career to the creation of such fables. Modern stories that carry the Aesopian tradition into our own time include Rudyard Kipling's *Just So Stories* (1902), James Thurber's *Fables for Our Time* (1940), and George Orwell's extended Aesopian fable, *Animal Farm* (1945).

The animal fable is not strictly a Western form. The use of animals to make moral lessons more palatable is worldwide. Many such tales appear in the literature of Africa, the American Indians, and the East; some of Aesop's tales are thought to have come from East Indian sources. We have included the fables that follow, however, to provide a contrast to the philosophic tales of Chuang Tzu; a sampler of these stories, representative of Taoism, another Eastern tradition, is offered in the World Context section.

Short and aphoristic, the fables of Aesop and the tales of Chuang Tzu take quite different postures toward reality and the way to live a better life. Aesop's tales might be described as confrontational: They present a conflict between two competing points of view. Their titles often identify the two sides in the struggle, as in "The Ant and the Grasshopper" or "The Dog and the Wolf," and the moral at the end makes explicit to the reader the reason for the winner's triumph. Chuang Tzu, by contrast, is an assimilationist. Where Aesop instructs, Chuang Tzu invites contemplation. His tales stress convergence and similarity rather than conflict and difference. The aim in the Taoist tale is harmony and assimilation, not victory. The story does not ask the reader to distinguish right from wrong points of view, but to blend differences into a larger, more holistic perspective. Stressing right action, the confrontational Aesopian fable teaches that the way to be is to do. The Taoist assimilationist fable, on the other hand, teaches that the way to do is to be.

Suggested Readings

G. K. Chesterton discusses the nature of the Aesopian fable and contrasts it with the fairy tale in his essay "Aesop's Fables" in *The Spice of Life and Other Essays* (1964). P. Gila Reinstein similarly contrasts the messages in Grimm's tales with those in Aesop in "Aesop and Grimm, Contrast in Ethical Codes and Contemporary Values" in *Children's Literature in Education,* n.s., 14 (Spring 1983) 44–53. The *Children's Literature Association Quarterly* included a special section in its Summer 1984 issue to celebrate the five-hundredth anniversary of Aesop in English; they included discussions of the tales, of the different translations and illustrations, and of the tradition of the fable in English. A scholarly discussion of the textual history of the fables can be found in B. E. Perry's *Studies in the Text History of the Life and Fables of Aesop* (1981).

Fables

Translated by Joseph Jacobs

The Wolf and the Lamb

Once upon a time a Wolf was lapping at a spring on a hillside, when, looking up, what should he see but a Lamb just beginning to drink a little lower down. "There's my supper," thought he, "if only I can find some excuse to seize it." Then he called out to the Lamb, "How dare you muddle the water from which I am drinking?"

"Nay, master, nay," said Lambikin; "if the water be muddy up there, I cannot be the cause of it, for it runs down from you to me."

"Well, then," said the Wolf, "why did you call me bad names this time last year?"

"That cannot be," said the Lamb; "I am only six months old."

"I don't care," snarled the Wolf; "if it was not you it was your father"; and with that he rushed upon the poor little Lamb and—

WARRA WARRA WARRA WARRA WARRA—

ate her all up. But before she died she gasped out—

"ANY EXCUSE WILL SERVE A TYRANT."

Androcles

A slave named Androcles once escaped from his master and fled to the forest. As he was wandering about there he came upon a Lion lying down moaning and groaning. At first he turned to flee, but finding that the Lion did not pursue him, he turned back and went up to him. As he came near, the Lion put out his paw, which was all swollen and bleeding, and Androcles found that a huge thorn had got into it, and was causing all the pain. He pulled out the thorn and bound up the paw of the Lion, who was soon able to rise and lick the hand of Androcles like a dog. Then the Lion took Androcles to his cave, and every day used to bring him meat from which to live. But shortly afterwards both Androcles and the Lion were captured, and the slave was sentenced to be thrown to the Lion, after the latter had been kept without food for several days. The Emperor and all his Court came to see the spectacle, and Androcles was led out into the middle of the arena. Soon the Lion was let loose from his den, and rushed bounding and roaring towards his victim. But as soon as he came near to Androcles he recognised his friend, and fawned upon him, and licked his hands like a friendly dog. The Emperor, surprised at this, summoned Androcles to him, who told him the whole story. Whereupon the slave was pardoned and freed, and the Lion let loose to his native forest.

"GRATITUDE IS THE SIGN OF NOBLE SOULS."

The Dog and the Wolf

A gaunt Wolf was almost dead with hunger when he happened to meet a House-dog who was passing by. "Ah, Cousin," said the Dog, "I knew how it would be; your irregular life will soon be the ruin of you. Why do you not work steadily as I do, and get your food regularly given to you?"

"I would have no objection," said the Wolf, "if I could only get a place."

"I will easily arrange that for you," said the Dog; "come with me to my master and you shall share my work."

So the Wolf and the Dog went towards the town together. On the way there the Wolf noticed that the hair on a certain part of the Dog's neck was very much worn away, so he asked him how that had come about.

"Oh, it is nothing," said the Dog. "That is only the place where the collar is put on at night to keep me chained up; it chafes a bit, but one soon gets used to it."

"Is that all?" said the Wolf. "Then good-bye to you, Master Dog."

"BETTER STARVE FREE THAN BE A FAT SLAVE."

The Horse, Hunter, and Stag

A quarrel had arisen between the Horse and the Stag, so the Horse came to a Hunter to ask his help to take revenge on the Stag. The Hunter agreed, but said: "If you desire to conquer the Stag, you must permit me to place this piece of iron between your jaws, so that I may guide you with these reins, and allow this saddle to be placed upon your back so that I may keep steady upon you as we follow after the enemy." The Horse agreed to the conditions, and the Hunter soon saddled and bridled him. Then with the aid of the Hunter the Horse soon overcame the Stag, and said to the Hunter: "Now, get off, and remove those things from my mouth and back."

"Not so fast, friend," said the Hunter. "I have now got you under bit and spur, and prefer to keep you as you are at present."

"IF YOU ALLOW MEN TO USE YOU FOR YOUR OWN PURPOSES, THEY WILL USE YOU FOR THEIRS."

THE LION AND THE STATUE

A Man and a Lion were discussing the relative strength of men and lions in general. The Man contended that he and his fellows were stronger than lions by reason of their greater intelligence. "Come now with me," he cried, "and I will soon prove that I am right." So he took him into the public gardens and showed him a statue of Hercules overcoming the Lion and tearing his mouth in two.

"That is all very well," said the Lion, "but proves nothing, for it was a man who made the statue."

"WE CAN EASILY REPRESENT THINGS AS WE WISH THEM TO BE."

THE ANT AND THE GRASSHOPPER

In a field one summer's day a Grasshopper was hopping about, chirping and singing to its heart's content. An Ant passed by, bearing along with great toil an ear of corn he was taking to the nest.

"Why not come and chat with me," said the Grasshopper, "instead of toiling and moiling in that way?"

"I am helping to lay up food for the winter," said the Ant, "and recommend you to do the same."

"Why bother about winter?" said the Grasshopper; "we have got plenty of food at present." But the Ant went on its way and continued its toil. When the winter came the Grasshopper had no food, and found itself dying of hunger, while it saw the ants distributing every day corn and grain from the stores they had collected in the summer. Then the Grasshopper knew

"IT IS BEST TO PREPARE FOR THE DAYS OF NECESSITY."

THE TREE AND THE REED

"Well, little one," said a Tree to a Reed that was growing at its foot, "why do you not plant your feet deeply in the ground, and raise your head boldly in the air as I do?"

"I am contented with my lot," said the Reed. "I may not be so grand, but I think I am safer."

"Safe!" sneered the Tree. "Who shall pluck me up by the roots or bow my head to the ground?" But it soon had to repent of its boasting, for a hurricane arose which tore it up from its roots, and cast it a useless log on the ground, while the little Reed, bending to the force of the wind, soon stood upright again when the storm had passed over.

"OBSCURITY OFTEN BRINGS SAFETY."

THE SHEPHERD'S BOY

There was once a young Shepherd Boy who tended his sheep at the foot of a mountain near a dark forest. It was rather lonely for him all day, so he thought upon a plan by which he could get a little company and some excitement. He rushed down towards the village calling out "Wolf, Wolf," and the villagers came out to meet him, and some of them stopped with him for a considerable time. This pleased the boy so much that a few days afterwards he tried the same trick, and again the villagers came to his help. But shortly after this a Wolf actually did come out from the forest, and began to worry the sheep, and the boy of course cried out "Wolf, Wolf," still louder than before. But this time the villagers, who had been fooled twice before, thought the boy was again deceiving them, and nobody stirred to come to his help. So the Wolf made a good meal off the boy's flock, and when the boy complained, the wise man of the village said:

"A LIAR WILL NOT BE BELIEVED, EVEN WHEN HE SPEAKS THE TRUTH."

THE MAN AND HIS TWO WIVES

In the old days, when men were allowed to have many wives, a middle-aged Man had one wife that was old and one that was young; each loved him very much, and desired to see him like herself. Now the Man's hair was turning grey, which the young Wife did not like, as it made him look too old for her husband. So every night she used to comb his hair and pick out the white ones. But the elder Wife saw her husband growing grey with great pleasure, for she did not like to be mistaken for his mother. So every morning she used to arrange his hair and pick out as many of the black ones as she could. The consequence was the Man soon found himself entirely bald.

"YIELD TO ALL AND YOU WILL SOON HAVE NOTHING TO YIELD."

THE TWO FELLOWS AND THE BEAR

Two Fellows were travelling together through a wood, when a Bear rushed out upon them. One of the travellers happened to be in front, and he seized hold of the branch of a tree, and hid himself among the leaves. The other, seeing no help for it, threw himself flat down upon the ground, with his face in the dust. The Bear, coming up to him, put his muzzle close to his ear, and sniffed and sniffed. But at last with a growl he shook his head and slouched off, for bears will not touch dead meat. Then the fellow in the tree came down to his comrade, and, laughing, said "What was it that Master Bruin whispered to you?"

"He told me," said the other,

"NEVER TRUST A FRIEND WHO DESERTS YOU AT A PINCH."

THE ASS'S BRAINS

The Lion and the Fox went hunting together. The Lion, on the advice of the Fox, sent a message to the Ass, proposing to make an alliance between their two families. The Ass came to the place of meeting, overjoyed at the prospect of a royal alliance. But when he came there the Lion simply pounced on the Ass, and said to the Fox: "Here is our dinner for to-day. Watch you here while I go and have a nap. Woe betide you if you touch my prey." The Lion went away and the Fox waited; but finding that his master did not return, ventured to take out the brains of the Ass and ate them up. When the Lion came back he soon noticed the absence of the brains, and asked the Fox in a terrible voice: "What have you done with the brains?"

"Brains, your Majesty! it had none, or it would never have fallen into your trap."

"WIT HAS ALWAYS AN ANSWER READY."

AESCHYLUS

[525–456 B.C.E.]

Rarely is a great poet a participant in a defining moment of his nation's history. We could say this of Virgil, present at the founding of the Roman Empire; Dante Alighieri, statesman and later exile of the city of Florence; John Milton, partisan of the Puritan cause in England; Walt Whitman, chronicler of the Civil War in the United States; and Vladimir Mayakovsky, first Soviet poet of the Russian Revolution. The Athenian tragedian Aeschylus must surely rate this distinction. A combatant in the victories over the Persians at Marathon in 490 B.C.E. and at Salamis and Plataea in 480–479 B.C.E., he watched Athens go on to develop the greatest civilization in ancient history; he even lived to see the beginning of the Age of Pericles in 461. His crowning triumph, the trilogy of plays called *The Oresteia,* came at the height of Athenian glory, winning the city's drama prize in 458 B.C.E.

Aeschylus and Greek Drama

Dramatically as well as politically, Aeschylus stood at a crossroads. He helped invent classical Greek drama, elevating it to a format approaching that of the modern theater. He took the earlier dramatic format, made up of the chorus and a single actor, and expanded it by limiting the size of the chorus to twelve and adding a second actor on stage. This changed the stage from an essentially static place in which the playwright recited the speeches of the hero to an active one in which professional actors played the roles the performance demanded.

The Oresteia

The Oresteia is composed of three plays: *Agamemnon,* the story of the murder of King Agamemnon by his wife Clytemnestra and her lover Aegisthus on his return from the Trojan War; *The Choephori,* the story of the return of Orestes, the son of Agamemnon, to avenge his father's murder; and *The Eumenides,* the story of the judgment of Orestes, in which he is declared innocent of the murder of his mother and her consort, and the blood-curse on the royal house is lifted. At the heart of *The Oresteia* is the idea that justice is a matter to be decided by the citizens of the state, not by an individual taking personal revenge nor by a priest class appointed to exact ritual punishment. The plays celebrate Athenian law, even giving it divine approval; the goddess of the city, Pallas Athena, renders the final verdict when the jury of citizens deadlocks. Our text includes two of the three plays in the trilogy, *Agamemnon* and *The Eumenides*.

In the background of *The Oresteia* is a story of family rivalry leading to a bloody cycle of revenge. The action concerns the House of Atreus in the city of Argos. In days past, Atreus had contested bitterly with his brother Thyestes for the throne of Argos. Greedy for power, Atreus murdered two of his brother's sons and served them up to Thyestes in a stew, thereby polluting him so that the citizens of Argos would never choose him as their king. But the surviving son of Thyestes, Aegisthus, has waited for his opportunity to seek revenge on Agamemnon, the son of Atreus and next ruler of Argos. In Agamemnon's absence during the Trojan War, Aegisthus, who is cowardly and devious, has formed an alliance with Agamemnon's wife and queen, Clytemnestra, and become her lover. Together they plot the death of Agamemnon upon his return.

Agamemnon

In the foreground of the play *Agamemnon* is King Agamemnon, hero of the Trojan War. He has joined his brother, King Menelaus of Sparta, in raising an army of Greeks after Menelaus' wife, Helen, was stolen by Paris, son of King Priam of Troy. Agamemnon thus becomes one of the two major battle leaders on the Greek side of the war. When his departure from Argos is frustrated by a becalmed sea, Agamemnon seeks a prophecy and discovers that the gods demand the sacrifice of his daughter, Iphigenia, in order for his ships to sail. He sacrifices his daughter and sets sail for Troy, leaving behind his wife, Clytemnestra, to mourn her daughter's death and plot revenge against her husband.

As the action begins, Agamemnon returns to Argos, greeted by Clytemnestra with more ceremony than he believes necessary. They argue, and then withdraw together. The chorus, which is constantly remembering and forgetting again the crimes that lie heavy on the land, hears Agamemnon's prisoner and concubine, the Trojan prophetess Cassandra, predict what is about to happen, but misinterprets her remarks. There is a scream from inside the door and Agamemnon's corpse is revealed. Clytemnestra and Aegisthus address the chorus, giving their reasons for the murder. The play ends with members of the chorus calling for the return of Orestes, the son of Agamemnon, to avenge his father's death and the usurpation of the state by Aegisthus.

The Choephori

In the play omitted here, *The Choephori,* Orestes returns. Spurred on by Apollo, he kills both his mother and Aegisthus. But a sense of guilt invades him: To avenge regicide, the murder of his father the king, he has committed matricide, the murder of his mother the queen. Furthermore, he has acted against the claims of both Aegisthus and Clytemnestra that *they* were in the right in murdering Agamemnon: Aegisthus in revenge against the House of Atreus for the murder of his brothers and pollution of his father, and Clytemnestra in revenge for the murder of her daughter, Iphigenia. Orestes, in killing the pair, is both an avenging hero and the perpetrator of fresh crimes; how will he account for his act? We pick up the action at the beginning of the third play, *The Eumenides*.

The Eumenides

The play opens at the temple of Apollo, where Orestes, his hands still dripping blood from the double killing, has gone seeking refuge from the twelve Furies, female monsters who pursue him with the knowledge of his guilt. The Furies prove to be the ancient upholders of vengeance who claim special jurisdiction in cases of a crime committed within a family. Apollo, whose powers are limited in this situation, sends Orestes to the temple of Athena, the goddess of wisdom. The Furies follow him and confront Athena with their case against him. They invite Athena to judge the case herself, but she decides instead to create a court of the citizens of Athens at whose head she will sit. This court of peers, a new innovation, is the centerpiece of the drama, since the play itself is presented for approval to the same Athenian citizenry.

At the trial, Orestes confesses to the killing of Clytemnestra, but pleads that he did so at the behest of Apollo. The rest of the case turns on the technical point of whether Orestes carries the blood of his mother Clytemnestra, since the fluid that formed him comes from the body of his father, Agamemnon. The citizen jury is evenly divided on the verdict, and Athena decides for Orestes. At the end of the play, peace is made with the Furies: Their traditional role is reconciled with the new system of law in Athens, and to placate them further Athena renames them the Eumenides, the "kindly ones." They will have their new home in Athens and exercise limited authority as the guardians of marriage, while the courts will decide in matters of law.

The intent of the plays, as mentioned before, is to celebrate the creation of the Athenian courts of law. Modern readers, however, have also seen in the plays an important treatment of the subject of women, in which the women come up losers more often than not. Cassandra, the prophetess unable to affect the outcome of what she sees, is killed during the murder of her earlier captor, Agamemnon. Clytemnestra, Agamemnon's wife, is held responsible for his murder despite her reason for the crime, the murder of her child. Orestes, on the other hand, is justified in murdering his mother because it is determined that the father's seed alone forms the blood of the offspring. The Furies, descendants of the goddesses of the past, lose their argument and are relegated to a secondary position in Athenian society. Athena, the goddess who is not born of woman, decides the case in favor of Orestes because he is a man! Given the state of society and the beliefs of the time, *The Oresteia* forms a convenient starting point for a discussion of the role of patriarchal ideas in ancient Western cultures.

Suggested Readings

Two recent translations of the plays offer somewhat different readings: Philip Vellacott's *Aeschylus: The Oresteian Tragedy* (1956), and Robert Fagles's *Aeschylus: The Oresteia* (1977). The standard edition is the three-volume translation and commentary by Hugh Lloyd-Jones, *Agamemnon, The Libation Bearers, The Eumenides* (1970). A good general introduction to the poet and his plays is John Herington's *Aeschylus* (1986). The reader should also refer to Marsh H. McCall's *Aeschylus: A Collection of Critical Essays* (1972). Recent works that treat the plays in the Greek context include Gerald Else's *The Origin and Early Form of Greek Tragedy* (1965), Anthony Podlecki's *The Political Background of Aeschylean Tragedy* (1966), and Brian Vickers's *Towards Greek Tragedy: Drama, Myth, Society* (1973).

The Oresteia: Agamemnon

Translated by Philip Vellacott

CHARACTERS:

A WATCHMAN
CHORUS *of twelve Elders of Argos*
CLYTEMNESTRA, *wife of Agamemnon*
A HERALD
AGAMEMNON, *King of Argos*
CASSANDRA, *a princess of Troy*
AEGISTHUS, *Clytemnestra's paramour, cousin to Agamemnon*
Soldiers attending Agamemnon; guards attending Aegisthus

It is night, a little before sunrise. On the roof of Atreus' palace a WATCHMAN *stands, or rises from a small mattress placed on the hewn stone. In front of the palace are statues of Zeus, Apollo, and Hermes; each with an altar before it.*

WATCHMAN:

O gods! grant me release from this long weary watch.
Release, O gods! Twelve full months now, night after night
Dog-like I lie here, keeping guard from this high roof
On Atreus' palace. The nightly conference of stars,
Resplendent rulers, bringing heat and cold in turn,
Studding the sky with beauty—I know them all, and watch them
Setting and rising; but the one light I long to see
Is a new star, the promised sign, the beacon-flare
To speak from Troy and utter one word, 'Victory!'—
Great news for Clytemnestra, in whose woman's heart 10
A man's will nurses hope.
Now once more, drenched with dew,
I walk about; lie down, but no dreams visit me.
Sleep's enemy, fear, stands guard beside me, to forbid
My eyes one instant's closing. If I sing some tune—
Since music's the one cure prescribed for heartsickness—
Why, then I weep, to think how changed this house is now
From splendour of old days, ruled by its rightful lord.
So may the gods be kind and grant release from trouble,
And send the fire to cheer this dark night with good news.
[*The beacon shines out.*]
O welcome beacon, kindling night to glorious day, 20
Welcome! You'll set them dancing in every street in Argos
When they hear your message. Ho there! Hullo! Call Clytemnestra!
The Queen must rise at once like Dawn from her bed, and welcome
The fire with pious words and a shout of victory,
For the town of Ilion's ours—that beacon's clear enough!
I'll be the first myself to start the triumphal dance.
Now I can say the gods have blessed my master's hand;
And for me too that beacon-light's a lucky throw.
Now Heaven bring Agamemnon safe to his home! May I
Hold his dear hand in mine! For the rest, I say no more; 30
My tongue's nailed down.[1] This house itself, if walls had words,
Would tell its story plainly. Well, I speak to those
Who understand me; to the rest—my door is shut.

[*He descends. Lights begin to appear in the palace. A cry of triumph is heard from* CLYTEMNESTRA *within, and is echoed by other women. Then from the palace a messenger hurries out towards the city; attendants follow, going in various directions, and carrying jars and bowls with oil and incense for sacrifice. Then* CLYTEMNESTRA *enters from the palace, with two attendants; she casts incense on the altars, and prays before the statue of Zeus. Day begins to break. From the city enter the* ELDERS OF ARGOS. *They do not yet see* CLYTEMNESTRA.]

CHORUS:

Ten years have passed since the strong sons of Atreus,
Menelaus and Agamemnon, both alike

[1] The literal meaning of the Greek is "A great ox stands on my tongue."

Honoured by Zeus with throned and sceptred power,
Gathered and manned a thousand Argive ships,
And with the youth of Hellas under arms
Sailed from these ports to settle scores with Priam.

Then loud their warlike anger cried, 40
As eagles cry, that wild with grief,
On some steep, lonely mountain-side
Above their robbed nest wheel and sail,
Oaring the airy waves, and wail
Their wasted toil, their watchful pride;
Till some celestial deity,
Zeus, Pan, Apollo,[2] hears on high
Their scream of wordless misery;
And pitying their forlorn estate
(Since air is Heaven's protectorate) 50
Sends a swift Fury to pursue
Marauding guilt with vengeance due.

So against Paris's guilty boast
Zeus, witness between guest and host,
Sends Atreus' sons for stern redress
Of his and Helen's wantonness.
Now Greece and Troy both pay their equal debt
Of aching limbs and wounds and sweat,
While knees sink low in gory dust,
And spears are shivered at first thrust. 60

Things are—as they are now; their end
Shall follow Fate's decree, which none can bend.
In vain shall Priam's altars burn,
His rich libations vainly flow
To gods above and powers below:
No gift, no sacrificial flame
Can soothe or turn
The wrath of Heaven from its relentless aim.

We were too old to take our share
With those who joined the army then. 70
We lean on sticks—in strength not men
But children; so they left us here.
In weakness youth and age are one:
The sap sleeps in the unripe bone
As in the withered. The green stalk
Grows without thorns: so, in the grey
And brittle years, old men must walk
Three-footed, weak as babes, and stray
Like dreams lost in the light of day.

---

[2]The gods care for the helpless young of animals. Cf. Calchas' address to Artemis, below. The parallel between these two passages suggests that the rape of Helen and the sacrifice of Iphigenia were both abhorrent to the gods.

[*Here the* CHORUS-LEADER *sees* CLYTEMNESTRA.]

Daughter of Tyndareos, Queen Clytemnestra, 80
What have you heard? What has happened? Why have you ordered
Sacrifice through the city? Is there news?
Altars of all the gods who guard our State,
Gods of the sky, powers of the lower earth,
Altars of town and country, blaze with offerings;
On every hand heaven-leaping flames implore
Anger to melt in gentleness—a glare
Enriched with holy ointment, balm so rare
As issues only from a royal store!
Why are these things? Be gracious, Queen: 90
Tell what you can, or what you may;
Be healer of this haunting fear
Which now like an enemy creeps near,
And now again, when hope has seen
These altars bright with promise, slinks away—
Tell us, that hope may lift the load
Which galls our souls by night and day,
Sick with the evil which has been,
The evil which our hearts forebode.[3]

[CLYTEMNESTRA *remains silent, her back turned to the* CHORUS.]

[*They continue, addressing the audience.*]

I am the man to speak, if you would hear 100
The whole tale from its hopeful starting-place—
That portent, which amazed our marching youth.
It was ten years ago—but I was there.[4]
The poet's grace, the singer's fire,
Grow with his years; and I can still speak truth
With the clear ring the gods inspire;—
How those twin monarchs of our warlike race,
Two leaders one in purpose, were sped forth—
Their vengeful spears in thousands pointing North
To Troy—by four wings' furious beat: 110
Two kings of birds, that seemed to bode
Great fortune to the kings of that great fleet.
Close to the palace, on spear-side of the road,
One tawny-feathered, one white in the tail,
Perched in full view, they ravenously tear
The body of a pregnant hare
Big with her burden, now a living prey
In the last darkness of their unborn day.[5]
Cry Sorrow, sorrow—yet let good prevail!
The army's learned Seer[6] saw this, and knew 120

---

[3]Past evil (the killing of Iphigenia) makes them apprehensive of the future. They now proceed to tell the story of the setting-out of the expedition.

[4]This line is inserted to make the situation clearer.

[5]The portent's primary meaning is the destruction of Troy, with its teeming population, by Agamemnon and Menelaus. There is also a secondary allusion to the sacrifice of Iphigenia. She was offered to Artemis, but "Artemis abominates the eagles' feast."

[6]Calchas, who was with the army throughout the ten years. He prescribed human sacrifice again when Troy was captured.

The devourers of the hare
For that relentless pair—
Different in nature, as the birds in hue—
The sons of Atreus; and in council of war
Thus prophesied: 'Your army, it is true,
In time shall make King Priam's town their prey;
Those flocks and herds Troy's priests shall slay
With prayers for safety of her wall
Perish in vain—Troy's violent doom shall swallow all.
Only, see to it, you who go 130
To bridle Trojan pride, that no
Anger of gods benight your day
And strike before your hulls are under way.
For virgin Artemis, whom all revere,
Hates with a deadly hate
The swift-winged hounds of Zeus who swooped to assail
Their helpless victim wild with fear
Before her ripe hour came;
Who dared to violate
(So warning spoke the priest) 140
The awe that parenthood must claim,
As for some rite performed in Heaven's name;
Yes, Artemis abominates the eagles' feast!'
Cry Sorrow, sorrow—yet let good prevail!

Still spoke on the prophet's tongue:
'Lovely child of Zeus, I pray,[7]
You who love the tender whelp
Of the ravening lion, and care
For the fresh-wild sucking young
Of fox and rat and hind and hare; 150
If ever by your heavenly help
Hope of good was brought to flower,
Bless the sign we saw to-day!
Cancel all its presaged ill,
All its promised good fulfil!
Next my anxious prayers entreat
Lord Apollo's healing power,
That his Sister may not plan
Winds to chain the Hellene fleet;
That her grievance may not crave 160
Blood to drench another grave
From a different sacrifice
Hallowed by no festal joy—
Blood that builds a tower of hate,
Mad blood raging to destroy
Its self-source, a ruthless Fate
Warring with the flesh of man;
Bloodshed bringing in its train

[7] Artemis. She and Apollo were the twin children of Leto by Zeus.

Kindred blood that flows again,
Anger still unreconciled 170
Poisoning a house's life
With darkness, treachery and strife,
Wreaking vengeance for a murdered child.'

So Calchas, from that parting prodigy
Auguring the royal house's destiny,
Pronounced his warning of a fatal curse,
With hope of better mingling fear of worse.
Let us too, echoing his uncertain tale,
Cry *Sorrow, sorrow—yet let good prevail!*

Let good prevail! 180
So be it! Yet, what is good? And who
Is God? How name him, and speak true?[8]
If he accept the name that men
Give him, Zeus I name him then.
I, still perplexed in mind,
For long have searched and weighed
Every hope of comfort or of aid:
Still I can find
No creed to lift this heaviness,
This fear that haunts without excuse— 190
No name inviting faith, no wistful guess,
Save only—Zeus.

The first of gods is gone,
Old Ouranos, once blown
With violence and pride;
His name shall not be known,
Nor that his dynasty once lived, and died.
His strong successor, Cronos, had his hour,
Then went his way, thrice thrown
By a yet stronger power. 200
Now Zeus is lord; and he
Who loyally acclaims his victory
Shall by heart's instinct find the universal key:

Zeus, whose will has marked for man
The sole way where wisdom lies;
Ordered one eternal plan:
Man must suffer to be wise.
Head-winds heavy with past ill
Stray his course and cloud his heart:
Sorrow takes the blind soul's part— 210
Man grows wise against his will.

[8]This question is inserted to make clear the sequence of thought, which is that "Let good prevail" assumes an understanding of what "good" is, and leads back to the more fundamental problem of God and so to the theme of the stanza.

For powers who rule from thrones above
By ruthlessness commend their love.

So was it then. Agamemnon, mortified,
Dared not, would not, admit to error; thought
Of his great Hellene fleet, and in his pride
Spread sail to the ill wind he should have fought.
Meanwhile his armed men moped along the shores,
And cursed the wind, and ate his dwindling stores;
Stared at white Chalkis' roofs day after day 220
Across the swell that churned in Aulis Bay.
And still from Strymon came that Northern blast,
While hulks and ropes grew rotten, mooring parted,
Deserters slunk away,
All ground their teeth, bored, helpless, hungry, thwarted.
The days of waiting doubled. More days passed.
The flower of warlike Hellas withered fast.

Then Calchas spoke again. The wind, he said,
Was sent by Artemis; and he revealed
Her remedy—a thought to crush like lead 230
The hearts of Atreus' sons, who wept, as weep they must,
And speechless ground their sceptres in the dust.

The elder king then spoke: 'What can I say?
Disaster follows if I disobey;
Surely yet worse disaster if I yield
And slaughter my own child, my home's delight,
In her young innocence, and stain my hand
With blasphemous unnatural cruelty,
Bathed in the blood I fathered! Either way,
Ruin! Disband the fleet, sail home, and earn 240
The deserter's badge—abandon my command,
Betray the alliance—now! The wind must turn,
There must be sacrifice, a maid must bleed—
Their chafing rage demands it—they are right!
May good prevail, and justify my deed!'

Then he put on
The harness of Necessity.[9]
The doubtful tempest of his soul
Veered, and his prayer was turned to blasphemy,
His offering to impiety. 250
Hence that repentance late and long
Which, since his madness passed, pays toll
For that one reckless wrong.
Shameless self-willed infatuation
Emboldens men to dare damnation,
And starts the wheels of doom which roll
Relentless to their piteous goal.

[9]This is the central paradox of Fate and free will. In *The Oresteia* and in other plays, Aeschylus insists that although an inherited curse may make a person's choice desperately hard, choice is still possible.

So Agamemnon, rather than retreat,
Endured to offer up his daughter's life
To help a war fought for a faithless wife 260
And pay the ransom for a storm-bound fleet.

Heedless of her tears,
Her cries of 'Father!' and her maiden years,
Her judges valued more
Their glory and their war.
A prayer was said. Her father gave the word.
Limp in her flowing dress
The priest's attendants held her high
Above the altar, as men hold a kid.
Her father spoke again, to bid 270
One bring a gag, and press
Her sweet mouth tightly with a cord,
Lest Atreus' house be cursed by some ill-omened cry.

Rough hands tear at her girdle, cast
Her saffron silks to earth. Her eyes
Search for her slaughterers; and each,
Seeing her beauty, that surpassed
A painter's vision, yet denies
The pity her dumb looks beseech,
Struggling for voice; for often in old days, 280
When brave men feasted in her father's hall,
With simple skill and pious praise
Linked to the flute's pure tone
Her virgin voice would melt the hearts of all,
Honouring the third libation near her father's throne.

The rest I did not see,
Nor do I speak of it...
But this I know:
What Calchas prophesies will be fulfilled.
The scale of Justice falls in equity:
The killer will be killed. 290

But now, farewell foreboding! Time may show,
But cannot alter, what shall be.
What help, then, to bewail
Troubles before they fall?
Events will take their way
Even as the prophet's words foreshadowed all.
For what is next at hand,
Let good prevail!
That is the prayer we pray—
We, who alone now stand 300
In Agamemnon's place, to guard this Argive land.

[*The day has broken.* THE QUEEN *now turns and stands facing the* ELDERS.]

CHORUS:
We come obedient to your bidding, Clytemnestra.
Our king and leader absent, and his throne unfilled,
Our duty pays his due observance to his wife.
Have you received some message? Do these sacrifices
Rise for good news, give thanks for long hope re-assured?
I ask in love; and will as loyally receive
Answer or silence.

CLYTEMNESTRA:
Good news, if the proverb's true,
Should break with sunrise from the kindly womb of night.
But here's a richer joy than you dared ever hope: 310
Our Argive men have captured Priam's town.

CHORUS:
Have *what?*
I heard it wrong—I can't believe it!

CLYTEMNESTRA:
Troy is ours!
Is that clear speaking?

CHORUS:
Happiness fills my eyes with tears.

CLYTEMNESTRA:
They show your loyalty.

CHORUS:
Have you some sure proof of this?

CLYTEMNESTRA:
I have indeed; unless a god has played me false.

CHORUS:
A god! Was it some dream you had, persuaded you?

CLYTEMNESTRA:
Dream! Am I one to air drowsy imaginings?

CHORUS:
Surely you feed yourself on unconfirmed report?

CLYTEMNESTRA:
You choose to criticize me as an ignorant girl!

CHORUS:
Well, then, when was Troy captured?

CLYTEMNESTRA:
In this very night 320
That brought to birth this glorious sun.

CHORUS:
What messenger
Could fly so fast from Troy to here?

CLYTEMNESTRA:
The god of fire!
Ida first launched his blazing beam; thence to this palace
Beacon lit beacon in relays of flame. From Ida
To Hermes' crag on Lemnos; from that island, third
To receive the towering torch was Athos, rock of Zeus;
There, as the blaze leapt the dark leagues, the watch in welcome
Leapt too, and a twin tower of brightness speared the sky,
Pointing athwart the former course; and in a stride

Crossing the Aegean, like the whip-lash of lightning, flew 330
The resinous dazzle, molten-gold, till the fish danced,
As at sunrise, enraptured with the beacon's glow,
Which woke reflected sunrise on Makistos' heights.
The watchman there, proof against sleep, surprise or sloth,
Rose faithful to the message; and his faggots' flame
Swept the wide distance to Euripus' channel, where
Its burning word was blazoned to the Messapian guards.
They blazed in turn, kindling their pile of withered heath,
And passed the signal on. The strong beam, still undimmed,
Crossed at one bound Asopus' plain, and like the moon 340
In brilliance, lighted on Cithaeron's crags, and woke
Another watch, to speed the flying token on.
On still the hot gleam hurtled, past Gorgopis' lake;
Made Aegiplanctus, stirred those watching mountaineers
Not to stint boughs and brushwood; generously they fed
Their beacon, and up burst a monstrous beard of fire,
Leapt the proud headland fronting the Saronic Gulf,
To lofty Arachnaeus, neighbour to our streets;
Thence on this Atreid palace the triumphant fire
Flashed, lineal descendant of the flame of Ida. 350

Such, Elders, was the ritual race my torchbearers,
Each at his faithful post succeeding each, fulfilled;
And first and last to run share equal victory.
Such, Elders, is my proof and token offered you,
A message sent to me from Troy by Agamemnon.

CHORUS:

Madam, we will in due course offer thanks to Heaven;
But now we want to savour wonder to the full,
And hear you speak at length: tell us your news again!

CLYTEMNESTRA:

Today the Greeks hold Troy! Her walls echo with cries
That will not blend. Pour oil and vinegar in one vessel, 360
You'll see them part and swirl, and never mix: so, there,
I think, down narrow streets a discord grates the ear—
Screams of the captured, shouts of those who've captured them,
The unhappy and the happy. Women of Troy prostrate
Over dead husbands, brothers; aged grandfathers
Mourning dead sons and grandsons, and remembering
Their very cries are slaves' cries now.... And then the victors:
After a night of fighting, roaming, plundering,
Hungry to breakfast, while their hosts lie quiet in dust;
No rules to keep, no order of place; each with the luck 370
That fell to him, quartered in captured homes of Troy,
Tonight, at last, rolled in dry blankets, safe from frost—
No going on guard—blissfully they'll sleep from dusk to dawn.

If in that captured town they are reverencing the gods
Whose home it was, and not profaning holy places,
The victors will avoid being vanquished in their turn.
Only, let no lust of unlawful plunder tempt

Our soldiers' hearts with wealth, to their own harm—there still
Remains the journey home: God grant we see them safe!
If the fleet sails free from the taint of sin, the gods 380
May grant them safely to retrace their outward course—
Those whom no wakeful anger of the forgotten dead[10]
Waits to surprise with vengeance. . . .
These are a woman's words.
May good prevail beyond dispute, in sight of all!
My life holds many blessings; I would enjoy them now.

CHORUS:
Madam, your words are like a man's, both wise and kind.
Now we have heard trustworthy proof from your own lips,
We will prepare ourselves again to praise the gods,
Whose gracious acts call for our most devout response.
[CLYTEMNESTRA *goes into the palace.*]

CHORUS:
Zeus, supreme of heavenly powers! 390
Friendly night, whose fateful hours
Built for Argos' warlike name
Bright imperishable fame!
Night in which a net was laid
Fast about the Trojan towers
Such that none of mortal flesh,
Great or little, could evade
Grim annihilation's deadly mesh!
This is the hand of Zeus! Zeus we revere,
Whose lasting law both host and guest must fear; 400
Who long since against Paris bent
His bow with careful aim, and sent
His vengeance flying not too near
Nor past the stars, but timed to pay
The debt of Justice on the appointed day.

'The hand of Zeus has cast
The proud from their high place!'
This we may say, and trace
That hand from first to last.
As Zeus foreknowing willed, 410
So was their end fulfilled.

One said, 'The gods disdain
To mark man's wanton way
Who tramples in the dust
Beauty of holy things.'
Impious! The truth shows plain:
Pride now has paid its debt, and they
Who laughed at Right and put their boastful trust

[10]As soon as he reaches home, a returning warrior must undergo ritual purification to guard himself against the vengeance of the spirits of those he has killed. The "forgotten dead" Clytemnestra is thinking of is Iphigenia, whom Agamemnon on his return will seem to have forgotten.

In arms and swollen wealth of kings,
Have gone their destined way. 420
A middle course is best,
Not poor nor proud; but this,
By no clear rule defined,
Eludes the unstable, undiscerning mind,
Whose aim will surely miss.
Thenceforth there is no way to turn aside;
When man has once transgressed,
And in his wealth and pride
Spurned the high shrine of Justice, nevermore
May his sin hope to hide 430
In that safe dimness he enjoyed before.[11]

Retreat cut off, the fiend Temptation
Forces him onward, the unseen
Effectual agent of Damnation;
When his fair freshness once has been
Blotched and defiled with grime, and he,
Like worthless bronze, which testing blows
Have blackened, lies despoiled, and shows
His baseness plain for all to see,
Then every cure renews despair; 440
A boy chasing a bird on wing,
He on his race and soil must bring
A deeper doom than flesh can bear;
The gods are deaf to every prayer;
If pity lights a human eye,
Pity by Justice's law must share
The sinner's guilt, and with the sinner die.
So, doomed, deluded, Paris came
To sit at his host's table, and seduce
Helen his wife, and shame 450
The house of Atreus and the law of Zeus.

Bequeathing us in Argos
Muster of shields and spears,
The din of forge and dockyard,
Lightly she crossed the threshold
And left her palace, fearless
Of what should wake her fears;
And took to Troy as dowry
Destruction, blood, and tears.
Here, in her home deserted, 460
The voice of guard and groom
With love and grief lamented:
'O house! O king! O pity!
O pillow softly printed
Where her loved head had rested!'

[11] The sinner is thought of as shunning the light, lest God should find him out.

There lies her husband fasting,
Dumb in his stricken room.
His thought across sea reaches
With longings, not reproaches;
A ghost will rule the palace, 470
A home become a tomb!
Her statue's sweet perfection
Torments his desolation;
Still his eyes' hunger searches—
That living grace is hardened
And lost that beauty's bloom.

Visions of her beset him
With false and fleeting pleasure
When dreams and dark are deep.
He sees her, runs to hold her; 480
And, through his fingers slipping,
Lightly departs his treasure,
The dream he cannot keep,
Wafted on wings that follow
The shadowy paths of sleep.

Such are the searching sorrows
This royal palace knows,
While through the streets of Argos
Grief yet more grievous grows,
With all our manhood gathered 490
So far from earth of Hellas;
As in each home unfathered,
Each widowed bed, the whetted
Sword of despair assails
Hearts where all hope has withered
And angry hate prevails.
They sent forth men to battle,
But no such men return;
And home, to claim their welcome,
Come ashes in an urn. 500

For War's a banker, flesh his gold.
There by the furnace of Troy's field,
Where thrust meets thrust, he sits to hold
His scale, and watch the spear-point sway;
And back to waiting homes he sends
Slag from the ore, a little dust
To drain hot tears from hearts of friends;
Good measure, safely stored and sealed
In a convenient jar—the just
Price for the man they sent away. 510
They praise him through their tears, and say,
'He was a soldier!' or, 'He died
Nobly, with death on every side!'
And fierce resentment mutters low,

'Yes—for another's wife!' And so
From grief springs gall, which fear must hide—
Let kings and their revenges go!
But under Ilion's wall the dead,
Heirs of her earth, lie chambered deep;
While she, whose living blood they shed, 520
Covers her conquerors in sleep.

A nation's voice, enforced with anger,
Strikes deadly as a public curse.
I wait for word of hidden danger,
And fear lest bad give place to worse.
God marks that man with watchful eyes
Who counts his killed by companies;
And when his luck, his proud success,
Forgets the law of righteousness,
Then the dark Furies launch at length 530
A counter-blow to crush his strength
And cloud his brightness, till the dim
Pit of oblivion swallows him.
In fame unmeasured, praise too high,
Lies danger: God's sharp lightnings fly
To stagger mountains. Then, I choose
Wealth that invites no rankling hate;
Neither to lay towns desolate,
Nor wear the chains of those who lose
Freedom and life to war and Fate. 540

[*The sound of women's voices excitedly shouting and cheering is heard. One or two* ELDERS *go out, and return immediately to report. The following remarks are made severally by various members of the* CHORUS.]

Since the beacon's news was heard
Rumour flies through every street.
Ought we to believe a word?
Is it some inspired deceit?
Childish, crack-brained fantasy!
Wing your hopes with such a tale,
Soon you'll find that fire can lie,
Facts can change, and trust can fail.
Women all are hasty-headed:
Beacons blaze—belief rejoices; 550
All too easily persuaded.
Rumour fired by women's voices,
As we know, is quickly spread;
—As we know, is quickly dead!

[*The* CHORUS *depart; and an interval representing the lapse of several days now takes place.*[12] *After the interval the* CHORUS *re-appear in great excitement.*]

---

[12] An interval is certainly indicated here. It is true that the action of most extant Greek plays is contained between dawn and dusk of one day, but this can hardly be said of the five extant plays of Aeschylus; only in *The Seven against Thebes* is the action in any way related to the passage of a day.

CHORUS:
We shall soon know whether this relay-race of flame,
This midnight torch-parade, this beacon-telegraph,
Told us the truth, or if the fire made fools of us—
All a delightful dream! Look! There's a herald coming
Up from the shore, wearing a crown of olive-leaves!
And, further off, a marching column of armed men, 560
Sheathed in hot dust, tells me this herald won't stand dumb
Or light a pinewood fire to announce the smoke of Troy!
Either his news doubles our happiness, or else—
The gods forbid all else! Good shows at first appearance,
Now may the proof be good! He who prays otherwise
For Argos—let him reap the folly of his soul!
[*Enter a* HERALD.]

HERALD:
Argos! Dear earth my fathers trod! After ten years
Today I have come home! All other hopes were false,
But this proves true! I dared not think my own land would
In death receive me to my due and dearest rest. 570
Now blest be Argos, and the sun's sweet light, and Zeus,
God of this realm, and Pythian Apollo, who no more
Aims against us the shafts of his immortal bow.
You fought us, Phoebus, by Scamander long enough:
Be Saviour now, be Healer; once, not twice, our death!
Gods of the city's gathering, hear my prayer; and thou,
Hermes, dear Guardian, Herald, every herald's god;
And you, heroes of old, whose blessing sent us forth,
Bless the returning remnant that the sword has spared!
O house of kings! Beloved walls! O august thrones! 580
You deities who watch the rising sun, watch now![13]
Welcome with shining eyes the royal architect
Of towering glories to adorn his ancient throne.
To you, and every Argive citizen, Agamemnon
Brings light in darkness; come, then, greet him royally,
As fits one in whose hands Zeus the Avenger's plough
Passed over Troy, to split her towers, scar and subdue
Her fields, and from her fair soil extirpate her seed.
So harsh a halter Atreus' elder son has thrown
Around Troy's neck, and now comes home victorious 590
To claim supremest honours among mortal men.
For neither Paris now, nor his accomplice town,
Can boast their deed was greater than their punishment.
Found guilty of theft and robbery, he has forfeited
His treasured spoil, destroyed his father's house and throne,
And made his people pay twice over for his sin.

CHORUS:
Herald of the Greek army, greeting! Welcome home!

HERALD:
Thanks. For ten years I've prayed for life; now I can die.

---

[13]The statues of Zeus, Apollo, and Hermes stand on the eastern or southeastern façade of the palace, facing the direction from which Agamemnon arrives.

CHORUS:
Longing for Argos, for your home, tormented you?
HERALD:
Cruelly; and now my cloak is wet with tears of joy. 600
CHORUS:
Your suffering had its happy side.
HERALD:
What do you mean?
CHORUS:
Your love and longing were returned. Is that not happy?
HERALD:
You mean that Argos longed for us, as we for her?
CHORUS:
Our hearts were dark with trouble. We missed and needed you.
HERALD:
What caused your trouble? An enemy?
CHORUS:
I learnt long ago,
Least said is soonest mended.
HERALD:
But was Argos threatened
In the king's absence?
CHORUS:
Friend, you said just now that death
Was dearly welcome. Our hearts echo what you felt.
HERALD:
Yes, I could die, now the war's over, and all well.
Time blurs the memory; some things one recalls as good, 610
Others as hateful. We're not gods; then why expect
To enjoy a lifetime of unbroken happiness?
To think what we went through! If I described it all,
The holes we camped in, dirt and weariness and sweat;
Or out at sea, with storms all night, trying to sleep
On a narrow board, with half a blanket; and all day,
Miserable and sick, we suffered and put up with it.
Then, when we landed, things were worse. We had to camp
Close by the enemy's wall, in the wet river-meadows,
Soaked with the dew and mist, ill from damp clothes, our hair 620
Matted like savages'. If I described the winter, when
In cruel snow-winds from Ida birds froze on the trees;
Or if I told of the fierce heat, when Ocean dropped
Waveless and windless to his noon-day bed, and slept...

Well, it's no time for moaning; all that's over now.
And those who died out there—it's over for them too;
No need to jump to orders; they can take their rest.
Why call the roll of those who were expendable,
And make the living wince from old wounds probed again?
Nor much hurrahing either, if we're sensible. 630
For us who've come safe home the good weighs heaviest,
And what we've suffered counts for less. The praise that's due,
Proudly inscribed, will show these words to the bright sun:

The Argive army conquered Troy,
And brought home over land and sea
These hard-won spoils, the pride and joy
Of ancient palaces, to be
Trophies of victory, and grace
The temples of the Hellene race.
Let Argos hear this, and receive her general home 640
With thanks and praise. Let Zeus, who gave us victory,
Be blest for his great mercy. I have no more to say.

CHORUS:
Well, I was wrong, I own it. Old and ready to learn
Is always young. But this great news is for the palace,
And chiefly Clytemnestra, whose wealth of joy we share.
[CLYTEMNESTRA *has appeared at the palace door.*]

CLYTEMNESTRA:
I sang for joy to hail this victory long ago,
When the first fiery midnight message told that Troy
Was sacked and shattered. Someone then took me to task:
'Beacons! So you believe them? Troy, you think, is taken?
Typical female hopefulness!' Remarks like these 650
Exposed my folly. Yet I made thankful sacrifice,
And throughout Argos women gathered to celebrate
Victory with songs of praise in temples of all the gods,
And feed their scented fires with rich flesh-offerings.
I have no need now to hear your detailed narrative;
I'll hear all from the king's own lips. But first, to greet
Fitly and soon my honoured husband's home-coming—
For to a wife what day is sweeter than when she,
Receiving by God's mercy her lord safe home from war,
Flings wide the gates in welcome?—take to him this message: 660
Let him come quickly; Argos longs for him; and he
Will find at home a wife as faithful as he left,[14]
A watch-dog at his door; knowing one loyalty;
To enemies implacable; in all ways unchanged.
No seal of his have I unsealed in these ten years.
Of pleasure found with other men, or any breath
Of scandal, I know no more than how to dip hot steel.
[*Exit* CLYTEMNESTRA *to the palace.*]

HERALD:
That's a strange boast—and more strange, as more full of truth.
Is it not scandal that a queen should speak such words?

CHORUS:
Strange? No! Her style eludes you. We interpret her. 670
A very proper statement—unimpeachable!
Now, Herald, tell us of our loved King Menelaus:
Has he come? Did he sail with you? Is he safely home?

HERALD:
That false good news you ask for—I can't give it you,
My friends; delusion would not comfort you for long.

---

[14]In this and the following lines, Clytemnestra uses her characteristic mixture of irony and extravagant lies, designed to baffle and disturb with innuendo.

CHORUS:
Telling a fair tale falsely cannot hide the truth;
When truth and good news part, the rift shows plain enough.

HERALD:
Then here it is: Menelaus has vanished, ship and all!

CHORUS:
You mean, he sailed with you from Troy, and then a storm
Fell on the fleet, and parted his ship from the rest? 680

HERALD:
Good marksman! An age of agony pointed in three words.

CHORUS:
But Menelaus—what was it thought had happened to him?
Is he given up for lost? Or may he yet survive?

HERALD:
No one can tell, for no one knows; except, perhaps,
The Sun, who fosters every earthly creature's life.

CHORUS:
You mean, I think, that when this storm had scourged our fleet
Some anger of the heavenly powers was satisfied?

HERALD:
Can it be right to foul this fair and holy day,
Blurting bad news? After our thanksgiving to the gods,
Such speech is out of place. When a man stands recounting 690
With bloodshot stare catastrophe and horror, an army dead,
The body of State staggered and gored, homes emptied, men
Blasted, lashed out of life by fire and sword, War's whips—
If such tales were my wares, this triumph-song of disaster
I bring, would suit well. But my news is victory,
Brought to a jubilant city—how can I countervail
Such good with sorrow, tell of the murderous armed alliance
Fate forged with angry gods to pursue and harass us?
For fire and water, age-old enemies, made league,
And pledged good faith in combined slaughter of Greek men. 700
One night a vicious swell rose with a gale from Thrace;
The sky was a mad shepherd tearing his own flock;
Ship against ship butted like rutting rams; mountains
Of wind and water leapt, surge swallowed and rain threshed.
At dawn, where were the ships? The bright sun beamed—we saw
The Aegean flowering thick with faces of dead Greeks
And scraps of wrecks...

Our hull had held, and we came through.
It was no mortal hand that gripped our helm that night:
Some god, by guile or intercession, saved our lives.
Fortune sat smiling on our prow; we sprang no leak, 710
Nor ran aground on rocks. In the next morning's light,
Stunned, sickened, still incredulous of our own luck,
We brooded, thinking of our maimed and battered fleet.
And they, if any still draw breath, now speak of us
As caught in the same fate we picture theirs.... But yet,
May best prove truest! For Menelaus, more than all else
Expect him home. If any searching shaft of sun

Sees him alive and well, by the providence of Zeus
Not yet resolved to exterminate this house—there's hope
That Menelaus will yet come safe to his own home. 720
And every word you have heard me speak is the plain truth.

[*The* MESSENGER *goes, in the direction from which he came.*]

CHORUS:

Who was the unknown seer whose voice—
Uttered at venture, but instinct
With prescience of what Fate decreed—
Guessing infallibly, made choice
Of a child's name, and deftly linked
Symbol with truth, and name with deed,
Naming, inspired, the glittering bride
Of spears, for whom men killed and died,
Helen, the Spoiler? On whose lips 730
Was born that fit and fatal name,
To glut the sea with spoil of ships,
Spoil souls with swords, a town with flame?[15]
The curtained softness of her bed
She left, to hear the Zephyr breathe
Gigantic in tall sails; and soon
Comes hue and cry—armed thousands fly
Tracing her trackless oar, and sheathe
Their keels in Simois' shingly bank,
Near fields where grass today grows rank 740
In soil by war's rich rain made red.

And anger—roused, relentless, sure—
Taught Troy that words have double edge,
That men and gods use *bond* and *pledge*
For love past limit, doom past cure:
Love seals the hearts of bride and groom;
And seal of love is seal of doom.
Loud rings the holy marriage-song
As kinsmen honour prince and bride;
The hour is theirs—but not for long. 750
Wrath, borne on Time's unhurrying tide,
Claims payment due for double wrong—
The outraged hearth, the god defied.[16]
And songs are drowned in tears, and soon
Must Troy the old learn a new tune;
On Paris, once her praise and pride,
She calls reproach, that his proud wooing
Has won his own and her undoing:
Her sons beset on every side,
Her life-blood mercilessly spilt— 760
Hers is the loss, and his the guilt.

---

[15]This does not mean that the name "Helen" originally meant "a destroyer"; but fancied derivations were a Greek pastime, and were felt to have dramatic significance.

[16]Zeus, guardian of the laws of hospitality, which Paris broke.

There was a shepherd once who reared at home
A lion's cub.[17] It shared with sucking lambs
Their milk—gentle, while bone and blood were young.
The children loved it; the old watched and smiled.
Often the shepherd held it like a child
High in his arms; and often it would seek
His hand with soft eyes and caressing tongue,
Tense with the force of hunger. But in time
It showed the nature of its kind. Repaying 770
Its debt for food and shelter, it prepared
A feast unbidden. Soon the nauseous reek
Of torn flesh filled the house; a bloody slime
Drenched all the ground from that unholy slaying,
While helpless weeping servants stood and stared.
The whelp once reared with lambs, now grown a beast,
Fulfils his nature as Destruction's priest!
And so to Troy there came
One in whose presence shone
Beauty no thought can name: 780
A still enchantment of sweet summer calm;
A rarity for wealth to dote upon;
Glances whose gentle fire
Bestowed both wound and balm;
A flower to melt man's heart with wonder and desire.
But time grew ripe, and love's fulfilment ran
Aside from that sweet course where it began.
She, once their summer joy,
Transmuted, now like a swift curse descended
On every home, on every life 790
Whose welcome once befriended
The outlaw wife;
A fiend sent by the god of host and guest,
Whose law her lover had transgressed,
To break his heart, and break the pride of Troy.

When Earth and Time were young,
A simple ancient saw
Phrased on the common tongue
Declared that man's good fortune, once mature,
Does not die childless, but begets its heir; 800
That from life's goodness grows, by Nature's law,
Calamity past cure
And ultimate despair.
I think alone; my mind
Rejects this general belief.
Sin, not prosperity, engenders grief;
For impious acts breed their own kind,
And evil's nature is to multiply.
The house whose ways are just in word and deed

[17]The gentle young creature is a symbol of Helen as Paris and the Trojans first saw her.

Still as the years go by 810
Sees lasting wealth and noble sons succeed.

So, by law of consequence,
Pride or Sin the Elder will,
In the man who chooses ill,
Breed a Younger Insolence.
Sin the Younger breeds again
Yet another unseen Power
Like the Powers that gave it birth:
Recklessness, whose force defies
War and violence, heaven and earth; 820
Whose menace like a black cloud lies
On the doomed house hour by hour,
Fatal with fear, remorse, and pain.

But Justice with her shining eyes
Lights the smoke-begrimed and mean
Dwelling; honours those who prize
Honour; searches far to find
All whose hearts and hands are clean;
Passes with averted gaze
Golden palaces which hide 830
Evil armed in insolence;
Power and riches close combined,
Falsely stamped with all men's praise,
Win from her no reverence.
Good and evil she will guide
To their sure end by their appointed ways.

[*Enter* AGAMEMNON *in his chariot, followed by another chariot bearing spoils of war and* CASSANDRA.]

CHORUS:

King! Heir of Atreus! Conqueror of Troy!
What greeting shall we bring? What shall we say
To voice our hearts' devotion,
Observe both truth and measure, 840
Be neither scant nor fulsome in our love?
Many, whose conscience is not innocent,
Attach high value to a show of praise.
As ill-luck finds on all sides
Eyes brimming with condolence
Where no true sting of sorrow pricks the heart,
So now some harsh embittered faces, forced
Into a seemly smile, will welcome you,
And hide the hearts of traitors
Beneath their feigned rejoicing. 850
Well, a wise shepherd knows his flock by face;
And a wise king can tell the flatterer's eye—
Moist, unctuous, adoring—
The expressive sign of loyalty not felt.
Now this I will not hide: ten years ago
When you led Greece to war for Helen's sake
You were set down as sailing

Far off the course of wisdom.
We thought you wrong, misguided, when you tried
To keep morale from sagging 860
In superstitious soldiers
By offering sacrifice to stop the storm.
Those times are past; you have come victorious home;
Now from our open hearts we wish you well.
Time and your own enquiries
Will show, among your people,
Who has been loyal, who has played you false.

AGAMEMNON:
First, Argos, and her native gods, receive from me
The conqueror's greeting on my safe return; for which,
As for the just revenge I wrought on Priam's Troy, 870
Heaven shares my glory. Supplications without end
Won Heaven's ear; Troy stood her trial; unfaltering
The immortals cast their votes into the urn of death,
Dooming Troy's walls to dust, her men to the sword's edge.
The acquitting urn saw hope alone come near, and pass,
Vanishing in each empty hand. Smoke, rising still,
Marks great Troy's fall; flames of destruction's sacrifice
Live yet; and, as they die, stirs from the settled ash
The wind-borne incense of dead wealth and luxury.

Now for this victory let our pious thanksgiving 880
Tell and re-tell Heaven's favour. We have made Troy pay
For her proud rape a woman's price. The Argive beast,
The lion rampant on all our shields, at dead of night
Sprang from the womb of the horse to grind that city's bones,
A ranked and ravening litter, that over wall and tower
Leaping, licked royal blood till lust was surfeited.

Thus to the gods I pay first my full salutation.
For your advice, I note it; I am of your mind,
And uphold your judgement. There are few whose inborn love
Warms without envy to a friend's prosperity. 890
Poison of jealousy laps the disappointed heart,
Doubling its grievance: pangs for its own losses match
With pangs for neighbours' wealth. Life and long observation
Taught me the look of men whose loving show, examined,
Proves but a shadow's shadow: I speak of what I know.
One man, Odysseus, who set sail unwillingly—
At this hour dead or living?—he alone, once yoked,
With good will shared my burden.

For affairs of State,
And this feared disaffection, we will set a day
For assembly and debate among our citizens, 900
And take wise counsel; where disease wants remedy,
Fire or the knife shall purge this body for its good.

Now to my home, to stand at my own altar-hearth
And give Heaven my first greeting, whose protecting power

Sent forth, and brought me home again. May Victory,
My guardian hitherto, walk constant at my side!

[*Enter* CLYTEMNESTRA *attended by maids holding a long drape of crimson silk.*]

CLYTEMNESTRA:

Elders and citizens of Argos! In your presence now
I will speak, unashamed, a wife's love for her husband.
With time dies diffidence. What I shall tell I learnt
Untaught, from my own long endurance, these ten years 910
My husband spent under the walls of Ilion.
First, that a woman should sit forlorn at home, unmanned,
Is a crying grief. Then, travellers, one on other's heels,
Dismay the palace, each with worse news than the last.
Why, if my lord received as many wounds as Rumour,
Plying from Troy to Argos, gave him, he is a net,
All holes! Or had he died each time report repeated
News of his death—see him, a second Geryon,
Boasting his monstrous right, his thrice-spread quilt of earth—
A grave for each death, each body! Many times despair 920
At a cruel message noosed my throat in a hung cord,
Which force against my will untied.

These fears explain
Why our child is not here to give you fitting welcome,
Our true love's pledge, Orestes. Have no uneasiness.
He is in Phocis, a guest of Strophius your well-tried friend,
Who warned me of peril from two sources: first, the risk
Threatening your life at Troy; then, if conspiracy
Matured to popular revolt in Argos, fear
Of man's instinct to trample on his fallen lord.
Such was his reasoning—surely free from all suspicion. 930

For me—the springing torrents of my tears are all
Drawn dry, no drop left; and my sleepless eyes are sore
With weeping by the lamp long lit for you in vain.
In dreams, the tenuous tremors of the droning gnat
Roused me from dreadful visions of more deaths for you
Than could be compassed in the hour that slept with me.

There is no dearer sight than shelter after storm;
No escape sweeter than from siege of circumstance.
Now, after siege and storm endured, my happy heart
Welcomes my husband, faithful watch-dog of his home, 940
Our ship's firm anchor, towering pillar that upholds
This royal roof; as dear, as to a father's hope
His longed-for son, a spring to thirsty travellers,
Or sight of land unlooked-for to men long at sea.

Such praise I hold his due; and may Heaven's jealousy
Acquit us; our past suffering has been enough.[18]

---

[18]She means, for the ears of the Chorus, "acquit Agamemnon and me for our abundant happiness in being reunited"; for the ears of the audience, "acquit Aegisthus and me for the success we hope to achieve by the removal of Agamemnon."

Now, dearest husband, come, step from your chariot.
But do not set to earth, my lord, the conquering foot
That trod down Troy. Servants, do as you have been bidden;
Make haste, carpet his way with crimson tapestries, 950
Spread silk before your master's feet; Justice herself
Shall lead him to a home he never hoped to see.
All other matters forethought, never lulled by sleep,
Shall order justly as the will of Heaven decrees.

[CLYTEMNESTRA*'s maids spread a path of crimson cloth from the chariot to the palace door.*]

AGAMEMNON:

Daughter of Leda, guardian of my house, your speech
Matches its theme, my absence; for both were prolonged.[19]
Praise fitly spoken should be heard on other lips.
And do not with these soft attentions woman me,
Nor prostrate like a fawning Persian mouth at me
Your loud addresses; not with your spread cloths invite 960
Envy of gods, for honours due to gods alone.
I count it dangerous, being mortal, to set foot
On rich embroidered silks. I would be reverenced
As man, not god. The praise of fame rings clear without
These frills and fancy foot-rugs; and the god's best gift
Is a mind free from folly. Call him fortunate
Whom the end of life finds harboured in tranquility.

CLYTEMNESTRA:

There is the sea—who shall exhaust the sea?—which teems
With purple dye costly as silver, a dark stream
For staining of fine stuffs, unceasingly renewed.[20] 970
This house has store of crimson, by Heaven's grace, enough
For one outpouring; you are no king of beggary!
Had oracles prescribed it, I would have dedicated
Twenty such cloths to trampling, if by care and cost
I might ensure safe journey's end for this one life.
Now you are come to your dear home, your altar-hearth,
The tree, its root refreshed, spreads leaf to the high beams
To veil us from the dog-star's heat. Your loved return
Shines now like Spring warmth after winter; but when Zeus
From the unripe grape presses his wine, then through the house 980
Heat dies, and coolness comes, as through this royal door
Enters its lord, perfected to receive his own.

AGAMEMNON:

I have said how I would enter with an easy mind.

CLYTEMNESTRA:

Tell me—not contrary to your resolve—one thing.

---

[19]The dramatic value of this vicious snub is not merely that it further whets Clytemnestra's appetite for revenge, but that it establishes Agamemnon as a formidable person, a worthy antagonist even for Clytemnestra.

[20][The translator has followed the edition of Professor A. Y. Campbell in moving this famous speech up 29 lines in the text. The purple dye of the sea is compared by Clytemnestra to the blood that has already stained the House of Atreus.]

AGAMEMNON:
Be sure I shall do nothing against my resolve.
CLYTEMNESTRA:
Might you have vowed to the gods, in danger, such an act?
AGAMEMNON:
Yes, if someone with knowledge had prescribed it me.
CLYTEMNESTRA:
Imagine Priam conqueror: what would he have done?
AGAMEMNON:
Walked on embroidered satin, I have little doubt.
CLYTEMNESTRA:
Then why humble your heart to men's censorious tongue? 990
AGAMEMNON:
Why indeed? Yet the people's voice speaks with great power.
CLYTEMNESTRA:
Greatness wins hate. Unenvied is unenviable.
AGAMEMNON:
It does not suit a woman to be combative.
CLYTEMNESTRA:
Yet it suits greatness also to accept defeat.
AGAMEMNON:
Why, here's a battle! What would you not give to win?
CLYTEMNESTRA:
Yield! You are victor: give me too my victory.
AGAMEMNON:
Since you're resolved—[*to an attendant*] Come kneel; untie my shoes; dismiss
These leathern slaves that smooth my path. And as I tread
This deep-sea treasure, may no watchful envious god
Glance from afar. It offends modesty, that I 1000
Should dare with unwashed feet to soil these costly rugs,
Worth weight for weight of silver, spoiling my own house!
But let that pass.

Take in this girl and treat her well.[21]
God will reward from heaven a gentle conqueror.
Slavery is a yoke no one bears willingly; and she
Came to me by the army's gift, of all Troy's wealth
The chosen jewel.
Now, since I have been subdued to obedience in this matter,
Treading on purple I will go into my house.
CLYTEMNESTRA:
Elelelelеu! 1010
[*a prolonged triumphant cry; which the* CHORUS *accept as a formal celebration of the victor's return, while only* CASSANDRA *understands its true meaning.* AGAMEMNON *walks alone along the purple path and enters the palace.*]
CLYTEMNESTRA:
Zeus, Zeus, Fulfiller! Now fulfil these prayers of mine;
And let thy will accomplish all that is thy will!
[CLYTEMNESTRA *enters the palace.* AGAMEMNON'S *chariot is taken away by attendants.* CASSANDRA *remains seated in the second chariot.*]

[21] Clytemnestra, who can impose her will on Agamemnon, fails to gain obedience from Cassandra.

CHORUS:

What is this persistent dread
Haunting, hovering to show
Signs to my foreboding soul,
While unbidden and unpaid
Throbs the prophet in my veins,
While persuasive confidence
That should rule the heart, and scorn
Fantasies of cloudy dreams, 1020
Trembles, and resigns her throne?
Once before, though far away,
My heart knew the pregnant hour,
When at Troy our sailors' shouts,
As they coiled their sheets astern,
Chimed with my triumphal song;
And the fleet set sail for home.

Then was guessing; now I see
With these eyes the fleet returned.
Yet my spirit knows again 1030
The foreboding hour; again
Sings, by untaught instinct, that
Sad, familiar, fatal dirge;
Yields her kingdom in the flesh,
Daunted with surmise, and feels
Pang and pulse of groin and gut,
Blood in riot, brain awhirl,
Nerve and tissue taut, and knows
Truth must prick, where flesh is sore.
Yet I pray, may time and truth 1040
Shame my fears; may prophecy
Vanish, and fulfilment fail!

When fortune flowers too lushly,
Decay, her envious neighbour,
Stands eager to invade;
Glory's brief hours are numbered,
And what has flowered must fade.
Bold in success, ambition
Sails on, where rocks lie hidden,
Strikes, and her debt is paid. 1050
Yet, debts may be compounded:
When Thracian storm-winds threaten,
The merchant, for his silver,
With pious prayers devotes
A tithe in ample measure;
Into the sea he slings it,
And safe his vessel floats.
The house that offers to the envious Powers
Its wealthy surplus will not fail and die;
Zeus to their prayers will bounteously reply, 1060
Bless each year's furrowed fields with sun and showers,
Bid harvests teem, and fear of famine fly.

But when, from flesh born mortal,
Man's blood on earth lies fallen,
A dark, unfading stain,
Who then by incantations
Can bid blood live again?
Zeus in pure wisdom ended
That sage's skill who summoned
Dead flesh to rise from darkness 1070
And live a second time;
Lest murder cheaply mended
Invite men's hands to crime.
Were I not sure that always
Events and causes hold
Sequence divinely ordered,
And next by last controlled,
Speech would forestall reluctance,
Voice thoughts I dare not fathom,
And leave no fear untold. 1080
But now my tongue mutters in darkness, sharing
The heart's distress, tormented with desire
To achieve some timely word, and still despairing;
While my dumb spirit smoulders with deep fire.

[CLYTEMNESTRA *comes to the palace door.*]

CLYTEMNESTRA:
You too, Cassandra there, do you hear me? Get indoors.
You may thank Zeus, this palace bears you no ill-will;
You shall stand near our sovereign altar, and partake,
With many other slaves, the cleansing ritual.
Then leave that chariot; do not be proud. They say
Heracles once was sold, and learnt to eat slaves' bread. 1090
If such misfortune falls, and there's no help for it—
A house of long-established wealth is generous;
Where meagre hopes reap opulence, it goes hard with slaves.
Here you shall have your due—what's customary, and more.

CHORUS:
It was to you she spoke. She waits. Was it not clear?
Since you're a captive in the toils of destiny
Obey, if you understand. Or do you choose defiance?

CLYTEMNESTRA:
If she's not crazed, she will obey; unless she speaks
Some weird unheard-of tongue, like swallows twittering.

CHORUS:
Come, now; her bidding is the best that's possible. 1100
Leave sitting in that chariot; obey, go in.

CLYTEMNESTRA:
I have no time to spend standing out here. Already
Victims for sacrifice wait at the central hearth.
If you understand what I have said, come in at once;
If not, [*to an attendant*] since she's a foreigner, explain by signs.

[*An attendant makes signs to* CASSANDRA *to enter the palace.*]

CHORUS:
It's clear enough the girl needs an interpreter.
She has the look of some wild creature newly trapped.

CLYTEMNESTRA:

Why, she is mad, hears only her own frenzied thoughts.
Has she not left her city levelled with the ground?—
Yet has not sense enough to accept her owner's bit 1110
Till she has frothed her rage out from a bloody mouth.
I will spend words no longer, to be thus ignored.

[CLYTEMNESTRA *goes into the palace.*]

CHORUS:

I feel pity, not anger. Come, poor girl, step down;
Yield to this hard necessity; wear your new yoke.

[CASSANDRA *steps down. She sees the statue of Apollo.*]

CASSANDRA:

O Apollo! Oh, oh! No, no, no, no! O Earth! O Apollo!

CHORUS:

Why name Apollo with this wail of agony?
He is no god of mourning, to be so invoked.

CASSANDRA:

Oh, oh! O horror! O Earth! O Apollo, Apollo!

CHORUS:

Again she utters blasphemy, to call Apollo,
Whose godhead may not stand in the same house with grief. 1120

CASSANDRA:

Apollo, Apollo! Leader of journeys, my destroyer!
All this way you have led me, to destroy me again!

CHORUS:

She is inspired to speak of her own sufferings.
The prophetic power stays with her even in slavery.

CASSANDRA:

Apollo, Apollo! Leader of journeys, my destroyer!
Where have you led me? Oh! what fearful house is this?

CHORUS:

Does not prophecy tell you this is Atreus' palace?
I tell you, then; so call it, and you will speak the truth.

CASSANDRA:

No! but a house that hates
The gods; whose very stones 1130
Bear guilty witness to a bloody act;
That hides within these gates
Remnants of bodies hacked,
And murdered children's bones!

CHORUS:

This prophetess goes to it like a keen-scented hound;
We know the trail she follows, and it leads to blood.

CASSANDRA:

To blood—I know. See there,
The witness that they bear—
Those children weeping for their own blood shed,
For their own tender flesh, 1140
That cruel, nameless dish
From which their father fed!

CHORUS:

We had all heard of your prophetic power; but this
Requires no prophecy to tell us of—

CASSANDRA:

Ah, ah!

Oh, shame! Conspiracy!
A heart obsessed with hate
And lurking to betray
Pollutes this house anew
With deadly injury
Where deepest love was due! 1150
Surprised, unarmed, how can he fight with Fate?
And help is far away.

CHORUS:

The first we understand—all Argos speaks of it;
But to this second prophecy I have no key.

CASSANDRA:

Shame on her! She will stand—
Would there were room for doubt!—
To cleanse her lawful lord
From guilt of war—and then—
How can I speak the word?
This cleansing ritual 1160
Shall serve his burial!
Despairing hands reach out,
Snared by a stronger hand!

CHORUS:

Still I am baffled by her riddling utterance;
What can one make of prophecy so recondite?

CASSANDRA:

There, there! O terror! What is this new sight?
A hunting-net, Death's weapon of attack!
And she who hunts is she who shared his bed.
Howl, Furies, howl, you bloody ravening pack,
Gorged with this house's blood, yet thirsting still; 1170
The victim bleeds: come, Fiends, and drink your fill!

CHORUS:

What fiends are these you call to bay at Death?
Your ghastly hymn has paled your cheek; and pale
The blood shrinks to your heart, as when men die
Sword-struck in battle, pulse and vision fail,
And life's warm colours fly;
See, how her utterance chokes her laboured breath!

CASSANDRA:

Help! Look, a nightmare! What? will cow gore bull,
The black-horned monarch? Save him, drag him away!
The treacherous water's poured, the lustral bath is full; 1180
She holds him in a trap made like a gown,—
She strikes! He crashes down!
Listen! It is treachery, treachery, I say!

CHORUS:

Although I claim no special skill in oracles,
Her words, I feel, augur no good. Yet, after all,
What good news ever comes to men through oracles?
Prophets find bad news useful. Why, the primary aim
Of all their wordy wisdom is to make men gape.

CASSANDRA:

O fear, and fear again!
O pity! Not alone 1190
He suffers; with his pain
Mingled I mourn my own!
Cruel Apollo! Why,
Why have you led me here?
Only that I may share
The death that he must die!

CHORUS:

She is insane, poor girl, or god-possessed,
And for herself alone she makes this wail,
Unwearied in her tuneless song;
As the shrill nightingale 1200
Unburdens her distracted breast,
Sobbing *Itun, Itun,* remembering all her wrong.[22]

CASSANDRA:

Bitter was her ordeal;
Yet by the kind gods' wish
The lovely robe she wears
Is feathered wings; and even
The plaint she pours to heaven,
Note answering note with tears,
Rings sweet. But I must feel
The parting of the flesh 1210
Before the whetted steel.

CHORUS:

Whence come these violent miseries, god-inspired
Yet void of meaning? Why with voice like doom
Intone these horrors in heart-searing words?
Who marked the oracular road
Whose evil terms you trace?

CASSANDRA [*changing from the shrill declamation of prophecy to the quiet sadness of mourning*]:

O Paris and his passion!
O marriage-bed that slew
His family and city!
O sweet Scamander river 1220
Our thirsting fathers knew,
By whose loved banks I grew!
But soon the dark Cocytus
And Acheron[23] shall echo
My prophecies, and witness
Whether my words are true.

CHORUS:

Paris's marriage! This is at last clear
To any child. Yet in her muttered fear

---

[22]The accusative case of *itus,* usually spelled *Itys* in English. He was the son of Procne, whom she herself killed to punish her husband Tereus for the rape of her sister Philomela. Philomela was afterwards turned into a nightingale, and "*itun, itun*" is supposed to represent her song.

[23]Two rivers of the lower world. The names mean respectively "river of wailing" and "river of grief."

Lies more than meets the sight:
With stunning pain, like a brute serpent's bite, 1230
Her whispered cry crashes upon my ear.

CASSANDRA:

O Ilion and her passion!
O city burnt and rased!
O fires my father kindled
To keep his towers defiant!
O blood of beasts he offered
From every herd that grazed!
Yet no propitiation
Could save her sons from dying
As I foretold they would; 1240
And I will join my brothers,
And soon the ground will welcome
My warm and flowing blood.

CHORUS:

Once more her utterance adds like to like.
Tell us, what god is he, so merciless,
Whose grievous hand can strike
Such deathly music from your mournful soul,
Arrows of prophecy whose course and goal
I seek, but cannot guess?

CASSANDRA:

Then listen. Now my prophecy shall no more peep 1250
From under shy veils like a new-made bride, but blow
A bounding gale towards the sunrise, on whose surge
A crime more fearful than my murder shall at once
Sweep into blazing light. Without more mystery
I will instruct you; but first testify how close
I scent the trail of bloody guilt incurred long since.
Under this roof live day and night a ghastly choir[24]
Venting their evil chant in hideous harmony;
Drunk with men's blood, boldly established here, they hold
Unbroken revel, Fiends of the blood royal, whom none 1260
Can exorcize. Drinking they sit, and with their songs
Drive folly first to crime; the crime performed, in turn
They spew out the defiler of his brother's bed!
Do I miss? Or has my arrow found a mark you know?
Or am I 'lying prophet', 'gypsy', 'tale-spinner'?
Come, on your oath, bear witness: the foul history
Of Atreus' palace, sin for sin, is known to me!

CHORUS:

The holiest oath could help but little. Yet I marvel
That you, bred overseas in a foreign tongue, unfold
Our city's past as truly as if you had been here. 1270

CASSANDRA:

Apollo, god of prophecy, gave me this office.

CHORUS:

Did *he* lust for your mortal body, though a god?

---

[24]Cassandra means the Furies, who would naturally haunt a house so steeped in crime.

CASSANDRA:
Yes. Until now I was ashamed to speak of it.
CHORUS:
We all are more reserved when we are prosperous.
CASSANDRA:
He urged me hard, made warmest protest of his love.
CHORUS:
And did you lie together? Had you child by him?
CASSANDRA:
I gave my word, and broke it—to the God of Words.[25]
CHORUS:
Already god-possessed with the prophetic art?
CASSANDRA:
I had foretold already the whole doom of Troy.
CHORUS:
Surely the god was angry? Did he punish you? 1280
CASSANDRA:
After my sin, no one believed one word I spoke.
CHORUS:
To us your prophecies seem all too credible.
CASSANDRA:
Oh! Oh!
Horror and sin! Again the anguish of true vision—
Yes, sin and horror!—racks and ravages my brain.
Look! See them sit, there on the wall, like forms in dreams,
Children butchered like lambs by their own kindred. See,
What do they carry in their hands? O piteous sight!
It is their own flesh—limb and rib and heart they hold,
Distinct and horrible, the food their father ate! 1290
I tell you, for this crime revenge grows hot: there lurks
In the home lair—as regent, say—a cowardly lion
Who plots against his master absent at the war;
While the Commander Lion who uprooted Troy,
Met by the fawning tongue, the bright obsequious ear,
Of the vile plotting she-hound, does not know what wounds
Venomed with hidden vengeance she prepares for him.
Female shall murder male: what kind of brazenness
Is that? What loathsome beast lends apt comparison?
A basilisk? Or Scylla's breed, living in rocks 1300
To drown men in their ships—a raging shark of hell,
Dreaming of steel thrust at her husband's unarmed flesh?
You heard her superb bluff, that cry of triumph, raised
As if for a hard battle won, disguised as joy
At his safe home-coming? You are incredulous—
No matter—I say, no matter; what will come will come.
Soon you will see with your own eyes, and pity me,
And wish my prophecy had not been half so true.

[25] A very common name for Apollo was Loxias, which has this meaning, being connected with the Greek *logos*, word, or *loxos*, ambiguous.

CHORUS:
Thyestes' feast of children's flesh we understand;
Horror gives place to wonder at your true account; 1310
The rest outstrips our comprehension; we give up.

CASSANDRA:
I say Agamemnon shall lie dead before your eyes.

CHORUS:
Silence, you wretched outcast—or speak wholesome words!

CASSANDRA:
No wholesome word can purge the poison of that truth.

CHORUS:
None, if it is to be; but may the gods forbid!

CASSANDRA:
You turn to prayer; others meanwhile prepare to kill.

CHORUS:
What man can be the source of such polluting sin?

CASSANDRA:
What man? You miss the main point of my prophecies.

CHORUS:
How could such murder be contrived? This baffles me.

CASSANDRA:
Yet I speak good Greek—all too good.

CHORUS:
The oracles 1320
Of Delphi are good Greek, but hard to understand.

CASSANDRA:
Oh, oh! For pity, Apollo! Where can I escape?
This death you send me is impatient, merciless!
She, this lioness in human form, who when her lord
Was absent paired with a wolf, will take my wretched life.
Like one who mixes medicine for her enemies,
Now, while she whets the dagger for her husband's heart,
She vows to drug his dram with a memory of me,
And make him pledge my safe arrival—in my blood.[26]

This robe—why should I wear what mocks me? Why still keep 1330
This sceptre, these oracular garlands round my neck?
Before I die I'll make an end of you . . . and you . . .
Go, with my curse, go! Thus I pay my debt to you!
[*trampling them on the ground*]
Go, make some other woman rich in misery!
And let Apollo see, and witness what I do—
He who once saw me in these same insignia
Scorned, jeered at like some gypsy quack, by enemies
And friends alike, called starveling, beggar, conjuror,
Pitiable wretch—all this I bore; and now Apollo,
Who gave a portion of his own prescience to me, 1340

[26]A safe arrival would be celebrated both by drinking and by libation to the gods. The cup Clytemnestra is preparing for Agamemnon is his death, mingled with Cassandra's.

Brings me from Ilion here to this death-reeking porch,
Where I shall never court crass unbelief again,
Where not my father's hearthstone but the slaughterer's block
Waits for me, warm already with a victim's blood.

Yet we shall not die unregarded by the gods.
A third shall come to raise our cause, a son resolved
To kill his mother, honouring his father's blood.
He, now a wandering exile, shall return to set
The apex on this tower of crime his race has built.
A great oath, sealed in sight of gods, binds him to exact 1350
Full penance for his father's corpse stretched dead in dust.

Why then should I lament? Am I so pitiable?
I have watched Fate unfold her pattern: Troy endured
What she endured; her captor now, by Heaven's decree,
Ends thus. I have done with tears. I will endure my death.
O gates of the dark world, I greet you as I come!
Let me receive, I pray, a single mortal stroke,
Sink without spasm, feel the warm blood's gentle ebb,
Embrace death for my comfort, and so close my eyes.

CHORUS:
O woman deep in wisdom as in suffering, 1360
You have told us much. Yet, if you have true foreknowledge
Of your own death, why, like an ox for sacrifice,
Move thus towards the altar with intrepid step?

CASSANDRA:
Friends, there is no escape, none—once the hour has come.

CHORUS:
Yet last to go gains longest time.

CASSANDRA:
This is the day.
Retreat wins little.

CHORUS:
Courage and destiny in you
Are proudly matched.

CASSANDRA:
The happy never hear such praise.

CHORUS:
Yet a brave death lends brightness to mortality.

CASSANDRA:
O father! O my brothers! All your brightness dead!...
I go. Now in the land of the defeated I 1370
Will mourn my end and Agamemnon's. I have lived.
[*She goes towards the door; then with a cry turns back.*]

CHORUS:
What is it? What do you see? What terror turns you back?
[CASSANDRA *gasps, with a sound of choking.*]

CHORUS:
You gasp, as if some nausea choked your very soul.

CASSANDRA:
There is a smell of murder. The walls drip with blood.

CHORUS:
The altar's ready. This is the smell of sacrifice.
CASSANDRA:
It is most like the air that rises from a grave.
CHORUS:
You mean the Syrian perfume sprinkled for the feast?
CASSANDRA:
I am not like a bird scared at an empty bush,
Trembling for nothing. Wait: when you shall see my death
Atoned with death, woman for woman; when in place 1380
Of him whom marriage cursed another man shall fall:
Then witness for me—these and all my prophecies
Were utter truth. This I request before I die.
CHORUS:
To die is sad; sadder, to know death fore-ordained.
CASSANDRA:
Yet one word more, a prophecy—or, if a dirge,
At least not mine alone. In this sun's light—my last—
I pray: when the sword's edge requites my captor's blood,
Then may his murderers, dying, with that debt pay too
For her they killed in chains, their unresisting prey!

Alas for human destiny! Man's happiest hours 1390
Are pictures drawn in shadow. Then ill fortune comes,
And with two strokes the wet sponge wipes the drawing out.
And grief itself's hardly more pitiable than joy.
[*She goes into the palace.*]
CHORUS:
Of fortune no man tastes his fill.
While pointing envy notes his store,
And tongues extol his happiness,
Man surfeited will hunger still.
For who grows weary of success,
Or turns good fortune from his door
Bidding her trouble him no more? 1400

Our king, whom Fortune loves to bless,
By the gods' will has taken Troy,
And honour crowns his safe return.
If now, for blood shed long ago,
In penance due his blood must flow,
And if his murderers must earn
Death upon death, and Fate stands so,
I ask, what mortal man can claim
That he alone was born to enjoy
A quiet life, and an untarnished name? 1410
[AGAMEMNON'S *voice is heard from inside the palace.*]
AGAMEMNON:
Help, help! I am wounded, murdered, here in the inner room!
CHORUS:
Hush, listen! Who cried 'Murder'? Do you know that voice?
AGAMEMNON:
Help, help again! Murder—a second, mortal blow!

CHORUS:

1. That groan tells me the deed is done. It was the king.
Come, let's decide together on the safest plan.
2. This is what I advise—to send a herald round
Bidding the citizens assemble here in arms.
3. Too slow. I say we should burst in at once, and catch
Murder in the act, before the blood dries on the sword.
4. I share your feeling—that is what we ought to do, 1420
Or something of that kind. Now is the time to act.
5. It's plain what this beginning points to: the assassins
Mean to establish a tyrannical regime.
6. Yes—while we talk and talk; but action, spurning sleep,
Tramples the gentle face of caution in the dust.
7. I can suggest no plan that might prove practical.
I say, let those who took this step propose the next.
8. I'm of the same opinion. If the king is dead,
I know no way to make him live by argument.
9. Then shall we patiently drag out our servile years 1430
Governed by these disgraces of our royal house?
10. No, no! Intolerable! Who would not rather die?—
A milder fate than living under tyranny!
11. Wait; not too fast. What is our evidence? Those groans?
Are we to prophesy from them that the king's dead?
12. We must be certain; this excitement's premature.
Guessing and certain knowledge are two different things.

CHORUS:

I find this view supported on all sides: that we
Make full enquiry what has happened to the king.

[*The palace doors open, revealing* CLYTEMNESTRA. *At her feet* AGAMEMNON *lies dead, in a silver bath, and wrapped in a voluminous purple robe. On his body lies* CASSANDRA, *also dead.*]

CLYTEMNESTRA:

I said, not long since, many things to match the time; 1440
All which, that time past, without shame I here unsay.
How else, when one prepares death for an enemy
Who seems a friend,—how else net round the deadly trap
High enough to forestall the victim's highest leap?
A great while I have pondered on this trial of strength.
At long last the pitched battle came, and victory:
Here where I struck I stand and see my task achieved.
Yes, this is my work, and I claim it. To prevent
Flight or resistance foiling death, I cast on him,
As one who catches fish, a vast voluminous net, 1450
That walled him round with endless wealth of woven folds;
And then I struck him, twice. Twice he cried out and groaned;
And then fell limp. And as he lay I gave a third
And final blow, my thanks for prayers fulfilled, to Zeus,
Lord of the lower region, Saviour—of dead men!
So falling he belched forth his life; with cough and retch
There spurted from him bloody foam in a fierce jet,
And spreading, spattered me with drops of crimson rain;
While I exulted as the sown cornfield exults
Drenched with the dew of heaven when buds burst forth in Spring. 1460

So stands the case, Elders of Argos. You may be
As you choose, glad or sorry; I am jubilant.
And, were it seemly over a *dead* man to pour
Thankoffering for safe journey, surely Justice here
Allows it, here demands it; so enriched a wine
Of wickedness this man stored in his house, and now
Returned, drains his own cursed cup to the last dregs.

CHORUS:
The brute effrontery of your speech amazes us.
To boast so shamelessly over your husband's corpse!

CLYTEMNESTRA:
You speak as to some thoughtless woman: you are wrong. 1470
My pulse beats firm. I tell what you already know:
Approve or censure, as you will; all's one to me.
This is my husband, Agamemnon, now stone dead;
His death the work of my right hand, whose craftsmanship
Justice acknowledges. There lies the simple truth.

CHORUS:
Vile woman! What unnatural food or drink,
Malignant root, brine from the restless sea,
Transformed you, that your nature did not shrink
From foulest guilt? Argos will execrate
Your nameless murder with one voice of hate, 1480
Revoke your portion with the just and free,
And drive you outlawed from our Argive gate.

CLYTEMNESTRA:
Yes! Now you righteously mulct *me* with banishment,
Award me public curses, roars of civic hate.
Why, once before, did you not dare oppose this man?
Who with as slight compunction as men butcher sheep,
When his own fields were white with flocks, must sacrifice
His child, and my own darling, whom my pain brought forth—
He killed her for a charm to stop the Thracian wind!
He was the one you should have driven from Argos; he, 1490
Marked with his daughter's blood, was ripe for punishment.
But *my* act shocks your ears, whets your judicial wrath!
Your threats doubtless rely on force—you have your men
And weapons: try your strength in fair fight against mine.
Win, and you may command me. If—please Heaven—you lose,
Old as you are, you shall be taught some wisdom yet.

CHORUS:
Such boasts show folly in a crafty mind.
So surely as your robe blazons your crime
In those red drops, shall your own head bow low
Under a bloody stroke. Wait but the time: 1500
Friendless, dishonoured, outcast, you shall find
Your debt fall due, and suffer blow for blow.

CLYTEMNESTRA:
Is it so? Then you shall hear the righteous oath I swear.
By Justice, guardian of my child, now perfected;
By her avenging Fury, at whose feet I poured
His blood: I have no fear that *his* avenger's tread
Shall shake this house, while my staunch ally now as then,

Aegisthus, kindles on my hearth the ancestral fire.
With such a shield, strength marches boldly on. Meanwhile,
He who was sweet to every Trojan Chryseis,[27] 1510
And soured my life, lies here; with him his prisoner,
His faithful soothsayer, who shared his berth, and knew
Sailors' lasciviousness; their ends both richly earned.
He—as you see him; she first, like the dying swan,
Sang her death-song, and now lies in her lover's clasp.
Brought as a variant to the pleasures of my bed,
She lends an added relish now to victory.

CHORUS:

Come, look on him, and weep.
O that some merciful swift fate,
Not wasting-sick nor wry with pain, 1520
Would bid me share his ever-endless sleep!
Low lies the kindly guardian of our State,
Who fought ten years to win
Redress for woman's sin;
Now by a woman slain.

Helen! Infatuate Helen! You who spilt
Beneath Troy's wall lives without number! You
Now on your house have fixed a lasting guilt
Which every age will tell anew.
Surely, that day you fled beyond recall, 1530
A curse of grief already grew
Deep-rooted in this royal hall.

CLYTEMNESTRA:

Is fact so gross a burden?
Put up no prayers for death;
Nor turn your spleen on Helen,
As if her act had ordered
The fate of fighting thousands
And robbed their souls of breath;
Or from her fault alone
Such cureless grief had grown. 1540

CHORUS:

Spirit of hate, whose strong curse weighs
Hard on the house and heirs of Tantalus,
Your power it is engenders thus
In woman's brain such evil art,
And darkens all my bitter days.
It is your hateful form I see rejoice,
Standing like crow on carrion; your voice
Whose execrable song affronts both ear and heart.

CLYTEMNESTRA:

You now speak more in wisdom,
Naming the thrice-gorged Fury 1550
That hates and haunts our race.

[27] The daughter of a priest of Apollo whom Agamemnon took for his concubine.

Hers is the thirst of slaughter,
Still slaked with feud and vengeance,
Till, with each wrong requited
A new thirst takes its place.

CHORUS:

This grievous power whose wrath you celebrate
With cursed truth, no royal house's fall,
No mad catastrophe, can ever sate.
O piteous mystery! Is Zeus not lord?
Zeus, Zeus, alas! doer and source of all? 1560
Could even this horror be, without his sovereign word?

Sad, silent king! How shall I mourn your death?
How find the heart's true word, to prove me friend?
Here where you spent your dying breath,
Caught by the ruthless falsehood of a wife,
In the foul spider's web fast bound you lie.
Unholy rest, and most ignoble end—
That man like beast should die
Pierced with a two-edged knife!

CLYTEMNESTRA:

This murder's mine, you clamour. 1570
I was his wife; but henceforth
My name from his be freed!
Dressed in my form, a phantom[28]
Of vengeance, old and bitter,
On that obscene host, Atreus,
For his abhorrent deed,
Has poured this blood in payment,
That here on Justice' altar
A man for babes should bleed.

CHORUS:

And are you guiltless? Some revengeful Power 1580
Stood, maybe, at your side; but of this blood
Who will, who could absolve you? Hour by hour
On his unyielding course the black-robed King,
Pressing to slaughter, swells the endless flood
Of crimson life by pride and hate released
From brothers' veins—till the due reckoning,
When the dried gore shall melt, and Ares bring
Justice at last for that unnatural feast.

Sad, silent king! How shall I mourn your death?
How find the heart's true word, to prove me friend? 1590
Here where you spent your dying breath,
Caught by the ruthless falsehood of a wife,
In the foul spider's web fast bound you lie.
Unholy rest, and most ignoble end—
That man like beast should die
Pierced with a two-edged knife!

[28]That is, I am but an instrument of the living curse that haunts our house.

CLYTEMNESTRA:

The guile I used to kill him
He used himself the first,
When he by guile uprooted
The tender plant he gave me, 1600
And made this house accurst.
When on my virgin daughter
His savage sword descended,
My tears in rivers ran;
If now by savage sword-thrust
His ageing days are ended,
Let shame and conscience ban
His boasts, where he pays forfeit
For wrong his guile began.

CHORUS:

Where, where lies Right? Reason despairs her powers, 1610
Mind numbly gropes, her quick resources spent.
Our throne endangered, and disaster near,
Where can I turn? I fear
Thunder that cracks foundations, blood-red showers;
The light rain slacks—the deluge is in store.
Justice, in harmony with Fate's intent,
Hardens her hold to shake the earth once more.

O earth, O earth! Would that some timely chance
Had laid me in your lap, before my eyes
Had seen him laid so low, 1620
Lord of this silver-walled inheritance!
Who will inter him? Who lament the dead?
Will *you* wear mourning for disguise?
Bewail the husband whom your own hand killed?
For his high glories offer gifts of lies?
Since Justice answers, No!
By whom shall tears of honest love be shed,
His graveside ritual of praise fulfilled?

CLYTEMNESTRA:

That question's not your business.
I felled him; I despatched him; 1630
And I will earth his bones.
No troops from house or city
Shall beat their breasts and lay him
In vaults of bronze and marble
With seemly civic groans.
But, as is fit, his daughter
Shall meet him near the porchway
Of those who perished young;
His loved Iphigenia
With loving arms shall greet him, 1640
And gagged and silent tongue.

CHORUS:

Reproach answers reproach; truth darkens still.
She strikes the striker; he who dared to kill

Pays the full forfeit. While Zeus holds his throne,
This maxim holds on earth: *the sinner dies.*
That is God's law. Oh, who can exorcize
This breeding curse, this canker that has grown
Into these walls, to plague them at its will?

CLYTEMNESTRA:

The sinner dies: you have reached the truth at last.
Now to the Powers that persecute 1650
Our race I offer a sworn pact:
With this harsh deed and bitter fact
I am content; let *them* forget the past,
Leave us for ever, and oppress
Some other house with murderous wickedness.
I ask no weight of wealth;
For me it will suffice
To purchase, at this price,
For our long sickness, health.

[*Enter* AEGISTHUS.]

AEGISTHUS:

O happy day, when Justice comes into her own! 1660
Now I believe that gods, who dwell above the earth,
See what men suffer, and award a recompense:
Here, tangled in a net the avenging Furies wove,
He lies, a sight to warm my heart; and pays his blood
In full atonement for his father's treacherous crime.

Here is the story plain. There was dispute between
Atreus, Agamemnon's father, who ruled Argos then,
And my father Thyestes, his own brother; whom
Atreus drove out from home and city. He came back;
Sat as a piteous suppliant at Atreus' hearth; 1670
Gained his request—in part: his own blood did not stain
His childhood's home. But Atreus, this man's father, gave
His guest, my father, a host's gift; a gift more full
Of eagerness than love. He feigned a feasting-day,
And amidst lavish meats served him his own sons' flesh.
The feet and the splayed fingers he concealed, putting
The other parts, unrecognizably chopped small,
Above them. Each guest had his table; and this dish
Was set before my father. He, in ignorance,
At once took that which prompted no close scrutiny, 1680
And tasted food from which, as you now see, our house
Has not recovered. Then he recognized, in all
Its loathsomeness, what had been done. With one deep groan,
Back from his chair, vomiting murdered flesh, he fell;
Cursed Pelops' race with an inexorable curse;
With his foot sent the table crashing wide, and screamed,
'So crash to ruin the whole house of Tantalus!'

That deed gave birth to what you now see here, this death.
I planned his killing, as was just: I was the third

Child of Thyestes, then a brat in baby-clothes; 1690
Spared, and sent off with my distracted father, till,
Full-grown, Justice restored me to my native land.
I, from a distance, plotted this whole evil snare,
And caught my man. Thus satisfied, I could die now,
Seeing Agamemnon in the trap of Justice, dead.

CHORUS:
Aegisthus, we acquit you of insults to the dead.
But since you claim that you alone laid the whole plot,
And thus, though absent, took his blood upon your hands,
I tell you plainly, your own life is forfeited;
Justice will curse you, Argive hands will stone you dead. 1700

AEGISTHUS:
So, this is how you lecture, from the lower deck,
The master on the bridge? Then you shall learn, though old,
How harsh a thing is discipline, when reverend years
Lack wisdom. Chains and the distress of hunger are
A magic medicine, of great power to school the mind.
Does not this sight bid you reflect? Then do not kick
Against the goad, lest you should stumble, and be hurt.

CHORUS:
You woman! While he went to fight, you stayed at home;
Seduced his wife meanwhile; and then, against a man
Who led an army, *you* could scheme this murder! Pah! 1710

AEGISTHUS:
You still use words that have in them the seed of tears.
Your voice is most unlike the voice of Orpheus: he
Bound all who heard him with delight; your childish yelps
Annoy us, and will fasten bonds on you yourselves.
With hard control you will prove more amenable.

CHORUS:
Control! Are we to see *you* king of Argos—you,
Who, after plotting the king's murder, did not dare
To lift the sword yourself?

AEGISTHUS:
To lure him to the trap
Was plainly woman's work; I, an old enemy,
Was suspect. Now, helped by his wealth, I will attempt 1720
To rule in Argos. The refractory shall not
Be fed fat like show-horses, but shall feel the yoke—
A heavy one. Hunger and darkness joined will soon
Soften resistance.

CHORUS:
Then, if you're so bold, why not
Yourself with your own hands plunder your enemy?
Instead, a woman, whose life makes this earth unclean
And flouts the gods of Argos, helped you murder him!
Oh, does Orestes live? Kind Fortune, bring him home,
To set against these two his sword invincible!

AEGISTHUS:
Then, since your treason's militant, you shall soon learn 1730
That it is foolish to insult authority.

Ready, there! Forward, guards! [*armed soldiers rush in*]
Here's work for you. Each man
Handle his sword.

CHORUS:
Our swords are ready. We can die.

AEGISTHUS:
'Die'! We accept the omen. Fortune hold the stakes!

CLYTEMNESTRA:
Stop, stop, Aegisthus, dearest! No more violence!
When this first harvest ripens we'll reap grief enough.
Crime and despair are fed to bursting; let us not
Plunge deeper still in blood. Elders, I beg of you,
Yield in good time to Destiny; go home, before
You come to harm; what we have done was fore-ordained. 1740
If our long agony finds here fulfilment, we,
Twice gored by Fate's long talons, welcome it. I speak
With woman's wisdom, if you choose to understand.

AEGISTHUS:
Then are these gross-tongued men to aim their pointed gibes
At random, and bluff out the fate they've richly earned?

CHORUS:
You'll find no Argive grovel at a blackguard's feet.

AEGISTHUS:
Enough! Some later day I'll settle scores with you.

CHORUS:
Not if Fate sets Orestes on the Argos road.

AEGISTHUS:
For men in exile hopes are meat and drink—I know.

CHORUS:
Rule on, grow fat defiling Justice—while you can. 1750

AEGISTHUS:
You are a fool; in time you'll pay me for those words.

CHORUS:
Brag blindly on—a cock that struts before his hen!

[*During these last lines the* CHORUS *have gone out two by two, the last man vanishing with the last insult, leaving* CLYTEMNESTRA *and* AEGISTHUS *alone.*]

CLYTEMNESTRA:
Pay no heed to this currish howling. You and I,
Joint rulers, will enforce due reverence for our throne.

The Oresteia: The Eumenides

Translated by Philip Vellacott

CHARACTERS:

THE PYTHIAN PRIESTESS
APOLLO
HERMES
ORESTES
THE GHOST OF CLYTEMNESTRA
CHORUS *of the Furies, or Eumenides*
ATHENE
Twelve Athenian Citizens
A number of Athenian women and girls

SCENE: *First at Delphi, at the Pythian*[1] *Oracle, or Temple of Apollo; then at Athens, in the Temple of Athene on the Acropolis.*

SCENE I: *Before the Pythian Oracle. The scene is curtained.* THE PYTHIAN PRIESTESS *enters below at one side, mounts by steps to the stage, and stands at the centre before the curtain.*

PRIESTESS:

First in my prayer of all the gods I reverence
Earth, first author of prophecy; Earth's daughter then,
Themis; who, legend tells, next ruled this oracle;
The third enthroned, succeeding by good-will, not force,
Phoebe—herself another Titan child of Earth—
In turn gave her prerogative, a birthday gift,
To her young namesake, Phoebus. From the Delian lake
Ringed with high rocks he came to the craft-crowded shores
Of Pallas; thence to Parnassus[2] and this holy seat.
And in his progress bands of Attic worshippers, 10
Hephaestus' sons,[3] builders of roads, escorted him,
Taming for pilgrims' passage ground untamed before.
So Phoebus came to Delphi; people and king alike
Paid him high honour; Zeus endowed his prescient mind
With heavenly wisdom, and established him as fourth
Successor to this throne, whence he, as Loxias,
Interprets to mankind his father's word and will.

These first my piety invokes. And I salute
With holy words Pallas Pronaia,[4] and the nymphs
Of the Corycian cave, where, in enchanted shelter, 20
Birds love to nest; where Bromius[5] too makes his home,
Since, once, he led his frenzied Bacchic army forth
To tear King Pentheus as a hare is torn by hounds.
Fountains of Pleistos, Delphi's river, next I name;
Poseidon; and, last, the supreme Fulfiller, Zeus.

Now on the seat of prophecy I take my place;
Heaven grant that this day's service far surpass in blessing
All former days! Let any Greek enquirer here,
As custom is, cast lots for precedence, and come.
As Phoebus guides my lips, so I pronounce his truth. 30

[*The* PRIESTESS *goes in between the curtains. After a short pause, her voice is heard in a cry of terror, and she reappears.*]

A fearful sight, a thing appalling to describe,
Drives me staggering and helpless out of Apollo's house.
My legs give way and tremble; hands must hold me up.

---

[1]The word is applied to Apollo, to his oracle, and to his priestess. It is derived from the Greek word meaning "to find out by inquiry," and refers to Apollo's oracular function.
[2]The mountain that rises close to Delphi.
[3]Erichthonius, mythical founder of Athens, was a son of Hephaestus.
[4]Pallas before the temple, or of the precincts.
[5]Dionysus.

How useless fear makes an old woman—like a child!
As I went towards the inner shrine, all hung with wreaths,
There on the navel-stone a suppliant was sitting,
A man polluted—blood still wet on hands that grasp
A reeking sword; yet on his head fresh olive-leaves,
Twined thickly with white wool, show heedful reverence.[6]
So far I can speak plainly. But beside this man, 40
Stretched upon benches, sleeping, a strange company
Of women—no, not women; Gorgons—yet, again,
They are not like Gorgons. Harpies I saw painted once,
Monsters robbing King Phineus of his feast; but these
Are wingless, black, utterly loathsome; their vile breath
Vents in repulsive snoring; from their eyes distils
A filthy rheum; their garb is wickedness to wear
In sight of the gods' statues or in human homes.
They are creatures of no race I ever saw; no land
Could breed them and not bear the curse of God and man. 50
I will go. Loxias is powerful, and this temple's his.
Men's tainted walls wait for his purifying power:
Let him—Priest, Prophet, Healer—now protect his own.

[*The* PRIESTESS *returns by the way that she came. The curtains open, revealing the Temple of Apollo. In the centre* ORESTES *sits by a rough stone altar—the 'Navel-Stone'. Beside him stand* APOLLO *and* HERMES. *Around them, asleep on benches or on the floor, lie the twelve* FURIES.]

APOLLO:
I will not fail you. Near at hand or far away,
I am your constant guardian and your enemies' dread.
Now for this one brief hour you see these ragers quiet,
These hunters caught in sleep; these ancient, ageless hags,
Whose presence neither god nor man nor beast can bear.
For sake of evil they were born; and evil is
The dark they dwell in, subterranean Tartarus; 60
Beings abhorred by men and by Olympian gods.
Then fly, and do not weaken. They will hound you yet
Through seas and island cities, over the vast continent,
Wherever the earth's face is hard with wanderers' feet.
Keep courage firm; nurse your appointed pain; and go
To Athens, city of Pallas. There with suppliant hands
Embrace her ancient image, and implore her help.
There I will set you judges; and with soothing pleas
I, who first bade you take your mother's life, will bring
From all your painful days final deliverance. 70

ORESTES:
Apollo, Lord! Knowledge of justice and of right
Is yours: let will prompt knowledge, and let care fulfil.
Your strength shall be my surety for your promised help.

APOLLO:
Remember, let no fear conquer your steadfast heart.
Go, Hermes, brother, as his guardian, and fulfil

---

[6]The proper equipment for a suppliant at an altar.

Your titular office. His protection is my care:
Shepherd him well. The outlaw has his sanctity,
Which Zeus regards, giving him Fortune for his guide.

[HERMES *leads* ORESTES *away;* APOLLO *retires into the temple. The* GHOST OF CLYTEMNESTRA *appears.*]

CLYTEMNESTRA:
Will you still sleep? Oh, wake! What use are you, asleep?
Since you so slight me, I am abused unceasingly 80
Among the other dead, for him I killed, and wander
Despised and shamed. I tell you truly, by them all
I am held guilty and condemned; while, for the blow
My own son struck, no angry voice protests. See here,
This wound under my heart, and say whose was the sword!
Look! For though daylight cannot see beyond the flesh,
The mind in sleep has eyes. Often for you my hand
Has poured wineless libations, sober soothing draughts;
Upon my hearth in midnight ritual—an hour
Given to no other god—banquets have burned for you. 90
Now all my gifts I see spurned underfoot; while he,
Like a fawn lightly leaping out of the sprung snare,
Has escaped away and gone, and mocks you to your shame.
Listen, you Powers of the deep earth, and understand!
Listen, I entreat you, for my plea is life and death!
Listen! In your dream I, Clytemnestra, call to you!

[*The* CHORUS *mutter restlessly, as dogs growl in sleep.*]

CLYTEMNESTRA:
You murmur; but your prey has vanished out of sight.
His friends are not like mine: they save him, while you sleep.

[*Again the* CHORUS *mutter.*]

CLYTEMNESTRA:
Will you not wake? Does grief not touch you? He has gone!
Orestes, who killed me, his mother, has escaped! 100

[*More excited cries come from the* CHORUS.]

CLYTEMNESTRA:
Still crying, still asleep? Quick now, wake and stand up!
To work! Evil's your province—evil waits for you!

[*The cries continue.*]

CLYTEMNESTRA:
Sleep and fatigue, two apt accomplices, have drained
All force from the she-dragons' rage.

CHORUS [*with still louder cries*]:
After him! Catch him, catch him, catch him, catch him, catch him! Take care, take care!

CLYTEMNESTRA:
In dreams you hunt your prey, baying like hounds whose thought
Will never rest; but what of deeds? Has weariness
Conquered and softened you with sleep, till you forget
My pain? Rise up, torment his heart with just reproach;
For whetted words goad the quick conscience. Storm at him 110
With hot blood-reeking blasts blown from your vaporous womb,
Wither his hope of respite, hunt him to the death!

[*As the* CHORUS *awake, the* GHOST OF CLYTEMNESTRA *vanishes.*]

CHORUS:

Come, wake; wake you too; wake each other; come, wake all!
Shake off your sleep, stand up. What could that warning mean?

[*They see that* ORESTES *has gone.*]

What has happened? Furies, we are foiled!
Who were ever mocked as we?
Who would bear such mockery?
Sleepless labour spent in vain!
Duty flouted, privilege despoiled!
See the empty snare—our prey 120
Vanished, fled, and free again!
While we slept our right was stolen away.

Phoebus, son of Zeus, are you a god?
You set honesty aside;
You, the younger, ride roughshod
Over elder Powers; you have defied
Justice for your altar's sake,
Saved a godless matricide
From appointed pain, to make
Mockery of motherhood: 130
Who can call such crooked dealing good?

Out of my dreams I heard
A sharp accusing word
That struck me to the deep heart's core,
As on an uphill road
The driver's firm-gripped goad
Strikes till the flesh is sore.
I feel the common scourge, Remorse,
Wielded in Fate's strong hand,
Whose cold and crushing force 140
None can withstand.

The fault's not ours. It lies
With younger gods who rise
In place of those that ruled before;
From stool to crown their throne
Is stained with gore.
See, how Earth's central sacred stone[7]
Has taken for its own
A grim pollution Justice must abhor!

Phoebus, for all your prophet's skill, 150
Your holy wisdom, by this deed
You of your own unprompted will
Have sullied your own altar's flames,
Infringing laws by gods decreed

[7] There was in the forecourt of the Delphic temple a stone, used as an altar, and said to be the central point of the earth. It was called Omphalos, "the navel."

And Destiny's primeval claims,[8]
To grant some mortal's passing need.

Fate's enemy, my enemy too,
Shall not give sanctuary to sin.
Orestes is accurst, and he,
Though he seek refuge with the dead, 160
Shall find no place where guilt is free;
Soon there shall come, of his own kin,
A like Avenger, to renew
Fate's curse upon his branded head.

[*Enter* APOLLO *from within the temple, carrying his bow and quiver.*]

APOLLO:

Out of this temple! I command you, go at once!
Quit my prophetic sanctuary, lest you feel
The gleaming snake that darts winged from my golden bow,
And painfully spew forth the black foam that you suck
From the sour flesh of murderers. What place have you
Within these walls? Some pit of punishments, where heads 170
Are severed, eyes torn out, throats cut, manhood unmanned,
Some hell of maimings, mutilations, stonings, where
Bodies impaled on stakes melt the mute air with groans—
Your place is there! Such are the feasts you love, for which
Heaven loathes you. Is not this the truth, proclaimed in you
By every feature? Find some blood-gorged lion's den,
There make your seemly dwelling, and no more rub off
Your foulness in this house of prayer and prophecy.
Away! Graze other fields, you flock unshepherded!
No god loves such as you![9]

CHORUS:

Now is my turn to speak. 180

You, Lord Apollo, you alone are answerable
To your own charge; what's done's your doing, first to last.

APOLLO:

How's this? So far inform me.

CHORUS;

It was your oracle
That bade him take his mother's life.

APOLLO:

My oracle
Bade him avenge his father.

CHORUS:

With his hand still red
He found you his protector.

APOLLO:

I commanded him
To fly for refuge to this temple.

---

[8]Literally, the three Fates.

[9]Apollo abuses the Furies as barbarous, and the barbarisms he mentions are horrors that Greeks usually associated with Oriental despotism. He means simply that the function of the Furies is "un-Hellenic," in contrast to the Hellenic use of courts and juries.

CHORUS:
We are here
As his appointed escort. Why revile us then?
APOLLO:
Your presence here is outrage.
CHORUS:
But it is no less
Our duty and our office.
APOLLO:
A high office, this. 190
Come, with due pride proclaim it.
CHORUS:
We hound matricides
To exile.
APOLLO:
And when wife kills husband, what of her?
CHORUS:
They are not kin; therefore such blood is not self-spilt.
APOLLO:
Then you dishonour and annul the marriage-bond
Of Zeus and Hera, that confirms all marriage-bonds;
And by your argument the sweetest source of joy
To mortals, Aphrodite, falls into contempt.
Marriage, that joins two persons in Fate's ordinance,
Guarded by justice, stands more sacred than an oath.
If, then, to one that kills the other you show grace, 200
All penalty remitted, and all wrath renounced,
You are unjust to persecute Orestes' life.
His crime, I know, you take most grievously to heart;
While for his mother's you show open leniency.
Pallas herself shall hear this case, and judge our pleas.
CHORUS:
I tell you, I will never let Orestes go.
APOLLO:
Pursue him, then; take all the pains you wish.
CHORUS:
Phoebus,
You shall not, even in word, curtail my privilege.
APOLLO:
Not as a gift would I accept your privilege.
CHORUS:
You are called great beside the throne of Zeus. 210
But I
Will trace him by his mother's blood, hound him to earth,
And sue for justice on him.
APOLLO:
He is my suppliant;
And I will stand by him and save him if I can.
Fierce anger stirs to action both in heaven and earth
If I forsake the guilty man who turned to me.
[*While* APOLLO *speaks the* CHORUS *have begun to leave the stage;* APOLLO *withdraws into the temple.*]

SCENE II: *The Temple of Athene in Athens, with a statue of the goddess before it.* ORESTES *enters and kneels before the statue.*

ORESTES:
Divine Athene! At Apollo's word I come.
Receive me graciously; though still a fugitive,
Not unclean now.[10] Long wandering through tribes and towns
Has cleansed my bloodstained hand, blunted the edge of guilt; 220
Welcoming homes have rubbed the foulness from my soul.
Now, my long journey over land and sea fulfilled,
Faithful to Loxias' bidding and his oracle,
Goddess, I approach your house, your holy effigy.
Here I will stay, to know the issue of my trial.

[*The* CHORUS *enter, following the track of* ORESTES.]

CHORUS:
This is his trail, I have it clear. Come, follow, where
The silent finger of pollution points the way.
Still by the scent we track him, as hounds track a deer
Wounded and bleeding. As a shepherd step by step
Searches a mountain, so have we searched every land, 230
Flown wingless over sea, swifter than sailing ships,
Always pursuing, till we gasp with weariness.
Now he is here, I know, crouched in some hiding-place.
The scent of mortal murder laughs in my nostrils—

Look there! See him! See him at last!
Watch every doorway, lest the murderer
Steal away and escape unpunished!
Once again he has found protection;
Closely clinging to the immortal
Goddess's image, thus he offers 240
His life for trial, for the deed of his hand.

No hope can rescue him.
A mother's blood once spilt
None can restore again;
In dust the fresh stream lies,
A parched, accusing stain.
You shall, for your soul's guilt,
Give us your blood to drink
Red from the living limb,
Our dear and deadly food, 250
Our labour's lawful prize.
Yes, while you still draw breath,
Your withered flesh shall sink,
In payment for her blood,
In penance for her pain,
Down to the world of death.

[10] In the first scene, his hands and sword were still wet with blood.

Mark this: not only you,
But every mortal soul
Whose pride has once transgressed
The law of reverence due 260
To parent, god, or guest,
Shall pay sin's just, inexorable toll.

Deep in the nether sky
Death rules the ways of man
With stern and strong control;
And there is none who can,
By any force or art,
Elude Death's watchful eye
Or his recording heart.

ORESTES:
Long taught by pain, learned in cleansing ritual, 270
I know when speech is lawful, when to hold my tongue;
And in this case a wise instructor bade me speak.
The blood upon my hand is drowsed and quenched; the stain
Of matricide washed clean, exorcized while yet fresh
At Phoebus' hearth with purgative blood-offerings.
It would take long to tell of all the friends whose homes
And hands have given me welcome without harm or taint.
And now from holy lips, with pure words, I invoke
Athene, ruler of this country, to my aid.
Thus she shall gain, without one blow, by just compact, 280
Myself, my country, and my Argive citizens
In loyal, lasting, unreserved confederacy.
Whether by the Tritonian lake, her Libyan home,
She stands—at rest, at war, a bulwark to her friends;[11]
Or with a warrior's eye in bold command surveys
The Phlegraean plain[12]—a god can hear me—let her now
Come in divine authority and save my soul!

CHORUS:
Neither Apollo nor Athene can have power
To save you. Lost, cast off, the very taste of joy
Forgotten, you will live the prey of vampire Powers, 290
A pale ghost. Do you spurn my words in silence—you,
To me assigned and dedicated? There's no need
To await knife and altar, for your living flesh
Shall feast us. Hear this song that binds you to our will.

Come, Furies, our resolve is set;
Let mime and measure tread their course,
That none who feels the maddening force
Of our dread music may forget
How all the varying fates that bind
Men's lives are by our will assigned. 300

---

[11]The Greek says "whether standing or sitting," and refers to statues of Athene, which were made sometimes in the one posture, sometimes in the other.

[12]The scene of the battle between gods and giants, in which Athene acted as a general.

We hold our judgement just and true:
The man whose open hands are pure
Anger of ours shall not pursue;
He lives untroubled and secure.
But when a sinner, such as he,
Burdened with blood so foully shed,
Covers his guilty hands for shame,
Then, bearing witness for the dead,
We at his judgement stand to claim
The price of blood unyieldingly. 310

Hear me, O brooding Night,
My mother, from whose womb
I came for punishment
Of all who live in light
Or grope beyond the tomb.
Phoebus would steal away
My office and my right,
My trapped and cowering prey
Whose anguish must atone
For sin so violent, 320
For blood that bore his own.

Now, by the altar,
Over the victim
Ripe for our ritual,
Sing this enchantment:
A song without music,
A sword in the senses,
A storm in the heart
And a fire in the brain;
A clamour of Furies 330
To paralyse reason,
A tune full of terror,
A drought in the soul!

Fate, whose all-powerful sway
Weaves out the world's design,
Decreed for evermore
This portion to be mine:
When for some murderous blow
The pangs of guilt surprise
Man's folly, from that day 340
Close at his side we go
Until the day he dies;
And Hope, that says, 'Below
The earth is respite', lies.

Now, by the altar,
Over the victim
Ripe for our ritual,
Sing this enchantment:

A song without music,
A sword in the senses, 350
A storm in the heart
And a fire in the brain:
A clamour of Furies
To paralyse reason,
A tune full of terror,
A drought in the soul!

The day we were begotten
These rights to us were sealed,
That against sin of mortals
Our hand should be revealed. 360
Immortals need not fear us;
Our feasts no god can share;
When white robes throng the temples
The darkness that we wear
Forbids our presence there.
Our chosen part is torment,
And great ones' overthrow;
When War turns home, and kinsman
Makes kinsman's life-blood flow,
Then in his strength we hunt him 370
And lay his glory low.

Our zeal assumes this office,
Our care and pains pursue it,
That gods may be exempt;
Zeus, free from taint or question,
Repels our gory presence
With loathing and contempt.
For him our dreaded footfall,
Launched from the height, leaps downward
With keen and crushing force, 380
Till helpless guilt, despairing,
Falls in his headlong course.

And so men's glories, towering to the sky,
Soon at our black-robed onset, the advance
Of vengeance beating in our fateful dance,
Fade under earth, and in dishonour die.

And in man's downfall his own hand's pollution,
Hovering round him like a misty gloom,
Pours deeper darkness on his mind's confusion,
While groaning ghosts intone his house's doom. 390

For Law lives on; and we, Law's holy few,
Law's living record of all evil done,
Resourceful and accomplishing, pursue
Our hateful task unhonoured; and no prayer
Makes us relent. All other gods must shun

The sunless glimmer of those paths we strew
With rocks, that quick and dead may stumble there.

So, Heaven's firm ordinance has now been told,
The task which Fate immutably assigned
To our devotion. Who will then withhold 400
Due fear and reverence? Though our dwelling lie
In subterranean caverns of the blind,
Our ancient privilege none dares deny.

[*Enter* ATHENE *from her temple.*]

ATHENE:

From far away I heard my name loudly invoked,
Beside Scamander, where I went in haste to claim
Land that the Achaean chieftains had allotted me,
An ample gift chosen from plunder won in war
And given entire to Theseus' sons to hold for ever.
And quickly, without toil of foot or wing, I came
Borne on my strident aegis, with the galloping winds 410
Harnessed before me.

This strange company I see
Here in my precincts moves me—not indeed to fear,
But to amazement. Who are you? I speak to all—
This man who clasps my statue as a suppliant,
And you—beings like none I know that earth brings forth,
Either of those seen among gods and goddesses—
Nor yet are you like mortals.—But I am unjust;
Reason forbids to slander others unprovoked.

CHORUS:

Daughter of Zeus, you shall hear all, and briefly told.
We are the children of primeval Night; we bear 420
The name of Curses in our home deep under earth.

ATHENE:

Your race I know, also your names in common speech.

CHORUS:

Maybe. Next you shall hear our office.

ATHENE:

Willingly—
If you would speak plain words.

CHORUS:

We drive out murderers.

ATHENE:

And where can such a fugitive find rest and peace?

CHORUS:

Only where joy and comfort are not current coin.

ATHENE:

And to such end your hue and cry pursues this man?

CHORUS:

Yes. He chose to become his mother's murderer.

ATHENE:

Was there not some compulsive power whose wrath he feared?

CHORUS:

And who has power to goad a man to matricide? 430

ATHENE:
One plea is now presented; two are to be heard.
CHORUS:
But he would ask no oath from us, nor swear himself.[13]
ATHENE:
You seek the form of justice, more than to be just.
CHORUS:
How so? Instruct me; you do not lack subtlety.
ATHENE:
Injustice must not win the verdict by mere oaths.
CHORUS:
Then try him fairly, and give judgement on the facts.
ATHENE:
You grant to me final decision in this case?
CHORUS:
We do; we trust your wisdom, and your father's name.
ATHENE:
It is your turn to speak, my friend. What will you say?
Your faith in justice sent you to my statue here, 440
A holy suppliant, like Ixion, at my hearth;
Therefore tell first your country, birth, and history;
Then answer to this charge; and let your speech be plain.
ORESTES:
Divine Athene, first from your last words I will
Set one great doubt at rest. My hand is not unclean;
I do not sit polluted at your statue's foot.
And I will tell you weighty evidence of this.
To a blood-guilty man the law forbids all speech,
Till blood-drops from some suckling beast are cast on him
By one whose office is to purge from homicide. 450
Long since, these rituals were all performed for me
In other temples; beasts were slain, pure water poured.
That question, then, I thus dispose of. For my birth,
I am of Argos, and you know my father well,
For you and he joined league to make the city of Troy
No city—Agamemnon, leader of that warlike fleet.
When he came home, he met a shameful death, murdered
By my black-hearted mother, with a cunning snare
Which first hid, then proclaimed the bloody act that felled
My father as he washed away the stains of war. 460

When, later, after years of exile I came home,
I killed my mother—I will not deny it—in
Just retribution for my father, whom I loved.
For this Apollo equally is answerable;
He told me of the tortures that would sear my soul
If I neglected vengeance on the murderers.

---

[13]In the preliminary inquiry, which an Athenian magistrate would conduct before referring the case to the appropriate court of law, the plaintiff would state on oath that he had suffered injury, and the defendant that he was innocent.

Whether or no I acted rightly, is for you
To judge; I will accept your word, for life or death.

ATHENE:

This is too grave a cause for any man to judge;
Nor, in a case of murder, is it right that I 470
Should by my judgement let the wrath of Justice loose;
The less so, since you came after full cleansing rites
As a pure suppliant to my temple, and since I
And Athens grant you sanctuary and welcome you.
But your accusers' claims are not to be dismissed;
And, should they fail to win their case, their anger falls
Like death and terror, blight and poison, on my land.
Hence my dilemma—to accept, or banish them;
And either course is peril and perplexity.
Then, since decision falls to me, I will choose out 480
Jurors of homicide, for a perpetual court,
In whom I vest my judgement. Bring your evidence,
Call witnesses, whose oaths shall strengthen Justice' hand.
I'll pick my wisest citizens, and bring them here
Sworn to give sentence with integrity and truth.

[*Exit* ATHENE, *to the city;* ORESTES *retires into the temple.*]

CHORUS:

Now true and false must change their names,
Old law and justice be reversed,
If new authority put first
The wrongful right this murderer claims.
His act shall now to every man 490
Commend the easy path of crime;
And parents' blood in after time
Shall gleam on children's hands accurst,
To pay the debt this day began.

The Furies' watchful rage shall sleep,
No anger hunt the guilty soul;
Murder shall flout my lost control;
And neighbours talk of wrongs, and weep,
And ask how flesh can more endure,
Or stem the swelling flood of ill, 500
Or hope for better times—while still
Each wretch commends some useless cure.

When stunned by hard misfortune,
On us let no man call,
Chanting the old entreaties,
'Come, swift, avenging Furies!
O sword of Justice, fall!'
Some parent, struck or slighted,
In loud and vain distress
Often will cry, a stranger 510
To the new wickedness,
Which soon shall reach and ruin
The house of Righteousness.

For fear, enforcing goodness,
Must somewhere reign enthroned,
And watch men's ways, and teach them,
Through self-inflicted sorrow,
That sin is not condoned.
What man, no longer nursing
Fear at his heart—what city, 520
Once fear is cast away,
Will bow the knee to Justice
As in an earlier day?

Seek neither licence, where no laws compel,
Nor slavery beneath a tyrant's rod;
Where liberty and rule are balanced well
Success will follow as the gift of God,
Though how He will direct it none can tell.
This truth is apt: the heart's impiety
Begets after its kind the hand's misdeed; 530
But when the heart is sound, from it proceed
Blessings long prayed for, and prosperity.

This above all I bid you: reverence
Justice' high altar; let no sight of gain
Tempt you to spurn with godless insolence
This sanctity. Cause and effect remain;
From sin flows sorrow. Then let man hold dear
His parents' life and honour, and revere
Each passing guest with welcome and defence.

Wealth and honour will attend 540
Love of goodness gladly held;
Virtue free and uncompelled
Fears no harsh untimely end.
But the man whose stubborn soul
Steers a rash defiant course
Flouting every law's control—
He in time will furl perforce,
Late repenting, when the blast
Shreds his sail and snaps his mast.

Helpless in the swirling sea, 550
Struggling hands and anguished cries
Plead with the unheeding skies;
And God smiles to note that he,
Changing folly for despair,
Boasts for fear, will not escape
Shipwreck on the stormy cape;
But, his former blessings thrown
On the reef of justice, there
Perishes unwept, unknown.

[ATHENE *returns, bringing with her twelve Athenian citizens.* APOLLO *comes from the temple, leading* ORESTES.]

ATHENE:

Summon the city, herald, and proclaim the cause; 560
Let the Tyrrhenian trumpet, filled with mortal breath,
Crack the broad heaven, and shake Athens with its voice.
And while the council-chamber fills, let citizens
And jurors all in silence recognize this court
Which I ordain today in perpetuity,
That now and always justice may be well discerned.

CHORUS:

Divine Apollo, handle what belongs to you.
Tell us, what right have you to meddle in this case?

APOLLO:

I came to answer that in evidence. This man
Has my protection by the law of suppliants. 570
I cleansed him from this murder; I am here to be
His advocate, since I am answerable for
The stroke that killed his mother. Pallas, introduce
This case, and so conduct it as your wisdom prompts.

ATHENE:

The case is open.

[*To the* LEADER OF THE CHORUS.] Since you are the accuser, speak.
The court must first hear a full statement of the charge.

CHORUS:

Though we are many, few words will suffice. [*To* ORESTES.] And you
Answer our questions, point for point. First, did you kill
Your mother?

ORESTES:

I cannot deny it. Yes, I did.

CHORUS:

Good; the first round is ours.

ORESTES:

It is too soon to boast: 580
I am not beaten.

CHORUS:

You must tell us, none the less,
How you dispatched her.

ORESTES:

With a sword I pierced her heart.

CHORUS:

On whose persuasion, whose advice?

ORESTES:

Apollo's. He
Is witness that his oracle commanded me.

CHORUS:

The god of prophecy commanded matricide?

ORESTES:

Yes; and he has not failed me from that day to this.

CHORUS:

If to-day's vote condemns you, you will change your words.

ORESTES:

I trust him. My dead father too will send me help.

CHORUS:

Yes, trust the dead now: your hand struck your mother dead.

ORESTES:
She was twice guilty, twice condemned.
CHORUS:
How so? Instruct 590
The court.
ORESTES:
She killed her husband, and my father too.
CHORUS:
Her death absolved her; you still live.
ORESTES:
But why was she
Not punished by you while she lived?
CHORUS:
The man she killed
Was not of her own blood.
ORESTES:
But I am of my mother's?
CHORUS:
Vile wretch! Did she not nourish you in her own womb?
Do you disown your mother's blood, which is your own?
ORESTES:
Apollo, now give evidence. Make plain to me
If I was right to kill her. That I struck the blow
Is true, I own it. But was murder justified?
Expound this point, and show me how to plead my cause. 600
APOLLO:
To you, august court of Athene, I will speak
Justly and truly, as befits a prophet-god.
I never yet, from my oracular seat, pronounced
For man, woman, or city any word which Zeus,
The Olympian Father, had not formally prescribed.
I bid you, then, mark first the force of justice here;
But next, even more, regard my father's will. No oath
Can have more force than Zeus, whose name has sanctioned it.[14]
CHORUS:
Then Zeus, you say, was author of this oracle
You gave Orestes—that his mother's claims should count 610
For nothing, till he had avenged his father's death?
APOLLO:
Zeus so ordained, and Zeus was right. For their two deaths
Are in no way to be compared. He was a king
Wielding an honoured sceptre by divine command.
A woman killed him: such death might be honourable—
In battle, dealt by an arrow from an Amazon's bow.
But you shall hear, Pallas and you who judge this case,
How Clytemnestra killed her husband. When he came
Home from the war, for the most part successful, and
Performed his ritual cleansing, she stood by his side; 620
The ritual ended, as he left the silver bath,

[14] Zeus was the guardian of oaths.

She threw on him a robe's interminable folds,
Wrapped, fettered him in an embroidered gown, and struck.

Such, jurors, was the grim end of this king, whose look
Was majesty, whose word commanded men and fleets.
Such was his wife who killed him—such that none of you,
Who sit to try Orestes, hears her crime unmoved.

CHORUS:
Zeus rates a father's death the higher, by your account.
Yet Zeus, when his own father Cronos became old,
Bound him with chains. Is there not contradiction here? 630
Observe this, jurors, on your oath.

APOLLO:
Execrable hags,
Outcasts of heaven! Chains may be loosed, with little harm,
And many ways to mend it. But when blood of man
Sinks in the thirsty dust, the life once lost can live
No more. For death alone my father has ordained
No healing spell; all other things his effortless
And sovereign power casts down or raises up at will.

CHORUS:
You plead for his acquittal: have you asked yourself
How one who poured out on the ground his mother's blood
Will live henceforth in Argos, in his father's house? 640
Shall he at public altars share in sacrifice?
Shall holy water lave his hands at tribal feasts?

APOLLO:
This too I answer; mark the truth of what I say.
The mother is not the true parent of the child
Which is called hers. She is a nurse who tends the growth
Of young seed planted by its true parent, the male.
So, if Fate spares the child, she keeps it, as one might
Keep for some friend a growing plant. And of this truth,
That father without mother may beget, we have
Present, as proof, the daughter of Olympian Zeus: 650
One never nursed in the dark cradle of the womb;
Yet such a being no god will beget again.

Pallas, I sent this man to supplicate your hearth;
He is but one of many gifts my providence
Will send, to make your city and your people great.
He and his city, Pallas, shall for ever be
Your faithful allies; their posterity shall hold
This pledge their dear possession for all future years.

ATHENE:
Shall I now bid the jurors cast each man his vote
According to his conscience? Are both pleas complete? 660

APOLLO:
I have shot every shaft I had; and wait to hear
The jurors' verdict.

ATHENE [*to the* CHORUS]:
Will this course content you too?

CHORUS [*to the jurors*]:
You have heard them and us. Now, jurors, as you cast
Your votes, let reverence for your oath guide every heart.

ATHENE:
Citizens of Athens! As you now try this first case
Of bloodshed, hear the constitution of your court.
From this day forward this judicial council shall
For Aegeus' race hear every trial of homicide.
Here shall be their perpetual seat, on Ares' Hill.
Here, when the Amazon army came to take revenge 670
On Theseus, they set up their camp, and fortified
This place with walls and towers as a new fortress-town
To attack the old, and sacrificed to Ares; whence
This rock is named Areopagus. Here, day and night,
Shall Awe, and Fear, Awe's brother, check my citizens
From all misdoing, while they keep my laws unchanged.
If you befoul a shining spring with an impure
And muddy dribble, you will come in vain to drink.
So, do not taint pure laws with new expediency.
Guard well and reverence that form of government 680
Which will eschew alike licence and slavery;
And from your polity do not wholly banish fear.
For what man living, freed from fear, will still be just?
Hold fast such upright fear of the law's sanctity,
And you will have a bulwark of your city's strength,
A rampart round your soil, such as no other race
Possesses between Scythia and the Peloponnese.
I here establish you a court inviolable,
Holy, and quick to anger, keeping faithful watch
That men may sleep in peace.

I have thus far extended 690
My exhortation, that Athens may remember it.
Now give your votes in uprightness, and judge this cause
With reverence for your oath. I have no more to say.

[*During the following dialogue the jurors rise in turn to vote. There are two urns, one of which is 'operative', the other 'inoperative'. Each juror has two pebbles, a black and a white. Into the 'operative' urn each drops a white pebble for acquittal or a black one for condemnation; then disposes of the other pebble in the other urn, and returns to his seat.*]

CHORUS:
I too advise you: do not act in scorn of us,
Your country's visitants, or you will find us harsh.

APOLLO:
I bid you fear my oracle and the word of Zeus,
And not make both unfruitful.

CHORUS [*to* APOLLO]:
Deeds of blood are not
For your protection. Henceforth you will prophesy
From a polluted shrine.

APOLLO:
Then what of Zeus? Did he
Suffer pollution, when he willed to purify 700
His suppliant Ixion, the first murderer?

CHORUS:
You argue; but if we should fail to win this case
We will infest the land with plagues unspeakable.

APOLLO:
You have as little honour amongst elder gods
As amongst us, the younger. I shall win this case.

CHORUS:
This recalls your behaviour in Admetus' house:
You bribed the Fates to let a mortal live again.

APOLLO:
Was it not right to help a man who worshipped me?
Undoubtedly; besides, Admetus' need was great.

CHORUS:
You mocked primeval goddesses with wine, to break 710
The ancient dispensation.

APOLLO:
Disappointment soon
Will make you vomit all your poison—harmlessly.

CHORUS:
You think your youth may tread my age into the dust.
When we have heard the verdict will be soon enough
To launch my anger against Athens. I will wait.

ATHENE:
My duty is to give the final vote. When yours
Are counted, mine goes to uphold Orestes' plea.
No mother gave me birth. Therefore the father's claim
And male supremacy in all things, save to give
Myself in marriage, wins my whole heart's loyalty. 720
Therefore a woman's death, who killed her husband, is,
I judge, outweighed in grievousness by his. And so
Orestes, if the votes are equal, wins the case.
Let those appointed bring the urns and count the votes.
[*Two of the jurors obey her.*]

ORESTES:
O bright Apollo, what verdict will be revealed?

CHORUS:
O Mother Night, O Darkness, look on us!

ORESTES:
To me
This moment brings despair and death, or life and hope.

CHORUS:
To us increase of honour, or disgrace and loss.

APOLLO:
The votes are out. Count scrupulously, citizens;
Justice is holy; in your division worship her. 730
Loss of a single vote is loss of happiness;
And one vote gained will raise to life a fallen house.
[*The votes are brought to* ATHENE. *The black and the white pebbles are even in number.* ATHENE *adds hers to the white.*]

ATHENE:
Orestes is acquitted of blood-guiltiness.
The votes are even.

ORESTES:

Pallas, Saviour of my house!
I was an exile; you have brought me home again.
Hellas can say of me, 'He is an Argive, as
He used to be, and holds his father's house and wealth
By grace of Pallas and Apollo, and of Zeus
The Saviour, the Fulfiller.' Zeus has shown respect
For my dead father, seeing my mother's advocates, 740
And has delivered me.

So now, before I turn
My steps to Argos, hear the oath I make to you,
Your country, and your people, for all future time:
No Argive king shall ever against Attica
Lead his embattled spears. If any man transgress
This oath of mine, I will myself rise from the grave
In vengeance, to perplex him with disastrous loss,
Clogging his marches with ill omens and despair,
Till all his soldiers curse the day they left their homes.
But if my oath is kept, and my posterity 750
Prove staunch and faithful allies to the Athenian State,
They shall enjoy my blessing. So, Pallas, farewell;
Farewell, citizens of Athens! May each struggle bring
Death to your foes, to you success and victory!

[*Exeunt* APOLLO *and* ORESTES.]

CHORUS:

The old is trampled by the new!
Curse on you younger gods who override
The ancient laws and rob me of my due!
Now to appease the honour you reviled
Vengeance shall fester till my full heart pours
Over this land on every side 760
Anger for insult, poison for my pain—
Yes, poison from whose killing rain
A sterile blight shall creep on plant and child
And pock the earth's face with infectious sores.
Why should I weep? Hear, Justice, what I do!
Soon Athens in despair shall rue
Her rashness and her mockery.
Daughters of Night and Sorrow, come with me,
Feed on dishonour, on revenge to be!

ATHENE:

Let me entreat you soften your indignant grief. 770
Fair trial, fair judgement, ended in an even vote,
Which brings to you neither dishonour nor defeat.
Evidence which issued clear as day from Zeus himself,
Brought by the god who bade Orestes strike the blow,
Could not but save him from all harmful consequence.
Then quench your anger; let not indignation rain
Pestilence on our soil, corroding every seed
Till the whole land is sterile desert. In return
I promise you, here in this upright land, a home,

And bright thrones in a holy cavern, where you shall 780
Receive for ever homage from our citizens.

CHORUS:

The old is trampled by the new!
Curse on you younger gods who override
The ancient laws and rob me of my due!
Now to appease the honour you reviled
Vengeance shall fester till my full heart pours
Over this land on every side
Anger for insult, poison for my pain—
Yes, poison from whose killing rain
A sterile blight shall creep on plant and child 790
And pock the earth's face with infectious sores.
Why should I weep? Hear, Justice, what I do!
Soon Athens in despair shall rue
Her rashness and her mockery.
Daughters of Night and Sorrow, come with me,
Feed on dishonour, on revenge to be!

ATHENE:

None has dishonoured you. Why should immortal rage
Infect the fields of mortal men with pestilence?
You call on Justice: I rely on Zeus. What need
To reason further? I alone among the gods 800
Know the sealed chamber's keys where Zeus's thunderbolt
Is stored. But force is needless; let persuasion check
The fruit of foolish threats before it falls to spread
Plague and disaster. Calm this black and swelling wrath;
Honour and dignity await you: share with me
A home in Athens. You will yet applaud my words,
When Attica's wide fields bring you their firstfruit gifts,
When sacrifice for childbirth and for marriage-vows
Is made upon your altars in perpetual right.

CHORUS:

O shame and grief, that such a fate 810
Should fall to me, whose wisdom grew
Within me when the world was new!
Must I accept, beneath the ground,
A nameless and abhorred estate?
O ancient Earth, see my disgrace!
While anguish runs through flesh and bone
My breathless rage breaks every bound.
O Night, my mother, hear me groan,
Outwitted, scorned and overthrown
By new gods from my ancient place! 820

ATHENE:

Your greater age claims my forbearance, as it gives
Wisdom far greater than my own; though to me too
Zeus gave discernment. And I tell you this: if you
Now make some other land your home, your thoughts will turn
With deep desire to Athens. For the coming age
Shall see her glory growing yet more glorious.
You, here possessing an exalted sanctuary

Beside Erechtheus'[15] temple, shall receive from all,
Both men and women, honours which no other land
Could equal. Therefore do not cast upon my fields 830
Whetstones of murder, to corrupt our young men's hearts
And make them mad with passions not infused by wine;
Nor plant in them the temper of the mutinous cock,
To set within my city's walls man against man
With self-destructive boldness, kin defying kin.
Let war be with the stranger, at the stranger's gate;
There let men fall in love with glory; but at home
Let no cocks fight.[16]

Then, goddesses, I offer you
A home in Athens, where the gods most love to live,
Where gifts and honours shall deserve your kind good-will. 840

CHORUS:

O shame and grief, that such a fate
Should fall to me, whose wisdom grew
Within me when the world was new!
Must I accept, beneath the ground,
A nameless and abhorred estate?
O ancient Earth, see my disgrace!
While anguish runs through flesh and bone
My breathless rage breaks every bound.
O Night, my mother, hear me groan,
Outwitted, scorned and overthrown 850
By new gods from my ancient place!

ATHENE:

I will not weary in offering you friendly words.
You shall not say that you, an elder deity,
Were by a younger Power and by these citizens
Driven dishonoured, homeless, from this land. But if
Holy Persuasion bids your heart respect my words
And welcome soothing eloquence, then stay with us!
If you refuse, be sure you will have no just cause
To turn with spleen and malice on our peopled streets.
A great and lasting heritage awaits you here; 860
Thus honour is assured and justice satisfied.

CHORUS:

What place, divine Athene, do you offer me?

ATHENE:

One free from all regret. Acceptance lies with you.

CHORUS:

Say I accept it: what prerogatives are mine?

ATHENE:

Such that no house can thrive without your favour sought.

CHORUS:

You promise to secure for me this place and power?

---

[15] The first king of Athens.

[16] This passage is plainly a stern warning against political disunity within Athens.

ATHENE:

I will protect and prosper all who reverence you.

CHORUS:

Your word is pledged for ever?

ATHENE:

Do I need to promise
What I will not perform?

CHORUS:

My anger melts. Your words
Move me.

ATHENE:

In Athens you are in the midst of friends. 870

CHORUS:

What blessings would you have me call upon this land?

ATHENE:

Such as bring victory untroubled with regret;
Blessing from earth and sea and sky; blessing that breathes
In wind and sunlight through the land; that beast and field
Enrich my people with unwearied fruitfulness,
And armies of brave sons be born to guard their peace.
Sternly weed out the impious, lest their rankness choke
The flower of goodness. I would not have just men's lives
Troubled with villainy. These blessings *you* must bring;
I will conduct their valiant arms to victory, 880
And make the name of Athens honoured through the world.

CHORUS:

I will consent to share Athene's home,
To bless this fortress of the immortal Powers
Which mighty Zeus and Ares
Chose for their habitation,
The pride and glory of the gods of Greece,
And guardian of their altars.
This prayer I pray for Athens,
Pronounce this prophecy with kind intent:
Fortune shall load her land with healthful gifts 890
From her rich earth engendered
By the sun's burning brightness.

ATHENE:

I will do my part, and win
Blessing for my city's life,
Welcoming within our walls
These implacable and great
Goddesses. Their task it is
To dispose all mortal ways.
He who wins their enmity
Lives accurst, not knowing whence 900
Falls the wounding lash of life.
Secret guilt his father knew
Hails him to their judgement-seat,
Where, for all his loud exclaims,
Death, his angry enemy,
Silent grinds him into dust.

CHORUS:

I have yet more to promise. No ill wind
Shall carry blight to make your fruit-trees fade;
No bud-destroying canker
Shall creep across your frontiers, 910
Nor sterile sickness threaten your supply.
May Pan give twin lambs to your thriving ewes
In their expected season;
And may the earth's rich produce
Honour the generous Powers with grateful gifts.

ATHENE:

Guardians of our city's wall,
Hear the blessings they will bring!
Fate's Avengers wield a power
Great alike in heaven and hell;
And their purposes on earth 920
They fulfil for all to see,
Giving, after their deserts,
Songs to some, to others pain
In a prospect blind with tears.

CHORUS:

I pray that no untimely chance destroy
Your young men in their pride;
And let each lovely virgin, as a bride,
Fulfil her life with joy.
For all these gifts, you sovereign gods, we pray,
And you, our sisters three, 930
Dread Fates, whose just decree
Chooses for every man his changeless way,
You who in every household have your place,
Whose visitations fall
With just rebuke on all—
Hear us, most honoured of the immortal race!

ATHENE:

Now, for the love that you perform
To this dear land, my heart is warm.
Holy Persuasion too I bless,
Who softly strove with harsh denial, 940
Till Zeus the Pleader came to trial
And crowned Persuasion with success.
Now good shall strive with good; and we
And they shall share the victory.

CHORUS:

Let civil war, insatiate of ill,
Never in Athens rage;
Let burning wrath, that murder must assuage,
Never take arms to spill,
In this my heritage,
The blood of man till dust has drunk its fill. 950
Let all together find
Joy in each other;
And each both love and hate with the same mind

As his blood-brother;
For this heals many hurts of humankind.

ATHENE:

These gracious words and promised deeds
Adorn the path where wisdom leads.
Great gain for Athens shall arise
From these grim forms and threatening eyes.
Then worship them with friendly heart, 960
For theirs is friendly. Let your State
Hold justice as her chiefest prize;
And land and city shall be great
And glorious in every part.

CHORUS:

City, rejoice and sing,
Who, blest and flourishing
With wealth of field and street,
Wise in your hour, and dear
To the goddess you revere,
Sit by the judgement-seat 970
Of heaven's all-judging king,
Who guards and governs well
Those favoured ones who dwell
Under her virgin wing.

ATHENE:

We wish you joy in turn. Now I must go
And guide you to your chambers in the rock,
Lit by the holy torches
Of these who shall escort you.
With eager haste and solemn sacrifice,
Come, enter this dear earth, there to repel 980
Harm from our homes and borders,
And bring us wealth and glory.
Sons of the Rock of Athens, lead their way,
Welcome these Residents within your walls;
They come to bless our city:
Let our good-will reward them.

CHORUS:

My blessings I repeat
On all whose homes are here,
To whom this rock is dear;
On temple and on street 990
Where gods and mortals meet.
And as with awe and fear
And humble hearts you greet
My presence as your guest,
So year succeeding year
Shall be more richly blest.

ATHENE:

I thank you for your prayers. Now by these torches' gleam
I and my maidens who attend my statue here
Come to escort you to your home beneath the ground.

Young women, children, a resplendent company,[17] 1000
Flower of the land of Theseus, with a reverend troop
Of elder women, dressed in robes of purple dye,
Shall go with you. Honour the Friendly Goddesses;
And let the flaring lights move on, that our new guests
In coming years may grace our land with wealth and peace.

[*During the last three speeches a procession has been gathering, with music and lighted torches, to escort the* CHORUS *from the stage; as they go, all sing together:*]

Pass onward to your home,
Great ones, lovers of honour,
Daughters of ancient Night,
Led by the friends your peace has won;
(And let every tongue be holy!) 1010

On to the deep of earth,
To the immemorial cavern,
Honoured with sacrifice,
Worshipped in fear and breathless awe;
(And let every tongue be holy!)

Come, dread and friendly Powers
Who love and guard our land;
And while devouring flame
Fills all your path with light,
Gather with gladness to your rest. 1020
And let every voice
Crown our song with a shout of joy!

Again let the wine be poured
By the glare of the crackling pine;
Now great, all-seeing Zeus
Guards the city of Pallas;
Thus God and Fate are reconciled.
Then let every voice
Crown our song with a shout of joy!

SOPHOCLES

[496–406 B.C.E.]

With Aeschylus and Euripides, Sophocles is considered one of the three greatest Greek tragedians. His tragedy steers a middle position between the high religious themes of Aeschylus and the topical social criticism of Euripides, focusing instead upon the dilemma of human beings caught between irreconcilable demands. Modulating between noble ambition and mean resignation, glorious pride and humiliating self-recognition, Sophocles' characters, such as Oedipus, Creon, and Antigone, are fraught with inner

[17] This suggests the great Panathenaic procession, the culminating event of a quarterly Athenian festival that in part honored "resident aliens" such as the Eumenides. Athenians prided themselves on the liberal welcome they extended to immigrants from other cities.

conflict and psychological blindnesses that lead them to intense suffering. Sophocles' awareness of the "ebb and flow / Of human misery," as Matthew Arnold called it in "Dover Beach," evokes even in modern readers a sense of sympathy and admiration before the spectacle of dignified suffering presented in the plays. Indeed, his tragic characters display what seems to be a timeless and universal condition for actors and spectators in the world: what Arnold called "the eternal note of sadness" inherent in human experience.

Life

Sophocles' life spanned the period from the end of the Persian Wars through the Peloponnesian War. Between the two wars Athens rose to the height of its political and cultural power during the Age of Pericles (461–429) before its decline after the great plague of 429 B.C.E., which killed a third of its population. Sophocles was born at Colonus, a suburb of Athens, in 496. A general, priest of Asclepius (god of medicine), and model citizen, Sophocles served in various civic and administrative posts and participated fully in the rise and decline of his city. The first notice we have of his public life is his participation in the chorus celebrating the Athenian naval victory over the Persians at Salamis in 480. In 468, Sophocles won his first victory as a playwright, when his *Triptolemus* took first place over Aeschylus at the festival of Dionysus. Sophocles was to enjoy at least eighteen more such victories in the course of his career, during which he produced more than 120 plays—only seven of which have come down to us.

Sophocles enjoyed the respect and admiration of his fellow Athenians, not only for his plays but for his public service and his reputation for fairness and affability. His even temper won him the friendship of Herodotus and Aristophanes, among others. In 443 Sophocles took charge of the imperial treasury, in 440 he was elected to be one of the ten *strategoi,* or generals, one of the highest positions of Athenian society, and he served with Pericles in the Samian War. During this time he was involved in forming a "company of the Educated" to promote discussion and criticism of literature. In later life Sophocles served his state as diplomat and ambassador, and was a priest of Halon, a minor god associated with Asclepius whose cult increased after the plague of 429. Sophocles died in 406, less than two years before a starving Athens surrendered to Sparta after the Athenian fleet, once the pride of the Aegean, was defeated at the Aegospotami.

Work

As a playwright, Sophocles was a conscientious craftsman and a technical innovator. He introduced the third actor into the plot, reduced the number of people in the chorus from fifty to twelve, and used painted backdrops for the first time. Such changes allow for more subtle and complex development of both plot and character, perhaps leading in part to Aristotle's tribute to Sophocles' craftsmanship in the *Poetics.* Aristotle chose *Oedipus the King,* Sophocles' greatest play, as the model tragedy for his *Poetics.* For Aristotle, the perfect tragedy must concentrate upon a single dramatic conflict, brought on by the major character's tragic flaw *(hamartia),* which gradually unfolds within the course of a single day's events. Like many of Sophocles' plays, *Oedipus the King* intertwines the concerns of public life with questions of fate and the personal struggles of people in power. Thus, the human individual is shown to be the site of a heroic contest between three contenders: religion, civic duty, and personal interest—the very stuff of which later great tragedies, such as those of Shakespeare and Chikamatsu, are made.

Antigone, the play we have selected here, epitomizes the tragic clash of contradictory values: the primarily religious and private obligations of Antigone as opposed to the primarily civic and public obligations of Creon. Performed around 441 B.C.E., *Antigone,* like *Oedipus the King* (430) and *Oedipus at Colonus* (409), invokes the familiar story of the curse upon the House of Thebes to dramatize the sweeping changes taking place in the fifth century in the political and cultural life of Athens, especially the move toward democracy, the decreasing role of religion, and the changing relations between men and women.

The story of the House of Thebes begins when Laïos (or Laius), the grandson of Cadmus, the founder of Thebes, abducted Chrysippus during a visit to Pelops, the grandson of Zeus. Laïos thus violated one of the most sacred of unwritten bonds, that between guest and host. An oracle warned Laïos that his punishment for this crime would be to die at the hands of his own son, the newborn child of Laïos and his wife, Iocastê (or Jocasta). To prevent the prophecy from being fulfilled, Laïos abandoned the infant, spiked through his ankles, upon Mount Cithaerus, where it was found by a goodhearted shepherd. This shepherd delivered the boy to the king and queen of Corinth, who named him Oedipus, which means *swollen foot.* What happens next Sophocles tells in *Oedipus the King.* Oedipus discovers that he has indeed unwittingly killed his true father and married Iocastê, his mother, who gave him two sons, Eteocles and Polyneices, and two daughters, Antigone and Ismene. When Oedipus and Iocastê learn the truth, Oedipus blinds himself and is banished, Iocastê kills herself in despair, and the throne of Thebes descends upon Creon, who assumes the role of regent until Eteocles and Polyneices are old enough to take power.

The story of Oedipus' banishment is told in Sophocles' *Oedipus at Colonus,* his last play as far as we know, written shortly before his death and performed posthumously. *Antigone* begins in the aftermath of the disagreement between Polyneices and Eteocles over sharing power at Thebes, though the chorus from time to time alludes to incidents from the larger legend of the House of Thebes. Because Eteocles backed out of an agreement to rule on alternate years, Polyneices has returned with seven Argive leaders to kill his brother, a story told in Aeschylus' *Seven against Thebes.* When the play opens, the two brothers are dead, and their uncle, Creon, has taken over as king of Thebes. Because he perceives Polyneices as a traitor to the *polis,* or city, Creon refuses to allow him a proper burial. Antigone, while recognizing that Polyneices has violated the legal code, insists that a higher and more ancient code—one that honors blood ties over civic duties—demands that he be buried.

Antigone has often been read as a struggle between two antagonistic but clear-cut opposites, usually as a play that pits the individual against the state. Tied to her brother by the sacred bonds of kinship, Antigone in this reading subverts the decree of Creon, who in the interest of civic order must deny her demand that her offending brother Polyneices receive a proper burial. Without proper burial a soul could not cross over the river Styx into the underworld, so Antigone's concern for Polyneices goes beyond a matter of mere formality or ritual. Thus, her religious responsibility for the destiny of her brother's soul stands in opposition to the civic law that must punish an enemy of the state.

Antigone, however, represents more than just the individual against the state. She is a symbol of a complex set of affiliations to the gods of the underworld and the household, to the ancient blood code of the family, and to women, who in fifth-century Athens did not enjoy the rights of citizenship granted to men. Creon has his own set of affiliations to the sky gods, to the new legal code ushered in under the auspices of Athene in Aeschylus' *Eumenides,* and to the patriarchy. The tragedy thus further dramatizes the transformations taking place in the democratization of Athens, which under Cleisthenes transferred power to districts established by law, not by kinship ties.

The tragedy does not rest easily even upon these more complex sets of oppositions, for it forces us to scrutinize both Antigone's and Creon's positions. Both Creon and Antigone are right, and both are wrong, so that the spectator must question seriously the values that each represents. Although Antigone swears to be bound by the blood code associated with the family and with faint traces of a matriarchal lineage, she nonetheless cruelly dismisses Ismene, who is both sister and woman. Moreover, although Creon declares that he has the interests of the state at heart, he ignores the advice and warnings from his people (embodied here by the chorus), his son Haemon, and the prophet Tiresias. Creon's refusal to bend mirrors Antigone's; her own unwillingness to compromise, though supported by the play, thus becomes suspect. Creon's unwillingness to listen to the voice of the people suggests that he is a tyrant, an outmoded political type who contradicts the democratic impetus of the new Athenian state. Yet despite his ultimate fall, his statements about the necessity of relinquishing the ties of blood in the interests of the *polis* or state were important to the very process of democratization that most Athenians would support. Thus, *Antigone* invites its spectators to place their most cherished interests into the crucible of high tragic art. The question of who is right, though settled, mirrors before its Athenian audience its own uncertainty about the costs of patriarchy and the demise of more ancient aristocratic systems of justice and codes of honor subverted by the process of democratic reform.

Further complicating the play is the question of destiny. As the curse on the House of Thebes unfolds, both Antigone and Creon—and one might add Ismene, Haemon, and even Eurydice—seem to be endowed with freedom of choice and are therefore in some measure the shapers of their own lives. Antigone rejects Ismene's argument, for example, that women should not contend with men, that by nature they must obey the stronger sex. Similarly, Tiresias reminds Creon that all human beings will err, but that once they recognize their error they can make amends. It is not certain whether Creon rejects Tiresias' advice, though in the final scene of the play the chorus seems to suggest that he does. Thus, Sophocles again holds two alternatives up before the audience: The willful actions of Creon and Antigone imply that human destiny is not sealed, that human actions and human decisions may indeed alter the course of events; on the other hand, the chorus repeats an older point of view, that fate determines the course of human life. Either way may lead to tragic consequences.

Antigone, whose name means *born to oppose,* remains fixed in her position throughout the play and experiences none of the dramatic crises visited upon Creon. Yet we see that Creon's inflexibility leads to the fall of his entire household. A dynamic character, Creon finally realizes that he has been too rigid; at this moment of recognition, or *anagnorisis,* Creon relents, but the reversal of his fortune has already gone too far in its course for him to save those who are dear to him. Because Creon, more than Antigone, goes through the classic phases of the tragic plot—pride, reversal, and recognition—it is worth considering whether he, rather than Antigone, is the tragic hero of the play. Knowing that they could have prevented the deaths that befall their loved ones, both Antigone and Creon achieve a considerable dignity and tragic loss that they would lack if they had been presented as mere playthings of the gods. So in both characters Sophocles may subtly question the consequences of secularization and the falling away from the gods that was taking place in his society. The greatest *hubris,* or tragic pride, may be to think that human beings can somehow sway the moral order of things. As Creon says in his final line, "Fate has brought all my pride to a thought of dust"; such despair, as in Shakespeare's King Lear, seems to be the price of wisdom.

Suggested Readings

Among the important general studies of Sophocles' tragedy in English are C. H. Whitman's *Sophocles, A Study in Heroic Humanism* (1951), S. M. Adams's *Sophocles the Playwright* (1957), and Bernard M. W. Knox's *The Heroic Temper* (1964); more recent general studies are Charles Segal's *Tragedy and Civilization* (1981), which includes an excellent reading of *Antigone* in the terms discussed here, and Ruth Scodel's *Sophocles* (1984). For discussions of Sophocles and Greek theater practices, see David Seale's *Vision and Stagecraft in Sophocles* (1982), and J. Michael Walton's *The Greek Sense of Theatre* (1985). R. F. Goheen's *The Imagery of Sophocles'* Antigone (1951) focuses upon *Antigone* in particular.

Antigone

Translated by Dudley Fitts and Robert Fitzgerald

PERSONS REPRESENTED:

ANTIGONE, *daughter of Oedipus and Iocastê*
ISMENE, *daughter of Oedipus and Iocastê*
EURYDICE, *Queen of Thebes*
CREON, *King of Thebes, brother of Iocastê*
HAIMON, *son of Creon*
TEIRESIAS, *a prophet*
A SENTRY
A MESSENGER
CHORUS

SCENE: *Before the palace of Creon, King of Thebes. A central double door, and two lateral doors. A platform extends the length of the façade, and from this platform three steps lead down into the* "orchestra," *or chorus-ground.* TIME: *Dawn of the day after the repulse of the Argive army from the assault on Thebes.*

Prologue

[ANTIGONE *and* ISMENE *enter from the central door of the Palace.*]

ANTIGONE:
Ismenê, dear sister,
You would think that we had already suffered enough
For the curse on Oedipus:[1]
I cannot imagine any grief
That you and I have not gone through. And now—
Have they told you of the new decree of our King Creon?

ISMENE:
I have heard nothing: I know
That two sisters lost two brothers, a double death
In a single hour; and I know that the Argive army
Fled in the night; but beyond this, nothing. 10

ANTIGONE:
I thought so. And that is why I wanted you
To come out here with me. There is something we must do.

ISMENE:
Why do you speak so strangely?

ANTIGONE:
Listen, Ismenê:
Creon buried our brother Eteoclês
With military honors, gave him a soldier's funeral,
And it was right that he should; but Polyneicês,
Who fought as bravely and died as miserably,—
They say that Creon has sworn
No one shall bury him, no one mourn for him, 20
But his body must lie in the fields, a sweet treasure
For carrion birds to find as they search for food.
That is what they say, and our good Creon is coming here

---

[1]Son of Laïos, King of Thebes, and Iocastê; through a series of events foretold in an oracle, Oedipus unknowingly killed his father, married his mother, and replaced his father as king. Learning the truth, as Ismene explains below, he blinded himself and was exiled to Colonus. Iocastê's brother Creon replaced Oedipus as king of Thebes.

To announce it publicly; and the penalty—
Stoning to death in the public square!
There it is,
And now you can prove what you are:
A true sister, or a traitor to your family.

ISMENE:
Antigonê, you are mad! What could I possibly do?

ANTIGONE:
You must decide whether you will help me or not.

ISMENE:
I do not understand you. Help you in what? 30

ANTIGONE:
Ismenê, I am going to bury him. Will you come?

ISMENE:
Bury him! You have just said the new law forbids it.

ANTIGONE:
He is my brother. And he is your brother, too.

ISMENE:
But think of the danger! Think what Creon will do!

ANTIGONE:
Creon is not strong enough to stand in my way.

ISMENE:
Ah sister!
Oedipus died, everyone hating him[2]
For what his own search brought to light, his eyes
Ripped out by his own hand; and Iocastê died,
His mother and wife at once: she twisted the cords 40
That strangled her life; and our two brothers died,
Each killed by the other's sword. And we are left:
But oh, Antigonê,
Think how much more terrible than these
Our own death would be if we should go against Creon
And do what he has forbidden! We are only women,
We cannot fight with men, Antigonê!
The law is strong, we must give in to the law
In this thing, and in worse. I beg the Dead
To forgive me, but I am helpless: I must yield 50
To those in authority. And I think it is dangerous business
To be always meddling.

ANTIGONE:
If that is what you think,
I should not want you, even if you asked to come.
You have made your choice, you can be what you want to be.
But I will bury him; and if I must die,
I say that this crime is holy: I shall lie down
With him in death, and I shall be as dear
To him as he to me.
It is the dead,
Not the living, who make the longest demands:

[2]In *Oedipus at Colonus*, which Sophocles wrote after *Antigone*, Oedipus receives a mysterious but honorable death, unlike that described here.

We die for ever . . .

You may do as you like, 60

Since apparently the laws of the gods mean nothing to you.

ISMENE:

They mean a great deal to me; but I have no strength
To break laws that were made for the public good.

ANTIGONE:

That must be your excuse, I suppose. But as for me,
I will bury the brother I love.

ISMENE:

Antigonê,

I am so afraid for you!

ANTIGONE:

You need not be:

You have yourself to consider, after all.

ISMENE:

But no one must hear of this, you must tell no one!
I will keep it a secret, I promise!

ANTIGONE:

Oh tell it! Tell everyone!

Think how they'll hate you when it all comes out 70
If they learn that you knew about it all the time!

ISMENE:

So fiery! You should be cold with fear.

ANTIGONE:

Perhaps. But I am doing only what I must.

ISMENE:

But can you do it? I say that you cannot.

ANTIGONE:

Very well: when my strength gives out, I shall do no more.

ISMENE:

Impossible things should not be tried at all.

ANTIGONE:

Go away, Ismenê:
I shall be hating you soon, and the dead will too,
For your words are hateful. Leave me my foolish plan:
I am not afraid of the danger; if it means death, 80
It will not be the worst of deaths—death without honor.

ISMENE:

Go then, if you feel that you must.
You are unwise,
But a loyal friend indeed to those who love you.

[*Exit into the Palace.* ANTIGONE *goes off, L. Enter the* CHORUS.]

PÁRODOS

Strophe 1

CHORUS:

Now the long blade of the sun, lying
Level east to west, touches with glory
Thebes of the Seven Gates. Open, unlidded

Eye of golden day! O marching light
Across the eddy and rush of Dircê's[3] stream,
Striking the white shields of the enemy 90
Thrown headlong backward from the blaze of morning!

CHORAGOS:
Polyneicês their commander
Roused them with windy phrases,
He the wild eagle screaming
Insults above our land,
His wings their shields of snow,
His crest their marshalled helms.

Antistrophe 1

CHORUS:
Against our seven gates in a yawning ring
The famished spears came onward in the night;
But before his jaws were sated with our blood, 100
Or pinefire took the garland of our towers,
He was thrown back; and as he turned, great Thebes—
No tender victim for his noisy power—
Rose like a dragon behind him,[4] shouting war.

CHORAGOS:
For God hates utterly
The bray of bragging tongues;
And when he beheld their smiling,
Their swagger of golden helms,
The frown of his thunder blasted
Their first man[5] from our walls. 110

Strophe 2

CHORUS:
We heard his shout of triumph high in the air
Turn to a scream; far out in a flaming arc
He fell with his windy torch, and the earth struck him.
And others storming in fury no less than his
Found shock of death in the dusty joy of battle.

CHORAGOS:
Seven captains at seven gates
Yielded their clanging arms to the god[6]
That bends the battle-line and breaks it.
These two only, brothers in blood,
Face to face in matchless rage, 120
Mirroring each the other's death,
Clashed in long combat.

[3]A river to the west of Thebes.

[4]The people of Thebes were said to descend from the teeth of a dragon slain by Cadmus, the city's founder.

[5]The giant Capaneus, a sworn enemy of Thebes; after Capaneus swore that he would raze Thebes, Zeus killed him.

[6]Zeus, the all-powerful chief of the gods.

Antistrophe 2

CHORUS:
But now in the beautiful morning of victory
Let Thebes of the many chariots sing for joy!
With hearts for dancing we'll take leave of war:
Our temples shall be sweet with hymns of praise,
And the long night shall echo with our chorus.

SCENE 1

CHORAGOS:
But now at last our new King is coming:
Creon of Thebes, Menoikeus' son.
In this auspicious dawn of his reign 130
What are the new complexities
That shifting Fate has woven for him?
What is his counsel? Why has he summoned
The old men to hear him?

[*Enter* CREON *from the Palace, C. He addresses the* CHORUS *from the top step.*]

CREON: Gentlemen: I have the honor to inform you that our Ship of State, which recent storms have threatened to destroy, has come safely to harbor at last, guided by the merciful wisdom of Heaven. I have summoned you here this morning because I know that I can depend upon you: your devotion to King Laïos was absolute; you never hesitated in your duty to our late ruler Oedipus; and when Oedipus died, your loyalty was transferred to his children. Unfortunately, as you 140 know, his two sons, the princes Eteoclês and Polyneicês, have killed each other in battle; and I, as the next in blood,[7] have succeeded to the full power of the throne.

I am aware, of course, that no Ruler can expect complete loyalty from his subjects until he has been tested in office. Nevertheless, I say to you at the very outset that I have nothing but contempt for the kind of Governor who is afraid, for whatever reason, to follow the course that he knows is best for the State; and as for the man who sets private friendship above the public welfare,—I have no use for him, either. I call God to witness that if I saw my country headed for ruin, I should not be afraid to speak out plainly; and I need hardly remind you that I would never have any dealings with an enemy of the people. No one 150 values friendship more highly than I; but we must remember that friends made at the risk of wrecking our Ship are not real friends at all.

These are my principles, at any rate, and that is why I have made the following decision concerning the sons of Oedipus: Eteoclês, who died as a man should die, fighting for his country, is to be buried with full military honors, with all the ceremony that is usual when the greatest heroes die; but his brother Polyneicês, who broke his exile to come back with fire and sword against his native city and the shrines of his fathers' gods, whose one idea was to spill the blood of his blood and sell his own people into slavery—Polyneicês, I say, is to have no burial: no man is to touch him or say the least prayer for him; he shall lie on the plain, 160 unburied; and the birds and the scavenging dogs can do with him whatever they like.

---

[7]Creon was first cousin of Laïos, the king of Thebes whom Oedipus murdered.

This is my command, and you can see the wisdom behind it. As long as I am King, no traitor is going to be honored with the loyal man. But whoever shows by word and deed that he is on the side of the State,—he shall have my respect while he is living, and my reverence when he is dead.

CHORAGOS:
If that is your will, Creon son of Menoikeus,
You have the right to enforce it: we are yours.

CREON:
That is my will. Take care that you do your part.

CHORAGOS:
We are old men: let the younger ones carry it out.

CREON:
I do not mean that: the sentries have been appointed. 170

CHORAGOS:
Then what is it that you would have us do?

CREON:
You will give no support to whoever breaks this law.

CHORAGOS:
Only a crazy man is in love with death!

CREON:
And death it is; yet money talks, and the wisest
Have sometimes been known to count a few coins too many.

[*Enter* SENTRY *from L.*]

SENTRY: I'll not say that I'm out of breath from running, King, because every time I stopped to think about what I have to tell you, I felt like going back. And all the time a voice kept saying, "You fool, don't you know you're walking straight into trouble?"; and then another voice: "Yes, but if you let somebody else get the news to Creon first, it will be even worse than that for you!" But good 180 sense won out, at least I hope it was good sense, and here I am with a story that makes no sense at all; but I'll tell it anyhow, because, as they say, what's going to happen's going to happen, and—

CREON:
Come to the point. What have you to say?

SENTRY:
I did not do it. I did not see who did it. You must not punish me for what someone else has done.

CREON:
A comprehensive defense! More effective, perhaps,
If I knew its purpose. Come: what is it?

SENTRY:
A dreadful thing . . . I don't know how to put it—

CREON:
Out with it!

SENTRY:
Well, then; 190
The dead man—
Polyneicês—

[*Pause. The* SENTRY *is overcome, fumbles for words.* CREON *waits impassively.*]

out there—
someone,—

New dust on the slimy flesh!

[*Pause. No sign from* CREON]

Someone has given it burial that way, and
Gone . . .

[*Long pause.* CREON *finally speaks with deadly control:*]

CREON:

And the man who dared do this?

SENTRY:

I swear I
Do not know! You must believe me!
Listen:
The ground was dry, not a sign of digging, no,
Not a wheeltrack in the dust, no trace of anyone.
It was when they relieved us this morning: and one of them,
The corporal, pointed to it.
There it was, 200
The strangest—
Look:
The body, just mounded over with light dust: you see?
Not buried really, but as if they'd covered it
Just enough for the ghost's peace. And no sign
Of dogs or any wild animal that had been there.

And then what a scene there was! Every man of us
Accusing the other: we all proved the other man did it,
We all had proof that we could not have done it.
We were ready to take hot iron in our hands,
Walk through fire, swear by all the gods, 210
It was not I!
I do not know who it was, but it was not I!

[CREON'S *rage has been mounting steadily, but the* SENTRY *is too intent upon his story to notice it*]

And then, when this came to nothing, someone said
A thing that silenced us and made us stare
Down at the ground: you had to be told the news,
And one of us had to do it! We threw the dice,
And the bad luck fell to me. So here I am,
No happier to be here than you are to have me:
Nobody likes the man who brings bad news.

CHORAGOS:

I have been wondering, King: can it be that the gods have done this? 220

CREON [*Furiously*]:

Stop!
Must you doddering wrecks
Go out of your heads entirely? "The gods!"
Intolerable!
The gods favor this corpse? Why? How had he served them?
Tried to loot their temples, burn their images,
Yes, and the whole State, and its law with it!
Is it your senile opinion that the gods love to honor bad men?
A pious thought!—
No, from the very beginning

There have been those who have whispered together, 230
Stiff-necked anarchists, putting their heads together,
Scheming against me in alleys. These are the men,
And they have bribed my own guard to do this thing.

[*Sententiously*]

Money!
There's nothing in the world so demoralizing as money.
Down go your cities,
Homes gone, men gone, honest hearts corrupted,
Crookedness of all kinds, and all for money!

[*To* SENTRY]

But you—!
I swear by God and by the throne of God,
The man who has done this thing shall pay for it! 240
Find that man, bring him here to me, or your death
Will be the least of your problems: I'll string you up
Alive, and there will be certain ways to make you
Discover your employer before you die;
And the process may teach you a lesson you seem to have missed:
The dearest profit is sometimes all too dear:
That depends on the source. Do you understand me?
A fortune won is often misfortune.

SENTRY:
King, may I speak?

CREON:
Your very voice distresses me.

SENTRY:
Are you sure that it is my voice, and not your conscience? 250

CREON:
By God, he wants to analyze me now!

SENTRY:
It is not what I say, but what has been done, that hurts you.

CREON:
You talk too much.

SENTRY:
Maybe; but I've done nothing.

CREON:
Sold your soul for some silver: that's all you've done.

SENTRY:
How dreadful it is when the right judge judges wrong!

CREON:
Your figures of speech
May entertain you now; but unless you bring me the man,
You will get little profit from them in the end.

[*Exit* CREON *into the Palace.*]

SENTRY:
"Bring me the man"—!
I'd like nothing better than bringing him the man! 260
But bring him or not, you have seen the last of me here.
At any rate, I am safe!

[*Exit* SENTRY]

Ode 1

Strophe 1

CHORUS:
Numberless are the world's wonders, but none
More wonderful than man; the stormgray sea
Yields to his prows, the huge crests bear him high;
Earth, holy and inexhaustible, is graven
With shining furrows where his plows have gone
Year after year, the timeless labor of stallions.

Antistrophe 1

The lightboned birds and beasts that cling to cover,
The lithe fish lighting their reaches of dim water, 270
All are taken, tamed in the net of his mind;
The lion on the hill, the wild horse windy-maned,
Resign to him; and his blunt yoke has broken
The sultry shoulders of the mountain bull.

Strophe 2

Words also, and thought as rapid as air,
He fashions to his good use; statecraft is his,
And his the skill that deflects the arrows of snow,
The spears of winter rain: from every wind
He has made himself secure—from all but one:
In the late wind of death he cannot stand. 280

Antistrophe 2

O clear intelligence, force beyond all measure!
O fate of man, working both good and evil!
When the laws are kept, how proudly his city stands!
When the laws are broken, what of his city then?
Never may the anárchic man find rest at my hearth,
Never be it said that my thoughts are his thoughts.

Scene 2

[*Re-enter* SENTRY *leading* ANTIGONE.]

CHORAGOS:
What does this mean? Surely this captive woman
Is the Princess, Antigonê. Why should she be taken?

SENTRY:
Here is the one who did it! We caught her
In the very act of burying him.—Where is Creon?

CHORAGOS:
Just coming from the house.

[*Enter* CREON, *C.*]

CREON:
What has happened?
Why have you come back so soon?

SENTRY [*Expansively*]:

O King,

A man should never be too sure of anything:
I would have sworn
That you'd not see me here again: your anger
Frightened me so, and the things you threatened me with; 10
But how could I tell then
That I'd be able to solve the case so soon?

No dice-throwing this time: I was only too glad to come!

Here is this woman. She is the guilty one:
We found her trying to bury him.
Take her, then; question her; judge her as you will.
I am through with the whole thing now, and glád óf it.

CREON:
But this is Antigonê! Why have you brought her here?

SENTRY:
She was burying him, I tell you!

CREON [*Severely*]:

Is this the truth?

SENTRY:
I saw her with my own eyes. Can I say more? 20

CREON:
The details: come, tell me quickly!

SENTRY:

It was like this:

After those terrible threats of yours, King,
We went back and brushed the dust away from the body.
The flesh was soft by now, and stinking,
So we sat on a hill to windward and kept guard.
No napping this time! We kept each other awake.
But nothing happened until the white round sun
Whirled in the center of the round sky over us:
Then, suddenly,
A storm of dust roared up from the earth, and the sky 30
Went out, the plain vanished with all its trees
In the stinging dark. We closed our eyes and endured it.
The whirlwind lasted a long time, but it passed;
And then we looked, and there was Antigonê!
I have seen
A mother bird come back to a stripped nest, heard
Her crying bitterly a broken note or two
For the young ones stolen. Just so, when this girl
Found the bare corpse, and all her love's work wasted,
She wept, and cried on heaven to damn the hands 40
That had done this thing.

And then she brought more dust

And sprinkled wine three times for her brother's ghost.

We ran and took her at once. She was not afraid,
Not even when we charged her with what she had done.

She denied nothing.
And this was a comfort to me,
And some uneasiness: for it is a good thing
To escape from death, but it is no great pleasure
To bring death to a friend.
Yet I always say
There is nothing so comfortable as your own safe skin!

CREON [*Slowly, dangerously*]:
And you, Antigonê, 50
You with your head hanging,—do you confess this thing?

ANTIGONE:
I do. I deny nothing.

CREON [*To* SENTRY]:
You may go.

[*Exit* SENTRY]

[*To* ANTIGONE:]

Tell me, tell me briefly:
Had you heard my proclamation touching this matter?

ANTIGONE:
It was public. Could I help hearing it?

CREON:
And yet you dared defy the law.

ANTIGONE:
I dared.
It was not God's proclamation. That final Justice
That rules the world below makes no such laws.

Your edict, King, was strong,
But all your strength is weakness itself against 60
The immortal unrecorded laws of God.
They are not merely now: they were, and shall be,
Operative for ever, beyond man utterly.

I knew I must die, even without your decree:
I am only mortal. And if I must die
Now, before it is my time to die,
Surely this is no hardship: can anyone
Living, as I live, with evil all about me,
Think Death less than a friend? This death of mine
Is of no importance; but if I had left my brother 70
Lying in death unburied, I should have suffered.
Now I do not.
You smile at me. Ah Creon,
Think me a fool, if you like; but it may well be
That a fool convicts me of folly.

CHORAGOS:
Like father, like daughter: both headstrong, deaf to reason!
She has never learned to yield.

CREON:
She has much to learn.
The inflexible heart breaks first, the toughest iron

Cracks first, and the wildest horses bend their necks
At the pull of the smallest curb.
Pride? In a slave?
This girl is guilty of a double insolence, 80
Breaking the given laws and boasting of it.
Who is the man here,
She or I, if this crime goes unpunished?
Sister's child, or more than sister's child,
Or closer yet in blood—she and her sister
Win bitter death for this!
[*To* SERVANTS:]
Go, some of you,
Arrest Ismenê. I accuse her equally.
Bring her: you will find her sniffling in the house there.

Her mind's a traitor: crimes kept in the dark
Cry for light, and the guardian brain shudders; 90
But how much worse than this
Is brazen boasting of barefaced anarchy!

ANTIGONE:
Creon, what more do you want than my death?

CREON:
Nothing.
That gives me everything.

ANTIGONE:
Then I beg you: kill me.
This talking is a great weariness: your words
Are distasteful to me, and I am sure that mine
Seem so to you. And yet they should not seem so:
I should have praise and honor for what I have done.
All these men here would praise me
Were their lips not frozen shut with fear of you. 100
[*Bitterly*]
Ah the good fortune of kings,
Licensed to say and do whatever they please!

CREON:
You are alone here in that opinion.

ANTIGONE:
No, they are with me. But they keep their tongues in leash.

CREON:
Maybe. But you are guilty, and they are not.

ANTIGONE:
There is no guilt in reverence for the dead.

CREON:
But Eteoclês—was he not your brother too?

ANTIGONE:
My brother too.

CREON:
And you insult his memory?

ANTIGONE [*Softly*]:
The dead man would not say that I insult it.

CREON:
He would: for you honor a traitor as much as him. 110
ANTIGONE:
His own brother, traitor or not, and equal in blood.
CREON:
He made war on his country. Eteoclês defended it.
ANTIGONE:
Nevertheless, there are honors due all the dead.
CREON:
But not the same for the wicked as for the just.
ANTIGONE:
Ah Creon, Creon,
Which of us can say what the gods hold wicked?
CREON:
An enemy is an enemy, even dead.
ANTIGONE:
It is my nature to join in love, not hate.
CREON [*Finally losing patience*]:
Go join them, then; if you must have your love,
Find it in hell! 120
CHORAGOS:
But see, Ismenê comes:
[*Enter* ISMENE, *guarded*]
Those tears are sisterly, the cloud
That shadows her eyes rains down gentle sorrow.
CREON:
You too, Ismenê,
Snake in my ordered house, sucking my blood
Stealthily—and all the time I never knew
That these two sisters were aiming at my throne!
Ismenê,
Do you confess your share in this crime, or deny it?
Answer me.
ISMENE:
Yes, if she will let me say so. I am guilty. 130
ANTIGONE [*Coldly*]:
No, Ismenê. You have no right to say so.
You would not help me, and I will not have you help me.
ISMENE:
But now I know what you meant; and I am here
To join you, to take my share of punishment.
ANTIGONE:
The dead man and the gods who rule the dead
Know whose act this was. Words are not friends.
ISMENE:
Do you refuse me, Antigonê? I want to die with you:
I too have a duty that I must discharge to the dead.
ANTIGONE:
You shall not lessen my death by sharing it.
ISMENE:
What do I care for life when you are dead? 140

ANTIGONE:
Ask Creon. You're always hanging on his opinions.
ISMENE:
You are laughing at me. Why, Antigonê?
ANTIGONE:
It's a joyless laughter, Ismenê.
ISMENE:
But can I do nothing?
ANTIGONE:
Yes. Save yourself. I shall not envy you.
There are those who will praise you; I shall have honor, too.
ISMENE:
But we are equally guilty!
ANTIGONE:
No more, Ismenê.
You are alive, but I belong to Death.
CREON [*To the* CHORUS]:
Gentlemen, I beg you to observe these girls:
One has just now lost her mind; the other,
It seems, has never had a mind at all. 150
ISMENE:
Grief teaches the steadiest minds to waver, King.
CREON:
Yours certainly did, when you assumed guilt with the guilty!
ISMENE:
But how could I go on living without her?
CREON:
You are.
She is already dead.
ISMENE:
But your own son's bride!
CREON:
There are places enough for him to push his plow.
I want no wicked women for my sons!
ISMENE:
O dearest Haimon, how your father wrongs you!
CREON:
I've had enough of your childish talk of marriage!
CHORAGOS:
Do you really intend to steal this girl from your son?
CREON:
No; Death will do that for me.
CHORAGOS:
Then she must die? 160
CREON [*Ironically*]:
You dazzle me.
—But enough of this talk!
[*To* GUARDS:]
You, there, take them away and guard them well:
For they are but women, and even brave men run
When they see Death coming.
[*Exeunt* ISMENE, ANTIGONE, *and* GUARDS]

Ode 2

Strophe 1

CHORUS:
Fortunate is the man who has never tasted God's vengeance!
Where once the anger of heaven has struck, that house is shaken
For ever: damnation rises behind each child
Like a wave cresting out of the black northeast,
When the long darkness under sea roars up
And bursts drumming death upon the windwhipped sand. 170

Antistrophe 1

I have seen this gathering sorrow from time long past
Loom upon Oedipus' children: generation from generation
Takes the compulsive rage of the enemy god.
So lately this last flower of Oedipus' line
Drank the sunlight! but now a passionate word
And a handful of dust have closed up all its beauty.

Strophe 2

What mortal arrogance
Transcends the wrath of Zeus?
Sleep cannot lull him, nor the effortless long months
Of the timeless gods: but he is young for ever, 180
And his house is the shining day of high Olympos.
All that is and shall be,
And all the past, is his.
No pride on earth is free of the curse of heaven.

Antistrophe 2

The straying dreams of men
May bring them ghosts of joy:
But as they drowse, the waking embers burn them;
Or they walk with fíxed éyes, as blind men walk.
But the ancient wisdom speaks for our own time:
Fate works most for woe 190
With Folly's fairest show.
Man's little pleasure is the spring of sorrow.

Scene 3

CHORAGOS:
But here is Haimon, King, the last of all your sons.[8]
Is it grief for Antigonê that brings him here,
And bitterness at being robbed of his bride?

[*Enter* HAIMON]

---

[8]Creon's first son was Megareus (see note 28).

CREON:
We shall soon see, and no need of diviners.
—Son,
You have heard my final judgment on that girl:
Have you come here hating me, or have you come
With deference and with love, whatever I do?

HAIMON:
I am your son, father. You are my guide.
You make things clear for me, and I obey you.
No marriage means more to me than your continuing wisdom. 10

CREON:
Good. That is the way to behave: subordinate
Everything else, my son, to your father's will.
This is what a man prays for, that he may get
Sons attentive and dutiful in his house,
Each one hating his father's enemies,
Honoring his father's friends. But if his sons
Fail him, if they turn out unprofitably,
What has he fathered but trouble for himself
And amusement for the malicious?
So you are right
Not to lose your head over this woman. 20
Your pleasure with her would soon grow cold, Haimon,
And then you'd have a hellcat in bed and elsewhere.
Let her find her husband in Hell!
Of all the people in this city, only she
Has had contempt for my law and broken it.

Do you want me to show myself weak before the people?
Or to break my sworn word? No, and I will not.
The woman dies.

I suppose she'll plead "family ties." Well, let her.
If I permit my own family to rebel, 30
How shall I earn the world's obedience?
Show me the man who keeps his house in hand,
He's fit for public authority.
I'll have no dealings
With law-breakers, critics of the government:
Whoever is chosen to govern should be obeyed—
Must be obeyed, in all things, great and small,
Just and unjust! O Haimon,
The man who knows how to obey, and that man only,
Knows how to give commands when the time comes.
You can depend on him, no matter how fast 40
The spears come: he's a good soldier, he'll stick it out.

Anarchy, anarchy! Show me a greater evil!
This is why cities tumble and the great houses rain down,
This is what scatters armies!

No, no: good lives are made so by discipline.
We keep the laws then, and the lawmakers,
And no woman shall seduce us. If we must lose,
Let's lose to a man, at least! Is a woman stronger than we?

CHORAGOS:
Unless time has rusted my wits,
What you say, King, is said with point and dignity. 50

HAIMON [*Boyishly earnest*]:
Father:
Reason is God's crowning gift to man, and you are right
To warn me against losing mine. I cannot say—
I hope that I shall never want to say!— that you
Have reasoned badly. Yet there are other men
Who can reason, too; and their opinions might be helpful.
You are not in a position to know everything
That people say or do, or what they feel:
Your temper terrifies them—everyone
Will tell you only what you like to hear. 60
But I, at any rate, can listen; and I have heard them
Muttering and whispering in the dark about this girl.
They say no woman has ever, so unreasonably,
Died so shameful a death for a generous act:
"She covered her brother's body. Is this indecent?
She kept him from dogs and vultures. Is this a crime?
Death?—She should have all the honor that we can give her!"
This is the way they talk out there in the city.
You must believe me:
Nothing is closer to me than your happiness. 70
What could be closer? Must not any son
Value his father's fortune as his father does his?
I beg you, do not be unchangeable:
Do not believe that you alone can be right.
The man who thinks that,
The man who maintains that only he has the power
To reason correctly, the gift to speak, the soul—
A man like that, when you know him, turns out empty.

It is not reason never to yield to reason!

In flood time you can see how some trees bend, 80
And because they bend, even their twigs are safe,
While stubborn trees are torn up, roots and all.
And the same thing happens in sailing:
Make your sheet fast, never slacken,—and over you go,
Head over heels and under: and there's your voyage.

Forget you are angry! Let yourself be moved!
I know I am young; but please let me say this:
The ideal condition

Would be, I admit, that men should be right by instinct;
But since we are all too likely to go astray, 90
The reasonable thing is to learn from those who can teach.

CHORAGOS:
You will do well to listen to him, King,
If what he says is sensible. And you, Haimon,
Must listen to your father.—Both speak well.

CREON:
You consider it right for a man of my years and experience
To go to school to a boy?

HAIMON:
It is not right
If I am wrong. But if I am young, and right,
What does my age matter?

CREON:
You think it right to stand up for an anarchist?

HAIMON:
Not at all. I pay no respect to criminals. 100

CREON:
Then she is not a criminal?

HAIMON:
The City would deny it, to a man.

CREON:
And the City proposes to teach me how to rule?

HAIMON:
Ah. Who is it that's talking like a boy now?

CREON:
My voice is the one voice giving orders in this City!

HAIMON:
It is no City if it takes orders from one voice.

CREON:
The State is the King!

HAIMON:
Yes, if the State is a desert.
[*Pause*]

CREON:
This boy, it seems, has sold out to a woman.

HAIMON:
If you are a woman: my concern is only for you.

CREON:
So? Your "concern"! In a public brawl with your father! 110

HAIMON:
How about you, in a public brawl with justice?

CREON:
With justice, when all that I do is within my rights?

HAIMON:
You have no right to trample on God's right.

CREON [*Completely out of control*]:
Fool, adolescent fool! Taken in by a woman!

HAIMON:
You'll never see me taken in by anything vile.

CREON:
Every word you say is for her!
HAIMON [*Quietly, darkly*]:
And for you.
And for me. And for the gods under the earth.
CREON:
You'll never marry her while she lives.
HAIMON:
Then she must die.—But her death will cause another.
CREON:
Another? 120
Have you lost your senses? Is this an open threat?
HAIMON:
There is no threat in speaking to emptiness.
CREON:
I swear you'll regret this superior tone of yours!
You are the empty one!
HAIMON:
If you were not my father,
I'd say you were perverse.
CREON:
You girlstruck fool, don't play at words with me!
HAIMON:
I am sorry. You prefer silence.
CREON:
Now, by God—!
I swear, by all the gods in heaven above us,
You'll watch it, I swear you shall!
[*To the* SERVANTS:]
Bring her out!
Bring the woman out! Let her die before his eyes! 130
Here, this instant, with her bridegroom beside her!
HAIMON:
Not here, no; she will not die here, King.
And you will never see my face again.
Go on raving as long as you've a friend to endure you.
[*Exit* HAIMON]

CHORAGOS:
Gone, gone.
Creon, a young man in a rage is dangerous!
CREON:
Let him do, or dream to do, more than a man can.
He shall not save these girls from death.
CHORAGOS:
These girls?
You have sentenced them both?
CREON:
No, you are right.
I will not kill the one whose hands are clean. 140
CHORAGOS:
But Antigonê?

CREON [*Somberly*]:
I will carry her far away
Out there in the wilderness, and lock her
Living in a vault of stone. She shall have food,
As the custom is, to absolve the State of her death.
And there let her pray to the gods of hell: [9]
They are her only gods:
Perhaps they will show her an escape from death,
Or she may learn,
though late,
That piety shown the dead is pity in vain.

[*Exit* CREON]

ODE 3

Strophe

CHORUS:
Love, unconquerable 150
Waster of rich men, keeper
Of warm lights and all-night vigil
In the soft face of a girl:
Sea-wanderer, forest-visitor!
Even the pure Immortals cannot escape you,
And mortal man, in his one day's dusk,
Trembles before your glory.

Antistrophe

Surely you swerve upon ruin
The just man's consenting heart,
As here you have made bright anger 160
Strike between father and son—
And none has conquered but Love!
A girl's glánce wórking the will of heaven:
Pleasure to her alone who mocks us,
Merciless Aphroditê. [10]

SCENE 4

CHORAGOS [*As* ANTIGONE *enters guarded*]:
But I can no longer stand in awe of this,
Nor, seeing what I see, keep back my tears.
Here is Antigonê, passing to that chamber
Where all find sleep at last.

[9] Hades, the king of the underworld.
[10] The goddess of love.

Strophe 1

ANTIGONE:

Look upon me, friends, and pity me
Turning back at the night's edge to say
Good-by to the sun that shines for me no longer;
Now sleepy Death
Summons me down to Acheron[11] that cold shore:
There is no bridesong there, nor any music. 10

CHORUS:

Yet not unpraised, not without a kind of honor,
You walk at last into the underworld;
Untouched by sickness, broken by no sword.
What woman has ever found your way to death?

Antistrophe 1

ANTIGONE:

How often I have heard the story of Niobê,[12]
Tantalos' wretched daughter, how the stone
Clung fast about her, ivy-close: and they say
The rain falls endlessly
And sifting soft snow; her tears are never done.
I feel the loneliness of her death in mine. 20

CHORUS:

But she was born of heaven, and you
Are woman, woman-born. If her death is yours,
A mortal woman's, is this not for you
Glory in our world and in the world beyond?

Strophe 2

ANTIGONE:

You laugh at me. Ah, friends, friends,
Can you not wait until I am dead? O Thebes,
O men many-charioted, in love with Fortune,
Dear springs of Dircê, sacred Theban grove,
Be witnesses for me, denied all pity,
Unjustly judged! and think a word of love 30
For her whose path turns
Under dark earth, where there are no more tears.

CHORUS:

You have passed beyond human daring and come at last
Into a place of stone where Justice sits.
I cannot tell
What shape of your father's guilt appears in this.

---

[11] The river of sorrow in the underworld.

[12] A princess married to Amphion, a king of Thebes; Niobê earned the wrath of the goddess Leto by boasting that Leto's two children—Apollo and Artemis—could not compare with Niobê's own fourteen children. To avenge the insult, Niobê's children were killed and Niobê was turned into a rock that cried perpetual tears.

Antistrophe 2

ANTIGONE:

You have touched it at last: that bridal bed
Unspeakable, horror of son and mother mingling:
Their crime, infection of all our family!
O Oedipus, father and brother! 40
Your marriage strikes from the grave to murder mine.[13]
I have been a stranger here in my own land:
All my life
The blasphemy of my birth has followed me.

CHORUS:

Reverence is a virtue, but strength
Lives in established law: that must prevail.
You have made your choice,
Your death is the doing of your conscious hand.

Epode

ANTIGONE:

Then let me go, since all your words are bitter,
And the very light of the sun is cold to me. 50
Lead me to my vigil, where I must have
Neither love nor lamentation; no song, but silence.

[CREON *interrupts impatiently*]

CREON:

If dirges and planned lamentations could put off death,
Men would be singing for ever.

[*To the* SERVANTS:]

Take her, go!

You know your orders: take her to the vault
And leave her alone there. And if she lives or dies,
That's her affair, not ours: our hands are clean.

ANTIGONE:

O tomb, vaulted bride-bed in eternal rock,
Soon I shall be with my own again
Where Persephonê[14] welcomes the thin ghosts underground: 60
And I shall see my father again, and you, mother,
And dearest Polyneicês—

dearest indeed

To me, since it was my hand
That washed him clean and poured the ritual wine:
And my reward is death before my time!

And yet, as men's hearts know, I have done no wrong,
I have not sinned before God. Or if I have,
I shall know the truth in death. But if the guilt

---

[13]Polyneicês had married the daughter of Adrastus, the Argive king, in order to guarantee the assistance of Argos in the war against Thebes.

[14]Queen of the underworld.

Lies upon Creon who judged me, then, I pray,
May his punishment equal my own.

CHORAGOS:

O passionate heart, 70

Unyielding, tormented still by the same winds!

CREON:

Her guards shall have good cause to regret their delaying.

ANTIGONE:

Ah! That voice is like the voice of death!

CREON:

I can give you no reason to think you are mistaken.

ANTIGONE:

Thebes, and you my fathers' gods,[15]
And rulers of Thebes, you see me now, the last
Unhappy daughter of a line of kings,
Your kings, led away to death. You will remember
What things I suffer, and at what men's hands,
Because I would not transgress the laws of heaven. 80

[*To the* GUARDS, *simply:*]

Come: let us wait no longer.

[*Exit* ANTIGONE, *L., guarded*]

ODE 4

Strophe 1

CHORUS:

All Danaê's[16] beauty was locked away
In a brazen cell where the sunlight could not come:
A small room, still as any grave, enclosed her.
Yet she was a princess too,
And Zeus in a rain of gold poured love upon her.
O child, child,
No power in wealth or war
Or tough sea-blackened ships
Can prevail against untiring Destiny! 90

Antistrophe 1

And Dryas' son[17] also, that furious king,
Bore the god's prisoning anger for his pride:
Sealed up by Dionysos in deaf stone,
His madness died among echoes.
So at the last he learned what dreadful power
His tongue had mocked:

---

[15]The house of Thebes charted its lineage to the gods.

[16]The daughter of Acrisius, an Argive king; because it was prophesied that he would die at the hand of Danaê's son, Acrisius ordered Danaê to be shut up in a tower. Here Zeus came to her in the form of a golden shower of rain, after which she gave birth to Perseus, who eventually killed Acrisius.

[17]Lycurgus, king of Thrace, who was imprisoned by the god Dionysus for trying to thwart the spread of the Dionysian sect.

For he had profaned the revels,
And fired the wrath of the nine
Implacable Sisters that love the sound of the flute.

Strophe 2

And old men tell a half-remembered tale 100
Of horror done where a dark ledge splits the sea
And a double surf beats on the gráy shóres:
How a king's new woman, sick
With hatred for the queen he had imprisoned,
Ripped out his two sons' eyes with her bloody hands
While grinning Arês watched the shuttle plunge
Four times: four blind wounds crying for revenge,[18]

Antistrophe 2

Crying, tears and blood mingled.—Piteously born,
Those sons whose mother was of heavenly birth!
Her father was the god of the North Wind 110
And she was cradled by gales,
She raced with young colts on the glittering hills
And walked untrammeled in the open light:
But in her marriage deathless Fate found means
To build a tomb like yours for all her joy.

Scene 5

[*Enter blind* TEIRESIAS, *led by a boy. The opening speeches of* TEIRESIAS *should be in singsong contrast to the realistic lines of* CREON.]

TEIRESIAS:
This is the way the blind man comes, Princes, Princes,
Lock-step, two heads lit by the eyes of one.

CREON:
What new thing have you to tell us, old Teiresias?

TEIRESIAS:
I have much to tell you: listen to the prophet, Creon.

CREON:
I am not aware that I have ever failed to listen.

TEIRESIAS:
Then you have done wisely, King, and ruled well.

CREON:
I admit my debt to you. But what have you to say?

TEIRESIAS:
This, Creon: you stand once more on the edge of fate.

[18]Phineas, a king of Thrace, divorced and imprisoned Cleopatra, daughter of Boreas (the north wind) and an Athenian princess, Orithyea. Phineas's new wife, Eidothea, blinded the two sons of Cleopatra as Arês, the god of war, looked on.

CREON:
What do you mean? Your words are a kind of dread.

TEIRESIAS:
Listen, Creon: 10
I was sitting in my chair of augury, at the place
Where the birds gather about me. They were all a-chatter,
As is their habit, when suddenly I heard
A strange note in their jangling, a scream, a
Whirring fury; I knew that they were fighting,
Tearing each other, dying
In a whirlwind of wings clashing. And I was afraid.
I began the rites of burnt-offering at the altar,
But Hephaistos failed me: instead of bright flame,
There was only the sputtering slime of the fat thigh-flesh 20
Melting: the entrails dissolved in gray smoke,
The bare bone burst from the welter. And no blaze!

This was a sign from heaven. My boy described it,
Seeing for me as I see for others.

I tell you, Creon, you yourself have brought
This new calamity upon us. Our hearths and altars
Are stained with the corruption of dogs and carrion birds
That glut themselves on the corpse of Oedipus' son.
The gods are deaf when we pray to them, their fire
Recoils from our offering, their birds of omen 30
Have no cry of comfort, for they are gorged
With the thick blood of the dead.
O my son,
These are no trifles! Think: all men make mistakes,
But a good man yields when he knows his course is wrong,
And repairs the evil. The only crime is pride.

Give in to the dead man, then: do not fight with a corpse—
What glory is it to kill a man who is dead?
Think, I beg you:
It is for your own good that I speak as I do.
You should be able to yield for your own good. 40

CREON:
It seems that prophets have made me their especial province.
All my life long
I have been a kind of butt for the dull arrows
Of doddering fortune-tellers!
No, Teiresias:
If your birds—if the great eagles of God himself
Should carry him stinking bit by bit to heaven,
I would not yield. I am not afraid of pollution:
No man can defile the gods.
Do what you will,
Go into business, make money, speculate
In India gold or that synthetic gold from Sardis, 50

Get rich otherwise than by my consent to bury him.
Teiresias, it is a sorry thing when a wise man
Sells his wisdom, lets out his words for hire!

TEIRESIAS:
Ah Creon! Is there no man left in the world—

CREON:
To do what?—Come, let's have the aphorism!

TEIRESIAS:
No man who knows that wisdom outweighs any wealth?

CREON:
As surely as bribes are baser than any baseness.

TEIRESIAS:
You are sick, Creon! You are deathly sick!

CREON:
As you say: it is not my place to challenge a prophet.

TEIRESIAS:
Yet you have said my prophecy is for sale. 60

CREON:
The generation of prophets has always loved gold.

TEIRESIAS:
The generation of kings has always loved brass.

CREON:
You forget yourself! You are speaking to your King.

TEIRESIAS:
I know it. You are a king because of me.

CREON:
You have a certain skill; but you have sold out.

TEIRESIAS:
King, you will drive me to words that—

CREON:
Say them, say them!
Only remember: I will not pay you for them.

TEIRESIAS:
No, you will find them too costly.

CREON:
No doubt. Speak:
Whatever you say, you will not change my will.

TEIRESIAS:
Then take this, and take it to heart! 70
The time is not far off when you shall pay back
Corpse for corpse, flesh of your own flesh.
You have thrust the child of this world into living night,
You have kept from the gods below the child that is theirs:
The one in a grave before her death, the other,
Dead, denied the grave. This is your crime:
And the Furies[19] and the dark gods of Hell
Are swift with terrible punishment for you.

[19]Female spirits who avenged crimes against the blood, such as patricide or matricide.

Do you want to buy me now, Creon?

Not many days,

And your house will be full of men and women weeping, 80

And curses will be hurled at you from far

Cities grieving for sons unburied, left to rot

Before the walls of Thebes.

These are my arrows, Creon: they are all for you.

[*To* BOY:]

But come, child: lead me home.

Let him waste his fine anger upon younger men.

Maybe he will learn at last

To control a wiser tongue in a better head.

[*Exit* TEIRESIAS]

CHORAGOS:

The old man has gone, King, but his words

Remain to plague us. I am old, too, 90

But I cannot remember that he was ever false.

CREON:

That is true. . . . It troubles me.

Oh it is hard to give in! but it is worse

To risk everything for stubborn pride.

CHORAGOS:

Creon: take my advice.

CREON:

What shall I do?

CHORAGOS:

Go quickly: free Antigonê from her vault

And build a tomb for the body of Polyneicês.

CREON:

You would have me do this?

CHORAGOS:

Creon, yes!

And it must be done at once: God moves

Swiftly to cancel the folly of stubborn men. 100

CREON:

It is hard to deny the heart! But I

Will do it: I will not fight with destiny.

CHORAGOS:

You must go yourself, you cannot leave it to others.

CREON:

I will go.

—Bring axes, servants:

Come with me to the tomb. I buried her, I

Will set her free.

Oh quickly!

My mind misgives—

The laws of the gods are mighty, and a man must serve them

To the last day of his life!

[*Exit* CREON]

PÆAN

Strophe 1

CHORAGOS:
God of many names
CHORUS:
O Iacchos
son
of Kadmeian Sémelê[20]
O born of the Thunder!
Guardian of the West
Regent
of Eleusis' plain[21]
O Prince of maenad Thebes
and the Dragon Field by rippling Ismenos:

110

Antistrophe 1

CHORAGOS:
God of many names
CHORUS:
the flame of torches
flares on our hills
the nymphs of Iacchos
dance at the spring of Castalia:[22]

from the vine-close mountain
come ah come in ivy:
Evohé evohé! sings through the streets of Thebes

Strophe 2

CHORAGOS:
God of many names
CHORUS:
Iacchos of Thebes
heavenly Child
of Sémelê bride of the Thunderer!
The shadow of plague is upon us:
come
with clement feet
oh come from Parnasos[23]
down the long slopes
across the lamenting water

120

[20]Sémelê, the mother of Bacchus (Iacchos or Dionysus), died when Zeus visited her in the form of a thunderbolt; her unborn infant lived on.

[21]Eleusis, on the coast of Attica, was the site of mystery rites for Persephone, goddess of the underworld, and her mother Demeter, goddess of the earth.

[22]A spring on Mount Parnassus (Parnasos), the waters of which were said to bring poetic inspiration.

[23]A mountain near Delphi whose two peaks were sacred to Apollo and Dionysus; the Corycian Cave, located on the mountain, was sacred to Pan and the woodland nymphs.

Antistrophe 2

CHORAGOS:

Iô Fire! Chorister of the throbbing stars!
O purest among the voices of the night!
Thou son of God, blaze for us!

CHORUS:

Come with choric rapture of circling Maenads[24]
Who cry *Iô Iacche!*
God of many names!

ÉXODOS

[*Enter* MESSENGER, *L.*]

MESSENGER:

Men of the line of Kadmos, you who live
Near Amphion's[25] citadel:
I cannot say
Of any condition of human life "This is fixed,
This is clearly good, or bad." Fate raises up,
And Fate casts down the happy and unhappy alike:

No man can foretell his Fate.
Take the case of Creon:
Creon was happy once, as I count happiness:
Victorious in battle, sole governor of the land,
Fortunate father of children nobly born.
And now it has all gone from him! Who can say 10
That a man is still alive when his life's joy fails?
He is a walking dead man. Grant him rich,
Let him live like a king in his great house:
If his pleasure is gone, I would not give
So much as the shadow of smoke for all he owns.

CHORAGOS:

Your words hint at sorrow: what is your news for us?

MESSENGER:

They are dead. The living are guilty of their death.

CHORAGOS:

Who is guilty? Who is dead? Speak!

MESSENGER:

Haimon.
Haimon is dead; and the hand that killed him
Is his own hand.

CHORAGOS:

His father's? or his own? 20

MESSENGER:

His own, driven mad by the murder his father had done.

---

[24]The Bacchae, or female worshippers of Dionysus.
[25]A ruler of Thebes; the power of his music raised the walls of the city.

CHORAGOS:
Teiresias, Teiresias, how clearly you saw it all!
MESSENGER:
This is my news: you must draw what conclusions you can from it.
CHORAGOS:
But look: Eurydicê, our Queen:
Has she overheard us?
[*Enter* EURYDICE *from the Palace, C.*]
EURYDICE:
I have heard something, friends:
As I was unlocking the gate of Pallas'[26] shrine,
For I needed her help today, I heard a voice
Telling of some new sorrow. And I fainted
There at the temple with all my maidens about me. 30
But speak again: whatever it is, I can bear it:
Grief and I are no strangers.
MESSENGER:
Dearest Lady,
I will tell you plainly all that I have seen.
I shall not try to comfort you: what is the use,
Since comfort could lie only in what is not true?
The truth is always best.
I went with Creon
To the outer plain where Polyneicês was lying,
No friend to pity him, his body shredded by dogs.
We made our prayers in that place to Hecatê[27]
And Pluto, that they would be merciful. And we bathed 40
The corpse with holy water, and we brought
Fresh-broken branches to burn what was left of it,
And upon the urn we heaped up a towering barrow
Of the earth of his own land.
When we were done, we ran
To the vault where Antigonê lay on her couch of stone.
One of the servants had gone ahead,
And while he was yet far off he heard a voice
Grieving within the chamber, and he came back
And told Creon. And as the King went closer,
The air was full of wailing, the words lost, 50
And he begged us to make all haste. "Am I a prophet?"
He said, weeping, "And must I walk this road,
The saddest of all that I have gone before?
My son's voice calls me on. Oh quickly, quickly!
Look through the crevice there, and tell me
If it is Haimon, or some deception of the gods!"

We obeyed; and in the cavern's farthest corner
We saw her lying:
She had made a noose of her fine linen veil

[26]Pallas Athene, goddess of war and of arts and crafts.
[27]Hecatê, goddess of the underworld, is associated with night and burial; Pluto is another name for Hades, king of the underworld.

And hanged herself. Haimon lay beside her, 60
His arms about her waist, lamenting her,
His love lost under ground, crying out
That his father had stolen her away from him.

When Creon saw him the tears rushed to his eyes
And he called to him: "What have you done, child? Speak to me.
What are you thinking that makes your eyes so strange?
O my son, my son, I come to you on my knees!"
But Haimon spat in his face. He said not a word,
Staring—
And suddenly drew his sword
And lunged. Creon shrank back, the blade missed; and the boy, 70
Desperate against himself, drove it half its length
Into his own side, and fell. And as he died
He gathered Antigonê close in his arms again,
Choking, his blood bright red on her white cheek.
And now he lies dead with the dead, and she is his
At last, his bride in the houses of the dead.

[*Exit* EURYDICE *into the Palace*]

CHORAGOS:
She has left us without a word. What can this mean?

MESSENGER:
It troubles me, too; yet she knows what is best,
Her grief is too great for public lamentation,
And doubtless she has gone to her chamber to weep 80
For her dead son, leading her maidens in his dirge.

CHORAGOS:
It may be so: but I fear this deep silence

[*Pause*]

MESSENGER:
I will see what she is doing. I will go in.

[*Exit* MESSENGER *into the Palace*]

[*Enter* CREON *with attendants, bearing* HAIMON'S *body*]

CHORAGOS:
But here is the King himself: oh look at him,
Bearing his own damnation in his arms.

CREON:
Nothing you say can touch me any more.
My own blind heart has brought me
From darkness to final darkness. Here you see
The father murdering, the murdered son—
And all my civic wisdom! 90

Haimon my son, so young, so young to die,
I was the fool, not you; and you died for me.

CHORAGOS:
That is the truth; but you were late in learning it.

CREON:
This truth is hard to bear. Surely a god
Has crushed me beneath the hugest weight of heaven.

And driven me headlong a barbaric way
To trample out the thing I held most dear.

The pains that men will take to come to pain!

[*Enter* MESSENGER *from the Palace*]

MESSENGER:
The burden you carry in your hands is heavy,
But it is not all: you will find more in your house. 100

CREON:
What burden worse than this shall I find there?

MESSENGER:
The Queen is dead.

CREON:
O port of death, deaf world,
Is there no pity for me? And you, Angel of evil,
I was dead, and your words are death again.
Is it true, boy? Can it be true?
Is my wife dead? Has death bred death?

MESSENGER:
You can see for yourself.

[*The doors are opened, and the body of* EURYDICE *is disclosed within.*]

CREON:
Oh pity!
All true, all true, and more than I can bear! 110
O my wife, my son!

MESSENGER:
She stood before the altar, and her heart
Welcomed the knife her own hand guided,
And a great cry burst from her lips for Megareus[28] dead,
And for Haimon dead, her sons; and her last breath
Was a curse for their father, the murderer of her sons.
And she fell, and the dark flowed in through her closing eyes.

CREON:
O God, I am sick with fear.
Are there no swords here? Has no one a blow for me?

MESSENGER:
Her curse is upon you for the deaths of both. 120

CREON:
It is right that it should be. I alone am guilty.
I know it, and I say it. Lead me in,
Quickly, friends.
I have neither life nor substance. Lead me in.

CHORAGOS:
You are right, if there can be right in so much wrong.
The briefest way is best in a world of sorrow.

CREON:
Let it come,
Let death come quickly, and be kind to me.
I would not ever see the sun again.

---

[28] Haimon's brother; he died willingly in the war to fulfill a prophesy and so to save Thebes from destruction.

CHORAGOS:
All that will come when it will; but we, meanwhile, 130
Have much to do. Leave the future to itself.
CREON:
All my heart was in that prayer!
CHORAGOS:
Then do not pray any more: the sky is deaf.
CREON:
Lead me away. I have been rash and foolish.
I have killed my son and my wife.
I look for comfort; my comfort lies here dead.
Whatever my hands have touched has come to nothing.
Fate has brought all my pride to a thought of dust.
[*As* CREON *is being led into the house, the* CHORAGOS *advances and speaks directly to the audience*]
CHORAGOS:
There is no happiness where there is no wisdom;
No wisdom but in submission to the gods. 140
Big words are always punished,
And proud men in old age learn to be wise.

EURIPIDES
[C. 480–406 B.C.E.]

Euripides, Aeschylus, and Sophocles make up the triumvirate of great Greek tragedians of the sixth and fifth centuries. Of the three, Euripides was the most unconventional and consequently the least esteemed and most satirized during his own lifetime. But Greek playgoers venerated him after his death, and twentieth-century audiences find his work eerily modern. His plays often shake themselves free of the formal conventions observed by Aeschylus and Sophocles; they are sometimes violent and shocking in the actions they depict; and they frequently concern themselves with human and divine aberration and irrationality. They feature fiery dramatic exchanges between opposing characters; they sharply question received ideas concerning war and justice, gods, and temporal rulers. Their endings are often tantalizingly ambiguous. More than any male Greek writer in any genre, Euripides gives great prominence to women. Whether the women are courageous and nurturing like Hecuba in *The Trojan Women* (415 B.C.E.), or witty and charming like the main character of *Helen* (412 B.C.E.), or terrifying like the title character of *Medea* (431 B.C.E.), they are fully realized and powerful figures.

LIFE

We know far fewer facts about Euripides than we do about Aeschylus and Sophocles, perhaps because he participated less in public life than they did. Aristotle does say that a Euripides was sent to negotiate a peace with Syracuse, and it may be the playwright he refers to, although Euripides by most accounts was a somber man who preferred to closet himself with his notable collection of books. Tradition has it that he was born on the day of the battle of Salamis in 480 B.C.E., but this date may represent the wishful thinking of a later biographer who wanted to make Euripides seem thoroughly Greek. If his plays are any indication, nationalism was scarcely his credo, and Euripides seems to have understood well what it meant to be the underdog, the gadfly, the outsider.

WORK

Euripides' career was long and productive. His first play, *The Daughters of Pelias,* was produced in 455, and his last, the *Bacchae,* in 405. Out of the eighty or ninety plays he wrote, his work won the prize at the Greater Dionysia only five times; in comparison, Sophocles won eighteen prizes over his lifetime. In 408 Euripides voluntarily left Athens and journeyed northeast to the court of Archelaus of Macedonia, where he was accorded great honor. Tradition has it that he died there, torn to pieces accidentally by his hosts' pack of hunting dogs, or else deliberately by a pack of wild women, but a Macedonian admirer named Adaeus provides a less dramatic story in the epitaph he composed for the playwright:

> Neither dogs slew thee, Euripides, nor the rage of women, . . . but death and old age, and under Macedonian Arethusa thou liest, honored by the friendship of Archelaus. Yet it is not this that I account thy tomb, but the altar of Dionysus, and the buskin-trodden stage.

Although his plays feature flying chariots drawn by dragons, as in *Medea,* strange prisoners transforming themselves into bulls, as in the *Bacchae,* and gods descending from heaven to solve impasses, as in the *Ion,* they are often described as more realistic than those of Aeschylus and Sophocles because his characters exhibit a wider and subtler range of human emotions. Among his contemporaries Euripides had the reputation of being able to make his kings, queens, gods, and warriors speak the language of everyday life, and he has the knack of making small homely details suggest a whole character for us. Among all the bedraggled and grieving and thirsty prisoners of war in *The Trojan Women,* only Helen contrives to get washwater so she can freshen up before she pleads for her life before Menelaus; at the beginning of *Medea,* the tutor describes how the old men sit gossiping and playing at dice beside the fountain in the marketplace; in the *Bacchae,* the elderly would-be orgiasts Tiresias and Cadmus wonder if it would be appropriate for them to ride up the steep mountain path to the wild Dionysian rites in their comfortable chariot. At such moments, we know we are in a Euripidean universe of realistic human behavior.

Nineteen of Euripides' plays survive. *Medea,* which we have chosen to represent his work, was produced in 431 B.C.E. Euripides could expect his audience to know by heart the earlier parts of the story of Medea and Jason, events he only alludes to throughout this play, which focuses on the violent end of their mutual passion and adventure. Jason's father, Aeson, is the rightful heir of the kingdom of Iolcus in Thessaly near the Black Sea, but when his half-brother Pelias usurps the throne, Jason is sent away for safekeeping to be educated by the wise centaur Chiron. When he becomes a man, he journeys back to Iolcus to try to argue for his family's right to the kingdom. But Pelias has been forewarned that he will die at the hands of a young relative wearing only one shoe, and when Jason arrives, Pelias sees that he has lost a sandal in his travels. Pelias tries to strike a wily bargain by agreeing that he will certainly restore the throne to Jason's family if Jason will only prove his worthiness by performing an impossible task. He commands Jason to fetch the golden fleece that grows upon sheep guarded by a ceaselessly vigilant dragon in Colchis, a land on the eastern coast of the Black Sea ruled by King Aietes. Jason sets about recruiting a company of sailor-heroes to accompany him on his quest. Just as comic-book superheroes of today team up to fight evil, he gathers in his fifty-man crew heroes from other myth cycles, such as Hercules, Orpheus, the twins Castor and Polydeuces, and assorted characters from *The Odyssey*. Together they will come to be called the Argonauts after the *Argo,* the trim oared ship especially built for their long voyage.

When the Argonauts anchor at Colchis after many harrowing adventures, Medea, Aietes' daughter, falls instantly in love with Jason. Aietes says he will give Jason the fleece if he can yoke two bullocks with brazen hooves and fiery breath, plow a field with them, and then sow the soil with the teeth of a dragon. From this strange seed will spring up a mighty army of men, whom the Argonauts will then have to defeat. Medea gives Jason and his men a magical ointment that makes them invulnerable for a day, and so they are able to accomplish Aietes' tasks. Aietes, growing alarmed at the prospect that he may actually have to give up the golden fleece, plots to ambush Jason and his friends in the night, but Medea overhears his plans and quietly leads Jason to the dragon's lair and enchants the creature into sleep so Jason can easily kill it. Then the lovers gather up the golden fleece and flee Colchis with the Argonauts. Aietes soon sails after them in pursuit, so to distract her father Medea kills and dismembers her younger brother and tosses the body into the sea, piece by piece, in front of Aietes' ship.

Back in Iolcus, when Jason learns that Pelias has murdered Aeson and that his mother has killed herself in her grief, he turns to Medea for magical revenge. She shows the daughters of Pelias an old ram, butchers it, and boils the meat with herbs in a cauldron, and soon a frisky lamb springs from the brew. She offers to rejuvenate Pelias in the same way, and his daughters eagerly cut him up and bring Medea the hacked-up corpse; this time, however, Medea leaves out the magical herbs and omits certain incantations, and Pelias stays quite dead. Pelias' son drives Jason and Medea from Iolcus, and they make their way to Corinth, where Medea bears their two sons. The play begins just after Jason has announced his plans to put Medea aside and make a profitable marriage to Glauce, the daughter of Creon, king of Corinth.

Medea's story has figured into many misogynist writings over the centuries, as it would seem to confirm the belief that if you give a woman power, especially magical powers, you have a monster on your hands. Indeed, defenses of Medea as a hapless woman who has been seduced, torn from her homeland, and then abandoned by a condescending, heartless ingrate all seem somewhat weak, given her unconscionable act of infanticide. It may be worthwhile to know that her character is derived from an even stronger figure, the mother-goddess of the Medes, an ancient Middle Eastern people who named themselves for her. As such a goddess, she would preside over life as well as death; in her different aspects, she would be the passionate lover, the tender, life-giving mother, and the deathcrone who comes at the end to lead human beings into the underworld. Perhaps some of her ancient significance hovers about Euripides' Medea, who makes love, gives birth, and strikes down with equal energy.

It is also interesting that similar stories of a wronged woman who kills her own children can be found in many widely separated cultures, ranging from ancient Mexico to Dravidian India and China; perhaps those stories are not so much about child abuse or women's innate evil as they are reflections of the male fear of dependency upon women as childbearers and nurturers; what if Mother, that radiant source of life and warmth, were to turn upon us? Such women are often depicted as outsiders to the culture in which the story is told, and the stories are often in part expressions of xenophobia. One insistent feature of the Medea story is its repeated contrast of West and East: Jason is a westerner, a rational Greek, from a land where men rule, whereas Medea is oriental, exotic, from a magic-ridden land noted for strong women; "in all Hellas there is not one woman / Who could have done it," rages Jason at lines 1214–15, referring to her string of murders, and it was probably very comforting for Greeks to think that was so.

The play also calls attention to certain legal issues involving women's lack of rights and power under Greek marriage laws; as an alien and a woman, Medea is especially without legal recourse, and the opportunistic Jason has the power to decide arbitrarily to dissolve their marriage and do with their sons as he sees fit. But it is difficult to see this as a primary focus of the play; one does not imagine Athenian citizens walking out of the theater engaged in heated discussions of women's rights. The delight and horror of the play really lie in watching the machinations of a woman of power who gradually evolves a plan, executes it, and gets away with it, escaping in her sun-god grandfather's chariot while Jason feebly shakes his fist at her from far below. In Greek myth she is not even punished in the afterlife but goes to Elysium, where she marries Achilles. Indeed, Achilles, whose sense of personal honor also looms large, might be a quite fitting mate for Medea. It is well to remember that, for the Greeks, a hero was not necessarily a good, kind person, but rather a strong one whose deeds are somehow on a grand scale.

Suggested Readings

Gilbert Murray's *Euripides and His Age* (1913) is still a comprehensive and readable introduction to Euripides' world. Erich Segal's *Euripides; A Collection of Critical Essays* (1968) gives a good range of modern critical thinking about the plays. Wolfgang Lederer's *The Fear of Women* (1968) is a psychiatrist's look at terrifying female figures such as witches, furies, and destructive goddesses, although it does not discuss Medea at length.

Medea

Translated by Philip Vellacott

CHARACTERS:

NURSE
TUTOR *to Medea's sons*
MEDEA
CHORUS *of Corinthian women*
CREON, *king of Corinth*
JASON
AEGEUS, *king of Athens*
MESSENGER
MEDEA'S TWO CHILDREN

SCENE: *Before Jason's house in Corinth*

NURSE:
If only they had never gone! If the Argo's hull
Never had winged out through the grey-blue jaws of rock
And on towards Colchis! If that pine on Pelion's slopes
Had never felt the axe, and fallen, to put oars
Into those heroes' hands, who went at Pelias' bidding
To fetch the golden fleece! Then neither would Medea,
My mistress, ever have set sail for the walled town
Of Iolcus, mad with love for Jason; nor would she,
When Pelias' daughters, at her instance, killed their father,
Have come with Jason and her children to live here 10
In Corinth; where, coming as an exile, she has earned
The citizens' welcome; while to Jason she is all

Obedience—and in marriage that's the saving thing,
When a wife obediently accepts her husband's will.[1]

But now her world has turned to enmity, and wounds her
Where her affection's deepest. Jason has betrayed
His own sons, and my mistress, for a royal bed,
For alliance with the king of Corinth. He has married
Glauce, Creon's daughter. Poor Medea! Scorned and shamed,
She raves, invoking every vow and solemn pledge 20
That Jason made her, and calls the gods as witnesses
What thanks she has received for her fidelity.
She will not eat; she lies collapsed in agony,
Dissolving the long hours in tears. Since first she heard
Of Jason's wickedness, she has not raised her eyes,
Or moved her cheek from the hard ground; and when her friends
Reason with her, she might be a rock or wave of the sea,
For all she hears—unless, maybe, she turns away
Her lovely head, speaks to herself alone, and wails
Aloud for her dear father, her own land and home, 30
Which she betrayed and left, to come here with this man
Who now spurns and insults her. Poor Medea! Now
She learns through pain what blessings they enjoy who are not
Uprooted from their native land. She hates her sons:
To see them is no pleasure to her. I am afraid
Some dreadful purpose is forming in her mind. She is
A frightening woman; no one who makes an enemy
Of her will carry off an easy victory.

Here come the boys, back from their running. They've no thought
Of this cruel blow that's fallen on their mother. Well, 40
They're young; young heads and painful thoughts don't go together.

[*Enter the* TUTOR *with* MEDEA'S TWO SONS.]

TUTOR:
Old nurse and servant of my mistress's house, tell me,
What are you doing, standing out here by the door,
All alone, talking to yourself, harping on trouble?
Eh? What does Medea say to being left alone?

NURSE:
Old friend, tutor of Jason's sons, an honest slave
Suffers in her own heart the blow that strikes her mistress.
It was too much, I couldn't bear it; I had to come
Out here and tell my mistress's wrongs to earth and heaven.

TUTOR:
Poor woman! Has she not stopped crying yet?

NURSE:
Stopped crying? 50
I envy you. Her grief's just born—not yet half-grown.

---

[1]The nurse alludes to the circumstances of Jason's voyage to capture the golden fleece and his early relationship with Medea.

TUTOR:

Poor fool—though she's my mistress and I shouldn't say it—
She had better save her tears. She has not heard the worst.

NURSE:

The worst? What now? Don't keep it from me. What has happened?

TUTOR:

Why, nothing's happened. I'm sorry I said anything.

NURSE:

Look—we're both slaves together: don't keep me in the dark.
Is it so great a secret? I can hold my tongue.

TUTOR:

I'd gone along to the benches where the old men play
At dice, next to the holy fountain of Peirene;
They thought I was not listening; and I heard one say 60
That Creon king of Corinth means to send these boys
Away from here—to banish them, and their mother too.
Whether the story's true I don't know. I hope not.

NURSE:

But surely Jason won't stand by and see his sons
Banished, even if he has a quarrel with their mother?

TUTOR:

Old love is ousted by new love. Jason's no friend
To this house.

NURSE:

Then we're lost, if we must add new trouble
To old, before we're rid of what we had already.

TUTOR:

But listen: it's no time to tell Medea this.
Keep quiet, say nothing about it.

NURSE:

Children, do you hear 70
What sort of father Jason is to you? My curse
On—No! No curse; he is my master. All the same,
He is guilty: he has betrayed those near and dear to him.

TUTOR:

What man's not guilty? It's taken you a long time to learn
That everybody loves himself more than his neighbour.
These boys are nothing to their father: he's in love.

NURSE:

Run into the house, boys. Everything will be all right.

[*The* CHILDREN *move away a little.*]

You do your best to keep them by themselves, as long
As she's in this dark mood; don't let them go to her.
I've watched her watching them, her eye like a wild bull's. 80
There's something that she means to do; and I know this:
She'll not relax her rage till it has found its victim.
God grant she strike her enemies and not her friends!

[MEDEA*'s voice is heard from inside the house.*]

MEDEA:

Oh, oh! What misery, what wretchedness!
What shall I do? If only I were dead!

NURSE:

There! You can hear; it is your mother
Racking her heart, racking her anger.
Quick, now, children, hurry indoors;
And don't go within sight of her,
Or anywhere near her; keep a safe distance. 90
Her mood is cruel, her nature dangerous,
Her will fierce and intractable.
Come on, now, in with you both at once.

[*The* CHILDREN *go in, and the* TUTOR *follows.*]

The dark cloud of her lamentations
Is just beginning. Soon, I know,
It will burst aflame as her anger rises.
Deep in passion and unrelenting,
What will she do now, stung with insult?

MEDEA [*indoors*]:

Do I not suffer? Am I not wronged? Should I not weep?
Children, your mother is hated, and you are cursed: 100
Death take you, with your father, and perish his whole house!

NURSE:

Oh, the pity of it! Poor Medea!
Your children—why, what have *they* to do
With their father's wickedness? Why hate *them?*
I am sick with fear for you, children, terror
Of what may happen. The mind of a queen
Is a thing to fear. A queen is used
To giving commands, not obeying them;
And her rage once roused is hard to appease.

To have learnt to live on the common level 110
Is better. No grand life for me,
Just peace and quiet as I grow old.
The middle way, neither great nor mean,
Is best by far, in name and practice.
To be rich and powerful brings no blessing;
Only more utterly
Is the prosperous house destroyed, when the gods are angry.

[*Enter the* CHORUS *of Corinthian women.*]

CHORUS:

I heard her voice, I heard
That unhappy woman from Colchis
Still crying, not calm yet. 120
Old Nurse, tell us about her.
As I stood by the door I heard her
Crying inside the palace.
And my own heart suffers too
When Jason's house is suffering;
For that is where my loyalty lies.

NURSE:

Jason's house? It no longer exists; all that is finished.
Jason is a prisoner in a princess's bed;

And Medea is in her room
Melting her life away in tears; 130
No word from any friend can give her comfort.

MEDEA [*still from indoors*]:

Come, flame of the sky,
Pierce through my head!
What do I gain from living any longer?
Oh, how I hate living! I want
To end my life, leave it behind, and die.

CHORUS:

O Zeus, and Earth, and Light,
Do you hear the chanted prayer
Of a wife in her anguish?

[*turning to the door and addressing* MEDEA]

What madness is this? The bed you long for— 140
Is it what others shrink from?
Is it death you demand?
Do not pray that prayer, Medea!
If your husband is won to a new love—
The thing is common; why let it anger you?
Zeus will plead your cause.
Check this passionate grief over your husband
Which wastes you away.

MEDEA:

Mighty Themis! Dread Artemis![2]
Do you see how I am used— 150
In spite of those great oaths I bound him with—
By my accursed husband?
Oh, may I see Jason and his bride
Ground to pieces in their shattered palace
For the wrong they have dared to do to me, unprovoked!
O my father, my city, you I deserted;
My brother I shamefully murdered!

NURSE:

Do you hear what my mistress is saying,
Clamouring to Themis, hearer of prayer,
And to Zeus, who is named guardian of men's oaths? 160
It is no trifling matter
That can end a rage like hers.

CHORUS:

I wish she would come out here and let us see her
And talk to her; if she would listen
Perhaps she would drop this fierce resentful spirit,
This passionate indignation.
As a friend I am anxious to do whatever I can.
Go, nurse, persuade her to come out to us.
Tell her we are all on her side.
Hurry, before she does harm—to those in there; 170
This passion of hers is an irresistible flood.

---

[2]Themis is a goddess of justice. Artemis is the goddess of wild animals, hunting, and childbirth.

NURSE:

I will. I fear I shall not persuade her;
Still, I am glad to do my best.
Yet as soon as any of us servants
Goes near to her, or tries to speak,
She glares at us like a mad bull
Or a lioness guarding her cubs.

[*The* NURSE *goes to the door, where she turns.*]

The men of old times had little sense;
If you called them fools you wouldn't be far wrong.
They invented songs, and all the sweetness of music, 180
To perform at feasts, banquets, and celebrations;
But no one thought of using
Songs and stringed instruments
To banish the bitterness and pain of life.
Sorrow is the real cause
Of deaths and disasters and families destroyed.
If music could cure sorrow it would be precious;
But after a good dinner why sing songs?
When people have fed full they're happy already.

[*The* NURSE *goes in.*]

CHORUS:

I heard her sobbing and wailing, 190
Shouting shrill, pitiful accusations
Against her husband who has betrayed her.
She invokes Themis, daughter of Zeus,
Who witnessed those promises which drew her
Across from Asia to Hellas, setting sail at night,
Threading the salt strait,
Key and barrier to the Pontic Sea.

[MEDEA *comes out. She is not shaken with weeping, but cool and self-possessed.*]

MEDEA:

Women of Corinth, I would not have you censure me,
So I have come. Many, I know, are proud at heart,
Indoors or out; but others are ill spoken of 200
As supercilious, just because their ways are quiet.
There is no justice in the world's censorious eyes.
They will not wait to learn a man's true character;
Though no wrong has been done them, one look—and they hate.
Of course a stranger must conform; even a Greek
Should not annoy his fellows by crass stubbornness.
I accept my place; but this blow that has fallen on me
Was not to be expected. It has crushed my heart.
Life has no pleasure left, dear friends. I want to die.
Jason was my whole life; he knows that well. Now he 210
Has proved himself the most contemptible of men.

Surely, of all creatures that have life and will, we women
Are the most wretched. When, for an extravagant sum,
We have bought a husband, we must then accept him as
Possessor of our body. This is to aggravate
Wrong with worse wrong. Then the great question: will the man

We get be bad or good? For women, divorce is not
Respectable; to repel the man, not possible.

Still more, a foreign woman, coming among new laws,
New customs, needs the skill of magic, to find out 220
What her home could not teach her, how to treat the man
Whose bed she shares. And if in this exacting toil
We are successful, and our husband does not struggle
Under the marriage yoke, our life is enviable.
Otherwise, death is better. If a man grows tired
Of the company at home, he can go out, and find
A cure for tediousness. We wives are forced to look
To one man only. And, they tell us, we at home
Live free from danger, they go out to battle: fools!
I'd rather stand three times in the front line than bear 230
One child.
But the same arguments do not apply
To you and me. You have this city, your father's home,
The enjoyment of your life, and your friends' company.
I am alone; I have no city; now my husband
Insults me. I was taken as plunder from a land
At the earth's edge. I have no mother, brother, nor any
Of my own blood to turn to in this extremity.

So, I make one request. If I can find a way
To work revenge on Jason for his wrongs to me,
Say nothing. A woman's weak and timid in most matters; 240
The noise of war, the look of steel, makes her a coward.
But touch her right in marriage, and there's no bloodier spirit.

CHORUS:
I'll do as you ask. To punish Jason will be just.
I do not wonder that you take such wrongs to heart.
[CREON *approaches*.]
But look, Medea; I see Creon, King of Corinth;
He must have come to tell you of some new decision.

CREON:
You there, Medea, scowling rage against your husband!
I order you out of Corinth; take your sons and go
Into exile. Waste no time; I'm here to see this order
Enforced. And I'm not going back into my palace 250
Until I've put you safe outside my boundaries.

MEDEA:
Oh! this is the cruel end of my accursed life!
My enemies have spread full sail; no welcoming shore
Waits to receive and save me. Ill-treated as I am,
Creon, I ask: for what offence do you banish me?

CREON:
I fear you. Why wrap up the truth? I fear that you
May do my daughter some irreparable harm.
A number of things contribute to my anxiety.
You're a clever woman, skilled in many evil arts;
You're barred from Jason's bed, and that enrages you. 260
I learn too from reports, that you have uttered threats

Of revenge on Jason and his bride and his bride's father.
I'll act first, then, in self-defence. I'd rather make you
My enemy now, than weaken, and later pay with tears.

MEDEA:

My reputation, yet again! Many times, Creon,
It has been my curse and ruin. A man of any shrewdness
Should never have his children taught to use their brains
More than their fellows. What do you gain by being clever?
You neglect your own affairs; and all your fellow citizens
Hate you. Those who are fools will call you ignorant 270
And useless, when you offer them unfamiliar knowledge.
As for those thought intelligent, if people rank
You above *them,* that is a thing they will not stand.
I know this from experience: because I am clever,
They are jealous; while the rest dislike me. After all,
I am not so clever as all that.

So you, Creon,
Are afraid—of what? Some harm that I might do to you?
Don't let *me* alarm you, Creon. I'm in no position—
A woman—to wrong a king. You have done me no wrong.
You've given your daughter to the man you chose. I hate 280
My husband—true; but you had every right to do
As you have done. So now I bear no grudge against
Your happiness: marry your daughter to him, and good luck
To you both. But let me live in Corinth. I will bear
My wrongs in silence, yielding to superior strength.

CREON:

Your words are gentle; but my blood runs cold to think
What plots you may be nursing deep within your heart.
In fact, I trust you so much less now than before.
A woman of hot temper—and a man the same—
Is a less dangerous enemy than one quiet and clever. 290
So out you go, and quickly; no more arguing.
I've made my mind up; you're my enemy. No craft
Of yours will find a way of staying in my city.

MEDEA:

I kneel to you, I beseech you by the young bride, your child.

CREON:

You're wasting words; you'll never make me change my mind.

MEDEA:

I beg you! Will you cast off pity, and banish me?

CREON:

I will: I have more love for my family than for you.

MEDEA:

My home, my country! How my thoughts turn to you now!

CREON:

I love my country too—next only to my daughter.

MEDEA:

Oh, what an evil power love has in people's lives! 300

CREON:

That would depend on circumstances, I imagine.

MEDEA:

Great Zeus, remember who caused all this suffering!

CREON:

Go, you poor wretch, take all my troubles with you! Go!

MEDEA:

I know what trouble is; I have no need of more.

CREON:

In a moment you'll be thrown out neck and crop. Here, men!

MEDEA:

No, no, not that! But, Creon, I have one thing to ask.

CREON:

You seem inclined, Medea, to give me trouble still.

MEDEA:

I'll go. [*She still clings to him.*] It was not *that* I begged.

CREON:

Then why resist?

Why will you not get out?

MEDEA:

This one day let me stay,
To settle some plan for my exile, make provision 310
For my two sons, since their own father is not concerned
To help them. Show some pity: you are a father too,
You should feel kindly towards them. For myself, exile
Is nothing. I weep for them; their fate is very hard.

CREON:

I'm no tyrant by nature. My soft heart has often
Betrayed me; and I know it's foolish of me now;
Yet none the less, Medea, you shall have what you ask.
But take this warning: if tomorrow's holy sun
Finds you or them inside my boundaries, you die.
That is my solemn word. Now stay here, if you must, 320
This one day. You can hardly in one day accomplish
What I am afraid of.

[*Exit* CREON.]

CHORUS:

Medea, poor Medea!
Your grief touches our hearts.
A wanderer, where can you turn?
To what welcoming house?
To what protecting land?
How wild with dread and danger
Is the sea where the gods have set your course!

MEDEA:

A bad predicament all round—yes, true enough; 330
But don't imagine things will end as they are now.
Trials are yet to come for this new-wedded pair;
Nor shall those nearest to them get off easily.

Do you think I would ever have fawned so on this man,
Except to gain my purpose, carry out my schemes?
Not one touch, not one word: yet he—oh, what a fool!
By banishing me at once he could have thwarted me
Utterly; instead, he allows me to remain one day.
Today three of my enemies I shall strike dead:
Father and daughter, and *my* husband. 340

I have in mind so many paths of death for them,
I don't know which to choose. Should I set fire to the house,
And burn the bridal chamber? Or creep up to their bed
And drive a sharp knife through their guts? There is one fear:
If I am caught entering the house, or in the act,
I die, and the last laugh goes to my enemies.
The best is the direct way, which most suits my bent:
To kill by poison.

So—say they are dead: what city will receive me then?
What friend will guarantee my safety, offer land 350
And home as sanctuary? None. I'll wait a little.
If some strong tower of help appears, I'll carry out
This murder cunningly and quietly. But if Fate
Banishes me without resource, I will myself
Take sword in hand, harden my heart to the uttermost,
And kill them both, even if I am to die for it.

For, by Queen Hecate,[3] whom above all divinities
I venerate, my chosen accomplice, to whose presence
My central hearth is dedicated, no one of them
Shall hurt me and not suffer for it! Let me work: 360
In bitterness and pain they shall repent this marriage,
Repent their houses joined, repent my banishment.

Come! Lay your plan, Medea; scheme with all your skill.
On to the deadly moment that shall test your nerve!
You see now where you stand. Your father was a king,
His father was the Sun-god: you must not invite
Laughter from Jason and his new allies, the tribe
Of Sisyphus.[4] You know what you must do. Besides—

[*She turns to the* CHORUS.]

We were born women—useless for honest purposes,
But in all kinds of evil skilled practitioners. 370

CHORUS:

Streams of the sacred rivers flow uphill;
Tradition, order, all things are reversed:
Deceit is *men's* device now,
Men's oaths are gods' dishonour.
Legend will now reverse our reputation;
A time comes when the female sex is honoured;
That old discordant slander
Shall no more hold us subject.
Male poets of past ages, with their ballads
Of faithless women, shall go out of fashion; 380
For Phoebus, Prince of Music,
Never bestowed the lyric inspiration

[3]A powerful moon goddess, associated with the female trinity of maiden, mother, and childbirth.
[4]Sisyphus was an earlier king of Corinth, an ancestor of Creon.

Through female understanding—
Or we'd find themes for poems,
We'd counter with our epics against man.
Oh, Time is old; and in his store of tales
Men figure no less famous
Or infamous than women.

So you, Medea, wild with love,
Set sail from your father's house, 390
Threading the Rocky Jaws of the eastern sea;
And here, living in a strange country,
Your marriage lost, your bed solitary,
You are driven beyond the borders,
An exile with no redress.
The grace of sworn oaths is gone;
Honour remains no more
In the wide Greek world, but is flown to the sky.
Where can you turn for shelter?
Your father's door is closed against you; 400
Another is now mistress of your husband's bed;
A new queen rules in your house.

[*Enter* JASON.]

JASON:

I have often noticed—this is not the first occasion—
What fatal results follow from ungoverned rage.
You could have stayed in Corinth, still lived in this house,
If you had quietly accepted the decisions
Of those in power. Instead, you talked like a fool; and now
You are banished. Well, your angry words don't upset *me;*
Go on as long as you like reciting Jason's crimes.
But after your abuse of the King and the princess 410
Think yourself lucky to be let off with banishment.
I have tried all the time to calm them down; but you
Would not give up your ridiculous tirades against
The royal family. So, you're banished. However, I
Will not desert a friend. I have carefully considered
Your problem, and come now, in spite of everything,
To see that you and the children are not sent away
With an empty purse, or unprovided. Exile brings
With it a train of difficulties. You no doubt
Hate me: but I could never bear ill-will to you. 420

MEDEA:

You filthy coward!—if I knew any worse name
For such unmanliness I'd use it—so, you've come!
You, my worst enemy, come to me! Oh, it's not courage,
This looking friends in the face after betraying them.
It is not even audacity; it's a disease,
The worst a man can have, pure shamelessness. However,
It is as well you came; to say what I have to say
Will ease my heart; to hear it said will make you wince.

I will begin at the beginning. When you were sent
To master the fire-breathing bulls, yoke them, and sow 430

The deadly furrow, then I saved your life; and that
Every Greek who sailed with you in the Argo knows.
The serpent that kept watch over the Golden Fleece,
Coiled round it fold on fold, unsleeping—it was I
Who killed it, and so lit the torch of your success.[5]
I willingly deceived my father; left my home;
With you I came to Iolcus by Mount Pelion,
Showing much love and little wisdom. There I put
King Pelias to the most horrible of deaths
By his own daughters' hands, and ruined his whole house. 440
And in return for this you have the wickedness
To turn me out, to get yourself another wife,
Even after I had borne you sons! If you had still
Been childless I could have pardoned you for hankering
After this new marriage. But respect for oaths has gone
To the wind. Do you, I wonder, think that the old gods
No longer rule? Or that new laws are now in force?
You must know you are guilty of perjury to me.

My poor right hand, which you so often clasped! My knees
Which you then clung to! How we are besmirched and mocked 450
By this man's broken vows, and all our hopes deceived!

Come, I'll ask your advice as if you were a friend.
Not that I hope for any help from you; but still,
I'll ask you, and expose your infamy. Where now
Can I turn? Back to my country and my father's house,
Which I betrayed to come with you? Or to Iolcus,
To Pelias's wretched daughters? What a welcome they
Would offer me, who killed their father! Thus it stands:
My friends at home now hate me; and in helping you
I have earned the enmity of those I had no right 460
To hurt. For my reward, you have made me the envy
Of Hellene women everywhere! A marvellous
Husband I have, and faithful too, in the name of pity;
When I'm banished, thrown out of the country without a friend,
Alone with my forlorn waifs. Yes, a shining shame
It will be to you, the new-made bridegroom, that your own sons,
And I who saved your life, are begging beside the road!

O Zeus! Why have you given us clear signs to tell
True gold from counterfeit; but when we need to know
Bad *men* from good, the flesh bears no revealing mark? 470

CHORUS:
The fiercest anger of all, the most incurable,
Is that which rages in the place of dearest love.

JASON:
I have to show myself a clever speaker, it seems.
This hurricane of recrimination and abuse

[5]Medea used her magic to assist Jason in his quest for the golden fleece.

Calls for good seamanship: I'll furl all but an inch
Of sail, and ride it out. To begin with, since you build
To such a height your services to me, I hold
That credit for my successful voyage was solely due
To Aphrodite, no one else divine or human.
I admit, you have intelligence; but, to recount 480
How helpless passion drove you then to save my life
Would be invidious; and I will not stress the point.
Your services, so far as they went, were well enough;
But in return for saving me you got far more
Than you gave. Allow me, in the first place, to point out
That you left a barbarous land to become a resident
Of Hellas; here you have known justice; you have lived
In a society where force yields place to law.
Moreover, here your gifts are widely recognized,
You are famous; if you still lived at the ends of the earth 490
Your name would never be spoken. Personally, unless
Life brings me fame, I long neither for hoards of gold,
Nor for a voice sweeter than Orpheus![6] Well, *you* began
The argument about my voyage; and that's my answer.

As for your scurrilous taunts against my marriage with
The royal family, I shall show you that my action
Was wise, not swayed by passion, and directed towards
Your interests and my children's.—No, keep quiet! When I
Came here from Iolcus as a stateless exile, dogged
And thwarted by misfortunes—why, what luckier chance 500
Could I have met, than marriage with the King's daughter?
It was not, as you resentfully assume, that I
Found your attractions wearisome, and was smitten with
Desire for a new wife; nor did I specially want
To raise a numerous family—the sons we have
Are enough, I'm satisfied; but I wanted to ensure
First—and the most important—that we should live well
And not be poor; I know how a poor man is shunned
By all his friends. Next, that I could bring up my sons
In a manner worthy of my descent; have other sons, 510
Perhaps, as brothers to your children; give them all
An equal place, and so build up a closely-knit
And prosperous family. *You* need no more children, do you?
While *I* thought it worth while to ensure advantages
For those I have, by means of those I hope to have.

Was such a plan, then, wicked? Even you would approve
If you could govern your sex-jealousy. But you women
Have reached a state where, if all's well with your sex-life,
You've everything you wish for; but when *that* goes wrong,
At once all that is best and noblest turns to gall. 520

---

[6]Orpheus was a legendary musician; his playing gained him entrance into the underworld. See Ovid's *Metamorphoses*, Book 10.

If only children could be got some other way,
Without the female sex! If women didn't exist,
Human life would be rid of all its miseries.

CHORUS:
Jason, you have set your case forth very plausibly.
But to my mind—though you may be surprised at this—
You are acting wrongly in thus abandoning your wife.

MEDEA:
No doubt I differ from many people in many ways.
To me, a wicked man who is also eloquent
Seems the most guilty of them all. He'll cut your throat
As bold as brass, because he knows he can dress up murder 530
In handsome words. He's not so clever after all.
You dare outface me now with glib high-mindedness!
One word will throw you: if you were honest, you ought first
To have won me over, not got married behind my back.

JASON:
No doubt, if I had mentioned it, you would have proved
Most helpful. Why, even now you will not bring yourself
To calm this raging temper.

MEDEA:
That was not the point;
But you're an ageing man, and an Asiatic wife
Was no longer respectable.

JASON:
Understand this:
It's not for the sake of any woman that I have made 540
This royal marriage, but, as I've already said,
To ensure your future, and to give my children brothers
Of royal blood, and build security for us all.

MEDEA:
I loathe your prosperous future; I'll have none of it,
Nor none of your security—it galls my heart.

JASON:
You know—you'll change your mind and be more sensible.
You'll soon stop thinking good is bad, and striking these
Pathetic poses when in fact you're fortunate.

MEDEA:
Go on, insult me: you have a roof over your head.
I am alone, an exile.

JASON:
It was your own choice. 550
Blame no one but yourself.

MEDEA:
My choice? What did I do?
Did I make you my wife and then abandon you?

JASON:
You called down wicked curses on the King and his house.

MEDEA:
I did. On your house too Fate sends me as a curse.

JASON:
I'll not pursue this further. If there's anything else
I can provide to meet the children's needs or yours,

Tell me; I'll gladly give whatever you want, or send
Letters of introduction, if you like, to friends
Who will help you.—Listen: to refuse such help is mad.
You've everything to gain if you give up this rage. 560

MEDEA:
Nothing would induce me to have dealings with your friends,
Nor to take any gift of yours; so offer none.
A lying traitor's gifts carry no luck.

JASON:
Very well.
I call the gods to witness that I have done my best
To help you and the children. You make no response
To kindness; friendly overtures you obstinately
Reject. So much the worse for you.

MEDEA:
Go! You have spent
Too long out here. You are consumed with craving for
Your newly-won bride. Go, enjoy her!

[*Exit* JASON.]

It may be—
And God uphold my words—that this your marriage-day 570
Will end with marriage lost, loathing and horror left.

CHORUS:
Visitations of love that come
Raging and violent on a man
Bring him neither good repute nor goodness.
But if Aphrodite descends in gentleness
No other goddess brings such delight.
Never, Queen Aphrodite,
Loose against me from your golden bow,
Dipped in sweetness of desire,
Your inescapable arrow! 580

Let Innocence, the gods' loveliest gift,
Choose me for her own;
Never may the dread Cyprian[7]
Craze my heart to leave old love for new,
Sending to assault me
Angry disputes and feuds unending;
But let her judge shrewdly the loves of women
And respect the bed where no war rages.

O my country, my home!
May the gods save me from becoming 590
A stateless refugee
Dragging out an intolerable life
In desperate helplessness!
That is the most pitiful of all griefs;

---

[7]One of Aphrodite's titles was "Cyprian" because Cyprus was a major center for her worship.

Death is better. Should such a day come to me
I pray for death first.
Of all pains and hardships none is worse
Than to be deprived of your native land.

This is no mere reflection derived from hearsay;
It is something we have seen. 600
You, Medea, have suffered the most shattering of blows;
Yet neither the city of Corinth
Nor any friend has taken pity on you.
May dishonour and ruin fall on the man
Who, having unlocked the secrets
Of a friend's frank heart, can then disown him!
He shall be no friend of mine.

[*Enter* AEGEUS.]

AEGEUS:
All happiness to you, Medea! Between old friends
There is no better greeting.

MEDEA:
All happiness to you,
Aegeus, son of Pandion the wise! Where have you come from? 610

AEGEUS:
From Delphi, from the ancient oracle of Apollo.

MEDEA:
The centre of the earth, the home of prophecy:
Why did you go?

AEGEUS:
To ask for children; that my seed
May become fertile.

MEDEA:
Why, have you lived so many years
Childless?

AEGEUS:
Childless I am; so some fate has ordained.

MEDEA:
You have a wife, or not?

AEGEUS:
I am married.

MEDEA:
And what answer
Did Phoebus give you about children?

AEGEUS:
His answer was
Too subtle for me or any human interpreter.

MEDEA:
Is it lawful for me to hear it?

AEGEUS:
Certainly; a brain
Like yours is what is needed.

MEDEA:
Tell me, since you may. 620

AEGEUS:
He commanded me 'not to unstop the wineskin's neck'—

MEDEA:
Yes—until when?
AEGEUS:
Until I came safe home again.
MEDEA:
I see. And for what purpose have you sailed to Corinth?
AEGEUS:
You know the King of Troezen, Pittheus, son of Pelops?
MEDEA:
Yes, a most pious man.
AEGEUS:
I want to ask his advice
About this oracle.
MEDEA:
He is an expert in such matters.
AEGEUS:
Yes, and my closest friend. We went to the wars together.
MEDEA:
I hope you will get all you long for, and be happy.
AEGEUS:
But you are looking pale and wasted: what is the matter?
MEDEA:
Aegeus, my husband's the most evil man alive. 630
AEGEUS:
Why, what's this? Tell me all about your unhappiness.
MEDEA:
Jason has betrayed me, though I never did him wrong.
AEGEUS:
What has he done? Explain exactly.
MEDEA:
He has taken
Another wife, and made her mistress of *my* house.
AEGEUS:
But such a thing is shameful! He has never dared—
MEDEA:
It is so. Once he loved me; now I am disowned.
AEGEUS:
Was he tired of you? Or did he fall in love elsewhere?
MEDEA:
Oh, passionately. He's not a man his friends can trust.
AEGEUS:
Well, if—as you say—he's a bad lot, let him go.
MEDEA:
It's royalty and power he's fallen in love with.
AEGEUS:
What? 640
Go on. Who's the girl's father?
MEDEA:
Creon, King of Corinth.
AEGEUS:
I see. Then you have every reason to be upset.

MEDEA:
It is the end of everything! What's more, I'm banished.

AEGEUS:
Worse still—extraordinary! Why, who has banished you?

MEDEA:
Creon has banished me from Corinth.

AEGEUS:
And does Jason
Accept this? How disgraceful!

MEDEA:
Oh, no! He protests.
But he's resolved to bear it bravely.—Aegeus, see,
I touch your beard as a suppliant, embrace your knees,
Imploring you to have pity on my wretchedness.
Have pity! I am an exile; let me not be friendless. 650
Receive me in Athens; give me a welcome in your house.
So may the gods grant you fertility, and bring
Your life to a happy close. You have not realized
What good luck chance has brought you. I know certain drugs
Whose power will put an end to your sterility.
I promise you shall beget children.

AEGEUS:
I am anxious,
For many reasons, to help you in this way, Medea;
First, for the gods' sake, then this hope you've given me
Of children—for I've quite despaired of my own powers.
This then is what I'll do: once you can get to Athens 660
I'll keep my promise and protect you all I can.
But I must make this clear first: I do not intend
To take you with me away from Corinth. If you come
Yourself to Athens, you shall have sanctuary there;
I will not give you up to anyone. But first
Get clear of Corinth without help; the Corinthians too
Are friends of mine, and I don't wish to give offence.

MEDEA:
So be it. Now confirm your promise with an oath,
And all is well between us.

AEGEUS:
Why? Do you not trust me?
What troubles you?

MEDEA:
I trust you; but I have enemies— 670
Not only Creon, but the house of Pelias.
Once you are bound by oaths you will not give me up
If they should try to take me out of your territory.
But if your promise is verbal, and not sworn to the gods,
Perhaps you will make friends with them, and agree to do
What they demand. I've no power on my side, while they
Have wealth and all the resources of a royal house.

AEGEUS:
Your forethought is remarkable; but since you wish it
I've no objection. In fact, the taking of an oath

Safeguards me; since I can confront your enemies 680
With a clear excuse; while *you* have full security.
So name your gods.

MEDEA:
Swear by the Earth under your feet,
By the Sun, my father's father, and the whole race of gods.

AEGEUS:
Tell me what I shall swear to do or not to do.

MEDEA:
Never yourself to expel me from your territory;
And, if my enemies want to take me away, never
Willingly, while you live, to give me up to them.

AEGEUS:
I swear by Earth, and by the burning light of the Sun,
And all the gods, to keep the words you have just spoken.

MEDEA:
I am satisfied. And if you break your oath, what then? 690

AEGEUS:
Then may the gods do to me as to all guilty men.

MEDEA:
Go now, and joy be with you. Everything is well.
I'll reach your city as quickly as I can, when I
Have carried out my purpose and achieved my wish.
[AEGEUS *clasps her hand and hurries off.*]

CHORUS:
May Hermes, protector of travellers, bring you
Safe to your home, Aegeus; may you accomplish
All that you so earnestly desire;
For your noble heart wins our goodwill.

MEDEA:
O Zeus! O Justice, daughter of Zeus! O glorious Sun!
Now I am on the road to victory; now there's hope! 700
I shall see my enemies punished as they deserve.
Just where my plot was weakest, at that very point
Help has appeared in this man Aegeus; he is a haven
Where I shall find safe mooring, once I reach the walls
Of the city of Athens. Now I'll tell you all my plans:
They'll not make pleasant hearing.
[*Medea's* NURSE *has entered; she listens in silence.*]
First I'll send a slave
To Jason, asking him to come to me; and then
I'll give him soft talk; tell him he has acted well,
Tell him I think this royal marriage which he has bought
With my betrayal is for the best and wisely planned. 710
But I shall beg that my children be allowed to stay.
Not that I would think of leaving sons of mine behind
On enemy soil for those who hate me to insult;
But in my plot to kill the princess they must help.
I'll send them to the palace bearing gifts, a dress
Of soft weave and a coronet of beaten gold.
If she takes and puts on this finery, both she

And all who touch her will expire in agony;
With such a deadly poison I'll anoint my gifts.

However, enough of that. What makes me cry with pain — 720
Is the next thing I have to do. I will kill my sons.
No one shall take my children from me. When I have made
Jason's whole house a shambles,[8] I will leave Corinth
A murderess, flying from my darling children's blood.
Yes, I can endure guilt, however horrible;
The laughter of my enemies I will not endure.

Now let things take their course. What use is life to me?
I have no land, no home, no refuge from despair.
My folly was committed long ago, when I
Was ready to desert my father's house, won over — 730
By eloquence from a Greek, whom with God's help I now
Will punish. He shall never see alive again
The sons he had from me. From his new bride he never
Shall breed a son; she by my poison, wretched girl,
Must die a hideous death. Let no one think of me
As humble or weak or passive; let them understand
I am of a different kind: dangerous to my enemies,
Loyal to my friends. To such a life glory belongs.

CHORUS:
Since you have told us everything, and since I want
To be your friend, and also to uphold the laws — 740
Of human life—I tell you, you must not do this!

MEDEA:
No other thing is possible. You have excuse
For speaking so: you have not been treated as I have.

CHORUS:
But—to kill your own children! Can you steel your heart?

MEDEA:
This is the way to deal Jason the deepest wound.

CHORUS:
This way will bring you too the deepest misery.

MEDEA:
Let be. Until it is done words are unnecessary.
Nurse! You are the one I use for messages of trust.
Go and bring Jason here. As you're a loyal servant,
And a woman, breathe no word about my purposes. — 750

[*Exit* NURSE.]

CHORUS:
The people of Athens, sons of Erechtheus, have enjoyed their prosperity
Since ancient times. Children of blessed gods,
They grew from holy soil unscorched by invasion.
Among the glories of knowledge their souls are pastured;
They walk always with grace under the sparkling sky.

---

[8] A slaughterhouse.

There long ago, they say, was born golden-haired Harmony,
Created by the nine virgin Muses[9] of Pieria.

They say that Aphrodite dips her cup
In the clear stream of the lovely Cephisus;[10]
It is she who breathes over the land the breath 760
Of gentle honey-laden winds; her flowing locks
She crowns with a diadem of sweet-scented roses,
And sends the Loves to be enthroned beside Knowledge,
And with her to create excellence in every art.

Then how will such a city,
Watered by sacred rivers,
A country giving protection to its friends—
How will Athens welcome
You, the child-killer
Whose presence is pollution? 770
Contemplate the blow struck at a child,
Weigh the blood you take upon you.
Medea, by your knees,
By every pledge or appeal we beseech you,
Do not slaughter your children!

Where will you find hardness of purpose?
How will you build resolution in hand or heart
To face horror without flinching?
When the moment comes, and you look at them—
The moment for you to assume the role of murderess— 780
How will you do it?
When your sons kneel to you for pity,
Will you stain your fingers with their blood?
Your heart will melt; you will know you cannot.

[*Enter* JASON *from the palace. Two maids come from the house to attend* MEDEA.]

JASON:

You sent for me: I have come. Although you hate me, I
Am ready to listen. You have some new request; what is it?

MEDEA:

Jason, I ask you to forgive the things I said.
You must bear with my violent temper; you and I
Share many memories of love. I have been taking
Myself to task. 'You are a fool,' I've told myself, 790
'You're mad, when people try to plan things for the best,
To be resentful, and pick quarrels with the King
And with your husband; what he's doing will help us all.
His wife is royal; her sons will be my sons' brothers.
Why not throw off your anger? What is the matter, since
The gods are making kind provision? After all

---

[9] The nine divine muses were associated with the various arts; Pieria is a region of Mount Olympus.
[10] A river that flows into the Saronic Gulf near Athens.

I have two children still to care for; and I know
We came as exiles, and our friends are few enough.'
When I considered this, I saw my foolishness;
I saw how useless anger was. So now I welcome 800
What you have done; I think you are wise to gain for us
This new alliance, and the folly was all mine.
I should have helped you in your plans, made it my pleasure
To get ready your marriage-bed, attend your bride.
But we women—I won't say we are bad by nature,
But we are what we are. You, Jason, should not copy
Our bad example, or match yourself with us, showing
Folly for folly. I give in; I was wrong just now,
I admit. But I have thought more wisely of it since.
Children, children! Are you indoors? Come out here.

[*The* CHILDREN *come out. Their* TUTOR *follows.*]

Children, 810

Greet your father, as I do, and put your arms round him.
Forget our quarrel, and love him as your mother does.
We have made friends; we are not angry any more.
There, children; take his hand.

[*She turns away in a sudden flood of weeping.*]

Forgive me; I recalled

What pain the future hides from us.

[*After embracing* JASON *the* CHILDREN *go back to* MEDEA.]

Oh children! Will you

All your lives long, stretch out your hands to me like this?
Oh, my tormented heart is full of tears and terrors.
After so long, I have ended my quarrel with your father;
And now, see! I have drenched this young face with my tears.

CHORUS:

I too feel fresh tears fill my eyes. May the course of evil 820
Be checked now, go no further!

JASON:

I am pleased, Medea,

That you have changed your mind; though indeed I do not blame
Your first resentment. Only naturally a woman
Is angry when her husband marries a second wife.
You have had wiser thoughts; and though it has taken time,
You have recognized the right decision. This is the act
Of a sensible woman. As for you, my boys, your father
Has taken careful thought, and, with the help of the gods,
Ensured a good life for you. Why, in time, I'm sure,
You with your brothers will be leading men in Corinth. 830
Only grow big and strong. Your father, and those gods
Who are his friends, have all the rest under control.
I want to see you, when you're strong, full-grown young men,
Tread down my enemies.

[*Again* MEDEA *breaks down and weeps.*]

What's this? Why these floods of tears?

Why are you pale? Did you not like what I was saying?
Why do you turn away?

MEDEA:

It is nothing. I was thinking
About these children.

JASON:

I'll provide for them. Cheer up.

MEDEA:

I will. It is not that I mean to doubt your word.
But women—are women; tears come naturally to us.

JASON:

Why do you grieve so over the children?

MEDEA:

I'm their mother. 840
When you just now prayed for them to live long, I wondered
Whether it would be so; and grief came over me.
But I've said only part of what I had to say;
Here is the other thing. Since Creon has resolved
To send me out of Corinth, I fully recognize
That for me too this course is best. If I lived here
I should become a trouble both to you and him.
People believe I bear a grudge against you all.
So I must go. But the boys—I would like *them* to be
Brought up in your care. Beg Creon to let them stay. 850

JASON:

I don't know if I can persuade him; but I'll try.

MEDEA:

Then—get your wife to ask her father to let them stay.

JASON:

Why, certainly; I'm pretty sure she'll win him over.

MEDEA:

She will, if she's like other women. But I too
Can help in this. I'll send a present to your wife—
The loveliest things to be found anywhere on earth.
The boys shall take them.—One of you maids, go quickly, bring
The dress and golden coronet.—They will multiply
Her happiness many times, when she can call her own
A royal, noble husband, and these treasures, which 860
My father's father the Sun bequeathed to his descendants.

[*A slave has brought a casket, which* MEDEA *now hands to her sons.*]

Boys, hold these gifts. Now carry them to the happy bride,
The princess royal; give them into her own hands.
Go! She will find them all that such a gift should be.

JASON:

But why deprive yourself of such things, foolish woman?
Do you think a royal palace is in want of dresses?
Or gold, do you suppose? Keep them, don't give them away.
If my wife values me at all she will yield to *me*
More than to costly presents, I am sure of that.

MEDEA:

Don't stop me. Gifts, they say, persuade even the gods; 870
With mortals, gold outweighs a thousand arguments.
The day is hers; from now on *her* prosperity
Will rise to new heights. She is royal and young. To buy

My sons from exile I would give life, not just gold.
Come, children, go both of you into this rich palace;
Kneel down and beg your father's new wife, and my mistress,
That you may not be banished. And above all, see
That she receives my present into her own hands.
Go quickly; be successful, and bring good news back,
That what your mother longs for has been granted you. 880

[*Exit* JASON *followed by the* CHILDREN *and the* TUTOR.]

CHORUS:

Now I have no more hope,
No more hope that the children can live;
They are walking to murder at this moment.
The bride will receive the golden coronet,
Receive her merciless destroyer;
With her own hands she will carefully fit
The adornment of death round her golden hair.

She cannot resist such loveliness, such heavenly gleaming;
She will enfold herself
In the dress and the wreath of wrought gold, 890
Preparing her bridal beauty
To enter a new home—among the dead.
So fatal is the snare she will fall into,
So inevitable the death that awaits her;
From its cruelty there is no escape.

And you, unhappy Jason, ill-starred in marriage,
You, son-in-law of kings:
Little you know that the favour you ask
Will seal your sons' destruction
And fasten on your wife a hideous fate. 900
O wretched Jason!
So sure of destiny, and so ignorant!

Your sorrow next I weep for, pitiable mother;
You, for jealousy of your marriage-bed,
Will slaughter your children;
Since, disregarding right and loyalty,
Your husband has abandoned you
And lives with another wife.

[*The* TUTOR *returns from the palace with the two* CHILDREN.]

TUTOR:

Mistress! These two boys are reprieved from banishment.
The princess took your gifts from them with her own hand, 910
And was delighted. They have no enemies in the palace.

[MEDEA *is silent.*]

Well, bless my soul!
Isn't that good news? Why do you stand there thunderstruck?

MEDEA [*to herself*]:

How cruel, how cruel!

TUTOR:

That's out of tune with the news I brought.

MEDEA:
How cruel life is!

TUTOR:
Have I, without knowing it,
Told something dreadful, then? I thought my news was good.

MEDEA:
Your news is what it is. I am not blaming you.

TUTOR:
Then why stand staring at the ground, with streaming eyes?

MEDEA:
Strong reason forces me to weep, old friend. The gods,
And my own evil-hearted plots, have led to this. 920

TUTOR:
Take heart, mistress; in time your sons will bring you home.

MEDEA:
Before then, I have others to send home.—Oh, gods!
[*She weeps.*]

TUTOR:
You're not the only mother parted from her sons.
We are all mortal; you must not bear grief so hard.

MEDEA:
Yes, friend. I'll follow your advice. Now go indoors
And get things ready for them, as on other days.
[*Exit* TUTOR. *The* CHILDREN *come to* MEDEA.]
O children, children! You have a city, and a home;
And when we have parted, there you both will stay for ever,
You motherless, I miserable. And I must go
To exile in another land, before I have had 930
My joy of you, before I have seen you growing up,
Becoming prosperous. I shall never see your brides,
Adorn your bridal beds, and hold the torches high.
My misery is my own heart, which will not relent.
All was for nothing, then—these years of rearing you,
My care, my aching weariness, and the wild pains
When you were born. Oh, yes, I once built many hopes
On you; imagined, pitifully, that you would care
For my old age, and would yourselves wrap my dead body
For burial. How people would envy me my sons! 940
That sweet, sad thought has faded now. Parted from you,
My life will be all pain and anguish. You will not
Look at your mother any more with these dear eyes.
You will have moved into a different sphere of life.

Dear sons, why are you staring at me so? You smile
At me—your last smile: why?
[*She weeps. The* CHILDREN *go from her a little, and she turns to the* CHORUS.]
Oh, what am I to do?
Women, my courage is all gone. Their young, bright faces—
I can't do it. I'll think no more of it. I'll take them
Away from Corinth. Why should I hurt *them,* to make
Their father suffer, when I shall suffer twice as much 950
Myself? I won't do it. I won't think of it again.
What is the matter with me? Are my enemies

To laugh at me? Am I to let them off scot free?
I must steel myself to it. What a coward I am,
Even tempting my own resolution with soft talk.
Boys, go indoors.

[*The* CHILDREN *go to the door, but stay there watching her.*]

If there is any here who finds it
Not lawful to be present at my sacrifice,
Let him see to it. My hand shall not weaken.

Oh, my heart, don't, don't do it! Oh, miserable heart,
Let them be! Spare your children! We'll all live together 960
Safely in Athens; and they will make you happy. . . . No!
No! No! By all the fiends of hate in hell's depths, no!
I'll not leave sons of mine to be the victims of
My enemies' rage. In any case there is no escape,
The thing's done now. Yes, now—the golden coronet
Is on her head, the royal bride is in her dress,
Dying, I know it. So, since I have a sad road
To travel, and send these boys on a still sadder road,
I'll speak to them. Come, children; give me your hand, dear son;
Yours too. Now we must say goodbye. Oh, darling hand, 970
And darling mouth; your noble, childlike face and body!
Dear sons, my blessing on you both—but there, not here!
All blessing here your father has destroyed. How sweet
To hold you! And children's skin is soft, and their breath pure.
Go! Go away! I can't look at you any longer;
My pain is more than I can bear.

[*The* CHILDREN *go indoors.*]

I understand
The horror of what I am going to do; but anger,
The spring of all life's horror, masters my resolve.

[MEDEA *goes to stand looking towards the palace.*]

CHORUS:

I have often engaged in arguments,
And become more subtle, and perhaps more heated, 980
Than is suitable for women;
Though in fact women too have intelligence,
Which forms part of our nature and instructs us—
Not all of us, I admit; but a certain few
You might perhaps find, in a large number of women—
A few not incapable of reflection;

And this is my opinion: those men or women
Who never had children of their own at all
Enjoy the advantage in good fortune
Over those who are parents. Childless people 990
Have no means of knowing whether children are
A blessing or a burden; but being without them
They live exempt from many troubles.

While those who have growing up in their homes
The sweet gift of children I see always

Burdened and worn with incessant worry,
First, how to rear them in health and safety,
And bequeath them, in time, enough to live on;
And then this further anxiety:
They can never know whether all their toil 1000
Is spent for worthy or worthless children.

And beyond the common ills that attend
All human life there is one still worse:
Suppose at last they are pretty well off,
Their children have grown up, and, what's more,
Are kind and honest: then what happens?
A throw of chance—and there goes Death
Bearing off your child into the unknown.

Then why should mortals thank the gods,
Who add to their load, already grievous, 1010
This one more grief, for their children's sake,
Most grievous of all?

MEDEA:
Friends, I have long been waiting for a message from the palace.
What is to happen next? I see a slave of Jason's
Coming, gasping for breath. He must bring fearful news.
[*Enter a* MESSENGER.]

MESSENGER:
Medea! Get away, escape! Oh, what a thing to do!
What an unholy, horrible thing! Take ship, or chariot,
Any means you can, but escape!

MEDEA:
Why should I escape?

MESSENGER:
She's dead—the princess, and her father Creon too,
They're both dead, by your poisons.

MEDEA:
Your news is excellent. 1020
I count you from today my friend and benefactor.

MESSENGER:
What? Are you sane, or raving mad? When you've committed
This hideous crime against the royal house, you're glad
At hearing of it? Do you not tremble at such things?

MEDEA:
I could make suitable reply to that, my friend.
But take your time now; tell me, how did they die? You'll give
Me double pleasure if their death was horrible.

MESSENGER:
When your two little boys came hand in hand, and entered
The palace with their father, where the wedding was,
We servants were delighted. We had all felt sorry 1030
To hear how you'd been treated; and now the word went round
From one to another, that you and Jason had made it up.
So we were glad to see the boys; one kissed their hand,

Another their fair hair. Myself, I was so pleased,
I followed with them to the princess's room. Our mistress—
The one we now call mistress in your place—before
She saw your pair of boys coming, had eyes only
For Jason; but seeing them she dropped her eyes, and turned
Her lovely cheek away, upset that they should come
Into her room. Your husband then began to soothe 1040
Her sulkiness, her girlish temper. 'You must not,'
He said, 'be unfriendly to our friends. Turn your head round,
And give up feeling angry. Those your husband loves
You must love too. Now take these gifts,' he said, 'and ask
Your father to revoke their exile for my sake.'
So, when she saw those lovely things, she was won over,
And agreed to all that Jason asked. At once, before
He and your sons were well out of the house, she took
The embroidered gown and put it round her. Then she placed
Over her curls the golden coronet, and began 1050
To arrange her hair in a bright mirror, smiling at
Her lifeless form reflected there. Then she stood up,
And to and fro stepped daintily about the room
On white bare feet, and many times she would twist back
To see how the dress fell in clear folds to the heel.

Then suddenly we saw a frightening thing. She changed
Colour; she staggered sideways, shook in every limb.
She was just able to collapse on to a chair,
Or she would have fallen flat. Then one of her attendants,
An old woman, thinking that perhaps the anger of Pan[11] 1060
Or some other god had struck her, chanted the cry of worship.
But then she saw, oozing from the girl's lips, white froth;
The pupils of her eyes were twisted out of sight;
The blood was drained from all her skin. The old woman knew
Her mistake, and changed her chant to a despairing howl.
One maid ran off quickly to fetch the King, another
To look for Jason and tell him what was happening
To his young bride; the whole palace was filled with a clatter
Of people running here and there.
All this took place
In a few moments, perhaps while a fast runner might run 1070
A hundred yards; and she lay speechless, with eyes closed.
Then she came to, poor girl, and gave a frightful scream,
As two torments made war on her together: first
The golden coronet round her head discharged a stream
Of unnatural devouring fire: while the fine dress
Your children gave her—poor miserable girl!—the stuff
Was eating her clear flesh. She leapt up from her chair,
On fire, and ran, shaking her head and her long hair
This way and that, trying to shake off the coronet.
The ring of gold was fitted close and would not move; 1080

[11]It was thought that the old nature-god Pan frightened some people, causing "panic."

The more she shook her head the fiercer the flame burned.
At last, exhausted by agony, she fell to the ground;
Save to her father, she was unrecognizable.
Her eyes, her face, were one grotesque disfigurement;
Down from her head dripped blood mingled with flame; her flesh,
Attacked by the invisible fangs of poison, melted
From the bare bone, like gum-drops from a pine-tree's bark—
A ghastly sight. Not one among us dared to touch
Her body. What we'd seen was lesson enough for us.

But suddenly her father came into the room. 1090
He did not understand, poor man, what kind of death
Had struck his child. He threw himself down at her side,
And sobbed aloud, and kissed her, and took her in his arms,
And cried, 'Poor darling child, what god destroyed your life
So cruelly? Who robs me of my only child,
Old as I am, and near my grave? Oh, let me die
With you, my daughter!' Soon he ceased his tears and cries,
And tried to lift his aged body upright; and then,
As ivy sticks to laurel-branches, so he stuck
Fast to the dress. A ghastly wrestling then began; 1100
He struggled to raise up his knee, she tugged him down.
If he used force, he tore the old flesh off his bones.
At length the King gave up his pitiful attempts;
Weakened with pain, he yielded, and gasped out his life.
Now, joined in death, daughter and father—such a sight
As tears were made for—they lie there.
To you, Medea,
I have no more to say. You will yourself know best
How to evade reprisal. As for human life,
It is a shadow, as I have long believed. And this
I say without hesitation: those whom most would call 1110
Intelligent, the propounders of wise theories—
Their folly is of all men's the most culpable.
Happiness is a thing no man possesses. Fortune
May come now to one man, now to another, as
Prosperity increases; happiness never.

[*Exit* MESSENGER.]

CHORUS:

Today we see the will of Heaven, blow after blow,
Bring down on Jason justice and calamity.

MEDEA:

Friends, now my course is clear: as quickly as possible
To kill the children and then fly from Corinth; not
Delay and so consign them to another hand 1120
To murder with a better will. For they must die,
In any case; and since they must, then I who gave
Them birth will kill them. Arm yourself, my heart: the thing
That you must do is fearful, yet inevitable.
Why wait, then? My accursed hand, come, take the sword;
Take it, and forward to your frontier of despair.
No cowardice, no tender memories; forget

That you once loved them, that of your body they were born.
For one short day forget your children; afterwards
Weep: though you kill them, they were your beloved sons. 1130
Life has been cruel to me.

[MEDEA *goes into the house.*]

CHORUS:

Earth, awake! Bright arrows of the Sun,
Look! Look down on the accursed woman
Before she lifts up a murderous hand
To pollute it with her children's blood!
For they are of your own golden race;
And for mortals to spill blood that grew
In the veins of gods is a fearful thing.
Heaven-born brightness, hold her, stop her,
Purge the palace of her, this pitiable 1140
Bloody-handed fiend of vengeance!

All your care for them lost! Your love
For the babes you bore, all wasted, wasted!
Why did you come from the blue Symplegades
That hold the gate of the barbarous sea?
Why must this rage devour your heart
To spend itself in slaughter of children?
Where kindred blood pollutes the ground
A curse hangs over human lives;
And murder measures the doom that falls 1150
By Heaven's law on the guilty house.

[*A child's scream is heard from inside the house.*]

CHORUS:

Do you hear? The children are calling for help.
O cursed, miserable woman!

CHILDREN'S VOICES:

Help, help! Mother, let me go!
Mother, don't kill us!

CHORUS:

Shall we go in?
I am sure we ought to save the children's lives.

CHILDREN'S VOICES:

Help, help, for the gods' sake! She is killing us!
We can't escape from her sword!

CHORUS:

O miserable mother, to destroy your own increase,
Murder the babes of your body!
Stone and iron you are, as you resolved to be. 1160

There was but one in time past,
One woman that I have heard of,
Raised hand against her own children.
It was Ino,[12] sent out of her mind by a god,

---

[12]Because Ino helped to raise Dionysus, son of Zeus and Semele, Zeus' wife Hera drove Ino mad.

When Hera, the wife of Zeus,
Drove her from her home to wander over the world.
In her misery she plunged into the sea
Being defiled by the murder of her children;
From the steep cliff's edge she stretched out her foot,
And so ended, 1170
Joined in death with her two sons.

What can be strange or terrible after this?
O bed of women, full of passion and pain,
What wickedness, what sorrow you have caused on the earth!

[*Enter* JASON, *running and breathless.*]

JASON:
You women standing round the door there! Is Medea
Still in the house?—vile murderess!—or has she gone
And escaped? I swear she must either hide in the deep earth
Or soar on wings into the sky's abyss, to escape
My vengeance for the royal house.—She has killed the King
And the princess! Does she expect to go unpunished? 1180

Well, I am less concerned with her than with the children.
Those who have suffered at her hands will make her suffer;
I've come to save my sons, before Creon's family
Murder them in revenge for this unspeakable
Crime of their mother's.

CHORUS:
Jason, you have yet to learn
How great your trouble is; or you would not have spoken so.

JASON:
What trouble? Is Medea trying to kill me too?

CHORUS:
Your sons are dead. Their mother has killed both your sons.

JASON:
What? Killed my sons? That word kills me.

CHORUS:
They are both dead.

JASON:
Where are they? Did she kill them out here, or indoors? 1190

CHORUS:
Open that door, and see them lying in their blood.

JASON:
Slaves, there! Unbar the doors! Open, and let me see
Two horrors: my dead sons, and the woman I will kill.

[JASON *batters at the doors.* MEDEA *appears above the roof, sitting in a chariot drawn by dragons, with the bodies of the two children beside her.*]

MEDEA:
Jason! Why are you battering at these doors, seeking
The dead children and me who killed them? Stop! Be quiet.
If you have any business with me, say what you wish.
Touch us you cannot, in this chariot which the Sun
Has sent to save us from the hands of enemies.

JASON:
You abomination! Of all women most detested
By every god, by me, by the whole human race! 1200
You could endure—a mother!—to lift sword against
Your own little ones; to leave me childless, my life wrecked.
After such murder do you outface both Sun and Earth—
Guilty of gross pollution? May the gods blast your life!
I am sane now; but I was mad before, when I
Brought you from your palace in a land of savages
Into a Greek home—you, a living curse, already
A traitor both to your father and your native land.
The vengeance due for your sins the gods have cast on me.
You had already murdered your brother at his own hearth 1210
When first you stepped on board my lovely Argo's hull.
That was your beginning. Then you became my wife, and bore
My children; now, out of mere sexual jealousy,
You murder them! In all Hellas there is not one woman
Who could have done it; yet in preference to them
I married you, chose hatred and murder for my wife—
No woman, but a tiger; a Tuscan Scylla[13]—but more savage.
Ah, what's the use? If I cursed you all day, no remorse
Would touch you, for your heart's proof against feeling. Go!
Out of my sight, polluted fiend, child-murderer! 1220
Leave me to mourn over my destiny: I have lost
My young bride; I have lost the two sons I begot
And brought up; I shall never see them alive again.

MEDEA:
I would if necessary have answered at full length
Everything you have said; but Zeus the father of all
Knows well what service I once rendered you, and how
You have repaid me. You were mistaken if you thought
You could dishonour my bed and live a pleasant life
And laugh at me. The princess was wrong too, and so
Was Creon, when he took you for his son-in-law 1230
And thought he could exile me with impunity.
So now, am I a tiger, Scylla?—Hurl at me
What names you please! I've reached your heart; and that is right.

JASON:
You suffer too; my loss is yours no less.

MEDEA:
It is true;
But my pain's a fair price, to take away your smile.

JASON:
O children, what a wicked mother Fate gave you!

MEDEA:
O sons, your father's treachery cost you your lives.

JASON:
It was not my hand that killed my sons.

MEDEA:
No, not your hand;
But your insult to me, and your new-wedded wife.

---

[13]Scylla was a sea-monster who attacked ships in the strait between Italy's mainland and Sicily.

JASON:
You thought *that* reason enough to murder them, that I 1240
No longer slept with you?
MEDEA:
And is that injury
A slight one, do you imagine, to a woman?
JASON:
Yes,
To a modest woman; but to you—the whole world lost.
MEDEA:
I can stab too: your sons are dead!
JASON:
Dead? No! They live—
To haunt your life with vengeance.
MEDEA:
Who began this feud?
The gods know.
JASON:
Yes—they know the vileness of your heart.
MEDEA:
Loathe on! Your bitter voice—how I abhor the sound!
JASON:
As I loathe yours. Let us make terms and part at once.
MEDEA:
Most willingly. What terms? What do you bid me do?
JASON:
Give me my sons for burial and mourning rites. 1250
MEDEA:
Oh, no! I will myself convey them to the temple
Of Hera Acraea; there in the holy precinct I
Will bury them with my own hand, to ensure that none
Of my enemies shall violate or insult their graves.
And I will ordain an annual feast and sacrifice
To be solemnized for ever by the people of Corinth,
To expiate this impious murder. I myself
Will go to Athens, city of Erechtheus, to make my home
With Aegeus son of Pandion. You, as you deserve,
Shall die an unheroic death, your head shattered 1260
By a timber from the Argo's hull. Thus wretchedly
Your fate shall end the story of your love for me.
JASON:
The curse of children's blood be on you!
Avenging Justice blast your being!
MEDEA:
What god will hear your imprecation,
Oath-breaker, guest-deceiver, liar?
JASON:
Unclean, abhorrent child-destroyer!
MEDEA:
Go home: your wife waits to be buried.
JASON:
I go—a father once; now childless.

MEDEA:
You grieve too soon. Old age is coming. 1270
JASON:
Children, how dear you were!
MEDEA:
To their mother; not to you.
JASON:
Dear—and you murdered them?
MEDEA:
Yes, Jason, to break your heart.
JASON:
I long to fold them in my arms;
To kiss their lips would comfort me.
MEDEA:
Now you have loving words, now kisses for them:
Then you disowned them, sent them into exile.
JASON:
For God's sake, let me touch their gentle flesh.
MEDEA:
You shall not. It is waste of breath to ask. 1280
JASON:
Zeus, do you hear how I am mocked,
Rejected, by this savage beast
Polluted with her children's blood?

But now, as time and strength permit,
I will lament this grievous day,
And call the gods to witness, how
You killed my sons, and now refuse
To let me touch or bury them.
Would God I had not bred them,
Or ever lived to see 1290
Them dead, you their destroyer!

[*During this speech the chariot has moved out of sight.*]

CHORUS:
Many are the Fates which Zeus in Olympus dispenses;
Many matters the gods bring to surprising ends.
The things we thought would happen do not happen;
The unexpected God makes possible;
And such is the conclusion of this story.

ARISTOPHANES

[C. 450–386 B.C.E.]

Imagine an entrepreneur who convinces a colony of birds to establish a kingdom between earth and sky where they can intercept the smoke from ritual sacrifices and thus "starve" the gods into submission. Or a school run by an ivory-tower Socrates who spends his days suspended in a basket from the ceiling because he needs that rarefied atmosphere to enable him to think. Or a dramatic contest in which the tragic playwrights Aeschylus and Euripides put their best lines on a scale, where they are weighed to determine which is the better dramatist. These are among the fantastic inventions of Aristophanes, the great comic dramatist of fifth-century Athens, whose works are the only surviving examples of Greek "Old Comedy." Although he used his comic inventiveness to satirize the politicians and cultural leaders of his day, to comment on topical issues, and, especially, to attack the Peloponnesian War between Athens and Sparta, Aristophanes' plays transcend their topicality and still provide trenchant and extravagant commentary on human foibles.

Life

Little is known of Aristophanes' life. He lived from about 450 to 386 B.C.E. and seems to have come from a well-to-do Athenian family, for his plays often take a traditional, aristocratic point of view as they criticize the democracy of Aristophanes' day. Most of his plays were written during the Peloponnesian War (431–404 B.C.E.), a war that Aristophanes opposed, blaming the leaders of democratic Athens for causing and prolonging it. Several of his extant eleven plays directly take up the issue of the war. The earliest, *The Archarnians* (425), attacked Athenian hawks as warmongers who persecute a farmer for making a private peace with the Spartans. *Peace* (421) shows another countryman, disgusted and ruined by the war, who goes up to heaven on the back of a gigantic dung beetle and discovers that the gods are gone and that War has imprisoned Peace in a cave and is about to grind up the Greek city-states in a mortar. The hero rescues Peace from the cave and takes back the Athenian council from the warmongers. *Lysistrata* (411), the most famous of Aristophanes' antiwar plays, describes the first women's strike for peace, as the women of the Greek city-states band together to end the war by withholding sexual favors from their warrior husbands. In several other plays, Aristophanes attacked Athenian politicians responsible for the war policy, especially Cleon, the ruling demagogue in Athens from 429 to 422. These attacks in *The Babylonians* (426) and *The Archarnians* led to prosecution by the government, perhaps for treason, but the punishment must have been light, for Aristophanes continued to write plays and he again attacked Cleon in *The Knights* in 423.

Work

Aristophanes' best-known plays in modern times have been those on social and cultural themes, many of which are as current today as they were in Aristophanes' own time. *The Clouds* (423) ridiculed the Sophists for training their students in rhetorical cleverness and encouraging them to use their knowledge for selfish and dishonest ends. *The Wasps* (422) satirized the litigiousness of the Athenians. In *The Frogs* (405), Aristophanes made literary controversy absurd. Although Aeschylus finally wins the contest with Euripides over which is the greater tragedian, both playwrights come in for their share of criticism in the course of their debate. The scheme of establishing a kingdom to challenge the gods in *The Birds* (414) was prompted by the disastrous Athenian invasion of Sicily, but it satirizes all grandiose imperialistic schemes and the jingoism that promotes them.

Aristophanes' best-known plays are examples of Old Comedy, a form that flourished in the fifth-century Greek theater. Because Aristophanes' plays are the only examples of the form that have survived, they define Old Comedy for us. These plays grew out of seasonal fertility rituals to Dionysus, the god of wine and vegetation, similar to those described by Euripides in the *Bacchae.* The animal choruses (the wasps, frogs, and birds, for example) play an important role. Each of the three main actors in the drama, masked and dressed in grotesquely padded costumes, displayed a conspicuous leather phallus. Coarse sexual humor, fantastic plots, explicit political satire, songs, and musical comedy, sometimes compared to songs of Gilbert and Sullivan, were all characteristic of the Old Comedy.

These plays typically have six parts: the Prologue, in which the main character develops a "happy idea," such as Lysistrata's scheme to organize the women against the war; the Parados, or entrance-song of the chorus; the Agon, a debate between those for and against the protagonist's happy idea, ending with the defeat of the opposition; the Parabasis, a second choral song in which the playwright addresses the audience directly on the issues of the play or on other topics; Episodes, which explore and apply the happy idea; and the Exode, a formal song that often leads to a feast, dance, or scene of revelry to close the play.

Aristophanes' later plays, less successful than those written during the Peloponnesian War, are examples of Middle Comedy, more realistic plays in which the chorus is less significant or absent and the coarse humor and political satire are more muted. One of these later plays, however, *Ecclesiazusae,* or *Women in Parliament* (392), is similar to *Lysistrata,* for it describes the women of Athens disguising themselves as men and voting themselves into power in the Assembly. There they establish a new regime where equality of the sexes and the communal ownership of property are the guiding principles. Through this feminist fantasy, Aristophanes turns the world upside down and makes visible the shortcomings of the established order. *Lysistrata* uses a similar situation to attack the Athenian involvement in the Peloponnesian War.

By the time the play was written, the war had gone on for twenty years and neither Athenian naval power nor the Spartan land armies could gain the upper hand. The Athenians were sick of the fighting and the political turmoil brought about by the war. Athens was split into bitterly contending factions of hawks and doves, and the democracy that Pericles so eloquently celebrated after the first year of the war had been undermined and replaced in 411 by an oligarchy. The war had also led to atrocities on both sides, to genocidal massacres, and to the enslavement of captured populations. In 413, the Athenian expedition to conquer Sicily and cut off Sparta from its western allies ended in failure. Two hundred Athenian ships were lost, virtually the whole navy, along with their crews of about 35,000 men and a land army including 4,000 Athenian soldiers. For Aristophanes, one of the moderate faction in Athens, the defeat in Sicily was a clarion call to challenge the extremism of the war party.

In characteristic fashion, Aristophanes begins with fantasy, imagining a new Athens ruled by women. Led by Lysistrata, the women take over the Acropolis, the "capitol hill" of Athens, and they promote similar rebellions in the other city-states. By doing so, they challenge the values of the male warrior culture and its sterile obsession with the war as "a serious business." The women propose an alternative set of values, expressed in the metaphor of weaving. They will wind the country and its citizens together into "a great ball, and then weave a stout cloak for the democracy." The women may scandalize the men by reducing state questions to matters of carding and weaving, but they do alter the course of the war.

Once they gain control of the Acropolis, the women seek to end the war by refusing to have sex with the men until the peace is signed. In the episodes that follow the Parabasis, Aristophanes plays out the effects of this scheme on both the women and their men in a series of sexual confrontations not far removed from the phallic comedy of the Dionysian rites. The final reconciliation, engineered by Lysistrata, takes place before the statue of the naked sex goddess Reconciliation, and the play ends with dancing and revelry in the Exode.

SUGGESTED READINGS

Two useful introductions to Aristophanes are Louis E. Lord's *Aristophanes: His Plays and Influence* (1963) and Lois Spatz's *Aristophanes* (1978). K. J. Dover discusses Greek theater of the fifth century and Aristophanes' use of fantasy and other dramatic techniques in *Aristophanic Comedy* (1972), a book that also includes a separate chapter on each of the plays. Victor Ehrenberg treats the character types and farcical elements in *The People of Aristophanes: A Sociology of the Old Comedy* (1962), and C. H. Whitman concentrates on the protagonists in *Aristophanes and the Comic Hero* (1964).

Lysistrata[1]

Translated by Charles T. Murphy

CHARACTERS IN THE PLAY

LYSISTRATA, CALONICE, MYRRHINE } *Athenian women*	THREE ATHENIAN WOMEN
LAMPITO, *a Spartan woman*	CINESIAS, *an Athenian, husband of* MYRRHINE
LEADER OF THE CHORUS OF OLD MEN	SPARTAN HERALD
CHORUS OF OLD MEN	SPARTAN AMBASSADORS
LEADER OF THE CHORUS OF OLD WOMEN	ATHENIAN AMBASSADORS
CHORUS OF OLD WOMEN	TWO ATHENIAN CITIZENS
ATHENIAN MAGISTRATE	CHORUS OF ATHENIANS
	CHORUS OF SPARTANS

SCENE: *in Athens, beneath the Acropolis. In the center of the stage is the Propylaea, or gate-way to the Acropolis; to one side is a small grotto, sacred to Pan. The Orchestra represents a slope leading up to the gate-way.*
It is early in the morning. LYSISTRATA *is pacing impatiently up and down.*

LYSISTRATA: If they'd been summoned to worship the God of Wine, or Pan, or to visit the Queen of Love, why, you couldn't have pushed your way through the streets for all the timbrels. But now there's not a single woman here—except my neighbour; here she comes. [*Enter* CALONICE] Good day to you, Calonice.

CALONICE: And to you, Lysistrata. [*noticing* LYSISTRATA*'s impatient air*] But what ails you? Don't scowl, my dear; it's not becoming to you to knit your brows like that.

LYSISTRATA [*sadly*]: Ah, Calonice, my heart aches; I'm so annoyed at us women. For among men we have a reputation for sly trickery—

CALONICE: And rightly too, on my word!

LYSISTRATA: —but when they were told to meet here to consider a matter of no small importance, they lie abed and don't come.

CALONICE: Oh, they'll come all right, my dear. It's not easy for a woman to get out, you know. One is working on her husband, another is getting up the maid, another has to put the baby to bed, or wash and feed it.

LYSISTRATA: But after all, there are other matters more important than all that.

---

[1]As is usual in ancient comedy, the leading characters have significant names. Lysistrata is "She who disbands the armies"; Myrrhine's name is chosen to suggest *myrton,* a Greek word meaning *pudenda muliebria;* Lampito is a celebrated Spartan name; Cinesias, although a real name in Athens, is chosen to suggest a Greek verb *kinein, to move,* then *to make love, to have intercourse,* and the name of his deme, Paionidai, suggests the verb *paiein,* which has about the same significance. [Translator's note]

CALONICE: My dear Lysistrata, just what is this matter you've summoned us women to consider? What's up? Something big?

LYSISTRATA: Very big.

CALONICE [*interested*]: Is it stout, too?

LYSISTRATA [*smiling*]: Yes indeed—both big and stout.

CALONICE: What? And the women still haven't come?

LYSISTRATA: It's not what you suppose; they'd have come soon enough for *that.* But I've worked up something, and for many a sleepless night I've turned it this way and that.

CALONICE [*in mock disappointment*]: Oh, I guess it's pretty fine and slender, if you've turned it this way and that.

LYSISTRATA: So fine that the safety of the whole of Greece lies in us women.

CALONICE: In us women? It depends on a very slender reed then.

LYSISTRATA: Our country's fortunes are in our hands; and whether the Spartans shall perish—

CALONICE: Good! Let them perish, by all means.

LYSISTRATA: —and the Boeotians shall be completely annihilated.

CALONICE: Not completely! Please spare the eels.[2]

LYSISTRATA: As for Athens, I won't use any such unpleasant words. But you understand what I mean. But if the women will meet here—the Spartans, the Boeotians, and we Athenians—then all together we will save Greece.

CALONICE: But what could women do that's clever or distinguished? We just sit around all dolled up in silk robes, looking pretty in our sheer gowns and evening slippers.

LYSISTRATA: These are just the things I hope will save us: these silk robes, perfumes, evening slippers, rouge, and our chiffon blouses.

CALONICE: How so?

LYSISTRATA: So never a man alive will lift a spear against the foe—

CALONICE: I'll get a silk gown at once.

LYSISTRATA: —or take up his shield—

CALONICE: I'll put on my sheerest gown!

LYSISTRATA: —or sword.

CALONICE: I'll buy a pair of evening slippers.

LYSISTRATA: Well then, shouldn't the women have come?

CALONICE: Come? Why, they should have *flown* here.

LYSISTRATA: Well, my dear, just watch: they'll act in true Athenian fashion—everything too late! And now there's not a woman here from the shore or from Salamis.[3]

CALONICE: They're coming, I'm sure; at daybreak they were laying—to their oars to cross the straits.

LYSISTRATA: And those I expected would be the first to come—the women of Acharnae[4]—they haven't arrived.

CALONICE: Yet the wife of Theagenes[5] means to come: she consulted Hecate about it. [*seeing a group of women approaching*] But look! Here come a few. And there are some more over here. Hurrah! Where do they come from?

LYSISTRATA: From Anagyra.[6]

CALONICE: Yes indeed! We've raised up quite a stink from Anagyra anyway.

---

[2] A delicacy from the Boeotian lakes.

[3] An island off the coast of Piraeus, the port of Athens.

[4] A town outside of Athens.

[5] A notoriously superstitious man.

[6] A foul-smelling marshy area south of Athens.

[*Enter* MYRRHINE *in haste, followed by several other women.*]

MYRRHINE [*breathlessly*]: Have we come in time, Lysistrata? What do you say? Why so quiet?

LYSISTRATA: I can't say much for you, Myrrhine, coming at this hour on such important business.

MYRRHINE: Why, I had trouble finding my girdle in the dark. But if it's so important, we're here now; tell us.

LYSISTRATA: No. Let's wait a little for the women from Boeotia and the Peloponnesus.

MYRRHINE: That's a much better suggestion. Look! Here comes Lampito now.

[*Enter* LAMPITO *with two other women.*]

LYSISTRATA: Greetings, my dear Spartan friend. How pretty you look, my dear. What a smooth complexion and well-developed figure! You could throttle an ox.

LAMPITO: Faith, yes, I think I could. I take exercises and kick my heels against my bum. [*She demonstrates with a few steps of the Spartan "bottom-kicking" dance.*]

LYSISTRATA: And what splendid breasts you have.

LAMPITO: La! You handle me like a prize steer.

LYSISTRATA: And who is this young lady with you?

LAMPITO: Faith, she's an Ambassadress from Boeotia.

LYSISTRATA: Oh yes, a Boeotian, and blooming like a garden too.

CALONICE [*lifting up her skirt*]: My word! How neatly her garden's weeded!

LYSISTRATA: And who is the other girl?

LAMPITO: Oh, she's a Corinthian swell.

MYRRHINE [*after a rapid examination*]: Yes indeed. She swells very nicely [*pointing*] here and here.

LAMPITO: Who has gathered together this company of women?

LYSISTRATA: I have.

LAMPITO: Speak up, then. What do you want?

MYRRHINE: Yes, my dear, do tell us what this important matter is.

LYSISTRATA: Very well, I'll tell you. But before I speak, let me ask you a little question.

MYRRHINE: Anything you like.

LYSISTRATA [*earnestly*]: Tell me: don't you yearn for the fathers of your children, who are away at the wars? I know you all have husbands abroad.

CALONICE: Why, yes; mercy me! my husband's been away for five months in Thrace keeping guard on—Eucrates.[7]

MYRRHINE: And mine for seven whole months in Pylus.

LAMPITO: And mine, as soon as ever he returns from the fray, readjusts his shield and flies out of the house again.

LYSISTRATA: And as for lovers, there's not even a ghost of one left. Since the Milesians revolted from us, I've not even seen an eight-inch dingus to be a leather consolation for us widows.[8] Are you willing, if I can find a way, to help me end the war?

MYRRHINE: Goodness, yes! I'd do it, even if I had to pawn my dress and—get drunk on the spot!

CALONICE: And I, even if I had to let myself be split in two like a flounder.

LAMPITO: I'd climb up Mt. Taygetus[9] if I could catch a glimpse of peace.

---

[7] An Athenian general of questionable loyalty.

[8] The Milesians, former allies of Athens, manufactured a leather dildo.

[9] A mountain near Sparta.

LYSISTRATA: I'll tell you, then, in plain and simple words. My friends, if we are going to force our men to make peace, we must do without—

MYRRHINE: Without what? Tell us.

LYSISTRATA: Will you do it?

MYRRHINE: We'll do it, if it kills us.

LYSISTRATA: Well then, we must do without sex altogether. [*general consternation*] Why do you turn away? Where go you? Why turn so pale? Why those tears? Will you do it or not? What means this hesitation?

MYRRHINE: I won't do it! Let the war go on.

CALONICE: Nor I! Let the war go on.

LYSISTRATA: So, my little flounder? Didn't you say just now you'd split yourself in half?

CALONICE: Anything else you like. I'm willing, even if I have to walk through fire. Anything rather than sex. There's nothing like it, my dear.

LYSISTRATA [*to* MYRRHINE]: What about you?

MYRRHINE [*sullenly*]: I'm willing to walk through fire, too.

LYSISTRATA: Oh vile and cursed breed! No wonder they make tragedies about us: we're naught but "love-affairs and bassinets." But you, my dear Spartan friend, if you alone are with me, our enterprise might yet succeed. Will you vote with me?

LAMPITO: 'Tis cruel hard, by my faith, for a woman to sleep alone without her nooky; but for all that, we certainly do need peace.

LYSISTRATA: O my dearest friend! You're the only real woman here.

CALONICE [*wavering*]: Well, if we do refrain from—[*shuddering*] what you say (God forbid!), would that bring peace?

LYSISTRATA: My goodness, yes! If we sit at home all rouged and powdered, dressed in our sheerest gowns, and neatly depilated, our men will get excited and want to take us; but if you don't come to them and keep away, they'll soon make a truce.

LAMPITO: Aye; Menelaus caught sight of Helen's naked breast and dropped his sword, they say.

CALONICE: What if the men give us up?

LYSISTRATA: "Flay a skinned dog," as Pherecrates says.

CALONICE: Rubbish! These make-shifts are no good. But suppose they grab us and drag us into the bedroom?

LYSISTRATA: Hold on to the door.

CALONICE: And if they beat us?

LYSISTRATA: Give in with a bad grace. There's no pleasure in it for them when they have to use violence. And you must torment them in every possible way. They'll give up soon enough; a man gets no joy if he doesn't get along with his wife.

MYRRHINE: If this is your opinion, we agree.

LAMPITO: As for our own men, we can persuade them to make a just and fair peace; but what about the Athenian rabble? Who will persuade them not to start any more monkey-shines?

LYSISTRATA: Don't worry. We guarantee to convince them.

LAMPITO: Not while their ships are rigged so well and they have that mighty treasure in the temple of Athene.

LYSISTRATA: We've taken good care for that too: we shall seize the Acropolis today. The older women have orders to do this, and while we are making our arrangements, they are to pretend to make a sacrifice and occupy the Acropolis.

LAMPITO: All will be well then. That's a very fine idea.

LYSISTRATA: Let's ratify this, Lampito, with the most solemn oath.

LAMPITO: Tell us what oath we shall swear.

LYSISTRATA: Well said. Where's our Policewoman? [*to a Scythian slave*] What are you gaping at? Set a shield upside-down here in front of me, and give me the sacred meats.

CALONICE: Lysistrata, what sort of an oath are we to take?

LYSISTRATA: What oath? I'm going to slaughter a sheep over the shield, as they do in Aeschylus.[10]

CALONICE: Don't, Lysistrata! No oaths about peace over a shield.

LYSISTRATA: What shall the oath be, then?

CALONICE: How about getting a white horse somewhere and cutting out its entrails for the sacrifice?

LYSISTRATA: White horse indeed!

CALONICE: Well then, how shall we swear?

MYRRHINE: I'll tell you: let's place a large black bowl upside-down and then slaughter—a flask of Thasian wine.[11] And then let's swear—not to pour in a single drop of water.

LAMPITO: Lord! How I like that oath!

LYSISTRATA: Someone bring out a bowl and a flask.

[*A slave brings the utensils for the sacrifice.*]

CALONICE: Look, my friends! What a big jar! Here's a cup that 'twould give me joy to handle. [*She picks up the bowl.*]

LYSISTRATA: Set it down and put your hands on our victim. [*as* CALONICE *places her hands on the flask*] O Lady of Persuasion and dear Loving Cup, graciously vouchsafe to receive this sacrifice from us women. [*She pours the wine into the bowl.*]

CALONICE: The blood has a good colour and spurts out nicely.

LAMPITO: Faith, it has a pleasant smell, too.

MYRRHINE: Oh, let me be the first to swear, ladies!

CALONICE: No, by our Lady! Not unless you're allotted the first turn.

LYSISTRATA: Place all your hands on the cup, and one of you repeat on behalf of all what I say. Then all will swear and ratify the oath. *I will suffer no man, be he husband or lover,*

CALONICE: *I will suffer no man, be he husband or lover,*

LYSISTRATA: *To approach me all hot and horny.* [*as* CALONICE *hesitates*] Say it!

CALONICE [*slowly and painfully*]: *To approach me all hot and horny.* O Lysistrata, I feel so weak in the knees!

LYSISTRATA: *I will remain at home unmated,*

CALONICE: *I will remain at home unmated,*

LYSISTRATA: *Wearing my sheerest gown and carefully adorned,*

CALONICE: *Wearing my sheerest gown and carefully adorned,*

LYSISTRATA: *That my husband may burn with desire for me.*

CALONICE: *That my husband may burn with desire for me.*

LYSISTRATA: *And if he takes me by force against my will,*

CALONICE: *And if he takes me by force against my will,*

LYSISTRATA: *I shall do it badly and keep from moving.*

CALONICE: *I shall do it badly and keep from moving.*

LYSISTRATA: *I will not stretch my slippers toward the ceiling,*

CALONICE: *I will not stretch my slippers toward the ceiling,*

LYSISTRATA: *Nor will I take the posture of the lioness on the knife-handle.*

---

[10] In *Seven against Thebes,* the warriors swear loyalty to each other and slaughter a bull so that the blood flows into the hollow of a shield.

[11] A strong wine from the island of Thasos.

CALONICE: *Nor will I take the posture of the lioness on the knife-handle.*
LYSISTRATA: *If I keep this oath, may I be permitted to drink from this cup,*
CALONICE: *If I keep this oath, may I be permitted to drink from this cup,*
LYSISTRATA: *But if I break it, may the cup be filled with water.*
CALONICE: *But if I break it, may the cup be filled with water.*
LYSISTRATA: Do you all swear to this?
ALL: I do, so help me!
LYSISTRATA: Come then, I'll just consummate this offering. [*She takes a long drink from the cup.*]
CALONICE [*snatching the cup away*]: Shares, my dear! Let's drink to our continued friendship.

[*A shout is heard from off-stage.*]

LAMPITO: What's that shouting?
LYSISTRATA: That's what I was telling you: the women have just seized the Acropolis. Now, Lampito, go home and arrange matters in Sparta; and leave these two ladies here as hostages. We'll enter the Acropolis to join our friends and help them lock the gates.
CALONICE: Don't you suppose the men will come to attack us?
LYSISTRATA: Don't worry about them. Neither threats nor fire will suffice to open the gates, except on the terms we've stated.
CALONICE: I should say not! Else we'd belie our reputation as unmanageable pests.

[LAMPITO *leaves the stage. The other women retire and enter the Acropolis through the Propylaea.*]

[*Enter the* CHORUS OF OLD MEN, *carrying fire-pots and a load of heavy sticks.*]

LEADER OF MEN:

Onward, Draces, step by step, though your shoulder's aching.
Cursèd logs of olive-wood, what a load you're making!

FIRST SEMI-CHORUS OF OLD MEN [*singing*]:

Aye, many surprises await a man who lives to a ripe old age;
For who could suppose, Strymodorus my lad, that the women
we've nourished (alas!),
Who sat at home to vex our days,
Would seize the holy image here,
And occupy this sacred shrine,
With bolts and bars, with fell design,
To lock the Propylaea?

LEADER:

Come with speed, Philourgus, come! to the temple hast'ning.
There we'll heap these logs about in a circle round them,
And whoever has conspired, raising this rebellion,
Shall be roasted, scorched, and burnt, all without exception,
Doomed by one unanimous vote—but first the wife of Lycon.[12]

SECOND SEMI-CHORUS [*singing*]:

No, no! by Demeter, while I'm alive, no woman shall mock at me.
Not even the Spartan Cleomenes,[13] our citadel first to seize,
Got off unscathed; for all his pride
And haughty Spartan arrogance,

[12] A woman of dubious reputation.
[13] A Spartan king who interfered in an Athenian civil dispute in 508 and briefly occupied the Acropolis.

He left his arms and sneaked away,
Stripped to his shirt, unkempt, unshav'd,
With six years' filth still on him.

LEADER:

I besieged that hero bold, sleeping at my station,
Marshalled at these holy gates sixteen deep against him.
Shall I not these cursèd pests punish for their daring,
Burning these Euripides-and-God-detested women?[14]
Aye! or else may Marathon overturn my trophy.[15]

FIRST SEMI-CHORUS [*singing*]:

There remains of my road
Just this brow of the hill;
There I speed on my way.
Drag the logs up the hill, though we've got no ass to help.
(God! my shoulder's bruised and sore!)
Onward still must we go.
Blow the fire! Don't let it go out
Now we're near the end of our road.

ALL [*blowing on the fire-pots*]: Whew! Whew! Drat the smoke!

SECOND SEMI-CHORUS [*singing*]:

Lord, what smoke rushing forth
From the pot, like a dog
Running mad, bites my eyes!
This must be Lemnos-fire.[16] What a sharp and stinging smoke!
Rushing onward to the shrine
Aid the gods. Once for all
Show your mettle, Laches my boy!
To the rescue hastening all!

ALL [*blowing on the fire-pots*]: Whew! Whew! Drat the smoke!

[*The chorus has now reached the edge of the orchestra nearest the stage, in front of the Propylaea. They begin laying their logs and fire-pots on the ground.*]

LEADER: Thank heaven, this fire is still alive. Now let's first put down these logs here and place our torches in the pots to catch; then let's make a rush for the gates with a battering-ram. If the women don't unbar the gate at our summons, we'll have to smoke them out.

Let me put down my load. Ouch! That hurts! [*to the audience*] Would any of the generals in Samos[17] like to lend a hand with this log? [*throwing down a log*] Well, *that* won't break my back any more, at any rate. [*turning to his fire-pot*] Your job, my little pot, is to keep those coals alive and furnish me shortly with a red-hot torch.

O mistress Victory, be my ally and grant me to rout these audacious women in the Acropolis.

[*While the men are busy with their logs and fires, the* CHORUS OF OLD WOMEN *enters, carrying pitchers of water.*]

LEADER OF WOMEN:

What's this I see? Smoke and flames? Is that a fire ablazing?
Let's rush upon them. Hurry up! They'll find us women ready.

---

[14] Aristophanes frequently represents Euripides as a misogynist.

[15] The old men are unbelievably boastful. If they were really alive at the time of Cleomenes' occupation in 508 and the Battle of Marathon in 490, they are very old men indeed.

[16] A volcanic island in the Aegean.

[17] An island off the coast of Asia Minor, headquarters for the Athenian fleet.

FIRST SEMI-CHORUS OF OLD WOMEN [*singing*]:
With wingèd foot onward I fly,
Ere the flames consume Neodice;
Lest Critylla be overwhelmed
By a lawless, accurst herd of old men.
I shudder with fear. Am I too late to aid them?
At break of the day filled we our jars with water
Fresh from the spring, pushing our way straight through the
crowds. Oh, what a din!
Mid crockery crashing, jostled by slave-girls,
Sped we to save them, aiding our neighbours,
Bearing this water to put out the flames.

SECOND SEMI-CHORUS OF OLD WOMEN [*singing*]:
Such news I've heard: doddering fools
Come with logs, like furnace-attendants,
Loaded down with three hundred pounds,
Breathing many a vain, blustering threat,
That all these abhorred sluts will be burnt to charcoal.
O goddess, I pray never may they be kindled;
Grant them to save Greece and our men; madness and war
help them to end.
With this as our purpose, golden-plumed Maiden,
Guardian of Athens, seized we thy precinct.
Be my ally, Warrior-maiden,
'Gainst these old men, bearing water with me.

[*The women have now reached their position in the orchestra, and their* LEADER *advances toward the* LEADER OF THE MEN.]

LEADER OF THE CHORUS OF OLD WOMEN: Hold on there! What's this, you utter scoundrels? No decent, God-fearing citizens would act like this.

LEADER OF THE CHORUS OF OLD MEN: Oho! Here's something unexpected: a swarm of women have come out to attack us.

LEADER OF THE CHORUS OF OLD WOMEN: What, do we frighten you? Surely you don't think we're too many for you. And yet there are ten thousand times more of us whom you haven't even seen.

LEADER OF THE CHORUS OF OLD MEN: What say, Phaedria? Shall we let these women wag their tongues? Shan't we take our sticks and break them over their backs?

LEADER OF THE CHORUS OF OLD WOMEN: Let's set our pitchers on the ground; then if anyone lays a hand on us, they won't get in our way.

LEADER OF THE CHORUS OF OLD MEN: By God! If someone gave them two or three smacks on the jaw, like Bupalus,[18] they wouldn't talk so much!

LEADER OF THE CHORUS OF OLD WOMEN: Go on, hit me, somebody! Here's my jaw! But no other bitch will bite a piece out of you before me.

LEADER OF THE CHORUS OF OLD MEN: Silence! or I'll knock out your—senility!

LEADER OF THE CHORUS OF OLD WOMEN: Just lay one finger on Stratyllis, I dare you!

LEADER OF THE CHORUS OF OLD MEN: Suppose I dust you off with this fist? What will you do?

LEADER OF THE CHORUS OF OLD WOMEN: I'll tear the living guts out of you with my teeth.

---

[18] A sixth-century sculptor.

LEADER OF THE CHORUS OF OLD MEN: No poet is more clever than Euripides: "There is no beast so shameless as a woman."

LEADER OF THE CHORUS OF OLD WOMEN: Let's pick up our jars of water, Rhodippe.

LEADER OF THE CHORUS OF OLD MEN: Why have you come here with water, you detestable slut?

LEADER OF THE CHORUS OF OLD WOMEN: And why have you come with fire, you funeral vault? To cremate yourself?

LEADER OF THE CHORUS OF OLD MEN: To light a fire and singe your friends.

LEADER OF THE CHORUS OF OLD WOMEN: And I've brought water to put out your fire.

LEADER OF THE CHORUS OF OLD MEN: What? You'll put out my fire?

LEADER OF THE CHORUS OF OLD WOMEN: Just try and see!

LEADER OF THE CHORUS OF OLD MEN: I wonder: shall I scorch you with this torch of mine?

LEADER OF THE CHORUS OF OLD WOMEN: If you've got any soap, I'll give you a bath.

LEADER OF THE CHORUS OF OLD MEN: Give *me* a bath, you stinking hag?

LEADER OF THE CHORUS OF OLD WOMEN: Yes—a bridal bath!

LEADER OF THE CHORUS OF OLD MEN: Just listen to her! What crust!

LEADER OF THE CHORUS OF OLD WOMEN: Well, I'm a free citizen.

LEADER OF THE CHORUS OF OLD MEN: I'll put an end to your bawling. [*The men pick up their torches.*]

LEADER OF THE CHORUS OF OLD WOMEN: You'll never do jury-duty again. [*The women pick up their pitchers.*]

LEADER OF THE CHORUS OF OLD MEN: Singe her hair for her!

LEADER OF THE CHORUS OF OLD WOMEN: Do your duty, water! [*The women empty their pitchers on the men.*]

LEADER OF THE CHORUS OF OLD MEN: Ow! Ow! For heaven's sake!

LEADER OF THE CHORUS OF OLD WOMEN: Is it too hot?

LEADER OF THE CHORUS OF OLD MEN: What do you mean "hot"? Stop! What are you doing?

LEADER OF THE CHORUS OF OLD WOMEN: I'm watering you, so you'll be fresh and green.

LEADER OF THE CHORUS OF OLD MEN: But I'm all withered up with shaking.

LEADER OF THE CHORUS OF OLD WOMEN: Well, you've got a fire; why don't you dry yourself?

[*Enter an Athenian* MAGISTRATE, *accompanied by four Scythian policemen.*]

ATHENIAN MAGISTRATE: Have these wanton women flared up again with their timbrels and their continual worship of Sabazius?[19] Is this another Adonis-dirge upon the roof-tops—which we heard not long ago in the Assembly? That confounded Demostratus[20] was urging us to sail to Sicily, and the whirling women shouted, "Woe for Adonis!" And then Demostratus said we'd best enroll the infantry from Zacynthus, and a tipsy woman on the roof shrieked, "Beat your breasts for Adonis!" And that vile and filthy lunatic forced his measure through. Such license do our women take.

---

[19]A religious cult worshipping the oriental deity Sabazius, similar to the Adonis cult. Both cults were suspect in the eyes of religious conservatives.

[20]Demostratus was one of the prominent supporters of the disastrous Athenian campaign in Sicily. He urged the Assembly to draft the inhabitants of the island of Zacynthus, allies of the Athenians, to the Athenian cause.

LEADER OF THE CHORUS OF OLD MEN: What if you heard of the insolence of these women here? Besides their other violent acts, they threw water all over us, and we have to shake out our clothes just as if we'd leaked in them.

ATHENIAN MAGISTRATE: And rightly, too, by God! For we ourselves lead the women astray and teach them to play the wanton; from these roots such notions blossom forth. A man goes into the jeweler's shop and says, "About that necklace you made for my wife, goldsmith: last night, while she was dancing, the fastening-bolt slipped out of the hole. I have to sail over to Salamis today; if you're free, do come around tonight and fit in a new bolt for her." Another goes to the shoe-maker, a strapping young fellow with manly parts, and says, "See here, cobbler, the sandal-strap chafes my wife's little—toe; it's so tender. Come around during the siesta and stretch it a little, so she'll be more comfortable." Now we see the results of such treatment: here I'm a special Councillor and need money to procure oars for the galleys; and I'm locked out of the Treasury by these women.

But this is no time to stand around. Bring up crow-bars there! I'll put an end to their insolence. [*to one of the policemen*] What are you gaping at, you wretch? What are you staring at? Got an eye out for a tavern, eh? Set your crow-bars here to the gates and force them open. [*retiring to a safe distance*] I'll help from over here.

[*The gates are thrown open and* LYSISTRATA *comes out followed by several other women.*]

LYSISTRATA: Don't force the gates; I'm coming out of my own accord. We don't need crow-bars here; what we need is good sound common-sense.

ATHENIAN MAGISTRATE: Is that so, you strumpet? Where's my policeman? Officer, arrest her and tie her arms behind her back.

LYSISTRATA: By Artemis, if he lays a finger on me, he'll pay for it, even if he is a public servant.

[*The policeman retires in terror.*]

ATHENIAN MAGISTRATE: You there, are you afraid? Seize her round the waist—and you, too. Tie her up, both of you!

FIRST WOMAN [*as the second policeman approaches* LYSISTRATA]: By Pandrosus,[21] if you but touch her with your hand, I'll kick the stuffings out of you.

[*The second policeman retires in terror.*]

ATHENIAN MAGISTRATE: Just listen to that: "kick the stuffings out." Where's another policeman? Tie *her* up first, for her chatter.

SECOND WOMAN: By the Goddess of the Light, if you lay the tip of your finger on her, you'll soon need a doctor.

[*The third policeman retires in terror.*]

ATHENIAN MAGISTRATE: What's this? Where's my policeman? Seize *her* too. I'll soon stop your sallies.

THIRD WOMAN: By the Goddess of Tauros,[22] if you go near her, I'll tear out your hair until it shrieks with pain.

[*The fourth policeman retires in terror.*]

ATHENIAN MAGISTRATE: Oh, damn it all! I've run out of policemen. But women must never defeat us. Others, let's charge them all together. Close up your ranks!

[*The policemen rally for a mass attack.*]

LYSISTRATA: By heaven, you'll soon find out that we have four companies of warrior-women, all fully equipped within!

ATHENIAN MAGISTRATE [*advancing*]: Twist their arms off, men!

---

[21] A mythical Athenian goddess.

[22] Artemis.

LYSISTRATA [*shouting*]:

To the rescue, my valiant women!
O sellers-of-barley-green-stuffs-and-eggs,
O sellers-of-garlic, ye keepers-of-taverns, and vendors-of-bread,
Grapple! Smite! Smash!
Won't you heap filth on them? Give them a tongue-lashing!

[*The women beat off the policemen.*]

Halt! Withdraw! No looting on the field.

ATHENIAN MAGISTRATE: Damn it! My police-force has put up a very poor show.

LYSISTRATA: What did you expect? Did you think you were attacking slaves? Didn't you know that women are filled with passion?

ATHENIAN MAGISTRATE: Aye, passion enough—for a good strong drink!

LEADER OF THE CHORUS OF OLD MEN:

O chief and leader of this land, why spend your words in vain?
Don't argue with these shameless beasts. You know not how we've fared:
A soapless bath they've given us; our clothes are soundly soaked.

LEADER OF THE CHORUS OF OLD WOMEN:

Poor fool! You never should attack or strike a peaceful girl.
But if you do, your eyes must swell. For I am quite content
To sit unmoved, like modest maids, in peace and cause no pain;
But let a man stir up my hive, he'll find me like a wasp.

CHORUS OF MEN [*singing*]:

O God, whatever shall we do with creatures like Womankind?
This can't be endured by any man alive. Question them!
Let us try to find out what this means.
To what end have they seized on this shrine,
This steep and rugged, high and holy,
Undefiled Acropolis?

LEADER OF THE CHORUS OF OLD MEN:

Come, put your questions; don't give in, and probe her every statement.
For base and shameful it would be to leave this plot untested.

ATHENIAN MAGISTRATE: Well then, first of all I wish to ask her this: for what purpose have you barred us from the Acropolis?

LYSISTRATA: To keep the treasure safe, so you won't make war on account of it.

ATHENIAN MAGISTRATE: What? Do we make war on account of the treasure?

LYSISTRATA: Yes, and you cause all our other troubles for it too. Peisander[23] and those greedy office-seekers keep things stirred up so they can find occasions to steal. Now let them do what they like: they'll never again make off with any of this money.

ATHENIAN MAGISTRATE: What will you do?

LYSISTRATA: What a question! We'll administer it ourselves.

ATHENIAN MAGISTRATE: *You* will administer the treasure?

LYSISTRATA: What's so strange in that? Don't we administer the household money for you?

ATHENIAN MAGISTRATE: That's different.

LYSISTRATA: How is it different?

ATHENIAN MAGISTRATE: We've got to make war with this money.

LYSISTRATA: But that's the very first thing: you mustn't make war.

[23] A corrupt politician and one of the leaders of the Athenian war party.

ATHENIAN MAGISTRATE: How else can we be saved?
LYSISTRATA: We'll save you.
ATHENIAN MAGISTRATE: *You?*
LYSISTRATA: Yes, we!
ATHENIAN MAGISTRATE: God forbid!
LYSISTRATA: We'll save you, whether you want it or not.
ATHENIAN MAGISTRATE: Oh! This is terrible!
LYSISTRATA: You don't like it, but we're going to do it none the less.
ATHENIAN MAGISTRATE: Good God! it's illegal!
LYSISTRATA: We *will* save you, my little man!
ATHENIAN MAGISTRATE: Suppose I don't want you to?
LYSISTRATA: That's all the more reason.
ATHENIAN MAGISTRATE: What business have you with war and peace?
LYSISTRATA: I'll explain.
ATHENIAN MAGISTRATE [*shaking his fist*]: Speak up, or you'll smart for it.
LYSISTRATA: Just listen, and try to keep your hands still.
ATHENIAN MAGISTRATE: I can't. I'm so mad I can't stop them.
FIRST WOMAN: Then you'll be the one to smart for it.
ATHENIAN MAGISTRATE: Croak to yourself, old hag! [*to* LYSISTRATA] Now then, speak up.
LYSISTRATA: Very well. Formerly we endured the war for a good long time with our usual restraint, no matter what you men did. You wouldn't let us say "boo," although nothing you did suited us. But we watched you well, and though we stayed at home we'd often hear of some terribly stupid measure you'd proposed. Then, though grieving at heart, we'd smile sweetly and say, "What was passed in the Assembly today about writing on the treaty-stone?"[24] "What's that to you?" my husband would say. "Hold your tongue!" And I held my tongue.
FIRST WOMAN: But I wouldn't have—not I!
ATHENIAN MAGISTRATE: You'd have been soundly smacked, if you hadn't kept still.
LYSISTRATA: So I kept still at home. Then we'd hear of some plan still worse than the first; we'd say, "Husband, how could you pass such a stupid proposal?" He'd scowl at me and say, "If you don't mind your spinning, your head will be sore for weeks. *War shall be the concern of Men*."[25]
ATHENIAN MAGISTRATE: And he was right, upon my word!
LYSISTRATA: Why right, you confounded fool, when your proposals were so stupid and we weren't allowed to make suggestions?

"There's not a *man* left in the country," says one. "No, not one," says another. Therefore all we women have decided in council to make a common effort to save Greece. How long should we have waited? Now, if you're willing to listen to our excellent proposals and keep silence for us in your turn, we still may save you.
ATHENIAN MAGISTRATE: We men keep silence for you? That's terrible; I won't endure it!
LYSISTRATA: Silence!
ATHENIAN MAGISTRATE: Silence for *you*, you wench, when you're wearing a snood? I'd rather die!
LYSISTRATA: Well, if that's all that bothers you—here! take my snood and tie it round your head. [*During the following words the women dress up the* MAGISTRATE *in*

[24]Treaties were inscribed on a stone and displayed in a public place.
[25]The final sentence repeats Hector's words to Andromache in *The Iliad,* Book 6.

women's garments.] And *now* keep quiet! Here, take this spinning-basket, too, and card your wool with robes tucked up, munching on beans. *War shall be the concern of Women!*

LEADER OF THE CHORUS OF OLD WOMEN:

Arise and leave your pitchers, girls; no time is this to falter.
We too must aid our loyal friends; our turn has come for action.

CHORUS OF WOMEN [*singing*]:

I'll never tire of aiding them with song and dance; never may
Faintness keep my legs from moving to and fro endlessly.
For I yearn to do all for my friends;
They have charm, they have wit, they have grace,
With courage, brains, and best of virtues—
Patriotic sapience.

LEADER OF THE CHORUS OF OLD WOMEN:

Come, child of manliest ancient dames, offspring of stinging nettles,
Advance with rage unsoftened; for fair breezes speed you onward.

LYSISTRATA: If only sweet Eros and the Cyprian Queen of Love shed charm over our breasts and limbs and inspire our men with amorous longing and priapic spasms, I think we may soon be called Peacemakers among the Greeks.

ATHENIAN MAGISTRATE: What will you do?

LYSISTRATA: First of all, we'll stop those fellows who run madly about the Market-place in arms.

FIRST WOMAN: Indeed we shall, by the Queen of Paphos.[26]

LYSISTRATA: For now they roam about the market, amid the pots and greenstuffs, armed to the teeth like Corybantes.[27]

ATHENIAN MAGISTRATE: That's what manly fellows ought to do!

LYSISTRATA: But it's so silly: a chap with a Gorgon-emblazoned shield buying pickled herring.

FIRST WOMAN: Why, just the other day I saw one of those long-haired dandies who command our cavalry ride up on horseback and pour into his bronze helmet the egg-broth he'd bought from an old dame. And there was a Thracian slinger too, shaking his lance like Tereus;[28] he'd scared the life out of the poor fig-peddler and was gulping down all her ripest fruit.

ATHENIAN MAGISTRATE: How can you stop all the confusion in the various states and bring them together?

LYSISTRATA: Very easily.

ATHENIAN MAGISTRATE: Tell me how.

LYSISTRATA: Just like a ball of wool, when it's confused and snarled: we take it thus, and draw out a thread here and a thread there with our spindles; thus we'll unsnarl this war, if no one prevents us, and draw together the various states with embassies here and embassies there.

ATHENIAN MAGISTRATE: Do you suppose you can stop this dreadful business with balls of wool and spindles, you nit-wits?

LYSISTRATA: Why, if *you* had any wits, you'd manage all affairs of state like our wool-working.

---

[26] Aphrodite.

[27] Armed priests of the goddess Cybele.

[28] A mythical king of Thrace.

ATHENIAN MAGISTRATE: How so?

LYSISTRATA: First you ought to treat the city as we do when we wash the dirt out of a fleece: stretch it out and pluck and thrash out of the city all those prickly scoundrels; aye, and card out those who conspire and stick together to gain office, pulling off their heads. Then card the wool, all of it, into one fair basket of goodwill, mingling in the aliens residing here, any loyal foreigners, and anyone who's in debt to the Treasury; and consider that all our colonies lie scattered round about like remnants; from all of these collect the wool and gather it together here, wind up a great ball, and then weave a good stout cloak for the democracy.

ATHENIAN MAGISTRATE: Dreadful! Talking about thrashing and winding balls of wool, when you haven't the slightest share in the war!

LYSISTRATA: Why, you dirty scoundrel, we bear more than twice as much as you. First, we bear children and send off our sons as soldiers.

ATHENIAN MAGISTRATE: Hush! Let bygones be bygones!

LYSISTRATA: Then, when we ought to be happy and enjoy our youth, we sleep alone because of your expeditions abroad. But never mind us married women: I grieve most for the maids who grow old at home unwed.

ATHENIAN MAGISTRATE: Don't men grow old, too?

LYSISTRATA: For heaven's sake! That's not the same thing. When a man comes home, no matter how grey he is, he soon finds a girl to marry. But woman's bloom is short and fleeting; if she doesn't grasp her chance, no man is willing to marry her and she sits at home a prey to every fortune-teller.

ATHENIAN MAGISTRATE [*coarsely*]: But if a man can still get it up—

LYSISTRATA: See here, you: what's the matter? Aren't you dead yet? There's plenty of room for you. Buy yourself a shroud and I'll make you a honey-cake.[29] [*handing him a copper coin for his passage across the Styx*] Here's your fare! Now get yourself a wreath.

[*During the following dialogue the women dress up the* MAGISTRATE *as a corpse.*]

FIRST WOMAN: Here, take these fillets.

SECOND WOMAN: Here, take this wreath.

LYSISTRATA: What do you want? What's lacking? Get moving; off to the ferry! Charon is calling you; don't keep him from sailing.

ATHENIAN MAGISTRATE: Am I to endure these insults? By God! I'm going straight to the magistrates to show them how I've been treated.

LYSISTRATA: Are you grumbling that you haven't been properly laid out? Well, the day after tomorrow we'll send around all the usual offerings early in the morning.

[*The* MAGISTRATE *goes out still wearing his funeral decorations.* LYSISTRATA *and the women retire into the Acropolis.*]

LEADER OF THE CHORUS OF OLD MEN: Wake, ye sons of freedom, wake! 'Tis no time for sleeping. Up and at them, like a man! Let us strip for action.

[*The* CHORUS OF MEN *remove their outer cloaks.*]

CHORUS OF MEN [*singing*]:

Surely there is something here greater than meets the eye;
For without a doubt I smell Hippias' tyranny.[30]
Dreadful fear assails me lest certain bands of Spartan men,

[29]The dead were provided with a honey-cake to throw to Cerberus, the guardian of the entrance to the underworld.

[30]The last tyrant in Athens, who was overthrown in 510 B.C.E.

Meeting here with Cleisthenes,[31] have inspired through treachery
All these god-detested women secretly to seize
Athens' treasure in the temple, and to stop that pay
Whence I live at my ease.

LEADER OF THE CHORUS OF OLD MEN: Now isn't it terrible for them to advise the state and chatter about shields, being mere women?

And they think to reconcile us with the Spartans—men who hold nothing sacred any more than hungry wolves. Surely this is a web of deceit, my friends, to conceal an attempt at tyranny. But they'll never lord it over me; I'll be on my guard and from now on, "The blade I bear / A myrtle spray shall wear." I'll occupy the market under arms and stand next to Aristogeiton.[32]

Thus I'll stand beside him. [*He strikes the pose of the famous statue of the tyrannicides, with one arm raised.*] And here's my chance to take this accurst old hag and—[*striking the* LEADER OF WOMEN] smack her on the jaw!

LEADER OF THE CHORUS OF OLD WOMEN: You'll go home in such a state your Ma won't recognize you!

Ladies all, upon the ground let us place these garments.

[*The* CHORUS OF WOMEN *remove their outer garments.*]

CHORUS OF WOMEN [*singing*]:

Citizens of Athens, hear useful words for the state.
Rightly; for it nurtured me in my youth royally.
As a child of seven years carried I the sacred box;[33]
Then I was a Miller-maid, grinding at Athene's shrine;
Next I wore the saffron robe and played Brauronia's Bear;
And I walked as Basket-bearer, wearing chains of figs,
As a sweet maiden fair.

LEADER OF THE CHORUS OF OLD WOMEN: Therefore, am I not bound to give good advice to the city? Don't take it ill that I was born a woman, if I contribute something better than our present troubles. I pay my share; for I contribute MEN. But you miserable old fools contribute nothing, and after squandering our ancestral treasure, the fruit of the Persian Wars, you make no contribution in return. And now, all on account of you, we're facing ruin.

What, muttering, are you? If you annoy me, I'll take this hard, rough slipper and—[*striking the* LEADER OF MEN] smack you on the jaw!

CHORUS OF MEN [*singing*]:

This is outright insolence! Things go from bad to worse.
If you're men with any guts, prepare to meet the foe.
Let us strip our tunics off! We need the smell of male
Vigour. And we cannot fight all swaddled up in clothes!

[*They strip off their tunics.*]

Come then, my comrades, on to the battle, ye who once to Leipsydrion[34] came;

---

[31] An effeminate Athenian, suspected of collaboration with the women.

[32] One of the heroes of Athenian democracy; he had assassinated Hipparchus, brother of the tyrant Hippias.

[33] The religious duties of an Athenian girl included carrying a sacred box containing relics connected with the worship of Athena, grinding flour for religious wafers, and wearing a saffron robe and participating in the rites of Artemis.

[34] The site where the heroes of Athenian democracy gathered to challenge Hippias.

Then ye were MEN. Now call back your youthful vigour.
With light, wingèd footstep advance,
Shaking old age from your frame.

LEADER OF THE CHORUS OF OLD MEN: If any of us give these wenches the slightest hold, they'll stop at nothing: such is their cunning.

They will even build ships and sail against us, like Artemisia.[35] Or if they turn to mounting, I count our Knights as done for: a woman's such a tricky jockey when she gets astraddle, with a good firm seat for trotting. Just look at those Amazons that Micon painted, fighting on horseback against men!

But we must throw them all in the pillory—[*seizing and choking the* LEADER OF WOMEN] grabbing hold of yonder neck!

CHORUS OF WOMEN [*singing*]:
'Ware my anger! Like a boar 'twill rush upon you men.
Soon you'll bawl aloud for help, you'll be so soundly trimmed!
Come, my friends, let's strip with speed, and lay aside these robes;
Catch the scent of women's rage. Attack with tooth and nail!

[*They strip off their tunics.*]

Now then, come near me, you miserable man! you'll never eat garlic or black beans again.
And if you utter a single hard word, in rage I will "nurse" you as once
The beetle requited her foe.[36]

LEADER OF THE CHORUS OF OLD WOMEN: For you don't worry me; no, not so long as my Lampito lives and our Theban friend, the noble Ismenia.

You can't do anything, not even if you pass a dozen—decrees! You miserable fool, all our neighbours hate you. Why, just the other day when I was holding a festival for Hecate, I invited as playmate from our neighbours the Boeotians a charming, well-bred Copaic—eel. But they refused to send me one on account of your decrees.

And you'll never stop passing decrees until I grab your foot and—[*tripping up the* LEADER OF MEN] toss you down and break your neck!

[*Here an interval of five days is supposed to elapse.* LYSISTRATA *comes out from the Acropolis.*]

LEADER OF THE CHORUS OF OLD WOMEN [*dramatically*]: Empress of this great emprise and undertaking,
Why come you forth, I pray, with frowning brow?

LYSISTRATA: Ah, these cursèd women! Their deeds and female notions make me pace up and down in utter despair.

LEADER OF THE CHORUS OF OLD WOMEN: Ah, what sayest thou?

LYSISTRATA: The truth, alas! the truth.

LEADER OF THE CHORUS OF OLD WOMEN: What dreadful tale hast thou to tell thy friends?

LYSISTRATA: 'Tis shame to speak, and not to speak is hard.

LEADER OF THE CHORUS OF OLD WOMEN: Hide not from me whatever woes we suffer.

LYSISTRATA: Well then, to put it briefly, we want—laying!

LEADER OF THE CHORUS OF OLD WOMEN: O Zeus, Zeus!

---

[35] Queen of Halicarnassus in Asia Minor, whose ships participated in Xerxes' invasion of Greece.

[36] In Aesop's fable, the beetle gets back at the eagle by breaking its eggs.

LYSISTRATA: Why call on Zeus? That's the way things are. I can no longer keep them away from the men, and they're all deserting. I caught one wriggling through a hole near the grotto of Pan, and another sliding down a rope, another deserting her post; and yesterday I found one getting on a sparrow's back to fly off to Orsilochus,[37] and had to pull her back by the hair. They're digging up all sorts of excuses to get home. Look, here comes one of them now. [*A woman comes hastily out of the Acropolis.*] Here you! Where are you off to in such a hurry?

FIRST WOMAN: I want to go home. My very best wool is being devoured by moths.

LYSISTRATA: Moths? Nonsense! Go back inside.

FIRST WOMAN: I'll come right back; I swear it. I just want to lay it out on the bed.

LYSISTRATA: Well, you won't lay it out, and you won't go home, either.

FIRST WOMAN: Shall I let my wool be ruined?

LYSISTRATA: If necessary, yes. [*Another woman comes out.*]

SECOND WOMAN: Oh dear! Oh dear! My precious flax! I left it at home all unpeeled.

LYSISTRATA: Here's another one, going home for her "flax." Come back here!

SECOND WOMAN: But I just want to work it up a little and then I'll be right back.

LYSISTRATA: No indeed! If you start this, all the other women will want to do the same. [*A third woman comes out.*]

THIRD WOMAN: O Eilithyia, goddess of travail, stop my labour till I come to a lawful spot![38]

LYSISTRATA: What's this nonsense?

THIRD WOMAN: I'm going to have a baby—right now!

LYSISTRATA: But you weren't even pregnant yesterday.

THIRD WOMAN: Well, I am today. O Lysistrata, do send me home to see a midwife, right away.

LYSISTRATA: What are you talking about? [*putting her hand on her stomach*] What's this hard lump here?

THIRD WOMAN: A little boy.

LYSISTRATA: My goodness, what have you got there? It seems hollow; I'll just find out. [*pulling aside her robe*] Why, you silly goose, you've got Athene's sacred helmet there. And you said you were having a baby!

THIRD WOMAN: Well, I *am* having one, I swear!

LYSISTRATA: Then what's this helmet for?

THIRD WOMAN: If the baby starts coming while I'm still in the Acropolis, I'll creep into this like a pigeon and give birth to it there.

LYSISTRATA: Stuff and nonsense! It's plain enough what you're up to. You just wait here for the christening of this—helmet.

THIRD WOMAN: But I can't sleep in the Acropolis since I saw the sacred snake.

FIRST WOMAN: And I'm dying for lack of sleep: the hooting of the owls[39] keeps me awake.

LYSISTRATA: Enough of these shams, you wretched creatures. You want your husbands, I suppose. Well, don't you think they want us? I'm sure they're spending miserable nights. Hold out, my friends, and endure for just a little while. There's an oracle that we shall conquer, if we don't split up. [*producing a roll of paper*] Here it is.

FIRST WOMAN: Tell us what it says.

LYSISTRATA: Listen.

"When in the length of time the Swallows shall gather together,

---

[37] Proprietor of a brothel.

[38] The Acropolis was sacred ground; to give birth there was considered sacrilegious.

[39] The sacred birds of Athena.

Fleeing the Hoopoe's amorous flight and the Cockatoo shunning,
Then shall your woes be ended and Zeus who thunders in heaven
Set what's below on top—"

FIRST WOMAN: What? Are we going to be on top?

LYSISTRATA: "But if the Swallows rebel and flutter away from the temple,
Never a bird in the world shall seem more wanton and worthless."

FIRST WOMAN: That's clear enough, upon my word!

LYSISTRATA: By all that's holy, let's not give up the struggle now. Let's go back inside. It would be a shame, my dear friends, to disobey the oracle.

[*The women all retire to the Acropolis again.*]

CHORUS OF MEN [*singing*]:

I have a tale to tell,
Which I know full well.
It was told me
In the nursery.

Once there was a likely lad,
Melanion they name him;
The thought of marriage made him mad,
For which I cannot blame him.

So off he went to mountains fair;
(No women to upbraid him!)
A mighty hunter of the hare,
He had a dog to aid him.

He never came back home to see
Detested women's faces.
He showed a shrewd mentality.
With him I'd fain change places!

ONE OF THE MEN [*to one of the women*]: Come here, old dame; give me a kiss.

WOMAN: You'll ne'er eat garlic, if you dare!

MAN: I want to kick you—just like this!

WOMAN: Oh, there's a leg with bushy hair!

MAN: Myronides and Phormio[40]
Were hairy—and they thrashed the foe.

CHORUS OF WOMEN [*singing*]:

I have another tale,
With which to assail
Your contention
'Bout Melanion.

Once upon a time a man
Named Timon left our city,

[40] Athenian generals.

To live in some deserted land.
(We thought him rather witty.)

He dwelt alone amidst the thorn;
In solitude he brooded.
From some grim Fury he was born:
Such hatred he exuded.

He cursed you men, as scoundrels through
And through, till life he ended.
He couldn't stand the sight of YOU!
But women he befriended.

WOMAN [*to one of the men*]: I'll smash your face in, if you like.
MAN: Oh no, please don't! You frighten me.
WOMAN: I'll lift my foot—and thus I'll strike.
MAN: Aha! Look there! What's that I see?
WOMAN: Whate'er you see, you cannot say
That I'm not neatly trimmed today.

[LYSISTRATA *appears on the wall of the Acropolis.*]

LYSISTRATA: Hello! Hello! Girls, come here quick!

[*Several women appear beside her.*]

WOMAN: What is it? Why are you calling?
LYSISTRATA: I see a man coming: he's in a dreadful state. He's mad with passion. O Queen of Cyprus, Cythera, and Paphos, just keep on this way!
WOMAN: Where is the fellow?
LYSISTRATA: There, beside the shrine of Demeter.
WOMAN: Oh yes, so he is. Who is he?
LYSISTRATA: Let's see. Do any of you know him?
MYRRHINE: Yes indeed. That's my husband, Cinesias.
LYSISTRATA: It's up to you, now: roast him, rack him, fool him, love him—and leave him! Do everything, except what our oath forbids.
MYRRHINE: Don't worry; I'll do it.
LYSISTRATA: I'll stay here to tease him and warm him up a bit. Off with you.

[*The other women retire from the wall. Enter* CINESIAS *followed by a slave carrying a baby.* CINESIAS *is obviously in great pain and distress.*]

CINESIAS [*groaning*]: Oh-h! Oh-h-h! This is killing me! O God, what tortures I'm suffering!
LYSISTRATA [*from the wall*]: Who's that within our lines?
CINESIAS: Me.
LYSISTRATA: A *man?*
CINESIAS [*pointing*]: A *man,* indeed!
LYSISTRATA: Well, go away!
CINESIAS: Who are you to send me away?
LYSISTRATA: The captain of the guard.
CINESIAS: Oh, for heaven's sake, call out Myrrhine for me.
LYSISTRATA: Call Myrrhine? Nonsense! Who are you?
CINESIAS: Her husband, Cinesias of Paionidai.
LYSISTRATA [*appearing much impressed*]: Oh, greetings, friend. Your name is not without honour here among us. Your wife is always talking about you, and whenever she takes an egg or an apple, she says, "Here's to my dear Cinesias!"
CINESIAS [*quivering with excitement*]: Oh, ye gods in heaven!

LYSISTRATA: Indeed she does! And whenever our conversations turn to men, your wife immediately says, "All others are mere rubbish compared with Cinesias."

CINESIAS [*groaning*]: Oh! Do call her for me.

LYSISTRATA: Why should I? What will you give me?

CINESIAS: Whatever you want. All I have is yours—and you see what I've got!

LYSISTRATA: Well then, I'll go down and call her. [*She descends.*]

CINESIAS: And hurry up! I've had no joy of life ever since she left home. When I go in the house, I feel awful: everything seems so empty and I can't enjoy my dinner. I'm in such a state all the time!

MYRRHINE [*from behind the wall*]: I *do* love him so. But he won't let me love him. No, no! Don't ask me to see him!

CINESIAS: O my darling, O Myrrhine honey, why do you do this to me? [MYRRHINE *appears on the wall.*] Come down here!

MYRRHINE: No, I won't come down.

CINESIAS: Won't you come, Myrrhine, when *I* call you?

MYRRHINE: No; you don't want me.

CINESIAS: *Don't want you?* I'm in agony!

MYRRHINE: I'm going now.

CINESIAS: Please don't! At least, listen to your baby. [*to the baby*] Here you, call your mamma! [*pinching the baby*]

BABY: Ma-ma! Ma-ma! Ma-ma!

CINESIAS [*to* MYRRHINE]: What's the matter with you? Have you no pity for your child, who hasn't been washed or fed for five whole days?

MYRRHINE: Oh, poor child; your father pays no attention to you.

CINESIAS: Come down then, you heartless wretch, for the baby's sake.

MYRRHINE: Oh, what it is to be a mother! I've got to come down, I suppose. [*She leaves the wall and shortly reappears at the gate.*]

CINESIAS [*to himself*]: She seems much younger, and she has such a sweet look about her. Oh, the way she teases me! And her pretty, provoking ways make me burn with longing.

MYRRHINE [*coming out of the gate and taking the baby*]: O my sweet little angel. Naughty papa! Here, let Mummy kiss you, Mamma's little sweetheart! [*She fondles the baby lovingly.*]

CINESIAS [*in despair*]: You heartless creature, why do you do this? Why follow these other women and make both of us suffer so? [*He tries to embrace her.*]

MYRRHINE: Don't touch me!

CINESIAS: You're letting all our things at home go to wrack and ruin.

MYRRHINE: I don't care.

CINESIAS: You don't care that your wool is being plucked to pieces by the chickens?

MYRRHINE: Not in the least.

CINESIAS: And you haven't celebrated the rites of Aphrodite for ever so long. Won't you come home?

MYRRHINE: Not on your life, unless you men make a truce and stop the war.

CINESIAS: Well then, if that pleases you, we'll do it.

MYRRHINE: Well then, if that pleases *you*, I'll come home—afterwards! Right now I'm on oath not to.

CINESIAS: Then just lie down here with me for a moment.

MYRRHINE: No—[*in a teasing voice*] and yet, I won't say I don't love you.

CINESIAS: You love me? Oh, do lie down here, Myrrhine dear!

MYRRHINE: What, you silly fool! in front of the baby?

CINESIAS [*hastily thrusting the baby at the slave*]: Of course not. Here—home! Take him, Manes! [*The slave goes off with the baby.*] See, the baby's out of the way. Now won't you lie down?

MYRRHINE: But where, my dear?
CINESIAS: Where? The grotto of Pan's a lovely spot.
MYRRHINE: How could I purify myself before returning to the shrine?
CINESIAS: Easily: just wash here in the Clepsydra.[41]
MYRRHINE: And then, shall I go back on my oath?
CINESIAS: On my head be it! Don't worry about the oath.
MYRRHINE: All right, then. Just let me bring out a bed.
CINESIAS: No, don't. The ground's all right.
MYRRHINE: Heavens, no! Bad as you are, I won't let you lie on the bare ground. [*She goes into the Acropolis.*]
CINESIAS: Why, she really loves me; it's plain to see.
MYRRHINE [*returning with a bed*]: There! Now hurry up and lie down. I'll just slip off this dress. But—let's see: oh yes, I must fetch a mattress.
CINESIAS: Nonsense! No mattress for me.
MYRRHINE: Yes indeed! It's not nice on the bare springs.
CINESIAS: Give me a kiss.
MYRRHINE [*giving him a hasty kiss*]: There! [*She goes.*]
CINESIAS [*in mingled distress and delight*]: Oh-h! Hurry back!
MYRRHINE [*returning with a mattress*]: Here's the mattress; lie down on it. I'm taking my things off now—but—let's see: you have no pillow.
CINESIAS: I don't *want* a pillow!
MYRRHINE: But I do. [*She goes.*]
CINESIAS: Cheated again, just like Heracles and his dinner!
MYRRHINE [*returning with a pillow*]: Here, lift your head. [*to herself, wondering how else to tease him*] Is that all?
CINESIAS: Surely that's all! Do come here, precious!
MYRRHINE: I'm taking off my girdle. But remember: don't go back on your promise about the truce.
CINESIAS: Hope to die, if I do.
MYRRHINE: You don't have a blanket.
CINESIAS [*shouting in exasperation*]: *I don't want one!* I WANT TO—
MYRRHINE: Sh-h! There, there, I'll be back in a minute. [*She goes.*]
CINESIAS: She'll be the death of me with these bed-clothes.
MYRRHINE [*returning with a blanket*]: Here, get up.
CINESIAS: I've got *this* up!
MYRRHINE: Would you like some perfume?
CINESIAS: Good heavens, no! I won't have it!
MYRRHINE: Yes, you shall, whether you want it or not. [*She goes.*]
CINESIAS: O lord! Confound all perfumes anyway!
MYRRHINE [*returning with a flask*]: Stretch out your hand and put some on.
CINESIAS [*suspiciously*]: By God, I don't much like this perfume. It smacks of shilly-shallying, and has no scent of the marriage-bed.
MYRRHINE: Oh dear! This is Rhodian perfume I've brought.
CINESIAS: It's quite all right, dear. Never mind.
MYRRHINE: Don't be silly! [*She goes out with the flask.*]
CINESIAS: Damn the man who first concocted perfumes!
MYRRHINE [*returning with another flask*]: Here, try this flask.
CINESIAS: I've got another one all ready for you. Come, you wretch, lie down and stop bringing me things.

---

[41] A spring on the Acropolis.

MYRRHINE: All right; I'm taking off my shoes. But, my dear, see that you vote for peace.

CINESIAS [*absently*]: I'll consider it. [MYRRHINE *runs away to the Acropolis.*] I'm ruined! The wench has skinned me and run away! [*chanting, in tragic style*] Alas! Alas! Deceived, deserted by this fairest of women, whom shall I—lay? Ah, my poor little child, how shall I nurture thee? Where's Cynalopex?[42] I needs must hire a nurse!

LEADER OF THE CHORUS OF OLD MEN [*chanting*]: Ah, wretched man, in dreadful wise beguiled, bewrayed, thy soul is sore distressed. I pity thee, alas! alas! What soul, what loins, what liver could stand this strain? How firm and unyielding he stands, with naught to aid him of a morning.

CINESIAS: O lord! O Zeus! What tortures I endure!

LEADER OF THE CHORUS OF OLD MEN: This is the way she's treated you, that vile and cursèd wanton.

LEADER OF THE CHORUS OF OLD WOMEN: Nay, not vile and cursèd, but sweet and dear.

LEADER OF THE CHORUS OF OLD MEN: Sweet, you say? Nay, hateful, hateful!

CINESIAS:

Hateful indeed! O Zeus, Zeus!
Seize her and snatch her away,
Like a handful of dust, in a mighty,
Fiery tempest! Whirl her aloft, then let her drop
Down to the earth, with a crash, as she falls—
On the point of this waiting
  Thingummybob! [*He goes out.*]

[*Enter a Spartan* HERALD, *in an obvious state of excitement, which he is doing his best to conceal.*]

HERALD: Where can I find the Senate or the Prytanes?[43] I've got an important message.

[*The Athenian* MAGISTRATE *enters.*]

ATHENIAN MAGISTRATE: Say there, are you a man or Priapus?[44]

HERALD [*in annoyance*]: I'm a herald, you lout! I've come from Sparta about the truce.

ATHENIAN MAGISTRATE: Is that a spear you've got under your cloak?

HERALD: No, of course not!

ATHENIAN MAGISTRATE: Why do you twist and turn so? Why hold your cloak in front of you? Did you rupture yourself on the trip?

HERALD: By gum, the fellow's an old fool.

ATHENIAN MAGISTRATE [*pointing*]: Why, you dirty rascal, you're all excited.

HERALD: Not at all. Stop this tom-foolery.

ATHENIAN MAGISTRATE: Well, what's that I see?

HERALD: A Spartan message-staff.

ATHENIAN MAGISTRATE: Oh, certainly! That's just the kind of message-staff I've got. But tell me the honest truth: how are things going in Sparta?

HERALD: All the land of Sparta is up in arms—and our allies are up, too. We need Pellene.[45]

ATHENIAN MAGISTRATE: What brought this trouble on you? A sudden Panic?

---

[42] A brothel-keeper.
[43] The executive committee of the Athenian Assembly.
[44] A fertility god whose phallic statue guarded gardens and orchards.
[45] A city held by Athens and claimed by Sparta; also a famous Athenian prostitute.

HERALD: No, Lampito started it and then all the other women in Sparta with one accord chased their husbands out of their beds.

ATHENIAN MAGISTRATE: How do you feel?

HERALD: Terrible. We walk around the city bent over like men lighting matches in a wind. For our women won't let us touch them until we all agree and make peace throughout Greece.

ATHENIAN MAGISTRATE: This is a general conspiracy of the women; I see it now. Well, hurry back and tell the Spartans to send ambassadors here with full powers to arrange a truce. And I'll go tell the Council to choose ambassadors from here; I've got a little something here that will soon persuade them!

HERALD: I'll fly there; for you've made an excellent suggestion.

[*The* HERALD *and the* MAGISTRATE *depart on opposite sides of the stage.*]

LEADER OF THE CHORUS OF OLD MEN:
No beast or fire is harder than womankind to tame,
Nor is the spotted leopard so devoid of shame.

LEADER OF THE CHORUS OF OLD WOMEN:
Knowing this, you dare provoke us to attack?
I'd be your steady friend, if you'd but take us back.

LEADER OF THE CHORUS OF OLD MEN:
I'll never cease my hatred keen of womankind.

LEADER OF THE CHORUS OF OLD WOMEN:
Just as you will. But now just let me help you find
That cloak you threw aside. You look so silly there
Without your clothes. Here, put it on and don't go bare.

LEADER OF THE CHORUS OF OLD MEN:
That's very kind, and shows you're not entirely bad.
But I threw off my things when I was good and mad.

LEADER OF THE CHORUS OF OLD WOMEN:
At last you seem a man, and won't be mocked, my lad.
If you'd been nice to me, I'd take this little gnat
That's in your eye and pluck it out for you, like that.

LEADER OF THE CHORUS OF OLD MEN:
So that's what's bothered me and bit my eye so long!
Please dig it out for me. I own that I've been wrong.

LEADER OF THE CHORUS OF OLD WOMEN:
I'll do so, though you've been a most ill-natured brat.
Ye gods! See here! A huge and monstrous little gnat!

LEADER OF THE CHORUS OF OLD MEN:
Oh, how that helps! For it was digging wells in me.
And now it's out, my tears can roll down hard and free.

LEADER OF THE CHORUS OF OLD WOMEN:
Here, let me wipe them off, although you're such a knave,
And kiss me.

LEADER OF THE CHORUS OF OLD MEN:
No!

LEADER OF THE CHORUS OF OLD WOMEN:
Whate'er you say, a kiss I'll have. [*She kisses him.*]

LEADER OF THE CHORUS OF OLD MEN:
Oh, confound these women! They've a coaxing way about them.
He was wise and never spoke a truer word, who said,
"We can't live with women, but we cannot live without them."
Now I'll make a truce with you. We'll fight no more; instead,

I will not injure you if you do me no wrong.
And now let's join our ranks and then begin a song.

COMBINED CHORUS [*singing*]:

Athenians, we're not prepared,
To say a single ugly word
About our fellow-citizens.
Quite the contrary: we desire but to say and to do
Naught but good. Quite enough are the ills now on hand.

Men and women, be advised:
If anyone requires
Money—minae two or three—,
We've got what he desires.

My purse is yours, on easy terms:
When Peace shall reappear,
Whate'er you've borrowed will be due.
So speak up without fear.

You needn't pay me back, you see,
If you can get a cent from me!

We're about to entertain
Some foreign gentlemen;
We've soup and tender, fresh-killed pork.
Come round to dine at ten.

Come early; wash and dress with care,
And bring the children, too.
Then step right in, no "by your leave."
We'll be expecting you.

Walk in as if you owned the place.
You'll find the door—shut in your face!

[*Enter a group of Spartan Ambassadors; they are in the same desperate condition as the Herald in the previous scene.*]

LEADER OF CHORUS: Here come the envoys from Sparta, sprouting long beards and looking for all the world as if they were carrying pig-pens in front of them.

Greetings, gentlemen of Sparta. Tell me, in what state have you come?

SPARTAN: Why waste words? You can plainly see what state we've come in!

LEADER OF CHORUS: Wow! You're in a pretty high-strung condition, and it seems to be getting worse.

SPARTAN: It's indescribable. Won't someone please arrange a peace for us—in any way you like.

LEADER OF CHORUS: Here come our own, native ambassadors, crouching like wrestlers and holding their clothes in front of them; this seems an athletic kind of malady.

[*Enter several Athenian Ambassadors.*]

ATHENIAN: Can anyone tell us where Lysistrata is? You see our condition.

LEADER OF CHORUS: Here's another case of the same complaint. Tell me, are the attacks worse in the morning?

ATHENIAN: No, we're always afflicted this way. If someone doesn't soon arrange this truce, you'd better not let me get my hands on—Cleisthenes!

LEADER OF CHORUS: If you're smart, you'll arrange your cloaks so none of the fellows who smashed the Hermae[46] can see you.

ATHENIAN: Right you are; a very good suggestion.

SPARTAN: Aye, by all means. Here, let's hitch up our clothes.

ATHENIAN: Greetings, Spartan. We've suffered dreadful things.

SPARTAN: My dear fellow, we'd have suffered still worse if one of those fellows had seen us in this condition.

ATHENIAN: Well, gentlemen, we must get down to business. What's your errand here?

SPARTAN: We're ambassadors about peace.

ATHENIAN: Excellent; so are we. Only Lysistrata can arrange things for us; shall we summon her?

SPARTAN: Aye, and Lysistratus too, if you like.

LEADER OF CHORUS: No need to summon her, it seems. She's coming out of her own accord.

[*Enter* LYSISTRATA *accompanied by a statue of a nude female figure, which represents Reconciliation.*]

Hail, noblest of women; now must thou be
A judge shrewd and subtle, mild and severe,
Be sweet yet majestic: all manners employ.
The leaders of Hellas, caught by thy love-charms,
Have come to thy judgment, their charges submitting.

LYSISTRATA: This is no difficult task, if one catch them still in amorous passion, before they've resorted to each other. But I'll soon find out. Where's Reconciliation? Go, first bring the Spartans here, and don't seize them rudely and violently, as our tactless husbands used to do, but as befits a woman, like an old, familiar friend; if they won't give you their hands, take them however you can. Then go fetch these Athenians here, taking hold of whatever they offer you. Now then, men of Sparta, stand here beside me, and you Athenians on the other side, and listen to my words.

I am a woman, it is true, but I have a mind; I'm not badly off in native wit, and by listening to my father and my elders, I've had a decent schooling.

Now I intend to give you a scolding which you both deserve. With one common font you worship at the same altars, just like brothers, at Olympia, at Thermopylae, at Delphi—how many more might I name, if time permitted;—and the Barbarians stand by waiting with their armies; yet you are destroying the men and towns of Greece.

ATHENIAN: Oh, this tension is killing me!

LYSISTRATA: And now, men of Sparta,—to turn to you—don't you remember how the Spartan Pericleidas came here once as a suppliant, and sitting at our altar, all pale with fear in his crimson cloak, begged us for an army?[47] For all Messene had attacked you and the god sent an earthquake too? Then Cimon went forth with four thousand hoplites and saved all Lacedaemon. Such was the aid you

---

[46] Small phallic statues of the god Hermes. Before the expedition to Sicily, rioters in Athens smashed many of these statues.

[47] In 464 the Spartans secured Athenian aid to put down a rebellion following an earthquake in Sparta.

received from Athens, and now you lay waste the country which once treated you so well.

ATHENIAN [*hotly*]: They're in the wrong, Lysistrata, upon my word, they are!

SPARTAN [*absently, looking at the statue of Reconciliation*]: We're in the wrong. What hips! How lovely they are!

LYSISTRATA: Don't think I'm going to let you Athenians off. Don't you remember how the Spartans came in arms when you were wearing the rough, sheepskin cloak of slaves and slew the host of Thessalians, the comrades and allies of Hippias?[48] Fighting with you on that day, alone of all the Greeks, they set you free and instead of a sheepskin gave your folk a handsome robe to wear.

SPARTAN [*looking at* LYSISTRATA]: I've never seen a more distinguished woman.

ATHENIAN [*looking at Reconciliation*]: I've never seen a more voluptuous body!

LYSISTRATA: Why then, with these many noble deeds to think of, do you fight each other? Why don't you stop this villainy? Why not make peace? Tell me, what prevents it?

SPARTAN [*waving vaguely at Reconciliation*]: We're willing, if you're willing to give up your position on yonder flank.

LYSISTRATA: What position, my good man?

SPARTAN: Pylus; we've been panting for it for ever so long.

ATHENIAN: No, by God! You shan't have it!

LYSISTRATA: Let them have it, my friend.

ATHENIAN: Then what shall we have to rouse things up?

LYSISTRATA: Ask for another place in exchange.

ATHENIAN: Well, let's see: first of all [*pointing to various parts of Reconciliation's anatomy*] give us Echinus here, this Maliac Inlet in back there, and these two Megarian legs.

SPARTAN: No, by heavens! You can't have *everything*, you crazy fool!

LYSISTRATA: Let it go. Don't fight over a pair of legs.

ATHENIAN [*taking off his cloak*]: I think I'll strip and do a little planting now.

SPARTAN [*following suit*]: And I'll just do a little fertilizing, by gosh!

LYSISTRATA: Wait until the truce is concluded. Now if you've decided on this course, hold a conference and discuss the matter with your allies.

ATHENIAN: Allies? Don't be ridiculous! They're in the same state we are. Won't all our allies want the same thing we do—to jump in bed with their women?

SPARTAN: Ours will, I know.

ATHENIAN: Especially the Carystians,[49] by God!

LYSISTRATA: Very well. Now purify yourselves, that your wives may feast and entertain you in the Acropolis; we've provisions by the basketfull. Exchange your oaths and pledges there, and then each of you may take his wife and go home.

ATHENIAN: Let's go at once.

SPARTAN: Come on, where you will.

ATHENIAN: For God's sake, let's hurry!

[*They all go into the Acropolis.*]

CHORUS [*singing*]:

Whate'er I have of coverlets
And robes of varied hue

---

[48]The Spartans had aided Athenian exiles in overthrowing the tyrant Hippias, thus establishing Athenian democracy. Hippias had required the exiles to wear sheepskins.

[49]Allies of the Athenians who were thought to be primitive and uninhibited.

And golden trinkets,—without stint
I offer them to you.

Take what you will and bear it home,
Your children to delight,
Or if your girl's a Basket-maid;
Just choose whate'er's in sight.

There's naught within so well secured
You cannot break the seal
And bear it off; just help yourselves;
No hesitation feel.

But you'll see nothing, though you try,
Unless you've sharper eyes than I!

If anyone needs bread to feed
A growing family,
I've lots of wheat and full-grown loaves;
So just apply to me.

Let every poor man who desires
Come round and bring a sack
To fetch the grain; my slave is there
To load it on his back.

But don't come near my door, I say:
Beware the dog, and stay away!

[*An* ATHENIAN *enters carrying a torch; he knocks at the gate.*]

ATHENIAN: Open the door! [*to the* CHORUS, *which is clustered around the gate*] Make way, won't you! What are you hanging around for? Want me to singe you with this torch? [*to himself*] No; it's a stale trick, I won't do it! [*to the audience*] Still, if I've got to do it to please you, I suppose I'll have to take the trouble.

[*A* SECOND ATHENIAN *comes out of the gate.*]

SECOND ATHENIAN: And I'll help you.

FIRST ATHENIAN [*waving his torch at the* CHORUS]: Get out! Go bawl your heads off! Move on there, so the Spartans can leave in peace when the banquet's over.

[*They brandish their torches until the* CHORUS *leaves the Orchestra.*]

SECOND ATHENIAN: I've never seen such a pleasant banquet: the Spartans are charming fellows, indeed they are! And we Athenians are very witty in our cups.

FIRST ATHENIAN: Naturally: for when we're sober we're never at our best. If the Athenians would listen to me, we'd always get a little tipsy on our embassies. As things are now, we go to Sparta when we're sober and look around to stir up trouble. And then we don't hear what they say—and as for what they *don't* say, we have all sorts of suspicions. And then we bring back varying reports about the mission. But this time everything is pleasant; even if a man should sing the Telamon-song when he ought to sing "Cleitagoras," we'd praise him and swear it was excellent.

[*The two* CHORUSES *return, as a* CHORUS OF ATHENIANS *and a* CHORUS OF SPARTANS.]

Here they come back again. Go to the devil, you scoundrels!

SECOND ATHENIAN: Get out, I say! They're coming out from the feast.

[*Enter the Spartan and Athenian envoys, followed by* LYSISTRATA *and all the women.*]

SPARTAN [*to one of his fellow-envoys*]: My good fellow, take up your pipes; I want to do a fancy two-step and sing a jolly song for the Athenians.

ATHENIAN: Yes, do take your pipes, by all means. I'd love to see you dance.

SPARTAN [*singing and dancing with the* CHORUS OF SPARTANS]:

These youths inspire
To song and dance, O Memory;
Stir up my Muse, to tell how we
And Athens' men, in our galleys clashing
At Artemisium,[50] 'gainst foemen dashing
In godlike ire,
Conquered the Persian and set Greece free.

Leonidas
Led on his valiant warriors
Whetting their teeth like angry boars.
Abundant foam on their lips was flow'ring,
A stream of sweat from their limbs was show'ring.
The Persian was
Numberless as the sand on the shores.

O Huntress[51] who slayest the beasts in the glade,
O Virgin divine, hither come to our truce,
Unite us in bonds which all time will not loose.
Grant us to find in this treaty, we pray,
An unfailing source of true friendship today,
And all of our days, helping us to refrain
From weaseling tricks which bring war in their train.
Then hither, come hither! O huntress maid.

LYSISTRATA: Come then, since all is fairly done, men of Sparta, lead away your wives, and you, Athenians, take yours. Let every man stand beside his wife, and every wife beside her man, and then, to celebrate our fortune, let's dance. And in the future, let's take care to avoid these misunderstandings.

CHORUS OF ATHENIANS [*singing and dancing*]:

Lead on the dances, your graces revealing.
Call Artemis hither, call Artemis' twin,
Leader of dances, Apollo the Healing,
Kindly God—hither! let's summon him in!
Nysian Bacchus call,
Who with his Maenads, his eyes flashing fire,

[50]Site of a naval battle where the Athenian fleet fought the Persians while the Spartans, led by Leonidas, fought the Persians on land at Thermopylae.

[51]Artemis.

Dances, and last of all
Zeus of the thunderbolt flaming, the Sire,
And Hera in majesty,
Queen of prosperity.

Come, ye Powers who dwell above
Unforgetting, our witnesses be
Of Peace with bonds of harmonious love—
The Peace which Cypris has wrought for me.
Alleluia! Io Paean!
Leap in joy—hurrah! hurrah!
'Tis victory—hurrah! hurrah!
Euoi! Euoi! Euai! Euai!

LYSISTRATA [*to the Spartans*]: Come now, sing a new song to cap ours.

CHORUS OF SPARTANS [*singing and dancing*]:
Leaving Taygetus fair and renown'd,
Muse of Laconia,[52] hither come:
Amyclae's god in hymns resound,
Athene of the Brazen Home,[53]
And Castor and Pollux, Tyndareus' sons,
Who sport where Eurotas[54] murmuring runs.

On with the dance! Heia! Ho!
All leaping along,
Mantles a-swinging as we go!
Of Sparta our song.
There the holy chorus ever gladdens,
There the beat of stamping feet,
As our winsome fillies, lovely maidens,
Dance, beside Eurotas' banks a-skipping,—
Nimbly go to and fro
Hast'ning, leaping feet in measures tripping,
Like the Bacchae's revels, hair a-streaming.
Leda's child, divine and mild,
Leads the holy dance, her fair face beaming.
On with the dance! as your hand
Presses the hair
Streaming away unconfined.
Leap in the air
Light as the deer; footsteps resound
Aiding our dance, beating the ground.
Praise Athene, Maid divine, unrivalled in her might,
Dweller in the Brazen Home, unconquered in the fight.

[*All go out singing and dancing.*]

---

[52]Laconia: the region of Sparta; Amyclae: part of Sparta.
[53]The Temple of Athena in Sparta was bronze-plated.
[54]The river in Sparta.

PLATO

[427?–347 B.C.E.]

SOCRATES

We have no works written by Socrates. He was a great teacher, but he didn't publish, so all we know about him comes from others, especially from the writings of his student Plato. Socrates plays the central role in many of Plato's dialogues, raising questions and focusing the issues under discussion. For Plato and his readers, and for us, Socrates represents the philosophic ideals of the Greeks, the belief in questioning as a way to truth, and the commitment to self understanding as the beginning of knowledge. The first of the three great ancient Greek philosophers—the other two were Plato and Aristotle (384–322 B.C.E.)—Socrates turned philosophy from speculation about the cosmos to questions about the conduct of human life. His own life became his most important work: like Jesus, in his life and his martyrdom, Socrates epitomized the most deeply held ideals of his culture.

LIFE OF SOCRATES

Born about 470, Socrates lived during a period of profound transformation in Athens. His early life was spent in the golden age of classical Athenian culture, the age of Pericles. Although we know little about this period in Socrates' life, he seems to have come from a prosperous family, one that was able to indulge his interest in learning and philosophical speculation. During these years, he may also have pursued questions about the origin and nature of the universe, the traditional subject of philosophical speculation in Greece. But by the beginning of the Peloponnesian War in 431, he had abandoned such questions to devote himself to the study of conduct.

Socrates' middle years coincided with the Peloponnesian War (431–404), the struggle between the city-states of the Greek Peninsula, led by Athens on one side and Sparta on the other. Although Athens had some important victories along the way, Sparta was the eventual winner. The political turmoil in Athens brought about by the war led to the fall of Athenian democracy and the emergence of oligarchic rule. In this heightened political context, Socrates' questions about justice, loyalty, and piety were not always well received, even though he served in the Athenian army and fought heroically in some of the battles. The years just before his death in 399 were troubled by the struggle between oligarchy and democracy in Athens. Although Socrates tried to avoid political involvement, he could not altogether escape this political turmoil, and politics may have played a part in his final condemnation. Socrates was neither political nor politic. In troubled times, he was a perfect candidate for martyrdom.

A "street teacher" known for his grotesque appearance—short and stout, with prominent eyes and a snub nose—and for such eccentricities as going barefoot year 'round, Socrates was sometimes linked with the Sophists, free-lance teachers who, for a fee, taught expedient and fashionable ideas to their pupils. In his *Apology,* Socrates is eager to distinguish himself from these popular teachers. He has no art to teach, he claims, nor any rhetorical cleverness to model for his followers. He is just a gadfly, asking innocent questions and seeking plain answers. If he is the wisest man in Athens, as the Delphic Oracle stated, it is only because he knows that he does not know anything. This stance of naive arrogance often annoyed those he questioned, especially when their arguments were held up to mockery. Although Socrates did not seek to explain the nature or origins of the cosmos, he did frequently challenge established truths and the conventional wisdom. When he asked what is justice, or piety, or wisdom, he often arrived at conclusions that rejected the generally accepted answers to these questions.

Socrates has often been compared to Jesus. Both were charismatic teachers who attracted a group of followers. Both believed absolutely in the truths they had a mission to tell. Both challenged the political and social institutions of their time and place. Both were models of the moral and committed life. And both became martyrs for their ideals, choosing to die rather than compromise the principles by which they lived. They differed most significantly, perhaps, in their ideals: Jesus taught love, compassion, and salvation as his essential truths; Socrates taught self-knowledge and good citizenship. Yet the ideals of both men comprise two central strands in the tapestry of the Western tradition.

Plato

Just as Jesus is largely known through the biographies of him in the four gospels, Socrates is known from Plato's dialogues. One of Socrates' students, Plato left Athens after Socrates' execution. When he returned about fourteen years later, he founded the Academy, a school that flourished in Athens until 529 C.E. There he taught for the remainder of his long life and wrote the dialogues for which he is famous. In many of these philosophic conversations, Socrates is the central figure, using the "Socratic method," the question-and-answer technique by which he pursues the truth about important questions. He tests big ideas by seeking clearer definitions. When he asks in the *Euthyphro,* for example, "What is piety?" Euthyphro answers that piety "is that which is dear to the gods, and impiety is that which is not dear to them." Then Socrates continues his questioning and gets Euthyphro to admit that because the gods disagree among themselves, there are contradictions in his definition. Moreover, the principle is no principle at all, for to define piety as "what is dear to the gods" does not identify what it is that makes it dear. Socrates gradually backs Euthyphro into a corner and by the end of their conversation, he has poked holes in Euthyphro's reasoning and he seems to be challenging any conventional, untested belief in the gods. Socrates has purged the definition of piety of its indefensible claims, but he has not really come up with a workable alternative. The Socratic method appeared to be more effective at undermining established opinions than in developing new ones, and it often angered those he questioned, for he seemed to be holding them, as well as their beliefs, up to ridicule. No wonder he was charged with impiety, with failing to pay due respect to the gods and do the things that were dear to them.

The critical side to the Socratic method is most apparent in Plato's early dialogues, such as the *Euthyphro* and the *Crito,* where Socrates challenges the views of those he questions. In the great dialogues of Plato's middle period, such as the *Symposium* or his masterwork, *The Republic,* Socrates also advances ideas of his own, and becomes the mouthpiece for Plato's philosophic ideals. We include a short section from *The Republic,* the famous "Allegory of the Cave," in which the Platonic doctrine of Ideas or Forms is given mythological expression. Plato is usually regarded as the first Western philosophic idealist, who believed that Reality resided in the realm of pure Ideas and that particular things or beings were simply imperfect manifestations of these perfect Ideas. Each individual man, for example, is simply one imperfect realization of the Idea of Man.

Scholars have debated whether these Platonic doctrines were also held by the real Socrates or whether the Socrates of the middle dialogues is a literary device that Plato uses as the mouthpiece for his own ideas. In any case, the historical Socrates becomes less important in Plato's later work and disappears altogether from some of Plato's late dialogues.

We include here the *Apology* and a section from the *Phaedo,* works that concentrate on the character of Socrates rather than on the ideas of Plato. The *Apology,* probably the most famous of Plato's writings, follows the question-and-answer method of most of the dialogues only in the brief section where Socrates questions Meletus about what constitutes the "improvement of youth." Most of the *Apology* summarizes Socrates' speeches in self-defense at his trial. There are two charges against him: that he corrupts the youth of Athens and that he has introduced new divinities. His three accusers, Meletus, Anytus, and Lycon, have made their case against him and as the *Apology* begins, Socrates is stating his defense. He must convince a jury of 501 citizens to vote for his acquittal. He begins by acknowledging the eloquence of his accusers and by pointing out that his presentation will be more informal because this is his first appearance in court and he is unaccustomed to orating. Then he takes up some old charges against him that he is a Sophist teaching for money and that he teaches cosmology.

Socrates opens his direct response to the current charges by telling of his quest to understand the meaning of the Delphic Oracle's assertion that he, a man who only knew that he knew nothing, was the wisest man in Athens. He describes how those he questioned—the politicians, poets, and artisans—proved to have no greater knowledge than he did, even though they professed to have answers to questions that Socrates could not answer. Finally he realized that his wisdom was that he knew he did not know, and he set out to show others that they were not as wise as they thought they were. His accusers are angry with him, he suggests, because they did not want their ignorance revealed.

There were also political reasons why Socrates was prosecuted. The democrats in power in Athens in 399 considered his belief that government should be led by trained experts subversive of democracy, and some of the most prominent of Socrates' disciples—Alcibiades, Critias, Plato, and Xenophon, for example—were members of the antidemocratic faction. In this charged political context in the aftermath of the loss to Sparta only a few years before, Socrates' arrogant questioning threatened the party in power.

Socrates offers no political compromises in his defense. He reaffirms his commitment to questioning and to teaching his fundamental truths that "virtue is knowledge" and that "the unexamined life is not worth living." He will not abandon his god-given role as a gadfly sent to sting the citizens of Athens to virtuous living. Defiant and uncompromising, he refuses to give the court an excuse for dismissing or reducing the charges against him. He will make no deals in exchange for his life. If he is allowed to live, he will continue to urge his fellow citizens to "know themselves."

Some readers have considered Socrates' uncompromising position a form of arrogance. Taking this elitist stance, they argue, Socrates rejects the compromises necessary in a democratic society and brings on himself a just punishment. But most view Socrates' death as unjust, the martyrdom of a principled and courageous man. In the final selection, an excerpt from the *Phaedo* that presents the moment of Socrates' execution by drinking hemlock, we see his courageous integrity as he faces death. True to his moral and philosophical positions, Socrates proves his piety by dying for his convictions.

Suggested Readings

W.K.C. Gutherie in *The Greek Philosophers: From Thales to Aristotle* (1950; 1975) places Socrates and Plato into their philosophic and cultural context, and Richard L. Levin and John Bremer in *The Question of Socrates* (1961) describe the historical Socrates from the various classical accounts about him. Coleman Phillopson discusses Socrates' last days in *The Trial of Socrates* (1928). Two applications of Socrates' ideas to modern issues can be found in Laszlo Versényi's *Socratic Humanism* (1963; 1979), which relates Socrates' ideas to modern existentialism, and in William K. Richmond's *Socrates and the Western World* (1954), which discusses the educational impact of Socrates. I. F. Stone's recent book on *The Trial of Socrates* (1988) provides a critical reading of Socrates' ideas and his trial.

Apology

Translated by Benjamin Jowett

How you, O Athenians, have been affected by my accusers, I cannot tell; but I know that they almost made me forget who I was—so persuasively did they speak; and yet they have hardly uttered a word of truth. But of the many falsehoods told by them, there was one which quite amazed me;—I mean when they said that you should be upon your guard and not allow yourselves to be deceived by the force of my eloquence. To say this, when they were certain to be detected as soon as I opened my lips and proved myself to be anything but a great speaker, did indeed appear to me most shameless—unless by the force of eloquence they mean the force of truth; for if such is their meaning, I admit that I am eloquent. But in how different a way from theirs! Well, as I was saying, they have scarcely spoken the truth at all; but from me you shall hear the whole truth: not, however, delivered after their manner in a set oration duly ornamented with words and phrases. No, by heaven! but I shall use the words and arguments which occur to me at the moment; for I am confident in the justice of my cause: at my time of life I ought not to be appearing before you, O men of Athens, in the character of a juvenile orator—let no one expect it of me. And I must beg of you to grant me a favour:—If I defend myself in my accustomed manner, and you hear me using the words which I have been in the habit of using in the agora[1] at the tables of the money-changers, or anywhere else, I would ask you not to be surprised, and not to interrupt me on this account. For I am more than seventy years of age, and appearing now for the first time in a court of law, I am quite a stranger to the language of the place; and therefore I would have you regard me as if I were really a stranger, whom you would excuse if he spoke in his native tongue, and after the fashion of his country:—Am I making an unfair request of you? Never mind the manner, which may or may not be good; but think only of the truth of my words, and give heed to that: let the speaker speak truly and the judge decide justly.

And first, I have to reply to the older charges and to my first accusers, and then I will go on to the later ones. For of old I have had many accusers, who have accused me falsely to you during many years; and I am more afraid of them than of Anytus and his associates, who are dangerous, too, in their own way. But far more dangerous are the others, who began when you were children, and took possession of your minds with their falsehoods, telling of one Socrates, a wise man, who speculated about the heaven above, and searched into the earth beneath, and made the worse appear the better cause.[2] The disseminators of this tale are the accusers whom I dread; for their hearers are apt to fancy that such enquirers do not believe in the existence of the gods. And they are many, and their charges against me are of ancient date, and they were made by them in the days when you were more impressible than

---

[1] The marketplace.

[2] Socrates is here answering older charges brought against him, specifically that he was a materialist who speculated about the physical world and that he was one of the Sophists who taught expeditious modes of argument rather than truth.

you are now—in childhood, or it may have been in youth—and the cause when heard went by default, for there was none to answer. And hardest of all, I do not know and cannot tell the names of my accusers; unless in the chance case of a Comic poet.[3] All who from envy and malice have persuaded you—some of them having first convinced themselves—all this class of men are most difficult to deal with; for I cannot have them up here, and cross-examine them, and therefore I must simply fight with shadows in my own defence, and argue when there is no one who answers. I will ask you then to assume with me, as I was saying, that my opponents are of two kinds; one recent, the other ancient: and I hope that you will see the propriety of my answering the latter first, for these accusations you heard long before the others, and much oftener.

Well, then, I must make my defence, and endeavor to clear away in a short time, a slander which has lasted a long time. May I succeed, if to succeed be for my good and yours, or likely to avail me in my cause! The task is not an easy one; I quite understand the nature of it. And so leaving the event with God, in obedience to the law I will now make my defence.

I will begin at the beginning, and ask what is the accusation which has given rise to the slander of me, and in fact has encouraged Meletus to prefer this charge against me. Well, what do the slanderers say? They shall be my prosecutors, and I will sum up their words in an affidavit: 'Socrates is an evil-doer, and a curious person, who searches into things under the earth and in heaven, and he makes the worse appear the better cause; and he teaches the aforesaid doctrines to others.' Such is the nature of the accusation: it is just what you have yourselves seen in the comedy of Aristophanes, who has introduced a man whom he calls Socrates, going about and saying that he walks in air, and talking a deal of nonsense concerning matters of which I do not pretend to know either much or little—not that I mean to speak disparagingly of any one who is a student of natural philosophy. I should be very sorry if Meletus could bring so grave a charge against me. But the simple truth is, O Athenians, that I have nothing to do with physical speculations. Very many of those here present are witnesses to the truth of this, and to them I appeal. Speak then, you who have heard me, and tell your neighbours whether any of you have ever known me hold forth in few words or in many upon such matters. . . . You hear their answer. And from what they say of this part of the charge you will be able to judge of the truth of the rest.

As little foundation is there for the report that I am a teacher, and take money; this accusation has no more truth in it than the other. Although, if a man were really able to instruct mankind, to receive money for giving instruction would, in my opinion, be an honour to him. There is Gorgias of Leontium, and Prodicus of Ceos, and Hippias of Elis,[4] who go the round of the cities, and are able to persuade the young men to leave their own citizens by whom they might be taught for nothing, and come to them whom they not only pay, but are thankful if they may be allowed to pay them. There is at this time a Parian[5] philosopher residing in Athens, of whom I have heard; and I came to hear of him in this way:—I came across a man who has spent a world of money on the Sophists, Callias, the son of Hipponicus, and knowing that he had sons, I asked him: 'Callias,' I said, 'if your two sons were foals or calves, there would be no difficulty in finding some one to

[3]Aristophanes, in *The Clouds,* satirized Socrates as a charlatan who promulgated extravagant theories about the physical world.

[4]Famous Sophists who taught rhetoric and logic.

[5]From Paros, an island in the Aegean.

put over them; we should hire a trainer of horses, or a farmer probably, who would improve and perfect them in their own proper virtue and excellence; but as they are human beings, whom are you thinking of placing over them? Is there any one who understands human and political virtue? You must have thought about the matter, for you have sons; is there any one?' 'There is,' he said. 'Who is he?' said I; 'and of what country? and what does he charge?' 'Evenus the Parian,' he replied; 'he is the man, and his charge is five minae.' Happy is Evenus, I said to myself; if he really has this wisdom, and teaches at such a moderate charge. Had I the same, I should have been very proud and conceited; but the truth is that I have no knowledge of the kind.

I dare say, Athenians, that some one among you will reply, 'Yes, Socrates, but what is the origin of these accusations which are brought against you; there must have been something strange which you have been doing? All these rumours and this talk about you would never have arisen if you had been like other men: tell us, then, what is the cause of them, for we should be sorry to judge hastily of you.' Now I regard this as a fair challenge, and I will endeavour to explain to you the reason why I am called wise and have such an evil fame. Please to attend then. And although some of you may think that I am joking, I declare that I will tell you the entire truth. Men of Athens, this reputation of mine has come of a certain sort of wisdom which I possess. If you ask me what kind of wisdom, I reply, wisdom such as may perhaps be attained by man, for to that extent I am inclined to believe that I am wise; whereas the persons of whom I was speaking have a superhuman wisdom, which I may fail to describe, because I have it not myself; and he who says that I have, speaks falsely, and is taking away my character. And here, O men of Athens, I must beg you not to interrupt me, even if I seem to say something extravagant. For the word which I will speak is not mine. I will refer you to a witness who is worthy of credit; that witness shall be the God of Delphi[6]—he will tell you about my wisdom, if I have any, and of what sort it is. You must have known Chaerephon; he was early a friend of mine, and also a friend of yours, for he shared in the recent exile of the people,[7] and returned with you. Well, Chaerephon, as you know, was very impetuous in all his doings, and he went to Delphi and boldly asked the oracle to tell him whether—as I was saying, I must beg you not to interrupt—he asked the oracle to tell him whether any one was wiser than I was, and the Pythian prophetess answered, that there was no man wiser. Chaerephon is dead himself; but his brother, who is in court, will confirm the truth of what I am saying.

Why do I mention this? Because I am going to explain to you why I have such an evil name. When I heard the answer, I said to myself, What can the god mean? and what is the interpretation of his riddle? for I know that I have no wisdom, small or great. What then can he mean when he says that I am the wisest of men? And yet he is a god, and cannot lie; that would be against his nature. After long consideration, I thought of a method of trying the question. I reflected that if I could only find a man wiser than myself, then I might go to the god with a refutation in my hand. I should say to him, 'Here is a man who is wiser than I am; but you said that I was the wisest.' Accordingly I went to one who had the reputation of wisdom, and observed him—his name I need not mention; he was a politician whom I selected for examination—and the result was as follows: When I began to talk with him, I

[6]The Oracle of Apollo at Delphi.

[7]After the defeat of Athens by Sparta in 404 B.C.E., the democratic leaders of Athens had gone into exile, driven out of the city by the Thirty Tyrants who ruled briefly until democracy was reestablished in 403 B.C.E.

could not help thinking that he was not really wise, although he was thought wise by many, and still wiser by himself; and thereupon I tried to explain to him that he thought himself wise, but was not really wise; and the consequence was that he hated me, and his enmity was shared by several who were present and heard me. So I left him, saying to myself, as I went away: Well, although I do not suppose that either of us knows anything really beautiful and good, I am better off than he is,—for he knows nothing, and thinks that he knows; I neither know nor think that I know. In this latter particular, then, I seem to have slightly the advantage of him. Then I went to another who had still higher pretensions to wisdom, and my conclusion was exactly the same. Whereupon I made another enemy of him, and of many others besides him.

Then I went to one man after another, being not unconscious of the enmity which I provoked, and I lamented and feared this: But necessity was laid upon me,—the word of God, I thought, ought to be considered first. And I said to myself, Go I must to all who appear to know, and find out the meaning of the oracle. And I swear to you, Athenians, by the dog I swear!—for I must tell you the truth—the result of my mission was just this: I found that the men most in repute were all but the most foolish; and that others less esteemed were really wiser and better. I will tell you the tale of my wanderings and of the 'Herculean' labours, as I may call them, which I endured only to find at last the oracle irrefutable. After the politicians, I went to the poets; tragic, dithyrambic, and all sorts. And there, I said to myself, you will be instantly detected; now you will find out that you are more ignorant than they are. Accordingly, I took them some of the most elaborate passages in their own writings, and asked what was the meaning of them—thinking that they would teach me something. Will you believe me? I am almost ashamed to confess the truth, but I must say that there is hardly a person present who would not have talked better about their poetry than they did themselves. Then I knew that not by wisdom do poets write poetry, but by a sort of genius and inspiration; they are like diviners or soothsayers who also say many fine things, but do not understand the meaning of them. The poets appeared to me to be much in the same case; and I further observed that upon the strength of their poetry they believed themselves to be the wisest of men in other things in which they were not wise. So I departed, conceiving myself to be superior to them for the same reason that I was superior to the politicians.

At last I went to the artisans, for I was conscious that I knew nothing at all, as I may say, and I was sure that they knew many fine things; and here I was not mistaken, for they did know many things of which I was ignorant, and in this they certainly were wiser than I was. But I observed that even the good artisans fell into the same error as the poets;—because they were good workmen they thought that they also knew all sorts of high matters, and this defect in them overshadowed their wisdom; and therefore I asked myself on behalf of the oracle, whether I would like to be as I was, neither having their knowledge nor their ignorance, or like them in both; and I made answer to myself and to the oracle that I was better off as I was.

This inquisition has led to my having many enemies of the worst and most dangerous kind, and has given occasion also to many calumnies. And I am called wise, for my hearers always imagine that I myself possess the wisdom which I find wanting in others: but the truth is, O men of Athens, that God only is wise; and by his answer he intends to show that the wisdom of men is worth little or nothing; he is not speaking of Socrates, he is only using my name by way of illustration, as if he said, He, O men, is the wisest, who, like Socrates, knows that his wisdom is in truth worth nothing. And so I go about the world, obedient to the god, and search and make enquiry into the wisdom of any one, whether citizen or stranger, who appears to be wise; and if he is not wise, then in vindication of the oracle I show him that he is not wise; and my occupation quite absorbs me, and I have no time to give either to any public matter of interest or to any concern of my own, but I am in utter poverty by reason of my devotion to the god.

There is another thing:—young men of the richer classes, who have not much to do, come about me of their own accord; they like to hear the pretenders examined, and they often imitate me, and proceed to examine others; there are plenty of persons, as they quickly discover, who think that they know something, but really know little or nothing; and then those who are examined by them instead of being angry with themselves are angry with me: This confounded Socrates, they say; this villainous misleader of youth!—and then if somebody asks them, Why, what evil does he practice or teach? they do not know, and cannot tell; but in order that they may not appear to be at a loss, they repeat the ready-made charges which are used against all philosophers about teaching things up in the clouds and under the earth, and having no gods, and making the worse appear the better cause; for they do not like to confess that their pretence of knowledge has been detected—which is the truth; and as they are numerous and ambitious and energetic, and are drawn up in battle array and have persuasive tongues, they have filled your ears with their loud and inveterate calumnies. And this is the reason why my three accusers, Meletus and Anytus and Lycon, have set upon me; Meletus, who has a quarrel with me on behalf of the poets; Anytus, on behalf of the craftsmen and politicians; Lycon, on behalf of the rhetoricians: and as I said at the beginning, I cannot expect to get rid of such a mass of calumny all in a moment. And this, O men of Athens, is the truth and the whole truth; I have concealed nothing, I have dissembled nothing. And yet, I know that my plainness of speech makes them hate me, and what is their hatred but a proof that I am speaking the truth?—Hence has arisen the prejudice against me; and this is the reason of it, as you will find out either in this or in any future enquiry.

I have said enough in my defence against the first class of my accusers; I turn to the second class. They are headed by Meletus, that good man and true lover of his country, as he calls himself. Against these, too, I must try to make a defence:—Let their affidavit be read: it contains something of this kind: It says that Socrates is a doer of evil, who corrupts the youth; and who does not believe in the gods of the state, but has other new divinities of his own. Such is the charge; and now let us examine the particular counts. He says that I am a doer of evil, and corrupt the youth; but I say, O men of Athens, that Meletus is a doer of evil, in that he pretends to be in earnest when he is only in jest, and is so eager to bring men to trial from a pretended zeal and interest about matters in which he really never had the smallest interest. And the truth of this I will endeavour to prove to you.

Come hither, Meletus, and let me ask a question of you. You think a great deal about the improvement of youth?

Yes, I do.

Tell the judges, then, who is their improver; for you must know, as you have taken the pains to discover their corrupter, and are citing and accusing me before them. Speak, then, and tell the judges who their improver is.—Observe, Meletus, that you are silent, and have nothing to say. But is not this rather disgraceful, and a very considerable proof of what I was saying, that you have no interest in the matter? Speak up, friend, and tell us who their improver is.

The laws.

But that, my good sir, is not my meaning. I want to know who the person is, who, in the first place, knows the laws.

The judges, Socrates, who are present in court.

What, do you mean to say, Meletus, that they are able to instruct and improve youth?

Certainly they are.

What, all of them, or some only and not others?

All of them.

By the goddess Here,[8] that is good news! There are plenty of improvers, then. And what do you say of the audience,—do they improve them?

Yes, they do.

And the senators?

Yes, the senators improve them.

But perhaps the members of the assembly corrupt them?—or do they too improve them?

They improve them.

Then every Athenian improves and elevates them; all with the exception of myself; and I alone am their corrupter? Is that what you affirm?

That is what I stoutly affirm.

I am very unfortunate if you are right. But suppose I ask you a question: How about horses? Does one man do them harm and all the world good? Is not the exact opposite the truth? One man is able to do them good, or at least not many;—the trainer of horses, that is to say, does them good, and others who have to do with them rather injure them? Is not that true, Meletus, of horses, or any other animals? Most assuredly it is; whether you and Anytus say yes or no. Happy indeed would be the condition of youth if they had one corrupter only, and all the rest of the world were their improvers. But you, Meletus, have sufficiently shown that you never had a thought about the young: your carelessness is seen in your not caring about the very things which you bring against me.

And now, Meletus, I will ask you another question—by Zeus I will: Which is better, to live among bad citizens, or among good ones? Answer, friend, I say; the question is one which may be easily answered. Do not the good do their neighbours good, and the bad do them evil?

Certainly.

And is there any one who would rather be injured than benefited by those who live with him? Answer, my good friend, the law requires you to answer—does any one like to be injured?

Certainly not.

And when you accuse me of corrupting and deteriorating the youth, do you allege that I corrupt them intentionally or unintentionally?

Intentionally, I say.

But you have just admitted that the good do their neighbours good, and evil do them evil. Now, is that a truth which your superior wisdom has recognized thus early in life, and am I, at my age, in such darkness and ignorance as not to know that if a man with whom I have to live is corrupted by me, I am very likely to be harmed by him; and yet I corrupt him, and intentionally, too—so you say, although neither I nor any other human being is ever likely to be convinced by you. But either I do not corrupt them, or I corrupt them unintentionally; and on either view of the case you lie. If my offence is unintentional, the law has no cognizance of unintentional offences: you ought to have taken me privately, and warned and admonished me; for if I had been better advised, I should have left off doing what I only did unintentionally—no doubt I should; but you would have nothing to say

[8]Hera, the queen of the gods.

to me and refused to teach me. And now you bring me up in this court, which is not a place of instruction, but of punishment.

It will be very clear to you, Athenians, as I was saying, that Meletus has no care at all, great or small, about the matter. But still I should like to know, Meletus, in what I am affirmed to corrupt the young. I suppose you mean, as I infer from your indictment, that I teach them not to acknowledge the gods which the state acknowledges, but some other new divinities or spiritual agencies in their stead. These are the lessons by which I corrupt the youth, as you say.

Yes, that I say emphatically.

Then, by the gods, Meletus, of whom we are speaking, tell me and the court, in somewhat plainer terms, what you mean! for I do not as yet understand whether you affirm that I teach other men to acknowledge some gods, and therefore that I do believe in gods, and am not an entire atheist—this you do not lay to my charge,—but only you say that they are not the same gods which the city recognizes—the charge is that they are different gods. Or, do you mean that I am an atheist simply, and a teacher of atheism?

I mean the latter—that you are a complete atheist.

What an extraordinary statement! Why do you think so, Meletus? Do you mean that I do not believe in the godhead of the sun or moon, like other men?

I assure you, judges, that he does not: for he says that the sun is stone, and the moon earth.[9]

Friend Meletus, you think that you are accusing Anaxagoras:[10] and you have but a bad opinion of the judges, if you fancy them illiterate to such a degree as not to know that these doctrines are found in the books of Anaxagoras the Clazomenian, which are full of them. And so, forsooth, the youth are said to be taught them by Socrates, when there are not unfrequently exhibitions of them at the theatre (price of admission one drachma at the most); and they might pay their money, and laugh at Socrates if he pretends to father these extraordinary views. And so, Meletus, you really think that I do not believe in any god?

I swear by Zeus that you believe absolutely in none at all.

Nobody will believe you, Meletus, and I am pretty sure that you do not believe yourself. I cannot help thinking, men of Athens, that Meletus is reckless and impudent, and that he has written this indictment in a spirit of mere wantonness and youthful bravado. Has he not compounded a riddle, thinking to try me? He said to himself:—I shall see whether the wise Socrates will discover my facetious contradiction, or whether I shall be able to deceive him and the rest of them. For he certainly does appear to me to contradict himself in the indictment as much as if he said that Socrates is guilty of not believing in the gods, and yet of believing in them—but this is not like a person who is in earnest.

I should like you, O men of Athens, to join me in examining what I conceive to be his inconsistency; and do you, Meletus, answer. And I must remind the audience of my request that they would not make a disturbance if I speak in my accustomed manner:

Did ever man, Meletus, believe in the existence of human things, and not of human beings? . . . I wish, men of Athens, that he would answer, and not be always trying to get up an interruption. Did ever any man believe in horsemanship, and not in horses? or in flute-playing, and not in flute-players? No, my friend; I will

[9]These are the older charges, that Socrates taught atheistic doctrines that challenged the worship of Apollo, god of the sun, and Artemis, goddess of the moon.

[10]A fifth-century materialist philosopher from Clazomenae.

answer to you and to the court, as you refuse to answer for yourself. There is no man who ever did. But now please to answer the next question: Can a man believe in spiritual and divine agencies, and not in spirits or demigods?

He cannot.

How lucky I am to have extracted that answer, by the assistance of the court! But then you swear in the indictment that I teach and believe in divine or spiritual agencies (new or old, no matter for that); at any rate, I believe in spiritual agencies,—so you say and swear in the affidavit; and yet if I believe in divine beings, how can I help believing in spirits or demigods;—must I not? To be sure I must; and therefore I may assume that your silence gives consent. Now what are spirits or demigods? Are they not either gods or the sons of gods?

Certainly they are.

But this is what I call the facetious riddle invented by you: the demigods or spirits are gods, and you say first that I do not believe in gods, and then again that I do believe in gods; that is, if I believe in demigods. For if the demigods are the illegitimate sons of gods, whether by the nymphs or by any other mothers, of whom they are said to be the sons—what human being will ever believe that there are no gods if they are the sons of gods? You might as well affirm the existence of mules and deny that of horses and asses. Such nonsense, Meletus, could only have been intended by you to make trial of me. You have put this into the indictment because you had nothing real of which to accuse me. But no one who has a particle of understanding will ever be convinced by you that the same men can believe in divine and superhuman things, and yet not believe that there are gods and demigods and heroes.

I have said enough in answer to the charge of Meletus: any elaborate defence is unnecessary; but I know only too well how many are the enmities which I have incurred, and this is what will be my destruction if I am destroyed;—not Meletus, nor yet Anytus, but the envy and detraction of the world, which has been the death of many good men, and will probably be the death of many more; there is no danger of my being the last of them.

Some one will say: And are you not ashamed, Socrates, of a course of life which is likely to bring you to an untimely end? To him I may fairly answer: There you are mistaken: a man who is good for anything ought not to calculate the chance of living or dying; he ought only to consider whether in doing anything he is doing right or wrong—acting the part of a good man or of a bad. Whereas, upon your view, the heroes who fell at Troy were not good for much, and the son of Thetis[11] above all, who altogether despised danger in comparison with disgrace; and when he was so eager to slay Hector, his goddess mother said to him, that if he avenged his companion Patroclus, and slew Hector, he would die himself—'Fate,' she said, in these or the like words, 'waits for you next after Hector;' he, receiving this warning, utterly despised danger and death, and instead of fearing them, feared rather to live in dishonour, and not to avenge his friend. 'Let me die forthwith,' he replies, 'and be avenged of my enemy, rather than abide here by the beaked ships, a laughing-stock and a burden of the earth.' Had Achilles any thought of death and danger? For wherever a man's place is, whether the place which he has chosen or that in which he has been placed by a commander, there he ought to remain in hour of danger; he should not think of death or of anything but of disgrace. And this, O men of Athens, is a true saying.

---

[11] Achilles; see Book 28 of *The Iliad* for the scene described here.

Strange, indeed, would be my conduct, O men of Athens, if I who, when I was ordered by the generals whom you chose to command me at Potidaea and Amphipolis and Delium,[12] remained where they placed me, like any other man, facing death—if now, when, as I conceive and imagine, God orders me to fulfil the philosopher's mission of searching into myself and other men, I were to desert my post through fear of death, or any other fear; that would indeed be strange, and I might justly be arraigned in court for denying the existence of the gods, if I disobeyed the oracle because I was afraid of death, fancying that I was wise when I was not wise. For the fear of death is indeed the pretence of wisdom, and not real wisdom, being a pretence of knowing the unknown; and no one knows whether death, which men in their fear apprehend to be the greatest evil, may not be the greatest good. Is not this ignorance of a disgraceful sort, the ignorance which is the conceit that man knows what he does not know? And in this respect only I believe myself to differ from men in general, and may perhaps claim to be wiser than they are:—that whereas I know but little of the world below, I do not suppose that I know: but I do know that injustice and disobedience to a better, whether God or man, is evil and dishonourable, and I will never fear or avoid a possible good rather than a certain evil. And therefore if you let me go now, and are not convinced by Anytus, who said that since I had been prosecuted I must be put to death (or if not that I ought never to have been prosecuted at all); and that if I escape now, your sons will all be utterly ruined by listening to my words—if you say to me, Socrates, this time we will not mind Anytus, and you shall be let off, but upon one condition, that you are not to enquire and speculate in this way any more, and that if you are caught doing so again you shall die:—if this was the condition on which you let me go, I should reply: Men of Athens, I honour and love you; but I shall obey God rather than you, and while I have life and strength I shall never cease from the practice and teaching of philosophy, exhorting any one whom I meet and saying to him after my manner: You, my friend,—a citizen of the great and mighty and wise city of Athens,—are you not ashamed of heaping up the greatest amount of money and honour and reputation, and caring so little about wisdom and truth and the greatest improvement of the soul, which you never regard or heed at all? And if the person with whom I am arguing, says: Yes, but I do care; then I do not leave him or let him go at once; but I proceed to interrogate and examine and cross-examine him, and if I think that he has no virtue in him, but only says that he has, I reproach him with undervaluing the greater, and overvaluing the less. And I shall repeat the same words to every one whom I meet, young and old, citizen and alien, but especially to the citizens, inasmuch as they are my brethren. For know that this is the command of God; and I believe that no greater good has ever happened in the state than my service to the God. For I do nothing but go around persuading you all, old and young alike, not to take thought for your persons or your properties, but first and chiefly to care about the greatest improvement of the soul. I tell you that virtue is not given by money, but that from virtue comes money and every other good of man, public as well as private. This is my teaching, and if this is the doctrine which corrupts the youth, I am a mischievous person. But if any one says that this is not my teaching, he is speaking an untruth. Wherefore, O men of Athens, I say to you, do as Anytus bids or not as Anytus bids, and either acquit me or not; but whichever you do, understand that I shall never alter my ways, not even if I have to die many times.

[12] The sites of three battles in which Socrates fought as a soldier.

Men of Athens, do not interrupt, but hear me; there was an understanding between us that you should hear me to the end: I have something more to say, at which you may be inclined to cry out; but I believe that to hear me will be good for you, and therefore I beg that you will not cry out. I would have you know, that if you kill such an one as I am, you will injure yourselves more than you will injure me. Nothing will injure me, not Meletus nor yet Anytus—they cannot, for a bad man is not permitted to injure a better than himself. I do not deny that Anytus may, perhaps, kill him, or drive him into exile, or deprive him of civil rights; and he may imagine, and others may imagine, that he is inflicting a great injury upon him: but there I do not agree. For the evil of doing as he is doing—the evil of unjustly taking away the life of another—is greater far.

And now, Athenians, I am not going to argue for my own sake, as you may think, but for yours, that you may not sin against the God by condemning me, who am his gift to you. For if you kill me you will not easily find a successor to me, who, if I may use such a ludicrous figure of speech, am a sort of gadfly, given to the state by God; and the state is a great and noble steed who is tardy in his motions owing to his very size, and requires to be stirred into life. I am that gadfly which God has attached to the state, and all day long and in all places am always fastening upon you, arousing and persuading and reproaching you. You will not easily find another like me, and therefore I would advise you to spare me. I dare say that you may feel out of temper (like a person who is suddenly awakened from sleep), and you think that you might easily strike me dead as Anytus advises, and then you would sleep on for the remainder of your lives, unless God in his care of you sent you another gadfly. When I say that I am given to you by God, the proof of my mission is this:—if I had been like other men, I should not have neglected all my own concerns or patiently seen the neglect of them during all these years, and have been doing yours, coming to you individually like a father or elder brother, exhorting you to regard virtue; such conduct, I say, would be unlike human nature. If I had gained anything, or if my exhortations had been paid, there would have been some sense in my doing so; but now, as you will perceive, not even the impudence of my accusers dares to say that I have ever exacted or sought pay of any one; of that they have no witness. And I have a sufficient witness to the truth of what I say—my poverty.

Some one may wonder why I go about in private giving advice and busying myself with the concerns of others, but do not venture to come forward in public and advise the state. I will tell you why. You have heard me speak at sundry times and in divers places of an oracle or sign which comes to me, and is the divinity which Meletus ridicules in the indictment. This sign, which is a kind of voice, first began to come to me when I was a child; it always forbids but never commands me to do anything which I am going to do. This is what deters me from being a politician. And rightly, as I think. For I am certain, O men of Athens, that if I had engaged in politics, I should have perished long ago, and done no good either to you or to myself. And do not be offended at my telling you the truth: for the truth is, that no man who goes to war with you or any other multitude, honestly striving against the many lawless and unrighteous deeds which are done in a state, will save his life; he who will fight for the right, if he would live even for a brief space, must have a private station and not a public one.

I can give you convincing evidence of what I say, not words only, but what you value far more—actions. Let me relate to you a passage of my own life which will prove to you that I should never have yielded to injustice from any fear of death, and that 'as I should have refused to yield' I must have died at once. I will tell you a tale of the courts, not very interesting perhaps, but nevertheless true. The only office of state which I ever held, O men of Athens, was that of senator:[13] the tribe Antiochis, which is my tribe, had the presidency at the trial of the generals who had not taken up the bodies of the slain after the battle of Arginusae; and you proposed to try them in a body, contrary to law, as you all thought afterwards; but at the time I was the only one of the Prytanes who was opposed to the illegality, and I gave my vote against you; and when the orators threatened to impeach and arrest me, and you called and shouted, I made up my mind that I would run the risk, having law and justice with me, rather than take part in your injustice because I feared imprisonment and death. This happened in the days of the democracy.[14] But when the oligarchy of the Thirty was in power, they sent for me and four others into the rotunda,[15] and bade us bring Leon the Salaminian from Salamis,[16] as they wanted to put him to death. This was a specimen of the sort of commands which they were always giving with the view of implicating as many as possible in their crimes; and then I showed, not in word only but in deed, that, if I may be allowed to use such an expression, I cared not a straw for death, and that my great and only care was lest I should do an unrighteous or unholy thing. For the strong arm of that oppressive power did not frighten me into doing wrong; and when we came out of the rotunda the other four went to Salamis and fetched Leon, but I went quietly home. For which I might have lost my life, had not the power of the Thirty shortly afterwards come to an end. And many will witness to my words.

Now do you really imagine that I could have survived all these years, if I had led a public life, supposing that like a good man I had always maintained the right and had made justice, as I ought, the first thing? No indeed, men of Athens, neither I nor any other man. But I have been always the same in all my actions, public as well as private, and never have I yielded any base compliance to those who are slanderously termed my disciples, or to any other. Not that I have any regular disciples. But if any one likes to come and hear me while I am pursuing my mission, whether he be young or old, he is not excluded. Nor do I converse only with those who pay; but any one, whether he be rich or poor, may ask and answer me and listen to my words; and whether he turns out to be a bad man or a good one, neither result can be justly imputed to me; for I never taught or professed to teach him anything. And if any one says that he has ever learned or heard anything from me in private which all the world has not heard, let me tell you that he is lying.

But I shall be asked, Why do people delight in continually conversing with you? I have told you already, Athenians, the whole truth about this matter: they like to hear the cross-examination of the pretenders to wisdom; there is amusement in it. Now this duty of cross-examining other men has been imposed upon me by God; and has been signified to me by oracles, visions, and in every way in which the will of divine power has ever intimated to any one. This is true, O Athenians; or, if not true, would be soon refuted. If I am or have been corrupting the youth, those of them who are now grown up and become sensible that I gave them bad advice in the days of their youth should come forward as accusers, and take their

[13]The Athenian Assembly was composed of 500 members, fifty from each of ten tribes. Each tribe led the Assembly for one-tenth of the year, during which time of leadership its members were known as Prytanes. Socrates, from the tribe of Antiochis, was serving as Prytane following the naval battle of Arginusae in 406 B.C.E., when several Athenian naval commanders were accused of neglecting the dead. Socrates refused to participate in the trial, held in the Assembly, which he deemed to be unjust.

[14]Socrates is giving two examples of his opposition to the government, one democratic and one the oligarchy of the Thirty Tyrants who ruled after Athens fell to Sparta.

[15]The circular building where the Prytanes met.

[16]An island off the coast near Athens, where Leon fled to escape prosecution.

revenge; or if they do not like to come themselves, some of their relatives, fathers, brothers, or other kinsmen, should say what evil their families have suffered at my hands. Now is their time. Many of them I see in the court. There is Crito, who is of the same age and of the same deme[17] with myself, and there is Critobulus his son, whom I also see. Then again there is Lysanias of Sphettus, who is the father of Aeschines—he is present; and also there is Antiphon of Cephisus, who is the father of Epigenes; and there are the brothers of several who have associated with me. There is Nicostratus the son of Theosdotides, and the brother of Theodotus (now Theodotus himself is dead, and therefore he, at any rate, will not seek to stop him); and there is Paralus the son of Demodocus, who had a brother Theages; and Adeimantus the son of Ariston, whose brother Plato[18] is present; and Aeantodorus, who is the brother of Apollodorus, whom I also see. I might mention a great many others, some of whom Meletus should have produced as witnesses in the course of his speech; and let him still produce them, if he has forgotten—I will make way for him. And let him say, if he has any testimony of the sort which he can produce. Nay, Athenians, the very opposite is the truth. For all these are ready to witness on behalf of the corrupter, of the injurer of their kindred, as Meletus and Anytus call me; not the corrupted youth only—there might have been a motive for that—but their uncorrupted elder relatives. Why should they too support me with their testimony? Why, indeed, except for the sake of truth and justice, and because they know that I am speaking the truth, and that Meletus is a liar.

Well, Athenians, this and the like of this is all the defence which I have to offer. Yet a word more. Perhaps there may be some one who is offended at me, when he calls to mind how he himself on a similar, or even a less serious occasion, prayed and entreated the judges with many tears, and how he produced his children in court, which was a moving spectacle, together with a host of relations and friends; whereas I, who am probably in danger of my life, will do none of these things. The contrast may occur to his mind, and he may be set against me, and vote in anger because he is displeased at me on this account. Now if there be such a person among you,—mind, I do not say that there is,—to him I may fairly reply: My friend, I am a man, and like other men, a creature of flesh and blood, and not 'of wood or stone,' as Homer says,[19] and I have a family, yes, and sons, O Athenians, three in number, one almost a man, and two others who are still young; and yet I will not bring any of them hither in order to petition you for an acquittal. And why not? Not from any self-assertion or want of respect for you. Whether I am or am not afraid of death is another question, of which I will not now speak. But, having regard to public opinion, I feel that such conduct would be discreditable to myself, and to you, and to the whole state. One who has reached my years, and who has a name for wisdom, ought not to demean himself. Whether this opinion of me be deserved or not, at any rate the world has decided that Socrates is in some way superior to other men. And if those among you who are said to be superior in wisdom and courage, and any other virtue, demean themselves in this way, how shameful is their conduct! I have seen men of reputation, when they have been condemned, behaving in the strangest manner: they seemed to fancy that they were going to suffer something dreadful if they died, and that they could be immortal if you only allowed them to live; and I think that such are a dishonour to the state,

[17] Precinct.

[18] The author of *Apology*.

[19] In Book 19 of *The Odyssey*, Penelope addresses these words to her husband, Odysseus, who is disguised as a beggar.

and that any stranger coming in would have said of them that the most eminent men of Athens, to whom the Athenians themselves give honour and command, are no better than women. And I say that these things ought not to be done by those of us who have a reputation; and if they are done, you ought not to permit them; you ought rather to show that you are far more disposed to condemn the man who gets up a doleful scene and makes the city ridiculous, than him who holds his peace.

But, setting aside the question of public opinion, there seems to be something wrong in asking a favour of a judge, and thus procuring an acquittal, instead of informing him and convincing him. For his duty is, not to make a present of justice, but to give judgment; and he has sworn that he will judge according to the laws, and not according to his own good pleasure; and we ought not to encourage you, nor should you allow yourself to be encouraged, in this habit of perjury—there can be no piety in that. Do not then require me to do what I consider dishonourable and impious and wrong, especially now, when I am being tried for impiety on the indictment of Meletus. For if, O men of Athens, by force of persuasion and entreaty I could overpower your oaths, then I should be teaching you to believe that there are no gods, and in defending should simply convict myself of the charge of not believing in them. But that is not so—far otherwise. For I do believe that there are gods, and in a sense higher than that which any of my accusers believe in them. And to you and to God I commit my cause, to be determined by you as is best for you and me.[20]

There are many reasons why I am not grieved, O men of Athens, at the vote of condemnation. I expected it, and am only surprised that the votes are so nearly equal; for I had thought that the majority against me would have been far larger; but now, had thirty votes gone over to the other side, I should have been acquitted. And I may say, I think, that I have escaped Meletus. I may say more; for without the assistance of Anytus and Lycon, any one may see that he would not have had a fifth part of the votes,[21] as the law requires, in which case he would have incurred a fine of a thousand drachmae.

And so he proposes death as the penalty. And what shall I propose on my part, O men of Athens? Clearly that which is my due. And what is my due? What return shall be made to the man who has never had the wit to be idle during his whole life; but has been careless of what the many care for—wealth, and family interests, and military offices, and speaking in the assembly, and magistracies, and plots, and parties. Reflecting that I was really too honest a man to be a politician and live, I did not go where I could do no good to you or to myself; but where I could do the greatest good privately to every one of you, thither I went, and sought to persuade every man among you that he must look to himself, and seek virtue and wisdom before he looks to his private interests, and look to the state before he looks to the interests of the state; and that this should be the order which he observes in all his actions. What shall be done to such an one? Doubtless some good thing, O men of Athens, if he has his reward; and the good should be of a kind suitable to him. What would be a reward suitable to a poor man who is your benefactor, and who desires

[20]The jurors cast their votes, 280 for conviction and 220 against. Next the jury must determine the sentence. Meletus demands death. Socrates is given an opportunity to propose a lighter sentence.

[21]A minimum vote of one-fifth of the Assembly, or 100 votes, was required to justify conducting a trial. By dividing the 280 votes among his three accusers, Socrates arrives at a figure that suggests his accusers have not met the minimum required.

leisure that he may instruct you? There can be no reward so fitting as maintenance in the Prytaneum,[22] O men of Athens, a reward which he deserves far more than the citizen who has won the prize at Olympia in the horse or chariot race, whether the chariots were drawn by two horses or by many. For I am in want, and he has enough; and he only gives you the appearance of happiness, and I give you the reality. And if I am to estimate the penalty fairly, I should say that maintenance in the Prytaneum is the just return.

Perhaps you think that I am braving you in what I am saying now, as in what I said before about the tears and prayers. But this is not so. I speak rather because I am convinced that I never intentionally wronged any one, although I cannot convince you—the time has been too short; if there were a law at Athens, as there is in other cities, that a capital cause should not be decided in one day, then I believe that I should have convinced you. But I cannot in a moment refute great slander; and, as I am convinced that I never wronged another, I will assuredly not wrong myself. I will not say of myself that I deserve any evil, or propose any penalty. Why should I? Because I am afraid of the penalty of death which Meletus proposes? When I do not know whether death is a good or an evil, why should I propose a penalty which would certainly be an evil? Shall I say imprisonment? And why should I live in prison, and be the slave of the magistrates of the year—of the Eleven?[23] Or shall the penalty be a fine, and imprisonment until the fine is paid? There is the same objection. I should have to lie in prison, for money I have none, and cannot pay. And if I say exile (and this may possibly be the penalty which you will affix), I must indeed be blinded by the love of life, if I am so irrational as to expect that when you, who are my own citizens, cannot endure my discourses and words, and have found them so grievous and odious that you will have no more of them, others are likely to endure me. No indeed, men of Athens, that is not very likely. And what a life should I lead, at my age, wandering from city to city, ever changing my place of exile, and always being driven out! For I am quite sure that wherever I go, there, as here, the young men will flock to me; and if I drive them away, their elders will drive me out at their request; and if I let them come, their fathers and friends will drive me out for their sakes.

Some one will say: Yes, Socrates, but cannot you hold your tongue, and then you may go into a foreign city, and no one will interfere with you? Now I have great difficulty in making you understand my answer to this. For if I tell you that to do as you say would be a disobedience to the God, and therefore that I cannot hold my tongue, you will not believe that I am serious; and if I say again that daily to discourse about virtue, and of those other things about which you hear me examining myself and others, is the greatest good of man, and that the unexamined life is not worth living, you are still less likely to believe me. Yet I say what is true, although a thing of which it is hard for me to persuade you. Also, I have never been accustomed to think that I deserve to suffer any harm. Had I money I might have estimated the offence at what I was able to pay, and not have been much the worse. But I have none, and therefore I must ask you to proportion the fine to my means. Well, perhaps I could afford a mina, and therefore I propose that penalty: Plato, Crito, Critobulus, and Apollodorus, my friends here, bid me say thirty minae, and they will be the sureties. Let thirty minae be the penalty; for which sum they will be ample security to you.[24]

---

[22] The place where the Prytanes honored the benefactors of Athens.
[23] The committee in charge of prisons and public executions.
[24] The jury now casts another split vote on the sentence, ruling for the death penalty.

Not much time will be gained, O Athenians, in return for the evil name which you will get from the detractors of the city, who will say that you killed Socrates, a wise man; for they will call me wise, even although I am not wise, when they want to reproach you. If you had waited a little while, your desire would have been fulfilled in the course of nature. For I am far advanced in years, as you may perceive, and not far from death. I am speaking now not to all of you, but only to those who have condemned me to death. And I have another thing to say to them: You think that I was convicted because I had no words of the sort which would have procured my acquittal—I mean, if I had thought fit to leave nothing undone or unsaid. Not so; the deficiency which led to my conviction was not of words—certainly not. But I had not the boldness or impudence or inclination to address you as you would have liked me to do, weeping and wailing and lamenting, and saying and doing many things which you have been accustomed to hear from others, and which, as I maintain, are unworthy of me. I thought at the time that I ought not to do anything common or mean when in danger: nor do I now repent of the style of my defence; I would rather die having spoken after my manner, than speak in your manner and live. For neither in war nor yet at law ought I or any man to use every way of escaping death. Often in battle there can be no doubt that if a man will throw away his arms, and fall on his knees before his pursuers, he may escape death; and in other dangers there are other ways of escaping death, if a man is willing to say and do anything. The difficulty, my friends, is not to avoid death, but to avoid unrighteousness; for that runs faster than death. I am old and move slowly, and the slower runner has overtaken me, and my accusers are keen and quick, and the faster runner, who is unrighteousness, has overtaken them. And now I depart hence condemned by you to suffer the penalty of death,—they too go their ways condemned by the truth to suffer the penalty of villainy and wrong; and I must abide by my award—let them abide by theirs. I suppose that these things may be regarded as fated,—and I think that they are well.

And now, O men who have condemned me, I would fain prophesy to you; for I am about to die, and in the hour of death men are gifted with prophetic power. And I prophesy to you who are my murderers, that immediately after my departure punishment far heavier than you have inflicted on me will surely await you. Me you have killed because you wanted to escape the accuser, and not to give an account of your lives. But that will not be as you suppose: far otherwise. For I say that there will be more accusers of you than there are now; accusers whom hitherto I have restrained: and as they are younger they will be more inconsiderate with you, and you will be more offended at them. If you think that by killing men you can prevent some one from censuring your evil lives, you are mistaken; that is not a way of escape which is either possible or honourable; the easiest and the noblest way is not to be disabling others, but to be improving yourselves. This is the prophecy which I utter before my departure to the judges who have condemned me.

Friends, who would have acquitted me, I would like also to talk with you about the thing which has come to pass, while the magistrates are busy, and before I go to the place at which I must die. Stay then a little, for we may as well talk with one another while there is time. You are my friends, and I should like to show you the meaning of this event which has happened to me. O my judges—for you I may truly call judges—I should like to tell you of a wonderful circumstance. Hitherto the divine faculty of which the internal oracle is the source has constantly been in the habit of opposing me even about trifles, if I was going to make a slip or error in any matter; and now as you see there has come upon me that which may be thought, and is generally believed to be, the last and worst evil. But the oracle made no sign of opposition, either when I was leaving my house in the morning, or when I was on my way to the court, or while I was speaking, at anything which I was going to say; and yet I have often been stopped in the middle of a speech, but now in nothing I either said or did touching the matter in hand has the oracle opposed me. What do I take to be the explanation of this silence? I will tell you. It is an intimation that what has happened to me is a good, and that those of us who think that death is an evil are in error. For the customary sign would surely have opposed me had I been going to evil and not to good.

Let us reflect in another way, and we shall see that there is great reason to hope that death is a good; for one of two things—either death is a state of nothingness and utter unconsciousness, or, as men say, there is a change and migration of the soul from this world to another. Now if you suppose that there is no consciousness, but a sleep like the sleep of him who is undisturbed even by dreams, death will be an unspeakable gain. For if a person were to select the night in which his sleep was undisturbed even by dreams, and were to compare with this the other days and nights of his life, and then were to tell us how many days and nights he had passed in the course of his life better and more pleasantly than this one, I think that any man, I will not say a private man, but even the great king will not find many such days or nights, when compared with the others. Now if death be of such a nature, I say that to die is gain; for eternity is then only a single night. But if death is the journey to another place, and there, as men say, all the dead abide, what good, O my friends and judges, can be greater than this? If indeed when the pilgrim arrives in the world below, he is delivered from the professors of justice in this world, and finds the true judges who are said to give judgment there, Minos and Rhadamanthus and Aeacus and Triptolemus,[25] and other sons of God who were righteous in their own life, that pilgrimage will be worth making. What would not a man give if he might converse with Orpheus and Musaeus and Hesiod[26] and Homer? Nay, if this be true, let me die again and again. I myself, too, shall have a wonderful interest in there meeting and conversing with Palamedes, and Ajax the son of Telamon, and any other ancient hero who has suffered death through an unjust judgment; and there will be no small pleasure, as I think, in comparing my own sufferings with theirs. Above all, I shall then be able to continue my search into true and false knowledge; as in this world, so also in the next and I shall find out who is wise, and who pretends to be wise, and is not. What would not a man give, O judges, to be able to examine the leader of the great Trojan expedition; or Odysseus or Sisyphus,[27] or numberless others, men and women too! What infinite delight would there be in conversing with them and asking them questions! In another world they do not put a man to death for asking questions: assuredly not. For besides being happier than we are, they will be immortal, if what is said is true.

Wherefore, O judges, be of good cheer about death, and know of a certainty, that no evil can happen to a good man, either in life or after death. He and his are not neglected by the gods; nor has my own approaching end happened by mere chance. But I see clearly that the time had arrived when it was better for me to die and be released from trouble; wherefore the oracle gave no sign. For which reason, also, I am not angry with my condemners, or with my accusers; they have done me no harm, although they did not mean to do me any good; and for this I may gently blame them.

[25] The four judges of the dead.

[26] Orpheus and Musaeus were legendary poets; Hesiod was a Greek poet of the eighth century B.C.E.

[27] Both Odysseus and Sisyphus were noted for their cunning.

Still I have a favour to ask of them. When my sons are grown up, I would ask you, O my friends, to punish them; and I would have you trouble them, as I have troubled you, if they seem to care about riches, or anything more than about virtue; or if they pretend to be something when they are really nothing,—then reprove them, as I have reproved you, for not caring about that for which they ought to care, and thinking that they are something when they are really nothing. And if you do this, both I and my sons will have received justice at your hands.

The hour of departure has arrived, and we go our ways—I to die, and you to live. Which is better God only knows.

FROM

Phaedo

Translated by Benjamin Jowett

PERSONS OF THE DIALOGUE:

PHAEDO, *who is the narrator of the Dialogue to Echecrates of Phlius*
SOCRATES
APOLLODORUS
SIMMIAS
CEBES
CRITO
ATTENDANT OF THE PRISON

SCENE: *The Prison of Socrates; Place of the Narration: Phlius*

[In this excerpt from the final pages of the *Phaedo*, Plato describes the execution of Socrates. The narrator, Phaedo, and several other friends of Socrates listen to the philosopher prove the immortality of the soul. The excerpt begins as Socrates concludes by describing the virtuous person's hopes for an afterlife.–ED.]

. . . A man of sense ought not to say, nor will I be very confident, that the description which I have given of the soul and her mansions is exactly true. But I do say that, inasmuch as the soul is shown to be immortal, he may venture to think, not improperly or unworthily, that something of the kind is true. The venture is a glorious one, and he ought to comfort himself with words like these, which is the reason why I lengthen out the tale. Wherefore, I say, let a man be of good cheer about his soul, who having cast away the pleasures and ornaments of the body as alien to him and working harm rather than good, has sought after the pleasures of knowledge; and has arrayed the soul, not in some foreign attire, but in her own proper jewels, temperance, and justice, and courage, and nobility, and truth—in these adorned she is ready to go on her journey to the world below, when her hour comes. You, Simmias and Cebes, and all other men, will depart at some time or other. Me already, as a tragic poet would say, the voice of fate calls. Soon I must drink the poison; and I think that I had better repair to the bath first, in order that the women may not have the trouble of washing my body after I am dead.

When he had done speaking, Crito said: And have you any commands for us, Socrates—anything to say about your children, or any other matter in which we can serve you?

Nothing particular, Crito, he replied: only, as I have always told you, take care of yourselves; that is a service which you may be ever rendering to me and mine and to all of us, whether you promise to do so or not. But if you have no thought for yourselves, and care not to walk according to the rule which I have prescribed for you, not now for the first time, however much you may profess or promise at the moment, it will be of no avail.

We will do our best, said Crito: And in what way shall we bury you?

In any way that you like; but you must get hold of me, and take care that I do not run away from you. Then he turned to us, and added with a smile:—I cannot make Crito believe that I am the same Socrates who has been talking and conducting the argument; he fancies that I am the other Socrates whom he will soon see, a dead body—and he asks, How shall he bury me? And though I have spoken many words in the endeavour to show that when I have drunk the poison I shall leave you and go to the joys of the blessed,—these words of mine, with which I was comforting you and myself, have had, as I perceive, no effect upon Crito. And therefore I want you to be surety for me to him now, as at the trial he was surety to the judges for me: but let the promise be of another sort; for he was surety for me to the judges that I would remain, and you must be my surety to him that I shall not remain, but go away and depart; and then he will suffer less at my death, and not be grieved when he sees my body being burned or buried. I would not have him sorrow at my hard lot, or say at the burial, Thus we lay out Socrates, or, Thus we follow him to the grave or bury him; for false words are not only evil in themselves, but they infect the soul with evil. Be of good cheer then, my dear Crito, and say that you are burying my body only, and do with that whatever is usual, and what you think best.

When he had spoken these words, he arose and went into a chamber to bathe; Crito followed him and told us to wait. So we remained behind, talking and thinking of the subject of discourse, and also of the greatness of our sorrow; he was like a father of whom we were being bereaved, and we were about to pass the rest of our lives as orphans. When he had taken the bath his children were brought to him—(he had two young sons and an elder one); and the women of his family also came, and he talked to them and gave them a few directions in the presence of Crito; then he dismissed them and returned to us.

Now the hour of sunset was near, for a good deal of time had passed while he was within. When he came out, he sat down with us again after his bath, but not much was said. Soon the jailer, who was the servant of the Eleven, entered and stood by him, saying:—To you, Socrates, whom I know to be the noblest and gentlest and best of all who ever came to this place, I will not impute the angry feelings of other men, who rage and swear at me, when, in obedience to the authorities, I bid them drink the poison—indeed, I am sure that you will not be angry with me; for others, as you are aware, and not I, are to blame. And so fare you well, and try to bear lightly what must needs be—you know my errand. Then bursting into tears he turned away and went out.

Socrates looked at him and said: I return your good wishes, and will do as you bid. Then turning to us, he said, How charming the man is: since I have been in prison he has always been coming to see me, and at times he would talk to me, and was as good to me as could be, and now see how generously he sorrows on my account. We must do as he says, Crito; and therefore let the cup be brought, if the poison is prepared: if not, let the attendant prepare some.

Yet, said Crito, the sun is still upon the hilltops, and I know that many a one has taken the draught late, and after the announcement has been made to him, he has eaten and drunk, and enjoyed the society of his beloved; do not hurry—there is time enough.

Socrates said: Yes, Crito, and they of whom you speak are right in so acting, for they think that they will be gainers by the delay; but I am right in not following their example, for I do not think that I should gain anything by drinking the poison a little later; I should only be ridiculous in my own eyes for sparing and saving a life which is already forfeit. Please then to do as I say, and not to refuse me.

Crito made a sign to the servant, who was standing by; and he went out, and having been absent for some time, returned with the jailer carrying the cup of poison. Socrates said: You, my good friend, who are experienced in these matters, shall give me directions how I am to proceed. The man answered: You have only to walk about until your legs are heavy, and then to lie down, and the poison will act. At the same time he handed the cup to Socrates, who in the easiest and gentlest manner, without the least fear or change of colour or feature, looking at the man with all his eyes, Echecrates, as his manner was, took the cup and said: What do you say about making a libation out of this cup to any god? May I, or not? The man answered: We only prepare, Socrates, just so much as we deem enough. I understand, he said: but I may and must ask the gods to prosper my journey from this to the other world—even so—and so be it according to my prayer. Then raising the cup to his lips, quite readily and cheerfully he drank off the poison. And hitherto most of us had been able to control our sorrow; but now when we saw him drinking, and saw too that he had finished the draught, we could no longer forbear, and in spite of myself my own tears were flowing fast; so that I covered my face and wept, not for him, but at the thought of my own calamity in having to part from such a friend. Nor was I the first; for Crito, when he found himself unable to restrain his tears, had got up, and I followed; and at that moment, Apollodorus, who had been weeping all the time, broke out in a loud and passionate cry which made cowards of us all. Socrates alone retained his calmness: What is this strange outcry? he said. I sent away the women mainly in order that they might not misbehave in this way, for I have been told that a man should die in peace. Be quiet then, and have patience. When we heard his words we were ashamed, and refrained our tears; and he walked about until, as he said, his legs began to fail, and then he lay on his back, according to the directions, and the man who gave him the poison now and then looked at his feet and legs; and after a while he pressed his foot hard, and asked him if he could feel; and he said, No; and then his leg, and so upwards and upwards, and showed us that he was cold and stiff. And he felt them himself, and said: When the poison reaches the heart, that will be the end. He was beginning to grow cold about the groin, when he uncovered his face, for he had covered himself up, and said—they were his last words—he said: Crito, I owe a cock to Asclepius; will you remember to pay the debt? The debt shall be paid, said Crito; is there anything else? There was no answer to this question; but in a minute or two a movement was heard, and the attendants uncovered him; his eyes were set, and Crito closed his eyes and mouth.

Such was the end, Echecrates, of our friend; concerning whom I may truly say, that of all the men of his time whom I have known, he was the wisest and justest and best.

The Republic

Translated by Benjamin Jowett

FROM BOOK 7
[THE ALLEGORY OF THE CAVE]

SPEAKERS IN THE DIALOGUE:

SOCRATES GLAUCON

And now, I said, let me show in a figure how far our nature is enlightened or unenlightened:—Behold! human beings living in an underground den, which has a mouth open towards the light and reaching all along the den; here they have been from their childhood, and have their legs and necks chained so that they cannot move, and can only see before them, being prevented by the chains from turning round their heads. Above and behind them a fire is blazing at a distance, and between the fire and the prisoners there is a raised way; and you will see, if you look, a low wall built along the way, like the screen which marionette players have in front of them, over which they show the puppets.

I see.

And do you see, I said, men passing along the wall carrying all sorts of vessels, and statues and figures of animals made of wood and stone and various materials, which appear over the wall? Some of them are talking, others silent.

You have shown me a strange image, and they are strange prisoners.

Like ourselves, I replied; and they see only their own shadows, or the shadows of one another, which the fire throws on the opposite wall of the cave?

True, he said; how could they see anything but the shadows if they were never allowed to move their heads?

And of the objects which are being carried in like manner they would only see the shadows?

Yes, he said.

And if they were able to converse with one another, would they not suppose that they were naming what was actually before them?

Very true.

And suppose further that the prison had an echo which came from the other side, would they not be sure to fancy when one of the passers-by spoke that the voice which they heard came from the passing shadow?

No question, he replied.

To them, I said, the truth would be literally nothing but the shadows of the images.

That is certain.

And now look again, and see what will naturally follow if the prisoners are released and disabused of their error. At first, when any of them is liberated and compelled suddenly to stand up and turn his neck round and walk and look towards the light, he will suffer sharp pains; the glare will distress him, and he will be unable to see the realities of which in his former state he had seen the shadows; and then conceive some one saying to him, that what he saw before was an illusion, but that now, when he is approaching nearer to being and his eye is turned towards more real existence, he has a clearer vision—what will be his reply? And you may further imagine that his instructor is pointing to the objects as they pass and requiring him to name them—will he not be perplexed? Will he not fancy that the shadows which he formerly saw are truer than the objects which are now shown to him?

Far truer.

And if he is compelled to look straight at the light, will he not have a pain in his eyes which will make him turn away to take refuge in the objects of vision which he can see, and which he will conceive to be in reality clearer than the things which are now being shown to him?

True, he said.

And suppose once more, that he is reluctantly dragged up a steep and rugged ascent, and held fast until he is forced into the presence of the sun himself, is he not likely to be pained and irritated? When he approaches the light his eyes will be dazzled, and he will not be able to see anything at all of what are now called realities.

Not all in a moment, he said.

He will require to grow accustomed to the sight of the upper world. And first he will see the shadows best, next the reflections of men and other objects in the water, and then the objects themselves; then he will gaze upon the light of the moon and the stars and the spangled heaven; and he will see the sky and the stars by night better than the sun or the light of the sun by day?

Certainly.

Last of all he will be able to see the sun, and not mere reflections of him in the water, but he will see him in his own proper place, and not in another; and he will contemplate him as he is.

Certainly.

He will then proceed to argue that this is he who gives the season and the years, and is the guardian of all that is in the visible world, and in a certain way the cause of all things which he and his fellows have been accustomed to behold?

Clearly, he said, he would first see the sun and then reason about him.

And when he remembered his old habitation, and the wisdom of the den and his fellow-prisoners, do you not suppose that he would felicitate himself on the change, and pity them?

Certainly, he would.

And if they were in the habit of conferring honours among themselves on those who were quickest to observe the passing shadows and to remark which of them went before, and which followed after, and which were together; and who were therefore best able to draw conclusions as to the future, do you think that he would care for such honours and glories, or envy the possessors of them? Would he not say with Homer,

> Better to be the poor servant of a poor master,

and to endure anything, rather than think as they do and live after their manner?

Yes, he said, I think that he would rather suffer anything than entertain these false notions and live in this miserable manner.

Imagine once more, I said, such an one coming suddenly out of the sun to be replaced in his old situation; would he not be certain to have his eyes full of darkness?

To be sure, he said.

And if there were a contest, and he had to compete in measuring the shadows with the prisoners who had never moved out of the den, while his sight was still weak, and before his eyes had become steady (and the time which would be needed to acquire this new habit of sight might be very considerable), would he not be ridiculous? Men would say of him that up he went and down he came without his eyes; and that it was better not even to think of ascending; and if any one tried to loose another and lead him up to the light, let them only catch the offender, and they would put him to death.

No question, he said.

This entire allegory, I said, you may now append, dear Glaucon, to the previous argument; the prison-house is the world of sight, the light of the fire is the sun, and you will not misapprehend me if you interpret the journey upwards to be the ascent of the soul into the intellectual world according to my poor belief, which, at your desire, I have expressed—whether rightly or wrongly God knows. But, whether true or false, my opinion is that in the world of knowledge the idea of good appears last of all, and is seen only with an effort; and, when seen, is also inferred to be the universal author of all things beautiful and right, parent of light and of the lord of light in this visible world, and the immediate source of reason and truth in the intellectual; and that this is the power upon which he who would act rationally either in public or private life must have his eye fixed.

I agree, he said, as far as I am able to understand you.

Moreover, I said, you must not wonder that those who attain to this beatific vision are unwilling to descend to human affairs; for their souls are ever hastening into the upper world where they desire to dwell; which desire of theirs is very natural, if our allegory may be trusted.

Yes, very natural.

And is there anything surprising in one who passes from divine contemplations to the evil state of man, misbehaving himself in a ridiculous manner; if, while his eyes are blinking and before he has become accustomed to the surrounding darkness, he is compelled to fight in courts of law, or in other places, about the images or the shadows of images of justice, and is endeavouring to meet the conceptions of those who have never yet seen absolute justice?

Anything but surprising, he replied.

Any one who has common sense will remember that the bewilderments of the eyes are of two kinds, and arise from two causes, either from coming out of the light or from going into the light, which is true of the mind's eye, quite as much as of the bodily eye; and he who remembers this when he sees any one whose vision is perplexed and weak, will not be too ready to laugh; he will first ask whether that soul of man has come out of the brighter life, and is unable to see because unaccustomed to the dark, or having turned from darkness to the day is dazzled by excess of light. And he will count the one happy in his condition and state of being, and he will pity the other; or, if he have a mind to laugh at the soul which comes from below into the light, there will be more reason in this than in the laugh which greets him who returns from above out of the light into the den.

That, he said, is a very just distinction.

But then, if I am right, certain professors of education must be wrong when they say that they can put a knowledge into the soul which was not there before, like sight into blind eyes.

They undoubtedly say this, he replied.

Whereas, our argument shows that the power and capacity of learning exists in the soul already; and that just as the eye was unable to turn from darkness to light without the whole body, so too the instrument of knowledge can only by the movement of the whole soul be turned from the world of becoming into that of being, and learn by degrees to endure the sight of being, and of the brightest and best of being, or in other words, of the good.

Very true.

And must there not be some art which will effect conversion in the easiest and quickest manner; not implanting the faculty of sight, for that exists already, but has been turned in the wrong direction, and is looking away from the truth?

Yes, he said, such an art may be presumed.

And whereas the other so-called virtues of the soul seem to be akin to bodily qualities, for even when they are not originally innate they can be implanted later by habit and exercise, the virtue of wisdom more than anything else contains a divine element which always remains, and by this conversion is rendered useful and profitable; or, on the other hand, hurtful and useless. Did you never observe the narrow intelligence flashing from the keen eye of a clever rogue—how eager he is, how clearly his paltry soul sees the way to his end; he is the reverse of blind, but his keen eye-sight is forced into the service of evil, and he is mischievous in proportion to his cleverness?

Very true, he said.

But what if there had been a circumcision of such natures in the days of their youth; and they had been severed from those sensual pleasures, such as eating and drinking, which, like leaden weights, were attached to them at their birth, and which drag them down and turn the vision of their souls upon the things that are below—if, I say, they had been released from these impediments and turned in the opposite direction, the very same faculty in them would have seen the truth as keenly as they see what their eyes are turned to now.

Very likely.

Yes, I said; and there is another thing which is likely, or rather a necessary inference from what has preceded, that neither the uneducated and uninformed of the truth, nor yet those who never make an end of their education, will be able ministers of State; not the former, because they have no single aim of duty which is the rule of all their actions, private as well as public; nor the latter, because they will not act at all except upon compulsion, fancying that they are already dwelling apart in the islands of the blest.

Very true, he replied.

Then, I said, the business of us who are the founders of the State will be to compel the best minds to attain that knowledge which we have already shown to be the greatest of all—they must continue to ascend until they arrive at the good; but when they have ascended and seen enough we must not allow them to do as they do now.

What do you mean?

I mean that they remain in the upper world: but this must not be allowed; they must be made to descend again among the prisoners in the den, and partake of their labours and honours, whether they are worth having or not.

But is not this unjust? he said; ought we to give them a worse life, when they might have a better?

You have again forgotten, my friend, I said, the intention of the legislator, who did not aim at making any one class in the State happy above the rest; the happiness was to be in the whole State, and he held the citizens together by persuasion and necessity, making them benefactors of the State, and therefore benefactors of one another; to this end he created them, not to please themselves, but to be his instruments in binding up the State.

True, he said, I had forgotten.

Observe, Glaucon, that there will be no injustice in compelling our philosophers to have a care and providence of others; we shall explain to them that in other States, men of their class are not obliged to share in the toils of politics: and this is reasonable, for they grow up at their own sweet will, and the government would rather not have them. Being self-taught, they cannot be expected to show any gratitude for a culture which they have never received. But we have brought you into the world to be rulers of the hive, kings of yourselves and of the other citizens, and have educated you far better and more perfectly than they have been educated, and you are better able to share in the double duty. Wherefore each of you, when his turn comes, must go down to the general underground abode, and get the habit of seeing in the dark. When you have acquired the habit, you will see ten thousand times better than the inhabitants of the den, and you will know what the several images are, and what they represent, because you have seen the beautiful and just and good in their truth. And thus our State which is also yours will be a reality, and not a dream only, and will be administered in a spirit unlike that of other States, in which men fight with one another about shadows only and are distracted in the struggle for power, which in their eyes is a great good. Whereas the truth is that the State in which the rulers are most reluctant to govern is always the best and most quietly governed, and the State in which they are most eager, the worst.

Quite true, he replied.

And will our pupils, when they hear this, refuse to take their turn at the toils of State, when they are allowed to spend the greater part of their time with one another in the heavenly light?

Impossible, he answered; for they are just men, and the commands which we impose upon them are just; there can be no doubt that every one of them will take office as a stern necessity, and not after the fashion of our present rulers of State.

Yes, my friend, I said; and there lies the point. You must contrive for your future rulers another and a better life than that of a ruler, and then you may have a well-ordered State; for only in the State which offers this, will they rule who are truly rich, not in silver and gold, but in virtue and wisdom, which are the true blessings of life. Whereas if they go to the administration of public affairs, poor and hungering after their own private advantage, thinking that hence they are to snatch the chief good, order there can never be; for they will be fighting about office, and the civil and domestic broils which thus arise will be the ruin of the rulers themselves and of the whole State.

Most true, he replied.

And the only life which looks down upon the life of political ambition is that of true philosophy. Do you know of any other?

Indeed, I do not, he said. . .

ARISTOTLE

[384–322 B.C.E.]

Aristotle's works, which number in the hundreds, cover nearly all the known fields of knowledge of his time. The essential point is not that Aristotle knew everything, but that he propounded the idea that the world is essentially rational, and that human reason can understand, analyze, and categorize the phenomena of the world. This view was in stark contrast to the views held in other cultures of his time—including some Greek ideas—which connected knowledge to divine sources.

Life

Aristotle was born the son of a physician in the north of Greece, in the town of Stagira in Macedonia. When he was seventeen, Aristotle studied at Plato's Academy in Athens and remained there twenty years, until Plato's death in 347 B.C.E. For the next several years he traveled about and was the tutor of young Alexander of Macedon, returning to Athens in 335 to found a school of philosophy, the Lyceum. Known also as the Peripatetic School because the students walked about on the grounds while Aristotle taught, this school became the first research institution in Greece devoted to science, literature, and philosophy. After Alexander's death in 323, anti-Macedonian feelings in Athens led Aristotle to retire on Macedonia's Chalcidian peninsula, where he died a year later, in 322 B.C.E.

Work

In the excerpt from *Metaphysics* that follows, Aristotle discusses the importance of reasoning. The selection from *The Nicomachean Ethics* fixes the source of moral virtues in the middle path, or mean, between two extremes. Courage, for example, is to be found in the mean between cowardice and rashness. We also include a selection from the *Poetics,* the first extended piece of literary criticism written in the West. In the *Poetics,*

Aristotle set out to describe the general nature of Greek literature. As with other fields of knowledge, Aristotle wanted to systematize literature by distinguishing between various kinds of literature and describing their basic principles and aims. In contrast to Plato, who questioned the moral impact of art, Aristotle discussed the positive influence of literature on human beings, especially the healthy effect of *catharsis,* the purgation of the emotions.

Aristotle's influence on Western culture has been immense. His philosophy was particularly important during the Middle Ages with the revival of learning in the twelfth and thirteenth centuries. Thomas Aquinas used Aristotelian philosophy to construct the theoretical basis of Medieval Christianity. After the rise of modern science, Aristotle's importance declined, but the example of his intellect and the compelling nature of his methodology continue to inspire thinkers to the present day. We might not all be Platonists or Aristotelians, as British romantic Samuel Taylor Coleridge maintained, but it is still common for modern intellectuals to seek refuge in the basic tenets of the Greek humanism fostered by these men.

SUGGESTED READINGS

An excellent introduction to the classical tradition is Werner Jaeger, *Paideia: The Ideals of Greek Culture,* 3 volumes (1939–1944). A good overview of Greek philosophy is Eduard Zeller, *Outlines of the History of Greek Philosophy* (1955). A thorough introduction to the *Poetics* is O. B. Hardison, Jr., *Aristotle's Poetics* (1968). For Aristotle's influence on criticism and literature, see Elder Olson, ed., *Aristotle's Poetics and English Literature: A Collection of Critical Essays* (1965).

Metaphysics

Translated by Philip Ellis Wheelwright

[ON PHILOSOPHICAL WISDOM]

All men by nature desire to know. An indication of this is the joy we take in our perceptions; which we cherish for their own sakes, quite apart from any benefits they may yield to us. It is especially true of sight, which we tend to prefer to all the other senses even when it points to no action, and even indeed when no action is in prospect; a preference explained by the greater degree to which sight promotes knowledge by revealing so many differences among things.

The Evolution of Reason

But while the other animals live by means of impressions and memories, with only a small amount of general experience, the human race lives also by art and reasoning. Memory is what gives rise to experience in men, for it is by having repeated memories of the same thing that our ability to have a single whole experience arises. At first sight experience seems much like knowledge and art, but it is truer to say that experience is the means through which science and art can be acquired; thus Polus rightly declares that "experience has produced art, inexperience chance."

No doubt the first discoverer of any art that went beyond man's ordinary sense-perceptions was admired by his fellows, not merely for whatever utility his discoveries may have had, but because his wisdom seemed to set him above others. And as further arts were discovered, some supplying the necessities of life, others its leisure moments, the discoverers of the latter were always considered wiser than the discoverers of the former, because theirs was a sort of knowledge that did not aim at utility. The next step, when all such discoveries had been made, was the discovery of the sciences that do not aim either at pleasure or at the necessities of life; and this first occurred in those places where men enjoyed leisure: which explains why the mathematical disciplines first arose in Egypt, because in that country the priestly caste was permitted to live in leisure.

The Nature of Wisdom

The aim of our present discussion is to inquire about wisdom, which is generally understood to deal with the basic determining factors and initiating principles. For the man of experience is agreed to be wiser than one who is limited to mere sense-awareness, the artist than the man of experience, the master-craftsman than the manual worker, and the contemplative sciences to partake of more wisdom than the productive sciences. From this progressive relation it becomes clear that wisdom is that kind of knowledge which concerns ultimate principles and reasons-why.[1]

The Motive of Philosophy

It is through wonder that men begin to philosophize, whether in olden times or today. First their wonder is stirred by difficulties of an obvious sort, and then gradually they proceed to inquire about weightier matters, like the changes of the moon, sun and stars, and the origin of the universe. Now the result of wonderment and perplexity is to feel oneself ignorant. If, then, it was to escape ignorance that men began to philosophize, it is evident that they were pursuing this sort of study in order to know and not from any motive of utility. An incidental confirmation of this view is that thinking began to be undertaken as a pastime and recreation at a period when all the main necessities of life had been supplied. Clearly, then, knowledge of the kind that is under discussion is not sought for the sake of any external advantage; but rather, as we call that man free who exists in and for himself and not for another, so we pursue this as the one free and independent study, because it is the only one that exists for the sake of itself.

The Paradox of Philosophy

Let it be noted, however, that the acquisition of such knowledge leads to a point of view which is in a way the reverse of that from which we began. Everyone begins, as we remarked earlier, by wondering that things should be as they are—whether the movements of marionettes, or the solstices, or the incommensurability of the diameter of a square with its side; because it seems remarkable to those who have not yet fathomed the reason-why, that there should exist no smallest common unit by which any two lengths could be measured. But in the end we come to the opposite point of view—which moreover is the better one, for surely the adage that "second thoughts are better thoughts" is most applicable in these cases where learning takes place. From the new standpoint there is nothing a geometer would so greatly wonder at as if the diameter *were* to be found commensurable.

The study of philosophic truth is difficult in one respect, easy in another. This is shown by the double fact that while no individual can grasp truth adequately, yet collectively we do not entirely fail. Each individual makes some report on the nature of things, and while this by itself contributes very little to the inquiry a

[1]Usually translated as "cause."

combination of all such reports amounts to a good deal. In so far as truth can be likened to the proverbial big door which even the poorest marksman cannot miss, it is easy; but the fact that we can know a large general truth and still not grasp some particular part of it shows how difficult truth-seeking really is. However, there are roughly two ways of accounting for a difficulty, and it may be that in the present case the reason for it lies not in the subject-matter but in ourselves, and that as bats' eyes are dimmed by daylight so the power of reason in our souls is dimmed by what is intrinsically most self-evident.

The Nicomachean Ethics

Translated by Philip Ellis Wheelwright

[The Doctrine of the Mean]

Differentia of Moral Virtue: Doctrine of the Mean

But to say that virtue is a disposition is not enough; we must specify what kind of a disposition it is.

The virtue, or excellence, of anything must be acknowledged to have a twofold effect on the thing to which it belongs: it renders the thing itself good, and causes it to perform its function well. The excellence of the eye, for instance, makes both the eye and its work good, for it is by the excellence of the eye that we see well. Likewise the proper excellence of horse at once makes a particular horse what he should be, and also makes him good at running and at carrying his rider and at facing the enemy. Hence, if this is universally true, the virtue or proper excellence of man will be just that formed disposition which both makes him good and enables him to perform his function well. We have already indicated how this is accomplished; but we may clarify the matter by examining wherein the nature of virtue consists.

Of everything that is both continuous and divisible it is possible to take a greater, a less, or an equal amount; and this may be true either objectively with respect to the thing in question or else relatively to ourselves. By equal I denote that which is a mean between excess and deficiency. By the objective mean I denote that which is equidistant from both extremes, and this will always be the same for everybody. By the mean that is relative to ourselves I denote that which is neither too much nor too little, and this is not one and the same for everybody. For instance, if ten is many and two is few, then six is the mean considered in terms of the object; for it exceeds and is exceeded by the same amount, and is therefore the mean of an arithmetical proportion. But the mean considered relatively to ourselves cannot be determined so simply: if ten pounds of food is too much for a certain man to eat and two pounds is too little, it does not follow that the trainer will prescribe six pounds, for this may be too much or too little for the man in question—too little for Milo the wrestler, too much for the novice at athletics. This is equally true of running and wrestling.

So it is that an expert in any field avoids excess and deficiency, and seeks and chooses the mean—that is, not the objective mean, but the mean relatively to himself. If, then, every sort of skill perfects its work in this way, by observing the mean and bringing its work up to this standard (which is the reason why people say of a good work of art that nothing could be either taken from it or added to it, implying that excellence is destroyed by excess or deficiency but is preserved by adherence to the mean; and good artists, we say, observe this standard in their work), and if furthermore virtue, like nature, is more exact and better than any art, it follows that virtue will have the property of aiming at the mean. I am speaking, of course, of moral virtue, for it is moral virtue that has to do with feelings and actions, and it is in respect of these that excess, deficiency, and moderation are possible. That is to say, we can feel fear, confidence, desire, anger, pity, and in general pleasure and pain, either too much or too little, and in either case not well; but to feel them at the right times, with reference to the right objects, toward the right people, with the right motive, and in the right manner, is to strike the mean, and therein to follow the best course—a mark of virtue. And in the same way our outward acts admit of excess, deficiency, and the proper mean. Now virtue has to do with feelings and also with outward acts; in both of these excess and deficiency are regarded as faults and are blamed, while a moderate amount is both praised and regarded as right—palpable signs of virtue. Virtue, then, is a kind of moderation, in that it aims at the mean. This conclusion is further confirmed by the fact that while there are numerous ways in which we can go wrong (for evil, according to the Pythagorean figure of speech, belongs to the class of the unlimited, good to that of the limited), there is only one way of going right. That is why the one is easy, the other hard—easy to miss the mark, but hard to hit it. And this offers further evidence that excess and deficiency are characteristic of vice while hitting the mean is characteristic of virtue: "for good is simple, badness manifold."

We may conclude, then, that virtue is an habitual disposition with respect to choice, the characteristic quality of which is moderation judged relatively to ourselves according to a determinate principle, *i.e.,* according to such a principle as a man of insight would use. The quality of moderation belongs to virtue in a double sense: as falling between two vices, the one of which consists in excess, the other in deficiency; and also in the sense that while these vices respectively fall short of and exceed the proper standard both of feelings and of actions, virtue both finds and chooses the mean. Hence, in respect of its essence and according to the definition of its basic nature, virtue is a state of moderation; but regarded in its relation to what is best and right it is an extreme.

Accordingly it is not every action nor every feeling to which the principle of the mean is applicable. There are some whose very names imply badness: *e.g.,* malevolence, shamelessness, envy, and among actions, adultery, theft, and murder. These and everything else like them are condemned as being bad in themselves and not merely when in excess or deficiency. To do right in performing them is therefore impossible; their performance is always wrong. Rightness or wrongness in any of them (*e.g.,* in adultery) does not depend on the rightness or wrongness of person and occasion and manner, but on the bare fact of doing it at all. It would be absurd to distinguish moderation, excess, and deficiency in action that is unjust or cowardly or profligate; for we should then have moderation of excess and deficiency, excess of excess, and deficiency of deficiency. The truth of the matter is that just as there can be no excess and deficiency of temperance and courage (for the proper mean is, in its own way, an extreme), so these opposite kinds of conduct likewise do not admit of moderation, excess, and deficiency: they are always wrong, no matter how they are done.

Difficulty of Attaining the Mean

We have now sufficiently shown that moral virtue consists in observance of a mean, and in what sense this is so: in the sense, namely, of holding a middle position between two vices, one of which involves excess and the other deficiency, and also in the sense of being the kind of a disposition which aims at the middle point both in feelings and in actions. This being the case, it is a hard thing to be good, for it is hard to locate the mean in particular instances; just as to locate the mean point (*i.e.*, the center) of a circle is not a thing that everybody can do, but only the man of science. So, too, anyone can get angry—that is easy—or spend money or give it away; but to do all this to the right person, to the right extent, at the right time, with the right motive, and in the right manner, is not a thing that everyone can do, and is not easy; and that is why good conduct is at once rare and praiseworthy and noble.

Accordingly, whoever aims at the mean should first of all strive to avoid that extreme which is more opposed to it, as in Calypso's advice to "keep the ship well clear of that foaming surf."[1] For of the two extremes one will be more of an evil, the other less; therefore, as it is hard to hit the exact mean, we ought to choose the lesser of the two evils and sail, as the saying goes, in the second best way, and this is accomplished most successfully in the manner stated. But we must bear in mind as well the errors to which we personally are prone. These will be different for different individuals, and each may discover them in his own case by noting the occasions on which he feels pleasure or pain. Having discovered them, let him bend himself in the opposite direction; for by steering wide of error we shall strike a middle course, as warped timber is straightened by bending it backwards. Especially and in all cases we must guard against pleasure and what is pleasant, because we cannot estimate it impartially. Hence we ought to feel toward pleasure as the elders of the people felt toward Helen, and on every occasion repeat their saying;[2] for if we dismiss pleasure thus we are less likely to go wrong.

Poetics

Translated by Samuel Henry Butcher

FROM

Chapter 6

Tragedy, then, is an imitation of an action that is serious, complete, and of a certain magnitude; in language embellished with every kind of artistic ornament, the several kinds being found in separate parts of the play; in the form of dramatic action, not of narrative; through pity and fear effecting the proper purification of these emotions.[1] By "language embellished," I mean language into which rhythm, harmony, and song enter. By "the several kinds in separate parts," I mean that some parts are rendered through the medium of verse alone, others again with the aid of song.

Now as tragic imitation implies persons acting, it necessarily follows, in the first place, that spectacular equipment will be a part of tragedy. Next, song and diction, for these are the medium of imitation. By diction, I mean the metrical arrangement of the words: as for song, it is a term whose sense everyone understands.

Again, tragedy is the imitation of an action, and an action implies personal actors, who necessarily possess certain distinctive qualities of character and thought; for

THE NICOMACHEAN ETHICS

[1] As related in the *Odyssey,* Odysseus followed Calypso's advice to steer toward the monstrous Scylla, rather than get caught by the whirlpool Charybdis.

[2] "She is wondrously like the immortal goddesses to look upon. But be that as it may, let her depart on the ships, rather than be left here as a bane to us and our children after us." (*Iliad,* Book 3, 158–60.)

POETICS

[1] The Greeks did not require an unhappy or "tragic" ending for their tragedies.

it is by these that we form our estimate of their actions and these two—thought and character—are the natural causes from which their actions spring, and on their actions all success or failure depends. Now, the imitation of the action is the plot; by plot I here mean the arrangement of the incidents. By character I mean that because of which we ascribe certain qualities to the actors. Thought is needed whenever they speak to prove a statement or declare a general truth. Every tragedy, therefore, must have six parts, which parts determine its quality—namely, plot, character, diction, thought, spectacle, song. . . .

But most important of all is the structure of the incidents. For tragedy is an imitation, not of men, but of action and life, of happiness and misery. And life consists of action, and its end is a mode of activity, not a quality. Now character determines men's qualities, but it is their actions that make them happy or wretched. The purpose of action in the tragedy, therefore, is not the representation of character: character comes in as contributing to the action. Hence the incidents and the plot are the end of the tragedy; and the end is the chief thing of all. So without action there cannot be a tragedy; there may be one without character. . . .

Again, you may string together a set of speeches expressive of character, and well finished in point of diction and thought, and not produce the essential tragic effect nearly so well as with a play which, however deficient in these respects, yet has a plot and artistically constructed incidents. Besides which, the most powerful elements of emotional interest in tragedy—reversal of the situation and recognition scenes—are parts of the plot. A further proof is that novices in the art attain to finish of diction and precision of portraiture before they can construct the plot. It is the same with almost all the early poets.

The plot, then, is the first principle, and, as it were, the soul of a tragedy: character holds the second place. A similar statement is true of painting. The most beautiful colors, laid on confusedly, will not give as much pleasure as a simple chalk outline of a portrait. Thus tragedy is the imitation of an action, and of actors mainly with a view to the action. . . .

The spectacle is, indeed, an attraction in itself, but of all the parts it is the least artistic, and connected least with the art of poetry. For the power of tragedy is felt even apart from representation and actors. Besides, the production of scenic effects is more a matter for the property man than for the poet.

FROM
CHAPTER 7

These principles being established, let us now discuss the proper structure of the plot, since this is the first and most important thing in tragedy.

Now, according to our definition, tragedy is an imitation of an action that is complete and whole and of a certain magnitude; for there may be a whole that is wanting in magnitude. A whole is that which has a beginning, a middle, and an end. A beginning is that which does not have to follow anything else, but after which something else naturally takes place. An end, on the contrary, is that which itself naturally follows something else, either by necessity or as a general rule, but has nothing coming after it. A middle is that which follows something else as some other thing follows it. A well-constructed plot must neither begin nor end at haphazard, but conform to these principles.

Again, a beautiful object, whether it be a living organism or any whole composed of parts, must not only have an orderly arrangement of parts, but must also be of a certain magnitude; for beauty depends on magnitude and order. Hence a very tiny creature cannot be beautiful; for the view of it is confused, the object being seen in an almost imperceptible moment of time. Nor, again, can one of vast size be beautiful; for as the eye cannot take it all in at once, the unity and sense of the whole is lost for the spectator; as it would be if there were a creature a thousand miles long. As, therefore, in the case of living bodies and organisms, a certain magnitude is necessary, and a magnitude which may be easily embraced in one view; so in the plot, a certain length is necessary, and length which can be easily embraced by the memory. . . . And to state the matter roughly, we may say that the proper length is such as to allow for a sequence of necessary or probable events that will bring about a change from calamity to good fortune, or from good fortune to calamity.

CHAPTER 8

Unity of plot does not, as some persons think, consist of having a single man as the hero. For infinitely various are the incidents in one man's life which cannot be reduced to unity; and so, too, there are many actions of one man out of which we cannot make one action. Hence the error, as it appears, of all poets who have composed a Heracleid, a Theseid,[2] or other poems of the kind. They imagine that as Heracles was one man, the story of Heracles must also be a unity. But Homer, as in all else he is of surpassing merit, here too—whether from art or natural genius—seems to have happily discerned the truth. In composing the *Odyssey* he did not include all the adventures of Odysseus—such as his wound on Parnassus, or his feigned madness at the mustering of the host[3]—incidents between which there was no necessary or probable connection: but he made the *Odyssey* and likewise the *Iliad* center around an action that in our sense of the word is one. As therefore, in the other imitative arts, the imitation is one when the object imitated is one, so the plot, being an imitation of an action, must imitate one action and that a whole, the structural union of the parts being such that, if any one of them is displaced or removed, the whole will be disjointed and disturbed. For a thing whose presence or absence makes no visible difference is not an organic part of the whole.

FROM CHAPTER 9

It is, moreover, evident from what has been said that it is not the function of the poet to relate what has happened but what may happen—what is possible according to the law of probability or necessity. The poet and the historian differ not by writing in verse or in prose. The work of Herodotus[4] might be put into verse, and it would still be a species of history, with meter no less than without it. The true difference is that one relates what has happened, the other what may happen. Poetry, therefore, is a more philosophical and a higher thing than history: for poetry tends to express the universal, history the particular. . . .

But even if a poet chances to take an historical subject, he is nonetheless a poet; for there is no reason why some events that have actually happened should not conform to the law of the probable and the possible, and in virtue of that aspect of them he is their poet or maker.

---

[2] A long narrative poem about the adventures of a figure such as Heracles or Theseus.

[3] Incidents that occurred before the opening of the *Iliad*.

[4] First Greek historian (c. 484–c. 425 B.C.E.).

Of all plots and actions the episodic are the worst. I call a plot "episodic" in which the episodes or acts succeed one another without probable or necessary sequence. Bad poets compose such pieces by their own fault, good poets, to please the players; for, as they write show pieces for competition, they stretch the plot beyond its capacity, and are often forced to break the natural continuity.

But again, tragedy is an imitation not only of a complete action, but of events inspiring fear or pity. Such an effect is best produced when the events come on us by surprise and when, at the same time, they follow as cause and effect. The wonder will then be greater than if they happened of themselves or merely by accident; for coincidences too are most marvelous when they have a look of design. We may instance the statue of Mitys at Argos, which fell upon his murderer while he was watching a festival, and killed him. Such events seem the result of more than chance. Plots, therefore, constructed on these principles are necessarily the best.

CHAPTER 10

Plots are either simple or complex, for the actions in real life, of which they are an imitation, are obviously either one or the other. An action which is one and continuous in the sense above defined, I call simple, when the change in the hero's fortune takes place without reversal of the situation and without recognition.

A complex action is one in which the change is accompanied by such a reversal, or by recognition, or by both. These all should arise from the internal structure of the plot, so that what follows should be the necessary or probable result of what went before. It makes a great difference whether the event is caused by or simply happens after the previous action.

FROM CHAPTER 11

Reversal of the situation is a change by which conditions in the play are transformed into their opposite, keeping always to our rule of probability or necessity. Thus in the Oedipus,[5] the messenger comes to cheer Oedipus and free him from his alarms about his mother, but by revealing who Oedipus really is produces the opposite effect. . . .

Recognition, as the name indicates, is a change from ignorance to knowledge, producing love or hate between the persons destined by the poet for good or bad fortune. The best form of recognition is coincident with a reversal of the situation, as in the Oedipus.

Even inanimate things of the most trivial kind may in a sense be objects of recognition. Again, we may recognize or discover whether a person has done a thing or not. But the recognition which is most intimately connected with the plot and action is, as we have said, the recognition of persons. This recognition, combined with a reversal, will produce either pity or fear; and actions producing these effects are those which, by our definition, tragedy represents. Moreover, it is upon such situations that the issue of good or bad fortune will depend. Recognition, then, being between persons, it may happen that one person only is recognized

---

[5]Aristotle admired *Oedipus Tyrannus,* the tragedy about the king of Thebes who discovers that he has unknowingly killed his father and married his mother.

by the other—when the latter is already known—or it may be necessary that the recognition should be on both sides. Thus Iphigenia is revealed to Orestes by the sending of the letter; but another act of recognition is required to make Orestes known to Iphigenia.[6]

Two parts, then, of the plot—reversal of the situation and recognition—turn upon surprises. A third part is the scene of suffering. The scene of suffering is a destructive or painful action, such as a death on the stage, bodily agony, wounds, and the like....

FROM
CHAPTER 14

Fear and pity may be aroused by spectacular means; but they may also result from the inner structure of the piece, which is the better way, and indicates a superior poet. For the plot ought to be so constructed that, even without the aid of the eye, he who hears the tale told will thrill with horror and melt to pity at what takes place. This is the impression we should receive from hearing the story of Oedipus. But to produce this effect by the mere spectacle is a less artistic method, and dependent on extraneous aids. Those who employ spectacular means to create a sense not of the terrible but of the merely monstrous are strangers to the purpose of tragedy; for we must not demand of tragedy any and every kind of pleasure, but only that which is proper to it. And since the pleasure the tragic poet should offer is that which comes from pity and fear through imitation, it is evident that this quality must be impressed on the incidents.

Let us then determine what circumstances strike us as terrible or pitiful.

Actions of this sort must happen between persons who are either friends or enemies or indifferent to one another. If an enemy kills an enemy, there is nothing to excite pity either in the act or the intention—except in so far as the suffering itself is pitiful. So too with indifferent persons. But when the tragic incident occurs between those who are near or dear to one another—if, for example, a brother kills, or intends to kill, a brother, a son his father, a mother her son, a son his mother, or any other deed of the kind is done—these are situations to be looked for by the poet. He may not indeed destroy the framework of the received legends—the fact, for instance, that Clytemnestra was slain by Orestes... but he ought to show invention of his own, and skillfully handle the traditional material....

Enough has now been said concerning the structure of the incidents and the right kind of plot.

FROM
CHAPTER 15

With regard to the characters there are four things to be aimed at. First, and most important, they must be good. Now any speech or action that manifests some kind of moral purpose will be expressive of character: the character will be good if the purpose is good. The goodness is possible in every class of persons. Even a woman

[6]Iphigenia and Orestes were children of Agamemnon and Clytemnestra; the family was involved in a series of tragic murders. Their stories were dramatized by Aeschylus and Euripides.

may be good, and also a slave, though the one is liable to be an inferior being, and the other quite worthless. The second thing to aim at is appropriateness. There is a type of manly valor, but manliness in a woman, or unscrupulous cleverness, is inappropriate. Thirdly, a character must be true to life: which is something different from goodness and appropriateness, as here described. The fourth point is consistency: for even though the person being imitated, who suggested the type, is inconsistent, still he must be consistently inconsistent.

As in the structure of the plot, so too in the portraiture of character, the poet should always aim at either the necessary or the probable. Thus a person of a given character should speak or act as it is necessary or probable that he would; just as this event should follow that as a necessary or probable consequence. It is therefore evident that the unraveling of the plot, no less than the complication, must arise out of the plot itself; it must not be brought about by supernatural interference—as in the *Medea.*[7] The supernatural should be employed only for events outside the drama—for past or future events, beyond the range of human knowledge, which need to be reported or foretold; for to the gods we ascribe the power of seeing all things. Within the action there must be nothing improbable. If the improbable cannot be excluded, it should be outside the field of the tragedy, as is the improbable element in the *Oedipus* of Sophocles.

Again, since tragedy is an imitation of persons above the common level, the example of good portrait painters should be followed. They, while reproducing the distinctive features of the original, make a likeness true to life and yet more beautiful. So too the poet, in representing men hot tempered or indolent or with other defects of character, should preserve the type and yet ennoble it. In this way Agathon and Homer have portrayed Achilles.[8]

These, then, are rules the poet should observe. Nor should he neglect those appeals to the eye, which, though not among the essentials, are the concomitants of poetry; for here too there is much room for error. But of this enough has been said in our published treatise[9]. . . .

CATULLUS

[C. 84–C. 54 B.C.E.]

The voice of the Roman lyric poet Catullus speaks directly to us across two thousand years. He addresses us in startlingly colloquial language, his tone ranging from leering to loving, from scornful sarcasm to warm affection and bitter grief. From the first century B.C.E. he reports on daily life among his friends, the rich and fast-living younger set in Julius Caesar's Rome, gossiping wickedly about bathhouse scandals, back-alley doings, and bisexual politics in the capital. He tells us who is incestuous or adulterous, who is a kleptomaniac, who writes terrible poetry. But there are private and tender moments, too, as when he thanks friends who have stood by him; or chronicles his aching love affair with Lesbia, the older woman whose flamboyance enchants him and breaks his heart; or when

[7] In Euripides' *Medea,* the heroine, angered by feelings of injustice, kills her two children, plots the death of her husband's new bride, and then escapes in a magic chariot.

[8] Agathon's plays have not survived; Homer portrays Achilles in the *Iliad.*

[9] Aristotle wrote a dialogue, *On Poets,* now lost.

he stands over the lonely grave of his beloved elder brother, who has died in the remote province of Bithynia. Like Sappho, the predecessor he revered and imitated, Catullus is a poet who has inspired almost every succeeding generation of poets to translate him anew.

LIFE

Like Sappho, Catullus grew up far from the intellectual center of the culture he lived in. He was born about 84 B.C.E. in the north of Italy, near Verona, the second son of a prosperous contractor for the Roman legions of Cisalpine Gaul. In Verona, Catullus was lucky enough to be taken into the circle gathered around the brilliant teacher Hellenist Valerius Cato. In one poem, he says he began to write when he was about sixteen. Brilliant, handsome, witty, and with a keen appetite for all sorts of experience, at some point Catullus made his way to Rome, which from that time on he regarded as his home. There he found companions among both the intellectuals and the most avid pleasure-seekers; if the great statesman Cicero was his friend, so were the full array of Gelliuses and Rufuses and Quintiuses and Balbuses who lust and drink and carouse through his poems. One person whom he and his friends seem to have regarded with mild dislike was Caesar himself, but this seems provoked more on grounds of personality than politics: "Caesar? What Caesar?" he jokes in one fragment.

Clodia Metelli, whom Catullus addresses in his poems as Lesbia in tribute to Sappho's island home, was the wife of the governor of Cisalpine Gaul. It is very likely that she came into his life while he was still living in Verona. She was about five years older than he, and already notorious for her commanding air, her charm, her caprices, and her sexual appetites; when her husband died in 59, rumors circulated that she had poisoned him to clear the way for an incestuous affair with her brother. Cicero wrote a polemic against her when one of his favorite pupils was accused of trying to poison her. What he has to say about her character is devastating: he reports, among many other things, that she would regularly go down to a garden on the banks of the Tiber where naked men were bathing in order to choose her lovers from among them. Cicero, an old-line conservative who believed Roman women should all be quiet, stately matrons, must have been galled to no end by the outspoken Clodia; she lived only a few houses away from Cicero, and enjoyed staging riotous salons for politicians opposed to him.

The very qualities in Clodia that so irked Cicero made Catullus fall helplessly in love with her. Their affair is chronicled in about forty poems that trace their relationship from its playful, ecstatic beginning through betrayal, jealousy, recriminations, reconciliations, and final contempt. Yet with all the heartbreak, it seems that Catullus does not wish to have forgone meeting and loving Clodia/Lesbia; she is the great experience of his life.

In 57, very likely at about the time that Catullus' love affair was ending, he received word that his much-loved elder brother had died in Bithynia, in what is now Turkey, while on a diplomatic mission. Catullus arranged for a political appointment and traveled to Bithynia in the entourage of the propraetor Memmius Gemellus. At some time during his tour of duty in Asia Minor, Catullus visited his brother's grave, an occasion commemorated movingly in one of his finest poems, 101, famous for its salutation to the dead, *Ave atque vale* ("Hail and farewell," here translated as "Goodbye, goodbye"). This death, perhaps linked in his mind with the death of his relationship with Lesbia, affected Catullus deeply. He had always lived at a riotous pace, as though he sensed death were close and he needed to cram in quickly all the experience he could. His brother's death seems to have confirmed what he had guessed about the imminence of mortality. He writes in another poem addressed to his brother, "You have darkened my mind."

Catullus remained in Bithynia for about a year, and then, homesick for Italy, he got himself released from service. He bought a yacht in which he sailed home through the

Adriatic and up the Po River to his family villa on the shores of Lake Garda. He returned to Rome one last time, where he may have resumed his affair with Lesbia. Soon after, though we do not know exactly when or how, Catullus died. He was about thirty.

Work

As a young poet, Catullus belonged to a bright group of Roman writers who called themselves the Neoterics, the "new poets." We know a few of their names, but Catullus' is the only body of work that has survived. The Neoterics were impatient with the ponderous high-mindedness and patriotic and mythological themes that characterized a good deal of Roman literature. They were far more taken by the racy, breezy Roman comedy that mocked pretentiousness and celebrated in colloquial language the everyday life of gossipy servants, lovesick young folk, feasting, and drinking. Catullus turns his poems away from epic themes and looks to the sophisticated urban life that teems before his eyes. Candor, wit, the intimacy of his voice, and the astonishing variety of his range characterize Catullus' work. That range is discernible even in the brief selection presented here. Lightly, lovingly, in poem 2 he describes his beloved sensuously playing with her tame sparrow, teasing it, cuddling it, feeding it; he says he wishes he might be her, able for a while to forget the pains of love, but it is clear that it is the petted sparrow he envies as well. And in poem 3, when the sparrow dies, his elegy for it begins in the mock-heroic tone of one making a great fuss over a trivial thing, but the poem deepens within a few lines into a genuine rage against the mortality that in the end will devour all lovely things, whether they are trivial or of great importance. Lesbia and her sparrow alike will one day be "lost in darkness / . . . a sad place / from which no one returns." Extravagantly, in poem 5, in the exuberance of first love, he and his sweetheart defy death with their wealth of infinitely multiplied embraces. Mockingly, in poem 25 he threatens to expose a male lover's habit of petty theft; in a raging fit of jealousy and despair, he rails in poem 37 at the crowds of young Roman men whom he imagines have all cuckolded him. Finally, in poem 101 he stands stricken beside a lonely grave in a far country, death offerings in his hands, surrounded by a vast silence. Paradoxically, it is perhaps his keen intuition of death's constant presence that enables Catullus to write these poems spilling over with all the beauty and decadence of Roman life.

Suggested Readings

Stuart G. P. Small's *Catullus: A Reader's Guide to the Poems* (1983) provides an excellent general introduction to Catullus' work. T. P. Wiseman's *Catullus and His World: A Reappraisal* (1985) looks at Catullus as a man of his times.

2: "Sparrow, O, sweet sparrow"

Translated by Horace Gregory

Sparrow, O, sweet sparrow,
love of my lady love,
she who's always nursing
you between her breasts and
feeding you her finger-tips;
she, that radiant lady,

delicious in her play with you,
for a while forgetting
all the deeper wounds of love . . .
I envy her. This pastime
would raise my heart from darkness.

3: "Dress now in sorrow, O all"

Translated by Horace Gregory

Dress now in sorrow, O all
you shades of Venus,
and your little cupids weep.

My girl has lost her darling sparrow;
he is dead, her precious toy
that she loved more than her two eyes,
O, honeyed sparrow following her
as a girl follows her mother,
never to leave her breast, but tripping
now here, now there, and always singing
his sweet falsetto
song to her alone.

Now he is gone; poor creature,
lost in darkness,
to a sad place
from which no one returns.

O ravenous hell!
My evil hatred rises against your power,
you that devour
all things beautiful;
and now this pitiful, broken sparrow,
who is the cause of my girl's grief,
making her eyes weary and red with sorrow.

5: "Come, Lesbia, let us live and love"

Translated by Horace Gregory

Come, Lesbia, let us live and love,
nor give a damn what sour old men say.
The sun that sets may rise again
but when our light has sunk into the earth,
it is gone forever.
            Give me a thousand kisses,
then a hundred, another thousand,

another hundred
          and in one breath
still kiss another thousand,
another hundred.
          O then with lips and bodies joined
many deep thousands;
          confuse
their number,
          so that poor fools and cuckolds (envious
even now) shall never
learn our wealth and curse us
with their
evil eyes.

25: "Sweet girlish Thallus"

Translated by Horace Gregory

Sweet girlish Thallus,[1] as soft to your caresses as a little Spanish rabbit,
delicate as down plucked from a goose, and languid as the fallen member
that decorates an old man—but O, a hungry Thallus, covetous, rapacious,
eager as roaring waves or sea gulls with their beaks wide for food—O give me
back my cloak, my Spanish napkins, my ancient Bithynian tablets, that you are
    now displaying—
fool—to show these things in public as yours alone! Drop them, your fingers
thick with glue to capture all things. I'll sear you,
your dainty little hips, your pretty hands, and I'll use
whips, inscribing phallus upon your flesh, O Thallus, broken, swaying,
lost in a violent storm,—little boat careering through a dark, angry ocean.

37: "Roadhouse and members of that bawdy fraternity"

Translated by Horace Gregory

Roadhouse and members of that bawdy fraternity
that roars behind the ninth pillar
from the temple where those two brothers, Castor and Pollux
wear their caps, signifying good fortune. Are you the only
men on earth fit to mount girls and ride them, the rest of us,
merely goats?
Come now, line up,
bent double in a circle, a hundred of you, or two hundred,
come, do you think I am not able to take on
two hundred of you in one grand bout of pederasty?
What's more I'll cover the front doors of your fine house
with nimble sketches of the phallus.

[1]Thallus has a reputation for petty thievery.

My girl has left me,
loved more than any woman born was she,
and I have fought, spilled blood for her,
but she has taken this house for a place to sleep and live.
O great and noble gentlemen, she's slept with all of you
to her dishonour, slept with pimps
that walk at night in darkest alley-ways,
and you, particularly, dainty, long-haired Egnatius,
son of a homosexual Spanish rabbit,
made handsome by an ancient Spanish custom,
your beard and teeth daily and delicately
bathed in Spanish urine.

101: "Dear brother, I have come these many miles"

Translated by Horace Gregory

Dear brother, I have come these many miles, through strange lands to this
Eastern Continent
to see your grave, a poor sad monument of what you were, O brother.
And I have come too late; you cannot hear me; alone now I must speak
to these few ashes that were once your body and expect no answer.
I shall perform an ancient ritual over your remains, weeping,
(this plate of lentils for dead men to feast upon, wet with my tears)
O brother, here's my greeting: here's my hand forever welcoming you
and I forever saying: good-bye, good-bye.

VIRGIL

[70–19 B.C.E.]

Publius Vergilius Maro achieved fame in his own lifetime as the poet of *The Eclogues* and *The Georgics* and was exalted after his death for his epic poem *The Aeneid.* This work, the story of the founding of Rome by descendants of the conquered city of Troy, recalls portions of the Greek epics of Homer, but goes beyond them to stress the theme of *pietas,* public virtue or duty, which Virgil thought lay at the core of Roman civilization. *The Aeneid* is believed to have been dedicated to Virgil's friend Octavian, the Emperor Augustus Caesar, the most powerful man in the world in the poet's time. The work survived its disappointed author's own command to burn it at his death. It subsequently influenced Dante in the writing of *The Divine Comedy,* and has come down to us as one of the great cultural monuments of Europe, especially celebrated in Germany, France, Italy, and England.

Life

Virgil was born in the northern city of Mantua (now Mantova) in a prosperous region that then marked the southern edge of Gaul. The provincial youth was educated at Cremona and Rome, but was never sent to Athens to receive the grounding in the Greek classics offered to Horace and other young Roman writers of the time. A shy and retiring figure, Virgil was never a rebel: He supported efforts to consolidate and stabilize Roman rule throughout his lifetime. This is not surprising when we recall that Virgil passed the first twenty years of his adult life surrounded by civil war. When he was twenty-one years of age, he and the others in his province were granted citizenship by Julius Caesar in the hope that they would support the embattled leader. After Caesar was assassinated in 44 B.C.E., Brutus, Cassius, Mark Antony, and Octavian struggled for power until 29 B.C.E., when Octavian returned victorious to Rome. Meanwhile, Virgil had already begun to address himself to the main business of the rest of his life: the writing of poetry of a national character.

WORK

Between 42 and 37 B.C.E., Virgil wrote *The Eclogues,* ten poems modeled after the pastoral poetry of the Greek writer Theocritus. *The Eclogues* were set in several locales, including the mythical Greek land of Arcadia, the reputed home of music and the contemplation of love, in contrast to Rome, the seat of strife and civil war. They addressed themselves to diverse subjects, including a homosexual love complaint, a lament over the warfare raking the countryside, and a vision of Justice returning to Italy in the form of a virgin goddess. *The Fourth Eclogue* has achieved fame because later Christian interpreters thought it heralded the coming of Christ.

Writing *The Georgics* took most of the next decade, from 36 through 29 B.C.E. Here Virgil imitated the ancient Greek writer Hesiod, author of *Works and Days,* a long didactic poem ostensibly devoted to farming, as well as the Roman poet Varro, author of a more literal-minded work titled *On Agriculture.* Virgil saw fit to add to his poem many passages touching on Roman political and moral life, contrasting, for example, the farmer's existence (hard-working and decent) with that of the city dweller (urbane and sometimes decadent). He even rather gracefully compared the life of the honest soldier such as Octavian to that of the poet such as himself, living in "inglorious ease."

Virgil began *The Aeneid* after the return of Octavian to Rome. Given Virgil's intention to produce an epic poem touching on the moral and political life of the Romans, fellow poets and probably even Octavian himself expected it would be a work in praise of the ruler's life. Instead, Virgil chose a subject suggested by Greek epic—the legendary flight of the last Trojan warriors from their doomed city and their eventual arrival on the shores of Italy—subtly linking the hero of the tale, Aeneas the Trojan, to Octavian, who was crowned Augustus Caesar in 27 B.C.E. In this way, Virgil could compose a national epic based on the founding of Rome while praising his patron and friend at the same time; and he could also use the story to point to lessons for the future. Thus the great patriotic poem doubled as a work of instruction.

Creating an epic poem was a more complicated matter for Virgil than it had been for Homer. In the first place, the form of composition was different, and this affected his treatment of the subject. While Homer used the oral-formulaic measure of Greek poetry to sing conventional praises of heroes and battles, Virgil was working on a written literary creation, subtler and more demanding in the ways it treated its subject and more likely to lead to thematic innovations. At the same time, the prevailing popular myth of the founding of Rome led Virgil to support the side in the Trojan War opposite from Homer's Achaean Greeks and to take a different view of the outcome than Homer did. The Romans believed they were the descendants of Trojans; from their admittedly biased perspective, the outcome of the Trojan War had been reversed a thousand years after the fall of Troy. The Romans had won, dominating as they did the Mediterranean and beyond, and carrying with them everywhere they went the highest values of ancient Greece. *The Aeneid,* therefore, amounts to a revisionist history of the Trojan War.

In Virgil's construction of the epic, the hero Aeneas, first prince of the Romans, had to be distinguished by his personal character. Consequently, Virgil endowed him with *pietas,* "public virtue" or "duty." The course taken by Aeneas was intended to demonstrate his spiritual growth, largely achieved when time and circumstance forced him to set aside all that he might hold dear in the world for the single goal of the founding of Lavinium, the ancient site of Roman civilization. But as we shall see, the story of his commitment leads us to examine the principal dilemma for Aeneas in the course of his wanderings: his encounter with Dido, Queen of Carthage.

THE AENEID

The Aeneid is divided into two parts: Books 1–6, describing the wanderings of Aeneas, and Books 7–12, telling of the battle for Italy. The first part is based roughly on *The Odyssey,* the second part on *The Iliad.* In this edition we have selected books 1–4 and 6 of the first part, leaving out Book 5, which is a description of athletic contests.

The poet's invocation in Book 1 finds him singing of "arms and a man," acts of war and the career of Aeneas, whose destiny brings him to the shores of Italy to found Lavinium. The poet puts the question immediately: Why must this prince, famed for his goodness, have to suffer so much to accomplish his goal? The opening lines thus brilliantly set the stage for the great themes of the work: Aeneas' destiny, his moral virtue, and the suffering he must endure.

In Book 1, the Trojans under Aeneas sail from Sicily to Italy on what appears to be the last leg of their fateful journey. Because of the goddess Juno's wrath, they encounter a storm at sea and are forced to land on the northern tip of Africa. Aeneas, battered by the storm, meets Queen Dido, who has recently led her people out of tribulation to this same shore to found the city of Carthage. Through a trick of the gods, Dido is made to fall in love with Aeneas. In Books 2 and 3, Aeneas tells Dido and her companions of his adventures, from the fall of Troy to the landing at Carthage. Hearing of his exploits while under the magical spell, Dido loves him all the more.

Dido is at the center of the action in Book 4. She roams Carthage like a stricken deer, wounded by love and careless of her commitment to her subjects. When Dido and Aeneas go hunting, they are separated from their followers by a storm; the flashes of lightning and shrieks of the nymphs from the mountain peak above them seem to mimic the ritual sounds of a Roman marriage. At least they do for Dido, who succumbs to Aeneas' embraces. After the couple returns to the city, Aeneas wears Dido's gift, a cloak she has embroidered in crimson and gold, and contributes to finishing the building of Carthage; but his emotional commitment to her remains ambiguous.

Seeing Aeneas' deviation from his duty to his people, Jupiter commands him to leave Carthage and continue his voyage. After hesitating, Aeneas begins to obey the command, not yet telling Dido what is taking place. When Dido finally confronts him and the two argue, Aeneas denies they were ever married, even symbolically, and Dido collapses in grief. As Aeneas sails away, Dido tricks her sister, Anna, into helping her commit suicide, which she does after a heart-rending series of speeches. The poet reminds us that ever since that day, there has been enmity between Rome and Carthage.

Aeneas encounters Dido again briefly in Book 6 when he visits the land of the dead. He assures her that he did not mean to leave her; in his eyes, he was as much a victim of Jupiter's command as she was a victim of his departure. But Dido will not speak to him and, eyes still on the ground, she leaves him. Aeneas' arrival in Carthage has brought about the destruction of Dido—a tragedy of the highest order. At the same time, we must remember the nature of Aeneas' calling. The head of the future Roman state, he is seemingly beyond moral judgment or even the pull of his own desires. He will do as he must, whatever the consequences. Yet Virgil shows him hesitating. The situation remains ambiguous, and we cannot help but think that Virgil intends it to be.

Two views have arisen concerning the characterization of Aeneas and Dido. The main sense of the text appears to be that Aeneas must serve the gods and found Lavinium, as is his destiny. His layover in Carthage leads to misfortune, brought about by the kind of foul play in heaven we have come to expect in classical epic. Aeneas is not to blame for the fate of Dido, and indeed there is something suspect in the way she falls ever more desperately in love with him, turning him from his true mission. The other reading, however, shifts the balance considerably. Here Aeneas commits a grievous error by dallying with Dido's feelings when he could not stay and be her true husband. He has wronged her and the tragic outcome is his own fault, which he must acknowledge for the rest of his life. This reading also calls into question the idea of *pietas,* which now appears neither pure nor innocent of consequences. Aeneas is a peculiarly isolated, estranged hero throughout Virgil's epic; one might almost call his loneliness "modern." The price of greatness, Virgil seems to tell us, is the surrender of our ordinary standards of moral conduct and our perpetual separation from those we love.

One might imagine what effect this tragedy would have had on the audience of Virgil's day. Dido's performance could be seen to reveal her tragic flaw, a species of pride. Her conduct belies the public-mindedness that should go with her role as queen of her people; instead, she succumbs to passion and lets it destroy her senses. In choosing love, both Dido and Aeneas allow the private realm of their lives to overwhelm the public one. But while Aeneas comprehends and corrects his action, Dido, the victim of her own passion, cannot. At the same time, one wonders what effect this story would have on Octavian. Perhaps it served as a warning against indiscretion. Did Virgil mean to instruct his friend to avoid excess—avoid even falling in love—to fulfill the callings of his public office?

The main purpose of Book 6 is not simply to conclude the story of Aeneas and Dido, but to move the action of the rest of the epic forward. Aeneas is granted a journey to the underworld, and visits those who will help him on his way to the conquest of Italy. The ghost of his father, Anchises, recently dead, shows him a long line of Roman heroes as yet unborn, including Octavius Caesar, and excites his mind with the desire for future fame. The principal art of the Romans, Anchises says, is in the rule of nations and the business of imposing peace. This is the message that Aeneas takes with him on his fateful voyage.

Our selection, limited to the first half of *The Aeneid,* has a different emphasis from that of the work as a whole; our excerpt subordinates the story of the founding of Rome to the love story of Aeneas and Dido, with its series of dramatic personal conflicts. In truth, however, the entire *Aeneid* deals with the conflict between preserving one's humanity and doing one's duty. Perhaps we should ask ourselves: In Western culture, what price have we paid for our perception that this conflict exists; and is our perception really true?

Suggested Readings

Because *The Aeneid* is one of the most popular books of all time, many translations and interpretations are available. Good modern translations include those of L. R. Lind (1962), F. O. Copley (1965), and Robert Fitzgerald (1965). Jasper Griffin's *Virgil* (1986) is a short, concise introduction to the poet and his work. A convenient recent introduction to Virgil's epic poem is K. W. Grandsen's *Virgil: The Aeneid* (1990). Modern interpretations include Brooks Otis's *Virgil: A Study in Civilized Poetry* (1963), Thomas Greene's *The Descent from Heaven: A Study in Epic Continuity* (1963), and W. A. Camps's *An Introduction to Virgil's Aeneid* (1969). A recent effort to study the more contradictory aspects of the work is W. R. Johnson's *Darkness Visible: A Study of Virgil's Aeneid* (1976). Some of the authors cited above are included in two selections of modern criticism: Steele Commager, ed., *Virgil: A Collection of Critical Essays* (1966); and Harold Bloom, ed., *Modern Critical Interpretations of the Aeneid* (1987).

The Aeneid

Translated by Frank O. Copley and Brooks Otis

Book 1
[Arriving in Carthage]

My song is arms and a man,[1] the first of Troy
to come to Italy and Lavinian shores,[2]
a fated fugitive, harried on land and sea
by heaven's huge might and Juno's endless hate,
pommeled by wars, till he could found the City
and bring his gods to Latium,[3] whence the race
of Latins, our Alban sires, and towering Rome.

Muse, tell me the causes: how was godhead wronged,
how injured the queen of heaven that she must force
through many a fall of fate and many a toil 10
that great, good man: can heaven hold such ill will?

A city once stood, a colony of Tyre,
Carthage, across from Italy and far
from Tiber's mouth, rich and agog for war,
a spot that Juno loved more than all worlds,
more even than Samos: here stood her arms and here
her chariot; throne of mankind it was to be
if Fate allowed; this was her cherished aim.
But men would spring of Trojan blood, she'd heard,
and some day lay her Carthage in the dust— 20
a race of world-wide kings, whose pride was war
and death for Libya: so ran the thread of Fate.

This she feared, remembering, too, that war
when first she fought for her dear Greece at Troy.
Still she recalled the anger and the pain
that sent her there: deep in her heart lay stored
the judgment of Paris,[4] the insult to her beauty,

---

[1]The introductory lines of *The Aeneid,* 1, 1–7, announcing the heroic theme, suggest parallel passages in Homer: *The Iliad,* 1, 1–7, on the wrath of Achilles; and *The Odyssey,* 1, 1–5, on the wanderings of Odysseus.

[2]Lavinia is the daughter of King Latinus, later to marry Aeneas.

[3]The area immediately around Rome, destination of the Trojan forces.

[4]Paris, son of Priam of Troy, judged Juno inferior in beauty to Venus, angering her. Later, under Venus' influence, Paris stole Helen from King Menelaus of Sparta, opening the Trojan War. The bitter enmity of Juno and Venus is a major theme of *The Aeneid.*

a hated people, a Ganymede raped to heaven.
Her anger flared; she drove all over the deep
the Trojan few that Achilles and Greece had spared, 30
and kept them far from Latium; year on year
they wandered, dogged by Fate, across the seas.[5]
Such matter it was to found our Roman race.

Scarce out of sight of Sicily they sailed on
lighthearted, while the bow cut through the waves,
when Juno, ever nursing her wounded heart,
thought thus: "What? Drop my design? Am I defeated,
and helpless to keep Troy's king from Italy?
Fate so decrees? Pallas could burn the ships
of Argos and drown their crewmen in the sea 40
for Ajax' lone offense—that lawless fool!
She threw Jove's shaft of lightning from the clouds,
shattered the fleet, and blew up the waves' wild roll.
Through Ajax' heart she drove a hissing flame,
whirled him away, and nailed him to a cliff.
But I, who stand here queen of heaven, to Jove
both wife and sister, all these years must fight
one single people. Who'll worship Juno now,
honor my altars, or come to me in prayer?"[6]

Turning these thoughts within her flaming heart 50
she came to Aeolia, home of clouds, a land
big with wild winds. Here Aeolus is king,
and keeps prisoned and locked in his vast cave
the battling storms and roaring hurricanes.
They curse and howl behind their granite bars
and moan at the bolts; he sits on his high throne,
scepter in hand, and holds them in constraint:
if he did not, they'd sweep the world away,
and whip sea, earth, and heaven through the air.

But Jove the almighty locked them in lightless caves 60
for fear of this, and piled a mountain range
upon them, and gave them a king with stern command
when to release and when to bolt and bar.
Juno then made her humble plea to him:

"Aeolus, you have power from father Jove
to calm the waves or whistle up the storm:
a people I hate are sailing the Tuscan sea,

---

[5]The command of Aeneas is prepared for in *The Iliad,* Book 20, where he is rescued after a battle with Achilles by the sea god Poseidon and it is determined that he will lead the Trojan remnants to exile. The wanderings of Aeneas depicted in Books 2–3 of *The Aeneid* borrow much of their incidental detail from the parallel adventures of Odysseus told in *The Odyssey,* Books 9–12.

[6]Ajax, son of Oileus, kidnapped Cassandra, daughter of Priam and a priestess of Athena, from the holy temple at Troy; in retribution, Athena killed him with a lightning bolt. Juno demands equal powers in dealing with Aeneas.

bringing to Italy Troy and her conquered gods.
Make your winds wild! Capsize and sink their ships!
Or scatter them, crews and corpses, over the deep! 70
Twice seven Nymphs I have of splendid form;
of these the loveliest, Deiopea,
I'll give you for your wife; she shall be yours
and, for the help you give, shall spend her years
with you, and make you father of stalwart sons."

Aeolus then: "My lady, you need only
work out your wish and speak: I must obey.
My throne, my scepter, all my power, my place
at the feasts of gods, you win from Jove for me
and make me ruler over cloud and storm." 80

With that he turned his spear and struck the mountain
full on the flank. The winds, in column formed,
rushed through the gap and roared across the world.
Down on the sea to stir it from its depths
fell East and South Winds, and with stormy squalls
the Sou'wester; on toward shore the combers rolled;
men shouted loud, and shrouds and tackle screamed.
Clouds ripped across the sky to steal the light
from Trojan eyes; black night fell over the sea.
The heavens thundered; lightning crackled and flashed; 90
wherever men looked they saw the face of death.
A chill swept over Aeneas; his limbs went weak;
he cried in grief and stretched his hands toward heaven,
calling aloud: "Oh, three times, four times blessed,
those men who died beneath the walls of Troy,
watched by their fathers! O Diomede, you bravest
of Greeks, why could you not have spilled my life
on Trojan soil? Why could I not have fallen
where Achilles laid Hector low, where tall Sarpedon
lies; where Simois rolls beneath his waves 100
the helmets, the shields of heroes, and those brave dead!"[7]

Amid his cries a screaming Northerly squall
set sails aback; the waves rose toward the stars.
Smashed were the oars; the vessel yawed and swung
broad-on; a craglike comber rose astern.
Some hung on the crests; some in the gaping troughs
saw bottom between the waves; the sand boiled up.
A Southerly drove three ships on hidden reefs
(Italians call them "The Altars"; far offshore
they lie, their great backs just awash); three more 110
an Easterly swept to a shallow (tragic sight!).
They grounded hard; the sand piled up around them.

[7]Our first picture of Aeneas shows him lamenting his fate. He wishes he had died nobly in defense of Troy rather than drown at sea, as seems probable, as a result of the storm.

One, with Orontes and his Lycian crew,
was swamped: Aeneas saw the huge sea rise
and crash on her quarterdeck; overboard went her helmsman
headfirst in the water; a moment she stood stock-still,
then spinning three times round sank in a flurry.
A few men bobbed up swimming in the swirl;
a spear, a plank, the flotsam wealth of Troy.
Ilioneus' stout ship and brave Achates', 120
the one that Abas rode, and old Aletes,
fell to the storm. Through weakened, gaping seams
they took in the deadly damp; their frames gave way.

Now Neptune heard the roaring, raving seas,
the wild wail of the winds, and felt the waters
come rolling from the deeps; in vast concern
he lifted his head serene above the flood.
He saw Aeneas' fleet strewn far and wide,
and Trojans battered and beaten by wind and wave.
Juno was angry—he knew his sister's work! 130
He called to the East and West Winds and addressed them:

"So sure of yourselves? So sure of kin and kind?
How dare you winds without my leave confound
heaven and earth and raise the waves so high?
You, whom—! But first I'd better calm the sea.
Next time you'll not pay penalty so light.
Go quickly now, and tell this to your king:
The sea's not his domain, not his the trident;
they're mine by lot. He has his pile of rocks,
a home for all you winds. Let Aeolus 140
play monarch there—and keep his winds locked up."

He spoke, and in a flash he calmed the swells,
swept off the cloud-rack, and brought back the sun.
Cymothoë then, and Triton, heaved the ships
off the sharp reef, while Neptune with his trident
cleared the great sandspit and broke up the waves;
his chariot wheels rolled lightly over the waters.
As when in some great nation the masses rise
in riot, and savage, ignoble hearts run wild;
now brands and stones, the weapons of madness, fly— 150
then, if some patriot stern and honor-laden
stands forth, the shouting ends, the people stop
to hear; his words bring back the public peace;
so ceased the roar of waters when their lord
looked out and rode beneath the open sky,
with skillful hand reining his car and steeds.

Bone-weary, the sons of Aeneas hurried for land—
the nearest shore; they raised the Libyan coast.
In a byway lies a bay; an island blocks
its entrance and behind it makes a lee 160

where every wave breaks to a gentle roll.
On either shore a rocky headland lifts
a rampart toward the sky; beneath those peaks
wide waters are silent; a sylvan backdrop hangs
rustling above a gloomy, lightless grove.
Ahead, a beetling cliff, at its base a cave
with a bubbling spring and seats of living rock,
home of the Nymphs. Here weary craft may rest
unheld by hawsers or the anchor's bite.
In sailed Aeneas with the seven ships 170
saved from his fleet; the Trojans leaped to land,
kissed the dear earth, and made the beach their own,
there to lay down their tired and salt-sick limbs.
Achates took his flint and struck a spark,
caught up the fire on leaves, and put dry tow
and tinder about it, then nursed it to a flame.
The men unloaded implements and supplies
all soaked in brine; dog-tired, they sorted out
the best, built up the fires, and cooked their meal.

Meanwhile Aeneas climbed the cliff and searched 180
the sea to the far horizon: could he find
the ships of Antheus riding out the storm?
Caicus on his quarterdeck? or Capys?
Not one ship was in sight, but on the shore
he saw three wandering stags; stretched out behind,
a whole herd followed browsing on the hills.
He stopped, and from Achates snatched the bow
and arrows that his faithful friend had brought.
First he shot down the leaders, who carried high
their antlered heads, then at the rest let fly 190
and sent them all stampeding through the woods,
nor stopped his archery till his shafts had laid
seven aground—for each ship one fat deer.[8]
Then back to the harbor to divide the spoils!
This called for wine, the casks that kind Acestes
gave them the day they sailed from Sicily.
Aeneas shared them out and spoke good cheer:
"This isn't the first time, men, that we've known trouble!
We've suffered worse, and God will end this, too!
You sailed close by those cliffs where Scylla raged 200
and roared; you saw the Cyclops and his home
on Aetna. Take courage, now! No fears nor sorrow!
Some day these memories, too, will bring a smile.
Whatever may happen, whatever perils we face,
it's on to Italy! Once there, we'll rest.

---

[8]Although there is precedent from *The Odyssey* for the hero to provide for his men, Aeneas is present as provider at every point in Virgil's narrative where his leadership is put to the test. His personal dedication is part of his *pietas*.

So God reveals; there Troy must rise again.
Hold hard and save yourselves for better days!"[9]

These were his words, though he was sick with care.
He forced a smile and kept his sorrows hidden.
The men made ready to cook their venison. 210
They stripped flesh from the bones and bared the entrails.
Some cut and spitted the pieces of fresh meat;
others set up the pots and tended fires.
Food restored strength. They lay back on the grass
and had their fill of wine and good fat meat.
With hunger appeased and dinner cleared away
they talked for hours, hung between hope and fear,
about the friends they'd lost: were they alive,
or were they gone and passed beyond recall?
Aeneas the good thought sadly of Orontes, 220
of Amycus and his fate, of Lycus' death
so cruel, of Gyas the brave, and brave Cloanthus.

Silence had fallen when Jove from heaven's height
looked out on sea and sail and level plain,
searching the coasts and nations; then on high
he stopped, and fixed his gaze on Libya's realm.
And as he pondered deeply, much concerned,
Venus, her eyes made bright by welling tears,
sadly addressed him: "Dear my lord, who rule
God and man forever, who hurl the thunder, 230
how could Aeneas, my son, offend you so?
How could the Trojans? They've seen so many die;
yet every door is locked, for Italy's sake.
In days to come, they were to give us Rome—
leaders, from blood of Troy recalled to life,
who'd hold beneath their sway all lands and seas:
you promised sure! What, sir, has turned your heart?
This helped me bear the fall and tearful wreck
of Troy: one fate I balanced by the other.
But there's no change! The same hard lot pursues them! 240
Dear lord and father, when will you grant them rest?
Antenor could slip through the Argive lines,
sail up the Adriatic, and find safety
far in Liburnia, past Timavus' wells,
where through nine mouths a roaring mountain torrent
floods over fields and plunges toward the sea.
Yes, he could build a town and make a home
for Trojans, name his nation, and set up
a Trojan standard. Now he rests in peace.
But we, your children, to whom you grant high heaven, 250
have lost our ships for one lone person's hate!

[9]The translation attempts to capture the optimism of Aeneas' speeches to his men.

We are betrayed and barred from Italy's shores!
Thus are the righteous honored and thrones restored?"

The universal father turned on her
the smile of peace that brings a clear, calm day.
He bent and kissed his daughter; then he spoke:
"No fear, Cytherea! Your people's fate remains
unchanged. You'll see the city and promised walls
of Lavinium; you shall carry to heaven's high stars
Aeneas the great and good: my heart's not turned. 260
But now (since care consumes you, I shall speak
more fully and reveal Fate's hidden page)
he'll wage hard war in Italy; savage tribes
he must defeat, and give them towns and laws.[10]
But once the Rutulans are pacified
the Latins shall know him king three seasons full.
Then young Ascanius, whom we name 'Iulus'
('Ilus' he was, in Ilium's royal days),
shall hold the throne while the long months roll round
through thirty years. He'll leave Lavinium 270
and build his seat of power at Alba Longa.
Here kings of Hector's lineage shall rule
three hundred years, till Ilia, priestess-queen,
shall lie with Mars and bear to him twin sons.
Then, glad of a nursing she-wolf's sheltering hide,
King Romulus shall found the walls of Mars,
and name his people 'Romans,' for himself.
For them I set no bounds of place or time;
rule without end I grant them. Juno, too,
whose harshness now frights earth and sky and sea, 280
shall come to better mind, and with me bless
the Romans, lords of the world, the toga'd race.
This is decreed. In time the day will come
when Phthia and proud Mycenae shall be slaves
to the sons of Priam, and Argos wear their yoke.
Of noble Trojan line shall spring a Caesar
(Ocean shall bound his power, the stars his fame)—
Julius, a name come down from great Iulus.
Laden one day with spoil of the East, he'll have
your welcome to heaven, and men will pray to him. 290
Hard hearts will soften then, and wars will cease;
old Faith and Vesta, Remus and his twin
will rule the world; tight bands of steel will close
the terrible temple of War, where Blood-Lust caged
will crouch on barbarous spears, bound hundredfold
with links of bronze, screaming and slavering blood."

---

[10]Through the vehicle of Jupiter's response to Athena's question, Virgil reveals the design of the gods: Aeneas will establish the society of the Romans in Italy after suffering hardship and fighting fierce battles. Jupiter goes on to summarize the legendary history of Rome.

So speaking, Jove sent Maia's son from heaven
to spread the lands and keeps of Carthage wide
in welcome to Trojans: Dido, untaught of fate,
must not repulse them.[11] Through large air he flew 300
and with quick wing-beats came to Libyan shores,
then did as ordered; the Tyrians, by God's will,
put off their savage ways; their leader and queen
conceived for men of Troy peace and good will.
Faithful Aeneas lay thinking all night long,
determined, soon as daylight came, to search
this unfamiliar land: Where had the wind
brought him? Who lived here? man? (he saw no homes)
or beast? He must find out and tell his men!
In a wooded cave beneath an overhang 310
he hid his ships where they were screened by trees
above and behind. Then with one friend, Achates,
he went forth, clasping in each hand a spear.
Out in the woods his mother came to meet him.[12]
She seemed a girl; her face and garb were those
of a Spartan maid or Thracian Harpalyce
whipping her horses to outrun Hebrus' current.
Over her shoulder a bow hung ready to hand;
her hair lay loose and scattered by the wind,
her flowing gown belted to bare her knee. 320
She hailed the men: "Tell me, sirs, have you seen
one of my sisters wandering down this way?
She'd have a quiver and spotted lynx-hide cape;
perhaps she was hot on the trail of a foam-flecked boar."

So Venus; and Venus' son replied to her:
"None of your sisters have I seen or heard,
O—what shall I call you? That's no mortal face,
that voice no girl's. You are a goddess, sure!
Sister of Phoebus? One of the Nymphs' descent?
Blessed be your name, whatever it is! But help us! 330
What land is this? On what coasts of the world
have we been tossed? Tell us, for we are lost.
Vast waves and winds have sent us hapless here.
We'll offer prayer and rich blood-sacrifice!"

Then Venus: "I am not worthy of such honor.
We girls of Tyre by custom bear the bow
and lace the scarlet boot high on the leg.
This land is Punic; of Tyre, our city and name;
around us are Libyans, people untamed by war.
Our queen is Dido; she left the city of Tyre 340

---

[11] Jupiter decrees that Dido and the Carthaginians will give Aeneas a peaceful reception; later Venus arranges the seduction of Dido by Aeneas. Thus, although she has the support of Juno, Dido is at the mercy of the most powerful faction of the gods throughout the ensuing action.

[12] Venus, the mother of Aeneas, is also the goddess of love. Her intervention on behalf of her son will lead to the seduction of Dido. Here she appears disguised, to the chagrin of Aeneas.

to escape her brother—a long and tortured tale
of cruel deception. Hear while I tell it briefly.
Her husband, Sychaeus, held the richest lands
in all Phoenicia; he was the man she loved,
her first, to whom her father gave her, a bride,
a virgin. But her brother, the king of Tyre,
Pygmalion, had no peer in monstrous crime.
The two men quarreled; blind for love of wealth
Pygmalion murdered Sychaeus at the altar,
catching him off his guard; his sister's love 350
left him unmoved. He kept the deed long hidden
and cheated the heartsick girl with empty hopes.
But as she slept, her husband's unlaid ghost
came to her, showing a face all strange and pale.
He told of the murder, bared his wounded breast,
and brought the whole foul story to the light.
'Hurry! Run! Leave your fatherland!' he urged,
'and for your help, look, here a treasure buried—
silver and gold, more than you ever knew!'
His words led Dido to prepare for flight. 360
She brought together those who loathed the tyrant
or feared him. Ships, it happened, stood complete;
they seized them, put the treasure aboard. To sea
went greedy Pygmalion's gold. A woman led them!
They came to the place where you shall see the walls
huge rising and the towers of Carthage-town.
Here they bought land—'as much as one bull's hide
enclosed'—for this is the place called 'The Purse.'
But who are you? From what coasts have you come?
Where are you going?" Aeneas at these words 370
heaved a deep sigh and drew speech from his heart:
"My lady, if I began with first-beginnings,
and you were free to hear our tale of toil,
day would lie locked in heaven before the end!
We are from ancient Troy—if to your ears has come
the name of Troy?—We'd traveled many a sea
when storms by sheer chance drove us to Libyan shores.
I am Aeneas the good; the gods I saved
ride in my ships. My name is known in heaven.
My goal is Italy, land of my fathers' line. 380
With twice ten ships I put to sea from Troy
to follow the path my goddess-mother showed me;
just seven, battered by wind and wave, remain.
I walk these Libyan wastes a helpless stranger
exiled by East and West." Venus could bear
no more, but spoke to end his sad account:

"Whoever you are, the love of heaven saved you
and brought you living to this Tyrian land.
Go now, and make your way to Dido's court.
Your men are safe, and changing winds have blown 390
your ships to safety. This I can tell you now,

unless I was taught to read the birds all wrong.
See there: twelve swans flying in joyful ranks;
Jove's eagle, swooping down from open sky
frightened and scattered them; now with lines new-formed
they've settled to earth or hover over the land.
As they in safety flapped their whistling wings
or soared in a flock to wreathe the sky with song,
just so your ships and men have come to port
or under full sail have reached the harbor's mouth. 400
Go now, and let this pathway guide your steps."

She turned to leave; a glow of light shone out
behind her head; her hair sent forth perfume
ambrosial; she let her train fall full-length down,
and walked in majesty divine! He knew
his mother, and as she hastened off he cried,
"What? Your son? Again so heartless to mock him—
you, too—with empty shows? Why was your hand
not laid in mine? Why could we not speak true?"
With this reproach he turned toward Dido's town. 410
But Venus walled the two in lightless air
and clothed them all about in heavy mist
so none could see them and no man had power
to hold them back or question why they came.
Then she flew off to Paphos, and with smiles
came home again, where incense wreathes her shrine
and hundred altars sweet with fresh-plucked blooms.

The two men meanwhile hurried down the path
and soon were climbing the highest hill that hangs
over the town and looks down on its walls. 420
Aeneas was awed: so vast, where once was camp-ground!
The wonder of gates, and avenues paved, and crowds!
Working like mad, those Tyrians; some at walls,
some toiled at forts, surveying, or hauling stone;
some marked out homesites and drew boundary lines.
They had their laws, their courts, their councilmen.
Here they were dredging a harbor; there they laid
a theater's undercroft, and cut tall columns
out of a quarry cliff to adorn the stage.
Like bees in June out in the blooming fields 430
busy beneath the sun, some teasing out
the new young workers, others pressing down
clear honey or making nectar burst the cells,
still others taking the loads brought in, while others
police the hive and drive off lazy drones:
the work hums on; the combs are sweet with thyme.
"O blessed by Fate! Your walls are building now!"
Aeneas said, as he watched the ramparts rise.
Walled in the cloud (a miracle!), he walked
among the workmen, and no one saw him come. 440

In mid-town was a pleasant, shady park,
marking the spot where Tyrians, tempest-tossed,
had dug to find, as Juno had foretold,
a horse's head—a sign that they should be
great soldiers and good farmers down the years.
Here Dido of Sidon built a temple to Juno,
a huge vault filled with wealth and holiness.
Above its steps the doorway was of bronze,
the beams bronze-nailed, the doors and hinges brazen.
Here in the park Aeneas saw a sight 450
that eased his fears and made him first dare hope
for safety, and take heart for all his troubles.
As he searched over the temple, stone by stone,
awaiting the queen, and wondering how this town
had come to be, amazed at the workmen's zeal
and skill, he saw, scene after scene, the war
at Troy, battles now famed through all the world:
the Atrides, Priam, and, savage to both, Achilles.[13]
His tears welled up. "What place, Achates, now,"
he said, "what land does not know all we suffered? 460
See: Priam! Here too the brave have their reward!
The world has tears; man's lot does touch the heart.
Put off your fears: our story will save us yet!"
Aeneas spoke, and let this empty show
nourish his grief and flood his face with tears.
He saw how men had fought the fight for Troy:
here Greeks retreating, here Trojans pressing hard,
here their allies, here plumed Achilles' car.
Nearby were Rhesus' snowy-canvassed tents—
(he knew them and wept!) his men, just fallen to sleep, 470
betrayed and butchered by bloody Diomede;
gone, too, his fiery team before they knew
the taste of Trojan feed or Xanthus' waters.
And here was Troilus, running, his weapons lost
(poor boy! he was no man to meet Achilles!),
his horses pulled him clinging to his car,
still gripping the reins; his head and shoulders dragged
over the ground; his spear wrote in the dust.
And here the women of Troy in sad parade
were bringing the robe to cruel Athena's temple 480
with humble prayer, beating their breasts in grief:
with stony eyes the goddess stared them down.
And there Achilles peddled the lifeless corpse
of Hector, dragged three times around Troy-walls.
Aeneas could not hold back a cry of pain
to see the car, the ransom, his dead friend,

[13]The battle scenes described here are taken from descriptions in *The Iliad* and later literature. Achilles, principal hero of the Achaeans, is "savage to both [sides]" because he holds a grudge against Agamemnon, leader of the Achaean forces.

and Priam stretching out defenseless hands.
He saw himself, surrounded by great Greeks,
and Memnon the Moor, with his Arabian troops.
And leading her crescent-shielded Amazons 490
Penthesilea fought madly amid the host.
One breast lay bare above the sword-belt clasp—
a warrior-maiden who dared to fight with men.

As Aeneas of Troy stood marveling at these sights,
unable to speak or turn his eyes away,
into the temple came Dido the beautiful,
the queen, with all her bodyguard around her.
As by Eurotas or on the height of Cynthus
Diana leads her dancing mountain-maids,
a thousand ringed about her; there she goes 500
quiver on back, head-high above them all
(no word betrays her mother's heartfelt joy)—
just so was Dido, and just so her joy
to see her people working, building, planning.[14]
She entered the temple; under its central dome
she took her place enthroned, walled by armed men.
There she sat judging, framing laws, assigning
work to her men by fair shares or by lot,
when all at once a crowd came rushing in.
Aeneas saw they had Sergestus, Antheus, 510
Cloanthus, and others whom the storm at sea
had scattered and carried away to distant shores.
Aeneas was speechless; Achates was struck hard
by joy and fear at once: they were afire
to greet their friends—but still, what did this mean?
Pretending calm, clothed in their cloud, they watched.
What had these men endured? Where were their ships?
Why were they here? Each ship had sent her man
to beg for mercy. Pleading, the group moved on.

Once they had entered and gained the right to speak, 520
Ilioneus, the oldest, pled in peace:
"My lady, Jove has let you found your city
and bring both right and rule to savage tribes.
We're Trojans, helpless, blasted by wind and wave.
We beg you: do us no wrong, nor burn our ships.
Spare a good people! Be merciful! Hear our plea!
We have not come in arms to scorch the earth
of Libya, to plunder your homes and load our ships.
The vanquished have no heart for such presumption.
There is a place called 'Westland' by the Greeks, 530
an ancient country, powerful, warlike, rich;

[14]Dido left her native Tyre with her followers after her brother, with whom she had shared the throne, murdered her husband and sought to murder her. The founder of Carthage, she is equal to Aeneas as the leader of her people and a builder of cities.

the Oenotri settled it; now, we hear, their sons
are calling it 'Italy' for their founder's name.
This was our goal.
But all of a sudden waves and rain and wind
drove us on unseen banks; squalls from the south
scattered our ships. Some sank; some hung on reefs
uncharted. We few swam here to your shores.
What kind of people are you? Civilized?
What laws are these? We have been kept from shore, 540
forbidden to land, and met with shows of force.
If men and mortal arms arouse your scorn,
be sure the gods take note of right and wrong.
Aeneas was our chief; he had no peer
in justice, goodness, and the arts of war.
If fate has saved him, if he lives and breathes,
and has not fallen to rest in heartless dark,
we have no fears. However great your kindness,
you'll not regret it. In Sicily, we have towns
and arms, for Acestes boasts his Trojan blood. 550
We're badly damaged: let us beach our craft,
shape timbers in your woods, and strip out oars;
then if we find our friends and chief, we'll sail
for Italy, Latium—Italy with a will!
But if it's finished, if our well-loved lord
is lost at sea, and hope of Iulus gone,
then let us cross to Sicily, whence we came.
Acestes will take us; he shall be our king."
Thus spoke Ilioneus; with one great shout
the sons of Troy assented. 560

Then with a gracious nod, Queen Dido answered:
"Put fear from your hearts, Trojans; dismiss your cares.
Our lot is hard, our kingdom new; for this
our laws are stern, our whole land under guard.
Who knows not Troy, knows not Aeneas' people,
those brave fighters, and that great holocaust?
We Punic folk are not so dull of heart;
the sun starts not his course so far from Tyre.
You're bound for the Westland, Saturn's wide domain?
or Sicily, and Acestes for your king? 570
I'll help you, keep you safe, and send you on.
Or will you settle here and share my realm?
The city I build is yours: pull up your ships.
Trojan, Tyrian, all shall be one to me.[15]
If only that same storm had forced your chief,
Aeneas, here too! I'll send out men to search

[15]Fearing attack from Tyre, Dido seeks to build an alliance with the Trojans to support her people. This will be one of her motivations for forming an attachment to Aeneas.

the shores and all the ends of Libyan land:
he may be safe, but in some backwood lost."

Her words set hearts a-beating in Achates
the brave and Lord Aeneas; they longed to burst 580
their cloud. Achates first was moved to speak:
"My lord, what thought arises in your heart?
Here we are safe; our ships and men are found.
One only is missing, but far at sea we saw
him drowned. The rest is as your mother told us."
Scarce had he spoken when their veiling cloud
burst all at once and turned to clearest air.
There stood Aeneas, splendid in bright light,
grand as a god, for Venus breathed on him
to give him strength and vigor, the glow of youth, 590
and made his eyes shine out with power and joy—
like ivory carved to beauty, like some work
of silver or Parian marble chased with gold.
His presence and his words burst on the queen
and all her men: "You want me? Here I am,
Aeneas the Trojan, saved from Libyan seas.
You pitied, you only, the terrible toil of Troy.
We few that Greece had left on land and sea
have suffered every blow, lost everything,
yet you would share your city, your home, with us! 600
My lady, how can we thank you, we and all
the sons of Troy, now scattered across the earth?
Oh, if the gods note goodness, if there are
such things as justice and hearts that know the right,
you shall be richly blessed. What happy year
bore you? What noble parents got you so?
While rivers run to sea, while shadows cross
the curving hills and fires feed the stars,
your name will live in honor and in praise
wherever the world may call me." With these words 610
he turned to greet Ilioneus, Serestus,
and the others, Gyas the brave, and brave Cloanthus.

Dido of Tyre, struck speechless at the sight
and at the man's misfortune, spoke at last:
"What happened, my lord? What ill luck dogged you here?
What dangers forced you onto rock and reef?
Are you Aeneas of Troy, Anchises' son?
Whom Venus in Phrygia bore by Simois' wave?
Yes! I remember! Teucer came to Tyre
driven from Salamis, searching for new realms: 620
'Would Belus help?' (Belus—my father—was then
reducing fertile Cyprus to his power.)
And since that time I've known the tale of Troy,
the city, your name, and all the Argive kings.
Teucer, who fought the Teucri, praised them high,

and loved to claim descent from Teucrian stock.[16]
Enter my home! My welcome to you all!
My fate, like yours, has harried me through great toil
and trouble, at last to place me in this land.
By evil schooled, I know what mercy means." 630

With that she led Aeneas to her palace
and called for prayers of thanks to all the gods.
Nor did she forget his men: down to the beach
she sent off twenty steers, a hundred hogs
(fat tuskers all), a hundred lambs and ewes,
and wine, god's gift of joy.
In the great hall splendor to ease a king
was set out, and a banquet was prepared;
the cloths were royal red, embroidered fine;
on tables massive plate, and golden cups 640
chased with historic scenes, the long, long line
of deeds heroic since the race began.

Aeneas, whose father-heart could not rest easy,
dispatched Achates to the ships, to tell
Ascanius the news and bring him back;
his every thought was for the son he loved.
"We need gifts, too," he said. "Bring what we saved
when Ilium fell—that coat all worked in gold,
the scarf bordered with yellow acanthus leaves
that Argive Helen wore, brought from Mycenae 650
when she set sail for Troy and wedded bliss
unlawful—they were her mother Leda's gifts;
yes, and the staff Ilione used to bear—
oldest of Priam's daughters—and her chain
of beads, her golden coronet, thick with gems."
Achates ran to the ships to speed compliance.

But Venus had new schemes at heart, new plans
devised: Cupid should change his face and form
and take Ascanius' place, to set the queen
afire with love and wrap her heart in flames.[17] 660
(Who could have faith in Tyre, the double-tongued?
Who could sleep sound with Juno on the rage?)
And so to winged Love she turned and spoke:
"Son, my strength, my power and might, dear son,
who only scorn our father's giant bolt,
help me, I beg you; grant me your godly aid.

---

[16]Teucer was a Greek warrior at Troy, son of King Telamon of Salamis, later exiled from his father's land; he first brought Dido word of the Trojan War. The legendary founder of Troy was also named Teucer; his descendants, the Trojans, were sometimes called "Teucri." Dido is playing on the names, suggesting she has heard an account of the battle sympathetic to the Trojans.

[17]Venus, jealous of Juno, sends her son, Cupid, to take the form of Ascanius, Aeneas' son, at Carthage to beguile Dido to fall in love with Aeneas. On the night of his arrival, Cupid tempts Dido. The next day, he returns to the gods, restoring the unsuspecting Ascanius to his place beside Aeneas.

Your brother, Aeneas—how on every sea
and strand he has been harried by Juno's hate,
you know, and you have often shared my grief.
Now Punic Dido holds him by her charms 670
entranced. I fear where Juno's gentleness
may end. Fate hinges here: she'll not be idle.
I shall prevent her schemes and ring the queen
with flames of passion, past all power to change;
love for Aeneas shall bind her to my side.
How may you help? Hear now what I have planned.
The little prince, my darling, soon will go
to Tyrian town at his dear father's call,
with gifts saved from the sea and flaming Troy.
He'll sleep; I'll hide him sleeping in my shrine 680
on Mount Cythera or holy Idalium:
he must not know our plan, nor intervene.
You change yourself—for just one night, no more—
to look like him, take his young face for yours:
when Dido smiles and holds you in her arms
(while princes feast and drink their royal wines)
and clasps you close to give a perfumed kiss,
breathe soft on her the poisoned flame of love."
Cupid obeyed his mother's word, stripped off
his wings, and gayly mocked Iulus' stride. 690
But Venus on Ascanius poured the peace
of sleep and took him cradled in her arms
to Mount Idalium, where soft marjoram
with blossoms breathing nectar wrapped him round.

Obeying his mother, Cupid carried gifts
to the Tyrians, happy to walk with good Achates.
When he arrived, Dido had found her place,
her golden couch, all hung with royal red;
then Lord Aeneas, and then the men of Troy
came in and took their seats on purpled thrones. 700
Slaves brought water for washing, put out bread
in baskets, and offered soft and fleecy napkins.
In kitchen fifty maids prepared the food,
each dish in order, and kept the hearth-fires bright;
a hundred others, paired with men to match,
waited on table and set the wine cups out.
The Tyrians came, too, crowding through the doors
to take their places and make holiday.
They admired Aeneas' gifts, admired Iulus
(his glow was a god's, his charming speech a show) 710
and the coat and scarf with yellow acanthus leaves.
Above all, the Punic queen, already doomed
to suffer much, looked and could not be filled;
both gifts and lad alike stirred up the flames.
The boy, his arms around Aeneas' neck,
kissed him and filled him with false-fathered love,
then ran to the queen; she looked and loved, and loved

again, and held him to her, unaware
what power to hurt lay there. He, with a mind
to Venus' orders, gently began to drive 720
Sychaeus out, and fill with a living love
a heart long unaroused and half forgetful.

As soon as the feasting lulled, they cleared the board,
set out the mixing bowls, and crowned the wine.
The noise of voices rose and filled the hall
to the gilded ceiling where the lamps hung down
alight, and flaming wicks drove out the dark.
Then Dido took her golden jeweled cup
and filled it full—the one that Belus used
and all his children. Silence fell. She prayed: 730
"Jove, whom we name the god of guest and host,
hallow this day for Tyre and Troy alike,
and bid our children keep its memory fresh!
Bless us, good Juno! Bacchus, give us joy!
Come, Tyrians, join us in our holiday!"
She spoke and poured libation on the table,
then—only then—just wet her lip with wine,
and passed to Bitias: "Drink!" He drained the cup,
wine, froth, and all, down to its golden base,
and handed it on. Iopas struck his lyre 740
a golden note, as Atlas the great had taught.
He sang the wandering moon, the toiling sun;
whence came mankind and beast, whence rain and fire,
Arcturus, the rain-stars, and the twin Triones,
why the sun hurries to dip below the seas
in winter, and why the nights must limp and lag.
The Tyrians cheered aloud; the Trojans joined them.
And Dido, too, prolonged the night with talk
and to her sorrow drank long draughts of love:
"Tell me of Priam, tell me! And Hector, too! 750
The son of Dawn—how blazoned was his shield?
Diomede's team—what breed? How tall Achilles?—
No, no, my lord! From the beginning tell
how the Greeks tricked you, how your city fell,
and how you lost your way—full seven years
have seen you wandering over land and sea."

BOOK 2
[THE FALL OF TROY]

All talking stopped; all faces turned to watch.
Aeneas looked out on the hall and then began:
"What? Know that sorrow again, my lady? What words
can tell how royal Troy, the throne of tears,
fell to the Greeks? I saw that tragedy
and in it played great part. Who'd tell that tale—
Myrmidon, Thracian, or cruel Ulysses' man—

and keep from tears? Now dewy night is fading
from heaven; the setting stars warn men to sleep.
But if you want so much to learn our fate, 10
to hear in a word how Troy travailed and died,
though memory makes me shrink and shudder with grief,
I'll try.[18]

"Broken by war, forced back by fate,
the Argive kings watched year on year slip by,
then built with help of Pallas' holy hand
a horse tall as a mountain, ribbed with pine—
'For a safe trip home,' they said. (The lie spread fast.)
They threw dice for a crew and slipped them in,
locking them deep inside that lightless cave
to fill the monster's womb with men-at-arms. 20

"Offshore lies Tenedos, famed and storied island,
rich and a power while Priam's throne held firm,
now only a bay where keels ride rough to anchor;
thus far they sailed, to hide by moldering piers.
We thought them gone with the wind and homeward bound.
All Troy shook off her shackled years of pain,
threw open the gates, ran out in joy to see
the empty Dorian camp, the vacant shore:
here tented the Thracians, here the cruel Achilles;
here lay the fleet, here ranged the ranks of war. 30
Some stopped to stare at Pallas' deadly gift,
amazed at a horse so huge. Up spoke Thymoetes:
'Inside the walls with it! Station it in our fort!'
(Treason? Or just the turn of fate for Troy?)
But Capys and all our wiser heads bade throw
this Grecian trick and generosity suspect
into the sea, or bring up fire and burn it,
or pierce it and see what hollow wombs might hide.
Divided, bewildered, the people turned here, turned there.

"Laocoon strode to the front. (With a crowd of priests 40
he'd run in fury and haste from Castle Hill.)
He shouted, 'You fools! You wretched, raving fools!
You think the enemy gone? Who left this 'gift'?
Greeks? And you trust it? This is our 'friend,' Ulysses?
That wooden thing holds Argives locked inside,
or else it's an engine built to attack our walls,
to spy on our homes and fall from above on us all.
There's treachery here. A horse? Don't trust it, Trojans!
Whatever it is, I fear Greeks even with gifts.'

[18]This opening serves several purposes. Dido, having reported her knowledge of the tale from a Greek warrior, may have spurred Aeneas to make an answer. Aeneas, for his part, is truly pained to retell the story of the fall of Troy; but his tale stirs the passion of Dido. The story itself is one of Virgil's great accomplishments, borrowing from *The Odyssey* and other sources.

"So speaking he heaved and hurled his heavy spear 50
against the creature's flank and vaulted paunch;
the shaft stood trembling; from that wounded womb
came a sound of moaning cavernous and hollow.
And had Fate and our hearts not been perverse,
we would have bloodied that Argive hiding-hole,
and Troy and Priam's towers would still be standing.

"Up came a man, hands bound behind his back,
dragged on by shepherds shouting, 'Where's the king?
We're Trojan; this stranger met us and surrendered!'
(He'd plotted and planned it so, to open Troy 60
to the Greeks—sure of himself—prepared both ways:
to turn his trick, or keep his day with death.)
From all sides, eager to see, our Trojan men
came rushing to ring the captive round with taunts.
Now hear how Greeks can lie; from this one crime
learn of them all!
We watched him. There he stood, unarmed and frightened,
looking from face to hostile Phrygian face:
'O gods!' he cried, 'what land will take me in?
What sea? What's left for one like me? What's left? 70
I have no place among the Greeks, and now
the Trojans call for my blood to slake their hate.'
His pitiful cry softened our hearts and dulled
our every impulse. What was his name? we asked.
What did he want? How dared he trust to capture?
At last he laid his fear aside and spoke:

"'I'll tell it all, my lord, yes, all, and tell
it true,' he said. 'I'm Greek. Be that confessed
first off. If Fortune molded Sinon luckless,
she shall not mold him foul and a liar, too.[19] 80
Has anyone told you—has word reached your ears
of Belus' son, Palamedes? Fame has called him
"the great." He hated war; for this, the Greeks
slandered, harried, and hounded the saintly man
down to his death. Now that he's gone, they mourn him.
I was his cousin. My father, a humble man,
sent me, no more than a boy, to be his aide.
While he stood king among the kings, full-fledged,
full-powered, I held my small lieutenancy
with honor; but Ulysses' craft and hate 90
(you know them!) sent him from this world of men.
That crushed me. I lived in darkness and in sorrow,
privately cursing my cousin's unjust fate.
Then like a fool I talked and swore revenge

[19]The figure of Sinon, Greek master of deceit, borrows from the figure of Odysseus. His supposed kinship with Palamedes, the warrior who advised Agamemnon to abandon the war against Troy, is strategically designed to win over the Trojans, as is his bluff soldier's speech.

if ever my luck should bring me home to Argos.
My silly boasting won me harsh ill will.
That was my downfall; from that hour Ulysses
brought charge after frightening charge, and spread dark hints
among the people, determined to see me dead.
He knew no rest until with Calchas' help— 100
but this is waste! Why tell unwelcome tales?
Why wait? If "Greek" means but one thing to you,
and the name is enough, exact the penalty now!
Ulysses would cheer, Agamemnon pay you well!'

"Then how we burned to question and inquire,
unschooled in crime so vile and Argive craft.
He trembled but talked on, with feigned concern:

"'Many times the Greeks had longed to abandon Troy
and run away home from the weary years of war;
and oh, that they had! Many times a blustery sea 110
blocked them, and storm winds frighted their departure.
And worst: when the wooden fabric stood complete—
that horse—all heaven flashed and roared and rained.
Worried, we sent Eurypylus off to seek
Apollo's will; and the word he brought was grim:
"With blood of a virgin slain you won the winds
when you set sail, you Greeks, for Trojan shores;
with blood you'll buy return: an Argive soul's
the price to pay." When this word reached the ranks
men's hearts went numb; an icy tremor ran 120
down through their bones: whom had Apollo claimed?
Riot was near when the Ithacan drew Calchas
into our midst. "Speak, priest," he said, "and tell
God's will." (Men prophesied that murder plot
was aimed at me. They watched but said no word.)
Ten days he held his tongue, guarding against
one word that might send some man to his death.
At last Ulysses' bluster brought him round
to speak, as planned, and mark me for the altar.
No one protested; indignation died, 130
now that one wretch was scape for all their fears.

The dreadful day drew near; the rites were readied—
salt meal and sacred ribbons for my head.
I ran from death—yes, ran. I broke my bonds
by dark of night; in muddy marsh and reeds
I lay and waited, praying that they would sail.
Now I've no hope to see the hills of home,
my little sons, the father that I love—
the Greeks may well assess on them the price
of my escape—their deaths acquit my sin. 140
And so, sir, by God's name and power and truth,
by all the honor that still lives unstained
in mortal man, have mercy on my pain;
have mercy on a heart unjustly used!"

"His tears won him a pardon and our pity.
Priam at once commanded him relieved
of shackle and chain, then spoke as to a friend:
'Whoever you are, you've lost your Greeks: forget them!
Be one of us! Now speak out, tell the truth:
Why the huge horse? Who moved to place it here? 150
What is it? An act of worship? A siege machine?'
Sinon had learned his lines; with Argive art
he sloughed his irons and raised his hands to heaven:
'O fires eternal, O power beyond blaspheme,
be witness,' he cried; 'O altar and unblessed blade
that I escaped, O ribbons I wore to die:
I solemnly renounce my Argive oaths
and curse the Greeks. No law, no loyalty
bids me beware of telling all I know.
And if I keep Troy free, then keep your word 160
and promise—if I speak truth and give full measure.
The Greeks went off to war with hope and trust
based full and forever on Pallas' help; then crime
and crime's inventor—Diomede and Ulysses—
sinfully wrested from her hallowed shrine
Pallas the Less. They killed the temple guards,
pulled down her idol, and with hands all blood
dared touch the virgin goddess' holy bands.
Thereafter nothing was certain. Argive hopes
faltered, their strength was gone, their goddess angry.[20] 170
No room for doubt! Tritonia gave clear sign:
scarce was her image based in camp, when fire
flashed from her staring eyes and salty sweat
ran over her limbs, and thrice (wonder to tell!)
she leaped up, shield in hand, and shook her spear.
"Run!" Calchas warned them. "Take to the seas at once!"—
Never could Argive power cut Troy down
till they went home to learn God's will, and brought
his blessing anew in curved keels over the sea.
And home they've gone, riding the wind to Greece. 180
They'll win God's favor again, recross the water,
and land here unforeseen—so spoke the prophet.
This horse is payment for their heinous crime:
for godhead wronged, for Pallas the Less defiled.
And Calchas bid them build it massive, tall,
beam upon beam, to tower toward the sky—
too wide for the gates, too huge to pass the walls
and by some ancient covenant save your people.
For if your hand should harm Minerva's gift
then death (on Calchas' head may that doom fall!) 190

---

[20]The story goes as follows: The seizure by Odysseus and Diomede of the Palladium (the statue of Pallas Athena) from inside her temple in Troy, along with the desecration of her temple, angered the goddess so much that she visited revenge upon the Greek forces she had supported hitherto. In order to propitiate the goddess, the Greeks built the Trojan Horse, abandoning it outside the gates of Troy. To please the goddess, it was up to the Trojans to bring the horse inside the walls, removing some of the fortification to fit it in.

would come to Priam's Trojans and his power.
But if by your hand it climbed within your city
then Asia would some day march on Grecian walls,
and in that war our grandsons groan and die.'

"Strategy, perjury vile! Sinon by craft
won our belief; tricks and counterfeit tears
took captive men whom Diomede, Achilles,
ten years, and a thousand ships had never tamed!

"Here something worse and far more frightful rose
to meet us and trouble our unsuspecting hearts. 200
Laocoon, chosen by lot as Neptune's priest,
was killing a great bull at his sacred shrine,
when out from Tenedos, over the quiet floods
(I shudder to tell it) two snakes, coil on huge coil
breasting the sea, came slithering toward the shore.
Their necks rose high in the troughs, their blood-red manes
crested the waves; their other parts behind
slid through the water, twin bodies winding vast.
The salt sea gurgled and foamed. Now they reached land.
Hot were their eyes, bloodshot and flecked with flame; 210
through hissing lips their tongues flicked in, flicked out.
Bloodless we fled the sight; they never wavered
but went for Laocoon; first his two young sons—
poor little boys!—they hugged in their twin coils
wrapping them round and tearing at leg and arm.
Laocoon leaped to the rescue, sword in hand;
the great snakes seized him, wrapped him round and round,
two scaly coils at his waist, two at his throat.
Above his head, their heads and necks rose high.
With his hands he tried to pry the loops apart, 220
while blood and venom soaked his sacred bands.
He screamed to make high heaven shudder—screamed
like a bloodied bull run roaring from the altar
to shake free of his neck an ill-aimed ax.
But those twin snakes slipped off toward Castle Hill
and escaped. They made for cruel Tritonia's shrine
and hid at her feet behind her circled shield.[21]

"We stood and shook while into every heart
fresh terror crept. 'He sinned and paid fair price,'
we said. 'Laocoon stabbed a sacred thing; 230
sin rode the spear he hurled against that flank.
Bring the horse home,' we cried, 'and let us pray,
pray to our lady of might.'
We cut through walls and flung our ramparts down.
All stripped for the work; under the horse's feet

[21] The scene of the destruction of Laocoon and his sons by the snakes is justly famous. A statue depicting it was created between 32 and 22 B.C.E.; it is housed at the Vatican museum.

we slipped rollers, and from its neck we rove
hempen halyards. Up rode the death machine,
big with armed men, while boys and virgin girls
sang hymns and joyed to lay hand to the lines.
Into mid-city the menacing mass rolled on. 240
O homeland, god-land, Troy! O Dardan walls
famed for your soldier sons! Four times it balked
at the sill, four times its belly rang with arms,
but we pushed on, forgetful, blind, and mad,
to set the luckless monster in our fort.
Even then Cassandra cried, 'Death! Men will die!'
but Apollo had bid the Trojans never heed her.
In festive mood (poor souls! this day would be
our last!), we banked our hallowed shrines with flowers.

"The vault of heaven turned; night rushed from Ocean 250
enfolding in vast darkness earth and sky
and Myrmidon guile; on the walls our sentries lay
scattered, wordless, weary, sound asleep.
Now came the Argive ships in battle line
from Tenedos under a silent, friendly moon,
heading for well-known shores. A torch flamed out
from the royal ship. Sinon, by unkind fates
preserved, slipped softly back the bolts of pine
and freed the Greeks from the womb. The opened horse
released them; glad from that wooden cave they poured. 260
Thessander, Sthenelus—lords—and dire Ulysses
let down a rope and slid, then Acamas, Thoas,
Machaon, next Neoptolemus, son of Achilles,
Menelaus, and he who laid the plot, Epeus.
They fell on a city buried in sleep and wine,
murdered the watch, threw open the gate, let in
their friends—a column of schemers, hand in hand.

"It was the hour when gentle sleep first comes,
welcome, by God's grace, welcome to weary men.
I dreamed, and there before my eyes stood Hector, 270
sorrowed and sad, his face a flood of tears.
He seemed as when the chariot dragged him: bruised,
bloody, dusty, thongs through his swollen feet.
O God! How he looked! How changed from that great man,
the Hector who wore Achilles' armor home,
who hurled into Argive ships our Trojan fire.
His beard all dirt, his hair was stiff with blood;
he wore each wound he'd earned before our walls—
our fathers' walls. I dreamed that I wept, too,
and hailed the man and let my grief pour out: 280
'O light of Troy! Dardania's hope unfailing!
What held you, Hector? Where have you been? How long
we waited! Your people—so many of them are dead;
our men, our city have borne so many trials!
We are weary! We see you—but what is wrong? Your face

is clouded dark: Why? Why do I see these wounds?'
He said no word, nor heeded my vain questions,
but with a groan drawn deep from a burdened heart,
'Run, goddess-born,' he cried; 'run from these flames!
Greece owns our walls; the towers of Troy are tumbling! 290
To country and king all debts are paid; my hand
had saved them, if any hand had power to save.
Her holy things, her gods, Troy trusts to you.
Take them to share your fate; find walls for them:
wander the wide sea over, then build them great.'
He spoke, and in my hands laid mighty Vesta,
her ribbons, and—from her inmost shrine—her fire.[22]

"And now from the walls came screams and cries and groans.
Louder and louder, although my father's house
was set far off, apart, well screened by trees, 300
came the noise of battle, the terrible clash of arms.
I shook off sleep, and to the highest peak
of the roof I climbed, and stopped and strained to hear:
as when a flame by wild winds driven falls
on a grain field, or a mountain stream in flood
sweeps farms, sweeps crops away and plowman's toil,
and topples trees; high on his cliff the shepherd,
hearing the thunderous noise, sits blank with fear.
Then all—the word of honor, the Argive lie—
came clear. Deiphobus' palace crashed and fell 310
in a holocaust roof-high; Ucalegon's next
caught fire; the straits reflected back the flames.
I heard men shouting, heard the trumpet-call.
Like a fool I seized my sword—what sense had swords?
But I was ablaze to round up men for war
and with them rush to the fort; a senseless wrath
propelled me: 'Glory!' I thought. 'To die in battle!'

"But here came Panthus escaping from Greek spears—
Panthus, priest of Apollo on Castle Hill—
arms full of holy things and beaten gods, 320
trailed by his grandson, panicking toward the gates.
'Panthus, how do we stand? What have we gained?'
He cut me off and answered with a groan:
'Dardania's end, her scapeless hour has come.
Trojan and Troy, we've had our day, our power,
our glory. A heartless Jove has handed all
to the Greeks. Our city is ashes! Greece is lord!
Tall stands the horse inside our fort, and births
her soldiers. Sinon, prancing his glory-dance,
sets fire on fire. Through gates flung wide, they come, 330

---

[22]The shade of Hector commends to Aeneas Vesta, the goddess of the hearth and fire with her eternal flame, and the Penates (household gods) of King Priam. Aeneas is to take them with him and establish a new city.

those myriads—all who marched from great Mycenae.
Posts have been set, spear locked with spear, to block
our streets; they stand, a line of shining steel,
blades ready for blood. Our first-line watch can scarce
form battle rank; they fight without command.'

"The words of Panthus and God's holy will
sent me toward flames and fighting, where Mars roared
his challenge, and battle cries rose up to heaven.
Friends joined me: Rhipeus and that champion,
Epytus, guided by moonlight; Hypanis, Dymas 340
fell in at my side, and young Coroebus, too,
the son of Mygdon, just now come to Troy,
fired with foolish passion for Cassandra
(accepted, he fought for Priam and his people—
unlucky youth, who would not heed the word
of his prophetic princess!).
I watched them boldly form a battle group,
then spoke to them: 'Good men, brave hearts—but brave
for nothing! If you feel you must fight on
and dare to the end, you see how fortune stands. 350
They've gone from every temple, every shrine,
the gods who blessed our power. You seek to save
a city in flames. But on to war! We'll die!
Sole hope of the vanquished is their hopelessness!'[23]
This fired their mad young hearts afresh. Like wolves
hot for a kill at murky midnight, blind,
driven by horrid belly-lust—their cubs
are waiting with blood-parched throats—through hostile arms
we rushed to death undoubted, held our way
through mid-town; night swung sable wings around us. 360
That night of ruin, night of death—who'd tell
its story or match our sorrows with his tears?
An ancient city, queen of the ages, fell;
the dead men lay by thousands in her streets,
in home and palace, at the hallowed gates
of gods. Nor only Trojans paid their lives;
sometimes courage returned to beaten hearts,
and Danaan victors died. Here grief heartrending,
terror, and death over all in countless forms.

"Androgeos first approached us, at the head 370
of a crowd of Greeks; mistakenly he thought
us comrades in arms and spoke to us as friends:
'Hurry, men! You are late! What held you back
so long? The rest have ripped and stripped and fired
Troy. Have you just now left the tall-sparred ships?'

[23]Seeing the defenders of Troy without command, Aeneas urges them to fight to the death. While this anticipates his later leadership of the Trojans, Aeneas appears to forget Hector's command that he protect the hearth gods and leave Troy.

He broke off then (our answers seemed not made
for trust) and sensed he'd fallen amid his foes.
He stopped, clapped hand to mouth, and stumbled back.
As one who, feeling his way through brambles, steps
on a sudden snake, jumps and shudders and runs 380
from head held high to strike, and hood spread wide—
just so Androgeos saw and jumped and fled.
Shield lapped to shield, we charged and hemmed them in.
On unknown ground, they panicked; one by one
we killed them. Fortune blessed our first assault.
Our luck now made Coroebus' heart beat high;
'Look! Fortune,' he said, 'has shown us how to win!
Success lies where she points the way: let's follow!
Let's take their shields and wear the Greek device
ourselves. Deceit or daring, who'd ask a foe? 390
Arms are here for the taking.' He spoke, and seized
Androgeos' plumed helmet and his shield
with its proud device, and buckled on his sword.
Rhipeus, Dymas and all their company
laughed as they took the spoil to arm themselves.
Under false signs we mingled with the Greeks
and many a battle joined while night was blind,
and sent to Orcus many a man of Greece.
Still others scattered and ran for trusted ship
and shore, while others in shame and terror climbed 400
the horse again, to cower in its vast belly.

" 'Man, trust not the gods except with their consent!'
Here, dragged by her long, long hair, came Priam's daughter,
holy and virgin, torn from Minerva's shrine;
in vain toward heaven she turned her burning eyes—
eyes, for her soft, young hands were bound with chains.
This sight Coroebus could not bear; his heart
went wild; he rushed against their ranks to die.
Behind him we charged in a body, sword by sword.
And now—disaster! Down from the temple's top 410
came Trojan spears to spill our wretched blood:
our arms and plumes had wrongly marked us Greeks.[24]
Then—for we'd seized the girl—the Argives roared
with fury, formed ranks and charged: Ajax the chief,
the twin Atridae, the whole Thessalian host;
as when sometimes the winds whirl till they burst
then crash head-on: Westerly, South, and East
rich with his Orient steeds; the woodlands wail
and Nereus stirs his deeps to foam and fury.
And those whom darkness and our stratagem 420
had put to flight pell-mell down every street

[24]Seeing Cassandra seized by Greeks from the shrine of Athena (Minerva), the Trojans led by Aeneas, wearing captured Greek uniforms, come to her rescue but are attacked in turn by Trojan defenders of the temple, who believe them to be Greeks.

now showed themselves; they first detected shields
and swords not ours, and caught our foreign speech.
Sheer numbers crushed us; first Coroebus fell
by hand of Peneleus at Minerva's altar;
and Rhipeus died, the justest man that lived
in Troy, unwavering servant of the right
(yet heaven forsook him); Hypanis died, and Dymas
transfixed by friends; not all your piety,
Panthus, could save you, nor Apollo's bands. 430
Ashes of Troy! Last flame of all I loved!
Bear witness that at your death I never shrank
from sword or sorrow, and had Fate so decreed
I had earned a death at Grecian hands![25] We ran,
Iphitus, Pelias, and I—one old and tired,
the other limping from Ulysses' wound—
straight toward the sound of war by Priam's palace.

"Here was huge battle to make all other strife
and death through all the city seem like nothing.
Here Mars ran wild, and Argives rushed the walls; 440
we saw them march the 'tortoise' toward the gates.
Up went the ladders next to the very doors;
men climbed the rungs; their left hands held their shields,
bulwark to blows; their right hands seized the roof.
Our Trojans on their side ripped loose and flung
whole towers and rooftrees; seeing the end had come,
as death approached they made these weapons serve.
Gilt beams, the glory that roofed their sires of old,
they tumbled down, while others bared their blades
and stood to the doors, a barricade of men. 450
Our strength came back; we ran toward Priam's walls
to help our friends and give the vanquished valor.

"There was a secret hall and door, a passage
between the royal mansions—a gate that none
would notice; often, while our throne held firm,
Andromache—poor thing!—had walked this way
taking her son to grandsire or to uncle.
Here I slipped in and climbed to the roof; there stood
our Trojans, hurling spear on useless spear.
On a steep gable stood a tower, the peak 460
of the palace, where we were wont to keep the watch
over Troy and Grecian fleet and Argive camp.
We hacked at this where tower and rooftop joined—
the fabric's weakest spot—and tore it loose
from its base and pushed it over; down it went
to crack and shatter and scatter its fragments far
over Argive troops. But more marched up, though stones
and weapons of every kind rained down.

[25] Aeneas defends himself against the charge that leaving Troy behind was an ignoble action.

"At the very door of the palace Pyrrhus pranced
with a flourish and brazen flash of spear and blade— 470
like a snake on foul herbs fed, come from his hole
all puffed from a long, cold winter under the soil.
Stripping his skin he turns out sleek and young
and ripples his liquid coils; he lofts his head
up toward the sun and flicks his three-forked tongue.
Periphas and Achilles' charioteer,
the squire Automedon, all the Scyrians, too,
charged the palace and tossed fire toward the roof.
Pyrrhus was leader; he seized a double ax,
chopped through the threshold and ripped out post and hinge, 480
fittings and all, then hacked at oaken beam
and panel to make a huge hole gaping wide.
There stood the house revealed, there stood its halls,
the home of Priam, of a long line of kings;
there at his doorway stood his bodyguard.
Inside the house rose cries and screams of terror
commingled, while the caverned inmost vaults
shrieked with the women; the outcry struck the stars.
Mothers in fright ran madly round the halls,
threw arms about the columns and kissed them close. 490
On pressed Pyrrhus, strong as his father; nor bolts
nor guards could hold him back. Crash! came the ram;
down fell the door; down tumbled post and hinge.
Force paved a way; in burst the Greeks to slaughter
the guard and fill the palace, wall to wall.
Not so from a broken dam a stream bursts forth
that foams and swirls and sweeps the dikes away;
its crest runs raging over field and plain
to bear off beast and barn. I saw blood drive
men mad: Achilles' son, the twin Atridae; 500
I saw Hecuba, her hundred daughters: Priam
fouling with blood the altar flame he'd blessed.
His fifty rooms, rich hope of a line of sons—
pillars of Orient gold, girt proud with spoils—
all fell. Where fire failed, the Argive ruled.

"Perhaps you wish to know how Priam died.[26]
There lay his city—lost, there lay the ruin
that was his palace, there at his hearth, a foe.
The old king threw his armor, long unused,
on his shaking shoulders—useless gesture!—bound 510
his sword at his waist, and rushed to fight and die.
Within the close, beneath heaven's naked pole,
stood a high altar; nearby an old bay tree
leaned toward it and wrapped the household gods in shade.

[26]The sack of Priam's castle was a favorite subject of Greek and Roman chroniclers; Virgil's treatment of the story is acknowledged as a masterpiece.

Here Hecuba and her daughters vainly fled
headlong (like doves before the black rain cloud)
and tight in a ring sat suppliant round the gods.
Then she saw Priam dressed in his young man's arms
and said, 'What dreadful madness, my poor lord,
led you to wear those weapons? Where will you charge? 520
This is no hour for help like yours, no time
for such defense—no, even were Hector here.
Come, stand by me; this altar shall shield us all,
or you will die with us.' So saying, she placed
the old man at her side on holy ground.

"Here now, escaped from Pyrrhus' blade, Polites,
a son of Priam, dashed through enemy lines,
ran down the cloisters and round the empty halls,
wounded. Enraged at having missed his aim,
Pyrrhus pursued him, caught him, and stabbed him down. 530
He crawled on, till before his parents' eyes
he fell, and with his blood coughed out his life.
Then Priam, though death already gripped him round,
could not hold back or check his angry words:
'You murderer!' he cried. 'You foul blasphemer!
If heaven has righteous gods to mark such acts,
oh, may they thank you well and pay the price
you've earned, who made me watch my own son die,
and with his death befouled a father's eyes.
Achilles—you lie, to say you are his son!— 540
never treated me so! I came a suppliant,
an enemy, yet he honored me and gave me
Hector's corpse to bury and sent me home.'
With that, the old king hurled his harmless spear
to touch and clang against the shield; it stopped
and dangled useless from the brazen boss.
Then Pyrrhus: 'Be my enemy! Tell your tale
to my father! Remember: call me barbarous
and name me "Neoptolemus, son unworthy"!
Now die!' He dragged him to the altar, faint 550
and slipping in the blood his son had shed.
His left hand gripped the old man's hair; his right
drew out a sword and sank it in his side.
So Priam died. His final, fated glance
fell on a Troy in ashes, on the ruins
of Pergama—sometime proud imperial power,
'of Asia, king.' On the strand his vast frame lies,
head torn from shoulders, a corpse without a name.

"For the first time then, a savage fear closed round me.
I froze. My own dear father's form rose up 560
as I watched the old king through that horrid wound
gasp out his life. Creusa—alone!—rose up:
my house—in ruins! My son, Iulus—where?

I turned about: What forces still remained?
Not a man! Heartsick and beaten, they had leaped
to the street or thrown themselves into the flames.[27]

"I alone survived—but no! By Vesta's shrine,
lurking wordless, in a dark corner hiding—
Helen! I saw her lighted by the flames
as I searched the ruins, looking everywhere. 570
She feared the fury of a vanquished Troy,
Greek vengeance, a deserted husband's wrath.
A fiendish curse alike to friend and foe,
hated, she'd sought asylum at the altar.
Flame burst in my heart as anger cried, 'Revenge,
for a country lost! Penalty, for her crimes!
Shall she, unscathed, see Sparta? Shall she march
in royal triumph through Mycenae's streets?
She, see her husband, her father's house, her children,
trailed by the women of Troy, her Orient slaves? 580
Yet death by the sword for Priam? Troy in flames?
A shore so often drenched in Trojan blood?
Never! Although men win no fame or glory
for woman punished (such victory earns no praise),
still to have stamped out sin, and made it pay
due price, is good; good, too, to fill the heart
with vengeful flame and vindicate the dead.'
Such the wild thoughts that swept my heart along
when—never before so clear for eye to see—
a vision shone through darkness, pure and bright: 590
my loving mother, goddess confessed, her form
and stature as in heaven. She seized my hand
and held me hard; her sweet lips spoke to me:
'My son, what pain has roused such unchecked wrath?
Are you mad, or have you lost all thought of me?
What? Not look first where your old father waits,
Anchises? See if yet Creusa lives,
your wife? Your son, Ascanius? All around them
Greeks walk their lines at will; but for my care,
flames or an enemy blade had borne them off. 600
No blame to Helen of Sparta's hated face;
no, nor to Paris: gods, the pitiless gods,
threw down the might and golden towers of Troy.[28]
Look, for I'll rip it all away—the cloud
that blocks and blunts your mortal sight, hung dank
and dark around you; you must never fear

---

[27]The death of Priam forces Aeneas to think of his own household: his father, Anchises; his wife, Creusa; and his son, Iulus (Ascanius).

[28]Seeing Helen of Troy in the ruins, Aeneas contemplates taking her life; he is stopped by his mother, Venus, who urges him to save his family. The future of Aeneas as a just and virtuous leader is at stake. Venus adds that Helen did not bring destruction upon Troy; the gods did.

a mother's precept or disobey her word.
Here where you see the masonry all tumbled,
stone upon stone, where dust and smoke boil up,
Neptune is rocking our walls, and with his trident 610
knocking their base-blocks loose; our homes and halls
he'll pull to the ground. There, at the Scaean gates,
Juno in blood-lust waves her columns on
from the ships with her drawn sword.
Look back! On Castle Hill Tritonia sits
in a cloud of flame, flashing her Gorgon head.
Our father himself gives comfort, power, and strength
to the Greeks—yes, hurls the gods against our arms.
Hurry, my son! Take flight! Call this work done!
I am always with you, to guide you safely home!' 620
She spoke, and hid herself in night's black shades.
There rose up faces full of death and hate
for Troy—a ghastly glory of gods.

"Then came collapse; I saw all Ilium fall
in flames—saw Neptune's Troy come crashing down.
As when on mountain top an ancient ash
is hacked by the steel; blow after blow falls
as farmers vie at the felling. The old tree leans,
her foliage shakes, she bows her stricken crown,
till bit by bit her wounds win out. She groans 630
her last and falls and strews the ridge with wreckage.

"Divine grace led me down through flame and foe
with ease; swords made away and flames fell back.

"Soon as I stepped inside my father's house
and ancient home, I sought him out and begged
he'd let me carry him off to the high hills.
He answered, No: his Troy was lost, and life
in exile not for him. 'You young in years
and blood,' said he, 'who yet own strength and sinew,
do you take thought for flight. 640
If heaven had wished me further years of life
they'd saved my home for me. Enough that once
I lived to see my city fall and die.
Just let me lie here; say farewell and leave me.
I'll find death by myself. The foe will say
"Too bad!" and strip my corpse. A grave's well lost.
I've lived unloved of heaven, useless, old,
for years, since Jove, the father of gods and men,
touched and scorched me with lightning's fiery breath.'[29]

[29] Anchises refuses at first to save himself. He is "unloved of heaven" (and was therefore struck by lightning) for sleeping with Venus. (Aeneas was the offspring of that union.)

"He spoke and stood his ground, unmoved, unmoving. 650
But we burst out in tears—my wife Creusa,
Ascanius, our whole house—'He must not ruin
us all, or hasten the death that threatens us.'
He would not change, or leave his chosen spot.
I turned to my arms with bitter prayer to die.
What plans could be; what fortune granted now?
'You think, sir, I could take one step and leave
you here? Monstrous! This, from a father's lips?
If by God's law our city must be destroyed,
and you are resolved to cap the death of Troy 660
with death of you and yours, that door stands wide:
Pyrrhus is coming bathed in Priam's blood—
son before father, father by altar slain.
For this you haled me, mother, through steel and flame,
that I might see the enemy in my house,
and you, Ascanius, and Creusa too,
heaped in one bloody sacrificial pile?
Arms, men! To arms! We're lost! Our last day calls us!
Back to the Greeks! I'll see the fight renewed
once more. We shall not all die unavenged!' 670

"I buckled my sword again and strapped my shield
to my left arm with care, then moved outside.
But there at the door my wife fell at my feet
and kissed them, and held Iulus out to me:
'You go to die? Take us, too—anywhere!
But if experience gives you faith in arms,
guard first your home. Abandon us? Your son,
your father, me—once called your wife? To whom?'

"While thus she pled and filled the house with sobs—
wonder to tell!—a miracle occurred. 680
There in our arms, before his parents' eyes,
Iulus' little cap, right at its peak,
seemed to shed light. A harmless flame licked down
to touch his hair and play about his brow.
In panic terror we slapped at his burning hair
and tried to quench the holy flame with water.
But Father Anchises smiled, and raising eyes
toward heaven, spread out his hands, and spoke in prayer:
'Almighty Jove, if any prayer can bend you,
look down and for our merit grant just this: 690
a sign, father! Confirm this omen for us!'

"Scarce had he spoken when with sudden crash
came thunder on the left; down the dark sky
a meteor fell in a burst of sparks and flame.
We watched it glide high over roof and hall
—so bright!—then bury itself in Ida's woods,

its path marked clear. Behind it, furrow and line
shed light and left a smoking reek of sulphur.
My father now was certain; he turned toward heaven,
hailed godhead, and adored the holy star: 700
'No hesitation now! Lead on! I'll follow,
gods of my fathers! Oh, save my house and line!
Yours was that sign; your will embraces Troy.
I yield, my son; I'll gladly share your way.'

"Just then through our walls we heard a louder noise
of fire and closer rolled the holocaust.
'Come then, dear father, and climb upon my back.
Ride on my shoulders; the load will not be heavy.
Whatever may happen, we'll share a single risk,
a single rescue. Iulus, little son, 710
walk by me! Wife, stay back, but trace my steps!
And all you others, listen to my words!
Outside the city is a hill and shrine
of Ceres, long unused; nearby, a cypress,
gnarled, and for years held sacred by our fathers.[30]
Each go your way; we'll meet at that one spot.
You, father, carry our holies and household gods.
Fresh come from all the fighting, blood, and death,
I dare not touch them till in running stream
I wash myself.' 720
With that I spread across my neck and shoulders
a cloak, and over that a lion's skin,
and lifted my burden; little Iulus seized
my right hand, following two steps to my one;
behind us, my wife. We moved through pitch-black plazas,
and I was afraid, though minutes before no spear
nor prowling Greek patrol had worried me.
I started at every breeze; at every sound
I stiffened, fearful alike for father and son.
And now I was near the gate, and clear, I thought, 730
of the streets, when all at once I caught the sound
of many marching feet. My father peered
through the night, and cried out, 'Hurry, son; they're coming.
I see their shields alight and the flash of blades.'
I panicked then, as some strange, unkind power
left me confused and mindless. Hurrying down
byways, I'd left familiar streets behind,
when Creusa—she was gone! Did cruel death take her?
Or had she lost her way? Or stopped to rest?
We've never known, nor ever seen her since. 740
I had not turned around nor marked her lost

---

[30]The debate whether to fight or flee ends with Aeneas lifting his father on his shoulders, taking his son by the hand, and commanding his wife to follow him. The dramatic departure is an example of *pietas,* especially duty toward the family.

until we reached the hill and ancient shrine
of Ceres. Here as we called the roll we found
her missing. Son nor husband—none had seen her.
Half mad, I railed at everyone, god and man:
What had I seen in captured town more cruel?
My son, my father, the household gods of Troy,
I left to my men, deep hidden in the hills.
I turned back to the city, armed again,
determined to take my chances, to go back 750
through all of Troy, and risk my life once more.
First to the walls and that half-hidden gate
where I'd gone out, I turned, and traced my steps
back through the night, my eyes' own light my guide;
no sound relieved the prickling sense of fear.
Then on to my house: Had she—had she perhaps
gone there? All doors were down, Greeks everywhere.
My house was wrapped in flames; wind-whipped they licked
at the roof, then raced in triumph toward the sky.
I ran to Priam's palace and the fort: 760
there on the empty porch of Juno's temple
a squad of sentries with Phoenix and Ulysses
were guarding the spoils. Here all the wealth of Troy,
ripped from her burning temples—holy tables,
wine bowls of solid gold, and captured vestments—
were heaped. Mothers and children, a long, long line,
terrified, stood nearby.
I even dared to shout. I filled the night
and dark streets with my sobbing cries: 'Creusa!'
No answer! 'Creusa!' I called, again, again. 770
I was pressing my search from house to endless house
when a luckless ghost, Creusa's very shade,
rose to my sight—her likeness, taller than life.
My hair stood up in terror; my voice stuck fast.
But then she spoke and banished all my fears:
'Why such indulgence of a pointless pain,
dear husband? Nothing but by the will of God
has happened. You were not meant to take Creusa
with you; so rules the lord of tall Olympus.
Go into exile; furrow the empty sea 780
to a western land of men and fertile fields,
where Tiber pours his gentle Tuscan stream.
There is your birthright: wealth, a throne, a queen.
You loved Creusa; but brush away your tears.
I'll catch no sight of Thessaly's haughty halls—
not I!—nor humbly serve the dames of Greece,
I, child of Dardanus, wife of Venus' son.
No; the mother of gods detains me here.
Farewell, and always love the son we share.'
With that, for all my tears, for all I hoped 790
to say, she turned to emptiness and air.
Three times I tried to fold her in my arms,
three times for nothing! The ghost-thing fled my grasp,

light as a breeze, most like the wings of sleep.
The night was gone when I rejoined my friends.[31]

"And here I stood in wonder at the crowd
of people newly come—mothers and men,
children, huddled for exile—poor, lost souls.
They'd brought what they could save; they'd brought their courage;
they'd follow the course I set, no matter where. 800
And now the dawn star rose from Ida's heights
to bring the day. Greek guards were everywhere,
at every gate. We knew no help could come.
Bearing my father, I started toward the hills."

Book 3
[Aeneas' Journey]

"With Asian power and Priam's tribe uprooted,
though blameless, by heaven's decree; with Ilium's pride
fallen, and Neptune's Troy all smoke and ash,
God's oracles drove us on to exile, on
to distant, lonely lands. We built a fleet
down by Antander and Ida's Phrygian peaks,
uncertain which way Fate led or where to stop.
We marshaled our men. When summer first came on
Anchises bade us trust our sails to fate.
With tears I left the shores and ports of home, 10
the land that once was Troy, and sailed away
with friends and son, with gods both small and great.

"Miles off, the land of Mars lay wide and flat
(Thracians farm it; Lycurgus was once its king),
friend and ally of Troy from ancient times
in our good days. I sailed there. Near the shore
I laid out a town (Fate frowned on my attempt)
and coined the name 'Aeneadae' from my name.[32]

"I offered prayer to Venus and to all gods
who bless new ventures, and for heaven's high king 20
I thought to slaughter a white bull by the shore.
Nearby was a mound, so happened; a dogwood tree
grew on its top, and myrtle thick with thorns.
As I stepped over to pull the greening shrubs
from the soil, to deck my altar with leaf boughs,
I saw a fearsome portent, strange to tell:

[31] What we make of Creusa's return as a ghost to tell Aeneas of his subsequent marriage and founding of a city depends on our understanding of her duty as wife, mother, and keeper of the household. While some pathos may be intended in her return, she is the one in the best position to enlighten Aeneas on his future responsibilities. Aeneas' attempt to embrace Creusa's ghost recalls a similar scene in Hades between Odysseus and his mother, in *The Odyssey,* Book 11.

[32] The attempt to found the city of Aeneadae is one of several false starts in Book 3. The bloody ground warns Aeneas of the treachery alive in Thrace.

The first bush that I broke loose from its root
and pulled from the ground oozed blood in dead black drops
and spotted the earth with gore. My hair stood up
in a chill; I shivered; my blood congealed with fear. 30
Trying again, I tugged the pliant stalk
next on, seeking the cause I could not see:
from its bark, too, the dark black blood ran down.
Puzzled, I muttered prayers to the rural Nymphs
and to Mars the father, who rules the Getic plains:
'Oh, bless this sign; may it rest light upon us!'
I attacked a third stalk then. Down on my knees
I pulled and worked and battled with the sand,
when—dare I tell it?—deep in the mound, I heard
a moan of sorrow, and words came to my ears: 40
'Aeneas, why tear at the tortured? Spare my tomb;
spare to pollute clean hands. I am of Troy,
no stranger to you. No plant has shed that blood.
Run from this heartless land, this greedy shore.
I'm Polydorus. Transfixed by steel, I grow
a crop of spears and a cover of pointed shafts.'
What should I do? Fear pressed upon my heart,
my hair stood up in terror, my voice stuck fast.

"This Polydorus had once been sent by Priam,
with sacks of gold, covertly, to the king 50
of Thrace for safety—trust in Trojan arms
was waning and our city ringed with steel.
When Ilium's power collapsed and Fortune left her,
this king joined Agamemnon's conquering arms;
defying the right, he killed Polydorus and seized
his gold. (To what do you not drive men's hearts,
damned money-lust!) When trembling left my limbs,
I summoned our chosen leaders—my father first—
told of the sign, and asked their views and votes.
They all agreed: to leave this land of crime, 60
where guest law was blasphemed, and put to sea.
We gave Polydorus new burial and piled high
his mound with earth; an altar to his ghost
stood dark with ribbons of grief and cypress wreaths;
round it the women of Troy let down their hair.
We brought up pitchers foaming with warm milk,
and plates of hallowed blood. His soul we laid
in the tomb and called his name that loud last time.

"Soon as we trusted the ocean, and winds brought peace
to the waters, and Auster called us soft to sea, 70
my men hauled down the ships and filled the shore.
We sailed from port; the lands and towns receded.
In mid-sea lies an isle much-loved and sacred
to the Nereids' mother and Neptune the Aegean.[33]

[33]The isle of Delos, traditionally held as the birthplace of Apollo and Diana.

It floated free until the archer-god
bound it to Gyaros and Myconos' cliffs,
to be a base for homes and mock the winds.
Here we found peace for the weary and safe haven;
on Apollo's ground we stepped out reverently.
Up ran King Anius—king at once and priest 80
of Apollo (he wore his bands and sacred crown
of laurel). He knew Anchises, an old, old friend.
He made us welcome and led us to his home.

"I prayed the god in a temple of moldered stone:
'Apollo, grant us a home, grant walls to the weary,
a city to last, a bloodline; save this second
Troy, these few that Achilles and Greece have spared.
Who will guide us, and where? Where shall we settle?
Grant, father, a sign; come and possess our hearts.'

"Scarce had I spoken when suddenly all things shook, 90
the temple the sacred laurel; the whole mount moved
around us. The shrine sprang open; the tripod clanged.
As we fell prostrate, a voice came to our ears:
'Oh, Dardans! Hardy men! The land that first
gave you and your fathers birth, with wealth and joy
will take you back. Look for your ancient mother.
Here shall Aeneas' line rule all the world—
his sons, their sons, the sons to be born of them.'
So Phoebus. My men raised shouts and cheers of joy
commingled. They asked in a body what walls these were, 100
where they must wander, where Phoebus bid return.
Then father, recalling the records of men long gone,
said, 'Hear me, you captains, and learn what we may hope.
Crete, island of Jove the king, lies in mid-sea;
there stands Mount Ida, and there our tribe was cradled.
Men live in a hundred cities there, rich realms.
Thence, if I read memory right, our sire,
Teucer the great, first sailed to Cape Rhoeteum
and chose that spot to rule. (No Troy yet stood,
nor walls of Pergama. Men lived in the hollows.) 110
Hence came great Cybele and her priests, their songs
and groves Idaean, their rite of silent prayer;
here lions learned to draw our lady's car.
Come, let us follow where the gods command;
pray to the winds, and make for Cnossus' throne.
It's no far course; if only Jove be with us,
three days will set our fleet on Cretan sands.'[34]
With that, he made due offering at the altar:
for Neptune, a bull; a bull for the lord Apollo,
and lambs—black for Tempest; for Zephyr, white. 120

[34]Anchises' interpretation of Apollo's prophecy is wrong. Aeneas follows his father without a challenge; but in the action of the poem, this is the beginning of Anchises' decline.

"Report ran that Idomeneus had been driven
from his father's throne, that Cretan shores were desert,
no foe in the palace, and empty, waiting homes.[35]
We left Ortygia's port and sped downwind,
past Naxos' Mount of Bacchus, green Donusa,
the Isle of Olives, white Paros, and the Sea
of the Circling Isles—waters thick-flecked with lands.
Sometimes we raced; loud rose the coxswain's cry:
'On, men, to Crete! To our ancestral home!'
As we sailed on, the wind rose brisk astern; 130
at last we raised the Curetes' ancient shore.
City we prayed for! I hurried to build its walls
and name it 'New Pergama,' to our people's joy;
I bade them love their homes and fortify them.
And now our hauled-out ships were nearly dry;
young couples married and worked their new-found farms.
I was granting titles and lands, when heaven turned foul
and dropped on our limbs a sudden, wretched rot;
trees wilted, too, and crops: the year brought death.
Men left sweet life or dragged themselves about 140
plague-stricken; Sirius scorched the sterile fields,
while pastures withered and blight denied us food.
'Back to Ortygia's oracle, back to Apollo!'
my father urged. 'Go pray for his good will!
What end to suffering? Whence does he bid us seek
help for our troubles? Where must we lay our course?'

"It was night, sleep held all creatures here on earth,
when—holy vision!—the Phrygian household gods
I'd brought with me from Troy, and from her flames
had rescued, seemed to rise before my eyes 150
as I lay sleeping. A bright light showed them clear
where through the window frames a full moon shone.
They spoke and with their words washed care away:
'What you would sail to Ortygia to learn,
Apollo will tell you here. Unasked, he sent us!
We followed you and your sword from flaming Troy,
and under you sailed over the swollen sea;
Some day we'll place your sons among the stars,
and bring your city power. For greatness, build
great walls! Your way is long, but grow not weary! 160
Move on! Apollo of Delos never meant
these shores, nor bade you make your home in Crete.
There is a place called "Westland" by the Greeks,
an ancient country, powerful, warlike, rich;
the Oenotri settled it; now, we hear, their sons
are calling it "Italy" for their founder's name.
Here is our rightful home; hence Dardanus sprang

[35]Caught in a storm at sea, Idomeneus promised to sacrifice the first creature he encountered on shore. It proved to be his son; as a consequence of doing so he was driven out of Crete, leaving it open for Aeneas.

and father Iasius, hero, first of our line.
Arise! Rejoice! Go tell your aged sire
our words! Have faith! Seek Corythus and the land 170
Ausonia! Jove forbids you Dicte's plain.'
Amazed at the sight and at this voice divine
(it was no dream; those gods were *there;* I saw
their features, ribbons, hair, their moving lips;
and icy sweat beaded my every limb),
I tore myself from bed and stretched my hands,
with a cry toward heaven, and sprinkled on the hearth
gifts virgin-pure. My office done, in joy
I told Anchises the story, straight and true.
He saw his error: two lines, two ancestors 180
confused, and two old place-names interchanged.
He spoke then: 'Son, by Ilium's fate beset,
Cassandra alone told me such things would be.
She said (I recall) this was ordained for us,
and often cried, "The Westland!" and "Italy's throne!"
But who'd have thought that Teucrians would leave
for lands in the West? Who'd heed Cassandra then?[36]
Phoebus has warned us; obey him and be wise.'
We heard his word and shouted our assent.
This home we abandoned, too (some stayed behind), 190
to course in hollow bark the boundless sea.

"Once we had gained the deep, and no more lands
were to be seen—sky only, and only sea—
a slatey rain cloud rose above my head
to bring us night and storm and shadowed squall.
The wind set waters rolling; waves rose up
huge, to scatter and toss us over the swirl.
Clouds covered the sky; a dripping night stole heaven
away; redoubled lightning split the murk.
Driven off course, we wandered waters unknown.[37] 200
Palinurus himself could not tell night from day,
nor call his course to mind, there in mid-sea.
Three days the sun was dimmed by blinding fog
as we wandered the deep; three nights there were no stars.
The fourth day brought us at last in sight of land
with mountains visible far, and coils of smoke.
We dropped the sails and leaped to oars; our men
heaved, swept, and churned blue water into foam.
I first from the waves found safety on those shores,
the Strophades (Greek for 'the Spinners'); the islands lie 210
in the broad Ionian, home of dread Celaeno
and Harpies all, since Phineus' house was locked
and they in terror fled their former feast.

[36]By a curse put upon her, Cassandra could see into the future but no one would believe her.

[37]The wanderings that follow parallel Odysseus' tales to some degree. Here, Aeneas encounters the prophetess Celaeno and her harpies; they appear in altered form in Aeschylus' *Eumenides*.

No monster grimmer than they, no plague more savage,
no wrath of God, has fled the shores of Styx.
They are women, but winged; the refuse of their bellies
is foul; their hands are taloned, and they wear
an endless pallor of hunger.
As we bore in and entered harbor, we saw
fat herds of cattle wandering over the fields, 220
and a flock of goats, unguarded, in the grass.
We attacked with steel and called on Jove himself
and the gods to share our booty; on the beach
we spread our couches and set out the rich, fat feast.
But here, from the hills, with a shriek and sudden swoop
the Harpies came; loudly they rattled their wings.
They tore at our meats and left their filthy prints
over all; they croaked, and stank like carrion death.
Once more in a pocket beneath a rocky ledge,
locked in by trees and awe-inspiring shade, 230
we set the tables and built fresh altar fires;
once more, from a different place, from unseen dens,
the noisy flock flew round and clawed their spoil;
their spittle fouled our feast. 'Men, fetch your arms,'
I shouted. 'We'll drive the fiendish creatures off!'
As ordered, they hid their swords in handy spots
under grass, and laid their shields in hiding-holes.
Then when the birds came shrieking down the shore,
Misenus from a hilltop gave a signal
on hollow brass. My men attacked—strange war!— 240
they strove with steel to stain those filthy birds.
But nothing pierced their plumage; never a wound
they got, but fled off flapping toward the stars,
leaving half-eaten meats fouled by their claws.
Alone on a spire of rock Celaeno settled
(that voice of doom) and from her throat broke speech:
'What, war? Slaughter our cows, stampede our steers,
and then make war, you sons of Laomedon,
and drive us guiltless from our native land?
Well then, hear this, and nail it to your heart— 250
the Almighty told it to Phoebus, Phoebus to me;
now I, chief of the Furies, declare it to you.
You sail for Italy and pray for winds:
you'll go to Italy, pass into her harbors,
but never wall your promised city round
till hunger, and guilt for what you murdered here,
shall make you gnaw your tables halfway through.'[38]
She spoke, and to the woods spread wing and fled.
My men shuddered. An icy fear congealed
their blood; their spirits fell. They'd fight no more, 260
but beg for peace, they said, with prayer and vow,
if those were goddesses or gruesome birds.

---

[38]Celaeno's prophecy is fulfilled in Book 7.

Anchises on the shore spread wide his hands,
called on the powers, and bade obeisance due:
'O gods, these threats forfend! Avert this fate!
Be kind! Preserve the faithful!' Then, 'Cut loose
the moorings!' he cried. 'Free lines, and let them run!'
The South Wind filled our sails; on foaming waves
we sped where wind and pilot laid our course.
Now in mid-sea we raised tree-clad Zacynthus, 270
Dulichium, Samë, Neritos steep and rocky;
we raced by Ithaca's cliffs, Laertes' realm,
and cursed the land that suckled cruel Ulysses.
Soon, too, Leucata's clouded mountain peaks
and Apollo, terror of sailors, came to view.
Here we sought rest, close by a little town.
The anchors went out; the fleet lay stern to shore.

"Thus, unexpectedly, we came to land;
we purged our stain and payed our vows to Jove,
then, there at Actium, staged the Trojan games. 280
Stripped and anointed, my men took part in sports
ancestral. (Joy! We'd slipped past all those towns
of Greeks! We'd escaped, though enemies hemmed us in!)
Meanwhile the sun rolled his great circle round,
and a wintry North Wind roughened and froze the waves.
On an entryway I nailed the curved bronze shield
huge Abas carried, and marked it with a verse:
This shield Aeneas, from the conquering Greeks,
then ordered, 'Man the thwarts and put to sea!'
My men vied at the stroke and swept the waters. 290
Phaeacia's airy towers soon dropped behind;
we skirted Epirus' shores and made the port
of Chaonia, near Buthrotum in the hills.

"Here came report, incredible to our ears,
that Helenus, Priam's son, was king in Greece,
possessing the throne of Pyrrhus and his wife—
Andromache gone to a man of Troy once more![39]
Speechless, my heart afire with passion strange
to address the king and hear so great a tale,
I walked from the harbor, leaving ship and shore. 300
At the city gates I chanced on funeral foods
and gifts in a grove by a counterfeit Simois;
Andromache there made offering to the dead
and called the ghosts to Hector's grass-grown mound—
empty, with twin altars—cause of her tears.
She saw me coming, saw my Trojan arms,
and thought me a phantom of madness and of fear.

---

[39] Pyrrhus, son of Achilles, took Helenus the prophet and Andromache, wife of Priam, as captives in the sack of Troy. Pyrrhus later joined the pair and ceded them part of his kingdom. Andromache's version of the story reveals her bitterness.

She looked and stiffened; the warmth fled from her limbs,
she tottered, but at long last she came to speech:
'Is this your face? Is this your voice I hear, 310
Aeneas? Are you alive? Or if you've lost
the light of life, where is Hector?' She burst out
in a flood of tears and frenzied sobs; I scarce
could put in a stumbling word, now here, now there:
'Living, yes—and a life of endless peril.
Never doubt: you see reality.
What fate caught you and cast you from estate
so regal? What fitting fortune came to you,
Hector's Andromache? Still the wife of Pyrrhus?'
She bowed her head and spoke as if in shame: 320
'Of Priam's daughters, call her only blessed
who died beneath the lofty walls of Troy
on hostile tomb. No lots were cast for her;
she was no war prize for some victor's bed.[40]
From a home in flames I sailed through many a sea
and bore, the merest slave, the proud contempt
of Achilles' half-grown son. Then he pursued
Hermione, Spartan princess, child of Leda,
and passed me on to Helenus—slave to slave.
Orestes, for his stolen bride enflamed 330
with love, and fury-driven for his crimes,
caught Pyrrhus and killed him at his father's shrine.
At Pyrrhus' death, a share in power passed
to Helenus; he has called this land "Chaonia"
for Chaon of Troy, these plains "Chaonian,"
and built in the hills a fort called "Ilium."
But say what winds, what fates have stayed your course?
You could not know the way: what guided you?
Your son—does he still draw the breath of life?
In Troy you kept him by you. 340
And does the boy still miss his poor lost mother?
Does he feel drawn toward ancient strength and courage
by Aeneas, his father, and by his uncle, Hector?'
She spoke in a flood of tears, and as she sobbed
long and in vain, down from the wall he came—
King Helenus, Priam's son, with all his guard.
He knew his kin and joyed to lead them home
with a word—then tears—then a word—then floods of tears.
As I walked, I saw it: a little Troy, a fort
just like the great one, and a dried-up stream 350
called 'Xanthus,' a Scaean Gate—I kissed that gate!
My people, too, all shared the city's welcome.
The king received them in his ample halls,
then in mid-court they drank a toast of wine,
and ate from golden plates, and raised their cups.

[40]Andromache refers to her daughter, Polyxena, whom the Greeks sacrificed at the tomb of Achilles.

"One day and then a second passed; then breezes
called to our canvas; a Southerly swelled our sails.
I went to our prophet and prince and thus inquired:
'Scion of Troy, God's prophet, who sense the will
of Phoebus in tripod and laurel, who know the stars 360
and the speech of birds, and the word of winged flight,
tell me (for all sound prophecy foretells
travel, and heaven's universal will
bids me seek Italy and her far-off lands;
only the Harpy sang of sacrilege
and strange forebodings, telling a carrion tale
of wrath and hunger), where lie my greatest dangers?
What course will carry me past all obstacles?'
Then Helenus, killing first the ritual calves,
prayed for God's peace, and from his hallowed head 370
untied the ribbons. He took me by the hand
and led me, filled with awe, to Phoebus' temple,
then spoke—a priest and voice of God—these words:

" 'Aeneas, we dare not doubt some greater power
sends you across the sea: so Jove allots
men's fate and turns the wheel of history.
I'll tell you a little, to help you cross strange waters
more safely to Ausonia, and come there
to harbor; all the rest the Fates forbid
me to know, or Juno says I may not tell.[41] 380
To begin: This Italy, which you think so close,
whose nearby ports you may invade at will,
lies land past distant land, down trackless ways.
First you must bend oar in Sicilian wave
and sail the circuit of Ausonian seas,
the pools of hell, and Circe's Aeaean isle,
before you'll see your city safely founded.
I'll tell you the signs; you lay them to your heart:
In an hour of trouble, beside a far-off stream
where oaks grow on the shore, you'll find a sow, 390
huge lying, having borne her thirty young—
white she will be, white babies at her teats.
Here build your city, find peace and labor's end.
For fated "gnawing of tables," have no fears:
Apollo will hearken, and fate will find a way.
But all these lands, these coasts of Italy
nearby, washed by this ocean and this tide:
Shun them! Vile Greeks infest their every town.
Here Locrians of Naryx laid their walls,
and here Idomeneus sat his army down 400

[41] Helenus tells Aeneas of his coming adventures, including meetings with Circe, Scylla, and Charybdis, from Homer's *Odyssey*. He adds, significantly, that Aeneas must appease Juno in order to progress to Italy, and that in the end he must visit Sibyl, prophetess of Apollo, whose reading of the leaves will direct him further.

on plains Salentine; here on ramparts rises
Petelia, Philoctetes' modest home.
No—cross the water, and when you come to land,
build altars on the shore and pay your vows;
but with a purple shawl veil head and hair,
that while the fires of holy office burn
no view of hostile face confuse the signs.
(Preserve this way of prayer, you and your people;
so may your sons in purity keep the rite.)
Then sail away; the wind will bring you close 410
to Sicily. Where Pelorus opens out,
bear off to port and follow coast and sea
the long way round. Shun starboard waves and shore.
These lands were once by earthquake ripped and riven
(long, long ago; such change time has wrought!).
They leaped apart, men say, though they had been
one mass before; in rushed a roaring sea
to cut Hesperian from Sicilian shores.
Now narrow waters ebb and flow between them.
The right shore Scylla guards; the left, Charybdis 420
insatiate. Thrice, in her maelstrom pit, she gulps
the floods deep down, then belches them again
up to the air, to splash the very stars.
But Scylla hides in lightless, caverned lair;
her lips reach out to suck ships to the reefs.
Human her face, her lovely breast a girl's—
so to her waist. Below, a shapeless fish,
a womb of wolves, tapered to dolphin's tail.
Better to pass the pillars of Pachynus,
taking the time to make the long course round, 430
than catch one glimpse of that vast-vaulted monster,
Scylla, and of the reefs where blue dogs bark.
Further, if Helenus has prophetic powers
worthy of trust, if God's truth fills his heart,
one thing, Aeneas, one thing before all else
I'll tell and advise you, again and again the same:
To Juno the queen make your first adorations;
to Juno, lady of power, chant willing prayers
and win her with humble gifts. So shall you gain
passage to Italy from Sicilian shores. 440
Once set down there, move on to Cumae's town,
her hallowed pools, Avernus' rustling groves.
There you'll find a prophetess: under a cliff
she sings of fate and writes her runes on leaves.
The leaves, with their recorded songs, she lays
in order and stores them deep within her cave;
they stay in place and never change their sequence.
But when some door is opened and a breeze,
the merest whisper, stirs the fragile leaves,
they flutter all over the cave. She never tries 450
to catch them, sort them out, or match the lines.
Men leave no wiser, and curse the Sibyl's see.

Count not too high the cost of tarrying here.
Though men complain, though breezes call you brisk
to sea and you could fill your canvas full,
still go to the lady, humbly beg her speak
and sing her runes, and let her words flow free.
The peoples of Italy, wars that are to be,
how best to shun each trial, or to bear,
she'll tell, and map your course to victory. 460
Thus far my voice may guide you. Go your way
and by your works exalt great Troy to heaven.'

"Thus spoke the prophet with the voice of love,
then ordered gifts heavy with ivory carved
and gold, sent to the ships, and crammed the holds
with silver ingots, cauldrons from Dodona,
a suit of mail, hook-linked and twilled with gold,
a shining helmet, peaked with horsehair plumes—
Neoptolemus' arms. Gifts for my father, too,
and horses he gave, and guides; 470
new oars for the ships, new armor for my men.

"Meanwhile Anchises bade the fleet make sail
to catch each minute of a favoring breeze.
With deep respect, Apollo's priest addressed him:
'Anchises, whom proud Venus deigned to wed,
heaven-blessed, twice rescued from a ruined Troy,
there lies your land, Ausonia! Sail there now!
But slip on down that coastline, as you must:
the shores Apollo names lie far beyond.
Blessed in the goodness of your son, sail on! 480
I'll say no more, nor block the rising winds.'
Andromache, too, sad at this last farewell,
brought garments pictured with a weft of gold;
for Ascanius, Trojan coats (he too was honored)
and piles of gifts of her weaving. Thus she spoke:
'These are for you, to call my hand to mind,
dear child, and witness to the lasting love
of Hector's wife. Take them, our parting gifts,
O image of Astyanax, all that's left me:
the eyes, the hands, the face—he bore them so, 490
and he'd be your age now, a boy like you.'
I turned to go, and tears flowed as I spoke:
'Be happy! Your trials are over, and you know
your fortune. We're hurried on from fate to fate.
You have found peace; you need not plow the sea
nor seek Ausonia, land that ever drops
below the horizon. You see Troy and Xanthus—
their likeness—built by your hands, and blessed, I pray,
more richly, and less in the path of Greeks.
If ever I enter Tiber and the lands 500
by Tiber, and see my people's promised walls,
that day shall see our towns, our nations, kin:

Hesperia to Epirus—one in blood
and one in fate; our hearts will build them both
one Troy. Be that our mandate to our sons!'

"We took to the seas close by Ceraunia
whence lies the shortest course to Italy.
The sun went down; black shadows hid the hills.
We found our posts, then stretched out by the waves
on earth's dear breast, there where the sand was dry, 510
and rested. Sleep flowed over our weary limbs.
The Hours had not yet borne Night to mid-course
when Palinurus, never the sluggard, rose
to listen for the breeze and test the winds.
He marked each star that crossed the silent night—
Arcturus, the rain stars, and the twin Triones,
and searched all round Orion, armed with gold.
Soon as he saw that heaven was at peace,
he sounded a clear signal. We broke our camp,
made way on course, and spread our winging sails. 520
The stars had fled, when, with the blush of Dawn,
we raised the misty hills and low shore line
of Italy. 'Italy, ho!' first cried Achates.
'Ho, Italy!' came my people's shout of joy.
Then Father Anchises crowned a mighty bowl
with flowers, filled it with wine, and standing high
on his quarterdeck, called the gods:
'O gods, who govern sea and land and storm,
grant us fair weather and a following wind!'
As he prayed, the gusts came faster; now we saw 530
a harbor, and on a hill Minerva's temple.
My men struck sail and turned our bows toward shore.
The harbor was bent to an arc by eastern waves;
athwart it, reefs in a mist of salty spray
hid it. Twin arms, like walls, came sweeping down
from a turreted cliff. The temple stood well back.
I saw first sign: Four horses in a field,
cropping the grass, each by itself, snow-white.
My father spoke: 'Host land, you bring us war.
The horse is accoutred for war; these beasts mean war. 540
Yet sometime, too, they learn to draw the cart,
these four-foot creatures, and wear the reins and yoke:
there's hope of peace.' We prayed to Pallas the holy,
clasher of arms, who first received our thanks
(at her altar we veiled our heads with Trojan shawls);
then heeding Helenus' earnest plea, we made
to Juno of Argos our due adorations.

"The minute our prayers and litanies were done,
we braced our yards and sheeted the canvas home,
then left these Greekish halls and suspect lands. 550
Tarentum next (called 'Home of Hercules'),
was seen facing Lacinia's sacred mount,

Fort Caulon, and Point Scylax, grave of ships.
Then far across the strait we saw Mount Aetna
and heard a distant roar of reefs and breakers
crashing, strange voicelike sounds along the shore.
The long waves leaped; the tide was roiled with sand.
Then said Anchises: 'See! This is Charybdis,
the rocks that Helenus sang, the dreadful reefs.
Put about, men! Stand to the oars, now, all together!' 560
They obeyed commands. Palinurus took the lead
with a 'Hard a-port!' athwart the howling waves;
with oar and sail the whole fleet swung to port.
Up one vast swirling slope we rode to heaven,
then dropped to hell as the wave slipped out from under.
Thrice reefs and hollow caverns gave a roar,
thrice we saw spume and spray that flecked the stars.
The wind, failing at sunset, left us tired;
not knowing our way, we put in to Cyclops land.[42]

"The harbor itself is windless, glassy, wide, 570
but near it Aetna's hideous ruin roars.
Sometimes toward heaven it hurls a dead-black cloud,
a pitchy swirl of smoke and glowing sparks,
and shoots out balls of flame that lick the stars;
sometimes it tears its own guts out and heaves
a vomit of boulders; up roll molten rocks
with groans and bubbles and seething, deep, deep down.
Men say Enceladus, scorched half dead by lightning,
lies underneath that mass, with Aetna huge
atop him breathing bursts of chimneyed flame; 580
whenever, wearied, he stirs, all Sicily
grumbles and shakes and veils her sky with smoke.
That night beneath the trees we saw and heard
things eerie, weird, and could assign no cause.
There were no fiery comets, no bright bands
of light at the pole; the sky was dark with clouds
and night foreboding wrapped the moon in mist.

"The next day's early light of dawn was rising
and Aurora had cleared the sky of dew and dark
when suddenly from the bush a strange, wild shape— 590
a man in hunger's final hour, all rags—
came running toward the beach, his hands outstretched.
We looked around: filth, stench, a ragged beard,
clothes pinned with thorns, but in all else a Greek,
sent once with his father's sword to fight at Troy.
Soon as he saw our Dardan dress, the arms
of Troy, he stumbled, terrified at the sight,
and checked his pace, then rushed on toward the shore

[42]In Virgil's version of the story of the Cyclops, the island on which the hideous one-eyed creatures live is beneath Mt. Aetna. The survivor of Odysseus' band is apparently Virgil's invention.

sobbing, gasping, praying: 'In heaven's name
and the gods', by light of day and breath of life, 600
save me, Trojans! Take me to any land!
That's all I ask. I know: I am a Greek;
my sword attacked the homes of Ilium.
For that, if I have done such hurt and wrong,
sprinkle the waves with me, or sink me deep.
I'll die—die gladly by the hand of man!'
With that he fell to his knees and seized my knees
and clung there. Who he was, of what line sprung,
we bade him tell, and what the fate that felled him.
With little ado Anchises gave his hand 610
to the fellow, and by that pledge brought courage back.
At last he laid aside his fear and spoke:
'I'm called Achaemenides, Ithacan, of the crew
of cursed Ulysses. My sire, Adamastus, sent me
to Troy (a poor man—would he had so remained!).
My shipmates, running in fear from savagery,
forgot me, left me behind, deep in the cave
of the Cyclops—house of gore and bloody feasts,
black, enormous—and he's so tall he knocks
the stars awry (God save earth from such horror!). 620
No man could stand to see him or hear him speak;
he lives on the guts and blood of luckless men.
I saw him! I saw him seize two of our muster
in his huge hand; then halfway up the cave
he smashed them against a rock; the place fair swam
with gore! I saw him gnaw their bleeding flesh—
muscles yet warm and twitching between his teeth!
But not unavenged: Ulysses stood no such thing,
nor lost his Ithacan wit, for all the danger.
The Cyclops, stuffed with food and drowned in wine, 630
soon bowed his head and fell to the floor, a bulk
elephantine, vomiting clots and bloody wine
and bits of flesh as he slept. We said our prayers,
threw dice for places, then all as one together
rushed him. With sharpened stake, we stabbed his eye
—just one, half hidden in his scowling brow,
huge as an Argive shield or Phoebus' lamp—
rejoicing to avenge our shipmates' ghosts.
But go, for pity, go, and cut your lines
from shore. 640
Now in his cave Polyphemus folds his sheep
and milks them; and like him, as huge as he,
a hundred others live along this shore,
each a foul Cyclops, wandering these high hills.
Three times the moon has filled her horns with light
while in the lonely woods where wild beasts lurk
I've dragged out a life, climbing up cliffs to watch
Cyclopes, trembling to hear them tramp and shout.
My food—poor stuff!—was berries and stony fruits
from trees, and a root or two ripped from the sod. 650

I've watched and watched; your fleet is the first I've seen
heading this way. To you, whatever may be,
I've turned. Enough, to escape these fiendish creatures!
Far better you took my life, however you will!'

"He scarce had spoken when high in the hills we saw
Polyphemus the shepherd, vast and lumpish, moving
among his sheep, and heading for shores he knew,
a horror, misshapen, huge, his eye put out.
A pine trunk guided his hand and steadied his step;
his woolly sheep came with him—they alone 660
were joy and solace in his pain.
Soon as he came to the sea where waves ran high
he washed from the pit of his eye the gouts of gore,
howling and grinding his teeth, then to mid-channel
strode out, and the wave had still not wet his flank.
Quickly we took our suppliant Greek (poor man!)
on board, and then in silence cut our lines,
put about, leaned on our oars, and raced away.
He heard our voices and whirled to track us down.
But when he found us past his power to reach, 670
and Ionian waves too deep for him to breast,
he raised a savage yell that set the sea
to shaking, frightened Italy's inmost heart,
and made the vaulted caves of Aetna roar.
The tribe of Cyclops heard, and from the woods
and hills rushed to the shore and filled the beach.
We saw the brethren of Aetna halt and scowl
in vain, despite their heads that reached to heaven,
a council of fright. They stood there towering high
like lofty oaks or cypresses cone-bearing— 680
some forest of Jove or woodland of Diana.
Sharp panic drove us to rush, to let the sheets
run free, and set the sails where blew the wind.
But Helenus had warned us not to course
'twixt Scylla and Charybdis—there the route
lay pinched between two deaths: We must put back!
Just then a Norther, blowing from Pelorus,
came down; I sailed past ports of living rock—
Pantagia, Megara, Thapsus flat and low.
These spots Achaemenides named, retracing now 690
his errant course, the crewman of cursed Ulysses.

"Athwart a Sicilian bay an island lies,
Plemyrium of the waves, its earlier name
Ortygia. Here, men say, the stream Alpheus,
comes up from hidden channels under the sea
to be 'Arethusa' and join Sicilian waves.
As bidden, we worshiped the local gods, and then
pushed past the fat, wet soil of swamp Helorus.
Thence we skirted the cliffs and jettied reefs
of Pachynus, then Camerina, by the Fates 700

decreed forever fixed; next, on to Gela
the monstrous, lying flat by laughing streams.
Thereafter Akragas on the hill displayed
her ramparts—breeder once of splendid steeds.
Past palmy Selinus we drove with freshening breeze,
and sounded our way through Lilybaeum's reefs.
Then Drepanum's harbor and its joyless shore
received us. Here after all those storms at sea
I lost my father, solace of every care
and blow, Anchises. Father, you left me wearied; 710
was it for this I'd saved you from those perils?
Not Helenus, for all his tales of terror,
nor foul Celaeno prophesied such grief.[43]
This was my final trial, my journey's end.
Thence I sailed; God brought me to your coasts."

Thus Lord Aeneas held them all intent,
telling his tale of travel, of God and fate.
At last he stopped, sank back, and made an end.

Book 4
[Aeneas and Dido]

Now Dido had felt the heavy slash of care,
the wound that grows in the vein, the lightless flame.[44]
Aeneas' great courage, the glory of his people,
coursed through her mind; fast in her heart lay fixed
his face, his words. She knew no rest or peace.
The next day's lamp of sun was lighting earth,
and Dawn had cleared the sky of dew and dark,
when she, sick soul, spoke to her loving sister:
"Anna! My dreams! They leave me tense with fear!
What strange outsider has come here to our home? 10
How proud his bearing! How brave his heart and hand!
I believe—not lightly—he is a child of gods.
Fear proves the soul debased; but he, though battered
by Fate, tells how he fought war after war.
Had I not fixed it firm within my heart
never to yield myself to marriage bond
since that first love left me cheated by death,
did I not sicken at thought of bed and torch,
to this one sin, this once, I might succumb.
No, Anna, I'll speak: Since poor Sychaeus died, 20
since brother drenched my house with husband's blood,
Aeneas alone has moved my heart and shaken

[43]The death of Anchises is not prophesied by Helenus or Celaeno, but Helenus has remarked that he was not allowed to speak all that he knew.

[44]In the first two lines of Book 4, Dido is introduced as a tragic figure; her "care" defines her, just as the arms of battle define Aeneas at the beginning of Book 1. Dido's wound is, of course, partly caused by the designs of Venus and her son, Cupid, recently poised on Dido's lap while disguised as Ascanius.

resolve. I mark the trace of long-dead flame.
But, oh, may the earth gape wide and deep for me,
or the father almighty blast me down to death,
to the paling ghosts of hell and the pit of night,
before I play honor false or break her laws.
The man who first knew union with me stole
my heart; let him keep and guard it in the tomb."[45]
She spoke; the well of her tears filled and ran over. 30

Then Anna: "Your sister loves you more than life:
why squander youth on endless, lonely grief,
with no sweet sons, without the gifts of love?
You think mere ashes, ghosts in the grave, will care?
So be it! You've mourned; you've turned all suitors down
in Libya, and Tyre before. You've scorned Iarbas
and all the chiefs that Africa, proud and rich,
parades: why battle a love that you've found good?
Have you forgotten whose lands you've settled here?
This side, Gaetulians (race untamed by war), 40
savage Numidians, and a barrier sea;
that side, the desert, thirst, the wild nomads
of Barca. Why tell of wars that rise in Tyre
or how your brother threatens?
I'm sure the gods have blessed the Trojans' course,
and Juno favored the wind that blew their ships.
Oh, what a city you'll see, what kingdoms rise,
with such a man! Allied with Trojan arms
Carthage will raise her glory to the sky.
Pray for the gods' forgiveness; give them gifts. 50
Be kind to our guest; weave tissues of delay:
'Winter—the sea is wild—the rains have come—
your ships are damaged—you cannot read the skies.'"[46]

Such talk inflamed her heart with uncurbed love,
gave hope to doubt, and let restraint go free.
First they went to altar and shrine to beg
God's peace; they made due rite of sacrifice:
sheep to Ceres, to Phoebus, to Father Bacchus,
and most to Juno, lady of marriage bonds.
Dido the beautiful lifted a cup of wine 60
and poured it between the horns of a pure white cow,
or danced where the gods watch over blood-rich altars.
Each day began with victims; she slit their throats,
and hung over living vitals to read the signs.
But priests are fools! What help from shrine and prayer
for her madness? Flames devoured her soft heart's-flesh;

---

[45]Dido's promise of widowhood contends with her unforeseen passion, as her mind moves back and forth.

[46]Anna's refreshing practicality points to the advantages to be had in detaining Aeneas. She sees an alliance between the two as the hope of Carthage.

the wound in her breast was wordless, but alive.
Fevered and ill-starred, Dido wandered wild
through all the town, like a doe trailing an arrow
that she, heedless in Cretan forest, caught 70
from a shepherd who shot but never knew his bolt
had flown to the mark; she ranges field and grove
of Dicte; the shaft of death clings to her flank.[47]
Now Dido escorted Aeneas from wall to wall,
showed him her Tyrian wealth, her city all built—
she'd start to speak, but in mid-word fall mute.
Again, at wane of day, she'd fill her hall
and ask to hear once more of Troy's travail,
and hang once more, madly, upon each word.
Then when they'd parted and the shadowed moon 80
had paled, and fading stars warned men to sleep,
in the empty hall she'd lie where he had lain,
hearing him, seeing him—gone, and she alone;
or hold Ascanius close, caught by his father's
likeness, in hope of eluding a sinful love.[48]
Her towers grew no taller; her army ceased
maneuvers and worked no more to strengthen port
and bastion for war: work hung half-done, walls stood
huge but unsteady; bare scaffolds met the sky.

As soon as Jove's dear wife knew Dido gripped 90
by the plague and grown too mad to heed report,
she, daughter of Saturn, spoke harsh words to Venus:
"What glorious praise, what rich return you've gained,
you and your son; such might, such fabled power,
now that by godhead twain one woman's conquered!
I'm not deceived: you feared my city, and me,
and hence held Carthage and her halls suspect.
Is there no limit? Why this vast rivalry?
Why not make peace for good, and carry through
the match you planned? You've gained your heart's desire: 100
Dido has drawn love's flame deep as her bones.
Why not join hands, join peoples, share the rule
between us? Let Dido serve her Trojan prince
and lay her dower—her Tyrians—in your hand."

Venus knew Juno spoke with veiled intent
to turn Italian power aside to Carthage.
Thus she replied: "To that, who but the mad
could object? Who'd choose to go to war with you?
If only success may crown our stratagem!
But I'm not sure of fate: would Jove allow 110
a single city for people of Tyre and Troy?

[47]From her morbid fascination with her sacrifices, to the naming of her love as madness, to the image of herself as a stricken deer, Dido is portrayed as wholly possessed by Venus' magic.
[48]Dido would pretend to be with Aeneas by cuddling his son.

Approve such mingled blood, such rule conjoint?
You are his wife: seek out his will. You may.
You lead, I'll follow." To her then Juno spoke:
"That shall be my concern. How best to meet
the need of the moment, hear, while I briefly tell.
A hunt is planned. Aeneas, and Dido with him,
are off to the woods soon as tomorrow's sun
rises and with his ray reveals the world.
They'll see the clouds turn black with hail and rain; 120
then as their beaters rush to encircle a dell,
I'll pour down floods and shake all heaven with thunder.
Their men will scatter in darkness and disappear.
Your prince of Troy and Dido both will come
to a cave. I'll be there, too. With your consent,
I'll join them in marriage and name her 'lawful wife.'
Their wedding this shall be." No adverse word
spoke Venus, but nodded. Such tactics made her smile.[49]

Meanwhile the Dawn arose and left the sea.
Out from the gates at sunrise young men ran 130
with nets and snares and broad-tipped hunting spears;
out galloped Moors with packs of keen-nosed hounds.
The queen was late; beside her hall the lords
of Carthage waited; there stood her horse, in gold
and purple caparison, nervous, champing the bit.
At last she came, surrounded by her vast guard,
wrapped in a scarlet cloak broidered with lace.
Gold was her quiver; gold held her plaited hair;
a brooch of gold fastened her purple gown.
In marched a Trojan group, Iulus too, 140
smiling and eager. Then, towering over all,
Aeneas joined them and brought their ranks together.
Like Apollo, leaving Lycia and streams of Xanthus,
in winter, to visit Delos, his mother's home!
He starts the dancing; gathering round his shrine,
islanders, mountaineers, painted plainsmen sing,
while he climbs Cynthus. He braids his flowing hair
and holds it in place with laurel and crown of gold;
his arrows clang at his back. So fresh, alive,
was Aeneas, so matchless the glory of his face. 150
They rode to the hills, to the wayless woods and marches.
Look! Down from a rocky ridge leaped mountain goats
to race downhill; on this side, where the plains
lay open, a line of antelopes flashed past
away from the hillsides, trailing a swirl of dust.
Ascanius—boy on a lively pony—loped
up hill, down dale, with a laugh past these, past those.

[49]The contention between Juno and Venus provides comic relief, but also reminds us what a pawn Dido is in their hands. The marriage as they envision it is a purely cynical affair.

Such nerveless beasts! He wished a foam-flecked boar
might come his way, or a lion charge from the hills.[50]

Now thunder roared and rumbled across the sky; 160
soon came black clouds, the hailstorm, and the rain.
The Tyrian people and men of Troy broke ranks,
and with them Venus' grandson ran for shelter—
anywhere! Rivers in spate rushed down the slopes.
The prince of Troy and Dido both had come
to a cave. The bride's attendants, Earth and Juno,
gave signal: lightning and empyrean flamed
in witness; high in the hills Nymphs made their moan.
That was the day, the first of death and first
of evil. Repute, appearance, nothing moved 170
the queen; she laid no plan to hide her love,
but called it marriage, with this word veiled her shame.[51]

At once Rumor went out through Libya's towns—
Rumor, than whom no evil thing is faster:
speed is her life; each step augments her strength.
Small, a shiver, at first, she soon rears high.
She walks aground; her head hides in the clouds.
Men say that Earth, in fury at the gods,
bore this last child, a sister to the Giants.
She is swift of foot and nimble on the wing, 180
a horror, misshapen, huge. Beneath each feather
there lies a sleepless eye (wonder to tell!),
and a tongue, and speaking lips, and ears erect.
By night she flies far over the shadowed world
gibbering; sleep never comes to rest her eyes.
By day she sits at watch high on a roof
or lofty tower, and terrifies great cities,
as much a vessel of slander as crier of truth.
This time she filled men's minds with varied gossip,
chuckling and chanting alike both false and true: 190
Aeneas had come, born of the blood of Troy;
Dido had deemed him worthy mate and man.
Now they were warming the winter with rich exchange,
forgetful of thrones, ensnared by shameful lust.
Such tales foul Rumor spread upon men's lips,
then turned her course straight off to King Iarbas,
heaped fire into his heart and raked his wrath.[52]

Iarbas, son of a Nymph by Hammon raped,
had raised in his broad realms a hundred shrines

---

[50]The entire scene breathes gaiety—a final gaiety—and youth. Ascanius, "boy on a lively pony," epitomizes the picture we see.

[51]As the storm breaks, Ascanius flees and nature takes over. Juno herself attends Dido, along with Earth, Fire, and Air. Juno creates the illusion of marriage and Dido accepts it wholeheartedly.

[52]The appearance of the allegorical figure Rumor serves as a bridge to the appearance of the jealous Iarbas, the Moor; it also distances us—as Aeneas is distanced—from the intensity of the moment.

to Jove, a hundred altars and vigil fires 200
with priests at endless prayer; the blood of beasts
fattened the soil, the doors were decked with flowers.
Maddened at heart, enflamed by bitter rumor
he stood at the altar amid the powers of heaven,
raised hands in suppliance, and prayed aloud:

"Almighty Jove, to whom the Moorish kind
on purple couches serve rich food and wine,
do you see this? Or are we fools to fear
your lightning bolt? Are cloud and fire blind,
that frighten our hearts, mere noise devoid of strength? 210
This woman, this immigrant in my bounds, who paid
to build her little town, to whom I granted
tidewater land on terms, rejects my hand
but takes my lord Aeneas to her throne.
And now that Paris and his half-male crew,
with perfumed hair and Persian caps chin-tied,
keeps what he stole, while I bring gifts to shrines—
your shrines—and worship empty shams of glory."[53]

As with hand on altar he made this prayer
the almighty heard; his eye turned toward the palace, 220
toward two in love forgetting their better fame.
He spoke to Mercury then with this command:
"Go, son, summon the Zephyrs and take flight.
Our prince of Troy dawdles in Carthage now
and takes no thought for cities assigned by fate.
Fly with the wind, bring him my word, and speak:
'Such not the man his lovely mother promised,
nor such twice saved by her from Argive arms,
but one to rule a country big with power—
Italy, land of the war cry—to pass on 230
the blood of Teucer, and bring worlds under law.'
If none of these great glories fires his heart
and for his own renown he'll spend no toil,
does he begrudge his son a fortress Rome?
What plans, what hopes hold him on foreign soil,
blind to Ausonia and Lavinia's land?
'Sail on!' That is all. Bring him this word from me."[54]

He ended. Mercury moved to carry out
the father's command. First he put on his sandals
golden, winged, that bear him swift as the wind 240
high over land and high above the sea,
then took his wand. With this he calls the ghosts
pale out of Orcus, or sends them sorrowing down,

---

[53]The anger of Iarbas praying to Jupiter is directed first at Dido for turning him down, then at Aeneas (and all the Trojan men) for supposed effeminacy and libertinism. Calling Aeneas by the hated name of Paris, he recalls the motive for the Trojan War.

[54]Jupiter heeds the prayer of Iarbas. He also wishes to remind Aeneas of his duty, both to the Trojans and his son.

grants sleep, withdraws it, unseals the eyes of death.
With it he drives the winds and sails the clouds.
Now flying he saw the cap and rugged flanks
of Atlas, whose granite shoulders prop the sky—
Atlas: his pine-clad head, forever crowned
with clouds, is buffeted by wind and rain.
A glacier clothes his back, and cascades course 250
down over his face; his beard bristles with ice.
Here Mercury hovering on both wings alike
stopped, then plummeted headlong toward the sea
just like a gull that, round the beaches, round
fish-haunted reefs, skims low across the waves.
So between earth and sky he flew along
toward Libya's sandy shore, cleaving the wind
eastward from Atlas—Mercury, son of Maia.
Soon as his winged feet touched settlement ground,
he saw Aeneas footing down forts and raising 260
new homes. The sword he wore was yellow-starred
with jasper, a cape of glowing Tyrian scarlet
hung from his shoulders—gifts the wealthy queen
had given, and broidered the cloth with thread of gold.[55]
Up stepped the god: "Aeneas! In Carthage now
do you lay foundations and plan a handsome town
for a wife? *Your* throne, *your* state—are they forgotten?
From shining Olympus *he* has sent me down—
the king of gods, whose nod makes heaven roll.
He bade me fly with the wind to bring his word: 270
what plans, what hopes hold you at leisure here?
If nothing of promised glory moves your heart,
and for your own renown you'll spend no toil,
what of your son? He's growing! Your heir, Iulus:
what of his hopes? A kingdom—Italy—Rome:
these are his due!" With this, the Cyllenian god
left mortal sight, nor waited for reply;
beyond the eye he vanished into air.

Aeneas was frightened out of speech and mind;
his hair stood up in terror, his voice stuck fast. 280
He burned to go, to flee this pleasant land;
God's word, God's great commands had struck him hard.
But what should he do? How dare he tell the queen?
She was mad for love: how could he start his plea?
His mind turned quickly here, turned quickly there,
darting in different ways all round about.
As he weighed the matter this seemed the better course:
he called Sergestus, Mnestheus, Serestus the brave:
"Not a word! Prepare to sail! Call out our people!
To battle stations, all: coin some excuse 290

[55] The ostentatiousness of Dido's gifts of the sword and cape stands in contrast to the plainness of Aeneas' duty, as Mercury explains it.

for these new orders." Meanwhile, let gentle Dido
know nothing, suspect no rupture of their love:
he now would test approaches, seek the time
and kindest way to tell her. Quickly all
in joy at his command obeyed his orders.[56]

But still the queen (who can deceive a lover?)
foretold the scheme, caught contemplated moves,
feared even where all was safe. Then Rumor came
to report the fleet outfitted and ready to sail.
Her passion burst control; savage, aflame, 300
she raced through town, as, at an elevation,
the Thyiad who feels the spur of Bacchic hymns
and dances, and hears Cithaeron shout by night.
At last she addressed Aeneas; her words burst forth:

"You lied! You thought you could conceal a wrong
so vast, and leave my land without one word?
Our love, your right hand given in pledge that day,
a Dido to suffer and die—are these no check?
What? Fit out your fleet beneath a winter sun,
and hurry across the sea while north winds howl, 310
hard-hearted man? Were it no foreign land,
no unknown home you sought, but Troy still stood,
would you send ships through storms like these to Troy?
You run from *me?* In tears, I seize your hand
(what other solace have I left myself?)
and beg you recall our marriage, our wedding day:
if I have served you well, if you have found
delight in me, have mercy! My house is crumbling!
If prayer can still be heard, change, change your heart!
You made the Libyan tribes, the Nomad kings, 320
yes, my own Tyrians, hate me; lost for you
were honor and good repute, my only path
to glory. Cast off, fit only to die, who'll have me,
you whom I entertained—no more say, 'married.'
What now? Wait till Pygmalion levels my walls,
or the Moor Iarbas drags me off in chains?
If only before your flight I had conceived
your child, if only a baby Aeneas played
here in my court, whose face might mirror yours,[57]
I'd feel less like one taken and discarded." 330
She finished. Aeneas, strengthened by Jove's words,
gazed steadily at her and suppressed his pain.
At last he briefly replied, "Speak! List them all—
your favors and courtesies! There is not one
I won't confess. I'll think of you with joy

[56] The men move "in joy"; they, like Dido's retainers, have barely tolerated the couple's love all along.

[57] Dido's passionate speech begins in rage at Aeneas' betrayal and ends in tearful pleading for a child of their love.

long as I think at all, and live, and breathe.
But now to the point. I did not mean (believe me!)
to slip away by stealth, nor ever feigned
the wedding torch, or made such league with you.
If fate had let me govern my own life 340
and heal my troubles in the way I willed,
I would be living in Troy with what remained
of my people; Priam's halls would still be standing;
and we, though beaten, had built our walls anew.
But Apollo Grynean sent me to Italy;
'Find Italy! Win her!' declared the oracles.
My love, my home, lie there. You are of Tyre,
yet Libyan Carthage holds you, hall and wall:
why take it ill that Trojans look for homes
in Italy? Strange lands we too may seek. 350
Whenever dewy night enshrouds the world
and fiery stars arise, Anchises' ghost,
murky and fearful, warns me in my dreams.
Ascanius, well-loved son: see how I wrong him,
cheating him of Hesperian land and throne!
Now comes a messenger from Jove himself
(I swear it!); he sped through air to bring command.
In the clear light of day I saw that god;
he entered these walls; my ears drank in his words.
Cease to enflame my heart and yours with plaints: 360
not by my choice I go to Italy."[58]

Even as he spoke she turned her face away.
Glancing now here, now there, she viewed the man
from head to foot, wordless. Then speech flared out:
"No goddess your mother, no Dardanus sired your kind,
you liar! No! Caucasus got you on those cliffs
of jagged granite, and tigers suckled you there!
Dissemble? Why? To await some greater wrong?
I wept; he made no sound, nor turned an eye.
I loved him; where were his tears, his sympathy? 370
What else shall I say? Juno, lady and queen,
Jove, son of Saturn, can be unmoved no longer.
Good faith is folly! I saved him, castaway
and helpless, I made him partner to my power.
He'd lost his ships, his men; I rescued them.
My madness flames like fire: 'Apollo' now,
'the oracles' now; now 'sent by Jove himself
a messenger comes through air with dread commands.'
This is the gods' life work! Such cares disturb
their peace! You're free; I'll not refute your claims. 380
Go! Find your Italian throne by wind and wave!

[58]Aeneas responds logically (some would say coldly) by stating that no marriage took place and that he is recalled by fate to settle in Italy. He invokes his family's need, and finally says the decision to go or not is not his to make.

Midway, I trust, if God has power, you'll drink
requital on a reef and scream for Dido!
There'll be no Dido, but a funeral flame
will follow, and when death sunders soul from flesh
my shade will haunt you till my price is paid.
I'll know! Report will reach my ghost in hell!"
She broke off in mid-speech and, sickened, fled
the light of day—ran from his sight, from him,
while he stood trembling, groping, conning a flood 390
of words. She fainted. Her people raised her up
and bore her to her room and to her bed.[59]

Aeneas the good,[60] though longing to ease her pain
with words of comfort and turn aside her care
(his groans came deep, for love had racked his heart),
obeyed God's orders and sought his fleet again.
Then truly his men fell to; the shore was filled
with hauling of ships. Out swam fresh-painted keels;
men loaded oars still green, and from the woods
brought spars half-hewn in haste. 400
"Move out!" they heard. "All hands!" "Look lively, now!"
(As when the ants, mindful of winter, attack
a heap of grain and carry it home across
the fields: black goes the column; they bear their prize
down narrow grassy lanes. Some push big kernels
with heave of shoulders; some close the line of march
and hurry stragglers. The path is a froth of toil.)
Dido! What did you feel to see all this?
What cries did you utter when from tower's top
you saw the shore all seething, saw the sea 410
churned up before your eyes, and heard the shouts!
Shameless love, where do you not drive men's hearts?
Again she went and wept and begged, for try
she must; her pride must bend the knee to love,
lest for failing to move she die in vain.

"Anna, you see them rushing round the shore:
the crews are mustered; the canvas calls the breeze;
the men have cheered as garlands dressed the spar.
Could I have known such sorrow was to come,
I could have borne it; but now in tears I beg 420
one favor, Anna, of you: that faithless man
was always with you, told you his secret thoughts;
you knew, as no one else, his gentler moods.

---

[59]Dido, in her reply, castigates Aeneas, then moves on to an interior monologue where she pleads her case against him as if he were not there. She turns again to prophesy doom for his ships, only to run away and faint.

[60]Aeneas is *pius*, "the good," exactly at the point he leaves Dido to do his duty. As R. G. Austin comments, "*Pius*, then, is a complex word, a sensitive symbol of adherence to a personal ideal of devotion, which may nevertheless bring pain and sorrow." Austin, ed., *Aeneidos: Liber Quartos* (1982), 122.

Go, bring to our heartless guest this humble plea:
I joined no Greeks; I took no oath at Aulis
of death to Trojans, I sent no ships to Troy,
I never harried his father Anchises' ghost.
Why will he lock his ears against my words?
Why haste? Let a broken heart win one last grace:
Await a safer passage and favoring winds! 430
I'll not ask now for the wedlock he betrayed,
or that he resign his darling Latin throne;
I beg for time, an hour of rest from madness,
till fortune teach me how to lose and grieve.
This favor the last your sister asks: be kind!
I'll pay my debt with death to make full measure."[61]

Such was her plea; such sorrows her grieving sister
reported, reported again. But nothing moved him;
no tears nor words could teach his heart to hear.
(Fate blocked the way; God closed his ears to pity.) 440
Like an oak tree, ancient, toughened by the years,
blasted by Alpine winds this way and that
contesting to uproot it; the North Wind howls,
the trunk is shaken, foliage strews the ground.
The tree holds hard; its crown lifts up toward heaven
far as its root grows down toward Tartarus.
Just so Aeneas, by pleas this side and that
assaulted, felt in his heart the thrust of care.
His mind stood firm; tears came, but came in vain.[62]

Then Dido, luckless, by fortune terrified, 450
invited death: to view heaven's vault was pain.
To strengthen her resolve to leave the light,
she saw, when she offered her gifts and censed the altars
(dreadful to tell!), the holy water turn black
and the wine pour down in horrid clots of gore.
She told none, not even Anna, what she'd seen.
Besides, in her house there stood a marble shrine
to her former husband, which she kept sacrosanct,
festooned with white wool bands and feast-day flowers:
from it she thought she heard her husband's voice 460
calling her, calling, when darkness gripped the world.
And on her roof a lonesome owl sang songs
of death; its mournful cry trailed off in sobs.
Then warnings of seers long dead came crowding back
to fill her with fright. She dreamed herself gone mad,

---

[61] Dido's disintegration begins. She pleads with her sister to beg for Aeneas' return, giving up all claims to him and seeking only time to adjust to his own departure. The last line of the passage is ambiguous: It could anticipate her suicide, but more likely means she would do anything to have Aeneas return, if only briefly.

[62] Another ambiguous line: Whose tears are these? Many readers, including St. Augustine, have thought they are the hidden tears of the stoic Aeneas.

with Aeneas in wild pursuit; then left alone
to travel, forever friendless, a long, long road,
seeking her Tyrians in an empty world,
like maddened Pentheus seeing the rank of Furies,
seeing twin suns and a double Thebes displayed; 470
or like Orestes racing across the stage
to escape a mother armed with torch and serpent—
and at Agamemnon's door the Dirae wait.

Filled with madness and prisoner of her pain,
she determined to die; and now, with how and when
planned in her mind, she addressed her tearful sister
(concealing intent behind a cloudless brow):
"Anna, I've found a way—applaud your sister!—
that will bring him back, or free me from my love.
Near to the ocean's edge and setting sun 480
lies African land's-end, where giant Atlas
bears on his back the spinning star-tricked wheel.
I've found a religious of that place—a Moor;
she served the Hesperides' temple, fed the snake,
and guarded the holy branches on the tree;
with honey and poppy she made the elixir of sleep.
She swears she can release what hearts she will
with spells, and freight still other hearts with care,
can stop the rivers and reverse the stars,
and raise the dead by night: you'll see the earth 490
groan at her feet and trees climb down the hills.
Sister, I tell you, by your life, by all
that's holy, I take to witchcraft against my will.
Slip into our inner courtyard and build there
a pyre; pile on it the arms that perjured man
hung in my house—take all he left, the bed
of marriage that brought me sorrow. I must destroy
his every devilish trace: so says my Moor."
This much, then silence, and her face turned pale.
Yet Anna did not suspect that these strange rites 500
were cover for death; her mind conceived no thought
so mad. Than when Sychaeus died: she feared
no worse, and did as asked.

In the inner court beneath the open sky
the pyre stood huge with pitch pine and with oak.
The queen hung garlands and wreathed the place with boughs
of death; atop, she laid his sword, his garments—
yes, and his image: she knew what she would do.
Ringed by altars the Moor let down her hair,
intoned the gods three hundred, Chaos, and Hell, 510
the Hecates three, Diana the triform virgin.
She sprinkled water labeled "from Avernus,"
selected hairy leaves by moonlight reaped
with brazen sickle (their milky juice turns black),
pulled out the membrane torn from a newborn foal

and snatched from its mother's mouth.[63]
Dido stepped to an altar, blessed her hands,
took meal, slipped off one shoe, unlatched her gown,
then, ready to die, begged gods and stars prophetic
to hear her prayer to any power just 520
and mindful, that cares for lovers wrongly matched.

It was night; all over the world the weary flesh
found peace in sleep; forests and savage seas
rested; in middle course the stars rolled on.
No sound from field, from herd, from painted birds
that swarm the liquid lakes or love the thorn
and thicket: they slept in silence of the night,
healing the heart of care, forgetting pain.
But never the broken-hearted, luckless queen
slipped off to sleep or took the night to eyes 530
and heart. Her torment doubled; desire rose
raging; she ebbed and flowed on waves of wrath.
At last she paused and pondered inner thoughts:
"What shall I do? I'm scorned! Shall I turn and try
my earlier suitors, and beg a Nomad's bed?
I have disdained their hand, how many times?
Well, then, to the Trojan fleet? Hurry to catch
their final word? Because they prized my help
and remember that musty favor with gratitude?
Granted the will, who'd let an unloved woman 540
tread his proud deck? You fool! You still don't know,
don't see, how the sons of Laomedon can lie?
Well—? Trail his jeering crews, a lovesick girl?
Or board ship with my Tyrians, rank on rank,
around me—men whom just now I saved from Sidon:
bid them make sail and put to sea once more?
No! Die as you've earned! Take steel and end your pains!
You, Anna, hurt by my tears, you topped my folly
with wrongful acts; you tossed me to our foe!
I had not the will to pass my life unwed, 550
unstained, like some wild creature, untouched by guilt.
I did not keep my oath to dead Sychaeus."
Such were the sorrows that broke forth from her breast.[64]

Aeneas knew he would go; on his tall ship,
his preparations made, he took his rest.
In his dreams a godly form appeared again,
just as before, and seemed to warn once more

[63]Dido has consulted an African witch and come back with a clay image of Aeneas for purposes of voodoo. The woman performs a ritual to cast a spell on Aeneas using hippomanes, a fleshy patch from the forehead of a newborn colt.

[64]Dido considers and rejects all possible sources of comfort, including her sister Anna. Finally she castigates herself for disloyalty to her dead husband. She is preparing herself for death where, as we later discover, she will join her husband in Hades.

(in all like Mercury, in voice, complexion,
in the flaxen hair and graceful limbs of youth):
"Goddess-born, can you sleep at such an hour, 560
and fail to see the dangers that surround you—
madman!—nor hear the favoring West Wind blow?
Dido devises malice and foul crime
(she knows she'll die) and roils her anger's waves.
Run! Leave in haste, while haste's within your power.
Soon you will see the ocean churned by ships,
the shore ablaze with savage torch and flames,
if Dawn shall touch you tarrying in this land.
Hurry, now! Ever a various, changeful thing
is woman." He spoke and mingled with black night. 570

This apparition terrified Aeneas.
He tore himself from sleep and harried his men
to haste: "Look lively, there, and man the thwarts!
Off buntlines! Quick! A god from heaven's height
again has bid us speed away and cut
our anchor-lines. We come, O sacred presence,
whoever you are! Again we obey your word.
Be with us in peace! Bless us! Show helpful stars
in heaven!" He spoke, and ripped his flashing sword
from sheath, and with the bared blade slashed the lines. 580
Like ardor held them all. They seized, they ran,
they emptied the beach; their vessels hid the sea.
Men heaved, churned up the foam, and swept the blue.

And now Aurora brought the dawn's new light
to earth, and left Tithonus' golden couch.
Dido was watching, and with the first pale gleam
she saw the fleet, yards squared and outward bound,
and marked the emptiness of shore and pier.
Three times and four she beat her lovely breast
and tore her golden hair: "What? Shall he go," 590
she said, "and mock my power—that foreigner![65]
There'll be no general muster? No pursuit?
Will no one hurry to launch my ships? Quick, men,
bring torches, hand out arms, lean on your oars!
What's this? Where am I? What madness warps my mind?
Fool! Has your sacrilege just struck you now?
It should have, the day you offered a throne! Such honor!
And he, they say, brings with him his fathers' gods;
his shoulders carried Anchises, tired and old!
Why couldn't I hack his flesh, tear it, and strew 600
the sea with it? Slaughter his people and his son—
serve up Ascanius at his father's table?
But battle had been uncertain? Grant it so,
why fear, when I meant to die? I'd have thrown fire

[65]Literally, upstart; a newcomer with no status.

and filled their camp with flame: father and son
and people had burned to death to make my pyre.
O Sun, who with your flame light all men's works;
you, Juno, who know my troubles and read them true;
Hecate, hailed at night by town and crossroad;
Dirae, gods of a Dido soon to die, 610
receive my prayer; turn sanction meet and right
upon these wrongs; hear me! If touch he must
on promised port and land—that man accursed!—
and so Jove's laws demand, this end is fixed.
But let brave people harass him with war.
Driven from home, torn from Iulus' arms,
let him beg for help, and see his people die
disgraced. Make him surrender under terms
unjust, and know no happy years of rule,
but die untimely, untombed, in miles of sand. 620
This is my final prayer, poured with my blood.
And you, my Tyrians, hate his race, his kind,
all and always. On my remains bestow
this office: no love, no peace between our peoples!
And from my grave let some avenger rise
to harry the Trojan settlers with fire and sword—
now, some day, whenever we have the power.
Shore against shore, I pray, wave against sea,
sword against sword, fight, father and son, forever!"[66]

So said she, and turned her thoughts this way and that, 630
seeking how soonest to end an unloved life.
To Barce then she spoke—Sychaeus' nurse
(her own lay buried in the fatherland):
"Dear nurse, bring Anna, my sister, here to me.
Tell her to hurry and wash in a running stream,
then bring the victims and holy things I showed her.
Come, both, with sacred ribbons in your hair.
I wish to do my office to Stygian Jove
(all duly prepared) to put an end to care
and lay that Trojan soul on funeral flames." 640

This much. In joy, the old nurse hobbled off.
Savage design drove Dido mad with fright.
Her eyes were wild and bloodshot; on her cheek
flush faded to pallor in terror of death so near.
She rushed to the inner court; madly she climbed
up the tall pyre and drew that Trojan sword,
gift that was never meant for such a use.
She saw his Trojan garment and their bed
well-known; then after a moment's tearful thought
lay down on the couch and spoke these final words: 650

---

[66]Dido's curse is a landmark speech. It ends with a prophecy of continual war between the Trojans (Romans) and Carthaginians.

"Here, trophies that I loved, while God allowed!
Oh, take my life and free me from my sorrow.
I've lived, and run the course that fate assigned;
in glory my shade now goes beneath the earth.
I built a splendid city and saw it walled,
avenged my husband, and made my brother pay—
blessed beyond measure, if only Dardan craft
had never touched upon these shores of mine."
She kissed the couch. "I'll die without revenge,
but die, and pass to darkness undismayed. 660
From shipboard let the heartless Trojan see
my flames! My death ride with him as he sails!"

While she yet spoke, her people saw her fall
crumpled upon the sword, the blade all frothed
with blood, her hands spattered. A scream rose high
in the hall; the city was stricken; Rumor ran wild.
Houses were filled with sobs and lamentations,
with keening of women: the din rose to the skies—
as if an enemy had burst in, and all
Carthage or ancient Tyre were falling, while flames 670
rolled to the roofs, through homes of gods and men.
Anna, half-dead with fear, came running fast:
her fingers tore her face; she beat her breast.
She pushed through the crowd, calling her sister's name:
"Dido, was this what it meant? You lied? to *me?*
Was this the purpose of pyre, altar, and flame?
You left me! What shall I say? You died, but scorned
to take me? You might have let me share your death:
one hour, one stroke of pain had served for two.
These hands helped build—this voice of mine helped call 680
our gods—oh, cruel!—that I must fail you now!
You've killed yourself and me, your people, the lords
of Sidon, and your own city! Oh, let me wash
your wounds, and if some faltering breath remains,
let my lips take it!" With that, she climbed the pyre
and cradled her dying sister in her arms,
cried as she used her dress to stop the blood.
Dido would open her heavy eyes again,
but failed. The gash hissed in her wounded breast.
Three times she raised herself up on one arm, 690
three times fell back, then with an errant eye
sought light in heaven, and moaned that she had found it.

Then Juno in pity for her lingering pain
and laggard death, sent Iris down from heaven
to free her struggling soul from limbs entwined.
(For not at her earned and fated hour she died,
but in a flash of fury, before her days:
Proserpina had not yet cut the lock
from her head, nor sentenced her to life below.)
But Iris flew down, dewy and golden-winged, 700

trailing against the sun a thousand colors.
She stopped over Dido's head: "This sacred lock
I carry to Dis, and from the flesh I free you."
With that she cut the wisp; at once all warmth
dispersed, and life retreated to the winds.[67]

Book 5
[Aeneas in Sicily]

[Aeneas, ignorant of Dido's death, sails to Sicily, where to commemorate his father's death he holds athletic games. In a succession of contests he demonstrates his fairness and concern for all his company, especially through the dispensing of gifts. Meanwhile, on the beaches, the Trojan women are beguiled by the goddess Iris to burn their men's ships so they may sail no more. Aeneas puts out the fires and decides to leave the dissenters behind in Sicily. Aeneas and his men finally sail for Italy, assured of safe passage by the gods, except for the helmsman Palinurus, who falls overboard and is lost at sea.]

Book 6
[Aeneas Visits the Underworld]

He spoke, and wept, and gave the ships free rein
until they raised Euboean Cumae's coasts.[68]
Seaward the bows were swung; the anchor's tooth
grounded the ships, their curving quarterdecks
curtained the strand. The young men dashed like flame
to Hesperian shores. Part sought the seeds of fire
hidden in veins of flint, part raided forests,
the wild beasts' homes, found brooks, and marked them out.
But Aeneas the good looked for Apollo's hill
and castle, and near it the awesome cave where hid 10
the Sibyl, the terrifier, whose heart and mind
the Delian seer filled with prophetic speech.
They came to Trivia's grove and golden halls.

Men say that Daedalus, fleeing Minos' power,
dared put his trust in air and widespread wings.
He sailed unwonted ways toward Arctic cold,
and settled lightly, at last, on Cumae's heights.
Safe landed, he made thank-offering first to Phoebus—
the wings he'd used—and built an awesome shrine:
on one door, Androgeos' death; the penalty, next, 20
paid by a sorrowing Athens every year:
seven of her sons; the urn and lots were shown.
On the other side, the isle of Crete rose high;
here a bull's cruel and furtive act of love
with Minos' daughter, their twoform hybrid child,
the Minotaur, monument to love profaned.

---

[67]The freeing of Dido's spirit is actually a relief, bringing the intervention of the gods to a fitting conclusion.

[68]Cumae is a Greek port town in Italy and site of the cave of the Sibyl, priestess of Apollo.

Next came that winding, wearying, hopeless house;
but Daedalus pitied a princess lost for love
and solved the riddle and puzzle of those halls,
with thread to guide blind feet. You, Icarus, too, 30
had shared in the masterpiece, had grief allowed.
Twice Daedalus tried to carve your fate in gold,
twice fell a father's hands.[69]
They had perused
each last detail, had not Achates joined them,
and with him the seer of Phoebus and Trivia,
Deiphobë, Glaucus' daughter. She hailed Aeneas:
"The hour allows no time for seeing sights!
Far better from virgin herd to slaughter bullocks
seven, and seven sheep, and make due prayer."
So speaking (the men at once performed the rites 40
as ordered), she called the Trojans to her shrine.

From Cumae's cliff was hewn a monstrous cave,
with hundred gaping mouths and hundred doors,
whence poured out hundred words, the Sibyl's answers.[70]
As they entered, the priestess cried, "Now hear your dooms!
'Tis the hour! Behold my god!" And as she spoke
there at the door her face and color changed,
her hair fell in a tangle; she choked, she gasped,
her heart swelled wild and savage; she seemed to grow
and utter inhuman sounds, as on her breathed 50
the power of God. "Trojan," she cried, "you lag?
Aeneas, you lag at prayers? No other power
can blast agape these temple doors." She spoke
no further word. Through hardened Trojan hearts
ran shock and chill; Aeneas was roused to pray:
"Phoebus, help ever-present in Troy's dark days,
who guided the Dardan shaft and hand of Paris
against Achilles, through countless seas that block
vast lands you led me, and to frontier tribes
Massylian—tracts that border on the Syrtes. 60
At last we've reached elusive Italy's coasts:
so far, no farther, let Troy's fate pursue us.
You too may lawfully show us mercy now,
you heavenly powers who hated Troy and all
our Dardan glory. And you, most holy seer,
who know the future, grant (the power I ask
is not unsanctioned) that for Trojan gods,
errant and battered, I find a Latin home.
To Phoebus and Trivia then I'll build a shrine
of marble, and name a day 'The Feast of Phoebus.' 70

[69]Virgil tells the story of Daedalus' connection with Cumae as a graceful way of introducing the designs on the temple walls and preparing us for a meeting with the Sibyl.

[70]The cave of the Sibyl at Cumae, approximately 400 feet long, is womblike in shape, descending straight down. It was dedicated about 500 B.C.E., apparently for religious purposes.

You too shall find a temple in my realm;
there I will place your lots and arcane dooms
proclaimed to my people, and men shall be ordained,
lady, to serve you.[71] Write no more on leaves,
lest wanton winds make nonsense of your songs:
let your lips speak!" He said no further word.

Not yet possessed by Phoebus, the weird fay danced
wild in the cave, if she might shake the god
free of her heart; he harassed all the more
her lips, her savage soul, suppressing, molding.[72] 80
And now the temple's hundred mouths gaped wide
of themselves; the Sibyl's answer rode the air:
"My son, you have passed all perils of the sea,
but ashore still worse await. To Latium's land
the sons of Troy shall come (this care dismiss),
but coming shall find no joy. War, terror, war,
I see, and Tiber foaming red with blood.
You'll face a Simois, Xanthus, Greeks encamped;
in Latium now a new Achilles lives,
he, too, a goddess' son. Troy's burden, Juno, 90
will never leave you; humble, in need, you'll plead
with every Italian tribe and town for help.
Cause of disaster again a foreign bride,
a match with a woman not of Troy.[73]
Still, never retreat! Gain boldness from disaster!
Where chance allows, march on! Salvation's path
(where least you'd think) a Greek town will reveal."

In words like these the Sibyl from her shrine
sang riddles of terror and bellowed in her cave,
wrapping the truth in darkness; such the rein 100
and spur Apollo gave her maddened heart.
Soon as her lips, deranged and wild, found rest,
Aeneas began: "Lady, no face of peril
will strike me strange or rise up unforetold;
I've seized and pondered all things in advance.
One favor! Men say the infernal king has here
his gate; here hell's dark, swampy rivers rise:
allow me to see my well-loved father's face;
show me the way, spread wide the holy doors.
Through flames and thousand flying spears I saved him 110
on these shoulders, with enemies all around.
He shared the route through all those seas with me
and bore the threats of ocean and of sky,
more than the old and ill have strength to bear.

---

[71] Aeneas' promise to build the Sibyl a holy shrine alludes to the collection of Sibyline books housed in a succession of Roman temples built by several rulers.

[72] The Sibyl is seen to be completely possessed by Apollo.

[73] Virgil compares Lavinia, Aeneas' future wife, and Helen of Troy.

Still more: he used to plead that I seek out
your door in humble access. Lady, have mercy
on father and son! All power is yours; not idly
did Hecate lay Avernus to your charge:
Orpheus could hale a wife's poor ghost from hell
by power of music and his Thracian lyre, 120
and Pollux, saving his twin by altern death,
could pass and repass that road. Why tell of Theseus
or Hercules? I too am of Jove's line."[74]

So he petitioned, with hand on altar laid.
The Sibyl replied: "O child of blood divine,
Anchises' son, descent to hell is easy:
all night, all day black Pluto's door stands wide.
To recall the step, escape to air and sky—
this, this is task and toil! Some few—those loved
of Jove, those heavenward rapt by valor's flame, 130
the sons of God—have done it. Between, all's forest
wrapped round with black Cocytus' coiling streams.
But if you have at heart such love and lust
twice to cross over Styx, hell's darkness twice
to behold, and this mad project gives you joy,
hear what is first to do. A dark tree hides
a bough whose pliant withes and leaves are gold,
to hell's queen sacred. Curtained by a grove
it lies locked in a shadowy, lightless vale.
But none may pass beneath this covering earth 140
till he has plucked the tree's gold-sprouted branch.
This must be brought to Pluto's lovely queen
as offering due. (Break one, a second grows
like it, with leaves and stems of purest gold.)
Search then the treetops; when you find it, pray
and pluck. The branch will come away with ease
if you are elect of Fate. If not, no force
of yours will break it, no cold steel hack it free.
Lastly: a friend lies now a lifeless corpse
(you did not know!); his death stains all your fleet 150
while you hang at my door to ask advice.
Now bring him home and lay him in the tomb.
Over black beasts; be this your first atonement.
Then shall you see the grove of Styx, those realms
where the living never tread." She spoke no more.[75]

Aeneas, with saddened face and downcast eye,
stepped from the cave, revolving in his heart
events beyond men's sight. Beside him walked

[74] Aeneas recites the names of those who have gone to the underworld before him and returned.

[75] In order to go below and return safely, Aeneas must first grasp the Golden Bough and then find and bury his recently drowned friend, Misenus. The origin of the Golden Bough is shrouded in mystery.

Achates the loyal, step by troubled step.
They spoke of many things, conjecturing much 160
what friend had died, whose body they must bury.
But high on the beach as they came in they found
Misenus, untimely taken off by death—
Misenus, son of Aeolus, best of all
at sounding the reveille or call to arms.
He had been Hector's man; by Hector's side
he'd marched to glory with trumpet and with spear.
But once Achilles had stripped his chief of life,
he'd joined Aeneas' corps, for he was brave
and a fighter, and would obey no lesser man. 170
But now with a conch he'd blared across the waves—
the fool!—and dared the gods contest his tunes.
Triton accepted and, if the tale be true,
caught him on foaming reefs and drowned him there.
Now, circling round, the company mourned his death,
Aeneas leading. Then, with tears, they turned
to the Sibyl's orders. Quickly they built a mound
and altar, and piled on logs to reach the sky.
They went to a wood, the wild beasts' mountain lair:
down came the pine, the oak rang to the ax, 180
the beech and holm were hewn and split to rail
and billet; great elms came rolling from the hills.

In this work, too, Aeneas took the lead,
urged on his men, and shared their tools and toil.
And yet discouragement circled through his heart
as he viewed the wood—so vast! He fell to prayer:
"Now be the golden bough revealed to us,
here in this endless wood! For all was true
that the seer has prophesied of poor Misenus."
Scarce had he spoken when before his face 190
a pair of doves came flying down the sky
and settled on the turf. Aeneas knew
his mother's birds, and said a joyful prayer:
"If path there be, lead me! Direct your flight
into the woods, where on the rich soil falls
the shade of the tree of wealth. Resolve my fears,
mother in heaven!" With that, he checked his pace
to see what signs they'd give, which way they'd go.
They stopped to feed, then flew on just so far
as could be seen by those who followed them. 200
Then as they reached Avernus' stinking throat,
they rose with a swoop and sailed through brighter air
to perch on the tree they loved, a pair at home;
but—strange!—through the branches came a flash of gold!
As in the winter's cold the mistletoe
grows leafy and green (no child of its parent tree)
and with its yellow fruit loops treetrunks round,
so in the darkness of the oak shone leaves

of gold, thin foil that tinkled in the breeze.
Aeneas seized the branch; it clung; he wrenched 210
it free and brought it to the Sibyl's home.

Meanwhile down on the shore the Trojans mourned
Misenus in thankless office for the dead.
They built his pyre with pitch pine and split oak,
like one great torch, and then with dull dark leaves
they screened its sides. In front they set the cypress,
the death tree; shining armor graced the top.
Some set bronze pots of water over flame
to boil, then washed the body and embalmed it.
They wailed the dead, then laid him on the bier, 220
and covered him with the purple robe he'd known
and loved. They lifted high his heavy bed—
sad office—and in our fathers' way applied
the torch with face averted. Up went the pyre:
incense, food, and oil and wine commingled.
When cinders crumbled and the flames died down,
they quenched the dust and thirsty ash with wine.
Corynaeus gathered the bones in a brazen urn;
he bore pure water three times round his friends,
sprinkling them with hyssop of fertile olive, 230
to wash them clean, then said the last farewell.
Aeneas the good piled high a mounded tomb
(placing upon it the man's arms, oar, and trumpet)
beneath the crag that men now call, for him,
"Mount Misenus," to keep his name forever.

This done, they turned to do the Sibyl's bidding.
There was a cave, deep, huge, and gaping wide,
rocky, guarded by night-black pools and woods;
above it hardly a bird could wing its way
safely, such were the vapors that poured forth 240
from that black throat, and rose toward heaven's vault
(and hence the Greeks have named it "Birdless Cavern").
Here the Sibyl began by bringing oxen
four, black-hided. She sluiced their heads with wine;
between their horns she snipped the tips of bristles
to lay as first fruits on her altar fires,
then called on Hecate, power of heaven and hell.
Acolytes plunged their knives and caught the blood
hot in their salvers. Aeneas killed a lamb,
black-fleeced, for the mother of Furies and her sister, 250
and for the queen of hell, a barren cow.
He built night-altars to the Stygian king
and laid bull's vitals whole upon the flames,
drenching the sizzling meats with olive oil.
Just before sunrise and the dawn's first light,
the earth beneath them bawled, the wooded hills
opened, and in the shadows she-wolves howled.
"Here comes our lady! Fall back, unhallowed souls!"

the seer cried. "Out of the grove! Out! Out with you!
Aeneas, start down the road! Unsheathe your sword! 260
Now you need courage and now a steadfast heart!"
With one mad shriek she entered the cavern's mouth;
she led, he followed, step for fearless step.

O gods who rule all souls! O silent shades!
Phlegethon, Chaos, regions of voiceless night!
Grant me apocalypse! Grant me right and power
to show things buried deep in earth and darkness![76]

They walked obscure through night's dark loneliness
past Pluto's empty halls and vacant thrones:
as one might walk through wood beneath a moon 270
malign and blotched, when Jove has hidden heaven
in shadow, and black night robs the world of color.
Right at the entrance, where hell's throat begins,
Sorrow, Vengeance, and Care have pitched their tents;
there live Diseases pale, and grim Old Age,
Fear, evil-counseling Hunger, shameful Want—
shapes terrible to see—and Death and Toil,
and Death's blood brother, Sleep, and Pleasures vile
even in thought. War, dealer of death, stands watch,
and Furies chambered in steel, while mad Sedition 280
leers through her bedlam braids of snakes and blood.

Midst all, an elm spreads wide her ancient boughs,
opaque and huge; men say this is the home
of Foolish Dreams: they cling beneath each leaf.
And there are wild beasts, monsters of mixed breed;
Centaurs and two-formed Scyllas haunt the doors,
Briareus hundred-handed, savage Hydra
horribly hissing, Chimaera armed with flame,
Gorgons, Harpies, the ghost of bodies three.
In sudden terror Aeneas drew his sword 290
and showed the charging creatures his bare blade;
and had his guide, who knew, not warned that these
were lives unsubstanced, flitting empty shapes,
he had attacked and wasted blows on shadows.

Here leads the road toward hell and Acheron,
that mud-dark stream, wide, swirling, sucking down,
sinking and rising to belch Cocytus' sands.
A frightful ferryman keeps the river-watch,
Charon, a ragged horror, whose thick white beard
lies matted upon his chin. His eyes are flames, 300
and knotted rags hang filthy from his frame.
He poles his craft himself, he tends its sail,

---

[76]The Sibyl rouses Aeneas to plunge into the underworld, and Virgil in turn invokes the gods of that region to grant him the appropriate powers of description.

and in its rusty hull he freights the dead—
old, but a god's old age is raw and green.[77]
Toward him the whole crowd rushed to the river bank—
mothers and husbands, those that had lived the lives
of bold, brave fighters, boys, unmarried girls,
young men cremated before a father's face—
as many as forest leaves that flutter down
at the first autumn frost, or as the birds 310
that flock to earth from sea when winter's cold
drives them across the deep to sunny lands.
They stood there begging to be first to cross,
their hands outstretched in love of the other shore.
The glowering boatman took now these, now those,
but drove back others and blocked them from the strand.
Aeneas, amazed and by the tumult moved,
said, "Tell me, why this gathering at the river?
What do the souls want? Why do some fall back
from shore, while others cross the lead-gray stream?" 320
Briefly the aged priestess spoke to him:
"Son of Anchises, prince of blood divine,
you see dark, deep Cocytus and swampy Styx,
names not even the gods dare take in vain.
The boatman: Charon; his passengers: the entombed.
Those others are all unburied, a hapless host;
they may not pass the shore, the hoarse, wild waters,
until their bones have found a home and rest.
A hundred years they flutter round this beach;
then finally they may approach the longed-for stream." 330
The son of Anchises checked his pace and stopped,
puzzled and grieved at death's inequities.
He saw, embittered for lack of funeral rites,
Orontes, the Lycian admiral, and Leucaspis.
These two, sailing the wind-swept seas from Troy,
were lost when a Norther sank them, ship and crew.[78]

Then toward them came the helmsman, Palinurus
(plotting his course from Libya by the stars
he'd slipped from his quarterdeck far out at sea);
Aeneas scarce recognized his face, so dark 340
and bitter. He spoke: "Palinurus, what god did this?
Who stole you from us and drowned you in mid-sea?
Tell me! I've never known Apollo lie
till this one message that betrayed my trust.
He said you'd be unharmed afloat, and come
to Italy. Is this then his word, his promise?"
Palinurus answered: "Apollo told no lie,
my lord Aeneas. I was not drowned at sea.

[77]Charon the boatman is a post-Homeric creation, with additional references in Greek, Italian, and Etruscan literature and art several centuries after Virgil's time.

[78]The crowd of the unburied dead, especially those drowned at sea, recalls Palinurus, washed overboard and left behind by Aeneas and his crew.

In a sudden lurch, the helm was cast adrift,
with me fast to it, for it was in my charge. 350
Overside I carried it. By all storms I swear
that for myself I feared not half so much
as that your ship, with helm and helmsman lost
overboard, might founder in the rising seas.
Three winter nights I drifted endless miles
of wind-torn water; when the fourth dawn came
from crest of a wave I raised the Italian coast.
I floated ashore by inches, made it safe,
and was clawing my way, slowed by dripping clothes,
uphill across sharp rocks, when tribesmen killed me. 360
(They did not know me, but thought I was fair game.)
And now I lie awash in wind and surf.
And so, by the sky, the light, the air we love,
by Anchises, by all you hope for young Iulus,
rescue me from this misery. Find the bay
of Velia and—for you can!—toss earth upon me.
Or, if your goddess mother show some way
(for not without the nod of heaven, I'm sure,
you sail the boundless pools and streams of hell),
give me a hand to cross the waves with you, 370
that here at last I find my peace, and rest."
Such was his plea, and this the seer's reply:
"Palinurus, whence this blasphemous desire?
Shall you, unburied, look on Styx, the stream
of stern requital—you, pass this beach unbidden?
Think not to change the law of God by prayer.
But hear! Note well! Be solaced, injured soul!
A nearby people, frightened by signs from heaven
all up and down their land, will bury your bones,
raise you a mound, do office for the dead, 380
and name that spot 'Palinurus' for all time."
These words resolved his care; for a time he ceased
to grieve, in joy that earth should bear his name.

They resumed their journey then and neared the stream.
But when the boatman saw them from the Styx
moving through voiceless trees on toward the shore,
he started up and challenged them, and shouted:
"You with the sword, who trespass toward my river,
halt! What are you doing here? Stop where you are!
This is the vale of Shades, Dreams, Night, and Sleep. 390
By law, no flesh may ride the boat of hell.
Alcides? Theseus? Pirithous? 'Twas no joy
to me to see them come and cross my swamp—
'Son of the gods'? 'Unconquered heroes'? Hah!
That first one snapped hell's watchdog to a leash
and dragged him whimpering from the royal door;
the others tried to kidnap Pluto's bride."
To him the Amphrysian seer gave brief reply:
"Here are no schemes like those (cease your concern),

nor does that sword mean war. Your ghostly guard 400
may bark forever to frighten bloodless ghosts,
your queen keep undefiled her uncle's house.
Aeneas of Troy, the good, the great in arms,
has come to the shadowy pit to find his father.
If goodness and greatness leave you unconcerned,
this bough" (she showed it, hidden in her gown)
"you'll know." His hostile, puffed-up fury died,
and with it, debate. He stood amazed and humbled
to see the wand of fate so long unseen;
he swung his dead-blue craft stern-on to shore. 410
The other souls who sat along the thwarts
he herded out and cleared the decks, then called
Aeneas aboard. With groans at his weight, the scow
took water at every ragged, gaping seam.
Slowly it ferried them, seer and man; still whole
it dropped them in foul muck and dry, grey reeds.

At once the world burst round them with wild barking,
for Cerberus crouched there, huge beside his cave.
But when the seer observed his snake-ruff rise,
she tossed him sleeping drugs tucked in a ball 420
of crumbs and honey. He stretched three greedy throats
and wildly gulped; his weird dog's-body crumpled
and sprawled from wall to wall across his cave.
Quickly Aeneas passed the sleeping guard,
and hurried away from the waters of no return.[79]

Now they heard voices, sobs, a strange vast noise
of ghostly babies crying: just at the door
of life they'd lost their share; pulled from the breast
they'd sunk in darkness down to bitter death.
Next, those whom perjured witness sent to die. 430
(Due process, here, and justice fix their homes:
Minos is judge; he draws the lots and holds
assize of the dead, to hear defense and charge.)
Next came the gloom-filled strip of suicides.
Sinless, they'd tossed their own dear lives away
for loathing of the light. Now, just to see
the sky, they'd gladly work for beggar's bread.
The law says no; the grim and loveless stream
prisons them: Styx enfolds them nine times round.[80]

Nearby, the plains ran wide in all directions; 440
these were the Fields of Mourning—such their name.
Here dwell Love's lepers: wasted, ulcered cruel,
they slink down private paths, and hide in thickets

[79] Cerberus, the "dog of Hades" in Homer, is described here in richer detail. Like Charon, he plays an even larger part in Dante's *Divine Comedy*.

[80] So far, Aeneas has encountered three groups of the prematurely dead: babies, the wrongfully executed, and suicides.

of myrtle; even death brings them no cure.
Aeneas saw Phaedra, Procris, Eriphylë
(tearfully showing the gash her son had made),
Evadne, Pasiphaë, Laodamia too,
all in a group, and Caeneus (once a boy,
but now by fate returned to woman's shape).
There too among tall trees walked Punic Dido, 450
faltering, for her wound still bled. Soon as
the lord of Troy came near and saw her darkly,
midst shadows—as one sees the young new moon
(or thinks he saw it) rising through the clouds—
he dropped a tear and spoke with gentle love:
"Poor Dido! Then the news I heard was true,
that with a sword you'd made an end of life?
Your death—was I its cause? By heaven and gods
I swear, by every oath that hell can muster,
unwillingly, Lady, I parted from your shore. 460
The law of God—the law that sends me now
through darkness, bramble, rot, and night profound—
imperious, drove me; nor could I have dreamed
that in my leaving I would hurt you so.
Wait! Let me see you! Do not shrink from me!
Why run? Fate will not let us speak again."
He talked; she watched him, but with eyes of hate
and scorn, for all his soothing words and tears,
then looked away, her gaze fixed on the ground.
He tried to plead; her face remained unchanged 470
as if she were carved of granite or of flint.
At last she drew erect and turned unsmiling
back to the shadowed grove where her first love,
Sychaeus, gave her comfort in his arms.
Aeneas, hard-struck by unkind fate, still watched her
and pitied and wept until she disappeared.[81]

The Sibyl led him farther. Soon they reached
Plain's-End, preserve where meet the great in arms.
Here Tydeus ran up, Parthenopaeus, too,
and Adrastus (poor, pale ghost!)—famed soldiers, all; 480
here, much bewailed on earth, the sons of Troy
fallen in war. Aeneas wept to see
that long parade: Glaucus, Thersilochus, Medon
(Antenor's sons), Polyboetes, priest of Ceres,
Idaeus, armed and gripping his chariot pole.
The souls thronged round him, pressing left and right.
Nor was one look enough; they tried to stop him,
to walk with him and learn why he had come.
But the Argive chiefs, Agamemnon's fighting men,

[81]Dido is a member of the fourth group of the prematurely dead, those abandoned by love. Aeneas weeps for her, as he did not at Carthage; Dido turns away. Suitably, she rejoins her murdered husband, careless of the one opportunity she will have to speak to Aeneas again.

soon as they saw Aeneas and caught the flash 490
of arms, panicked. Some turned their backs and ran,
as once they ran to the ships; some gibbered and squeaked:
a jaw slack-fallen was all their battle cry.

Here too he saw Deiphobus, Priam's son,
his body one bloody wound, his lips hacked off—
his lips and both his hands; his ears were torn
from his head, his nose was lopped—unkindest cut.
He hardly knew him, for he cowered and tried
to hide his gashes. Aeneas addressed him gently:
"Deiphobus! Captain! Prince of Teucer's line! 500
Who felt impelled to such bloodthirsty blows?
Who thought himself so free? On that last night,
I heard, you killed Greeks till you fell exhausted
to die on your dead all helter-skelter piled.
On Cape Rhoeteum I raised your cenotaph—
I took that time—and thrice invoked your ghost.
Your name and armor mark the spot; I found
no trace of you to bury before I sailed."
Deiphobus answered: "You left no work undone;
you paid me every due the dead may ask. 510
Fate and that murdering she-devil from Sparta
gave me these wounds: these are her souvenirs.
That final night: you know how gay we were,
such fools! You must remember all too well.
Even as that deadly horse came bounding up
Troy's hill, its belly big with men-at-arms,
she led our women in the fire dance round,
'to honor God.' She held the biggest torch
and from a high point signaled to the Greeks.
I'd come home tired, worried, dead for rest, 520
to my ill-starred bedroom; there I lay in sleep
so sweet, so deep—most like the peace of death.
My noble wife now stripped my house of weapons;
from under my pillow she even slipped my sword.
She called Menelaus in, threw wide my door—
thinking this lovely gift would please her darling
and make him forget old tales and ugly talk.
In short, the two burst in (he had a friend
to abet his crime, Ulysses): God give the Greeks
as much, if I may justly ask revenge![82] 530
But you're alive! Come, tell me now: What chance
has brought you? Did you lose your course at sea?
Did God command? Tell, by what blow of fate
you've come to this grim, sunless, fogbound place?"

As they talked, Aurora with her rosy team
had passed the mid-point of her course in heaven,

---

[82]The story of the death of Deiphobus at the hands of the jealous Menelaus is post-Homeric.

and the time allowed might all have been so spent,
had not the Sibyl uttered admonition:
"Night's coming, Aeneas; we're wasting time on tears.
The road splits here and leads in two directions. 540
The right fork stretches beneath the wall of Dis
to Elysium: this is our route. Left runs the road
to Tartarus, where the vile atone their crimes."
Deiphobus then: "Don't chide me, reverend lady!
I'm going—back to my company, back to night.
Go, glory of Troy! Have better luck than I!"
With that last word he turned and walked away.

Aeneas looked quickly round. To the left, he saw
a cliff; at its base, broad battlements triple-walled.
A river of swirling flame flowed all around— 550
Phlegethon, rolling a rubble of grinding rocks.
A gate rose huge, by granite columns flanked;
no mortal power—not even gods at war—
had strength to force it. Its tower of steel stood tall,
and at its gate, Tisiphone, bloody-garbed,
kept sleepless watch eternal, night and day.
From here came forth wild screams, the savage whistle
of whips, the hiss of irons, the rattle of chains.
Aeneas stopped short. He listened and turned pale:
"What shapes of sin are here? Speak, Sibyl! What pains 560
pursue them? The noise is deafening to my ears!"
Then spoke the holy seer: "Great prince of Troy,
no guiltless man may pass the door of sin.
When Hecate laid Avernus to my charge
she showed me the place, and how God punishes.
This kingdom of torment Rhadamanthus rules;
he hears and chastens fraud; all must confess
their sins committed on earth and tucked away
for atonement (death seemed pleasantly remote).
At the word 'Guilty!' Tisiphone lifts her lash 570
and leaps to snap it; her left hand holds out snakes
poised to strike; she summons her savage sisters.
Then only the hellish gates are opened wide
on shrieking hinges. You see what kind of guard
sits at the entry? What shape patrols the door?
Inside is the Hydra's post; her fifty mouths
gape still more black and monstrous. Then the pit
opens toward darkness downward twice as far
as eye looks up toward heaven and Olympus.
Down at the bottom the ancient sons of Earth, 580
the Titans, wallow where the lightning hurled them.
I saw the sons of Aloeus, giant twins,
who attacked high heaven and tried to tear it down
barehanded, and pull Jove from his royal throne—
saw Salmoneus in torment of the damned
for mocking the flame and thunderbolt of Jove.
Driving a four-horse team and shaking a torch

he'd marched in pride through Greece and down the streets
of Elis, demanding honors due a god,
the fool: he'd made a lightning bolt of brass 590
and fashioned his horses' hooves to drum like thunder.
But the father almighty massed his clouds and whirled
his bolt—no pitch pine and no smoky flame
of torch; a fireball rode the pretender down.
Tityus, too, the child of Earth all-mother,
was there to see: his body filled a field
nine acres broad; with curving beak, a vulture
fed on his deathless liver (fertile food
for pain), probing his vitals, making his ribs
her home; his flesh, reborn, could never rest. 600
Why tell of the Lapiths, Pirithous, and Ixion,

. . .

over whom a black flint, ever about to fall,
hangs menacing. Brightly shines the wedding couch,
deep-cushioned, gilded; royal is the feast
he sees laid out. But there she lies, the worst
of the Furies, and will not let him touch the food:
she jumps to her feet, lifts up her torch, and snarls.

"They too come here who, living, loathed a brother,
drove out a father, or tricked a poor man's trust;
who, finding wealth, sat lonely brooding on it 610
with never a share for a neighbor (legion, they!);
and those for adultery killed, and those who raised
rebellion, heedless of oath and service due;
here they are jailed and wait their dooms. Don't ask
what doom, what shape, what lot entraps them there.
Some roll great boulders; some, spread-eagled, hang
on whirling wheels. One sits, forever sits:
Theseus the luckless; one—poor, wretched Phlegyas—
repeats in the gloom his warning to all men:
'Hear this: learn justice; never scorn the gods!' 620
Here is the man who for a tyrant's gold
enslaved his country; here, the peddler of laws;
here, one who raped his child and called it marriage:
all monsters of insolence, monsters in success.
Had I a hundred tongues, a hundred mouths,
and chords of steel, I could not tell the forms
of all their crimes, nor list the penalties."

When Phoebus' aged seer had thus concluded,
"Come now," she said. "Move on! Complete your task!
Let's hurry! I see the walls forged on the hearths 630
of the Cyclops. There's the arch and there the gate,
where we must place our gift, as we were ordered."
Then, walking together over a lightless road,
they covered the mid-space and approached the door.

Aeneas stood close and with fresh water sprinkled
his body, then set the bough against the door.

Thus with their liturgy to the goddess ended,
they came to the place of joy, the pleasant lawns,
the groves of the lucky, and the blessed homes.[83]
These lands are clothed in larger air and light 640
the color of life; they see their sun, their stars.
Here, figures were training on the grassy grounds,
some playing games, some wrestling in the ring,
and some were treading the dance and singing songs.
There stood, in his poet's gown, the priest of Thrace,
playing his instrument of seven strings
(he plucked with fingers now, and now with plectrum).
Here, Teucer's ancient line, his splendid sons,
greathearted heroes, born in happier days:
Ilus, Assaracus, Dardanus, founder of Troy. 650
Aeneas was startled: there lay cars and arms
at rest, spears stacked, and horses running free
grazing the field. The joy the living knew
in arms and car, their love of grooming horses
to sleekness, followed them beyond the grave.
Aeneas saw others about him on the grass,
feasting and singing cheerful songs of praise.
Above them hung sweet bays, and from a hill
Eridanus tumbled his waters through the grove.

Here were the band who for their country bled, 660
here priests who in the world led saintly lives,
prophets of truth, who spoke as God would speak,
those whose discoveries made a better world,
those who by doing good earned men's remembrance.
Each one wore snow-white bands about his head.
The Sibyl addressed them as they gathered round,
Musaeus first (the crowd surrounded him
and watched him towering shoulder-high above them):
"Tell us, O blessed souls, tell, best of bards,
where we may find Anchises? To see him 670
we came and crossed the floods of Erebus."
Then from the great man came this brief reply:
"None has a place assigned. We live in groves;
our beds are the riverbanks and fields made fresh
by springs. But if you wish so much to find him,
climb up this hill; I'll set you on your way."
He walked ahead, and from the hilltop showed them
the garden land. They left the summit then.

[83] They reach Elysium, bathed in light, the place of eternal play and happiness. The "priest of Thrace" is Orpheus. Elysium is also the home of Anchises.

Deep in a grassy valley stood the souls
mustered for life on earth. With eye alert 680
Anchises surveyed them, checking off the roll
of all his cherished line: his sons, their sons,
their luck, their destinies, their works and ways.
But when, across the fields, he saw Aeneas
coming, he stretched out both his hands for joy;
tears washed his cheeks; words tumbled from his lips:
"You've come at last! Your father waited long
for love to conquer hardship! Oh, my son!
Do I see your face? And may we talk once more?
I knew it would happen! In my heart I knew! 690
I reckoned the hours with care and told them right.
Over what lands, what endless seas you traveled,
harried by countless dangers, and now you've come!
In Libya, disaster was close: I feared for you."
Aeneas replied: "Father, your tear-stained face,
so often in my mind, compelled me here.
Our fleet is in Tuscan waters! Give me your hand,
let me embrace you, father: don't slip away!"
So speaking, he let the tears course down his face.
Three times he tried to fold him in his arms; 700
three times an empty shade escaped his grasp,
light as the air, most like the wings of sleep.[84]

Just then, far down a slope, Aeneas saw
a grove apart, with foliage thick and rustling:
this was the haven of peace, where Lethe flowed:
about it flitted the nations of mankind
like bees in a meadow on a summer's day
(they stop at bright-hued blooms and cluster close
around white lilies; their humming fills the field).
At the sight Aeneas was puzzled and stopped short: 710
"What did this mean? What river," he asked, "was that?
Who were those people that swarmed about its banks?"
Then Lord Anchises: "Those are souls whose fate
binds them to flesh once more. At Lethe's wave
they drink and forget past years of care and fear.
I've longed to show them to you and tell their names—
the line of my children, the number of my heirs—
that you may rejoice with me for Italy found."
"What, father? Must I think men's souls rise up
from here to the air, and to the sluggish flesh 720
return? Poor fools! Whence this mad lust for life?"
"I'll speak at once, dear son, and ease your mind,"
Anchises answered, and told the order of things.

"To begin: the heavens, the earth, the watery wastes,
the lucent globe of moon, the sun, the stars,

[84]These lines repeat the scene in Book 2 where Aeneas tries to embrace the shade of Creusa, his wife.

exist through inward spirit. Their total mass
by mind is permeated: hence their motion.
From mind and spirit comes life—of man, of beast,
of bird, of monsters under the foam-flecked seas.
Life is from heaven—a seed of fire that glows 730
bright, so far as flesh cannot repress it,
or earthly, death-bound bodies dull its glow.
From flesh come fear, desire, pain, and joy:
its pitch-dark prison blinds us to the light.
And even on that last day when life departs,
not all our evil, all the body's foul
corruption leaves us: deep ingrained, in ways
past comprehension, much has hardened fast.
Our souls, then, suffer pain, and pay the price
for wrongs done years before: some, like a cloak 740
laid off, hang to the winds; some lose their stains
by flood and swirl, or cautery of fire.
We suffer, each, our ghostly selves, then pass—
some few—to gain Elysium's fields of joy.
The years go by; Time makes his cycle just,
our hardened filth is sloughed; intelligence
pure, as of heaven, is left, and breath, and fire.
After a thousand circling years, God calls
these souls to Lethe in a long parade
to gain forgetfulness, then view the sky 750
once more, and wish to put on flesh again."

Anchises spoke no more, and led his son
and the Sibyl, too, deep into the rustling throng,
then up on a mound where they could see the files
approaching and watch the faces as they passed.

"Now you shall see the glory that awaits
the children of Troy and their Italian sons—
all souls of splendor, who shall bear our name.
Hear their story, and learn your destiny.
That young man—see him, leaning on his staff?— 760
by lot will be the first to rise to light
and air with blood of Italy in his veins.
His name is Alban, 'Silvius,' your last child,
born in your old age to your wife, Lavinia,
bred in the forest, king and sire of kings;
through him our line shall rule in Alba Longa.
Next him is Procas, pride of the race of Troy,
and Capys and Numitor and—named after you—
Aeneas Silvius, famed alike for valor
and goodness—if ever he gain the Alban throne. 770
What fine young men! Look at the strength they show!
See how they wear the oak-leaf civil crown!
They'll found Fidenae, Gabii, Nomentum,
and build Collatia's castle on the hills,

Bola, Cora, Pometii, and Castrum.
(Great names they'll be; now they are land unnamed.)

"There's Romulus, son of Mars; with Numitor
he'll take his stand (through Ilia, his mother,
he's of our blood): see, on his head, twin plumes,
sign of a father's favor, mark divine. 780
With him Rome will begin her march to glory,
to world-wide rule, to spirit that rivals heaven.
She'll throw one wall around her seven hills;
she shall be rich in sons, like that great mother
who, mural-crowned, rides through the Eastern world,
god-bearer triumphant; a hundred sons of sons,
all gods, a heavenly host, are in her arms.
But look, now! Look! Here comes your family,
your Roman children: Caesar and all the sons
of Iulus who'll come beneath the vault of heaven. 790
Here is the man you've heard so often promised:
Augustus, son of godhead. He'll rebuild
a golden age in Latium, land where once
Saturn was king. Past India, past the Moor
he'll spread his rule to zones beyond the stars,
beyond the ecliptic, where Atlas carries heaven,
and bears on his back the spinning, star-tricked wheel.
Against Augustus' advent, even now
God's oracles have panicked Eastern steppes
and roiled the outlets of the seven-twinned Nile. 800
Not even Hercules crossed so much land
to shoot the bronze-hoofed hind, or bring back peace
to Erymanthan groves, or frighten Lerna;
nor Bacchus, when he drove his tiger team,
with vines for reins, in glory down from Nysa.
(And still we hesitate to fight and win,
or fear to make our stand in Italy?)

"But who is that? He wears the olive crown
and carries hallows. White hair and beard—I know him:
that king whose code gave Rome a base of law. 810
He'll come from little Cures, poor-man's land,
but rise to royal heights. Succeeding him,
Tullus will shatter our peace and lead to war
a people soft, unused to battle line
and glory. Ancus next—a boastful man,
too much enamored of the people's whims.
And there the Tarquins—see?—and their avenger,
Brutus the proud, who'll give us back our power.
He first will rule as consul, first will take
the axes; when his sons rise in revolt, 820
in liberty's name he'll see them put to death
(unhappy father, however the tale be told!)
bested by love of country and lust for praise.

"See—back there!—Decius, Drusus, and Torquatus
the savage headsman, Camillus with his standards,
and, just this way, two souls in armor bright,
full of good will while night entombs them here;
but oh, if they see the light, what wars, what strife
they'll set afoot, what battle lines and death:
from Gaul and the Alps the father-in-law will march 830
against the son with Eastern legions massed.
(Children, never grow hardened to wars like those;
against your homeland raise no hostile hand!
Oh, take the lead, show mercy, child of heaven,
throw down that sword, son of my blood!)

"That man will slaughter Greeks and conquer Corinth,
then ride in triumph up high Capitol Hill;
this one will pull Agamemnon's Argos down,
and a king who boasts the blood of brave Achilles—
vengeance for Troy and Pallas' fane defiled! 840
Who'd pass by Cato or Cossus without a word?
Who the Gracchi, or those twin thunderbolts,
the Scipios, bane of Libya? Who Fabricius,
whose need spelled might, or Regulus, sower of seed?
The Fabii rush me, yet he'll be their greatest
'who lone by laggard tactics saves our state.'
Others will forge the bronze to softer breath,
no doubt, and bring the sculptured stone to life,
show greater eloquence, and with their rule
map out the skies and tell the rising stars: 850
you, Roman, remember: Govern! Rule the world!
These are your arts! Make peace man's way of life;
spare the humble but strike the braggart down."
So Lord Anchises; then to their wonder, added:
"See, there: Marcellus, splendid in the spoils
of war, in victory tall above his troops.
In the great conflict, he'll set Rome aright
once more, bring down rebellious Gaul and Carthage,
and a third time offer captured arms to Mars."

Beside him, Aeneas saw, there walked a man 860
handsome and young, with armor shining bright,
but brow not joyful, face and eyes downcast.
"Who, father, walks there at Marcellus' side?
His son? Some other of his glorious line?
See how his friends press close! There's greatness there,
yet shadows black as night hang round his head."[85]

Anchises answered as tears rose in his eyes:
"Seek not to know your people's vastest grief!

[85]From among the throng of Trojans destined to live again as Romans, the final figure is Marcellus, son-in-law of Octavian (Augustus Caesar), Virgil's patron and friend.

The world will see him—only that, for Fate
will grant no more. The gods had deemed 870
our power too great, if we had kept this gift.
Mars' people, in his field, beside his city—
how they will grieve! What mourners you will see,
Tiber, as you glide past that new-raised mound!
No child of Trojan blood will raise such hopes
among his Latin sires, nor rouse such pride
of offspring in the land of Romulus.
Ah, loyalty, ancient honor, hand unbeaten
in battle! If he'd gone out to fight, no man
had dared to face him, whether he went on foot 880
or spurred a foaming horse against the foe.
Poor boy! If you should break the bars of fate,
you'll be Marcellus. Bring lilies! Fill my hands!
I'll scatter scarlet blooms: so much, at least,
I'll give a grandson's ghost, and do my office,
though vain."[86] Thus over all that place they walked,
through broad and airy fields, and saw the sights.
After Anchises had shown his son each thing
and fired his heart with love of fame to come,
then he recounted wars that must be waged, 890
told of the Rutuli, of Latium's city,
and how he'd bear, or how escape, each blow.

Twin are the gates of sleep; men say that one
is of horn, a ready exit for real shades;
the other is white, of flawless ivory:
this way the dead send false dreams to the world.
Anchises' tale was told. Taking his son
and the Sibyl, he sent them through the ivory gate.[87]
Aeneas made for the ships and joined his friends.
Then straight upshore he sailed to Port Caieta. 900
Out went the anchors; the fleet lay stern to shore.

OVID

[43 B.C.E.–18 C.E.]

Publius Ovidius Naso, better known as Ovid, was the last of a new wave of poets who challenged the assumptions of previous writers such as Cicero and Lucretius whose works focused primarily upon serious matters of the state and religion. Like Catullus, the greatest lyric poet of the earlier generation, Ovid turned to love and private feeling for his subject matter. Most important, however, Ovid was a great storyteller. When he decided to

[86] Anchises' lament for Marcellus is an example of the classical "literature of grief."

[87] The usual explanation for Anchises' sending Aeneas and the Sibyl through the Gate of Ivory is that, not being ghosts, they cannot leave an underworld they have never entered. A more conjectural reading is that Aeneas has witnessed a view of the future that is to some extent a fiction—Virgil's wish or his duty to tell—and not reality.

retell the major Greek and Roman myths about transformation and love, he produced one of the most influential and readable works of all Latin literature, the *Metamorphoses.* This encyclopedic collection of tales, loosely organized around the motif of changing form, has served readers from his time down to our own as a sourcebook for stories about figures such as Apollo and Daphne, Echo and Narcissus, Orpheus and Eurydice, Midas, and even the heroes of the Trojan War. Despite the scandal attached to his name and his cavalier attitude toward the "serious" poets of the earlier age, Ovid brilliantly managed to satisfy what Horace claimed to be the highest purpose of poetry: to please and to instruct.

To understand Ovid's place in literature it is useful to review the historical situation from which his work emerged. Social disorder and rivalry between the two highest ranking officers of Rome, Pompey and Julius Caesar, led Rome to a civil war that lasted from 49 B.C.E. to 45 B.C.E. Caesar's brilliant outmaneuvering of his opponents placed him in a position of absolute power as Consul of Rome, which he turned into a dictatorship. Despite his introduction of certain political and cultural reforms, including the use of the solar calendar that we still use today and that was devised with the assistance of Egyptian astronomers, a group of conspirators, including Marcus Junius Brutus and Gaius Cassius, cut short Caesar's reign. Caesar was succeeded by his nineteen-year-old grandnephew Gaius Octavius, who joined forces in 43 B.C.E. with Marc Antony and Marcus Lepidus to form what is called the Second Triumvirate.

By 36 B.C.E. Octavian and Antony stood alone as leaders of Rome, but they could not suppress their rivalry. The two leaders divided Rome into two parts, with Octavian presiding over Italy and the West and Antony over the East, which at that time included Egypt under Cleopatra. The events that followed have become a part of Western legend. Although Antony married Octavian's sister Octavia in order to settle the conflict between the two leaders, he left her for Cleopatra, renewing the antagonism between him and Octavian. War broke out, and in 30 B.C.E. when Octavian defeated the Egyptian forces, Antony and Cleopatra committed suicide.

Octavian's victory finally ended the bitter fighting that had divided Rome for most of the century, and it ushered in the *Pax Romana* that brought peace to the Mediterranean—at least for a while. To honor Octavian, the Roman senate conferred upon him the title Augustus, the name posterity has given the era of his reign; as *princeps* or "chief citizen," Augustus ruled with almost absolute authority. The Augustan Age brought political and social stability to Rome, whose citizens had been worn down by the ongoing civil strife. Moreover, Augustus, in the interests of civil order, attempted to regulate strictly the morality of the citizens, the wealthier of whom had earned a reputation for extravagance, luxury, and vice. Even his own daughter, Julia, was not safe from exile for adultery, and given the voyeuristic celebration of love in Ovid's *Amores, Ars Amatoria,* and other poems, it is perhaps no surprise that Ovid himself was banished from Rome in 9 C.E.

Although Augustus enjoyed little success in controlling the moral behavior of Roman citizens, he did manage to improve and protect trade, increase the standard of living even for the working class, and gradually secure control of the entire Iberian Peninsula. Most importantly for our purposes, Augustus, with the help of his minister Gaius Maecenas, patronized the arts to create what some call the golden age of Latin literature. This was the age of the epic poet Virgil, the great satirist Horace, the historian Livy, and the renegade love poet Ovid.

LIFE

One year after Caesar's assassination on the celebrated Ides of March in 44 B.C.E., Publius Ovidius Naso, more commonly known as Ovid, was born in Sulmo, a town just east of Rome. Ovid was born into a family of distinction and nobility, a fact he often flaunts in his love poetry. His father prepared him for a life of public service, although Ovid was drawn early on toward writing poetry. Pursuing his studies in rhetoric and grammar, Ovid tells us that his writing always turned out in verse, so even though he tried his hand at minor government posts and became a member of the "Court of the Hundred" where he helped to oversee civil and criminal cases, he gave up civil service at twenty-four so he could follow his Muse—or perhaps one should say his Muses. Living on the small but respectable family fortune, Ovid went through two very brief and very disastrous marriages before finally finding the right match on his third attempt. He lived in Rome and was part of the literary circle that included writers of elegiac love poetry, including Gallus, Tibullus, and Propertius, whom he describes as his models and sometime companions. Virgil and Horace, who were older than Ovid, were also in Rome at this time, but his relationship to them—other than that he respected their work even as he departed from their style—is not entirely clear. All of these poets were trying to find a more authentically Roman voice and gradually to release themselves from the hold that Greek models exercised on the earlier generation of Latin poets. Gallus, Tibullus, and Propertius, in particular, were realizing the potential of the erotic love elegy they had inherited from Catullus, but Ovid, above them all, caught the attention of his contemporaries by making the form a vehicle for ever more personal and playfully wanton purposes than those of his peers and predecessors.

WORK

His first work, *Amores* (*Loves*), published in 13 B.C.E., rather boldly declares its affiliation to Cupid and rejects the epic hexameter verse for elegiac couplets, for which he jokes "Arms and violent wars, all in hexameters, / I was preparing to sound, when I heard a snicker from Cupid; / What had the rascal done, but taken one foot away" (I: 2–4). Unlike Catullus or Propertius, Ovid portrays himself as a sort of armed participant in the game of love, a voyeur who muses upon the trials of the spurned suitor, rather than the hapless victim of unrequited love. Riding on the popularity of his first book, Ovid took this cavalier attitude even farther in the *Ars Amatoria* or *Art of Love* and its sequel, *Remedia Amores* (*The Cure for Love*). The former is a kind of instruction book for lovers, written in two books as a how-to manual for men, with a third book for women added later; the latter follows logically from the first, for it recommends strategies for the love-bitten to get out of love. Given the aims of Augustus to rectify the lax morals of Rome, it's not too surprising, perhaps, that he would cast a cold eye on Ovid's light treatment of love and the questionable behavior that these books recommended. Another work of this period, the *Heroides,* differs from the others in that it takes the form of epistles from mythological heroines to their lost or parted lovers—Ariadne to Theseus, Medea to Jason, and Dido to Aeneas, for example. Here Ovid showed that he was capable of greater seriousness than the earlier works suggested.

Despite the success of these works, we tend to appreciate Ovid today for his *Metamorphoses,* a work that combines the interest in love and lovers with a more serious purpose of exploring the idea of mutability or change. As he tells us, "My intention is to tell of bodies changed / To different forms" (I: 1–2). Moreover, the *Metamorphoses* marks a novel treatment of myth, for Ovid's interest in the gods and goddesses, nymphs, satyrs, and naiads that frolic through his great work is clearly literary. Ovid takes great pleasure in embellishing a story when it suits his purpose, elaborating and fabricating when necessary to produce lively and entertaining tales out of the stock mythological material he inherited from tradition.

In the *Metamorphoses,* Ovid writes in hexameter verse, the verse Latin and Greek writers use for epic poetry, and indeed his poem is of epic proportions, containing fifteen books in all, which tell nearly 250 stories. In addition, he uses many epic devices such as catalogues, digressions, and epic similes, although the poem lacks the central hero and the unifying plot of epics such as *The Odyssey* and *The Aeneid*. Instead we have a series of short tales drawn from mythology and from a mythologized version of history, beginning with the story of creation and ending with the apotheosis of Caesar. Thus, like Virgil, Ovid paid poetic tribute to the glory of Rome. Another work, the unfinished *Fasti* (*Feast Days*), celebrates the important feast days of the Roman calendar. Despite the quantity of material it contains, however, the *Metamorphoses* remains more than just an encyclopedia of related tales, for Ovid attempts to link them by providing sometimes gratuitous connections between the stories. Rolfe Humphries's excellent verse translation of the stories, brilliantly written in a vibrant, witty, and economical style, generates a vital poetic momentum that carries the reader forward.

The *Fasti* remained unfinished, perhaps because it was interrupted by Ovid's exile to Tomi, on the Black Sea, where he spent the last ten years of his life. Augustus had more than Ovid's poetry in mind when he banished the poet, for Ovid was involved directly or indirectly with the scandal surrounding Augustus' daughter Julia's adultery. Once at Tomi, Ovid wrote mostly epistolary verse intended to defend himself and to win favor so that he could return to Rome. The *Tristia* and the *Epistulae ex Ponto,* works of this period, give a biographical account of Ovid's life and claim that he had not lived the life outlined in his youthful writings. Nonetheless, his suit did not succeed, and Ovid died in 18 C.E., away from his beloved Rome and from his family.

SUGGESTED READINGS

Ovid's life and the historical background to his work are detailed in H. Fraenkel's *Ovid: A Poet Between Two Worlds* (1945) and L. P. Wilkinson's *Ovid Surveyed* (1962). For a general introduction to his work, see Sara Mack's *Ovid* (1988) and the section on Ovid in E. J. Kenney's *The Cambridge History of Classical Literature,* vol. 2 (1982). Works that focus primarily upon the *Metamorphoses* include Brooks Otis's *Ovid as an Epic Poet* (1966, 1970), Charles P. Segal's *Landscape in Ovid's Metamorphoses* (1969), and G. K. Galinsky's *Ovid's Metamorphoses: An Introduction to the Basic Aspects* (1974).

Metamorphoses

Translated by Rolfe Humphries

BOOK 1

My intention is to tell of bodies changed
To different forms; the gods, who made the changes,
Will help me—or I hope so—with a poem
That runs from the world's beginning to our own days.[1]

The Creation

Before the ocean was, or earth, or heaven,
Nature was all alike, a shapelessness,
Chaos, so-called, all rude and lumpy matter,

[1] In Book 15, Julius Caesar, assassinated in 44 B.C.E., is transformed into a star.

Nothing but bulk, inert, in whose confusion
Discordant atoms warred: there was no sun
To light the universe; there was no moon 10
With slender silver crescents filling slowly;
No earth hung balanced in surrounding air;
No sea reached far along the fringe of shore.
Land, to be sure, there was, and air, and ocean,
But land on which no man could stand, and water
No man could swim in, air no man could breathe,
Air without light, substance forever changing,
Forever at war: within a single body
Heat fought with cold, wet fought with dry, the hard
Fought with the soft, things having weight contended 20
With weightless things.
Till God, or kindlier Nature,
Settled all argument, and separated
Heaven from earth, water from land, our air
From the high stratosphere, a liberation
So things evolved, and out of blind confusion
Found each its place, bound in eternal order.
The force of fire, that weightless element,
Leaped up and claimed the highest place in heaven;
Below it, air; and under them the earth
Sank with its grosser portions; and the water, 30
Lowest of all, held up, held in, the land.

Whatever god it was, who out of chaos
Brought order to the universe, and gave it
Division, subdivision, he molded earth,
In the beginning, into a great globe,
Even on every side, and bade the waters
To spread and rise, under the rushing winds,
Surrounding earth; he added ponds and marshes,
He banked the river-channels, and the waters
Feed earth or run to sea, and that great flood 40
Washes on shores, not banks. He made the plains
Spread wide, the valleys settle, and the forest
Be dressed in leaves; he made the rocky mountains
Rise to full height, and as the vault of Heaven
Has two zones, left and right, and one between them
Hotter than these, the Lord of all Creation
Marked on the earth the same design and pattern.
The torrid zone too hot for men to live in,
The north and south too cold, but in the middle
Varying climate, temperature and season. 50
Above all things the air, lighter than earth,
Lighter than water, heavier than fire,
Towers and spreads; there mist and cloud assemble,
And fearful thunder and lightning and cold winds,
But these, by the Creator's order, held
No general dominion; even as it is,
These brothers brawl and quarrel; though each one

Has his own quarter, still, they come near tearing
The universe apart. Eurus is monarch
Of the lands of dawn, the realms of Araby, 60
The Persian ridges under the rays of morning.
Zephyrus holds the west that glows at sunset,
Boreas, who makes men shiver, holds the north,
Warm Auster governs in the misty southland,
And over them all presides the weightless ether,
Pure without taint of earth.
These boundaries given,
Behold, the stars, long hidden under darkness,
Broke through and shone, all over the spangled heaven,
Their home forever, and the gods lived there,
And shining fish were given the waves for dwelling 70
And beasts the earth, and birds the moving air.

But something else was needed, a finer being,
More capable of mind, a sage, a ruler,
So Man was born, it may be, in God's image,
Or Earth, perhaps, so newly separated
From the old fire of Heaven, still retained
Some seed of the celestial force which fashioned
Gods out of living clay and running water.
All other animals look downward; Man,
Alone, erect, can raise his face toward Heaven. 80

The Four Ages

The Golden Age was first, a time that cherished
Of its own will, justice and right; no law.
No punishment, was called for; fearfulness
Was quite unknown, and the bronze tablets held
No legal threatening; no suppliant throng
Studied a judge's face; there were no judges,
There did not need to be. Trees had not yet
Been cut and hollowed, to visit other shores.
Men were content at home, and had no towns
With moats and walls around them; and no trumpets 90
Blared out alarums; things like swords and helmets
Had not been heard of. No one needed soldiers.
People were unaggressive, and unanxious;
The years went by in peace. And Earth, untroubled,
Unharried by hoe or plowshare, brought forth all
That men had need for, and those men were happy,
Gathering berries from the mountain sides,
Cherries, or blackcaps, and the edible acorns.
Spring was forever, with a west wind blowing
Softly across the flowers no man had planted, 100
And Earth, unplowed, brought forth rich grain; the field,
Unfallowed, whitened with wheat, and there were rivers
Of milk, and rivers of honey, and golden nectar
Dripped from the dark-green oak-trees.

After Saturn[2]
Was driven to the shadowy land of death,
And the world was under Jove, the Age of Silver
Came in, lower than gold, better than bronze.
Jove made the springtime shorter, added winter,
Summer, and autumn, the seasons as we know them.
That was the first time when the burnt air glowed 110
White-hot, or icicles hung down in winter.
And men built houses for themselves; the caverns,
The woodland thickets, and the bark-bound shelters
No longer served; and the seeds of grain were planted
In the long furrows, and the oxen struggled
Groaning and laboring under the heavy yoke.

Then came the Age of Bronze, and dispositions
Took on aggressive instincts, quick to arm,
Yet not entirely evil. And last of all
The Iron Age succeeded, whose base vein 120
Let loose all evil: modesty and truth
And righteousness fled earth, and in their place
Came trickery and slyness, plotting, swindling,
Violence and the damned desire of having.
Men spread their sails to winds unknown to sailors,
The pines came down their mountain-sides, to revel
And leap in the deep waters, and the ground,
Free, once, to everyone, like air and sunshine,
Was stepped off by surveyors. The rich earth,
Good giver of all the bounty of the harvest, 130
Was asked for more; they dug into her vitals,
Pried out the wealth a kinder lord had hidden
In Stygian[3] shadow, all that precious metal,
The root of evil. They found the guilt of iron,
And gold, more guilty still. And War came forth
That uses both to fight with; bloody hands
Brandished the clashing weapons. Men lived on plunder.
Guest was not safe from host, nor brother from brother,
A man would kill his wife, a wife her husband,
Stepmothers, dire and dreadful, stirred their brews 140
With poisonous aconite, and sons would hustle
Fathers to death, and Piety lay vanquished,
And the maiden Justice, last of all immortals,
Fled from the bloody earth.
Heaven was no safer.
Giants attacked the very throne of Heaven,
Piled Pelion on Ossa,[4] mountain on mountain
Up to the very stars. Jove struck them down
With thunderbolts, and the bulk of those huge bodies

---

[2]An ancient Roman fertility god, ruler of the Golden Age, and father of Jove, who overthrew him.
[3]In the underworld, associated with the Styx, the river that marks the threshold to Hades.
[4]Mountains in Thessaly, in central Greece.

Lay on the earth, and bled, and Mother Earth,
Made pregnant by that blood, brought forth new bodies, 150
And gave them, to recall her older offspring,
The forms of men. And this new stock was also
Contemptuous of gods, and murder-hungry
And violent. You would know they were sons of blood.

Jove's Intervention

And Jove was witness from his lofty throne
Of all this evil, and groaned as he remembered
The wicked revels of Lycaon's[5] table,
The latest guilt, a story still unknown
To the high gods. In awful indignation
He summoned them to council. No one dawdled. 160
Easily seen when the night skies are clear,
The Milky Way shines white. Along this road
The gods move toward the palace of the Thunderer,
His royal halls, and, right and left, the dwellings
Of other gods are open, and guests come thronging.
The lesser gods live in a meaner section,
An area not reserved, as this one is,
For the illustrious Great Wheels of Heaven.
(Their Palatine Hill,[6] if I might call it so.)

They took their places in the marble chamber 170
Where high above them all their king was seated,
Holding his ivory sceptre, shaking out
Thrice, and again, his awful locks, the sign
That made the earth and stars and ocean tremble,
And then he spoke, in outrage: "I was troubled
Less for the sovereignty of all the world
In that old time when the snake-footed giants
Laid each his hundred hands on captive Heaven.
Monstrous they were, and hostile, but their warfare
Sprung from one source, one body. Now, wherever 180
The sea-gods roar around the earth, a race
Must be destroyed, the race of men. I swear it!
I swear by all the Stygian rivers gliding
Under the world, I have tried all other measures.
The knife must cut the cancer out, infection
Averted while it can be, from our numbers.
Those demigods, those rustic presences,
Nymphs, fauns, and satyrs, wood and mountain dwellers,
We have not yet honored with a place in Heaven,
But they should have some decent place to dwell in, 190
In peace and safety. Safety? Do you reckon
They will be safe, when I, who wield the thunder,
Who rule you all as subjects, am subjected
To the plottings of the barbarous Lycaon?"

---

[5]A king of Arcadia, the primitive and mountainous region of the Peloponnese.
[6]The hill in Rome where Caesar Augustus lived.

They burned, they trembled. Who was this Lycaon,
Guilty of such rank infamy? They shuddered
In horror, with a fear of sudden ruin,
As the whole world did later, when assassins
Struck Julius Caesar down, and Prince Augustus
Found satisfaction in the great devotion 200
That cried for vengeance, even as Jove took pleasure,
Then, in the gods' response. By word and gesture
He calmed them down, awed them again to silence,
And spoke once more:

The Story of Lycaon

"He has indeed been punished.
On that score have no worry. But what he did,
And how he paid, are things that I must tell you.
I had heard the age was desperately wicked,
I had heard, or so I hoped, a lie, a falsehood,
So I came down, as man, from high Olympus,
Wandered about the world. It would take too long 210
To tell you how widespread was all that evil.
All I had heard was grievous understatement!
I had crossed Maenala, a country bristling
With dens of animals, and crossed Cyllene,
And cold Lycaeus'[7] pine woods. Then I came
At evening, with the shadows growing longer,
To an Arcadian palace, where the tyrant
Was anything but royal in his welcome.
I gave a sign that a god had come, and people
Began to worship, and Lycaon mocked them, 220
Laughed at their prayers, and said: 'Watch me find out
Whether this fellow is a god or mortal,
I can tell quickly, and no doubt about it.'
He planned, that night, to kill me while I slumbered;
That was his way to test the truth. Moreover,
And not content with that, he took a hostage,
One sent by the Molossians,[8] cut his throat,
Boiled pieces of his flesh, still warm with life,
Broiled others, and set them before me on the table.
That was enough. I struck, and the bolt of lightning 230
Blasted the household of that guilty monarch.
He fled in terror, reached the silent fields,
And howled, and tried to speak. No use at all!
Foam dripped from his mouth; bloodthirsty still, he turned
Against the sheep, delighting still in slaughter,
And his arms were legs, and his robes were shaggy hair,
Yet he is still Lycaon, the same grayness,
The same fierce face, the same red eyes, a picture
Of bestial savagery. One house has fallen,

---

[7] Maenala, Cyllene, and Lycaeus are mountains in Arcadia.
[8] A tribe from Epeirus, along the Adriatic coast of Greece, noted for its barbarism.

But more than one deserves to. Fury reigns 240
Over all the fields of Earth. They are sworn to evil,
Believe it. Let them pay for it, and quickly!
So stands my purpose."
Part of them approved
With words and added fuel to his anger,
And part approved with silence, and yet all
Were grieving at the loss of humankind,
Were asking what the world would be, bereft
Of mortals: who would bring their altars incense?
Would earth be given the beasts, to spoil and ravage?
Jove told them not to worry; he would give them 250
Another race, unlike the first, created
Out of a miracle; he would see to it.

He was about to hurl his thunderbolts
At the whole world, but halted, fearing Heaven
Would burn from fire so vast, and pole to pole
Break out in flame and smoke, and he remembered
The fates had said that some day land and ocean,
The vault of Heaven, the whole world's mighty fortress,
Besieged by fire, would perish. He put aside
The bolts made in Cyclopean[9] workshops; better, 260
He thought, to drown the world by flooding water.

The Flood

So, in the cave of Aeolus,[10] he prisoned
The North-wind, and the West-wind, and such others
As ever banish cloud, and he turned loose
The South-wind, and the South-wind came out streaming
With dripping wings, and pitch-black darkness veiling
His terrible countenance. His beard is heavy
With rain-cloud, and his hoary locks a torrent,
Mists are his chaplet, and his wings and garments
Run with the rain. His broad hands squeeze together 270
Low-hanging clouds, and crash and rumble follow
Before the cloudburst, and the rainbow, Iris,
Draws water from the teeming earth, and feeds it
Into the clouds again. The crops are ruined,
The farmers' prayers all wasted, all the labor
Of a long year, comes to nothing.
And Jove's anger,
Unbounded by his own domain, was given
Help by his dark-blue brother. Neptune[11] called
His rivers all, and told them, very briefly,
To loose their violence, open their houses, 280

[9] One-eyed giants who worked under Vulcan, the artisan god of fire, as metalworkers.

[10] King of Aeolia, an island northeast of Sicily, in charge of governing the winds; he eventually came to be identified as the god of the winds.

[11] God of the sea, recognized typically by his trident, a three-pronged spear.

Pour over embankments, let the river horses
Run wild as ever they would. And they obeyed him.
His trident struck the shuddering earth; it opened
Way for the rush of waters. The leaping rivers
Flood over the great plains. Not only orchards
Are swept away, not only grain and cattle,
Not only men and houses, but altars, temples,
And shrines with holy fires. If any building
Stands firm, the waves keep rising over its roof-top,
Its towers are under water, and land and ocean 290
Are all alike, and everything is ocean,
An ocean with no shore-line.
Some poor fellow
Seizes a hill-top; another, in a dinghy,
Rows where he used to plough, and one goes sailing
Over his fields of grain or over the chimney
Of what was once his cottage. Someone catches
Fish in the top of an elm-tree, or an anchor
Drags in green meadow-land, or the curved keel brushes
Grape-arbors under water. Ugly sea-cows
Float where the slender she-goats used to nibble 300
The tender grass, and the Nereids[12] come swimming
With curious wonder, looking, under water,
At houses, cities, parks, and groves. The dolphins
Invade the woods and brush against the oak-trees;
The wolf swims with the lamb; lion and tiger
Are borne along together; the wild boar
Finds all his strength is useless, and the deer
Cannot outspeed that torrent; wandering birds
Look long, in vain, for landing-place, and tumble,
Exhausted, into the sea. The deep's great license 310
Has buried all the hills, and new waves thunder
Against the mountain-tops. The flood has taken
All things, or nearly all, and those whom water,
By chance, has spared, starvation slowly conquers.

Deucalion and Pyrrha

Phocis, a fertile land, while there was land,
Marked off Oetean from Boeotian fields.[13]
It was ocean now, a plain of sudden waters.
There Mount Parnassus lifts its twin peaks skyward,
High, steep, cloud-piercing. And Deucalion came there
Rowing his wife. There was no other land, 320
The sea had drowned it all. And here they worshipped
First the Corycian nymphs and native powers,
Then Themis,[14] oracle and fate-revealer.

[12] Sea nymphs.

[13] A region north of the Gulf of Corinth and site of Delphi and Mt. Parnassus; Phocis divides the region of Boeotia, site of Thebes, from Oeta, a mountain range in southern Thessaly.

[14] Corycus is a sacred cave above Delphi on Mt. Parnassus. Themis, goddess of order and justice, held the oracle at Delphi until Apollo took it over.

There was no better man than this Deucalion,
No one more fond of right; there was no woman
More scrupulously reverent than Pyrrha.
So, when Jove saw the world was one great ocean,
Only one woman left of all those thousands,
And only one man left of all those thousands,
Both innocent and worshipful, he parted 330
The clouds, turned loose the North-wind, swept them off,
Showed earth to heaven again, and sky to land,
And the sea's anger dwindled, and King Neptune
Put down his trident, calmed the waves, and Triton,[15]
Summoned from far down under, with his shoulders
Barnacle-strewn, loomed up above the waters,
The blue-green sea-god, whose resounding horn
Is heard from shore to shore. Wet-bearded, Triton
Set lip to that great shell, as Neptune ordered,
Sounding retreat, and all the lands and waters 340
Heard and obeyed. The sea has shores; the rivers,
Still running high, have channels; the floods dwindle,
Hill-tops are seen again; the trees, long buried,
Rise with their leaves still muddy. The world returns.

Deucalion saw that world, all desolation,
All emptiness, all silence, and his tears
Rose as he spoke to Pyrrha: "O my wife,
The only woman, now, on all this earth,
My consort and my cousin and my partner
In these immediate dangers, look! Of all the lands 350
To East or West, we two, we two alone,
Are all the population. Ocean holds
Everything else; our foothold, our assurance,
Are small as they can be, the clouds still frightful.
Poor woman—well, we are not all alone—
Suppose you had been, how would you bear your fear?
Who would console your grief? My wife, believe me,
Had the sea taken you, I would have followed.
If only I had the power, I would restore
The nations as my father did, bring clay 360
To life with breathing.[16] As it is, we two
Are all the human race, so Heaven has willed it,
Samples of men, mere specimens."
They wept,
And prayed together, and having wept and prayed,
Resolved to make petition to the goddess
To seek her aid through oracles. Together
They went to the river-water, the stream Cephisus,
Still far from clear, but flowing down its channel,
And they took river-water, sprinkled foreheads,

[15]Son of Neptune.
[16]Prometheus, who according to one legend made human beings from clay.

Sprinkled their garments, and they turned their steps 370
To the temple of the goddess, where the altars
Stood with the fires gone dead, and ugly moss
Stained pediment and column. At the stairs
They both fell prone, kissed the chill stone in prayer:
"If the gods' anger ever listens
To righteous prayers, O Themis, we implore you,
Tell us by what device our wreck and ruin
May be repaired. Bring aid, most gentle goddess,
To sunken circumstance."
And Themis heard them,
And gave this oracle: "Go from the temple, 380
Cover your heads, loosen your robes, and throw
Your mother's bones behind you!" Dumb, they stood
In blank amazement, a long silence, broken
By Pyrrha, finally: she would not do it!
With trembling lips she prays whatever pardon
Her disobedience might merit, but this outrage
She dare not risk, insult her mother's spirit
By throwing her bones around. In utter darkness
They voice the cryptic saying over and over,
What can it mean? They wonder. At last Deucalion 390
Finds the way out: "I might be wrong, but surely
The holy oracles would never counsel
A guilty act. The earth is our great mother,
And I suppose those bones the goddess mentions
Are the stones of earth; the order means to throw them,
The stones, behind us."
She was still uncertain,
And he by no means sure, and both distrustful
Of that command from Heaven; but what damage,
What harm, would there be in trying? They descended,
Covered their heads, loosened their garments, threw 400
The stones behind them as the goddess ordered.
The stones—who would believe it, had we not
The unimpeachable witness of Tradition?—
Began to lose their hardness, to soften, slowly,
To take on form, to grow in size, a little,
Become less rough, to look like human beings,
Or anyway as much like human beings
As statues do, when the sculptor is only starting,
Images half blocked out. The earthy portion,
Damp with some moisture, turned to flesh, the solid 410
Was bone, the veins were as they always had been.
The stones the man had thrown turned into men,
The stones the woman threw turned into women,
Such being the will of God. Hence we derive
The hardness that we have, and our endurance
Gives proof of what we have come from.
Other forms
Of life came into being, generated
Out of the earth: the sun burnt off the dampness,

Heat made the slimy marshes swell; as seed
Swells in a mother's womb to shape and substance, 420
So new forms came to life. When the Nile river
Floods and recedes and the mud is warmed by sunshine,
Men, turning over the earth, find living things,
And some not living, but nearly so, imperfect,
On the verge of life, and often the same substance
Is part alive, part only clay. When moisture
Unites with heat, life is conceived; all things
Come from this union. Fire may fight with water,
But heat and moisture generate all things,
Their discord being productive. So when earth, 430
After that flood, still muddy, took the heat,
Felt the warm fire of sunlight, she conceived,
Brought forth, after their fashion, all the creatures,
Some old, some strange and monstrous.
One, for instance,
She bore unwanted, a gigantic serpent,
Python by name, whom the new people dreaded,
A huge bulk on the mountain-side. Apollo,
God of the glittering bow, took a long time
To bring him down, with arrow after arrow
He had never used before except in hunting 440
Deer and the skipping goats. Out of the quiver
Sped arrows by the thousand, till the monster,
Dying, poured poisonous blood on those black wounds.
In memory of this, the sacred games,
Called Pythian, were established, and Apollo
Ordained for all young winners in the races,
On foot or chariot, for victorious fighters,
The crown of oak. That was before the laurel,
That was before Apollo wreathed his forehead
With garlands from that tree, or any other. 450

Apollo and Daphne

Now the first girl Apollo loved was Daphne,
Whose father was the river-god Peneus,
And this was no blind chance, but Cupid's malice.
Apollo, with pride and glory still upon him
Over the Python slain, saw Cupid bending
His tight-strung little bow. "O silly youngster,"
He said, "What are you doing with such weapons?
Those are for grown-ups! The bow is for my shoulders;
I never fail in wounding beast or mortal,
And not so long ago I slew the Python 460
With countless darts; his bloated body covered
Acre on endless acre, and I slew him!
The torch, my boy, is enough for you to play with,
To get the love-fires burning. Do not meddle
With honors that are mine!" And Cupid answered:
"Your bow shoots everything, Apollo—maybe—
But mine will fix you! You are far above

All creatures living, and by just that distance
Your glory less than mine." He shook his wings,
Soared high, came down to the shadows of Parnassus, 470
Drew from his quiver different kinds of arrows,
One causing love, golden and sharp and gleaming,
The other blunt, and tipped with lead, and serving
To drive all love away, and this blunt arrow
He used on Daphne, but he fired the other,
The sharp and golden shaft, piercing Apollo
Through bones, through marrow, and at once he loved
And she at once fled from the name of lover,
Rejoicing in the woodland hiding places
And spoils of beasts which she had taken captive, 480
A rival of Diana,[17] virgin goddess.
She had many suitors, but she scorned them all;
Wanting no part of any man, she travelled
The pathless groves, and had no care whatever
For husband, love, or marriage. Her father often
Said, "Daughter, give me a son-in-law!" and "Daughter,
Give me some grandsons!" But the marriage torches
Were something hateful, criminal, to Daphne,
So she would blush, and put her arms around him,
And coax him: "Let me be a virgin always; 490
Diana's father said she might. Dear father!
Dear father—please!" He yielded, but her beauty
Kept arguing against her prayer. Apollo
Loves at first sight; he wants to marry Daphne,
He hopes for what he wants—all wishful thinking!—
Is fooled by his own oracles. As stubble
Burns when the grain is harvested, as hedges
Catch fire from torches that a passer-by
Has brought too near, or left behind in the morning,
So the god burned, with all his heart, and burning 500
Nourished that futile love of his by hoping.
He sees the long hair hanging down her neck
Uncared for, says, "But what if it were combed?"
He gazes at her eyes—they shine like stars!
He gazes at her lips, and knows that gazing
Is not enough. He marvels at her fingers,
Her hands, her wrists, her arms, bare to the shoulder,
And what he does not see he thinks is better.
But still she flees him, swifter than the wind,
And when he calls she does not even listen: 510
"Don't run away, dear nymph! Daughter of Peneus,
Don't run away! I am no enemy,
Only your follower: don't run away!
The lamb flees from the wolf, the deer the lion,
The dove, on trembling wing, flees from the eagle.
All creatures flee their foes. But I, who follow,

[17] A goddess of wild animals, eventually associated with the Greek Artemis, goddess of the hunt.

Am not a foe at all. Love makes me follow,
Unhappy fellow that I am, and fearful
You may fall down, perhaps, or have the briars
Make scratches on those lovely legs, unworthy 520
To be hurt so, and I would be the reason.
The ground is rough here. Run a little slower,
And I will run, I promise, a little slower.
Or wait a minute: be a little curious
Just who it is you charm. I am no shepherd,
No mountain-dweller, I am not a ploughboy,
Uncouth and stinking of cattle. You foolish girl,
You don't know who it is you run away from,
That must be why you run. I am lord of Delphi
And Tenedos and Claros and Patara.[18] 530
Jove is my father. I am the revealer
Of present, past and future; through my power
The lyre and song make harmony; my arrow
Is sure in aim—there is only one arrow surer,
The one that wounds my heart. The power of healing
Is my discovery; I am called the Healer
Through all the world: all herbs are subject to me.
Alas for me, love is incurable
With any herb; the arts which cure the others
Do me, their lord, no good!"
He would have said 540
Much more than this, but Daphne, frightened, left him
With many words unsaid, and she was lovely
Even in flight, her limbs bare in the wind,
Her garments fluttering, and her soft hair streaming,
More beautiful than ever. But Apollo,
Too young a god to waste his time in coaxing,
Came following fast. When a hound starts a rabbit
In an open field, one runs for game, one safety,
He has her, or thinks he has, and she is doubtful
Whether she's caught or not, so close the margin, 550
So ran the god and girl, one swift in hope,
The other in terror, but he ran more swiftly,
Borne on the wings of love, gave her no rest,
Shadowed her shoulder, breathed on her streaming hair.
Her strength was gone, worn out by the long effort
Of the long flight; she was deathly pale, and seeing
The river of her father, cried "O help me,
If there is any power in the rivers,
Change and destroy the body which has given
Too much delight!" And hardly had she finished, 560
When her limbs grew numb and heavy, her soft breasts
Were closed with delicate bark, her hair was leaves,
Her arms were branches, and her speedy feet
Rooted and held, and her head became a tree top,

[18] These are oracular shrines associated with Apollo.

Everything gone except her grace, her shining.
Apollo loved her still. He placed his hand
Where he had hoped and felt the heart still beating
Under the bark; and he embraced the branches
As if they still were limbs, and kissed the wood,
And the wood shrank from his kisses, and the god 570
Exclaimed: "Since you can never be my bride,
My tree at least you shall be! Let the laurel
Adorn, henceforth, my hair, my lyre, my quiver:
Let Roman victors, in the long procession,
Wear laurel wreaths for triumph and ovation.
Beside Augustus' portals let the laurel
Guard and watch over the oak, and as my head
Is always youthful, let the laurel always
Be green and shining!" He said no more. The laurel,
Stirring, seemed to consent, to be saying *Yes*. 580

There is a grove in Thessaly, surrounded
By woodlands with steep slopes; men call it Tempe.
Through this the Peneus River's foamy waters
Rise below Pindus mountain. The cascades
Drive a fine smoky mist along the tree tops,
Frail clouds, or so it seems, and the roar of the water
Carries beyond the neighborhood. Here dwells
The mighty god himself,[19] his holy of holies
Is under a hanging rock; it is here he gives
Laws to the nymphs, laws to the very water. 590
And here came first the streams of his own country
Not knowing what to offer, consolation
Or something like rejoicing: crowned with poplars
Sperchios came, and restless Enipeus,
Old Apidanus, Aeas, and Amphrysos[20]
The easy-going. And all the other rivers
That take their weary waters into oceans
All over the world, came there, and only one
Was absent, Inachus,[21] hiding in his cavern,
Salting his stream with tears, oh, most unhappy, 600
Mourning a daughter lost. Her name was Io,
Who might, for all he knew, be dead or living,
But since he can not find her anywhere
He thinks she must be nowhere, and his sorrow
Fears for the worst.

Jove and Io

Jove had seen Io coming
From the river of her father, and had spoken:
"O maiden, worthy of the love of Jove,

[19] Peneus.
[20] All rivers in Thessaly.
[21] The main river of Argos.

And sure to make some lover happy in bed,
Come to the shade of these deep woods" (he showed them)
"Come to the shade, the sun is hot and burning, 610
No beasts will hurt you there, I will go with you,
If a god is at your side, you will walk safely
In the very deepest woods. I am a god,
And no plebeian godling, either, but the holder
Of Heaven's scepter, hurler of the thunder.
Oh, do not flee me!" She had fled already
Leaving Lyrcea's plains, and Lerna's meadows,[22]
When the god hid the lands in murk and darkness
And stayed her flight, and took her.
Meanwhile Juno
Looked down on Argos: what could those clouds be doing 620
In the bright light of day? They were not mists
Rising from rivers or damp ground. She wondered,
Took a quick look round to see her husband,
Or see where he might be—she knew his cheating!
So when she did not find him in the heaven,
She said, "I am either wrong, or being wronged,"
Came gliding down from Heaven, stood on earth,
Broke up the clouds. But Jove, ahead of time,
Could tell that she was coming; he changed Io
Into a heifer, white and shining, lovely 630
Even in altered form, and even Juno
Looked on, though hating to, with admiration,
And asked whom she belonged to, from what pasture,
As if she did not know! And Jove, the liar,
To put a stop to questions, said she had sprung
Out of the earth, full-grown. Then Juno asked him,
"Could I have her, as a present?" What could he do?
To give his love away was surely cruel,
To keep her most suspicious. Shame on one side
Says *Give her up!* and love says *Don't!* and shame 640
Might have been beaten by love's argument,
But then, if he refused his wife the heifer,
So slight a present—if he should refuse it,
Juno might think perhaps it was no heifer!

Her rival thus disposed of, still the goddess
Did not at once abandon all suspicion.
Afraid of Jove, and worried over his cheating,
She turned her over to the keeping of Argus
Who had a hundred eyes; two at a time,
No more than two, would ever close in slumber, 650
The rest kept watch. No matter how he stood,
Which way he turned, he always looked at Io,
Always had Io in sight. He let her graze
By daylight, but at sundown locked her in,

[22]Both are places in Argos.

Hobbled and haltered. She would feed on leaves
And bitter grasses, and her couch, poor creature,
Was ground, not always grassy, and the water
She drank was muddy, often. When she wanted
To reach toward Argus her imploring arms,
She had no arms to reach with; when she tried 660
To plead, she only lowed, and her own voice
Filled her with terror. When she came to the river,
Her father's, where she used to play, and saw,
Reflected in the stream, her jaws and horns,
She fled in panic. None of her sisters knew her,
And Inachus, her father, did not know her,
But following them, she let them pet and praise her.
Old Inachus pulled grass and gave it to her,
And she licked his hand and tried to give it kisses,
Could not restrain her tears. If she could talk, 670
She would ask for help, and tell her name and sorrow,
But as it was, all she could do was furrow
The dust with one forefoot, and make an I,
And then an O beside it, spelling her name,
Telling the story of her changed condition.
Her father knew her, cried, "Alas for me!"
Clung to her horns and snowy neck, poor heifer,
Crying, "Alas for me! I have sought you, daughter,
All over the world, and now that I have found you,
I have found a greater grief. You do not answer, 680
And what you think is sighing comes out mooing!
And all the while I, in my ignorance, counted
On marriage for you, wanting, first, a son,
Then, later, grandsons; now your mate must be
Selected from some herd, your son a bullock.
Not even death can end my heavy sorrow.
It hurts to be a god; the door of death,
Shut in my face, prolongs my grief forever."
And both of them were weeping, but their guardian,
Argus the star-eyed, drove her from her father 690
To different pasture-land, and sat there, watching,
Perched on a mountain-top above the valley.
Jove could not bear her sorrows any longer;
He called his son, born of the shining Pleiad,[23]
Told him *Kill Argus!* And Mercury came flying
On winged sandals, wearing the magic helmet,
Bearing the sleep-producing wand, and lighted
On earth, and put aside the wings and helmet
Keeping the wand. With this he plays the shepherd
Across the pathless countryside, a driver 700
Of goats, collected somewhere, and he goes
Playing a little tune on a pipe of reeds,
And this new sound is wonderful to Argus.

[23]Maia, one of the seven daughters of Atlas and Pleïone, who were transformed into stars.

"Whoever you are, come here and sit beside me,"
He says, "This rock is in the shade; the grass
Is nowhere any better." And Mercury joins him,
Whiling the time away with conversation
And soothing little melodies, and Argus
Has a hard fight with drowsiness; his eyes,
Some of them, close, but some of them stay open. 710
To keep himself awake by listening,
He asks about the pipe of reeds, how was it
This new invention came about?
The god
Began the story: "On the mountain slopes
Of cool Arcadia, a woodland nymph
Once lived, with many suitors, and her name
Was Syrinx. More than once the satyrs chased her,
And so did other gods of field or woodland,
But always she escaped them, virgin always
As she aspired to be, one like Diana, 720
Like her in dress and calling, though her bow
Was made of horn, not gold, but even so,
She might, sometimes, be taken for the goddess.
Pan,[24] with a wreath of pine around his temples,
Once saw her coming back from Mount Lycaeus,
And said—" and Mercury broke off the story
And then went on to tell what Pan had told her,
How she said *No,* and fled, through pathless places,
Until she came to Ladon's river, flowing
Peaceful along the sandy banks, whose water 730
Halted her flight, and she implored her sisters
To change her form, and so, when Pan had caught her
And thought he held a nymph, it was only reeds
That yielded in his arms, and while he sighed,
The soft air stirring in the reeds made also
The echo of a sigh. Touched by this marvel,
Charmed by the sweetness of the tone, he murmured
This much I have! and took the reeds, and bound them
With wax, a tall and shorter one together,
And called them Syrinx, still.
And Mercury 740
Might have told more, but all the eyes of Argus,
He saw, had closed, and he made the slumber deeper
With movements of the wand, and then he struck
The nodding head just where it joins the shoulder,
Severed it with the curving blade, and sent it
Bloody and rolling over the rocks. So Argus
Lay low, and all the light in all those eyes
Went out forever, a hundred eyes, one darkness.
And Juno took the eyes and fastened them

---

[24]An Arcadian shepherd-god, ruler of woodlands and meadows; with goat legs and horns, he sported with nymphs and played to them on the syrinx, or shepherd's pipe.

On the feathers of a bird of hers, the peacock, 750
So that the peacock's tail is spread with jewels,
And Juno, very angry, sent a fury
To harass Io, to drive her mad with terror,
In flight all over the world. At last a river
Halted her flight, the Nile, and when she came there
She knelt beside the stream, lifted her head,
The only gesture she could make of praying,
And seemed, with groans and tears and mournful lowing,
To voice complaint to Jove, to end her sorrows,
And he was moved to pity; embracing Juno 760
He begged her: "End this punishment; hereafter
Io, I swear, will never cause you anguish,"
And what he swore he called the Styx to witness.
And Juno was appeased. Io became
What once she was, again; the bristles vanish,
The horns are gone, the great round eyes grow smaller,
The gaping jaws are narrower, the shoulders
Return, she has hands again, and toes and fingers,
The only sign of the heifer is the whiteness.
She stands erect, a nymph again, still fearful 770
That speech may still be mooing, but she tries
And little by little gains back the use of language.
Now people, robed in linen, pay her homage,
A very goddess, and a son is born,
Named Epaphus, the seed of Jove; his temples
Are found beside his mother's in many cities.
His boon companion was young Phaethon,
Son of the Sun-god, given to speaking proudly,
Boasting about his parentage, till one day
Epaphus said: "You are a silly fellow, 780
Believing every word your mother tells you,
And all swelled up about your phony father!"
Phaethon flushed, made no retort, but carried
The insult to his mother, the nymph Clymene,
And told her: "Mother, to make it all the worse,
There was nothing I could answer back. I tell you
It is shameful for a fellow with any spirit,
And I think I have plenty, to have to listen
To such insulting slanders, and have no answer.
Give me some proof that my father was the Sun-god, 790
Really and truly!" He put his arms about her,
Pleading, imploring, in his own name, his brother's,
His married sisters', for complete assurance.
Clymene, moved, by her son's prayers, or maybe
By anger at her damaged reputation,
Stretched out both arms to Heaven, raised her eyes
To the bright sun, and cried: "By that bright splendor
Which hears and sees us both, I swear, my son,
You are his son too, the son of that great presence
Whom you behold with me, the radiant ruler 800
Of all the world. If I am lying to you,

May I never see his light again, this day
Be the last time I ever look upon him.
And you can find his house with no great trouble;
His rising is not far from here: go thither,
Ask him yourself!" And Phaethon, delighted,
Already imagining himself in Heaven,
Crosses beyond his own frontiers to India,
The nearest land to the starry fires of Heaven,
And comes, exulting, to his father's palace. 810

. . .

Book 10

The Story of Orpheus and Eurydice

So Hymen left there, clad in saffron robe,
Through the great reach of air, and took his way
To the Ciconian country, where the voice
Of Orpheus called him, all in vain.[25] He came there,
True, but brought with him no auspicious words,
No joyful faces, lucky omens. The torch
Sputtered and filled the eyes with smoke; when swung,
It would not blaze: bad as the omens were,
The end was worse, for as the bride went walking
Across the lawn, attended by her naiads, 10
A serpent bit her ankle, and she was gone.
Orpheus mourned her to the upper world,
And then, lest he should leave the shades untried,
Dared to descend to Styx, passing the portal
Men call Taenarian.[26] Through the phantom dwellers,
The buried ghosts, he passed, came to the king
Of that sad realm, and to Persephone,
His consort, and he swept the strings, and chanted:
"Gods of the world below the world, to whom
All of us mortals come, if I may speak 20
Without deceit, the simple truth is this:
I came here, not to see dark Tartarus,[27]
Nor yet to bind the triple-throated monster[28]
Medusa's offspring, rough with snakes. I came
For my wife's sake, whose growing years were taken
By a snake's venom. I wanted to be able
To bear this; I have tried to. Love has conquered.
This god is famous in the world above,
But here, I do not know. I think he may be
Or is it all a lie, that ancient story 30

---

[25]Hymen, god of marriage, has just left Greece and arrived in Ciconia, a territory in Thrace.

[26]Taenarum, a cape on the southern Peloponnesus, thought to be an entrance to Hades, the underworld.

[27]The farthest region in Hades, where the rebellious Titans were imprisoned.

[28]Cerberus, the three-headed dog that guarded the entrance to Hades. Hercules once bound Cerberus and carried him to the upper world.

Of an old ravishment,[29] and how he brought
The two of you together? By these places
All full of fear, by this immense confusion,
By this vast kingdom's silences, I beg you,
Weave over Eurydice's life, run through too soon.
To you we all, people and things, belong,
Sooner or later, to this single dwelling
All of us come, to our last home; you hold
Longest dominion over humankind.
She will come back again, to be your subject, 40
After the ripeness of her years; I am asking
A loan and not a gift. If fate denies us
This privilege for my wife, one thing is certain:
I do not want to go back either; triumph
In the death of two."
And with his words, the music
Made the pale phantoms weep: Ixion's wheel
Was still, Tityos' vultures left the liver,
Tantalus tried no more to reach for the water,
And Belus' daughters rested from their urns,
And Sisyphus[30] climbed on his rock to listen. 50
That was the first time ever in all the world
The Furies wept.[31] Neither the king nor consort
Had harshness to refuse him, and they called her,
Eurydice. She was there, limping a little
From her late wound, with the new shades of Hell.
And Orpheus received her, but one term
Was set: he must not, till he passed Avernus,[32]
Turn back his gaze, or the gift would be in vain.

They climbed the upward path, through absolute silence,
Up the steep murk, clouded in pitchy darkness, 60
They were near the margin, near the upper land,
When he, afraid that she might falter, eager to see her,
Looked back in love, and she was gone, in a moment.
Was it he, or she, reaching out arms and trying
To hold or to be held, and clasping nothing
But empty air? Dying the second time,
She had no reproach to bring against her husband,
What was there to complain of? One thing, only:
He loved her. He could hardly hear her calling
Farewell! when she was gone.

---

[29] Ovid alludes to the story of Pluto's abduction of Persephone told in Book 5.

[30] These are all sinners facing eternal tortures. Ixion was chained to a fiery wheel that turned endlessly; Tityos suffered the pain of vultures constantly feeding on his liver; Tantalus stood chin deep in water that receded whenever he tried to drink it, while above him fruit dangled just out of reach; Belus' daughters had to carry water in pitchers punctured with holes; and Sisyphus continually pushed a huge boulder to the top of a hill only to see it roll back down.

[31] Female spirits who avenged crimes against blood kin, especially against fathers and mothers; sometimes thought to inflict the tortures in Hades.

[32] A poisonous lake near the entrance to the underworld.

The double death 70
Stunned Orpheus, like the man who turned to stone
At sight of Cerberus, or the couple of rock,
Olenos and Lethaea,[33] hearts so joined
One shared the other's guilt, and Ida's mountain,
Where rivers run, still holds them, both together.
In vain the prayers of Orpheus and his longing
To cross the river once more; the boatman Charon
Drove him away. For seven days he sat there
Beside the bank, in filthy garments, and tasting
No food whatever. Trouble, grief, and tears 80
Were all his sustenance. At last, complaining
The gods of Hell were cruel, he wandered on
To Rhodope and Haemus,[34] swept by the north winds,
Where, for three years, he lived without a woman
Either because marriage had meant misfortune
Or he had made a promise. But many women
Wanted this poet for their own, and many
Grieved over their rejection. His love was given
To young boys only, and he told the Thracians
That was the better way: *enjoy that springtime,* 90
Take those first flowers!
There was a hill, and on it
A wide-extending plain, all green, but lacking
The darker green of shade, and when the singer
Came there and ran his fingers over the strings,
The shade came there to listen. The oak-tree came,
And many poplars, and the gentle lindens,
The beech, the virgin laurel, and the hazel
Easily broken, the ash men use for spears,
The shining silver-fir, the ilex bending
Under its acorns, the friendly sycamore, 100
The changing-colored maple, and the willows
That love the river-waters, and the lotus
Favoring pools, and the green boxwood came,
Slim tamarisks, and myrtle, and viburnum
With dark-blue berries, and the pliant ivy,
The tendrilled grape, the elms, all dressed with vines,
The rowan-trees, the pitch-pines, and the arbute
With the red fruit, the palm, the victor's triumph,
The bare-trunked pine with spreading leafy crest,
Dear to the mother of the gods since Attis[35] 110
Put off his human form, took on that likeness,
And the cone-shaped cypress joined them, now a tree,
But once a boy, loved by the god Apollo
Master of lyre and bow-string, both together.

---

[33]When Olenos, Lethaea's husband, offered to take on her punishment for offending the gods by bragging of her beauty, both were turned to stone.

[34]Mountains in Thrace.

[35]A youth associated with the Phrygian mother goddess Cybele; in a fit of madness inspired by the jealous goddess, he castrated himself and was transformed into a pine tree.

The Story of Ganymede, a Very Brief One

The king of the gods once loved a Trojan boy
Named Ganymede; for once, there was something found
That Jove would rather have been than what he was.
He made himself an eagle, the only bird
Able to bear his thunderbolts, went flying
On his false wings, and carried off the youngster 120
Who now, though much against the will of Juno,
Tends to the cups of Jove and serves his nectar.

The Story of Apollo and Hyacinthus

There was another boy, who might have had
A place in Heaven, at Apollo's order,
Had Fate seen fit to give him time, and still
He is, in his own fashion, an immortal.
Whenever spring drives winter out, and the Ram
Succeeds the wintry Fish, he springs to blossom
On the green turf. My father[36] loved him dearly,
This Hyacinthus, and left Delphi for him, 130
Outward from the world's center, on to Sparta,
The town that has no walls, and Eurotas River.
Quiver and lyre were nothing to him there,
No more than his own dignity; he carried
The nets for fellows hunting, and held the dogs
In leash for them, and with them roamed the trails
Of the rough mountain ridges. In their train
He fed the fire with long association.
It was noon one day: Apollo, Hyacinthus,
Stripped, rubbed themselves with oil, and tried their skill 140
At discus-throwing. Apollo sent the missile
Far through the air, so far it pierced the clouds,
A long time coming down, and when it fell
Proved both his strength and skill, and Hyacinthus,
All eager for his turn, heedless of danger,
Went running to pick it up, before it settled
Fully to earth. It bounded once and struck him
Full in the face, and he grew deadly pale
As the pale god caught up the huddled body,
Trying to warm the dreadful chill that held it, 150
Trying to staunch the wound, to keep the spirit
With healing herbs, but all the arts were useless,
The wound was past all cure. So, in a garden,
If one breaks off a violet or poppy
Or lilies, bristling with their yellow stamens,
And they droop over, and cannot raise their heads,
But look on earth, so sank the dying features,
The neck, its strength all gone, lolled on the shoulder.
'Fallen before your time, O Hyacinthus,'
Apollo cried, 'I see your wound, my crime: 160

[36] Apollo.

You are my sorrow, my reproach; my hand
Has been your murderer. But how am I
To blame? Where is my guilt, except in playing
With you, in loving you? I cannot die
For you, or with you either; the law of Fate
Keeps us apart: it shall not! You will be
With me forever, and my songs and music
Will tell of you, and you will be reborn
As a new flower whose markings will spell out
My cries of grief, and there will come a time 170
When a great hero's name will be the same
As this flower's markings.' So Apollo spoke,
And it was truth he told, for on the ground
The blood was blood no longer; in its place
A flower grew, brighter than any crimson,
Like lilies with their silver changed to crimson.
That was not all; Apollo kept the promise
About the markings, and inscribed the flower
With his own grieving words: *Ai, Ai*
The petals say, Greek for *Alas!*[37] In Sparta, 180
Even to this day, they hold their son in honor,
And when the day comes round, they celebrate
The rites for Hyacinthus, as did their fathers.

Two Incidents of Venus' Anger

Amathus, a town of Cyprus, is rich in metals,
But never ask that town about her daughters,
Whose foreheads once bore horns, or the other ones,
Turned, later, into stone. The former had
An altar at their gates, sacred to Jove,
The god of host and guest: if any stranger
Had seen it, stained with blood, he would suppose 190
That sheep or calves were slain there, and how wrong
He would have been! That blood came from the murder,
Always, of innocent guests. Venus, offended,
Prepared to leave her Cyprian plains and cities,
And then reflected: 'But these lovely regions
Are not at fault, the cities are not guilty.
Let these Horned Girls, these wicked creatures, rather
Pay for their sins by exile or by death
Or by some punishment halfway between,
Let us say, a change of body.' As she wondered 200
What change, her eyes fell on the horns they carried:
Those they might keep. They were big women by nature,
Let them be bulls!

"And even so, the others,
The foul Propoetides, would not acknowledge
Venus and her divinity, and her anger

---

[37]Ovid puns here on the Greek spelling for Ajax (*Aias*), the Trojan War hero who killed himself after losing the prize of Achilles' armor to Odysseus.

Made whores of them, the first such women ever
To sell their bodies, and in shamelessness
They hardened, even their blood was hard, they could not
Blush any more; it was no transition, really,
From what they were to actual rock and stone. 210

The Story of Pygmalion

One man, Pygmalion, who had seen these women
Leading their shameful lives, shocked at the vices
Nature has given the female disposition
Only too often, chose to live alone,
To have no woman in his bed. But meanwhile
He made, with marvelous art, an ivory statue,
As white as snow, and gave it greater beauty
Than any girl could have, and fell in love
With his own workmanship. The image seemed
That of a virgin, truly, almost living, 220
And willing, save that modesty prevented,
To take on movement. The best art, they say,
Is that which conceals art, and so Pygmalion
Marvels, and loves the body he has fashioned.
He would often move his hands to test and touch it,
Could this be flesh, or was it ivory only?
No, it could not be ivory. His kisses,
He fancies, she returns; he speaks to her,
Holds her, believes his fingers almost leave
An imprint on her limbs, and fears to bruise her. 230
He pays her compliments, and brings her presents
Such as girls love, smooth pebbles, winding shells,
Little pet birds, flowers with a thousand colors,
Lilies, and painted balls, and lumps of amber.
He decks her limbs with dresses, and her fingers
Wear rings which he puts on, and he brings a necklace,
And earrings, and a ribbon for her bosom,
And all of these become her, but she seems
Even more lovely naked, and he spreads
A crimson coverlet for her to lie on, 240
Takes her to bed, puts a soft pillow under
Her head, as if she felt it, calls her *Darling,*
My darling love!

"And Venus' holiday
Came round, and all the people of the island
Were holding festival, and snow-white heifers,
Their horns all tipped with gold, stood at the altars,
Where incense burned, and, timidly, Pygmalion
Made offering, and prayed: 'If you can give
All things, O gods, I pray my wife may be—
(He almost said, *My ivory girl,* but dared not)— 250
One like my ivory girl.' And golden Venus
Was there, and understood the prayer's intention,
And showed her presence, with the bright flame leaping
Thrice on the altar, and Pygmalion came
Back where the maiden lay, and lay beside her,

And kissed her, and she seemed to glow, and kissed her,
And stroked her breast, and felt the ivory soften
Under his fingers, as wax grows soft in sunshine,
Made pliable by handling. And Pygmalion
Wonders, and doubts, is dubious and happy, 260
Plays lover again, and over and over touches
The body with his hand. It is a body!
The veins throb under the thumb. And oh, Pygmalion
Is lavish in his prayer and praise to Venus,
No words are good enough. The lips he kisses
Are real indeed, the ivory girl can feel them,
And blushes and responds, and the eyes open
At once on lover and heaven, and Venus blesses
The marriage she has made. The crescent moon
Fills to full orb, nine times, and wanes again, 270
And then a daughter is born, a girl named Paphos,
From whom the island later takes its name.

The Story of Adonis

Time, in its stealthy gliding, cheats us all
Without our notice; nothing goes more swiftly
Than do the years. That little boy, whose sister
Became his mother, his grandfather's son,
Is now a youth, and now a man, more handsome
Than he had ever been, exciting even
The goddess Venus, and thereby avenging
His mother's passion. Cupid, it seems, was playing, 280
Quiver on shoulder, when he kissed his mother,
And one barb grazed her breast; she pushed him away,
But the wound was deeper than she knew; deceived,
Charmed by Adonis' beauty, she cared no more
For Cythera's shores nor Paphos' sea-ringed island,
Nor Cnidos, where fish teem, nor high Amathus,[38]
Rich in its precious ores. She stays away
Even from Heaven, Adonis is better than Heaven.
She is beside him always; she has always,
Before this time, preferred the shadowy places, 290
Preferred her ease, preferred to improve her beauty
By careful tending, but now, across the ridges,
Through woods, through rocky places thick with brambles,
She goes, more like Diana than like Venus,
Bare-kneed and robes tucked up. She cheers the hounds,
Hunts animals, at least such timid creatures
As deer and rabbits; no wild boars for her,
No wolves, no bears, no lions. And she warns him
To fear them too, as if there might be good
In giving him warnings. 'Be bold against the timid, 300
The running creatures, but against the bold ones
Boldness is dangerous. Do not be reckless.

---

[38] These places were the favorite earthly haunts of Venus.

I share whatever risk you take; be careful!
Do not attack those animals which Nature
Has given weapons, lest your thirst for glory
May cost me dear. Beauty and youth and love
Make no impression on bristling boars and lions,
On animal eyes and minds. The force of lightning
Is in the wild boar's tusks, and tawny lions
Are worse than thunderbolts. I hate and fear them.' 310
He asks her why. She answers, 'I will tell you,
And you will wonder at the way old crime
Leads to monstrosities. I will tell you sometime,
Not now, for I am weary, all this hunting
Is not what I am used to. Here's a couch
Of grassy turf, and a canopy of poplar,
I would like to lie there with you.' And she lay there,
Making a pillow for him of her breast,
And kisses for her story's punctuation.

Venus Tells Adonis the Story of Atalanta

You may have heard (she said) about a girl 320
Who could outrun the swiftest men. The story
Is very true: she really could outrun them.
It would be hard to say, though, whether her speed
Or beauty earned more praise. She was very lovely.
She asked the oracle, one day, to give her
Advice on marriage. "You don't need a husband,"
The god replied, "Avoid that habit! Still,
I know you will not: you will keep your life,
And lose yourself." So Atalanta, frightened,
Lived in the shadowy woods, a single woman, 330
Harshly rejecting urgent throngs of suitors.
"No one gets me who cannot beat me running,
Race me!" she told them, "Wife and marriage-chamber
Go to the winner, but the slow ones get
The booby-prize of death. Those are my terms."
The terms were harsh, but beauty has such power
That those harsh terms were met by many suitors,
Foolhardy fellows. Watching the cruel race,
Hippomenes had some remarks to make:
"Is any woman worth it? These young men 340
Strike me as very silly." But when he saw her,
Her face, her body naked, with such beauty
As mine is, or as yours would be, Adonis,
If you were woman, he was struck with wonder,
Threw up his hands and cried: "I beg your pardon,
Young men, I judged you wrongly; I did not know
The value of the prize!" And he caught fire
From his own praising, hoped that no young runner
Would beat her, feared they might, was worried, jealous.
"Why don't I try?" he thought, "God helps the bold." 350
And, swifter than his thought, the girl sped by
On winged feet, swifter than Scythian arrow,

Yet not too swift for a young man's admiration,
And running made her lovelier: the breeze
Bore back the streaming pinions of her sandals,
Her hair was tossed back over ivory shoulders,
The colored ribbons fluttered at her knees,
And a light flush came over her girlish body
The way a crimson awning, over marble,
Tints it in pastel color. As he watched her, 360
She crossed the finish line, received the crown
Of victory, and the beaten suitors, groaning,
Were led away to death.
'Hippomenes,
Undaunted, came from the crowd; he fixed his eyes
On Atalanta, and he made his challenge:
"This is too easy, beating all these turtles!
Race against me!" he said, "If you are beaten
It will be no disgrace. Megareus is my father,
Whose grandfather was Neptune, and that makes me
Great-grandson of the king of all the oceans. 370
Nor is my worth inferior to my race.
Beat me, and you will have something to boast of!"
Listening, looking almost tenderly
At that young man, she wondered, in confusion,
Which would be better, to win or lose. "What god"
She thought, "So hates the young and handsome
He wants to ruin this one, tempting him
To risk his precious life to marry me?
I do not think I am worth it. I am not moved
By his beauty (though I could be); I am moved 380
Because he seems so young: he does not move me,
Only his age. What of his manly courage,
His nerve, his claim to proud descent, his love
For me, so great a love that death, he claims,
Is an advantage if he cannot have me?
Go while you may, O stranger, flee this marriage,
There is too much blood upon it. Any girl
Would marry you, and wisely. Why do I care,
Why worry for him, when I have slain so many?
Let him look out for himself, or let him die 390
Since the death of all those others has not warned him,
Since life is such a bore! Is he to die
Because he wants to live with me? Is death
To be the price of love? I shall be hated
In victory. It is not my fault. Poor fellow,
I wish you would forget it but, since you are crazy,
I wish at least you could run a little faster!
He looks like a girl, almost. I wish he had never
Laid eyes on me. He should have lived. If I
Were luckier, if the fates allowed me marriage, 400
He was the only one I would have taken
To bed with any pleasure." Atalanta
Was green in love, untutored—she did not know
What she was doing, and loved, and did not know it.

Meanwhile the people and her father, restless,
Were clamoring for the race. Hippomenes
Called me in supplication: "O, may Venus
Be near, I pray, assist my daring, favor
The love she gave me!" And a gentle breeze
Bore this soft prayer my way; it moved my heart, 410
I own, and there was little time to aid him.
There is a field the natives call Tamasus,
The richest part of Cyprus, which the ancients
Hallowed for me, and built my temples there,
And in a field there stands a golden tree,
Shining with golden leaves and branches rustling
With the soft click of gold, and golden apples
Are the fruit of that golden tree. I came from there
With three such apples in my hand, and no one
Saw me except Hippomenes, and I 420
Told him how he should use them.

'The trumpets sounded
The start: the pair, each crouching low, shot forward,
Skimming the sand with flying feet, so lightly
They could run on waves and never wet their sandals,
They could run on fields of grain and never bend them.
He heard them cheering: "Go, Hippomenes,
Lean to the work, use all your strength: go, go,
You are sure to win!" I could not tell you whether
The cheering pleased him more, or Atalanta.
How many times, when she could have passed, she lingered, 430
Slowed down to see his face, and, most unwilling,
Sprinted ahead! And now his breathing labored,
Came in great sobbing gasps, and the finish line
Was a long way off, and he tossed one golden apple,
The first one, down. She looked at it with wonder,
Eager to have the shining fruit, she darted
Out of the course, and picked it up, still rolling,
The golden thing. He gained the lead again
As all the people roared applause. She passed him
Again, and once again lost ground to follow 440
The toss of the second apple, and once more
Caught up and sprinted past him. "O be near me,
Gift-bringing Goddess, help me now!" he cried,
And this time threw the last third apple farther,
Angling it off the course, way to one side.
She hesitated, only for a moment,
Whether to chase it, but I made her do it,
And made the fruit weigh more, so she was hindered
Both by the burden and her own delay.
To run my story quickly, as the race 450
Was run, the girl was beaten, and the winner
Led off his prize.

'Do you not think, Adonis,
He should have brought me incense, or at least
Given me thanks? He did not. I was angry:

Once slighted, I should not again be slighted.
I told myself I would make examples of them.
One day they were going by a temple, hidden
In the deep woods; in ancient times Echion
Had consecrated this to Cybele
In payment of a vow. Their trip was long, 460
And they were tired, or thought so, but I drove
Hippomenes half crazy with the passion
To take his wife. He saw, beside the temple,
A dimly-lighted cavern, roofed with rock,
A chapel it was, really, where the priesthood
Had placed for worship their old wooden idols.
He could not wait, here he took Atalanta,
And the gods turned their eyes away; Cybele,
The tower-crowned Mother, had at first the impulse
To drown them, for their guilt, in the Stygian waters, 470
But that seemed much too easy. So their necks
Grew rough with tawny manes, their fingers, hooked,
Were claws, their arms were legs, their chests grew heavy,
Their tails swept over the sandy ground, and anger
Blazed in their features, they conversed in growling,
Took to the woods to couple: they were lions,
Frightful to all but Cybele, whose bridle
And bit they champed in meekness. Do not hunt them,
Adonis: let all beasts alone, which offer
Breasts to the fight, not backs, or else your daring 480
Will be the ruin of us both.'

The Fate of Adonis

"Her warning
Was given, and the goddess took her way,
Drawn by her swans through air. But the young hunter
Scorned all such warnings, and one day, it happened,
His hounds, hard on the trail, roused a wild boar,
And as he rushed from the wood, Adonis struck him
A glancing blow, and the boar turned, and shaking
The spear from the side, came charging at the hunter,
Who feared, and ran, and fell, and the tusk entered
Deep in the groin, and the youth lay there dying 490
On the yellow sand, and Venus, borne through air
In her light swan-guided chariot, still was far
From Cyprus when she heard his groans, and, turning
The white swans from their course, came back to him,
Saw, from high air, the body lying lifeless
In its own blood, and tore her hair and garments,
Beat her fair breasts with cruel hands, came down
Reproaching Fate. 'They shall not have it always
Their way,' she mourned, 'Adonis, for my sorrow,
Shall have a lasting monument: each year 500
Your death will be my sorrow, but your blood
Shall be a flower. If Persephone
Could change to fragrant mint the girl called Mentha,

Cinyras' son, my hero, surely also
Can be my flower.' Over the blood she sprinkled
Sweet-smelling nectar, and as bubbles rise
In rainy weather, so it stirred, and blossomed,
Before an hour, as crimson in its color
As pomegranates are, as briefly clinging
To life as did Adonis, for the winds 510
Which gave a name to the flower, anemone,
The wind-flower, shake the petals off, too early,
Doomed all too swift and soon."

REPRESENTATIVE TEXTS OF ANCIENT ISRAEL AND CHRISTENDOM

THE OLD TESTAMENT

[C. 10TH CENTURY–2ND CENTURY B.C.E.]

The King James Version

The Bible is probably the single most influential book in Western history, translated into most, if not all, the written languages on earth. As a history of ancient Judaism and early Christianity, the Bible covers a period of about 2,000 years, and for about 2,000 years the Bible, with its belief in a Father-God, a code of ethics, depictions of gender roles, its view of history, and its prophecies for the future, has had an impact on all aspects of Western society. Although science has challenged the truth of certain portions of the Bible, it is, nevertheless, the basic religious document of over a billion people throughout the world today, while the Islamic followers of the Koran number some 800 million.

The word *Bible,* from the Greek *biblia,* means "little books," and indeed it is a collection of little books: thirty-nine in the Old Testament and twenty-seven in the New Testament. When we use the title "Old Testament," we are reflecting a Christian point of view that divides the Bible into the Old Testament—which contains the old covenant between God and his people—and the New Testament—which describes a new covenant established by Jesus and his followers. For religious Jews, there is only one covenant. What Christians call the Old Testament, Jews call *Tanak,* a word in which the consonants stand for the three major groups of books in the Hebrew Bible: *Torah* (The Law), *Nebi'im* (The Prophets), and *Ketubim* (The Writings)—TNK, or *Tanak.*

The authorship of the Bible was once thought to be a simple matter; some scholars, even into the twentieth century, thought that Moses wrote the Torah and Job, that Joshua wrote the book of Joshua, that Samuel wrote Samuel, Judges, and Ruth—in other words, the names of biblical books indicated their authorship. But over the years, textual scholars noted stylistic differences, inconsistencies, and chronological problems in the writings. A basic difference, for example, is found in the first two creation stories in Genesis, where the names for God differ. In the nineteenth century, a document theory arose that stated that there were four major historical narrations that were combined by editors to constitute the Pentateuch (first five books), Joshua, Samuel, and Kings: the "J" document, about 900 B.C.E.; the "E" document, about 700 B.C.E.; the "D" document, about 650 B.C.E.; and the "P", about 500 B.C.E. These various strands were joined together and officially recognized around 400 B.C.E. by Ezra or the school of Ezra. The entire Hebrew Bible was finally canonized at the Council of Jamnia, 90 C.E. It is generally assumed that all the writers and editors were male.

The Hebrew Bible contains a wide variety of literature written primarily in Hebrew: myth, folk tales, history, poetry, drama, short story, biography, philosophy, prophecy. Through various kinds of literature, the Hebrew Bible records a people's struggle to understand an all-powerful, complex, seemingly contradictory deity, Yahweh, and then to live up to the terms of a series of agreements or covenants with this exacting deity. On one hand, Yahweh is a god of violence and destruction, wiping out cities, flooding the world, demanding death without mercy for his enemies. But another side of Yahweh is revealed in the terms of the covenant: The fruits of the peoples' obedience and loyalty will be the blessings bestowed on the chosen ones of Israel if they remain faithful. Yahweh is very much like a stern but loving father who both reprimands and rewards his children.

The Old Testament is also a historical record of rebellion and backsliding, as the Hebrews continually stray from the straight and narrow path into embracing the religion of their neighbors or their conquerors. In *This Is My God*, Herman Wouk summarizes this theme:

> The Hebrew Bible read as living literature is a tragic epic with a single long plot: the tale of the fall of a hero through his weaknesses. The hero is Israel, a people given a destiny almost too high for human beings, the charge of God's law. . . . Unlike all other epic tragedies, it does not end in death. The hero has eternal life, and the prospect of ages of pain, in which to rise at long last to the destiny which he cannot escape.

The Jewish focus on preserving monotheism and a comprehensive code of ethics was shaped by poets and prophets in the life of the people and was formulated into basic concepts that permeated Western civilization.

GENESIS, EXODUS, JOSHUA

The first five books of the Bible are called the Pentateuch or the Torah (the Law). They constitute the most important portion of scripture to Orthodox Jews. The Torah was originally divided into books because it was too long for a single roll of papyrus or parchment. The most important writer of this section is identified as the "J" writer because he uses Jahweh (or Yahweh) for God's name. This writer constructed a national epic that begins with the creation of the world and the first humans in Genesis 2:5. Using the folk materials of his day, the "J" writer tells about how humans were tempted by a talking snake and rebelled against Yahweh, causing him to curse the natural world, inflict pain on women in childbirth, and drive these first ancestors out of Eden. He describes the founding of tribal identity under a series of patriarchs and the escape from Egyptian bondage under a heroic leader called Moses. After receiving an ethical code from their god on Mt. Sinai, the Hebrews triumphantly enter the land of Canaan, which had been promised to their first patriarch, Abraham. With the central themes of obedience, rebellion, and reconciliation, this story became the founding story of the nation of Israel and of the Jews, in the same way that the Trojan War story for the Greeks and the story of Aeneas for the Romans were founding tales.

The themes of rebellion and conflict are continued in the origin stories of the first murder and the birth of giants. Yahweh's wrath is exhibited in the universal flood, the razing of the tower of Babel, and the destruction of Sodom and Gomorrah. Palestine was situated between two great cultures, Mesopotamia and Egypt, and their literatures influenced Bible stories. In particular, the basic ingredients of the Babylonian flood story from the second millennium B.C.E. shaped the biblical version.

Chapter 12 of Genesis begins the second stage of the epic with the stories of the tribal fathers, the rivalry between brothers, and the conflict between fathers and sons. Scholars tend to interpret these legendary stories of the patriarchs Abraham, Isaac, Jacob, and Joseph as histories of whole clans or tribes over a period of some 600 years, 1900–1300 B.C.E. They present the patriarchal patterns of conflict within tribal families as exemplifying the rivalries between the Semitic tribes of nomads, who were migrating from the Arabian peninsula into the Fertile Crescent and formulating their religion and culture. The biblical writer stresses the unique identity of the Hebrews and their role as chosen by a personal deity who entered into a series of covenants with the founding fathers and promised them a prosperous future.

According to the Bible, Abraham, the first patriarch, came from Ur of the Chaldees, an ancient Sumerian city in Mesopotamia, sometime around 1900 B.C.E. His journey apparently represents the movement of Amorites into the southern portion of Canaan. The stories about Abraham and his descendants are full of family twists and unexpected ironies, as concubines assist their own sons in the competition for the patriarchal inheritance. Jacob wins a wrestling match with an angel and Joseph shows his brilliance interpreting dreams and managing an empire.

In 1700 B.C.E., a number of Canaanite and Amorite tribes moved farther on to Egypt, where they were known as Hyksos (foreign chiefs). The migration of Joseph and his brothers southward into Egypt reflects this historical event. Egyptians eventually enslaved the Hyksos interlopers, a fact to which the story of the Hebrew slaves at the beginning of the book of Exodus may allude.

The book of Exodus describes the emergence of an extraordinary leader, Moses, who was the real founder of Judaism and was primarily responsible for the transition of the Hebrew people from tribal to national culture. Moses is believed to have led his people out of slavery in Egypt sometime in the thirteenth century B.C.E., during the nineteenth Egyptian Dynasty ruled by the famous pharaohs Seti (1308–1290 B.C.E.) and Ramses II (1290–1223 B.C.E.). The song of Miriam, dating from the thirteenth century B.C.E., celebrates a victory over the Egyptian chariots and is probably the oldest piece of literature in the Bible.

> I will sing unto the Lord, for he hath triumphed gloriously:
> The horse and his rider hath he thrown into the sea.

During the forty years of wandering in the Sinai desert (the exact route is uncertain), Moses prepared his followers for settling down in Canaan—the Promised Land—by transforming tribal groups with various deities into a more or less unified group under the worship of a single God, Yahweh. Moses provided the Israelites with a fundamental religious code, as symbolized by the receiving of the Ten Commandments at Mt. Sinai and detailed in Leviticus and Deuteronomy. The laws, which were influenced by the Babylonian Code of Hammurabi and the Hittite legal system, circumscribed the Hebrews' sacred calling as the chosen people of Yahweh and provided them with a legal foundation for communal life and eventually nationhood.

The book of Joshua, named after the successor to Moses, concludes the "J" epic with the migration of the Hebrews into Canaan and an idealized description of the absolute victories over Canaanite towns. Yahweh's origin as a tribal deity is revealed in the book of Deuteronomy (chapters 6, 7, and 20), where he prescribes ruthless treatment for defeated populations. Overall, the exodus pattern—from slavery through migration to Promised

Land—served later as an inspirational model and narrative pattern for Christians as well as Jews; it was a beacon of hope for numerous groups down through the ages who were living in bondage and looked forward to some new dispensation.

Job

The book of Job is considered to be one of the great masterpieces of Western literature, although its literary form is difficult to classify. Dating probably from the sixth century B.C.E., the book is a series of dialogues on the nature of God and of divine justice. Even though, in general, the book belongs to the wisdom tradition of the ancient Near East, it is unusual because it calls into question the validity of conventional wisdom that the good, pious person would ultimately be rewarded in this lifetime with a large family and material prosperity, while the evil person would be punished. The problem with this view is simply that experience provides contradictory evidence: Some good or innocent people suffer and some evil people prosper.

It is around this basic issue of cosmic justice that the author of Job creates his debate, which is framed at the beginning and end by prose folk material from an earlier age. The book begins with a description of the righteous man named Job and a discussion in a fictional land between God and Satan—the "accuser"—who wonders whether Job's piety depends on his wealth. The two of them then test Job. When Job is finally deprived of all the good things of his life, including his own health, he makes his complaint to God about his treatment, and three friends respond in the first cycle of speeches. His friends, in effect, reaffirm conventional wisdom, which argues that God is just and that Job must have sinned in order to have deserved his suffering.

As Job reaffirms his innocence and becomes increasingly isolated in his position, he demands that he be allowed to make his case in person with God and hear God's response. The climax of the book arrives when God breaks his silence and responds in a whirlwind to Job's request with a discourse on power. The meaning and appropriateness of God's response has been the subject of discussion ever since. Because God does not answer Job's questions directly, it appears as if the author of the book of Job is suggesting a faith in a transcendent deity whose connection to this world cannot be readily understood or experienced by ordinary humans.

Psalms

The 150 poems that constitute the book of Psalms represent a broad spectrum of emotions and attitudes. The word "psalm" means a song sung to a harp, indicating that the book of Psalms was originally a hymnbook for temple services and for private prayers and meditations. Both Jews and Christians treasure this collection and many people have memorized individual psalms for consolation and strength. Stories about martyrs to the faith often mention the psalm that the persecuted recited before his or her death. Martin Luther used psalms to create his hymnbook and Johann Sebastian Bach set a number of psalms to music.

Although as many as seventy-three psalms have been ascribed to David, the authorship of most of the psalms is unknown. Most were probably written after the Babylonian captivity, between 400 and 100 B.C.E. There are various types of psalms: royal psalms, associated with enthronement and the kingship of God; psalms of praise and thanksgiving; psalms of lament and confession. Most of them are known for their concrete imagery and their emotional sincerity.

Included in this text is probably the most famous psalm of all, Psalm 23. Its lyric beauty and comforting message have made it a favorite for millions of people generation after generation.

The King James Bible

The King James, or Authorized Version, completed in 1611, has been chosen for the Bible selections. As the most significant literary translation of the Bible, it influenced numerous English writers and was brought to the United States by the Pilgrims. Strangely enough, this version was the result of a group effort: James I appointed fifty-four scholars, who worked together to produce a new translation. These translators were not only scholars but literary stylists, so they produced not only a religious document but a work of literature known for its majestic style and poetic interludes.

Suggested Readings

Bernhard Anderson's *Understanding the Old Testament* (1986) is a good place for a student to begin. Stephen L. Harris provides a nonsectarian approach in *Understanding the Bible* (1992). The literary qualities are emphasized in Mary Ellen Chase, *The Bible and the Common Reader* (1952) and Richard G. Moulton, *A Short Introduction to the Literature of the Bible* (1903). The five volumes of George A. Buttrick et al., eds., *The Interpreter's Dictionary of the Bible* (1962, 1976) and the twelve volumes of George A. Buttrick et al., eds., *The Interpreter's Bible* (1952) provide ample commentary. A stimulating, humanistic interpretation of the Hebrew Bible is in Erich Fromm, *You Shall Be as Gods: A Radical Interpretation of the Old Testament and Its Tradition* (1966). Harold S. Kushner's *When Bad Things Happen to Good People* (1981) is a personal, fascinating inquiry into divine justice in the Book of Job. A fine appreciation of the Psalms is found in Samuel Terrien, *The Psalms and Their Meaning Today* (1952).

[Origin Stories]

Genesis 1–11

Chapter 1[1]

In the beginning God created the heaven and the earth.[2] And the earth was without form, and void, and darkness was upon the face of the deep: and the spirit of God moved upon the face of the waters. And God said, "Let there be light": and there was light. And God saw the light, that it was good: and God divided the light from the darkness. And God called the light Day, and the darkness he called Night: and the evening and the morning were the first day.

[1] Verse numbers have been specified only for chapters where verses have been omitted.

[2] Chapter 1 and the first paragraph of Chapter 2 tell the Priestly story of creation; God is designated in Hebrew as *Elohim*.

And God said, "Let there be a firmament[3] in the midst of the waters: and let it divide the waters from the waters." And God made the firmament, and divided the waters which were under the firmament from the waters which were above the firmament: and it was so. And God called the firmament Heaven: and the evening and the morning were the second day.

And God said, "Let the waters under the heaven be gathered together unto one place, and let the dry land appear": and it was so. And God called the dry land Earth, and the gathering together of the waters called he Seas: and God saw that it was good. And God said, "Let the earth bring forth grass, the herb yielding seed, and the fruit tree yielding fruit after his kind, whose seed is in itself, upon the earth": and it was so. And the earth brought forth grass, and herb yielding seed after his kind, and the tree yielding fruit, whose seed was in itself, after his kind: and God saw that it was good. And the evening and the morning were the third day.

And God said, "Let there be lights in the firmament of the heaven, to divide the day from the night: and let them be for signs and for seasons, and for days and years. And let them be for lights in the firmament of the heaven, to give light upon the earth": and it was so. And God made two great lights: the greater light to rule the day, and the lesser light to rule the night: he made the stars also. And God set them in the firmament of the heaven, to give light upon the earth: and to rule over the day, and over the night, and to divide the light from the darkness: and God saw that it was good. And the evening and the morning were the fourth day.

And God said, "Let the waters bring forth abundantly the moving creature that hath life, and fowl that may fly above the earth in the open firmament of heaven." And God created great whales, and every living creature that moveth, which the waters brought forth abundantly after their kind, and every winged fowl after his kind: and God saw that it was good. And God blessed them, saying, "Be fruitful, and multiply, and fill the waters in the seas, and let fowl multiply in the earth." And the evening and the morning were the fifth day.

And God said, "Let the earth bring forth the living creature after his kind, cattle, and creeping thing, and beast of the earth after his kind": and it was so. And God made the beast of the earth after his kind, and cattle after their kind, and every thing that creepeth upon the earth after his kind: and God saw that it was good.

And God said, "Let us[4] make man[5] in our image, after our likeness: and let them have dominion over the fish of the sea, and over the fowl of the air, and over the cattle, and over all the earth, and over every creeping thing that creepeth upon the earth." So God created man in his own image, in the image of God created he him; male and female created he them. And God blessed them, and God said unto them, "Be fruitful, and multiply, and replenish the earth, and subdue it, and have dominion over the fish of the sea, and over the fowl of the air, and over every living thing that moveth upon the earth."

And God said, "Behold, I have given you every herb bearing seed which is upon the face of all the earth, and every tree, in the which is the fruit of a tree yielding seed; to you it shall be for meat: and to every beast of the earth, and to every fowl of the air, and to every thing that creepeth upon the earth, wherein there is life, I

---

[3]The firmament is the solid dome of the sky.

[4]The *us* and *our* probably refer to members of God's heavenly court.

[5]The Hebrew for *man* is *adam,* referring to mankind.

have given every green herb for meat": and it was so. And God saw every thing that he had made: and behold, it was very good. And the evening and the morning were the sixth day.

Chapter 2

Thus the heavens and the earth were finished, and all the host of them. And on the seventh day God ended his work which he had made. And he rested on the seventh day from all his work which he had made. And God blessed the seventh day, and sanctified it: because that in it he had rested from all his work which God created and made.

These[6] are the generations of the heavens and of the earth when they were created, in the day that the Lord God[7] made the earth and the heavens, and every plant of the field before it was in the earth, and every herb of the field before it grew: for the Lord God had not caused it to rain upon the earth, and there was not a man to till the ground. But there went up a mist from the earth, and watered the whole face of the ground. And the Lord God formed man of the dust of the ground,[8] and breathed into his nostrils the breath of life; and man became a living soul.

And the Lord God planted a garden eastward in Eden; and there he put the man whom he had formed. And out of the ground made the Lord God to grow every tree that is pleasant to the sight and good for food: the tree of life also in the midst of the garden, and the tree of knowledge of good and evil. And a river went out of Eden to water the garden, and from thence it was parted, and became into four heads. The name of the first is Pison: that is it which compasseth the whole land of Havilah, where there is gold. And the gold of that land is good: there is bdellium and the onyx stone. And the name of the second river is Gihon: the same is it that compasseth the whole land of Ethiopia. And the name of the third river is Hiddekel: that is it which goeth toward the east of Assyria: and the fourth river is Euphrates. And the Lord God took the man, and put him into the garden of Eden, to dress it and to keep it. And the Lord God commanded the man, saying, "Of every tree of the garden thou mayest freely eat. But of the tree of the knowledge of good and evil, thou shalt not eat of it: for in the day that thou eatest thereof thou shalt surely die."

And the Lord God said, "It is not good that the man should be alone: I will make him an help meet for him." And out of the ground the Lord God formed every beast of the field, and every fowl of the air, and brought them unto Adam, to see what he would call them: and whatsoever Adam called every living creature, that was the name thereof. And Adam gave names to all cattle, and to the fowl of the air, and to every beast of the field: but for Adam there was not found an help meet for him. And the Lord God caused a deep sleep to fall upon Adam, and he slept: and he took one of his ribs, and closed up the flesh instead thereof. And the rib which the Lord God had taken from man, made he a woman, and brought her unto the man. And Adam said, "This is now bone of my bones, and flesh of my flesh: she shall be called woman,[9] because she was taken out of man."[10] Therefore

---

[6]This begins the second creation account and is from the "J" account; God is designated as *Jehovah* (Hebrew *Yahweh*). The order of events in this version differ from the first version.

[7]Lord God: In Hebrew, *Yahweh Elohim.*

[8]A pun is intended linking *man* (Hebrew *adam*) to *ground* (Hebrew *adamah*).

[9]Woman: in Hebrew, *ishshah.*

[10]Man: in Hebrew, *ish.*

shall a man leave his father and his mother, and shall cleave unto his wife: and they shall be one flesh. And they were both naked, the man and his wife, and were not ashamed.

Chapter 3

Now the serpent was more subtle than any beast of the field which the Lord God had made, and he said unto the woman, "Yea, hath God said, 'Ye shall not eat of every tree of the garden'?" And the woman said unto the serpent, "We may eat of the fruit of the trees of the garden: but of the fruit of the tree which is in the midst of the garden, God hath said, 'Ye shall not eat of it, neither shall ye touch it, lest ye die.'" And the serpent said unto the woman, "Ye shall not surely die. For God doth know that in the day ye eat thereof, then your eyes shall be opened: and ye shall be as gods, knowing good and evil." And when the woman saw that the tree was good for food, and that it was pleasant to the eyes, and a tree to be desired to make one wise, she took of the fruit thereof, and did eat, and gave also unto her husband with her, and he did eat. And the eyes of them both were opened, and they knew that they were naked, and they sewed fig leaves together, and made themselves aprons. And they heard the voice of the Lord God walking in the garden in the cool of the day: and Adam and his wife hid themselves from the presence of the Lord God, amongst the trees of the garden.

And the Lord God called unto Adam, and said unto him, "Where art thou?" And he said, "I heard thy voice in the garden: and I was afraid, because I was naked, and I hid myself." And he said, "Who told thee that thou wast naked? Hast thou eaten of the tree whereof I commanded thee that thou shouldst not eat?" And the man said, "The woman whom thou gavest to be with me, she gave me of the tree, and I did eat." And the Lord God said unto the woman, "What is this that thou hast done?" And the woman said, "The serpent beguiled me, and I did eat." And the Lord God said unto the serpent, "Because thou hast done this, thou art cursed above all cattle, and above every beast of the field: upon thy belly shalt thou go, and dust shalt thou eat, all the days of thy life. And I will put enmity between thee and the woman, and between thy seed and her seed: it shall bruise thy head, and thou shalt bruise his heel." Unto the woman he said, "I will greatly multiply thy sorrow and thy conception. In sorrow thou shalt bring forth children: and thy desire shall be to thy husband, and he shall rule over thee." And unto Adam he said, "Because thou hast hearkened unto the voice of thy wife, and hast eaten of the tree, of which I commanded thee, saying, 'Thou shalt not eat of it': cursed is the ground for thy sake: in sorrow shalt thou eat of it all the days of thy life. Thorns also and thistles shall it bring forth to thee: and thou shalt eat the herb of the field. In the sweat of thy face shalt thou eat bread, till thou return unto the ground: for out of it wast thou taken, for dust thou art, and unto dust shalt thou return." And Adam called his wife's name Eve,[11] because she was the mother of all living. Unto Adam also, and to his wife, did the Lord God make coats of skins, and clothed them.

And the Lord God said, "Behold, the man is become as one of us, to know good and evil. And now, lest he put forth his hand, and take also of the tree of life, and eat and live for ever—": therefore the Lord God sent him forth from the garden of Eden, to till the ground from whence he was taken. So he drove out the man: and he placed at the east of the garden of Eden cherubim, and a flaming sword which turned every way, to keep the way of the tree of life.

[11] *Eve* means *life*.

Chapter 4:1–17, 25–26

And Adam[12] knew[13] Eve his wife, and she conceived, and bare Cain, and said, "I have gotten a man from the Lord." And she again bare his brother Abel, and Abel was a keeper of sheep, but Cain was a tiller of the ground. And in process of time it came to pass, that Cain brought of the fruit of the ground an offering unto the Lord. And Abel, he also brought of the firstlings of his flock, and of the fat thereof: and the Lord had respect unto Abel and to his offering. But unto Cain and to his offering he had not respect: and Cain was very wroth, and his countenance fell. And the Lord said unto Cain, "Why art thou wroth? And why is thy countenance fallen? If thou doest well, shalt thou not be accepted? and if thou doest not well, sin lieth at the door: and unto thee shall be his desire, and thou shalt rule over him." And Cain talked with Abel his brother: and it came to pass when they were in the field, that Cain rose up against Abel his brother, and slew him.

And the Lord said unto Cain, "Where is Abel thy brother?" And he said, "I know not: am I my brother's keeper?" And he said "What hast thou done? the voice of thy brother's blood crieth unto me from the ground. And now art thou cursed from the earth, which hath opened her mouth to receive thy brother's blood from thy hand. When thou tillest the ground, it shall not henceforth yield unto thee her strength: a fugitive and a vagabond shalt thou be in the earth." And Cain said unto the Lord, "My punishment is greater than I can bear. Behold, thou hast driven me out this day from the face of the earth, and from thy face shall I be hid, and I shall be a fugitive, and a vagabond in the earth: and it shall come to pass, that every one that findeth me shall slay me." And the Lord said unto him, "Therefore whosoever slayeth Cain, vengeance shall be taken on him sevenfold." And the Lord set a mark upon Cain, lest any finding him should kill him.

And Cain went out from the presence of the Lord, and dwelt in the land of Nod,[14] on the east of Eden. And Cain knew his wife, and she conceived and bare Enoch, and he builded a city, and called the name of the city after the name of his son, Enoch. . . . And Adam knew his wife again, and she bare a son, and called his name Seth: "For God," said she, "hath appointed me another seed instead of Abel, whom Cain slew." And to Seth, to him also there was born a son, and he called his name Enos: then began men to call upon the name of the Lord.

Chapter 5:5[15]

And the days of Adam, after he had begotten Seth, were eight hundred years: and he begat sons and daughters. And all the days that Adam lived were nine hundred and thirty years: and he died.

Chapter 6

And it came to pass, when men began to multiply on the face of the earth, and daughters were born unto them, that the sons of God saw the daughters of men, that they were fair, and they took them wives of all which they chose. And the Lord said, "My spirit shall not always strive with men, for that he also is flesh: yet his days shall be an hundred and twenty years." There were giants in the earth in those days: and also after that, when the sons of God came in unto the daughters of

[12] Adam: used for the first time as a name.

[13] Knew: as in sexual intercourse.

[14] The land of wandering.

[15] Chapter 5 contains genealogies, descendants of Adam and Eve.

men, and they bare children to them, the same became mighty men, which were of old, men of renown.[16]

And God saw that the wickedness of men was great in the earth, and that every imagination of the thoughts of his heart was only evil continually. And it repented the Lord that he had made man on the earth, and it grieved him at his heart. And the Lord said, "I will destroy man, whom I have created, from the face of the earth: both man and beast, and the creeping thing, and the fowls of the air: for it repenteth me that I have made them."[17] But Noah found grace in the eyes of the Lord.

These are the generations of Noah: Noah was a just man, and perfect in his generations, and Noah walked with God. And Noah begat three sons: Shem, Ham, and Japheth. The earth also was corrupt before God; and the earth was filled with violence. And God looked upon the earth, and behold, it was corrupt: for all flesh had corrupted his way upon the earth. And God said unto Noah, "The end of all flesh is come before me; for the earth is filled with violence through them; and behold, I will destroy them with the earth."

"Make thee an ark of gopher wood:[18] rooms shalt thou make in the ark, and shalt pitch it within and without with pitch. And this is the fashion which thou shalt make it of: the length of the ark shall be three hundred cubits,[19] the breadth of it fifty cubits, and the height of it thirty cubits. A window shalt thou make to the ark, and in a cubit shalt thou finish it above; and the door of the ark shalt thou set in the side thereof: with lower, second, and third stories shalt thou make it. And behold, I, even I do bring a flood of waters upon the earth, to destroy all flesh wherein is the breath of life from under heaven, and every thing that is in the earth shall die. But with thee will I establish my covenant:[20] and thou shalt come into the ark, thou, and thy sons, and thy wife, and thy sons' wives with thee. And of every living thing of all flesh, two of every sort shalt thou bring into the ark, to keep them alive with thee: they shall be male and female. Of fowls after their kind, and of cattle after their kind, of every creeping thing of the earth after his kind, two of every sort shall come unto thee, to keep them alive. And take thou unto thee of all food that is eaten, and thou shalt gather it to thee; and it shall be for food, for thee, and for them." Thus did Noah; according to all that God commanded him, so did he.

Chapter 7

And the Lord said unto Noah, "Come thou and all thy house into the ark: for thee have I seen righteous before me in this generation. Of every clean beast thou shalt take to thee by sevens, the male and his female: and of beasts that are not clean, by two, the male and his female. Of fowls also of the air, by sevens, the male and the female; to keep seed alive upon the face of all the earth. For yet seven days, and I will cause it to rain upon the earth forty days and forty nights: and every living substance that I have made will I destroy from off the face of the earth." And Noah did according unto all that the Lord commanded him. And Noah was six hundred years old when the flood of waters was upon the earth.

And Noah went in, and his sons, and his wife, and his sons' wives with him, into the ark, because of the waters of the flood. Of clean beasts, and of beasts that

---

[16] A folk explanation for a race of giants.

[17] The story of the flood in Genesis is similar to the earlier flood story in *The Epic of Gilgamesh*.

[18] Gopher wood: cypress.

[19] Cubit: approximately 18 inches.

[20] Covenant: This is the first of several agreements between God and mankind; after the flood this covenant is sealed with a rainbow.

are not clean, and of fowls, and of every thing that creepeth upon the earth, there went in two and two unto Noah into the ark, the male and the female, as God had commanded Noah. And it came to pass after seven days, that the waters of the flood were upon the earth.

In the six hundredth year of Noah's life, in the second month, the seventeenth day of the month, the same day were all the fountains of the great deep broken up, and the windows of heaven were opened. And the rain was upon the earth forty days and forty nights. In the selfsame day entered Noah, and Shem, and Ham, and Japheth, the sons of Noah, and Noah's wife, and the three wives of his sons with them, into the ark, they, and every beast after his kind, and all the cattle after their kind, and every creeping thing that creepeth upon the earth after his kind, and every fowl after his kind, every bird of every sort. And they went in unto Noah into the ark, two and two of all flesh wherein is the breath of life. And they that went in, went in male and female of all flesh, as God had commanded him: and the Lord shut him in.

And the flood was forty days upon the earth, and the waters increased, and bare up the ark, and it was lifted up above the earth. And the waters prevailed, and were increased greatly upon the earth: and the ark went upon the face of the waters. And the waters prevailed exceedingly upon the earth, and all the high hills that were under the whole heaven were covered. Fifteen cubits upward did the waters prevail; and the mountains were covered. And all flesh died that moved upon the earth, both of fowl, and of cattle, and of beast, and of every creeping thing that creepeth upon the earth, and every man. All in whose nostrils was the breath of life, of all that was in the dry land, died. And every living substance was destroyed which was upon the face of the ground, both man and cattle, and the creeping things, and the fowl of the heaven; and they were destroyed from the earth: and Noah only remained alive, and they that were with him in the ark. And the waters prevailed upon the earth an hundred and fifty days.

Chapter 8

And God remembered Noah, and every living thing, and all the cattle that was with him in the ark: and God made a wind to pass over the earth, and the waters assuaged. The fountains also of the deep and the windows of heaven were stopped, and the rain from heaven was restrained. And the waters returned from off the earth continually: and after the end of the hundred and fifty days the waters were abated. And the ark rested in the seventh month, on the seventeenth day of the month, upon the mountains of Ararat.[21] And the waters decreased continually until the tenth month: in the tenth month, on the first day of the month, were the tops of the mountains seen.

And it came to pass at the end of forty days, that Noah opened the window of the ark which he had made. And he sent forth a raven, which went forth to and fro, until the waters were dried up from off the earth. Also he sent forth a dove from him, to see if the waters were abated from off the face of the ground. But the dove found no rest for the sole of her foot, and she returned unto him into the ark: for the waters were on the face of the whole earth. Then he put forth his hand, and took her, and pulled her in unto him, into the ark. And he stayed yet other seven days; and again he sent forth the dove out of the ark. And the dove came in to him in the evening, and lo, in her mouth was an olive leaf plucked off: so Noah knew

[21] Ararat is a region in Armenia.

that the waters were abated from off the earth. And he stayed yet other seven days, and sent forth the dove, which returned not again unto him any more.

And it came to pass in the six hundredth and one year, in the first month, the first day of the month, the waters were dried up from off the earth: and Noah removed the covering of the ark, and looked, and behold, the face of the ground was dry. And in the second month, on the seven and twentieth day of the month, was the earth dried.

And God spake unto Noah, saying, "Go forth of the ark, thou, and thy wife, and thy sons and thy sons' wives with thee: bring forth with thee every living thing that is with thee, of all flesh, both of fowl, and of cattle, and of every creeping thing that creepeth upon the earth, that they may breed abundantly in the earth, and be fruitful, and multiply upon the earth." And Noah went forth, and his sons, and his wife, and his sons' wives with him: every beast, every creeping thing, and every fowl, and whatsoever creepeth upon the earth, after their kinds, went forth out of the ark.

And Noah builded an altar unto the Lord, and took of every clean beast, and of every clean fowl, and offered burnt offerings on the altar. And the Lord smelled a sweet savour, and the Lord said in his heart, "I will not again curse the ground any more for man's sake; for the imagination of man's heart is evil from his youth: neither will I again smite any more every thing living, as I have done. While the earth remaineth, seedtime and harvest, and cold and heat, and summer and winter, and day and night shall not cease."

Chapter 9

And God blessed Noah, and his sons, and said unto them, "Be fruitful and multiply, and replenish the earth. And the fear of you and the dread of you shall be upon every beast of the earth, and upon every fowl of the air, upon all that moveth upon the earth, and upon all the fishes of the sea; into your hand are they delivered. Every moving thing that liveth shall be meat for you; even as the green herb have I given you all things. But flesh with the life thereof, which is the blood thereof, shall you not eat. And surely your blood of your lives will I require: at the hand of every beast will I require it, and at the hand of man, at the hand of every man's brother will I require the life of man. Whoso sheddeth man's blood, by man shall his blood be shed: for in the image of God made he man. And you, be ye fruitful and multiply, bring forth abundantly in the earth, and multiply therein."

And God spake unto Noah, and to his sons with him, saying, "And I, behold, I establish my covenant with you and with your seed after you: and with every living creature that is with you, of the fowl, of the cattle, and of every beast of the earth with you, from all that go out of the ark, to every beast of the earth. And I will establish my covenant with you, neither shall all flesh be cut off any more by the waters of a flood, neither shall there any more be a flood to destroy the earth." And God said, "This is the token of the covenant which I make between me and you, and every living creature that is with you, for perpetual generations. I do set my bow in the cloud, and it shall be for a token of a covenant between me and the earth.[22] And it shall come to pass, when I bring a cloud over the earth, that the bow shall be seen in the cloud. And I will remember my covenant, which is between me and you, and every living creature of all flesh: and the waters shall no more become a flood to destroy all flesh. And the bow shall be in the cloud; and I

[22]Among ancient peoples, the rainbow was used by God to shoot lightning; here it is a sign of the covenant.

will look upon it, that I may remember the everlasting covenant between God and every living creature of all flesh that is upon the earth." And God said unto Noah, "This is the token of the covenant which I have established between me and all flesh that is upon the earth."

And the sons of Noah that went forth of the ark were Shem, and Ham, and Japheth: and Ham is the father of Canaan. These are the three sons of Noah: and of them was the whole earth overspread. And Noah began to be an husbandman, and he planted a vineyard. And he drank of the vine, and was drunken, and he was uncovered within his tent. And Ham, the father of Canaan, saw the nakedness of his father, and told his two brethren without. And Shem and Japheth took a garment, and laid it upon both their shoulders, and went backward, and covered the nakedness of their father, and their faces were backward, and they saw not their father's nakedness. And Noah awoke from his wine, and knew what his younger son had done unto him. And he said, "Cursed be Canaan:[23] a servant of servants shall he be unto his brethren." And he said, "Blessed be the Lord God of Shem, and Canaan shall be his servant. God shall enlarge Japheth, and he shall dwell in the tents of Shem, and Canaan shall be his servant." And Noah lived after the flood three hundred and fifty years. And all the days of Noah were nine hundred and fifty years, and he died.

Chapter 10:1, 32 [24]

Now these are the generations of the sons of Noah, Shem, Ham, and Japheth: and unto them were sons born after the flood. . . . And by these were the nations divided in the earth after the flood.

Chapter 11:1–9, 31–32

And the whole earth was of one language, and of one speech.[25] And it came to pass, as they journeyed from the east, that they found a plain in the land of Shinar, and they dwelt there. And they said one to another, "Go to, let us make brick, and burn them thoroughly." And they had brick for stone, and slime had they for mortar. And they said, "Go to, let us build us a city and a tower, whose top may reach unto heaven, and let us make us a name, lest we be scattered abroad upon the face of the whole earth." And the Lord came down to see the city and the tower, which the children of men builded. And the Lord said, "Behold, the people is one, and they have all one language: and this they begin to do: and now nothing will be restrained from them, which they have imagined to do. Go to, let us go down, and there confound their language, that they may not understand one another's speech." So the Lord scattered them abroad from thence upon the face of all the earth: and they left off to build the city. Therefore is the name of it called Babel, because the Lord did there confound the language of all the earth: and from thence did the Lord scatter them abroad upon the face of all the earth. . . .

And Terah took Abram his son, and Lot the son of Haran his son's son, and Sarai his daughter in law, his son Abram's wife, and they went forth with them from Ur of the Chaldees, to go into the land of Canaan: and they came unto Haran, and dwelt there. And the days of Terah were two hundred and five years: and Terah died in Haran.

---

[23]The guilt is shifted from Ham to Canaan, perhaps to justify later subjugation of the Canaanites.

[24]Chapter 10 contains genealogies.

[25]The Tower of Babel explains the existence of diverse languages; the tower itself alludes to the *ziggurats*, or stepped pyramids, of Babylon.

[Abraham and Isaac]

GENESIS 12–13, 16–19, 21–22

Chapter 12

Now the Lord had said unto Abram, "Get thee out of thy country, and from thy kindred, and from thy father's house, unto a land that I will show thee. And I will make of thee a great nation, and I will bless thee, and make thy name great; and thou shalt be a blessing. And I will bless them that bless thee, and curse him that curseth thee: and in thee shall all families of the earth be blessed."[26] So Abram departed, as the Lord had spoken unto him, and Lot went with him: and Abram was seventy and five years old when he departed out of Haran. And Abram took Sarai his wife, and Lot his brother's son, and all their substance that they had gathered, and the souls that they had gotten in Haran, and they went forth to go into the land of Canaan: and into the land of Canaan they came.

And Abram passed through the land, unto the place of Sichem, unto the plain of Moreh. And the Canaanite was then in the land. And the Lord appeared unto Abram, and said, "Unto thy seed will I give this land": and there builded he an altar unto the Lord, who appeared unto him. And he removed from thence unto a mountain on the east of Bethel, and pitched his tent, having Bethel on the west, and Hai on the east: and there he builded an altar unto the Lord, and called upon the name of the Lord. And Abram journeyed, going on still toward the south.

And there was a famine in the land, and Abram went down into Egypt to sojourn there: for the famine was grievous in the land. And it came to pass when he was come near to enter into Egypt, that he said unto Sarai his wife, "Behold now, I know that thou art a fair woman to look upon. Therefore it shall come to pass, when the Egyptians shall see thee, that they shall say, 'This is his wife': and they will kill me, but they will save thee alive. Say, I pray thee, thou art my sister, that it may be well with me for thy sake; and my soul shall live because of thee."

And it came to pass that, when Abram was come into Egypt, the Egyptians beheld the woman, that she was very fair. The princes also of Pharaoh saw her, and commended her before Pharaoh: and the woman was taken into Pharaoh's house. And he entreated Abram well for her sake: and he had sheep, and oxen, and he-asses, and menservants, and maidservants, and she-asses, and camels. And the Lord plagued Pharaoh and his house with great plagues, because of Sarai Abram's wife. And Pharaoh called Abram, and said, "What is this that thou hast done unto me? Why didst thou not tell me that she was thy wife? Why saidst thou, 'She is my sister'? so I might have taken her to me to wife: now therefore behold thy wife, take her, and go thy way." And Pharaoh commanded his men concerning him: and they sent him away, and his wife, and all that he had.

Chapter 13

And Abram went up out of Egypt, he, and his wife, and all that he had, and Lot with him, into the south. And Abram was very rich in cattle, in silver, and in gold. And he went on his journeys from the south, even to Bethel, unto the place where his tent had been at the beginning, between Bethel and Hai: unto the place of the altar, which he had made there at the first: and there Abram called on the name of the Lord.

---

[26]This is a statement of the covenant made with Abraham and the Hebrews; the terms of the covenant evolve, forming a central theme in the Old Testament.

And Lot also, which went with Abram, had flocks, and herds, and tents. And the land was not able to bear them, that they might dwell together: for their substance was great, so that they could not dwell together. And there was a strife between the herdmen of Abram's cattle and the herdmen of Lot's cattle: and the Canaanite and the Perizzite dwelled then in the land. And Abram said unto Lot, "Let there be no strife, I pray thee, between me and thee, and between my herdmen and thy herdmen: for we be brethren. Is not the whole land before thee? Separate thyself, I pray thee, from me: if thou wilt take the left hand, then I will go to the right: or if thou depart to the right hand, then I will go to the left." And Lot lifted up his eyes, and beheld all the plain of Jordan, that it was well watered everywhere, before the Lord destroyed Sodom and Gomorrah, even as the garden of the Lord, like the land of Egypt, as thou comest unto Zoar. Then Lot chose him all the plain of Jordan: and Lot journeyed east; and they separated themselves the one from the other. Abram dwelled in the land of Canaan, and Lot dwelled in the cities of the plain, and pitched his tent toward Sodom. But the men of Sodom were wicked, and sinners before the Lord exceedingly.

And the Lord said unto Abram, after that Lot was separated from him, "Lift up now thine eyes, and look from the place where thou art, northward, and southward, and eastward, and westward. For all the land which thou seest, to thee will I give it, and to thy seed for ever. And I will make thy seed as the dust of the earth: so that if a man can number the dust of the earth, then shall thy seed also be numbered. Arise, walk through the land, in the length of it, and in the breadth of it: for I will give it unto thee." Then Abram removed his tent, and came and dwelt in the plain of Mamre, which is in Hebron, and built there an altar unto the Lord.[27]

• • •

Chapter 16

Now Sarai Abram's wife bare him no children: and she had an handmaid, an Egyptian, whose name was Hagar. And Sarai said unto Abram, "Behold now, the Lord hath restrained me from bearing: I pray thee go in unto my maid: it may be that I may obtain children by her": and Abram hearkened to the voice of Sarai. And Sarai Abram's wife took Hagar her maid, the Egyptian, after Abram had dwelt ten years in the land of Canaan, and gave her to her husband Abram, to be his wife.

And he went in unto Hagar, and she conceived: and when she saw that she had conceived, her mistress was despised in her eyes. And Sarai said unto Abram, "My wrong be upon thee: I have given my maid into thy bosom, and when she saw that she had conceived, I was despised in her eyes: the Lord judge between me and thee." But Abram said unto Sarai, "Behold, thy maid is in thy hand; do to her as it pleaseth thee." And when Sarai dealt hardly with her, she fled from her face.

And the angel of the Lord found her by a fountain of water in the wilderness, by the fountain in the way to Shur: and he said, "Hagar, Sarai's maid, whence camest thou? and whither wilt thou go?" And she said, "I flee from the face of my mistress Sarai." And the angel of the Lord said unto her, "Return to thy mistress, and submit thyself under her hands." And the angel of the Lord said unto her, "I will multiply thy seed exceedingly, that it shall not be numbered for multitude." And the angel of the Lord said unto her, "Behold, thou art with child, and shalt bear a son, and shalt call his name Ishmael; because the Lord hath heard thy affliction. And he will be a wild man; his hand will be against every man, and every man's hand against him: and he shall dwell in the presence of all his brethren." And she called the name of the Lord that spake unto her, "Thou God seest me": for she said, "Have I also

[27]Chapters 14 and 15 describe wars with regional kingdoms.

here looked after him that seeth me?" Wherefore the well was called Beer-lahai-roi: behold, it is between Kadesh and Bered.

And Hagar bare Abram a son: and Abram called his son's name, which Hagar bare, Ishmael.[28] And Abram was fourscore and six years old when Hagar bare Ishmael to Abram.

Chapter 17

And when Abram was ninety years old and nine, the Lord appeared to Abram, and said unto him, "I am the almighty God, walk before me, and be thou perfect. And I will make my covenant between me and thee, and will multiply thee exceedingly." And Abram fell on his face, and God talked with him, saying, "As for me, behold, my covenant is with thee, and thou shalt be a father of many nations. Neither shall thy name any more be called Abram, but thy name shall be Abraham: for a father of many nations have I made thee. And I will make thee exceeding fruitful, and I will make nations of thee, and kings shall come out of thee. And I will establish my covenant between me and thee, and thy seed after thee, in their generations for an everlasting covenant, to be a God unto thee, and to thy seed after thee. And I will give unto thee, and to thy seed after thee, the land wherein thou art a stranger, all the land of Canaan, for an everlasting possession, and I will be their God."

And God said unto Abraham, "Thou shalt keep my covenant therefore, thou, and thy seed after thee, in their generations. This is my covenant, which ye shall keep between me and you, and thy seed after thee: every man child among you shall be circumcised.[29] And ye shall circumcise the flesh of your foreskin; and it shall be a token of the covenant betwixt me and you. And he that is eight days old shall be circumcised among you, every man child in your generations, he that is born in the house, or bought with money of any stranger, which is not of thy seed. He that is born in thy house, and he that is bought with thy money, must needs be circumcised: and my covenant shall be in your flesh for an everlasting covenant. And the uncircumcised man child whose flesh of his foreskin is not circumcised, that soul shall be cut off from his people: he hath broken my covenant."

And God said unto Abraham, "As for Sarai thy wife, thou shalt not call her name Sarai, but Sarah shall her name be. And I will bless her, and give thee a son also of her: yea I will bless her, and she shall be a mother of nations; kings of people shall be of her." Then Abraham fell upon his face, and laughed, and said in his heart, "Shall a child be born unto him that is an hundred years old? and shall Sarah that is ninety years old, bear?" And Abraham said unto God, "O that Ishmael might live before thee." And God said, "Sarah thy wife shall bear thee a son indeed, and thou shalt call his name Isaac: and I will establish my covenant with him for an everlasting covenant, and with his seed after him. And as for Ishmael, I have heard thee: behold, I have blessed him, and will make him fruitful, and will multiply him exceedingly: twelve princes shall he beget, and I will make him a great nation. But my covenant will I establish with Isaac, which Sarah shall bear unto thee at this set time in the next year." And he left off talking with him, and God went up from Abraham.

And Abraham took Ishmael his son, and all that were born in his house, and all that were bought with his money, every male among the men of Abraham's house, and circumcised the flesh of their foreskin, in the selfsame day, as God had said

---

[28]Ishmael is the ancestor of the Bedouin.

[29]God's covenant requires name changes (Abram to Abraham and Sarai to Sarah) and circumcision.

unto him. And Abraham was ninety years old and nine when he was circumcised in the flesh of his foreskin. And Ishmael his son was thirteen years old when he was circumcised in the flesh of his foreskin. In the selfsame day was Abraham circumcised, and Ishmael his son. And all the men of his house, born in the house, and bought with money of the stranger, were circumcised with him.

Chapter 18

And the Lord appeared unto him in the plains of Mamre: and he sat in the tent door, in the heat of the day. And he lifted up his eyes and looked, and lo, three men stood by him: and when he saw them, he ran to meet them from the tent door, and bowed himself toward the ground, and said, "My Lord, if now I have found favour in thy sight, pass not away, I pray thee, from thy servant: let a little water, I pray you, be fetched, and wash your feet, and rest yourselves under the tree: and I will fetch a morsel of bread; and comfort ye your hearts, after that ye shall pass on: for therefore are you come to your servant." And they said, "So do, as thou hast said." And Abraham hastened into the tent, unto Sarah, and said, "Make ready quickly three measures of fine meal, knead it, and make cakes upon the hearth." And Abraham ran unto the herd, and fetched a calf, tender and good, and gave it unto a young man: and he hasted to dress it. And he took butter, and milk, and the calf which he had dressed, and set it before them; and he stood by them under the tree: and they did eat.

And they said unto him, "Where is Sarah thy wife?" And he said, "Behold, in the tent." And he said, "I will certainly return unto thee according to the time of your life; and lo, Sarah thy wife shall have a son." And Sarah heard it in the tent door, which was behind him. Now Abraham and Sarah were old, and well stricken in age: and it ceased to be with Sarah after the manner of women. Therefore Sarah laughed within herself, saying, "After I am waxed old shall I have pleasure, my lord being old also?" And the Lord said unto Abraham, "Wherefore did Sarah laugh, saying, 'Shall I of a surety bear a child, which am old?' Is any thing too hard for the Lord? At the time appointed will I return unto thee, according to the time of life, and Sarah shall have a son." Then Sarah denied, saying, "I laughed not": for she was afraid. And he said, "Nay, but thou didst laugh."

And the men rose up from thence, and looked toward Sodom: and Abraham went with them, to bring them on the way. And the Lord said, "Shall I hide from Abraham that thing which I do; seeing that Abraham shall surely become a great and mighty nation, and all the nations of the earth shall be blessed in him? For I know him, that he will command his children, and his household after him, and they shall keep the way of the Lord, to do justice and judgment, that the Lord may bring upon Abraham that which he hath spoken of him." And the Lord said, "Because the cry of Sodom and Gomorrah is great, and because their sin is very grievous: I will go down now, and see whether they have done altogether according to the cry of it, which is come unto me: and if not, I will know." And the men turned their faces from thence, and went toward Sodom: but Abraham stood yet before the Lord.

And Abraham drew near, and said, "Wilt thou also destroy the righteous with the wicked? Peradventure there be fifty righteous within the city; wilt thou also destroy, and not spare the place for the fifty righteous that are therein? That be far from thee, to do after this manner, to slay the righteous with the wicked; and that the righteous should be as the wicked, that be far from thee: shall not the judge of all the earth do right?" And the Lord said, "If I find in Sodom fifty righteous within the city, then I will spare all the place for their sakes." And Abraham answered, and said, "Behold now, I have taken upon me to speak unto the Lord, which am but dust and ashes. Peradventure there shall lack five of the fifty righteous: wilt thou destroy all the city for lack of five?" And he said, "If I find there forty and five, I will not destroy it." And he spake unto him yet again, and said, "Peradventure there shall be forty found there." And he said, "I will not do it for forty's sake." And he said unto him, "Oh let not the Lord be angry, and I will speak: peradventure there shall thirty be found there." And he said, "I will not do it, if I find thirty there." And he said, "Behold now, I have taken upon me to speak unto the Lord: peradventure there shall be twenty found there." And he said, "I will not destroy it for twenty's sake." And he said, "Oh let not the Lord be angry, and I will speak yet but this once: peradventure ten shall be found there." And he said, "I will not destroy it for ten's sake." And the Lord went his way, as soon as he had left communing with Abraham: and Abraham returned unto his place.

Chapter 19

And there came two angels to Sodom at even, and Lot sat in the gate of Sodom: and Lot seeing them rose up to meet them, and he bowed himself with his face toward the ground. And he said, "Behold now my lords, turn in, I pray you, into your servant's house, and tarry all night, and wash your feet, and ye shall rise up early and go on your ways." And they said, "Nay: but we will abide in the street all night." And he pressed upon them greatly, and they turned in unto him, and entered into his house: and he made them a feast, and did bake unleavened bread, and they did eat.

But before they lay down, the men of the city, even the men of Sodom, compassed the house round, both old and young, all the people from every quarter. And they called unto Lot, and said unto him, "Where are the men which came in to thee this night? bring them out unto us, that we may know them." And Lot went out at the door unto them, and shut the door after him, and said, "I pray you, brethren, do not so wickedly. Behold now, I have two daughters, which have not known man; let me, I pray you, bring them out unto you, and do ye to them as is good in your eyes: only unto these men do nothing: for therefore came they under the shadow of my roof." And they said, "Stand back." And they said again, "This one fellow came in to sojourn, and he will needs be a judge: now will we deal worse with thee than with them." And they pressed sore upon the man, even Lot, and came near to break the door. But the men put forth their hand, and pulled Lot into the house to them, and shut to the door. And they smote the men that were at the door of the house with blindness, both small and great: so that they wearied themselves to find the door.

And the men said unto Lot, "Hast thou here any besides? Son in law, and thy sons, and thy daughters, and whatsoever thou hast in the city, bring them out of this place. For we will destroy this place, because the cry of them is waxen great before the face of the Lord: and the Lord hath sent us to destroy it." And Lot went out, and spake unto his sons in law, which married his daughters, and said, "Up, get ye out of this place: for the Lord will destroy this city": but he seemed as one that mocked unto his sons in law.

And when the morning arose, then the angels hastened Lot, saying, "Arise, take thy wife, and thy two daughters, which are here, lest thou be consumed in the iniquity of the city." And while he lingered, the men laid hold upon his hand, and upon the hand of his wife, and upon the hand of his two daughters, the Lord being merciful unto him: and they brought him forth, and set him without the city.

And it came to pass, when they had brought them forth abroad, that he said, "Escape for thy life, look not behind thee, neither stay thou in all the plain: escape to the mountain, lest thou be consumed." And Lot said unto them, "Oh, not so, my Lord. Behold now, thy servant hath found grace in thy sight, and thou hast magnified thy mercy, which thou hast showed unto me in saving my life, and I cannot escape to the mountain, lest some evil take me, and I die. Behold now, this city is near to flee unto, and it is a little one. Oh, let me escape thither (is it not a little one?), and my soul shall live." And he said unto him, "See, I have accepted thee concerning this thing also, that I will not overthrow this city, for the which thou hast spoken. Haste thee, escape thither: for I cannot do any thing till thou be come thither": therefore the name of the city was called Zoar.

The sun was risen upon the earth when Lot entered into Zoar. Then the Lord rained upon Sodom and upon Gomorrah brimstone and fire from the Lord out of heaven. And he overthrew those cities, and all the plain, and all the inhabitants of the cities, and that which grew upon the ground. But his wife looked back from behind him, and she became a pillar of salt.

And Abraham got up early in the morning to the place where he stood before the Lord. And he looked toward Sodom and Gomorrah, and toward all the land of the plain, and beheld, and lo, the smoke of the country went up as the smoke of a furnace. And it came to pass, when God destroyed the cities of the plain, that God remembered Abraham, and sent Lot out of the midst of the overthrow, when he overthrew the cities in the which Lot dwelt.

And Lot went up out of Zoar, and dwelt in the mountain, and his two daughters with him: for he feared to dwell in Zoar, and he dwelt in a cave, he and his two daughters. And the firstborn said unto the younger, "Our father is old, and there is not a man in the earth to come in unto us after the manner of all the earth. Come, let us make our father drink wine, and we will lie with him, that we may preserve seed of our father." And they made their father drink wine that night, and the firstborn went in, and lay with her father: and he perceived not when she lay down, nor when she arose. And it came to pass on the morrow, that the firstborn said unto the younger, "Behold, I lay yesternight with my father: let us make him drink wine this night also, and go thou in, and lie with him, that we may preserve seed of our father." And they made their father drink wine that night also, and the younger arose, and lay with him: and he perceived not when she lay down, nor when she arose. Thus were both the daughters of Lot with child by their father. And the firstborn bare a son, and called his name Moab: the same is the father of the Moabites unto this day. And the younger, she also bare a son, and called his name Ben-ammi: the same is the father of the children of Ammon unto this day.[30]

• • •

Chapter 21:1–21

And the Lord visited Sarah as he had said, and the Lord did unto Sarah as he had spoken. For Sarah conceived, and bare Abraham a son in his old age, at the set time of which God had spoken to him. And Abraham called the name of his son that was born unto him, whom Sarah bare to him, Isaac. And Abraham circumcised his son Isaac, being eight days old, as God had commanded him. And Abraham was an hundred years old when his son Isaac was born unto him. And Sarah said, "God hath made me to laugh, so that all that hear will laugh with me." And she said, "Who would have said unto Abraham that Sarah should have given children suck? for I have borne him a son in his old age." And the child grew, and was weaned: and Abraham made a great feast the same day that Isaac was weaned.

And Sarah saw the son of Hagar the Egyptian, which she had borne unto Abraham, mocking. Wherefore she said unto Abraham, "Cast out this bondwoman

[30]Chapter 20 relates an encounter with Abimelech, king of Gerar.

and her son: for the son of this bondwoman shall not be heir with my son, even with Isaac." And the thing was very grievous in Abraham's sight, because of his son.

And God said unto Abraham, "Let it not be grievous in thy sight because of the lad, and because of thy bondwoman. In all that Sarah hath said unto thee, hearken unto her voice: for in Isaac shall thy seed be called. And also of the son of the bondwoman will I make a nation, because he is thy seed." And Abraham rose up early in the morning, and took bread, and a bottle of water, and gave it unto Hagar (putting it on her shoulder), and the child, and sent her away: and she departed, and wandered in the wilderness of Beer-sheba. And the water was spent in the bottle, and she cast the child under one of the shrubs. And she went, and sat her down over against him, a good way off, as it were a bowshot: for she said, "Let me not see the death of the child." And she sat over against him, and lifted up her voice, and wept. And God heard the voice of the lad, and the angel of God called to Hagar out of heaven, and said unto her, "What aileth thee, Hagar? fear not: for God hath heard the voice of the lad, where he is. Arise, lift up the lad, and hold him in thine hand: for I will make him a great nation." And God opened her eyes, and she saw a well of water, and she went, and filled the bottle with water, and gave the lad drink. And God was with the lad, and he grew, and dwelt in the wilderness, and became an archer. And he dwelt in the wilderness of Paran: and his mother took him a wife out of the land of Egypt.

• • •

Chapter 22:1–19

And it came to pass after these things, that God did tempt Abraham, and said unto him, "Abraham": and he said, "Behold, here I am." And he said, "Take now thy son, thine only son Isaac, whom thou lovest, and get thee into the land of Moriah; and offer him there for a burnt offering upon one of the mountains which I will tell thee of." And Abraham rose up early in the morning, and saddled his ass, and took two of his young men with him, and Isaac his son, and clave the wood for the burnt offering, and rose up, and went unto the place of which God had told him. Then on the third day Abraham lifted up his eyes, and saw the place afar off. And Abraham said unto his young men, "Abide you here with the ass, and I and the lad will go yonder and worship, and come again to you." And Abraham took the wood of the burnt offering, and laid it upon Isaac his son: and he took the fire in his hand, and a knife: and they went both of them together. And Isaac spake unto Abraham his father, and said, "My father": and he said, "Here am I, my son." And he said, "Behold the fire and the wood: but where is the lamb for a burnt offering?" And Abraham said, "My son, God will provide himself a lamb for a burnt offering": so they went both of them together. And they came to the place which God had told him of, and Abraham built an altar there, and laid the wood in order, and bound Isaac his son, and laid him on the altar upon the wood. And Abraham stretched forth his hand, and took the knife to slay his son. And the angel of the Lord called unto him out of heaven, and said, "Abraham, Abraham." And he said, "Here am I." And he said, "Lay not thine hand upon the lad, neither do thou any thing unto him: for now I know that thou fearest God, seeing thou hast not withheld thy son, thine only son from me." And Abraham lifted up his eyes, and looked, and behold, behind him a ram caught in a thicket by his horns: and Abraham went and took the ram, and offered him up for a burnt offering in the stead of his son. And Abraham called the name of that place Jehovah-jireh, as it is said to this day, "In the mount of the Lord it shall be seen."

And the angel of the Lord called unto Abraham out of heaven the second time, and said, "By myself have I sworn, saith the Lord, for because thou hast done this thing, and hast not withheld thy son, thine only son, that in blessing I will bless thee, and in multiplying I will multiply thy seed as the stars of the heaven, and as the sand which is upon the sea shore, and thy seed shall possess the gate of his enemies. And in thy seed shall all the nations of the earth be blessed, because thou hast obeyed my voice." So Abraham returned unto his young men, and they rose up, and went together to Beer-sheba, and Abraham dwelt at Beer-sheba.

[Joseph and His Brothers[31]]

GENESIS 37, 39–47

Chapter 37

And Jacob dwelt in the land wherein his father was a stranger, in the land of Canaan. These are the generations of Jacob: Joseph, being seventeen years old, was feeding the flock with his brethren, and the lad was with the sons of Bilhah, and with the sons of Zilpah, his father's wives: and Joseph brought unto his father their evil report. Now Israel loved Joseph more than all his children, because he was the son of his old age: and he made him a coat of many colours. And when his brethren saw that their father loved him more than all his brethren, they hated him, and could not speak peaceably unto him. And Joseph dreamed a dream, and he told it his brethren, and they hated him yet the more. And he said unto them, "Hear, I pray you, this dream which I have dreamed. For behold, we were binding sheaves in the field, and lo, my sheaf arose, and also stood upright; and behold, your sheaves stood round about, and made obeisance to my sheaf." And his brethren said to him, "Shalt thou indeed reign over us? or shalt thou indeed have dominion over us?" And they hated him yet the more, for his dreams, and for his words.

And he dreamed yet another dream, and told it his brethren, and said, "Behold, I have dreamed a dream more: and behold, the sun and the moon, and the eleven stars made obeisance to me." And he told it to his father, and to his brethren: and his father rebuked him, and said unto him, "What is this dream that thou hast dreamed? Shall I, and thy mother, and thy brethren indeed come to bow down ourselves to thee to the earth?" And his brethren envied him: but his father observed the saying.

And his brethren went to feed their father's flock in Shechem. And Israel said unto Joseph, "Do not thy brethren feed the flock in Shechem? Come, and I will send thee unto them": and he said to him, "Here am I." And he said to him, "Go, I pray thee, see whether it be well with thy brethren, and well with the flocks, and bring me word again": so he sent him out of the vale of Hebron, and he came to Shechem.

And a certain man found him, and behold, he was wandering in the field, and the man asked him, saying, "What seekest thou?" And he said, "I seek my brethren: tell me, I pray thee, where they feed their flocks." And the man said, "They are departed hence: for I heard them say, 'Let us go to Dothan.'" And Joseph went after his brethren, and found them in Dothan. And when they saw him afar off, even before he came near unto them, they conspired against him, to slay him. And they said one to another, "Behold, this dreamer cometh. Come now therefore, and let us slay him, and cast him into some pit, and we will say, 'Some evil beast hath devoured him': and we shall see what will become of his dreams." And Reuben

---

[31] Isaac had two sons, Jacob and Esau. Jacob, whose name was changed to Israel at Bethel, had twelve sons and one daughter. Jacob's wife Rachel bore Joseph and Benjamin.

heard it, and he delivered him out of their hands, and said, "Let us not kill him." And Reuben said unto them, "Shed no blood, but cast him into this pit that is in the wilderness, and lay no hand upon him"; that he might rid him out of their hands, to deliver him to his father again.

And it came to pass when Joseph was come unto his brethren, that they stripped Joseph out of his coat, his coat of many colours that was on him. And they took him, and cast him into a pit: and the pit was empty, there was no water in it. And they sat down to eat bread: and they lifted up their eyes and looked, and behold, a company of Ishmaelites came from Gilead, with their camels, bearing spicery and balm and myrrh, going to carry it down to Egypt. And Judah said unto his brethren, "What profit is it if we slay our brother, and conceal his blood? Come, and let us sell him to the Ishmaelites, and let not our hand be upon him: for he is our brother, and our flesh"; and his brethren were content. Then there passed by Midianites merchantmen; and they drew and lifted up Joseph out of the pit, and sold Joseph to the Ishmaelites for twenty pieces of silver: and they brought Joseph into Egypt.[32]

And Reuben returned unto the pit, and behold, Joseph was not in the pit: and he rent his clothes. And he returned unto his brethren and said, "The child is not, and I, whither shall I go?" And they took Joseph's coat, and killed a kid of the goats, and dipped the coat in the blood. And they sent the coat of many colours, and they brought it to their father, and said, "This have we found: know now whether it be thy son's coat or no." And he knew it, and said, "It is my son's coat: an evil beast hath devoured him; Joseph is without doubt rent in pieces." And Jacob rent his clothes, and put sackcloth upon his loins, and mourned for his son many days. And all his sons and all his daughters rose up to comfort him: but he refused to be comforted: and he said, "For I will go down into the grave unto my son, mourning"; thus his father wept for him. And the Midianites sold him into Egypt unto Potiphar, an officer of Pharaoh's, and captain of the guard.[33]

• • •

Chapter 39

And Joseph[34] was brought down to Egypt, and Potiphar, an officer of Pharaoh, captain of the guard, an Egyptian, bought him of the hand of the Ishmaelites, which had brought him down thither. And the Lord was with Joseph, and he was a prosperous man, and he was in the house of his master the Egyptian. And his master saw that the Lord was with him, and that the Lord made all that he did to prosper in his hand. And Joseph found grace in his sight, and he served him; and he made him overseer over his house, and all that he had he put into his hand. And it came to pass from the time that he had made him overseer in his house, and over all that he had, that the Lord blessed the Egyptian's house for Joseph's sake: and the blessing of the Lord was upon all that he had in the house, and in the field. And he left all that he had in Joseph's hand: and he knew not aught he had, save the bread which he did eat: and Joseph was a goodly person, and well-favoured.

And it came to pass after these things, that his master's wife cast her eyes upon Joseph, and she said, "Lie with me." But he refused, and said unto his master's wife, "Behold, my master wotteth not what is with me in the house, and he hath

[32]The confusion between Ishmaelites and Midianites in this passage suggests that two accounts were fused by an editor.

[33]Chapter 38 interrupts the narrative with an account of Judah and Tamar.

[34]The story of Joseph is similar to an Egyptian story, "The Story of Two Brothers." An extended account of Joseph can be found in the Koran.

committed all that he hath to my hand. There is none greater in this house than I: neither hath he kept back any thing from me but thee, because thou art his wife: how then can I do this great wickedness, and sin against God?" And it came to pass, as she spake to Joseph day by day, that he hearkened not unto her, to lie by her, or to be with her. And it came to pass about this time, that Joseph went into the house to do his business, and there was none of the men of the house there within. And she caught him by his garment, saying, "Lie with me": and he left his garment in her hand, and fled, and got him out.

And it came to pass, when she saw that he had left his garment in her hand, and was fled forth, that she called unto the men of her house, and spake unto them, saying, "See, he hath brought in an Hebrew unto us, to mock us: he came in unto me to lie with me, and I cried with a loud voice. And it came to pass when he heard that I lifted up my voice and cried, that he left his garment with me, and fled, and got him out." And she laid up his garment by her, until her lord came home. And she spake unto him according to these words, saying, "The Hebrew servant which thou hast brought unto us came in unto me to mock me. And it came to pass as I lifted up my voice and cried, that he left his garment with me, and fled out." And it came to pass when his master heard the words of his wife, which she spake unto him, saying, "After this manner did thy servant to me," that his wrath was kindled. And Joseph's master took him, and put him into the prison, a place where the king's prisoners were bound: and he was there in the prison.

But the Lord was with Joseph, and showed him mercy, and gave him favour in the sight of the keeper of the prison. And the keeper of the prison committed to Joseph's hand all the prisoners that were in the prison, and whatsoever they did there, he was the doer of it: the keeper of the prison looked not to any thing that was under his hand, because the Lord was with him: and that which he did, the Lord made it to prosper.

Chapter 40

And it came to pass after these things, that the butler of the king of Egypt, and his baker, had offended their lord the king of Egypt. And Pharaoh was wroth against two of his officers, against the chief of the butlers, and against the chief of the bakers. And he put them in ward in the house of the captain of the guard, into the prison, the place where Joseph was bound. And the captain of the guard charged Joseph with them, and he served them, and they continued a season in ward.

And they dreamed a dream both of them, each man his dream in one night, each man according to the interpretation of his dream, the butler and the baker of the king of Egypt, which were bound in the prison. And Joseph came in unto them in the morning, and looked upon them, and behold, they were sad. And he asked Pharaoh's officers that were with him in the ward of his lord's house, saying, "Wherefore look ye so sadly today?" And they said unto him, "We have dreamed a dream, and there is no interpreter of it." And Joseph said unto them, "Do not interpretations belong to God? tell me them, I pray you." And the chief butler told his dream to Joseph, and said to him, "In my dream, behold, a vine was before me: and in the vine were three branches, and it was as though it budded, and her blossoms shot forth; and the clusters thereof brought forth ripe grapes. And Pharaoh's cup was in my hand, and I took the grapes and pressed them into Pharaoh's cup: and I gave the cup into Pharaoh's hand." And Joseph said unto him, "This is the interpretation of it: the three branches are three days: yet within three days shall Pharaoh lift up thine head, and restore thee unto thy place, and thou shalt deliver Pharaoh's cup into his hand, after the former manner when thou wast his butler. But think on me when it shall be well with thee, and show kindness, I pray thee, unto me, and make mention of me unto Pharaoh, and bring me out of this house. For indeed I was stolen away out of the land of the Hebrews: and here also have I done nothing that they should put me into the dungeon."

When the chief baker saw that the interpretation was good, he said unto Joseph, "I also was in my dream, and behold, I had three white baskets on my head. And in the uppermost basket there was of all manner of bake-meats for Pharaoh, and the birds did eat them out of the basket upon my head." And Joseph answered, and said, "This is the interpretation thereof: the three baskets are three days: yet within three days shall Pharaoh lift up thy head from off thee, and shall hang thee on a tree, and the birds shall eat thy flesh from off thee.

And it came to pass the third day, which was Pharaoh's birthday, that he made a feast unto all his servants: and he lifted up the head of the chief butler and of the chief baker among his servants. And he restored the chief butler unto his butlership again, and he gave the cup into Pharaoh's hand. But he hanged the chief baker, as Joseph had interpreted to them. Yet did not the chief butler remember Joseph, but forgot him.

Chapter 41

And it came to pass at the end of two full years, that Pharaoh dreamed: and behold, he stood by the river. And behold, there came up out of the river seven well-favoured kine[35] and fat-fleshed, and they fed in a meadow. And behold, seven other kine came up after them out of the river, ill-favoured and lean-fleshed, and stood by the other kine, upon the brink of the river. And the ill-favoured and lean-fleshed kine did eat up the seven well-favoured and fat kine: so Pharaoh awoke. And he slept and dreamed the second time: and behold, seven ears of corn came up upon one stalk, rank[36] and good. And behold, seven thin ears and blasted with the east wind sprang up after them. And the seven thin ears devoured the seven rank and full ears: and Pharaoh awoke, and behold, it was a dream. And it came to pass in the morning, that his spirit was troubled, and he sent and called for all the magicians of Egypt, and all the wise men thereof: and Pharaoh told them his dream; but there was none that could interpret them unto Pharaoh.

Then spake the chief butler unto Pharaoh, saying, "I do remember my faults this day. Pharaoh was wroth with his servants, and put me in ward, in the captain of the guard's house, both me and the chief baker. And we dreamed a dream in one night, I and he: we dreamed each man according to the interpretation of his dream. And there was there with us a young man, an Hebrew, servant to the captain of the guard: and we told him, and he interpreted to us our dreams, to each man according to his dream he did interpret. And it came to pass, as he interpreted to us, so it was; me he restored unto mine office, and him he hanged."

Then Pharaoh sent and called Joseph, and they brought him hastily out of the dungeon: and he shaved himself, and changed his raiment, and came in unto Pharaoh. And Pharaoh said unto Joseph, "I have dreamed a dream, and there is none that can interpret it: and I have heard say of thee that thou canst understand a dream to interpret it." And Joseph answered Pharaoh, saying, "It is not in me: God shall give Pharaoh an answer of peace." And Pharaoh said unto Joseph, "In my dream, behold, I stood upon the bank of the river. And behold, there came up out of the river seven kine, fat-fleshed and well-favoured, and they fed in a meadow.

---

[35]Kine: cows.

[36]Rank: full or ripe.

And behold, seven other kine came up after them, poor and very ill-favoured and lean-fleshed, such as I never saw in all the land of Egypt for badness. And the lean and the ill-favoured kine did eat up the first seven fat kine. And when they had eaten them up, it could not be known that they had eaten them, but they were still ill-favoured, as at the beginning: so I awoke. And I saw in my dream, and behold, seven ears came up in one stalk, full and good. And behold, seven ears, withered, thin, and blasted with the east wind, sprang up after them. And the thin ears devoured the seven good ears: and I told this unto the magicians, but there was none that could declare it to me."

And Joseph said unto Pharaoh, "The dream of Pharaoh is one; God hath showed Pharaoh what he is about to do. The seven good kine are seven years: and the seven good ears are seven years: the dream is one. And the seven thin and ill-favoured kine that came up after them are seven years; and the seven empty ears blasted with the east wind shall be seven years of famine. This is the thing which I have spoken unto Pharaoh: what God is about to do he showeth unto Pharaoh. Behold, there come seven years of great plenty throughout all the land of Egypt. And there shall arise after them seven years of famine, and all the plenty shall be forgotten in the land of Egypt: and the famine shall consume the land. And the plenty shall not be known in the land, by reason of that famine following: for it shall be very grievous. And for that the dream was doubled unto Pharaoh twice, it is because the thing is established by God: and God will shortly bring it to pass. Now therefore let Pharaoh look out a man discreet and wise, and set him over the land of Egypt. Let Pharaoh do this, and let him appoint officers over the land, and take up the fifth part of the land of Egypt in the seven plenteous years. And let them gather all the food of those good years that come, and lay up corn under the hand of Pharaoh, and let them keep food in the cities. And that food shall be for store to the land against the seven years of famine, which shall be in the land of Egypt, that the land perish not through the famine."

And the thing was good in the eyes of Pharaoh, and in the eyes of all his servants. And Pharaoh said unto his servants, "Can we find such a one as this is, a man in whom the spirit of God is?" And Pharaoh said unto Joseph, "Forasmuch as God hath showed thee all this, there is none so discreet and wise as thou art. Thou shalt be over my house, and according unto thy word shall all my people be ruled: only in the throne will I be greater than thou." And Pharaoh said unto Joseph, "See, I have set thee over all the land of Egypt." And Pharaoh took off his ring from his hand, and put it upon Joseph's hand, and arrayed him in vestures of fine linen, and put a gold chain about his neck. And he made him to ride in the second chariot which he had: and they cried before him, "Bow the knee": and he made him ruler over all the land of Egypt. And Pharaoh said unto Joseph, "I am Pharaoh, and without thee shall no man lift up his hand or foot in all the land of Egypt." And Pharaoh called Joseph's name Zaphnath-paaneah, and he gave him to wife Asenath the daughter of Poti-pherah, priest of On: and Joseph went out over all the land of Egypt.

(And Joseph was thirty years old when he stood before Pharaoh king of Egypt.) And Joseph went out from the presence of Pharaoh, and went throughout all the land of Egypt. And in the seven plenteous years the earth brought forth by handfuls. And he gathered up all the food of the seven years, which were in the land of Egypt, and laid up the food in the cities: the food of the field, which was round about every city, laid he up in the same. And Joseph gathered corn as the sand of the sea, very much, until he left numbering: for it was without number. And unto Joseph were born two sons, before the years of famine came: which Asenath the daughter of Poti-pherah, priest of On, bare unto him. And Joseph called the name of the firstborn Manasseh:[37] "For God," said he, "hath made me forget all my toil, and all my father's house." And the name of the second called he Ephraim:[38] "For God hath caused me to be fruitful in the land of my affliction."

And the seven years of plenteousness, that was in the land of Egypt, were ended. And the seven years of dearth began to come according as Joseph had said, and the dearth was in all lands: but in all the land of Egypt there was bread. And when all the land of Egypt was famished, the people cried to Pharaoh for bread: and Pharaoh said unto all the Egyptians, "Go unto Joseph: what he saith to you, do." And the famine was over all the face of the earth; and Joseph opened all the storehouses, and sold unto the Egyptians: and the famine waxed sore in the land of Egypt. And all countries came into Egypt to Joseph, for to buy corn, because that the famine was so sore in all lands.

Chapter 42

Now when Jacob saw that there was corn in Egypt, Jacob said unto his sons, "Why do ye look one upon another?" And he said, "Behold, I have heard that there is corn in Egypt: get you down thither and buy for us from thence, that we may live, and not die." And Joseph's ten brethren went down to buy corn in Egypt. But Benjamin, Joseph's brother, Jacob sent not with his brethren: for he said, "Lest peradventure mischief befall him." And the sons of Israel came to buy corn among those that came: for the famine was in the land of Canaan. And Joseph was the governor over the land, and he it was that sold to all the people of the land: and Joseph's brethren came, and bowed down themselves before him with their faces to the earth.

And Joseph saw his brethren, and he knew them, but made himself strange unto them, and spake roughly unto them; and he said unto them, "Whence come ye?" And they said, "From the land of Canaan, to buy food." And Joseph knew his brethren, but they knew not him. And Joseph remembered the dreams which he dreamed of them, and said unto them, "Ye are spies: to see the nakedness of the land you are come." And they said unto him, "Nay, my lord, but to buy food are thy servants come. We are all one man's sons; we are true men: thy servants are no spies." And he said unto them, "Nay: but to see the nakedness of the land you are come." And they said, "Thy servants are twelve brethren, the sons of one man in the land of Canaan: and behold, the youngest is this day with our father, and one is not." And Joseph said unto them, "That is it that I spake unto you, saying, 'Ye are spies.' Hereby ye shall be proved: by the life of Pharaoh ye shall not go forth hence, except your youngest brother come hither. Send one of you, and let him fetch your brother, and ye shall be kept in prison, that your words may be proved, whether there be any truth in you: or else by the life of Pharaoh surely ye are spies." And he put them all together into ward three days. And Joseph said unto them the third day, "This do, and live: for I fear God. If ye be true men, let one of your brethren be bound in the house of your prison: go ye, carry corn for the famine of your houses. But bring your youngest brother unto me, so shall your words be verified, and ye shall not die": and they did so.

And they said one to another, "We are verily guilty concerning our brother, in that we saw the anguish of his soul, when he besought us, and we would not hear: therefore is this distress come upon us." And Reuben answered them, saying, "Spake I not unto you, saying, 'Do not sin against the child,' and ye would not

[37] Causing to forget.
[38] Fruitfulness.

hear? therefore behold also, his blood is required."[39] And they knew not that Joseph understood them: for he spake unto them by an interpreter. And he turned himself about from them and wept, and returned to them again, and communed with them, and took from them Simeon, and bound him before their eyes.

Then Joseph commanded to fill their sacks with corn, and to restore every man's money into his sack, and to give them provision for the way: and thus did he unto them. And they laded their asses with the corn, and departed thence. And as one of them opened his sack to give his ass provender in the inn, he espied his money: for behold, it was in his sack's mouth. And he said unto his brethren, "My money is restored, and lo, it is even in my sack": and their heart failed them, and they were afraid, saying one to another, "What is this that God hath done unto us?"

And they came unto Jacob their father, unto the land of Canaan, and told him all that befell unto them, saying, "The man who is the lord of the land spake roughly to us, and took us for spies of the country. And we said unto him, 'We are true men; we are no spies. We be twelve brethren, sons of our father: one is not, and the youngest is this day with our father in the land of Canaan.' And the man the lord of the country said unto us, 'Hereby shall I know that ye are true men: leave one of your brethren here with me, and take food for the famine of your households, and be gone. And bring your youngest brother unto me: then shall I know that you are no spies, but that you are true men: so will I deliver you your brother, and ye shall traffic in the land.' "

And it came to pass as they emptied their sacks, that behold, every man's bundle of money was in his sack: and when both they and their father saw the bundles of money, they were afraid. And Jacob their father said unto them, "Me have ye bereaved of my children: Joseph is not, and Simeon is not, and ye will take Benjamin away: all these things are against me." And Reuben spake unto his father, saying, "Slay my two sons, if I bring him not to thee: deliver him into my hand, and I will bring him to thee again." And he said, "My son shall not go down with you, for his brother is dead, and he is left alone: if mischief befall him by the way in the which ye go, then shall ye bring down my gray hairs with sorrow to the grave."

Chapter 43

And the famine was sore in the land. And it came to pass when they had eaten up the corn which they had brought out of Egypt, their father said unto them, "Go again, buy us a little food." And Judah spake unto him, saying, "The man did solemnly protest unto us, saying, 'Ye shall not see my face, except your brother be with you.' If thou wilt send our brother with us, we will go down and buy thee food. But if thou wilt not send him, we will not go down: for the man said unto us, 'Ye shall not see my face, except your brother be with you.' " And Israel said, "Wherefore dealt ye so ill with me, as to tell the man whether ye had yet a brother?" And they said, "The man asked us straitly of our state, and of our kindred, saying, 'Is your father yet alive? have ye another brother?' and we told him according to the tenor of these words: could we certainly know that he would say, 'Bring your brother down'?" And Judah said unto Israel his father, "Send the lad with me, and we will arise and go, that we may live, and not die, both we, and thou, and also our little ones. I will be surety for him; of my hand shalt thou require him: if I bring him not unto thee, and set him before thee, then let me bear the blame for ever. For except we had lingered, surely now we had returned this second time." And their father Israel said unto them, "If it must be so now, do this: take of the best

[39] An exchange is necessary for the presumed killing of Joseph.

fruits in the land in your vessels, and carry down the man a present, a little balm, and a little honey, spices, and myrrh, nuts, and almonds. And take double money in your hand, and the money that was brought again in the mouth of your sacks: carry it again in your hand; peradventure it was an oversight. Take also your brother, and arise, go again unto the man. And God Almighty give you mercy before the man, that he may send away your other brother, and Benjamin: if I be bereaved of my children, I am bereaved."

And the men took that present, and they took double money in their hand, and Benjamin, and rose up, and went down to Egypt, and stood before Joseph. And when Joseph saw Benjamin with them, he said to the ruler of his house, "Bring these men home, and slay,[40] and make ready: for these men shall dine with me at noon." And the man did as Joseph bade: and the man brought the men into Joseph's house. And the men were afraid, because they were brought into Joseph's house, and they said, "Because of the money that was returned in our sacks at the first time are we brought in, that he may seek occasion against us, and fall upon us, and take us for bondmen, and our asses." And they came near to the steward of Joseph's house, and they communed with him at the door of the house, and said, "O sir, we came indeed down at the first time to buy food. And it came to pass when we came to the inn, that we opened our sacks, and behold, every man's money was in the mouth of his sack, our money in full weight: and we have brought it again in our hand. And other money have we brought down in our hands to buy food: we cannot tell who put our money in our sacks." And he said, "Peace be to you, fear not: your God, and the God of your father, hath given you treasure in your sacks: I had your money." And he brought Simeon out unto them. And the man brought the men into Joseph's house, and gave them water, and they washed their feet, and he gave their asses provender. And they made ready the present against Joseph came at noon: for they heard that they should eat bread there.

And when Joseph came home, they brought him the present which was in their hand into the house, and bowed themselves to him to the earth. And he asked them of their welfare, and said, "Is your father well, the old man of whom ye spake? Is he yet alive?" And they answered, "Thy servant our father is in good health, he is yet alive": and they bowed down their heads, and made obeisance. And he lifted up his eyes, and saw his brother Benjamin, his mother's son, and said, "Is this your younger brother, of whom ye spake unto me?" and he said, "God be gracious unto thee, my son." And Joseph made haste: for his bowels did yearn upon his brother: and he sought where to weep, and he entered into his chamber, and wept there. And he washed his face, and went out, and refrained himself, and said, "Set on bread." And they set on for him by himself, and for them by themselves, and for the Egyptians which did eat with him by themselves: because the Egyptians might not eat bread with the Hebrews: for that is an abomination unto the Egyptians. And they sat before him, the firstborn according to his birthright, and the youngest according to his youth: and the men marvelled one at another. And he took and sent messes[41] unto them from before him: but Benjamin's mess was five times so much as any of theirs. And they drunk, and were merry with him.

Chapter 44

And he commanded the steward of his house, saying, "Fill the men's sacks with food, as much as they can carry, and put every man's money in his sack's mouth. And put my cup, the silver cup, in the sack's mouth of the youngest, and his corn

[40] Slay a beast for food.

[41] Portions.

money": and he did according to the word that Joseph had spoken. As soon as the morning was light, the men were sent away, they, and their asses. And when they were gone out of the city, and not yet far off, Joseph said unto his steward, "Up, follow after the men; and when thou dost overtake them, say unto them, 'Wherefore have ye rewarded evil for good? Is not this it in which my lord drinketh? and whereby indeed he divineth?[42] ye have done evil in so doing.' "

And he overtook them, and he spake unto them these same words. And they said unto him, "Wherefore saith my lord these words? God forbid that thy servants should do according to this thing. Behold, the money which we found in our sacks' mouths we brought again unto thee out of the land of Canaan: how then should we steal out of thy lord's house silver or gold? With whomsoever of thy servants it be found, both let him die, and we also will be my lord's bondmen." And he said, "Now also let it be according unto your words: he with whom it is found shall be my servant: and ye shall be blameless." Then they speedily took down every man his sack to the ground, and opened every man his sack. And he searched, and began at the eldest, and left at the youngest: and the cup was found in Benjamin's sack. Then they rent their clothes, and laded every man his ass, and returned to the city.

And Judah and his brethren came to Joseph's house (for he was yet there): and they fell before him on the ground. And Joseph said unto them, "What deed is this that ye have done? wot ye not that such a man as I can certainly divine?" And Judah said, "What shall we say unto my lord? what shall we speak? or how shall we clear ourselves? God hath found out the iniquity of thy servants: behold, we are my lord's servants, both we, and he also with whom the cup is found." And he said, "God forbid that I should do so: but the man in whose hand the cup is found, he shall be my servant; and as for you, get you up in peace unto your father."

Then Judah came near unto him, and said, "Oh my lord, let thy servant, I pray thee, speak a word in my lord's ears, and let not thine anger burn against thy servant: for thou art even as Pharaoh. My lord asked his servants, saying, 'Have ye a father, or a brother?' And we said unto my lord, 'We have a father, an old man, and a child of his old age, a little one: and his brother is dead, and he alone is left of his mother, and his father loveth him.' And thou saidst unto thy servants, 'Bring him down unto me, that I may set mine eyes upon him.' And we said unto my lord, 'The lad cannot leave his father: for if he should leave his father, his father would die.' And thou saidst unto thy servants, 'Except your youngest brother come down with you, you shall see my face no more.' And it came to pass when we came up unto thy servant my father, we told him the words of my lord. And our father said, 'Go again, and buy us a little food.' And we said, 'We cannot go down: if our youngest brother be with us, then will we go down: for we may not see the man's face, except our youngest brother be with us.' And thy servant my father said unto us, 'Ye know that my wife bare me two sons. And the one went out from me, and I said, "Surely he is torn in pieces": and I saw him not since. And if ye take this also from me, and mischief befall him, ye shall bring down my gray hairs with sorrow to the grave.' Now therefore when I come to thy servant my father, and the lad be not with us (seeing that his life is bound up in the lad's life), it shall come to pass, when he seeth that the lad is not with us, that he will die, and thy servants shall bring down the gray hairs of thy servant our father with sorrow to the grave. For thy servant became surety for the lad unto my father, saying, 'If I bring him not unto thee, then I shall bear the blame to my father for ever.' Now therefore, I pray

[42] The same cup that is used for drinking is used for divination.

thee, let thy servant abide instead of the lad a bondman to my lord, and let the lad go up with his brethren. For how shall I go up to my father, and the lad be not with me, lest peradventure I see the evil that shall come on my father?"

Chapter 45

Then Joseph could not refrain himself before all them that stood by him: and he cried, "Cause every man to go out from me"; and there stood no man with him, while Joseph made himself known unto his brethren. And he wept aloud: and the Egyptians and the house of Pharaoh heard. And Joseph said unto his brethren, "I am Joseph; doth my father yet live?" and his brethren could not answer him: for they were troubled at his presence. And Joseph said unto his brethren, "Come near to me, I pray you": and they came near; and he said, "I am Joseph your brother, whom ye sold into Egypt. Now therefore be not grieved, nor angry with yourselves, that ye sold me hither: for God did send me before you to preserve life. For these two years hath the famine been in the land: and yet there are five years in the which there shall neither be earing[43] nor harvest. And God sent me before you to preserve you a posterity in the earth, and to save your lives by a great deliverance. So now it was not you that sent me hither, but God: and he hath made me a father to Pharaoh, and lord of all his house, and a ruler throughout all the land of Egypt. Haste you, and go up to my father, and say unto him, 'Thus saith thy son Joseph, "God hath made me lord of all Egypt; come down unto me, tarry not. And thou shalt dwell in the land of Goshen, and thou shalt be near unto me, thou, and thy children, and thy children's children, and thy flocks, and thy herds, and all that thou hast. And there will I nourish thee (for yet there are five years of famine), lest thou, and thy household, and all that thou hast, come to poverty." ' And behold, your eyes see, and the eyes of my brother Benjamin, that it is my mouth that speaketh unto you. And you shall tell my father of all my glory in Egypt, and of all that you have seen, and ye shall haste and bring down my father hither." And he fell upon his brother Benjamin's neck, and wept: and Benjamin wept upon his neck. Moreover he kissed all his brethren, and wept upon them: and after that his brethren talked with him.

And the fame thereof was heard in Pharaoh's house, saying, "Joseph's brethren are come": and it pleased Pharaoh well, and his servants. And Pharaoh said unto Joseph, "Say unto thy brethren, 'This do ye, lade your beasts and go, get you unto the land of Canaan. And take your father, and your households, and come unto me; and I will give you the good of the land of Egypt, and ye shall eat the fat of the land.' Now thou art commanded, this do ye: take you wagons out of the land of Egypt for your little ones, and for your wives, and bring your father, and come. Also regard not your stuff: for the good of all the land of Egypt is yours." And the children of Israel did so: and Joseph gave them wagons, according to the commandment of Pharaoh, and gave them provision for the way. To all of them he gave each man changes of raiment; but to Benjamin he gave three hundred pieces of silver, and five changes of raiment. And to his father he sent after this manner: ten asses laden with the good things of Egypt, and ten she-asses laden with corn and bread and meat for his father by the way. So he sent his brethren away, and they departed: and he said unto them, "See that ye fall not out by the way."

And they went up out of Egypt, and came into the land of Canaan unto Jacob their father, and told him, saying, "Joseph is yet alive, and he is governor over all the land of Egypt." And Jacob's heart fainted, for he believed them not. And they told him all the words of Joseph, which he had said unto them: and when he saw

[43]Ploughing.

the wagons which Joseph had sent to carry him, the spirit of Jacob their father revived. And Israel said, "It is enough; Joseph my son is yet alive: I will go and see him before I die."

Chapter 46:1–7, 27–34

And Israel took his journey with all that he had, and came to Beer-sheba, and offered sacrifices unto the God of his father Isaac. And God spake unto Israel in the visions of the night, and said, "Jacob, Jacob." And he said, "Here am I." And he said, "I am God, the God of thy father, fear not to go down into Egypt: for I will there make of thee a great nation. I will go down with thee into Egypt; and I will also surely bring thee up again: and Joseph shall put his hand upon thine eyes." And Jacob rose up from Beer-sheba: and the sons of Israel carried Jacob their father, and their little ones, and their wives, in the wagons which Pharaoh had sent to carry him. And they took their cattle, and their goods, which they had gotten in the land of Canaan, and came into Egypt, Jacob, and all his seed with him: his sons, and his sons' sons with him, his daughters, and his sons' daughters, and all his seed brought he with him into Egypt. . . . All the souls of the house of Jacob, which came into Egypt, were threescore and ten.

And he sent Judah before him unto Joseph, to direct his face unto Goshen, and they came into the land of Goshen. And Joseph made ready his chariot, and went up to meet Israel his father, to Goshen, and presented himself unto him: and he fell on his neck, and wept on his neck a good while. And Israel said unto Joseph, "Now let me die, since I have seen thy face, because thou art yet alive." And Joseph said unto his brethren, and unto his father's house, "I will go up, and show Pharaoh, and say unto him, 'My brethren, and my father's house, which were in the land of Canaan, are come unto me. And the men are shepherds, for their trade hath been to feed cattle: and they have brought their flocks, and their herds, and all that they have.' And it shall come to pass when Pharaoh shall call you, and shall say, 'What is your occupation?' that ye shall say, 'Thy servants' trade hath been about cattle, from our youth even until now, both we, and also our fathers': that ye may dwell in the land of Goshen; for every shepherd is an abomination unto the Egyptians."

Chapter 47:1–12

Then Joseph came and told Pharaoh, and said, "My father and my brethren, and their flocks, and their herds, and all that they have, are come out of the land of Canaan: and behold, they are in the land of Goshen." And he took some of his brethren, even five men, and presented them unto Pharaoh. And Pharaoh said unto his brethren, "What is your occupation?" And they said unto Pharaoh, "Thy servants are shepherds, both we and also our fathers." They said moreover unto Pharaoh, "For to sojourn in the land are we come: for thy servants have no pasture for their flocks, for the famine is sore in the land of Canaan: now therefore we pray thee, let thy servants dwell in the land of Goshen." And Pharaoh spake unto Joseph, saying, "Thy father and thy brethren are come unto thee. The land of Egypt is before thee: in the best of the land make thy father and brethren to dwell, in the land of Goshen let them dwell: and if thou knowest any man of activity amongst them, then make them rulers over my cattle." And Joseph brought in Jacob his father, and set him before Pharaoh: and Jacob blessed Pharaoh. And Pharaoh said unto Jacob, "How old art thou?" And Jacob said unto Pharaoh, "The days of the years of my pilgrimage are an hundred and thirty years: few and evil have the days of the years of my life been, and have not attained unto the days of the years of the life of my fathers, in the days of their pilgrimage." And Jacob blessed Pharaoh, and went out from before Pharaoh.

And Joseph placed his father, and his brethren, and gave them a possession in the land of Egypt, in the best of the land, in the land of Rameses, as Pharaoh had commanded. And Joseph nourished his father and his brethren, and all his father's household, with bread, according to their families.

WESTERN TEXTS OF ANCIENT ISRAEL AND CHRISTENDOM

THE OLD TESTAMENT

[C. 10TH CENTURY—2ND CENTURY B.C.E]

The King James Version

[Moses and the Exodus]

EXODUS 1–15[1]

Chapter 1

Now these are the names of the children of Israel, which came into Egypt, every man and his household came with Jacob. Reuben, Simeon, Levi, and Judah, Issachar, Zebulun, and Benjamin, Dan, and Naphtali, Gad, and Asher. And all the souls that came out of the loins of Jacob were seventy souls: for Joseph was in Egypt already. And Joseph died, and all his brethren, and all that generation.

And the children of Israel were fruitful, and increased abundantly, and multiplied, and waxed exceeding mighty, and the land was filled with them. Now there arose up a new king over Egypt, which knew not Joseph. And he said unto his people, "Behold, the people of the children of Israel are more and mightier than we. Come on, let us deal wisely with them, lest they multiply, and it come to pass that, when there falleth out any war, they join also unto our enemies, and fight against us, and so get them up out of the land." Therefore they did set over them taskmasters to afflict them with their burdens: and they built for Pharaoh treasure cities, Pithom and Raamses. But the more they afflicted them, the more they multiplied and grew: and they were grieved because of the children of Israel. And the Egyptians made the children of Israel to serve with rigour. And they made their lives bitter with hard bondage, in mortar, and in brick, and in all manner of service in the field: all their service wherein they made them serve was with rigour.

And the king of Egypt spake to the Hebrew midwives (of which the name of the one was Shiphrah, and the name of the other Puah), and he said, "When ye do the office of a midwife to the Hebrew women, and see them upon the stools,[2] if

[1] The story of the exodus begins c. 1300 B.C.E., several hundred years after the Joseph story in *Genesis*. The "new king" might belong to the Nineteenth Dynasty in Egypt.

[2] Birth stools.

it be a son, then ye shall kill him: but if it be a daughter, then she shall live." But the midwives feared God, and did not as the king of Egypt commanded them, but saved the men children alive. And the king of Egypt called for the midwives, and said unto them, "Why have ye done this thing, and have saved the men children alive?" And the midwives said unto Pharaoh, "Because the Hebrew women are not as the Egyptian women: for they are lively, and are delivered ere the midwives come in unto them." Therefore God dealt well with the midwives: and the people multiplied and waxed very mighty. And it came to pass, because the midwives feared God, that he made them houses. And Pharaoh charged all his people, saying, "Every son that is born, ye shall cast into the river, and every daughter ye shall save alive."

Chapter 2

And there went a man of the house of Levi, and took to wife a daughter of Levi. And the woman conceived, and bare a son: and when she saw him that he was a goodly child, she hid him three months. And when she could not longer hide him, she took for him an ark of bulrushes, and daubed it with slime, and with pitch, and put the child therein, and she laid it in the flags by the river's brink.[3] And his sister stood afar off, to wit what would be done to him.

And the daughter of Pharaoh came down to wash herself at the river, and her maidens walked along by the river side: and when she saw the ark among the flags, she sent her maid to fetch it. And when she had opened it, she saw the child: and behold, the babe wept. And she had compassion on him, and said, "This is one of the Hebrews' children." Then said his sister to Pharaoh's daughter, "Shall I go and call to thee a nurse of the Hebrew women, that she may nurse the child for thee?" And Pharaoh's daughter said to her, "Go." And the maid went and called the child's mother. And Pharaoh's daughter said unto her, "Take this child away, and nurse it for me, and I will give thee thy wages." And the woman took the child, and nursed it. And the child grew, and she brought him unto Pharaoh's daughter, and he became her son. And she called his name Moses: and she said, "Because I drew him out of the water."[4]

And it came to pass in those days, when Moses was grown, that he went out unto his brethren, and looked on their burdens, and he spied an Egyptian smiting an Hebrew, one of his brethren. And he looked this way and that way, and when he saw that there was no man, he slew the Egyptian, and hid him in the sand. And when he went out the second day, behold, two men of the Hebrews strove together: and he said to him that did the wrong, "Wherefore smitest thou thy fellow?" And he said, "Who made thee a prince and a judge over us? intendest thou to kill me, as thou killedst the Egyptian?" And Moses feared, and said, "Surely this thing is known." Now when Pharaoh heard this thing, he sought to slay Moses. But Moses fled from the face of Pharaoh, and dwelt in the land of Midian: and he sat down by a well. Now the priest of Midian had seven daughters, and they came and drew water, and filled the troughs to water their father's flock. And the shepherds came and drove them away: but Moses stood up and helped them, and watered their flock. And when they came to Reuel[5] their father, he said, "How is it that you are come so soon today?" And they said, "An Egyptian delivered us out of the hand of the shepherds, and also drew water enough for us, and watered the flock." And he said unto his daughters, "And where is he? why is it that ye have left the man?

[3]"Moses' birth resembles the birth story of Sargon of Akkad (c. 2300 B.C.E); "Flag" means iris."

[4]A folk explanation is given for Moses' name; actually, *Moses* is Egyptian for "has begotten a child."

[5]Called Jethro in Exodus 3:1, Reuel probably introduces Moses to Yahweh.

Call him, that he may eat bread." And Moses was content to dwell with the man, and he gave Moses Zipporah his daughter. And she bare him a son, and he called his name Gershom: for he said, "I have been a stranger in a strange land."

And it came to pass in process of time, that the king of Egypt died[6] and the children of Israel sighed by reason of the bondage, and they cried, and their cry came up unto God, by reason of the bondage. And God heard their groaning, and God remembered his covenant with Abraham, with Isaac, and with Jacob. And God looked upon the children of Israel, and God had respect unto them.

Chapter 3

Now Moses kept the flock of Jethro his father in law, the priest of Midian: and he led the flock to the backside of the desert, and came to the mountain of God, even to Horeb. And the angel of the Lord appeared unto him, in a flame of fire out of the midst of a bush, and he looked, and behold, the bush burned with fire, and the bush was not consumed. And Moses said "I will now turn aside, and see this great sight, why the bush is not burnt." And when the Lord saw that he turned aside to see, God called unto him out of the midst of the bush, and said, "Moses, Moses." And he said, "Here am I." And he said, "Draw not nigh hither: put off thy shoes from off thy feet, for the place whereon thou standest is holy ground." Moreover he said, "I am the God of thy father, the God of Abraham, the God of Isaac, and the God of Jacob." And Moses hid his face: for he was afraid to look upon God.

And the Lord said, "I have surely seen the affliction of my people which are in Egypt, and have heard their cry, by reason of their taskmasters: for I know their sorrows, and I am come down to deliver them out of the hand of the Egyptians, and to bring them up out of that land, unto a good land and a large, unto a land flowing with milk and honey, unto the place of the Canaanites, and the Hittites, and the Amorites, and the Perizzites, and the Hivites, and the Jebusites. Now therefore behold, the cry of the children of Israel is come unto me: and I have also seen the oppression wherewith the Egyptians oppress them. Come now therefore, and I will send thee unto Pharaoh, that thou mayest bring forth my people the children of Israel out of Egypt."

And Moses said unto God, "Who am I, that I should go unto Pharaoh, and that I should bring forth the children of Israel out of Egypt?" And he said, "Certainly I will be with thee, and this shall be a token unto thee, that I have sent thee: when thou hast brought forth the people out of Egypt, ye shall serve God upon this mountain." And Moses said unto God, "Behold, when I come unto the children of Israel, and shall say unto them, 'The God of your fathers hath sent me unto you'; and they shall say to me, 'What is his name?' what shall I say unto them?" And God said unto Moses, "I AM THAT I AM":[7] and he said, "Thus shalt thou say unto the children of Israel, 'I AM hath sent me unto you.' " And God said moreover unto Moses, "Thus shalt thou say unto the children of Israel, 'The Lord God of your fathers, the God of Abraham, the God of Isaac, and the God of Jacob, hath sent me unto you: this is my name for ever, and this is my memorial unto all generations.' Go and gather the elders of Israel together, and say unto them, 'The Lord God of your fathers, the God of Abraham, of Isaac, and of Jacob,

[6]The *king* was probably Seti I; the oppressive building program was continued by Ramses II.

[7]The divine name, Yahweh, (in Hebrew, YHWH, often read as Jehovah) is derived from the verb "to be," and is also rendered as "I cause to happen what I cause to happen," indicating a God active in human history.

appeared unto me, saying, "I have surely visited you, and seen that which is done to you in Egypt. And I have said, I will bring you up out of the affliction of Egypt, unto the land of the Canaanites, and the Hittites, and the Amorites, and the Perizzites, and the Hivites, and the Jebusites, unto a land flowing with milk and honey." ' And they shall hearken to thy voice: and thou shalt come, thou and the elders of Israel, unto the king of Egypt, and you shall say unto him, 'The Lord God of the Hebrews hath met with us: and now let us go (we beseech thee) three days' journey into the wilderness, that we may sacrifice to the Lord our God.'

"And I am sure that the king of Egypt will not let you go, no, not by a mighty hand. And I will stretch out my hand, and smite Egypt with all my wonders which I will do in the midst thereof: and after that he will let you go. And I will give this people favour in the sight of the Egyptians, and it shall come to pass that when ye go, ye shall not go empty: but every woman shall borrow of her neighbour, and of her that sojourneth in her house, jewels of silver, and jewels of gold, and raiment: and ye shall put them upon your sons, and upon your daughters, and ye shall spoil the Egyptians."

Chapter 4

And Moses answered, and said, "But behold, they will not believe me, nor hearken unto my voice: for they will say, 'The Lord hath not appeared unto thee.' " And the Lord said unto him, "What is that in thine hand?" And he said, "A rod." And he said, "Cast it on the ground." And he cast it on the ground, and it became a serpent: and Moses fled from before it. And the Lord said unto Moses, "Put forth thine hand, and take it by the tail": and he put forth his hand, and caught it, and it became a rod in his hand: "That they may believe that the Lord God of their fathers, the God of Abraham, the God of Isaac, and the God of Jacob, hath appeared unto thee."

And the Lord said furthermore unto him, "Put now thine hand into thy bosom." And he put his hand into his bosom: and when he took it out, behold, his hand was leprous as snow. And he said, "Put thine hand into thy bosom again." And he put his hand into his bosom again, and plucked it out of his bosom, and behold, it was turned again as his other flesh. "And it shall come to pass, if they will not believe thee, neither hearken to the voice of the first sign, that they will believe the voice of the latter sign. And it shall come to pass, if they will not believe also these two signs, neither hearken unto thy voice, that thou shalt take of the water of the river, and pour it upon the dry land: and the water which thou takest out of the river shall become blood upon the dry land."

And Moses said unto the Lord, "O my Lord, I am not eloquent, neither heretofore, nor since thou hast spoken unto thy servant: but I am slow of speech, and of a slow tongue." And the Lord said unto him, "Who hath made man's mouth? or who maketh the dumb or deaf, or the seeing, or the blind? have not I the Lord? Now therefore go, and I will be with thy mouth, and teach thee what thou shalt say." And he said, "O my Lord, send, I pray thee, by the hand of him whom thou wilt send." And the anger of the Lord was kindled against Moses, and he said, "Is not Aaron the Levite thy brother? I know that he can speak well. And also behold, he cometh forth to meet thee: and when he seeth thee, he will be glad in his heart. And thou shalt speak unto him, and put words in his mouth, and I will be with thy mouth, and with his mouth, and will teach you what ye shall do. And he shall be thy spokesman unto the people: and he shall be, even he shall be to thee instead of a mouth, and thou shalt be to him instead of God. And thou shalt take this rod in thine hand, wherewith thou shalt do signs."

And Moses went and returned to Jethro his father in law, and said unto him, "Let me go, I pray thee, and return unto my brethren, which are in Egypt, and see whether they be yet alive." And Jethro said to Moses, "Go in peace." And the Lord said unto Moses in Midian, "Go, return into Egypt: for all the men are dead which sought thy life." And Moses took his wife, and his sons, and set them upon an ass, and he returned to the land of Egypt. And Moses took the rod of God in his hand. And the Lord said unto Moses, "When thou goest to return into Egypt, see that thou do all those wonders before Pharaoh, which I have put in thine hand: but I will harden his heart, that he shall not let the people go. And thou shalt say unto Pharaoh, 'Thus saith the Lord, "Israel is my son, even my firstborn. And I say unto thee, Let my son go, that he may serve me: and if thou refuse to let him go, behold, I will slay thy son, even thy firstborn." ' "

And it came to pass by the way in the inn, that the Lord met him, and sought to kill him. Then Zipporah took a sharp stone, and cut off the foreskin of her son,[8] and cast it at his feet, and said, "Surely a bloody husband art thou to me." So he let him go: then she said, "A bloody husband thou art, because of the circumcision."

And the Lord said to Aaron, "Go into the wilderness to meet Moses." And he went, and met him in the mount of God, and kissed him. And Moses told Aaron all the words of the Lord, who had sent him, and all the signs which he had commanded him.

And Moses and Aaron went, and gathered together all the elders of the children of Israel. And Aaron spake all the words which the Lord had spoken unto Moses, and did the signs in the sight of the people. And the people believed: and when they heard that the Lord had visited the children of Israel, and that he had looked upon their affliction, then they bowed their heads and worshipped.

Chapter 5

And afterward Moses and Aaron went in, and told Pharaoh, "Thus saith the Lord God of Israel, 'Let my people go, that they may hold a feast unto me in the wilderness.' " And Pharaoh said, "Who is the Lord, that I should obey his voice to let Israel go? I know not the Lord, neither will I let Israel go." And they said, "The God of the Hebrews hath met with us: let us go, we pray thee, three days' journey into the desert, and sacrifice unto the Lord our God, lest he fall upon us with pestilence, or with the sword." And the king of Egypt said unto them, "Wherefore do ye, Moses and Aaron, let[9] the people from their works? get you unto your burdens." And Pharaoh said, "Behold, the people of the land now are many, and you make them rest from their burdens." And Pharaoh commanded the same day the taskmasters of the people, and their officers, saying, "Ye shall no more give the people straw to make brick, as heretofore: let them go and gather straw for themselves. And the tale[10] of the bricks, which they did make heretofore, you shall lay upon them: you shall not diminish aught thereof: for they be idle; therefore they cry, saying, 'Let us go and sacrifice to our God.' Let there more work be laid upon the men, that they may labour therein, and let them not regard vain words."

And the taskmasters of the people went out, and their officers, and they spake to the people, saying, "Thus saith Pharaoh, 'I will not give you straw. Go ye, get you straw where you can find it: yet not aught of your work shall be diminished.' "

---

[8]The implication of this story is that the practice of circumcision had been abandoned for a time.
[9]Hinder.
[10]Number.

So the people were scattered abroad throughout all the land of Egypt, to gather stubble instead of straw. And the taskmasters hasted them, saying, "Fulfill your works, your daily tasks, as when there was straw." And the officers of the children of Israel, which Pharaoh's taskmasters had set over them, were beaten, and demanded,[11] "Wherefore have ye not fulfilled your task, in making brick both yesterday and today, as heretofore?"

Then the officers of the children of Israel came and cried unto Pharaoh, saying, "Wherefore dealest thou thus with thy servants? There is no straw given unto thy servants, and they say to us, 'Make brick': and behold, thy servants are beaten: but the fault is in thine own people." But he said, "Ye are idle, ye are idle: therefore ye say, 'Let us go and do sacrifice to the Lord.' Go therefore now and work: for there shall no straw be given you, yet shall ye deliver the tale of bricks." And the officers of the children of Israel did see that they were in evil case, after it was said, "Ye shall not minish[12] aught from your bricks of your daily task."

And they met Moses and Aaron, who stood in the way, as they came forth from Pharaoh. And they said unto them, "The Lord look upon you, and judge, because ye have made our savour to be abhorred in the eyes of Pharaoh, and in the eyes of his servants, to put a sword in their hand to slay us." And Moses returned unto the Lord, and said, "Lord, wherefore hast thou so evil entreated this people? why is it that thou hast sent me? For since I came to Pharaoh to speak in thy name, he hath done evil to this people, neither hast thou delivered thy people at all."

Chapter 6:1–13

Then the Lord said unto Moses, "Now shalt thou see what I will do to Pharaoh: for with a strong hand shall he let them go, and with a strong hand shall he drive them out of his land." And God spake unto Moses, and said unto him, "I am the Lord. And I appeared unto Abraham, unto Isaac, and unto Jacob, by the name of God Almighty, but by my name JEHOVAH was I not known to them. And I have also established my covenant with them, to give them the land of Canaan, the land of their pilgrimage, wherein they were strangers. And I have also heard the groaning of the children of Israel, whom the Egyptians keep in bondage: and I have remembered my covenant. Wherefore say unto the children of Israel, 'I am the Lord, and I will bring you out from under the burdens of the Egyptians, and I will rid you out of their bondage: and I will redeem you with a stretched out arm, and with great judgments. And I will take you to me for a people, and I will be to you a God: and ye shall know that I am the Lord your God, which bringeth you out from under the burdens of the Egyptians. And I will bring you in unto the land concerning the which I did swear to give it, to Abraham, to Isaac, and to Jacob, and I will give it you for an heritage: I am the Lord.' "

And Moses spake so unto the children of Israel: but they hearkened not unto Moses, for anguish of spirit, and for cruel bondage. And the Lord spake unto Moses, saying, "Go in, speak unto Pharaoh king of Egypt, that he let the children of Israel go out of his land." And Moses spake before the Lord, saying, "Behold, the children of Israel have not hearkened unto me: how then shall Pharaoh hear me, who am of uncircumcised lips?" And the Lord spake unto Moses and unto Aaron, and gave them a charge unto the children of Israel, and unto Pharaoh king of Egypt, to bring the children of Israel out of the land of Egypt.

---

[11] Asked.

[12] Diminish.

Chapter 7

And the Lord said unto Moses, "See, I have made thee a god to Pharaoh, and Aaron thy brother shall be thy prophet. Thou shalt speak all that I command thee, and Aaron thy brother shall speak unto Pharaoh, that he send the children of Israel out of his land. And I will harden Pharaoh's heart, and multiply my signs and my wonders in the land of Egypt. But Pharaoh shall not hearken unto you, that I may lay my hand upon Egypt, and bring forth mine armies, and my people the children of Israel, out of the land of Egypt, by great judgments. And the Egyptians shall know that I am the Lord, when I stretch forth mine hand upon Egypt, and bring out the children of Israel from among them." And Moses and Aaron did as the Lord commanded them, so did they. And Moses was fourscore years old, and Aaron fourscore and three years old, when they spake unto Pharaoh.

And the Lord spake unto Moses, and unto Aaron, saying, "When Pharaoh shall speak unto you, saying, 'Show a miracle for you': then thou shalt say unto Aaron, 'Take thy rod and cast it before Pharaoh, and it shall become a serpent.' "

And Moses and Aaron went in unto Pharaoh, and they did so as the Lord had commanded: and Aaron cast down his rod before Pharaoh, and before his servants, and it became a serpent. Then Pharaoh also called the wise men and the sorcerers: now the magicians of Egypt, they also did in like manner with their enchantments. For they cast down every man his rod, and they became serpents: but Aaron's rod swallowed up their rods. And he hardened Pharaoh's heart, that he hearkened not unto them, as the Lord had said.

And the Lord said unto Moses, "Pharaoh's heart is hardened: he refuseth to let the people go. Get thee unto Pharaoh in the morning, lo, he goeth out unto the water, and thou shalt stand by the river's brink against[13] he come: and the rod which was turned to a serpent shalt thou take in thine hand. And thou shalt say unto him, 'The Lord God of the Hebrews hath sent me unto thee, saying, "Let my people go, that they may serve me in the wilderness": and behold, hitherto thou wouldest not hear.' Thus saith the Lord, 'In this thou shalt know that I am the Lord: behold, I will smite with the rod that is in my hand upon the waters which are in the river, and they shall be turned to blood. And the fish that is in the river shall die, and the river shall stink, and the Egyptians shall loathe to drink of the water of the river.' "

And the Lord spake unto Moses, "Say unto Aaron, 'Take thy rod, and stretch out thine hand upon the waters of Egypt, upon their streams, upon their rivers, and upon their ponds, and upon all their pools of water, that they may become blood, and that there may be blood throughout all the land of Egypt, both in vessels of wood, and in vessels of stone.' " And Moses and Aaron did so, as the Lord commanded: and he lifted up the rod and smote the waters that were in the river, in the sight of Pharaoh, and in the sight of his servants: and all the waters that were in the river were turned to blood. And the fish that was in the river died: and the river stank, and the Egyptians could not drink of the water of the river: and there was blood throughout all the land of Egypt. And the magicians of Egypt did so with their enchantments: and Pharaoh's heart was hardened, neither did he hearken unto them, as the Lord had said. And Pharaoh turned and went into his house, neither did he set his heart to this also. And all the Egyptians digged round about the river for water to drink: for they could not drink of the water of the river. And seven days were fulfilled after that the Lord had smitten the river.

[13]Until.

Chapter 8

And the Lord spake unto Moses, "Go unto Pharaoh, and say unto him, 'Thus saith the Lord, "Let my people go, that they may serve me." And if thou refuse to let them go, behold, I will smite all thy borders with frogs. And the river shall bring forth frogs abundantly, which shall go up and come into thine house, and into thy bedchamber, and upon thy bed, and into the house of thy servants, and upon thy people, and into thine ovens, and into thy kneading troughs. And the frogs shall come up both on thee, and upon thy people, and upon all thy servants.' "

And the Lord spake unto Moses, "Say unto Aaron, 'Stretch forth thine hand with thy rod over the streams, over the rivers, and over the ponds, and cause frogs to come up upon the land of Egypt.' "And Aaron stretched out his hand over the waters of Egypt, and the frogs came up, and covered the land of Egypt. And the magicians did so with their enchantments, and brought up frogs upon the land of Egypt.

Then Pharaoh called for Moses, and Aaron, and said, "Entreat the Lord, that he may take away the frogs from me, and from my people: and I will let the people go, that they may do sacrifice unto the Lord." And Moses said unto Pharaoh, "Glory over me: when shall I entreat for thee, and for thy servants, and for thy people, to destroy the frogs from thee, and thy houses, that they may remain in the river only?" And he said, "Tomorrow." And he said, "Be it according to thy word: that thou mayest know that there is none like unto the Lord our God. And the frogs shall depart from thee, and from thy houses, and from thy servants, and from thy people; they shall remain in the river only." And Moses and Aaron went out from Pharaoh, and Moses cried unto the Lord because of the frogs which he had brought against Pharaoh. And the Lord did according to the word of Moses: and the frogs died out of the houses, out of the villages, and out of the fields. And they gathered them together upon heaps, and the land stank. But when Pharaoh saw that there was respite, he hardened his heart, and hearkened not unto them, as the Lord had said.

And the Lord said unto Moses, "Say unto Aaron, 'Stretch out thy rod, and smite the dust of the land, that it may become lice throughout all the land of Egypt.' " And they did so: for Aaron stretched out his hand with his rod, and smote the dust of the earth, and it became lice, in man and in beast: all the dust of the land became lice throughout all the land of Egypt. And the magicians did so with their enchantments to bring forth lice, but they could not: so there were lice upon man and upon beast. Then the magicians said unto Pharaoh, "This is the finger of God." And Pharaoh's heart was hardened, and he hearkened not unto them, as the Lord had said.

And the Lord said unto Moses, "Rise up early in the morning, and stand before Pharaoh: lo, he cometh forth to the water, and say unto him, 'Thus saith the Lord, "Let my people go, that they may serve me. Else, if thou wilt not let my people go, behold, I will send swarms of flies upon thee, and upon thy servants, and upon thy people, and into thy houses: and the houses of the Egyptians shall be full of swarms of flies, and also the ground whereon they are. And I will sever in that day the land of Goshen in which my people dwell, that no swarms of flies shall be there, to the end thou mayest know that I am the Lord in the midst of the earth. And I will put a division between my people and thy people: tomorrow shall this sign be." ' " And the Lord did so: and there came a grievous swarm of flies into the house of Pharaoh, and into his servants' houses, and into all the land of Egypt: the land was corrupted by reason of the swarm of flies.

And Pharaoh called for Moses and for Aaron, and said, "Go ye, sacrifice to your God in the land." And Moses said, "It is not meet so to do; for we shall sacrifice the abomination of the Egyptians to the Lord our God: lo, shall we sacrifice the abomination[14] of the Egyptians before their eyes, and will they not stone us? We will go three days' journey into the wilderness, and sacrifice to the Lord our God, as he shall command us." And the Pharaoh said, "I will let you go that ye may sacrifice to the Lord your God in the wilderness: only you shall not go very far away: entreat for me." And Moses said, "Behold, I go out from thee, and I will entreat the Lord that the swarms of flies may depart from Pharaoh, from his servants, and from his people tomorrow: but let not Pharaoh deal deceitfully any more in not letting the people go to sacrifice to the Lord." And Moses went out from Pharaoh, and entreated the Lord: and the Lord did according to the word of Moses: and he removed the swarms of flies from Pharaoh, from his servants, and from his people: there remained not one. And Pharaoh hardened his heart at this time also, neither would he let the people go.

Chapter 9

Then the Lord said unto Moses, "Go in unto Pharaoh, and tell him, 'Thus saith the Lord God of the Hebrews, "Let my people go, that they may serve me. For if thou refuse to let them go, and wilt hold them still, behold, the hand of the Lord is upon thy cattle which is in the field, upon the horses, upon the asses, upon the camels, upon the oxen, and upon the sheep: there shall be a very grievous murrain.[15] And the Lord shall sever between the cattle of Israel and the cattle of Egypt, and there shall nothing die of all that is the children's of Israel."'" And the Lord appointed a set time, saying, "Tomorrow the Lord shall do this thing in the land." And the Lord did that thing on the morrow; and all the cattle of Egypt died, but of the cattle of the children of Israel died not one. And Pharaoh sent, and behold, there was not one of the cattle of the Israelites dead. And the heart of Pharaoh was hardened, and he did not let the people go.

And the Lord said unto Moses and unto Aaron, "Take to you handfuls of ashes of the furnace, and let Moses sprinkle it toward the heaven, in the sight of Pharaoh: and it shall become small dust in all the land of Egypt, and shall be a boil breaking forth with blains[16] upon man, and upon beast, throughout all the land of Egypt." And they took ashes of the furnace, and stood before Pharaoh, and Moses sprinkled it up toward heaven: and it became a boil breaking forth with blains upon man and upon beast. And the magicians could not stand before Moses, because of the boils: for the boil was upon the magicians, and upon all the Egyptians. And the Lord hardened the heart of Pharaoh, and he hearkened not unto them, as the Lord had spoken unto Moses.

And the Lord said unto Moses, "Rise up early in the morning, and stand before Pharaoh, and say unto him, 'Thus saith the Lord God of the Hebrews, "Let my people go, that they may serve me. For I will at this time send all my plagues upon thine heart, and upon thy servants, and upon thy people: that thou mayest know that there is none like me in all the earth. For now I will stretch out my hand, that I may smite thee and thy people with pestilence, and thou shalt be cut off from the earth. And in very deed for this cause have I raised thee up, for to show in thee my power, and that my name may be declared throughout all the earth. As yet exaltest thou thyself against my people, that thou wilt not let them go? Behold, tomorrow about this time I will cause it to rain a very grievous hail, such as hath not been in Egypt, since the foundation thereof even until now. Send therefore now, and gather

[14]The abomination seems to imply an unstated Egyptian taboo such as animal sacrifices, but it is unclear.
[15]A plague affecting cattle.
[16]Sores.

thy cattle, and all that thou hast in the field: for upon every man and beast which shall be found in the field, and shall not be brought home, the hail shall come down upon them, and they shall die.'" " He that feared the word of the Lord amongst the servants of Pharaoh made his servants and his cattle flee into the houses. And he that regarded not the word of the Lord left his servants and his cattle in the field.

And the Lord said unto Moses, "Stretch forth thine hand toward heaven, that there may be hail in all the land of Egypt, upon man and upon beast, and upon every herb of the field, throughout the land of Egypt." And Moses stretched forth his rod toward heaven, and the Lord sent thunder and hail, and the fire ran along upon the ground, and the Lord rained hail upon the land of Egypt. So there was hail, and fire mingled with the hail, very grievous, such as there was none like it in all the land of Egypt, since it became a nation. And the hail smote throughout all the land of Egypt all that was in the field, both man and beast: and the hail smote every herb of the field, and brake every tree of the field. Only in the land of Goshen where the children of Israel were, was there no hail.

And Pharaoh sent, and called for Moses and Aaron, and said unto them, "I have sinned this time: the Lord is righteous, and I and my people are wicked. Entreat the Lord (for it is enough) that there be no more mighty thunderings and hail, and I will let you go, and ye shall stay no longer." And Moses said unto him, "As soon as I am gone out of the city, I will spread abroad my hands unto the Lord, and the thunder shall cease, neither shall there be any more hail: that thou mayest know how that the earth is the Lord's. But as for thee and thy servants, I know that ye will not yet fear the Lord God." And the flax and the barley was smitten: for the barley was in the ear, and the flax was bolled:[17] but the wheat and the rye were not smitten: for they were not grown up. And Moses went out of the city from Pharaoh, and spread abroad his hands unto the Lord: and the thunders and hail ceased, and the rain was not poured upon the earth. And when Pharaoh saw that the rain and the hail and the thunders were ceased, he sinned yet more, and hardened his heart, he and his servants. And the heart of Pharaoh was hardened, neither would he let the children of Israel go, as the Lord had spoken by Moses.

Chapter 10

And the Lord said unto Moses, "Go in unto Pharaoh: for I have hardened his heart, and the heart of his servants, that I might show these my signs before him: and that thou mayest tell in the ears of thy son, and of thy son's son, what things I have wrought in Egypt, and my signs which I have done amongst them, that ye may know how that I am the Lord." And Moses and Aaron came in unto Pharaoh, and said unto him, "Thus saith the Lord God of the Hebrews, 'How long wilt thou refuse to humble thyself before me? Let my people go, that they may serve me. Else, if thou refuse to let my people go, behold, tomorrow will I bring the locusts into thy coast. And they shall cover the face of the earth, that one cannot be able to see the earth, and they shall eat the residue of that which is escaped, which remaineth unto you from the hail, and shall eat every tree which groweth for you out of the field. And they shall fill thy houses, and the houses of all thy servants, and the houses of all the Egyptians, which neither thy fathers, nor thy fathers' fathers have seen, since the day that they were upon the earth unto this day.'" And he turned himself, and went out from Pharaoh. And Pharaoh's servants said unto him, "How long shall this man be a snare unto us? Let the men go, that they may serve the Lord their God: knowest thou not yet that Egypt is destroyed?" And Moses and Aaron were brought again unto Pharaoh: and he said unto them, "Go, serve

[17]In bud.

the Lord your God: but who are they that shall go?" And Moses said, "We will go with our young, and with our old, with our sons and with our daughters, with our flocks and with our herds will we go: for we must hold a feast unto the Lord." And he said unto them, "Let the Lord be so with you, as I will let you go, and your little ones. Look to it, for evil is before you. Not so: go now ye that are men, and serve the Lord, for that you did desire."[18] And they were driven out from Pharaoh's presence.

And the Lord said unto Moses, "Stretch out thine hand over the land of Egypt for the locusts, that they may come up upon the land of Egypt, and eat every herb of the land, even all that the hail hath left." And Moses stretched forth his rod over the land of Egypt, and the Lord brought an east wind upon the land all that day, and all that night: and when it was morning, the east wind brought the locusts. And the locusts went up over all the land of Egypt, and rested in all the coasts of Egypt: very grievous were they: before them there were no such locusts as they, neither after them shall be such. For they covered the face of the whole earth, so that the land was darkened, and they did eat every herb of the land, and all the fruit of the trees which the hail had left, and there remained not any green thing in the trees, or in the herbs of the field, through all the land of Egypt.

Then Pharaoh called for Moses and Aaron in haste: and he said, "I have sinned against the Lord your God, and against you. Now therefore forgive, I pray thee, my sin only this once, and entreat the Lord your God, that he may take away from me this death only." And he went out from Pharaoh, and entreated the Lord. And the Lord turned a mighty strong west wind, which took away the locusts, and cast them into the Red Sea: there remained not one locust in all the coasts of Egypt. But the Lord hardened Pharaoh's heart, so that he would not let the children of Israel go.

And the Lord said unto Moses, "Stretch out thine hand toward heaven, that there may be darkness over the land of Egypt, even darkness which may be felt." And Moses stretched forth his hand toward heaven: and there was a thick darkness in all the land of Egypt three days. They saw not one another, neither rose any from his place for three days: but all the children of Israel had light in their dwellings.

And Pharaoh called unto Moses, and said, "Go ye, serve the Lord: only let your flocks and your herds be stayed: let your little ones also go with you." And Moses said, "Thou must give us also sacrifices, and burnt offerings, that we may sacrifice unto the Lord our God. Our cattle also shall go with us: there shall not an hoof be left behind: for thereof must we take to serve the Lord our God; and we know not with what we must serve the Lord, until we come thither."

But the Lord hardened Pharaoh's heart, and he would not let them go. And Pharaoh said unto him, "Get thee from me, take heed to thyself: see my face no more: for in that day thou seest my face, thou shalt die." And Moses said, "Thou hast spoken well, I will see thy face again no more."

Chapter 11

And the Lord said unto Moses, "Yet will I bring one plague more upon Pharaoh, and upon Egypt; afterwards he will let you go hence: when he shall let you go, he shall surely thrust you out hence altogether. Speak now in the ears of the people, and let every man borrow of his neighbour, and every woman of her neighbour, jewels of silver, and jewels of gold." And the Lord gave the people favour in the sight of the Egyptians. Moreover the man Moses was very great in the land of Egypt, in the sight of Pharaoh's servants, and in the sight of the people. And Moses said,

[18]The New English Bible translates the last sentence as, "No, your menfolk may go and worship the Lord, for that is all you asked."

"Thus saith the Lord, 'About midnight will I go out into the midst of Egypt. And all the firstborn in the land of Egypt shall die, from the firstborn of Pharaoh that sitteth upon his throne, even unto the firstborn of the maidservant that is behind the mill, and all the firstborn of beasts. And there shall be a great cry throughout all the land of Egypt, such as there was none like it, nor shall be like it any more. But against any of the children of Israel shall not a dog move his tongue, against man or beast: that ye may know how that the Lord doth put a difference between the Egyptians and Israel. And all these thy servants shall come down unto me, and bow down themselves unto me, saying, "Get thee out, and all the people that follow thee": and after that I will go out.'" And he went out from Pharaoh in a great anger. And the Lord said unto Moses, "Pharaoh shall not hearken unto you, that my wonders may be multiplied in the land of Egypt." And Moses and Aaron did all these wonders before Pharaoh: and the Lord hardened Pharaoh's heart, so that he would not let the children of Israel go out of his land.

Chapter 12

And the Lord spake unto Moses and Aaron in the land of Egypt, saying, "This month shall be unto you the beginning of months: it shall be the first month of the year to you.

"Speak ye unto all the congregation of Israel, saying, 'In the tenth day of this month they shall take to them every man a lamb, according to the house of their fathers, a lamb for an house. And if the household be too little for the lamb, let him and his neighbour next unto his house take it according to the number of the souls: every man according to his eating shall make your count for the lamb. Your lamb shall be without blemish, a male of the first year: ye shall take it out from the sheep or from the goats. And ye shall keep it up until the fourteenth day of the same month: and the whole assembly of the congregation of Israel shall kill it in the evening. And they shall take of the blood and strike it on the two side posts and on the upper door post of the houses wherein they shall eat it. And they shall eat the flesh in that night roast with fire, and unleavened bread, and with bitter herbs they shall eat it. Eat not of it raw, nor sodden at all with water, but roast with fire: his head, with his legs, and with the purtenance thereof. And ye shall let nothing of it remain until the morning: and that which remaineth of it until the morning ye shall burn with fire.[19]

" 'And thus shall ye eat it: with your loins girded, your shoes on your feet, and your staff in your hand: and ye shall eat it in haste: it is the Lord's Passover. For I will pass through the land of Egypt this night, and will smite all the firstborn in the land of Egypt, both man and beast, and against all the gods of Egypt I will execute judgment: I am the Lord. And the blood shall be to you for a token upon the houses where you are: and when I see the blood, I will pass over you, and the plague shall not be upon you to destroy you, when I smite the land of Egypt. And this day shall be unto you for a memorial: and you shall keep it a feast to the Lord, throughout your generations: you shall keep it a feast by an ordinance for ever. Seven days shall ye eat unleavened bread, even the first day ye shall put away leaven out of your houses: for whosoever eateth leavened bread, from the first day until the seventh day, that soul shall be cut off from Israel. And in the first day there shall be an holy convocation, and in the seventh day there shall be an holy convocation to you: no manner of work shall be done in them, save that which every man must eat, that only may be done of you. And ye shall observe the feast of unleavened bread: for

[19]This section describes one of the most important Jewish religious festivals, Passover. Passover initiates the exodus, which provided a pattern of liberation from slavery for numerous peoples, Jews and non-Jews.

in this selfsame day have I brought your armies out of the land of Egypt; therefore shall ye observe this day in your generations by an ordinance for ever.

" 'In the first month, on the fourteenth day of the month at even, ye shall eat unleavened bread until the one and twentieth day of the month at even. Seven days shall there be no leaven found in your houses: for whosoever eateth that which is leavened, even that soul shall be cut off from the congregation of Israel, whether he be a stranger, or born in the land. Ye shall eat nothing leavened: in all your habitations shall ye eat unleavened bread.' "

Then Moses called for all the elders of Israel, and said unto them, "Draw out and take you a lamb, according to your families, and kill the Passover.[20] And ye shall take a bunch of hyssop, and dip it in the blood that is in the basin, and strike the lintel and the two side posts with the blood that is in the basin: and none of you shall go out at the door of his house until the morning. For the Lord will pass through to smite the Egyptians: and when he seeth the blood upon the lintel, and on the two side posts, the Lord will pass over the door, and will not suffer the destroyer to come in unto your houses to smite you. And ye shall observe this thing for an ordinance to thee and to thy sons for ever. And it shall come to pass when ye be come to the land, which the Lord will give you, according as he hath promised, that ye shall keep this service. And it shall come to pass, when your children shall say unto you, 'What mean ye by this service?' that ye shall say, 'It is the sacrifice of the Lord's Passover, who passed over the houses of the children of Israel in Egypt, when he smote the Egyptians, and delivered our houses.' " And the people bowed the head, and worshipped. And the children of Israel went away, and did as the Lord had commanded Moses and Aaron, so did they.

And it came to pass that at midnight the Lord smote all the firstborn in the land of Egypt, from the firstborn of Pharaoh that sat on his throne, unto the firstborn of the captive that was in the dungeon, and all the firstborn of cattle. And Pharaoh rose up in the night, he and all his servants, and all the Egyptians; and there was a great cry in Egypt: for there was not a house where there was not one dead.

And he called for Moses and Aaron by night, and said, "Rise up, and get you forth from amongst my people, both you and the children of Israel: and go, serve the Lord, as ye have said. Also take your flocks and your herds, as ye have said: and be gone, and bless me also." And the Egyptians were urgent upon the people that they might send them out of the land in haste: for they said, "We be all dead men." And the people took their dough before it was leavened, their kneading troughs being bound up in their clothes upon their shoulders. And the children of Israel did according to the word of Moses: and they borrowed of the Egyptians jewels of silver, and jewels of gold, and raiment. And the Lord gave the people favour in the sight of the Egyptians, so that they lent unto them such things as they required: and they spoiled the Egyptians.

And the children of Israel journeyed from Rameses to Succoth, about six hundred thousand on foot that were men, besides children. And a mixed multitude went up also with them, and flocks and herds, even very much cattle. And they baked unleavened cakes of the dough, which they brought forth out of Egypt; for it was not leavened: because they were thrust out of Egypt, and could not tarry, neither had they prepared for themselves any victual.

Now the sojourning of the children of Israel, who dwelt in Egypt, was four hundred and thirty years. And it came to pass at the end of the four hundred and thirty years, even the selfsame day it came to pass, that all the hosts of the Lord

[20]Passover lamb.

went out from the land of Egypt. It is a night to be much observed unto the Lord, for bringing them out from the land of Egypt: this is that night of the Lord to be observed of all the children of Israel, in their generations.

And the Lord said unto Moses and Aaron, "This is the ordinance of the Passover: there shall no stranger eat thereof. But every man's servant that is bought for money, when thou hast circumcised him, then shall he eat thereof. A foreigner and an hired servant shall not eat thereof. In one house shall it be eaten, thou shalt not carry forth aught of the flesh abroad out of the house, neither shall ye break a bone thereof. All the congregation of Israel shall keep it. And when a stranger shall sojourn with thee, and will keep the Passover to the Lord, let all his males be circumcised, and then let him come near, and keep it: and he shall be as one that is born in the land: for no uncircumcised person shall eat thereof. One law shall be to him that is homeborn, and unto the stranger that sojourneth among you." Thus did all the children of Israel: as the Lord commanded Moses and Aaron, so did they. And it came to pass the selfsame day, that the Lord did bring the children of Israel out of the land of Egypt by their armies.[21]

Chapter 13

And the Lord spake unto Moses, saying, "Sanctify unto me all the firstborn, whatsoever openeth the womb, among the children of Israel, both of man and of beast: it is mine."

And Moses said unto the people, "Remember this day, in which ye came out from Egypt, out of the house of bondage: for by strength of hand the Lord brought you out from this place: there shall no leavened bread be eaten. This day came ye out, in the month Abib.[22]

"And it shall be when the Lord shall bring thee into the land of the Canaanites, and the Hittites, and the Amorites, and the Hivites, and the Jebusites, which he sware unto thy fathers to give thee, a land flowing with milk and honey, that thou shalt keep this service in this month. Seven days thou shalt eat unleavened bread, and in the seventh day shall be a feast to the Lord. Unleavened bread shall be eaten seven days: and there shall no leavened bread be seen with thee: neither shall there be leaven seen with thee in all thy quarters.

"And thou shalt show thy son in that day, saying, 'This is done because of that which the Lord did unto me, when I came forth out of Egypt. And it shall be for a sign unto thee, upon thine hand, and for a memorial between thine eyes, that the Lord's law may be in thy mouth: for with a strong hand hath the Lord brought thee out of Egypt. Thou shalt therefore keep this ordinance in his season from year to year.'

"And it shall be when the Lord shall bring thee into the land of the Canaanites as he sware unto thee, and to thy fathers, and shall give it thee: that thou shalt set apart unto the Lord all that openeth the matrix, and every firstling that cometh of a beast which thou hast, the males shall be the Lord's. And every firstling of an ass thou shalt redeem with a lamb: and if thou wilt not redeem it, then thou shalt break his neck, and all the first born of man amongst thy children shalt thou redeem.

"And it shall be when thy son asketh thee in time to come, saying, 'What is this?' that thou shalt say unto him, 'By strength of hand the Lord brought us out

---

[21] In their tribal units.

[22] The Hebrew month of Nisan: March–April.

from Egypt, from the house of bondage. And it came to pass when Pharaoh would hardly let us go, that the Lord slew all the firstborn in the land of Egypt, both the firstborn of man, and the firstborn of beast: therefore I sacrifice to the Lord all that openeth the matrix, being males: but all the firstborn of my children I redeem. And it shall be for a token upon thine hand, and for frontlets between thine eyes. For by strength of hand the Lord brought us forth out of Egypt.' "

And it came to pass when Pharaoh had let the people go, that God led them not through the way of the land of the Philistines, although that was near: for God said, "Lest peradventure the people repent when they see war, and they return to Egypt": but God led the people about through the way of the wilderness of the Red Sea: and the children of Israel went up harnessed[23] out of the land of Egypt. And Moses took the bones of Joseph with him: for he had straitly[24] sworn the children of Israel, saying, "God will surely visit you, and ye shall carry up my bones away hence with you."

And they took their journey from Succoth, and encamped in Etham, in the edge of the wilderness. And the Lord went before them by day in a pillar of cloud to lead them the way; and by night in a pillar of fire, to give them light; to go by day and night. He took not away the pillar of the cloud by day, nor the pillar of fire by night, from before the people.

Chapter 14

And the Lord spake unto Moses, saying, "Speak unto the children of Israel, that they turn and encamp before Pi-hahiroth, between Migdol and the sea, over against Baal-zephon: before it shall ye encamp by the sea. For Pharaoh will say of the children of Israel, 'They are entangled in the land, the wilderness hath shut them in.' And I will harden Pharaoh's heart, that he shall follow after them, and I will be honoured upon Pharaoh, and upon all his host, that the Egyptians may know that I am the Lord." And they did so.

And it was told the king of Egypt, that the people fled: and the heart of Pharaoh and of his servants was turned against the people, and they said, "Why have we done this, that we have let Israel go from serving us?" And he made ready his chariot, and took his people with him. And he took six hundred chosen chariots, and all the chariots of Egypt, and captains over every one of them. And the Lord hardened the heart of Pharaoh king of Egypt, and he pursued after the children of Israel: and the children of Israel went out with an high hand. But the Egyptians pursued after them (all the horses and chariots of Pharaoh, and his horsemen, and his army) and overtook them encamping by the sea, beside Pi-hahiroth, before Baal-zephon.

And when Pharaoh drew nigh, the children of Israel lifted up their eyes, and behold, the Egyptians marched after them, and they were sore afraid: and the children of Israel cried out unto the Lord. And they said unto Moses, "Because there were no graves in Egypt, hast thou taken us away to die in the wilderness? Wherefore hast thou dealt thus with us, to carry us forth out of Egypt? Is not this the word that we did tell thee in Egypt, saying, 'Let us alone, that we may serve the Egyptians?' For it had been better for us to serve the Egyptians, than that we should die in the wilderness."

And Moses said unto the people, "Fear ye not, stand still, and see the salvation of the Lord, which he will show to you today: for the Egyptians whom ye have seen

[23]Possibly "the fifth generation of Israelites" or "equipped for battle."

[24]Strictly.

today, ye shall see them again no more for ever. The Lord shall fight for you, and ye shall hold your peace."

And the Lord said unto Moses, "Wherefore criest thou unto me? Speak unto the children of Israel, that they go forward: but lift thou up thy rod, and stretch out thine hand over the sea, and divide it: and the children of Israel shall go on dry ground through the midst of the sea. And I, behold, I will harden the hearts of the Egyptians, and they shall follow them: and I will get me honour upon Pharaoh, and upon all his host, upon his chariots, and upon his horsemen. And the Egyptians shall know that I am the Lord, when I have gotten me honour upon Pharaoh, upon his chariots, and upon his horsemen."

And the angel of God, which went before the camp of Israel, removed and went behind them, and the pillar of the cloud went from before their face, and stood behind them. And it came between the camp of the Egyptians and the camp of Israel, and it was a cloud and darkness to them, but it gave light by night to these: so that the one came not near the other all the night. And Moses stretched out his hand over the sea, and the Lord caused the sea to go back by a strong east wind all that night, and made the sea dry land, and the waters were divided. And the children of Israel went into the midst of the sea upon the dry ground, and the waters were a wall unto them on their right hand, and on their left.

And the Egyptians pursued, and went in after them, to the midst of the sea, even all Pharaoh's horses, his chariots, and his horsemen. And it came to pass, that in the morning watch the Lord looked unto the host of the Egyptians, through the pillar of fire and of the cloud, and troubled the host of the Egyptians, and took off their chariot wheels, that they drave them heavily: so that the Egyptians said, "Let us flee from the face of Israel: for the Lord fighteth for them against the Egyptians."

And the Lord said unto Moses, "Stretch out thine hand over the sea, that the waters may come again upon the Egyptians, upon their chariots, and upon their horsemen." And Moses stretched forth his hand over the sea, and the sea returned to his strength when the morning appeared: and the Egyptians fled against it: and the Lord overthrew the Egyptians in the midst of the sea. And the waters returned, and covered the chariots, and the horsemen, and all the host of Pharaoh that came into the sea after them: there remained not so much as one of them. But the children of Israel walked upon dry land, in the midst of the sea, and the waters were a wall unto them on their right hand, and on their left. Thus the Lord saved Israel that day out of the hand of the Egyptians: and Israel saw the Egyptians dead upon the sea shore. And Israel saw that great work which the Lord did upon the Egyptians: and the people feared the Lord, and believed the Lord, and his servant Moses.

Chapter 15

Then sang Moses and the children of Israel this song[25] unto the Lord, and spake, saying, "I will sing unto the Lord: for he hath triumphed gloriously, the horse and his rider hath he thrown into the sea.

The Lord is my strength and song, and he is become my salvation: he is my God, and I will prepare him an habitation, my father's God, and I will exalt him.

[25] This song and Miriam's song, which immediately follows, are two of the oldest pieces of literature in the Bible.

The Lord is a man of war: the Lord is his name.

Pharaoh's chariots and his host hath he cast into the sea: his chosen captains also are drowned in the Red Sea.

The depths have covered them: they sank into the bottom as a stone.

Thy right hand, O Lord, is become glorious in power, thy right hand, O Lord, hath dashed in pieces the enemy.

And in the greatness of thine excellency thou hast overthrown them that rose up against thee: thou sentest forth thy wrath, which consumed them as stubble.

And with the blast of thy nostrils the waters were gathered together: the floods stood upright as an heap, and the depths were congealed in the heart of the sea.

The enemy said, 'I will pursue, I will overtake, I will divide the spoil: my lust shall be satisfied upon them: I will draw my sword, mine hand shall destroy them.'

Thou didst blow with thy wind, the sea covered them, they sank as lead in the mighty waters.

Who is like unto thee, O Lord, amongst the gods? who is like thee, glorious in holiness, fearful in praises, doing wonders!

Thou stretchedst out thy right hand, the earth swallowed them.

Thou in thy mercy hast led forth the people which thou hast redeemed: thou hast guided them in thy strength unto thy holy habitation.

The people shall hear, and be afraid: sorrow shall take hold on the inhabitants of Palestina,

Then the dukes of Edom shall be amazed: the mighty men of Moab, trembling shall take hold upon them: all the inhabitants of Canaan shall melt away.

Fear and dread shall fall upon them, by the greatness of thine arm then shall be as still as a stone, till thy people pass over, O Lord, till the people pass over, which thou hast purchased.

Thou shalt bring them in, and plant them in the mountain of thine inheritance, in the place, O Lord, which thou hast made for thee to dwell in, in the sanctuary, O Lord, which thy hands have established.

The Lord shall reign for ever and ever.

For the horse of Pharaoh went in with his chariots and with his horsemen into the sea, and the Lord brought again the waters of the sea upon them: but the children of Israel went on dry land in the midst of the sea."

And Miriam the prophetess, the sister of Aaron, took a timbrel in her hand, and all the women went out after her, with timbrels and with dances. And Miriam answered them, "Sing ye to the Lord, for he hath triumphed gloriously: the horse and his rider hath he thrown into the sea." So Moses brought Israel from the Red Sea, and they went out into the wilderness of Shur: and they went three days in the wilderness, and found no water.

And when they came to Marah, they could not drink of the waters of Marah, for they were bitter: therefore the name of it was called Marah. And the people murmured against Moses, saying, "What shall we drink?" And he cried unto the Lord: and the Lord showed him a tree, which when he had cast into the waters, the waters were made sweet: there he made for them a statute and an ordinance, and there he proved them, and said, "If thou wilt diligently hearken to the voice of the Lord thy God, and wilt do that which is right in his sight, and wilt give ear to his commandments, and keep all his statutes, I will put none of these diseases upon thee, which I have brought upon the Egyptians: for I am the Lord that healeth thee."

And they came to Elim, where were twelve wells of water, and threescore and ten palm trees, and they encamped there by the waters.

[The Law at Mt. Sinai]

Exodus 19–20

Chapter 19

In the third month when the children of Israel were gone forth out of the land of Egypt, the same day came they into the wilderness of Sinai. For they were departed from Rephidim, and were come to the desert of Sinai, and had pitched in the wilderness, and there Israel camped before the mount. And Moses went up unto God: and the Lord called unto him out of the mountain, saying, "Thus shalt thou say to the house of Jacob, and tell the children of Israel: 'Ye have seen what I did unto the Egyptians, and how I bare you on eagles' wings, and brought you unto myself. Now therefore, if ye will obey my voice indeed, and keep my covenant, then ye shall be a peculiar treasure unto me above all people: for all the earth is mine. And ye shall be unto me a kingdom of priests, and an holy nation.' These are the words which thou shalt speak unto the children of Israel."

And Moses came and called for the elders of the people, and laid before their faces all these words which the Lord commanded him. And all the people answered together, and said, "All that the Lord hath spoken we will do." And Moses returned the words of the people unto the Lord. And the Lord said unto Moses, "Lo, I come unto thee in a thick cloud, that the people may hear when I speak with thee, and believe thee for ever": and Moses told the words of the people unto the Lord.

And the Lord said unto Moses, "Go unto the people, and sanctify them today and tomorrow, and let them wash their clothes. And be ready against the third day: for the third day the Lord will come down in the sight of all the people, upon mount Sinai. And thou shalt set bounds unto the people round about, saying, 'Take heed to yourselves, that ye go not up into the mount, or touch the border of it: whosoever toucheth the mount shall be surely put to death. There shall not a hand touch it, but he shall surely be stoned, or shot through; whether it be beast or man, it shall not live': when the trumpet soundeth long, they shall come up to the mount."

And Moses went down from the mount unto the people, and sanctified the people; and they washed their clothes. And he said unto the people, "Be ready against the third day: come not at your wives."

And it came to pass on the third day in the morning, that there were thunders and lightnings, and a thick cloud upon the mount, and the voice of the trumpet exceeding loud, so that all the people that was in the camp trembled. And Moses brought forth the people out of the camp to meet with God, and they stood at the nether part of the mount. And mount Sinai was altogether on a smoke, because the Lord descended upon it in fire: and the smoke thereof ascended as the smoke of a furnace, and the whole mount quaked greatly. And when the voice of the trumpet sounded long, and waxed louder and louder, Moses spake, and God answered him by a voice. And the Lord came down upon mount Sinai, on the top of the mount: and the Lord called Moses up to the top of the mount, and Moses went up. And the Lord said unto Moses, "Go down, charge the people, lest they break through unto the Lord to gaze, and many of them perish. And let the priests also, which come near to the Lord, sanctify themselves, lest the Lord break forth upon them." And Moses said unto the Lord, "The people cannot come up to mount Sinai: for thou chargedst us, saying, 'Set bounds about the mount, and sanctify it.' " And the Lord said unto him, "Away, get thee down, and thou shalt come up, thou, and Aaron with thee: but let not the priests and the people break through, to come up unto the Lord, lest he break forth upon them." So Moses went down unto the people, and spake unto them.

Chapter 20

And God spake all these words, saying, "I am the Lord thy God, which have brought thee out of the land of Egypt, out of the house of bondage:[1]

Thou shalt have no other gods before me.

Thou shalt not make unto thee any graven image, or any likeness of any thing that is in heaven above, or that is in the earth beneath, or that is in the water under the earth. Thou shalt not bow down to them, nor serve them: for I the Lord thy God am a jealous God, visiting the iniquity of the fathers upon the children, unto the third and fourth generation of them that hate me: and showing mercy unto thousands of them that love me, and keep my commandments.

Thou shalt not take the name of the Lord thy God in vain: for the Lord will not hold him guiltless that taketh his name in vain.

Remember the sabbath day, to keep it holy. Six days shalt thou labour, and do all thy work: but the seventh day is the sabbath of the Lord thy God: in it thou shalt not do any work, thou, nor thy son, nor thy daughter, thy manservant, nor thy maidservant, nor thy cattle, nor thy stranger that is within thy gates: for in six days the Lord made heaven and earth, the sea, and all that in them is, and rested the seventh day: wherefore the Lord blessed the sabbath day, and hallowed it.

Honour thy father and thy mother: that thy days may be long upon the land, which the Lord thy God giveth thee.

Thou shalt not kill.

Thou shalt not commit adultery.

Thou shalt not steal.

Thou shalt not bear false witness against thy neighbour.

Thou shalt not covet thy neighbour's house, thou shalt not covet thy neighbour's wife, nor his manservant, nor his maidservant, nor his ox, nor his ass, nor any thing that is thy neighbour's."

And all the people saw the thunderings, and the lightnings, and the noise of the trumpet, and the mountain smoking: and when the people saw it, they removed, and stood afar off. And they said unto Moses, "Speak thou with us, and we will hear: but let not God speak with us, lest we die." And Moses said unto the people, "Fear not: for God is come to prove you, and that his fear may be before your faces, that ye sin not." And the people stood afar off, and Moses drew near unto the thick darkness where God was.

And the Lord said unto Moses, "Thus thou shalt say unto the children of Israel, 'Ye have seen that I have talked with you from heaven. Ye shall not make with me gods of silver, neither shall ye make unto you gods of gold. An altar of earth thou shalt make unto me, and shalt sacrifice thereon thy burnt offerings, and thy peace offerings, thy sheep, and thine oxen: in all places where I record my name I will come unto thee, and I will bless thee. And if thou wilt make me an altar of stone, thou shalt not build it of hewn stone: for if thou lift up thy tool upon it, thou hast

[1] Obeying the Ten Commandments becomes the necessary condition for entering into a covenant with God and receiving his blessings.

polluted it. Neither shalt thou go up by steps unto mine altar, that thy nakedness be not discovered thereon.' "[2]

[The Golden Calf]

Exodus 32

And when the people saw that Moses delayed to come down out of the mount, the people gathered themselves together unto Aaron, and said unto him, "Up, make us gods which shall go before us: for as for this Moses, the man that brought us up out of the land of Egypt, we wot not what is become of him." And Aaron said unto them, "Break off the golden earrings which are in the ears of your wives, of your sons, and of your daughters, and bring them unto me." And all the people brake off the golden earrings which were in their ears, and brought them unto Aaron. And he received them at their hand, and fashioned it with a graving tool, after he had made it a molten calf:[1] and they said, "These be thy gods, O Israel, which brought thee up out of the land of Egypt." And when Aaron saw it, he built an altar before it, and Aaron made proclamation, and said, "Tomorrow is the feast of the Lord." And they rose up early on the morrow, and offered burnt offerings, and brought peace offerings: and the people sat down to eat and to drink, and rose up to play.

And the Lord said unto Moses, "Go, get thee down: for thy people which thou broughtest out of the land of Egypt have corrupted themselves. They have turned aside quickly out of the way which I commanded them: they have made them a molten calf, and have worshipped it, and have sacrificed thereunto, and said, 'These be thy gods, O Israel, which have brought thee up out of the land of Egypt.' " And the Lord said unto Moses, "I have seen this people, and behold, it is a stiffnecked people. Now therefore let me alone, that my wrath may wax hot against them, and that I may consume them: and I will make of thee a great nation." And Moses besought the Lord his God, and said, "Lord, why doth thy wrath wax hot against thy people, which thou hast brought forth out of the land of Egypt, with great power, and with a mighty hand? Wherefore should the Egyptians speak and say, 'For mischief did he bring them out, to slay them in the mountains, and to consume them from the face of the earth'? Turn from thy fierce wrath, and repent of this evil against thy people. Remember Abraham, Isaac, and Israel thy servants, to whom thou swarest by thine own self, and saidst unto them, 'I will multiply your seed as the stars of heaven: and all this land that I have spoken of will I give unto your seed, and they shall inherit it for ever.' " And the Lord repented of the evil which he thought to do unto his people.

And Moses turned, and went down from the mount, and the two tables of the testimony were in his hand: the tables were written on both their sides; on the one side, and on the other they were written. And the tables were the work of God; and the writing was the writing of God, graven upon the tables. And when Joshua heard the noise of the people as they shouted, he said unto Moses, "There is a noise of war in the camp." And he said, "It is not the voice of them that shout for

---

[2]The next chapters contain detailed applications of the law and instructions for building the Tabernacle and for religious practice.

[THE GOLDEN CALF]

[1]The worship of the golden calf reflects both Egyptian and Canaanite practices.

mastery, neither is it the voice of them that cry for being overcome: but the noise of them that sing do I hear."

And it came to pass, as soon as he came nigh unto the camp, that he saw the calf, and the dancing: and Moses' anger waxed hot, and he cast the tables out of his hands, and brake them beneath the mount. And he took the calf which they had made, and burnt it in the fire, and ground it to powder, and strewed it upon the water, and made the children of Israel drink of it. And Moses said unto Aaron, "What did this people unto thee, that thou hast brought so great a sin upon them?" And Aaron said, "Let not the anger of my lord wax hot: thou knowest the people, that they are set on mischief. For they said unto me, 'Make us gods which shall go before us: for as for this Moses, the man that brought us up out of the land of Egypt, we wot not what is become of him.' And I said unto them, 'Whosoever hath any gold, let them break it off': so they gave it me: then I cast it into the fire, and there came out this calf."

And when Moses saw that the people were naked (for Aaron had made them naked unto their shame amongst their enemies), then Moses stood in the gate of the camp, and said, "Who is on the Lord's side? let him come unto me." And all the sons of Levi gathered themselves together unto him. And he said unto them, "Thus saith the Lord God of Israel, 'Put every man his sword by his side, and go in and out from gate to gate throughout the camp, and slay every man his brother, and every man his companion, and every man his neighbour.' " And the children of Levi did according to the word of Moses; and there fell of the people that day about three thousand men. For Moses had said, "Consecrate yourselves today to the Lord, even every man upon his son, and upon his brother, that he may bestow upon you a blessing this day."

And it came to pass on the morrow, that Moses said unto the people, "Ye have sinned a great sin: and now I will go up unto the Lord; peradventure I shall make an atonement for your sin." And Moses returned unto the Lord, and said, "Oh, this people have sinned a great sin, and have made them gods of gold. Yet now, if thou wilt forgive their sin; and if not, blot me, I pray thee, out of thy book, which thou hast written." And the Lord said unto Moses, "Whosoever hath sinned against me, him will I blot out of my book. Therefore now go, lead the people unto the place of which I have spoken unto thee: behold, mine angel shall go before thee; nevertheless in the day when I visit, I will visit their sin upon them." And the Lord plagued the people, because they made the calf, which Aaron made.[2]

[The Promised Land and Jericho]

JOSHUA 1-3, 6[1]

Chapter 1

Now after the death of Moses the servant of the Lord it came to pass, that the Lord spake unto Joshua the son of Nun, Moses' minister, saying, "Moses my servant is dead; now therefore arise, go over this Jordan, thou, and all this people, unto

[2]The covenant is renewed when the commandments are again written on two tablets of stone. The final chapters of Exodus detail further laws and describe the construction of the Tabernacle.

[THE PROMISED LAND AND JERICHO]

[1]The people of Israel journey from the Sinai to the Jordan River. After Moses dies, Joshua is appointed as his successor. The following excerpt describes the destruction of Jericho and the initial occupation of Canaan.

the land which I do give to them, even to the children of Israel. Every place that the sole of your foot shall tread upon, that have I given unto you, as I said unto Moses. From the wilderness and this Lebanon even unto the great river, the river Euphrates, all the land of the Hittites, and unto the great sea toward the going down of the sun, shall be your coast. There shall not any man be able to stand before thee all the days of thy life: as I was with Moses, so I will be with thee: I will not fail thee, nor forsake thee. Be strong and of a good courage: for unto this people shalt thou divide for an inheritance the land, which I sware unto their fathers to give them. Only be thou strong and very courageous, that thou mayest observe to do according to all the law, which Moses my servant commanded thee: turn not from it to the right hand or to the left, that thou mayest prosper whithersoever thou goest. This book of the law shall not depart out of thy mouth; but thou shalt meditate therein day and night, that thou mayest observe to do according to all that is written therein: for then thou shalt make thy way prosperous, and then thou shalt have good success. Have not I commanded thee? Be strong and of a good courage; be not afraid, neither be thou dismayed: for the Lord thy God is with thee whithersoever thou goest."

Then Joshua commanded the officers of the people, saying, "Pass through the host, and command the people, saying, 'Prepare you victuals; for within three days ye shall pass over this Jordan, to go in to possess the land, which the Lord your God giveth you to possess it.' "

And to the Reubenites, and to the Gadites, and to half the tribe of Manasseh, spake Joshua, saying, "Remember the word which Moses the servant of the Lord commanded you, saying, 'The Lord your God hath given you rest, and hath given you this land.' Your wives, your little ones, and your cattle, shall remain in the land which Moses gave you on this side Jordan; but ye shall pass before your brethren armed, all the mighty men of valour, and help them. Until the Lord have given your brethren rest, as he hath given you, and they also have possessed the land which the Lord your God giveth them: then ye shall return unto the land of your possession, and enjoy it, which Moses the Lord's servant gave you on this side Jordan toward the sunrising."

And they answered Joshua, saying, "All that thou commandest us we will do, and whithersoever thou sendest us, we will go. According as we hearkened unto Moses in all things, so will we hearken unto thee: only the Lord thy God be with thee, as he was with Moses. Whosoever he be that doth rebel against thy commandment, and will not hearken unto thy words in all that thou commandest him, he shall be put to death: only be strong and of a good courage."

Chapter 2

And Joshua the son of Nun sent out of Shittim two men to spy secretly, saying, "Go view the land, even Jericho." And they went, and came into an harlot's house, named Rahab, and lodged there. And it was told the king of Jericho, saying, "Behold, there came men in hither to night of the children of Israel to search out the country." And the king of Jericho sent unto Rahab, saying, "Bring forth the men that are come to thee, which are entered into thine house: for they be come to search out all the country." And the woman took the two men, and hid them, and said thus, "There came men unto me, but I wist not whence they were. And it came to pass about the time of shutting of the gate, when it was dark, that the men went out: whither the men went I wot not: pursue after them quickly; for ye shall overtake them." But she had brought them up to the roof of the house, and hid them with the stalks of flax, which she had laid in order upon the roof. And the men pursued after them the way to Jordan unto the fords: and as soon as they which pursued after them were gone out, they shut the gate.

And before they were laid down, she came up unto them upon the roof; and she said unto the men, "I know that the Lord hath given you the land, and that your terror is fallen upon us, and that all the inhabitants of the land faint because of you. For we have heard how the Lord dried up the water of the Red sea for you, when ye came out of Egypt; and what ye did unto the two kings of the Amorites, that were on the other side Jordan, Sihon and Og, whom ye utterly destroyed. And as soon as we had heard these things, our hearts did melt, neither did there remain any more courage in any man, because of you: for the Lord your God, he is God in heaven above, and in earth beneath. Now therefore, I pray you, swear unto me by the Lord, since I have shewed you kindness, that ye will also shew kindness unto my father's house, and give me a true token, and that ye will save alive my father, and my mother, and my brethren, and my sisters, and all that they have, and deliver our lives from death." And the men answered her, "Our life for yours, if ye utter not this our business. And it shall be, when the Lord hath given us the land, that we will deal kindly and truly with thee."

Then she let them down by a cord through the window: for her house was upon the town wall, and she dwelt upon the wall. And she said unto them, "Get you to the mountain, lest the pursuers meet you; and hide yourselves there three days, until the pursuers be returned: and afterward may ye go your way." And the men said unto her, "We will be blameless of this thine oath which thou hast made us swear. Behold, when we come into the land, thou shalt bind this line of scarlet thread in the window which thou didst let us down by: and thou shalt bring thy father, and thy mother, and thy brethren, and all thy father's household, home unto thee. And it shall be, that whosoever shall go out of the doors of thy house into the street, his blood shall be upon his head, and we will be guiltless: and whosoever shall be with thee in the house, his blood shall be on our head, if any hand be upon him. And if thou utter this our business, then we will be quit of thine oath which thou hast made us to swear." And she said, "According unto your words, so be it." And she sent them away, and they departed: and she bound the scarlet line in the window.

And they went, and came unto the mountain, and abode there three days, until the pursuers were returned: and the pursuers sought them throughout all the way, but found them not. So the two men returned, and descended from the mountain, and passed over, and came to Joshua the son of Nun, and told him all things that befell them. And they said unto Joshua, "Truly the Lord hath delivered into our hands all the land; for even all the inhabitants of the country do faint because of us."

Chapter 3

And Joshua rose early in the morning; and they removed from Shittim, and came to Jordan, he and all the children of Israel, and lodged there before they passed over. And it came to pass after three days, that the officers went through the host. And they commanded the people, saying, "When ye see the ark of the covenant of the Lord your God, and the priests the Levites bearing it, then ye shall remove from your place, and go after it. Yet there shall be a space between you and it, about two thousand cubits by measure: come not near unto it, that ye may know the way by which ye must go: for ye have not passed this way heretofore." And Joshua said unto the people, "Sanctify yourselves: for to morrow the Lord will do wonders among you." And Joshua spake unto the priests, saying, "Take up the ark of the covenant, and pass over before the people." And they took up the ark of the covenant, and went before the people.

And the Lord said unto Joshua, "This day will I begin to magnify thee in the sight of all Israel, that they may know that, as I was with Moses, so I will be with thee. And thou shalt command the priests that bear the ark of the covenant, saying, 'When ye are come to the brink of the water of Jordan, ye shall stand still in Jordan.'" And Joshua said unto the children of Israel, "Come hither, and hear the words of the Lord your God." And Joshua said, "Hereby ye shall know that the living God is among you, and that he will without fail drive out from before you the Canaanites, and the Hittites, and the Hivites, and the Perizzites, and the Girgashites, and the Amorites, and the Jebusites. Behold, the ark of the covenant of the Lord of all the earth passeth over before you into Jordan. Now therefore take you twelve men out of the tribes of Israel, out of every tribe a man. And it shall come to pass, as soon as the soles of the feet of the priests that bear the ark of the Lord, the Lord of all the earth, shall rest in the waters of Jordan, that the waters of Jordan shall be cut off from the waters that come down from above; and they shall stand upon an heap."

And it came to pass, when the people removed from their tents, to pass over Jordan, and the priests bearing the ark of the covenant before the people. And as they that bare the ark were come unto Jordan, and the feet of the priests that bare the ark were dipped in the brim of the water, (for Jordan overfloweth all his banks all the time of harvest,) that the waters which came down from above stood and rose up upon an heap very far from the city Adam, that is beside Zaretan: and those that came down toward the sea of the plain, even the salt sea, failed, and were cut off: and the people passed over right against Jericho. And the priests that bare the ark of the covenant of the Lord stood firm on dry ground in the midst of Jordan, and all the Israelites passed over on dry ground, until all the people were passed clean over Jordan.

. . .

Chapter 6

Now Jericho was straitly shut up because of the children of Israel: none went out, and none came in. And the Lord said unto Joshua, "See, I have given into thine hand Jericho, and the king thereof, and the mighty men of valour. And ye shall compass the city, all ye men of war, and go round about the city once. Thus shalt thou do six days. And seven priests shall bear before the ark seven trumpets of rams' horns: and the seventh day ye shall compass the city seven times, and the priests shall blow with the trumpets. And it shall come to pass, that when they make a long blast with the ram's horn, and when ye hear the sound of the trumpet, all the people shall shout with a great shout; and the wall of the city shall fall down flat, and the people shall ascend up every man straight before him."

And Joshua the son of Nun called the priests, and said unto them, "Take up the ark of the covenant, and let seven priests bear seven trumpets of rams' horns before the ark of the Lord." And he said unto the people, "Pass on, and compass the city, and let him that is armed pass on before the ark of the Lord."

And it came to pass, when Joshua had spoken unto the people, that the seven priests bearing the seven trumpets of rams' horns passed on before the Lord, and blew with the trumpets: and the ark of the covenant of the Lord followed them.

And the armed men went before the priests that blew with the trumpets, and the rereward[2] came after the ark, the priests going on, and blowing with the trumpets. And Joshua had commanded the people, saying, "Ye shall not shout, nor make any noise with your voice, neither shall any word proceed out of your mouth, until the day I bid you shout; then shall ye shout." So the ark of the Lord compassed the city, going about it once: and they came into the camp, and lodged in the camp.

[2]Rearguard.

And Joshua rose early in the morning, and the priests took up the ark of the Lord. And seven priests bearing seven trumpets of rams' horns before the ark of the Lord went on continually, and blew with the trumpets: and the armed men went before them; but the rereward came after the ark of the Lord, the priests going on, and blowing with the trumpets. And the second day they compassed the city once, and returned into the camp: so they did six days. And it came to pass on the seventh day, that they rose early about the dawning of the day, and compassed the city after the same manner seven times: only on that day they compassed the city seven times. And it came to pass at the seventh time, when the priests blew with their trumpets, Joshua said unto the people, "Shout; for the Lord hath given you the city. And the city shall be accursed, even it, and all that are therein, to the Lord: only Rahab the harlot shall live, she and all that are with her in the house, because she hid the messengers that we sent. And ye, in any wise keep yourselves from the accursed thing, lest ye make yourselves accursed, when ye take of the accursed thing, and make the camp of Israel a curse, and trouble it. But all the silver, and gold, and vessels of brass and iron, are consecrated unto the Lord: they shall come into the treasury of the Lord."

So the people shouted when the priests blew with the trumpets: and it came to pass, when the people heard the sound of the trumpet, and the people shouted with a great shout, that the wall fell down flat, so that the people went up into the city, every man straight before him, and they took the city. And they utterly destroyed all that was in the city, both man and woman, young and old, and ox, and sheep, and ass, with the edge of the sword. But Joshua had said unto the two men that had spied out the country, "Go into the harlot's house, and bring out thence the woman, and all that she hath, as ye sware unto her." And the young men that were spies went in, and brought out Rahab, and her father, and her mother, and her brethren, and all that she had; and they brought out all her kindred, and left them without the camp of Israel. And they burnt the city with fire, and all that was therein: only the silver, and the gold, and the vessels of brass and of iron, they put into the treasury of the house of the Lord. And Joshua saved Rahab the harlot alive, and her father's household, and all that she had; and she dwelleth in Israel even unto this day; because she hid the messengers, which Joshua sent to spy out Jericho.

And Joshua adjured them at that time, saying, "Cursed be the man before the Lord, that riseth up and buildeth this city Jericho: he shall lay the foundation thereof in his firstborn, and in his youngest son shall he set up the gates of it." So the Lord was with Joshua; and his fame was noised throughout all the country.[3]

[The Trials of Job]

Job 1–19, 29–31, 38–42

Chapter 1

There was a man in the land of Uz, whose name was Job, and that man was perfect and upright, and one that feared God, and eschewed evil. And there were born unto him seven sons and three daughters. His substance also was seven thousand sheep, and three thousand camels, and five hundred yoke of oxen, and five hundred she-asses, and a very great household; so that this man was the greatest

---

[3]The destruction of Jericho might be compared with the treatment of Troy in the Trojan War. The rest of the Book of Joshua describes the further conquest of Palestine.

of all the men of the east. And his sons went and feasted in their houses, every one his day, and sent and called for their three sisters to eat and to drink with them. And it was so, when the days of their feasting were gone about, that Job sent and sanctified them, and rose up early in the morning, and offered burnt offerings according to the number of them all: for Job said, "It may be that my sons have sinned, and cursed God in their hearts." Thus did Job continually.

Now there was a day when the sons of God came to present themselves before the Lord, and Satan[1] came also among them. And the Lord said unto Satan, "Whence comest thou?" Then Satan answered the Lord, and said, "From going to and fro in the earth, and from walking up and down in it." And the Lord said unto Satan, "Hast thou considered my servant Job, that there is none like him in the earth, a perfect and an upright man, one that feareth God, and escheweth evil?" Then Satan answered the Lord, and said, "Doth Job fear God for nought? Hast not thou made an hedge about him, and about his house, and about all that he hath on every side? thou hast blessed the work of his hands, and his substance is increased in the land. But put forth thine hand now, and touch all that he hath, and he will curse thee to thy face." And the Lord said unto Satan, "Behold, all that he hath is in thy power, only upon himself put not forth thine hand." So Satan went forth from the presence of the Lord.

And there was a day when his sons and his daughters were eating and drinking wine in their eldest brother's house: and there came a messenger unto Job, and said, "The oxen were plowing, and the asses feeding beside them, and the Sabeans fell upon them, and took them away: yea, they have slain the servants with the edge of the sword, and I only am escaped alone to tell thee." While he was yet speaking, there came also another, and said, "The fire of God is fallen from heaven, and hath burnt up the sheep, and the servants, and consumed them, and I only am escaped alone to tell thee." While he was yet speaking, there came also another, and said, "The Chaldeans made out three bands, and fell upon the camels, and have carried them away, yea, and slain the servants with the edge of the sword, and I only am escaped alone to tell thee." While he was yet speaking, there came also another, and said, "Thy sons and thy daughters were eating and drinking wine in their eldest brother's house. And behold, there came a great wind from the wilderness, and smote the four corners of the house, and it fell upon the young men, and they are dead, and I only am escaped alone to tell thee." Then Job arose, and rent his mantle, and shaved his head, and fell down upon the ground, and worshipped, and said, "Naked came I out of my mother's womb, and naked shall I return thither: the Lord gave, and the Lord hath taken away, blessed be the name of the Lord." In all this Job sinned not, nor charged God foolishly.

Chapter 2

Again there was a day when the sons of God came to present themselves before the Lord, and Satan came also among them to present himself before the Lord. And the Lord said unto Satan, "From whence comest thou?" And Satan answered the Lord, and said, "From going to and fro in the earth, and from walking up and down in it." And the Lord said unto Satan, "Hast thou considered my servant Job, that there is none like him in the earth, a perfect and an upright man, one that feareth God, and escheweth evil? and still he holdeth fast his integrity, although thou movedst me against him, to destroy him without cause." And Satan answered the Lord, and said, "Skin for skin,[2] yea all that a man hath, will he give for his life.

[1] Literally "adversary" or "accuser," and not the evil being that the name Satan is associated with later.
[2] An expression meaning "value for value."

But put forth thine hand now, and touch his bone and his flesh, and he will curse thee to thy face." And the Lord said unto Satan, "Behold, he is in thine hand, but save his life."

So went Satan forth from the presence of the Lord, and smote Job with sore boils, from the sole of his foot unto his crown. And he took him a potsherd to scrape himself withal; and he sat down among the ashes.

Then said his wife unto him, "Dost thou still retain thine integrity? curse God, and die." But he said unto her, "Thou speakest as one of the foolish women speaketh; what? shall we receive good at the hand of God, and shall we not receive evil?" In all this did not Job sin with his lips.

Now when Job's three friends heard of all this evil that was come upon him, they came every one from his own place: Eliphaz the Temanite, and Bildad the Shuhite, and Zophar the Naamathite; for they had made an appointment together to come to mourn with him, and to comfort him. And when they lifted up their eyes afar off, and knew him not, they lifted up their voice, and wept; and they rent every one his mantle, and sprinkled dust upon their heads toward heaven. So they sat down with him upon the ground seven days and seven nights, and none spake a word unto him; for they saw that his grief was very great.

Chapter 3

After this, opened Job his mouth, and cursed his day. And Job spake, and said,

"Let the day perish wherein I was born, and the night in which it was said, 'There is a man-child conceived.'

Let that day be darkness, let not God regard it from above, neither let the light shine upon it.

Let darkness and the shadow of death stain it, let a cloud dwell upon it, let the blackness of the day terrify it.

As for that night, let darkness seize upon it, let it not be joined unto the days of the year, let it not come into the number of the months.

Lo, let that night be solitary, let no joyful voice come therein.

Let them curse it that curse the day, who are ready to raise up their mourning.

Let the stars of the twilight thereof be dark, let it look for light but have none, neither let it see the dawning of the day:

Because it shut not up the doors of my mother's womb, nor hid sorrow from mine eyes.

Why died I not from the womb? why did I not give up the ghost when I came out of the belly?

Why did the knees prevent[3] me? or why the breasts, that I should suck?

For now should I have lain still and been quiet, I should have slept; then had I been at rest,

With kings and counsellors of the earth, which built desolate places for themselves,

Or with princes that had gold, who filled their houses with silver:

Or as an hidden untimely birth, I had not been; as infants which never saw light.

There the wicked cease from troubling: and there the weary be at rest.

There the prisoners rest together, they hear not the voice of the oppressor.

The small and great are there, and the servant is free from his master.

Wherefore is light given to him that is in misery, and life unto the bitter in soul?

---

[3]Receive.

Which long for death, but it cometh not, and dig for it more than for hid treasures:

Which rejoice exceedingly, and are glad when they can find the grave?

Why is light given to a man, whose way is hid, and whom God hath hedged in?

For my sighing cometh before I eat, and my roarings are poured out like the waters.

For the thing which I greatly feared is come upon me, and that which I was afraid of is come unto me.

I was not in safety, neither had I rest, neither was I quiet: yet trouble came."

Chapter 4

Then Eliphaz the Temanite answered, and said,

"If we assay to commune with thee, wilt thou be grieved? But who can withhold himself from speaking?

Behold, thou hast instructed many, and thou hast strengthened the weak hands.

Thy words have upholden him that was falling, and thou hast strengthened the feeble knees.

But now it is come upon thee, and thou faintest; it toucheth thee, and thou art troubled.

Is not this thy fear, thy confidence, thy hope, and the uprightness of thy ways?

Remember, I pray thee, who ever perished, being innocent? or where were the righteous cut off?

Even as I have seen, they that plow iniquity, and sow wickedness, reap the same.[4]

By the blast of God they perish, and by the breath of his nostrils are they consumed.

The roaring of the lion, and the voice of the fierce lion, and the teeth of the young lions, are broken.

The old lion perisheth for lack of prey, and the stout lion's whelps are scattered abroad.

Now a thing was secretly brought to me, and mine ear received a little thereof.

In thoughts from the visions of the night, when deep sleep falleth on men:

Fear came upon me, and trembling, which made all my bones to shake.

Then a spirit passed before my face: the hair of my flesh stood up.

It stood still, but I could not discern the form thereof: an image was before mine eyes, there was silence, and I heard a voice saying,

'Shall mortal man be more just than God? shall a man be more pure than his maker?

'Behold, he put no trust in his servants; and his angels he charged with folly:

'How much less on them that dwell in houses of clay, whose foundation is in the dust, which are crushed before the moth.

'They are destroyed from morning to evening: they perish for ever, without any regarding it.

'Doth not their excellency which is in them go away? they die, even without wisdom.'"

Chapter 5

"Call now, if there be any that will answer thee, and to which of the saints wilt thou turn?

For wrath killeth the foolish man, and envy slayeth the silly one. I have seen the foolish taking root: but suddenly I cursed his habitation.

---

[4]Conventional wisdom held that the good prosper and that the evil are punished.

His children are far from safety, and they are crushed in the gate, neither is there any to deliver them.

Whose harvest the hungry eateth up, and taketh it even out of the thorns, and the robber swalloweth up their substance.

Although affliction cometh not forth of the dust, neither doth trouble spring out of the ground:

Yet man is born unto trouble, as the sparks fly upward.

I would seek unto God, and unto God would I commit my cause:

Which doeth great things and unsearchable: marvelous things without number.

Who giveth rain upon the earth, and sendeth waters upon the fields:

To set up on high those that be low; that those which mourn may be exalted to safety.

He disappointeth the devices of the crafty, so that their hands cannot perform their enterprise.

He taketh the wise in their own craftiness: and the counsel of the froward is carried headlong.

They meet with darkness in the daytime, and grope in the noonday as in the night.

But he saveth the poor from the sword, from their mouth, and from the hand of the mighty.

So the poor hath hope, and iniquity stoppeth her mouth.

Behold, happy is the man whom God correcteth: therefore despise not thou the chastening of the Almighty.

For he maketh sore, and bindeth up: he woundeth, and his hands make whole.[5]

He shall deliver thee in six troubles, yea in seven there shall no evil touch thee.

In famine he shall redeem thee from death: and in war from the power of the sword.

Thou shalt be hid from the scourge of the tongue: neither shalt thou be afraid of destruction when it cometh.

At destruction and famine thou shalt laugh: neither shalt thou be afraid of the beasts of the earth.

For thou shalt be in league with the stones of the field: and the beasts of the field shall be at peace with thee.

And thou shalt know that thy tabernacle[6] shall be in peace; and thou shalt visit thy habitation, and shalt not sin.

Thou shalt know also that thy seed shall be great, and thine offspring as the grass of the earth.

Thou shalt come to thy grave in a full age, like as a shock of corn cometh in, in his season.

Lo this, we have searched it, so it is; hear it, and know thou it for thy good."

Chapter 6

But Job answered, and said,

"Oh that my grief were thoroughly weighed, and my calamity laid in the balances together.

For now it would be heavier than the sand of the sea, therefore my words are swallowed up.[7]

---

[5]In wisdom literature, God uses discipline (in Hebrew, *muser*) to educate and correct.

[6]Tent.

[7]Job replies that his misfortunes are unjust. In another translation, "For they would outweigh the sands of the sea: what wonder if my words are wild?"

For the arrows of the Almighty are within me, the poison whereof drinketh up my spirit: the terrors of God do set themselves in array against me.

Doth the wild ass bray when he hath grass? or loweth the ox over his fodder?

Can that which is unsavoury be eaten without salt? or is there any taste in the white of an egg?

The things that my soul refused to touch are as my sorrowful meat.

O that I might have my request! and that God would grant me the thing that I long for!

Even that it would please God to destroy me, that he would let loose his hand, and cut me off.

Then should I yet have comfort, yea I would harden myself in sorrow; let him not spare, for I have not concealed the words of the holy One.

What is my strength, that I should hope? and what is mine end, that I should prolong my life?

Is my strength the strength of stones? or is my flesh of brass?

Is not my help in me? and is wisdom driven quite from me?

To him that is afflicted pity should be showed from his friend; but he forsaketh the fear of the Almighty.

My brethren have dealt deceitfully as a brook, and as the stream of brooks they pass away,

Which are blackish by reason of the ice, and wherein the snow is hid:

What time they wax warm, they vanish: when it is hot, they are consumed out of their place.

The paths of their way are turned aside; they go to nothing, and perish.

The troops of Tema looked, the companies of Sheba waited for them.

They were confounded because they had hoped;[8] they came thither, and were ashamed.

For now ye are nothing; ye see my casting down, and are afraid.

Did I say, 'Bring unto me'? or 'Give a reward for me of your substance'?

Or 'Deliver me from the enemy's hand,' or 'Redeem me from the hand of the mighty'?

Teach me, and I will hold my tongue: and cause me to understand wherein I have erred.

How forcible are right words? but what doth your arguing reprove?

Do ye imagine to reprove words, and the speeches of one that is desperate, which are as wind?

Yea, ye overwhelm the fatherless, and you dig a pit for your friend.

Now therefore be content, look upon me, for it is evident unto you if I lie.

Return, I pray you, let it not be iniquity; yea return again: my righteousness is in it.

Is there iniquity in my tongue? cannot my taste discern perverse things?

Chapter 7

"Is there not an appointed time to man upon earth? are not his days also like the days of an hireling?

As a servant earnestly desireth the shadow,[9] and as an hireling looketh for the reward of his work:

---

[8]The springs they planned on were dry.

[9]The end of the working day at night.

So am I made to possess months of vanity, and wearisome nights are appointed to me.

When I lie down, I say, 'When shall I arise, and the night be gone?' and I am full of tossings to and fro, unto the dawning of the day.

My flesh is clothed with worms and clods of dust, my skin is broken, and become loathsome.

My days are swifter than a weaver's shuttle, and are spent without hope.

O remember that my life is wind: mine eye shall no more see good.

The eye of him that hath seen me shall see me no more: thine eyes are upon me, and I am not.

As the cloud is consumed and vanisheth away: so he that goeth down to the grave shall come up no more.

He shall return no more to his house: neither shall his place know him any more.

Therefore I will not refrain my mouth, I will speak in the anguish of my spirit, I will complain in the bitterness of my soul.

Am I a sea, or a whale, that thou settest a watch over me?

When I say, 'My bed shall comfort me, my couch shall ease my complaint':

Then thou scarest me with dreams, and terrifiest me through visions:

So that my soul chooseth strangling, and death rather than my life.

I loathe it, I would not live alway: let me alone, for my days are vanity.

What is man, that thou shouldest magnify him? and that thou shouldest set thine heart upon him?

And that thou shouldest visit him every morning, and try him every moment?

How long wilt thou not depart from me? nor let me alone till I swallow down my spittle?

I have sinned: what shall I do unto thee, O thou preserver of men? why hast thou set me as a mark against thee, so that I am a burden to myself?

And why dost thou not pardon my transgression, and take away mine iniquity? for now shall I sleep in the dust, and thou shalt seek me in the morning, but I shall not be."

Chapter 8

Then answered Bildad the Shuhite, and said,

"How long wilt thou speak these things? and how long shall the words of thy mouth be like a strong wind?

Doth God pervert judgment? or doth the Almighty pervert justice?

If thy children have sinned against him, and he have cast them away for their transgression:

If thou wouldst seek unto God betimes, and make thy supplication to the Almighty:

If thou wert pure and upright, surely now he would awake for thee, and make the habitation of thy righteousness prosperous.

Though thy beginning was small, yet thy latter end should greatly increase.

For inquire, I pray thee, of the former age, and prepare thyself to the search of their fathers.

(For we are but of yesterday, and know nothing, because our days upon earth are a shadow.)

Shall not they teach thee, and tell thee, and utter words out of their heart?

Can the rush grow up without mire?[10] can the flag grow without water?

---

[10] Marsh.

Whilst it is yet in his greenness, and not cut down, it withereth before any other herb.

So are the paths of all that forget God, and the hypocrite's hope shall perish:

Whose hope shall be cut off, and whose trust shall be a spider's web.

He shall lean upon his house, but it shall not stand: he shall hold it fast, but it shall not endure.

He is green before the sun, and his branch shooteth forth in his garden.

His roots are wrapped about the heap, and seeth the place of stones.

If he destroy him from his place, then it shall deny him, saying, 'I have not seen thee.'

Behold, this is the joy of his way, and out of the earth shall others grow.

Behold, God will not cast away a perfect man, neither will he help the evildoers:

Till he fill thy mouth with laughing, and thy lips with rejoicing.

They that hate thee shall be clothed with shame, and the dwelling place of the wicked shall come to nought."

Chapter 9

Then Job answered, and said,

"I know it is so of a truth: but how should man be just with God?

If he will contend with him, he cannot answer him one of a thousand.[11]

He is wise in heart, and mighty in strength: who hath hardened himself against him, and hath prospered?

Which removeth the mountains, and they know not: which overturneth them in his anger:

Which shaketh the earth out of her place, and the pillars thereof tremble:

Which commandeth the sun, and it riseth not: and sealeth up the stars:

Which alone spreadeth out the heavens, and treadeth upon the waves of the sea:

Which maketh Arcturus, Orion, and Pleiades, and the chambers of the south:

Which doeth great things past finding out, yea and wonders without number.

Lo, he goeth by me, and I see him not: he passeth on also, but I perceive him not.

Behold, he taketh away, who can hinder him? who will say unto him, 'What doest thou?'

If God will not withdraw his anger, the proud helpers do stoop under him.

How much less shall I answer him, and choose out my words to reason with him?

Whom, though I were righteous, yet would I not answer, but I would make supplication to my judge.

If I had called, and he had answered me, yet would I not believe that he had hearkened unto my voice:

For he breaketh me with a tempest, and multiplieth my wounds without cause.

He will not suffer me to take my breath, but filleth me with bitterness.

If I speak of strength, lo, he is strong: and if of judgment, who shall set me a time to plead?

If I justify myself, mine own mouth shall condemn me: If I say, 'I am perfect,' it shall also prove me perverse.

Though I were perfect, yet would I not know my soul: I would despise my life.

This is one thing, therefore I said it: 'He destroyeth the perfect and the wicked.'

If the scourge slay suddenly, he will laugh at the trial of the innocent.

---

[11] One question in a thousand.

The earth is given into the hand of the wicked: he covereth the faces of the judges thereof; if not, where, and who is he?

Now my days are swifter than a post:[12] they flee away, they see no good.

They are passed away as the swift ships, as the eagle that hasteth to the prey.

If I say, 'I will forget my complaint, I will leave off my heaviness, and comfort myself';

I am afraid of all my sorrows, I know that thou wilt not hold me innocent.

If I be wicked, why then labour I in vain?

If I wash myself with snow-water, and make my hands never so clean:

Yet shalt thou plunge me in the ditch, and mine own clothes shall abhor me.

For he is not a man as I am, that I should answer him, and we should come together in judgment.

Neither is there any daysman[13] betwixt us, that might lay his hand upon us both.

Let him take his rod away from me, and let not his fear terrify me:

Then would I speak, and not fear him; but it is not so with me."

Chapter 10

"My soul is weary of my life, I will leave my complaint upon myself; I will speak in the bitterness of my soul.

I will say unto God, 'Do not condemn me; show me wherefore thou contendest with me.

Is it good unto thee that thou shouldest oppress? that thou shouldest despise the work of thine hands? and shine upon the counsel of the wicked?

Hast thou eyes of flesh? or seest thou as man seeth?

Are thy days as the days of man? are thy years as man's days,

That thou inquirest after mine iniquity, and searchest after my sin?

Thou knowest that I am not wicked, and there is none that can deliver out of thine hand.

Thine hands have made me and fashioned me together round about; yet thou dost destroy me.

Remember, I beseech thee, that thou hast made me as the clay, and wilt thou bring me into dust again?

Hast thou not poured me out as milk, and curdled me like cheese?

Thou hast clothed me with skin and flesh, and hast fenced me with bones and sinews.

Thou hast granted me life and favour, and thy visitation hath preserved my spirit.

And these things hast thou hid in thine heart; I know that this is with thee.

If I sin, then thou markest me, and thou wilt not acquit me from mine iniquity.

If I be wicked, woe unto me; and if I be righteous, yet will I not lift up my head: I am full of confusion, therefore see thou mine affliction:

For it increaseth: thou huntest me as a fierce lion: and again thou showest thyself marvelous upon me.

Thou renewest thy witnesses against me, and increasest thine indignation upon me; changes and war are against me.

Wherefore then hast thou brought me forth out of the womb? Oh that I had given up the ghost, and no eye had seen me!

I should have been as though I had not been, I should have been carried from the womb to the grave.

---

[12] Messenger.

[13] Arbiter.

Are not my days few? cease then, and let me alone that I may take comfort a little,

Before I go whence I shall not return, even to the land of darkness and the shadow of death,

A land of darkness, as darkness itself, and of the shadow of death, without any order, and where the light is as darkness.' "

Chapter 11

Then answered Zophar the Naamathite, and said,

"Should not the multitude of words be answered? and should a man full of talk be justified?

Should thy lies make men hold their peace? and when thou mockest, shall no man make thee ashamed?

For thou hast said, 'My doctrine is pure, and I am clean in thine eyes.'

But O that God would speak, and open his lips against thee,

And that he would show thee the secrets of wisdom, that they are double to that which is: know therefore that God exacteth of thee less than thine iniquity deserveth.

Canst thou by searching find out God? canst thou find out the Almighty unto perfection?

It is as high as heaven, what canst thou do? deeper than hell, what canst thou know?

The measure thereof is longer than the earth, and broader than the sea.

If he cut off, and shut up, or gather together, then who can hinder him?

For he knoweth vain men: he seeth wickedness also, will he not then consider it?

For vain man would be wise, though man be born like a wild ass's colt.

If thou prepare thine heart, and stretch out thine hands toward him:

If iniquity be in thine hand, put it far away, and let not wickedness dwell in thy tabernacles.

For then shalt thou lift up thy face without spot, yea thou shalt be steadfast, and shalt not fear:

Because thou shalt forget thy misery, and remember it as waters that pass away:

And thine age shall be clearer than the noonday; thou shalt shine forth, thou shalt be as the morning.

And thou shalt be secure because there is hope, yea thou shalt dig[14] about thee, and thou shalt take thy rest in safety.

Also thou shalt lie down, and none shall make thee afraid; yea many shall make suit unto thee.

But the eyes of the wicked shall fail, and they shall not escape, and their hope shall be as the giving up of the ghost."

Chapter 12

And Job answered, and said,

"No doubt but ye are the people, and wisdom shall die with you.

But I have understanding as well as you, I am not inferior to you: yea who knoweth not such things as these?

---

[14]In another translation: "You will be confident, because there is hope; sure of protection, you will lie down in confidence."

I am as one mocked of his neighbour, who calleth upon God, and he answereth him: the just upright man is laughed to scorn.

He that is ready to slip with his feet is as a lamp despised in the thought of him that is at ease.

The tabernacles of robbers prosper, and they that provoke God are secure, into whose hand God bringeth abundantly.

But ask now the beasts, and they shall teach thee; and the fowls of the air, and they shall tell thee.

Or speak to the earth, and it shall teach thee; and the fishes of the sea shall declare unto thee.

Who knoweth not in all these that the hand of the Lord hath wrought this?

In whose hand is the soul of every living thing, and the breath of all mankind.

Doth not the ear try words? and the mouth taste his meat?

With the ancient is wisdom, and in length of days understanding.

With him is wisdom and strength, he hath counsel and understanding.

Behold, he breaketh down, and it cannot be built again: he shutteth up a man, and there can be no opening.

Behold, he withholdeth the waters, and they dry up: also he sendeth them out, and they overturn the earth.

With him is strength and wisdom: the deceived and the deceiver are his.

He leadeth counsellors away spoiled, and maketh the judges fools.

He looseth the bond of kings, and girdeth their loins with a girdle.

He leadeth princes away spoiled, and overthroweth the mighty.

He removeth away the speech of the trusty, and taketh away the understanding of the aged.

He poureth contempt upon princes, and weakeneth the strength of the mighty.

He discovereth deep things out of darkness, and bringeth out to light the shadow of death.

He increaseth the nations and destroyeth them: he enlargeth the nations, and straiteneth them again.

He taketh away the heart of the chief of the people of the earth, and causeth them to wander in a wilderness where there is no way.

They grope in the dark without light, and he maketh them to stagger like a drunken man.

Chapter 13

"Lo, mine eye hath seen all this, mine ear hath heard and understood it.

What ye know, the same do I know also, I am not inferior unto you.

Surely I would speak to the Almighty, and I desire to reason with God.

But ye are forgers of lies, ye are all physicians of no value.

O that you would altogether hold your peace, and it should be your wisdom.

Hear now my reasoning, and hearken to the pleadings of my lips.

Will you speak wickedly for God? and talk deceitfully for him?

Will ye accept[15] his person? will ye contend for God?

Is it good that he should search you out? or as one man mocketh another, do ye so mock him?

He will surely reprove you, if ye do secretly accept persons.[16]

Shall not his excellency make you afraid? and his dread fall upon you?

Your remembrances are like unto ashes, your bodies to bodies of clay.

---

[15]Respect.

[16]In another translation: "He will most surely expose you if you take his part by falsely accusing me."

Hold your peace, let me alone that I may speak, and let come on me what will.
Wherefore do I take my flesh in my teeth, and put my life in mine hand?
Though he slay me, yet will I trust in him: but I will maintain mine own ways before him.
He also shall be my salvation: for an hypocrite shall not come before him.
Hear diligently my speech, and my declaration with your ears.
Behold now, I have ordered my cause, I know that I shall be justified.
Who is he that will plead with me? for now if I hold my tongue, I shall give up the ghost.
Only do not two things unto me: then will I not hide myself from thee.
Withdraw thine hand far from me, and let not thy dread make me afraid.
Then call thou, and I will answer: or let me speak, and answer thou me.
How many are mine iniquities and sins? make me to know my transgression and my sin.
Wherefore hidest thou thy face, and holdest me for thine enemy?
Wilt thou break a leaf driven to and fro? and wilt thou pursue the dry stubble?
For thou writest bitter things against me, and makest me to possess the iniquities of my youth.
Thou puttest my feet also in the stocks, and lookest narrowly unto all my paths; thou settest a print upon the heels of my feet.
And he, as a rotten thing, consumeth, as a garment that is moth-eaten."

Chapter 14

"Man that is born of a woman is of few days, and full of trouble.
He cometh forth like a flower, and is cut down: he fleeth also as a shadow, and continueth not.
And dost thou open thine eyes upon such an one, and bringest me into judgment with thee?
Who can bring a clean thing out of an unclean? not one.
Seeing his days are determined, the number of his months are with thee, thou hast appointed his bounds that he cannot pass.
Turn from him that he may rest, till he shall accomplish, as an hireling, his day.
For there is hope of a tree, if it be cut down, that it will sprout again, and that the tender branch thereof will not cease.
Though the root thereof wax old in the earth, and the stock thereof die in the ground:
Yet through the scent of water it will bud, and bring forth boughs like a plant.
But man dieth, and wasteth away; yea, man giveth up the ghost, and where is he?
As the waters fail from the sea, and the flood decayeth and dryeth up:
So man lieth down, and riseth not: till the heavens be no more, they shall not awake, nor be raised out of their sleep.
O that thou wouldest hide me in the grave, that thou wouldest keep me secret, until thy wrath be past, that thou wouldest appoint me a set time, and remember me.
If a man die, shall he live again? All the days of my appointed time will I wait, till my change come.
Thou shalt call, and I will answer thee: thou wilt have a desire to[17] the work of thine hands.

[17] For.

For now thou numberest my steps: dost thou not watch over my sin?
My transgression is sealed up in a bag, and thou sewest up mine iniquity.
And surely the mountain falling cometh to nought: and the rock is removed out of his place.
The waters wear the stones, thou washest away the things which grow out of the dust of the earth, and thou destroyest the hope of man.
Thou prevailest for ever against him, and he passeth: thou changest his countenance, and sendest him away.
His sons come to honour, and he knoweth it not; and they are brought low, but he perceiveth it not of them.
But his flesh upon him shall have pain, and his soul within him shall mourn."

Chapter 15

Then answered Eliphaz the Temanite, and said,
"Should a wise man utter vain knowledge, and fill his belly with the east wind?
Should he reason with unprofitable talk? or with speeches wherewith he can do no good?
Yea thou castest off fear, and restrainest prayer before God.
For thy mouth uttereth thine iniquity, and thou choosest the tongue of the crafty.
Thine own mouth condemneth thee, and not I: yea thine own lips testify against thee.
Art thou the first man that was born? or wast thou made before the hills?
Hast thou heard the secret of God? and dost thou restrain wisdom to thyself?
What knowest thou that we know not? what understandest thou which is not in us?
With us are both the grayheaded and very aged men, much elder than thy father.
Are the consolations of God small with thee? is there any secret thing with thee?
Why doth thine heart carry thee away? and what do thine eyes wink at,
That thou turnest thy spirit against God, and lettest such words go out of thy mouth?
What is man, that he should be clean? and he which is born of a woman, that he should be righteous?
Behold, he putteth no trust in his saints, yea, the heavens are not clean in his sight.
How much more abominable and filthy is man, which drinketh iniquity like water?
I will show thee, hear me, and that which I have seen I will declare,
Which wise men have told from their fathers, and have not hid it:
Unto whom alone the earth was given, and no stranger passed among them.
The wicked man travaileth with pain all his days, and the number of years is hidden to the oppressor.
A dreadful sound is in his ears; in prosperity the destroyer shall come upon him.
He believeth not that he shall return out of darkness, and he is waited for of the sword.
He wandereth abroad for bread, saying, 'Where is it?' he knoweth that the day of darkness is ready at his hand.
Trouble and anguish shall make him afraid; they shall prevail against him, as a king ready to the battle.
For he stretcheth out his hand against God, and strengtheneth himself against the Almighty.

He runneth upon him, even on his neck, upon the thick bosses of his bucklers:[18]

Because he covereth his face with his fatness, and maketh collops of fat[19] on his flanks.

And he dwelleth in desolate cities, and in houses which no man inhabiteth, which are ready to become heaps.

He shall not be rich, neither shall his substance continue, neither shall he prolong the perfection thereof upon the earth.

He shall not depart out of darkness, the flame shall dry up his branches, and by the breath of his mouth shall he go away.

Let not him that is deceived trust in vanity: for vanity shall be his recompense.

It shall be accomplished before his time, and his branch shall not be green.

He shall shake off his unripe grape as the vine, and shall cast off his flower as the olive.

For the congregation of hypocrites shall be desolate, and fire shall consume the tabernacles of bribery.

They conceive mischief, and bring forth vanity, and their belly prepareth deceit."

Chapter 16

Then Job answered, and said,

"I have heard many such things: miserable comforters are ye all.

Shall vain words have an end? or what emboldeneth thee that thou answerest?

I also could speak as ye do: if your soul were in my soul's stead, I could heap up words against you, and shake mine head at you.

But I would strengthen you with my mouth, and the moving of my lips should assuage your grief.

Though I speak, my grief is not assuaged: and though I forbear, what am I eased?

But now he hath made me weary: thou hast made desolate all my company.

And thou hast filled me with wrinkles, which is a witness against me: and my leanness rising up in me beareth witness to my face.

He teareth me in his wrath, who hateth me: he gnasheth upon me with his teeth; mine enemy sharpeneth his eyes upon me.

They have gaped upon me with their mouth, they have smitten me upon the cheek reproachfully, they have gathered themselves together against me.

God hath delivered me to the ungodly, and turned me over into the hands of the wicked.

I was at ease, but he hath broken me asunder: he hath also taken me by my neck, and shaken me to pieces, and set me up for his mark.

His archers compass me round about, he cleaveth my reins asunder, and doth not spare; he poureth out my gall upon the ground.

He breaketh me with breach upon breach, he runneth upon me like a giant.

I have sewed sackcloth upon my skin, and defiled my horn in the dust.

My face is foul with weeping, and on mine eyelids is the shadow of death;

Not for any injustice in mine hands: also my prayer is pure.

O earth, cover not thou my blood, and let my cry have no place.

Also now, behold, my witness is in heaven, and my record is on high.

My friends scorn me: but mine eye poureth out tears unto God.

O that one might plead for a man with God, as a man pleadeth for his neighbour.

When a few years are come, then I shall go the way whence I shall not return."

---

[18]In another translation: " . . . charging him head down, with the full weight of his bossed shield."

[19]Bulges with fat.

Chapter 17

"My breath is corrupt, my days are extinct, the graves are ready for me.

Are there not mockers with me? and doth not mine eye continue in their provocation?

Lay down now, put me in a surety with thee; who is he that will strike hands[20] with me?

For thou hast hid their heart from understanding: therefore shalt thou not exalt them.

He that speaketh flattery to his friends, even the eyes of his children shall fail.

He hath made me also a byword of the people, and aforetime I was as a tabret.[21]

Mine eye also is dim by reason of sorrow, and all my members are as a shadow.

Upright men shall be astonished at this, and the innocent shall stir up himself against the hypocrite.

The righteous also shall hold on his way, and he that hath clean hands shall be stronger and stronger.

But as for you all, do you return, and come now, for I cannot find one wise man among you.

My days are past, my purposes are broken off, even the thoughts of my heart:

They change the night into day: the light is short because of darkness.

If I wait, the grave is mine house: I have made my bed in the darkness.

I have said to corruption, 'Thou art my father': to the worm, 'Thou art my mother, and my sister.'

And where is now my hope? as for my hope, who shall see it?

They shall go down to the bars of the pit, when our rest together is in the dust."

Chapter 18

Then answered Bildad the Shuhite, and said,

"How long will it be ere you make an end of words? Mark, and afterwards we will speak.

Wherefore are we counted as beasts, and reputed vile in your sight?

He teareth himself in his anger: shall the earth be forsaken for thee? and shall the rock be removed out of his place?

Yea, the light of the wicked shall be put out, and the spark of his fire shall not shine.

The light shall be dark in his tabernacle, and his candle shall be put out with him.

The steps of his strength shall be straitened, and his own counsel shall cast him down.

For he is cast into a net by his own feet, and he walketh upon a snare.

The gin[22] shall take him by the heel, and the robber shall prevail against him.

The snare is laid for him in the ground, and a trap for him in the way.

Terrors shall make him afraid on every side, and shall drive him to his feet.

His strength shall be hunger-bitten, and destruction shall be ready at his side.

It shall devour the strength of his skin: even the firstborn of death shall devour his strength.

---

[20]Shake hands, meaning "who will defend me before God?"

[21]A timbrel or tambourine.

[22]Snare.

His confidence shall be rooted out of his tabernacle, and it shall bring him to the king of terrors.

It shall dwell in his tabernacle, because it is none of his: brimstone shall be scattered upon his habitation.

His roots shall be dried up beneath: and above shall his branch be cut off.

His remembrance shall perish from the earth, and he shall have no name in the street.

He shall be driven from light into darkness, and chased out of the world.

He shall neither have son nor nephew among his people, nor any remaining in his dwellings.

They that come after him shall be astonished at his day, as they that went before were affrighted.

Surely such are the dwellings of the wicked, and this is the place of him that knoweth not God."

Chapter 19

Then Job answered, and said,

"How long will ye vex my soul, and break me in pieces with words?

These ten times have ye reproached me: you are not ashamed that you make yourselves strange to me.

And be it indeed that I have erred, mine error remaineth with myself.

If indeed ye will magnify yourselves against me, and plead against me my reproach:

Know now that God hath overthrown me, and hath compassed me with his net.

Behold, I cry out of wrong, but I am not heard: I cry aloud, but there is no judgment.

He hath fenced up my way that I cannot pass; and he hath set darkness in my paths.

He hath stripped me of my glory, and taken the crown from my head.

He hath destroyed me on every side, and I am gone: and mine hope hath he removed like a tree.

He hath also kindled his wrath against me, and he counteth me unto him as one of his enemies.

His troops come together, and raise up their way against me, and encamp round about my tabernacle.

He hath put my brethren far from me, and mine acquaintance are verily estranged from me.

My kinsfolk have failed, and my familiar friends have forgotten me.

They that dwell in mine house, and my maids, count me for a stranger: I am an alien in their sight.

I called my servant, and he gave me no answer: I entreated him with my mouth.

My breath is strange to my wife, though I entreated for the children's sake of mine own body.

Yea, young children despised me; I arose, and they spake against me.

All my inward friends abhorred me: and they whom I loved are turned against me.

My bone cleaveth to my skin, and to my flesh, and I am escaped with the skin of my teeth.

Have pity upon me, have pity upon me, O ye my friends; for the hand of God hath touched me.

Why do ye persecute me as God, and are not satisfied with my flesh?

Oh that my words were now written, oh that they were printed in a book!

That they were graven with an iron pen and lead in the rock for ever!

For I know that my redeemer liveth, and that he shall stand at the latter day upon the earth:

And though after my skin worms destroy this body, yet in my flesh shall I see God:

Whom I shall see for myself, and mine eyes shall behold, and not another, though my reins be consumed within me.

But ye should say, 'Why persecute we him?' seeing the root of the matter is found in me.

Be ye afraid of the sword: for wrath bringeth the punishments of the sword, that ye may know there is a judgment."[23]

. . .

Chapter 29

Moreover Job continued his parable, and said,

"O that I were as in months past, as in the days when God preserved me:

When his candle shined upon my head, and when by his light I walked through darkness:

As I was in the days of my youth, when the secret of God was upon my tabernacle:

When the Almighty was yet with me, when my children were about me:

When I washed my steps with butter, and the rock poured me out rivers of oil:

When I went out to the gate through the city, when I prepared my seat in the street.

The young men saw me, and hid themselves: and the aged arose, and stood up.

The princes refrained talking, and laid their hand on their mouth.

The nobles held their peace, and their tongue cleaved to the roof of their mouth.

When the ear heard me, then it blessed me, and when the eye saw me, it gave witness to me:

Because I delivered the poor that cried, and the fatherless, and him that had none to help him.

The blessing of him that was ready to perish came upon me: and I caused the widow's heart to sing for joy.

I put on righteousness, and it clothed me: my judgment was as a robe and a diadem.

I was eyes to the blind, and feet was I to the lame.

I was a father to the poor: and the cause which I knew not, I searched out.

And I brake the jaws of the wicked, and plucked the spoil out of his teeth.

Then I said, 'I shall die in my nest, and I shall multiply my days as the sand.'

My root was spread out by the waters, and the dew lay all night upon my branch.

My glory was fresh in me, and my bow was renewed in my hand.

Unto me men gave ear, and waited, and kept silence at my counsel.

After my words they spake not again, and my speech dropped upon them,

And they waited for me as for the rain, and they opened their mouth wide as for the latter rain.

If I laughed on them, they believed it not, and the light of my countenance they cast not down.

I chose out their way, and sat chief, and dwelt as a king in the army, as one that comforteth the mourners."

---

[23]The round of speeches in chapters 20–28 generally repeats earlier arguments.

Chapter 30

"But now they that are younger than I have me in derision, whose fathers I would have disdained to have set with the dogs of my flock.

Yea whereto might the strength of their hands profit me, in whom old age was perished?[24]

For want and famine they were solitary: flying into the wilderness in former time desolate and waste:

Who cut up mallows by the bushes, and juniper roots for their meat.

They were driven forth from among men (they cried after them, as after a thief),

To dwell in the cliffs of the valleys, in caves of the earth, and in the rocks.

Among the bushes they brayed: under the nettles they were gathered together.

They were children of fools, yea children of base men: they were viler than the earth.

And now am I their song, yea I am their byword.

They abhor me, they flee far from me, and spare not to spit in my face.

Because he hath loosed my cord and afflicted me, they have also let loose the bridle before me.

Upon my right hand rise the youth, they push away my feet, and they raise up against me the ways of their destruction.

They mar my path, they set forward my calamity, they have no helper.

They came upon me as a wide breaking in of waters: in the desolation they rolled themselves upon me.

Terrors are turned upon me: they pursue my soul as the wind: and my welfare passeth away as a cloud.

And now my soul is poured out upon me: the days of affliction have taken hold upon me:

My bones are pierced in me in the night season: and my sinews take no rest.

By the great force of my disease is my garment changed: it bindeth me about as the collar of my coat.

He hath cast me into the mire, and I am become like dust and ashes.

I cry unto thee, and thou dost not hear me: I stand up, and thou regardest me not.

Thou art become cruel to me: with thy strong hand thou opposest thyself against me.

Thou liftest me up to the wind: thou causest me to ride upon it, and dissolvest my substance.

For I know that thou wilt bring me to death, and to the house appointed for all living.

Howbeit he will not stretch out his hand to the grave, though they cry in his destruction.

Did not I weep for him that was in trouble? was not my soul grieved for the poor?

When I looked for good, then evil came unto me: and when I waited for light, there came darkness.

My bowels boiled and rested not: the days of affliction prevented me.

I went mourning without the sun: I stood up, and I cried in the congregation.

I am a brother to dragons, and a companion to owls.

---

[24] Who had become weak with age.

My skin is black upon me, and my bones are burnt with heat.

My harp[25] also is turned to mourning, and my organ into the voice of them that weep."

Chapter 31

"I made a covenant with mine eyes; why then should I think upon a maid?

For what portion of God is there from above? and what inheritance of the Almighty from on high?

Is not destruction to the wicked? and a strange punishment to the workers of iniquity?

Doth not he see my ways, and count all my steps?

If I have walked with vanity, or if my foot hath hasted to deceit:

Let me be weighed in an even balance, that God may know mine integrity.

If my step hath turned out of the way, and mine heart walked after mine eyes, and if any blot hath cleaved to my hands:

Then let me sow, and let another eat, yea let my offspring be rooted out.

If mine heart have been deceived by a woman, or if I have laid wait at my neighbour's door:

Then let my wife grind unto another, and let others bow down upon her.

For this is an heinous crime, yea, it is an iniquity to be punished by the judges.

For it is a fire that consumeth to destruction, and would root out all mine increase.

If I did despise the cause of my manservant, or of my maidservant, when they contended with me:

What then shall I do when God riseth up? and when he visiteth, what shall I answer him?

Did not he that made me in the womb, make him? and did not one fashion us in the womb?

If I have withheld the poor from their desire, or have caused the eyes of the widow to fail:

Or have eaten my morsel myself alone, and the fatherless hath not eaten thereof:

(For from my youth he was brought up with me as with a father, and I have guided her from my mother's womb.)

If I have seen any perish for want of clothing, or any poor without covering:

If his loins have not blessed me, and if he were not warmed with the fleece of my sheep:

If I have lifted up my hand against the fatherless, when I saw my help in the gate:[26]

Then let mine arm fall from my shoulder blade, and mine arm be broken from the bone.

For destruction from God was a terror to me: and by reason of his highness I could not endure.

If I have made gold my hope, or have said to the fine gold, 'Thou art my confidence':

If I rejoiced because my wealth was great, and because mine hand had gotten much:

[25] Flute.

[26] In the court.

If I beheld the sun when it shined, or the moon walking in brightness:

And my heart hath been secretly enticed, or my mouth hath kissed my hand.[27]

This also were an iniquity to be punished by the judge: for I should have denied the God that is above.

If I rejoiced at the destruction of him that hated me, or lifted up myself when evil found him:

(Neither have I suffered my mouth to sin by wishing a curse to his soul.)

If the men of my tabernacle said not, 'Oh that we had of his flesh! we cannot be satisfied.'

The stranger did not lodge in the street: but I opened my doors to the traveler.

If I covered my transgressions, as Adam, by hiding mine iniquity in my bosom:

Did I fear a great multitude, or did the contempt of families terrify me, that I kept silence, and went not out of the door?

O that one would hear me! Behold, my desire is that the Almighty would answer me, and that mine adversary had written a book.

Surely I would take it upon my shoulder, and bind it as a crown to me.

I would declare unto him the number of my steps, as a prince would I go near unto him.

If my land cry against me, or that the furrows likewise thereof complain:

If I have eaten the fruits thereof without money, or have caused the owners thereof to lose their life:

Let thistles grow instead of wheat, and cockle instead of barley." The words of Job are ended.[28]

. . .

Chapter 38

Then the Lord answered Job out of the whirlwind, and said, "Who is this that darkeneth counsel by words without knowledge?

Gird up now thy loins like a man; for I will demand of thee, and answer thou me.

Where wast thou when I laid the foundations of the earth? declare, if thou hast understanding.

Who hath laid the measures thereof, if thou knowest? or who hath stretched the line upon it?

Whereupon are the foundations thereof fastened? or who laid the cornerstone thereof;

When the morning stars sang together, and all the sons of God shouted for joy?

Or who shut up the sea with doors, when it brake forth as if it had issued out of the womb?

When I made the cloud the garment thereof, and thick darkness a swaddling band for it,

And brake up for it my decreed place, and set bars and doors,

And said, 'Hitherto shalt thou come, but no further: and here shall thy proud waves be stayed'?

Hast thou commanded the morning since thy days? and caused the day-spring to know his place,

[27] Acts of homage.

[28] Chapters 32–37 are considered a later interpretation; a young man, Elihu, repeats earlier ideas.

That it might take hold of the ends of the earth, that the wicked might be shaken out of it?

It is turned as clay to the seal,[29] and they stand as a garment.

And from the wicked their light is withholden, and the high arm shall be broken.

Hast thou entered into the springs of the sea? or hast thou walked in the search of the depth?

Have the gates of death been opened unto thee? or hast thou seen the doors of the shadow of death?

Hast thou perceived the breadth of the earth? Declare if thou knowest it all.

Where is the way where light dwelleth? and as for darkness, where is the place thereof,

That thou shouldest take it to the bound thereof, and that thou shouldest know the paths to the house thereof?

Knowest thou it, because thou wast then born? or because the number of thy days is great?

Hast thou entered into the treasures of the snow? or hast thou seen the treasures of the hail,

Which I have reserved against the time of trouble, against the day of battle and war?

By what way is the light parted, which scattereth the east wind upon the earth?

Who hath divided a watercourse for the overflowing of waters? or a way for the lightning of thunder,

To cause it to rain on the earth, where no man is: on the wilderness wherein there is no man;

To satisfy the desolate and waste ground, and to cause the bud of the tender herb to spring forth?

Hath the rain a father? or who hath begotten the drops of dew?

Out of whose womb came the ice? and the hoary frost of heaven, who hath gendered it?

The waters are hid as with a stone, and the face of the deep is frozen.

Canst thou bind the sweet influences of Pleiades? or loose the bands of Orion?

Canst thou bring forth Mazzaroth[30] in his season, or canst thou guide Arcturus with his sons?

Knowest thou the ordinances of heaven? canst thou set the dominion thereof in the earth?

Canst thou lift up thy voice to the clouds, that abundance of waters may cover thee?

Canst thou send lightnings, that they may go, and say unto thee, 'Here we are'?

Who hath put wisdom in the inward parts? or who hath given understanding to the heart?

Who can number the clouds in wisdom? or who can stay the bottles of heaven,

When the dust groweth into hardness, and the clods cleave fast together?

Wilt thou hunt the prey for the lion? or fill the appetite of the young lions,

When they couch in their dens, and abide in the covert to lie in wait?

Who provideth for the raven his food? when his young ones cry unto God, they wander for lack of meat."

---

[29]"As clay under a seal," so that the creation might be highlighted.

[30]Probably a constellation.

Chapter 39

"Knowest thou the time when the wild goats of the rock bring forth? or canst thou mark when the hinds do calve?

Canst thou number the months that they fufill? or knowest thou the time when they bring forth?

They bow themselves, they bring forth their young ones, they cast out their sorrows.

Their young ones are in good liking, they grow up with corn: they go forth, and return not unto them.

Who hath sent out the wild ass free? or who hath loosed the bands of the wild ass?

Whose house I have made the wilderness, and the barren land his dwellings.

He scorneth the multitude of the city, neither regardeth he the crying of the driver.

The range of the mountains is his pasture, and he searcheth after every green thing.

Will the unicorn[31] be willing to serve thee? or abide by thy crib?

Canst thou bind the unicorn with his band in the furrow? or will he harrow the valleys after thee?

Wilt thou trust him because his strength is great? or wilt thou leave thy labour to him?

Wilt thou believe him that he will bring home thy seed? and gather it into thy barn?

Gavest thou the goodly wings unto the peacocks, or wings and feathers unto the ostrich?

Which leaveth her eggs in the earth, and warmeth them in the dust,

And forgetteth that the foot may crush them, or that the wild beast may break them.

She is hardened against her young ones, as though they were not hers: her labour is in vain without fear:

Because God hath deprived her of wisdom, neither hath he imparted to her understanding.

What time she lifteth up herself on high, she scorneth the horse and his rider.

Hast thou given the horse strength? hast thou clothed his neck with thunder?

Canst thou make him afraid as a grasshopper? the glory of his nostrils is terrible.

He paweth in the valley, and rejoiceth in his strength: he goeth on to meet the armed men.

He mocketh at fear, and is not affrighted: neither turneth he back from the sword.

The quiver rattleth against him, the glittering spear and the shield.

He swalloweth the ground with fierceness and rage: neither believeth he that it is the sound of the trumpet.

He saith among the trumpets, 'Ha, ha': and he smelleth the battle afar off, the thunder of the captains, and the shouting.

Doth the hawk fly by thy wisdom, and stretch her wings toward the south?

Doth the eagle mount up at thy command? and make her nest on high?

She dwelleth and abideth on the rock, upon the crag of the rock, and the strong place.

---

[31] Probably a wild ox.

From thence she seeketh the prey, and her eyes behold afar off.

Her young ones also suck up blood: and where the slain are, there is she."

Chapter 40

Moreover the Lord answered Job, and said,

"Shall he that contendeth with the Almighty instruct him? he that reproveth God, let him answer it."

Then Job answered the Lord, and said,

"Behold, I am vile, what shall I answer thee? I will lay my hand upon my mouth.

Once have I spoken, but I will not answer: yea twice, but I will proceed no further."

Then answered the Lord unto Job out of the whirlwind, and said,

"Gird up thy loins now like a man: I will demand of thee, and declare thou unto me.

Wilt thou also disannul my judgment? wilt thou condemn me, that thou mayest be righteous?

Hast thou an arm like God? or canst thou thunder with a voice like him?

Deck thyself now with majesty and excellency, and array thyself with glory and beauty.

Cast abroad the rage of thy wrath: and behold every one that is proud, and abase him.

Look on every one that is proud, and bring him low: and tread down the wicked in their place.

Hide them in the dust together, and bind their faces in secret.

Then will I also confess unto thee, that thine own right hand can save thee.

Behold now behemoth,[37] which I made with thee, he eateth grass as an ox.

Lo now, his strength is in his loins, and his force is in the navel of his belly.

He moveth his tail like a cedar: the sinews of his stones[33] are wrapped together.

His bones are as strong pieces of brass: his bones are like bars of iron.

He is the chief of the ways of God: he that made him can make his sword to approach unto him.

Surely the mountains bring him forth food, where all the beasts of the field play.

He lieth under the shady trees, in the covert of the reed, and fens.

The shady trees cover him with their shadow: the willows of the brook compass him about.

Behold, he drinketh up a river, and hasteth not: he trusteth that he can draw up Jordan into his mouth.

He taketh it with his eyes: his nose pierceth through snares."

Chapter 41

"Canst thou draw out leviathan[34] with an hook? or his tongue with a cord which thou lettest down?

Canst thou put an hook into his nose? or bore his jaw through with a thorn?

Will he make many supplications unto thee? will he speak soft words unto thee?

Will he make a covenant with thee? wilt thou take him for a servant for ever?

Wilt thou play with him as with a bird? or wilt thou bind him for thy maidens?

Shall the companions make a banquet of him? shall they part him among the merchants?

---

[37] Probably a hippopotamus or crocodile.

[33] Thighs; testicles.

[34] Probably a whale.

Canst thou fill his skin with barbed irons? or his head with fish spears?

Lay thine hand upon him, remember the battle: do no more.

Behold, the hope of him is in vain: shall not one be cast down even at the sight of him?

None is so fierce that dare stir him up: who then is able to stand before me?

Who hath prevented me that I should repay him? whatsoever is under the whole heaven is mine.

I will not conceal his parts, nor his power, nor his comely proportion.

Who can discover the face of his garment? or who can come to him with his double bridle?

Who can open the doors of his face? his teeth are terrible round about.

His scales are his pride, shut up together as with a close seal.

One is so near to another that no air can come between them.

They are joined one to another, they stick together, that they cannot be sundered.

By his neesings[35] a light doth shine, and his eyes are like the eyelids of the morning.

Out of his mouth go burning lamps, and sparks of fire leap out.

Out of his nostrils goeth smoke, as out of a seething pot or caldron.

His breath kindleth coals, and a flame goeth out of his mouth.

In his neck remaineth strength, and sorrow is turned into joy before him.

The flakes of his flesh are joined together: they are firm in themselves, they cannot be moved.

His heart is as firm as a stone, yea as hard as a piece of the nether millstone.

When he raiseth up himself, the mighty are afraid: by reason of breakings they purify themselves.[36]

The sword of him that layeth at him cannot hold: the spear, the dart, nor the habergeon.[37]

He esteemeth iron as straw, and brass as rotten wood.

The arrow cannot make him flee: slingstones are turned with him into stubble.

Darts are counted as stubble: he laugheth at the shaking of a spear.

Sharp stones are under him: he spreadeth sharp pointed things upon the mire.

He maketh the deep to boil like a pot: he maketh the sea like a pot of ointment.

He maketh a path to shine after him; one would think the deep to be hoary.[38]

Upon earth there is not his like, who is made without fear.

He beholdeth all high things: he is a king over all the children of pride."

Chapter 42

Then Job answered the Lord, and said,

"I know that thou canst do every thing, and that no thought can be withholden from thee.

Who is he that hideth counsel without knowledge? therefore have I uttered that I understood not, things too wonderful for me, which I knew not.

Hear, I beseech thee, and I will speak: I will demand of thee, and declare thou unto me.

[35] Sneezings.

[36] In another translation: "When he raises himself, strong men take fright, bewildered at the lashings of his tail."

[37] A coat of mail.

[38] White.

I have heard of thee by the hearing of the ear: but now mine eye seeth thee.
Wherefore I abhor myself, and repent in dust and ashes."

And it was so, that after the Lord had spoken these words unto Job, the Lord said to Eliphaz the Temanite, "My wrath is kindled against thee, and against thy two friends: for ye have not spoken of me the thing that is right, as my servant Job hath. Therefore take unto you now seven bullocks, and seven rams, and go to my servant Job, and offer up for yourselves a burnt offering, and my servant Job shall pray for you, for him will I accept: lest I deal with you after your folly, in that ye have not spoken of me the thing which is right, like my servant Job." So Eliphaz the Temanite, and Bildad the Shuhite, and Zophar the Naamathite went, and did according as the Lord commanded them: the Lord also accepted Job. And the Lord turned the captivity of Job,[39] when he prayed for his friends: also the Lord gave Job twice as much as he had before.

Then came there unto him all his brethren, and all his sisters, and all they that had been of his acquaintance before, and did eat bread with him in his house: and they bemoaned him, and comforted him over all the evil that the Lord had brought upon him: every man also gave him a piece of money, and every one an earring of gold. So the Lord blessed the latter end of Job more than his beginning: for he had fourteen thousand sheep, and six thousand camels, and a thousand yoke of oxen, and a thousand she-asses. He had also seven sons, and three daughters. And he called the name of the first Jemima, and the name of the second Kezia, and the name of the third Keren-happuch. And in all the land were no women found so fair as the daughters of Job: and their father gave them inheritance among their brethren. After this lived Job an hundred and forty years, and saw his sons, and his sons' sons, even four generations. So Job died, being old, and full of days.

Psalms

Psalm 6: "O Lord, rebuke me not in thine anger"

O Lord, rebuke me not in thine anger, neither chasten me in thy hot displeasure.

Have mercy upon me, O Lord, for I am weak: O Lord, heal me, for my bones are vexed.

My soul is also sore vexed: but thou, O Lord, how long?

Return, O Lord, deliver my soul: oh save me, for thy mercies' sake.

For in death there is no remembrance of thee: in the grave who shall give thee thanks?

I am weary with my groaning, all the night make I my bed to swim:[1] I water my couch with my tears.

Mine eye is consumed because of grief; it waxeth old because of all mine enemies.

Depart from me, all ye workers of iniquity; for the Lord hath heard the voice of my weeping.

The Lord hath heard my supplication; the Lord will receive my prayer.

Let all mine enemies be ashamed and sore vexed: let them return and be ashamed suddenly.

. . .

---

[39]"The Lord showed favor to Job."

PSALMS

[1]In another translation: " . . . my pillow is wet with tears."

Psalm 19: "The heavens declare the glory of God"

The heavens declare the glory of God: and the firmament showeth his handiwork.

Day unto day uttereth speech, and night unto night showeth knowledge.

There is no speech nor language, where their voice is not heard.

Their line is gone out through all the earth, and their words to the end of the world: in them hath he set a tabernacle for the sun,

Which is as a bridegroom coming out of his chamber, and rejoiceth as a strong man to run a race.

His going forth is from the end of the heaven, and his circuit unto the ends of it: and there is nothing hid from the heat thereof.

The law of the Lord is perfect, converting the soul: the testimony of the Lord is sure, making wise the simple.

The statutes of the Lord are right, rejoicing the heart: the commandment of the Lord is pure, enlightening the eyes.

The fear of the Lord is clean, enduring for ever: the judgments of the Lord are true, and righteous altogether.

More to be desired are they than gold, yea, than much fine gold: sweeter also than honey, and the honeycomb.

Moreover by them is thy servant warned: and in keeping of them there is great reward.

Who can understand his errors? cleanse thou me from secret faults.

Keep back thy servant also from presumptuous sins, let them not have dominion over me: then shall I be upright, and I shall be innocent from the great transgression.

Let the words of my mouth, and the meditation of my heart, be acceptable in thy sight, O Lord, my strength, and my redeemer.

. . .

Psalm 23: "The Lord is my shepherd, I shall not want"

The Lord is my shepherd, I shall not want.

He maketh me to lie down in green pastures: he leadeth me beside the still waters.

He restoreth my soul: he leadeth me in the paths of righteousness, for his name's sake.

Yea though I walk through the valley of the shadow of death, I will fear no evil: for thou art with me, thy rod and thy staff they comfort me.

Thou preparest a table before me, in the presence of mine enemies: thou anointest my head with oil, my cup runneth over.

Surely goodness and mercy shall follow me all the days of my life: and I will dwell in the house of the Lord for ever.

. . .

Psalm 121: "I will lift up mine eyes unto the hills, from whence cometh my help"

I will lift up mine eyes unto the hills, from whence cometh my help.

My help cometh from the Lord, which made heaven and earth.

He will not suffer thy foot to be moved: he that keepeth thee will not slumber.

Behold, he that keepeth Israel shall neither slumber nor sleep.

The Lord is thy keeper: the Lord is thy shade upon thy right hand.

The sun shall not smite thee by day, nor the moon by night.

The Lord shall preserve thee from all evil: he shall preserve thy soul.

The Lord shall preserve thy going out, and thy coming in, from this time forth and even for evermore.

. . .

Psalm 137: "By the rivers of Babylon, there we sat down"

By the rivers of Babylon,[2] there we sat down, yea we wept, when we remembered Zion.

We hanged our harps upon the willows, in the midst thereof.

For there they that carried us away captive required of us a song, and they that wasted us required of us mirth: saying, "Sing us one of the songs of Zion."

How shall we sing the Lord's song in a strange land?

If I forget thee, O Jerusalem, let my right hand forget her cunning.

If I do not remember thee, let my tongue cleave to the roof of my mouth; if I prefer not Jerusalem above my chief joy.

Remember, O Lord, the children of Edom,[3] in the day of Jerusalem, who said, "Rase it, rase it: even to the foundation thereof."

O daughter of Babylon, who art to be destroyed: happy shall he be that rewardeth thee, as thou hast served us.

Happy shall he be that taketh and dasheth thy little ones against the stones.

THE NEW TESTAMENT

[1ST CENTURY–2ND CENTURY C.E.]

The King James Version

A collection of documents from the early Christian community, written in the first two centuries after Jesus, the New Testament brings together the Hebraic and Hellenic strands of Western culture. It centers on the life and teachings of a Jewish prophet, yet it was written down in Greek. The message of the New Testament replaces the old law and the old covenant between Moses, the Jewish people, and God with a new covenant and a new law. Instead of a religion restricted to God's chosen people, the new covenant was put forth as one with all humankind, and Christianity proclaimed itself to be a world religion for all people.

The twenty-seven books of the New Testament were all written in less than a century, beginning about 50 C.E. with Paul's early letters. They embody the evangelistic mission of Christianity. Shortly before his death in 29 C.E., Jesus instructed his followers to "go into all the world and preach the gospel," and the books of the New Testament reflect various aspects of this mission. From its beginnings as a sect in Jerusalem after Jesus' death, Christianity soon spread throughout the Mediterranean. Saint Stephen, the first Christian martyr, who was killed about 34 C.E., prophesied the destruction of the Temple in Jerusalem and prompted a persecution of the Christians. Those fleeing this persecution scattered and established churches in other places, especially at Antioch, a center of early Christian evangelism. In these new religious centers, Gentile converts soon outnumbered the Jewish members of the sect, and Christianity concentrated on extending its message beyond the Jewish community in Palestine. Paul's letters, the earliest documents in the New Testament, recount his missionary activities in the fifth decade of the first century as he established and encouraged new churches. The gospels and the other later books of the New Testament reflect the growing need in these early churches for historical, ethical,

[2]In 586 B.C.E., the Jews were taken away into exile in Babylon, the beginning of the Diaspora.

[3]The Edomites assisted the Babylonians in the capture and destruction of Jerusalem.

and theological documents explaining a movement that was reaching far beyond its place of origin. Written in Greek, the international language of the day, the New Testament exported the Christian message from Palestine to the whole Mediterranean world.

Shorter and less varied than the Old Testament, the New Testament includes four major kinds of writing: biography, history, letters, and apocalyptic vision. The first four books, the Gospels of Matthew, Mark, Luke, and John, tell the life of Jesus from different perspectives. Mark, generally believed to be the first of the gospels, written around 65 or 70 C.E., is also the shortest and most matter-of-fact. In Mark, Jesus is presented realistically, even journalistically, by a writer who may have been present during the last week of Jesus' ministry and who traveled with Paul on one of his missionary journeys. Although he may have been an eyewitness to some of the events he describes, Mark probably based most of his gospel on oral stories about Jesus that circulated in the Christian community. His plain and vigorous style matches the simple, unembellished story that he tells. Because many of the episodes and teachings in Mark's biography reappear in the gospels of Matthew and Luke, scholars believe that these two later accounts—written between 80 and 95 C.E.—were based on Mark's work. Because they tell essentially the same story and work from a common outline or synopsis of Jesus' life, these three gospels are often referred to as the synoptic gospels. By comparing the three and noting their differences and similarities, scholars have been able to date their composition and establish the authorship and intent of each. Both Matthew and Luke are longer than Mark and the added material in the two later gospels has distinct similarities, leading scholars to posit a second source, a lost "Q Document," that both later writers used along with Mark. Matthew is significantly concerned with placing Jesus into a Jewish context, so his gospel is sometimes called the Jewish gospel. He traces Jesus' genealogy back to David, presents him as the Messiah, and often relates his teachings to those of the Old Testament. Luke is more literary. A physician who addresses his work to a largely gentile audience, he presents Jesus as a human and heroic figure. The fourth gospel is very different from the other three. Writing much later, about 130 C.E., John is less interested in biography than are his three predecessors. Instead, his gospel develops a spiritual interpretation of Jesus' life and message.

The Acts of the Apostles, the fifth book of the New Testament, is also thought to be by Luke. A work of church history, it describes the evangelistic efforts of the early apostles and the formation of the early Christian Church. These subjects are important as well in the letters of Paul and other early apostles that make up about half of the New Testament. Although they do not appear first in the New Testament as it has come down to us, Paul's letters were the first written. The ones we have were composed in the decade between 50 and 60 C.E. Most of them are addressed to the fledgling churches in Asia Minor, Greece, and Italy that Paul helped to establish and that he visited on his evangelistic journeys around the Mediterranean. Paul's life and missionary work are described in the book of Acts. He began his life as Saul of Tarsus—a city in Cilicia in what is now Turkey—the son of parents who were Pharisees, strict followers of Jewish laws. Saul became an enforcer of these laws and a persecutor especially of the followers of "the way," the new Christian sect. But as he was traveling on the road from Jerusalem to Damascus, he was blinded by a light from heaven and converted to Christianity. Under his Christian name, Paul became the most important of the Christian apostles. His missionary work moved the center of Christianity from Jerusalem to Antioch and his message combined the ethical dimension of Judaism with elements from Greek and Oriental mystery religions. His letters, written before the gospels and addressed to a gentile rather than a Jewish audience, take up practical matters having to do with church organization, ethical and moral issues, and points of theology and belief. They develop the doctrine of the early Christian Church.

The last book of the twenty-seven in the established canon of the New Testament, "The Revelation of St. John the Divine," is an example of apocalyptic writing, for it presents a cryptic vision of the future, especially of the final days, the second coming of Christ, and the last judgment. If the Bible is viewed as a single work presenting a spiritual

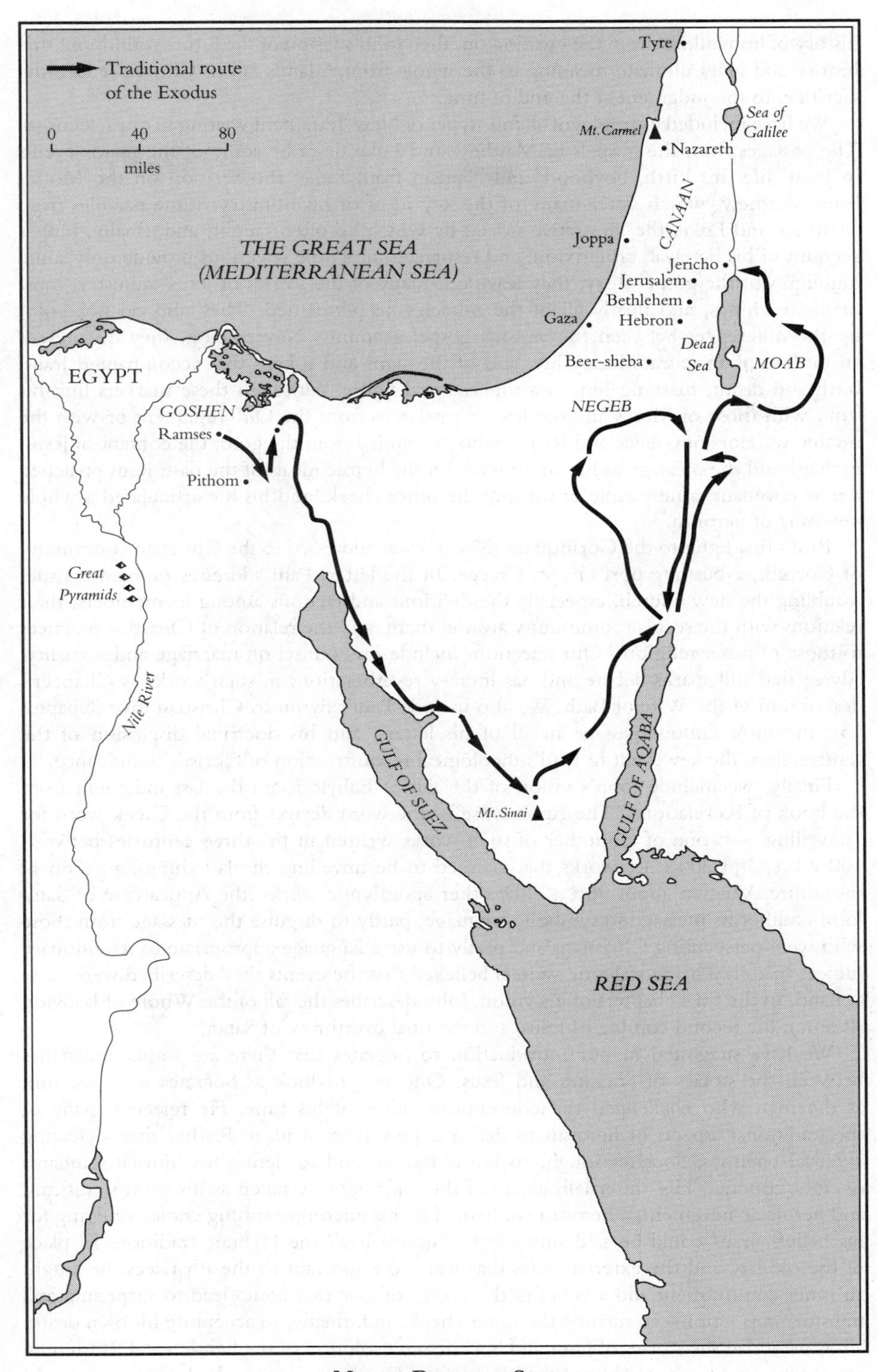
Traditional route
of the Exodus
0
40
80
miles
Tyre
Sea of
Galilee
Mt. Carmel
Nazareth
CANAAN
Joppa
THE GREAT SEA
(MEDITERRANEAN SEA)
Jericho
Jerusalem
Bethlehem
Gaza
Hebron
Dead
Sea
MOAB
Beer-sheba
EGYPT
GOSHEN
NEGEB
Ramses
Pithom
Great
Pyramids
Nile River
GULF OF SUEZ
GULF OF AQABA
Mt. Sinai
RED SEA

Major Biblical Sites

history of humankind from the creation on, then John's vision of the future rounds out that history and gives ultimate meaning to the whole from Adam's fall to Christ's redeeming sacrifice, to the judgment at the end of time.

We have included examples of all four types of New Testament writing in our selections. The passages from the gospels of Matthew and Luke describe some of the major events in Jesus' life: his birth, boyhood, and baptism from Luke; the Sermon on the Mount from Matthew, which states many of the key ideas of his ministry; some parables from Matthew and Luke, the illustrative stories by which he often taught; and, finally, Luke's account of his betrayal, crucifixion, and resurrection. These selections provide only some highlights of the gospel story; they leave out many of the stories of Jesus' ministry, most of his teachings, and nearly all of the miracles he performed. They also do not point up the differences between the various gospel accounts. Nevertheless, they do present an outline of an extraordinary life, and of the signs and tokens that accompanied Jesus' birth and death, marking him as a supernatural figure. Although these markers link his story with those of Moses and the Jewish patriarchs from the Old Testament or with the mythic warriors of Greece and Rome who descended from the gods, the content of Jesus' message and the message of his life broke with the heroic ideals of the past. Jesus preached a new covenant, a new ethic of turning the other cheek, and his life articulated a whole new way of heroism.

Paul's first letter to the Corinthians (57 C.E.) was addressed to the Christian community of Corinth, a bustling port city in Greece. In the letter, Paul addresses numerous issues troubling the new church, especially the divisions and factions among its members, their relations with the secular community around them, and the relation of Christian practices to those of other religions. Our selections include his counsel on marriage and sexuality, advice that still sparks debate and has literary reverberations in such works as Chaucer's description of the Wife of Bath. We also include Paul's hymn to Christian love (Chapter 13), the most famous passage in all of his letters, and his doctrinal discussion of the resurrection, the key event in Paul's theological reconstruction of Christ's significance.

Finally, we include John's vision of the fall of Babylon and the last judgment from the book of Revelation. "The Apocalypse"—the word derives from the Greek word for "unveiling"—is one of a number of such works written in the three centuries between 100 B.C.E. and 200 C.E., works that claimed to be unveiling the last things, a vision of the future. Written about 96 C.E. like other apocalyptic works, the Apocalypse of Saint John codifies its message in symbolic language, partly to disguise the message from those who were persecuting Christians and partly to use a language appropriate to its visionary subject matter. The apocalyptic writers believed that the events they described were close at hand. In the final chapters of his vision, John describes the fall of the Whore of Babylon (Rome), the second coming of Jesus, and the final overthrow of Satan.

We have suggested in our introduction to Socrates that there are some similarities between the stories of Socrates and Jesus. One way to look at Socrates is to see him as the man who challenged the conventional ideas of his time. He rejected many of the traditional aspects of heroism to define a new type of ideal. Rather than defeating external enemies, Socrates sought to know himself and to define for himself standards of right conduct. His "internalization" of the self might be taken as his most significant and heroic achievement, a heroism confirmed by his uncompromising choice of dying for his beliefs. Jesus could be said similarly to "internalize" the Hebraic tradition. In place of the old law and the external rules that were so important to the Pharisees, he taught an inner commitment and a belief in the power of love that could lead to surprising and transforming action—to turning the other cheek, and, finally, to accepting his own death. Thus we see in the stories of Jesus and Socrates an evolution of the heroic ideal. Both men revise their traditions, modifying the ideals of the Greek warriors or the Hebrew patriarchs in some interestingly similar ways. In both cases, their revisions become more widespread than the traditions they modify.

The New Testament tells more than the story of Jesus, for it places that story into historical and prophetic contexts. From a Christian point of view, the New Testament fulfills the Old, so that many Christian readings of the Bible find foreshadowings, or "types," of Christ in the Old Testament patriarchs. Adam and Joseph and Moses are matched by Jesus; he becomes the "antitype" who completes their historical roles and gives ultimate meaning to their stories. Such "typological" readings see the Bible as much more than a loosely connected collection of miscellaneous songs, histories, myths, and stories by many different writers from many different epochs. They see it as a unified story revealing all of human history. Whatever position one takes on these views of the Bible, one cannot deny its significance in Western culture. It has not only given us a fund of stories, an anthology of literature, and a handbook of ethics. It has constituted for the West, as Northrop Frye has called it, "the great code," the cosmic diagram of promise and fulfillment through which we plot our history and tell the stories of our lives.

Suggested Readings

We have used the King James Version of the New Testament, even though it is sometimes archaic and occasionally ambiguous and confusing. This translation, done at the behest of King James I of England in 1611 and the standard English translation for more than three centuries, is so ingrained in our language and literature that it defines "biblical language" for the English-speaking reader. There are, however, many more recent translations of the Bible that are based on more authoritative sources and cast in a more contemporary idiom. We especially recommend the Revised Standard Version (1952, 1989) and the New English Bible among modern translations. The Oxford Bible provides a fully annotated text explaining both internal connections within the Bible and the historical and cultural contexts. For background and critical works on the Bible, see the recommendations for additional reading in our introduction to the Old Testament. Among the countless introductions to the New Testament, we call attention to two: Howard Clark Kee, Franklin W. Young, and Karlfried Froehlich, *Understanding the New Testament* (1957, 1973), and A. M. Hunter, *Introducing the New Testament* (1945, 1957). Morton Scott Enslin's *Christian Beginnings* (1938, 1956) provides a detailed account of the historical and theological contexts that produced the New Testament. Northrop Frye's *The Great Code: The Bible and Literature* (1981) traces the importance of the Bible in Western culture.

[The Birth, Youth, and Baptism of Jesus]

Luke 1–3

Chapter 1:5–80

There was in the days of Herod,[1] the king of Judæa, a certain priest named Zacharias, of the course[2] of Abia: and his wife was of the daughters of Aaron, and her name was Elisabeth. And they were both righteous before God, walking in all

---

[1]Ruler of Palestine, including Judea or southern Palestine, under authority from Augustus Caesar, the Roman Emperor.

[2]A division of the priesthood.

the commandments and ordinances of the Lord blameless. And they had no child, because that Elisabeth was barren, and they both were now well stricken in years.

And it came to pass, that while he executed the priest's office before God in the order of his course, according to the custom of the priest's office, his lot was to burn incense when he went into the temple of the Lord. And the whole multitude of the people were praying without at the time of incense. And there appeared unto him an angel of the Lord standing on the right side of the altar of incense. And when Zacharias saw him, he was troubled, and fear fell upon him. But the angel said unto him, "Fear not, Zacharias: for thy prayer is heard; and thy wife Elisabeth shall bear thee a son, and thou shalt call his name John. And thou shalt have joy and gladness; and many shall rejoice at his birth. For he shall be great in the sight of the Lord, and shall drink neither wine nor strong drink; and he shall be filled with the Holy Ghost, even from his mother's womb. And many of the children of Israel shall he turn to the Lord their God. And he shall go before him in the spirit and power of Elias,[3] to turn the hearts of the fathers to the children, and the disobedient to the wisdom of the just; to make ready a people prepared for the Lord." And Zacharias said unto the angel, "Whereby shall I know this? for I am an old man, and my wife well stricken in years." And the angel answering said unto him, "I am Gabriel, that stand in the presence of God; and am sent to speak unto thee, and to shew thee these glad tidings. And, behold, thou shalt be dumb, and not able to speak, until the day that these things shall be performed, because thou believest not my words, which shall be fulfilled in their season." And the people waited for Zacharias, and marvelled that he tarried so long in the temple. And when he came out, he could not speak unto them: and they perceived that he had seen a vision in the temple: for he beckoned unto them, and remained speechless. And it came to pass, that, as soon as the days of his ministration were accomplished, he departed to his own house.

And after those days his wife Elisabeth conceived, and hid herself five months, saying, "Thus hath the Lord dealt with me in the days wherein he looked on me, to take away my reproach among men."

And in the sixth month the angel Gabriel was sent from God unto a city of Galilee, named Nazareth, to a virgin espoused to a man whose name was Joseph, of the house of David; and the virgin's name was Mary. And the angel came in unto her, and said, "Hail, thou that art highly favoured, the Lord is with thee: blessed art thou among women." And when she saw him, she was troubled at his saying, and cast in her mind what manner of salutation this should be. And the angel said unto her, "Fear not, Mary: for thou hast found favour with God. And, behold, thou shalt conceive in thy womb, and bring forth a son, and shalt call his name JESUS.[4] He shall be great, and shall be called the Son of the Highest: and the Lord God shall give unto him the throne of his father David: and he shall reign over the house of Jacob for ever; and of his kingdom there shall be no end." Then said Mary unto the angel, "How shall this be, seeing I know not a man?" And the angel answered and said unto her, "The Holy Ghost shall come upon thee, and the power of the Highest shall overshadow thee: therefore also that holy thing which shall be born of thee shall be called the Son of God. And, behold, thy cousin Elisabeth, she hath also conceived a son in her old age: and this is the sixth month with her, who was called barren. For with God nothing shall be impossible." And Mary said, "Behold

[3]According to the prophesy in Malachi 4, Elijah was to come and prepare the way for the Messiah.
[4]The name Jesus, the Greek form of the Hebrew Yeshua or Joshua, means "he shall serve."

the handmaid of the Lord; be it unto me according to thy word." And the angel departed from her.

And Mary arose in those days, and went into the hill country with haste, into a city of Juda; and entered into the house of Zacharias, and saluted Elisabeth. And it came to pass, that, when Elisabeth heard the salutation of Mary, the babe leaped in her womb; and Elisabeth was filled with the Holy Ghost: and she spake out with a loud voice, and said, "Blessed art thou among women, and blessed is the fruit of thy womb. And whence is this to me, that the mother of my Lord should come to me? For, lo, as soon as the voice of thy salutation sounded in mine ears, the babe leaped in my womb for joy. And blessed is she that believed: for there shall be a performance of those things which were told her from the Lord." And Mary said,

"My soul doth magnify the Lord,
And my spirit hath rejoiced in God my Saviour.
For he hath regarded the low estate of his handmaiden:
For, behold, from henceforth all generations shall call me blessed.
For he that is mighty hath done to me great things;
And holy is his name.
And his mercy is on them that fear him
From generation to generation.
He hath shewed strength with his arm;
He hath scattered the proud in the imagination of their hearts.
He hath put down the mighty from their seats,
And exalted them of low degree.
He hath filled the hungry with good things;
And the rich he hath sent empty away.
He hath holpen his servant Israel,
In remembrance of his mercy;
As he spake to our fathers,
To Abraham, and to his seed for ever."

And Mary abode with her about three months, and returned to her own house.

Now Elisabeth's full time came that she should be delivered; and she brought forth a son. And her neighbours and her cousins heard how the Lord had shewed great mercy upon her; and they rejoiced with her. And it came to pass, that on the eighth day they came to circumcise the child; and they called him Zacharias, after the name of his father. And his mother answered and said, "Not so; but he shall be called John." And they said unto her, "There is none of thy kindred that is called by this name." And they made signs to his father, how he would have him called. And he asked for a writing table, and wrote, saying, "His name is John." And they marvelled all. And his mouth was opened immediately, and his tongue loosed, and he spake, and praised God. And fear came on all that dwelt round about them: and all these sayings were noised abroad throughout all the hill country of Judæa. And all they that heard them laid them up in their hearts, saying, "What manner of child shall this be!" And the hand of the Lord was with him.

And his father Zacharias was filled with the Holy Ghost, and prophesied, saying,

"Blessed be the Lord God of Israel;
For he hath visited and redeemed his people,
And hath raised up an horn of salvation for us
In the house of his servant David;
As he spake by the mouth of his holy prophets,
Which have been since the world began:
That we should be saved from our enemies,
And from the hand of all that hate us;

To perform the mercy promised to our fathers,
And to remember his holy covenant;
The oath which he sware to our father Abraham,
That he would grant unto us, that we being delivered out of
the hand of our enemies
Might serve him without fear,
In holiness and righteousness before him,
All the days of our life.
And thou, child, shalt be called the prophet of the Highest:
For thou shalt go before the face of the Lord
To prepare his ways;
To give knowledge of salvation unto his people
By the remission of their sins,
Through the tender mercy of our God;
Whereby the dayspring[5] from on high hath visited us,
To give light to them that sit in darkness and in the shadow of death,
To guide our feet into the way of peace."

And the child grew, and waxed strong in spirit, and was in the deserts till the day of his shewing unto Israel.

Chapter 2

And it came to pass in those days, that there went out a decree from Cæsar Augustus, that all the world[6] should be taxed. (And this taxing was first made when Cyrenius was governor of Syria.) And all went to be taxed, every one into his own city. And Joseph also went up from Galilee, out of the city of Nazareth, into Judæa, unto the city of David, which is called Bethlehem; (because he was of the house and lineage of David:) to be taxed with Mary his espoused wife, being great with child. And so it was, that, while they were there, the days were accomplished that she should be delivered. And she brought forth her firstborn son, and wrapped him in swaddling clothes, and laid him in a manger; because there was no room for them in the inn.

And there were in the same country shepherds abiding in the field, keeping watch over their flock by night. And, lo, the angel of the Lord came upon them, and the glory of the Lord shone round about them: and they were sore afraid. And the angel said unto them, "Fear not: for, behold, I bring you good tidings of great joy, which shall be to all people. For unto you is born this day in the city of David a Saviour, which is Christ the Lord. And this shall be a sign unto you; Ye shall find the babe wrapped in swaddling clothes, lying in a manger." And suddenly there was with the angel a multitude of the heavenly host praising God, and saying,

"Glory to God in the highest,
And on earth peace,
Good will toward men."

And it came to pass, as the angels were gone away from them into heaven, the shepherds said one to another, "Let us now go even unto Bethlehem, and see this thing which is come to pass, which the Lord hath made known unto us." And they came with haste, and found Mary, and Joseph, and the babe lying in a manger. And when they had seen it, they made known abroad the saying which was told them concerning this child. And all they that heard it wondered at those things which

---

[5]The sunrise, or the Messiah.
[6]That is, the Roman Empire.

were told them by the shepherds. But Mary kept all these things, and pondered them in her heart. And the shepherds returned, glorifying and praising God for all the things that they had heard and seen, as it was told unto them.

And when eight days were accomplished for the circumcising of the child, his name was called JESUS, which was so named of the angel before he was conceived in the womb.

And when the days of her purification according to the law of Moses were accomplished, they brought him to Jerusalem, to present him to the Lord; (as it is written in the law of the Lord, "Every male that openeth the womb shall be called holy to the Lord;")[7] and to offer a sacrifice according to that which is said in the law of the Lord, "A pair of turtledoves, or two young pigeons." And, behold, there was a man in Jerusalem, whose name was Simeon; and the same man was just and devout, waiting for the consolation of Israel: and the Holy Ghost was upon him. And it was revealed unto him by the Holy Ghost, that he should not see death, before he had seen the Lord's Christ. And he came by the Spirit into the temple: and when the parents brought in the child Jesus, to do for him after the custom of the law, then took he him up in his arms, and blessed God, and said,

> "Lord, now lettest thou thy servant depart
> In peace, according to thy word:
> For mine eyes have seen thy salvation,
> Which thou hast prepared before the face of all people;
> A light to lighten the Gentiles, and the glory of thy people Israel."

And Joseph and his mother marvelled at those things which were spoken of him. And Simeon blessed them, and said unto Mary his mother, "Behold, this child is set for the fall and rising again of many in Israel; and for a sign which shall be spoken against; (yea, a sword shall pierce through thy own soul also,) that the thoughts of many hearts may be revealed." And there was one Anna, a prophetess, the daughter of Phanuel, of the tribe of Aser: she was of a great age, and had lived with an husband seven years from her virginity; and she was a widow of about fourscore and four years, which departed not from the temple, but served God with fastings and prayers night and day. And she coming in that instant gave thanks likewise unto the Lord, and spake of him to all them that looked for redemption in Jerusalem. And when they had performed all things according to the law of the Lord, they returned into Galilee, to their own city Nazareth.

And the child grew, and waxed strong in spirit, filled with wisdom: and the grace of God was upon him.

Now his parents went to Jerusalem every year at the feast of the passover. And when he was twelve years old, they went up to Jerusalem after the custom of the feast. And when they had fulfilled the days, as they returned, the child Jesus tarried behind in Jerusalem; and Joseph and his mother knew not of it. But they, supposing him to have been in the company, went a day's journey; and they sought him among their kinsfolk and acquaintance. And when they found him not, they turned back again to Jerusalem, seeking him. And it came to pass, that after three days they found him in the temple, sitting in the midst of the doctors,[8] both hearing them, and asking them questions. And all that heard him were astonished at his understanding and answers. And when they saw him, they were amazed: and his mother said unto him, "Son, why hast thou thus dealt with us? behold, thy father

[7]See Exodus 13:2.
[8]Rabbis, teachers.

and I have sought thee sorrowing." And he said unto them, "How is that ye sought me? wist ye not that I must be about my Father's business?" And they understood not the saying which he spake unto them. And he went down with them, and came to Nazareth, and was subject unto them: but his mother kept all these sayings in her heart.

And Jesus increased in wisdom and stature, and in favour with God and man.

Chapter 3:1–22

Now in the fifteenth year of the reign of Tiberius Cæsar,[9] Pontius Pilate being governor of Judæa, and Herod being tetrarch of Galilee, and his brother Philip tetrarch of Ituræa and of the region of Trachonitis, and Lysanias the tetrarch of Abilene, Annas and Caiaphas being the high priests, the word of God came unto John the son of Zacharias in the wilderness. And he came into all the country about Jordan, preaching the baptism of repentance for the remission of sins; as it is written in the book of the words of Esaias the prophet, saying,

"The voice of one crying in the wilderness,
'Prepare ye the way of the Lord,
Make his paths straight.
Every valley shall be filled,
And every mountain and hill shall be brought low;
And the crooked shall be made straight,
And the rough ways shall be made smooth;
And all flesh shall see the salvation of God.' "

Then said he to the multitude that came forth to be baptized of him, "O generation of vipers, who hath warned you to flee from the wrath to come? Bring forth therefore fruits worthy of repentance, and begin not to say within yourselves, 'We have Abraham to our father': for I say unto you, that God is able of these stones to raise up children unto Abraham. And now also the axe is laid unto the root of the trees: every tree therefore which bringeth not forth good fruit is hewn down, and cast into the fire." And the people asked him, saying, "What shall we do then ?" He answereth and saith unto them, "He that hath two coats, let him impart to him that hath none; and he that hath meat, let him do likewise." Then came also publicans to be baptized, and said unto him, "Master, what shall we do?" And he said unto them, "Exact no more than that which is appointed you." And the soldiers likewise demanded of him, saying, "And what shall we do?" And he said unto them, "Do violence to no man, neither accuse any falsely; and be content with your wages."

And as the people were in expectation, and all men mused in their hearts of John, whether he were the Christ, or not; John answered, saying unto them all, "I indeed baptize you with water; but one mightier than I cometh, the latchet of whose shoes I am not worthy to unloose: he shall baptize you with the Holy Ghost and with fire: whose fan[10] is in his hand, and he will throughly purge his floor, and will gather the wheat into his garner; but the chaff he will burn with fire unquenchable."

And many other things in his exhortation preached he unto the people. But Herod the tetrarch, being reproved by him for Herodias his brother Philip's wife,[11]

[9] 26 or 27 C.E.
[10] A tool used to separate the wheat from the chaff.
[11] John had objected that Herod's marriage to Herodias, his brother Philip's wife, was unlawful.

and for all the evils which Herod had done, added yet this above all, that he shut up John in prison.

Now when all the people were baptized, it came to pass, that Jesus also being baptized, and praying, the heaven was opened, and the Holy Ghost descended in a bodily shape like a dove upon him, and a voice came from heaven, which said, "Thou art my beloved Son; in thee I am well pleased."

[The Teachings of Jesus: The Sermon on the Mount]

MATTHEW 5–7

Chapter 5

And seeing the multitudes, he went up into a mountain: and when he was set, his disciples came unto him: and he opened his mouth, and taught them, saying,

"Blessed are the poor in spirit: for theirs is the kingdom of heaven.

"Blessed are they that mourn: for they shall be comforted.

"Blessed are the meek: for they shall inherit the earth.

"Blessed are they which do hunger and thirst after righteousness: for they shall be filled.

"Blessed are the merciful: for they shall obtain mercy.

"Blessed are the pure in heart: for they shall see God.

"Blessed are the peacemakers: for they shall be called the children of God.

"Blessed are they which are persecuted for righteousness' sake: for theirs is the kingdom of heaven. Blessed are ye, when men shall revile you, and persecute you, and shall say all manner of evil against you falsely, for my sake. Rejoice, and be exceeding glad: for great is your reward in heaven: for so persecuted they the prophets which were before you.

"Ye are the salt of the earth: but if the salt have lost his savour, wherewith shall it be salted?[12] It is thenceforth good for nothing, but to be cast out, and to be trodden under foot of men. Ye are the light of the world. A city that is set on an hill cannot be hid. Neither do men light a candle, and put it under a bushel,[13] but on a candlestick; and it giveth light unto all that are in the house. Let your light so shine before men, that they may see your good works, and glorify your Father which is in heaven.

"Think not that I am come to destroy the law, or the prophets: I am not come to destroy, but to fulfil. For verily I say unto you, Till heaven and earth pass, one jot or one tittle shall in no wise pass from the law, till all be fulfilled. Whosoever therefore shall break one of these least commandments, and shall teach men so, he shall be called the least in the kingdom of heaven: but whosoever shall do and teach them, the same shall be called great in the kingdom of heaven. For I say unto you, that except your righteousness shall exceed the righteousness of the scribes and Pharisees,[14] ye shall in no case enter into the kingdom of heaven.

"Ye have heard that it was said by them of old time, 'Thou shalt not kill; and whosoever shall kill shall be in danger of the judgment': but I say unto you, that whosoever is angry with his brother without a cause shall be in danger of the

[12]Regain its taste.

[13]A bushel basket.

[14]Scribes, official interpreters of the Hebrew scriptures; Pharisees, a Jewish sect that insisted on strict observance of the Mosaic law.

judgment: and whosoever shall say to his brother, 'Raca,'[15] shall be in danger of the council: but whosoever shall say, 'Thou fool,' shall be in danger of hell fire. Therefore if thou bring thy gift to the altar, and there rememberest that thy brother hath aught against thee; leave there thy gift before the altar, and go thy way; first be reconciled to thy brother, and then come and offer thy gift. Agree with thine adversary quickly, whiles thou art in the way with him; lest at any time the adversary deliver thee to the judge, and the judge deliver thee to the officer, and thou be cast into prison. Verily I say unto thee, Thou shalt by no means come out thence, till thou hast paid the uttermost farthing.

"Ye have heard that it was said by them of old time, 'Thou shalt not commit adultery': but I say unto you, that whosoever looketh on a woman to lust after her hath committed adultery with her already in his heart. And if thy right eye offend thee, pluck it out, and cast it from thee: for it is profitable for thee that one of thy members should perish, and not that thy whole body should be cast into hell. And if thy right hand offend thee, cut it off, and cast it from thee: for it is profitable for thee that one of thy members should perish, and not that thy whole body should be cast into hell. It hath been said, 'Whosoever shall put away his wife, let him give her a writing of divorcement': but I say unto you, that whosoever shall put away his wife, saving for the cause of fornication, causeth her to commit adultery: and whosoever shall marry her that is divorced committeth adultery.

"Again, ye have heard that it hath been said by them of old time, 'Thou shalt not forswear thyself, but shalt perform unto the Lord thine oaths': but I say unto you, Swear not at all; neither by heaven; for it is God's throne: nor by the earth; for it is his footstool: neither by Jerusalem; for it is the city of the great King. Neither shalt thou swear by thy head, because thou canst not make one hair white or black. But let your communication be, 'Yea, yea'; 'Nay, nay': for whatsoever is more than these cometh of evil.

"Ye have heard that it hath been said, 'An eye for an eye, and a tooth for a tooth': but I say unto you, that ye resist not evil: but whosoever shall smite thee on thy right cheek, turn to him the other also. And if any man will sue thee at the law, and take away thy coat, let him have thy cloke also. And whosoever shall compel thee to go a mile, go with him twain.[16] Give to him that asketh thee, and from him that would borrow of thee turn not thou away.

"Ye have heard that it hath been said, 'Thou shalt love thy neighbour, and hate thine enemy'. But I say unto you, Love your enemies, bless them that curse you, do good to them that hate you, and pray for them which despitefully use you, and persecute you; that ye may be the children of your Father which is in heaven: for he maketh his sun to rise on the evil and on the good, and sendeth rain on the just and on the unjust. For if ye love them which love you, what reward have ye? do not even the publicans[17] the same? And if ye salute your brethren only, what do ye more than others? do not even the publicans so? Be ye therefore perfect, even as your Father which is in heaven is perfect."

Chapter 6

"Take heed that ye do not your alms before men, to be seen of them: otherwise ye have no reward of your Father which is in heaven.

"Therefore when thou doest thine alms, do not sound a trumpet before thee, as the hypocrites do in the synagogues and in the streets, that they may have

---

[15] Blockhead.

[16] Two.

[17] Tax collectors.

glory of men. Verily I say unto you, They have their reward. But when thou doest alms, let not thy left hand know what thy right hand doeth: that thine alms may be in secret: and thy Father which seeth in secret himself shall reward thee openly.

"And when thou prayest, thou shalt not be as the hypocrites are: for they love to pray standing in the synagogues and in the corners of the streets, that they may be seen of men. Verily I say unto you, They have their reward. But thou, when thou prayest, enter into thy closet, and when thou hast shut thy door, pray to thy Father which is in secret; and thy Father which seeth in secret shall reward thee openly. But when ye pray, use not vain repetitions, as the heathen do: for they think that they shall be heard for their much speaking. Be not ye therefore like unto them: for your Father knoweth what things ye have need of, before ye ask him. After this manner therefore pray ye: 'Our Father which art in heaven, Hallowed be thy name. Thy kingdom come. Thy will be done in earth, as it is in heaven. Give us this day our daily bread. And forgive us our debts, as we forgive our debtors. And lead us not into temptation, but deliver us from evil: For thine is the kingdom, and the power, and the glory, for ever. Amen.' For if ye forgive men their trespasses, your heavenly Father will also forgive you: but if ye forgive men not their trespasses, neither will your Father forgive your trespasses.

"Moreover when ye fast, be not, as the hypocrites, of a sad countenance: for they disfigure their faces, that they may appear unto men to fast. Verily I say unto you, They have their reward. But thou, when thou fastest, anoint thine head, and wash thy face; that thou appear not unto men to fast, but unto thy Father which is in secret: and thy Father, which seeth in secret, shall reward thee openly.

"Lay not up for yourselves treasures upon earth, where moth and rust doth corrupt, and where thieves break through and steal: but lay up for yourselves treasures in heaven, where neither moth nor rust doth corrupt, and where thieves do not break through nor steal: for where your treasure is, there will your heart be also. The light of the body is the eye: if therefore thine eye be single,[18] thy whole body shall be full of light. But if thine eye be evil, thy whole body shall be full of darkness. If therefore the light that is in thee be darkness, how great is that darkness! No man can serve two masters: for either he will hate the one, and love the other; or else he will hold to the one, and despise the other. Ye cannot serve God and mammon.[19] Therefore I say unto you, Take no thought for your life, what ye shall eat, or what ye shall drink; nor yet for your body, what ye shall put on. Is not the life more than meat, and the body than raiment? Behold the fowls of the air: for they sow not, neither do they reap, nor gather into barns; yet your heavenly Father feedeth them. Are ye not much better then they? Which of you by taking thought can add one cubit unto his stature? And why take ye thought for raiment? Consider the lilies of the field, how they grow; they toil not, neither do they spin: and yet I say unto you, that even Solomon in all his glory was not arrayed like one of these. Wherefore, if God so clothe the grass of the field, which to day is, and to morrow is cast into the oven, shall he not much more clothe you, O ye of little faith? Therefore take no thought, saying, 'What shall we eat?' or, 'What shall we drink?' or, 'Wherewithal shall we be clothed?' (for after all these things do the Gentiles seek:) for your heavenly Father knoweth that ye have need of all these things. But seek ye first the kingdom of God, and his righteousness; and all these things

[18] Healthy.
[19] Wealth; money.

shall be added unto you. Take therefore no thought for the morrow: for the morrow shall take thought for the things of itself. Sufficient unto the day is the evil thereof."

Chapter 7

"Judge not, that ye be not judged. For with what judgment ye judge, ye shall be judged: and with what measure ye mete, it shall be measured to you again. And why beholdest thou the mote[20] that is in thy brother's eye, but considerest not the beam that is in thine own eye? Or how wilt thou say to thy brother, 'Let me pull out the mote out of thine eye'; and, behold, a beam is in thine own eye? Thou hypocrite, first cast out the beam out of thine own eye; and then shalt thou see clearly to cast out the mote out of thy brother's eye.

"Give not that which is holy unto the dogs, neither cast ye your pearls before swine, lest they trample them under their feet, and turn again and rend you.

"Ask, and it shall be given you; seek, and ye shall find; knock, and it shall be opened unto you: for every one that asketh receiveth; and he that seeketh findeth; and to him that knocketh it shall be opened. Or what man is there of you, whom if his son ask bread, will he give him a stone? Or if he ask a fish, will he give him a serpent? If ye then, being evil, know how to give good gifts unto your children, how much more shall your Father which is in heaven give good things to them that ask him? Therefore all things whatsoever ye would that men should do to you, do ye even so to them: for this is the law and the prophets.

"Enter ye in at the strait gate: for wide is the gate, and broad is the way, that leadeth to destruction, and many there be which go in thereat: because strait is the gate, and narrow is the way, which leadeth unto life, and few there be that find it.

"Beware of false prophets, which come to you in sheep's clothing, but inwardly they are ravening wolves. Ye shall know them by their fruits. Do men gather grapes of thorns, or figs of thistles? Even so every good tree bringeth forth good fruit; but a corrupt tree bringeth forth evil fruit. A good tree cannot bring forth evil fruit, neither can a corrupt tree bring forth good fruit. Every tree that bringeth not forth good fruit is hewn down, and cast into the fire. Wherefore by their fruits ye shall know them. Not every one that saith unto me, 'Lord, Lord,' shall enter into the kingdom of heaven; but he that doeth the will of my Father which is in heaven. Many will say to me in that day, 'Lord, Lord, have we not prophesied in thy name? and in thy name have cast out devils? and in thy name done many wonderful works?' And then will I profess unto them, I never knew you: depart from me, ye that work iniquity. Therefore whosoever heareth these sayings of mine, and doeth them, I will liken him unto a wise man, which built his house upon a rock: and the rain descended, and the floods came, and the winds blew, and beat upon that house; and it fell not: for it was founded upon a rock. And every one that heareth these sayings of mine, and doeth them not, shall be likened unto a foolish man, which built his house upon the sand: and the rain descended, and the floods came, and the winds blew, and beat upon that house; and it fell: and great was the fall of it."

And it came to pass, when Jesus had ended these sayings, the people were astonished at his doctrine: for he taught them as one having authority, and not as the scribes.

[20]Speck.

[The Teachings of Jesus: Parables]

Matthew 13, 25

Chapter 13:1–23

The same day went Jesus out of the house, and sat by the sea side. And great multitudes were gathered together unto him, so that he went into a ship, and sat; and the whole multitude stood on the shore. And he spake many things unto them in parables, saying, "Behold, a sower went forth to sow; and when he sowed, some seeds fell by the way side, and the fowls came and devoured them up: some fell upon stony places, where they had not much earth: and forthwith they sprung up, because they had no deepness of earth: and when the sun was up, they were scorched; and because they had no root, they withered away. And some fell among thorns; and the thorns sprung up, and choked them: but others fell into good ground, and brought forth fruit, some an hundredfold, some sixtyfold, some thirtyfold. Who hath ears to hear, let him hear."

And the disciples came, and said unto him, "Why speakest thou unto them in parables?" He answered and said unto them, "Because it is given unto you to know the mysteries of the kingdom of heaven, but to them it is not given. For whosoever hath, to him shall be given, and he shall have more abundance: but whosoever hath not, from him shall be taken away even that he hath. Therefore speak I to them in parables: because they seeing see not; and hearing they hear not, neither do they understand. And in them is fulfilled the prophecy of Esaias,[21] which saith,

> 'By hearing ye shall hear, and shall not understand;
> And seeing ye shall see, and shall not perceive:
> For this people's heart is waxed gross,
> And their ears are dull of hearing,
> And their eyes they have closed;
> Lest at any time they should see with their eyes,
> And hear with their ears,
> And should understand with their heart,
> And should be converted,
> And I should heal them.'

But blessed are your eyes, for they see: and your ears, for they hear. For verily I say unto you, that many prophets and righteous men have desired to see those things which ye see, and have not seen them; and to hear those things which ye hear, and have not heard them. Hear ye therefore the parable of the sower. When any one heareth the word of the kingdom, and understandeth it not, then cometh the wicked one, and catcheth away that which was sown in his heart. This is he which received seed by the way side. But he that received the seed into stony places, the same is he that heareth the word, and anon with joy receiveth it; yet hath he not root in himself, but dureth for a while: for when tribulation or persecution ariseth because of the word, by and by he is offended.[22] He also that received seed among the thorns is he that heareth the word; and the care of this world, and the deceitfulness of riches, choke the word, and he becometh unfruitful. But he that received seed into the good ground is he that heareth the word, and understandeth it; which also beareth fruit, and bringeth forth, some an hundredfold, some sixty, some thirty."

---

[21] Isaiah 5:9–10.

[22] Falls away.

Chapter 25:14–30

"For the kingdom of heaven is as a man travelling into a far country, who called his own servants, and delivered unto them his goods. And unto one he gave five talents,[23] to another two, and to another one; to every man according to his several ability; and straightway took his journey. Then he that had received the five talents went and traded with the same, and made them other five talents. And likewise he that had received two, he also gained other two. But he that had received one went and digged in the earth, and hid his lord's money. After a long time the lord of those servants cometh, and reckoned with them. And so he that had received five talents came and brought other five talents, saying, 'Lord, thou deliveredst unto me five talents: behold, I have gained beside them five talents more.' His lord said unto him, 'Well done, thou good and faithful servant: thou has been faithful over a few things, I will make thee ruler over many things: enter thou into the joy of thy lord.' He also that had received two talents came and said, 'Lord, thou deliveredst unto me two talents: behold, I have gained two other talents beside them.' His lord said unto him, 'Well done, good and faithful servant; thou hast been faithful over a few things, I will make thee ruler over many things: enter thou into the joy of thy lord.' Then he which had received the one talent came and said, 'Lord, I knew thee that thou art an hard man, reaping where thou hast not sown, and gathering where thou hast not strawed: and I was afraid, and went and hid thy talent in the earth: lo, there thou hast that is thine.' His lord answered and said unto him, 'Thou wicked and slothful servant, thou knewest that I reap where I sowed not, and gather where I have not strawed: thou oughtest therefore to have put my money to the exchangers, and then at my coming I should have received mine own with usury.[24] Take therefore the talent from him, and give it unto him which hath ten talents. For unto every one that hath shall be given, and he shall have abundance: but from him that hath not shall be taken away even that which he hath. And cast ye the unprofitable servant into outer darkness: there shall be weeping and gnashing of teeth.' "

LUKE 10, 15

Chapter 10:25–37

And, behold, a certain lawyer stood up, and tempted him, saying, "Master, what shall I do to inherit eternal life?" He said unto him, "What is written in the law? how readest thou?" And he answering said, "Thou shalt love the Lord thy God with all thy heart, and with all thy soul, and with all thy strength, and with all thy mind; and thy neighbour as thyself." And he said unto him, "Thou hast answered right: this do, and thou shalt live." But he, willing to justify himself, said unto Jesus, "And who is my neighbour?" And Jesus answering said, "A certain man went down from Jerusalem to Jericho, and fell among thieves, which stripped him of his raiment, and wounded him, and departed, leaving him half dead. And by chance there came down a certain priest that way: and when he saw him, he passed by on the other side. And likewise a Levite,[25] when he was at the place, came and looked on him, and passed by on the other side. But a certain Samaritan,[26] as he journeyed, came where he was: and when he saw him, he had compassion on him, and went to

[23] A large sum of money; one talent equaled more than fifteen years' wages for a laborer.
[24] Interest.
[25] A lay associate of the priest.
[26] A foreigner, not expected to show sympathy to a Jew.

him, and bound up his wounds, pouring in oil and wine, and set him on his own beast, and brought him to an inn, and took care of him. And on the morrow when he departed, he took out two pence, and gave them to the host, and said unto him, 'Take care of him; and whatsoever thou spendest more, when I come again, I will repay thee.' Which now of these three, thinkest thou, was neighbour unto him that fell among the thieves?" And he said, "He that shewed mercy on him." Then said Jesus unto him, "Go, and do thou likewise."

Chapter 15:11–32

And he said, "A certain man had two sons: and the younger of them said to his father, 'Father, give me the portion of goods that falleth to me.' And he divided unto them his living. And not many days after the younger son gathered all together, and took his journey into a far country, and there wasted his substance with riotous living. And when he had spent all, there arose a mighty famine in that land; and he began to be in want. And he went and joined himself to a citizen of that country; and he sent him into his fields to feed swine. And he would fain have filled his belly with the husks that the swine did eat: and no man gave unto him. And when he came to himself, he said, 'How many hired servants of my father's have bread enough and to spare, and I perish with hunger! I will arise and go to my father, and will say unto him, Father, I have sinned against heaven, and before thee, and am no more worthy to be called thy son: make me as one of thy hired servants.' And he arose, and came to his father. But when he was yet a great way off, his father saw him, and had compassion, and ran, and fell on his neck, and kissed him. And the son said unto him, 'Father, I have sinned against heaven, and in thy sight, and am no more worthy to be called thy son.' But the father said to his servants, 'Bring forth the best robe, and put it on him; and put a ring on his hand, and shoes on his feet: and bring hither the fatted calf, and kill it; and let us eat, and be merry: for this my son was dead, and is alive again; he was lost, and is found.' And they began to be merry. Now his elder son was in the field: and as he came and drew nigh to the house, he heard musick and dancing. And he called one of the servants, and asked what these things meant. And he said unto him, 'Thy brother is come; and thy father hath killed the fatted calf, because he hath received him safe and sound.' And he was angry, and would not go in: therefore came his father out, and intreated him. And he answering said to his father, 'Lo, these many years do I serve thee, neither transgressed I at any time thy commandment: and yet thou never gavest me a kid, that I might make merry with my friends: but as soon as this thy son was come, which hath devoured thy living with harlots, thou hast killed for him the fatted calf.' And he said unto him, 'Son, thou art ever with me, and all that I have is thine. It was meet that we should make merry, and be glad: for this thy brother was dead, and is alive again; and was lost, and is found.' "

[The Betrayal, Trial, Crucifixion, and Resurrection of Jesus]

LUKE 22–24

Chapter 22:1–34, 39–71

Now the feast of unleavened bread drew nigh, which is called the Passover. And the chief priests and scribes sought how they might kill him; for they feared the people.

Then entered Satan into Judas surnamed Iscariot, being of the number of the twelve. And he went his way, and communed with the chief priests and captains, how he might betray him unto them. And they were glad, and covenanted to give him money. And he promised, and sought opportunity to betray him unto them in the absence of the multitude.

Then came the day of unleavened bread, when the passover must be killed. And he sent Peter and John, saying, "Go and prepare us the passover, that we may eat." And they said unto him, "Where wilt thou that we prepare?" And he said unto them, "Behold, when ye are entered into the city, there shall a man meet you; bearing a pitcher of water; follow him into the house where he entereth in. And ye shall say unto the goodman of the house, 'The Master saith unto thee, Where is the guestchamber, where I shall eat the passover with my disciples?' And he shall shew you a large upper room furnished: there make ready." And they went, and found as he had said unto them: and they made ready the passover.

And when the hour was come, he sat down, and the twelve apostles with him. And he said unto them, "With desire I have desired to eat this passover with you before I suffer: for I say unto you, I will not any more eat thereof, until it be fulfilled in the kingdom of God." And he took the cup, and gave thanks, and said, "Take this, and divide it among yourselves: for I say unto you, I will not drink of the fruit of the vine, until the kingdom of God shall come." And he took bread, and gave thanks, and brake it, and gave unto them, saying, "This is my body which is given for you: this do in remembrance of me." Likewise also the cup after supper, saying, "This cup is the new testament in my blood, which is shed for you. But, behold, the hand of him that betrayeth me is with me on the table. And truly the Son of man goeth, as it was determined: but woe unto that man by whom he is betrayed!" And they began to enquire among themselves, which of them it was that should do this thing.

And there was also a strife among them, which of them should be accounted the greatest. And he said unto them, "The kings of the Gentiles exercise lordship over them; and they that exercise authority upon them are called benefactors. But ye shall not be so: but he that is greatest among you, let him be as the younger; and he that is chief, as he that doth serve. For whether is greater, he that sitteth at meat, or he that serveth? is not he that sitteth at meat? but I am among you as he that serveth. Ye are they which have continued with me in my temptations. And I appoint unto you a kingdom, as my Father hath appointed unto me; that ye may eat and drink at my table in my kingdom, and sit on thrones judging the twelve tribes of Israel." And the Lord said, "Simon, Simon, behold, Satan hath desired to have you, that he may sift you as wheat: but I have prayed for thee, that thy faith fail not: and when thou art converted, strengthen thy brethren." And he said unto him, "Lord, I am ready to go with thee, both into prison, and to death." And he said, "I tell thee, Peter, the cock shall not crow this day, before that thou shalt thrice deny that thou knowest me." . . .

And he came out, and went, as he was wont, to the mount of Olives; and his disciples also followed him. And when he was at the place, he said unto them, "Pray that ye enter not into temptation." And he was withdrawn from them about a stone's cast, and kneeled down, and prayed, saying, "Father, if thou be willing, remove this cup from me: nevertheless not my will, but thine, be done." And there appeared an angel unto him from heaven, strengthening him. And being in an agony he prayed more earnestly: and his sweat was as it were great drops of blood falling down to the ground. And when he rose up from prayer, and was come to his disciples, he found them sleeping for sorrow, and said unto them, "Why sleep ye? rise and pray, lest ye enter into temptation."

And while he yet spake, behold a multitude, and he that was called Judas, one of the twelve, went before them, and drew near unto Jesus to kiss him. But Jesus said unto him, "Judas, betrayest thou the Son of man with a kiss?" When they which were about him saw what would follow, they said unto him, "Lord, shall we smite with the sword?" And one of them smote the servant of the high priest, and cut off his right ear. And Jesus answered and said, "Suffer ye thus far."[27] And he touched his ear, and healed him. Then Jesus said unto the chief priests, and captains of the temple, and the elders, which were come to him, "Be ye come out, as against a thief, with swords and staves? When I was daily with you in the temple, ye stretched forth no hands against me: but this is your hour, and the power of darkness."

Then took they him, and led him, and brought him into the high priest's house. And Peter followed afar off. And when they had kindled a fire in the midst of the hall, and were set down together, Peter sat down among them. But a certain maid beheld him as he sat by the fire, and earnestly looked upon him, and said, "This man was also with him." And he denied him, saying, "Woman, I know him not." And after a little while another saw him, and said, "Thou art also of them." And Peter said, "Man, I am not." And about the space of one hour after another confidently affirmed, saying, "Of a truth this fellow also was with him: for he is a Galilæan." And Peter said, "Man, I know not what thou sayest." And immediately, while he yet spake, the cock crew. And the Lord turned, and looked upon Peter. And Peter remembered the word of the Lord, how he had said unto him, "Before the cock crow, thou shalt deny me thrice." And Peter went out, and wept bitterly.

And the men that held Jesus mocked him, and smote him. And when they had blindfolded him, they struck him on the face, and asked him, saying, "Prophesy, who is it that smote thee?" And many other things blasphemously spake they against him.

And as soon as it was day, the elders of the people and the chief priests and the scribes came together, and led him into their council, saying, "Art thou the Christ? tell us." And he said unto them, "If I tell you, ye will not believe: and if I also ask you, ye will not answer me, nor let me go. Hereafter shall the Son of man sit on the right hand of the power of God." Then said they all, "Art thou then the Son of God?" And he said unto them, "Ye say that I am." And they said, "What need we any further witness? for we ourselves have heard of his own mouth."

Chapter 23

And the whole multitude of them arose, and led him unto Pilate. And they began to accuse him, saying, "We found this fellow perverting the nation, and forbidding to give tribute to Cæsar, saying that he himself is Christ a King." And Pilate asked him, saying, "Art thou the King of the Jews?" And he answered him and said, "Thou sayest it." Then said Pilate to the chief priests and to the people, "I find no fault in this man." And they were the more fierce, saying, "He stirreth up the people, teaching throughout all Jewry, beginning from Galilee to this place." When Pilate heard of Galilee, he asked whether the man were a Galilæan. And as soon as he knew that he belonged unto Herod's jurisdiction, he sent him to Herod, who himself also was at Jerusalem at that time.

And when Herod saw Jesus, he was exceeding glad: for he was desirous to see him of a long season, because he had heard many things of him; and he hoped to have seen some miracle done by him. Then he questioned with him in many words; but he answered him nothing. And the chief priests and scribes stood and

[27] "No more of this."

vehemently accused him. And Herod with his men of war set him at nought, and mocked him, and arrayed him in a gorgeous robe, and sent him again to Pilate. And the same day Pilate and Herod were made friends together: for before they were at enmity between themselves.

And Pilate, when he had called together the chief priests and the rulers and the people, said unto them, "Ye have brought this man unto me, as one that perverteth the people: and, behold, I, having examined him before you, have found no fault in this man touching those things whereof ye accuse him: no, nor yet Herod: for I sent you to him; and, lo, nothing worthy of death is done unto him. I will therefore chastise him, and release him." (For of necessity he must release one unto them at the feast.) And they cried out all at once, saying, "Away with this man, and release unto us Barabbas": (who for a certain sedition made in the city, and for murder, was cast into prison.) Pilate therefore, willing to release Jesus, spake again to them. But they cried, saying, "Crucify him, crucify him." And he said unto them the third time, "Why, what evil hath he done? I have found no cause of death in him: I will therefore chastise him, and let him go." And they were instant with loud voices, requiring that he might be crucified. And the voices of them and of the chief priests prevailed. And Pilate gave sentence that it should be as they required. And he released unto them him that for sedition and murder was cast into prison, whom they had desired; but he delivered Jesus to their will.

And as they led him away, they laid hold upon one Simon, a Cyrenian,[28] coming out of the country, and on him they laid the cross, that he might bear it after Jesus.

And there followed him a great company of people, and of women, which also bewailed and lamented him. But Jesus turning unto them said, "Daughters of Jerusalem, weep not for me, but weep for yourselves, and for your children. For, behold, the days are coming, in the which they shall say, 'Blessed are the barren, and the wombs that never bare, and the paps which never gave suck.' Then shall they begin to say to the mountains, 'Fall on us'; and to the hills, 'Cover us.' For if they do these things in a green tree, what shall be done in the dry?"

And there were also two other, malefactors, led with him to be put to death.

And when they were come to the place, which is called Calvary, there they crucified him, and the malefactors, one on the right hand, and the other on the left. Then said Jesus, "Father, forgive them; for they know not what they do." And they parted his raiment, and cast lots. And the people stood beholding. And the rulers also with them derided him, saying, "He saved others; let him save himself, if he be Christ, the chosen of God." And the soldiers also mocked him, coming to him, and offering him vinegar, and saying, "If thou be the king of the Jews, save thyself." And a superscription also was written over him in letters of Greek, and Latin, and Hebrew, THIS IS THE KING OF THE JEWS.

And one of the malefactors which were hanged railed on him, saying, "If thou be Christ, save thyself and us." But the other answering rebuked him, saying, "Dost not thou fear God, seeing thou art in the same condemnation? And we indeed justly; for we receive the due reward of our deeds: but this man hath done nothing amiss." And he said unto Jesus, "Lord, remember me when thou comest into thy kingdom." And Jesus said unto him, "Verily I say unto thee, To day shalt thou be with me in paradise."

And it was about the sixth hour, and there was a darkness over all the earth until the ninth hour. And the sun was darkened, and the veil of the temple was rent in the midst. And when Jesus had cried with a loud voice, he said, "Father,

---

[28] A North African.

into thy hands I commend my spirit": and having said thus, he gave up the ghost. Now when the centurion saw what was done, he glorified God, saying, "Certainly this was a righteous man." And all the people that came together to that sight, beholding the things which were done, smote their breasts, and returned. And all his acquaintance, and the women that followed him from Galilee, stood afar off, beholding these things.

And, behold, there was a man named Joseph, a counsellor;[29] and he was a good man, and a just: (the same had not consented to the counsel and deed of them;) he was of Arimathæa, a city of the Jews: who also himself waited for the kingdom of God. This man went unto Pilate, and begged the body of Jesus. And he took it down, and wrapped it in linen, and laid it in a sepulchre that was hewn in stone, wherein never man before was laid. And that day was the preparation, and the sabbath drew on. And the women also, which came with him from Galilee, followed after, and beheld the sepulchre, and how his body was laid. And they returned, and prepared spices and ointments; and rested the sabbath day according to the commandment.

Chapter 24

Now upon the first day of the week, very early in the morning, they came unto the sepulchre, bringing the spices which they had prepared, and certain others with them. And they found the stone rolled away from the sepulchre. And they entered in, and found not the body of the Lord Jesus. And it came to pass, as they were much perplexed thereabout, behold, two men stood by them in shining garments: and as they were afraid, and bowed down their faces to the earth, they said unto them, "Why seek ye the living among the dead? He is not here, but is risen: remember how he spake unto you when he was yet in Galilee, saying, 'The Son of man must be delivered into the hands of sinful men, and be crucified, and the third day rise again.' " And they remembered his words, and returned from the sepulchre, and told all these things unto the eleven, and to all the rest. It was Mary Magdalene, and Joanna, and Mary the mother of James, and other women that were with them, which told these things unto the apostles. And their words seemed to them as idle tales, and they believed them not. Then arose Peter, and ran unto the sepulchre; and stooping down, he beheld the linen clothes laid by themselves, and departed, wondering in himself at that which was come to pass.

And, behold, two of them went that same day to a village called Emmaus, which was from Jerusalem about threescore furlongs.[30] And they talked together of all these things which had happened. And it came to pass, that, while they communed together and reasoned, Jesus himself drew near, and went with them. But their eyes were holden that they should not know him. And he said unto them, "What manner of communications are these that ye have one to another, as ye walk, and are sad?" And the one of them, whose name was Cleopas, answering said unto him, "Art thou only a stranger in Jerusalem, and hast not known the things which are come to pass there in these days?" And he said unto them, "What things?" And they said unto him, "Concerning Jesus of Nazareth, which was a prophet mighty in deed and word before God and all the people: and how the chief priests and our rulers delivered him to be condemned to death, and have crucified him. But we trusted that it had been he which should have redeemed Israel: and beside all this, to day is the third day since these things were done. Yea, and certain women

[29] A member of the Sanhedrin, the Jewish high court.

[30] About seven miles.

also of our company made us astonished, which were early at the sepulchre; and when they found not his body, they came, saying, that they had also seen a vision of angels, which said that he was alive. And certain of them which were with us went to the sepulchre, and found it even so as the women had said: but him they saw not." Then he said unto them, "O fools, and slow of heart to believe all that the prophets have spoken: ought not Christ to have suffered these things, and to enter into his glory?" And beginning at Moses and all the prophets, he expounded unto them in all the scriptures the things concerning himself. And they drew nigh unto the village, whither they went: and he made as though he would have gone further. But they constrained him, saying, "Abide with us: for it is toward evening, and the day is far spent." And he went in to tarry with them. And it came to pass, as he sat at meat with them, he took bread, and blessed it, and brake, and gave to them. And their eyes were opened, and they knew him; and he vanished out of their sight. And they said one to another, "Did not our heart burn within us, while he talked with us by the way, and while he opened to us the scriptures?" And they rose up the same hour, and returned to Jerusalem, and found the eleven gathered together, and them that were with them, saying, "The Lord is risen indeed, and hath appeared to Simon." And they told what things were done in the way, and how he was known of them in breaking of bread.

And as they thus spake, Jesus himself stood in the midst of them, and saith unto them, "Peace be unto you." But they were terrified and affrighted, and supposed that they had seen a spirit. And he said unto them, "Why are ye troubled? and why do thoughts arise in your hearts? Behold my hands and my feet, that it is I myself: handle me, and see; for a spirit hath not flesh and bones, as ye see me have." And when he had thus spoken, he shewed them his hands and his feet. And while they yet believed not for joy, and wondered, he said unto them, "Have ye here any meat?" And they gave him a piece of a broiled fish, and of an honeycomb. And he took it, and did eat before them.

And he said unto them, "These are the words which I spake unto you, while I was yet with you, that all things must be fulfilled, which were written in the law of Moses, and in the prophets, and in the psalms, concerning me." Then opened he their understanding, that they might understand the scriptures, and said unto them, "Thus it is written, and thus it behoved Christ to suffer, and to rise from the dead the third day: and that repentance and remission of sins should be preached in his name among all nations, beginning at Jerusalem. And ye are witnesses of these things. And, behold, I send the promise of my Father upon you: but tarry ye in the city of Jerusalem, until ye be endued with power from on high."

And he led them out as far as to Bethany, and he lifted up his hands, and blessed them. And it came to pass, while he blessed them, he was parted from them, and carried up into heaven. And they worshipped him, and returned to Jerusalem with great joy: and were continually in the temple, praising and blessing God. Amen.

[Paul: On the Christian Life]

First Corinthians 1, 7, 11–13, 15

Chapter 1:1–9

Paul, called to be an apostle of Jesus Christ through the will of God, and Sosthenes our brother, unto the church of God which is at Corinth, to them that are sanctified in Christ Jesus, called to be saints, with all that in every place call upon the name of Jesus Christ our Lord, both theirs and ours: Grace be unto you, and peace, from God our Father, and from the Lord Jesus Christ.

I thank my God always on your behalf, for the grace of God which is given you by Jesus Christ; that in every thing ye are enriched by him, in all utterance, and in all knowledge; even as the testimony of Christ was confirmed in you: so that ye come behind[31] in no gift; waiting for the coming of our Lord Jesus Christ: who shall also confirm you unto the end, that ye may be blameless in the day of our Lord Jesus Christ. God is faithful, by whom ye were called unto the fellowship of his Son Jesus Christ our Lord.

. . .

Chapter 7

Now concerning the things whereof ye wrote unto me: It is good for a man not to touch a woman. Nevertheless, to avoid fornication, let every man have his own wife, and let every woman have her own husband. Let the husband render unto the wife due benevolence:[32] and likewise also the wife unto the husband. The wife hath not power of her own body, but the husband: and likewise also the husband hath not power of his own body, but the wife. Defraud[33] ye not one the other, except it be with consent for a time, that ye may give yourselves to fasting and prayer; and come together again, that Satan tempt you not for your incontinency. But I speak this by permission, and not of commandment.[34] For I would that all men were even as I myself.[35] But every man hath his proper gift of God, one after this manner, and another after that.

I say therefore to the unmarried and widows, It is good for them if they abide even as I. But if they cannot contain, let them marry: for it is better to marry than to burn. And unto the married I command, yet not I, but the Lord, Let not the wife depart from her husband: but and if she depart, let her remain unmarried, or be reconciled to her husband: and let not the husband put away his wife. But to the rest speak I, not the Lord: If any brother hath a wife that believeth not, and she be pleased to dwell with him, let him not put her away. And the woman which hath an husband that believeth not, and if he be pleased to dwell with her, let her not leave him. For the unbelieving husband is sanctified by the wife, and the unbelieving wife is sanctified by the husband: else were your children unclean; but now are they holy. But if the unbelieving depart, let him depart. A brother or a sister[36] is not under bondage in such cases: but God hath called us to peace. For what knowest thou, O wife, whether thou shalt save thy husband? or how knowest thou, O man, whether thou shalt save thy wife? But as God hath distributed to every man, as the Lord hath called every one, so let him walk. And so ordain I in all churches. Is any man called[37] being circumcised? let him not become uncircumcised. Is any called in uncircumcision? let him not be circumcised. Circumcision is nothing, and uncircumcision is nothing, but the keeping of the commandments of God. Let every man abide in the same calling[38] wherein he was called. Art thou called being

---

[31] Are lacking.
[32] Her conjugal rights.
[33] Deprive.
[34] As a concession, and not as a commandment.
[35] Paul was unmarried.
[36] That is, the Christian partner.
[37] That is, at the time of his call to Christianity.
[38] Condition.

a servant? care not for it: but if thou mayest be made free, use it rather. For he that is called in the Lord, being a servant, is the Lord's freeman: likewise also he that is called, being free, is Christ's servant. Ye are bought with a price; be not ye the servants of men. Brethren, let every man, wherein he is called, therein abide with God.

Now concerning virgins I have no commandment of the Lord: yet I give my judgment, as one that hath obtained mercy of the Lord to be faithful. I suppose therefore that this is good for the present distress, I say, that it is good for a man so to be. Art thou bound unto a wife? seek not to be loosed. Art thou loosed from a wife? seek not a wife. But and if thou marry, thou hast not sinned; and if a virgin marry, she hath not sinned. Nevertheless such shall have trouble in the flesh: but I spare you. But this I say, brethren, the time is short: it remaineth, that both they that have wives be as though they had none; and they that weep, as though they wept not; and they that rejoice, as though they rejoiced not; and they that buy, as though they possessed not; and they that use this world, as not abusing it: for the fashion of this world passeth away.[39] But I would have you without carefulness.[40] He that is unmarried careth for the things that belong to the Lord, how he may please the Lord: but he that is married careth for the things that are of the world, how he may please his wife. There is difference also between a wife and a virgin. The unmarried woman careth for the things of the Lord, that she may be holy both in body and in spirit: but she that is married careth for the things of the world, how she may please her husband. And this I speak for your own profit; not that I may cast a snare upon you, but for that which is comely,[41] and that ye may attend upon the Lord without distraction. But if any man think that he behaveth himself uncomely toward his virgin, if she pass the flower of her age, and need so require, let him do what he will, he sinneth not: let them marry. Nevertheless he that standeth stedfast in his heart, having no necessity, but hath power over his own will, and hath so decreed in his heart that he will keep his virgin, doeth well. So then he that giveth her in marriage doeth well; but he that giveth her not in marriage doeth better. The wife is bound by the law as long as her husband liveth; but if her husband be dead, she is at liberty to be married to whom she will; only in the Lord. But she is happier if she so abide, after my judgment: and I think also that I have the Spirit of God.

. . .

Chapter 11:1–16

Be ye followers of me, even as I also am of Christ. Now I praise you, brethren, that ye remember me in all things, and keep the ordinances, as I delivered them to you. But I would have you know, that the head of every man is Christ; and the head of the woman is the man; and the head of Christ is God. Every man praying or prophesying, having his head covered, dishonoureth his head. But every woman that prayeth or prophesieth with her head uncovered dishonoureth her head: for that is even all one as if she were shaven. For if the woman be not covered, let her also be shorn: but if it be a shame for a woman to be shorn or shaven, let her be covered. For a man indeed ought not to cover his head, forasmuch as he is the image and glory of God: but the woman is the glory of the man. For the man

[39] That is, the end of the world is near.
[40] Free from anxiety.
[41] Proper.

is not of the woman; but the woman of the man. Neither was the man created for the woman; but the woman for the man. For this cause ought the woman to have power[42] on her head because of the angels. Nevertheless neither is the man without[43] the woman, neither the woman without the man, in the Lord. For as the woman is of the man, even so is the man also by the woman; but all things of God. Judge in yourselves: is it comely that a woman pray unto God uncovered? Doth not even nature itself teach you, that, if a man have long hair, it is a shame unto him? But if a woman have long hair, it is a glory to her: for her hair is given her for a covering. But if any man seem to be contentious, we have no such custom, neither the churches of God. . . .

Chapter 12

Now concerning spiritual gifts, brethren, I would not have you ignorant. Ye know that ye were Gentiles, carried away unto these dumb idols, even as ye were led. Wherefore I give you to understand, that no man speaking by the Spirit of God calleth Jesus accursed: and that no man can say that Jesus is the Lord, but by the Holy Ghost.

Now there are diversities of gifts, but the same Spirit. And there are differences of administrations, but the same Lord. And there are diversities of operations, but it is the same God which worketh all in all. But the manifestation of the Spirit is given to every man to profit withal. For to one is given by the Spirit the word of wisdom; to another the word of knowledge by the same Spirit; to another faith by the same Spirit; to another the gifts of healing by the same Spirit; to another the working of miracles; to another prophecy; to another discerning of spirits; to another divers kinds of tongues; to another the interpretation of tongues: but all these worketh that one and the selfsame Spirit, dividing to every man severally as he will.

For as the body is one, and hath many members, and all the members of that one body, being many, are one body: so also is Christ. For by one Spirit are we all baptized into one body, whether we be Jews or Gentiles, whether we be bond or free; and have been all made to drink into one Spirit. For the body is not one member, but many. If the foot shall say, "Because I am not the hand, I am not of the body"; is it therefore not of the body? And if the ear shall say, "Because I am not the eye, I am not of the body"; is it therefore not of the body? If the whole body were an eye, where were the hearing? If the whole were hearing, where were the smelling? But now hath God set the members every one of them in the body, as it hath pleased him. And if they were all one member, where were the body? But now are they many members, yet but one body. And the eye cannot say unto the hand, "I have no need of thee": nor again the head to the feet, "I have no need of you." Nay, much more those members of the body, which seem to be more feeble, are necessary: and those members of the body, which we think to be less honourable, upon these we bestow more abundant honour; and our uncomely parts have more abundant comeliness. For our comely parts have no need: but God hath tempered the body together, having given more abundant honour to that part which lacked: that there should be no schism in the body; but that the members should have the same care one for another. And whether one member suffer, all the members suffer with it; or one member be honoured, all the members rejoice with it. Now ye are the body of Christ, and members in particular. And God hath set some in the church, first apostles, secondarily prophets, thirdly teachers, after that

---

[42] A symbol of authority.

[43] Independent of.

miracles, then gifts of healings, helps, governments, diversities of tongues. Are all apostles? are all prophets? are all teachers? are all workers of miracles? Have all the gifts of healing? do all speak with tongues? do all interpret? But covet[44] earnestly the best gifts: and yet shew I unto you a more excellent way.

Chapter 13

Though I speak with the tongues of men and of angels, and have not charity, I am become as sounding brass, or a tinkling cymbal.[45] And though I have the gift of prophecy, and understand all mysteries, and all knowledge; and though I have all faith, so that I could remove mountains, and have not charity, I am nothing. And though I bestow all my goods to feed the poor, and though I give my body to be burned, and have not charity, it profiteth me nothing. Charity suffereth long, and is kind; charity envieth not; charity vaunteth not itself, is not puffed up, doth not behave itself unseemly, seeketh not her own, is not easily provoked, thinketh no evil; rejoiceth not in iniquity, but rejoiceth in the truth; beareth all things, believeth all things, hopeth all things, endureth all things. Charity never faileth: but whether there be prophecies, they shall fail; whether there be tongues, they shall cease; whether there be knowledge, it shall vanish away. For we know in part, and we prophesy in part. But when that which is perfect is come, then that which is in part shall be done away. When I was a child, I spake as a child, I understood as a child, I thought as a child: but when I became a man, I put away childish things. For now we see through a glass,[46] darkly; but then face to face: now I know in part; but then shall I know even as also I am known. And now abideth faith, hope, charity, these three; but the greatest of these is charity.

• • •

Chapter 15

Moreover, brethren, I declare unto you the gospel which I preached unto you, which also ye have received, and wherein ye stand; by which also ye are saved, if ye keep in memory what I preached unto you, unless ye have believed in vain. For I delivered unto you first of all that which I also received, how that Christ died for our sins according to the scriptures; and that he was buried, and that he rose again the third day according to the scriptures: and that he was seen of Cephas, then of the twelve: after that, he was seen of above five hundred brethren at once; of whom the greater part remain unto this present, but some are fallen asleep.[47] After that, he was seen of James; then of all the apostles. And last of all he was seen of me also, as of one born out of due time. For I am the least of the apostles, that am not meet to be called an apostle, because I persecuted the church of God. But by the grace of God I am what I am: and his grace which was bestowed upon me was not in vain; but I laboured more abundantly than they all: yet not I, but the grace of God which was with me. Therefore whether it were I or they, so we preach, and so ye believed.

Now if Christ be preached that he rose from the dead, how say some among you that there is no resurrection of the dead? But if there be no resurrection of the dead, then is Christ not risen: and if Christ be not risen, then is our preaching vain, and your faith is also vain. Yea, and we are found false witnesses of God; because we have testified of God that he raised up Christ: whom he raised not up, if so be that the dead rise not. For if the dead rise not, then is not Christ raised: and if Christ be

[44]Strive for.

[45]The gong and the cymbal were instruments used in pagan worship.

[46]Mirror.

[47]That is, many are still alive, but some are dead.

not raised, your faith is vain; ye are yet in your sins. Then they also which are fallen asleep in Christ[48] are perished. If in this life only[49] we have hope in Christ, we are of all men most miserable.

But now is Christ risen from the dead, and become the firstfruits of them that slept. For since by man came death, by man came also the resurrection of the dead. For as in Adam all die, even so in Christ shall all be made alive. But every man in his own order: Christ the firstfruits; afterward they that are Christ's at his coming. Then cometh the end, when he shall have delivered up the kingdom to God, even the Father; when he shall have put down all rule and all authority and power. For he must reign, till he hath put all enemies under his feet. The last enemy that shall be destroyed is death. For he hath put all things under his feet. But when he saith all things are put under him, it is manifest that he is excepted, which did put all things under him. And when all things shall be subdued unto him, then shall the Son also himself be subject unto him that put all things under him, that God may be all in all.

Else what shall they do which are baptized for the dead,[50] if the dead rise not at all? why are they then baptized for the dead? And why stand we in jeopardy every hour? I protest by your rejoicing which I have in Christ Jesus our Lord, I die daily. If after the manner of men I have fought with beasts at Ephesus, what advantageth it me, if the dead rise not? let us eat and drink; for to morrow we die. Be not deceived: evil communications corrupt good manners.[51] Awake to righteousness, and sin not; for some have not the knowledge of God: I speak this to your shame.

But some man will say, "How are the dead raised up? and with what body do they come?" Thou fool, that which thou sowest is not quickened, except it die: and that which thou sowest, thou sowest not that body that shall be, but bare grain,[52] it may chance of wheat, or of some other grain: but God giveth it a body as it hath pleased him, and to every seed his own body. All flesh is not the same flesh: but there is one kind of flesh of men, another flesh of beasts, another of fishes, and another of birds. There are also celestial bodies, and bodies terrestrial: but the glory of the celestial is one, and the glory of the terrestrial is another. There is one glory of the sun, and another glory of the moon, and another glory of the stars: for one star differeth from another star in glory. So also is the resurrection of the dead. It is sown in corruption; it is raised in incorruption: it is sown in dishonour; it is raised in glory: it is sown in weakness; it is raised in power: it is sown a natural body; it is raised a spiritual body. There is a natural body, and there is a spiritual body. And so it is written, "The first man Adam was made a living soul; the last Adam was made a quickening spirit." Howbeit that was not first which is spiritual, but that which is natural; and afterward that which is spiritual. The first man is of the earth, earthy: the second man is the Lord from heaven. As is the earthy, such are they also that are earthy: and as is the heavenly, such are they also that are heavenly. And as we have borne the image of the earthy, we shall also bear the image of the heavenly.

Now this I say, brethren, that flesh and blood cannot inherit the kingdom of God; neither doth corruption inherit incorruption. Behold, I shew you a mystery; We shall not all sleep, but we shall all be changed, in a moment, in the twinkling of an eye, at the last trump: for the trumpet shall sound, and the dead shall be raised incorruptible, and we shall be changed. For this corruptible must put on incorruption, and this mortal must put on immortality. So when this corruptible

---

[48] That is, Christians who have died.

[49] And not after death as well.

[50] Apparently Christians were baptized on behalf of loved ones who had died without being baptized.

[51] That is, "Evil companions corrupt good morals."

[52] That is, bare seed.

shall have put on incorruption, and this mortal shall have put on immortality, then shall be brought to pass the saying that is written, "Death is swallowed up in victory." O death, where is thy sting? O grave, where is thy victory? The sting of death is sin; and the strength of sin is the law. But thanks be to God, which giveth us the victory through our Lord Jesus Christ. Therefore, my beloved brethren, be ye stedfast, unmoveable, always abounding in the work of the Lord, forasmuch as ye know that your labour is not in vain in the Lord.

[The Last Judgment]

The Revelation of St. John the Divine 18–22

Chapter 18

And after these things I saw another angel come down from heaven, having great power; and the earth was lightened with his glory. And he cried mightily with a strong voice, saying,

"Babylon[53] the great is fallen, is fallen,
And is become the habitation of devils,
And the hold of every foul spirit,
And a cage of every unclean and hateful bird.
For all nations have drunk of the wine of the wrath of her fornication,
And the kings of the earth have committed fornication with her,
And the merchants of the earth are waxed rich through the abundance of her delicacies."

And I heard another voice from heaven, saying,

"Come out of her, my people,
That ye be not partakers of her sins,
And that ye receive not of her plagues.
For her sins have reached unto heaven,
And God hath remembered her iniquities.
Reward her even as she rewarded you,
And double unto her double according to her works:
In the cup which she hath filled fill to her double.
How much she hath glorified herself, and lived deliciously,
So much torment and sorrow give her:
For she saith in her heart, 'I sit a queen,
And am no widow, and shall see no sorrow.'
Therefore shall her plagues come in one day,
Death, and mourning, and famine;
And she shall be utterly burned with fire:
For strong is the Lord God who judgeth her.
And the kings of the earth, who have committed fornication and lived deliciously with her,
Shall bewail her, and lament for her,
When they shall see the smoke of her burning,
Standing afar off for the fear of her torment,
Saying, 'Alas, alas, that great city Babylon, that mighty city!

[53] In the Old Testament Babylon is the worldly city, opposed to the Israelites and their God. Following that symbolism, here, in the early Christian period, Babylon is Rome, the seat of worldly power opposed to the Christians.

For in one hour is thy judgment come.'
And the merchants of the earth shall weep and mourn over her;
For no man buyeth their merchandise any more:
The merchandise of gold, and silver,
And precious stones, and of pearls,
And fine linen, and purple, and silk, and scarlet,
And all thyine wood, and all manner vessels of ivory,
And all manner vessels of most precious wood,
And of brass, and iron, and marble,
And cinnamon, and odours,
And ointments, and frankincense,
And wine, and oil, and fine flour, and wheat,
And beasts, and sheep, and horses, and chariots,
And slaves, and souls of men.
And the fruits that thy soul lusted after are departed from thee,
And all things which were dainty and goodly are departed from thee,
And thou shalt find them no more at all.
The merchants of these things, which were made rich by her,
Shall stand afar off for the fear of her torment,
Weeping and wailing, and saying,
'Alas, alas, that great city,
That was clothed in fine linen, and purple, and scarlet,
And decked with gold, and precious stones, and pearls!
For in one hour so great riches is come to nought.'
And every shipmaster, and all the company in ships,
And sailors, and as many as trade by sea,
Stood afar off, and cried
When they saw the smoke of her burning, saying,
'What city is like unto this great city!'
And they cast dust on their heads,
And cried, weeping and wailing, saying,
'Alas, alas, that great city,
Wherein were made rich all that had ships in the sea by reason of her costliness!
For in one hour is she made desolate.'
Rejoice over her, thou heaven,
And ye holy apostles and prophets;
For God hath avenged you on her."

And a mighty angel took up a stone like a great millstone, and cast it into the sea, saying,

"Thus with violence shall that great city Babylon be thrown down, and shall be found no more at all.
And the voice of harpers, and musicians, and of pipers, and trumpeters, shall be heard no more at all in thee;
And no craftsman, of whatsoever craft he be, shall be found any more in thee;
And the sound of a millstone shall be heard no more at all in thee;
And the light of a candle shall shine no more at all in thee;
And the voice of the bridegroom and of the bride shall be heard no more at all in thee:
For thy merchants were the great men of the earth;
For by thy sorceries were all nations deceived.
And in her was found the blood of prophets, and of saints,
And of all that were slain upon the earth."

Chapter 19

And after these things I heard a great voice of much people in heaven, saying, "Alleluia; Salvation, and glory, and honour, and power, unto the Lord our God: for true and righteous are his judgments: for he hath judged the great whore, which did corrupt the earth with her fornication, and hath avenged the blood of his servants at her hand." And again they said, "Alleluia." And her smoke rose up for ever and ever. And the four and twenty elders and the four beasts fell down and worshipped God that sat on the throne, saying, "Amen; Alleluia." And a voice came out of the throne, saying, "Praise our God, all ye his servants, and ye that fear him, both small and great." And I heard as it were the voice of a great multitude, and as the voice of many waters, and as the voice of mighty thunderings, saying, "Alleluia: for the Lord God omnipotent reigneth. Let us be glad and rejoice, and give honour to him: for the marriage of the Lamb[54] is come, and his wife hath made herself ready. And to her was granted that she should be arrayed in fine linen, clean and white: for the fine linen is the righteousness of saints." And he saith unto me, "Write, Blessed are they which are called unto the marriage supper of the Lamb." And he saith unto me, "These are the true sayings of God." And I fell at his feet to worship him. And he said unto me, "See thou do it not: I am thy fellowservant, and of thy brethren that have the testimony of Jesus: worship God: for the testimony of Jesus is the spirit of prophecy."

And I saw heaven opened, and behold a white horse; and he that sat upon him was called Faithful and True, and in righteousness he doth judge and make war. His eyes were as a flame of fire, and on his head were many crowns; and he had a name written, that no man knew, but he himself. And he was clothed with a vesture dipped in blood: and his name is called The Word of God. And the armies[55] which were in heaven followed him upon white horses, clothed in fine linen, white and clean. And out of his mouth goeth a sharp sword, that with it he should smite the nations: and he shall rule them with a rod of iron: and he treadeth the winepress of the fierceness and wrath of Almighty God. And he hath on his vesture and on his thigh a name written, KING OF KINGS, AND LORD OF LORDS.

And I saw an angel standing in the sun; and he cried with a loud voice, saying to all the fowls that fly in the midst of heaven, "Come and gather yourselves together unto the supper of the great God; that ye may eat the flesh of kings, and the flesh of captains, and the flesh of mighty men, and the flesh of horses, and of them that sit on them, and the flesh of all men, both free and bond, both small and great."

And I saw the beast,[56] and the kings of the earth, and their armies, gathered together to make war against him that sat on the horse, and against his army. And the beast was taken, and with him the false prophet that wrought miracles before him, with which he deceived them that had received the mark of the beast, and them that worshipped his image. These both were cast alive into a lake of fire burning with brimstone. And the remnant were slain with the sword of him that sat upon the horse, which sword proceeded out of his mouth: and all the fowls were filled with their flesh.

Chapter 20

And I saw an angel come down from heaven, having the key of the bottomless pit and a great chain in his hand. And he laid hold on the dragon, that old serpent, which is the Devil, and Satan, and bound him a thousand years, and cast him into the bottomless pit, and shut him up, and set a seal upon him, that he should deceive the nations no more, till the thousand years should be fulfilled: and after that he must be loosed a little season.

[54]The Lamb is Christ; his wife is the Church.
[55]The angelic host.
[56]The Antichrist.

And I saw thrones, and they sat upon them, and judgment was given unto them: and I saw the souls of them that were beheaded for the witness of Jesus, and for the word of God, and which had not worshipped the beast, neither his image, neither had received his mark upon their foreheads, or in their hands; and they lived and reigned with Christ a thousand years. But the rest of the dead lived not again until the thousand years were finished. This is the first resurrection. Blessed and holy is he that hath part in the first resurrection: on such the second death hath no power, but they shall be priests of God and of Christ, and shall reign with him a thousand years.

And when the thousand years are expired, Satan shall be loosed out of his prison, and shall go out to deceive the nations which are in the four quarters of the earth, Gog and Magog, to gather them together to battle: the number of whom is as the sand of the sea. And they went up on the breadth of the earth, and compassed the camp of the saints about, and the beloved city:[57] and fire came down from God out of heaven, and devoured them. And the devil that deceived them was cast into the lake of fire and brimstone, where the beast and the false prophet are, and shall be tormented day and night for ever and ever.

And I saw a great white throne, and him that sat on it, from whose face the earth and the heaven fled away; and there was found no place for them. And I saw the dead, small and great, stand before God; and the books were opened: and another book was opened, which is the book of life: and the dead were judged out of those things which were written in the books, according to their works. And the sea gave up the dead which were in it; and death and hell delivered up the dead which were in them: and they were judged every man according to their works. And death and hell were cast into the lake of fire. This is the second death. And whosoever was not found written in the book of life was cast into the lake of fire.

Chapter 21

And I saw a new heaven and a new earth: for the first heaven and the first earth were passed away; and there was no more sea. And I John saw the holy city, new Jerusalem, coming down from God out of heaven, prepared as a bride adorned for her husband. And I heard a great voice out of heaven saying, "Behold, the tabernacle of God is with men, and he will dwell with them, and they shall be his people, and God himself shall be with them, and be their God. And God shall wipe away all tears from their eyes; and there shall be no more death, neither sorrow, nor crying, neither shall there be any more pain: for the former things are passed away." And he that sat upon the throne said, "Behold, I make all things new." And he said unto me, "Write: for these words are true and faithful." And he said unto me, "It is done. I am Alpha and Omega, the beginning and the end. I will give unto him that is athirst of the fountain of the water of life freely. He that overcometh shall inherit all things; and I will be his God, and he shall be my son. But the fearful, and unbelieving, and the abominable, and murderers, and whoremongers, and sorcerers, and idolaters, and all liars, shall have their part in the lake which burneth with fire and brimstone: which is the second death."

And there came unto me one of the seven angels which had the seven vials full of the seven last plagues, and talked with me, saying, "Come hither, I will shew thee the bride, the Lamb's wife." And he carried me away in the spirit to a great and high mountain, and shewed me that great city, the holy Jerusalem, descending out of heaven from God, having the glory of God: and her light was like unto a

[57] Jerusalem.

stone most precious, even like a jasper stone, clear as crystal; and had a wall great and high, and had twelve gates, and at the gates twelve angels, and names written thereon, which are the names of the twelve tribes of the children of Israel: on the east three gates; on the north three gates; on the south three gates; and on the west three gates. And the wall of the city had twelve foundations, and in them the names of the twelve apostles of the Lamb. And he that talked with me had a golden reed to measure the city, and the gates thereof, and the wall thereof. And the city lieth foursquare, and the length is as large as the breadth: and he measured the city with the reed, twelve thousand furlongs.[58] The length and the breadth and the height of it are equal. And he measured the wall thereof, an hundred and forty and four cubits,[59] according to the measure of a man, that is, of the angel. And the building of the wall of it was of jasper: and the city was pure gold, like unto clear glass. And the foundations of the wall of the city were garnished with all manner of precious stones. The first foundation was jasper; the second, sapphire; the third, a chalcedony; the fourth, an emerald; the fifth, sardonyx; the sixth, sardius; the seventh, chrysolite; the eighth, beryl; the ninth, a topaz; the tenth, a chrysoprasus; the eleventh, a jacinth; the twelfth, an amethyst. And the twelve gates were twelve pearls; every several gate was of one pearl: and the street of the city was pure gold, as it were transparent glass. And I saw no temple therein: for the Lord God Almighty and the Lamb are the temple of it. And the city had no need of the sun, neither of the moon, to shine in it: for the glory of God did lighten it, and the Lamb is the light thereof. And the nations of them which are saved shall walk in the light of it: and the kings of the earth do bring their glory and honour into it. And the gates of it shall not be shut at all by day: for there shall be no night there. And they shall bring the glory and honour of the nations into it. And there shall in no wise enter into it any thing that defileth, neither whatsoever worketh abomination, or maketh a lie: but they which are written in the Lamb's book of life.

Chapter 22

And he shewed me a pure river of water of life, clear as crystal, proceeding out of the throne of God and of the Lamb. In the midst of the street of it, and on either side of the river, was there the tree of life, which bare twelve manner of fruits, and yielded her fruit every month: and the leaves of the tree were for the healing of the nations. And there shall be no more curse: but the throne of God and of the Lamb shall be in it; and his servants shall serve him: and they shall see his face; and his name shall be in their foreheads. And there shall be no night there; and they need no candle, neither light of the sun; for the Lord God giveth them light: and they shall reign for ever and ever.

And he said unto me, "These sayings are faithful and true: and the Lord God of the holy prophets sent his angel to shew unto his servants the things which must shortly be done. Behold, I come quickly: blessed is he that keepeth the sayings of the prophecy of this book."

And I John saw these things, and heard them. And when I had heard and seen, I fell down to worship before the feet of the angel which shewed me these things. Then saith he unto me, "See thou do it not: for I am thy fellowservant, and of thy brethren the prophets, and of them which keep the sayings of this book: worship God."

---

[58]Fifteen hundred miles.

[59]Seventy-five yards.

And he saith unto me, "Seal not the sayings of the prophecy of this book: for the time is at hand. He that is unjust, let him be unjust still: and he which is filthy, let him be filthy still: and he that is righteous, let him be righteous still: and he that is holy, let him be holy still. And, behold, I come quickly; and my reward is with me, to give every man according as his work shall be. I am Alpha and Omega, the beginning and the end, the first and the last. Blessed are they that do his commandments, that they may have right to the tree of life, and may enter in through the gates into the city. For without are dogs, and sorcerers, and whoremongers, and murderers, and idolaters, and whosoever loveth and maketh a lie.

"I Jesus have sent mine angel to testify unto you these things in the churches. I am the root and the offspring of David, and the bright and morning star."

And the Spirit and the bride say, "Come." And let him that heareth say, "Come." And let him that is athirst come. And whosoever will, let him take the water of life freely.

For I testify unto every man that heareth the words of the prophecy of this book, If any man shall add unto these things, God shall add unto him the plagues that are written in this book: and if any man shall take away from the words of the book of this prophecy, God shall take away his part out of the book of life, and out of the holy city, and from the things which are written in this book.

He which testifieth these things saith, "Surely I come quickly." Amen. Even so, come, Lord Jesus.

The grace of our Lord Jesus Christ be with you all. Amen.

THE WORLD CONTEXT

THE DESCENT OF INANNA

[C. 2000 B.C.E.]

The oldest text in these volumes, *The Descent of Inanna,* was set down by scribes in about 2000 B.C.E.; stylistic elements of repetition and formulaic phrasing in the text suggest that far older oral versions must have existed, and Inanna's story may easily go back to 3500 B.C.E., or even earlier. The story of Inanna comes to us from ancient Sumer, a kingdom of agricultural people who flourished in the plains they irrigated along the Tigris and Euphrates rivers in the southern part of what is now Iraq, between present-day Baghdad and the Persian Gulf. Ancient Sumer came into being sometime about the fifth millennium and lasted until 1750 B.C.E., when Hammurabi, king of Babylon, conquered Sumer and made it a part of Babylonia. So highly regarded was Sumer's culture that even after the Babylonian conquest, the learned language of writers and scholars continued to be Sumerian, just as classical Greek and Latin and Sanskrit were honored long after they ceased to be spoken by everyday people.

In contrast with the Jewish and Christian and Islamic sacred texts that replaced Sumerian stories, the chief actors in *The Descent of Inanna* are not a male god and an assemblage of desert patriarchs, but rather the shining Inanna—Queen of Heaven and Earth, Goddess of Love and Beauty, she of the Morning and Evening Star—and her grim shadow-sister

Ereshkigal, Queen of the Great Below. These sisters are incarnations of the Triple Goddess who, in her three aspects of fresh maiden, ripe lover-mother, and frightening death-crone, was once worshipped under different names over most of the world. In most cultures she was eradicated or demoted to secondary status as the consort of a male deity. Yet the literature of those cultures still bears traces of her, even if only in the form of sensuous nature worship; in fearful representations of bloodthirsty female revenge-spirits; in reverent adorations of female figures such as the Christian Madonna or the Muslim Fatima; in celebrations or excoriations of the Goddess's human sisters such as Eve, Helen of Troy, Clytemnestra, Deirdre, the Wife of Bath, Dante's Beatrice, and Petrarch's Laura. It is fitting both thematically and chronologically for our first world-text to be a story that deals openly and primarily with the Goddess.

Scholars have pieced together Inanna's story, or the outlines of it, from fragments of clay tablets inscribed with cuneiform writing that were unearthed at various sites in Iraq, many toward the close of the nineteenth century. Most such tablets are administrative and business documents, inventories, and records, but about six thousand tablets and fragments are inscribed with Sumerian literary texts dating from about the second millennium B.C.E. These texts encompass the same sort of rich variety to be found in the Old Testament—they include myths, hymns of praise to deities, epic histories, lamentations, and wisdom literature. In 1983 Samuel Noah Kramer, the great scholar of Sumerian literature, was able to write, "Many a text is still lying buried in the tells of southern Iraq, awaiting the spade of the lucky future excavator"; after the aerial bombardment of Baghdad and its environs in the early 1990s, it is to be hoped that Kramer's words hold true.

The literary texts that have been recovered and deciphered tell stories that predate Hebrew and Greek literature by about a thousand years. These interconnecting Sumerian mythic and historic stories tell of the earliest-known epic hero, Gilgamesh, and relate a version of the flood story upon which the Genesis story seems to have been modeled. From more than four hundred lines of text inscribed on thirty different tablets and fragments, Samuel Noah Kramer and other scholars have assembled the cycle of stories about the goddess called Inanna, named Ishtar and Isis in later cultures.

In the earliest parts of the story from the Sumerian tablets, Inanna is an adolescent goddess laying claim to her own powers first by witnessing the growth of a special tree, and then by encouraging the human hero Gilgamesh to make a bed for her out of it; these episodes are echoed in Homer's *Odyssey* and in the tree of the knowledge of good and evil in the Genesis garden. Inanna then challenges an elder generation of parental god-figures such as Enki, Sumerian sea-god and god of wisdom. After Enki has been enticed into a beer-drinking bout, he lets his guard down, and with drunken generosity the old god grants Inanna guardianship of the *me*. The *me* are not easily described; there are more than one hundred of them listed, and the texts suggest there are many more; the *me* do not easily fit into any category. The best way to describe them might be to say they are the qualities and characteristics and skills of human civilization, for good or for ill. They include such diverse gifts as the attributes and duties of kingship and the priesthood; the techniques of sexual pleasure, arts and crafts, agriculture, cookery, and oratory; and abstractions such as truth, fear, comfort, and the ability to make choices.

Inanna's story goes on to show her as a young fertility goddess discovering her own allure and sexuality. She falls in love with the shepherd Dumuzi, woos and is wooed by him in sensual words that clearly parallel parts of the biblical *Song of Songs,* joyously sleeps with him, and then begins to learn that the intensity of romance does not necessarily last forever.

The Descent of Inanna, the part of the story-cycle we use here, was recorded on fourteen separate tablets and fragments, and contains a good many lacunae (gaps in the text) and mysterious references to beings or objects or customs we can only guess about. The story recounts one of many similar journeys to the underworld or kingdom of death made by mythological heroes in cultures around the world; Persephone, Attis, Orpheus, Osiris, and Jesus are among the many other figures from the Mediterranean and Middle East who make such a descent and return. In part, such descents into the darkness concern the agricultural cycle: spring flowering, summer fruition, harvest, the apparent death of winter dormancy, and the renewal of spring. *The Descent of Inanna* may in part describe an actual ritual wherein priestesses staged Inanna's descent, death, and return, thereby ensuring another season of fertility in the fields and homes of Sumer. Here, it is the Goddess who must die and be reborn; in many other versions, it is a god-king who must die and be reborn. In a later part of the story not included here, once Inanna has escaped the underworld she makes her husband Dumuzi substitute for her, but as in other fertility stories a bargain is struck so that he must remain in the underworld for only half of each year; when Dumuzi ascends, the new shoots and buds and leaves come with him, and spring returns to the land.

But the descent story is not only about the eternal return of spring. It may suggest how people experience alternating periods of flagging energy and renewed strength. It is a story about the human quest for the kind of knowledge that adds to our spiritual power, and it hints about where that knowledge lies. Inanna, already Queen of Heaven and Earth, knows somehow that all her honor and glory is not enough, just as apparently happy and successful people in every age and culture often ask, "Is this all?" In the face of grief, disappointment, fear, or simply a sense of something lacking, we may retreat deeply into our own psyches, descend into the psychological depths to do battle with our own demons, who are almost always aspects of ourselves. In the depths we experience pain and shock. One common experience is the humiliation of learning, as Inanna learns, that outward trappings and honors and titles and definitions of who-I-am mean nothing in that place of ultimate trial. And there, like many before and after her, Inanna experiences a death of self; no one ever emerges from such an ordeal exactly the same person. Indeed, death or permanent shattering despair are very possible outcomes of daring to explore the depths. But Inanna says to us that with luck, courage, and good helpers, we may eventually emerge from those experiences with new power and hope and heightened understanding. We will dare to behold Ereshkigal, who is the worst there is. We will acknowledge that she lies within us, that she is a part of us; we will experience the worst she can do to us; and yet we will prove to ourselves that her power over us can be broken. That is a story worth knowing, a great gift from Sumer.

Suggested Readings

Inanna, Queen of Heaven and Earth: Her Stories and Hymns from Sumer (1983) is a rich collaboration by the Sumerian scholar Samuel Noah Kramer and the storyteller Diane Wolkstein, who polishes and reshapes the texts of the tablets into a smooth, connected narrative; good essays by Kramer on the history of Sumer and the recovery and translation of the texts, and interpretive materials by Wolkstein, are included. Wolkstein also performs the Inanna stories on an excellent videotape available from Cloudstone Productions.

The Descent of Inanna

Translated by Samuel Noah Kramer

From the "great above" she set her mind toward the "great below,"
The *goddess,* from the "great above" she set her mind toward the "great below,"
Inanna, from the "great above" she set her mind toward the "great below."

My lady abandoned heaven, abandoned earth,
To the nether world she descended,
Inanna abandoned heaven, abandoned earth,
To the nether world she descended,
Abandoned lordship, abandoned ladyship,
To the nether world she descended.

In Erech she abandoned Eanna, 10
To the nether world she descended,
In Badtibira she abandoned Emushkalamma,
To the nether world she descended,
In Zabalam she abandoned Giguna,
To the nether world she descended,
In Adab she abandoned Esharra,
To the nether world she descended,
In Nippur she abandoned Baratushgarra,
To the nether world she descended,
In Kish she abandoned Hursagkalamma, 20
To the nether world she descended,
In Agade she abandoned Eulmash,
To the nether world she descended.[1]

The seven divine decrees she fastened at the side,
She sought out the divine decrees, placed them at her hand,
All the decrees she set up at (her) waiting foot, 30
The *shugurra,* the crown of the plain, she put upon her head,
Radiance she placed upon her countenance,
The . . . rod of lapis lazuli she gripped in (her) hand,
Small lapis lazuli stones she tied about her neck,
Sparkling . . . stones she fastened to her breast,
A gold ring she gripped in her hand,
A . . . breastplate she bound about her breast,
All the garments of ladyship she *arranged* about her body,
. . . *ointment* she put on her face.

"In Eridu upon thy entering the house of Enki,[2]
Weep before Enki:
'O father Enki, let not thy daughter be *put to death* in the nether world,
Let not thy good metal be *ground up* into the dust of the nether world,
Let not thy good lapis lazuli be *broken up* into the stone of the stone-worker, 40
Let not thy *boxwood* be *cut up* into the wood of the wood-worker,
Let not the maid Inanna be *put to death* in the nether world.'

"Father Enki, the lord of wisdom,
Who knows the food of life, who knows the water of life,
He will surely bring me to life."

Inanna walked toward the nether world,
To her messenger Ninshubur she says:

[1]In this passage Inanna abandons the temples in her seven major cities, giving up her earthly powers.
[2]Enki is the Sumerian god of water and of wisdom.

"Go, Ninshubur,
The word which I have commanded thee . . ."

When Inanna had arrived at the lapis lazuli palace of the nether world, 50
At the door of the nether world she acted evilly,
In the palace of the nether world she spoke evilly:
"Open the house, gatekeeper, open the house,
Open the house, Neti, open the house, all alone I would enter."

Neti, the chief gatekeeper of the nether world,
Answers the pure Inanna:
"Who pray art thou?"

"I am the queen of heaven, the place where the sun rises."

"If thou art the queen of heaven, the place where the sun rises,
Why pray hast thou come to the land of no return? 60
On the road whose traveller returns not how has thy heart led thee?"

The pure Inanna answers him:
"My elder sister Ereshkigal,[3]
Because her husband, the lord Gugalanna, had been killed,
To witness the funeral rights,
. . . ; so be it."

Neti, the chief gatekeeper of the nether world,
Answers the pure Inanna:
"*Stay,* Inanna, to my queen let me speak,
To my queen Ereshkigal let me speak . . . let me speak." 70

Neti, the chief gatekeeper of the nether world,
Enters the house of his queen Ereshkigal and says to her:
"O my queen, a maid,
Like a god . . . ,
The door . . . ,
. . . ,
In Eanna . . . ,
The seven divine decrees she has fastened at the side,
She has sought out the divine decrees, has placed them at her hand,
All the decrees she has set up at (her) waiting foot, 80
The *shugurra,* the crown of the plain, she has put upon her head,
Radiance she has placed upon her countenance,
The . . . rod of lapis lazuli she has gripped in (her) hand,
Small lapis lazuli stones she has tied about her neck,
Sparkling . . . stones she has fastened to her breast,
A gold ring she has gripped in her hand,
A . . . breastplate she has bound about her breast,

[3]Ereshkigal, Inanna's sister and the queen of the underworld, is represented in Sumerian myth as spiteful, jealous, and unfulfilled.

All her garments of ladyship she has *arranged* about her body,
. . . *ointment* she has put on her face."

Then Ereshkigal . . . , 90
Answers Neti, her chief gatekeeper:
"Come, Neti, chief gatekeeper of the nether world,
Unto the word which I command thee, give ear.
Of the seven gates of the nether world, open their locks,
Of the gate Ganzir, the 'face' of the nether world, define its rules;
Upon her (Inanna's) entering,
Bowed low . . . let her . . . "

Neti, the chief gatekeeper of the nether world,
Honored the word of his queen.
Of the seven gates of the nether world, he opened their locks, 100
Of the gate Ganzir, the 'face' of the nether world, he defined its rules.
To the pure Inanna he says:
"Come, Inanna, enter."

Upon her entering the first gate,
The *shugurra*, the "crown of the plain" of her head, was removed.
"*What, pray, is this?*"
"Extraordinarily, O Inanna, have the decrees of the nether world been perfected,
O Inanna, *do not question* the rites of the nether world."

Upon her entering the second gate,
The . . . rod of lapis lazuli was removed. 110
"*What, pray, is this?*"
"Extraordinarily, O Inanna, have the decrees of the nether world been perfected,
O Inanna, *do not question* the rites of the nether world."

Upon her entering the third gate,
The small lapis lazuli stones of her neck were removed.
"*What, pray, is this?*"
"Extraordinarily, O Inanna, have the decrees of the nether world been perfected,
O Inanna, *do not question* the rites of the nether world."

Upon her entering the fourth gate,
The sparkling . . . stones of her breast were removed. 120
"*What, pray, is this?*"
"Extraordinarily, O Inanna, have the decrees of the nether world been perfected,
O Inanna, *do not question* the rites of the nether world."

Upon her entering the fifth gate,
The gold ring of her hand was removed.
"*What, pray, is this?*"
"Extraordinarily, O Inanna, have the decrees of the nether world been perfected,
O Inanna, *do not question* the rites of the nether world."

Upon her entering the sixth gate,
The . . . breastplate of her breast was removed. 130
"*What, pray, is this?*"

"Extraordinarily, O Inanna, have the decrees of the nether world been perfected,
O Inanna, *do not question* the rites of the nether world."

Upon her entering the seventh gate,
All the garments of ladyship of her body were removed.
"*What, pray, is this?*"
"Extraordinarily, O Inanna, have the decrees of the nether world been perfected,
O Inanna, *do not question* the rites of the nether world."

Bowed low . . .

The pure Ereshkigal seated herself upon her throne, 140
The Anunnaki, the seven judges,pronounced judgment before her,
They fastened (their) eyes upon her, the eyes of death,
At their word, the word which tortures the spirit,

. . . ,
The sick woman was turned into a *corpse,*
The *corpse* was hung from a *stake.*

After three days and three nights had passed,
Her messenger Ninshubur,
Her messenger of favorable words,
Her carrier of supporting words, 150
Fills the heaven *with complaints for her,*
Cried for her in the assembly shrine,
Rushed about for her in the house of the gods,
Lowered his eye for her, *lowered* his mouth for her,
With . . . he *lowered* his great . . . for her,
Like a pauper in a single garment he dressed for her,
To the Ekur, the house of Enlil,[4] all alone he directed his step.

Upon his entering the Ekur, the house of Enlil,
Before Enlil he weeps:
"O father Enlil, let not thy daughter be *put to death* in the nether world, 160
Let not thy good metal be *ground up* into the dust of the nether world,
Let not thy good lapis lazuli be *broken up* into the stone of the stone-worker,
Let not thy *boxwood* be *cut up* into the wood of the wood-worker,
Let not the maid Inanna be *put to death* in the nether world."

Father Enlil answers Ninshubur:
"My daughter, in the 'great above' . . . , in the 'great below' . . . ,
Inanna, in the 'great above' . . . , in the 'great below' . . . ,
The decrees of the nether world, the . . . decrees, to their place . . . ,
Who, pray, *to* their place . . . ?"

Father Enlil stood not by him in this matter, he went to Ur. 170

[4]Enlil is the Sumerian god of the air.

In Ur upon his entering the house of the . . . of the land,
The Ekishshirgal, the house of Nanna,[5] Before Nanna he weeps:
"O father Nanna, let not thy daughter be *put to death* in the nether world,
Let not thy good metal be *ground up* into the dust of the nether world,
Let not thy good lapis lazuli be *broken up* into the stone of the stone-worker,
Let not thy *boxwood* be *cut up* into the wood of the wood-worker,
Let not the maid Inanna be *put to death* in the nether world."

Father Nanna answers Ninshubur:
"My daughter in the 'great above' . . . , in the 'great below' . . . , 180
Inanna, in the 'great above' . . . , in the 'great below' . . . ,
The decrees of the nether world, the . . . decrees, to their place . . . ,
Who, pray, *to* their place . . . ?"

Father Nanna stood not by him in this matter, he went to Eridu.

In Eridu upon his entering the house of Enki,
Before Enki he weeps:
"O father Enki, let not thy daughter be *put to death* in the nether world,
Let not thy good metal be *ground up* into the dust of the nether world
Let not thy good lapis lazuli be *broken up* into the stone of the stone-worker,
Let not thy *boxwood* be *cut up* into the wood of the wood-worker, 190
Let not the maid Inanna be *put to death* in the nether world."

Father Enki answers Ninshubur:
"What now has my daughter done! I am troubled,
What now has Inanna done! I am troubled,
What now has the queen of all lands done! I am troubled,
What now has the hierodule of heaven done! I am troubled."

. . . *he brought forth dirt* (and) fashioned the *kurgarru,*
. . . *he brought forth dirt* (and) fashioned the *kalaturru,*[6]
To the *kurgarru* he gave the food of life,
To the *kalaturru* he gave the water of life,
Father Enki says to the *kalaturru* and *kurgarru*: 200
. . . (nineteen lines destroyed)
"*Upon the corpse hung from a stake direct the fear of the rays of fire,*
Sixty times the food of life, *sixty times* the water of life, sprinkle upon it,
Verily Inanna will arise."

. . . (twenty-four (?) lines destroyed)
Upon the corpse hung from a stake they directed the fear of the rays of fire,
Sixty times the food of life, *sixty times* the water of life, they sprinkled upon it,
Inanna arose.

Inanna ascends from the nether world,
The Anunnaki fled, 210

---

[5]Nanna is the Sumerian moon god.

[6]The kurgarru and the kalaturru are spirits who are able to restore Inanna to life; in the missing lines, it may be that they ingratiate themselves with Ereshkigal by sympathizing with her complaints.

(And) whoever of the nether world that had descended peacefully to the nether world;
When Inanna ascends from the nether world,
Verily the dead *hasten ahead of her.*

Inanna ascends from the nether world,
The small *demons* like . . . reeds,
The large demons like tablet styluses,
Walked at her side.
Who walked in front of her, being without . . . , held a staff in the hand,
Who walked at her side, being without . . . , carried a weapon on the loin.
They who *preceded* her, 220
They who *preceded* Inanna,
(Were beings who) know not food, who know not water,
Who eat not sprinkled flour,
Who drink not libated *wine,*
Who take away the wife from the loins of man,
Who take away the child from the breast of the nursing mother.

Inanna ascends from the nether world;
Upon Inanna's ascending from the nether world,
Her messenger Ninshubur threw himself at her feet,
Sat in the dust, dressed in *dirt.* 230
The demons say to the pure Inanna:
"O Inanna, *wait before* thy city, *we would bring him to thee.*"

The pure Inanna answers the demons:
"(He is) my messenger of favorable words,
My carrier of supporting words,
He *fails* not my directions,
He delays not my commanded word,
He *fills* heaven *with complaints for me,*
In the assembly shrine he cried out for me,
In the house of the gods he rushed about for me, 240
He *lowered* his eye for me, he *lowered* his mouth for me,
With . . . he *lowered* his great . . . for me,
Like a pauper in a single garment he dressed for me,
To the Ekur, the house of Enlil,
In Ur, to the house of Nanna,
In Eridu, to the house of Enki (he directed his step),
He brought me to life."

"Let us *precede* her, in Umma to the Sigkurshagga let us precede her."

In Umma, from the Sigkurshagga,
Shara[7] threw himself at her feet, 250
Sat in the dust, dressed in *dirt.*
The demons say to the pure Inanna:
"O Inanna, *wait before* thy city, we would bring him to thee."

---

[7]Shara is Inanna's son.

The pure Inanna answers the demons:
(Inanna's answer is destroyed)

"Let us *precede* her, in Badtibira to the Emushkalamma let us *precede* her."

In Badtibira from the Emushkalamma,
. . . threw themselves at her feet,
Sat in the dust, dressed in *dirt*.
The demons say to the pure Inanna: 260
"O Inanna, *wait before* thy city, we would bring them to thee."

The pure Inanna answers the demons:
(Inanna's answer is destroyed; the end of the poem is wanting).

THE EPIC OF GILGAMESH

[STANDARD VERSION, C. 7TH CENTURY B.C.E.]

SOURCES OF THE EPIC

In the mid-nineteenth century, a young English archaeologist, Austen Henry Layard, and a Turkish archaeologist, Hormuzd Rassam, made a discovery that eventually revolutionized the history of Western literature; in their excavations along the Tigris River in Mesopotamia, they found at Nineveh the ancient library of the last great Assyrian king, Assurbanipal (seventh century B.C.E.). The library, which had been buried in sand since the fall of Nineveh in the late seventh century B.C.E., consisted of some 25,000 broken clay tablets written in a wedge-shaped writing called cuneiform. As these tablets were slowly translated, scholars learned that most of them were business records, but they also discovered fragments of two great literary works, the Babylonian *Epic of Creation* and the *Epic of Gilgamesh*. Earlier versions of these two works predated both Homer's epics and the Bible by more than 1,000 years. In 1872 George Smith, who had been assisting in the translation of the tablets, made an announcement that immediately received attention from students of the Bible: The tablets include an account of the flood that bears unmistakable resemblances to the account in Genesis. Either the writer of the biblical version was acquainted with the Babylonian account in some form or another, or the two accounts drew upon a common source.

Since the late 1800s, other versions of the Gilgamesh story have been found, and it is safe to conclude that the *Epic of Gilgamesh* was widely known and extremely popular for hundreds, if not thousands, of years, before it was lost under the sands of Mesopotamia. The name Gilgamesh is actually found in Sumerian lists of kings after a flood, and it is believed that he reigned in the city of Uruk on the Euphrates River about 2500 B.C.E. Stories about him were passed down orally until poets around 2100 B.C.E. began to record some of his adventures. These stories were written in Akkadian and shaped into epic form during the Old Babylonian period between 1900 B.C.E. and 1600 B.C.E., whereas the Standard Version of the epic comes from Assurbanipal's library.

THE STORY OF GILGAMESH

The introductory section of the epic poem celebrates the feats that made Gilgamesh famous and gave him a place in history. He was a wise king, known for his building projects, especially for the great wall circling the city. The stories in this epic about this legendary figure cluster around two major events in his life: Gilgamesh's friendship with Enkidu and his grand journey to the edge of the world in search of immortality.

Characteristic of most great heroes down through the ages, Gilgamesh is of mixed parentage, divine and human, which sets him apart from ordinary men and raises his destiny to a cosmic plane. As an untested king, Gilgamesh's youthful energy creates a problem: He is using an antiquated custom to claim first sexual rights to brides and other women in Uruk. He also alienates sons from their fathers. The people are fed up and cry out to the father of the gods, Anu, for assistance. Anu provides for the creation of Enkidu, a young man capable of challenging Gilgamesh and diverting him from his previous life-style.

Because Enkidu initially lives with animals and frees them from traps, he comes to the attention of trappers, who complain about him. The translated text says that a temple prostitute is used to domesticate Enkidu, but the word "prostitute" has a negative connotation for a woman who was probably a temple priestess, familiar with the time-honored arts of sexuality and well suited to initiate Enkidu into carnal mysteries. After six days and seven nights of love-making, Enkidu finds himself estranged from the animals and ready to enter civilized society in order to confront Gilgamesh, who knows of Enkidu from his dreams, an important source of visionary knowledge for the Sumerians.

After they test each other's strength in a wrestling match, Enkidu and Gilgamesh become close friends and soul-mates, reminiscent of other famous friendships from antiquity, such as Achilles and Patroclus from Homer's *Iliad*, and David and Jonathan from the Bible, male friendships described by Plato as deeper than those between men and women. In some ways, however, they appear to be opposites: Gilgamesh is a civilized ruler and Enkidu is a wild, hairy man of nature; Gilgamesh is at home in the court, Enkidu roams with the animals. If Gilgamesh represents the urban male, then Enkidu complements him by being the natural man, the man of instinct and intuition. It would not be extreme to suggest that the two of them together represent wholeness and health, almost as if Enkidu were a psychological extension or alter ego of Gilgamesh.

Together they are better prepared to face their first challenge—a rite of passage for young warriors coming of age. They confront the giant Humbaba, who dwells in cedar forests on the other side of the mountains. The defeat of this giant symbolizes the extension of civilization, and it gives the two men the confidence to return to Uruk as independent, self-reliant warriors. The first part of the epic reaches a climax when Gilgamesh encounters the goddess Ishtar, who asks him to be her lover. This is not a simple request for sexual pleasure; she represents the earth's fertility and is proposing that Gilgamesh become the year-king. As such, he symbolizes the annual vegetative cycle and must be sacrificed to the Great Mother in order to guarantee the harvest at the end of the season. Gilgamesh's negative response includes a litany of Ishtar's former lovers, all of whom were sacrificed in some manner. Gilgamesh's rejection of this role amounts to a major turning point in masculine consciousness. Freed from the annual round of the Mother Goddess, Gilgamesh is charting a new destiny for the patriarchal hero as a solitary individual meeting challenges on his own and searching for personal answers.

Feeling rejected and angry, Ishtar tries to punish the young warriors with the Bull of Heaven, which is killed in what amounts to the first bullfight in literature. As a final insult, Enkidu tears out the bull's right thigh (symbolic of genitals?) and flings it in Ishtar's face.

A price must be paid, however, for the destruction of Humbaba and the Bull of Heaven, for the humiliation of Ishtar and the old religion. The two heroes, after all, have defied the gods and created a new independence for humans. In some sense they have gone too far, which is always the initial implication of extending psychological boundaries and developing a new consciousness. The Greek story of Prometheus explores a similar transition from old to new with tragic consequences, as does the Renaissance tale of Faustus. Enkidu must die, not a glorious death in battle, but a withering away in illness. In Enkidu's dreams, we see a vivid picture of the Sumerian land of the dead, where the deceased resemble bats residing in dust and darkness. The real price therefore of individual consciousness is not the death of a hero, but dread of death itself, which drives Gilgamesh to question his own mortality and to seek answers in a faraway land.

Following the path of the sun, Gilgamesh embarks on his great journey to find Utnapishtim, the one mortal who has been granted immortality by the gods. Although it is impossible to determine the exact influence that *Gilgamesh* had on later works of literature in Greece and Israel, a number of patterns or motifs in *Gilgamesh* later appear as standard fare in epic works. At the thresholds to the other side of the mountains, Gilgamesh must confront guardians who are a mixture of human and animal, signifying their allegiances to two worlds. He meets a mysterious woman in a paradisal garden. She assists him in dealing with Urshanabi the ferryman, a time-honored occupation. To reach Utnapishtim they must cross the waters of death or chaos. Finally, Gilgamesh accomplishes his goal by questioning Utnapishtim about mortality.

There are two parts to Utnapishtim's answer. First, he explains that the essence of life is change. Then he tells Gilgamesh his life story, which largely is the story of the flood, complete with ark, rains, and birds as emissaries. Gilgamesh, however, is more complex than Noah; he is a wise man. Gilgamesh does not learn how to get immortality from the gods, as did Utnapishtim, but he is given a plant for eternal youth, which is stolen and eaten by a snake, a tale possibly to explain a snake's capacity for rebirth through shedding skins.

Although it is impossible to conclude with certainty about the lessons learned by Gilgamesh from Siduri and Utnapishtim, it appears that the advice consists of a gentle kind of hedonism, the kind found in the biblical Ecclesiastes: Although one cannot completely understand the mysteries of life, the essence of life is change, and death is the end result; one should accept this and live life to its fullest. Gilgamesh returned to Uruk with the necessary lessons for becoming a great king, about whom stories were told generation after generation. Furthermore, it is remarkable that the personality of that king, captured in literature of such antiquity, should seem so contemporary, so relevant to questions about the meaning of life faced today.

Suggested Readings

Alexander Heidel discusses *Gilgamesh* and the Bible in *The Gilgamesh Epic and Old Testament Parallels* (1963). A fine new translation of *Gilgamesh* and other literary works are in Stephanie Dalley, *Myths from Mesopotamia* (1991). Important background information can be found in Thorkild Jacobsen, *The Treasure of Darkness: A History of Mesopotamian Religion* (1976) and in Samuel Noah Kramer, *Sumerian Mythology* (1944). An insightful discussion of *Gilgamesh* and the transition from neolithic to Sumerian civilization is in William Irwin Thompson, *The Time Falling Bodies Take to Light: Mythology, Sexuality & the Origins of Culture* (1981).

The Epic of Gilgamesh

Translated by N. K. Sandars

Prologue
Gilgamesh King in Uruk

I will proclaim to the world the deeds of Gilgamesh. This was the man to whom all things were known; this was the king who knew the countries of the world. He was wise, he saw mysteries and knew secret things, he brought us a tale of the days before the flood. He went on a long journey, was weary, worn-out with labour, returning he rested, he engraved on a stone the whole story.

When the gods created Gilgamesh they gave him a perfect body. Shamash[1] the glorious sun endowed him with beauty, Adad the god of the storm endowed him with courage, the great gods made his beauty perfect, surpassing all others, terrifying like a great wild bull. Two thirds they made him god and one third man.

In Uruk[2] he built walls, a great rampart, and the temple of blessed Eanna[3] for the god of the firmament Anu,[4] and for Ishtar the goddess of love. Look at it still today: the outer wall where the cornice runs, it shines with the brilliance of copper; and the inner wall, it has no equal. Touch the threshold, it is ancient. Approach Eanna the dwelling of Ishtar, our lady of love and war, the like of which no latter-day king, no man alive can equal. Climb upon the wall of Uruk; walk along it, I say; regard the foundation terrace and examine the masonry: is it not burnt brick and good? The seven sages[5] laid the foundations.

1
The Coming of Enkidu

Gilgamesh went abroad in the world, but he met with none who could withstand his arms till he came to Uruk. But the men of Uruk muttered in their houses, 'Gilgamesh sounds the tocsin for his amusement, his arrogance has no bounds by day or night. No son is left with his father, for Gilgamesh takes them all, even the children; yet the king should be a shepherd to his people. His lust leaves no virgin to her lover, neither the warrior's daughter nor the wife of the noble; yet this is the shepherd of the city, wise, comely, and resolute.'

The gods heard their lament, the gods of heaven cried to the Lord of Uruk, to Anu the god of Uruk: 'A goddess made him, strong as a savage bull, none can withstand his arms. No son is left with his father, for Gilgamesh takes them all; and is this the king, the shepherd of his people? His lust leaves no virgin to her lover, neither the warrior's daughter nor the wife of the noble.' When Anu had heard their lamentation the gods cried to Aruru, the goddess of creation, 'You made him, O Aruru, now create his equal; let it be as like him as his own reflection, his second

---

[1]Shamash is also the god of law and the husband of Ishtar, Queen of Heaven and goddess of love and fertility.

[2]An important city in southern Babylonia; after the flood it was the seat of a dynasty of kings. Gilgamesh was the fifth and most famous king of this dynasty.

[3]A temple precinct sacred to Anu and Ishtar.

[4]Father of the gods and the firmament and god of the firmament or "Great Above."

[5]Wise men who brought civilization to the seven oldest cities of Mesopotamia.

self, stormy heart for stormy heart. Let them contend together and leave Uruk in quiet.'

So the goddess conceived an image in her mind, and it was of the stuff of Anu of the firmament. She dipped her hands in water and pinched off clay, she let it fall in the wilderness, and noble Enkidu was created. There was virtue in him of the god of war, of Ninurta himself. His body was rough, he had long hair like a woman's; it waved like the hair of Nisaba, the goddess of corn. His body was covered with matted hair like Samuqan's, the god of cattle. He was innocent of mankind; he knew nothing of the cultivated land.

Enkidu ate grass in the hills with the gazelle and lurked with wild beasts at the water-holes; he had joy of the water with the herds of wild game. But there was a trapper who met him one day face to face at the drinking-hole, for the wild game had entered his territory. On three days he met him face to face, and the trapper was frozen with fear. He went back to his house with the game that he had caught, and he was dumb, benumbed with terror. His face was altered like that of one who has made a long journey. With awe in his heart he spoke to his father: 'Father, there is a man, unlike any other, who comes down from the hills. He is the strongest in the world, he is like an immortal from heaven. He ranges over the hills with wild beasts and eats grass; he ranges through your land and comes down to the wells. I am afraid and dare not go near him. He fills in the pits which I dig and tears up my traps set for the game; he helps the beasts to escape and now they slip through my fingers.'

His father opened his mouth and said to the trapper, 'My son, in Uruk lives Gilgamesh; no one has ever prevailed against him, he is strong as a star from heaven. Go to Uruk, find Gilgamesh, extol the strength of this wild man. Ask him to give you a harlot, a wanton[6] from the temple of love; return with her, and let her woman's power overpower this man. When next he comes down to drink at the wells she will be there, stripped naked; and when he sees her beckoning he will embrace her, and then the wild beasts will reject him.'

So the trapper set out on his journey to Uruk and addressed himself to Gilgamesh saying, 'A man unlike any other is roaming now in the pastures; he is as strong as a star from heaven and I am afraid to approach him. He helps the wild game to escape; he fills in my pits and pulls up my traps.' Gilgamesh said, 'Trapper, go back, take with you a harlot, a child of pleasure. At the drinking-hole she will strip, and when he sees her beckoning he will embrace her and the game of the wilderness will surely reject him.'

Now the trapper returned, taking the harlot with him. After a three days' journey they came to the drinking-hole, and there they sat down; the harlot and the trapper sat facing one another and waited for the game to come. For the first day and for the second day the two sat waiting, but on the third day the herds came; they came down to drink and Enkidu was with them. The small wild creatures of the plains were glad of the water, and Enkidu with them, who ate grass with the gazelle and was born in the hills; and she saw him, the savage man, come from far-off in the hills. The trapper spoke to her: 'There he is. Now, woman, make your breasts bare, have no shame, do not delay but welcome his love. Let him see you naked, let him possess your body. When he comes near uncover yourself and lie with him; teach him, the savage man, your woman's art, for when he murmurs love to you the wild beasts that shared his life in the hills will reject him.'

[6]"Harlot" or "wanton" has a negative connotation for someone who is probably a temple priestess of Ishtar.

She was not ashamed to take him, she made herself naked and welcomed his eagerness; as he lay on her murmuring love she taught him the woman's art. For six days and seven nights they lay together, for Enkidu had forgotten his home in the hills; but when he was satisfied he went back to the wild beasts. Then, when the gazelle saw him, they bolted away; when the wild creatures saw him they fled. Enkidu would have followed, but his body was bound as though with a cord, his knees gave way when he started to run, his swiftness was gone. And now the wild creatures had all fled away; Enkidu was grown weak, for wisdom was in him, and the thoughts of a man were in his heart. So he returned and sat down at the woman's feet, and listened intently to what she said. 'You are wise, Enkidu, and now you have become like a god. Why do you want to run wild with the beasts in the hills? Come with me. I will take you to strong-walled Uruk, to the blessed temple of Ishtar and of Anu, of love and of heaven: there Gilgamesh lives, who is very strong, and like a wild bull he lords it over men.'

When she had spoken Enkidu was pleased; he longed for a comrade, for one who would understand his heart. 'Come, woman, and take me to that holy temple, to the house of Anu and of Ishtar, and to the place where Gilgamesh lords it over the people. I will challenge him boldly, I will cry out aloud in Uruk, "I am the strongest here, I have come to change the old order, I am he who was born in the hills, I am he who is strongest of all." '

She said, 'Let us go, and let him see your face. I know very well where Gilgamesh is in great Uruk. O Enkidu, there all the people are dressed in their gorgeous robes, every day is holiday, the young men and the girls are wonderful to see. How sweet they smell! All the great ones are roused from their beds. O Enkidu, you who love life, I will show you Gilgamesh, a man of many moods; you shall look at him well in his radiant manhood. His body is perfect in strength and maturity; he never rests by night or day. He is stronger than you, so leave your boasting. Shamash the glorious sun has given favours to Gilgamesh, and Anu of the heavens, and Enlil, and Ea the wise has given him deep understanding. I tell you, even before you have left the wilderness, Gilgamesh will know in his dreams that you are coming.'

Now Gilgamesh got up to tell his dream to his mother, Ninsun, one of the wise gods. 'Mother, last night I had a dream. I was full of joy, the young heroes were round me and I walked through the night under the stars of the firmament, and one, a meteor of the stuff of Anu, fell down from heaven. I tried to lift it but it proved too heavy. All the people of Uruk came round to see it, the common people jostled and the nobles thronged to kiss its feet; and to me its attraction was like the love of woman. They helped me, I braced my forehead and I raised it with thongs and brought it to you, and you yourself pronounced it my brother.'

Then Ninsun, who is well-beloved and wise, said to Gilgamesh, 'This star of heaven which descended like a meteor from the sky; which you tried to lift, but found too heavy, when you tried to move it it would not budge, and so you brought it to my feet; I made it for you, a goad and spur, and you were drawn as though to a woman. This is the strong comrade, the one who brings help to his friend in his need. He is the strongest of wild creatures, the stuff of Anu; born in the grass-lands and the wild hills reared him; when you see him you will be glad; you will love him as a woman and he will never forsake you. This is the meaning of the dream.'

Gilgamesh said, 'Mother, I dreamed a second dream. In the streets of strong-walled Uruk there lay an axe; the shape of it was strange and the people thronged round. I saw it and was glad. I bent down, deeply drawn towards it; I loved it like a woman and wore it at my side.' Ninsun answered, 'That axe, which you saw, which drew you so powerfully like love of a woman, that is the comrade whom I give you, and he will come in his strength like one of the host of heaven. He is the brave companion who rescues his friend in necessity.' Gilgamesh said to his mother, 'A friend, a counsellor has come to me from Enlil, and now I shall befriend and counsel him.' So Gilgamesh told his dreams; and the harlot retold them to Enkidu.

And now she said to Enkidu, 'When I look at you you have become like a god. Why do you yearn to run wild again with the beasts in the hills? Get up from the ground, the bed of a shepherd.' He listened to her words with care. It was good advice that she gave. She divided her clothing in two and with the one half she clothed him and with the other herself; and holding his hand she led him like a child to the sheepfolds, into the shepherds' tents. There all the shepherds crowded round to see him, they put down bread in front of him, but Enkidu could only suck the milk of wild animals. He fumbled and gaped, at a loss what to do or how he should eat the bread and drink the strong wine. Then the woman said, 'Enkidu, eat bread, it is the staff of life; drink the wine, it is the custom of the land.' So he ate till he was full and drank strong wine, seven goblets. He became merry, his heart exulted and his face shone. He rubbed down the matted hair of his body and anointed himself with oil. Enkidu had become a man; but when he had put on man's clothing he appeared like a bridegroom. He took arms to hunt the lion so that the shepherds could rest at night. He caught wolves and lions and the herdsmen lay down in peace; for Enkidu was their watchman, that strong man who had no rival.

He was merry living with the shepherds, till one day lifting his eyes he saw a man approaching. He said to the harlot, 'Woman, fetch that man here. Why has he come? I wish to know his name.' She went and called the man saying, 'Sir, where are you going on this weary journey?' The man answered, saying to Enkidu, 'Gilgamesh has gone into the marriage-house and shut out the people. He does strange things in Uruk, the city of great streets. At the roll of the drum work begins for the men, and work for the women. Gilgamesh the king is about to celebrate marriage with the Queen of Love, and he still demands to be first with the bride, the king to be first and the husband to follow, for that was ordained by the gods from his birth, from the time the umbilical cord was cut. But now the drums roll for the choice of the bride and the city groans.' At these words Enkidu turned white in the face. 'I will go to the place where Gilgamesh lords it over the people, I will challenge him boldly, and I will cry aloud in Uruk, "I have come to change the old order, for I am the strongest here."'

Now Enkidu strode in front and the woman followed behind. He entered Uruk, that great market, and all the folk thronged round him where he stood in the street in strong-walled Uruk. The people jostled; speaking of him they said, 'He is the spit of Gilgamesh.' 'He is shorter.' 'He is bigger of bone.' 'This is the one who was reared on the milk of wild beasts. His is the greatest strength.' The men rejoiced: 'Now Gilgamesh has met his match. This great one, this hero whose beauty is like a god, he is a match even for Gilgamesh.'

In Uruk the bridal bed was made, fit for the goddess of love. The bride waited for the bridegroom, but in the night Gilgamesh got up and came to the house. Then Enkidu stepped out, he stood in the street and blocked the way. Mighty Gilgamesh came on and Enkidu met him at the gate. He put out his foot and prevented Gilgamesh from entering the house, so they grappled, holding each other like bulls. They broke the doorposts and the walls shook, they snorted like bulls locked together. They shattered the doorposts and the walls shook. Gilgamesh bent his knee with his foot planted on the ground and with a turn Enkidu was thrown. Then immediately his fury died. When Enkidu was thrown he said to Gilgamesh, 'There is not another like you in the world. Ninsun, who is as strong as a wild ox in the byre, she was the mother who bore you, and now you are raised above all men, and Enlil has given you the kingship, for your strength surpasses the strength of men.' So Enkidu and Gilgamesh embraced and their friendship was sealed.

2
The Forest Journey

Enlil[7] of the mountain, the father of the gods, had decreed the destiny of Gilgamesh. So Gilgamesh dreamed and Enkidu said, 'The meaning of the dream is this. The father of the gods has given you kingship, such is your destiny, everlasting life is not your destiny. Because of this do not be sad at heart, do not be grieved or oppressed. He has given you power to bind and to loose, to be the darkness and the light of mankind. He has given you unexampled supremacy over the people, victory in battle from which no fugitive returns, in forays and assaults from which there is no going back. But do not abuse this power, deal justly with your servants in the palace, deal justly before Shamash.'

The eyes of Enkidu were full of tears and his heart was sick. He sighed bitterly and Gilgamesh met his eye and said, 'My friend, why do you sigh so bitterly?' But Enkidu opened his mouth and said, 'I am weak, my arms have lost their strength, the cry of sorrow sticks in my throat, I am oppressed by idleness.' It was then that the lord Gilgamesh turned his thoughts to the Country of the Living; on the Land of Cedars the lord Gilgamesh reflected. He said to his servant Enkidu, 'I have not established my name stamped on bricks as my destiny decreed; therefore I will go to the country where the cedar is felled. I will set up my name in the place where the names of famous men are written, and where no man's name is written yet I will raise a monument to the gods. Because of the evil that is in the land, we will go to the forest and destroy the evil; for in the forest lives Humbaba[8] whose name is "Hugeness," a ferocious giant.' But Enkidu sighed bitterly and said, 'When I went with the wild beasts ranging through the wilderness I discovered the forest; its length is ten thousand leagues in every direction. Enlil has appointed Humbaba to guard it and armed him in sevenfold terrors, terrible to all flesh is Humbaba. When he roars it is like the torrent of the storm, his breath is like fire, and his jaws are death itself. He guards the cedars so well that when the wild heifer stirs in the forest, though she is sixty leagues distant, he hears her. What man would willingly walk into that country and explore its depths? I tell you, weakness overpowers whoever goes near it: it is not an equal struggle when one fights with Humbaba; he is a great warrior, a battering-ram. Gilgamesh, the watchman of the forest never sleeps.'

Gilgamesh replied: 'Where is the man who can clamber to heaven? Only the gods live for ever with glorious Shamash, but as for us men, our days are numbered, our occupations are a breath of wind. How is this, already you are afraid! I will go first although I am your lord, and you may safely call out, "Forward, there is nothing to fear!" Then if I fall I leave behind me a name that endures; men will say of me, "Gilgamesh has fallen in fight with ferocious Humbaba." Long after the child has been born in my house, they will say it, and remember.' Enkidu spoke again to Gilgamesh, 'O my lord, if you will enter that country, go first to the hero Shamash, tell the Sun God, for the land is his. The country where the cedar is cut belongs to Shamash.'

---

[7] As god of earth, wind, and spirit, Enlil is the active manifestation of Anu.

[8] A nature divinity, guardian spirit of the forest.

Gilgamesh took up a kid, white without spot, and a brown one with it; he held them against his breast, and he carried them into the presence of the sun. He took in his hand his silver sceptre and he said to glorious Shamash, 'I am going to that country, O Shamash, I am going; my hands supplicate, so let it be well with my soul and bring me back to the quay of Uruk. Grant, I beseech, your protection, and let the omen be good.' Glorious Shamash answered, 'Gilgamesh, you are strong, but what is the Country of the Living to you?'

'O Shamash, hear me, hear me, Shamash, let my voice be heard. Here in the city man dies oppressed at heart, man perishes with despair in his heart. I have looked over the wall and I see the bodies floating on the river, and that will be my lot also. Indeed I know it is so, for whoever is tallest among men cannot reach the heavens, and the greatest cannot encompass the earth. Therefore I would enter that country: because I have not established my name stamped on brick as my destiny decreed, I will go to the country where the cedar is cut. I will set up my name where the names of famous men are written; and where no man's name is written I will raise a monument to the gods.' The tears ran down his face and he said, 'Alas, it is a long journey that I must take to the Land of Humbaba. If this enterprise is not to be accomplished, why did you move me, Shamash, with the restless desire to perform it? How can I succeed if you will not succour me? If I die in that country I will die without rancour, but if I return I will make a glorious offering of gifts and of praise to Shamash.'

So Shamash accepted the sacrifice of his tears; like the compassionate man he showed him mercy. He appointed strong allies for Gilgamesh, sons of one mother, and stationed them in the mountain caves. The great winds he appointed: the north wind, the whirlwind, the storm and the icy wind, the tempest and the scorching wind. Like vipers, like dragons, like a scorching fire, like a serpent that freezes the heart, a destroying flood and the lightning's fork, such were they and Gilgamesh rejoiced.

He went to the forge and said, 'I will give orders to the armourers; they shall cast us our weapons while we watch them.' So they gave orders to the armourers and the craftsmen sat down in conference. They went into the groves of the plain and cut willow and box-wood; they cast for them axes of nine score pounds, and great swords they cast with blades of six score pounds each one, with pommels and hilts of thirty pounds. They cast for Gilgamesh the axe 'Might of Heroes' and the bow of Anshan;[9] and Gilgamesh was armed and Enkidu; and the weight of the arms they carried was thirty score pounds.

The people collected and the counsellors in the streets and in the market-place of Uruk; they came through the gate of seven bolts and Gilgamesh spoke to them in the market-place: 'I, Gilgamesh, go to see that creature of whom such things are spoken, the rumour of whose name fills the world. I will conquer him in his cedar wood and show the strength of the sons of Uruk, all the world shall know of it. I am committed to this enterprise: to climb the mountain, to cut down the cedar, and leave behind me an enduring name.' The counsellors of Uruk, the great market, answered him, 'Gilgamesh, you are young, your courage carries you too far, you cannot know what this enterprise means which you plan. We have heard that Humbaba is not like men who die, his weapons are such that none can stand against them; the forest stretches for ten thousand leagues in every direction; who would willingly go down to explore its depths? As for Humbaba, when he roars it is like the torrent of the storm, his breath is like fire and his jaws are death itself.

[9]A district in southwest Persia, probably the source of wood for making bows.

Why do you crave to do this thing, Gilgamesh? It is no equal struggle when one fights with Humbaba, that battering-ram.'

When he heard these words of the counsellors Gilgamesh looked at his friend and laughed, 'How shall I answer them; shall I say I am afraid of Humbaba, I will sit at home all the rest of my days?' Then Gilgamesh opened his mouth again and said to Enkidu, 'My friend, let us go to the Great Palace, to Egalmah,[10] and stand before Ninsun the queen. Ninsun is wise with deep knowledge, she will give us counsel for the road we must go.' They took each other by the hand as they went to Egalmah, and they went to Ninsun the great queen. Gilgamesh approached, he entered the palace and spoke to Ninsun. 'Ninsun, will you listen to me; I have a long journey to go, to the Land of Humbaba, I must travel an unknown road and fight a strange battle. From the day I go until I return, till I reach the cedar forest and destroy the evil which Shamash abhors, pray for me to Shamash.'

Ninsun went into her room, she put on a dress becoming to her body, she put on jewels to make her breast beautiful, she placed a tiara on her head and her skirts swept the ground. Then she went up to the altar of the Sun, standing upon the roof of the palace; she burnt incense and lifted her arms to Shamash as the smoke ascended: 'O Shamash, why did you give this restless heart to Gilgamesh, my son; why did you give it? You have moved him and now he sets out on a long journey to the Land of Humbaba, to travel an unknown road and fight a strange battle. Therefore from the day that he goes till the day he returns, until he reaches the cedar forest, until he kills Humbaba and destroys the evil thing which you, Shamash, abhor, do not forget him; but let the dawn, Aya, your dear bride, remind you always, and when day is done give him to the watchman of the night to keep him from harm.' Then Ninsun the mother of Gilgamesh extinguished the incense, and she called to Enkidu with this exhortation: 'Strong Enkidu, you are not the child of my body, but I will receive you as my adopted son; you are my other child like the foundlings they bring to the temple. Serve Gilgamesh as a foundling serves the temple and the priestess who reared him. In the presence of my women, my votaries and hierophants, I declare it.' Then she placed the amulet for a pledge round his neck, and she said to him, 'I entrust my son to you; bring him back to me safely.'

And now they brought to them the weapons, they put in their hands the great swords in their golden scabbards, and the bow and the quiver. Gilgamesh took the axe, he slung the quiver from his shoulder, and the bow of Anshan, and buckled the sword to his belt; and so they were armed and ready for the journey. Now all the people came and pressed on them and said, 'When will you return to the city?' The counsellors blessed Gilgamesh and warned him, 'Do not trust too much in your own strength, be watchful, restrain your blows at first. The one who goes in front protects his companion; the good guide who knows the way guards his friend. Let Enkidu lead the way, he knows the road to the forest, he has seen Humbaba and is experienced in battles; let him press first into the passes, let him be watchful and look to himself. Let Enkidu protect his friend, and guard his companion, and bring him safe through the pitfalls of the road. We, the counsellors of Uruk entrust our king to you, O Enkidu; bring him back safely to us.' Again to Gilgamesh they said, 'May Shamash give you your heart's desire, may he let you see with your eyes the thing accomplished which your lips have spoken; may he open a path for you where it is blocked, and a road for your feet to tread. May he open the mountains for your

[10]The palace home of the goddess Ninsun.

crossing, and may the nighttime bring you the blessings of night, and Lugulbanda,[11] your guardian god, stand beside you for victory. May you have victory in the battle as though you fought with a child. Wash your feet in the river of Humbaba to which you are journeying; in the evening dig a well, and let there always be pure water in your water-skin. Offer cold water to Shamash and do not forget Lugulbanda.'

Then Enkidu opened his mouth and said, 'Forward, there is nothing to fear. Follow me, for I know the place where Humbaba lives and the paths where he walks. Let the counsellors go back. Here is no cause for fear.' When the counsellors heard this they sped the hero on his way. 'Go, Gilgamesh, may your guardian god protect you on the road and bring you safely back to the quay of Uruk.'

After twenty leagues they broke their fast; after another thirty leagues they stopped for the night. Fifty leagues they walked in one day; in three days they had walked as much as a journey of a month and two weeks. They crossed seven mountains before they came to the gate of the forest. Then Enkidu called out to Gilgamesh, 'Do not go down into the forest; when I opened the gate my hand lost its strength.' Gilgamesh answered him, 'Dear friend, do not speak like a coward. Have we got the better of so many dangers and travelled so far, to turn back at last? You, who are tried in wars and battles, hold close to me now and you will feel no fear of death; keep beside me and your weakness will pass, the trembling will leave your hand. Would my friend rather stay behind? No, we will go down together into the heart of the forest. Let your courage be roused by the battle to come; forget death and follow me, a man resolute in action, but one who is not foolhardy. When two go together each will protect himself and shield his companion, and if they fall they leave an enduring name.'

Together they went down into the forest and they came to the green mountain. There they stood still, they were struck dumb; they stood still and gazed at the forest. They saw the height of the cedar, they saw the way into the forest and the track where Humbaba was used to walk. The way was broad and the going was good. They gazed at the mountain of cedars, the dwelling-place of the gods and the throne of Ishtar. The hugeness of the cedar rose in front of the mountain, its shade was beautiful, full of comfort; mountain and glade were green with brushwood.

There Gilgamesh dug a well before the setting sun. He went up the mountain and poured out fine meal on the ground and said, 'O mountain, dwelling of the gods, bring me a favourable dream.' Then they took each other by the hand and lay down to sleep; and sleep that flows from the night lapped over them. Gilgamesh dreamed, and at midnight sleep left him, and he told his dream to his friend. 'Enkidu, what was it that woke me if you did not? My friend, I have dreamed a dream. Get up, look at the mountain precipice. The sleep that the gods sent me is broken. Ah, my friend, what a dream I have had! Terror and confusion; I seized hold of a wild bull in the wilderness. It bellowed and beat up the dust till the whole sky was dark, my arm was seized and my tongue bitten. I fell back on my knee; then someone refreshed me with water from his water-skin.'

Enkidu said, 'Dear friend, the god to whom we are travelling is no wild bull, though his form is mysterious. That wild bull which you saw is Shamash the Protector; in our moment of peril he will take our hands. The one who gave water from his water-skin, that is your own god who cares for your good name, your Lugulbanda. United with him, together we will accomplish a work the fame of which will never die.'

---

[11] The third king in the King-list, the hero of several poems, and the spirit guardian of Gilgamesh.

Gilgamesh said, 'I dreamed again. We stood in a deep gorge of the mountain, and beside it we two were like the smallest of swamp flies; and suddenly the mountain fell, it struck me and caught my feet from under me. Then came an intolerable light blazing out, and in it was one whose grace and whose beauty were greater than the beauty of this world. He pulled me out from under the mountain, he gave me water to drink and my heart was comforted, and he set my feet on the ground.'

Then Enkidu the child of the plains said, 'Let us go down from the mountain and talk this thing over together.' He said to Gilgamesh the young god, 'Your dream is good, your dream is excellent, the mountain which you saw is Humbaba. Now, surely, we will seize and kill him, and throw his body down as the mountain fell on the plain.'

The next day after twenty leagues they broke their fast, and after another thirty they stopped for the night. They dug a well before the sun had set and Gilgamesh ascended the mountain. He poured out fine meal on the ground and said, 'O mountain, dwelling of the gods, send a dream for Enkidu, make him a favourable dream.' The mountain fashioned a dream for Enkidu; it came, an ominous dream; a cold shower passed over him, it caused him to cower like the mountain barley under a storm of rain. But Gilgamesh sat with his chin on his knees till the sleep which flows over all mankind lapped over him. Then, at midnight, sleep left him; he got up and said to his friend, 'Did you call me, or why did I wake? Did you touch me, or why am I terrified? Did not some god pass by, for my limbs are numb with fear? My friend, I saw a third dream and this dream was altogether frightful. The heavens roared and the earth roared again, daylight failed and darkness fell, lightnings flashed, fire blazed out, the clouds lowered, they rained down death. Then the brightness departed, the fire went out, and all was turned to ashes fallen about us. Let us go down from the mountain and talk this over, and consider what we should do.'

When they had come down from the mountain Gilgamesh seized the axe in his hand: he felled the cedar. When Humbaba heard the noise far off he was enraged; he cried out, 'Who is this that has violated my woods and cut down my cedar?' But glorious Shamash called to them out of heaven, 'Go forward, do not be afraid.' But now Gilgamesh was overcome by weakness, for sleep had seized him suddenly, a profound sleep held him; he lay on the ground, stretched out speechless, as though in a dream. When Enkidu touched him he did not rise, when he spoke to him he did not reply. 'O Gilgamesh, Lord of the plain of Kullab,[12] the world grows dark, the shadows have spread over it, now is the glimmer of dusk. Shamash has departed, his bright head is quenched in the bosom of his mother Ningal. O Gilgamesh, how long will you lie like this, asleep? Never let the mother who gave you birth be forced in mourning into the city square.'

At length Gilgamesh heard him; he put on his breastplate, 'The Voice of Heroes,' of thirty shekels' weight; he put it on as though it had been a light garment that he carried, and it covered him altogether. He straddled the earth like a bull that snuffs the ground and his teeth were clenched. 'By the life of my mother Ninsun who gave me birth, and by the life of my father, divine Lugulbanda, let me live to be the wonder of my mother, as when she nursed me on her lap.' A second time he said to him, 'By the life of Ninsun my mother who gave me birth, and by the life of my father, divine Lugulbanda, until we have fought this man, if man he is, this god, if god he is, the way that I took to the Country of the Living will not turn back to the city.'

---

[12]Part of Uruk.

Then Enkidu, the faithful companion, pleaded, answering him, 'O my lord, you do not know this monster and that is the reason you are not afraid. I who know him, I am terrified. His teeth are dragon's fangs, his countenance is like a lion, his charge is the rushing of the flood, with his look he crushes alike the trees of the forest and reeds in the swamp. O my Lord, you may go on if you choose into this land, but I will go back to the city. I will tell the lady your mother all your glorious deeds till she shouts for joy: and then I will tell the death that followed till she weeps for bitterness.' But Gilgamesh said, 'Immolation and sacrifice are not yet for me, the boat of the dead shall not go down, nor the three-ply cloth be cut for my shrouding. Not yet will my people be desolate, nor the pyre be lit in my house and my dwelling burnt on the fire. Today, give me your aid and you shall have mine: what then can go amiss with us two? All living creatures born of the flesh shall sit at last in the boat of the West, and when it sinks, when the boat of Magilum[13] sinks, they are gone; but we shall go forward and fix our eyes on this monster. If your heart is fearful throw away fear; if there is terror in it throw away terror. Take your axe in your hand and attack. He who leaves the fight unfinished is not at peace.'

Humbaba came out from his strong house of cedar. Then Enkidu called out, 'O Gilgamesh, remember now your boasts in Uruk. Forward, attack, son of Uruk, there is nothing to fear.' When he heard these words his courage rallied; he answered, 'Make haste, close in, if the watchman is there do not let him escape to the woods where he will vanish. He has put on the first of his seven splendours[14] but not yet the other six, let us trap him before he is armed.' Like a raging wild bull he snuffed the ground; the watchman of the woods turned full of threatenings, he cried out. Humbaba came from his strong house of cedar. He nodded his head and shook it, menacing Gilgamesh; and on him he fastened his eye, the eye of death. Then Gilgamesh called to Shamash and his tears were flowing, 'O glorious Shamash, I have followed the road you commanded but now if you send no succour how shall I escape?' Glorious Shamash heard his prayer and he summoned the great wind, the north wind, the whirlwind, the storm and the icy wind, the tempest and the scorching wind; they came like dragons, like a scorching fire, like a serpent that freezes the heart, a destroying flood and the lightning's fork. The eight winds rose up against Humbaba, they beat against his eyes; he was gripped, unable to go forward or back. Gilgamesh shouted, 'By the life of Ninsun my mother and divine Lugulbanda my father, in the Country of the Living, in this Land I have discovered your dwelling; my weak arms and my small weapons I have brought to this Land against you, and now I will enter your house.'

So he felled the first cedar and they cut the branches and laid them at the foot of the mountain. At the first stroke Humbaba blazed out, but still they advanced. They felled seven cedars and cut and bound the branches and laid them at the foot of the mountain, and seven times Humbaba loosed his glory on them. As the seventh blaze died out they reached his lair. He slapped his thigh in scorn. He approached like a noble wild bull roped on the mountain, a warrior whose elbows are bound together. The tears started to his eyes and he was pale, 'Gilgamesh, let me speak. I have never known a mother, no, nor a father who reared me. I was born of the mountain, he reared me, and Enlil made me the keeper of this forest. Let me go free, Gilgamesh, and I will be your servant, you shall be my lord; all the trees of the forest that I tended on the mountain shall be yours. I will cut them down and build you a palace.' He took him by the hand and led him to his house, so that the heart

---

[13]Possibly the "boat of the dead."

[14]Unclear, but probably natural armaments like winds.

of Gilgamesh was moved with compassion. He swore by the heavenly life, by the earthly life, by the underworld itself: 'O Enkidu, should not the snared bird return to its nest and the captive man return to his mother's arms?' Enkidu answered, 'The strongest of men will fall to fate if he has no judgement. Namtar, the evil fate that knows no distinction between men, will devour him. If the snared bird returns to its nest, if the captive man returns to his mother's arms, then you my friend will never return to the city where the mother is waiting who gave you birth. He will bar the mountain road against you, and make the pathways impassable.'

Humbaba said, 'Enkidu, what you have spoken is evil: you, a hireling, dependent for your bread! In envy and for fear of a rival you have spoken evil words.' Enkidu said, 'Do not listen, Gilgamesh: this Humbaba must die. Kill Humbaba first and his servants after.' But Gilgamesh said, 'If we touch him the blaze and the glory of light will be put out in confusion, the glory and glamour will vanish, its rays will be quenched.' Enkidu said to Gilgamesh, 'Not so, my friend. First entrap the bird, and where shall the chicks run then? Afterwards we can search out the glory and the glamour, when the chicks run distracted through the grass.'

Gilgamesh listened to the word of his companion, he took the axe in his hand, he drew the sword from his belt, and he struck Humbaba with a thrust of the sword to the neck, and Enkidu his comrade struck the second blow. At the third blow Humbaba fell. Then there followed confusion for this was the guardian of the forest whom they had felled to the ground. For as far as two leagues the cedars shivered when Enkidu felled the watcher of the forest, he at whose voice Hermon and Lebanon used to tremble. Now the mountains were moved and all the hills, for the guardian of the forest was killed. They attacked the cedars, the seven splendours of Humbaba were extinguished. So they pressed on into the forest bearing the sword of eight talents. They uncovered the sacred dwellings of the Anunnaki[15] and while Gilgamesh felled the first of the trees of the forest Enkidu cleared their roots as far as the banks of Euphrates. They set Humbaba before the gods, before Enlil; they kissed the ground and dropped the shroud and set the head before him. When he saw the head of Humbaba, Enlil raged at them. 'Why did you do this thing? From henceforth may the fire be on your faces, may it eat the bread that you eat, may it drink where you drink.' Then Enlil took again the blaze and the seven splendours that had been Humbaba's: he gave the first to the river, and he gave to the lion, to the stone of execration, to the mountain and to the dreaded daughter of the Queen of Hell.

O Gilgamesh, king and conqueror of the dreadful blaze; wild bull who plunders the mountain, who crosses the sea, glory to him, and from the brave the greater glory is Enki's![16]

3
Ishtar and Gilgamesh, and the Death of Enkidu

Gilgamesh washed out his long locks and cleaned his weapons; he flung back his hair from his shoulders; he threw off his stained clothes and changed them for new. He put on his royal robes and made them fast. When Gilgamesh had put

[15] Gods of the underworld and judges of the dead.

[16] God of sweet water and wisdom.

on the crown, glorious Ishtar lifted her eyes, seeing the beauty of Gilgamesh. She said, 'Come to me Gilgamesh, and be my bridegroom; grant me seed of your body, let me be your bride and you shall be my husband. I will harness for you a chariot of lapis lazuli and of gold, with wheels of gold and horns of copper; and you shall have mighty demons of the storm for draftmules. When you enter our house in the fragrance of cedar-wood, threshold and throne will kiss your feet. Kings, rulers, and princes will bow down before you; they shall bring you tribute from the mountains and the plain. Your ewes shall drop twins and your goats triplets; your pack-ass shall outrun mules; your oxen shall have no rivals, and your chariot horses shall be famous far-off for their swiftness.'

Gilgamesh opened his mouth and answered glorious Ishtar, 'If I take you in marriage, what gifts can I give in return? What ointments and clothing for your body? I would gladly give you bread and all sorts of food fit for a god. I would give you wine to drink fit for a queen. I would pour out barley to stuff your granary; but as for making you my wife—that I will not. How would it go with me? Your lovers have found you like a brazier which smoulders in the cold, a backdoor which keeps out neither squall of wind nor storm, a castle which crushes the garrison, pitch that blackens the bearer, a water-skin that chafes the carrier, a stone which falls from the parapet, a battering-ram turned back from the enemy, a sandal that trips the wearer. Which of your lovers did you ever love for ever? What shepherd of yours has pleased you for all time? Listen to me while I tell the tale of your lovers. There was Tammuz,[17] the lover of your youth, for him you decreed wailing, year after year. You loved the many-coloured roller, but still you struck and broke his wing; now in the grove he sits and cries, "kappi, kappi, my wing, my wing." You have loved the lion tremendous in strength: seven pits you dug for him, and seven. You have loved the stallion magnificent in battle, and for him you decreed whip and spur and a thong, to gallop seven leagues by force and to muddy the water before he drinks; and for his mother Silili[18] lamentations. You have loved the shepherd of the flock; he made meal-cake for you day after day, he killed kids for your sake. You struck and turned him into a wolf; now his own herd-boys chase him away, his own hounds worry his flanks. And did you not love Ishullanu,[19] the gardener of your father's palm-grove? He brought you baskets filled with dates without end; every day he loaded your table. Then you turned your eyes on him and said, "Dearest Ishullanu, come here to me, let us enjoy your manhood, come forward and take me, I am yours." Ishullanu answered, "What are you asking from me? My mother has baked and I have eaten; why should I come to such as you for food that is tainted and rotten? For when was a screen of rushes sufficient protection from frosts?" But when you had heard his answer you struck him. He was changed to a blind mole deep in the earth, one whose desire is always beyond his reach. And if you and I should be lovers, should not I be served in the same fashion as all these others whom you loved once?'

When Ishtar heard this she fell into a bitter rage, she went up to high heaven. Her tears poured down in front of her father Anu, and Antum her mother. She said, 'My father, Gilgamesh has heaped insults on me, he has told over all my abominable behaviour, my foul and hideous acts.' Anu opened his mouth and said, 'Are you a father of gods? Did not you quarrel with Gilgamesh the king, so now he has related your abominable behaviour, your foul and hideous acts.'

[17]God of vegetation who is born in the spring and dies in the fall.
[18]Perhaps a divine mare.
[19]The gardener of Anu.

Ishtar opened her mouth and said again, 'My father, give me the Bull of Heaven to destroy Gilgamesh. Fill Gilgamesh, I say, with arrogance to his destruction; but if you refuse to give me the Bull of Heaven I will break in the doors of hell and smash the bolts; there will be confusion of people, those above with those from the lower depths. I shall bring up the dead to eat food like the living; and the hosts of dead will outnumber the living.' Anu said to great Ishtar, 'If I do what you desire there will be seven years of drought throughout Uruk when corn will be seedless husks. Have you saved grain enough for the people and grass for the cattle?' Ishtar replied. 'I have saved grain for the people, grass for the cattle; for seven years of seedless husks there is grain and there is grass enough.'

When Anu heard what Ishtar had said he gave her the Bull of Heaven to lead by the halter down to Uruk. When they reached the gates of Uruk the Bull went to the river; with his first snort cracks opened in the earth and a hundred young men fell down to death. With his second snort cracks opened and two hundred fell down to death. With his third snort cracks opened, Enkidu doubled over but instantly recovered, he dodged aside and leapt on the Bull and seized it by the horns. The Bull of Heaven foamed in his face, it brushed him with the thick of its tail. Enkidu cried to Gilgamesh, 'My friend, we boasted that we would leave enduring names behind us. Now thrust in your sword between the nape and the horns.' So Gilgamesh followed the Bull, he seized the thick of its tail, he thrust the sword between the nape and the horns and slew the Bull. When they had killed the Bull of Heaven they cut out its heart and gave it to Shamash, and the brothers rested.

But Ishtar rose up and mounted the great wall of Uruk; she sprang on to the tower and uttered a curse: 'Woe to Gilgamesh, for he has scorned me in killing the Bull of Heaven.' When Enkidu heard these words he tore out the Bull's right thigh and tossed it in her face saying, 'If I could lay my hands on you, it is this I should do to you, and lash the entrails to your side.' Then Ishtar called together her people, the dancing and singing girls, the prostitutes of the temple, the courtesans. Over the thigh of the Bull of Heaven she set up lamentation.

But Gilgamesh called the smiths and the armourers, all of them together. They admired the immensity of the horns. They were plated with lapis lazuli two fingers thick. They were thirty pounds each in weight, and their capacity in oil was six measures, which he gave to his guardian god, Lugulbanda. But he carried the horns into the palace and hung them on the wall. Then they washed their hands in Euphrates, they embraced each other and went away. They drove through the streets of Uruk where the heroes were gathered to see them, and Gilgamesh called to the singing girls, 'Who is most glorious of the heroes, who is most eminent among men?' 'Gilgamesh is the most glorious of heroes, Gilgamesh is most eminent among men.' And now there was feasting, and celebrations and joy in the palace, till the heroes lay down saying, 'Now we will rest for the night.'

When the daylight came Enkidu got up and cried to Gilgamesh, 'O my brother, such a dream I had last night. Anu, Enlil, Ea and heavenly Shamash took counsel together, and Anu said to Enlil, "Because they have killed the Bull of Heaven, and because they have killed Humbaba who guarded the Cedar Mountain one of the two must die." Then glorious Shamash answered the hero Enlil, "It was by your command they killed the Bull of Heaven, and killed Humbaba, and must Enkidu die although innocent?" Enlil flung round in rage at glorious Shamash, "You dare to say this, you who went about with them every day like one of themselves!" '

So Enkidu lay stretched out before Gilgamesh; his tears ran down in streams and he said to Gilgamesh, 'O my brother, so dear as you are to me, brother, yet they will take me from you.' Again he said, 'I must sit down on the threshold of the dead and never again will I see my dear brother with my eyes.'

While Enkidu lay alone in his sickness he cursed the gate as though it was living flesh, 'You there, wood of the gate, dull and insensible, witless, I searched for you over twenty leagues until I saw the towering cedar. There is no wood like you in our land. Seventy-two cubits high and twenty-four wide, the pivot and the ferrule and the jambs are perfect. A master craftsman from Nippur has made you; but O, if I had known the conclusion! If I had known that this was all the good that would come of it, I would have raised the axe and split you into little pieces and set up here a gate of wattle instead. Ah, if only some future king had brought you here, or some god had fashioned you. Let him obliterate my name and write his own, and the curse fall on him instead of on Enkidu.'

With the first brightening of dawn Enkidu raised his head and wept before the Sun God, in the brilliance of the sunlight his tears streamed down. 'Sun God, I beseech you, about that vile Trapper, that Trapper of nothing because of whom I was to catch less than my comrade; let him catch least, make his game scarce, make him feeble, taking the smaller of every share, let his quarry escape from his nets.'

When he had cursed the Trapper to his heart's content he turned on the harlot. He was roused to curse her also. 'As for you, woman, with a great curse I curse you! I will promise you a destiny to all eternity. My curse shall come on you soon and sudden. You shall be without a roof for your commerce, for you shall not keep house with other girls in the tavern, but do your business in places fouled by the vomit of the drunkard. Your hire will be potter's earth, your thievings will be flung into the hovel, you will sit at the cross-roads in the dust of the potter's quarter, you will make your bed on the dunghill at night, and by day take your stand in the wall's shadow. Brambles and thorns will tear your feet, the drunk and the dry will strike your cheek and your mouth will ache. Let you be stripped of your purple dyes, for I too once in the wilderness with my wife had all the treasure I wished.'

When Shamash heard the words of Enkidu he called to him from heaven: 'Enkidu, why are you cursing the woman, the mistress who taught you to eat bread fit for gods and drink wine of kings? She who put upon you a magnificent garment, did she not give you glorious Gilgamesh for your companion, and has not Gilgamesh, your own brother, made you rest on a royal bed and recline on a couch at his left hand? He has made the princes of the earth kiss your feet, and now all the people of Uruk lament and wail over you. When you are dead he will let his hair grow long for your sake, he will wear a lion's pelt and wander through the desert.'

When Enkidu heard glorious Shamash his angry heart grew quiet, he called back the curse and said, 'Woman, I promise you another destiny. The mouth which cursed you shall bless you! Kings, princes and nobles shall adore you. On your account a man though twelve miles off will clap his hand to his thigh and his hair will twitch. For you he will undo his belt and open his treasure and you shall have your desire; lapis lazuli, gold and carnelian from the heap in the treasury. A ring for your hand and a robe shall be yours. The priest will lead you into the presence of the gods. On your account a wife, a mother of seven, was forsaken.'

As Enkidu slept alone in his sickness, in bitterness of spirit he poured out his heart to his friend. 'It was I who cut down the cedar, I who levelled the forest, I who slew Humbaba and now see what has become of me. Listen, my friend, this is the dream I dreamed last night. The heavens roared, and earth rumbled back an answer; between them stood I before an awful being, the sombre-faced man-bird; he had directed on me his purpose. His was a vampire face, his foot was a lion's foot, his hand was an eagle's talon. He fell on me and his claws were in my hair, he held me fast and I smothered; then he transformed me so that my arms became wings covered with feathers. He turned his stare towards me, and he led me away to the palace of Irkalla, the Queen of Darkness,[20] to the house from which none who enters ever returns, down the road from which there is no coming back.

'There is the house whose people sit in darkness; dust is their food and clay their meat. They are clothed like birds with wings for covering, they see no light, they sit in darkness. I entered the house of dust and I saw the kings of the earth, their crowns put away for ever; rulers and princes, all those who once wore kingly crowns and ruled the world in the days of old. They who had stood in the place of the gods like Anu and Enlil, stood now like servants to fetch baked meats in the house of dust, to carry cooked meat and cold water from the water-skin. In the house of dust which I entered were high priests and acolytes, priests of the incantation and of ecstasy; there were servers of the temple, and there was Etana, that king of Kish whom the eagle carried to heaven in the days of old. I saw also Samuqan, god of cattle, and there was Ereshkigal the Queen of the Underworld; and Belit-Sheri squatted in front of her, she who is recorder of the gods and keeps the book of death. She held a tablet from which she read. She raised her head, she saw me and spoke: "Who has brought this one here?" Then I awoke like a man drained of blood who wanders alone in a waste of rushes; like one whom the bailiff has seized and his heart pounds with terror.'

Gilgamesh had peeled off his clothes, he listened to his words and wept quick tears, Gilgamesh listened and his tears flowed. He opened his mouth and spoke to Enkidu: 'Who is there in strong-walled Uruk who has wisdom like this? Strange things have been spoken, why does your heart speak strangely? The dream was marvellous but the terror was great; we must treasure the dream whatever the terror; for the dream has shown that misery comes at last to the healthy man, the end of life is sorrow.' And Gilgamesh lamented, 'Now I will pray to the great gods, for my friend had an ominous dream.'

This day on which Enkidu dreamed came to an end and he lay stricken with sickness. One whole day he lay on his bed and his suffering increased. He said to Gilgamesh, the friend on whose account he had left the wilderness, 'Once I ran for you, for the water of life, and I now have nothing.' A second day he lay on his bed and Gilgamesh watched over him but the sickness increased. A third day he lay on his bed, he called out to Gilgamesh, rousing him up. Now he was weak and his eyes were blind with weeping. Ten days he lay and his suffering increased, eleven and twelve days he lay on his bed of pain. Then he called to Gilgamesh, 'My friend, the great goddess cursed me and I must die in shame. I shall not die like a man fallen in battle; I feared to fall, but happy is the man who falls in the battle, for I must die in shame.' And Gilgamesh wept over Enkidu. With the first light of dawn he raised his voice and said to the counsellors of Uruk:

'Hear me, great ones of Uruk,
I weep for Enkidu, my friend,
Bitterly moaning like a woman mourning
I weep for my brother.
O Enkidu, my brother,
You were the axe at my side,
My hand's strength, the sword in my belt,
The shield before me,
A glorious robe, my fairest ornament;
An evil Fate has robbed me.

[20]She is also called Ereshkigal.

The wild ass and the gazelle
That were father and mother,
All long-tailed creatures that nourished you
Weep for you,
All the wild things of the plain and pastures;
The paths that you loved in the forest of cedars
Night and day murmur.
Let the great ones of strong-walled Uruk
Weep for you;
Let the finger of blessing
Be stretched out in mourning;
Enkidu, young brother. Hark,
There is an echo through all the country
Like a mother mourning.
Weep all the paths where we walked together;
And the beasts we hunted, the bear and hyena,
Tiger and panther, leopard and lion,
The stag and the ibex, the bull and the doe.
The river along whose banks we used to walk,
Weeps for you,
Ula of Elam and dear Euphrates
Where once we drew water for the water-skins.
The mountain we climbed where we slew the Watchman,
Weeps for you.
The warriors of strong-walled Uruk
Where the Bull of Heaven was killed,
Weep for you.
All the people of Eridu
Weep for you Enkidu.
Those who brought grain for your eating
Mourn for you now;
Who rubbed oil on your back
Mourn for you now;
Who poured beer for your drinking
Mourn for you now.
The harlot who anointed you with fragrant ointment
Laments for you now;
The women of the palace, who brought you a wife,
A chosen ring of good advice,
Lament for you now.
And the young men your brothers
As though they were women
Go long-haired in mourning.
What is this sleep which holds you now?
You are lost in the dark and cannot hear me.'

He touched his heart but it did not beat, nor did he lift his eyes again. When Gilgamesh touched his heart it did not beat. So Gilgamesh laid a veil, as one veils the bride, over his friend. He began to rage like a lion, like a lioness robbed of her whelps. This way and that he paced round the bed, he tore out his hair and strewed it around. He dragged off his splendid robes and flung them down as though they were abominations.

In the first light of dawn Gilgamesh cried out, 'I made you rest on a royal bed, you reclined on a couch at my left hand, the princes of the earth kissed your feet. I will cause all the people of Uruk to weep over you and raise the dirge of the dead. The joyful people will stoop with sorrow; and when you have gone to the earth I will let my hair grow long for your sake, I will wander through the wilderness in the skin of a lion.' The next day also, in the first light, Gilgamesh lamented; seven days and seven nights he wept for Enkidu, until the worm fastened on him. Only then he gave him up to the earth, for the Anunnaki, the judges, had seized him.

Then Gilgamesh issued a proclamation through the land, he summoned them all, the coppersmiths, the goldsmiths, the stone-workers, and commanded them, 'Make a statue of my friend.' The statue was fashioned with a great weight of lapis lazuli for the breast and of gold for the body. A table of hard-wood was set out, and on it a bowl of carnelian filled with honey, and a bowl of lapis lazuli filled with butter. These he exposed and offered to the Sun; and weeping he went away.

4
The Search for Everlasting Life

Bitterly Gilgamesh wept for his friend Enkidu; he wandered over the wilderness as a hunter, he roamed over the plains; in his bitterness he cried, 'How can I rest, how can I be at peace? Despair is in my heart. What my brother is now, that shall I be when I am dead. Because I am afraid of death I will go as best I can to find Utnapishtim[21] whom they call the Faraway, for he has entered the assembly of the gods.' So Gilgamesh travelled over the wilderness, he wandered over the grasslands, a long journey, in search of Utnapishtim, whom the gods took after the deluge; and they set him to live in the land of Dilmun, in the garden of the sun; and to him alone of men they gave everlasting life.

At night when he came to the mountain passes Gilgamesh prayed: 'In these mountain passes long ago I saw lions, I was afraid and I lifted my eyes to the moon; I prayed and my prayers went up to the gods, so now, O moon god Sin, protect me.' When he had prayed he lay down to sleep, until he was woken from out of a dream. He saw the lions round him glorying in life; then he took his axe in his hand, he drew his sword from his belt, and he fell upon them like an arrow from the string, and struck and destroyed and scattered them.

So at length Gilgamesh came to Mashu, the great mountains about which he had heard many things, which guard the rising and the setting sun. Its twin peaks are as high as the wall of heaven and its paps reach down to the underworld. At its gate the Scorpions stand guard, half man and half dragon; their glory is terrifying, their stare strikes death into men, their shimmering halo sweeps the mountains that guard the rising sun. When Gilgamesh saw them he shielded his eyes for the length of a moment only; then he took courage and approached. When they saw him so undismayed the Man-Scorpion called to his mate, 'This one who comes to us now is flesh of the gods.' The mate of the Man-Scorpion answered, 'Two thirds is god but one third is man.'

Then he called to the man Gilgamesh, he called to the child of the gods: 'Why have you come so great a journey; for what have you travelled so far, crossing the dangerous waters; tell me the reason for your coming?' Gilgamesh answered, 'For Enkidu; I loved him dearly, together we endured all kinds of hardships; on his account I have come, for the common lot of man has taken him. I have wept for him day and night, I would not give up his body for burial, I thought my friend would come back because of my weeping. Since he went, my life is nothing; that is why I have travelled here in search of Utnapishtim my father; for men say he

[21] A wise king and priest of Shurrupak who survived the primordial flood and was taken by the gods to live in Dilmun, the Sumerian garden paradise. He is similar to the biblical Noah.

has entered the assembly of the gods, and has found everlasting life. I have a desire to question him concerning the living and the dead.' The Man-Scorpion opened his mouth and said, speaking to Gilgamesh, 'No man born of woman has done what you have asked, no mortal man has gone into the mountain; the length of it is twelve leagues of darkness; in it there is no light, but the heart is oppressed with darkness. From the rising of the sun to the setting of the sun there is no light.' Gilgamesh said, 'Although I should go in sorrow and in pain, with sighing and with weeping, still I must go. Open the gate of the mountain.' And the Man-Scorpion said, 'Go, Gilgamesh, I permit you to pass through the mountain of Mashu and through the high ranges; may your feet carry you safely home. The gate of the mountain is open.'

When Gilgamesh heard this he did as the Man-Scorpion had said, he followed the sun's road to his rising, through the mountain. When he had gone one league the darkness became thick around him, for there was no light, he could see nothing ahead and nothing behind him. After two leagues the darkness was thick and there was no light, he could see nothing ahead and nothing behind him. After three leagues the darkness was thick, and there was no light, he could see nothing ahead and nothing behind him. After four leagues the darkness was thick and there was no light, he could see nothing ahead and nothing behind him. At the end of five leagues the darkness was thick and there was no light, he could see nothing ahead and nothing behind him. At the end of six leagues the darkness was thick and there was no light, he could see nothing ahead and nothing behind him. When he had gone seven leagues the darkness was thick and there was no light, he could see nothing ahead and nothing behind him. When he had gone eight leagues Gilgamesh gave a great cry, for the darkness was thick and he could see nothing ahead and nothing behind him. After nine leagues he felt the north wind on his face, but the darkness was thick and there was no light, he could see nothing ahead and nothing behind him. After ten leagues the end was near. After eleven leagues the dawn light appeared. At the end of twelve leagues the sun streamed out.

There was the garden of the gods; all round him stood bushes bearing gems. Seeing it he went down at once, for there was fruit of carnelian with the vine hanging from it, beautiful to look at; lapis lazuli leaves hung thick with fruit, sweet to see. For thorns and thistles there were haematite and rare stones, agate, and pearls from out of the sea. While Gilgamesh walked in the garden by the edge of the sea Shamash saw him, and he saw that he was dressed in the skins of animals and ate their flesh. He was distressed, and he spoke and said, 'No mortal man has gone this way before, nor will, as long as the winds drive over the sea.' And to Gilgamesh he said, 'You will never find the life for which you are searching.' Gilgamesh said to glorious Shamash, 'Now that I have toiled and strayed so far over the wilderness, am I to sleep, and let the earth cover my head for ever? Let my eyes see the sun until they are dazzled with looking. Although I am no better than a dead man, still let me see the light of the sun.'

Beside the sea she lives, the woman of the vine, the maker of wine; Siduri[22] sits in the garden at the edge of the sea, with the golden bowl and the golden vats that the gods gave her. She is covered with a veil; and where she sits she sees Gilgamesh coming towards her, wearing skins, the flesh of the gods in his body, but despair in his heart, and his face like the face of one who has made a long journey. She looked, and as she scanned the distance she said in her own heart, 'Surely this is some felon; where is he going now?' And she barred her gate against him with the cross-bar

[22] A divine wine-maker who has advice for Gilgamesh.

and shot home the bolt. But Gilgamesh, hearing the sound of the bolt, threw up his head and lodged his foot in the gate; he called to her, 'Young woman, maker of wine, why do you bolt your door; what did you see that made you bar your gate? I will break in your door and burst in your gate, for I am Gilgamesh who seized and killed the Bull of Heaven, I killed the watchman of the cedar forest, I overthrew Humbaba who lived in the forest, and I killed the lions in the passes of the mountain.'

Then Siduri said to him, 'If you are that Gilgamesh who seized and killed the Bull of Heaven, who killed the watchman of the cedar forest, who overthrew Humbaba that lived in the forest, and killed the lions in the passes of the mountain, why are your cheeks so starved and why is your face so drawn? Why is despair in your heart and your face like the face of one who has made a long journey? Yes, why is your face burned from heat and cold, and why do you come here wandering over the pastures in search of the wind?'

Gilgamesh answered her, 'And why should not my cheeks be starved and my face drawn? Despair is in my heart and my face is the face of one who has made a long journey, it was burned with heat and with cold. Why should I not wander over the pastures in search of the wind? My friend, my younger brother, he who hunted the wild ass of the wilderness and the panther of the plains, my friend, my younger brother who seized and killed the Bull of Heaven and overthrew Humbaba in the cedar forest, my friend who was very dear to me and who endured dangers beside me, Enkidu my brother, whom I loved, the end of mortality has overtaken him. I wept for him seven days and nights till the worm fastened on him. Because of my brother I am afraid of death, because of my brother I stray through the wilderness and cannot rest. But now, young woman, maker of wine, since I have seen your face do not let me see the face of death which I dread so much.'

She answered, 'Gilgamesh, where are you hurrying to? You will never find that life for which you are looking. When the gods created man they allotted to him death, but life they retained in their own keeping. As for you, Gilgamesh, fill your belly with good things; day and night, night and day, dance and be merry, feast and rejoice. Let your clothes be fresh, bathe yourself in water, cherish the little child that holds your hand, and make your wife happy in your embrace; for this too is the lot of man.'

But Gilgamesh said to Siduri, the young woman, 'How can I be silent, how can I rest, when Enkidu whom I love is dust, and I too shall die and be laid in the earth. You live by the sea-shore and look into the heart of it; young woman, tell me now, which is the way to Utnapishtim, the son of Ubara-Tutu? What directions are there for the passage; give me, oh, give me directions. I will cross the Ocean if it is possible; if it is not I will wander still farther in the wilderness.' The wine-maker said to him, 'Gilgamesh, there is no crossing the Ocean; whoever has come, since the days of old, has not been able to pass that sea. The Sun in his glory crosses the Ocean, but who beside Shamash has ever crossed it? The place and the passage are difficult, and the waters of death are deep which flow between. Gilgamesh, how will you cross the Ocean? When you come to the waters of death what will you do? But Gilgamesh, down in the woods you will find Urshanabi,[23] the ferryman of Utnapishtim; with him are the holy things, the things of stone. He is fashioning the serpent prow of the boat. Look at him well, and if it is possible, perhaps you will cross the waters with him; but if it is not possible, then you must go back.'

---

[23] A boatman comparable to the Greek Charon.

When Gilgamesh heard this he was seized with anger. He took his axe in his hand, and his dagger from his belt. He crept forward and he fell on them like a javelin. Then he went into the forest and sat down. Urshanabi saw the dagger flash and heard the axe, and he beat his head, for Gilgamesh had shattered the tackle of the boat in his rage. Urshanabi said to him, 'Tell me, what is your name? I am Urshanabi, the ferryman of Utnapishtim the Faraway.' He replied to him, 'Gilgamesh is my name, I am from Uruk, from the house of Anu.' Then Urshanabi said to him, 'Why are your cheeks so starved and your face drawn? Why is despair in your heart and your face like the face of one who has made a long journey; yes, why is your face burned with heat and with cold, and why do you come here wandering over the pastures in search of the wind?'

Gilgamesh said to him, 'Why should not my cheeks be starved and my face drawn? Despair is in my heart, and my face is the face of one who has made a long journey. I was burned with heat and with cold. Why should I not wander over the pastures? My friend, my younger brother who seized and killed the Bull of Heaven, and overthrew Humbaba in the cedar forest, my friend who was very dear to me, and who endured dangers beside me, Enkidu my brother whom I loved, the end of mortality has overtaken him. I wept for him seven days and nights till the worm fastened on him. Because of my brother I am afraid of death, because of my brother I stray through the wilderness. His fate lies heavy upon me. How can I be silent, how can I rest? He is dust and I too shall die and be laid in the earth for ever. I am afraid of death, therefore, Urshanabi, tell me which is the road to Utnapishtim? If it is possible I will cross the waters of death; if not I will wander still farther through the wilderness.'

Urshanabi said to him, 'Gilgamesh, your own hands have prevented you from crossing the Ocean; when you destroyed the tackle of the boat you destroyed its safety.' Then the two of them talked it over and Gilgamesh said, 'Why are you so angry with me, Urshanabi, for you yourself cross the sea by day and night, at all seasons you cross it.' 'Gilgamesh, those things you destroyed, their property is to carry me over the water, to prevent the waters of death from touching me. It was for this reason that I preserved them, but you have destroyed them, and the *urnu* snakes with them. But now, go into the forest, Gilgamesh; with your axe cut poles, one hundred and twenty, cut them sixty cubits long, paint them with bitumen, set on them ferrules and bring them back.'

When Gilgamesh heard this he went into the forest, he cut poles one hundred and twenty; he cut them sixty cubits long, he painted them with bitumen, he set on them ferrules, and he brought them to Urshanabi. Then they boarded the boat, Gilgamesh and Urshanabi together, launching it out on the waves of Ocean. For three days they ran on as it were a journey of a month and fifteen days, and at last Urshanabi brought the boat to the waters of death. Then Urshanabi said to Gilgamesh, 'Press on, take a pole and thrust it in, but do not let your hands touch the waters. Gilgamesh, take a second pole, take a third, take a fourth pole. Now, Gilgamesh, take a fifth, take a sixth and seventh pole. Gilgamesh, take an eighth, and ninth, a tenth pole. Gilgamesh, take an eleventh, take a twelfth pole.' After one hundred and twenty thrusts Gilgamesh had used the last pole. Then he stripped himself, he held up his arms for a mast and his covering for a sail. So Urshanabi the ferryman brought Gilgamesh to Utnapishtim, whom they call the Faraway, who lives in Dilmun at the place of the sun's transit, eastward of the mountain. To him alone of men the gods had given everlasting life.

Now Utnapishtim, where he lay at ease, looked into the distance and he said in his heart, musing to himself, 'Why does the boat sail here without tackle and mast; why are the sacred stones destroyed, and why does the master not sail the boat?

That man who comes is none of mine; where I look I see a man whose body is covered with skins of beasts. Who is this who walks up the shore behind Urshanabi, for surely he is no man of mine?' So Utnapishtim looked at him and said, 'What is your name, you who come here wearing the skins of beasts, with your cheeks starved and your face drawn? Where are you hurrying to now? For what reason have you made this great journey, crossing the seas whose passage is difficult? Tell me the reason for your coming.'

He replied, 'Gilgamesh is my name. I am from Uruk, from the house of Anu.' Then Utnapishtim said to him, 'If you are Gilgamesh, why are your cheeks so starved and your face drawn? Why is despair in your heart and your face like the face of one who has made a long journey? Yes, why is your face burned with heat and cold; and why do you come here, wandering over the wilderness in search of the wind?'

Gilgamesh said to him, 'Why should not my cheeks be starved and my face drawn? Despair is in my heart and my face is the face of one who has made a long journey. It was burned with heat and with cold. Why should I not wander over the pastures? My friend, my younger brother who seized and killed the Bull of Heaven and overthrew Humbaba in the cedar forest, my friend who was very dear to me and endured dangers beside me, Enkidu, my brother whom I loved, the end of mortality has overtaken him. I wept for him seven days and nights till the worm fastened on him. Because of my brother I am afraid of death; because of my brother I stray through the wilderness. His fate lies heavy upon me. How can I be silent, how can I rest? He is dust and I shall die also and be laid in the earth for ever.' Again Gilgamesh said, speaking to Utnapishtim, 'It is to see Utnapishtim whom we call the Faraway that I have come this journey. For this I have wandered over the world, I have crossed many difficult ranges, I have crossed the seas, I have wearied myself with travelling; my joints are aching, and I have lost acquaintance with sleep which is sweet. My clothes were worn out before I came to the house of Siduri. I have killed the bear and hyena, the lion and panther, the tiger, the stag and the ibex, all sorts of wild game and the small creatures of the pastures. I ate their flesh and I wore their skins; and that was how I came to the gate of the young woman, the maker of wine, who barred her gate of pitch and bitumen against me. But from her I had news of the journey; so then I came to Urshanabi the ferryman, and with him I crossed over the waters of death. Oh, father Utnapishtim, you who have entered the assembly of the gods, I wish to question you concerning the living and the dead, how shall I find the life for which I am searching?'

Utnapishtim said, 'There is no permanence. Do we build a house to stand for ever, do we seal a contract to hold for all time? Do brothers divide an inheritance to keep for ever, does the flood-time of rivers endure? It is only the nymph of the dragon-fly who sheds her larva and sees the sun in his glory. From the days of old there is no permanence. The sleeping and the dead, how alike they are, they are like a painted death. What is there between the master and the servant when both have fulfilled their doom? When the Anunnaki, the judges, come together, and Mammetun the mother of destinies, together they decree the fates of men. Life and death they allot but the day of death they do not disclose.'

Then Gilgamesh said to Utnapishtim the Faraway, 'I look at you now, Utnapishtim, and your appearance is no different from mine; there is nothing strange in your features. I thought I should find you like a hero prepared for battle, but you lie here taking your ease on your back. Tell me truly, how was it that you came to enter the company of the gods and to possess everlasting life?' Utnapishtim said to Gilgamesh, 'I will reveal to you a mystery, I will tell you a secret of the gods.'

5
The Story of the Flood

'You know the city Shurrupak, it stands on the banks of Euphrates? That city grew old and the gods that were in it were old. There was Anu, lord of the firmament, their father, and warrior Enlil their counsellor, Ninurta the helper, and Ennugi watcher over canals; and with them also was Ea. In those days the world teemed, the people multiplied, the world bellowed like a wild bull, and the great god was aroused by the clamour. Enlil heard the clamour and he said to the gods in council, "The uproar of mankind is intolerable and sleep is no longer possible by reason of the babel." So the gods agreed to exterminate mankind. Enlil did this, but Ea because of his oath warned me in a dream. He whispered their words to my house of reeds, "Reed-house, reed-house! Wall, O wall, hearken reed-house, wall reflect; O man of Shurrupak, son of Ubara-Tutu; tear down your house and build a boat, abandon possessions and look for life, despise worldly goods and save your soul alive. Tear down your house, I say, and build a boat. These are the measurements of the barque as you shall build her: let her beam equal her length, let her deck be roofed like the vault that covers the abyss; then take up into the boat the seed of all living creatures."

'When I had understood I said to my lord, "Behold, what you have commanded I will honour and perform, but how shall I answer the people, the city, the elders?" Then Ea opened his mouth and said to me, his servant, "Tell them this: I have learnt that Enlil is wrathful against me, I dare no longer walk in his land nor live in his city; I will go down to the Gulf to dwell with Ea my lord. But on you he will rain down abundance, rare fish and shy wild-fowl, a rich harvest-tide. In the evening the rider of the storm will bring you wheat in torrents."

'In the first light of dawn all my household gathered round me, the children brought pitch and the men whatever was necessary. On the fifth day I laid the keel and the ribs, then I made fast the planking. The ground-space was one acre, each side of the deck measured one hundred and twenty cubits, making a square. I built six decks below, seven in all, I divided them into nine sections with bulk-heads between. I drove in wedges where needed, I saw to the punt-poles, and laid in supplies. The carriers brought oil in baskets, I poured pitch into the furnace and asphalt and oil; more oil was consumed in caulking, and more again the master of the boat took into his stores. I slaughtered bullocks for the people and every day I killed sheep. I gave the shipwrights wine to drink as though it were river water, raw wine and red wine and oil and white wine. There was feasting then as there is at the time of the New Year's festival; I myself anointed my head. On the seventh day the boat was complete.

'Then was the launching full of difficulty; there was shifting of ballast above and below till two thirds was submerged. I loaded into her all that I had of gold and of living things, my family, my kin, the beast of the field both wild and tame, and all the craftsmen. I sent them on board, for the time that Shamash had ordained was already fulfilled when he said, "In the evening, when the rider of the storm sends down the destroying rain, enter the boat and batten her down." The time was fulfilled, the evening came, the rider of the storm sent down the rain. I looked out at the weather and it was terrible, so I too boarded the boat and battened her down. All was now complete, the battening and the caulking; so I handed the tiller to Puzur-Amurri the steersman, with the navigation and the care of the whole boat.

'With the first light of dawn a black cloud came from the horizon; it thundered within where Adad, lord of the storm, was riding. In front over hill and plain Shullat and Hanish, heralds of the storm, led on. Then the gods of the abyss rose up; Nergal pulled out the dams of the nether waters, Ninurta the war-lord threw down the dykes, and the seven judges of hell, the Anunnaki, raised their torches, lighting the land with their livid flame. A stupor of despair went up to heaven when the god of the storm turned daylight to darkness, when he smashed the land like a cup. One whole day the tempest raged, gathering fury as it went, it poured over the people like the tides of battle; a man could not see his brother nor the people be seen from heaven. Even the gods were terrified at the flood, they fled to the highest heaven, the firmament of Anu; they crouched against the walls, cowering like curs. Then Ishtar the sweet-voiced Queen of Heaven cried out like a woman in travail: "Alas the days of old are turned to dust because I commanded evil; why did I command this evil in the council of all the gods? I commanded wars to destroy the people, but are they not my people, for I brought them forth? Now like the spawn of fish they float in the ocean." The great gods of heaven and of hell wept, they covered their mouths.

'For six days and six nights the winds blew, torrent and tempest and flood overwhelmed the world, tempest and flood raged together like warring hosts. When the seventh day dawned the storm from the south subsided, the sea grew calm, the flood was stilled; I looked at the face of the world and there was silence, all mankind was turned to clay. The surface of the sea stretched as flat as a roof-top; I opened a hatch and the light fell on my face. Then I bowed low, I sat down and I wept, the tears streamed down my face, for on every side was the waste of water. I looked for land in vain, but fourteen leagues distant there appeared a mountain, and there the boat grounded; on the mountain of Nisir the boat held fast, she held fast and did not budge. One day she held, and a second day on the mountain of Nisir she held fast and did not budge. A third day, and a fourth day she held fast on the mountain and did not budge; a fifth day and a sixth day she held fast on the mountain. When the seventh day dawned I loosed a dove and let her go. She flew away, but finding no resting-place she returned. Then I loosed a swallow, and she flew away but finding no resting-place she returned. I loosed a raven, she saw that the waters had retreated, she ate, she flew around, she cawed, and she did not come back. Then I threw everything open to the four winds, I made a sacrifice and poured out a libation on the mountain top. Seven and again seven cauldrons I set up on their stands, I heaped up wood and cane and cedar and myrtle. When the gods smelled the sweet savour, they gathered like flies over the sacrifice. Then, at last, Ishtar also came, she lifted her necklace with the jewels of heaven that once Anu had made to please her. "O you gods here present, by the lapis lazuli round my neck I shall remember these days as I remember the jewels of my throat; these last days I shall not forget. Let all the gods gather round the sacrifice, except Enlil. He shall not approach this offering, for without reflection he brought the flood; he consigned my people to destruction."

'When Enlil had come, when he saw the boat, he was wrath and swelled with anger at the gods, the host of heaven, "Has any of these mortals escaped? Not one was to have survived the destruction." Then the god of the wells and canals Ninurta opened his mouth and said to the warrior Enlil, "Who is there of the gods that can devise without Ea? It is Ea alone who knows all things." Then Ea opened his mouth and spoke to warrior Enlil, "Wisest of gods, hero Enlil, how could you so senselessly bring down the flood?

Lay upon the sinner his sin,
Lay upon the transgressor his transgression,
Punish him a little when he breaks loose,
Do not drive him too hard or he perishes;
Would that a lion had ravaged mankind

Rather than the flood,
Would that a wolf had ravaged mankind
Rather than the flood,
Would that famine had wasted the world
Rather than the flood,
Would that pestilence had wasted mankind
Rather than the flood.

It was not I that revealed the secret of the gods; the wise man learned it in a dream. Now take your counsel what shall be done with him."

'Then Enlil went up into the boat, he took me by the hand and my wife and made us enter the boat and kneel down on either side, he standing between us. He touched our foreheads to bless us saying, "In time past Utnapishtim was a mortal man; henceforth he and his wife shall live in the distance at the mouth of the rivers." Thus it was that the gods took me and placed me here to live in the distance, at the mouth of the rivers.'

6
THE RETURN

Utnapishtim said, 'As for you, Gilgamesh, who will assemble the gods for your sake, so that you may find that life for which you are searching? But if you wish, come and put it to the test: only prevail against sleep for six days and seven nights.' But while Gilgamesh sat there resting on his haunches, a mist of sleep like soft wool teased from the fleece drifted over him, and Utnapishtim said to his wife, 'Look at him now, the strong man who would have everlasting life, even now the mists of sleep are drifting over him.' His wife replied, 'Touch the man to wake him, so that he may return to his own land in peace, going back through the gate by which he came.' Utnapishtim said to his wife, 'All men are deceivers, even you he will attempt to deceive; therefore bake loaves of bread, each day one loaf, and put it beside his head; and make a mark on the wall to number the days he has slept.'

So she baked loaves of bread, each day one loaf, and put it beside his head, and she marked on the wall the days that he slept; and there came a day when the first loaf was hard, the second loaf was like leather, the third was soggy, the crust of the fourth had mould, the fifth was mildewed, the sixth was fresh, and the seventh was still on the embers. Then Utnapishtim touched him and he woke. Gilgamesh said to Utnapishtim the Faraway, 'I hardly slept when you touched and roused me.' But Utnapishtim said, 'Count these loaves and learn how many days you slept, for your first is hard, your second like leather, your third is soggy, the crust of your fourth has mould, your fifth is mildewed, your sixth is fresh and your seventh was still over the glowing embers when I touched and woke you.' Gilgamesh said, 'What shall I do, O Utnapishtim, where shall I go? Already the thief in the night has hold of my limbs, death inhabits my room; wherever my foot rests, there I find death.'

Then Utnapishtim spoke to Urshanabi the ferryman: 'Woe to you Urshanabi, now and for ever more you have become hateful to this harbourage; it is not for you, nor for you are the crossings of this sea. Go now, banished from the shore. But this man before whom you walked, bringing him here, whose body is covered with foulness and the grace of whose limbs has been spoiled by wild skins, take him to the washing-place. There he shall wash his long hair clean as snow in the water, he shall throw off his skins and let the sea carry them away, and the beauty of his body shall be shown, the fillet on his forehead shall be renewed, and he shall be given clothes to cover his nakedness. Till he reaches his own city and his journey is accomplished, these clothes will show no sign of age, they will wear like a new garment.' So Urshanabi took Gilgamesh and led him to the washing-place, he washed his long hair as clean as snow in the water, he threw off his skins, which the sea carried away, and showed the beauty of his body. He renewed the fillet on his forehead, and to cover his nakedness gave him clothes which would show no sign of age, but would wear like a new garment till he reached his own city, and his journey was accomplished.

Then Gilgamesh and Urshanabi launched the boat on to the water and boarded it, and they made ready to sail away; but the wife of Utnapishtim the Faraway said to him, 'Gilgamesh came here wearied out, he is worn out; what will you give him to carry him back to his own country?' So Utnapishtim spoke, and Gilgamesh took a pole and brought the boat in to the bank. 'Gilgamesh, you came here a man wearied out, you have worn yourself out; what shall I give you to carry you back to your own country? Gilgamesh, I shall reveal a secret thing, it is a mystery of the gods that I am telling you. There is a plant that grows under the water, it has a prickle like a thorn, like a rose; it will wound your hands, but if you succeed in taking it, then your hands will hold that which restores his lost youth to a man.'

When Gilgamesh heard this he opened the sluices so that a sweet-water current might carry him out to the deepest channel; he tied heavy stones to his feet and they dragged him down to the water-bed. There he saw the plant growing; although it pricked him he took it in his hands; then he cut the heavy stones from his feet, and the sea carried him and threw him on to the shore. Gilgamesh said to Urshanabi the ferryman, 'Come here, and see this marvellous plant. By its virtue a man may win back all his former strength. I will take it to Uruk of the strong walls; there I will give it to the old men to eat. Its name shall be "The Old Men Are Young Again"; and at last I shall eat it myself and have back all my lost youth.' So Gilgamesh returned by the gate through which he had come, Gilgamesh and Urshanabi went together. They travelled their twenty leagues and then they broke their fast; after thirty leagues they stopped for the night.

Gilgamesh saw a well of cool water and he went down and bathed; but deep in the pool there was lying a serpent, and the serpent sensed the sweetness of the flower. It rose out of the water and snatched it away, and immediately it sloughed its skin and returned to the well. Then Gilgamesh sat down and wept, the tears ran down his face, and he took the hand of Urshanabi; 'O Urshanabi, was it for this that I toiled with my hands, is it for this I have wrung out my heart's blood? For myself I have gained nothing; not I, but the beast of the earth has joy of it now. Already the stream has carried it twenty leagues back to the channels where I found it. I found a sign and now I have lost it. Let us leave the boat on the bank and go.'

After twenty leagues they broke their fast, after thirty leagues they stopped for the night; in three days they had walked as much as a journey of a month and fifteen days. When the journey was accomplished they arrived at Uruk, the strong-walled city. Gilgamesh spoke to him, to Urshanabi the ferryman, 'Urshanabi, climb up on to the wall of Uruk, inspect its foundation terrace, and examine well the brickwork; see if it is not of burnt bricks; and did not the seven wise men lay these foundations? One third of the whole is city, one third is garden, and one third is field, with the precinct of the goddess Ishtar. These parts and the precinct are all Uruk.'

This too was the work of Gilgamesh, the king, who knew the countries of the world. He was wise, he saw mysteries and knew secret things, he brought us a tale of the days before the flood. He went a long journey, was weary, worn out with labour, and returning engraved on a stone the whole story.

7
The Death of Gilgamesh

The destiny was fulfilled which the father of the gods, Enlil of the mountain, had decreed for Gilgamesh: 'In nether-earth the darkness will show him a light: of mankind, all that are known, none will leave a monument for generations to come to compare with his. The heroes, the wise men, like the new moon have their waxing and waning. Men will say, "Who has ever ruled with might and with power like him?" As in the dark month, the month of shadows, so without him there is no light. O Gilgamesh, this was the meaning of your dream. You were given the kingship, such was your destiny, everlasting life was not your destiny. Because of this do not be sad at heart, do not be grieved or oppressed; he has given you power to bind and to loose, to be the darkness and the light of mankind. He has given unexampled supremacy over the people, victory in battle from which no fugitive returns, in forays and assaults from which there is no going back. But do not abuse this power, deal justly with your servants in the palace, deal justly before the face of the Sun.'

The king has laid himself down and will not rise again,
The Lord of Kullab will not rise again;
He overcame evil, he will not come again;
Though he was strong of arm he will not rise again;

He had wisdom and a comely face, he will not come again;
He is gone into the mountain, he will not come again;
On the bed of fate he lies, he will not rise again,
From the couch of many colours he will not come again.

The people of the city, great and small, are not silent; they lift up the lament, all men of flesh and blood lift up the lament. Fate has spoken; like a hooked fish he lies stretched on the bed, like a gazelle that is caught in a noose. Inhuman Namtar is heavy upon him, Namtar that has neither hand nor foot, that drinks no water and eats no meat.

For Gilgamesh, son of Ninsun, they weighed out their offerings; his dear wife, his son, his concubine, his musicians, his jester, and all his household; his servants, his stewards, all who lived in the palace weighed out their offerings for Gilgamesh the son of Ninsun, the heart of Uruk. They weighed out their offerings to Ereshkigal, the Queen of Death, and to all the gods of the dead. To Namtar, who is fate, they weighed out the offering. Bread for Neti the Keeper of the Gate, bread for Ningizzida the god of the serpent, the lord of the Tree of Life; for Dumuzi[24] also, the young shepherd, for Enki and Ninki, for Endukugga and Nindukugga,[25] for Enmul and Ninmul, all the ancestral gods, forbears of Enlil. A feast for Shulpae the god of feasting. For Samuqan, god of the herds, for the mother Ninhursag, and the gods of creation in the place of creation, for the host of heaven, priest and priestess weighed out the offering of the dead.

Gilgamesh, the son of Ninsun, lies in the tomb. At the place of offerings he weighed the bread-offering, at the place of libation he poured out the wine. In those days the lord Gilgamesh departed, the son of Ninsun, the king, peerless, without an equal among men, who did not neglect Enlil his master. O Gilgamesh, lord of Kullab, great is thy praise.

---

[24] The Sumerian version of Tammuz.
[25] Gods of the underworld.

THE TAOISTS

[7TH OR 5TH CENTURY B.C.E.–4TH CENTURY B.C.E]

According to one legend, Lao Tzu, the founder of Taoism, was an older contemporary of Confucius (551–479 B.C.E.). The two men constructed two very different schools of thought during a period of history when feudalism was decaying and the commoner was emerging. The ideas of Confucius and Lao Tzu were almost totally opposite to one another. Confucius' ideas are generally approachable by Western readers, with his emphasis on respecting a hierarchy of loyalties, deliberately living according to prescribed ethical standards, and transforming society through political action. Lao Tzu is less accessible with his individual, subjective truth, his doctrine of inaction, and a life lived in harmony with the Tao ("the Way"). Ssu-ma Ch'ien (c. 145–89 B.C.E.), in his *Historical Records,* tells about a visit that Confucius made to Lao Tzu in order to inquire about the rules of propriety. Lao Tzu told Confucius to get rid of his pride and his desires. Confucius reported back to his pupils: "I know birds can fly, fish can swim, and animals can run. That which runs can be trapped, that which swims can be netted, and that which flies can be shot. As to the dragon, I don't know how it rides on the winds and clouds and ascends to heaven. Lao Tzu, whom I saw today, is indeed like a dragon."

Some scholars believe that Taoism arose in the fifth century B.C.E. as a response to the dominant role of Confucian philosophy and politics in China and a desire to return to an earlier period of Chinese history when life was simpler and people lived closer to nature. The history of Taoism becomes further complicated in the second century C.E. when a split occurred between philosophical Taoism, which is rational, contemplative, and nonsectarian, and religious Taoism, which is cultic and uses alchemy to achieve immortality. The sampling of texts below comes from the philosophical Taoism associated with Lao Tzu and Chuang Tzu, a tradition that profoundly altered the consciousness of ancient China and has attracted millions of followers around the globe.

LAO TZU

Very few details are known with certainty about Lao Tzu's life. Nothing is known about his parents, his childhood, or his education. There is no agreement about whether Lao Tzu (literally, "the old philosopher") lived in the seventh or the fifth century B.C.E. One legend states that he was immaculately conceived and another legend that he was born already an old man with white hair and beard. It was thought that for most of his life he lived a secluded life as an ordinary bookkeeper of the imperial archives in the province of Honan. The most famous incident of his life occurs near the end of it. Ssu-ma Ch'ien in his *Historical Records* summarizes his career:

> Lao Tzu practiced the Way and its Virtue. He learned to do his work in self-effacement and anonymity. For a long time he lived in Chou, and when he saw that it was breaking up, he left [riding a water buffalo]. At the frontier, the official Yin Hsi said: "Since, sir, you are retiring, I urge you to write me a book." So Lao Tzu wrote a book in two parts, explaining the Way and its Virtue in something over five thousand words. Then he went away. No one knows where he died.

The book is the *Tao Te Ching.*

One of the difficulties of dealing with the poems in the *Tao Te Ching* is that the book does not make allowances for foreigners or beginners by starting with simple explanations or definitions and then gradually progressing to the complex conclusions; it does not begin with the creation of the world as in the Old Testament or with heroic biography as in the

New Testament—both of which provide places of orientation for later teachings. The *Tao Te Ching* begins with what seems to be a series of conclusions about the *Tao,* a word for which we have no English equivalent. Nor do we have a clear concept for the *Tao.*

The Chinese written character for *tao* is a combination of two characters, one for "head" and the other for "going." The two together have been translated as the "conscious path," "the way," "the flow," or even "God." The second word in the title, *te,* means "virtue" and the third, *ching,* means "classic" or "text." Altogether the title is something like *The Classic of the Way and Its Virtue,* or simply *The Way of Life.* The first two lines of the very first poem in the book have been translated in our version as "Existence is beyond the power of words / To define." A literal translation would be, "Tao can tao not eternal Tao," or "Way can speak-about not eternal Way." Here are a few other versions:

> The Way that can be described is not the eternal Way.
>
> The Flow that can be followed is not the real Flow.
>
> God (the great everlasting infinite First Cause from whom all things in heaven and earth proceed) can neither be defined nor named.
>
> There are ways but the Way is uncharted.

The complexity of Taoism's central tenet is not a deliberate attempt to mystify and confuse the reader, but a recognition of the nature of consciousness and our attempts to reduce reality to words and definitions in order to conceptualize and then to categorize them. Despite the fact that wars have been fought over the "correct" name of God, language is a distinctly human construct that can only approximate or point to the ultimate, ineffable reality.

Lao Tzu's first poem concludes with, "From wonder into wonder / Existence opens." This kind of writing fits into the category of proverbs or aphorisms, kernels of truth meant for meditation and contemplation. Pithy sayings were used in the wisdom tradition of the Middle East and were characteristic of the way that Jesus often spoke. Although the truths of Taoism are stated simply, their meanings tend to be personal and subjective. This kind of speaking or writing is not necessarily meant to be easily understood the first time one hears or reads it. Most of Lao Tzu's poems demand repeated readings; furthermore, the meanings change as one's circumstances change, or as one grows older and gains more experience. Explaining Lao Tzu's poems to others can be difficult.

One way to approach the idea of the *Tao* is to imagine that the world is one great, interrelated system, that all the parts fit together harmoniously, and that this whole system is moving through time, simply flowing along like a vast river, just about the way it should be, with overall purpose and meaning. We might call this flow "the natural way," and then Lao Tzu advises us:

> Those who flow as life flows know
> They need no other force:
> They feel no wear, they feel no tear,
> They need no mending, no repair. (#15)

It is obvious from this use of metaphors that the Taoists thought of water as providing a close analogy to the Tao. Water has tremendous power to support objects and carry them along, and with a strong current one learns not to thrash about or go upstream, but to swim with the flow and to adjust one's own movements according to the nature of the current. The only thing a person must do to be happy is to go along with this grand movement or flow, to let the flow in and out. The Chinese character for a swimmer means "one who knows the nature of water."

The ancient Chinese described the two poles of this natural rhythm, the ebb and flow, as *yin* and *yang*: *Yin* is associated with darkness and enclosure, withdrawal and winter; *yang* is associated with light and openness, expansiveness and summer. At times *yin* is linked to the feminine and *yang* to the masculine, but the use of these terms can be deceiving, since in no way are they tied to gender or sex. *Yin* and *yang* are simply metaphors for describing a changing, reciprocal flow from one side to another, just as the day flows from light to dark and back again, and the seasons flow from life to death and back again. It is important to remember that *yin* and *yang* are not irreconcilable opposites, in the sense that Christians use the terms "good" and "evil" as labels for making either-or distinctions about people or things. Taoism recognizes the necessity of embracing both poles of the rhythm, both the light and the dark, both the external and the internal. It is essentially a question of merging with the rhythm that is at the heart of the universe, as if life were a dance.

It seems so simple, but why then does there appear to be such disharmony and unhappiness around us? The early Taoist philosophers suggested that we get into trouble when we actively try to control our lives by making arbitrary choices and dominating our surroundings, instead of going with the flow. Because human consciousness perceives only a small portion, a fragment of the whole, we do not see how everything is connected and meaningful. People attempt to make adjustments in the world system without understanding it. When we step outside the natural flow of nature and attempt to manipulate and construct a better system, we interject conflicting systems of values, and ultimately confusion and disorder. The ancient Taoists prized the state of *wu wei,* which literally means "inaction," but seems to suggest a way of doing without egotistical effort or motives of gain—don't force it, take it easy.

Instead of modeling their lives after symbols of strength and hierarchy—the warrior, the mountain, the spear, the blacksmith, the king—the founders of Taoism valued images that are supple and illustrate participating or assimilating: images such as water, infant, female, valley, dancing, swimming.

> Man, born tender and yielding,
> Stiffens and hardens in death.
> All living growth is pliant,
> Until death transfixes it. (#76)

CHUANG TZU

According to Ssu-ma Ch'ien (*Historical Records*), Chuang Tzu was a native of Meng, served as an official in the lacquer garden, and lived at the same time as King Hui (370–319 B.C.E.) of Liang. Very little is known about Chuang Tzu's life, but there is no doubt about the enormous influence of his writings. He wrote a book in 100,000 words, mostly in the form of fables and anecdotes, parables and aphorisms, which his editors divided into thirty-three sections.

Chuang Tzu's emphasis is more mystical than Lao Tzu's in the sense that the object of his writings seems to be to free his readers from all the stuff that keeps them from merging with the grand scheme of nature. By changing consciousness, Chuang Tzu expects to change lives. He tells a story of a man who visits Lao Tzu for answers to his life. When Lao Tzu asks him why he brought a crowd of people along with him, the man turns around and literally sees no one behind him. The implication is that we carry tremendous amounts of psychological baggage with us: old ideas, training, advice, guilt, shame—almost as if we were literally carrying parents, teachers, priests on our backs, or just behind us in a long procession. It is this burden of stuff that we must leave behind in order to be free.

In order to entice us into a freer state, Chuang Tzu uses humor, illogical perceptions, debates, and incisive metaphors. Chuang Tzu's swimmer explains that he is able to stay afloat because of his nature, not because of some special technique. An entirely different analogy is provided by the butcher who does not hack at the ox carcass but finds "the spaces between the joints" for cutting up the ox and preserving the edge on his knives. As in the story about the swimmer, the butcher's technique has a literal meaning, but it also symbolizes how one might live, sliding between life's joints rather than hacking at them. The Taoist philosophy meets a critical test with the death of Chuang Tzu's wife; when one might expect grief and protestations about fate, Chuang Tzu responds with both honesty and clarity. "The Death of Lao Tan" contains similar insights.

Suggested Readings

Readable, concise introductions to Taoism can be found in Huston Smith, *The Religions of Man* (1958), Joseph Gaer, *What the Great Religions Believe* (1963), and Arthur Waley, *Three Ways of Thought in Ancient China* (1939). A fine introduction to Lao Tzu is in Wing-tsit Chan, ed., *The Way of Lao Tzu* (1963); an introduction to Chuang Tzu is provided by Herbert Giles, *Chuang Tzu: Taoist Philosopher and Chinese Mystic* (1961).

LAO TZU

[7th or 5th century B.C.E.]

Tao Te Ching

Translated by Witter Bynner

1: "Existence is beyond the power of words"

Existence is beyond the power of words
To define:
Terms may be used
But are none of them absolute.
In the beginning of heaven and earth there were no words,
Words came out of the womb of matter;
And whether a man dispassionately
Sees to the core of life
Or passionately
Sees the surface,
The core and the surface
Are essentially the same,
Words making them seem different
Only to express appearance.
If name be needed, wonder names them both:
From wonder into wonder
Existence opens.

15: "Long ago the land was ruled with a wisdom"

Long ago the land was ruled with a wisdom
Too fine, too deep, to be fully understood
And, since it was beyond men's full understanding,
Only some of it has come down to us, as in these sayings:
'Alert as a winter-farer on an icy stream,'
'Wary as a man in ambush,'
'Considerate as a welcome guest,'
'Selfless as melting ice,'
'Green as an uncut tree,'
'Open as a valley,'
And this one also, 'Roiled as a torrent.'
Why roiled as a torrent?
Because when a man is in turmoil how shall he find peace
Save by staying patient till the stream clears?
How can a man's life keep its course
If he will not let it flow?
Those who flow as life flows know
They need no other force:
They feel no wear, they feel no tear,
They need no mending, no repair.

16: "Be utterly humble"

Be utterly humble
And you shall hold to the foundation of peace.
Be at one with all these living things which, having arisen and flourished,
Return to the quiet whence they came,
Like a healthy growth of vegetation
Falling back upon the root.
Acceptance of this return to the root has been called 'quietism,'
Acceptance of quietism has been condemned as 'fatalism.'
But fatalism is acceptance of destiny
And to accept destiny is to face life with open eyes,
Whereas not to accept destiny is to face death blindfold.
He who is open-eyed is open-minded,
He who is open-minded is open-hearted,
He who is open-hearted is kingly,
He who is kingly is godly,
He who is godly is useful,
He who is useful is infinite,
He who is infinite is immune,
He who is immune is immortal.

19: "Rid of formalized wisdom and learning"

Rid of formalized wisdom and learning
People would be a hundredfold happier,
Rid of conventionalized duty and honor

People would find their families dear,
Rid of legalized profiteering
People would have no thieves to fear.
These methods of life have failed, all three,
Here is the way, it seems to me:
Set people free,
As deep in their hearts they would like to be,
From private greeds
And wanton needs.

20: "Leave off fine learning!"

Leave off fine learning! End the nuisance
Of saying yes to this and perhaps to that,
Distinctions with how little difference!
Categorical this, categorical that,
What slightest use are they!
If one man leads, another must follow,
How silly that is and how false!
Yet conventional men lead an easy life
With all their days feast-days,
A constant spring visit to the Tall Tower,
While I am a simpleton, a do-nothing,
Not big enough yet to raise a hand,
Not grown enough to smile,
A homeless, worthless waif.
Men of the world have a surplus of goods,
While I am left out, owning nothing.
What a booby I must be
Not to know my way round,
What a fool!
The average man is so crisp and so confident
That I ought to be miserable
Going on and on like the sea,
Drifting nowhere.
All these people are making their mark in the world,
While I, pig-headed, awkward,
Different from the rest,
Am only a glorious infant still nursing at the breast.

28: "One who has a man's wings"

'One who has a man's wings
And a woman's also
Is in himself a womb of the world'
And, being a womb of the world,
Continuously, endlessly,
Gives birth;
One who, preferring light,
Prefers darkness also

Is in himself an image of the world
And, being an image of the world,
Is continuously, endlessly
The dwelling of creation;
One who is highest of men
And humblest also
Is in himself a valley of the world,
And, being a valley of the world,
Continuously, endlessly
Conducts the one source
From which vessels may be usefully filled;
Servants of the state are such vessels,
To be filled from undiminishing supply.

29: "Those who would take over the earth"

Those who would take over the earth
And shape it to their will
Never, I notice, succeed.
The earth is like a vessel so sacred
That at the mere approach of the profane
It is marred
And when they reach out their fingers it is gone.
For a time in the world some force themselves ahead
And some are left behind,
For a time in the world some make a great noise
And some are held silent,
For a time in the world some are puffed fat
And some are kept hungry,
For a time in the world some push aboard
And some are tipped out:
At no time in the world will a man who is sane
Over-reach himself,
Over-spend himself,
Over-rate himself.

36: "He who feels punctured"

He who feels punctured
Must once have been a bubble,
He who feels unarmed
Must have carried arms,
He who feels belittled
Must have been consequential,
He who feels deprived
Must have had privilege,
Whereas a man with insight
Knows that to keep under is to endure.

What happens to a fish pulled out of a pond?
Or to an implement of state pulled out of a scabbard?
Unseen, they survive.

42: "Life, when it came to be"

Life, when it came to be,
Bore one, then two, then three
Elements of things;
And thus the three began
—Heaven and earth and man—
To balance happenings:
Cool night behind, warm day ahead,
For the living, for the dead.
Though a commoner be loth to say
That he is only common clay,
Kings and princes often state
How humbly they are leading,
Because in true succeeding
High and low correlate.
It is an ancient thought,
Which many men have taught,
That he who over-reaches
And tries to live by force
Shall die thereby of course,
And is what my own heart teaches.

43: "As the soft yield of water cleaves obstinate stone"

As the soft yield of water cleaves obstinate stone,
So to yield with life solves the insoluble:
To yield, I have learned, is to come back again.
But this unworded lesson,
This easy example,
Is lost upon men.

47: "There is no need to run outside"

There is no need to run outside
For better seeing,
Nor to peer from a window. Rather abide
At the center of your being;
For the more you leave it, the less you learn.
Search your heart and see
If he is wise who takes each turn:
The way to do is to be.

74: "Death is no threat to people"

Death is no threat to people
Who are not afraid to die;
But even if these offenders feared death all day,
Who should be rash enough
To act as executioner?
Nature is executioner.
When man usurps the place,
A carpenter's apprentice takes the place of the master:
And 'an apprentice hacking with the master's axe
May slice his own hand.'

81: "Real words are not vain"

Real words are not vain,
Vain words not real;
And since those who argue prove nothing
A sensible man does not argue.
A sensible man is wiser than he knows,
While a fool knows more than is wise.
Therefore a sensible man does not devise resources:
The greater his use to others
The greater their use to him,
The more he yields to others
The more they yield to him.
The way of life cleaves without cutting:
Which, without need to say,
Should be man's way.

CHUANG TZU

[4th century b.c.e.]

from

The Writings of Chuang Tzu

Translated by Burton Watson

[Gamecocks]

Chi Hsing-tzu was training gamecocks for the king. After ten days the king asked if they were ready.

"Not yet. They're too haughty and rely on their nerve."

Another ten days and the king asked again.

"Not yet. They still respond to noises and movements."

Another ten days and the king asked again.

"Not yet. They still look around fiercely and are full of spirit."

Another ten days and the king asked again.

"They're close enough. Another cock can crow and they show no sign of change. Look at them from a distance and you'd think they were made of wood. Their virtue is complete. Other cocks won't dare face up to them, but will turn and run."

[The Ailanthus Tree]

Hui Tzu said to Chuang Tzu, "I have a big tree named ailanthus. Its trunk is too gnarled and bumpy to apply a measuring line to, its branches too bent and twisty to match up to a compass or square. You could stand it by the road and no carpenter would look at it twice. Your words, too, are big and useless, and so everyone alike spurns them!"

Chuang Tzu said, "Maybe you've never seen a wildcat or a weasel. It crouches down and hides, watching for something to come along. It leaps and races east and west, not hesitating to go high or low—until it falls into the trap and dies in the net. Then again there's the yak, big as a cloud covering the sky. It certainly knows how to be big, though it doesn't know how to catch rats. Now you have this big tree and you're distressed because it's useless. Why don't you plant it in Not-Even-Anything Village, or the field of Broad-and-Boundless, relax and do nothing by its side, or lie down for a free and easy sleep under it? Axes will never shorten its life, nothing can ever harm it. If there's no use for it, how can it come to grief or pain?"

[Transformations]

Master Ssu, Master Yü, Master Li, and Master Lai were all four talking together. "Who can look upon inaction as his head, on life as his back, and on death as his rump?" they said. "Who knows that life and death, existence and annihilation, are all a single body? I will be his friend!"

The four men looked at each other and smiled. There was no disagreement in their hearts and so the four of them became friends.

All at once Master Yü fell ill. Master Ssu went to ask how he was. "Amazing!" said Master Yü. "The Creator is making me all crookedy like this! My back sticks up like a hunchback and my vital organs are on top of me. My chin is hidden in my navel, my shoulders are up above my head, and my pigtail points at the sky. It must be some dislocation of the yin and yang!"

Yet he seemed calm at heart and unconcerned. Dragging himself haltingly to the well, he looked at his reflection and said, "My, my! So the Creator is making me all crookedy like this!"

"Do you resent it?" asked Master Ssu.

"Why no, what would I resent? If the process continues, perhaps in time he'll transform my left arm into a rooster. In that case I'll keep watch on the night. Or perhaps in time he'll transform my right arm into a crossbow pellet and I'll shoot down an owl for roasting. Or perhaps in time he'll transform my buttocks into cartwheels. Then, with my spirit for a horse, I'll climb up and go for a ride. What need will I ever have for a carriage again?

"I received life because the time had come; I will lose it because the order of things passes on. Be content with this time and dwell in this order and then neither sorrow nor joy can touch you. In ancient times this was called the 'freeing of the bound.' There are those who cannot free themselves, because they are bound by things. But nothing can ever win against Heaven—that's the way it's always been. What would I have to resent?"

Suddenly Master Lai grew ill. Gasping and wheezing, he lay at the point of death. His wife and children gathered round in a circle and began to cry. Master Li, who had come to ask how he was, said, "Shoo! Get back! Don't disturb the process of change!"

Then he leaned against the doorway and talked to Master Lai. "How marvelous the Creator is! What is he going to make out of you next? Where is he going to send you? Will he make you into a rat's liver? Will he make you into a bug's arm?"

Master Lai said, "A child, obeying his father and mother, goes wherever he is told, east or west, south or north. And the yin and yang—how much more are they to a man than father or mother! Now that they have brought me to the verge of death, if I should refuse to obey them, how perverse I would be! What fault is it of theirs? The Great Clod burdens me with form, labors me with life, eases me in old age, and rests me in death. So if I think well of my life, for the same reason I must think well of my death. When a skilled smith is casting metal, if the metal should leap up and say, 'I insist upon being made into a Mo-yeh!' he would surely regard it as very inauspicious metal indeed. Now, having had the audacity to take on human form once, if I should say, 'I don't want to be anything but a man! Nothing but a man!', the Creator would surely regard me as a most inauspicious sort of person. So now I think of heaven and earth as a great furnace, and the Creator as a skilled smith. Where could he send me that would not be all right? I will go off to sleep peacefully, and then with a start I will wake up."

[Walking Two Roads]

What is acceptable we call acceptable; what is unacceptable we call unacceptable. A road is made by people walking on it; things are so because they are called so. What makes them so? Making them so makes them so. What makes them not so? Making them not so makes them not so. Things all must have that which is so; things all must have that which is acceptable. There is nothing that is not so, nothing that is not acceptable.

For this reason, whether you point to a little stalk or a great pillar, a leper or the beautiful Hsi-shih, things ribald and shady or things grotesque and strange, the Way makes them all into one. Their dividedness is their completeness; their completeness is their impairment. No thing is either complete or impaired, but all are made into one again. Only the man of far-reaching vision knows how to make them into one. So he has no use [for categories], but relegates all to the constant. The constant is the useful; the useful is the passable; the passable is the successful; and with success, all is accomplished. He relies upon this alone, relies upon it and does not know he is doing so. This is called the Way.

But to wear out your brain trying to make things into one without realizing that they are all the same—this is called "three in the morning." What do I mean by "three in the morning"? When the monkey trainer was handing out acorns, he said, "You get three in the morning and four at night." This made all the monkeys furious. "Well, then," he said, "you get four in the morning and three at night." The monkeys were all delighted. There was no change in the reality behind the words, and yet the monkeys responded with joy and anger. Let them, if they want to. So the sage harmonizes with both right and wrong and rests in Heaven the Equalizer. This is called walking two roads.

[The Swimmer]

Confucius was seeing the sights at Lü-liang, where the water falls from a height of thirty fathoms and races and boils along for forty li, so swift that no fish or other water creature can swim in it. He saw a man dive into the water and, supposing that the man was in some kind of trouble and intended to end his life, he ordered his disciples to line up on the bank and pull the man out. But after the man had gone a couple of hundred paces, he came out of the water and began strolling along the base of the embankment, his hair streaming down, singing a song. Confucius ran after him and said, "At first I thought you were a ghost, but now I see you're a man. May I ask if you have some special way of staying afloat in the water?"

"I have no way. I began with what I was used to, grew up with my nature, and let things come to completion with fate. I go under with the swirls and come out with the eddies, following along the way the water goes and never thinking about myself. That's how I can stay afloat."

Confucius said, "What do you mean by saying that you began with what you were used to, grew up with your nature, and let things come to completion with fate?"

"I was born on the dry land and felt safe on the dry land—that was what I was used to. I grew up with the water and felt safe in the water—that was my nature. I don't know why I do what I do—that's fate."

[Woodworker]

Woodworker Ch'ing carved a piece of wood and made a bell stand, and when it was finished, everyone who saw it marveled, for it seemed to be the work of gods or spirits. When the marquis of Lu saw it, he asked, "What art is it you have?"

Ch'ing replied, "I am only a craftsman—how would I have any art? There is one thing, however. When I am going to make a bell stand, I never let it wear out my energy. I always fast in order to still my mind. When I have fasted for three days, I no longer have any thought of congratulations or rewards, of titles or stipends. When I have fasted for five days, I no longer have any thought of praise or blame, of skill or clumsiness. And when I have fasted for seven days, I am so still that I forget I have four limbs and a form and body. By that time, the ruler and his court no longer exist for me. My skill is concentrated and all outside distractions fade away. After that, I go into the mountain forest and examine the Heavenly nature of the trees. If I find one of superlative form, and I can see a bell stand there, I put my hand to the job of carving; if not, I let it go. This way I am simply matching up 'Heaven' with 'Heaven.' That's probably the reason that people wonder if the results were not made by spirits."

[Death of Chuang Tzu's Wife]

Chuang Tzu's wife died. When Hui Tzu went to convey his condolences, he found Chuang Tzu sitting with his legs sprawled out, pounding on a tub and singing. "You lived with her, she brought up your children and grew old," said Hui Tzu. "It should be enough simply not to weep at her death. But pounding on a tub and singing—this is going too far, isn't it?"

Chuang Tzu said, "You're wrong. When she first died, do you think I didn't grieve like anyone else? But I looked back to her beginning and the time before she was born. Not only the time before she was born, but the time before she had a body. Not only the time before she had a body, but the time before she had a spirit. In the midst of the jumble of wonder and mystery a change took place and she had a spirit. Another change and she had a body. Another change and she was born. Now there's been another change and she's dead. It's just like the progression of the four seasons, spring, summer, fall, winter.

"Now she's going to lie down peacefully in a vast room. If I were to follow after her bawling and sobbing, it would show that I don't understand anything about fate. So I stopped."

[The Job Offer]

Once, when Chuang Tzu was fishing in the P'u River, the king of Ch'u sent two officials to go and announce to him: "I would like to trouble you with the administration of my realm."

Chuang Tzu held on to the fishing pole and, without turning his head, said, "I have heard that there is a sacred tortoise in Ch'u that has been dead for three thousand years. The king keeps it wrapped in cloth and boxed, and stores it in the ancestral temple. Now would this tortoise rather be dead and have its bones left behind and honored? Or would it rather be alive and dragging its tail in the mud?"

"It would rather be alive and dragging its tail in the mud," said the two officials.

Chuang Tzu said, "Go away! I'll drag my tail in the mud!"

[Yüan-Ch'u Bird]

When Hui Tzu was prime minister of Liang, Chuang Tzu set off to visit him. Someone said to Hui Tzu, "Chuang Tzu is coming because he wants to replace you as prime minister!" With this Hui Tzu was filled with alarm and searched all over the state for three days and three nights trying to find Chuang Tzu. Chuang Tzu then came to see him and said, "In the south there is a bird called the Yüan-ch'u—I wonder if you've ever heard of it? The Yüan-ch'u rises up from the South Sea and flies to the North Sea, and it will rest on nothing but the Wu-t'ung tree, eat nothing but the fruit of the Lien, and drink only from springs of sweet water. Once there was an owl who had gotten hold of a half-rotten old rat, and as the Yüan-ch'u passed by, it raised its head, looked up at the Yüan-ch'u, and said, 'Shoo!' Now that you have this Liang state of yours, are you trying to shoo me?"

[Happiness]

Is there such a thing as supreme happiness in the world or isn't there? Is there some way to keep yourself alive or isn't there? What to do, what to rely on, what to avoid, what to stick by, what to follow, what to leave alone, what to find happiness in, what to hate?

This is what the world honors: wealth, eminence, long life, a good name. This is what the world finds happiness in: a life of ease, rich food, fine clothes, beautiful sights, sweet sounds. This is what it looks down on: poverty, meanness, early death, a bad name. This is what it finds bitter: a life that knows no rest, a mouth that gets no rich food, no fine clothes for the body, no beautiful sights for the eye, no sweet sounds for the ear.

People who can't get these things fret a great deal and are afraid—this is a stupid way to treat the body. People who are rich wear themselves out rushing around on business, piling up more wealth than they could ever use—this is a superficial way to treat the body. People who are eminent spend night and day scheming and wondering if they are doing right—this is a shoddy way to treat the body. Man lives his life in company with worry, and if he lives a long while, till he's dull and doddering, then he has spent that much time worrying instead of dying, a bitter lot indeed! This is a callous way to treat the body.

Men of ardor are regarded by the world as good, but their goodness doesn't succeed in keeping them alive. So I don't know whether their goodness is really good or not. Perhaps I think it's good—but not good enough to save their lives. Perhaps I think it's no good—but still good enough to save the lives of others. So I say, if your loyal advice isn't heeded, give way and do not wrangle. Tzu-hsü wrangled and lost his body. But if he hadn't wrangled, he wouldn't have made a name. Is there really such a thing as goodness or isn't there?

What ordinary people do and what they find happiness in—I don't know whether such happiness is in the end really happiness or not. I look at what ordinary people find happiness in, what they all make a mad dash for, racing around as though they couldn't stop—they all say they're happy with it. I'm not happy with it and I'm not unhappy with it. In the end is there really happiness or isn't there?

I take inaction to be true happiness, but ordinary people think it is a bitter thing. I say: the highest happiness has no happiness, the highest praise has no praise. The world can't decide what is right and what is wrong. And yet inaction can decide this. The highest happiness, keeping alive—only inaction gets you close to this!

Let me try putting it this way. The inaction of Heaven is its purity, the inaction of earth is its peace. So the two inactions combine and all things are transformed and brought to birth. Wonderfully, mysteriously, there is no place they come out of. Mysteriously, wonderfully, they have no sign. Each thing minds its business and all grow up out of inaction. So I say, Heaven and earth do nothing and there is nothing that is not done. Among men, who can get hold of this inaction?

[What Fish Enjoy]

Chuang Tzu and Hui Tzu were strolling along the dam of the Hao River when Chuang Tzu said, "See how the minnows come out and dart around where they please! That's what fish really enjoy!"

Hui Tzu said, "You're not a fish—how do you know what fish enjoy?"

Chuang Tzu said, "You're not I, so how do you know I don't know what fish enjoy?"

Hui Tzu said, "I'm not you, so I certainly don't know what you know. On the other hand, you're certainly not a fish—so that still proves you don't know what fish enjoy!"

Chuang Tzu said, "Let's go back to your original question, please. You asked me *how* I know what fish enjoy—so you already knew I knew it when you asked the question. I know it by standing here beside the Hao."

[Cutting Up the Ox]

Cook Ting was cutting up an ox for Lord Wen-hui. At every touch of his hand, every heave of his shoulder, every move of his feet, every thrust of his knee—zip! zoop! He slithered the knife along with a zing, and all was in perfect rhythm, as though he were performing the dance of the Mulberry Grove or keeping time to Ching-shou music.

"Ah, this is marvelous!" said Lord Wen-hui. "Imagine skill reaching such heights!"

Cook Ting laid down his knife and replied, "What I care about is the Way, which goes beyond skill. When I first began cutting up oxen, all I could see was the ox itself. After three years I no longer saw the whole ox. And now—now I go at it by spirit and don't look with my eyes. Perception and understanding have come to a stop and spirit moves where it wants. I go along with the natural makeup, strike in the big hollows, guide the knife through the big openings, and follow things as they are. So I never touch the smallest ligament or tendon, much less a main joint.

"A good cook changes his knife once a year—because he cuts. A mediocre cook changes his knife once a month—because he hacks. I've had this knife of mine for nineteen years and I've cut up thousands of oxen with it, and yet the blade is as good as though it had just come from the grindstone. There are spaces between the joints, and the blade of the knife has really no thickness. If you insert what has no thickness into such spaces, then there's plenty of room—more than enough for the blade to play about in. That's why after nineteen years the blade of my knife is still as good as when it first came from the grindstone.

"However, whenever I come to a complicated place, I size up the difficulties, tell myself to watch out and be careful, keep my eyes on what I'm doing, work very slowly, and move the knife with the greatest subtlety, until—flop! the whole thing comes apart like a clod of earth crumbling to the ground. I stand there holding the knife and look all around me, completely satisfied and reluctant to move on, and then I wipe off the knife and put it away."

"Excellent!" said Lord Wen-hui. "I have heard the words of Cook Ting and learned how to care for life!"

[The Death of Lao Tan]

When Lao Tan died, Ch'in Shih went to mourn for him; but after giving three cries, he left the room.

"Weren't you a friend of the Master?" asked Lao Tan's disciples.

"Yes."

"And you think it's all right to mourn him this way?"

"Yes," said Ch'in Shih. "At first I took him for a real man, but now I know he wasn't. A little while ago, when I went in to mourn, I found old men weeping for him as though they were weeping for a son, and young men weeping for him as though they were weeping for a mother. To have gathered a group like *that,* he must have done something to make them talk about him, though he didn't ask them to talk, or make them weep for him, though he didn't ask them to weep. This is to hide from Heaven, turn your back on the true state of affairs, and forget what you were born with. In the old days, this was called the crime of hiding from Heaven. Your master happened to come because it was his time, and he happened to leave because things follow along. If you are content with the time and willing to follow along, then grief and joy have no way to enter in. In the old days, this was called being freed from the bonds of God.

"Though the grease burns out of the torch, the fire passes on, and no one knows where it ends."

[Penumbra and Shadow]

Penumbra said to Shadow, "A little while ago you were walking and now you're standing still; a little while ago you were sitting and now you're standing up. Why this lack of independent action?"

Shadow said, "Do I have to wait for something before I can be like this? Does what I wait for also have to wait for something before it can be like this? Am I waiting for the scales of a snake or the wings of a cicada? How do I know why it is so? How do I know why it isn't so?"

[The Dream and the Butterfly]

Once Chuang Chou dreamt he was a butterfly, a butterfly flitting and fluttering around, happy with himself and doing as he pleased. He didn't know he was Chuang Chou. Suddenly he woke up and there he was, solid and unmistakable Chuang Chou. But he didn't know if he was Chuang Chou who had dreamt he was a butterfly, or a butterfly dreaming he was Chuang Chou. Between Chuang Chou and a butterfly there must be *some* distinction! This is called the Transformation of Things.

[The Wasted Gourd]

Hui Tzu said to Chuang Tzu, "The king of Wei gave me some seeds of a huge gourd. I planted them, and when they grew up, the fruit was big enough to hold five piculs. I tried using it for a water container, but it was so heavy I couldn't lift it. I split it in half to make dippers, but they were so large and unwieldy that I couldn't dip them into anything. It's not that the gourds weren't fantastically big—but I decided they were no use and so I smashed them to pieces."

Chuang Tzu said, "You certainly are dense when it comes to using big things! In Sung there was a man who was skilled at making a salve to prevent chapped hands, and generation after generation his family made a living by bleaching silk in water. A traveler heard about the salve and offered to buy the prescription for a hundred measures of gold. The man called everyone to a family council. 'For generations we've been bleaching silk and we've never made more than a few measures of gold,' he said. 'Now, if we sell our secret, we can make a hundred measures in one morning. Let's let him have it!' The traveler got the salve and introduced it to the king of Wu, who was having trouble with the state of Yüeh. The king put the man in charge of his troops, and that winter they fought a naval battle with the men of Yüeh and gave them a bad beating. A portion of the conquered territory was awarded to the man as a fief. The salve had the power to prevent chapped hands in either case; but one man used it to get a fief, while the other one never got beyond silk bleaching—because they used it in different ways. Now you had a gourd big enough to hold five piculs. Why didn't you think of making it into a great tub so you could go floating around the rivers and lakes, instead of worrying because it was too big and unwieldy to dip into things! Obviously you still have a lot of underbrush in your head!"

BHAGAVAD GITA

[C. 1ST CENTURY C.E.]

Tucked into the midst of India's greatest epic, a mammoth collection of tales, legends, and philosophical discourses called the *Mahabharata* (c. 400 B.C.E.–400 C.E.), appears an extended dialogue between Prince Arjuna, an epic hero like Hector or Achilles, and Lord Krishna, who like Christ is an incarnation of the divine spirit. Called the *Bhagavad Gita,* the *Song of God,* this segment of the great epic constitutes India's single most important document of philosophy and religion, for the dialogue attempts to synthesize the religious, social, and moral codes present in a transitional moment of Indian thought and history. In his *Hinduism and Buddhism,* Ananda Coomaraswamy calls the *Gita,* as it is often known, "a compendium of the whole Vedic doctrine to be found in the earlier Vedas, Brahmanas, and Upanishads," which provides the nucleus from which all later developments of Indian religion evolve.

Indo-Aryan invaders of the Indus River valley in about 1500 B.C.E. found themselves among a highly structured and deeply spiritual people who had developed a standardized system of weights and measures, a pictographic script, and thriving cities such as Harappa; these ancient people of India supplemented their living from the land by sea trade with Mesopotamia. Although the Indo-Aryan invaders originally shared a common culture with the Achaeans and Dorians of ancient Greece and Rome, they adapted their ways in light of the indigenous traditions of the Indus River valley, even as they imposed upon it. Thus, they developed a culture significantly different from that of their ancestors, whose descendants produced Greco-Roman culture. Modern Indian spirituality rests upon the foundations of Indo-Aryan sacred texts such as the *Rig Veda* (c. 1200 B.C.E.), one of the oldest Indo-European literary/philosophical works, and the *Upanishads* (c. 400 B.C.E.).

Between the *Rig Veda* and the *Upanishads* one can see a transformation in spiritual thought from a pantheistic and this-worldly orientation to a more metaphysical and otherworldly approach in the *Upanishads.* The *Rig Veda* focuses upon rituals and prayers that lead to acceptance of earthly life; its gods, like the gods of early Greece, are personifications of natural forces. The *Upanishads,* however, mark a turn away from the phenomenal world of nature; its doctrines advocate a renunciation of the world and focus upon the inner life and transcendental spirit. Thus, Vedic songs of praise to Agni, the god of fire, Indra, god of thunder, and Soma, god of the intoxicating moonplant, give way in the *Upanishads* to speculative poems about Brahman, the universal soul and creative spirit, Atman, the individual soul that partakes of the universal, Vishnu, the preserver, and Shiva, the destructive force. This reformation of ideas was brought about in part by a reaction against the Brahman priesthood, which exploited the Vedic teachings to amass vast tracts of land and to exercise special privileges over members of the lower castes.

The *Mahabharata* and the *Ramayana,* the great epics of Indian literature, are compendiums of legendary lore, philosophical poems and tales, hymns, and prayers passed down from the most ancient oral traditions to their first written manifestations sometime around the fourth century B.C.E. By the fourth century B.C.E., the Indo-Aryans had given up their tribal organization and formed kingdoms that eventually led to the Maurya and the

Gupta empires (c. 321–c. 200 B.C.E. and c. 320–550 C.E., respectively). The latter was a great period of cultural efflorescence in India, which saw the consolidation of the great texts such as the *Mahabharata* and the *Ramayana,* as well as the life of Kalidasa, India's greatest classical playwright, who like Aeschylus and Sophocles based his plays upon ancient lore. Although the *Bhagavad Gita,* which is part of the *Mahabharata,* dates from sometime in the first or second century C.E., we know it only in the form it took at the hands of Gupta writers.

A poem of about 200,000 lines, the *Mahabharata* is almost seven times longer than *The Iliad* and *The Odyssey* combined. Unlike the Homeric epics, the *Mahabharata* is an encyclopedic assemblage of many closely related stories, with interspersed mythic, genealogical, and philosophical tales about the descendants of King Bharata, a legendary ancestor of the Indo-Aryans. Like *The Iliad,* nonetheless, this national epic tells the story of an ancient war, in this case between two sets of cousins, the five sons of Pandu (the Pandavas) and the hundred sons of Dhritarashtra (the Kauravas). The *Bhagavad Gita* takes place in the ancient kingdom of Kurukshetra just before the battle between the cousins begins. Arjuna, the epic hero and the leader of the righteous but exiled Pandavas, surveys the scene with his charioteer Krishna, the incarnation of the god Vishnu. Looking out upon his cousins, Arjuna loses heart for the battle, so Krishna councils him in his duties or *dharma* as a noble warrior. In the course of his counsel, Krishna reveals to him the higher truth of the universe, the place of human action in the overall scheme of things, and the nature of divinity. Dating from the time of the *Upanishads,* the *Gita* attempts to reconcile the older Vedic vision with the newer one, rather in the same way that Homeric epics or classical Greek tragedy synthesize the mythology of an older, oral culture with the philosophical needs of their own time. The *Gita* embraces the epic and heroic realm of action, even as it demonstrates that those actions take their meaning only in the transcendental realm of the supreme spirit or pure self.

It is thought that the caste system, which had evolved by 500 B.C.E., originated in the Aryan attempt to legitimate what they thought was their racial superiority over the people of color, known as *Dasyas,* who occupied the lands before their arrival. Like the Greek term *barbaros,* from which we derive *barbarian, Dasyas* is a term of exclusion applied to all foreigners. As set down in the Laws of Manu, "All tribes of the world that do not belong to those born from the mouth, the arms, the thighs and the feet of Brahman, are called Dasyus, whether they speak the language of the Mlecchas or that of the Aryans." Within the legitimate social order, as Lord Krishna explains in Book Four of the *Gita,* mankind is created in four classes or castes: "The Four Caste Rule was formed by Me, according to the division of powers and works" (IV.13). The *Sudras,* at the bottom of the four-tiered structure, were excluded from the rituals and citizenship enjoyed by the *Vaishyas* (farmers), *Kshatriyas* (warriors), and *Brahmans* (priests) who, in ascending order, ranked above them. Within this strict hierarchy, each person must perform the particular duties of his or her caste, to follow the traditions of *dharma,* duty or law, in order to achieve the common good.

Recognizing the importance of the caste system helps to understand the *Bhagavad Gita,* which proclaims that the greatest happiness is to perform one's *dharma* according to one's assigned station in life. Any mixing of such duties, as Lord Krishna advises Arjuna, yields confusion and subverts the moral and spiritual order: "Better one's own duty without excellence than the duty of another well followed out. Death in one's own duty is better; the duty of another is full of danger" (III.35). According to the law of *karma,* actions in a past life determine one's caste position in the present; but if one lives according to *dharma* one may move out of that caste, or—ultimately—out of the system altogether by achieving *Nirvana,* a oneness with God that releases the soul from the great wheel of birth and rebirth. Lord Krishna: "Even continuing to perform all works, taking refuge in Me, through My grace he gains that everlasting home" (XVIII.56).

Although our reading of the story is enriched by an understanding of the philosophical and religious background of the *Bhagavad Gita,* it can also be appreciated from a literary perspective. The dialogue itself, while engaging the most abstract concepts, never loses sight of the dramatic situation in which the conversation takes place. The spiritual import of Krishna's teachings reflects upon Arjuna's worldly dilemma, reminding us that our own actions and intentions, our individual reality, take part in a greater spiritual unfolding.

SUGGESTED READINGS

Helpful commentaries and general introductions to the text and backgrounds of the *Bhagavad Gita* may be found in Franklin Edgerton's *The Bhagavad Gita,* G. A. Feuerstein's *Introduction to the Bhagavad-Gita* (1974), Robert N. Minor's *Bhagavad-Gita* (1982), and R. C. Zaehner's *The Bhagavad-Gita* (1969). More specialized studies include Phulgenda Sinha's *The Gita as it Was* (1986) and J. A. B. van Buitenen's *Ramanuja on the Bhagavad-Gita* (1968). Sarveapalli Radhakrishnan discusses the philosophical traditions of India in *Indian Philosophy* (1966); Heinrich Zimmer's survey of Indian philosophy, *Philosophies of India* (1951), includes a fine chapter on the *Gita.* Barend A. Van Nooten's *The Mahabharata* (1971) offers a historical introduction and outline of each chapter of the great epic; for a lively, condensed retelling of the *Mahabharata,* see R. K. Narayan's modern rendering of the epic.

Bhagavad Gita

Translated by Charles Johnston

BOOK 1[1] [THE MEETING BETWEEN KRISHNA AND ARJUNA]

DHRITARASHTRA SAID:

On the field of the law, on Kuru's field assembled and ready to fight, what did my people,[2] O Sanjaya, and the Pandu host?

SANJAYA SAID:

King Duryodhana,[3] beholding the Pandu army drawn up for battle, coming to Drona, his instructor, addressed to him this word:

Behold, O instructor, this mighty host of the sons of Pandu, marshaled by thy wise pupil, Drupada's son;[4]

Heroes are here, mighty archers, equal to Bhima and Arjuna[5] in battle, Yuyudhana and Virata, and Drupada of the great chariot;

Dhrishtaketu and Chekitana, and Kashi's valorous king; Purujit and Kuntibhoja and Shaivya, bull of men:

[1] The original text is written in quatrains.

[2] The blind King Dhritarashtra asks his bard and charioteer, Sanjaya, to tell him about the war between Dhritarashtra's nephews, the Pandavas, and his sons, the Kauravas (also called the Kurus).

[3] Dhritarashtra's eldest son, the leader of the Kauravas and an embodiment here of disorder and evil.

[4] Drishtadyumna, the commander in chief of the Pandavas. Drona is priest and master of the martial arts who has taught his skills to both the Pandavas and the Kaurava brothers.

[5] Prince Bhima and Arjuna are two of Pandu's sons; the other brothers are Yudhishthira, whom Dhritarashtra had named heir apparent to the throne of Hastinapur, and so inflamed Duryodhana's jealousy; Nakäla; and Sahadeva. The names that follow, as in the Homeric epic, are a catalogue of the heroes in the Pandava army, and farther below, in the Kaurava army.

The victorious Yudhamanyu and Uttamaujas the valorous, Subhadra's son and the sons of Draupadi, with great chariots all.
Hear now, best of the Twice-born, who are our chiefest men, my army's captains; that thou mayest know their names, I tell them to thee;
Thyself and Bhishma,[6] Karna and Kripa, conqueror in battle, Ashvatthama and Vikarna, and Somadatta's son;
And many other heroes who give their lives for me, variously armed, all skilled in war.
Our force which Bhishma leads is inadequate; their force which Bhima commands is strong; 10
Therefore, do ye all support Bhishma, holding the several places allotted to you, O worthy warriors!
Then enkindling his ardor the elder Kuru, the martial grandsire,[7] loudly blew his conch-shell, sounding the lion note.
Thereupon sounded conches, drums, great drums, cymbals and trumpets, the sound grew to a tumult.
Then standing together in their great chariot yoked with white horses, Krishna, slayer of Madhu,[8] and Arjuna, son of Pandu, blew their god-like conches.
He of the flowing hair blew the conch called Fivefold, and the conqueror of wealth blew the God-given; and he of the wolf-maw, terrible in deeds, blew the Reed-note;[9]
King Yudhishthira, the son of Kunti,[10] blew Unending-victory; Nakula and Sahadeva blew the conches Well-sounding and Pearl-flowered;
And the mighty archer, the king of Kashi, and Shikhandin of the great chariot, Dhrishtadyumna, Virata and Satyaka's unvanquished son;
Drupada and the sons of Draupadi, his daughter, O monarch, and Subhadra's son of mighty arms, blew their conches on all hands, on this side and on that;
And the sound pierced the hearts of Dhritarashtra's sons; the din made heaven and earth resound.
Then Pandu's son,[11] he of the monkey-banner, looking toward the sons of Dhritarashtra set over against him, while the arrows were already falling, grasped his bow; 20
And thus, O monarch, he spoke to him of the flowing hair: Draw up my chariot, O unfallen one, between the two armies;
That I may view those ranged against us ready to fight, with whom I must do battle in this clash of war;
That I may see those who are about to fight, gathered here to work the will of Dhritarashtra's evil-minded son in battle!

---

[6]Dhritarashtra's father, leader of the Kaurava forces; Bhishma, related to both the Pandava leaders and the Kaurava brothers, fights on the side of the Kauravas out of his sense of *dharma,* or duty. He had tried to reconcile the two parties, but failed.

[7]Bhishma; as father of Dhritarashtra, he was the grand uncle of both Duryodhana and Arjuna. As the story is placed in the larger context of the *Mahabharata,* Bhishma has fallen to the arrows of Arjuna; the *Gita* offers a spiritual justification of his death at the hands of his kin—it is a soldier's *dharma* to fight, no matter who the opponent.

[8]A demon.

[9]Krishna, Arjuna, and Bhima, respectively.

[10]The wife of Pandu and mother of the Pandavas; she is also named Prithā.

[11]Arjuna.

SANJAYA SAID:

Krishna of the flowing hair, thus addressed by Arjuna of the crested locks, O son of Bharata,[12] stopping the most excellent chariot between the two armies,

In face of Bhishma and Drona and all the rulers of the earth, spoke thus: Behold the Kurus assembled here, O son of Prithä!

Prithä's son beheld standing there fathers and grandfathers, instructors, uncles, brothers, sons, grandsons and companions,

Fathers-in-law and dear friends in both armies. He, the son of Kunti, viewing all these near kinsmen standing opposed, filled with supreme pity, desponding, spoke thus:

ARJUNA SAID:

Seeing my own kindred here, O Krishna, desiring battle, ranged against each other,

My limbs sink under me, my mouth dries up, trembling besets my body, and my flesh creeps;

My bow Gandiva slips from my hand, my skin burns with fever; I cannot stand, my heart is confused; 30

I see contrary omens, O thou of the flowing hair, nor can I look for the better part, if I slay my kindred in battle.

I want not victory, Krishna, nor the kingdom nor its pleasures; for what profit is the kingdom to us, thou lord of the earth; what are feasts, or even life itself?

They for whose sake a kingdom is sought, and its feasts and pleasures, even they are drawn up against us, staking their lives and wealth in battle:

Instructors, fathers, sons and grandsires, uncles, fathers-in-law, grandsons, wives' brothers, kinsmen.

These would I not kill, though killed myself, O slayer of Madhu, even for the kingdom of the three worlds, much less for this earth;

If we strike down the sons of Dhritarashtra, what joy shall we find, thou arouser of men? Sin will follow us if we slay these usurpers.

Therefore, we must not slay the sons of Dhritarashtra, our kinsmen. How can we be happy, if we kill our own kin, O slayer of Madhu?

Even if they, their hearts blinded by greed, see not the evil of family strife, and the crime of the hatred of friends;

How shall we fail to turn back from this sin, we who do see the evil of family strife, O arouser of men?

For when the family is cut off, the immemorial rites of the family perish, and when the rites perish, lawlessness overtakes the whole family; 40

Overtaken by lawlessness, O Krishna, the women of the family are led astray; when the women are led astray, descendant of Vrishni,[13] there comes mingling of races;

And mingling of races makes for hell for the slayers of family and for their family; for their departed fathers fall, cut off from the offerings of rice-cakes and water.

Through these sins of those who slay their kindred, thus causing impurity of race, the immemorial birth rites and family rites are overthrown;

---

[12]Here an aside to remind us that Sanjaya is telling the story to Dhritarashtra. Bharata is the legendary King from whom the Pandavas and the Kauravas are descended. Elsewhere in the text, "O Bharata" will refer at times to Arjuna, at others to Dhritarashtra.

[13]Krishna was born to Devaki, the wife of Vasudeva, in the family of the Vrishni.

And for the sons of men whose family rites fail, thou arouser of men, a place in hell is certain. Thus we have heard from our fathers!

Woe is me! We are set on doing a great evil, since through lust of the kingdom and its pleasures, we are ready to slay our own kin.

If Dhritarashtra's sons, weapon in hand, should slay me in battle, weaponless and unresisting, that would be far more easy to bear!

SANJAYA SAID:

Thus speaking Arjuna sank on the floor of the chariot, in the midst of the host, dropping his bow and his arrows, his heart shaken with sorrow.

BOOK 2 [YOGA]

SANJAYA SAID:

To him thus full of distress, his eyes perplexed and filled with tears, despondent, the slayer of Madhu spoke this word:

THE MASTER SAID:

Whence has this faint-heartedness in trouble come upon thee, unseemly for a noble, not bringing heaven, inglorious, O Arjuna?

Fall not into impotence, O son of Prithä, for this beseems thee not! Put away this mean faint-heartedness, and arise, O consumer of the foe!

ARJUNA SAID:

How can I fight against Bhishma, how against Drona, with my arrows, O slayer of Madhu, for they are both worthy of honor, O slayer of the foe!

Rather than slay these great ones, worthy of all honor, it were better to eat the bread of beggars in this world; for slaying them, even though they seek my possessions, I should eat feasts sprinkled with blood!

Nor do we know which is heavier for us, whether we conquer or whether they conquer us; for Dhritarashtra's sons are here facing us, slaying whom we should not wish to live.

Overwhelmed with pity and fear of sin I ask thee, for my vision of duty is obscured. Which is better? Tell me clearly! I am thy disciple! Teach me! I appeal to thee!

For I see no way to drive away my grief and this fever in all my powers, though gaining wealth and mastery of the earth without a rival, or even overlordship of the gods!

SANJAYA SAID:

He of the crested locks, consumer of the foe, thus addressing him of the flowing hair, saying to the lord of the earth: I will not fight! was silent.

To him Krishna of the flowing hair replied, smiling as it were, O son of Bharata, as he sank there despondent between the two armies: 10

THE MASTER SAID:

Thou hast grieved for those who need no grief, and thou speakest words of wisdom! The wise grieve neither for the dead nor for the living;

For never was I not, nor thou, nor these princes of men; nor shall we all ever cease to be, in the time to come.

As the lord of the body in the body here finds boyhood, youth and age, so is there the gaining of another body; the wise err not concerning this.

These things of matter, that bring us cold, heat, pleasure, pain, come and go again; they last not; therefore endure them, O son of Bharata!

Whom these perturb not, O bull of men, equal in pain and pleasure, wise, he builds for immortality.
For the unreal there is no being, nor any end of being for the real; the truth as to these two is seen by those who behold reality.
But know That to be imperishable whereby all this is stretched forth; and none can cause the destruction of the everlasting.
These temporal bodies are declared to belong to the eternal lord of the body, imperishable, immeasurable; therefore fight, O son of Bharata!
He who sees him as slayer, or who thinks of him as slain, both understand not; he slays not nor is slain.
He is never born nor dies, nor will he, having being, evermore cease to be; unborn, eternal, immemorial, this Ancient is not slain when the body is slain. 20
He who knows this imperishable, eternal, unborn, and passing not away, how can that man, O son of Prithä, slay any, or cause any to be slain?
As putting off worn out garments, a man takes others new, so putting off worn-out bodies, the lord of the body enters others new.
Swords cut him not, nor may fire burn him, O son of Bharata, waters wet him not, nor dry winds parch.
He may not be cut nor burned nor wet nor withered; he is eternal, all-present, firm, unshaken, everlasting.
He is called unmanifest, unimaginable, unchanging; therefore, knowing him thus, deign not to grieve!
But even if thou thinkest of him as ever born, ever dying, yet deign not, therefore, to grieve for him, O mighty armed one!
For certain is the death of what is born, and certain is the birth of what dies; therefore, deign not to grieve in a matter that is inevitable.
The beginnings of things are unmanifest, their mid course is manifest, O son of Bharata; their ending is unmanifest; what cause is here for lamentation?
One sees him as marvelous, another speaks of him as marvelous, another hears of him as marvelous, yet even hearing, one knows him not.
This lord of the body dwells ever immortal in the body of each, O son of Bharata; therefore, deign not to grieve even for all beings! 30

Or having regard to thy duty, deign not to shrink back! For nothing is better for a warrior than a righteous battle.
And such a battle has come to thee of its own accord, a very door of heaven wide opened; happy the warriors, son of Prithä, who find such a fight as this!
But if thou shalt not fight this righteous fight, then failing in duty and honor, thou wilt incur sin;
And men will tell of thy lasting dishonor, and for one who has stood in honor, ill-fame is worse than death.
The warriors in their chariots will think thou hast retreated from the battle through fear, and thou shalt come to light esteem among those who held thee high.
Many unspeakable words will thy enemies speak of thee, impeaching thy manhood. What fate could be more grievous than that?
Either, slain, thou wilt gain heaven, or, conquering, thou wilt enjoy the earth; therefore, arise, O son of Kunti, determined to do battle!
Making equal good and ill fortune, gain and loss, victory and defeat; gird thyself for the fight, for thus thou shalt not fall into sin!

[This thought is declared to thee according to Sankhya; now hear it according to Yoga.[14] Held by this thought, O son of Prithä, thou shalt free thyself from the bond of works.]

Here is no loss of advantage, nor any going back; even a little of this law saves from the great fear. 40

The thought whose essence is determination is single, O rejoicer of the Kurus! Many-branched and endless are the thoughts of the undetermined.

[This is a flowery word which the unwise declare, who delight in the letter of the Vedas, O son of Prithä, and say there is nothing else,

[They who are full of desire and eager for heaven; this word offering rebirth and the reward of works, abounding in special rites making for feasts and lordship;

[The thought of those who are set on feasts and lordship, whose minds are carried away thereby, has not determination as its essence, nor is it set in soul-vision;

[The Vedas have the Three Powers[15] as their object; be thou above the Three Powers, O Arjuna! Be free from duality, ever standing in the real, without desire of possessions, full of the Soul;

[As much use as there is in a well, when the whole land is flooded, so much use is there in all the Vedas for a Knower of the Eternal who possesses wisdom.]

Thy right is to the work, but never to its fruits; let not the fruit of thy work be thy motive, nor take refuge in abstinence from works.

Standing in union with the Soul carry out thy work, putting away attachment, O conqueror of wealth; equal in success and failure, for equalness is called union with the Soul.

For work is far lower than union in soul-vision, O conqueror of wealth; find refuge in soul-vision, for pitiful are those whose motive is the fruit of their works.

He who is united in soul-vision offers up even here both things well done and ill done; therefore, gird thyself for union with the Soul, for this union brings success in works. 50

For the possessors of wisdom, united in soul-vision, giving up the fruit of works, freed from the bondage of rebirth, reach the home where no sorrow dwells.

When thy soul shall pass beyond the forest of delusion, thou shalt no more regard what shall be taught or what has been taught.

When withdrawn from traditional teaching, thy soul shall stand steadfast, firm in soul-vision, then shalt thou regain union with the Soul.

ARJUNA SAID:

What is the description of one firm in perception, of one firm in soul-vision, O thou of the flowing hair? He who is firm in soul, how does he speak? How does he sit? How does he go?

---

[14]Sankhya, along with Yoga, are two of the six major schools of thought in Indian philosophy. Here Sankhya and Yoga, roughly equivalent to theory and practice, are contrasted.

[15]These are the three *gunas: sattva,* or potential consciousness; *rajas,* the source of action; and *tamas,* that which resists action.

THE MASTER SAID:

When he offers up all desires that dwell in the heart, O son of Prithä, in soul rejoicing in the Soul, then he is said to be firm in perception.

Whose heart is untroubled in sorrows, who in pleasures is unallured, from whom lust and fear and wrath have gone, that silent one is declared to be firm in soul.

He who is free from over-fondness, meeting glory and gloom alike, who exults not nor hates, his perception is set firm.

When as a tortoise withdraws its limbs on all sides, he withdraws his powers from things of sense, his perception is set firm.

Things of sense withdraw from the lord of the body who tastes them not; even the desire for them falls away from him who has seen the desireless Supreme.

Even when a wise man strives, O son of Kunti, the turbulent powers swiftly steal away his heart; 60

Controlling them all let him remain united, intent upon Me; for of him who controls his powers, the perception is set firm.

In the man who broods on things of sense, attachment to them springs up; from attachment is born desire, from desire wrath takes birth;

From wrath comes delusion, from delusion loss of recollection, from loss of recollection comes loss of soul-vision, through loss of soul-vision he perishes.

But who among things of sense uses his powers freed from lust and hate, and controlled by the Soul, with soul well-disposed he enters into peace.

In peace there comes the ending of all sorrows, for the soul of inspiration swiftly enfolds him whose heart is full of peace.

There is no soul-vision for him who is not united, nor is there any divine experience for him; without experience of the divine, there is no rest, and what happiness can there be without rest?

For when his emotion follows the powers in their action it carries his perception away, as the wind carries a boat away to sea.

Therefore, of him, O mighty armed one, whose powers are altogether withheld from things of sense, the perception is set firm.

He who has attained self-mastery wakes where is night for all beings, and where all beings wake is night for the silent seer.

As the waters enter the ocean, ever filled yet standing unmoved, whom all desires so enter, he gains peace, not he who lusts after desires. 70

The man who, offering up all desires, walks without allurement, without the sense of possessing, without self-reference, he enters into peace.

This is the God-like resting-place, O son of Prithä, nor will he who has gained it be led away; dwelling in this at the time of the end, he wins union with the Eternal.

BOOK 3 [KARMA]

ARJUNA SAID:

If soul-vision be deemed by thee greater than work, O arouser of men, then why dost thou engage me in a terrible deed, O thou of flowing hair?

With confused speech thou deludest my thought, as it were; then declare one thing clearly, whereby I may gain the better way.

THE MASTER SAID:

[In this world a twofold rule was declared by me of old, O sinless one: by union through wisdom for the Sankhyas; by union through works, for the followers of Yoga.]

Not by withholding from works does a man reach freedom from works, nor through renunciation alone does he win supreme success.

For none ever for an instant even remains without working works; for he is made to work works involuntarily, through the Powers born of Nature.

He who, restraining the powers of action, dwells remembering in mind the objects of sense, such a one, wholly deluded, is called a false ascetic.

But he who, controlling the sense-powers by the mind, Arjuna, enters through his powers of action on union through works, he, detached, gains excellence.

Do the work that is laid on thee, for work is better than ceasing from works; nor could thy bodily life proceed, if thou didst cease from works.

Except by work done through sacrifice, this world is bound by works; therefore, do thou, son of Kunti, carry out thy work to that end, free from attachment.

Putting forth beings united with sacrifice, the Lord of beings declared of old: By this shall ye increase and multiply; let this be your cow of plenty, granting your wishes. 10

Nourish the gods through this; may the gods also nourish you! Thus mutually nourishing each other, ye shall gain happiness supreme.

For the gods, nourished by sacrifice, will grant you the feasts that you wish. He who eats, not giving to them of what they give, is a thief indeed.

The righteous, who eat what is left from the sacrifice, are freed from all sins. The sinful eat sin, who prepare food for themselves alone.

From food are born beings; from the Rain lord is born food; from sacrifice is born the Rain lord; sacrifice is born of works;

Know that works are born of Brahma;[16] Brahma is born of the Everlasting. Therefore the all-present Brahma is set firm for ever in sacrifice.

He who makes not to revolve the wheel thus set revolving, sinful of life, making a pleasure-ground of the senses, he, son of Prithä, lives in vain.

But the son of man who, rejoicing in the Soul, delighting in the Soul, finds contentment, verily, in the Soul, for him no work remains to be done.

There is no gain to him through work done, nor through what is left undone in this world below; nor among all beings is there any whom he need beg for any boon.

Therefore detached carry out ever the work that is to be done; for the man who accomplishes his work detached wins the supreme.

For through works did Janaka[17] and his like achieve supreme success. And deign thou also to work, having regard to the host of the people. 20

Whatever the best does, that lesser folk do also; what example he sets, that the world follows after.

For Me, son of Prithä, nothing remains that should be done throughout the three worlds, nor aught to gain that I have not gained; yet I engage in works.

---

[16]The Absolute or Supreme Self; though the term also means *Veda* (The Teachings) and Nature, thus providing a composite symbol of Spirit, Mind, and Nature.

[17]King of Videha, a philosopher king known for his generosity.

For if I should not engage in works unceasingly, even for a moment,—since all beings put forth their energy in obedience to mine—

These worlds would sink away, were I not to carry on works, and I should cause confusion among them, and bring destruction to these beings.

As the unwise work, attached to their work, O son of Bharata, so let the wise man work detached, working for the order of mankind.

Let him not cause a breach in the understanding of the unwise, who are attached to works, but rather let the wise man lead them in all works, engaging in them in union with the Soul.

Works are being wrought on all hands by the Powers of Nature; only when the soul is deluded by egotism, does one think himself to be the doer.

But he who knows the truth, O mighty armed one, as to the separateness of the Powers and works, understanding that the Powers work in the Powers, is not attached.

Those who are deluded by the Powers of Nature become attached to the works of the Powers; they see not the whole, and are slow of understanding; let not him who sees the whole cause them to waver.

In Me renouncing all works, through perception of oneness with the Over-soul, without expectation or sense of possession, fight thou, thy fever gone! 30

The sons of man who follow ever after this mind of Mine, full of faith, without cavil, they indeed are freed by their works.

But they who cavil, and follow not this mind of Mine, know them, led astray from all wisdom, as lost through lack of understanding.

The wise ever strives conformably with his nature; beings follow their nature,—what will constraint avail?

Lust and hate are lodged in the object of every sense; let him not come under their sway, for they lie in wait about his path.

Better one's own duty without excellence than the duty of another well followed out. Death in one's own duty is better; the duty of another is full of danger.

ARJUNA SAID:

Then under whose yoke does man here commit sin, unwillingly even, O descendant of Vrishni, as though compelled by force?

THE MASTER SAID:

It is lust, it is wrath, born of the Power of Passion; the great consumer, the great evil,—know this to be the enemy.

As flame is wrapped by smoke, as a mirror is veiled by rust, as the germ is enwrapped by the womb, so is this enveloped by that;

Wisdom is enveloped by that eternal enemy of the wise, whose form is Desire, O son of Kunti, an insatiate fire.

The sense-powers, the emotions, the understanding are its dwelling place; through them Desire deludes the lord of the body, enveloping wisdom. 40

Therefore in the beginning restraining the sense-powers, O bull of the Bharatas, do thou put away this evil, destroyer of wisdom and knowledge both.

They say the sense-powers are higher than objects; than the sense-powers emotion is higher; than emotion understanding is higher; but higher than understanding is He.

Thus awaking to Him who is above understanding, establishing thy soul on the Soul, slay the enemy, O mighty armed one, whose form is Desire, who is hard to overcome.

BOOK 4 [KNOWLEDGE]

THE MASTER SAID:

This imperishable teaching of union I declared to the Solar lord.[18] The Solar lord imparted it to Manu, and Manu told it to Ikshvaku.

Thus the Rajanya sages knew it, handed down from Master to disciple. This teaching of union has been lost in the world through long lapse of time, O consumer of the foe.

This same immemorial teaching of union I have declared to thee to-day; for thou art my beloved, my companion; and this secret doctrine is the most excellent treasure.

ARJUNA SAID:

Later was thy birth, O noble one, earlier the birth of the Solar lord. How then may I understand this, that thou hast declared it in the beginning?

THE MASTER SAID:

Many are My past births and thine also, Arjuna; I know them all, but thou knowest them not, O consumer of the foe.

Though I am the Unborn, the Soul that passes not away, though I am the lord of beings, yet as lord over My nature I become manifest, through the magical power of the Soul.

For whenever there is a withering of the Law, O son of Bharata, and an uprising of lawlessness on all sides, then I manifest Myself.

For the salvation of the righteous, and the destruction of such as do evil; for the firm establishing of the Law I come to birth in age after age.

He who thus perceives My birth and work as divine, as in truth it is, leaving the body, he goes not to rebirth; he goes to Me, Arjuna.

Rid of rage and fear and wrath, become like Me, taking refuge in Me, many made pure by the fire of wisdom have entered My being. 10

In whatever way men approach Me, in that way I love them; in all ways the sons of man follow My way, O son of Prithā.

Desiring the success of their works, they worship the deities here; for quickly in the world of men success comes, born of works.

The Four Caste Rule[19] was formed by Me, according to the division of powers and works; know Me as its maker, I who forever am above all works.

Works smear Me not, nor am I allured by reward of works; he who thus knows Me well, such a one is not bound by works.

Thus knowing, those of old who sought liberation engaged in works. Do thou therefore that same work which was done of old by the men of old.

As to what is work, and what not work, even seers have been deceived; therefore I shall declare work to thee, knowing which thou shalt go free from darkness.

One must understand works; one must understand also what is forbidden; and one must understand abstinence from works; the way of works is hard to trace.

He who sees abstinence from work in work, and work in abstinence from work, he is wise among the sons of man; he possesses union, and has accomplished the whole work.

---

[18]Vivasvat, a sun god and father of the seventh Manu from whom human beings are descended; Ikshvaku is a sun god.

[19]The four castes are the Brahmans, or elite; the Kshatriyas, or warriors; the Vaishyas, or merchants; and the Sudras, or servants.

He whose initiatives are all devoid of lust and false imaginings, the wise say that that sage has burned up works in the fire of wisdom.
Giving up attachment to the reward of works, ever content, not seeking boons, though thoroughly wrapped up in work, such a one engages not in work.
Without expectations, with imagination well ruled, ceasing from all grasping, with the body only engaging in work, he incurs no sin.
Content with what comes of its own accord, beyond the opposites, without sense of ownership, equal in success and failure, though engaging in works he is not bound.
Works fall away from him, whose attachment is gone, who is set free, whose thought rests in wisdom, who works for sacrifice alone.
The Eternal[20] is the offering, the Eternal is the sacrificial butter, the Eternal is in the fire, by the Eternal is the sacrifice made: the Eternal, verily, is to be approached by that sacrifice, by him intent on the work of the Eternal.
Some who seek union worship through sacrifice to the gods; but others offer self-sacrifice as a sacrifice in the fire of the Eternal.
Others offer up hearing and the other powers in the fire of self-control; others offer sound and other things of sense in the fire of the powers.
Yet others offer all the works of the powers and the works of the life-force in the fire of control by the soul, the fire that wisdom kindles.
There are sacrificers of wealth, sacrificers through fervor, sacrificers for union, sacrificers through study and wisdom, well-ruled, firm in their vows.
So others offer the life-breath in the downward breath, or the downward breath in the life-breath, guarding the ways of the life-breath and the downward breath, devoted to breath-control.
Others restrained in food, offer the life-breath in the life-breath; all these knowers of sacrifice, through sacrifice wear away their darkness.
They who eat the ambrosial leavings of the sacrifice go to the immemorial Eternal. Not this world even belongs to him who sacrifices not, how then the other world, O best descendant of Kuru?
Thus are many forms of sacrifice set forth before the Eternal. Know them all to be born of works; thus knowing, thou shalt be set free.
Better than the sacrifice of wealth is the sacrifice of wisdom, O consumer of the foe! Each and every work is consummated in wisdom.
Seek for wisdom with obeisance, questioning and service; the wise, who know the truth, will point the way of wisdom to thee;
Knowing which, thou shalt not again come to confusion, O son of Pandu; and by it thou shalt behold all beings without reserve in the Soul, and thus in Me.
Even though thou art the chief sinner among all sinners, thou shalt cross to the further side of evil in the boat of all-knowledge.
As a kindled fire reduces the fuel to ashes, Arjuna, so does the fire of wisdom reduce to ashes all works.
For no purifier can be found equal to wisdom; he who is perfected in union in due time finds that within his own soul.
He who is full of faith gains wisdom, seeking after it with powers controlled; gaining wisdom, in no long time he enters the supreme peace.

[20]Brahman; see note 16.

But the unknowing, who has no faith, who is full of doubt, falls; neither this world, nor the world beyond, nor happiness are for him who is full of doubt. 40

Works bind not him who offers up works through wisdom, who by wisdom has cut through all doubt, who is full of the Soul, O conqueror of wealth.

Therefore with the Soul's sword of wisdom cutting through every doubt born of unwisdom that dwells in the heart, arise and go forward to union, son of Bharata!

BOOK 5 [RENUNCIATION]

ARJUNA SAID:

Thou praisest renunciation of works, O Krishna, and again union with the Soul; tell me with certainty which of these two is better!

THE MASTER SAID:

Renunciation and union through works both make for the supreme goal; but of these two union through works is more excellent than renunciation of works.

He should be known as ever renouncing, who hates not nor desires; for he who is without these opposites, O mighty armed one, is happily freed from bondage.

Children, not wise men, speak of Sankhya and Yoga as different; he who has perfectly mastered one finds the fruit of both.

The goal that is gained by the Sankhyas, is also reached by the followers of Yoga; who sees Sankhya and Yoga as one, he indeed sees!

But renunciation, O mighty armed one, is hard to attain for him who is without union; the master of silence, who is joined in union, in no long time attains the Eternal.

Joined in union, purified in soul, self-conquered, lord of all his powers, his soul made one with the Soul of all beings, even though working, he is not stained.

He who is joined in union, who truly knows, understands that he engages not at all in work, though seeing, hearing, touching, smelling, eating, walking, sleeping, breathing,

Conversing, putting forth, grasping, opening or closing his eyes; he understands that the powers are working with the objects of the powers.

Who works, putting all works on the Eternal, giving up attachment, is not stained by sin, as the lotus leaf by water. 10

With body, with mind, with understanding, with pure powers the followers of union do work, free from attachment, to make themselves clean.

He who is united, giving up the fruit of works, wins perfect peace; the ununited, attached to the fruit of his works, is bound by the force of his desire.

Renouncing all works in mind, lord of himself, the lord of the body dwells content in the nine-doored abode, neither working nor the cause of work.

The Lord of the world makes neither actorship nor works, nor attachment to the fruit of works; self-existent Nature acts in these.

The Lord receives not the sin nor the good deeds of any; wisdom is concealed by unwisdom; through this the people are led astray.

But in whom unwisdom is destroyed by the wisdom of the Soul, for them wisdom sunlike illumines the Supreme.

With thought fixed on That, with soul set on That, making That their rule, going forward toward That, they go the Way that has no return, by wisdom rid of all their sins.

A Brahman full of wisdom and virtue, a cow, an elephant, a dog or a feeder of dogs: in these the wise behold no difference.

Even in this world they have conquered rebirth, whose minds are set firm in Oneness; the Eternal is one and faultless, therefore they are set firm in the Eternal.

Let him not exult when he meets happiness, let him not grieve when he meets sorrow; firm in soul-vision, undeluded, knowing the Eternal, he stands firm in the Eternal. 20

When with soul detached from contact of outer things, he finds all happiness in the Soul, joined in union with the Eternal, he reaches everlasting joy.

For delights born of contact with outer things are wombs of pain; they have their beginning and their ending, son of Kunti; in them the wise finds no delight.

He who even here, before the liberation from the body, is able to withstand the impetuous rush of desire and wrath, he is united, he is the happy man.

Who finds his joy within, his paradise within, his light within, that master of union, becomes the Eternal, wins Nirvana,[21] union with the Eternal.

The seers win Nirvana, union with the Eternal, whose sins are worn away, who have cut the knot of separateness, who are self-mastered, who delight in the weal of all beings.

Nirvana, union with the Eternal, has come nigh to those who are rid of desire and wrath, who have gained control, who control their thoughts, who have beheld the Soul.

Putting away external contacts, fixing the vision between the brows, making the inbreathing and outbreathing in the nostrils equal,

Controlling the powers and mind and thought, master of silence, bent on liberation, free from longing, fear and wrath, such a one is ever free.

Knowing Me to be the enjoyer of sacrifice and fervor, mighty Lord of all the world, lover of all beings, he reaches peace.

. . .

Book 18 [Conclusion]

ARJUNA SAID:

The truth of Renunciation, O mighty-armed one, I would learn of Thee, and of Resignation, with their difference, O Thou demon-slayer of flowing locks!

THE MASTER SAID:

The renouncing of works done through desire, sages have called Renunciation; and the wise have declared that ceasing from all desire of personal reward for one's work is Resignation.

Some of those who follow after knowledge have declared that every work is to be abandoned, as being faulty; but others say that works of sacrifice, gifts and penance are not to be abandoned.

[21] The cessation of bodily action in a union with the Eternal; a state of spiritual ecstasy.

Learn therefore from Me the certain truth concerning Resignation, O best descendant of Bharata; for Resignation, O tiger of men, is declared to be of three kinds.

Works of sacrifice, gifts and penance are not to be abandoned, but are to be performed; for sacrifice, gifts and penance are the purifiers of those who seek wisdom.

But even these works are to be performed with abandonment of attachment and the desire of reward; this, O son of Prithä, is My sure and excellent decision.

But the renunciation of necessary work is not right; the ceasing from such work comes of delusion, and is declared to be the fruit of Darkness.

Whoever ceases from any work through fear of bodily weariness, and saying: "it is painful," he, making the renunciation of Passion, does not gain the fruit of renunciation.

Whatever necessary work is done, O Arjuna, from the thought that it ought to be done, without attachment or desire of reward, this is held to be the renunciation of Substance.

He hates not unhappy work, nor is attached to happy work, the wise renouncer, who is pervaded by Substance, whose doubts are cut. 10

For it is impossible for an embodied being to abandon all work without exception; but he who has given up the love of reward, he indeed has made the true renunciation.

The fruit of works is threefold, desirable, or undesirable, or mixed; it follows those who have not abandoned desire, but not those who have made renunciation.

Learn from Me, O mighty-armed one, these five causes, which are declared in the Sankhya teaching, for the accomplishment of all works:

They are: the material instrument, the doer, the organ of whatever kind, the different impulses, and, fifthly, Destiny.

Whatever work a man initiates, by body, speech or mind, whether it be righteous or the contrary, these are its five causes.

As this is so, whoever views the Self, the lonely one, as the doer, he, confused in thought, sees not rightly through defect of understanding.

Whose nature is not selfish, whose vision is not stained, even though he slays the whole world, such a one kills not, nor is he subject to bondage.

The knowing, the thing to be known, the knower, make the threefold driving-power of works; the organ, the thing done, the doer, make the threefold content of works.

The knowing, the thing done, and the doer, divided threefold according to the powers, are declared according to the enumeration of the powers. Hear thou rightly these:

The knowledge whereby one eternal nature is perceived in all beings, undivided though beings are divided, know that knowledge to be of Substance. 20

But the knowledge which sees in all beings various natures according to their variety, know that knowledge to be of Force.

But the knowledge which attaches itself to one thing, as though that were the whole, lacking the right motive, without true perception, narrow, know that to be of Darkness.

The work that is done because it is necessary, without attachment, without lust or hate, by one who seeks no reward, is declared to be the work of Substance.

But work done by one seeking his desire, and selfishly, and with abundant toil, is declared to be the work of Force.

What work is begun without regard for consequences for the loss it may cause, or injury to others, or waste of power, through delusion, this is declared to be of Darkness.

The doer who is free from attachment, without vanity, who has firmness and will, who is not changed by success or failure, such a one is declared to be of Substance.

The doer who is full of desire, who seeks the reward of his works, who is greedy, who harms others and is impure, who falls into exultation or sorrow, is famed to be of Force.

The doer who is without union, brutish, conceited, malignant, unfair, slothful, despondent, temporising, is declared to be of Darkness.

Hear thou the division of understanding and of firmness, threefold according to the powers, declared completely according to their differences, O conqueror of wealth.

The understanding which knows action and abstention, what is to be done, what left undone, what is to be feared and what not, and also bondage and freedom, that, O son of Prithä, is of Substance. 30

The understanding which distinguishes not truly between law and lawlessness, what should and should not be done is of Force, O son of Prithä.

The understanding which, enwrapped in darkness, sees the unlawful as lawful, and all things as opposite to their true nature, that, O son of Prithä, is of Darkness.

The firmness whereby one firmly holds the emotional nature, and the actions of the life-powers, unwavering in union, that, O son of Prithä, is the firmness of Substance.

But the firmness, O Arjuna, whereby one desiring reward holds firmly to duty, desire, riches, that, O son of Prithä is the firmness of Force.

But the firmness through which one of foolish mind will not let go dreams, fears, grief, despondency, arrogance, that, O son of Prithä, is of Darkness.

Hear now from Me the three kinds of happiness, O bull of the Bharatas, through following which one finds delight, and makes an end of pain.

That which at the beginning is as poison, but in the outcome is like nectar, that is the happiness of Substance, springing from clear vision of the Soul.

The happiness which springs from the union of the senses with the objects of desire, in the beginning like nectar, but in the outcome like poison, that is declared to be the happiness of Force.

The happiness which, in the beginning, and to the end, causes blindness to the Soul, springing from sleep, sloth, negligence, that is declared to be of Darkness.

Neither on earth, nor in heaven, nor among the gods is there any being which is free from these three powers born of Nature. 40

The works of Brahman, Kshatriya, Vaishya and Shudra,[22] O consumer of the foe, are apportioned according to the powers inherent in the character of each.

Peace, control, penance, purity, patience, and also rectitude, wisdom, knowledge, affirmative faith, are the Brahman's work, according to his nature.

[22]The four castes; see note 19.

Heroism, fire, firmness, skill, and refusal to flee in battle, giving of gifts, governing, are the works of the Kshatriya, according to his nature.

Ploughing, tending cattle, commerce, are the natural work of the Vaishya; work which consists in service is the natural work of the Shudra.

By devotion each to his own work, every man gains true success; how each finds success through devotion to his own work, learn thou:

From Whom all beings come, by Whom all this is stretched forth, Him honoring, each by his own work, the son of man finds success.

Better is one's own duty even without excellence than the duty of another well carried out; doing the work imposed by one's own nature, he incurs no sin.

Let not a man withdraw from his natural work, O son of Kunti, even if it be faulty; for all initiatives are subject to fault, as fire is wrapped in smoke.

With thought everywhere unattached, self-conquered, from longing free, through renunciation he gains supreme success, free from bondage to works.

And how, having gained success, he gains the Eternal, learn thou of Me, hearing briefly, O son of Kunti, what is the supreme seat of wisdom. 50

With soul-vision kept pure, firmly self-controlled, detached from sounds and other sense-objects, and discarding lust and hate;

Seeking solitude, eating little, with speech, body and mind controlled, given up to union through soul-vision, following ever after dispassion;

Getting free from vanity, violence, pride, lust, wrath, avarice, without desire of possessions, full of peace, he builds for union with the Eternal.

Become one with the Eternal, with soul at peace, he grieves not nor desires; equal toward all beings, he gains highest love of Me.

Through love he learns Me truly, how great and what I am; then knowing Me truly, he straightway enters that Supreme.

Even continuing to perform all works, taking refuge in Me, through My grace he gains that everlasting home.

In heart renouncing all works in Me, devoted to Me, following after union through soul-vision, keep thy heart ever set on Me.

With heart set on Me, through My grace thou shalt cross through all rough places. But if through vanity thou wilt not hearken to Me, thou shalt perish.

When through self-assertion thou thinkest: "I will not fight!" thy determination is a delusion, for Nature will constrain thee.

Bound, O son of Kunti, by thine own natural work, what thou desirest not to do through thy delusion, thou shalt do against thy will. 60

The Lord dwells in the heart of every creature, O Arjuna, through His divine power moving all beings, as though guided by mechanism.

Take refuge in Him with thy whole heart, O descendant of Bharata; through His grace thou shalt gain supreme peace, the everlasting resting-place.

Thus to thee that wisdom which is more secret than all secrets is declared by Me; fully pondering on it, as thou desirest, so do!

Hear further My ultimate word, most secret of all; thou art exceeding dear to Me, therefore will I speak what is good for thee.

Set thy heart on Me, full of love for Me, sacrificing to Me, make obeisance to Me, and thou shalt come to Me; this is truth I promise thee, for thou art dear to Me.

Putting aside all other duties, come for refuge to Me alone; grieve not, for I shall set thee free from all sins.

This is never to be told by thee to him who is without fervor, without love, to him who seeks not to hear it, or who cavils at Me.
Whosoever shall declare this supreme secret in the company of those who love Me, showing the highest love for Me, he shall certainly come to Me.
Nor does any among mankind do aught dearer to Me than he; nor shall any in the world be dearer to Me than he.
And whosoever shall study this righteous converse of Me and thee, such a one sacrifices to Me the sacrifice of wisdom; such is My thought. 70
And whosoever shall hear it, full of faith and without cavil, he also, set free, will gain the shining worlds of those of holy works.
Say then, O son of Prithä, whether thou hast listened in singleness of heart; say whether thy delusion of unwisdom is destroyed, O conquerer of wealth!

ARJUNA SAID:
Gone is my delusion; I have come to right remembrance through Thy grace, O unfallen one! I stand, with my doubts gone. I shall fulfil thy word!

SANJAYA SAID:
Thus did I hear the converse of the son of Vasudeva[23] and the mighty-souled son of Prithä, marvelous, causing the hair to stand erect with wonder.
Through Vyasa's[24] grace I heard this supreme secret, this union, from the Lord of union, Krishna himself, relating it.
O king, ever and anon remembering this marvelous converse, this holy talk between him of the flowing locks and Arjuna, I exult again and again.
And ever and anon remembering Vishnu's[25] marvelous form, great dismay comes on me, O king, and I exult again and again.
Wherever are Krishna, Lord of union, and Prithä's son, bearer of the bow, there are fortune, victory, blessing and steadfast law; this I maintain.

THUS THE BHAGAVAD GITA IS COMPLETED.
MAY IT BE WELL WITH ALL BEINGS!

BACKGROUND TEXTS

HESIOD
[8TH CENTURY B.C.E.]

Western culture owes a great debt to a Greek poet who lived in roughly the same era as Homer but was interested in very different kinds of myths and stories. Homer focused primarily on the Uranian deities that became a part of the Olympic pantheon, a divine community gathered around Zeus, often resembling the Mycenean city-state with its patriarchal, feudal trappings. Homer avoided those stories that Hesiod collected and

[23]Kunti's brother; he is the father of Krishna.
[24]The sage and bard who is the legendary author of the *Bhagavad Gita.*
[25]Krishna stands in relation to Vishnu as Christ to God; he is the incarnate form of the supreme being.

preserved: the stories about old, powerful goddesses such as Styx and Hecate, about the rebellions against Zeus and the creation of woman, about the chthonic, nocturnal worlds of sacrifice and spells, about sex, fertility, and death.

Details about Hesiod's life are very sketchy. He was probably born in the region of Boeotia, in the town of Ascra. Evidence of his life as a farmer can be found in one of his important poems, *Works and Days*, in which he gives his brother Perses advice about living an upright life and provides him with maxims about farming. In his other major work, the *Theogony*, Hesiod describes how the Muses visited him while he was tending sheep on Mount Helicon and inspired him to write *Works and Days*. It is believed that Hesiod was murdered and buried at Oenoe.

We have provided an excerpt from the *Theogony*, which means "the generations of the gods." In this work Hesiod attempts to provide some coherence for a collection of creation stories and short sketches of deities. Hesiod believes that life is difficult and that women are dangerous to men; these views have their roots in the family dynamics of the first generations of the gods. In line with most primitive mythology, Hesiod reports that creation began with an existent material world. Gaia, or Earth as the physical world, gave birth to the first sky god, Uranus. Uranus (Sky) and Gaia (Earth) mated and produced the Titans and many other deities. Uranus hated his children and hid them back in Gaia's body. Groaning in pain, Gaia hatched a plan for revenge; Cronos, one of the sons, castrated his father one night with a flint knife. This pattern of father–son conflict was repeated in succeeding generations, becoming a divine model for the patriarchal family and a theme later for Greek drama.

Becoming the next ruler of the universe, Cronos married his sister Rhea and they created the first generation of Olympian deities. Because of the cycle of violence that he initiated, Cronos feared the birth of a son, and he swallowed each of his children after birth. Again the wife rebelled and, assisted by Gaia and Uranus, she substituted a swaddled stone for the baby Zeus, which Cronos swallowed. The grown Zeus overthrew his father and the Titans and released his siblings. Fearing a repetition of the pattern of the rebellious son and afraid of being dethroned, Zeus swallowed Metis, who was pregnant and the potential mother of the next ruler. Athena was born out of Zeus' head and joined forces with him. The important story of Prometheus' struggle with Zeus over the ritual of sacrifice and the possession of fire extended the pattern of rebellion and conflict.

Hesiod is the first poet in Greece to recognize the persuasive power of speaking directly to his audience, the men of his time. In *Works and Days*, Hesiod explains how the world has gradually deteriorated through a series of ages, from the Golden Age of peace and plenty to the Silver and then the Bronze. Recognizing that they lived in the Iron Age of warfare and family strife, Hesiod warns his readers about the consequences of conflict and injustice. In this role, Hesiod has often been compared to the prophets of Israel.

FROM

Theogony

Translated by H. G. Evelyn-White

. . . Verily at the first Chaos came to be, but next wide-bosomed Earth, the ever-sure foundation of all the deathless ones who hold the peaks of snowy Olympus, and dim Tartarus in the depth of the wide-pathed Earth, and Eros (Love), fairest among the deathless gods, who unnerves the limbs and overcomes the mind and wise counsels of all gods and all men within them. From Chaos came forth Erebus and black Night; but of Night were born Aether and Day, whom she conceived and bare from union in love with Erebus. And Earth first bare starry Heaven, equal to herself, to cover her on every side, and to be an ever-sure abiding-place for the blessed gods. And she brought forth long Hills, graceful haunts of the goddess-Nymphs who dwell amongst the glens of the hills. She bare also the fruitless deep with his raging swell, Pontus, without sweet union of love. But afterwards she lay with Heaven and bare deep-swirling Oceanus, Coeus and Crius and Hyperion and Iapetus, Theia and Rhea, Themis and Mnemosyne and gold-crowned Phoebe and lovely Tethys. After them was born Cronos the wily, youngest and most terrible of her children, and he hated his lusty sire.

And again, she bare the Cyclopes, overbearing in spirit, Brontes, and Steropes and stubborn-hearted Arges, who gave Zeus the thunder and made the thunderbolt: in all else they were like the gods, but one eye only was set in the midst of their foreheads. And they were surnamed Cyclopes (Orb-eyed) because one orbed eye was set in their foreheads. Strength and might and craft were in their works.

And again, three other sons were born of Earth and Heaven, great and doughty beyond telling, Cottus and Briareos and Gyes, presumptuous children. From their shoulders sprang an hundred arms, not to be approached, and each had fifty heads upon his shoulders on their strong limbs, and irresistible was the stubborn strength that was in their great forms. For of all the children that were born of Earth and Heaven, these were the most terrible, and they were hated by their own father from the first. And he used to hide them all away in a secret place of Earth so soon as each was born, and would not suffer them to come up into the light: and Heaven rejoiced in his evil doing. But vast Earth groaned within, being straitened, and she thought a crafty and an evil wile. Forthwith she made the element of grey flint and shaped a great sickle, and told her plan to her dear sons. And she spoke, cheering them, while she was vexed in her dear heart:

"My children, gotten of a sinful father, if you will obey me, we should punish the vile outrage of your father; for he first thought of doing shameful things."

So she said; but fear seized them all, and none of them uttered a word. But great Cronos the wily took courage and answered his dear mother:

"Mother, I will undertake to do this deed, for I reverence not our father of evil name, for he first thought of doing shameful things."

So he said: and vast Earth rejoiced greatly in spirit, and set and hid him in an ambush, and put in his hands a jagged sickle, and revealed to him the whole plot.

And Heaven came, bringing on night and longing for love, and he lay about Earth spreading himself full upon her. Then the son from his ambush stretched forth his left hand and in his right took the great long sickle with jagged teeth, and swiftly lopped off his own father's members and cast them away to fall behind him. And not vainly did they fall from his hand; for all the bloody drops that gushed forth Earth received, and as the seasons moved round she bare the strong Erinyes and the great Giants with gleaming armour, holding long spears in their hands and the Nymphs whom they call Meliae all over the boundless earth. And so soon as he had cut off the members with flint and cast them from the land into the surging sea, they were swept away over the main a long time: and a white foam spread around them from the immortal flesh, and in it there grew a maiden. First she drew near holy Cythera, and from there, afterwards, she came to sea-girt Cyprus, and came forth an awful and lovely goddess, and grass grew up about her beneath her shapely feet. Her gods and men call Aphrodite, and the foam-born goddess and rich-crowned Cytherea, because she grew amid the foam, and Cytherea because she reached Cythera, and Cyprogenes because she was born in billowy Cyprus, and

Philommedes because she sprang from the members. And with her went Eros, and comely Desire followed her at her birth at the first and as she went into the assembly of the gods. This honour she has from the beginning, and this is the portion allotted to her amongst men and undying gods,—the whisperings of maidens and smiles and deceits with sweet delight and love and graciousness.

But these sons whom he begot himself great Heaven used to call Titans (Strainers) in reproach, for he said that they strained and did presumptuously a fearful deed, and that vengeance for it would come afterwards. . . .

HERODOTUS

[C. 480–C. 425 B.C.E.]

Along with Thucydides and Xenophon, Herodotus, who lived sometime between 480 and 425 B.C.E., was one of the three earliest historians in the West. The chronicler of the Persian Wars, Herodotus is one of two "Fathers of History" (Thucydides is the other), although he has also been called the "Father of Lies" because he records much second-hand material. His work predates that of two other early Greek historians, Thucydides (c. 460–c. 399 B.C.E.) and Xenophon (434–355 B.C.E.); these three were the first writers in the West to think of history as more than a mere collection of records and documents. Combining literary and rhetorical talent with interpretation and analysis, Herodotus, Thucydides, and Xenophon turned the writing of history into a specialized craft, a focused discipline attempting to leave behind an account of the past.

Herodotus first lived under Persian rule in Halicarnassus in Asia Minor. Later he moved to Athens, which, along with Sparta, had defended Greece against the Persian attempt to invade the Peninsula between 490 and 479. Due to the Persian occupation of his city, Herodotus was denied the rights of citizenship and the political career that a well-born man would have expected. Possibly because of this, he traveled extensively as a young man, visiting most of the known world, including Egypt, Mesopotamia, Palestine, the area around the Black Sea, and the north coast of Africa. After spending some years in Athens, where he probably knew Thucydides and Sophocles, Herodotus moved to Thurii, a new colony in what is now southern Italy, where he finished writing the *Histories* and where—at least according to one tradition—he died around 425 B.C.E.

The *Histories* (which means "inquiries"), as his work is called, is divided into nine books that describe the history of Persia and Greece up through the Persian Wars (490–479). In addition to giving an account of major events, Herodotus sought to understand and describe the life, manners, and customs of the Persians, as well as the Greeks, and in doing so he creates a detailed panorama of the ways of the East and the West in the ancient world. His cultural history and his account of the Persian Wars contains much that is substantially embellished if not invented by the writer, but the *Histories,* nonetheless, reports lively and detailed accounts of events and characters. Despite his open celebration of the Athenian victory and Athenian democracy, to which he attributes Athens' triumph, Herodotus paints the Persian society and its leaders with admirable objectivity.

The selection we include here comes from Book I of the *Histories,* in which Herodotus describes an encounter between Solon, the first important constitutional reformer of Athens, and Croesus, the fabulously wealthy king of Lydia, in what is now western Turkey. As Plutarch first noted, the meeting between Solon and Croesus could never have taken place, thus demonstrating Herodotus' penchant for mixing legend and fable with accounts of what actually took place. His purpose in staging this meeting, however, is to demonstrate the difference between the East and the West. Solon's speech emphasizes the transience of human life and the fragility and uncertainty of human happiness.

FROM

The Persian Wars

Translated by George Rawlinson

[Solon on Happiness]

When all these conquests had been added to the Lydian empire, and the prosperity of Sardis was now at its height, there came thither, one after another, all the sages of Greece living at the time, and among them Solon, the Athenian. He was on his travels, having left Athens to be absent ten years, under the pretense of wishing to see the world, but really to avoid being forced to repeal any of the laws which, at the request of the Athenians, he had made for them. Without his sanction the Athenians could not repeal them, as they had bound themselves under a heavy curse to be governed for ten years by the laws which should be imposed on them by Solon.

On this account, as well as to see the world, Solon set out upon his travels, in the course of which he went to Egypt to the court of Amasis, and also came on a visit to Croesus at Sardis. Croesus received him as his guest, and lodged him in the royal palace. On the third or fourth day after, he bade his servants conduct Solon over his treasuries, and show him all their greatness and magnificence. When he had seen them all, and, so far as time allowed, inspected them, Croesus addressed this question to him. "Stranger of Athens, we have heard much of thy wisdom and of thy travels through many lands, from love of knowledge and a wish to see the world. I am curious therefore to inquire of thee, whom, of all the men that thou hast seen, thou deemest the most happy?" This he asked because he thought himself the happiest of mortals: but Solon answered him without flattery, according to his true sentiments, "Tellus of Athens, sire." Full astonishment at what he heard, Croesus demanded sharply, "And wherefore dost thou deem Tellus happiest?" To which the other replied, "First, because his country was flourishing in his days, and he himself had sons both beautiful and good, and he lived to see children born to each of them, and these children all grew up; and further because, after a life spent in what our people look upon as comfort, his end was surpassingly glorious. In a battle between the Athenians and their neighbors near Eleusis, he came to the assistance of his countrymen, routed the foe, and died upon the field most gallantly. The Athenians gave him a public funeral on the spot where he fell, and paid him the highest honors."

Thus did Solon admonish Croesus by the example of Tellus, enumerating the manifold particulars of his happiness. When he had ended, Croesus inquired a second time, who after Tellus seemed to him the happiest, expecting that at any rate, he would be given the second place. "Cleobis and Bito," Solon answered; "they were of Argive race; their fortune was enough for their wants, and they were besides endowed with so much bodily strength that they had both gained prizes at the Games. Also this tale is told of them:—There was a great festival in honor of the goddess Hera at Argos, to which their mother must needs be taken in a car. Now the oxen did not come home from the field in time: so the youths, fearful of being too late, put the yoke on their own necks, and themselves drew the car in which their mother rode. Five and forty furlongs did they draw her, and stopped before the temple. This deed of theirs was witnessed by the whole assembly of worshipers, and then their life closed in the best possible way. Herein, too, God showed forth most evidently, how much better a thing for man death is than life. For the Argive men, who stood around the car, extolled the vast strength of the youths; and the Argive women extolled the mother who was blessed with such a pair of sons; and the mother herself, overjoyed at the deed and at the praises it had won, standing straight before the image, besought the goddess to bestow on Cleobis and Bito, the sons who had so mightily honored her, the highest blessing to which mortals can attain. Her prayer ended, they offered sacrifice and partook of the holy banquet, after which the two youths fell asleep in the temple. They never woke more, but so passed from the earth. The Argives, looking on them as among the best of men, caused statues of them to be made, which they gave to the shrine at Delphi."

When Solon had thus assigned these youths the second place, Croesus broke in angrily, "What, stranger of Athens, is my happiness, then, so utterly set at nought by thee, that thou dost not even put me on a level with private men?"

"Oh! Croesus," replied the other, "thou askedst a question concerning the condition of man, of one who knows that the power above us is full of jealousy, and fond of troubling our lot. A long life gives one to witness much, and experience much oneself, that one would not choose. Seventy years I regard as the limit of the life of man. In these seventy years are contained, without reckoning intercalary months, twenty-five thousand and two hundred days. Add an intercalary month to every other year, that the seasons may come round at the right time, and there will be, besides the seventy years, thirty-five such months, making an addition of one thousand and fifty days. The whole number of the days contained in the seventy years will thus be twenty-six thousand two hundred and fifty, whereof not one but will produce events unlike the rest. Hence man is wholly accident. For thyself, oh! Croesus, I see that thou art wonderfully rich, and art the lord of many nations; but with respect to that whereon thou questionest me, I have no answer to give, until I hear that thou hast closed thy life happily. For assuredly he who possesses great store of riches is no nearer happiness than he who has what suffices for his daily needs, unless it so hap that luck attend upon him, and so he continue in the enjoyment of all his good things to the end of life. For many of the wealthiest men have been unfavored of fortune, and many whose means were moderate have had excellent luck. Men of the former class excel those of the latter but in two respects; these last excel the former in many. The wealthy man is better able to content his desires, and to bear up against a sudden buffet of calamity. The other has less ability to withstand these evils (from which, however, his good luck keeps him clear), but he enjoys all these following blessings: he is whole of limb, a stranger to disease, free from misfortune, happy in his children, and comely to look upon. If, in addition to all this, he end his life well, he is of a truth the man of whom thou art in search, the man who may rightly be termed happy. Call him, however, until he die, not happy but fortunate. Scarcely, indeed, can any man unite all these advantages: as there is no country which contains within it all that it needs, but each, while it possesses some things, lacks others, and the best country is that which contains the most; so no single human being is complete in every respect—something is always lacking. He who unites the greatest number of advantages, and retaining them to the day of his death, then dies peaceably, that man alone, sire, is, in my judgment, entitled to bear the name of 'happy.' But in every matter it behoves us to mark well the end: for oftentimes God gives men a gleam of happiness, and then plunges them into ruin."

Such was the speech which Solon addressed to Croesus, a speech which brought him neither largess nor honor. The king saw him depart with much indifference, since he thought that a man must be an arrant fool who made no account of present good, but bade men always wait and mark the end.

THUCYDIDES

[C. 460–C. 399 B.C.E.]

Along with Herodotus (c. 480–c. 425 B.C.E.), Thucydides is the other great historian of classical Greece, one of the two "Fathers of History." His *History of the Peloponnesian War* describes Athens at the high point of its democratic golden age and traces its decline as the sustained conflict with Sparta and its allies weakened Athenian alliances and undermined its democratic ideals.

Herodotus had written in his *Histories* a sweeping account of the emergence of Greece as a nation and of its struggle to separate itself from Asia, from the time of the Trojan War (c. 1200 B.C.E.) to the Persian Wars in the fifth century. Thucydides took a different approach. He did not attempt to create a panorama of the past, but rather a detailed record of his own time. His *History of the Peloponnesian War* is a strictly chronological account of the wars between the Athenian empire and Sparta and its allies between 431 and 404 B.C.E. Thucydides did not finish his history, however, for it breaks off abruptly in 411, more than six years before the end of the war.

Legend has it that this sudden conclusion resulted from Thucydides' death by assassination, but the story is a product of speculation, for little is known of Thucydides' life beyond what he alludes to in his history. We do know that he commanded the Athenian naval forces at the Battle of Amphipolis in 424 and as a result of the defeat he suffered there, he was banished from Athens for twenty years. During this period in exile, presumably, he had time to write his history of the war.

Thucydides was also a more documentary historian than Herodotus. Writing about the events of his own time, he seems to have kept careful notes of things as they happened, and, even though he lacked the news accounts and tape recorders of the contemporary historian, he recreated speeches and debates from memory and from oral sources, which he included verbatim in his record. As an exile, he was also in the unusual position of having access to sources from both sides in the conflict, so he was able to achieve an extraordinary degree of objectivity. Because he was writing before the end of the war, without the benefit of hindsight, Thucydides produced a dramatic and objective narrative of the events and controversies of the period with insightful portraits of the statesmen and generals, as well as an analysis of the psychological, economic, and moral forces at work.

The passage that follows, Pericles' famous Funeral Oration commemorating the Athenian dead after the first year of the war (430 B.C.E.), illustrates Thucydides' dramatic method. Even though he had to reconstruct it, he presents the speech in Pericles' own words. The speech itself is much more than a funeral oration. Pericles uses the occasion to celebrate Athens and its democratic ideals, for which he is remembered as the great champion during the "Age of Pericles," from 461 to 429 B.C.E. His defense of majority rule, political equality, the recognition of merit, tolerance, and individualism have made this speech a classic statement of democratic values.

FROM

The Peloponnesian War

Translated by Benjamin Jowett

[PERICLES' FUNERAL ORATION]

In the same winter the Athenians gave a funeral at the public cost to those who had first fallen in this war. It was a custom of their ancestors, and the manner of it is as follows. Three days before the ceremony, the bones of the dead are laid out in a tent which has been erected; and their friends bring to their relatives such offerings as they please. In the funeral procession cypress coffins are borne on wagons, one for each tribe, the bones of the deceased being placed in the coffin of their tribe. Among these is carried one empty bier decked for the missing, that is, for those whose bodies could not be recovered. Any citizen or stranger who pleases joins in the procession: and the female relatives are there to wail at the burial. The dead are laid in the public sepulchre in the most beautiful suburb of the city, in which those who fall in war are always buried—with the exception of those slain at Marathon, who for their singular and extraordinary valour were interred on the spot where they fell. After the bodies have been laid in the earth, a man chosen by the state, of approved wisdom and eminent reputation, pronounces over them an appropriate panegyric, after which all retire. Such is the manner of the burying; and throughout the whole of the war, whenever the occasion arose, the established custom was observed. Meanwhile these were the first that had fallen, and Pericles, son of Xanthippus, was chosen to pronounce their eulogium. When the proper time arrived, he advanced from the sepulchre to an elevated platform in order to be heard by as many of the crowd as possible, and spoke as follows:

"Most of my predecessors in this place have commended him who made this speech part of the law, telling us that it is well that it should be delivered at the burial of those who fall in battle. For myself, I should have thought that the worth which had displayed itself in deeds would be sufficiently rewarded by honours also shown by deeds, such as you now see in this funeral prepared at the people's cost. And I could have wished that the reputations of many brave men were not to be imperilled in the mouth of a single individual, to stand or fall according as he spoke well or ill. For it is hard to speak properly upon a subject where it is even difficult to convince your hearers that you are speaking the truth. On the one hand, the friend who is familiar with every fact of the story may think that some point has not been set forth with that fullness which he wishes and knows it to deserve; on the other, he who is a stranger to the matter may be led by envy to suspect exaggeration if he hears anything above his own nature. For men can endure to hear others praised only so long as they can severally persuade themselves of their own ability to equal the actions recounted: when this point is passed, envy comes in and with it incredulity. However, since our ancestors have stamped this custom with their approval, it becomes my duty to obey the law and to try to satisfy your several wishes and opinions as best I may.

"I shall begin with our ancestors: it is both just and proper that they should have the honour of the first mention on an occasion like the present. They dwelt in the country without break in the succession from generation to generation, and handed it down free to the present time by their valour. And if our more remote ancestors deserve praise, much more do our own fathers, who added to their inheritance the empire which we now possess, and spared no pains to be able to leave their acquisitions to us of the present generation. Lastly, there are few parts of our dominions that have not been augmented by those of us here, who are still more or less in the vigour of life; and the mother country has been furnished by us with everything that can enable her to depend on her own resources whether for war or for peace. That part of our history which tells of the military achievements which gave us our several possessions, or of the ready valour with which either we or our fathers stemmed the tide of Hellenic or foreign aggression, is a theme too familiar to my hearers for me to dilate on, and I shall therefore pass it by. But by what road we reached our position, under what form of government our greatness grew, out of what national habits it sprang—these are subjects which I may pursue before I proceed to my panegyric upon these men; for I think them to be themes upon which on the present occasion a speaker may properly dwell, and to which the whole assemblage, whether citizens or foreigners, may listen with advantage.

"Our constitution does not copy the laws of neighbouring states; we are rather a pattern to others than imitators ourselves. Its administration favours the many instead of the few; this is why it is called a democracy. If we look to the laws, they afford equal justice to all in their private differences; if to social standing, advancement in public life falls to reputation for capacity, class considerations not being allowed to interfere with merit; nor again does poverty bar the way: if a man is able to serve the state, he is not hindered by the obscurity of his condition. The freedom which we enjoy in our government extends also to our ordinary life. There, far from exercising a jealous surveillance over each other, we do not feel called upon to be angry with our neighbour for doing what he likes, or even to indulge in those injurious looks which cannot fail to be offensive, although they inflict no positive penalty. But all this ease in our private relations does not make us lawless as citizens. Against this fear is our chief safeguard, teaching us to obey the magistrates and the laws, particularly such as regard the protection of the injured, whether they are actually on the statute book, or belong to that code which, although unwritten, yet cannot be broken without acknowledged disgrace.

"Further, we provide plenty of means for the mind to refresh itself from business. We celebrate games and sacrifices all the year round, and the elegance of our private establishments forms a daily source of pleasure and helps to banish our cares; and the magnitude of our city draws the produce of the world into our harbour, so that to the Athenian the fruits of other countries are as familiar a luxury as those of his own.

"If we turn to our military policy, there also we differ from our antagonists. We throw open our city to the world, and never by alien acts exclude foreigners from any opportunity of learning or observing, although the eyes of an enemy may occasionally profit by our liberality; we trust less in system and policy than in the native spirit of our citizens; and in education, where our rivals from their very cradles by a painful discipline seek after manliness, at Athens we live exactly as we please, and yet are just as ready to encounter every legitimate danger. In proof of this it may be noticed that the Lacedæmonians do not invade our country alone, but bring with them all their confederates, while we Athenians advance unsupported into the territory of a neighbour, and fighting upon a foreign soil usually vanquish with ease men who are defending their homes. Our united force was never yet encountered by any enemy, because we have at once to attend to our marine and to despatch our citizens by land upon a hundred different services; thus wherever they engage with some such fraction of our strength, a success against a detachment is magnified into a victory over the nation, and a defeat into a reverse suffered at the hands of our entire people. And yet if with habits not of labour but of ease, and courage not of art but of nature, we are still willing to encounter danger, we have the double advantage of escaping the experience of hardships in anticipation and of facing them in the hour of need as fearlessly as those who are never free from them.

"Nor are these the only points in which our city is worthy of admiration. We cultivate refinement without extravagance and knowledge without effeminacy; wealth we employ more for use than for show, and place the real disgrace of poverty not in owning to the fact but in declining the struggle against it. Our public men have, besides politics, their private affairs to attend to, and our ordinary citizens, though occupied with the pursuits of industry, are still fair judges of public matters; for, unlike any other nation, regarding him who takes no part in these duties not as unambitious but as useless, we Athenians are able to judge at all events if we cannot originate, and instead of looking on discussion as a stumbling-block in the way of action, we think it an indispensable preliminary to any wise action at all. Again, in our enterprises we present the singular spectacle of daring and deliberation, each carried to its highest point, and both united in the same persons, although usually decision is the fruit of ignorance, hesitation of reflection. But the palm of courage will surely be adjudged most justly to those who best know the difference between hardship and pleasure and yet are never tempted to shrink from danger. In generosity we are equally singular, acquiring our friends by conferring, not by receiving, favours. Yet, of course, the doer of the favour is the firmer friend of the two, in order by continued kindness to keep the recipient in his debt, while the debtor feels less keenly from the very consciousness that the return he makes will be a payment, not a free gift. And it is only the Athenians who, fearless of consequences, confer their benefits not from calculations of expediency, but in the confidence of liberality.

"In short, I say that as a city we are the school of Hellas; and I doubt if the world can produce a man, who where he has only himself to depend upon, is equal to so many emergencies, and graced by so happy a versatility as the Athenian. And that this is no mere boast thrown out for the occasion, but plain matter of fact, the power of the state acquired by these habits proves. For Athens alone of her contemporaries is found when tested to be greater than her reputation, and alone gives no occasion to her assailants to blush at the antagonist by whom they have been worsted, or to her subjects to question her title by merit to rule. Rather, the admiration of the present and succeeding ages will be ours, since we have not left our power without witness, but have shown it by mighty proofs; and far from needing a Homer for our panegyrist, or other of his craft whose verses might charm for the moment only for the impression which they gave to melt at the touch of fact, we have forced every sea and land to be the highway of our daring, and everywhere, whether for evil or for good, have left imperishable monuments behind us. Such is the Athens for which these men, in the assertion of their resolve not to lose her, nobly fought and died; and well may every one of their survivors be ready to suffer in her cause.

"Indeed if I have dwelt at some length upon the character of our country, it has been to show that our stake in the struggle is not the same as theirs who have no such blessings to lose, and also that the panegyric of the men over whom I am now speaking might be by definite proofs established. That panegyric is now in a great measure complete; for the Athens that I have celebrated is only what the heroism of these and their like have made her, men whose fame, unlike that of most Hellenes, will be found to be only commensurate with their deserts. And if a test of worth be wanted, it is to be found in their closing scene, and this not only in the cases in which it set the final seal upon their merit, but also in those in which it gave the first intimation of their having any. For there is justice in the claim that steadfastness in his country's battles should be as a cloak to cover a man's other imperfections; for the good action has blotted out the bad, and his merit as a citizen more than outweighed his demerits as an individual. But none of these allowed either wealth with its prospect of future enjoyment to unnerve his spirit, or poverty with its hope of a day of freedom and riches to tempt him to shrink from danger. No, holding that vengeance upon their enemies was more to be desired than any personal blessings, and reckoning this to be the most glorious of hazards, they joyfully determined to accept the risk, to make sure of their vengeance and to let their wishes wait; and while committing to hope the uncertainty of final success, in the business before them they thought fit to act boldly and trust in themselves. Thus choosing to die resisting, rather than to live submitting, they fled only from dishonour, but met danger face to face, and after one brief moment, while at the summit of their fortune, escaped, not from their fear, but from their glory.

"So died these men as became Athenians. You, their survivors, must determine to have as unaltering a resolution in the field, though you may pray that it may have a happier issue. And not contented with ideas derived only from words of the advantages which are bound up with the defence of your country, though these would furnish a valuable text to a speaker even before an audience so alive to them as the present, you must yourselves realize the power of Athens, and feed your eyes upon her from day to day, till love of her fills your hearts; and then when all her greatness shall break upon you, you must reflect that it was by courage, sense of duty, and a keen feeling of honour in action that men were enabled to win all this, and that no personal failure in an enterprise could make them consent to deprive their country of their valour, but they laid it at her feet as the most glorious contribution that they could offer. For this offering of their lives made in common by them all they each of them individually received that renown which never grows old, and for a sepulchre, not so much that in which their bones have been deposited, but that noblest of shrines wherein their glory is laid up to be eternally remembered upon every occasion on which deed or story shall call for its commemoration. For heroes have the whole earth for their tomb; and in lands far from their own, where the column with its epitaph declares it, there is enshrined in every breast a record unwritten with no tablet to preserve it, except that of the heart. These take as your model, and judging happiness to be the fruit of freedom and freedom of valour, never decline the dangers of war. For it is not the miserable that would most justly be unsparing of their lives; these have nothing to hope for: it is rather they to whom continued life may bring reverses as yet unknown, and to whom a fall, if it came, would be most tremendous in its consequences. And surely, to a man of spirit, the degradation of cowardice must be immeasurably more grievous than the unfelt death which strikes him in the midst of his strength and patriotism!

"Comfort, therefore, not condolence, is what I have to offer to the parents of the dead who may be here. Numberless are the chances to which, as they know, the life of man is subject; but fortunate indeed are they who draw for their lot a death so glorious as that which has caused your mourning, and to whom life has been so exactly measured as to terminate in the happiness in which it has been passed. Still I know that this is a hard saying, especially when those are in question of whom you will constantly be reminded by seeing in the homes of others blessings of which once you also boasted: for grief is felt not so much for the want of what we have never known, as for the loss of that to which we have been long accustomed. Yet you who are still of an age to beget children must bear up in the hope of having others in their stead; not only will they help you to forget those whom you have lost, but will be to the state at once a reinforcement and a security; for never can a fair or just policy be expected of the citizen who does not, like his fellows, bring to the decision the interests and apprehensions of a father. And those of you who have passed your prime must congratulate yourselves with the thought that the best part of your life was fortunate, and that the brief span that remains will be cheered by the fame of the departed. For it is only the love of honour that never grows old; and honour it is, not gain, as some would have it, that rejoices the heart of age and helplessness.

"Turning to the sons or brothers of the dead, I see an arduous struggle before you. When a man is gone, all are wont to praise him, and should your merit be ever so transcendent, you will still find it difficult not merely to overtake, but even to approach their renown. The living have envy to contend with, while those who are no longer in our path are honoured with a goodwill into which rivalry does not enter. On the other hand, if I must say anything on the subject of female excellence to those of you who will now be in widowhood, it will be all comprised in this brief exhortation. Great will be your glory in not falling short of your natural character; and greatest will be hers who is least talked of among the men whether for good or for bad.

"My task is now finished. I have performed it to the best of my ability, and in words, at least, the requirements of the law are now satisfied. If deeds be in question, those who are here interred have received part of their honours already, and for the rest, their children will be brought up till manhood at the public expense: the state thus offers a valuable prize as the garland of victory in this race of valour, for the reward both of those who have fallen and their survivors. And where the rewards for merit are greatest, there are found the best citizens.

"And now that you have brought to a close your lamentations for your relatives, you may depart."

CONFUCIUS

[551–479 B.C.E.]

Like Socrates and Jesus, Confucius left behind no writings of his own. What we know in English as *The Analects of Confucius,* as their first translator James Legge called them, is a compendium of collected aphoristic tales and sayings handed down from Confucius' earliest followers and students; *Lun Yü,* as this collection is known in Chinese, literally means "Selected Sayings." Confucius was the most profoundly influential thinker in Asia, for his teachings gave rise to a sociophilosophical system that has endured for more than 2,000 years. By the second century B.C.E., Confucianism had become official doctrine in China, and it remains so today, having survived attempts to discredit it or to reduce it to apologist dogma. Despite the inherent conservativism of Confucianism, which emphasizes filial piety, dutiful respect for authority, and deference to tradition, it has influenced various democratic movements in the East and the West. Sun Yat-sen, for example, called Confucius and his best-known disciple, Mencius, fathers of the Chinese Revolution.

The life of Confucius has been obscured by the layers of legend that have grown up around his name. He was born in 551 B.C.E. in the feudal province of Lu, in eastern China north of the Yangtze River, probably to a family of the lower aristocracy, although legend has it that he sprung from more humble origins. Kong Fuzi, or Master Kung (Latinized to Confucius), became a philosopher teacher after intensive study of the traditional *Five Classics,* a collection of poems, lore, and documents rooted in the ancient history of China. As *The Analects* report him to have said, "At fifteen I wanted to learn. At thirty I had a foundation. At forty, a certitude. At fifty, knew the orders of heaven. At sixty, was ready to listen to them. At seventy, could follow my own heart's desire without overstepping the law" (II.iv). Apparently before he achieved certitude he began teaching, for he had begun teaching just before his mother's death, when he was twenty-three years old. After a three-year period of grieving, he resumed his teaching and traveled from court to court trying to teach the way to right government and right living.

Confucius lived during the Eastern Zhou dynasty (771–256 B.C.E.), an age of great importance to Chinese culture. It was a time of great social and technological change during which the arts and letters flourished despite the lack of a strong central government. In this era, the power of feudal lords overshadowed that of the kings descended from the Zhou invaders, who had overthrown the ancient Shang dynasty. Once the center of political power, these traditional leaders had been reduced to nominal roles as spiritual leaders. Most importantly for Confucianism, it was a time of instability when the system that had held China intact began to break down; with a weakened central power, rivalries arose among the competing provincial lords. In the last years of his life, Confucius traveled to the courts of these once vassal lords, unsuccessfully trying to convince them to accept his ways and to convert them into philosopher-kings, an ideal he held in common with Plato. Thus, the practical piety, filial obligation, and respect for tradition that Confucius taught arose in part from his intention to preserve the foundering integrity of Chinese society.

The selections from *The Analects* here give a fair sample of the basic tenets of Confucius' thought: its focus upon the matters of this world; its celebration of the family as the central pillar of political and social life; and its emphasis upon practicing a middle way that leads to moral propriety and social responsibility. Above all, Confucius taught that people should set aside self-interest for the good of others—their immediate family, their province, and their state. Right conduct at home, achieved through observing ritual and basing action in moral principle, would lead ultimately to a balanced individual, family, and state.

The Analects

Translated by Arthur Waley

FROM

Book 1

1. The Master said, To learn and at due times to repeat what one has learnt, is that not after all a pleasure? That friends should come to one from afar, is this not after all delightful? To remain unsoured even though one's merits are unrecognized by others, is that not after all what is expected of a gentleman?

2. Master Yu said, Those who in private life behave well towards their parents and elder brothers, in public life seldom show a disposition to resist the authority of their superiors. And as for such men starting a revolution, no instance of it has ever occurred. It is upon the trunk that a gentleman works. When that is firmly set up, the Way grows. And surely proper behaviour towards parents and elder brothers is the trunk of Goodness?

3. The Master said, 'Clever talk and a pretentious manner' are seldom found in the Good.

4. Master Tsêng said, Every day I examine myself on these three points: in acting on behalf of others, have I always been loyal to their interests? In intercourse with my friends, have I always been true to my word? Have I failed to repeat the precepts that have been handed down to me?

5. The Master said, A country of a thousand war-chariots cannot be administered unless the ruler attends strictly to business, punctually observes his promises, is economical in expenditure, shows affection towards his subjects in general, and uses the labour of the peasantry only at the proper times of year.

6. The Master said, A young man's duty is to behave well to his parents at home and to his elders abroad, to be cautious in giving promises and punctual in keeping them, to have kindly feelings towards everyone, but seek the intimacy of the Good. If, when all that is done, he has any energy to spare, then let him study the polite arts.

7. Tzu-hsia said, A man who

> Treats his betters as betters,
> Wears an air of respect,
> Who into serving father and mother
> Knows how to put his whole strength,

Who in the service of his prince will lay down his life,
Who in intercourse with friends is true to his word—

others may say of him that he still lacks education, but I for my part should certainly call him an educated man.

8. The Master said, If a gentleman is frivolous, he will lose the respect of his inferiors and lack firm ground upon which to build up his education. First and foremost he must learn to be faithful to his superiors, to keep promises, to refuse the friendship of all who are not like him. And if he finds he has made a mistake, then he must not be afraid of admitting the fact and amending his ways.

9. Master Tsêng said, When proper respect towards the dead is shown at the End and continued after they are far away the moral force (*tê*) of a people has reached its highest point.

10. Tzu-Ch'in said to Tzu-kung, When our Master arrives in a fresh country he always manages to find out about its policy. Does he do this by asking questions, or do people tell him of their own accord? Tzu-kung said, Our Master gets things by being cordial, frank, courteous, temperate, deferential. That is our Master's way of enquiring—a very different matter, certainly, from the way in which enquiries are generally made.

11. The Master said, While a man's father is alive, you can only see his intentions; it is when his father dies that you discover whether or not he is capable of carrying them out. If for the whole three years of mourning he manages to carry on the household exactly as in his father's day, then he is a good son indeed. . . .

FROM

Book 2

. . . 5. Mêng I Tzu asked about the treatment of parents. The Master said, Never disobey! When Fan Ch'ih was driving his carriage for him, the Master said, Mêng asked me about the treatment of parents and I said, Never disobey! Fan Ch'ih said, In what sense did you mean it? The Master said, While they are alive, serve them according to ritual. When they die, bury them according to ritual and sacrifice to them according to ritual.

6. Mêng Wu Po asked about the treatment of parents. The Master said, Behave in such a way that your father and mother have no anxiety about you, except concerning your health.

7. Tzu-yu asked about the treatment of parents. The Master said, 'Filial sons' nowadays are people who see to it that their parents get enough to eat. But even dogs and horses are cared for to that extent. If there is no feeling of respect, wherein lies the difference?

8. Tzu-hsia asked about the treatment of parents. The Master said, It is the demeanour that is difficult. Filial piety does not consist merely in young people undertaking the hard work, when anything has to be done, or serving their elders first with wine and food. It is something much more than that. . . .

13. Tzu-kung asked about the true gentleman. The Master said, He does not preach what he practises till he has practised what he preaches.

14. The Master said, A gentleman can see a question from all sides without bias. The small man is biased and can see a question only from one side.

15. The Master said, 'He who learns but does not think, is lost.' He who thinks but does not learn is in great danger.

16. The Master said, He who sets to work upon a different strand destroys the whole fabric.

17. The Master said, Yu, shall I teach you what knowledge is? When you know a thing, to recognize that you know it, and when you do not know a thing, to recognize that you do not know it. That is knowledge. . . .

19. Duke Ai asked, What can I do in order to get the support of the common people? Master K'ung replied, If you 'raise up the straight and set them on top of the crooked,' the commoners will support you. But if you raise the crooked and set them on top of the straight, the commoners will not support you.

20. Chi K'ang-tzu asked whether there were any form of encouragement by which he could induce the common people to be respectful and loyal. The Master said, Approach them with dignity, and they will respect you. Show piety towards your parents and kindness toward your children, and they will be loyal to you. Promote those who are worthy, train those who are incompetent; that is the best form of encouragement. . . .

FROM BOOK 6

. . . 27. The Master said, How transcendent is the moral power of the Middle Use! That it is but rarely found among the common people is a fact long admitted.

28. Tzu-kung said, If a ruler not only conferred wide benefits upon the common people, but also compassed the salvation of the whole State, what would you say of him? Surely, you would call him Good? The Master said, It would no longer be a matter of 'Good.' He would without doubt be a Divine Sage. Even Yao and Shun could hardly criticize him. As for Goodness—you yourself desire rank and standing; then help others to get rank and standing. You want to turn your own merits to account; then help others to turn theirs to account—in fact, the ability to take one's own feelings as a guide—that is the sort of thing that lies in the direction of Goodness. . . .

FROM BOOK 8

. . . 4. When Master Tsêng was ill, Mêng Ching Tzu came to see him. Master Tsêng spoke to him saying, When a bird is about to die its song touches the heart. When a man is about to die, his words are of note. There are three things that a gentleman, in following the Way, places above all the rest: from every attitude, every gesture that he employs he must remove all trace of violence or arrogance; every look that he composes in his face must betoken good faith; from every word that he utters, from every intonation, he must remove all trace of coarseness or impropriety. As to the ordering of ritual vessels and the like, there are those whose business it is to attend to such matters.

5. Master Tsêng said, Clever, yet not ashamed to consult those less clever than himself; widely gifted, yet not ashamed to consult those with few gifts; having, yet seeming not to have; full, yet seeming empty; offended against, yet never contesting—long ago I had a friend whose ways were such as this. . . .

FROM BOOK 9

. . . 7. The Master said, Do I regard myself as a possessor of wisdom? Far from it. But if even a simple peasant comes in all sincerity and asks me a question, I am ready to thrash the matter out, with all its pros and cons, to the very end. . . .

FROM
Book 11

. . . 3. The Master said, Hui was not any help to me; he accepted everything I said. . . .

11. Tzu-lu asked how one should serve ghosts and spirits. The Master said, Till you have learnt to serve men, how can you serve ghosts? Tzu-lu then ventured upon a question about the dead. The Master said, Till you know about the living, how are you to know about the dead? . . .

FROM
Book 13

. . . 6. The Master said, If the ruler himself is upright, all will go well even though he does not give orders. But if he himself is not upright, even though he gives orders, they will not be obeyed. . . .

21. The Master said, If I cannot get men who steer a middle course to associate with, I would far rather have the impetuous and hasty. For the impetuous at any rate assert themselves; and the hasty have this at least to be said for them, that there are things they leave undone. . . .

FROM
Book 14

. . . 5. The Master said, One who has accumulated moral power (*tê*) will certainly also possess eloquence; but he who has eloquence does not necessarily possess moral power. A Good Man will certainly also possess courage; but a brave man is not necessarily Good. . . .

13. Tzu-lu asked what was meant by 'the perfect man.' The Master said, If anyone had the wisdom of Tsang Wu Chung, the uncovetousness of Mêng Kung Ch'o, the valour of Chuang Tzu of P'ien and the dexterity of Jan Ch'iu, and had graced these virtues by the cultivation of ritual and music, then indeed I think we might call him 'a perfect man.'

He said, But perhaps to-day we need not ask all this of the perfect man. One who, when he sees a chance of gain, stops to think whether to pursue it would be right; when he sees that (his prince) is in danger, is ready to lay down his life; when the fulfilment of an old promise is exacted, stands by what he said long ago—him indeed I think we might call 'a perfect man.' . . .

FROM
Book 15

. . . 14. The Master said, To demand much from oneself and little from others is the way (for a ruler) to banish discontent. . . .

20. The Master said, 'The demands that a gentleman makes are upon himself; those that a small man makes are upon others.'

21. The Master said, A gentleman is proud, but not quarrelsome, allies himself with individuals, but not with parties. . . .

23. Tzu-kung asked saying, Is there any single saying that one can act upon all day and every day? The Master said, Perhaps the saying about consideration: 'Never do to others what you would not like them to do to you.' . . .

DEAD SEA SCROLLS

[2ND CENTURY B.C.E.–1ST CENTURY C.E.]

In 1947, two young shepherds accidentally discovered a cave in the Qumran hills near the Dead Sea in Palestine, and in the cave they found some ancient scrolls in clay jars. When the archeological and biblical value of the scrolls was recognized, extensive exploration of other caves in the region turned up other scrolls. Then the task of editing and translating began. Ten complete scrolls were found along with thousands of fragments from six hundred manuscripts. Except for the book of Esther, the documents contain biblical texts from the entire Hebrew Bible and are 1,000 years older than the previous extant codices. Most of the documents are nonbiblical writings by a Jewish sect who left them behind in caves when they were defeated by the Romans and forced to abandon the site just before the destruction of the temple and the fall of Jerusalem in 70 C.E. Called the Qumran community, after the place on the Dead Sea where they built their settlement, members of the sect withdrew into monastic piety from what they considered to be a wicked society some time in the second half of the second century B.C.E. This group is believed by many scholars to have been the Essenes, whose existence is described by the Jewish historian Josephus and the Roman Pliny the Elder.

Following the apocalyptic tradition of Daniel in the Hebrew Bible, the Qumran community interpreted the political unrest of the region in the first century B.C.E. as preparation for the final battle between the forces of good and evil, between the Sons of Light and the Sons of Darkness. The excerpt is from what is called the War Rule or War Scroll and was found among the documents in the cave. It describes the military preparations for fighting a group called the Kittim, who are the occupying Romans but are also symbolic of the final foe, the armies of Satan, since the battle will involve the whole cosmos and not just Palestine.

It has been surmised that John the Baptist was a member of the Qumran community, and, because they followed a Teacher of Righteousness, it is possible that Jesus of Nazareth visited the community and learned from it. The apocalyptic scheme of history was reinforced by the Book of Revelations in the Christian Bible; its dualistic view of reality has been revived through the ages whenever Christians have felt the end of the world is near.

Dead Sea Scrolls

Translated by G. Vermes

[WAR OF SONS OF LIGHT AND SONS OF DARKNESS]

1

For the M[aster. The Rule of] War on the unleashing of the attack of the sons of light against the company of the sons of darkness, the army of Satan: against the band of Edom, Moab, and the sons of Ammon, and [against the army of the sons of the East and] the Philistines, and against the bands of the Kittim of Assyria and their allies the ungodly of the Covenant

The sons of Levi, Judah, and Benjamin, the exiles in the desert, shall battle against them in . . . all their bands when the exiled sons of light return from the Desert of the Peoples to camp in the Desert of Jerusalem; and after the battle they shall go up from there (to Jerusalem?).

[The king] of the Kittim [shall enter] into Egypt, and in his time he shall set out in great wrath to wage war against the kings of the north, that his fury may destroy and cut off the horn of [the nations].

This shall be a time of salvation for the people of God, an age of dominion for all the members of His company, and of everlasting destruction for all the company of Satan. The confusion of the sons of Japheth shall be [great] and Assyria shall fall unsuccoured. The dominion of the Kittim shall come to an end and iniquity shall be vanquished, leaving no remnant; [for the sons] of darkness there shall be no escape. [The seasons of righteous]ness shall shine over all the ends of the earth; they shall go on shining until all the seasons of darkness are consumed and, at the season appointed by God, His exalted greatness shall shine eternally to the peace, blessing, glory, joy, and long life of all the sons of light.

On the day when the Kittim fall, there shall be battle and terrible carnage before the God of Israel, for that shall be the day appointed from ancient times for the battle of destruction of the sons of darkness. At that time, the assembly of gods and the hosts of men shall battle, causing great carnage; on the day of calamity, the sons of light shall battle with the company of darkness amid the shouts of a mighty multitude and the clamour of gods and men to [make manifest] the might of God. And it shall be a time of [great] tribulation for the people which God shall redeem; of all its afflictions none shall be as this, from its sudden beginning until its end in eternal redemption.

On the day of their battle against the Kittim [they shall set out for] carnage. In three lots shall the sons of light brace themselves in battle to strike down iniquity, and in three lots shall Satan's host gird itself to thrust back the company [of God. And when the hearts of the detach]ments of foot-soldiers faint, then shall the might of God fortify [the heart of the sons of light]. And with the seventh lot, the mighty hand of God shall bring down [the army of Satan, and all] the angels of his kingdom, and all the members [of his company in everlasting destruction]. . . .

2

. . . the fifty-two heads of family in the congregation.

They shall rank the chief Priests below the High Priest and his vicar. And the twelve chief Priests shall minister at the daily sacrifice before God, whereas the twenty-six leaders of the priestly divisions shall minister in their divisions.

Below them, in perpetual ministry, shall be the chiefs of the Levites to the number of twelve, one for each tribe. The leaders of their divisions shall minister each in his place.

Below them shall be the chiefs of the tribes together with the heads of family of the congregation. They shall attend daily at the gates of the Sanctuary, whereas the leaders of their divisions, with their numbered men, shall attend at their appointed times, on new moons and on Sabbaths and on all the days of the year, their age being fifty years and over.

These are the men who shall attend at holocausts and sacrifices to prepare sweet-smelling incense for the good pleasure of God, to atone for all His congregation, and to satisfy themselves perpetually before Him at the table of glory. They shall arrange all these things during the season of the year of Release.

During the remaining thirty-three years of the war, the men of renown, those summoned to the Assembly, together with all the heads of family of the congregation, shall choose for themselves fighting-men for all the lands of the nations. They shall arm for themselves warriors from all the tribes of Israel to enter the army year by year when they are summoned to war. But they shall arm no man for entry into the army during the years of Release, for they are Sabbaths of rest for Israel. In the thirty-five years of service, the war shall be fought during six; the whole congregation shall fight it together.

And during the remaining twenty-nine years the war shall be divided. During the first year they shall fight against Aram-Naharaim; during the second, against the sons of Lud; during the third, against the remnant of the sons of Aram, against Uz and Hul and Togar and Mesha beyond the Euphrates; during the fourth and fifth, they shall fight against the sons of Arphakshad; during the sixth and seventh, against all the sons of Assyria and Persia and the East as far as the Great Desert; during the eighth year they shall fight against the sons of Elam; during the ninth, against the sons of Ishmael and Keturah. In the ten years which follow, the war shall be divided against all the sons of Ham according to [their clans and in their ha]bitations; and during the ten years which remain, the war shall be divided against all [the sons of Japhethin] their habitations.

3

[The Rule for the trumpets of Summons and the trumpe]ts of Alarm according to all their duties

. . . [the trumpets of Summons shall sound for disposal in] . . . battle formations and to summon the foot-soldiers to advance when the gates of war shall open; and the trumpets of Alarm shall sound for massacre, and for ambush, and for pursuit when the enemy shall be smitten, and for withdrawal from battle.

On the trumpets calling the congregation they shall write, *The Called of God.*

On the trumpets calling the chiefs they shall write, *The Princes of God.*

On the trumpets of the levies they shall write, *The Army of God.*

On the trumpets of the men of renown and of the heads of family of the congregation gathered in the house of Assembly they shall write, *Summoned by God to the Council of Holiness.*

On the trumpets of the camps they shall write, *The Peace of God in the Camps of His Saints.*

And on the trumpets for breaking camp they shall write, *The mighty Deeds of God shall crush the Enemy, putting to Flight all those who hate Righteousness and bringing Shame on those who hate Him.*

On the trumpets for battle formations they shall write, *Formations of the Divisions of God for the Vengeance of His Wrath on the Sons of Darkness.*

On the trumpets summoning the foot-soldiers to advance towards the enemy formations when the gates of war are opened they shall write, *Reminder of Vengeance in God's appointed Time.*

On the trumpets of massacre they shall write, *The mighty Hand of God in War shall cause all the ungodly Slain to fall.*

On the trumpets of ambush they shall write, *The Mysteries of God shall undo Wickedness.*

On the trumpets of pursuit they shall write, *God has smitten all the Sons of Darkness; His Fury shall not end until they are utterly consumed.*

On the trumpets of withdrawal, when they withdraw from battle to the formation, they shall write, *God has reassembled.*

On the trumpets of return from battle against the enemy when they journey to the congregation in Jerusalem they shall write, *Rejoicings of God in the peaceful Return.*

THE GOSPEL OF MARY

[2ND CENTURY C.E.]

In December 1945, two brothers from Nag Hammadi in northern Egypt were digging for nitrates to enrich their fields when they unearthed a large jar containing twelve leather-bound papyrus books and the fragments of a thirteenth. These thirteen books proved to contain fifty-two Gnostic religious writings, some of them duplicates of one another. All the texts were in Coptic, the language spoken in Egypt during the first few centuries C.E. By various paths the books found their way into the hands of antiquities dealers, and by the 1950s all of them, now called the Nag Hammadi Library, were safely reunited in Cairo's Coptic Museum. These texts are of great importance, for they give us some insight into certain radical, feminist, and visionary early Christian sects that were largely silenced by the more conservative and patriarchal branches of Christianity.

Gnostos simply means "knowledge," especially secret knowledge revealed only to adepts, visionaries, or initiates; Gnostic is a general term loosely applied to a number of mystery cults, both Christian and non-Christian, that lasted from around the time of Christ until well beyond the Middle Ages. Most Christian Gnostics were dualistic; Gnostics believed in a primordial female power, sometimes called Silence, who paired with the male Logos, or Word, referred to in the cryptic opening verses of *The Gospel of John.* Gnostics believed as well that the material world was corrupt and had been created by a demiurge, a secondary God inferior to the Silence and the Logos who had somehow ensnared pure spirit in matter; thus, the creator-god of Genesis would be essentially an evil force. They also retained from older pagan mystery cults the figure of a Great Mother who was usually thought of as the daughter of Silence and who was often identified as Wisdom (Sophia). The young God-King, like Jesus, who dies to redeem the corrupt world was at once Sophia's son and her husband; hence, among Christian Gnostic sects, Mary the mother of Jesus and Mary Magdalene, Jesus' follower and close friend, were seen not as two people, but as different aspects of one female principle, two sides of Sophia. Given such beliefs, it is not surprising that Gnostic sects usually accorded women a good deal of authority and respect, allowing them to serve as priests and bishops and prophets; they were permitted to baptize, to heal, and to preach. The more conservative Christians who became the recognized Church regarded Gnostics with horror and sought to root them out; many of the heresies identified by the Church through the Middle Ages were essentially Gnostic beliefs.

The Gospel of Mary, one of the Nag Hammadi texts, was originally composed in Greek around the second century C.E.; there are two other very fragmentary Greek manuscripts in existence. The Nag Hammadi *Gospel of Mary* is actually the beginning and end of a manuscript with a gap of four missing pages at a crucial point in the text. *The Gospel of Mary* falls into two distinct parts. In the first, the risen Christ speaks to his disciples, explaining in terms that may be borrowed from *Romans* 7 the basic Gnostic idea that sin is not really a question of people committing moral wrongs, but simply a given condition of creation, a state in which the pure spirit is encased in a corrupt material world; eventually, matter and spirit will be sorted out, and sin will cease to exist. After Jesus leaves, Mary Magdalene comforts the grief-stricken disciples.

In the second part, Mary, at Peter's behest, describes a conversation between herself and Jesus that took place before the crucifixion; she is represented here as his favorite and most adept disciple, "an apostle to the apostles," as the Gnostic saying went. She recalls asking Jesus a question about how visions are perceived; the manuscript breaks off as he begins to explain that visions are seen not with the "soul" or the "spirit"—the distinction the Gospel is making between these two terms is unclear—but rather with the mind, which lies between the two. When the manuscript resumes, Mary is in the middle of reporting Jesus' account of how the freed soul rises past the "four powers," perhaps the four elements of Earth, Air, Fire, and Water, and attains blessed silence. As Mary herself falls silent, Andrew accuses her of having "strange ideas," and Peter says he doubts Jesus would entrust to a woman any revelation he kept from his male disciples. Mary weeps to think Peter could call her a liar, and then Levi rebukes Peter, reminding him that Mary was indeed Jesus' favorite, and urges all to go forth and preach the gospels.

Whether or not the confrontation between Mary, Andrew, and Peter is based on a real incident, this suppressed Gospel is thought-provoking and very human in its enactment of gender-based jealousies at work even among those who knew Jesus best. It is also valuable for its presentation of Mary Magdalene as not merely a repentant woman who hovers on the edge of the crowd of male disciples, but as a central figure, a role only hinted at in all four canonical gospels, where Mary Magdalene and other women are the first people Jesus appears to after his resurrection.

The Gospel of Mary

Translated by George W. MacRae and R. McL. Wilson; edited by Douglas M. Parrott

. . . will matter then be [destroyed] or not?" The Savior said, "All natures, all formations, all creatures exist in and with one another, and they will be resolved again into their own roots. For the nature of matter is resolved into the (roots) of its nature alone. He who has ears to hear, let him hear."

Peter said to him, "Since you have explained everything to us, tell us this also: What is the sin of the world?" The Savior said, "There is no sin, but it is you who make sin when you do the things that are like the nature of adultery, which is called 'sin.' That is why the Good came into your midst, to the (essence) of every nature, in order to restore it to its root." Then he continued and said, "That is why you [become sick] and die, for [. . .] of the one who [. . . He who] understands, let him understand. [Matter gave birth to] a passion that has no equal, which proceeded from (something) contrary to nature. Then there arise a disturbance in the whole body. That is why I said to you, 'Be of good courage,' and if you are discouraged (be) encouraged in the presence of the different forms of nature. He who has ears to hear, let him hear."

When the blessed one had said this, he greeted them all, saying, "Peace be with you. Receive my peace to yourselves. Beware that no one lead you astray, saying, 'Lo here!' or 'Lo there!' For the Son of Man is within you. Follow after him! Those who seek him will find him. Go then and preach the gospel of the kingdom. Do not lay down any rules beyond what I appointed for you, and do not give a law like the lawgiver lest you be constrained by it." When he had said this, he departed.

But they were grieved. They wept greatly, saying, "How shall we go to the gentiles and preach the gospel of the kingdom of the Son of Man? If they did not spare him, how will they spare us?" Then Mary stood up, greeted them all, and said to her brethren, "Do not weep and do not grieve nor be irresolute, for his grace will be entirely with you and will protect you. But rather let us praise his greatness, for he has prepared us and made us into men." When Mary said this, she turned their hearts to the Good, and they began to discuss the words of the [Savior].

Peter said to Mary, "Sister, we know that the Savior loved you more than the rest of women. Tell us the words of the Savior which you remember—which you know (but) we do not, nor have we heard them." Mary answered and said, "What is hidden from you I will proclaim to you." And she began to speak to them these words: "I," she said, "I saw the Lord in a vision and I said to him, 'Lord, I saw you today in a vision.' He answered and said to me, 'Blessed are you, that you did not waver at the sight of me. For where the mind is, there is the treasure.' I said to him, 'Lord, now does he who sees the vision see it ⟨through⟩ the soul ⟨or⟩ through the spirit?' The Savior answered and said, 'He does not see through the soul nor through the spirit, but the mind which [is] between the two—that is [what] sees the vision and it is [. . .].' (pp. 11–14 missing)

"[. . .] it. And desire that, 'I did not see you descending, but now I see you ascending. Why do you lie, since you belong to me?' The soul answered and said, 'I saw you. You did not see me nor recognize me. I served you as a garment, and you did not know me.' When it had said this, it went away rejoicing greatly.

"Again it came to the third power, which is called ignorance. [It (the power)] questioned the soul saying, 'Where are you going? In wickedness are you bound. But you are bound; do not judge!' And the soul said, 'why do you judge me although I have not judged? I was bound though I have not bound. I was not recognized. But I have recognized that the All is being dissolved, both the earthly (things) and the heavenly.'

When the soul had overcome the third power, it went upwards and saw the fourth power, (which) took seven forms. The first form is darkness, the second desire, the third ignorance, the fourth is the excitement of death, the fifth is the kingdom of the flesh, the sixth is the foolish wisdom of flesh, the seventh is the wrathful wisdom. These are the seven [powers] of wrath. They ask the soul, 'Whence do you come, slayer of men, or where are you going, conqueror of space?' The soul answered and said, 'What binds me has been slain, and what surrounds me has been overcome, and my desire has been ended, and ignorance has died. In a [world] I was released from a world, [and] in a type from a heavenly type, and (from) the fetter of oblivion which is transient. From this time on will I attain to the rest of the time, of the season, of the aeon, in silence.' "

When Mary had said this, she fell silent, since it was to this point that the Savior had spoken with her. But Andrew answered and said to the brethren, "Say what you (wish to) say about what she has said. I at least do not believe that the Savior said this. For certainly these teachings are strange ideas." Peter answered and spoke concerning these same things. He questioned them about the Savior: "Did he really speak with a woman without our knowledge (and) not openly? Are we to turn about and all listen to her? Did he prefer her to us?"

Then Mary wept and said to Peter, "My brother Peter, what do you think? Do you think that I thought this up myself in my heart, or that I am lying about the Savior?" Levi answered and said to Peter, "Peter, you have always been hot-tempered. Now I see you contending against the woman like the adversaries. But if the Savior made her worthy, who are you indeed to reject her? Surely the Savior knows her very well. That is why he loved her more than us. Rather let us be ashamed and put on the perfect man and acquire him for ourselves as he commanded us, and preach the gospel, not laying down any other rule or other law beyond what the Savior said." When [. . .] and they began to go forth [to] proclaim and to preach.

THE MIDDLE AGES

The Pilgrimage of Life

TIME LINE FOR THE MIDDLE AGES

Date	*History and Politics*
300–400	313 Emperor Constantine grants protection to Christianity.
	325 Council of Nicaea condemns Arian heresy.
	330 Constantinople founded as capital of Eastern Empire.
	376 Visigoths cross Danube.
400–500	
	410 Alaric the Visigoth sacks Rome.
	430 Vandals sack Hippo in North Africa.
	452 Attila the Hun advances on Rome; Pope Leo I protects city.
	476 Germanic general Odavacar deposes last Roman Emperor.
	481 Clovis becomes King of Franks.
	493 Theodoric the Ostrogoth conquers Italy, unites Visigoths and Ostrogoths against Eastern Empire.
500–600	
	527 Justinian becomes Eastern Emperor, directs reconquest of Western Empire. Height of Byzantine expansion.
	571 Birth of Muhammad in Mecca on Arabian Peninsula.
	590 Pope Gregory the Great encourages conversion missions and rise of Benedictine monasticism.
600–700	622 Muhammad's *Hegira* (flight to Medina); first year of Muslim calendar.
	632 Death of Muhammad; Islamic conquest begins in Syria, Persia, and Egypt.
	661 Umayyads defeat Ali, son-in-law of Muhammad, in Muslim civil war; Islamic conquest continues in North Africa and Iberian Peninsula.
	687 Pepin II, mayor of Franks; rise of Carolingian dynasty.
700–800	

Science, Culture, and Technology	***Literature***
c. 300 Mayan mathematicians discover the zero; widespread use of paper in China; Palace of Diocletian in Split; harp is main musical instrument, used by bardic singers across Europe.	
	400 St. Augustine, *The Confessions.*
c. 400 Development of Runic alphabet among Germanic tribes of Europe.	c. 400 St. Jerome's biblical commentaries, foundation for medieval Christian humanism; Macrobius, *Commentary on the Dream of Scipio.*
425 University of Constantinople founded by Theodosius II.	426 St. Augustine, *The City of God.*
c. 500 Metal stirrups brought to Europe during raids by Avars; Irish monasteries develop centers of learning, art, culture.	
537 Hagia Sophia, cathedral in Constantinople.	523 Boethius, *The Consolation of Philosophy.*
548 San Vitale, cathedral in Ravenna.	
570 Abacus invented in China.	c. 560 Cassiodorus, *Introduction to Divine and Human Readings.*
c. 600 Gregorian chant collected in Europe; windmills invented in Persia.	c. 600 Pope Gregory the Great, *Pastoral Care;* Welsh poets Taliesin and Aneirin.
	651 The Koran.
c. 700 Gunpowder invented in China; Arabs bring lute and rebec (stringed instrument) into Iberian Peninsula.	c. 700 Irish sagas, including *The Tain.*

(*Continued on next page*)

TIME LINE FOR THE MIDDLE AGES (Continued)

Date	*History and Politics*
700–800 *(cont.)*	
	732 Charles Martel, mayor of Franks, defeats Arabs at Tours; Muslim advance in Europe is halted.
	750 Abbasids overthrow Umayyad dynasty; Muslim capital moves to Baghdad; Islamic conquest continues in China, India, and Indonesia.
	751 Pepin III, King of Franks, throws support to Rome.
	768 Charlemagne, King of Franks; military campaigns to south, east, and northeast expand Frankish Empire.
800–900	800 Charlemagne crowned Holy Roman Emperor by Pope Leo III.
	837 Vikings begin to sack major European cities.
	843 Partition of Frankish Empire; decline of Carolingian dynasty.
	867 Division of Christianity between Roman Catholicism and Eastern Orthodox Church.
900–1000	911 Normandy established in northern France.
1000–1100	c. 1000 Leif Eriksson visits North America.
	1066 William of Normandy conquers England; Angevin dynasty begins.
	1085 Christians recapture Toledo from Muslims.
	1095 Byzantine Emperor asks Pope Urban II for aid against Seljuk Turks; Urban II preaches First Crusade.
	1099 Crusaders sack Jerusalem, massacre inhabitants.
1100–1200	1112 St. Bernard begins monastic life; becomes most important spiritual authority of twelfth century.

Science, Culture, and Technology	*Literature*
c. 700 Lindisfarne Gospels, British illuminated manuscript; Burgundian and Frankish metallurgy, especially decorated swords.	
726 Iconoclastic period begins in the Byzantine Empire.	732 Bede, *Ecclesiastical History of the English People.*
781 Alcuin brings cultural renewal to court of Charlemagne; Carolingian renaissance.	c. 750 Anglo-Saxon epic *Beowulf;* Li Po, poet of the T'ang dynasty.
783 Arab paper made for first time in Baghdad.	
c. 800 Jabir, the father of Arabic chemistry; height of Arabic music with romantic composer Harrun al-Rashid; Baghdad Academy of Science; Book of Kells, Irish illuminated manuscript.	
c. 850 First use of term *algebra* by Al-Khwarizmi, Arabic mathematician.	830 Einhard, *Life of Charlemagne.*
	891 *Anglo-Saxon Chronicle* commissioned by Alfred the Great.
c. 900 Muslims introduce cotton and silk manufacture into Iberian Peninsula; Cordoba a center of scientific learning.	
c. 950 Romanesque Abbey of Cluny constructed.	
c. 980 Gerbert, later Pope Sylvester II, introduces astrolabe, arabic numerals into Europe from Cordoba.	
c. 1000 Medical texts produced in India and China.	c. 1022 Murasaki Shikibu, *The Tale of Genji;* Ibn Hazm, *The Dove's Necklace.*
	c. 1050 Rise of the cathedral schools; increased access to the Latin classics.
c. 1080 Bayeux Tapestry, depicting Norman Conquest of 1066.	
c. 1100 Troubadours, professional musicians, sing to harp accompaniment in courts in the south of France; use of metal salts in glassmaking improves stained-glass windows.	c. 1100 *Song of Roland.*
	1132 Abelard, *History of My Misfortunes.*

(*Continued on next page*)

TIME LINE FOR THE MIDDLE AGES (Continued)

Date	*History and Politics*
1100–1200 *(cont.)*	
	1154 Henry II, King of England and Duke of Normandy, presides over Angevin culture.
	1187 Jerusalem recaptured by Saladin.
1200–1300	1205 Fourth Crusade results in sack of Constantinople and partial destruction of the Byzantine Empire.
	1206 Genghis Khan becomes ruler of Mongols; invades China, Persia, and southern Russia.
	1208 Albigensian Crusade against heretics in south of France. Inquisition begins shortly thereafter.
	1210 St. Francis of Assisi founds Franciscan Order.
	1216 St. Dominic founds Dominican Order.
	1244 Jerusalem falls to Turks.
	1271 Venetian trader Marco Polo visits China.
	1291 Fall of Acre signals end of Crusader states in Asia Minor.
1300–1400	1309 Pope Clement V vacates Rome, settles in Avignon.
	1337 Hundred Years' War between England and France begins.

Science, Culture, and Technology	***Literature***
c. 1140 Bishop Suger rebuilds choir of St. Denis cathedral; first true Gothic architecture.	c. 1140 Geoffrey of Monmouth, *History of the Kings of England.*
c. 1150 Coal used for smelting ore in Liège; alcohol distilled from wine in Salerno.	c. 1150 Rise of allegorical interpretation of secular literature. Bernard Silvestris on Virgil's *Aeneid.*
c. 1163 Construction of Notre Dame Cathedral, Paris; first use of flying buttresses.	c. 1160 Period of chivalric romance, including the stories of King Arthur; romances of Tristan and Isolde from Celtic, French, and German sources; *Breton lais* of Marie de France.
	1165–1180 Arthurian romances of Chrétien de Troyes.
	1169 Averroes begins commentary on Aristotle.
1174 Construction of Canterbury Cathedral.	1174 Andreas Capellanus, *The Art of Courtly Love.*
	c. 1180 Chrétien de Troyes, *Perceval, or the Quest of the Holy Grail.*
1195 Construction of Chartres Cathedral.	1185 Ibn Jubayr, *Travels;* Usamah Ibn Munqidh, *The Book of Reflections.*
c. 1200 Formation of Universities of Paris and Oxford.	c. 1200 Translations into Latin of the works of Aristotle on natural history, metaphysics, ethics, politics.
	c. 1230 Guillaume de Lorris, first part of *Romance of the Rose.*
c. 1248 Saint-Chapelle, Paris, St. Louis' chapel.	1273 St. Thomas Aquinas, *Summa Theologica.*
1252 Gold currencies introduced in Florence, Genoa.	c. 1275 Jean de la Meun, continuation of *Romance of the Rose.*
c. 1280 Cimabue, Florentine painter, begins realism in depiction of holy subjects.	1298 Marco Polo, *Travels.*
c. 1300 Giotto, Florentine painter, portrays nature realistically in *Saint Francis and the Birds.*	1321 Dante, *The Divine Comedy.*
	c. 1330 Anonymous, *Little Flowers of St. Francis.*
	1353 Boccaccio, *The Decameron.*

(*Continued on next page*)

TIME LINE FOR THE MIDDLE AGES (Continued)

Date	*History and Politics*
1300–1400 *(cont.)*	1348 The Black Death in Europe.
	1378 Great Schism creates rival popes in Avignon and Rome.
1400–1500	

INTRODUCTION

THE CONCEPT OF THE EUROPEAN MIDDLE AGES was first formulated during the Italian Renaissance, when scholars wished to account for the period between the classical age of Greece and Rome and the time of their own "rebirth." In most European languages, the period is still spoken of as the Middle Age; the term was pluralized in English in the nineteenth century. We now recognize four periods of political and cultural history within the Middle Ages: the Dark Ages, from the fifth century to the late eighth or early ninth; the period of feudalism, from about 800 to 1100; the High Middle Ages, from 1100 to about 1300; and a period of transition beginning at different times in different places but spreading through most of Europe in the fourteenth century.

So what we call the Middle Ages is a period of about a thousand years when certain historical developments led to the establishment of Europe as a political entity. For our purposes, three major events define the period: the emergence of Christianity as a world religion, occurring principally in the Dark Ages; the steady transformation of society from feudalism to the growth of towns and cities in the High Middle Ages; and the creation of Europe itself as a political region distinct from and sometimes hostile to its neighbors, especially from the beginning of the Crusades to near the end of the medieval period.

Broadly speaking, the literature of the Middle Ages follows these historical periods and the events that define them. The earliest literature reflects the emergence of Christianity as a world religion. It includes the Latin literature of the Church as well as preservations of the heroic literature of the original societies, often with Christian overlays. The next period of literature reflects the interests of the courts of the feudal period and beyond, from feudal epic to Arthurian romance and the courtly love poetry of Provence. The literature of the High Middle Ages reflects the rise of towns and the new education provided in the cathedral schools and universities. This literature includes translations of some Greek and Latin classics that had not been taught in the Christian monastic schools. Finally, the literature of European emergence and self-awareness reflects a broader, more cosmopolitan outlook, including stories from many lands and cultures and from religious and secular sources alike. Here, also for the first time, women appear as major voices in European writing.

Science, Culture, and Technology	*Literature*
	1357 *Mandeville's Travels.*
	c. 1375 *Sir Gawain and the Green Knight.*
	c. 1386 Chaucer, *Canterbury Tales.*
	1405 Christine de Pizan, *The Book of the City of Ladies.*
	1438 Margery Kempe, *The Book of Margery Kempe.*
	c. 1500 *Everyman.*

One theme that predominates throughout the Middle Ages is that of the pilgrimage of humanity through this world, anticipating the possibility of salvation in the next. Two great practitioners of this theme whose work we emphasize are St. Augustine, whose *Confessions* was written in 400 C.E., at the beginning of our period, and the Italian poet Dante, whose *Divine Comedy* was completed early in the fourteenth century, near its end. The universe described by both writers is essentially Christian; both also show the drama of the individual soul in realistic, not merely allegorical, terms, in a way that the reader can understand and apply to living in the present. The same theme of the pilgrimage of life is repeated in a number of other texts, including Chaucer's *Canterbury Tales,* the *Travels* attributed to Mandeville, and the English morality play *Everyman.*

The Medieval Period

The Dark Ages

As the Western Roman Empire began to disintegrate during the third century, the Roman people turned to a number of mystery religions for spiritual comfort. Cults grew up in celebration of the goddess Isis from Egypt, the god Mithras from Persia, and various manifestations of the Earth Mother from Asia Minor. Until the end of the third century, the Christian Church uneasily shared territory with its Eastern rivals. However, the Christians had certain advantages in winning followers, including the strength of their conversion mission as first practiced by St. Paul and his followers. The *ecumenism* of Christianity—its openness to prevailing political currents and its desire to expand its circle of believers—became the key to its success, both with the general population and with sponsoring governments.

Popular support for Christianity continued to increase as Roman authority waned. Around 300 C.E., the Emperor Diocletian's last-ditch attempt to wipe out the religion altogether failed on such a scale that, in 313, Emperor Constantine granted the Christian church his official protection; he had already converted to Christianity himself. At the Council of Nicaea in 325, the way was opened to make Christianity the official religion of the Empire. What was needed now to solidify the Christian position was the reconciliation of the Graeco-Roman and Christian traditions. It took three great leaders of the Church—St. Ambrose, St. Jerome, and St. Augustine—to accomplish this, principally by admitting classical learning into the realm of the Christian faith.

Each of these towering figures of the late fourth and early fifth centuries was a man of many parts—administrator, scholar, writer, champion of the faith. St. Ambrose of Milan (c. 340–397) vigorously fought the Arian heresy, which taught that Christ was not God but a man; he even opposed the Emperor when necessary in order to defend the sanctity of the Roman Catholic Church. St. Jerome (c. 340–420) directed the copying of Greek and Roman classics and produced the first great translation of the Hebraic and Greek Bible into Latin prose—the Latin Vulgate. St. Augustine (354–430) served as Bishop of Hippo in North Africa, where he completed his monumental Christian writings, *The Confessions* (400) and *The City of God* (426). At the time of Augustine's death, Hippo lay under siege and the remaining Western Roman Empire was being torn apart. Although Roman political power was nearing its end, the three great fathers of the Church had preserved what they needed of classical culture and adapted it to Christian purposes. Thus by the early fifth century, while tribal societies fought to consolidate their positions all over the continent, the victory of Christianity as the dominant religious and cultural force was virtually complete.

The greater Roman world of the third and fourth centuries was a frightening place to live. Even in the better days of Empire, the system of military rule was never matched by an economic plan for the development of the provinces; as Roman control expanded, its economy stagnated. Cities declined due to the lack of trade to support them. The military authority itself weakened, especially in the Germanic regions, so that increasingly the soldiers in the provinces were Romanized Germans. Slowly the Germanic tribes, first described by the historian Tacitus in the first century C.E., gathered strength and overcame the Roman defenders. For several hundred years, waves of invaders from the west, north, and east swept Roman territory. Life was uniformly hard and cruel in the warrior societies, but a new system of ethics, justice, and social organization was slowly taking shape, combining ancient tribal custom with Roman practices. Eventually the new possessors of the land established a degree of stability: These were the Ostrogoths in what was later Italy, the Visigoths in what was later southern France and Spain, and the Germanic tribes to the north, including the Anglo-Saxons in what had been Roman and Celtic Britain. Meanwhile, the Catholic Church learned how to adapt to the challenges of the Germanic order. After Pope Leo I (440–461) consolidated his authority in Rome, the Frankish king Clovis (481–511) extended protection to the Church and some of the old Roman estates in his realm.

The next great leader of the Church, Pope Gregory the Great (590–604), further consolidated Catholic authority. He wrote a treatise on practical theology (pastoral care) and compiled the liturgy of the Church (Gregorian chant). He encouraged the Benedictine order of monks, following the simple precepts of the Benedictine Rule, to undertake conversion missions throughout Europe. For the next 500 years, the Benedictines would lead the European monastic movement, converting tribes and whole nations to Christ, educating future monks and the children of rich landowners, and establishing islands of order amid the tumult of contending powers. In fact, the Benedictines and similar monastic orders preserved most of what remains of barbarian culture by copying poetry and prose writings in the ancient languages. In this way, for example, on the British Isles many Germanic poems, including the heroic epic *Beowulf,* were saved.

The Latin culture of the period of Gregory the Great was on the whole very rudimentary, due to the practical needs of the conversion missions. At the same time, the old Germanic culture never died; instead it found a new basis of expression in the Christian environment. We can glimpse this process at work in the early conversion stories. During the reign of Pope Gregory, a mission was sent to England. The British historian

Bede reports that one elder who favored Christianity tried to persuade his king to convert by using traditional Anglo-Saxon eloquence.

> This sparrow flies swiftly in one door of the hall, and out through another. While he is inside, he is safe from the winter storms; but after a few moments of comfort, he vanishes from sight into the wintry world from which he came. Even so, man appears on earth for a little while; but of what went before this life or of what follows, we know nothing. Therefore, if this new teaching has brought any more certain knowledge, it seems only right that we should follow it.[1]

Politically, the European continent just emerging from Roman authority was still largely unconscious of itself. A parallel situation existed among the peoples of the Arabian Peninsula until the early seventh century, when the prophet Muhammad, born at Mecca in 571 C.E. and driven out of his native city in 622, preached to and converted the citizens of Medina, creating a new religion and political state. Taking up arms, he conquered Mecca in 630 and added other small Arabic states until his death in 632. His community became the basis of the nation of Islam, soon to lead holy wars to the north through Syria, Persia, and Egypt, into North Africa and across the Mediterranean to the Iberian Peninsula (now Portugal and Spain). Europe could not halt Islam's advance to the north for a hundred years, until the battle at Tours in 732; by then, the Christian world trembled at the might of Muhammadism.

The Christian counterforce to Muhammadism started humbly in the old Frankish kingdom. The Carolingian dynasty named itself after the Frankish leader Charles Martel, who ruled from 714 to 741. Though impoverished, thoroughly rural, dependent on a crudely efficient system of agriculture, and centered far in the north, the Carolingians under Martel managed to lead the attack against the Islamic forces at Tours and subsequently extended the borders of the Frankish state. But the historic moment of uniting the Franks with the Papacy would be reserved for Charles Martel's grandson Charlemagne (742–814), a giant of a man and a great king. Under his authority, the Frankish holdings were extended into what is now Spain, Italy, Bavaria, Austria, and Northern Germany. A minor battle against the Basques in the Pyrenees in 778, which caused the death of one of Charlemagne's lords, eventually led to the great epic of feudal society, *The Song of Roland.* The work was written down late in the eleventh century.

The Formation of Europe

Charlemagne was crowned Holy Roman Emperor on Christmas Day in 800 C.E. in his northern capitol at Aachen (Aix-la-Chapelle). Whatever we make of the contention of his biographer that he was taken by surprise by the appearance of Pope Leo III for his coronation, the event served the interests of both Rome and the Carolingians. It marked an unprecedented moment in history: the restoration—at least in name—of the Roman Empire, the formal joining of Church and State, the consecration of Europe as an idea, and the start of a cultural renaissance through which learning and the arts would come to their fullest flower in 500 years. The moment of glory, however, was brief; after the death of the great king, the Frankish kingdom would stall again. Only the Carolingian cultural renaissance would survive over a long period; primarily due to its influence, what some modern historians still call the Dark Ages finally ended.

The grandiose conception of an empire stretching from the North Sea to the Mediterranean faltered due to the poverty of the entire area, the development of separate local cultures with their own languages and customs, and the fragmentation brought about by

---

[1] Bede, *Ecclesiastical History of the English People,* Leo Sherley-Price, translated and revised by R. E. Latham (1990), 129–130.

the Viking raids and other incursions of the ninth and tenth centuries. Since the dissolution of the Roman Empire, trading opportunities were limited, roads were poorly developed, and towns were few and primitive. Efforts to raise taxes from local barons were hampered by inefficiency and by the poverty of the estates. On top of this, invaders from the north, principally the Danes and Vikings, attacked outposts near the sea and isolated, unguarded monasteries, occupying territory in what is now called Normandy. England resisted the early Viking attacks with a good measure of success, only to fall victim to the Norman Invasion of 1066, in which Norman French troops seized the throne and significantly changed the direction of British language, culture, and society.

The Carolingian cultural renaissance is important both for what it accomplished and for what it deferred. Under the direction of Charlemagne, barely literate himself, scholars were brought in from throughout Europe to begin an ambitious program of cultural reclamation. The Bible was purged of earlier corruptions, schools were established under the royal court, delinquent monasteries were scrutinized and abuses corrected, and the Benedictine Rule was expanded to facilitate reform. Still, the "renaissance" was essentially conservative in character; for instance, Charlemagne prohibited the writing of love poems in the vernacular by women in the religious orders, and few original works of literary or philosophical merit were produced. Latin hymns and secular lyrics did develop rapidly in the monasteries and paved the way for a broader vernacular literature later on.

Feudalism and the Crusades

In the ninth and tenth centuries, as the Carolingian Empire fragmented, Europe was developing a feudal system, largely so the baronial estates could defend themselves against raids and the harshness of economic circumstances. Within each feudal enclave was a landed class of knights who pledged, along with their lesser vassals and serfs, to defend the lord of the manor. Ties of obedience were created and a culture grew out of this vertical system of loyalties. A world view based on such ties was necessarily a limited one; the typical literature of the day emphasized rigidly determined knightly virtues, conceived as service to the lord and faith in God, to be maintained even in the harshest battle.

It should be emphasized, however, that European feudal society as a whole, especially in the Frankish kingdoms, was never static. It began with the weakening of the Carolingian Empire in the ninth century and started to collapse with the First Crusade in 1095. Feudal society had depended on the fragmentation of Europe into small political entities. The coming of the Crusades meant the expansion of Christendom, and with it the military reorganization of Europe.

The new warfare between the Christians and Muslims actually began early in the eleventh century when Muslim control of the Iberian Peninsula began to crumble. As the century ended, Christian forces in what was later Spain began recapturing the major cities (the effort would take well over a hundred more years to complete). Meanwhile, deep in Asia Minor, a force of Seljuk Turks interfered with Christian pilgrims traveling to Jerusalem, and the ruler of Constantinople, powerless to stop the raiders, asked for western aid. Following a fiery sermon by Pope Urban II, the First Crusade was launched in 1095 to occupy and pacify the Holy Land. Once begun, it took a direction of its own. The capture of Jerusalem from the Muslims in 1099 followed one of the worst massacres in human history; commentators reported that for days the streets of the city ran with Muslim blood.

The impact of the First Crusade was as much economic as it was religious or political. By gaining control of a vast area in Asia Minor, the crusaders secured the Mediterranean as a trade route deep into the Orient. This new opportunity led in turn to the southern European recovery in the period to follow. In hindsight, the First Crusade appears to have been a rather cynically managed affair. It is clear that blood-lust, prejudice, and greed inflamed the hearts of the early crusaders as much as religious zeal. Even so, the

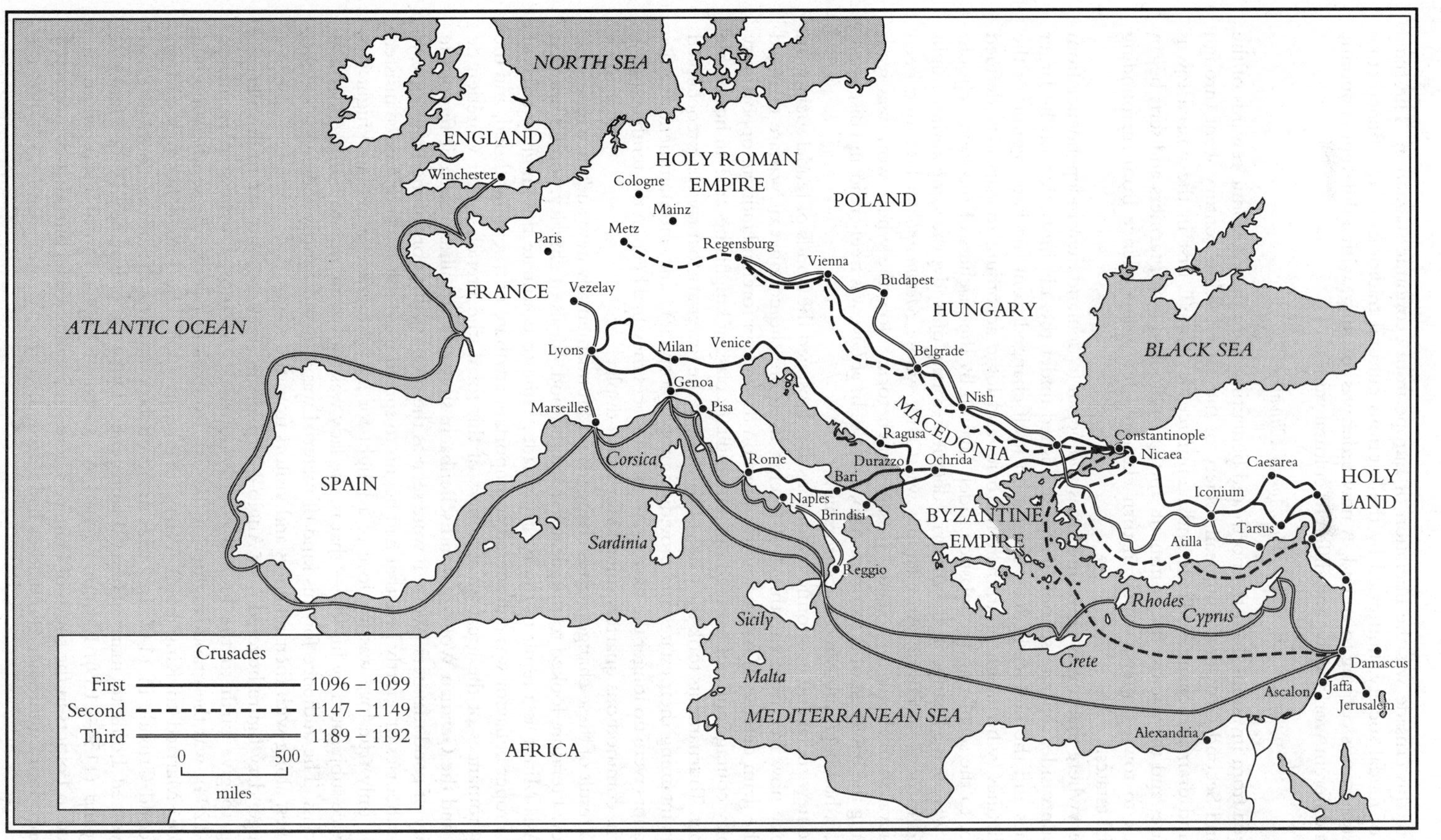

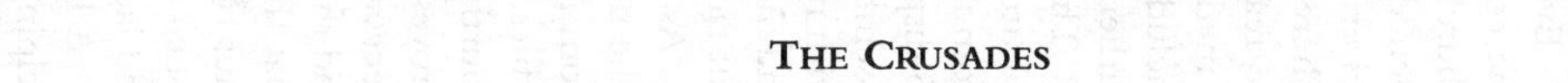
THE CRUSADES

result of this crusade was the liberation of Europe from economic stagnation. The fixed order of feudal society, buttressed by the cautious cultural traditions of the Benedictine monasteries, was coming to an end. A new order was forming, with a different economic base, a different world view, and different cultural values.

The Age of Chivalry

Freed from invasions from the north and benefiting from the economic rewards of the First and Second Crusades, European society of the early twelfth century went through swift and dramatic changes. Trade and commerce developed, first in the coastal towns and cities and then across the continent. In the landlocked areas, farmers and serfs began to flock to town centers, which in turn clamored for independence from surrounding baronial estates.

Everywhere that towns grew into cities and began to demand their independence from the countryside, separate schools were established under the administration of the larger churches and the new cathedrals. Education itself changed from the hard regime of the Benedictines, who taught grammar, rhetoric, and logic according to narrowly defined criteria, to the secular and scholastic models favored by the teachers of the town schools. There was even a change in the material deemed worthy of study; the same author might be read in new selections. An example was Ovid, whose *Metamorphoses* had long been a medieval sourcebook for selected passages of rhetoric. Now the whole work was read, including the bawdiest of the stories. Also, Ovid's *Art of Love* was freely read and discussed; earlier, it had been subjected to censorship.

The new social and economic conditions also loosened the bonds of feudal society. In a Europe now free from the threat of foreign invasion, the conduct of warfare changed from the grim defense of native soil to an option to serve in foreign lands, an opportunity to display courage and noble breeding. The military class of knights became an honorable assembly. Tournaments took the place of battles and the lower aristocracy was preoccupied with maintaining their estates and providing proper hospitality and entertainment. Castles and manors were no longer the narrow, fortified spaces they had been in the tenth century, but rich, commodious quarters suitable for lavish display.

As a result of these changes, tastes changed and a fundamentally new audience emerged. The new literature looked to the idealized knighthood. Ideals of chivalry, some imported from Asia Minor as a result of the First Crusade, came to dominate the knightly code of ethics. Proper behavior was considered an important attribute of true knighthood, and the courtly romances of the great practitioners of this form, the French writer Chrétien de Troyes and the German Wolfram von Eschenbach, stressed with almost didactic fervor the necessity of good manners. Women were seen as the proper educators of men in courtesy, and the theories of courtly love that had begun to spread from the south of France insisted that the only true love was the love of a knight for his aristocratic lady. The knight was thus twice subjugated by his love—that is, the lady was above him due to both gender and social class. The audience for this kind of material was a mixed courtly society of knights and ladies, along with their retainers and visitors from the towns.

A legendary figure hovered over Anglo-Norman and French court life in this period, helping to give birth to the French courtly romance. Eleanor, Duchess of Aquitaine (1122–1204), was the granddaughter of the first troubadour poet in the southern French province. Married to King Louis VII of France in 1137, she joined her husband on the Second Crusade in 1147. In 1152, tiring of the confining life of the court in Paris, she divorced Louis to marry Henry Plantagenet, Duke of Normandy, later Henry II of England (1154–1189). Eleanor reigned as Queen of England until 1170, when she returned to Poitiers in the south of France. There she established a court that consolidated the troubadour culture her grandfather had initiated.

Before Eleanor's residency in England, the stories of the legendary King Arthur already had been immortalized in Geoffrey of Monmouth's largely fictitious *History of the Kings of England* (1140). Borrowing heavily from Celtic legends, Geoffrey made Arthur a British king of the fifth century who extended his empire to Ireland, northern Europe, and Gaul—precisely the Norman territory of Geoffrey's day. Geoffrey's Arthur lived in a supernatural realm populated by fairies, magicians, and fantasy knights of Celtic chivalry. In this atmosphere laden with the miraculous, knights were easily separated from their feudal ties to experience new adventures. It is no exaggeration to say that Geoffrey of Monmouth gave the Anglo-Norman court of Henry II and Eleanor its Camelot.

The New Spirituality and the Decline of the Papacy

In a very different way, the Catholic Church also benefited from the new economic and social order. Saint Bernard of Clairvaux (1090–1153), a Cistercian monk who preached the call to the Second Crusade, led a conservative reform movement that emphasized a mystical association with God. He became the arbiter of morals in the second quarter of the twelfth century, fighting a temporarily successful battle against some of the new scholastic teaching of the period. Following Bernard's example, two religious orders rose at the beginning of the next century: the Dominicans and the Franciscans. Both observed strict poverty; the Dominicans emphasized their preaching mission and the Franciscans were known for the simplicity and piety attributed to their founder, St. Francis of Assisi (1182–1226). The story of St. Francis's spiritual sufferings and his concern for the condition of the poor made him a popular favorite of the thirteenth century. The *Little Flowers of St. Francis* (c. 1330), collected after his death, paved the way for his canonization as a saint by the Church.

In the late thirteenth century, the new European monarchies, built around strong nation-states such as England and France, began to clamor for control of the Church. The inauguration of Pope Clement V in 1305 marked the beginning of the period of decline in papal authority: Under attack from various heads of state, Clement moved the Papacy from Rome to Avignon in the south of France. It would remain there without a Roman alternative until 1376.

The new spirituality and the decay of the Papacy were major concerns of the Italian poet Dante Alighieri (1265-1321), a Florentine exile who completed his masterpiece, *The Divine Comedy,* early in the fourteenth century. Dante's visionary poem describing a dreamer's visit to Hell, Purgatory, and Heaven deals harshly with the secular world. Great lords, popes, and citizens of Florence people Dante's Hell, providing the poet considerable opportunity for satire. Dante's vision, both personal and symbolic, rests solidly on the Christian world view of the Middle Ages, although it is written near the end of the medieval period.

End of an Era

The medieval world of the late thirteenth and early fourteenth centuries saw great turmoil and change. The Italian cities were the first to fully reflect and respond to the new economic boom. The boom spread to the north in the late fourteenth century, but so did a number of new social problems: religious fanaticism, epidemics, and political unrest. The ultimate disaster was the Black Death of 1348–1349, a pandemic that carried off a third of the population of Europe.

Europe of the later fourteenth century inherited many opportunities and problems from the recent past. The opening of trade through the Mediterranean in the thirteenth century gave the economy of Europe a solid base and ensured the durability of goods and services for centuries. The decline of the Papacy, beginning with the defection to Avignon and leading to the Great Schism of 1378–1415 in which rival popes reigned in Avignon and Rome, was a precondition for the rise of Protestantism in the fifteenth and early sixteenth centuries. Both the new prosperity and the decline of Catholicism strengthened the hand of developing governments in the new nations of England, France, and Spain. Late in the fifteenth century, these states would develop strong monarchies that would dominate European political life for centuries to come. This rise in the secular powers and decline of the role of the Catholic Church in European politics also meant a new mental climate in which the state, the city, and the individual became the dominant moral and cultural forces, and the ideals of the Church and the feudal and courtly society it had supported fell away.

Even amidst the chaos of the fourteenth century, the increasingly secularized writers enjoyed a new position. Authors such as Giovanni Boccaccio, Geoffrey Chaucer, and Christine de Pizan already had one foot in the Renaissance. They were individuals, expressing themselves not merely as witnesses to divine truth, nor only because they were attached to courts or religious institutions that expected it of them, but partly out of personal motivation. They were still Christians, but not in quite the same sense an earlier medieval writer would have been. Above all, they possessed a new perspective on the passing of a millennium—a thousand years in which, by and large, the City of God had taken precedence over the City of Man.

Medieval European Literature

The Creation of Europe

There is another way besides the historical to look at the formation of European experience: that is to see it as a text Europe wrote about itself, emphasizing points it wanted to stress and leaving out others it preferred to suppress. In this sense, "Europe" came about as a result of a series of victorious political and cultural struggles on the part of the Christian inheritors of Greek and Roman civilization against other indigenous peoples and their cultures. In most areas conquered by the Christian Europeans, the conquered were assimilated. The case of Islam, however, was different. The Christian incursion into Islamic territory at the end of the eleventh century was eventually repulsed, with the result that the Islamic contribution to European culture was marginalized and suppressed. We therefore study Islam as a separate society that interacted with Europe for several centuries.

European Cultural Texts

Every society has its myths and texts, cultural themes that are important to its growth and survival. For the Germanic tribal societies involved in the final struggles with the Roman Empire, there were heroic stories of larger-than-life human figures, including epics such as *Beowulf.* Typically in these stories, which are pagan in origin and celebrate the collective life of the tribal community, the hero saves his people from monsters or leads them into battle, the outcome of which is governed by Fate. There is often an elegaic tone to these works, since no man lives forever and even the greatest of heroes and societies weakens and dies. Works of this Heroic Age are an important precondition for later European literature. They endure later in altered form in what we shall call quest literature.

The Christian literature of the Middle Ages, which can be said to begin with St. Augustine's *Confessions,* includes a variety of literary types: saints' lives, spiritual autobiographies and other stories designed for edification, accounts of conversion missions, and accounts of pilgrimages. They share the perspective that this life is a journey toward God and the promise of salvation. Humankind is thus seen as a traveler in this life, *homo viator,* awaiting word of salvation in the next. Although this literature may appear pessimistic concerning the state of the world, it is optimistic in that it holds out hope for a life beyond. Once we understand this concept, we can speak of all medieval Christian literature as pilgrimage literature—not simply literature about pilgrimages, but literature viewing life itself as a physical and spiritual journey leading to a hoped-for end. Thus, we have selected the subheading "The Pilgrimage of Life" for this section.

In the history of European literature, the quest literature of paganism gradually merges into the pilgrimage literature of Christianity. The late eleventh century, the period of the all-out Christian attack on the Muslim armies in Spain and Asia Minor, marks the transition period. The epic poem *The Song of Roland* retains some of the system of values of the older heroic epic, but now the hero, completely human, fights and dies with the name of God on his lips, and his opponent is a pagan infidel, not a monster. This is the literature of the Church Militant, suitable for the armies of Europe as they ride off under the banner of the Pope to the First Crusade. What is new is what the knights are fighting for: the glory of God and the destruction of the heathen.

The next stage of literary development marks a real departure. The courtly literature of the twelfth century is romance; the hero is still a knight, but the harsh realities of the struggle for existence are reduced and he often exists in a world made up partly of fantasy and partly of the rules of social decorum, or chivalry. The religious parallel to romance literature comes in stories of holy pilgrimages and mystical experiences, where again the behavior of the individual characters is very important and is intended to present an example of proper behavior for the audience. (It is interesting that as a young man St. Francis of Assisi was an avid reader of medieval romances of chivalry; after his death, the accounts of his life carry a distinctly "romance" flavor.) Sometimes the courtly romance and the literature of Christian pilgrimage come close together. In the romance of *Perceval* by Chrétien de Troyes, for example, the young knight Perceval goes in quest of the Holy Grail, the most spiritual of objects.

In the later medieval period, the theme of love emerges and modifies the quest or pilgrimage story. There are treatises on love, theories of love, and accounts of both sublimated and sexual love, even in religious settings. (Abelard's *History of My Misfortunes,* written around 1132, tells the story of his seduction of young Heloise, left in his care; their love affair; and his later castration at the hands of members of her family. Although his autobiography was not available to the public until the thirteenth century, the story was well known in his lifetime.) Some of the great expressions of the love story in the Middle Ages come in the Breton *lais*, the French and German romances, and the Provençal lyrics of the twelfth century. As has already been noted, this literature emerges at the time when monastic Christianity loses its hold on the educational process and previously suppressed works find their way into the curricula of the church schools and the universities. At the same time, literacy is extended to a larger portion of the population. Thus, the rise of the love story in the twelfth century goes hand in hand with the decline of censorship and the availability of at least a minimum level of education.

It should be noted that the conception of love in the twelfth century is different from that in the twentieth century, because it reflects a different cultural tradition. Medieval conventions of love are closely connected with medieval ideas of social class. As the court priest Andreas Capellanus tells us late in the twelfth century, love is understood differently when it takes place between members of the nobility, the peasantry, or the clergy (the latter is deemed immoral, and Capellanus does not even admit the possibility of homosexual love, whatever class he is speaking of). For the nobility, love is a complicated matter, with distinctions of rank and custom to be observed. Love among the peasantry, on the other hand, is bawdy and direct; Capellanus views it as animal passion with no human qualities whatever. We can still see this distinction observed in the work of Chaucer in the fourteenth century, between the secular romance of knights and ladies and the popular stories of the urban or rural poor.

There are other transformations in the subject matter of literature near the end of the Middle Ages, reflecting the beginnings of what might be called the *individualization* of literary experience. Although Chaucer writes in familiar medieval forms and genres and uses the frame of the holy pilgrimage for his most famous collection of stories, his interest in the human personality is more modern than medieval. The same is true of his Italian predecessor, Boccaccio. And although fifteenth-century English mystic Margery Kempe goes on a pilgrimage of her own, her account of it, like that of the rest of her life, is so blunt and realistic that it transforms the literary genre it occupies. After Margery Kempe, it is hard to find pilgrimage literature in the old sense at all—so much has the personality of the narrator and the other characters come to dominate the original purpose of the journey. Only in the drama, such as the morality play *Everyman,* written and performed around 1500, do we see the old idea of the pilgrimage of life intact, and even here the realistically portrayed individual begins to emerge from the allegory of the soul facing the call of Death.

Non-Western Literature

The non-Western literature included here is from three distinct cultures: Islam, China, and Japan. Whereas Islamic culture was Europe's self-defined enemy from the eighth through the thirteenth century, Chinese culture was unknown to Europe until the later thirteenth century, and Japanese culture remained foreign until comparatively modern times.

The medieval Islamic literature familiar to us in the West can be divided into two periods. The first is that of the Koran, the revelations of Allah to the sixth-century prophet Muhammad that were gathered during the seventh century. In many ways the Koran is comparable to the Old Testament, reflecting the parallels as well as the polarities between the Arabic and Judeo-Christian cultures. The Islamic followers of the Koran and the Christian crusaders of the eleventh and twelfth centuries were mirror-images of one another, each group equating its own beliefs with universal truth and justice and damning the other as the infidel. The second period of Islamic literature comes from the eleventh and twelfth centuries, the time of the Islamic retreat from the Iberian Peninsula as well as the contact between the two societies in the first two Crusades. Our three selections from this literature are from different dates and places. *The Dove's Necklace* (1022), a treatise on love by a young scholar from Cordoba, Ibn Hazm, stresses love's secrecy, its hidden signs and powers, as well as the rules under which it should be conducted. This work may have influenced the poetry of the troubadours in neighboring Provence a century later. *The Book of Reflections* by Usamah Ibn Munqidh of Syria in Asia Minor, written around 1185, gives a vivid account of the manners and morals of the crusading Christian Franks from the point of view of an urbane ninety-year-old Muslim diplomat. The *Travels* of Ibn Jubayr, a diplomatic aide in Granada, written in 1185, gives an Islamic version of a holy pilgrimage, which we find preserved in Christian versions in a number of other texts, notably the *Travels* ascribed to Sir John Mandeville in 1357.

The opening of the Orient to medieval Europe occurred in stages, first through the Crusades and later through trade routes along the Mediterranean. Although Marco Polo visited China as early as 1271, attaching himself for a decade to the royal house of the Emperor Kublai Khan, and European conversion missions traveled to China repeatedly in the fourteenth century, Europe did not yet show conspicuous interest in oriental culture. The most visible sign of European interest in China, in fact, came over two centuries later, when Italian navigator Christopher Columbus proposed to King Ferdinand and Queen Isabella of Spain the opening of a new trade route across the Atlantic Ocean.

Our Chinese and Japanese texts stand completely outside the European tradition. The poems of Li Po (701–762) from the Golden T'ang era show the author's deep feeling for nature, his love of the common people, and the deceptive simplicity of his literary style. Nothing in the West could be compared to Li Po's poetic idiom until the birth of Provençal poetry in the twelfth century, and even that is a rather poor comparison: Li Po's designs on his audience are more subtle than those of the European poets. The Japanese selection, from *The Tale of Genji* by Murasaki Shikibu (c. 978–1030), reflects the period of growing independence of Japanese culture from Chinese influences and its own Age of Chivalry, which is earlier and more refined than its European counterpart. In its sophisticated treatment of courtly love according to the principle of *mono no aware,* or sensitivity to things, this selection compares favorably with the Islamic love treatise of Ibn Hazm or the Western courtly love literature of the twelfth century.

THE CONFESSIONS AND *THE DIVINE COMEDY*

Our two thematic texts for this period are noteworthy for both their similarities and differences. Both are works of Christian pilgrimage literature, influenced to a greater or lesser degree by classical literature. Saint Augustine, one of the first writers of the medieval tradition, was a leading exponent of Christian doctrine for all who followed him. His view of reality was conditioned both by the importance he put on his own experience and his willingness to see himself as a *type* of humankind in search of salvation, seeking the knowledge of God while still living in the world. For Augustine, there was no contradiction between his autobiographical impulse and his allegorical imagination. Indeed, to him all of history flowed from one moment, the sacrifice of Christ on the cross, which made salvation possible. Dante Alighieri, writing nine hundred years later, still shared an Augustinian vision of salvation, and his dream vision reflects the Augustinian literary tradition as well. The differences in the texts have largely to do with the purposes and perspectives of the authors. Whereas Augustine wrote primarily as a bishop concerned with the religious edification of his flock, Dante wrote with a more complicated design, standing half inside and half outside his subject, conscious of his partial separation from both the Church and the body politic due to his equivocal position as a spiritual and political exile from the city-state of Florence in the fourteenth century.

The Confessions is a highly important text not only because Augustine recounts his own search for salvation, but because he defends his beliefs by arguing polemically against all opposing beliefs. In his highly dramatized personal account, opponents such as the Manichaeans are shown to commit not only error, but sin. By defining the enemy in this manner, Augustine establishes a new system of moral absolutes, providing among other things a theological framework that will justify Christian activity for centuries to come. Thus Augustine's spiritual absolutism lies behind not only the conversion missions of Gregory the Great in the sixth century, but the Crusades of the eleventh and twelfth centuries as well. Augustinian theology was not successfully challenged, in fact, until the rise of scholastic philosophy in the universities in the twelfth century.

Dante in *The Divine Comedy,* noting the captivity of the Papacy and the depravity of people everywhere at the end of the Middle Ages, stands at the other end of the medieval millennium, asking what has become of Christian Europe under its popes and kings, its creeds and dynasties. Any belief in the actions of the papal armies and the holy wars ended in the exhaustion of the Crusades; Dante witnessed this in his own lifetime. For the individual soul there remained the hope of salvation; the doctrine of Grace was still intact. But what had man, acting in the name of God, made of man? It was the secular Dante, the inquisitor of historical practices, who sent shivers up the spines of the Augustinians of his time by asking questions they could no longer answer.

For a moment, let us consider Augustine and Dante as men. Both are individuals bent on spiritual pilgrimage. Augustine takes us with him as he grows up, falls under certain influences, turns toward the Christian faith, experiences conversion in his garden, and resolves to write about it for the good of all humanity. Dante, following the more literary model of the epic in a conscious imitation of the Latin poet Virgil, moves through the uncharted territory of Hell, Purgatory, and Heaven, entertaining the world of the flesh and the spirit, showing us the fallen spirits of the dead who are allowed to speak from their positions of ruin, and finally leading us to the picture of salvation at the end of his poem. Like Augustine's autobiographical experiment in *The Confessions,* Dante's epic is a great tour de force, bringing us closer to God through purely literary representation. *The Divine Comedy* is in many ways the summation of the medieval story, the age's ultimate pursuit of spiritual truth and its boldest attempt to reveal what lies beyond death. Interestingly enough, in both these works the author is the hero of his own adventure; few other medieval writers would have had the audacity or the talent to write in such a manner.

In medieval literature, there is a constant fear concerning the fickleness of fortune and the possibility of untimely death. St. Augustine, beginning the millennium with the barbarians at the gates of Hippo, contrasts the chaos he sees around him to the bliss awaiting the saved in the City of God. At the other end of the period, Boccaccio sets the telling of the tales of *The Decameron* in a country estate where travelers have come to escape the Black Death. It is, of course, the business of the Church to contrast life's uncertainty with the prospect of eternal life in heaven, but the darker rendering of this theme, expressed in the formula *memento mori* (remember to die), had a distinctly popular appeal: It recurs in countless songs and stories throughout the period.

In view of this fear of death and the disruption of life, the existence of so much medieval pilgrimage literature may seem odd or contradictory. To put it simply, one might have thought that discretion consisted of playing it safe and staying at home, on both a physical and allegorical level. But from St. Augustine seeking salvation to Beowulf struggling against the dragon to the knight pursuing the Holy Grail to Christine de Pizan envisioning a new city of women, medieval Europe found its best cultural expression in its dreams of the future. Perhaps the logic of this is best described as a cycle: While life leads to death, death leads to the promise of a new life. The definition of new life and what it might become, however, was changing in the late medieval period and would continue to change in the Renaissance.

Suggested Readings

Writings on medieval history and culture are legion. This introduction follows to some degree the historical outline in C. Warren Hollister's *Medieval Europe,* 5th ed. (1982), although it varies frequently in interpretation. Another standard text, Norman F. Cantor's *The Civilization of the Middle Ages* (1993), was helpful in areas such as the rise of the individual. Other useful reference works include Erich Auerbach, *Mimesis: The Representation of Reality in Western Literature* (1953); Marc Bloch, *Feudal Society* (1963); Ernst R. Curtius, *European Literature and the Latin Middle Ages* (1953); Etienne Gilson, *A History of Christian Philosophy in the Middle Ages* (1956); Charles H. Haskins, *The Renaissance of the 12th Century* (1957); Friedrich Heer, *The Medieval World* (1961); Johan Huizinga, *The Waning of the Middle Ages* (1969); C. S. Lewis, *The Discarded Image: An Introduction to Medieval and Renaissance Literature* (1964); Henri Pirenne, *Medieval Cities: Their Origins and the Revival of Trade* (1969) and *Mohammed and Charlemagne* (1955); Eileen Power, *Medieval Women* (1975); R. W. Southern, *The Making of the Middle Ages* (1953); and Karl Vossler, *Medieval Culture* (1958). Standard guides to the literature of the period include Boris Ford, *Medieval Literature,* Part I: *Chaucer and the Alliterative Tradition* (1982), and Part II: *The European Inheritance* (1984); and W. T. H. Jackson, *Medieval Literature* (1966).

REPRESENTATIVE TEXTS

ST. AUGUSTINE

[354–430]

In the centuries following St. Augustine's death, Western Europe as we know it slowly rose out of the ashes of the Roman Empire. When it did, it could claim a Christian culture based on classical foundations. Along with his contemporaries St. Anselm and St. Jerome, St. Augustine had helped to build this model for the future. Beyond this, St. Augustine offered a reading of Christian theology that, following the Pauline epistles, saw individual, historical man traveling on a spiritual pilgrimage toward God and salvation in heaven. This theme of the *homo viator* (the traveler through life) is taken up in one way or another by writer after writer all through the Middle Ages and even beyond. The medieval part of the story begins with St. Augustine's *Confessions*.

LIFE

By the time Aurelius Augustinus was born in Roman North Africa in 354, Christianity had established itself as the official religion of the declining Roman Empire. Emperor Constantine had offered protection to Christianity in 313; the Council of Nicaea had confirmed the ties between Church and Empire in 325. This did not necessarily mean, however, that a young man of promising abilities would become a Christian. Despite the pleadings of his mother, Monica, young Augustine spent years choosing among rival beliefs and philosophies. For nine years, while he taught rhetoric in the schools, he followed Manicheism, a dualistic creed emphasizing a sharp division between Good and Evil. He studied other ideas as well, and finally came under the influence of Neoplatonism, especially concerning matters of the spirit. Finally, in 384, Augustine attended the sermons of St. Ambrose of Milan and began to pay attention to Christian teachings, especially regarding the interpretation of the Bible. Through reading the Epistles of St. Paul he began to understand the doctrine of grace. In 387, at the age of 32, he was baptised a Christian by St. Ambrose.

After the death of his mother the following year, he entered monastic life, becoming the Bishop of Hippo in his native North Africa in 396. From then on he devoted himself to serving his diocese and writing his great theological works, including *The Confessions* (397–400) and *The City of God* (413–426). In his later years, the Roman Empire rapidly disintegrated; Rome was sacked by Alaric and the Goths in 410, and Hippo itself lay under siege by the Vandals at the time of Augustine's death in 430. In fact, Augustine's bones were moved twice in subsequent centuries to protect them from desecration: from Hippo, under attack by the Vandals again, to the island of Sardinia in 497; and from there, under Saracen attack, to Italy in 721–722.

WORK

Keys to Interpretation

Augustine's writings are too extensive to summarize here. His *Confessions* charts his own progress from a prodigal son living a life of waste and profligacy to a Christian convert living under the grace of God, and ends with several chapters expounding Christian doctrine and interpreting the Scriptures in praise of God. *The City of God,* written to demonstrate the primacy of the heavenly city over fallen Rome, elaborates on the doctrine of the grace necessary for salvation. His other mature works take up issues that Augustine had wrestled with as a convert, such as the doctrine of the Trinity, the nature of evil, the authority of the priesthood, and the relationship between free will and determinism. A notable feature in all Augustine's writings is the desire lying behind the work: Augustine writes to solve problems, state beliefs, and influence those who must follow him in life. In doing so he establishes a personal bond with the reader.

A crucial factor in Augustine's work is his use of scriptural interpretation. The very core of *The Confessions*—its dual status as the first true autobiography in the Western tradition and the first description in detail of the journey of the Christian soul toward God—is dependent on the kind of scriptural interpretation expounded to the young Augustine by St. Ambrose. Basically, this doctrine holds that everything in the Old Testament is a "figure" of the New Testament; everything under the Old Law is fulfilled in the New Law of Christ. For example, Exodus, the story of the deliverance of the Jewish people from slavery, is the "figure" of which the story of the Redemption of humankind by Christ is the fulfillment. Applied to the case of the individual, Augustine is not only himself; his story is a "figure" of humankind seeking fulfillment in salvation. (To some degree, every medieval writer after Augustine is subject to this kind of interpretation, though one should retain common sense enough to see a real hero slaying a real dragon before one begins to allow a spiritual interpretation.)

The reader of St. Augustine will also notice the rhetorical energy of *The Confessions.* Even in translation one cannot help but hear the cadences and rhythms of Augustinian style, which borrows heavily from the rich verbal effects of late classical Latin. Trained in the art of argument, Augustine embraced classical rhetoric as a means of promoting Christian doctrine. Often the energy of his prose comes in the form of questions; at other times, he displays the force of his argument in repetitions of sound and sense:

> Who will bring to my mind the sins of my infancy? For in your sight no man is clean of sin, not even the infant who has lived but a day upon earth. Who will bring this to my mind? (I, 7)
>
> Therefore, I defiled the very source of friendship by the filth of concupiscence, and its clear waters I befouled with the lust of hell. Yet foul and vicious as I was, with overflowing vanity, I took pride in being refined and cultured. (III, 1)

The Pattern of The Confessions

The Confessions covers autobiographical ground from childhood to Augustine's struggles over his faith to his Christian conversion. The first part of the work ends with the death of his mother, Monica, in 388, when Augustine himself was 33. Three chapters follow on Christian doctrine, with a final chapter giving a scriptural interpretation of the book of Genesis. In terms of Catholic religious practice, the work echoes the sacrament of confession by its multiple confessions touching on sin, faith, and the praise of God. First, Augustine confesses his sins: the Original Sin of the child; his sins of the flesh, which begin in adolescence; his sins of misguided faith as a young man; and the sin of pride, which holds him back from conversion. Second, Augustine acknowledges his faith in God, which leads him to conversion. Third, in the closing chapters of the work, Augustine manifests his praise of God by expounding doctrine on such matters as Memory, Time and Eternity, Form and Matter, and finally the Creation.[1]

In the early chapters of *The Confessions,* we encounter Augustine's extreme consciousness of sin. There is, for instance, the passage in which he states that as a child he loved the classical romances too much: "I wept over the dead Dido, who sought her end by the

[1]John K. Ryan, *The Confessions of St. Augustine* (1960), 29.

sword. I forsook you [God], and I followed after your lowest creatures" (I, 13). At the age of 16, he tells us "the madness of lust . . . took me completely under its scepter, and I clutched it with both hands" (II, 2). At the same age, he slipped into a walled garden and stole pears from a neighbor's tree. "Those pears I gathered solely that I might steal," he relates, "for if I put any of that fruit in my mouth, my sin was its seasoning" (II, 6). The details of his sins—some palpable, some we would think of as the product of a guilty conscience—are everywhere, with interpretations never far behind. It should not surprise us that St. Augustine was one of the major exponents of the doctrine of Original Sin in the early debates of the Church.

In his twenties, the self-described young "sensualist" would rise in the intellectual world of Carthage, where he conducted his studies. At first, he tells us, he found the Holy Scriptures "unworthy of comparison with the nobility of Cicero's writings" (III, 5), and a bishop his mother had sent to speak to him found him still unripe for religious instruction (III, 12). But finally he traveled to Rome and then to Milan, where he met Bishop Ambrose and became a catechumen in the Catholic faith (V, 14). After some further agonizing, he was led by his reading of the Platonists to the Epistles of Paul.

Now, with the benefit of both his learning and his new exposure to Christianity, Augustine moved toward the point of conversion. The most famous passage in *The Confessions* begins in Augustine's backyard in Milan. There, in a small garden attached to his house, he found himself driven by "the tumult in my breast" (VIII, 8). Excoriating himself for his sins, uncertain of where to turn with his faith, he found himself interrupted by a new sound:

> And lo, I heard from a nearby house, a voice like that of a boy or a girl, I know not which, chanting and repeating over and over, "Take up and read, take up and read." (VIII, 12)

Opening his book of the Epistles of Paul, Augustine read the first passage on which his eyes fell:

> Not in rioting and drunkenness, not in chambering and impurities, not in strife and envying; but put you on the Lord Jesus Christ, and make not provision for the flesh in its concupiscences. (Romans 13:13–14. Cited in VIII, 12)

His conversion followed. The ties between the Bible, the message of Paul, and the living Augustine had been joined. Augustine hoped that in the same way his own book would serve many other Christians, leading them to the Bible so that it might perform its intended office.

The confession of faith comes throughout the book, interspersed within the autobiography. The work is written directly to God, so that it represents half of a dialogue: Augustine frequently addresses God in the second person as "you." Book VIII, including the narrative of the conversion, is the penultimate book of the autobiographical portion of *The Confessions.* The confession of praise begins with Book X, after the death of Monica, Augustine's mother. Here the author begins a new invocation to God, as in Book I. The new confession begins: "Not with doubtful but with sure knowledge do I love you, O Lord" (X, 6). The business of the next several books—Memory, Time and Eternity, Form and Matter—is primarily spiritual, and its treatment has often been thought of as a fine example of Christian Neoplatonism. Book XIII, on the Creation, is only very loosely an interpretation of Genesis: it draws together the themes of *The Confessions* into an acknowledgement of faith by praising God. Thus *The Confessions* ends as it began, in the spirit of divine witness.

The Historical Legacy

There are several reasons why Augustine's spiritual autobiography is so important. In the first place, it is the account of a journey, literally from place to place but also spiritually from the darkness of sin to the light of salvation, in an autobiographical form that was to find many adherents in later literature. Second, it is a pattern, or figure, of conversion sent out to the souls of other men awaiting their own fulfillment in their coming to Christ. Third, following in the Pauline tradition, it marks the beginning of a long historical epoch in which conversion missions to the heathen populations would determine the fate of a continent and beyond.

At its simplest level, Augustine's tale of salvation is autobiography. Thus he helped to create a literary form that has come down to the modern period. In the Middle Ages, autobiography was largely restricted to religious authors writing for the edification of the laity. With the expansion of literature to the middle class at the beginning of the Renaissance, authors of various backgrounds recounted their lives, and they have done so ever since. At the same time, pseudo-autobiographical forms developed in fiction. These included the picaresque novel, a tale of adventure on the road; the novel of development, in which the hero is shown going through the stages of life from childhood to maturity or death; and the epistolary novel, a series of letters often confessional in form. In some way all these later forms borrow their concentration on the speaking self and their penchant for self-examination from *The Confessions.*

As a pattern for spiritual conversion, *The Confessions* enjoyed a tremendous popularity all through the Middle Ages. Copies in monasteries and the rise of derivative works such as Abelard's *History of My Misfortunes* (1132) attest to this fact. Toward the end of the medieval period we also see noteworthy poems of spiritual pilgrimage on the Augustinian model: These include Dante's epic *Divine Comedy,* finished in 1321; the English consolatory poem *Pearl,* written about 1375; and the English spiritual monologue *Piers Plowman,* written about the same time. Later literary works on pilgrimage and conversion follow the Augustinian model to one degree or another; a famous example is *Pilgrim's Progress* (1675).

The relationship between Augustine's groundbreaking narrative, rich in the language and imagery of the Pauline epistles, and the conversion missions to the multitudes of pagan Europe requires some comment. The spirit of personal witness and the drama of conversion that we see portrayed in St. Augustine's *Confessions* no doubt influenced the decision of Gregory the Great to send monks to the corners of the known world to convert the heathen populations at the beginning of the sixth century; we may say further that the success of the conversion missions in general influenced the departure of the three ships of Columbus in 1492, bringing Catholic Europeans to confront and eventually dominate the vast indigenous population in the New World; and this general influence echoes down to our own times, when evangelism still plays its role in the religious and political enterprises of the twentieth century. Conversion, an act of personal affirmation of faith speeded by the grace of God, has had the same appeal whether one thinks of an individual life or the potential for converting a continent. If it works for one, it should work for all, and for a Christian it carries a revolutionary thrust.

Thus the conversion of St. Augustine, grounded in the Epistles of Paul, was not only a personal story; it became a pattern for the rest of the world to follow, sometimes of its own volition and sometimes not. As we shall see, conversion and the journey to God as Augustine understood them would profoundly shape the thousand years that made up the rest of the Middle Ages.

Suggested Readings

One text of *The Confessions* with sound introductory material and apparatus is *Confessions,* trans. R. S. Pine-Coffin (1961). Peter Brown's *Augustine of Hippo* (1967) is the standard modern biography. Sources for an understanding of Augustine's thought include Dom Cuthbert Butler's *Western Mysticism* (1934), Herbert Deane's *The Political and Social*

Ideal of St. Augustine (1963), and Etienne Gilson's *The Christian Philosophy of St. Augustine* (1960). A more specialized study of the doctrine of grace is Gerhard Ladner's *The Idea of Reform* (1959). For a study of scriptural interpretation as practiced by St. Augustine and others, see Erich Auerbach's "Figura," in *Scenes from the Drama of European Literature* (1959), pp. 11–78.

The Confessions

Translated by John K. Ryan

Book I
Childhood

Chapter 1
God and the Soul

(1) You are great, O Lord, and greatly to be praised: great is your power and to your wisdom there is no limit.[1] And man, who is a part of your creation, wishes to praise you, man who bears about within himself his mortality, who bears about within himself testimony to his sin and testimony that you resist the proud.[2] Yet man, this part of your creation, wishes to praise you. You arouse him to take joy in praising you, for you have made us for yourself, and our heart is restless until it rests in you.[3] Lord, grant me to know and understand which is first, to call upon you or to praise you, and also which is first, to know you or to call upon you? But how does one who does not know you call upon you? For one who does not know you might call upon another instead of you. Or must you rather be called upon so that you may be known? Yet "how shall they call upon him in whom they have not believed? Or how shall they believe without a preacher?"[4] "And they shall praise the Lord that seek him,"[5] for they that seek him find him,[6] and finding him they shall praise him. Lord, let me seek you by calling upon you, and let me call upon you by believing in you, for you have been preached to us. Lord, my faith calls upon you, that faith which you have given to me, which you have breathed into me by the incarnation of your Son and through the ministry of your preacher.[7]

Chapter 2
God Omnipresent

(2) How shall I call upon my God, my God and my Lord, since, in truth, when I call upon him, I call him into myself? What place is there within me where my God can come? How can God come into me, God who made heaven and earth?[8] O Lord my God, is there anything in me that can contain you? In truth, can heaven and earth, which you have made and in which you have made me, contain you? Or because without you whatever is would not be, does it hold that whatever exists contains you? Since I do indeed exist, and yet would not be unless you were in me, why do I beg that you come to me? I am not now in hell, yet you are even there.

---

[1]Cf. Ps. 144:3; Ps. 146:5. [All notes to *The Confessions* are translator's notes.]

[2]Cf. Jas. 4:6; I Pet. 5:5; Prov. 3:34.

[3]"Our heart is restless until it rests in you" sums up Augustine's whole teaching on man's relation to God. It is perhaps the most quoted line in *The Confessions*.

[4]Cf. Rom. 10:14. [5]Ps. 21:27. [6]Cf. Matt. 7:7.

[7]The preacher was St. Ambrose (c. 339–397), Bishop of Milan.

[8]Gen. 1:1.

For "if I descend into hell, you are present."[9] Therefore, my God, I would not be, I would in no wise be, unless you were in me. Or rather, I would not be unless I were in you, "from whom, by whom, and in whom are all things."[10] Even so, O Lord, even so. To what place do I call you, since I am in you? Or from what place can you come to me? Where can I go beyond heaven and earth, so that there you may come to me, my God, who have said, "I fill heaven and earth?"[11]

Chapter 3
God's Immensity

(3) Do heaven and hell therefore contain you, since you fill them? Or do you fill them, and does there yet remain something further, since they do not contain you? Where then do you diffuse what remains of you after heaven and hell have been filled? Or do you who contain all things have no need to be contained by anything further, since you fill all the things you fill by containing them? The vessels that are filled by you do not restrict you, for even if they are shattered, you are not poured forth. When you are poured upon us,[12] you are not cast down, but you raise us up;[13] you are not scattered about, but you gather us up. You fill all things, and you fill them all with your entire self. But since all things cannot contain you in your entirety, do they then contain a part of you, and do all things simultaneously contain the same part? Or do single things contain single parts, greater things containing greater parts and smaller things smaller parts? Is one part of you greater, therefore, and another smaller? Or are you entire in all places, and does no one thing contain you in your entirety?

Chapter 4
Divine Attributes

(4) What, then, is my God? What, I ask, unless the Lord God? Who is Lord but the Lord? Or who is God but our God?[14]

Most high, most good, most mighty, most almighty; most merciful and most just; most hidden and most present; most beautiful and most strong; stable and incomprehensible; unchangeable, yet changing all things; never new, and never old, yet renewing all things;[15] leading proud men into senility, although they know it not;[16] ever active, and ever at rest; gathering in, yet needing nothing; supporting, fulfilling, and protecting things; creating, nourishing, and perfecting them; searching them out, although nothing is lacking in you.

You love, but are not inflamed with passion; you are jealous, yet free from care; you repent, but do not sorrow; you grow angry, but remain tranquil. You change your works, but do not change your plan; you take back what you find, although you never lost it; you are never in want, but you rejoice in gain; you are never covetous, yet you exact usury. Excessive payments are made to you, so that you may be our debtor—yet who has anything that is not yours? You pay debts, although you owe no man anything; you cancel debts, and lose nothing. What have we said, my God, my life, my holy delight? Or what does any man say when he speaks of you? Yet woe to those who keep silent concerning you, since even those who speak much are as the dumb.

---

[9]Cf. Ps. 138:8: "If I ascend into heaven you are there; if I descend into hell, you are present." Cf. also Amos 9:2.

[10]Cf. Rom. 11:36. [11]Jer. 23:24.

[12]Cf. Acts 2:17; Joel 2:28.

[13]Cf. Ps. 145:8. [14]Cf. Ps. 17:32. [15]Cf. Wisd. 7:27. [16]Cf. Job 9:5.

Chapter 5
Augustine's Prayer

(5) Who will give me help, so that I may rest in you? Who will help me, so that you will come into my heart and inebriate it, to the end that I may forget my evils and embrace you, my one good? What are you to me? Have pity on me, so that I may speak! What am I myself to you, that you command me to love you, and grow angry and threaten me with mighty woes unless I do? Is it but a small affliction if I do not love you? Unhappy man that I am, in your mercy, O Lord my God, tell me what you are to me. "Say to my soul: I am your salvation."[17] Say this, so that I may hear you. Behold, my heart's ears are turned to you, O Lord: open them, and "say to my soul: I am your salvation." I will run after that voice, and I will catch hold of you. Do not hide your face from me.[18] Lest I die, let me die, so that I may see it.

(6) Too narrow is the house of my soul for you to enter into it: let it be enlarged by you. It lies in ruins; build it up again. I confess and I know that it contains things that offend your eyes. Yet who will cleanse it? Or upon what other than you shall I call? "From my secret sins cleanse me, O Lord, and from those of others spare your servant."[19] I believe, and therefore I speak out.[20] Lord, all this you know. Have I not accused myself to you, my God, of my sins, and have you not forgiven the iniquity of my heart?[21] I do not contend in judgment with you[22] who are truth itself. I do not deceive myself, lest my iniquity lie to itself.[23] Therefore, I do not contend in judgment with you, for "if you, O Lord, will mark iniquities: Lord, who shall stand it?"[24]

Chapter 6
The Infant Augustine

(7) Yet grant me to plead before your mercy, grant me who am dust and ashes[25] to speak, for behold, it is not a man who makes mock of me but your mercy that I address. Perhaps even you deride me, but when you have turned towards me, you will have mercy on me.[26] What do I want to say, Lord, except that I do not know whence I came into what I may call a mortal life or a living death. Whence I know not. Your consolation and your mercies[27] have raised me up, as I have heard from the parents of my flesh, for by one and in the other you fashioned me in time. I myself do not remember this. Therefore, the comfort of human milk nourished me, but neither my mother nor my nurses filled their own breasts. Rather, through them you gave me an infant's food in accordance with your law and out of the riches that you have distributed even down to the lowest level of things. You gave me to want no more than you gave, and you gave to those who nursed me the will to give what you gave to them. By an orderly affection they willingly gave me what they possessed so abundantly from you. It was good for them that my good should come from them; yet it was not from them but through them. For from you, O God, come all good things, and from you, my God, comes all my salvation. This I afterwards observed when you cried out to me by means of those things which you bestow both inwardly and outwardly. For at that time I knew how to seek

---

[17] Ps. 34:3.
[18] Cf. Ps. 142:7; Exod. 33:20; Deut. 31:17.
[19] Ps. 18:13–14. [20] Cf. Ps. 115:10. [21] Cf. Ps. 31:5. [22] Cf. Job 9:3.
[23] Cf. Ps. 26:12. [24] Ps. 129:3.
[25] Cf. Gen. 18:27; Ecclus. 10:9.
[26] Cf. Jer. 12:15.
[27] Cf. Ps. 93:19; 68:17.

the breast, to be satisfied with pleasant things, and to cry at my bodily hurts, but nothing more.

(8) Later on, I began to laugh, at first when asleep and then when awake. This has been told to me concerning myself, and I believe it, since we see other infants acting thus, although I do not remember such acts of my own. Then little by little I perceived where I was, and I wished to make my wants known to those who could satisfy them. Yet I could not do so, because the wants were within me, while those outside could by no sensible means penetrate into my soul. So I tossed my limbs about and uttered sounds, thus making such few signs similar to my wishes as I could, and in such fashion as I could, although they were not like the truth. When they would not obey me, either because they did not understand or because it would be harmful, I grew angry at older ones who were not subject to me and at children for not waiting on me, and took it out on them by crying. That infants are of this sort I have since learned from those whom I have been able to observe. That I was such a one they have unwittingly taught me better than my nurses who knew me.

(9) But see, my infancy is dead long ago, and I still live. Lord, you who live forever and in whom nothing dies—since before the beginning of the ages, and before anything that can even be called "before," you are, and you are God and Lord of all that you have created, and with you stand the causes of all impermanent things and with you abide the unchanging sources of all changing things, and in you live the sempiternal reasons of all unreasoning and temporal things—tell to me, your suppliant, O God, in your mercy, tell to me, your wretched servant, whether my infancy followed another age of mine that was already dead. Or was it that time which I passed within my mother's womb? Of that time something has been told to me, and I have seen pregnant women. What was there even before this, my joy, my God? Was I anywhere, or anyone? I have no one to tell me this, neither father nor mother could do so, nor the experience of others, nor my own memory. Do you laugh at me for questioning you of such things? Do you command me to praise you and confess to you only for what I know?

(10) I confess to you, O Lord of heaven and earth,[28] and I utter praise to you for my first being and my infancy, which I do not remember. You have endowed man so that he can gather these things concerning himself from others, and even on the words of weak women believe much about himself. For even then I had being and lived, and already at the close of my infancy I looked for signs by which I could make known my meaning to others. Where except from you, O Lord, could come such a living being? Who has the art and power to make himself? Is there any channel, through which being and life flow into us, that comes from any source but you, Lord, who made us? In you being and life are not different things, because supreme being and supreme life are one and the same. You are supreme and you are not changed.[29] Nor is this present day spent in you—and yet it is spent in you, for in you are all these times. Unless you contained them, they would have no way of passing on. And because your years do not fail,[30] your years are this every day. No matter how many have already been our days and the days of our fathers, they have all passed through this single present day of yours, and from it they have taken their measures and their manner of being. And others still shall also pass away and receive their measures and their manner of being. "But you are the Selfsame,"[31] and all things of tomorrow and all beyond, and all things of yesterday and all things before, you shall make into today, and you have already made them into today.

[28]Cf. Matt. 11:25. [29]Cf. Mal. 3:6. [30]Ps. 101:28. [31]Ibid.

What matters it to me if someone does not understand this? Let him too rejoice and say, "What is this?"[32] Let him rejoice even at this, and let him love to find you while not finding it out, rather than, while finding it out, not to find you.

Chapter 7
The Psychology of Infancy

(11) Graciously hear me, O God. Woe to the sins of men! Yet a man says this, and you have mercy upon him, for you have made him, but the sin that is in him you have not made. Who will bring to my mind the sins of my infancy? For in your sight no man is clean of sin,[33] not even the infant who has lived but a day upon earth. Who will bring this to my mind? Does not each little child now do this, for in him I now perceive what I do not remember about myself? How then did I sin at that age? Was it because I cried out as I tried to mouth the breast? Indeed if I did so now—not of course as one gaping for the breast, but for food fitting to my years—I would be laughed at and most justly blamed. Hence at that time I did reprehensible things, but because I could not understand why anyone should blame me, neither custom nor reason allowed me to be blamed. As we grow up, we root out such things and throw them aside. Yet I have never seen anyone knowingly throw aside the good when he purges away the bad.

But even then were these things good: to try to get by crying even what would be harmful if it were given to me, to be bitterly resentful at freemen, elders, my parents, and many other prudent people who would not indulge my whims, when I struck at them and tried to hurt them as far as I could because they did not obey orders that would be obeyed only to my harm? Thus it is not the infant's will that is harmless, but the weakness of infant limbs. I myself have seen and have had experience with a jealous little one; it was not yet able to speak, but it was pale and bitter in face as it looked at another child nursing at the same breast.

Who is unaware of such things? Mothers and nurses claim to make up for them by some sort of correctives. Yet is it really innocence not to allow another child to share in that richly flowing fountain of milk, although it is in great need of help and derives life from that sole source of food? These things are easily put up with, not because they are of little or no account, but because they will disappear with increase in age. This you can prove from the fact that the same things cannot be borne with patience when detected in an older person.

(12) Therefore, O Lord my God, you have given to the infant life and a body, which, as we see, you have thus furnished with senses, equipped with limbs, beautified with a shapely form, and, for its complete good and protection, have endowed with all the powers of a living being. For all such things you command me to praise you and to confess you, and to "sing to your name, O Most High."[34] For you are God, all-powerful and good, even if you made only such things. For no other can do this but you, the One, from whom is every measure, you, the absolute Form,[35] who give form to all things and govern all things by your law.

Therefore, O Lord, this age which I do not remember to have lived, which I have taken on trust from others, which I conclude myself to have passed from observing other infants, although such testimonies are most probable, this age I hesitate to join to this life of mine which I have lived in this world. In so far as it belongs to the dark regions of forgetfulness, it is like that which I lived in my mother's womb.

[32] Cf. Exod. 16:15; Ecclus. 39:26.
[33] Cf. Job 25:4. [34] Cf. Ps. 91:2.
[35] God is referred to as the One and the supreme Form or Beauty in terms of Plotinian philosophy.

But "if I was conceived in iniquity," and if my mother nourished me within her womb in sins,[36] where, I beseech you, O Lord my God, where or when was your servant innocent? But, see, I now set aside that period. What matters that now to me of which I recall no trace?

Chapter 8
The Growth of Speech

(13) Did I not advance from infancy and come into boyhood? Or rather, did it not come upon me and succeed to my infancy? Yet infancy did not depart: for where did it go? Still, it was no more, for I was no longer an infant, one who could not speak, but now I was a chattering boy. I remembered this, and afterwards I reflected on how I learned to talk. Grown up men did not teach me by presenting me with words in any orderly form of instruction, as they did my letters a little later. But I myself, with that mind which you, my God, gave me, wished by means of various cries and sounds and movements of my limbs to express my heart's feelings, so that my will would be obeyed. However, I was unable to express all that I wished or to all to whom I wished. I pondered over this in memory: when they named a certain thing and, at that name, made a gesture towards the object, I observed that object and inferred that it was called by the name they uttered when they wished to show it to me. That they meant this was apparent by their bodily gestures, as it were by words natural to all men, which are made by change of countenance, nods, movements of the eyes and other bodily members, and sounds of the voice, which indicate the affections of the mind in seeking, possessing, rejecting, or avoiding things. So little by little I inferred that the words set in their proper places in different sentences, that I heard frequently, were signs of things. When my mouth had become accustomed to these signs, I expressed by means of them my own wishes. Thus to those among whom I was I communicated the signs of what I wished to express. I entered more deeply into the stormy society of human life, although still dependent on my parents' authority and the will of my elders.

. . .

Chapter 12
Good out of Evil

(19) In boyhood itself, when there was less to be feared in my regard than from youth, I did not love study and hated to be driven to it. Yet I was driven to it, and good was thus done to me, but I myself did not do good. I would have learned nothing unless forced to it. No one does good against his will, even if what he does is good. Nor did those who drove me on do well: the good was done to me by you, my God. They did not see to what use I would put what they forced me to learn, beyond satisfying the insatiable desires of a rich beggary and a base glory. But you, before whom the hairs of our head are numbered,[37] turned to my advantage the error of all those who kept me at my studies. The error of myself, who did not want to study, you used for my chastisement. For I, so small a boy and yet so great a sinner, was not unworthy of punishment. Thus by means of men who did not do well you did well for me, and out of my sinning you justly imposed punishment on me. You have ordered it, and so it is, that every disordered mind should be its own punishment.

---

[36]Cf. Ps. 50:7. [37]Cf. Matt. 10:30.

Chapter 13
Studies in Greek and Latin

(20) Why I detested the Greek language when I was taught it as a little boy I have not yet fully discovered. I liked Latin very much, not the parts given by our first teachers but what the men called grammarians teach us.[38] The first stages of our education, when we learn reading, writing, and arithmetic, I considered no less a burden and punishment than all the Greek courses. Since I was but "flesh, and a wind that goes and does not return,"[39] where could this come from except from sin and vanity of life? Better indeed, because more certain, were those first studies by which there was formed and is formed in me what I still possess, the ability to read what I find written down and to write what I want to, than the later studies wherein I was required to learn by heart I know not how many of Aeneas's wanderings, although forgetful of my own, and to weep over Dido's death, because she killed herself for love, when all the while amid such things, dying to you, O God my life, I most wretchedly bore myself about with dry eyes.

(21) Who can be more wretched than the wretched one who takes no pity on himself, who weeps over Dido's death, which she brought to pass by love for Aeneas,[40] and who does not weep over his own death, brought to pass by not loving you, O God, light of my heart, bread for the inner mouth of my soul, power wedding together my mind and the bosom of my thoughts? I did not love you, and I committed fornication against you,[41] and amid my fornications from all sides there sounded the words, "Well done! Well done!"[42] Love of this world is fornication against you,[43] but "Well done! Well done!" is said, so that it will be shameful for a man to be otherwise. I did not weep over these facts, but I wept over the dead Dido "who sought her end by the sword."[44] I forsook you, and I followed after your lowest creatures, I who was earth, turning to earth. If I had been forbidden to read those tales, I would have grieved because I could not read what would cause me to grieve. Such folly is deemed a higher and more profitable study than that by which I learned to read and write.

(22) Now let my God cry out in my soul, and let your truth say to me, "It is not so. It is not so." Far better is that earlier teaching. See how I am readier to forget the wanderings of Aeneas and all such tales than to read and write. True it is that curtains hang before the doors of the grammar schools, but they do not symbolize some honored mystery but rather a cloak for error. Let not men whom I no longer fear inveigh against me when I confess to you, my God, what my soul desires, and when I acquiesce in a condemnation of my evil ways, so that I may love your ways, which are good.[45] Let not these buyers and sellers of literature inveigh against me if I put this question to them: "Did Aeneas ever come to Carthage, as the poet says?" For if I do, the more unlearned will answer that they do not know; the more learned will even deny that it is true. But if I ask them with what letters the name Aeneas is spelled, all who have learned this much will give the right answer

---

[38]The "first teachers" taught the three R's; the *grammatici* gave more advanced courses, such as composition, rhetoric, and literature.

[39]Ps. 77:39.

[40]As Dido was the legendary queen of Carthage, her story must have been a favorite in African schools.

[41]Cf. Osee 9:1; 4:12.

[42]Ps. 39:16. [43]Cf. Jas. 4:4.

[44]Vergil, *Aeneid*, iv, 457.

[45]Cf. Jer. 18:11.

in accordance with that agreement and convention by which men have established these characters among themselves. Again, if I should ask which of these would be forgotten with greater inconvenience to our life, to read and write or those poetic fables, who does not discern the answer of every man who has not completely lost his mind? Therefore, as a boy I sinned when I preferred these inane tales to more useful studies, or rather when I hated the one and loved the other. But then, "One and one are two, and two and two are four" was for me a hateful chant, while the wooden horse full of armed men, the burning of Troy, and Creusa's ghost[46] were most sweet but empty spectacles.

. . .

Book II
Augustine's Sixteenth Year

Chapter 1
The Depths of Vice

(1) I wish to bring back to mind my past foulness and the carnal corruptions of my soul. This is not because I love them, but that I may love you, my God. Out of love for your love I do this. In the bitterness of my remembrance, I tread again my most evil ways, so that you may grow sweet to me, O sweetness that never fails, O sweetness happy and enduring, which gathers me together again from that disordered state in which I lay in shattered pieces, wherein, turned away from you, the one, I spent myself upon the many.[47] For in my youth, I burned to get my fill of hellish things. I dared to run wild in different darksome ways of love. My comeliness wasted away.[48] I stank in your eyes, but I was pleasing to myself and I desired to be pleasing to the eyes of men.

Chapter 2
Love and Lust

(2) What was there to bring me delight except to love and be loved? But that due measure between soul and soul, wherein lie the bright boundaries of friendship, was not kept. Clouds arose from the slimy desires of the flesh and from youth's seething spring. They clouded over and darkened my soul, so that I could not distinguish the calm light of chaste love from the fog of lust. Both kinds of affection burned confusedly within me and swept my feeble youth over the crags of desire and plunged me into a whirlpool of shameful deeds. Your wrath was raised above me, but I knew it not. I had been deafened by the clanking chains of my mortality, the penalty of my pride of soul. I wandered farther away from you, and you let me go. I was tossed about and spilt out in my fornications; I flowed out and boiled over in them, but you kept silent. Ah, my late-found joy! you kept silent at that time,[49] and farther and farther I went from you, into more and more fruitless seedings of sorrow, with a proud dejection and a weariness without rest.

(3) Who might have tempered my misery, turned to good use the fleeting beauties of those lowest things, and put limits to their delights, so that youth's flood might have spent itself on the shore of married life, if rest in such pleasures could not be gained by the end of begetting children, as your law, O Lord, prescribes?

---

[46] Cf. *Aeneid*, ii, 772.
[47] The phrases "the one" and "the many" are from Neoplatonic philosophy.
[48] Cf. Dan. 10:8. [49] Cf. Isa. 42:14.

Even so do you fashion the offspring of our mortality, for you have power to stretch forth a gentle hand and soften those thorns that had no place in your paradise.[50] For your omnipotence is not far from us, even when we are far from you. Or I might have listened more heedfully to your voice as it sounded from the clouds: "Nevertheless, such shall have tribulation of the flesh. But I spare you."[51] "It is good for a man not to touch a woman."[52] And again: "He that is without a wife is solicitous for the things that belong to God, how he may please God. But he that is with a wife is solicitous for the things of this world, how he may please his wife."[53] I should have listened more heedfully to these words, and having thus been made a eunuch for the sake of the kingdom of heaven,[54] I would have looked with greater joy to your embraces.

(4) But I, poor wretch, foamed over: I followed after the sweeping tide of passions and I departed from you. I broke all your laws, but I did not escape your scourges. For what mortal man can do that? You were always present to aid me, merciful in your anger, and charging with the greatest bitterness and disgust all my unlawful pleasures, so that I might seek after pleasure that was free from disgust, to the end that, when I could find it, it would be in none but you, Lord, in none but you. For you fashion sorrow into a lesson to us.[55] You smite so that you may heal. You slay us, so that we may not die apart from you.[56]

Where was I in that sixteenth year of my body's age, and how long was I exiled from the joys of your house? Then it was that the madness of lust, licensed by human shamelessness but forbidden by your laws, took me completely under its scepter, and I clutched it with both hands. My parents took no care to save me by marriage from plunging into ruin. Their only care was that I should learn to make the finest orations and become a persuasive speaker.

Chapter 3
A Year of Idleness

(5) In that year my studies were interrupted, with my return from Madauros,[57] the nearby city in which I had already resided to take up the study of literature and oratory, while the money for the longer journey to Carthage was being raised, more by the determination than by the finances of my father, a moderately well-off burgess[58] of Thagaste. To whom do I tell these things? Not to you, my God, but before you I tell them to my own kind, to mankind, or to whatever small part of it may come upon these books of mine. Why do I tell these things? It is that I myself and whoever else reads them may realize from what great depths we must cry unto you.[59] And what is closer to your ears than a contrite heart and a life of faith?[60]

Who at that time did not praise and extol my father because, beyond the resources of his own estate, he furnished his son with everything needed for this long sojourn

---

[50] Cf. Gen. 3:18; Matt. 22:30.

[51] I Cor. 7:28. [52] I Cor. 7:1. [53] I Cor. 7:32, 33. [54] Cf. Matt. 19:12.

[55] Cf. Ps. 93:20: "... who frame labor in commandment."

[56] Cf. Deut. 32:39.

[57] Madauros, or Madaura, the present-day Mdaourouch, was about twenty miles from Thagaste. In Augustine's boyhood it was still largely pagan, and he must have been adversely affected by his surroundings and companions.

[58] Patricius, Augustine's father, had the rights of a Roman citizen. He had some property, but apparently not too much. As a member of the municipal curia, he incurred expenses that must have been a serious burden to him.

[59] Cf. Ps. 129:1.

[60] Cf. Hab. 2:4; Rom. 1:17; Gal. 3:11; Heb. 10:38.

to be made for purposes of study? No such provision was made for their sons by many far richer citizens. But meanwhile this same father took no pains as to how I was growing up before you, or as to how chaste I was, as long as I was cultivated in speech, even though I was left a desert, uncultivated for you, O God, who are the one true and good Lord of that field which is my heart.[61]

(6) During the idleness of that sixteenth year, when, because of lack of money at home, I lived with my parents and did not attend school, the briars of unclean desires spread thick over my head, and there was no hand to root them out. Moreover, when my father saw me at the baths, he noted how I was growing into manhood and was clothed with stirring youth. From this, as it were, he already took pride in his grandchildren, and found joy in telling it to my mother. He rejoiced over it in that intoxication, wherein this world, from the unseen wine of its own perverse will, tending down towards lower things, forgets you, its creator, and loves your creature more than yourself.[62] But you had already begun to build your temple within my mother's breast and to lay there the foundations of your holy dwelling place. My father, indeed, was still a catechumen, and that a recent one. But she was moved by a holy fear and trembling, and although I was not yet baptized she feared the crooked ways on which walk those who turn their back on you and not their face towards you.[63]

(7) Ah, woe to me! Do I dare to say that you, my God, remained silent when I departed still farther from you? Did you in truth remain silent to me at that time? Whose words but yours were those that you sang in my ears by means of my mother, your faithful servant? Yet none of them sank deep into my heart, so that I would fulfill them. It was her wish, and privately she reminded me and warned me with great solicitude, that I should keep from fornication, and most of all from adultery with any man's wife. Such words seemed to be only a woman's warnings, which I should be ashamed to bother with. But they were your warnings, and I knew it not. I thought that you kept silent and that only she was speaking, whereas through her you did not remain silent to me. In her person you were despised[64] by me, by me, her son, "the son of your handmaid,"[65] and your servant.

But I did not know this, and I ran headlong with such great blindness that I was ashamed to be remiss in vice in the midst of my comrades. For I heard them boast of their disgraceful acts, and glory in them all the more, the more debased they were. There was pleasure in doing this, not only for the pleasure of the act, but also for the praise it brought. What is worthy of censure if not vice? But lest I be put to scorn, I made myself more depraved than I was. Where there was no actual deed, by which I would be on equal footing with the most abandoned, I pretended that I had done what I had not done, lest I be considered more contemptible because I was actually more innocent, and lest I be held a baser thing because more chaste than the others.

(8) See with what companions I ran about the streets of Babylon, and how I wallowed in its mire as though in cinnamon and precious ointments![66] That I might cling even more firmly to its very navel, my invisible enemy crushed me under foot and seduced me, for I was easy to seduce. The mother of my flesh, who had fled from the center of Babylon,[67] but lingered in other parts of the city, just as she had warned me against unchastity, so also had some concern over what her husband had

[61] Cf. I Cor. 3:9. [62] Cf. Rom. 1:25. [63] Cf. Jer. 2:27.
[64] Cf. I Thess. 4:8; II Sam. 12:9.
[65] Ps. 115:16. [66] Cf. Cant. 4:14.
[67] Cf. Jer. 50:8; 51:6. Babylon is here used as a synonym for a city of idolatry and vice.

said about me, to restrain within the bounds of married love, if it could not be cut back to the quick, what she knew to be a present disease and a future danger. Yet she took no final care for this, because of fear that my prospects would be hindered by the impediment of a wife. These were not those hopes of the life to come which my mother herself had, but those hopes for learning, which, as I knew, both parents desired too much: he, because he almost never thought of you, and only of vain things for me; she, because she thought that the usual studies would be not only no obstacle but even of some help to me in attaining to you. Thus recalling things as far as I can, I conjecture that such were my parents' attitudes. Meanwhile, the lines of liberty at play were loosened over me beyond any just severity and the result was dissolution and various punishments. In all these things, my God, there was a mist that darkened for me the serene light of your truth, and my "iniquity came forth as it were from fatness."[68]

Chapter 4
The Stolen Fruit

(9) Surely, Lord, your law punishes theft, as does that law written on the hearts of men, which not even iniquity itself blots out. What thief puts up with another thief with a calm mind? Not even a rich thief will pardon one who steals from him because of want. But I willed to commit theft, and I did so, not because I was driven to it by any need, unless it were by poverty of justice, and dislike of it, and by a glut of evil-doing. For I stole a thing of which I had plenty of my own and of much better quality. Nor did I wish to enjoy that thing which I desired to gain by theft, but rather to enjoy the actual theft and the sin of theft.

In a garden nearby to our vineyard there was a pear tree, loaded with fruit that was desirable neither in appearance nor in taste. Late one night to which hour, according to our pestilential custom, we had kept up our street games, a group of very bad youngsters set out to shake down and rob this tree. We took great loads of fruit from it, not for our own eating, but rather to throw it to the pigs; even if we did eat a little of it, we did this to do what pleased us for the reason that it was forbidden.

Behold my heart, O Lord, behold my heart upon which you had mercy in the depths of the pit. Behold, now let my heart tell you what it looked for there, that I should be evil without purpose and that there should be no cause for my evil but evil itself. Foul was the evil, and I loved it. I loved to go down to death. I loved my fault, not that for which I did the fault, but I loved my fault itself. Base in soul was I, and I leaped down from your firm clasp even towards complete destruction, and I sought nothing from the shameful deed but shame itself!

Chapter 5
Why Men Sin

(10) There is a splendor in beautiful bodies, both in gold and silver and in all things. For the sense of touch, what is suitable to it affords great pleasure, and for each of the other senses there is a just adaptation of bodily things. Worldly honor, too, and the power to command and to rule over others have their own appeal, and from them issues greed for revenge. But even to gain all these objects, we must not depart from you, O Lord, or fall away from your law. This life which we live here has its own allurements, which come from its own particular mode of beauty and its

[68]Ps. 72:7.

agreement with all these lower beauties. The friendship of men, bound together by a loving tie, is sweet because of the unity that it fashions among many souls. With regard to all these things, and others of like nature, sins are committed when, out of an immoderate liking for them, since they are the least goods, we desert the best and highest goods, which are you, O Lord our God, and your truth and your law. These lower goods have their delights, but none such as my God, who has made all things, for in him the just man finds delight, and he is the joy of the upright of heart.[69]

(11) When there is discussion concerning a crime and why it was committed, it is usually held that there appeared possibility that the appetites would obtain some of these goods, which we have termed lower, or there was fear of losing them. These things are beautiful and fitting, but in comparison with the higher goods, which bring happiness, they are mean and base. A man commits murder: why did he do so? He coveted his victim's wife or his property; or he wanted to rob him to get money to live on; or he feared to be deprived of some such thing by the other; or he had been injured, and burned for revenge. Would anyone commit murder without reason and out of delight in murder itself? Who can believe such a thing? Of a certain senseless and utterly cruel man[70] it was said that he was evil and cruel without reason. Nevertheless, a reason has been given, for he himself said, "I don't want to let my hand or will get out of practice through disuse."[71] Why did he want that? Why so? It was to the end that after he had seized the city by the practice of crime, he would attain to honors, power, and wealth, and be free from fear of the law and from trouble due to lack of wealth or from a guilty conscience. Therefore, not even Catiline himself loved his crimes, but something else, for sake of which he committed them.

Chapter 6
The Anatomy of Evil

(12) What was it that I, a wretch, loved in you, my act of theft, my deed of crime done by night, done in the sixteenth year of my age? You were not beautiful, for you were but an act of thievery. In truth, are you anything at all, that I may speak to you? The fruit we stole was beautiful, for it was your creation, O most beautiful of all beings, creator of all things, God the good, God the supreme good and my true good. Beautiful was the fruit, but it was not what my unhappy soul desired. I had an abundance of better pears, but those pears I gathered solely that I might steal. The fruit I gathered I threw away, devouring in it only iniquity, and that I rejoiced to enjoy. For if I put any of that fruit into my mouth, my sin was its seasoning. But now, O Lord my God, I seek out what was in that theft to give me delight, and lo, there is no loveliness in it. I do not say such loveliness as there is in justice and prudence, or in man's mind, and memory, and senses, and vigorous life, nor that with which the stars are beautiful and glorious in their courses, or the land and the sea filled with their living kinds, which by new births replace those that die, nor even that flawed and shadowy beauty found in the vices that deceive us.

(13) For pride imitates loftiness of mind, while you are the one God, highest above all things. What does ambition seek, except honor and glory, while you alone are to be honored above all else and are glorious forever? The cruelty of the mighty desires to be feared: but who is to be feared except the one God, and from

[69] Cf. Ps. 63:11.

[70] Augustine refers to Lucius Sergius Catiline (c. 108–62 B.C.E.) against whom Cicero delivered four powerful orations.

[71] Cf. Sallust, *De Catilina*, xvi.

his power what can be seized and stolen away, and when, or where, or how, or by whom? The caresses of the wanton call for love; but there is naught more caressing than your charity, nor is anything to be loved more wholesomely than your truth, which is beautiful and bright above all things. Curiosity pretends to be a desire for knowledge, while you know all things in the highest degree. Ignorance itself and folly are cloaked over with the names of simplicity and innocence, because nothing more simple than you can be found. What is more innocent than you, whereas to evil men their own works are hostile? Sloth seeks rest as it were, but what sure rest is there apart from the Lord? Luxury of life desires to be called plenty and abundance; you are the fullness and the unfailing plenty of incorruptible pleasure. Prodigality casts but the shadow of liberality, while you are the most affluent giver of all good things. Avarice desires to possess many things, and you possess all things. Envy contends for excellence: what is more excellent than you? Anger seeks vengeance: who takes vengeance with more justice than you?[72] Fear shrinks back at sudden and unusual things threatening what it loves, and is on watch for its own safety. But for you what is unusual or what is sudden? Or who can separate you from what you love? Where, except with you, is there firm security? Sadness wastes away over things now lost in which desire once took delight. It did not want this to happen, whereas from you nothing can be taken away.

(14) Thus the soul commits fornication when it is turned away from you and, apart from you, seeks such pure, clean things as it does not find except when it returns to you. In a perverse way, all men imitate you who put themselves far from you, and rise up in rebellion against you. Even by such imitation of you they prove that you are the creator of all nature, and that therefore there is no place where they can depart entirely from you.

What, therefore, did I love in that theft of mine, in what manner did I perversely or viciously imitate my Lord? Did it please me to go against your law, at least by trickery, for I could not do so with might? Did it please me that as a captive I should imitate a deformed liberty, by doing with impunity things illicit bearing a shadowy likeness of your omnipotence? Behold, your servant flees from his Lord and follows after a shadow![73] O rottenness! O monstrous life and deepest death! Could a thing give pleasure which could not be done lawfully, and which was done for no other reason but because it was unlawful?

Chapter 7
Grace That Keeps and Heals

(15) "What shall I render to the Lord,"[74] for he recalls these things to my memory, but my soul is not made fearful by them? Lord, I will love you, and give thanks to you, and confess to your name,[75] since you have forgiven me so many evils and so many impious works. To your grace and to your mercy I ascribe it that you have dissolved my sins as if they were ice. To your grace I ascribe also whatsoever evils I have not done. For what evil is there that I, who even loved the crime for its own sake, might not have done? I confess that you have forgiven me all my sins, both those which I have done by my own choice and those which, under your guidance, I have not committed.

Who is the man who will reflect on his weakness, and yet dare to credit his chastity and innocence to his own powers, so that he loves you the less, as if he had little need for that mercy by which you forgive sins to those who turn to you.

---

[72]Cf. Rom. 12:19.
[73]Cf. Job 7:2, as known to Augustine.
[74]Ps. 115:12. [75]Cf. Ps. 53:8.

There may be someone who has been called by you, and has heeded your voice, and has shunned those deeds which he now hears me recalling and confessing of myself. Let him not laugh to scorn a sick man who has been healed by that same physician who gave him such aid that he did not fall ill, or rather that he had only a lesser ill. Let him therefore love you just as much, nay even more. For he sees that I have been rescued from such depths of sinful disease by him who, as he also sees, has preserved him from the same maladies.

. . .

Book III
Later Youth

Chapter 1
A Student at Carthage

(1) I came to Carthage, where a caldron of shameful loves seethed and sounded about me on every side.[76] I was not yet in love, but I was in love with love, and by a more hidden want I hated myself for wanting little. I sought for something to love, for I was in love with love; I hated security, and a path free from snares.[77] For there was a hunger within me from a lack of that inner food, which is yourself, my God. Yet by that hunger I did not hunger, but was without desire for incorruptible food, not because I was already filled with it, but because the more empty I was, the more distaste I had for it. Therefore, my soul did not grow healthy, but it was ulcered over, and it cast outside itself and in its misery was avid to be scratched by the things of sense,[78] things that would not be loved if they lacked all soul. To love and to be loved was sweet to me, and all the more if I enjoyed my loved one's body.

Therefore, I defiled the very source of friendship by the filth of concupiscence, and its clear waters I befouled with the lust of hell. Yet foul and vicious as I was, with overflowing vanity, I took pride in being refined and cultured. I plunged headlong into love, whose captive I desired to be. But my God, my mercy, with how much gall did you sprinkle all that sweetness of mine, and how good you were to do it![79] For I was loved, and I had gained love's bond of joy. But in my joy I was bound about with painful chains of iron, so that I might be scourged by burning rods of jealousy, and suspicion, and fear, and anger, and quarreling.

Chapter 2
A Lover of Shows

(2) The theater enraptured me, for its shows were filled with pictures of my own miseries and with tinder for my fires. Why is it that a man likes to grieve over doleful and tragic events which he would not want to happen to himself? The spectator likes to experience grief at such scenes, and this very sorrow is a pleasure to him. What is this but a pitiable folly? For the more a man is moved by these things, the less free is he from such passions. However, when he himself experiences it, it is usually called misery; when he experiences it with regard to others, it is called mercy.[80] But what sort of mercy is to be shown to these unreal things upon the stage? The auditor is not aroused to go to the aid of the others; he is only asked

---

[76]In the Latin, *sartago,* here translated as caldron, repeats the sound of *Carthago,* as we would say, "London, a dungeon." Carthage was notorious for vice.

[77]Cf. Wisd. 14:11. [78]Cf. Job 2:7, 8.

[79]Cf. Plato, *Gorgias,* 509, for this thought.

[80]Mercy, or compassion.

to grieve over them. Moreover, he will show greater approval of the author of such representations, the greater the grief he feels. But if men's misfortunes, whether fictitious or of ancient times, are put on in such manner that the spectator does not feel sorrow, then he leaves in disgust and with disapproval. If grief is aroused in him, he remains in the theater, full of attention and enjoying himself.

(3) Tears and sorrow, therefore, are objects of love. Certainly, every man likes to enjoy himself. But while no man wants to be wretched, does he nevertheless want to be merciful? Now since mercy cannot exist apart from grief, is it for this sole reason that grief is loved? This also has friendship as its source and channel. But where does it go? Where does it flow? Why does it run down into a torrent of boiling pitch,[81] into those immense surges of loathsome lusts? For into these it is changed, and by its own choice it is turned from the purity of heaven into something distorted and base. Shall mercy, therefore, be cast aside? By no means. At certain times, therefore, sorrows may be loved. But shun uncleanness, O my soul! With God as my keeper, the God of our fathers, worthy to be praised and exalted above all forever,[82] shun uncleanness!

Today still I feel compassion, but in those days at the theater I felt joy together with the lovers when by shameful means they had joy in one another, although those things were only pretended in the show, and when they lost each other, I became sad like one who feels compassion. Both situations gave me delight. But now I have more pity for one who rejoices in a shameful deed than for one who has suffered, so to speak, damage to a pernicious pleasure or loss of some vile joy. This is surely the truer mercy, and sorrow finds no delight in it. Although any man who sorrows over a sinner is commended for his act of charity, yet one who shows fraternal mercy prefers rather that there be no occasion for his sorrow. If there is a good will that is at the same time bad-willed, which cannot be, then only a truly and sincerely merciful man can wish that there might be some unfortunates, so that he could show mercy to them. Hence, a certain kind of sorrow can be commended, but none can be loved. Such mercy is yours, O Lord God, for you love our souls with a purity of love more deep and wide than that we have for ourselves, and you are unalterably merciful, because you suffer no wound from sorrow. "And for these things who is sufficient."[83]

(4) But in my wretchedness at that time I loved to feel sorrow, and I sought out opportunities for sorrow. In the false misery of another man as it was mimicked on the stage, that actor's playing pleased me most and had the strongest attraction for me which struck tears from my eyes. What wonder was it that I, an unhappy sheep straying from your flock and impatient of your protection, should be infected with loathsome sores? Hence came my love for such sorrows, by which I was not pierced deep down—for I did not like to suffer such things, but only to look at them—and by which, when they were heard and performed, I was scratched lightly, as it were. As a result, as though from scratches made by fingernails, there followed a burning tumor and horrid pus and wasting away. Such was my life, but was it truly life, my God?

Chapter 3
The Wreckers

(5) Your faithful mercy hovered above me but from afar. Upon what great evils did I waste myself, and what a sacrilegious desire for knowledge did I pursue, so that it might bring me, a deserter from you, down into the depths of apostasy and into

[81]Cf. Isa. 34:9. [82]Cf. Dan. 3:52. [83]II. Cor. 2:16.

the deceitful service of demons! To them I made a sacrifice of my evil deeds, by all of which you scourged me. Even during the celebration of your mysteries, within the walls of your church, I dared to desire and to arrange an affair for procuring the fruit of death. Hence you scourged me with heavy punishments, but nothing in proportion to my faults, O you my most mighty mercy, my God, my refuge from those terrible dangers amid which I wandered, too proud of neck, so that I might depart far from you, loving my own ways and not yours, loving a fugitive's freedom!

(6) Moreover, my studies, which were called honorable, were directed to the practice of law, so that I might excel at it and become so much the more distinguished because so much the more crafty. So great is the blindness of men, who even glory in their blindness! I was already the leading student in the school of rhetoric, and in my pride I rejoiced and I was swollen up with vanity. However, I was much more reserved than others, as you know, O Lord. I kept entirely apart from the acts of wreckage which were perpetrated by the wreckers—this cruel and diabolical name is a sort of emblem of their sophistication—among whom I lived with a sort of shameless shame, since I was not one of them. I associated with them and sometimes took pleasure in their friendship. But I always abhorred their deeds, that is, their acts of wreckage, by which they wantonly mocked at the natural shyness of the new students. By their coarse tricks they overturned this modesty, and thus they provided for their own perverted fun. Nothing is more like the acts of demons than their conduct. How could they be better named than as wreckers? For they themselves had been altogether overturned and perverted in the first instance by devils who laugh at them and through trickery secretly seduce them in the very way in which they love to deride and trick others.

Chapter 4
Cicero's Influence

(7) Among such associates of my callow youth I studied the treatises on eloquence, in which I desired to shine, for a damnable and inflated purpose, directed towards empty human joys. In the ordinary course of study I came upon a book by a certain Cicero,[84] whose tongue almost all men admire but not his heart. This work contains his exhortation to philosophy and is called *Hortensius*. This book changed my affections. It turned my prayers to you, Lord, and caused me to have different purposes and desires. All my vain hopes forthwith became worthless to me, and with incredible ardor of heart I desired undying wisdom. I began to rise up,[85] so that I might return to you. I did not use that book to sharpen my tongue: that I seemed to purchase with the money my mother gave to me, since I was in my nineteenth year and my father had died two years before. I did not use it, then, to sharpen my tongue, nor did it impress me by its way of speaking but rather by what it spoke.

(8) How I burned, O my God, how I burned with desire to fly away from earthly things and upwards to you, and yet I did not know what you would do with me! For with you there is wisdom.[86] Love of wisdom has the name philosophy in Greek, and that book set me on fire for it. There are some who may lead others astray by means of philosophy, coloring and falsifying their errors with that great, and beauteous, and honest name. Almost all such men, both of Cicero's time and of earlier periods, are marked out and refuted in that book. There also he makes

[84]Cicero was, of course, a familiar author to Augustine. Apparently, he says, "a certain Cicero" to indicate detachment from a pagan author.

[85]Cf. Luke 15:18–20 for the parable of the prodigal son.

[86]Cf. Job 12:13.

clear the salutary warning of your Spirit, given to us through your good and devout servant: "Beware lest any man deceive you through philosophy and vain deceit, according to the tradition of man, according to the elements of the world, and not according to Christ: For in him dwells all the fulness of the Godhead corporeally."[87] At that time, as you, the light of my heart, do know, these apostolic words were not yet known to me. But I was delighted with the exhortation only because by its argument I was stirred up and enkindled and set aflame to love, and pursue, and attain and catch hold of, and strongly embrace not this or that sect, but wisdom itself, whatsoever it might be. In so great a blaze only this checked me, that Christ's name was not in it. For this name, O Lord, according to your mercy,[88] this name of my Savior, your Son, my tender heart had holily drunken in with my mother's milk and kept deep down within itself. Whatever lacked this name, no matter how learned and polished and veracious it was, could not wholly capture me.

Chapter 5
Introduction to Sacred Scripture

(9) I accordingly decided to turn my mind to the Holy Scriptures and to see what they were like. And behold, I see something within them that was neither revealed to the proud nor made plain to children, that was lowly on one's entrance but lofty on further advance, and that was veiled over in mysteries. None such as I was at that time could enter into it, nor could I bend my neck for its passageways. When I first turned to that Scripture, I did not feel towards it as I am speaking now, but it seemed to me unworthy of comparison with the nobility of Cicero's writings. My swelling pride turned away from its humble style, and my sharp gaze did not penetrate into its inner meaning. But in truth it was of its nature that its meaning would increase together with your little ones, whereas I disdained to be a little child and, puffed up with pride, I considered myself to be a great fellow.

Chapter 6
The Manichees

(10) And so I fell in with certain men,[89] doting in their pride, too carnal-minded and glib of speech, in whose mouth were the snares of the devil[90] and a very birdlime confected by mixing together the syllables of your name, and the name of our Lord Jesus Christ, and the name of the Paraclete, our comforter, the Holy Spirit.[91] These names were never absent from their mouths, but were only the tongue's sound and clatter, while their hearts were empty of truth. Yet they were always saying, "Truth! Truth!" Many times they said it to me, but it was never inside them. They spoke falsehoods, not only of you, who are truly truth, but even of the elements of this world, your creation. With regard to such matters, for love of you, O my Father, supremely good, beauty of all things beautiful,[92] I should have given over even those philosophers who speak the truth. O Truth, Truth, how intimately did even the very marrow of my mind sigh for you, while these men boomed forth your name at me so many times and in so many ways, by the voice alone and by books many and huge! Such were the platters on which the sun and the moon, your beauteous works, but still only your works and not you yourself, and not even chief among your works, were brought to me while I hungered for you. For your

---

[87]Col. 2:8, 9. [88]Cf. Ps. 24:7.
[89]The Manichaeans, or Manichees.
[90]Cf. I Tim. 3:7; 6:9; II Tim. 2:26.
[91]Cf. John 14:16 and 26.
[92]Cf. Plotinus, *The Enneads,* 6, 9, 4.

spiritual works are above those corporeal things, bright and heavenly though these latter be.

But I hungered and thirsted not for those higher works, but for yourself, O Truth, "with whom there is no change or shadow of alteration."[93] But still they put before me on those platters splendid fantasies. Far better were it to love the sun itself, for the sun is at least true to our eyes, than those false images which deceive the mind by means of our eyes. Yet because I thought that they were you, I fed upon them, not avidly indeed, because you did not taste in my mouth as you are in truth—for you were not those empty figments—nor did I receive nourishment from them, but rather was I myself exhausted by them. Food in dreams is very like the food of waking men, but sleepers are not fed by it: they merely sleep. But those fantasies were in nowise similar to you, as you have now told me, because they were corporeal fantasies, false bodies, and real bodies, whether in the heavens or on earth, which we see by bodily sight, are more certain than they. These things we behold in common with beasts of the field and birds of the air, and they are more certain than those which we conjure up in imagination. Again, there is more certainty when we fashion mental images of these real things than when by means of them we picture other vaster and unlimited bodies that do not exist at all. On such empty phantoms was I fed—and yet I was not fed.

. . .

Chapter 9
God's Judgments and Ours

(17) Along with base deeds and crimes and so many other iniquities there are the sins of those who are making progress. These sins are reprehended by good judges in the light of the rule of perfection, but they are praised out of a hope of fruit, as is the blade for the grain. There are certain things that seem like vice or crime, but are not sins, because they neither offend you, our Lord God, nor human society. Instances are when a man gathers for a time certain things suitable to his needs, and it is uncertain whether he does this out of greediness; or when certain acts are punished by proper authority with a view to correcting them, and it is uncertain whether this was done out of a desire to inflict harm. Hence many things which would seem fit to be disapproved by men have been approved by your testimony, and many things praised by men have been condemned by you as judge. For often the outward appearance of the deed is one thing, while the mind of the doer and unknown circumstances at the time are another. But when you suddenly command some unusual and unforeseen deed, even one you had once forbidden, and although you for a time keep secret the reason for your command, who can doubt that it must be done, although it may be against the law of some human society, since only that human society which serves you is just? Happy are they who know that it was you who gave the command. For by your servants all things are done either to show what is needful at present or to foretell the future.

Chapter 10
The Superstition of the Manichees

(18) I was ignorant of such things, and I mocked at those holy men, your servants and prophets. But what did I accomplish when I derided them, except that I should become a thing of scorn to you? For slowly, little by little, I was led on to such follies as to believe that a fig weeps when it is plucked and that the mother tree

[93]Jas. 1:17.

sheds milky tears. And if some "saint"[94] ate this fig—providing, forsooth, that it was picked not by his but by another's sinful hand—then he would digest it in his stomach, and from it he would breathe forth angels! While he groaned and retched in prayer, he would even breathe forth bits of God! And those bits of the most high and true God would have remained bound up in that piece of fruit, unless they had been let loose by the teeth and belly of an elected saint! In my wretched state I believed that more mercy should be shown to the fruits of the earth than to men, for whose sake they were brought forth. If a non-Manichee who was sorely hungry begged a mouthful I would think it was like condemning it to capital punishment to give it to him.

Chapter 11
Monica's Dream

(19) "You put forth your hand from on high,"[95] and you drew my soul out[96] of that pit of darkness, when before you my mother, your faithful servant, wept more for me than mothers weep over their children's dead bodies. By that spirit of faith which she had from you, she saw my death, and you graciously heard her, O Lord. Graciously you heard her, and you did not despise her tears when they flowed down from her eyes and watered the earth beneath, in whatsoever place she prayed. Graciously you heard her. For whence was that dream by which you consoled her, so that she consented to live with me and to share the same table with me in my home? For this she had begun to be unwilling to do, turning her back on my errors and detesting them. She saw herself standing upon a certain wooden rule,[97] and coming towards her a young man, splendid, joyful, and smiling upon her, although she grieved and was crushed with grief. When he asked her the reasons for her sorrow and her daily tears—he asked, as is the custom, not for the sake of learning but of teaching[98]—she replied that she lamented for my perdition. Then he bade her rest secure, and instructed her that she should attend and see that where she was, there was I also. And when she looked there she saw me standing on the same rule. Whence was this, but that your ears were inclined towards her heart,[99] O you, the good omnipotent, who so care for each one of us as if you care for him alone, and who care for all as for each single person?

(20) Whence too was this, that when she had narrated the vision to me and I attempted to distort it to mean rather that she should not despair of becoming what I already was, she immediately replied without any hesitation: "No!" she said. "It was not said to me, 'Where he is, there also are you,' but 'Where you are, there also is he.' " I confess to you, Lord, that my memory of this, as best I can recall it, and I often spoke of it, is that I was more disturbed by your answer to me through my mother—for she was not disturbed by the likely-seeming falsity of my interpretation and quickly saw what was to be seen, which I certainly did not see before she spoke—than by the dream itself. By this dream the joy of that holy woman, to be fulfilled so long afterwards, was predicted much beforehand so as to bring

[94] Among the Manichaeans, the saints or elect were supposed to follow a higher rule of life than the auditors or hearers, such as Augustine. Among their duties, the auditors were to serve the saints. The particles of light within the saints' food were held to be released by digestion, as Augustine scathingly describes in this passage.

[95] Ps. 143:7. [96] Cf. Ps. 85:13.

[97] A wooden measuring rod, which was figuratively the rule of faith.

[98] For Augustine's theory of questions as a form of teaching, cf. his dialogue *On the Teacher.* Also John 21:5; Acts 1:11.

[99] Cf. Ps. 10:17.

consolation in her then present solicitude. For almost nine years passed, in which I wallowed "in the mire of the deep"[100] and in the darkness of error, and although I often strove to rise out of it, I was all the more grievously thrust down again. But all the while, that chaste, devout, and sober widow, one such as those you love, already livelier in hope, but no less assiduous in weeping and mourning, ceased not in all her hours of prayer to lament over me before you. Her prayers entered into your sight,[101] but you still abandoned me to turn yet again in that darkness.

Chapter 12
A Bishop's Prophecy

(21) Meanwhile, you gave my mother another answer that I recall, although I pass over many things because I hasten to those which most urge me to confess to you, and there are many things that I do not remember. You gave her another answer, then, through one of your priests, a certain bishop brought up in the Church and well trained in your books. When that woman besought him that he would deign to talk with me, refute my errors, correct my evil beliefs, and teach me good ones—for he was accustomed to do this for those whom he found to be properly disposed—he refused, very prudently indeed, as I later understood. He told her that I was as yet lacking in docility, that I was puffed up by the novelty of that heresy, and that I had already unsettled many unlearned men with numerous trifling questions, just as she had indicated to him. "But let him be," he said. "Only pray to the Lord in his behalf. He will find out by reading what is the character of that error and how great is its impiety."

At the same time also, he narrated how he himself as a little child had been handed over to the Manichees by his deluded mother, and how he had not only read through almost all their books but had even copied them out, and how it had appeared to him, although he had no one to argue with him and convince him, that he must flee from this sect, and so he had fled from it. When he had spoken these words, and she still would not keep quiet, but by her entreaties and flowing tears urged him all the more to see me and discuss matters with me, he became a little vexed and said: "Go away from me now. As you live, it is impossible that the son of such tears should perish." As she was often wont to recall in her conversations with me, she took this as if it had sounded forth from heaven.

Book IV
Augustine the Manichean

Chapter 1
The Teacher as Seducer

(1) For the same period of nine years, from the nineteenth year of my age to the twenty-eighth, we[102] were seduced and we seduced others, deceived and deceiving by various desires, both openly by the so-called liberal arts[103] and secretly[104] in the name of a false religion, proud in the one, superstitious in the other, and everywhere

[100] Ps. 68:3. [101] Cf. Ps. 87:3.

[102] Augustine here says "we" because he is writing of himself and others who were both teachers by profession and Manichees in religion.

[103] Cf. II Tim. 2:13. The *doctrinae liberales,* here translated as liberal arts, taught by Augustine included rhetoric and literature and also philosophy, mathematics, and music.

[104] The Manichean religion had been proscribed both by pagan emperors in earlier times and later by the Church. In Augustine's day the Manichees still flourished.

vain. On the one hand, we pursued an empty fame and popularity even down to the applause of the playhouse, poetical competitions, and contests for garlands of grass, foolish plays on the stage, and unbridled lusts. On the other hand, as we desired to be cleansed from all such defilements by the help of men who wanted to be styled "the elect" and "the saints," we brought them food from which, in the workshop of their own bellies, they would fabricate angels and gods through whom we would be set free.[105] Such things did I pursue and do in company with my friends who were deceived by me and with me.

Let proud men, who have not yet for their good been cast down and broken by you, my God, laugh me to scorn, but in your praise let me confess my shame to you. Permit me, I beseech you, and enable me to follow around in present recollection the windings of my past errors, and to offer them up to you as a sacrifice of jubilation. For without you, what am I to myself but the leader of my own destruction? What am I, when all is well with me, except one sucking your milk and feeding on you, the incorruptible food?[106] What manner of man is any man, since he is but a man? Let the strong and mighty laugh us to scorn, and let us, the weak and needy,[107] confess ourselves to you.

• • •

Chapter 4
The Death of a Friend

(7) During those years, when I first began to teach—it was in the town in which I was born—I gained a friend, my equal in age, flowering like me with youth, and very dear to me because of community of interests. As a boy, he had grown up with me, we had gone to school together, and had played games together. But in childhood he was not such a friend as he became later on, and even later on ours was not a true friendship, for friendship cannot be true unless you solder it together among those who cleave to one another by the charity "poured forth in our hearts by the Holy Spirit, who is given to us."[108] Yet it was sweet to us, made fast as it was by our ardor in like pursuits. I had turned him away from the true faith, which he did not hold faithfully and fully as a youth, and towards those superstitious and pernicious fables because of which my mother wept over me. This man was now wandering with me in spirit, and my soul could not endure to be without him. But behold, you were close at the back of those fleeing from you, you who are at once the God of vengeance[109] and the fount of mercy, who in a marvelous manner convert us to yourself. Behold, you took the man from this life when he had scarce completed a year in my friendship, sweet to me above every sweetness of that life of mine.

(8) What one man can number all your praises which he has felt in himself alone?[110] What was it that you did at that time, my God, and how unsearchable are the depths of your judgments?[111] Tormented by fever, he lay for a long time senseless in a deadly sweat, and when his life was despaired of, he was baptized while unconscious. For this I cared nothing and I presumed that his soul would retain rather what it had taken from me and not what had been done to his unconscious body. But it turned out far different: he was revived and regained his strength. Immediately, upon my first chance to speak to him, and I could do this just as soon as he could talk, since I had not left him, as we relied so much upon one another,

---

[105]The elect among the Manichees renounced marriage and abstained from meat and wine.
[106]Cf. John 6:27. [107]Cf. Ps. 73:21. [108]Rom. 5:5. [109]Cf. Ps. 93:1.
[110]Cf. Ps. 105:2.
[111]Cf. Ps. 35:7; Rom. 11:33.

I tried to make jokes with him, just as though he would joke with me about that baptism which he had received when he was far away in mind and sense. He had already learned that he had received it. But he was horrified at me as if I were an enemy, and he warned me with a swift and admirable freedom that if I wished to remain his friend, I must stop saying such things to him. I was struck dumb and was disturbed, but I concealed all my feelings until he would grow well again and would be fit in health and strength. Then I would deal with him as I wished. But he was snatched away from my madness, so that he might be kept with you for my consolation. After a few days, while I was absent, he was attacked again by the fever and died.

(9) My heart was made dark by sorrow, and whatever I looked upon was death.[112] My native place was a torment to me, and my father's house was a strange unhappiness. Whatsoever I had done together with him was, apart from him, turned into a cruel torture. My eyes sought for him on every side, and he was not given to them. I hated all things, because they no longer held him. Nor could they now say to me, "Here he comes," as they did in his absence from them when he lived. To myself I became a great riddle, and I questioned my soul as to why it was sad and why it afflicted me so grievously,[113] and it could answer me nothing. If I said to it, "Hope in God," it did right not to obey me, for the man, that most dear one whom she had lost, was more real and more good to her than the fantasy[114] in which she was bade to hope. Only weeping was sweet to me, and it succeeded to my friend in my soul's delights.

Chapter 5
A Sweet Sorrow

(10) Lord, these things have now passed away and time has eased my wound. Am I able to hearken to you, who are truth, and to turn my heart's ear to your mouth, that you may tell me why weeping is sweet to those in misery? Is it that you, although present in all places, have flung our misery far away from yourself, and do you abide unchanged in yourself, while we are spun about in our trials? Yet unless we could weep into your ears, no trace of hope would remain for us. Whence is it, then, that sweet fruit is plucked from life's bitterness, from mourning and weeping, from sighing and lamenting? Does sweetness lie there because we hope that you will graciously hear us? This rightly holds for our prayers, since they contain our desire of attaining to you. But does it hold for that grief and mourning over what was lost, with which I was overwhelmed? I did not hope that he would come back to life, nor did I beg for that by my tears; I only sorrowed and wept, for I was wretched and I had lost my joy. Or is weeping itself a bitter thing, and does it give us pleasure because of distaste for things in which we once took joy, but only at such times as we shrink back from them?

Chapter 6
His Love for the Lost Friend

(11) Why do I speak of these things? For now is not the time for questioning, but for confessing to you. Wretched was I, and wretched is every soul that is

[112]Cf. Lam. 5:17.

[113]Cf. Ps. 41:6 and 12; Ps. 42:5.

[114]The conception of God held by Augustine as a Manichee was but a fantasy, without power to give him hope or comfort.

bound fast by friendship for mortal things, that is torn asunder when it loses them, and then first feels the misery by which it is wretched even before it loses those things. Such was I at that time, and I wept most bitterly and I found rest in my bitterness. So wretched was I that I held that life of wretchedness to be more dear to me than my friend himself. For although I wished to change it, yet I was more unwilling to lose it than I was to lose my friend. I do not know whether I would have wished its loss, even for his sake, as is told of Orestes and Pylades, if it is not a fiction, who wished to die together for one another, since to them not to live together was worse than death. But in me there had arisen I know not what sort of affection, one far different from theirs, for most heavily there weighed upon me both weariness of life and fear of dying.[115] I believe that the more I loved him, the more did I hate and fear death, which had taken him away from me, as my cruelest enemy. I thought that it would speedily devour all men, since it had been able to devour him. All this I was, and I remember it.

Behold my heart, my God, behold what is within it! See this, for I remember it, O you who are my hope, who cleanse me from the uncleanness of such affections, who direct my eyes to you and pluck my feet out of the snare.[116] I marveled that other men should live, because he, whom I had loved as if he would never die, was dead. I marveled more that I, his second self, could live when he was dead. Well has someone said of his friend that he is half of his soul.[117] For I thought that my soul and his soul were but one soul in two bodies.[118] Therefore, my life was a horror to me, because I would not live as but a half. Perhaps because of this I feared to die, lest he whom I had loved so much should wholly die.

Chapter 7
Departure from Thagaste

(12) O madness, which does not know how to love men, as men should be loved! O foolish man, who so rebelliously endures man's lot! Such was I at that time. Therefore I raged, and sighed, and wept, and became distraught, and there was for me neither rest nor reason. I carried about my pierced and bloodied soul, rebellious at being carried by me, but I could find no place where I might put it down. Not in pleasant groves, not in games and singing, not in sweet-scented spots, not in rich banquets, not in the pleasures of the bedchamber, not even in books and in poetry did it find rest. All things grew loathsome, even the very light itself; and whatsoever was not he was base and wearisome to me—all except groans and tears, for in them alone was found a little rest. But when my soul was withdrawn from these, a mighty burden of misery weighed me down. To you, O Lord, ought it to have been lifted up,[119] to be eased by you. I knew it, but I willed it not, nor was I able to will it, and this the more because for me, when I thought upon you, you were not something solid and firm. For to me then you were not what you are, but an empty phantom, and my error was my god. If I attempted to put my burden there, so that it might rest, it hurtled back upon me through the void, and I myself remained an unhappy place where I could not abide and from which I could depart. For where could my heart fly to, away from my heart? Where could I fly to,

[115]Cf. Seneca, *Moral Epistles,* iv, i, 6.
[116]Cf. Ps. 24:15.
[117]Horace, *Odes* I, 3, 8.
[118]Cf. Ovid, *Tristia,* 4, 4, 72.
[119]Cf. Ps. 241.

apart from my own self?[120] Where would I not pursue myself? But still I fled from my native town. Less often would my eyes seek him where they were not used to seeing him, and from Thagaste I came to Carthage.[121]

Chapter 8
The Healing Powers of Time and Change

(13) Time does not take time off, nor does it turn without purpose through our senses: it works wondrous effects in our minds. See how it came and went from day to day, and by coming and going it planted in me other hopes and other memories, and little by little they filled me up again with my former sources of delight. My sorrow gave way to them, but to it succeeded not new sorrows, but yet causes of new sorrows. Why did that sorrow penetrate so easily into my deepest being, unless because I had poured out my soul upon the sand by loving a man soon to die as though he were one who would never die? Most of all, the solace of other friends restored and revived me, and together with them I loved what I loved in place of you. This was a huge fable and a long-drawn-out lie, and by its adulterous fondling, our soul, itching in its ears,[122] was corrupted.

But that fable did not die for me, even when one of my friends would die. There were other things done in their company which more completely seized my mind: to talk and to laugh with them; to do friendly acts of service for one another; to read well-written books together; sometimes to tell jokes and sometimes to be serious; to disagree at times, but without hard feelings, just as a man does with himself; and to keep our many discussions pleasant by the very rarity of such differences; to teach things to the others and to learn from them; to long impatiently for those who were absent, and to receive with joy those joining us. These and similar expressions, proceeding from the hearts of those who loved and repaid their comrades' love, by way of countenance, tongue, eyes, and a thousand pleasing gestures, were like fuel to set our minds ablaze and to make but one out of many.

Chapter 9
A Higher Love

(14) This is what we love in our friends, and love in such wise that a man's conscience condemns him if he does love one who returns his love, or if he does not return the love of one who loved him first, seeking nothing from that person but signs of good will. Hence the mourning, if anyone should die, the shadows cast by sorrow, the heart drenched in tears, the sweetness turned all bitter, and from the lost life of the dead, death for the living.

But blessed is the man who loves you,[123] and his friend in you, and his enemy for your sake. For he alone loses no dear one to whom all are dear in him who is not lost. But who is this unless our God, the God who made heaven and earth[124] and fills all things because by filling them he made them?[125] No man loses you except one who forsakes you, and if he forsakes you, where does he go or where does he flee, except from you well-pleased back to you all wrathful? Where does he find your law but in his own punishment? "And your law is the truth,"[126] and you are the truth.[127]

. . .

[120] Cf. Horace, *Carmina* 2, 16, 19.

[121] Augustine left Thagaste secretly, without telling anyone except his wealthy friend Romanianus, with whom he had been living after his break with Monica, his mother. The year was 376.

[122] Cf. II Tim. 4:3: "For there shall be a time when they will not endure sound doctrine; but, according to their own desires, they will heap to themselves teachers, having itching ears."

[123] Cf. Tob. 13:18. [124] Cf. Gen. 1:1; 2:1. [125] Cf. Jer. 23:24. [126] Ps. 118:142.

[127] Cf. John 14:6.

Book V
At Rome and Milan

Chapter 8
A Road to Rome

(14) You worked within me, then, so that I might be persuaded to go to Rome, and to teach there rather than at Carthage. How I was persuaded to do this I will not neglect to confess to you, for in all this both the most hidden depths of your providence and your mercy, most near at hand to give us help, must be thought upon and proclaimed. I did not want to go to Rome because greater stipends and greater honors were promised to me by friends who urged me on to this, although such things also influenced my mind at that time. The greatest and almost the sole reason was because I had heard that young men studied there in more a peaceful way and were kept quiet by the restraints of a better order and discipline.[128] They were not allowed to rush insolently and at random into the classroom of a teacher with whom they were not enrolled, nor were they let in at all unless he gave permission. On the other hand, at Carthage there is a foul, unrestrained license among the students. They break in boldly and, looking almost like madmen, they disrupt whatever order a teacher has established for his students' benefit. With strange recklessness they do many injurious things that would be punished by law, unless they had custom as their patron. This very custom displays them to be the more wretched in that they do, with permission as it were, what will never be permitted by your eternal law. They think that they act with impunity, whereas they are punished by the very blindness in which they act, and they suffer incomparably greater evils than they inflict. Thus, manners that I did not want for myself as a student I was forced to endure in others when I became a teacher. Hence I was pleased to go where such things were not done, as all who knew the situation told me. But you, "my hope and my portion in the land of the living,"[129] to the end that I would change my residence on earth for the sake of my soul's salvation, put goads to me at Carthage by which I would be turned away from there, and at Rome you set allurements before me by which I would be drawn thither. All this you did by means of men who loved a dead life, and in the one case did senseless deeds and in the other made empty promises. To correct my steps[130] you secretly made use of both their perversity and my own. For those who disturbed my peace were blinded by a foul frenzy, and those who called me to another course savored of earth.[131] But I myself, who in the one city detested true misery, in the other sought false felicity.

(15) Why I went from the one place and went to the other you knew, O God, but you did not reveal it to me or to my mother, who bitterly bewailed my journey and followed me even down to the seashore. But I deceived her, although she held onto me by force, so that she might either call me back or make the journey with me. I pretended that I had a friend whom I would not leave until a fair wind came and he could sail away. Thus I lied to my mother—to such a mother!—and slipped away from her. This deed also you have forgiven me in your mercy, and you preserved me, all full of execrable filth, from waters of the sea and kept me safe for the waters of your grace.[132] For when I would be washed clean by that water, then also would be dried up those rivers flowing down from my mother's eyes, by which, before you and in my behalf, she daily watered the ground beneath her face.

---

[128]At Rome there were laws governing students.

[129]Ps. 141:6.

[130]Cf. Ps. 39:3; Prov. 20:24.

[131]Cf. Phil. 3:19: "... who mind earthly things."

[132]The reference is to the waters of baptism.

Yet she refused to return without me, and I was hardly able to persuade her to spend the night in a place close by our ship, an oratory built in memory of Blessed Cyprian.[133] During the night I secretly set out; she did not, but remained behind, praying and weeping. What was it, my God, that she sought from you with so many tears, except that you would not let me sail away. But in your deepest counsels you heard the crux of her desire: you had no care for what she then sought, so that you might do for me what she forever sought. The wind blew and filled our sails, and the shore receded from our sight. On that shore in the morning she stood, wild with grief, and with complaints and groans she filled your ears. But you rejected such things, since you carried me away on my own desires so as to put an end to those desires, and thus the carnal affection that was in her was beaten by the just scourge of sorrow. For she loved me to be present with her, after the custom of mothers, but much more than many mothers. She did not know how great a joy you would fashion for her out of my absence. She knew nothing of this, and therefore she wept and lamented. By such torments the remnant of Eve within her was made manifest, and with groans she sought what she had brought forth with groans.[134] Yet after her denunciation of my falsity and cruelty, she turned again to beseech you in prayer for me. She went back home, and I went on to Rome.

Chapter 9
Sickness at Rome

(16) But behold, there I was caught under the scourge of bodily sickness, and I was on the verge of going down to hell, carrying with me all the sins that I had committed against you, against myself, and against others, many and great they were, and beyond that bond of original sin, in which we all die in Adam.[135] You had not yet forgiven me any of them in Christ, nor had he destroyed upon his cross the enmities[136] that I had contracted against you by my sins. How would he destroy them on the cross of a phantom, which was what I then believed him to be?[137] As false, therefore, as his bodily death seemed to me, so true was the death of my soul. As true as was the death of his body, so false was the life of my soul, which did not believe in his bodily death.

My fever grew worse within me: I was now about to depart and to perish. Where would I have gone, if I had then left this world, except into the fire and torment that were worthy of my deeds, according to the truth of your dispensation? Of all this my mother knew nothing, yet far away she continued to pray for me. But you are present in all places, and you graciously heard her where she was, and you had mercy on me where I was, so that I regained my bodily health, although still diseased within my sacrilegious heart. Nor in so great a danger did I desire your baptism: I had been better disposed as a boy, when I had begged for it of my mother's piety, as I have already recorded and confessed. But I had grown in my shame, and, a very madman, I scoffed at the healing remedies of you who did not

[133] St. Cyprian, bishop and martyr. A convert, probably in his mature years, he was baptized c. 246 and about two years later became bishop of Carthage. He was martyred on August 14, 258, during the Decian persecution.

[134] Cf. Gen. 3:16: "To the woman [Eve] also he said: I will multiply thy sorrows, and thy conceptions: in sorrow shalt thou bring forth children."

[135] Cf. I Cor. 15:22: "And as in Adam all die, so also in Christ all shall be made alive."

[136] Cf. Eph. 2:16: ". . . and might reconcile to God in one body by the cross, killing the enmities in himself."

[137] As a Manichean, Augustine believed that what died upon the Cross was a phantom, an evil spirit pretending to be Christ.

let me as such a man die a twofold death.[138] If my mother's heart had been struck by that wound, it would never have been healed. I cannot tell clearly enough what love she had for me, and how with greater anguish she brought me forth in spirit than she had given me birth in the flesh.[139]

(17) Hence, I cannot see how she would ever have been healed, if my death in such a state had pierced through and through the bowels of her love.[140] Where would have been such mighty prayers, sent up so often and without ceasing? Nowhere, except with you! But would you, O God of mercies, have despised the contrite and humbled heart[141] of so chaste and sober a widow, generous in almsgiving, faithful and helpful to your holy ones, letting no day pass without an offering at your altar, going without fail to church twice a day, in the morning and at evening, not for empty stories and old wives' tales, but that she might hear you in your instructions and that you might hear her in her prayers? Could you, by whose gift she was such, despise and reject from your help those tears, by which she sought from you not gold and silver or any changing, fleeting good but the salvation of her son's soul? By no means, O Lord! Yes, you were present to help her, and you graciously heard her, and you did this in the order in which you had predestined it to be done. Far be it that you would deceive her by those visions and by your answers to her, both those I have already recounted and those I have not recounted. She kept them faithfully in her breast, and, always at prayer, she would urge them upon you as if they were your own signed bonds. For since your mercy endures forever,[142] you vouchsafe, to those in whom you forgive all debts,[143] to become even a debtor by your promises.

. . .

Chapter 12
Dishonest Students at Rome

(22) I began to devote myself busily to the purpose for which I had come to Rome, namely, to teach rhetoric. I first gathered together in the house some students with whom and through whom I began to gain a reputation. See now how I learned that certain things are done in Rome which I had not suffered from in Africa. It became manifest to me that the wreckage wrought there by abandoned young men was not done here. "But yet," men told me, "to evade paying their teacher, many young men conspire together and all at once transfer themselves from one teacher to another. They are false to their own word, and out of love for money they hold justice in contempt." My heart hated these men, but not with "a perfect hatred."[144] For perhaps I hated them because of what I was to suffer at their hands, rather than because they did unjust things to other men. In truth such men are vile in character; they fornicate against you[145] out of love for passing, temporary trifles and filthy lucre, which defiles the hand that seizes it, and by embracing a fleeting world, and by despising you who abide forever, who call back to yourself and forgive the human soul, which though once sunk in harlotries has now returned to you.

But now I hate such depraved and perverse men, although I can love them when they have been corrected, so that they may prize above money the doctrine itself

[138] A twofold death: of both body and soul.
[139] Cf. Gal. 4:19.
[140] Cf. Phil. 2:1; Col. 3:12.
[141] Cf. Ps. 50:19.
[142] Cf. Ps. 118:1; Ps. 137:8.
[143] Cf. Matt. 18:32. [144] Ps. 138:22. [145] Cf. Ps. 72:27.

which they learn, and above that last, yourself, O God, the truth, and the fullness of all sure good, and peace most chaste. But at that time, because of self-regard, I was more unwilling to suffer at the hands of evil men than I was willing that they become good men for your sake.

Chapter 13
A New Career at Milan

(23) Afterwards a message was sent from Milan[146] to Rome, addressed to the prefect of the city, asking that a rhetoric master be secured for Milan and stating that his transportation would be at public expense. I applied for the position through the offices of those very men, drunk as they were with Manichean follies, to get free from whom I was leaving, although neither I nor they knew that. The result was that after I had been tested by a public discourse that had been prescribed, Symmachus,[147] who was then prefect, sent me there. I came to Milan, and to Ambrose,[148] its bishop, a man famed throughout the world as one of its very best men, and your devout worshiper. By his eloquent sermons in those days he zealously provided your people with the fat of your wheat,[149] the gladness of your oil,[150] and the sobering intoxication of your wine.[151] All unknowing, I was led to him by you, so that through him I might be led, while fully knowing it, to you.

That man of God[152] received me in fatherly fashion, and as an exemplary bishop he welcomed my pilgrimage. I began to love him, at first not as a teacher of the truth, which I utterly despaired of finding in your Church, but as a man who was kindly disposed towards me. I listened carefully to him as he preached to the people, not with the intention I should have had, but to try out his eloquence, as it were, and to see whether it came up to its reputation, or whether it flowed forth with greater or less power than was asserted of it. I hung eagerly on his words, but I remained uninterested in his subject matter or contemptuous of it. With the sweetness of his discourse I was delighted, which, although more learned, was less lively and entertaining than was that of Faustus. This applies to his style of speaking, for with regard to their subjects there was no comparison. The one man went wandering about among his Manichean fallacies, whereas the other taught salvation in a most salutary way. But "salvation is far from sinners,"[153] and such was I at that time. Yet little by little I was drawing closer to you, although I did not know it.

Chapter 14
The Influence of St. Ambrose's Preaching

(24) Although I was not anxious to learn what he said, but merely to hear how he said it—for such bootless concern remained with me, although I had no hope that any way lay open for a man to come to you—yet at the same time with the words, which I loved, there also entered into my mind the things themselves, to which I was indifferent. Nor was I able to separate them from one another, and

---

[146] At that time Milan was the usual seat of the emperors of the West.

[147] Symmachus (c. 340–402) was famous as the greatest orator of his time, and it was seemingly as such rather than as an official that he was asked to choose a professor of rhetoric for Milan.

[148] St. Ambrose (c. 337–April 4, 397) came from one of the greatest Roman families, the Aurelii. He was great as a preacher, writer, administrator, and fearless defender of the faith. He is one of the four great Latin doctors of the Church. He presents a striking contrast to St. Augustine.

[149] Cf. Ps. 80:17; Ps. 147:14.

[150] Cf. Ps. 44:8; Ps. 4:8.

[151] A quotation from St. Ambrose's hymn *Splendor Paternae Gloriae*. Cf. Eph. 5:18.

[152] Cf. Deut. 33:1.

[153] Ps. 118:155.

when I opened up my heart to receive the eloquence with which he spoke, there likewise entered, although only by degrees, the truths that he spoke. At first it began to appear that what he said could be defended. I now judged that the Catholic faith, for which I had thought nothing could be said against the Manichean objectors, could be maintained without being ashamed of it. This was especially the case after I had heard various passages in the Old Testament explained most frequently by way of allegory, by which same passages I was killed when I had taken them literally.[154] Hence when many passages in those books were explained spiritually, I now blamed my own despair, in which I had believed that the law and the prophets could in no way be upheld against those who hated them and scoffed at them.

(25) Yet for all that I did not think that the Catholic way must be held to by myself, even though it could have its learned defenders who would fully and not absurdly refute objections made to it. Nor did I think that what I had previously held was to be condemned, for both parties seemed to be equal in their defenses. Thus while the Catholic position did not seem to be overthrown, neither did it appear to be the victor. I then earnestly applied my mind to see if it were possible, by means of sure arguments, to convict the Manicheans of falsity. For if I were only able to conceive a spiritual substance, then forthwith all those stratagems would be foiled and cast out of my mind. But this I was unable to do.

But with regard to the structure of this world, and every nature that our bodily senses can perceive, as I more and more reflected on and compared things, I came to the conclusion that the philosophers had held much more probable opinions. After the manner of the Academics (as they supposedly are) I doubted everything and wavered in the midst of all things. Yet I resolved that the Manicheans must be abandoned. Even in my skeptical period I did not see how I could persist in a sect above which I now placed many philosophers. But because these philosophers were without the saving name of Christ, I refused utterly to commit the cure of my soul's sickness to them. Therefore, I determined to continue as a catechumen[155] in the Catholic Church, commended to me by my parents, until something certain would enlighten me, by which I might direct my course.

Book VI
Years of Struggle

Chapter 1
The Widow's Son

(1) "My hope from my youth,"[156] where were you, and where had you gone?[157] Was it not you who created me, and made me different from the beasts of the field, and made me wiser than the birds of the air?[158] But I walked in darkness, and upon a slippery way,[159] and I sought for you outside myself, but I did not find you, the God of my heart.[160] I went down into the depth of the sea,[161] and I lost confidence, and I despaired of finding the truth.

---

[154] Cf. II Cor. 3:6: "For the letter kills, but the spirit quickeneth." Augustine was killed, that is, brought into serious error and mortal sin, when he took in a literal sense passages that should have been interpreted in a figurative or spiritual sense.

[155] Augustine considers himself to be a catechumen in view of his initial enrollment by his mother.

[156] Ps. 70:5. [157] Cf. Ps. 10:1.

[158] Cf. Job 35:10, 11.

[159] Cf. Ps. 34:6; Isa. 50:10.

[160] Cf. Ps. 72:26. [161] Cf. Ps. 67:23.

But now my mother, strong in her love, had come to me, for she had followed me over land and sea, kept safe by you through all her perils. In the midst of storms at sea, she reassured the sailors themselves, by whom inexperienced travelers upon the deep are accustomed to be comforted, and promised them that they would reach port in safety, for you had promised this to her in a vision.[162] She found me in great danger because of my despair at ever finding the truth. Yet when I told her that I was no longer a Manichean, although not a Catholic Christian, she did not leap with joy, as if she had heard something unexpected. The reason was that she had already been assured with regard to that aspect of my wretched state, in which she bewailed me as one dead, but yet destined to be brought back to life by you. In thought she put me before you on a bier, so that you might say to a widow's son, "Young man, I say to you, arise!"[163] Then would he revive, and begin to speak, and you would deliver him to his mother. Therefore, her heart did not pound in turbulent exultation when she heard that what she daily implored you with her tears to do was already done in so great a part. For although I had not yet attained to the truth, I had now been rescued from falsehood. Rather, she was all the more certain that you, who had promised the whole, would grant what still remained. Hence most calmly and with a heart filled with confidence, she replied to me how she believed in Christ that before she departed from this life she would see me a faithful Catholic. This much she said to me. But to you, O fountain of mercies, she multiplied her prayers and tears, so that you would speed your help[164] and enlighten my darkness.[165] More zealously still she would hasten to the church, and she would hang on the words of Ambrose, as on "a fountain of water springing up into life everlasting."[166] For she loved that man as though he were an angel of God,[167] because she had learned that through him I had been brought in the meantime to the wavering, doubtful state in which I then was. She felt sure that through this state I was to pass from sickness to health, with a more acute danger intervening, through that paroxysm, as it were, which doctors call the crisis.

Chapter 2
Outworn Customs

(2) One time when she had brought to the saints' memorial shrines pottage and bread and wine, as was her custom in Africa, she was forbidden to do this by the doorkeeper. As soon as she learned that this prohibition came from the bishop, she accepted it in so devout and obedient a manner that I myself wondered at how easily she became an accuser of her custom rather than an objector to his command.[168] Addiction to wine did not capture her will, nor did a love of wine arouse her to a hatred of truth, as it does so many men and women who object to sober praise, just as the intoxicated object to a watery drink. But when she brought her basket of festival foods, which were to be merely tasted and then shared with others, she never set out more than a single small cup, diluted to suit her own sober taste, from which she would take a little for sake of courtesy. If there were many memorials of the dead that seemed fit to be honored in this manner, she carried around the same cup, which she would set out in all shrines. This cupful, which had become very

[162]Cf. Acts 27:21–26. [163]Luke 7:14.
[164]Cf. Ps. 69:2. [165]Cf. Ps. 17:29.
[166]John 4:14. [167]Cf. Gal. 4:14.
[168]Following St. Ambrose's example, Augustine later helped to stop the custom in Africa. The objections were twofold, as he indicates: there were associations with pagan customs and they were the occasion of drinking and revelry.

watery and tepid, she would share in small portions with those present. In those places she sought devotion and not pleasure.

As soon as she found that by order of that famous preacher and patron of devotion such things were not to be done, not even by those who would do them in a sober fashion, so that no opportunity would be offered for sots to get drunk, and because such tributes to the dead were too much like Gentile superstitions, she most willingly gave them up. Instead of a basket filled with the fruits of the earth, she learned to bring to the martyrs' memorials a breast filled with purer oblations. Thus she would give what she could to the poor, and thus would the communication of the Lord's body be celebrated in those places where, in imitation of his passion, the martyrs were immolated and received their crowns.

Yet it seems to me, O Lord my God, and so stands my heart on this matter in your sight, that perhaps it would not have been easy for my mother to forego that custom, if it had been forbidden by someone whom she did not love as she loved Ambrose. She loved him greatly because of my salvation, while he loved her because of her most devout life, in which, so fervent in spirit[169] among her good works, she frequented the church. Hence when he saw me, he would often break forth in her praise, and congratulate me for having such a mother. But he did not know what sort of son she had, for I doubted all things, and I thought that the way to life[170] could not be found.

Chapter 3
The Example and Words of St. Ambrose

(3) I had not yet groaned in prayer for you to come to my help, but my mind was intent on questioning and restless for argument. Ambrose himself I believed to be a happy man, as the world judges such things, because so many powerful persons showed him honor. His celibacy alone appeared to me to be a hard thing. But what hopes he held, what struggles against temptations arising from his exalted station, what comforts amid adversities, how sweet the joys of that secret mouth within his heart as it fed upon and savored again the bread you gave him—such things I could not guess at, nor had I any experience of them.

He did not know the passions that seethed within me, nor my pit of danger. Yet I was unable to ask of him what I wanted and in the way I wanted, for crowds of busy men, to whose troubles he was a slave, shut me away from both his ear and his mouth. When he was not with them, and this was but a little while, he either refreshed his body with needed food or his mind with reading. When he read, his eyes moved down the pages and his heart sought out their meaning, while his voice and tongue remained silent. Often when we were present—for no one was forbidden entry, and it was not his custom to have whoever came announced to him—we saw him reading to himself, and never otherwise. After sitting for a long time in silence—who would dare to annoy a man so occupied?—we would go away. We thought that in that short time which he obtained for refreshing his mind, free from the din of other men's problems, he did not want to be summoned to some other matter. We thought too that perhaps he was afraid, if the author he was reading had expressed things in an obscure manner, then it would be necessary to explain it for some perplexed but eager listener, or to discuss some more difficult questions, and if his time were used up in such tasks, he would be able to read fewer books than he wished to. However, need to save his voice, which easily grew

[169]Cf. Acts 18:25; Rom. 12:11.
[170]Cf. Prov. 6:23; 10:17; 15:10.

hoarse, was perhaps the more correct reason why he read to himself. But with whatever intention he did it, that man did it for a good purpose.[171]

(4) Certainly, no opportunity was given me to ask what I desired to ask of so holy an oracle of yours, his breast, unless the matter could be heard quickly. But my surging passions needed full leisure in him to whom they might be poured out, but this they never found. I heard him, indeed, every Sunday as he was "rightly handling the word of truth"[172] before the people. More and more was I convinced that all the knots of the wily calumnies that those men who had deceived us wove against the sacred books could be loosened. When I found that "man was made by you to your image,"[173] was understood by your spiritual sons, whom you had regenerated by grace in our Catholic Mother, not as though they believed and thought of you as limited by the shape of the human body—although what a spiritual substance would be like I did not surmise even in a weak and obscure manner[174]—I blushed joyfully because I had barked for so many years, not against the Catholic faith but against the fantasies of a carnal imagination. Rash and irreverent had I been in that I talked about and condemned things I should have inquired into and learned about. But you, most high and most near at hand, most secret and most present, in whom there are no members, some greater and others smaller, who are everywhere whole and entire, who are never confined in place, and who surely are not in our corporeal shape, you have yet made man to your own image.[175] And behold, from head to foot he is contained in space!

Chapter 4
Errors Refuted; Truth Not Yet Found

(5) Therefore, since I did not understand how this, your image, should subsist, I should have knocked[176] and proposed the question, "How is this to be believed?" instead of insultingly opposing it, as if it were believed as I thought. So much the more sharply did concern over what I could hold with certainty gnaw at my very vitals, so much the more shame did I feel at being so long deluded and deceived by a promise of certainties and for gabbling in childish error and ardor over so many uncertainties as if they were certain.[177] That they were false afterwards became clear to me. Certain it was that they were uncertain, and that at one time they had been taken for certain by me, when with blind belligerence I would attack your Catholic Church, although I had not yet discovered that it teaches true doctrines, and that it does not teach those with which I had seriously charged it. Thus I was in the course of being refuted and converted. I rejoiced, my God, that the one only Church, the body of your Only-begotten Son,[178] in which the name of Christ had been put upon me as an infant, had no place for such infantile nonsense. Nor in its sound doctrine would it maintain one that would confine you, the creator of all things, in a space, however high and wide, yet bounded on every side by the shape of human members.

(6) I rejoiced also that the ancient scriptures of the law and the prophets were now set before me for reading, not with that eye which once looked on them as absurdities, when I argued as if your saints understood them in that way, whereas in truth they did not thus understand them. I was glad when I often heard Ambrose

[171] The present passage is reported to be one of the few descriptions of silent reading in ancient literature. The detail with which Augustine describes St. Ambrose's custom indicates how unusual silent reading must have been.

[172] II Tim. 2:15. [173] Cf. Gen. 9:6. [174] Cf. I Cor. 13:12. [175] Cf. Gen. 1:26.

[176] Cf. Matt. 7:7: "Knock, and it shall be opened to you."

[177] Augustine's Manichean errors.

[178] Cf. Col. 1:18–24.

speaking in his sermons to the people as though he most earnestly commended it as a rule that "the letter kills, but the spirit quickens."[179] For he would draw aside the veil of mystery and spiritually lay open things that interpreted literally seemed to teach unsound doctrine. He would say nothing that caused me difficulty, although he would state things which I did not as yet know to be true. I held back my heart from all assent, fearing to fall headlong, and died all the more from that suspense. I wished to be made just as certain of things that I could not see, as I was certain that seven and three make ten. I was not so mad as to think that even this last could not be known, but I wanted other things to be known with the same certainty, whether bodily things that were not present to my senses, of spiritual things, which I did not know how to conceive except in a corporeal way. By believing I could have been healed, so that my mind's clearer sight would be directed in some way to your truth, which endures forever[180] and is lacking in nothing. But as often happens, just as a man who has had trouble with a poor physician fears to entrust himself even to a good one, so it was with my soul's health. In truth, it could never be healed except by believing, but lest it believe what was false, it refused to be cured and it resisted the hands of you who have compounded the remedies of faith, and have applied them to the diseases of the whole world, and to them you have given great efficacy.

Chapter 5
The Authority of the Scriptures

(7) From that time forward I preferred Catholic teaching. I thought that on its part it was more moderate and not at all deceptive to command men to believe what was not demonstrated, either because it was a matter that could be demonstrated, but perhaps not to everyone, or because it was indemonstratable, than for others to make a mockery of credulity by rash promises of sure knowledge, and then commanding that so many most fabulous and absurd things be accepted on trust because they could not be demonstrated. Then, little by little, O Lord, with a most mild and merciful hand you touched and calmed my heart. I considered how countless were the things that I believed, although I had not seen them nor was I present when they took place. Such were so many events in human history, so many things about places and cities that I had not seen, so many things about my friends, so many things about physicians, so many things about countless other men. Unless we believed these things, nothing at all could be done in this life. Lastly, I thought of how I held with fixed and unassailable faith that I was born of certain parents, and this I could never know unless I believed it by hearing about them. By all this you persuaded me that not those who believe in your books, which you have established with such mighty authority among almost all nations, but those who do not believe in them are the ones to be blamed, and not to be given a hearing, if they should perhaps say to me: "How do you know that these are the books of the one true and most truthful God, dispensed by his Spirit to the human race?" This truth most above all was to be believed, for no hostile and slanderous questions, so many of which I had read in philosophers who contradict one another, could extort from me the answer that I would at any time believe that you do not exist, whatsoever might be your nature (for this I did not know), or that the governance of human affairs did not belong to you.

(8) Sometimes I believed this more strongly and at other times in a more feeble way. But always I believed both that you are and that you have care for us, although I did not know either what must be thought concerning your substantial being or

---

[179] II Cor. 3:6. [180] Cf. Ps. 116:2.

what way led up to you or back to you. Therefore, since we were too weak to find the truth by pure reason, and for that cause we needed the authority of Holy Writ, I now began to believe that in no wise would you have given such surpassing authority throughout the whole world to that Scripture, unless you wished that both through it you be believed in and through it you be sought. Now that I had heard many things in those writings explained in a probable manner, I referred the absurdity that used there to cause me difficulty to the depths of their mysteries. To me, that authority seemed all the more venerable and worthy of inviolable faith, because they were easy for everyone to read and yet safeguarded the dignity of their hidden truth within a deeper meaning, by words completely clear and by a lowly style of speech making itself accessible to all men, and drawing the attention of those who are not light of heart.[181] Thus it can receive all men into its generous bosom, and by narrow passages lead on to you a small number of them,[182] although these are more numerous than if it did not stand out with such lofty authority and if it had not attracted throngs into the bosom of its holy humility.

I thought over these things, and you were present to me. I uttered sighs, and you gave ear to me. I wavered back and forth, and you guided me. I wandered upon the broad way[183] of the world, but you did not forsake me.

. . .

Book VIII
The Grace of Faith

Chapter 1
Truth Seen but Not Followed

(1) With thanksgiving let me remember, O my God, all your mercies to me and let me confess them to you. Let my bones be filled with your love, and let them say to you: "Lord, who is like unto you?[184] You have broken my bonds. I will sacrifice to you the sacrifice of praise."[185] I will narrate how you broke them asunder. And when they hear these things, let all who adore you say: "Blessed be the Lord, in heaven and on earth. Great and wonderful is his name."[186]

Your words had stuck fast in the depths of my heart, and on every side I was encompassed by you. I was now certain that you are eternal life, although I saw it only "in a glass, in a dark manner."[187] Yet all my doubts concerning incorruptible substance, and that every other substance comes from it, had been removed from me. It was not to be more certain concerning you, but to be more steadfast in you that I desired. But in my temporal life all things were uncertain, and my heart had to be cleansed of the old leaven.[188] The way, the Savior himself, had become pleasing, but as yet I was loath to tread its narrow passes. You put it into my mind, and it seemed good to my sight, to turn to Simplicianus,[189] who appeared to me to be a good servant of yours, for in him your grace shone bright. I had also heard that from his youth he had lived most devoutly in your service. At that time he had grown old, and because of long years spent in following your way with such

---

[181] Cf. Ecclus. 19:4.

[182] Augustine makes a contrast between the many and the few (cf. Matt. 7:13,14 and 20:16), but it is to the effect that the simplicity of the Scriptures has an appeal to all men, while a smaller number are led on to a deeper study of them.

[183] Cf. Matt. 7:13. [184] Ps. 34:10. [185] Ps. 115:16, 17. [186] Cf. Ps. 75:2.

[187] I Cor. 13:12. [188] Cf. I Cor. 5:7.

[189] Simplicianus succeeded St. Ambrose as Bishop of Milan in 397. Augustine dedicated his work *De divinis quaestionibus* to him.

good zeal, I thought that he was one who had experienced many things and learned many things. In truth, he was such a one. Hence I wished that after I had discussed my problems with him, he would show me the proper manner for one affected like me to walk in your way.

(2) I saw that the Church was full of men, of whom one went this way, another that. I was displeased with the course I followed in the world, and with my desires no longer aflame with hope of honor and wealth, as they had been, to bear so grievous a bondage was a very great burden to me. In comparison with your sweetness and the beauty of your house, which I loved,[190] those things no longer gave me delight, but I was still tightly bound by love of women. However, your apostle did not forbid me to marry, although he exhorted me to something better, especially wishing that all men would be like himself.[191] But I was weaker and chose the softer place. For this one thing I was tossed all about in other ways: I was faint and I wasted away with withering cares. For in other matters, which I had no wish to endure, I was forced to adapt myself to that conjugal life, which I had given myself to and by which I was therefore restricted.

From the mouth of your truth I had learned that there are eunuchs who made themselves such for the kingdom of heaven, but he also says, "He that can take it, let him take it."[192] Surely "all men are vain in whom there is not the knowledge of God: and who by these good things that are seen could not understand, could not find, him who is."[193] I was no longer in that vanity! I had passed beyond it, and by the testimony of the whole creation I had found you our creator, and your Word, who is God with you, and who is one God with you, through whom you created all things.

There is another class of impious men, who "knowing God, have not glorified him as God, or given thanks."[194] Into this group also I had fallen, but your right hand[195] raised me up, and took me out of it, and you placed me where I might grow strong again. For you have said to man: "Behold, piety is wisdom,"[196] and "Do not desire to appear wise,"[197] "for professing themselves to be wise, they became fools."[198] But I had now found the good pearl, and this I must buy, after selling all that I had.[199] Yet still I hesitated.

Chapter 2
The Conversion of Victorinus

(3) I went, then, to Simplicianus, the father, as to his reception of grace,[200] of Ambrose, the then bishop, and by him loved as a father. To him I recounted the winding ways of my errors. When I recorded how I had read certain books of the Platonists, translated into the Latin language by Victorinus,[201] sometime professor of rhetoric at Rome, who, I had heard, had died a Christian, he congratulated me because I had not fallen in with the writings of other philosophers, full of fallacies and deceits according to the elements of this world,[202] whereas in the works of the Platonists God and his Word are introduced in all manners. Thereupon, in order to exhort me to accept Christ's humility, "hidden from the wise and revealed to little ones,"[203] he spoke of Victorinus himself, whom he had known intimately when

[190]Cf. Ps. 25:8. [191]Cf. I Cor. 7:27–35. [192]Matt. 19:12. [193]Wisd. 13:1.
[194]Rom. 1:21. [195]Cf. Ps. 17:36. [196]Cf. Job 28:28. [197]Cf. Prov. 3:7.
[198]Rom. 1:22. [199]Cf. Matt. 13:46.

[200]Simplicianus was St. Ambrose's "spiritual father," i.e., he was very close to him, and may have instructed and baptized him.

[201]Gaius Marius Victorinus, the great fourth-century rhetorician, was of African origin.

[202]Cf. Col. 2:8. [203]Matt. 11:25.

he was in Rome. He told me certain things about him that I will not pass over in silence, as they involve an instance of that great praise of your grace[204] which must be confessed to you. For that aged man, most learned and most highly skilled in all liberal studies, had read through and passed judgment on many philosophical works and had been the teacher of many noble senators. He had even merited and obtained a statue in the Roman forum as a memorial of his outstanding teaching, which citizens of this world deem a great honor. Right up to his old age, he had been a worshiper of idols and a communicant in sacrilegious rites, with which almost the entire Roman nobility was then inflated. By such rites they inspired the people with the cult of Osiris, and every kind of god, monsters, and barking Anubis, which at one time had borne arms against Neptune and Venus, and against Minerva.[205] These gods, whom Rome had once conquered, she now adored. Over the course of many years, the aged Victorinus himself had defended them with thunderous and terrifying eloquence. But now he did not blush to become the child of your Christ and a newborn infant at your font,[206] to bend his neck under the yoke of humility, and to lower his brow before the reproach of the cross.[207]

(4) Lord, Lord, you who have bowed down the heavens and have descended, you who have touched the mountains and they have smoked,[208] by what means did you wend your way into his breast? He used to read Holy Writ, as Simplicianus has said, and he studiously searched into and examined all Christian writings. He said to Simplicianus, not openly, but privately and as a friend, "You should know that I am already a Christian." But he answered, "I will not believe it, nor will I reckon you among Christians, unless I see you in the Church of Christ." The other laughed and said, "Is it walls, then, that make men Christians?" He often said that he was already a Christian; Simplicianus just as often made his reply; and just as often he made his joke about the walls. He was afraid of offending his friends, the proud worshipers of demons. He thought that from their lofty seat of honor in Babylon,[209] as from cedars of Lebanon, which the Lord had not yet broken down,[210] the heavy weight of their enmity would rush down upon him.

Afterwards, through reading and longing, he drank in strength. He feared that he would be denied by Christ before the angels if he now feared to confess him before men.[211] He saw himself as guilty of a great crime by being ashamed of the mysteries of the humility of your Word, while not being ashamed of the sacrilegious rites of proud demons, which he had proudly imitated and accepted. He put aside shame from vanity and became modest before the truth. Suddenly and unexpectedly, he said to Simplicianus, who has himself described it, "Let us go to the church. I wish to become a Christian." Unable to contain himself for joy, Simplicianus went with him. There he was granted the initial sacraments of instruction, and not long after he gave in his name, so that he might be reborn in baptism. Rome stood in wonder, and the Church rejoiced. The proud saw, and were angry; they gnashed their teeth, and pined away.[212] But the Lord God was the hope of his servant, and he had no regard for vanities and lying follies.[213]

(5) At length the hour came for him to make his profession of faith.[214] At Rome, those who are about to approach your grace usually deliver this profession from an elevated place, in the sight of your faithful people, in set words which they have learned and committed to memory. To Victorinus, he said, the priests gave

[204]Cf. Eph. 1:6. [205]Cf. *Aeneid,* viii, 698–99. [206]Cf. John 3:5. [207]Cf. Gal. 5:11.
[208]Cf. Ps. 143:5. [209]Babylon, i.e., pagan Rome. [210]Cf. Ps. 28:5. [211]Cf. Luke 12:9.
[212]Cf. Ps. 111:10. [213]Cf. Ps. 39:5.
[214]A public recitation of the Apostles' creed.

permission to make the profession in private, as it was the custom to allow this to those who looked as if they would be self-conscious and upset. However, he preferred to make profession of his salvation in the sight of that holy throng. What he taught in his school of rhetoric was not salvation, and yet he taught it publicly. How much less, then, should he dread your meek flock when he affirmed your Word, since he had never dreaded to pronounce his own words before throngs of madmen! Hence, when he arose to make his profession, all who knew him uttered his name to one another with a murmur of congratulation. And who among them did not know him? A suppressed sound issued from the mouths of all those who rejoiced together, "Victorinus! Victorinus!" Suddenly, as they saw him, they gave voice to their joy, and just as suddenly they became silent in order to hear him. He pronounced the true faith with splendid confidence, and they all desired to clasp him to their hearts. By their love and joy they clasped him to themselves. Those were the hands by which they clasped him.

. . .

Chapter 5
The Inner Conflict

(10) When Simplicianus, your servant, related to me all this concerning Victorinus, I was on fire to imitate him, and it was for this reason that he had told it to me. Afterwards he added to it how in Emperor Julian's time a law was passed by which Christians were forbidden to teach literature and oratory, and how he obeyed the law, and chose rather to give up his school for words than your Word, by which you make eloquent the tongues of infants.[215] Then he appeared to me to have been no more courageous than fortunate, since he found opportunity to devote himself to you alone. For this very thing did I sigh, bound as I was, not by another's irons but by my own iron will. The enemy[216] had control of my will, and out of it he fashioned a chain and fettered me with it. For in truth lust is made out of a perverse will, and when lust is served, it becomes habit, and when habit is not resisted, it becomes necessity. By such links, joined one to another, as it were—for this reason I have called it a chain—a harsh bondage held me fast. A new will, which had begun within me, to wish freely to worship you and find joy in you, O God, the sole sure delight, was not yet able to overcome that prior will, grown strong with age. Thus did my two wills, the one old, the other new, the first carnal, and the second spiritual, contend with one another, and by their conflict they laid waste my soul.

(11) Thus I understood from my own experience what I had read, how "the flesh lusts against the spirit, and the spirit against the flesh."[217] I was in both camps, but I was more in that which I approved within myself than in that other which I disapproved within me. For now, in the latter, it was not so much myself, since in large part I suffered it against my will rather than did it voluntarily. Yet it was by me that this habit had been made so warlike against me, since I had come willingly to this point where I now willed not. Who can rightly argue against it, when just punishment comes upon the sinner? Nor did I any longer have that former excuse, in which I used to look upon myself as unable to despise the world and to serve you, because knowledge of the truth was still uncertain to me. Now indeed it was

---

[215] Cf. Ps. 8:3; Wisd. 10:21; Matt. 21:16.
[216] The enemy, Satan.
[217] Gal 5:17.

certain to me. Yet I was still bound to the earth, and I refused to become your soldier.[218] I was afraid to be lightened of all my heavy burden, even as I should have feared to be encumbered by it.

(12) Thus by the burdens of this world I was sweetly weighed down, just as a man often is in sleep. Thoughts wherein I meditated upon you were like the efforts of those who want to arouse themselves but, still overcome by deep drowsiness, sink back again. Just as no man would want to sleep forever, and it is the sane judgment of all men that it is better to be awake, yet a man often defers to shake off sleep when a heavy languor pervades all his members, and although the time to get up has come, he yields to it with pleasure even although it now irks him. In like manner, I was sure that it was better for me to give myself up to your love than to give in to my own desires. However, although the one way appealed to me and was gaining mastery, the other still afforded me pleasure and kept me victim. I had no answer to give to you when you said to me, "Rise, you who sleep, and arise from the dead, and Christ will enlighten you."[219] When on all sides you showed me that your words were true, and I was overcome by your truth, I had no answer whatsoever to make, but only those slow and drowsy words, "Right away. Yes, right away." "Let me be for a little while." But "Right away—right away" was never right now, and "Let me be for a little while" stretched out for a long time.

In vain was I delighted with your law according to the inward man, when another law in my members fought against the law of my mind, and led me captive in the law of sin which was in my members.[220] For the law of sin is force of habit, whereby the mind is dragged along and held fast, even against its will, but still deservedly so, since it was by its will that it had slipped into the habit. Unhappy man that I was! Who would deliver me from the body of this death, unless your grace through Jesus Christ our Lord?[221]

. . .

Chapter 8
In the Garden

(19) Then, during that great struggle in my inner house, which I had violently raised up against my own soul in our chamber,[222] in my heart, troubled both in mind and in countenance, I turn upon Alypius and cry out to him: "What is the trouble with us? What is this? What did you hear? The unlearned rise up and take heaven by storm,[223] and we, with all our erudition but empty of heart, see how we wallow in flesh and blood! Are we ashamed to follow, because they have gone on ahead of us? Is it no shame to us not even to follow them?" I said some such words, and my anguish of mind tore me from him, while astounded he looked at me and kept silent. I did not speak in my usual way. My brow, cheeks, eyes, color, and tone of voice spoke of my state of mind more than the words that I uttered.

Attached to our lodging there was a little garden; we had the use of it, as of the whole house, for our host, the owner of the house, did not live in it. The tumult within my breast hurried me out into it, where no one would stop the raging combat that I had entered into against myself, until it would come to such an end as you knew of, but as I knew not. I suffered from a madness that was to bring health, and I was in a death agony that was to bring life: for I knew what a thing of evil I was, but I did not know the good that I would be after but a little while. I rushed, then, into the garden, and Alypius followed in my steps. Even when he

---

[218]Cf. II Tim. 2:4. [219]Eph. 5:14. [220]Cf. Rom. 7:22, 23. [221]Cf. Rom. 7:24, 25.
[222]Cf. Isa. 26:20; Matt. 6:6.
[223]Cf. Matt. 11:12.

was present, I was not less alone—and how could he desert me when I was reduced to such a state? We sat down as far as we could from the house. Suffering from a most fearful wound, I quaked in spirit, angered by a most turbulent anger, because I did not enter into your will and into a covenant with you,[224] my God. For all my bones cried out[225] to me to enter into that covenant, and by their praises they lifted me up to the skies. Not by ships, or in chariots, or on foot do we enter therein; we need not go even so far as I had gone from the house to the place where we were sitting. For not only to go, but even to go in thither was naught else but the will to go, to will firmly and finally, and not to turn and toss, now here, now there, a struggling, half-maimed will, with one part rising upwards and another falling down.

(20) Finally, in the shifting tides of my indecision, I made many bodily movements, such as men sometimes will to make but cannot, whether because they lack certain members or because those members are bound with chains, weakened by illness, or hindered in one way or another. If I tore my hair, and beat my forehead, if I locked my fingers together and clasped my knees, I did so because I willed it. But I could have willed this and yet not done it, if the motive power of my limbs had not made its response. Therefore I did many things in which to will was not the same as the ability to act. Yet I did not do that which I wanted to do with an incomparably greater desire, and could have done as soon as I willed to act, for immediately, when I made that act of will, I would have willed with efficacy. In such an act the power to act and the will itself are the same, and the very act of willing is actually to do the deed. Yet it was not done: it was easier for the body to obey the soul's most feeble command, so that its members were moved at pleasure, than for the soul to obey itself and to accomplish its own high will wholly within the will.

Chapter 9
The Two Wills

(21) Whence comes this monstrous state?[226] Why should it be? Let your mercy shine forth, and let me inquire, if perchance man's hidden penalties and the darkest sufferings of the sons of Adam may be able to give me an answer. Whence comes this monstrous state? Why should it be? Mind commands body, and it obeys forthwith. Mind gives orders to itself, and it is resisted. Mind gives orders for the hand to move, and so easy is it that command can scarce be distinguished from execution. Yet mind is mind, while hand is body. Mind commands mind to will: there is no difference here, but it does not do so. Whence comes this monstrous state? Why should it be? I say that it commands itself to will a thing: it would not give this command unless it willed it, and yet it does not do what it wills.

It does not will it in its entirety: for this reason it does not give this command in its entirety. For it commands a thing only in so far as it wills it, and in so far as what it commands is not done, to that extent it does not will it. For the will commands that there be a will, and that this be itself, and not something else. But the complete will does not give the command, and therefore what it commands is not in being. For if it were a complete will, it would not command it to be, since the thing would already be in being. Therefore, it is no monstrous thing partly to will a thing and partly not to will it, but it is a sickness in the mind. Although it is supported by truth, it does not wholly rise up, since it is heavily encumbered by habit. Therefore there are two wills, since one of them is not complete, and what is lacking in one of them is present in the other.

---

[224] Cf. Ezech. 16:8. [225] Cf. Ps. 34:10.

[226] St. Augustine struggles in this chapter with most difficult psychological problems, involving the nature of the will and its acts.

Chapter 10
Man's Single Nature

(22) Let them perish from before your face,[227] O God, even as vain talkers and seducers[228] of men's minds perish who detect in the act of deliberation two wills at work, and then assert that in us there are two natures of two minds, one good, the other evil.[229] They themselves are truly evil, when they think such evil things. They will become good, if they come to know true doctrines and assent to the truth, so that your apostle may say to them, "For you were heretofore darkness, but now light in the Lord."[230] But they wish to be light, not in the Lord, but in themselves, and they think the soul's nature to be that which God is. Thus they are made into a deeper darkness, for in horrid pride they have turned back farther from you, from you who are "the true light which enlightens every man that comes into this world."[231] Take heed of what you say, and blush for shame, but "come to him and be enlightened, and your faces shall not be confounded."[232]

As for me, when I deliberated upon serving the Lord my God, as I had long planned to do, it was I myself who willed it and I myself who did not will it. It was I myself. I neither willed it completely, nor did I refrain completely from willing it. Therefore, I was at war within myself, and I was laid waste by myself. This devastation was made against my will indeed, and yet it revealed not the nature of a different mind within me, but rather the punishment of my own nature. Therefore, it is no more I that did it, but sin that dwells in me,[233] sin that issues from punishment of a more voluntary sin, for I was Adam's son.[234]

(23) If there are as many contrary natures as there are conflicting wills, there will now be not only two natures but many of them. If a man deliberates whether he should go to the Manicheans' meeting place or to the theater, they cry out: "See, there are two natures: the good one draws him this way, while the evil one leads him back there! For whence else is this hesitation between the opposing wills?" I answer that both of them are evil, both that which draws him to them and that which draws him back to the theater. But they do not believe a will that leads them to be anything but good. What results? If one of us debates within himself and wavers between two contending wills—whether he should go to the theater or to our church—must not those men likewise waver as to their answer? Either they will admit what they do not want to, viz., that he goes to our church out of a good will, as those who receive its sacraments and are obligated by them enter into it, or else they will suppose that two evil natures and two evil minds conflict within one man. But then what they are accustomed to say, that one nature is good and the other evil, will not be true. Or else they will be converted to the truth, and they will not deny that when a man deliberates, a single soul wavers between different wills.

(24) Therefore, when they perceive two conflicting wills within one man, let them no longer say that two contrary minds, deriving from two contrary substances and from two contrary principles, contend together, one good, the other evil. For you, the God of truth, condemn them, and contradict and refute them, as in cases where both wills are bad. For instance, a man deliberates whether he should murder

[227]Cf. Ps. 57:3. [228]Cf. Titus 1:10.
[229]That is, the Manicheans, with their extreme dualism of two natures, one good, the other evil.
[230]Eph. 5:8. [231]John 1:9. [232]Ps. 33:6. [233]Cf. Rom. 7:17.
[234]Because of his greater gifts of nature and grace, the sin by which Adam fell was committed with more freedom than any of the sins committed by his descendants. Hence Augustine indicates that his own wrongdoing, voluntary as it is, issues from Adam's still "more voluntary sin" and is part of the punishment incurred by that sin.

another by poison or with a sword; whether he should seize this or that part of another man's land, when he cannot take both; whether he should purchase pleasure out of lust or save his money out of avarice; whether he should go to the circus or to the theater, if both are showing on the same day. To this last I add a third choice, whether he should rob another man's house, if he has the chance. And I add a fourth, whether he should commit adultery, if an opportunity opens up at the same time. Let us suppose that all these occur together at exactly the same time, and that all are equally desired but cannot be carried out simultaneously. They rend asunder the mind, with these four wills opposing one another, or even with many more, in accordance with the great range of things that are desired. Yet the Manicheans are not accustomed to assert that there is such a great multitude of diverse substances.

So also with regard to wills that are good. I ask of them whether it is good to find delight in reading the apostle, whether it is good to take delight out of a sober psalm, whether it is good to discourse on the Gospel? To each of these questions they will answer, "It is good." What now? If, therefore, all these offer delight at one and the same time, do not diverse wills perplex a man's heart while it deliberates which thing we would seize upon before all others? All of them are good, but all strive with one another, until one is chosen, and there is fixed upon it a single complete will, whereas it had been divided into many wills. So also, when eternity above delights us and the pleasure found in a temporal good holds us fast from below, it is the same soul that wills this course or that, but not with its whole will. Therefore, it is rent asunder by grievous hurt as long as it prefers the first because of its truth but does not put away the other because of habit.

Chapter 11
The Voice of Continence

(25) Thus I was sick and tormented, and I upbraided myself much more bitterly than ever before.[235] I twisted and turned in my chain, until it might be completely broken, although now I was scarcely held by it, but still held by it I was. Within the hidden depths of my soul, O Lord, you urged me on. By an austere mercy you redoubled the scourges[236] of fear and shame, lest I should give in again, and lest that thin little remaining strand should not be broken through but should grow strong again and bind me yet more firmly.

Within myself I said: "Behold, let it be done now, now let it be done," and by those words I was already moving on to a decision. By then I had almost made it, and yet I did not make it. Still, I did not slip back into my former ways, but close by I stood my ground and regained my breath. Again I tried, and I was but a little away from my goal, just a little away from it, and I all but reached it and laid hold of it. Yet I was not quite there, and I did not reach it, and I did not catch hold of it. I still hesitated to die to death and to live to life, for the ingrown worse had more power over me than the untried better. The nearer came that moment in time when I was to become something different, the greater terror did it strike into me. Yet it did not strike me back, nor did it turn me away, but it held me in suspense.

(26) My lovers of old, trifles of trifles and vanities of vanities,[237] held me back. They plucked at my fleshy garment, and they whispered softly: "Do you cast us

---

[235]This chapter is a marvelous display of Augustine's powers of psychological analysis and vivid description.

[236]Cf. *Aeneid,* v, 457.

[237]Cf. Eccles. 1:2.

off?" and "From that moment we shall no more be with you forever and ever!" and again, "From that moment no longer will this thing and that be allowed to you, forever and ever!" What did they suggest by what I have called "this thing and that," what, O my God, did they suggest? May your mercy turn away all that from your servant's soul! What filth did they suggest! What deeds of shame! But now by far less than half did I hear them. For now it was not as if they were openly contradicting me, face to face, but as if they were muttering behind my back, and as if they were furtively picking at me as I left them, to make me look back again. Yet they did delay me, for I hesitated to tear myself away, and shake myself free of them, and leap over to that place where I was called to be. For an overpowering habit kept saying to me, "Do you think that you can live without them?"

(27) But now it asked this in a very feeble voice. For from that way in which I had set my face and where I trembled to pass, there appeared to me the chaste dignity of continence, serene and joyous, but in no wanton fashion, virtuously alluring, so that I would come to her and hesitate no longer. To lift me up and embrace me, she stretched forth her holy hands, filled with varied kinds of good examples. Many were the boys and girls, there too a host of youths, men and women of every age, grave widows and aged virgins, and in all these continence herself was in no wise barren but a fruitful mother[238] of children, of joys born of you, O Lord, her spouse.

She smiled upon me with an enheartening mockery, as if to say: "Cannot you do what these youths and these maidens do? Or can these youths and these maidens do this of themselves, and not rather in the Lord their God? The Lord their God gave me to them. Why do you stand on yourself, and thus stand not at all? Cast yourself on him. Have no fear. He will not draw back and let you fall. Cast yourself trustfully on him: he will receive you and he will heal you." I felt great shame, for I still heard the murmurings of those trifles, and still I delayed and hung there in suspense. Again she smiled, as if to say: "Turn deaf ears to those unclean members of yours upon the earth, so that they may be mortified. They tell you of delights, but not as does the law of the Lord your God."[239] This debate within my heart was solely of myself against myself. But Alypius, standing close by my side, silently awaited the outcome of my strange emotion.

Chapter 12
The Voice as of a Child

(28) But when deep reflection had dredged out of the secret recesses of my soul all my misery and heaped it up in full view of my heart, there arose a mighty storm, bringing with it a mighty downpour of tears. That I might pour it all forth with its own proper sounds, I arose from Alypius's side—to be alone seemed more proper to this ordeal of weeping—and went farther apart, so that not even his presence would be a hindrance to me. Such was I at that moment, and he sensed it, for I suppose that I had said something in which the sound of my voice already appeared to be choked with weeping. So I had arisen, while he, in deep wonder, remained there where we were sitting. I flung myself down, how I do not know, under a certain fig tree, and gave free rein to my tears.[240] The floods burst from my eyes, an acceptable sacrifice to you.[241] Not indeed in these very words but to this effect

[238] Cf. Ps. 112:9. [239] Cf. Ps. 118:85. [240] Cf. *Aeneid,* vii, 499. [241] Cf. Ps. 50:19.

I spoke many things to you: "And you, O Lord, how long?[242] How long, O Lord, will you be angry forever?[243] Remember not our past iniquities."[244] For I felt that I was held by them, and I gasped forth these mournful words, "How long, how long? Tomorrow and tomorrow? Why not now? Why not in this very hour an end to my uncleanness?"

(29) Such words I spoke, and with most bitter contrition I wept within my heart. And lo, I heard from a nearby house, a voice like that of a boy or a girl, I know not which, chanting and repeating over and over, "Take up and read. Take up and read." Instantly, with altered countenance, I began to think most intently whether children made use of any such chant in some kind of game, but I could not recall hearing it anywhere. I checked the flow of my tears and got up, for I interpreted this solely as a command given to me by God to open the book and read the first chapter I should come upon. For I had heard how Anthony had been admonished by a reading from the Gospel at which he chanced to be present, as if the words read were addressed to him: "Go, sell what you have, and give to the poor, and you shall have treasure in heaven, and come, follow me,"[245] and that by such a portent he was immediately converted to you.

So I hurried back to the spot where Alypius was sitting, for I had put there the volume of the apostle when I got up and left him. I snatched it up, opened it, and read in silence the chapter on which my eyes first fell: "Not in rioting and drunkenness, not in chambering and impurities, not in strife and envying; but put you on the Lord Jesus Christ, and make not provision for the flesh in its concupiscences."[246] No further wished I to read, nor was there need to do so. Instantly, in truth, at the end of this sentence, as if before a peaceful light streaming into my heart, all the dark shadows of doubt fled away.

(30) Then, having inserted my finger, or with some other mark, I closed the book, and, with a countenance now calm, I told it all to Alypius. What had taken place in him, which I did not know about, he then made known to me. He asked to see what I had read: I showed it to him, and he looked also at what came after what I had read for I did not know what followed. It was this that followed: "Now him that is weak in the faith take unto you,"[247] which he applied to himself and disclosed to me. By this admonition he was strengthened, and by a good resolution and purpose, which were entirely in keeping with his character, wherein both for a long time and for the better he had greatly differed from me, he joined me without any painful hesitation.

Thereupon we went in to my mother; we told her the story, and she rejoiced. We related just how it happened. She was filled with exultation and triumph, and she blessed you, "who are able to do above that which we ask or think."[248] She saw that through me you had given her far more than she had long begged for by her piteous tears and groans. For you had converted me to yourself, so that I would seek neither wife nor ambition in this world, for I would stand on that rule of faith where, so many years before, you had showed me to her. You turned her mourning into a joy[249] far richer than that she had desired, far dearer and purer than that she had sought in grandchildren born of my flesh.[250]

. . .

[242]Ps. 6:4. [243]Ps. 78:5. [244]Ps. 78:8. [245]Matt. 19:21.
[246]Rom. 13:13, 14. [247]Rom. 14:1. [248]Cf. Eph. 3:20. [249]Cf. Ps. 29:12.
[250]Monica had made efforts to arrange a lawful marriage for her son. Cf. *Confessions,* Book 6, ch. 13.

Book IX
The New Catholic

Chapter 1
A Soul Set Free

(1) "O Lord, I am your servant; I am your servant and the son of your handmaid. You have broken my bonds: I will sacrifice to you the sacrifice of praise."[251] Grant that my heart and my tongue may praise you. Grant that all my bones may say, "Lord who is like unto you?"[252] Grant that they may speak, and deign to answer me and "say to my soul: I am your salvation."[253]

Who am I, and what am I? Is there any evil that is not found in my acts, or if not in my acts, in my words, or if not in my words, in my will? But you, O Lord, are good and merciful, and your right hand has had regard for the depth of my death, and from the very bottom of my heart it has emptied out an abyss of corruption. This was the sum of it: not to will what I willed and to will what you willed.

But throughout these long years where was my free will? Out of what deep and hidden pit was it called forth in a single moment, wherein to bend my neck to your mild yoke and my shoulders to your light burden,[254] O Christ Jesus,[255] "my helper and my redeemer?"[256] How sweet did it suddenly become to me to be free of the sweets of folly: things that I once feared to lose it was now joy to put away. You cast them forth from me, you the true and highest sweetness, you cast them forth, and in their stead you entered in, sweeter than every pleasure, but not to flesh and blood, brighter than every light, but deeper within me than any secret retreat, higher than every honor, but not to those who exalt themselves. Now was my mind free from the gnawing cares of favor-seeking, of striving for gain, of wallowing in the mire, and of scratching lust's itchy sore. I spoke like a child to you, my light, my wealth, my salvation, my Lord God.

Chapter 2
End of a Worldly Career

(2) In your sight I resolved not to make a boisterous break, but gently to withdraw the service of my tongue from the language marts. Thus youths who did not meditate on your law,[257] or on your peace, but on foolish lies and court quarrels, would no longer pry from my mouth weapons for their madness. Happily, very few days still remained before the vintage vacation.[258] I resolved to endure them, so that I might leave in correct fashion, and, since I had now been ransomed by you, not to put myself up for sale again. Hence our plan was known to you, but it was not known to men, with the exception of our friends. We had agreed among ourselves, that it should not be spread everywhere, even though to us who were now mounting up from the vale of tears[259] and were singing a gradual canticle[260] you had given sharp arrows and consuming coals against a deceitful tongue.[261] For

[251] Ps. 115:16, 17. [252] Ps. 34:10. [253] Ps. 34:3. [254] Cf. Matt. 11:30.

[255] This is the only passage where Christ is addressed directly. Three times Augustine prays in the familiar formula "through Christ." Cf. Book 11, chs. 2 and 22.

[256] Ps. 18:15 [257] Cf. Ps. 118:70.

[258] About the time of Augustine's conversion the Emperors Theodosius and Valentinian II decreed the times for court and perhaps for school vacations. The vintage vacation extended from August 22 to October 15. There were also Easter (two weeks) and New Year (three days) vacation.

[259] Cf. Ps. 83:7.

[260] Pss. 119–133 are traditionally called "gradual psalms."

[261] Cf. Ps. 119:3, 4.

such a tongue, while seeming to counsel us, would oppose us, and out of fondness would devour us, as it does its food.

(3) Your love pierced our heart like an arrow,[262] and we bore within us your words, transfixing our inmost parts. The examples set by your servants, whom you had turned from black to shining bright, and from death to life, brought together in the bosom of our thought, set fire to our heavy torpor and burned it away, so that we would not turn towards lower things. So strong a fire did they enkindle in us that all the hostile blasts from deceitful tongues would only inflame us more fiercely and not put out that fire.

But truly for your name's sake, which you have hallowed throughout the earth, our vow and our resolution might even find men to give them praise. Therefore, it seemed like outward show if we would not wait for the vacation time that was now so near, but would leave early a public profession, practiced before the eyes of all men. The result would be that all who regarded my act and noted how close was that day of the vintage holidays which I wished to anticipate, would do a great deal of talking, to the effect that I wanted to look like a big man. Further, what would it have profited me for them to think and argue about my state of mind and "for our good to be evil spoken of?"[263]

(4) Moreover, it happened that in that very summer, because of too much literary work, my lungs had begun to weaken and it was difficult for me to breathe deeply. By pains in my chest they showed that they were injured, and it was impossible to make clear or extended use of my voice. This fact first disturbed me, as it was forcing me almost of necessity to put down my burden of teaching, or surely, to interrupt it, even if I were to be cured and recover. But when a complete will to remain still and see that you are the Lord[264] arose and was made firm in me—you know all this, my God—I even began to be glad that this not untrue excuse was at hand. It would lessen the opposition of men who, for the sake of their freeborn sons, were willing that I should never be free. Full of such joy, then, I endured that space of time until it had run its course—whether there were twenty days I am not sure—yet they were endured by sheer strength. The desire for profit, by which I used to bear this heavy trial, was gone from me, and I would have continued in it completely crushed if patience had not succeeded to it. Some of your servants, my brethren, may say that I sinned in this matter, in that, with a heart now completely in your service, I allowed myself to sit for even a single hour in that chair of lies. I do not debate with them on this. But have not you, most merciful Lord, by your sacred waters pardoned and wiped away this sin along with my other horrid and deadly deeds?

. . .

Chapter 5
Resignation of a Professorship

(13) When the vintage vacation was ended, I sent word to the citizens of Milan that they should arrange for another seller of words for their students. This was both because I had chosen to serve you and because I was no longer equal to that profession by reason of difficulty in breathing and the pain in my chest. By letters I made known to your bishop, Ambrose, that holy man, both my former errors and my present intention, so that he could advise me as to which of your books it would

---

[262]This passage is probably the immediate basis for Augustine's symbol in Christian art, a heart pierced by an arrow.
[263]Rom. 14:16. [264]Cf. Ps. 45:11.

be best for me to read, to the end that I would become more prepared and better fitted to receive so great a grace. He recommended the prophet Isaias: I believe it was because he is a more manifest prophet of the gospel and of the calling of the Gentiles than are the other writers. But in fact I did not understand the first lesson in this book, and thinking the whole work to be similar, I put it aside to be taken up again when I was better accustomed to the Lord's mode of speech.

Chapter 6
Baptism, Easter 387

(14) When the time arrived for me to give in my name,[265] we left the country and returned to Milan.[266] Alypius likewise resolved to be born again in you, in company with me, for he was now clothed with that humility which befits your sacraments. Valiantly had he brought his body into subjection, even to the point that, with unusual daring, he would tread the icy Italian ground with bare feet. We also joined to ourselves the boy Adeodatus, born of me in the flesh out of my sin. Well had you made him: he was almost fifteen years old, and in power of mind he surpassed many grave and learned men. O Lord my God, creator of all things and most powerful to reform our deformities, to you do I confess your gifts. For in that boy I owned nothing but the sin. That he was brought up by us in your discipline, to that you and none other inspired us. Your gifts I confess to you. There is one of our books which is entitled *On the Teacher,*[267] and in it he speaks with me. You know that his are all the ideas which are inserted there, as from the person of the one talking with me, when he was in his sixteenth year. I had experience of many still more wonderful things in him. To me his power of mind was a source of awe. Who except you is the worker of such marvels?

Quickly you took his life away from the earth, and now I remember him with a more peaceful mind, for I have no fear for anything in his childhood or youth, and none at all for him as a man. We joined him to us, of equal age in your grace, to be instructed in your discipline. We were baptized, and anxiety over our past life fled away from us. In those days I could not take my fill of meditating with wondrous sweetness on the depths of your counsel concerning the salvation of mankind. How greatly did I weep during hymns and canticles, keenly affected by the voices of your sweet-singing Church! Those voices flowed into my ears, and your truth was distilled into my heart, and from that truth holy emotions overflowed, and the tears ran down, and amid those tears all was well with me.

Chapter 7
Saints Gervase and Protase

(15) The Church in Milan had not long before begun to worship with this form of consolation and exhortation, wherein with great fervor the brethren sing together in voice and heart. For it was only a year, or not much more, since Justina, the mother of the boy king,[268] Valentinian, had persecuted your man Ambrose in favor

[265] At the approach of Lent, catechumens who wished to be baptized gave in their names and were examined in the catechism.

[266] While awaiting baptism in Milan, Augustine wrote several books, including *On the Immortality of the Soul.*

[267] This profound and beautiful dialogue, in which Augustine considers problems of semantics along with those of teaching and others, was written at Thagaste.

[268] Augustine uses the term *rex* (king) for Valentinian as a synonym for *imperator* (emperor) and the adjective *regia* (royal) for Justina. They have been translated literally here, as it may be thought that Augustine uses them in a somewhat pejorative sense.

of her heresy, to which she had been seduced by the Arians.[269] A devout people, who were prepared to suffer death together with their bishop, your servant, kept watch in the church. Therein, living in prayer, my mother, your handmaid, held a first place amid these cares and watchings. Ourselves, still cold to the warmth of your Spirit, were nevertheless stirred by the astonished and disturbed city. At that time it was established that, after the custom of the Eastern lands, hymns and canticles should be sung, so that the people would not become weak through the tedium and sorrow. From then up to the present day that custom has been maintained, with many, or almost all, of your congregations taking it up throughout other parts of the world.

(16) At that same time you revealed by a vision to your aforenamed prelate the place in which the bodies of the martyrs Protase and Gervase[270] lay hidden, which for so many years you had stored away uncorrupted in your secret treasure house. In due time you would bring them forth from that place so as to restrain the mad rage of a woman, yes, a woman of royal rank. When they were discovered and dug up, and with fitting honors transferred into the Ambrosian basilica, not only were those tormented by unclean spirits healed, while those same demons confessed themselves, but also a certain citizen,[271] very well known throughout the city, who had been blind for many years, asked and heard the reason for the people's joy and tumult, and then leaped up and demanded that his guide lead him thither. Brought there, he begged to be admitted so that he might touch the bier with his handkerchief, for precious in your sight is the death of your saints.[272] When he had done this and touched the cloth to his eyes, they were immediately opened. From that place the story spread abroad. From there, your praises grew bright and shone forth. From there, the mind of that hostile woman, although not turned to sound belief, was yet restrained from the fury of persecution. "Thanks be to you, my God."[273] Whence and whither have you led my recollection so that I confess also these things to you, mighty deeds that I had almost passed over in forgetfulness? Yet even then, when the odor of your ointments was so fragrant, we did not run after you.[274] Therefore, I wept the more at the singing of your hymns. For long had I sighed after you, and at length I breathed in you, as far as breath may enter into this house of grass.[275]

Chapter 8
Monica's Youth

(17) You "who make men to dwell of one mind in a house,"[276] joined with us Evodius,[277] a young man of our own city, who had served as a special agent. He had been converted to you before we were, and he had been baptized. Having given up

---

[269]The Empress Justina Augusta was the wife of Valentinian I and mother of Valentinian Augustus II. Early in 385 she ordered St. Ambrose to give over a church within the city to the Arians, but he refused. The struggle came to a climax in Holy Week 386 when she ordered him to leave Milan. He refused to do so and conducted services in the basilica as usual. In Easter Week Justina's troops besieged Ambrose in the basilica, but the movement collapsed when many of the soldiers joined him. Justina died a Catholic in 388 in Thessalonica.

[270]Sts. Gervase and Protase, Milanese martyrs, probably of the second century. Their remains, clothed in priestly vestments and with the palms of martyrdom in their hands, still rest under the altar of the Church of St. Ambrose in Milan.

[271]Severus, a butcher by trade.

[272]Cf. Ps. 115:15. [273]Luke 18:11. [274]Cf. Cant. 1:3. [275]Cf. Isa. 40:6.

[276]Cf. Ps. 67:7.

[277]Evodius was a member of Augustine's community in Thagaste and later became Bishop of Uzala in 396.

his secular service, he girded himself for yours. We were together, and we planned to dwell together in our holy resolution. We made investigations as to what place would be best fitted to us for your service, and together we were returning back to Africa.[278] When we were at Ostia on the Tiber, my mother died.[279]

I omit many things, as I am making great haste. Accept my confessions and acts of thanksgiving, O my God, for countless things, even those I pass over in silence. But I will not pass over whatever my soul brings to birth concerning that handmaiden of yours, who brought me to birth, both in her flesh, so that I was born into this temporal light, and in her heart, that I might be born into eternal light. Not of her gifts, but of your gifts in her, will I speak. She neither made herself nor did she educate herself: you created her. Neither her father nor her mother knew what sort of woman would be made from them. The rod of your Christ, the rule of your only Son, in a faithful home, in a good member of your Church, instructed her "in your fear."[280] But for her training she was wont to praise not so much her mother's diligence as that of a certain age-worn maidservant who had carried her father about when he was an infant, as little ones are usually carried on the backs of older girls. Because of this service and because of her advanced age and excellent habits, she was held in high esteem by the masters of a Christian house. For these reasons also she was put in charge of her master's daughters and she took diligent care of them. When necessary, she restrained them strictly with a holy severity, and she taught them with prudence and sobriety. Outside the hours when they were properly fed at their parents' table, she did not permit them to drink water, even though they were parched with thirst. She thus forestalled a bad habit, and she added these sound words: "You drink water now, because you cannot get at the wine. When you come to be married, and are made mistresses of storerooms and cellars, water will be distasteful to you, but the habit of drinking will persist." By this form of teaching and by her authority to give orders, she restrained the greediness of their tender age and turned the girls' thirst towards a virtuous moderation, so that even then they would not want to do what they should not do.

(18) Nevertheless, there crept on her, as your handmaid told me, her son, there crept on her a love of wine. For when her parents, according to custom, ordered her as a sober girl to fetch wine out of the cask, she would dip a cup into the opening at the top before she poured the wine into a pitcher. Then she would take just a little sip with the tip of her lips, since the taste kept her from taking more. She did this not out of a desire for drink, but from a sort of excess of those youthful spirits which blow off in absurd actions and which parental firmness usually suppresses in our childhood years. Thus by adding to that daily little bit each day another little bit—for "he who contemns small things falls by little and little"[281]—she had fallen into the habit of greedily drinking her little cups almost full up with wine. Where then was the wise old woman, and where was her stern prohibition? Did anything avail against a secret disease, Lord, unless your medicine kept watch over us?[282] Father and mother and protectors are absent, yet you are present, you who have created us, who have called us, who work good towards the salvation of souls even through men placed over us. My God, what did you do at that time? How did you cure her? Whence did you heal her? Was it not that you brought out of another soul, a hard and sharp reproach, like a surgeon's knife out of your secret

[278]Monica's desire to be buried with her husband very likely figured in this return to Africa.

[279]The exact date of St. Monica's death is unknown. Apparently she died before November 387. Ostia is part of Rome.

[280]Ps. 5:8. [281]Ecclus. 19:1. [282]Cf. Jer. 31:28.

stores, and by one stroke you cut away all that foul matter? A maidservant, with whom she used to go down to the cellar, quarreled with her little mistress, the two being all alone, as it so happened. She threw this fault at her with most bitter insults, and called her a winebibber. Wounded through and through by this taunt, she beheld her own foul state, and immediately condemned it and cast if off. Just as fawning friends pervert us, so also quarrelsome enemies often correct us. Yet you repay them, not according to what you did through them, but according to what they themselves had a will to do. For that wrathful servant desired to provoke her little mistress, not to cure her. Therefore, she did this in private, either because the time and place of the quarrel so found them or perhaps because she was afraid that she would get into trouble for reporting it so late. But you, O Lord, ruler of things in heaven and on earth, who turn to your uses the deeps of the torrent, and give order to the turbulent flood of the ages, by means of madness in one soul you even heal another. This is to the end that no man who observes this may attribute it to his own powers, when some other man, whom he wishes to correct, is corrected by his words.

Chapter 9
Monica, Wife of Patricius

(19) Brought up modestly and soberly in this manner, and made subject by you to her parents rather than by her parents to you, when she arrived at a marriageable age, she was given to a husband and served "him as her lord."[283] She strove to win him to you,[284] speaking to him about you through her conduct, by which you made her beautiful, an object of reverent love, and a source of admiration to her husband. She endured offenses against her marriage bed in such wise that she never had a quarrel with her husband over this matter. She looked forward to seeing your mercy upon him, so that he would believe in you and be made chaste. But in addition to this, just as he was remarkable for kindness, so also was he given to violent anger. However, she had learned to avoid resisting her husband when he was angry, not only by deeds but even by words. When she saw that he had curbed his anger and become calm and that the time was opportune, then she explained what she had done, if he happened to have been inadvertently disturbed.

In fine, when many wives, who had better-tempered husbands but yet bore upon their faces signs of disgraceful beatings, in the course of friendly conversation criticized their husbands' conduct, she would blame it all on their tongues. Thus she would give them serious advice in the guise of a joke. From the time, she said, they heard what are termed marriage contracts read to them, they should regard those documents as legal instruments making them slaves. Hence, being mindful of their condition, they should not rise up in pride against their lords. Women who knew what a sharp-tempered husband she had to put up with marveled that it was never reported or revealed by any sign that Patricius[285] had beaten his wife or that they had differed with one another in a family quarrel, even for a single day. When they asked her confidentially why this was so, she told them of her policy, which I have described above. Those who acted upon it, found it to be good advice and were thankful for it; those who did not act upon it, were kept down and abused.

(20) By her good services and by perseverance in patience and meekness, she also won over her mother-in-law who at first was stirred up against her by the whispered

---

[283] Eph. 5:21. [284] Cf. I Pet. 3:1.

[285] The first mention of his father's name. Augustine does not use his own name at all throughout *The Confessions*.

stories of malicious servants. She told her son about the meddling tongues of the servants, by which peace within the house had been disturbed between herself and her daughter-in-law, and asked him to punish them. Afterwards, both to obey his mother and to improve discipline within his household and promote peace among its members, he punished by whippings the servants who had been exposed, in accordance with the advice of her who had exposed them. Afterwards she promised that the same reward might be expected by whoever tried to please her by telling any evil tale about her daughter-in-law. Since nobody thereafter dared to do this, they lived together with extraordinary harmony and good will.

(21) Moreover, upon that good handmaiden of yours, in whose womb you created me, "my God, my mercy,"[286] you bestowed this great gift: wherever she could, she showed herself to be a great peacemaker between persons who were at odds and in disagreement. When she heard from either side many very bitter things, like something a swollen, undigested discord often vomits up, when a rough mass of hatred is belched out in biting talk to a present friend about an absent enemy, she would never betray a thing to either of them about the other except what would help towards their reconciliation. This might have seemed a small thing to me, if from sad experience I had not known unnumbered throngs who, through some kind of horrid wide-spreading sinful infection, not only report the words of angry enemies to angry enemies, but even add things they did not say. On the contrary, to a man who is a man it should be a little thing not to stir up or increase men's enmities by evil speaking, or else he even strives to extinguish them by speaking well of others. Such was she, and she had you as her inward teacher in the school of her heart.

(22) Finally, towards the very end of his earthly life, she gained her husband for you. After he became one of the faithful, she did not have to complain of what she had endured from him when he was not yet a believer. She was also a servant of your servants.[287] Whosoever among them knew her greatly praised you, and honored you, and loved you in her, because they recognized your presence in her heart, for the fruit of her holy life bore witness to this. She had been the wife of one husband; she repaid the duty she owed to her parents; she had governed her house piously; she had testimony for her good works;[288] she had brought up children, being as often in labor in birth of them[289] as she saw them straying from you. Lastly, Lord, of all of us, your servants—for out of your gift you permit us to speak—who, before she fell asleep[290] in you already lived together, having received the graces of your baptism, she took care as though she had been mother to us all, and she served us as though she had been a daughter to all of us.

Chapter 10
The Vision at Ostia

(23) With the approach of that day on which she was to depart from this life, a day that you knew, although it was unknown to us, it came about, as you yourself ordered it, so I believe, in your secret ways, that she and I stood leaning out from a certain window, where we could look into the garden within the house we had taken at Ostia on the Tiber, where, removed from crowds, we were resting up, after the hardships of a long journey, in preparation for the voyage. We were alone, conversing together most tenderly, "forgetting those things that are behind, and stretching forth to those that are before."[291] We inquired of one another "in the

[286] Ps. 58:18. [287] Cf. Gen. 9:25. [288] Cf. I Tim. 5:4, 9, 10. [289] Cf. Gal. 4:9.
[290] Cf. John 11:13. [291] Phil. 3:13.

present truth,"[292] which truth you are, as to what the eternal life of the saints would be like, "which eye has not seen, nor ear heard, nor has it entered into the heart of a man."[293] But we were straining out with the heart's mouth for those supernal streams flowing from your fountain, "the fountain of life," which is "with you,"[294] so that, being sprinkled with it according to our capacity, we might in some measure think upon so great a subject.

(24) When our discourse had been brought to the point that the highest delight of fleshly senses, in the brightest corporeal light, when set against the sweetness of that life seemed unworthy not merely of comparison with it, but even of remembrance, then, raising ourselves up with a more ardent love to the Selfsame, we proceeded step by step through all bodily things up to that heaven whence shine the sun and the moon and the stars down upon the earth. We ascended higher yet by means of inward thought and discourse and admiration of your works, and we came up to our own minds. We transcended them, so that we attained to the region of abundance that never fails,[295] in which you feed Israel[296] forever upon the food of truth, and where life is that Wisdom by which all these things are made, both which have been and which are to be. And this Wisdom itself is not made, but it is such as it was, and so it will be forever. Nay, rather, to have been and to be in the future do not belong to it, but only to be, for it is eternal. And while we discourse of this and pant after it, we attain to it in a slight degree by an effort of our whole heart. And we sighed for it, and we left behind, bound to it, "the first-fruits of the spirit,"[297] and we turned back again to the noise of our mouths, where a word both begins and ends. But what is there like to your Word, our Lord, remaining in himself without growing old, and yet renewing all things?[298]

(25) Therefore we said: If for any man the tumult of the flesh fell silent, silent the images of earth, and of the waters, and of the air; silent the heavens; silent for him the very soul itself, and he should pass beyond himself by not thinking upon himself; silent his dreams and all imagined appearances, and every tongue, and every sign; and if all things that come to be through change should become wholly silent to him—for if any man can hear, then all these things say to him, "We did not make ourselves,"[299] but he who endures forever made us[300]—if when they have said these words, they then become silent, for they have raised up his ear to him who made them, and God alone speaks, not through such things but through himself, so that we hear his Word, not uttered by a tongue of flesh, nor by an angel's voice,[301] "nor by the sound of thunder,"[302] nor by the riddle of a similitude,[303] but by himself whom we love in these things, himself we hear without their aid,—even as we then reached out and in swift thought attained to that eternal Wisdom which abides over all things—if this could be prolonged, and other visions of a far inferior kind could be withdrawn, and this one alone ravish, and absorb, and hide away its beholder within its deepest joys, so that sempiternal life might be such as was that moment of understanding for which we sighed, would it not be this: "Enter into the joy of your Lord?"[304] When shall this be? When "we shall all rise again, but we shall not all be changed."[305]

(26) Such things I said, although not in this manner and in these words. Yet, O Lord, you know that on that day when we were speaking of such things, and this

---

[292]II Pet. 1:12. [293]I Cor. 2:9.
[294]Ps. 35:10. [295]Cf. Ezech. 34:14.
[296]Cf. Ps. 77:71. [297]Rom. 8:23. [298]Cf. Wisd. 7:27. [299]Ps. 99:3.
[300]Cf. Ecclus. 18:1. [301]Cf. Gen. 22:11. [302]Ps. 76:18.
[303]Cf. I Cor. 13:12; Num. 12:8.
[304]Matt. 25:21. [305]I Cor. 15:51.

world with all its delights became contemptible to us in the course of our words, my mother said: "Son, for my own part, I now find no delight in anything in this life. What I can still do here, and why I am here, I do not know, now that all my hopes in this world have been accomplished. One thing there was, for which I desired to linger a little while in this life, that I might see you a Catholic Christian before I died. God has granted this to me in more than abundance, for I see you his servant, with even earthly happiness held in contempt. What am I doing here?"

Chapter 11
The Death of St. Monica

(27) What I said to her in answer to this I do not entirely recall, for scarcely five days later, or not much more, she fell sick of fever. One day, as she lay ill, she lost consciousness and for a little while she was withdrawn from all present things. We rushed to her, but she quickly regained her senses. She looked at me and my brother as we stood there, and said to us, after the manner of one seeking something. "Where was I?" Then, gazing at us who were struck dumb with grief, she said, "Here you put your mother."[306] I remained silent and stopped my weeping. But my brother said, as if wishing a happier lot for her, that she should die not in a foreign land but in her own country. When she heard this, she stared reproachfully at him with an anxious countenance, because he was concerned about such things. Then she looked at me and said, "See what he says!" Presently she said to both of us: "Put this body away anywhere. Don't let care about it disturb you. I ask only this of you, that you remember me at the altar of the Lord, wherever you may be." When she had expressed this wish in what words she could manage, she fell silent and was racked with increasing sickness.

(28) I thought of your gifts, O God unseen,[307] which you instill into the hearts of your faithful and from which come wonderful fruits, and I rejoiced and gave thanks to you. I recalled what I already knew, how concerned she had always felt over her burial place, which she had arranged and prepared for herself next to her husband's body. They had lived together in great harmony, and hence she wished—so little is the human mind able to grasp the things of God—this too to be added to her happiness and remembered by men: that after a journey across the sea it had been granted to her that the earth of the two wedded ones have joint covering of earth.

At what time, out of the fullness of your bounty, this vain wish began to fade from her heart I do not know. I marveled and rejoiced over the fact that she had thus revealed it to me, although in our conversation at the window, when she said, "What do I still do here?" it did not appear that she wanted to die in her native land. I also heard later on that already, while we were at Ostia, one day when I was absent, she talked with a mother's confidence to certain friends of mine about contempt of this life and the advantages of death. They were amazed at the woman's strength, which you had given to her, and asked if she did not fear leaving her body so far from her own city. She replied, "Nothing is far from God. I need not fear that he will not know where to raise me up at the end of the world."

So, on the ninth day of her illness, in the fifty-sixth year of her life and in the thirty-third year of mine, this devout and holy soul was set loose from the body.

---

[306] Augustine apparently wants to give Monica's exact words, which we here translate literally.
[307] Cf. Col. 1:15.

Chapter 12
Monica's Burial; Augustine's Grief

(29) I closed her eyes, and a mighty sorrow welled up from the depths of my heart and overflowed into tears. At the same time, by a powerful command of my mind, my eyes drank up their source until it was dry. Most ill was it with me in such an agony! When she breathed her last, the boy Adeodatus burst out in lamentation, but he was hushed by all of us and fell silent. In like manner, something childish in me, which was slipping forth in tears, was by a youthful voice, my heart's own voice, checked, and it grew silent. We did not think it fitting to solemnize that funeral with tearful cries and groans, for it is often the custom to bewail by such means the wretched lot of those who die, or even their complete extinction. But she did not die in misery, nor did she meet with total death. This we knew by sure evidence and proofs given by her good life and by her "unfeigned faith."[308]

(30) What was it, therefore, that grieved me so heavily, if not the fresh wound wrought by the sudden rupture of our most sweet and dear way of life together? I took joy indeed from her testimony, when in that last illness she mingled her endearments with my dutiful deeds and called me a good son. With great love and affection she recalled that she had never heard me speak a harsh or disrespectful word to her. Yet, O my God who made us! what comparison was there between the honor she had from me and the services that she rendered to me? When I was bereft of such great consolation, my heart was wounded through and my life was as if ripped asunder. For out of her life and mine one life had been made.

(31) After the boy had been stopped from weeping, Evodius took up the psalter and began to sing a psalm. The whole household answered him in the psalm, "I will sing of mercy and judgment unto you, O Lord."[309] When they heard what had happened, many of the brethren and devout women gathered there. According to custom, those whose duty it was made ready the burial. At the same time, in that part of the house where I could do so, I discussed a subject suitable to such a time with those who thought that I should not be left alone. By so true a salve I soothed a torment known to me alone. The others knew nothing of it; they listened attentively to me, and they thought that I was free from all sense of sorrow. But in your ears, where none of them could hear, I upbraided the weakness of my affection, and I held back the flood of sorrow. It gave way a little before me, but I was again swept away by its violence, although not as far as to burst into tears, nor to any change of expression. But I knew what it was I crushed down within my heart. Because it distressed me greatly that these human feelings had such sway over me, for this needs must be according to due order and our allotted state, I sorrowed over my sorrow with an added sorrow, and I was torn by a twofold sadness.

(32) Lo, when her body was carried away, we went out,[310] and we returned without tears. Not even in those prayers we poured forth to you when the sacrifice of our redemption was offered up in her behalf, with the corpse already placed beside the grave before being lowered into it, as is the custom of that place,[311] not even during those prayers did I shed tears. But all day long in secret, heavy was my sorrow, and with a troubled mind I besought you as best I could to heal my

[308] I Tim. 1:5. [309] Ps. 100:1.
[310] Terence, *Andria,* 1, i, 90.
[311] It was a custom in Italy for Mass to be offered for the dead person at the grave.

anguish. You did not do so, and it was, I think, to impress upon my memory by this one lesson how strong is the bond of any habit, even upon a mind that no longer feeds upon deceptive words. I also thought it good to go and bathe, as I had heard that the baths (*balnea*) are so-called because the Greeks say βαλανεῖον, meaning that it drives anxiety from the mind. See, O Father of orphans, this fact too do I confess to your mercy, for after I had bathed I was the same as before I bathed. Bitter grief did not pour like sweat out of my heart. But then I slept, and I woke up, and I found that my sorrow had in no small part been eased. As I lay alone on my bed, I remembered those truthful verses of your own Ambrose. For you are

> God, creator of all things, ruler of the sky,
> Who clothe the day with beauteous light, the night with grateful sleep,
> That rest may weakened limbs restore for labor's needs,
> And ease our weary minds, and free our worried hearts from grief.

(33) Little by little, I regained my former thoughts about your handmaid, about the devout life she led in you, about her sweet and holy care for us, of which I was so suddenly deprived. I took comfort in weeping in your sight over her and for her, over myself and for myself. I gave way to the tears that I had held back, so that they poured forth as much as they wished. I spread them beneath my heart, and it rested upon them, for at my heart were placed your ears, not the ears of a mere man, who would interpret with scorn my weeping.

Now, Lord, I confess to you in writing. Let him read it who wants to, let him interpret it as he wants. If he finds a sin in it, that I wept for my mother for a small part of an hour, for that mother now dead to my eyes who for so many years had wept for me so that I might live in your eyes, let him not laugh me to scorn. But rather, if he is a man of large charity, let him weep over my sins before you, the Father of all brothers of your Christ.

Chapter 13
Remembrance in Prayer

(34) But now, with a heart healed from that wound, for which afterwards I blamed my merely natural feelings, I pour out to you, our God, in behalf of her who was your handmaid, a far different kind of tears. These tears flow from a spirit shaken by thought of the dangers besetting every soul "that dies in Adam." She had been made to live in Christ[312] even while not yet released from the flesh, and she had so lived as to give praise of your name by her faith and conduct. Still, I dare not say that from the time you regenerated her by baptism no word had issued from her mouth contrary to your commandment. By the Truth, your Son, it has been said, "Whosoever shall say to his brother, 'Thou fool,' shall be in danger of hell fire."[313] Woe even to such life of men as can be praised if you should set aside mercy and examine that life carefully.[314] But because you are not rigorous in searching out sins, we confidently hope to find a place with you. Yet if a man numbers his true merits before you, what else does he number before you except your own gifts? Ah, if men would know themselves to be but men, and if he who glories would glory in the Lord.[315]

---

[312] Cf. I Cor. 15:22. "And as in Adam all die, so also in Christ shall all be made alive."
[313] Matt. 5:22–23. [314] Cf. Ps. 129:3. [315] Cf. II Cor. 10:17.

(35) Therefore, O my praise[316] and my life, O God of my heart,[317] I put aside for a while her good deeds, for which I give thanks to you with joy, and I now beseech you in behalf of my mother's sins. Hear me for the sake of him who is the medicine of our wounds, of him who hung upon the tree, of him who now sits at your right hand and makes intercession for us.[318] I know that she was merciful to others and that from her heart she forgave her debtors their debts. Do you also forgive her her debts,[319] if she contracted any in so many years after receiving the water of salvation? Forgive her, Lord, forgive her, I beseech you. Enter not into judgment with her.[320] Let your mercy be exalted above your justice,[321] for your words are true, and you have promised mercy to the merciful.[322] Such you made them to be, for you will have mercy on whom you will have mercy, and you will show mercy to whom you will show mercy.[323]

(36) I believe that you have already done what I ask, but accept, O Lord, "the free offerings of my mouth."[324] For when the day of her dissolution was at hand,[325] she did not think of having her body richly clothed or embalmed with spices. She did not desire a carefully chosen monument, nor did she care for a grave in her own land. Such things she did not enjoin upon us, but she desired only that she be remembered at your altar, which she had served without the loss of a single day. For she knew that from it would be dispensed that holy Victim by whom "the handwriting of the decree that was against us, which was contrary to us,"[326] was blotted out, through whose sacrifice was vanquished that enemy who counted up our offenses and sought what he could lay against us, but found nothing in him[327] in whom we conquer. Who shall pour back into him his innocent blood? Who shall repay him the price by which he bought us, so as to take us from him? By the bond of faith your handmaid bound her soul to this sacrament of our redemption. Let no one sever her from your protection. Let neither the lion nor the dragon[328] put himself between you and her by force or fraud. She will not answer that she owes no debt, lest she be convicted and seized by her crafty accuser. She will answer that her sins have been forgiven by him to whom no one can return that price which he who owed nothing returned for us.

(37) Therefore, may she rest in peace, together with that husband before whom and after whom she had no other, whom she obeyed with patience, bringing forth fruit[329] to you so that she might win him also to you. Inspire, O my Lord, my God, inspire your servants my brethren, your sons my masters, whom with voice and heart and pen I serve, so that as many of them as read these words may at your altar remember Monica,[330] your handmaid, together with Patricius, sometime her husband, by whose flesh you brought me into this life, how I know not. May they with devout affection remember them who were my parents in this passing light, my brethren under you our Father in our Catholic Mother, and my fellow citizens in that eternal Jerusalem, which your pilgrim people sigh after from their setting forth even to their return,[331] so that, more abundantly than through my own prayers, my mother's last request of me may be granted through the prayers of many, occasioned by these confessions.

---

[316] Cf. Ps. 117:14. [317] Cf. Ps. 72:26. [318] Cf. Rom. 8:34. [319] Cf. Matt. 6:12.
[320] Cf. Ps. 142:2. [321] Cf. Jas. 2:13. [322] Cf. Matt. 5:7.
[323] Cf. Rom. 9:15; Exod. 33:19.
[324] Ps. 118:108. [325] Cf. II Tim. 4:6. [326] Col. 2:14. [327] Cf. John 14:30
[328] Cf. Ps. 90:13. [329] Cf. Luke 8:15.
[330] This is the only place in *The Confessions* in which Monica is named.
[331] Cf. Heb. 11:10–16.

DANTE ALIGHIERI

[1265–1321]

If we use the word *epic* to mean a lengthy and elevated poem that deals with serious issues in a vast or cosmic setting, then Dante's *The Divine Comedy* certainly qualifies. The heroes of his extended narrative are not Homer's or Virgil's warriors of the battlefield, but they are certainly warriors of the spirit, redefining the arena of adventure for the Middle Ages and later. Dante's pilgrim travels the physical and spiritual universe from the underworld of Hell to the outer reaches of Heaven, all of which was systematized by a single world view and system of values found in the medieval Roman Catholic Church. With Satan at the center and God on the circumference of the universe, the relative good or evil of an individual can be measured by his or her proximity to one or the other. Dante's pilgrimage has also been read as an allegorical journey of the soul or a psychological descent into the darkness within. Multiple possibilities make *The Divine Comedy* as interesting and profound today as it was in the fourteenth century.

LIFE

Very little is known about Dante's early life in Florence or about his parents, although his father probably gained some wealth as a money changer; his mother died when he was young. Nothing is known about Dante's formal education, but his writings suggest that he studied the standard classical and medieval works of literature, rhetoric, and theology. Because of his evident talents he was entertained in the leading families of Florence. He married Gemma Donati in about 1285 and they had at least three children, one of whom, Pietro, became an important commentator on the *Comedy*.

Undoubtedly the most important event of Dante's early life was his encounter with Beatrice Portinari. He first saw her when they were both nine years old. He fell in love with her at first sight and, although he saw her only a few times and they married other persons, she had a tremendous impact on his life, an influence that might seem unusual to a modern audience. Beatrice was married to Simone di' Bardi and died in 1290. It was perhaps her death at such an early age that allowed Dante to idealize her, to transform her into a spiritual symbol of inspiration for the sake of his writings and his own growth as a person. Influenced by the courtly love lyrics of the troubadours in twelfth-century France, especially those concerning love for a married woman, Dante began his apprenticeship as a writer by composing prose and poetry celebrating Beatrice. By 1294 he had written thirty-one poems with prose commentary focusing on his devotion to Beatrice. He published them in a collection titled *La Vita Nuova (The New Life).* In this work Beatrice, whose name means "she who blesses," was already becoming a religious, transcendent figure, capable of transformative power. Later she played an even more important role in the *Comedy*.

As a young man, Dante became actively involved in the political affairs of Florence, which had been turbulent and divisive throughout the thirteenth century. The Guelphs, who supported the Papacy, and the Ghibellines, who supported the Holy Roman Empire, were engaged in a civil war. On the side of the Guelphs, Dante probably participated in two decisive battles in 1289, Campaldinoa and the taking of Caprona, in which the Ghibellines were finally vanquished. The Guelphs then split over the issue of papal influence in Florence. Dante was a member of the White Guelphs, who sought to preserve an independent republic in Florence, whereas the aristocratic Blacks sought power for themselves through collaboration with Pope Boniface VIII. Dante became one of the six guild representatives who governed the city and, when the Pope made encroachments into Florentine politics with threats of excommunication and confiscation of possessions, Dante and two others were sent on a mission to Rome in 1301 to query the Pope about his plans.

Dante never returned to Florence. In a coup d'état, the Blacks gained power and took measures to eliminate the leaders of the Whites. When Dante chose not to return to face charges, he was sentenced to two years of exile and a large fine. This penalty was subsequently enlarged to permanent exile with the threat of being burned alive should he return to Florence. In very poignant lines in *The Paradiso* (Canto 17), Dante later described the painful existence of an exile:

> All that you held most dear you will put by
> and leave behind you; and this is the arrow
> the longbow of your exile first lets fly.
>
> You will come to learn how bitter as salt and stone
> is the bread of others, how hard the way that goes
> up and downstairs that never are your own.

As an exiled intellectual, Dante temporarily linked up with other exiled Whites and some Ghibellines; after becoming disillusioned with their plans, he wandered from town to town in Italy, finding temporary lodgings with a variety of patrons. His studies produced several treatises. *Il Convivio (The Banquet*, c. 1304–1307) was an extension of the autobiographical, philosophical elements of *La Vita Nuova*, plus an explanation of Dante's literary views. *De vulgari eloquentia (The Illustrious Vernacular)*, written in Latin during the same period, defends the use of Italian in serious literature and explores the role of the Italian writer in contemporary society. Later, the *Comedy* was written in vernacular Italian, leading to a broader audience and the promotion of cultural identity. Both *Convivio* and *De vulgari eloquentia* remained unfinished. A pamphlet, *Monarchia* (between 1308 and 1317), placed hope for healing Italy's afflictions and divisiveness in a clear separation of powers between church and state and the investiture of two powerful leaders, a secular emperor and a sacred pope. Crowned in 1308, the new emperor Henry VII began to unite Italy, giving possible substance to Dante's vision, but Florence rebuffed him and he died suddenly in 1313.

Work

All of the learning and living that underlay his early writing reasserted itself in the complex fabric of the *Comedy,* to which Dante devoted himself for the rest of his life, from 1312 until his death in 1321. Published before the completion of the whole work, the first two parts of Dante's *Comedy* were immediately recognized as part of a great work of literature. With it Dante hoped to gain an honorable return to his beloved Florence, but that did not happen. After finishing the last cantos of *The Paradiso,* he died in Ravenna and was buried there in 1321. Dante's masterpiece became known as *The Divine Comedy* in the sixteenth century.

Dante called his monumental work a comedy because it has a happy ending. The story is essentially a pilgrimage by a person named Dante through the three spiritual realms of the Catholic world—Hell, Purgatory, and Heaven—during the Easter season. Because of the importance of the Trinity in Christian theology, the number three plays a key role in Dante's elaborate design. Each of the major divisions of the work points to a person of the Trinity and contains 33 cantos: *The Inferno,* identified with God the Father and judgment, includes one additional canto as a general introduction; the salvific acts of the

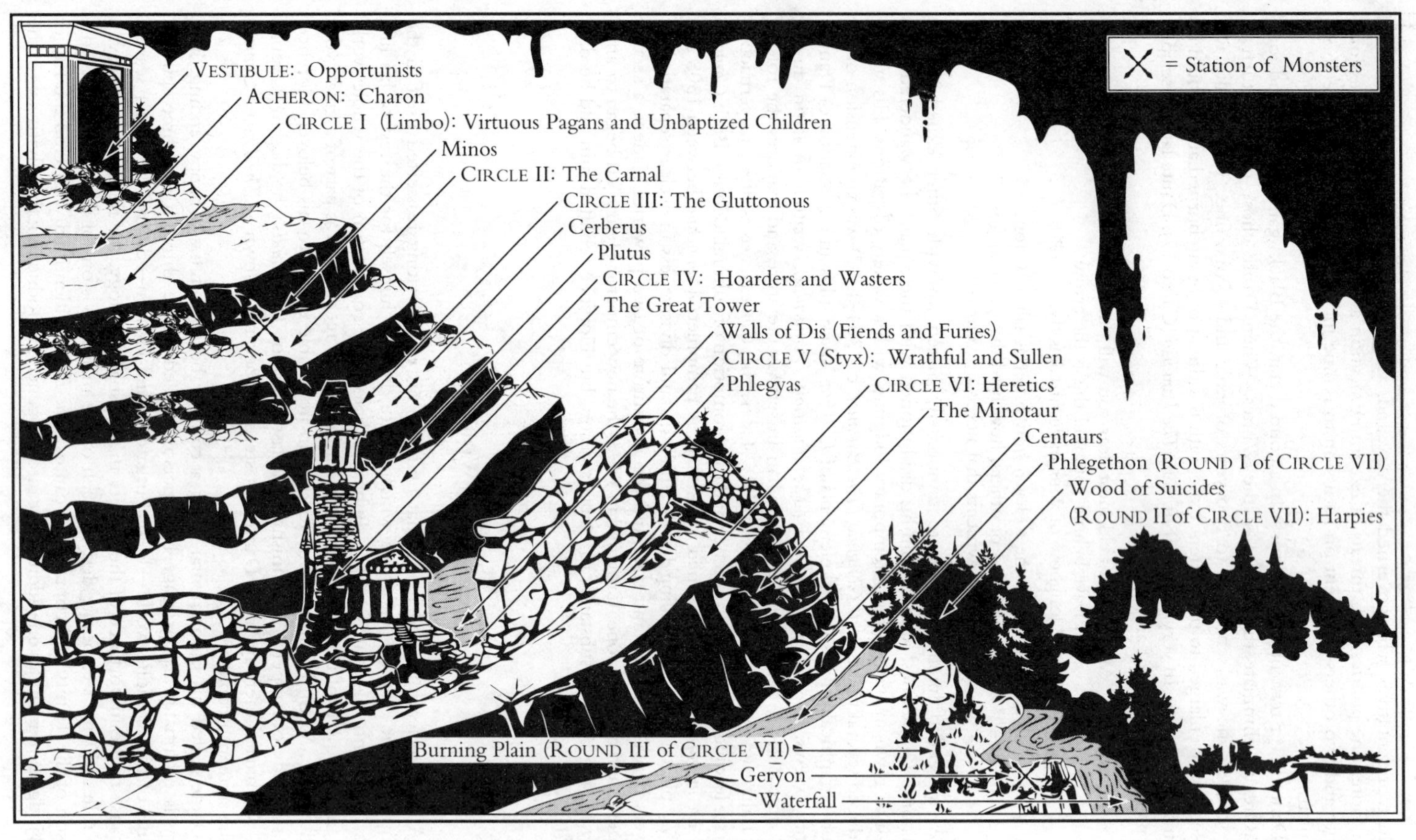
VESTIBULE: Opportunists
ACHERON: Charon
CIRCLE I (Limbo): Virtuous Pagans and Unbaptized Children
Minos
CIRCLE II: The Carnal
CIRCLE III: The Gluttonous
Cerberus
Plutus
CIRCLE IV: Hoarders and Wasters
The Great Tower
Walls of Dis (Fiends and Furies)
CIRCLE V (Styx): Wrathful and Sullen
Phlegyas
CIRCLE VI: Heretics
The Minotaur
Centaurs
Phlegethon (ROUND I of CIRCLE VII)
Wood of Suicides
(ROUND II of CIRCLE VII): Harpies
Burning Plain (ROUND III of CIRCLE VII)
Geryon
Waterfall
= Station of Monsters

THE FIRST SEVEN CIRCLES OF INFERNO

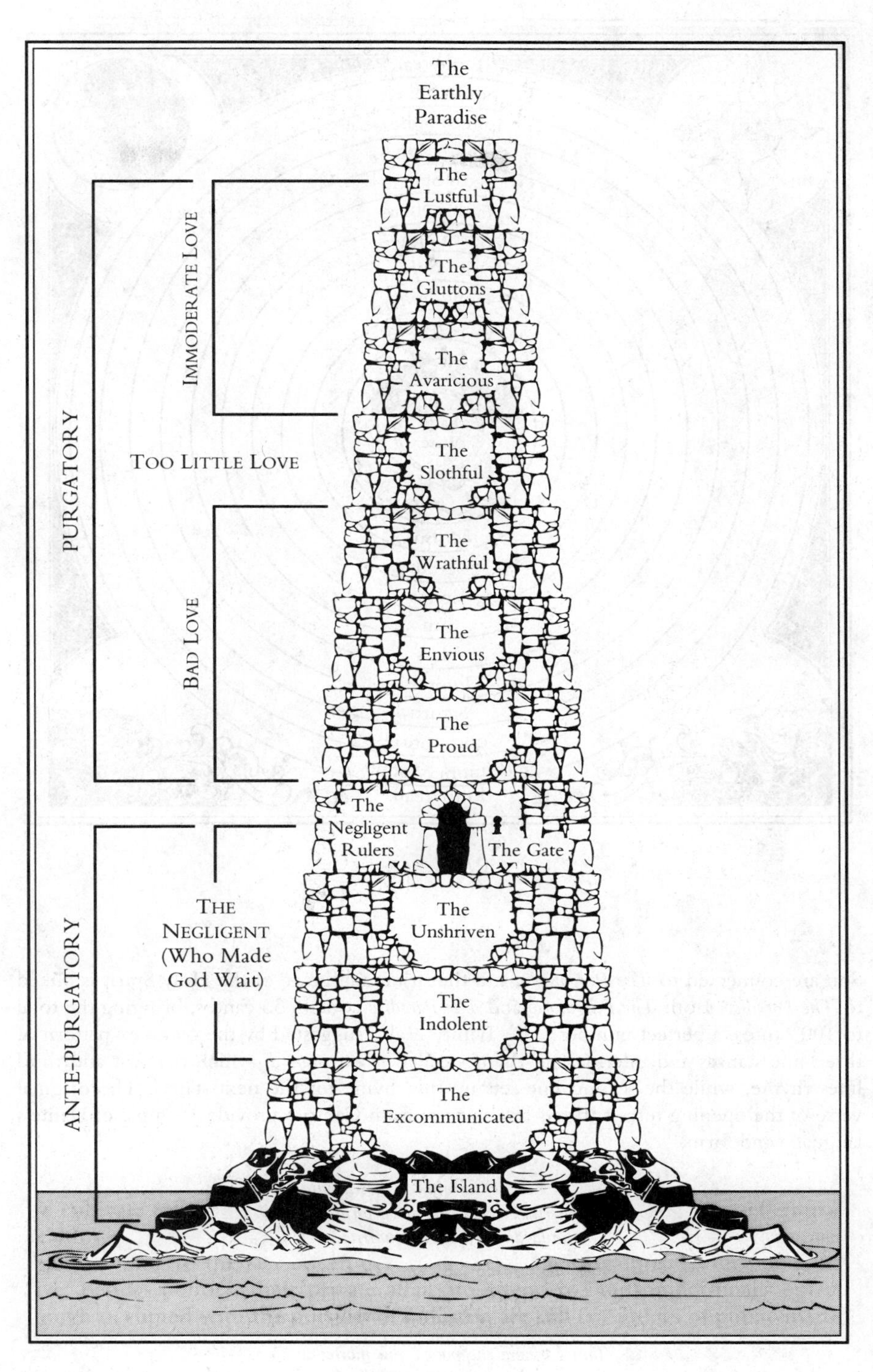
The Earthly Paradise
The Lustful
The Gluttons
The Avaricious
The Slothful
The Wrathful
The Envious
The Proud
The Negligent Rulers
The Gate
The Unshriven
The Indolent
The Excommunicated
The Island
PURGATORY
IMMODERATE LOVE
TOO LITTLE LOVE
BAD LOVE
ANTE-PURGATORY
THE NEGLIGENT (Who Made God Wait)

PURGATORY

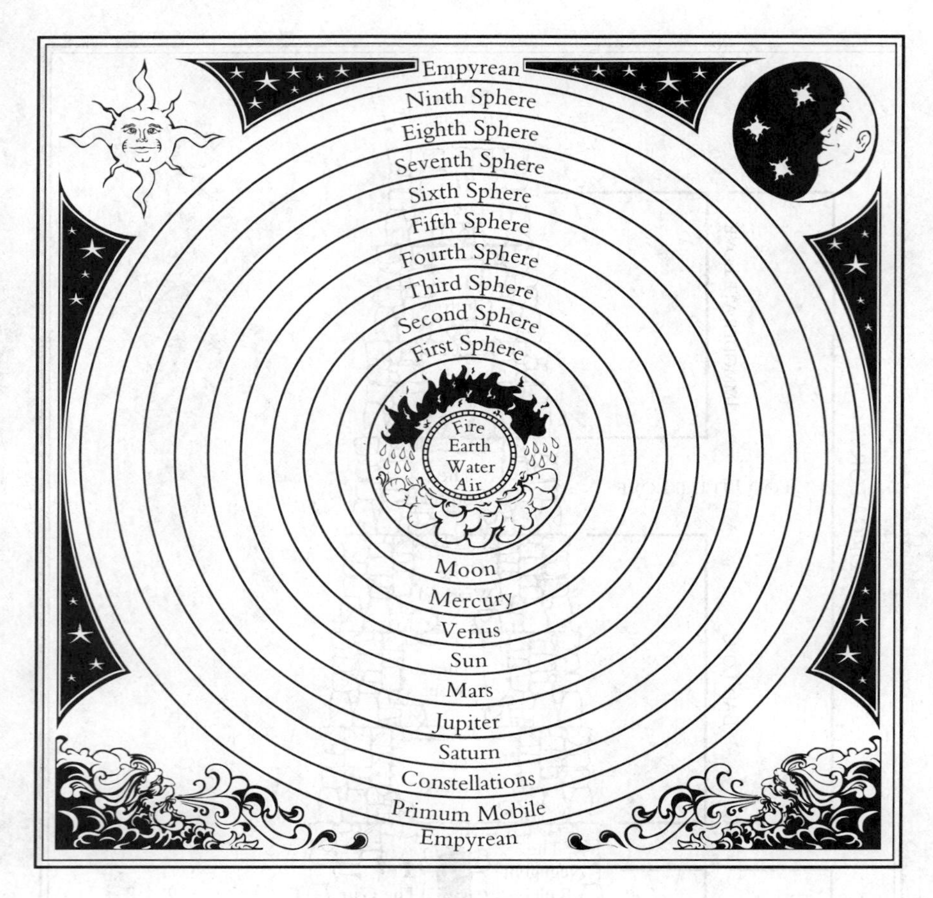

PARADISE

Son are connected to *The Purgatorio*; and the sustaining grace of the Holy Spirit is linked to *The Paradiso*. Both *The Purgatorio* and *The Paradiso* contain 33 cantos, bringing the total to 100 cantos, a perfect number. The Trinity is also suggested by the complex pattern of three-line stanzas and interlocking rhymes called *terza rima*, in which the first and third lines rhyme, while the second line sets up the rhyme for the next stanza. The original verse of the opening tercets (three-line stanzas) from Canto 1 provide a sample of Dante's language and form.

Nel mezzo del cammin di nostra vita
mi ritrovai per una selva oscura,
chè la diritta via era smarrita.

Ah quanto a dir qual era è cosa dura
esta selva selvaggia e aspra e forte
che nel pensier rinnova la paura!

Tant'è amara che poco è più morte;
ma per trattar del ben ch'io vi trovai,
dirò dell'altre cose ch' i' v'ho scorte.

Because Italian offers so many possibilities for rhyme, *terza rima* is nearly impossible to duplicate in Engish; our translation follows a modified version of this pattern. But the essential point about Dante's intricate construction of the work is that its complexity is a continual unfolding of God's own masterful plan for the world.

The poem begins on the evening of Maundy Thursday with Dante lost in the woods. At dawn on Good Friday, he fortunately meets Virgil, who serves as his guide through Hell, an enormous funnel-shaped region extending from the earth's surface deep into the center of the earth. It is divided into three major divisions and nine separate circles, beginning with the mildest kinds of sins at the top and descending into the worst. The first book takes us through Hell, and ends on Easter morning when Dante and Virgil arrive at Purgatory, which is a mountain on an island in the sea, divided into three areas, Ante-Purgatory, Purgatory proper, and the Earthly Paradise at the summit. Here Virgil's job as guide must end because Purgatory is as far as reason can carry the individual pilgrim; to advance further toward God, divine intervention of some kind is necessary. Beatrice, who sent Virgil to be Dante's guide on the first stage of his pilgrimage, takes over now and leads him through the three regions of Paradise: the seven planets of ancient astronomy, the circles of fixed stars, and the Empyrean or highest Heaven, which they witness at sunset on the Thursday after Easter.

Because sin is always more interesting to hear about than goodness, and because Dante's punishments are so imaginative, *The Inferno* is the most popular section of the work to a modern audience. Canto 1 begins with a rather commonplace statement about the pilgrim Dante who, at thirty-five years of age, has gone astray and found himself in a "dark wood," a different kind of beginning from those found in Homer's epics or Virgil's *Aeneid*, in which a grand theme is announced. As a very visual poet, Dante begins with what seems to be an ordinary situation in accordance with the manner of his narrator, who is a simplified, at times more naïve, version of himself. Dante's style, however, becomes more elevated as he progresses upward in *The Purgatorio* and *The Paradiso*. The literal level of the poem's meaning follows the dramatic adventures of this Dante as he journeys through the three realms, encountering various sinners and saints from the ancient world and contemporary Italy, learning from their lives, and progressing from confusion to spiritual illumination.

The first lines of *The Inferno*, however, begin to hint of another layer of meaning, symbolic or allegorical, because the pilgrim is at the age when questions traditionally arise about one's spiritual condition; a "dark wood" mirrors the inner confusion and fear people may experience when they reach mid-life. When Dante sees the sunrise and decides to climb the Mount of Joy where he confronts three symbolic animals, it is clear that Dante the poet is deliberately using symbolic language to indicate multiple levels of interpretation. The notes provided with the text assist modern readers to unravel Dante's complex creation, but they do not exhaust possible meanings of the many events.

The three animals that rebuff Dante represent the three major kinds of sins—incontinence, violence, and fraud—and also point to the three divisions of Hell. Enter Virgil, who explains that he has been sent to guide Dante through a descent into Hell and an ascent through Purgatory, where he will be replaced by Beatrice. Several reasons explain the choice of Virgil for a guide. Virgil sought to unify the Roman Empire with his great epic, even as Dante's poem was for all of Italy and not just for Florence. In addition, Virgil had written the *Fourth Eclogue,* which seemed to many Christians to predict the advent of a child Messiah and, in Book 4 of *The Aeneid*, he had described a descent into Hades, which qualified him as an appropriate guide.

In Canto 3, the two poets pass the Gate of Hell and view for the first time a scene depicting the principle used by Dante to punish sinners, *contra passo,* or symbolic retribution. The idea of fitting punishments to different sins makes Dante's Hell more just, more picturesque, and altogether different from most other pictures of Hell, where general horrors engulf the entire group of sinners. Because the wishy-washy opportunists and the cowardly took no moral stand in life for either good or evil, they are adrift in Hell. Regardless of our modern understanding of why people commit evil acts, Dante's view was consistent with medieval theology, which held that individuals choose sin and therefore can be awarded punishments as individuals, regardless of their family or social situations.

The first circle of Hell in Canto 4 is for Virtuous Pagans. As moderns we might sympathize with the likes of Homer, Horace, Ovid, and Lucan, but the medieval Christian view was clear on this point: Jesus alone was the gateway to Heaven. Thus the noble and virtuous pagans are held here at the threshold. The first souls guilty of carnal sin are found in Canto 5. Those who are led by their desires are blown about by the winds of desire. Dante's method of depicting sinners is to present appropriate examples who would be known to his readers and then to develop more complete portraits of just a few of them. He does not analyze the sin abstractly, but rather he vividly shows how people following their desires and yielding to temptation can drift into damnation, as is the case with the most famous couple in *The Divine Comedy*, Paolo and Francesca. Despite their sin, their story is told with a great deal of sensitivity and sympathy.

The first of several political prophecies about Florence is uttered in Canto 6 by the glutton Ciacco the Hog, who is buried in swill. In subsequent cantos, Dante forthrightly locates his political enemies in various circles of Hell. Cantos 10 and 11, for Heretics, serve as an intermediary locale between the upper Hell for sins of incontinence and the lower Hell for violence and fraud. After witnessing the instigators of war boiling in blood, we are shown the memorable wood of the suicides in Canto 13, where The Violent Against Themselves are punished and the souls are denied human form. Even though the Church considered suicide a sin, Pier delle Vigne's narrative can elicit sympathy. In Canto 15, Brunetto Latini, Dante's teacher and mentor, is also treated with delicacy and respect, despite the fact that the sin of homosexuality is acknowledged and punished with a burning rain. This canto is a reminder to the reader that Hell is filled with humans who might not appear to be evil, but who have hidden sins. With certain cases, however, Dante seems to be torn between the justice of a particular punishment and his sympathy with the vagaries of human nature; after all, most of us are a mixture of noble sentiments and carnal weaknesses.

In Canto 17, Virgil and Dante descend into the third section of Hell—for premeditated fraud—on the back of Geryon, a marvelous monster with the face of a man and a serpent's body. The eighth circle of Hell is divided into ten trenches, the Malebolge, with different kinds of sinners having to do with fraud. Dante's artistic genius is shown in the details of the punishments and their varieties. The Simoniacs are upside down in holes with their feet on fire. The fortune tellers and sorcerers walk backward with their heads turned backward. It is a little strange to find Ulysses (Odysseus), whom Homer describes as quick-witted and clever, as far down as Bolgia Eight (Canto 26), the place for evil counselors. But Italians traced their ancestry back to the Trojans, and Odysseus was the architect for the wooden horse, which led to the destruction of Troy. Hidden in a great flame, a proud Ulysses recounts his exploration of the Western ocean. His death by shipwreck on Purgatory Mountain is a symbolic statement that courage and intelligence alone cannot attain salvation.

The climax of *The Inferno* occurs in the last three cantos, when the poets reach the ninth circle of Hell. Here the sinners are so far from the warmth of God's love that they are frozen in a lake of ice, symbolic of the condition of their hearts. One of the lasting images of this section is Ugolino gnawing on the skull of Ruggieri in Canto 33, in which Ugolino tells their story of betrayal and infamy. The great pathos associated with the starvation of children makes this episode one of the most memorable in the entire poem. In the final canto we meet the master of evil himself, Satan, with his great flapping wings and a treacherous threesome in his mouths: Judas Iscariot, Brutus, and Cassius. For modern readers, Brutus and Cassius may not meet the same standard of evil as the betrayer of Jesus, nor does the portrait of Satan inspire fear.

From the beginning of *The Purgatorio*, there is a joyful, hopeful tone, totally different from the dark despair of *The Inferno*. Just as Dante the pilgrim learned about avoiding sin in *The Inferno*, he now learns about the virtues that result from purging the seven deadly sins on the seven ledges in the middle of Purgatory. These ledges plus Ante-Purgatory and the Earthly Paradise add up to nine. In the cantos we have selected, Dante and Virgil have been joined by Statius, a first-century Roman poet who, unlike Virgil, is redeemed by his faith and his purification in Purgatory. In Canto 27, the poets cross through a wall of fire, a multilayered symbol of transformation, into the Earthly Paradise, where Dante experiences freedom of action associated with being purged of sin. Virgil the virtuous pagan, having reached a place where he "can discern nothing further," gives his farewell speech. Cantos 28 and 29 show Dante learning about the Earthly Paradise. Finally in Canto 30 we are introduced to the epitome of beauty and virtue, the veiled Beatrice, who becomes Dante's next guide:

> My soul—such years had passed since last it saw
> that lady and stood trembling in her presence,
> stupefied by the power of holy awe—

Beatrice scolds Dante for lapsing into material desires, which is perhaps a confession by the poet of his own waywardness. After Dante has been bathed in the river Lethe, washing away all memory of sin, he is allowed to look at Beatrice without her veil and is blinded by the sight. His virtues are strengthened by drinking from the waters of the Eunoe and then he is ready to experience the celestial Paradise.

As the final section of *The Divine Comedy*, *The Paradiso* is a celebration of the starry heavens of an earth-centered cosmos, as understood by medieval astronomy. As Dante and Beatrice ascend from planet to planet, various redeemed souls provide scientific explanations for the heavenly bodies. Appropriate Christian doctrines are also discussed. The seven planets plus the circle of fixed stars and the *primum mobile* equal nine; the Empyrean or Heaven is the tenth, a symbol of unity and the totality of the universe. Our selection includes the last three cantos of *The Paradiso*, where the saints of the Catholic Church are arranged in a mystic white rose with God at its center.

Canto 32 identifies the thrones of the most blessed; Beatrice returns to her eternal throne and St. Bernard becomes Dante's final guide to a climactic, beatific vision. The final canto begins with a beautiful prayer to the Virgin, paying tribute to her loving qualities and asking her to intercede for Dante. The culminating vision of God represents a difficult task for the poet: to describe that which by definition transcends words themselves—that is, the ineffable. Dante's answer to this dilemma is to focus on the effect of the vision on the human witness, rather than to strain a series of adjectives in a direct description. The result of Dante's artistry is the experience of merging with the divine, the final and ultimate goal, after all, of the medieval pilgrim.

Translators of Dante face tremendous challenges; about his translation, John Ciardi says:

> One of the main sources of the tone of Dante's speech is his revolt from the Sicilian School of Elegance. Nothing would be more misleading than to say that Dante's language is simple. Overwhelmingly, however, it seeks to avoid elegance simply for the sake of elegance. And overwhelmingly it is a spoken tongue.
>
> I have labored therefore for something like idiomatic English in the present rendering.

The characteristics of Dante's Italian become the guidelines for any adequate rendering of *The Divine Comedy* into English.

Suggested Readings

A good biography of Dante is Monroe Sterns, *Dante: Poet of Love* (1965). A general introduction to Dante's life and works is Carlo Golino, *Dante Alighieri* (1979). A book connecting Dante to his age is K. Vossler, *Medieval Culture: An Introduction to Dante and His Times* (1929). Two works by Dorothy Sayers provide important background, *Introductory Papers on Dante* (1954) and *Further Papers on Dante* (1957). A variety of views on Dante's work can be found in John Freccero, ed., *Dante: A Collection of Critical Essays* (1965). Philosophical views of Dante are developed in Erich Auerbach, *Dante: Poet of the Secular World* (1961) and George Santayana, *Three Philosophical Poets* (1927).

The Divine Comedy

Translated by John Ciardi

The Inferno

Canto 1

The Dark Wood of Error: Midway in his allotted threescore years and ten, Dante comes to himself with a start and realizes that he has strayed from the True Way into the Dark Wood of Error (Worldliness). As soon as he has realized his loss, Dante lifts his eyes and sees the first light of the sunrise (the Sun is the Symbol of Divine Illumination) lighting the shoulders of a little hill (the Mount of Joy). It is the Easter Season, the time of resurrection, and the sun is in its equinoctial rebirth. This juxtaposition of joyous symbols fills Dante with hope and he sets out at once to climb directly up the Mount of Joy, but almost immediately his way is blocked by the Three Beasts of Worldliness: the Leopard of Malice and Fraud, the Lion of Violence and Ambition, and the She-Wolf of Incontinence. These beasts, and especially the She-Wolf, drive him back despairing into the darkness of error. But just as all seems lost, a figure appears to him. It is the shade of Virgil, Dante's symbol of Human Reason.

Virgil explains that he has been sent to lead Dante from error. There can, however, be no direct ascent past the beasts: the man who would escape them must go a longer and harder way. First he must descend through Hell (The Recognition of Sin), then he must ascend through Purgatory (The Renunciation of Sin), and only then may he reach the pinnacle of joy and come to the Light of God. Virgil offers to guide Dante, but only as far as Human Reason can go. Another guide (Beatrice, symbol of Divine Love) must take over for the final ascent, for Human Reason is self-limited. Dante submits himself joyously to Virgil's guidance and they move off.

Midway in our life's journey,[1] I went astray
  from the straight road and woke to find myself
  alone in a dark wood. How shall I say
what wood that was! I never saw so drear,
  so rank, so arduous a wilderness!
  Its very memory gives a shape to fear.
Death could scarce be more bitter than that place!
  But since it came to good, I will recount
  all that I found revealed there by God's grace.

---

[1]The biblical life span is threescore years and ten. The action opens in Dante's thirty-fifth year, i.e., 1300 C.E. [All notes to *The Divine Comedy* are the translator's.]

How I came to it I cannot rightly say, 10
so drugged and loose with sleep had I become
when I first wandered there from the True Way.
But at the far end of that valley of evil
whose maze had sapped my very heart with fear
I found myself before a little hill
and lifted up my eyes. Its shoulders glowed
already with the sweet rays of that planet[2]
whose virtue leads men straight on every road,
and the shining strengthened me against the fright
whose agony had wracked the lake of my heart 20
through all the terrors of that piteous night.
Just as a swimmer, who with his last breath
flounders ashore from perilous seas, might turn
to memorize the wide water of his death—
so did I turn, my soul still fugitive
from death's surviving image, to stare down
that pass that none had ever left alive.
And there I lay to rest from my heart's race
till calm and breath returned to me. Then rose
and pushed up that dead slope at such a pace 30
each footfall rose above the last.[3] And lo!
almost at the beginning of the rise
I faced a spotted Leopard, all tremor and flow
and gaudy pelt. And it would not pass, but stood
so blocking my every turn that time and again
I was on the verge of turning back to the wood.
This fell at the first widening of the dawn
as the sun was climbing Aries with those stars
that rode with him to light the new creation.[4]
Thus the holy hour and the sweet season 40
of commemoration did much to arm my fear
of that bright murderous beast with their good omen.
Yet not so much but what I shook with dread
at sight of a great Lion that broke upon me
raging with hunger, its enormous head

---

[2]The sun. Ptolemaic astronomers considered it a planet. It is also symbolic of God as He who lights man's way.

[3]The literal rendering would be: "So that the fixed foot was ever the lower." "Fixed" has often been translated "right" and an ingenious reasoning can support that reading, but a simpler explanation offers itself and seems more competent: Dante is saying that he climbed with such zeal and haste that every footfall carried him above the last despite the steepness of the climb. At a slow pace, on the other hand, the rear foot might be brought up only as far as the forward foot.

[4]The medieval tradition had it that the sun was in Aries at the time of the Creation. The significance of the astronomical and religious conjunction is an important part of Dante's intended allegory. It is just before dawn of Good Friday C.E. 1300 when he awakens in the Dark Wood. Thus his new life begins under Aries, the sign of creation, at dawn (rebirth), and in the Easter season (resurrection). Moreover the moon is full and the sun is in the equinox, conditions that did not fall together on any Friday of 1300. Dante is obviously constructing poetically the perfect Easter as a symbol of his new awakening.

held high as if to strike a mortal terror
into the very air. And down his track,
a She-Wolf drove upon me, a starved horror
ravening and wasted beyond all belief.[5]
She seemed a rack for avarice, gaunt and craving. 50
Oh many the souls she has brought to endless grief!
She brought such heaviness upon my spirit
at sight of her savagery and desperation,
I died from every hope of that high summit.
And like a miser—eager in acquisition
but desperate in self-reproach when Fortune's wheel
turns to the hour of his loss—all tears and attrition
I wavered back; and still the beast pursued,
forcing herself against me bit by bit
till I slid back into the sunless wood. 60
And as I fell to my soul's ruin, a presence
gathered before me on the discolored air,
the figure of one who seemed hoarse from long silence.
At sight of him in that friendless waste I cried:
"Have pity on me, whatever thing you are,
whether shade or living man." And it replied:
"Not man, though man I once was, and my blood
was Lombard, both my parents Mantuan.
I was born, though late, *sub Julio,*[6] and bred
in Rome under Augustus in the noon 70
of the false and lying gods. I was a poet
and sang of old Anchises' noble son[7]
who came to Rome after the burning of Troy.
But you—why do *you* return to these distresses
instead of climbing that shining Mount of Joy
which is the seat and first cause of man's bliss?"
"And are you then that Virgil and that fountain
of purest speech?" My voice grew tremulous:
"Glory and light of poets! now may that zeal
and love's apprenticeship that I poured out 80
on your heroic verses serve me well!
For you are my true master and first author,
the sole maker from whom I drew the breath
of that sweet style whose measures have brought me honor.
See there, immortal sage, the beast I flee.
For my soul's salvation, I beg you, guard me from her,
for she has struck a mortal tremor through me."
And he replied, seeing my soul in tears:
"He must go by another way who would escape
this wilderness, for that mad beast that fleers 90

---

[5]These three beasts undoubtedly are taken from Jeremiah 5:6. Many additional and incidental interpretations have been advanced for them, but the central interpretation must remain as noted. They foreshadow the three divisions of Hell (incontinence, violence, and fraud) which Virgil explains at length in Canto 11, 16–111.

[6]In the reign of Julius Caesar.

[7]Aeneas.

before you there, suffers no man to pass.
  She tracks down all, kills all, and knows no glut,
  but, feeding, she grows hungrier than she was.
She mates with any beast, and will mate with more
  before the Greyhound[8] comes to hunt her down.
  He will not feed on lands nor loot, but honor
and love and wisdom will make straight his way.
  He will rise between Feltro and Feltro, and in him
  shall be the resurrection and new day
of that sad Italy for which Nisus died, 100
  and Turnus, and Euryalus, and the maid Camilla.[9]
  He shall hunt her through every nation of sick pride
till she is driven back forever to Hell
  whence Envy first released her on the world.
  Therefore, for your own good, I think it well
you follow me and I will be your guide
  and lead you forth through an eternal place.
  There you shall see the ancient spirits tried
in endless pain, and hear their lamentation
  as each bemoans the second death[10] of souls. 110
  Next you shall see upon a burning mountain
souls in fire and yet content in fire,
  knowing that whensoever it may be
  they yet will mount into the blessed choir.
To which, if it is still your wish to climb,
  a worthier spirit shall be sent to guide you.
  With her shall I leave you, for the King of Time,
who reigns on high, forbids me to come there
  since, living, I rebelled against his law.[11]
  He rules the waters and the land and air 120
and there holds court, his city and his throne.
  Oh blessed are they he chooses!" And I to him:
  "Poet, by that God to you unknown,
lead me this way. Beyond this present ill
  and worse to dread, lead me to Peter's gate[12]
  and be my guide through the sad halls of Hell."
And he then: "Follow." And he moved ahead
in silence, and I followed where he led.

---

[8]Almost certainly refers to Can Grande della Scala (1290–1329), great Italian leader born in Verona, which lies between the towns of Feltre and Montefeltro.

[9]All were killed in the war between the Trojans and the Latians when, according to legend, Aeneas led the survivors of Troy into Italy. Nisus and Euryalus (*Aeneid* 9) were Trojan comrades-in-arms who died together. Camilla (*Aeneid* 11) was the daughter of the Latian king and one of the warrior women. She was killed in a horse charge against the Trojans after displaying great gallantry. Turnus (*Aeneid* 12) was killed by Aeneas in a duel.

[10]Damnation. "This is the second death, even the lake of fire" (Revelation 20:14).

[11]Salvation is only through Christ in Dante's theology. Virgil lived and died before the establishment of Christ's teachings in Rome, and cannot therefore enter Heaven.

[12]The gate of Purgatory. (*The Purgatorio* 9, 76ff.) The gate is guarded by an angel with a gleaming sword. The angel is Peter's vicar (Peter, the first Pope, symbolized all Popes, Christ's vicar on earth) and is entrusted with the two great keys. Some commentators argue that this is the gate of Paradise, but Dante mentions no gate beyond this one in his ascent to Heaven. It should be remembered, too, that those who pass the gate of Purgatory have effectively entered Heaven.

Canto 2

The Descent: It is evening of the first day (Friday). Dante is following Virgil and finds himself tired and despairing. How can he be worthy of such a vision as Virgil has described? He hesitates and seems about to abandon his first purpose.

To comfort him Virgil explains how Beatrice descended to him in Limbo and told him of her concern for Dante. It is she, the symbol of Divine Love, who sends Virgil to lead Dante from error. She has come into Hell itself on this errand, for Dante cannot come to Divine Love unaided; Reason must lead him. Moreoever Beatrice has been sent with the prayers of the Virgin Mary (Compassion), and of Saint Lucia (Divine Light). Rachel (the Contemplative Life) also figures in the heavenly scene which Virgil recounts.

Virgil explains all this and reproaches Dante: how can he hesitate longer when such heavenly powers are concerned for him, and Virgil himself has promised to lead him safely?

Dante understands at once that such forces cannot fail him, and his spirits rise in joyous anticipation.

The light was departing. The brown air drew down
all the earth's creatures, calling them to rest
from their day-roving, as I, one man alone,
prepared myself to face the double war
of the journey and the pity, which memory
shall here set down, nor hesitate, nor err.
O Muses! O High Genius! Be my aid!
O Memory, recorder of the vision,
here shall your true nobility be displayed!
Thus I began: "Poet, you who must guide me, 10
before you trust me to that arduous passage,
look to me and look through me—can I be worthy?
You sang how the father of Sylvius,[13] while still
in corruptible flesh won to that other world,
crossing with mortal sense the immortal sill.
But if the Adversary of all Evil
weighing his consequence and who and what
should issue from him, treated him so well—
that cannot seem unfitting to thinking men,
since he was chosen father of Mother Rome 20
and of her Empire by God's will and token.
Both, to speak strictly, were founded and foreknown
as the established Seat of Holiness
for the successors of Great Peter's throne.

[13] Aeneas. Lines 13–30 are a fair example of the way in which Dante absorbed pagan themes into his Catholicism. According to Virgil, Aeneas is the son of mortal Anchises and of Venus. Venus, in her son's interest, secures a prophecy and a promise from Jove to the effect that Aeneas is to found a royal line that shall rule the world. After the burning of Troy, Aeneas is directed by various signs to sail for the Latian lands (Italy) where his destiny awaits him. After many misadventures, he is compelled (like Dante) to descend to the underworld of the dead. There he finds his father's shade, and there he is shown the shades of the great kings that are to stem from him (*Aeneid* 6, 921ff.). Among them are Romulus, Julius Caesar, and Augustus Caesar. The full glory of the Roman Empire is also foreshadowed to him. Dante, however, continues the Virgilian theme and includes in the predestination not only the Roman Empire but the Holy Roman Empire and its Church. Thus what Virgil presented as an arrangement of Jove, a concession to the son of Venus, becomes part of the divine scheme of the Catholic God, and Aeneas is cast as a direct forerunner of Peter and Paul.

In that quest, which your verses celebrate,
he learned those mysteries from which arose
his victory and Rome's apostolate.
There later came the chosen vessel, Paul,
bearing the confirmation of that Faith
which is the one true door to life eternal. 30
But I—how should I dare? By whose permission?
I am not Aeneas. *I* am not Paul.
Who could believe me worthy of the vision?
How, then, may I presume to this high quest
and not fear my own brashness? You are wise
and will grasp what my poor words can but suggest."
As one who unwills what he wills, will stay
strong purposes with feeble second thoughts
until he spells all his first zeal away—
so I hung back and balked on that dim coast 40
till thinking had worn out my enterprise,
so stout at starting and so early lost.
"I understand from your words and the look in your eyes,"
that shadow of magnificence answered me,
"your soul is sunken in that cowardice
that bears down many men, turning their course
and resolution by imagined perils,
as his own shadow turns the frightened horse.
To free you of this dread I will tell you all
of why I came to you and what I heard 50
when first I pitied you. I was a soul
among the souls of Limbo,[14] when a Lady
so blessed and so beautiful, I prayed her
to order and command my will, called to me.
Her eyes were kindled from the lamps of Heaven.
Her voice reached through me, tender, sweet, and low.
An angel's voice, a music of its own:
'O gracious Mantuan whose melodies
live in earth's memory and shall live on
till the last motion ceases in the skies, 60
my dearest friend, and fortune's foe, has strayed
onto a friendless shore and stands beset
by such distresses that he turns afraid
from the True Way, and news of him in Heaven
rumors my dread he is already lost.
I come, afraid that I am too-late risen.
Fly to him and with your high counsel, pity,
and with whatever need be for his good
and soul's salvation, help him, and solace me.
It is I, Beatrice, who send you to him. 70
I come from the blessed height for which I yearn.
Love called me here. When amid Seraphim

[14]See Canto 4, lines 31–45, where Virgil explains his state in Hell.

I stand again before my Lord, your praises
shall sound in Heaven.' She paused, and I began:
'O Lady of that only grace that raises
feeble mankind within its mortal cycle
above all other works God's will has placed
within the heaven of the smallest circle;[15]
so welcome is your command that to my sense,
were it already fulfilled, it would yet seem tardy. 80
I understand, and am all obedience.
But tell me how you dare to venture thus
so far from the wide heaven of your joy
to which your thoughts yearn back from this abyss.'
'Since what you ask,' she answered me, 'probes near
the root of all, I will say briefly only
how I have come through Hell's pit without fear.
Know then, O waiting and compassionate soul,
that is to fear which has the power to harm,
and nothing else is fearful even in Hell. 90
I am so made by God's all-seeing mercy
your anguish does not touch me, and the flame
of this great burning has no power upon me.
There is a Lady in Heaven so concerned
for him I send you to, that for her sake
the strict decree is broken. She has turned
and called Lucia[16] to her wish and mercy
saying: "Thy faithful one is sorely pressed;
in his distresses I commend him to thee."
Lucia, that soul of light and foe of all 100
cruelty, rose and came to me at once
where I was sitting with the ancient Rachel,[17]
saying to me: "Beatrice, true praise of God,
why dost thou not help him who loved thee so
that for thy sake he left the vulgar crowd?
Dost thou not hear his cries? Canst thou not see
the death he wrestles with beside that river
no ocean can surpass for rage and fury?"
No soul of earth was ever as rapt to seek
its good or flee its injury as I was— 110
when I had heard my sweet Lucia speak—

---

[15]The moon. "Heaven" here is used in its astronomical sense. All within that circle is the earth. According to the Ptolemaic system the earth was the center of creation and was surrounded by nine heavenly spheres (nine heavens) concentrically placed around it. The moon was the first of these, and therefore the smallest. A cross section of this universe could be represented by drawing nine concentric circles (at varying distances about the earth as a center). Going outward from the center these circles would indicate, in order, the spheres of: the Moon, Mercury, Venus, the Sun, Mars, Jupiter, Saturn, the Fixed Stars, and the Primum Mobile. Beyond the Primum Mobile lies the Empyrean.

[16]Allegorically she represents Divine Light. Her name in Italian inevitably suggests *luce* (light), and she is the patron saint of eyesight.

[17]Represents the Contemplative Life.

to descend from Heaven and my blessed seat
  to you, laying my trust in that high speech
  that honors you and all who honor it.'
She spoke and turned away to hide a tear
  that, shining, urged me faster. So I came
  and freed you from the beast that drove you there,
blocking the near way to the Heavenly Height.
  And now what ails you? Why do you lag? Why
  this heartsick hesitation and pale fright 120
when three such blessed Ladies lean from Heaven
  in their concern for you and my own pledge
  of the great good that waits you has been given?"
As flowerlets drooped and puckered in the night
  turn up to the returning sun and spread
  their petals wide on his new warmth and light—
just so my wilted spirits rose again
  and such a heat of zeal surged through my veins
  that I was born anew. Thus I began:
"Blesséd be that Lady of infinite pity, 130
  and blesséd be thy taxed and courteous spirit
  that came so promptly on the word she gave thee.
Thy words have moved my heart to its first purpose.
  My Guide! My Lord! My Master! Now lead on:
  one will shall serve the two of us in this."
He turned when I had spoken, and at his back
I entered on that hard and perilous track.

Canto 3

The Vestibule of Hell—The Opportunists: The Poets pass the Gate of Hell and are immediately assailed by cries of anguish. Dante sees the first of the souls in torment. They are the Opportunists, those souls who in life were neither for good nor evil but only for themselves. Mixed with them are those outcasts who took no sides in the Rebellion of the Angels. They are neither in Hell nor out of it. Eternally unclassified, they race round and round pursuing a wavering banner that runs forever before them through the dirty air; and as they run they are pursued by swarms of wasps and hornets, who sting them and produce a constant flow of blood and putrid matter which trickles down the bodies of the sinners and is feasted upon by loathsome worms and maggots who coat the ground.

The law of Dante's Hell is the law of symbolic retribution. As they sinned so are they punished. They took no sides, therefore they are given no place. As they pursued the ever-shifting illusion of their own advantage, changing their courses with every changing wind, so they pursue eternally an elusive, ever-shifting banner. As their sin was a darkness, so they move in darkness. As their own guilty conscience pursued them, so they are pursued by swarms of wasps and hornets. And as their actions were a moral filth, so they run eternally through the filth of worms and maggots which they themselves feed.

Dante recognizes several, among them Pope Celestine V, but without delaying to speak to any of these souls, the Poets move on to Acheron, the first of the rivers of Hell. Here the newly arrived souls of the damned gather and wait for monstrous Charon to ferry them over to punishment. Charon recognizes Dante as a living man and angrily refuses him passage. Virgil forces Charon to serve them, but Dante swoons with terror, and does not reawaken until he is on the other side.

I AM THE WAY INTO THE CITY OF WOE.
  I AM THE WAY TO A FORSAKEN PEOPLE.
  I AM THE WAY INTO ETERNAL SORROW.

SACRED JUSTICE MOVED MY ARCHITECT.
I WAS RAISED HERE BY DIVINE OMNIPOTENCE,
PRIMORDIAL LOVE AND ULTIMATE INTELLECT.
ONLY THOSE ELEMENTS TIME CANNOT WEAR[18]
WERE MADE BEFORE ME, AND BEYOND TIME I STAND.[19]
ABANDON ALL HOPE YE WHO ENTER HERE.[20]
These mysteries I read cut into stone 10
above a gate. And turning I said: "Master,
what is the meaning of this harsh inscription?"
And he then as initiate to novice:
"Here must you put by all division of spirit
and gather your soul against all cowardice.
This is the place I told you to expect.
Here you shall pass among the fallen people,
souls who have lost the good of intellect."
So saying, he put forth his hand to me,
and with a gentle and encouraging smile 20
he led me through the gate of mystery.
Here sighs and cries and wails coiled and recoiled
on the starless air, spilling my soul to tears.
A confusion of tongues and monstrous accents toiled
in pain and anger. Voices hoarse and shrill
and sounds of blows, all intermingled, raised
tumult and pandemonium that still
whirls on the air forever dirty with it
as if a whirlwind sucked at sand. And I,
holding my head in horror, cried: "Sweet Spirit, 30
what souls are these who run through this black haze?"
And he to me: "These are the nearly soulless
whose lives concluded neither blame nor praise.
They are mixed here with that despicable corps
of angels who were neither for God nor Satan,
but only for themselves. The High Creator
scourged them from Heaven for its perfect beauty,
and Hell will not receive them since the wicked
might feel some glory over them." And I:
"Master, what gnaws at them so hideously 40
their lamentation stuns the very air?"
"They have no hope of death," he answered me,
"and in their blind and unattaining state
their miserable lives have sunk so low
that they must envy every other fate.
No word of them survives their living season.
Mercy and Justice deny them even a name.
Let us not speak of them: look, and pass on."

---

[18]The Angels, the Empyrean, and the First Matter are the elements time cannot wear, for they will last to all time. Man, however, in his mortal state, is not eternal. The Gate of Hell, therefore, was created before man.

[19]So odious is sin to God that there can be no end to its just punishment.

[20]The admonition, of course, is to the damned and not to those who come on Heaven-sent errands.

I saw a banner there upon the mist.
  Circling and circling, it seemed to scorn all pause. 50
  So it ran on, and still behind it pressed
a never-ending rout of souls in pain.
  I had not thought death had undone so many
  as passed before me in that mournful train.
And some I knew among them; last of all
  I recognized the shadow of that soul
  who, in his cowardice, made the Great Denial.[21]
At once I understood for certain: these
  were of that retrograde and faithless crew
  hateful to God and to His enemies. 60
These wretches never born and never dead
  ran naked in a swarm of wasps and hornets
  that goaded them the more the more they fled,
and made their faces stream with bloody gouts
  of pus and tears that dribbled to their feet
  to be swallowed there by loathsome worms and maggots.
Then looking onward I made out a throng
  assembled on the beach of a wide river,
  whereupon I turned to him: "Master, I long
to know what souls these are, and what strange usage 70
  makes them as eager to cross as they seem to be
  in this infected light." At which the Sage:
"All this shall be made known to you when we stand
  on the joyless beach of Acheron." And I
  cast down my eyes, sensing a reprimand
in what he said, and so walked at his side
  in silence and ashamed until we came
  through the dead cavern to that sunless tide.
There, steering toward us in an ancient ferry
  came an old man[22] with a white bush of hair, 80
  bellowing: "Woe to you depraved souls! Bury
here and forever all hope of Paradise:
  I come to lead you to the other shore,
  into eternal dark, into fire and ice.
And you who are living yet, I say begone
  from these who are dead." But when he saw me stand
  against his violence he began again:

[21] This is almost certainly intended to be Celestine V, who became Pope in 1294. He was a man of saintly life, but allowed himself to be convinced by a priest named Benedetto that his soul was in danger since no man could live in the world without being damned. In fear for his soul he withdrew from all worldly affairs and renounced the papacy. Benedetto promptly assumed the mantle himself and became Boniface VIII, a Pope who became for Dante a symbol of all the worst corruptions of the church. Dante also blamed Boniface and his intrigues for many of the evils that befell Florence. We shall learn in Canto 19 that the fires of Hell are waiting for Boniface in the pit of the Simoniacs, and further evidence of his corruption is found in Canto 27. Celestine's great guilt is that his cowardice (in selfish terror for his own welfare) served as the door through which so much evil entered the church.

[22] Charon. He is the ferryman of dead souls across the Acheron in all classical mythology.

"By other windings and by other steerage
  shall you cross to that other shore. Not here! Not here!
  A lighter craft than mine must give you passage."[23] 90
And my Guide to him: "Charon, bite back your spleen:
  this has been willed where what is willed must be,
  and is not yours to ask what it may mean."
The steersman of that marsh of ruined souls,
  who wore a wheel of flame around each eye,
  stifled the rage that shook his woolly jowls.
But those unmanned and naked spirits there
  turned pale with fear and their teeth began to chatter
  at sound of his crude bellow. In despair
they blasphemed God,[24] their parents, their time on earth, 100
  the race of Adam, and the day and the hour
  and the place and the seed and the womb that gave them birth.
But all together they drew to that grim shore
  where all must come who lose the fear of God.
  Weeping and cursing they come for evermore,
and demon Charon with eyes like burning coals
  herds them in, and with a whistling oar
  flails on the stragglers to his wake of souls.
As leaves in autumn loosen and stream down
  until the branch stands bare above its tatters 110
  spread on the rustling ground, so one by one
the evil seed of Adam in its Fall
  cast themselves, at his signal, from the shore
  and streamed away like birds who hear their call.
So they are gone over that shadowy water,
  and always before they reach the other shore
  a new noise stirs on this, and new throngs gather.
"My son," the courteous Master said to me,
  "all who die in the shadow of God's wrath
  converge to this from every clime and country. 120
And all pass over eagerly, for here
  Divine Justice transforms and spurs them so
  their dread turns wish: they yearn for what they fear.[25]
No soul in Grace comes ever to this crossing;
  therefore if Charon rages at your presence
  you will understand the reason for his cursing."
When he had spoken, all the twilight country
  shook so violently, the terror of it
  bathes me with sweat even in memory:

---

[23]Charon recognizes Dante not only as a living man but as a soul in grace, and knows, therefore, that the Internal Ferry was not intended for him. He is probably referring to the fact that souls destined for Purgatory and Heaven assemble not at his ferry point, but on the banks of the Tiber, from which they are transported by an Angel.

[24]The souls of the damned are not permitted to repent, for repentance is a divine grace.

[25]Hell (allegorically Sin) is what the souls of the damned really wish for. Hell is their actual and deliberate choice, for divine grace is denied to none who wish for it in their hearts. The damned must, in fact, deliberately harden their hearts to God in order to become damned. Christ's grace is sufficient to save all who wish for it.

the tear-soaked ground gave out a sigh of wind 130
  that spewed itself in flame on a red sky,
  and all my shuttered senses left me. Blind,
like one whom sleep comes over in a swoon,
I stumbled into darkness and went down.[26]

Canto 4

Circle One: Limbo—The Virtuous Pagans: Dante wakes to find himself across Acheron. The Poets are now on the brink of Hell itself, which Dante conceives as a great funnel-shaped cave lying below the northern hemisphere with its bottom point at the earth's center. Around this great circular depression runs a series of ledges, each of which Dante calls a Circle. Each circle is assigned to the punishment of one category of sin.

As soon as Dante's strength returns, the Poets begin to cross the First Circle. Here they find the Virtuous Pagans. They were born without the light of Christ's revelation, and, therefore, they cannot come into the light of God, but they are not tormented. Their only pain is that they have no hope.

Ahead of them Dante sights a great dome of light, and a voice trumpets through the darkness welcoming Virgil back, for this is his eternal place in Hell. Immediately the great Poets of all time appear—Homer, Horace, Ovid, and Lucan. They greet Virgil, and they make Dante a sixth in their company.

With them Dante enters the Citadel of Human Reason and sees before his eyes the Master Souls of Pagan Antiquity gathered on a green, and illuminated by the radiance of Human Reason. This is the highest state man can achieve without God, and the glory of it dazzles Dante, but he knows also that it is nothing compared to the glory of God.

A monstrous clap of thunder broke apart
  the swoon that stuffed my head; like one awakened
  by violent hands, I leaped up with a start.
And having risen; rested and renewed,
  I studied out the landmarks of the gloom
  to find my bearings there as best I could.
And I found I stood on the very brink of the valley
  called the Dolorous Abyss, the desolate chasm
  where rolls the thunder of Hell's eternal cry,
so depthless-deep and nebulous and dim 10
  that stare as I might into its frightful pit
  it gave me back no feature and no bottom.
Death-pale,[27] the Poet spoke: "Now let us go
  into the blind world waiting here below us.
  I will lead the way and you shall follow."
And I, sick with alarm at his new pallor,
  cried out, "How can I go this way when you
  who are my strength in doubt turn pale with terror?"

---

[26]This device (repeated at the end of Canto 5) serves a double purpose. The first is technical: Dante uses it to cover a transition. We are never told how he crossed Acheron, for that would involve certain narrative matters he can better deal with when he crosses Styx in Canto 7. The second is to provide a point of departure for a theme that is carried through the entire descent: the theme of Dante's emotional reaction to Hell. These two swoons early in the descent show him most susceptible to the grief about him. As he descends, pity leaves him, and he even goes so far as to add to the torments of one sinner. The allegory is clear: we must harden ourselves against every sympathy for sin.

[27]Virgil is most likely affected here by the return to his own place in Hell. "The pain of these below" then (line 19) would be the pain of his own group in Limbo (the Virtuous Pagans) rather than the total of Hell's suffering.

And he: "The pain of these below us here,
drains the color from my face for pity,
and leaves this pallor you mistake for fear.
Now let us go, for a long road awaits us."
So he entered and so he led me in
to the first circle and ledge of the abyss.
No tortured wailing rose to greet us here
but sounds of sighing rose from every side,
sending a tremor through the timeless air,
a grief breathed out of untormented sadness,
the passive state of those who dwelled apart,
men, women, children—a dim and endless congress.
And the Master said to me: "You do not question
what souls these are that suffer here before you?
I wish you to know before you travel on
that these were sinless. And still their merits fail,
for they lacked Baptism's grace, which is the door
of the true faith *you* were born to. Their birth fell
before the age of the Christian mysteries,
and so they did not worship God's Trinity
in fullest duty. I am one of these.
For such defects are we lost, though spared the fire
and suffering Hell in one affliction only:
that without hope we live on in desire."
I thought how many worthy souls there were
suspended in that Limbo, and a weight
closed on my heart for what the noblest suffer.
"Instruct me, Master and most noble Sir,"
I prayed him then, "better to understand
the perfect creed that conquers every error:
has any, by his own or another's merit,
gone ever from this place to blessedness?"
He sensed my inner question and answered it:
"I was still new to this estate of tears
when a Mighty One[28] descended here among us,
crowned with the sign of His victorious years.
He took from us the shade of our first parent,[29]
of Abel, his pure son, of ancient Noah,
of Moses, the bringer of law, the obedient.
Father Abraham, David the King,
Israel[30] with his father and his children,
Rachel,[31] the holy vessel of His blessing,
and many more He chose for elevation
among the elect. And before these, you must know,
no human soul had ever won salvation."

[28] Christ. His name is never directly uttered in Hell. *Descended here:* The legend of the Harrowing of Hell is apocryphal. It is based on I Peter 3:19: "He went and preached unto the spirits in prison." The legend is that Christ in the glory of His resurrection descended into Limbo and took with Him to Heaven the first human souls to be saved. The event would, accordingly, have occurred in C.E. 33 or 34. Virgil died in 19 B.C.E.

[29] Adam.

[30] Another name for Jacob; his father was Isaac.

[31] Wife of Jacob.

We had not paused as he spoke, but held our road
and passed meanwhile beyond a press of souls
crowded about like trees in a thick wood.
And we had not traveled far from where I woke
when I made out a radiance before us
that struck away a hemisphere of dark.
We were still some distance back in the long night, 70
yet near enough that I half-saw, half-sensed,
what quality of souls lived in that light.
"O ornament of wisdom and of art,
what souls are these whose merit lights their way
even in Hell. What joy sets them apart?"
And he to me: "The signature of honor
they left on earth is recognized in Heaven
and wins them ease in Hell out of God's favor."
And as he spoke a voice rang on the air:
"Honor the Prince of Poets; the soul and glory 80
that went from us returns. He is here! He is here!"
The cry ceased and the echo passed from hearing;
I saw four mighty presences come toward us
with neither joy nor sorrow in their bearing.
"Note well," my Master said as they came on,
"that soul that leads the rest with sword in hand
as if he were their captain and champion.
It is Homer, singing master of the earth.
Next after him is Horace, the satirist,
Ovid is third, and Lucan is the fourth. 90
Since all of these have part in the high name
the voice proclaimed, calling me Prince of Poets,
the honor that they do me honors them."
So I saw gathered at the edge of light
the masters of that highest school whose song
outsoars all others like an eagle's flight.
And after they had talked together a while,
they turned and welcomed me most graciously,
at which I saw my approving Master smile.
And they honored me far beyond courtesy, 100
for they included me in their own number,
making me sixth in that high company.
So we moved toward the light, and as we passed
we spoke of things as well omitted here
as it was sweet to touch on there. At last
we reached the base of a great Citadel
circled by seven towering battlements
and by a sweet brook flowing round them all.[32]

---

[32]The most likely allegory is that the Citadel represents philosophy (that is, human reason without the light of God) surrounded by seven walls that represent the seven liberal arts, or the seven sciences, or the seven virtues. Note that Human Reason makes a light of its own, but that it is a light in darkness and forever separated from the glory of God's light. The *sweet brook flowing* round them all has been interpreted in many ways. Clearly fundamental, however, is the fact that it divides those in the Citadel (those who wish to know) from those in the outer darkness.

This we passed over as if it were firm ground.[33]
Through seven gates I entered with those sages 110
and came to a green meadow blooming round.
There with a solemn and majestic poise
stood many people gathered in the light,
speaking infrequently and with muted voice.
Past that enameled green we six withdrew
into a luminous and open height
from which each soul among them stood in view.
And there directly before me on the green
the master souls of time were shown to me.
I glory in the glory I have seen![34] 120
Electra stood in a great company
among whom I saw Hector and Aeneas
and Caesar in armor with his falcon's eye.
I saw Camilla, and the Queen Amazon
across the field. I saw the Latian King
seated there with his daughter by his throne.
And the good Brutus who overthrew the Tarquin:
Lucrezia, Julia, Marcia, and Cornelia;
and, by himself apart, the Saladin.
And raising my eyes a little I saw on high 130
Aristotle, the master of those who know,
ringed by the great souls of philosophy.
All wait upon him for their honor and his.
I saw Socrates and Plato at his side
before all others there. Democritus

---

[33]Since Dante still has his body, and since all others in Hell are incorporeal shades, there is a recurring narrative problem in *The Inferno* (and through the rest of the *Commedia*): how does flesh act in contact with spirit? In *The Purgatorio* Dante attempts to embrace the spirit of Casella and his arms pass through him as if he were empty air. In the Third Circle, below (Canto 6, 34–36), Dante steps on some of the spirits lying in the slush and his foot passes right through them. (The original lines offer several possible readings of which I have preferred this one.) And at other times Virgil, also a spirit, picks Dante up and carries him bodily. It is clear, too, that Dante means the spirits of Hell to be weightless. When Virgil steps into Phlegyas' bark (Canto 8) it does not settle into the water, but it does when Dante's living body steps aboard. There is no narrative reason why Dante should not sink into the waters of this stream and Dante follows no fixed rule in dealing with such phenomena, often suiting the physical action to the allegorical need. Here, the moat probably symbolizes some requirement (The Will to Know) which he and the other poets meet without difficulty.

[34]The inhabitants of the citadel fall into three main groups: 1. *The heroes and heroines:* All of these it must be noted were associated with the Trojans and their Roman descendants. The Electra Dante mentions here is not the sister of Orestes (see Euripides' *Electra*) but the daughter of Atlas and the mother of Dardanus, the founder of Troy. 2. *The philosophers:* Most of this group is made up of philosophers whose teachings were, at least in part, acceptable to church scholarship. Democritus, however, "who ascribed the world to chance," would clearly be an exception. The group is best interpreted, therefore, as representing the highest achievements of Human Reason unaided by Divine Love. *Plato and Aristotle:* Through a considerable part of the Middle Ages Plato was held to be the fountainhead of all scholarship, but in Dante's time practically all learning was based on Aristotelian theory as interpreted through the many commentaries. *Linus:* The Italian is "Lino" and for it some commentators read "Livio" (Livy). 3. *The naturalists:* They are less well known today. In Dante's time their place in scholarship more or less corresponded to the role of the theoretician and historian of science in our universities. *Avicenna* (his major work was in the eleventh century) and *Averrhoës* (twelfth century) were Arabian philosophers and physicians especially famous in Dante's time for their commentaries on Aristotle. *Great Commentary:* Has the force of a title, i.e., The Great Commentary as distinguished from many lesser commentaries. *The Saladin:* This is the famous Saladin who was defeated by Richard the Lion-Heart, and whose great qualities as a ruler became a legend in medieval Europe.

who ascribes the world to chance, Diogenes,
  and with him there Thales, Anaxagoras,
  Zeno, Heraclitus, Empedocles.
And I saw the wise collector and analyst—
  Dioscorides I mean. I saw Orpheus there, 140
  Tully, Linus, Seneca the moralist,
Euclid the geometer, and Ptolemy,
  Hippocrates, Galen, Avicenna,
  and Averrhoës of the Great Commentary.
I cannot count so much nobility;
  my longer theme pursues me so that often
  the word falls short of the reality.
The company of six is reduced by four.
  My Master leads me by another road
  out of that serenity to the roar 150
and trembling air of Hell. I pass from light
into the kingdom of eternal night.

Canto 5

Circle Two—The Carnal: The Poets leave Limbo and enter the Second Circle. Here begin the torments of Hell proper, and here, blocking the way, sits Minos, the dread and semi-bestial judge of the damned who assigns to each soul its eternal torment. He orders the Poets back; but Virgil silences him as he earlier silenced Charon, and the Poets move on.

They find themselves on a dark ledge swept by a great whirlwind, which spins within it the souls of the Carnal, those who betrayed reason to their appetites. Their sin was to abandon themselves to the tempest of their passions: so they are swept forever in the tempest of Hell, forever denied the light of reason and of God. Virgil identifies many among them. Semiramis is there, and Dido, Cleopatra, Helen, Achilles, Paris, and Tristan. Dante sees Paolo and Francesca swept together, and in the name of love he calls to them to tell their sad story. They pause from their eternal flight to come to him, and Francesca tells their history while Paolo weeps at her side. Dante is so stricken by compassion at their tragic tale that he swoons once again.

So we went down to the second ledge alone;
  a smaller circle[35] of so much greater pain
  the voice of the damned rose in a bestial moan.
There Minos[36] sits, grinning, grotesque, and hale.
  He examines each lost soul as it arrives
  and delivers his verdict with his coiling tail.
That is to say, when the ill-fated soul
  appears before him it confesses all,
  and that grim sorter of the dark and foul
decides which place in Hell shall be its end, 10
  then wraps his twitching tail about himself
  one coil for each degree it must descend.

---

[35]The pit of Hell tapers like a funnel. The circles of ledges accordingly grow smaller as they descend.

[36]The son of Europa and of Zeus who descended to her in the form of a bull. Minos became a mythological king of Crete, so famous for his wisdom and justice that after death his soul was made judge of the dead. Virgil presents him fulfilling the same office at Aeneas's descent to the underworld. Dante, however, transforms him into an irate and hideous monster with a tail. The transformation may have been suggested by the form Zeus assumed for the rape of Europa—the monster is certainly bullish enough here—but the obvious purpose of the brutalization is to present a figure symbolic of the guilty conscience of the wretches who come before it to make their confessions.

The soul descends and others take its place:
each crowds in its turn to judgment, each confesses,
each hears its doom and falls away through space.
"O you who come into this camp of woe,"
cried Minos when he saw me turn away
without awaiting his judgment, "watch where you go
once you have entered here, and to whom you turn!
Do not be misled by that wide and easy passage!" 20
And my Guide to him: "That is not your concern;
it is his fate to enter every door.
This has been willed where what is willed must be,
and is not yours to question. Say no more."
Now the choir of anguish, like a wound,
strikes through the tortured air. Now I have come
to Hell's full lamentation, sound beyond sound.
I came to a place stripped bare of every light
and roaring on the naked dark like seas
wracked by a war of winds. Their hellish flight 30
of storm and counterstorm through time foregone,
sweeps the souls of the damned before its charge.
Whirling and battering it drives them on,
and when they pass the ruined gap of Hell[37]
through which we had come, their shrieks begin anew.
There they blaspheme the power of God eternal.
And this, I learned, was the never ending flight
of those who sinned in the flesh, the carnal and lusty
who betrayed reason to their appetite.
As the wings of wintering starlings bear them on 40
in their great wheeling flights, just so the blast
wherries these evil souls through time foregone.
Here, there, up, down, they whirl and, whirling, strain
with never a hope of hope to comfort them,
not of release, but even of less pain.
As cranes go over sounding their harsh cry,
leaving the long streak of their flight in air,
so come these spirits, wailing as they fly.
And watching their shadows lashed by wind, I cried:
"Master, what souls are these the very air 50
lashes with its black whips from side to side?"
"The first of these whose history you would know,"
he answered me, "was Empress of many tongues.[38]
Mad sensuality corrupted her so
that to hide the guilt of her debauchery
she licensed all depravity alike,
and lust and law were one in her decree.

---

[37]See note to Canto 4, line 53. At the time of the Harrowing of Hell a great earthquake shook the underworld, shattering rocks and cliffs. Ruins resulting from the same shock are noted in Canto 12, 34, and Canto 21, 112ff. At the beginning of Canto 24, the Poets leave the *bolgia* of the Hypocrites by climbing the ruined slabs of a bridge that was shattered by this earthquake.

[38]Semiramis, a legendary queen of Assyria who assumed full power at the death of her husband, Ninus.

She is Semiramis of whom the tale is told
how she married Ninus and succeeded him
to the throne of that wide land the Sultans hold. 60
The other is Dido;[39] faithless to the ashes
of Sichaeus, she killed herself for love.
The next whom the eternal tempest lashes
is sense-drugged Cleopatra. See Helen[40] there,
from whom such ill arose. And great Achilles,[41]
who fought at last with love in the house of prayer.
And Paris. And Tristan." As they whirled above
he pointed out more than a thousand shades
of those torn from the mortal life by love.
I stood there while my Teacher one by one 70
named the great knights and ladies of dim time;
and I was swept by pity and confusion.
At last I spoke: "Poet, I should be glad
to speak a word with those two swept together
so lightly on the wind and still so sad."[42]
And he to me: "Watch them. When next they pass,
call to them in the name of love that drives
and damns them here. In that name they will pause."
Thus, as soon as the wind in its wild course
brought them around, I called: "O wearied souls! 80
if none forbid it, pause and speak to us."
As mating doves that love calls to their nest
glide through the air with motionless raised wings,
borne by the sweet desire that fills each breast—
Just so those spirits turned on the torn sky
from the band where Dido whirls across the air;
such was the power of pity in my cry.
"O living creature, gracious, kind, and good,
going this pilgrimage through the sick night,
visiting us who stained the earth with blood, 90

[39]Queen and founder of Carthage. She had vowed to remain faithful to her husband, Sichaeus, but she fell in love with Aeneas. When Aeneas abandoned her she stabbed herself on a funeral pyre she had had prepared. According to Dante's own system of punishments, she should be in the Seventh Circle (Canto 13) with the suicides. The only clue Dante gives to the tempering of her punishment is his statement that "she killed herself for love." Dante always seems readiest to forgive in that name.

[40]She was held responsible for the Trojan War; the wife of King Meneleus of Sparta, she ran away with the visiting prince Paris from Troy.

[41]He is placed among this company because of his passion for Polyxena, the daughter of Priam. For love of her, he agreed to desert the Greeks and to join the Trojans, but when he went to the temple for the wedding (according to the legend Dante has followed) he was killed by Paris.

[42]Paolo and Francesca. In 1275 Giovanni Malatesta of Rimini, called Giovanni the Lame, a somewhat deformed but brave and powerful warrior, made a political marriage with Francesca, daughter of Guido da Polenta of Ravenna. Francesca came to Rimini and there an amour grew between her and Giovanni's younger brother Paolo. Despite the fact that Paolo had married in 1269 and had become the father of two daughters by 1275, his affair with Francesca continued for many years. It was sometime between 1283 and 1286 that Giovanni surprised them in Francesca's bedroom and killed both of them. Around these facts the legend has grown that Paolo was sent by Giovanni as his proxy to the marriage, that Francesca thought he was her real bridegroom and accordingly gave him her heart irrevocably at first sight. The legend obviously increases the pathos, but nothing in Dante gives it support.

were the King of Time our friend, we would pray His peace
on you who have pitied us. As long as the wind
will let us pause, ask of us what you please.
The town where I was born lies by the shore
where the Po descends into its ocean rest
with its attendant streams in one long murmur.
Love, which in gentlest hearts will soonest bloom
seized my lover with passion for that sweet body
from which I was torn unshriven to my doom.
Love, which permits no loved one not to love, 100
took me so strongly with delight in him
that we are one in Hell, as we were above.[43]
Love led us to one death. In the depths of Hell
Caïna waits for him[44] who took our lives."
This was the piteous tale they stopped to tell.
And when I had heard those world-offended lovers
I bowed my head. At last the Poet spoke:
"What painful thoughts are these your lowered brow covers?"
When at length I answered, I began: "Alas!
What sweetest thoughts, what green and young desire 110
led these two lovers to this sorry pass."
Then turning to those spirits once again,
I said: "Francesca, what you suffer here
melts me to tears of pity and of pain.
But tell me: in the time of your sweet sighs
by what appearances found love the way
to lure you to his perilous paradise?"
And she: "The double grief of a lost bliss
is to recall its happy hour in pain.
Your Guide and Teacher knows the truth of this. 120
But if there is indeed a soul in Hell
to ask of the beginning of our love
out of his pity, I will weep and tell:
On a day for dalliance we read the rhyme
of Lancelot,[45] how love had mastered him.
We were alone with innocence and dim time.[46]
Pause after pause that high old story drew
our eyes together while we blushed and paled;
but it was one soft passage overthrew

[43]At many points of *The Inferno* Dante makes clear the principle that the souls of the damned are locked so blindly into their own guilt that none can feel sympathy for another, or find any pleasure in the presence of another. The temptation of many readers is to interpret this line romantically: i.e., that the love of Paolo and Francesca survives Hell itself. The more Dantean interpretation, however, is that they add to one another's anguish (a) as mutual reminders of their sin, and (b) as insubstantial shades of the bodies for which they once felt such great passion.

[44]Giovanni Malatesta was still alive at the writing. His fate is already decided, however, and upon his death, his soul will fall to Caïna, the first ring of the last circle (Canto 32), where lie those who performed acts of treachery against their kin.

[45]The story of Lancelot and Guinevere (of Arthurian legend) exists in many forms. The details Dante makes use of are from an Old French version.

[46]The original simply reads "We were alone, suspecting nothing." "Dim time" is rhyme-forced, but not wholly outside the legitimate implications of the original, I hope. The old courtly romance may well be thought of as happening in the dim ancient days. The apology, of course, comes after the fact: one does the possible then argues for justification, and there probably is none.

our caution and our hearts. For when we read 130
how her fond smile was kissed by such a lover,
he who is one with me alive and dead
breathed on my lips the tremor of his kiss.
That book, and he who wrote it, was a pander.[47]
That day we read no further." As she said this,
the other spirit, who stood by her, wept
so piteously, I felt my senses reel
and faint away with anguish. I was swept
by such a swoon as death is, and I fell,
as a corpse might fall, to the dead floor of Hell. 140

Canto 6

Circle Three—The Gluttons: Dante recovers from his swoon and finds himself in the Third Circle. A great storm of putrefaction falls incessantly, a mixture of stinking snow and freezing rain, which forms into a vile slush underfoot. Everything about this Circle suggests a gigantic garbage dump. The souls of the damned lie in the icy paste, swollen and obscene, and Cerberus, the ravenous three-headed dog of Hell, stands guard over them, ripping and tearing them with his claws and teeth.

These are the Gluttons. In life they made no higher use of the gifts of God than to wallow in food and drink, producers of nothing but garbage and offal. Here they lie through all eternity, themselves like garbage, half-buried in fetid slush, while Cerberus slavers over them as they in life slavered over their food.

As the Poets pass, one of the speakers sits up and addresses Dante. He is Ciacco, the Hog, a citizen of Dante's own Florence. He recognizes Dante and asks eagerly for news of what is happening there. With the foreknowledge of the damned, Ciacco then utters the first of the political prophecies that are to become a recurring theme of *The Inferno.* The Poets then move on toward the next Circle, at the edge of which they encounter the monster Plutus.

My senses had reeled from me out of pity
for the sorrow of those kinsmen and lost lovers.
Now they return, and waking gradually,
I see new torments and new souls in pain
about me everywhere. Wherever I turn
away from grief I turn to grief again.
I am in the Third Circle of the torments.
Here to all time with neither pause nor change
the frozen rain of Hell descends in torrents.
Huge hailstones, dirty water, and black snow 10
pour from the dismal air to putrefy
the putrid slush that waits for them below.
Here monstrous Cerberus,[48] the ravening beast,
howls through his triple throats like a mad dog
over the spirits sunk in that foul paste.
His eyes are red, his beard is greased with phlegm,
his belly is swollen, and his hands are claws
to rip the wretches and flay and mangle them.

---

[47]"Galeotto," the Italian word for "pander," is also the Italian rendering of the name of Gallehault, who in the French romance Dante refers to here, urged Lancelot and Guinevere on to love.

[48]In classical mythology Cerberus appears as a three-headed dog. His master was Pluto, king of the Underworld. Cerberus was placed at the Gate of the Underworld to allow all to enter, but none to escape. His three heads and his ravenous disposition make him an apt symbol of gluttony. *Like a mad dog:* Dante seems clearly to have visualized him as a half-human monster. The beard (line 16) suggests that at least one of his three heads is human, and many illuminated manuscripts so represent him.

And they, too, howl like dogs in the freezing storm,
turning and turning from it as if they thought 20
one naked side could keep the other warm.
When Cerberus discovered us in that swill
his dragon-jaws yawned wide, his lips drew back
in a grin of fangs. No limb of him was still.
My Guide bent down and seized in either fist
a clod of the stinking dirt that festered there
and flung them down the gullet of the beast.
As a hungry cur will set the echoes raving
and then fall still when he is thrown a bone,
all of his clamor being in his craving, 30
so the three ugly heads of Cerberus,
whose yowling at those wretches deafened them,
choked on their putrid sops and stopped their fuss.
We made our way across the sodden mess
of souls the rain beat down, and when our steps
fell on a body, they sank through emptiness.
All those illusions of being seemed to lie
drowned in the slush; until one wraith among them
sat up abruptly and called as I passed by:
"O you who are led this journey through the shade 40
of Hell's abyss, do you recall this face?
You had been made before I was unmade."[49]
And I: "Perhaps the pain you suffer here
distorts your image from my recollection.
I do not know you as you now appear."
And he to me: "Your own city, so rife
with hatred that the bitter cup flows over
was mine too in that other, clearer life.
Your citizens nicknamed me Ciacco, The Hog:
gluttony was my offense, and for it 50
I lie here rotting like a swollen log.
Nor am I lost in this alone; all these
you see about you in this painful death
have wallowed in the same indecencies."
I answered him: "Ciacco, your agony
weighs on my heart and calls my soul to tears;
But tell me, if you can, what is to be
for the citizens of that divided state,
and whether there are honest men among them,
and for what reasons we are torn by hate." 60
And he then: "After many words given and taken
it shall come to blood; White shall rise over Black
and rout the dark lord's force, battered and shaken.
Then it shall come to pass within three suns
that the fallen shall arise, and by the power
of one now gripped by many hesitations

[49]That is, "you were born before I died." The further implication is that they must have seen one another in Florence, a city one can still walk across in twenty minutes, and around in a very few hours. Dante certainly would have known everyone in Florence.

Black shall ride on White for many years,
  loading it down with burdens and oppressions
  and humbling of proud names and helpless tears.
Two are honest, but none will heed them. There, 70
  pride, avarice, and envy are the tongues
  men know and heed, a Babel of despair."[50]
Here he broke off his mournful prophecy.
  And I to him: "Still let me urge you on
  to speak a little further and instruct me:
Farinata and Tegghiaio, men of good blood,
  Jacopo Rusticucci, Arrigo, Mosca,[51]
  and the others who set their hearts on doing good—
where are they now whose high deeds might be-gem
  the crown of kings? I long to know their fate. 80
  Does Heaven soothe or Hell envenom them?"
And he: "They lie below in a blacker lair.
  A heavier guilt draws them to greater pain.
  If you descend so far you may see them there.
But when you move again among the living,
  oh speak my name to the memory of men![52]
  Having answered all, I say no more." And giving
his head a shake, he looked up at my face
  cross-eyed, then bowed his head and fell away
  among the other blind souls of that place. 90
And my Guide to me: "He will not wake again
  until the angel trumpet sounds the day
  on which the host shall come to judge all men.
Then shall each soul before the seat of Mercy
  return to its sad grave and flesh and form
  to hear the edict of Eternity."
So we picked our slow way among the shades
  and the filthy rain, speaking of life to come.
  "Master," I said, "when the great clarion fades

---

[50]This is the first of the political prophecies that are to become a recurring theme of *The Inferno.* (It is the second if we include the political symbolism of the Greyhound in Canto 1.) Dante is, of course, writing after these events have all taken place. At Easter time of 1300, however, the events were in the future. The Whites and the Blacks of Ciacco's prophecy should not be confused with the Guelphs and the Ghibellines. The internal strife between the Guelphs and the Ghibellines ended with the total defeat of the Ghibellines. By the end of the thirteenth century that strife had passed. But very shortly a new feud began in Florence between White Guelphs and Black Guelphs. A rather gruesome murder perpetrated by Focaccio de' Cancellieri became the cause of new strife between two branches of the Cancellieri family. On May 1 of 1300 the White Guelphs (Dante's party) drove the Black Guelphs from Florence in bloody fighting. Two years later, however ("within three suns"), the Blacks, aided by Dante's detested Boniface VIII, returned and expelled most of the prominent Whites, among them Dante; for he had been a member of the Priorate (City Council) that issued a decree banishing the leaders of both sides. This was the beginning of Dante's long exile from Florence.

[51]Farinata will appear in Canto 10 among the Heretics, Tegghiaio and Jacopo Rusticucci, in Canto 16 with the homosexuals, Mosca in Canto 28 with the sowers of discord. Arrigo does not appear again and he has not been positively identified. Dante probably refers here to Arrigo (or Oderigo) dei Fifanti, one of those who took part in the murder of Buondelmonte (Canto 28, 106, note).

[52]Excepting those shades in the lowest depths of Hell whose sins are so shameful that they wish only to be forgotten, all of the damned are eager to be remembered on earth. The concept of the family name and of its survival in the memories of men were matters of first importance among Italians of Dante's time, and expressions of essentially the same attitude are common in Italy today.

into the voice of thundering Omniscience, 100
what of these agonies? Will they be the same,
or more, or less, after the final sentence?"
And he to me: "Look to your science[53] again
where it is written: the more a thing is perfect
the more it feels of pleasure and of pain.
As for these souls, though they can never soar
to true perfection, still in the new time
they will be nearer it than they were before."
And so we walked the rim of the great ledge
speaking of pain and joy, and of much more 110
that I will not repeat, and reached the edge
where the descent begins. There, suddenly,
we came on Plutus, the great enemy.

Canto 7

Circle Four—The Hoarders and the Wasters; Circle Five—The Wrathful and the Sullen: Plutus menaces the Poets, but once more Virgil shows himself more powerful then the rages of Hell's monsters. The Poets enter the Fourth Circle and find what seems to be a war in progress.

The sinners are divided into two raging mobs, each soul among them straining madly at a great boulder-like weight. The two mobs meet, clashing their weights against one another, after which they separate, pushing the great weights apart, and begin over again.

One mob is made up of the Hoarders, the other of the Wasters. In life, they lacked all moderation in regulating their expenses; they destroyed the light of God within themselves by thinking of nothing but money. Thus in death, their souls are encumbered by dead weights (mundanity) and one excess serves to punish the other. Their souls, moreover, have become so dimmed and awry in their fruitless rages that there is no hope of recognizing any among them.

The Poets pass on while Virgil explains the function of Dame Fortune in the Divine Scheme. As he finishes (it is past midnight now of Good Friday) they reach the inner edge of the ledge and come to a Black Spring which bubbles murkily over the rocks to form the Marsh of Styx, which is the Fifth Circle, the last station of the Upper Hell.

Across the marsh they see countless souls attacking one another in the foul slime. These are the Wrathful and the symbolism of their punishment is obvious. Virgil also points out to Dante certain bubbles rising from the slime and informs him that below that mud lie entombed the souls of the Sullen. In life they refused to welcome the sweet light of the Sun (Divine Illumination) and in death they are buried forever below the stinking waters of the Styx, gargling the words of an endless chant in a grotesque parody of singing a hymn.

"Papa Satán, Papa Satán, aleppy,"[54]
Plutus[55] clucked and stuttered in his rage;
and my all-knowing Guide, to comfort me:

---

[53] "Science" to those of Dante's time meant specifically "the writings of Aristotle and the commentaries upon them."

[54] Virgil, the all-knowing, may understand these words, but no one familiar with merely human languages has deciphered them. In Canto 31 the monster Nimrod utters a similar meaningless jargon, and Virgil there cites it as evidence of the dimness of his mind. Gibberish is certainly a characteristic appropriate to monsters, and since Dante takes pains to make the reference to Satan apparent in the gibberish, it is obviously infernal and debased, and that is almost certainly all he intended. The word "papa" as used here probably means "Pope" rather than "father." "Il papa santo" is the Pope. "Papa Satán" would be his opposite. In the original the last word is "aleppe." On the assumption that jargon translates jargon I have twisted it a bit to rhyme with "me."

[55] In Greek mythology, Plutus was the God of Wealth. Many commentators suggest that Dante confused him with Pluto, the son of Saturn and God of the Underworld. But in that case, Plutus would be identical with Lucifer himself and would require a central place in Hell, whereas the classical function of Plutus as God of Material Wealth makes him the ideal overseer of the miserly and the prodigal.

"Do not be startled, for no power of his,
however he may lord it over the damned,
may hinder your descent through this abyss."
And turning to that carnival of bloat
cried: "Peace, you wolf of Hell. Choke back your bile
and let its venom blister your own throat.
Our passage through this pit is willed on high 10
by that same Throne that loosed the angel wrath
of Michael on ambition and mutiny."
As puffed out sails fall when the mast gives way
and flutter to a self-convulsing heap—
so collapsed Plutus into that dead clay.
Thus we descended the dark scarp of Hell
to which all the evil of the Universe
comes home at last, into the Fourth Great Circle
and ledge of the abyss. O Holy Justice,
who could relate the agonies I saw! 20
What guilt is man that he can come to this?
Just as the surge Charybdis[56] hurls to sea
crashes and breaks upon its countersurge,
so these shades dance and crash eternally.
Here, too, I saw a nation of lost souls,
far more than were above: they strained their chests
against enormous weights, and with mad howls
rolled them at one another. Then in haste
they rolled them back, one party shouting out:
"Why do you hoard?" and the other: "Why do you waste?" 30
So back around that ring they puff and blow,
each faction to its course, until they reach
opposite sides, and screaming as they go
the madmen turn and start their weights again
to crash against the maniacs. And I,
watching, felt my heart contract with pain.
"Master," I said, "what people can these be?
And all those tonsured ones there on our left—
is it possible they *all* were of the clergy?"
And he: "In the first life beneath the sun 40
they were so skewed and squinteyed in their minds
their misering or extravagance mocked all reason.
The voice of each clamors its own excess
when lust meets lust at the two points of the circle
where opposite guilts meet in their wretchedness.
These tonsured wraiths of greed were priests indeed,
and popes and cardinals, for it is in these
the weed of avarice sows its rankest seed."
And I to him: "Master, among this crew
surely I should be able to make out 50
the fallen image of some soul I knew."

[56] A famous whirlpool in the Straits of Sicily.

And he to me: "This is a lost ambition.
  In their sordid lives they labored to be blind,
  and now their souls have dimmed past recognition.
All their eternity is to butt and bray:
  one crew will stand tight-fisted, the other stripped
  of its very hair at the bar of Judgment Day.
Hoarding and squandering wasted all their light
  and brought them screaming to this brawl of wraiths.
  You need no words of mine to grasp their plight. 60
Now may you see the fleeting vanity
  of the goods of Fortune for which men tear down
  all that they are, to build a mockery.
Not all the gold that is or ever was
  under the sky could buy for one of these
  exhausted souls the fraction of a pause."
"Master," I said, "tell me—now that you touch
  on this Dame Fortune[57]—what *is* she, that she holds
  the good things of the world within her clutch?"
And he to me: "O credulous mankind, 70
  is there one error that has wooed and lost you?
  Now listen, and strike error from your mind:
That king whose perfect wisdom transcends all,
  made the heavens and posted angels on them
  to guide the eternal light that it might fall
from every sphere to every sphere the same.
  He made earth's splendors by a like decree
  and posted as their minister this high Dame,
the Lady of Permutations. All earth's gear
  she changes from nation to nation, from house to house, 80
  in changeless change through every turning year.
No mortal power may stay her spinning wheel.
  The nations rise and fall by her decree.
  None may foresee where she will set her heel:[58]
she passes, and things pass. Man's mortal reason
  cannot encompass her. She rules her sphere
  as the other gods[59] rule theirs. Season by season
her changes change her changes endlessly,
  and those whose turn has come press on her so,
  she must be swift by hard necessity. 90
And this is she so railed at and reviled
  that even her debtors in the joys of time
  blaspheme her name. Their oaths are bitter and wild,
but she in her beatitude does not hear.
  Among the Primal Beings of God's joy
  she breathes her blessedness and wheels her sphere.

---

[57] A central figure in medieval mythology. She is almost invariably represented as a female figure holding an ever-revolving wheel symbolic of Chance. Dante incorporates her into his scheme of the Universe, ranking her among the angels, and giving her a special office in the service of the Catholic God.

[58] A literal translation of the original would be "She is hidden like a snake in the grass." To avoid the comic overtone of that figure in English, I have substituted another figure which I believe expresses Dante's intent without destroying his tone.

[59] Dante can only mean here "the other angels and ministers of God."

But the stars that marked our starting fall away.[60]
We must go deeper into greater pain,
for it is not permitted that we stay."
And crossing over to the chasm's edge 100
we came to a spring[61] that boiled and overflowed
through a great crevice worn into the ledge.
By that foul water, black from its very source,
we found a nightmare path among the rocks,
and followed the dark stream along its course.
Beyond its rocky race and wild descent
the river floods and forms a marsh called Styx,[62]
a dreary swampland, vaporous and malignant.
And I, intent on all our passage touched,
made out a swarm of spirits in that bog 110
savage with anger, naked, slime-besmutched.
They thumped at one another in that slime
with hands and feet, and they butted, and they bit
as if each would tear the other limb from limb.
And my kind Sage: "My son, behold the souls
of those who lived in wrath. And do you see
the broken surfaces of those water-holes
on every hand, boiling as if in pain?
There are souls beneath that water. Fixed in slime
they speak their piece, end it, and start again: 120
'Sullen were we in the air made sweet by the Sun;
in the glory of his shining our hearts poured
a bitter smoke. Sullen were we begun;
sullen we lie forever in this ditch.'
This litany they gargle in their throats
as if they sang, but lacked the words and pitch."
Then circling on along that filthy wallow,
we picked our way between the bank and fen,
keeping our eyes on those foul souls that swallow
the slime of Hell. And so at last we came 130
to the foot of a Great Tower that has no name.[63]

Canto 8

Circle Five: Styx—The Wrathful, Phlegyas; Circle Six: Dis—The Fallen Angels: The Poets stand at the edge of the swamp, and a mysterious signal flames from the great tower. It is answered from the darkness of the other side, and almost immediately the Poets see Phlegyas, the Boatman

[60]It is now past midnight of Good Friday.

[61]All the waters of Hell derive from one source (see Canto 14, 12ff.). This black spring must therefore be the waters of Acheron boiling out of some subterranean passage.

[62]The river Styx figures variously in classic mythology, but usually (and in later myths always) as a river of the Underworld. Dante, to heighten his symbolism, makes it a filthy marsh. This marsh marks the first great division of Hell. Between Acheron and Styx are punished the sins of Incontinence (the Sins of the She-Wolf). This is the Upper Hell. Beyond Styx rise the flaming walls of the infernal city of Dis, within which are punished Violence and Fraud (the Sins of the Lion, and the Sins of the Leopard).

[63]No special significance need be attributed to the Tower. It serves as a signaling point for calling the ferryman from Dis.

of Styx, racing toward them across the water, fast as a flying arrow. He comes avidly, thinking to find new souls for torment, and he howls with rage when he discovers the Poets. Once again, however, Virgil conquers wrath with a word and Phlegyas reluctantly gives them passage.

As they are crossing, a muddy soul rises before them. It is Filippo Argenti, one of the Wrathful. Dante recognizes him despite the filth with which he is covered, and he berates him soundly, even wishing to see him tormented further. Virgil approves Dante's disdain and, as if in answer to Dante's wrath, Argenti is suddenly set upon by all the other sinners present, who fall upon him and rip him to pieces.

The boat meanwhile has sped on, and before Argenti's screams have died away, Dante sees the flaming red towers of Dis, the Capital of Hell. The great walls of the iron city block the way to the Lower Hell. Properly speaking, all the rest of Hell lies within the city walls, which separate the Upper and the Lower Hell.

Phlegyas deposits them at a great Iron Gate which they find to be guarded by the Rebellious Angels. These creatures of Ultimate Evil, rebels against God Himself, refuse to let the Poets pass. Even Virgil is powerless against them, for Human Reason by itself cannot cope with the essence of Evil. Only Divine Aid can bring hope. Virgil accordingly sends up a prayer for assistance and waits anxiously for a Heavenly Messenger to appear.

Returning to my theme,[64] I say we came
to the foot of a Great Tower; but long before
we reached it through the marsh, two horns of flame
flared from the summit, one from either side,
and then, far off, so far we scarce could see it
across the mist, another flame replied.
I turned to that sea of all intelligence
saying: "What is this signal and counter-signal?
Who is it speaks with fire across this distance?"
And he then: "Look across the filthy slew: 10
you may already see the one they summon,
if the swamp vapors do not hide him from you."
No twanging bowspring ever shot an arrow
that bored the air it rode dead to the mark
more swiftly than the flying skiff whose prow
shot toward us over the polluted channel
with a single steersman at the helm who called:
"So, do I have you at last, you whelp of Hell?"
"Phlegyas,[65] Phlegyas," said my Lord and Guide,
"this time you waste your breath: you have us only 20
for the time it takes to cross to the other side."

[64]There is evidence that Dante stopped writing for a longer or shorter period between the seventh and eighth Cantos. None of the evidence is conclusive but it is quite clear that the plan of *The Inferno* changes from here on. Up to this point the Circles have been described in one canto apiece. If this was Dante's original plan, Hell would have been concluded in five more cantos, since there are only Nine Circles in all. But in the later journey the Eighth Circle alone occupies thirteen cantos. Dante's phrase may be simply transitional, but it certainly marks a change in the plan of the poem.

[65]Mythological King of Boeotia. He was the son of Ares (Mars) by a human mother. Angry at Apollo, who had seduced his daughter (Aesculapius was born of this union), he set fire to Apollo's temple at Delphi. For this offense, the God killed him and threw his soul into Hades under sentence of eternal torment. Dante's choice of a ferryman is especially apt. Phlegyas is the link between the Wrathful (to whom his paternity relates him) and the Rebellious Angels who menaced God (as he menaced Apollo).

Phlegyas, the madman, blew his rage among
those muddy marshes like a cheat deceived,
or like a fool at some imagined wrong.
My Guide, whom all the fiend's noise could not nettle,
boarded the skiff, motioning me to follow:
and not till I stepped aboard did it seem to settle[66]
into the water. At once we left the shore,
that ancient hull riding more heavily
than it had ridden in all of time before. 30
And as we ran on that dead swamp, the slime
rose before me, and from it a voice cried:[67]
"Who are you that come here before your time?"
And I replied: "If I come, I do not remain.
But you, who are *you*, so fallen and so foul?"
And he: "I am one who weeps." And I then:
"May you weep and wail to all eternity,
for I know you, hell-dog, filthy as you are."
Then he stretched both hands to the boat, but warily
the Master shoved him back, crying, "Down! Down! 40
with the other dogs!" Then he embraced me saying:
"Indignant spirit, I kiss you as you frown.
Blessed be she who bore you.[68] In world and time
this one was haughtier yet. Not one unbending
graces his memory. Here is his shadow in slime.
How many living now, chancellors of wrath,
shall come to lie here yet in this pigmire,
leaving a curse to be their aftermath!"
And I: "Master, it would suit my whim
to see the wretch scrubbed down into the swill 50
before we leave this stinking sink and him."
And he to me: "Before the other side
shows through the mist, you shall have all you ask.
This is a wish that should be gratified."
And shortly after, I saw the loathsome spirit
so mangled by a swarm of muddy wraiths
that to this day I praise and thank God for it.

[66]Because of his living weight.

[67]Filippo Argenti, one of the Adimari family, who were bitter political enemies of Dante. Dante's savagery toward him was probably intended in part as an insult to the family. He pays them off again in *The Paradiso* when he has Cacciaguida call them "The insolent gang that makes itself a dragon to chase those who run away, but is sweet as a lamb to any who show their teeth—or their purse."

[68]These were Luke's words to Christ. To have Virgil apply them to Dante after such violence seems shocking, even though the expression is reasonably common in Italian. But Dante does not use such devices lightly. The *Commedia,* it must be remembered, is a vision of the progress of man's soul toward perfection. In being contemptuous of Wrath, Dante is purging it from his soul. He is thereby growing nearer to perfection, and Virgil, who has said nothing in the past when Dante showed pity for other sinners (though Virgil will later take him to task for daring to pity those whom God has shut off from pity), welcomes this sign of relentless rejection. Only by a ruthless enmity toward evil may the soul be purified, and as Christ is the symbol of ultimate perfection by rejection of Evil, so the birth of that rejection in Dante may aptly be greeted by the words of Luke, for it is from this that the soul must be reborn. Righteous indignation, moreover (*giusto sdegno*), is one of the virtues Christ practiced (e.g., against the money changers) and is the golden mean of right action between the evil extremes of wrath and sullenness.

"After Filippo Argenti!" all cried together.
  The maddog Florentine wheeled at their cry
  and bit himself for rage. I saw them gather. 60
And there we left him. And I say no more,
  But such a wailing beat upon my ears,
  I strained my eyes ahead to the far shore.
"My son," the Master said, "the City called Dis[69]
  lies just ahead, the heavy citizens,
  the swarming crowds of Hell's metropolis."
And I then: "Master, I already see
  the glow of its red mosques,[70] as if they came
  hot from the forge to smolder in this valley."
And my all-knowing Guide: "They are eternal 70
  flues to eternal fire[71] that rages in them
  and makes them glow across this lower Hell."
And as he spoke we entered the vast moat
  of the sepulchre. Its wall seemed made of iron
  and towered above us in our little boat.
We circled through what seemed an endless distance
  before the boatman ran his prow ashore
  crying: "Out! Out! Get out! This is the entrance."
Above the gates more than a thousand shades
  of spirits purged from Heaven for its glory[72] 80
  cried angrily: "Who is it that invades
Death's Kingdom in his life?" My Lord and Guide
  advanced a step before me with a sign
  that he wished to speak to some of them aside.
They quieted somewhat, and one called, "Come,
  but come alone. And tell that other one,
  who thought to walk so blithely through death's kingdom,
he may go back along the same fool's way
  he came by. Let him try his living luck.
  You who are dead can come only to stay." 90
Reader, judge for yourself, how each black word
  fell on my ears to sink into my heart:
  I lost hope of returning to the world.
"O my beloved Master, my Guide in peril,
  who time and time again[73] have seen me safely
  along this way, and turned the power of evil,
  stand by me now," I cried, "in my heart's fright.

---

[69]Pluto, King of the Underworld of ancient mythology, was sometimes called Dis. This, then, is his city, the metropolis of Satan. Within the city walls lies all the Lower Hell; within it fire is used for the first time as a torment of the damned; and at its very center Satan himself stands fixed forever in a great ice cap.

[70]To a European of Dante's time a mosque would seem the perversion of a church, the impious counterpart of the House of God, just as Satan is God's impious counterpart. His city is therefore architecturally appropriate, a symbolism that becomes all the more terrible when the mosques are made of red-hot iron.

[71]The fires of Hell are all within Dis.

[72]The Rebellious Angels. We have already seen, on the other side of Acheron, the Angels who sinned by refusing to take sides.

[73]A literal translation of the original would read "more than seven times." "Seven" is used here as an indeterminate number indicating simply "quite a number of times." Italians makes rather free use of such numbers.

And if the dead forbid our journey to them,
let us go back together toward the light."
My Guide then, in the greatness of his spirit: 100
"Take heart. Nothing can take our passage from us
when such a power has given warrant for it.
Wait here and feed your soul while I am gone
on comfort and good hope; I will not leave you
to wander in this underworld alone."
So the sweet Guide and Father leaves me[74] here,
and I stay on in doubt with yes and no
dividing all my heart to hope and fear.
I could not hear my Lord's words, but the pack
that gathered round him suddenly broke away 110
howling and jostling and went pouring back,
slamming the towering gate hard in his face.
That great Soul stood alone[75] outside the wall.
Then he came back; his pain showed in his pace.
His eyes were fixed upon the ground, his brow
had sagged from its assurance. He sighed aloud:
"Who has forbidden me the halls of sorrow?"
And to me he said: "You need not be cast down
by my vexation, for whatever plot
these fiends may lay against us, we will go on. 120
This insolence of theirs is nothing new:
they showed it once at a less secret gate[76]
that still stands open for all that they could do—
the same gate where you read the dead inscription;
and through it at this moment a Great One[77] comes.
Already he has passed it and moves down
ledge by dark ledge. He is one who needs no guide,
and at his touch all gates must spring aside."

. . .

Canto 11

Circle Six—The Heretics: The Poets reach the inner edge of the Sixth Circle and find a great jumble of rocks that had once been a cliff, but which has fallen into rubble as the result of the great earthquake that shook Hell when Christ died. Below them lies the Seventh Circle, and so fetid is the air that arises from it that the Poets cower for shelter behind a great tomb until their breaths can grow accustomed to the stench.

Dante finds an inscription on the lid of the tomb labeling it as the place in Hell of Pope Anastasius.

Virgil takes advantage of the delay to outline in detail the Division of the Lower Hell, a theological discourse based on *The Ethics* and *The Physics* of Aristotle with subsequent medieval

[74]Dante shifts tenses more freely than English readers are accustomed to.

[75]Virgil's allegorical function as Human Reason is especially important to an interpretation of this passage.

[76]The Gate of Hell. According to an early medieval tradition, these demons gathered at the outer gate to oppose the descent of Christ into Limbo at the time of the Harrowing of Hell, but Christ broke the door open and it has remained so ever since. The service of the Mass for Holy Saturday still sings *Hodie portas mortis et seras pariter Salvator noster disrupit.* (On this day our Saviour broke open the door of the dead and its lock as well.)

[77]A Messenger of Heaven. He is described in Canto 9.

interpretations. Virgil explains also why it is that the Incontinent are not punished within the walls of Dis, and rather ingeniously sets forth the reasons why Usury is an act of Violence against Art, which is the child of Nature and hence the Grandchild of God. (By "Art," Dante means the arts and crafts by which man draws from nature, i.e., Industry.)

As he concludes he rises and urges Dante on. By means known only to Virgil, he is aware of the motion of the stars and from them he sees that it is about two hours before Sunrise of Holy Saturday.

We came to the edge of an enormous sink
rimmed by a circle of great broken boulders.[78]
Here we found ghastlier gangs. And here the stink
thrown up by the abyss so overpowered us
that we drew back, cowering behind the wall
of one of the great tombs; and standing thus,
I saw an inscription in the stone, and read:
"I guard Anastasius, once Pope,
he whom Photinus[79] led from the straight road."
"Before we travel on to that blind pit 10
we must delay until our sense grows used
to its foul breath, and then we will not mind it,"
my Master said. And I then: "Let us find
some compensation for the time of waiting."
And he: "You shall see I have just that in mind.
My son," he began, "there are below this wall
three smaller circles,[80] each in its degree
like those you are about to leave, and all
are crammed with God's accurst. Accordingly,
that you may understand their sins at sight, 20
I will explain how each is prisoned, and why.
Malice is the sin most hated by God.
And the aim of malice is to injure others
whether by fraud or violence. But since fraud
is the vice of which man alone is capable,
God loathes it most. Therefore, the fraudulent
are placed below, and their torment is more painful.
The first below are the violent. But as violence
sins in three persons, so is that circle formed
of three descending rounds of crueler torments. 30
Against God, self, and neighbor is violence shown.
Against their persons and their goods, I say,
as you shall hear set forth with open reason.

[78]These boulders were broken from the earthquake that shook Hell at the death of Christ.

[79]Anastasius II was Pope from 496 to 498. This was the time of schism between the Eastern (Greek) and Western (Roman) churches. Photinus, deacon of Thessalonica, was of the Greek church and held to the Acacian heresy, which denied the divine paternity of Christ. Dante follows the report that Anastasius gave communion to Photinus, thereby countenancing his heresy. Dante's sources, however, had probably confused Anastasius II, the Pope, with Anastasius I, who was Emperor from 491 to 518. It was the Emperor Anastasius who was persuaded by Photinus to accept the Acacian heresy.

[80]The Poets are now at the cliff that bounds the Sixth Circle. Below them lie Circles Seven, Eight, and Nine. They are smaller in circumference, being closer to the center, but they are all intricately subdivided, and will be treated at much greater length than were the Circles of Upper Hell.

Murder and mayhem are the violation
of the person of one's neighbor: and of his goods;
harassment, plunder, arson, and extortion.
Therefore, homicides, and those who strike
in malice—destroyers and plunderers—all lie
in that first round, and like suffers with like.
A man may lay violent hands upon his own 40
person and substance; so in that second round
eternally in vain repentance moan
the suicides and all who gamble away
and waste the good and substance of their lives
and weep in that sweet time when they should be gay.
Violence may be offered the deity
in the heart that blasphemes and refuses Him
and scorns the gifts of Nature, her beauty and bounty.
Therefore, the smallest round brands with its mark
both Sodom and Cahors,[81] and all who rail 50
at God and His commands in their hearts' dark.
Fraud, which is a canker to every conscience,
may be practiced by a man on those who trust him,
and on those who have reposed no confidence.
The latter mode seems only to deny
the bond of love which all men have from Nature;
therefore within the second circle lie
simoniacs, sycophants, and hypocrites,
falsifiers, thieves, and sorcerers,
grafters, pimps, and all such filthy cheats. 60
The former mode of fraud not only denies
the bond of Nature, but the special trust
added by bonds of friendship or blood-ties.
Hence, at the center point of all creation,[82]
in the smallest circle, on which Dis is founded,
the traitors lie in endless expiation."
"Master," I said, "the clarity of your mind
impresses all you touch; I see quite clearly
the orders of this dark pit of the blind.
But tell me: those who lie in the swamp's bowels, 70
those the wind blows about, those the rain beats,
and those who meet and clash with such mad howls[83]—
why are *they* not punished in the rust-red city[84]
if God's wrath be upon them? and if it is not,
why must they grieve through all eternity?"

---

[81] Both these cities are used as symbols for the sins that are said to have flourished within them. Sodom (Genesis 19) is, of course, identified with unnatural sex practices. Cahors, a city in southern France, was notorious in the Middle Ages for its usurers.

[82] In the Ptolemaic system the earth was the center of the Universe. In Dante's geography, the bottom of Hell is the center of the earth.

[83] These are, of course, the sinners of the Upper Hell.

[84] Dis. All of Lower Hell is within the city walls.

And he: "Why does your understanding stray
so far from its own habit? or can it be
your thoughts are turned along some other way?
Have you forgotten that your *Ethics*[85] states
the three main dispositions of the soul 80
that lead to those offenses Heaven hates—
incontinence, malice, and bestiality?
and how incontinence offends God least
and earns least blame from Justice and Charity?
Now if you weigh this doctrine and recall
exactly who they are whose punishment
lies in that upper Hell outside the wall,
you will understand at once why they are confined
apart from these fierce wraiths, and why less anger
beats down on them from the Eternal Mind." 90
"O sun which clears all mists from troubled sight,
such joy attends your rising that I feel
as grateful to the dark as to the light.
Go back a little further," I said, "to where
you spoke of usury as an offense
against God's goodness. How is that made clear?"
"Philosophy makes plain by many reasons,"
he answered me, "to those who heed her teachings,
how all of Nature,—her laws, her fruits, her seasons,—
springs from the Ultimate Intellect and Its art: 100
and if you read your *Physics*[86] with due care,
you will note, not many pages from the start,
that Art strives after her by imitation,
as the disciple imitates the master;
Art, as it were, is the Grandchild of Creation.
By this, recalling the Old Testament
near the beginning of Genesis, you will see
that in the will of Providence, man was meant
to labor and to prosper. But usurers,
by seeking their increase in other ways, 110
scorn Nature in herself and her followers.
But come, for it is my wish now to go on:
the wheel turns and the Wain lies over Caurus,[87]
the Fish are quivering low on the horizon,
and there beyond us runs the road we go
down the dark scarp into the depths below."

[85] *The Ethics* of Aristotle.

[86] *The Physics* of Aristotle.

[87] The Wain is the constellation of the Great Bear. Caurus was the northwest wind in classical mythology. Hence the constellation of the Great Bear now lies in the northwest. The Fish is the constellation and zodiacal sign of Pisces. It is just appearing over the horizon. The next sign of the zodiac is Aries. We know from Canto 1 that the sun is in Aries, and since the twelve signs of the zodiac each cover two hours of the day, it must now be about two hours before dawn. It is, therefore, approximately 4:00 A.M. of Holy Saturday. The stars are not visible in Hell, but throughout *The Inferno* Virgil reads them by some special power which Dante does not explain.

Canto 12

Circle Seven: Round One—The Violent Against Neighbors: The Poets begin the descent of the fallen rock wall, having first to evade the Minotaur, who menaces them. Virgil tricks him and the Poets hurry by.

Below them they see the River of Blood, which marks the First Round of the Seventh Circle as detailed in the previous Canto. Here are punished the Violent Against Their Neighbors, great war-makers, cruel tyrants, highwaymen—all who shed the blood of their fellowmen. As they wallowed in blood during their lives, so they are immersed in the boiling blood forever, each according to the degree of his guilt, while fierce Centaurs patrol the banks, ready to shoot with their arrows any sinner who raises himself out of the boiling blood beyond the limits permitted him. Alexander the Great is here, up to his lashes in the blood, and with him Attila, the Scourge of God. They are immersed in the deepest part of the river, which grows shallower as it circles to the other side of the ledge, then deepens again.

The Poets are challenged by the Centaurs, but Virgil wins a safe conduct from Chiron, their chief, who assigns Nessus to guide them and to bear them across the shallows of the boiling blood. Nessus carries them across at the point where it is only ankle deep and immediately leaves them and returns to his patrol.

The scene that opened from the edge of the pit
  was mountainous, and such a desolation
  that every eye would shun the sight of it:
a ruin like the Slides of Mark[88] near Trent
  on the bank of the Adige, the result of an earthquake
  or of some massive fault in the escarpment—
for, from the point on the peak where the mountain split
  to the plain below, the rock is so badly shattered
  a man at the top might make a rough stair of it.[89]
Such was the passage down the steep, and there 10
  at the very top, at the edge of the broken cleft,
  lay spread the Infamy of Crete,[90] the heir
of bestiality and the lecherous queen
  who hid in a wooden cow. And when he saw us,
  he gnawed his own flesh in a fit of spleen.
And my Master mocked: "How you do pump your breath!
  Do you think, perhaps, it is the Duke of Athens,
  who in the world above served up your death?
Off with you, monster; this one does not come
  instructed by your sister, but of himself 20
  to observe your punishment in the lost kingdom."

---

[88] *Li Slavoni di Marco* are about two miles from Rovereto (between Verona and Trent) on the left bank of the River Adige.

[89] I am defeated in all attempts to convey Dante's emphasis in any sort of a verse line. The sense of the original: "It might provide some sort of a way down for one who started at the top, but (by implication) would not be climbable from below."

[90] This is the infamous Minotaur of classical mythology. His mother was Pasiphaë, wife of Minos, the King of Crete. She conceived an unnatural passion for a bull, and in order to mate with it, she crept into a wooden cow. From this union the Minotaur was born, half-man, half-beast. King Minos kept him in an ingenious labyrinth from which he could not escape. When Androgeos, the son of King Minos, was killed by the Athenians, Minos exacted an annual tribute of seven maidens and seven youths. These were annually turned into the labyrinth and there were devoured by the Minotaur. The monster was finally killed by Theseus, Duke of Athens. He was aided by Ariadne, daughter of Minos (and half-sister of the monster). She gave Theseus a ball of cord to unwind as he entered the labyrinth and a sword with which to kill the Minotaur.

As a bull that breaks its chains just when the knife
has struck its death-blow, cannot stand nor run
but leaps from side to side with its last life—
so danced the Minotaur, and my shrewd Guide
cried out: "Run now! While he is blind with rage!
Into the pass, quick, and get over the side!"
So we went down across the shale and slate
of that ruined rock, which often slid and shifted
under me at the touch of living weight. 30
I moved on, deep in thought; and my Guide to me:
"You are wondering perhaps about this ruin
which is guarded by the beast upon whose fury
I played just now. I should tell you that when last
I came this dark way to the depths of Hell,
this rock had not yet felt the ruinous blast.[91]
But certainly, if I am not mistaken,
it was just before the coming of Him who took
the souls from Limbo, that all Hell was shaken
so that I thought the universe felt love 40
and all its elements moved toward harmony,
whereby the world of matter, as some believe,
has often plunged to chaos.[92] It was then,
that here and elsewhere in the pits of Hell,
the ancient rock was stricken and broke open.
But turn your eyes to the valley; there we shall find
the river of boiling blood[93] in which are steeped
all who struck down their fellow men." Oh blind!
Oh ignorant, self-seeking cupidity
which spurs us so in the short mortal life 50
and steeps us so through all eternity!
I saw an arching fosse that was the bed
of a winding river circling through the plain
exactly as my Guide and Lord had said.
A file of Centaurs[94] galloped in the space
between the bank and the cliff, well armed with arrows,
riding as once on earth they rode to the chase.
And seeing us descend, that straggling band
halted, and three of them moved out toward us,
their long bows and their shafts already in hand. 60

---

[91]According to Matthew 27:51, an earthquake shook the earth at the moment of Christ's death. These stones, Dante lets us know, were broken off in that earthquake. We shall find other effects of the same shock in the Eighth Circle. It is worth noting also that both the Upper (see Canto 5, 34) and the Lower Hell begin with evidences of this ruin.

[92]The Greek philosopher Empedocles taught that the universe existed by the counterbalance (discord or mutual repulsion) of its elements. Should the elemental matter feel harmony (love or mutual attraction) all would fly together into chaos.

[93]Phlegethon, the river that circles through the First Round of the Seventh Circle, then sluices through the Wood of the Suicides (the Second Round) and the Burning Sands (Third Round) to spew over the Great Cliff into the Eighth Circle, and so, eventually, to the bottom of Hell (Cocytus).

[94]Creatures of classical mythology, half-horse, half-men. They were skilled and savage hunters, creatures of passion and violence. Like the Minotaur, they are symbols of the bestial-human, and as such, they are fittingly chosen as the tormentors of these sinners.

And one of them cried out while still below:
"To what pain are you sent down that dark coast?
Answer from where you stand, or I draw the bow!"
"Chiron[95] is standing there hard by your side;
our answer will be to him. This wrath of yours
was always your own worst fate," my Guide replied.
And to me he said: "That is Nessus, who died in the wood
for insulting Dejanira.[96] At his death
he plotted his revenge in his own blood.
The one in the middle staring at his chest 70
is the mighty Chiron, he who nursed Achilles:
the other is Pholus,[97] fiercer than all the rest.
They run by that stream in thousands, snapping their bows
at any wraith who dares to raise himself
out of the blood more than his guilt allows."
We drew near those swift beasts. In a thoughtful pause
Chiron drew an arrow, and with its notch
he pushed his great beard back along his jaws.
And when he had thus uncovered the huge pouches
of his lips, he said to his fellows: "Have you noticed 80
how the one who walks behind moves what he touches?
That is not how the dead go." My good Guide,
already standing by the monstrous breast
in which the two mixed natures joined, replied:
"It is true he lives; in his necessity
I alone must lead him through this valley.
Fate brings him here, not curiosity.
From singing Alleluia the sublime
spirit[98] who sends me came. He is no bandit.
Nor am I one who ever stooped to crime. 90
But in the name of the Power by which I go
this sunken way across the floor of Hell,
assign us one of your troop whom we may follow,
that he may guide us to the ford, and there
carry across on his back the one I lead,
for he is not a spirit to move through air."
Chiron turned his head on his right breast[99]
and said to Nessus: "Go with them, and guide them,
and turn back any others that would contest

---

[95]The son of Saturn and of the nymph Philira. He was the wisest and most just of the Centaurs and reputedly was the teacher of Achilles and of other Greek heroes to whom he imparted great skill in bearing arms, medicine, astronomy, music, and augury. Dante places him far down in Hell with the others of his kind, but though he draws Chiron's coarseness, he also grants him a kind of majestic understanding.

[96]Nessus carried travelers across the River Evenus for hire. He was hired to ferry Dejanira, the wife of Hercules, and tried to abduct her, but Hercules killed him with a poisoned arrow. While Nessus was dying, he whispered to Dejanira that a shirt stained with his poisoned blood would act as a love charm should Hercules' affections stray. When Hercules fell in love with Iole, Dejanira sent him a shirt stained with the Centaur's blood. The shirt poisoned Hercules and he died in agony.

[97]A number of classical poets mention Pholus but very little else is known of him.

[98]Beatrice.

[99]The right is the side of virtue and honor. In Chiron it probably signifies his human side as opposed to his bestial side.

their passage." So we moved beside our guide 100
along the bank of the scalding purple river
in which the shrieking wraiths were boiled and dyed.
Some stood up to their lashes in that torrent,
and as we passed them the huge Centaur said:
"These were the kings of bloodshed and despoilment.
Here they pay for their ferocity.
Here is Alexander.[100] And Dionysius,
who brought long years of grief to Sicily.
That brow you see with the hair as black as night
is Azzolino;[101] and that beside him, the blonde, 110
is Opizzo da Esti,[102] who had his mortal light
blown out by his own stepson." I turned then
to speak to the Poet but he raised a hand:
"Let him be the teacher now, and I will listen."
Further on, the Centaur stopped beside
a group of spirits steeped as far as the throat
in the race of boiling blood, and there our guide
pointed out a sinner who stood alone:
"That one before God's altar pierced a heart
still honored on the Thames."[103] And he passed on. 120
We came in sight of some who were allowed
to raise the head and all the chest from the river,
and I recognized many there. Thus, as we followed
along the stream of blood, its level fell
until it cooked no more than the feet of the damned.
And here we crossed the ford to deeper Hell.
"Just as you see the boiling stream grow shallow
along this side," the Centaur said to us
when we stood on the other bank, "I would have you know
that on the other, the bottom sinks anew 130
more and more, until it comes again
full circle to the place where the tyrants stew.
It is there that Holy Justice spends its wrath
on Sextus[104] and Pyrrhus through eternity,
and on Attila,[105] who was a scourge on earth:

---

[100] Alexander the Great. *Dionysius:* Dionysius I (d. 367 B.C.E.) and his son, Dionysius II (d. 343), were tyrants of Sicily. Both were infamous as prototypes of the bloodthirsty and exorbitant ruler. Dante may intend either or both.

[101] Ezzelino da Romano, Count of Onora (1194–1259). The cruelest of the Ghibelline tyrants. In 1236 Frederick II appointed Ezzelino his vicar in Padua. Ezzelino became especially infamous for his bloody treatment of the Paduans, whom he slaughtered in great numbers.

[102] Marquis of Ferrara (1264–1293). The account of his life is confused. One must accept Dante's facts as given.

[103] The sinner indicated is Guy de Montfort. His father, Simon de Montfort, was a leader of the barons who rebelled against Henry III and was killed at the battle of Evesham (1265) by Prince Edward (later Edward I). In 1271, Guy (then Vicar General of Tuscany) avenged his father's death by murdering Henry's nephew (who was also named Henry). The crime was openly committed in a church at Viterbo. The murdered Henry's heart was sealed in a casket and sent to London, where it was accorded various honors.

[104] Probably the younger son of Pompey the Great. His piracy is mentioned in Lucan (*Pharsalia* VI. 420–422). *Pyrrhus:* Pyrrhus, the son of Achilles, was especially bloodthirsty at the sack of Troy. Pyrrhus, King of Epirus (319–372 B.C.E.), waged relentless and bloody war against the Greeks and Romans. Either may be intended.

[105] King of the Huns from 433 to 453. He was called the Scourge of God.

and everlastingly milks out the tears
of Rinier da Corento and Rinier Pazzo,[106]
those two assassins who for many years
stalked the highways, bloody and abhorred."
And with that he started back across the ford. 140

Canto 13

Circle Seven: Round Two—The Violent Against Themselves: Nessus carries the Poets across the river of boiling blood and leaves them in the Second Round of the Seventh Circle, the Wood of the Suicides. Here are punished those who destroyed their own lives and those who destroyed their substance.

The souls of the Suicides are encased in thorny trees whose leaves are eaten by the odious Harpies, the overseers of these damned. When the Harpies feed upon them, damaging their leaves and limbs, the wound bleeds. Only as long as the blood flows are the souls of the trees able to speak. Thus, they who destroyed their own bodies are denied a human form; and just as the supreme expression of their lives was self-destruction, so they are permitted to speak only through that which tears and destroys them. Only through their own blood do they find voice. And to add one more dimension to the symbolism, it is the Harpies—defilers of all they touch—who give them their eternally recurring wounds.

The Poets pause before one tree and speak with the soul of Pier delle Vigne. In the same wood they see Jacomo da Sant' Andrea and Lano da Siena, two famous Squanderers and Destroyers of Goods, pursued by a pack of savage hounds. The hounds overtake Sant' Andrea, tear him to pieces and go off carrying his limbs in their teeth, a self-evident symbolic retribution for the violence with which these sinners destroyed their substance in the world. After this scene of horror, Dante speaks to an Unknown Florentine Suicide whose soul is inside the bush which was torn by the hound pack when it leaped upon Sant' Andrea.

Nessus had not yet reached the other shore
when we moved on into a pathless wood
that twisted upward from Hell's broken floor.
Its foliage was not verdant, but nearly black.
The unhealthy branches, gnarled and warped and tangled,
bore poison thorns instead of fruit. The track
of those wild beasts that shun the open spaces
men till between Cecina and Corneto
runs through no rougher nor more tangled places.[107]
Here nest the odious Harpies[108] of whom my Master 10
wrote how they drove Aeneas and his companions
from the Strophades with prophecies of disaster.
Their wings are wide, their feet clawed, their huge bellies
covered with feathers, their necks and faces human.
They croak eternally in the unnatural trees.

[106] Both were especially bloodthirsty robber-barons of the thirteenth century.

[107] The reference here is to the Maremma district of Tuscany which lies between the mountains and the sea. The river Cecina is the northern boundary of this district; Corneto is on the river Marta, which forms the southern boundary. It is a wild district of marsh and forest.

[108] These hideous birds with the faces of malign women were often associated with the Erinyes (Furies). Their original function in mythology was to snatch away the souls of men at the command of the Gods. Later, they were portrayed as defilers of food, and, by extension, of everything they touched. The islands of the Strophades were their legendary abode. Aeneas and his men landed there and fought with the Harpies, who drove them back and pronounced a prophecy of unbearable famine upon them.

"Before going on, I would have you understand,"
  my Guide began, "we are in the second round
  and shall be till we reach the burning sand.[109]
Therefore look carefully and you will see
  things in this wood, which, if I told them to you
  would shake the confidence you have placed in me."
I heard cries of lamentation rise and spill
  on every hand, but saw no souls in pain
  in all that waste; and, puzzled, I stood still.
I think perhaps he thought that I was thinking[110]
  those cries rose from among the twisted roots
  through which the spirits of the damned were slinking
to hide from us. Therefore my Master said:
  "If you break off a twig, what you will learn
  will drive what you are thinking from your head."
Puzzled, I raised my hand a bit and slowly
  broke off a branchlet from an enormous thorn:
  and the great trunk of it cried: "Why do you break me?"
And after blood had darkened all the bowl
  of the wound, it cried again: "Why do you tear me?
  Is there no pity left in any soul?
Men we were, and now we are changed to sticks;
  well might your hand have been more merciful
  were we no more than souls of lice and ticks."
As a green branch with one end all aflame
  will hiss and sputter sap out of the other
  as the air escapes—so from that trunk there came
words and blood together, gout by gout.
  Startled, I dropped the branch that I was holding
  and stood transfixed by fear, half turned about
to my Master, who replied: "O wounded soul,
  could he have believed before what he has seen
  in my verses only,[111] you would yet be whole,
for his hand would never have been raised against you.
  But knowing this truth could never be believed
  till it was seen, I urged him on to do
what grieves me now; and I beg to know your name,
  that to make you some amends in the sweet world
  when he returns, he may refresh your fame."
And the trunk: "So sweet those words to me that I
  cannot be still, and may it not annoy you
  if I seem somewhat lengthy in reply.

---

[109] The Third Round of this Circle.

[110] The original is *"Cred' io ch'ei credette ch'io credesse."* This sort of word play was considered quite elegant by medieval rhetoricians and by the ornate Sicilian School of poetry. Dante's style is based on a rejection of all such devices in favor of a sparse and direct diction. The best explanation of this unusual instance seems to be that Dante is anticipating his talk with Pier delle Vigne, a rhetorician who, as we shall see, delights in this sort of locution.

[111] The *Aeneid*, Book 3, describes a similar bleeding plant. There, Aeneas pulls at a myrtle growing on a Thracian hillside. It bleeds where he breaks it and a voice cries out of the ground. It is the voice of Polydorus, son of Priam and friend of Aeneas. He had been treacherously murdered by the Thracian king.

I am he who held both keys to Frederick's heart,[112]
locking, unlocking with so deft a touch
that scarce another soul had any part
in his most secret thoughts. Through every strife
I was so faithful to my glorious office
that for it I gave up both sleep and life.
That harlot, Envy, who on Caesar's[113] face
keeps fixed forever her adulterous stare,
the common plague and vice of court and palace,
inflamed all minds against me. These inflamed
so inflamed him that all my happy honors
were changed to mourning. Then, unjustly blamed,
my soul, in scorn, and thinking to be free
of scorn in death, made me at last, though just,
unjust to myself. By the new roots[114] of this tree
I swear to you that never in word or spirit
did I break faith to my lord and emperor
who was so worthy of honor in his merit.
If either of you return to the world, speak for me,
to vindicate in the memory of men
one who lies prostrate from the blows of Envy."
The Poet stood. Then turned. "Since he is silent,"
he said to me, "do not you waste this hour,
if you wish to ask about his life or torment."
And I replied: "Question him for my part,
on whatever you think I would do well to hear;
I could not, such compassion chokes my heart."
The Poet began again: "That this man may
with all his heart do for you what your words
entreat him to, imprisoned spirit, I pray,
tell us how the soul is bound and bent
into these knots, and whether any ever
frees itself from such imprisonment."
At that the trunk blew powerfully, and then
the wind became a voice that spoke these words:
"Briefly is the answer given: when
out of the flesh from which it tore itself,
the violent spirit comes to punishment,
Minos assigns it to the seventh shelf.

60

70

80

90

[112]Pier delle Vigne (1190–1249). A famous and once-powerful minister of Emperor Frederick II. He enjoyed Frederick's whole confidence until 1247 when he was accused of treachery and was imprisoned and blinded. He committed suicide to escape further torture. Pier delle Vigne was famous for his eloquence and for his mastery of the ornate Provençal-inspired Sicilian School of Italian Poetry, and Dante styles his speech accordingly. It is worth noting, however, that the style changes abruptly in the middle of line 72. There, his courtly preamble finished, delle Vigne speaks from the heart, simply and passionately. *Who held both keys:* The phrasing unmistakably suggests the Papal keys; delle Vigne may be suggesting that he was to Frederick as the Pope is to God.

[113]Frederick II was of course Caesar of the Roman Empire, but in this generalized context "Caesar" seems to be used as a generic term for any great ruler, i.e., "The harlot, Envy, never turns her attention from those in power."

[114]Pier delle Vigne had only been in Hell fifty-one years, a short enough time on the scale of eternity.

It falls into the wood, and landing there,
 wherever fortune flings it,[115] it strikes root,
 and there it sprouts, lusty as any tare,
shoots up a sapling, and becomes a tree. 100
 The Harpies, feeding on its leaves then, give it
 pain and pain's outlet simultaneously.[116]
Like the rest, we shall go for our husks on Judgment Day,
 but not that we may wear them, for it is not just
 that a man be given what he throws away.
Here shall we drag them and in this mournful glade
 our bodies will dangle to the end of time,
 each on the thorns of its tormented shade."
We waited by the trunk, but it said no more;
 and waiting, we were startled by a noise 110
 that grew through all the wood. Just such a roar
and trembling as one feels when the boar and chase
 approach his stand, the beasts and branches crashing
 and clashing in the heat of the fierce race.
And there on the left, running so violently
 they broke off every twig in the dark wood,
 two torn and naked wraiths went plunging by me.
The leader cried, "Come now, O Death! Come now!"
 And the other, seeing that he was outrun,
 cried out: "Your legs were not so ready, Lano,[117] 120
in the jousts at the Toppo." And suddenly in his rush,
 perhaps because his breath was failing him,
 he hid himself inside a thorny bush
and cowered among its leaves. Then at his back,
 the wood leaped with black bitches, swift as greyhounds
 escaping from their leash, and all the pack
sprang on him; with their fangs they opened him
 and tore him savagely, and then withdrew,
 carrying his body with them, limb by limb.
Then, taking me by the hand across the wood, 130
 my Master led me toward the bush. Lamenting,
 all its fractures blew out words and blood:
"O Jacomo da Sant' Andrea!"[118] it said,
 "what have you gained in making me your screen?
 What part had I in the foul life you led?"
And when my Master had drawn up to it
 he said: "Who were you, who through all your wounds
 blow out your blood with your lament, sad spirit?"

---

[115] Just as the soul of the suicide refused to accept divine regulation of its mortal life span, so eternal justice takes no special heed of where the soul falls.

[116] Suicide also gives pain and its outlet simultaneously.

[117] Lano da Siena, a famous squanderer. He died at the ford of the river Toppo near Arezzo in 1287 in a battle against the Aretines. Boccaccio writes that he deliberately courted death having squandered all his great wealth and being unwilling to live on in poverty. Thus his companion's jeer probably means: "You were not so ready to run then, Lano: why are you running now?"

[118] A Paduan with an infamous lust for laying waste his own goods and those of his neighbors; arson was his favorite prank. On one occasion, to celebrate the arrival of certain noble guests, he set fire to all the workers' huts and outbuildings of his estate. He was murdered in 1239, probably by assassins hired by Ezzolino (for whom see Canto 12).

And he to us: "You who have come to see
how the outrageous mangling of these hounds
has torn my boughs and stripped my leaves from me, 140
O heap them round my ruin! I was born
in the city that tore down Mars and raised the Baptist.[119]
On that account the God of War has sworn
her sorrow shall not end. And were it not
that something of his image still survives
on the bridge across the Arno, some have thought
those citizens who of their love and pain
afterwards rebuilt it from the ashes
left by Attila,[120] would have worked in vain. 150
I am one who has no tale to tell:
I made myself a gibbet of my own lintel."

Canto 14

Circle Seven: Round Three—The Violent Against God, Nature, and Art: Dante, in pity, restores the torn leaves to the soul of his countryman and the Poets move on to the next round, a great Plain of Burning Sand upon which there descends an eternal slow Rain of Fire. Here, scorched by fire from above and below, are three classes of sinners suffering differing degrees of exposure to the fire. The Blasphemers (the Violent Against God) are stretched supine upon the sand, the Sodomites (the Violent Against Nature) run in endless circles, and the Usurers (the Violent Against Art, which is the Grandchild of God) huddle on the sands.

The Poets find Capaneus stretched out on the sands, the chief sinner of that place. He is still blaspheming God. They continue along the edge of the Wood of the Suicides and come to a blood-red rill which flows boiling from the Wood and crosses the burning plain. Virgil explains the miraculous power of its waters and discourses on the Old Man of Crete and the origin of all the rivers of Hell.

The symbolism of the burning plain is obviously centered in sterility (the desert image) and wrath (the fire image). Blasphemy, sodomy, and usury are all unnatural and sterile actions: thus the unbearing desert is the eternity of these sinners; and thus the rain, which in nature should be fertile and cool, descends as fire. Capaneus, moreover, is subjected not to the wrath of nature (the sands below) and the wrath of God (the fire from above), but is tortured most by his own inner violence, which is the root of blasphemy.

Love of that land that was our common source
moved me to tears; I gathered up the leaves
and gave them back. He was already hoarse.
We came to the edge of the forest where one goes
from the second round to the third, and there we saw
what fearful arts the hand of Justice knows.
To make these new things wholly clear, I say
we came to a plain whose soil repels all roots.
The wood of misery rings it the same way

---

[119]Florence. Mars was the first patron of the city and when the Florentines were converted to Christianity, they pulled down his equestrian statue and built a church on the site of his temple. The statue of Mars was placed on a tower beside the Arno. When Totila (see note to line 150) destroyed Florence the tower fell into the Arno and the statue with it. Legend has it that Florence could never have been rebuilt had not the mutilated statue been rescued. It was placed on the Ponte Vecchio but was carried away in the flood of 1333.

[120]Dante confuses Attila with Totila, King of the Ostrogoths (d. 552). He destroyed Florence in 542. Attila (d. 453), King of the Huns, destroyed many cities of northern Italy, but not Florence.

the wood itself is ringed by the red fosse. 10
We paused at its edge: the ground was burning sand,
just such a waste as Cato marched across.[121]
O endless wrath of God: how utterly
thou shouldst become a terror to all men
who read the frightful truths revealed to me!
Enormous herds of naked souls I saw,
lamenting till their eyes were burned of tears;
they seemed condemned by an unequal law,
for some were stretched supine upon the ground,
some squatted with their arms about themselves, 20
and others without pause roamed round and round.
Most numerous were those that roamed the plain.
Far fewer were the souls stretched on the sand,
but moved to louder cries by greater pain.
And over all that sand on which they lay
or crouched or roamed, great flakes of flame fell slowly
as snow falls in the Alps on a windless day.
Like those Alexander met in the hot regions
of India, flames raining from the sky
to fall still unextinguished on his legions: 30
whereat he formed his ranks, and at their head
set the example, trampling the hot ground
for fear the tongues of fire might join and spread[122]—
just so in Hell descended the long rain
upon the damned, kindling the sand like tinder
under a flint and steel, doubling the pain.
In a never-ending fit upon those sands,
the arms of the damned twitched all about their bodies,
now here, now there, brushing away the brands.
"Poet," I said, "master of every dread 40
we have encountered, other than those fiends
who sallied from the last gate of the dead—
who is that wraith who lies along the rim
and sets his face against the fire in scorn,
so that the rain seems not to mellow him?"
And he himself,[123] hearing what I had said
to my Guide and Lord concerning him, replied:
"What I was living, the same am I now, dead.
Though Jupiter wear out his sooty smith
from whom on my last day he snatched in anger 50
the jagged thunderbolt he pierced me with;

---

[121] In 47 B.C.E., Cato of Utica led an army across the Libyan desert. Lucan described the march in *Pharsalia* IX, 587ff.

[122] This incident of Alexander the Great's campaign in India is described in *De Meteoris* of Albertus Magnus and was taken by him with considerable alteration from a letter reputedly sent to Aristotle by Alexander.

[123] Capaneus, one of the seven captains who warred on Thebes. As he scaled the walls of Thebes, Capaneus defied Jove to protect them. Jove replied with a thunderbolt that killed the blasphemer with his blasphemy still on his lips. (Statius, *Thebiad* X, 845ff.)

though he wear out the others one by one
who labor at the forge at Mongibello[124]
crying again 'Help! Help! Help me, good Vulcan!'
as he did at Phlegra[125] and hurl down endlessly
with all the power of Heaven in his arm,
small satisfaction would he win from me."
At this my Guide spoke with such vehemence
as I had not heard from him in all of Hell:
"O Capaneus, by your insolence 60
you are made to suffer as much fire inside
as falls upon you. Only your own rage
could be fit torment for your sullen pride."
Then he turned to me more gently. "That," he said,
"was one of the Seven who laid siege to Thebes.
Living, he scorned God, and among the dead
he scorns Him yet. He thinks he may detest
God's power too easily, but as I told him,
his slobber is a fit badge for his breast.
Now follow me; and mind for your own good 70
you do not step upon the burning sand,
but keep well back along the edge of the wood."
We walked in silence then till we reached a rill
that gushes from the wood;[126] it ran so red
the memory sends a shudder through me still.
As from the Bulicame[127] springs the stream
the sinful women keep to their own use;
so down the sand the rill flowed out in steam.
The bed and both its banks were petrified,
as were its margins; thus I knew at once 80
our passage through the sand lay by its side.
"Among all other wonders I have shown you
since we came through the gate denied to none,
nothing your eyes have seen is equal to
the marvel of the rill by which we stand,
for it stifles all the flames above its course
as it flows out across the burning sand."
So spoke my Guide across the flickering light,
and I begged him to bestow on me the food
for which he had given me the appetite. 90

---

[124] Mt. Etna. Vulcan was believed to have his smithy inside the volcano.

[125] At the battle of Phlegra in Thessaly the Titans tried to storm Olympus. Jove drove them back with the help of the thunderbolts Vulcan forged for him.

[126] The rill, still blood-red and still boiling, is the overflow of Phlegethon which descends across the Wood of the Suicides and the Burning Plain to plunge over the Great Cliff into the Eighth Circle. It is clearly a water of marvels, for it not only petrifies the sands over which it flows, but its clouds of steam quench all the flames above its course.

[127] A hot sulphur spring near Viterbo. The choice is strikingly apt, for the waters of the Bulicame not only boil and steam but have a distinctly reddish tint as a consequence of their mineral content. A part of the Bulicame flows out through what was once a quarter reserved to prostitutes; and they were given special rights to the water, since they were not permitted to use the public baths.

"In the middle of the sea, and gone to waste,
there lies a country known as Crete," he said,
"under whose king the ancient world was chaste.
Once Rhea[128] chose it as the secret crypt
and cradle of her son; and better to hide him,
her Corybantes raised a din when he wept.
An ancient giant[129] stands in the mountain's core.
He keeps his shoulder turned toward Damietta,
and looks toward Rome as if it were his mirror.
His head is made of gold; of silverwork 100
his breast and both his arms, of polished brass
the rest of his great torso to the fork.
He is of chosen iron from there down,
except that his right foot is terra cotta;
it is this foot he rests more weight upon.
Every part except the gold is split
by a great fissure from which endless tears
drip down and hollow out the mountain's pit.
Their course sinks to this pit from stone to stone,
becoming Acheron, Phlegethon, and Styx. 110
Then by this narrow sluice they hurtle down
to the end of all descent, and disappear
into Cocytus.[130] You shall see what sink that is
with your own eyes. I pass it in silence here."
And I to him: "But if these waters flow
from the world above, why is this rill met only
along this shelf?" And he to me: "You know
the place is round, and though you have come deep
into the valley through the many circles,
always bearing left along the steep, 120
you have not traveled any circle through
its total round; hence when new things appear
from time to time, that hardly should surprise you."

[128]Wife of Saturn (Cronos) and mother of Jove (Zeus). It had been prophesied to Saturn that one of his own children would dethrone him. To nullify the prophecy Saturn devoured each of his children at birth. On the birth of Jove, Rhea duped Saturn by letting him bolt down a stone wrapped in baby clothes. After this tribute to her husband's appetite she hid the infant on Mount Ida in Crete. There she posted her Corybantes (or Bacchantes) as guards and instructed them to set up a great din whenever the baby cried. Thus Saturn would not hear him. The Corybantic dances of the ancient Greeks were based on the frenzied shouting and clashing of swords on shields with which the Corybantes protected the infant Jove.

[129]This is the Old Man of Crete. The original of this figure occurs in Daniel 2:32–34, where it is told by Daniel as Nebuchadnezzar's dream. Dante follows the details of the original closely but adds a few of his own and a totally different interpretation. In Dante each metal represents one of the ages of humanity, each deteriorating from the Golden Age of Innocence. The left foot, terminating the Age of Iron, is the Holy Roman Empire. The right foot, of terra cotta, is the Roman Catholic Church, a more fragile base than the left, but the one upon which the greater weight descends. The tears of the woes of humanity are a Dantean detail: they flow down the great fissure that defaces all but the Golden Age. Thus, starting in woe, they flow through humanity's decline, into the hollow of the mountain and become the waters of all Hell. Dante's other major addition is the site and position of the figure: equidistant from the three continents, the Old Man stands at a sort of center of Time, his back turned to Damietta in Egypt (here symbolizing the East, the past, the birth of religion) and fixes his gaze upon Rome (the West, the future, the Catholic Church). It is certainly the most elaborately worked single symbol in *The Inferno*.

[130]The frozen lake that lies at the bottom of Hell. (See Cantos 32–34.)

And I: "Where shall we find Phlegethon's course?
  And Lethe's? One you omit, and of the other
  you only say the tear-flood is its source."
"In all you ask of me you please me truly,"
  he answered, "but the red and boiling water
  should answer the first question you put to me,
and you shall stand by Lethe, but far hence: 130
  there, where the spirits go to wash themselves
  when their guilt has been removed by penitence."
And then he said: "Now it is time to quit
  this edge of shade: follow close after me
  along the rill, and do not stray from it;
for the unburning margins form a lane,
  and by them we may cross the burning plain."

Canto 15

Circle Seven: Round Three—The Violent Against Nature: Protected by the marvelous powers of the boiling rill, the Poets walk along its banks across the burning plain. The Wood of the Suicides is behind them; the Great Cliff at whose foot lies the Eighth Circle is before them.

They pass one of the roving bands of Sodomites. One of the sinners stops Dante, and with great difficulty the Poet recognizes him under his baked features as Ser Brunetto Latino. This is a reunion with a dearly loved man and writer, one who had considerably influenced Dante's own development, and Dante addresses him with great and sorrowful affection, paying him the highest tribute offered to any sinner in *The Inferno.* Brunetto prophesies Dante's sufferings at the hands of the Florentines, gives an account of the souls that move with him through the fire, and finally, under Divine Compulsion, races off across the plain.

We go by one of the stone margins now
  and the steam of the rivulet makes a shade above it,
  guarding the stream and banks from the flaming snow.
As the Flemings in the lowland between Bruges
  and Wissant, under constant threat of the sea,
  erect their great dikes to hold back the deluge;
as the Paduans along the shores of the Brent
  build levees to protect their towns and castles
  lest Chiarentana drown in the spring torrent[131]—
to the same plan, though not so wide nor high,[132] 10
  did the engineer, whoever he may have been,
  design the margin we were crossing by.
Already we were so far from the wood
  that even had I turned to look at it,
  I could not have made it out from where I stood,
when a company of shades came into sight
  walking beside the bank. They stared at us
  as men at evening by the new moon's light

[131] Dante compares the banks of the rill of Phlegethon to the dikes built by the Flemings to hold back the sea, and to those built by the Paduans to hold back the spring floods of the river Brent. Chiarentana (Latin: Clarentana) was a Duchy of the Middle Ages. Its territory included the headwaters of the Brent (Brenta).

[132] Their width is never precisely specified, but we shall see when Dante walks along speaking to Ser Brunetto (line 40) that their height is about that of a man.

stare at one another when they pass by
  on a dark road, pointing their eyebrows toward us 20
  as an old tailor squints at his needle's eye.
Stared at so closely by that ghostly crew,
  I was recognized by one[133] who seized the hem
  of my skirt and said: "Wonder of wonders! You?"
And I, when he stretched out his arm to me,
  searched his baked features closely, till at last
  I traced his image from my memory
in spite of the burnt crust, and bending near
  to put my face closer to his, at last
  I answered: "Ser Brunetto, are *you* here?" 30
"O my son! may it not displease you," he cried,
  "if Brunetto Latino leave his company
  and turn and walk a little by your side."
And I to him: "With all my soul I ask it.
  Or let us sit together, if it please him
  who is my Guide and leads me through this pit."
"My son!" he said, "whoever of this train
  pauses a moment, must lie a hundred years
  forbidden to brush off the burning rain.
Therefore, go on; I will walk at your hem,[134] 40
  and then rejoin my company, which goes
  mourning eternal loss in eternal flame."
I did not dare descend to his own level
  but kept my head inclined, as one who walks
  in reverence meditating good and evil.
"What brings you here before your own last day?
  What fortune or what destiny?" be began.
  "And who is he that leads you this dark way?"
"Up there in the happy life I went astray
  in a valley," I replied, "before I had reached 50
  the fullness of my years. Only yesterday
at dawn I turned from it. This spirit showed
  himself to me as I was turning back,
  and guides me home again along this road."

---

[133] *Ser Brunetto Latino:* or Latini. (Born between 1210 and 1230, died 1294.) A prominent Florentine Guelph who held, among many other posts, that of notary, whence the title *Ser* (sometimes *Sere*). He was not Dante's schoolmaster as many have supposed—he was much too busy and important a man for that. Dante's use of the word "master" is to indicate spiritual indebtedness to Brunetto and his works. It is worth noting that Dante addresses him in Italian as "voi" instead of using the less respectful "tu" form. Farinata is the only other sinner so addressed in *The Inferno*. Brunetto's two principal books, both of which Dante admired, were the prose *Livre dou Tresor* (*The Book of the Treasure*) and the poetic *Tesoretto* (*The Little Treasure*). Dante learned a number of his devices from the allegorical journey that forms the *Tesoretto*. Dante's surprise at finding Brunetto here is worth puzzling about. So too is the fact that he did not ask Ciacco about him (Canto 6) when he mentioned other prominent Florentines. One speculation is that Dante had not intended to place him in Hell, and that he found reason to believe him guilty of this sin only years after Brunetto's death (*The Inferno* was written between 1310 and 1314, in all probability). This answer is not wholly satisfactory.

[134] See also line 10. Dante is standing on the dike at approximately the level of Brunetto's head and he cannot descend because of the rain of fire and the burning sands.

And he: "Follow your star, for if in all
of the sweet life I saw one truth shine clearly,
you cannot miss your glorious arrival.
And had I lived to do what I meant to do,
I would have cheered and seconded your work,
observing Heaven so well disposed toward you. 60
But that ungrateful and malignant stock[135]
that came down from Fiesole of old
and still smacks of the mountain and the rock,
for your good works will be your enemy.
And there is cause: the sweet fig is not meant
to bear its fruit beside the bitter sorb-tree.[136]
Even the old adage calls them blind,[137]
an envious, proud, and avaricious people:
see that you root their customs from your mind.
It is written in your stars and will come to pass, 70
that your honours shall make both sides hunger for you:[138]
but the goat shall never reach to crop that grass.
Let the beasts of Fiesole[139] devour their get
like sows, but never let them touch the plant,
if among their rankness any springs up yet,
in which is born again the holy seed
of the Romans who remained among their rabble
when Florence made a new nest for their greed."
"Ah, had I all my wish," I answered then,
"you would not yet be banished from the world 80
in which you were a radiance among men,
for that sweet image, gentle and paternal,
you were to me in the world when hour by hour
you taught me how man makes himself eternal,
lives in my mind, and now strikes to my heart;
and while I live, the gratitude I owe it
will speak to men out of my life and art.
What you have told me of my course, I write
by another text I save to show a Lady[140]
who will judge these matters, if I reach her height. 90

[135]The ancient Etruscan city of Fiesole was situated on a hill about three miles north of the present site of Florence. According to legend, Fiesole had taken the side of Catiline in his war with Julius Caesar. Caesar destroyed the town and set up a new city called Florence on the Arno, peopling it with Romans and Fiesolans. The Romans were the aristocracy of the new city, but the Fiesolans were a majority. Dante ascribes the endless bloody conflicts of Florence largely to the internal strife between these two strains. His scorn of the Fiesolans is obvious in this passage. Dante proudly proclaimed his descent from the Roman strain.

[136]A species of tart apple.

[137]The source of this proverbial expression, "Blind as a Florentine," can no longer be traced with any assurance, though many incidents from Florentine history suggest possible sources.

[138]Brunetto can scarcely mean that both sides will hunger to welcome the support of a man of Dante's distinction. Rather that both sides will hunger to destroy him. (See also lines 94–95. Dante obviously accepts this as another dark prophecy.)

[139]The Fiesolans themselves.

[140]Beatrice.

This much I would have you know: so long, I say,
as nothing in my conscience troubles me
I am prepared for Fortune, come what may.
Twice already[141] in the eternal shade
I have heard this prophecy; but let Fortune turn
her wheel as she please, and the countryman his spade."
My guiding spirit paused at my last word
and, turning right about, stood eye to eye
to say to me: "Well heeded is well heard."
But I did not reply to him, going on 100
with Ser Brunetto to ask him who was with him
in the hot sands, the best-born and best known.
And he to me: "Of some who share this walk
it is good to know; of the rest let us say nothing,
for the time would be too short for so much talk.
In brief, we all were clerks and men of worth,
great men of letters, scholars of renown;
all by the one same crime defiled on earth.
Priscian[142] moves there along the wearisome
sad way, and Francesco d'Accorso,[143] and also there, 110
if you had any longing for such scum,
you might have seen that one the Servant of Servants[144]
sent from Arno to the Bacchiglione
where he left his unnatural organ[145] wrapped in cerements.
I would say more, but there across the sand
a new smoke rises and new people come,
and I must run to be with my own band.
Remember my *Treasure,* in which I still live on:
I ask no more." He turned then, and he seemed,
across that plain, like one of those who run 120
for the green cloth[146] at Verona; and of those,
more like the one who wins, than those who lose.

. . .

[141]The prophecies of Ciacco (Canto 6) and of Farinata (Canto 10) are the other two places at which Dante's exile and suffering are foretold. Dante replies that come what may he will remain true to his purpose through all affliction; and Virgil turns to look proudly at his pupil, uttering a proverb: "*Bene ascolta chi la nota,*" "Well heeded is well heard."

[142]Latin grammarian and poet of the first half of the sixth century.

[143]A Florentine scholar. He served as a professor at Bologna and, from 1273 to 1280, at Oxford. He died in Bologna in 1294.

[144]"The Servant of Servants" was Dante's old enemy, Boniface VIII. *Servus servorum* is technically a correct papal title, but there is certainly a touch of irony in Dante's application of it in this context. In 1295 Boniface transferred Bishop Andrea de'Mozzi from the Bishopric of Florence (on the Arno) to that of Vicenza (on the Bacchiglione). The transference was reputedly brought about at the request of the Bishop's brother, Tommaso de'Mozzi of Florence, who wished to remove from his sight the spectacle of his brother's stupidity and unnatural vices.

[145]The original, *mal protesi nervi,* contains an untranslatable word-play. *Nervi* may be taken as "the male organ" and *protesi* for "erected"; thus the organ aroused to passion for unnatural purposes (*mal*). Or *nervi* may be taken as "nerves" and *mal protesi* for "dissolute." Taken in context, the first rendering strikes me as more Dantean.

[146]On the first Sunday of Lent all the young men of Verona ran a race for the prize of green cloth. The last runner in was given a live rooster and was required to carry it through the town.

Canto 17

Circle Seven: Round Three—The Violent Against Art: The monstrous shape lands on the brink and Virgil salutes it ironically. It is Geryon, the Monster of Fraud. Virgil announces that they must fly down from the cliff on the back of this monster. While Virgil negotiates for their passage, Dante is sent to examine the Usurers (The Violent Against Art).

These sinners sit in a crouch along the edge of the burning plain that approaches the cliff. Each of them has a leather purse around his neck, and each purse is blazoned with a coat of arms. Their eyes, gushing with tears, are forever fixed on these purses. Dante recognizes none of these sinners, but their coats of arms are unmistakably those of well-known Florentine families.

Having understood who they are and the reason for their present condition, Dante cuts short his excursion and returns to find Virgil mounted on the back of Geryon. Dante joins his Master and they fly down from the great cliff.

Their flight carries them from the Hell of the Violent and the Bestial (The Sins of the Lion) into the Hell of the Fraudulent and Malicious (The Sins of the Leopard).

"Now see the sharp-tailed beast[147] that mounts the brink.
He passes mountains, breaks through walls and weapons.
Behold the beast that makes the whole world stink."
These were the words my Master spoke to me;
then signaled the weird beast to come to ground
close to the sheer end of our rocky levee.
The filthy prototype of Fraud drew near
and settled his head and breast upon the edge
of the dark cliff, but let his tail hang clear.
His face was innocent of every guile, 10
benign and just in feature and expression;
and under it his body was half reptile.
His two great paws were hairy to the armpits;
all his back and breast and both his flanks
were figured with bright knots and subtle circlets:
never was such a tapestry of bloom
woven on earth by Tartar or Turk,[148]
nor by Arachne[149] at her flowering loom.
As a ferry sometimes lies along the strand,
part beached and part afloat; and as the beaver,[150] 20
up yonder in the guzzling Germans'[151] land,

---

[147]A mythical king of Spain represented as a giant with three heads and three bodies. He was killed by Hercules, who coveted the king's cattle. A later tradition represents him as killing and robbing strangers whom he lured into his realm. It is probably on this account that Dante chose him as the prototype of Fraud, though in a radically altered bodily form. Some of the details of Dante's Geryon may be drawn from Revelation 9:9–20, but most of them are almost certainly his own invention: a monster with the general shape of a dragon but with the tail of a scorpion, hairy arms, a gaudily marked reptilian body, and the face of a just and honest man. The careful reader will note that the gaudily spotted body suggests the Leopard; the hairy paws, the Lion; and that the human face represents the essentially human nature of Fraud, which thus embodies corruption of the Appetite, of the Will, and of the Intellect.

[148]These were the most skilled weavers of Dante's time.

[149]She was so famous as a spinner and weaver that she challenged Minerva to a weaving contest. There are various accounts of what happened in the contest, but all of them end with the goddess so moved to anger that she changed Arachne into a spider.

[150]Dante's description of the beaver is probably drawn from some old bestiary or natural history. It may be based on the medieval belief that the beaver fished by crouching on the bank, scooping the fish out with its tail.

[151]The heavy drinking of the Germans was proverbial in the Middle Ages and far back into antiquity.

squats halfway up the bank when a fight is on—
just so lay that most ravenous of beasts
on the rim which bounds the burning sand with stone.
His tail twitched in the void beyond that lip,
thrashing, and twisting up the envenomed fork
which, like a scorpion's stinger, armed the tip.
My Guide said: "It is time now we drew near
that monster." And descending on the right[152]
we moved ten paces outward to be clear 30
of sand and flames. And when we were beside him,
I saw upon the sand a bit beyond us
some people[153] crouching close beside the brim.
The Master paused. "That you may take with you
the full experience of this round," he said,
"go now and see the last state of that crew.
But let your talk be brief, and I will stay
and reason with this beast till you return,
that his strong back may serve us on our way."
So further yet along the outer edge 40
of the seventh circle I moved on alone.
And came to the sad people of the ledge.
Their eyes burst with their grief; their smoking hands
jerked about their bodies, warding off
now the flames and now the burning sands.
Dogs in summer bit by fleas and gadflies,
jerking their snouts about, twitching their paws
now here, now there, behave no otherwise.
I examined several faces there among
that sooty throng, and I saw none I knew; 50
but I observed that from each neck there hung
an enormous purse, each marked with its own beast
and its own colors like a coat of arms.
On these their streaming eyes appeared to feast.
Looking about, I saw one purse display
azure on or, a kind of lion;[154] another,
on a blood red field, a goose whiter than whey.[155]
And one that bore a huge and swollen sow
azure on field argent[156] said to me:
"What are you doing in this pit of sorrow? 60

---

[152]The Poets had crossed on the right bank of the rill. In the course of Geryon's flight they will be carried to the other side of the falls, thus continuing their course to the left. It should be noted that inside the walls of Dis, approaching the second great division of Hell (as here the third) they also moved to the right. No satisfactory reason can be given for these exceptions.

[153]The Usurers. Virgil explains in Canto 11 why they sin against Art, which is the Grandchild of God. They are the third and final category of the Violent against God and His works.

[154]The arms of the Gianfigliazzi of Florence were a lion azure on a field of gold. The sinner bearing this purse must be Catello di Rosso Gianfigliazzi, who set up as a usurer in France and was made a knight on his return to Florence.

[155]A white goose on a red field was the arms of the noble Ghibelline family of the Ubriachi, or Ebriachi, of Florence. The wearer is probably Ciappo Ubriachi, a notorious usurer.

[156]These are the arms of the Scrovegni of Padua. The bearer is probably Reginaldo Scrovegni.

Leave us alone! And since you have not yet died,
  I'll have you know my neighbor Vitaliano[157]
  has a place reserved for him here at my side.
A Paduan among Florentines, I sit here
  while hour by hour they nearly deafen me
  shouting: 'Send us the sovereign cavalier[158]
with the purse of the three goats!' " He half arose,
  twisted his mouth, and darted out his tongue
  for all the world like an ox licking his nose.
And I, afraid that any longer stay 70
  would anger him who had warned me to be brief,
  left those exhausted souls without delay.
Returned, I found my Guide already mounted
  upon the rump of that monstrosity.
  He said to me: "Now must you be undaunted:
this beast must be our stairway to the pit:
  mount it in front, and I will ride between
  you and the tail, lest you be poisoned by it."
Like one so close to the quartanary chill[159]
  that his nails are already pale and his flesh trembles 80
  at the very sight of shade or a cool rill—
so did I tremble at each frightful word.
  But his scolding filled me with that shame that makes
  the servant brave in the presence of his lord.
I mounted the great shoulders of that freak
  and tried to say "Now help me to hold on!"
  But my voice clicked in my throat and I could not speak.
But no sooner had I settled where he placed me
  than he, my stay, my comfort, and my courage
  in other perils, gathered and embraced me. 90
Then he called out: "Now, Geryon, we are ready:
  bear well in mind that his is living weight
  and make your circles wide and your flight steady."
As a small ship slides from its beaching or its pier,
  backward, backward—so that monster slipped
  back from the rim. And when he had drawn clear
he swung about, and stretching out his tail
  he worked it like an eel, and with his paws
  he gathered in the air, while I turned pale.

---

[157]Vitaliano di Iacopo Vitaliani, another Paduan.

[158]Giovanni di Buiamonte was esteemed in Florence as "the sovereign cavalier" and was chosen for many high offices. He was a usurer and a gambler who lost great sums at play. Dante's intent is clearly to bewail the decay of standards which permits Florence to honor so highly a man for whom Hell is waiting so dismally. Buiamonte was of the Becchi family whose arms were three black goats on a gold field. "Becchi" in Italian is the plural form of the word for "goat."

[159]Quartan fever is an ague that runs a four-day cycle with symptoms roughly like those of malaria. At the approach of the chill, Dante intends his figure to say, any thought of coolness strikes terror into the shivering victim.

I think there was no greater fear the day 100
Phaeton[160] let loose the reins and burned the sky
along the great scar of the Milky Way,
nor when Icarus,[161] too close to the sun's track
felt the wax melt, unfeathering his loins,
and heard his father cry "Turn back! Turn back!"—
than I felt when I found myself in air,
afloat in space with nothing visible
but the enormous beast that bore me there.
Slowly, slowly, he swims on through space,
wheels and descends, but I can sense it only 110
by the way the wind blows upward past my face.
Already on the right I hear the swell
and thunder of the whirlpool. Looking down
I leaned my head out and stared into Hell.
I trembled again at the prospect of dismounting
and cowered in on myself, for I saw fires
on every hand, and I heard a long lamenting.
And then I saw—till then I had but felt it—
the course of our down-spiral to the horrors
that rose to us from all sides of the pit. 120
As a flight-worn falcon[162] sinks down wearily
though neither bird nor lure has signalled it,
the falconer crying out: "What! spent already!"—
then turns and in a hundred spinning gyres
sulks from her master's call, sullen and proud—
so to that bottom lit by endless fires
the monster Geryon circled and fell,
setting us down at the foot of the precipice
of ragged rock on the eighth shelf of Hell.
And once freed of our weight, he shot from there 130
into the dark like an arrow into air.

Canto 18

Circle Eight (Malebolge)—The Fraudulent and Malicious; Bolgia One—The Panderers and Seducers; Bolgia Two—The Flatterers: Dismounted from Geryon, the Poets find themselves in the Eighth Circle, called Malebolge (the Evil Ditches). This is the upper half of the Hell of the Fraudulent and Malicious. Malebolge is a great circle of stone that slopes like an amphitheater. The slopes are divided into ten concentric ditches; and within these ditches, each with his own kind, are punished those guilty of Simple Fraud.

A series of stone dikes runs like spokes from the edge of the great cliff face to the center of the place, and these serve as bridges.

---

[160] Son of Apollo who drove the chariot of the sun. Phaeton begged his father for a chance to drive the chariot himself but he lost control of the horses and Zeus killed him with a thunderbolt for fear the whole earth would catch fire. The scar left in the sky by the runaway horses is marked by the Milky Way.

[161] Daedalus, the father of Icarus, made wings for himself and his son and they flew into the sky, but Icarus, ignoring his father's commands, flew too close to the sun. The heat melted the wax with which the wings were fastened and Icarus fell into the Aegean and was drowned.

[162] Falcons, when sent aloft, were trained to circle until sighting a bird, or until signaled back by the lure (a stuffed bird). Flight-weary, Dante's metaphoric falcon sinks bit by bit, rebelling against his training and sulking away from his master in wide slow circles. The weighed, slow, downward flight of Geryon is powerfully contrasted with his escaping bound into the air once he has deposited his burden.

The Poets bear left toward the first ditch, and Dante observes below him and to his right the sinners of the first bolgia, the Panderers and Seducers. These make two files, one along either bank of the ditch, and are driven at an endless fast walk by horned demons who hurry them along with great lashes. In life these sinners goaded others on to serve their own foul purposes; so in Hell are they driven in their turn. The horned demons who drive them symbolize the sinners' own vicious natures, embodiments of their own guilty consciences. Dante may or may not have intended the horns of the demons to symbolize cuckoldry and adultery.

The Poets see Venedico Caccianemico and Jason in the first pit, and pass on to the second, where they find the souls of the Flatterers sunk in excrement, the true equivalent of their false flatteries on earth. They observe Alessio Interminelli and Thaïs, and pass on.

There is in Hell a vast and sloping ground
 called Malebolge,[163] a lost place of stone
 as black as the great cliff that seals it round.
Precisely in the center of that space
 there yawns a well extremely wide and deep.[164]
 I shall discuss it in its proper place.
The border that remains between the well-pit
 and the great cliff forms an enormous circle,
 and ten descending troughs are cut in it,
offering a general prospect like the ground 10
 that lies around one of those ancient castles
 whose walls are girded many times around
by concentric moats. And just as, from the portal,
 the castle's bridges run from moat to moat
 to the last bank; so from the great rock wall
across the embankments and the ditches, high
 and narrow cliffs run to the central well,
 which cuts and gathers them like radii.
Here, shaken from the back of Geryon,
 we found ourselves. My Guide kept to the left 20
 and I walked after him. So we moved on.
Below, on my right, and filling the first ditch
 along both banks, new souls in pain appeared,
 new torments, and new devils black as pitch.
All of these sinners were naked; on our side
 of the middle they walked toward us; on the other,
 in our direction, but with swifter stride.
Just so the Romans, because of the great throng
 in the year of the Jubilee, divide the bridge[165]
 in order that the crowds may pass along, 30
so that all face the Castle as they go
 on one side toward St. Peter's, while on the other,
 all move along facing toward Mount Giordano.

[163] *Bolgia* in Italian equals "ditch" or "pouch." That combination of meanings is not possible in a single English word, but it is well to bear in mind that Dante intended both meanings: not only a ditch of evil, but a pouch full of it, a filthy treasure of ill-gotten souls.

[164] This is the final pit of Hell, and in it are punished the Treacherous (those Guilty of Compound Fraud). Cantos 29–34 deal with this part of Hell.

[165] Boniface VIII had proclaimed 1300 a Jubilee Year, and consequently throngs of pilgrims had come to Rome. Since the date of the vision is also 1300, the Roman throngs are moving back and forth across the Tiber via Ponte Castello Sant' Angelo at the very time Dante is watching the sinners in Hell.

And everywhere along that hideous track
  I saw horned demons with enormous lashes
  move through those souls, scourging them on the back.
Ah, how the stragglers of that long rout stirred
  their legs quick-march at the first crack of the lash!
  Certainly no one waited a second, or third!
As we went on, one face in that procession 40
  caught my eye and I said: "That sinner there:
  It is certainly not the first time I've seen that one."
I stopped, therefore, to study him, and my Guide
  out of his kindness waited, and even allowed me
  to walk back a few steps at the sinner's side.
And that flayed spirit, seeing me turn around,
  thought to hide his face, but I called to him:
  "You there, that walk along with your eyes on the ground—
if those are not false features, then I know you
  as Venedico Caccianemico of Bologna:[166] 50
  what brings you here among this petty crew?"
And he replied: "I speak unwillingly,
  but something in your living voice, in which
  I hear the world again, stirs and compels me.
It was I who brought the fair Ghisola 'round
  to serve the will and lust of the Marquis,
  however sordid that old tale may sound.
There are many more from Bologna who weep away
  eternity in this ditch; we fill it so
  there are not as many tongues that are taught to say 60
'sipa'[167] in all the land that lies between
  the Reno and the Saveno, as you must know
  from the many tales of our avarice and spleen."
And as he spoke, one of those lashes fell
  across his back, and a demon cried, "Move on,
  you pimp, there are no women here to sell."
Turning away then, I rejoined my Guide.
  We came in a few steps to a raised ridge
  that made a passage to the other side.
This we climbed easily, and turning right 70
  along the jagged crest, we left behind
  the eternal circling of those souls in flight.
And when we reached the part at which the stone
  was tunneled for the passage of the scourged,
  my Guide said, "Stop a minute and look down
on these other misbegotten wraiths of sin.
  You have not seen their faces, for they moved
  in the same direction we were headed in."

---

[166]To win the favor of the Marquis Obbizo da Este of Ferrara, Caccianemico acted as the procurer of his own sister Ghisola, called "la bella" or "Ghisolabella."

[167]Bolognese dialect for *si,* i.e., "yes." Bologna lies between the Savena and the Reno. This is a master taunt at Bologna as a city of panderers and seducers, for it clearly means that the Bolognese then living on earth were fewer in number than the Bolognese dead who had been assigned to this *bolgia.*

So from that bridge we looked down on the throng
 that hurried toward us on the other side. 80
 Here, too, the whiplash hurried them along.
And the good Master, studying that train,
 said: "Look there, at that great soul that approaches
 and seems to shed no tears for all his pain—
what kingliness moves with him even in Hell!
 It is Jason,[168] who by courage and good advice
 made off with the Colchian Ram. Later it fell
that he passed Lemnos, where the women of wrath,
 enraged by Venus' curse that drove their lovers
 out of their arms, put all their males to death. 90
There with his honeyed tongue and his dishonest
 lover's wiles, he gulled Hypsipyle,
 who, in the slaughter, had gulled all the rest.
And there he left her, pregnant and forsaken.
 Such guilt condemns him to such punishment;
 and also for Medea is vengeance taken.
All seducers march here to the whip.
 And let us say no more about this valley
 and those it closes in its stony grip."
We had already come to where the walk 100
 crosses the second bank, from which it lifts
 another arch, spanning from rock to rock.
Here we heard people whine in the next chasm,
 and knock and thump themselves with open palms,
 and blubber through their snouts as if in a spasm.
Steaming from that pit, a vapour rose
 over the banks, crusting them with a slime
 that sickened my eyes and hammered at my nose.
That chasm sinks so deep we could not sight
 its bottom anywhere until we climbed 110
 along the rock arch to its greatest height.
Once there, I peered down; and I saw long lines
 of people in a river of excrement
 that seemed the overflow of the world's latrines.
I saw among the felons of that pit
 one wraith who might or might not have been tonsured—
 one could not tell, he was so smeared with shit.
He bellowed: "You there, why do you stare at me
 more than at all the others in this stew?"
 And I to him: "Because if memory 120

---

[168] Leader of the Argonauts. He carried off the Colchian Ram (i.e., The Golden Fleece). "The good advice" that helped him win the fleece was given by Medea, daughter of the King of Colchis, whom Jason took with him and later abandoned for Creusa ("Also for Medea is vengeance taken"). In the course of his very Grecian life, Jason had previously seduced Hypsipyle and deserted her to continue his voyage after the fleece. She was one of the women of Lemnos whom Aphrodite, because they no longer worshiped her, cursed with a foul smell which made them unbearable to their husbands and lovers. The women took their epic revenge by banding together to kill all their males, but Hypsipyle managed to save her father, King Thoas, by pretending to the women that she had already killed him.

serves me, I knew you when your hair was dry.
You are Alessio Interminelli da Lucca.[169]
That's why I pick you from this filthy fry."
And he then, beating himself on his clown's head:
"Down to this have the flatteries I sold
the living sunk me here among the dead."
And my Guide prompted then: "Lean forward a bit
and look beyond him, there—do you see that one
scratching herself with dungy nails, the strumpet
who fidgets to her feet, then to a crouch? 130
It is the whore Thaïs[170] who told her lover
when he sent to ask her, 'Do you thank me much?'
'Much? Nay, past all believing!' And with this
let us turn from the sight of this abyss."

Canto 19

Circle Eight: Bolgia Three—The Simoniacs: Dante comes upon the Simoniacs (sellers of ecclesiastic favors and offices) and his heart overflows with the wrath he feels against those who corrupt the things of God. This bolgia is lined with round tube-like holes and the sinners are placed in them upside down with the soles of their feet ablaze. The heat of the blaze is proportioned to their guilt.

The holes in which these sinners are placed are debased equivalents of the baptismal fonts common in the cities of Northern Italy and the sinners' confinement in them is temporary: as new sinners arrive, the souls drop through the bottom of their holes and disappear eternally into the crevices of the rock.

As always, the punishment is a symbolic retribution. Just as the Simoniacs made a mock of holy office, so are they turned upside down in a mockery of the baptismal font. Just as they made a mockery of the holy water of baptism, so is their hellish baptism by fire, after which they are wholly immersed in the crevices below. The oily fire that licks at their soles may also suggest a travesty on the oil used in Extreme Unction (last rites for the dying).

Virgil carries Dante down an almost sheer ledge and lets him speak to one who is the chief sinner of that place, Pope Nicholas III. Dante delivers himself of another stirring denunciation of those who have corrupted church office, and Virgil carries him back up the steep ledge toward the Fourth Bolgia.

O Simon Magus![171] O you wretched crew
who follow him, pandering for silver and gold
the things of God which should be wedded to
love and righteousness! O thieves for hire,
now must the trump of judgment sound your doom
here in the third fosse of the rim of fire!

---

[169] One of the noble family of the Interminelli or Interminei, a prominent White family of Lucca. About all that is known of Alessio is the fact that he was still alive in 1295.

[170] The flattery uttered by Thaïs is put into her mouth by Terence in his *Eunuchus* (act 2, sc. 1, lines 1–2). Thaïs' lover had sent her a slave, and later sent a servant to ask if she thanked him much. *Magnas vero agere gratias Thaïs mihi?* The servant reported her as answering *Ingentes!* Cicero later commented on the passage as an example of immoderate flattery, and Dante's conception of Thaïs probably springs from this source. (*De Amicitia,* 26.)

[171] Simon the Samarian magician (cf. Acts 8:9–24) from whom the word "Simony" derives. Upon his conversion to Christianity he offered to buy the power to administer the Holy Ghost and was severely rebuked by Peter.

We had already made our way across
  to the next grave, and to that part of the bridge[172]
  which hangs above the mid-point of the fosse.
O Sovereign Wisdom, how Thine art doth shine 10
  in Heaven, on Earth, and in the Evil World![173]
  How justly doth Thy power judge and assign!
I saw along the walls and on the ground
  long rows of holes cut in the livid stone;
  all were cut to a size, and all were round.
They seemed to be exactly the same size
  as those in the font of my beautiful San Giovanni,
  built to protect the priests who come to baptize;[174]
(one of which, not so long since, I broke open
  to rescue a boy who was wedged and drowning in it. 20
  Be this enough to undeceive all men.)[175]
From every mouth a sinner's legs stuck out
  as far as the calf. The soles were all ablaze
  and the joints of the legs quivered and writhed about.
Withes and tethers would have snapped in their throes.
  As oiled things blaze upon the surface only,
  so did they burn from the heels to the points of their toes.
"Master," I said, "who is that one in the fire
  who writhes and quivers more than all the others?[176]
  From him the ruddy flames seem to leap higher." 30
And he to me: "If you wish me to carry you down
  along that lower bank, you may learn from him
  who he is, and the evil he has done."
And I: "What you will, I will. You are my lord
  and know I depart in nothing from your wish;
  and you know my mind beyond my spoken word."
We moved to the fourth ridge, and turning left
  my Guide descended by a jagged path
  into the strait and perforated cleft.
Thus the good Master bore me down the dim 40
  and rocky slope, and did not put me down
  till we reached the one whose legs did penance for him.
"Whoever you are, sad spirit," I began,
  "who lie here with your head below your heels
  and planted like a stake—speak if you can."

---

[172]The Center point, obviously the best observation point. *The next grave:* The next *bolgia.*

[173]Hell.

[174]It was the custom in Dante's time to baptize only on Holy Saturday and on Pentecost. These occasions were naturally thronged, therefore, and to protect the priests a special font was built in the Baptistry of San Giovanni with marble stands for the priests, who were thus protected from both the crowds and the water in which they immersed those to be baptized. The Baptistry is still standing, but the font is no longer in it. A similar font still exists, however, in the Baptistry at Pisa.

[175]In these lines Dante is replying to a charge of sacrilege that had been rumored against him. One day a boy playing in the baptismal font became jammed in the marble tube and could not be extricated. To save the boy from drowning, Dante took it upon himself to smash the tube.

[176]The fire is proportioned to the guilt of the sinner. These are obviously the feet of the chief sinner of this *bolgia.* In a moment we shall discover that he is Pope Nicholas III.

I stood like a friar who gives the sacrament
to a hired assassin, who, fixed in the hole,
recalls him, and delays his death a moment.[177]
"Are you there already, Boniface?[178] Are you there
already?" he cried. "By several years the writ 50
has lied. And all that gold, and all that care—
are you already sated with the treasure
for which you dared to turn on the Sweet Lady
and trick and pluck and bleed her at your pleasure?"
I stood like one caught in some raillery,
not understanding what is said to him,
lost for an answer to such mockery.
Then Virgil said, "Say to him: 'I am not he,
I am not who you think.' " And I replied
as my good Master had instructed me. 60
The sinner's feet jerked madly; then again
his voice rose, this time choked with sighs and tears,
and said at last: "What do you want of me then?
If to know who I am drives you so fearfully
that you descend the bank to ask it, know
that the Great Mantle[179] was once hung upon me.
And in truth I was a son of the She-Bear,[180]
so sly and eager to push my whelps ahead,
that I pursed wealth above, and myself here.[181]
Beneath my head are dragged all who have gone 70
before me in buying and selling holy office;
there they cower in fissures of the stone.
I too shall be plunged down when that great cheat
for whom I took you comes here in his turn.
Longer already have I baked my feet
and been planted upside-down, than he shall be
before the west sends down a lawless Shepherd[182]
of uglier deeds to cover him and me.

---

[177] Persons convicted of murdering for hire were sometimes executed by being buried alive upside down. If the friar were called back at the last moment, he should have to bend over the hole in which the man is fixed upside down awaiting the first shovelful of earth.

[178] The speaker is Pope Nicholas III, Giovanni Gaetano degli Orsini, Pope from 1277 to 1280. His presence here is self-explanatory. He is awaiting the arrival of his successor, Boniface VIII, who will take his place in the stone tube and who will in turn be replaced by Clement V, a Pope even more corrupt than Boniface. With the foresight of the damned he had read the date of Boniface's death (1303) in the Book of Fate. Mistaking Dante for Boniface, he thinks his foresight has erred by three years, since it is now 1300.

[179] Of the Papacy.

[180] Nicholas's family name, degli Orsini, means in Italian "of the bear cubs."

[181] A play on the second meaning of *bolgia* (i.e., "purse"). "Just as I put wealth in my purse when alive, so am I put in this foul purse now that I am dead."

[182] Clement V, Pope from 1305 to 1314. He came from Gascony (the West) and was involved in many intrigues with the King of France. It was Clement V who moved the Papal See to Avignon, where it remained until 1377. He is compared to Jason (see Maccabees 4:7ff.), who bought an appointment as High Priest of the Jews from King Antiochus and thereupon introduced pagan and venal practices into the office in much the same way as Clement used his influence with Philip of France to secure and corrupt his high office. Clement will succeed Boniface in Hell because Boniface's successor, Benedictus XI (1303–1304), was a good and holy man.

He will be a new Jason of the Maccabees;
and just as that king bent to his high priests' will, 80
so shall the French king do as this one please."
Maybe—I cannot say—I grew too brash
at this point, for when he had finished speaking
I said: "Indeed! Now tell me how much cash
our Lord required of Peter in guarantee
before he put the keys into his keeping?
Surely he asked nothing but 'Follow me!'
Nor did Peter, nor the others, ask silver or gold
of Matthew when they chose him for the place
the despicable and damned apostle sold.[183] 90
Therefore stay as you are; this hole well fits you—
and keep a good guard on the ill-won wealth
that once made you so bold toward Charles of Anjou.[184]
And were it not that I am still constrained
by the reverence I owe to the Great Keys[185]
you held in life, I should not have refrained
from using other words and sharper still;
for this avarice of yours grieves all the world,
tramples the virtuous, and exalts the evil.
Of such as you was the Evangelist's[186] vision 100
when he saw She who Sits upon the Waters
locked with the Kings of earth in fornication.
She was born with seven heads and ten enormous
and shining horns strengthened and made her glad
as long as love and virtue pleased her spouse.
Gold and silver are the gods you adore!
In what are you different from the idolater,
save that he worships one, and you a score?
Ah Constantine, what evil marked the hour—
not of your conversion, but of the fee 110
the first rich Father[187] took from you in dower!"
And as I sang him this tune, he began to twitch
and kick both feet out wildly, as if in rage
or gnawed by conscience—little matter which.

---

[183] Upon the expulsion of Judas from the band of Apostles, Matthias was chosen in his place.

[184] The seventh son of Louis VIII of France. Charles became King of Naples and of Sicily largely through the good offices of Pope Urban IV and later of Clement IV. Nicholas III withdrew the high favor his predecessors had shown Charles, but the exact nature and extent of his opposition are open to dispute. Dante probably believed, as did many of his contemporaries, that Nicholas instigated the massacre called the Sicilian Vespers, in which the Sicilians overthrew the rule of Charles and held a general slaughter of the French who had been their masters. The Sicilian Vespers, however, was a popular and spontaneous uprising, and it did not occur until Nicholas had been dead for two years.

[185] Of the Papacy.

[186] St. John the Evangelist. His vision of She who sits upon the waters is set forth in Revelation 17. The Evangelist intended it as a vision of Pagan Rome, but Dante interprets it as a vision of the Roman Church in its simoniacal corruption. The seven heads are the seven sacraments; the ten horns the ten commandments.

[187] Silvester (Pope from 314 to 355). Before him the Popes possessed nothing, but when Constantine was converted and Catholicism became the official religion of the Empire, the Church began to acquire wealth. Dante and the scholars of his time believed, according to a document called "The Donation of Constantine," that the Emperor had moved his Empire to the East in order to leave sovereignty of the West to the Church. The document was not shown to be a forgery until the fifteenth century.

And I think, indeed, it pleased my Guide: his look
was all approval as he stood beside me
intent upon each word of truth I spoke.
He approached, and with both arms he lifted me,
and when he had gathered me against his breast,
remounted the rocky path out of the valley, 120
nor did he tire of holding me clasped to him,
until we reached the topmost point of the arch
which crosses from the fourth to the fifth rim
of the pits of woe. Arrived upon the bridge,
he tenderly set down the heavy burden
he had been pleased to carry up that ledge
which would have been hard climbing for a goat.
Here I looked down on still another moat.

. . .

Canto 26

Circle Eight: Bolgia Eight—The Evil Counselors: Dante turns from the Thieves toward the Evil Counselors of the next Bolgia, and between the two he addresses a passionate lament to Florence prophesying the griefs that will befall her from these two sins. At the purported time of the Vision, it will be recalled, Dante was a Chief Magistrate of Florence and was forced into exile by men he had reason to consider both thieves and evil counselors. He seems prompted, in fact, to say much more on this score, but he restrains himself when he comes in sight of the sinners of the next Bolgia, for they are a moral symbolism, all men of gift who abused their genius, perverting it to wiles and stratagems. Seeing them in Hell he knows his must be another road: his way shall not be by deception.

So the Poets move on and Dante observes the Eighth Bolgia in detail. Here the Evil Counselors move about endlessly, hidden from view inside great flames. Their sin was to abuse the gifts of the Almighty, to steal his virtues for low purposes. And as they stole from God in their lives and worked by hidden ways, so are they stolen from sight and hidden in the great flames which are their own guilty consciences. And as, in most instances at least, they sinned by glibness of tongue, so are the flames made into a fiery travesty of tongues.

Among the others, the Poets see a great doubleheaded flame, and discover that Ulysses and Diomede are punished together within it. Virgil addresses the flame, and through its wavering tongue Ulysses narrates an unforgettable tale of his last voyage and death.

Joy to you, Florence, that your banners swell,
beating their proud wings over land and sea,
and that your name expands through all of Hell!
Among the thieves I found five who had been
your citizens, to my shame; nor yet shall you
mount to great honor peopling such a den!
But if the truth is dreamed of toward the morning,[188]
you soon shall feel what Prato[189] and the others
wish for you. And were that day of mourning

[188] A semi-proverbial expression. It was a common belief that those dreams that occur just before waking foretell the future. "Morning" here would equal both "the rude awakening" and the potential "dawn of a new day."

[189] Not the neighboring town (which was on good terms with Florence) but Cardinal Niccolo da Prato, papal legate from Benedict XI to Florence. In 1304 he tried to reconcile the warring factions, but found that neither side would accept mediation. Since none would be blessed, he cursed all impartially and laid the city under an interdict (i.e., forbade the offering of the sacraments). Shortly after this rejection by the Church, a bridge collapsed in Florence, and later a great fire broke out. Both disasters cost many lives, and both were promptly attributed to the Papal curse.

already come it would not be too soon. 10
So may it come, since it must! for it will weigh
more heavily on me as I pass my noon.
We left that place. My Guide climbed stone by stone
the natural stair by which we had descended
and drew me after him. So we passed on,
and going our lonely way through that dead land
among the crags and crevices of the cliff,
the foot could make no way without the hand.
I mourned among those rocks, and I mourn again
when memory returns to what I saw: 20
and more than usually I curb the strain
of my genius, lest it stray from Virtue's course;
so if some star, or a better thing, grant me merit,
may I not find the gift cause for remorse.
As many fireflies as the peasant sees
when he rests on a hill and looks into the valley
(where he tills or gathers grapes or prunes his trees)
in that sweet season when the face of him
who lights the world rides north, and at the hour
when the fly yields to the gnat and the air grows dim— 30
such myriads of flames I saw shine through
the gloom of the eighth abyss when I arrived
at the rim from which its bed comes into view.
As he the bears avenged[190] so fearfully
beheld Elijah's chariot depart—
the horses rise toward heaven—but could not see
more than the flame, a cloudlet in the sky,
once it had risen—so within the fosse
only those flames, forever passing by
were visible, ahead, to right, to left; 40
for though each steals a sinner's soul from view
not one among them leaves a trace of the theft.
I stood on the bridge, and leaned out from the edge;
so far, that but for a jut of rock I held to
I should have been sent hurtling from the ledge
without being pushed. And seeing me so intent,
my Guide said: "There are souls within those flames;
each sinner swathes himself in his own torment."
"Master," I said, "your words make me more sure,
but I had seen already that it was so 50
and meant to ask what spirit must endure
the pains of that great flame which splits away
in two great horns, as if it rose from the pyre
where Eteocles and Polynices lay?"[191]

---

[190]Elisha saw Elijah transported to Heaven in a fiery chariot. Later he was mocked by some children, who called out tauntingly that he should "Go up" as Elijah had. Elisha cursed the children in the name of the Lord, and bears came suddenly upon the children and devoured them. (2 Kings 2:11–24.)

[191]Eteocles and Polynices, sons of Oedipus, succeeded jointly to the throne of Thebes, and came to an agreement whereby each one would rule separately for a year at a time. Eteocles ruled the first year and when he refused to surrender the throne at the appointed time, Polynices led the Seven against Thebes in a bloody war. In single combat the two brothers killed one another. Statius (*Thebaid* XII, 429ff.) wrote that their mutual hatred was so great that when they were placed on the same funeral pyre the very flame of their burning drew apart in two great raging horns.

He answered me: "Forever round this path
Ulysses and Diomede[192] move in such dress,
united in pain as once they were in wrath;
there they lament the ambush of the Horse
which was the door through which the noble seed
of the Romans issued from its holy source; 60
there they mourn that for Achilles slain
sweet Deidamia weeps even in death;
there they recall the Palladium in their pain."
"Master," I cried, "I pray you and repray
till my prayer becomes a thousand—if these souls
can still speak from the fire, oh let me stay
until the flame draws near! Do not deny me:
You see how fervently I long for it!"
And he to me: "Since what you ask is worthy,
it shall be. But be still and let me speak; 70
for I know your mind already, and they perhaps
might scorn your manner of speaking, since they were Greek."
And when the flame had come where time and place
seemed fitting to my Guide, I heard him say
these words to it: "O you two souls who pace
together in one flame!—if my days above
won favor in your eyes, if I have earned
however much or little of your love
in writing my High Verses, do not pass by,
but let one of you[193] be pleased to tell where he, 80
having disappeared from the known world, went to die."
As if it fought the wind, the greater prong
of the ancient flame began to quiver and hum;
then moving its tip as if it were the tongue
that spoke, gave out a voice above the roar.
"When I left Circe,"[194] it said, "who more than a year
detained me near Gaëta long before
Aeneas came and gave the place that name,
not fondness for my son, nor reverence
for my aged father, nor Penelope's[195] claim 90

[192]They suffer here for their joint guilt in counseling and carrying out many stratagems which Dante considered evil, though a narrator who was less passionately a partisan of the Trojans might have thought their actions justifiable methods of warfare. Their first sin was the stratagem of the Wooden Horse, as a result of which Troy fell and Aeneas went forth to found the Roman line. The second evil occurred at Scyros. There Ulysses discovered Achilles in female disguise, hidden by his mother, Thetis, so that he would not be taken off to the war. Deidamia was in love with Achilles and had borne him a son. When Ulysses persuaded her lover to sail for Troy, she died of grief. The third count is Ulysses' theft of the sacred statue of Pallas from the Palladium. Upon the statue, it was believed, depended the fate of Troy. Its theft, therefore, would result in Troy's downfall.

[193]Ulysses. He is the figure in the larger horn of the flame (which symbolizes that his guilt, as leader, is greater than that of Diomede). His memorable account of his last voyage and death is purely Dante's invention.

[194]She changed Ulysses' men to swine and kept him a prisoner, though with rather exceptional accommodations. *Gaëta:* Southeastern Italian coastal town. According to Virgil (*Aeneid* 7, 1ff.) it was earlier named Caieta by Aeneas in honor of his aged nurse.

[195]Ulysses' wife.

to the joys of love, could drive out of my mind
the lust to experience the far-flung world
and the failings and felicities of mankind.
I put out on the high and open sea
with a single ship and only those few souls
who stayed true when the rest deserted me.
As far as Morocco and as far as Spain
I saw both shores;[196] and I saw Sardinia
and the other islands of the open main.
I and my men were stiff and slow with age 100
when we sailed at last into the narrow pass[197]
where, warning all men back from further voyage,
Hercules' Pillars rose upon our sight.
Already I had left Ceuta on the left;
Seville[198] now sank behind me on the right.
'Shipmates,' I said, 'who through a hundred thousand
perils have reached the West, do not deny
to the brief remaining watch our senses stand
experience of the world beyond the sun.
Greeks! You were not born to live like brutes, 110
but to press on toward manhood and recognition!'
With this brief exhortation I made my crew
so eager for the voyage I could hardly
have held them back from it when I was through;
and turning our stern toward morning, our bow toward night,
we bore southwest out of the world of man;
we made wings of our oars for our fool's flight.
That night we raised the other pole ahead
with all its stars, and ours had so declined
it did not rise out of its ocean bed.[199] 120
Five times since we had dipped our bending oars
beyond the world, the light beneath the moon
had waxed and waned, when dead upon our course
we sighted, dark in space, a peak so tall
I doubted any man had seen the like.[200]
Our cheers were hardly sounded, when a squall
broke hard upon our bow from the new land:
three times it sucked the ship and the sea about
as it pleased Another to order and command.
At the fourth, the poop rose and the bow went down 130
till the sea closed over us and the light was gone."

. . .

[196] Of the Mediterranean.

[197] The straits of Gibraltar, formerly called the Pillars of Hercules. They were presumed to be the western limit beyond which no man could navigate.

[198] In Dante's time this was the name given to the general region of Spain. Having passed through the Straits, the men are now in the Atlantic. *Ceuta:* In Africa, opposite Gibraltar.

[199] They drove south across the equator, observed the southern stars, and found that the North Star had sunk below the horizon.

[200] Purgatory. They sight it after five months of passage. According to Dante's geography, the Northern hemisphere is land and the Southern is all water except for the Mountain of Purgatory, which rises above the surface at a point directly opposite Jerusalem.

Canto 28

Circle Eight: Bolgia Nine—The Sowers of Discord: The Poets come to the edge of the Ninth Bolgia and look down at a parade of hideously mutilated souls. These are the Sowers of Discord, and just as their sin was to rend asunder what God had meant to be united, so are they hacked and torn through all eternity by a great demon with a bloody sword. After each mutilation the souls are compelled to drag their broken bodies around the pit and to return to the demon, for in the course of the circuit their wounds knit in time to be inflicted anew. Thus is the law of retribution observed, each sinner suffering according to his degree.

Among them Dante distinguishes three classes with varying degrees of guilt within each class. First come the Sowers of Religious Discord. Mahomet is chief among them, and appears first, cleft from crotch to chin, with his internal organs dangling between his legs. His son-in-law, Ali, drags on ahead of him, cleft from top-knot to chin. These reciprocal wounds symbolize Dante's judgment that, between them, these two sum up the total schism between Christianity and Mohammedanism. The revolting details of Mahomet's condition clearly imply Dante's opinion of that doctrine. Mahomet issues an ironic warning to another schismatic, Fra Dolcino.

Next come the Sowers of Political Discord, among them Pier da Medicina, the Tribune Curio, and Mosca dei Lamberti, each mutilated according to the nature of his sin.

Last of all is Bertrand de Born, Sower of Discord Between Kinsmen. He separated father from son, and for that offense carries his head separated from his body, holding it with one hand by the hair, and swinging it as if it were a lantern to light his dark and endless way. The image of Bertrand raising his head at arm's length in order that it might speak more clearly to the Poets on the ridge is one of the most memorable in *The Inferno.* For some reason that cannot be ascertained, Dante makes these sinners quite eager to be remembered in the world, despite the fact that many who lie above them in Hell were unwilling to be recognized.

Who could describe, even in words set free
 of metric and rhyme and a thousand times retold,
 the blood and wounds that now were shown to me!
At grief so deep the tongue must wag in vain;
 the language of our sense and memory
 lacks the vocabulary of such pain.
If one could gather all those who have stood
 through all of time on Puglia's[201] fateful soil
 and wept for the red running of their blood
in the war of the Trojans;[202] and in that long war 10
 which left so vast a spoil of golden rings,
 as we find written in Livy, who does not err;[203]
along with those whose bodies felt the wet
 and gaping wounds of Robert Guiscard's lances;[204]
 with all the rest whose bones are gathered yet

[201]I have used the modern name but some of the events Dante narrates took place in the ancient province of Apulia. The southeastern area of Italy is the scene of all the fighting Dante mentions in the following passage. It is certainly a bloody total of slaughter that Dante calls upon to illustrate his scene.

[202]The Romans (descended from the Trojans) fought the native Samnites in a long series of raids and skirmishes from 343 to 290 B.C.E.

[203]The Punic Wars (264–146 B.C.E.). Livy writes that in the battle of Cannae (216 B.C.E.) so many Romans fell that Hannibal gathered three bushels of gold rings from the fingers of the dead and produced them before the Senate at Carthage.

[204]Dante places Guiscard (1015–1085) in *The Paradiso* among the Warriors of God. He fought the Greeks and Saracens in their attempted invasion of Italy.

at Ceperano where every last Pugliese
turned traitor;[205] and with those from Tagliacozzo
where Alardo won without weapons[206]—if all these
were gathered, and one showed his limbs run through,
another his lopped off, that could not equal 20
the mutilations of the ninth pit's crew.
A wine tun when a stave or cant-bar starts
does not split open as wide as one I saw
split from his chin to the mouth with which man farts.
Between his legs all of his red guts hung
with the heart, the lungs, the liver, the gall bladder,
and the shriveled sac that passes shit to the bung.
I stood and stared at him from the stone shelf;
he noticed me and opening his own breast
with both hands cried: "See how I rip myself! 30
See how Mahomet's mangled and split open!
Ahead of me walks Ali[207] in his tears,
his head cleft from the top-knot to the chin.
And all the other souls that bleed and mourn
along this ditch were sowers of scandal and schism:
as they tore others apart, so are they torn.
Behind us, warden of our mangled horde,
the devil who butchers us and sends us marching
waits to renew our wounds with his long sword
when we have made the circuit of the pit; 40
for by the time we stand again before him
all the wounds he gave us last have knit.
But who are you that gawk down from that sill—
probably to put off your own descent
to the pit you are sentenced to for your own evil?"
"Death has not come for him, guilt does not drive
his soul to torment," my sweet Guide replied.
"That he may experience all while yet alive
I, who am dead, must lead him through the drear
and darkened halls of Hell, from round to round: 50
and this is true as my own standing here."
More than a hundred wraiths who were marching under
the sill on which we stood, paused at his words
and stared at me, forgetting pain in wonder.

[205] In 1266 the Pugliese under Manfred, King of Sicily, were charged with holding the pass at Ceperano against Charles of Anjou. The Pugliese, probably under Papal pressure, allowed the French free passage, and Charles went on to defeat Manfred at Benevento. Manfred himself was killed in that battle.

[206] At Tagliacozzo (1268) in a continuation of the same strife, Charles of Anjou used a stratagem suggested to him by Alardo de Valéry and defeated Conradin, nephew of Manfred. "Won without weapons" is certainly an overstatement: what Alardo suggested was a simple but effective concealment of reserve troops. When Conradin seemed to have carried the day and was driving his foes before him, the reserve troops broke on his flank and rear, and defeated Conradin's out-positioned forces.

[207] Ali succeeded Mahomet to the Caliphate, but not until three of the disciples had preceded him. Mahomet died in 632, and Ali did not assume the Caliphate until 656.

"And if you do indeed return to see
the sun again, and soon, tell Fra Dolcino[208]
unless he longs to come and march with me
he would do well to check his groceries
before the winter drives him from the hills
and gives the victory to the Novarese." 60
Mahomet, one foot raised, had paused to say
these words to me. When he had finished speaking
he stretched it out and down, and moved away.
Another—he had his throat slit, and his nose
slashed off as far as the eyebrows, and a wound
where one of his ears had been—standing with those
who stared at me in wonder from the pit,
opened the grinning wound of his red gullet
as if it were a mouth, and said through it:
"O soul unforfeited to misery 70
and whom—unless I take you for another—
I have seen above in our sweet Italy;
if ever again you see the gentle plain
that slopes down from Vercelli to Marcabò,[209]
remember Pier da Medicina in pain,
and announce this warning to the noblest two
of Fano, Messers Guido and Angiolello:
that unless our foresight sees what is not true
they shall be thrown from their ships into the sea
and drown in the raging tides near La Cattolica 80
to satisfy a tyrant's treachery.[210]
Neptune never saw so gross a crime
in all the seas from Cyprus to Majorca,
not even in pirate raids, nor the Argive time.[211]
The one-eyed traitor,[212] lord of the demesne
whose hill and streams one who walks here beside me
will wish eternally he had never seen,
will call them to a parley, but behind
sweet invitations he will work it so
they need not pray against Focara's wind." 90

---

[208] In 1300 Fra Dolcino took over the reformist order called the Apostolic Brothers, who preached, among other things, the community of property and of women. Clement V declared them heretical and ordered a crusade against them. The brotherhood retired with its women to an impregnable position in the hills between Novara and Vercelli, but their supplies gave out in the course of a year-long siege, and they were finally starved out in March of 1307. Dolcino and Margaret of Trent, his "Sister in Christ," were burned at the stake at Vercelli the following June.

[209] Vercelli is the most western town in Lombardy. Marcabò stands near the mouth of the Po.

[210] Malatestino da Rimini (see [Canto 27]), in a move to annex the city of Fano, invited Guido del Cassero and Angioletto da Carignano, leading citizens of Fano, to a conference at La Cattolica, a point on the Adriatic midway between Fano and Rimini. At Malatestino's orders the two were thrown overboard off Focara, a headland swept by such dangerous currents that approaching sailors used to offer prayers for a safe crossing.

[211] The Greeks were raiders and pirates. *Cyprus . . . Majorca:* These islands are at opposite ends of the Mediterranean.

[212] Malatestino.

And I to him: "If you would have me bear
your name to time, show me the one who found
the sight of that land so harsh, and let me hear
his story and his name." He touched the cheek
of one nearby, forcing the jaws apart,
and said: "This is the one; he cannot speak.
This outcast settled Caesar's doubts that day
beside the Rubicon by telling him:
'A man prepared is a man hurt by delay.'"
Ah, how wretched Curio[213] seemed to me 100
with a bloody stump in his throat in place of the tongue
which once had dared to speak so recklessly!
And one among them with both arms hacked through
cried out, raising his stumps on the foul air
while the blood bedaubed his face: "Remember, too,
Mosca dei Lamberti,[214] alas, who said
'A thing done has an end!' and with those words
planted the fields of war with Tuscan dead."
"And brought about the death of all your clan!"
I said, and he, stung by new pain on pain, 110
ran off; and in his grief he seemed a madman.
I stayed to watch those broken instruments,
and I saw a thing so strange I should not dare
to mention it without more evidence
but that my own clear conscience strengthens me,
that good companion that upholds a man
within the armor of his purity.
I saw it there; I seem to see it still—
a body without a head, that moved along
like all the others in that spew and spill. 120
It held the severed head by its own hair,
swinging it like a lantern in its hand;
and the head looked at us and wept in its despair.
It made itself a lamp of its own head,
and they were two in one and one in two;
how this can be, He knows who so commanded.
And when it stood directly under us
it raised the head at arm's length toward our bridge
the better to be heard, and swaying thus
it cried: "O living soul in this abyss, 130
see what a sentence has been passed upon me,
and search all Hell for one to equal this!

[213]This is the Roman Tribune Curio, who was banished from Rome by Pompey and joined Caesar's forces, advising him to cross the Rubicon, which was then the boundary between Gaul and the Roman Republic. The crossing constituted invasion, and thus began the Roman Civil War. The Rubicon flows near Rimini.

[214]Dante had asked Ciacco (Canto 6) for news of Mosca as a man of good works. Now he finds him, his merit canceled by his greater sin. Buondelmonte del Buondelmonti had insulted the honor of the Amidei by breaking off his engagement to a daughter of that line in favor of a girl of the Donati. When the Amidei met to discuss what should be done, Mosca spoke for the death of Buondelmonte. The Amidei acted upon his advice and from that murder sprang the bloody feud between the Guelphs and Ghibellines of Florence.

When you return to the world, remember me:
I am Bertrand de Born,[215] and it was I
who set the young king on to mutiny,
son against father, father against son
as Achitophel[216] set Absalom and David;
and since I parted those who should be one
in duty and in love, I bear my brain
divided from its source within this trunk; 140
and walk here where my evil turns to pain,
an eye for an eye to all eternity:
thus is the law of Hell observed in me."

. . .

Canto 32

Circle Nine: Cocytus—Compound Fraud; Round One: Caïna—The Treacherous to Kin; Round Two: Antenora—The Treacherous to Country: At the bottom of the well Dante finds himself on a huge frozen lake. This is Cocytus, the Ninth Circle, the fourth and last great water of Hell, and here, fixed in the ice, each according to his guilt, are punished sinners guilty of Treachery Against Those to Whom They Were Bound by Special Ties. The ice is divided into four concentric rings marked only by the different positions of the damned within the ice.

This is Dante's symbolic equivalent of the final guilt. The treacheries of these souls were denials of love (which is God) and of all human warmth. Only the remorseless dead center of the ice will serve to express their natures. As they denied God's love, so are they furthest removed from the light and warmth of His Sun. As they denied all human ties, so are they bound only by the unyielding ice.

The first round is Caïna, named for Cain. Here lie those who were treacherous against blood ties. They have their necks and heads out of the ice and are permitted to bow their heads—a double boon since it allows them some protection from the freezing gale and, further, allows their tears to fall without freezing their eyes shut. Here Dante sees Alessandro and Napoleone degli Alberti, and he speaks to Camicion, who identifies other sinners of this round.

The second round is Antenora, named for Antenor, the Trojan who was believed to have betrayed his city to the Greeks. Here lie those guilty of Treachery to Country. They, too, have their heads above the ice, but they cannot bend their necks, which are gripped by the ice. Here Dante accidentally kicks the head of Bocca Degli Abbati and then proceeds to treat him with a savagery he had shown to no other soul in Hell. Bocca names some of his fellow traitors, and the Poets pass on to discover two heads frozen together in one hole. One of them is gnawing the nape of the other's neck.

If I had rhymes as harsh and horrible
as the hard fact of the final dismal hole
which bears the weight of all the steeps of Hell,
I might more fully press the sap and substance
from my conception; but since I must do
without them, I begin with some reluctance.
For it is no easy undertaking, I say,
to describe the bottom of the Universe;
nor is it for tongues that only babble child's play.

[215](1140–1215), a great knight and master of the troubadours of Provence. He is said to have instigated a quarrel between Henry II of England and his son Prince Henry, called "The Young King" because he was crowned within his father's lifetime.

[216]One of David's counselors, who deserted him to assist the rebellious Absalom. (II Samuel 15–17.)

But may those Ladies of the Heavenly Spring[217]
who helped Amphion wall Thebes, assist my verse, 10
that the word may be the mirror of the thing.
O most miscreant rabble, you who keep
the stations of that place whose name is pain,
better had you been born as goats or sheep!
We stood now in the dark pit of the well,
far down the slope below the Giant's feet,
and while I still stared up at the great wall,
I heard a voice cry: "Watch which way you turn:
take care you do not trample on the heads 20
of the forworn and miserable brethren."
Whereat I turned and saw beneath my feet
and stretching out ahead, a lake so frozen
it seemed to be made of glass. So thick a sheet
never yet hid the Danube's winter course,
nor, far away beneath the frigid sky,
locked the Don up in its frozen source:
for were Tanbernick and the enormous peak
of Pietrapana[218] to crash down on it,
not even the edges would so much as creak. 30
The way frogs sit to croak, their muzzles leaning
out of the water, at the time and season
when the peasant woman dreams of her day's gleaning[219]—
Just so the livid dead are sealed in place
up to the part at which they blushed for shame,
and they beat their teeth like storks. Each holds his face
bowed toward the ice, each of them testifies
to the cold with his chattering mouth, to his heart's grief
with tears that flood forever from his eyes.
When I had stared about me, I looked down 40
and at my feet I saw two clamped together
so tightly that the hair of their heads had grown
together. "Who are you," I said, "who lie
so tightly breast to breast?" They strained their necks,
and when they had raised their heads as if to reply,
the tears their eyes had managed to contain
up to that time gushed out, and the cold froze them
between the lids, sealing them shut again
tighter than any clamp grips wood to wood,
and mad with pain, they fell to butting heads 50
like billy-goats in a sudden savage mood.
And a wraith who lay to one side and below,
and who had lost both ears to frostbite, said,
his head still bowed: "Why do you watch us so?

---

[217]The Muses. They so inspired Amphion's hand upon the lyre that the music charmed blocks of stone out of Mount Cithaeron, and the blocks formed themselves into the walls of Thebes.

[218]There is no agreement on the location of the mountain Dante called Tanbernick. Pietrapana, today known as *la Pania,* is in Tuscany.

[219]The summer.

If you wish to know who they are[220] who share one doom,
they owned the Bisenzio's valley with their father,
whose name was Albert. They spring from one womb,
and you may search through all Caïna's crew
without discovering in all this waste
a squab more fit for the aspic than these two; 60
not him whose breast and shadow a single blow
of the great lance of King Arthur pierced with light;[221]
nor yet Focaccia[222] nor this one fastened so
into the ice that his head is all I see,
and whom, if you are Tuscan, you know well—
his name on the earth was Sassol Mascheroni.[223]
And I—to tell you all and so be through—
was Camicion de' Pazzi.[224] I wait for Carlin
beside whose guilt my sins will shine like virtue."
And leaving him,[225] I saw a thousand faces 70
discolored so by cold, I shudder yet
and always will when I think of those frozen places.
As we approached the center of all weight,
where I went shivering in eternal shade,
whether it was my will, or chance, or fate,
I cannot say, but as I trailed my Guide
among those heads, my foot struck violently
against the face of one.[226] Weeping, it cried:
"Why do you kick me? If you were not sent
to wreak a further vengeance for Montaperti, 80
why do you add this to my other torment?"
"Master," I said, "grant me a moment's pause
to rid myself of a doubt concerning this one;
then you may hurry me at your own pace."
The Master stopped at once, and through the volley
of foul abuse the wretch poured out, I said:
"Who are you who curse others so?" And he:

[220] Alessandro and Napoleone, Counts of Mangona. Among other holdings, they inherited a castle in the Val di Bisenzio. They seemed to have been at odds on all things and finally killed one another in a squabble over their inheritance and their politics (Alessandro was a Guelph and Napoleone a Ghibelline).

[221] Mordred, King Arthur's traitorous nephew. He tried to kill Arthur, but the king struck him a single blow of his lance, and when it was withdrawn, a shaft of light passed through the gaping wound and split the shadow of the falling traitor.

[222] Of the Cancellieri of Pistoia. He murdered his cousin (among others) and may have been the principal cause of a great feud that divided the Cancellieri, and split the Guelphs into the White and Black parties.

[223] Of the Toschi of Florence. He was appointed guardian of one of his nephews and murdered him to get the inheritance for himself.

[224] Alberto Camicion de' Pazzi of Valdarno. He murdered a kinsman. *Carlin:* Carlino de' Pazzi, relative of Alberto. He was charged with defending for the Whites the castle of Piantravigne in Valdarno but surrendered it for a bribe. He belongs therefore in the next lower circle, Antenora, as a traitor to his country, and when he arrives there his greater sin will make Alberto seem almost virtuous by comparison.

[225] These words mark the departure from Caïna to Antenora.

[226] Bocca degli Abbati, a traitorous Florentine. At the battle of Montaperti (cf. Farinata, Canto 10) he hacked off the hand of the Florentine standard bearer. The calvary, lacking a standard around which it could rally, was soon routed.

"And who are *you* who go through the dead larder
of Antenora kicking the cheeks of others
so hard, that were you alive, you could not kick harder?" 90
"I *am* alive," I said, "and if you seek fame,
it may be precious to you above all else
that my notes on this descent include your name."
"Exactly the opposite is my wish and hope,"
he answered. "Let me be; for it's little you know
of how to flatter on this icy slope."
I grabbed the hair of his dog's-ruff and I said:
"Either you tell me truly who you are,
or you won't have a hair left on your head."
And he: "Not though you snatch me bald. I swear 100
I will not tell my name nor show my face.
Not though you rip until my brain lies bare."
I had a good grip on his hair; already
I had yanked out more than one fistful of it,
while the wretch yelped, but kept his face turned from me;
when another said: "Bocca, what is it ails you?
What the Hell's wrong?[227] Isn't it bad enough
to hear you bang your jaws? Must you bark too?"
"Now filthy traitor, say no more!" I cried,
"for to your shame, be sure I shall bear back 110
a true report of you." The wretch replied:
"Say anything you please but go away.
And if you *do* get back, don't overlook
that pretty one who had so much to say
just now. Here he laments the Frenchman's price.
'I saw Buoso da Duera,[228] you can report,
'where the bad salad is kept crisp on ice.'
And if you're asked who else was wintering here,
Beccheria,[229] whose throat was slit by Florence,
is there beside you. Gianni de' Soldanier[230] 120
is further down, I think, with Ganelon,[231]
and Tebaldello,[232] who opened the gates of Faenza
and let Bologna steal in with the dawn."

---

[227] In the circumstances, a monstrous pun. The original is "*qual diavolo ti tocca?*" (what devil touches, or molests, you?), a standard colloquialism for "what's the matter with you?" A similar pun occurs in line 117: "kept crisp (cool) on ice." Colloquially "*stare fresco*" (to be or to remain cool) equals "to be left out in the cold," that is, to be out of luck.

[228] Of Cremona. In 1265 Charles of Anjou marched against Manfred and Naples (see Canto 19), and Buoso da Duera was sent out in charge of a Ghibelline army to oppose the passage of one of Charles' armies, but accepted a bribe and let the French pass unopposed. The event took place near Parma.

[229] Tesauro dei Beccheria of Pavia, Abbot of Vallombrosa and Papal Legate (of Alexander IV) in Tuscany. The Florentine Guelphs cut off his head in 1258 for plotting with the expelled Ghibellines.

[230] A Florentine Ghibelline of ancient and noble family. In 1265, however, during the riots that occurred under the Two Jovial Friars, he deserted his party and became a leader of the commoners (Guelphs). In placing him in Antenora, Dante makes no distinction between turning on one's country and turning on one's political party, not at least if the end is simply for power.

[231] It was Ganelon who betrayed Roland to the Saracens.

[232] Tebaldello de' Zambrasi of Faenza. At dawn on November 13, 1280, he opened the city gates and delivered Faenza to the Bolognese Guelphs in order to revenge himself on the Ghibelline family of the Lambertazzi who, in 1274, had fled from Bologna to take refuge in Faenza.

Leaving him then, I saw two souls together
in a single hole, and so pinched in by the ice
that one head made a helmet for the other.
As a famished man chews crusts—so the one sinner
sank his teeth into the other's nape
at the base of the skull, gnawing his loathsome dinner.
Tydeus in his final raging hour 130
gnawed Menalippus' head[233] with no more fury
than this one gnawed at skull and dripping gore.
"You there," I said, "who show so odiously
your hatred for that other, tell me why
on this condition: that if in what you tell me
you seem to have a reasonable complaint
against him you devour with such foul relish,
I, knowing who you are, and his soul's taint,
may speak your cause to living memory,
God willing the power of speech be left to me." 140

Canto 33

Circle Nine: Cocytus—Compound Fraud; Round Two: Antenora—The Treacherous to Country; Round Three: Ptolomea—The Treacherous to Guests and Hosts: In reply to Dante's exhortation, the sinner who is gnawing his companion's head looks up, wipes his bloody mouth on his victim's hair, and tells his harrowing story. He is Count Ugolino and the wretch he gnaws is Archbishop Ruggieri. Both are in Antenora for treason. In life they had once plotted together. Then Ruggieri betrayed his fellow-plotter and caused his death, by starvation, along with his four "sons." In the most pathetic and dramatic passage of *The Inferno,* Ugolino details how their prison was sealed and how his "sons" dropped dead before him one by one, weeping for food. His terrible tale serves only to renew his grief and hatred, and he has hardly finished it before he begins to gnaw Ruggieri again with renewed fury. In the immutable Law of Hell, the killer-by-starvation becomes the food of his victim.

The Poets leave Ugolino and enter Ptolomea, so named for the Ptolomaeus of Maccabees, who murdered his father-in-law at a banquet. Here are punished those who were Treacherous Against the Ties of Hospitality. They lie with only half their faces above the ice and their tears freeze in their eye sockets, sealing them with little crystal visors. Thus even the comfort of tears is denied them. Here Dante finds Friar Alberigo and Branca D'Oria, and discovers the terrible power of Ptolomea: so great is its sin that the souls of the guilty fall to its torments even before they die, leaving their bodies still on earth, inhabited by Demons.

The sinner raised his mouth from his grim repast
and wiped it on the hair of the bloody head
whose nape he had all but eaten away. At last
he began to speak: "You ask me to renew
a grief so desperate that the very thought
of speaking of it tears my heart in two.
But if my words may be a seed that bears
the fruit of infamy for him I gnaw,
I shall weep, but tell my story through my tears.
Who you may be, and by what powers you reach 10
into this underworld, I cannot guess,
but you seem to me a Florentine by your speech.

[233]Statius recounts in the *Thebaid* that Tydeus killed Menalippus in battle but fell himself mortally wounded. As he lay dying he had Menalippus' head brought to him and fell to gnawing it in his dying rage.

I was Count Ugolino,[234] I must explain;
  this reverend grace is the Archbishop Ruggieri:
  now I will tell you why I gnaw his brain.
That I, who trusted him, had to undergo
  imprisonment and death through his treachery,
  you will know already.[235] What you cannot know—
that is, the lingering inhumanity
  of the death I suffered—you shall hear in full: 20
  then judge for yourself if he has injured me.
A narrow window in that coop[236] of stone
  now called the Tower of Hunger for my sake
  (within which others yet must pace alone)
had shown me several waning moons already[237]
  between its bars, when I slept the evil sleep
  in which the veil of the future parted for me.
This beast[238] appeared as master of a hunt
  chasing the wolf and his whelps across the mountain
  that hides Lucca from Pisa.[239] Out in front 30
of the starved and shrewd and avid pack he had placed
  Gualandi and Sismondi and Lanfranchi[240]
  to point his prey. The father and sons had raced
a brief course only when they failed of breath
  and seemed to weaken; then I thought I saw
  their flanks ripped open by the hounds' fierce teeth.
Before the dawn, the dream still in my head,
  I woke and heard my sons,[241] who were there with me,
  cry from their troubled sleep, asking for bread.
You are cruelty itself if you can keep 40
  your tears back at the thought of what foreboding
  stirred in my heart; and if you do not weep,
at what are you used to weeping?—The hour when food
  used to be brought, drew near. They were now awake,
  and each was anxious from his dream's dark mood.
And from the base of that horrible tower I heard
  the sound of hammers nailing up the gates:
  I stared at my sons' faces without a word.

---

[234]Count of Donoratico and a member of the Guelph family della Gherardesca. He and his nephew, Nino de' Visconti, led the two Guelph factions of Pisa. In 1288 Ugolino intrigued with Archbishop Ruggieri degli Ubaldini, leader of the Ghibellines, to get rid of Visconti and to take over the command of all the Pisan Guelphs. The plan worked, but in the consequent weakening of the Guelphs, Ruggieri saw his chance and betrayed Ugolino, throwing him into prison with his sons and his grandsons. In the following year the prison was sealed up and they were left to starve to death.

[235]News of Ugolino's imprisonment and death would certainly have reached Florence. *What you cannot know:* No living man could know what happened after Ugolino and his sons were sealed in the prison and abandoned.

[236]Dante uses the word *muda,* in Italian signifying a stone tower in which falcons were kept in the dark to moult. From the time of Ugolino's death it became known as The Tower of Hunger.

[237]Ugolino was jailed late in 1288. He was sealed in to starve early in 1289.

[238]Ruggieri.

[239]These two cities would be in view of one another were it not for Monte San Giuliano.

[240]Three Pisan nobles, Ghibellines and friends of the Archbishop.

[241]Actually two of the boys were grandsons and all were considerably older than one would gather from Dante's account. Anselm, the younger grandson, was fifteen. The others were really young men and were certainly old enough for guilt despite Dante's charge in line 90.

I did not weep: I had turned stone inside.
They wept. 'What ails you, Father, you look so strange,' 50
my little Anselm, youngest of them, cried.
But I did not speak a word nor shed a tear:
not all that day nor all that endless night,
until I saw another sun appear.
When a tiny ray leaked into that dark prison
and I saw staring back from their four faces
the terror and the wasting of my own,
I bit my hands in helpless grief. And they,
thinking I chewed myself for hunger, rose
suddenly together. I heard them say: 60
'Father, it would give us much less pain
if you ate us: it was you who put upon us
this sorry flesh; now strip it off again.'
I calmed myself to spare them. Ah! hard earth,
why did you not yawn open? All that day
and the next we sat in silence. On the fourth,
Gaddo, the eldest, fell before me and cried,
stretched at my feet upon that prison floor:
'Father, why don't you help me?' There he died.
And just as you see me, I saw them fall 70
one by one on the fifth day and the sixth.
Then, already blind, I began to crawl
from body to body shaking them frantically.
Two days I called their names, and they were dead.
Then fasting overcame my grief and me."[242]
His eyes narrowed to slits when he was done,
and he seized the skull again between his teeth
grinding it as a mastiff grinds a bone.
Ah, Pisa! foulest blemish on the land
where "si" sounds sweet and clear,[243] since those nearby you 80
are slow to blast the ground on which you stand,
may Caprara and Gorgona[244] drift from place
and dam the flooding Arno at its mouth
until it drowns the last of your foul race!
For if to Ugolino falls the censure
for having betrayed your castles,[245] you for your part

---

[242] That is, he died. Some interpret the line to mean that Ugolino's hunger drove him to cannibalism. Ugolino's present occupation in Hell would certainly support that interpretation but the fact is that cannibalism is the one major sin Dante does not assign a place to in Hell. So monstrous would it have seemed to him that he must certainly have established a special punishment for it. Certainly he could hardly have relegated it to an ambiguity. Moreover, it would be a sin of bestiality rather than of fraud, and as such it would be punished in the Seventh Circle.

[243] Italy.

[244] These two islands near the mouth of the Arno were Pisan possessions in 1300.

[245] In 1284, Ugolino gave up certain castles to Lucca and Florence. He was at war with Genoa at the time and it is quite likely that he ceded the castles to buy the neutrality of these two cities, for they were technically allied with Genoa. Dante, however, must certainly consider the action as treasonable, for otherwise Ugolino would be in Caïna for his treachery to Visconti.

should not have put his sons to such a torture:
you modern Thebes![246] those tender lives you spilt—
Brigata, Uguccione, and the others
I mentioned earlier—were too young for guilt! 90
We passed on further,[247] where the frozen mine
entombs another crew in greater pain;
these wraiths are not bent over, but lie supine.
Their very weeping closes up their eyes;
and the grief that finds no outlet for its tears
turns inward to increase their agonies:
for the first tears that they shed knot instantly
in their eye-sockets, and as they freeze they form
a crystal visor above the cavity.
And despite the fact that standing in that place 100
I had become as numb as any callus,
and all sensation had faded from my face,
somehow I felt a wind begin to blow,
whereat I said: "Master, what stirs this wind?
Is not all heat extinguished here below?"[248]
And the Master said to me: "Soon you will be
where your own eyes will see the source and cause
and give you their own answer to the mystery."
And one of those locked in that icy mall
cried out to us as we passed: "O souls so cruel 110
that you are sent to the last post of all,
relieve me for a little from the pain
of this hard veil; let my heart weep a while
before the weeping freeze my eyes again."
And I to him: "If you would have my service,
tell me your name; then if I do not help you
may I descend to the last rim of the ice."[249]
"I am Friar Alberigo,"[250] he answered therefore,
"the same who called for the fruits from the bad garden.
Here I am given dates for figs full store." 120
"What! Are you dead already?" I said to him.
And he then: "How my body stands in the world
I do not know. So privileged is this rim

---

[246]Thebes, as a number of the foregoing notes will already have made clear, was the site of some of the most hideous crimes of antiquity.

[247]Marks the passage into Ptolomea.

[248]Dante believed (rather accurately, by chance) that all winds resulted from "exhalations of heat." Cocytus, however, is conceived as wholly devoid of heat, a metaphysical absolute zero. The source of the wind, as we discover in the next Canto, is Satan himself.

[249]Dante is not taking any chances; he has to go on to the last rim in any case. The sinner, however, believes him to be another damned soul and would interpret the oath quite otherwise than as Dante meant it.

[250]Of the Manfredi of Faenza. He was another Jovial Friar. In 1284 his brother Manfred struck him in the course of an argument. Alberigo pretended to let it pass, but in 1285 he invited Manfred and his son to a banquet and had them murdered. The signal to the assassins was the words: "Bring in the fruit." "Friar Alberigo's bad fruit" became a proverbial saying.

of Ptolomea, that often souls fall to it
before dark Atropos[251] has cut their thread.
And that you may more willingly free my spirit
of this glaze of frozen tears that shrouds my face,
I will tell you this: when a soul betrays as I did,
it falls from flesh, and a demon takes its place,
ruling the body till its time is spent. 130
The ruined soul rains down into this cistern.
So, I believe, there is still evident
in the world above, all that is fair and mortal
of this black shade who winters here behind me.
If you have only recently crossed the portal
from that sweet world, you surely must have known
his body: Branca D'Oria[252] is its name,
and many years have passed since he rained down."
"I think you are trying to take me in," I said,
"Ser Branca D'Oria is a living man; 140
he eats, he drinks, he fills his clothes and his bed."
"Michel Zanche had not yet reached the ditch
of the Black Talons," the frozen wraith replied,
"there where the sinners thicken in hot pitch,
when this one left his body to a devil,
as did his nephew and second in treachery,
and plumbed like lead through space to this dead level.
But now reach out your hand, and let me cry."
And I did not keep the promise I had made,
for to be rude to him was courtesy. 150
Ah, men of Genoa! souls of little worth,
corrupted from all custom of righteousness,
why have you not been driven from the earth?
For there beside the blackest soul of all
Romagna's evil plain, lies one of yours
bathing his filthy soul in the eternal
glacier of Cocytus for his foul crime,
while he seems yet alive in world and time!

Canto 34

Ninth Circle: Cocytus—Compound Fraud; Round Four: Judecca—The Treacherous to Their Masters; The Center: Satan: "On march the banners of the King," Virgil begins as the Poets face the last depth. He is quoting a medieval hymn, and to it he adds the distortion and perversion of all that lies about him. "On march the banners of the King—of Hell." And there before them, in an infernal parody of Godhead, they see Satan in the distance, his great wings beating like a windmill. It is their beating that is the source of the icy wind of Cocytus, the exhalation of all evil.

All about him in the ice are strewn the sinners of the last round, Judecca, named for Judas Iscariot. These are the Treacherous to Their Masters. They lie completely sealed in the ice, twisted and distorted into every conceivable posture. It is impossible to speak to them, and the Poets move on to observe Satan.

[251] The Fate who cuts the thread of life.

[252] A Genoese Ghibelline. His sin is identical in kind to that of Friar Alberigo. In 1275 he invited his father-in-law, Michel Zanche, to a banquet and had him and his companions cut to pieces. He was assisted in the butchery by his nephew.

He is fixed into the ice at the center to which flow all the rivers of guilt; and as he beats his great wings as if to escape, their icy wind only freezes him more surely into the polluted ice. In a grotesque parody of the Trinity, he has three faces, each a different color, and in each mouth he clamps a sinner whom he rips eternally with his teeth. Judas Iscariot is in the central mouth: Brutus and Cassius in the mouths on either side.

Having seen all, the Poets now climb through the center, grappling hand over hand down the hairy flank of Satan himself—a last supremely symbolic action—and at last, when they have passed the center of all gravity, they emerge from Hell. A long climb from the earth's center to the Mount of Purgatory awaits them, and they push on without rest, ascending along the sides of the river Lethe, till they emerge once more to see the stars of Heaven, just before dawn on Easter Sunday.

"On march the banners of the King of Hell,"[253]
my Master said. "Toward us. Look straight ahead:
can you make him out at the core of the frozen shell?"
Like a whirling windmill seen afar at twilight,
or when a mist has risen from the ground—
just such an engine rose upon my sight
stirring up such a wild and bitter wind
I cowered for shelter at my Master's back,
there being no other windbreak I could find.
I stood now where the souls of the last class 10
(with fear my verses tell it) were covered wholly;
they shone below the ice like straws in glass.
Some lie stretched out; others are fixed in place
upright, some on their heads, some on their soles;
another, like a bow, bends foot to face.
When we had gone so far across the ice
that it pleased my Guide to show me the foul creature[254]
which once had worn the grace of Paradise,
he made me stop, and, stepping aside, he said:
"Now see the face of Dis! This is the place 20
where you must arm your soul against all dread."
Do not ask, Reader, how my blood ran cold
and my voice choked up with fear. I cannot write it:
this is a terror that cannot be told.
I did not die, and yet I lost life's breath:
imagine for yourself what I became,
deprived at once of both my life and death.
The Emperor of the Universe of Pain
jutted his upper chest above the ice;
and I am closer in size to the great mountain 30
the Titans make around the central pit,
than they to his arms. Now, starting from this part,
imagine the whole that corresponds to it!
If he was once as beautiful as now
he is hideous, and still turned on his Maker,
well may he be the source of every woe!

[253]The hymn (*Vexilla regis prodeunt*) was written in the sixth century by Venantius Fortunatus, Bishop of Poitiers. The original celebrates the Holy Cross, and is part of the service for Good Friday to be sung at the moment of uncovering the cross.

[254]Satan.

With what a sense of awe I saw his head
towering above me! for it had three faces:
one was in front, and it was fiery red;
the other two, as weirdly wonderful, 40
merged with it from the middle of each shoulder
to the point where all converged at the top of the skull;
the right was something between white and bile;
the left was about the color that one finds
on those who live along the banks of the Nile.
Under each head two wings rose terribly,
their span proportioned to so gross a bird:
I never saw such sails upon the sea.
They were not feathers—their texture and their form
were like a bat's wings—and he beat them so 50
that three winds blew from him in one great storm:
it is these winds that freeze all Cocytus.
He wept from his six eyes, and down three chins
the tears ran mixed with bloody froth and pus.[255]
In every mouth he worked a broken sinner
between his rake-like teeth. Thus he kept three
in eternal pain at his eternal dinner.
For the one in front the biting seemed to play
no part at all compared to the ripping: at times
the whole skin of his back was flayed away. 60
"That soul that suffers most," explained my Guide,
"is Judas Iscariot, he who kicks his legs
on the fiery chin and has his head inside.
Of the other two, who have their heads thrust forward,
the one who dangles down from the black face
is Brutus: note how he writhes without a word.
And there, with the huge and sinewy arms,[256] is the soul
of Cassius.—But the night is coming on[257]
and we must go, for we have seen the whole."
Then, as he bade, I clasped his neck, and he, 70
watching for a moment when the wings
were opened wide, reached over dexterously
and seized the shaggy coat of the king demon;
then grappling matted hair and frozen crusts
from one tuft to another, clambered down.
When we reached the joint where the great thigh
merges into the swelling of the haunch,
my Guide and Master, straining terribly,
turned his head to where his feet had been
and began to grip the hair as if he were climbing; 80
so that I thought we moved toward Hell again.

---

[255] The gore of the sinners he chews which is mixed with his slaver.

[256] The Cassius who betrayed Caesar was more generally described in terms of Shakespeare's "lean and hungry look." Another Cassius is described by Cicero (*Catiline* III) as huge and sinewy. Dante probably confused the two.

[257] It is now Saturday evening.

"Hold fast!" my Guide said, and his breath came shrill[258]
with labor and exhaustion. "There is no way
but by such stairs to rise above such evil."
At last he climbed out through an opening
in the central rock, and he seated me on the rim;
then joined me with a nimble backward spring.
I looked up, thinking to see Lucifer
as I had left him, and I saw instead
his legs projecting high into the air. 90
Now let all those whose dull minds are still vexed
by failure to understand what point it was
I had passed through, judge if I was perplexed.
"Get up. Up on your feet," my Master said.
"The sun already mounts to middle tierce,[259]
and a long road and hard climbing lie ahead."
It was no hall of state we had found there,
but a natural animal pit hollowed from rock
with a broken floor and a close and sunless air.
"Before I tear myself from the Abyss," 100
I said when I had risen, "O my Master,
explain to me my error in all this:
where is the ice? and Lucifer—how has he
been turned from top to bottom: and how can the sun
have gone from night to day so suddenly?"
And he to me: "You imagine you are still
on the other side of the center where I grasped
the shaggy flank of the Great Worm of Evil
which bores through the world—you *were* while I climbed down,
but when I turned myself about, you passed 110
the point to which all gravities are drawn.
You are under the other hemisphere where you stand;
the sky above us is the half opposed
to that which canopies the great dry land.
Under the mid-point of that other sky
the Man who was born sinless and who lived
beyond all blemish, came to suffer and die.
You have your feet upon a little sphere
which forms the other face of the Judecca.
There it is evening when it is morning here. 120
And this gross Fiend and Image of all Evil
who made a stairway for us with his hide
is pinched and prisoned in the ice-pack still.
On this side he plunged down from heaven's height,
and the land that spread here once hid in the sea
and fled North to our hemisphere for fright;

[258]Cf. Canto 23, 85, where the fact that Dante breathes indicates to the Hypocrites that he is alive. Virgil's breathing is certainly a contradiction.

[259]In the canonical day tierce is the period from about six to nine A.M. Middle tierce, therefore, is seven-thirty. In going through the center point, they have gone from night to day. They have moved ahead twelve hours.

and it may be that moved by that same fear,
the one peak[260] that still rises on this side
fled upward leaving this great cavern here.
Down there, beginning at the further bound 130
of Beelzebub's dim tomb, there is a space
not known by sight, but only by the sound
of a little stream[261] descending through the hollow
it has eroded from the massive stone
in its endlessly entwining lazy flow."
My Guide and I crossed over and began
to mount that little known and lightless road
to ascend into the shining world again.
He first, I second, without thought of rest
we climbed the dark until we reached the point 140
where a round opening brought in sight the blest
and beauteous shining of the Heavenly cars.
And we walked out once more beneath the Stars.[262]

The Purgatorio

Canto 27

The Seventh Cornice—The Angel of Chastity; The Wall of Fire; The Earthly Paradise—The Angel Guardian: A little before sunset of the third day on the Mountain the Poets come to the further limit of the Seventh Cornice and are greeted by the Angel of Chastity, who tells them they must pass through the wall of fire. Dante recoils in terror, but Virgil persuades him to enter in Beatrice's name.

They are guided through the fire by a chant they hear coming from the other side. Emerging, they find it is sung by the Angel Guardian of the Earthly Paradise, who stands in a light so brilliant that Dante cannot see him.

The Angel hurries them toward the ascent, but night overtakes them, and the Poets lie down to sleep, each on the step on which he finds himself. (For Statius it will be the last sleep, since there is no night in Heaven.) There, just before dawn, Dante has a prophetic dream of Leah and Rachel, which foreshadows the appearance, above, of Matilda and Beatrice.

Day arrives; the Poets rise and race up the rest of the ascent until they come in sight of the Earthly Paradise. Here Virgil speaks his last words, for the Poets have now come to the limit of Reason, and Dante is now free to follow his every impulse, since all will to sin in him has been purged away.

As the day stands when the Sun begins to glow
over the land where his Maker's blood was shed,
and the scales of Libra ride over the Ebro,

[260] The Mount of Purgatory.

[261] Lethe. In classical mythology, the river of forgetfulness, from which souls drank before being born. In Dante's symbolism it flows down from Purgatory, where it has washed away the memory of sin from the souls who are undergoing purification. That memory it delivers to Hell, which draws all sin to itself.

[262] As part of his total symbolism Dante ends each of the three divisions of the *Commedia* with this word. Every conclusion of the upward soul is toward the stars, God's shining symbols of hope and virtue. It is just before dawn of Easter Sunday that the Poets emerge—a further symbolism.

while Ganges' waters steam in the noonday glare[1]—
so it stood, the light being nearly faded,
when we met God's glad Angel[2] standing there
on the rocky ledge beyond the reach of the fire,
and caroling *"Beati mundo corde"*[3]
in a voice to which no mortal could aspire.
Then: "Blessèd ones, till by flame purified 10
no soul may pass this point. Enter the fire
and heed the singing from the other side."
These were his words to us when we had come
near as we could, and hearing them, I froze
as motionless as one laid in his tomb.
I lean forward over my clasped hands and stare
into the fire, thinking of human bodies
I once saw burned,[4] and once more see them there.
My kindly escorts heard me catch my breath
and turned, and Virgil said: "Within that flame 20
there may be torment, but there is no death.
Think well, my son, what dark ways we have trod...
I guided you unharmed on Geryon:[5]
shall I do less now we are nearer God?
Believe this past all doubt: were you to stay
within that womb of flame a thousand years,
it would not burn a single hair away.
And if you still doubt my sincerity,
but reach the hem of your robe into the flame:
your hands and eyes will be your guarantee. 30
My son, my son, turn here with whole assurance.
Put by your fears and enter to your peace."
And I stood fixed, at war with my own conscience.
And seeing me still stubborn, rooted fast,
he said, a little troubled: "Think, my son,
you shall see Beatrice when this wall is past."
As Pyramus, but one breath from the dead,
opened his eyes when he heard Thisbe's name,[6]
and looked at her, when the mulberry turned red—

---

[1]It is shortly before sunset of the third day on the Mountain. Dante's details here are the reverse of those given at the opening of Canto 2. *The land where his Maker's blood was shed:* Jerusalem. *The Ebro:* For Spain.

[2]The Angel of Chastity. He is standing on the narrow rocky path outside the wall of fire.

[3]"Blessed are the pure in heart [for they shall see God]." (Matthew 5:8.)

[4]Dante must mean as a witness at an execution. Burnings at the stake generally took place in public squares. They were a rather common spectacle. Dante's sentence of exile, it is relevant to note, decreed that he was to be burned if taken on Florentine territory.

[5]The Monster of Fraud. See *The Inferno,* 17.

[6]Famous tragic lovers of Babylon. Ovid (*Metamorphoses,* IV. 55–166) tells their story. At a tryst by a mulberry (which in those days bore white fruit) Thisbe was frightened by a lion and ran off, dropping her veil. The lion, his jaws bloody from a recent kill, tore at the veil, staining it with blood. Pyramus, arriving later, saw the stained veil, concluded that Thisbe was dead, and stabbed himself. Thisbe, returning, found him and cried to him to open his eyes for his Thisbe. At that name Pyramus opened his eyes, looked at her, and died. Thisbe, invoking the tree to darken in their memory, thereupon stabbed herself. (Cf. Shakespeare's *A Midsummer Night's Dream.*) The mulberry roots drank their blood and the fruit turned red ever after.

just so my hard paralysis melted from me, 40
and I turned to my Leader at that name
which wells forever in my memory;
at which he wagged his head, as at a child
won over by an apple. Then he said:
"Well, then, what are we waiting for?" and smiled.
He turned then and went first into the fire,
requesting Statius, who for some time now
had walked between us, to bring up the rear.
Once in the flame, I gladly would have cast
my body into boiling glass to cool it 50
against the measureless fury of the blast.
My gentle father, ever kind and wise,
strengthened me in my dread with talk of Beatrice,
saying: "I seem already to see her eyes."
From the other side, to guide us, rose a paean,
and moving toward it, mindless of all else,
we emerged at last where the ascent began.
There I beheld a light[7] that burned so brightly
I had to look away; and from it rang:
"Venite benedicti patris mei."[8] 60
"Night falls," it added, "the sun sinks to rest;
do not delay but hurry toward the height
while the last brightness lingers in the west."
Straight up through the great rock-wall lay the way
on such a line that, as I followed it,
my body blocked the sun's last level ray.
We had only climbed the first few stairs as yet
when I and my two sages saw my shadow[9]
fade from me; and we knew the sun had set.
Before the vast sweep of the limned horizon 70
could fade into one hue and night win all
the immeasurable air to its dominion,
each made the step on which he stood his bed,
for the nature of the Mount not only stopped us
but killed our wish to climb, once day had fled.
As goats on a rocky hill will dance and leap,
nimble and gay, till they find grass, and then,
while they are grazing, grow as tame as sheep
at ease in the green shade when the sun is high
and the shepherd stands by, leaning on his staff, 80
and at his ease covers them with his eye—
and as the herdsman beds down on the ground,
keeping his quiet night watch by his flock
lest it be scattered by a wolf or hound;
just so we lay there, each on his stone block,
I as the goat, they as my guardians,
shut in on either side by walls of rock.

---

[7] This is the Angel Guardian of the Earthly Paradise.
[8] "Come ye blessèd of my Father." (Matthew 25:34.)
[9] Virgil and Statius, of course, cast none.

I could see little ahead—rock blocked the way—
but through that little I saw the stars grow larger,
brighter than mankind sees them. And as I lay, 90
staring and lost in thought, a sleep came on me—
the sleep that oftentimes presents the fact
before the event, a sleep of prophecy.
At the hour, I think, when Venus, first returning
out of the east, shone down upon the mountain[10]—
she who with fires of love comes ever-burning—
I dreamed I saw a maiden innocent
and beautiful, who walked a sunny field
gathering flowers, and caroling as she went:
"Say I am Leah if any ask my name, 100
and my white hands weave garlands wreath on wreath
to please me when I stand before the frame
of my bright glass. For this my fingers play
among these blooms. But my sweet sister Rachel[11]
sits at her mirror motionless all day.
To stare into her own eyes endlessly
is all her joy, as mine is in my weaving.
She looks, I do. Thus live we joyously."
Now eastward the new day rayed Heaven's dome
(the sweeter to the returning wanderer 110
who wakes from each night's lodging nearer home),
and the shadows fled on every side as I
stirred from my sleep and leaped upon my feet,
seeing my Lords already standing by.
"This is the day your hungry soul shall be
fed on the golden apples men have sought
on many different boughs so ardently."
These were the very words which, at the start,
my Virgil spoke to me, and there have never
been gifts as dear as these were to my heart. 120
Such waves of yearning to achieve the height
swept through my soul, that at each step I took
I felt my feathers growing for the flight.
When we had climbed the stairway to the rise
of the topmost step, there with a father's love
Virgil turned and fixed me with his eyes.
"My son," he said, "you now have seen the torment
of the temporal and the eternal fires;
here, now, is the limit of my discernment.
I have led you here by grace of mind and art; 130
now let your own good pleasure be your guide;
you are past the steep ways, past the narrow part.

[10]It is the hour before dawn, in which the truth is dreamed.

[11]Leah and Rachel were, respectively, the first- and second-born daughters of Laban and the first and second wives of Jacob. Many authors before Dante had interpreted them as representing the Active and the Contemplative Life of the Soul. Leah's white hands *(le belle mani)* symbolize the Active Life, as Rachel's eyes (lines 104–108) symbolize the Contemplative Life.

See there the sun that shines upon your brow,
the sweet new grass, the flowers, the fruited vines
which spring up without need of seed or plow.
Until those eyes come gladdened which in pain
moved me to come to you and lead your way,
sit there at ease or wander through the plain.
Expect no more of me in word or deed:
here your will is upright, free, and whole, 140
and you would be in error not to heed
whatever your own impulse prompts you to:
lord of yourself I crown and mitre you."[12]

Canto 28

The Earthly Paradise—Lethe: It is the morning of the Wednesday after Easter, Dante's fourth day on the Mountain, and having been crowned Lord of Himself by Virgil, Dante now takes the lead for the first time, wandering at his leisure into The Sacred Wood of the Earthly Paradise until his way is blocked by the waters of Lethe.

His feet stopped, Dante sends his eyes on to wander that Wood and there suddenly appears to him a solitary lady singing and gathering flowers. She is Matilda, who symbolizes The Active Life of the Soul.

In reply to Dante's entreaty, Matilda approaches to the other bank of the river. So standing, three paces across from him, she offers to answer all that Dante wishes to ask. Dante replies that he is in some confusion about the sources of the wind and the water of the Earthly Paradise. Matilda promises to dispel the mists from his understanding and proceeds to explain in great detail The Natural Phenomena of The Earthly Paradise, which is to say, the source of the wind, the vegetation, and the water. She further explains the special powers of the water of Lethe and of Eunoë and concludes with some remarks on the errors of the ancient poets in the location of the Earthly Paradise. At her last words, Dante turns to his two ancient poets to see how they are taking her remarks. Finding them smiling, he turns back once more to Matilda.

Eager now to explore in and about
the luxuriant holy forest evergreen
that softened the new light, I started out,
without delaying longer, from the stair
and took my lingering way into the plain
on ground that breathed a fragrance to the air.
With no least variation in itself
and with no greater force than a mild wind,
the sweet air stroked my face on that sweet shelf,
and at its touch the trembling branches swayed, 10
all bending toward that quarter into which
the holy mountain cast its morning shade;
yet not so far back that in any part
of that sweet wood the small birds in the tops
had reason to stop practicing their art;

[12] Crown as king of your physical self and mitre (as a bishop) as lord of your soul.

but bursting with delight those singing throngs
within their green tents welcomed the new breeze
that murmured a sweet burden of their songs
like that one hears gathering from bough to bough
of the pine wood there on Chiassi's shore 20
when Aeolus lets the Sirocco blow.
I had already come, slow bit by bit,
so far into that ancient holy wood
I could not see where I had entered it;
when I came upon a stream that blocked my way.
To my left it flowed, its wavelets bending back
the grasses on its banks as if in play.
The purest waters known to man would seem
to have some taint of sediment within them
compared to those, for though that holy stream 30
flows darkly there, its surface never lit
in its perpetual shade by any shaft
of sun or moon, nothing could hide in it.
My feet stopped, but my eyes pursued their way
across that stream, to wander in delight
the variousness of everblooming May.
And suddenly—as rare sights sometimes do,
the wonder of them driving from the mind
all other thoughts—I saw come into view
a lady, all alone, who wandered there 40
singing, and picking flowers from the profusion
with which her path was painted everywhere.
"Fair lady who—if outward looks and ways
bear, as they ought, true witness to the heart—
have surely sunned yourself in Love's own rays,
be pleased," I said to her, "to draw as near
the bank of this sweet river as need be
for me to understand the song I hear.
You make me see in my imagining
Persephone as she appeared that day 50
her mother lost a daughter; she, the Spring."
As a dancer, keeping both feet on the ground
and close together, hardly putting one
before the other, spins herself around—
so did she turn to me upon the red
and yellow flowerlets, virgin modesty
making her lower her eyes and bow her head.
And she did all I asked, for she came forward
till I not only heard the melody
of what she sang, but made out every word. 60
And when she stood where the bright grasses are
bathed and bent by the waves of the clear river,
she raised her eyes—and gave my soul a star.
I cannot think so glorious a ray
shot out of Venus' eyes that time her son
wounded her inadvertently in play.

There, on the other bank, smiling she stood
    and gathered to her arms more of the flowers
    that sprang up without seeds in that high wood.
The stream between us was three paces wide, 70
    but the Hellespont where Persian Xerxes crossed
    to leave a dire example to all pride,
in its raging between Sestos and Abydos,
    caused less hate in Leander than this in me,
    for not dividing so that I might cross.
"You are newcomers, and perhaps you find
    because I smile," she said, "here in this place
    chosen to be the nest of humankind,
some doubt that makes you wonder at the sight.
    To pierce such mists as gather on your thoughts 80
    the psalm, *Delectasti me,* will give you light.
And you in front who first entreated me,
    speak if you would know more. I came prepared
    to answer you as fully as need be."
"The way the wood hums and the waters flow,"
    I said then, "are at odds with the conclusions
    I drew from what I heard a while ago."
"I shall explain from what cause," she replied,
    "these things that have confused your mind proceed,
    and thus brush its obscuring mist aside. 90
That Highest Good which only Itself can please
    made man good, and for goodness, and It gave him
    this place as earnest of eternal peace.
But man defaulted. All too brief his stay.
    Defaulted, and exchanged for tears and toil
    his innocent first laughter and sweet play.
When vapors of the earth and water meet
    a storm is born, below there. Now these vapors
    reach up, as far as possible, toward heat.
To guard man from such warring elements 100
    this mountain soared so high that no earth vapor
    could rise above the gate of penitence.
Now since the air revolves in one conjoint
    and perfect circuit with The Primal Motion,
    unless its wheel is broken at some point;
here at this altitude, where it goes round
    in its pure state, it strikes the foliage
    which, being dense, is made to give off sound.
The stricken plant impregnates the pure air
    with its particular powers, which are then borne 110
    on the great wheel and scattered everywhere;
and the other earth, according to the powers
    of soil and climate in its various zones,
    conceives and bears its various fruits and flowers.
When this is understood there, no man need
    believe it strange when plants take root and spring
    out of the earth without apparent seed.

Know, too, the sacred soil on which you stand
  is bursting-full of species of all sorts,
  and bears fruits never picked by human hand. 120
The water you see here is from no source
  that needs replenishment from cloudy vapors,
  like streams that rise and fall: with constant force
it leaves a fountain that receives again,
  from God's Will, every drop that it pours forth
  to the two streams it sends across this plain.
On this side, it removes as it flows down
  all memory of sin; on that, it strengthens
  the memory of every good deed done.
It is called Lethe here: Eunoë there. 130
  And one must drink first this and then the other
  to feel its powers. No sweetness can compare
with the savor of these waters. And although
  you may at once, and with no more instruction,
  drink your soul's fill from the eternal flow,
let me bestow one thing more for good measure.
  Though I exceed my promise, I cannot think
  what I add now will meet with your displeasure.
Those ancients who made songs to celebrate
  man's Age of Gold, placed probably on Parnassus 140
  this perfect garden of his first pure state.
Here mankind lived its innocent first days.
  Here is the Eternal Spring and every fruit.
  This is the nectar that the poets praise."
She paused, I turned around to face my lords,
  the poets whose strains had honored ancient song,
  and saw they had received her final words
with smiles that lingered yet upon their faces;
then turned back to that lady of glad graces.

Canto 29

The Earthly Paradise—The Banks of Lethe—The Heavenly Pageant: Chanting a blessing on those whose sins are forgiven, Matilda moves upstream along one bank of Lethe, and Dante keeps pace with her on the other side. A glorious light and a sweet melody grow on the air, filling Dante with such rapture that he cries out against Eve's daring, through which such joys were lost to mankind.

Soon thereafter he sees the approach of The Heavenly Pageant. It is led by Seven Golden Candelabra that paint a Seven-Striped Rainbow on the sky. Behind them come Twenty-Four Elders (the Books of the Old Testament), and behind them Four Beasts (the Four Gospels), who guard A Triumphal Chariot (the Church), drawn by a Griffon (Christ). At the right wheel of the Chariot dance The Three Theological Virtues; at its left wheel, The Four Cardinal Virtues. This group is followed, in order, by Two Elders representing Luke as the author of Acts and Paul as the author of the fourteen epistles; by Four Elders representing James, Peter, John, and Jude as authors of the four Catholic epistles; and finally by A Single Elder representing John as the author of Revelation.

When the Chariot reaches a point directly across from Dante, a thunderclap resounds, and the entire pageant halts upon that signal.

Her words done, she began her song again—
Beati quorum tecta sunt peccata[13]—
as if in love when love is free of pain.
As nymphs of old went wandering alone
through the deep-shaded woodlands, some pursuing,
and others seeking to evade, the Sun;
so, then, she started up the riverside
and, on my own bank, I kept pace with her,
matching her little steps with shortened stride.
Some fifty paces each we moved this way, 10
when both banks curved as one;[14] and now I found
my face turned to the cradle of the day.[15]
Nor had we gone as far again, all told,
beyond the curve, when she turned to me, saying:
"Dear brother, look and listen." And behold!—
through all that everlasting forest burst
an instantaneous flood of radiance.
I took it for a lightning-flash at first.
But lightning comes and goes. The light I saw
not only stayed on but grew more resplendent. 20
"What can this be?" I asked myself in awe.
And a sweet melody filled the bright air—
so sweet that I reproached in righteous zeal[16]
Eve's fatal recklessness. How could she dare?—
one woman alone, made but a moment since—
all heaven and earth obedient—to refuse
the one veil willed by High Omnipotence;
beneath which, had she stayed God's acolyte,
I should have known before then, and for longer
those raptures of ineffable delight. 30
My soul hung tranced in joy beyond all measure
and yearning for yet more, as I moved on
through those first fruits of the eternal pleasure;[17]
when, under the green boughs that spread before us
the air became a blaze, and the sweet sound
we had been hearing grew into a chorus.
O holy, holy Virgins, if for you[18]
I ever suffered vigils, cold, or fasts,
occasion spurs me now to claim my due.

---

[13]This is Dante's elision of Psalms 32:1: "Blessed are they [whose transgression is forgiven] whose sins are covered."

[14]Note the regularity (constancy, perfection) of the river's curve.

[15]The East.

[16]For having thrown away the glory of the Earthly Paradise by refusing to endure the one veil (of ignorance) under which, had Eve been dutiful, Dante would have known his present bliss since birth (hence, "before then, and for longer").

[17]The joys of Heaven. The joys of the Earthly Paradise are the first fruits of the great harvest to come.

[18]Dante is about to describe the entrance of the Heavenly Pageant, a spectacle of such splendor that it is difficult to conceive, let alone put into rhyme. For his great effort, therefore, he summons all the Muses from Helicon, calling upon Urania to preside, since she is the Muse of Astronomy, hence of heavenly things. (Her name in Greek means, literally, "the heavenly one.") *O holy, holy Virgins:* The Nine Muses. *with your full choir:* With all the other Muses.

Empty all Helicon! Now is the time! 40
Urania, help me here with your full choir,
to bring things scarce conceivable to rhyme!
I saw next, far ahead, what I believed[19,20]
were seven golden trees (at such a distance
and in such light the eye can be deceived);
but in a while, when I had drawn so near
that chance resemblances confused by distance
no longer made false images appear,
that power that reaps for reason's mill could see
that they were candelabra;[21] and in the chant 50
it heard that word *Hosanna!*[22] ringing free.
Above the gold array flamed seven times seven
candles more lucent than the mid-month moon
at midnight in the calm of clearest heaven.
I turned about, amazed at what I saw,
to my good Virgil,[23] and he answered me
in silence, with a look of equal awe.[24]

---

[19]The Pageant Dante now describes is an allegory of the Church Triumphant in the form of a religious procession or a formal masque in which devout mummers present themselves in allegorical guises. The center of the Pageant is the Chariot of The Church Triumphant, guarded by the Four Gospels, and attended on the right by the Three Theological Graces and on the left by the Four Cardinal Virtues. The Chariot itself is drawn by the Griffon, who represents the twofold nature of Christ as Man-and-God. Before this central group walk twenty-four Elders representing the books of the Old Testament. Behind the central group walk seven Elders representing the books of the New Testament. The entire procession is led by seven enormous Candelabra whose candles trail a rainbow canopy across the sky representing the Seven Gifts of the Spirit under which the Church moves.

Dante has not presented any allegory of such formality up to this point, and some readers have thought the allegory of the Pageant stiff and lifeless. One should bear in mind, however, that Dante is beginning to deal, now, not with reason but with revelation, and that the increased formality of his allegory here is apt to its content, and apt again in its resemblance to the rituals of the Church whose triumph he is representing. Note too, as distinct from the rest of Dante's allegory, that these figures do not enter as themselves (St. John, for example, appears in three guises) but as heavenly beings made up to represent others.

[20]Dante sees in the distance what he takes to be seven trees of gold. Drawing nearer, he sees they are, in reality, enormous candelabra. At that point too, he is close enough to make out that the word being sung by the chorus (line 36) which was first heard as a distant melody (line 21) is "Hosanna!" *chance resemblances:* Of the bases of the candelabra to tree trunks. *that power that reaps for reason's mill:* The discernment of the senses through which reason draws the data of nature from which it derives its concepts.

[21]On the Mountain the Lord specified to Moses the exact form of the seven-branched candelabrum of pure gold which was to be an essential part of the tabernacle (Exodus 25:31–37). In Revelation 1:12, John had a vision of seven candelabra and interpreted them as seven churches (1:20). Later (4:5) he interprets them as the Seven Gifts of the Holy Spirit (wisdom, understanding, counsel, might, knowledge, piety, and fear of the Lord). As the Candelabra advance in the van of the procession, their candles paint the sky overhead with a seven-striped rainbow that represents these Gifts. Thus, the Candelabra may be taken as the light and glory of God from which issue the Seven Gifts of the Holy Spirit. The Church follows where the Candelabra lead.

[22]Literally, "Save, we pray!" On Palm Sunday as Christ was about to enter Jerusalem, he was hailed at Bethphage on the Mount of Olives with the words "Hosannah to the son of David!" (Matthew 21:9.) The chant is especially apt in that Christ, as the Griffon, is about to enter in triumph.

[23]A new and much more familiar form of address signifying Dante's new state. Dante has always referred to Virgil with titles of honor and superiority.

[24]Allegorically: Dante, out of old habit, turns to Reason for an explanation, but finds that Reason itself is overawed. Virgil has already explained (Canto 27, 129) that he has passed the limit of his understanding.

I turned back then to those sublimities
that were approaching at so slow a pace
that new brides[25] might outdistance them with ease. 60
The lady cried: "Why have you set your mind
so fixedly upon those living lights
that you do not observe what comes behind?"
Then I saw people walking[26] like attendants
behind their lords, and clothed in robes so white
earth has no snow of such a pure resplendence.
Upon my left the polished river shone
bright as a mirror, and when I looked in
I saw my left side there, perfectly drawn.
And when I had moved close enough to be 70
kept at a distance by no more than water,
I halted my slow steps, better to see.
I saw the flames advance, leaving the air
painted behind, as if by massive strokes,
or by bright pennons they were trailing there;
thus, all the trailing heavens were aglow
with seven bands of light of the same color
as Delia's girdle or Apollo's bow.[27]
Those bands stretched back further than I could see,[28]
and the distance separating side from side 80
came to ten paces, as it seemed to me.
And there, advancing two by two beneath
that seven-striped sky came four-and-twenty elders,
each crowned in glory with a lily-wreath.
And all sang with one voice, triumphantly:
"Blessèd art thou among the daughters of Adam!
Blessèd thy beauty to eternity!"
And when those souls elect, as in a dream,
had left behind the flowers and the new grass
that shone before me, there across the stream, 90
as star follows on star in the serene
of heaven's height, there came on at their backs
four beasts, and these wore wreaths of living green.[29]

---

[25]Walking back from the altar. Hence, at a very slow pace. But even that pace would easily outdistance this procession.

[26]These are the figures made up as four and twenty elders who represent the books of the Old Testament as counted by St. Jerome in his *Gallican Psalter* (the twelve minor prophets are counted as one book, and so are Ezra-Nehemiah, I and II Kings, I and II Samuel, and I and II Chronicles). Thus the elders represent all Revelation before Christ. They wear white robes and wreaths of lilies as symbols of the purity of their faith. John has a vision of them in Revelation 4:4–5, and explains them, there, as the Twelve Patriarchs and the Twelve Apostles. In his vision they wore crowns of gold. Their song (lines 86–87) is an adaptation of the words used by Gabriel and Elisabeth in addressing Mary at the time of the Annunciation. (Luke 1:28, 42.)

[27]The rainbow-colored halo around the moon. Delia was another name for Diana, the moon goddess. *Apollo's bow:* The rainbow. Apollo was, of course, the Sun.

[28]Allegorically, the Gifts of the Holy Spirit stretch further back into time than any man can reckon. *ten paces:* May certainly be taken as the Ten Commandments in which the Seven Gifts of the Holy Spirit were revealed, and through which they may be enjoyed.

[29]They represent the Four Gospels of Matthew, Mark, Luke, and John that follow immediately upon the Old Testament. Their wreaths of living green signify Hope. The wings may be taken as signifying the speed with which the Gospels spread through the world. The fact that there are three pairs of wings obviously suggests the Trinity, and the eyes may be taken as Omniscience which is able to see past, present, and future. That much stated, Dante refers the reader to Ezekiel 1:4–14, for a detailed description, except that they are there described as having only four wings, and Dante follows John (Revelation 4:8) in giving them six.

Each had three pairs of wings, and every pair
was full of eyes. Were Argus[30] living yet,
his eyes would be most like what I saw there.
I cannot spend my rhymes as liberally
as I should like to in describing them,
for, Reader, other needs are pressing me:
but read Ezekiel where he sets forth 100
how they appeared to him in a great storm
of wind and cloud and fire out of the North;
and such as he recounts, such did I see;
except that in the number of their wings
John differs with him, and agrees with me.
Within the space they guarded there came on
a burnished two-wheeled chariot in triumph,[31]
and harnessed to the neck of a great Griffon[32]
whose wings, upraised into the bands of light,
inclosed the middle one so perfectly 110
they cut no part of those to left or right.
Higher than sight its wing-tips soared away.
Its bird-like parts were gold; and white the rest
with blood-red markings. Will it serve to say
Rome never saw such a caparison,
no, not for Africanus, nor yet Augustus?
The Sun's own would seem shabby by comparison;
yes, even the Sun's own chariot, which strayed[33]
and was destroyed in fire by Jove's dark justice
that day the frightened Earth devoutly prayed. 120
Beside the right wheel, dancing in a gyre,[34]
three maidens came. The first one was so red
she would be barely visible in fire.

---

[30]Jove made love to Io. Juno, in wifely jealousy, turned Io into a cow and set Argus of the hundred eyes to watch her. Mercury, sent by Jove, caused Argus to fall into an enchanted sleep and cut his head off. Juno set Argus' eyes in the tail of the peacock. Dante makes the point that the peacock's eyes, bright as they are, are dead, whereas the eyes in the feathers of these beasts are alive.

[31]Within the square guarded by the Four Gospel Beasts the Church is represented by a chariot so splendid that Rome never saw its equal, not even in the triumphs of Scipio Africanus or of Augustus. The very chariot of the Sun could not compare with it. Its two wheels may best be taken as representing the Old and the New Testament. It is drawn by the Griffon that represents Christ, and it is flanked by the Theological Virtues and the Cardinal Virtues.

[32]A mythical figure with the fore parts of an eagle and the hind parts of a lion, here meant to represent the dual role of Christ as God and Man, his birdlike part divine, his lionlike part animal, hence human, and the unity of the two a symbol of his incarnation as the Word. His upraised wings, their tips soaring higher than the sight of man can follow, extend into the seven-striped heaven and enclose the central stripe representing Might as the central Gift of the Holy Spirit and as a symbol of His triumph. The Griffon's coloration is probably suggested by Song of Solomon 5:10–11: "My beloved is white and ruddy, the chiefest among ten thousand. His head is as the most fine gold."

[33]The Chariot of the Sun was driven by Apollo. One day Phaëthon, Apollo's son, tried to drive it, but could not manage the horses. The chariot swerved from its path, scorching the sky and threatening to destroy the Earth. In terror Earth prayed to Jove for deliverance, and Jove destroyed the chariot with a thunderbolt. The scar left on the sky by Phaëthon's course became the Milky Way.

[34]*The Three Theological Virtues.* They are Caritas (Christian Love), Faith, and Hope. Caritas is so red she could scarcely be seen in a fire. Hope is green, and Faith pure white. They dance in a ring at the Chariot's right wheel, and Faith and Caritas take turns leading the dance, while Hope (who cannot move except as Faith and Caritas direct) follows. Note that it is Caritas ("And the greatest of these is Charity") that sings the song to which they dance.

The second looked as if both flesh and bone
were made of flawless emerald. The third
seemed a new snow no slightest wind has blown.
And now the white one led the dance, and now
the red: and from the song the red one sang
the others took their measure, fast or slow.
Beside the left wheel, dancing in a flame[35] 130
of purple robes, and led by one who had
three eyes within her head, four glad nymphs came.
Behind these seven came on, side by side,[36]
two elders, different in dress, but both
by the same massive bearing dignified.
One showed he was a follower of the art
of great Hippocrates,[37] whom Nature made
to heal the creatures dearest to her heart.
The other, his counterpart,[38] carried a blade
so sharp and bright that at the sight of it, 140
even across the stream, I was afraid.
Next I saw four who walked with humble mien.
And last of all, one who moved in a trance,
as if asleep but his face was firm and keen.
These seven were robed like the first twenty-four
in flowing robes of white, but, for their crowns,
it was not wreaths of lilies that they wore,
but roses and whatever blooms most red.
One would have sworn, seeing them at a distance,
that they were wearing flames about the head. 150
And when the chariot had reached the place
across from me, I heard a thunderclap
that seemed a signal to those souls in grace,
for there, in unison with the exalted
first flaming standards,[39] all that pageant halted.

Canto 30

The Earthly Paradise—Beatrice; Virgil Vanishes: The procession [of the Heavenly Pageant] halts and the Prophets turn to the chariot and sing "Come, my bride, from Lebanon." They are summoning Beatrice, who appears on the left side of the chariot, half-hidden from view by

[35] *The Four Cardinal (or Natural) Virtues.* They are Prudence, Justice, Fortitude, and Temperance. They are dressed in the Imperial Purple, for they represent the Classical Virtues. Prudence, who leads them in their dance, has three eyes symbolizing that it is her duty to look at and consider the past, present, and the future. Note, too, that the Classical and the Theological Virtues *must* go together if the soul is to develop.

[36] *The Seven Elders.* These represent the remaining books of the New Testament (aside from the Four Gospels). Note that it is the books, not the persons, that are represented, for John appears three times in this procession; first as the Gospel, next as the Epistles, and finally as Revelation. Thus the first two are Acts and the Fourteen Epistles. The next four are the Catholic Epistles. And the final single figure is Revelation. They wear wreaths of brightest red to signify the ardor of Caritas.

[37] Luke, as the author of Acts. In Colossians 4:14, Paul describes him as "the beloved physician." He is the doctor of souls, as Hippocrates was the doctor of bodies.

[38] The figure is Paul. The sword he carries may symbolize his martyrdom by a sword, or more aptly "the sword of the Spirit, which is the word of God." (Ephesians 6:17.) Thus he is here the taker rather than the healer of lives, as presented in the Epistles.

[39] The candelabra that led the procession like pennons. *in unison:* The rear and the van of the procession stopped at the same instant.

showers of blossoms poured from above by a hundred angels. Dante, stirred by the sight, turns to Virgil to express his overflowing emotions, and discovers that Virgil has vanished.

Because he bursts into tears at losing Virgil, Dante is reprimanded by Beatrice. The Angel Choir overhead immediately breaks into a Psalm of Compassion, but Beatrice, still severe, answers by detailing Dante's offenses in not making proper use of his great gifts. It would violate the ordering of the Divine Decree, she argues, to let Dante drink the waters of Lethe, thereby washing all memory of sin from his soul, before he had shed the tears of a real repentance.

When the Septentrion of the First Heaven,[40]
which does not rise nor set, and which has never
been veiled from sight by any mist but sin,
and which made every soul in that high court
know its true course (just as the lower Seven
direct the helmsman to his earthly port),
had stopped; the holy prophets,[41] who till then
had walked between the Griffon and those lights,
turned to the car like souls who cry "Amen."
And one among them[42] who seemed sent from Heaven 10
clarioned: *"Veni, sponsa, de Libano,"*[43]
three times, with all the others joining in.
As, at the last trump every saint shall rise
out of the grave, ready with voice new-fleshed
to carol *Alleluliah* to the skies;
just so, above the chariot, at the voice
of such an elder, rose a hundred Powers
and Principals[44] of the Eternal Joys,
all saying together: *"Benedictus qui venis"*;[45]
then, scattering flowers about on every side: 20
"Manibus o date lilia plenis."[46]
Time and again at daybreak I have seen
the eastern sky glow with a wash of rose
while all the rest hung limpid and serene,
and the Sun's face rise tempered from its rest
so veiled by vapors that the naked eye
could look at it for minutes undistressed.
Exactly so, within a cloud of flowers
that rose like fountains from the angels' hands
and fell about the chariot in showers, 30

[40]The Septentrion is the seven stars of the Big Dipper. Here Dante means the seven candelabra [of the Heavenly Pageant]. They are the Septentrion of the First Heaven (the empyrean) as distinct from the seven stars of the dipper, which occur lower down in the Sphere of the Fixed Stars.

[41]The twenty-four elders who represent the books of the Old Testament. *Griffon:* A mythical figure with the fore parts of an eagle and the hind parts of a lion, here meant to represent the dual role of Christ as God and Man.

[42]The Song of Songs.

[43]"Come [with me] from Lebanon, my spouse." Song of Songs 4:8. This cry, reechoed by choirs of angels, summons Beatrice.

[44]Angels.

[45]"Blessed is he who cometh." (Matthew 21:9.)

[46]"Oh, give lilies with full hands." These are the words of Anchises in honor of Marcellus (*Aeneid* 6, 883). Thus they are not only apt to the occasion but their choice is a sweetly conceived last literary compliment to Virgil before he vanishes.

a lady[47] came in view: an olive crown
wreathed her immaculate veil, her cloak was green,
the colors of live flame played on her gown.
My soul—such years had passed since last it saw[48]
that lady and stood trembling in her presence,
stupefied by the power of holy awe—
now, by some power that shone from her above
the reach and witness of my mortal eyes,
felt the full mastery of enduring love.
The instant I was smitten by the force, 40
which had already once transfixed my soul
before my boyhood years had run their course,
I turned left with the same assured belief
that makes a child run to its mother's arms
when it is frightened or has come to grief,
to say to Virgil: "There is not within me
one drop of blood unstirred. I recognize
the tokens of the ancient flame." But he,
he had taken his light from us. He had gone.
Virgil had gone. Virgil, the gentle Father 50
to whom I gave my soul for its salvation!
Not all that sight of Eden lost to view
by our First Mother could hold back the tears
that stained my cheeks so lately washed with dew.[49]
"Dante,[50] do not weep yet, though Virgil goes.
Do not weep yet, for soon another wound
shall make you weep far hotter tears than those!"
As an admiral takes his place at stern or bow
to observe the handling of his other ships
and spur all hands to do their best—so now, 60
on the chariot's left side, I saw appear
when I turned at the sound of my own name
(which, necessarily, is recorded here),
that lady who had been half-veiled from view
by the flowers of the angel-revels. Now her eyes
fixed me across the stream, piercing me through.
And though the veil she still wore, held in place
by the wreathed flowers of wise Minerva's leaves,[51]
let me see only glimpses of her face,
her stern and regal bearing made me dread 70
her next words, for she spoke as one who saves
the heaviest charge till all the rest are read.
"Look at me well. I am she. I am Beatrice.
How dared you make your way to this high mountain?
Did you not know that here man lives in bliss?"

---

[47] Beatrice. She is dressed in the colors of Faith (white), Hope (green), and Caritas (red).
[48] Beatrice died in 1290. Thus Dante has passed ten years without sight of her.
[49] By Virgil, 1, 124.
[50] This is the only point in the *Commedia* at which Dante mentions his own name.
[51] The olive crown.

I lowered my head and looked down at the stream.
  But when I saw myself reflected there,
  I fixed my eyes upon the grass for shame.
I shrank as a wayward child in his distress
  shrinks from his mother's sternness, for the taste 80
  of love grown wrathful is a bitterness.
She paused. At once the angel chorus sang
  the blessed psalm: *"In te, Domine, speravi."*
  As far as *"pedes meos"* their voices rang.[52]
As on the spine of Italy the snow
  lies frozen hard among the living rafters[53]
  in winter when the northeast tempests blow;
then, melting if so much as a breath stir
  from the land of shadowless noon,[54] flows through itself
  like hot wax trickling down a lighted taper— 90
just so I froze, too cold for sighs or tears
  until I heard that choir whose notes are tuned
  to the eternal music of the spheres.
But when I heard the voice of their compassion
  plead for me more than if they had cried out:
  "Lady, why do you treat him in this fashion?";
the ice, which hard about my heart had pressed,
  turned into breath and water, and flowed out
  through eyes and throat in anguish from my breast.
Still standing at the chariot's left side, 100
  she turned to those compassionate essences
  whose song had sought to move her, and replied:
"You keep your vigil in the Eternal Day
  where neither night nor sleep obscures from you
  a single step the world takes on its way;
but I must speak with greater care that he
  who weeps on that far bank may understand
  and feel a grief to match his guilt. Not only
by the workings of the spheres that bring each seed
  to its fit end according to the stars 110
  that ride above it, but by gifts decreed
in the largesse of overflowing Grace,
  whose rain has such high vapors for its source
  our eyes cannot mount to their dwelling place;
this man, potentially was so endowed
  from early youth that marvelous increase
  should have come forth from every good he sowed.
But richest soil the soonest will grow wild
  with bad seed and neglect. For a while I stayed him
  with glimpses of my face. Turning my mild 120

---

[52]In mercy the angel chorus sings Psalm 31:1–8, beginning "In thee, O Lord, do I put my trust" and continuing as far as "thou has set my feet in a large room."

[53]The trees. *The spine of Italy:* the Apennines.

[54]Africa. In equatorial regions the noonday sun is at the zenith over each point twice a year. Its rays then fall straight down and objects cast no shadows.

and youthful eyes into his very soul,
I let him see their shining, and I led him
by the straight way, his face to the right goal.
The instant I had come upon the sill
of my second age,[55] and crossed and changed my life,
he left me and let others shape his will.
When I rose from the flesh into the spirit,
to greater beauty and to greater virtue,
he found less pleasure in me and less merit.
He turned his steps aside from the True Way, 130
pursuing the false images of good
that promise what they never wholly pay.
Not all the inspiration I won by prayer
and brought to him in dreams and meditations
could call him back, so little did he care.
He fell so far from every hope of bliss
that every means of saving him had failed
except to let him see the damned. For this
I visited the portals of the dead
and poured my tears and prayers before that spirit 140
by whom his steps have, up to now, been led.
The seal Almighty God's decree has placed
on the rounds of His creation would be broken
were he to come past Lethe and to taste
the water that wipes out the guilty years
without some scot of penitential tears!"[56]

Canto 31

The Earthly Paradise—Lethe; Beatrice, Matilda: Beatrice continues her reprimand, forcing Dante to confess his faults until he swoons with grief and pain at the thought of his sin. He wakes to find himself in Lethe, held in the arms of Matilda, who leads him to the other side of the stream and there immerses him that he may drink the waters that wipe out all memory of sin.

Matilda then leads him to the Four Cardinal Virtues, who dance about him and lead him before the Griffon, where he may look into the eyes of Beatrice. In them Dante sees, in a First Beatific Vision, the radiant reflection of the Griffon, who appears now in his human and now in his godly nature.

The Three Theological Virtues now approach and beg that Dante may behold the smile of Beatrice. Beatrice removes her veil, and in a Second Beatific Vision, Dante beholds the splendor of the unveiled shining of Divine Love.

"You, there, who stand upon the other side[57]—"
(turning to me now, who had thought the edge
of her discourse was sharp, the point) she cried

[55] Beatrice's womanhood. When she had reached the full bloom of youth Dante turned from her and wrote to his *donna gentile.* [The *donna gentile* (noble or gentle lady) is not identified by name.] Allegorically, he turned from divine "sciences" to an overreliance upon philosophy (the human "sciences"). For this sin he must suffer.

[56] In passing Lethe and drinking its waters, the soul loses all memory of guilt. This, therefore, is Dante's last opportunity to do penance. *Scot:* payment.

[57] Of Lethe. But also the other side of the immortal life, i.e., still living.

without pause in her flow of eloquence,
"Speak up! Speak up! Is it true? To such a charge
your own confession must give evidence."
I stood as if my spirit had turned numb:
the organ of my speech moved, but my voice
died in my throat before a word could come.
Briefly she paused, then cried impatiently: 10
"What are you thinking? Speak up, for the waters[58]
have yet to purge sin from your memory."
Confusion joined to terror forced a broken
"yes" from my throat, so weak that only one
who read my lips would know that I had spoken.
As an arbalest will snap when string and bow
are drawn too tight by the bowman, and the bolt
will strike the target a diminished blow[59]—
so did I shatter, strengthless and unstrung,
under her charge, pouring out floods of tears, 20
while my voice died in me on the way to my tongue.
And she: "Filled as you were with the desire
I taught you for That Good beyond which nothing
exists on earth to which man may aspire,
what yawning moats or what stretched chain-lengths[60] lay
across your path to force you to abandon
all hope of pressing further on your way?
What increase or allurement seemed to show
in the brows of others that you walked before them
as a lover walks below his lady's window?" 30
My breath dragged from me in a bitter sigh;
I barely found a voice to answer with;
my lips had trouble forming a reply.
In tears I said: "The things of the world's day,
false pleasures and enticements, turned my steps
as soon as you had ceased to light my way."
And she: "Had you been silent, or denied
what you confess, your guilt would still be known
to Him from Whom no guilt may hope to hide.
But here, before our court, when souls upbraid 40
themselves for their own guilt in true remorse,
the grindstone is turned back against the blade.[61]
In any case that you may know your crime
truly and with true shame and so be stronger
against the Siren's song another time,

[58]Of Lethe.

[59]The figure is a bit confusing. Dante seems to say that the bolt (corresponding to an arrow) of a crossbow strikes the target with less force when the bow snaps. He does not stop to consider that the bolt may miss the target entirely. Nevertheless, the intent of his figure is clear enough.

[60]These were, of course, defensive military measures. The moats guarded castles. The chains were strung to block roads, bridges, and gates.

[61]Turning the grindstone away from the blade sharpens it. Turning it back against the blade dulls it. Thus Beatrice is saying that when a soul openly confesses in true repentance what could not in any case be hidden from God, the sword of Justice is blunted, i.e., no longer cuts as deeply.

control your tears and listen with your soul
  to learn how my departure from the flesh
  ought to have spurred you to the higher goal.
Nothing in Art or Nature could call forth
  such joy from you, as sight of that fair body 50
  which clothed me once and now sifts back to earth.
And if my dying turned that highest pleasure
  to very dust, what joy could still remain
  in mortal things for you to seek and treasure?
At the first blow you took from such vain things
  your every thought should have been raised to follow
  my flight above decay. Nor should your wings
have been weighed down by any joy below—
  love of a maid,[62] or any other fleeting
  and useless thing—to wait a second blow. 60
The fledgling waits a second shaft, a third;
  but nets[63] are spread and the arrow sped in vain
  in sight or hearing of the full-grown bird."
As a scolded child, tongue tied for shame, will stand
  and recognize his fault, and weep for it,
  bowing his head to a just reprimand,
so did I stand. And she said: "If to hear me
  grieves you, now raise your beard and let your eyes
  show you a greater cause for misery."[64]
The blast that blows from Libya's hot sand, 70
  or the Alpine gale, overcomes less resistance
  uprooting oaks than I, at her command,
overcame then in lifting up my face;
  for when she had referred to it as my "beard"
  I sensed too well the venom of her phrase.
When I had raised my eyes with so much pain,
  I saw those Primal Beings, now at rest,
  who had strewn blossoms round her thick as rain;
and with my tear-blurred and uncertain vision
  I saw Her turned to face that beast which is 80
  one person in two natures without division.[65]
Even veiled and across the river from me
  her face outshone its first-self[66] by as much
  as she outshone all mortals formerly.
And the thorns of my repentance pricked me so
  that all the use and substance of the world
  I most had loved, now most appeared my foe.
Such guilty recognition gnawed my heart
  I swooned for pain; and what I then became
  she best knows who most gave me cause to smart. 90

[62]Dante mentions another maiden in some of his songs but in an indefinite way. No specific reference can be attached to these words.

[63]Sometimes used for trapping birds.

[64]The sight of her accompanied by the guilty knowledge that he had turned away from so much beauty and perfection.

[65]The Griffon. He is the masque of Christ and represents His two aspects as man and God.

[66]Her mortal self.

When I returned to consciousness at last
  I found the lady who had walked alone[67]
  bent over me. "Hold fast!" she said, "Hold fast!"
She had drawn me into the stream up to my throat,
  and pulling me behind her, she sped on
  over the water, light as any boat.
Nearing the sacred bank, I heard her say
  in tones so sweet I cannot call them back,
  much less describe them here: *"Asperges me."*[68]
Then the sweet lady took my head between 100
  her open arms, and embracing me, she dipped me
  and made me drink the waters that make clean.
Then raising me in my new purity
  she led me to the dance of the Four Maidens;[69]
  each raised an arm and so joined hands above me.
"Here we are nymphs; stars are we in the skies.
  Ere Beatrice went to earth we were ordained
  her handmaids. We will lead you to her eyes;
but that your own may see what joyous light
  shines in them, yonder Three,[70] who see more deeply, 110
  will sharpen and instruct your mortal sight."
Thus they sang, then led me to the Griffon.
  Behind him, Beatrice waited. And when I stood
  at the Griffon's breast, they said in unison:
"Look deep, look well, however your eyes may smart.
  We have led you now before those emeralds[71]
  from which Love shot his arrows through your heart."
A thousand burning passions, every one
  hotter than any flame, held my eyes fixed
  to the lucent eyes she held fixed on the Griffon. 120
Like sunlight in a glass the twofold creature
  shone from the deep reflection of her eyes,
  now in the one, now in the other nature.
Judge, Reader, if I found it passing strange
  to see the thing unaltered in itself
  yet in its image working change on change.
And while my soul in wonder and delight
  was savoring that food which in itself
  both satisfies and quickens appetite,[72]

[67] Matilda, who appears in Canto 28, having been foreshadowed by Leah in Dante's dream (27). She may be taken to symbolize the Active Life of the Soul.

[68] *Asperges me hyssopo, et mundabor; lavabis me, et super nivem dealbabor.* ("Purge me with hyssop, and I shall be clean; wash me, and I shall be whiter than snow.") Psalm 51:7. These are the words the priest utters when he sprinkles holy water over the confessed sinner to absolve him.

[69] The Four Cardinal Virtues: Justice, Prudence, Fortitude, and Temperance. In their present manifestation they are nymphs. In another manifestation they are the four stars Dante saw above him when he arrived at the base of the mountain. (Canto 1, 23, note.)

[70] The Theological Virtues: Faith, Hope, and Charity (i.e., *Caritas*).

[71] The eyes of Beatrice. Dante may have intended to describe them as green (hazel) but more likely his choice of words here is meant only to signify "jewel bright." Green is, of course, the color of Hope, and an allegorical significance may be implied in that.

[72] "They that eat me shall yet be hungry, and they that drink me shall yet be thirsty." (Ecclesiasticus 24:21.)

the other Three, whose bearing made it clear 130
they were of higher rank, came toward me dancing
to the measure of their own angelic air.
"Turn, Beatrice, oh turn the eyes of grace,"
was their refrain, "upon your faithful one
who comes so far to look upon your face.
Grant us this favor of your grace: reveal
your mouth to him, and let his eyes behold
the Second Beauty,[73] which your veils conceal."
O splendor of the eternal living light!
who that has drunk deep of Parnassus' waters,[74] 140
or grown pale in the shadow of its height,
would not, still, feel his burdened genius fail
attempting to describe in any tongue
how you appeared when you put by your veil
in that free air open to heaven and earth
whose harmony is your shining shadowed forth!

Canto 32

The Earthly Paradise—Beatrice Unveiled; Departure of the Heavenly Pageant; Transformation of the Chariot: Beatrice unveils and for the first time in ten years Dante looks upon her face. When he recovers from that blinding sight, Dante finds the Heavenly Pageant has wheeled about and is heading east. Dante and Statius follow the Chariot to The Tree of Good and Evil, which rises to vast heights but bears neither leaves nor flowers. The Griffon ties the pole of the Chariot to the Tree, and the Tree immediately breaks into leaf and flower. The Heavenly Pageant greets this wonder with a hymn unknown to mortals. Overpowered by the singing, Dante sleeps.

He awakens to find himself, as he believes at first, alone with Matilda. The Heavenly Pageant has, in fact, departed, but as Dante soon learns, Beatrice has remained behind to guard the Chariot and the Seven Nymphs have remained to attend her. She is seated upon the ground, on the roots of the tree and under its shade.

Dante then witnesses an allegorical masque of the Corruption of the Church through Wealth. First an Eagle (the Roman Empire) attacks the tree and the Chariot. Then a Fox (heresy). Then the Eagle returns and covers the Chariot with its feathers. Immediately a Dragon (Satan) rips at the chariot's foundation. The Chariot then covers itself with the feathers (riches) and is converted into a Monstrous Beast on which rides a Harlot (the corrupted Papacy) attended by a Giant (the French Monarchy) that beats the harlot and drags the monster into the woods and out of sight.

My eyes were fixed with such intensity
on quenching, at long last, their ten years' thirst
that every sense but sight abandoned me.
Tranced by the holy smile that drew me there
into the old nets, I forgot all else—
my eyes wore blinders, and I could not care.

---

[73]The smile of Beatrice (Divine Love). Dante was led to the First Beauty by the Four Cardinal Virtues. Now the Three Theological Virtues, as higher beings, lead him to the second, and higher, beauty, which is the joy of Divine Love in receiving the purified soul.

[74]The fountain of Castalia. To drink from it is to receive poetic gifts. To grow pale in the shadow of Parnassus signifies to labor at mastering the art of poetry.

When suddenly my gaze was wrenched away
and forced to turn left to those goddesses:
"He stares too fixedly," I heard them say.[75]
And as a man is blinded by the light 10
when he has looked directly at the sun,
just so I found that I had lost my sight.
When I could make out lesser (I mean, of course,
"less sensible objects") as compared to the greater
from which I had been called away by force,
I saw the legion of those souls in grace
had turned right-wheel-about, and marched back now
with the sun and the seven torches in its face.[76]
As forward troops when they are giving ground
turn under their shields,[77] and their standards face about 20
before the rest of the column has turned round—
just so the vanguard of that heavenly force[78]
had all gone by before the chariot
had swung its pole around to the new course.
Then to their wheels the ladies turned together,
and the Griffon once more pulled the sacred car,
not ruffling so much as a single feather.
Statius and I followed across that park
with the lady who had led me through the ford,
behind the wheel that turned the lesser arc.[79] 30
We marched across the sacred wood which she
who heeded a forked tongue had left deserted,
our steps timed by angelic melody.
We had moved on, I think, about as far
as three good bowshots, end to end, might reach,
when Beatrice descended[80] from the car.

---

[75]Beatrice had died in 1290. Dante has not, therefore, seen her for ten years, and the sight of her unveiled face so draws him into the old nets (of love) that he loses track of all else until he is brought to his senses by overhearing the Three Maidens charge him with overdoing. For it is immoderate (*non è bello,* i.e., it is not an Aristotelian mean of good conduct) to stare so intensely, even at the vision of eternal beauty, if in so doing a man loses sight of the other gifts of God. Bear in mind, too, that Dante is staring with his earthly memory of the other Beatrice. The Heavenly Beatrice has not yet been truly revealed to him. That revelation will take place in the next Canto.

[76]The Heavenly Pageant came originally from the east. It passed Dante, executed a right-wheel-about, and is now returning, face to the east. Accordingly, it now has in its face the light of the sun as well as that of the candelabra.

[77]Troops turning in retreat within range of the enemy held their shields over their heads for protection.

[78]The twenty-four elders.

[79]The right. In making a right turn, it would swing through the lesser arc. The poets, therefore, are walking behind the Three Theological Virtues.

[80]In this masque, Beatrice has entered in a chariot that represents the Church Triumphant. The procession is now moving to the tree that represents the Civil Authority of the Holy Roman Empire. Her descent in order to approach on foot signifies the humility the Church should display before civil authority, as commanded by Paul (Romans 13: 1): "Let every soul be subject unto the higher powers. For there is no power but of God: the powers that be are ordained of God." To this, as Dante's image of the ideal Church, contrast his lament for the evils that befell the Church when it grew rich and arrogant (*The Inferno,* 19, 109–111, and note), and the final allegory of the present Canto.

"Adam!" I heard all murmur, censuring him.
  Then they all formed a circle round a tree
  that bore no leaf nor flower on any limb.
It soared so high that even in woods like those 40
  the Indians know it would have seemed a wonder;
  and the crown spread out the more the more it rose.
"Blessèd art thou, Griffon, whose beak hath rent
  no morsel of the sweet wood of this tree,
  for it grips the belly with a raging torment!"
—So shouted all the others as they stood
  about the tree. And the two-natured being:
  "Thus is preserved the seed of every good!"
Then he drew up before the widowed mast
  the chariot's pole, and what came from the tree 50
  he gave it back, and tied the two stems fast.
As in the spring on earth, when the great light
  falls mingled with the rays of those sweet stars
  that follow Pisces into Heaven's height,
the trees begin to swell, then burgeon full,
  each one in its own hue, before the Sun
  harnesses his team beneath the Bull—
just so the boughs that had been bare before
  took color, turning something less than rose
  and more than violet as they bloomed once more.[81] 60
The hymn I heard those blessèd souls sing then
  is not sung here, nor did I understand it;
  nor did I hear it through to the Amen.

[81] *The Tree of Good and Evil.* This passage contains an elaborate conception, difficult in itself, and made more difficult by much of Dante's phrasing in what is certainly his least attractive style. The tree, to begin with, is instantly recognizable, by its resemblance to its offshoot on the ledge below, as the original Tree of Good and Evil. It is for this reason that all souls murmur against Adam at sight of it. Then, in a second symbolism, the tree is made to represent the Holy Roman Empire, towering so high (and spreading wider as it soars) that no tree in the Indian forests (the comparison is from Virgil) could equal it. (The comparison to Indian forests implies, of course, the superiority of the Christian empire.) But though enormous, the tree is, by itself, barren. When Christ (the Griffon) approaches the tree, all praise Him for not having eaten (peculiar diet) the sweet-tasting wood (the material riches of the Empire), for by His holy poverty in this world, He escaped the bellyache of corruption (with which the Church has been plagued ever since it grew rich). The Griffon replies that only so (in holy poverty) can the seed of goodness be preserved. To understand the Griffon's next action, it is necessary to know that the true cross, according to legend, had been cut from the Tree of Good and Evil. The Griffon draws the Chariot (the Church) to the tree and binds fast to the tree "what came from it," i.e., the pole of the chariot. Thus one may understand that the pole the Griffon has been pulling (and what draws the Church forward) is the true cross. This interpretation is disputed but does have the virtue of being coherent. Now with the Church securely bound to the Empire by the true cross, the tree that had been barren breaks into bloom, turning (lines 59–60) something less than rose and more than violet (i.e., the Imperial purple). For good measure, Dante throws in a legendary reference and several astrological ones. Sense of lines 52–57: "As in the spring on earth, when the great light falls mingled with the rays of those sweet stars [of Aries, the sign in which the sun rides from March 21 to April 19] that follow Pisces [the zodiacal sign immediately preceding Aries] . . . the trees begin to swell, then burgeon full . . . before the Sun [Apollo, the charioteer of the Sun] harnesses his team [to bear the Sun across the sky] beneath the Bull [Taurus, the sign the Sun enters on April 20]."

Could I portray the eyes of Argus here,
  lulled one by one by drowsy tales of Syrinx,[82]
  that time their pitiless watch cost him so dear,
as a painter paints his model, I would try
  to show exactly how I fell asleep.
  But who can image drowsiness? Not I.
Therefore, I pass to my waking,[83] and declare 70
  a radiance tore the veil of sleep; a voice
  cried out: "Arise! What are you doing there?"
When they were shown the flowering of that Tree[84]
  that makes the angels hungry for Its fruit
  and sets a feast in Heaven eternally,
Peter, John, and James, awe-stricken, fell
  into a sleep from which they were recalled
  by the same word that broke a greater spell;
and saw their company reduced, as both
  Moses and Elijah vanished from them; 80
  and saw the Master's robe change back to cloth.[85]
Just so did I awaken from my dream
  to find, bent over me, the compassionate lady[86]
  who had conducted me along the stream.

---

[82]Argus (called Panoptes, or "the all-seeing") had a hundred eyes all over his body. When Jupiter was smitten by Io, Juno changed the girl into a cow and sent Argus to keep watch over her. Jupiter, in his turn, sent Mercury to lull Argus to sleep either by the magic of his flute or, in the version Dante follows, by a kind of Arabian Nights series of tales about Syrinx, who was loved by Pan, and who was changed into a reed by her sisters to save her from Pan's pursuit. His watch cost him dear because Mercury, after lulling him to sleep, cut off his head. Juno set the eyes of her dead gamekeeper into the tail of the peacock, the bird sacred to her. (Canto 29, 95, note.)

[83]The strains of the heavenly hymn lull Dante into a blissful sleep, which may be taken as symbolizing the serenity of the Kingdom. A radiance reaches through his closed eyes and he awakens to hear a voice cry "Arise!" This is the word with which Christ called Lazarus, among others, from the "greater spell" of death. Obviously, therefore, Dante's awakening symbolizes one more release from mortal error into eternal life. Opening his eyes, Dante finds Matilda bending over him. It was she who cried to him, and at first Dante thinks that all the others have left and that he is alone with her. Dante then compares his experience to that of Peter, John, and James at the Transfiguration. "And after six days Jesus taketh with him Peter, and James, and John his brother, and bringeth them up into a high mountain apart, and he was transfigured before them: and his face did shine as the sun, and his garments became white as the light . . . they fell on their face, and were sore afraid. And Jesus came and touched them and said, Arise, and be not afraid. And lifting up their eyes, they saw no one, save Jesus only." (Matthew 17:1–8.) See also Luke 9:28–36, especially, "Now Peter and they that were with him were heavy with sleep: but when they were fully awake, they saw his glory, and the two men that stood with him." Basing his account on these two passages, Dante adds his own allegory. The vision that is shown to the disciples becomes a vision of Christ as the Mystic Tree of Heaven (which is, of course, another aspect of the Tree of Good and Evil). The vision, however, is not of the fruit of the tree but of its flowers (line 73). It is, therefore, the vision of the flowering promise of Christ, from which will follow the fruit of eternal rejoicing. The vision is especially apt since, during Dante's sleep, Christ (the Griffon) has reascended to Heaven with most of the Heavenly Procession. There Dante shall follow him in *The Paradiso,* and there the fruit of felicity awaits.

[84]Christ.

[85]Back to its mortal state, as it was before the Transfiguration.

[86]Matilda.

Fearful[87] I cried out, "Beatrice! Where is she?"
And the lady: "She is seated on the roots
of the new foliage,[88] as you can see,
encircled by the seven shining Graces.
The others mount to Heaven behind the Griffon,
intoning sweeter and profounder praises." 90
If she said more, her words were lost on me,
for now my eyes were fixed once more on Beatrice,
my senses closed to all that was not she.
She sat on the bare earth alone, left there
to guard the chariot that the Biformed Beast
had fastened to the tree with such great care.
A living cloister ringing her about,
the Seven Nymphs stood, holding in their hands
those candles no wind ever shall blow out.
"Here briefly in this forest shall you dwell; 100
and evermore, with me, be of that Rome
in which Christ is a Roman. Hence, look well
there at the great car, and that you may be
a light to the dark world, when you return
set down exactly all that you shall see."
Thus Beatrice; and I, devoutly bent
at the feet of her commands, turned mind and eye
as she had willed, in all obedient.
No flash from densest clouds when the rains fall
from the remotest reaches of the sky 110
ever shot down as fast out of the squall[89]
as did the bird of Jove[90] that I saw break
down through the tree, ripping the flowers, the leaves,
even the bark, with its fierce claws and beak.
He struck the chariot a tremendous blow,
at which it lurched like a storm-battered ship,
now rolled to port, now starboard, to and fro.

---

[87]Seeing only Matilda by him, Dante is afraid that Beatrice has left.

[88]As Christ, after his Transfiguration, resumed his earthly appearance, so Beatrice, having entered as the figure of revelation aboard the triumphal chariot, is now seated upon the ground. Beatrice is seated *on* the ground and *under* the new foliage (that sprang from the touch of Christ—the Griffon). Let the tree in this aspect symbolize the Holy Roman Empire, and the roots Rome. The chariot, of course, represents the Church. It rests on the roots (Rome) and is tied to the tree (the Empire). Beatrice (Divine Love) is left on earth to guard the chariot under the protective shade of the tree, while the Griffon (Christ) ascends to Heaven followed by the rest of the Heavenly Train, which is singing a hymn that is sweeter and profounder than earth can understand. Beatrice is left on earth encircled and attended by the Seven Nymphs (the Three Theological Virtues and the Four Cardinal Virtues).

[89]Dante's meteorological figure here is based on the belief that the highest reaches of the sky are the domain of fire. The highest clouds, therefore, being closest to the sphere of fire would be especially subject to fiery influences and would give forth the most powerful lightning flashes.

[90]The eagle. See Ezekiel 17, the Parable of the Eagles and the Cedar. There, the eagle represents the Babylonian persecution of the Jews. Here, Dante clearly enough intends its attack to symbolize the Roman persecution of the early Christians.

Next came a fox,[91] so gaunt and angular
it seemed to know no fit food; and it pounced
upon the cab of the triumphal car. 120
But threatening all its filthy sins with woe
my lady sent it reeling back from there
as fast as such a bag of bones could go.
Then, through the tree, I saw the bird descend
once more into the car, and shed its plumes
to feather it in gold from end to end.
And from the sky, as if a heart let slip
all of its grief in one sound, a voice cried:
"O what a load you bear, my little ship!"[92]
Then, as I watched, I saw a fissure split 130
the earth between the two wheels, and a dragon[93]
rise to the car and sink its tail in it.
Much as an angry wasp draws back its stinger,
it drew its tail back, ripping the car's floor
and wandered off as if it meant to linger.[94]
Like rich soil left to weeds, what then remained
covered itself with feathers, which no doubt
had been intended to burnish what they stained.
And both the wheels and the pole were overgrown,
and all the car to the last part, and all 140
in less time than the lips part for a moan.
So changed, the holy ark began to sprout
heads from its various parts: three from the pole,
one from each corner. Seven in all grew out.
The three were horned like oxen, but the four
were each armed with a single evil horn.
No one had seen the monster's like before.[95]

[91]Usually taken to represent the heresies that threatened the early Church and that were repelled by the divine wisdom of the Church Fathers.

[92]The Eagle of Imperial Rome returns and covers the car (the Church) with its feathers (riches) and a voice from Heaven cries out in grief. The grief is clearly for the evils that descended upon the Church when it grew rich. Dante must certainly have had the Donation of Constantine (see *The Inferno,* 19, 109–111, and note) in mind in the first feathering of the car. The second gift of the eagle would then symbolize the whole process whereby the temporal wealth of the Empire passed so largely into the hands of the Church.

[93]Satan.

[94]Having broken the floor of the car (the foundation of the Church, once it has been weakened by wealth), Satan would certainly not run away, but rather remain to see what other mischief he could do, wandering off only very slowly.

[95]"And I saw a woman sitting upon a scarlet-colored beast full of the names of blasphemy, having seven heads and ten horns." (Revelation 17:3.) The Seven Heads have been interpreted in endless ingenious ways. Let them be taken as representing the Seven Deadly Sins. They thus took root in the Church as soon as it covered itself with wealth. The first three of the seven are Pride, Wrath, and Avarice. Being the worst sins, they sprout from the pole (i.e., they come before the others). And since they represent offenses against both God and one's neighbors, they are represented as having two horns. The four lesser sins (Apathy, Envy, Gluttony, and Lust) offend God but not necessarily one's neighbors and they are, therefore, represented as having single horns. Thus the total of ten horns.

Secure as a great fortress on a crag,
  an ungirt harlot rode the beast, her eyes
  darting with avarice.[96] Beside that hag, 150
and ready to risk all to keep her his,
  a giant[97] strode erect, and as they passed,
  from time to time the two exchanged a kiss.
But when she turned her hungry eyes on me,[98]
  her savage lover in a bestial rage
  whipped her from head to foot unmercifully.
Then in a jealous fit the brute untied
  the monster from the tree, and dragged it off[99]
  into the woods, far toward the other side,
until between me and the doxie queen 160
on her weird beast, he made the trees a screen.

Canto 33

The Earthly Paradise—Eunoë; Dante's Purification Completed: The Seven Nymphs sing a hymn of sorrow for the grief of the Church, and Beatrice answers with Christ's words announcing his resurrection. All then move onward, Beatrice summoning Dante to her side as they walk on.

Beatrice begins her discourse with an obscurely worded prophecy of the Deliverance of the Church. In much simpler language, she then utters her Final Reproach to Dante for having so lost sight of the truth.

Just as she finishes, the train halts before the Great Spring from which flow the waters of both Lethe and Eunoë. At Beatrice's command, the Seven Nymphs lead Dante forward and he drinks the Waters of Eunoë. By drinking the waters of Lethe, Dante has already forgotten all sin and error; now every good is strengthened in him. Thus is his Final Purification completed, and Dante rises "perfect, pure, and ready for the stars."

"Deus, venerunt gentes"[100]—the Holy Seven,
  in alternating chorus through their tears,
  first three, then four,[101] raised a sweet chant to Heaven;

[96] She represents the Papacy as it existed under Boniface VIII and Clement V, the two popes Dante most charges with corruption. (See *The Inferno,* 19, and note to 77–79.) "Ungirt" (Dante uses *sciolta,* "untied, unbound") should be understood to imply both lewdness (immodesty of dress) and lack of restraint (knowing no bounds). *her eyes darting with avarice:* looking everywhere for plunder.

[97] The French monarchy, and especially Philip the Fair (Philip IV, 1268–1314, crowned in 1285), who made the Papacy his puppet.

[98] The question here is why the giant beats the harlot for looking at Dante. Again, many answers have been suggested, but two seem most to the point. If Dante is taken here as representing Italy, the whipping can only refer to Philip's humiliation of Boniface VIII (Canto 20, 85–93, note), and the harlot's covetous glance at Dante-as-Italy would represent Boniface's intrigues with various rulers. It was these intrigues that put him most at odds with Philip. On the other hand, Dante may be taken to represent the typical Christian who looks to the Church for guidance. The allegory would then be saying that every time the corrupt Church is stirred by a wish to return to its true pastoral mission, the French kings whip her and drag her back to sin.

[99] In 1304 Philip engineered the election of Clement V and transferred the Papal Seat (dragged it off) to Avignon.

[100] Psalm 79, the lamentation for the destruction of Jerusalem. "O God, the heathen are come into thine inheritance; thy holy temple have they defiled; they have laid Jerusalem on heaps." So have the later unbelievers despoiled and defiled the Church.

[101] The Seven Nymphs sing the psalm antiphonally, the Three Theological Virtues singing first (they being higher in the scale of things), and then the Four Cardinal Virtues.

and Beatrice, when she heard them mourn such loss
sighed with a grief so deep that even Mary
could not have changed more[102] at the foot of the cross.
But when the other virgins in their choir
fell still for her reply, she rose erect
in holy zeal, and said, as if afire:
"Modicum et non videbitis me; 10
et iterum, dearly beloved sisters,
modicum, et vos videbitis me."[103]
Then placing the Seven before her, she moved ahead
with a nod to me, to the Lady,[104] and to the Sage
that had remained, to follow where she led.
So she strolled on, and she had not yet laid
her tenth step[105] on the sward, when she turned round
and struck my eyes with her eyes[106] as she said
with a serene tranquillity:[107] "Draw near,
that you may, if I wish to speak to you 20
as we move on, be better placed to hear."
When I was, as I should be, at her side,[108]
she said: "Dear brother, why are you not moved
to question me as we move on?—Tongue-tied,
like one who knows his station is beneath
that of the presences in which he stands,
and cannot drag his voice across his teeth,[109]
so did I, with a voice almost choked through,
manage to say: "My Lady, all my need
and all that is my good is known to you." 30
And she to me: "My wish is that you break
the grip of fear and shame, and from now on
no longer speak like one but half awake.[110]

---

[102]The comparison is not a hyperbole. Beatrice, mourning for the crucifixion of the Church, would endure the same grief Mary suffered at the crucifixion of her son, Christ and the Church being one.

[103]"A little while and ye shall not see me; and again a little while, and ye shall see me [because I go to the Father]." (John 16:16.) These are Christ's words to his disciples, announcing his resurrection. Beatrice speaks them afire with her holy zeal in reply to the mournful psalm. She is saying, in effect, that the triumph of the True Faith shall be seen again. On one level her words may be taken to mean that the pure in heart shall rise above the corruption of the Church to see Christ again in Heaven. More likely, Dante meant that the Church shall be purged until Christ is once more truly visible in its workings.

[104]Matilda. *the Sage that had remained:* Statius. The other Sage, Virgil, has departed.

[105]Every number mentioned by Dante invites allegorical conjecture, and many have taken the "ten" here to refer to the Ten Commandments. The interpretation seems doubtful, however, especially since the actual steps taken were not yet ten.

[106]Dante takes this forceful way of emphasizing the power of her eyes. (The Lamps of Heaven?)

[107]The change in Beatrice is not a matter of feminine mood. When Dante still had upon himself a stain of neglect, Beatrice berated him for it. But he has now done fit penance and the stain has been removed, thereby removing all cause for anger.

[108]Dante's whole progress up to this time has been, as it should be the object of every soul, to stand beside Divine Love.

[109]It is characteristic of Dante that a certain pungency should creep into his phrasing even at such sublime moments.

[110]Dante has achieved purification, and all memory of sin has been washed from him by the waters of Lethe. He must yet drink of the waters of Eunoë, which will strengthen every good memory in him. Because he has not yet been so strengthened, he still speaks, partly, with the habituated fears and confusions of his former ways. It is these fears and confusions Beatrice is telling him to put by.

The cart the dragon broke was, and is not;
let him whose fault that is believe God's wrath
will not be calmed by soup, however hot.[111]
The eagle you saw shed its plumes back there
to make the cart a monster and a prey
will not remain forever without heir;[112]
for certain as my words, my eyes foresee, 40
already nearing, the unstayable stars[113]
that bring the time in which, by God's decree,
five hundred, ten, and five[114] shall be the sign
of one who comes to hunt down and destroy
the giant and his thievish concubine.
My prophecy, being obscure as those
of Themis and the Sphinx, may fail to move you,
since all such words hide what they should disclose
but soon now, like an Oedipus reborn,
events themselves shall solve the dark enigma, 50
and without loss of either sheep or corn.[115]
Note my words well, and when you give them breath[116]
repeat them as I said them, to the living
whose life is no more than a race toward death.

---

[111] Beatrice now refers to the allegory that concluded Canto 32, assuring Dante, as in her answer to the psalm, that a dawn of righteousness is approaching. *was, and is not:* These are the words of John, Revelation 17:8: "The beast thou sawest was, and is not." *soup:* In some parts of ancient Greece a murderer could protect himself from all vengeance if for nine successive days he ate soup on the grave of his victim. In Florence it became a custom to stand guard for nine days over the grave of a murdered man to see that no one ate soup upon it. The reference is a strange one, but Dante's intent is, clearly, that no such simple rite will ward off the vengeance of God.

[112] The eagle is, of course, the Roman Empire. The true heir of the Caesars, who will restore order and goodness, will come at last. Dante thought of Frederick II as the last real heir of the Caesars.

[113] Nothing can stay the stars in their courses. Beatrice foresees propitious stars already near at hand. (God's wrath will not be stayed: cf. lines 35-36.)

[114] As Beatrice says in the next tercet, she is speaking in the veiled tongue of prophecy, and her words hide what they should disclose. Whatever the numerological significance Dante intended by the number, it cannot be identified. Since Dante could make himself clear enough when he wanted to, and since he goes on to have Beatrice say that her meaning is hidden, it follows, as a fair guess, that Dante deliberately kept his reference vague.

[115] The basic sense of this passage is: "Though my way of speaking is obscure, events themselves will soon make clear my meaning." It is the mythological references that may confuse the modern reader. *Themis:* Daughter of Gaea (Earth) and Uranus (Heaven). She was the second wife of Zeus, and later, no longer as his wife, became his Goddess of Law and Order. She was noted for the obscurity of her oracles. *the Sphinx:* A monster with the head of an innocent maiden and the body of a savage beast. One of the oracles of Themis. She waited for travelers on a rock near Thebes and killed them when they failed to solve her famous riddle: "What walks on four legs in the morning, on two at noon, and on three at night?" *Oedipus:* The ill-fated King of Thebes answered properly that the riddle meant a man in the three stages of his life (for he crawls on all fours as an infant, walks on two legs in the middle of his life, and totters on two legs and a cane thereafter). The Sphinx was so enraged on hearing the right answer that she killed herself. (Dante's text reads not "Oedipus" but "the Naiads." The Naiads had no connection with the riddle. Dante's error follows a corrupt text of Ovid's *Metamorphoses,* VII, 759, which reads "Naiades"—the Naiads—for "Laiades"—son of Laius, i.e., *Oepidus.*) *without loss of either sheep or corn:* Themis, to avenge her oracle, sent a monstrous beast to ravage the flocks and fields of Thebes.

[116] This phrase is my own invention, forced upon the text by the, to me, clear necessity to render line 54 with "death" as the rhyme. I hope the rendering will seem at least approximately Dantean: since the words thus far have been spoken only by Beatrice, a spirit, they have not yet been given breath, as they will be when Dante repeats them with his mortal voice.

And when you come to write them down, make clear
what you have seen of the Tree, now twice-despoiled[117]
since all-creating God first raised it here.
All those who rob or break those boughs commit
a blasphemy-in-deed,[118] offending God
who sacred to Himself created it. 60
For just one bite, the First Soul's[119] tears were spilt
five thousand years and more,[120] yearning for Him
who suffered in His own flesh for that guilt.
Your wits must be asleep not to have known
that a particular reason[121] must account
for its great height and its inverted crown.
Had not your idle thoughts been to your brain
an Elsan water,[122] and your pleasure in them
a Pyramus to the mulberry's new stain,
those two facts surely should have made you see 70
the justice of God's interdict shine forth
as the moral meaning[123] of the form of the Tree.
It is my wish—because I see your mind
turned into stone;[124] and like a stone, so darkened
that the light of what I tell you strikes it blind—
that you bear back, if not in writing, then
in outline, what I say, as pilgrims wreathe
their staffs with palm[125] to show where they have been."
And I to her: "As pressed wax will retain
a faithful imprint of the signet ring, 80
so is your seal imprinted on my brain.
But why do your desired words fly so high
above my power to follow their intent
that I see less and less the more I try?"

---

[117] Dante probably meant the Fall as the first despoilment of the tree, and the corruption of the Church as the second.

[118] As distinct from blasphemy-in-word and blasphemy-in-thought.

[119] Adam's.

[120] According to Genesis 5:5, Adam lived 930 years on earth. According to *Paradiso,* 26, 118, he then waited in Limbo for 4,302 years. Dante follows, in this, the chronology of the ecclesiastical historian Eusebius, who set Christ's birth in the year 5200 since the Creation. Christ's death, therefore (and the Harrowing of Hell, for which see *Inferno,* 4, 53, note), would have occurred in the year 5232.

[121] The tree is enormously tall and broadens toward the crown (hence "inverted"). The "particular reason" for such a form must have been to make the fruit inaccessible to man. The story of Genesis, however, indicates that Eve certainly had no trouble getting her apple. It must follow that the tree has grown since Genesis. According to the chronology of Eusebius, the year 1300 would be the year 6500 since Creation—time enough for the knowledge of good and evil to show some substantial growth rings.

[122] The Elsa, a river of Tuscany, is so rich in lime that at some points along its course objects left in its waters will either petrify or become coated. So Dante's idle thoughts (seemingly flowing *around* his brain more than *through* it) have petrified his intellect. *a Pyramus to the mulberry's new stain:* The blood of Pyramus (and Thisbe) stained the mulberry red. (See Canto 27, 37ff., note.) So Dante's delight in his idle thoughts has stained his intellect. Lines 73–75, below, further explain Dante's meaning here.

[123] The form of the tree symbolizes its essential nature. Interpreted in the moral sense (as distinct, for example, from the allegorical narrative, or anagogical senses) the two main facts of the tree's form (its great height and inverted crown) express how far above and beyond man is the final understanding of Good and Evil. Hence the justice of God's interdict in forbidding man what lies beyond his grasp.

[124] As if by Elsan waters. *so darkened:* As was the mulberry.

[125] The palm grows in the Holy Land. Returning pilgrims wreathed their staffs with palm to prove they had been there.

"They fly so high," she said, "that you may know
what school you followed,[126] and how far behind
the truth I speak its feeble doctrines go;
and see that man's ways, even at his best,
are far from God's as earth is from the heaven
whose swiftest wheel turns above all the rest."[127] 90
"But," I replied, "I have no recollection
of ever having been estranged from you.
Conscience does not accuse me of defection."
And she then with a smile: "If, as you say
you lack that memory, then call to mind
how you drank Lethe's waters here today.
As certainly as smoke betrays the fire,
this new forgetfulness of your wish to stray
betrays the sinfulness of that desire.
But I assure you that I shall select 100
the simplest words that need be from now on
to make things clear to your dull intellect."[128]
Now with a brighter flame and slower pace[129]
the sun was holding its meridian height,
which varies round the world from place to place,[130]
when suddenly—as one who leads a line
of travelers as their escort will stop short
at a strange sight or an unusual sign—
so stopped the Seven at an edge of shade
pale as a shadow cast by a cold peak 110
on a cold stream deep in an Alpine glade.
And there ahead of them, in a single flow,
Tigris and Euphrates[131] seemed to rise
and part as friends who linger as they go.
"O light and glory of mankind," I cried,
"what is this flood that pours forth from one source
and then parts from itself to either side?"[132]
In answer to that prayer I heard the name
"Matilda" and "ask her." Who spoke up then
as one does who absolves himself to blame: 120

---

[126]The school of philosophy, whose error lies in placing its dependence on reason as an end, and which cannot, therefore, comprehend the mysteries of faith.

[127]The Primum Mobile, uppermost of the nine spheres. Since all the spheres turn together, the outermost must move most swiftly.

[128]Dante protests that he has no recollection of ever having been estranged from Beatrice, despite the fact that he had relied more heavily on human philosophy than on divine love. Beatrice, smiling, points out that he has just drunk the waters of Lethe, whose powers wipe away all memory of sin. Since they have wiped out the memory of his estrangement, it follows that the estrangement was sinful.

[129]To an observer the sun seems brightest at its noon height and seems to move most slowly then. (Its slowness is an illusion, as is the speed with which it seems to set once it has touched the horizon, but its brightness can be accounted for by the fact that its rays travel a vertical, and hence shortest, course through the atmosphere at noon.)

[130]In one sense, the sun is always at the meridian: it is always noon somewhere on the earth.

[131]The Tigris flows through Turkey and Iraq (ancient Chaldea) to join the Euphrates, which rises in Armenia and flows into the Persian Gulf. Genesis, 2:10ff., identifies the Euphrates as one of the four rivers of Eden, all of which rise from the same source. The rivers of Dante's Earthly Paradise are Lethe and Eunoë. They "seem to rise" as if they were Tigris and Euphrates rising from a single spring.

[132]The two rivers flow off in opposite directions, just as their powers, rising from one source, work in opposite ways to achieve one good.

"This, and much more, I have this very day
explained to him, and Lethe certainly
could not have washed that memory away."[133]
And Beatrice: "Perhaps a greater care,
as often happens, dims his memory
and his mind's eye. But see Eunoë there—
lead him, as is your custom, to the brim
of that sweet stream, and with its holy waters
revive the powers that faint and die in him."
Then as a sweet soul gladly shapes its own 130
good will to the will of others, without protest,
as soon as any sign has made it known,
so the sweet maid, taking me by the hand
and saying in a modest voice to Statius,
"Come you with him," obeyed the good command.
Reader, had I the space to write at will,
I should, if only briefly, sing a praise
of that sweet draught. Would I were drinking still!
But I have filled all of the pages planned
for this, my second, canticle, and Art 140
pulls at its iron bit with iron hand.
I came back from those holiest waters new,
remade, reborn, like a sun-wakened tree
that spreads new foliage to the Spring dew
in sweetest freshness, healed of Winter's scars;
perfect, pure, and ready for the Stars.[134]

The Paradiso

Canto 30

Ascent to the Empyrean; [1] *The Empyrean—Praise of Beatrice's Beauty; The River of Light; The Mystic Rose; The Throne of Henry VII; Dununciation of Evil Popes:* The great theme is drawing to a close. Here in the Empyrean, Beatrice is at last at home, her beauty made perfect, and Dante utters a lofty Praise of Beatrice.

[133]There being nothing sinful in it.

[134]Dante ends each canticle with the word "stars," a fixed architectural device, and one that any rendition must preserve at whatever cost. Unfortunately for English renditions, the cost of forcing a rhyme for "stars" is great, and I have had to take considerable liberties. More closely rendered, these lines read: "I came back from that holiest wave [flood] made new like new trees renewed with new foliage, pure and prepared to mount to the stars."

THE PARADISO

[1]Heretofore the glories of the heavens have shone like stars in glorious night. In the Empyrean, God (the Sun) shines forever in the fullness of His glorious day, obscuring all other heavenly bodies except as they reflect His Light. The ascent into the Empyrean, therefore, is a dawning, and Dante's figure for it is based on an earthly dawn. When the sun is at its noon height over India (about 6000 miles away) dawn is just beginning in Italy and the Earth's shadow is almost a level line (level bed) out into space (i.e., nearly perpendicular to a line dropped from the zenith). Then the stars directly overhead begin to fade, the dimmest first, then the brighter. Then as dawn (Aurora, the serving maid of Apollo, the Sun) draws nearer, all the stars go out, even the loveliest and brightest. Just so nine rings of the three trinities of Angelic beings fade as Dante and Beatrice ascend into the first dawning of the direct vision of God. Obviously the dimmer outer rings would fade first, then the others in order.

Beatrice promises Dante a Vision of Both Hosts of Paradise. He is blinded by a new radiance, hears a voice announce that he shall be given new powers, and immediately he sees a Vision of a River of Light. As in the Terrestrial Paradise, he is commanded to drink. No sooner is his face submerged in the water than the vision grows circular and re-forms as a Vision of the Mystic Rose.

When, as may be, the sun's noon heat is shed
six thousand miles away, while, where we are,
earth's shadow makes an almost level bed;
when, at our zenith, the sky begins to show
such changes that a star or two begins
to fade from the eyes of watchers here below;
and as the sun's most radiant serving maid
comes nearer yet, and heaven puts out its lamps
one by one, till the loveliest, too, must fade—
just so that Triumph that forever races 10
around the blinding ray of the fixed Point
that seems embraced by what Itself embraces,[2]
faded from sight, degree by slow degree;
at which I turned my eyes from the lost vision
to Beatrice, as love commanded me.
If all that I have said of her below
were gathered now into a single paean,
that would be scant praise of her beauty now.
The beauty I saw there transcends all measure
of mortal minds. I think only her Maker 20
can wholly comprehend so great a treasure.
Here I concede defeat. No poet known,
comic or tragic, challenged by his theme
to show his power, was ever more outdone.[3]
As feeblest eyes, struck by the sun, go blind,
so the remembrance of my lady's smile
strikes every recognition from my mind.
From the first day I looked upon her face
in this life, to this present sight of her,
my song has followed her to sing her praise. 30
But here I must no longer even try
to walk behind her beauty. Every artist,
his utmost done, must put his brushes by.

---

[2]The Angel Rings seem to contain God within their rounds, whereas it is God who contains them and all else.

[3]As Dante ascended each new heaven and became more able to perceive, Beatrice grew more beautiful (was able to reveal more of herself to his senses). Now fully disclosed in the direct light of the Empyrean she surpasses conception: only God can realize her full beauty. On another level it is only natural that Dante stand inarticulate before the full beauty of Divine Revelation. What religious man could think himself equal to describing the entire beauty of Revelation? (Such inarticulateness is all the more effective when it overtakes a man who boasted of his powers in *The Inferno,* 4, 100–102; 25, 91–99; 32, 7–9; and in *The Paradiso,* 2, 1–18.)

So do I leave her to a clarion
of greater note than mine,[4] which starts to draw
its long and arduous theme to a conclusion.
She, like a guide who has his goal in sight
began to speak again: "We have ascended
from the greatest sphere [5] to the heaven of pure light.
Light of the intellect, which is love unending; 40
love of the true good, which is wholly bliss;
bliss beyond bliss, all other joys transcending;
here shall you see both hosts of Paradise, [6]
one of them [7] in the aspect you shall see
when you return the day all bodies rise."
As a flash of lightning striking on our sight
destroys our visual spirits, [8] so that the eye
cannot make out even a brighter light;
just so, an aureole burst all about me,
swathing me so completely in its veil 50
that I was closed in light and could not see.
"The Love that keeps this Heaven ever the same [9]
greets all who enter with such salutation,
and thus prepares the candle for His flame."[10]
No sooner had these few words penetrated
my hearing than I felt my powers increase
beyond themselves; transcendant and elated,
my eyes were lit with such new-given sight
that they were fit to look without distress
on any radiance, however bright. 60
I saw a light that was a river flowing
light within light between enameled banks
painted with blossoms of miraculous spring;
and from the river as it glowed and rolled
live sparks shot forth to settle on the flowers.
They seemed like rubies set in bands of gold;[11]

---

[4]Does Dante mean that a greater poet will follow to sing the full beauty of Beatrice? He has just said that only God can fully realize her beauty. I think it is no accident that Dante says "clarion" rather than "lyre." The Day of Judgment will be announced by a clarion call, and on that day the souls of all mortals may look upon Beatrice in her full beauty. Dante's "clarion" must occupy itself with drawing its long and arduous theme to a conclusion.

[5]The Primum Mobile. *heaven of pure light:* The Empyrean.

[6]The Angels and the Blessèd.

[7]The Blessèd. Those who once wore mortal bodies which shall be returned to them on Judgment Day. Within the Mystic Rose Dante does see the radiances of the Blessèd with their lineaments etched upon them. He is offered this sight as a special dispensation in a climactic act of *caritas.*

[8]Canto 26, 70–72.

[9]*The Love*: God. *that keeps his Heaven ever the same:* All the other heavens rotate in constant change. The Empyrean, reflecting God's unchanging and unchangeable perfection, is always the same.

[10]Dante has several times been blinded by the light that prepared him for better vision. Here the candle of his soul is put out by the splendor of the Empyrean to be relit by the light of God Himself.

[11]As Dante makes clear in line 95, the sparks are Angels and the flowers, the Blessèd. The river may be taken as the endless flowering of God's grace. Some religious commentators suggest that the two banks represent the Church. As verified by lines 76–78, the rubies of line 66 should be taken to be Angels and the bands of gold as the Blessèd.

and then, as if the fragrance overthrew
their senses, they dove back into the river;
and as one dove in there, out another flew.
"The flame of high desire that makes you yearn 70
for greater knowledge of these things you see
pleases me more the more I see it burn.
But only this same water satisfies
such thirst as yours. You must bend down and drink."
—So spoke the sun and pole-star of my eyes.
And added: "The river and the jewels[12] you see
dart in and out of it, and the smiling flowers
are dim foretastes of their reality.
Not that these fruits are in their natures tart
and unformed, but that you still lack the vision 80
of such high things. The defect is on your part."
No babe in arms[13] that ever wakened hungry
for having slept too long could turn its face
to its dear mother's milk more eagerly
than I bent down to drink in Paradise
of the sweet stream that flows its grace to us,
so to make better mirrors[14] of our eyes.
No sooner were my eyes' eaves[15] sweetly drowned
in that bright stream to drink, than it appeared
to widen and change form till it was round. 90
I have seen masqueraders here below
shed the disguises that had hidden them
and show their true appearances. Just so,
the sparks and spring flowers changed before my eyes
into a greater festival, and I saw[16]
the vision of both courts of Paradise.
O splendor of God eternal through which I saw
the supreme triumph of the one true kingdom,
grant me the power to speak forth what I saw!

---

[12]Dante says "topazes" and the topaz was believed to have the power of reflecting things without distortion, certainly a relevant suggestion in context, though "topazes" here does not accord with "rubies" in line 66.

[13]"Except ye be converted and become as little children, ye shall not enter into the kingdom of heaven" (Matthew 18:3).

[14]The better to reflect God.

[15]His eyelashes. Dante has, of course, plunged his face into the river. It may seem odd to say that he drank with his eyes, but note that this is a river of light, and that it is to wash the last mortal weakness from his eyes that Dante is drinking. Also consider the common idiom: "My eyes drank in the sight of it."

[16]Now and then in *The Paradiso* Dante says "I saw." More often he uses some such phrase as "there appeared to me" or "it manifested itself." Such phrasing is deliberate. "I saw" implies an action of the speaker's own powers. Heaven, however, is a gift of grace: Dante does not see it through his own powers; rather it manifests itself to him as an act of love, and does so not in its true essence but in manifestations graspable by Dante's mortal mind. Here, however, Dante uses "I saw" as one of his rare triple rhymings on the same word. In Dante an unusual device always indicates unusual stress. It occurs, moreover, at one of the great climaxes of the poem. For Dante has just experienced the first direct revelation of God. Until he drank from the stream he could not see things with the spontaneous intuition of heavenly souls, who partake directly of the mind of God. Now he, too, has achieved the beginnings of Paradisal power. This is the true rebirth, the spiritual enlargement to which the entire journey has been directed. And soon now, as Virgil left him below, Beatrice will leave him to take her throne among the hosts of the Blessèd, though in a larger sense she will be with him forever, both her soul and Dante's being contained in God.

There in Heaven, a lamp shines in whose light 100
the Creator is made visible to His creature,
whose one peace lies in having Him in sight.
That lamp forms an enormous circle, such
that its circumference, fitted to the Sun
as a bright belt, would be too large by much.
It is made up entirely of the reflection
of rays that strike the top of the first-moved sphere,
imparting to it all its power[17] and motion.
And as a slope shines in the looking glass
of a lake below it, as if to see itself 110
in its time of brightest flower and greenest grass;
so, tier on tier, mounting within that light,[18]
there glowed, reflected in more than a thousand circles,
all those who had won return[19] to Heaven's height.
And if so vast a nimbus can be bound
within its lowest tier, what then must be
the measure[20] of this rose at its topmost round?
Nor were my eyes confounded by that sea
and altitude of space, but took in all,
both number and quality, of that ecstasy. 120
There, far and near cause neither loss nor gain,
for where God rules directly, without agents,
the laws that govern nature do not pertain.[21]
Into the gold of the rose[22] that blooms eternal,
rank on rank, in incenses of praise
it sends up to the Sun forever vernal—
I, yearning to speak and silent—Beatrice drew me,
and said: "Now see how many are in the convent
of the white robes. Behold our far-flung city.

---

[17]Virtue. The ability to influence what lies below it. *motion:* Its own rapid revolution.

[18]*The Mystic Rose.* As ever in Paradise, the heavenly beings manifest themselves to Dante at the highest level he is capable of grasping at each point of his development. At every stage they have sent their manifestations down to him as an act of love. They themselves remain forever in the direct presence of God. Now, his vision at last approaching perfection, Dante sees them in their supreme heavenly state, ranked tier on tier in a huge stadium that gives forth the appearance of an enormous white rose basking in the eternal springtime of the direct light of God. Note, however, that he sees the rose not directly (even at this point he is not yet ready) but as a vision reflected in the sea of God's light. For purposes of placing Dante in relation to it, the rose may be thought of as an immense, truncated, inverted, floating cone marked off in many tiers. The tier first reflected to Dante from that sea of light is the bottom one, the upper tiers being only partially visible at this point. The nimbus of the bottom tier (lines 115–116) is far greater than the circumference of the Sun (lines 104–105).

[19]The loyal angels, having never left, would not have won return.

[20]There are more than a thousand tiers. If the lowest is greater by far than the circumference of the Sun, what must be the dimensions of its upper ring, a thousand steps up from such magnitude?

[21]On earth we see near things in detail and far things indistinctly. The laws of nature, however, are God's agencies and have no force where God rules without intermediaries. So, despite the galactic dimensions of the rose, Dante sees all in minute detail, not only each being in that multitude, but the quality of each one's ecstasy.

[22]The central corona of the rose, from which the petals grow, is always golden, or so it was in Dante's time, though some modern hybrids no longer have a golden center. *Beatrice drew me:* If the Mystic Rose is conceived as a vast circular stadium, Dante and Beatrice are now in the center of the arena looking up at the tiers.

And see the benches—every one a throne— 130
how every rank of them is filled so full
that few are wanted before all is done.[23]
That great throne with the crown already set
above it draws your eyes. To it shall come—
before your own call to this nuptial banquet—
the soul, already anointed,[24] of Henry the Great,[25]
who will come to Italy to bring law and order
before the time is ripe to set things straight.
Tranced in blind greed, your ever deepening curse,
you[26] have become as mindless as an infant 140
who screams with hunger, yet pushes away his nurse.
The prefect[27] of the holy court will be
a man who will profess his cause in public
while working to defeat it secretly.[28]
But after that God will not long permit[29]
his simony, he shall be stuffed away
where Simon Magus, headfirst in the pit,[30]
pays for his guilt. There, paying for his own,
he shall force the guilt of Alagna[31] further down."

Canto 31

The Empyrean—The Mystic Rose; The Angel Host; Beatrice Leaves Dante; St. Bernard: The Second Soldiery of the Church Triumphant is the Angel Host, and Dante now receives a vision of them as a swarm of bees in eternal transit between God and the Rose.

Dante turns from that rapturous vision to speak to Beatrice and finds in her place a reverend elder. It is St. Bernard, who will serve as Dante's guide to the ultimate vision of God. Bernard shows Dante his last vision of Beatrice, who has resumed her throne among the blessed. Across the vastness of Paradise, Dante sends his soul's prayer of thanks to her. Beatrice smiles down at Dante a last time, then turns her eyes forever to the eternal Fountain of God.

Bernard, the most faithful of the worshippers of the Virgin, promises Dante the final vision of God through the Virgin's intercession. Accordingly, he instructs Dante to raise his eyes to her throne. Dante obeys and burns with bliss at the vision of her splendor.

---

[23]As with so many other revelationists, Dante believes God will not long endure the evils of mankind and that the trump of Judgment will soon sound.

[24]As Holy Roman Emperor.

[25]Henry VII of Luxemburg, Emperor 1308–1313. He was not, strictly speaking, referred to as Henry the Great, but I have been forced to call him that for purposes of rhyme. In *The Purgatorio* Dante says Henry came too late. Here he says he came before the time was ripe. In either case the result was the same and Dante attributes Henry's failure to the evil designs of the bad popes Beatrice now goes on to denounce before the full court of Heaven. It is certainly relevant, here, to note that Dante placed his one hope of returning to Florence on the outcome of Henry's efforts to settle the hatreds of Italian politics.

[26]You Italians.

[27]The Pope. *The holy court:* Rome, the Vatican. Here Dante intends Clement V, who worked to defeat Henry's policy, though he professed to support it.

[28]I have found it necessary to translate the intent rather than the phrasing of Dante's lines here. Literally rendered, they would read: "Who will not walk with him the same road openly and covertly," a strange figure that has Clement walking beside Henry on two separate roads at the same time.

[29]Clement died eight months after Henry, on April 20, 1314.

[30]With the Simoniacs in the Third Bolgia of the Eighth Circle (*The Inferno,* Canto 19). There the sinners are stuffed head-first into a tubelike baptismal font, their feet kicking the air, their soles aflame. As each replaces his successor in selling holy office, the earlier tenant is shoved down into some undescribed lower pit, sealed from the eyes of all.

[31]Boniface VIII. He was born at Alagna (or, variantly, Anagna).

Then, in the form of a white rose, the host
of the sacred soldiery[32] appeared to me,
all those whom Christ in his own blood espoused.
But the other host (who soar, singing and seeing
His glory, who to will them to his love
made them so many in such blissful being,
like a swarm of bees who in one motion dive
into the flowers, and in the next return
the sweetness of their labors to the hive)
flew ceaselessly to the many-petaled rose 10
and ceaselessly returned into that light
in which their ceaseless love has its repose.
Like living flame their faces seemed to glow.[33]
Their wings were gold. And all their bodies shone[34]
more dazzling white than any earthly snow.
On entering the great flower they spread about them,
from tier to tier, the ardor and the peace
they had acquired in flying close to Him.
Nor did so great a multitude in flight
between the white rose and what lies above it 20
block in the least the glory of that light;
for throughout all the universe God's ray
enters all things according to their merit,
and nothing has the power to block its way.
This realm of ancient bliss shone, soul on soul,
with new and ancient beings, and every eye
and every love was fixed upon one goal.
O Threefold Light which, blazoned in one star,
can so content their vision with your shining,
look down upon us in the storm we are! 30
If the barbarians (coming from that zone
above which Helice[35] travels every day
wheeling in heaven with her belovèd son)

---

[32]In Canto 30, 43, Beatrice promised that Dante would see both hosts of Paradise. The first host is of the sacred soldiery, those who were once mortal and who were redeemed by Christ. They are seated upon the thrones of the Mystic Rose in which are gathered eternally the essences of all those heavenly souls that manifested themselves to Dante in the various spheres below, moved by *caritas* to reveal themselves to Dante at the various levels of his developing understanding. How these souls could be eternally within the Rose while yet manifesting themselves to Dante in the various spheres is, of course, one of the mysteries to be grasped only by revelation. The essential point is that Dante becomes better able to see; the vision of Heaven unfolds to him ever more clearly and ever more profoundly. The second soldiery is of the angels who never left Heaven. They soar above the Rose like Heavenly bees, in constant motion between the Rose and the radiance of God. Unlike earthly bees, however, it is from God, the mystical hive of grace, that they bring the sweetness to the flower, bearing back to God, of course, the bliss of the souls of Heaven. (See lines 16–18.) The first host is more emphatically centered on the aspect of God as the Son; the second, on the aspect of God as the Father.

[33]See the vision of God and Heaven in Ezekiel 1:14ff.

[34]See the similar vision in Daniel 10:4ff.

[35]The nymph Helice attracted Zeus and was turned into a bear by the jealous Hera. Zeus translated his nymph to heaven as Ursa Major, the constellation of the Great Bear which contains the Big Dipper. Arcas, her son by Zeus, was translated to Ursa Minor, within which he forms the Little Dipper. The two dippers, being near the pole, are always above the horizon in the northland, the zone from which the barbarians came.

looking at Rome, were stupefied to see
her works in those days when the Lateran[36]
outshone all else built by humanity;
What did I feel on reaching such a goal
from human to blest, from time to eternity,
from Florence to a people just and whole[37]—
by what amazement was I overcome? 40
Between my stupor and my new-found joy
my bliss was to hear nothing and be dumb.
And as a pilgrim at the shrine of his vow
stares, feels himself reborn, and thinks already
how he may later describe it[38] —just so now
I stood and let my eyes go wandering out
into that radiance from rank to rank,
now up, now down, now sweeping round about.
I saw faces that compelled love's charity
lit by Another's lamp and their own smiles, 50
and gestures graced by every dignity.
Without having fixed on any part, my eyes
already had taken in and understood
the form and general plan of Paradise:
and—my desire rekindled—I wheeled about
to question my sweet lady on certain matters
concerning which my mind was still in doubt.
One thing I expected; another greeted me:
I thought to find Beatrice there; I found instead
an elder[39] in the robes of those in glory. 60
His eyes and cheeks were bathed in the holy glow
of loving bliss; his gestures, pious grace.
He seemed a tender father standing so.
"She—where is she?" I cried in sudden dread.
"To lead you to the goal of all your wish
Beatrice called me from my place," he said;
"And if you raise your eyes you still may find her
in the third circle down[40] from the highest rank
upon the throne her merit has assigned her."

---

[36]Today a section of old Rome. Here Dante uses it to signify Rome in general.

[37]This is Dante's last mention of Florence. Note that Florence has not improved but that on the universal scale it has become too insignificant for the sort of denunciation he once heaped upon it.

[38]It was a custom of the pious, as thanks for an answered prayer, to win forgiveness of sins, or as a testimony of faith, to vow a journey to a stated shrine or temple. Such pilgrimages were often dangerous. Travel was rare in the Middle Ages, and the pilgrim returned from far shrines was much sought after for the hopefully miraculous, and in any case rare, news he brought back. How could Dante, having traveled to the Infinite Summit, fail to think ahead to the way he would speak his vision to mankind?

[39]St. Bernard (1090–1153), the famous Abbot of Clairvaux, a contemplative mystic and author. Under him the Cistercian Order (a branch of the Benedictines with a stricter rule than the original order) flourished and spread. All Cistercian monasteries are especially dedicated to the Virgin, and St. Bernard is particularly identified with her worship.

[40]In the Mystic Rose, Mary sits in the topmost tier, Eve directly below her, Rachel (the Contemplative Life) below Eve. Beatrice sits to the right of Rachel. In Dante, of course, every mention of three must suggest trinity, but the reader is left to decide for himself the significance of the Mary–Eve–Rachel trinity.

Without reply I looked up to that height 70
  and saw her draw an aureole round herself
  as she reflected the Eternal Light.
No mortal eye, though plunged to the last bounds
  of the deepest sea, has ever been so far
  from the topmost heaven to which the thunder sounds
as I was then from Beatrice; but there
  the distance did not matter, for her image
  reached me unblurred by any atmosphere.
"O lady in whom my hope shall ever soar
  and who for my salvation suffered even 80
  to set your feet upon Hell's broken floor;[41]
through your power and your excellence alone
  have I recognized the goodness and the grace
  inherent in the things I have been shown.
You have led me from my bondage and set me free
  by all those roads, by all those loving means
  that lay within your power and charity.
Grant me your magnificence that my soul,
  which you have healed, may please you when it slips
  the bonds of flesh and rises to its goal." 90
Such was my prayer, and she—far up a mountain,
  as it appeared to me—looked down and smiled.
  Then she turned back to the Eternal Fountain.
And the holy Elder said: "I have been sent
  by prayer and sacred love to help you reach
  the perfect consummation of your ascent.
Look round this garden, therefore, that you may
  by gazing at its radiance, be prepared
  to lift your eyes up to the Trinal Ray.
The Queen of Heaven, for whom in whole devotion 100
  I burn with love, will grant us every grace
  because I am Bernard, her faithful one."
As a stranger afar—a Croat,[42] if you will—
  comes to see our Veronica,[43] and awed
  by its ancient fame, can never look his fill,
but says to himself as long as it is displayed:
  "My Lord, Jesus Christ, true God, and is this then
  the likeness of thy living flesh portrayed?"—
just so did I gaze on the living love
  of him who in this world, through contemplation, 110
  tasted the peace which ever dwells above.[44]

---

[41]As she did when she descended to Limbo (as, of course, a manifestation) to summon Virgil.

[42]Probably used here in a generic sense to signify the native of any far-off Christian land, but Croatia, aside from lying at one of the outer limits of Christianity, was also known for the ardor of its religious belief.

[43]From *vera icon,* the true image. Certainly the most famous relic in St. Peter's, the Veronica was the handkerchief of the faithful follower ever after known as St. Veronica. She gave it to Jesus to wipe the blood from his face on the road to Calvary, and what was believed to be the true likeness of Jesus was believed to have appeared on what was believed to be the cloth in what was believed to be His own blood.

[44]According to legend, Bernard was rewarded for his holiness by being permitted a vision of Heaven's blessedness while he was yet on earth.

"Dear son of Grace," he said, "you cannot know
this state of bliss while you yet keep your eyes
fixed only on those things that lie below;
rather, let your eyes mount to the last round
where you shall see the Queen to whom this realm
is subject and devoted, throned and crowned."
I looked up: by as much as the horizon
to eastward in the glory of full dawn
outshines the point at which the sun went down;[45] 120
by so much did one region on the height
to which I raised my eyes out of the valley
outshine the rays of every other light.
And as the sky is brightest in that region
where we on earth expect to see the shaft
of the chariot so badly steered by Phaeton,
while to one side and the other it grows dim—
just so that peaceful oriflamme lit the center
and faded equally along either rim.[46]
And in the center, great wings spread apart, 130
more than a thousand festive angels shone,
each one distinct in radiance and in art.[47]
I saw there, smiling at this song and sport,
her whose beauty entered like a bliss
into the eyes of all that sainted court.
And even could my speech match my conception,
yet I would not dare make the least attempt
to draw her delectation and perfection.
Bernard, seeing my eyes so fixed and burning
with passion on his passion, turned his own 140
up to that height with so much love and yearning
that the example of his ardor sent
new fire through me, making my gaze more ardent.

Canto 32

The Empyrean—St. Bernard; The Virgin Mary; The Thrones of the Blessed: His eyes fixed blissfully on the vision of the Virgin Mary, Bernard recites the orders of the Mystic Rose, identifying the thrones of the most blessed.

Mary's Throne is on the topmost tier of the Heavenly Stadium. Directly across from it rises the Throne of John the Baptist. From her throne to the central arena (the Yellow of the Rose) descends a Line of Christian Saints. These two radii form a diameter that divides

[45]The comparison is not, as careless readers sometimes take it to be, between a dawn and a sunset (whose brightnesses would be approximately equal) but between the eastern and western horizons at dawn. Bright as Heaven is, Mary outshines it as the east outshines the west at daybreak.

[46]The shaft of the chariot of the Sun would project ahead of the horses. It would, therefore, be the first point of light of the new dawn, that moment when light glows on the eastern rim while the horizon to north and south is still dark. Thus Mary not only outshines all heaven as the east at daybreak outshines the west, but even at the uppermost tier of the blessed, those radiances at either side of her are dim by comparison.

[47]Motion. No two angel beings are exactly equal in their brightness, nor in the speed of their flight. These festive angels are, of course, another manifestation of the Angel Hierarchy.

the stadium. On one side are throned Those Who Believed in Christ to Come; on the other, Those who Believed in Christ Descended. The lower half of the Rose contains, on one side, the Pre-Christian Children Saved by Love, and on the other, the Christian Children Saved by Baptism.

Through all these explanations, Bernard has kept his eyes fixed in adoration upon the Virgin. Having finished his preliminary instruction of Dante, Bernard now calls on him to join in a prayer to the Virgin.

Still rapt in contemplation,[48] the sainted seer
assumed the vacant office of instruction,
beginning with these words I still can hear:
"The wound that Mary healed with balm so sweet
was first dealt and then deepened by that being
who sits in such great beauty at her feet.[49]
Below her, in the circle sanctified
by the third rank of loves, Rachel is throned
with Beatrice, as you see, there at her side.
Sarah[50] and Rebecca and Judith and she[51] 10
who was the great-grandmother of the singer
who for his sins cried, 'Lord, have mercy on me!'—
as I go down the great ranks tier by tier,
naming them for you in descending order,
petal by petal, you shall see them clear.
And down from the seventh, continuing from those
in the first six tiers, a line of Hebrew women
forms a part in the tresses of the rose.[52]
Arranged to form a wall thus, they divide
all ranks according to the view of Christ 20
that marked the faith of those on either side.
On this side, where the flower is in full bloom[53]
to its last petal, are arranged all those
whose faith was founded upon Christ to Come;
on that, where the half circles show the unblended
gaps of empty seats, are seated those
whose living faith was fixed on Christ Descended.

---

[48]Of the Virgin. His eyes have not left her. Nor do they turn again to Dante. *The vacant office of instruction:* Formerly held by Beatrice. *I still can hear:* A rhyme-forced addition, not in Dante's text.

[49]Mary, Mother of God, sits in the uppermost tier. At her feet in the second tier sits Eve, Mother of Man. *The wound:* Original sin. *Balm so sweet:* Jesus. *Dealt:* The first fault, Eve's disobedience. *Deepened:* Her seduction of Adam, thus spreading sin to all mankind. *In such great beauty:* Eve, having been created directly by God, was perfect in her beauty.

[50]Wife of Abraham. Hebrews, 11:11–14, cites her as the mother (by miraculous fertility in her old age) of the Jews who foresaw Christ's coming and believed in him. *Rebecca:* Wife of Isaac. *Judith:* She killed Holofernes and freed the Jews.

[51]Ruth: great-grandmother of David ("that singer"). *Who for his sins:* His lust for Bathsheba, wife of Uriah. In order to marry Bathsheba, David sent Uriah to his death in the first line of battle. David's lament is in Psalm 50.

[52]As if the rose were a head of hair and that vertical row of Hebrew women formed a part in it. In the next line the part becomes a wall.

[53]That half of the rose-stadium that holds the pre-Christian believers would naturally be completely filled. On the other side there are thrones waiting for those who have yet to win salvation through Christ Descended. Dante, in fact, is laboring to earn one of them for himself. The Day of Judgment will be upon mankind when the last throne is filled, for Heaven will then be complete.

And as, on this side, the resplendent throne
of Heaven's Lady, with the thrones below it,
establishes the line of that division; 30
so, facing hers, does the throned blessedness
of the Great John[54] who, ever holy, bore
the desert, martyrdom, and Hell's distress;
and under him, forming that line are found
Francis, Benedict, Augustine,[55] and others
descending to this center round by round.
Now marvel at all-foreseeing profundity:
this garden shall be complete when the two aspects
of the one faith have filled it equally.
And know that below that tier that cuts the two 40
dividing walls at their centerpoint, no being
has won his seat of glory by his own virtue,
but by another's, under strict condition;
for all of these were spirits loosed from flesh
before they had matured to true volition.[56]
You can yourself make out their infant graces:
you need no more than listen to their treble
and look attentively into their faces.
You do not speak now: many doubts confound you.[57]
Therefore, to set you free I shall untie 50
the cords in which your subtle thoughts have bound you.
Infinite order rules in this domain.
Mere accidence can no more enter in
than hunger can, or thirst, or grief, or pain.
All you see here is fixed by the decree
of the eternal law, and is so made
that the ring goes on the finger perfectly.
These, it follows, who had so short a pause
in the lower life are not ranked higher or lower
among themselves without sufficient cause. 60
The king in whom this realm abides unchanging
in so much love and bliss that none dares will
increase of joy, creating and arranging
the minds of all in the glad Paradise
of His own sight, grants them degrees of grace
as He sees fit. Here let the effect suffice.[58]

[54]The Baptist. He denounced Herod Antipos and was beheaded two years before the Crucifixion. He had to wait in Limbo for two years, therefore, till Christ came for him at the Resurrection.

[55]St. Francis of Assisi (1181?–1226), founder of the Franciscan order; St. Benedict (c. 480–547), founder of the Benedictine Order; St. Augustine (354–430).

[56]The lower half of the rose-stadium contains the blessed infants, the souls of those who died before they had achieved the true volition of reason and faith. Salvation is granted them not directly through belief in Christ but through the faith and prayers of their parents, relatives, and others of the faithful who interceded for them.

[57]The infants are ranked in tiers that indicate degrees of heavenly merit. But if they were saved through no merit of their own, how can one be more worthy than the other? Such is Dante's doubt, which Bernard goes on to set at rest by telling him, in essence, that God knows what He is doing.

[58]The cause is buried in God's mind. The effect must speak for itself.

Holy Scripture clearly and expressly
notes this effect upon those twins who fought
while still within their mother.[59] So we see
how the Supreme light fittingly makes fair 70
its aureole by granting them their graces
according to the color of their hair.[60]
Thus through no merit of their works and days
they are assigned their varying degrees
by variance only in original grace.
In the first centuries of man's creation
their innocence and the true faith of their parents
was all they needed to achieve salvation.
When the first age of man had run its course,
then circumcision was required of males, 80
to give their innocent wings sufficient force.
But when the age of grace came to mankind
then, unless perfectly baptized in Christ,
such innocents went down among the blind.[61]
Look now on her who most resembles Christ,[62]
for only the great glory of her shining
can purify your eyes to look on Christ."
I saw such joy rain down upon that face[63]—
borne to it by those blest Intelligences
created thus to span those heights of space— 90
that through all else on the long road I trod
nothing had held my soul so fixed in awe,
nor shown me such resemblances to God.
The self-same Love that to her first descended[64]
singing *"Ave Maria, gratia plena"*
stood before her with its wings extended.
Thus rang the holy chant to Heaven's Queen
and all the blessèd court joined in the song,
and singing, every face grew more serene.
"O holy Father, who endures for me 100
the loss of being far from the sweet place
where fate has raised your throne eternally,
who is that angel who with such desire
gazes into the eyes of our sweet Queen,
so rapt in love he seems to be afire?"

---

[59]Jacob and Esau. According to Genesis 25:21ff., they were at odds while still in their mother's womb. (Cf. the legend of Polyneices and Eteocles, twin sons of Oedipus and Jocasta.) Dante follows St. Paul (Romans 9:11–13) in interpreting the division between Jacob and Esau as a working of God's unfathomable will. "Even as it is written, Jacob I loved, but Esau I hated." Man can note the will of God in such matters ("the effect") but cannot plumb its causes.

[60]For what may seem to be superficial reasons, Esau (Genesis 25:25) was red-headed.

[61]Among the souls of Hell. Such infants were assigned to Limbo.

[62]The Virgin Mary.

[63]Mary's.

[64]The archangel Gabriel, the Angel of the Annunciation. Dante seems to conceive of Gabriel suspended in air before her, repeating the blissful chant of the Annunciation as he had first hymned it in Nazareth.

Thus did I seek instruction from that Great One
who drew the beauty of his light from Mary
as the morning star draws beauty from the sun.
And he: "As much as angel or soul can know
of exultation, gallantry, and poise 110
there is in him; and we would have it so,
for it was he who brought the victory[65]
to Mary when the Son of God had willed
to bear the weight of human misery.
But let your eyes go where my words point out
among this court, and note the mighty peers
of the empire of the just and the devout.
Those two whose bliss it is to sit so close
to the radiance of the Empress of All Joy
are the two eternal roots of this our rose:[66] 120
The one just to the left of her blessedness
is the father whose unruly appetite
left man the taste for so much bitterness;
and on her right, that ancient one you see
is the father of Holy Church to whom Christ gave
the twin keys to this flower of timeless beauty.
And that one who in his prophetic sight
foretold the evil days of the Sweet Bride
won by the spear and nails,[67] sits on his right.
While by the other father and first man 130
sits the great leader to whom manna fell
to feed an ingrate and rebellious clan.[68]
Across the circle from Peter, behold Anna.[69]
She feels such bliss in looking at her daughter
she does not move her eyes to sing 'Hosanna!'
And opposite the father of us all
sits Lucy,[70] who first urged your lady to you
when you were blindly bent toward your own fall.
But the time allowed for this dream vision flies.
As a tailor must cut the gown from what cloth is given, 140
just so must we move on, turning our eyes
to the Primal Love, that as your powers advance
with looking toward him, you may penetrate
as deep as may be through His radiance.

[65](Dante says "the palm.") Of God's election, that she bear the promised Messiah.

[66]Adam and St. Peter. Adam as Father of Mankind, Peter as Father of the Church. Note that Peter has the place of honor on the right.

[67]St. John the Evangelist. His *Apocalypse* was received as the prophetic book in which the entire history of the Church is foretold. He sits on Peter's right.

[68]Moses.

[69]Ste. Anna, Ste. Anne, mother of the Virgin. Her position directly across the circle from Peter's puts her to the right of John the Baptist. *Does not move her eyes to sing 'Hosanna!':* Like all the other heavenly beings, she constantly sings the praise of God. All others, naturally enough, look up as they sing. She, however, is so filled with bliss by the sight of Mary that she does not turn her eyes from her blessed daughter.

[70]See *The Inferno* Canto 2, 97–100. It was she who first sent Beatrice to rescue Dante from the Dark Wood of Error. She sits opposite Adam. She would, accordingly, be to the left of John the Baptist.

But lest you should fall backward when you flare
your mortal wings, intending to mount higher,
remember grace must be acquired through prayer.
Therefore I will pray that blessèd one[71]
who has the power to aid you in your need.
See that you follow me with such devotion 150
your heart adheres to every word I say."
And with those words the saint began to pray.

Canto 33

The Empyrean—St. Bernard; Prayer to the Virgin; The Vision of God: St. Bernard offers a lofty prayer to the Virgin, asking her to intercede in Dante's behalf, and in answer Dante feels his soul swell with new power and grow calm in rapture as his eyes are permitted the direct vision of God.

There can be no measure of how long the vision endures. It passes, and Dante is once more mortal and fallible. Raised by God's presence, he had looked into the Mystery and had begun to understand its power and majesty. Returned to himself, there is no power in him capable of speaking the truth of what he saw. Yet the impress of the truth is stamped upon his soul, which he now knows will return to be one with God's love.

"Virgin Mother, daughter of thy son;
humble beyond all creatures and more exalted;
predestined turning point of God's intention;
thy merit so ennobled human nature
that its divine Creator did not scorn
to make Himself the creature of His creature.
The Love that was rekindled in Thy womb
sends forth the warmth of the eternal peace
within whose ray this flower has come to bloom.
Here, to us, thou art the noon and scope 10
of Love revealed; and among mortal men,
the living fountain of eternal hope.
Lady, thou art so near God's reckonings
that who seeks grace and does not first seek thee
would have his wish fly upward without wings.
Not only does thy sweet benignity
flow out to all who beg, but oftentimes
thy charity arrives before the plea.
In thee is pity, in thee munificence,
in thee the tenderest heart, in thee unites 20
all that creation knows of excellence!
Now comes this man who from the final pit
of the universe up to this height has seen,
one by one, the three lives of the spirit.
He prays to thee in fervent supplication
for grace and strength, that he may raise his eyes
to the all-healing final revelation.
And I, who never more desired to see
the vision myself than I do that he may see It,
add my own prayer, and pray that it may be 30

[71] Mary.

enough to move you to dispel the trace
of every mortal shadow by thy prayers
and let him see revealed the Sum of Grace.
I pray thee further, all-persuading Queen,
keep whole the natural bent of his affections[72]
and of his powers after his eyes have seen.
Protect him from the stirrings of man's clay;[73]
see how Beatrice and the blessèd host
clasp reverent hands to join me as I pray."
The eyes[74] that God reveres and loves the best 40
glowed on the speaker, making clear the joy
with which true prayer is heard by the most blest.
Those eyes turned then to the Eternal Ray,
through which, we must indeed believe, the eyes
of others do not find such ready way.
And I, who neared the goal of all my nature,
felt my soul, at the climax of its yearning,
suddenly, as it ought, grow calm with rapture.
Bernard then, smiling sweetly, gestured to me
to look up, but I had already become 50
within myself all he would have me be.[75]
Little by little as my vision grew
it penetrated further through the aura
of the high lamp which in Itself is true.[76]
What then I saw is more than tongue can say.
Our human speech is dark before the vision.
The ravished memory swoons and falls away.
As one who sees in dreams and wakes to find
the emotional impression of his vision
still powerful while its parts fade from his mind— 60
just such am I, having lost nearly all
the vision itself, while in my heart I feel
the sweetness of it yet distill and fall.
So, in the sun, the footprints fade from snow.
On the wild wind that bore the tumbling leaves
the Sybil's oracles were scattered so.[77]
O Light Supreme who doth Thyself withdraw
so far above man's mortal understanding,
lend me again some glimpse of what I saw;

---

[72]Bernard is asking Mary to protect Dante lest the intensity of the vision overpower his faculties.

[73]Protect him from the stirrings of base human impulse, especially from pride, for Dante is about to receive a grace never before granted to any man and the thought of such glory might well move a mere mortal to a hubris that would turn glory to sinfulness.

[74]Of Mary.

[75]That is, "But I had already fixed my entire attention upon the vision of God." But if so, how could Dante have seen Bernard's smile and gesture? Eager students like to believe they catch Dante in a contradiction here. Let them bear in mind that Dante is looking directly at God, as do the souls of Heaven, who thereby acquire—insofar as they are able to contain it—God's own knowledge. As a first stirring of that heavenly power, therefore, Dante is sharing God's knowledge of St. Bernard.

[76]The light of God is the one light whose source is Itself. All others are a reflection of this.

[77]The Cumean Sybil (Virgil describes her in *Aeneid* 3, 441ff.) wrote her oracles on leaves, one letter to a leaf, then sent her message scattering on the wind. Presumably, the truth was all contained in that strew, could one only gather all the leaves and put the letters in the right order.

make Thou my tongue so eloquent it may 70
of all Thy glory speak a single clue
to those who follow me in the world's day;
for by returning to my memory
somewhat, and somewhat sounding in these verses,
Thou shalt show man more of Thy victory.
So dazzling was the splendor of that Ray,
that I must certainly have lost my senses
had I, but for an instant, turned away.[78]
And so it was, as I recall, I could
the better bear to look, until at last 80
my vision made one with the Eternal Good.
Oh grace abounding that had made me fit
to fix my eyes on the eternal light
until my vision was consumed in it!
I saw within Its depth how It conceives
all things in a single volume bound by Love,
of which the universe is the scattered leaves;
substance,[79] accident, and their relation
so fused that all I say could do no more
than yield a glimpse of that bright revelation. 90
I think I saw the universal form
that binds these things,[80] for as I speak these words
I feel my joy swell and my spirits warm.
Twenty-five centuries since Neptune saw
the Argo's keel have not moved all mankind,
recalling that adventure, to such awe
as I felt in an instant. My tranced being
stared fixed and motionless upon that vision,
ever more fervent to see in the act of seeing.
Experiencing that Radiance, the spirit 100
is so indrawn it is impossible
even to think of ever turning from It.
For the good which is the will's ultimate object
is all subsumed in It; and, being removed,
all is defective which in It is perfect.
Now in my recollection of the rest
I have less power to speak than any infant
wetting its tongue yet at its mother's breast;
and not because that Living Radiance bore
more than one semblance, for It is unchanging 110
and is forever as it was before;
rather, as I grew worthier to see,
the more I looked, the more unchanging semblance
appeared to change with every change in me.

[78]How can a light be so dazzling that the beholder would swoon if he looked away for an instant? Would it not be, rather, in looking at, not away from, the overpowering vision that the viewer's senses would be overcome? So it would be on earth. But now Dante, with the help of all heaven's prayers, is in the presence of God and strengthened by all he sees. It is by being so strengthened that he can see yet more.

[79]Matter, all that exists in itself. *Accident:* All that exists as a phase of matter.

[80]Substance and accident.

Within the depthless deep and clear existence
  of that abyss of light three circles shown—
  three in color, one in circumference:
the second from the first, rainbow from rainbow;
  the third, an exhalation of pure fire
  equally breathed forth by the other two. 120
But oh how much my words miss my conception,
  which is itself so far from what I saw
  that to call it feeble would be rank deception!
O Light Eternal fixed in Itself alone,
  by Itself alone understood, which from Itself
  loves and glows, self-knowing and self-known;
that second aureole which shone forth in Thee,
  conceived as a reflection of the first—
  or which appeared so to my scrutiny—
seemed in Itself of Its own coloration 130
  to be painted with man's image. I fixed my eyes
  on that alone in rapturous contemplation.
Like a geometer wholly dedicated
  to squaring the circle, but who cannot find,
  think as he may, the principle indicated—
so did I study the supernal face.
  I yearned to know just how our image merges
  into that circle, and how it there finds place;
but mine were not the wings for such a flight.
  Yet, as I wished, the truth I wished for came
  cleaving my mind in a great flash of light.
Here my powers rest from their high fantasy,
  but already I could feel my being turned—
  instinct and intellect balanced equally
as in a wheel whose motion nothing jars—
by the Love that moves the Sun and the other stars.

WESTERN TEXTS

BARDIC POETRY
[5TH CENTURY–8TH CENTURY]

The selections grouped under Irish, Welsh, and Old English poetry originate within three centuries: the fifth century, when Christian missionaries converted and partially colonized Ireland; the sixth century, when Anglo-Saxon invaders destroyed Celtic strongholds in Wales and northern Britain; and the seventh century, when Gregory the Great sent missionaries to convert the Anglo-Saxons. In each case, the native cultures were overcome by an invading force, either political or military, while efforts peculiar to the region helped to ensure the preservation of the literature of the native peoples.

The Irish Tradition

In Ireland, Christian missionaries of the fifth century encountered the survivors of the old pagan culture, including the *file,* poets who served as the kings' counselors. Many Irish legends and sagas were already of great antiquity, going back to the invasion of the Celts in the first century B.C.E. The scribes in the monasteries recorded the literature of Ireland in the sixth and seventh centuries, intending to incorporate it into a broader Christian framework. But the monasteries were sacked during the Danish invasions of the ninth and tenth centuries and the poetic records scattered, not to be recovered until the twelfth century. It is then that we find, in fragmented form, such treasures as the "Exile of the Sons of Uisliu."

The great Irish epic, The Ulster Cycle, includes the legendary story of the *Tain Bo Cualnge* (*The Cattle Raid of Cooley*). Of all the stories connected to the *Tain,* the most famous is "Exile of the Sons of Uisliu," the account of the birth, life, and death of Derdriu (Deidre), the beautiful woman whose changing fortunes led the lords of Ireland into fratricidal battle. The story of Derdriu is one of the "pre-tales" of the epic account of the legendary battle between the Ulstermen and the men of Connacht for the magical bull of Connacht. The purpose of the pre-tales is to explain the background of the battle of Cooley. This tale centers on the deeds of Conchobor, king of Ulster, concerning the young woman Derdriu, the sons of the Ulsterman Uisliu, and the Ulster heroes Fergus, Dubthach, and Cormac. The tale explains why Fergus, Dubthach, and Cormac develop a deadly hatred for Conchobor and eventually turn against him, fighting for the men of Connacht.

As the story opens, Conchobor defies a prophecy warning him against Derdriu, the infant daughter of his court storyteller. He raises Derdriu himself, keeping her apart from the other men of Ulster, and when she is old enough he takes her to his bed. But Derdriu does not agree to this arrangement. She encounters Noisiu, one of the sons of Uisliu, while he is tending cattle and binds him to an oath to take her as his wife. When his brothers hear of it, they decide to support the couple and they all leave Conchobor's castle together. Later the same sons of Uisliu make overtures of peace to Conchobor, which he appears to accept. He even sends three heroes—Fergus, Dubthach, and his own son Cormac—to accompany them as safe conduct on their return. But he plots treachery instead, and detains the hero Fergus at a feast while he encourages a former retainer, Eogan mac Durthacht, to attack and kill the sons of Uisliu. In the ensuing battle, the three heroes, angry at Conchobor's deception, fight against him. Later Fergus, Dubthach, and Cormac join forces with the king and queen of Connacht in defiance of Conchobor, their former lord.

Meanwhile, Conchobor takes Derdriu captive again. For a year she mourns the death of Noisiu and refuses Conchobor's advances. Finally, while being driven to a fair, she escapes both Conchobor and the treacherous Eogan mac Durthacht by dashing her head against a stone.

The story is not only an economically told tale of the passion, rage, and retribution that swept through the kingdom of Ulster; it is also a great world-myth of a woman's defiance. From the start, Derdriu assumes a larger-than-life position as the woman who will bring ruin to the Ulstermen. First as Conchobor's captive and later as Noisiu's wife, she challenges the order of society in an effort to have her own way. After she brings death and destruction on the sons of Uisliu, she achieves a kind of victory only by the ferocious enactment of her own suicide. The splendor and terror of her resistance have not been lost on later generations: In the twentieth century, her indomitable will has been memorialized by the Irish poet William Butler Yeats and the playwright John M. Synge.

THE WELSH TRADITION

The story of the collection of Welsh heroic saga is even more circuitous because the materials originally came from two Celtic kingdoms in what is now Scotland: Rheged, the capital of which was probably Carlisle, and Gododdin, the capital of which was Edinburgh, 100 miles further north. The rulers of these and associated kingdoms were referred to as "Men of the North." Until sometime in the sixth century, they had remained in continuous contact with their kin in Wales; then tribes of invading Angles established themselves across the north of England, cutting off access to Wales.

Late in the sixth century, stories of Urien, king of Rheged, and his royal court were made into heroic songs and elegies that became identified with the poet Taliesin. These and later poems also attributed to Taliesin were finally assembled near the end of the thirteenth century in the *Book of Taliesin*. Meanwhile, in the early seventh century, the massacre of 300 supporters of the kingdom of Gododdin was memorialized, supposedly by the poet Aneirin, in the epic poem *The Gododdin*. This poem and other works attributed to Aneirin were collected in the *Book of Aneirin* around 1250 C.E. Together, the works ascribed to Taliesin and Aneirin are the most important remains of Welsh bardic poetry.

The poems included here date back as far as the Anglo-Saxon invasion in the sixth century. Taliesin and Aneirin are known as the earliest of the *Cynfeirrd,* the master bards of the Welsh tradition. Welsh Scholar Gwyn Jones defines a bardic poet:

> The bard, we might say, is the poet as public figure. It is his business to maintain a leader's fame, retail tribal triumphs and disasters, persuade and foretell, convey to his hearers that accepted corpus of lore and precept relating to animals, weather, crops, human nature and behavior which involves man in the visible and palpable world, and to set forth repeatedly and unequivocably in the compressed verse-forms, bare syntax, and severely stylized diction common to his kind the cherished beliefs of a hierarchical and war-waging society: valour, loyalty, service, reward.[1]

As we shall see, the Anglo-Saxon tradition (and others besides) also had bards. In fact, the courtly poet survived as a fixture of society, though in changing form, all the way through the Middle Ages.

The first reference to Taliesin and Aneirin comes in Nennius' *History of the Britons* at the beginning of the ninth century, where they are described as "renowned in British poetry." Nennius puts the reign of King Urien of Rheged, the subject of Taliesin's poetry, within the period 572–592. Because the date of the battle memorialized in *The Gododdin,* attributed to Aneirin, was 600, we can assign the activity of the two legendary poets to the end of the sixth century and the beginning of the seventh century, respectively.

Taliesin

Taliesin appears to have begun his career in Wales and then traveled north to join the court of King Urien around 580. There he wrote poems in praise of Urien and his son Owain, along with other rulers of North Britain. *The Battle of Argoed Llwyfain* is a

[1] Gwyn Jones, *The Oxford Book of Welsh Verse in English* (1977), xviii–xix.

dramatized narrative of a battle between King Urien with his son Owain and the Saxon king identified as Fflamddwyn (Flame Bearer)—possibly Deodric of Anglia. The poem begins as Fflamddwyn arrogantly asks Urien and Owain for hostages as pledges of their peaceful intentions. Owain responds that no descendant of Coel, the tribal patriarch, would dishonor himself by giving hostages. Urien adds that there will be no talk of peace; only war will come to the Saxons. In the conclusion, we are told that the crows fattened themselves on the blood of the fallen and that the poet will praise the victor until the end of his days. The poem is marked by its realistic reporting of the events of the day.

The *Death Song for Owain ab Urien* is written in one of the complicated metrical patterns frequently employed in later Welsh poetry. The movement of the four-line stanzas, heavily rhymed in the original, plays off against the poet's economical use of imagery. The reference to Owain as Rheged's prince suggests that the son lived long enough to succeed Urien as king; the prayer at the end is in keeping with the Christian piety of sixth-century Britain. The solemn ending, mingling pagan and Christian beliefs, reminds a reader familiar with Old English literature of the ending of *Beowulf.*

Aneirin

We know little more of Aneirin than of Taliesin. A manuscript of *The Gododdin* attributes the work to "the son of Dwywai." This would put Aneirin in the royal courts of the North because Dwywai was a northern prince. The only other evidence we have about the author and the work is their mention in Welsh poetry of the first half of the seventh century, indicating that *The Gododdin* was known in the North within a quarter century of its composition.

The Gododdin celebrates the gathering of a host of 300 men by the king of Gododdin, Mynyddog the Wealthy, for the purpose of fighting the Saxons at the town of Catraeth in North Yorkshire. Catraeth was an important strategic location in the kingdom of Rheged. In the poem, King Mynyddog recruits the 300 warriors, most of them hand-picked from his own kingdom, by holding a year-long mead-feast for them in his castle in Edinburgh. The feast establishes a bond of obligation between the king and the warriors; it is described as "bitter," referring to the massacre that is its outcome.

The Gododdin has been called the unique exposition of the heroic ideal in Welsh literature. It celebrates 80 of the 300 warriors by name. Its forceful language, fierce partisanship, and celebration of warfare seem to anticipate similar features in the French *Song of Roland,* composed at the end of the twelfth century. When it was recited by the Welsh court bard, *The Gododdin* must have seemed compelling indeed.

The Anglo-Saxon Tradition

Two centuries after the Anglo-Saxons first waged war against the Celtic inhabitants of Britain, their own culture came into contact with Christian missionaries and was Latinized in the process. A significant body of Old English literature was saved from oblivion, thanks to the efforts of some of the monasteries and the intervention of enlightened lords such as King Alfred the Great (871–899). What remains of Old English poetry comes from manuscripts of the tenth century, although its sources are even older. The oldest Old English poem in existence, *Widsith, the Minstrel,* probably dates from the seventh century. Other poems were probably composed or assembled between the eighth and tenth centuries; they include *The Cotton MS. Maxims,* a collection of sayings; the elegiac pieces *The Wanderer* and *The Ruin;* and the monologues *The Wife's Lament* and *The Husband's Message.*

The earliest Old English poem included here expands our definition of the bardic tradition. *Widsith, the Minstrel* dates back to the seventh century and catalogues the wanderings of a bard in Europe centuries before, from the court of Eormanric the Goth (c. 375) to that of Aelfwine in Italy (c. 568). He tells of the hardships of the road ("bereft of my kinsmen, far from my folk") but also the joys of patronage ("the giving of rings, the shining jewels"). The conclusion of the poem blends pagan and Christian imagery as the poet describes the honor one receives by coming to a good end ("He who earns praise / Has under heaven the greatest glory").

The *Cotton MS. Maxims,* bardic sayings intended for a noble audience, were written down by a monastic scribe in the tenth century. They combine several elements: predictions about the political life of the community, seasonal lore and observation of natural events, and traditional sayings concerning ethics and proper behavior. The text has a Christian ending that was probably added after the rest of the composition was complete.

Some longer poems, also written down in the tenth century, reflect back on earlier times even when they have a Christian coloring. *The Wanderer* begins as a lament over the loss of a lord and protector. The themes of exile, the loss of companions, the desolation of landscape and ruined dwellings, and bitter, death-dealing cold all haunt the Wanderer, who ends by lamenting the end of the culture to which warriors such as he have traditionally belonged. But there is a new development in the poem: The wanderer recedes and the "wise man," who understands the transience of human affairs, begins to take over. The ending adds the hope of eternal salvation.

The Ruin is a shorter poem on a similar theme. Instead of focusing on the speaker, the poet describes the ruins of a city. Anglo-Saxon communities often grew up around the remains of Roman cities, so the poem has an eerily literal quality. The dazzling description of ruined public baths near the end is regarded as a tour de force, using the poetic vocabulary of Old English to its heights.

The dramatic monologues *The Wife's Lament* and *The Husband's Message* may be companion pieces. The plot of these poems, assuming they have a common origin, is as follows: The kinsmen of a lord, jealous of his wife and her prerogatives, have engineered his rejection of his mate. The lord has gone off to sea, leaving his former wife defenseless, and through his family's conniving she now lives in a cave under a tree in the forest. She grieves for her lord and expresses her undying love for him. Meanwhile, a message is sent from the lord across the sea to his wife to join him. The message is spoken by the magical staff he has sent her; the personified staff tells how he was cut from a sapling that grew near the seacoast. At the end of the poem are five runic letters, coded symbols understood only by the wife, conveying the husband's message. While possessing a remarkable degree of psychological sophistication, these poems also lack the usual Christian references. One might find Celtic origins in such details as the talking staff.

Suggested Readings

Cultural histories of the Irish, Welsh, and Anglo-Saxon traditions include Robin Flower's *The Irish Tradition* (1947); Myles Dillon's "The Celtic Languages and the Beginnings of Literature" and "Welsh Literature" in Myles Dillon and N. K. Chadwick, *The Celtic Realms* (1967); and David M. Zesmer's "The Old English Period" in *Guide to English Literature: From Beowulf through Chaucer* (1961). A masterful early study that stressed the similarities between the ancient cultures is H. M. Chadwick's *The Heroic Age* (1912; repr. 1967).

The present version of "Exile of the Sons of Uisliu" is the result of a fine modern translation by the poet Thomas Kinsella in *The Tain* (1969). For the fullest version of the epic, see Cecile O'Rahilly's *Tain Bo Cualnge from the Book of Leinster* (1967). General works of scholarship and criticism in early Irish culture include T. F. O'Rahilly's *Early Irish History and Mythology* (1946), Robin Flower's *The Irish Tradition* (1947), and Myles Dillon's *Early Irish Literature* (1948).

Early Welsh literature is more accessible now than any time since the Norman Conquest. The work of the two legendary poets of the Cynfeirdd can be approached through modern translations: Sir Ifor Williams, ed., *The Poems of Taliesin* (1968), and A. O. H. Jarman, ed., *Aneirin: Y Gododdin* (1988). Broader collections include J. P. Clancy, ed., *The Earliest Welsh Poetry* (1970) and Gwyn Jones, ed., *The Oxford Book of Welsh Poetry in English* (1977). A rich discussion of the ancient poets can be found in A. O. H. Jarman's *The Cynfeirdd: Early Welsh Poets and Poetry* (1981).

Translations of Old English poetry include R. K. Gordon's *Anglo Saxon Poetry* (1926; reprinted 1974) and Charles W. Kennedy's *An Anthology of Old English Poetry* (1960). There are a number of commentaries: Recent ones include Stanley B. Greenfield in *The Interpretation of Old English Poems* (1972) and Derek Pearsall in *Old English and Middle English Poetry* (1977).

ANONYMOUS

[6TH CENTURY–7TH CENTURY]

Exile of the Sons of Uisliu

Translated from the Old Irish by Thomas Kinsella

What caused the exile of the sons of Uisliu? It is soon told.

The men of Ulster were drinking in the house of Conchobor's storyteller, Fedlimid mac Daill. Fedlimid's wife was overseeing everything and looking after them all. She was full with child. Meat and drink were passed round, and a drunken uproar shook the place. When they were ready to sleep the woman went to her bed. As she crossed the floor of the house the child screamed in her womb and was heard all over the enclosure. At that scream everyone in the house started up, ready to kill. Sencha mac Ailella said:

'No one move! Bring the woman here. We'll see what caused this noise.'

So the woman was brought before them. Her husband Fedlimid said:

'Woman,
what was that fierce shuddering sound
furious in your troubled womb?
The weird uproar at your waist
hurts the ears of all who hear it.
My heart trembles at some great terror
or some cruel injury.'

She turned distracted to the seer Cathbad:

'Fair-faced Cathbad, hear me
—prince, pure, precious crown,
grown huge in druid spells.
I can't find the fair words
that would shed the light of knowledge
for my husband Fedlimid,

even though it was the hollow
of my own womb that howled.
No woman knows what her womb bears.'

Then Cathbad said:

'A woman with twisted yellow tresses,
green-irised eyes of great beauty
and cheeks flushed like the foxglove
howled in the hollow of your womb.
I say that whiter than the snow
is the white treasure of her teeth;
Parthian-red, her lip's lustre.
Ulster's chariot-warriors
will deal many a blow for her.
There howled in your troubled womb
a tall, lovely, long-haired woman.
Heroes will contend for her,
high kings beseech on her account;
then, west of Conchobor's kingdom
a heavy harvest of fighting men.
High queens will ache with envy
to see those lips of Parthian-red
opening on her pearly teeth,
and see her pure perfect body.'

Cathbad placed his hand on the woman's belly and the baby wriggled under it.

'Yes,' he said, 'there is a girl there. Derdriu shall be her name. She will bring evil.'

Then the daughter was born and Cathbad said:

'Much damage, Derdriu, will follow
your high fame and fair visage:
Ulster in your time tormented,
demure daughter of Fedlimid.

And later, too, jealousy
will dog you, woman like a flame,
and later still—listen well—
the three sons of Uisliu exiled.

Then again, in your lifetime,
a bitter blow struck in Emain.
Remorse later for that ruin
wrought by the great son of Roech;

Fergus exiled out of Ulster
through your fault, fatal woman,
and the much-wept deadly wound
of Fiachna, Conchobor's son.

Your fault also, fatal woman,
Gerrce felled, Illadan's son,
and a crime that no less cries out,
the son of Durthacht, Eogan, struck.

> Harsh, hideous deeds done
> in anger at Ulster's high king,
> and little graves everywhere
> —a famous tale, Derdriu.'

'Kill the child!' the warriors said.

'No,' Conchobor said. 'The girl will be taken away tomorrow. I'll have her reared for me. This woman I'll keep to myself.'

The men of Ulster didn't dare speak against him.

And so it was done. She was reared by Conchobor and grew into the loveliest woman in all Ireland. She was kept in a place set apart, so that no Ulsterman might see her until she was ready for Conchobor's bed. No one was allowed in the enclosure but her foster-father and her foster-mother, and Leborcham, tall and crooked, a satirist, who couldn't be kept out.

One day in winter, the girl's foster-father was skinning a milk-fed calf on the snow outside, to cook it for her. She saw a raven drinking the blood on the snow. She said to Leborcham:

'I could desire a man who had those three colours there: hair like the raven, cheeks like blood and his body like snow.'

'Good luck and success to you!' Leborcham said. 'He isn't too far away, but close at hand—Noisiu, Uisliu's son.'

'I'll be ill in that case,' she said, 'until I see him.'

This man Noisiu was chanting by himself one time near Emain, on the rampart of the stronghold. The chanting of the sons of Uisliu was very sweet. Every cow or beast that heard it gave two thirds more milk. Any person hearing it was filled with peace and music. Their deeds in war were great also: if the whole province of Ulster came at them at once, they could put their three backs together and not be beaten, their parrying and defence were so fine. Besides this they were swift as hounds in the chase, killing the wild beasts in flight.

While Noisiu was out there alone, therefore, she slipped out quickly to him and made as though to pass him and not recognize him.

'That is a fine heifer going by,' he said.

'As well it might,' she said. 'The heifers grow big where there are no bulls.'

'You have the bull of this province all to yourself,' he said, 'the king of Ulster.'

'Of the two,' she said, 'I'd pick a game young bull like you.'

'You couldn't,' he said. 'There is Cathbad's prophecy.'

'Are you rejecting me?'

'I am,' he said.

Then she rushed at him and caught the two ears of his head.

'Two ears of shame and mockery,' she said, 'if you don't take me with you.'

'Woman, leave me alone!' he said.

'You will do it,' she said, binding him.

A shrill cry escaped him at that. The men of Ulster nearby, when they heard it, started up ready to kill. Uisliu's other sons went out to quieten their brother.

'What is wrong?' they said. 'Whatever it is, Ulstermen shouldn't kill each other for it.'

He told them what had happened.

'Evil will come of this,' the warriors said. 'But even so, you won't be shamed as long as we live. We can bring her with us to some other place. There's no king in Ireland who would deny us a welcome.'

They decided on that. They left that night, with three times fifty warriors and three times fifty women and the same of hounds and menials. Derdriu was among them, mingling with the rest.

They travelled about Ireland for a long time, under protection. Conchobor tried to destroy them often with ambushes and treachery. They went round southwestward from the red cataract at Es Ruaid, and to the promontory at Benn Etair, northeastward. But still the men of Ulster pursued them until they crossed the sea to the land of Alba.

They settled there in the waste places. When the mountain game failed them they turned to take the people's cattle. A day came when the people of Alba went out to destroy them. Then they offered themselves to the king of Alba, who accepted them among his people as hired soldiers. They set their houses on the green. They built their houses so that no one could see in at the girl in case there might be killing on her account.

It happened that a steward came looking around their house early one morning. He saw the couple sleeping. Then he went and woke the king:

'I never found a woman fit for you until today,' he said. 'There is a woman with Noisiu mac Uislenn who is fit for a king over the Western World. If you have Noisiu killed, you can have the woman to sleep with,' the steward said.

'No,' the king said, 'but go and ask her every day in secret.'

He did this, but every day he came she told Noisiu about it that night. Since nothing could be done with her, the sons of Uisliu were ordered into all kinds of traps and dangerous battles to have them killed. But they were so hard in the carnage that nothing came of it.

They tried her one last time. Then the men of Alba were called together to kill them. She told Noisiu this.

'Go away from here,' she said. 'If you don't leave here this night, you will be dead tomorrow.'

So they left that night and reached an island in the sea.

This news reached Ulster.

'Conchobor,' everyone said, 'it would be shameful if the sons of Uisliu fell in enemy lands by the fault of a bad woman. Better to forgive and protect them—to save their lives and let them come home—than for enemies to lay them low.'

'Let them come,' Conchobor said. 'Send for them, with guarantees of safety.'

This news was brought to them.

'It is welcome,' they said. 'We'll go if Fergus comes as a pledge of safety, and Dubthach and Conchobor's son Cormac.'

Then they went down with the messengers to the sea.

So they were brought back to Ireland. But Fergus was stopped through Conchobor's cunning. He was invited to a number of ale feasts and, by an old oath, couldn't refuse. The sons of Uisliu had sworn they would eat no food in Ireland until they ate Conchobor's food first, so they were bound to go on. Fiacha, Fergus's son, went on with them, while Fergus and Dubthach stayed behind. The sons of Uisliu came to the green at Emain. Eogan mac Durthacht, king of Fernmag, was there: he had come to make peace with Conchobor, with whom he had long been at enmity. He had been chosen to kill them. Conchobor's hired soldiers gathered around him so that the sons of Uisliu couldn't reach him. They stood in the middle of the green. The women settled on the ramparts of Emain.

Eogan crossed the green with his men. Fergus's son came and stood at Noisiu's side. Eogan welcomed Noisiu with the hard thrust of a great spear that broke his back. Fergus's son grasped Noisiu in his two arms and pulled him down and threw himself across him, and Noisiu was finished off through Fergus's son's body. Then the slaughter broke out all over the green. No one left except by spike of spear or slash of sword. Derdriu was brought over to Conchobor and stood beside him with her hands bound at her back.

Fergus was told of this, and Dubthach and Cormac. They came at once and did mighty deeds. Dubthach killed Maine, Conchobor's son. Fiachna, son of Conchobor's daughter Fedelm, was killed with a single thrust. Fergus killed Traigthrén, Traiglethan's son, and his brother. Conchobor was outraged, and on a day soon afterward battle was joined between them, and three hundred among the men of Ulster fell. Before morning Dubthach had massacred the girls of Ulster and Fergus had burned Emain.

Then they went to Connacht, to Ailill and Medb—not that this was a home from home for Ulstermen, but that they knew these two would protect them. A full three thousand the exiles numbered. For sixteen years they made sure that weeping and trembling never died away in Ulster; there was weeping and trembling at their hands every single night.

She was kept a year by Conchobor. In that time she never gave one smile, nor took enough food or sleep, nor lifted up her head from her knees. If they sent musicians to her, she would say this following poem:

'Sweet in your sight the fiery stride
of raiding men returned to Emain.
More nobly strode the three proud
sons of Uisliu toward their home:

Noisiu bearing the best mead
—I would wash him by the fire—
Ardán, with a stag or a boar,
Anle, shouldering his load.

The son of Nes, battle-proud,
drinks, you say, the choicest mead.
Choicer still—a brimming sea—
I have taken frequently.

Modest Noisiu would prepare
a cooking-pit in the forest floor.
Sweeter then than any meat
the son of Uisliu's, honey-sweet.

Though for you the times are sweet
with pipers and with trumpeters,
I swear today I can't forget
that I have known far sweeter airs.

Conchobor your king may take delight
in pipers and in trumpeters
—I have known a sweeter thing,
the three sons' triumphant song.

Noisiu's voice a wave roar,
a sweet sound to hear forever;
Ardán's bright baritone;
Anle, the hunter's, high tenor.

Noisiu: his grave-mound is made
and mournfully accompanied.
The highest hero—and I poured
the deadly drink when he died.

His cropped gold fleece I loved,
and fine form—a tall tree.
Alas, I needn't watch today,
nor wait for the son of Uisliu.

I loved the modest, mighty warrior,
loved his fitting, firm desire,
loved him at daybreak as he dressed
by the margin of the forest.

Those blue eyes that melted women,
and menaced enemies, I loved;
then, with our forest journey done,
his chanting through the dark woods.

I don't sleep now,
nor redden my fingernails.
What have I to do with welcomes?
The son of Indel will not come.

I can't sleep,
lying there half the night.
These crowds—I am driven out of my mind.
I can neither eat nor smile.

What use for welcome have I now
with all these nobles crowding Emain?
Comfortless, no peace nor joy,
nor mansion nor pleasant ornament.'

If Conchobor tried to soothe her, she would chant this following poem:

'Conchobor, what are you thinking, you
that piled up sorrow over woe?
Truly, however long I live,
I can't spare you much love.

The thing most dear to me in the world,
the very thing I most loved,
your harsh crime took from me.
I won't see him till I die.

I feel his lack, wearily,
the son of Uisliu. All I see—
black boulders on fair flesh
so bright once among the others.

Red-cheeked, sweet as the river-brink;
red-lipped; brows beetle-black;
pearly teeth gleaming bright
with a noble snowy light.

His figure easiest to find,
bright among Alba's fighting-men
—a border made of red gold
matched his handsome crimson cloak.

A soft multitude of jewels
in the satin tunic—itself a jewel:
for decoration, all told,
fifty ounces of light gold.

He carried a gold-hilted sword
and two javelins sharply tipped,
a shield rimmed with yellow gold
with a knob of silver at the middle.

Fergus did an injury
bringing us over the great sea.
How his deeds of valour shrank
when he sold honour for a drink!

If all Ulster's warriors
were gathered on this plain, Conchobor,
I would gladly give them all
for Noisiu, son of Uisliu.

Break my heart no more today.
In a short while I'll be no more.
Grief is heavier than the sea,
if you were but wise, Conchobor.'

'What do you see that you hate most?' Conchobor said.

'You, of course,' she said, 'and Eogan mac Durthacht!'

'Go and live for a year with Eogan, then,' Conchobor said.

Then he sent her over to Eogan.

They set out the next day for the fair of Macha. She was behind Eogan in the chariot. She had sworn that two men alive in the world together would never have her.

'This is good, Derdriu,' Conchobor said. 'Between me and Eogan you are a sheep eyeing two rams.'

A big block of stone was in front of her. She let her head be driven against the stone, and made a mass of fragments of it, and she was dead.

TALIESIN

[LATE 6TH CENTURY]

The Battle of Argoed Llwyfain

Translated from the Old Welsh by Anthony Conran

There was a great battle Saturday morning
From when the sun rose until it grew dark.
The fourfold hosts of Fflamddwyn invaded.
Goddau and Rheged gathered in arms,
Summoned from Argoed as far as Arfynydd—
They might not delay by so much as a day.

With a great swaggering din, Fflamddwyn shouted,
'Are these the hostages come? Are they ready?'
To him then Owain, scourge of the eastlands,
'They've not come, no! They're not, nor shall they be ready! 10
And a whelp of Coel would indeed be afflicted
Did he have to give any man as a hostage!'

And Urien, lord of Erechwydd, shouted,
'If they would meet us now for our kinsfolk,
High on the hilltop let's raise our ramparts,
Carry our faces over the shield rims,
Raise up our spears, men, over our heads
And set upon Fflamddwyn in the midst of his hosts
And slaughter him, ay, and all that go with him!'

There was many a corpse beside Argoed Llwyfain; 20
  From warriors ravens grew red,
And with their leader a host attacked.
For a whole year I shall sing to their triumph.

And when I'm grown old, with death hard upon me,
I'll not be happy save to praise Urien.

Death Song for Owain ab Urien

Translated from the Old Welsh by Anthony Conran

God, consider the soul's need
  Of Owain son of Urien!
Rheged's prince, secret in loam:
  No shallow work, to praise him!

A strait grave, a man much praised,
  His whetted spear the wings of dawn:

That lord of bright Llwyfenydd,
Where is his peer?

Reaper of enemies; strong of grip;
One kind with his fathers; 10
Owain, to slay Fflamddwyn,
Thought it no more than sleep.

Sleepeth the wide host of England
With light in their eyes,
And those that had not fled
Were braver than were wise.

Owain dealt them doom
As the wolves devour sheep;
That warrior, bright of harness,
Gave stallions for the bard. 20

Though he hoarded wealth like a miser,
For his soul's sake he gave it.
God, consider the soul's need
Of Owain son of Urien.

ANEIRIN

[EARLY 7TH CENTURY]

FROM

The Gododdin

Translated from the Old Welsh by Joseph P. Clancy

Men went to Catraeth, keen their war-band.
Pale mead their portion, it was poison.
Three hundred under orders to fight.
And after celebration, silence.
Though they went to churches for shriving,
True is the tale, death confronted them.

Men went to Catraeth at dawn:
Their high spirits lessened their life-spans.
They drank mead, gold and sweet, ensnaring;
For a year the minstrels were merry. 10
Red their swords, let the blades remain
Uncleansed, white shields and four-sided spearheads,
Before Mynyddawg Mwynfawr's men.

. . .

Gododdin's war-band on shaggy mounts,
Steeds the hue of swans, in full harness,
Fighting for Eidin's treasure and mead.

On Mynyddawg's orders
Shields were battered to bits,
Sword-blades descended
On pallid cheeks. 20
They loved combat, broad line of attack:
They bore no disgrace, men who stood firm.

Man's mettle, youth's years,
Courage for combat:
Swift thick-maned stallions
Beneath a fine stripling's thighs,
Broad lightweight buckler
On a slim steed's crupper,
Glittering blue blades,
Gold-bordered garments. 30
Never will there be
Bitterness between us:
Rather I make of you
Song that will praise you.
The blood-soaked field
Before the marriage-feast,
Foodstuff for crows
Before the burial.
A dear comrade, Owain;
Vile, his cover of crows. 40
Ghastly to me that ground,
Slain, Marro's only son.

. . .

Warriors rose together, formed ranks.
With a single mind they assaulted.
Short their lives, long their kinsmen long for them.
Seven times their sum of English they slew:
Their fighting turned wives into widows;
Many a mother with tear-filled eyelids.

Because of wine-feast and mead-feast they charged,
Men famed in fighting, heedless of life. 50
Bright ranks around cups, they joined to feast.
Wine and mead and bragget, these were theirs.
From Mynyddawg's banquet, grief-stricken my mind,
Many I lost of my true comrades.
Of three hundred champions who charged on Catraeth,
It is tragic, but one man came back.

. . .

Three hundred golden-torqued men attacked:
Contending for the land was cruel.
Although they were being slain, they slew;
Till the world ends, they will be honoured. 60
Of the comrades who went together,
Tragic, but a single man returned.

ANONYMOUS

[7TH CENTURY]

Widsith, the Minstrel

Translated from the Old English by Charles W. Kennedy

Widsith spoke, his word-hoard unlocked,
Who most had traveled of men on earth
Among many peoples, and prospered in hall
With splendid treasure. His forebears sprang
From the Myrging tribe. In his earliest travels
With Ealhild he went, fair weaver of peace,
From the East out of Angle to Eormanric's home,
Who was prince of the Goths, fierce breaker of pledges.
Many a tale he told of his travels:
"Much have I learned of the rulers of men! 10
A prince must live by custom and law,
Each after other ruling the realm,
Who wishes his power to prosper and thrive.
Of them was Hwala a while the best,
And Alexander greatest of all
Of the race of men; he prospered most
Of all I have heard of over the earth.
Attila ruled the Huns, Eormanric the Goths,
Becca the Banings, Gifica the Burgundians;
Caesar ruled the Greeks, Caelic the Finns, 20
Hagena the Holmrygir, Heoden the Glomman;
Witta ruled the Swabians, Wada the Hælsings,
Meaca the Myrgings, Mearchealf the Hundings;
Theodoric ruled the Franks, Thyle the Rondings,
Breca the Brondings, Billing the Wernas;
Oswine ruled the Eowas, Gefwulf the Jutes,
Finn, son of Folcwalda, the Frisian folk.
Sighere longest governed the Sea Danes;
Hnæf ruled the Hocings, Helm the Wulfings....
"I have fared through many a foreign land 30
Over spacious earth, knowing weal and woe,
Bereft of my kinsmen, far from my folk,
Widely wandering over the world.
Many a song and many a story
I can tell in the mead-hall, recounting to men
How princes and nobles graced me with gifts.
I was with the Huns, and with the Hrethgoths,
With Swedes I was, and with Geats, and with South-Danes....
"I was in Italy also with Ælfwine
Who of all mankind as ever I heard 40
Had the easiest hand in the earning of praise,
And the readiest heart in the giving of rings,
The shining jewels, Eadwine's son....

"I was with Eormanric, and all the while
The king of the Goths was gracious and kind.
He gave me a ring, the ruler of cities,
Worth six hundred sceats counted in cost
Of shilling pieces of smelted gold.
To Eadgils I gave it, my gracious lord,
To requite his kindness when home I came. 50
For the lord of the Myrgings had granted me land,
The holding and home of my father before me.
"And Ealhild also gave me a ring,
The fair folk-queen, the daughter of Eadwine.
To many a people her praise I published
Whenever in song my task was to tell
Of a gold-decked queen most kind under heaven,
Best and most gracious in giving of gifts.
There Scilling and I in echoing strains
Before our dear lord lifted our songs. 60
Loud to the harp the lay resounded;
And many a noble who knew aright
Said he had never heard better song." . . .
Widely they wander, as Fate may guide,
The strolling singers who roam the world
Telling their need, returning their thanks,
And always finding, or south or north,
Some great one skilled in knowledge of song
Who is open-handed in giving of gifts,
Who seeks for honor and strives for fame 70
Till all things vanish, light and life
Passing together. He who earns praise
Has under heaven the greatest glory.

ANONYMOUS
[8TH CENTURY–10TH CENTURY]

Cotton MS. Maxims

Translated from the Old English by Charles W. Kennedy

King must rule kingdom. Cities are seen from afar,
Cunning handwork of giants who inhabit this earth,
Wondrous work of wallstones. Wind is swiftest in air,
Thunder at times is loudest. Great are the glories of Christ.
Wyrd is mightiest, winter is coldest,
Spring is frostiest, longest cold;
Summer is sunniest, sun is hottest,
Autumn most glorious giving to man
The fruits of the year that God brings forth.

Truth is clearest,   treasure is dearest,   10
Gold most precious,   age most wise;
Years make prudent   who suffers long.
Woe is close clinging;   clouds drift by.
Good companions   encourage a prince
To glory in battle   and giving of gifts.
Eorl must have courage;   edge against helm
Survives the sword-play.   Hawk on glove
The wild one waits.   Wolf in the forest,
Beastly lone-goer.   Boar in the wood,
Mighty of tusk.   Good man at home   20
Harvests renown.   Spear for the hand
Garnished with gold.   Gem for the ring
Ample and wide.   Stream in the waves
Shall mix with the sea.   Mast for the ship,
The sailyard fastened.   Sword on lap,
A lordly blade.   In mound dragon bideth,
Old guarder of gold.   Fish in water
Must spawn its kind.   King in the hall
Must hand out rings.   Bear on the heath
Roams old and fierce.   River from hills   30
Flows down flood-gray.   Army must be gathered,
A band of the brave.   Faith for an eorl,
Wisdom for man.   Woods of the world
Must bud with blossoms.   Hills of earth
Must gleam with green.   God in heaven
Is judge of deeds.   Door in the hall
Is mouth of the building.   Boss on shield
Is the fingers' guard.   Birds above
Soar in the air.   In deep pool salmon
Swims with the trout.   Showers from heaven   40
Mingled with wind   sweep over the world.
Thief goes in darkness.   Ghost on the fen
Is alone in the land.   In secret a woman
Will haste to her friend   if she has no wish
To prosper with husband,   purchased with rings.
Sea shall be salt;   water and air
Shall flow in floods   around all lands.
Cattle on earth   shall bear and bring forth.
Stars shine bright   by the Maker's command.
Good against evil;   youth against age;   50
Life against death;   light against darkness;
Army against army;   foe against foe;
Hostile with hostile   shall always fight
Contending for land   and avenging wrongs.
A wise man must ponder   this world's strife;
Outlaw must hang,   paying the price
That he wronged mankind.
God alone knows
Where the soul passes   and all the spirits
Who after their death-days   go before God.

They abide their judgment in the Father's bosom; 60
Their future fate is secret and hid;
God alone knows, the Saviour Father.
And none returns ever, hither under roof,
To tell men for truth of God's decree,
Or the home of the victor-folk, where He Himself dwells.

ANONYMOUS

[8TH CENTURY–10TH CENTURY]

The Wanderer

Translated from the Old English by Charles W. Kennedy

Oft to the Wanderer, weary of exile,
Cometh God's pity, compassionate love,
Though woefully toiling on wintry seas
With churning oar in the icy wave,
Homeless and helpless he fled from Fate.
Thus saith the Wanderer mindful of misery,
Grievous disasters, and death of kin:
"Oft when the day broke, oft at the dawning,
Lonely and wretched I wailed my woe.
No man is living, no comrade left, 10
To whom I dare fully unlock my heart.
I have learned truly the mark of a man
Is keeping his counsel and locking his lips,
Let him think what he will! For, woe of heart
Withstandeth not Fate; a failing spirit
Earneth no help. Men eager for honor
Bury their sorrow deep in the breast.
"So have I also, often in wretchedness
Fettered my feelings, far from my kin,
Homeless and hapless, since days of old, 20
When the dark earth covered my dear lord's face,
And I sailed away with sorrowful heart,
Over wintry seas, seeking a gold-lord,
If far or near lived one to befriend me
With gift in the mead-hall and comfort for grief.
"Who bears it, knows what a bitter companion,
Shoulder to shoulder, sorrow can be,
When friends are no more. His fortune is exile,
Not gifts of fine gold; a heart that is frozen,
Earth's winsomeness dead. And he dreams of the hall-men, 30
The dealing of treasure, the days of his youth,
When his lord bade welcome to wassail and feast.
But gone is that gladness, and never again
Shall come the loved counsel of comrade and king.

"Even in slumber his sorrow assaileth,
And, dreaming he claspeth his dear lord again,
Head on knee, hand on knee, loyally laying,
Pledging his liege as in days long past.
Then from his slumber he starts lonely-hearted,
Beholding gray stretches of tossing sea, 40
Sea-birds bathing, with wings outspread,
While hailstorms darken, and driving snow.
Bitterer then is the bane of his wretchedness,
The longing for loved one: his grief is renewed.
The forms of his kinsmen take shape in the silence;
In rapture he greets them; in gladness he scans
Old comrades remembered. But they melt into air
With no word of greeting to gladden his heart.
Then again surges his sorrow upon him;
And grimly he spurs his weary soul 50
Once more to the toil of the tossing sea.
"No wonder therefore, in all the world,
If a shadow darkens upon my spirit
When I reflect on the fates of men—
How one by one proud warriors vanish
From the halls that knew them, and day by day
All this earth ages and droops unto death.
No man may know wisdom till many a winter
Has been his portion. A wise man is patient,
Not swift to anger, nor hasty of speech, 60
Neither too weak, nor too reckless, in war,
Neither fearful nor fain, nor too wishful of wealth,
Nor too eager in vow— ere he know the event.
A brave man must bide when he speaketh his boast
Until he know surely the goal of his spirit.
"A wise man will ponder how dread is that doom
When all this world's wealth shall be scattered and waste
As now, over all, through the regions of earth,
Walls stand rime-covered and swept by the winds.
The battlements crumble, the wine-halls decay; 70
Joyless and silent the heroes are sleeping
Where the proud host fell by the wall they defended.
Some battle launched on their long, last journey;
One a bird bore o'er the billowing sea;
One the gray wolf slew; one a grieving eorl
Sadly gave to the grave's embrace.
The Warden of men hath wasted this world
Till the sound of music and revel is stilled,
And these giant-built structures stand empty of life.
"He who shall muse on these mouldering ruins, 80
And deeply ponder this darkling life,
Must brood on old legends of battle and bloodshed,
And heavy the mood that troubles his heart:
'Where now is the warrior? Where is the war horse?
Bestowal of treasure, and sharing of feast?
Alas! the bright ale-cup, the byrny-clad warrior,

The prince in his splendor —those days are long sped
In the night of the past, as if they never had been!'
And now remains only, for warriors' memorial,
A wall wondrous high with serpent shapes carved. 90
Storms of ash-spears have smitten the eorls,
Carnage of weapon, and conquering Fate.
"Storms now batter these ramparts of stone;
Blowing snow and the blast of winter
Enfold the earth; night-shadows fall
Darkly lowering, from the north driving
Raging hail in wrath upon men.
Wretchedness fills the realm of earth,
And Fate's decrees transform the world.
Here wealth is fleeting, friends are fleeting, 100
Man is fleeting, maid is fleeting;
All the foundation of earth shall fail!"

Thus spake the sage in solitude pondering.
Good man is he who guardeth his faith.
He must never too quickly unburden his breast
Of its sorrow, but eagerly strive for redress;
And happy the man who seeketh for mercy
From his heavenly Father, our Fortress and Strength.

ANONYMOUS

[8TH CENTURY–10TH CENTURY]

The Ruin

Translated from the Old English by Charles W. Kennedy

Wondrous this masonry wasted by Fate!
Giant-built battlements shattered and broken!
The roofs are in ruin, the towers are wrecked,
The frost-covered bastions battered and fallen.
Rime whitens mortar; the cracking walls
Have sagged and toppled, weakened by Time.
The clasp of earth and the clutch of the grave
Grip the proud builders, long perished and gone,
While a hundred generations have run.
Hoary with lichen and ruddy of hue 10
This wall has outlasted, unshaken by storm,
Reign after reign; now ravaged and wrecked
The lofty arch is leveled in ruin. . . .
Firmly the builder laid the foundations,
Cunningly bound them with iron bands;
Stately the palaces, splendid the baths,
Towers and pinnacles pointing on high;
Many a mead-hall rang with their revelry,

Many a court with the clangor of arms,
Till Fate the all-leveling laid them low. 20
A pestilence rose and corpses were rife,
And death laid hold on the warrior-host.
Then their bulwarks were broken, their fortresses fell,
The hands to restore them were helpless and still.
Desolate now are the courts, and the dome,
With arches discolored, is stripped of its tiles.
Where of old once the warrior walked in his pride,
Gleaming with gold and wanton with wine,
Splendidly shining in glittering mail,
The structure lies fallen and scattered in ruin. 30
Around him he saw a treasure of silver,
Riches of pearl and precious stones,
In a shining city of far-flung sway.
There stood courts of stone, with a gushing spring
Of boiling water in welling floods,
And a wall embosomed in gleaming embrace
The spot where the hot baths burst into air.

ANONYMOUS
[8TH CENTURY–10TH CENTURY]

The Wife's Lament

Translated from the Old English by Charles W. Kennedy

A song I sing of sorrow unceasing,
The tale of my trouble, the weight of my woe,
Woe of the present, and woe of the past,
Woe never-ending of exile and grief,
But never since girlhood greater than now.
First, the pang when my lord departed,
Far from his people, beyond the sea;
Bitter the heartache at break of dawn,
The longing for rumor in what far land
So weary a time my loved one tarried. 10
Far I wandered then, friendless and homeless,
Seeking for help in my heavy need.
With secret plotting his kinsmen purposed
To wedge us apart, wide worlds between,
And bitter hate. I was sick at heart.
Harshly my lord bade lodge me here.
In all this land I had few to love me,
Few that were loyal, few that were friends.
Wherefore my spirit is heavy with sorrow
To learn my beloved, my dear man and mate 20
Bowed by ill-fortune and bitter in heart,
Is masking his purpose and planning a wrong.
With blithe hearts often of old we boasted

That nought should part us save death alone;
All that has failed and our former love
Is now as if it had never been!
Far or near where I fly there follows
The hate of him who was once so dear.
In this forest-grove they have fixed my abode
Under an oak in a cavern of earth, 30
An old cave-dwelling of ancient days,
Where my heart is crushed by the weight of my woe.
Gloomy its depths and the cliffs that o'erhang it,
Grim are its confines with thorns overgrown—
A joyless dwelling where daily the longing
For an absent loved one brings anguish of heart.
Lovers there are who may live their love,
Joyously keeping the couch of bliss,
While I in my earth-cave under the oak
Pace to and fro in the lonely dawn. 40
Here must I sit through the summer-long day,
Here must I weep in affliction and woe;
Yet never, indeed, shall my heart know rest
From all its anguish, and all its ache,
Wherewith life's burdens have brought me low.
Ever man's years are subject to sorrow,
His heart's thoughts bitter, though his bearing be blithe;
Troubled his spirit, beset with distress—
Whether all wealth of the world be his lot,
Or hunted by Fate in a far country 50
My beloved is sitting soul-weary and sad,
Swept by the storm, and stiff with the frost,
In a wretched cell under rocky cliffs
By severing waters encircled about—
Sharpest of sorrows my lover must suffer
Remembering always a happier home.
Woeful his fate whose doom is to wait
With longing heart for an absent love.

ANONYMOUS

[8TH CENTURY–10TH CENTURY]

The Husband's Message

Translated from the Old English by Charles W. Kennedy

In the sand I grew, by the rocky sea-wall
Near the surf firm-rooted in fixed abode.
Few were the men who beheld my refuge
In the lonely reaches beside the sea;
Only the dark wave at the day's dawning

Sportively bound me   in flowing embrace.
Little I weened   that I, who was voiceless,
Should ever hold speech,   or discourse at the feast.
That is a marvel   amazing the mind
Of those who know little   of such-like things   10
How a knife's sharp edge,   and a strong hand's skill,
Steel's keen point,   and man's cunning craft,
Purposely planned me,   assigned me my part
To give thee a message   that we two may grasp,
To utter it boldly,   yet so that no other
May publish abroad   the words I report.
To thine ear only   I tell the tale
How first as a sapling   I flourished and grew. . . .
In the hold of a ship,   o'er the salt sea-streams,
Where my liege lord sent me   oft I have sailed.   20
Now in a bark's bosom   here am I borne.
Now shalt thou learn   of my lord's loyal love;
His enduring affection   I dare to affirm.
Lady ring-laden,   he bade me implore thee,
Who carved this wood,   that thou call to mind
The pledges you plighted   before you were parted,
While still in the same land   together you shared
A lordly home   and the rapture of love,
Before a feud   drove him far from his folk.
He it is bids me   eagerly urge   30
When from the hill slope,   out of the wood,
Thou hearest the cuckoo   plaintively calling,
Haste thee to ship   on the tossing sea.
Let no living man, then,   delay thee in sailing,
Stay thee in leaving   or stop thee in flight.
Spread thy sail   on the home of the sea-mew,
Take seat in thy galley,   and steer away south
To where o'er the sea-lane   thy lover awaits.
No greater bliss   could his heart engage
In all the world   —'twas his word to me—   40
If God the Almighty   would grant you two
To dwell together   and deal out gifts,
To tried retainers,   of treasure and rings.
He hath abundance   of beaten gold. . . .
Now in a far land   my lord holds in fee
Home and fair fields   though here once of old,
Fated and lonely,   need forced him to flight,
Launching his ship   on the lanes of the deep,
Churning the sea-streams   in haste to escape.
Now his troubles are over   and all distress,   50
He lacks no wealth   that the heart may wish,
Jewels and horses   and joys of the hall,
Nor any fair treasure   that earth can afford.
O Prince's daughter!   if he may possess thee,
To add to the pledges   ye plighted of old,
Here S and R   together I set,

EA, W, and D, by oath to declare
That while life lasts so long he'll be faithful
To lover's vow and to true love's pledge
Which often ye plighted in days of old. 60

BEOWULF

[8TH CENTURY]

The English epic poem *Beowulf* is renowned as one of the great world stories. Coming down to us in a unique manuscript written by two West Saxon scribes of the late tenth century, it probably dates in written composition from some time in the eighth century, either around 700 C.E. in Northumbria, or later in the century in Mercia. Its original compiler was possibly a minor religious officer; this would help explain the many Christian overlays in the poem. On the other hand, the two stories that make up the epic are earlier in origin, probably dating back, like *Widsith, the Minstrel,* to northern Europe in the fifth or sixth century.

THE ORAL POETIC TRADITION AND CHRISTIAN ELEMENTS IN *BEOWULF*

Beowulf belongs principally to the oral poetic tradition common to many early societies. It may be compared in structure to such distant works as the Sumerian epic *Gilgamesh* and the Greek Homeric epics *The Iliad* and *The Odyssey.* Like them, it includes a hero who is stronger and wiser than other men, but fated by mortality; his adversaries, also superhuman in strength, who ultimately come from monster stories; a social ethic that emphasizes the desirability of winning good repute among men and the moral and ethical status of the lord as protector; and a belief system in which no one is secure before fate and no one knows what lies after death.

The oral poetic tradition and the Christian elements that were later introduced into the poem coexist uneasily in the text. Viewed historically, *Beowulf* reflects three distinct cultures: the ancient folk culture of monsters and demons that existed among the Scandinavians and north Germans before the Germanic invasions of England; the Germanic culture brought to England by the invasions of the sixth century, marked by its practicality and high ethical standards; and the Christian culture of the written composer of the poem, reflecting the influence of the British conversion missions of the seventh century and emphasizing such nonpagan ideals as humility. One of the most obvious clashes between the Germanic and Christian cultures comes at the end of the poem, when Beowulf is eulogized in both his Christian and pagan aspects: "mildest, most gentle, most eager for fame."

In its reception by audiences over the last several centuries, *Beowulf* has been acclaimed first of all for its rich, dramatic storytelling, which emerges once scholarly questions concerning the readings of difficult passages are cleared up. It has also been viewed as a treasure-trove of mythological lore, primarily German and Scandinavian, but also Celtic (suggesting early influence from European sources or later Welsh or Irish influence). When comparative mythology was in vogue at the beginning of the twentieth century, scholars found analogues to the dragon and monster stories in many mythologies. More recently, British scholars have sought to show how much Christianity influences the poem, not only in passing references but in its deep structure. Finally, the ethical and moral nature of the poem has received attention, especially as we reexamine so-called primitive stories and rediscover how pertinent many of their concerns still are to us in modern times.

Examining the Narrative

Because of the circumnavigations of the epic story, a certain amount of summary may be in order. Particularly important for our purposes are themes and incidents touching on the nature of Beowulf, his retainers, and the other actors in the story, including the monsters and the dragon.

In the first half of the story, the young Geatish lord Beowulf hears of the tribulations experienced in the great hall named Heorot, presided over by King Hrothgar in the land of the Danes. The hall has been subjected for twelve years to bloodthirsty raids by Grendel, a human-like monster who kills and eats many of the lords. Against the advice of his uncle Hygelac, Beowulf sets sail with a small band of supporters from his home in southern Sweden to come to the aid of the friendly Danes. According to the conventions of hospitality of the day, the heroes are warmly greeted by the lords of Heorot, with the exception of Unferth, who insults Beowulf by reflecting on his prowess. After getting the better of Unferth in an exchange of remarks and vowing to fight Grendel hand-to-hand, Beowulf retires for the night with his retinue in Heorot hall.

Overnight, Grendel arrives and feasts on one of the men. Beowulf grapples with him, and finally succeeds in tearing off the monster's arm at the shoulder. The mortally wounded Grendel flees; in the morning, Beowulf and his men track his bloody footprints back to the pool where he lives, and where he has now sunk and died. The survivors at Heorot celebrate Beowulf's feat of glory with a great feast, and his deed is also memorialized in song. But the same night, another monster invades the hall. This female monster attacks and kills Aeschere, the friend of King Hrothgar, leading Beowulf once more to pledge his vengeance. This time the battle is fought at the evil pool, underwater, with strong suggestions of the kind of descent into the underworld found in other oral epic stories. Beowulf finally kills Grendel's mother with one of her own great swords, purging the evil of Heorot's hall.

At the celebration of the second killing, Beowulf meets the young Danish hero Wealhtheow and his bride Freawaru, daughter of King Hrothgar, and is given many rich gifts. Accepting the farewell of the old king, he returns to the kingdom of the Geats, where he shares his riches with King Hygelac and his wife Hygd. He is in turn given a great hall and land of his own, and the first part of the epic ends.

Noteworthy in this long portion of the poem, two-thirds of its total length, is the attention given to the deeds of valor of the energetic young hero and his service for the good of his Danish companions. Beowulf is the exemplary young warrior, a rising hero who is justly celebrated in the dazzling, if endangered, court of Heorot Hall. A far different world is depicted in the final episode, in which the world of the aging Beowulf's own people is in eclipse and the heroic age itself is coming to an end.

The second part begins with a swift account of the declining fortunes of the Geats over the next fifty years. The poet also introduces the dragon and tells of his discovery of the ancient treasure, abandoned by a royal house 300 years before. The dragon, disturbed by the theft of a drinking cup by a fugitive from the court of Beowulf, vows revenge and, flying by night, burns down the dwellings of Beowulf's followers as well as Beowulf's stronghold. Beowulf, though aware of his own coming destruction, pursues the dragon. He takes twelve retainers, including the slave who stole the flagon; the allusion to the Twelve Disciples and Judas is intentional. Beowulf tells his men at the entrance to the dragon's earthen barrow to await the outcome of the battle. He gives his battle cry and the dragon emerges from the cavern.

When Beowulf encounters the dragon, his old sword Naegling and his other defenses fail him. Seeing this, his retainers all flee into the forest, but the youthful Wiglaf, who rebukes his comrades for deserting their master, tells Beowulf to take heart, and joins the battle. Finally the dragon bites Beowulf on the neck, giving him a death-wound. Wiglaf strikes the dragon a mortal blow, though he is burned in the process, and Beowulf cuts the monster in two. Beowulf feels the poison taking effect and commands Wiglaf to bring the treasure to him where he lies outside the cavern. He rejoices in having won it for his people and commands Wiglaf to build a burial mound on which he shall be cremated. He gives Wiglaf his collar, ring, helmet, and byrny, calling him the last of his royal line. The cowardly retainers return and Wiglaf again rebukes them. A messenger brings back to the people the story of Beowulf's death, mingling it with forebodings about the future; he fears the Geats' destruction at the hands of the Swedish enemy. The Geats prepare both Beowulf and the treasure for cremation and final burial. Wiglaf gives the oratory over the barrow. The cremation accomplished, the people build a great mound over the site. It is fitting, the poet concludes, to mourn such a great king.

Whereas the first long portion of the poem emphasized the youthfulness of the hero and his society, the episode of the dragon fight shows all such societies in decay. The elegiac tone of this portion of the work is unmistakable. At the same time, in this portion the Christian flavoring is the strongest. If one world is in decline, by inference another is on the rise. The dying Beowulf is the best possible hero of the older type–what Christian theologians called the "virtuous pagan," honorable among men but born too soon for salvation.

The form of the poem presents some difficulties to the reader in any existing translation. Verse translations that keep the alliterative, four-stress rhythm of the original lines are preferable, although they may present seemingly incomprehensible passages from time to time. This translation, by Charles W. Kennedy, is by no means the newest, but it preserves faithfully some of the feel (as well as the difficulty) of the original. More than most poetry, *Beowulf* richly repays a close reading of the text in collaboration with the instructor and the notes.

Suggested Readings

Anyone wishing to consult the Anglo-Saxon text should see Frederick Klaeber's *Beowulf and the Fight at Finnsburg*, 3rd ed., (1950), with its excellent introduction and notes; a more modern edition is C. L. Wrenn's *Beowulf and the Finnsburg Fragment*, revised by W. F. Bolton (1973). Our translation, Charles W. Kennedy's *Beowulf: The Oldest English Epic* (1940), contains a useful introduction for the general reader. See also Frederick Rebsamen's *Beowulf: A Verse Translation* (1992), a recent effort with a lively introduction and a brief bibliography. General backgrounds to the poem may be found in the systematic modern study by Arthur G. Brodeur, *The Art of Beowulf* (1959), and the comprehensive review of scholarship, R. W. Chambers's *Beowulf: An Introduction to the Poem*, 3rd ed., revised by C. L. Wrenn (1958). Other important studies include J. R. R. Tolkien, "*Beowulf*: The Monsters and the Critics" (1936), available in many collections; Dorothy Whitelock, *The Audience of Beowulf* (1951); and Kenneth Sisam, *The Structure of Beowulf* (1965).

Beowulf

Translated by Charles W. Kennedy

The Danish Court and the Raids of Grendel

Lo! we have listened to many a lay
Of the Spear-Danes' fame, their splendor of old,
Their mighty princes, and martial deeds!
Many a mead-hall Scyld, son of Sceaf,
Snatched from the forces of savage foes.[1]
From a friendless foundling, feeble and wretched,
He grew to a terror as time brought change.
He throve under heaven in power and pride
Till alien peoples beyond the ocean
Paid toll and tribute. A good king he! 10
To him thereafter an heir was born,
A son of his house, whom God had given
As stay to the people; God saw the distress
The leaderless nation had long endured.
The Giver of glory, the Lord of life,
Showered fame on the son of Scyld;
His name was honored, Beowulf known,[2]
To the farthest dwellings in Danish lands.
So must a young man strive for good
With gracious gifts from his father's store, 20
That in later seasons, if war shall scourge,
A willing people may serve him well.
'Tis by earning honor a man must rise
In every state. Then his hour struck,
And Scyld passed on to the peace of God.
As their leader had bidden, whose word was law
In the Scylding realm which he long had ruled,
His loving comrades carried him down
To the shore of ocean; a ring-prowed ship,
Straining at anchor and sheeted with ice, 30
Rode in the harbor, a prince's pride.
Therein they laid him, their well-loved lord,
Their ring-bestower, in the ship's embrace,
The mighty prince at the foot of the mast
Amid much treasure and many a gem
From far-off lands. No lordlier ship
Have I ever heard of, with weapons heaped,
With battle-armor, with bills and byrnies.[3]

---

[1]Scyld arrived as a child on the shores of the Danes and became their king; at death he was sent out to sea with a rich hoard of treasure. "Mystery surrounds him, signalizing a being of supernatural, divine origin." (Klaeber, *Beowulf,* 121).

[2]This Beowulf, son of the legendary Scyld the Dane, is not to be confused with the young hero of the poem, a Geat who comes to support the Danes in their need.

[3]We are better able to visualize this burial description due to the discovery of so-called ship burials (cenotaphs or memorials) in recent times, especially the Sutton Hoo burial discovered in 1939. The treasure described here includes bills (swords) and byrnies (breast coverings of ringed metal).

On the ruler's breast lay a royal treasure
As the ship put out on the unknown deep. 40
With no less adornment they dressed him round,
Or gift of treasure, than once they gave
Who launched him first on the lonely sea
While still but a child. A golden standard
They raised above him, high over head,
Let the wave take him on trackless seas.
Mournful their mood and heavy their hearts;
Nor wise man nor warrior knows for a truth
Unto what haven that cargo came.
Then Beowulf ruled o'er the Scylding realm, 50
Beloved and famous, for many a year—
The prince, his father, had passed away—
Till, firm in wisdom and fierce in war,
The mighty Healfdene held the reign,
Ruled, while he lived, the lordly Scyldings.
Four sons and daughters were seed of his line,
Heorogar and Hrothgar,[4] leaders of hosts,
And Halga, the good. I have also heard
A daughter was Onela's consort and queen,
The fair bed-mate of the Battle-Scylfing. 60
To Hrothgar was granted glory in war,
Success in battle; retainers bold
Obeyed him gladly; his band increased
To a mighty host. Then his mind was moved
To have men fashion a high-built hall,
A mightier mead-hall than man had known,
Wherein to portion to old and young
All goodly treasure that God had given,
Save only the folk-land, and lives of men.
His word was published to many a people 70
Far and wide o'er the ways of earth
To rear a folk-stead richly adorned;
The task was speeded, the time soon came
That the famous mead-hall was finished and done.
To distant nations its name was known,
The Hall of the Hart; and the king kept well
His pledge and promise to deal out gifts,
Rings at the banquet. The great hall rose
High and horn-gabled, holding its place
Till the battle-surge of consuming flame 80
Should swallow it up; the hour was near
That the deadly hate of a daughter's husband
Should kindle to fury and savage feud.[5]
Then an evil spirit who dwelt in the darkness
Endured it ill that he heard each day
The din of revelry ring through the hall,

---

[4]Hrothgar is one of three sons of Healfdene, in the third generation after Scyld.

[5]The poet describes the burning of Heorot Hall just after he has told of its construction. The burning is the result of a feud between the Danes and the Heathobards that occurs despite Hrothgar's attempts at diplomacy.

The sound of the harp, and the scop's sweet song.[6]
A skillful bard sang the ancient story
Of man's creation; how the Maker wrought
The shining earth with its circling waters; 90
In splendor established the sun and moon
As lights to illumine the land of men;
Fairly adorning the fields of earth
With leaves and branches; creating life
In every creature that breathes and moves.
So the lordly warriors lived in gladness,
At ease and happy, till a fiend from hell
Began a series of savage crimes.
They called him Grendel, a demon grim
Haunting the fen-lands, holding the moors, 100
Ranging the wastes, where the wretched wight
Made his lair with the monster kin;
He bore the curse of the seed of Cain
Whereby God punished the grievous guilt
Of Abel's murder. Nor ever had Cain
Cause to boast of that deed of blood;
God banished him far from the fields of men;
Of his blood was begotten an evil brood,
Marauding monsters and menacing trolls,
Goblins and giants who battled with God 110
A long time. Grimly He gave them reward!
Then at the nightfall the fiend drew near
Where the timbered mead-hall towered on high,
To spy how the Danes fared after the feast.
Within the wine-hall he found the warriors
Fast in slumber, forgetting grief,
Forgetting the woe of the world of men.
Grim and greedy the gruesome monster,
Fierce and furious, launched attack,
Slew thirty spearmen asleep in the hall, 120
Sped away gloating, gripping the spoil,
Dragging the dead men home to his den.
Then in the dawn with the coming of daybreak
The war-might of Grendel was widely known.
Mirth was stilled by the sound of weeping;
The wail of the mourner awoke with day.
And the peerless hero, the honored prince,
Weighed down with woe and heavy of heart,
Sat sorely grieving for slaughtered thanes,[7]
As they traced the track of the cursed monster. 130
From that day onward the deadly feud
Was a long-enduring and loathsome strife.
Not longer was it than one night later
The fiend returning renewed attack

---

[6]Grendel, an evil spirit, is disturbed by the rejoicing in Heorot. The rejoicing is a song of the Creation, while Grendel is descended from Cain. Cf. Genesis 6:4, "There were giants in the earth in those days, and also afterward, when the sons of God had relations with the daughters of men, who bore children to them."

[7]Liege-lords under feudal authority.

With heart firm-fixed in the hateful war,
Feeling no rue for the grievous wrong.
'Twas easy thereafter to mark the men
Who sought their slumber elsewhere afar,
Found beds in the bowers, since Grendel's hate
Was so boldly blazoned in baleful signs. 140
He held himself at a safer distance
Who escaped the clutch of the demon's claw.
So Grendel raided and ravaged the realm,
One against all, in an evil war
Till the best of buildings was empty and still.
'Twas a weary while! Twelve winters' time
The lord of the Scyldings had suffered woe,
Sore affliction and deep distress.
And the malice of Grendel, in mournful lays,
Was widely sung by the sons of men, 150
The hateful feud that he fought with Hrothgar—
Year after year of struggle and strife,
An endless scourging, a scorning of peace
With any man of the Danish might.
No strength could move him to stay his hand,
Or pay for his murders; the wise knew well
They could hope for no halting of savage assault.
Like a dark death-shadow the ravaging demon,
Night-long prowling the misty moors,
Ensnared the warriors, wary or weak. 160
No man can say how these shades of hell
Come and go on their grisly rounds.
With many an outrage, many a crime,
The fierce lone-goer, the foe of man,
Stained the seats of the high-built house,
Haunting the hall in the hateful dark.
But throne or treasure he might not touch,
Finding no favor or grace with God.
Great was the grief of the Scylding leader,
His spirit shaken, while many a lord 170
Gathered in council considering long
In what way brave men best could struggle
Against these terrors of sudden attack.
From time to time in their heathen temples
Paying homage they offered prayer
That the Slayer of souls would send them succor
From all the torment that troubled the folk.
Such was the fashion and such the faith
Of their heathen hearts that they looked to hell,
Not knowing the Maker, the mighty Judge, 180
Nor how to worship the Wielder of glory,
The Lord of heaven, the God of hosts.[8]
Woe unto him who in fierce affliction

[8] Although Hrothgar is a devout Christian, it appears that his principal knights, when faced with danger, return to pagan practices.

Shall plunge his soul in the fiery pit
With no hope of mercy or healing change;
But well with the soul that at death seeks God,
And finds his peace in his Father's bosom.
 The son of Healfdene was heavy-hearted,
Sorrowfully brooding in sore distress,
Finding no help in a hopeless strife; 190
Too bitter the struggle that stunned the people,
The long oppression, loathsome and grim.

The Coming of Beowulf

 Then tales of the terrible deeds of Grendel
Reached Hygelac's thane in his home with the Geats; [9]
Of living strong men he was the strongest,
Fearless and gallant and great of heart.
He gave command for a goodly vessel
Fitted and furnished; he fain would sail
Over the swan-road[10] to seek the king
Who suffered so sorely for need of men. 200
And his bold retainers found little to blame
In his daring venture, dear though he was;
They viewed the omens, and urged him on.
Brave was the band he had gathered about him,
Fourteen stalwarts seasoned and bold,
Seeking the shore where the ship lay waiting,
A sea-skilled mariner sighting the landmarks.
Came the hour of boarding; the boat was riding
The waves of the harbor under the hill.
The eager mariners mounted the prow; 210
Billows were breaking, sea against sand.
In the ship's hold snugly they stowed their trappings,
Gleaming armor and battle-gear;
Launched the vessel, the well-braced bark,
Seaward bound on a joyous journey.
Over breaking billows, with bellying sail
And foamy beak, like a flying bird
The ship sped on, till the next day's sun
Showed sea-cliffs shining, towering hills
And stretching headlands. The sea was crossed, 220
The voyage ended, the vessel moored.
And the Weder people waded ashore
With clatter of trappings and coats of mail;
Gave thanks to God that His grace had granted
Sea-paths safe for their ocean-journey.
 Then the Scylding coast-guard watched from the sea-cliff
Warriors bearing their shining shields,

---

[9]Beowulf, the hero of the poem, the son of Ecgtheow, is the thane of his uncle Hygelac, the ruler of the Geats or Weders. The Geats flourished in Sweden in the sixth century C.E.

[10]Swan-road, a beautiful kenning (poetic metaphor) for the sea.

Their gleaming war-gear, ashore from the ship.
His mind was puzzled, he wondered much
What men they were. On his good horse mounted, 230
Hrothgar's thane made haste to the beach,
Boldly brandished his mighty spear
With manful challenge: 'What men are you,
Carrying weapons and clad in steel,
Who thus come driving across the deep
On the ocean-lanes in your lofty ship?
Long have I served as the Scylding outpost,
Held watch and ward at the ocean's edge
Lest foreign foemen with hostile fleet
Should come to harry our Danish home, 240
And never more openly sailed to these shores
Men without password, or leave to land.
I have never laid eyes upon earl on earth
More stalwart and sturdy than one of your troop,
A hero in armor; no hall-thane he
Tricked out with weapons, unless looks belie him,
And noble bearing. But now I must know
Your birth and breeding, nor may you come
In cunning stealth upon Danish soil.
You distant-dwellers, you far sea-farers, 250
Hearken, and ponder words that are plain:
'Tis best you hasten to have me know
Who your kindred and whence you come.'
The lord of the seamen gave swift reply,
The prince of the Weders unlocked his word-hoard:[11]
'We are sprung of a strain of the Geatish stock,
Hygelac's comrades and hearth-companions.
My father was famous in many a folk-land,
A leader noble, Ecgtheow his name!
Many a winter went over his head 260
Before death took him from home and tribe;
Well nigh every wise man remembers him well
Far and wide on the ways of earth.
With loyal purpose we seek your lord,
The prince of your people, great Healfdene's son.
Be kindly of counsel; weighty the cause
That leads us to visit the lord of the Danes;
Nor need it be secret, as far as I know!
You know if it's true, as we've heard it told,
That among the Scyldings some secret scather, 270
Some stealthy demon in dead of night,
With grisly horror and fiendish hate
Is spreading unheard-of havoc and death.
Mayhap I can counsel the good, old king
What way he can master the merciless fiend,
If his coil of evil is ever to end

[11] Another kenning, suggesting the speech of a poet or important leader.

And feverish care grow cooler and fade—
Or else ever after his doom shall be
Distress and sorrow while still there stands
This best of halls on its lofty height.' 280
Then from the saddle the coast-guard spoke,
The fearless sentry: 'A seasoned warrior
Must know the difference between words and deeds,
If his wits are with him. I take your word
That your band is loyal to the lord of the Scyldings.
Now go your way with your weapons and armor,
And I will guide you; I'll give command
That my good retainers may guard your ship,
Your fresh-tarred floater, from every foe,
And hold it safe in its sandy berth, 290
Till the curving prow once again shall carry
The loved man home to the land of the Geat.
To hero so gallant shall surely be granted
To come from the swordplay sound and safe.'
Then the Geats marched on; behind at her mooring,
Fastened at anchor, their broad-beamed boat
Safely rode on her swinging cable.
Boar-heads glittered on glistening helmets
Above their cheek-guards, gleaming with gold;[12]
Bright and fire-hardened the boar held watch 300
Over the column of marching men.
Onward they hurried in eager haste
Till their eyes caught sight of the high-built hall,
Splendid with gold, the seat of the king,
Most stately of structures under the sun;
Its light shone out over many a land.
The coast-guard showed them the shining hall,
The home of heroes; made plain the path;
Turned his horse; gave tongue to words:
'It is time to leave you! The mighty Lord 310
In His mercy shield you and hold you safe
In your bold adventure. I'll back to the sea
And hold my watch against hostile horde.'

Beowulf's Welcome at Hrothgar's Court

The street had paving of colored stone;
The path was plain to the marching men.
Bright were their byrnies, hard and hand-linked;
In their shining armor the chain-mail sang
As the troop in their war-gear tramped to the hall.
The sea-weary sailors set down their shields,
Their wide, bright bucklers along the wall, 320

---

[12]The helmets are fashioned in the shape of a boar's head. The boar was sacred to the Old Norse deity Freyr, and is without doubt a magical symbol of protection.

And sank to the bench. Their byrnies rang.
Their stout spears stood in a stack together
Shod with iron and shaped of ash.
'Twas a well-armed troop! Then a stately warrior
Questioned the strangers about their kin:
'Whence come you bearing your burnished shields,
Your steel-gray harness and visored helms,
Your heap of spears? I am Hrothgar's herald,
His servant-thane. I have never seen strangers,
So great a number, of nobler mien. 330
Not exiles, I ween, but high-minded heroes
In greatness of heart have you sought out Hrothgar.'
Then bold under helmet the hero made answer,
The lord of the Weders, manful of mood,
Mighty of heart: 'We are Hygelac's men,
His board-companions; Beowulf is my name.
I will state my mission to Healfdene's son,
The noble leader, your lordly prince,
If he will grant approach to his gracious presence.'
And Wulfgar answered, the Wendel prince, 340
Renowned for merit in many a land,
For war-might and wisdom: 'I will learn the wish
Of the Scylding leader, the lord of the Danes,
Our honored ruler and giver of rings,
Concerning your mission, and soon report
The answer our leader thinks good to give.'
He swiftly strode to where Hrothgar sat
Old and gray with his earls about him;
Crossed the floor and stood face to face
With the Danish king; he knew courtly custom. 350
Wulfgar saluted his lord and friend:
'Men from afar have fared to our land
Over ocean's margin—men of the Geats,
Their leader called Beowulf—seeking a boon,
The holding of parley, my prince, with thee.
O gracious Hrothgar, refuse not the favor!
In their splendid war-gear they merit well
The esteem of earls; he's a stalwart leader
Who led this troop to the land of the Danes.'
Hrothgar spoke, the lord of the Scyldings: 360
'Their leader I knew when he was still a lad.
His father was Ecgtheow; Hrethel the Geat
Gave him in wedlock his only daughter.
Now is their son come, keen for adventure,
Finding his way to a faithful friend.
Sea-faring men who have voyaged to Geatland
With gifts of treasure as token of peace,
Say that his hand-grip has thirty men's strength.
God, in His mercy, has sent him to save us—
So springs my hope—from Grendel's assaults. 370
For his great courage I'll load him with gifts!
Make haste now, marshal the men to the hall,
And give them welcome to Danish ground.'

Then to the door went the well-known warrior,
Spoke from the threshold welcoming words:
'The Danish leader, my lord, declares
That he knows your kinship; right welcome you come,
You stout sea-rovers, to Danish soil.
Enter now, in your shining armor
And vizored helmets, to Hrothgar's hall. 380
But leave your shields and the shafts of slaughter
To wait the issue and weighing of words.'
Then the bold one rose with his band round him,
A splendid massing of mighty thanes;
A few stood guard as the Geat gave bidding
Over the weapons stacked by the wall.
They followed in haste on the heels of their leader
Under Heorot's roof. Full ready and bold
The helmeted warrior strode to the hearth;
Beowulf spoke; his byrny glittered, 390
His war-net woven by cunning of smith:
'Hail! King Hrothgar! I am Hygelac's thane,
Hygelac's kinsman. Many a deed
Of honor and daring I've done in my youth.
This business of Grendel was brought to my ears
On my native soil. The sea-farers say
This best of buildings, this boasted hall,
Stands dark and deserted when sun is set,
When darkening shadows gather with dusk.
The best of my people, prudent and brave, 400
Urged me, King Hrothgar, to seek you out;
They had in remembrance my courage and might.
Many had seen me come safe from the conflict,
Bloody from battle; five foes I bound
Of the giant kindred, and crushed their clan.[13]
Hard-driven in danger and darkness of night
I slew the nicors that swam the sea,[14]
Avenged the woe they had caused the Weders,
And ended their evil—they needed the lesson!
And now with Grendel, the fearful fiend, 410
Single-handed I'll settle the strife!
Prince of the Danes, protector of Scyldings,
Lord of nations, and leader of men,
I beg one favor—refuse me not,
Since I come thus faring from far-off lands—
That I may alone with my loyal earls,
With this hardy company, cleanse Hart-Hall.
I have heard that the demon in proud disdain
Spurns all weapons; and I too scorn—
May Hygelac's heart have joy of the deed— 420
To bear my sword, or sheltering shield,

---

[13]"The fight against giants, five of whom were bound, seems reminiscent of folk-tales" (Klaeber, *Beowulf*, 143).

[14]Sea-serpents. See 1.549 and ff.

Or yellow buckler, to battle the fiend.
With hand-grip only I'll grapple with Grendel;
Foe against foe I'll fight to the death,
And the one who is taken must trust to God's grace!
The demon, I doubt not, is minded to feast
In the hall unaffrighted, as often before,
On the force of the Hrethmen, the folk of the Geats.
No need then to bury the body he mangles!
If death shall call me, he'll carry away 430
My gory flesh to his fen-retreat
To gorge at leisure and gulp me down,
Soiling the marshes with stains of blood.
There'll be little need longer to care for my body!
If the battle slays me, to Hygelac send
This best of corselets that covers my breast,
Heirloom of Hrethel, and Wayland's work,
Finest of byrnies. Fate goes as Fate must!'[15]

Hrothgar spoke, the lord of the Scyldings:
'Deed of daring and dream of honor 440
Bring you, friend Beowulf, knowing our need!
Your father once fought the greatest of feuds,
Laid Heatholaf low, of the Wylfing line;
And the folk of the Weders refused him shelter
For fear of revenge. Then he fled to the South-Danes,
The Honor-Scyldings beyond the sea.
I was then first governing Danish ground,
As a young lad ruling the spacious realm,
The home-land of warriors. Heorogar was dead,
The son of Healfdene no longer living, 450
My older brother, and better than I!
Thereafter by payment composing the feud,
O'er the water's ridge I sent to the Wylfing
Ancient treasure; he swore me oaths![16]
It is sorrow sore to recite to another
The wrongs that Grendel has wrought in the hall,
His savage hatred and sudden assaults.
My war-troop is weakened, my hall-band is wasted;
Fate swept them away into Grendel's grip.
But God may easily bring to an end 460
The ruinous deeds of the ravaging foe.
Full often my warriors over their ale-cups
Boldly boasted, when drunk with beer,
They would bide in the beer-hall the coming of battle,
The fury of Grendel, with shining swords.
Then in the dawn, when the daylight strengthened,
The hall stood reddened and reeking with gore,
Bench-boards wet with the blood of battle;

---

[15]Beowulf's speech is purely conventional, stressing his prowess, his eagerness for fame, and his acquiescence to Fate as the final arbiter. Many such speeches will follow.

[16]Hrothgar as a younger man helped negotiate a truce, ending a feud with the Geats and king Ecgtheow, Beowulf's father. Friendly relations have existed between the Danes and the Geats since that time.

And I had the fewer of faithful fighters,
Beloved retainers, whom Death had taken. 470
Sit now at the banquet, unbend your mood,
Speak of great deeds as your heart may spur you!'
Then in the beer-hall were benches made ready
For the Geatish heroes. Noble of heart,
Proud and stalwart, they sat them down
And a beer-thane served them; bore in his hands
The patterned ale-cup, pouring the mead,
While the scop's sweet singing was heard in the hall.
There was joy of heroes, a host at ease,
A welcome meeting of Weder and Dane. 480

Unferth Taunts Beowulf

Then out spoke Unferth, Ecglaf's son,
Who sat at the feet of the Scylding lord,
Picking a quarrel—for Beowulf's quest,
His bold sea-voyaging, irked him sore;
He bore it ill that any man other
In all the earth should ever achieve
More fame under heaven than he himself:
'Are you the Beowulf that strove with Breca
In a swimming match in the open sea,
Both of you wantonly tempting the waves, 490
Risking your lives on the lonely deep
For a silly boast? No man could dissuade you,
Nor friend nor foe, from the foolhardy venture
Of ocean-swimming; with outstretched arms
You clasped the sea-stream, measured her streets,
With plowing shoulders parted the waves.
The sea-flood boiled with its wintry surges,
Seven nights you toiled in the tossing sea;
His strength was the greater, his swimming the stronger!
The waves upbore you at break of day 500
To the stretching beach of the Battle-Ræmas;
And Breca departed, beloved of his people,
To the land of the Brondings, the beauteous home,
The stronghold fair, where he governed the folk,
The city and treasure; Beanstan's son
Made good his boast to the full against you!
Therefore, I ween, worse fate shall befall,
Stout as you are in the struggle of war,
In deeds of battle, if you dare to abide
Encounter with Grendel at coming of night.'[17] 510
Beowulf spoke, the son of Ecgtheow:
'My good friend Unferth, addled with beer

[17]Unferth's attack on Beowulf rests on two points: Beowulf 's "foolhardy venture" and the fact that he lost the contest. The name Unferth means "mar-peace," and this figure has often been compared to the "wicked counselors" of Norse legend.

Much have you made of the deeds of Breca!
I count it true that I had more courage,
More strength in swimming than any other man.
In our youth we boasted—we were both of us boys—
We would risk our lives in the raging sea.
And we made it good! We gripped in our hands
Naked swords, as we swam in the waves,
Guarding us well from the whales' assault. 520
In the breaking seas he could not outstrip me,
Nor would I leave him. For five nights long
Side by side we strove in the waters
Till racing combers wrenched us apart,
Freezing squalls, and the falling night,
And a bitter north wind's icy blast.
Rough were the waves; the wrath of the sea-fish
Was fiercely roused; but my firm-linked byrny,
The gold-adorned corselet that covered my breast,
Gave firm defense from the clutching foe. 530
Down to the bottom a savage sea-beast
Fiercely dragged me and held me fast
In a deadly grip; none the less it was granted me
To pierce the monster with point of steel.
Death swept it away with the swing of my sword.
  The grisly sea-beasts again and again
Beset me sore; but I served them home
With my faithful blade as was well-befitting.
They failed of their pleasure to feast their fill
Crowding round my corpse on the ocean-bottom! 540
Bloody with wounds, at the break of day,
They lay on the sea-beach slain with the sword.
No more would they cumber the mariner's course
On the ocean deep. From the east came the sun,
Bright beacon of God, and the seas subsided;
I beheld the headlands, the windy walls.
Fate often delivers an undoomed earl
If his spirit be gallant! And so I was granted
To slay with the sword-edge nine of the nicors.
I have never heard tell of more terrible strife 550
Under dome of heaven in darkness of night,
Nor of man harder pressed on the paths of ocean.
But I freed my life from the grip of the foe
Though spent with the struggle. The billows bore me,
The swirling currents and surging seas,
To the land of the Finns. And little I've heard
Of any such valiant adventures from you!
Neither Breca nor you in the press of battle
Ever showed such daring with dripping swords—
Though I boast not of it! But you stained your blade 560
With blood of your brothers, your closest of kin;
And for that you'll endure damnation in hell,
Sharp as you are! I say for a truth,
Son of Ecglaf, never had Grendel

Wrought such havoc and woe in the hall,
That horrid demon so harried your king,
If your heart were as brave as you'd have men think![18]
But Grendel has found that he never need fear
Revenge from your people, or valiant attack
From the Victor-Scyldings; he takes his toll, 570
Sparing none of the Danish stock.
He slays and slaughters and works his will
Fearing no hurt at the hands of the Danes!
But soon will I show him the stuff of the Geats,
Their courage in battle and strength in the strife;
Then let him who may go bold to the mead-hall
When the next day dawns on the dwellings of men,
And the sun in splendor shines warm from the south.'
Glad of heart was the giver of treasure,
Hoary-headed and hardy in war; 580
The lordly leader had hope of help
As he listened to Beowulf's bold resolve.

There was revel of heroes and high carouse,
Their speech was happy; and Hrothgar's queen,
Of gentle manners, in jewelled splendor
Gave courtly greeting to all the guests.
The high-born lady first bore the beaker
To the Danish leader, lord of the land,
Bade him be blithe at the drinking of beer;
Beloved of his people, the peerless king 590
Joined in the feasting, had joy of the cup.
Then to all alike went the Helming lady
Bearing the beaker to old and young,
Till the jewelled queen with courtly grace
Paused before Beowulf, proffered the mead.
She greeted the Geat and to God gave thanks,
Wise of word, that her wish was granted;
At last she could look to a hero for help,
Comfort in evil. He took the cup,
The hardy warrior, at Wealhtheow's hand 600
And, eager for battle, uttered his boast;
Beowulf spoke, the son of Ecgtheow:
'I had firm resolve when I set to sea
With my band of earls in my ocean-ship,
Fully to work the will of your people
Or fall in the struggle slain by the foe.
I shall either perform deeds fitting an earl
Or meet in this mead-hall the coming of death!'
Then the woman was pleased with the words he uttered,
The Geat-lord's boast; the gold-decked queen 610
Went in state to sit by her lord.

[18] Beowulf's response is particularly vehement; the fact that there is no response suggests the rhetorical nature of this boasting.

Beowulf Slays Grendel

In the hall as of old were brave words spoken,
There was noise of revel; happy the host
Till the son of Healfdene would go to his rest.
He knew that the monster would meet in the hall
Relentless struggle when light of the sun
Was dusky with gloom of the gathering night,
And shadow-shapes crept in the covering dark,
Dim under heaven. The host arose.
Hrothgar graciously greeted his guest, 620
Gave rule of the wine-hall, and wished him well,
Praised the warrior in parting words:
'Never to any man, early or late,
Since first I could brandish buckler and sword,
Have I trusted this ale-hall save only to you!
Be mindful of glory, show forth your strength,
Keep watch against foe! No wish of your heart
Shall go unfulfilled if you live through the fight.'
Then Hrothgar withdrew with his host of retainers,
The prince of the Scyldings, seeking his queen, 630
The bed of his consort. The King of Glory
Had established a hall-watch, a guard against Grendel,
Dutifully serving the Danish lord,
The land defending from loathsome fiend.
The Geatish hero put all his hope
In his fearless might and the mercy of God!
He stripped from his shoulders the byrny of steel,
Doffed helmet from head; into hand of thane
Gave inlaid iron, the best of blades;
Bade him keep well the weapons of war. 640
Beowulf uttered a gallant boast,
The stalwart Geat, ere he sought his bed:
'I count myself nowise weaker in war
Or grapple of battle than Grendel himself.
Therefore I scorn to slay him with sword,
Deal deadly wound, as I well might do!
Nothing he knows of a noble fighting,
Of thrusting and hewing and hacking of shield,
Fierce as he is in the fury of war.
In the shades of darkness we'll spurn the sword 650
If he dares without weapon to do or to die.
And God in His wisdom shall glory assign,
The ruling Lord, as He deems it right.'
Then the bold in battle bowed down to his rest,
Cheek pressed pillow; the peerless thanes
Were stretched in slumber round their lord.
Not one had hope of return to his home,
To the stronghold or land where he lived as a boy.
For they knew how death had befallen the Danes,
How many were slain as they slept in the wine-hall. 660
But the wise Lord wove them fortune in war,

Gave strong support to the Weder people;
They slew their foe by the single strength
Of a hero's courage. The truth is clear,
God rules forever the race of men.
  Then through the shades of enshrouding night
The fiend came stealing; the archers slept
Whose duty was holding the horn-decked hall—
Though one was watching—full well they knew
No evil demon could drag them down 670
To shades under ground if God were not willing.
But the hero watched awaiting the foe,
Abiding in anger the issue of war.
  From the stretching moors, from the misty hollows,
Grendel came creeping, accursed of God,
A murderous ravager minded to snare
Spoil of heroes in high-built hall.
Under clouded heavens he held his way
Till there rose before him the high-roofed house,
Wine-hall of warriors gleaming with gold. 680
Nor was it the first of his fierce assaults
On the home of Hrothgar; but never before
Had he found worse fate or hardier hall-thanes!
Storming the building he burst the portal,
Though fastened of iron, with fiendish strength;
Forced open the entrance in savage fury
And rushed in rage o'er the shining floor.
A baleful glare from his eyes was gleaming
Most like to a flame. He found in the hall
Many a warrior sealed in slumber, 690
A host of kinsmen. His heart rejoiced;
The savage monster was minded to sever
Lives from bodies ere break of day,
To feast his fill of the flesh of men.
But he was not fated to glut his greed
With more of mankind when the night was ended!
  The hardy kinsman of Hygelac waited
To see how the monster would make his attack.
The demon delayed not, but quickly clutched
A sleeping thane in his swift assault, 700
Tore him in pieces, bit through the bones,
Gulped the blood, and gobbled the flesh,
Greedily gorged on the lifeless corpse,
The hands and the feet. Then the fiend stepped nearer,
Sprang on the Sea-Geat lying outstretched,
Clasping him close with his monstrous claw.
But Beowulf grappled and gripped him hard,
Struggled up on his elbow; the shepherd of sins
Soon found that never before had he felt
In any man other in all the earth 710
A mightier hand-grip; his mood was humbled,
His courage fled; but he found no escape!
He was fain to be gone; he would flee to the darkness,

The fellowship of devils. Far different his fate
From that which befell him in former days!
The hardy hero, Hygelac's kinsman,
Remembered the boast he had made at the banquet;
He sprang to his feet, clutched Grendel fast,
Though fingers were cracking, the fiend pulling free.
The earl pressed after; the monster was minded 720
To win his freedom and flee to the fens.
He knew that his fingers were fast in the grip
Of a savage foe. Sorry the venture,
The raid that the ravager made on the hall.
  There was din in Heorot. For all the Danes,
The city-dwellers, the stalwart Scyldings,
That was a bitter spilling of beer!
The walls resounded, the fight was fierce,
Savage the strife as the warriors struggled.
The wonder was that the lofty wine-hall 730
Withstood the struggle, nor crashed to earth,
The house so fair; it was firmly fastened
Within and without with iron bands
Cunningly smithied; though men have said
That many a mead-bench gleaming with gold
Sprang from its sill as the warriors strove.
The Scylding wise men had never weened
That any ravage could wreck the building,
Firmly fashioned and finished with bone,
Or any cunning compass its fall, 740
Till the time when the swelter and surge of fire
Should swallow it up in a swirl of flame.
  Continuous tumult filled the hall;
A terror fell on the Danish folk
As they heard through the wall the horrible wailing,
The groans of Grendel, the foe of God
Howling his hideous hymn of pain,
The hell-thane shrieking in sore defeat.
He was fast in the grip of the man who was greatest
Of mortal men in the strength of his might, 750
Who would never rest while the wretch was living,
Counting his life-days a menace to man.
  Many an earl of Beowulf brandished
His ancient iron to guard his lord,
To shelter safely the peerless prince.
They had no knowledge, those daring thanes,
When they drew their weapons to hack and hew,
To thrust to the heart, that the sharpest sword,
The choicest iron in all the world,
Could work no harm to the hideous foe. 760
On every sword he had laid a spell,
On every blade; but a bitter death
Was to be his fate; far was the journey
The monster made to the home of fiends.

Then he who had wrought such wrong to men,
With grim delight as he warred with God,
Soon found that his strength was feeble and failing
In the crushing hold of Hygelac's thane.
Each loathed the other while life should last!
There Grendel suffered a grievous hurt, 770
A wound in the shoulder, gaping and wide;
Sinews snapped and bone-joints broke,
And Beowulf gained the glory of battle.
Grendel, fated, fled to the fens,
To his joyless dwelling, sick unto death.
He knew in his heart that his hours were numbered,
His days at an end. For all the Danes
Their wish was fulfilled in the fall of Grendel.
The stranger from far, the stalwart and strong,
Had purged of evil the hall of Hrothgar, 780
And cleansed of crime; the heart of the hero
Joyed in the deed his daring had done.
The lord of the Geats made good to the East-Danes
The boast he had uttered; he ended their ill,
And all the sorrow they suffered long
And needs must suffer—a foul offense.
The token was clear when the bold in battle
Laid down the shoulder and dripping claw—
Grendel's arm—in the gabled hall!

The Joy of the Danes and the Lay of Sigemund

When morning came, as they tell the tale, 790
Many a warrior hastened to hall,
Folk-leaders faring from far and near
Over wide-running ways, to gaze at the wonder,
The trail of the demon. Nor seemed his death
A matter of sorrow to any man
Who viewed the tracks of the vanquished monster
As he slunk weary-hearted away from the hall,
Doomed and defeated and marking his flight
With bloody prints to the nicors' pool.
The crimson currents bubbled and heaved 800
In eddying reaches reddened with gore;
The surges boiled with the fiery blood.
But the monster had sunk from the sight of men.
In that fenny covert the cursed fiend
Not long thereafter laid down his life,
His heathen spirit; and hell received him.
Then all the comrades, the old and young,
The brave of heart, in a blithesome band
Came riding their horses home from the mere.
Beowulf's prowess was praised in song; 810
And many men stated that south or north,

Over all the world, or between the seas,
Or under the heaven, no hero was greater,
More worthy of rule. But no whit they slighted
The gracious Hrothgar, their good old king.
Time and again they galloped their horses,
Racing their roans where the roads seemed fairest;
Time and again a gleeman chanted,
A minstrel mindful of saga and lay.
He wove his words in a winsome pattern, 820
Hymning the burden of Beowulf's feat,
Clothing the story in skillful verse.

All tales he had ever heard told he sang of Sigemund's glory,
Deeds of the Wælsing forgotten, his weary roving and wars,
Feuds and fighting unknown to men, save Fitela only,
Tales told by uncle to nephew when the two were companions,
What time they were bosom-comrades in battle and bitter strife.
Many of monster blood these two had slain with the sword-edge;
Great glory Sigemund gained that lingered long after death,
When he daringly slew the dragon that guarded the hoard of gold. 830
Under the ancient rock the warrior ventured alone,
No Fitela fighting beside him; but still it befell
That his firm steel pierced the worm, the point stood fast in the wall;
The dragon had died the death! And the hero's daring
Had won the treasure to have and to hold as his heart might wish.
Then the Wælsing loaded his sea-boat, laid in the breast of the ship
Wondrous and shining treasure; the worm dissolved in the heat.[19]
Sigemund was strongest of men in his deeds of daring,
Warrior's shield and defender, most famous in days of old
After Heremod's might diminished, his valor and vigor in war, 840
Betrayed in the land of the Jutes to the hands of his foemen, and slain.
Too long the surges of sorrow swept over his soul; in the end
His life was a lingering woe to people and princes.
In former days his fate was mourned by many a warrior
Who had trusted his lord for protection from terror and woe,
Had hoped that the prince would prosper, wielding his father's wealth,
Ruling the tribe and the treasure, the Scylding city and home.
Hygelac's kinsman had favor and friendship of all mankind,
But the stain of sin sank deep into Heremod's heart.[20]

Time and again on their galloping steeds 850
Over yellow roads they measured the mile-paths;
Morning sun mounted the shining sky
And many a hero strode to the hall,

[19] The stories of Sigemund and his companion Fitela go back to Norse legend, especially the *Volsungasaga*, where Fitela is actually the son of Sigemund and helps him destroy the hall of their bitter enemy. The story of the dragon-fight may belong more properly to Sigfrid, another son of Sigemund, in Norse and Germanic legend; here it foreshadows Beowulf's own desperate encounter with the dragon at the end of the poem.

[20] The story of Heremod is intended to show how a great warrior can turn into a bad king, a burden to his people who comes to a miserable end.

Stout of heart, to behold the wonder.
The worthy ruler, the warder of treasure,
Set out from the bowers with stately train;
The queen with her maidens paced over the mead-path.
Then spoke Hrothgar; hasting to hall
He stood at the steps, stared up at the roof
High and gold-gleaming; saw Grendel's hand: 860
'Thanks be to God for this glorious sight!
I have suffered much evil, much outrage from Grendel,
But the God of glory works wonder on wonder.
I had no hope of a haven from sorrow
While this best of houses stood badged with blood,
A woe far-reaching for all the wise
Who weened that they never could hold the hall
Against the assaults of devils and demons.
But now with God's help this hero has compassed
A deed our cunning could no way contrive. 870
Surely that woman may say with truth,
Who bore this son, if she still be living,
Our ancient God showed favor and grace
On her bringing-forth! O best of men,
I will keep you, Beowulf, close to my heart
In firm affection; as son to father
Hold fast henceforth to this foster-kinship.
You shall know not want of treasure or wealth
Or goodly gift that your wish may crave,
While I have power. For poorer deeds 880
I have granted guerdon,[21] and graced with honor
Weaker warriors, feebler in fight.
You have done such deeds that your fame shall flourish
Through all the ages! God grant you still
All goodly grace as He gave before.'
Beowulf spoke, the son of Ecgtheow:
'By the favor of God we won the fight,
Did the deed of valor, and boldly dared
The might of the monster. I would you could see
The fiend himself lying dead before you! 890
I thought to grip him in stubborn grasp
And bind him down on the bed of death,
There to lie straining in struggle for life,
While I gripped him fast lest he vanish away.
But I might not hold him or hinder his going
For God did not grant it, my fingers failed.
Too savage the strain of his fiendish strength!
To save his life he left shoulder and claw,
The arm of the monster, to mark his track.
But he bought no comfort; no whit thereby 900
Shall the wretched ravager racked with sin,
The loathsome spoiler, prolong his life.

[21]Bounteous rewards.

A deep wound holds him in deadly grip,
In baleful bondage; and black with crime
The demon shall wait for the day of doom
When the God of glory shall give decree.'
  Then slower of speech was the son of Ecglaf,
More wary of boasting of warlike deeds,
While the nobles gazed at the grisly claw,
The fiend's hand fastened by hero's might 910
On the lofty roof. Most like to steel
Were the hardened nails, the heathen's hand-spurs,
Horrible, monstrous; and many men said
No tempered sword, no excellent iron,
Could have harmed the monster or hacked away
The demon's battle-claw dripping with blood.

The Feast and the Lay of Finnsburg

  In joyful haste was Heorot decked
And a willing host of women and men
Gaily dressed and adorned the guest-hall.
Splendid hangings with sheen of gold 920
Shone on the walls, a glorious sight
To eyes that delight to behold such wonders.
The shining building was wholly shattered
Though braced and fastened with iron bands;
Hinges were riven; the roof alone
Remained unharmed when the horrid monster,
Foul with evil, slunk off in flight,
Hopeless of life. It is hard to flee
The touch of death, let him try who will;
Necessity urges the sons of men, 930
The dwellers on earth, to their destined place
Where the body, bound in its narrow bed,
After the feasting is fast in slumber.
  Soon was the time when the son of Healfdene
Went to the wine-hall; he fain would join
With happy heart in the joy of feasting.
I never have heard of a mightier muster
Of proud retainers round their prince.
All at ease they bent to the benches,
Had joy of the banquet; their kinsmen bold, 940
Hrothgar and Hrothulf, happy of heart,
In the high-built hall drank many a mead-cup.
The hall of Hrothgar was filled with friends;
No treachery yet had troubled the Scyldings.
Upon Beowulf, then, as a token of triumph,
Hrothgar bestowed a standard of gold,
A banner embroidered, a byrny and helm.
In sight of many, a costly sword
Before the hero was borne on high;

Beowulf drank of many a bowl. 950
No need for shame in the sight of heroes
For gifts so gracious! I never have heard
Of many men dealing in friendlier fashion,
To others on ale-bench, richer rewards,
Four such treasures fretted with gold!
On the crest of the helmet a crowning wreath,
Woven of wire-work, warded the head
Lest tempered swordblade, sharp from the file,
Deal deadly wound when the shielded warrior
Went forth to battle against the foe. 960
Eight horses also with plated headstalls
The lord of heroes bade lead into hall;
On one was a saddle skillfully fashioned
And set with jewels, the battle-seat
Of the king himself, when the son of Healfdene
Would fain take part in the play of swords;
Never in fray had his valor failed,
His kingly courage, when corpses were falling.
And the prince of the Ingwines gave all these gifts
To the hand of Beowulf, horses and armor; 970
Bade him enjoy them! With generous heart
The noble leader, the lord of heroes,
Rewarded the struggle with steeds and with treasure,
So that none can belittle, and none can blame,
Who tells the tale as it truly happened.
Then on the ale-bench to each of the earls
Who embarked with Beowulf, sailing the sea-paths,
The lord of princes dealt ancient heirlooms,
Gift of treasure, and guerdon of gold
To requite his slaughter whom Grendel slew, 980
As he would have slain others, but all-wise God
And the hero's courage had conquered Fate.[22]
The Lord ruled over the lives of men
As He rules them still. Therefore understanding
And a prudent spirit are surely best!
He must suffer much of both weal and woe
Who dwells here long in these days of strife.
Then song and revelry rose in the hall;
Before Healfdene's leader the harp was struck
And hall-joy wakened; the song was sung, 990
Hrothgar's gleeman rehearsed the lay
Of the sons of Finn when the terror befell them:

Hnæf of the Scyldings, the Half-Dane, fell in the Frisian slaughter;
Nor had Hildeburh cause to acclaim the faith of the Jutish folk,
Blameless, bereft of her brothers in battle, and stripped of her sons

---

[22]One of many passages in the poem where the Christian God is seen to triumph over the older conception of Fate.

Who fell overcome by their fate and wounded with spears![23]
Not for nothing Hoc's daughter bewailed death's bitter decree,
In the dawn under morning skies, when she saw the slaughter of kinsmen
In the place where her days had been filled with the fairest delights of the world.
Finn's thanes were slain in the fight, save only a few; 1000
Nor could he do battle with Hengest or harry his shattered host;
And the Frisians made terms with the Danes, a truce, a hall for their dwelling,
A throne, and a sharing of rights with the sons of the Jutes,
And that Finn, the son of Folcwalda, each day would honor the Danes,
The host of Hengest, with gifts, with rings and guerdon of gold,
Such portion of plated treasure as he dealt to the Frisian folk
When he gladdened their hearts in the hall. So both were bound by the truce.
And Finn swore Hengest with oaths that were forceful and firm
He would rightfully rule his remnant, follow his council's decree,
And that no man should break the truce, or breach it by word or by will, 1010
Nor the lordless in malice lament they were fated to follow
The man who had murdered their liege; and, if ever a Frisian
Fanned the feud with insolent speech, the sword should avenge it.
  Then a funeral pyre was prepared, and gold was drawn from the hoard,
The best of the Scylding leaders was laid on the bier;
In the burning pile was a gleaming of blood-stained byrnies,
The gilded swine and the boar-helm hard from the hammer,
Many a warrior fated with wounds and fallen in battle.
And Hildeburh bade that her son be laid on the bier of Hnæf,
His body consumed in the surging flame at his uncle's shoulder. 1020
Beside it the lady lamented, singing her mournful dirge.
The hero was placed on the pyre; the greatest of funeral flames
Rolled with a roar to the skies at the burial barrow.
Heads melted and gashes gaped, the mortal wounds of the body,
Blood poured out in the flames; the fire, most greedy of spirits,
Swallowed up all whom battle had taken of both their peoples.
Their glory was gone! The warriors went to their homes,
Bereft of their friends, returning to Friesland, to city and stronghold.
  Then Hengest abode with Finn all the slaughter-stained winter,
But his heart longed ever for home, though he could not launch on the sea 1030
His ring-stemmed ship, for the billows boiled with the storm,
Strove with the wind, and the winter locked ocean in bonds of ice;
Till a new Spring shone once more on the dwellings of men,
The sunny and shining days which ever observe their season.
The winter was banished afar, and fair the bosom of earth.
Then the exile longed to be gone, the guest from his dwelling,
But his thoughts were more on revenge than on voyaging over the wave,
Plotting assault on the Jutes, renewal of war with the sword.

---

[23] The Finn episode in *Beowulf* is summarized: A tribe of Danes under king Hnaef and his chief thane, Hengest, visit the Frisian court of Finn, son of Folcwalda. Fighting breaks out and many are killed on both sides, including Hnaef. After a truce is declared, angry Danish soldiers under Hengest kill Finn and rout his followers. Between the two parties stands Hildeburh, wife of Finn and sister of Hnaef. The poet's sympathy is with the Danes. The entire narrative is Germanic in its ethical orientation: its praise of the *comitatus*, its glorification of battle and of the tragic conflict of duties. Hildeburh, the queen of Finn, may be compared with Wealhtheow, the queen of Hrothgar, who serves the visiting Geats in the great hall of Heorot as the lay is sung.

So he spurned not the naked hint when Hunlafing laid in his lap
The battle-flasher, the best of blades, well known to the Jutes! 1040
In his own home death by the sword befell Finn, the fierce-hearted,
When Guthlaf and Oslaf requited the grim attack,
The woe encountered beyond the sea, the sorrow they suffered,
Nor could bridle the restive spirits within their breasts!
Then the hall was reddened with blood and bodies of foemen,
Finn killed in the midst of his men, and the fair queen taken.
The Scylding warriors bore to their ships all treasure and wealth,
Such store as they found in the home of Finn of jewels and gems.
And the noble queen they carried across the sea-paths,
Brought her back to the Danes, to her own dear people. 1050

So the song was sung, the lay recited,
The sound of revelry rose in the hall.
Stewards poured wine from wondrous vessels;
And Wealhtheow, wearing a golden crown,
Came forth in state where the two were sitting,
Courteous comrades, uncle and nephew,
Each true to the other in ties of peace.
Unferth, the orator, sat at the feet
Of the lord of the Scyldings; and both showed trust
In his noble mind, though he had no mercy 1060
On kinsmen in swordplay. The Scylding queen spoke:
'My sovereign lord, dispenser of treasure,
Drink now of this flagon, have joy of the feast!
Speak to the Geats, O gold-friend of men,
In winning words as is well-befitting;
Be kind to the Geat-men and mindful of gifts
From the gold you have garnered from near and far.
You have taken as son, so many have told me,
This hardy hero. Heorot is cleansed,
The gleaming gift-hall. Rejoice while you may 1070
In lavish bounty, and leave to your kin
People and kingdom when time shall come,
Your destined hour, to look on death.
I know the heart of my gracious Hrothulf,
That he'll safely shelter and shield our sons
When you leave this world, if he still is living.
I know he will favor with gracious gifts
These boys of ours, if he bears in mind
The many honors and marks of love
We bestowed upon him while he still was a boy.'[24] 1080
She turned to the bench where her boys were sitting,
Hrethric and Hrothmund, the sons of heroes,
The youth together; there the good man sat,
Beowulf of the Geats, beside the two brothers.
Then the cup was offered with gracious greeting,

[24]Hrothulf is the son of Halga and nephew of Hrothgar. The whole passage is ironic; the audience knows that after the death of Hrothgar, Hrothulf will commit treachery against the family.

And seemly presents of spiraled gold,
A corselet, and rings, and the goodliest collar
Of all that ever were known on earth.
I have never heard tell of a worthier treasure
In the hoarding of heroes beneath the sky 1090
Since Hama bore off to the shining city
The Brosings' jewel, setting and gems,
Fled from Eormanric's cruel craft
And sought the grace of eternal glory.
Hygelac, the Geat, grandson of Swerting
Wore the ring in the last of his raids,
Guarding the spoil under banner in battle,
Defending the treasure. Overtaken by Fate,
In the flush of pride he fought with the Frisians
And met disaster. The mighty prince 1100
Carried the ring o'er the cup of the waves,
The precious jewel, and sank under shield.
Then his body fell into Frankish hands,
His woven corselet and jewelled collar,
And weaker warriors plundered the dead
After the carnage and welter of war.
The field of battle was covered with corpses
Of Geats who had fallen, slain by the sword.[25]
The sound of revelry rose in the hall;
Wealhtheow spoke to the warrior host: 1110
'Take, dear Beowulf, collar and corselet,
Wear these treasures with right good will!
Thrive and prosper and prove your might!
Befriend my boys with your kindly counsel;
I will remember and I will repay.
You have earned the undying honor of heroes
In regions reaching as far and wide
As the windy walls that the sea encircles.
May Fate show favor while life shall last!
I wish you wealth to your heart's content; 1120
In your days of glory be good to my sons!
Here each hero is true to other,
Gentle of spirit, loyal to lord,
Friendly thanes and a folk united,
Wine-cheered warriors who do my will.'

THE TROLL-WIFE AVENGES GRENDEL

Then she went to her seat. At the fairest of feasts
Men drank of the wine-cup, knowing not Fate,
Nor the fearful doom that befell the earls

[25] This circuitous aside traces the path of the golden neck-ring Hrothgar gives Beowulf. Beowulf on his return to the land of the Geats gives it to his uncle and king, Hygelac, who wears it during his fatal battle with the Frisians.

When darkness gathered, and gracious Hrothgar
Sought his dwelling and sank to rest. 1130
A host of heroes guarded the hall
As they oft had done in the days of old.
They stripped the benches and spread the floor
With beds and bolsters. But one of the beer-thanes
Bowed to his hall-rest doomed to death.
They set at their heads their shining shields,
Their battle-bucklers; and there on the bench
Above each hero his towering helmet,
His spear and corselet hung close at hand.
It was ever their wont to be ready for war 1140
At home or in field, as it ever befell
That their lord had need. 'Twas a noble race!
Then they sank to slumber. But one paid dear
For his evening rest, as had often happened
When Grendel haunted the lordly hall
And wrought such ruin, till his end was come,
Death for his sins; it was easily seen,
Though the monster was slain, an avenger survived
Prolonging the feud, though the fiend had perished.
The mother of Grendel, a monstrous hag, 1150
Brooded over her misery, doomed to dwell
In evil waters and icy streams
From ancient ages when Cain had killed
His only brother, his father's son.
Banished and branded with marks of murder
Cain fled far from the joys of men,
Haunting the barrens, begetting a brood
Of grisly monsters; and Grendel was one,
The fiendish ogre who found in the hall
A hero on watch, and awaiting the fray. 1160
The monster grappled; the Geat took thought
Of the strength of his might, that marvelous gift
Which the Lord had given; in God he trusted
For help and succor and strong support,
Whereby he humbled the fiend from hell,
Destroyed the demon; and Grendel fled,
Harrowed in heart and hateful to man,
Deprived of joy, to the place of death.
But rabid and raging his mother resolved
On a dreadful revenge for the death of her son! 1170
She stole to the hall where the Danes were sleeping,
And horror fell on the host of earls
When the dam[26] of Grendel burst in the door.
But the terror was less as the war-craft is weaker,
A woman's strength, than the might of a man
When the hilted sword, well shaped by the hammer,
The blood-stained iron of tempered edge,

[26]Mother.

Hews the boar from the foeman's helmet.
Then in the hall was the hard-edged blade,
The stout steel, brandished above the benches; 1180
Seizing their shields men stayed not for helmet
Or ample byrny, when fear befell.
As soon as discovered, the hag was in haste
To fly to the open, to flee for her life.
One of the warriors she swiftly seized,
Clutched him fast and made off to the fens.
He was of heroes the dearest to Hrothgar,
The best of comrades between two seas;
The warrior brave, the stout-hearted spearman,
She slew in his sleep. Nor was Beowulf there; 1190
But after the banquet another abode
Had been assigned to the glorious Geat.
There was tumult in Heorot. She tore from its place
The blood-stained claw. Care was renewed!
It was no good bargain when both in turn
Must pay the price with the lives of friends!
  Then the white-haired warrior, the aged king,
Was numb with sorrow, knowing his thane
No longer was living, his dearest man dead.
Beowulf, the brave, was speedily summoned, 1200
Brought to the bower; the noble prince
Came with his comrades at dawn of day
Where the wise king awaited if God would award
Some happier turn in these tidings of woe.
The hero came tramping into the hall
With his chosen band—the boards resounded—
Greeted the leader, the Ingwine lord,
And asked if the night had been peaceful and pleasant.
  Hrothgar spoke, the lord of the Scyldings:
'Ask not of pleasure; pain is renewed 1210
For the Danish people. Æschere is dead!
Dead is Yrmenlaf's elder brother!
He was my comrade, closest of counsellors,
My shoulder-companion as side by side
We fought for our lives in the welter of war,
In the shock of battle when boar-helms crashed.
As an earl should be, a prince without peer,
Such was Æschere, slain in the hall
By the wandering demon! I know not whither
She fled to shelter, proud of her spoil, 1220
Gorged to the full. She avenged the feud
Wherein yesternight you grappled with Grendel
And savagely slew him because so long
He had hunted and harried the men of my folk.
He fell in the battle and paid with his life.
But now another fierce ravager rises
Avenging her kinsman, and carries it far,
As it seems to many a saddened thane
Who grieves in his heart for his treasure-giver.

This woe weighs heavy! The hand lies still 1230
That once was lavish of all delights.
  Oft in the hall I have heard my people,
Comrades and counsellors, telling a tale
Of evil spirits their eyes have sighted,
Two mighty marauders who haunt the moors.
One shape, as clearly as men could see,
Seemed woman's likeness, and one seemed man,
An outcast wretch of another world,
And huger far than a human form.
Grendel my countrymen called him, not knowing 1240
What monster-brood spawned him, what sire begot.
Wild and lonely the land they live in,
Wind-swept ridges and wolf-retreats,
Dread tracts of fen where the falling torrent
Downward dips into gloom and shadow
Under the dusk of the darkening cliff.
Not far in miles lies the lonely mere
Where trees firm-rooted and hung with frost
Overshroud the wave with shadowing gloom.
And there a portent appears each night, 1250
A flame in the water; no man so wise
Who knows the bound of its bottomless depth.
The heather-stepper, the horned stag,
The antlered hart hard driven by hounds,
Invading that forest in flight from afar
Will turn at bay and die on the brink
Ere ever he'll plunge in that haunted pool.
'Tis an eerie spot! Its tossing spray
Mounts dark to heaven when high winds stir
The driving storm, and the sky is murky, 1260
And with foul weather the heavens weep.
On your arm only rests all our hope!
Not yet have you tempted those terrible reaches
The region that shelters that sinful wight.
Go if you dare! I will give requital
With ancient treasure and twisted gold,
As I formerly gave in guerdon of battle,
If out of that combat you come alive.'[27]
  Beowulf spoke, the son of Ecgtheow:
'Sorrow not, brave one! Better for man 1270
To avenge a friend than much to mourn.
All men must die; let him who may
Win glory ere death. That guerdon is best
For a noble man when his name survives him.
Then let us rise up, O ward of the realm,
And haste us forth to behold the track
Of Grendel's dam. And I give you pledge
She shall not in safety escape to cover,

[27]Hrothgar's offer of more treasure is appropriate to the cultural practices of the time.

To earthy cavern, or forest fastness,
Or gulf of ocean, go where she may. 1280
This day with patience endure the burden
Of every woe, as I know you will.'
Up sprang the ancient, gave thanks to God
For the heartening words the hero had spoken.

BEOWULF SLAYS THE TROLL-WIFE

Quickly a horse was bridled for Hrothgar,
A mettlesome charger with braided mane;
In royal splendor the king rode forth
Mid the trampling tread of a troop of shieldmen.
The tracks lay clear where the fiend had fared
Over plain and bottom and woodland path, 1290
Through murky moorland making her way
With the lifeless body, the best of thanes
Who of old with Hrothgar had guarded the hall.
By a narrow path the king pressed on
Through rocky upland and rugged ravine,
A lonely journey, past looming headlands,
The lair of monster and lurking troll.
Tried retainers, a trusty few,
Advanced with Hrothgar to view the ground.
Sudden they came on a dismal covert 1300
Of trees that hung over hoary stone,
Over churning water and bloodied wave.
Then for the Danes was the woe the deeper,
The sorrow sharper for Scylding earls,
When they first caught sight, on the rocky sea-cliff,
Of slaughtered Æschere's severed head.
The water boiled in a bloody swirling
With seething gore as the spearmen gazed.
The trumpet sounded a martial strain;
The shield-troop halted. Their eyes beheld 1310
The swimming forms of strange sea-dragons,
Dim serpent shapes in the watery depths,
Sea-beasts sunning on headland slopes;
Snakelike monsters that oft at sunrise
On evil errands scour the sea.
Startled by tumult and trumpet's blare,
Enraged and savage, they swam away;
But one the lord of the Geats brought low,
Stripped of his sea-strength, despoiled of life,
As the bitter bow-bolt pierced his heart. 1320
His watery-speed grew slower, and ceased,
And he floated, caught in the clutch of death.
Then they hauled him in with sharp-hooked boar-spears,
By sheer strength grappled and dragged him ashore,
A wondrous wave-beast; and all the array
Gathered to gaze at the grisly guest.

Beowulf donned his armor for battle,
Heeded not danger; the hand-braided byrny,
Broad of shoulder and richly bedecked,
Must stand the ordeal of the watery depths.[28] 1330
Well could that corselet defend the frame
Lest hostile thrust should pierce to the heart.
Or blows of battle beat down the life.
A gleaming helmet guarded his head
As he planned his plunge to the depths of the pool
Through the heaving waters—a helm adorned
With lavish inlay and lordly chains,
Ancient work of the weapon-smith
Skillfully fashioned, beset with the boar,
That no blade of battle might bite it through. 1340
Not the least or the worst of his war-equipment
Was the sword the herald of Hrothgar loaned
In his hour of need—Hrunting its name—
An ancient heirloom, trusty and tried;
Its blade was iron, with etched design,
Tempered in blood of many a battle.
Never in fight had it failed the hand
That drew it during the perils of war,
The rush of the foe. Not the first time then
That its edge must venture on valiant deeds. 1350
But Ecglaf's stalwart son was unmindful
Of words he had spoken while heated with wine,
When he loaned the blade to a better swordsman.
He himself dared not hazard his life
In deeds of note in the watery depths;
And thereby he forfeited honor and fame.[29]
Not so with that other undaunted spirit
After he donned his armor for battle.
Beowulf spoke, the son of Ecgtheow:
'O gracious ruler, gold-giver to men, 1360
As I now set forth to attempt this feat,
Great son of Healfdene, hold well in mind
The solemn pledge we plighted of old,
That if doing your service I meet my death
You will mark my fall with a father's love.
Protect my kinsmen, my trusty comrades,
If battle take me. And all the treasure
You have heaped on me bestow upon Hygelac,
Hrothgar beloved! The lord of the Geats,
The son of Hrethel, shall see the proof, 1370

---

[28]For this battle, Beowulf arms himself. The byrny, the helmet, and especially the sword Hrunting are described in detail.

[29]Unferth is compared unfavorably to Beowulf, "the better swordsman." A few lines later, Beowulf prays that the sword Hrunting be returned to Unferth if he fails at his task. It is the sword that fails, not Beowulf, but nonetheless he returns it to Unferth graciously and without a word of blame.

Shall know as he gazes on jewels and gold,
That I found an unsparing dispenser of bounty,
And joyed, while I lived, in his generous gifts.
Give back to Unferth the ancient blade,
The sword-edge splendid with curving scrolls,
For either with Hrunting I'll reap rich harvest
Of glorious deeds, or death shall take me.'

After these words the prince of the Weders
Awaited no answer, but turned to the task,
Straightway plunged in the swirling pool. 1380
Nigh unto a day he endured the depths
Ere he first had view of the vast sea-bottom.
Soon she found, who had haunted the flood,
A ravening hag, for a hundred half-years,
Greedy and grim, that a man was groping
In daring search through the sea-troll's home.
Swift she grappled and grasped the warrior
With horrid grip, but could work no harm,
No hurt to his body; the ring-locked byrny
Cloaked his life from her clutching claw; 1390
Nor could she tear through the tempered mail
With her savage fingers. The she-wolf bore
The ring-prince down through the watery depths
To her den at the bottom; nor could Beowulf draw
His blade for battle, though brave his mood.
Many a sea-beast, strange sea-monsters,
Tasked him hard with their menacing tusks,
Broke his byrny and smote him sore.

Then he found himself in a fearsome hall
Where water came not to work him hurt, 1400
But the flood was stayed by the sheltering roof.
There in the glow of firelight gleaming
The hero had view of the huge sea-troll.
He swung his war-sword with all his strength,
Withheld not the blow, and the savage blade
Sang on her head its hymn of hate.
But the bold one found that the battle-flasher
Would bite no longer, nor harm her life.
The sword-edge failed at his sorest need.
Often of old with ease it had suffered 1410
The clash of battle, cleaving the helm,
The fated warrior's woven mail.
That time was first for the treasured blade
That its glory failed in the press of the fray.
But fixed of purpose and firm of mood
Hygelac's earl was mindful of honor;
In wrath, undaunted, he dashed to earth
The jewelled sword with its scrolled design,
The blade of steel; staked all on strength,
On the might of his hand, as a man must do 1420
Who thinks to win in the welter of battle
Enduring glory; he fears not death.

The Geat-prince joyed in the straining struggle,
Stalwart-hearted and stirred to wrath,
Gripped the shoulder of Grendel's dam
And headlong hurled the hag to the ground.
But she quickly clutched him and drew him close,
Countered the onset with savage claw.
The warrior staggered, for all his strength,
Dismayed and shaken and borne to earth. 1430
She knelt upon him and drew her dagger,
With broad bright blade, to avenge her son,
Her only issue. But the corselet's steel
Shielded his breast and sheltered his life
Withstanding entrance of point and edge.
Then the prince of the Geats would have gone his journey,
The son of Ecgtheow, under the ground;
But his sturdy breast-net, his battle-corselet,
Gave him succor, and holy God,
The Lord all-wise, awarded the mastery; 1440
Heaven's Ruler gave right decree.
Swift the hero sprang to his feet;
Saw mid the war-gear a stately sword,
An ancient war-brand of biting edge,
Choicest of weapons worthy and strong,
The work of giants, a warrior's joy,
So heavy no hand but his own could hold it,
Bear to battle or wield in war.
Then the Scylding warrior, savage and grim,
Seized the ring-hilt and swung the sword, 1450
Struck with fury, despairing of life,
Thrust at the throat, broke through the bone-rings;
The stout blade stabbed through her fated flesh.
She sank in death; the sword was bloody;
The hero joyed in the work of his hand.
The gleaming radiance shimmered and shone
As the candle of heaven shines clear from the sky.
Wrathful and resolute Hygelac's thane
Surveyed the span of the spacious hall;
Grimly gripping the hilted sword 1460
With upraised weapon he turned to the wall.
The blade had failed not the battle-prince;
A full requital he firmly planned
For all the injury Grendel had done
In numberless raids on the Danish race,
When he slew the hearth-companions of Hrothgar,
Devoured fifteen of the Danish folk
Clasped in slumber, and carried away
As many more spearmen, hideous spoil.
All this the stout-heart had stern requited; 1470
And there before him bereft of life
He saw the broken body of Grendel
Stilled in battle, and stretched in death,
As the struggle in Heorot smote him down.

The corpse sprang wide as he struck the blow,
The hard sword-stroke that severed the head.
  Then the tried retainers, who there with Hrothgar
Watched the face of the foaming pool,
Saw that the churning reaches were reddened,
The eddying surges stained with blood. 1480
And the gray, old spearmen spoke of the hero,
Having no hope he would ever return
Crowned with triumph and cheered with spoil.
Many were sure that the savage sea-wolf
Had slain their leader. At last came noon.
The stalwart Scyldings forsook the headland;
Their proud gold-giver departed home.
But the Geats sat grieving and sick in spirit,
Stared at the water with longing eyes,
Having no hope they would ever behold 1490
Their gracious leader and lord again.
  Then the great sword, eaten with blood of battle,
Began to soften and waste away
In iron icicles, wonder of wonders,
Melting away most like to ice
When the Father looses the fetters of frost,
Slackens the bondage that binds the wave,
Strong in power of times and seasons;
He is true God! Of the goodly treasures
From the sea-cave Beowulf took but two, 1500
The monster's head and the precious hilt
Blazing with gems; but the blade had melted,
The sword dissolved, in the deadly heat,
The venomous blood of the fallen fiend.

Beowulf Returns to Heorot

  Then he who had compassed the fall of his foes
Came swimming up through the swirling surge.
Cleansed were the currents, the boundless abyss,
Where the evil monster had died the death
And looked her last on this fleeting world.
With sturdy strokes the lord of the seamen 1510
To land came swimming, rejoiced in his spoil,
Had joy of the burden he brought from the depths.
And his mighty thanes came forward to meet him,
Gave thanks to God they were granted to see
Their well-loved leader both sound and safe.
From the stalwart hero his helmet and byrny
Were quickly loosened; the lake lay still,
Its motionless reaches reddened with blood.
Fain of heart men fared o'er the footpaths,
Measured the ways and the well-known roads. 1520
From the sea-cliff's brim the warriors bore

The head of Grendel, with heavy toil;
Four of the stoutest, with all their strength,
Could hardly carry on swaying spear
Grendel's head to the gold-decked hall.
Swift they strode, the daring and dauntless,
Fourteen Geats, to the Hall of the Hart;
And proud in the midst of his marching men
Their leader measured the path to the mead-hall.
The hero entered, the hardy in battle, 1530
The great in glory, to greet the king;
And Grendel's head by the hair was carried
Across the floor where the feasters drank—
A terrible sight for lord and for lady—
A gruesome vision whereon men gazed!
  Beowulf spoke, the son of Ecgtheow:
'O son of Healfdene, lord of the Scyldings!
This sea-spoil wondrous, whereon you stare,
We joyously bring you in token of triumph!
Barely with life surviving the battle, 1540
The war under water, I wrought the deed
Weary and spent; and death had been swift
Had God not granted His sheltering strength.
My strong-edged Hrunting, stoutest of blades,
Availed me nothing. But God revealed—
Often His arm has aided the friendless—
The fairest of weapons hanging on wall,
An ancient broadsword; I seized the blade,
Slew in the struggle, as fortune availed,
The cavern-warders. But the war-brand old, 1550
The battle-blade with its scrolled design,
Dissolved in the gush of the venomous gore;
The hilt alone I brought from the battle.
The record of ruin, and slaughter of Danes,
These wrongs I avenged, as was fitting and right.
Now I can promise you, prince of the Scyldings,
Henceforth in Heorot rest without rue
For you and your nobles; nor need you dread
Slaughter of follower, stalwart or stripling,
Or death of earl, as of old you did.' 1560
Into the hand of the aged leader,
The gray-haired hero, he gave the hilt,
The work of giants, the wonder of gold.
At the death of the demons the Danish lord
Took in his keeping the cunning craft,
The wondrous marvel, of mighty smiths;
When the world was freed of the ravaging fiend,
The foe of God, and his fearful dam
Marked with murder and badged with blood,
The bound hilt passed to the best of kings 1570
Who ever held sceptre beside two seas,
And dealt out treasure in Danish land!

Hrothgar spoke, beholding the hilt,
The ancient relic whereon was etched
An olden record of struggle and strife,
The flood that ravaged the giant race,
The rushing deluge of ruin and death.
That evil kindred were alien to God,
But the Ruler avenged with the wrath of the deep!
On the hilt-guards, likewise, of gleaming gold 1580
Was rightly carven in cunning runes,
Set forth and blazoned, for whom that blade,
With spiral tooling and twisted hilt,
That fairest of swords, was fashioned and smithied.[30]
Then out spoke Hrothgar, Healfdene's son,
And all the retainers were silent and still:
'Well may he say, whose judgment is just,
Recalling to memory men of the past,
That this earl was born of a better stock!
Your fame, friend Beowulf, is blazoned abroad 1590
Over all wide ways, and to every people.
In manful fashion have you showed your strength,
Your might and wisdom. My word I will keep,
The plighted friendship we formerly pledged.
Long shall you stand as a stay to your people,
A help to heroes, as Heremod was not
To the Honor-Scyldings, to Ecgwela's sons!
Not joy to kindred, but carnage and death,
He wrought as he ruled o'er the race of the Danes.
In savage anger he slew his comrades, 1600
His table-companions, till, lawless and lone,
An odious outcast, he fled from men.
Though God had graced him with gifts of strength,
Over all men exalting him, still in his breast
A bloodthirsty spirit was rooted and strong.
He dealt not rings to the Danes for glory;
His lot was eternal torment of woe,
And lasting affliction. Learn from his fate!
Strive for virtue! I speak for your good;
In the wisdom of age I have told the tale.[31] 1610
'Tis a wondrous marvel how mighty God
In gracious spirit bestows on men
The gift of wisdom, and goodly lands,
And princely power! He rules over all!
He suffers a man of lordly line
To set his heart on his own desires,
Awards him fullness of worldly joy,
A fair home-land, and the sway of cities,

[30] There has been much discussion about the magical sword of Grendel's mother, which is covered with Runic inscriptions. See Chambers, *Beowulf: An Introduction*, 468 ff.

[31] Hrothgar returns to the story of Heremod, the bad king, as a warning against pride.

The wide dominion of many a realm,
An ample kingdom, till, cursed with folly, 1620
The thoughts of his heart take no heed of his end.
He lives in luxury, knowing not want,
Knowing no shadow of sickness or age;
No haunting sorrow darkens his spirit,
No hatred or discord deepens to war;
The world is sweet, to his every desire,
And evil assails not—until in his heart
Pride overpowering gathers and grows!
The warder slumbers, the guard of his spirit;
Too sound is that sleep, too sluggish the weight 1630
Of worldly affairs, too pressing the Foe,
The Archer who looses the arrows of sin.
Then is his heart pierced, under his helm,
His soul in his bosom, with bitter dart.
He has no defense for the fierce assaults
Of the loathsome Fiend. What he long has cherished
Seems all too little! In anger and greed
He gives no guerdon of plated rings.
Since God has granted him glory and wealth
He forgets the future, unmindful of Fate. 1640
But it comes to pass in the day appointed
His feeble body withers and fails;
Death descends, and another seizes
His hoarded riches and rashly spends
The princely treasure, imprudent of heart.
Beloved Beowulf, best of warriors,
Avoid such evil and seek the good,
The heavenly wisdom. Beware of pride!
Now for a time you shall feel the fullness
And know the glory of strength, but soon 1650
Sickness or sword shall strip you of might,
Or clutch of fire, or clasp of flood,
Or flight of arrow, or bite of blade,
Or relentless age; or the light of the eye
Shall darken and dim, and death on a sudden,
O lordly ruler, shall lay you low.
A hundred half-years I've been head of the Ring-Danes,
Defending the folk against many a tribe
With spear-point and sword in the surges of battle
Till not one was hostile 'neath heaven's expanse. 1660
But a loathsome change swept over the land,
Grief after gladness, when Grendel came,
That evil invader, that ancient foe!
Great sorrow of soul from his malice I suffered;
But thanks be to God who has spared me to see
His bloody head at the battle's end!
Join now in the banquet; have joy of the feast,
O mighty in battle! And the morrow shall bring
Exchange of treasure in ample store.'

Happy of heart the Geat leader hastened, 1670
Took seat at the board as the good king bade.
Once more, as of old, brave heroes made merry
And tumult of revelry rose in the hall.
Then dark over men the night shadows deepened;
The host all rose, for Hrothgar was minded,
The gray, old Scylding, to go to his rest.
On Beowulf too, after labor of battle,
Came limitless longing and craving for sleep.
A hall-thane graciously guided the hero,
Weary and worn, to the place prepared, 1680
Serving his wishes and every want
As befitted a mariner come from afar.
The stout-hearted warrior sank to his rest;
The lofty building, splendid and spacious,
Towered above him. His sleep was sound
Till the black-coated raven, blithesome of spirit,
Hailed the coming of Heaven's bliss.

The Parting of Beowulf and Hrothgar

Then over the shadows uprose the sun.
The Geats were in haste, and eager of heart
To depart to their people. Beowulf longed 1690
To embark in his boat, to set sail for his home.
The hero tendered the good sword Hrunting
To the son of Ecglaf, bidding him bear
The lovely blade; gave thanks for the loan,
Called it a faithful friend in the fray,
Bitter in battle. The greathearted hero
Spoke no word in blame of the blade!
Arrayed in war-gear, and ready for sea,
The warriors bestirred them; and, dear to the Danes,
Beowulf sought the high seat of the king. 1700
The gallant in war gave greeting to Hrothgar;
Beowulf spoke, the son of Ecgtheow:
'It is time at last to tell of our longing!
Our homes are far, and our hearts are fain
To seek again Hygelac over the sea.
You have welcomed us royally, harbored us well
As a man could wish; if I ever can win
Your affection more fully, O leader of heroes,
Swift shall you find me to serve you again!
If ever I learn, o'er the levels of ocean, 1710
That neighboring nations beset you sore,
As in former days when foemen oppressed,
With thanes by the thousand I will hasten to help.
For I know that Hygelac, lord of the Geats,
Prince of the people, though young in years,

Will favor and further by word and deed
That my arm may aid you, and do you honor,
With stout ash-spear and succor of strength
In the press of need. And if princely Hrethric
Shall purpose to come to the court of the Geats, 1720
He will find there a legion of loyal friends.
That man fares best to a foreign country
Who himself is stalwart and stout of heart.'
Hrothgar addressed him, uttered his answer:
'Truly, these words has the Lord of wisdom
Set in your heart, for I never have harkened
To speech so sage from a man so young.
You have strength, and prudence, and wisdom of word!
I count it true if it come to pass
That point of spear in the press of battle, 1730
Or deadly sickness, or stroke of sword,
Shall slay your leader, the son of Hrethel,
The prince of your people, and you still live,
The Sea-Geats could have no happier choice
If you would be willing to rule the realm,
As king to hold guard o'er the hoard and the heroes.
The longer I know you, the better I like you,
Beloved Beowulf! You have brought it to pass
That between our peoples a lasting peace
Shall bind the Geats to the Danish-born; 1740
And strife shall vanish, and war shall cease,
And former feuds, while I rule this realm.
And many a man, in the sharing of treasure,
Shall greet another with goodly gifts
O'er the gannet's bath. And the ring-stemmed ship
Shall bear over ocean bountiful riches
In pledge of friendship. Our peoples, I know,
Shall be firm united toward foe and friend,
Faultless in all things, in fashion of old.'
Then the son of Healfdene, shelter of earls, 1750
Bestowed twelve gifts on the hero in hall,
Bade him in safety with bounty of treasure
Seek his dear people, and soon return.
The peerless leader, the Scylding lord,
Kissed the good thane and clasped to his bosom
While tears welled fast from the old man's eyes.
Both chances he weighed in his wise, old heart,
But greatly doubted if ever again
They should meet at council or drinking of mead.
Nor could Hrothgar master—so dear was the man— 1760
His swelling sorrow; a yearning love
For the dauntless hero, deep in his heart,
Burned through his blood. Beowulf, the brave,
Prizing his treasure and proud of the gold,
Turned away, treading the grassy plain.
The ring-stemmed sea-goer, riding at anchor,

Awaited her lord. There was loud acclaim
Of Hrothgar's gifts, as they went their way.
He was a king without failing or fault,
Till old age, master of all mankind, 1770
Stripped him of power and pride of strength.

Beowulf Returns to Geatland

Then down to the sea came the band of the brave,
The host of young heroes in harness of war,
In their woven mail; and the coast-warden viewed
The heroes' return, as he heeded their coming!
No uncivil greeting he gave from the sea-cliff
As they strode to ship in their glistening steel;
But rode toward them and called their return
A welcome sight for their Weder kin.
There on the sand the ring-stemmed ship, 1780
The broad-bosomed bark, was loaded with war-gear,
With horses and treasure; the mast towered high
Over the riches of Hrothgar's hoard.
A battle-sword Beowulf gave to the boatwarden
Hilted with gold; and thereafter in hall
He had the more honor because of the heirloom,
The shining treasure. The ship was launched.
Cleaving the combers of open sea
They dropped the shoreline of Denmark astern.
A stretching sea-cloth, a bellying sail, 1790
Was bent on the mast; there was groaning of timbers;
A gale was blowing; the boat drove on.
The foamy-necked plunger plowed through the billows,
The ring-stemmed ship through the breaking seas,
Till at last they sighted the sea-cliffs of Geatland,
The well-known headlands; and, whipped by the wind,
The boat drove shoreward and beached on the sand.
Straightway the harbor-watch strode to the seashore;
Long had he watched for the well-loved men,
Scanning the ocean with eager eyes! 1800
The broad-bosomed boat he bound to the shingle
With anchor ropes, lest the rip of the tide
Should wrench from its mooring the comely craft.
From the good ship Beowulf bade them bear
The precious jewels and plated gold,
The princely treasure. Not long was the path
That led to where Hygelac, son of Hrethel,
The giver of treasure, abode in his home
Hard by the sea-wall, hedged by his thanes.
Spacious the castle, splendid the king 1810
On his high half-seat; youthful was Hygd,
Wise and well-born—though winters but few
Hæreth's daughter had dwelt at court.

She was noble of spirit, not sparing in gifts
Of princely treasure to the people of the Geats.

Of the pride of Thryth, and her crimes, the fair folk-queen was free;
Thryth, of whose liegemen none dared by day, save only her lord,
Lift up his eyes to her face, lest his fate be a mortal bondage,
Seizure and fetters and sword, a blow of the patterned blade
Declaring his doom, and proclaiming the coming of death.[32] 1820
That is no way of a queen, nor custom of lovely lady,
Though peerless her beauty and proud, that a weaver of peace
Should send a dear man to his death for a feigned affront.
But the kinsman of Hemming at last made an end of her evil.
For men at the drinking of mead tell tale of a change,
How she wrought less ruin and wrong when, given in marriage
Gleaming with jewels and gold, to the high-born hero and young,
Over the fallow flood she sailed, at her father's bidding
Seeking the land of Offa, and there while she lived,
Famed for goodness, fulfilled her fate on the throne. 1830
She held high love for her lord, the leader of heroes,
The best, I have heard, of mankind or the children of men
Between the two seas; for Offa, the stalwart, was honored
For his gifts and his greatness in war. With wisdom he governed;
And from him Eomær descended, Hemming's kinsman, grandson of Garmund,
Stalwart and strong in war, and the helper of heroes.

Then the hero strode with his stalwart band
Across the stretches of sandy beach,
The wide sea-shingle. The world-candle shone,
The hot sun hasting on high from the south. 1840
Marching together they made their way
To where in his stronghold the stout young king,
Ongentheow's slayer, protector of earls,
Dispensed his treasure. Soon Hygelac heard
Of the landing of Beowulf, bulwark of men,
That his shoulder-companion had come to his court
Sound and safe from the strife of battle.
The hall was prepared, as the prince gave bidding,
Places made ready for much travelled men.
And he who came safe from the surges of battle 1850
Sat by the side of the king himself,
Kinsman by kinsman; in courtly speech
His liege lord greeted the loyal thane
With hearty welcome. And Hæreth's daughter
Passed through the hall-building pouring the mead,
With courtesy greeting the gathered host,
Bearing the cup to the hands of the heroes.
In friendly fashion in high-built hall

[32]Hygd, wife of Hygelac, is wise beyond her years, in contrast to Thryth, a violent young woman later reformed by marriage to King Offa. This rather convoluted discussion of queenly behavior is an epic convention.

Hygelac questioned his comrade and thane;
For an eager longing burned in his breast 1860
To hear from the Sea-Geats the tale of their travels.
'How did you fare in your far sea-roving,
Beloved Beowulf, in your swift resolve
To sail to the conflict, the combat in Heorot,
Across the salt waves? Did you soften at all
The sorrows of Hrothgar, the weight of his woe?
Deeply I brooded with burden of care
For I had no faith in this far sea-venture
For one so beloved. Long I implored
That you go not against the murderous monster, 1870
But let the South Danes settle the feud
Themselves with Grendel. To God be thanks
That my eyes behold you unharmed and unhurt.'
Beowulf spoke, the son of Ecgtheow:
'My dear lord Hygelac, many have heard
Of that famous grapple 'twixt Grendel and me,
The bitter struggle and strife in the hall
Where he formerly wrought such ruin and wrong,
Such lasting sorrow for Scylding men!
All that I avenged! Not any on earth 1880
Who longest lives of that loathsome brood,
No kin of Grendel cloaked in his crime,
Has cause to boast of that battle by night!
First, in that country, I fared to the hall
With greeting for Hrothgar; Healfdene's kinsman
Learned all my purpose, assigned me a place
Beside his own son. 'Twas a happy host!
I never have seen under span of heaven
More mirth of heroes sitting at mead!
The peerless queen, the peace-pledge of peoples, 1890
Passed on her round through the princely hall;
There was spurring of revels, dispensing of rings,
Ere the noble woman went to her seat.
At times in the host the daughter of Hrothgar
Offered the beaker to earls in turn;
Freawaru men called her, the feasters in hall,
As she held out to heroes the well-wrought cup.
Youthful and gleaming with jewels of gold
To the fair son of Froda the maiden is plighted.[33]
For the Scylding leader, the lord of the land, 1900
Deems it wise counsel, accounting it gain,
To settle by marriage the murderous feud,
The bloody slaughter! But seldom for long

[33]Picking up an earlier strand in the narrative, Beowulf guesses correctly that Hrothgar's attempt to resolve the feud between the Danes and Heathobards by marrying his daughter Freawaru to the Heathobard prince Ingeld will fail. He prophesies the murder of one of Freawaru's attendants by a Heathobard, followed by war between the two groups. Implicit in this long digression is criticism of Hrothgar for relying too much on diplomacy, too little on practical responses to dangerous situations.

Does the spear go ungrasped when a prince has perished,
Though the bride in her beauty be peerless and proud!
Ill may it please the Heathobard prince
And all his thanes, when he leads his lady
Into the hall, that a Danish noble
Should be welcomed there by the Heathobard host.
For on him shall flash their forefathers' heirlooms, 1910
Hard-edged, ring-hilted, the Heathobards' hoard
When of old they had war-might, nor wasted in battle
Their lives and the lives of their well-loved thanes.
Then an aged spearman shall speak at the beer-feast,
The treasure beholding with sorrow of heart,
Remembering sadly the slaughter of men,
Grimly goading the young hero's spirit,
Spurring to battle, speaking this word:
"Do you see, my lord, the sword of your father,
The blade he bore to the last of his fights, 1920
The pride of his heart as, under his helmet,
The Scyldings slew him, the savage Danes,
When Withergyld fell, and after the slaughter,
The fall of heroes, they held the field?
And now a son of those bloody butchers,
Proud in his trappings, tramps into hall
And boasts of the killing, clothed with the treasure
That is yours by your birthright to have and to hold?"
Over and over the old man will urge him,
With cutting reminders recalling the past 1930
Till it comes at last that the lady's thane,
For the deeds of his father, shall forfeit his life
In a bloody slaughter, slain by the sword,
While the slayer goes scatheless knowing the land.
On both sides then shall sword-oaths be broken
When hate boils up within Ingeld's heart,
And his love of his lady grows cooler and lessens
Because of his troubles. I count not true
Heathobard faith, nor their part in the peace,
Nor their friendship firm to the Danish folk. 1940
I must now speak on, dispenser of treasure,
Further of Grendel, till fully you know
How we fared in that fierce and furious fight!
When the jewel of heaven had journeyed o'er earth,
The wrathful demon, the deadly foe,
Stole through the darkness spying us out
Where still unharmed we guarded the gold-hall.
But doom in battle and bitter death
Were Handscio's fate! He was first to perish
Though girded with weapon and famous in war. 1950
Grendel murdered him, mangled his body,
Bolted the dear man's bloody corpse.
No sooner for that would the slaughterous spirit,
Bloody of tooth and brooding on evil,
Turn empty-handed away from the hall!

The mighty monster made trial of my strength
Clutching me close with his ready claw.
Wide and wondrous his huge pouch hung
Cunningly fastened, and fashioned with skill
From skin of dragon by devil's craft. 1960
Therein the monster was minded to thrust me
Sinless and blameless, and many beside.
But it might not be, when I rose in wrath,
And fronted the hell-fiend face to face.
Too long is the tale how I took requital
On the cursed foe for his every crime,
But the deeds I did were a lasting honor,
Beloved prince, to your people's name.
He fled away, and a fleeting while
Possessed his life and the world's delights; 1970
But he left in Heorot his severed hand,
A bloody reminder to mark his track.
Humbled in spirit and wretched in heart
Down he sank to the depths of the pool.

When the morrow fell, and we feasted together,
The Scylding ruler rewarded me well
For the bloody strife, in guerdon bestowing
Goodly treasure of beaten gold.
There was song and revel. The aged Scylding
From well-stored mind spoke much of the past. 1980
A warrior sang to the strains of the glee-wood,
Sometimes melodies mirthful and joyous,
Sometimes lays that were tragic and true.
And the great-hearted ruler at times would tell
A tale of wonder in fitting words.
Heavy with years the white-haired warrior
Grieved for his youth and the strength that was gone;
And his heart was moved by the weight of his winters
And many a memory out of the past.
All the long day we made merry together 1990
Till another night came to the children of men,
And quickly the mother of Grendel was minded
To wreak her vengeance; raging with grief
She came to the hall where the hate of the Weders
Had slain her son. But the hideous hag
Avenged his killing; with furious clutch
She seized a warrior—the soul of Æschere,
Wise and aged, went forth from the flesh!
Not at all could the Danes, when the morrow dawned,
Set brand to his body or burn on the bale 2000
Their well-loved comrade. With fiendish clasp
She carried his corpse through the fall of the force.
That was to Hrothgar, prince of the people,
Sorest of sorrows that ever befell!
For your sake the sad-hearted hero implored me
To prove my valor and, venturing life,
To win renown in the watery depths.

He promised reward. Full well is it known
How I humbled the horrible guard of the gulf.
Hand to hand for a space we struggled 2010
Till the swirling eddies were stained with blood;
With cleaving sword-edge I severed the head
Of Grendel's hag in that hall of strife.
Not easily thence did I issue alive,
But my death was not fated; not yet was I doomed!
Then the son of Healfdene, the shelter of earls,
Gave many a treasure to mark the deed.
The good king governed with courtly custom;
In no least way did I lose reward,
The meed of my might; but he gave me treasure, 2020
Healfdene's son, to my heart's desire.
These riches I bring you, ruler of heroes,
And warmly tender with right good will.
Save for you, King Hygelac, few are my kinsmen,
Few are the favors but come from you.'
Then he bade men bring the boar-crested headpiece,
The towering helmet, and steel-gray sark,
The splendid war-sword, and spoke this word:
'The good king Hrothgar gave me this gift,
This battle-armor, and first to you 2030
Bade tell the tale of his friendly favor.
He said King Heorogar, lord of the Scyldings,
Long had worn it, but had no wish
To leave the mail to his manful son,
The dauntless Heoroweard, dear though he was!
Well may you wear it! Have joy of it all.'
As I've heard the tale, he followed the trappings
With four bay horses, matched and swift,
Graciously granting possession of both,
The steeds and the wealth. 'Tis the way of a kinsman, 2040
Not weaving in secret the wiles of malice
Nor plotting the fall of a faithful friend.
To his kinsman Hygelac, hardy in war,
The heart of the nephew was trusty and true;
Dear to each was the other's good!
To Hygd, as I've heard, he presented three horses
Gaily saddled, slender and sleek,
And the gleaming necklace Wealhtheow gave,
A peerless gift from a prince's daughter.
With the gracious guerdon, the goodly jewel, 2050
Her breast thereafter was well bedecked.
So the son of Ecgtheow bore himself bravely,
Known for his courage and courteous deeds,
Strove after honor, slew not his comrades
In drunken brawling; nor brutal his mood.
But the bountiful gifts which the Lord God gave him
He held with a power supreme among men.
He had long been scorned, when the sons of the Geats
Accounted him worthless; the Weder lord

Held him not high among heroes in hall. 2060
Laggard they deemed him, slothful and slack.
But time brought solace for all his ills![34]
Then the battle-bold king, the bulwark of heroes,
Bade bring a battle-sword banded with gold,
The heirloom of Hrethel; no sharper steel,
No lovelier treasure, belonged to the Geats.
He laid the war-blade on Beowulf's lap,
Gave him a hall and a stately seat
And hides seven thousand. Inherited lands
Both held by birth-fee, home and estate. 2070
But one held rule o'er the spacious realm,
And higher therein his order and rank.

THE FIRE-DRAGON AND THE TREASURE

It later befell in the years that followed
After Hygelac sank in the surges of war,
And the sword slew Heardred under his shield
When the Battle-Scylfings, those bitter fighters,
Invaded the land of the victor-folk
Overwhelming Hereric's nephew in war,
That the kingdom came into Beowulf's hand.[35]
For fifty winters he governed it well, 2080
Aged and wise with the wisdom of years,
Till a fire-drake flying in darkness of night
Began to ravage and work his will.
On the upland heath he guarded a hoard,
A stone barrow lofty. Under it lay
A path concealed from the sight of men.
There a thief broke in on the heathen treasure,
Laid hand on a flagon all fretted with gold,
As the dragon discovered, though cozened in sleep
By the pilferer's cunning. The people soon found 2090
That the mood of the dragon was roused to wrath!
Not at all with intent, of his own free will,
Did he ravish the hoard, who committed the wrong;
But in dire distress the thrall of a thane,
A guilty fugitive fleeing the lash,
Forced his way in. There a horror befell him![36]

---

[34]Klaeber comments, "The introduction of the commonplace story of the sluggish youth is not very convincing" (*Beowulf*, 207).

[35]This transition covering fifty years may have been added by the composer of the final version; the whole dragon fight is separate in time and spirit from the first two-thirds of the existing poem. At the same time, there is considerable foreshadowing of the events in the final section, beginning with the story of Hygelac's last battle, discussed above.

[36]There has been some controversy as to the status of the thief. He is either a *thegn* (warrior) or a *theow* (slave). Klaeber takes the latter view, and reads the passage: "A slave, a fugitive from justice, stole a costly vessel from the dragon's hoard, and upon presenting it to his master—one of Beowulf's men—obtained his pardon. The vessel was then sent to Beowulf himself." (*Beowulf*, 208).

Yet the wretched exile escaped from the dragon,
Swift in retreat when the terror arose.
A flagon he took. There, many such treasures
Lay heaped in that earth-hall where the owner of old 2100
Had carefully hidden the precious hoard,
The countless wealth of a princely clan.[37]
Death came upon them in days gone by
And he who lived longest, the last of his line,
Guarding the treasure and grieving for friend,
Deemed it his lot that a little while only
He too might hold that ancient hoard.
A barrow new-built near the ocean billows
Stood cunningly fashioned beneath the cliff;
Into the barrow the ring-warden bore 2110
The princely treasure, the precious trove
Of golden wealth, and these words he spoke:
'Keep thou, O Earth, what men could not keep—
This costly treasure—it came from thee!
Baleful slaughter has swept away,
Death in battle, the last of my blood;
They have lived their lives; they have left the mead-hall.
Now I have no one to wield the sword,
No one to polish the plated cup,
The precious flagon—the host is fled. 2120
The hard-forged helmet fretted with gold
Shall be stripped of its inlay; the burnishers sleep
Whose charge was to brighten the battle-masks.
Likewise the corselet that countered in war
Mid clashing of bucklers the bite of the sword—
Corselet and warrior decay into dust;
Mailed coat and hero are moveless and still.
No mirth of gleewood, no music of harp,
No good hawk swinging in flight through the hall;
No swift steed stamps in the castle yard; 2130
Death has ravished an ancient race.'
So sad of mood he bemoaned his sorrow,
Lonely and sole survivor of all,
Restless by day and wretched by night
Till the clutch of death caught at his heart.
Then the goodly treasure was found unguarded
By the venomous dragon enveloped in flame,
The old naked night-foe flying in darkness,
Haunting the barrows; a bane that brings
A fearful dread to the dwellers of earth. 2140
His wont is to hunt out a hoard under ground
And guard heathen gold, growing old with the years.
But no whit for that is his fortune more fair!

---

[37]The next stage of the narrative traces the history of the treasure hoard. Once the property of "a princely clan," it falls under the care of a last survivor, a "ring-warden" who buries it in a barrow by the sea. The dragon finds it and keeps it for 300 years until the thief steals the cup and brings down the wrath of the monster.

For three hundred winters this waster of peoples
Held the huge treasure-hall under the earth
Till the robber aroused him to anger and rage,
Stole the rich beaker and bore to his master,
Imploring his lord for a compact of peace.
So the hoard was robbed and its riches plundered;
To the wretch was granted the boon that he begged; 2150
And his liege-lord first had view of the treasure,
The ancient work of the men of old.
Then the worm awakened and war was kindled,
The rush of the monster along the rock,
When the fierce one found the tracks of the foe;
He had stepped too close in his stealthy cunning
To the dragon's head. But a man undoomed
May endure with ease disaster and woe
If he has His favor who wields the world.
Swiftly the fire-drake sought through the plain 2160
The man who wrought him this wrong in his sleep.
Inflamed and savage he circled the mound,
But the waste was deserted—no man was in sight.
The worm's mood was kindled to battle and war;
Time and again he returned to the barrow
Seeking the treasure-cup. Soon he was sure
That a man had plundered the precious gold.
Enraged and restless the hoard-warden waited
The gloom of evening. The guard of the mound
Was swollen with anger; the fierce one resolved 2170
To requite with fire the theft of the cup.
Then the day was sped as the worm desired;
Lurking no longer within his wall
He sallied forth surrounded with fire,
Encircled with flame. For the folk of the land
The beginning was dread as the ending was grievous
That came so quickly upon their lord.
Then the baleful stranger belched fire and flame,
Burned the bright dwellings—the glow of the blaze
Filled hearts with horror. The hostile flier 2180
Was minded to leave there nothing alive.
From near and from far the war of the dragon,
The might of the monster, was widely revealed
So that all could see how the ravaging scather
Hated and humbled the Geatish folk.
Then he hastened back ere the break of dawn
To his secret den and the spoil of gold.
He had compassed the land with a flame of fire,
A blaze of burning; he trusted the wall,
The sheltering mound, and the strength of his might— 2190
But his trust betrayed him! The terrible news
Was brought to Beowulf, told for a truth,
That his home was consumed in the surges of fire,
The goodly dwelling and throne of the Geats.
The heart of the hero was heavy with anguish,

The greatest of sorrows; in his wisdom he weened
He had grievously angered the Lord Everlasting,
Blamefully broken the ancient law.
Dark thoughts stirred in his surging bosom,
Welled in his breast, as was not his wont. 2200
The flame of the dragon had levelled the fortress,
The people's stronghold washed by the wave.
But the king of warriors, prince of the Weders,
Exacted an ample revenge for it all.
The lord of warriors and leader of earls
Bade work him of iron a wondrous shield,
Knowing full well that wood could not serve him
Nor linden defend him against the flame.[38]
The stalwart hero was doomed to suffer
The destined end of his days on earth; 2210
Likewise the worm, though for many a winter
He had held his watch o'er the wealth of the hoard.
The ring-prince scorned to assault the dragon
With a mighty army, or host of men.
He feared not the combat, nor counted of worth
The might of the worm, his courage and craft,
Since often aforetime, beset in the fray,
He had safely issued from many an onset,
Many a combat and, crowned with success,
Purged of evil the hall of Hrothgar 2220
And crushed out Grendel's loathsome kin.

Nor was that the least of his grim engagements
When Hygelac fell, great Hrethel's son;
When the lord of the people, the prince of the Geats,
Died of his wounds in the welter of battle,
Perished in Friesland, smitten with swords.[39]
Thence Beowulf came by his strength in swimming;
Thirty sets of armor he bore on his back
As he hasted to ocean. The Hetware men
Had no cause to boast of their prowess in battle 2230
When they gathered against him with linden shields.
But few of them ever escaped his assault
Or came back alive to the homes they had left;
So the son of Ecgtheow swam the sea-stretches,
Lonely and sad, to the land of his kin.
Hygd then tendered him kingdom and treasure,
Wealth of riches and royal throne,
For she had no hope with Hygelac dead

---

[38]Beowulf, hearing of the destruction of his ancestral home, first asks God whether he has offended Him, then prepares for action by having a metal shield built.

[39]Here we pick up the account of Beowulf 's actions following the death of Hygelac in battle against the Frisians. First, he swims across the sea to the battlefield, bearing thirty sets of armor on his back, and kills many of the enemy. Then he returns, but refuses to stand in place of Heardred, Hygelac's son, instead becoming his loyal supporter. On Heardred's death, he finally becomes prince of the Geats, avenging the Geats on Heardred's foes. His strength, bravery, and princely demeanor are praised.

That her son could defend the seat of his fathers
From foreign foemen. But even in need, 2240
No whit the more could they move the hero
To be Heardred's liege, or lord of the land.
But he fostered Heardred with friendly counsel,
With honor and favor among the folk,
Till he came of age and governed the Geats.
Then the sons of Ohthere fleeing in exile
Sought out Heardred over the sea.
They had risen against the lord of the Scylfings,
Best of the sea-kings, bestower of rings,
An illustrious prince in the land of the Swedes. 2250
So Heardred fell. For harboring exiles
The son of Hygelac died by the sword.
Ongentheow's son, after Heardred was slain,
Returned to his home, and Beowulf held
The princely power and governed the Geats.
He was a good king, grimly requiting
In later days the death of his prince.
Crossing the sea with a swarming host
He befriended Eadgils, Ohthere's son,
In his woe and affliction, with weapons and men; 2260
He took revenge in a savage assault,
And slew the king. So Ecgtheow's son
Had come in safety through all his battles,
His bitter struggles and savage strife,
To the day when he fought with the deadly worm.
With eleven comrades, kindled to rage
The Geat lord went to gaze on the dragon.
Full well he knew how the feud arose,
The fearful affliction; for into his hold
From hand of finder the flagon had come. 2270
The thirteenth man in the hurrying throng
Was the sorrowful captive who caused the feud.[40]
With woeful spirit and all unwilling
Needs must he guide them, for he only knew
Where the earth-hall stood near the breaking billows
Filled with jewels and beaten gold.
The monstrous warden, waiting for battle,
Watched and guarded the hoarded wealth.
No easy bargain for any of men
To seize that treasure! The stalwart king, 2280
Gold-friend of Geats, took seat on the headland,
Hailed his comrades and wished them well.
Sad was his spirit, restless and ready,
And the march of Fate immeasurably near;
Fate that would strike, seek his soul's treasure,

[40]Beowulf sets out with a company of eleven men to seek the dragon. The twelfth in the company is the thief—an allusion to Judas among Jesus' twelve disciples.

And deal asunder the spirit and flesh.
Not long was his life encased in the body!
  Beowulf spoke, the son of Ecgtheow:
'Many an ordeal I endured in youth,
And many a battle. I remember it all. 2290
I was seven winters old when the prince of the people,
The lord of the treasure-hoard, Hrethel the king,
From the hand of my father had me and held me,
Recalling our kinship with treasure and feast.[41]
As long as he lived I was no less beloved,
As thane in his hall, than the sons of his house,
Herebeald and Hæthcyn and Hygelac, my lord.
For the eldest brother the bed of death
Was foully fashioned by brother's deed
When Hæthcyn let fly a bolt from his horn-bow, 2300
Missed the mark, and murdered his lord;
Brother slew brother with bloody shaft—
A tragic deed and beyond atonement,
A foul offense to sicken the heart!
Yet none the less was the lot of the prince
To lay down his soul and his life, unavenged.
  Even so sad and sorrowful is it,
And bitter to bear, to an old man's heart,
Seeing his young son swing on the gallows.
He wails his dirge and his wild lament 2310
While his son hangs high, a spoil to the raven;
His aged heart can contrive no help.
Each dawn brings grief for the son that is gone
And his heart has no hope of another heir,
Seeing the one has gone to his grave.
In the house of his son he gazes in sorrow
On wine-hall deserted and swept by the wind,
Empty of joy. The horsemen and heroes
Sleep in the grave. No sound of the harp,
No welcoming revels as often of old! 2320
He goes to his bed with his burden of grief;
To his spirit it seems that dwelling and land
Are empty and lonely, lacking his son.
  So the helm of the Weders yearned after Herebeald
And welling sadness surged in his heart.
He could not avenge the feud on the slayer
Nor punish the prince for the loathsome deed,
Though he loved him no longer, nor held him dear.
Because of this sorrow that sore befell
He left life's joys for the heavenly light, 2330

---

[41]Speaking to his men before fighting the dragon, Beowulf recounts the history of the house of Hrethel, father of Herebeald, Haethcyn, and Hygelac, including the accidental slaying of Herebeald by Haethcyn, the death of Hrethel, the war between the Swedes and Geats, and the succession of Hygelac to the throne. He ends by describing his own victories in battle, concluding with the killing of the Frankish warrior Daeghrefn, probably the slayer of Hygelac himself, "before the host."

Granting his sons, as a good man will,
Cities and land, when he went from the world.
  Then across the wide water was conflict and war,
A striving and struggle of Swedes and Geats,
A bitter hatred, when Hrethel died.
Ongentheow's sons were dauntless and daring,
Cared not for keeping of peace overseas;
But often around Hreosnabeorh slaughtered and slew.
My kinsmen avenged the feud and the evil,
As many have heard, though one of the Weders 2340
Paid with his life—a bargain full bitter!
Hæthcyn's fate was to fall in the fight.
It is often recounted, a kinsman with sword-edge
Avenged in the morning the murderer's deed
When Ongentheow met Eofor. Helm split asunder;
The aged Scylfing sank down to his death.
The hand that felled him remembered the feud
And drew not back from the deadly blow.
  For all the rich gifts that Hygelac gave me
I repaid him in battle with shining sword, 2350
As chance was given. He granted me land,
A gracious dwelling and goodly estate.
Nor needed he seek of the Gifths, or the Spear-Danes,
Or in Swedish land, a lesser in war
To fight for pay; in the press of battle
I was always before him alone in the van.
So shall I bear me while life-days last,
While the sword holds out that has served me well
Early and late since I slew Dæghrefn,
The Frankish hero, before the host. 2360
He brought no spoil from the field of battle,
No corselet of mail to the Frisian king.
Not by the sword the warden of standards,
The stalwart warrior, fell in the fight.
My battle-grip shattered the bones of his body
And silenced the heart-beat. But now with the sword,
With hand and hard blade, I must fight for the treasure.'

Beowulf and Wiglaf Slay the Dragon

  For the last time Beowulf uttered his boast:
'I came in safety through many a conflict
In the days of my youth; and now even yet, 2370
Old as I am, I will fight this feud,
Do manful deeds, if the dire destroyer
Will come from his cavern to meet my sword.'
The king for the last time greeted his comrades,
Bold helmet-bearers and faithful friends:
'I would bear no sword nor weapon to battle
With the evil worm, if I knew how else
I could close with the fiend, as I grappled with Grendel.

From the worm I look for a welling of fire,
A belching of venom, and therefore I bear 2380
Shield and byrny. Not one foot's space
Will I flee from the monster, the ward of the mound.
It shall fare with us both in the fight at the wall
As Fate shall allot, the lord of mankind.
Though bold in spirit, I make no boast
As I go to fight with the flying serpent.
Clad in your corselets and trappings of war,
By the side of the barrow abide you to see
Which of us twain may best after battle
Survive his wounds. Not yours the adventure, 2390
Nor the mission of any, save mine alone,
To measure his strength with the monstrous dragon
And play the part of a valiant earl.
By deeds of daring I'll gain the gold
Or death in battle shall break your lord.'[42]
Then the stalwart rose with his shield upon him,
Bold under helmet, bearing his sark
Under the stone-cliff; he trusted the strength
Of his single might. Not so does a coward!
He who survived through many a struggle, 2400
Many a combat and crashing of troops,
Saw where a stone-arch stood by the wall
And a gushing stream broke out from the barrow.
Hot with fire was the flow of its surge,
Nor could any abide near the hoard unburned,
Nor endure its depths, for the flame of the dragon.
Then the lord of the Geats in the grip of his fury
Gave shout of defiance; the strong-heart stormed.
His voice rang out with the rage of battle,
Resounding under the hoary stone. 2410
Hate was aroused; the hoard-warden knew
'Twas the voice of a man. No more was there time
To sue for peace; the breath of the serpent,
A blast of venom, burst from the rock.
The ground resounded; the lord of the Geats
Under the barrow swung up his shield
To face the dragon; the coiling foe
Was gathered to strike in the deadly strife.
The stalwart hero had drawn his sword,
His ancient heirloom of tempered edge; 2420
In the heart of each was fear of the other!
The shelter of kinsmen stood stout of heart
Under towering shield as the great worm coiled;
Clad in his war-gear he waited the rush.
In twisting folds the flame-breathing dragon
Sped to its fate. The shield of the prince

[42]Beowulf orders his men to crouch behind the side of the barrow to await the outcome of his battle with the dragon. Instead, they flee when the fight begins, except for Wiglaf.

For a lesser while guarded his life and his body
Than heart had hoped. For the first time then
It was not his portion to prosper in war;
Fate did not grant him glory in battle! 2430
Then lifted his arm the lord of the Geats
And smote the worm with his ancient sword
But the brown edge failed as it fell on bone,
And cut less deep than the king had need
In his sore distress. Savage in mood
The ward of the barrow countered the blow
With a blast of fire; wide sprang the flame.
The ruler of Geats had no reason to boast;
His unsheathed iron, his excellent sword,
Had weakened as it should not, had failed in the fight. 2440
It was no easy journey for Ecgtheow's son
To leave this world and against his will
Find elsewhere a dwelling! So every man shall
In the end give over this fleeting life.
  Not long was the lull. Swiftly the battlers
Renewed their grapple. The guard of the hoard
Grew fiercer in fury. His venomous breath
Beat in his breast. Enveloped in flame
The folk-leader suffered a sore distress.
No succoring band of shoulder-companions, 2450
No sons of warriors aided him then
By valor in battle. They fled to the forest
To save their lives; but a sorrowful spirit
Welled in the breast of one of the band.
The call of kinship can never be stilled
In the heart of a man who is trusty and true.
  His name was Wiglaf, Weohstan's son,
A prince of the Scylfings, a peerless thane,
Ælfhere's kinsman; he saw his king
Under his helmet smitten with heat. 2460
He thought of the gifts which his lord had given,
The wealth and the land of the Wægmunding line
And all the folk-rights his father had owned;
Nor could he hold back, but snatched up his buckler,
His linden shield and his ancient sword,
Heirloom of Eanmund, Ohthere's son,
Whom Weohstan slew with the sword in battle,
Wretched and friendless and far from home.
The brown-hewed helmet he bore to his kinsmen,
The ancient blade and the byrny of rings. 2470
These Onela gave him—his nephew's arms—
Nor called for vengeance, nor fought the feud,
Though Weohstan had slaughtered his brother's son.
He held the treasures for many half-years,
The byrny and sword, till his son was of age
For manful deeds, as his father before him.
Among the Geats he gave him of war-gear
Countless numbers of every kind;

Then, full of winters, he left the world,
Gave over this life. And Wiglaf, the lad, 2480
Was to face with his lord the first of his battles,
The hazard of war. But his heart did not fail
Nor the blade of his kinsman weaken in war,
As the worm soon found when they met in the fight!
Wiglaf spoke in sorrow of soul,
With bitter reproach rebuking his comrades:[43]
'I remember the time, as we drank in the mead-hall,
When we swore to our lord who bestowed these rings
That we would repay for the war-gear and armor,
The hard swords and helmets, if need like this 2490
Should ever befall him. He chose us out
From all the host for this high adventure,
Deemed us worthy of glorious deeds,
Gave me these treasures, regarded us all
As high-hearted bearers of helmet and spear—
Though our lord himself, the shield of his people,
Thought single-handed to finish this feat,
Since of mortal men his measure was most
Of feats of daring and deeds of fame.
Now is the day that our lord has need 2500
Of the strength and courage of stalwart men.
Let us haste to succor his sore distress
In the horrible heat and the merciless flame.
God knows I had rather the fire should enfold
My body and limbs with my gold-friend and lord.
Shameful it seems that we carry our shields
Back to our homes ere we harry the foe
And ward the life of the Weder king.
Full well I know it is not his due
That he alone, of the host of the Geats, 2510
Should suffer affliction and fall in the fight.
One helmet and sword, one byrny and shield,
Shall serve for us both in the storm of strife.'
Then Wiglaf dashed through the deadly reek
In his battle-helmet to help his lord.
Brief were his words: 'Beloved Beowulf,
Summon your strength, remember the vow
You made of old in the years of youth
Not to allow your glory to lessen
As long as you lived. With resolute heart, 2520
And dauntless daring, defend your life
With all your force. I fight at your side!'[44]
Once again the worm, when the words were spoken,
The hideous foe in a horror of flame,

---

[43]Here Wiglaf reminds the other warriors of their obligation to their liege-lord and to the Geats as a tribal body. He will repeat his reproof of the warriors when they return after Beowulf dies (2699–2724).

[44]Klaeber finds "a singular lack of propriety in making young Wiglaf administer fatherly advice to Beowulf" (*Beowulf*, 218). But it may be intended as the speech of a young warrior, proud at heart, seeking fame for the first time. It does not seem out of keeping with other boastful speeches in the poem.

Rushed in rage at the hated men.
Wiglaf's buckler was burned to the boss
In the billows of fire; his byrny of mail
Gave the young hero no help or defense.
But he stoutly pressed on under shield of his kinsman
When his own was consumed in the scorching flame. 2530
Then the king once more was mindful of glory,
Swung his great sword-blade with all his might
And drove it home on the dragon's head.
But Nægling broke, it failed in the battle,
The blade of Beowulf, ancient and gray.
It was not his lot that edges of iron
Could help him in battle; his hand was too strong,
Overtaxed, I am told, every blade with its blow.
Though he bore a wondrous hard weapon to war,
No whit the better was he thereby! 2540
A third time then the terrible scather,
The monstrous dragon inflamed with the feud,
Rushed on the king when the opening offered,
Fierce and flaming; fastened its fangs
In Beowulf's throat; he was bloodied with gore;
His life-blood streamed from the welling wound.
As they tell the tale, in the king's sore need
His shoulder-companion showed forth his valor,
His craft and courage, and native strength.
To the head of the dragon he paid no heed, 2550
Though his hand was burned as he helped his king.
A little lower the stalwart struck
At the evil beast, and his blade drove home
Plated and gleaming. The fire began
To lessen and wane. The king of the Weders
Summoned his wits; he drew the dagger
He wore on his corselet, cutting and keen,
And slit asunder the worm with the blow.
So they felled the foe and wrought their revenge;
The kinsmen together had killed the dragon. 2560
So a man should be when the need is bitter!
That was the last fight Beowulf fought;
That was the end of his work in the world.

Beowulf's Death

The wound which the dragon had dealt him began
To swell and burn; and soon he could feel
The baneful venom inflaming his breast.
The wise, old warrior sank down by the wall
And stared at the work of the giants of old,
The arches of stone and the standing columns
Upholding the ancient earth-hall within. 2570
His loyal thane, the kindest of comrades,
Saw Beowulf bloody and broken in war;

In his hands bore water and bathed his leader,
And loosened the helm from his dear lord's head.
Beowulf spoke, though his hurt was sore,
The wounds of battle grievous and grim.
Full well he weened that his life was ended,
And all the joy of his years on earth;
That his days were done, and Death most near:
'My armor and sword I would leave to my son 2580
Had Fate but granted, born of my body,
An heir to follow me after I'm gone.
For fifty winters I've ruled this realm,
And never a lord of a neighboring land
Dared strike with terror or seek with sword.
In my life I abode by the lot assigned,
Kept well what was mine, courted no quarrels,
Swore no false oaths. And now for all this
Though my hurt is grievous, my heart is glad.
When life leaves body, the Lord of mankind 2590
Cannot lay to my charge the killing of kinsmen!
Go quickly, dear Wiglaf, to gaze on the gold
Beneath the hoar stone. The dragon lies still
In the slumber of death, despoiled of his hoard.
Make haste that my eyes may behold the treasure,
The gleaming jewels, the goodly store,
And, glad of the gold, more peacefully leave
The life and the realm I have ruled so long.'[45]
Then Weohstan's son, as they tell the tale,
Clad in his corselet and trappings of war, 2600
Hearkened at once to his wounded lord.
Under roof of the barrow he broke his way.
Proud in triumph he stood by the seat,
Saw glittering jewels and gold on the ground,
The den of the dragon, the old dawn-flier,
And all the wonders along the walls.
Great bowls and flagons of bygone men
Lay all unburnished and barren of gems,
Many a helmet ancient and rusted,
Many an arm-ring cunningly wrought. 2610
Treasure and gold, though hid in the ground,
Override man's wishes, hide them who will![46]
High o'er the hoard he beheld a banner,
Greatest of wonders, woven with skill,
All wrought of gold; its radiance lighted
The vasty ground and the glittering gems.
But no sign of the worm! The sword-edge had slain him.
As I've heard the tale, the hero unaided

[45]Beowulf, acting according to custom, asks to see the treasure as the rightful spoils of victory, which he will leave for his people. Later he describes it as a "dower of riches" (2641).

[46]The poet notes that such treasures often "override man's wishes," suggesting that love of gold leads to tragedy.

Rifled those riches of giants of old,
The hoard in the barrow, and heaped in his arms 2620
Beakers and platters, picked what he would
And took the banner, the brightest of signs.
The ancient sword with its edge of iron
Had slain the worm who watched o'er the wealth,
In the midnight flaming, with menace of fire
Protecting the treasure for many a year
Till he died the death. Then Wiglaf departed
In haste returning enriched with spoil.
He feared, and wondered if still he would find
The lord of the Weders alive on the plain, 2630
Broken and weary and smitten with wounds.
With his freight of treasure he found the prince,
His dear lord, bloody and nigh unto death.
With water he bathed him till words broke forth
From the hoard of his heart and, aged and sad,
Beowulf spoke, as he gazed on the gold:
'For this goodly treasure whereon I gaze
I give my thanks to the Lord of all,
To the Prince of glory, Eternal God,
Who granted me grace to gain for my people 2640
Such dower of riches before my death.
I gave my life for this golden hoard.
Heed well the wants, the need of my people;
My hour is come, and my end is near.
Bid warriors build, when they burn my body,
A stately barrow on the headland's height.
It shall be for remembrance among my people
As it towers high on the Cape of the Whale,
And sailors shall know it as Beowulf's Barrow,
Sea-faring mariners driving their ships 2650
Through fogs of ocean from far countries.'[47]
Then the great-hearted king unclasped from his throat
A collar of gold, and gave to his thane;
Gave the young hero his gold-decked helmet,
His ring and his byrny, and wished him well.
'You are the last of the Wægmunding line.
All my kinsmen, earls in their glory,
Fate has sent to their final doom,
And I must follow.' These words were the last
The old king spoke ere the pyre received him, 2660
The leaping flames of the funeral blaze,
And his breath went forth from his bosom, his soul
Went forth from the flesh, to the joys of the just.
  Then bitter it was for Beowulf's thane
To behold his loved one lying on earth
Suffering sore at the end of life.

[47] The high funeral mound is a common motif in epic poetry, occurring in *The Iliad*, *The Odyssey*, and *The Aeneid* as well.

The monster that slew him, the dreadful dragon,
Likewise lay broken and brought to his death.
The worm no longer could rule the hoard,
But the hard, sharp sword, the work of the hammer, 2670
Had laid him low; and the winged dragon
Lay stretched near the barrow, broken and still.
No more in the midnight he soared in air,
Disclosing his presence, and proud of his gold;
For he sank to earth by the sword of the king.
But few of mankind, if the tales be true,
Has it prospered much, though mighty in war
And daring in deed, to encounter the breath
Of the venomous worm or plunder his wealth
When the ward of the barrow held watch o'er the mound. 2680
Beowulf bartered his life for the treasure;
Both foes had finished this fleeting life.
  Not long was it then till the laggards in battle
Came forth from the forest, ten craven in fight,
Who had dared not face the attack of the foe
In their lord's great need. The shirkers in shame
Came wearing their bucklers and trappings of war
Where the old man lay. They looked upon Wiglaf.
Weary he sat by the side of his leader
Attempting with water to waken his lord. 2690
It availed him little; the wish was vain!
He could not stay his soul upon earth,
Nor one whit alter the will of God.
The Lord ruled over the lives of men
As He rules them still. With a stern rebuke
He reproached the cowards whose courage had failed.
Wiglaf addressed them, Weohstan's son;
Gazed sad of heart on the hateful men:
'Lo! he may say who would speak the truth
That the lord who gave you these goodly rings, 2700
This warlike armor wherein you stand—
When oft on the ale-bench he dealt to his hall-men
Helmet and byrny, endowing his thanes
With the fairest he found from near or from far—
That he grievously wasted these trappings of war
When battle befell him. The king of the folk
Had no need to boast of his friends in the fight.
But the God of victory granted him strength
To avenge himself with the edge of the sword
When he needed valor. Of little avail 2710
The help I brought in the bitter battle!
Yet still I strove, though beyond my strength,
To aid my kinsman. And ever the weaker
The savage foe when I struck with my sword;
Ever the weaker the welling flame!
Too few defenders surrounded our ruler
When the hour of evil and terror befell.
Now granting of treasure and giving of swords,

Inherited land-right and joy of the home,
Shall cease from your kindred. And each of your clan 2720
Shall fail of his birthright when men from afar
Hear tell of your flight and your dastardly deed.
Death is better for every earl
Than life besmirched with the brand of shame!'

The Messenger Foretells the Doom of the Geats

Then Wiglaf bade tell the tidings of battle
Up over the cliff in the camp of the host
Where the linden-bearers all morning long
Sat wretched in spirit, and ready for both,
The return, or the death, of their dear-loved lord.
Not long did he hide, who rode up the headland, 2730
The news of their sorrow, but spoke before all:[48]
'Our leader lies low, the lord of the Weders,
The king of the Geats, on the couch of death.
He sleeps his last sleep by the deeds of the worm.
The dreadful dragon is stretched beside him
Slain with dagger-wounds. Not by the sword
Could he quell the monster or lay him low.
And Wiglaf is sitting, Weohstan's son,
Bent over Beowulf, living by dead.
Death watch he keeps in sorrow of spirit 2740
Over the bodies of friend and foe.

Now comes peril of war when this news is rumored abroad,
The fall of our king known afar among Frisians and Franks!
For a fierce feud rose with the Franks when Hygelac's warlike host
Invaded the Frisian fields, and the Hetware vanquished the Geats,
Overcame with the weight of their hordes, and Hygelac fell in the fray;
It was not his lot to live on dispensing the spoils of war.
And never since then of the Franks had we favor or friend.
And I harbor no hope of peace or faith from the Swedish folk,
For well is it known of men that Ongentheow slew with the sword 2750
Hæthcyn, the son of Hrethel, near Ravenswood, in the fight
When the Swedish people in pride swept down on the Geats.[49]
And Ohthere's aged father, old and a terror in battle,
Made onslaught, killing their king, and rescued his queen,
Ohthere's mother and Onela's, aged, bereft of her gold.
He followed the flying foe till, lordless and lorn,
They barely escaped into Ravenswood. There he beset them,

---

[48]Wiglaf dispatches a rider to the camp of Beowulf's followers to tell them the news. After doing so briefly and describing the mourning of Wiglaf, the messenger adds what he fears will be the political consequences of Beowulf's death. For similar ruminations, see the Old English *Cotton MS. Maxims* in the Bardic Literature section.

[49]Midway in his speech, the messenger describes the battle of Ravenswood, in which Haethcyn, son of Hrethel, is killed by Ongentheow, a king of the Swedes; Wulf, a Geatish prince and liege of Hygelac, kills Ongentheow in return. Klaeber notes that this is "the only detailed account of a real battle in *Beowulf*" (*Beowulf*, 223).

A wretched remnant of war, and weary with wounds.
And all the long hours of the night he thundered his threats
That some on the morrow he would slay with the edge of the sword, 2760
And some should swing on the gallows for food for the fowls!
But hope returned with the dawn to the heavy-hearted
When they heard the sound of the trumpets and Hygelac's horn,
As the good king came with his troops marching up on their track.
Then was a gory meeting of Swedes and Geats;
On all sides carnage and slaughter, savage and grim,
As the struggling foemen grappled and swayed in the fight.
And the old earl Ongentheow, crestfallen and cowed,
Fled with his men to a fastness, withdrew to the hills.
He had tasted Hygelac's strength, the skill of the hero in war, 2770
And he had no hope to resist or strive with the sea-men,
To save his hoard from their hands, or his children, or wife.
So the old king fled to his fortress; but over the plain
Hygelac's banners swept on in pursuit of the Swedes,
Stormed to the stronghold's defenses, and old Ongentheow
Was brought to bay with the sword, and subject to Eofor's will!
Wulf, son of Wonred, in wrath then struck with his sword,
And the blood in streams burst forth from under the old man's hair.
Yet the aged Scylfing was all undaunted and answered the stroke
With a bitter exchange in the battle; and Wonred's brave son 2780
Could not requite the blow, for the hero had cleft his helmet,
And, covered with blood, he was forced to bow; he fell to the earth.
But his death was not doomed, and he rallied, though the wound was deep.
Then Hygelac's hardy thane, when his brother lay low,
Struck with his ancient blade, a sturdy sword of the giants,
Cut through the shield-wall, cleaving the helmet. The king,
The folk-defender, sank down. He was hurt unto death.
Then were many that bound Wulf's wounds when the fight was won,
When the Geats held the ground of battle; as booty of war
Eofor stripped Ongentheow of iron byrny and helm, 2790
Of sword-blade hilted and hard, and bore unto Hygelac
The old man's trappings of war. And Hygelac took the treasures,
Promising fair rewards, and this he fulfilled.
The son of Hrethel, the king of the Geats, when he came to his home,
Repaid with princely treasure the prowess of Eofor and Wulf;
Gave each an hundred thousand of land and linked rings,
And none could belittle or blame. They had won the honor in war.
He gave to Eofor also the hand of his only daughter
To be a pledge of good will, and the pride of his home.

This is the fighting and this the feud, 2800
The bitter hatred, that breeds the dread
Lest the Swedish people should swarm against us
Learning our lord lies lifeless and still.
His was the hand that defended the hoard,
Heroes, and realm against ravaging foe,
By noble counsel and dauntless deed.
Let us go quickly to look on the king
Who brought us treasure, and bear his corpse
To the funeral pyre. The precious hoard

Shall burn with the hero. There lies the heap 2810
Of untold treasure so grimly gained,
Jewels and gems he bought with his blood
At the end of life. All these at the last
The flames shall veil and the brands devour.[50]
No man for remembrance shall take from the treasure,
Nor beauteous maiden adorn her breast
With gleaming jewel; bereft of gold
And tragic-hearted many shall tread
A foreign soil, now their lord has ceased
From laughter and revel and rapture of joy. 2820
Many a spear in the cold of morning
Shall be borne in hand uplifted on high.
No sound of harp shall waken the warrior,
But the dusky raven despoiling the dead
Shall clamor and cry and call to the eagle
What fare he found at the carrion-feast
The while with the wolf he worried the corpses.'

So the stalwart hero had told his tidings,
His fateful message; nor spoke amiss
As to truth or telling. The host arose; 2830
On their woeful way to the Eagles' Ness
They went with tears to behold the wonder.
They found the friend, who had dealt them treasure
In former days, on the bed of death,
Stretched out lifeless upon the sand.
The last of the good king's days was gone;
Wondrous the death of the Weder prince!
They had sighted first, where it lay outstretched,
The monstrous wonder, the loathsome worm,
The horrible fire-drake, hideous-hued, 2840
Scorched with the flame. The spread of its length
Was fifty foot-measures! Oft in the night
It sported in air, then sinking to earth
Returned to its den. Now moveless in death
It had seen the last of its earthly lair.
Beside the dragon were bowls and beakers,
Platters lying, and precious swords
Eaten with rust, where the hoard had rested
A thousand winters in the womb of earth.
That boundless treasure of bygone men, 2850
The golden dower, was girt with a spell
So that never a man might ravage the ring-hall
Save as God himself, the Giver of victory—
He is the Shelter and Shield of men—
Might allow such man as seemed to Him meet,
Might grant whom He would, to gather the treasure.[51]

---

[50]The burning of the treasure appears to be against Beowulf's dying wish, stated above. It was not, however, alien to pagan practice. In the poem, the treasure is actually buried in the funeral mound.

[51]The spell that prohibits use of the treasure appears to come as an afterthought; it may help to justify the destruction of the hoard along with the cremation of Beowulf.

His way of life, who had wickedly hoarded
The wealth of treasure beneath the wall,
Had an evil end, as was widely seen.
Many the dragon had sent to death,[52]
But in fearful fashion the feud was avenged! 2860
'Tis a wondrous thing when a warlike earl
Comes to the close of his destined days,
When he may no longer among his kinsmen
Feast in the mead-hall. So Beowulf fared
When he sought the dragon in deadly battle!
Himself he knew not what fate was in store
Nor the coming end of his earthly life.
The lordly princes who placed the treasure
Had cursed it deep to the day of doom, 2870
That the man who plundered and gathered the gold
Might pay for the evil imprisoned in hell,
Shackled in torment and punished with pain,
Except the invader should first be favored
With the loving grace of the Lord of all![53]
Then spoke Wiglaf, Weohstan's son:
'Often for one man many must sorrow
As has now befallen the folk of the Geats.
We could not persuade the king by our counsel,
Our well-loved leader, to shun assault 2880
On the dreadful dragon guarding the gold;
To let him lie where he long had lurked
In his secret lair till the world shall end.
But Beowulf, dauntless, pressed to his doom.
The hoard was uncovered; heavy the cost;
Too strong the fate that constrained the king!
I entered the barrow, beholding the hoard
And all the treasure throughout the hall;
In fearful fashion the way was opened,
An entrance under the wall of earth. 2890
Of the hoarded treasure I heaped in my arms
A weighty burden, and bore to my king.
He yet was living; his wits were clear.
Much the old man said in his sorrow;
Sent you greeting, and bade you build
In the place of burning a lofty barrow,
Proud and peerless, to mark his deeds;
For he was of all men the worthiest warrior
In all the earth, while he still might rule
And wield the wealth of his lordly land. 2900
Let us haste once more to behold the treasure,
The gleaming wonders beneath the wall.
I will show the way that you all may see

[52]What Kennedy translates as "many" is literally "one and few others." A disputed line, possibly a poetic understatement. It may simply say that the dragon killed Beowulf alone.

[53]The attempt to treat the curse morally makes the situation all the more confusing. Was Beowulf killed by the curse or would he have been granted the right to the treasure by divine grace?

And closely scan the rings and the gold.
Let the bier be ready, the pyre prepared,
When we come again to carry our lord,
Our leader beloved, where long he shall lie
In the kindly care of the Lord of all.'

BEOWULF'S FUNERAL

Then the son of Weohstan, stalwart in war,
Bade send command to the heads of homes 2910
To bring from afar the wood for the burning
Where the good king lay: 'Now glede shall devour,
As dark flame waxes, the warrior prince
Who has often withstood the shower of steel
When the storm of arrows, sped from the string,
Broke over shield, and shaft did service,
With feather-fittings guiding the barb.'
Then the wise son of Weohstan chose from the host
Seven thanes of the king, the best of the band;
Eight heroes together thy hied to the barrow 2920
In under the roof of the fearful foe;
One of the warriors leading the way
Bore in his hand a burning brand.
They cast no lots who should loot the treasure
When they saw unguarded the gold in the hall
Lying there useless; little they scrupled
As quickly they plundered the precious store.
Over the sea-cliff into the ocean
They tumbled the dragon, the deadly worm,
Let the sea-tide swallow the guarder of gold. 2930
Then a wagon was loaded with well-wrought treasure,
A countless number of every kind;
And the aged warrior, the white-haired king,
Was borne on high to the Cape of the Whale.
The Geat folk fashioned a peerless pyre
Hung round with helmets and battle-boards,
With gleaming byrnies as Beowulf bade.
In sorrow of soul they laid on the pyre
Their mighty leader, their well-loved lord.
The warriors kindled the bale on the barrow, 2940
Wakened the greatest of funeral fires.
Dark o'er the blaze the wood-smoke mounted;
The winds were still, and the sound of weeping
Rose with the roar of the surging flame
Till the heat of the fire had broken the body.
With hearts that were heavy they chanted their sorrow,
Singing a dirge for the death of their lord;
And an aged woman with upbound locks
Lamented for Beowulf, wailing in woe.
Over and over she uttered her dread 2950
Of sorrow to come, of bloodshed and slaughter,

Terror of battle, and bondage, and shame.
The smoke of the bale-fire rose to the sky!
  The men of the Weder folk fashioned a mound
Broad and high on the brow of the cliff,
Seen from afar by seafaring men.
Ten days they worked on the warrior's barrow
Inclosing the ash of the funeral flame
With a wall as worthy as wisdom could shape.
They bore to the barrow the rings and the gems, 2960
The wealth of the hoard the heroes had plundered.
The olden treasure they gave to the earth,
The gold to the ground, where it still remains
As useless to men as it was of yore.
Then round the mound rode the brave in battle,
The sons of warriors, twelve in a band,
Bemoaning their sorrow and mourning their king.
They sang their dirge and spoke of the hero
Vaunting his valor and venturous deeds.
So is it proper a man should praise 2970
His friendly lord with a loving heart,
When his soul must forth from the fleeting flesh.
So the folk of the Geats, the friends of his hearth,
Bemoaned the fall of their mighty lord;
Said he was kindest of worldly kings,
Mildest, most gentle, most eager for fame.

THE SONG OF ROLAND

[LATE 11TH CENTURY]

For a French audience at the end of the eleventh century, the dawn of the First Crusade, *The Song of Roland* must have represented entertainment of the highest order: a heroic epic in the service of the Catholic Church honoring the renewed fighting against the Moslems by recalling a legendary battle fought by a lord of Charlemagne over three hundred years before. But the poem also marked an ending, the last time that the ideal of knighthood could exist within such a seemingly irreproachable social and moral framework. Soon the last memory of the Holy Roman Empire would die, and the Crusades themselves would become tarnished monuments to politics and greed. The new ideal of chivalry and the courtly romances that were to follow soon after these events would be of a totally different character.

Only scraps of information remain about the historical Roland. In Einhard's biography of Charlemagne, an account of the Frankish king's wars in Spain relates that the Basques of the northern Pyrenees ambushed a rear guard of Charlemagne's army, "forced them down into the valley beneath, joined battle with them and killed them to the last man." In this battle some of the Frankish nobility died, including "Roland, Lord of the Breton Marches." The date, available from a separate source, was August 15, 778.

Massacres, of course, are the stuff of legend, but we lose track of the story of Roland until it resurfaces more than 300 years later as Roland's battle against the Saracens. In this version, Roland is accompanied by his friend Oliver, the Archbishop Turpin, and others, and he is hounded by his enemy, the traitor Ganelon. These figures, some historical and some not, must have been included in an older cycle of stories already known to a French audience. What is certainly new is the poem's association with the more recent Moslem enemy, including certain features of Spanish Saracen life nearly contemporary to the poet.

The plot of *The Song of Roland* is simple. Due to the connivance of the traitor Ganelon with the enemy, the rear guard of Charlemagne's army under the leadership of the young Count Roland is separated from the main force and attacked. Roland, too proud to call for help, refuses to blow on the horn Olifant until the situation is hopeless and all of his forces are to be massacred. Finally, Charlemagne orders a counterattack against the enemy, buries Roland and his company of knights, and captures, arraigns, and executes the traitors. The outcome is no mystery: the poet even reminds the listener of the main lines of the plot as the poem progresses.

The Song of Roland is a patriotic poem and a paean to the spirit of the Crusades. It elevates, with its stately and intentionally repetitious stanzas, the figure of Roland as the exemplary Frankish Christian knight, emphasizing his courage, his steadfastness, his faith in God, and his role as a defender of the crown and the Catholic Church. Roland is also firmly fixed within a larger hierarchy: He is the Christian warrior just as Charlemagne is the Christian king. It is for this reason that the epic does not end with the death of Roland; the rest of the poem, which details the rout of the Saracens and the capture, torture, and execution of Ganelon and his men, bloodily confirms the restoration of the authority of Charlemagne and Christianity. At its end, the aged Charlemagne plucks his beard and cries out, "How weary is my life!" but then rises out of bed to rescue another Christian king held under siege by the Saracens.

In the rigidly moral and ethical framework of the knightly epic, every character stands for a specific virtue and may also by implication have specific faults. Roland is strong, but he is often rash; his courage does not contain an equal measure of wisdom. Oliver, his friend, though lacking Roland's strength, is the wiser: He angrily upbraids Roland for not calling for help sooner than he does. Ganelon, meanwhile, is the villain, led by his jealousy, his false pride, and his desire for revenge to betray not only Roland, but the Frankish kingdom.

The work is organized in *laisses,* stanzas of ten-syllable lines with the concluding line sometimes repeated in part for emphasis. The action moves briskly if one tolerates this device of incremental repetition. The rhetoric of the poem is concentrated in a manner unique among major works of Western literature. There is an iconographic quality about the portraits of the leading figures, as if they had just stepped down from stained-glass windows or emerged from illuminations in manuscripts. The picture of Charlemagne, for instance, is dignified, economical, and rather conventional, but he retains certain stylistic idiosyncracies as well, such as the habit of stroking his beard. In the depiction of the characters, there is high artistry in the brief rendering of emotional states, such as Ganelon's anger at Roland or the encounter between Roland and Oliver over the blowing of the battle horn Olifant. The gestures of the characters are often larger than life, as we can see most tellingly in the case of Roland, who literally blows his brains out while sounding Olifant. The realism is marked, with the violence and gore of the battlefield perhaps unparalleled in epic poetry. At the same time, the poem rises to heights of dignity, such as the burial of Roland and his peers by the grieving king. Perhaps the most famous rhetorical feature of the poem is also the simplest: its method of presenting the opposition of two qualities within a single line, as when the poet states "Roland is good, and Oliver is wise" (St. 87) or "Pagans are wrong and Christians are right" (St. 79).

In cutting this poem to manageable size for anthology presentation, we have reduced the plot to the story of Roland alone and curtailed somewhat the repetition of language. In part this marks our acquiescence to modern taste. But one should still try to recapture the world of the original story imaginatively. *Roland* was recited out loud to a company of knights in the close quarters of a small feudal castle against a setting of light and shadows, and the language of the Old French casts a spell heightened by repetition. If possible, the modern reader should go back to the full version and even try, with a flat pronunciation of all syllables, reading stanzas of the Old French original. The work still conveys a sense of danger and dignity that is present only if the ear is the trusted medium of its reception.

Suggested Readings

There are many good modern translations of this work. Three besides the current translation that have special merit are the versions by Dorothy L. Sayers (1957), Patricia Terry (1965), and D. D. R. Owen (1972). Owen is also the author of a wonderful illustrated account of the poem, *The Legend of Roland: A Pageant of the Middle Ages* (1973). Recent studies of the work in English include Eugene Vance's *Reading the Song of Roland* (1970) and Robert Francis Cook's *The Sense of the Song of Roland* (1987). There are very illuminating sections on *The Song of Roland* in two of the best books about medieval culture and society: on its literary style, in Erich Auerbach's *Mimesis* (1953), pp. 83–107, and on its historical implications, in R. W. Southern's *The Making of the Middle Ages* (1953), pp. 241–246.

The Song of Roland

Translated and annotated by Frederick Goldin

1

Charles the King, our emperor, the Great,
has been in Spain for seven full years,
has conquered the high land down to the sea.
There is no castle that stands against him now,
no wall, no citadel left to break down—
except Saragossa, high on a mountain.
King Marsilion holds it, who does not love God,
who serves Mahumet and prays to Apollin.
He cannot save himself: his ruin will find him there. AOI.[1]

2

King Marsilion was in Saragossa. 10
He has gone forth into a grove, beneath its shade,
and he lies down on a block of blue marble,
twenty thousand men, and more, all around him.
He calls aloud to his dukes and his counts:
"Listen, my lords, to the troubles we have.
The Emperor Charles of the sweet land of France

[1] AOI: these three mysterious letters appear at certain moments throughout the text, 180 times in all. No one has ever adequately explained them, but every reader feels their effect.

has come into this country to destroy us.
I have no army able to give him battle,
I do not have the force to break his force.
Now act like my wise men: give me counsel, 20
save me, save me from death, save me from shame!"
No pagan there has one word to say to him
except Blancandrin, of the castle of Valfunde.

3

One of the wisest pagans was Blancandrin,
brave and loyal, a great mounted warrior,
a useful man, the man to aid his lord;
said to the King: "Do not give way to panic.
Do this: send Charles, that wild, terrible man,
tokens of loyal service and great friendship:
you will give him bears and lions and dogs, 30
seven hundred camels, a thousand molted hawks,
four hundred mules weighed down with gold and silver,
and fifty carts, to cart it all away:
he'll have good wages for his men who fight for pay.
Say he's made war long enough in this land:
let him go home, to France, to Aix,[2] at last—
come Michaelmas[3] you will follow him there,
say you will take their faith, become a Christian,
and be his man with honor, with all you have.
If he wants hostages, why, you'll send them, 40
ten, or twenty, to give him security.
Let us send him the sons our wives have borne.
I'll send my son with all the others named to die.
It is better that they should lose their heads
than that we, Lord, should lose our dignity
and our honors—and be turned into beggars!" AOI.

4

Said Blancandrin: "By this right hand of mine
and by this beard that flutters on my chest,
you will soon see the French army disband,
the Franks will go to their own land, to France. 50
When each of them is in his dearest home,
King Charles will be in Aix, in his chapel.
At Michaelmas he will hold a great feast—
that day will come, and then our time runs out,
he'll hear no news, he'll get no word from us.
This King is wild, the heart in him is cruel:
he'll take the heads of the hostages we gave.

[2]Aix: Aachen (Aix-la-Chapelle), capital of Charlemagne's empire.
[3]Michaelmas: either September 29 or October 16.

It is better, Lord, that they lose their heads
than that we lose our bright, our beautiful Spain—
and nothing more for us but misery and pain!" 60
The pagans say: "It may be as he says."

5

King Marsilion brought his counsel to end,
then he summoned Clarin of Balaguét,
Estramarin and Eudropin, his peer,
and Priamun, Guarlan, that bearded one,
and Machiner and his uncle Maheu,
and Joüner, Malbien from over-sea,
and Blancandrin, to tell what was proposed.
From the worst of criminals he called these ten.
"Barons, my lords, you're to go to Charlemagne; 70
he's at the siege of Cordres, the citadel.
Olive branches are to be in your hands—
that signifies peace and humility.
If you've the skill to get me an agreement,
I will give you a mass of gold and silver
and lands and fiefs, as much as you could want."
Say the pagans: "We'll benefit from this!" AOI.

. . .

8

The Emperor is secure and jubilant:
he has taken Cordres, broken the walls,
knocked down the towers with his catapults. 80
And what tremendous spoils his knights have won—
gold and silver, precious arms, equipment.
In the city not one pagan remained
who is not killed or turned into a Christian.
The Emperor is in an ample grove,
Roland and Oliver are with him there,
Samson the Duke and Ansëis the fierce,
Geoffrey d'Anjou, the King's own standard-bearer;
and Gerin and Gerer, these two together always,
and the others, the simple knights, in force: 90
fifteen thousand from the sweet land of France.
The warriors sit on bright brocaded silk;
they are playing at tables to pass the time,
the old and wisest men sitting at chess,
the young light-footed men fencing with swords.
Beneath a pine, beside a wild sweet-briar,
there was a throne, every inch of pure gold.
There sits the King, who rules over sweet France.
His beard is white, his head flowering white.
That lordly body! the proud fierce look of him!— 100
if someone should come here asking for him,

there'd be no need to point out the King of France.
The messengers dismounted, and on their feet
they greeted him in all love and good faith.

9

Blancandrin spoke, he was the first to speak,
said to the King: "Greetings, and God save you,
that glorious God whom we all must adore.
Here is the word of the great king Marsilion:
he has looked into this law of salvation,
wants to give you a great part of his wealth,
bears and lions and hunting dogs on chains, 110
seven hundred camels, a thousand molted hawks,
four hundred mules packed tight with gold and silver,
and fifty carts, to cart it all away;
and there will be so many fine gold bezants,
you'll have good wages for the men in your pay.
You have stayed long—long enough!—in this land,
it is time to go home, to France, to Aix.
My master swears he will follow you there."
The Emperor holds out his hands toward God,
bows down his head, begins to meditate. AOI. 120

10

The Emperor held his head bowed down;
never was he too hasty with his words:
his custom is to speak in his good time.
When his head rises, how fierce the look of him;
he said to them: "You have spoken quite well.
King Marsilion is my great enemy.
Now all these words that you have spoken here—
how far can I trust them? How can I be sure?"
The Saracen: "He wants to give you hostages.
How many will you want? ten? fifteen? twenty? 130
I'll put my son with the others named to die.
You will get some, I think, still better born.
When you are at home in your high royal palace,
at the great feast of Saint Michael-in-Peril,[4]
the lord who nurtures me will follow you,
and in those baths—the baths God made for you—
my lord will come and want to be made Christian."
King Charles replies: "He may yet save his soul." AOI.

. . .

[4]Saint Michael-in-Peril: The epithet "in the peril of the sea" was applied to the famous sanctuary of Saint Michael on the Normandy coast because it could only be reached on foot at low tide, and pilgrims were endangered by the incoming tide; eventually the phrase was applied to the saint himself.

12

The Emperor goes forth beneath a pine,
calls for his barons to complete his council: 140
Ogier the Duke, and Archbishop Turpin,
Richard the Old, and his nephew Henri;
from Gascony, the brave Count Acelin,
Thibaut of Reims, and his cousin Milun;
and Gerer and Gerin, they were both there,
and there was Count Roland, he came with them,
and Oliver, the valiant and well-born;
a thousand Franks of France, and more, were there.
Ganelon came, who committed the treason.
Now here begins the council that went wrong. AOI. 150

13

"Barons, my lords," said Charles the Emperor,
"King Marsilion has sent me messengers,
wants to give me a great mass of his wealth,
bears and lions and hunting dogs on chains,
seven hundred camels, a thousand molting hawks,
four hundred mules packed with gold of Araby,
and with all that, more than fifty great carts;
but also asks that I go back to France:
he'll follow me to Aix, my residence,
and take our faith, the one redeeming faith, 160
become a Christian, hold his march[5] lands from me.
But what lies in his heart? I do not know."
And the French say: "We must be on our guard!" AOI.

14

The Emperor has told them what was proposed.
Roland the Count will never assent to that,
gets to his feet, comes forth to speak against it;
says to the King: "Trust Marsilion—and suffer!
We came to Spain seven long years ago,
I won Noples for you, I won Commibles,
I took Valterne and all the land of Pine, 170
and Balaguer and Tudela and Seville.
And then this king, Marsilion, played the traitor:
he sent you men, fifteen of his pagans—
and sure enough, each held an olive branch;
and they recited just these same words to you.
You took counsel with all your men of France;
they counseled you to a bit of madness:

[5] March: a frontier province or territory.

you sent two Counts across to the Pagans,
one was Basan, the other was Basile.
On the hills below Haltille, he took their heads. 180
They were your men. Fight the war you came to fight!
Lead the army you summoned on to Saragossa!
Lay siege to it all the rest of your life!
Avenge the men that this criminal murdered!" AOI.

15

The Emperor held his head bowed down with this,
and stroked his beard, and smoothed his mustache down,
and speaks no word, good or bad, to his nephew.
The French keep still, all except Ganelon:
he gets to his feet and comes before King Charles,
how fierce he is as he begins his speech; 190
said to the King: "Believe a fool—me or
another—and suffer! Protect your interest!
When Marsilion the King sends you his word
that he will join his hands and be your man,[6]
and hold all Spain as a gift from your hands
and then receive the faith that we uphold—
whoever urges that we refuse this peace,
that man does not care, Lord, what death we die.
That wild man's counsel must not win the day here—
let us leave fools, let us hold with wise men!" AOI. 200

16

And after that there came Naimon the Duke—
no greater vassal in that court than Naimon—
said to the King: "You've heard it clearly now,
Count Ganelon has given you your answer:
let it be heeded, there is wisdom in it.
King Marsilion is beaten in this war,
you have taken every one of his castles,
broken his walls with your catapults,
burnt his cities and defeated his men.
Now when he sends to ask you to have mercy, 210
it would be a sin to do still more to him.
Since he'll give you hostages as guarantee,
this great war must not go on, it is not right."
And the French say: "The Duke has spoken well." AOI.

[6]He will join his hands: part of the gesture of homage; the lord enclosed the joined hands of his vassal with his own hands.

17

"Barons, my lords, whom shall we send down there,
to Saragossa, to King Marsilion?"
Naimon replies, "I'll go, if you grant it!
At once, my lord! give me the glove and the staff."
The King replies: "You're a man of great wisdom:
now by my beard, now by this mustache of mine, 220
you will not go so far from me this year; or ever.
Go take your seat when no one calls on you."

18

"Barons, my lords, whom can we send down there,
to this Saracen who holds Saragossa?"
Roland replies: "I can go there! No trouble!"
"No, no, not you!" said Oliver the Count,
"that heart in you is wild, spoils for a fight,
how I would worry—you'd fight with them, I know.
Now I myself could go, if the King wishes."
The King replies: "Be still, the two of you! 230
Not you, not he—neither will set foot there.
Now by this beard, as sure as you see white,
let no man here name one of the Twelve Peers!"
The French keep still, see how he silenced them.

19

Turpin of Reims has come forth from the ranks,
said to the King: "Let your Franks have a rest.
You have been in this land for seven years,
the many pains, the struggles they've endured!
I'm the one, Lord, give me the glove and the staff,
and I'll go down to this Saracen of Spain 240
and then I'll see what kind of man we have."
The Emperor replies to him in anger:
"Now you go back and sit on that white silk
and say no more unless I command it!" AOI.

20

"My noble knights," said the Emperor Charles,
choose me one man:[7] a baron from my march,
to bring my message to King Marsilion."

[7]Charlemagne wants them to choose a baron from an outlying region and not one of the Twelve Peers, the circle of his dearest men.

And Roland said: "Ganelon, my stepfather."
The French respond: "Why, that's the very man!
pass this man by and you won't send a wiser." 250
And hearing this Count Ganelon began to choke,
pulls from his neck the great furs of marten
and stands there now, in his silken tunic,
eyes full of lights, the look on him of fury,
he has the body, the great chest of a lord;
stood there so fair, all his peers gazed on him;
said to Roland: "Madman, what makes you rave?
Every man knows I am your stepfather,
yet you named me to go to Marsilion.
Now if God grants that I come back from there, 260
you will have trouble: I'll start a feud with you,
it will go on till the end of your life."
Roland replies: "What wild words—all that blustering!
Every man knows that threats don't worry me.
But we need a wise man to bring the message:
if the King wills, I'll gladly go in your place."

21

Ganelon answers: "You will not go for me. AOI.
You're not my man, and I am not your lord.
Charles commands me to perform this service:
I'll go to Marsilion in Saragossa. 270
And I tell you, I'll play a few wild tricks
before I cool the anger in me now."
When he heard that, Roland began to laugh. AOI.

22

Ganelon sees: *Roland laughing at him!*
and feels such pain he almost bursts with rage,
needs little more to go out of his mind;
says to the Count: "I have no love for you,
you *made* this choice fall on me, and that was wrong.
Just Emperor, here I am, before you.
I have one will: to fulfill your command." 280

23

"I know now I must go to Saragossa. AOI.
Any man who goes there cannot return.
And there is this: I am your sister's husband,
have a son by her, the finest boy there can be,
Baldewin," says he, "who will be a good man.

To him I leave my honors, fiefs, and lands.
Protect my son: these eyes will never see him."
Charles answers him: "That tender heart of yours!
You have to go, I have commanded it."

24

And the King said: "Ganelon, come forward, AOI. 290
come and receive the staff and the glove.
You have heard it: the Franks have chosen you."
Said Ganelon: "Lord, it's Roland who did this.
In all my days I'll have no love for him,
or Oliver, because he's his companion,
or the Twelve Peers, because they love him so.
I defy them, here in your presence, Lord."
And the King said: "What hate there is in you!
You will go there, for I command you to."
"I can go there, but I'll have no protector. AOI. 300
Basile had none, nor did Basan his brother."

. . .

27

Count Ganelon goes away to his camp.
He chooses, with great care, his battle-gear,
picks the most precious arms that he can find.
The spurs he fastened on were golden spurs;
he girds his sword, Murgleis, upon his side;
he has mounted Tachebrun, his battle horse,
his uncle, Guinemer, held the stirrup.
And there you would have seen brave men in tears,
his men, who say: "Baron, what bad luck for you! 310
All your long years in the court of the King,
always proclaimed a great and noble vassal!
Whoever it was doomed you to go down there—
Charlemagne himself will not protect that man.
Roland the Count should not have thought of this—
and you the living issue of a mighty line!"
And then they say: "Lord, take us there with you!"
Ganelon answers: "May the Lord God forbid!
It is better that I alone should die
    than so many good men and noble knights.
You will be going back, Lords, to sweet France: 320
go to my wife and greet her in my name,
and Pinabel, my dear friend and peer,
and Baldewin, my son, whom you all know:
give him your aid, and hold him as your lord."
And he starts down the road; he is on his way. AOI.

28

Ganelon rides to a tall olive tree,
there he has joined the pagan messengers.
And here is Blancandrin, who slows down for him:
with what great art they speak to one another.
Said Blancandrin: "An amazing man, Charles! 330
conquered Apulia, conquered all of Calabria,
crossed the salt sea on his way into England,
won its tribute, got Peter's pence[8] for Rome:
what does he want from us here in our march?"
Ganelon answers: "That is the heart in him.
There'll never be a man the like of him." AOI.

29

Said Blancandrin: "The Franks are a great people.
Now what great harm all those dukes and counts do
to their own lord when they give him such counsel:
they torment him, they'll destroy him, and others." 340
Ganelon answers: "Well, now, I know no such man
except Roland, who'll suffer for it yet.
One day the Emperor was sitting in the shade:
his nephew came, still wearing his hauberk,
he had gone plundering near Carcassonne;
and in his hand he held a bright red apple:
'Dear Lord, here, take,' said Roland to his uncle;
'I offer you the crowns of all earth's kings.'
Yes, Lord, that pride of his will destroy him,
for every day he goes riding at death. 350
And *should* someone kill him, we would have peace." AOI.

30

Said Blancandrin: "A wild man, this Roland!
wants to make every nation beg for his mercy
and claims a right to every land on earth!
But what men support him, if that is his aim?"
Ganelon answers: "Why, Lord, the men of France.
They love him so, they will never fail him.
He gives them gifts, masses of gold and silver,
mules, battle horses, brocaded silks, supplies.
And it is all as the Emperor desires: 360
he'll win the lands from here to the Orient." AOI.

[8] Peter's pence: a tribute of one penny per house "for the use of Saint Peter," that is, for the Pope in Rome.

31

Ganelon and Blancandrin rode on until
each pledged his faith to the other and swore
they'd find a way to have Count Roland killed.
They rode along the paths and ways until,
in Saragossa, they dismount beneath a yew.
There was a throne in the shade of a pine,
covered with silk from Alexandria.
There sat the king who held the land of Spain,
and around him twenty thousand Saracens. 370
There is no man who speaks or breathes a word,
poised for the news that all would like to hear.
Now here they are: Ganelon and Blancandrin.

32

Blancandrin came before Marsilion,
his hand around the fist of Ganelon,
said to the King: "May Mahumet save you,
and Apollin, whose sacred laws we keep!
We delivered your message to Charlemagne:
when we finished, he raised up both his hands
and praised his god. He made no other answer. 380
Here he sends you one of his noble barons,
a man of France, and very powerful.
You'll learn from him whether or not you'll have peace."
"Let him speak, we shall hear him," Marsilion answers. AOI.

33

But Ganelon had it all well thought out.
With what great art he commences his speech,
a man who knows his way about these things;
said to the King: "May the Lord God save you,
that glorious God, whom we must all adore.
Here is the word of Charlemagne the King: 390
you are to take the holy Christian faith;
he will give you one half of Spain in fief.
If you refuse, if you reject this peace,
you will be taken by force, put into chains,
and then led forth to the King's seat at Aix;
you will be tried; you will be put to death:
you will die there, in shame, vilely, degraded."
King Marsilion, hearing this, was much shaken.
In his hand was a spear, with golden feathers.
He would have struck, had they not held him back. AOI. 400

• • •

36

Now Ganelon drew closer to the King
and said to him: "You are wrong to get angry,
for Charles, who rules all France, sends you this word:
you are to take the Christian people's faith;
he will give you one half of Spain in fief,
the other half goes to his nephew: Roland—
quite a partner you will be getting there!
If you refuse, if you reject this peace,
he will come and lay siege to Saragossa;
you will be taken by force, put into chains, 410
and brought straight on to Aix, the capital.
No saddle horse, no war horse for you then,
no he-mule, no she-mule for you to ride:
you will be thrown on some miserable dray;
you will be tried, and you will lose your head.
Our Emperor sends you this letter."
He put the letter in the pagan's right fist.

37

Marsilion turned white; he was enraged;
he breaks the seal, he's knocked away the wax,
runs through the letter, sees what is written there: 420
"Charles sends me word, this king who rules in France:
I'm to think of his anger and his grief—
he means Basan and his brother Basile,
I took their heads in the hills below Haltille;
if I want to redeem the life of my body,
I must send him my uncle: the Algalife.[9]
And otherwise he'll have no love for me."
Then his son came and spoke to Marsilion,
said to the King: "Ganelon has spoken madness.
He crossed the line, he has no right to live. 430
Give him to me, I will do justice on him."
When he heard that, Ganelon brandished his sword;
he runs to the pine, set his back against the trunk.

38

King Marsilion went forth into the orchard,
he takes with him the greatest of his men;
Blancandrin came, that gray-haired counselor,
and Jurfaleu, Marsilion's son and heir,
the Algalife, uncle and faithful friend.
Said Blancandrin: "Lord, call the Frenchman back.

---

[9]The Algalife: the Caliph.

He swore to me to keep faith with our cause." 440
And the King said: "Go, bring him back here, then."
He took Ganelon's right hand by the fingers,
leads him into the orchard before the King.
And there they plotted that criminal treason. AOI.

39

Said Marsilion: "My dear Lord Ganelon,
that was foolish, what I just did to you,
I showed my anger, even tried to strike you.
Here's a pledge of good faith, these sable furs,
the gold alone worth over five hundred pounds:
I'll make it all up before tomorrow night." 450
Ganelon answers: "I will not refuse it.
May it please God to reward you for it." AOI.

40

Said Marsilion: "I tell you, Ganelon,
I have a great desire to love you dearly.
I want to hear you speak of Charlemagne.
He is so old, he's used up all his time—
from what I hear, he is past two hundred!
He has pushed his old body through so many lands,
taken so many blows on his buckled shield,
made beggars of so many mighty kings: 460
when will he lose the heart for making war?"
Ganelon answers: "Charles is not one to lose heart.
No man sees him, no man learns to know him
who does not say: the Emperor is great.
I do not know how to praise him so highly
that his great merit would not surpass my praise.
Who could recount his glory and his valor?
God put the light in him of such lordliness,
he would choose death before he failed his barons."

41

Said the pagan: "I have reason to marvel 470
at Charlemagne, a man so old and gray—
he's two hundred years old, I hear, and more;
he has tortured his body through so many lands,
and borne so many blows from lance and spear,
made beggars of so many mighty kings:
when will he lose the heart for making war?"
"Never," said Ganelon, "while his nephew lives,
he's a fighter, there's no vassal like him
under the vault of heaven. And he has friends.

There's Oliver, a good man, his companion.
And the Twelve Peers, whom Charles holds very dear, 480
form the vanguard, with twenty thousand knights.
Charles is secure, he fears no man on earth." AOI.

42

Said the pagan: "Truly, how I must marvel
at Charlemagne, who is so gray and white—
over two hundred years, from what I hear;
gone through so many lands a conqueror,
and borne so many blows from strong sharp spears,
killed and conquered so many mighty kings:
when will he lose the heart for making war?"
"Never," said Ganelon, "while one man lives: Roland! 490
no man like him from here to the Orient!
There's his companion, Oliver, a brave man.
And the Twelve Peers, whom Charles holds very dear,
form the vanguard, with twenty thousand Franks.
Charles is secure, he fears no man alive." AOI.

43

"Dear Lord Ganelon," said Marsilion the King,
"I have my army, you won't find one more handsome:
I can muster four hundred thousand knights!
With this host, now, can I fight Charles and the French?"
Ganelon answers: "No, no, don't try that now, 500
you'd take a loss: thousands of your pagans!
Forget such foolishness, listen to wisdom:
send the Emperor so many gifts
there'll be no Frenchman there who does not marvel.
For twenty hostages—those you'll be sending—
he will go home: home again to sweet France!
And he will leave his rear-guard behind him.
There will be Roland, I do believe, his nephew,
and Oliver, brave man, born to the court.
These Counts are dead, if anyone trusts me. 510
Then Charles will see that great pride of his go down,
he'll have no heart to make war on you again." AOI.

44

"Dear Lord Ganelon," said Marsilion the King,
"What must I do to kill Roland the Count?"
Ganelon answers: "Now I can tell you that.
The King will be at Cize, in the great passes,
he will have placed his rear-guard at his back:
there'll be his nephew, Count Roland, that great man,

and Oliver, in whom he puts such faith,
and twenty thousand Franks in their company. 520
Now send one hundred thousand of your pagans
against the French—let them give the first battle.
The French army will be hit hard and shaken.
I must tell you: your men will be martyred.
Give them a second battle, then, like the first.
One will get him, Roland will not escape.
Then you'll have done a deed, a noble deed,
and no more war for the rest of your life!" AOI.

. . .

46

Marsilion said, "Why talk. . . .
No plan has any worth which one. . . .[10] 530
Now swear to me that you will betray Roland."
Ganelon answers: "Let it be as you wish."
On the relics in his great sword Murgleis
he swore treason and become a criminal. AOI.

. . .

52

Marsilion took Ganelon by the shoulder
and said to him: "You're a brave man, a wise man.
Now by that faith you think will save your soul,
take care you do not turn your heart from us.
I will give you a great mass of my wealth,
ten mules weighed down with fine Arabian gold; 540
and come each year, I'll do the same again.
Now you take these, the keys to this vast city:
present King Charles with all of its great treasure;
then get me Roland picked for the rear-guard.
Let me find him in some defile or pass,
I will fight him, a battle to the death."
Ganelon answers: "It's high time that I go."
Now he is mounted, and he is on his way. AOI.

53

The Emperor moves homeward, he's drawing near.
Now he has reached the city of Valterne: 550
Roland had stormed it, destroyed it, and it stood
from that day forth a hundred years laid waste.
Charles is waiting for news of Ganelon

[10]529, 530: Parts of these lines are unintelligible in the manuscript.

and the tribute from Spain, from that great land.
In the morning, at dawn, with the first light,
Count Ganelon came to the Christian camp. AOI.

54

The Emperor rose early in the morning,
the King of France, and has heard mass and matins.
On the green grass he stood before his tent.
Roland was there, and Oliver, brave man, 560
Naimon the Duke, and many other knights.
Ganelon came, the traitor, the foresworn.
With what great cunning he commences his speech;
said to the King: "May the Lord God save you!
Here I bring you the keys to Saragossa.
And I bring you great treasure from that city,
and twenty hostages, have them well guarded.
And good King Marsilion sends you this word:
Do not blame him concerning the Algalife:
I saw it all myself, with my own eyes:
four hundred thousand men, and all in arms, 570
their hauberks on, some with their helms laced on,
swords on their belts, the hilts enameled gold,
who went with him to the edge of the sea.
They are in flight: it is the Christian faith—
they do not want it, they will not keep its law.
They had not sailed four full leagues out to sea
when a high wind, a tempest swept them up.
They were all drowned; you will never see them;
if he were still alive, I'd have brought him.
As for the pagan King, Lord, believe this: 580
before you see one month from this day pass,
he'll follow you to the Kingdom of France
and take the faith—he will take your faith, Lord,
and join his hands and become your vassal.
He will hold Spain as a fief from your hand."
Then the King said: "May God be thanked for this.
You have done well, you will be well rewarded."
Throughout the host they sound a thousand trumpets.
The French break camp, strap their gear on their pack-horses.
They take the road to the sweet land of France. AOI. 590

. . .

58

The day goes by, and the bright dawn arises.
Throughout that host. . . .[11]
The Emperor rides forth with such fierce pride.

[11] Second hemistich of line 592 is unintelligible in the manuscript.

"Barons, my lords," said the Emperor Charles,
"look at those passes, at those narrow defiles—
pick me a man to command the rear-guard."
Ganelon answers: "Roland, here, my stepson.
You have no baron as great and brave as Roland."
When he hears that, the King stares at him in fury;
and said to him: "You are the living devil, 600
a mad dog—the murderous rage in you!
And who will precede me, in the vanguard?"
Ganelon answers, "Why, Ogier of Denmark,
you have no baron who could lead it so well."

59

Roland the Count, when he heard himself named,
knew what to say, and spoke as a knight must speak:
"Lord Stepfather, I have to cherish you!
You have had the rear-guard assigned to me.
Charles will not lose, this great King who rules France,
I swear it now, one palfrey, one war horse—
while I'm alive and know what's happening— 610
one he-mule, one she-mule that he might ride,
Charles will not lose one sumpter, not one pack horse
that has not first been bought and paid for with swords."
Ganelon answers: "You speak the truth, I know." AOI.

60

When Roland hears he will lead the rear-guard,
he spoke in great fury to his stepfather:
"Hah! you nobody, you base-born little fellow,
and did you think the glove would fall from my hands
as the staff fell from yours before King Charles?" AOI.[12]

61

"Just Emperor," said Roland, that great man, 620
"give me the bow that you hold in your hand.
And no man here, I think, will say in reproach
I let it drop, as Ganelon let the staff drop
from his right hand, when he should have taken it."
The Emperor bowed down his head with this,
he pulled his beard, he twisted his mustache,
cannot hold back, tears fill his eyes, he weeps.

. . .

[12]Ganelon had let fall a glove, not a staff (*laisse* 25). For this and other less objective reasons, some editors have questioned the authenticity of this *laisse*. In line 623, an editor tried to make the text more consistent by adding the reference to the staff.

64

Roland the Count mounted his battle horse. AOI.
Oliver came to him, his companion.
And Gerin came, and the brave Count Gerer, 630
and Aton came, and there came Berenger,
and Astor came, and Anseïs, fierce and proud,
and the old man Gerard of Roussillon,
and Gaifier, that great and mighty duke.
Said the Archbishop: "I'm going, by my head!"
"And I with you," said Gautier the Count,
"I am Count Roland's man and must not fail him."
And together they choose twenty thousand men. AOI.

65

Roland the Count summons Gautier de l'Hum:
"Now take a thousand Franks from our land, France, 640
and occupy those passes and the heights there.
The Emperor must not lose a single man." AOI.
Gautier replies: "Lord, I'll fight well for you."
And with a thousand French of France, their land,
Gautier rides out to the hills and defiles;
will not come down, for all the bad news, again,
till seven hundred swords have been drawn out.
King Almaris of the Kingdom of Belferne
gave them battle that day, and it was bitter.

66

High are the hills, the valleys tenebrous, 650
the cliffs are dark, the defiles mysterious.
That day, and with much pain, the French passed through.
For fifteen leagues around one heard their clamor.
When they reach Tere Majur, the Land of Fathers,
they beheld Gascony, their lord's domain.
Then they remembered: their fiefs, their realms, their honors,
remembered their young girls, their gentle wives:
not one who does not weep for what he feels.
Beyond these others King Charles is in bad straits:
his nephew left in the defiles of Spain! 660
feels the pity of it; tears break through. AOI.

67

And the Twelve Peers are left behind in Spain,
and twenty thousand Franks are left with them.
They have no fear, they have no dread of death.

The Emperor is going home to France.
Beneath his cloak, his face shows all he feels.
Naimon the Duke is riding beside him;
and he said to the King: "What is this grief?"
And Charles replies: "Whoever asks me, wrongs me.
I feel such pain, I cannot keep from wailing. 670
France will be destroyed by Ganelon.
Last night I saw a vision brought by angels:
the one who named my nephew for the rear-guard
shattered the lance between my fists to pieces.
I have left him in a march among strangers.
If I lose him, God! I won't find his like." AOI.

68

King Charles the Great cannot keep from weeping.
A hundred thousand Franks feel pity for him;
and for Roland, an amazing fear.
Ganelon the criminal has betrayed him; 680
got gifts for it from the pagan king,
gold and silver, cloths of silk, gold brocade,
mules and horses and camels and lions.
Marsilion sends for the barons of Spain,
counts and viscounts and dukes and almaçurs,
and the emirs, and the sons of great lords:
four hundred thousand assembled in three days.
In Saragossa he has them beat the drums,
they raise Mahumet upon the highest tower:
no pagan now who does not worship him 690
and adore him. Then they ride, racing each other,
search through the land, the valleys, the mountains;
and then they saw the banners of the French.
The rear-guard of the Twelve Companions
will not fail now, they'll give the pagans battle.

. . .

79

They arm themselves in Saracen hauberks,
all but a few are lined with triple mail;
they lace on their good helms of Saragossa,
gird on their swords, the steel forged in Vienne;
they have rich shields, spears of Valencia, 700
and gonfanons of white and blue and red.
They leave the mules and riding horses now,
mount their war horses and ride in close array.
The day was fair, the sun was shining bright,
all their armor was aflame with the light;
a thousand trumpets blow: that was to make it finer.

That made a great noise, and the men of France heard.
Said Oliver: "Companion, I believe
we may yet have a battle with the pagans."
Roland replies: "Now may God grant us that. 710
We know our duty: to stand here for our King.
A man must bear some hardships for his lord,
stand everything, the great heat, the great cold,
lose the hide and hair on him for his good lord.
Now let each man make sure to strike hard here:
let them not sing a bad song about us!
Pagans are wrong and Christians are right!
They'll make no bad example of me this day!" AOI.

80

Oliver climbs to the top of a hill,
looks to his right, across a grassy vale, 720
sees the pagan army on its way there;
and called down to Roland, his companion:
"That way, toward Spain: the uproar I see coming!
All their hauberks, all blazing, helmets like flames!
It will be a bitter thing for our French.
Ganelon knew, that criminal, that traitor,
when he marked us out before the Emperor."
"Be still, Oliver," Roland the Count replies.
"He is my stepfather—my stepfather.
I won't have you speak one word against him."

81

Oliver has gone up upon a hill, 730
sees clearly now: the kingdom of Spain,
and the Saracens assembled in such numbers:
helmets blazing, bedecked with gems in gold,
those shields of theirs, those hauberks sewn with brass,
and all their spears, the gonfanons affixed;
cannot begin to count their battle corps,
there are too many, he cannot take their number.
And he is deeply troubled by what he sees.
He made his way quickly down from the hill,
came to the French, told them all he had seen. 740

82

Said Oliver: "I saw the Saracens,
no man on earth ever saw more of them—
one hundred thousand, with their shields, up in front,
helmets laced on, hauberks blazing on them,

the shafts straight up, the iron heads like flames—
you'll get a battle, nothing like it before.
My lords, my French, may God give you the strength.
Hold your ground now! Let them not defeat us!"
And the French say: "God hate the man who runs!
We may die here, but no man will fail you." AOI. 750

83

Said Oliver: "The pagan force is great;
from what I see, our French here are too few.
Roland, my companion, sound your horn then,
Charles will hear it, the army will come back."
Roland replies: "I'd be a fool to do it.
I would lose my good name all through sweet France.
I will strike now, I'll strike with Durendal,
the blade will be bloody to the gold from striking!
These pagan traitors came to these passes doomed!
I promise you, they are marked men, they'll die." AOI. 760

84

"Roland, Companion, now sound the olifant,
Charles will hear it, he will bring the army back,
the King will come with all his barons to help us."
Roland replies: "May it never please God
that my kin should be shamed because of me,
or that sweet France should fall into disgrace.
Never! Never! I'll strike with Durendal,
I'll strike with this good sword strapped to my side,
you'll see this blade running its whole length with blood.
These pagan traitors have gathered here to die. 770
I promise you, they are all bound for death." AOI.

85

"Roland, Companion, sound your olifant now,
Charles will hear it, marching through those passes.
I promise you, the Franks will come at once."
Roland replies: "May it never please God
that any man alive should come to say
that pagans—pagans!—once made me sound this horn:
no kin of mine will ever bear that shame.
Once I enter this great battle coming
and strike my thousand seven hundred blows, 780
you'll see the bloody steel of Durendal.
These French are good—they will strike like brave men.
Nothing can save the men of Spain from death."

86

Said Oliver: "I see no blame in it—
I watched the Saracens coming from Spain,
the valleys and mountains covered with them,
every hillside and every plain all covered,
hosts and hosts everywhere of those strange men—
and here we have a little company."
Roland replies: "That whets my appetite. 790
May it not please God and his angels and saints
to let France lose its glory because of me—
let me not end in shame, let me die first.
The Emperor loves us when we fight well."

87

Roland is good, and Oliver is wise,
both these vassals men of amazing courage:
once they are armed and mounted on their horses,
they will not run, though they die for it, from battle.
Good men, these Counts, and their words full of spirit.
Traitor pagans are riding up in fury. 800
Said Oliver: "Roland, look—the first ones,
on top of us—and Charles is far away.
You did not think it right to sound your olifant:
if the King were here, we'd come out without losses.
Now look up there, toward the passes of Aspre—
you can see the rear-guard: it will suffer.
No man in that detail will be in another."
Roland replies: "Don't speak such foolishness—
shame on the heart gone coward in the chest.
We'll hold our ground, we'll stand firm—we're the ones! 810
We'll fight with spears, we'll fight them hand to hand!" AOI.

88

When Roland sees that there will be a battle,
it makes him fiercer than a lion or leopard;
shouts to the French, calls out to Oliver:
"Lord, companion: friend, do not say such things.
The Emperor, who left us these good French,
had set apart these twenty thousand men:
he knew there was no coward in their ranks.
A man must meet great troubles for his lord,
stand up to the great heat and the great cold, 820
give up some flesh and blood—it is his duty.
Strike with the lance, I'll strike with Durendal—
it was the King who gave me this good sword!
If I die here, the man who gets it can say:
it was a noble's, a vassal's, a good man's sword."

89

And now there comes the Archbishop Turpin.
He spurs his horse, goes up into a mountain,
summons the French; and he preached them a sermon:
"Barons, my lords, Charles left us in this place.
We know our duty: to die like good men for our King. 830
Fight to defend the holy Christian faith.
Now you will have a battle, you know it now,
you see the Saracens with your own eyes.
Confess your sins, pray to the Lord for mercy.
I will absolve you all, to save your souls.
If you die here, you will stand up holy martyrs,
you will have seats in highest Paradise."
The French dismount, cast themselves on the ground;
the Archbishop blesses them in God's name.
He commands them to do one penance: strike. 840

90

The French arise, stand on their feet again;
they are absolved, released from all their sins:
the Archbishop has blessed them in God's name.
Now they are mounted on their swift battle horses,
bearing their arms like faithful warriors;
and every man stands ready for the battle.
Roland the Count calls out to Oliver:
"Lord, Companion, you knew it, you were right,
Ganelon watched for his chance to betray us,
got gold for it, got goods for it, and money. 850
The Emperor will have to avenge us now.
King Marsilion made a bargain for our lives,
but still must pay, and that must be with swords." AOI.

91

Roland went forth into the Spanish passes
on Veillantif, his good swift-running horse.
He bears his arms—how they become this man!—
grips his lance now, hefting it, working it,
now swings the iron point up toward the sky,
the gonfanon all white laced on above—
the golden streamers beat down upon his hands: 860
a noble's body, the face aglow and smiling.
Close behind him his good companion follows;
the men of France hail him: their protector!
He looks wildly toward the Saracens,
and humbly and gently to the men of France;
and spoke a word to them, in all courtesy:
"Barons, my lords, easy now, keep at a walk.

These pagans are searching for martyrdom.
We'll get good spoils before this day is over,
no king of France ever got such treasure!" 870
And with these words, the hosts are at each other. AOI.

92

Said Oliver: "I will waste no more words.
You did not think it right to sound your olifant,
there'll be no Charles coming to your aid now.
He knows nothing, brave man, he's done no wrong;
those men down there—they have no blame in this.
Well, then, ride now, and ride with all your might!
Lords, you brave men, stand your ground, hold the field!
Make up your minds, I beg you in God's name,
to strike some blows, take them and give them back! 880
Here we must not forget Charlemagne's war cry."
And with that word the men of France cried out.
A man who heard that shout: Munjoie! Munjoie!
would always remember what manhood is.
Then they ride, God! look at their pride and spirit!
and they spur hard, to ride with all their speed,
come on to strike—what else would these men do?
The Saracens kept coming, never fearing them.
Franks and pagans, here they are, at each other.

93

Marsilion's nephew is named Aëlroth. 890
He rides in front, at the head of the army,
comes on shouting insults against our French:
"French criminals, today you fight our men.
One man should have saved you: he betrayed you.
A fool, your King, to leave you in these passes.
This is the day sweet France will lose its name,
and Charlemagne the right arm of his body."
When he hears that—God!—Roland is outraged!
He spurs his horse, gives Veillantif its head.
The Count comes on to strike with all his might, 900
smashes his shield, breaks his hauberk apart,
and drives: rips through his chest, shatters the bones,
knocks the whole backbone out of his back,
casts out the soul of Aëlroth with his lance;
which he thrusts deep, makes the whole body shake,
throws him down dead, lance straight out, from his horse;[13]
he has broken his neck; broken it in two.
There is something, he says, he must tell him:

[13]Lance straight out (*pleine sa hanste,* "with his full lance"): the lance is held, not thrown, and used to knock the enemy from his horse. To throw one's weapons is savage and ignoble.

"Clown! Nobody! Now you know Charles is no fool,
he never was the man to love treason. 910
It took his valor to leave us in these passes!
France will not lose its name, sweet France! today.
Brave men of France, strike hard! The first blow is ours!
We're in the right, and these swine in the wrong!" AOI.

. . .

104

The battle is fearful and wonderful
and everywhere. Roland never spares himself,
strikes with his lance as long as the wood lasts:
the fifteenth blow he struck, it broke, was lost.
Then he draws Durendal, his good sword, bare,
and spurs his horse, comes on to strike Chernuble, 920
smashes his helmet, carbuncles shed their light,
cuts through the coif, through the hair on his head,
cut through his eyes, through his face, through that look,
the bright, shining hauberk with its fine rings,
down through the trunk to the fork of his legs,
through the saddle, adorned with beaten gold,
into the horse; and the sword came to rest:
cut through the spine, never felt for the joint;
knocks him down, dead, on the rich grass of the meadow;
then said to him: "You were doomed when you started, 930
Clown! Nobody! Let Mahum help you now.
No pagan swine will win this field today."

105

Roland the Count comes riding through the field,
holds Durendal, that sword! it carves its way!
and brings terrible slaughter down on the pagans.
To have seen him cast one man dead on another,
the bright red blood pouring out on the ground,
his hauberk, his two arms, running with blood,
his good horse—neck and shoulders running with blood!
And Oliver does not linger, he strikes! 940
and the Twelve Peers, no man could reproach them;
and the brave French, they fight with lance and sword.
The pagans die, some simply faint away!
Said the Archbishop: "Bless our band of brave men!"
Munjoie! he shouts—the war cry of King Charles. AOI.

106

Oliver rides into that battle-storm,
his lance is broken, he holds only the stump;
comes on to strike a pagan, Malsarun;

and he smashes his shield, all flowers and gold,
sends his two eyes flying out of his head, 950
and his brains come pouring down to his feet;
casts him down, dead, with seven hundred others.
Now he has killed Turgis and Esturguz,
and the shaft bursts, shivers down to his fists.
Count Roland said: "Companion, what are you doing?
Why bother with a stick in such a battle?
Iron and steel will do much better work!
Where is your sword, your Halteclere—that name!
Where is that crystal hilt, that golden guard?"
"Haven't had any time to draw it out, 960
been so busy fighting," said Oliver. AOI.

. . .

110

The battle is fearful and full of grief.
Oliver and Roland strike like good men,
the Archbishop, more than a thousand blows,
and the Twelve Peers do not hang back, they strike!
the French fight side by side, all as one man.
The pagans die by hundreds, by thousands:
whoever does not flee finds no refuge from death,
like it or not, there he ends all his days.
And there the men of France lose their greatest arms; 970
they will not see their fathers, their kin again,
or Charlemagne, who looks for them in the passes.
Tremendous torment now comes forth in France,
a mighty whirlwind, tempests of wind and thunder,
rains and hailstones, great and immeasurable,
bolts of lightning hurtling and hurtling down:
it is, in truth, a trembling of the earth.
From Saint Michael-in-Peril to the Saints,[14]
from Besançon to the port of Wissant,
there is no house whose veil of walls does not crumble. 980
A great darkness at noon falls on the land,
there is no light but when the heavens crack.
No man sees this who is not terrified,
and many say: "The Last Day! Judgment Day!
The end! The end of the world is upon us!"
They do not know, they do not speak the truth:
it is the worldwide grief for the death of Roland.

. . .

[14]It is clear that these four points mark out the France of the tenth century, the realm of the last Carolingians.

112

King Marsilion comes along a valley
with all his men, the great host he assembled:
twenty divisions, formed and numbered by the King, 990
helmets ablaze with gems beset in gold,
and those bright shields, those hauberks sewn with brass.
Seven thousand clarions sound the pursuit,
and the great noise resounds across that country.
Said Roland then: "Oliver, Companion, Brother,
that traitor Ganelon has sworn our deaths:
it is treason, it cannot stay hidden,
the Emperor will take his terrible revenge.
We have this battle now, it will be bitter,
no man has ever seen the like of it. 1000
I will fight here with Durendal, this sword,
and you, my companion, with Halteclere—
we've fought with them before, in many lands!
how many battles have we won with these two!
Let no one sing a bad song of our swords." AOI.

. . .

114

Turpin the Archbishop begins the battle.
He rides the horse that he took from Grossaille,
who was a king this priest once killed in Denmark.
Now this war horse is quick and spirited,
his hooves high-arched, the quick legs long and flat, 1010
short in the thigh, wide in the rump, long in the flanks,
and the backbone so high, a battle horse!
and that white tail, the yellow mane on him,
the little ears on him, the tawny head!
No beast on earth could ever run with him.
The Archbishop—that valiant man!—spurs hard,
he will attack Abisme, he will not falter,
strikes on his shield, a miraculous blow:
a shield of stones, of amethysts, topazes,
esterminals, carbuncles all on fire— 1020
a gift from a devil, in Val Metas,
sent on to him by the Amiral Galafre.
There Turpin strikes, he does not treat it gently—
after that blow, I'd not give one cent for it;
cut through his body, from one side to the other,
and casts him down dead in a barren place.
And the French say: "A fighter, that Archbishop!
Look at him there, saving souls with that crozier!"

. . .

127

Roland the Count calls out to Oliver:
"Lord, Companion, now you have to agree 1030
the Archbishop is a good man on horse,
there's none better on earth or under heaven,
he knows his way with a lance and a spear."
The Count replies: "Right! Let us help him then."
And with these words the Franks began anew,
the blows strike hard, and the fighting is bitter;
there is a painful loss of Christian men.
To have seen them, Roland and Oliver,
these fighting men, striking down with their swords,
the Archbishop with them, striking with his lance! 1040
One can recount the number these three killed:
it is written—in charters, in documents;
the Geste tells it: it was more than four thousand.
Through four assaults all went well with our men;
then comes the fifth, and that one crushes them.
They are all killed, all these warriors of France,
all but sixty, whom the Lord God has spared:
they will die too, but first sell themselves dear. AOI.

128

Count Roland sees the great loss of his men,
calls on his companion, on Oliver: 1050
"Lord, Companion, in God's name, what would you do?
All these good men you see stretched on the ground.
We can mourn for sweet France, fair land of France!
a desert now, stripped of such great vassals.
Oh King, and friend, if only you were here!
Oliver, Brother, how shall we manage it?
What shall we do to get word to the King?"
Said Oliver: "I don't see any way.
I would rather die now than hear us shamed." AOI.

129

And Roland said: "I'll sound the olifant, 1060
Charles will hear it, drawing through the passes,
I promise you, the Franks will return at once."
Said Oliver: "That would be a great disgrace,
a dishonor and reproach to all your kin,
the shame of it would last them all their lives.
When I urged it, you would not hear of it;
you will not do it now with my consent.

It is not acting bravely to sound it now—
look at your arms, they are covered with blood."
The Count replies: "I've fought here like a lord."[15] AOI. 1070

130

And Roland says: "We are in a rough battle.
I'll sound the olifant, Charles will hear it."
Said Oliver: "No good vassal would do it.
When I urged it, friend, you did not think it right.
If Charles were here, we'd come out with no losses.
Those men down there—no blame can fall on them."
Oliver said: "Now by this beard of mine,
If I can see my noble sister, Aude,
once more, you will never lie in her arms!" AOI.

131

And Roland said: "Why are you angry at me?" 1080
Oliver answers: "Companion, it is your doing.
I will tell you what makes a vassal good:
it is judgment, it is never madness;
restraint is worth more than the raw nerve of a fool.
Frenchmen are dead because of your wildness.
And what service will Charles ever have from us?
If you had trusted me, my lord would be here,
we would have fought this battle through to the end,
Marsilion would be dead, or our prisoner.
Roland, your prowess—had we never seen it!
And now, dear friend, we've seen the last of it.
No more aid from us now for Charlemagne, 1090
a man without equal till Judgment Day,
you will die here, and your death will shame France.
We kept faith, you and I, we were companions;
and everything we were will end today.
We part before evening, and it will be hard." AOI.

132

Turpin the Archbishop hears their bitter words,
digs hard into his horse with golden spurs

[15] Some have found these lines difficult. Oliver means: We have fought this far—look at the enemy's blood on your arms: It is too late, it would be a disgrace to summon help when there is no longer any chance of being saved. Roland thinks that is the one time when it is not a disgrace.

and rides to them; begins to set them right:
"You, Lord Roland, and you, Lord Oliver,
I beg you in God's name do not quarrel.
To sound the horn could not help us now, true, 1100
but still it is far better that you do it:
let the King come, he can avenge us then—
these men of Spain must not go home exulting!
Our French will come, they'll get down on their feet,
and find us here—we'll be dead, cut to pieces.
They will lift us into coffins on the backs of mules,
and weep for us, in rage and pain and grief,
and bury us in the courts of churches;
and we will not be eaten by wolves or pigs or dogs."
Roland replies, "Lord, you have spoken well." AOI. 1110

133

Roland has put the olifant to his mouth,
he sets it well, sounds it with all his strength.
The hills are high, and that voice ranges far,
they heard it echo thirty great leagues away.
King Charles heard it, and all his faithful men.
And the King says: "Our men are in a battle."
And Ganelon disputed him and said:
"Had someone else said that, I'd call him liar!" AOI.

134

And now the mighty effort of Roland the Count:
he sounds his olifant; his pain is great, 1120
and from his mouth the bright blood comes leaping out,
and the temple bursts in his forehead.
That horn, in Roland's hands, has a mighty voice:
King Charles hears it drawing through the passes.
Naimon heard it, the Franks listen to it.
And the King said: "I hear Count Roland's horn;
he'd never sound it unless he had a battle."
Says Ganelon: "Now no more talk of battles!
You are old now, your hair is white as snow,
the things you say make you sound like a child. 1130
You know Roland and that wild pride of his—
what a wonder God has suffered it so long!
Remember? he took Noples without your command:
the Saracens rode out, to break the siege;
they fought with him, the great vassal Roland.
Afterwards he used the streams to wash the blood
from the meadows: so that nothing would show.
He blasts his horn all day to catch a rabbit,
he's strutting now before his peers and bragging—

who under heaven would dare meet him on the field? 1140
So now: ride on! Why do you keep on stopping?
The Land of Fathers lies far ahead of us." AOI.

135

The blood leaping from Count Roland's mouth,
the temple broken with effort in his forehead,
he sounds his horn in great travail and pain.
King Charles heard it, and his French listen hard.
And the King said: "That horn has a long breath!"
Naimon answers: "It is a baron's breath.
There is a battle there, I know there is.
He betrayed him! and now asks you to fail him! 1150
Put on your armor! Lord, shout your battle cry,
and save the noble barons of your house!
You hear Roland's call. He is in trouble."

136

The Emperor commanded the horns to sound,
the French dismount, and they put on their armor:
their hauberks, their helmets, their gold-dressed swords,
their handsome shields; and take up their great lances,
the gonfalons of white and red and blue.
The barons of that host mount their war horses
and spur them hard the whole length of the pass; 1160
and every man of them says to the other:
"If only we find Roland before he's killed,
we'll stand with him, and then we'll do some fighting!"
What does it matter what they say? They are too late.

137

It is the end of day, and full of light,
arms and armor are ablaze in the sun,
and fire flashes from hauberks and helmets,
and from those shields, painted fair with flowers,
and from those lances, those gold-dressed gonfanons.
The Emperor rides on in rage and sorrow, 1170
the men of France indignant and full of grief.
There is no man of them who does not weep,
they are in fear for the life of Roland.
The King commands: seize Ganelon the Count!
and gave him over to the cooks of his house;
summons the master cook, their chief, Besgun:
"Guard him for me like the traitor he is:
he has betrayed the barons of my house."

Besgun takes him, sets his kitchen comrades,
a hundred men, the best, the worst, on him; 1180
and they tear out his beard and his mustache,
each one strikes him four good blows with his fist;
and they lay into him with cudgels and sticks,
put an iron collar around his neck
and chain him up, as they would chain a bear;
dumped him, in dishonor, on a packhorse,
and guard him well till they give him back to Charles.

138

High are the hills, and tenebrous, and vast, AOI.
the valleys deep, the raging waters swift;
to the rear, to the front, the trumpets sound: 1190
they answer the lone voice of the olifant.
The Emperor rides on, rides on in fury,
the men of France in grief and indignation.
There is no man who does not weep and wail,
and they pray God: protect the life of Roland
till they come, one great host, into the field
and fight at Roland's side like true men all.
What does it matter what they pray? It does no good.
They are too late, they cannot come in time. AOI.

139

King Charles the Great rides on, a man in wrath, 1200
his great white beard spread out upon his hauberk.[16]
All the barons of France ride spurring hard,
there is no man who does not wail, furious
not to be with Roland, the captain count,
who stands and fights the Saracens of Spain,
so set upon, I cannot think his soul abides.
God! those sixty men who stand with him, what men!
No king, no captain ever stood with better. AOI.

140

Roland looks up on the mountains and slopes,
sees the French dead, so many good men fallen, 1210
and weeps for them, as a great warrior weeps:

[16]The beard spread out upon the hauberk is a gesture of defiance toward the enemy.

"Barons, my lords, may God give you his grace,
may he grant Paradise to all your souls,
make them lie down among the holy flowers.
I never saw better vassals than you.
All the years you've served me, and all the times,
the mighty lands you conquered for Charles our King!
The Emperor raised you for this terrible hour!
Land of France, how sweet you are, native land,
laid waste this day, ravaged, made a desert. 1220
Barons of France, I see you die for me,
and I, your lord—I cannot protect you.
May *God* come to your aid, that God who never failed.
Oliver, brother, now I will not fail *you*.
I will die here—of grief, if no man kills me.
Lord, Companion, let us return and fight."

141

Roland returned to his place on the field,
strikes—a brave man keeping faith—with Durendal,
struck through Faldrun de Pui, cut him to pieces,
and twenty-four of the men they valued most; 1230
no man will ever want his vengeance more!
As when the deer turns tail before the dogs,
so the pagans flee before Roland the Count.
Said the Archbishop: "You! Roland! What a fighter!
Now that's what every knight must have in him
who carries arms and rides on a fine horse:
he must be strong, a savage, when he's in battle;
for otherwise, what's he worth? Not four cents!
Let that four-cent man be a monk in some minster,
and he can pray all day long for our sins." 1240
Roland replies: "Attack, do not spare them!"
And with that word the Franks began again.
There was a heavy loss of Christian men.

142

When a man knows there'll be no prisoners,
what will that man not do to defend himself!
And so the Franks fight with the fury of lions.
Now Marsilion, the image of a baron,
mounted on that war horse he calls Gaignun,
digs in his spurs, comes on to strike Bevon,
who was the lord of Beaune and of Dijon; 1250
smashes his shield, rips apart his hauberk,
knocks him down, dead, no need to wound him more.

And then he killed Yvorie and Yvon,
and more: he killed Gerard of Rousillon.
Roland the Count is not far away now,
said to the pagan: "The Lord God's curse on you!
You kill my companions, how you wrong me!
You'll feel the pain of it before we part,
you will learn my sword's name by heart today";
comes on to strike—the image of a baron. 1260
He has cut off Marsilion's right fist;
now takes the head of Jurfaleu the blond—
the head of Jurfaleu! Marsilion's son.
The pagans cry: "Help, Mahumet! Help us!
Vengeance, our gods, on Charles! the man who set
these criminals on us in our own land,
they will not quit the field, they'll stand and die!"
And one said to the other: "Let *us* run then."
And with that word, some hundred thousand flee.
Now try to call them back: they won't return. AOI. 1270

143

What does it matter? If Marsilion has fled,
his uncle has remained: the Algalife,
who holds Carthage, Alfrere, and Garmalie,
and Ethiopia: a land accursed;
holds its immense black race under his power,
the huge noses, the enormous ears on them;
and they number more than fifty thousand.
These are the men who come riding in fury,
and now they shout that pagan battle cry.
And Roland said: "Here comes our martyrdom; 1280
I see it now: we have not long to live.
But let the world call any man a traitor
who does not make them pay before he dies!
My lords, attack! Use those bright shining swords!
Fight a good fight for your deaths and your lives,
let no shame touch sweet France because of us!
When Charles my lord comes to this battlefield
and sees how well we punished these Saracens,
finds fifteen of their dead for one of ours,
I'll tell you what he will do: he will bless us." AOI.

144

When Roland sees that unbelieving race, 1290
those hordes and hordes blacker than blackest ink—
no shred of white on them except their teeth—
then said the Count: "I see it clearly now,
we die today: it is there before us.

Men of France, strike! I will start it once more."
Said Oliver: "God curse the slowest man."
And with that word, the French strike into battle.

. . .

146

Oliver feels: he has been struck to death;
grips Halteclere, that steel blade shining, strikes
on the gold-dressed pointed helm of the Algalife, 1300
sends jewels and flowers crackling down to the earth,
into the head, into the little teeth;
draws up his flashing sword, casts him down, dead,
and then he says: "Pagan, a curse on you!
If only I could say Charles has lost nothing—
but no woman, no lady you ever knew
will hear you boast, in the land you came from,
that you could take one thing worth a cent from me,
or do me harm, or do any man harm";
then cries out to Roland to come to his aid. AOI. 1310

147

Oliver feels he is wounded to death,
will never have his fill of vengeance, strikes,
as a baron strikes, where they are thickest,
cuts through their lances, cuts through those buckled shields,
through feet, through fists, through saddles, and through flanks.
Had you seen him, cutting the pagans limb
from limb, casting one corpse down on another,
you would remember a brave man keeping faith.
Never would he forget Charles' battle-cry,
Munjoie! he shouts, that mighty voice ringing; 1320
calls to Roland, to his friend and his peer:
"Lord, Companion, come stand beside me now.
We must part from each other in pain today." AOI.

148

Roland looks hard into Oliver's face,
it is ashen, all its color is gone,
the bright red blood streams down upon his body,
Oliver's blood spattering on the earth.
"God!" said the Count, "I don't know what to do,
Lord, Companion, your fight is finished now.
There'll never be a man the like of you. 1330
Sweet land of France, today you will be stripped

of good vassals, laid low, a fallen land!
The Emperor will suffer the great loss";
faints with that word, mounted upon his horse. AOI.

149

Here is Roland, lords, fainted on his horse,
and Oliver the Count, wounded to death:
he has lost so much blood, his eyes are darkened—
he cannot see, near or far, well enough
to recognize a friend or enemy:
struck when he came upon his companion, 1340
strikes on his helm, adorned with gems in gold,
cuts down straight through, from the point to the nasal,[17]
but never harmed him, he never touched his head.
Under this blow, Count Roland looked at him;
and gently, softly now, he asks of him:
"Lord, Companion, do you mean to do this?
It is Roland, who always loved you greatly.
You never declared that we were enemies."
Said Oliver: "Now I hear it is you—
I don't see you, may the Lord God see you. 1350
Was it you that I struck? Forgive me then."
Roland replies: "I am not harmed, not harmed,
I forgive you, Friend, here and before God."
And with that word, each bowed to the other.
And this is the love, lords, in which they parted.

150

Oliver feels: death pressing hard on him;
his two eyes turn, roll up into his head,
all hearing is lost now, all sight is gone;
gets down on foot, stretches out on the ground,
cries out now and again: *mea culpa!* 1360
his two hands joined, raised aloft toward heaven,
he prays to God: grant him His Paradise;
and blesses Charles, and the sweet land of France,
his companion, Roland, above all men.
The heart fails him, his helmet falls away,
the great body settles upon the earth.
The Count is dead, he stands with us no longer.
Roland, brave man, weeps for him, mourns for him,
you will not hear a man of greater sorrow.

[17]Nasal: the nosepiece protruding down from the cone-shaped helmet.

151

Roland the Count, when he sees his friend dead, 1370
lying stretched out, his face against the earth,
softly, gently, begins to speak the regret:[18]
"Lord, Companion, you were brave and died for it.
We have stood side by side through days and years,
you never caused me harm, I never wronged you;
when you are dead, to be alive pains me."
And with that word the lord of marches faints
upon his horse, which he calls Veillantif.
He is held firm by his spurs of fine gold,
whichever way he leans, he cannot fall. 1380

152

Before Roland could recover his senses
and come out of his faint, and be aware,
a great disaster had come forth before him:
the French are dead, he has lost every man
except the Archbishop, and Gautier de l'Hum,
who has come back, down from that high mountain:
he has fought well, he fought those men of Spain.
His men are dead, the pagans finished them;
flees now down to these valleys, he has no choice,
and calls on Count Roland to come to his aid: 1390
"My noble Count, my brave lord, where are you?
I never feared whenever you were there.
It is Walter: I conquered Maëlgut,
my uncle is Droün, old and gray: your Walter
and always dear to you for the way I fought;
and I have fought this time: my lance is shattered,
my good shield pierced, my hauberk's meshes broken;
and I am wounded, a lance struck through my body.
I will die soon, but I sold myself dear."
And with that word, Count Roland has heard him, 1400
he spurs his horse, rides spurring to his man. AOI.

153

Roland in pain, maddened with grief and rage:
rushes where they are thickest and strikes again,
strikes twenty men of Spain, strikes twenty dead,

[18] To speak the regret: what follows is a formal and customary lament for the dead.

and Walter six, and the Archbishop five.
The pagans say: "Look at those criminals!
Now take care, Lords, they don't get out alive,
only a traitor will not attack them now!
Only a coward will let them save their skins!"
And then they raise their hue and cry once more, 1410
rush in on them, once more, from every side. AOI.

154

Count Roland was always a noble warrior,
Gautier de l'Hum is a fine mounted man,
the Archbishop, a good man tried and proved:
not one of them will ever leave the others;
strike, where they are thickest, at the pagans.
A thousand Saracens get down on foot,
and forty thousand more are on their mounts:
and I tell you, not one will dare come close,
they throw, and from afar, lances and spears, 1420
wigars and darts, mizraks, javelins, pikes.
With the first blows they killed Gautier de l'Hum
and struck Turpin of Reims, pierced through his shield,
broke the helmet on him, wounded his head;
ripped his hauberk, shattered its rings of mail,
and pierced him with four spears in his body,
the war horse killed under him; and now there comes
great pain and rage when the Archbishop falls. AOI.

155

Turpin of Reims, when he feels he is unhorsed,
struck to the earth with four spears in his body, 1430
quickly, brave man, leaps to his feet again;
his eyes find Roland now, he runs to him
and says one word: "See! I'm not finished yet!
What good vassal ever gives up alive!";
and draws Almace, his sword, that shining steel!
and strikes, where they are thickest, a thousand blows, and more.
Later, Charles said: Turpin had spared no one;
he found four hundred men prostrate around him,
some of them wounded, some pierced from front to back,
some with their heads hacked off. So says the Geste, 1440
and so says one who was there, on that field,
the baron Saint Gilles,[19] for whom God performs miracles,

[19]Saint Gilles of Provence. These lines explain how the story of Rencesvals could be told after all who had fought there died.

who made the charter setting forth these great things
in the Church of Laon. Now any man
who does not know this much understands nothing.

156

Roland the Count fights well and with great skill,
but he is hot, his body soaked with sweat;
has a great wound in his head, and much pain,
his temple broken because he blew the horn.
But he must know whether King Charles will come;
draws out the olifant, sounds it, so feebly. 1450
The Emperor drew to a halt, listened.
"Seigneurs," he said, "it goes badly for us—
My nephew Roland falls from our ranks today.
I hear it in the horn's voice: he hasn't long.
Let every man who wants to be with Roland
ride fast! Sound trumpets! Every trumpet in this host!"
Sixty thousand, on these words, sound, so high
the mountains sound, and the valleys resound.
The pagans hear: it is no joke to them;
cry to each other: "We're getting Charles on us!" 1460

157

The pagans say: "The Emperor is coming, AOI.
listen to their trumpets—it is the French!
If Charles comes back, it's all over for us,
if Roland lives, this war begins again
and we have lost our land, we have lost Spain."
Some four hundred, helmets laced on, assemble,
some of the best, as they think, on that field.
They storm Roland, in one fierce, bitter attack.
And now Count Roland has some work on his hands. AOI.

. . .

160

Say the pagans: "We were all born unlucky! 1470
The evil day that dawned for us today!
We have lost our lords and peers, and now comes Charles—
that Charlemagne!—with his great host. Those trumpets!
that shrill sound on us—the trumpets of the French!
And the loud roar of that Munjoie! This Roland
is a wild man, he is too great a fighter—
What man of flesh and blood can ever hope
to bring him down? Let us cast at him, and leave him there."

And so they did: arrows, wigars, darts,
lances and spears, javelots dressed with feathers; 1480
struck Roland's shield, pierced it, broke it to pieces,
ripped his hauberk, shattered its rings of mail,
but never touched his body, never his flesh.
They wounded Veillantif in thirty places,
struck him dead, from afar, under the Count.
The pagans flee, they leave the field to him.
Roland the Count stood alone, on his feet. AOI.

161

The pagans flee, in bitterness and rage,[20]
strain every nerve running headlong toward Spain,
and Count Roland has no way to chase them, 1490
he has lost Veillantif, his battle horse;
he has no choice, left alone there on foot.
He went to the aid of Archbishop Turpin,
unlaced the gold-dressed helmet, raised it from his head,
lifted away his bright, light coat of mail,
cut his under tunic into some lengths,
stilled his great wounds with thrusting on the strips;
then held him in his arms, against his chest,
and laid him down, gently, on the green grass;
and softly now Roland entreated him: 1500
"My noble lord, I beg you, give me leave:
our companions, whom we have loved so dearly,
are all dead now, we must not abandon them.
I want to look for them, know them once more,
and set them in ranks, side by side, before you."
Said the Archbishop: "Go then, go and come back.
The field is ours, thanks be to God, yours and mine."

162

So Roland leaves him, walks the field all alone,
seeks in the valleys, and seeks in the mountains.
He found Gerin, and Gerer his companion, 1510
and then he found Berenger and Otun,
Anseïs and Sansun, and on that field
he found Gerard the Old of Roussillon;
and carried them, brave man, all, one by one,
came back to the Archbishop with these French dead,
and set them down in ranks before his knees.
The Archbishop cannot keep from weeping,

[20]This respite granted to Roland and Turpin after the pagans have fled and before these heroes die is an act of overwhelming grace, one of the poem's many lyrical arrests, and the sign of the two men's blessedness.

raises his hand and makes his benediction;
and said: "Lords, Lords, it was your terrible hour.
May the Glorious God set all your souls 1520
among the holy flowers of Paradise!
Here is my own death, Lords, pressing on me,
I shall not see our mighty Emperor."

163

And Roland leaves, seeks in the field again;
he has found Oliver, his companion,
held him tight in his arms against his chest;
came back to the Archbishop, laid Oliver
down on a shield among the other dead.
The Archbishop absolved him, signed him with the Cross.
And pity now and rage and grief increase; 1530
and Roland says: "Oliver, dear companion,
you were the son of the great duke Renier,
who held the march of the vale of Runers.
Lord, for shattering lances, for breaking shields,
for making men great with presumption weak with fright,
for giving life and counsel to good men,
for striking fear in that unbelieving race,
no warrior on earth surpasses you."

164

Roland the Count, when he sees his peers dead,
and Oliver, whom he had good cause to love, 1540
felt such grief and pity, he begins to weep;
and his face lost its color with what he felt:
a pain so great he cannot keep on standing,
he has no choice, falls fainting to the ground.
Said the Archbishop: "Baron, what grief for you."

165

The Archbishop, when he saw Roland faint,
felt such pain then as he had never felt;
stretched out his hand and grasped the olifant.
At Rencesvals there is a running stream:
he will go there and fetch some water for Roland; 1550
and turns that way, with small steps, staggering;
he is too weak, he cannot go ahead,
he has no strength: all the blood he has lost.
In less time than a man takes to cross a little field
that great heart fails, he falls forward, falls down;
and Turpin's death comes crushing down on him.

. . .

167

Roland the Count sees the Archbishop down,
sees the bowels fallen out of his body,
and the brain boiling down from his forehead.
Turpin has crossed his hands upon his chest 1560
beneath the collarbone, those fine white hands.
Roland speaks the lament, after the custom
followed in his land: aloud, with all his heart:
"My noble lord, you great and well-born warrior,
I commend you today to the God of Glory,
whom none will ever serve with a sweeter will.
Since the Apostles no prophet the like of you
arose to keep the faith and draw men to it.[21]
May your soul know no suffering or want,
and behold the gate open to Paradise." 1570

168

Now Roland feels that death is very near.
His brain comes spilling out through his two ears;
prays to God for his peers: let them be called;
and for himself, to the angel Gabriel;
took the oliphant: there must be no reproach!
took Durendal his sword in his other hand,
and farther than a crossbow's farthest shot
he walks toward Spain, into a fallow land,
and climbs a hill: there beneath two fine trees
stand four great blocks of stone, all are of marble; 1580
and he fell back, to earth, on the green grass,
has fainted there, for death is very near.

169

High are the hills, and high, high are the trees;
there stand four blocks of stone, gleaming of marble.
Count Roland falls fainting on the green grass,
and is watched, all this time, by a Saracen:
who has feigned death and lies now with the others,
has smeared blood on his face and on his body;
and quickly now gets to his feet and runs—
a handsome man, strong, brave, and so crazed with pride 1590
that he does something mad and dies for it:
laid hands on Roland, and on the arms of Roland,
and cried: "Conquered! Charles's nephew conquered!
I'll carry this sword home to Arabia!"
As he draws it, the Count begins to come round.

[21] Compare Deuteronomy 34:10.

170

Now Roland feels: *someone taking his sword!*
opened his eyes, and had one word for him:
"I don't know you, you aren't one of ours";
grasps that olifant that he will never lose,
strikes on the helm beset with gems in gold, 1600
shatters the steel, and the head, and the bones,
sent his two eyes flying out of his head,
dumped him over stretched out at his feet dead;
and said: "You nobody! how could you dare
lay hands on me—rightly or wrongly: how?
Who'll hear of this and not call you a fool?
Ah! the bell-mouth of the olifant is smashed,
the crystal and the gold fallen away."

171

Now Roland the Count feels: his sight is gone;
gets on his feet, draws on his final strength, 1610
the color on his face lost now for good.
Before him stands a rock; and on that dark rock
in rage and bitterness he strikes ten blows:
the steel blade grates, it will not break, it stands unmarked.
"Ah!" said the Count, "Blessed Mary, your help!
Ah Durendal, good sword, your unlucky day,
for I am lost and cannot keep you in my care.
The battles I have won, fighting with you,
the mighty lands that holding you I conquered,
that Charles rules now, our King, whose beard is white! 1620
Now you fall to another: it must not be
a man who'd run before another man!
For a long while a good vassal held you:
there'll never be the like in France's holy land."

172

Roland strikes down on that rock of Cerritania:
the steel blade grates, will not break, stands unmarked.
Now when he sees he can never break that sword,
Roland speaks the lament, in his own presence:
"Ah Durendal, how beautiful and bright!
so full of light, all on fire in the sun!
King Charles was in the vales of Moriane 1630
when God sent his angel and commanded him,
from heaven, to give you to a captain count.
That great and noble King girded it on me.
And with this sword I won Anjou and Brittany,
I won Poitou, I won Le Maine for Charles,
and Normandy, that land where men are free,

I won Provence and Aquitaine with this,
and Lombardy, and every field of Romagna,
I won Bavaria, and all of Flanders,
all of Poland, and Bulgaria, for Charles, 1640
Constantinople, which pledged him loyalty,
and Saxony, where he does as he wills;
and with this sword I won Scotland and Ireland,
and England, his chamber, his own domain—
the lands, the nations I conquered with this sword,
for Charles, who rules them now, whose beard is white!
Now, for this sword, I am pained with grief and rage:
Let it not fall to pagans! Let me die first!
Our Father God, save France from that dishonor."

173

Roland the Count strikes down on a dark rock, 1650
and the rock breaks, breaks more than I can tell,
and the blade grates, but Durendal will not break,
the sword leaped up, rebounded toward the sky.
The Count, when he sees that sword will not be broken,
softly, in his own presence, speaks the lament:
"Ah Durendal, beautiful, and most sacred,
the holy relics in this golden pommel!
Saint Peter's tooth and blood of Saint Basile,
a lock of hair of my lord Saint Denis,
and a fragment of blessed Mary's robe: 1660
your power must not fall to the pagans,
you must be served by Christian warriors.
May no coward ever come to hold you!
It was with you I conquered those great lands
that Charles has in his keeping, whose beard is white,
the Emperor's lands, that make him rich and strong."

174

Now Roland feels: death coming over him,
death descending from his temples to his heart.
He came running underneath a pine tree
and there stretched out, face down, on the green grass, 1670
lays beneath him his sword and the olifant.
He turned his head toward the Saracen hosts,
and this is why: with all his heart he wants
King Charles the Great and all his men to say,
he died, that noble Count, a conqueror;
makes confession, beats his breast often, so feebly,
offers his glove, for all his sins, to God. AOI.

175

Now Roland feels that his time has run out;
he lies on a steep hill, his face toward Spain;
and with one of his hands he beat his breast: 1680
"Almighty God, *mea culpa* in thy sight,[22]
forgive my sins, both the great and the small,
sins I committed from the hour I was born
until this day, in which I lie struck down."
And then he held his right glove out to God.
Angels descend from heaven and stand by him. AOI.

176

Count Roland lay stretched out beneath a pine;
he turned his face toward the land of Spain,
began to remember many things now:
how many lands, brave man, he had conquered; 1690
and he remembered: sweet France, the men of his line,
remembered Charles, his lord, who fostered him:
cannot keep, remembering, from weeping, sighing;
but would not be unmindful of himself:
he confesses his sins, prays God for mercy:
"Loyal Father, you who never failed us,
who resurrected Saint Lazarus from the dead,
and saved your servant Daniel from the lions:
now save the soul of me from every peril
for the sins I committed while I still lived." 1700
Then he held out his right glove to his Lord:
Saint Gabriel took the glove from his hand.
He held his head bowed down upon his arm,
he is gone, his two hands joined, to his end.
Then God sent him his angel Cherubin
and Saint Michael, angel of the sea's Peril;
and with these two there came Saint Gabriel:
they bear Count Roland's soul to Paradise.

177

Roland is dead, God has his soul in heaven.
The Emperor rides into Rencesvals; 1710
there is no passage there, there is no track,
no empty ground, not an elle, not one foot,
that does not bear French dead or pagan dead.

[22]See Psalm 51:4.

King Charles cries out: "Dear Nephew, where are you?
Where is the Archbishop? Count Oliver?
Where is Gerin, his companion Gerer?
Where is Otun, where is Count Berenger,
Yves and Yvoire, men I have loved so dearly?
What has become of Engeler the Gascon,
Sansun the Duke, and Anseïs, that fighter? 1720
Where is Gerard the Old of Roussillon,
and the Twelve Peers, whom I left in these passes?"
And so forth—what's the difference? No one answered.
"God!" said the King, "how much I must regret
I was not here when the battle began";
pulls his great beard, a man in grief and rage.
His brave knights weep, their eyes are filled with tears,
twenty thousand fall fainting to the ground;
Duke Naimon feels the great pity of it.

178

There is no knight or baron on that field 1730
who does not weep in bitterness and grief;
for they all weep: for their sons, brothers, nephew,
weep for their friends, for their sworn men and lords;
the mass of them fall fainting to the ground.
Here Naimon proved a brave and useful man:
he was the first to urge the Emperor:
"Look ahead there, two leagues in front of us,
you can see the dust rising on those wide roads:
the pagan host—and how many they are!
After them now! Ride! Avenge this outrage!" 1740
"Oh! God!" said Charles, "look how far they have gotten!
Lord, let me have my right, let me have honor,
they tore from me the flower of sweet France."
The King commands Gebuïn and Othon,
Thibaut of Reims and Count Milun his cousin:
"Now guard this field, the valleys, the mountains,
let the dead lie, all of them, as they are,
let no lion, let no beast come near them,
let no servant, let no groom come near them,
I command you, let no man come near these dead 1750
until God wills we come back to this field."
And they reply, gently, and in great love:
"Just Emperor, dear Lord, we shall do that."
They keep with them a thousand of their knights. AOI.

179

The Emperor has his high-pitched trumpets sound,
and then he rides, brave man, with his great host.

They made the men of Spain show them their heels,
and they keep after them, all as one man.
When the King sees the twilight faltering,
he gets down in a meadow on the green grass, 1760
lies on the ground, prays to the Lord his God
to make the sun stand still for him in heaven,
hold back the night, let the day linger on.
Now comes the angel always sent to speak with Charles;[23]
and the angel at once commanded him:
"Charles, ride: God knows. The light will not fail you.
God knows that you have lost the flower of France.
You can take vengeance now on that criminal race."
The Emperor, on that word, mounts his horse. AOI.

180

God made great miracles for Charlemagne, 1770
for on that day in heaven the sun stood still.
The pagans flee, the Franks keep at their heels,
catch up with them in the Vale Tenebrous,
chase them on spurring hard to Saragossa,
and always killing them, striking with fury;
cut off their paths, the widest roads away:
the waters of the Ebro lie before them,
very deep, an amazing sight, and swift;
and there is no boat, no barge, no dromond, no galley.
They call on Tervagant, one of their gods. 1780
Then they jump in, but no god is with them:
those in full armor, the ones who weigh the most,
sank down, and they were many, to the bottom;
the others float downstream: the luckiest ones,
who fare best in those waters, have drunk so much,
they all drown there, struggling, it is amazing.
The French cry out: "Curse the day you saw Roland!" AOI.

181

When Charlemagne sees all the pagans dead,
many struck down, the great mass of them drowned—
the immense spoils his knights win from that battle!— 1790
the mighty King at once gets down on foot,
lies on the ground, and gives thanks to the Lord.
When he stands up again, the sun has set.
Said the Emperor: "It is time to make camp.

[23]The angel always sent to speak with Charles: Gabriel.

It is late now to return to Rencesvals;
our horses are worn out, they have no strength—
take off their saddles, the bridles on their heads,
let them cool down and rest in these meadows."
The Franks reply: "Yes, as you well say, Lord." AOI.

182

The Emperor commands them to make camp. 1800
The French dismount into that wilderness;
they have removed the saddles from their horses,
and the bridles, dressed in gold, from their heads,
free them to the meadows and the good grass;
and that is all the care they can give them.
Those who are weary sleep on the naked earth;
and all sleep, they set no watch that night.

. . .

203

On that morning, at the first light of dawn,
Charlemagne the Emperor woke from his sleep.
Saint Gabriel, who guards him in the Lord's name, 1810
raises his hand and signs him with the Cross.
The King arises, and he lays down his arms,
and so, throughout the host, all men disarm.
Then they mount up and ride with all their strength
on these long ways and on these great wide roads.
And they shall see the fearful numbers of the dead
at Rencesvals, where the great battle was. AOI.

204

King Charles has reached the field of Rencesvals;
and comes upon the dead, and weeps for them;
said to the French: "Seigneurs, keep at a walk, 1820
for I must ride ahead by myself now:
it is for my nephew, I would find him.
I was at Aix one day, at a high feast,
there were my valiant knights, all of them boasting
of great assaults, the battles they would fight.
There was one thing that I heard Roland say:
he said he would not die in a strange land
before he'd passed beyond his men and peers,
he'd turn his face toward the enemies' land
and so, brave man, would die a conqueror." 1830

Farther ahead than one could hurl a stick,
beyond them all, he has gone up a hill.

205

The Emperor, as he looks for his nephew,
found in the meadow grass many fair flowers
so bright and red with the blood of our barons;
and he is moved, he cannot keep from weeping.
He came beneath two trees and knew it was
Roland who struck those blows on the three rocks;
and sees his nephew stretched out on the green grass.
Who would wonder at his rage and sorrow?— 1840
gets down on foot; he has come running hard,
and takes in his two hands Roland the Count,
and falls fainting, choked with grief, on his body.

206

The Emperor recovered from his faint.
Naimon the Duke, and Acelin the Count,
Gefrei d'Anjou, and Tierri his brother
help the King up, help him stand beneath a pine.
The King looks on the ground, sees his nephew;
and he begins, most gently, the regret:
"Roland, dear friend, God have mercy on you. 1850
No man has seen a warrior like you
for fighting on till the great battle ends.
This is the fall and the death of my honor."
Charlemagne faints, cannot hold out against it. AOI.

207

King Charles the Great recovered from his faint,
his four barons raise him up with their hands;
looks on the ground, sees where his nephew lies,
Roland's body, vivid with life, its color gone,
his eyes rolled up, overflowing with shadows;
speaks the lament, in love and loyalty: 1860
"Roland, dear friend, God set your soul in the flowers
of Paradise, among his Glorious!
Lord, the black hour of your coming to Spain!
No day will pass that I feel no pain for you.
My strength will fail, and my joy in my strength,
I'll have no man to uphold my honor;
under heaven I cannot find one friend;

there's all my kin, but where is the like of you!"—
pulls at his hair, pulls with his two hands full.
A hundred thousand Franks feel the grief of this, 1870
the tears they weep are bitter, and they all weep. AOI.

208

"Roland, dear friend, I shall go back to France:
when I am in Laon,[24] my own domain,
alien vassals will come from many realms,
and they will ask: 'Where is the captain Count?'
I shall tell them: dead in the land of Spain!
And I shall rule my land henceforth in grief,
no day will pass that I do not weep and mourn."

209

"Dear friend, brave man, Roland, your fair young life!
And when I am in Aix, in my chapel, 1880
vassals will come, and they will ask for news.
I shall tell them: Amazing, terrible news!
My nephew's dead, who led me to my conquests.
Then the Saxons will rise up against me,
Hungarians, Bulgars, infidel races,
men of Romagna, Apulia, Palermo,
nations of Africa and Califerne;
then begins the season of my pains and losses.
Who will rise with your strength to lead my hosts
when you are dead, who always captained us? 1890
Sweet land of France, made a wasteland today!
The pain, the rage I feel! Let me not live!";
and falls to tearing out his great white beard,
and tears with both his hands the hair on his head.
A hundred thousand Franks fall to the earth.

210

"Dear friend, Roland, the end of your good life!
Now may your soul be set in Paradise!
What man killed you? Killing you he shamed sweet France.[25]
I live on, wanting to die, I feel such pain
for the men of my house, who died for me. 1900

---

[24]Laon: the capital of the last Carolingians.

[25]No man killed Roland. He died because his temples burst from the effort of blowing the horn. France is not ruined or dishonored.

May God grant me, may blessed Mary's Son,
before I reach the great defiles of Cize,
grant that my soul part today from my body
and take its place beside my warriors' souls,
and my flesh be buried beside their flesh";
and weeps, tears fill his eyes, pulls his white beard.
Duke Naimon said: "The great grief of Charlemagne." AOI.

211

"Lord Emperor," said Geoffrey of Anjou,
"do not linger in this pain and grief, come,
let our men be sought out across the field, 1910
whom the pagans of Spain killed in this battle;
let them be borne into a common grave."
And the King said: "So be it. Sound your horn." AOI.

212

Geoffrey d'Anjou sounded his high-pitched horn.
The French dismount, Charles has commanded it.
And all their killed in battle, the friends they found,
they bore at once into a common grave.
Now bishops and abbots in great number,
monks, canons, tonsured priests stand in our ranks:
they absolved them, and blessed them in God's name, 1920
and set burning myrrh and thymiama,
and censed their dead, in Rencesvals, with great ardor,
and buried them, when they were blessed, in great honor,
and left them then: what more could they do there? AOI.

213

The Emperor commands: prepare Roland,
and Oliver, and Archbishop Turpin;
has their bodies opened in his presence,
the hearts received in cloths of silk brocade,
and laid in a coffin of white marble.
Then they took the remains of these good men, 1930
and they wrapped the three lords in deerskin shrouds,
their bodies washed in spiced and fragrant wine.
The King commands Thibaut and Gebuïn,
Milun the Count, and Othon the Marquis:
"Escort these dead in three carts on their journey";
spread over them rich cloths of Eastern silk. AOI.

LATIN LYRIC

[9TH CENTURY–12TH CENTURY]

The medieval Latin lyric derives from the composing of Latin hymns in the early Middle Ages. The earliest Christian hymns were written in strict quantitative measure, observing the formalities of Old Latin poetry; later hymns dropped the elongated vowels of classical Latin and were governed by stress accents, just as vernacular speech was by that time. By the end of the sixth century, Latin hymns were already being composed in the popular measures of the common language, and must have had a distinctly "modern" sound. Eventually other forms of Latin poetry followed this adaptation to the sounds and rhythms of the developing Romance languages.

The best-preserved medieval Latin poetry was written inside monastery walls for the monks who lived there. One such writer was Alcuin (735–804), a British scholar famed as Charlemagne's tutor. After retiring to a monastery at Tours in 796, Alcuin wrote on grammar and other subjects, but also wrote Latin verses. One of his finest poems, a lament for a cuckoo, was actually addressed to a young monk, a recently departed favorite of the monastery. The language of affection used in the poem expresses the chaste love of the monks for their former brother. The same language is apparent in the beautiful and dignified elegy for Alcuin himself, written in 804 by his pupil Fredugis.

Another product of monastic education was Walafrid Strabo (800–849), a pupil at the school at Fulda and later a tutor of the future emperor Charles the Bald. Strabo eventually became Abbot of Reichenau, the town where he had grown up in poverty. Well regarded in his day, Strabo has left us a variety of poems: included are a complaint over his student days of exile at Fulda, a tasteful dedication of a book on gardening, and an elegy to a friend who died young. The love language in the latter poem, unlike that of the monks at Tours, appears to be of a sexual nature.

Some of the most gifted medieval Latin poets emerged from the European borderlands. Sedulius Scottus (fl. 847–874) left Ireland owing either to fear of the Danish invasions or, as Strabo once remarked, to "the Irish fashion of going away." He may have enjoyed the patronage of Charles the Bald in 848. He worked as a resident poet at Liège, writing greetings to visitors, songs for the seasons, and what he called "saturated songs" or drinking poems. Sedulius was a great grumbler and also one of the first medieval poets to publicly request money. Although he wrote in formal Latin quantitative measures—already an oddity for his day—in spirit he was close to the traveling poets, or *vagantes,* who were soon to follow him. Two of his poems are included here: a lyric celebrating Easter Sunday and a poem to his bishop requesting money for wine.

The finest Latin poetry of the late tenth and early eleventh centuries is preserved in a manuscript called the Cambridge Songs. These mostly anonymous, extremely varied lyrics—copied by a traveler and brought to Canterbury from somewhere along the Rhine in Germany—include a number of short masterpieces. Printed here are a seduction song, "Come, sweetheart, come," and a mournful love song, "Softly the west wind blows," which was written by a woman.

Latin poetry distanced itself from the monasteries in the eleventh and twelfth centuries as opportunities for young men increased in the church and cathedral schools, the town guilds, and the baronial courts. Once it was thought that poems of this period were chiefly written by *vagantes,* "wandering scholars" in training for the priesthood who had somehow slipped the bonds of religious obligation and taken to the road. Now it seems more likely that many levels of medieval society produced the new Latin secular poetry, which criticized everything previously held above blame, including the state. Certainly the new learning of the church schools contributed to this state of mind, with its access to the more satirical and licentious works of Roman poets such as Horace, Ovid, Petronius, and Martial.

This poetry was sometimes called Goliardic, named after the legendary poet Golias, described in a later work as "a glutton of words." Little evidence can be found of a real-life "society of Goliards," drunken and sensual, surviving outside the law, an order of beggars with twenty-eight kinds of tramps; but individual poets who wrote disruptive songs and ballads in the twelfth century may have been rewarded for their pains, and without begging. The best of these known to us is The Archpoet of Cologne (fl. 1161–1165), who left a collection of his work including the extraordinary poem "Confession."

The "Confession," preserved in a collection called *The Carmina Burana,* is the angry, blasphemous, greedy, and at times comical statement of a new man, the professional poet set loose on society while surviving on more or less obscure donations. The poem, which goes so far as to blaspheme the Mass, anticipates some of the best writing of late medieval and Renaissance Europe. It has even been equated with certain poems of the modern revolutionary spirit.

Suggested Readings

There are several excellent anthologies of medieval Latin poetry. Helen Waddell's *Medieval Latin Lyrics* (1929) is still unsurpassed for the quality of the translations. *Latin Poetry in Verse Translation* (1957), edited by L. R. Lind, covers the field from Early Latin to the seventeenth century, with an enlightening medieval section. George F. Whicher's *The Goliard Poets* (1949) and David Parlett's *Selections from the Carmina Burana* (1986) are good specialized collections. For anyone with a classical language background, F. Brittain's *The Medieval Latin and Romance Lyric* (1951) is still the best survey of the field.

ALCUIN

[735–804]

Lament for the Cuckoo

Translated by Helen Waddell

O cuckoo that sang to us and art fled,
    Where'er thou wanderest, on whatever shore
Thou lingerest now, all men bewail thee dead,
    They say our cuckoo will return no more.
Ah, let him come again, he must not die,
    Let him return with the returning spring,
And waken all the songs he used to sing.
    But will he come again? I know not, I.

I fear the dark sea breaks above his head,
    Caught in the whirlpool, dead beneath the waves. 10

Sorrow for me, if that ill god of wine
 Hath drowned him deep where young things find their graves.
But if he lives yet, surely he will come,
 Back to the kindly nest, from the fierce crows.
Cuckoo, what took you from the nesting place?
 But will he come again? That no man knows.

If you love songs, cuckoo, then come again,
 Come again, come again, quick, pray you come.
Cuckoo, delay not, hasten thee home again,
 Daphnis who loveth thee longs for his own. 20
Now spring is here again, wake from thy sleeping,
 Alcuin the old man thinks long for thee.
Through the green meadows go the oxen grazing;
 Only the cuckoo is not. Where is he?

FREDUGIS
[EARLY 9TH CENTURY]

Lament for Alcuin
Translated by Helen Waddell

O little house, O dear and sweet my dwelling,
O little house, for ever fare thee well!
The trees stand round thee with their sighing branches,
A little flowering wood for ever fair,
A field in flower where one can gather herbs
To cure the sick;
Small streams about thee, all their banks in flower,
And there the happy fisher spreads his nets.
And all thy cloisters smell of apple orchards,
And there are lilies white and small red roses, 10
And every bird sings in the early morning,
Praising the God who made him in his singing.
And once the Master's kind voice sounded in thee,
Reading the books of old philosophy,
And at set times the holy hymn ascended
From hearts and voices both alike at peace.
O little house, my song is broke with weeping,
And sorrow is upon me for your end.
Silent the poets' songs, stilled in a moment,
And thou art passed beneath a stranger's hand. 20
No more shall Angilbert or Alcuin come,
Or the boys sing their songs beneath thy roof.
So passes all the beauty of the earth.

WALAFRID STRABO

[800–849]

The Wandering Scholar

Translated by Helen Waddell

Sister, my Muse, weep thou for me I pray.
Wretched am I that ever went away
From my own land, and am continually
Ashamed and poor.

Fool that I was, a scholar I would be,
For learning's sake I left my own country,
No luck have I and no man cares for me,
Exiled and strange.

'Tis bitter frost and I am poorly happed,
I cannot warm my hands, my feet are chapped, 10
My very face shudders when I go out
To brave the cold.

Even in the house it is as cold as snow,
My frozen bed's no pleasure to me now,
I'm never warm enough in it to go
To quiet sleep.

I think perhaps if I had any sense,
Even a little smattering pretence
Of wisdom, I could put up some defence,
Warmed by my wits. 20

Alas, my father, if thou wert but here,
At whose behest thy scholar came so far,
I think there is no hurt that could come near
His foolish heart.

Of Gardening

Translated by Helen Waddell

A very paltry gift, of no account,
My father, for a scholar like to thee,
But Strabo sends it to thee with his heart.
So might you sit in the small garden close
In the green darkness of the apple trees
Just where the peach tree casts its broken shade,

And they would gather you the shining fruit
With the soft down upon it; all your boys,
Your little laughing boys, your happy school,
And bring huge apples clasped in their two hands. 10
Something the book may have of use to thee.
Read it, my father, prune it of its faults,
And strengthen with thy praise what pleases thee.
And may God give thee in thy hands the green
Unwithering palm of everlasting life.

To the Cleric Liutger

Translated by T. Stehling

My dear, you come suddenly, and suddenly too you leave;
I hear, I do not see. Yet I do see inwardly, and inwardly
I embrace you even as you flee from me—in body but not in faithfulness.
For just as I have been sure, so am I now, and so will I always be
That I am cherished in your heart, and you in mine. May passing time
Never persuade me or you of anything else.
If you can visit me, it will be enough to see my dear one.
But at other times, write me, write me anything; I have known your sorrows
And reflect on them with grief; grief is the world's province.
The things you consider bright and happy flee all the faster into clouds 10
And sad shadows. Like a bird that hovers above the world,
Now climbing, now falling, so is the wheel of the world in its turning.

SEDULIUS SCOTTUS

[FLOURISHED 847–874]

Easter Sunday

Translated by Helen Waddell

Last night did Christ the Sun rise from the dark,
  The mystic harvest of the fields of God,
And now the little wandering tribes of bees
  Are brawling in the scarlet flowers abroad.
The winds are soft with birdsong; all night long
  Darkling the nightingale her descant told,
And now inside church doors the happy folk
  The Alleluia chant a hundredfold.
O father of thy folk, be thine by right
The Easter joy, the threshold of the light. 10

He Complains to Bishop Hartgar of Thirst

Translated by Helen Waddell

The standing corn is green, the wild in flower,
  The vines are swelling, 'tis the sweet o' the year,
Bright-winged the birds, and heaven shrill with song,
  And laughing sea and earth and every star.

But with it all, there's never a drink for me,
  No wine, nor mead, nor even a drop of beer.
Ah, how hath failed that substance manifold,
  Born of the kind earth and the dewy air!

I am a writer, I, a musician, Orpheus the second,
  And the ox that treads out the corn, and your well-wisher I, 10
I am your champion armed with the weapons of wisdom and logic,
  Muse, tell my lord bishop and father his servant is dry.

ANONYMOUS

[10TH CENTURY]

"Come, sweetheart, come"

Translated by Helen Waddell

Come, sweetheart, come,
  Dear as my heart to me,
Come to the room
  I have made fine for thee.

Here there be couches spread,
  Tapestry tented,
Flowers for thee to tread,
  Green herbs sweet scented.

Here is the table spread,
  Love, to invite thee, 10
Clear is the wine and red,
  Love, to delight thee.

Sweet sounds the viol,
  Shriller the flute,
A lad and a maiden
  Sing to the lute.

He'll touch the harp for thee,
  She'll sing the air,

They will bring wine for thee,
  Choice wine and rare. 20

Yet for this care not I,
  'Tis what comes after,
Not all this lavishness,
  But thy dear laughter.

Mistress mine, come to me,
  Dearest of all,
Light of mine eyes to me,
  Half of my soul.

Alone in the wood
  I have loved hidden places, 30
Fled from the tumult,
  And crowding of faces.

Now the snow's melting,
  Out the leaves start,
The nightingale's singing,
  Love's in the heart.

Dearest, delay not,
  Ours love to learn,
I live not without thee,
  Love's hour is come. 40

What boots delay, Love,
  Since love must be?
Make no more stay, Love,
  I wait for thee.

ANONYMOUS

[11TH CENTURY]

"Softly the west wind blows"

Translated by Helen Waddell

Softly the west wind blows;
Gaily the warm sun goes;
The earth her bosom sheweth,
And with all sweetness floweth.

Goes forth the scarlet spring,
Clad with all blossoming,
Sprinkles the fields with flowers,
Leaves on the forest

Dens for four-footed things,
Sweet nests for all with wings. 10
On every blossomed bough
Joy ringeth now.

I see it with my eyes,
I hear it with my ears,
But in my heart are sighs,
And I am full of tears.

Alone with thought I sit,
And blench, remembering it;
Sometimes I lift my head,
I neither hear nor see. 20

Do thou, O Spring most fair,
Squander thy care
On flower and leaf and grain.
—Leave me alone with pain!

THE ARCHPOET
[FLOURISHED 1161–1165]

Confession

Translated by Helen Waddell

Seething over inwardly
With fierce indignation,
In my bitterness of soul,
Hear my declaration.
I am of one element,
Levity my matter,
Like enough a withered leaf
For the winds to scatter.

Since it is the property
Of the sapient
To sit firm upon a rock,
It is evident
That I am a fool, since I
Am a flowing river,
Never under the same sky,
Transient for ever.

Hither, thither, masterless
Ship upon the sea,
Wandering through the ways of air,
Go the birds like me. 10

Bound am I by ne'er a bond,
   Prisoner to no key,
Questing go I for my kind,
   Find depravity.

Never yet could I endure
   Soberness and sadness,
Jests I love and sweeter than
   Honey find I gladness.
Whatsoever Venus bids
   Is a joy excelling,
Never in an evil heart
   Did she make her dwelling.

Down the broad way do I go,
   Young and unregretting,
Wrap me in my vices up,
   Virtue all forgetting,
Greedier for all delight
   Than heaven to enter in:
Since the soul in me is dead,
   Better save the skin. 20

Pardon, pray you, good my lord,
   Master of discretion,
But this death I die is sweet,
   Most delicious poison.
Wounded to the quick am I
   By a young girl's beauty:
She's beyond my touching? Well,
   Can't the mind do duty?

Hard beyond all hardness, this
   Mastering of Nature:
Who shall say his heart is clean,
   Near so fair a creature?
Young are we, so hard a law,
   How should we obey it?
And our bodies, they are young,
   Shall they have no say in't?

Sit you down amid the fire,
   Will the fire not burn you?
To Pavia come, will you
   Just as chaste return you? 30
Pavia, where Beauty draws
   Youth with finger-tips,
Youth entangled in her eyes,
   Ravished with her lips.

Let you bring Hippolytus,
   In Pavia dine him,

Never more Hippolytus
  Will the morning find him.
In Pavia not a road
  But leads to venery,
Nor among its crowding towers
  One to chastity.

Yet a second charge they bring:
  I'm for ever gaming.
Yea, the dice hath many a time
  Stripped me to my shaming.
What an if the body's cold,
  If the mind is burning,
On the anvil hammering,
  Rhymes and verses turning? 40

Look again upon your list.
  Is the tavern on it?
Yea, and never have I scorned,
  Never shall I scorn it,
Till the holy angels come,
  And my eyes discern them,
Singing for the dying soul,
  Requiem aeternam.

For on this my heart is set:
  When the hour is nigh me,
Let me in the tavern die,
  With a tankard by me,
While the angels looking down
  Joyously sing o'er me,
Deus sit propitius
  Huic potatori.

'Tis the fire that's in the cup
  Kindles the soul's torches,
'Tis the heart that drenched in wine
  Flies to heaven's porches. 50
Sweeter tastes the wine to me
  In a tavern tankard
Than the watered stuff my Lord
  Bishop hath decanted.

Let them fast and water drink,
  All the poets' chorus,
Fly the market and the crowd
  Racketing uproarious:
Sit in quiet spots and think,
  Shun the tavern's portal,
Write, and never having lived,
  Die to be immortal.

Never hath the spirit of
  Poetry descended,
Till with food and drink my lean
  Belly was distended,
But when Bacchus lords it in
  My cerebral story,
Comes Apollo with a rush,
  Fills me with his glory. 60

Unto every man his gift.
  Mine was not for fasting.
Never could I find a rhyme
  With my stomach wasting.
As the wine is, so the verse:
  'Tis a better chorus
When the landlord hath a good
  Vintage set before us.

Good my lord, the case is heard,
  I myself betray me.
And affirm myself to be
  All my fellows say me.
See, they in thy presence are:
  Let whoe'er hath known
His own heart and found it
  clean,
  Cast at me the stone.

PROVENÇAL POETRY

[11TH CENTURY–13TH CENTURY]

The rise of vernacular love poetry in the south of France, especially in Provence, cannot be dated precisely, but by 1100 certain courts were already hearing poems devoted to the affairs of the day, *lais* of Celtic origin, and love poems of several types. The first professional courtly poet, or *troubadour*, known to us is Guillaume IX, Duke of Aquitaine and Count of Poitiers (1071–1127), who apparently proved more successful in the love-jousts he recorded in his poetry than in the fighting he did in the Crusades. Guillaume composed love poems in two different styles: refined and bawdy. Eventually, as *troubadour* poetry developed, the sophisticated poetry of *amour courtois*, or courtly love, won out over the rough *pastourelles*, records of sexual conquest. The poetry of Bernart de Ventadorn (fl. 1150–1180) is often said to have marked the turning point in this triumph of "good" poetry over "bad."

Apart from their intrinsic interest, the more refined love poems served as a form of instruction in manners to young knights and other retainers of the court. This effort to entertain and educate at the same time was eventually buttressed by books on the art of love; one such work, *The Art of Courtly Love*, was written at Poitiers between 1174 and 1186 by the monk Andreas Capellanus under the patronage of Eleanor of Aquitaine. The new love literature dictated the sublimation of sexual impulses, the cultivation of romantic sensibilities, and familiarity with the legalistic vocabulary associated with the "claim" of love. One effect of this poetry was the elevation of women, putting the ladies of the court on a pedestal. Most scholars agree that in the Middle Ages this was a considerable advance for the women at court, surrounded as they were by a hitherto unruly and unmannerly knighthood.

The troubadour poets of southern France of the twelfth and thirteenth centuries came from a variety of backgrounds. Some were princes: Besides Guillaume, there was Thibaut de Champagne, King of Navarre. Some were the knights-at-arms who followed princes. Some were ladies of the court, participating in contests of wits with the male poets. But for the most part, the poets were followers of the court, beneficiaries of a good education who had been trained in the poetic tradition. A young man might seek the position of *jongleur,* the musician who performed the music of the troubadour composer, and rise later to the master's position. What mattered were one's talent and the ability to make connections at court once installed there.

Professional troubadours who enjoyed the patronage of the court were expected to celebrate the major events of the community of which they were a part. They might be asked to provide entertainment by singing lays about heroes and heroines of romance. They also composed *cansos,* or love songs, sometimes addressed to the lady of the court, probably performed in front of her husband as well as the rest of the company. Finally, they composed *sirventes,* personal or political pieces, ruminations on the state of society. Some of the latter compositions reveal an interesting facet of the troubadours: their self-identification as a class of poets, defined by the economic character of their profession. This tendency to discuss their own circumstances in their poetry increased as the theme of love became more stale.

Guillaume IX, Duke of Aquitaine

Guillaume IX, Duke of Aquitaine, is known for his deeds as well as his songs. The lord of an immense domain and the leader of a disastrous Crusade, he was also a notorious seducer of women and a constant irritation to the Church. His songs range from bawdy backroom ballads to showpieces of courtly devotion. The song "My companions, I am going to make a *vers* that is refined" is the raucous account of a man with two lovers, whom he compares to "good and noble horses"; his problem is that they will not abide by the arrangement. The women live in two castles within his domain; one is married to another man, although the poet boasts that he has first rights to her. The poem is characterized by its chauvinist point of view and its conspicuous bad taste: For instance, the poet pointedly names the two women, exposing their identities and destroying their reputations.

A world apart from this poem is the one beginning "Now when we see the meadows once again," one of the early defining texts of the doctrine of courtly love, addressed to a mixed audience of lords and ladies. Here Guillaume both practices and preaches the art of sublimation. He rebukes himself for having wanted love so much that he has frequently lost it, and he acknowledges that he will never gain love without first obeying its laws. This time he is careful to conceal the identity of his beloved.

Marcabru

Marcabru (fl. 1129–1150), who although he was low-born enjoyed for a time the patronage of Guillaume IX, could not have been more different from his prince in approach or inspiration. His poems attack the practitioners of courtly love as for the most part hypocritical and depraved, while defending what he calls true love, the love of friendship. Modestly, Marcabru depicts himself as a flawed person who cannot live up to his own ideals. The poem describing an encounter with a grieving woman, "By the fountain in the orchard," keeps a high moral tone despite the inappropriate desires confessed by the narrator.

Bernart de Ventadorn

Little is known for certain about Bernart de Ventadorn (fl. 1150–1180), although his songs frequently dramatize his life. One of the most prolific of the troubadours, he also seems to have struggled constantly against the conventionality of the poetry. The poem "My heart is so full of joy" shares with the work of Guillaume IX a certain outrageousness, as when he says he could go about naked because love protects him from the wind, or asserts that he would not exchange this love for all the wealth in Pisa. De Ventadorn's assertion that by keeping at a distance from his beloved he has really won the battle (having conquered the power of her image) is a clever rendering of a familiar theme. These ponderings in the middle of the poem give more excitement to the somewhat conventional exhortations at the end.

Raimbaut, Count of Orange

Raimbaut, Count of Orange (fl. 1162–1173), inherited some of the rich lands of Montpellier and Vaucluse. Known for his immense virtuosity and for his habit of calling attention to it in his work, he never achieved his full promise, dying young in an epidemic. The poem "Listen, Lords" is a direct address to an audience of his peers, wittily arguing that he doesn't know what kind of song he is singing because he doesn't know what effect his pursuit is having on his lady. It ends, characteristically, on a note of self-praise.

Countess of Dia

The Countess of Dia (fl. 1160) was reputed to have had an affair with Raimbaut, but the life histories of these poets are full of doubtful claims. The first and probably the best of the female singers, she was equally capable in the common song and the courtly lyric, as our two selections show. The poem "I've lately been in great distress" is earthy and direct, with nothing held back, including the fact that she would infinitely prefer having her lover in her husband's place. The poem "Of things I'd rather keep in silence I must sing," giving a messenger instructions about what to say to a lover who has spurned her, stays within the conventions of courtly love; she reminds her lover of their past relationship and demands that he respond to her with more courtesy in the future, warning him at the same time against the excessive pride that may be his undoing.

Bertran de Born

Bertran de Born (fl. 1180–1195), a minor nobleman, took sides against King Henry II of England and his son, Richard Lionheart, and was later blamed by Dante and others for having stirred up trouble among members of the royal family. It is doubtful that his poems could have had the powerful effect Dante allows them, but it is true that a characteristic of his work is its strong advocacy for one side or another in contentions among the members of the warrior class. The poem "I shall make a half *sirventes* about both kings" anticipates a battle in language as fresh as today's news; his acceptance of the outcome in advance, whatever its effect on his life and fortunes may be, is typical of his work.

PEIRE VIDAL

Peire Vidal (fl. 1180–1205) was another poet who infused his art with his energetic involvement in politics. The son of a furrier, he traveled among courts in the turbulent years at the end of the twelfth century while many of his patrons died, some in battle with one another. His poem "With my breath I draw toward me the air" is a tour de force; it celebrates the far country of Provence, and then the beautiful body of his beloved, without so much as a pause when he changes the subject.

SUGGESTED READINGS

Many works have been written about the poetry of Provence, the first great vernacular poetry of Europe, but they are sometimes difficult to locate, and good translations are surprisingly few. Frederick Goldin, ed., *Lyrics of the Troubadours and Trouveres* (1973), offers the verse translations included here, along with a good introduction and notes. Another selection by Alan R. Press, *Anthology of Troubadour Lyric Poetry* (1971), has original texts, prose translations, rather sparse introductions, and no notes. Robert S. Briffault, *The Troubadours* (1965), offers a lively but rather speculative interpretation of the poetry. Two general articles with good insights are Peter Dronke, "Transformations of Medieval Love Lyric," in his book *The Medieval Lyric* (1968), pp. 109–66; and Ingeborg Glier, "Troubadours and Minnesang," in Boris Ford, ed., *Medieval Literature: The European Inheritance* (1984), Vol. 1, part 2, pp. 167–87.

GUILLAUME IX, DUKE OF AQUITAINE

[1071–1127]

"My companions, I am going to make a *vers* that is refined"

Translated by Frederick Goldin

My companions,[1] I am going to make a *vers* that is refined,
and it will have more foolishness than sense,
and it will all be mixed with love and joy and youth.

Whoever does not understand it, take him for a peasant,
whoever does not learn it deep in his heart.
It is hard for a man to part from love that he finds to his desire.

I have two good and noble horses for my saddle,
they are good, adroit in combat, full of spirit,
but I cannot keep them both, one can't stand the other.

If I could tame them as I wish, 10
I would not want to put my equipment anywhere else,
for I'd be better mounted then than any man alive.

---

[1]By addressing the poem to his male friends, Guillaume helps to establish its unmannerly type, despite his disclaimer that it is "refined."

One of them was the fastest of the mountain horses,
but for a long time now it has been so fierce and shy,
so touchy, so wild, it fights off the currycomb.

The other was nurtured down there around Confolens,
and you never saw a prettier one, I know.
I won't get rid of that one, not for gold or silver.

I gave it to its master as a grazing colt;
but I reserved the right 20
that for every year he had it, I got it for more than a hundred.

You knights, counsel me in this predicament,
no choice ever caused me more embarrassment:
I can't decide which one to keep, Na Agnes or Na Arsen.[2]

Of Gimel I have the castle and the fief,
and with Niol I show myself proud to everyone,
for both are sworn to me and bound by oath.

"Now when we see the meadows once again"

Translated by Frederick Goldin

Now when we see the meadows once again
in flower and the orchards turning green,
streams and fountains running clear,
the breezes and the winds,
it is right that each man celebrate the joy
that makes him rejoice.

Now I must not say anything but good of Love.
Why do I get not one bit of it?
Maybe I wasn't meant for more.
And yet how freely 10
it gives great joy to any man who upholds
its rules.

This is the way it has always been with me:
I never had the joy of what I loved,
and I never will, as I never did.
For I am aware,
I do many things and my heart says,
"It is all nothing."

And so I know less than anyone what pleasure is,
because I want what I cannot have. 20
And yet, one wise saying tells me
the certain truth:

[2] "Na" means "domina," an address to a lady.

"When the heart is good, its power is good,
if a man knows patience."

Surely no one can ever be Love's
perfect man unless he gives it homage in humility
and is obliging to strangers
and acquaintances,
and to all the people of that realm
obedient. 30

A man who wants to be a lover
must meet many people with obedience,
and must know how to do
the things that fit in court,
and must keep, in court, from speaking
like a vulgar man.

Concerning this *vers* I tell you a man is all the more noble
as he understands it, and he gets more praise;
and all the strophes are built exactly
on the same meter, 40
and the melody, which I myself am happy about,
is fine and good.

Let my *vers*, since I myself do not,
appear before her,
Mon Esteve, and let it be the witness
for my praise.

MARCABRU

[FLOURISHED 1129–1150]

"By the fountain in the orchard"

Translated by Frederick Goldin

By the fountain in the orchard,
where the grass is green down to the sandy banks,
in the shade of a planted tree,
in a pleasant setting of white flowers
and the ancient song of the new season,
I found her alone, without a companion,
this girl who does not want my company.

She was a young girl, and beautiful,
the daughter of a castle lord.
And just as I reckoned the birds 10
must be filling her with joy, and the green things,
in this sweet new time,

and she would gladly hear my little speech,
suddenly her whole manner changed.

Her eyes welled up beside the fountain,
and she sighed from the depths of her heart,
"Jesus," she said, "King of the world,
because of You my grief increases,
I am undone by your humiliation,[1]
for the best men of this whole world 20
are going off to serve you, that is your pleasure.

"With you departs my so
handsome, gentle, valiant, noble friend;
here, with me, nothing of him remains but the great distress,
the frequent desiring, and the tears.
Ai! damn King Louis,
he gave the orders and the sermons,
and grief invaded my heart."

When I heard how she was losing heart,
I came up to her beside the clear stream. 30
"Beautiful one," I said, "with too much weeping
your face grows pale, the color fades;
you have no reason to despair, now,
for He who makes the woods burst into leaf
has the power to give you joy in great abundance."

"Lord," she said, "I do believe
that God may pity me
in the next world, time without end,
like many other sinners,
but here He wrests from me the one thing 40
that made my joy increase. Nothing matters now,
for he has gone so far away."

BERNART DE VENTADORN

[FLOURISHED 1150–1180]

"My heart is so full of joy"

Translated by Frederick Goldin

My heart is so full of joy
it changes every nature.
The winter that comes to me
is white red yellow flowers;
my good luck grows

[1] God was humiliated, the lady says, by the capture of Jerusalem in 1147, during a Crusade led by King Louis VII of France.

with the wind and the rain,
and so my song mounts up, rises,
and my worth increases.
I have such love in my heart,
such joy, such sweetness, 10
the ice I see is a flower,
the snow, green things that grow.

I could walk around undressed,
naked in my shirt,
for perfect love protects me
from the cold north wind.
But a man is a fool when he does things out of measure
and doesn't hold himself with courtesy.
Therefore I have kept a watch upon myself
ever since I begged her, 20
my most beautiful, for love,
and I await such honor
that in place of her riches
I don't want Pisa.

Let her make me keep my distance from her love—
there's still one thing I'm sure of:
I have conquered nothing less
than her beautiful image.
Cut off from her like this I have
such bliss, 30
that the day I see her again,
not having seen her will not weigh on me.
My heart stays close to Love,
my spirit runs to it there,
but my body is here, in another place,
far from her, in France.

I get good hope from her;
but that does me little good,
because she holds me like this, poised
like a ship on the wave. 40
I don't know where to take cover
from the sad thoughts that pull me down.
The whole night long I toss and turn
on the edge of the bed.
I bear more pain from love
than Tristan the lover,
who suffered many sorrows
for Isolt the blonde.

Ah, God! couldn't I be a swallow
and fly through the air 50
and come in the depths of the night
into her dwelling there.
O gentle lady, o joyful,
your lover dies.

I fear the heart will melt within me
if this lasts a little longer.
Lady, for your love
I join my hands and worship.
Beautiful body of the colors of youth,
what suffering you make me bear. 60

For in this world no enterprise
so draws my thought,
that when I hear any talk of her
my heart does not turn to it
and my face light up,
so that no matter what you hear me saying,
you will always think
I want to laugh.
I love her so with such good love,
that many time I weep for it, 70
because for me the sighs

have a sweeter taste.
Go, messenger, run,
and tell her, the one most beautiful,
of the pain and the sorrow
I bear for her, and the willing death.

RAIMBAUT D'ORANGE

[FLOURISHED 1162–1173]

"Listen, Lords . . . but I don't know what"

Translated by Frederick Goldin

Listen, Lords . . . but I don't know what
to call this thing I'm about to declaim.
Vers? Estribot? Sirventes? It's none
of these. I can't think up a name,
and don't know how I'd compose such a thing
if I could not finish it and claim
that no one ever saw the like of it made by any man or
woman in our century or in the other which
has passed.[1]

Call me a madman if you like,
it would not make me leave my vow,
Lords, to tell you what I feel. 10

[1] By stating his confusion over what kind of poem he is writing, and by the breakdown of metrical form at the end of the first stanza, the poet is parodying certain inept songs, probably those of Guillaume IX.

Let no one blame me. I would not set
a penny on this whole Creation,
compared to what I see right now,
and I'll tell you why: because if I started this thing for
 you and did not bring it off, you'd take me
 for
 a fool: because I prefer six cents in my fist to
 a thousand suns in the sky.

Let my friend never fear he may have done
a thing that weighs on me, I pray:
if he will not help me in my need at once,
let him offer me help after long delay.
But she that conquered me alone
deceives me as though it were child's play. 20
I say all this because of one lady who makes me pine
 away with beautiful words and a long expectation, I don't know why—Lords, can she be
 good to me?

It's been a good four months—that's more
than a thousand years to me, yes,
since she promised me and swore
to give me what I long for most.
Lady, my heart is your prisoner,
therefore sweeten my bitterness.
Help me, God, *in nomine Patris et Filii et Spiritus*
 sancti! Madam, how will it all turn out?

You make me frolic in my wrath,
you make me sing with joyful rage; 30
and I have left three such as have
no peer, save you, in our age.
Joglar they call me, I go singing
mad with love, in courtly ways.
Lady, you can do as you please about it, as Na Ayma
 did with the shoulder bone, she stuck it
 where
 she liked.[2]

Now I conclude my Whatdoyoucallit,
for that is how I've had it baptized;
since I've never heard of a similar thing,
I use the name that I devised;
whoever likes it, let him sing, 40
once he has it memorized,
and if anyone asks him who made it, he can say: one
 who
 can do anything, and do it well, when he
 wants to.

[2]Na Ayma must be a lady known to the court. The reference is obscene.

COUNTESS OF DIA

[FLOURISHED 1160]

"I've lately been in great distress"

Translated by Magda Bogin

I've lately been in great distress
over a knight who once was mine,
and I want it known for all eternity
how I loved him to excess.
Now I see I've been betrayed
because I wouldn't sleep with him;
night and day my mind won't rest
to think of the mistake I made.

How I wish just once I could caress
that chevalier with my bare arms, 10
for he would be in ecstasy
if I'd just let him lean his head against my breast.
I'm sure I'm happier with him
than Blancaflor with Floris.
My heart and love I offer him,
my mind, my eyes, my life.

Handsome friend, charming and kind,
when shall I have you in my power?
If only I could lie beside you for an hour
and embrace you lovingly— 20
know this, that I'd give almost anything
to have you in my husband's place,
but only under the condition
that you swear to do my bidding.

"Of things I'd rather keep in silence I must sing"

Translated by Magda Bogin

Of things I'd rather keep in silence I must sing:
so bitter do I feel toward him
whom I love more than anything.
With him my mercy and fine manners are in vain,
my beauty, virtue and intelligence.
For I've been tricked and cheated
as if I were completely loathesome.

There's one thing, though, that brings me recompense:
I've never wronged you under any circumstance,
and I love you more than Seguin loved Valensa. 10
At least in love I have my victory,

since I surpass the worthiest of men.
With me you always act so cold,
but with everyone else you're so charming.

I have good reason to lament
when I feel your heart turn adamant
toward me, friend: it's not right another love
take you away from me, no matter what she says.
Remember how it was with us in the beginning
of our love! May God not bring to pass 20
that I should be the one to bring it to an end.

The great renown that in your heart resides
and your great worth disquiet me,
for there's no woman near or far
who wouldn't fall for you if love were on her mind.
But you, my friend, should have the acumen
to tell which one stands out above the rest.
And don't forget the stanzas we exchanged.

My worth and noble birth should have some weight,
my beauty and especially my noble thoughts; 30
so I send you, there on your estate,
this song as messenger and delegate.
I want to know, my handsome noble friend,
why I deserve so savage and so cruel a fate.
I can't tell whether it's pride or malice you intend.

But above all, messenger, make him comprehend
that too much pride has undone many men.

BERTRAN DE BORN

[FLOURISHED 1180–1195]

"I shall make a half *sirventes* about both kings"

Translated by Frederick Goldin

I shall make a half *sirventes* about both kings,[1]
for soon we shall see who will have more riders:
the valiant king of Castile, En Alfons,
who is coming, I hear, and will want soldiers for pay;
Richard will pay by the bushel and the pail
gold and silver, and he thinks he is lucky
to pay out and give, and he wants no treaties,
no, he wants war more than a hawk wants quail.

[1]Alfonso VIII of Castile and Richard Lionheart. The poet is attempting to remain neutral, but fears the outcome.

If both of the kings are brave and spirited,
soon we shall see the fields bestrewn with fragments, 10
helms and shields and swords and saddlebows,
and corpses cloven through the trunk to the cinctures,
and the coursers we shall see running wild,
and in sides and breasts many lances,
and joy and weeping and grief and celebration:
the loss will be great, but the winnings will be greater.

Trumpets and tabors, ensigns and pennons,
banners and horses white and black
we shall soon see, and life will be good,
we shall pillage the stores of the usurers, 20
and on the roads the sumpters will not go

safely in the light, nor the burgher without wondering,
nor any merchant traveling from France,
no, but he will be rich who will gladly take.

If the King comes, I put my faith in God
I shall be alive or in pieces.

And if I am alive, it will be great luck,
and if I am dead, a great deliverance.

PEIRE VIDAL
[FLOURISHED 1180–1205]

"With my breath I draw toward me the air"

Translated by Frederick Goldin

With my breath I draw toward me the air
that I feel coming from Provence;
everything that comes from there rejoices me,
so that when I hear good of it
I listen smiling,
and for every word demand a hundred:
so much it pleases me when I hear good of it.

For no one knows so sweet a country
as from the Rhône to Vence,
enclosed between the sea and the Durance, 10
and nowhere knows a joy so pure that shines.
And so among those noble people
I have left my rejoicing heart
with her who brings laughter back to the afflicted.

For a man cannot draw bad luck
the day he thinks of her,

for joy is born in her and comes forth to us.
And whoever praises her
and whatever he says, he tells no lie:
for there's no arguing: she's the best
and the gentlest beheld in this world. 20

And if I can do or say a thing or two,
let the thanks be hers, for she
gave me the understanding and the craft,
because of her I am courtly, and a poet.
And everything I do that is fitting
I infer from her beautiful body,
and even these words of longing, rising from my heart.

MARIE DE FRANCE

[SECOND HALF OF THE 12TH CENTURY]

We know surprisingly little about Marie de France. She is believed to have written in the latter half of the twelfth century, and it is certain that she composed or translated into Norman French a significant body of literature: a book of English fables, a Latin saint's life, and twelve short verse romances, or *lais,* at the least. We know from her prefaces that she translated material "into romance" (the vernacular language) so that the work might "be understood and available to the layman." She is referred to by a contemporary as

> Lady Marie, who wrote in rhyme and composed the verses of *lais* which are not at all true. And so is she much praised because of it and the rhyme loved everywhere; for all love it greatly and hold it dear—counts, barons, and knights.[1]

LIFE

Since several of Marie's works came from English sources and the surviving manuscripts were found in England, it is generally believed that she was a member of the Anglo-Norman, or Angevin, aristocracy who lived part of her life in England. The *noble reis* (noble king) to whom she dedicated her *lais* was probably King Henry II of England, who reigned 1154–1189. Marie herself has been identified with Mary, Abbess of Shaftesbury from 1181 to 1215, a natural sister of Henry. This is an interesting possibility, because Shaftesbury was the seat of King Alfred the Great, whom Marie identifies as the author of the fables she translates, as well as a key locale of the Arthurian revival under Henry II.

WORK

Whoever she was, Marie de France displayed a remarkable literary background for any age. She was familiar with such classics as Aesop's *Fables* and Ovid's *Metamorphoses.* She was also well acquainted with the Anglo-Norman and Latin literature of her day, including the epic poem *Brut,* Geoffrey of Monmouth's *History of the Kings of Britain,* and various

[1] Cited in Emanuel Mickel, Jr., *Marie de France* (1974), 15. The writer is Denis Piramus.

romances. At the same time, the originality of her own work has often been noted. Her *Breton lais* do not resemble existing French versions of earlier Latin stories, such as *Pyramus and Thisbe,* or later epics such as the *Romance of Thebes*. Nor do they resemble the short romance *Tristan* by Thomas of Britain or the anonymous romance *Floris and Blanchefleur.* She herself, however, almost certainly influenced the master French *romancier,* Chrétien de Troyes.

The word *lai,* originally meaning a melody with or without lyrics celebrating a tale of adventure, came to mean in Marie's use a narrative poem recited at court. Marie claims her *lais* are based on Breton (Celtic) legends, though she would not have required first-hand knowledge of such an esoteric tradition. The main innovations of her poems are their extremely condensed structure and the sophistication of the narrator's voice. They are also marked by "signatures," often the titles of the works, utilizing romantic symbols such as the nightingale, the swan, or in our case the honeysuckle.

Although the subject matter of the *lais* is love, Marie takes no position on the subject, but shows respect for her sources, understanding the role of the artist as bound by the conventions of her "matter." Yet she often conveys a sense of mystery in her writing. In *The Lay of Chevrefoil,* derived from the Tristan legends, she presents love in its simplest yet most elusive aspect, as that which exists and therefore cannot be questioned, a power that makes us both greater and less than ourselves. In the sweep of passion, danger or even death may result from an unguarded moment; but sometimes luck is on the side of the lovers after all.

Of all the medieval stories of love, the story of Tristan and Isolt is the purest and most tragic. Preserved in a number of surviving sources, it derives from a rich body of Celtic legend. In the simplest version, Tristan is a knight in the court of his uncle, King Mark of Cornwall, sent by the king to woo and bring back Isolt, a young girl in Ireland. On their journey to King Mark's court, Tristan and Isolt are tricked into drinking a magic potion that fills them both with undeniable yearning. After many tests of will, they consummate their love and are captured and brought before the king for judgment. He banishes them from his kingdom; but later, he seeks them in the forest and finds them sleeping with Tristan's sword between them. He forgives Isolt and takes the couple back. Finally, however, Tristan is again forced into exile and is wounded. Isolt comes seeking him, but is too late: he has died waiting for her. She dies beside him. King Mark, repentant, buries them in a chapel, over which a vine and a rose intertwine. Though it has been briefly requited, their love is forever unfulfilled; unbidden and unsanctified, criminalized by the king's law, it exists only in a world of possibility.

In the *Lay of Chevrefoil,* Marie de France suggests the theme of unfulfilled love with the most economy possible. She uses elements of the familiar legend, including the king's anger, the envy of the court, and the necessity that the lovers meet in secret. Their love is symbolized by the image of the honeysuckle and the hazel tree, two plants that require each other in order to survive. The *lai* centers on the happy moment that the lovers share in the forest despite the odds against them. Their encounter is made possible not so much by craft or guile as by their perfect, intuitive understanding of each other's thoughts. Isolt is not even named in this version: calling her only "the queen," Marie emphasizes both the impossibility and the fragile truth of their love.

Suggested Readings

For most of this century, the *lais* of Marie de France were neglected; fortunately, in recent years they have received sympathetic attention. The best modern rendering of the poems is *The Lais of Marie de France,* translated with an introduction by Robert Hanning and Joan Ferrante (1978). Brief scholarly studies include Emanuel J. Mickel, Jr., *Marie de France* (1974), or, in even shorter compass, Paula Clifford, *Marie de France: Lais* (1982). For the original French text see Alfred Ewert, ed., *Marie de France: Lais,* in Blackwell's French Texts Series (1969).

The Lay of Chevrefoil (The Honeysuckle)

Translated by Robert Hanning and Joan Ferrante

I should like very much
to tell you the truth
about the *lai* men call *Chevrefoil*—
why it was composed and where it came from.
Many have told and recited it to me
and I have found it in writing,
about Tristan and the queen
and their love that was so true,
that brought them much suffering
and caused them to die the same day. 10
King Mark was annoyed,
angry at his nephew Tristan;
he exiled Tristan from his land
because of the queen whom he loved.
Tristan returned to his own country,
South Wales, where he was born,
he stayed a whole year;
he couldn't come back.
Afterward he began to expose himself
to death and destruction. 20
Don't be surprised at this:
for one who loves very faithfully
is sad and troubled
when he cannot satisfy his desires.
Tristan was sad and worried,
so he set out from his land.
He traveled straight to Cornwall,
where the queen lived,
and entered the forest all alone—
he didn't want anyone to see him; 30
he came out only in the evening
when it was time to find shelter.
He took lodging that night,
with peasants, poor people.
He asked them for news
of the king—what he was doing.
They told him they had heard
that the barons had been summoned by ban.
They were to come to Tintagel
where the king wanted to hold his court; 40
at Pentecost they would all be there,

there'd be much joy and pleasure,
and the queen would be there too.
Tristan heard and was very happy;
she would not be able to go there
without his seeing her pass.
The day the king set out,
Tristan also came to the woods
by the road he knew
their assembly must take. 50
He cut a hazel tree in half,
then he squared it.
When he had prepared the wood,
he wrote his name on it with his knife.
If the queen noticed it—
and she should be on the watch for it,
for it had happened before
and she had noticed it then—
she'd know when she saw it,
that the piece of wood had come from her love. 60
This was the message of the writing
that he had sent to her:
he had been there a long time,
had waited and remained
to find out and to discover
how he could see her,
for he could not live without her.
With the two of them it was just
as it is with the honeysuckle
that attaches itself to the hazel tree: 70
when it has wound and attached
and worked itself around the trunk,
the two can survive together;
but if someone tries to separate them,
the hazel dies quickly
and the honeysuckle with it.
"Sweet love, so it is with us:
You cannot live without me, nor I without you."
The queen rode along;
she looked at the hillside 80
and saw the piece of wood; she knew what it was,
she recognized all the letters.
The knights who were accompanying her,
who were riding with her,
she ordered to stop:
she wanted to dismount and rest.
They obeyed her command.
She went far away from her people
and called her girl
Brenguein, who was loyal to her. 90
She went a short distance from the road;
and in the woods she found him

whom she loved more than any living thing.
They took great joy in each other.
He spoke to her as much as he desired,
she told him whatever she liked.
Then she assured him
that he would be reconciled with the king—
for it weighed on him
that he had sent Tristan away; 100
he'd done it because of the accusation.
Then she departed, she left her love,
but when it came to the separation,
they began to weep.
Tristan went to Wales,
to wait until his uncle sent for him.
For the joy that he'd felt
from his love when he saw her,
by means of the stick he inscribed
as the queen had instructed, 110
and in order to remember the words,
Tristan, who played the harp well,
composed a new *lai* about it.
I shall name it briefly:
in English they call it *Goat's Leaf*
the French call it *Chevrefoil.*
I have given you the truth
about the *lai* that I have told here.

GIOVANNI BOCCACCIO

[1313–1375]

Like Chaucer's *Canterbury Tales,* Boccaccio's *Decameron* (1353) is a collection of stories enclosed within a frame narrative. The frame differs from Chaucer's, for Boccaccio's storytellers are not religious pilgrims, but rather a group of sophisticated young people who have retreated to the countryside to escape a plague that has swept through Florence. Also unlike Chaucer's tales, which are mainly in verse, Boccaccio's are all written in prose. Together they constitute the most important work of prose fiction of the time. In the vernacular Italian of his day, Boccaccio tells earthy and realistic stories about love in all its aspects.

Boccaccio's realism, his use of prose, and his secular frame narrative have led some commentators to describe him as a Renaissance writer who has broken away from the spiritual preoccupations of the Middle Ages. Such a view may exaggerate the spirituality of the medieval mind and ignore its worldliness. If we choose to place *The Decameron* among works of the Middle Ages, it is important to recognize that Boccaccio lived during an age of transition. He is in many ways much like his friend and contemporary, Petrarch (1304–1374), whom we include among the defining figures of the Renaissance. Both men and their work remind us that the divisions between historical periods are arbitrary and that life has a continuity that historical distinctions sometimes misrepresent.

LIFE

Boccaccio was born in 1313, the son of a Florentine businessman and a French mother. Although he spent much of his childhood in Florence, he went to Naples when he was about fourteen to study commerce. But business bored him and he turned for a time to canon law before becoming what he really wanted to be—a poet. In Naples he wrote his first poems and, as legend has it, met his Fiammetta, the woman who, like Dante's Beatrice and Petrarch's Laura, inspired his adoration and his poetry. After he returned to Florence in 1340, Boccaccio's work took a more realistic turn, culminating in his masterwork, *The Decameron*, which was completed in 1353. In the 1350s he also met Petrarch and they became close friends. Under Petrarch's influence, Boccaccio turned from the vernacular prose fiction of *The Decameron* to more scholarly works written in Latin. In his later years he compiled classical myths, composed short biographies of famous men and women, and wrote a biography of Dante and a commentary on *The Divine Comedy*. In 1373 he was appointed to the Dante Chair in Florence. He died in 1375.

WORK

The title of *The Decameron*, which suggests its form, literally translates as "the work of ten days." It collects the daily tales of seven women and three men who retreat from Florence to the country to escape the ravages of a plague in the city. Altogether, they tell 100 stories during their retreat, all generally concerned with the theme of love. On each day one of the ten is the "queen" or "king" for that day, and she or he may set a more specific thematic agenda. Day Three, for example, ruled by Neifile, a virginal young woman, is devoted to tales "told of those who by their wits obtained something they greatly desired or regained something they had lost." On Day Four, Filostrato's day, he orders the others to tell tales "of those whose love had an unhappy ending."

The frame in *The Decameron* is less developed than that in Chaucer's Canterbury pilgrimage, but it does more than simply establish an excuse for the tale-telling. The plague from which the young people are fleeing is described in vivid detail in the opening to the first day, and the account is historical. Boccaccio lived through the Black Death that ravaged Florence in the spring of 1348. The frame thus establishes a measure of truth against which to judge the fictions of the storytelling. It reminds us of death and the transience of life and raises questions about the spiritual dimensions of the human condition. The prologue implicitly asks us to consider whether the storytellers represent one or another of the reactions to the plague that the narrator describes. Even the most frivolous tales are told against this contrasting historical backdrop. Insofar as the stories can make us forget their menacing context, they become celebrations of the power of imagination to release us from mortal limitation.

Boccaccio took most of his stories from others, reworking traditional tales, jokes, historical anecdotes, and earlier literature. The power of his work is not in the ideas for the stories, but in the telling of them. His use of realistic detail, dialogue, and quick strokes of characterization give the individual tales a life of their own. If Chaucer is memorable for his frame and for his diverse cast of storytellers and their interactions, Boccaccio is memorable for the tales his tellers tell. Indeed, his name has come down in history as a by-word for a prolific and inventive storyteller; for example, Tirso de Molina called Cervantes "the Castilian Boccaccio."

The three tales that we include suggest the range in Boccaccio's storytelling. We have an example of Boccaccio's influence on later writers in the tale of the three rings (Day One, Tale Three), a story reworked in Gotthold Lessing's *Nathan the Wise*. In Boccaccio's version, the tale places wisdom in a contest with cleverness, as the wise Jew Melchisedech eludes the trap that the clever Saladin sets for him. Nevertheless the contest seals their friendship and Saladin gets the money he needs, even though he has been bested. Lessing turns this tale into an Enlightenment parable on religious tolerance. He shifts the emphasis from the contest between the two men to the meaning of its outcome.

Boccaccio is also famous—perhaps notorious—as a teller of bawdy tales. In this regard, he is clearly a man of his time: for Boccaccio, Chaucer, and their contemporaries, the divisions between body and spirit and sexual ecstasy and spiritual rapture were not so marked as they have later become. But Boccaccio's comments in the epilogue to *The Decameron* suggest that some of his racy stories offended even his medieval readers. The tale of Alibeck and Rustico (Day Three, Tale Ten) is a wonderful example of Boccaccio's ability to turn a bawdy joke with blasphemous possibilities into a study of character and a celebration of human vitality. The story begins as a racy parody of the many saints' lives, such as Saint Anthony's, telling of going into the wilderness and overcoming temptations of the flesh. Boccaccio does not simply turn such stories on their head: Even though Rustico hypocritically breaks his vows by putting the devil in hell, he does not do so without struggle; and Alibeck's innocence blesses her unusual service to God and her later marriage.

The third tale, the tragic story of Prince Tancred who "murders" his daughter, reveals a very different dimension of Boccaccio's storytelling genius. An unusual love triangle centers the story, linking the two lovers—the young widow Ghismonda and the page Guiscardo—and Ghismonda's father, the jealous ruler Tancred. With brief strokes, Boccaccio brings each of the characters to life, especially the independent Ghismonda, whose eloquent defense of her love challenges Tancred's patriarchal assumptions. In pursuing the doomed relationships between them, Boccaccio unsettles conventional notions about the role of fathers, about independent and assertive women, and about love across class lines. In the way that he explores these relationships and issues, he seems surprisingly modern.

Suggested Readings

Thomas Bergin's *Boccaccio* (1982) is a good recent account of the author's life. Judith Powers Serafini-Sauli's *Giovanni Boccaccio* (1982) and Vittore Branca's *Boccaccio: The Man and His Works* (1976) provide critical introductions to Boccaccio and his works. Discussions of *The Decameron* in particular can be found in Yvonne Rodax's *The Real and the Ideal in the Novella of Italy, France and England*, ch. 2 (1968), and Giuseppe Mazzotta's *The World at Play in Boccaccio's "Decameron"* (1986).

The Decameron

Translated by Richard Aldington

The First Day

[Here begins the first day of *The Decameron,* wherein, after the author has showed the reasons why certain persons gathered to tell tales, they treat of any subject pleasing to them, under the rule of Pampinea.]

Most gracious ladies, knowing that you are all by nature pitiful, I know that in your judgment this work will seem to have a painful and sad origin. For it brings to mind the unhappy recollection of that late dreadful plague, so pernicious to all who saw or heard of it. But I would not have this frighten you from reading further, as though you were to pass through nothing but sighs and tears in your reading. This dreary opening will be like climbing a steep mountain side to a most beautiful and delightful valley, which appears the more pleasant in proportion to the difficulty of the ascent. The end of happiness is pain, and in like manner misery ends in unexpected happiness.

This brief fatigue (I say brief, because it occupies only a few words) is quickly followed by pleasantness and delight, as I promised you above; which, if I had not promised, you would not expect perhaps from this opening. Indeed, if I could have taken you by any other way than this, which I know to be rough, I would gladly have done so; but since I cannot otherwise tell you how the tales you are about to read came to be told, I am forced by necessity to write in this manner.

In the year 1348 after the fruitful incarnation of the Son of God, that most beautiful of Italian cities, noble Florence, was attacked by deadly plague. It started in the East either through the influence of the heavenly bodies or because God's just anger with our wicked deeds sent it as a punishment to mortal men; and in a few years killed an innumerable quantity of people. Ceaselessly passing from place to place, it extended its miserable length over the West. Against this plague all human wisdom and foresight were vain. Orders had been given to cleanse the city of filth, the entry of any sick person was forbidden, much advice was given for keeping healthy; at the same time humble supplications were made to God by pious persons in processions and otherwise. And yet, in the beginning of the spring of the year mentioned, its horrible results began to appear, and in a miraculous manner. The symptoms were not the same as in the East, where a gush of blood from the nose was the plain sign of inevitable death; but it began both in men and women with certain swellings in the groin or under the armpit. They grew to the size of a small apple or an egg, more or less, and were vulgarly called tumours. In a short space of time these tumours spread from the two parts named all over the body. Soon after this the symptoms changed and black or purple spots appeared on the arms or thighs or any other part of the body, sometimes a few large ones, sometimes many little ones. These spots were a certain sign of death, just as the original tumour had been and still remained.

No doctor's advice, no medicine could overcome or alleviate this disease. An enormous number of ignorant men and women set up as doctors in addition to those who were trained. Either the disease was such that no treatment was possible or the doctors were so ignorant that they did not know what caused it, and consequently could not administer the proper remedy. In any case very few recovered; most people died within about three days of the appearance of the tumours described above, most of them without any fever or other symptoms.

The violence of this disease was such that the sick communicated it to the healthy who came near them, just as a fire catches anything dry or oily near it. And it even went further. To speak to or go near the sick brought infection and a common death to the living; and moreover, to touch the clothes or anything else the sick had touched or worn gave the disease to the person touching.

What I am about to tell now is a marvelous thing to hear; and if I and others had not seen it with our own eyes I would not dare to write it, however much I was willing to believe and whatever the good faith of the person from whom I heard it. So violent was the malignancy of this plague that it was communicated, not only from one man to another, but from the garments of a sick or dead man to animals of another species, which caught the disease in that way and very quickly died of it. One day among other occasions I saw with my own eyes (as I said just now) the rags left lying in the street of a poor man who had died of the plague; two pigs came along and, as their habit is, turned the clothes over with their snouts and then munched at them, with the result that they both fell dead almost at once on the rags, as if they had been poisoned.

From these and similar or greater occurrences, such fear and fanciful notions took possession of the living that almost all of them adopted the same cruel policy, which was entirely to avoid the sick and everything belonging to them. By so doing, each one thought he would secure his own safety.

Some thought that moderate living and the avoidance of all superfluity would preserve them from the epidemic. They formed small communities, living entirely separate from everybody else. They shut themselves up in houses where there were no sick, eating the finest food and drinking the best wine very temperately, avoiding all excess, allowing no news or discussion of death and sickness, and passing the time in music and suchlike pleasures. Others thought just the opposite. They thought the sure cure for the plague was to drink and be merry, to go about singing and amusing themselves, satisfying every appetite they could, laughing and jesting at what happened. They put their words into practice, spent day and night going from tavern to tavern, drinking immoderately, or went into other people's houses, doing only those things which pleased them. This they could easily do because everyone felt doomed and had abandoned his property, so that most houses became common property and any stranger who went in made use of them as if he had owned them. And with all this bestial behaviour, they avoided the sick as much as possible.

In this suffering and misery of our city, the authority of human and divine laws almost disappeared, for, like other men, the ministers and the executors of the laws were all dead or sick or shut up with their families, so that no duties were carried out. Every man was therefore able to do as he pleased.

Many others adopted a course of life midway between the two just described. They did not restrict their victuals so much as the former, nor allow themselves to be drunken and dissolute like the latter, but satisfied their appetites moderately. They did not shut themselves up, but went about, carrying flowers or scented herbs or perfumes in their hands, in the belief that it was an excellent thing to comfort the brain with such odours; for the whole air was infected with the smell of dead bodies, of sick persons and medicines.

Others again held a still more cruel opinion, which they thought would keep them safe. They said that the only medicine against the plaguestricken was to go right away from them. Men and women, convinced of this and caring about nothing but themselves, abandoned their own city, their own houses, their dwellings, their relatives, their property, and went abroad or at least to the country round Florence, as if God's wrath in punishing men's wickedness with this plague would not follow them but strike only those who remained within the walls of the city, or as if they thought nobody in the city would remain alive and that its last hour had come.

Not everyone who adopted any of these various opinions died, nor did all escape. Some when they were still healthy had set the example of avoiding the sick, and, falling ill themselves, died untended.

One citizen avoided another, hardly any neighbour troubled about others, relatives never or hardly ever visited each other. Moreover, such terror was struck into the hearts of men and women by this calamity, that brother abandoned brother, and the uncle his nephew, and the sister her brother, and very often the wife her husband. What is even worse and nearly incredible is that fathers and mothers refused to see and tend their children, as if they had not been theirs.

Thus, a multitude of sick men and women were left without any care except from the charity of friends (but these were few), or the greed of servants, though not many of these could be had even for high wages. Moreover, most of them were coarse-minded men and women, who did little more than bring the sick what they asked for or watch over them when they were dying. And very often these servants lost their lives and their earnings. Since the sick were thus abandoned by neighbours, relatives and friends, while servants were scarce, a habit sprang up which had never been heard of before. Beautiful and noble women, when they fell sick, did not scruple to take a young or old manservant, whoever he might be, and with no sort of shame, expose every part of their bodies to these men as if they had been women, for they were compelled by the necessity of their sickness to do so. This, perhaps, was a cause of looser morals in those women who survived.

In this way many people died who might have been saved if they had been looked after. Owing to the lack of attendants for the sick and the violence of the plague, such a multitude of people in the city died day and night that it was stupefying to hear of, let alone to see. From sheer necessity, then, several ancient customs were quite altered among the survivors.

The custom had been (as we still see it today), that women relatives and neighbours should gather at the house of the deceased, and there lament with the family. At the same time the men would gather at the door with the male neighbours and other citizens. Then came the clergy, few or many according to the dead person's rank; the coffin was placed on the shoulders of his friends and carried with funeral pomp of lighted candles and dirges to the church which the deceased had chosen before dying. But as the fury of the plague increased, this custom wholly or nearly disappeared, and new customs arose. Thus, people died, not only without having a number of women near them, but without a single witness. Very few indeed were honoured with the piteous laments and bitter tears of their relatives, who, on the contrary, spent their time in mirth, feasting and jesting. Even the women abandoned womanly pity and adopted this custom for their own safety. Few were they whose bodies were accompanied to church by more than ten or a dozen neighbours. Nor were these grave and honourable citizens but grave-diggers from the lowest of the people who got themselves called sextons, and performed the task for money. They took up the bier and hurried it off, not to the church chosen by the deceased but to the church nearest, preceded by four or six of the clergy with few candles and often none at all. With the aid of the grave-diggers, the clergy huddled the bodies away in any grave they could find, without giving themselves the trouble of a long or solemn burial service.

The plight of the lower and most of the middle classes was even more pitiful to behold. Most of them remained in their houses, either through poverty or in hopes of safety, and fell sick by thousands. Since they received no care and attention, almost all of them died. Many ended their lives in the streets both at night and during the day; and many others who died in their houses were only known to be dead because the neighbours smelled their decaying bodies. Dead bodies filled every corner. Most of them were treated in the same manner by the survivors, who were more concerned to get rid of their rotting bodies than moved by charity towards the dead. With the aid of porters, if they could get them, they carried the bodies out of the houses and laid them at the doors, where every morning quantities of the dead might be seen. They then were laid on biers, or, as these were often lacking, on tables.

Often a single bier carried two or three bodies, and it happened frequently that a husband and wife, two or three brothers, or father and son were taken off on the same bier. It frequently happened that two priests, each carrying a cross, would go out followed by three or four biers carried by porters; and where the priests thought there was one person to bury, there would be six or eight, and often, even more. Nor were these dead honoured by tears and lighted candles and mourners, for things had reached such a pass that people cared no more for dead men than we care for dead goats. Thus it plainly appeared that what the wise had not learned to endure with patience through the few calamities of ordinary life, became a matter of indifference even to the most ignorant people through the greatness of this misfortune.

Such was the multitude of corpses brought to the churches every day and almost every hour that there was not enough consecrated ground to give them burial, especially since they wanted to bury each person in the family grave, according to the old custom. Although the cemeteries were full they were forced to dig huge trenches, where they buried the bodies by hundreds. Here they stowed them away like bales in the hold of a ship and covered them with a little earth, until the whole trench was full.

Not to pry any further into all the details of the miseries which afflicted our city, I shall add that the surrounding country was spared nothing of what befell Florence. The villages on a smaller scale were like the city; in the fields and isolated farms the poor wretched peasants and their families were without doctors and any assistance, and perished in the highways, in their fields and houses, night and day, more like beasts than men. Just as the townsmen became dissolute and indifferent to their work and property, so the peasants, when they saw that death was upon them, entirely neglected the future fruits of their past labours both from the earth and from cattle, and thought only of enjoying what they had. Thus it happened that cows, asses, sheep, goats, pigs, fowls and even dogs, those faithful companions of man, left the farms and wandered at their will through the fields, where the wheat crops stood abandoned, unreaped and ungarnered. Many of these animals seemed endowed with reason, for, after they had pastured all day, they returned to the farms for the night of their own free will, without being driven.

Returning from the country to the city, it may be said that such was the cruelty of Heaven, and perhaps in part of men, that between March and July more than one hundred thousand persons died within the walls of Florence, what between the violence of the plague and the abandonment in which the sick were left by the cowardice of the healthy. And before the plague it was not thought that the whole city held so many people.

Oh, what great palaces, how many fair houses and noble dwellings, once filled with attendants and nobles and ladies, were emptied to the meanest servant! How many famous names and vast possessions and renowned estates were left without an heir! How many gallant men and fair ladies and handsome youths, whom Galen, Hippocrates and Æsculapius themselves would have said were in perfect health, at noon dined with their relatives and friends, and at night supped with their ancestors in the next world!

But it fills me with sorrow to go over so many miseries. Therefore, since I want to pass over all I can leave out, I shall go on to say that when our city was in this condition and almost emptied of inhabitants, one Tuesday morning the venerable church of Santa Maria Novella had scarcely any congregation for divine service except (as I have heard from a person worthy of belief) seven young women in the mourning garments suitable to the times, who were all related by ties of blood, friendship or neighbourship. None of them was older than twenty-eight or younger than eighteen; all were educated and of noble blood, fair to look upon, well-mannered and of graceful modesty.

I should tell you their real names if I had not a good reason for not doing so, which is that I would not have any of them blush in the future for the things they say and hearken to in the following pages. The laws are now strict again, whereas then, for the reasons already shown, they were very lax, not only for persons of their age but for those much older. Nor would I give an opportunity to the envious (always ready to sneer at every praiseworthy life) to attack the virtue of these modest ladies with vulgar speech. But so that you may understand without confusion what each one says, I intend to give them names wholly or partly suitable to the qualities of each.

The first and eldest I shall call Pampinea, the second Fiammetta, the third Filomena, the fourth Emilia, the fifth Lauretta, the sixth Neifile, and the last Elisa (or "the virgin") for a very good reason. They met, not by arrangement, but by chance, in the same part of the church, and sat down in a circle. After many sighs they ceased to pray and began to talk about the state of affairs and other things. After a short space of silence, Pampinea said:

"Dear ladies, you must often have heard, as I have, that to make a sensible use of one's reason harms nobody. It is natural for everybody to aid, preserve and defend his life as far as possible. And this is so far admitted that to save their own lives men often kill others who have done no harm. If this is permitted by the laws which are concerned with the general good, it must certainly be lawful for us to take any reasonable means for the preservation of our lives. When I think of what we have been doing this morning and still more on former days, when I remember what we have been saying, I perceive and you must perceive that each of us goes in fear of her life. I do not wonder at this, but, since each of us has a woman's judgment, I do wonder that we do not seek some remedy against what we dread.

"In my opinion we remain here for no other purpose than to witness how many bodies are buried, or listen whether the friars here (themselves reduced almost to nothing) sing their offices at the canonical hours, or to display by our clothes the quantity and quality of our miseries to anyone who comes here. If we leave this church we see the bodies of the dead and the sick being carried about. Or we see those who had been exiled from the city by the authority of the laws for their crimes, deriding this authority because they know the guardians of the law are sick or dead, and running loose about the place. Or we see the dregs of the city battening on our blood and calling themselves sextons, riding about on horseback in every direction and insulting our calamities with vile songs. On every side we hear nothing but "So-and-so is dead" or "So-and-so is dying." And if there were anyone left to weep we should hear nothing but piteous lamentations. I do not know if it is the same in your homes as in mine. But if I go home there is nobody left there but one of my maids, which fills me with such horror that the hair stands upon my head. Wherever I go or sit at home I seem to see the ghosts of the departed, not with the faces as I knew them but with dreadful looks which terrify me.

"I am ill at ease here and outside of here and at home; the more so since nobody who has the strength and ability to go away (as we have) now remains here, except ourselves. The few that remain (if there are any), according to what I see and hear, do anything which gives them pleasure or pleases their appetites, both by day and night, whether they are alone or in company, making no distinction between right and wrong. Not only laymen, but those cloistered in convents have broken their oaths and given themselves up to the delights of the flesh, and thus in trying to escape the plague by doing what they please, they have become lascivious and dissolute.

"If this is so (and we may plainly see it is) what are we doing here? What are we waiting for? What are we dreaming about? Are we less eager and active than other citizens in saving our lives? Are they less dear to us than to others? Or do we think that our lives are bound to our bodies with stronger chains than other people's, and so believe that we need fear nothing which might harm us? We were and are deceived. How stupid we should be to believe such a thing! We may see the plainest proofs from the number of young men and women who have died of this cruel plague.

"I do not know if you think as I do, but in my opinion if we, through carelessness, do not want to fall into this calamity when we can escape it, I think we should do well to leave this town, just as many others have done and are doing. Let us avoid the wicked examples of others like death itself, and go and live virtuously in our country houses, of which each of us possesses several. There let us take what happiness and pleasure we can, without ever breaking the rules of reason in any manner.

"There we shall hear the birds sing, we shall see the green hills and valleys, the wheat-fields rolling like a sea, and all kinds of trees. We shall see the open Heavens which, although now angered against man, do not withhold from us their eternal beauties that are so much fairer to look upon than the empty walls of our city. The air will be fresher there, we shall find a greater plenty of those things necessary to life at this time, and fewer troubles. Although the peasants are dying like the townsmen, still, since the houses and inhabitants are fewer, we shall see less of them and feel less misery. On the other hand I believe we are not abandoning anybody here. Indeed we can truthfully say that we are abandoned, since our relatives have either died or fled from death and have left us alone in this calamity as if we were nothing to them.

"If we do what I suggest, no blame can fall upon us; if we fail to do it, the result may be pain, trouble and perhaps death. Therefore I think that we should do well to take our servants and all things necessary, and go from one house to another, enjoying whatever merriment and pleasure these times allow. Let us live in this way (unless death comes upon us) until we see what end Heaven decrees to this plague. And remember that going away virtuously will not harm us so much as staying here in wickedness will harm others."

The other ladies listened to what Pampinea said, praised her advice, and in their eagerness to follow it began to discuss details, as if they were going to leave at once. But Filomena, who was a most prudent young woman, said:

"Ladies, although what Pampinea says is excellent advice, we must not rush off at once, as you seem to wish. Remember we are all women; and any girl can tell you how women behave together and conduct themselves without the direction of some man. We are fickle, wayward, suspicious, faint-hearted and cowardly. So if we have no guide but ourselves I greatly suspect that this company will very soon break up, without much honour to ourselves. Let us settle this matter before we start."

Elisa then broke in:

"Indeed men are a woman's head and we can rarely succeed in anything without their help; but how can we find any men? Each of us knows that most of her menfolk are dead, while the others are away, we know not where, flying with their companions from the end we wish to escape. To ask strangers would be unbecoming; for, if we mean to go away to save our lives we must take care that scandal and annoyance do not follow us where we are seeking rest and amusement."

While the ladies were thus arguing, three young men came into the church, the youngest of whom was not less than twenty-five. They were lovers whose love could not be quenched or even cooled by the horror of the times, the loss of relatives and friends, or even fear for themselves. The first was named Pamfilo, the second Filostrato, the third Dioneo. They were pleasant, well-mannered men, and in this public calamity they sought the consolation of looking upon the ladies they loved. These ladies happened to be among our seven, while some of the others were related to one or other of the three men. They no sooner came into sight than the ladies saw them; whereupon Pampinea said with a smile:

"See how Fortune favours our plan at once by sending us these valiant and discreet young men, who will gladly act as our guides and servants if we do not refuse to accept them for such duties."

Neifile then became crimson, for she was one of the ladies beloved by one of the young men, and said:

"For God's sake, Pampinea, be careful what you are saying. I know quite well that nothing but good can be said of any of them and I am sure they could achieve greater things than this. I also think that their company would be fitting and pleasant, not only to us, but to ladies far more beautiful and charming than we are. But it is known to everyone that they are in love with some of us women here; and so, if we take them with us, I am afraid that blame and infamy will fall upon us, through no fault of ours or theirs."

Then said Filomena:

"What does that matter? If I live virtuously, my conscience never pricks me, whatever people may say. God and the truth will fight for me. If these men would come with us, then indeed, as Pampinea said, fortune would be favourable to our plan of going away."

The others not only refrained from censuring what she said, but agreed by common consent that the men should be spoken to, told their plan, and asked if they would accompany the ladies on their expedition. Without more ado, Pampinea, who was related to one of them, arose and went towards them where they stood looking at the ladies, saluted them cheerfully, told them the plan, and begged them in the name of all the ladies to accompany them out of pure and fraternal affection.

At first the young men thought this was a jest. But when they saw the lady was speaking seriously, they said they were willing to go. And in order to start without delay they at once gave the orders necessary for departure. Everything necessary was made ready, and word was sent on ahead to the place they were going. At dawn next morning, which was Wednesday, the ladies with some of their servants, and the young men with a man servant each, left the city and set out. They had not gone more than two miles when they came to the first place where they were to stay.

This estate was on slightly raised ground, at some distance from any main road, with many trees and plants, fair to look upon. At the top of the rise was a country mansion with a large inner courtyard. It had open colonnades, galleries and rooms, all beautiful in themselves and ornamented with gay paintings. Roundabout were lawns and marvelous gardens and wells of cool water. There were cellars of fine wines, more suitable to wine connoisseurs than to sober and virtuous ladies. The whole house had been cleaned, the beds were prepared in the rooms, and every corner was strewn with the flowers of the season and fresh rushes. All of which the company beheld with no little pleasure.

They all sat down to discuss plans, and Dioneo, who was a most amusing young man and full of witticisms, remarked:

"Ladies, your good sense, rather than our foresight, has brought us here. I do not know what you are thinking of doing with your troubles here, but I dropped mine inside the gates of the city when I left it with you a little time ago. Therefore, either you must make up your minds to laugh and sing and amuse yourselves with me (that is, to the extent your dignity allows), or you must let me go back to my troubles and stay in the afflicted city."

Pampinea, who had driven away her woes in the same way, cheerfully replied:

"Dioneo, you speak well, let us amuse ourselves, for that was the reason why we fled from our sorrows. But when things are not organised they cannot long continue.

And, since I began the discussion which brought this fair company together and since I wish our happiness to continue, I think it necessary that one of us should be made chief, whom the others will honour and obey, and whose duty shall be to regulate our pleasures. Now, so that everyone—both man and woman—may experience the cares as well as the pleasures of ruling and no one feel any envy at not sharing them, I think the weight and honour should be given to each of us in turn for one day. The first shall be elected by all of us. At vespers he or she shall choose the ruler for the next day, and so on. While their reigns last these rulers shall arrange where and how we are to spend our time."

These words pleased them all and they unanimously elected her for the first day. Filomena ran to a laurel bush, whose leaves she had always heard were most honourable in themselves and did great honour to anyone crowned with them, plucked off a few small branches and wove them into a fair garland of honour. When this was placed on the head of any one of them, it was a symbol of rule and authority over the rest so long as the party remained together.

Pampinea, thus elected queen, ordered silence. She then sent for the three servants of the young men and the four women servants the ladies had brought, and said:

"To set a first example to you all which may be bettered and thus allow our gathering to live pleasantly and orderly and without shame and to last as long as we desire, I appoint Dioneo's servant Parmeno as my steward, and hand over to him the care of the whole family and of everything connected with the dining hall. Pamfilo's servant Sirisco shall be our treasurer and buyer, and carry out Parmeno's instructions. Tindaro shall wait on Filostrato and Dioneo and Pamfilo in their rooms, when the other two servants are occupied with their new duties. Filomena's servant Licisca and my own servant Misia shall remain permanently in the kitchen and carefully prepare the food which Parmeno sends them. Lauretta's Chimera and Fiammetta's Stratilia shall take care of the ladies' rooms and see that the whole house is clean. Moreover we will and command that everyone who values our good grace shall bring back only cheerful news, wherever he may go or return from, and whatever he may hear or see."

Having given these orders, which were approved by everyone, she jumped gaily to her feet and said:

"Here are gardens and lawns and other delicious places, where each of us can wander and enjoy them at will. But let everyone be here at the hour of Tierce so that we can eat together while it is still cool."

The company of gay young men and women, thus given the queen's permission, went off together slowly through the gardens, talking of pleasant matters, weaving garlands of different leaves, and singing love songs. After the time allotted by the queen had elapsed they returned to the house and found that Parmeno had carefully carried out the duties of his office. Entering a ground floor room decorated everywhere with broom blossoms, they found tables covered with white cloths and set with glasses which shone like silver. They washed their hands and, at the queen's command, all sat down in the places allotted them by Parmeno. Delicately cooked food was brought, exquisite wines were at hand, and the three men servants waited at table. Everyone was delighted to see things so handsome and well arranged, and they ate merrily with much happy talk.

All the ladies and young men could dance and many of them could play and sing; so, when the tables were cleared, the queen called for musical instruments. At her command Dioneo took a lute and Fiammetta a viol, and began to play a dance tune. The queen sent the servants to their meal, and then with slow steps danced with the two young men and the other ladies. After that, they began to sing gay and charming songs.

In this way they amused themselves until the queen thought it was time for the siesta. So, at the queen's bidding, the three young men went off to their rooms (which were separated from the ladies') and found them filled with flowers as the dining hall had been. And similarly with the women. So they all undressed and went to sleep.

Not long after the hour of Nones the queen arose and made the other women and the young men also get up, saying that it was harmful to sleep too long during the daytime. Then they went out to a lawn of thick green grass entirely shaded from the sun. A soft breeze came to them there. The queen made them sit down in a circle on the grass, and said:

"As you see, the sun is high and the heat great, and nothing can be heard but the cicadas in the olive trees. To walk about at this hour would be foolish. Here it is cool and lovely, and, as you see, there are games of chess and draughts which everyone can amuse himself with, as he chooses. But, if my opinion is followed, we shall not play games, because in games the mind of one of the players must necessarily be distressed without any great pleasure to the other player or the onlookers. Let us rather spend this hot part of the day in telling tales, for thus one person can give pleasure to the whole company. When each of us has told a story, the sun will be going down and the heat less, and we can then go walking anywhere we choose for our amusement. If this pleases you (for here I am ready to follow your pleasure) let us do it. If it does not please you, let everyone do as he likes until evening."

The women and men all favoured the telling of stories.

"Then if it pleases you," said the queen, "on this first day I order that everyone shall tell his tale about any subject he likes."

She then turned to Pamfilo, who was seated on her right, and ordered him to begin with a tale. Hearing this command, Pamfilo at once began as follows, while all listened.

. . .

The First Day
Third Tale

[By means of a tale about three rings, a Jew named Melchisedech escapes a trap laid for him by Saladin.]

When Neifile was silent, her tale was praised by them all; and then, at the queen's command, Filomena began to speak as follows:

Neifile's tale brings back to my mind a dangerous adventure which once happened to a Jew. Now since God and the truth of our faith have already been well dealt with among us, we should not be forbidden to come down to the adventures and actions of men. I shall tell you this tale, and when you have heard it perhaps you will become more cautious in answering the questions which are put to you. You must be aware, my loving friends, that stupidity often drags people out of happiness into the greatest misery, while good sense saves the wise man from the greatest dangers and puts him in complete security. That stupidity brings people from happiness to misery may be seen from many examples, which I do not intend to relate now, seeing that a thousand instances of it occur every day. But, as I have promised, I will briefly show you by a little tale how wisdom may be the cause of joy.

Such was the valour of Saladin that not only did he rise from the people to be Sultan of Babylon but he won many victories over Saracen and Christian Kings. He found one day that he had spent the whole of his treasure in divers wars and magnificent displays, while something had occurred which made him need a large sum of money. He did not know where to get it as speedily as he needed, when he remembered a rich Jew named Melchisedech who lent money at usury in Alexandria; and Saladin thought that this Jew could be of use to him if he wanted. But the Jew was so miserly that he would never do it of his own free will, while Saladin did not wish to use force. Since necessity pressed him, Saladin tried to think of some means whereby the Jew would come to his aid, and finally decided that he would devise some colourable pretext for compelling Melchisedech. So he sent for the Jew, received him in a friendly way, made him sit down, and then said:

"Worthy man, I have heard from many people that you are very wise, and that you have a deep understanding of God's ways. So I should very much like to know from you which of the three Laws you think the true one—Judaism, Mohammedanism or Christianity?"

The Jew, who really was a wise man, saw at once that Saladin intended to catch him by his words in order to draw him into a dispute. So he thought he must not praise one of the three above another, otherwise Saladin would attain his object. So he sharpened his wits, like a man who needs to make an answer which will not entrap him, realised excellently beforehand what he ought to say, and said:

"My Lord, you have asked me a very good question, but if I am to tell you what I think about it I shall have to relate a little story, which you will now hear.

"If I err not, I remember that I have often heard that once upon a time there was a great and rich man who possessed a most beautiful and valuable ring among the other very precious jewels in his treasure. Being desirous to do honour to it on account of its value and beauty and to make it a perpetual heirloom among his descendants, he commanded that whichever of his sons should be found in possession of the ring, which he would leave to him, should be looked upon as his heir, and that all his other children should reverence and honour this son as the greatest among them.

"The son to whom the ring was left gave similar orders to his descendants, and acted as his predecessor had done. In short, this ring passed from hand to hand through many succeeding generations, and finally came into the hands of a man who had three fine and virtuous sons who were all very obedient to their father. For which reason he loved all three of them equally. The young men knew the custom attached to the ring and each was desirous to be the most honoured, and therefore each of them to the best of his ability besought the father—now grown old—to leave him the ring when he died.

"The worthy man, who loved them all three equally, did not himself know which of the three he would choose to leave the ring, and, as he had promised it to each of them, he thought he would satisfy all three. So he caused a good artist secretly to make two other rings, which were so much like the first that even the man who had made them could scarcely tell which was the real one. When the old man was dying, he secretly gave one of the rings to each of his sons. And after their father's death, each of them claimed the honour and the inheritance, and each denied it to the others; and to prove that they were acting rightly, each one brought forth his own ring. And the rings were found to be so much alike that no one could tell which was the true one, so the question as to which was the father's real heir remained unsettled and is not settled yet.

"My Lord, I say it is the same with the three Laws given by God our Father to three peoples, concerning which you have questioned me. Each of them thinks it has the inheritance, the true Law, and carries out His Commandments; but which does have it is a question as far from being settled as that of the rings."

Saladin perceived that the Jew had most skilfully avoided the snare which he had woven to catch his feet. And therefore he decided to tell the man of his necessity and to find out whether he would aid him. And this Saladin did, telling the Jew what he had thought of doing if the Jew had not replied so discreetly.

The Jew freely put at Saladin's disposal all the money he needed, and Saladin afterwards repaid him in full. Moreover, Saladin gave him very great gifts and always looked upon him as a friend and kept the Jew near his person in great and honourable state.

. . .

The Third Day
Tenth Tale

[Alibech becomes a hermit, and the monk Rustico teaches her how to put the devil in hell. She is afterwards taken away and becomes the wife of Neerbale.]

Dioneo had listened closely to the queen's story, and, when it was over and only he remained to tell a story, he did not wait to be commanded, but smilingly began as follows:

Most gracious ladies, perhaps you have never heard how the devil is put into hell; and so, without departing far from the theme upon which you have all spoken today, I shall tell you about it. Perhaps when you have learned it, you also will be able to save your souls, and you may also discover that although love prefers to dwell in gay palaces and lovely rooms rather than in poor huts, yet he sometimes makes his power felt among thick woods and rugged mountains and desert caves. Whereby we may well perceive that all of us are subject to his power.

Now, to come to my story—in the city of Capsa in Barbery there lived a very rich man who possessed among other children a pretty and charming daughter, named Alibech. She was not a Christian, but she heard many Christians in her native town crying up the Christian Faith and service to God, and one day she asked one of them how a person could most effectively serve God. The reply was that those best serve God who fly furthest from the things of this world, like the hermits who had departed to the solitudes of the Thebaid Desert.

The girl was about fourteen and very simple minded. Urged by a mere childish enthusiasm and not by a well ordered desire, she secretly set out next morning quite alone, without saying a word to anyone, to find the Thebaid Desert. Her enthusiasm lasted several days and enabled her with great fatigue to reach those solitudes. In the distance she saw a little hut with a holy man standing at its entrance. He was amazed to see her there, and asked her what she was seeking. She replied that by God's inspiration she was seeking to serve Him, and begged the hermit to show her the right way to do so. But the holy man saw she was young and pretty, and feared that if he kept her with him he might be tempted of the devil. So he praised her good intentions, gave her some roots and wild apples to eat and some water to drink, and said:

"Daughter, not far from here dwells a holy man who is a far greater master of what you are seeking than I am; go to him."

And so he put her on the way. When she reached him, she was received with much the same words, and passing further on came to the cell of a young hermit named Rustico, to whom she made the same request as to the others. To test his spiritual strength, Rustico did not send her away, but took her into his cell. And when night came, he made her a bed of palm leaves and told her to sleep there.

Almost immediately after this, temptation began the struggle with his spiritual strength, and the hermit found that he had greatly over-estimated his powers of resistance. After a few assaults of the demon he shrugged his shoulders and surrendered. Putting aside holy thoughts and prayers and macerations, he began to think of her beauty and youth, and then pondered how he should proceed with her so that she should not perceive that he obtained what he wanted from her like a dissolute man. First of all he sounded her by certain questions, and discovered that she had never lain with a man and appeared to be very simple minded. He then saw how he could bring her to his desire under pretext of serving God. He began by eloquently showing how the devil is the enemy of the Lord God, and then gave her to understand that the service most pleasing to God is to put the devil back into hell, to which the Lord God has condemned him. The girl asked how this was done, and Rustico replied:

"You shall soon know. Do what you see me do."

He then threw off the few clothes he had and remained stark naked, and the girl imitated him. He kneeled down as if to pray and made her kneel exactly opposite him. As he gazed at her beauty, Rustico's desire became so great that the resurrection of the flesh occurred. Alibech looked at it with amazement, and said:

"Rustico, what is that thing I see sticking out in front of you which I haven't got?"

"My daughter," said Rustico, "that is the devil I spoke of. Do you see? He gives me so much trouble at this moment that I can scarcely endure him."

Said the girl:

"Praised be God! I see I am better off than you are, since I haven't such a devil."

"You speak truly," said Rustico, "but instead of this devil you have something else which I haven't."

"What's that?" said Alibech.

"You've got hell," replied Rustico, "and I believe God sent you here for the salvation of my soul, because this devil gives me great trouble, and if you will take pity upon me and let me put him into hell, you will give me the greatest comfort and at the same time will serve God and please Him, since, as you say, you came here for that purpose."

In all good faith the girl replied: "Father, since I have hell in me, let it be whenever you please."

Said Rustico: "Blessings upon you, my daughter. Let us put him in now so that he will afterwards depart from me."

So saying, he took the girl to one of their beds, and showed her how to lie so as to imprison the thing accursed of God. The girl had never before put any devil into her hell and at first felt a little pain, and exclaimed to Rustico:

"O father! This devil must certainly be wicked and the enemy of God, for even when he is put back into hell he hurts it."

"Daughter," said Rustico, "it will not always be so."

To prevent this from happening, Rustico put it into hell six times, before he got off the bed, and so purged the devil's pride that he was glad to rest a little. Thereafter he returned often and the obedient girl was always glad to take him in; and then the game began to give her pleasure, and she said to Rustico:

"I see that the good men of Capsa spoke the truth when they told me how sweet a thing is the service of God. I certainly do not remember that I ever did anything which gave me so much delight and pleasure as I get from putting the devil into hell. I think that everyone is a fool who does anything but serve God."

Thus it happened that she would often go to Rustico, and say:

"Father, I came here to serve God and not to remain in idleness. Let us put the devil in hell."

And once as they were doing it, she said:

"Rustico, I don't know why the devil ever goes out of hell. If he liked to remain there as much as hell likes to receive and hold him, he would never leave it."

The girl's frequent invitations to Rustico and their mutual pleasures in the service of God so took the stuffing out of his doublet that he now felt chilly where another man would have been in a sweat. So he told the girl that the devil must not be chastened or put into hell except when pride made him lift his head. "And we," he said, "have so quelled his rage that he prays God to be left in peace." And in this way he silenced the girl for a time. But when she found that Rustico no longer asked her to put the devil in hell, she said one day:

"Rustico, your devil may be chastened and give you no more trouble, but my hell is not. You should therefore quench the raging of my hell with your devil, as I helped you to quell the pride of your devil with my hell."

Rustico, who lived on nothing but roots and water, made a poor response to this invitation. He told her that many devils would be needed to soothe her hell, but that he would do what he could. In this way he satisfied her hell a few times, but so seldom that it was like throwing a bean in a lion's mouth. And the girl, who thought they were not serving God as much as she wanted, kept murmuring.

Now, while there was this debate between the excess of desire in Alibech's hell and the lack of potency in Rustico's devil, a fire broke out in Capsa, and burned Alibech's father with all his children and servants. So Alibech became heir to all his property. A young man named Neerbale, who had spent all his money in riotous living, heard that she was still alive and set out to find her, which he succeeded in doing before the Court took over her father's property as that of a man who had died without heirs. To Rustico's great relief, but against her will, Neerbale brought her back to Capsa and married her, and together they inherited her large patrimony. But before Neerbale had lain with her, certain ladies one day asked her how she had served God in the desert. She replied that her service was to put the devil in hell, and that Neerbale had committed a great sin by taking her away from such service. The ladies asked:

"And how do you put the devil in hell?"

Partly in words and partly by gestures, the girl told them. At this they laughed so much that they are still laughing, and said:

"Be not cast down, my child, they know how to do that here, and Neerbale will serve the Lord God with you in that way."

As they told it up and down the city, it passed into a proverb that the service most pleasing to God is to put the devil into hell. And this proverb crossed the seas and remains until this day.

Therefore, young ladies, when you seek God's favour, learn to put the devil in hell, because this is most pleasing to God and to all parties concerned, and much good may come of it.

Dioneo's tale moved the chaste ladies to laughter hundreds of times, so apt and amusing did they find his words. When he had finished, the queen knew that the end of her reign had come, and therefore took the laurel wreath from her head and placed it upon Filostrato's, saying pleasantly:

"We shall soon find out if the wolf can guide the flock, as well as the flock has guided the wolves."

Filostrato laughingly replied:

"If my advice were followed, the wolves would have showed the flock how to put the devil in hell, as Rustico taught Alibech; and so they would not be called wolves, where you would not be the flock. However, since the rule now falls to me, I shall begin my reign."

Said Neifile:

"Filostrato, in trying to teach us, you might have learned wisdom, as Masetto da Lamporecchio learned it from the nuns, and you might have regained your speech when your bones were rattling together from exhaustion!"

Filostrato, finding the ladies' sickles were as good as his shafts, ceased jesting, and occupied himself with the government of his kingdom. Calling the steward, he made enquiries into everything, and gave orders to ensure the well being and satisfaction of the band during his kingship. He then turned to the ladies and said:

"Amorous ladies, to my own misfortune—although I was quite aware of my disease—I have always been one of Love's subjects owing to the beauty of one of you. To be humble and obedient to her and to follow all her whims as closely as I could, was all of no avail to me, and I was soon abandoned for another. Thus I go from bad to worse, and believe I shall until I die. Tomorrow then it is my pleasure that we tell tales on a theme in conformity with my own fate—that is, about those persons whose love ended unhappily. In the long run I expect a most unhappy end for myself, and the person who gave me the nickname of Filostrato, or the Victim of Love, knew what she was doing."

So saying, he rose to his feet, and gave them all leave to depart until supper time.

The garden was so delightful and so beautiful that they all chose to remain there, since no greater pleasure could be found elsewhere. The sun was now not so hot, and therefore some of them began to chase the deer and rabbits and other animals which had annoyed them scores of times by leaping in among them while they were seated. Dioneo and Fiammetta began to sing the song of Messer Guglielmo and the Lady of Vergiu. Filomena and Pamfilo played chess. Thus, with one thing and another, time passed so quickly that supper time arrived long before they expected. The tables were set round the fountain, and there they ate their evening meal with the utmost pleasure.

When they rose from table, Filostrato would not depart from the path followed by the preceding queens, and so ordered Lauretta to dance and sing a song. And she said:

"My lord, I do not know any songs of other persons, and I do not remember any of my own which are fitting for this merry band. But if you wish to have one of those I remember, I will gladly sing it."

"Nothing of yours could be anything but fair and pleasing," said the king, "so sing it just as it is."

Then to the accompaniment of the others, Lauretta sang as follows in a sweet but rather plaintive voice:

> No helpless lady has such cause to weep as I, who vainly sigh, alas, for love.
>
> He who moves the heavens and all the stars made me for His delight so fair, so sweet, so gracious and so lovely that I might show to every lofty mind some trace of that high Beauty which ever dwells within His presence. But a weak man, who knew not Beauty, found me undelightful and scorned me.
>
> Once there was one who held me dear, and in my early years took me into his arms and to his thoughts, being quite conquered by my eyes. And time, that flies so swiftly, he spent in serving me; and I in courtesy made him worthy of me. But now, alas, he is taken from me.
>
> Then came a proud presumptuous man, who thought himself both noble and valorous, and made me his, but through false belief became most jealous of me. And

then, alas, I came near to despair, for I saw that I, who came into the world to pleasure many, was possessed by one alone.

I curse my luckless fate that ever I said "yes" to man, and changed to a wife's garb. I was so gay in my old plain maiden's dress! Now in these finer clothes I lead so sad a life, reputed less than chaste. O hapless wedding feast! Would I had died before I knew the fate it held for me!

O my first love, with whom I was so happy, who now in Heaven do stand before Him who created it, have pity on me. I cannot forget you for another. Let me feel that the flame wherewith you burned for me is not extinct, and pray that I may soon return to you.

Here ended Lauretta's song, which was noted carefully by them all, but interpreted differently. Some understood it in the Milanese sense—that it is better to be a good pig than a pretty girl. Others were of a better, more sublime and truer understanding, but of this I shall not now speak.

After this the king had many torches brought and made them sing other songs as they sat on the grass and flowers, until the rising stars began to turn towards the west. Then, thinking it time for sleep, he said good night and sent each one to his room.

[End of the Third Day]

The Fourth Day
First Tale

[Tancred, Prince of Salerno, murders his daughter's lover and sends her the heart in a gold cup. She pours poison on it, which she drinks; and so dies.]

Our king has given us a sad theme for tale-telling today, thinking that as we came here to enjoy ourselves it is befitting to speak of the tears of others, which cannot be heard without pity either by the teller or the listeners. Perhaps he did this to temper the happiness we have had in the past few days. But, whatever his motive, it is not for me to change his good pleasure, and so I shall tell you a piteous story of misadventure, worthy of your tears.

Tancred, Prince of Salerno, was a humane and kindly man, except that in his old age he stained his hands with the blood of lovers. In the whole of his life he had no child but one daughter, and it would have been happier for him if he had not had her. This girl was as much beloved by her father as any daughter ever was, and long after she had reached marriageable age this tender love of his prevented him from marrying her to anyone. At length he gave her to a son of the Duke of Capua, who died soon after the marriage; and she returned home a widow. In face and body she was most beautiful, and young and merry and perhaps cleverer than a woman should be. She lived with her father in great luxury like a great lady, and, when she saw that her father loved her so much that he cared little about marrying her again, while she thought it immodest to ask him to do so, she determined that if she could she would secretly have a valiant lover.

Many men, both nobles and others, frequented her father's Court. She observed the manners and behaviour of many of these men, among them a young servant of her father's named Guiscardo, a man of humble birth but whose virtues and noble bearing pleased her so much that she fell secretly in love with him, and the more she saw him the more she admired him. The young man, who was no novice, soon perceived this and took her so deep into his heart that he could think of scarcely anything but his love for her.

Since they both were secretly in love with each other, the young widow desired nothing so much as to be alone with him, and, as she would trust nobody in this love affair, she thought of a new device for telling him where to meet her. She wrote him a letter telling him what he had to do the next day in order to be with her, and then put it into a hollow stick, which she laughingly gave him, saying:

"Make a bellows of this tonight for your servant to blow the fire."

Guiscardo took it, and realised that she would not have given it to him and have spoken these words without some reason. When he got to his lodging he looked at the stick, saw it was hollow and found her letter, which he read. When he discovered what he was to do, he was the happiest man alive, and prepared to meet her in the way she had arranged.

Near the Prince's palace was a cave, hollowed out of a hill in the remote past, and dimly lighted by a small opening cut in the hill-side. The cave had been so long abandoned that this opening was almost covered over with brambles and other plants. A secret stairway, secured by a very strong door, led to the cave from one of the rooms in the palace where the lady had her apartments. This stairway had been disused so long that scarcely anyone remembered its existence. But Love, from whose eyes nothing secret can be hidden, brought it to the remembrance of this enamoured lady.

To avoid anyone's knowing about all this, she exerted her wits for many days until she had succeeded in opening the door. Having opened it, she entered the cave alone and saw the outer entrance, and afterwards told Guiscardo to find some means of entering it, telling him about how far it was from the ground. Guiscardo immediately prepared a rope with knots and loops so that he could climb up and descend. The next night he wrapped himself in a leather skin as protection against the brambles and, without allowing anyone to know about it, went to the cave entrance. There he fitted one of the rope loops round a strong tree stump which had grown up in the mouth of the cave entrance, and so let himself down into the cave, and waited for the lady.

Next day, under pretence of taking a siesta, she sent away her women and shut herself up alone in her room. Then, opening the door, she got into the cave where she found Guiscardo; and together they made much of one another. They afterwards went to her room and remained together with the greatest delight for a large portion of that day. They made the necessary arrangements to keep their love secret; Guiscardo returned to the cave, she locked the door, and returned to her waiting women. When night came Guiscardo climbed up his rope and got out by the same opening he had come in, and returned home. Having thus learned this way, he returned often in the course of time.

But Fortune, envious of this prolonged and deep delight, changed the lovers' joy into piteous lament by a grievous happening.

Tancred was sometimes accustomed to go alone to his daughter's room to talk to her for a time, and then depart. One day he went there while his daughter (whose name was Ghismonda) was in a garden with all her women. Unwilling to disturb her pleasure he went into the room unseen and unheard, and finding the windows of the room shut and the bed-curtains drawn, sat down at the foot of the bed on a low stool. He leaned his head on the bed, drew the curtain round him, as if he had been hiding himself, and went to sleep. As misfortune would have it, Ghismonda had bidden Guiscardo come that day, and therefore left her women in the garden and softly entered the room where Tancred was asleep. She locked the door without noticing that he was there, and opened the other door for Guiscardo, who was waiting for her. They went to bed together, as usual, and while they were playing together and taking their delight, Tancred awoke and saw and heard what his daughter and Guiscardo were doing. In his distress he nearly made an outcry, but then determined to remain silent and hidden if he could, so that he could carry out with less shame what he had already determined to do.

The two lovers remained a long time together, as they were accustomed to do, without noticing Tancred; and when they thought it was time they got out of bed, Guiscardo returned to the cave, and she went out of the room. Tancred, although he was an old man, climbed out of a window into the garden, and returned to his own apartment almost dead with grief.

That night, by Tancred's orders, Guiscardo was arrested by two men as he came out of the cave opening still wrapped in the leather skin, and was secretly taken to Tancred. And when Tancred saw him, he said almost in tears:

"Guiscardo, my kindness to you has not merited the outrage and shame you have done me, as this day I saw with my own eyes."

But to this the only reply Guiscardo made was:

"Love is more powerful than either you or I."

Tancred then ordered that he should be closely guarded in a neighbouring room; which was done. The next day, while Ghismonda was still ignorant of what had happened, Tancred went to his daughter's room as usual after dinner, having turned over all kinds of thoughts in his mind. He had her called, locked himself in with her, and said to her in tears:

"Ghismonda, I thought I knew your virtue and modesty so well that, whatever had been said to me, it would never have come into my mind (if I had not seen it with my own eyes) that you would have yielded to any man who was not your husband, or even have thought of doing so. Whenever I think of it I shall always grieve during that short space of life left me in my old age.

"Since you had to come to this disgrace, would to God that you had taken a man who was worthy of your noble blood. But among all the men in my Court you chose Guiscardo, a young man of the basest extraction, bred in my Court from childhood, almost out of charity. You have plunged my mind in the greatest perplexity, and I do not know what to do. Last night I had Guiscardo arrested when he came out of the cave opening, and I have him in prison; and I know what I shall do with him. But God knows what I am to do with you. On the one hand, I am urged by the love I feel for you, which is greater than any father ever felt for a daughter. On the other hand, I am urged by my indignation at your folly. The one urges me to forgive you, the other to punish you against my natural feeling. But before I make up my mind, I should like to hear what you have to say."

So saying he bowed his head, and wept like a beaten child. As Ghismonda listened to her father, she saw that her secret love was discovered, and that Guiscardo was in prison. This caused her inexpressible grief, which she was very near to showing by tears and shrieks, as most women do. But her lofty love conquered this weak feeling, she kept her countenance with marvellous strength of mind, and made up her mind that before she made any prayer for herself, she would not remain alive since she saw Guiscardo was already as good as dead. So she faced her father, not like a weeping woman detected in a fault, but like a brave and unconcerned one, and replied to him unperturbed, with a clear and open visage:

"Tancred, I am not prepared either to deny or to supplicate, because the former would not avail me and I do not want to avail myself of the latter. Moreover, I do not mean to make your love and gentleness of service to me, but to confess the truth, to defend my fame with good reasons and then with deeds to follow boldly the greatness of my soul. It is true that I have loved and do love Guiscardo. As long as I live—which will not be long—I shall love him. And if there is love after death, I shall continue to love him then. I was not drawn to this love so much by my womanish weakness as by your neglecting to marry me and by his virtues.

"Since you are flesh and blood, Tancred, you should know that you begot a daughter of flesh and blood, not of stone or iron. You should have remembered now and earlier, although you are now an old man, what and how powerful are the laws of youth. Although you spent the best years of your manhood in warfare, yet you should know the power of idleness and luxury upon the old as well as upon the young.

"Now, I was begotten by you and so am of flesh and blood, and I have not lived so long that I am yet old. My youth and my flesh are the reasons why I am filled with amorous desires; and they have been greatly increased by my marriage, which showed what pleasure there is in satisfying these desires. I could not resist them, but yielded to them, as a young woman would do; and fell in love. As far as I could, I endeavoured to avoid shame to you and to me in doing what I was drawn to do by natural sin. Compassionate Love and kindly Fortune found and showed me a secret way to reach my desires, without anyone else knowing. Nor do I make any denial of all this, however you may have learned it or whoever told you.

"I did not take Guiscardo at a venture, as many women would have done, but I chose him above all others deliberately and with forethought, and he and I have long enjoyed our desires. Whereby it appears from your bitter reproof that, in addition to my sin of loving, you think (following, in this, rather common opinion than the truth) that I have erred in addition by choosing a man of low birth, as if you thought you need not be angry if I had chosen a nobleman. Here you should not reprove my error but that of Fortune, who often lifts the unworthy on high and casts down the most worthy.

"But let us leave all this, and look at the principles of things. You will see that we all have the same flesh, and that all souls were created by the same Creator with equal powers, equal strength and equal virtues. It was virtue which first introduced differences among us who were born and are born equal. Those who were most virtuous and most devoted themselves to virtue were called noble, and the others remained commoners. And although this law has been glossed over by contrary custom, yet it is neither repealed nor broken by Nature and good manners. Therefore, he who lives virtuously manifests himself noble; and if such a man is called other than noble, the fault rests not with him but with those who call him ignoble.

"Consider all your nobles, examine their virtues, their manners, their behaviour; and then look upon Guiscardo. If you will pass judgment without prejudice, you will see that Guiscardo is most noble, and that all your nobles are peasants. Concerning the virtue and valour of Guiscardo I shall trust nobody's judgment save that of your words and my own eyes. Whoever praised him so much as you have praised him for all worthy deeds befitting a valiant man? And certainly you were not wrong. If my eyes did not deceive me, you never praised him for anything which I did not see him perform better than your words could express. If I was deceived here, I was deceived by you.

"Will you now say that I chose a man of base condition? You would speak falsely. You may say he is a poor man, and that is granted—to your shame, since you left one of your bravest servants in such a state. Poverty takes away nobleness from no man, but wealth does.

"Many Kings, many great Princes, were once poor. Many of those who plough and watch herds were once rich.

"Now, concerning your doubt as to what you should do to me—hesitate no further, if you are determined to be cruel, to do in your old age what you did not do in your youth. Wreak your cruelty upon me, for I will use no supplication to you, and it was I who was the real cause of this sin, if sin there is. And I tell you that if you do not do to me what you have done or may do to Guiscardo, my own hands shall perform it upon myself.

"Go, weep with women, and if you must be cruel and think we have deserved death, kill him and me with the same stroke."

The Prince saw his daughter's greatness of soul, but he did not believe she was as resolute as her words sounded. So he departed from her, and determined to use no cruelty upon her person but to cool her hot love with other punishment. He therefore commanded the two men who were guarding Guiscardo to strangle him the next night without any noise, to cut out his heart and send it to him. And they did as they were ordered.

Next day, the Prince sent for a large handsome gold cup and put Guiscardo's heart into it. This he sent to his daughter by a trusted servant, with orders to give it to her and to say: "Your father sends you this to console you for what you most loved, even as you consoled him for what he loved most."

When her father left her, Ghismonda did not abandon her desperate resolution, but sent for poisonous herbs and roots and distilled them with water, to have poison ready in case what she feared should happen. When the servant came with the Prince's present, and repeated his words, she took the cup with a firm countenance, opened it, saw the heart, and knew for certain that it was Guiscardo's heart. She turned her face to the servant, and said:

"Gold alone is a fitting burial place for such a heart. Herein my father has done wisely."

So saying, she carried it to her mouth and kissed it and then said:

"Always, in every respect my father's love has been most tender towards me, and herein more than ever. For this princely present I render him the highest thanks, as I ought to do."

And then, holding the cup tightly, she gazed upon the heart, and said:

"Ah! Thou most sweet dwelling-place of all my delight, cursed be the cruelty of him who has made me look upon you with the eyes of my head! It was enough for me to gaze upon you hourly with the eyes of my spirit. You have run your race, you are now free from all that Fortune imposed upon you. You have reached that bourn to which all men run. You have left the labours and miseries of the world, and from your enemy have you received that burial your valour deserved. Nothing is lacking to your funeral rites, save only the tears of her you loved so dearly in your life. That you might have them, God inspired my pitiless father to send you to me. Those tears I shall give you, although I had determined to die dry-eyed and with a calm face. And when I have wept for you, I shall straightway act in such a way that my soul shall be joined with yours, and do you accept that soul which of old was so dear to you. In what company could I go more gladly or more securely to an unknown land than with your soul? I am certain that it is yet here, and looks upon the place of its delight and mine. And since I am certain your soul loves me, let it wait for mine by which it is so deeply beloved."

So saying, she bowed weeping over the cup, and with no womanish outcries shed as many tears as if she had had a fountain of water in her head, kissing the dead heart an infinite number of times, so that it was a marvel to behold. Her women did not know whose heart it was, and did not understand her words, but all were filled with pity and began to weep, and pityingly but in vain asked her the cause of her lamentations, and strove to comfort her as best they could. But when she felt she had lamented long enough, she raised her head and dried her eyes, and said:

"O most beloved heart, I have performed all my duties to you; nothing now remains for me to do, save to come with my soul to bear company with yours."

So saying, she took the phial containing the poison she had made, and poured it into the cup where the heart was wet with her tears. Fearlessly she lifted it to her mouth and drank; and having drunk, she lay down on her bed and arranged her body as modestly as she could, and placed the heart of her dead lover upon her heart, and thus awaited death without uttering a word.

Her women, having heard and seen these things, sent word of them to Tancred, although they did not know that she had drunk poison. Dreading what might happen, Tancred came at once to his daughter's room, and reached it just as she had laid herself down upon the bed. He tried to comfort her with sweet words too late; and seeing to what extremity she was come, he began piteously to weep. And the lady said:

"Tancred, spare your tears for a fate less longed for than this of mine; give them not to me, for I do not want them. Whoever saw anyone but you weep over what he willed should happen. And yet, if any of the love you once felt for me is still alive, grant me one last gift—although it displeased you that I lived secretly and silently with Guiscardo, let my body lie openly with his in the place where you have cast it."

The agony of his weeping prevented the Prince from replying. Then she felt her end was come, and holding the dead heart to her bosom, she said:

"God be with you, and let me go."

She veiled her eyes and all sense left her and she departed this sad life.

Such, as you have heard, was the sad end of the love of Guiscardo and Ghismonda. Tancred wept much and repented too late of his cruelty; and, amid the general grief of all Salerno, buried them both honourably in the same grave.

. . .

Conclusion

Most noble ladies, for whose delight I have given myself over to this long task, I believe that with the aid of divine grace it is more through your pious prayers than any merit of mine that I have carried out what I promised to do at the beginning of this work. So now, after giving thanks, first to God and then to you, I shall rest my pen and weary hand. I know that these tales can expect no more immunity than any others, as I think I showed in the beginning of the Fourth Day; and so before I rest, I mean to reply to certain objections which might be made by you or others.

Some of you may say that in writing these tales I have taken too much license, by making ladies sometimes say and often listen to matters which are not proper to be said or heard by virtuous ladies. This I deny, for there is nothing so unchaste but may be said chastely if modest words are used; and this I think I have done.

But suppose it to be true—and I shall not strive with you, for you are certain to win—I reply that I have many arguments ready. First, if there is any license in some of them, the nature of the stories demanded it; and if any understanding person looks at them with a reasonable eye he will see that they could not be related otherwise, unless I had altered them entirely. And if there are a few words rather freer than suits the prudes, who weigh words more than deeds and take more pains to appear than to be good, I say that I should no more be reproved for having written them than other men and women are reproved for daily saying "hole," "peg," "mortar," "pestle," "sausage," "Bologna sausage," and the like things. My pen should be allowed no less power than is permitted the painter's brush; the painters are not censured for allowing Saint Michele to slay the serpent with a sword or lance and Saint Giorgio to kill the dragon as he pleases. They make Christ male and Eve female, and they fasten sometimes with one nail, sometimes with two, the feet of Him who died for the human race on the Cross.

In addition, anyone can see that these things were not told in church, where everything should be treated with reverent words and minds (although you will find plenty of license in the stories of the church); nor were they told in a school of philosophers, where virtue is as much required as anywhere else; nor among churchmen or other philosophers in any place; but they were told in gardens, in pleasure places, by young people who were old enough not to be led astray by stories, and at a time when everyone threw his cap over the mill and the most virtuous were not reproved for it.

But, such as they are, they may be amusing or harmful, like everything else, according to the persons who listen to them. Who does not know that wine is a most excellent thing, if we may believe Cinciglione and Scolaio, while it is harmful to a man with a fever? Are we to say wine is wicked because it is bad for those who are feverish? Who does not know that fire is most useful and even necessary to mankind? And because it sometimes destroys houses, villages and towns, shall we say it is bad? Weapons defend the safety of those who wish to live in peace, but they also kill men, not through any wrong in them but through the wickedness of those who use them ill.

No corrupt mind ever understands words healthily. And just as such people do not enjoy virtuous words, so the well-disposed cannot be harmed by words which are somewhat less than virtuous, any more than mud can sully sunlight or earthy filth the beauty of the skies.

What books, what words, what letters are more holy, more worthy, more to be revered than those of the divine Scripture? Yet many people by perversely interpreting them have sent themselves and others to perdition. Everything in itself is good for something, and if wrongly used may be harmful in many ways; and I say the same of my tales. Whoever wants to turn them to bad counsel or bad ends will not be forbidden by the tales themselves, if by any chance they contain such things and are twisted and turned to produce them. Those who want utility and good fruits from them, will not find them denied; nor will the tales ever be thought anything but useful and virtuous if they are read at the times and to the persons for which they are intended.

Those who have to say paternosters and play the hypocrite to their confessor can leave them alone; my tales will run after nobody asking to be read. And yet bigots say and even do such little trifles from time to time!

There will also be people to say that if some of the tales here were absent it would be all the better. Granted. But I could only write down the tales which were related; if they had told better ones, I should have written them down better. But suppose that I was both the inventor and the scribe (which I was not), I say that I am not ashamed that they are not all good, because there is no one, save God alone, who can do everything well and perfectly. Charlemagne, who first devised the Paladins, could not make enough of them to form an army. In a multitude of things we must be prepared to find diverse qualities. No field was ever so well cultivated that it contained no nettles, briars and thorns mingled with better plants.

Moreover, since I was speaking to simple young women such as most of you are, it would have been folly for me to go seeking and striving to find such exquisite things and to take pains to speak with great measure. However, those who read these tales can leave those they dislike and read those they like. I do not want to deceive anybody, and so all these tales bear written at the head a title explaining what they contain.

I suppose some people will say that some of the tales are too long. I reply that for those who have something else to do it is folly to read the tales, even when they are short. A long time has passed between the day when I began to write and now when I have come to the end of my labours; but I have not forgotten that I said my work is offered to those ladies who are unoccupied, and not to others. To those who read for pastime, no tale can be too long if it succeeds in its object. Brevity befits students, who labour to spend time usefully, not to make it pass; but not you, ladies, who have unoccupied all that time you do not spend in love pleasures. None of you has studied at Athens, Bologna or Paris; and so one must chatter a little more volubly for you than for those who have sharpened their wits by study.

I have no doubt that others will say that the things related are too full of jests and jokes, and that it ill befits a grave and weighty man to write such things. To them I must offer thanks and do thank them that they are so zealously tender of my good fame. But I shall reply to their objection. I confess I am weighty, and have often weighed myself. But, speaking to those who have not weighed me, I must observe that I am not grave but so light that I float in water. Considering that the friars' sermons, which are made to censure men's sins, are full of jokes and jests and railleries, I think that such things do not go ill in my tales, which are written to drive away ladies' melancholy. However, if the tales make them laugh too much, they can easily cure that by reading the lamentations of Jeremiah, the passion of the Saviour and the penitence of Mary Magdalene.

Who can doubt that there will be others who will say that I have a wicked poisonous tongue, because in some places I have written the truth about the friars? I mean to pardon those who say that, because it cannot be believed but that they are moved except by just cause, since the friars are good men who avoid poverty for the love of God, and do good service to the ladies and say nothing about it. And if they did not all smell a little of the goat, their company would be most pleasant.

Yet I confess that there is no stability in the things of this world and that everything changes. So may it have chanced with my tongue. I do not trust my own judgment, which I always avoid in matters concerning myself, but one of my women neighbours the other day told me I have the best and sweetest tongue in the world. But, to speak the truth, when that happened there were not many of my tales left to finish. And so let what I have said suffice as a reply to those who make these objections.

I leave it to every lady to say and think what she pleases; for me it is time to end my words, giving thanks humbly to Him who by His aid and after so much labour has brought me to the desired end.

And you, fair ladies, rest in peace in His grace; and if in reading any of these tales you find any pleasure, remember me.

JOHN MANDEVILLE

[14TH CENTURY]

In order to appreciate the importance of *Mandeville's Travels,* a work attributed to an English knight that was apparently written in French in 1357 and subsequently translated into English, we need to look at both the tradition upon which the book rested and its subsequent authority and popularity. Its sources include both legendary matter in ancient texts and contemporaneous accounts of travel to the Holy Land and the Orient. The book is thus both part of a long tradition and as fresh as a daily newspaper. The success of *Mandeville's Travels,* its favorable reception by a world audience, is startling. It is credited with helping to popularize the idea of a round, navigable world. It may have encouraged Christopher Columbus to set out for India by sailing west from Europe; along with Marco Polo's *Travels,* it lay on the captain's desk in his ship's room when he first sighted land on October 12, 1492. Finally, as a master account of discoveries and wonders, *Mandeville's Travels* influenced other writers down to the nineteenth century, even though what had passed for fact in the original work gradually acquired the status of fairy tales. Curiously, this English translation of a French original was also hailed through five centuries as the first great work of English prose, although internal evidence now suggests that its author and its translator were not even the same person.

Life

Who was John Mandeville? Was a man by this name the author of the work we know as *Mandeville's Travels*? An answer to this apparently straightforward question still eludes us. Claims in early editions of the *Travels* as well as other writings suggest that Sir John Mandeville, Knight, fled persecution in England in 1322 after having killed a member of the landed aristocracy, and assumed the name of a physician, Jean de Bourgogne, in Liège, Flanders, perhaps dying there in 1372. Another tradition argues the reverse, that "Mandeville" never existed and that the Liège physician was the author–compiler of the *Travels,* an account of journeys he had never actually taken. A more recent opinion suggests that neither of the first two stories is true, and that all we can say about the work is that it appears to have been written in Liège and based primarily on works compiled and translated into French by a monk in 1351. Whatever the case, two cities lay claim to the historical Mandeville: St. Albans, England, as the city of his birth and eventual return; and Liège, as his place of residence and death. The remains buried in Liège in a cloistered graveyard were visited by admirers until the French Revolution, when all evidence of the burial place was destroyed.

Work

All we can be sure of, then, is the book, a charming compilation of stories of travel to the Holy Land and the Orient that was already translated not only into English but into every major European language by the end of the fourteenth century, and later served as inspiration not only for Columbus but for such British and European writers as Chaucer, Cervantes, Johnson, and Montaigne. The book followed others of its type: the *Travels* of Marco Polo (1298) and a collection of travel accounts to the Middle East, Orient, and Holy Land translated into French by Jean Le Long, a monk cloistered near Liège, in 1351. This collection contained an account by a Franciscan friar, Odoric de Portenone, originally published in 1330, and an account of the Holy Land by William of Boldensele first published in 1336.

The use of sources in *Mandeville's Travels* is both conventional and innovative. Traditional sources supply accounts of natural wonders and fabulous creatures, just as in other medieval travel literature. Far more important than these bits of lore, however, is the contemporary travel literature. Here the author carefully edits accounts of real journeys to produce a tone of constantly increasing curiosity and discovery. He also uses other accounts of the Orient connected with the Crusades, mindful of his audience's fascination with the religious, cultural, and material riches thought to exist in the relatively inaccessible regions to the east.

In his approach to travel literature, the author is primarily secular, not religious. Thus his appeal is first to curiosity and a sense of adventure, second to piety or devotion, setting him in marked contrast to the pilgrims in the Islamic tradition such as Ibn Jubayr, whose journey to Mecca is recounted later in this volume. At the same time, his interest in human behavior makes the customs and practices of people different from himself seem worthy of comment, even when his own understanding or those of his sources is limited. He tends to credit pagans with a "natural religion"—indeed, he is one of the first writers to see religious belief as a matter of impulse rather than doctrine. It is partly for this reason that he is later praised for his tolerance and clarity, and is well regarded by authors of similar disposition, such as Chaucer. Along with this open-mindedness, however, his careful attention to his source materials enables him to extract meanings that may have been lost on their original authors, even such real travelers as Marco Polo. Mandeville has an eye for the defining moment, the perfect example, and the exemplary story necessary to move his account along. His stylistic influence can be seen in such later English works as Defoe's *Robinson Crusoe* and Swift's *Gulliver's Travels*.

The author's reliance on written sources, especially the works of Odoric and William of Boldensele, is so extensive that critics have tended to characterize *all* of his work as literary borrowing. But certain descriptions in the book, such as a monastery near Mount Sinai, the source of the oil supply in the region, or a field for jousting at Constantinople, do not appear to be dependent on earlier sources. Also, his account of travel to Jerusalem seems to take issue with the narrative of William of Boldensele written in 1336, as if our author has seen the same sights but not in the same way. From these and other observations, scholar Josephine Waters Bennett argues that Mandeville, whoever he was, really may have traveled to the Holy Land and the Near East, although he relies far more often on existing authority than on his own experience—this is a habit common to many medieval writers.

It remains to ask why the *Travels* was written. The author himself states as his reason that no recent "general passage or voyage over the sea" to the Orient has taken place, and therefore "many men desire to hear speak of the Holy Land." He lived when the Christian defeat at Acre in 1291 had signaled the receding of European influence in the Near East and when a new Crusade was becoming increasingly improbable. His occasional attacks on the Moslem infidel are conventional; despite some opinion to the contrary, the *Travels* does not appear to be even remotely viable as Crusade propaganda. It is, however, dependent on earlier literature of the Crusades; one suspects, therefore, that it is designed to appeal to an audience fascinated with recent history (perhaps as literature of the Western frontier still fascinates American audiences). A more difficult question is whether the *Travels* was seen as a practical travel guide in the modern sense. One suspects that it was intended more for its literary than for its practical value. Although trade routes to the Orient certainly existed in the author's time and one could undertake a pilgrimage with guides or companions, the majority of the author's audience was likely to be at the hearthside rather than pilgrimage-bound. On the other hand, it may have rekindled an interest in pilgrimages; Chaucer's figure of the Knight in *The Canterbury Tales* suggests this.

The selection presented here covers the approach to the holy city of Jerusalem and discusses its landmarks and monuments. The author follows scriptural references wherever possible, but he also makes use of other traditions, such as the legend of the Dry Tree, which will bloom again when the Jews and infidels are converted. Once in Jerusalem, when he describes the Church of the Holy Sepulchre and the Temple of Our Lord, he is following his contemporary sources carefully. Even so, there are characteristic touches of liberality and charm. On entering the Temple, the author notes the reverence shown by the Saracens and says he "thought that we should do as much worship and reverence thereto as any of the misbelieving men should, and as great compunction in heart to have."

Suggested Readings

Our edition of this work is *The Travels of Sir John Mandeville* (1900; repr. 1964). The Middle English version is very accessible in the excellent edition by M. C. Seymour, *Mandeville's Travels* (1967). Modern attempts to unravel the question of authorship and other matters include Malcolm Letts, *Sir John Mandeville: The Man and His Book* (1944) and Josephine Waters Bennett, *The Rediscovery of Sir John Mandeville* (1954).

The Travels of Sir John Mandeville

Chapter 9

Of the Desert between the Church of Saint Catherine and Jerusalem. Of the Dry Tree; and how Roses came first into the World

Now, after that men have visited those holy places, then will they turn toward Jerusalem. And then will they take leave of the monks, and recommend themselves to their prayers. And then they give the pilgrims of their victuals for to pass with the deserts toward Syria. And those deserts dure well a thirteen journeys.

In that desert dwell many of Arabians, that men clepe Bedouins and Ascopards, and they be folk full of all evil conditions. And they have none houses, but tents, that they make of skins of beasts, as of camels and of other beasts that they eat; and there beneath these they couch them and dwell in place where they may find water, as on the Red Sea or elsewhere: for in that desert is full great default of water, and often-time it falleth that where men find water at one time in a place it faileth another time; and for that skill they make none habitations there. These folk that I speak of, they till not the land, and they labour nought; for they eat no bread, but if it be any that dwell nigh a good town, that go thither and eat bread sometime. And they roast their flesh and their fish upon the hot stones against the sun. And they be strong men and well-fighting; and there so is much multitude of that folk, that they be without number. And they ne reck of nothing, ne do not but chase after beasts to eat them. And they reck nothing of their life, and therefore they fear not the sultan, ne no other prince; but they dare well war with them, if they do anything that is grievance to them. And they have often-times war with the sultan, and, namely, that time that I was with him. And they bear but one shield and one spear, without other arms; and they wrap their heads and their necks with a great quantity of white linen cloth; and they be right felonous and foul, and of cursed kind.

And when men pass this desert, in coming toward Jerusalem, they come to Bersabe (Beersheba), that was wont to be a full fair town and a delectable of Christian men; and yet there be some of their churches. In that town dwelled Abraham the patriarch, a long time. That town of Bersabe founded Bersabe (Bathsheba), the wife of Sir Uriah the Knight, on the which King David gat Solomon the Wise, that was king after David upon the twelve kindreds of Jerusalem and reigned forty year.

And from thence go men to the city of Hebron, that is the mountance of twelve good mile. And it was clept sometime the Vale of Mamre, and some-time it was clept the Vale of Tears, because that Adam wept there an hundred year for the death of Abel his son, that Cain slew. Hebron was wont to be the principal city of the Philistines, and there dwelled some time the giants. And that city was also sacerdotal, that is to say, sanctuary of the tribe of Judah; and it was so free, that men received there all manner of fugitives of other places for their evil deeds. In Hebron Joshua, Caleb and their company came first to aspy, how they might win the land of Behest. In Hebron reigned first king David seven year and a half; and in Jerusalem he reigned thirty-three year and a half.

And in Hebron be all the sepultures of the patriarchs, Adam, Abraham, Isaac, and of Jacob; and of their wives, Eve, Sarah and Rebecca, and of Leah; the which sepultures the Saracens keep full curiously, and have the place in great reverence for the holy fathers, the patriarchs that lie there. And they suffer no Christian man to enter into that place, but if it be of special grace of the sultan; for they hold Christian men and Jews as dogs, and they say, that they should not enter into so holy place. And men clepe that place, where they lie, Double Spelunk, or Double Cave, or Double Ditch, forasmuch as that one lieth above that other. And the Saracens clepe that place in their language, *Karicarba,* that is to say, 'The Place of Patriarchs.' And the Jews clepe that place *Arboth.* And in that same place was Abraham's house, and there he sat and saw three persons, and worshipped but one; as holy writ saith, *Tres vidit et unum adoravit,* that is to say, 'He saw three and worshipped one': and of those same received Abraham the angels into his house.

And right fast by that place is a cave in the rock, where Adam and Eve dwelled when they were put out of Paradise; and there got they their children. And in that same place was Adam formed and made, after that some men say: (for men were wont for to clepe that place the field of Damascus, because that it was in the lordship of Damascus), and from thence was he translated into Paradise of delights, as they say; and after that he was driven out of Paradise he was there left. And the same day that he was put in Paradise, the same day he was put out, for anon he sinned. There beginneth the Vale of Hebron, that dureth nigh to Jerusalem. There the angel commanded Adam that he should dwell with his wife Eve, of the which he gat Seth; of which tribe, that is to say kindred, Jesu Christ was born.

In that valley is a field, where men draw out of the earth a thing that men clepe cambile, and they eat it instead of spices, and they bear it to sell. And men may not make the hole or the cave, where it is taken out of the earth, so deep or so wide, but that it is, at the year's end, full again up to the sides, through the grace of God.

And two mile from Hebron is the grave of Lot, that was Abraham's brother.

And a little from Hebron is the mount of Mamre, of the which the valley taketh his name. And there is a tree of oak, that the Saracens clepe *Dirpe,* that is of Abraham's time: the which men clepe the Dry Tree. And they say that it hath been there since the beginning of the world, and was some-time green and bare leaves, unto the time that our Lord died on the cross, and then it dried: and so did all the trees that were then in the world. And some say, by their prophecies, that a lord, a prince of the west side of the world, shall win the Land of Promission that is the Holy Land with help of Christian men, and he shall do sing a mass under that dry tree; and then the tree shall wax green and bear both fruit and leaves, and through that miracle many Saracens and Jews shall be turned to Christian faith: and, therefore, they do great worship thereto, and keep it full busily. And, albeit so, that it be dry, natheles yet he beareth great virtue, for certainly he that hath a little thereof upon him, it healeth him of the falling evil, and his horse shall not be a-foundered: and many other virtues it hath; wherefore men hold it full precious.

From Hebron men go to Bethlehem in half a day, for it is but five mile; and it is full fair way, by plains and woods full delectable. Bethlehem is a little city, long and narrow and well walled, and in each side enclosed with good ditches: and it was wont to be clept Ephrata, as holy writ saith, *Ecce, audivimus eum in Ephrata,* that is to say, 'Lo, we heard him in Ephrata.' And toward the east end of the city is a full fair church and a gracious, and it hath many towers, pinacles and corners, full strong and curiously made; and within that church be forty-four pillars of marble, great and fair.

And between the city and the church is the field *Floridus,* that is to say, the 'field flourished.' For as much as a fair maiden was blamed with wrong, and slandered that she had done fornication; for which cause she was demned to death, and to be burnt in that place, to the which she was led. And, as the fire began to burn about her, she made her prayers to our Lord, that as wisely as she was not guilty of that sin, that he would help her and make it to be known to all men, of his merciful grace. And when she had thus said, she entered into the fire, and anon was the fire quenched and out; and the brands that were burning became red rose-trees, and the brands that were not kindled became white rose-trees, full of roses. And these were the first rose-trees and roses, both white and red, that ever any man saw; and thus was this maiden saved by the grace of God. And therefore is that field clept the field of God flourished, for it was full of roses.

Also beside the choir of the church, at the right side, as men come downward sixteen degrees, is the place where our Lord was born, that is full well dight of marble, and full richly painted with gold, silver, azure and other colours. And three paces beside is the crib of the ox and the ass. And beside that is the place where the star fell, that led the three kings, Jaspar, Melchior and Balthazar: but men of Greece clepe them thus, *Galgalath, Malgalath,* and *Seraphie,* and the Jews clepe them, in this manner, in Hebrew, *Appelius, Amerrius,* and *Damasus*. These three kings offered to our Lord, gold, incense and myrrh, and they met together through miracle of God; for they met together in a city in Ind, that men clepe Cassak, that is a fifty-three journeys from Bethlehem; and they were at Bethlehem the thirteenth day; and that was the fourth day after that they had seen the star, when they met in that city, and thus they were in nine days from that city at Bethlehem, and that was great miracle.

Also, under the cloister of the church, by eighteen degrees at the right side, is the charnel of the Innocents, where their bones lie. And before the place where our Lord was born is the tomb of Saint Jerome, that was a priest and a cardinal, that translated the Bible and the Psalter from Hebrew into Latin: and without the minster is the chair that he sat in when he translated it. And fast beside that church, a sixty fathom, is a church of Saint Nicholas, where our Lady rested her after she was lighted of our Lord; and forasmuch as she had too much milk in her paps, that grieved her, she milked them on the red stones of marble, so that the traces may yet be seen, in the stones, all white.

And ye shall understand, that all that dwell in Bethlehem be Christian men.

And there be fair vines about the city, and great plenty of wine, that the Christian men have do let make. But the Saracens ne till not no vines, ne they drink no wine: for their books of their law, that Mahomet betoke them, which they clepe their *Al Koran,* and some clepe it *Mesaph,* and in another language it is clept *Harme,* and the same book forbiddeth them to drink wine. For in that book, Mahomet cursed all those that drink wine and all them that sell it: for some men say, that he slew once an hermit in his drunkenness, that he loved full well; and therefore he cursed wine and them that drink it. But his curse be turned on to his own head, as holy writ saith, *Et in verticem ipsius iniquitas ejus descendet,* that is for to say, 'His wickedness shall turn and fall in his own head.'

And also the Saracens bring forth no pigs, nor they eat no swine's flesh, for they say it is brother to man, and it was forbidden by the old law; and they hold him all accursed that eat thereof. Also in the land of Palestine and in the land of Egypt, they eat but little or none of flesh of veal or of beef, but if be so old, that he may no more travel for old; for it is forbidden, and for because they have but few of them; therefore they nourish them for to ere their lands.

In this city of Bethlehem was David the king born; and he had sixty wives, and the first wife was called Michal; and also he had three hundred lemans.

And from Bethlehem unto Jerusalem is but two mile; and in the way to Jerusalem half a mile from Bethlehem is a church, where the angel said to the shepherds of the birth of Christ. And in that way is the tomb of Rachel, that was Joseph's mother, the patriarch; and she died anon after that she was delivered of her son Benjamin. And there she was buried of Jacob her husband, and he let set twelve great stones on her, in token that she had born twelve children. In the same way, half mile from Jerusalem, appeared the star to the three kings. In that way also be many churches of Christian men, by the which men go towards the city of Jerusalem.

CHAPTER 10

Of the Pilgrimages in Jerusalem, and of the Holy Places thereabout

After, for to speak of Jerusalem the holy city: ye shall understand, that it stands full fair between hills, and there be no rivers ne wells, but water cometh by conduit from Hebron. And ye shall understand, that Jerusalem of old time, unto the time of Melchisadech, was clept Jebus; and after it was clept Salem, unto the time of King David, that put these two names together, and clept it Jebusalem; and after that, King Solomon clept it Jerosolomye; and after that, men clept it Jerusalem, and so it is clept yet.

And about Jerusalem is the kingdom of Syria. And there beside is the land of Palestine, and beside it is Ascalon, and beside that is the land of Maritaine. But Jerusalem is in the land of Judea, and it is clept Judea, for that Judas Maccabeus was king of that country; and it marcheth eastward to the kingdom of Arabia; on the south side to the land of Egypt; and on the west side to the Great Sea; on the north side, towards the kingdom of Syria and to the sea of Cyprus. In Jerusalem was wont to be a patriarch; and archbishops and bishops about in the country. About Jerusalem be these cities: Hebron, at seven mile; Jericho, at six mile; Beersheba, at eight mile; Ascalon, at seventeen mile; Jaffa, at sixteen mile; Ramath, at three mile; and Bethlehem, at two mile. And a two mile from Bethlehem, toward the south, is the Church of St. Karitot, that was abbot there, for whom they made much dole amongst the monks when he should die; and yet they be in mourning in the wise that they made their lamentation for him the first time; and it is full great pity to behold.

This country and land of Jerusalem hath been in many divers nations' hands, and often, therefore, hath the country suffered much tribulation for the sin of the people that dwell there. For that country hath been in the hands of all nations; that is to say, of Jews, of Canaanites, Assyrians, Persians, Medes, Macedonians, of Greeks, Romans, of Christian men, of Saracens, Barbarians, Turks, Tartars, and of many other divers nations; for God will not that it be long in the hands of traitors ne of sinners, be they Christian or other. And now have the heathen men held that land in their hands forty year and more; but they shall not hold it long, if God will.

And ye shall understand, that when men come to Jerusalem, their first pilgrimage is to the Church of the Holy Sepulchre, where our Lord was buried, that is without the city on the north side; but it is now enclosed in with the town wall. And there is a full fair church, all round, and open above, and covered with lead; and on the west side is a fair tower and an high for bells, strongly made.

And in the midst of the church is a tabernacle, as it were a little house, made with a low little door, and that tabernacle is made in manner of half a compass, right curiously and richly made of gold and azure and other rich colours full nobly made. And in the right side of that tabernacle is the sepulchre of our Lord; and the tabernacle is eight foot long, and five foot wide, and eleven foot in height. And it is not long sith the sepulchre was all open, that men might kiss it and touch it; but for pilgrims that came thither pained them to break the stone in pieces or in powder, therefore the soldan hath do make a wall about the sepulchre that no man may touch it: but in the left side of the wall of the tabernacle is, well the height of a man, a great stone to the quantity of a man's head, that was of the holy sepulchre; and that stone kiss the pilgrims that come thither. In that tabernacle be no windows, but it is all made light with lamps that hang before the sepulchre. And there is a lamp that hangeth before the sepulchre, that burneth light; and on the Good Friday it goeth out by himself, [and lighteth again by himself] at that hour that our Lord rose from death to life.

Also within the church, at the right side, beside the choir of the church, is the mount of Calvary, where our Lord was put on the cross; and it is a rock of white colour and a little medled with red. And the cross was set in a mortise in the same rock. And on that rock dropped the wounds of our Lord when he was pined on the cross. And that is clept Golgotha.

And men go up to that Golgotha by degrees; and in the place of that mortise was Adam's head found after Noah's flood, in token that the sins of Adam should be bought in that same place. And upon that rock made Abraham sacrifice to our Lord. And there is an altar; and before that altar lie Godefray de Bouillon and Baldwin, and other Christian kings of Jerusalem.

And there, nigh where our Lord was crucified, is this written in Greek:

'Ο Θεὸς βασιλεὺς ἡμῶν πρὸ αἰώνων εἰργύσατο σωτηρίαν ἐν μέσῳ τῆς γῆς;

that is to say, in Latin,—

Deus Rex noster ante secula operatus est salutem, in medio terrae;

that is to say,—

This God our King, before the worlds, hath wrought health in midst of the earth.

And also on that rock, where the cross was set, is written within the rock these words:

'Ο εἴδεις, ἐστὶ βάσις τῆς πίστεως ὅλης τοῦ κόσμου τούτου;

that is to say, in Latin,—

Quod vides, est fundamentum totius fidei mundi hujus;

that is to say,—

That thou seest, is the ground of all the faith of this world.

And ye shall understand, that when our Lord was done upon the cross, he was thirty-three year and three months of old. And the prophecy of David saith thus: *Quadraginta annis proximus fui generationi huic;* that is to say, 'Forty year was I neighbour to this kindred.' And thus should it seem that the prophecies were not true. But they be both true; for in old time men made a year of ten months, of the which March was the first and December was the last. But Gaius, that was Emperor of Rome, put these two months thereto, January and February, and ordained the year of twelve months; that is to say, 365 days, without leap year, after the proper course of the sun. And therefore, after counting of ten months of the year, he died in the fortieth year, as the prophet said. And after the year of twelve months, he was of age thirty-three year and three months.

Also, within the mount of Calvary, on the right side, is an altar, where the pillar lieth that our Lord Jesu was bounden to when he was scourged. And there beside be four pillars of stone, that always drop water; and some men say that they weep for our Lord's death. And nigh that altar is a place under earth forty-two degrees of deepness, where the holy cross was found, by the wit of Saint Helen, under a rock where the Jews had hid it. And that was the very cross assayed; for they found three crosses, one of our Lord, and two of the two thieves; and Saint Helen proved them by a dead body that arose from death to life, when that it was laid on it, that our Lord died on. And thereby in the wall is the place where the four nails of our Lord were hid: for he had two in his hands and two in his feet. And, of one of these, the Emperor of Constantinople made a bridle to his horse to bear him in battle; and, through virtue thereof, he overcame his enemies, and won all the land of Asia the less, that is to say, Turkey, Armenia the less and the more, and from Syria to Jerusalem, from Arabia to Persia, from Mesopotamia to the kingdom of Aleppo, from Egypt the high and the low and all the other kingdoms unto the depth of Ethiopia, and into Ind the less that then was Christian.

And there were in that time many good holy men and holy hermits, of whom the book of Fathers' lives speaketh, and they be now in Paynims' and Saracens' hands: but when God Almighty will, right as the lands were lost through sin of Christian men, so shall they be won again by Christian men through help of God.

And in midst of that church is a compass, in the which Joseph of Arimathea laid the body of our Lord when he had taken him down off the cross; and there he washed the wounds of our Lord. And that compass, say men, is the midst of the world.

And in the church of the sepulchre, on the north side, is the place where our Lord was put in prison (for he was in prison in many places); and there is a part of the chain that he was bounden with; and there he appeared first to Mary Magdalene when he was risen, and she wend that he had been a gardener.

In the church of Saint Sepulchre was wont to be canons of the order of Saint Augustine, and had a prior, but the patriarch was their sovereign.

And without the doors of the church, on the right side as men go upward eighteen grees, said our Lord to his mother, *Mulier, ecce Filius tuus;* that is to say, Woman, lo! thy Son! And after that he said to John, his disciple, *Ecce mater tua;* that is to say, Lo! behold thy mother! And these words he said on the cross. And on these grees went our Lord when he bare the cross on his shoulder. And under these grees is a chapel, and in that chapel sing priests, Indians, that is to say, priests of Ind, not after our law, but after theirs; and alway they make their sacrament of the altar, saying, *Pater Noster* and other prayers therewith; with the which prayers they say the words that the sacrament is made of, for they ne know not the additions that many popes have made; but they sing with good devotion. And there near, is the place where that our Lord rested him when he was weary for bearing of the cross.

And ye shall understand that before the church of the sepulchre is the city more feeble than in any other part, for the great plain that is between the church and the city. And toward the east side, without the walls of the city, is the vale of Jehosaphat that toucheth to the walls as though it were a large ditch. And above that vale of Jehosaphat, out of the city, is the church of Saint Stephen where he was stoned to death. And there beside, is the Golden Gate, that may not be opened, by the which gate our Lord entered on Palm-Sunday upon an ass: and the gate opened against him when he would go unto the temple; and yet appear the steps of the ass's feet in three places of the degrees that be of full hard stone.

And before the church of Saint Sepulchre, toward the south, at 200 paces, is the great hospital of Saint John, of which the hospitallers had their foundation. And within the palace of the sick men of that hospital be 124 pillars of stone. And in the walls of the house, without the number above-said, there be fifty-four pillars that bear up the house. And from that hospital to go toward the east is a full fair church, that is clept *Nôtre Dame la Grande.* And then is there another church right nigh, that is clept *Nôtre Dame de Latine.* And there were Mary Cleophas and Mary Magdalene, and tore their hair when our Lord was pained in the cross.

Chapter 11

Of the Temple of our Lord. Of the Cruelty of King Herod. Of the Mount Sion. Of Probatica Piscina; and of Natatorium Siloe

And from the church of the sepulchre, toward the east, at eight score paces, is *Templum Domini.* It is right a fair house, and it is all round and high, and covered with lead. And it is well paved with white marble. But the Saracens will not suffer no Christian man ne Jews to come therein, for they say that none so foul sinful men should not come in so holy place: but I came in there and in other places there I would, for I had letters of the soldan with his great seal, and commonly other men have but his signet. In the which letters he commanded, of his special grace, to all his subjects, to let me see all the places, and to inform me pleinly all the mysteries of every place, and to conduct me from city to city, if it were need, and buxomly to receive me and my company, and for to obey to all my requests reasonable if they were not greatly against the royal power and dignity of the soldan or of his law. And to others, that ask him grace, such as have served him, he ne giveth not but his signet, the which they make to be borne before them hanging on a spear. And the folk of the country do great worship and reverence to his signet or seal, and kneel thereto as lowly as we do to *Corpus Domini.* And yet men do full greater reverence to his letters; for the admiral and all other lords that they be shewed to, before or they receive them, they kneel down; and then they take them and put them on their heads; and after, they kiss them and then they read them, kneeling with great reverence; and then they offer them to do all that the bearer asketh.

And in this *Templum Domini* were some-time canons regulars, and they had an abbot to whom they were obedient; and in this temple was Charlemagne when that the angel brought him the prepuce of our Lord Jesus Christ of his circumcision; and after, King Charles let bring it to Paris into his chapel, and after that he let bring it to Peyteres, and after that to Chartres.

And ye shall understand, that this is not the temple that Solomon made, for that temple dured not but 1102 year. For Titus, Vespasian's son, Emperor of Rome, had laid siege about Jerusalem for to discomfit the Jews; for they put our Lord to death, without leave of the emperor. And, when he had won the city, he burnt the temple and beat it down, and all the city, and took the Jews and did them to death—1,100,000; and the others he put in prison and sold them to servage,—thirty for one penny; for they said they bought Jesu for thirty pennies, and he made of them better cheap when he gave thirty for one penny.

And after that time, Julian Apostate, that was emperor, gave leave to the Jews to make the temple of Jerusalem, for he hated Christian men. And yet he was christened, but he forsook his law, and became a renegade. And when the Jews had made the temple, came an earthquaking, and cast it down (as God would) and destroyed all that they had made.

And after that, Adrian, that was Emperor of Rome, and of the lineage of Troy, made Jerusalem again and the temple in the same manner as Solomon made it. And he would not suffer no Jews to dwell there, but only Christian men. For although it were so that he was not christened, yet he loved Christian men more than any other nation save his own. This emperor let enclose the church of Saint Sepulchre, and walled it within the city; that, before, was without the city, long time before. And he would have changed the name of Jerusalem, and have clept it Aelia; but that name lasted not long.

Also, ye shall understand, that the Saracens do much reverence to that temple, and they say, that that place is right holy. And when they go in they go bare-foot, and kneel many times. And when my fellows and I saw that, when we came in we did off our shoes and came in bare-foot, and thought that we should do as much worship and reverence thereto, as any of the misbelieving men should, and as great compunction in heart to have.

This temple is sixty-four cubits of wideness, and as many in length; and of height it is six score cubits. And it is within, all about, made with pillars of marble. And in the middle place of the temple be many high stages, of fourteen degrees of height, made with good pillars all about: and this place the Jews call *Sancta Sanctorum;* that is to say, 'Holy of Hallows.' And, in that place, cometh no man save only their prelate, that maketh their sacrifice. And the folk stand all about, in diverse stages, after they be of dignity or of worship, so that they all may see the sacrifice. And in that temple be four entries, and the gates be of cypress, well made and curiously dight: and within the east gate our Lord said, 'Here is Jerusalem.' And in the north side of that temple, within the gate, there is a well, but it runneth nought, of the which holy writ speaketh of and saith, *Vidi aquam egredientem de templo;* that is to say, 'I saw water come out of the temple.'

And on that other side of the temple there is a rock that men clepe Moriach, but after it was clept Bethel, where the ark of God with relics of Jews were wont to be put. That ark or hutch with the relics Titus led with him to Rome, when he had discomfited all the Jews. In that ark were the Ten Commandments, and of Aaron's yard, and Moses' yard with the which he made the Red Sea depart, as it had been a wall, on the right side and on the left side, whiles that the people of Israel passed the sea dry-foot: and with that yard he smote the rock, and the water came out of it: and with that yard he did many wonders. And therein was a vessel of gold full of manna, and clothing and ornaments and the tabernacle of Aaron, and a tabernacle square of gold with twelve precious stones, and a box of jasper green with four figures and eight names of our Lord, and seven candlesticks of gold, and twelve pots of gold, and four censers of gold, and an altar of gold, and four lions of gold upon the which they bare cherubin of gold twelve spans long, and the circle of swans of heaven with a tabernacle of gold and a table of silver, and two trumps of silver, and seven barley loaves and all the other relics that were before the birth of our Lord Jesu Christ.

And upon that rock was Jacob sleeping when he saw the angels go up and down by a ladder, and he said, *Vere locus iste sanctus est, et ego ignorabam;* that is to say, 'Forsooth this place is holy, and I wist it nought.' And there an angel held Jacob still, and turned his name, and clept him Israel. And in that same place David saw the angel that smote the folk with a sword, and put it up bloody in the sheath. And in that same rock was Saint Simeon when he received our Lord into the temple. And in this rock he set him when the Jews would have stoned him; and a star came down and gave him light. And upon that rock preached our Lord often-time to the people. And out that said temple our Lord drove out the buyers and the sellers. And upon that rock our Lord set him when the Jews would have stoned him;

and the rock clave in two, and in that cleaving was our Lord hid, and there came down a star and gave light and served him with clarity. And upon that rock sat our Lady, and learned her psalter. And there our Lord forgave the woman her sins, that was found in avowtry. And there was our Lord circumcised. And there the angels shewed tidings to Zacharias of the birth of Saint Baptist his son. And there offered first Melchisadech bread and wine to our Lord, in token of the sacrament that was to come. And there fell David praying to our Lord and to the angel that smote the people, that he would have mercy on him and on the people: and our Lord heard his prayer, and therefore would he make the temple in that place, but our Lord forbade him by an angel; for he had done treason when he let slay Uriah the worthy knight, for to have Bathsheba his wife. And therefore, all the purveyance that he had ordained to make the temple with he took it Solomon his son, and he made it. And he prayed our Lord, that all those that prayed to him in that place with good heart—that he would hear their prayer and grant it them if they asked it rightfully: and our Lord granted it him, and therefore Solomon clept that temple the Temple of Counsel and of Help of God.

And without the gate of that temple is an altar where Jews were in wont to offer doves and turtles. And between the temple and that altar was Zacharias slain. And upon the pinnacle of that temple was our Lord brought for to be tempted of the enemy, the fiend. And on the height of that pinnacle the Jews set Saint James, and cast him down to the earth, that first was Bishop of Jerusalem. And at the entry of that temple, toward the west, is the gate that is clept *Porta Speciosa.* And nigh beside that temple, upon the right side, is a church, covered with lead, that is clept Solomon's School.

And from that temple towards the south, right nigh, is the temple of Solomon, that is right fair and well polished. And in that temple dwell the Knights of the Temple that were wont to be clept Templars; and that was the foundation of their order, so that there dwelled knights and in *Templo Domini* canons regulars.

From that temple toward the east, a six score paces, in the corner of the city, is the bath of our Lord; and in that bath was wont to come water from Paradise, and yet it droppeth. And there beside is our Lady's bed. And fast by is the temple of Saint Simeon, and without the cloister of the temple, toward the north, is a full fair church of Saint Anne, our Lady's mother; and there was our Lady conceived; and before that church is a great tree that began to grow the same night. And under that church, in going down by twenty-two degrees, lieth Joachim, our Lady's father, in a fair tomb of stone; and there beside lay some-time Saint Anne, his wife; but Saint Helen let translate her to Constantinople. And in that church is a well, in manner of a cistern, that is clept *Probatica Piscina,* that hath five entries. Into that well angels were wont to come from heaven and bathe them within. And what man, that first bathed him after the moving of the water, was made whole of what manner of sickness that he had. And there our Lord healed a man of the palsy that lay thirty-eight year, and our Lord said to him, *Tolle grabatum tuum et ambula,* that is to say, 'Take thy bed and go.' And there beside was Pilate's house.

And fast by is King Herod's house, that let slay the innocents. This Herod was over-much cursed and cruel. For first he let slay his wife that he loved right well; and for the passing love that he had to her when he saw her dead, he fell in a rage and out of his wit a great while; and sithen he came again to his wit. And after he let slay his two sons that he had of that wife. And after that he let slay another of his wives, and a son that he had with her. And after that he let slay his own mother; and he would have slain his brother also, but he died suddenly. And after that he did all the harm that he could or might. And after he fell into sickness; and when he felt that he should die, he sent after his sister and after all the lords of his land; and when they were come he let command them to prison. And then he said to his sister, he wist well that men of the country would make no sorrow for his death; and therefore he made his sister swear that she should let smite off all the heads of the lords when he were dead; and then should all the land make sorrow for his death, and else, nought; and thus he made his testament. But his sister fulfilled not his will. For, as soon as he was dead, she delivered all the lords out of prison and let them go, each lord to his own, and told them all the purpose of her brother's ordinance. And so was this cursed king never made sorrow for, as he supposed for to have been. And ye shall understand, that in that time there were three Herods, of great name and fame for their cruelty. This Herod, of which I have spoken of was Herod Ascalonite; and he that let behead Saint John the Baptist was Herod Antipas; and he that let smite off Saint James's head was Herod Agrippa, and he put Saint Peter in prison.

Also, furthermore, in the city is the church of Saint Saviour; and there is the left arm of John Chrisostome, and the more part of the head of Saint Stephen. And on that other side in the street, toward the south as men go to Mount Sion, is a church of Saint James, where he was beheaded.

And from that church, a six score paces, is the Mount Sion. And there is a fair church of our Lady, where she dwelled; and there she died. And there was wont to be an abbot of canons regulars. And from thence was she borne of the apostles unto the vale of Jehosaphat. And there is the stone that the angel brought to our Lord from the mount of Sinai, and it is of that colour that the rock is of Saint Catherine. And there beside is the gate where through our Lady went, when she was with child, when she went to Bethlehem. Also at the entry of the Mount Sion is a chapel. And in that chapel is the stone, great and large, with the which the sepulchre was covered with, when Joseph of Arimathea had put our Lord therein; the which stone the three Marys saw turn upward when they came to the sepulchre the day of his resurrection, and there found an angel that told them of our Lord's uprising from death to life. And there also is a stone in the wall, beside the gate, of the pillar that our Lord was scourged at. And there was Annas's house, that was bishop of the Jews in that time. And there was our Lord examined in the night, and scourged and smitten and villainous entreated. And in that same place Saint Peter forsook our Lord thrice or the cock crew. And there is a part of the table that he made his supper on, when he made his maundy with his disciples, when he gave them his flesh and his blood in form of bread and wine.

And under that chapel, thirty-two degrees, is the place where our Lord washed his disciples' feet, and yet is the vessel where the water was. And there beside that same vessel was Saint Stephen buried. And there is the altar where our Lady heard the angels sing mass. And there appeared first our Lord to his disciples after his resurrection, the gates enclosed, and said to them, *Pax vobis!* that is to say, 'Peace to you!' And on that mount appeared Christ to Saint Thomas the apostle and bade him assay his wounds; and then believed he first, and said, *Dominus meus et Deus meus!* that is to say 'My Lord and my God!' In the same church, beside the altar, were all the apostles on Whitsunday, when the Holy Ghost descended on them in likeness of fire. And there made our Lord his pasque with his disciples. And there slept Saint John the evangelist upon the breast of our Lord Jesu Christ, and saw sleeping many heavenly privities.

Mount Sion is within the city, and it is a little higher than the other side of the city; and the city is stronger on that side than on that other side. For at the foot of the Mount Sion is a fair castle and a strong that the soldan let make. In the Mount Sion were buried King David and King Solomon, and many other kings, Jews of Jerusalem. And there is the place where the Jews would have cast up the body of our Lady when the apostles bare the body to be buried in the vale of Jehosaphat. And there is the place where Saint Peter wept full tenderly after that he had forsaken our Lord. And a stone's cast from that chapel is another chapel, where our Lord was judged, for that time was there Caiaphas's house. From that chapel, to go toward the east, at seven score paces, is a deep cave under the rock, that is clept the Galilee of our Lord, where Saint Peter hid him when he had forsaken our Lord. *Item,* between the Mount Sion and the Temple of Solomon is the place where our Lord raised the maiden in her father's house.

Under the Mount Sion, toward the vale of Jehosaphat, is a well that is clept *Natatorium Siloe.* And there was our Lord washed after his baptism; and there made our Lord the blind man to see. And there was y-buried Isaiah the prophet. Also, straight from *Natatorium Siloe,* is an image, of stone and of old ancient work, that Absalom let make, and because thereof men clepe it the hand of Absalom. And fast by is yet the tree of elder that Judas hanged himself upon, for despair that he had, when he sold and betrayed our Lord. And there beside was the synagogue, where the bishops of Jews and the Pharisees came together and held their council; and there cast Judas the thirty pence before them, and said that he had sinned betraying our Lord. And there nigh was the house of the apostles Philip and Jacob Alphei. And on that other side of Mount Sion, toward the south, beyond the vale a stone's cast, is Aceldama; that is to say, the field of blood, that was bought for the thirty pence, that our Lord was sold for. And in that field be many tombs of Christian men, for there be many pilgrims graven. And there be many oratories, chapels and hermitages, where hermits were wont to dwell. And toward the east, an hundred paces, is the charnel of the hospital of Saint John, where men were wont to put the bones of dead men.

Also from Jerusalem, toward the west, is a fair church, where the tree of the cross grew. And two mile from thence is a fair church, where our Lady met with Elizabeth, when they were both with child; and Saint John stirred in his mother's womb, and made reverence to his Creator that he saw not. And under the altar of that church is the place where Saint John was born. And from that church is a mile to the castle of Emmaus: and there also our Lord shewed him to two of his disciples after his resurrection. Also on that other side, 200 paces from Jerusalem, is a church, where was wont to be the cave of the lion. And under that church, at thirty degrees of deepness, were interred 12,000 martyrs, in the time of King Cosdroe that the lion met with, all in a night, by the will of God.

Also from Jerusalem, two mile, is the Mount Joy, a full fair place and a delicious; and there lieth Samuel the prophet in a fair tomb. And men clepe it Mount Joy, for it giveth joy to pilgrims' hearts, because that there men see first Jerusalem.

Also between Jerusalem and the mount of Olivet is the vale of Jehosaphat, under the walls of the city, as I have said before. And in the midst of the vale is a little river that men clepe *Torrens Cedron,* and above it, overthwart, lay a tree (that the cross was made of) that men yede over on. And fast by it is a little pit in the earth, where the foot of the pillar is yet interred; and there was our Lord first scourged, for he was scourged and villainously entreated in many places. Also in the middle place of the vale of Jehosaphat is the church of our Lady: and it is of forty-three degrees under the earth unto the sepulchre of our Lady. And our Lady was of age, when she died, seventy-two year. And beside the sepulchre of our Lady is an altar, where our Lord forgave Saint Peter all his sins. And from thence, toward the west, under an altar, is a well that cometh out of the river of Paradise. And wit well, that that church is full low in the earth, and some is all within the earth. But I suppose well, that it was not so founded. But for because that Jerusalem hath often-time been destroyed and the walls abated and beten down and tumbled into the vale, and that they have been so filled again and the ground enhanced; and for that skill is the church so low within the earth. And, natheles, men say there commonly, that the earth hath so been cloven sith the time that our Lady was there buried; and yet men say there, that it waxeth and groweth every day, without doubt. In that church were wont to be monks black, that had their abbot.

And beside that church is a chapel, beside the rock that hight Gethsemane. And there was our Lord kissed of Judas; and there was he taken of the Jews. And there left our Lord his disciples, when he went to pray before his passion, when he prayed and said, *Pater, si fieri potest, transeat a me calix iste;* that is to say, 'Father, if it may be, do let this chalice go from me': and, when he came again to his disciples, he found them sleeping. And in the rock within the chapel yet appear the fingers of our Lord's hand, when he put them in the rock, when the Jews would have taken him.

And from thence, a stone's cast towards the south, is another chapel, where our Lord sweat drops of blood. And there, right nigh, is the tomb of King Jehosaphat, of whom the vale beareth the name. This Jehosaphat was king of that country, and was converted by an hermit, that was a worthy man and did much good. And from thence, a bow draught towards the south, is the church, where Saint James and Zachariah the prophet were buried.

And above the vale is the mount of Olivet; and it is clept so for the plenty of olives that grow there. That mount is more high than the city of Jerusalem is; and, therefore, may men upon that mount see many of the streets of the city. And between that mount and the city is not but the vale of Jehosaphat that is not full large. And from that mount styed our Lord Jesu Christ to heaven upon Ascension Day; and yet there sheweth the shape of his left foot in the stone. And there is a church where was wont to be an abbot and canons regulars. And a little thence, twenty-eight paces, is a chapel; and therein is the stone on the which our Lord sat, when he preached the eight blessings and said thus: *Beati pauperes spiritu:* and there he taught his disciples the *Pater Noster;* and wrote with his finger in a stone. And there nigh is a church of Saint Mary Egyptian, and there she lieth in a tomb. And from thence toward the east, a three bow shot, is Bethphage, to the which our Lord sent Saint Peter and Saint James for to seek the ass upon Palm-Sunday, and rode upon that ass to Jerusalem.

And in coming down from the mount of Olivet, toward the east, is a castle that is clept Bethany. And there dwelt Simon leprous, and there harboured our Lord: and after he was baptised of the apostles and was clept Julian, and was made bishop; and this is the same Julian that men clepe to for good harbourage, for our Lord harboured with him in his house. And in that house our Lord forgave Mary Magdalene her sins: there she washed his feet with her tears, and wiped them with her hair. And there served Saint Martha our Lord. There our Lord raised Lazarus from death to life, that was dead four days and stank, that was brother to Mary Magdalene and to Martha. And there dwelt also Mary Cleophas. That castle is well a mile long from Jerusalem. Also in coming down from the mount of Olivet is the place where our Lord wept upon Jerusalem. And there beside is the place where our Lady appeared to Saint Thomas the apostle after her assumption, and gave him her girdle. And right nigh is the stone where our Lord often-time sat upon when he preached; and upon that same he shall sit at the day of doom, right as himself said.

Also after the mount of Olivet is the mount of Galilee. There assembled the apostles when Mary Magdalene came and told them of Christ's uprising. And there, between the Mount Olivet and the Mount Galilee, is a church, where the angel said to our Lady of her death.

Also from Bethany to Jericho was sometime a little city, but it is now all destroyed, and now is there but a little village. That city took Joshua by miracle of God and commandment of the angel, and destroyed it, and cursed it and all them that bigged it again. Of that city was Zaccheus the dwarf that clomb up into the sycamore tree for to see our Lord, because he was so little he might not see him for the people. And of that city was Rahab the common woman that escaped alone with them of her lineage: and she often-time refreshed and fed the messengers of Israel, and kept them from many great perils of death; and, therefore, she had good reward, as holy writ saith: *Qui accipit prophetam in nomine meo, mercedem prophetae accipiet;* that is to say, 'He that taketh a prophet in my name, he shall take meed of the prophet.' And so had she. For she prophesied to the messengers, saying, *Novi quod Dominus tradet vobis terram hanc;* that is to say, 'I wot well, that our Lord shall betake you this land': and so he did. And after, Salomon, Naasson's son, wedded her, and from that time was she a worthy woman, and served God well.

Also from Bethany go men to flom Jordan by a mountain and through desert. And it is nigh a day journey from Bethany, toward the east, to a great hill, where our Lord fasted forty days. Upon that hill the enemy of hell bare our Lord and tempted him, and said, *Dic ut lapides isti panes fiant;* that is to say, 'Say, that these stones be made loaves.' In that place, upon the hill, was wont to be a fair church; but it is all destroyed, so that there is now but an hermitage, that a manner of Christian men hold, that be clept Georgians, for Saint George converted them. Upon that hill dwelt Abraham a great while, and therefore men clepe it Abraham's Garden. And between the hill and this garden runneth a little brook of water that was wont to be bitter; but, by the blessing of Elisha the prophet, it became sweet and good to drink. And at the foot of this hill, toward the plain, is a great well, that entereth into flom Jordan.

From that hill to Jericho, that I spake of before, is but a mile in going toward flom Jordan. Also as men go to Jericho sat the blind man crying, *Jesu, Fili David, miserere mei;* that is to say, 'Jesu, David's Son, have mercy on me.' And anon he had his sight. Also, two mile from Jericho, is flom Jordan. And, an half mile more nigh, is a fair church of Saint John the Baptist, where he baptised our Lord. And there beside is the house of Jeremiah the prophet.

GEOFFREY CHAUCER

[C. 1340–1400]

For a vivid, lively, and delightful portrayal of medieval life in all its fullness and diversity, no writer has exceeded Geoffrey Chaucer. While mastering the tales of courtly love and heroic deeds popular in France and Italy, Chaucer turned his attention to the great variety of people from all walks of life in his greatest work, *The Canterbury Tales*. Taking us from the ribald and bawdy to the pious and chaste, Chaucer's *Canterbury Tales* truly merits its reputation as a tour de force that embodies the high, the middle, and the low. This panoramic story about a group of travelers on their way to Canterbury embraces both the spirit of the tavern and the spirit of the cathedral. Moreover, in the individual portraits of each traveler—from the noble Knight to the base Miller, the lanky Clerk to the robust Franklin, the delicate Prioress to the earthy Wife of Bath—Chaucer presents us with unique and complex characters with all their vices and virtues, as well as a picture of fourteenth-century England and its moral, social, philosophical, and spiritual concerns.

Life

Geoffrey Chaucer was born in London about 1340 into a family of French descent who had made their fortune in trade. The poet's father, John Chaucer, was a property owner, vintner, and deputy to the King's Butler, and he had served with Edward III at Antwerp. The young Geoffrey was most likely educated in London, where he learned Latin, French, and Italian, though whether he studied with a tutor or at a school can only be guessed. By 1357, when he was in his teens, Chaucer had entered into the service of Lionel, the third son of Edward III. Soon he found himself serving in the army of Edward III in France, where he was captured in battle at Rheims. Here he was held captive for nearly six months, then ransomed in March 1360, to return to England where he served as a messenger between England and France.

Not long thereafter, Chaucer married Philippa Pan, who had been in the service of John of Gaunt's second wife, Constance of Castile. Sometime during this decade Chaucer began his first major literary project, the translation of *The Romance of the Rose* by Guillaume de Lorris, completed by Jean de Meun. Although most of it is lost, this translation is important, for many of Chaucer's early works borrow plots, motifs, and form—such as the dream vision—from this and other French romances. In 1367, Chaucer was a king's yeoman, then esquire, engaged in diplomatic missions to Spain, France, Flanders, and Italy. On his first mission to Italy, in 1372, Chaucer was thought to have met Petrarch, but no definitive evidence exists for such a meeting. On this and a later mission to Italy in 1378, Chaucer acquired Italian books and had the opportunity to familiarize himself with important Italian works, including Dante's *Divine Comedy,* Petrarch's poetry, and the works of Boccaccio.

In June 1374, Chaucer was appointed Controller of the Custom and Subsidy, where he was in charge of keeping records of the wool trade. Ten years later he was appointed Controller of the Petty Customs, and held both offices for two years until 1386 when he resigned to serve as justice of the peace in Kent, where he was elected as one of the Knights of the Shire. By this time, the young Richard II's court was being challenged by an opposition party under the leadership of the Duke of Gloucester, and Chaucer's fortunes took a brief but painful turn for the worse. Gloucester executed some of Chaucer's friends at court; Chaucer's wife died in 1387; and in May 1388, he was forced to sell his annuities. A grand decade of increasing personal prosperity had come to an abrupt end. In May 1389, however, Richard recovered his power, and in July Chaucer was appointed Clerk of the Works, in which position he was responsible for the maintenance of various properties of the Crown, including those at Westminster and the Tower of London.

All this time, Chaucer had kept his property at Kent, and as far as we know, moved back and forth from London as duty called. When Richard II was removed from power and replaced by Henry IV, Chaucer, pressed for money, wrote a brief lyric called the "Complaint to His Purse," asking for more financial support and a "butt of wine." The new king promptly honored this request for patronage, enabling Chaucer to live out his final years in relative security and comfort. About a year before his death, Chaucer leased a home near Westminster Abbey; he died October 25, 1400.

Work

It should be clear from the sketch of his life that Chaucer, one of the greatest of English poets, cultivated his literary interests while performing the duties of the various public offices he held. His diplomatic missions helped to broaden the scope of Chaucer's poetry, influenced as it was by Latin, French, and Italian literature, especially great works such as the *Romance of the Rose* and perhaps Boccaccio's *Decameron.* Chaucer's early poems, *The Book of the Duchess* and *The Parliament of the Fowls,* adopt familiar motifs from continental models, though even here Chaucer demonstrates his genius for innovation. His first long poem, *The Book of the Duchess,* is an elegy, likely written sometime soon after the death of John of Gaunt's first wife, Blanche, Duchess of Lancaster, in 1369. The poem takes the form of a dream, suggested by the narrator's reading of "A romaunce." As in other early poems, the influence of Ovid is evident in the mythic apparatus of the poem involving the intervention of Juno and Morpheus. *The House of Fame* (c. 1374–1386), a second, though unfinished, long poem, uses the dream convention for comic purposes; it is a vision of love in which a series of parties petition the goddess Fame, whose blessing will confer upon them a good name. As in the classical journey to the underworld in *The Aeneid* or in *The Divine Comedy,* to which the poem often alludes, the poet requires a guide, in this case an eagle, to lead him to the house of Fame and to explain to him the nature of the celestial journey and other spiritual matters.

Birds play an even more important role in *The Parliament of Fowls,* written sometime between 1375 and 1385. The poem is a dream poem in which Chaucer constructs an elaborate poetic version of the popular beast fable to demonstrate the difficulties of love. The poem invokes the popular tradition that birds choose their mates on St. Valentine's Day. The speaker falls asleep lamenting his ill fate at love, has a vision of a garden similar to that in the *Romance of the Rose,* and witnesses the competition among three eagles who vie for the love of a "formel," or female. The poem may have been written for an actual marriage—that of Richard II and Anne of Bohemia has been proposed, among others—but scholars argue over the actual parties involved. Such bird fables are found not only in medieval and Latin literature but in Islamic literature as well; the most famous of such Islamic tales is the *Conference of the Birds* by Fared ud-din Attar.

Chaucer's greatest love poem, *Troilus and Criseyde* (c. 1385), tells the story of the romance between Troilus, a hero from the Trojan War, and Cressida, who does not appear in classical literature but derives from medieval stories. Boccaccio's *Il Filostrato* was Chaucer's most immediate source for the story, which tells how Troilus, hoping to win out over his rival Diomedes (also of *Iliad* fame), engages the services of the older matchmaker Pandarus to win the love of Cressida. Like *The Parliament of Fowls, Troilus and Criseyde* reviews the conventions of courtly love but gives them more serious treatment.

Chaucer planned two other long poems: *The Legend of Good Women,* for which he completed in the late 1380s a Prologue and nine stories, including the story of Cleopatra; and his greatest poem, *The Canterbury Tales,* begun in 1386 and left unfinished at his death. Though incomplete, this delightful set of tales consists of a Prologue and twenty-four stories in over 170,000 lines of verse. Modeled in part on Boccaccio's *Decameron, The Canterbury Tales* consists of a framing story about a socially heterogeneous group of travelers making a pilgrimage to Canterbury, "the hooly blesful martir for to seke." Every year groups of pilgrims made the journey from London to Canterbury, the shrine of Saint Thomas à Becket, the former Archbishop of Canterbury, who was murdered in the cathedral in 1170. To entertain one another along the way, Harry Bailly, the host for the journey and the proprietor of the Tabard Inn, where it begins, proposes that each of the twenty-nine pilgrims tell four stories, two on the way to Canterbury and two on the return home. Chaucer's actual intention was most likely to complete only the stories on the way to the shrine, in itself a prodigious task. Whatever the author's plan, what Chaucer accomplished was to produce a compendium of remarkably diverse tales in a variety of literary genres that opens up to the reader the social, philosophical, and religious world of fourteenth-century England.

The framing story of the meeting of the pilgrims at the Tabard Inn provides structural unity to the successive tales told by each traveler. Along the way the travelers engage in friendly banter, prankish jesting, and downright disputes, sometimes motivated by occupational rivalry, jealousy, and gender differences. The Miller, for example, tells a bawdy story about Nicolaus the clerk who tricks John the carpenter and sleeps with his wife. Offended, the Reeve, a carpenter, replies with an equally salacious story about

Symkyn the greedy miller, who cheats two clerks out of some grain they've brought to be ground; they take revenge on him by sleeping with his wife and daughter, and to top it off, his wife clubs him over the head at the end of the tale.

Among the travelers is Chaucer the pilgrim, an innocent observer through whose eyes and ears his fellow travelers display their true character. Chaucer the author, however, is anything but naive, and the combined perspectives of the General Prologue, each teller's prologue, and their tales create a complex and multifaceted portrait of each character. Although some characters—such as the Knight, the Parson, or the Nun's Priest—display values consistent with their occupations and command our respect, others—such as the Pardoner, the Summoner, and the Friar—betray contradictions between their professed values and their real actions and intentions. The Monk, for example, loves to hunt, and the Friar is overly fond of riches; worst of them all is the Pardoner, who is an outright hypocrite. This "portrait gallery of pilgrims," as the General Prologue is sometimes called, displays English society in all its diversity. While the narrator in the General Prologue gives us a vivid, often ironic, description of each character, their actions and quibbles throughout the journey and particularly the tales that they tell paint a highly complex portrait that opens multiple perspectives on the travelers.

Often an important ironic connection exists between the tale and the teller; even the form in which the pilgrims frame their tales indicates something about their character, taste, social position, and education. Thus the knight, for example, tells the tale of two heroes, Palamon and Arcite, who compete for the love of a beautiful, idealized woman, Emelye. In perfect compatibility with his position and interests, the Knight's tale is told in the form of a romance. The Second Nun, on the other hand, retells the legend of St. Cecilia in the form of a saint's life. Most interesting are those tales that fall in ironic relation to their teller, such as the Pardoner's tale, discussed below. Other literary forms included in this remarkable compendium include the fabliaux, or popular tale, the beast fable, and even a sermon.

In addition to the General Prologue, we include "The Pardoner's Prologue and Tale" and "The Wife of Bath's Prologue and Tale." "The Pardoner's Tale" retells a story familiar in the Middle Ages of three men whose greed and lack of trust lead them to kill one another. Because the Pardoner reveals in his prologue that he is guilty of avarice, the story reflects on his hypocrisy; and yet the Pardoner recognizes the moral gap between his *exemplum* and his own actions. As he says, "though myself be gilty in that synne, / Yet kan I maken oother folk to twynne / From avarice." His frank admission of guilt and insistence that his story can nonetheless turn others from sin and cause them to repent raises the question of whether a bad man can tell a moral tale. The Pardoner claims that he can.

In contrast to the Pardoner, the Wife of Bath tells a story completely compatible with her character. Many readers see the Wife of Bath, with her worldly ways, self-assured contentiousness, and resolute independence, as the most colorful, vital, and engaging character in the poem. In her prologue, she single-handedly takes the offensive against the doctrine of celibacy and against those who would appeal to church doctrine to legitimate their abuse of, and contempt for, women. The Wife of Bath's prologue argues that women deserve to be respected and declares their independence from male tyranny. This argument is enhanced by the Wife's vital and earthy celebration of love and sexuality. She proudly boasts that "Housbondes at chirche dore I have had fyve," and that she is ruled by both Venus and Mars:

> For certes, I am al Venerien
> In feelynge, and myn herte is marcien.
> Venus me yaf my lust, my likerousnesse,
> And mars yaf me my sturdy hardynesse.

Her boldness and tenacity derive in part from her experience of the world, which she claims provides a more powerful authority upon which to base judgment than do books, with their false doctrines and wrongheaded assumptions about women. As she puts it: "Experience, though noon auctoritee / Were in this world, is right ynogh for me / To speke of wo that is in marriage."

The Wife of Bath's tale is one of a series of tales sometimes called the "marriage group" that show marriage in a variety of forms. The story she tells takes the form of a popular romance about the handsome knight and the loathsome lady. The knight, who commits rape, will be pardoned for his act if he can discover what it is that women most desire. The loathsome lady promises to tell him provided that he marry her. What the knight learns is that women above all want "sovereynetee / As wel over hir housbond as hir love / And for to been in maistrie hym above"; that is, sovereignty over their husbands and lovers, and to be above them in mastery. When the knight finally submits to love the old hag, she transforms into a beautiful young woman and the story ends well for both parties.

We should add a word about Chaucer's English. As you can see from the quoted passages above and the short selection that follows, the language of Chaucer's day was quite different from our own. Although it is recognizable to the modern reader as English, changes in sound, meaning, spelling, and grammar between the fourteenth and seventeenth centuries render Chaucer's text difficult today without careful study. The final "e" sounds in the original text, for example, though gradually phased out of the spoken language in Chaucer's time, were still pronounced to capture rhyme and meter. Initial consonants such as the "k" in "knight" are pronounced, and the "gh" in "knight" or "drought" is pronounced as "ch," as in the German *nach.* Most other consonant sounds in Chaucer's language are similar to modern English, but long vowel sounds differ from those of modern English. As a general rule, long vowels in Chaucer's language should be sounded as they are in Spanish, French, and German today.

The following example, the famous opening passage from the General Prologue, should be compared with Theodore Morrison's translation, used for our text. As you can see, even the best of translations cannot fully capture the delightful rhythm and melody of Chaucer's verse; it is well worth the effort to learn to read Chaucer in the original.

Whan that Aprill with his shoures soote
The droghte of March hath perced to the roote,
And bathed every veyne in swich licour
Of which vertu engendred is the flour;
Whan Zephirus eek with his sweete breeth
Inspired hath in every holt and heeth
The tendre croppes, and the yonge sonne
Hath in the Ram his halve cours yronne,
And smale fowele maken melodye,
That slepen al the nyght with open yë
(So priketh hem nature in hir corages),—
Thanne longen folk to goon on pilgrimages,
And palmeres for to seken straunge strondes,
To ferne halwes, kowthe in sondry londes;
And specially from every shires ende
Of Engelond to Cuanterbury they wende,
The hooly blisful martir for to seke,
That ham hath holpen whan that they were seeke.

Suggested Readings

A standard edition of Chaucer's works in Middle English, complete with notes and helpful commentaries, is *The Riverside Chaucer,* Third edition (1987), general editor Larry D. Benson. Derek Pearsall's *The Life of Geoffrey Chaucer: A Critical Biography* (1992) and

Donald R. Howard's *Chaucer: His Life, His Works, His World* (1987) review in fine detail Chaucer's life and work; Derek S. Brewer's *Chaucer and His World* (1978) surveys the fourteenth-century background. G. L. Kittredge's *Chaucer and His Poetry* (1915) remains a classic study of Chaucer's work in general. For *The Canterbury Tales* in particular, see Donald R. Howard's *The Idea of the Canterbury Tales* (1976), Derek Pearsall's *The Canterbury Tales* (1985), and P. G. Ruggiers's *The Art of the Canterbury Tales* (1965).

The Canterbury Tales

Translated by Theodore Morrison

FROM

General Prologue

As soon as April pierces to the root
The drought of March, and bathes each bud and shoot
Through every vein of sap with gentle showers
From whose engendering liquor spring the flowers;
When zephyrs have breathed softly all about
Inspiring every wood and field to sprout,
And in the zodiac the youthful sun
His journey halfway through the Ram has run;[1]
When little birds are busy with their song
Who sleep with open eyes the whole night long 10
Life stirs their hearts and tingles in them so,
Then off as pilgrims people long to go,
And palmers[2] to set out for distant strands
And foreign shrines renowned in many lands.
And specially in England people ride
To Canterbury[3] from every countryside
To visit there the blessed martyred saint
Who gave them strength when they were sick and faint.
In Southwark at the Tabard one spring day
It happened, as I stopped there on my way, 20
Myself a pilgrim with a heart devout
Ready for Canterbury to set out,
At night came all of twenty-nine assorted
Travelers, and to that same inn resorted,
Who by a turn of fortune chanced to fall
In fellowship together, and they were all
Pilgrims who had it in their minds to ride
Toward Canterbury. The stable doors were wide,
The rooms were large, and we enjoyed the best,
And shortly, when the sun had gone to rest, 30
I had so talked with each that presently
I was a member of their company

[1]The sun is in Aries, the Ram, from mid March to early April.
[2]Pilgrims.
[3]A city sixty miles southeast of London; site of Canterbury Cathedral, the shrine of St Thomas à Becket ("the blessed martyred saint"), who was murdered there in 1170.

And promised to rise early the next day
To start, as I shall show, upon our way.
 But none the less, while I have time and space,
Before this tale has gone a further pace,
I should in reason tell you the condition
Of each of them, his rank and his position,
And also what array they all were in;
And so then, with a knight I will begin. 40
 A Knight was with us, and an excellent man,
Who from the earliest moment he began
To follow his career loved chivalry,
Truth, openhandedness, and courtesy.
He was a stout man in the king's campaigns
And in that cause had gripped his horse's reins
In Christian lands and pagan through the earth,
None farther, and always honored for his worth.
He was on hand at Alexandria's fall.
He had often sat in precedence to all 50
The nations at the banquet board in Prussia.
He had fought in Lithuania and in Russia,
No Christian knight more often; he had been
In Moorish Africa at Benmarin,
At the siege of Algeciras in Granada,
And sailed in many a glorious armada
In the Mediterranean, and fought as well
At Ayas and Attalia when they fell
In Armenia and on Asia Minor's coast.
Of fifteen deadly battles he could boast, 60
And in Algeria, at Tremessen,
Fought for the faith and killed three separate men
In single combat. He had done good work
Joining against another pagan Turk
With the king of Palathia. And he was wise,
Despite his prowess, honored in men's eyes,
Meek as a girl and gentle in his ways.
He had never spoken ignobly all his days
To any man by even a rude inflection.
He was a knight in all things to perfection. 70
He rode a good horse, but his gear was plain,
For he had lately served on a campaign.
His tunic was still spattered by the rust
Left by his coat of mail, for he had just
Returned and set out on his pilgrimage.
 His son was with him, a young Squire, in age
Some twenty years as near as I could guess.
His hair curled as if taken from a press.
He was a lover and would become a knight.
In stature he was of a moderate height 80
But powerful and wonderfully quick.
He had been in Flanders, riding in the thick
Of forays in Artois and Picardy,
And bore up well for one so young as he,
Still hoping by his exploits in such places

To stand the better in his lady's graces.
He wore embroidered flowers, red and white,
And blazed like a spring meadow to the sight.
He sang or played his flute the livelong day.
He was as lusty as the month of May. 90
His coat was short, its sleeves were long and wide.
He sat his horse well, and knew how to ride,
And how to make a song and use his lance,
And he could write and draw well, too, and dance.
So hot his love that when the moon rose pale
He got no more sleep than a nightingale.
He was modest, and helped whomever he was able,
And carved as his father's squire at the table.
But one more servant had the Knight beside,
Choosing thus simply for the time to ride: 100
A Yeoman, in a coat and hood of green.
His peacock-feathered arrows, bright and keen,
He carried under his belt in tidy fashion.
For well-kept gear he had a yeoman's passion.
No draggled feather might his arrows show,
And in his hand he held a mighty bow.
He kept his hair close-cropped, his face was brown.
He knew the lore of woodcraft up and down.
His arm was guarded from the bowstring's whip
By a bracer, gaily trimmed. He had at hip 110
A sword and buckler, and at his other side
A dagger whose fine mounting was his pride,
Sharp-pointed as a spear. His horn he bore
In a sling of green, and on his chest he wore
A silver image of St. Christopher,
His patron, since he was a forester.
There was also a Nun, a Prioress,
Whose smile was gentle and full of guilelessness.
"By St. Loy!" was the worst oath she would say.
She sang mass well, in a becoming way, 120
Intoning through her nose the words divine,
And she was known as Madame Eglantine.
She spoke good French, as taught at Stratford-Bow,[4]
For the Parisian French she did not know.
She was schooled to eat so primly and so well
That from her lips no morsel ever fell.
She wet her fingers lightly in the dish
Of sauce, for courtesy was her first wish.
With every bite she did her skillful best
To see that no drop fell upon her breast. 130
She always wiped her upper lip so clean
That in her cup was never to be seen
A hint of grease when she had drunk her share.
She reached out for her meat with comely air.
She was a great delight, and always tried
To imitate court ways, and had her pride,

[4]A convent in Middlesex, near London.

Both amiable and gracious in her dealings.
As for her charity and tender feelings,
She melted at whatever was piteous.
She would weep if she but came upon a mouse 140
Caught in a trap, if it were dead or bleeding.
Some little dogs that she took pleasure feeding
On roasted meat or milk or good wheat bread
She had, but how she wept to find one dead
Or yelping from a blow that made it smart,
And all was sympathy and loving heart.
Neat was her wimple in its every plait,
Her nose well formed, her eyes as gray as slate.
Her mouth was very small and soft and red.
She had so wide a brow I think her head 150
Was nearly a span broad, for certainly
She was not undergrown, as all could see.
She wore her cloak with dignity and charm,
And had her rosary about her arm,
The small beads coral and the larger green,
And from them hung a brooch of golden sheen,
On it a large A and a crown above;
Beneath, "All things are subject unto love."
A Priest accompanied her toward Canterbury,
And an attendant Nun, her secretary. 160
There was a Monk, and nowhere was his peer,
A hunter, and a roving overseer.
He was a manly man, and fully able
To be an abbot. He kept a hunting stable,
And when he rode the neighborbood could hear
His bridle jingling in the wind as clear
And loud as if it were a chapel bell.
Wherever he was master of a cell
The principles of good St. Benedict,
For being a little old and somewhat strict, 170
Were honored in the breach, as past their prime.
He lived by the fashion of a newer time.
He would have swapped that text for a plucked hen
Which says that hunters are not holy men,
Or a monk outside his discipline and rule
Is too much like a fish outside his pool;
That is to say, a monk outside his cloister.
But such a text he deemed not worth an oyster.
I told him his opinion made me glad.
Why should he study always and go mad, 180
Mewed in his cell with only a book for neighbor?
Or why, as Augustine commanded, labor
And sweat his hands? How shall the world be served?
To Augustine be all such toil reserved!
And so he hunted, as was only right.
He had greyhounds as swift as birds in flight.
His taste was all for tracking down the hare,
And what his sport might cost he did not care.
His sleeves I noticed, where they met his hand,
Trimmed with gray fur, the finest in the land. 190

His hood was fastened with a curious pin
Made of wrought gold and clasped beneath his chin,
A love knot at the tip. His head might pass,
Bald as it was, for a lump of shining glass,
And his face was glistening as if anointed.
Fat as a lord he was, and well appointed.
His eyes were large, and rolled inside his head
As if they gleamed from a furnace of hot lead.
His boots were supple, his horse superbly kept.
He was a prelate to dream of while you slept. 200
He was not pale nor peaked like a ghost.
He relished a plump swan as his favorite roast.
He rode a palfrey brown as a ripe berry.
A Friar was with us, a gay dog and a merry,
Who begged his district with a jolly air.
No friar in all four orders[5] could compare
With him for gallantry; his tongue was wooing.
Many a girl was married by his doing,
And at his own cost it was often done.
He was a pillar, and a noble one, 210
To his whole order. In his neighborhood
Rich franklins[6] knew him well, who served good food,
And worthy women welcomed him to town;
For the license that his order handed down,
He said himself, conferred on him possession
Of more than a curate's power of confession.
Sweetly the list of frailties he heard,
Assigning penance with a pleasant word.
He was an easy man for absolution
Where he looked forward to a contribution, 220
For if to a poor order a man has given
It signifies that he has been well shriven,
And if a sinner let his purse be dented
The Friar would stake his oath he had repented.
For many men become so hard of heart
They cannot weep, though conscience makes them smart.
Instead of tears and prayers, then, let the sinner
Supply the poor friars with the price of dinner.
For pretty women he had more than shrift.
His cape was stuffed with many a little gift, 230
As knives and pins and suchlike. He could sing
A merry note, and pluck a tender string,
And had no rival at all in balladry.
His neck was whiter than a fleur-de-lis,[7]
And yet he could have knocked a strong man down.
He knew the taverns well in every town.
The barmaids and innkeepers pleased his mind
Better than beggars and lepers and their kind.
In his position it was unbecoming
Among the wretched lepers to go slumming. 240

---

[5]The monastic orders: Franciscan, Dominican, Carmelite, and Augustinian.
[6]Landowners or country gentlemen who were not noblemen.
[7]Lily.

It mocks all decency, it sews no stitch
To deal with such riffraff; but with the rich,
With sellers of victuals, that's another thing.
Wherever he saw some hope of profiting,
None so polite, so humble. He was good,
The champion beggar of his brotherhood.
Should a woman have no shoes against the snow,
So pleasant was his *"In principio"*[8]
He would have her widow's mite before he went.
He took in far more than he paid in rent 250
For his right of begging within certain bounds.
None of his brethren trespassed on his grounds!
He loved as freely as a half-grown whelp.
On arbitration-days[9] he gave great help,
For his cloak was never shiny nor threadbare
Like a poor cloistered scholar's. He had an air
As if he were a doctor or a pope.
It took stout wool to make his semicope[10]
That plumped out like a bell for portliness.
He lisped a little in his rakishness 260
To make his English sweeter on his tongue,
And twanging his harp to end some song he'd sung
His eyes would twinkle in his head as bright
As the stars twinkle on a frosty night.
Hubert this gallant Friar was by name.
Among the rest a Merchant also came.
He wore a forked beard and a beaver hat
From Flanders. High up in the saddle he sat,
In figured cloth, his boots clasped handsomely,
Delivering his opinions pompously, 270
Always on how his gains might be increased.
At all costs he desired the sea policed
From Middleburg in Holland to Orwell.
He knew the exchange rates, and the time to sell
French currency, and there was never yet
A man who could have told he was in debt
So grave he seemed and hid so well his feelings
With all his shrewd engagements and close dealings.
You'd find no better man at any turn;
But what his name was I could never learn. 280
There was an Oxford Student too, it chanced,
Already in his logic well advanced.
He rode a mount as skinny as a rake,
And he was hardly fat. For learning's sake
He let himself look hollow and sober enough.
He wore an outer coat of threadbare stuff,
For he had no benefice for his enjoyment

[8]"In the beginning"—the opening phrase of the gospel of St. John; the friar uses Latin ostentatiously to puff up his authority.
[9]Special days for settling disputes.
[10]A cape or jacket.

And was too unworldly for some lay employment.
He much preferred to have beside his bed
His twenty volumes bound in black or red 290
All packed with Aristotle from end to middle
Than a sumptuous wardrobe or a merry fiddle.
For though he knew what learning had to offer
There was little coin to jingle in his coffer.
Whatever he got by touching up a friend
On books and learning he would promptly spend
And busily pray for the soul of anybody
Who furnished him the wherewithal for study.
His scholarship was what he truly heeded.
He never spoke a word more than was needed, 300
And that was said with dignity and force,
And quick and brief. He was of grave discourse,
Giving new weight to virtue by his speech,
And gladly would he learn and gladly teach.
There was a Lawyer, cunning and discreet,
Who had often been to St. Paul's porch to meet
His clients. He was a Sergeant of the Law,
A man deserving to be held in awe,
Or so he seemed, his manner was so wise.
He had often served as Justice of Assize 310
By the king's appointment, with a broad commission,
For his knowledge and his eminent position.
He had many a handsome gift by way of fee.
There was no buyer of land as shrewd as he.
All ownership to him became fee simple.[11]
His titles were never faulty by a pimple.
None was so busy as he with case and cause,
And yet he seemed much busier than he was.
In all cases and decisions he was schooled
That were of record since King William[12] ruled. 320
No one could pick a loophole or a flaw
In any lease or contract he might draw.
Each statute on the books he knew by rote.
He traveled in a plain, silk-belted coat.
A Franklin traveled in his company.
Whiter could never daisy petal be
Than was his beard. His ruddy face gave sign
He liked his morning sop of toast in wine.
He lived in comfort, as he would assure us,
For he was a true son of Epicurus[13] 330
Who held the opinion that the only measure
Of perfect happiness was simply pleasure.
Such hospitality did he provide,
He was St. Julian[14] to his countryside.

[11] Ownership without legal restrictions.
[12] William the Conqueror (ruled 1066–1087 C.E.).
[13] Greek philosopher (341–270 B.C.E.); taught that refined pleasure was the greatest good.
[14] Patron saint of hospitality.

His bread and ale were always up to scratch.
He had a cellar none on earth could match.
There was no lack of pasties in his house,
Both fish and flesh, and that so plenteous
That where he lived it snowed of meat and drink.
With every dish of which a man can think, 340
After the various seasons of the year,
He changed his diet for his better cheer.
He had coops of partridges as fat as cream,
He had a fishpond stocked with pike and bream.
Woe to his cook for an unready pot
Or a sauce that wasn't seasoned and spiced hot!
A table in his hall stood on display
Prepared and covered through the livelong day.
He presided at court sessions for his bounty
And sat in Parliament often for his county. 350
A well-wrought dagger and a purse of silk
Hung at his belt, as white as morning milk.
He had been a sheriff and county auditor.
On earth was no such rich proprietor!

. . .

With us came also an astute Physician.
There was none like him for a disquisition 400
On the art of medicine or surgery,
For he was grounded in astrology.
He kept his patient long in observation,
Choosing the proper hour for application
Of charms and images by intuition
Of magic, and the planets' best position.
For he was one who understood the laws
That rule the humors, and could tell the cause
That brought on every human malady,
Whether of hot or cold, or moist or dry. 410
He was a perfect medico, for sure.
The cause once known, he would prescribe the cure,
For he had his druggists ready at a motion
To provide the sick man with some pill or potion—
A game of mutual aid, with each one winning.
Their partnership was hardly just beginning!
He was well versed in his authorities,
Old Aesculapius, Dioscorides,
Rufus, and old Hippocrates, and Galen,
Haly, and Rhazes, and Serapion, 420
Averroës, Bernard, Johannes Damascenus,
Avicenna, Gilbert, Gaddesden, Constantinus.[15]
He urged a moderate fare on principle,
But rich in nourishment, digestible;
Of nothing in excess would he admit.

[15] Ancient and medieval medical authorities from Greece, Arabia, and England.

He gave but little heed to Holy Writ.
His clothes were lined with taffeta; their hue
Was all of blood red and of Persian blue,
Yet he was far from careless of expense.
He saved his fees from times of pestilence, 430
For gold is a cordial, as physicians hold,
And so he had a special love for gold.
  A worthy woman there was from near the city
Of Bath, but somewhat deaf, and more's the pity.
For weaving she possessed so great a bent
She outdid the people of Ypres and of Ghent.[16]
No other woman dreamed of such a thing
As to precede her at the offering,
Or if any did, she fell in such a wrath
She dried up all the charity in Bath. 440
She wore fine kerchiefs of old-fashioned air,
And on a Sunday morning, I could swear,
She had ten pounds of linen on her head.
Her stockings were of finest scarlet-red,
Laced tightly, and her shoes were soft and new.
Bold was her face, and fair, and red in hue.
She had been an excellent woman all her life.
Five men in turn had taken her to wife,
Omitting other youthful company—
But let that pass for now! Over the sea 450
She had traveled freely; many a distant stream
She crossed, and visited Jerusalem
Three times. She had been at Rome and at Boulogne,
At the shrine of Compostella, and at Cologne.[17]
She had wandered by the way through many a scene.
Her teeth were set with little gaps between.
Easily on her ambling horse she sat.
She was well wimpled, and she wore a hat
As wide in circuit as a shield or targe.[18]
A skirt swathed up her hips, and they were large. 460
Upon her feet she wore sharp-roweled spurs.
She was a good fellow; a ready tongue was hers.
All remedies of love she knew by name,
For she had all the tricks of that old game.
  There was a good man of the priest's vocation,
A poor town Parson of true consecration,
But he was rich in holy thought and work.
Learned he was, in the truest sense a clerk
Who meant Christ's gospel faithfully to preach
And truly his parishioners to teach. 470
He was a kind man, fully of industry,
Many times tested by adversity

[16]Cities in Flanders renowned for their textiles.
[17]Shrines famous during the Middle Ages.
[18]A small shield.

And always patient. If tithes[19] were in arrears,
He was loth to threaten any man with fears
Of excommunication; past a doubt
He would rather spread his offering about
To his poor flock, or spend his property.
To him a little meant sufficiency.
Wide was his parish, with houses far asunder,
But he would not be kept by rain or thunder, 480
If any had suffered a sickness or a blow,
From visiting the farthest, high or low,
Plodding his way on foot, his staff in hand.
He was a model his flock could understand,
For first he did and afterward he taught.
That precept from the Gospel he had caught,
And he added as a metaphor thereto,
"If the gold rusts, what will the iron do?"
For if a priest is foul, in whom we trust,
No wonder a layman shows a little rust. 490
A priest should take to heart the shameful scene
Of shepherds filthy while the sheep are clean.
By his own purity a priest should give
The example to his sheep, how they should live.
He did not rent his benefice[20] for hire,
Leaving his flock to flounder in the mire,
And run to London, happiest of goals,
To sing paid masses in St. Paul's for souls,
Or as chaplain from some rich guild take his keep,
But dwelt at home and guarded well his sheep 500
So that no wolf should make his flock miscarry.
He was a shepherd, and not a mercenary.
And though himself a man of strict vocation
He was not harsh to weak souls in temptation,
Not overbearing nor haughty in his speech,
But wise and kind in all he tried to teach.
By good example and just words to turn
Sinners to heaven was his whole concern.
But should a man in truth prove obstinate,
Whoever he was, of rich or mean estate, 510
The Parson would give him a snub to meet the case.
I doubt there was a priest in any place
His better. He did not stand on dignity
Nor affect in conscience too much nicety,
But Christ's and his disciples' word he sought
To teach, and first he followed what he taught.
There was a Plowman with him on the road,
His brother, who had forked up many a load
Of good manure. A hearty worker he,
Living in peace and perfect charity. 520
Whether his fortune made him smart or smile,
He loved God with his whole heart all the while

[19]Regular offerings to the church.
[20]His appointment as pastor.

And his neighbor as himself. He would undertake,
For every luckless poor man, for the sake
Of Christ to thresh and ditch and dig by the hour
And with no wage, if it was in his power.
His tithes on goods and earnings he paid fair.
He wore a coarse, rough coat and rode a mare.
There also were a Manciple, a Miller,
A Reeve, a Summoner, and a Pardoner, 530
And I—this makes our company complete.
As tough a yokel as you care to meet
The Miller was. His big-beefed arms and thighs
Took many a ram put up as wrestling prize.
He was a thick, squat-shouldered lump of sins.
No door but he could heave it off its pins
Or break it running at it with his head.
His beard was broader than a shovel, and red
As a fat sow or fox. A wart stood clear
Atop his nose, and red as a pig's ear 540
A tuft of bristles on it. Black and wide
His nostrils were. He carried at his side
A sword and buckler. His mouth would open out
Like a great furnace, and he would sing and shout
His ballads and jokes of harlotries and crimes.
He could steal corn and charge for it three times,
And yet was honest enough, as millers come,
For a miller, as they say, has a golden thumb.
In white coat and blue hood this lusty clown,
Blowing his bagpipes, brought us out of town. 550
The Manciple was of a lawyers' college,
And other buyers might have used his knowledge
How to be shrewd provisioners, for whether
He bought on cash or credit, altogether
He managed that the end should be the same:
He came out more than even with the game.
Now isn't it an instance of God's grace
How a man of little knowledge can keep pace
In wit with a whole school of learned men?
He had masters to the number of three times ten 560
Who knew each twist of equity and tort;
A dozen in that very Inn of Court
Were worthy to be steward of the estate
To any of England's lords, however great,
And keep him to his income well confined
And free from debt, unless he lost his mind,
Or let him scrimp, if he were mean in bounty;
They could have given help to a whole county
In any sort of case that might befall;
And yet this Manciple could cheat them all! 570
The Reeve was a slender, fiery-tempered man.
He shaved as closely as a razor can.
His hair was cropped about his ears, and shorn
Above his forehead as a priest's is worn.
His legs were very long and very lean.
No calf on his lank spindles could be seen.

But he knew how to keep a barn or bin,
He could play the game with auditors and win.
He knew well how to judge by drought and rain
The harvest of his seed and of his grain. 580
His master's cattle, swine, and poultry flock,
Horses and sheep and dairy, all his stock,
Were altogether in this Reeve's control.
And by agreement, he had given the sole
Accounting since his lord reached twenty years.
No man could ever catch him in arrears.
There wasn't a bailiff, shepherd, or farmer working
But the Reeve knew all his tricks of cheating and shirking.
He would not let him draw an easy breath.
They feared him as they feared the very death. 590
He lived in a good house on an open space,
Well shaded by green trees, a pleasant place.
He was shrewder in acquisition than his lord.
With private riches he was amply stored.
He had learned a good trade young by work and will.
He was a carpenter of first-rate skill.
On a fine mount, a stallion, dappled gray,
Whose name was Scot, he rode along the way.
He wore a long blue coat hitched up and tied
As if it were a friar's, and at his side 600
A sword with rusty blade was hanging down.
He came from Norfolk, from nearby the town
That men call Bawdswell. As we rode the while,
The Reeve kept always hindmost in our file.
A Summoner in our company had his place.
Red as the fiery cherubim his face.
He was pocked and pimpled, and his eyes were narrow.
He was lecherous and hot as a cock sparrow.
His brows were scabby and black, and thin his beard.
His was a face that little children feared. 610
Brimstone or litharge bought in any quarter,
Quicksilver, ceruse, borax, oil of tartar,
No salve nor ointment that will cleanse or bite
Could cure him of his blotches, livid white,
Or the nobs and nubbins sitting on his cheeks.
He loved his garlic, his onions, and his leeks.
He loved to drink the strong wine down blood-red.
Then would he bellow as if he had lost his head,
And when he had drunk enough to parch his drouth,
Nothing but Latin issued from his mouth. 620
He had smattered up a few terms, two or three,
That he had gathered out of some decree—
No wonder; he heard law Latin all the day,
And everyone knows a parrot or a jay
Can cry out "Wat" or "Poll" as well as the pope;
But give him a strange term, he began to grope.
His little store of learning was paid out,
So *"Questio quod juris"*[21] he would shout.

[21] "The question is, what law?," i.e., what law applies?

He was a goodhearted bastard and a kind one.
If there were better, it was hard to find one. 630
He would let a good fellow, for a quart of wine,
The whole year round enjoy his concubine
Scot-free from summons, hearing, fine, or bail,
And on the sly he too could flush a quail.
If he liked a scoundrel, no matter for church law.
He would teach him that he need not stand in awe
If the archdeacon threatened with his curse—
That is, unless his soul was in his purse,
For in his purse he would be punished well.
"The purse," he said, "is the archdeacon's hell." 640
Of course I know he lied in what he said.
There is nothing a guilty man should so much dread
As the curse that damns his soul, when, without fail,
The church can save him, or send him off to jail.
He had the young men and girls in his control
Throughout the diocese; he knew the soul
Of youth, and heard their every last design.
A garland big enough to be the sign
Above an alehouse balanced on his head,
And he made a shield of a great round loaf of bread. 650
There was a Pardoner of Rouncivalle[22]
With him, of the blessed Mary's hospital,
But now come straight from Rome (or so said he).
Loudly he sang, "Come hither, love, to me,"
While the Summoner's counterbass trolled out profound—
No trumpet blew with half so vast a sound.
This Pardoner had hair as yellow as wax,
But it hung as smoothly as a hank of flax.
His locks trailed down in bunches from his head,
And he let the ends about his shoulders spread, 660
But in thin clusters, lying one by one.
Of hood, for rakishness, he would have none,
For in his wallet he kept it safely stowed.
He traveled, as he thought, in the latest mode,
Disheveled. Save for his cap, his head was bare,
And in his eyes he glittered like a hare.
A Veronica[23] was stitched upon his cap,
His wallet lay before him in his lap
Brimful of pardons from the very seat
In Rome. He had a voice like a goat's bleat. 670
He was beardless and would never have a beard.
His cheek was always smooth as if just sheared.
I think he was a gelding or a mare;
But in his trade, from Berwick down to Ware,
No pardoner could beat him in the race,
For in his wallet he had a pillow case

[22] A religious house and hospital outside of London.

[23] A copy of the veil of St. Veronica, said to have imprinted the image of Christ's face when he used it to wipe his face on the way to the Crucifiction.

Which he represented as Our Lady's veil;
He said he had a piece of the very sail
St. Peter, when he fished in Galilee
Before Christ caught him, used upon the sea. 680
He had a latten[24] cross embossed with stones
And in a glass he carried some pig's bones,
And with these holy relics, when he found
Some village parson grubbing his poor ground,
He would get more money in a single day
Than in two months would come the parson's way.
Thus with his flattery and his trumped-up stock
He made dupes of the parson and his flock.
But though his conscience was a little plastic
He was in church a noble ecclesiastic. 690
Well could he read the Scripture or saint's story,
But best of all he sang the offertory,
For he understood that when this song was sung,
Then he must preach, and sharpen up his tongue
To rake in cash, as well he knew the art,
And so he sang out gaily, with full heart.
Now I have set down briefly, as it was,
Our rank, our dress, our number, and the cause
That made our sundry fellowship begin
In Southwark, at this hospitable inn 700
Known as the Tabard, not far from the Bell.
But what we did that night I ought to tell,
And after that our journey, stage by stage,
And the whole story of our pilgrimage.
But first, in justice, do not look askance
I plead, nor lay it to my ignorance
If in this matter I should use plain speech
And tell you just the words and style of each
Reporting all their language faithfully.
For it must be known to you as well as me 710
That whoever tells a story after a man
Must follow him as closely as he can.
If he takes the tale in charge, he must be true
To every word, unless he would find new
Or else invent a thing or falsify.
Better some breadth of language than a lie!
He may not spare the truth to save his brother.
He might as well use one word as another.
In Holy Writ Christ spoke in a broad sense,
And surely his word is without offense. 720
Plato, if his are pages you can read,
Says let the word be cousin to the deed.
So I petition your indulgence for it
If I have cut the cloth just as men wore it,
Here in this tale, and shown its very weave.
My wits are none too sharp, you must believe.

[24] A metal alloy.

Our Host gave each of us a cheerful greeting
And promptly of our supper had us eating.
The victuals that he served us were his best.
The wine was potent, and we drank with zest. 730
Our Host cut such a figure, all in all,
He might have been a marshal in a hall.
He was a big man, and his eyes bulged wide.
No sturdier citizen lived in all Cheapside,[25]
Lacking no trace of manhood, bold in speech,
Prudent, and well versed in what life can teach,
And with all this he was a jovial man.
And so when supper ended he began
To jolly us, when all our debts were clear.
"Welcome," he said. "I have not seen this year 740
So merry a company in this tavern as now,
And I would give you pleasure if I knew how.
And just this very minute a plan has crossed
My mind that might amuse you at no cost.
"You go to Canterbury—may the Lord
Speed you, and may the martyred saint reward
Your journey! And to while the time away
You mean to talk and pass the time of day,
For you would be as cheerful all alone
As riding on your journey dumb as stone. 750
Therefore, if you'll abide by what I say,
Tomorrow, when you ride off on your way,
Now, by my father's soul, and he is dead,
If you don't enjoy yourselves, cut off my head!
Hold up your hands, if you accept my speech."
Our counsel did not take us long to reach.
We bade him give his orders at his will.
"Well, sirs," he said, "then do not take it ill,
But hear me in good part, and for your sport,
Each one of you, to make our journey short, 760
Shall tell two stories, as we ride, I mean,
Toward Canterbury; and coming home again
Shall tell two other tales he may have heard
Of happenings that some time have occurred.
And the one of you whose stories please us most,
Here in this tavern, sitting by this post
Shall sup at our expense while we make merry
When we come riding home from Canterbury.
And to cheer you still the more, I too will ride
With you at my own cost, and be your guide. 770
And if anyone my judgment shall gainsay
He must pay for all we spend along the way.
If you agree, no need to stand and reason.
Tell me, and I'll be stirring in good season."
This thing was granted, and we swore our pledge
To take his judgment on our pilgrimage,
His verdict on our tales, and his advice.

[25] A commercial street in London.

He was to plan a supper at a price
Agreed upon; and so we all assented
To this command, and we were well contented. 780
The wine was fetched; we drank, and went to rest.
 Next morning, when the dawn was in the east,
Up sprang our Host, who acted as our cock,
And gathered us together in a flock,
And off we rode, till presently our pace
Had brought us to St. Thomas' watering place.
And there our host began to check his horse.
"Good sirs," he said, "you know your promise, of course.
Shall I remind you what it was about?
If evensong and matins don't fall out, 790
We'll soon find who shall tell us the first tale.
But as I hope to drink my wine and ale,
Whoever won't accept what I decide
Pays everything we spend along the ride.
Draw lots, before we're farther from the Inn.
Whoever draws the shortest shall begin.
Sir Knight," said he, "my master, choose your straw.
Come here, my lady Prioress, and draw,
And you, Sir Scholar, don't look thoughtful, man!
Pitch in now, everyone!" So all began 800
To draw the lots, and as the luck would fall
The draw went to the Knight, which pleased us all.
And when this excellent man saw how it stood,
Ready to keep his promise, he said, "Good!
Since it appears that I must start the game,
Why then, the draw is welcome, in God's name.
Now let's ride on, and listen, what I say."
And with that word we rode forth on our way,
And he, with his courteous manner and good cheer,
Began to tell his tale, as you shall hear. 810

. . .

Prologue to the Wife of Bath's Tale

"Experience, though all authority
Was lacking in the world, confers on me
The right to speak of marriage, and unfold
Its woes. For, lords, since I was twelve years old
—Thanks to eternal God in heaven alive—
I have married at church door no less than five
Husbands, provided that I can have been
So often wed, and all were worthy men.
But I was told, indeed, and not long since,
That Christ went to a wedding only once 10
At Cana, in the land of Galilee.
By this example he instructed me
To wed once only—that's what I have heard!
Again, consider now what a sharp word,
Beside a well, Jesus, both God and man,

Spoke in reproving the Samaritan:
'Thou hast had five husbands'—this for a certainty
He said to her—'and the man that now hath thee
Is not thy husband.' True, he spoke this way,
But what he meant is more than I can say 20
Except that I would ask why the fifth man
Was not a husband to the Samaritan?
To just how many could she be a wife?
I have never heard this number all my life
Determined up to now. For round and round
Scholars may gloze, interpret, and expound,
But plainly, this I know without a lie,
God told us to increase and multiply.
That noble text I can well understand.
My husband—this too I have well in hand— 30
Should leave both father and mother and cleave to me.
Number God never mentioned, bigamy,
No, nor even octogamy; why do men
Talk of it as a sin and scandal, then?
"Think of that monarch, wise King Solomon.[26]
It strikes me that *he* had more wives than one!
To be refreshed, God willing, would please me
If I got it half as many times as he!
What a gift he had, a gift of God's own giving,
For all his wives! There isn't a man now living 40
Who has the like. By all that I make out
This king had many a merry first-night bout
With each, he was so thoroughly alive.
Blessed be God that I have married five,
And always, for the money in his chest
And for his nether purse, I picked the best.
In divers schools ripe scholarship is made,
And various practice in all kinds of trade
Makes perfect workmen, as the world can see.
Five husbands have had turns at schooling me. 50
Welcome the sixth, whenever I am faced
With yet another. I don't mean to be chaste
At all costs. When a spouse of mine is gone,
Some other Christian man shall take me on,
For then, says the Apostle,[27] I'll be free
To wed, in God's name, where it pleases me.
To marry is no sin, as we can learn
From him; better to marry than to burn,
He says. Why should I care what obloquy
Men heap on Lamech[28] and his bigamy? 60
Abraham was, by all that I can tell,
A holy man; so Jacob was as well,

---

[26] Solomon had 700 wives and 300 concubines (1 Kings 2:3).

[27] St. Paul, who recommends in 1 Corinthians 7:8–9 that celibacy is preferable to marriage, marriage to promiscuity.

[28] A man with two wives (Genesis 4: 19–24).

And each of them took more than two as brides,
And many another holy man besides.
Where, may I ask, in any period,
Can you show in plain words that Almighty God
Forbade us marriage? Point it out to me!
Or where did he command virginity?
The Apostle, when he speaks of maidenhood,
Lays down no law. This I have understood 70
As well as you, milords, for it is plain.
Men may advise a woman to abstain
From marriage, but mere counsels aren't commands.
He left it to our judgment, where it stands.
Had God enjoined us all to maidenhood
Then marriage would have been condemned for good.
But truth is, if no seed were ever sown,
In what soil could virginity be grown?
Paul did not dare command a thing at best
On which his Master left us no behest. 80
"But now the prize goes to virginity.
Seize it whoever can, and let us see
What manner of man shall run best in the race!
But not all men receive this form of grace
Except where God bestows it by his will.
The Apostle was a maid, I know; but still,
Although he wished all men were such as he,
It was only *counsel* toward virginity.
To be a wife he gave me his permission,
And so it is no blot on my condition 90
Nor slander of bigamy upon my state
If when my husband dies I take a mate.
A man does virtuously, St. Paul has said,
To touch no woman—meaning in his bed.
For fire and fat are dangerous friends at best.
You know what this example should suggest.
Here is the nub: he held virginity
Superior to wedded frailty,
And frailty I call it unless man
And woman both are chaste for their whole span. 100
"I am not jealous if maidenhood outweighs
My marriages; I grant it all the praise.
It pleases them, these virgins, flesh and soul
To be immaculate. I won't extol
My own condition. In a lord's household
You know that every vessel can't be gold.
Some are of wood, and serve their master still.
God calls us variously to do his will.
Each has his proper gift, of all who live,
Some this, some that, as it pleases God to give. 110
"To be virgin is a high and perfect course,
And continence is holy. But the source
Of all perfection, Jesus, never bade
Each one of us to go sell all he had
And give it to the poor; he did not say

That all should follow him in this one way.
He spoke to those who would live perfectly,
And by your leave, lords, that is not for me!
The flower of my best years I find it suits
To spend on the acts of marriage and its fruits. 120
"Tell me this also: why at our creation
Were organs given us for generation,
And for what profit were we creatures made?
Believe me, not for nothing! Ply his trade
Of twisting texts who will, and let him urge
That they were only given us to purge
Our urine; say without them we should fail
To tell a female rightly from a male
And that's their only object—say you so?
It won't work, as experience will show. 130
Without offense to scholars, I say this,
They were given us for both these purposes,
That we may both be cleansed, I mean, and eased
Through intercourse, where God is not displeased.
Why else in books is this opinion met,
That every man should pay his wife his debt?
Tell me with what a man should hope to pay
Unless he put his instrument in play?
They were supplied us, then, for our purgation,
But they were also meant for generation. 140
"But none the less I do not mean to say
That all those who are furnished in this way
Are bound to go and practice intercourse.
The world would then grant chastity no force.
Christ was a maid, yet he was formed a man,
And many a saint, too, since the world began,
And yet they lived in perfect chastity.
I am not spiteful toward virginity.
Let virgins be white bread of pure wheat-seed.
Barley we wives are called, and yet I read 150
In Mark, and tell the tale in truth he can,
That Christ with barley bread cheered many a man.[29]
In the state that God assigned to each of us
I'll persevere. I'm not fastidious.
In wifehood I will use my instrument
As freely by my Maker it was lent.
If I hold back with it, God give me sorrow!
My husband shall enjoy it night and morrow
When it pleases him to come and pay his debt.
But a husband, and I've not been thwarted yet, 160
Shall always be my debtor and my slave.
From tribulation he shall never save
His flesh, not for as long as I'm his wife!
I have the power, during all my life,

---

[29]The miracle of feeding 5,000 people with five loaves and two fishes (Mark 8:1–21; John 6:9).

Over his very body, and not he.
For so the Apostle has instructed me,
Who bade men love their wives for better or worse.
It pleases me from end to end, that verse!"
The Pardoner, before she could go on,
Jumped up and cried, "By God and by St. John, 170
Upon this topic you preach nobly, Dame!
I was about to wed, but now, for shame,
Why should my body pay a price so dear?
I'd rather not be married all this year!"
"Hold on," she said. "I haven't yet begun.
You'll drink a keg of this before I'm done,
I promise you, and it won't taste like ale!
And after I have told you my whole tale
Of marriage, with its fund of tribulation—
And I'm the expert of my generation, 180
For I myself, I mean, have been the whip—
You can decide then if you want a sip
Out of the barrel that I mean to broach.
Before you come too close in your approach,
Think twice. I have examples, more than ten!
'The man who won't be warned by other men,
To other men a warning he shall be.'
These are the words we find in Ptolemy.
You can read them right there in his *Almagest*."[30]
"Now, Madame, if you're willing, I suggest," 190
Answered the Pardoner, "as you began,
Continue with your tale, and spare no man.
Teach us your practice—we young men need a guide."
"Gladly, if it will please you," she replied.
"But first I ask you, if I speak my mind,
That all this company may be well inclined,
And will not take offense at what I say.
I only mean it, after all, in play.
"Now, sirs, I will get onward with my tale.
If ever I hope to drink good wine or ale, 200
I'm speaking truth: the husbands I have had,
Three of them have been good, and two were bad.
The three were kindly men, and rich, and old.
But they were hardly able to uphold
The statute which had made them fast to me.
You know well what I mean by this, I see!
So help me God, I can't help laughing yet
When I think of how at night I made them sweat,
And I thought nothing of it, on my word!
Their land and wealth they had by then conferred 210
On me, and so I safely could neglect
Tending their love or showing them respect.
So well they loved me that by God above
I hardly set a value on their love.

[30]This aphorism appears not in the *Almagest,* but in a collection of Ptolemy's writings.

A woman who is wise is never done
Busily winning love when she has none,
But since I had them wholly in my hand
And they had given me their wealth and land,
Why task myself to spoil them or to please
Unless for my own profit and my ease? 220
I set them working so that many a night
They sang a dirge, so grievous was their plight!
They never got the bacon, well I know,
Offered as prize to couples at Dunmow[31]
Who live a year in peace without repentance!
So well I ruled them, by my law and sentence,
They were glad to bring me fine things from the fair
And happy when I spoke with a mild air,
For God knows I could chide outrageously.
"Now judge if I could do it properly! 230
You wives who understand and who are wise,
This is the way to throw dust in their eyes.
There isn't on the earth so bold a man
He can swear false or lie as a woman can.
I do not urge this course in every case,
Just when a prudent wife is caught off base;
Then she should swear the parrot's mad who tattled
Her indiscretions, and when she's once embattled
Should call her maid as witness, by collusion.
But listen, how I threw them in confusion: 240
" 'Sir dotard, this is how you live?' I'd say.
'How can my neighbor's wife be dressed so gay?
She carries off the honors everywhere.
I sit at home. I've nothing fit to wear.
What were you doing at my neighbor's house?
Is she so handsome? Are you so amorous?
What do you whisper to our maid? God bless me,
Give up your jokes, old lecher. They depress me.
When I have a harmless friend myself, you balk
And scold me like a devil if I walk 250
For innocent amusement to his house.
You drink and come home reeling like a souse
And sit down on your bench, worse luck, and preach.
Taking a wife who's poor—this is the speech
That you regale me with—costs grievously,
And if she's rich and of good family,
It is a constant torment, you decide,
To suffer her ill humor and her pride.
And if she's fair, you scoundrel, you destroy her
By saying that every lecher will enjoy her; 260
For chastity at best has frail protections
If a woman is assailed from all directions.
" 'Some want us for our wealth, so you declare,
Some for our figure, some think we are fair,

---

[31] A town in southeastern England that awarded such a prize for couples who had no quarrels or doubts about marriage for a year after their wedding.

Some want a woman who can dance or sing,
Some want kindness, and some philandering,
Some look for hands and arms well turned and small.
Thus, by your tale, the devil may take us all!
Men cannot keep a castle or redoubt
Longer, you tell me, than it can hold out. 270
Or if a woman's plain, you say that she
Is one who covets each man she may see,
For at him like a spaniel she will fly
Until she finds some man that she can buy.
Down to the lake goes never a goose so gray
But it will have a mate, I've heard you say.
It's hard to fasten—this too I've been told—
A thing that no man willingly will hold.
Wise men, you tell me as you go to bed,
And those who hope for heaven should never wed. 280
I hope wild lightning and a thunderstroke
Will break your wizened neck! You say that smoke
And falling timbers and a railing wife
Drive a man from his house. Lord bless my life!
What ails an old man, so to make him chide?
We cover our vices till the knot is tied,
We wives, you say, and then we trot them out.
Here's a fit proverb for a doddering lout!
An ox or ass, you say, a hound or horse,
These we examine as a matter of course. 290
Basins and also bowls, before we buy them,
Spoons, spools, and such utensils, first we try them,
And so with pots and clothes, beyond denial;
But of their wives men never make a trial
Until they are married. After that, you say,
Old fool, we put our vices on display.
"'I am in a pique if you forget your duty
And fail, you tell me, to praise me for my beauty,
Or unless you are always doting on my face
And calling me "fair dame" in every place, 300
Or unless you give a feast on my birthday
To keep me in good spirits, fresh and gay,
Or unless all proper courtesies are paid
To my nurse and also to my chambermaid,
And my father's kin with all their family ties—
You say so, you old barrelful of lies!
"'Yet just because he has a head of hair
Like shining gold, and squires me everywhere,
You have a false suspicion in your heart
Of Jenkin, our apprentice. For my part 310
I wouldn't have him if you died tomorrow!
But tell me this, or go and live in sorrow:
That chest of yours, why do you hide the keys
Away from me? It's my wealth, if you please,
As much as yours. Will you make a fool of me,
The mistress of our house? You shall not be
Lord of my body and my wealth at once!
No, by St. James himself, you must renounce

One or the other, if it drives you mad!
Does it help to spy on me? You would be glad 320
To lock me up, I think, inside your chest.
"Enjoy yourself, and go where you think best,"
You ought to say; "I won't hear tales of malice.
I know you for a faithful wife, Dame Alice."
A woman loves no man who keeps close charge
Of where she goes. We want to be at large.
Blessed above all other men was he,
The wise astrologer, Don Ptolemy,
Who has this proverb in his *Almagest:*
"Of all wise men his wisdom is the best 330
Who does not care who has the world in hand."
Now by this proverb you should understand,
Since you have plenty, it isn't yours to care
Or fret how richly other people fare,
For by your leave, old dotard, you for one
Can have all you can take when day is done.
The man's a niggard to the point of scandal
Who will not lend his lamp to light a candle;
His lamp won't lose although the candle gain.
If you have enough, you ought not to complain. 340
"'You say, too, if we make ourselves look smart,
Put on expensive clothes and dress the part,
We lay our virtue open to disgrace.
And then you try to reinforce your case
By saying these words in the Apostle's name:
"In chaste apparel, with modesty and shame,
So shall you women clothe yourselves," said he,
"And not in rich coiffure or jewelry,
Pearls or the like, or gold, or costly wear."[32]
Now both your text and rubric, I declare, 350
I will not follow as I would a gnat!
"'You told me once that I was like a cat,
For singe her skin and she will stay at home,
But if her skin is smooth, the cat will roam.
No dawn but finds her on the neighbors calling
To show her skin, and go off caterwauling.
If I am looking smart, you mean to say,
I'm off to put my finery on display.
"'What do you gain, old fool, by setting spies?
Though you beg Argus[33] with his hundred eyes 360
To be my bodyguard, for all his skill
He'll keep me only by my own free will.
I know enough to blind him, as I live!
"'There are three things, you also say, that give
Vexation to this world both south and north,
And you add that no one can endure the fourth.

---

[32]Timothy 2:9.

[33]In Greek mythology, a giant with a hundred eyes; the goddess Hera had him spy on her husband, Zeus, who had amorous designs on beautiful Io.

Of these catastrophes a hateful wife—
You precious wretch, may Christ cut short your life!—
Is always reckoned, as you say, for one.
Is this your whole stock of comparison, 370
And why in all your parables of contempt
Can a luckless helpmate never be exempt?
You also liken woman's love to hell,
To barren land where water will not dwell.
I've heard you call it an unruly fire;
The more it burns, the hotter its desire
To burn up everything that burned will be.
You say that just as worms destroy a tree
A wife destroys her spouse, as they have found
Who get themselves in holy wedlock bound.' 380
"By these devices, lords, as you perceive,
I got my three old husbands to believe
That in their cups they said things of this sort,
And all of it was false; but for support
Jenkin bore witness, and my niece did too.
These innocents, Lord, what I put them through!
God's precious pains! And they had no recourse,
For I could bite and whinny like a horse.
Though in the wrong, I kept them well annoyed,
Or oftentimes I would have been destroyed! 390
First to the mill is first to grind his grain.
I was always the first one to complain,
And so our peace was made; they gladly bid
For terms to settle things they never did!
"For wenching I would scold them out of hand
When they were hardly well enough to stand.
But this would tickle a man; it would restore him
To think I had so great a fondness for him!
I'd vow when darkness came and out I stepped,
It was to see the girls with whom he slept. 400
Under this pretext I had plenty of mirth!
Such wit as this is given us at our birth.
Lies, tears, and needlework the Lord will give
In kindness to us women while we live.
And thus in one point I can take just pride:
In the end I showed myself the stronger side.
By sleight or strength I kept them in restraint,
And chiefly by continual complaint.
In bed they met their grief in fullest measure.
There I would scold; I would not do their pleasure. 410
Bed was a place where I would not abide
If I felt my husband's arm across my side
Till he agreed to square accounts and pay,
And after that I'd let him have his way.
To every man, therefore, I tell this tale:
Win where you're able, all is up for sale.
No falcon by an empty hand is lured.
For victory their cravings I endured
And even feigned a show of appetite.
And yet in old meat I have no delight; 420

It made me always rail at them and chide them,
For though the pope himself sat down beside them
I would not give them peace at their own board.
No, on my honor, I paid them word for word.
Almighty God so help me, if right now
I had to make my last will, I can vow
For every word they said to me, we're quits.
For I so handled the contest by my wits
That they gave up, and took it for the best,
Or otherwise we should have had no rest. 430
Like a mad lion let my husband glare,
In the end he got the worst of the affair.
"Then I would say, 'My dear, you ought to keep
In mind how gentle Wilkin looks, our sheep.
Come here, my husband, let me kiss your cheek!
You should be patient, too; you should be meek.
Of Job and of his patience when you prate
Your conscience ought to show a cleaner slate.
He should be patient who so well can preach.
If not, then it will fall on me to teach 440
The beauty of a peaceful wedded life.
For one of us must give in, man or wife,
And since men are more reasonable creatures
Than women are, it follows that *your* features
Ought to exhibit patience. Why do you groan?
You want my body yours, and yours alone?
Why, take it all! Welcome to every bit!
But curse you, Peter, unless you cherish it!
Were I inclined to peddle my *belle chose,*[34]
I could go about dressed freshly as a rose. 450
But I will keep it for your own sweet tooth.
It's your fault if we fight. By God, that's truth!'
"This was the way I talked when I had need.
But now to my fourth husband I'll proceed.
"This fourth I married was a roisterer.
He had a mistress, and my passions were,
Although I say it, strong; and altogether
I was young and stubborn, pert in every feather.
If anyone took up his harp to play,
How I could dance! I sang as merry a lay 460
As any nightingale when of sweet wine
I had drunk my draft. Metellius, the foul swine,
Who beat his spouse until he took her life
For drinking wine, had I only been his wife,
He'd never have frightened me away from drinking!
But after a drink, Venus gets in my thinking,
For just as true as cold engenders hail
A thirsty mouth goes with a thirsty tail.
Drinking destroys a woman's last defense
As lechers well know by experience. 470

[34]"Beautiful thing" (French).

"But, Lord Christ, when it all comes back to me,
Remembering my youth and jollity,
It tickles me to the roots. It does me good
Down to this very day that while I could
I took my world, my time, and had my fling.
But age, alas, that poisons everything
Has robbed me of my beauty and my pith.
Well, let it go! Good-by! The devil with
What cannot last! There's only this to tell:
The flour is gone, I've only chaff to sell. 480
Yet I'll contrive to keep a merry cheek!
But now of my fourth husband I will speak.
"My heart was, I can tell you, full of spite
That in another he should find delight.
I paid him for this debt; I made it good.
I furnished him a cross of the same wood,
By God and by St. Joce—in no foul fashion,
Not with my flesh; but I put on such passion
And rendered him so jealous, I'll engage
I made him fry in his own grease for rage! 490
On earth, God knows, I was his purgatory;
I only hope his soul is now in glory.
God knows it was a sad song that he sung
When the shoe pinched him; sorely was he wrung!
Only he knew, and God, the devious system
By which outrageously I used to twist him.
He died when I came home from Jerusalem.
He is buried near the chancel, under the beam
That holds the cross. His tomb is less ornate
Than the sepulcher where Darius[35] lies in state 500
And which the paintings of Appelles graced
With subtle work. It would have been a waste
To bury him lavishly. Farewell! God save
His soul and give him rest! He's in his grave.
"And now of my fifth husband let me tell.
God never let his soul go down to hell
Though he of all five was my scourge and flail!
I feel it on my ribs, right down the scale,
And ever shall until my dying day.
And yet he was so full of life and gay 510
In bed, and could so melt me and cajole me
When on my back he had a mind to roll me,
What matter if on every bone he'd beaten me!
He'd have my love, so quickly he could sweeten me.
I loved him best, in fact; for as you see,
His love was a more arduous prize for me.
We women, if I'm not to tell a lie,
Are quaint in this regard. Put in our eye
A thing we cannot easily obtain,
All day we'll cry about it and complain. 520
Forbid a thing, we want it bitterly,

[35] Legendary king of Persia (c. 521–486 B.C.E.), notorious for his wealth.

But urge it on us, then we turn and flee.
We are chary of what we hope that men will buy.
A throng at market makes the prices high;
Men set no value on cheap merchandise,
A truth all women know if they are wise.
"My fifth, may God forgive his every sin,
I took for love, not money. He had been
An Oxford student once, but in our town
Was boarding with my good friend, Alison. 530
She knew each secret that I had to give
More than our parish priest did, as I live!
I told her my full mind, I shared it all.
For if my husband pissed against a wall
Or did a thing that might have cost his life,
To her, and to another neighbor's wife,
And to my niece, a girl whom I loved well,
His every thought I wouldn't blush to tell.
And often enough I told them, be it said.
God knows I made his face turn hot and red 540
For secrets he confided to his shame.
He knew he only had himself to blame.
"And so it happened once that during Lent,
As I often did, to Alison's I went,
For I have loved my life long to be gay
And to walk out in April or in May
To hear the talk and seek a favorite haunt.
Jenkin the student, Alice, my confidante,
And I myself into the country went.
My husband was in London all that Lent. 550
I had the greater liberty to see
And to be seen by jolly company.
How could I tell beforehand in what place
Luck might be waiting with a stroke of grace?
And so I went to every merrymaking.
No pilgrimage was past my undertaking.
I was at festivals, and marriages,
Processions, preachings, and at miracle plays,
And in my scarlet clothes I made a sight.
Upon that costume neither moth nor mite 560
Nor any worm with ravening hunger fell.
And why, you ask? It was kept in use too well.
"Now for what happened. In the fields we walked,
The three of us, and gallantly we talked,
The student and I, until I told him he,
If I became a widow, should marry me.
For I can say, and not with empty pride,
I have never failed for marriage to provide
Or other things as well. Let mice be meek;
A mouse's heart I hold not worth a leek. 570
He has one hole to scurry to, just one,
And if that fails him, he is quite undone.
"I let this student think he had bewitched me.
(My mother with this piece of guile enriched me!)

All night I dreamed of him—this too I said;
He was killing me as I lay flat in bed;
My very bed in fact was full of blood;
But still I hoped it would result in good,
For blood betokens gold, as I have heard.
It was a fiction, dream and every word, 580
But I was following my mother's lore
In all this matter, as in many more.
"Sirs—let me see; what did I mean to say?
Aha! By God, I have it! When he lay,
My fourth, of whom I've spoken, on his bier,
I wept of course; I showed but little cheer,
As wives must do, since custom has its place,
And with my kerchief covered up my face.
But since I had provided for a mate,
I did not cry for long, I'll freely state. 590
And so to church my husband on the morrow
Was borne away by neighbors in their sorrow.
Jenkin, the student, was among the crowd,
And when I saw him walk, so help me God,
Behind the bier, I thought he had a pair
Of legs and feet so cleanly turned and fair
I put my heart completely in his hold.
He was in fact some twenty winters old
And I was forty, to confess the truth;
But all my life I've still had a colt's tooth. 600
My teeth were spaced apart; that was the seal
St. Venus printed, and became me well.
So help me God, I was a lusty one,
Pretty and young and rich, and full of fun.
And truly, as my husbands have all said,
I was the best thing there could be in bed.
For I belong to Venus in my feelings,
Though I bring the heart of Mars to all my dealings.
From Venus come my lust and appetite,
From Mars I get my courage and my might, 610
Born under Taurus, while Mars stood therein.
Alas, alas, that ever love was sin!
I yielded to my every inclination
Through the predominance of my constellation;
This made me so I never could withhold
My chamber of Venus, if the truth be told,
From a good fellow; yet upon my face
Mars left his mark, and in another place.
For never, so may Christ grant me intercession,
Have I yet loved a fellow with discretion, 620
But always I have followed appetite,
Let him be long or short or dark or light.
I never cared, as long as he liked me,
What his rank was or how poor he might be.
"What should I say, but when the month ran out,
This jolly student, always much about,
This Jenkin married me in solemn state.

To him I gave land, titles, the whole slate
Of goods that had been given me before;
But my repentance afterward was sore! 630
He wouldn't endure the pleasures I held dear.
By God, he gave me a lick once on the ear,
When from a book of his I tore a leaf,
So hard that from the blow my ear grew deaf.
I was stubborn as a lioness with young,
And by the truth I had a rattling tongue,
And I would visit, as I'd done before,
No matter what forbidding oath he swore.
Against this habit he would sit and preach me
Sermons enough, and he would try to teach me 640
Old Roman stories, how for his whole life
The man Sulpicius Gallus left his wife
Only because he saw her look one day
Bareheaded down the street from his doorway.
"Another Roman he told me of by name
Who, since his wife was at a summer's game
Without his knowledge, thereupon forsook
The woman. In his Bible he would look
And find that proverb of the Ecclesiast
Where he enjoins and makes the stricture fast 650
That men forbid their wives to rove about.
Then he would quote me this, you needn't doubt:
'Build a foundation over sands or shallows,
Or gallop a blind horse across the fallows,
Let a wife traipse to shrines that some saint hallows,
And you are fit to swing upon the gallows.'
Talk as he would, I didn't care two haws
For his proverbs or his venerable saws.
Set right by him I never meant to be.
I hate the man who tells my faults to me, 660
And more of us than I do, by your pleasure.
This made him mad with me beyond all measure.
Under his yoke in no case would I go.
"Now, by St. Thomas, I will let you know
Why from that book of his I tore a leaf,
For which I got the blow that made me deaf.
"He had a book, *Valerius,* he called it,
And Theophrastus,[36] and he always hauled it
From where it lay to read both day and night
And laughed hard at it, such was his delight. 670
There was another scholar, too, at Rome
A cardinal, whose name was St. Jerome;
He wrote a book against Jovinian.
In the same book also were Tertullian,
Chrysippus, Trotula, Abbess Héloïse
Who lived near Paris; it contained all these,
Bound in a single volume, and many a one

[36]Walter Map's *Letter of Valerius Concerning Not Marrying* and Theophrastus's *Book Concerning Marriage* are two misogynist treatises in Jenkin's library.

Besides; the Parables of Solomon
And Ovid's *Art of Love*.[37] On such vacation
As he could snatch from worldly occupation 680
He dredged this book for tales of wicked wives.
He knew more stories of their wretched lives
Than are told about good women in the Bible.
No scholar ever lived who did not libel
Women, believe me; to speak well of wives
Is quite beyond them, unless it be in lives
Of holy saints; no woman else will do.
Who was it painted the lion,[38] tell me who?
By God, if women had only written stories
Like wits and scholars in their oratories, 690
They would have pinned on men more wickedness
Than the whole breed of Adam can redress.
Venus's children clash with Mercury's;
The two work evermore by contraries.
Knowledge and wisdom are of Mercury's giving,
Venus loves revelry and riotous living,
And with these clashing dispositions gifted
Each of them sinks when the other is uplifted.
Thus Mercury falls, God knows, in desolation
In the sign of Pisces, Venus's exaltation, 700
And Venus falls when Mercury is raised.
Thus by a scholar no woman can be praised.
The scholar, when he's old and cannot do
The work of Venus more than his old shoe,
Then sits he down, and in his dotage fond
Writes that no woman keeps her marriage bond!
"But now for the story that I undertook—
To tell how I was beaten for a book.
"Jenkin, one night, who never seemed to tire
Of reading in his book, sat by the fire 710
And first he read of Eve, whose wickedness
Delivered all mankind to wretchedness
For which in his own person Christ was slain
Who with his heart's blood bought us all again.
'By this,' he said, 'expressly you may find
That woman was the loss of all mankind.'
"He read me next how Samson lost his hair.
Sleeping, his mistress clipped it off for fair;
Through this betrayal he lost both his eyes.
He read me then—and I'm not telling lies— 720
How Deianeira, wife of Hercules,
Caused him to set himself on fire. With these
He did not overlook the sad to-do
Of Socrates with *his* wives—he had two.

---

[37] St. Jerome's *Reply to Jovinian* accused women of licentiousness; Tertullian wrote treatises on modesty; Chrysippus is a misogynist mentioned in Jerome. Trotula was a female doctor, and Heloise (Eloise) is the infamous lover of Abelard. Ovid's *Art of Love* and the Parables of Solomon are two other scandalous texts.

[38] Aesop tells of a lion who, when shown a picture of a man killing a lion, remarks that lions would draw a picture of the reverse.

Xantippe emptied the pisspot on his head.
This good man sat as patient as if dead.
He wiped his scalp; he did not dare complain
Except to say 'With thunder must come rain.'
"Pasiphaë,[39] who was the queen of Crete,
For wickedness he thought her story sweet. 730
Ugh! That's enough, it was a grisly thing,
About her lust and filthy hankering!
And Clytemnestra[40] in her lechery
Who took her husband's life feloniously,
He grew devout in reading of her treason.
And then he told me also for what reason
Unhappy Amphiaraus[41] lost his life.
My husband had the story of *his* wife,
Eriphyle, who for a clasp of gold
Went to his Grecian enemies and told 740
The secret of her husband's hiding place,
For which at Thebes he met an evil grace.
Livia and Lucilia,[42] he went through
Their tale as well; they killed their husbands, too.
One killed for love, the other killed for hate.
At evening Livia, when the hour was late,
Poisoned her husband, for she was his foe.
Lucilia doted on her husband so
That in her lust, hoping to make him think
Ever of her, she gave him a love-drink 750
Of such a sort he died before the morrow.
And so at all turns husbands come to sorrow!
"He told me then how one Latumius,
Complaining to a friend named Arrius,
Told him that in his garden grew a tree
On which his wives had hanged themselves, all three,
Merely for spite against their partnership.
'Brother,' said Arrius, 'let me have a slip
From this miraculous tree, for, begging pardon,
I want to go and plant it in my garden.' 760
"Then about wives in recent times he read,
How some had murdered husbands lying abed
And all night long had let a paramour
Enjoy them with the corpse flat on the floor;
Or driven a nail into a husband's brain
While he was sleeping, and thus he had been slain;
And some had given them poison in their drink.
He told more harm than anyone can think,
And seasoned his wretched stories with proverbs
Outnumbering all the blades of grass and herbs 770

---

[39]Wife of Minos, King of Crete; angered at Minos, Poseidon caused Pasiphaë to fall in love with a bull, after which she gave birth to the Minotaur, part human and part beast.

[40]Clytemnestra killed her husband, King Agamemnon, on his return from the Trojan War.

[41]Knowing that only her brother Adrastus would survive the war against Thebes, Eriphyle, the wife of Argive warrior Amphiaraus, forced him to go into that battle.

[42]Notorious Roman women who killed their husbands; Lucilia's husband was the poet Lucretius.

On earth. 'Better a dragon for a mate,
Better,' he said, 'on a lion's whims to wait
Than on a wife whose way it is to chide.
Better,' he said, 'high in the loft to bide
Than with a railing wife down in the house.
They always, they are so contrarious,
Hate what their husbands like,' so he would say.
'A woman,' he said, 'throws all her shame away
When she takes off her smock.' And on he'd go:
'A pretty woman, unless she's chaste also, 780
Is like a gold ring stuck in a sow's nose.'
Who could imagine, who would half suppose
The gall my heart drank, raging at each drop?
"And when I saw that he would never stop
Reading all night from his accursed book,
Suddenly, in the midst of it, I took
Three leaves and tore them out in a great pique,
And with my fist I caught him on the cheek
So hard he tumbled backward in the fire.
And up he jumped, he was as mad for ire 790
As a mad lion, and caught me on the head
With such a blow I fell down as if dead.
And seeing me on the floor, how still I lay,
He was aghast, and would have fled away,
Till I came to at length, and gave a cry.
'Have you killed me for my lands? Before I die,
False thief,' I said, 'I'll give you a last kiss!'
"He came to me and knelt down close at this,
And said, 'So help me God, dear Alison,
I'll never strike you. For this thing I have done 800
You are to blame. Forgive me, I implore.'
So then I hit him on the cheek once more
And said, 'Thus far I am avenged, you thief.
I cannot speak. Now I shall die for grief.'
But finally, with much care and ado,
We reconciled our differences, we two.
He let me have the bridle in my hand
For management of both our house and land.
To curb his tongue he also undertook,
And on the spot I made him burn his book. 810
And when I had secured in full degree
By right of triumph the whole sovereignty,
And he had said, 'My dear, my own true wife,
Do as you will as long as you have life;
Preserve your honor and keep my estate,'
From that day on we had settled our debate.
I was as kind, God help me, day and dark
As any wife from India to Denmark,
And also true, and so he was to me.
I pray the Lord who sits in majesty 820
To bless his soul for Christ's own mercy dear.
And now I'll tell my tale, if you will hear."
"Dame," laughed the Friar, "as I hope for bliss,
It was a long preamble to a tale, all this!"

"God's arms!" the Summoner said, "it is a sin,
Good people, how friars are always butting in!
A fly and a friar will fall in every dish
And every question, whatever people wish.
What do you know, with your talk about 'preambling'?
Amble or trot or keep still or go scrambling, 830
You interrupt our pleasure."
"You think so,
Sir Summoner?" said the Friar. "Before I go,
I'll give the people here a chance or two
For a laugh at summoners, I promise you."
"Curse on your face," the Summoner said, "curse me,
If I don't tell some stories, two or three,
On friars, before I get to Sittingborne,[43]
With which I'll twist your heart and make it mourn,
For you have lost your temper, I can see."
"Be quiet," cried our Host, "immediately," 840
And ordered, "Let the woman tell her tale.
You act like people who've got drunk on ale.
Do, Madame, tell us. That is the best measure."
"All ready, sir," she answered "at your pleasure,
With the license of this worthy Friar here."
"Madame, tell on," he said. "You have my ear."

The Wife of Bath's Tale

In the old days when King Arthur ruled the nation,
Whom Welshmen speak of with such veneration,
This realm we live in was a fairy land.
The fairy queen danced with her jolly band
On the green meadows where they held dominion.
This was, as I have read, the old opinion;
I speak of many hundred years ago.
But no one sees an elf now, as you know,
For in our time the charity and prayers
And all the begging of these holy friars 10
Who swarm through every nook and every stream
Thicker than motes of dust in a sunbeam,
Blessing our chambers, kitchens, halls, and bowers,
Our cities, towns, and castles, our high towers,
Our villages, our stables, barns, and dairies,
They keep us all from seeing any fairies,
For where you might have come upon an elf
There now you find the holy friar himself
Working his district on industrious legs
And saying his devotions while he begs. 20
Women are safe now under every tree.
No incubus is there unless it's he,
And all they have to fear from him is shame.
It chanced that Arthur had a knight who came
Lustily riding home one day from hawking,

[43] A town forty miles north of London.

And in his path he saw a maiden walking
Before him, stark alone, right in his course.
This young knight took her maidenhead by force,
A crime at which the outcry was so keen
It would have cost his neck, but that the queen, 30
With other ladies, begged the king so long
That Arthur spared his life, for right or wrong,
And gave him to the queen, at her own will,
According to her choice, to save or kill.
She thanked the king, and later told this knight,
Choosing her time, "You are still in such a plight
Your very life has no security.
I grant your life, if you can answer me
This question: what is the thing that most of all
Women desire? Think, or your neck will fall 40
Under the ax! If you cannot let me know
Immediately, I give you leave to go
A twelvemonth and a day, no more, in quest
Of such an answer as will meet the test.
But you must pledge your honor to return
And yield your body, whatever you may learn."
The knight sighed; he was rueful beyond measure.
But what! He could not follow his own pleasure.
He chose at last upon his way to ride
And with such answer as God might provide 50
To come back when the year was at the close.
And so he takes his leave, and off he goes.
He seeks out every house and every place
Where he has any hope, by luck or grace,
Of learning what thing women covet most.
But it seemed he could not light on any coast
Where on this point two people would agree,
For some said wealth and some said jollity,
Some said position, some said sport in bed
And often to be widowed, often wed. 60
Some said that to a woman's heart what mattered
Above all else was to be pleased and flattered.
That shaft, to tell the truth, was a close hit.
Men win us best by flattery, I admit,
And by attention. Some say our greatest ease
Is to be free and do just as we please,
And not to have our faults thrown in our eyes,
But always to be praised for being wise.
And true enough, there's not one of us all
Who will not kick if you rub us on a gall. 70
Whatever vices we may have within,
We won't be taxed with any fault or sin.
Some say that women are delighted well
If it is thought that they will never tell
A secret they are trusted with, or scandal.
But that tale isn't worth an old rake handle!
We women, for a fact, can never hold
A secret. Will you hear a story told?
Then witness Midas! For it can be read

In Ovid that he had upon his head 80
Two ass's ears that he kept out of sight
Beneath his long hair with such skill and sleight
That no one else besides his wife could guess.
He loved her well, and trusted her no less.
He begged her not to make his blemish known,
But keep her knowledge to herself alone.
She swore that never, though to save her skin,
Would she be guilty of so mean a sin,
And yet it seemed to her she nearly died
Keeping a secret locked so long inside. 90
It swelled about her heart so hard and deep
She was afraid some word was bound to leap
Out of her mouth, and since there was no man
She dared to tell, down to a swamp she ran—
Her heart, until she got there, all agog—
And like a bittern booming in the bog
She put her mouth close to the watery ground:
"Water, do not betray me with your sound!
I speak to you, and you alone," she said.
"Two ass's ears grow on my husband's head! 100
And now my heart is whole, now it is out.
I'd burst if I held it longer, past all doubt."
Safely, you see, awhile you may confide
In us, but it will out; we cannot hide
A secret. Look in Ovid if you care
To learn what followed; the whole tale is there.
This knight, when he perceived he could not find
What women covet most, was low in mind;
But the day had come when homeward he must ride,
And as he crossed a wooded countryside 110
Some four and twenty ladies there by chance
He saw, all circling in a woodland dance,
And toward this dance he eagerly drew near
In hope of any counsel he might hear.
But the truth was, he had not reached the place
When dance and all, they vanished into space.
No living soul remained there to be seen
Save an old woman sitting on the green,
As ugly a witch as fancy could devise.
As he approached her she began to rise 120
And said, "Sir knight, here runs no thoroughfare.
What are you seeking with such anxious air?
Tell me! The better may your fortune be.
We old folk know a lot of things," said she.
"Good mother," said the knight, "my life's to pay,
That's all too certain, if I cannot say
What women covet most. If you could tell
That secret to me, I'd requite you well."
"Give me your hand," she answered. "Swear me true
That whatsoever I next ask of you, 130
You'll do it if it lies within your might
And I'll enlighten you before the night."
"Granted, upon my honor," he replied.

"Then I dare boast, and with no empty pride,
Your life is safe," she told him. "Let me die
If the queen herself won't say the same as I.
Let's learn if the haughtiest of all who wear
A net or coverchief upon their hair
Will be so forward as to answer 'no'
To what I'll teach you. No more; let us go." 140
With that she whispered something in his ear,
And told him to be glad and have no fear.
When they had reached the court, the knight declared
That he had kept his day, and was prepared
To give his answer, standing for his life.
Many the wise widow, many the wife,
Many the maid who rallied to the scene,
And at the head as justice sat the queen.
Then silence was enjoined; the knight was told
In open court to say what women hold 150
Precious above all else. He did not stand
Dumb like a beast, but spoke up at command
And plainly offered them his answering word
In manly voice, so that the whole court heard.
"My liege and lady, most of all," said he,
"Women desire to have the sovereignty
And sit in rule and government above
Their husbands, and to have their way in love.
That is what most you want. Spare me or kill
As you may like; I stand here by your will." 160
No widow, wife, or maid gave any token
Of contradicting what the knight had spoken.
He should not die; he should be spared instead;
He was worthy of his life, the whole court said.
The old woman whom the knight met on the green
Sprang up at this. "My sovereign lady queen,
Before your court has risen, do me right!
It was I who taught this answer to the knight,
For which he pledged his honor in my hand,
Solemnly, that the first thing I demand, 170
He would do it, if it lay within his might.
Before the court I ask you, then, sir knight,
To take me," said the woman, "as your wife,
For well you know that I have saved your life.
Deny me, on your honor, if you can."
"Alas," replied this miserable man,
"That was my promise, it must be confessed.
For the love of God, though, choose a new request!
Take all my wealth, and let my body be."
"If that's your tune, then curse both you and me," 180
She said. "Though I am ugly, old, and poor,
I'll have, for all the metal and the ore
That under earth is hidden or lies above,
Nothing, except to be your wife and love."
"My love? No, my damnation, if you can!
Alas," he said, "that any of my clan
Should be so miserably misallied!"

All to no good; force overruled his pride,
And in the end he is constrained to wed,
And marries his old wife and goes to bed. 190
Now some will charge me with an oversight
In failing to describe the day's delight,
The merriment, the food, the dress at least.
But I reply, there was no joy nor feast;
There was only sorrow and sharp misery.
He married her in private, secretly,
And all day after, such was his distress,
Hid like an owl from his wife's ugliness.
Great was the woe this knight had in his head
When in due time they both were brought to bed. 200
He shuddered, tossed, and turned, and all the while
His old wife lay and waited with a smile.
"Is every knight so backward with a spouse?
Is it," she said, "a law in Arthur's house?
I am your love, your own, your wedded wife,
I am the woman who has saved your life.
I have never done you anything but right.
Why do you treat me this way the first night?
You must be mad, the way that you behave!
Tell me my fault, and as God's love can save, 210
I will amend it, truly, if I can."
"Amend it?" answered this unhappy man.
"It can never be amended, truth to tell.
You are so loathsome and so old as well,
And your low birth besides is such a cross
It is no wonder that I turn and toss.
God take my woeful spirit from my breast!"
"Is this," she said, "the cause of your unrest?"
"No wonder!" said the knight. "It truly is."
"Now sir," she said, "I could amend all this 220
Within three days, if it should please me to,
And if you deal with me as you should do.
"But since you speak of that nobility
That comes from ancient wealth and pedigree,
As if *that* constituted gentlemen,
I hold such arrogance not worth a hen!
The man whose virtue is pre-eminent,
In public and alone, always intent
On doing every generous act he can,
Take him—he is the greatest gentleman! 230
Christ wills that we should claim nobility
From him, not from old wealth or family.
Our elders left us all that they were worth
And through their wealth and blood we claim high birth,
But never, since it was beyond their giving,
Could they bequeath to us their virtuous living;
Although it first conferred on them the name
Of gentlemen, they could not leave that claim!
"Dante the Florentine on this was wise:
'Frail is the branch on which man's virtues rise'— 240
Thus runs his rhyme—'God's goodness wills that we

Should claim from him alone nobility.'[44]
Thus from our elders we can only claim
Such temporal things as men may hurt and maim.
"It is clear enough that true nobility
Is not bequeathed along with property,
For many a lord's son does a deed of shame
And yet, God knows, enjoys his noble name.
But though descended from a noble house
And elders who were wise and virtuous, 250
If he will not follow his elders, who are dead,
But leads, himself, a shameful life instead,
He is not noble, be he duke or earl.
It is the churlish deed that makes the churl.
And therefore, my dear husband, I conclude
That though my ancestors were rough and rude,
Yet may Almighty God confer on me
The grace to live, as I hope, virtuously.
Call me of noble blood when I begin
To live in virtue and to cast out sin. 260
"As for my poverty, at which you grieve,
Almighty God in whom we all believe
In willful poverty chose to lead his life,
And surely every man and maid and wife
Can understand that Jesus, heaven's king,
Would never choose a low or vicious thing.
A poor and cheerful life is nobly led;
So Seneca and others have well said.
The man so poor he doesn't have a stitch,
If he thinks himself repaid, I count him rich. 270
He that is covetous, he is the poor man,
Pining to have the things he never can.
It is of cheerful mind, true poverty.
Juvenal[45] says about it happily:
'The poor man as he goes along his way
And passes thieves is free to sing and play.'
Poverty is a good we loathe, a great
Reliever of our busy worldly state,
A great amender also of our minds
As he that patiently will bear it finds. 280
And poverty, for all it seems distressed,
Is a possession no one will contest.
Poverty, too, by bringing a man low,
Helps him the better both God and self to know.
Poverty is a glass where we can see
Which are our true friends, as it seems to me.
So, sir, I do not wrong you on this score;
Reproach me with my poverty no more.
"Now, sir, you tax me with my age; but, sir,
You gentlemen of breeding all aver 290

---

[44] *Purgatorio,* Canto 7.
[45] Roman satiric poet (c. 60–140 C.E.); see *Satires* X for the quote.

That men should not despise old age, but rather
Grant an old man respect, and call him 'father.'
   "If I am old and ugly, as you have said,
You have less fear of being cuckolded,
For ugliness and age, as all agree,
Are notable guardians of chastity.
But since I know in what you take delight,
I'll gratify your worldly appetite.
   "Choose now, which of two courses you will try:
To have me old and ugly till I die 300
But evermore your true and humble wife,
Never displeasing you in all my life,
Or will you have me rather young and fair
And take your chances on who may repair
Either to your house on account of me
Or to some other place, it well may be.
Now make your choice, whichever you prefer."
   The knight took thought, and sighed, and said to her
At last, "My love and lady, my dear wife,
In your wise government I put my life. 310
Choose for yourself which course will best agree
With pleasure and honor, both for you and me.
I do not care, choose either of the two;
I am content, whatever pleases you."
   "Then have I won from you the sovereignty,
Since I may choose and rule at will?" said she.
   He answered, "That is best, I think, dear wife."
   "Kiss me," she said. "Now we are done with strife,
For on my word, I will be both to you,
That is to say, fair, yes, and faithful too. 320
May I die mad unless I am as true
As ever wife was since the world was new.
Unless I am as lovely to be seen
By morning as an empress or a queen
Or any lady between east and west,
Do with my life or death as you think best.
Lift up the curtain, see what you may see."
   And when the knight saw what had come to be
And knew her as she was, so young, so fair,
His joy was such that it was past compare. 330
He took her in his arms and gave her kisses
A thousand times on end; he bathed in blisses.
And she obeyed him also in full measure
In everything that tended to his pleasure.
   And so they lived in full joy to the end.
And now to all us women may Christ send
Submissive husbands, full of youth in bed,
And grace to outlive all the men we wed.
And I pray Jesus to cut short the lives
Of those who won't be governed by their wives; 340
And old, ill-tempered niggards who hate expense,
God promptly bring them down with pestilence!

Words of the Host to the Pardoner

"Now my fine friend," he said, "you Pardoner,
Be quick, tell us a tale of mirth or fun."
"By St. Ninian," he said, "it shall be done,
But at this tavern here, before my tale,
I'll just go in and have some bread and ale."
The proper pilgrims in our company
Cried quickly, "Let him speak no ribaldry!
Tell us a moral tale, one to make clear
Some lesson to us, and we'll gladly hear."
"Just as you wish," he said. "But I must think 10
Of something edifying while I drink."

Prologue to the Pardoner's Tale

"In churches," said the Pardoner, "when I preach,
I use, milords, a lofty style of speech
And ring it out as roundly as a bell,
Knowing by rote all that I have to tell.
My text is ever the same, and ever was:
Radix malorum est cupiditas.[46]
"First I inform them whence I come; that done,
I then display my papal bulls, each one.
I show my license first, my body's warrant,
Sealed by the bishop, for it would be abhorrent 10
If any man made bold, though priest or clerk,
To interrupt me in Christ's holy work.
And after that I give myself full scope.
Bulls in the name of cardinal and pope,
Of bishops and of patriarchs I show.
I say in Latin some few words or so
To spice my sermon; it flavors my appeal
And stirs my listeners to greater zeal.
Then I display my cases made of glass
Crammed to the top with rags and bones. They pass 20
For relics with all the people in the place.
I have a shoulder bone in a metal case,
Part of a sheep owned by a holy Jew.
'Good men,' I say, 'heed what I'm telling you:
Just let this bone be dipped in any well
And if cow, calf, or sheep, or ox should swell
From eating a worm, or by a worm be stung,
Take water from this well and wash its tongue
And it is healed at once. And furthermore
Of scab and ulcers and of every sore 30
Shall every sheep be cured, and that straightway,
That drinks from the same well. Heed what I say:
If the good man who owns the beasts will go,
Fasting, each week, and drink before cockcrow

[46]"Greed is the root of evil" (1 Timothy 6:10).

Out of this well, his cattle shall be brought
To multiply—that holy Jew so taught
Our elders—and his property increase.
"'Moreover, sirs, this bone cures jealousies.
Though into a jealous madness a man fell,
Let him cook his soup in water from this well, 40
He'll never, though for truth he knew her sin,
Suspect his wife again, though she took in
A priest, or even two of them or three.
"'Now here's a mitten that you all can see.
Whoever puts his hand in it shall gain,
When he sows his land, increasing crops of grain,
Be it wheat or oats, provided that he bring
His penny or so to make his offering.
"'There is one word of warning I must say,
Good men and women. If any here today 50
Has done a sin so horrible to name
He daren't be shriven of it for the shame,
Or if any woman, young or old, is here
Who has cuckolded her husband, be it clear
They may not make an offering in that case
To these my relics; they have no power nor grace.
But any who is free of such dire blame,
Let him come up and offer in God's name
And I'll absolve him through the authority
That by the pope's bull has been granted me.' 60
"By such hornswoggling I've won, year by year,
A hundred marks since being a pardoner.
I stand in my pulpit like a true divine,
And when the people sit I preach my line
To ignorant souls, as you have heard before,
And tell skullduggeries by the hundred more.
Then I take care to stretch my neck well out
And over the people I nod and peer about
Just like a pigeon perching on a shed.
My hands fly and my tongue wags in my head 70
So busily that to watch me is a joy.
Avarice is the theme that I employ
In all my sermons, to make the people free
In giving pennies—especially to me.
My mind is fixed on what I stand to win
And not at all upon correcting sin.
I do not care, when they are in the grave,
If souls go berry-picking that I could save.
Truth is that evil purposes determine,
And many a time, the origin of a sermon: 80
Some to please people and by flattery
To gain advancement through hypocrisy,
Some for vainglory, some again for hate.
For when I daren't fight otherwise, I wait
And give him a tongue-lashing when I preach.
No man escapes or gets beyond the reach
Of my defaming tongue, supposing he

Has done a wrong to my brethren or to me.
For though I do not tell his proper name,
People will recognize him all the same. 90
By sign and circumstance I let them learn.
Thus I serve those who have done us an ill turn.
Thus I spit out my venom under hue
Of sanctity, and seem devout and true!
"But to put my purpose briefly, I confess
I preach for nothing but for covetousness.
That's why my text is still and ever was
Radix malorum est cupiditas.
For by this text I can denounce, indeed,
The very vice I practice, which is greed. 100
But though that sin is lodged in my own heart,
I am able to make other people part
From avarice, and sorely to repent,
Though that is not my principal intent.
"Then I bring in examples, many a one,
And tell them many a tale of days long done.
Plain folk love tales that come down from of old.
Such things their minds can well report and hold.
Do you think that while I have the power to preach
And take in silver and gold for what I teach 110
I shall ever live in willful poverty?
No, no, that never was my thought, certainly.
I mean to preach and beg in sundry lands.
I won't do any labor with my hands,
Nor live by making baskets. I don't intend
To beg for nothing; that is not my end.
I won't ape the apostles; I must eat,
I must have money, wool, and cheese, and wheat,
Though I took it from the meanest wretch's tillage
Or from the poorest widow in a village, 120
Yes, though her children starved for want. In fine,
I mean to drink the liquor of the vine
And have a jolly wench in every town.
But, in conclusion, lords, I will get down
To business: you would have me tell a tale.
Now that I've had a drink of corny ale,
By God, I hope the thing I'm going to tell
Is one that you'll have reason to like well.
For though myself a very sinful man,
I can tell a moral tale, indeed I can, 130
One that I use to bring the profits in
While preaching. Now be still, and I'll begin."

THE PARDONER'S TALE

There was a company of young folk living
One time in Flanders, who were bent on giving
Their lives to follies and extravagances,
Brothels and taverns, where they held their dances

With lutes, harps, and guitars, diced at all hours,
And also ate and drank beyond their powers,
Through which they paid the devil sacrifice
In the devil's temple with their drink and dice,
Their abominable excess and dissipation.
They swore oaths that were worthy of damnation; 10
It was grisly to be listening when they swore.
The blessed body of our Lord they tore—
The Jews, it seemed to them, had failed to rend
His body enough—and each laughed at his friend
And fellow in sin. To encourage their pursuits
Came comely dancing girls, peddlers of fruits,
Singers with harps, bawds and confectioners
Who are the very devil's officers
To kindle and blow the fire of lechery
That is the follower of gluttony. 20
Witness the Bible, if licentiousness
Does not reside in wine and drunkenness!
Recall how drunken Lot, unnaturally,
With his two daughters lay unwittingly,
So drunk he had no notion what he did.[47]
Herod, the stories tell us, God forbid,
When full of liquor at his banquet board
Right at his very table gave the word
To kill the Baptist, John, though guiltless he.[48]
Seneca[49] says a good word, certainly. 30
He says there is no difference he can find
Between a man who has gone out of his mind
And one who carries drinking to excess,
Only that madness outlasts drunkenness.
O gluttony, first cause of mankind's fall,
Of our damnation the cursed original
Until Christ bought us with his blood again!
How dearly paid for by the race of men
Was this detestable iniquity!
This whole world was destroyed through gluttony. 40
Adam our father and his wife also
From paradise to labor and to woe
Were driven for that selfsame vice, indeed.
As long as Adam fasted—so I read—
He was in heaven; but as soon as he
Devoured the fruit of that forbidden tree
Then he was driven out in sorrow and pain.
Of gluttony well ought we to complain!
Could a man know how many maladies
Follow indulgences and gluttonies 50
He would keep his diet under stricter measure
And sit at table with more temperate pleasure.
The throat is short and tender is the mouth,

[47] Genesis 19:30–36.
[48] Mark 6:17–29.
[49] Roman stoic philosopher, dramatist, and statesman (c. 4 B.C.E.–65 C.E.).

And hence men toil east, west, and north, and south,
In earth, and air, and water—alas to think—
Fetching a glutton dainty meat and drink.
  This is a theme, O Paul, that you well treat:
"Meat unto belly, and belly unto meat,
God shall destroy them both," as Paul has said.[50]
When a man drinks the white wine and the red— 60
This is a foul word, by my soul, to say,
And fouler is the deed in every way—
He makes his throat his privy through excess.
  The Apostle says, weeping for piteousness,
"There are many of whom I told you—at a loss
I say it, weeping—enemies of Christ's cross,
Whose belly is their god; their end is death."[51]
O cursed belly! Sack of stinking breath
In which corruption lodges, dung abounds!
At either end of you come forth foul sounds. 70
Great cost it is to fill you, and great pain!
These cooks, how they must grind and pound and strain
And transform substance into accident
To please your cravings, though exorbitant!
From the hard bones they knock the marrow out.
They'll find a use for everything, past doubt,
That down the gullet sweet and soft will glide.
The spiceries of leaf and root provide
Sauces that are concocted for delight,
To give a man a second appetite. 80
But truly, he whom gluttonies entice
Is dead, while he continues in that vice.
  O drunken man, disfigured is your face,
Sour is your breath, foul are you to embrace!
You seem to mutter through your drunken nose
The sound of "Samson, Samson," yet God knows
That Samson never indulged himself in wine.[52]
Your tongue is lost, you fall like a stuck swine,
And all the self-respect that you possess
Is gone, for of man's judgment, drunkenness 90
Is the very sepulcher and annihilation.
A man whom drink has under domination
Can never keep a secret in his head.
Now steer away from both the white and red,
And most of all from that white wine keep wide
That comes from Lepe. They sell it in Cheapside
And Fish Street.[53] It's a Spanish wine, and sly
To creep in other wines that grow nearby,
And such a vapor it has that with three drinks
It takes a man to Spain; although he thinks 100
He is home in Cheapside, he is far away
At Lepe. Then "Samson, Samson" will he say!

---

[50] 1 Corinthians 6:13.
[51] St. Paul; Philippians 3:18–19.
[52] Judges 13–16.
[53] Market streets in London.

By God himself, who is omnipotent,
All the great exploits in the Old Testament
Were done in abstinence, I say, and prayer.
Look in the Bible, you may learn it there.
Attila,[54] conqueror of many a place,
Died in his sleep in shame and in disgrace
Bleeding out of his nose in drunkenness.
A captain ought to live in temperateness! 110
And more than this, I say, remember well
The injunction that was laid on Lemuel—
Not Samuel, but Lemuel, I say!
Read in the Bible; in the plainest way
Wine is forbidden to judges and to kings.[55]
This will suffice; no more upon these things.
Now that I've shown what gluttony will do,
Now I will warn you against gambling, too;
Gambling, the very mother of low scheming,
Of lying and forswearing and blaspheming 120
Against Christ's name, of murder and waste as well
Alike of goods and time; and, truth to tell,
With honor and renown it cannot suit
To be held a common gambler by repute.
The higher a gambler stands in power and place,
The more his name is lowered in disgrace.
If a prince gambles, whatever his kingdom be,
In his whole government and policy
He is, in all the general estimation,
Considered so much less in reputation. 130
Stilbon, who was a wise ambassador,
From Lacedaemon once to Corinth bore
A mission of alliance.[56] When he came
It happened that he found there at a game
Of hazard all the great ones of the land,
And so, as quickly as it could be planned,
He stole back, saying, "I will not lose my name
Nor have my reputation put to shame
Allying you with gamblers. You may send
Other wise emissaries to gain your end, 140
For by my honor, rather than ally
My countrymen to gamblers, I will die.
For you that are so gloriously renowned
Shall never with this gambling race be bound
By will of mine or treaty I prepare."
Thus did this wise philosopher declare.
Remember also how the Parthians'[57] lord
Sent King Demetrius, as the books record,
A pair of golden dice, by this proclaiming
His scorn, because that king was known for gaming, 150
And the king of Parthia therefore held his crown

---

[54]Leader of the Huns, who invaded Europe in the fifth century C.E.
[55]Lemuel's mother told him that kings should not drink wine (Proverbs 31:4).
[56]Lacedaemon (Sparta) and Corinth are ancient city-states in Greece.
[57]The Parthians, from Persia, defeated the Romans in 53 B.C.E.

Devoid of glory, value, or renown.
Lords can discover other means of play
More suitable to while the time away.
Now about oaths I'll say a word or two,
Great oaths and false oaths, as the old books do.
Great swearing is a thing abominable,
And false oaths yet more reprehensible.
Almighty God forbade swearing at all,
Matthew be witness; but specially I call 160
The holy Jeremiah on this head.
"Swear thine oaths truly, do not lie," he said.
"Swear under judgment, and in righteousness."[58]
But idle swearing is a great wickedness.
Consult and see, and he that understands
In the first table of the Lord's commands
Will find the second of his commandments this:
"Take not the Lord's name idly or amiss."
If a man's oaths and curses are extreme,
Vengeance shall find his house, both roof and beam. 170
"By the precious heart of God," and "By his nails"—
"My chance is seven, by Christ's blood at Hailes,[59]
Yours five and three." "Cheat me, and if you do,
By God's arms, with this knife I'll run you through!"—
Such fruit comes from the bones, that pair of bitches:
Oaths broken, treachery, murder. For the riches
Of Christ's love, give up curses, without fail,
Both great and small!—Now, sirs, I'll tell my tale.
These three young roisterers of whom I tell
Long before prime had rung from any bell 180
Were seated in a tavern at their drinking,
And as they sat, they heard a bell go clinking
Before a corpse being carried to his grave.
One of these roisterers, when he heard it, gave
An order to his boy: "Go out and try
To learn whose corpse is being carried by.
Get me his name, and get it right. Take heed."
"Sir," said the boy, "there isn't any need.
I learned before you came here, by two hours.
He was, it happens, an old friend of yours, 190
And all at once, there on his bench upright
As he was sitting drunk, he was killed last night.
A sly thief, Death men call him, who deprives
All the people in this country of their lives,
Came with his spear and smiting his heart in two
Went on his business with no more ado.
A thousand have been slaughtered by his hand
During this plague. And, sir, before you stand
Within his presence, it should be necessary,
It seems to me, to know your adversary. 200
Be evermore prepared to meet this foe.
My mother taught me thus; that's all I know."

[58]Matthew 5:34; Jeremiah 4:2.
[59]An abbey in Gloucester said to have some of Christ's blood.

"Now by St. Mary," said the innkeeper,
"This child speaks truth. Man, woman, laborer,
Servant, and child the thief has slain this year
In a big village a mile or more from here.
I think it is his place of habitation.
It would be wise to make some preparation
Before he brought a man into disgrace."
"God's arms!" this roisterer said. "So that's the case! 210
Is it so dangerous with this thief to meet?
I'll look for him by every path and street,
I vow it, by God's holy bones! Hear me,
Fellows of mine, we are all one, we three.
Let each of us hold up his hand to the other
And each of us become his fellow's brother.
We'll slay this Death, who slaughters and betrays.
He shall be slain whose hand so many slays,
By the dignity of God, before tonight!"
The three together set about to plight 220
Their oaths to live and die each for the other
Just as though each had been to each born brother.
And in their drunken frenzy up they get
And toward the village off at once they set
Which the innkeeper had spoken of before,
And many were the grisly oaths they swore.
They rent Christ's precious body limb from limb—
Death shall be dead, if they lay hands on him!
When they had hardly gone the first half mile,
Just as they were about to cross a stile, 230
An old man, poor and humble, met them there.
The old man greeted them with a meek air
And said, "God bless you, lords, and be your guide."
"What's this?" the proudest of the three replied.
"Old beggar, I hope you meet with evil grace!
Why are you all wrapped up except your face?
What are you doing alive so many a year?"
The old man at these words began to peer
Into this gambler's face. "Because I can,
Though I should walk to India, find no man," 240
He said, "in any village or any town,
Who for my age is willing to lay down
His youth. So I must keep my old age still
For as long a time as it may be God's will.
Nor will Death take my life from me, alas!
Thus like a restless prisoner I pass
And on the ground, which is my mother's gate,
I walk and with my staff both early and late
I knock and say, 'Dear mother, let me in!
See how I vanish, flesh, and blood, and skin! 250
Alas, when shall my bones be laid to rest?
I would exchange with you my clothing chest,
Mother, that in my chamber long has been
For an old haircloth rag to wrap me in.'
And yet she still refuses me that grace.
All white, therefore, and withered is my face.

"But, sirs, you do yourselves no courtesy
To speak to an old man so churlishly
Unless he had wronged you either in word or deed.
As you yourselves in Holy Writ may read, 260
'Before an aged man whose head is hoar
Men ought to rise.'[60] I counsel you, therefore,
No harm nor wrong here to an old man do,
No more than you would have men do to you
In your old age, if you so long abide.
And God be with you, whether you walk or ride!
I must go yonder where I have to go."
"No, you old beggar, by St. John, not so,"
Said another of these gamblers. "As for me,
By God, you won't get off so easily! 270
You spoke just now of that false traitor, Death,
Who in this land robs all our friends of breath.
Tell where he is, since you must be his spy,
Or you will suffer for it, so say I
By God and by the holy sacrament.
You are in league with him, false thief, and bent
On killing us young folk, that's clear to my mind."
"If you are so impatient, sirs, to find
Death," he replied, "turn up this crooked way,
For in that grove I left him, truth to say, 280
Beneath a tree, and there he will abide.
No boast of yours will make him run and hide.
Do you see that oak tree? Just there you will find
This Death, and God, who bought again mankind,
Save and amend you!" So said this old man;
And promptly each of these three gamblers ran
Until he reached the tree, and there they found
Florins of fine gold, minted bright and round,
Nearly eight bushels of them, as they thought.
And after Death no longer then they sought. 290
Each of them was so ravished at the sight,
So fair the florins glittered and so bright,
That down they sat beside the precious hoard.
The worst of them, he uttered the first word.
"Brothers," he told them, "listen to what I say.
My head is sharp, for all I joke and play.
Fortune has given us this pile of treasure
To set us up in lives of ease and pleasure.
Lightly it comes, lightly we'll make it go.
God's precious dignity! Who was to know 300
We'd ever tumble on such luck today?
If we could only carry this gold away,
Home to my house, or either one of yours—
For well you know that all this gold is ours—
We'd touch the summit of felicity.
But still, by daylight that can hardly be.
People would call us thieves, too bold for stealth,

[60] Leviticus 19:32.

And they would have us hanged for our own wealth.
It must be done by night, that's our best plan,
As prudently and slyly as we can. 310
Hence my proposal is that we should all
Draw lots, and let's see where the lot will fall,
And the one of us who draws the shortest stick
Shall run back to the town, and make it quick,
And bring us bread and wine here on the sly,
And two of us will keep a watchful eye
Over this gold; and if he doesn't stay
Too long in town, we'll carry this gold away
By night, wherever we all agree it's best."
One of them held the cut out in his fist 320
And had them draw to see where it would fall,
And the cut fell on the youngest of them all.
At once he set off on his way to town,
And the very moment after he was gone
The one who urged this plan said to the other:
"You know that by sworn oath you are my brother.
I'll tell you something you can profit by.
Our friend has gone, that's clear to any eye,
And here is gold, abundant as can be,
That we propose to share alike, we three. 330
But if I worked it out, as I could do,
So that it could be shared between us two,
Wouldn't that be a favor, a friendly one?"
The other answered, "How that can be done,
I don't quite see. He knows we have the gold.
What shall we do, or what shall he be told?"
"Will you keep the secret tucked inside your head?
And in a few words," the first scoundrel said,
"I'll tell you how to bring this end about."
"Granted," the other told him. "Never doubt, 340
I won't betray you, that you can believe."
"Now," said the first, "we are two, as you perceive,
And two of us must have more strength than one.
When he sits down, get up as if in fun
And wrestle with him. While you play this game
I'll run him through the ribs. You do the same
With your dagger there, and then this gold shall be
Divided, dear friend, between you and me.
Then all that we desire we can fulfill,
And both of us can roll the dice at will." 350
Thus in agreement these two scoundrels fell
To slay the third, as you have heard me tell.
The youngest, who had started off to town,
Within his heart kept rolling up and down
The beauty of these florins, new and bright.
"O Lord," he thought, "were there some way I might
Have all this treasure to myself alone,
There isn't a man who dwells beneath God's throne
Could live a life as merry as mine should be!"
And so at last the fiend, our enemy, 360
Put in his head that he could gain his ends

If he bought poison to kill off his friends.
Finding his life in such a sinful state,
The devil was allowed to seal his fate.
For it was altogether his intent
To kill his friends, and never to repent.
So off he set, no longer would he tarry,
Into the town, to an apothecary,
And begged for poison; he wanted it because
He meant to kill his rats; besides, there was 370
A polecat living in his hedge, he said,
Who killed his capons; and when he went to bed
He wanted to take vengeance, if he might,
On vermin that devoured him by night.
    The apothecary answered, "You shall have
A drug that as I hope the Lord will save
My soul, no living thing in all creation,
Eating or drinking of this preparation
A dose no bigger than a grain of wheat,
But promptly with his death-stroke he shall meet. 380
Die, that he will, and in a briefer while
Than you can walk the distance of a mile,
This poison is so strong and virulent."
    Taking the poison, off the scoundrel went,
Holding it in a box, and next he ran
To the neighboring street, and borrowed from a man
Three generous flagons. He emptied out his drug
In two of them, and kept the other jug
For his own drink; he let no poison lurk
In that! And so all night he meant to work 390
Carrying off the gold. Such was his plan,
And when he had filled them, this accursed man
Retraced his path, still following his design,
Back to his friends with his three jugs of wine.
    But why dilate upon it any more?
For just as they had planned his death before,
Just so they killed him, and with no delay.
When it was finished, one spoke up to say:
"Now let's sit down and drink, and we can bury
His body later on. First we'll be merry," 400
And as he said the words, he took the jug
That, as it happened, held the poisonous drug,
And drank, and gave his friend a drink as well,
And promptly they both died. But truth to tell,
In all that Avicenna[61] ever wrote
He never described in chapter, rule, or note
More marvelous signs of poisoning, I suppose,
Than appeared in these two wretches at the close.
Thus they both perished for their homicide,
And thus the traitorous poisoner also died. 410
    O sin accursed above all cursedness,
O treacherous murder, O foul wickedness,

[61] Persian philosopher and physician (980–1037 C.E.) who interpreted Aristotle and wrote influential medical treatises.

O gambling, lustfulness, and gluttony,
Traducer of Christ's name by blasphemy
And monstrous oaths, through habit and through pride!
Alas, mankind! Ah, how may it betide
That you to your Creator, he that wrought you
And even with his precious heart's blood bought you,
So falsely and ungratefully can live?
  And now, good men, your sins may God forgive 420
And keep you specially from avarice!
My holy pardon will avail in this,
For it can heal each one of you that brings
His pennies, silver brooches, spoons, or rings.
Come, bow your head under this holy bull!
You wives, come offer up your cloth or wool!
I write your names here in my roll, just so.
Into the bliss of heaven you shall go!
I will absolve you here by my high power,
You that will offer, as clean as in the hour 430
When you were born. —Sirs, thus I preach. And now
Christ Jesus, our souls' healer, show you how
Within his pardon evermore to rest,
For that, I will not lie to you, is best.
  But in my tale, sirs, I forgot one thing.
The relics and the pardons that I bring
Here in my pouch, no man in the whole land
Has finer, given me by the pope's own hand.
If any of you devoutly wants to offer
And have my absolution, come and proffer 440
Whatever you have to give. Kneel down right here,
Humbly, and take my pardon, full and clear,
Or have a new, fresh pardon if you like
At the end of every mile of road we strike,
As long as you keep offering ever newly
Good coins, not counterfeit, but minted truly.
Indeed it is an honor I confer
On each of you, an authentic pardoner
Going along to absolve you as you ride.
For in the country mishaps may betide— 450
One or another of you in due course
May break his neck by falling from his horse.
Think what security it gives you all
That in this company I chanced to fall
Who can absolve you each, both low and high,
When the soul, alas, shall from the body fly!
By my advice, our Host here shall begin,
For he's the man enveloped most by sin.
Come, offer first, Sir Host, and once that's done,
Then you shall kiss the relics, every one, 460
Yes, for a penny! Come, undo your purse!
  "No, no," said he. "Then I should have Christ's curse!
I'll do nothing of the sort, for love or riches!
You'd make me kiss a piece of your old britches
And for a saintly relic make it pass
Although it had the tincture of your ass.

By the cross St. Helen found in the Holy Land,
I wish I had your balls here in my hand
For relics! Cut 'em off, and I'll be bound
If I don't help you carry them around. 470
I'll have the things enshrined in a hog's turd!"
The Pardoner did not answer; not a word,
He was so angry, could he find to say.
"Now," said our Host, "I will not try to play
With you, nor any other angry man."
Immediately the worthy Knight began,
When he saw that all the people laughed, "No more,
This has gone far enough. Now as before,
Sir Pardoner, be gay, look cheerfully,
And you, Sir Host, who are so dear to me, 480
Come, kiss the Pardoner, I beg of you,
And Pardoner, draw near, and let us do
As we've been doing, let us laugh and play."
And so they kissed, and rode along their way.

CHRISTINE DE PIZAN
[C. 1365–C. 1430]

As Chaucer's Wife of Bath's stories about her fifth husband suggest, misogynist literature abounded in Europe during the Middle Ages. Misogynist diatribes and assumptions in books were so commonplace that they went nearly unremarked by male readers and often by female readers as well. Stereotypes such as these from Jean de Meun's *Romance of the Rose* were typical:

> All women are, have been, and e'er will be
> In thought if not in deed, unvirtuous,
> Though some may hesitate to do the act,
> None can restrain their wish.

If a book portrayed women as deceitful, spendthrift, vain, greedy, lustful betrayers, well, that was simply the way things were; everyone, even the most learned writers, said so. Surely there must have been many real women who, like the fictional Wife of Bath, spoke out against the complacent slander, but Christine de Pizan, a young widow and mother of three, was the first European woman to take issue in print and in an accessible vernacular language with the drearily familiar litanies of women's vices and moral deformities. Stung into action by reading yet one more smug and badly written attack upon her sex, she began to create her extraordinary work, *The Book of the City of Ladies,* a comprehensive history and defense of womankind that is at once deeply medieval in its allegorical form and surprisingly modern in a number of the feminist issues it fearlessly raises, issues such as rape and the physical abuse of women. The book had fallen from notice by the mid-sixteenth century, but for about a century and a half after its appearance in 1405 it was a popular and influential text: de Pizan was read by writers of succeeding generations such as Alain Chartier, Marguerite de Navarre, and François Rabelais. Significantly, a number of women rulers during the Renaissance—Marguerite of Austria, Mary of Hungary, Anne of Brittany, among them—are known to have possessed manuscripts of her work.

Life

Christine de Pizan was born in Venice to Italian parents in about 1365. Her mother was well-born; her father, the physician Tommaso de Pizzano, was serving as an astrological consultant to the Venetian Republic at the time of his daughter's birth; astrology was then still a respected science considered closely allied to both medicine and astronomy. De Pizan was about four when her father accepted a post as royal astrologer at the Parisian court of Charles V, a skilled and enlightened ruler. Raised in that secure atmosphere of intellectual warmth and light, she grew to identify herself as French; she spent the rest of her life in France, and although she must surely have felt herself to be always slightly on the outside, today she is considered a French writer.

Tommaso de Pizzano observed that his daughter was intellectually gifted and eager to learn, and she tells us in *The Book of the City of Ladies* that despite her mother's protests he saw to it that she received some education, though how or what she was taught is not clear. She mentions a "natural inclination" to the sciences that was thwarted by her mother's desire to keep her busy "with spinning and silly girlishness," but adds that even her mother's efforts could not deprive her of love for the knowledge she had managed "to gather in little droplets." Certainly as an adult writer she exhibits a wide range of knowledge, not only of literary matters, but of such subjects as politics, mythography, and history; she even wrote a learned treatise on arms and weaponry.

Whatever education she received, at the age of about fifteen she married Étienne du Castel, a promising young university graduate who was appointed a secretary to the king. By all evidence their marriage was a supremely happy one; after his death, de Pizan would write that no other man in her judgment could surpass Étienne "in kindness, peacefulness, loyalty, and true love." But shadows began to gather as Charles V died later in the first year of de Pizan's marriage. Until his son, Charles VI, reached his majority, France was ruled by Charles' rivalrous uncles, Philip, the Duke of Burgundy, and Louis II, the Duke of Bourbon, around whom opposing factions gathered. France would remain unstable throughout their regency and Charles VI's reign. De Pizan's beloved father died in 1387, and three years later, in 1390, in the tenth year of their marriage, her husband died suddenly while on a diplomatic mission with Charles VI, the weak young king. At twenty-five, de Pizan found herself a grieving widow faced with supporting her mother, her own three children, and a niece, for her father had lost most of the family money before his death, and the estates of both father and husband proved to be tied up in complex lawsuits that would take nearly fifteen years to untangle.

Precipitated into a daunting world of unscrupulous lawyers and creditors and pressing need, de Pizan proved a capable and courageous head of household. She decided to make her living as a writer, and set out on a determined course of self-education and the promotion of her work; she is often called the first professional writer in Europe. By 1393, the heartfelt elegaic poetry she had written when she was freshly bereaved gave way to the chivalric forms of love poetry that were enjoying a nostalgic revival, as she produced rondeaus, ballades, and virelais, the kind of conventional verse she knew would find a popular audience. This skill earned her a place at the court of the Duke of Orléans, and later at the court of his rival, the Duke of Burgundy. Of necessity, she gravitated toward whichever court could offer the most help and protection to her and her family. The Duke of Burgundy found a place for one of her adolescent sons at court and also commissioned Christine to write the biography of his brother, Charles V, her first prose work, which she published in 1404.

Between 1399 and 1403, de Pizan became involved in an ongoing debate among learned authorities over the misogyny of *The Romance of the Rose.* This long poem was begun in about 1225 by a poet named Guillaume de Lorris, who set out to tell the allegorical story of one Amant, a lover who seeks to win a beautiful Rose. De Lorris' text breaks off before Amant succeeds in his quest. About fifty years later, Jean de Meun, hoping to capitalize on the popularity of the old poem, wrote a much-admired expansion and continuation of the *Romance,* weaving into his new material many accounts of women's deceptions, treacheries, and weaknesses. De Pizan deplored the influence the poem's sour view of women might have upon young men. Many scholars entered into the fray, siding with de Pizan or defending de Meun; although she had not begun the quarrel, she became one of the most famous of its participants, especially when she presented a copy of the letters she and others had exchanged on the subject to Queen Isabeau of Bavaria in 1402.

De Pizan had been turning her hand to longer narrative poetry since about 1400. Now, in response to *The Romance of the Rose* and to countless works of lesser literary merit, she began her master work, *The Book of the City of Ladies,* which appeared in 1405. In that same year she also wrote *Christine's Vision (Avision-Christine),* a surrealistic semi-autobiographical dream vision that also has much to say about the condition of her beloved France.

In the summer of that year, the instability that had long threatened France began to gather to a head as the two rival dukedoms of Orléans and Burgundy began to battle openly. From 1405 until the end of her life, probably between 1429 and 1431, de Pizan's writings show her being drawn more and more into questions of politics and government. She produced whole books on subjects pertaining to statecraft: *The Book of the Body Politic* (1406–1407); *Feats of Arms and Chivalry* (1410), published anonymously because no one would credit a woman with being an expert on that masculine subject; and *The Book of Peace* (1414). From the convent she prudently entered in about 1418 as Paris became more wracked by factional disturbances, she penned letters to ruling monarchs advising them to exercise their roles as peacemakers, protesting abuses in government, and urging that princes be adequately educated to fit them for their tasks. She was stirred by the appearance of Joan of Arc, the heroic young woman who came forward from the peasantry in 1429 to lead the siege of Orléans and ensure the coronation of Charles VII; her last known work, *The Poem of Joan of Arc,* fittingly celebrates this female warrior, and was apparently composed before Joan's enemies brought her to the stake in 1431.

WORK

The Book of the City of Ladies, excerpted here, begins like many medieval dream visions, including *The Divine Comedy,* in an hour of despair. But here is a uniquely *female* hour of despair, as the narrator Christine struggles with the sexist ideas even she has unthinkingly absorbed, and contrasts what authorities say of women with what experience teaches her of women's goodness. She questions how a good God might have willfully shaped such imperfect creatures as women are said to be and, finally, cries out to ask God why he did not let her be born a man so that she might serve him better. Through her downcast eyes she suddenly sees a ray of light spread over her lap, and she raises her eyes to the three allegorical figures of Reason, Rectitude, and Justice. They have come to guide her in building the shining City of Ladies, and she need never again lower her head in shame and weeping on account of her gender. In turn, each of the great ladies instructs her, refuting sexist canards largely by example, telling story after story of women who were warriors, queens, scholars, poets, prophets, loyal daughters and wives, and blessed saints. If much of her material is borrowed from Boccaccio, and her governing metaphor of the blessed community comes from St. Augustine's *City of God,* de Pizan's organization and intent as well as her woman's voice and stance transform these borrowings into her own unique work. Her pen, she tells us, is her trowel; her ink is her mortar. Every story told in her text, every portrait of a good woman, is another stone in the walls of this city that is at once a fair dwelling place and a well-defended citadel, for Christine de Pizan's City is nothing less than the reconstructed history of her sex, built from the ground up. Within that storied City, her own contemporary female readers, the spirits of their foremothers, and the generations of the daughters yet to be born may safely go about their affairs in a place where they are not raped, where they are not beaten, where they are not enlisted against one another, and where they are not ravaged by vicious stereotypes. Here in the City of Ladies, says de Pizan, they shall be judged fairly and their good deeds honored in the land.

Suggested Readings

The only available English translation of de Pizan's *The Book of the City of Ladies* is the excellent one by Earl Jeffrey Richards (1982), which is accompanied by a useful foreword by Marina Warner. Charity Cannon Willard's *Christine de Pizan: Her Life and Works* (1984) is an excellent critical biography; Diane Bornstein has edited a collection of essays, *Ideals for Women in the Works of Christine de Pizan* (1981), that consider a variety of feminist issues in de Pizan.

The Book of the City of Ladies

Translated by Earl Jeffrey Richards

Book I

1

[Here begins the book of the City of Ladies, whose first chapter tells why and for what purpose this book was written.]

One day as I was sitting alone in my study surrounded by books on all kinds of subjects, devoting myself to literary studies, my usual habit, my mind dwelt at length on the weighty opinions of various authors whom I had studied for a long time. I looked up from my book, having decided to leave such subtle questions in peace and to relax by reading some light poetry. With this in mind, I searched for some small book. By chance a strange volume came into my hands, not one of my own, but one which had been given to me along with some others. When I held it open and saw from its title page that it was by Mathéolus,[1] I smiled, for though I had never seen it before, I had often heard that like other books it discussed respect for women. I thought I would browse through it to amuse myself. I had not been reading for very long when my good mother called me to refresh myself with some supper, for it was evening. Intending to look at it the next day, I put it down. The next morning, again seated in my study as was my habit, I remembered wanting to examine this book by Mathéolus. I started to read it and went on for a little while. Because the subject seemed to me not very pleasant for people who do not enjoy lies, and of no use in developing virtue or manners, given its lack of integrity in diction and theme, and after browsing here and there and reading the end, I put it down in order to turn my attention to more elevated and useful study. But just the

[1]Mathéolus (fl. 1300) wrote a conventional tirade against women in Ovidian verse entitled *The Book of the Lamentations of Mathéolus*.

sight of this book, even though it was of no authority, made me wonder how it happened that so many different men—and learned men among them—have been and are so inclined to express both in speaking and in their treatises and writings so many wicked insults about women and their behavior. Not only one or two and not even just this Mathéolus (for this book had a bad name anyway and was intended as a satire) but, more generally, judging from the treatises of all philosophers and poets and from all the orators—it would take too long to mention their names—it seems that they all speak from one and the same mouth. They all concur in one conclusion: that the behavior of women is inclined to and full of every vice. Thinking deeply about these matters, I began to examine my character and conduct as a natural woman and, similarly, I considered other women whose company I frequently kept, princesses, great ladies, women of the middle and lower classes, who had graciously told me of their most private and intimate thoughts, hoping that I could judge impartially and in good conscience whether the testimony of so many notable men could be true. To the best of my knowledge, no matter how long I confronted or dissected the problem, I could not see or realize how their claims could be true when compared to the natural behavior and character of women. Yet I still argued vehemently against women, saying that it would be impossible that so many famous men—such solemn scholars, possessed of such deep and great understanding, so clear-sighted in all things, as it seemed—could have spoken falsely on so many occasions that I could hardly find a book on morals where, even before I had read it in its entirety, I did not find several chapters or certain sections attacking women, no matter who the author was. This reason alone, in short, made me conclude that, although my intellect did not perceive my own great faults and, likewise, those of other women because of its simpleness and ignorance, it was however truly fitting that such was the case. And so I relied more on the judgment of others than on what I myself felt and knew. I was so transfixed in this line of thinking for such a long time that it seemed as if I were in a stupor. Like a gushing fountain, a series of authorities, whom I recalled one after another, came to mind, along with their opinions on this topic. And I finally decided that God formed a vile creature when He made woman, and I wondered how such a worthy artisan could have deigned to make such an abominable work which, from what they say, is the vessel as well as the refuge and abode of every evil and vice. As I was thinking this, a great unhappiness and sadness welled up in my heart, for I detested myself and the entire feminine sex, as though we were monstrosities in nature. And in my lament I spoke these words:

"Oh, God, how can this be? For unless I stray from my faith, I must never doubt that Your infinite wisdom and most perfect goodness ever created anything which was not good. Did You yourself not create woman in a very special way and since that time did You not give her all those inclinations which it pleased You for her to have? And how could it be that You could go wrong in anything? Yet look at all these accusations which have been judged, decided, and concluded against women. I do not know how to understand this repugnance. If it is so, fair Lord God, that in fact so many abominations abound in the female sex, for You Yourself say that the testimony of two or three witnesses lends credence, why shall I not doubt that this is true? Alas, God, why did You not let me be born in the world as a man, so that all my inclinations would be to serve You better, and so that I would not stray in anything and would be as perfect as a man is said to be? But since Your kindness has not been extended to me, then forgive my negligence in Your service, most fair Lord God, and may it not displease You, for the servant who receives fewer gifts from his lord is less obliged in his service." I spoke these words to God in my lament and a great deal more for a very long time in sad reflection, and in my folly I considered myself most unfortunate because God had made me inhabit a female body in this world.

2

[Here Christine describes how three ladies appeared to her and how the one who was in front spoke first and comforted her in her pain.]

So occupied with these painful thoughts, my head bowed in shame, my eyes filled with tears, leaning on the pommel of my chair's armrest, I suddenly saw a ray of light fall on my lap, as though it were the sun. I shuddered then, as if wakened from sleep, for I was sitting in a shadow where the sun could not have shone at that hour. And as I lifted my head to see where this light was coming from, I saw three crowned ladies standing before me, and the splendor of their bright faces shone on me and throughout the entire room. Now no one would ask whether I was surprised, for my doors were shut and they had still entered. Fearing that some phantom had come to tempt me and filled with great fright, I made the Sign of the Cross on my forehead.

Then she who was the first of the three smiled and began to speak, "Dear daughter, do not be afraid, for we have not come here to harm or trouble you but to console you, for we have taken pity on your distress, and we have come to bring you out of the ignorance which so blinds your own intellect that you shun what you know for a certainty and believe what you do not know or see or recognize except by virtue of many strange opinions. You resemble the fool in the prank who was dressed in women's clothes while he slept; because those who were making fun of him repeatedly told him he was a woman, he believed their false testimony more readily than the certainty of his own identity. Fair daughter, have you lost all sense? Have you forgotten that when fine gold is tested in the furnace, it does not change or vary in strength but becomes purer the more it is hammered and handled in different ways? Do you not know that the best things are the most debated and the most discussed? If you wish to consider the question of the highest form of reality, which consists in ideas or celestial substances, consider whether the greatest philosophers who have lived and whom you support against your own sex have ever resolved whether ideas are false and contrary to the truth. Notice how these same philosophers contradict and criticize one another, just as you have seen in the *Metaphysics* where Aristotle takes their opinions to task and speaks similarly of Plato and other philosophers. And note, moreover, how even Saint Augustine and the Doctors of the Church have criticized Aristotle in certain passages, although he is known as the prince of philosophers in whom both natural and moral philosophy attained their highest level. It also seems that you think that all the words of the philosophers are articles of faith, that they could never be wrong. As far as the poets of whom you speak are concerned, do you not know that they spoke on many subjects in a fictional way and that often they mean the contrary of what their words openly say? One can interpret them according to the grammatical figure of *antiphrasis,* which means, as you know, that if you call something bad, in fact, it is good, and also vice versa. Thus I advise you to profit from their works and to interpret them in the manner in which they are intended in those passages where they attack women. Perhaps this man, who called himself Mathéolus in his own book, intended it in such a way, for there are many things which, if taken literally, would be pure heresy. As for the attack against the estate of marriage—which is a holy estate, worthy and ordained by God—made not only by Mathéolus but also by others and even by the *Romance of the Rose*[2] where greater credibility is averred because of the authority of its author, it is evident and proven by experience that the contrary of the evil which they posit and claim to be found in this estate through the obligation and fault of women is true. For where has the husband ever been found who would allow his wife to have authority to abuse and insult him as a matter of course, as these authorities maintain? I believe that, regardless of what you might have read, you will never see such a husband with your own eyes, so badly colored are these lies. Thus, in conclusion, I tell you, dear friend, that simplemindedness has prompted you to hold such an opinion. Come back to yourself, recover your senses, and do not trouble yourself anymore over such absurdities. For you know that any evil spoken of women so generally only hurts those who say it, not women themselves."

3

[Here Christine tells how the lady who had said this showed her who she was and what her character and function were and told her how she would construct a city with the help of these same three ladies.]

The famous lady spoke these words to me, in whose presence I do not know which one of my senses was more overwhelmed: my hearing from having listened to such worthy words or my sight from having seen her radiant beauty, her attire, her reverent comportment, and her most honored countenance. The same was true of the others, so that I did not know which one to look at, for the three ladies resembled each other so much that they could be told apart only with difficulty, except for the last one, for although she was of no less authority than the others, she had so fierce a visage that whoever, no matter how daring, looked in her eyes would be afraid to commit a crime, for it seemed that she threatened criminals unceasingly. Having stood up out of respect, I looked at them without saying a word, like someone too overwhelmed to utter a syllable. Reflecting on who these beings could be, I felt much admiration in my heart and, if I could have dared, I would have immediately asked their names and identities and what was the meaning of the different scepters which each one carried in her right hand, which were of fabulous richness, and why they had come here. But since I considered myself unworthy to address these questions to such high ladies as they appeared to me, I did not dare to, but continued to keep my gaze fixed on them, half-afraid and half-reassured by the words which I had heard, which had made me reject my first impression. But the most wise lady who had spoken to me and who knew in her mind what I was thinking, as one who has insight into everything, addressed my reflections, saying:

"Dear daughter, know that God's providence, which leaves nothing void or empty, has ordained that we, though celestial beings, remain and circulate among the people of the world here below, in order to bring order and maintain in balance those institutions we created according to the will of God in the fulfillment of various offices, that God whose daughters we three all are and from whom we were born. Thus it is my duty to straighten out men and women when they go astray and to put them back on the right path. And when they stray, if they have enough understanding to see me, I come to them quietly in spirit and preach to them, showing them their error and how they have failed, I assign them the causes,

[2] See the headnote to de Pizan for the significance of this text in de Pizan's life.

and then I teach them what to do and what to avoid. Since I serve to demonstrate clearly and to show both in thought and deed to each man and woman his or her own special qualities and faults, you see me holding this shiny mirror which I carry in my right hand in place of a scepter. I would thus have you know truly that no one can look into this mirror, no matter what kind of creature, without achieving clear self-knowledge. My mirror has such great dignity that not without reason is it surrounded by rich and precious gems, so that you see, thanks to this mirror, the essences, qualities, proportions, and measures of all things are known, nor can anything be done well without it. And because, similarly, you wish to know what are the offices of my other sisters whom you see here, each will reply in her own person about her name and character, and this way our testimony will be all the more certain to you. But now I myself will declare the reason for our coming. I must assure you, as we do nothing without good cause, that our appearance here is not at all in vain. For, although we are not common to many places and our knowledge does not come to all people, nevertheless you, for your great love of investigating the truth through long and continual study, for which you come here, solitary and separated from the world, you have deserved and deserve, our devoted friend, to be visited and consoled by us in your agitation and sadness, so that you might also see clearly, in the midst of the darkness of your thoughts, those things which taint and trouble your heart.

"There is another greater and even more special reason for our coming which you will learn from our speeches: in fact we have come to vanquish from the world the same error into which you had fallen, so that from now on, ladies and all valiant women may have a refuge and defense against the various assailants, those ladies who have been abandoned for so long, exposed like a field without a surrounding hedge, without finding a champion to afford them an adequate defense, notwithstanding those noble men who are required by order of law to protect them, who by negligence and apathy have allowed them to be mistreated. It is no wonder then that their jealous enemies, those outrageous villains who have assailed them with various weapons, have been victorious in a war in which women have had no defense. Where is there a city so strong which could not be taken immediately if no resistance were forthcoming, or the law case, no matter how unjust, which was not won through the obstinance of someone pleading without opposition? And the simple, noble ladies, following the example of suffering which God commands, have cheerfully suffered the great attacks which, both in the spoken and the written word, have been wrongfully and sinfully perpetrated against women by men who all the while appealed to God for the right to do so. Now it is time for their just cause to be taken from Pharaoh's hands, and for this reason, we three ladies whom you see here, moved by pity, have come to you to announce a particular edifice built like a city wall, strongly constructed and well founded, which has been predestined and established by our aid and counsel for you to build, where no one will reside except all ladies of fame and women worthy of praise, for the walls of the city will be closed to those women who lack virtue."

4

[Here the lady explains to Christine the city which she has been commissioned to build and how she was charged to help Christine build the wall and enclosure, and then gives her name.]

"Thus, fair daughter, the prerogative among women has been bestowed on you to establish and build the City of Ladies. For the foundation and completion of this City you will draw fresh waters from us as from clear fountains, and we will bring you sufficient building stone, stronger and more durable than any marble with cement could be. Thus your City will be extremely beautiful, without equal, and of perpetual duration in the world.

"Have you not read that King Tros founded the great city of Troy with the aid of Apollo, Minerva, and Neptune, whom the people of that time considered gods, and also how Cadmus founded the city of Thebes with the admonition of the gods? And yet over time these cities fell and have fallen into ruin. But I prophesy to you, as a true sybil,[3] that this City, which you will found with our help, will never be destroyed, nor will it ever fall, but will remain prosperous forever, regardless of all its jealous enemies. Although it will be stormed by numerous assaults, it will never be taken or conquered.

"Long ago the Amazon kingdom was begun through the arrangement and enterprise of several ladies of great courage who despised servitude, just as history books have testified. For a long time afterward they maintained it under the rule of several queens, very noble ladies whom they elected themselves, who governed them well and maintained their dominion with great strength. Yet, although they were strong and powerful and had conquered a large part of the entire Orient in the course of their rule and terrified all the neighboring lands (even the Greeks, who were then the flower of all countries in the world, feared them), nevertheless, after a time, the power of this kingdom declined, so that as with all earthly kingdoms, nothing but its name has survived to the present. But the edifice erected by you in this City which you must construct will be far stronger, and for its founding I was commissioned, in the course of our common deliberation, to supply you with durable and pure mortar to lay the sturdy foundations and to raise the lofty walls all around, high and thick, with mighty towers and strong bastions, surrounded by moats with firm blockhouses, just as is fitting for a city with a strong and lasting defense. Following our plan, you will set the foundations deep to last all the longer, and then you will raise the walls so high that they will not fear anyone. Daughter, now that I have told you the reason for our coming and so that you will more certainly believe my words, I want you to learn my name, by whose sound alone you will be able to learn and know that, if you wish to follow my commands, you have in me an administrator so that you may do your work flawlessly. I am called Lady Reason; you see that you are in good hands. For the time being then, I will say no more."

5

[Here Christine tells how the second lady told her name and what she served as and how she would aid her in building the City of Ladies.]

When the lady above finished her speech, before I could resume, the second lady began as follows: "I am called Rectitude and reside more in Heaven than on Earth, but as the radiance and splendor of God and messenger of His goodness, I often visit the just and exhort them to do what is right, to give to each person what is his according to his capacity, to say and uphold the truth, to defend the rights of the poor and the innocent, not to hurt anyone through usurpation, to uphold the reputation of those unjustly accused. I am the shield and defense of the servants of God. I resist the power and might of evil-doers. I give rest to workers and reward those who act well. Through me, God reveals to His friends His secrets; I am their advocate in Heaven. This shining ruler which you see me carry in my right

[3]The sybils were female oracular spirits of the classical world; medieval revisionists claimed the sybils had prophesied the coming of Christ.

hand instead of a scepter is the straight ruler which separates right from wrong and shows the difference between good and evil: who follows it does not go astray. It is the rod of peace which reconciles the good and where they find support and which beats and strikes down evil. What should I tell you about this? All things are measured by this ruler, for its powers are infinite. It will serve you to measure the edifice of the City which you have been commissioned to build, and you will need it for constructing the façade, for erecting the high temples, for measuring the palaces, houses, and all public buildings, the streets and squares, and all things proper to help populate the City. I have come as your assistant, and this will be my duty. Do not be uneasy about the breadth and long circuit of the walls, for with God's help and our assistance you will build fair and sturdy mansions and inns without leaving anything vague, and you will people the City with no trouble."

6

[Here Christine tells how the third lady told her who she was and her function and how she would help build the high roofs of the towers and palaces and would bring to her the Queen, accompanied by noble ladies.]

Afterward, the third lady spoke and said, "My friend Christine, I am Justice, the most singular daughter of God, and my nature proceeds purely from His person. My residence is found in Heaven, on Earth, or in Hell: in Heaven, for the glory of the saints and blessed souls; on Earth, for the apportionment to each man of the good or evil which he has deserved; in Hell, for the punishment of the evil. I do not bend anywhere, for I have not friend nor enemy nor changeable will; pity cannot persuade me nor cruelty move me. My duty is only to judge, to decide, and to dispense according to each man's just deserts. I sustain all things in their condition, nothing could be stable without me. I am in God and God is in me, and we are as one and the same. Who follows me cannot fail, and my way is sure. I teach men and women of sound mind who want to believe in me to chastise, know, and correct themselves, and to do to others what they wish to have done to themselves, to distribute wealth without favor, to speak the truth, to flee and hate lies, to reject all viciousness. This vessel of fine gold which you see me hold in my right hand, made like a generous measure, God, my Father, gave me, and it serves to measure out to each his rightful portion. It carries the sign of the fleur-de-lis of the Trinity, and in all portions it measures true, nor can any man complain about my measure. Yet the men of the Earth have other measures which they claim depend upon and derive from mine, but they are mistaken. Often they measure in my shadow, and their measure is not always true but sometimes too much for some and too little for others. I could give a rather long account of the duties of my office, but, put briefly, I have a special place among the Virtues, for they are all based on me. And of the three noble ladies whom you see here, we are as one and the same, we could not exist without one another; and what the first disposes, the second orders and initiates, and then I, the third, finish and terminate it. Thus I have been appointed by the will of us three ladies to perfect and complete your City, and my job will be to construct the high roofs of the towers and of the lofty mansions and inns which will all be made of fine shining gold. Then I will populate the City for you with worthy ladies and the mighty Queen whom I will bring to you. Hers will be the honor and prerogative among all other women, as well as among the most excellent women. And in this condition I will turn the City over to you, completed with your help, fortified and closed off with strong gates which I will search for in Heaven, and then I will place the keys in your hands."

. . .

Book II

44

[Refuting those men who claim women want to be raped, Rectitude gives several examples, and first of all, Lucretia.]

Then I, Christine, spoke as follows, "My lady, I truly believe what you are saying, and I am certain that there are plenty of beautiful women who are virtuous and chaste and who know how to protect themselves well from the entrapments of deceitful men.[4] I am therefore troubled and grieved when men argue that many women want to be raped and that it does not bother them at all to be raped by men even when they verbally protest. It would be hard to believe that such great villainy is actually pleasant for them."

She answered, "Rest assured, dear friend, chaste ladies who live honestly take absolutely no pleasure in being raped. Indeed, rape is the greatest possible sorrow for them. Many upright women have demonstrated that this is true with their own credible examples, just like Lucretia, the noblest Roman woman, supreme in chastity among Roman women, wife of a nobleman named Tarquin Collatinus. Now, when another man, Tarquin the Proud, son of King Tarquin, was greatly taken with love for this noble Lucretia, he did not dare to tell her because of the great chastity he saw in her, and, despairing of achieving his goal with presents or entreaties, he considered how he could have her through ruse. Claiming to be a close friend of her husband, he managed to gain entrance into her house whenever he wished, and once, knowing her husband was not at home, he went there and the noble lady received him with the honors due to someone whom she thought to be a close friend of her husband. However, Tarquin, who had something altogether different on his mind, succeeded in entering Lucretia's bedroom and frightened her terribly. Put briefly, after trying to coax her for a long time with promises, gifts, and favors, he saw that entreaties were getting him nowhere. He drew his sword and threatened to kill her if she made a sound and did not submit to his will. She answered that he should go ahead and kill her, for she would rather die then consent. Tarquin, realizing that nothing would help him, concocted a great malice, saying that he would publicly declare that he had found her with one of his sergeants. In brief, he so scared her with this threat (for she thought that people would believe him) that finally she suffered his rape. Lucretia, however, could not patiently endure this great pain, so that when daylight came she sent for her husband, her father, and her close relatives who were among the most powerful people in Rome, and, weeping and sobbing, confessed to them what had happened to her. Then, as her husband and relatives, who saw that she was overwhelmed with grief, were comforting her, she drew a knife from under her robe and said, 'This is how I absolve myself of sin and show my innocence. Yet I cannot free myself from the torment nor extricate myself from the pain. From now on no woman will ever live shamed and disgraced by Lucretia's example.' Having said this, she forcibly plunged the knife into her breast and collapsed dead before her husband and friends. They rushed like madmen to attack Tarquin. All Rome was moved to this cause, and they drove out the king and would have killed his son if they had found him. Never again was there a king in Rome. And because of this outrage perpetrated on Lucretia, so some claim, a law was enacted whereby a man would be executed for raping a woman, a law which is fitting, just, and holy."

---

[4]Rectitude has just been citing examples of women who were at once beautiful and chaste.

MARGERY KEMPE

[C. 1373–C. 1438]

Chaucer's Wife of Bath, deploring the misogynistic literature her fifth husband collects, fervently wishes that "By Godde, wommen had writen stories." About fifty years after Chaucer created the Wife, a real woman did so—a woman who in her own way was every bit as feisty, courageous, and pilgrimage-loving as the Wife, albeit one who actively sought celibacy instead of toothsome young husbands.

Margery Kempe was a young, illiterate middle-class housewife in the prosperous fifteenth-century English town of King's Lynn when she began having the mystical visual and auditory experiences that turned her from worldly pride to fervent Christian belief. When she was more than sixty years old, "this creature," as she referred to herself, began to dictate the story of her life to scribes. Except for a compendium of brief excerpts, *The Book of Margery Kempe* was lost until 1934, when a copy was discovered in a private library in England. Her associative, pungent account is noted for being the first autobiography written in English, but it is an invaluable document for other reasons as well. Because Margery Kempe chose not to join a religious order, but to live her spiritual adventures in the secular world, her memoirs afford us glimpses of the realities of everyday life in bustling ports and at pilgrimage sites across Europe and the Near East. Feminists and theologians value what she has to tell us first-hand about being a medieval woman mystic. Above all, *The Book of Margery Kempe* gives us a lively self-portrait of a bumbling, stubborn, passionate fifteenth-century woman determined to live in the way she is convinced God wants her to live, despite the pressures exerted upon her by family, church, and society to lead a more conventional existence.

LIFE

Margery Kempe was born about 1373 into a prominent family at King's Lynn, Norfolk, where her father served five times as mayor. Her book skips over her childhood completely to begin with her marriage at twenty to John Kempe, a man who, as she was quick to point out, was not nearly so honored nor so successful a citizen as her father. Her first pregnancy and childbirth were difficult and precipitated a mental and spiritual crisis that may well have been what we now call postpartum psychosis, a circumstance that once inclined many critics and theologians to dismiss her experiences and her text as "hysterical." Kempe's own more holistic view of her early illness was that it resulted in part from her confessor scolding her too sharply before she had quite finished enumerating all her sins. Childbirth had brought a sense of her mortality home to her, and, caught between her fear of the stern cleric and her fear of dying unconfessed and entering into eternal damnation, she was disturbed for some months. She was rescued from her despair by the intervention of Jesus, who appeared to her "clad in a mantle of purple silk." He sat down on her sickbed and gently rebuked her for forsaking him, even though, as he assured her, he had never forsaken her.

This timely vision healed Kempe from her madness, but she describes herself as persisting for some time in an excessive attachment to the things of this world. She loved to flaunt her fashionable, brightly colored clothing, she prided herself on her distinguished family, and she valued above all the high opinion of her neighbors. In an attempt to make more money she started her own brewing business and later tried her hand at running a grain mill. Both enterprises failed mysteriously. Her ale, though carefully prepared, would not ferment properly, and ordinarily docile work horses refused to turn her millstones.

She interpreted these calamities as signs from God telling her to abandon her worldly pride and ambition, and she dated her entrance into "the way of everlasting life" from that point.

During the first twenty years of her marriage, while she bore John Kempe fourteen children, Margery Kempe's religious visions grew in frequency and intensity, although at least one worldly appetite remained strong within her. At times, she says, the Devil tempted her with "the snare of lechery," though that lust was not directed toward her husband; in Chapter 4 of her *Book,* she recounts the awkward incident of a failed adulterous tryst. Further, she continually begged her husband to let her be celibate, but he doggedly insisted upon his conjugal rights until, as she records in Chapter 11, husband and wife sat down together in the shade of a wayside cross on a sweltering summer day and after much wrangling and bargaining arrived at a compromise. They agreed that Margery might sleep alone if in return she would pay off John's debts and abandon her practice of fasting on Fridays in order to keep him company at meals. At some forty years of age, she at last became free to seek the style of spiritual life she longed for.

Kempe made her first and longest overseas pilgrimage to Jerusalem in 1413. While she was atop Mount Calvary, the site of the crucifixion, she was visited by her first "crying." Weeping had previously played a part in her religious experiences, when she felt remorse for her sins, when she empathized as she witnessed in visions the trials of the Holy Family, and when she rejoiced in the sound of the heavenly music she was sometimes able to hear. But these tears in Jerusalem were of a new order—violent, copious, accompanied by loud screams, and clearly beyond Kempe's control. Indeed, her disruptive behavior often embarrassed her, especially when it caused her to be forcibly removed from churches where someone was trying to preach a sermon. Even close friends were alienated by her prodigious weeping, some believing she was shamming, others that she had a disorder akin to epilepsy, whose victims in the Middle Ages were made outcasts. More than once she sought counsel about how to deal with these visitations of weeping, which lasted over a ten-year period. Perhaps Kempe recalled the advice the renowned English mystic and theologian Dame Julian of Norwich had given to her in the days they spent together before Kempe's first pilgrimage and the onset of her cryings: "Set all your trust in God and fear not the language of the world," Julian had told her, "for the more spite, shame, and reproof you have in the world, the more is your merit in the sight of God." And Christ himself explained to her that her tears were to be understood as a mark of his love and as a way to convey to other mortals the sufferings of the Virgin Mary.

Margery Kempe continued to be a controversial figure among her contemporaries, disturbing to people in religious orders and members of the laity—disturbing, at least, to those who did not deem her a holy woman touched by God's special grace. She was questioned, threatened, and even arrested a number of times on suspicion of heresy, but no accusation ever stuck. Dressed in bridal white and wearing a wedding ring inscribed in Latin *Jesus Christ is my Love,* she pilgrimaged and wept and roared her way across Europe and the Middle East, buttonholing people to tell them of her visions, such as the ceremony in which she saw herself wed to Jesus, and her attendance in turn at the births of both the Virgin Mary and Jesus. Fearlessly, she preached to hostile crowds and confronted distinguished members of the clergy with their shortcomings and imperfections of faith. In about 1431, when her husband was paralyzed in an accident, she went back to live with him and nursed him until his death. She died in King's Lynn sometime after 1438, when she is last mentioned in public records.

Modern feminist scholars point out that Margery Kempe's style of spirituality—her tears as her major sign of God's grace and the intensely domestic quality of her visions of the Holy Family, encompassing marriage and childbirth and domestic scenes in the household in Nazareth—although common among women, was not confined to that gender. Monks and friars, especially Franciscans, also practiced the "affective piety" of compassionate tears and meditated upon the everyday lives of Jesus and his earthly parents. But her way of life does have particular parallels among other holy women of Europe about whom she would have known. Saint Birgitta of Sweden (1303–1373) and Dorothea of Montaux (1347–1394), for example, also experienced great conflict over issues of sexuality and their married lives; Hildegarde of Bingen (1098–1179), another visionary like Kempe, had also dared despite her gender to rebuke male clerics for their faults.

Work

Kempe's candid narrative of her life exhibits certain features that are often found in women's writing. She follows an associative rather than a strictly chronological framework, and emotional connections, rather than linear organization, often determine the order in which she narrates events. Her prose is also very personal and particular, sprinkled with gossipy anecdotes and homely details. We know the fabric and color of Christ's robe when he appears to her, and how hot it was on that day when she and her husband argued toward a compromise about sex; we know that the slab at Jerusalem upon which Jesus' crucified body was said to have been laid out was made of marble, and that the cup in which she was given wine while visiting a poor household in Rome was stoneware. For all her spiritual intensity, Kempe's relish for the physical world, with its weather, terrain, and texture and all its curious variety, shines through her narrative and perhaps suggests why this extraordinary woman chose to pursue her idiosyncratic vocation outside convent walls.

Suggested Readings

A fine comprehensive study of Margery Kempe's life and work is Clarissa W. Atkinson's *Mystic and Pilgrim: The Book and the World of Margery Kempe* (1983).

The Book of Margery Kempe

Translated by W. Butler-Bowden

Chapter 1

Her marriage and illness after childbirth. She recovers.

When this creature was twenty years of age, or some deal more, she was married to a worshipful burgess (of Lynne) and was with child within a short time, as nature would. And after she had conceived, she was belaboured with great accesses[1] till the child was born and then, what with the labour she had in childing, and the sickness going before, she despaired of her life, weening she might not live. And

[1]Attacks of pain.

then she sent for her ghostly father,[2] for she had a thing on her conscience which she had never shewn before that time in all her life. For she was ever hindered by her enemy, the devil, evermore saying to her that whilst she was in good health she needed no confession, but to do penance by herself alone and all should be forgiven, for God is merciful enough. And therefore this creature oftentimes did great penance in fasting on bread and water, and other deeds of alms with devout prayers, save she would not shew that in confession.

And when she was at any time sick or dis-eased, the devil said in her mind that she should be damned because she was not shriven of that default. Wherefore after her child was born, she, not trusting to live, sent for her ghostly father, as is said before, in full will to be shriven of all her lifetime, as near as she could. And when she came to the point for to say that thing which she had so long concealed, her confessor was a little too hasty and began sharply to reprove her, before she had fully said her intent, and so she would no more say for aught he might do. Anon, for the dread she had of damnation on the one side, and his sharp reproving of her on the other side, this creature went out of her mind and was wondrously vexed and laboured with spirits for half a year, eight weeks and odd days.

And in this time she saw, as she thought, devils opening their mouths all inflamed with burning waves of fire, as if they would have swallowed her in, sometimes ramping at her, sometimes threatening her, pulling her and hauling her, night and day during the aforesaid time. Also the devils cried upon her with great threatenings, and bade her that she should forsake Christendom, her faith, and deny her God, His Mother and all the Saints in Heaven, her good works and all good virtues, her father, her mother and all her friends. And so she did. She slandered her husband, her friends and her own self. She said many a wicked word, and many a cruel word; she knew no virtue nor goodness; she desired all wickedness; like as the spirits tempted her to say and do, so she said and did. She would have destroyed herself many a time at their stirrings and have been damned with them in Hell, and in witness thereof, she bit her own hand so violently, that the mark was seen all her life after.

And also she rived the skin on her body against her heart with her nails spitefully, for she had no other instruments, and worse she would have done, but that she was bound and kept with strength day and night so that she might not have her will. And when she had long been laboured in these and many other temptations, so that men weened she should never have escaped or lived, then on a time as she lay alone and her keepers were from her, Our Merciful Lord Jesus Christ, ever to be trusted, worshipped be His Name, never forsaking His servant in time of need, appeared to His creature who had forsaken Him, in the likeness of a man, most seemly, most beauteous and most amiable that ever might be seen with man's eye, clad in a mantle of purple silk, sitting upon her bedside, looking upon her with so blessed a face that she was strengthened in all her spirit, and said to her these words:—

'Daughter, why hast thou forsaken Me, and I forsook never thee?'

And anon, as He said these words, she saw verily how the air opened as bright as any lightning. And He rose up into the air, not right hastily and quickly, but fair and easily, so that she might well behold Him in the air till it was closed again.

And anon this creature became calmed in her wits and reason, as well as ever she was before, and prayed her husband as soon as he came to her, that she might have the keys of the buttery to take her meat and drink as she had done before. Her

---

[2]Spiritual advisor; a priest.

maidens and her keepers counselled him that he should deliver her no keys, as they said she would but give away such goods as there were, for she knew not what she said, as they weened.

Nevertheless, her husband ever having tenderness and compassion for her, commanded that they should deliver to her the keys; and she took her meat and drink as her bodily strength would serve her, and knew her friends and her household and all others that came to see how Our Lord Jesus Christ had wrought His grace in her, so blessed may He be, Who ever is near in tribulation. When men think He is far from them, He is full near by His grace. Afterwards, this creature did all other occupations as fell to her to do, wisely and soberly enough, save she knew not verily the call of Our Lord.

FROM

CHAPTER 2

Her worldly pride. Her attempt at brewing and milling, and failure at both. She amends her ways.

When this creature had thus graciously come again to her mind, she thought that she was bound to God and that she would be His servant. Nevertheless, she would not leave her pride or her pompous array, which she had used beforetime, either for her husband, or for any other man's counsel. Yet she knew full well that men said of her full much villainy, for she wore gold pipes on her head, and her hoods, with the tippets, were slashed. Her cloaks also were slashed and laid with divers colours between the slashes, so that they should be the more staring to men's sight, and herself the more worshipped.

And when her husband spoke to her to leave her pride, she answered shrewdly and shortly, and said that she was come of worthy kindred—he should never have wedded her—for her father was sometime Mayor of the town of N . . . and afterwards he was alderman of the High Guild of the Trinity in N. . . . And therefore she would keep the worship of her kindred whatever any man said.

She had full great envy of her neighbours, that they should be as well arrayed as she. All her desire was to be worshipped by the people. She would not take heed of any chastisement, nor be content with the goods that God had sent her, as her husband was, but ever desired more and more.

Then for pure covetousness, and to maintain her pride, she began to brew, and was one of the greatest brewers in the town of N . . . for three years or four, till she lost much money, for she had never been used thereto. For, though she had ever such good servants, cunning in brewing, yet it would never succeed with them. For when the ale was fair standing under barm[3] as any man might see, suddenly the barm would fall down, so that all the ale was lost, one brewing after another, so that her servants were ashamed and would not dwell with her.

Then this creature thought how God had punished her aforetime—and she could not take heed—and now again, by the loss of her goods. Then she left and brewed no more.

Then she asked her husband's mercy because she would not follow his counsel aforetime, and she said that her pride and sin were the cause of all her punishing, and that she would amend and that she had trespassed with good will.

---

[3]The foam or head on top of the ale.

Yet she left not the world altogether, for she now bethought herself of a new housewifery. She had a horse-mill. She got herself two good horses and a man to grind men's corn, and thus she trusted to get her living. This enterprise lasted not long, for in a short time after, on Corpus Christi Eve,[4] befell this marvel. This man, being in good health of body, and his two horses sturdy and gentle, had pulled well in the mill beforetime, and now he took one of these horses and put him in the mill as he had done before, and this horse would draw no draught in the mill for anything the man might do. The man was sorry and essayed with all his wits how he should make this horse pull. Sometimes he led him by the head, sometimes he beat him, sometimes he cherished him and all availed not, for he would rather go backward than forward. Then this man set a sharp pair of spurs on his heels and rode on the horse's back to make him pull, and it was never the better. When the man saw it would work in no way, he set up this horse again in the stable, and gave him corn, and he ate well and freshly. And later he took the other horse and put him in the mill, and like his fellow did, so did he, for he would not draw for anything the man might do. Then the man forsook his service and would no longer remain with the aforesaid creature. Anon, it was noised about the town of N . . . that neither man nor beast would serve the said creature.

Then some said she was accursed; some said God took open vengeance on her; some said one thing and some said another. Some wise men, whose minds were more grounded in the love of Our Lord, said that it was the high mercy of Our Lord Jesus Christ that called her from the pride and vanity of the wretched world.

Then this creature, seeing all these adversities coming on every side, thought they were the scourges of Our Lord that would chastise her for her sin. Then she asked God's mercy, and forsook her pride, her covetousness, and the desire that she had for the worship of the world, and did great bodily penance, and began to enter the way of everlasting life as shall be told hereafter.

Chapter 3

Her vision of Paradise. She desires to live apart from her husband. Does penance and wears a haircloth.

On a night, as this creature lay in her bed with her husband, she heard a sound of melody so sweet and delectable, that she thought she had been in Paradise, and therewith she started out of her bed and said:—

'Alas, that ever I did sin! It is full merry in Heaven.'

This melody was so sweet that it surpassed all melody that ever might be heard in this world, without any comparison, and caused her, when she heard any mirth or melody afterwards, to have full plenteous and abundant tears of high devotion, with great sobbings and sighings after the bliss of Heaven, not dreading the shames and the spites of this wretched world. Ever after this inspiration, she had in her mind the mirth and the melody that was in Heaven, so much, that she could not well restrain herself from speaking thereof, for wherever she was in any company she would say oftentimes:—'It is full merry in Heaven.'

And they that knew her behaviour beforetime, and now heard her speaking so much of the bliss of Heaven, said to her:—

[4]The night before the Church feast of Corpus Christi, held in honor of the Eucharist and celebrated on the Thursday following Trinity Sunday, the eighth Sunday after Easter.

'Why speak ye so of the mirth that is in Heaven? Ye know it not, and ye have not been there, any more than we.' And were wroth with her, for she would not hear nor speak of worldly things as they did, and as she did beforetime.

And after this time she had never desired to commune fleshly with her husband, for the debt of matrimony was so abominable to her that she would rather, she thought, have eaten or drunk the ooze and the muck in the gutter than consent to any fleshly communing, save only for obedience.

So she said to her husband:—'I may not deny you my body, but the love of my heart and my affections are withdrawn from all earthly creatures, and set only in God.'

He would have his will and she obeyed, with great weeping and sorrowing that she might not live chaste. And oftentimes this creature counselled her husband to live chaste, and said that they often, she knew well, had displeased God by their inordinate love, and the great delectation they each had in using the other, and now it was good that they should, by the common will and consent of them both, punish and chastise themselves wilfully by abstaining from the lust of their bodies. Her husband said it was good to do so, but he might not yet. He would when God willed. And so he used her as he had done before. He would not spare her. And ever she prayed to God that she might live chaste; and three or four years after, when it pleased Our Lord, he made a vow of chastity, as shall be written afterwards, by leave of Jesus.

And also, after this creature heard this heavenly melody, she did great bodily penance. She was shriven sometimes twice or thrice on a day, and specially of that sin she so long had (hid), concealed and covered, as is written in the beginning of the book.

She gave herself up to great fasting and great watching; she rose at two or three of the clock, and went to church, and was there at her prayers unto the time of noon and also all the afternoon. Then she was slandered and reproved by many people, because she kept so strict a life. She got a hair-cloth from a kiln, such as men dry malt on, and laid it in her kirtle as secretly and privily as she might, so that her husband should not espy it. Nor did he, and she lay by him every night in his bed and wore the hair-cloth every day, and bore children in the time.

Then she had three years of great labour with temptations which she bore as meekly as she could, thanking Our Lord for all His gifts, and was as merry when she was reproved, scorned and japed for Our Lord's love, and much more merry than she was beforetime in the worship of the world. For she knew right well she had sinned greatly against God and was worthy of more shame and sorrow than any man could cause her, and despite of the world was the right way Heavenwards, since Christ Himself had chosen that way. All His apostles, martyrs, confessors and virgins, and all that ever came to Heaven, passed by the way of tribulation, and she, desiring nothing so much as Heaven, then was glad in her conscience when she believed that she was entering the way that would lead her to the place she most desired.

And this creature had contrition and great compunction with plenteous tears and many boisterous sobbings for her sins and for her unkindness against her Maker. She repented from her childhood for unkindness, as Our Lord would put it in her mind, full many a time. Then, beholding her own wickedness, she could but sorrow and weep and ever pray for mercy and forgiveness. Her weeping was so plenteous and continuing, that many people thought she could weep and leave off, as she liked. And therefore many men said she was a false hypocrite, and wept before the world for succour and worldly goods. Then full many forsook her that loved her before while she was in the world, and would not know her. And ever, she thanked God for all, desiring nothing but mercy and forgiveness of sin.

CHAPTER 4

Her temptation to adultery with a man, who, when she consents, rejects her.

The first two years when this creature was thus drawn to Our Lord, she had great quiet in spirit from any temptations. She could well endure to fast, and it did not trouble her. She hated the joys of the world. She felt no rebellion in her flesh. She was so strong, as she thought, that she dreaded no devil in Hell, as she did such great bodily penance. She thought that she loved God more than He did her. She was smitten with the deadly wound of vainglory, and felt it not, for she many times desired that the crucifix should loosen His hands from the Cross, and embrace her in token of love. Our Merciful Lord Jesus Christ, seeing this creature's presumption, sent her, as is written before, three years of great temptations, one of the hardest of which I purpose to write as an example to those who come after, so that they should not trust in themselves, or have joy in themselves, as she had. For, no dread, our ghostly enemy sleepeth not, but he full busily searcheth our complexions and dispositions and where he findeth us most frail, there, by Our Lord's sufferance, he layeth his snare, which no man may escape by his own power.

So he laid before this woman the snare of lechery, when she believed that all fleshly lust had wholly been quenched in her. And so for a long time she was tempted with the sin of lechery, for aught that she could do. Yet she was often shriven, she wore her hair-cloth, and did great bodily penance and wept many a bitter tear, and prayed full often to Our Lord that He should preserve her and keep her, so that she should not fall into temptation, for she thought she would rather be dead than consent thereto. All this time she had no lust to commune with her husband; but it was very painful and horrible unto her.

In the second year of her temptation, it so fell that a man whom she loved well, said unto her on St. Margaret's Eve[5] before evensong that, for anything, he would lie by her and have his lust of his body, and she should not withstand him, for if he did not have his will that time, he said he would anyhow have it another time; she should not choose. And he did it to see what she would do, but she thought that he had meant it in full earnest at that time, and said but little thereto. So they parted then and both went to hear evensong, for her church was that of Saint Margaret. This woman was so laboured with the man's words that she could not hear her evensong, nor say her Paternoster, or think any other good thought, but was more troubled than ever she was before.

The devil put into her mind that God had forsaken her, or else she would not be so tempted. She believed the devil's persuasion, and began to consent because she could think no good thought. Therefore thought she that God had forsaken her, and when evensong was done, she went to the man aforesaid, so that he could have his lust, as she thought he had desired, but he made such simulation that she could not know his intent, and so they parted asunder for that night. This creature was so laboured and vexed all that night, that she never knew what she might do. She lay by her husband, and to commune with him was so abominable to her that she could not endure it, and yet it was lawful unto her, in lawful time, if she would. But ever she was laboured with the other man, to sin with him inasmuch as he had spoken to her. At last, through the importunity of temptation, and lack of discretion, she was

[5]This Saint Margaret's feast falls on July 20. Margaret of Antioch was one of the most popular saints in the Middle Ages, although she may be entirely fictional. Ironically (given Margery's temptation falling on St. Margaret's Eve), she was a virgin martyr, the Christian daughter of a pagan priest at Antioch who was punished for refusing to sleep with a man chosen for her. Satan, in the form of a dragon, swallowed her, but the fiend exploded when she made the sign of the cross inside his belly.

overcome and consented in her mind, and went to the man to know if he would then consent to her, and he said he never would, for all the gold in this world; he would rather be hewn as small as flesh for the pot.

She went away all shamed and confused in herself at seeing his stability and her own instability. Then thought she of the grace that God had given her before; how she had had two years of great quiet in her soul, repenting of her sin with many bitter tears of compunction, and a perfect will never again to turn to her sin, but rather to die. Now she saw how she had consented in her will to do sin, and then fell she half into despair. She thought she must have been in Hell for the sorrow she felt. She thought she was worthy of no mercy, for her consent was so wilfully done, nor ever worthy to do Him service, because she was so false to Him. Nevertheless she was shriven many times and often, and did whatever penance her confessor would enjoin her to do, and was governed by the rules of the Church. That grace, God gave his creature, blessed may He be, but He withdrew not her temptation, but rather increased it, as she thought.

Therefore she thought He had forsaken her, and dared not trust to His mercy, but was afflicted with horrible temptations to lechery and despair all the next year following. But Our Lord, of His mercy, as she said herself, gave her each day for the most part two hours of sorrow for her sins, with many bitter tears. Afterwards, she was laboured with temptation to despair as she was before, and was as far from feelings of grace, as they that never felt any, and that she could not bear, and so she gave away to despair. But for the time that she felt grace, her labours were so wonderful that she could evil fare with them, but ever mourned and sorrowed as though God had forsaken her.

. . .

Chapter 11

On the way back from York, she and her husband argue as to their carnal relationship to each other.

It befell on a Friday on Midsummer Eve in right hot weather, as this creature was coming from York-ward carrying a bottle with beer in her hand, and her husband a cake in his bosom, that he asked his wife this question:—

'Margery, if there came a man with a sword, who would strike off my head, unless I should commune naturally with you as I have done before, tell me on your conscience—for ye say ye will not lie—whether ye would suffer my head to be smitten off, or whether ye would suffer me to meddle with you again, as I did at one time?'

'Alas, sir,' said she, 'why raise this matter, when we have been chaste these eight weeks?'

'For I will know the truth of your heart.'

And then she said with great sorrow:—'Forsooth, I would rather see you being slain, than that we should turn again to our uncleanness.'

And he replied:—'Ye are no good wife.'

She then asked her husband what was the cause that he had not meddled with her for eight weeks, since she lay with him every night in his bed. He said he was made so afraid when he would have touched her, that he dare do no more.

'Now, good sir, amend your ways, and ask God's mercy, for I told you nearly three years ago that ye[6] should be slain suddenly, and now is this the third year, and

[6]"Your lust."

so I hope I shall have my desire. Good sir, I pray you grant me what I ask, and I will pray for you that ye shall be saved through the mercy of Our Lord Jesus Christ, and ye shall have more reward in Heaven than if ye wore a hair-cloth or a habergeon.[7] I pray you, suffer me to make a vow of chastity at what bishop's hand God wills.'

'Nay,' he said, 'that I will not grant you, for now may I use you without deadly sin, and then might I not do so.'

Then she said to him:—'If it be the will of the Holy Ghost to fulfil what I have said, I pray God that ye may consent thereto; and if it be not the will of the Holy Ghost, I pray God ye never consent to it.'

Then they went forth towards Bridlington in right hot weather, the creature having great sorrow and dread for her chastity. As they came by a cross, her husband sat down under the cross, calling his wife to him and saying these words unto her:—'Margery, grant me my desire, and I shall grant you your desire. My first desire is that we shall lie together in bed as we have done before; the second, that ye shall pay my debts, ere ye go to Jerusalem; and the third, that ye shall eat and drink with me on the Friday as ye were wont to do.'

'Nay, sir,' said she, 'to break the Friday, I will never grant you whilst I live.'

'Well,' said he, 'then I shall meddle with you again.'

She prayed him that he would give her leave to say her prayers, and he granted it kindly. Then she knelt down beside a cross in the field and prayed in this manner, with a great abundance of tears:—

'Lord God, Thou knowest all things. Thou knowest what sorrow I have had to be chaste in my body to Thee all these three years, and now might I have my will, and dare not for love of Thee. For if I should break that manner of fasting which Thou commandest me to keep on the Friday, without meat or drink, I should now have my desire. But, Blessed Lord, Thou knowest that I will not contravene Thy will, and much now is my sorrow unless I find comfort in Thee. Now, Blessed Jesus, make Thy will known to me unworthy, that I may follow it thereafter and fulfil it with all my might.'

Then Our Lord Jesus Christ with great sweetness, spoke to her, commanding her to go again to her husband, and pray him to grant her what she desired, 'And he shall have what he desireth. For, my dearworthy daughter, this was the cause that I bade thee fast, so that thou shouldst the sooner obtain and get thy desire, and now it is granted to thee. I will no longer that thou fast. Therefore I bid thee in the Name of Jesus, eat and drink as thy husband doth.'

Then this creature thanked Our Lord Jesus Christ for His grace and goodness, and rose up and went to her husband, saying to him:—

"Sir, if it please you, ye shall grant me my desire, and ye shall have your desire. Grant me that ye will not come into my bed, and I grant you to requite your debts ere I go to Jerusalem. Make my body free to God so that ye never make challenge to me, by asking any debt of matrimony. After this day, whilst ye live, I will eat and drink on the Friday at your bidding.'

Then said her husband:—'As free may your body be to God, as it hath been to me.'

This creature thanked God, greatly rejoicing that she had her desire, praying her husband that they should say three Paternosters in worship of the Trinity for the great grace that He had granted them. And so they did, kneeling under a cross, and afterwards they ate and drank together in great gladness of spirit. This was on

[7] A coat of mail that could be worn for penance as well as for armor.

a Friday on Midsummer's Eve. Then went they forth Bridlingtonward and also to many other countries and spoke with God's servants, both anchorites and recluses, and many others of Our Lord's lovers, with many worthy clerks, doctors of divinity and bachelors also, in divers places. And this creature, to many of them, shewed her feelings and her contemplations, as she was commanded to do, to find out if any deceit were in her feelings.

. . .

FROM
CHAPTER 18

At Norwich she visits a White Friar, William Sowthfeld, and an anchoress, Dame Jelyan.

This creature was charged and commanded in her soul that she should go to a White Friar, in the same city of Norwich, called William Sowthfeld, a good man and a holy liver, to shew him the grace that God wrought in her, as she had done to the good Vicar before. She did as she was commanded and came to the friar on a forenoon, and was with him in a chapel a long time, and shewed him her meditations, and what God had wrought in her soul, to find out if she were deceived by any illusion or not.

This good man, the White Friar, ever whilst she told him her feelings, holding up his hands, said:—'Jesu Mercy and gramercy.'

'Sister,' he said, 'dread not for your manner of living, for it is the Holy Ghost working plenteously His grace in your soul. Thank Him highly for His goodness, for we all be bound to thank Him for you, Who now in our days will inspire His grace in you, to the help and comfort of us all, who are supported by your prayers and by such others as ye be. And we are preserved from many mischiefs and diseases which we should suffer, and worthily, for our trespass. Never were such good creatures amongst us. Blessed be Almighty God for His goodness. And therefore, sister, I counsel you that ye dispose yourself to receive the gifts of God as lowly and meekly as ye can, and put no obstacle or objection against the goodness of the Holy Ghost, for He may give His gifts where He will, and of unworthy He maketh worthy, of sinful He maketh rightful. His mercy is ever ready unto us, unless the fault be in ourselves, for He dwelleth not in a body subject to sin. He flieth all false feigning and falsehood: He asketh of us a lowly, a meek and a contrite heart, with a good will. Our Lord sayeth Himself:—"My Spirit shall rest upon a meek man, a contrite man, and one dreading My words."

'Sister, I trust to Our Lord that ye have these conditions either in your will or your affection, or else in both, and I believe not that Our Lord suffereth them to be deceived endlessly, that set all their trust in Him, and seek and desire nothing but Him only, as I hope ye do. And therefore believe fully that Our Lord loveth you and worketh His grace in you. I pray God to increase it and continue it to His everlasting worship, for His mercy.'

The aforesaid creature was much comforted both in body and in soul by this good man's words, and greatly strengthened in her faith.

Then she was bidden by Our Lord to go to an anchoress in the same city, named Dame Jelyan,[8] and so she did, and showed her the grace that God put into her soul, of compunction, contrition, sweetness and devotion, compassion with holy meditation and high contemplation, and full many holy speeches and dalliance that

[8]Julian of Norwich (1342–?), a Christian recluse and seer who recorded her visionary experiences or "showings," which emphasized God as a maternal figure.

Our Lord spake to her soul; and many wonderful revelations, which she shewed to the anchoress to find out if there were any deceit in them, for the anchoress was expert in such things, and good counsel could give.

The anchoress, hearing the marvellous goodness of Our Lord, highly thanked God with all her heart for His visitation, counselling this creature to be obedient to the will of Our Lord God and to fulfil with all her might whatever He put into her soul, if it were not against the worship of God, and profit of her fellow Christians, for if it were, then it were not the moving of a good spirit, but rather of an evil spirit. 'The Holy Ghost moveth ne'er a thing against charity, for if He did, He would be contrary to His own self for He is all charity. Also He moveth a soul to all chasteness, for chaste livers are called the Temple of the Holy Ghost, and the Holy Ghost maketh a soul stable and steadfast in the right faith, and the right belief.

'And a double man in soul is ever unstable and unsteadfast in all his ways. He that is ever doubting is like the flood of the sea which is moved and born about with the wind, and that man is not likely to receive the gifts of God.

'Any creature that hath these tokens may steadfastly believe that the Holy Ghost dwelleth in his soul. And much more when God visiteth a creature with tears of contrition, devotion, and compassion, he may and ought to believe that the Holy Ghost is in his soul. Saint Paul saith that the Holy Ghost asketh for us with mourning and weeping unspeakable, that is to say, He maketh us to ask and pray with mourning and weeping so plenteously that the tears may not be numbered. No evil spirit may give these tokens, for Saint Jerome saith that tears torment more the devil than do the pains of Hell. God and the devil are ever at odds and they shall never dwell together in one place, and the devil hath no power in a man's soul.

'Holy Writ saith that the soul of a rightful man is the seat of God, and so I trust, sister, that ye be. I pray God grant you perseverance. Set all your trust in God and fear not the language of the world, for the more despite, shame and reproof that ye have in the world, the more is your merit in the sight of God. Patience is necessary to you, for in that shall ye keep your soul.'

Much was the holy dalliance that the anchoress and this creature had by communing in the love of Our Lord Jesus Christ the many days that they were together. . . .

FROM

Chapter 26

She starts from Yarmouth on her way to the Holy Land. She has trouble with her companions owing to her weeping and piety. She reaches Constance.

When the time came that this creature should visit those holy places where Our Lord was quick and dead, as she had by revelation years before, she prayed the parish priest of the town where she was dwelling, to say for her in the pulpit, that, if any man or woman claimed any debt from her husband or herself, they should come and speak with her ere she went, and she, with the help of God would make a settlement with each of them, so that they should hold themselves content. And so she did.

Afterwards, she took her leave of her husband and of the holy anchorite, who had told her, before, the process of her going and the great dis-ease that she would suffer by the way, and when all her fellowship forsook her, how a broken-backed man would lead her forth in safety, through the help of Our Lord.

And so it befell indeed, as shall be written afterward.

Then she took her leave . . . of other friends. Then she went forth to Norwich, and offered at the Trinity, and afterwards she went to Yarmouth and offered at an image of Our Lady, and there she took her ship.

And next day they came to a great town called Zierikzee, where Our Lord of His high goodness visited this creature with abundant tears of contrition for her own sins, and sometime for other men's sins also. And especially she had tears of compassion in mind of Our Lord's Passion. And she was houselled each Sunday where there was time and place convenient thereto, with great weeping and boisterous sobbing, so that many men marvelled and wondered at the great grace that God had wrought in His creature.

This creature had eaten no flesh and drunk no wine for four years ere she went out of England, and so now her ghostly father charged her, by virtue of obedience, that she should both eat flesh and drink wine. And so she did a little while; afterwards she prayed her confessor that he would hold her excused if she ate no flesh, and suffer her to do as she would for such time as pleased him.

And soon after, through the moving of some of her company, her confessor was displeased because she ate no flesh, and so were many of the company. And they were most displeased because she wept so much and spoke always of the love and goodness of Our Lord, as much at the table as in other places. And therefore shamefully they reproved her, and severely chid her, and said they would not put up with her as her husband did when she was at home and in England.

And she answered meekly to them:—'Our Lord, Almighty God, is as great a Lord here as in England, and as good cause have I to love Him here as there, blessed may He be.'

At these words, her fellowship was angrier than before, and their wrath and unkindness to this creature was a matter of great grief, for they were held right good men and she desired greatly their love, if she might have it to the pleasure of God.

And then she said to one of them specially:—'Ye cause me much shame and great grievance.'

He answered her anon:—'I pray God that the devil's death may overcome thee soon and quickly,' and many more cruel words he said to her than she could repeat.

And soon after some of the company in whom she trusted best, and her own maiden also, said she could no longer go in their fellowship. And they said that they would take away her maiden from her, so that she should no strumpet be, in her company. And then one of them, who had her gold in keeping, left her a noble with great anger and vexation to go where she would and help herself as she might, for with them, they said, she should no longer abide; and they forsook her that night.

Then, on the next morning, there came to her one of their company, a man who loved her well, praying her that she would go to his fellows and meeken[9] herself to them, and pray them that she might go still in their company till she came to Constance.

And so she did, and went forth with them till she came to Constance with great discomfort and great trouble, for they did her much shame and much reproof as they went, in divers places. They cut her gown so short that it came but little beneath her knee, and made her put on a white canvas, in the manner of a sacken apron, so that she should be held a fool and the people should not make much of

[9]Behave meekly, with humility.

her or hold her in repute. They made her sit at the table's end, below all the others, so that she ill durst speak a word.

And, notwithstanding all their malice, she was held in more worship than they were, wherever they went.

And the good man of the house where they were hostelled, though she sat lowest at the table's end, would always help her before them all as well as he could, and sent her from his own table such service as he had, and that annoyed her fellowship full evil.

As they went by the way Constance-ward, it was told them that they would be robbed and have great discomfort unless they had great grace.

Then this creature came to a church and went in to make her prayer, and she prayed with all her heart, with great weeping and many tears, for help and succour against their enemies.

Then Our Lord said to her mind:—'Dread thee naught, daughter, thy fellowship shall come to no harm whilst thou art in their company.'

And so, blessed may Our Lord be in all His works, they went forth in safety to Constance.

Chapter 27

At Constance, the Papal legate befriends her. She meets William Wever, of Devonshire. She goes to Bologna and Venice.

When this creature and her fellowship had come to Constance, she heard tell of an English friar, a master of divinity, and the Pope's legate, who was in that city. Then she went to that worshipful man and shewed him her life from the beginning till that hour, as nigh as she might in confession, because he was the Pope's legate and a worshipful clerk.

And afterwards she told him what discomfort she had with her fellowship. She told him also what grace God gave her of contrition and compunction, of sweetness and devotion and of many divers revelations that God had revealed to her, and the fear that she had of illusions and deceits of her ghostly enemies, of which she lived in great dread, desiring to put them away, and to feel none, if she might withstand them.

And when she had spoken, the worshipful clerk gave her words of great comfort, and said it was the work of the Holy Ghost, commanding and charging her to obey them and receive them when God should give them and to have no doubts, for the devil hath no power to work such grace in a soul. And also he said that he would support her against the evil will of her fellowship.

Afterwards, when it pleased her fellowship, they prayed this worthy doctor to dinner, and the doctor told the aforesaid creature, warning her to sit at the meat in his presence as she did in his absence, and to keep the same manner of behaviour as she kept when he was not there.

When the time had come for them to sit at meat, every man took his place as he liked; the worshipful legate and doctor sat first, and then the others, and, at the last, the said creature at the board's end, sitting and speaking no word, as she was wont to do, when the legate was not there.

Then the legate said to her:—

'Why are ye no merrier?'

And she sat still and answered not, as he himself had commanded her to do.

When they had eaten, the company made great complaint against this creature to the legate, and said that, utterly, she could no longer be in their company, unless he commanded her to eat flesh as they did and stop her weeping, and that she should not talk so much of holiness.

Then the worshipful doctor said:—'Nay, sirs, I will not make her eat flesh whilst she can abstain and be the better disposed to Our Lord. If one of you made a vow to go to Rome barefoot, I would not dispense him of his vow whilst he could fulfil it, nor will I bid her to eat flesh whilst our Lord giveth her strength to abstain. As for her weeping, it is not in my power to restrain it, for it is the gift of the Holy Ghost. As for her speaking, I will pray her to cease till she cometh where men will hear her with better will than ye do.'

The company was wroth, and in great anger. They gave her over to the legate and said utterly that they would no more associate with her. He full benignly and kindly received her as though she had been his mother, and received her gold, about twenty pounds, and yet one of them withheld wrongfully about sixteen pounds.

And they withheld also her maiden, and would not let her go with her mistress, notwithstanding that she had promised her mistress and assured her that she would not forsake her for any need.

And the legate made arrangements for this creature and made her his charge as if she had been his mother.

Then this creature went into a church and prayed Our Lord that He would provide her with a leader.

And anon Our Lord spoke to her and said:—

'Thou shalt have right good help and a good leader.'

Immediately afterwards there came to her an old man with a white beard. He was from Devonshire, and said:—

'Damsel, will ye pray me for God's love, and for Our Lady's, to go with you and be your guide, for your countrymen have forsaken you?'

She asked, what was his name?

He said:—'My name is William Wever.'

She prayed him, by the reverence of God and of Our Lady, that he would help her at her need, and she would well reward him for his labour, and so they agreed.

Then went she to the legate and told him how well Our Lord had ordained for her, and took her leave of him and of her company who so unkindly had rejected her, and also of her maiden who was bounden to have gone with her. She took her leave with full heavy face and rueful, having great grief in as much as she was in a strange country, and knew not the language, or the man who would lead her, either.

And so the man and she went forth in great dread and gloom. As they went together, the man said to her:—

'I am afraid thou wilt be taken from me, and I shall be beaten for thee, and lose my jacket.'

She said:—'William, dread you not. God will keep us right well.'

And this creature had every day mind of the Gospel which telleth of the woman that was taken in adultery, and brought before Our Lord.

And she prayed:—'Lord, as thou drove away her enemies, so drive away mine enemies, and keep well my chastity that I vowed to Thee, and let me never be defiled, for if I am, Lord, I make my vow, that I will never come back to England whilst I live.'

Then they went forth day by day and met with many jolly men. And they said no evil word to this creature, but gave her and her man meat and drink, and the good wives where they were housed, laid her in their own beds for God's love, in many places where they came.

And Our Lord visited her with great grace of ghostly comfort as she went by the way. And so God brought her forth till she came to Bologna. And after she had come there, there came thither also her other fellowship, which had forsaken her before. And when they heard say that she had come to Bologna ere they had, then had they great wonder, and one of their fellowship came to her praying her to go to his fellowship and try if they would receive her again into their fellowship. And so she did.

'If ye will go in our fellowship, ye must make a new covenant, and that is this—ye shall not speak of the Gospel where we are, but shall sit still and make merry, as we do, both at meat and at supper.'

She consented and was received again into their fellowship. Then went they forth to Venice and dwelt there thirteen weeks; and this creature was houselled every Sunday in a great house of nuns, and had great cheer among them, where Our Lord Jesus Christ visited this creature with great devotion and plenteous tears, so that the good ladies of the place were much marvelled thereof.

Afterwards, it happened, as this creature sat at meat with her fellowship, that she repeated a text of the Gospel that she had learnt beforetime with other good words, and then her fellowship said she had broken covenant. And she said:—

'Yea, sirs, forsooth I may no longer keep your covenant, for I must needs speak of My Lord Jesus Christ, though all this world had forbidden it me.'

Then she took to her chamber and ate alone for six weeks, unto the time that Our Lord made her so sick that she weened to have been dead, and then suddenly He made her whole again. And all the time her maiden let her alone and made the company's meat and washed their clothes, and, to her mistress, under whom she had taken service, she would no deal attend.

FROM

CHAPTER 28

She sails from Venice and reaches Jerusalem. Much trouble owing to her crying.

Also this company, which had put the aforesaid creature from their table, so that she should no longer eat amongst them, engaged a ship for themselves to sail in. They bought vessels for their wine, and obtained bedding for themselves, but nothing for her. Then she, seeing their unkindness, went to the same man where they had been, and bought herself bedding as they had done, and came where they were and shewed them what she had done, purposing to sail with them in that ship which they had chartered.

Afterwards, as this creature was in contemplation, Our Lord warned her in her mind that she should not sail in that ship, and He assigned her to another ship, a galley, that she should sail in. Then she told this to some of the company, and they told it forth to their fellowship, and then they durst not sail in the ship they had chartered. So they sold away their vessels which they had got for their wines, and were right fain to come to the galley where she was, and so, though it was against her will, she went forth with them in their company, for they durst not otherwise do.

When it was time to make their beds, they locked up her clothes, and a priest, who was in their company, took away a sheet from the aforesaid creature, and said it was his. She took God to witness that it was her sheet. Then the priest swore a great oath, by the book in his hand, that she was as false as she might be, and despised her and strongly rebuked her.

And so she had ever much tribulation till she came to Jerusalem. And ere she came there, she said to them that she supposed they were grieved with her.

'I pray you, Sirs, be in charity with me, for I am in charity with you, and forgive me that I have grieved you by the way. And if any of you have in anything trespassed against me, God forgive it you, and I do.'

So they went forth into the Holy Land till they could see Jerusalem. And when this creature saw Jerusalem, riding on an ass, she thanked God with all her heart, praying Him for His mercy that, as He had brought her to see His earthly city of Jerusalem, He would grant her grace to see the blissful city of Jerusalem above, the city of Heaven. Our Lord Jesus Christ, answering her thought, granted her to have her desire.

Then for the joy she had, and the sweetness she felt in the dalliance with Our Lord, she was on the point of falling off her ass, for she could not bear the sweetness and grace that God wrought in her soul. Then two pilgrims, Duchemen, went to her, and kept her from falling; one of whom was a priest, and he put spices in her mouth to comfort her, thinking she had been sick. And so they helped her on to Jerusalem, and when she came there, she said:—

'Sirs, I pray you be not displeased though I weep sore in this holy place where Our Lord Jesus Christ was quick and dead.'

Then went they to the temple in Jerusalem and they were let in on the same day at evensong time, and abode there till the next day at evensong time. Then the friars lifted up a cross and led the pilgrims about from one place to another where Our Lord suffered . . . His Passion, every man and woman bearing a wax candle in one hand. And the friars always, as they went about, told them what Our Lord suffered in every place. The aforesaid creature wept and sobbed as plenteously as though she had seen Our Lord with her bodily eye, suffering His Passion at that time. Before her in her soul she saw Him verily by contemplation, and that caused her to have compassion. And when they came up on to the Mount of Calvary, she fell down because she could not stand or kneel, and rolled and wrested with her body, spreading her arms abroad, and cried with a loud voice as though her heart would have burst asunder; for, in the city of her soul, she saw verily and clearly how Our Lord was crucified. Before her face, she heard and saw, in her ghostly sight, the mourning of Our Lady, of Saint John, and Mary Magdalene and of many others that loved Our Lord.

And she had such great compassion and such great pain, at seeing Our Lord's pain that she could not keep herself from crying and roaring though she should have died for it. And this was the first cry that ever she cried in any contemplation. And this manner of crying endured many years after this time, for aught any man might do, and therefore, suffered she much despite and much reproof. The crying was so loud and so wonderful that it made the people astounded unless they had heard it before, or unless they knew the cause of the crying. And she had them so often that they made her right weak in her bodily might, and especially if she heard of Our Lord's Passion.

And sometimes, when she saw the crucifix, or if she saw a man with a wound, or a beast, whichever it were, or if a man beat a child before her, or smote a horse or other beast with a whip, if she saw it or heard it, she thought she saw Our Lord being beaten or wounded, just as she saw it in the man or the beast either in the field or the town, and by herself alone as well as amongst the people.

First when she had her cryings in Jerusalem, she had them often, and in Rome also. And when she came home to England, first at her coming home, it came but seldom, as it were once a month, then once a week, afterwards daily, and once she had fourteen in one day, and another day she had seven, and so on, as God would visit her, sometimes in church, sometimes in the street, sometimes in her chamber, sometimes in the fields, whenever God would send them, for she never knew the time nor the hour when they would come. And they never came without passing great sweetness of devotion and high contemplation. And as soon as she perceived that she would cry, she would keep it in as much as she might that the people should not hear it, to their annoyance. For some said that a wicked spirit vexed her; some said it was a sickness; some said she had drunk too much wine; some banned her; some wished she was in the harbour; some wished she was on the sea in a bottomless boat; and thus each man as he thought. Other ghostly men loved her and favoured her the more. Some great clerks said Our Lady cried never so, nor any saint in Heaven, but they knew full little what she felt, nor would they believe that she could not stop crying if she wished.

And therefore when she knew that she would cry, she kept it in as long as she might, and did all she could to withstand it or put it away, till she waxed as livid as any lead, and ever it would labour in her mind more and more till the time it broke out. And when the body might no longer endure the ghostly labour, but was overcome with the unspeakable love that wrought so fervently in her soul, then she fell down and cried wondrous loud, and the more she laboured to keep it in or put it away, so much the more would she cry, and the louder. Thus she did on the Mount of Calvary, as is written before.

Thus she had as very contemplation in the sight of her soul, as if Christ had hung before her bodily eye in His Manhood. And when through the dispensation of the high mercy of Our Sovereign Saviour Christ Jesus, it was granted to this creature to behold so verily His precious tender body, all rent and torn with scourges, fuller of wounds than ever was a dove-house of holes, hanging on the Cross with the crown of thorns upon His head, His beautiful hands, His tender feet nailed to the hard tree, the rivers of blood flowing out plenteously from every member, the grisly and grievous wound in His precious side shedding blood and water for her love and her salvation, then she fell down and cried with a loud voice, wonderfully turning and wresting her body on every side, spreading her arms abroad as if she would have died, and could not keep herself from crying, and from these bodily movements for the fire of love that burnt so fervently in her soul with pure pity and compassion.

It is not to be marvelled at, if this creature cried and made wondrous faces and expressions, when we may see each day with the eye both men and women, some for the loss of worldly goods, some for affection of their kindred, or worldly friendships, through over much study and earthly affection, and most of all for inordinate love and fleshly affection, if their friends are parted from them, they will cry and roar and wring their hands as if they had no wits or senses, and yet know they well that they are displeasing God.

And, if a man counsel them to leave or cease their weeping and crying, they will say that they cannot; they loved their friend so much, and he was so gentle and so kind to them, that they may in no way forget him. How much more might they weep, cry, and roar, if their most beloved friends were with violence taken in their sight and with all manner of reproof, brought before the judge, wrongfully condemned to death, and especially so spiteful a death as Our Merciful Lord suffered for our sake. How would they suffer it? No doubt they would both cry and roar and avenge themselves if they might, or else men would say they were no friends.

Alas! Alas! for sorrow that the death of a creature, who hath often sinned and trespassed against their Maker, shall be so immeasurably mourned and sorrowed. And it is an offence to God, and a hindrance to the souls beside them.

And the compassionate death of Our Saviour by which we are all restored to life, is not kept in mind by us unworthy and unkind wretches, nor do we support Our Lord's own secretaries whom He hath endued with love, but rather detract and hinder them as much as we may.

CHAPTER 29

She visits the Holy Sepulchre, Mount Sion and Bethlehem.

When this creature with her fellowship came to the grave where Our Lord was buried, anon, as she entered that holy place, she fell down with her candle in her hand, as if she would have died for sorrow. And later she rose up again with great weeping and sobbing, as though she had seen Our Lord buried even before her.

Then she thought she saw Our Lady in her soul, how she mourned and how she wept for her Son's death, and then was Our Lady's sorrow her sorrow.

And so, wherever the friars led them in that holy place, she always wept and sobbed wonderfully, and especially when she came where Our Lord was nailed on the Cross. There cried she, and wept without measure, so that she could not restrain herself.

Also they came to a stone of marble that Our Lord was laid on when He was taken down from the Cross, and there she wept with great compassion, having mind of Our Lord's Passion.

Afterwards she was houselled on the Mount of Calvary, and then she wept, she sobbed, she cried so loud that it was a wonder to hear it. She was so full of holy thoughts and meditations and holy contemplations on the Passion of Our Lord Jesus Christ, and holy dalliance that Our Lord Jesus Christ spoke to her soul, that she could never express them after, so high and so holy were they. Much was the grace that Our Lord shewed to this creature whilst she was three weeks in Jerusalem.

Another day, early in the morning, they went again amongst great hills, and their guides told her where Our Lord bore the Cross on His back, and where His Mother met with Him, and how she swooned and fell down and He fell down also. And so they went forth all the forenoon till they came to Mount Sion. And ever this creature wept abundantly, all the way that she went, for compassion of Our Lord's Passion. On Mount Sion is a place where Our Lord washed His disciples' feet and, a little therefrom, He made His Maundy[10] with His disciples.

And therefore this creature had great desire to be houselled in that holy place where Our Merciful Lord Christ Jesus first consecrated His precious Body in the form of bread, and gave it to His disciples. And so she was, with great devotion and plenteous tears and boisterous sobbings, for in this place is plenary remission,[11] and so there is in four other places in the Temple. One is on the Mount of Calvary; another at the grave where Our Lord was buried; the third is at the marble stone that His precious Body was laid on, when It was taken from the Cross; the fourth is where the Holy Cross was buried; and in many other places in Jerusalem.

And when this creature came to the place where the apostles received the Holy Ghost, Our Lord gave her great devotion. Afterwards she went to the place where

[10]The ceremony of washing the feet; see John 13:1–16.

[11]To pilgrimage to certain especially holy sites remits all temporal punishment incurred through previously committed sins.

Our Lady was buried, and as she knelt on her knees the time of two masses, Our Lord Jesus Christ said to her:—

'Thou comest not hither, daughter, for any need except merit and reward, for thy sins were forgiven thee ere thou came here and therefore thou comest here for the increasing of thy reward and thy merit. And I am well pleased with thee, daughter, for thou standest under obedience to Holy Church, and because thou wilt obey thy confessor and follow his counsel who, through authority of Holy Church, hath absolved thee of thy sins and dispensed thee so that thou shouldst not go to Rome and Saint James unless thou wilt thine own self. Notwithstanding all this, I command thee in the Name of Jesus, daughter, that thou go visit these holy places and do as I bid thee, for I am above Holy Church, and I shall go with thee and keep thee right well.'

Then Our Lady spoke to her soul in this manner, saying:—

'Daughter, well art thou blessed, for my Son Jesus shall flow so much grace into thee that all the world shall wonder at thee. Be not ashamed, my dearworthy daughter, to receive the gifts that my Son shall give thee, for I tell thee in truth, they shall be great gifts that He shall give thee. And therefore, my dearworthy daughter, be not ashamed of Him that is thy God, thy Lord and thy love, any more than I was, when I saw Him hanging on the Cross—my sweet Son, Jesus—to cry and to weep for the pain of my sweet Son Jesus Christ. Mary Magdalene was not ashamed to cry and weep for my Son's love. Therefore, daughter, if thou will be partaker in our love, thou must be partaker in our sorrow.'

This sweet speech and dalliance had this creature at Our Lady's grave, and much more than she could ever repeat.

Afterwards she rode on an ass to Bethlehem, and when she came to the temple and the crib where Our Lord was born, she had great devotion, much speech and dalliance in her soul, and high ghostly comfort with much weeping and sobbing, so that her fellows would not let her eat in their company, and therefore she ate her meat by herself alone.

And then the Grey Friars, who had led her from place to place, received her to them and set her with them at the meat so that she should not eat alone. And one of the friars asked one of her fellowship if she were the woman of England whom, they had heard said, spoke with God. And when this came to her knowledge, she knew well that it was the truth that Our Lord said to her, ere she went out of England:—

'Daughter, I will make all the world to wonder at thee, and many a man and many a woman shall speak of Me for love of thee, and worship Me in thee.'

. . .

Chapter 89

On her feelings. The end of the treatise through the death of the first writer of it.

Also, while the aforesaid creature was occupied about the writing of this treatise, she had many holy tears and weeping, and oftentimes there came a flame of fire about her breast, full hot and delectable; and also he that was her writer could not sometimes keep himself from weeping.

And often in the meantime, when the creature was in church, Our Lord Jesus Christ with His Glorious Mother and many saints also came into her soul and thanked her, saying that they were well pleased with the writing of this book. And also she heard many times a voice of a sweet bird singing in her ear, and oftentimes she heard sweet sounds and melodies that passed her wit to tell of. And she was many times sick while this treatise was in writing, and, as soon as she would go about the writing of this treatise, she was hale and whole suddenly, in a manner; and often she was commanded to make herself ready in all haste.

And, on a time, as she lay in her prayers in the church at the time of Advent before Christmas, she thought in her heart she would that God of His goodness would make Master Aleyn[12] to say a sermon as well as he could; and as quickly as she had thought thus, she heard Our Sovereign Lord Christ Jesus saying in her soul:—

'Daughter, I wot right well what thou thinkest now of Master Aleyn, and I tell thee truly that he shall say a right holy sermon; and look that thou believest steadfastly the words that he shall preach, as though I preached them Myself, for they shall be words of great solace and comfort to thee, for I shall speak in him.'

When she heard this answer, she went and told it to her confessor and to two other priests that she trusted much on; and when she had told them her feeling, she was full sorry for dread whether he should speak as well as she had felt or not, for revelations be hard sometimes to understand.

And sometimes those that men think were revelations, are deceits and illusions, and therefore it is not expedient to give readily credence to every stirring, but soberly abide, and pray if it be sent of God. Nevertheless, as to this feeling of this creature, it was very truth, shewn in experience, and her dread and her gloom turned into great ghostly comfort and gladness.

Sometimes she was in great gloom for her feelings, when she knew not how they should be understood, for many days together, for dread that she had of deceits and illusions, so that she thought she would that her head had been smitten from her body till God of His goodness declared them to her mind.

For sometimes, what she understood bodily was to be understood ghostly, and the dread that she had of her feelings was the greatest scourge that she had on earth; and especially when she had her first feelings; and that dread made her full meek, for she had no joy in the feeling till she knew by experience whether it was true or not.

But ever blessed may God be, for He made her always more mighty and more strong in His love and in His dread, and gave her increase of virtue with perseverance.

Here endeth this treatise, for God took him to His mercy, that wrote the copy of this book, and, though he wrote it not clearly nor openly to our manner of speaking, he, in his manner of writing and spelling made true sense, which, through the help of God and of herself that had all this treatise in feeling and working, is truly drawn out of the copy into this little book.

EVERYMAN

[C. 1500]

The play *Everyman,* or *The Calling of Everyman,* is thought to be the English reworking of a Dutch original, *Elckerlijc,* first published in Delft in 1495. Although the authorship of the English play is unknown, because of the similarity between the two works it is nowadays assumed either that they are creations of the same author or that the English version is a translation of the Dutch. The earliest edition of the English version dates

[12] A doctor of divinity well known in the region of King's Lynn and Norwich.

from 1508 to 1525, and there is no record of its performance in the sixteenth century, but like its Dutch predecessor it was popular in its printed form (the title page refers to it as made "in the *manner* of a moral play"). Its great appeal for audiences since the Middle Ages is due to the simplicity and directness of its story, which concerns the reluctant journey of an individual who has been summoned by Death. The latter part of the play deals with how Everyman may hope to attain salvation, which he does at the end. The English play with which *Everyman* is most often compared is Marlowe's tragedy *Dr. Faustus,* composed a century later; both dramas center on the state of an individual's soul and the choices that he must make concerning salvation.

For a long time, it was theorized that *Everyman* and other medieval morality and mystery plays descended directly from the liturgy of the Catholic Church. The simplest version of this theory holds that the drama moved physically from the altar to the front porch of the church and outside to a raised platform. Recent scholarship suggests a much more complicated process in which medieval drama was performed by professional actors who may have been located outside the confines of the church from the beginning. This does not, however, rule out the complicated interaction between Catholic liturgy, biblical story, and popular versions of devotional literature in a variety of forms and what we now think of as medieval drama. Whatever the evolutionary progress of this kind of drama, its reliance on Catholic doctrine is easy to see. What is so fascinating to the modern reader, however, is the extent to which the religious subject matter of the plays has been colored by realistic renderings of the human beings involved in the action, even when they are portrayed allegorically.

One of the major thematic elements of *Everyman* comes from its characteristic structure as a journey. Everyman is summoned by Death to travel to life's conclusion. The theme of travel is common in late fourteenth-century English literature: Chaucer's *Canterbury Tales,* the description of a pilgrimage, and Langland's long poem *Piers Plowman,* the narrative of a traveler across the English landscape, are famous examples. In this case, the journey is an allegorical one. Everyman will shed certain properties as he goes along: his Fellowship; his Kindred and Cousin; his Worldly Goods; his Discretion, Strength, and Beauty; and his Five Senses. Only Good Deeds and Knowledge will remain with him, Good Deeds to follow his body into the grave and Knowledge to take him to the gates of Heaven. This then is an allegory of Holy Dying, a journey in which the traveler gives up his trust in the things of this world while holding on to his good deeds and preparing himself through his religious knowledge for salvation.

This journey is enclosed in a frame. In the opening scene, God addresses the audience, noting that Everyman has behaved unnaturally, withholding himself from God by his sins. Having offered mercy and hearing no response, God now must deal out justice. For this he summons Death, commanding him to visit Everyman and call him to judgment; Death obeys and the journey of Everyman begins. At the end of the play, when Everyman's body has descended into the grave and his soul has risen to heaven, a character called the doctor appears; he is the learned doctor, or theologian, who explains to the audience that although Everyman's physical and worldly attributes have forsaken him, his Good Deeds have stayed to protect him. Because Everyman's accounts—his reckoning of good deeds—have proved sound, he is saved after all. The symmetry of the frame—God's command at the beginning and the doctor's explanation at the end—encloses the journey of Everyman, which is the subject of the rest of the play.

The dramatic action centers on the theme of riches. When Death first spies Everyman, he is walking alone, his mind on "fleshly lusts and his treasure." When Death summons Everyman, he tells him to bring along his book of accounts because God demands a "reckoning," regarding particularly "how thou hast spent thy life." Everyman ponders over the state of his affairs and tries to bribe Death to give him more time to get his books in order (he estimates that it will take him twelve more years). Death, of course, refuses the bribe. It is in this context of the contrast between worldly riches and the heavenly good that the rest of the drama is played out. At long last, Good Deeds is the true wealth Everyman finds he can rely on.

Everyman borrows both its structure and some of its topics from the religious literature available to the late Middle Ages. The structure of the play is like that of a sermon, with an introduction in which the main text is offered; a middle, which is the telling of an illustrative tale; and a closing interpretation in the light of holy doctrine. Many of the themes taken up in the course of the play repeat the standard themes of medieval religious lyric—the journey through life, the inevitability of death, the omnipresence of sin, the uncertainty of the state of the soul facing judgment, and the mystery of God's mercy. One scholar has pointed out how closely the action of the play follows the parable of the talents in Matthew 25:14–30, in which a man gives his servants differing amounts of coins and then expects them to give him back what was given to them, plus interest. Interpreted figuratively, the parable is a meditation on God's grace, which anticipates a strict accounting in the end.

One of the easiest features of the play to recognize, though one of the most difficult to describe, is its evocation of human personality and its use of gesture. Everyman is a real human being, gnashing his teeth in fear of Death, embracing Fellowship in the hope that it will save him, and voicing his dismay at the withdrawal of the Five Senses and his disbelief that Good Deeds will follow him into the grave. His gestures of denial, fear, and despair win us over: We recognize him through his actions as much as his words. The drama of whether Everyman will be saved carries us to the end because we know him by then as a real sinner; will his good deeds balance out his sins in the final accounting? We, as much as he, thrill with relief when Knowledge assures him, "Everyman, I will go with thee, and be thy guide." Almost despite ourselves, we are caught up in his drama; at heart we know it may be ours as well.

Suggested Readings

Everyman is available in many drama collections; the most frequently referred to, A. C. Cawley, ed., *Everyman and Medieval Miracle Plays* (revised 1974), has a good introduction. An even broader collection, with interesting texts for comparison, is John Gassner, ed., *Medieval and Tudor Drama* (1971).

Until recently, scholarship focused on the supposed rise of medieval drama from liturgical services in the Catholic Church. The key studies, Edmund K. Chambers's *The Medieval Stage* (1903) and Karl Young's *The Drama of the Medieval Church* (1933), are summarized in Hardin Craig's *English Religious Drama of the Middle Ages* (1955). More recent scholarship has focused on the history of the medieval stage separate from the celebration of the liturgy. See O. B. Hardison's *Christian Rite and Christian Drama in the Middle Ages* (1965) and Richard Southern's *The Medieval Theatre in the Round* (1957), which shows how a medieval English morality play, *The Castle of Perseverance,* may have been staged.

The best scholarship on the morality plays themselves is still in the form of articles. Among the most enlightening are Richard Axton's "The Morality Tradition," in Boris Ford, ed., *The New Pelican Guide to English Literature: Medieval Literature,* vol. I, part 1 (1982), 340–352; and, on *Everyman,* Lawrence V. Ryan's "Doctrine and Dramatic Structure in *Everyman,*" in Edward Vasta, ed., *Middle English Survey: Critical Essays* (1965), 283–308; and V. A. Kolve's "*Everyman* and the Parable of the Talents," in Jerome Taylor and Alan H. Nelson, eds., *Medieval English Drama* (1972), 316–340.

Everyman[1]

CHARACTERS:

GOD
MESSENGER
DEATH
EVERYMAN
FELLOWSHIP
KINDRED
COUSIN
GOODS
GOOD DEEDS
KNOWLEDGE
CONFESSION
BEAUTY
STRENGTH
DISCRETION
FIVE WITS
ANGEL
DOCTOR

Here Beginneth a Treatise how the High Father of Heaven Sendeth Death to Summon Every Creature to Come and Give Account of their Lives in this World, and is in Manner of a Moral Play.

[*Enter* MESSENGER *as a Prologue.*]

MESSENGER:

I pray you all give your audience,
And hear this matter with reverence,
By figure a moral play.
The *Summoning of Everyman* called it is,
That of our lives and ending shows
How transitory we be all day.
This matter is wondrous precious,
But the intent of it is more gracious,
And sweet to bear away.
The story saith: Man, in the beginning (10)
Look well, and take good heed to the ending,
Be you never so gay!
Ye think sin in the beginning full sweet,
Which in the end causeth the soul to weep,
When the body lieth in clay.
Here shall you see how Fellowship and Jollity,
Both Strength, Pleasure, and Beauty,
Will fade from thee as flower in May;
For ye shall hear how our Heaven King
Calleth Everyman to a general reckoning. (20)
Give audience, and hear what he doth say.

[*Exit.*]

[GOD *speaketh.*]

GOD:

I perceive, here in my majesty,
How that all creatures be to me unkind,
Living without dread in worldly prosperity.
Of ghostly sight[2] the people be so blind,
Drowned in sin, they know me not for their God.

---

[1]Our text is reproduced from Sylvan Barnet, Morton Berman, and William Burton, eds., *The Genius of the Early English Theater* (1962).

[2]Spiritual understanding.

In worldly riches is all their mind;
They fear not my rightwiseness,[3] the sharp rod.
My law that I showed, when I for them died,
They forget clean, and shedding of my blood red; 30
I hanged between two,[4] it cannot be denied;
To get them life I suffered to be dead;
I healed their feet, with thorns hurt was my head.
I could do no more than I did, truly;
And now I see the people do clean forsake me.
They use the seven deadly sins damnable,
As pride, covetise, wrath, and lechery
Now in the world be made commendable;
And thus they leave of angels, the heavenly company.
Every man liveth so after his own pleasure, 40
And yet of their life they be nothing sure.
I see the more that I them forbear
The worse they be from year to year.
All that liveth appaireth[5] fast;
Therefore I will, in all the haste,
Have a reckoning of every man's person;
For, and[6] I leave the people thus alone
In their life and wicked tempests,
Verily they will become much worse than beasts;
For now one would by envy another up eat; 50
Charity they do all clean forget.
I hoped well that every man
In my glory should make his mansion,
And thereto I had them all elect.
But now I see, like traitors deject,
They thank me not for the pleasure that I to them meant,
Nor yet for their being that I them have lent.
I proffered the people great multitude of mercy,
And few there be that asketh it heartily.
They be so cumbered with worldly riches 60
That needs on them I must do justice,
On every man living, without fear.
Where art thou, Death, thou mighty messenger?

[*Enter* DEATH.]

DEATH:

Almighty God, I am here at your will,
Your commandment to fulfill.

GOD:

Go thou to Everyman,[7]
And show him, in my name,

---

[3]Righteousness.

[4]Was crucified between two others.

[5]Grows worse.

[6]If.

[7]Everyman has a double aspect, as humankind in general and as the individual representative of humankind. Up to now, God has been speaking of all humankind; the Everyman we see in the play, however, will be individualized.

A pilgrimage he must on him take,
Which he in no wise may escape;
And that he bring with him a sure reckoning 70
Without delay or any tarrying.

[GOD *withdraws.*]

DEATH:

Lord, I will in the world go run overall,
And cruelly outsearch both great and small.
Every man will I beset that liveth beastly
Out of God's laws, and dreadeth not folly.
He that loveth riches I will strike with my dart,[8]
His sight to blind, and from heaven to depart[9]—
Except that alms be his good friend—
In hell for to dwell, world without end.
Lo, yonder I see Everyman walking. 80
Full little he thinketh on my coming;
His mind is on fleshly lusts and his treasure,
And great pain it shall cause him to endure
Before the Lord, Heaven King.

[*Enter* EVERYMAN.]

Everyman, stand still! Whither art thou going
Thus gaily? Hast thou thy Maker forget?

EVERYMAN:

Why askest thou?
Wouldest thou wit?[10]

DEATH:

Yea, sir; I will show you:
In great haste I am sent to thee 90
From God out of his majesty.

EVERYMAN:

What, sent to me?

DEATH:

Yea, certainly.
Though thou have forget him here,
He thinketh on thee in the heavenly sphere,
As, ere we depart, thou shalt know.

EVERYMAN:

What desireth God of me?

DEATH:

That shall I show thee:
A reckoning he will needs have
Without any longer respite. 100

EVERYMAN:

To give a reckoning longer leisure I crave;
This blind matter troubleth my wit.[11]

---

[8]The image of death with his arrow, or "dart," is a commonplace of medieval iconography, in both art and literature.

[9]Death will separate the sinner from the hope of heaven.

[10]What is it you would know?

[11]This unexpected development has confused me.

DEATH:

On thee thou must take a long journey;
Therefore thy book of count with thee thou bring,
For turn again thou cannot by no way.[12]
And look thou be sure of thy reckoning,
For before God thou shalt answer, and show
Thy many bad deeds, and good but a few;
How thou hast spent thy life, and in what wise,
Before the chief Lord of paradise. 110
Have ado that we were in that way,[13]
For, wit thou well, thou shalt make none attorney.[14]

EVERYMAN:

Full unready I am such reckoning to give.
I know thee not. What messenger art thou?

DEATH:

I am Death, that no man dreadeth,
For every man I rest, and no man spareth;[15]
For it is God's commandment
That all to me shall be obedient.

EVERYMAN:

O Death, thou comest when I had thee least in mind!
In thy power it lieth me to save; 120
Yet of my good will I give thee, if thou will be kind;[16]
Yea, a thousand pound shalt thou have,
And defer this matter till another day.

DEATH:

Everyman, it may not be, by no way.
I set not by gold, silver, nor riches,
Ne by pope, emperor, king, duke, ne princes;
For, and I would receive gifts great,
All the world I might get;
But my custom is clean contrary.
I give thee no respite. Come hence, and not tarry. 130

EVERYMAN:

Alas, shall I have no longer respite?
I may say Death giveth no warning!
To think on thee, it maketh my heart sick,
For all unready is my book of reckoning.
But twelve year and I might have abiding,[17]
My counting-book I would make so clear
That my reckoning I should not need to fear.
Wherefore, Death, I pray thee, for God's mercy,
Spare me till I be provided of remedy.

---

[12]Bring your accounts with you, for there is no escape.
[13]Make haste: Let us be on our way.
[14]Know well that no one shall take your place.
[15]I am Death, who fears no man, for I arrest (detain) everyone without exception.
[16]Everyman offers Death a bribe from his worldly goods. "Kind" has also the meaning of "natural."
[17]If I had twelve years' delay. (Everyman is pleading for a stay of execution.)

DEATH:

Thee availeth not to cry, weep, and pray; 140
But haste thee lightly[18] that thou were gone that journey,
And prove thy friends, if thou can;
For, wit thou well, the tide[19] abideth no man,
And in the world each living creature
For Adam's sin must die of nature.[20]

EVERYMAN:

Death, if I should this pilgrimage take,
And my reckoning surely make,
Show me, for Saint Charity,[21]
Should I not come again shortly?

DEATH:

No, Everyman; and thou be once there, 150
Thou mayst never more come here,
Trust me verily.

EVERYMAN:

O gracious God in the high seat celestial,
Have mercy on me in this most need!
Shall I have no company from this vale terrestrial
Of mine acquaintance, that way me to lead?

DEATH:

Yea, if any be so hardy
That would go with thee and bear thee company.
Hie thee that thou were gone to God's magnificence,
Thy reckoning to give before his presence. 160
What, weenest thou thy life is given thee,
And thy worldly goods also?[22]

EVERYMAN:

I had wend so, verily.

DEATH:

Nay, nay; it was but lent thee;
For as soon as thou art go,
Another a while shall have it, and then go therefro,
Even as thou hast done.
Everyman, thou art mad! Thou hast thy wits five,
And here on earth will not amend thy life;
For suddenly I do come. 170

EVERYMAN:

O wretched caitiff,[23] whither shall I flee,
That I might scape this endless sorrow?
Now, gentle Death, spare me till tomorrow,
That I may amend me
With good advisement.[24]

---

[18] Quickly.
[19] Time.
[20] According to the law of Nature.
[21] In the name of Holy Charity.
[22] Did you suppose that your life and worldly goods were given to you unconditionally?
[23] Prisoner; anyone in a miserable condition. Everyman is speaking of himself.
[24] Preparation.

DEATH:

Nay, thereto I will not consent,
Nor no man will I respite;
But to the heart suddenly I shall smite
Without any advisement.
And now out of thy sight I will me hie. 180
See thou make thee ready shortly,
For thou mayst say this is the day
That no man living may scape away.

[*Exit* DEATH.]

EVERYMAN:

Alas, I may well weep with sighs deep!
Now have I no manner of company
To help me in my journey, and me to keep;
And also my writing is full unready.
How shall I do now for to excuse me?
I would to God I had never be get![25]
To my soul a full great profit it had be; 190
For now I fear pains huge and great.
The time passeth. Lord, help, that all wrought!
For though I mourn it availeth nought.
The day passeth, and is almost ago.
I wot not well what for to do.
To whom were I best my complaint to make?
What and I to Fellowship thereof spake,
And showed him of this sudden chance?
For in him is all mine affiance;[26]
We have in the world so many a day 200
Be good friends in sport and play.
I see him yonder certainly.
I trust that he will bear me company;
Therefore to him will I speak to ease my sorrow.
Well met, good Fellowship, and good morrow!

[FELLOWSHIP *speaketh.*]

FELLOWSHIP:

Everyman, good morrow, by this day!
Sir, why lookest thou so piteously?
If any thing be amiss, I pray thee me say,
That I may help to remedy.

EVERYMAN:

Yea, good Fellowship, yea; 210
I am in great jeopardy.

FELLOWSHIP:

My true friend, show to me your mind;
I will not forsake thee to my life's end
In the way of good company.

EVERYMAN:

That was well spoken, and lovingly.

---

[25] I wish to God I had never been conceived.
[26] Trust.

FELLOWSHIP:
Sir, I must needs know your heaviness;
I have pity to see you in any distress.
If any have you wronged, ye shall revenged be,
Though I on the ground be slain for thee,
Though that I know before that I should die. 220

EVERYMAN:
Verily, Fellowship, gramercy.[27]

FELLOWSHIP:
Tush! by thy thanks I set not a straw.
Show me your grief, and say no more.

EVERYMAN:
If I my heart should to you break,
And then you to turn your mind from me,
And would not me comfort when ye hear me speak,
Then should I ten times sorrier be.

FELLOWSHIP:
Sir, I say as I will do, indeed.

EVERYMAN:
Then be you a good friend at need!
I have found you true here before. 230

FELLOWSHIP:
And so ye shall evermore;
For, in faith, and thou go to hell,
I will not forsake thee by the way.

EVERYMAN:
Ye speak like a good friend; I believe you well.
I shall deserve it, and I may.

FELLOWSHIP:
I speak of no deserving, by this day!
For he that will say, and nothing do,
Is not worthy with good company to go;
Therefore show me the grief of your mind,
As to your friend most loving and kind. 240

EVERYMAN:
I shall show you how it is:
Commanded I am to go a journey—
A long way, hard and dangerous—
And give a strait count, without delay,
Before the high Judge, Adonai.[28]
Wherefore, I pray you, bear me company,
As ye have promised, in this journey.

FELLOWSHIP:
That is matter indeed. Promise is duty;
But, and I should take such a voyage on me,
I know it well, it should be to my pain. 250
Also it maketh me afeard, certain.

---

[27] Many thanks (literally "grant you mercy").
[28] God.

But let us take counsel here as well as we can,
For your words would fear[29] a strong man.

EVERYMAN:
Why, ye said if I had need
Ye would me never forsake, quick ne dead,
Though it were to hell, truly.

FELLOWSHIP:
So I said, certainly,
But such pleasures be set aside, the sooth to say.
And also, if we took such a journey,
When should we come again? 260

EVERYMAN:
Nay, never again, till the day of doom.

FELLOWSHIP:
In faith, then will not I come there!
Who hath you these tidings brought?

EVERYMAN:
Indeed, Death was with me here.

FELLOWSHIP:
Now, by God that all hath bought,
If Death were the messenger,
For no man that is living today
I will not go that loath journey—
Not for the father that begat me!

EVERYMAN:
Ye promised otherwise, pardie.[30] 270

FELLOWSHIP:
I wot well I said so, truly.
And yet if thou wilt eat, and drink, and make good cheer,
Or haunt to women the lusty company,
I would not forsake you while the day is clear,
Trust me verily.

EVERYMAN:
Yea, thereto ye would be ready!
To go to mirth, solace, and play,
Your mind will sooner apply,
Than to bear me company in my long journey.

FELLOWSHIP:
Now, in good faith, I will not that way. 280
But and thou will murder, or any man kill,
In that I will help thee with a good will.

EVERYMAN:
O, that is a simple advice indeed!
Gentle fellow, help me in my necessity;
We have loved long, and now I need;
And now, gentle Fellowship, remember me.

FELLOWSHIP:
Whether ye have loved me or no,
By Saint John, I will not with thee go.

---

[29] Make afraid. [30] By God.

EVERYMAN:
Yet, I pray thee, take the labor, and do so much for me
To bring me forward, for Saint Charity, 290
And comfort me till I come without the town.[31]

FELLOWSHIP:
Nay, and thou would give me a new gown,
I will not a foot with thee go;
But, and thou had tarried, I would not have left thee so.[32]
And as now God speed thee in thy journey,
For from thee I will depart as fast as I may.

EVERYMAN:
Whither away, Fellowship? Will you forsake me?

FELLOWSHIP:
Yea, by my fay! To God I betake thee.[33]

EVERYMAN:
Farewell, good Fellowship; for thee my heart is sore.
Adieu for ever! I shall see thee no more. 300

FELLOWSHIP:
In faith, Everyman, farewell now at the end,
For you I will remember that parting is mourning.

[*Exit* FELLOWSHIP.]

EVERYMAN:
Alack! shall we thus depart indeed—
Ah, Lady, help!—without any more comfort?
Lo, Fellowship forsaketh me in my most need.
For help in this world whither shall I resort?
Fellowship here before with me would merry make,
And now little sorrow for me doth he take.
It is said, "In prosperity men friends may find,
Which in adversity be full unkind." 310
Now whither for succor shall I flee,
Sith that Fellowship hath forsaken me?
To my kinsmen I will, truly,
Praying them to help me in my necessity.
I believe that they will do so,
For "kind will creep where it may not go."[34]
I will go say, for yonder I see them go.
Where be ye now, my friends and kinsmen?

[*Enter* KINDRED *and* COUSIN.]

KINDRED:
Here be we now at your commandment.
Cousin, I pray you show us your intent 320
In any wise, and do not spare.

COUSIN:
Yea, Everyman, and to us declare
If ye be disposed to go any whither;
For, wit you well, we will live and die together.

---

[31] At least take on the task of guiding me to the outskirts of town.
[32] But if you had stayed here, I would not have abandoned you.
[33] Yes, by my faith! (The tone is ironic.) I commend you to God.
[34] Kinship will crawl where it is forbidden to walk (relatives will not desert one another).

KINDRED:
In wealth and woe we will with you hold,
For over his kin a man may be bold.[35]
EVERYMAN:
Gramercy, my friends and kinsmen kind.
Now shall I show you the grief of my mind:
I was commanded by a messenger,
That is a high king's chief officer; 330
He bade me go a pilgrimage, to my pain,
And I know well I shall never come again;
Also I must give a reckoning strait,
For I have a great enemy that hath me in wait,
Which intendeth me for to hinder.
KINDRED:
What account is that which ye must render?
That would I know.
EVERYMAN:
Of all my works I must show
How I have lived and my days spent;
Also of ill deeds that I have used 340
In my time sith life was me lent;
And of all virtues that I have refused.
Therefore, I pray you, go thither with me
To help to make mine account, for Saint Charity.
COUSIN:
What, to go thither? Is that the matter?
Nay, Everyman, I had liefer fast bread and water
All this five year and more.[36]
EVERYMAN:
Alas, that ever I was bore!
For now shall I never be merry,
If that you forsake me. 350
KINDRED:
Ah, sir, what, ye be a merry man!
Take good heart to you, and make no moan.
But one thing I warn you, by Saint Anne—
As for me, ye shall go alone.
EVERYMAN:
My Cousin, will you not with me go?
COUSIN:
No, by Our Lady! I have the cramp in my toe.
Trust not to me, for, so God me speed,
I will deceive you in your most need.
KINDRED:
It availeth not us to tice.[37]
Ye shall have my maid with all my heart; 360

[35] A man may have confidence in his family.
[36] I would rather dine on bread and water for five years.
[37] We should not try to entice you. (Because Kindred offers his companion in his place, it appears he is doing just that.)

She loveth to go to feasts, there to be nice,
And to dance, and abroad to start.
I will give her leave to help you in that journey,
If that you and she may agree.

EVERYMAN:
Now show me the very effect of your mind:
Will you go with me, or abide behind?

KINDRED:
Abide behind? Yea, that will I, and I may!
Therefore farewell till another day.

[*Exit* KINDRED.]

EVERYMAN:
How should I be merry or glad?
For fair promises men to me make, 370
But when I have most need they me forsake.
I am deceived; that maketh me sad.

COUSIN:
Cousin Everyman, farewell now,
For verily I will not go with you.
Also of mine own an unready reckoning
I have to account; therefore I make tarrying.
Now God keep thee, for now I go.

[*Exit* COUSIN.]

EVERYMAN:
Ah, Jesus, is all come hereto?
Lo, fair words maketh fools fain;[38]
They promise, and nothing will do certain. 380
My kinsmen promised me faithfully
For to abide with me steadfastly;
And now fast away do they flee.
Even so Fellowship promised me.
What friend were best me of to provide?
I lose my time here longer to abide.
Yet in my mind a thing there is:
All my life I have loved riches;
If that my Good now help me might,
He would make my heart full light. 390
I will speak to him in this distress.
Where art thou, my Goods and riches?

GOODS [*within*]:
Who calleth me? Everyman? What! hast thou haste?
I lie here in corners, trussed and piled so high,
And in chests I am locked so fast,
Also sacked in bags. Thou mayst see with thine eye
I cannot stir; in packs low I lie.
What would ye have? Lightly me say.

EVERYMAN:
Come hither, Good, in all the haste thou may,
For of counsel I must desire thee. 400

[*Enter* GOODS.]

[38] Fair words make fools glad.

GOODS:

Sir, and ye in the world have sorrow or adversity,
That can I help you to remedy shortly.

EVERYMAN:

It is another disease that grieveth me;
In this world it is not, I tell thee so.
I am sent for another way to go,
To give a strait count general
Before the highest Jupiter of all;
And all my life I have had joy and pleasure in thee,
Therefore, I pray thee, go with me;
For, peradventure, thou mayst before God Almighty 410
My reckoning help to clean and purify;
For it is said ever among
That "money maketh all right that is wrong."

GOODS:

Nay, Everyman, I sing another song.
I follow no man in such voyages;
For, and I went with thee,
Thou shouldst fare much the worse for me;
For because on me thou did set thy mind,
Thy reckoning I have made blotted and blind,
That thine account thou cannot make truly— 420
And that hast thou for the love of me.

EVERYMAN:

That would grieve me full sore,
When I should come to that fearful answer.
Up, let us go thither together.

GOODS:

Nay, not so! I am too brittle, I may not endure.
I will follow no man one foot, be ye sure.

EVERYMAN:

Alas, I have thee loved, and had great pleasure
All my life-days on good and treasure.

GOODS:

That is to thy damnation, without lesing,[39]
For my love is contrary to the love everlasting. 430
But if thou had me loved moderately during,
As to the poor to give part of me,
Then shouldst thou not in this dolor be,
Nor in this great sorrow and care.

EVERYMAN:

Lo, now was I deceived ere I was ware,
And all I may wite misspending of time.[40]

GOODS:

What, weenest thou that I am thine?

---

[39]Without lying. (Worldly Goods is correct; unlike Fellowship, Kindred, and Cousin, he expresses no guile.)

[40]Everyman claims that he has been deceived into misspending his time; Worldly Goods, like those before him, will point out that nothing in this world is permanent, but only a loan from God.

EVERYMAN:
I had wend so.
GOODS:
Nay, Everyman, I say no.
As for a while I was lent thee; 440
A season thou hast had me in prosperity.
My condition is man's soul to kill;
If I save one, a thousand I do spill.
Weenest thou that I will follow thee?
Nay, not from this world, verily.
EVERYMAN:
I had wend otherwise.
GOODS:
Therefore to thy soul Good is a thief;
For when thou art dead, this is my guise—
Another to deceive in this same wise
As I have done thee, and all to his soul's reprief. 450
EVERYMAN:
O false Good, cursed may thou be,
Thou traitor to God, that hast deceived me
And caught me in thy snare!
GOODS:
Mary! thou brought thyself in care,
Whereof I am right glad;
I must needs laugh, I cannot be sad.
EVERYMAN:
Ah, Good, thou hast had long my heartly love;
I gave thee that which should be the Lord's above.
But wilt thou not go with me indeed?
I pray thee truth to say. 460
GOODS:
No, so God me speed!
Therefore farewell, and have good day.
[*Exit* GOODS.]
EVERYMAN:
O, to whom shall I make my moan
For to go with me in that heavy journey?
First Fellowship said he would with me gone—
His words were very pleasant and gay,
But afterward he left me alone.
Then spake I to my kinsmen, all in despair,
And also they gave me words fair—
They lacked no fair speaking, 470
But all forsook me in the ending.
Then went I to my Goods, that I loved best,
In hope to have comfort, but there had I least;
For my Goods sharply did me tell
That he bringeth many into hell.
Then of myself I was ashamed,
And so I am worthy to be blamed.
Thus may I well myself hate.
Of whom shall I now counsel take?
I think that I shall never speed 480

Till that I go to my Good Deed.
But, alas, she is so weak
That she can neither go[41] nor speak.
Yet will I venture on her now.
My Good Deeds, where be you?
[GOOD DEEDS *speaks from the ground.*]

GOOD DEEDS:
Here I lie, cold in the ground.
Thy sins hath me sore bound,
That I cannot stir.

EVERYMAN:
O Good Deeds, I stand in fear!
I must you pray of counsel, 490
For help now should come right well.

GOOD DEEDS:
Everyman, I have understanding
That ye be summoned account to make
Before Messias, of Jerusalem King;
And you do by me,[42] that journey with you will I take.

EVERYMAN:
Therefore I come to you, my moan to make.
I pray you that ye will go with me.

GOOD DEEDS:
I would full fain, but I cannot stand, verily.

EVERYMAN:
Why, is there anything on you fall?

GOOD DEEDS:
Yea, sir, I may thank you of all;[43] 500
If ye had perfectly cheered me,
Your book of count full ready had be.
Look, the books of your works and deeds eke![44]
Behold how they lie under the feet
To your soul's heaviness.

EVERYMAN:
Our Lord Jesus help me!
For one letter here I cannot see.[45]

GOOD DEEDS:
There is a blind reckoning in time of distress.

EVERYMAN:
Good Deeds, I pray you help me in this need,
Or else I am for ever damned indeed; 510
Therefore help me to make reckoning
Before the Redeemer of all thing,
That King is, and was, and ever shall.

GOOD DEEDS:
Everyman, I am sorry of your fall,
And fain would I help you, and I were able.

EVERYMAN:
Good Deeds, your counsel I pray you give me.

---

[41] Get about.
[42] If you abide by me.
[43] For everything. [44] Also.
[45] I cannot see a single letter.

GOOD DEEDS:
That shall I do verily;
Though that on my feet I may not go,
I have a sister that shall with you also,
Called Knowledge, which shall with you abide, 520
To help you to make that dreadful reckoning.
[*Enter* KNOWLEDGE.]

KNOWLEDGE:
Everyman, I will go with thee, and be thy guide,
In thy most need to go by thy side.

EVERYMAN:
In good condition I am now in every thing,
And am wholly content with this good thing,
Thanked be God my creator.

GOOD DEEDS:
And when she hath brought you there
Where thou shalt heal thee of thy smart,[46]
Then go you with your reckoning and your Good Deeds together,
For to make you joyful at heart 530
Before the Blessed Trinity.

EVERYMAN:
My Good Deeds, gramercy!
I am well content, certainly,
With your words sweet.

KNOWLEDGE:
Now go we together lovingly
To Confession, that cleansing river.

EVERYMAN:
For joy I weep; I would we were there!
But, I pray you give me cognition
Where dwelleth that holy man, Confession?

KNOWLEDGE:
In the house of salvation: 540
We shall find him in that place,
That shall us comfort, by God's grace.
[KNOWLEDGE *leads* EVERYMAN *to* CONFESSION.]
Lo, this is Confession. Kneel down and ask mercy,
For he is in good conceit with God Almighty.[47]

EVERYMAN:
O glorious fountain, that all uncleanness doth clarify,
Wash from me the spots of vice unclean,
That on me no sin may be seen.
I come with Knowledge for my redemption,
Redempt with heart and full contrition;
For I am commanded a pilgrimage to take, 550
And great accounts before God to make.
Now I pray you, Shrift, mother of salvation,[48]
Help my Good Deeds for my piteous exclamation.

---

[46] Pain.
[47] He is well thought of by God.
[48] Shrift: confession (the modern "to make short shrift"). Though allegorized as a male figure, Confession is also seen as the "mother of salvation."

CONFESSION:

I know your sorrow well, Everyman.
Because with Knowledge ye come to me,
I will you comfort as well as I can,
And a precious jewel I will give thee,
Called penance, voider of adversity;
Therewith shall your body chastised be,
With abstinence and perseverance in God's service. 560
Here shall you receive that scourge of me,
Which is penance strong that ye must endure,
To remember thy Savior was scourged for thee
With sharp scourges, and suffered it patiently;
So must thou, ere thou scape that painful pilgrimage.
Knowledge, keep him in this voyage,
And by that time Good Deeds will be with thee.
But in any wise be siker of mercy,
For your time draweth fast, and ye will saved be.[49]
Ask God mercy, and he will grant truly. 570
When with the scourge of penance man doth him bind,
The oil of forgiveness then shall he find.

EVERYMAN:

Thanked be God for his gracious work!
For now I will my penance begin;
This hath rejoiced and lighted my heart,
Though the knots be painful and hard within.

KNOWLEDGE:

Everyman, look your penance that ye fulfill,
What pain that ever it to you be;
And Knowledge shall give you counsel at will
How your account ye shall make clearly. 580

EVERYMAN:

O eternal God, O heavenly figure,
O way of rightwiseness, O goodly vision,
Which descended down in a virgin pure
Because he would every man redeem,
Which Adam forfeited by his disobedience,
O blessed Godhead, elect and high divine,
Forgive my grievous offense;
Here I cry thee mercy in this presence.
O ghostly treasure, O ransomer and redeemer,
Of all the world hope and conductor, 590
Mirror of joy, and founder of mercy,
Which enlumineth heaven and earth thereby,
Hear my clamorous complaint, though it late be;
Receive my prayers, unworthy of thy benignity.
Though I be a sinner most abominable,
Yet let my name be written in Moses' table.
O Mary, pray to the Maker of all thing,
Me for to help at my ending,
And save me from the power of my enemy,

[49]But if in any way you are sure of receiving mercy, you will be saved, for your time draws near.

For Death assaileth me strongly. 600
And, Lady, that I may by mean of thy prayer
Of your Son's glory to be partner,
By the means of his passion, I it crave.
I beseech you help my soul to save.
Knowledge, give me the scourge of penance;
My flesh therewith shall give acquittance.[50]
I will now begin, if God give me grace.

KNOWLEDGE:
Everyman, God give you time and space!
Thus I bequeath you in the hands of our Savior.
Now may you make your reckoning sure. 610

EVERYMAN:
In the name of the Holy Trinity,
My body sore punished shall be.
Take this, body, for the sin of the flesh! [*Scourges himself.*]
Also thou delightest to go gay and fresh,
And in the way of damnation thou did me bring;
Therefore suffer now strokes of punishing.
Now of penance I will wade the water clear,
To save me from purgatory, that sharp fire.
[GOOD DEEDS *rises from the floor.*]

GOOD DEEDS:
I thank God, now I can walk and go,
And am delivered of my sickness and woe. 620
Therefore with Everyman I will go, and not spare;
His good works I will help him to declare.

KNOWLEDGE:
Now, Everyman, be merry and glad!
Your Good Deeds cometh now; ye may not be sad.
Now is your Good Deeds whole and sound,
Going upright upon the ground.

EVERYMAN:
My heart is light, and shall be evermore;
Now will I smite faster than I did before.

GOOD DEEDS:
Everyman, pilgrim, my special friend,
Blessed be thou without end; 630
For thee is preparate the eternal glory.
Ye have me made whole and sound,
Therefore I will bide by thee in every stound.[51]

EVERYMAN:
Welcome, my Good Deeds! Now I hear thy voice,
I weep for very sweetness of love.

KNOWLEDGE:
Be no more sad, but ever rejoice;
God seeth thy living in his throne above.
Put on this garment to thy behove,

---

[50] Satisfaction.
[51] Moment of suffering.

Which is wet with your tears,
Or else before God you may it miss, 640
When ye to your journey's end come shall.

EVERYMAN:
Gentle Knowledge, what do ye it call?

KNOWLEDGE:
It is a garment of sorrow;
From pain it will you borrow;[52]
Contrition it is,
That getteth forgiveness;
It pleaseth God passing well.

GOOD DEEDS:
Everyman, will you wear it for your heal?

EVERYMAN:
Now blessed be Jesu, Mary's Son,
For now have I on true contrition. 650
And let us go now without tarrying.
Good Deeds, have we clear our reckoning?

GOOD DEEDS:
Yea, indeed, I have here.

EVERYMAN:
Then I trust we need not fear.
Now, friends, let us not part in twain.

KNOWLEDGE:
Nay, Everyman, that will we not, certain.

GOOD DEEDS:
Yet must thou lead with thee
Three persons of great might.

EVERYMAN:
Who should they be?

GOOD DEEDS:
Discretion and Strength they hight,[53] 660
And thy Beauty may not abide behind.

KNOWLEDGE:
Also ye must call to mind
Your Five Wits[54] as for your counselors.

GOOD DEEDS:
You must have them ready at all hours.

EVERYMAN:
How shall I get them hither?

KNOWLEDGE:
You must call them all together,
And they will hear you incontinent.

EVERYMAN:
My friends, come hither and be present,
Discretion, Strength, my Five Wits, and Beauty.

[*Enter* BEAUTY, STRENGTH, DISCRETION, *and* FIVE WITS.]

---

[52]Redeem.

[53]Are named.

[54]Five Senses. By assembling Discretion, Strength, Beauty, and the Five Senses, Everyman is calling up the last physical characteristics to leave him before death.

BEAUTY:
Here at your will we be all ready. 670
What will ye that we should do?

GOOD DEEDS:
That ye would with Everyman go,
And help him in his pilgrimage.
Advise you, will ye with him or not in that voyage?

STRENGTH:
We will bring him all thither,
To his help and comfort, ye may believe me.

DISCRETION:
So will we go with him all together.

EVERYMAN:
Almighty God, loved may thou be!
I give thee laud that I have hither brought
Strength, Discretion, Beauty, and Five Wits. Lack I nought. 680
And my Good Deeds, with Knowledge clear,
All be in my company at my will here.
I desire no more to my business.

STRENGTH:
And I, Strength, will by you stand in distress,
Though thou would in battle fight on the ground.

FIVE WITS:
And though it were through the world round,
We will not depart for sweet ne sour.

BEAUTY:
No more will I unto death's hour,
Whatsoever thereof befall.

DISCRETION:
Everyman, advise you first of all; 690
Go with a good advisement and deliberation.
We all give you virtuous monition
That all shall be well.

EVERYMAN:
My friends, harken what I will tell:
I pray God reward you in his heavenly sphere.
Now harken, all that be here,
For I will make my testament
Here before you all present:
In alms half my good I will give with my hands twain
In the way of charity with good intent, 700
And the other half still shall remain
In queth, to be returned there it ought to be.[55]
This I do in despite of the fiend of hell,
To go quite out of his peril
Ever after and this day.

KNOWLEDGE:
Everyman, harken what I say:
Go to Priesthood, I you advise,
And receive of him in any wise

[55] After giving away half his belongings as an act of charity, Everyman holds the other half in bequest, to go where it is determined it should. This is a formal will.

The holy sacrament and ointment together.
Then shortly see ye turn again hither; 710
We will all abide you here.

FIVE WITS:
Yea, Everyman, hie you that ye ready were.
There is no emperor, king, duke, ne baron,
That of God hath commission
As hath the least priest in the world being;
For of the blessed sacraments pure and benign
He bareth the keys, and thereof hath the cure
For man's redemption—it is ever sure—
Which God for our soul's medicine
Gave us out of his heart with great pain 720
Here in this transitory life, for thee and me.
The blessed sacraments seven there be:
Baptism, confirmation, with priesthood good,
And the sacrament of God's precious flesh and blood,
Marriage, the holy extreme unction, and penance.
These seven be good to have in remembrance,
Gracious sacraments of high divinity.

EVERYMAN:
Fain would I receive that holy body,
And meekly to my ghostly father I will go.

FIVE WITS:
Everyman, that is the best that ye can do. 730
God will you to salvation bring,
For priesthood exceedeth all other thing:
To us Holy Scripture they do teach,
And converteth man from sin heaven to reach;
God hath to them more power given
Than to any angel that is in heaven.
With five words[56] he may consecrate,
God's body in flesh and blood to make,
And handleth his Maker between his hands.
The priest bindeth and unbindeth all bands, 740
Both in earth and in heaven.[57]
Thou ministers all the sacraments seven;
Though we kissed thy feet, thou were worthy;
Thou art surgeon that cureth sin deadly;
No remedy we find under God
But all only priesthood.[58]
Everyman, God gave priests that dignity,
And setteth them in his stead among us to be.
Thus be they above angels in degree.

[*Exit* EVERYMAN *to receive the last sacraments from the priest.*]

KNOWLEDGE:
If priests be good, it is so, surely. 750
But when Jesus hanged on the cross with great smart,

---

[56] "For this is my body," spoken at the offering at communion.

[57] A reference to Matthew 16:19, that whatever St. Peter bound or dissolved on Earth will be honored in Heaven.

[58] All except the priesthood.

There he gave out of his blessed heart
The same sacrament in great torment.
He sold them not to us, that Lord omnipotent.
Therefore Saint Peter the apostle doth say
That Jesu's curse hath all they
Which God their Savior do buy or sell,
Or they for any money do take or tell.
Sinful priests giveth the sinners example bad;
Their children sitteth by other men's fires, I have heard; 760
And some haunteth women's company
With unclean life, as lusts of lechery:
These be with sin made blind.

FIVE WITS:
I trust to God no such may we find.
Therefore let us priesthood honor,
And follow their doctrine for our souls' succor.
We be their sheep, and they shepherds be,
By whom we all be kept in surety.
Peace, for yonder I see Everyman come,
Which hath made true satisfaction. 770

GOOD DEEDS:
Methink it is he indeed.

[*Re-enter* EVERYMAN.]

EVERYMAN:
Now Jesu be your alder speed!
I have received the sacrament for my redemption,
And then mine extreme unction.
Blessed be all they that counseled me to take it!
And now, friends, let us go without longer respite;
I thank God that ye have tarried so long.
Now set each of you on this rod your hand,[59]
And shortly follow me.
I go before there I would be; God be our guide! 780

STRENGTH:
Everyman, we will not from you go
Till ye have done this voyage long.

DISCRETION:
I, Discretion, will bide by you also.

KNOWLEDGE:
And though this pilgrimage be never so strong,
I will never part you fro.

STRENGTH:
Everyman, I will be as sure by thee
As ever I did by Judas Maccabee.[60]

[*They go together to the grave.*]

EVERYMAN:
Alas, I am so faint I may not stand;
My limbs under me doth fold.

---

[59] He commands each of them to touch the Cross.
[60] I Maccabees 3:19.

Friends, let us not turn again to this land, 790
Not for all the world's gold;
For into this cave must I creep
And turn to earth, and there to sleep.

BEAUTY:
What, into this grave? Alas!

EVERYMAN:
Yea, there shall ye consume, more and less.

BEAUTY:
And what, should I smother here?

EVERYMAN:
Yea, by my faith, and never more appear.
In this world live no more we shall,
But in heaven before the highest Lord of all.

BEAUTY:
I cross out all this! Adieu, by Saint John! 800
I take my cap in my lap, and am gone.

EVERYMAN:
What, Beauty, whither will ye?

BEAUTY:
Peace, I am deaf; I look not behind me,
Not and thou wouldest give me all the gold in thy chest.

[*Exit* BEAUTY.]

EVERYMAN:
Alas, whereto may I trust?
Beauty goeth fast away from me;
She promised with me to live and die.

STRENGTH:
Everyman, I will thee also forsake and deny;
Thy game liketh me not at all.

EVERYMAN:
Why, then, ye will forsake me all? 810
Sweet Strength, tarry a little space.

STRENGTH:
Nay, sir, by the rood of grace!
I will hie me from thee fast,
Though thou weep till thy heart to-brast.

EVERYMAN:
Ye would ever bide by me, ye said.

STRENGTH:
Yea, I have you far enough conveyed.
Ye be old enough, I understand,
Your pilgrimage to take on hand;
I repent me that I hither came.

EVERYMAN:
Strength, you to displease I am to blame; 820
Yet promise is debt, this ye well wot.

STRENGTH:
In faith, I care not.
Thou art but a fool to complain;
You spend your speech and waste your brain.
Go, thrust thee into the ground!

[*Exit* STRENGTH.]

EVERYMAN:
I had wend surer I should you have found.
He that trusteth in his Strength
She him deceiveth at the length.
Both Strength and Beauty forsaketh me;
Yet they promised me fair and lovingly. 830

DISCRETION:
Everyman, I will after Strength be gone;
As for me, I will leave you alone.

EVERYMAN:
Why, Discretion, will ye forsake me?

DISCRETION:
Yea, in faith, I will go from thee,
For when Strength goeth before
I follow after evermore.

EVERYMAN:
Yet, I pray thee, for the love of the Trinity,
Look in my grave once piteously.

DISCRETION:
Nay, so nigh will I not come;
Farewell, everyone! 840

[*Exit* DISCRETION.]

EVERYMAN:
O, all thing faileth, save God alone—
Beauty, Strength, and Discretion;
For when Death bloweth his blast,
They all run from me full fast.

FIVE WITS:
Everyman, my leave now of thee I take;
I will follow the other, for here I thee forsake.

EVERYMAN:
Alas, then may I wail and weep,
For I took you for my best friend.

FIVE WITS:
I will no longer thee keep;
Now farewell, and there an end. 850

[*Exit* FIVE WITS.]

EVERYMAN:
O Jesu, help! All hath forsaken me.

GOOD DEEDS:
Nay, Everyman; I will bide with thee.
I will not forsake thee indeed;
Thou shalt find me a good friend at need.

EVERYMAN:
Gramercy, Good Deeds! Now may I true friends see.
They have forsaken me, every one;
I loved them better than my Good Deeds alone.
Knowledge, will ye forsake me also?

KNOWLEDGE:
Yea, Everyman, when ye to Death shall go;
But not yet, for no manner of danger. 860

EVERYMAN:
Gramercy, Knowledge, with all my heart.

KNOWLEDGE:
Nay, yet I will not from hence depart
Till I see where ye shall be come.
EVERYMAN:
Methink, alas, that I must be gone
To make my reckoning and my debts pay,
For I see my time is nigh spent away.
Take example, all ye that this do hear or see,
How they that I loved best do forsake me,
Except my Good Deeds that bideth truly.
GOOD DEEDS:
All earthly things is but vanity: 870
Beauty, Strength, and Discretion do man forsake,
Foolish friends, and kinsmen, that fair spake—
All fleeth save Good Deeds, and that am I.
EVERYMAN:
Have mercy on me, God most mighty;
And stand by me, thou mother and maid, Holy Mary.
GOOD DEEDS:
Fear not; I will speak for thee.
EVERYMAN:
Here I cry God mercy.
GOOD DEEDS:
Short our end, and minish our pain;
Let us go and never come again.
EVERYMAN:
Into thy hands, Lord, my soul I commend; 880
Receive it, Lord, that it be not lost.
As thou me boughtest, so me defend,
And save me from the fiend's boast,
That I may appear with that blessed host
That shall be saved at the day of doom.
In manus tuas, of might's most
For ever, *commendo spiritum meum.*[61]

[EVERYMAN *and* GOOD DEEDS *descend into the grave.*]

KNOWLEDGE:
Now hath he suffered that we all shall endure;[62]
The Good Deeds shall make all sure.
Now hath he made ending. 890
Methinketh that I hear angels sing,
And make great joy and melody
Where Everyman's soul received shall be.
ANGEL:
Come, excellent elect spouse, to Jesu!
Here above thou shalt go
Because of thy singular virtue.
Now the soul is taken the body fro,
Thy reckoning is crystal clear.
Now shalt thou in to the heavenly sphere,

---

[61] See Luke 23:46 and line 880, above: "Into thy hands I commend my spirit."

[62] The line "Now hath he suffered that we all shall endure" refers first of all to Christ's redemption; but Everyman, by his performance of penance and confession, has also become a type for the rest of humankind to emulate.

Unto the which all ye shall come 900
That liveth well before the day of doom.

[*Exit* KNOWLEDGE.]

[*Enter* DOCTOR.]

DOCTOR:

This moral men may have in mind.
Ye hearers, take it of worth, old and young,
And forsake Pride, for he deceiveth you in the end;
And remember Beauty, Five Wits, Strength, and Discretion,
They all at the last do every man forsake,
Save his Good Deeds, there doth he take.[63]
But beware, and they be small
Before God, he hath no help at all;
None excuse may be there for every man. 910
Alas, how shall he do then?
For after death amends may no man make,
For then mercy and pity doth him forsake.
If his reckoning be not clear when he doth come,
God will say: *"Ite, maledicti, in ignem eternum."*[64]
And he that hath his account whole and sound,
High in heaven he shall be crowned;
Unto which place God bring us all thither,
That we may live body and soul together.
Thereto help the Trinity! 920
Amen, say ye, for Saint Charity.

Thus Endeth this Moral Play of Everyman.

THE WORLD CONTEXT

THE KORAN

[651–652]

The Koran is the sacred book of Islam, the third major religion to originate in the Middle East. After the Bible, the Koran, or *Qur'an,* which means "book" or "reading" in Arabic, is probably the most influential book in the world. The Koran is a series of revelations from God, or Allah, to the prophet Muhammad (c. 570–632 C.E.) about living a moral life. Believed to be the final revelation by Allah to humankind, the Koran reviles idolatry, exalts monotheism, praises righteousness, and promises a glorious afterlife for believers and hellfire for the unredeemed. The Koran, however, was much more than a series of spiritual admonitions for its early believers; it became the clarion call to heterogeneous, nomadic tribes of the Arabian Peninsula to unite in conquest, a call

[63] Except for his Good Deeds; those he takes there.
[64] Matthew 25:41: "Depart, you accursed, into the fire eternal."

that eventually extended the nation of Islam far beyond its original borders. Today Islam is a major force in world politics. It is very popular in Eastern developing nations and numbers over 800 million adherents worldwide.

Born in Mecca to a poor clan of the Quraish tribe, Muhammad was orphaned as a child. As a young man he worked for his uncle as a camel driver on caravans, but he also spent time alone thinking. Marriage to a rich widow, Khadijah, brought him four daughters, the management of her caravans, and more time for reflection and meditation. In 611 C.E., while in the desert hills outside of Mecca, he had a vision from the angel Gabriel, who said:

> Recite thou, in the name of thy Lord who created—
> Created man from Clots of Blood—
> Recite thou! For thy Lord is the Most Beneficent,
> Who hath taught the use of the pen—
> Hath taught Man that which he knoweth not.

This was the first fragment of the Koran. After an intermission of two to three years, the visions began again, sometimes in dreams and sometimes in daytime reveries, and over a period of twenty-two years the entire Koran was transmitted to Muhammad. He recited the verses to his followers, who memorized them; eventually the verses were written down by scribes on everything from parchment, leather, and palm leaves to camel shoulder blades and ribs. After much tribal conflict, Muhammad and a small band of followers were forced to relocate in Medina in 622, where they supported themselves with raids on caravans to and from Mecca. Muhammad's defeat of armies from Mecca led to a large number of converts, and by the time of his death in 632, the religion of Islam was firmly established with a large following.

Under the Caliph Othman, Zaid ibn Thabit, Muhammad's secretary, collected Muhammad's texts and then in 651–652 C.E. edited them into 114 suras, or chapters, thereby creating the official version of the Koran in Arabic. All alternative texts were destroyed at that time, firmly fixing the canonical version that has been passed down, virtually without alteration, to the present time. Each of the 114 suras is titled with a word such as "Women" or "Jonah" that suggests its contents; the suras vary in length from a few words to 286 verses, and, although the shortest suras tend to be the earliest, the longest suras come first in the Koran.

Most of the suras we have selected include stories of figures recognizable to Western audiences, such as Abraham, Moses, Jonah, and Jesus. Parallels between the Bible and the Koran exist in part because the Koran is indebted to Jewish and Christian writings, as well as to apocryphal and folk traditions. Both Arabs and Jews trace their lineage to a common ancestor, Abraham, although the Arabs descended from Abraham's son by Hagar, Ishmael. The literature of the Koran is written from the point of view of God addressing various audiences, such as believers or unbelievers, all of humankind, or just Muhammad. Nevertheless Muhammad appears to have put the stamp of his own imagination on the prose literature in the Koran and on the writing style of the whole work, giving it a poetic fervor. There is a compelling urgency in the repetitious, impassioned exhortations to ethical reform that must have reassured his early followers and intimidated his enemies.

The Koran is not held together by narrative threads or cultural histories, such as we find in the Bible. The first sura is like the Lord's Prayer of the Muslims and is used with all Muslim worship and formal negotiations. Sura 2 is a reminder that Muslims recognize the tradition of Judaism and Christianity, although they regard Jesus as a human prophet, whom the prophet Muhammad has superseded. Sura 4 establishes the social hierarchy in Muslim society regarding the relationships of men and women. In Suras 10 and 12 we meet figures from the Bible; the story of Joseph in the Koran contains some new details and twists in the plot. Sura 19 mentions the birth of John the Baptist and Jesus' conception and birth. Suras 55 and 56 deal with the Day of Judgment and with the delights of heaven. Sura 112, thought by some scholars to be the last sura, contains the essence of the Koran by reaffirming the omnipotence and unity of Allah.

Muslims (which in Arabic means "ones who submit") believe that the Koran completes the revelations given earlier to Moses and Jesus, and represents the final revelation from God. Often referred to as "The Noble Qur'an" or "The Book," the Koran provides the necessary spiritual, ethical, and social guidelines for all of a Muslim's life. Like the study of the Torah for Jews, the most important activity for a Muslim is the study of God's word in the Koran. A person who memorizes the entire Koran is called Hafiz, someone who "guards" the Book in his heart. It has been used to define Arabic grammar and to establish legal codes for the courtroom. With the authority of the Koran, armies of Muslims have engaged in wars with neighboring peoples, converting large numbers of them to Islam.

Although the early spread of Islam was heavily dependent on the sword, the message of the Koran reaches out to the downtrodden and the poor. The essential simplicity and beauty of the Islamic faith appeals to those who seek a direct relationship with Allah wherever one is, without a reliance on an intermediary priesthood or on a special place of worship such as a church or synagogue. All men are equal before Allah (although women are considered inferior to men). The Five Pillars of the Faith are clear and make Islam accessible to a wide variety of peoples: The first duty is to recite the creed, "There is no God but Allah, and Muhammad is His Prophet." Muslims are to acknowledge the oneness of Allah in prayer five times each day, reciting the opening verses of the Koran, known as *Al-Fatitah.* They must practice charity and help the needy; they are to fast in the month of Ramadan and to make a pilgrimage to Mecca at least once in a lifetime, if possible. Someone who acknowledges the unity of God and practices the four duties is called a *Mu'min,* or believer. A person who disagrees with these pillars is a *kafir,* or infidel. In time the Koran was supplemented by a body of sayings and accepted practices called the Traditions (*Hadith*), a manual of daily prescriptions for prayer, almsgiving, diet, burial, fasting, and so forth.

Within a century after Muhammad's death, the message of Islam dominated the region from Spain across North Africa to India.

SUGGESTED READINGS

Translations of the Koran with introductory material have been made by G. Sale (1734), E. H. Palmer (1880), and N. J. Dawood (1965). For extended studies of the Koran, see A. J. Arberry's *Koran Interpreted,* 2 vols. (1955), and H. A. Ali's *The Student's Qur'an* (1961).

The Koran

Translated by J. M. Rodwell

SURA 1: [THE OPENING]

[Mecca]

In the Name of God, the Compassionate, the Merciful[1]
Praise be to God, Lord of the worlds!
The compassionate, the merciful!
King on the day of reckoning!
Thee *only* do we worship, and to Thee do we cry for help.
Guide Thou us on the straight path,
The path of those to whom Thou hast been gracious;—with whom thou art not angry, and who go not astray.

[1]According to Islamic law, this phrase must precede most formal tasks.

FROM

SURA 2: THE COW

[Medina]

In the Name of God, the Compassionate, the Merciful

ELIF. LAM. MIM.[2] No doubt is there about this Book: It is a guidance to the God-fearing,

Who believe in the unseen, who observe prayer, and out of what we have bestowed on them, expend *for God;*

And who believe in what hath been sent down to thee, and in what hath been sent down before thee, and full faith have they in the life to come:

These are guided by their Lord; and with these it shall be well.

As to the infidels, alike is it to them whether thou warn them or warn them not—they will not believe:

Their hearts and their ears hath God sealed up; and over their eyes is a covering. For them, a severe chastisement!

And some there are who say, "We believe in God, and in the latter day:" Yet are they not believers!

Fain would they deceive God and those who have believed; but they deceive themselves only, and know it not.

Diseased are their hearts! And that disease hath God increased to them. There's a sore chastisement, for that they treated their *prophet* as a liar!

And when it is said to them, "Cause not disorders in the earth:" they say, "Nay, rather do we set them right."

Is it not that they are themselves the authors of disorder? But they perceive it not!

And when it is said to them, "Believe as other men have believed;" they say, "Shall we believe as the fools have believed?" Is it not that they are themselves the fools? But they know it not!

And when they meet the faithful they say, "We believe;" but when they are apart with their Satans[3] they say, "Verily we hold with you, and *at them* we only mock."

God shall mock at them, and keep them long in their rebellion, wandering in perplexity.

These are they who have purchased error at the price of guidance: but their traffic hath not been gainful, neither are they guided at all.

They are like one who kindleth a fire, and when it hath thrown its light on all around him. . . . God taketh away their light and leaveth them in darkness—they cannot see!—

Deaf, dumb, blind: therefore they shall not retrace their steps *from error!*

Or like *those who, when there cometh* a storm-cloud out of the Heaven, big with darkness thunder and lightning, thrust their fingers into their ears because of the thunder-clap, for fear of death! God is round about the infidels.

The lightning almost snatcheth away their eyes! So oft as it gleameth on them they walk on in it, but when darkness closeth upon them, they stop! And if God pleased, of their ears and of their eyes would he surely deprive them:—verily God is Almighty! O men *of Mecca* adore your Lord, who hath created you and those who were before you: haply ye will fear Him

Who hath made the earth a bed for you, and the heaven a covering, and hath caused water to come down from heaven, and by it hath brought forth fruits for your sustenance! Do not then wittingly give peers to God.

---

[2]That is, at the command of Muhammad.

[3]The Jews and Christians who are hostile to Muhammad's mission.

And if ye be in doubt as to that which we have sent down to our servant, then produce a Sura like it, and summon your witnesses, beside God, if ye are men of truth:

But if ye do it not, and never shall ye do it, then fear the fire prepared for the infidels, whose fuel is men and stones:

But announce to those who believe and do the things that are right, that for them are gardens 'neath which the rivers flow! So oft as they are fed therefrom with fruit for sustenance, they shall say, "This same was our sustenance of old:" And they shall have its like given to them. Therein shall they have wives of *perfect* purity, and therein shall they abide for ever.

Verily God is not ashamed to set forth as well the instance of a gnat as of any nobler object: for as to those who have believed, they know it to be the truth from their Lord; but as to the unbelievers, they will say, "What meaneth God by this comparison?" Many will He mislead by such *parables* and many guide: but none will He mislead thereby except the wicked,

Who, after its establishment, violate the covenant of God, and cut in sunder what God hath bidden to be joined, and act disorderly on the Earth. These are they who shall suffer loss!

How can ye withhold faith from God? Ye were dead and He gave you life; next He will cause you to die; next He will restore you to life: next shall ye return to Him!

He it is who created for you all that is on Earth, then proceeded to the Heaven, and into seven[4] Heavens did He fashion it: and He knoweth all things.

When thy Lord said to the angels, "Verily, I am about to place one in my stead on earth," they said, "Wilt thou place there one who will do ill therein and shed blood, when we celebrate thy praise and extol thy holiness?" God said, "Verily, I know what ye know not."

And he taught Adam the names of all things, and then set them before the angels, and said, "Tell me the names of these, if ye are endued with wisdom."

They said, "Praise be to Thee! We have no knowledge but what Thou hast given us to know. Thou! Thou art the Knowing, the Wise."

He said, "O Adam, inform them of their names." And when he had informed them of their names, He said, "Did I not say to you that I know the hidden things of the Heavens and of the Earth, and that I know what ye bring to light, and what ye hide?"

And when we said to the angels, "Bow down and worship Adam," then worshipped they all, save Eblis.[5] He refused and swelled with pride, and became one of the unbelievers.

And we said, "O Adam! dwell thou and thy wife in the Garden, and eat ye plentifully therefrom wherever ye list; but to this tree come not nigh, lest ye become of the transgressors."

But Satan made them slip from it, and caused their banishment from the place in which they were. And we said, "Get ye down, the one of you an enemy to the other: and there shall be for you in the earth a dwelling-place, and a provision for a time."

And words *of prayer* learned Adam from his Lord: and God turned to him; for He loveth to turn, the Merciful.

---

[4]The number of heavens is possibly borrowed from the Talmud or a source depending upon it.

[5]An evil one.

We said, "Get ye down from it, all together: and if Guidance shall come to you from me, whoso shall follow my guidance, on them shall come no fear, neither shall they be grieved:

But they who shall not believe, and treat our signs as falsehoods, these shall be inmates of the fire; in it shall they remain for ever."

O children of Israel! remember my favour wherewith I shewed favour upon you, and be true to your covenant with me; I will be true to my covenant with you; me therefore, revere me! and believe in what I have sent down confirming your Scriptures, and be not the first to disbelieve it, neither for a mean price barter my signs: me therefore, fear ye me!

And clothe not the truth with falsehood, and hide not the truth when ye know it:

And observe prayer and pay the legal impost, and bow down with those who bow.

Will ye enjoin what is right upon others, and forget yourselves? Yet ye read the Book: will ye not understand?

And seek help with patience and prayer: a hard duty indeed is this, but not to the humble,

Who bear in mind that they shall meet their Lord, and that unto Him shall they return.

O children of Israel! remember my favour wherewith I shewed favour upon you; for verily to you above all human beings have I been bounteous.

And fear ye the day when soul shall not satisfy for soul at all, nor shall any intercession be accepted from them, nor shall any ransom be taken, neither shall they be helped.

And *remember* when we rescued you from the people of Pharaoh, who had laid on you a cruel chastisement. They slew your male children, and let only your females live: and in this was a great trial from your Lord:

And when we parted the sea for you, and saved you, and drowned the people of Pharaoh, while ye were looking on:

And when we were in treaty with Moses forty nights: then during his absence took ye the calf and acted wickedly:

Yet after this we forgave you, that ye might be grateful:

And when we gave Moses the Book and the Illumination in order to your guidance:

And *remember* when Moses said to his people, "O my people! verily ye have sinned to your own hurt, by your taking the calf *to worship it:* Be turned then to your creator, and slay the guilty among you; this will be best for you with your creator:" Then turned He unto you, for He is the one who turneth, the Merciful:

And when ye said, "O Moses! we will not believe thee until we see God plainly;" the thunderbolt fell upon you while ye were looking on:

Then we raised you to life after ye had been dead, that haply ye might give thanks:

And we caused the clouds to overshadow you, and we sent down manna and quails upon you;—"Eat of the good things we have given you for sustenance;"—and they injured not us but they injured themselves.

And when we said, "Enter this city,[6] and eat therefrom plentifully at your will, and enter the gate with prostrations, and say, 'Forgiveness;' and we will pardon you your sins, and give an increase to the doers of good:"—

[6]Either Jericho or Jerusalem.

But the evil-doers changed that word into another than that spoken to them, and we sent down upon those evil-doers wrath from heaven, for that they had done amiss:

And when Moses asked drink for his people, we said, "Strike the rock with thy rod;" and from it there gushed twelve fountains: each tribe knew their drinking-place:—"Eat and drink," said we, "of what God hath supplied, and do no wrong on the earth by licentious deeds:"

And when ye said, "O Moses! we will not put up with one sort of food: pray, therefore, thy Lord for us, that He would bring forth for us of that which the earth groweth, its herbs and its cucumbers and its garlic and its lentils and its onions:" He said, "What! will ye exchange that which is worse for what is better? Get ye down into Egypt;—for ye shall have what ye have asked:" Vileness and poverty were stamped upon them, and they returned with wrath from God: This, for that they disbelieved the signs of God, and slew the Prophets[7] unjustly: this, for that they rebelled and transgressed!

Verily, they who believe (Muslims), and they who follow the Jewish religion, and the Christians, and the Sabeites[8]—whoever of these believeth in God and the last day, and doeth that which is right, shall have their reward with their Lord: fear shall not come upon them, neither shall they be grieved.

Call to mind also when we entered into a covenant with you, and lifted up the mountain over you:—"Take hold," *said we,* "on what we have revealed to you, with resolution, and remember what is therein, that ye may fear:"

But after this ye turned back, and but for God's grace and mercy toward you, ye had surely been of the lost! Ye know too those of you who transgressed on the Sabbath, and to whom we said, "Be *changed into* scouted apes:"

And we made them a warning to those of their day, and to those who came after them, and a caution to the God-fearing:

And when Moses said to his people, "Verily, God bids you sacrifice a COW;"[9] they said, "Makest thou a jest of us?" He said, "God keep me from being one of the foolish." They said, "Call on thy Lord for us that He would make plain to us what she is." He said, "God saith, 'She is a cow neither old nor young, *but* of the middle age—between *the two:*' do therefore what ye are bidden."

They said, "Call on your Lord for us, that he would make plain to us what is her colour." He said, "God saith, 'She is a fawn-coloured cow; her colour is very bright; she rejoiceth the beholders.' "

They said, "Call on thy Lord for us that He would make plain to us what cow it is—for to us are cows alike,—and verily, if God please, we shall be guided rightly:"

He said, "God saith, 'She is a cow not worn by ploughing the earth or watering the field, sound, no blemish in her.' " They said, "Now hast thou brought the truth:" Then they sacrificed her; Yet nearly had they done it not:

And when ye slew a man, and strove among yourselves about him, God brought to light what he had hidden:

For we said, "Strike *the corpse* with part of her." So God giveth life to the dead, and sheweth you his signs, that haply ye may understand.

Then after that your hearts became hard like rocks, or harder still: for verily, from rocks have rivers gushed; others, verily, have been cleft, and water hath issued from them; and others, verily, have sunk down through fear of God: And God is not regardless of your actions.

---

[7]The meaning is unclear.

[8]Christians residing at the mouth of the Euphrates.

[9]The cow was to be sacrificed so that a miracle might take place on the corpse.

Desire ye then that for your sakes *the Jews* should believe? Yet a part of them heard the word of God, and then, after they had understood it, perverted it, and knew that they did so.

And when they fall in with the faithful, they say, "We believe;" but when they are apart one with another, they say, "Will ye acquaint them with what God hath revealed to you, that they may dispute with you about it in the presence of your Lord?" Understand ye their aim?

Know they not that God knoweth what they hide, as well as what they bring to light?

But there are illiterates among them who are unacquainted with the Book,[10] but with lies only, and have but vague fancies. Woe to those who with their own hands transcribe the Book corruptly, and then say, "This is from God," that they may sell it for some mean price! Woe then to them for that which their hands have written! and, Woe to them for the gains which they have made!

And they say, "Hell fire shall not touch us, but for a few days:" SAY: Have ye received such a promise from God? for God will not revoke his promise: or, Speak ye of God that which ye know not? . . .

FROM
SURA 4: WOMEN

[Medina]

In the Name of God, the Compassionate, the Merciful

O men! fear your Lord, who hath created you of one man (*nafs,* soul), and of him created his wife, and from these twain hath spread abroad so many men and WOMEN. And fear ye God, in whose name ye ask mutual favours,—and reverence the wombs *that bare you.* Verily is God watching over you!

And give to the orphans their property; substitute not worthless things of your own for their valuable ones, and devour not their property after adding it to your own; for this is a great crime.

And if ye are apprehensive that ye shall not deal fairly with orphans, then, of *other* women who seem good in your eyes, marry *but* two, or three, or four; and if ye *still* fear that ye shall not act equitably, then one only; or the slaves whom ye have acquired: this will make justice on your part easier. Give women their dowry freely; but if of themselves they give up aught thereof to you, then enjoy it as convenient, and profitable:

And entrust not to the incapable the substance which God hath placed with you for their support; but maintain them therewith, and clothe them, and speak to them with kindly speech.

And make trial of orphans until they reach the age of marriage; and if ye perceive in them a sound judgment, then hand over their substance to them; but consume ye it not wastefully, or *by* hastily *entrusting it to them;*

Because they are growing up. And let the rich *guardian* not even touch it; and let him who is poor use it for his support (eat of it) with discretion.

And when ye make over their substance to them, then take witnesses in their presence: God also maketh a sufficient account.

Men ought to have a part of what their parents and kindred leave; and women a part of what their parents and kindred leave: whether it be little or much, let them have a stated portion.

---

[10] The Koran.

And when they who are of kin are present at the divison, and the orphans and the poor, let them too have a share; and speak to them with kindly speech.

And let those be afraid *to wrong the orphans*, who, should they leave behind them weakly offspring, would be solicitous on their account. Let them, therefore, fear God, and let them propose what is right.

Verily they who swallow the substance of the orphan wrongfully, shall swallow down only fire into their bellies, and shall burn in the flame!

With regard to your children, God commandeth you to give the male the portion of two females; and if they be females more than two, then they shall have two-thirds of that which *their father* hath left: but if she be an only daughter, she shall have the half; and the father and mother of the deceased shall each of them have a sixth part of what he hath left, if he have a child; but if he have no child, and his parents be his heirs, then his mother shall have the third: and if he have brethren, his mother shall have the sixth, after paying the bequests he shall have bequeathed, and his debts. As to your fathers, or your children, ye know not which of them is the most advantageous to you. This is the law of God. Verily, God is Knowing, Wise!

Half of what your wives leave shall be yours, if they have no issue; but if they have issue, then a fourth of what they leave shall be yours, after paying the bequests they shall bequeath, and debts.

And your wives shall have a fourth part of what ye leave, if ye have no issue; but if ye have issue, then they shall have an eighth part of what ye leave, after paying the bequests ye shall bequeath, and debts.

If a man or a woman make a distant relation their heir, and he or she have a brother or a sister, each of these two shall have a sixth; but if there are more than this, then shall they be sharers in a third, after payment of the bequests he shall have bequeathed, and debts,

Without loss to any one. This is the ordinance of God, and God is Knowing, Gracious!

These are the precepts of God; and whoso obeyeth God and his prophet, him shall God bring into gardens beneath whose *shades* the rivers flow, therein to abide for ever: and this, the great blessedness!

And whoso shall rebel against God and his apostle, and shall break His bounds, him shall God place in the fire to abide therein for ever; and his shall be a shameful torment.

If any of your women be guilty of whoredom, then bring four witnesses against them from among yourselves; and if they bear witness *to the fact*, shut them up within their houses till death release them, or God make some way for them.

And if two men among you commit the same crime, then punish them both; but if they turn and amend, then let them be: for God is He who turneth, Merciful!

With God himself will the repentance of those who have done evil ignorantly, and then turn speedily *unto Him*, be accepted. These! God will turn unto them: for God is Knowing, Wise!

But no *place of* repentance shall there be for those who do evil, until, when death is close to one of them, he saith, "Now verily am I turned to God;" nor to those who die unbelievers. These! we have made ready for them a grievous torment!

O believers! it is not allowed you to be heirs of your wives against their will; nor to hinder them from marrying, in order to take from them part of the dowry you had given them, unless they have been guilty of undoubted lewdness; but associate kindly with them: for if ye are estranged from them, haply ye are estranged from that in which God hath placed abundant good.

And if ye be desirous to exchange one wife for another, and have given one of them a talent, make no deduction from it. Would ye take it by slandering her, and with manifest wrong?

How, moreover, could ye take it, when one of you hath gone in unto the other, and they have received from you a strict bond of union?

And marry not women whom your fathers have married: for this is a shame, and hateful, and an evil way:—though what is past may be allowed.

Forbidden to you are your mothers, and your daughters, and your sisters, and your aunts, both on the father and mother's side, and your nieces on the brother and sister's side, and your foster-mothers, and your foster-sisters, and the mothers of your wives, and your step-daughters who are your wards, born of your wives to whom ye have gone in: (but if ye have not gone in unto them, it shall be no sin in you to marry them;) and the wives of your sons who proceed out of your loins; and ye may not have two sisters; except where it is already done. Verily, God is Indulgent, Merciful!

Forbidden to you also are married women, except those who are in your hands as slaves: This is the law of God for you. And it is allowed you, beside this, to seek out wives by means of your wealth, with modest conduct, and without fornication. And give those with whom ye have cohabited their dowry. This is the law. But it shall be no crime in you to make agreements over and above the law. Verily, God is Knowing, Wise!

And whoever of you is not rich enough to marry free believing women, then let him marry such of your believing maidens as have fallen into your hands as slaves; God well knoweth your faith. Ye are sprung the one from the other. Marry them, then, with the leave of their masters, and give them a fair dower: but let them be chaste and free from fornication, and not entertainers of lovers.

If after marriage they commit adultery, then inflict upon them half the penalty enacted for free married women. This *law* is for him among you who is afraid of doing wrong:[11] but if ye abstain,[12] it will be better for you. And God is Lenient, Merciful.

God desireth to make this known to you, and to guide you into the ways of those who have been before you, and to turn Him unto you in mercy. And God is Knowing, Wise!

God desireth *thus* to turn him unto you: but they who follow their own lusts, desire that with great swerving should ye swerve! God desireth to make your burden light: for man hath been created weak.

O believers! devour not each other's substance in mutual frivolities;[13] unless there be a trafficking among you by your own consent: and commit not suicide:—of a truth God is merciful to you.

And whoever shall do this maliciously and wrongfully, we will in the end cast him into the fire; for this is easy with God.

If ye avoid the great sins which ye are forbidden, we will blot out your faults, and we will cause you to enter *Paradise* with honourable entry.

Covet not the gifts by which God hath raised some of you above others. The men shall have a portion according to their deserts, and the women a portion according to their deserts. Of God, therefore, ask his gifts. Verily, God hath knowledge of all things.

---

[11]By marrying without adequate means of supporting a free wife or by remaining single.

[12]From marrying slaves.

[13]Gambling, usury, etc.

To every one have we appointed kindred, as heirs of what parents and relatives, and those with whom ye have joined right hands in contract, leave. Give therefore, to each their portion. Verily, God witnesseth all things.

Men are superior to women on account of the qualities with which God hath gifted the one above the other, and on account of the outlay they make from their substance for them. Virtuous women are obedient, careful, during *the husband's* absence, because God hath of them been careful.[14] But chide those for whose refractoriness ye have cause to fear; remove them into beds apart, and scourge them: but if they are obedient to you, then seek not occasion against them: verily, God is High, Great!

And if ye fear a breach between man and wife, then send a judge chosen from his family, and a judge chosen from her family: if they are desirous of agreement, God will effect a reconciliation between them; verily, God is knowing, apprised of all!

Worship God, and join not aught with Him in worship. Be good to parents, and to kindred, and to orphans, and to the poor, and to a neighbour, whether kinsman or new-comer, and to a fellow traveller, and to the wayfarer, and to the slaves whom your right hands hold; verily, God loveth not the proud, the vain boaster,

Who are niggardly themselves, and bid others be niggards, and hide away what God of his bounty hath given them. We have made ready a shameful chastisement for the unbelievers,

And for those who bestow their substance in alms to be seen of men, and believe not in God and in the last day. Whoever hath Satan for his companion, an evil companion hath he!

But what *blessedness would be* theirs, if they should believe in God and in the last day, and bestow alms out of what God hath vouchsafed them; for God taketh knowledge of them!

God truly will not wrong any one of the weight of a mote; and if there be any good deed, he will repay it doubly; and from his presence shall be given a great recompense.

How! when we shall bring up against them witnesses from all peoples, and when we shall bring thee up as a witness against these? On that day they who were Infidels and rebelled against the prophet, shall wish that the earth were levelled with them! But nothing shall they hide from God.

O ye true believers, come not to prayer when ye are drunken, but wait till ye can understand what ye utter; nor when ye are polluted, unless ye be travelling on the road, until ye have washed you. If ye be sick, or on a journey, or have come from the unclean place, or have touched a woman, and ye find not water, then rub pure sand, and bathe your face and your hands with it: verily, God is Lenient, Merciful. . . .

FROM

SURA 10: JONAH

[Mecca]

. . . Recite to them the history of Noah, when he said to his people,—If, O my people! my abode with you, and my reminding you of the signs of God, be grievous to you, yet in God is my trust: Muster, therefore, your designs and your

[14] By providing them with a home and a husband.

false gods, and let not your design be carried on by you in the dark: then come to some decision about me, and delay not.

And if ye turn your backs on me, yet ask I no reward from you: my reward is with God alone, and I am commanded to be of the Muslims.

But they treated him as a liar: therefore we rescued him and those who were with him in the ark, and we made them to survive the others; and we drowned those who charged our signs with falsehood. See, then, what was the end of these warned ones!

Then after him, we sent Apostles to their peoples, and they came to them with credentials; but they would not believe in what they had denied aforetime: Thus seal we up the hearts of the transgressors!

Then sent we, after them, Moses and Aaron to Pharaoh and his nobles with our signs; but they acted proudly and were a wicked people:

And when the truth came to them from us, they said, "Verily, this is clear sorcery."

Moses said: "What! say ye of the truth after it hath come to you, 'Is this sorcery?' But sorcerers shall not prosper."

They said: "Art thou come to us to pervert us from the faith in which we found our fathers, and that you twain shall bear rule in this land? But we believe you not."

And Pharaoh said: "Fetch me every skilled magician." And when the magicians arrived, Moses said to them, "Cast down what ye have to cast."

And when they had cast them down, Moses said, "Verily, God will render vain the sorceries which ye have brought to pass: God prospereth not the work of the evildoers.

"And by his words will God verify the Truth, though the impious be averse to it."

And none believed on Moses but a race among his own people, through fear of Pharaoh and his nobles, lest he should afflict them: For of a truth mighty was Pharaoh in the land, and one who committed excesses.

And Moses said: "O my people! if ye believe in God, then put your trust in Him—if ye be Muslims."

And they said: "In God put we our trust. O our Lord! abandon us not to trial from that unjust people,

"And deliver us by thy mercy from the unbelieving people."

Then thus revealed we to Moses and to his brother: "Provide houses for your people in Egypt, and *in* your houses make a Kebla, and observe prayer and proclaim good tidings to the believers."

And Moses said: "O our Lord! thou hast indeed given to Pharaoh and his nobles splendour and riches in this present life: O our Lord! that they may err from thy way! O our Lord! confound their riches, and harden their hearts that they may not believe till they see the dolorous torment."

He said: "The prayer of you both is heard: pursue ye both therefore the straight path, and follow not the path of those who have no knowledge."

And we led the children of Israel through the sea; and Pharaoh and his hosts followed them in eager and hostile sort until, when the drowning overtook him, he said, "I believe that there is no God but he on whom the children of Israel believe, and I am one of the Muslims."

"Yes, now," *said God:* "but thou hast been rebellious hitherto, and wast one of the wicked doers.

"But this day will we rescue thee with thy body that thou mayest be a sign to those who shall be after thee: but truly, most men are of our signs regardless!"

Moreover, we prepared a settled abode for the children of Israel, and provided them with good things: nor did they fall into variance till the knowledge (the Law)

came to them: Truly thy Lord will decide between them on the day of Resurrection concerning that in which they differed.

And if thou art in doubt as to what we have sent down to thee, inquire at those who have read the Scriptures before thee. Now hath the truth come unto thee from thy Lord: be not therefore of those who doubt.

Neither be of those who charge the signs of God with falsehood, lest thou be of those who perish.

Verily they against whom the decree of thy Lord is pronounced, shall not believe,

Even though every kind of sign come unto them, till they behold the dolorous torment!

Were it otherwise, any city, had it believed, might have found its safety in its faith. But it was so, only with the people of JONAS. When they believed, we delivered them from the penalty of shame in this world, and provided for them for a time.

But if thy Lord had pleased, verily all who are in the earth would have believed together. What! wilt thou compel men to become believers?

No soul can believe but by the permission of God: and he shall lay his wrath on those who will not understand.

SAY: Consider ye whatever is in the Heavens and on the Earth: but neither signs, nor warners, avail those who will not believe!

What then can they expect but the like of such days *of wrath* as befel those who flourish before them? SAY: WAIT; I too will wait with you:

Then will we deliver our apostles and those who believe. Thus is it binding on us to deliver the faithful.

SAY: O men! if ye are in doubt as to my religion, verily I worship not what ye worship beside God; but I worship God who will cause you to die: and I am commanded to be a believer.

And set thy face toward true religion, sound in faith, and be not of those who join other gods with God:

Neither invoke beside God that which can neither help nor hurt thee: for if thou do, thou wilt certainly then be one of those who act unjustly.

And if God lay the touch of trouble on thee, none can deliver thee from it but He: and if He will thee any good, none can keep back his boons. He will confer them on such of his servants as he chooseth: and He is the Gracious, the Merciful!

SAY: O men! now hath the truth come unto you from your Lord. He therefore who will be guided, will be guided only for his own behoof: but he who shall err will err only against it; and I am not your guardian!

And follow what is revealed to thee: and persevere steadfastly till God shall judge, for He is the best of Judges.

. . .

SURA 12: JOSEPH

[Mecca]

In the Name of God, the Compassionate, the Merciful

ELIF. LAM. RA.[15] These are signs of the clear Book.

An Arabic Koran have we sent it down, that ye might understand it.

In revealing to thee this Koran, one of the most beautiful of narratives will we narrate to thee, of which thou hast hitherto been regardless.

[15] The meaning of these Arabic letters is unclear.

When Joseph said to his Father, "O my Father! verily I beheld eleven stars and the sun and the moon—beheld them make obeisance to me!"

He said, "O my son! tell not thy vision to thy brethren, lest they plot a plot against thee: for Satan is the manifest foe of man.

"It is thus that thy Lord shall choose thee and will teach thee the interpretation of dark sayings, and will perfect his favours on thee and on the family of Jacob, as of old he perfected it on thy fathers Abraham and Isaac; verily thy Lord is Knowing, Wise!"

Now in JOSEPH and his brethren are signs for the enquirers;

When they said, "Surely better loved by our Father, than we, who are more in number, is Joseph and his brother; verily, our father hath clearly erred.

"Slay ye Joseph! or drive him to some other land, and on you alone shall your father's face be set! and after this, ye shall live as upright persons."

One of them said, "Slay not Joseph, but cast him down to the bottom of the well: if ye do so, some wayfarers will take him up."

They said, "O our Father! why dost thou not entrust us with Joseph? indeed we mean him well.

"Send him with us to-morrow that he may enjoy himself and sport: we will surely keep him safely."

He said, "Verily, your taking him away will grieve me; and I fear lest while ye are heedless of him the wolf devour him."

They said, "Surely if the wolf devour him, and we so many, we must in that case be weak indeed."

And when they went away with him they agreed to place him at the bottom of the well. And We revealed to him, "Thou wilt yet tell them of this their deed, when they shall not know thee."

And they came at nightfall to their father weeping.

They said, "O our Father! of a truth, we went to run races, and we left Joseph with our clothes, and the wolf devoured him: but thou wilt not believe us even though we speak the truth."

And they brought his shirt with false blood upon it. He said, "Nay, but yourselves have managed this affair. But patience is seemly: and the help of God is to be implored that I may bear what you tell me."

And wayfarers came and sent their drawer of water, and he let down his bucket. "Good news!" said he, "This is a youth!" And they kept his case secret, to make merchandise of him. But God knew what they did.

And they sold him for a paltry price—for some dirhems counted down, and at no high rate did they value him.

And he who bought him—an Egyptian—said to his wife, "Treat him hospitably; haply he may be useful to us, or we may adopt him as a son." Thus did we settle Joseph in the land, and we instructed him in the interpretation of dark sayings, for God is equal to his purpose; but most men know it not.

And when he had reached his age of strength we bestowed on him judgment and knowledge; for thus do we recompense the well doers.

And she in whose house he was conceived a passion for him, and she shut the doors and said, "Come hither." He said, "God keep me! Verily, my lord hath given me a good home: and the injurious shall not prosper."

But she longed for him; and he had longed for her had he not seen a token from his lord. Thus we averted evil and defilement from him, for he was one of our sincere servants.

And they both made for the door, and she rent his shirt behind; and at the door they met her lord. "What," said she, "shall be the recompense of him who would do evil to thy family, but a prison or a sore punishment?"

He said, "She solicited me to evil." And a witness out of her own family witnessed: "If his shirt be rent in front she speaketh truth, and he is a liar:

"But if his shirt be rent behind, she lieth and he is true."

And when his lord saw his shirt torn behind, he said, "This is one of your devices! verily your devices are great!

"Joseph! leave this affair. And thou, *O wife*, ask pardon for thy crime, for thou hast sinned."

And in the city, the women said, "The wife of the Prince hath solicited her servant: he hath fired her with his love: but we clearly see her manifest error."

And when she heard of their cabal, she sent to them and got ready a banquet for them, and gave each one of them a knife, and said, "*Joseph* shew thyself to them." And when they saw him they were amazed at him, and cut their hands[16] and said, "God keep us! This is no man! This is no other than a noble angel!"

She said, "This is he about whom ye blamed me. I wished him to yield to my desires, but he stood firm. But if he obey not my command, he shall surely be cast into prison, and become one of the despised."

He said, "O my Lord! I prefer the prison to compliance with their bidding: but unless thou turn away their snares from me, I shall play the youth with them, and become one of the unwise."

And his Lord heard him and turned aside their snares from him: for he is the Hearer, the Knower.

Yet resolved they, even after they had seen the signs *of his innocence,* to imprison him for a time.

And there came into the prison with him two youths. Said one of them, "Methought in my dream that I was pressing grapes." And the other said, "I dreamed that I was carrying bread on my head, of which the birds did eat. Declare to us the interpretation of this, for we see thou art a virtuous person."

He said, "There shall not come to you *in a dream* any food wherewith ye shall be fed, but I will acquaint you with its interpretation ere it come to pass to you. This is *a part* of that which my Lord hath taught me: for I have abandoned the religion of those who believe not in God and who deny the life to come;

"And I follow the religion of my fathers, Abraham and Isaac and Jacob. We may not associate aught with God. This is of God's bounty towards us and towards mankind: but the greater part of mankind are not thankful.

"O my two fellow prisoners! are sundry lords best, or God, the One, the Mighty?

"Ye worship beside him mere names which ye have named, ye and your fathers, for which God hath not sent down any warranty. Judgment belongeth to God alone. He hath bidden you worship none but Him. This is the right faith: but most men know it not.

"O my two fellow prisoners! as to one of you, he will serve wine unto his Lord: but as to the other, he will be crucified and the birds shall eat from off his head. The matter is decreed concerning which ye enquire."

And he said unto him who he judged would be set at large, "Remember me with thy lord." But Satan caused him to forget the remembrance of his Lord, so he remained some years in prison.

And the King said, "Verily, I saw *in a dream* seven fat kine which seven lean devoured; and seven green ears and other withered. O nobles, teach me my vision, if a vision ye are able to expound."

[16]Surprised at his beauty, they cut their hands rather than their food.

They said, "They are confused dreams, nor know we aught of the unravelling of dreams."

And he of the twain who had been set at large, said, "I will tell you the interpretation; let me go for it."

"Joseph, man of truth! teach us of the seven fat kine which seven lean devoured, and of the seven green ears, and other withered, that I may return to the men, and that they may be informed."

He said, "Ye shall sow seven years as is your wont, and the corn which ye reap leave ye in its ear, except a little of which ye shall eat.

"Then after that shall come seven grievous years which shall eat what ye have stored for them, except a little which ye shall have kept.

"Then shall come after this a year, in which men shall have rain, and in which they shall press the grape."

And the King said, "Bring him to me." And when the messenger came to Joseph he said, "Go back to thy lord, and ask him what meant the women who cut their hands, for my lord well knoweth the snare they laid."

Then said the Prince to the women, "What was your purpose when ye solicited Joseph?" They said, "God keep us! we know not any ill of him." The wife of the Prince said, "Now doth the truth appear. It was I who would have led him into unlawful love, and he is one of the truthful."

"By this" (said Joseph) "may my lord know that I did not in his absence play him false, and that God guideth not the machinations of deceivers.

"Yet I hold not myself clear, for the heart is prone to evil, save theirs on whom my Lord hath mercy; for gracious is my Lord, Merciful."

And the King said, "Bring him to me: I will take him for my special service." And when he had spoken with him he said, "From this day shalt thou be with us, invested with place and trust."

He said, "Set me over the granaries of the land, I will be their prudent keeper!"

Thus did we stablish Joseph in the land that he might house himself therein at pleasure. We bestow our favours on whom we will, and suffer not the reward of the righteous to perish.

And truly the recompense of the life to come is better, for those who have believed and feared God.

And Joseph's brethren came and went in to him and he knew them, but they recognised him not.

And when he had provided them with their provision, he said, "Bring me your brother from your father. See ye not that I fill the measure, and am the best of hosts?

But if ye bring him not to me, then no measure of corn shall there be for you from me, nor shall ye come near me."

They said, "We will ask him of his father, and we will surely do it."

Said he to his servants, "Put their money into their camel-packs, that they may perceive it when they have returned to their family: haply they will come back to us."

And when they returned to their father, they said, "O, our father! corn is withholden from us: send, therefore, our brother with us and we shall have our measure; and all care of him will we take."

He said, "Shall I entrust you with him otherwise than as I before entrusted you with his brother? But God is the best guardian, and of those who shew compassion He is the most compassionate."

And when they opened their goods they found their money had been returned to them. They said, "O, our father, what more can we desire? Here is our money returned to us; we will provide corn for our families, and will take care of our brother, and shall receive a camel's burden more of corn. This is an easy quantity."[17]

He said, "I will not send him with you but on your oath before God that ye will, indeed, bring him back to me, unless hindrances encompass you." And when they had given him their pledge, he said, "God is witness of what we say."

And he said, "O, my sons! Enter not by one gate, but enter by different gates. Yet can I not help you against aught decreed by God: judgment belongeth to God alone. In Him put I my trust, and in Him let the trusting trust."

And when they entered as their father had bidden them, it did not avert from them anything decreed of God; but it only *served to satisfy* a desire in the soul of Jacob which he had charged them to perform; for he was possessed of knowledge which we had taught him; but most men have not that knowledge.

And when they came in to Joseph, he took his brother to him. He said, "Verily, I am thy brother. Be not thou grieved for what they did."

And when he had provided them with their provisions, he placed his drinking cup in his brother's camel-pack. Then a crier cried after them, "O travellers! ye are surely thieves."

They turned back to them and said, "What is that ye miss?"

"We miss," said they, "the prince's cup. For him who shall restore it, a camel's load of corn! I pledge myself for it."

They said, "By God! ye know certainly that we came not to do wrong in the land and we have not been thieves."

"What," said *the Egyptians,* "shall be the recompense of him *who hath stolen it,* if ye be found liars?"

They said, "That he in whose camel-pack it shall be found be given up to you in satisfaction for it. Thus recompense we the unjust."

And Joseph began with their sacks, before the sack of his brother, and then from the sack of his brother he drew it out. This strategem did we suggest to Joseph. By the King's law he had no power to seize his brother, had not God pleased. We uplift into grades *of wisdom* whom we will. And there is one knowing above every one else endued with knowledge.

They said, "If he steal, a brother of his hath stolen heretofore." But Joseph kept his secret, and did not discover it to them. Said he, *aside,* "Ye are in the worse condition. And God well knoweth what ye state."

They said, "O Prince! Verily he hath a very aged father; in his stead, therefore, take one of us, for we see that thou art a generous person."

He said, "God forbid that we should take but him with whom our property was found, for then should we act unjustly."

And when they despaired of Benjamin, they went apart for counsel. The eldest of them said, "Know ye not how that your father hath taken a pledge from you before God, and how formerly ye failed in duty with regard to Joseph? I will not quit the land till my father give me leave, or God decide for me; for of those who decide is He the best.

"Return ye to your father and say, 'O our father! Verily, thy son hath stolen: we bear witness only of what we know: we could not guard against the unforeseen.

"Enquire for thyself in the city where we have been, and of the caravan with which we have arrived; and we are surely speakers of the truth.'"

He said, "Nay, ye have arranged all this among yourselves: But patience is seemly: God, may be, will bring them back to me together; for he is the Knowing, the Wise."

[17] Easy for the king to provide.

And he turned away from them and said, "Oh! how I am grieved for Joseph!" and his eyes became white with grief, for he bore a silent sorrow.

They said, "By God thou wilt only cease to think of Joseph when thou art at the point of death, or dead."

He said, "I only plead my grief and my sorrow to God: but I know from God what ye know not:[18]

"Go, my sons, and seek tidings of Joseph and his brother, and despair not of God's mercy, for none but the unbelieving despair of the mercy of God."

And when they came in to Joseph, they said, "O Prince, distress hath reached us and our family, and little is the money that we have brought. But give us full measure, and bestow it as alms, for God will recompense the almsgivers."

He said, "Know ye what ye did to Joseph and his brother in your ignorance?"

They said, "Canst thou indeed be Joseph?" He said, "I am Joseph, and this is my brother. Now hath God been gracious to us. For whoso feareth God and endureth.... God verily will not suffer the reward of the righteous to perish!"

They said, "By God! now hath God chosen thee above us, and we have indeed been sinners!"

He said, "No blame be on you this day. God will forgive you, for He is the most merciful of those who shew mercy.

"Go ye with this my shirt and throw it on my father's face, and he shall recover his sight: and bring me all your family."

And when the caravan was departed, their father said, "I surely perceive the smell of Joseph: think ye that I dote?"

They said, "By God, it is thy old mistake."

And when the bearer of good tidings came, he cast it on his face, and Jacob's eyesight returned.

Then he said, "Did I not tell you that I knew from God what ye knew not?"

They said, "Our father, ask pardon for our crimes for us, for we have indeed been sinners."

He said, "I will ask your pardon of my Lord, for he is Gracious, Merciful."

And when they came into Joseph he took his parents[19] to him, and said, "Enter ye Egypt, if God will, secure."

And he raised his parents to the seat of state, and they fell down bowing themselves unto him. Then said he, "O my father, this is the meaning of my dream of old. My Lord hath now made it true, and he hath surely been gracious to me, since he took me forth from the prison, and hath brought you up out of the desert, after that Satan had stirred up strife between me and my brethren; for my Lord is gracious to whom He will; for He is the Knowing, the Wise.

"O my Lord, thou hast given me dominion, and hast taught me to expound dark sayings. Maker of the Heavens and of the Earth! My guardian art thou in this world and in the next! Cause thou me to die a Muslim, and join me with the just."

This is one of the secret histories which we reveal unto thee. Thou wast not present with Joseph's brethren when they conceived their design and laid their plot: but the greater part of men, though thou long for it, will not believe.

Thou shalt not ask of them any recompense for this *message*. It is simply an instruction for all mankind.

And many as are the signs in the Heavens and on the Earth, yet they will pass them by, and turn aside from them:

[18]That is, that Joseph is still alive.

[19]Joseph's mother was dead, so "parents" has been a source of debate.

And most of them believe not in God, without also joining other deities with Him.

What! Are they sure that the overwhelming chastisement of God shall not come upon them, or that that Hour shall not come upon them suddenly, while they are unaware?

SAY: This is my way: resting on a clear proof, I call you to God, I and whoso followeth me: and glory be to God! I am not one of those who add other deities to Him.

Never before thee have we sent any but men, chosen out of the people of the cities, to whom we made revelations. Will they not journey through the land, and see what hath been the end of those who were before them? But the mansions of the next life shall be better for those who fear God. Will they not then comprehend?

When at last the Apostles lost all hope, and deemed that they were reckoned as liars, our aid reached them, and we delivered whom we would; but our vengeance was not averted from the wicked.

Certainly in their histories is an example for men of understanding. This is no new tale of fiction, but a confirmation of previous scriptures, and an explanation of all things, and guidance and mercy to those who believe.

. . .

FROM

SURA 19: MARY

[Mecca]

In the Name of God, the Compassionate, the Merciful

KAF. HA. YA. AIN. SAD.[20] A recital of thy Lord's mercy to his servant Zachariah;

When he called upon his Lord with secret calling,

And said: "O Lord, verily my bones are weakened, and the hoar hairs glisten on my head,

"And never, Lord, have I prayed to thee with ill success.

"But now I have fears for my kindred after me; and my wife is barren:

"Give me, then, a successor as thy special gift, who shall be my heir and an heir of the family of Jacob: and make him, Lord, well pleasing to thee."

—"O Zachariah! verily we announce to thee a son,—his name John: That name We have given to none before him."

He said: "O my Lord! how when my wife is barren shall I have a son, and when I have now reached old age, failing in my powers?"

He said: "So shall it be. Thy Lord hath said, Easy is this to me, for I created thee aforetime when thou wast nothing."

He said: "Vouchsafe me, O my Lord! a sign." He said: "Thy sign shall be that for three nights, though sound in health, thou speakest not to man."

And he came forth from the sanctuary to his people, and made signs to them to sing praises morn and even.

We said: "O John! receive the Book with purpose of heart:"—and We bestowed on him wisdom while yet a child;

And mercifulness from Ourself, and purity; and pious was he, and duteous to his parents; and not proud, rebellious.

And peace was on him on the day he was born, and the day of his death, and *shall be* on the day when he shall be raised to life!

[20] Meaning unclear.

And make mention in the Book, of Mary, when she went apart from her family, eastward,

And took a veil *to shroud herself* from them: and we sent our spirit[21] to her, and he took before her the form of a perfect man.

She said: "I fly for refuge from thee to the God of Mercy! If thou fearest Him, *begone from me*."

He said: "I am only a messenger of thy Lord, that I may bestow on thee a holy son."

She said: "How shall I have a son, when man hath never touched me? and I am not unchaste."

He said: "So shall it be. Thy Lord hath said: 'Easy is this with me;' and we will make him a sign to mankind, and a mercy from us. For it is a thing decreed."

And she conceived him, and retired with him to a far-off place.

And the throes came upon her by the trunk of a palm. She said: "Oh, would that I had died ere this, and been a thing forgotten, forgotten quite!"

And one cried to her from below her:[22] "Grieve not thou, thy Lord hath provided a streamlet at thy feet:—

"And shake the trunk of the palm-tree toward thee: it will drop fresh ripe dates upon thee.

"Eat then and drink, and be of cheerful eye: and shouldst thou see a man,

"Say,—Verily, I have vowed abstinence to the God of mercy.—To no one will I speak this day."

Then came she with the babe to her people, bearing him. They said, "O Mary! now hast thou done a strange thing!

"O sister of Aaron![23] Thy father was not a man of wickedness, nor unchaste thy mother."

And she made a sign *to them, pointing* towards the babe. They said, "How shall we speak with him who is in the cradle, an infant?"

It said, "Verily, I am the servant of God; He hath given me the Book, and He hath made me a prophet;

"And He hath made me blessed wherever I may be, and hath enjoined me prayer and almsgiving so long as I shall live;

"And to be duteous to her that bare me: and he hath not made me proud, depraved.

"And the peace of God was on me the day I was born, and will be the day I shall die, and the day I shall be raised to life."

This is Jesus, the son of Mary; this is a statement of the truth concerning which they doubt.

It beseemeth not God to beget a son. Glory be to Him when he decreeth a thing, He only saith to it, Be, and it Is.

And verily, God is my Lord and your Lord; adore Him then. This is the right way.

But the Sects have fallen to variance among themselves *about Jesus:* but woe, because of the assembly of a great day, to those who believe not!

Make them hear, make them behold the day when they shall come before us! But the offenders this day are in a manifest error.

---

[21] Gabriel.

[22] Either the baby who was just born or Gabriel.

[23] The identity of this Aaron is unclear, for there appears to be confusion of this Mary with the Miriam of the Exodus period.

Warn them of the day of sighing when the decree shall be accomplished, while they are *sunk* in heedlessness and while they believe not.

Verily, we will inherit the earth and all who are upon it. To us shall they be brought back.

Make mention also in the Book of Abraham; for he was a man of truth, a Prophet.

When he said to his Father, "O my Father! why dost thou worship that which neither seeth nor heareth, nor profiteth thee aught?

"O my Father! verily now hath knowledge come to me which hath not come to thee. Follow me therefore—I will guide thee into an even path.

"O my Father! worship not Satan, for Satan is a rebel against the God of Mercy.

"O my Father! indeed I fear lest a chastisement from the God of Mercy light upon thee, and thou become Satan's vassal."

He said, "Castest thou off my Gods, O Abraham? If thou forbear not, I will surely stone thee. Begone from me for a length of time."

He said, "Peace be on thee! I will pray my Lord for thy forgiveness, for he is gracious to me:

"But I will separate myself from you, and the gods ye call on beside God, and on my Lord will I call. Haply, my prayers to my Lord will not be with ill success."

And when he had separated himself from them and that which they worshipped beside God, we bestowed on him Isaac and Jacob, and each of them we made a prophet:

And we bestowed gifts on them in our mercy, and gave them the lofty tongue of truth."

And commemorate Moses in "the Book;" for he was a man of purity: moreover he was an Apostle, a Prophet:

From the right side of the mountain we called to him, and caused him to draw nigh to us for secret converse:

And we bestowed on him in our mercy his brother Aaron, a Prophet.

And commemorate Ismael in "the Book;" for he was true to his promise, and was an Apostle, a Prophet;

And he enjoined prayer and almsgiving on his people, and was well pleasing to his Lord.

And commemorate Edris[24] in "the Book;" for he was a man of truth, a Prophet:

And we uplifted him to a place on high.

These are they among the prophets of the posterity of Adam, and among those whom we bare with Noah, and among the posterity of Abraham and Israel, and among those whom we have guided and chosen, to whom God hath shewed favour. When the signs of the God of Mercy were rehearsed to them, they bowed them down worshipping and weeping. . . .

Sura 55: The Merciful

[Mecca]

In the Name of God, the Compassionate, the Merciful

The God of MERCY hath taught the Koran,

Hath created man,

Hath taught him articulate speech.

[24]Enoch.

The Sun and the Moon have each their times,
And the plants and the trees bend in adoration.
And the Heaven, He hath reared it on high, and hath appointed the balance;
That in the balance ye should not transgress.
Weigh therefore with fairness, and scant not the balance.
And the Earth, He hath prepared it for the living tribes:
Therein are fruits, and the palms with sheathed clusters,
And the grain with its husk, and the fragrant plants,
Which then of the bounties of your Lord will ye twain[25] deny?
He created man of clay like that of the potter.
And He created the djinn of pure fire:
Which then of the bounties, etc.
He is the Lord of the East,
He is the Lord of the West:
Which, etc.
He hath let loose the two seas which meet each other:
Yet between them is a barrier which they overpass not:
Which, etc.
From each he bringeth up pearls both great and small:
Which, etc.
And His are the ships towering up at sea like mountains:
Which, etc.
All on the earth shall pass away,
But the face of thy Lord shall abide resplendent with majesty and glory:
Which, etc.

To Him maketh suit all that is in the Heaven and the Earth. Every day doth some new work employ Him:

Which, etc.
We will find leisure *to judge* you, O ye men and djinn:
Which, etc.

O company of djinn and men, if ye can overpass the bounds of the Heavens and the Earth, then overpass them. But by *our* leave only shall ye overpass them:

Which, etc.

A bright flash of fire shall be hurled at you both, and molten brass, and ye shall not defend yourselves from it:

Which, etc.

When the Heaven shall be cleft asunder, and become rose red, like stained leather:

Which, etc.
On that day shall neither man nor djinn be asked of his sin:
Which, etc.

By their tokens shall the sinners be known, and they shall be seized by their forelocks and their feet:

Which, etc.
"This is Hell which sinners treated as a lie."
To and fro shall they pass between it and the boiling water:
Which, etc.
But for those who dread the majesty of their Lord shall be two gardens:
Which, etc.
With o'erbranching trees in each:

---

[25] Men and djinn.

Which, etc.
In each two fountains flowing:
Which, etc.
In each two kinds of every fruit:
Which, etc.
On couches with linings of brocade shall they recline, and the fruit of the two gardens shall be within easy reach:
Which, etc.
Therein shall be the damsels with retiring glances, whom nor man nor djinn hath touched before them:
Which, etc.
Like jacynths and pearls:
Which, etc.
Shall the reward of good be aught but good?
Which, etc.
And beside these shall be two other gardens:[26]
Which, etc.
Of a dark green:
Which, etc.
With gushing fountains in each:
Which, etc.
In each fruits and the palm and the pomegranate:
Which, etc.
In each, the fair, the beauteous ones:
Which, etc.
With large dark eyeballs, kept close in their pavilions:
Which, etc.
Whom man hath never touched, nor any djinn:
Which, etc.
Their spouses on soft green cushions and on beautiful carpets shall recline:
Which, etc.
Blessed be the name of thy Lord, full of majesty and glory.

Sura 56: The Inevitable

[Mecca]

In the name of God, the Compassionate, the Merciful
When the day that must come shall have come suddenly,
None shall treat that sudden coming as a lie:
Day that shall abase! Day that shall exalt!
When the earth shall be shaken with a shock,
And the mountains shall be crumbled with a crumbling,
And shall become scattered dust,
And into three bands shall ye be divided:
Then the people of the right hand—Oh! how happy shall be the people of the right hand!

[26]One for men and the other for Genii.

And the people of the left hand—Oh! how wretched shall be the people of the left hand!

And they who were foremost *on earth*—the foremost still.

These are they who shall be brought nigh to God,

In gardens of delight;

A crowd of the former

And few of the latter generations;

On inwrought couches

Reclining on them face to face:

Aye-blooming youths go round about to them

With goblets and ewers and a cup of flowing wine;

Their brows ache not from it, nor fails the sense:

And with such fruits as shall please them best,

And with flesh of such birds, as they shall long for:

And theirs shall be the Houris, with large dark eyes, like pearls hidden in their shells,

In recompense of their labours past.

No vain discourse shall they hear therein, nor charge of sin,

But only the cry, "Peace! Peace!"

And the people of the right hand—oh! how happy shall be the people of the right hand!

Amid thornless sidrahs[27]

And talh[28] trees clad with fruit,

And in extended shade,

And by flowing waters,

And with abundant fruits,

Unfailing, unforbidden,

And on lofty couches.

Of a *rare* creation have we created the Houris,

And we have made them ever virgins,

Dear to their spouses, of equal age *with them*,

For the people of the right hand,

A crowd of the former,

And a crowd of the latter generations.

But the people of the left hand—oh! how wretched shall be the people of the left hand!

Amid pestilential winds and in scalding water,

And in the shadow of a black smoke,

Not cool, and horrid to behold.

For they truly, ere this, were blessed with worldy goods,

But persisted in heinous sin,

And were wont to say,

"What! after we have died, and become dust and bones, shall we be raised?

"And our fathers, the men of yore?"

SAY: Aye, the former and the latter:

Gathered shall they all be for the time of a known day.

Then ye, O ye the erring, the gainsaying,

[27] A special tree in paradise; on its leaves are written the names of the human race.
[28] Probably the banana.

Shall surely eat of the tree Ez-zakkoum,
And fill your bellies with it,
And thereupon shall ye drink boiling water,
And ye shall drink as the thirsty camel drinketh.
This shall be their repast in the day of reckoning!

. . .

SURA 71: NOAH

[Mecca]

In the Name of God, the Compassionate, the Merciful

We sent NOAH to his people, and said to him, "Warn thou thy people ere there come on them an afflictive punishment."

He said, "O my people! I come to you a plain-spoken warner:

"Serve God and fear Him, and obey me:

"Your sins will He forgive you, and respite you till the fixed Time; for when God's fixed Time hath come, it shall not be put back. Would that ye knew this!"

He said, "Lord I have cried to my people night and day; and my cry doth but make them flee from me the more.

"So oft as I cry to them, that thou mayest forgive them, they thrust their fingers into their ears, and wrap themselves in their garments, and persist *in their error,* and are disdainfully disdainful.

"Then I cried aloud to them:

"Then again spake I with plainness, and in private did I secretly address them:

"And I said, 'Beg forgiveness of your Lord, for He is ready to forgive.

"He will send down the very Heaven upon you in plenteous rains;

"And will increase you in wealth and children; and will give you gardens, and will give you watercourses:—

"What hath come to you that ye hope not for goodness from the hand of God?

"For He it is who hath formed you by successive steps.

"See ye not how God hath created the seven heavens one over the other?

"And He hath placed therein the moon as a light, and hath placed *there* the sun as a torch;

"And God hath caused you to spring forth from the earth like a plant;

"Hereafter will He turn you back into it again, and will bring you forth anew—

"And God hath spread the earth for you like a carpet,

"That ye may walk therein along spacious paths.' "

Said Noah, "O my Lord! they rebel against me, and they follow those whose riches and children do but aggravate their ruin."

And they plotted a great plot;

And they said, "Forsake not your Gods; forsake not Wadd nor Sowah,

"Nor Yaghuth and Yahuk and Nesr;"[29]

And they caused many to err;—and thou, too, O Muhammad! shalt be the means of increasing only error in the wicked—

Because of their sins they were drowned, and made to go into the Fire;

And they found that they had no helper save God.

And Noah said, "Lord, leave not one single family of Infidels on the Earth:

---

[29] These idols were worshipped in Mecca before they were destroyed by Muhammad.

"For if thou leave them they will beguile thy servants and will beget only sinners, infidels.

"O my Lord, forgive me, and my parents, and every one who, being a believer, shall enter my house, and believers men and women: and add to the wicked nought but perdition."

. . .

SURA 112: THE UNITY

[Mecca]

In the Name of God, the Compassionate, the Merciful

SAY: He is God alone:
God the eternal!
He begetteth not, and He is not begotten;
And there is none like unto Him.

IBN HAZM

[994–1064]

The expansion of Islam into the Iberian Peninsula took place between 644 and 661, ending thirty years after the death of Muhammad. After Charles Martel finally stopped the northward progress of the Muslim forces near Poitou in 732, the Franks attempted a series of counterattacks across and around the Pyrenees, ending with the retreat of Charlemagne from Spain in 778. For the next 300 years skirmishes between Frankish and Muslim forces were inconclusive, until Muslim control of the peninsula began to crumble in the eleventh century.

LIFE

Ibn Hazm, a systematic philosopher who eventually wrote an encyclopedic work comparing the religions of the West and Asia Minor, lived in difficult times. The sack of his native city of Cordoba by Berber tribesmen in 1012, the death of his father later the same year, and the death of his first love a year later led to his decision to dedicate himself to serious studies as a response to an unstable world. It may seem odd, then, that he accepted a request less than a decade later to write a treatise on love, but he states that he was following a moral precept that suggests that those who have grieved excessively should perform an apparently light task in order to strengthen the soul for hard work ahead. He completed the treatise, entitled *Tawq al-Hamamah*, or *The Dove's Necklace*, in 1022, before reaching the age of thirty.

WORK

Ibn Hazm's philosophy of love drew upon Greek sources, especially the writings of Plato. Ibn Hazm stresses the spiritual aspect of love that Plato develops in his *Symposium*, an emphasis that had become commonplace in the education of the Muslim upper classes as early as the ninth century. But although Platonic idealism and the monotheism of Islam

("There is no god but God") were often seen as complementary philosophical positions, the cult of Sufism, which situated the love of God *within* the person, was sometimes viewed as a dangerous heresy because it threatened to idealize God out of existence. Under threat of repression, the Sufi poets of the tenth century began to conceal their doctrine of divine love in their poems. The poets of worldly love, already saturated in Platonic idealism, were quick to seize on this ethic of concealment. Thus the ideal of love that Muslim culture began to express in Ibn Hazm's day stressed particular values: It is not too much to say that the love poetry of the time borrowed the language of heresy. This ideal of refined and sublimated behavior was given a name: the practice of *adab*.

The young philosopher thus borrowed from an existing tradition when he wrote about love's secrecy, its hidden signs, its power and authority. Love also clearly had a basis in gender and class: It was to be practiced by educated men of the upper class. It did *not* discriminate as to the gender of the love object: Man or woman would do.

There are obvious affinities between the philosophy of love developed in the treatise by Ibn Hazm, *The Dove's Necklace*, and the love ethic of Provençal poetry as it began to be performed in the courts of the south of France less than a century later. Nor is the transmission of the idea across antagonistic cultures a mystery: Frequent encounters across the Pyrenees between Muslim and Christian meant cultural contact. For these reasons, the reader should compare *The Dove's Necklace* with Provençal lyric poetry, the *lais* of Marie de France, French romances, and the *Art of Courtly Love* by Andreas Capellanus.

Suggested Readings

The most recent translation of *The Dove's Necklace* is *The Ring of the Dove*, A. J. Arberry, trans. (1953). The classic discussion of the Islamic influence on Western ideas of romantic love is in Denis de Rougement's *Love in the Western World* (1956). Connections between Arabic culture and Provençal poetry are explored in Robert S. Briffault's *The Troubadours* (1965).

FROM

The Dove's Necklace

Translated by A. J. Arberry

Love has certain signs which the intelligent man quickly detects and the shrewd man readily recognizes. Of these the first is the brooding gaze: the eye is the wide gateway of the soul, the scrutinizer of its secrets, conveying its most private thoughts and giving expression to its deepest-hid feelings. You will see the lover gazing at the beloved unblinkingly; his eyes follow the loved one's every movement, withdrawing as he withdraws, inclining as he inclines, just as the chameleon's stare shifts with the shifting of the sun.

The lover will direct his conversation to the beloved even when he purports, however earnestly, to address another: the affection is apparent to anyone with eyes to see. When the loved one speaks, the lover listens with rapt attention to his every word; he marvels at everything the beloved says, however extraordinary and absurd his observations may be; he believes him implicitly even when he is clearly lying, agrees with him though he is obviously in the wrong, testifies on his behalf for all that he may be unjust, follows after him however he may proceed and whatever line of argument he may adopt. The lover hurries to the spot where the beloved is at the moment, endeavours to sit as near to him as possible, sidles up close to him, lays aside all occupations that might oblige him to leave his company, makes light of any matter, however weighty, that would demand his parting from him, is very slow to move when he takes his leave of him.

Other signs of love are that sudden confusion and excitement betrayed by the lover when he unexpectedly sees the one he loves coming upon him unawares, that agitation which overmasters him on beholding someone who resembles his beloved or on hearing his name suddenly pronounced. A man in love will give prodigally, to the limit of his capacity, in a way that formerly he would have refused; as if he were the one receiving the donation, he the one whose happiness is the object in view; all this in order that he may show off his good points, and make himself desirable. How often has the miser opened his purse-strings, the scowler relaxed his frown, the coward leapt heroically into the fray, the clod suddenly become sharp-witted, the boor turned into the perfect gentleman, the stinker transformed into the elegant dandy, the sloucher smartened up, the decrepit recaptured his lost youth, the godly gone wild, the self-respecting kicked over the traces—and all because of love!

All these signs are to be observed even before the fire of love is properly kindled, ere its conflagration truly bursts forth, its blaze waxes fierce, its flames leap up. But when the fire really takes a hold and is firmly established, then you will see the secret whispering, the unconcealed turning away from all present but the beloved.

Other outward signs and tokens of love are the following, which are apparent to all having eyes in their heads: abundant and exceeding cheerfulness at finding oneself with the beloved in a narrow space, and a corresponding depression on being together in a wide expanse; to engage in a playful tug of war for anything the one or the other lays hold of; much clandestine winking; leaning sideways and supporting oneself against the object of one's affection; endeavouring to touch his hand and whatever part of his body one can reach, while engaged in conversation; and drinking the remainder of what the beloved has left in his cup, seeking out the very spot against which his lips were pressed.

There are also contrary signs that occur according to casual provocations and accidental incitements and a variety of motivating causes and stimulating thoughts. Opposites are of course likes, in reality; when things reach the limit of contrariety, and stand at the furthest bounds of divergency, they come to resemble one another. This is decreed by God's omnipotent power, in a manner that baffles entirely the human imagination. Thus, when ice is pressed a long time in the hand, it finally produces the same effect as fire. We find that extreme joy and extreme sorrow kill equally; excessive and violent laughter sends the tears coursing from the eyes. It is a very common phenomenon in the world about us. Similarly with lovers: when they love each other with an equal ardour and their mutual affection is intensely strong, they will turn against one another without any valid reason, each purposely contradicting the other in whatever he may say; they quarrel violently over the smallest things, each picking up every word that the other lets fall and wilfully misinterpreting it. All these devices are aimed at testing and proving what each is seeking in the other.

Now the difference between this sham, and real aversion and contrariness born of deep-seated hatred and inveterate contention, is that lovers are very quickly reconciled after their disputes. You will see a pair of lovers seeming to have reached the extreme limit of contrariety, to the point that you would reckon not to be mended even in the instance of a person of most tranquil spirit and wholly exempt from rancour, save after a long interval, and wholly irreparable in the case of a quarrelsome man; yet in next to no time you will observe them to have become the best of friends once more; silenced are those mutual reproaches, vanished that disharmony; forthwith they are laughing again and playfully sporting together. The same scene may be enacted several times at a single session. When you see a pair of lovers behaving in such a fashion, let no doubt enter your mind, no uncertainty invade your thoughts; you may be sure without hesitation, and convinced as by an unshakable certainty, that there lies between them a deep and hidden secret—the secret of true love. Take this then for a sure test, a universally valid experiment: it is the product only of an equal partnership in love and a true concord of hearts. I myself have observed it frequently.

Another sign is when you find the lover almost entreating to hear the loved one's name pronounced, taking an extreme delight in speaking about him, so that the subject is a positive obsession with him; nothing so much rejoices him, and he is not in the least restrained by the fear that someone listening may realize what he is about, and someone present will understand his true motives. Love for a thing renders you blind and deaf. If the lover could so contrive that in the place where he happens to be there should be no talk of anything but his beloved, he would never leave that spot for any other in the whole world.

It can happen that a man sincerely affected by love will start to eat his meal with an excellent appetite; yet the instant the recollection of his loved one is excited, the food sticks in his throat and chokes his gullet. It is the same if he is drinking or talking—he begins to converse with you gaily enough, then all at once he is invaded by a chance thought of his dear one. You will notice the change in his manner of speaking, the instantaneous failure of his conversational powers; the sure signs are his long silences, the way he stares at the ground, his extreme taciturnity. One moment he is all smiles, lightly gesticulating; the next he has become completely boxed up, sluggish, distrait, rigid, too weary to utter a single word, irritated by the most innocent question.

Love's signs also include a fondness for solitude and a pleasure in being alone, as well as a wasting of the body not accompanied by any fever or ache preventing free activity and liberty of movement. The walk is also an unerring indication and never-deceiving sign of an inward lassitude of spirit. Sleeplessness too is a common affliction of lovers; the poets have described this condition frequently, relating how they watch the stars, and giving an account of the night's interminable length.

Another sign of love is that you will see the lover loving his beloved's kith and kin and the intimate ones of his household, to such an extent that they are nearer and dearer to him than his own folk, himself, and all his familiar friends.

Weeping is a well-known sign of love, except that men differ very greatly from one another in this particular. Some are ready weepers; their tear-ducts are always overflowing, and their eyes respond immediately to their emotions, the tears rolling down at a moment's notice. Others are dry-eyed and barren of tears; to this category I myself belong. This is the result of my habit of eating frankincense to abate the palpitation from which I have suffered since childhood. I will be afflicted by some shocking blow, and at once feel my heart to be splitting and breaking into fragments; I have a choking sensation in my heart more bitter than colocynth, that prevents me from getting my words out properly, and sometimes well nigh suffocates me. My eyes therefore respond to my feelings but rarely, and then my tears are exceedingly sparse.

You will see the lover, when unsure of the constancy of his loved one's feelings for him, perpetually on his guard in a way that he never troubled to be before; he polishes his language, he refines his gestures and his glances, particularly if he has the misfortune and mischance to be in love with one given to making unjust accusations, or of a quarrelsome disposition.

Another sign of love is the way the lover pays attention to the beloved; remembering everything that falls from his lips; searching out all the news about him, so that nothing small or great that happens to him may escape his knowledge;

in short, following closely his every movement. Upon my life, sometimes you will see a complete dolt under these circumstances become most keen, a careless fellow turn exceedingly quick-witted.

One of the strangest origins of passion is when a man falls in love through merely hearing the description of the other party, without ever having set eyes on the beloved. In such a case he will progress through all the accustomed stages of love; there will be the sending to and fro of messengers, the exchange of letters, the anxiety, the deep emotion, the sleeplessness; and all this without actual sight of the object of affection. Stories, descriptions of beautiful qualities, and the reporting of news about the fair one have a manifest effect on the soul; to hear a girl's voice singing behind a wall may well move the heart to love, and preoccupy the mind.

All this has occurred to more than one man. In my opinion, however, such a love is a tumbledown building without any foundations. If a man's thoughts are absorbed by passionate regard for one whom he has never seen, the inevitable result is that whenever he is alone with his own reflections, he will represent to himself a purely imaginary picture of the person whose identity he keeps constantly before his mind; no other being than this takes shape in his fantasy; he is completely carried away by his imagination, and visualizes and dreams of her only. Then if some day he actually sees the object of his fanciful passion, either his love is confirmed or it is wholly nullified. Both these alternatives have actually happened and been known.

This kind of romance usually takes place between veiled ladies of guarded palaces and aristocratic households, and their male kinsfolk; the love of women is more stable in these cases than that of men, because women are weak creatures and their natures swiftly respond to this sort of attraction, which easily masters them completely.

Often it happens that love fastens itself to the heart as the result of a single glance. This variety of love is divided into two classes. The first class is the contrary of what we have just been describing, in that a man will fall head over heels in love with a mere form, without knowing who that person may be, what her name is, or where she lives. This sort of thing happens frequently enough.

The second class is the contrary of what we shall be describing in the chapter next following, if God wills. This is for a man to form an attachment at first sight with a young lady whose name, place of abode and origin are known to him. The difference here is the speed or tardiness with which the affair passes off. When a man falls in love at first sight, and forms a sudden attachment as the result of a fleeting glance, that proves him to be little steadfast, and proclaims that he will as suddenly forget his romantic adventure; it testifies to his fickleness and inconstancy. So it is with all things; the quicker they grow, the quicker they decay; while on the other hand slow produced is slow consumed.

Some men there are whose love becomes true only after long converse, much contemplation, and extended familiarity. Such a one is likely to persist and to be steadfast in his affection, untouched by the passage of time; what enters with difficulty goes not out easily. That is my own way in these matters, and it is confirmed by Holy Tradition. For God, as we are informed by our teachers, when He commanded the Spirit to enter Adam's body, that was like an earthen vessel—and the Spirit was afraid, and sorely distressed—said to it, "Enter in unwillingly, and come forth again unwillingly!"

I have myself seen a man of this description who, whenever he sensed within himself the beginnings of a passionate attachment, or conceived a penchant for some form whose beauty he admired, at once employed the device of shunning that person and giving up all association with him, lest his feelings become more intense and the affair get beyond his control, and he find himself completely stampeded. This proves how closely love cleaves to such people's hearts, and once it lays hold of them never looses its grip.

I indeed marvel profoundly at all those who pretend to fall in love at first sight; I cannot easily prevail upon myself to believe their claims, and prefer to consider such love as merely a kind of lust. As for thinking that that sort of attachment can really possess the inmost heart and penetrate the veil of the soul's recess, that I cannot under any circumstances credit. Love has never truly gripped my bowels, save after a long lapse of time and constant companionship with the person concerned, sharing with him all that while my every occupation, be it earnest or frivolous. So I am alike in consolation and in passion; I have never in my life forgotten any romance, and my nostalgia for every former attachment is such that I well nigh choke when I drink and suffocate when I eat. The man who is not so constituted quickly finds complete relief and is at rest again; I have never wearied of anything once I have known it, and neither have I hastened to feel at home with it on first acquaintance. Similarly, I have never longed for a change for change's sake, in any of the things that I have possessed; I am speaking here not only of friends and comrades, but also of all the other things a man uses—clothes, riding-beast, food, and so on.

Life holds no joy for me, and I do nothing but hang my head and feel utterly cast down, ever since I first tasted the bitterness of being separated from those I love. It is an anguish that constantly revisits me, an agony of grief that ceases not for a moment to assail me. My remembrance of past happiness has abated for me every joy that I may look for in the future. I am a dead man, though counted among the living, slain by sorrow and buried by sadness, entombed while yet a dweller on the face of this mortal earth. God be praised, whatever be the circumstances that befall us; there is indeed no other God but He!

As for what transpires at first blush as a result of certain accidental circumstances—physical admiration, and visual enchantment which does not go beyond mere external forms—and this is the very secret and meaning of carnal desire; when carnal desire moreover becomes so overflowing that it surpasses these bounds, and when such an overflow coincides with a spiritual union in which the natural instincts share equally with the soul, the resulting phenomenon is called passionate love. Herein lies the root of the error which misleads a man into asserting that he loves two persons, or is passionately enamoured of two entirely different individuals. All this is to be explained as springing out of carnal desire, as we have just described; it is called love only metaphorically, and not in the true meaning of the term. As for the true lover, his yearning of the soul is so excessive as to divert him from all his religious and mundane occupations; how then should he have room to busy himself with a second love affair?

Know now—may God exalt you!—that love exercises an effective authority, a decisive sovereignty over the soul; its commands cannot be opposed; its ordinances may not be flouted; its rule is not to be transgressed; it demands unwavering obedience, and against its dominion there is no appeal. Love untwists the firmest plaits and looses the tightest strands; it dissolves that which is most solid, undoes that which is most firm; it penetrates the deepest recesses of the heart, and makes lawful things most strictly forbidden.

I have known many men whose discrimination was beyond suspicion, men not to be feared deficient in knowledge, or wanting in taste, or lacking in discernment, who nevertheless described their loved ones as possessing certain qualities not by any means admired by the general run of mankind or approved according to the accepted canons of beauty. Yet those qualities had become an obsession with them, the sole object of their passion, and the very last word (as they thought) in elegance. Thereafter their loved ones vanished, either into oblivion, or by separation, or jilting, or through some other accident to which love is always liable; but those men never lost their admiration for the curious qualities which provoked their approval of them, neither did they ever afterwards cease to prefer these above other attributes that are in reality superior to them.

Let me add a personal touch. In my youth I loved a slave-girl who happened to be a blonde; from that time I have never admired brunettes, not though their dark tresses set off a face as resplendent as the sun, or the very image of beauty itself. I find this taste to have become a part of my whole make-up and constitution since those early days; my soul will not suffer me to acquire any other, or to love any type but that. This very same thing happened to my father also (God be pleased with him!), and he remained faithful to his first preference until the term of his earthly life was done.

Were it not that this world below is a transitory abode of trial and trouble, and paradise a home where virtue receives its reward, secure from all annoyances, I would have said that union with the beloved is that pure happiness which is without alloy, and gladness unsullied by sorrow the perfect realization of hopes and the complete fulfillment of one's dreams.

I have tested all manner of pleasures, and known every variety of joy; and I have found that neither intimacy with princes, nor wealth acquired, nor finding after lacking, nor returning after long absence, nor security after fear, and repose in a safe refuge—none of these things so powerfully affects the soul as union with the beloved, especially if it come after long denial and continual banishment. For then the flame of passion waxes exceeding hot, and the furnace of yearning blazes up, and the fire of eager hope rages ever more fiercely.

The fresh springing of herbs after the rains, the glitter of flowers when the night clouds have rolled away in the hushed hour between dawn and sunrise, the plashing of waters as they run through the stalks of golden blossoms, the exquisite beauty of white castles encompassed by verdant meadows—not lovelier is any of these than union with the well-beloved, whose character is virtuous, and laudable her disposition, whose attributes are evenly matched in perfect beauty. Truly that is a miracle of wonder surpassing the tongues of the eloquent, and far beyond the range of the most cunning speech to describe: the mind reels before it, and the intellect stands abashed.

USAMAH IBN MUNQIDH

[1095–1190]

Urbane and loquacious, Usamah Ibn Munqidh wrote his memoirs, *The Book of Reflections*, when he was ninety. In this work he recounts a vast number of stories about his long association with the Franks, providing vivid and revealing anecdotes of cross-cultural contact in the twelfth century.

Usamah was an upper-class officer and gentleman of Syria, well-educated and positioned to be in contact with his Frankish peers after hostilities between the Franks and Muslims cooled in the latter half of the twelfth century. He records for the Muslim reader a series of quick vignettes of the Franks: doctors, military men, other professionals, and such commoners as he encountered. He reveals the horror that he says he felt as a cultivated Muslim in the presence of these crude and unsophisticated Europeans, giving modern readers from the West an unforgettable picture of what some of their ancestors looked like to the "other side."

Suggested Readings

The complete text of Usamah's autobiography is available in a translation by Philip K. Hitti, *An Arab-Syrian Gentleman and Warrior in the Period of the Crusades* (1929).

FROM

The Book of Reflections

Translated by Philip K. Hitti

Mysterious are the works of the Creator, the author of all things! When one comes to recount cases regarding the Franks, he cannot but glorify Allah (exalted is he!) and sanctify him, for he sees them as animals possessing the virtues of courage and fighting, but nothing else, just as animals have only the virtues of strength and carrying loads. I shall now give some instances of their doings and their curious mentality.

In the army of King Fulk, son of Fulk, was a Frankish reverend knight who had just arrived from their land in order to make the holy pilgrimage and then return home. He was of my intimate fellowship and kept such constant company with me that he began to call me "my brother." Between us were mutual bonds of amity and friendship. When he resolved to return by sea to his homeland, he said to me:

"My brother, I am leaving for my country and I want thee to send with me thy son (my son, who was then fourteen years old, was at that time in my company) to our country, where he can see the knights and learn wisdom and chivalry. When he returns, he will be like a wise man."

Thus there fell upon my ears words which would never come out of the head of a sensible man; for even if my son were to be taken captive, his captivity could not bring him a worse misfortune than carrying him into the lands of the Franks. However, I said to the man:

"By thy life, this has been exactly my idea. But the only thing that prevented me from carrying it out was the fact that his grandmother, my mother, is so fond of him that she did not this time let him come out with me until she exacted an oath from me to the effect that I would return him to her."

Thereupon he asked, "Is thy mother still alive?" "Yes," I replied. "Well," said he, "disobey her not."

A case illustrating their curious medicine is the following:

The lord of al-Munayṭirah wrote to my uncle asking him to dispatch a physician to treat certain sick persons among his people. My uncle sent him a Christian physician named Thābit. Thābit was absent but ten days when he returned. So we said to him, "How quickly hast thou healed thy patients!" He said:

They brought before me a knight in whose leg an abscess had grown, and a woman afflicted with imbecility. To the knight I applied a small poultice until the abscess opened and became well; and the woman I put on diet and made her humor wet. Then a Frankish physician came to them and said, "This man knows nothing about treating them." He then said to the knight, "Which wouldst thou prefer, living with one leg or dying with two?" The latter replied, "Living with one leg." The physician said, "Bring me a strong knight and a sharp ax." A knight came with the ax. And I was standing by. Then the physician laid the leg of the patient on a block of wood and bade the knight strike his leg with the ax and chop it off at one blow. Accordingly he struck it—while I was looking on—one blow, but the leg was not severed. He dealt another blow, upon which the marrow of the leg flowed out and the patient died on the spot. He then examined the woman and said, "This is a woman in whose head there is a devil which has possessed her. Shave off her hair." Accordingly they shaved it off and the woman began once more to eat their ordinary diet—garlic and mustard. Her imbecility took a turn for the worse. The physician then said, "The devil has penetrated through her head." He therefore took a razor, made a deep cruciform incision on it, peeled off the skin at the middle of the incision until the bone of the skull was exposed, and rubbed it with salt. The woman also expired instantly. Thereupon I asked them whether my services were needed any longer, and when they replied in the negative I returned home, having learned of their medicine what I knew not before.

I have, however, witnessed a case of their medicine which was quite different from that.

The king of the Franks had for treasurer a knight named Bernard [*barnād*], who (may Allah's curse be upon him!) was one of the most accursed and wicked among the Franks. A horse kicked him in the leg, which was subsequently infected and which opened in fourteen different places. Every time one of these cuts would close in one place, another would open in another place. All this happened while I was praying for his perdition. Then came to him a Frankish physician and removed from the leg all the ointments which were on it and began to wash it with very strong vinegar. By this treatment all the cuts were healed and the man became well again. He was up again like a devil.

Another case illustrating their curious medicine is the following:

In Shayzar we had an artisan named abu-al-Fath, who had a boy whose neck was afflicted with scrofula. Every time a part of it would close, another part would open. This man happened to go to Antioch on business of his, accompanied by his son. A Frank noticed the boy and asked his father about him. Abu-al-Fath replied, "This is my son." The Frank said to him, "Wilt thou swear by thy religion that if I prescribe to thee a medicine which will cure thy boy, thou wilt charge nobody fees for prescribing it thyself? In that case, I shall prescribe to thee a medicine which will cure the boy." The man took the oath and the Frank said:

"Take uncrushed leaves of glasswort, burn them, then soak the ashes in olive oil and sharp vinegar. Treat the scrofula with them until the spot on which it is growing is eaten up. Then take burnt lead, soak it in ghee butter [*samn*] and treat him with it. That will cure him."

The father treated the boy accordingly, and the boy was cured. The sores closed, and the boy returned to his normal condition of health.

I have myself treated with this medicine many who were afflicted with such disease, and the treatment was successful in removing the cause of the complaint.

Everyone who is a fresh emigrant from the Frankish lands is ruder in character than those who have become acclimatized and have held long association with the Moslems. Here is an illustration of their rude character.

Whenever I visited Jerusalem I always entered the Aqṣa Mosque, beside which stood a small mosque which the Franks had converted into a church. When I used to enter the Aqṣa Mosque, which was occupied by the Templars [*al-dāwiyyah*], who were my friends, the Templars would evacuate the little adjoining mosque so that I might pray in it. One day I entered this mosque, repeated the first formula, "Allah is great," and stood up in the act of praying, upon which one of the Franks rushed on me, got hold of me and turned my face eastward, saying, "This is the way thou shouldst pray!" A group of Templars hastened to him, seized him and repelled him from me. I resumed my prayer. The same man, while the others were otherwise busy, rushed once more on me and turned my face eastward, saying, "This is the way thou shouldst pray!" The Templars again came in to him and expelled him. They apologized to me, saying, "This is a stranger who has only recently arrived from the land of the Franks and he has never before seen anyone praying except eastward." Thereupon I said to myself, "I have had enough prayer." So I went out, and have ever been surprised at the conduct of this devil of a man, at the change in the color of his face, his trembling, and his sentiment at the sight of one praying towards the *qiblah*.

I saw one of the Franks come to al-Amīr Muʿīn-al-Dīn (may Allah's mercy rest upon his soul!) when he was in the Dome of the Rock, and say to him, "Dost thou want to see God as a child?" Muʿīn-al-Dīn said, "Yes." The Frank walked ahead of us until he showed us the picture of Mary with Christ (may peace be upon him!) as an infant in her lap. He then said, "This is God as a child." But Allah is exalted far above what the infidels say about him!

The Franks are void of all zeal and jealousy. One of them may be walking along with his wife. He meets another man who takes the wife by the hand and steps aside to converse with her while the husband is standing on one side waiting for his wife to conclude the conversation. If she lingers too long for him, he leaves her alone with the conversant and goes away.

Here is an illustration which I myself witnessed:

When I used to visit Nāblus, I always took lodging with a man named Muʿizz, whose home was a lodging house for the Moslems. The house had windows which opened to the road, and there stood opposite to it on the other side of the road a house belonging to a Frank who sold wine for the merchants. He would take some wine in a bottle and go around announcing it by shouting, "So and so, the merchant, has just opened a cask full of this wine. He who wants to buy some of it will find it in such and such a place." The Frank's pay for the announcement made would be the wine in that bottle. One day this Frank went home and found a man with his wife in the same bed. He asked him, "What could have made thee enter into my wife's room?" The man replied, "I was tired, so I went in to rest." "But how," asked he, "didst thou get into my bed?" The other replied, "I found a bed that was spread, so I slept in it." "But," said he, "my wife was sleeping together with thee!" The other replied, "Well, the bed is hers. How could I therefore have prevented her from using her own bed?" "By the truth of my religion," said the husband, "if thou shouldst do it again, thou and I would have a quarrel." Such was for the Frank the entire expression of his disapproval and the limit of his jealousy.

Another illustration:

We had with us a bath-keeper named Sālim, originally an inhabitant of al-Maʿarrah, who had charge of the bath of my father (may Allah's mercy rest upon his soul!). This man related the following story:

"I once opened a bath in al-Maʿarrah in order to earn my living. To this bath there came a Frankish knight. The Franks disapprove of girding a cover around one's waist while in the bath. So this Frank stretched out his arm and pulled off my cover from my waist and threw it away. He looked and saw that I had recently shaved off my pubes. So he shouted, 'Sālim!' As I drew near him he stretched his hand over my pubes and said, 'Sālim, good! By the truth of my religion, do the same for me.' Saying this, he lay on his back and I found that in that place the hair was like his beard. So I shaved it off. Then he passed his hand over the place and, finding it smooth, he said, 'Sālim, by the truth of my religion, do the same to madame [*al-dāma*]' (*al-dāma* in their language means the lady), referring to his wife. He then said to a servant of his, 'Tell madame to come here.' Accordingly the servant went and brought her and made her enter the bath. She also lay on her back. The knight repeated, 'Do what thou hast done to me.' So I shaved all that hair while her husband was sitting looking at me. At last he thanked me and handed me the pay for my service."

Consider now this great contradiction! They have neither jealousy nor zeal, but they have great courage, although courage is nothing but the product of zeal and of ambition to be above ill repute.

Here is a story analogous to the one related above:

I entered the public bath in Ṣūr [Tyre] and took my place in a secluded part. One of my servants thereupon said to me, "There is with us in the bath a woman." When I went out, I sat on one of the stone benches and behold! the woman who was in the bath had come out all dressed and was standing with her father just opposite me. But I could not be sure that she was a woman. So I said to one of my companions, "By Allah, see if this is a woman," by which I meant that he should ask about her. But he went, as I was looking at him, lifted the end of her robe and looked carefully at her. Thereupon her father turned toward me and said, "This is my daughter. Her mother is dead and she has nobody to wash her hair. So I took her in with me to the bath and washed her head." I replied, "Thou hast well done! This is something for which thou shalt be rewarded [by Allah]!"

A curious case relating to their medicine is the following, which was related to me by William of Bures [*kilyām dabūr*], the lord of Ṭabarayyah [Tiberias], who was one of the principal chiefs among the Franks. It happened that William had accompanied al-Amīr Muʿīn-al-Dīn (may Allah's mercy rest upon his soul!) from ʿAkka to Ṭabarayyah when I was in his company too. On the way William related to us the following story in these words:

"We had in our country a highly esteemed knight who was taken ill and was on the point of death. We thereupon came to one of our great priests and said to him, 'Come with us and examine so and so, the knight.' 'I will,' he replied, and walked along with us, while we were assured in ourselves that if he would only lay his hand on him the patient would recover. When the priest saw the patient, he said, 'Bring me some wax.' We fetched him a little wax, which he softened and shaped like the knuckles of fingers, and he stuck one in each nostril. The knight died on the spot. We said to him, 'He is dead.' 'Yes,' he replied, 'he was suffering great pain, so I closed up his nose that he might die and get relief.'

Let this go and let us resume the discussion regarding Harim.

We shall now leave the discussion of their treatment of the orifices of the body to something else.

I found myself in Ṭabarayyah at the time the Franks were celebrating one of their feasts. The cavaliers went out to exercise with lances. With them went out two decrepit, aged women whom they stationed at one end of the race course. At the other end of the field they left a pig which they had scalded and laid on a rock. They then made the two aged women run a race while each one of them was accompanied by a detachment of horsemen urging her on. At every step they took, the women would fall down and rise again, while the spectators would laugh. Finally one of them got ahead of the other and won that pig for a prize.

I attended one day a duel in Nāblus between two Franks. The reason for this was that certain Moslem thieves took by surprise one of the villages of Nāblus. One of the peasants of that village was charged with having acted as guide for the thieves when they fell upon the village. So he fled away. The king sent and arrested his children. The peasant thereupon came back to the king and said, "Let justice be done in my case. I challenge to a duel the man who claimed that I guided the thieves to the village." The king then said to the tenant who held the village in fief, "Bring forth someone to fight the duel with him." The tenant went to his village, where a blacksmith lived, took hold of him and ordered him to fight the duel. The tenant became thus sure of the safety of his own peasants, none of whom would be killed and his estate ruined.

I saw this blacksmith. He was a physically strong young man, but his heart failed him. He would walk a few steps and then sit down and ask for a drink. The one who had made the challenge was an old man, but he was strong in spirit and he would rub the nail of his thumb against that of the forefinger in defiance, as if he was not worrying over the duel. Then came the viscount [*al-biskund*], i.e., the seignior of the town, and gave each one of the two contestants a cudgel and a shield and arranged the people in a circle around them.

The two met. The old man would press the blacksmith backward until he would get him as far as the circle, then he would come back to the middle of the arena. They went on exchanging blows until they looked like pillars smeared with blood. The contest was prolonged and the viscount began to urge them to hurry, saying, "Hurry on." The fact that the smith was given to the use of the hammer proved now of great advantage to him. The old man was worn out and the smith gave him a blow which made him fall. His cudgel fell under his back. The smith knelt down over him and tried to stick his fingers into the eyes of his adversary, but could not do it because of the great quantity of blood flowing out. Then he rose up and hit his head with the cudgel until he killed him. They then fastened a rope around the neck of the dead person, dragged him away and hanged him. The lord who brought the smith now came, gave the smith his own mantle, made him mount the horse behind him, and rode off with him. This case illustrates the kind of jurisprudence and legal decisions the Franks have—may Allah's curse be upon them!

I once went in the company of al-Amīr Muʿīn-al-Dīn (may Allah's mercy rest upon his soul!) to Jerusalem. We stopped at Nāblus. There a blind man, a Moslem, who was still young and was well dressed, presented himself before al-Amīr carrying fruits for him and asked permission to be admitted into his service in Damascus. The Amīr consented. I inquired about this man and was informed that his mother had been married to a Frank whom she had killed. Her son used to practice ruses against the Frankish pilgrims and co-operate with his mother in assassinating them. They finally brought charges against him and tried his case according to the Frankish way of procedure.

They installed a huge cask and filled it with water. Across it they set a board of wood. They then bound the arms of the man charged with the act, tied a rope around his shoulders, and dropped him into the cask, their idea being that in case he was innocent, he would sink in the water and they would then lift him up with the rope so that he might not die in the water; and in case he was guilty, he would not sink in the water. This man did his best to sink when they dropped him into the water, but he could not do it. So he had to submit to their sentence against him—may Allah's curse be upon them! They pierced his eyeballs with red-hot awls.

Later this same man arrived in Damascus. Al-Amīr Muʿīn-al-Dīn (may Allah's mercy rest upon his soul!) assigned him a stipend large enough to meet all his needs and said to a slave of his, "Conduct him to Burhān-al-Dīn al-Balkhi (may Allah's mercy rest upon his soul!) and ask him on my behalf to order somebody to teach this man the Koran and something of Moslem jurisprudence." Hearing that, the blind man remarked, "May triumph and victory be thine! But this was never my thought." "What didst thou think I was going to do for thee?" asked Muʿīn-al-Dīn. The blind man replied, "I thought thou wouldst give me a horse, a mule and a suit of armor and make me a knight." Muʿīn-al-Dīn then said, "I never thought that a blind man could become a knight."

Among the Franks are those who have become acclimatized and have associated long with the Moslems. These are much better than the recent comers from the Frankish lands. But they constitute the exception and cannot be treated as a rule.

Here is an illustration. I dispatched one of my men to Antioch on business. There was in Antioch at that time al-Ra'īs Theodoros Sophianos [*tādrus ibn-al-ṣaffi*], to whom I was bound by mutual ties of amity. His influence in Antioch was supreme. One day he said to my man, "I am invited by a friend of mine who is a Frank. Thou shouldst come with me so that thou mayest see their fashions." My man related the story in the following words:

"I went along with him and we came to the home of a knight who belonged to the old category of knights who came with the early expeditions of the Franks. He had been by that time stricken off the register and exempted from service, and possessed in Antioch an estate on the income of which he lived. The knight presented an excellent table, with food extraordinarily clean and delicious. Seeing me abstaining from food, he said, 'Eat, be of good cheer! I never eat Frankish dishes, but I have Egyptian women cooks and never eat except their cooking. Besides, pork never enters my home.' I ate, but guardedly, and after that we departed.

"As I was passing in the market place, a Frankish woman all of a sudden hung to my clothes and began to mutter words in their language, and I could not understand what she was saying. This made me immediately the center of a big crowd of Franks. I was convinced that death was at hand. But all of a sudden that same knight approached. On seeing me, he came and said to that woman, 'What is the matter between thee and this Moslem?' She replied, 'This is he who has killed my brother Hurso [ʿ*urs*].' This Hurso was a knight in Afāmiyah who was killed by someone of the army of Hamāh. The Christian knight shouted at her, saying, 'This is a bourgeois [*burjāsi*] (i.e., a merchant) who neither fights nor attends a fight.' He also yelled at the people who had assembled, and they all dispersed. Then he took me by the hand and went away. Thus the effect of that meal was my deliverance from certain death."

IBN JUBAYR

[LATE 12TH CENTURY]

The *Koran* says this of the Ka'bah, the "first house appointed for men," at Mecca: "Whoever enters it shall be secure, and pilgrimage to the House is incumbent upon men for the sake of Allah" (Sura III, 97). From the beginnings of the faith to the present day, every Muslim of sufficient means has been commanded to travel there at least once in a lifetime. (Muhammad made his journey in the tenth year of the Moslem calendar.) Rituals must be seen to: the declaration of intent, the *ihram* or wearing of the robes of modesty, the prayer upon entering the house, and so on. At certain times of year, throngs of pilgrims gather before the Mountain of Arafat, symbolizing the believers of the world before Allah. The road to Mecca is thus the road to salvation.

For Ibn Jubayr, secretary to the Muslim governor of Granada, the journey to Mecca in 1183 was a form of penitence for the drinking of wine, which his reckless employer had forced upon him. Once on his journey, he kept copious notes, which he fashioned into a journal after his return to Spain in 1185. His travel account has been celebrated since that time for its remarkable clarity, humanity, and descriptive powers.

The portion of Ibn Jubayr's account we have printed here spans the summer month of Jumada'l-Ula of the Muslim calendar year 579 (1183) and concerns his journey to Mecca. We are swept up in the bounteous detail Ibn Jubayr provides about his surroundings. He describes the approach to Mecca and the holy site, the Ka'bah. The chapter describing the House begins with the new moon, "the most auspicious our eyes had seen in all that had passed our life." The inside space is described in loving detail, with attention given to such matters as the kissing of the Black Stone and the appearance of the khatib, or preacher, at the prayer on Fridays.

The reader should compare this selection with Mandeville's treatment of the city of Jerusalem. The Christian author has compiled a careful description of the city from a variety of sources, yielding a public view with a certain detachment, like a postcard. Ibn Jubayr, passionately respectful of his subject, makes his much more private document the mirror of his faith, conveying through his clear descriptions the feelings of his soul.

Suggested Readings

The attractive translation of this work is provided by R. J. C. Broadhurst, *The Travels of Ibn Jubayr* (1952). This unique modern edition contains a short, useful introduction, excellent notes, and a glossary.

The Travels of Ibn Jubayr

Translated by R. J. C. Broadhurst

FROM

The Month of Rabi' al-Akhir (579) [July 24–August 21, 1183]

May God let us know His favour

At eventide on Tuesday the 11th of the month, being the 2nd of August, we left Jiddah, after the pilgrims had guaranteed each other (for payment), and their names had been recorded in a register kept by the governor of the city. . . .

We passed on our way that night until we arrived at al-Qurayn, with the rising of the sun. This place is a staging post for pilgrims and a place of their encampment. There they put on the *ihram,*[1] and there they rest throughout the day of their arrival. . . . In this place is a well of sweet spring water, and by reason of it the pilgrims do not need to supply themselves with water save for the night on which they travel to it. Throughout the daylight hours of Wednesday we stayed resting at al-Qurayn, but when evening had come, we left it in the pilgrim garb to perform

[1]Prohibition. Several aspects of this ritual are the wearing of pilgrim garb denoting modesty before Allah, strict observation of chastity, and other prohibitions regarding such matters as covering the head and killing animals.

the *'Umrah,'*[2] and marched throughout the night. With the dawn, we came near to the Haram, and descended as the light was about to spread.

We entered Mecca—God protect it—at the first hour of Thursday the 13th of Rabi', being the 4th of August, by the 'Umrah Gate. As we marched that night, the full moon had thrown its rays upon the earth, the night had lifted its veil, voices struck the ears with the *Talbiyat,*[3] from all sides, and tongues were loud in invocation, humbly beseeching God to grant them their requests, sometimes redoubling their *Talbiyat,* and sometimes imploring with prayers. Oh night most happy, the bride of all the nights of life, the virgin of the maidens of time.

And so, at the time and on the day we have mentioned, we came to God's venerable Haram, the place of sojourn of Abraham the Friend (of God), and found the Ka'bah, the Sacred House, the unveiled bride conducted (like a bride to her groom) to the supreme felicity of heaven, encompassed by the deputations of the All-Merciful. We performed the *tawaf*[4] of the new arrival, and then prayed at the revered Maqam.[5] We clung to the covering of the Ka'bah near the Multazam, which is between the Black Stone and the door, and is a place where prayers are answered. We entered the dome of Zamzam and drank of its waters which is 'to the purpose for which it is drunk,' as said the Prophet—may God bless and preserve him—and then performed the *sa'i*[6] between al-Safa and al-Marwah. After this we shaved and entered a state of *halal.*[7] Praise be to God for generously including us in the pilgrimage to Him and for making us to be of those on whose behalf the prayers of Abraham reach. Sufficient He is for us and the best Manager. We took lodging in Mecca at a house called al-Halal near to the Haram and the Bab al-Suddah, one of its gates, in a room having many domestic conveniences and overlooking the Haram and the sacred Ka'bah.

FROM

THE MONTH OF JUMADA 'L-ULA (579) [AUGUST 22–SEPTEMBER 20, 1183]

May God let us know His favour

The new moon rose on the night of Monday the 22nd of August, when we had been in Mecca—may God Most High exalt it—eighteen days. The new moon of this month was the most auspicious our eyes had seen in all that had passed of our life. It rose after we had already entered the seat of the venerable enclosure, the sacred Haram of God, the dome in which is the maqam of Abraham, the place from whence the Prophet's mission (was sent out), and the alighting place of the faithful spirit Gabriel with inspiration and revelation. May God with His power and strength

---

[2]Lesser Pilgrimage, the journey to Mecca including the sevenfold circumambulation of the Ka'bah and the ritual run between al-Marwah and al-Safa; performed any time of the year except the three days of the *Hajj,* or Greater Pilgrimage.

[3]"Waiting for orders," the cry pilgrims are supposed to utter as they approach Mecca. It begins, "Here I am, oh God, here I am."

[4]The rite of the sevenfold circumambulation of the Ka'bah, an ancient practice preserved by Muhammad.

[5]*Maqam* can refer either to the sacred stone on which Abraham stood when he built the temple of Ka'bah, or the building that formerly housed this stone. In this text, the building is referred to by the word *Maqam,* the stone by the word *maqam.*

[6]The ritual run between al-Marwah and al-Safa, recalling the course run by Hagar, mother of Ishmael, until the angel Gabriel delivered water to her son who was dying of thirst. Pilgrims to Mecca must complete this course seven times.

[7]Release, here meaning release from the prohibitions of *ihram.*

inspire us to thanks for His favour and make us sensible of that amount of privilege He has made our portion, finally accepting us (into Paradise) and rewarding us with the accustomed generosity of His beneficent works, and giving us of His gracious help and support. There is no God but He.

A description of the Sacred Mosque and the Ancient House
May God bless and exalt it

The venerable House has four corners and is almost square. The custodians of the House . . . informed me that its height, on the side which faces the Gate al-Safa and which extends from the Black Stone to the Yemen Corner, is twenty-nine cubits. The remaining sides are twenty-eight cubits because of the slope of the roof towards the water-spout.

The principal corner is the one containing the Black Stone. There the circumambulation begins, the circumambulator drawing back (a little) from it so that all of his body might pass by it, the blessed House being on his left. The first thing that is met after that is the 'Iraq corner, which faces the north, then the Syrian corner which faces west, then the Yemen corner which faces south, and then back to the Black corner which faces east. That completes one single course. The door of the blessed House is on the side between the 'Iraq corner and the Black Stone corner, and is close to the Stone at a distance of barely ten spans. That part of the side of the House which is between them is called the Multazam: a place where prayers are answered.

The venerable door is raised above the ground eleven and a half spans. It is of silver gilt and of exquisite workmanship and beautiful design, holding the eyes for its excellence and in emotion for the awe God has clothed His House in. After the same fashion are the two posts, and the upper lintel over which is a slab of pure gold about two spans long. The door has two large silver staples on which is hung the lock. It faces to the east, and is eight spans wide and thirteen high. The thickness of the wall in which it turns is five spans. The inside of the blessed House is overlaid with variegated marbles, and the walls are all variegated marbles. (The ceiling) is sustained by three teak pillars of great height, four paces apart, and punctuating the length of the House, and down its middle. One of these columns, the first, faces the centre of the side enclosed by the two Yemen corners, and is three paces distant from it. The third column, the last, faces the side enclosed by the 'Iraq and Syrian corners.

The whole circuit of the upper half of the House is plated with silver, thickly gilt, which the beholder would imagine, from its thickness, to be a sheet of gold. It encompasses the four sides and covers the upper half of the walls. The ceiling of the House is covered by a veil of coloured silk.

The outside of the Ka'bah, on all its four sides, is clothed in coverings of green silk with cotton warps; and on their upper parts is a band of red silk on which is written the verse, 'Verily the first House founded for mankind was that at Mecca' (Koran III, 96). The name of the Imam al-Nasir li Din Ilah, in depth three cubits, encircles it all. On these coverings there has been shaped remarkable designs resembling handsome pulpits, and inscriptions entertaining the name of God Most High and calling blessings on Nasir, the aforementioned 'Abbaside (Caliph) who had ordered its instalment. With all this, there was no clash of colour. The number of covers on all four sides is thirty-four, there being eighteen on the two long sides, and sixteen on the two short sides.

The Ka'bah has five windows of 'Iraq glass, richly stained. One of them is in the middle of the ceiling, and at each corner is a window, one of which is not seen because it is beneath the vaulted passage described later. Between the pillars (hang) thirteen vessels, of silver save one that is gold.

The first thing which he who enters at the door will find to his left is the corner outside which is the Black Stone. Here are two chests containing Korans. Above them in the corner are two small silver doors like windows set in the angle of the corner, and more than a man's stature from the ground. In the angle which follows, the Yemen, it is the same, but the doors have been torn out and only the wood to which they were attached remains. In the Syrian corner it is the same and the small doors remain. It is the same in the 'Iraq corner, which is to the right of him who enters. In the 'Iraq corner is a door called the Bab al-Rahmah [Door of Mercy, usually called the Door of Repentance, Bab al-Taubah] from which ascent is made to the roof of the blessed House. It leads to a vaulted passage connecting with the roof of the House and having in it a stairway and, at its beginning, the vault containing the venerable maqam. Because of this passage the Ancient House has five corners. The height of both its sides is two statures and it encloses the 'Iraq corner with the halves of each of those two sides. Two-thirds of the circuit of this passage is dressed with pieces of coloured silk, as if it had been previously wrapped in them and then set in place.

This venerable maqam that is inside the passage is the maqam of Abraham—God's blessings on our Prophet and on him—and is a stone covered with silver. Its height is three spans, its width two and its upper part is larger than the lower. If it is not frivolous to draw the comparison it is like a large potter's oven, its middle being narrower than its top or bottom. We gazed upon it and were blessed by touching and kissing it. The water of Zamzam was poured for us into the imprints of the two blessed feet [of Abraham who stood on this stone when he built the Ka'bah], and we drank it—may God profit us by it. The traces of both feet are visible, as are the traces of the honoured and blessed big toes. Glory to God who softened the stone beneath the tread so that it left its trace as no trace of foot is left in the soft sand. Glory to God who made it a manifest sign. The contemplation of this maqam and the venerable House is an awful sight which distracts the senses in amazement, and ravishes the heart and mind. You will see only reverent gazes, flowing tears, eyes dissolved in weeping, and tongues in humble entreaty to Great and Glorious God.

Between the venerable door and the 'Iraq corner is a basin twelve spans long, five and a half spans wide, and about one in depth. It runs from opposite the door post, on the side of the 'Iraq corner, towards that corner, and is the mark of the place of the maqam at the time of Abraham—on whom be (eternal) happiness—until the Prophet—may God bless and preserve him—moved it to the place where now it is a place of worship. The basin remained as a conduit for the water of the House when it is washed. It is a blessed spot and is said to be one of the pools of Paradise, with men crowding to pray at it. Its bottom is spread with soft white sand.

The place of the venerated Maqam, behind which prayers are said, faces the space between the blessed door and the 'Iraq corner, well towards the side of the door. Over it is a wooden dome, a man's stature or more high, angulated and sharp-edged, of excellent modelling, and having four spans from one angle to another. It was erected on the place where once was the maqam, and around it is a stone projection built on the edge like an oblong basin about a span deep, five paces long, and three paces wide. The maqam was put into the place we have described in the blessed House as a measure of safety. Between the maqam and the side of the House opposite it lie seventeen paces, a pace being three spans. The place of the Maqam also has a dome made of steel and placed beside the dome of Zamzam. During the months of the pilgrimage, when many men have assembled and those from 'Iraq and Khurasan have arrived, the wooden dome is removed and the steel dome put in its place that it might better support the press of men.

From the corner containing the Black Stone to the 'Iraq corner is scarcely fifty-four spans. From the Black Stone to the ground is six spans, so that the tall man must bend to it and the short man raise himself (to kiss it). From the 'Iraq corner to the Syrian corner is scarcely forty-eight spans, and that is through the inside of the Hijr; but around it from the one corner to the other is forty paces or almost one hundred and twenty spans. The *tawaf* moves outside. (The distance from) the Syrian corner to the Yemen corner is the same as that from the Black corner to the 'Iraq corner for they are opposite sides. From the Yemen to the Black is the same, inside the Hijr, as from the 'Iraq to the Syrian for they are opposite sides.

The place of circumambulation is paved with wide stones like marble and very beautiful, some black, some brown and some white. They are joined to each other, and reach nine paces from the House save in the part facing the Maqam where they reach out to embrace it. The remainder of the Haram, including the colonnades, is wholly spread with white sand. The place of circumambulation for the women is at the edge of the paved stones.

Between the 'Iraq corner and the beginning of the wall of the Hijr is the entrance to the Hijr; it is four paces wide, that is six cubits exactly, for we measured it by hand.... Opposite this entrance, at the Syrian corner, is another of the same size. Between that part of the wall of the House which is under the Mizab [waterspout] and the wall of the Hijr opposite, following the straight line which cuts through the middle of the aforementioned Hijr, lie forty spans. The distance from entrance to entrance is sixteen paces, which is forty-eight spans. This place, I mean the surroundings of the wall (of the Ka'bah, under the Mizab), is all tessellated marble, wonderfully joined...with bands of gilded copper worked into its surface like a chess-board, being interlaced with each other and with shapes of *mihrabs*. When the sun strikes them, such light and brightness shine from them that the beholder conceives them to be gold, dazzling the eyes with their rays. The height of the marble wall of this Hijr is five and a half spans and its width four and a half. Inside the Hijr is a wide paving, round which the Hijr bends as it were in two-thirds of a circle. It is laid with tessellated marble, cut in discs the size of the palm of the hand, of a dinar and more minute than that, and joined with remarkable precision. It is composed with wonderful art, is of singular perfection, beautifully inlaid and checkered, and is superbly set and laid. The beholder will see bendings, inlays, mosaics of tiles, chess-board forms and the like, of various forms and attributes, such as will fix his gaze for their beauty. Or let his looks roam from the carpet of flowers of many colours to the mihrabs over which bend arches of marble, and in which are these forms we have described and the arts we have mentioned.

Beside it are two slabs of marble adjacent to the wall of the Hijr opposite the Mizab, on which art has worked such delicate leaves, branches, and trees as could not be done by skilled hands cutting with scissors from paper. It is a remarkable sight.... Facing the waterspout, in the middle of the Hijr and the centre of the marble wall, is a marble slab of most excellent chiselling with a cornice round it bearing an inscription in striking black in which is written, '(This is) among the things ordered to be done by the servant and Caliph of God Abu 'l-'Abbas Ahmad al-Nasir li dini Ilah, Prince of the Faithful, in the year 576 [1180]'.

The Mizab is on the top of the wall which overlooks the Hijr. It is of gilded copper and projects four cubits over the Hijr, its breadth being a span. This place under the waterspout is also considered as being a place where, by the favour of God Most High, prayers are answered. The Yemen corner is the same. The wall connecting this place with the Syrian corner is called The Place of Refuge.

Underneath the waterspout, and in the court of the Hijr near to the wall of the blessed House, is the tomb of Ishmael—may God bless and preserve him. Its mark is a slab of green marble, almost oblong and in the form of a mihrab. Beside it is a round green slab of marble, and both are remarkable tō look upon. There are spots on them both which turns them from their colour to something of yellow so that they are like a mosaic of colours, and I compare them to the spots that are left in the crucible after the gold has been melted in it. Beside this tomb, and on the side towards the 'Iraq corner, is the tomb of his mother Hagar—may God hold her in His favour—its mark being a green stone a span and a half wide. Men are blessed by praying in these two places in the Hijr, and men are right to do so, for they are part of the Ancient House and shelter the two holy and venerated bodies. May God cast His light upon them and advantage with their blessings all who pray over them. Seven spans lie between the two holy tombs.

The dome of the Well of Zamzam is opposite the Black Corner, and lies twenty-four paces from it. The Maqam, which we have already mentioned and behind which prayers are said, is to the right of this dome, from the corner of which to the other is ten paces. The inside of the dome is paved with pure white marble. The orifice of the blessed well is in the centre of the dome deviating towards the wall which faces the venerated House. Its depth is eleven statures of a man as we measured it, and the depth of the water is seven statures, as it is said. The door of this dome faces east, and the door of the dome of 'Abbas and that of the Jewish dome face north. The angle of that side of the dome named after the Jews, which faces the Ancient House, reaches the left corner of the back wall of the 'Abbaside corner which faces east. Between them lies that amount of deviation. Beside the dome of the Well of Zamzam and behind it stands the qabbat al-Sharab [the dome of drinking], which was erected by 'Abbas—may God hold him in His favour. Beside this 'Abbaside dome, obliquely to it, is the dome named after the Jews. These two domes are used as storerooms for pious endowments made to the blessed House, such as Korans, books, candlesticks, and the like. The 'Abbaside dome is still called al-Sharabiyyah because it was a place of drinking for the pilgrims; and there, until to-day, the water of Zamzam is put therein to cool in earthenware jars and brought forth at eventide for the pilgrims to drink. These jars are called *dawraq* and have one handle only. The orifice of the Well of Zamzam is of marble stones so well joined, with lead poured into the interstices, that time will not ravage them. The inside of the orifice is similar, and round it are lead props attached to it to reinforce the strength of the binding and the lead overlay. These props number thirty-two, and their tops protrude to hold the brim of the well round the whole of the orifice. The circumference of the orifice is forty spans, its depth four spans and a half, and its thickness a span and a half. Round the inside of the dome runs a trough of width one span, and depth about two spans and raised five spans from the ground, and it is filled with water for the ritual ablutions. Around it runs a stone block on which men mount to perform the ablutions.

The blessed Black Stone is enchased in the corner facing east. The depth to which it penetrates it is not known, but it is said to extend two cubits into the wall. Its breadth is two-thirds of a span, its length one span and a finger joint. It has four pieces, joined together, and it is said that it was the Carmathians—may God curse them—who broke it. Its edges have been braced with a sheet of silver whose white shines brightly against the black sheen and polished brilliance of the Stone, presenting the observer a striking spectacle which will hold his looks. The Stone, when kissed, has a softness and moistness which so enchants the mouth that he who puts his lips to it would wish them never to be removed. This is one of the special favours of Divine Providence, and it is enough that the Prophet—may God bless and preserve him—declare to be a covenant of God on earth. May God profit us by the kissing and touching of it. By His favour may all who yearn fervently for it be brought to it. In the sound piece of the stone, to the right of him who presents himself to kiss it, is a small white spot that shines and appears like a mole on the blessed surface. Concerning this white mole, there is a tradition that he who looks upon it clears his vision, and when kissing it one should direct one's lips as closely as one can to the place of the mole.

The sacred Mosque is encompassed by colonnades in three (horizontal) ranges on three rows of marble columns so arranged as to make it like a single colonnade. Its measurement in length is four hundred cubits, its width three hundred, and its area is exactly forty-eight *maraja*. The area between the colonnades is great, but at the time of the Prophet—may God bless and preserve him—it was small and the dome of Zamzam was outside it. Facing the Syrian corner, wedged in the ground, is the capital of a column which at first was the limit of the Haram. Between this capital and the Syrian corner are twenty-two paces. The Ka'bah is in the centre (of the Haram) and its four sides run directly to the east, south, north and west. The number of the marble columns, which myself I counted, is four hundred and seventy-one, excluding the stuccoed column that is in the Dar al-Nadwah (House of Counsel), which was added to the Haram. This is within the colonnade which runs from the west to the north and is faced by the Maqam and the 'Iraq corner. It has a large court and is entered from the colonnade. Against the whole length of this colonnade are benches under vaulted arches where sit the copyists, the readers of the Koran, and some who ply the tailor's trade.

The Haram enfolds rings of students sitting around their teachers, and learned men. Along the wall of the colonnade facing it are also benches under arches in the same fashion. This is the colonnade which runs from the south to the east. In the other colonnades, the benches against the walls have no arches over them. The buildings now in the Haram are at the height of perfection. At Abraham's Gate is another entrance from the colonnade which runs from the west to the south and has also stuccoed columns. I found in the writing of Abu Ja'far ibn ['Ali] al-Fanaki al-Qurtubi, the jurisprudent and traditionalist, that the number of columns was four hundred and eighty; for I had not counted those outside the Safa Gate.

. . .

The Haram has seven minarets. Four are at each corner, another is at the Dar al-Nadwah, and another at the Safa Gate indicates the Gate and is the smallest of them, no one being able to climb up to it for its narrowness. The seventh stands at the Abraham Gate which we shall mention later.

The Safa Gate faces the Black corner in the colonnade which runs from the south to the east. In the middle of the colonnade which is opposite the door are two columns facing the aformentioned corner and bearing this engraved inscription: 'The Servant of God Muhammad al-Mahdi, Prince of the Faithful—may God have him in His favour—ordered the erection of these two columns to indicate the path of the Messenger of God—may God bless and preserve him—to al-Safa, that the pilgrims to the House of God and those that dwell therein might follow him. (Done) by the hand of Yaqtin ibn Musa and Ibrahim ibn Salih in the year 167 [A.D. 783].'

On the door of the holy Ka'bah is engraved in gold, with graceful characters long and thick, that hold the eyes for their form and beauty, this writing: 'This is amongst those things erected by order of the servant and Caliph of God, the Imam Abu 'Abdullah Muhammad al-Muqtafi li Amri Ilah, Prince of the Faithful. May God bless him and the Imams his righteous ancestors, perpetuating for him the prophetic inheritance and making it an enduring word for his prosperity until the Day of Resurrection. In the year 550 [A.D. 1155].' In this wise (was it written) on the faces of the two door-leaves. These two noble door-leaves are enclosed by a thick band of silver gilt, excellently carved, which rises to the blessed lintel, passes over it and then goes round the sides of the two door-leaves. Between them, when they are closed together, is a sort of broad strip of silver gilt which runs the length of the doors and is attached to the door-leaf which is to the left of him who enters the House.

The *Kiswah* of the sacred Ka'bah is of green silk as we have said. There are thirty-four pieces: nine on the side between the Yemen and Syrian corners, nine also on the opposite side between the Black corner and the 'Iraq corner, and eight on both the side between the 'Iraq and Syrian corners and on that between the Yemen and the Black. Together they come to appear as one single cover comprehending the four sides. The lower part of the Ka'bah is surrounded by a projecting border built of stucco, more than a span in depth and two spans or a little more in width, inside which is wood, not discernible. Into this are driven iron pegs which have at their ends iron rings that are visible. Through these is inserted a rope of hemp, thick and strongly made, which encircles the four sides, and which is sewn with strong, twisted, cotton, thread to a girdle, like that of the *sirwal* [the Arab cotton bloomers], fixed to the hems of the covers. At the juncture of the covers at the four corners, they are sewn together for more than a man's stature, and above that they are brought together by iron hooks engaged in each other. At the top, round the sides of the terrace, runs another projecting border to which the upper parts of the covers are attached with iron rings, after the fashion described. Thus the blessed *Kiswah* is sewn top and bottom, and firmly buttoned, being never removed save at its renewal year by year. Glory to God who perpetuates its honour until the Day of Resurrection. There is no God but He. . . .

LI PO

[701–762]

Sometimes called the "Fallen Immortal" because of his literary precociousness and genius, Li Po ranks with Tu Fu and Wang Wei as one of the greatest poets of the celebrated Golden T'ang era in China. Li Po, known in Japan as the great master Rihaku, exerted a profound influence on Chinese and Japanese literature, and through the translations of Ezra Pound and Arthur Waley, on American poets of the beat generation. Because of Li Po's deep feeling for nature, his brash disregard for convention, and his love of the common people, his poetry had often been compared to that of European romantic poets such as Goethe and Wordsworth. As in these poets, a melancholy strain of loss and regret tempers even his most celebratory poems, and scenes of conviviality and union with nature are often revisited through the eyes of a poet who can only count these scenes among his memories.

The T'ang dynasty (618–906), the golden age of China, began when Li Shih-min set up his father on the Dragon Throne, recently abandoned by Emperor Yang Ti. When his father proved unfit to rule, Li Shih-min succeeded him, taking the name of Emperor T'ai Tsung. Although a Confucian bureaucracy tended to the everyday affairs of the state, the Emperor enjoyed absolute authority, and T'ai Tsung sidestepped the bureaucrats in selecting key officials, thereby strengthening his authority and power. Above all, T'ai Tsung wanted to expand and promote Chinese culture; he accomplished this in part by first securing the borders and then by founding the Ch'ang-an Academy, a renowned center of learning that drew students from as far away as the Middle East.

T'ai Tsung was succeeded in 635 by his son Kao Tsung, a ruler with little of his father's merit, skill, or ambition, and whose most significant step was to bring the soon-to-be empress Wu Tse-t'ien into the royal household. When Kao Tsung died in 684, Wu Tse-t'ien effectively managed China, becoming empress in 690. For the next fifteen years, despite whispered tales of scandal and intrigue at the court in Ch'ang-an, China enjoyed unprecedented peace and prosperity. Turing this time Ch'ang-an, the capital city on the Wei River in Shensi Province, was a center of trade from Central Asia, and a city bustling with merchants, travelers, and intellectuals representing various countries and creeds, including Buddhists, Confucianists, Jews, Christians, and Moslems. Under Empress Wu, poetry stood alongside Confucian and Buddhist texts as required subjects for the civil service examinations all officials had to take. As a consequence of the flourishing of literature and scholarship during this time, Ch'ang-an with its academy, its libraries, and its reputation as a center for learning ranked with Alexandria and Constantinople as one of the key intellectual centers of the early Middle Ages.

Shortly after Empress Wu's reign ended, Hsüan-tsung, himself a poet, took over the throne, which he held until the rebellion of An Lu-shan in 755 set off a series of civil wars that would plague China for the next 150 years, and that crippled and in 907 finally brought down the T'ang dynasty. Nonetheless, the literary brilliance of that era still shines in the prodigious anthology of T'ang poetry that was compiled in the early eighteenth century. Among the almost 50,000 poems by more than 2,200 poets that appear in *The Complete T'ang Poems,* those written by Li Po, Wang Wei, Tu Fu, and their junior, Po Chü–i, whose poetry records with some bitterness the decline of the age, stand out among the conventional imitations written by the many court officials whose work makes up the bulk of that encyclopedic compendium.

LIFE

Li Po was born, probably in Chinese Turkestan west of Kansu, in 701 just before the end of the reign of Empress Wu. His family apparently had a remote ancestor, Li Kao, in common with the Imperial family, although near the end of the Shui Dynasty (c. 610) one of his relatives was banished to the western region for some unknown crime or for political reasons. Little is known of Li Po's life. He seems to have spent his childhood in Szechwan, where he studied the Confucian classics and practiced swordsmanship, poetry, and other gentlemanly arts. In his mid-twenties he left home to travel throughout northern and central China, taking advantage of the improved roads and bridges and greater assurance of safety made possible by the T'ang dynasty. Li Po's penchant for traveling continued throughout his life, and the numerous poems thanking friends for hospitality and the number of places mentioned in his poetry testify to his love of being on the road. After taking up residence in Yun Meng, Li Po married the granddaughter of a former prime minister (although this story may be apocryphal), and eventually moved to Shansi, where his testimony saved a young soldier, Kuo Tzu-i, from court martial; twenty years later Kuo Tzu-i would return the favor. Sometimes called the "Old Wine Genius," Li Po lost the first of his four wives because he spent too much time with a group of fellow poets who came to be called the "Six Idlers of the Bamboo Valley."

In his extensive travels, Li Po had occasion to meet and befriend many important people, among them the Taoist priests Wu Yun and Ho Chi-chang—from whom Li Po received the name "Banished Immortal"—as well as the emperor himself, Hsüan-tsung, who granted Li Po patronage and appointed him to the prestigious Han-lin Academy. In the service of Hsüan-tsung, Li Po was commissioned to write various commemorative poems, tributes, and even edicts, all of which were written in poetry. In the short time he was in the service of the court (742–744), Li Po amplified his reputation for drunkenness, giving rise to numerous stories (some apocryphal) about his life. Tu Fu, who wrote a number of poems praising and jesting with his friendly rival, names Li Po among the "Eight Immortals of the Wine Cup," in which he quips, "Does his Majesty know that his humble servant is a drunken angel."

After leaving Ch'ang-an, Li Po used Shantung as a base for continuing travels. When in 755 the revolt of An Lu-shan forced the Emperor to flee the capital, Li Po, who was in the service of one of the emperor's sons, was arrested and sentenced to death. His life was spared by Kuo Tzu-i, who was now Minister of War, and Li Po was banished to southwestern China. Eventually an amnesty enabled him to return to the region of the lower Yangtze, where he died in 762. Legend has it that Li Po drowned in a drunken stupor, falling off a boat as he tried to embrace the moon reflected in the water, but it is more likely that he died of pneumonia or another natural cause.

Work

If we apply to China the Western split between the tavern and the cathedral, between worldly pleasures and otherworldly ecstasy, Li Po's poetry would place him most at home in the first category. Although he studied Taoism, his poems celebrate—often with a pensive, melancholy sense of regret and longing—wine, romance, love, and friendship. Given his high-spirited rebellion against poetic and social conventions and his emphasis upon worldly indulgence, Li Po's poetry stands in direct conflict with the hierarchical conformity of the Confucian tradition in China. Unlike his friend and contemporary Tu Fu, whose poetry embraces the humility and discipline of Confucianism, or Wang Wei, whose poetry engages the serenity and calm asceticism of Buddhism, Li Po's poetry is boastful, reckless, and iconoclastic—qualities that have made him one of China's best-known poets and have earned him from time to time the disfavor of state-commissioned *literati*—Confucianist and Communist—interested in enforcing conformity.

We have selected here some of Li Po's most celebrated poems, primarily drawn from his *yüeh-fu* poems, his occasional poetry. The *yüeh-fu* are poems modeled after old songs, and the best known of Li Po's poems in this genre is "Hard Road to Shu," sometimes translated as "Szechwan Road." Of his many songs, we include here examples of the drinking songs and occasional poems about leaving friends and lovers, which show the romantic side of his character. Although he is considered technically to be a less proficient poet than Tu Fu, Li Po's originality and sometimes arrogant individualism have made him one of the most popular of Chinese poets, from his time down to our own, in Asia and in the West.

Robert Frost once said, "Poetry is what gets lost in translation," and most poets and editors wholeheartedly agree. Poetry works upon the senses as well as upon the intellect, and rhythms, rhymes, balance, and colloquialism inevitably are muted, if not lost altogether, even in the best translations. Some translators try especially hard to preserve the integrity of the structure, form, rhythms, and music of a poem, while others attempt to do justice to its subtle innuendoes or capture the literal meaning of the words. Selecting translations always vexes editors, but the difficulty of selection becomes particularly acute when it comes to poems translated into English from non-European languages such as Sanskrit, Chinese, or Japanese, which have very different sound structures, grammatical features, and systems of writing. Unlike English, the Chinese poetic language is paratactic. That is, in Chinese the relationships between words are not fixed down so tightly by articles, linking words, and indicators of tense, agency, and number as they are in English. In a special edition of *Ironwood* on translating Chinese, Yip Wai-lim gives the example of *sung-feng,* a common poetic phrase that literally means "pine-wind." Should the English translator render the phrase as "wind in the pine," "the wind in the pines," "the wind blowing through the pine trees," or "pine wind"? Each translator of even the shortest Chinese poem faces endless decisions like this, and we've chosen a relatively simple example.

Look at the first four lines of Li Po's "Drinking Alone under the Moon" in the two translations that follow the Chinese version below. The first translation by Jerome Seaton, the complete version of which we include in our selection, renders the poem more literally than the second. Seaton's version captures the grammatical essence of the Chinese, as it juxtaposes concrete images that elicit an abstract sense of isolation and loneliness.

李白　月下獨酌

花間一壺酒
獨酌無相親
舉杯邀明月
對影成三人

Among the flowers, a jug of wine.
Drinking alone, no companion.
Raise the cup, invite bright moon.
And my shadow, that makes three.

Here are the same lines from the equally effective and respectable translation by Professor Irving Yu-cheng Lo.

A pot of wine among the flowers:
I drink alone, no kith or kin near.
I raise my cup to invite the moon to join me;
It and my shadow make a party of three.

Notice that Professor Lo's translation supplies the pronoun "I" that we would expect to find in an English poem about loneliness, thereby privatizing the experience more than it would appear to be in the original Chinese. Nonetheless, readers of Chinese have remarked that Li Po's style does indeed point quite dramatically to a private voice. Thus, Professor Lo tries to capture something from the Chinese that would be lost in a more literal translation.

In comparing Professor Lo's version of these lines to those of Jerome Seaton, you can see not only the great variety of possibilities for the translator, but you can get a sense of what may be lost in translations. It is not a question here of which translation is better or more accurate, but a question of what the translator chooses to capture from the original. For Li Po's work we have drawn upon a variety of respected, but different, translations to allow you to experience the range of Li Po's work as it has been rendered into English and to let you decide for yourself which you prefer.

Suggested Readings

The most thorough study of Li Po and his contemporaries is Stephen Owen's *The Great Age of Chinese Poetry* (1981); Arthur Waley's *Poetry and Career of Li Po* (1950) remains an important early study and translation of selected poems of Li Po into English. Arthur Cooper's *Li Po and Tu Fu* (1973) contains an excellent and comprehensive introduction to Li Po's poetry, its social background, and its place in the history of Chinese poetry and poetics. Further analysis of Chinese poetics and the problems of translating Li Po, as well as many other poets, appears in Wai-lim Yip's *Chinese Poetry: Major Modes and Genres* (1976). A useful survey of Chinese literature in general is Wu-chi Liu's *An Introduction to Chinese Literature* (1966).

Bring the Wine!

Translated by Burton Watson

Have you never seen the Yellow River[1] waters descending from
 the sky,
racing restless toward the ocean, never to return?
Have you never seen
bright mirrors in high halls, the white-haired ones lamenting,
their black silk of morning by evening turned to snow?
If life is to have meaning, seize every joy you can;
do not let the golden cask sit idle in the moonlight!
Heaven gave me talents and meant them to be used;
gold scattered by the thousand comes home to me again. 10
Boil the mutton, roast the ox—we will be merry,
at one bout no less than three hundred cups.
Master Ts'en![2]
Scholar Tan-ch'iu![3]
Bring wine and no delay!
For you I'll sing a song—
be pleased to bend your ears and hear.
Bells and drums, food rare as jade—these aren't worth prizing;
all I ask is to be drunk forever, never to sober up!
Sages and worthies from antiquity—all gone into silence; 20
only the great drinkers have left a name behind.
The Prince of Ch'en once feasted in the Hall of Calm Delight;
wine, ten thousand coins a cask, flowed for his revelers' joy.
Why does my host tell me the money has run out?
Buy more wine at once—my friends have cups to be refilled!
My dappled mount,

[1]Hwang Ho, one of China's major rivers, flowing from northern China into the Yellow Sea; it has been called "The River of Death" and "China's Sorrow" because of its frequent devastating floods.
[2]The poet Ts'en Ts'an (715–770).
[3]Yüan Tan-ch'iu, a Taoist friend of Li Po.

my furs worth a thousand—
call the boy, have him take them and barter for fine wine!
Together we'll wash away ten thousand years of care.

Drinking Alone under the Moon

Translated by Jerome P. Seaton

Among the flowers, a jug of wine.
Drinking alone, no companion.
Raise the cup, invite bright moon.
And my shadow, that makes three.
The moon knows nothing of drinking.
My shadow merely follows me.
I will go with moon and shadow,
Joyful, till spring end.
I sing, the moon dances.
I dance, my shadow tumbles. 10
Sober, we share our joy.
Drunk, each goes his way.
Forever bound, to ramble free,
To meet again, in the Milky Way.

Drinking with a Friend, among the Mountains

Translated by Jerome P. Seaton

Together, we drink; the mountain flowers open.
A cup, a cup, and one more cup.
Drunk, I'd sleep; you go.
Tomorrow, come again: Do bring your lute.

Calling on a Taoist Priest in Tai-t'ien Mountain[1]

Translated by Joseph J. Lee

A dog barks amid the sound of water;
Peach blossoms tinged by dew take on a deeper
tone.
In the dense woods at times I see deer;
By the brook I hear no bells at noon.
Wild bamboos divide the blue haze; 5
Tumbling waterfalls hang from the green cliff.
No one can tell me where you are,
Saddened, I lean against the pines.

[1] Tai-t'ien Mountain, sacred to the Taoists, is where the legendary Liu Ch'en was said to have met with divine maidens.

Searching for Master Yung

Translated by Jerome P. Seaton

So many cliffs, jade blue to scour the sky,
I've rambled, years uncounted,
Brushed aside the clouds, and sought the Ancient Way,[1]
Or leaned against a tree and listened to streams flow.
Sunwarmed blossoms: the blue ox sleeps. 5
Tall pines: the white cranes resting.
Words came, with the river sunset.
Alone, I came down, through the cold mist.

Seeing Off a Friend

Translated by Jerome P. Seaton

Green mountains border Northern Rampart.
Clear water curls by Eastern Wall.
Here, we'll make our parting.
There, lonely brambles stretch ten thousand *li*.
Floating clouds: the traveler's thoughts. 5
Falling sun: the old friend's feelings.
Touch hands, and now you go,
Muffled sighs, and the post horse, neighing.

Ballad of Ch'ang-kan[1]

Translated by Jerome P. Seaton

My hair barely covered my forehead then.
My play was plucking flowers by the gate.
You would come on your bamboo horse,
Riding circles round my bench, and pitching green
plums.
Growing up together here, in Ch'ang-kan. 5
Two little ones; no thought of what would come.
At fourteen I became your wife,
Blushing and timid, unable to smile,
Bowing my head, face to dark wall.
You called a thousand times, without one answer. 10
At fifteen I made up my face,
And swore that our dust and ashes should be one,
To keep faith like "the Man at the Pillar."[2]

SEARCHING FOR MASTER YUNG

[1]The Tao, the unnameable way of truth.

BALLAD OF CH'ANG-KAN

[1]This poem is well known in Ezra's Pound's translation as "The Sailor's Wife." Ch'ang-kan was a port town on the Yangtze, China's longest river, in what is now Nan-king.

[2]This line alludes to a sixth-century story about Wei Sheng, who arranged to meet his lover by a pillar and was drowned as the river rose and she failed to arrive.

How could I have known I'd climb the Watch Tower?
For when I was sixteen you journeyed far,
To Chü-t'ang Gorge, by Yan-yü Rocks.[3]
In the fifth month, there is no way through.
There the apes call, mournful to the heavens.

By the gate, the footprints that you left,
Each one greens with moss, 20
So deep I cannot sweep them.
The falling leaves, the autumn's wind is early,
October's butterflies already come,
In pairs to fly above the western garden's grass.
Wounding the heart of the wife who waits,
Sitting in sadness, bright face growing old.
Sooner or later, you'll come down from San-pa,[4]
Send me a letter, let me know.
I'll come out to welcome you, no matter how far,
All the way to Long Wind Sands.[5] 30

Sent to My Two Little Children in the East of Lu[1]

Translated by Burton Watson

Wu land mulberry leaves grow green,
already Wu silkworms have slept three times.
I left my family in the east of Lu;
who sows our fields there on the dark side of Mt. Kuei?[2]
Spring chores too long untended,
river journeys that leave me dazed—
south winds blow my homing heart;
it soars and comes to rest before the wine tower.
East of the tower a peach tree grows,
branches and leaves brushed with blue mist, 10
a tree I planted myself,
parted from it these three years.
The peach now is tall as the tower
and still my journey knows no return.
P'ing-yang, my darling girl,
picks blossoms, leaning by the peach,
picks blossoms and does not see me;
her tears flow like a welling fountain.
The little boy, named Po-ch'in,

[3]One of the dangerous Yangtze Gorges, stretching for a few hundred miles near the T'ang resort of Pai-ti, City of the White Emperor. The Yan-yü Rocks lie mid-river in the Gorges and pose a hazard to navigation.

[4]A district far north along the Yangtze in Shu, or Szechuan.

[5]A northern port town along the Yangtze.

SENT TO MY TWO LITTLE CHILDREN IN THE EAST OF LU

[1]Lu refers to Jen-ch'eng in Shantung, where Li Po had left his family while traveling in the south, which he refers to here as Wu.

[2]Mt. Gui is in Shantung near Li Po's home.

is shoulder high to his elder sister;
side by side they walk beneath the peach—
who will pat them with loving hands?
I lose myself in thoughts of them;
day by day care burns out my heart.
On this piece of cut silk I'll write my far-away thoughts
and send them floating down the river Wen-yang.[3]

The Road to Shu Is Hard[1]

Translated by Irving Y. Lo

Alas! behold! how steep! how high!
The road to Shu is hard, harder than climbing to the heavens.
The two kings Ts'an-ts'ung and Yü-fu[2]
Opened up this land in the dim past;
Forty-eight thousand years since that time,
Sealed off from the frontier region of Ch'in![3]
The Great White Peak[4] blocks the west approach, a bird track,
Just wide enough to be laid across the top of Mount Omei.[5]
Earth tottered, mountain crumbled, brave men perished,
And then came stone hanging-bridges, sky-ascending ladder interlocked. 10
Above, on the highest point, the Six-Dragon Peak curls around the sun;
Below, the gushing, churning torrents turn rivers around.[6]
White geese cannot fly across,
And gibbons in despair give up climbing.
How the Mud Mountain twists and turns!
Nine bends within a hundred steps, zigzagging up the cliffside
To where one can touch the stars, breathless!
Beating my breast, I heave a long sigh and sit down.

May I ask if you expect to return, traveling so far west?
Terrifying road, inaccessible mountain peaks lie ahead, 20
Where one sees only dismal birds howling in ancient woods
Where the female and the male fly around and around.
One also hears cuckoos crying beneath the moon at night,
Grief overfills the empty mountain.
The road to Shu is hard, harder than climbing to the heavens;
Just hearing these words turns one's cheeks pale.

---

[3]A river in Shantung.

THE ROAD TO SHU IS HARD

[1]Shu refers to what is now Szechuan, the southwestern province of China, where Li Po grew up.

[2]Gods of silkworm breeding and fishing and two of the legendary rulers of ancient Shu.

[3]A province, now called Shensi, neighboring Szechuan. It is from Ch'in, whose king conquered his neighboring rivals in the third century B.C.E., that the name *China* comes.

[4]T'ai Po mountain lies between Ch'in and Shu; T'ai Po also refers to the planet Venus, with which Li Po was associated by name.

[5]A sacred mountain in southern Szechuan.

[6]Li Po refers here to a Chinese legend about the king of Ch'in, who promised the ruler of Shu five young women for marriage. The king of Shu sent five men to bring back the young women, and on the way they were attacked by a huge snake; during the fight that ensued, the mountains collapsed and all the men died. The women were then transformed into five mountains.

Peak upon peak less than a foot from the sky,
Where withered pines hang inverted from sheer cliffs,
Where cataracts and roaring torrents make noisy clamor,
Dashing upon rocks, a thunderclap from ten thousand glens. 30
An impregnable place like this—
I sigh and ask why should anyone come here from far away?
There the Dagger Peak[7] stands erect and sharp:
With one man guarding the pass,
Ten thousand people can't advance.
Should those on guard prove untrustworthy,
They could have turned into leopards and wolves.
Mornings, one runs away from fierce tigers;
Evenings, one runs away from long snakes—
They gnash their fangs, suck human blood, 40
And maul people down like hemp.
The Brocade City[8] might be a place for pleasure,
But it's far better to hurry home.
The road to Shu is hard, harder than climbing to the heavens.
Sideways I look westward and heave a long sigh.

T'ien-mu Mountain Ascended in a Dream[1]

Translated by Wu-chi Liu

Sea voyagers talk about fairy islands,
Lost in mists and waves, and hard to reach.
The men of Yüeh[2] speak of the T'ien-mu Mountain,
Sometimes it can be seen when clouds gather or disperse.
T'ien-mu Mountain links to the horizon and extends heavenward—
Its majesty surpassing the five sacred peaks and overshadowing Mount
Ch'ih-ch'eng.[3]
Nearby, the T'ien-t'ai Mountain,[4] five hundred thousand feet high,
Appears to sink low, leaning to the southeast.

How I would like to dream of Wu and Yüeh,
And fly one night with the moon over Mirror Lake! 10
The lake-moon shines on my shadow
And takes me to Shimmering Stream.

---

[7]A pass in the mountains between Ch'in and Shu.

[8]The capital city of Szechuan, so named for the legend that when a faithful woman washed a Buddhist monk's robe in the water there, the river filled up with flowers; this marks the beginning of the making of silk brocades at Shu, an industry that still continues.

T'IEN-MU MOUNTAIN ASCENDED IN A DREAM

[1]T'ien-mu, "Heaven's Matron," is a sacred mountain near the sea in Chekiang; the fairy isles of line one are the Islands of Ying, the home of immortals in the eastern sea.

[2]The ancient kingdoms of Yüeh and Wu (see line 9) were, respectively, north and south of the Yangtze.

[3]The legendary Five Peaks, formed during the creation, upon which the heavens are balanced; Mt. Ch'ih-ch'eng, "Red Rampart," is a famous mountain.

[4]Heaven's Terrace, another famous mountain southeast of T'ien-mu.

The place Lord Hsieh[5] lodged is still here,
Where blue waters ripple and gibbons cry.
Wearing Lord Hsieh's clogs,
I scale the mountain among azure clouds.

Halfway up appears the sun in the sea;
In midair is heard the Cock of Heaven.[6]
Among thousands of crags and ravines, the road meanders.
Lured by flowers, I lean on a rock and suddenly it becomes dark. 20
Bears roar, dragons chant—the thundering cascade;
Deep woods quake with fear and towering ridges tremble.
Clouds turn dark with a hint of rain;
On the placid waters mists rise.
Lightning flashes and thunder rumbles;
Crags and peaks crash and crumble.
The stone gate in the fairy cave
Splits asunder with a shattering sound;
Its blue depth is vast, the bottom is invisible.
The sun and moon shine on the Towers of Gold and Silver; 30
Clad in rainbow raiments and riding on the wind,
The Lords of Clouds[7] descend in long processions,
Tigers playing the zither and phoenixes drawing the carriages;
The fairies stand in rows like a field of hemp.
Suddenly startled, my soul shivers;
Dazed, I awake in fright and I heave a long sigh.

At this moment, I am conscious only of my pillow and mat;
Gone are the mists and clouds of a while ago—
Likewise are the pleasures of this world;
Since ancient times, myriad affairs vanish like waters flowing east. 40
Taking leave of you, I have no date for return.
I would tend a white deer on the green cliff
And ride it whenever I go to visit famous mountains.
How could I lower my eyebrows, bend my waist to serve those with
power and wealth,
And deny myself the joys of a smiling face and a buoyant heart?

Summer Day in the Mountains

Translated by Burton Watson

Too lazy to wave the white plume fan,
stripped to the waist in the green wood's
midst,
I loose my headcloth, hang it on a stony wall,
bare my topknot for the pine winds to riffle.

[5]The poet Hsieh Ling-yün (385–433), who was Prince of K'ang-lo; he invented a kind of crampon for use in climbing mountains.
[6]The golden pheasant.
[7]A god celebrated in early shaman songs of the ancient anthology of Chinese poetry, the *Chu Ci.*

Sitting Alone in Ching-t'ing Mountain

Translated by Irving Y. Lo

Flocks of birds fly high and vanish;
A single cloud, alone, calmly drifts on.
Never tired of looking at each other—
Only the Ching-t'ing Mountain and me.

MURASAKI SHIKIBU, LADY MURASAKI

[C. 978–C. 1030]

The Tale of Genji (c. 1022 C.E.), often considered to be Japan's greatest classic and a masterpiece of prose fiction, is sometimes said to be the world's first psychological novel, remarkable for its subtle and dramatic evocation of character. Although the early form of Japanese in which it was written makes the original inaccessible to the modern Japanese reader, all Japanese recognize Genji, much as English readers recognize King Arthur and Sir Lancelot, or French readers recognize Roland. Indeed, throughout the nearly one thousand years since *The Tale of Genji* first appeared, literary echoes and images of Lady Murasaki and the shining prince Genji have appeared in later novels and poems and on screen paintings and porcelains. As its earliest translator into English noted, even European readers may recognize Lady Murasaki from the familiar motif in Japanese art of the lady at the writing desk, pen in hand, with the moon reflected from a lake in the background.

The era in which Lady Murasaki produced *The Tale of Genji* is known as the late Heian period (794–1186), which dates from the removal of the imperial family from the old capital of Nara to what is now Kyoto. The Heian era, during which Japanese artists and intellectuals became more independent of Chinese cultural influences, was marked by peace, prosperity, and relative isolation. During this period of stability, the Japanese aristocracy fostered a way of life characterized by elegance, luxury, and refinement. The aristocracy itself was divided into three groups, at the center of which was the imperial court at Kyoto, the "City of Peace." The "cloud dwellers" of the Court lived in virtual exclusion from members of the lower aristocracy, the provincial governors, and the ordinary people of Japan. Their life was governed by a complex system of distinctions that involved intricate attention to detail and style in everything from performing ceremonies, such as the Chrysanthemum Festival, through composing highly elevated and conventional poems (*waka*) in Chinese, to balancing fine shades of color and perfume for their fine robes. Dominated by the ruling Fujiwara clan, the court nobles cultivated a refined set of manners and ritual practices in accordance with the courtly tradition known as *miyabi*. A fine aesthetic sensibility permeated the speech, dress, and deportment of these courtiers, who transformed the business of governance into a subtle art of indirection and suggestion. This "rule of taste," as one historian of the era calls it, laid the groundwork for much of the subtlety embodied in later Japanese culture. Eventually such delicacy and refinement disintegrated into complacency and dissipation that made the court aristocracy vulnerable to the provincial lords, whom the court held in low esteem but upon whom they depended for military protection. One of these provincial lords, Minamoto Yoritomo, in his role as shogun (commander-in-chief), effectively took over power from the emperor at Kyoto in the twelfth century—the age of the *samurai* warlords.

While the profusion of luxury ultimately weakened the political and moral authority of the court, it conversely encouraged the cultivation of letters and music, especially works that centered on court life and the aristocracy. Great Heian classics such as *The Tales of Ise, The Pillow Book* of Sei Shonagon, and *The Tale of Genji* present a detailed picture of life among the Fujiwara nobility as observed from the perspective of courtly women. Typically, the writers of *monogatari,* or tales, such as Lady Murasaki, and of miscellaneous reflections, such as Sei Shonagon, deftly portray the psychological and personal dimensions of courtly life. *The Tales of Ise* and *The Tale of Genji,* in particular, recount the romantic affairs of their courtly heroes, and *The Pillow Book*—a sort of poetic diary—records the everyday life of a lady-in-waiting at Court, including her numerous romances. Japanese women of the aristocracy could legally inherit and manage their own property, a right unknown to European and later Japanese women until the twentieth century; nevertheless, with a few notable exceptions, such as Lady Murasaki's Empress Akiko, women were excluded by property law and tradition from active participation in the administrative activities of the court. Occupying a kind of country behind walls and protected within these walls by strategically placed screens, these women nonetheless had occasion to observe the fine details of life behind the scenes at court. Nevertheless, while the emphasis upon personal conflicts, love, and domestic incidents that characterize *The Pillow Book* and *The Tale of Genji* may result from the constricted sphere of action prescribed for women of the court, marriage played a key role in extending the power of the Fujiwara clan and was itself a key and strategic matter of politics. Through one of the ironies of history, because women did not receive training in writing Chinese characters—the official literary style, proficiency in which earned their male cohorts distinction and rank—these women wrote in Japanese characters called *kana,* and *kana* allowed them to capture the language as it was spoken. The great *nikki* (diaries) and *monogatari* (tales) written by Heian women thus established a native literary tradition.

Life

Murasaki Shikibu, the author of *The Tale of Genji,* was destined for the court life, for her father was a minor court official assigned to the Board of Rites (Shikibu) and a member of a branch of the ruling Fujiwara clan. She was born around 978 C.E. in Kyoto. Like that of many European women before the nineteenth century, Murasaki's education focused upon "accomplishments" that would increase her value to men, skills such as a fine hand in writing, the rote memorization of classical poetry, and skill in playing music on the *koto* or *biwa,* both stringed instruments. Nonetheless, like some of her European counterparts, Lady Murasaki broke through these limitations, in part by eavesdropping on her brother's Chinese lessons. By her own account, she excelled her brother in Chinese, but propriety forced her to conceal her abilities. When she was in her early twenties, Lady Murasaki experienced two tragedies: the death of her older sister, with whom she was close, and the death of her husband of only two years, Fujiwara Jobutaka. After briefly joining her father, who had accepted a governorship in the northern province of Echigo, Lady Murasaki returned with her only child to Kyoto, where she began writing *The Tale of Genji.* At Kyoto she served as attendant to the Empress Akiko, whose residence at the imperial palace gave the writer firsthand experience of the complex rivalries and the sometimes comic, other times tragic, consequences of her mistress's naiveté and strict standards of moral conduct. Critics have noted many parallels between Murasaki's recorded accounts of her years with Akiko in the *Murasaki Shikibu Nikki* (*Lady Murasaki's Diary*) and incidents that occur in *The Tale of Genji.* With Akiko, Lady Murasaki managed to turn her surreptitious learning of Chinese to good use, for the princess also wanted to learn this language, forbidden to women under Confucian tenets that relegated women to a subordinate place in the intellectual hierarchy. Although the court, including the Emperor, apparently admired *The Tale of Genji,* Lady Murasaki's diary notes that after hearing some passages from her story the Emperor announced that "This lady has been reading the Annals of Japan," giving rise to a rumor that she prided herself on her learning and earning her the nickname "Dame Annals." Little is known of Lady Murasaki's life after 1010, the year her *Diary* ends. *The Tale of Genji* was completed by 1022, and we know that a Lady Murasaki participated in ceremonies at the birth of the emperor Go-Ryozen in 1025. It is thought that she died around 1030.

WORK

Spanning fifty-four chapters, *The Tale of Genji* divides into two distinct parts. The first forty-one chapters focus on the life of prince Genji, and the last chapters, which take place after Genji's death, turn to the love relations of two young men introduced earlier, Niou and Kaoru, the illegitimate son of Genji's wife. Only a reading of the complete novel allows one to appreciate fully the richness and complexity of *The Tale of Genji,* but its episodic structure enables the reader to appreciate its poetic style and the sensitivity of its characters even in a single chapter. In the chapter we have selected here, "Yugao," or "Evening Faces," we follow the young seventeen-year-old prince, accompanied by his loyal servant, Koremitsu, on a visit to Genji's old nurse, Koremitsu's mother, who is now a Buddhist nun. While visiting the dying nursemaid, Genji is attracted to a beautiful visitor in her neighbor's house in the poor neighborhood. Genji calls this woman Evening Faces, after the white flowers of the Yugao; like those flowers, she is "hapless" but beautiful, and somewhat out of place in the shabby surroundings of the neighborhood. The gift of a suggestive poem on a scented fan that ultimately leads to the meeting of Genji and Evening Faces captures the spirit of the elaborate indirection upon which Lady Murasaki's culture prided itself. Although the mysterious young woman ranks far beneath Genji socially, the amorous prince determines to meet her and eventually wins her affection. It was common among the men of the middle to lower aristocracy in Heian Japan to have more than one wife: a primary wife and two or three secondary wives. As we know from *The Pillow Book,* amorous affairs at court were commonplace, despite the predominant Confucianism of the Heian era and its emphasis upon simplicity. Indeed, as one historian of the era suggests, a man with only one or two wives would earn reproach and would be thought to be antisocial or indelicate. Although we cannot be certain, the kind of affair in "Evening Faces" would not likely result in a secondary marriage, but women as well as men engaged in such romantic encounters; the woman of "Evening Faces," for example, had already attracted the interest of Genji's brother-in-law, Tō no Chūjō.

As in so much of court life, what was emphasized in these affairs—and especially in the story here—was not sexual conquest, but the display of refined feeling, delicacy of manners, and appreciation of beauty among those involved. This kind of social aesthetics known as *mono no aware,* or "sensitivity to things," cultivates a kind of exquisite delight, tempered by a feeling for the pathos and fragility of the beautiful. Lady Murasaki's novel masterfully evokes this complex feeling, and in the story here the young woman's unexpected death heightens the melancholy aspect of the romantic tale.

Despite the openness of polygamy and of romantic encounters, jealousy appears to have been rather common. This chapter literally raises the specter of such jealousy when Genji is visited in the dream by the spirit of another of his paramours, the lady from Rokujō. Although we don't learn about her in detail until a later chapter, it appears here that Genji's desire for the lady from Rokujō has cooled. As he begins this brief affair with Evening Faces, the jilted lover haunts him and appears to take the life of his new love. In her supernatural or demonic form called the *hannya,* the jealous woman is reminiscent of the Greek furies.

While the spirit of the lady from Rokujō seems to suffocate Evening Faces, we should not read this passage too literally, for Murasaki's interest is in Genji's response to the young woman's death, which he sees as the consequence of some action in a previous life. This instance of the doctrine of *karma* and Genji's allusion to an afterlife among the "highest summits of the Pure Land" allude to the Tendai Buddhism that permeates the religious dimensions of the novel. A complex and syncretic system, Tendai Buddhism teaches that all things of this world are fleeting, that human beings are caught up in a cycle of death and reincarnation from which, through right practice and the grace of Amida Buddha, they can escape into a land of purity and bliss. In the "Evening Faces" chapter, Genji begins to grasp the transience and fragility of life and reflects on the promise of a life beyond; his tragic, if problematic, response to death demonstrates both his aesthetic sensibility and his deep feeling. The chapter suggests that the joy of love—especially secret love, as here—like life, mixes melancholy with its joy, and is given only to be taken away.

As Earl Miner has suggested in the essay mentioned below, Genji's heroism derives from his "artistic command of life." He is much closer to the unrequited knights of European courtly romances, whose code of conduct and display of honor count more to their credit, than he is to such heroes as Achilles and Beowulf, who earn their glory in physical combat. Genji does not engage in martial competition, nor does he act in accordance with any doctrine of chivalry. In Japan, that kind of hero would arise in the next generation of Japanese literature, in works such as the *Tales of the Heike,* which celebrates the heroic deeds of the Heike clan in the age of the *samurai.*

Suggested Readings

For more reading on the Heian period and Lady Murasaki, see George Sansom's *A History of Japan to 1334* (1958) and Ivan Morris's *The World of the Shining Prince* (1964). Mary Ellen Waithe discusses the philosophical importance of Lady Murasaki in *A History of Women Philosophers,* vol. 2 (1989). Jin'ichi Konishi's *A History of Japanese Literature,* vol. 2 (translated by Aileen Gatten, 1986) provides an overview of *The Tale of Genji* and places it in the context of other tales. Norma Field studies the importance of love in *The Splendor of Longing in The Tale of Genji* (1987). Earl Miner's "The Heroine: Identity, Recurrence, Destiny" in *Ukifune: Love in The Tale of Genji* (1982), edited by Andrew Pekarik, discusses certain parallels between our story and a similar episode in the famous "Ukifune" chapter.

The Tale of Genji

Translated by Edward G. Seidensticker

Chapter 4: Evening Faces

On his way from court to pay one of his calls at Rokujō,[1] Genji stopped to inquire after his old nurse, Koremitsu's mother, at her house in Gojō.[2] Gravely ill, she had become a nun. The carriage entrance was closed. He sent for Koremitsu and while he was waiting looked up and down the dirty, cluttered street. Beside the nurse's house was a new fence of plaited cypress. The four or five narrow shutters

[1] Although we learn little of her until a later chapter, Genji is on his way to meet Lady Rokujō, an older woman who is highly jealous of Genji's other lovers. Rokujō is also where Genji builds a fabulous mansion.

[2] A town southwest of Osaka.

above had been raised, and new blinds, white and clean, hung in the apertures. He caught outlines of pretty foreheads beyond. He would have judged, as they moved about, that they belonged to rather tall women. What sort of women might they be? His carriage was simple and unadorned and he had no outrunners. Quite certain that he would not be recognized, he leaned out for a closer look. The hanging gate, of something like trelliswork, was propped on a pole, and he could see that the house was tiny and flimsy. He felt a little sorry for the occupants of such a place—and then asked himself who in this world had more than a temporary shelter. A hut, a jeweled pavilion, they were the same. A pleasantly green vine was climbing a board wall. The white flowers, he thought, had a rather self-satisfied look about them.

" 'I needs must ask the lady far off yonder,' " he said, as if to himself.

An attendant came up, bowing deeply. "The white flowers far off yonder are known as 'evening faces,' "[3] he said. "A very human sort of name—and what a shabby place they have picked to bloom in."

It was as the man said. The neighborhood was a poor one, chiefly of small houses. Some were leaning precariously, and there were "evening faces" at the sagging eaves.

"A hapless sort of flower. Pick one off for me, would you?"

The man went inside the raised gate and broke off a flower. A pretty little girl in long, unlined yellow trousers of raw silk came out through a sliding door that seemed too good for the surroundings. Beckoning to the man, she handed him a heavily scented white fan.

"Put it on this. It isn't much of a fan, but then it isn't much of a flower either."

Koremitsu, coming out of the gate, passed it on to Genji.

"They lost the key, and I have had to keep you waiting. You aren't likely to be recognized in such a neighborhood, but it's not a very nice neighborhood to keep you waiting in."

Genji's carriage was pulled in and he dismounted. Besides Koremitsu, a son and a daughter, the former an eminent cleric, and the daughter's husband, the governor of Mikawa, were in attendance upon the old woman. They thanked him profusely for his visit.

The old woman got up to receive him. "I did not at all mind leaving the world, except for the thought that I would no longer be able to see you as I am seeing you now. My vows seem to have given me a new lease on life, and this visit makes me certain that I shall receive the radiance of Lord Amitābha with a serene and tranquil heart." And she collapsed in tears.

Genji was near tears himself. "It has worried me enormously that you should be taking so long to recover, and I was very sad to learn that you have withdrawn from the world. You must live a long life and see the career I make for myself. I am sure that if you do you will be reborn upon the highest summits of the Pure Land. I am told that it is important to rid oneself of the smallest regret for this world."

Fond of the child she has reared, a nurse tends to look upon him as a paragon even if he is a half-wit. How much prouder was the old woman, who somehow gained stature, who thought of herself as eminent in her own right for having been permitted to serve him. The tears flowed on.

Her children were ashamed for her. They exchanged glances. It would not do to have these contortions taken as signs of a lingering affection for the world.

---

[3] The Japanese name for this flowering gourd is *Yugao*.

Genji was deeply touched. "The people who were fond of me left me when I was very young. Others have come along, it is true, to take care of me, but you are the only one I am really attached to. In recent years there have been restrictions upon my movements, and I have not been able to look in upon you morning and evening as I would have wished, or indeed to have a good visit with you. Yet I become very depressed when the days go by and I do not see you. 'Would that there were on this earth no final partings.'" He spoke with great solemnity, and the scent of his sleeve, as he brushed away a tear, quite flooded the room.

Yes, thought the children, who had been silently reproaching their mother for her want of control, the fates had been kind to her. They too were now in tears.

Genji left orders that prayers and services be resumed. As he went out he asked for a torch, and in its light examined the fan on which the "evening face" had rested. It was permeated with a lady's perfume, elegant and alluring. On it was a poem in a disguised cursive hand that suggested breeding and taste. He was interested.

> "I think I need not ask whose face it is,
> So bright, this evening face, in the shining dew."

"Who is living in the house to the west?" he asked Koremitsu. "Have you perhaps had occasion to inquire?"

At it again, thought Koremitsu. He spoke somewhat tartly. "I must confess that these last few days I have been too busy with my mother to think about her neighbors."

"You are annoyed with me. But this fan has the appearance of something it might be interesting to look into. Make inquiries, if you will, please, of someone who knows the neighborhood."

Koremitsu went in to ask his mother's steward, and emerged with the information that the house belonged to a certain honorary vice-governor. "The husband is away in the country, and the wife seems to be a young woman of taste. Her sisters are out in service here and there. They often come visiting. I suspect the fellow is too poorly placed to know the details."

His poetess would be one of the sisters, thought Genji. A rather practiced and forward young person, and, were he to meet her, perhaps vulgar as well—but the easy familiarity of the poem had not been at all unpleasant, not something to be pushed away in disdain. His amative propensities, it will be seen, were having their way once more.

Carefully disguising his hand, he jotted down a reply on a piece of notepaper and sent it in by the attendant who had earlier been of service.

> "Come a bit nearer, please. Then might you know
> Whose was the evening face so dim in the twilight."

Thinking it a familiar profile, the lady had not lost the opportunity to surprise him with a letter, and when time passed and there was no answer she was left feeling somewhat embarrassed and disconsolate. Now came a poem by special messenger. Her women became quite giddy as they turned their minds to the problem of replying. Rather bored with it all, the messenger returned empty-handed. Genji made a quiet departure, lighted by very few torches. The shutters next door had been lowered. There was something sad about the light, dimmer than fireflies, that came through the cracks.

At the Rokujō house, the trees and the plantings had a quiet dignity. The lady herself was strangely cold and withdrawn. Thoughts of the "evening faces" quite left him. He overslept, and the sun was rising when he took his leave. He presented such a fine figure in the morning light that the women of the place understood well enough why he should be so universally admired. On his way he again passed those shutters, as he had no doubt done many times before. Because of that small incident he now looked at the house carefully, wondering who might be within.

"My mother is not doing at all well, and I have been with her," said Koremitsu some days later. And, coming nearer: "Because you seemed so interested, I called someone who knows about the house next door and had him questioned. His story was not completely clear. He said that in the Fifth Month or so someone came very quietly to live in the house, but that not even the domestics had been told who she might be. I have looked through the fence from time to time myself and had glimpses through blinds of several young women. Something about their dress suggests that they are in the service of someone of higher rank. Yesterday, when the evening light was coming directly through, I saw the lady herself writing a letter. She is very beautiful. She seemed lost in thought, and the women around her were weeping."

Genji had suspected something of the sort. He must find out more.

Koremitsu's view was that while Genji was undeniably someone the whole world took seriously, his youth and the fact that women found him attractive meant that to refrain from these little affairs would be less than human. It was not realistic to hold that certain people were beyond temptation.

"Looking for a chance to do a bit of exploring, I found a small pretext for writing to her. She answered immediately, in a good, practiced hand. Some of her women do not seem at all beneath contempt."

"Explore very thoroughly, if you will. I will not be satisfied until you do."

The house was what the guardsman would have described as the lowest of the low, but Genji was interested. What hidden charms might he not come upon!

He had thought the coldness of the governor's wife, the lady of "the locust shell," quite unique. Yet if she had proved amenable to his persuasions the affair would no doubt have been dropped as a sad mistake after that one encounter. As matters were, the resentment and the distinct possibility of final defeat never left his mind. The discussion that rainy night would seem to have made him curious about the several ranks. There had been a time when such a lady would not have been worth his notice. Yes, it had been broadening, that discussion! He had not found the willing and available one, the governor of Iyo's daughter, entirely uninteresting, but the thought that the stepmother must have been listening coolly to the interview was excruciating. He must await some sign of her real intentions.

The governor of Iyo returned to the city. He came immediately to Genji's mansion. Somewhat sunburned, his travel robes rumpled from the sea voyage, he was a rather heavy and displeasing sort of person. He was of good lineage, however, and, though aging, he still had good manners. As they spoke of his province, Genji wanted to ask the full count of those hot springs, but he was somewhat confused to find memories chasing one another through his head. How foolish that he should be so uncomfortable before the honest old man! He remembered the guardsman's warning that such affairs are unwise, and he felt sorry for the governor. Though he resented the wife's coldness, he could see that from the husband's point of view it was admirable. He was upset to learn that the governor meant to find a suitable husband for his daughter and take his wife to the provinces. He consulted the lady's young brother upon the possibility of another meeting. It would have been difficult even with the lady's cooperation, however, and she was of the view that to receive a gentleman so far above her would be extremely unwise.

Yet she did not want him to forget her entirely. Her answers to his notes on this and that occasion were pleasant enough, and contained casual little touches that made him pause in admiration. He resented her chilliness, but she interested him. As for the stepdaughter, he was certain that she would receive him hospitably enough however formidable a husband she might acquire. Reports upon her arrangements disturbed him not at all.

Autumn came. He was kept busy and unhappy by affairs of his own making, and he visited Sanjō infrequently. There was resentment.

As for the affair at Rokujō, he had overcome the lady's resistance and had his way, and, alas, he had cooled toward her. People thought it worthy of comment that his passions should seem so much more governable than before he had made her his. She was subject to fits of despondency, more intense on sleepless nights when she awaited him in vain. She feared that if rumors were to spread the gossips would make much of the difference in their ages.

On a morning of heavy mists, insistently roused by the lady, who was determined that he be on his way, Genji emerged yawning and sighing and looking very sleepy. Chūjō, one of her women, raised a shutter and pulled a curtain aside as if urging her lady to come forward and see him off. The lady lifted her head from her pillow. He was an incomparably handsome figure as he paused to admire the profusion of flowers below the veranda. Chūjō followed him down a gallery. In an aster robe that matched the season pleasantly and a gossamer train worn with clean elegance, she was a pretty, graceful woman. Glancing back, he asked her to sit with him for a time at the corner railing. The ceremonious precision of the seated figure and the hair flowing over her robes were very fine.

He took her hand.

> "Though loath to be taxed with seeking fresher blooms,
> I feel impelled to pluck this morning glory."

"Why should it be?"

She answered with practiced alacrity, making it seem that she was speaking not for herself but for her lady:

> "In haste to plunge into the morning mists,
> You seem to have no heart for the blossoms here."

A pretty little page boy, especially decked out for the occasion, it would seem, walked out among the flowers. His trousers wet with dew, he broke off a morning glory for Genji. He made a picture that called out to be painted.

Even persons to whom Genji was nothing were drawn to him. No doubt even rough mountain men wanted to pause for a time in the shade of the flowering tree, and those who had basked even briefly in his radiance had thoughts, each in accordance with his rank, of a daughter who might be taken into his service, a not ill-formed sister who might perform some humble service for him. One need not be surprised, then, that people with a measure of sensibility among those who had on some occasion received a little poem from him or been treated to some little kindness found him much on their minds. No doubt it distressed them not to be always with him.

I had forgotten: Koremitsu gave a good account of the fence peeping to which he had been assigned. "I am unable to identify her. She seems determined to hide herself from the world. In their boredom her women and girls go out to the long gallery at the street, the one with the shutters, and watch for carriages. Sometimes the lady who seems to be their mistress comes quietly out to join them. I've not had a good look at her, but she seems very pretty indeed. One day a carriage with outrunners went by. The little girls shouted to a person named Ukon that she must come in a hurry. The captain[4] was going by, they said. An older woman came out and motioned to them to be quiet. How did they know? she asked, coming out toward the gallery. The passage from the main house is by a sort of makeshift bridge. She was hurrying and her skirt caught on something, and she stumbled and almost fell off. 'The sort of thing the god of Katsuragi[5] might do,' she said, and seems to have lost interest in sightseeing. They told her that the man in the carriage was wearing casual court dress and that he had a retinue. They mentioned several names, and all of them were undeniably Lord Tō no Chūjō's guards and pages."

"I wish you had made positive identification." Might she be the lady of whom Tō no Chūjō had spoken so regretfully that rainy night?

Koremitsu went on, smiling at this open curiosity. "I have as a matter of fact made the proper overtures and learned all about the place. I come and go as if I did not know that they are not all equals. They think they are hiding the truth and try to insist that there is no one there but themselves when one of the little girls makes a slip."

"Let me have a peep for myself when I call on your mother."

Even if she was only in temporary lodgings, the woman would seem to be of the lower class for which his friend had indicated such contempt that rainy evening. Yet something might come of it all. Determined not to go against his master's wishes in the smallest detail and himself driven by very considerable excitement, Koremitsu searched diligently for a chance to let Genji into the house. But the details are tiresome, and I shall not go into them.

Genji did not know who the lady was and he did not want her to know who he was. In very shabby disguise, he set out to visit her on foot. He must be taking her very seriously, thought Koremitsu, who offered his horse and himself went on foot.

"Though I do not think that our gentleman will look very good with tramps for servants."

To make quite certain that the expedition remained secret, Genji took with him only the man who had been his intermediary in the matter of the "evening faces" and a page whom no one was likely to recognize. Lest he be found out even so, he did not stop to see his nurse.

The lady had his messengers followed to see how he made his way home and tried by every means to learn where he lived; but her efforts came to nothing. For all his secretiveness, Genji had grown fond of her and felt that he must go on seeing her. They were of such different ranks, he tried to tell himself, and it was altogether too frivolous. Yet his visits were frequent. In affairs of this sort, which can muddle the senses of the most serious and honest of men, he had always kept himself under tight control and avoided any occasion for censure. Now, to a most astonishing degree, he would be asking himself as he returned in the morning from a visit how he could wait through the day for the next. And then he would rebuke himself. It was madness, it was not an affair he should let disturb him. She was of an extraordinarily gentle and quiet nature. Though there was a certain vagueness about her, and indeed an almost childlike quality, it was clear that she knew something about men. She did not appear to be of very good family. What was there about her, he asked himself over and over again, that so drew him to her?

[4]Tō no Chūjō, the head of the Fujiwara clan and Genji's brother-in-law, is a friend and rival whose actions in the novel both parallel and contrast with Genji's; in this case, he is a former lover of Evening Faces.

[5]This god was so ugly that he would come out only at night to work on a bridge he had been ordered to build.

He took great pains to hide his rank and always wore travel dress, and he did not allow her to see his face. He came late at night when everyone was asleep. She was frightened, as if he were an apparition from an old story. She did not need to see his face to know that he was a fine gentleman. But who might he be? Her suspicions turned to Koremitsu. It was that young gallant, surely, who had brought the strange visitor. But Koremitsu pursued his own little affairs unremittingly, careful to feign indifference to and ignorance of this other affair. What could it all mean? The lady was lost in unfamiliar speculations.

Genji had his own worries. If, having lowered his guard with an appearance of complete unreserve, she were to slip away and hide, where would he seek her? This seemed to be but a temporary residence, and he could not be sure when she would choose to change it, and for what other. He hoped that he might reconcile himself to what must be and forget the affair as just another dalliance; but he was not confident.

On days when, to avoid attracting notice, he refrained from visiting her, his fretfulness came near anguish. Suppose he were to move her in secret to Nijō. If troublesome rumors were to arise, well, he could say that they had been fated from the start. He wondered what bond in a former life might have produced an infatuation such as he had not known before.

"Let's have a good talk," he said to her, "where we can be quite at our ease."

"It's all so strange. What you say is reasonable enough, but what you do is so strange. And rather frightening."

Yes, she might well be frightened. Something childlike in her fright brought a smile to his lips. "Which of us is the mischievous fox spirit?[6] I wonder. Just be quiet and give yourself up to its persuasions."

Won over by his gentle warmth, she was indeed inclined to let him have his way. She seemed such a pliant little creature, likely to submit absolutely to the most outrageous demands. He thought again of Tō no Chūjō's "wild carnation," of the equable nature his friend had described that rainy night. Fearing that it would be useless, he did not try very hard to question her. She did not seem likely to indulge in dramatics and suddenly run off and hide herself, and so the fault must have been Tō no Chūjō's. Genji himself would not be guilty of such negligence—though it did occur to him that a bit of infidelity might make her more interesting.

The bright full moon of the Eighth Month came flooding in through chinks in the roof. It was not the sort of dwelling he was used to, and he was fascinated. Toward dawn he was awakened by plebeian voices in the shabby houses down the street.

"Freezing, that's what it is, freezing. There's not much business this year, and when you can't get out into the country you feel like giving up. Do you hear me, neighbor?"

He could make out every word. It embarrassed the woman that, so near at hand, there should be this clamor of preparation as people set forth on their sad little enterprises. Had she been one of the stylish ladies of the world, she would have wanted to shrivel up and disappear. She was a placid sort, however, and she seemed to take nothing, painful or embarrassing or unpleasant, too seriously. Her manner elegant and yet girlish, she did not seem to know what the rather awful clamor up and down the street might mean. He much preferred this easygoing bewilderment to a show of consternation, a face scarlet with embarrassment. As

[6]Foxes disguised as humans were said to seduce unsuspecting people.

if at his very pillow, there came the booming of a foot pestle, more fearsome than the stamping of the thunder god, genuinely earsplitting. He did not know what device the sound came from, but he did know that it was enough to awaken the dead. From this direction and that there came the faint thump of fulling hammers against coarse cloth; and mingled with it—these were sounds to call forth the deepest emotions—were the calls of geese flying overhead. He slid a door open and they looked out. They had been lying near the veranda. There were tasteful clumps of black bamboo just outside and the dew shone as in more familiar places. Autumn insects sang busily, as if only inches from an ear used to wall crickets at considerable distances. It was all very clamorous, and also rather wonderful. Countless details could be overlooked in the singleness of his affection for the girl. She was pretty and fragile in a soft, modest cloak of lavender and a lined white robe. She had no single feature that struck him as especially beautiful, and yet, slender and fragile, she seemed so delicately beautiful that he was almost afraid to hear her voice. He might have wished her to be a little more assertive, but he wanted only to be near her, and yet nearer.

"Let's go off somewhere and enjoy the rest of the night. This is too much."

"But how is that possible?" She spoke very quietly. "You keep taking me by surprise."

There was a newly confiding response to his offer of his services as guardian in this world and the next. She was a strange little thing. He found it hard to believe that she had had much experience of men. He no longer cared what people might think. He asked Ukon to summon his man, who got the carriage ready. The women of the house, though uneasy, sensed the depth of his feelings and were inclined to put their trust in him.

Dawn approached. No cocks were crowing. There was only the voice of an old man making deep obeisance to a Buddha, in preparation, it would seem, for a pilgrimage to Mitake.[7] He seemed to be prostrating himself repeatedly and with much difficulty. All very sad. In a life itself like the morning dew, what could he desire so earnestly?

"Praise to the Messiah to come," intoned the voice.

"Listen," said Genji. "He is thinking of another world.

"This pious one shall lead us on our way
As we plight our troth for all the lives to come."

The vow exchanged by the Chinese emperor and Yang Kuei-fei seemed to bode ill, and so he preferred to invoke Lord Maitreya, the Buddha of the Future; but such promises are rash.

"So heavy the burden I bring with me from the past,
I doubt that I should make these vows for the future."

It was a reply that suggested doubts about his "lives to come."

The moon was low over the western hills. She was reluctant to go with him. As he sought to persuade her, the moon suddenly disappeared behind clouds in a lovely dawn sky. Always in a hurry to be off before daylight exposed him, he lifted her easily into his carriage and took her to a nearby villa. Ukon was with them. Waiting for the caretaker to be summoned, Genji looked up at the rotting gate and the ferns that trailed thickly down over it. The groves beyond were still dark, and the mist and the dews were heavy. Genji's sleeve was soaking, for he had raised the blinds of the carriage.

---

[7] A shrine south of Nara in the Yoshino mountains.

"This is a novel adventure, and I must say that it seems like a lot of trouble.

> "And did it confuse them too, the men of old,
> This road through the dawn, for me so new and strange?

"How does it seem to you?"

She turned shyly away.

> "And is the moon, unsure of the hills it approaches,
> Foredoomed to lose its way in the empty skies?"

"I am afraid."

She did seem frightened, and bewildered. She was so used to all those swarms of people, he thought with a smile.

The carriage was brought in and its traces propped against the veranda while a room was made ready in the west wing. Much excited, Ukon was thinking about earlier adventures. The furious energy with which the caretaker saw to preparations made her suspect who Genji was. It was almost daylight when they alighted from the carriage. The room was clean and pleasant, for all the haste with which it had been readied.

"There are unfortunately no women here to wait upon His Lordship." The man, who addressed him through Ukon, was a lesser steward who had served in the Sanjō mansion of Genji's father-in-law. "Shall I send for someone?"

"The last thing I want. I came here because I wanted to be in complete solitude, away from all possible visitors. You are not to tell a soul."

The man put together a hurried breakfast, but he was, as he had said, without serving women to help him.

Genji told the girl that he meant to show her a love as dependable as "the patient river of the loons." He could do little else in these strange lodgings.

The sun was high when he arose. He opened the shutters. All through the badly neglected grounds not a person was to be seen. The groves were rank and overgrown. The flowers and grasses in the foreground were a drab monotone, an autumn moor. The pond was choked with weeds, and all in all it was a forbidding place. An outbuilding seemed to be fitted with rooms for the caretaker, but it was some distance away.

"It is a forbidding place," said Genji. "But I am sure that whatever devils emerge will pass me by."

He was still in disguise. She thought it unkind of him to be so secretive, and he had to agree that their relationship had gone beyond such furtiveness.

> "Because of one chance meeting by the wayside
> The flower now opens in the evening dew.

"And how does it look to you?"

> "The face seemed quite to shine in the evening dew,
> But I was dazzled by the evening light."

Her eyes turned away. She spoke in a whisper.

To him it may have seemed an interesting poem.

As a matter of fact, she found him handsomer than her poem suggested, indeed frighteningly handsome, given the setting.

"I hid my name from you because I thought it altogether too unkind of you to be keeping your name from me. Do please tell me now. This silence makes me feel that something awful might be coming."

"Call me the fisherman's daughter." Still hiding her name, she was like a little child.

"I see. I brought it all on myself? A case of *warekara*?"[8]

And so, sometimes affectionately, sometimes reproachfully, they talked the hours away.

Koremitsu had found them out and brought provisions. Feeling a little guilty about the way he had treated Ukon, he did not come near. He thought it amusing that Genji should thus be wandering the streets, and concluded that the girl must provide sufficient cause. And he could have had her himself, had he not been so generous.

Genji and the girl looked out at an evening sky of the utmost calm. Because she found the darkness in the recesses of the house frightening, he raised the blinds at the veranda and they lay side by side. As they gazed at each other in the gathering dusk, it all seemed very strange to her, unbelievably strange. Memories of past wrongs quite left her. She was more at ease with him now, and he thought her charming. Beside him all through the day, starting up in fright at each little noise, she seemed delightfully childlike. He lowered the shutters early and had lights brought.

"You seem comfortable enough with me, and yet you raise difficulties."

At court everyone would be frantic. Where would the search be directed? He thought what a strange love it was, and he thought of the turmoil the Rokujō lady was certain to be in. She had every right to be resentful, and yet her jealous ways were not pleasant. It was that sad lady to whom his thoughts first turned. Here was the girl beside him, so simple and undemanding; and the other was so impossibly forceful in her demands. How he wished he might in some measure have his freedom.

It was past midnight. He had been asleep for a time when an exceedingly beautiful woman appeared by his pillow.

"You do not even think of visiting me, when you are so much on my mind. Instead you go running off with someone who has nothing to recommend her, and raise a great stir over her. It is cruel, intolerable." She seemed about to shake the girl from her sleep. He awoke, feeling as if he were in the power of some malign being. The light had gone out. In great alarm, he pulled his sword to his pillow and awakened Ukon. She too seemed frightened.

"Go out to the gallery and wake the guard. Have him bring a light."

"It's much too dark."

He forced a smile. "You're behaving like a child."

He clapped his hands and a hollow echo answered. No one seemed to hear. The girl was trembling violently. She was bathed in sweat and as if in a trance, quite bereft of her senses.

"She is such a timid little thing," said Ukon, "frightened when there is nothing at all to be frightened of. This must be dreadful for her."

Yes, poor thing, thought Genji. She did seem so fragile, and she had spent the whole day gazing up at the sky.

"I'll go get someone. What a frightful echo. You stay here with her." He pulled Ukon to the girl's side.

The lights in the west gallery had gone out. There was a gentle wind. He had few people with him, and they were asleep. They were three in number: a young man who was one of his intimates and who was the son of the steward here, a court page, and the man who had been his intermediary in the matter of the "evening faces." He called out. Someone answered and came up to him.

---

[8]Genji's phrase contains an allusion to a classic poem from the *Kokinshū:* "The grass the fishermen take, the *warekara:* / 'I did it myself.' I shall weep but I shall not hate you." Lady Murasaki often uses such allusions. Commentaries and annotated editions of *Genji* exist in Japanese; here, we cite only instances essential to understanding the meaning of a phrase.

"Bring a light. Wake the other, and shout and twang your bowstrings. What do you mean, going to sleep in a deserted house? I believe Lord Koremitsu was here."

"He was. But he said he had no orders and would come again at dawn."

An elite guardsman, the man was very adept at bow twanging. He went off with a shouting as of a fire watch. At court, thought Genji, the courtiers on night duty would have announced themselves, and the guard would be changing. It was not so very late.

He felt his way back inside. The girl was as before, and Ukon lay face down at her side.

"What is this? You're a fool to let yourself be so frightened. Are you worried about the fox spirits that come out and play tricks in deserted houses? But you needn't worry. They won't come near me." He pulled her to her knees.

"I'm not feeling at all well. That's why I was lying down. My poor lady must be terrified."

"She is indeed. And I can't think why."

He reached for the girl. She was not breathing. He lifted her and she was limp in his arms. There was no sign of life. She had seemed as defenseless as a child, and no doubt some evil power had taken possession of her. He could think of nothing to do. A man came with a torch. Ukon was not prepared to move, and Genji himself pulled up curtain frames to hide the girl.

"Bring the light closer."

It was a most unusual order. Not ordinarily permitted at Genji's side, the man hesitated to cross the threshold.

"Come, come, bring it here! There is a time and place for ceremony."

In the torchlight he had a fleeting glimpse of a figure by the girl's pillow. It was the woman in his dream. It faded away like an apparition in an old romance. In all the fright and horror, his confused thoughts centered upon the girl. There was no room for thoughts of himself.

He knelt over her and called out to her, but she was cold and had stopped breathing. It was too horrible. He had no confidant to whom he could turn for advice. It was the clergy one thought of first on such occasions. He had been so brave and confident, but he was young, and this was too much for him. He clung to the lifeless body.

"Come back, my dear, my dear. Don't do this awful thing to me." But she was cold and no longer seemed human.

The first paralyzing terror had left Ukon. Now she was writhing and wailing. Genji remembered a devil a certain minister had encountered in the Grand Hall.

"She can't possibly be dead." He found the strength to speak sharply. "All this noise in the middle of the night—you must try to be a little quieter." But it had been too sudden.

He turned again to the torchbearer. "There is someone here who seems to have had a very strange seizure. Tell your friend to find out where Lord Koremitsu is spending the night and have him come immediately. If the holy man is still at his mother's house, give him word, very quietly, that he is to come too. His mother and the people with her are not to hear. She does not approve of this sort of adventure."

He spoke calmly enough, but his mind was in a turmoil. Added to grief at the loss of the girl was horror, quite beyond describing, at this desolate place. It would be past midnight. The wind was higher and whistled more dolefully in the pines. There came a strange, hollow call of a bird. Might it be an owl? All was silence, terrifying solitude. He should not have chosen such a place—but it was too late now. Trembling violently, Ukon clung to him. He held her in his arms, wondering if she might be about to follow her lady. He was the only rational one present, and he could think of nothing to do. The flickering light wandered here and there. The upper parts of the screens behind them were in darkness, the lower parts fitfully in the light. There was a persistent creaking, as of someone coming up behind them. If only Koremitsu would come. But Koremitsu was a nocturnal wanderer without a fixed abode, and the man had to search for him in numerous places. The wait for dawn was like the passage of a thousand nights. Finally he heard a distant crowing. What legacy from a former life could have brought him to this mortal peril? He was being punished for a guilty love, his fault and no one else's, and his story would be remembered in infamy through all the ages to come. There were no secrets, strive though one might to have them. Soon everyone would know, from his royal father down, and the lowest court pages would be talking; and he would gain immortality as the model of the complete fool.

Finally Lord Koremitsu came. He was the perfect servant who did not go against his master's wishes in anything at any time; and Genji was angry that on this night of all nights he should have been away, and slow in answering the summons. Calling him inside even so, he could not immediately find the strength to say what must be said. Ukon burst into tears, the full horror of it all coming back to her at the sight of Koremitsu. Genji too lost control of himself. The only sane and rational one present, he had held Ukon in his arms, but now he gave himself up to his grief.

"Something very strange has happened," he said after a time. "Strange—'unbelievable' would not be too strong a word. I wanted a priest—one does when these things happen—and asked your reverend brother to come."

"He went back up the mountain yesterday. Yes, it is very strange indeed. Had there been anything wrong with her?"

"Nothing."

He was so handsome in his grief that Koremitsu wanted to weep. An older man who has had everything happen to him and knows what to expect can be depended upon in a crisis; but they were both young, and neither had anything to suggest.

Koremitsu finally spoke. "We must not let the caretaker know. He may be dependable enough himself, but he is sure to have relatives who will talk. We must get away from this place."

"You aren't suggesting that we could find a place where we would be less likely to be seen?"

"No, I suppose not. And the women at her house will scream and wail when they hear about it, and they live in a crowded neighborhood, and all the mob around will hear, and that will be that. But mountain temples are used to this sort of thing. There would not be much danger of attracting attention." He reflected on the problem for a time. "There is a woman I used to know. She has gone into a nunnery up in the eastern hills. She is very old, my father's nurse, as a matter of fact. The district seems to be rather heavily populated, but the nunnery is off by itself."

It was not yet full daylight. Koremitsu had the carriage brought up. Since Genji seemed incapable of the task, he wrapped the body in a covering and lifted it into the carriage. It was very tiny and very pretty, and not at all repellent. The wrapping was loose and the hair streamed forth, as if to darken the world before Genji's eyes.

He wanted to see the last rites through to the end, but Koremitsu would not hear of it. "Take my horse and go back to Nijō, now while the streets are still quiet."

He helped Ukon into the carriage and himself proceeded on foot, the skirts of his robe hitched up. It was a strange, bedraggled sort of funeral procession, he thought, but in the face of such anguish he was prepared to risk his life. Barely conscious, Genji made his way back to Nijō.

"Where have you been?" asked the women. "You are not looking at all well."

He did not answer. Alone in his room, he pressed a hand to his heart. Why had he not gone with the others? What would she think if she were to come back to life? She would think that he had abandoned her. Self-reproach filled his heart to breaking. He had a headache and feared he had a fever. Might he too be dying? The sun was high and still he did not emerge. Thinking it all very strange, the women pressed breakfast upon him. He could not eat. A messenger reported that the emperor had been troubled by his failure to appear the day before.

His brothers-in-law came calling.

"Come in, please, just for a moment." He received only Tō no Chūjō and kept a blind between them. "My old nurse fell seriously ill and took her vows in the Fifth Month or so. Perhaps because of them, she seemed to recover. But recently she had a relapse. Someone came to ask if I would not call on her at least once more. I thought I really must go and see an old and dear servant who was on her deathbed, and so I went. One of her servants was ailing, and quite suddenly, before he had time to leave, he died. Out of deference to me they waited until night to take the body away. All this I learned later. It would be very improper of me to go to court with all these festivities coming up, I thought, and so I stayed away. I have had a headache since early this morning—perhaps I have caught cold. I must apologize."

"I see. I shall so inform your father. He sent out a search party during the concert last night, and really seemed very upset." Tō no Chūjō turned to go, and abruptly turned back. "Come now. What sort of brush did you really have? I don't believe a word of it."

Genji was startled, but managed a show of nonchalance. "You needn't go into the details. Just say that I suffered an unexpected defilement. Very unexpected, really."

Despite his cool manner, he was not up to facing people. He asked a younger brother-in-law to explain in detail his reasons for not going to court. He got off a note to Sanjō with a similar explanation.

Koremitsu came in the evening. Having announced that he had suffered a defilement, Genji had callers remain outside, and there were few people in the house. He received Koremitsu immediately.

"Are you sure she is dead?" He pressed a sleeve to his eyes.

Koremitsu too was in tears. "Yes, I fear she is most certainly dead. I could not stay shut up in a temple indefinitely, and so I have made arrangements with a venerable priest whom I happen to know rather well. Tomorrow is a good day for funerals."

"And the other woman?"

"She has seemed on the point of death herself. She does not want to be left behind by her lady. I was afraid this morning that she might throw herself over a cliff. She wanted to tell the people at Gojō, but I persuaded her to let us have a little more time."

"I am feeling rather awful myself and almost fear the worst."

"Come, now. There is nothing to be done and no point in torturing yourself. You must tell yourself that what must be must be. I shall let absolutely no one know, and I am personally taking care of everything."

"Yes, to be sure. Everything is fated. So I tell myself. But it is terrible to think that I have sent a lady to her death. You are not to tell your sister, and you must be very sure that your mother does not hear. I would not survive the scolding I would get from her."

"And the priests too: I have told them a plausible story." Koremitsu exuded confidence.

The women had caught a hint of what was going on and were more puzzled than ever. He had said that he had suffered a defilement, and he was staying away from court; but why these muffled lamentations?

Genji gave instructions for the funeral. "You must make sure that nothing goes wrong."

"Of course. No great ceremony seems called for."

Koremitsu turned to leave.

"I know you won't approve," said Genji, a fresh wave of grief sweeping over him, "but I will regret it forever if I don't see her again. I'll go on horseback."

"Very well, if you must." In fact Koremitsu thought the proposal very ill advised. "Go immediately and be back while it is still early."

Genji set out in the travel robes he had kept ready for his recent amorous excursions. He was in the bleakest despair. He was on a strange mission and the terrors of the night before made him consider turning back. Grief urged him on. If he did not see her once more, when, in another world, might he hope to see her as she had been? He had with him only Koremitsu and the attendant of that first encounter. The road seemed a long one.

The moon came out, two nights past full. They reached the river. In the dim torchlight, the darkness off towards Mount Toribe was ominous and forbidding; but Genji was too dazed with grief to be frightened. And so they reached the temple.

It was a harsh, unfriendly region at best. The board hut and chapel where the nun pursued her austerities were lonely beyond description. The light at the altar came dimly through cracks. Inside the hut a woman was weeping. In the outer chamber two or three priests were conversing and invoking the holy name in low voices. Vespers seemed to have ended in several temples nearby. Everything was quiet. There were lights and there seemed to be clusters of people in the direction of Kiyomizu. The grand tones in which the worthy monk, the son of the nun, was reading a sutra brought on what Genji thought must be the full flood tide of his tears.

He went inside. The light was turned away from the corpse. Ukon lay behind a screen. It must be very terrible for her, thought Genji. The girl's face was unchanged and very pretty.

"Won't you let me hear your voice again?" He took her hand. "What was it that made me give you all my love, for so short a time, and then made you leave me to this misery?" He was weeping uncontrollably.

The priests did not know who he was. They sensed something remarkable, however, and felt their eyes mist over.

"Come with me to Nijō," he said to Ukon.

"We have been together since I was very young. I never left her side, not for a single moment. Where am I to go now? I will have to tell the others what has happened. As if this weren't enough, I will have to put up with their accusations." She was sobbing. "I want to go with her."

"That is only natural. But it is the way of the world. Parting is always sad. Our lives must end, early or late. Try to put your trust in me." He comforted her with the usual homilies, but presently his real feelings came out. "Put your trust in me—when I fear I have not long to live myself." He did not after all seem likely to be much help.

"It will soon be light," said Koremitsu. "We must be on our way."

Looking back and looking back again, his heart near breaking, Genji went out. The way was heavy with dew and the morning mists were thick. He scarcely knew where he was. The girl was exactly as she had been that night. They had exchanged robes and she had on a red singlet of his. What might it have been in other lives that had brought them together? He managed only with great difficulty to stay in his saddle. Koremitsu was at the reins. As they came to the river Genji fell from his horse and was unable to remount.

"So I am to die by the wayside? I doubt that I can go on."

Koremitsu was in a panic. He should not have permitted this expedition, however strong Genji's wishes. Dipping his hands in the river, he turned and made supplication to Kiyomizu. Genji somehow pulled himself together. Silently invoking the holy name, he was seen back to Nijō.

The women were much upset by these untimely wanderings. "Very bad, very bad. He has been so restless lately. And why should he have gone out again when he was not feeling well?"

Now genuinely ill, he took to his bed. Two or three days passed and he was visibly thinner. The emperor heard of the illness and was much alarmed. Continuous prayers were ordered in this shrine and that temple. The varied rites, Shinto and Confucian and Buddhist, were beyond counting. Genji's good looks had been such as to arouse forebodings. All through the court it was feared that he would not live much longer. Despite his illness, he summoned Ukon to Nijō and assigned her rooms near his own. Koremitsu composed himself sufficiently to be of service to her, for he could see that she had no one else to turn to. Choosing times when he was feeling better, Genji would summon her for a talk, and she soon was accustomed to life at Nijō. Dressed in deep mourning, she was a somewhat stern and forbidding young woman, but not without her good points.

"It lasted such a very little while. I fear that I will be taken too. It must be dreadful for you, losing your only support. I had thought that as long as I lived I would see to all your needs, and it seems sad and ironical that I should be on the point of following her." He spoke softly and there were tears in his eyes. For Ukon the old grief had been hard enough to bear, and now she feared that a new grief might be added to it.

All through the Nijō mansion there was a sense of helplessness. Emissaries from court were thicker than raindrops. Not wanting to worry his father, Genji fought to control himself. His father-in-law was extremely solicitous and came to Nijō every day. Perhaps because of all the prayers and rites the crisis passed—it had lasted some twenty days—and left no ill effects. Genji's full recovery coincided with the final cleansing of the defilement. With the unhappiness he had caused his father much on his mind, he set off for his apartments at court. For a time he felt out of things, as if he had come back to a strange new world.

By the end of the Ninth Month he was his old self once more. He had lost weight, but emaciation only made him handsomer. He spent a great deal of time gazing into space, and sometimes he would weep aloud. He must be in the clutches of some malign spirit, thought the women. It was all most peculiar.

He would summon Ukon on quiet evenings. "I don't understand it at all. Why did she so insist on keeping her name from me? Even if she *was* a fisherman's daughter it was cruel of her to be so uncommunicative. It was as if she did not know how much I loved her."

"There was no reason for keeping it secret. But why should she tell you about her insignificant self? Your attitude seemed so strange from the beginning. She used to say that she hardly knew whether she was waking or dreaming. Your refusal to identify yourself, you know, helped her guess who you were. It hurt her that you should belittle her by keeping your name from her."

"An unfortunate contest of wills. I did not want anything to stand between us; but I must always be worrying about what people will say. I must refrain from things my father and all the rest of them might take me to task for. I am not permitted the smallest indiscretion. Everything is exaggerated so. The little incident of the 'evening faces' affected me strangely and I went to very great trouble to see her. There must have been a bond between us. A love doomed from the start to be fleeting—why should it have taken such complete possession of me and made me find her so precious? You must tell me everything. What point is there in keeping secrets now? I mean to make offerings every week, and I want to know in whose name I am making them."

"Yes, of course—why have secrets now? It is only that I do not want to slight what she made so much of. Her parents are dead. Her father was a guards captain.

She was his special pet, but his career did not go well and his life came to an early and disappointing end. She somehow got to know Lord Tō no Chūjō—it was when he was still a lieutenant. He was very attentive for three years or so, and then about last autumn there was a rather awful threat from his father-in-law's house. She was ridiculously timid and it frightened her beyond all reason. She ran off and hid herself at her nurse's in the western part of the city. It was a wretched little hovel of a place. She wanted to go off into the hills, but the direction she had in mind has been taboo since New Year's. So she moved to the odd place where she was so upset to have you find her. She was more reserved and withdrawn than most people, and I fear that her unwillingness to show her emotions may have seemed cold."

So it was true. Affection and pity welled up yet more strongly.

"He once told me of a lost child. Was there such a one?"

"Yes, a very pretty little girl, born two years ago last spring."

"Where is she? Bring her to me without letting anyone know. It would be such a comfort. I should tell my friend Tō no Chūjō, I suppose, but why invite criticism? I doubt that anyone could reprove me for taking in the child. You must think up a way to get around the nurse."

"It would make me very happy if you were to take the child. I would hate to have her left where she is. She is there because we had no competent nurses in the house where you found us."

The evening sky was serenely beautiful. The flowers below the veranda were withered, the songs of the insects were dying too, and autumn tints were coming over the maples. Looking out upon the scene, which might have been a painting, Ukon thought what a lovely asylum she had found herself. She wanted to avert her eyes at the thought of the house of the "evening faces." A pigeon called, somewhat discordantly, from a bamboo thicket. Remembering how the same call had frightened the girl in that deserted villa, Genji could see the little figure as if an apparition were there before him.

"How old was she? She seemed so delicate, because she was not long for this world, I suppose."

"Nineteen, perhaps? My mother, who was her nurse, died and left me behind. Her father took a fancy to me, and so we grew up together, and I never once left her side. I wonder how I can go on without her. I am almost sorry that we were so close. She seemed so weak, but I can see now that she was a source of strength."

"The weak ones do have a power over us. The clear, forceful ones I can do without. I am weak and indecisive by nature myself, and a woman who is quiet and withdrawn and follows the wishes of a man even to the point of letting herself be used has much the greater appeal. A man can shape and mold her as he wishes, and becomes fonder of her all the while."

"She was exactly what you would have wished, sir." Ukon was in tears. "That thought makes the loss seem greater."

The sky had clouded over and a chilly wind had come up. Gazing off into the distance, Genji said softly:

> "One sees the clouds as smoke that rose from the pyre,
> And suddenly the evening sky seems nearer."

Ukon was unable to answer. If only her lady were here! For Genji even the memory of those fulling blocks was sweet.

"In the Eighth Month, the Ninth Month, the nights are long,"[9] he whispered, and lay down.

---

[9]Genji quotes here from the T'ang dynasty Chinese poet Po Chü-i.

The young page, brother of the lady of the locust shell, came to Nijō from time to time, but Genji no longer sent messages for his sister. She was sorry that he seemed angry with her and sorry to hear of his illness. The prospect of accompanying her husband to his distant province was a dreary one. She sent off a note to see whether Genji had forgotten her.

"They tell me you have not been well.

> "Time goes by, you ask not why I ask not.
> Think if you will how lonely a life is mine.

"I might make reference to Masuda Pond."[10]

This was a surprise; and indeed he had not forgotten her. The uncertain hand in which he set down his reply had its own beauty.

"Who, I wonder, lives the more aimless life.

> "Hollow though it was, the shell of the locust
> Gave me strength to face a gloomy world.

"But only precariously."

So he still remembered "the shell of the locust." She was sad and at the same time amused. It was good that they could correspond without rancor. She wished no further intimacy, and she did not want him to despise her.

As for the other, her stepdaughter, Genji heard that she had married a guards lieutenant. He thought it a strange marriage and he felt a certain pity for the lieutenant. Curious to know something of her feelings, he sent a note by his young messenger.

"Did you know that thoughts of you had brought me to the point of expiring?

> "I bound them loosely, the reeds beneath the eaves,[11]
> And reprove them now for having come undone."

He attached it to a long reed.

The boy was to deliver it in secret, he said. But he thought that the lieutenant would be forgiving if he were to see it, for he would guess who the sender was. One may detect here a note of self-satisfaction.

Her husband was away. She was confused, but delighted that he should have remembered her. She sent off in reply a poem the only excuse for which was the alacrity with which it was composed:

> "The wind brings words, all softly, to the reed,
> And the under leaves are nipped again by the frost."

It might have been cleverer and in better taste not to have disguised the clumsy handwriting. He thought of the face he had seen by lamplight. He could forget neither of them, the governor's wife, seated so primly before him, or the younger woman, chattering on so contentedly, without the smallest suggestion of reserve. The stirrings of a susceptible heart suggested that he still had important lessons to learn.

Quietly, forty-ninth-day services[12] were held for the dead lady in the Lotus Hall on Mount Hiei. There was careful attention to all the details, the priestly robes and the scrolls and the altar decorations. Koremitsu's older brother was a priest of

---

[10] An allusion to the following lines from the *Shūishū:* "Long the roots of the Masuda water shield, / Longer still the aimless, sleepless nights."

[11] "Reeds beneath the eaves," Nokiba no ogi, is the girl's name.

[12] According to Buddhist tradition, a dead spirit exists in a sort of limbo for forty-nine days before being reincarnated.

considerable renown, and his conduct of the services was beyond reproach. Genji summoned a doctor of letters with whom he was friendly and who was his tutor in Chinese poetry and asked him to prepare a final version of the memorial petition. Genji had prepared a draft. In moving language he committed the one he had loved and lost, though he did not mention her name, to the mercy of Amitābha.

"It is perfect, just as it is. Not a word needs to be changed." Noting the tears that refused to be held back, the doctor wondered who might be the subject of these prayers. That Genji should not reveal the name, and that he should be in such open grief—someone, no doubt, who had brought a very large bounty of grace from earlier lives.

Genji attached a poem to a pair of lady's trousers which were among his secret offerings:

> "I weep and weep as today I tie this cord.
> It will be untied in an unknown world to come."

He invoked the holy name with great feeling. Her spirit had wandered uncertainly these last weeks. Today it would set off down one of the ways of the future.

His heart raced each time he saw Tō no Chūjō. He longed to tell his friend that "the wild carnation" was alive and well; but there was no point in calling forth reproaches.

In the house of the "evening faces," the women were at a loss to know what had happened to their lady. They had no way of inquiring. And Ukon too had disappeared. They whispered among themselves that they had been right about that gentleman, and they hinted at their suspicions to Koremitsu. He feigned complete ignorance, however, and continued to pursue his little affairs. For the poor women it was all like a nightmare. Perhaps the wanton son of some governor, fearing Tō no Chūjō, had spirited her off to the country? The owner of the house was her nurse's daughter. She was one of three children and related to Ukon. She could only long for her lady and lament that Ukon had not chosen to enlighten them. Ukon for her part was loath to raise a stir, and Genji did not want gossip at this late date. Ukon could not even inquire after the child. And so the days went by bringing no light on the terrible mystery.

Genji longed for a glimpse of the dead girl, if only in a dream. On the day after the services he did have a fleeting dream of the woman who had appeared that fatal night. He concluded, and the thought filled him with horror, that he had attracted the attention of an evil spirit haunting the neglected villa.

Early in the Tenth Month the governor of Iyo left for his post, taking the lady of the locust shell with him. Genji chose his farewell presents with great care. For the lady there were numerous fans, and combs of beautiful workmanship, and pieces of cloth (she could see that he had had them dyed specially) for the wayside gods. He also returned her robe, "the shell of the locust."

> "A keepsake till we meet again, I had hoped,
> And see, my tears have rotted the sleeves away."

There were other things too, but it would be tedious to describe them. His messenger returned empty-handed. It was through her brother that she answered his poem.

> "Autumn comes, the wings of the locust are shed.
> A summer robe returns, and I weep aloud."

She had remarkable singleness of purpose, whatever else she might have. It was the first day of winter. There were chilly showers, as if to mark the occasion, and the skies were dark. He spent the day lost in thought.

"The one has gone, to the other I say farewell.
They go their unknown ways. The end of autumn."

He knew how painful a secret love can be.

I had hoped, out of deference to him, to conceal these difficult matters; but I have been accused of romancing, of pretending that because he was the son of an emperor he had no faults. Now, perhaps, I shall be accused of having revealed too much.

BACKGROUND TEXTS

BEDE

[DIED 735]

Medieval Britain was a land twice conquered and twice colonized, first by Republican Rome and then by the Germanic tribes who replaced the departing Romans. After the first conquest, at the hands of Julius Caesar in 54 B.C.E., the Celtic Britons intermarried with the conquerors, producing a Romanized Britain that lasted until the fifth century C.E. Then it fell to the Germanic invaders, who eventually identified themselves as Anglo-Saxons. The religion of the Roman Britons was an early form of Christianity, adapted by the native priests from the practices of the Romans themselves. The religion of the Anglo-Saxons did not come with them; it came a hundred years later, by order of Pope Gregory in 597 C.E., in the form of a conversion mission led by St. Augustine (not to be confused with the earlier Bishop of Hippo). The missionaries worked so successfully among the Anglo-Saxon kings that by the middle of the seventh century their influence had penetrated all the way to the Scottish border. The second version of the Roman Catholic religion was officially recognized in England in 669 by the Synod of Whitby, held in Northumbria.

Bede, later called "Bede the Venerable" to connote respect for his age and wisdom, was a product of Northumbrian culture and the leading scholar of his age. Given up to God by his family as a young boy, he spent his lifetime in the Benedictine abbey of Jarrow, where he wrote prodigiously. His most famous work is the encyclopedic *Ecclesiastical History of the English People*, which he completed several years before his death in 735. The first historian to record dates by the Christian calendar, Bede accounted for the successful conversion mission from its arrival on English shores in 597 to 731 C.E., pulling together details and narrating incidents with remarkable clarity and candor. Primarily a moral historian intent on showing the effects of good and evil in the world, Bede concentrated on exemplary stories of the clergy and Anglo-Saxon nobility. He was not without prejudice: in particular, he hated "false monasteries" where the Christian calendar was not strictly followed—in other words, where the practices of the old Church of the first period of colonization were still adhered to.

The *Ecclesiastical History* traces the arrival of the Germanic invaders, portraying the conquering tribes of the fifth century in a state of pagan darkness and disunity. Subsequent chapters on the Angles, strongest of the Germanic tribes, show them wreaking "God's just punishment on the sins of the nation" and winning territorial control. Bede's account of the arrival of the conversion mission (I, 23) describes the horror of the monks at the barbarity of the British inhabitants. But despite their pleas, Pope Gregory refuses to let the monks return to Rome, stating that "it is better not to begin a good work than to abandon it once it is begun." In a subsequent chapter (II, 2), St. Augustine, supported by the kings of Northumbria, prophesies the punishment of the rebellious British clergy. Sure enough, after his death the Northumbrian kings single out the British monks at the battle of Carlegion, utterly destroying them before turning to attack their British defenders.

Bede reflects the special position of Northumbria in some of his other stories. A famous one (II, 13) involves the conversion of King Edwin in 627 C.E., over a century before the writing of the *Ecclesiastical History*. An advisor to the king compares life on earth to the passing of a sparrow through a great hall and into darkness again; if the new religion offers the hope of salvation, why not try it? In answer, King Edwin accepts the new religion and personally destroys the pagan altars he formerly dedicated. A final selection (IV, 24), again from Northumbria, tells the story of the monk Caedmon, skillful in composing religious poems in his native tongue. Because we have verses attributed to Caedmon from other sources, we are able to verify the fact that he was one of the great poets of his day.

Ecclesiastical History of the English People

Translated by Leo Sherley-Price, revised by R. E. Latham

Book I

Chapter 23

The holy Pope Gregory sends Augustine and other monks to preach to the English nation, and encourages them in a letter to persevere in their mission [596 C.E.]

In the year of our Lord 582, Maurice, fifty-fourth in succession from Augustus, became Emperor, and ruled for twenty-one years. In the tenth year of his reign, Gregory, an eminent scholar and administrator, was elected Pontiff of the apostolic Roman see, and ruled it for thirteen years, six months, and ten days. In the fourteenth year of this Emperor, and about the one hundred and fiftieth year after the coming of the English to Britain, Gregory was inspired by God to send his servant Augustine with several other God-fearing monks to preach the word of God to the English nation. Having undertaken this task in obedience to the Pope's command and progressed a short distance on their journey, they became afraid, and began to consider returning home. For they were appalled at the idea of going to a barbarous, fierce, and pagan nation, of whose very language they were ignorant. They unanimously agreed that this was the safest course, and sent back Augustine—who was to be consecrated bishop in the event of their being received by the English—so that he might humbly request the holy Gregory to recall them from so dangerous, arduous, and uncertain a journey. In reply, the Pope wrote them a letter of encouragement, urging them to proceed on their mission to preach God's word, and to trust themselves to his aid. This letter ran as follows:

'Gregory, servant of the servants of God, to the servants of our Lord. My very dear sons, it is better never to undertake any high enterprise than to abandon it when once begun. So with the help of God you must carry out this holy task which you have begun. Do not be deterred by the troubles of the journey or by what men say. Be constant and zealous in carrying out this enterprise which, under

God's guidance, you have undertaken: and be assured that the greater the labour, the greater will be the glory of your eternal reward. When Augustine your leader returns, whom we have appointed your abbot, obey him humbly in all things, remembering that whatever he directs you to do will always be to the good of your souls. May Almighty God protect you with His grace, and grant me to see the result of your labours in our heavenly home. And although my office prevents me from working at your side, yet because I long to do so, I hope to share in your joyful reward. God keep you safe, my dearest sons.

'Dated the twenty-third of July, in the fourteenth year of the reign of the most pious Emperor Maurice Tiberius Augustus, and the thirteenth year after his Consulship: the fourteenth indiction.'

BOOK II

Chapter 2

Augustine urges the British bishops to cement Catholic unity, and performs a miracle in their presence. Retribution follows their refusal [603 C.E.]

Meanwhile, with the aid of King Ethelbert, Augustine summoned the bishops and teachers of the nearest British province to a conference at a place still known to the English as Augustine's Oak, which lies on the border between the Hwiccas and the West Saxons. He began by urging them to establish brotherly relations with him in Catholic unity, and to join with him in God's work of preaching the Gospel to the heathen.

Now the Britons did not keep Easter at the correct time, but between the fourteenth and twentieth days of the moon—a calculation depending on a cycle of eighty-four years. Furthermore, certain other of their customs were at variance with the universal practice of the Church. But despite protracted discussions, neither the prayers nor the advice nor the censures of Augustine and his companions could obtain the compliance of the Britons, who stubbornly preferred their own customs to those in universal use among Christian Churches. Augustine then brought this lengthy and fruitless conference to a close, saying: 'Let us ask our Lord, *who makes men to be of one mind* in His Father's house, to grant us a sign from heaven and show us which tradition is to be followed, and by what roads we are to hasten our steps towards His kingdom. Bring in some sick person, and let the beliefs and practice of those who can heal him be accepted as pleasing to God and to be followed by all.' On the reluctant agreement of his opponents, a blind Englishman was led in and presented to the British priests, from whose ministry he obtained no healing or benefit. Then Augustine, as the occasion demanded, knelt in prayer to the Father of our Lord Jesus Christ, imploring that the man's lost sight be restored and prove the means of bringing the light of spiritual grace to the minds of countless believers. Immediately the blind man's sight was restored, and all acknowledged Augustine as the true herald of the light of Christ. The Britons declared that, while they had learnt that what Augustine taught was the true way of righteousness, they could not abandon their ancient customs without the consent and approval of their own people, and therefore asked that a second and fuller conference might be held.

This was arranged, and seven British bishops and many very learned men are said to have attended, who came mainly from their most famous monastery which the English call Bancornaburg, then ruled by Abbot Dinoot. Those summoned to this council first visited a wise and prudent hermit, and enquired of him whether they should abandon their own traditions at Augustine's demand. He answered: 'If he is a man of God, follow him.' 'But how can we be sure of this?' they asked. 'Our Lord says, *Take My yoke upon you and learn of Me, for I am meek and lowly in heart,*' he replied. 'Therefore if Augustine is meek and lowly in heart, it shows that he bears the yoke of Christ himself, and offers it to you. But if he is haughty and unbending, then he is not of God, and we should not listen to him.' Then they asked, 'But how can we know even this?' 'Arrange that he and his followers arrive first at the place appointed for the conference,' answered the hermit. 'If he rises courteously as you approach, rest assured that he is the servant of Christ and do as he asks. But if he ignores you and does not rise, then, since you are in the majority, do not comply with his demands.'

The British bishops carried out his suggestion, and it happened that Augustine remained seated in his chair. Seeing this, they became angry, accusing him of pride and taking pains to contradict all that he said. Augustine then declared: 'There are many points on which your customs conflict with ours, or rather with those of the universal Church. Nevertheless, if you will agree with me on three points, I am ready to countenance all your other customs, although they are contrary to our own. These points are: to keep Easter at the correct time; to complete the Sacrament of Baptism, by which we are reborn to God, according to the rites of the holy, Roman, and apostolic Church; and to join with us in preaching the word of God to the English.' But the bishops refused these things, nor would they recognize Augustine as their archbishop, saying among themselves that if he would not rise to greet them in the first instance, he would have even less regard for them once they submitted to his authority. Whereupon Augustine, that man of God, is said to have answered with a threat that was also a prophecy: if they refused to accept peace with fellow-Christians, they would be forced to accept war at the hands of enemies; and if they refused to preach to the English the way of life, they would eventually suffer at their hands the penalty of death. And, by divine judgement, all these things happened as Augustine foretold.

Some while after this, the powerful king Ethelfrid, whom I have already mentioned, raised a great army at the City of Legions—which the English call Legacestir, but which the Britons more correctly named Carlegion—and made a great slaughter of the faithless Britons. Before battle was joined, he noticed that their priests were assembled apart in a safer place to pray for their soldiers, and he enquired who they were and what they had come there to do. Most of these priests came from the monastery of Bangor, where there are said to have been so many monks that although it was divided into seven sections, each under its own head, none of these sections contained less than three hundred monks, all of whom supported themselves by manual work. Most of these monks, who had kept a three-day fast, had gathered to pray at the battle, guarded by a certain Brocmail, who was there to protect them from the swords of the barbarians while they were intent on prayer. As soon as King Ethelfrid was informed of their purpose, he said: 'If they are crying to their God against us, they are fighting against us even if they do not bear arms.' He therefore directed his first attack against them, and then destroyed the rest of the accursed army, not without heavy loss to his own forces. It is said that of the monks who had come to pray about twelve hundred perished in this battle, and only fifty escaped by flight. Brocmail and his men took to their heels at the first assault, leaving those whom they should have protected unarmed and exposed to the sword-strokes of the enemy. Thus, long after his death, was fulfilled Bishop Augustine's prophecy that the faithless Britons, who had rejected the offer of eternal salvation, would incur the punishment of temporal destruction.

. . .

Chapter 13

Edwin holds a council with his chief men about accepting the Faith of Christ. The high priest destroys his own altars [627 C.E.]

When he heard this, the king answered that it was his will as well as his duty to accept the Faith that Paulinus taught, but said that he must still discuss the matter with his principal advisers and friends, so that, if they were in agreement with him, they might all be cleansed together in Christ the Fount of Life. Paulinus agreed, and the king kept his promise. He summoned a council of the wise men, and asked each in turn his opinion of this strange doctrine and this new way of worshipping the godhead that was being proclaimed to them.

Coifi, the chief Priest, replied without hesitation: 'Your Majesty, let us give careful consideration to this new teaching; for I frankly admit that, in my experience, the religion that we have hitherto professed seems valueless and powerless. None of your subjects has been more devoted to the service of our gods than myself; yet there are many to whom you show greater favour, who receive greater honours, and who are more successful in all their undertakings. Now, if the gods had any power, they would surely have favoured myself, who have been more zealous in their service. Therefore, if on examination you perceive that these new teachings are better and more effectual, let us not hesitate to accept them.'

Another of the king's chief men signified his agreement with this prudent argument, and went on to say: 'Your Majesty, when we compare the present life of man on earth with that time of which we have no knowledge, it seems to me like the swift flight of a single sparrow through the banqueting-hall where you are sitting at dinner on a winter's day with your thegns and counsellors. In the midst there is a comforting fire to warm the hall; outside, the storms of winter rain or snow are raging. This sparrow flies swiftly in through one door of the hall, and out through another. While he is inside, he is safe from the winter storms; but after a few moments of comfort, he vanishes from sight into the wintry world from which he came. Even so, man appears on earth for a little while; but of what went before this life or of what follows, we know nothing. Therefore, if this new teaching has brought any more certain knowledge, it seems only right that we should follow it.' The other elders and counsellors of the king, under God's guidance, gave similar advice.

Coifi then added that he wished to hear Paulinus' teaching about God in greater detail; and when, at the king's bidding, this had been given, he exclaimed: 'I have long realized that there is nothing in our way of worship; for the more diligently I sought after truth in our religion, the less I found. I now publicly confess that this teaching clearly reveals truths that will afford us the blessings of life, salvation, and eternal happiness. Therefore, Your Majesty, I submit that the temples and altars that we have dedicated to no advantage be immediately desecrated and burned.' In short, the king granted blessed Paulinus full permission to preach, renounced idolatry, and professed his acceptance of the Faith of Christ. And when he asked the Chief Priest who should be the first to profane the altars and shrines of the idols, together with the enclosures that surrounded them, Coifi replied: 'I will do this myself; for now that the true God has granted me knowledge, who more suitably than I can set a public example and destroy the idols that I worshipped in ignorance?' So he formally renounced his empty superstitions and asked the king to give him arms and a stallion—for hitherto it had not been lawful for the Chief Priest to carry arms or to ride anything but a mare—and, thus equipped, he set out to destroy the idols. Girded with a sword and with a spear in his hand, he mounted the king's stallion and rode up to the idols. When the crowd saw him, they thought he had gone mad; but without hesitation, as soon as he reached the shrine, he cast into it the spear he carried and thus profaned it. Then, full of joy at his knowledge of the worship of the true God, he told his companions to set fire to the shrine and its enclosures and destroy them. The site where these idols once stood is still shown, not far east of York, beyond the river Derwent, and is known today as Goodmanham. Here it was that the Chief Priest, inspired by the true God, desecrated and destroyed the altars that he had himself dedicated.

Book IV

Chapter 24

A brother of the monastery is found to possess God's gift of poetry [680 C.E.]

In this monastery of Streanaeshalch lived a brother singularly gifted by God's grace. So skilful was he in composing religious and devotional songs that, when any passage of Scripture was explained to him by interpreters, he could quickly turn it into delightful and moving poetry in his own English tongue. These verses of his have stirred the hearts of many folk to despise the world and aspire to heavenly things. Others after him tried to compose religious poems in English, but none could compare with him; for he did not acquire the art of poetry from men or through any human teacher but received it as a free gift from God. For this reason he could never compose any frivolous or profane verses; but only such as had a religious theme fell fittingly from his devout lips. He had followed a secular occupation until well advanced in years without ever learning anything about poetry. Indeed it sometimes happened at a feast that all the guests in turn would be invited to sing and entertain the company; then, when he saw the harp coming his way, he would get up from table and go home.

On one such occasion he had left the house in which the entertainment was being held and went out to the stable where it was his duty that night to look after the beasts. There when the time came he settled down to sleep. Suddenly in a dream he saw a man standing beside him who called him by name. 'Caedmon,' he said, 'sing me a song.' 'I don't know how to sing,' he replied. 'It is because I cannot sing that I left the feast and came here.' The man who addressed him then said: 'But you shall sing to me.' 'What should I sing about?' he replied. 'Sing about the Creation of all things,' the other answered. And Caedmon immediately began to sing verses in praise of God the Creator that he had never heard before, and their theme ran thus:

> Praise we the Fashioner now of Heaven's fabric,
> The majesty of his might and his mind's wisdom,
> Work of the world-warden, worker of all wonders,
> How he the Lord of Glory everlasting,
> Wrought first for the race of men Heaven as a rooftree,
> Then made he Middle Earth to be their mansion.

This is the general sense, but not the actual words that Caedmon sang in his dream; for verses, however masterly, cannot be translated literally from one language into another without losing much of their beauty and dignity. When Caedmon awoke, he remembered everything that he had sung in his dream, and soon added more verses in the same style to a song truly worthy of God.

Early in the morning he went to his superior the reeve, and told him about this gift that he had received. The reeve took him before the abbess, who ordered him to give an account of his dream and repeat the verses in the presence of many learned men, so that a decision might be reached by common consent as to their quality and origin. All of them agreed that Caedmon's gift had been given him by our Lord. And they explained to him a passage of scriptual history or doctrine and asked him to render it into verse if he could. He promised to do this, and returned next morning with excellent verses as they had ordered him. The abbess was delighted that God had given such grace to the man, and advised him to abandon secular life and adopt the monastic state. And when she had admitted him into the Community as a brother, she ordered him to be instructed in the events of sacred history. So Caedmon stored up in his memory all that he learned, and like one of the clean animals chewing the cud, turned it into such melodious verse that his delightful renderings turned his instructors into auditors. He sang of the creation of the world, the origin of the human race, and the whole story of Genesis. He sang of Israel's exodus from Egypt, the entry into the Promised Land, and many other events of scriptural history. He sang of the Lord's Incarnation, Passion, Resurrection, and Ascension into heaven, the coming of the Holy Spirit, and the teaching of the Apostles. He also made poems on the terrors of the Last Judgement, the horrible pains of Hell, and the joys of the Kingdom of Heaven. In addition to these, he composed several others on the blessings and judgements of God, by which he sought to turn his hearers from delight in wickedness and to inspire them to love and do good. For Caedmon was a deeply religious man, who humbly submitted to regular discipline and hotly rebuked all who tried to follow another course. And so he crowned his life with a happy end.

For, when the time of his death drew near, he felt the onset of physical weakness for fourteen days, but not seriously enough to prevent his walking or talking the whole time. Close by there was a house to which all who were sick or likely to die were taken. Towards nightfall on the day when he was to depart this life, Caedmon asked his attendant to prepare a resting-place for him in this house. The attendant was surprised at this request from a man who did not appear likely to die yet; nevertheless, he did as he was asked. So Caedmon went to the house, and conversed and jested cheerfully with those who were already there; and when it was past midnight, he asked: 'Is the Eucharist in the house?' 'Why do you want the Eucharist?' they enquired; 'you are not likely to die yet, when you are talking so cheerfully to us and seem to be in perfect health.' 'Nevertheless,' he said, 'bring me the Eucharist.' And taking It in his hands, Caedmon asked whether they were all charitably disposed towards him, and whether they had any complaint or ill-feeling against him. They replied that they were all most kindly disposed towards him, and free from all bitterness. Then in turn they asked him to clear his heart of bitterness towards them. At once he answered: 'Dear sons, my heart is at peace with all the servants of God.' Then, when he had fortified himself with the heavenly Viaticum, he prepared to enter the other life, and asked how long it would be before the brothers were roused to sing God's praises in the Night Office. 'Not long,' they replied. 'Good, then let us wait until then,' he answered; and signing himself with the holy Cross, he laid his head on the pillow and passed away quietly in his sleep. So, having served God with a simple and pure mind, and with tranquil devotion, he left the world and departed to his presence by a tranquil death. His tongue, which had sung so many inspiring verses in praise of his Maker, uttered its last words in his praise as he signed himself with the Cross and commended his soul into his hands. For, as I have already said, Caedmon seems to have had a premonition of his death.

HISTORY OF THE FIRST CRUSADE

[EARLY 12TH CENTURY]

From an anonymous French *History of the First Crusade* comes the first description of the Muslim enemy on the field of battle from the viewpoint of a Christian Crusader.

The First Crusade was preached and set into motion by Pope Urban II, addressing the French aristocracy in Clermont in 1095. Urban called for Christian vengeance on the Turks for atrocities they had supposedly committed and the expulsion of the infidel from Jerusalem. He concluded, "Undertake this journey for the remission of your sins, with the assurance of the imperishable glory of the kingdom of Heaven." So the desire for revenge and the drive for possession of the Holy Land—combined with a promise of salvation for the fallen soldier—led to two hundred years of Christian invasions into Syria and the Holy Land.

Initially successful, the Crusaders established a series of states in conquered territory; but by the time of the Second Crusade in 1147, it was already clear that Muslim resistance was capable of throwing back the attackers in the end. Jerusalem, captured by the Christians in 1099, was finally recaptured by Saladin in 1187. In 1204, during the Fourth Crusade, the Christians diverted around the Holy Land and sacked Constantinople, destroying what remained of the Byzantine Empire in the process. In 1291, the last Christian stronghold in Syria fell and the Crusades came to an end.

Our account of the First Crusade mingles realistic scenes that show respect for the prowess of the enemy with religious rhetoric betraying unreasoning prejudice against the states of Islam. Surprisingly, it is candid about what we would call Christian atrocities: the robbing of the graves of the Turkish dead at Antioch and the sacking of Marra and Jerusalem. Nothing, not even cannibalism, escapes notice. Accounts such as this one provide some of the most appalling revelations in Western history.

FROM

History of the First Crusade

Translated by James B. Ross

The First Contact of Crusaders and Turks

Impressions of the People and the Country in Anatolia

The first day of our departure from the city [Constantinople], we reached a bridge and we stayed there two days. The third day our men rose before dawn and, since it was still night, they did not see well enough to hold to the same route, and they divided into two corps which were separated by two days' march. In the first group were Bohemond, Robert of Normandy, the prudent Tancred and many others; in the second were the count of St. Giles, Duke Godfrey, the bishop of Puy, Hugh the Great, the count of Flanders and many others.

The third day [July 1, 1097], the [Seljuk] Turks violently burst upon Bohemond and his companions. At once the Turks began to shriek, scream, and cry out in high voices, repeating some diabolical sound in their own language. The wise Bohemond, seeing the innumerable Turks at a distance, shrieking and crying out in demoniac voices, at once ordered all the knights to dismount and the tents to be pitched quickly. Before the tents were pitched, he said to all the soldiers: "Lords, and valiant soldiers of Christ, here we are confronted on all sides by a difficult battle.

Let all the knights advance bravely and let the foot soldiers quickly and carefully pitch the tents."

When all this was done, the Turks had already surrounded us on all sides, fighting, throwing javelins and shooting arrows marvellously far and wide. And we, although we did not know how to resist them nor to endure the weight of so great an enemy, nevertheless we met that encounter with united spirit. And our women on that day were a great help to us, in bearing drinking water to our fighters and perhaps also in always comforting those fighting and defending. The wise Bohemond sent word forthwith to the others, that is, to the count of St. Giles, to Duke Godfrey, Hugh the Great, the bishop of Puy and all the other knights of Christ, to hasten and come quickly to the battle, saying, "If today they wish to fight, let them come bravely." . . .

Our men wondered greatly whence could have sprung such a great multitude of Turks, Arabs, Saracens, and others too numerous to count, for almost all the mountains and hills and valleys and all the plains, both within and without, were covered entirely by that excommunicated race. There was among us a quiet exchange of words, praising God and taking counsel and saying: "Be unanimous in every way in the faith of Christ and the victory of the holy cross, for today, if it pleases God, you will all become rich." . . .

On the approach of our knights, the Turks, Arabs, Saracens, Angulans [unidentifiable], and all the barbarous peoples fled quickly through the passes of the mountains and the plains. The number of the Turks, Persians, Paulicians, Saracens, Angulans, and other pagans was three hundred and sixty thousand, without counting the Arabs, whose number no one knows except God alone. They fled extremely quickly to their tents but were not allowed to remain there long. Again they resumed their flight and we pursued them, killing them during one whole day; and we took much booty, gold, silver, horses, asses, camels, sheep, cows, and many other things which we do not know. If the Lord had not been with us in this battle, if He had not quickly sent us the other division, none of ours would have escaped, because from the third hour up to the ninth hour the battle continued. But God all-powerful, pious and merciful, who did not permit His knights to perish nor to fall into the hands of the enemy, sent aid to us rapidly. But two of our knights died there honourably . . . and other knights and foot soldiers whose names I do not know, found death there.

Who will ever be wise or learned enough to describe the prudence, the military skill, and the fortitude of the Turks? They thought to terrorize the race of the Franks by the threats of their arrows, as they have terrorized the Arabs, Saracens and Armenians, Syrians and Greeks. But, if it pleases God, they will never prevail over such a great people as ours. In truth they say they are of the race of the Franks and that no man, except the Franks and themselves, ought rightly to be called a knight. Let me speak the truth which no one will dare to contest; certainly, if they had always been firm in the faith of Christ and holy Christianity, if they had been willing to confess one Lord in three persons, and the Son of God born of a virgin, who suffered, rose from the dead, ascended into heaven in the sight of His disciples and sent the consolation of the Holy Spirit, and if they had believed in right mind and faith that He reigns in heaven and on earth, no one could have been found more powerful or courageous or gifted in war; and nevertheless, by the grace of God, they were conquered by our men. This battle took place on the first of July. . . .

And we kept going on [July–August, 1097], pursuing the most iniquitous Turks who fled each day before us. . . . And we pursued them through deserts and a land without water or inhabitants from which we scarcely escaped and got out alive. Hunger and thirst pressed us on all sides, and there was almost nothing for us to eat, except the thorns which we pulled and rubbed between our hands; on such food we lived miserably. In that place there died most of our horses, so that many of our knights became foot soldiers; and from lack of horses, cattle took the place of war steeds and in this extreme necessity goats, sheep, and dogs were used by us for carrying.

Then we began to enter an excellent region, full of nourishment for the body, of delights and all kinds of good things, and soon we approached Iconium. The inhabitants of this country [probably Armenians] persuaded and warned us to carry with us skins full of water, because for the journey one day thence there is a great dearth of water. We did so until we came to a certain river and there we camped for two days. . . .

We . . . penetrated into a diabolic mountain [in the Antitaurus], so high and so narrow that no one dared to go before another on the path which lay open on the mountain; there the horses plunged down and one packhorse dragged over another. On all sides the knights were in despair; they beat their breasts in sorrow and sadness, wondering what to do with themselves and their arms. They sold their shields and their best coats of mail with helmets for only three or five pennies or for anything at all; those who failed to sell them, threw them away for nothing and proceeded. . . .

Finally [October, 1097] our knights reached the valley in which is situated the royal city of Antioch, which is the capital of all Syria and which the Lord Jesus Christ gave to St. Peter, prince of the apostles, in order that he might recall it to the cult of the holy faith, he who lives and reigns with God the Father in the unity of the Holy Spirit, God through all the ages. Amen. . . .

At the Siege of Antioch

The next day [March 7, 1098], at dawn, some Turks went forth from the city and collected all the fetid corpses of the Turkish dead which they could find on the bank of the river and buried them at the mosque beyond the bridge, before the gate of the city. With the bodies they buried cloaks, bezants [gold coins], pieces of gold, bows, arrows, and many other objects which we cannot name. Our men, hearing that the Turks had buried their dead, all prepared themselves and hastened to the diabolic edifice. They ordered the tombs to be dug up and broken, and dragged from the burial places. They threw all the corpses into a certain ditch and carried the severed heads to our tents so that the number of them should be known exactly. . . . At this sight the Turks mourned exceedingly and were sad unto death for on that day they did nothing in their sorrow except weep and utter cries. . . .

The Taking of Marra

The Saracens, seeing that our men had sapped the wall, were struck with terror and fled within the city. All this took place on Saturday at the hour of vespers, at sunset, December 11th [1098]. Bohemond sent word by an interpreter to the Saracen chiefs that they with their wives and children and other belongings should take refuge in a palace which is above the gate and he himself would protect them from sentence of death.

Then all our men entered the city and whatever of value they found in the houses or hiding places each one took for his own. When day came, wherever they found anyone of the enemy, either man or woman, they killed him. No corner of the city was empty of Saracen corpses, and no one could go through the streets of the city without stepping on these corpses. At length Bohemond seized those whom he had ordered to go to the palace and took from them everything they had, gold, silver, and other ornaments; some he had killed, others he ordered to be led to Antioch to be sold.

Now the stay of the Franks in this city was one month and four days, during which the bishop of Orange died. There were some of our men who did not find there what they needed, both because of the long stay and the pressure of hunger, for outside the city they could find nothing to take. They sawed open the bodies of the dead because in their bellies they found bezants hidden; others cut the flesh in strips and cooked them for eating. . . .

The Sack of Jerusalem

Entering the city [July 15, 1099], our pilgrims pursued and killed Saracens up to the Temple of Solomon, in which they had assembled and where they gave battle to us furiously for the whole day so that their blood flowed throughout the whole temple. Finally, having overcome the pagans, our knights seized a great number of men and women, and they killed whom they wished and whom they wished they let live. . . . Soon the crusaders ran throughout the city, seizing gold, silver, horses, mules, and houses full of all kinds of goods.

Then rejoicing and weeping from extreme joy our men went to worship at the sepulchre of our Saviour Jesus and thus fulfilled their pledge to Him. . . .

Then, our knights decided in council that each one should give alms with prayers so that God should elect whom He wished to reign over the others and rule the city. They also ordered that all the Saracen dead should be thrown out of the city because of the extreme stench, for the city was almost full of their cadavers. The live Saracens dragged the dead out before the gates and made piles of them, like houses. No one has ever heard of or seen such a slaughter of pagan peoples since pyres were made of them like boundary marks, and no one except God knows their number.

ANDREAS CAPELLANUS

[FLOURISHED 1170–1186]

We know little of the life of Andreas Capellanus, and we are not even sure what he thought of the famous treatise on love that he produced. Apparently a monk attached to the glittering court of Poitiers in the south of France, he was probably commissioned to write *The Art of Courtly Love* (literally *The Art of Honest Loving*) by Marie of Champagne, daughter of Eleanor of Aquitaine, at the court Marie and Eleanor frequented. This book, completed in 1174, brought together several principal themes: definitions of love derived from Ovid's *Art of Love* and *Remedies for Love;* sample "cases" of love that summarized love disputes heard at Marie's court; and a short retraction in which Andreas appears to take back much of what he has said in the rest of his work. The meaning of this little book often has been debated.

The court of Poitiers, the ancestral seat of Countess Eleanor of Aquitaine, was one of the capitals of the troubador tradition of Provençal poetry, which had started with Eleanor's grandfather, Guillaume IX of Aquitaine, a century before. Eleanor, returning home from her tempestuous marriage to Henry II of England in 1170, apparently decreed a celebration of courtly love throughout her realm. She and her daughter, Marie of Champagne, patronized various scholars and artists, encouraging them to enlarge on this doctrine and promote its significance. Two of those who were encouraged in this respect were Andreas Capellanus and the poet Chrétien de Troyes, who lists Marie as the patron of his romance *Lancelot*.

Andreas dedicates his work to a young friend Walter, a "new recruit of Love" who has "recently been wounded by an arrow of his." He proposes to describe ways in which a "state of love between two lovers may be kept unharmed and likewise how those who do not love may get rid of the darts of Venus that are fixed in their hearts." The topic he proposes, then, sounds like an updating of Ovid's *Art* and *Remedies* of love. But unlike Ovid, Andreas does not propose to write a textbook on seduction. In fact, his definition of love appears to be very chaste. Love is "an inborn suffering derived from the sight of and excessive meditation upon the beauty of the opposite sex, which causes one to wish above all things the embraces of the other." Basically, Andreas advises temperance: a subordination of passion to civil behavior in a love that, in any case, can occur only between a man and a woman who are social equals.

Andreas follows with a description of how to keep love. It should be, first of all, a secret. It may be increased by the difficulty of its attainment or decreased by its ease of access. It is often broken by a failure to maintain loyalty or by its revelation to others. In this part of his work, Andreas sometimes appears to be defining the nature of passion rather than the civil behavior he had advocated previously.

Finally, Andreas writes on "the rejection of love," in which he advises his friend Walter to ignore the pursuit of carnal love and pursue the love of God, which will lead to salvation. The point of writing the book, he now says, is "not because we consider it advisable for you or any other man to fall in love, but for fear lest you might think us stupid. . . . For God is more pleased with a man who is able to sin and does not, than with a man who has no opportunity to sin."

Modern scholars have had considerable difficulty with Andreas Capellanus' writings, finding them contradictory and yet ascribing great importance to what he writes, especially for our understanding of near contemporaries of his such as Marie de France, Chrétien de Troyes, and the troubador poets. We will not discuss the problems of *The Art of Courtly Love* in detail, but several points might be raised. First, Andreas is writing a treatise to commemorate a hundred years of the cult of love in the south of France, and (except at the end of his treatise) his words are more descriptive of prevailing and sometimes contradictory opinions than they are prescriptive of what they ought to be. Second, because he is following Ovid, sometimes he repeats his source and sometimes he disagrees; sometimes Ovid even disagrees with himself. Consistency was not a strong point of most medieval writers, nor of their classical models. Third, the attitude of caution he presents in several places appears to be genuine. If he really is writing a treatise on the subject "for fear lest you might think us stupid," then this is an older man telling a younger one what he knows about a notoriously difficult and dangerous subject. The value of this little book for the modern reader is thus neither as a definitive guide to the ideas on love of the period nor as a logical revision of Ovid to conform to the ideas of the Middle Ages, but as another interesting look into the medieval mind, with results we find expressed nowhere else in quite the same way.

The Art of Courtly Love

Translated by John J. Parry

Book I
Introduction to the Treatise on Love

We must first consider what love is, whence it gets its name, what the effect of love is, between what persons love may exist, how it may be acquired, retained, increased, decreased, and ended, what are the signs that one's love is returned, and what one of the lovers ought to do if the other is unfaithful.

Chapter 1
What Love Is

Love is a certain inborn suffering derived from the sight of and excessive meditation upon the beauty of the opposite sex, which causes each one to wish above all things the embraces of the other and by common desire to carry out all of love's precepts in the other's embrace.

That love is suffering is easy to see, for before the love becomes equally balanced on both sides there is no torment greater, since the lover is always in fear that his love may not gain its desire and that he is wasting his efforts. He fears, too, that rumors of it may get abroad, and he fears everything that might harm it in any way, for before things are perfected a slight disturbance often spoils them. If he is a poor man, he also fears that the woman may scorn his poverty; if he is ugly, he fears that she may despise his lack of beauty or may give her love to a more handsome man; if he is rich, he fears that his parsimony in the past may stand in his way. To tell the truth, no one can number the fears of one single lover. This kind of love, then, is a suffering which is felt by only one of the persons and may be called "single love." But even after both are in love the fears that arise are just as great, for each of the lovers fears that what he has acquired with so much effort may be lost through the effort of someone else, which is certainly much worse for a man than if, having no hope, he sees that his efforts are accomplishing nothing, for it is worse to lose the things you are seeking than to be deprived of a gain you merely hope for. The lover fears, too, that he may offend his loved one in some way; indeed he fears so many things that it would be difficult to tell them.

That this suffering is inborn I shall show you clearly, because if you will look at the truth and distinguish carefully you will see that it does not arise out of any action; only from the reflection of the mind upon what it sees does this suffering come. For when a man sees some woman fit for love and shaped according to his taste, he begins at once to lust after her in his heart; then the more he thinks about her the more he burns with love, until he comes to a fuller meditation. Presently he begins to think about the fashioning of the woman and to differentiate her limbs, to think about what she does, and to pry into the secrets of her body, and he desires to put each part of it to the fullest use. Then after he has come to this complete meditation, love cannot hold the reins, but he proceeds at once to action; straightway he strives to get a helper to find an intermediary. He begins to plan how he may find favor with her, and he begins to seek a place and a time opportune for talking; he looks upon a brief hour as a very long year, because he cannot do anything fast enough to suit his eager mind. It is well known that many things happen to him in this manner. This inborn suffering comes, therefore, from seeing and meditating. Not every kind of meditation can be the cause of love, an excessive one is required; for a restrained thought does not, as a rule, return to the mind, and so love cannot arise from it.

Chapter 2
Between What Persons Love May Exist

Now, in love you should note first of all that love cannot exist except between persons of opposite sexes. Between two men or two women love can find no place, for we see that two persons of the same sex are not at all fitted for giving each other the exchanges of love or for practicing the acts natural to it. Whatever nature forbids, love is ashamed to accept.

Chapter 3
What the Effect of Love Is

Now it is the effect of love that a true lover cannot be degraded with any avarice. Love causes a rough and uncouth man to be distinguished for his handsomeness; it can endow a man even of the humblest birth with nobility of character; it blesses the proud with humility; and the man in love becomes accustomed to performing many services gracefully for everyone. O what a wonderful thing is love, which makes a man shine with so many virtues and teaches everyone, no matter who he is, so many good traits of character! There is another thing about love that we should not praise in few words: it adorns a man, so to speak, with the virtue of chastity, because he who shines with the light of one love can hardly think of embracing another woman, even a beautiful one. For when he thinks deeply of his beloved the sight of any other woman seems to his mind rough and rude.

Chapter 4
What Persons Are Fit for Love

We must now see what persons are fit to bear the arms of love. You should know that everyone of sound mind who is capable of doing the work of Venus may be wounded by one of love's arrows unless prevented by age, or blindness, or excess of passion.

An excess of passion is a bar to love, because there are men who are slaves to such passionate desire that they cannot be held in the bonds of love—men who, after they have thought long about some woman or even enjoyed her, when they see another woman straightway desire her embraces, and they forget about the services they have received from their first love and they feel no gratitude for them. Men of this kind lust after every woman they see; their love is like that of a shameless dog. They should rather, I believe, be compared to asses, for they are moved only by that low nature which shows that men are on the level of the other animals rather than by that true nature which sets us apart from all the other animals by the difference of reason.

Chapter 5
In What Manner Love May Be Acquired, and in How Many Ways

It remains next to be seen in what ways love may be acquired.

A beautiful figure wins love with very little effort, especially when the lover who is sought is simple, for a simple lover thinks that there is nothing to look for in one's beloved besides a beautiful figure and face and a body well cared for.

But a wise woman will seek as a lover a man of praiseworthy character—not one who anoints himself all over like a woman or makes a rite of the care of the body, for it does not go with a masculine figure to adorn oneself in womanly fashion or to be devoted to the care of the body.

Likewise, if you see a woman too heavily rouged you will not be taken in by her beauty unless you have already discovered that she is good company besides, since a woman who puts all her reliance on her rouge usually doesn't have any particular gifts of character. As I said about men, so with women—I believe you should not seek for beauty so much as for excellence of character. For since all of us human beings are derived originally from the same stock and all naturally claim the same ancestor, it was not beauty or care of the body or even abundance of possessions, but excellence of character alone which first made a distinction of nobility among men and led to the difference of class.

Character alone, then, is worthy of the crown of love. Many times fluency of speech will incline to love the hearts of those who do not love, for an elaborate line of talk on the part of the lover usually sets love's arrows a-flying and creates a presumption in favor of the excellent character of the speaker. How this may be I shall try to show you as briefly as I can.

To this end I shall first explain to you that one woman belongs to the middle class, a second to the simple nobility, and a third to the higher nobility. So it is with men: one is of the middle class, another of the nobility, a third of the higher nobility, and a fourth of the very highest nobility. What I mean by a woman of the middle class is clear enough to you; a noblewoman is one descended from an untitled nobleman [vavasor] or a lord, or is the wife of one of these, while a woman of the higher nobility is descended from great lords. The same rules apply to men, except that a man married to a woman of higher or lower rank than himself does not change his rank. A married woman changes her status to match that of her husband, but a man can never change his nobility by marriage. In addition, among men we find one rank more than among women, since there is a man more noble than any of these, that is, the clerk.

• • •

Chapter 9
The Love of Peasants

If you should, by some chance, fall in love with a peasant woman, be careful to puff her up with lots of praise, and then, when you find a convenient place, do not hesitate to take what you seek and to embrace her by force. For you can hardly soften their outward inflexibility so far that they will grant you their embraces quietly or permit you to have the solaces you desire unless first you use a little compulsion as a convenient cure for their shyness. We do not say these things, however, because we want to persuade you to love such women, but only so that, if through lack of caution you should be driven to love them, you may know, in brief compass, what to do.

Book II
How Love May Be Retained

Chapter 1
How Love, When It Has Been Acquired, May Be Kept

Now since we have already said enough about acquiring love, it is not unfitting that we should next see and describe how this love may be retained after it has once been acquired. The man who wants to keep his love affair for a long time untroubled should above all things be careful not to let it be known to any outsider, but should keep it hidden from everybody; because when a number of people begin to get wind of such an affair, it ceases to develop naturally and even loses what progress it has already made. Furthermore a lover ought to appear to his beloved wise in every respect and restrained in his conduct, and he should do nothing disagreeable that might annoy her. And if inadvertently he should do something improper that offends her, let him straightway confess with downcast face that he has done wrong, and let him give the excuse that he lost his temper or make some other suitable explanation that will fit the case. And every man ought to be sparing of praise of his beloved when he is among other men; he should not spend a great deal of time in places where she is. When he is with other men, if he meets her in a group of women, he should not try to communicate with her by signs, but should treat her almost like a stranger lest some person spying on their love might have opportunity to spread malicious gossip. Lovers should not even nod to each other unless they are sure that nobody is watching them. Every man should also wear things that his beloved likes and pay a reasonable amount of attention to his appearance—not too much because excessive care for one's looks is distasteful to everybody and leads people to despise the good looks that one has. If the lover is lavish in giving, that helps him retain a love he has acquired, for all lovers ought to despise all worldly riches and should give alms to those who have need of them. Also, if the lover is one who is fitted to be a warrior, he should see to it that his courage is apparent to everybody, for it detracts very much from the good character of a man if he is timid in a fight. A lover should always offer his services and obedience freely to every lady, and he ought to root out all his pride and be very humble. Then, too, he must keep in mind the general rule that lovers must not neglect anything that good manners demand or good breeding suggests, but they should be very careful to do everything of this sort. Love may also be retained by indulging in the sweet and delightful solaces of the flesh, but only in such manner and in such number that they may never seem wearisome to the loved one. Let the lover strive to practice gracefully and manfully any act or mannerism which he has noticed is pleasing to his beloved. A clerk should not, of course, affect the manners or the dress of the laity, for no one is likely to please his beloved, if she is a wise woman, by wearing strange clothing or by practicing manners that do not suit his status. Furthermore a lover should make every attempt to be constantly in the company of good men and to avoid completely the society of the wicked. For association with the vulgar makes a lover who joins them a thing of contempt to his beloved.

Chapter 2
How Love, Once Consummated, May Be Increased

We shall attempt to show you in a few words how love may be increased after it has been consummated. Now in the first place it is said to increase if the lovers see each other rarely and with difficulty; for the greater the difficulty of exchanging solaces, the more do the desire for them and the feeling of love increase. Love increases, too, if one of the lovers shows that he is angry at the other; for the lover falls at once into a great fear that this feeling which has arisen in his beloved may last forever. Love increases, likewise, if one of the lovers feels real jealousy, which is called, in fact, the nurse of love. Even if he does not suffer from real jealousy, but from a shameful suspicion, still by virtue of this his love always increases and grows more powerful. Love increases, too, if it happens to last after it has been made public; ordinarily it does not last, but begins to fail just as soon as it is revealed. Again, if one of the lovers dreams about the other, that gives rise to love, or if love already exists it increases it. So, too, if you know that someone is trying to win your beloved away from you, that will no doubt increase your love and you will begin to feel more affection for her. I will go further and say that even though you know perfectly well that some other man is enjoying the embraces of your beloved, this will make you begin to value her solaces all the more, unless your greatness of soul and nobility of mind keep you from such wickedness. When you have gone to some other place or are about to go away—that increases your love, and so do the scoldings and beatings that lovers suffer from their parents, for not only does a scolding lecture cause love to increase after it is perfected, but it even gives a perfect reason for beginning a love affair that has not yet started. Frequent dwelling with delight on the thought of the beloved is of value in increasing love; so is the sight of her eyes when you are by yourselves and fearful, and her eager acceptance of a demand for the acts of love. Love is greatly intensified by a carriage and a way of walking that please the beloved, by a readiness to say pretty things, by a pleasant manner of speaking, and by hearing men sing the praises of the loved one.

Chapter 3
In What Ways Love May Be Decreased

Now let us see in what ways love may be decreased. Too many opportunities for exchanging solaces, too many opportunities of seeing the loved one, too much chance to talk to each other all decrease love, and so does an uncultured appearance or manner of walking on the part of the lover or the sudden loss of his property. Love decreases, too, if the woman finds that her lover is foolish and indiscreet, or if he seems to go beyond reasonable bounds in his demands for love, or if she sees that he has no regard for her modesty and will not forgive her bashfulness. Love decreases, too, if the woman considers that her lover is cowardly in battle, or sees that he is unrestrained in his speech or spoiled by the vice of arrogance.

Other things which weaken love are blasphemy against God or His saints, mockery of the ceremonies of the Church, and a deliberate withholding of charity from the poor. We find that love decreases very sharply if one is unfaithful to his friend, or if he brazenly says one thing while he deceitfully conceals a different idea in his heart. Love decreases, too, if the lover piles up more wealth than is proper, or if he is too ready to go to law over trifles.

Chapter 4
How Love May Come to an End

Now having treated briefly of the lessening of love we shall try next to add for you an explanation of how it may come to an end. First of all we see that love comes to an end if one of the lovers breaks faith or tries to break faith with the other, or if he is found to go astray from the Catholic religion. It comes to an end also after it has been openly revealed and made known to men. So, too, if one of the lovers has plenty of money and does not come to the aid of the other who is in great need and lacks a great many things, then love usually becomes very cheap and comes to an ignominious end. An old love also ends when a new one begins, because no one can love two people at the same time. Furthermore, inequality of love and a fraudulent and deceitful duplicity of heart always drive out love, for a deceitful lover, no matter how worthy he is otherwise, ought to be rejected by any woman. Again, if by some chance one of the lovers becomes incapable of carrying out love's duties, love can no longer last between them and deserts them and deserts them completely. Likewise if one of the lovers becomes insane or develops a sudden timidity, love flees and becomes hateful.

You may, however, ask whether a love once ended can ever come to life again. If this failure of love comes from ignorance of some particular thing, there is no doubt but that it may be revived; however, where it grows out of some misdeed of the lover or of some defect in his nature, we cannot remember any case where it has revived, although we do not say that it cannot, except perhaps in cases where this failure is due to some defect in the lover's nature. And if love should at some time happen to come to life again, we do not think that the lovers would have perfect confidence in each other.

Chapter 5
Indications That One's Love Is Returned

Now that we have thus disposed of these questions and have, in a short space, finished them up, let us add to them a discussion of how to find out whether one's love is returned. There are many ways in which a lover can find out the faith of his beloved and test her feelings. If you see that your loved one is missing all sorts of opportunities to meet you or is putting false obstacles in your path, you cannot hope long to enjoy her love. So, too, if you find her, for no reason at all, growing half-hearted about giving you the usual solaces, you may see that her faith is wavering. If you find that she keeps out of your sight more than she was accustomed to do, her feelings are not very stable; and if she tries to hide from your faithful messenger, there is no doubt that she has turned you adrift in the mighty waves and that her love for you is only feigned. If at the very moment of delight when she is offering you her sweet solaces the act is more wearisome to her than usual, you need not doubt that she has no love for you. So, too, if she finds more fault with you than usual or demands things that she has not been in the habit of demanding, you may know that your love will not last much longer. Again, if when she is with you or someone else she frequently talks about what you did and what the other man did, without making any distinction between you, or if on some clever pretext she asks what sort of man he is or what sort of character he has, you may know that she is thinking about the love of the other man. Moreover, if you find that she is paying more attention to the care of her person than she had been doing, either her love for you is growing or she is interested in the love of someone else.

Chapter 6
If One of the Lovers Is Unfaithful to the Other

If one of the lovers should be unfaithful to the other, and the offender is the man, and he has an eye to a new love affair, he renders himself wholly unworthy of his former love, and she ought to deprive him completely of her embraces.

But what if he should be unfaithful to his beloved,—not with the idea of finding a new love, but because he has been driven to it by an irresistible passion for another woman? What, for instance, if chance should present to him an unknown woman in a convenient place or what if at a time when Venus is urging him on to that which I am talking about he should meet with a little strumpet or somebody's servant girl? Should he, just because he played with her in the grass, lose the love of his beloved? We can say without fear of contradiction that just for this a lover is not considered unworthy of the love of his beloved unless he indulges in so many excesses with a number of women that we may conclude that he is overpassionate. But if whenever he becomes acquainted with a woman he pesters her to gain his end, or if he attains his object as a result of his efforts, then rightly he does deserve to be deprived of his former love, because there is strong presumption that he has acted in this way with an eye toward a new one, especially where he has strayed with a woman of the nobility or otherwise of an honorable estate.

I know that once when I sought advice I got the answer that a true lover can never desire a new love unless he knows that for some definite and sufficient reason the old love is dead; we know from our own experience that this rule is very true. We have fallen in love with a woman of the most admirable character, although we have never had, or hope to have, any fruit of this love. For we are compelled to pine away for love of a woman of such lofty station that we dare not say one word about it, nor dare we throw ourself upon her mercy, and so at length we are forced to find our body shipwrecked. But although rashly and without foresight we have fallen into such great waves in this tempest, still we cannot think about a new love or look for any other way to free ourself.

But since you are making a special study of the subject of love, you may well ask whether a man can have a pure love for one woman and a mixed or common love with another. We will show you, by an unanswerable argument, that no one can feel affection for two women in this fashion. For although pure love and mixed love may seem to be very different things, if you will look at the matter properly you will see that pure love, so far as its substance goes, is the same as mixed love and comes from the same feeling of the heart. The substance of the love is the same in each case, and only the manner and form of loving are different, as this illustration will make clear to you. Sometimes we see a man with a desire to drink his wine unmixed, and at another time his appetite prompts him to drink only water or wine and water mixed; although his appetite manifests itself differently, the substance of it is the same and unchanged. So likewise when two people have long been united by pure love and afterwards desire to practice mixed love, the substance of the love remains the same in them, although the manner and form and the way of practicing it are different.

Chapter 7
Various Decisions in Love Cases

Now then, let us come to various decisions in cases of love:

I. A certain knight loved his lady beyond all measure and enjoyed her full embrace, but she did not love him with equal ardor. He sought to leave her, but she, desiring to retain him in his former status, opposed his wish. In this affair the Countess of Champagne gave this response: "It is considered very unseemly for a woman to seek to be loved and yet to refuse to love. It is silly for anybody disrespectfully to ask of others what she herself wholly refuses to give to others."

II. A certain man asked the Lady Ermengarde of Narbonne to make clear where there was the greater affection—between lovers or between married people. The lady gave him a logical answer. She said: "We consider that marital affection and the true love of lovers are wholly different and arise from entirely different sources, and so the ambiguous nature of the word prevents the comparison of the things and we have to place them in different classes. Comparisons of more or less are not valid when things are grouped together under an ambiguous heading and the comparison is made in regard to that ambiguous term. It is no true comparison to say that a name is simpler than a body or that the outline of a speech is better arranged than the delivery."

III. The same man asked the same lady this question. A certain woman had been married, but was now separated from her husband by a divorce, and her former husband sought eagerly for her love. In this case the lady replied: "If any two people have been married and afterwards separate in any way, we consider love between them wholly wicked."

IV. A certain knight was in love with a woman who had given her love to another man, but he got from her this much hope of her love—that if it should ever happen that she lost the love of her beloved, then without a doubt her love would go to this man. A little while after this the woman married her lover. The other knight then demanded that she give him the fruit of the hope she had granted him, but this she absolutely refused to do, saying that she had not lost the love of her lover. In this affair the Queen gave her decision as follows: "We dare not oppose the opinion of the Countess of Champagne, who ruled that love can exert no power between husband and wife. Therefore we recommend that the lady should grant the love she has promised."

V. The Queen was also asked which was preferable: the love of a young man or of one advanced in years. She answered this question with wonderful subtlety by saying, "We distinguish between a good and a better love by the man's knowledge and his character and his praiseworthy manners, not by his age. But as regards that natural instinct of passion, young men are usually more eager to gratify it with older women than with young ones of their own age; those who are older prefer to receive the embraces and kisses of young women rather than of the older ones. But on the other hand a woman whether young or somewhat older likes the embraces and solaces of young men better than those of older ones. The explanation of this fact seems to be a physiological one."

Chapter 8
The Rules of Love

Let us come now to the rules of love, and I shall try to present to you very briefly those rules which the King of Love is said to have proclaimed with his own mouth and to have given in writing to all lovers. . . .

These are the rules.

I. Marriage is no real excuse for not loving.
II. He who is not jealous cannot love.
III. No one can be bound by a double love.
IV. It is well known that love is always increasing or decreasing.
V. That which a lover takes against his will of his beloved has no relish.
VI. Boys do not love until they arrive at the age of maturity.
VII. When one lover dies, a widowhood of two years is required of the survivor.
VIII. No one should be deprived of love without the very best of reasons.
IX. No one can love unless he is impelled by the persuasion of love.
X. Love is always a stranger in the home of avarice.
XI. It is not proper to love any woman whom one should be ashamed to seek to marry.
XII. A true lover does not desire to embrace in love anyone except his beloved.
XIII. When made public love rarely endures.
XIV. The easy attainment of love makes it of little value; difficulty of attainment makes it prized.
XV. Every lover regularly turns pale in the presence of his beloved.
XVI. When a lover suddenly catches sight of his beloved his heart palpitates.
XVII. A new love puts to flight an old one.
XVIII. Good character alone makes any man worthy of love.
XIX. If love diminishes, it quickly fails and rarely revives.
XX. A man in love is always apprehensive.
XXI. Real jealousy always increases the feeling of love.
XXII. Jealousy, and therefore love, are increased when one suspects his beloved.
XXIII. He whom the thought of love vexes, eats and sleeps very little.
XXIV. Every act of a lover ends in the thought of his beloved.
XXV. A true lover considers nothing good except what he thinks will please his beloved.
XXVI. Love can deny nothing to love.
XXVII. A lover can never have enough of the solaces of his beloved.
XXVIII. A slight presumption causes a lover to suspect his beloved.
XXIX. A man who is vexed by too much passion usually does not love.

XXX. A true lover is constantly and without intermission possessed by the thought of his beloved.

XXXI. Nothing forbids one woman being loved by two men or one man by two women.

ST. FRANCIS OF ASSISI

[1182–1226]

St. Francis of Assisi is one of those figures who can be said to have changed history as much by who he was as by what he did. His initial devotion to the ideals of chivalry mark him as a product of the new education that swept Europe in the twelfth century. His conversion to Christianity in 1206 was accompanied by activities characteristic of his entire later career: the preaching of simple sermons, service to the poor, and acts of generosity to others. Drawing a brotherhood around him, he wrote a rule for them in 1210 and became deacon of their order, declining the priesthood. For a decade he traveled to the corners of the world, attempting to convert heathens and present himself for martyrdom. He returned to Assisi in 1220 to unite his quarrelsome order on its original basis, and practiced piety and simplicity for the remainder of his life. He received many religious visions and the holy stigmata, and died a legend in 1226. He was canonized almost immediately, memorialized in paintings by Giotto and other famous artists throughout Italy, and commemorated in Dante's *Divine Comedy* a century later. Almost forgotten during the Reformation, he re-emerged as a great saint in recent times, and remains the paragon of holiness for Catholics around the world today.

Two biographies of St. Francis were begun but never completed in the century after his death. Finally, Brother Ugolino compiled the legends surrounding his life with the help of James of Massa, an elderly lay brother who had known many of his original followers. The Latin original of *The Little Flowers of St. Francis* was published in 1330; the beloved Italian translation followed soon after. The work was printed in 1476, only to suffer attacks from Protestant reformers and later from rationalists; it came back to light with new editions in 1718 and 1822, and its popularity has continued to increase in this century.

The Canticle of Brother Sun is a famous song attributed to St. Francis, an example of the simplicity of Franciscan piety. Our selection from *The Little Flowers* tells the story of how the Franciscans were given Mount Alverna, the site of their monastery, and includes several stories of St. Francis besieged by devils and confronted by the people of the town. The scene at the end, picturing St. Francis in celebration with the birds, is the subject of a painting by Giotto about the time *The Little Flowers* was compiled.

The Canticle of Brother Sun

Translated by Raphael Brown

Most High Almighty Good Lord,
Yours are the praises, the glory, the honor, and all blessings!
To You alone, Most High, do they belong,
And *no man is worthy* to mention You.

Be praised, my Lord, with all Your creatures,
Especially Sir Brother Sun,

By whom You give us the light of day!
And he is beautiful and radiant with great splendor.
Of You, Most High, he is a symbol!

Be praised, my Lord, for Sister Moon and the Stars!
In the sky You formed them bright and lovely and fair.

Be praised, my Lord, for Brother Wind
And for the Air and cloudy and clear and all Weather,
By which You give sustenance to Your creatures!

Be praised, my Lord, for Sister Water,
Who is very useful and humble and lovely and chaste!

Be praised, my Lord, for Brother Fire,
By whom You give us light at night,
And he is beautiful and merry and mighty and strong!

Be praised, my Lord, for our Sister Mother Earth,
Who sustains and governs us,
And produces fruits with colorful flowers and leaves!

Be praised, my Lord, for those who forgive for love of You
And endure infirmities and tribulations.
Blessed are those who shall endure them in peace,
For by You, Most High, they will be crowned!

Be praised, my Lord, for our Sister Bodily Death,
From whom no living man can escape!
Woe to those who shall die in mortal sin!
Blessed are those whom she will find in Your most holy will,
For the Second Death will not harm them.

Praise and bless my Lord and thank Him
And serve Him with great humility!

ANONYMOUS

The Little Flowers of Saint Francis

Translated by Raphael Brown

THE CONSIDERATIONS ON THE HOLY STIGMATA

In this part we shall contemplate with devout consideration the glorious, sacred, and holy Stigmata of our blessed Father St. Francis which he received from Christ on the holy Mount Alverna. And because those Stigmata were five, like the five Wounds of Our Lord Jesus Christ, therefore this treatise shall have Five Considerations.

The First will be about the way St. Francis came to the holy Mount Alverna.

The Second will be about the life he lived and the conversation he had with his companions on that holy mountain.

The Third will be about the apparition of the Seraph and the imprinting of the most holy Stigmata.

The Fourth will be about St. Francis' going down from Mount Alverna after he had received the holy Stigmata and about his return to St. Mary of the Angels.

The Fifth will be about certain apparitions and revelations which were given after the death of St. Francis to some holy friars and to other pious persons concerning those glorious Stigmata.

The First Consideration: How Count Orlando of Chiusi Gave Mount Alverna to St. Francis

Regarding the First Consideration, you should know that St. Francis, some time before he had the Stigmata of the Savior, moved by an inspiration from God, left the Valley of Spoleto to go to the Romagna with his companion Brother Leo.

And on their way they passed by the foot of the castle and walled village of Montefeltro, where at that time a great banquet and festival were being held to celebrate the knighting of one of the Counts of Montefeltro. When St. Francis heard from the villagers about the festivity that was taking place, and that many noblemen had gathered there from various districts, he said to Brother Leo: "Let's go up to that festival, for with God's help we will gather some good spiritual fruit."

Among the noblemen who had come to that meeting was a great and wealthy Count from Tuscany named Orlando of Chiusi in Casentino who, because of the marvelous things he had heard about the holiness and miracles of St. Francis, had a great devotion for him and wanted very much to see him and hear him preach.

St. Francis arrived at that village and entered and went to the square where all those noblemen were assembled. And in fervor of spirit he climbed onto a low wall and began to preach, taking as the theme of his sermon these words in Italian: "So great is the good which I expect that all pain is to me a delight." And under the dictation of the Holy Spirit he preached on this theme so devoutly and so profoundly—proving its truth by the various sufferings and martyrdoms of the holy Apostles and Martyrs, and by the severe penances of the holy Confessors, and by the many tribulations and temptations of the holy Virgins and of the other Saints—that everyone stood there gazing attentively at him, listening to him as though an angel of God were speaking. Among them, Count Orlando was touched to the heart by God through the marvelous preaching of St. Francis, and he decided to have a talk with him after the sermon about the state of his soul.

Therefore, when the sermon was over, he took St. Francis aside and said to him: "Father, I would like to speak to you about the salvation of my soul."

But St. Francis, who was very tactful, answered: "I am glad. But this morning go and honor your friends, since they invited you to the festival, and have dinner with them, and after dinner we will talk together as much as you wish."

Count Orlando therefore went to dine, and after dinner he returned to St. Francis and had a long talk with him about the state and salvation of his soul. And at the end Count Orlando said to St. Francis: "Brother Francis, I have a mountain in Tuscany which is very solitary and wild and perfectly suited for someone who wants to do penance in a place far from people or who wants to live a solitary life. It is called Mount Alverna. If that mountain should please you and your companions, I would gladly give it to you for the salvation of my soul."

Now St. Francis had a most intense desire to find some solitary place where he could conveniently devote himself to contemplation. So when he heard this offer, he first praised God who provides for His little sheep, and then he thanked Count

Orlando, saying: "Sire, when you go home, I will send two of my companions to you, and you can show them that mountain. And if it seems suitable for prayer and penance, I very gladly accept your charitable offer."

And after he said that, St. Francis left. And when he had ended his journey, he returned to St. Mary of the Angels.

And likewise Count Orlando, after the knighting festival was over, returned to his castle named Chiusi, which is a mile away from Mount Alverna.

After St. Francis had returned to St. Mary of the Angels, he sent two of his companions to Count Orlando. They searched for him, but because they did not know that part of the country they had great difficulty in finding his castle. When they arrived, he was very glad to see them, and he welcomed them with great joy and kindness, as though they were angels of God.

And wishing to show them Mount Alverna, he sent about fifty armed men with them, perhaps to protect them from wild animals. With this escort the friars climbed up Mount Alverna and explored it for a place where they might set up a house to live in. Finally they came to a part of the mountain where there was a small plateau that was very suitable for prayer and contemplation. And they decided in the name of the Lord to make their dwelling and that of St. Francis in that place.

With the help of the armed men who accompanied them, they cut down some branches with swords and built a little hut with the branches.

And having thus in the name of God accepted and taken possession of Mount Alverna and of the friars' Place on that mountain, with the count's permission, they left and went back to St. Francis.

And when they came to him, they told him that the place was very solitary and suitable for contemplation. And they told him in detail how they had taken possession of it.

On hearing this news St. Francis was very happy. And praising and thanking God, he said to those friars with a joyful expression: "My sons, our Lent of St. Michael the Archangel is approaching. I firmly believe that it is the will of God that we spend that Lent up on Mount Alverna, which has been prepared for us by Divine Providence, so that for the honor and glory of God and the glorious Virgin Mary and the holy angels, we may merit from Christ to consecrate that blessed mountain with penance."

Then, having said that, St. Francis took with him Brother Masseo of Marignano of Assisi, who was a man of great wisdom and eloquence, and Brother Angelo Tancredi of Rieti, who was a man of very noble birth and had been a knight in the world, and Brother Leo, who was a man of the greatest simplicity and purity, because of which St. Francis loved him very much and used to reveal nearly all his secrets to him.

With those three friars St. Francis began to pray. And when their prayer was finished, he commended himself and the above-mentioned friars to the prayers of the friars who were staying behind. And with those three, in the name of Jesus Christ Crucified, he set out for Mount Alverna.

And as they were leaving, St. Francis called one of his three companions—Brother Masseo—and said to him: "Brother Masseo, you are to be our guardian and our superior on this journey. And while traveling and stopping together, we will follow our custom: either we will say the office or we will talk about God or we will keep silence. And we will not take any thought about eating or sleeping, but when the time for overnight rest comes we will beg for a little bread, and we will stop and rest in the place which God will prepare for us."

Then those three companions nodded. And making the Sign of the Cross, they set out.

And the first evening they came to a Place of the friars, and they stayed there overnight.

The second evening, because of bad weather and because they were tired and were unable to reach any Place of the friars or any village or house, when night came on with bad weather, they sought shelter in an abandoned and uninhabited church. And they lay down to rest there.

While his companions were sleeping, St. Francis began to pray. And he was persevering in prayer when, during the first watch of the night, a great number of the fiercest devils came with very great noise and tumult, and they began to attack and persecute him. One took hold of him here, another there. One pulled him down, another up. One threatened him with one thing, another scolded him for something else. And so they strove to disturb his praying in different ways.

But they were not able to do so because God was with him. And when St. Francis had endured those attacks of the devils for some time, he began to cry out in a loud voice: "You damned spirits, you can do only what the hand of God allows you. And therefore in the name of Almighty God I tell you to do to my body whatever God allows you. I will gladly endure it since I have no enemy worse than my body. And so if you take revenge on my enemy for me, you do me a very great favor."

Then the devils seized him with great violence and fury, and began to drag him around the church and to hurt him and persecute him much more than before.

And then St. Francis cried out and said: "My Lord Jesus Christ, I thank You for the great love and charity which You are showing me, because it is a sign of great love when the Lord punishes His servant well for all his faults in this world, so that he may not be punished for them in the next world. And I am prepared to endure with joy every pain and every adversity which You, my God, wish to send me for my sins."

Then the devils, having been humiliated and defeated by his endurance and patience, went away.

And in fervor of spirit St. Francis came out of the church and entered into a forest that was nearby. And there he gave himself to prayer. And praying and weeping and beating his breast, he sought Jesus Christ, the spouse and delight of his soul. And at last he found Him in the secret depths of his heart. And he spoke to Him reverently as to his Lord. Then he answered Him as his Judge. Next he entreated Him as a father. Then he talked with Him as with a friend.

During that night and in that forest, his companions, after they awoke, stood listening and wondering what he was doing. And they saw and heard him devoutly praying with tears and cries to God to have mercy on sinners. And they also saw and heard him weeping aloud over the Passion of Christ, as if he were seeing it with his own eyes.

That same night they saw him praying with his arms crossed on his chest, raised up above the ground and suspended in the air for a long time, surrounded by a bright cloud.

And so he spent that whole night in holy contemplation without sleeping.

The next morning, as his companions knew that, owing to his exhaustion and lack of sleep during the night, St. Francis was too weak to be able to continue the journey on foot, they went to a poor local peasant and asked him, for the love of God, to lend his donkey for their Father, Brother Francis, who could not travel on foot. Hearing Brother Francis mentioned, the man asked them: "Are you friars of that Brother Francis of Assisi about whom people say so much good?"

The friars answered, "Yes," and that it was really for him that they were asking for the donkey.

Then with great devotion and care this good man saddled the donkey and led it to St. Francis, and with great reverence helped him get into the saddle.

Then they continued their journey, the peasant walking with them behind his donkey. And after they had gone a while, he said to St. Francis: "Tell me, are you Brother Francis of Assisi?"

St. Francis answered that he was.

"Well, then," said the peasant, "try to be as good as everyone thinks you are, because many people have great faith in you. So I urge you: never let there be anything in you different from what they expect of you."

When St. Francis heard these words, he did not mind being admonished by a peasant, and he did not say to himself, as many proud fellows who wear the cowl nowadays would say, "Who is this brute who admonishes me?" But he immediately got off the donkey and threw himself on his knees before the farmer and humbly kissed his feet, thanking him for having deigned to admonish him so charitably.

Then his companions and the peasant very devoutly helped him to his feet and set him on the donkey again. And they traveled on.

When they had climbed about halfway up the mountain, because the summer heat was very great and the path was long and steep, the peasant began to suffer intensely from thirst, and he called ahead to St. Francis: "I am dying of thirst. If I don't have something to drink, I'll suffocate in a minute!"

So St. Francis immediately got off the donkey and began to pray. And he remained kneeling on the ground, raising his hands toward Heaven, until he knew by revelation that God had granted his prayer. Then he said to the peasant: "Run quickly to that rock, and there you will find running water which Christ in His mercy has just caused to flow from the rock."

The man ran to the place which St. Francis had shown him, and found a very fine spring that had been made to flow through the hard rock by the power of St. Francis' prayer. And he drank all he wanted, and felt better.

And it truly seems that that spring was produced by a divine miracle through the prayers of St. Francis, because neither before nor afterward was any spring ever seen there or anywhere nearby.

After he had done this, St. Francis, with his companions and the peasant, gave thanks to God for having shown them this miracle. And then they traveled on.

And as they drew near to the peak that forms Mount Alverna itself, it pleased St. Francis to rest for a while under a certain oak tree standing by the path that is still there now.

While resting under the oak tree St. Francis began to study the location and the scenery. And when he was absorbed in this contemplation, a great number of all kinds of birds came flying down to him with joyful songs, and twittering and fluttering their wings. And they surrounded St. Francis in such a way that some of them settled on his head and others on his shoulders and others on his knees, and still others on his arms and lap and on his hands and around his feet. They all showed great joy by their tuneful singing and happy movements, as if they were rejoicing at his coming and inviting and persuading him to stay there.

Seeing this, his companions and the peasant were greatly surprised. St. Francis rejoiced in spirit and said to them: "My dear Brothers, I believe it is pleasing to Our Lord Jesus Christ that we accept a Place and live a while on this solitary mountain, since our little brothers and sisters the birds show such joy over our coming."

After saying these words, he arose and they journeyed on. And at last they came to the spot which his companions had first selected, where until then there was nothing but a very poor little hut made of tree-branches.

To the glory of God and of His Most Holy Name. Amen.

And this is the end of the First Consideration, namely, how St. Francis came to the holy Mount Alverna.

THE RENAISSANCE

Power

and

Discovery

TIME LINE FOR THE RENAISSANCE

Date	*History and Politics*
1300–1325	
	c. 1305 Golden Age of African kingdom of Mali in the Sudan.
	1309 Papacy moves to Avignon.
	c. 1312 Uzbeg converts Mongol Empire of the Golden Horde to Islam.
	1320 Turkish Tughluk dynasty founded in northern India.
1325–1350	1325 Aztecs found Tenochtitlán on Lake Texcoco.
	1337 Hundred Years' War between England and France begins.
	1348 Black Death in Europe.
1350–1375	
1375–1400	1378 Rival popes in Rome and Avignon.
	1398 Tamerlane, after conquering Central Asia, conquers Delhi.
1400–1425	1403 Beginning of Chinese commercial naval expeditions to India and Africa.
	1405 Florence buys Pisa for seaport.
	1410 Henry the Navigator urges exploration of the coast of Africa.
	1415 Henry V wins at Agincourt.
	1417 Papal schism ends.
	1420 Henry V recognized as heir to French throne.
1425–1450	1429–1431 Jeanne d'Arc's campaign, trial, and execution.
	1434 Medicis begin sixty-year domination of Florence.

Science, Culture, and Technology

1300 First European use of gunpowder.

1305 Giotto frescoes at Arena Chapel, Padua, show natural perspective and realistic detail.

1373 Lock gates developed on Dutch waterways.

1386 Weight-driven clocks, invented in China, appear in Europe.

c. 1390 Arab astronomers construct observatories.

1392 Renewed contact with China and Korea introduces art of painting in Japan at beginning of Ashikaga period.

1403 Ghiberti's doors of Florence Baptistry link Gothic, Renaissance styles.

c. 1415 Duc de Berry commissions *Très Riches Heures* from Limbourg brothers; Brunelleschi experiments with perspective.

1419 Brunelleschi, Foundling Hospital in Florence, often called first example of Renaissance architecture.

1435 Donatello finishes *David*.

Literature

c. 1330 Petrarch begins writing the *Canzoniere* to Laura.

c. 1340 Persian mystic poet Hafiz writing in ghazal form.

c. 1360 Rise of Nō drama in Japan.

1440 Rhymed version of *Ramayana* in Bengali by Kirttivasa.

(*Continued on next page*)

TIME LINE FOR THE RENAISSANCE (Continued)

Date	***History and Politics***
1450–1475	1453 Turks capture Constantinople.
	1455 English Wars of the Roses begin.
	1462 Ivan the Great becomes tsar.
1475–1500	1476 Inca Empire extends into Bolivia, Chile.
	1478 Spanish Inquisition punishes Jews, Muslims, heretics.
	1492 Columbus's first transatlantic voyage, landfall; Spain captures Granada, expels 200,000 Jews.
	1494 Charles VIII of France invades Italy.
1500–1525	
	1513 Balboa reaches Pacific Ocean.
	1517 Luther's *Ninety-Five Theses.*
	1519 Cortés begins two-year conquest of Aztec Empire; Nanak founds Sikhism.
	1520 Portuguese traders come to China.
	1521 Fall of Tenochtitlán.
1525–1550	1526 Babur founds Mogul Empire in North India.
	1527 Charles V, the Holy Roman Emperor, takes Rome.
	1531 Pizarro captures Inca ruler Atahualpa.
	1540 Ignatius Loyola founds Jesuit order.
	1541 John Calvin founds puritan theocracy at Geneva; Cartier in Québec; de Soto reaches the Mississippi.
	1542 Portuguese first Europeans to reach Japan.
	1545 The Council of Trent.
	1549 Jesuit missionaries in Japan.

Science, Culture, and Technology	***Literature***
c. 1450 Gutenberg begins to print with movable type, invented in fifteenth-century Korea.	c. 1450 Persian mystic Jami writing romantic Sufi verse.
1456 First printed Bible; quadrants used at sea to determine latitude.	
1469 Publication of Pliny's *Natural History*, first printed scientific book.	
c. 1470 Josquin Des Pres composing polyphonic sacred songs.	
1475 Muzzle-loading rifles made.	
c. 1482 Sangallo builds first Renaissance villa for Pope Leo.	1486 Pico della Mirandola, *On the Dignity of Man*.
	1492 Columbus keeps log of his first transatlantic voyage.
1501 Michaelangelo begins *David*.	c. 1500 Commedia dell'arte developing in Italy from earlier folk drama.
1506 Leonardo da Vinci finishes *Mona Lisa*.	
1512 Michaelangelo finishes Sistine Chapel ceiling.	
c. 1520 Painters of Chinese Wu school work on pen-and-ink landscape, genre painting.	
1530 Copernicus writes *Concerning the Revolutions of the Celestial Spheres;* published in 1543.	1528 Castiglione, *The Courtier*.
1532 Jean Mouton, *A Mass,* published; first printed sheet music that incorporates staff, notes, text.	1532 Machiavelli, *The Prince;* Ariosto, *Orlando Furioso*.
	1549 Manifesto of La Pleiade, group of seven French poets including Pierre de Ronsard, Joachim du Bellay.

(*Continued on next page*)

TIME LINE FOR THE RENAISSANCE (Continued)

Date	*History and Politics*
1550–1575	
	1558 Elizabeth I ascends English throne.
	1562 Slave trade from West Africa to the Spanish West Indies begins in earnest.
	1574 Portuguese colonize Angola.
1575–1600	1579 Sir Francis Drake claims California for Queen Elizabeth I.
	1587 Hidayoshi expels missionaries from Japan.
	1588 England defeats the Spanish Armada.
	1598 Juan de Oñate begins to colonize New Mexico.
1600–1625	1603 Edo period begins in Japan; Samuel de Champlain explores the Saint Lawrence.
	1607 First permanent English colony founded at Jamestown.
	1608 Confucianism introduced as official religion of Japan.
	1612 English East India Company surpasses Portugal in trade with India.
	1618–1648 Thirty Years' War.
	1620 *Mayflower* arrives in Massachusetts.
1625–1650	
	1637 Japan closes off all foreign trade and contact.
	1642 English Civil War begins.
	1649 Charles I executed; Commonwealth established under Cromwell.
1650–1675	1660 Restoration of English monarchy.
1675–1700	1675 Metacomet (King Philip) leads Algonquin uprising in New England.
	1680 Pueblos drive Spanish from New Mexico.

Science, Culture, and Technology

c. 1600 Dutch lens-grinders make first telescopes and microscopes.

1628 Harvey publishes treatise on the circulatory system.

1633 Galileo recants belief in his own theories (which Pope John Paul II will accept in 1992).

Literature

c. 1550 Wu Ch'êng-ên, *Monkey*.

1552 Rabelais completes *Gargantua* and *Pantagruel*.

1558 Marguerite de Navarre, *The Heptameron*.

1562 Cellini, *Autobiography*.

1575 Realistic novel *The Golden Lotus* appears in China.

1580–1588 Montaigne, *Essays*.

c. 1592 Marlowe, *Doctor Faustus*.

1605 Cervantes, *Don Quixote*.

1610 Ben Jonson, *The Alchemist*.

1611 Shakespeare, *The Tempest;* The King James Bible.

1621 Bacon, *The New Atlantis*.

1630 Tirso de Molina, *The Love-Rogue of Seville*.

1635 Calderon, *Life Is a Dream*.

1637 Corneille, *Le Cid*.

1667 John Milton, *Paradise Lost*.

1686 Sor Juana Inés de la Cruz, *The Divine Narcissus*.

INTRODUCTION

IMAGINE A SCHEMATIC MAP OF WESTERN EUROPE upon which the countries appear uniformly flat, gray, and featureless. Suddenly, a tiny pinprick of light blinks on nearly a third of the way down the Italian boot, in the neighborhood of Florence. Pulsing outward from that center in Tuscany, light slowly washes over the whole map, now miraculously revealing both color and detail: The Alps, the Pyrenees, great rivers and cities and ancient ruins come into view, and printed names appear—Venice, Avignon, Paris, Toledo, Prague, Rotterdam, Wittenberg, London. The Renaissance has begun.

This representation provided by an educational film of the 1950s may be simplistic, but it is not entirely amiss. For one thing, the image of gradually spreading light to suggest the advance of the Renaissance seems appropriate, however elementary. Again and again, the people who lived during the Renaissance and who helped to shape it spoke in terms of walking abroad in a new light. Erasmus of Rotterdam exclaimed, "Immortal God, what an age I see dawning! Why can I not grow young again?"; Rabelais, through his giant character Gargantua, exulted, "Out of the sick Gothic night our eyes are opened to the glorious touch of the sun." Moreover, the ways of thinking we associate with the Renaissance—the desire to recover the classical past, the impulse to relish and explore the physical and temporal world, the passion for discovery and invention, the interest in personal knowledge and power and in charismatic individuals challenging institutions—all these phenomena did not appear simultaneously all over Europe. The spirit of the time began in Italy and spread northward, eastward, and westward across the Atlantic; our earliest Renaissance texts in this volume are fourteenth-century Italian, our latest ones seventeenth-century texts from Russia and Mexico.

Again, the film is not amiss in singling out Florence, for Florence throughout the fourteenth century was an extraordinary city. For all its ongoing political intrigue, Renaissance Florence actually was a relatively stable republic governed by a council of representatives rather than by a single tyrannical ruler, and Florentines were proud that at the turn of the fourteenth century they had been able to resist the military encroachments of the Duke of Milan, who was trying to reunite all Italy, calling himself a "new Caesar." During the fourteenth century, Florence replaced Genoa as the center of the European banking system; in the fifteenth century it became the seat of power for noble families such as the Medicis, who were bankers, secular and religious leaders, and patrons of the arts. Florence was the ancestral home of Petrarch and the birthplace of Boccaccio, Machiavelli, and many of the famous painters, sculptors, and architects of the Italian Renaissance. The artists Masaccio, Giotto, Fra Angelico, Botticelli, Leonardo da Vinci, Donatello, Michaelangelo, and Cellini, among many others, were Florentines. Artists such as Raphael who were not born there spoke of pilgrimaging to Florence to "wash their garments in the Arno," the river that flows through the city, meaning that they wished to partake of the Florentine spirit of innovation and discovery. Not every intellectual, political, and artistic movement of the fifteenth century arose in Florence, but Florence attracted, fostered, and encouraged people who were innovative, creative, and inquiring. For Europeans from the fourteenth century onward, Florence was indeed "the new Athens," the center for enlightened political, intellectual, and artistic leadership.

THE AGE OF THE RENAISSANCE

Like almost every term or description invented to try to distinguish a historical and cultural period, the notion of the Renaissance has been surrounded by controversy concerning what it was, when it happened, and even whether it happened at all. Perhaps the most important thing is that many people who actually lived during the centuries we

THE CITY-STATES OF RENAISSANCE ITALY

designate as the Renaissance believed they were intellectually and spiritually freer to look to both the past and the future than their medieval forebears had been. The physical and social worlds beckoned to them, and they welcomed the chance to exercise their curiosity and test their own strengths in those worlds. The dual theme we have chosen to represent the Renaissance, therefore, is Power and Discovery.

Renaissance people thought about themselves in a way that was genuinely new in the history of the European human psyche; they were acutely aware of and interested in their own potential for creative thought and action. For them, there was a great deal more to accomplish than simply to live a Christian life and go to heaven, although they hoped to achieve that end as well. For them, the world was not merely an assemblage of temptations, but an arena that was both wonderful in its own right and, like the human soul, a legitimate theater for exploration. In reviving the old and in creating and discovering the new, in looking more toward the temporal world and its pleasures, people also inevitably became more interested in and indulgent toward human power. The hero most interesting to the Renaissance intellectual was not the Christian soul making its way toward the heavenly city; instead, it was the man—rarely the woman—who operated from a power base in the secular city and exercised his abilities to manipulate, control, and theorize about all manner of materials, people, enterprises, and kingdoms. In an early expression of this new interest, Coluccio Salutati, the Chancellor of Florence in the 1390s, exhorted in a letter a friend who feared the growing secularization of society,

> Do not believe, my friend, that to flee the crowd, to avoid the sight of beautiful things, to shut one's self up in a cloister, is the way to perfection. In fleeing the world, you may topple down from heaven to earth, whereas I, remaining among earthly things, shall be able to lift my heart securely up to heaven. In striving and working, in caring for your family, your friends, your city which comprises all, you cannot but follow the right way to please God.

During the Renaissance, the world Salutati recommended so heartily to his friend seemed to grow larger and more interesting all the time. It is still astonishing to consider the great changes occurring in different arenas from the fourteenth through the seventeenth centuries—changes in the visual arts, politics, science, religion, navigation, geographical exploration, and literature that would alter radically the world St. Augustine, Dante, and Boccaccio once knew.

We begin discussing particular facets of the Renaissance with the visual arts because the word *Renaissance,* which means *rebirth,* was originally applied to the period in 1550 by Giorgio Vasari, often called the first art historian. Vasari spoke of how the painters and sculptors of his own time were recovering classical aesthetics and techniques and rediscovering ways to see and to depict nature accurately. Art, he contended, had been debased ever since the fall of Rome, but his contemporaries might now rejoice to "follow the progress of her second birth to the high perfection which she has once more attained in these her days." In keeping with a growing interest in the secular world, Vasari's contemporaries and succeeding generations were indeed recovering ways to represent nature in realistic proportion, and they were learning once again to pay attention, as classical sculptors had, to the individual features and the emotional state of the human subject. The artists of the fifteenth century were not just recovering techniques, but also discovering how to do things classical artists had not been able to do. For example, they learned to work with perspective on two-dimensional surfaces to create the illusion of three-dimensional space with more and more accuracy. Moreover, they experimented boldly with chiaroscuro, the play of light and shadow upon solid surfaces, a realistic technique that lent flashes and shadings of drama and emotion to a painted scene.

As technique and subject matter changed for artists during the Renaissance, so did the individual person's pride in creation. During the Middle Ages, most people thought of painting and sculpture as crafts rather than as arts. Art was often created by people in guilds or religious orders, and many artists remained as anonymous as the individual weavers in a weaving shop. Many artists of the Middle Ages are known simply as the artist or master of such-and-such a town or religious community, as the collective weavers, seamstresses, carvers, sculptors, or illuminators of a particular town or court where an art work originated. During the Renaissance, male artists gradually began to claim more individual recognition; sometimes they even became secular heroes. Benvenuto Cellini may have been an exceptionally self-conscious and self-congratulatory artist, but his account of his casting of Perseus illustrates not only the Renaissance interest in classical themes and techniques but also the way the Renaissance understood talent and personality as a means to power in a temporal world.

The major political trend across Europe during the Renaissance was a gradual turning away from European peoples' conception of themselves as a population loosely united, whether as tribal peoples roughly converted and united under the Papacy or under the Holy Roman Empire, or as a "Christendom" at war with Arabic "pagans." Instead, Europeans began to think of themselves more and more as having particular national identities. With the exception of Italy, which remained a loose federation of city-states until the nineteenth century, most major European countries during the Renaissance became increasingly nationalistic, drawing diverse tribal and political factions together under charismatic and powerful monarchs. Spain, for example, became a united and intensely Catholic nation under the joint rule of Ferdinand V and Isabella I between 1474 and 1504; in 1492, the fateful year of Columbus's voyage under their aegis, these monarchs oversaw the fall of Granada, the last Moorish stronghold in Europe, and banished all Jews who would not convert to Christianity. Later, under Charles I (r. 1516–1556), Spain enjoyed a Golden Age when its economy was greatly enriched by the wealth of the Americas; arts and intellectual life flourished under his patronage. England, after enduring decades of factional wars, found a new central stability under the Tudor monarchs, shakily at first under the popular Henry VIII, who reigned from 1509 to 1547, and then spectacularly under his daughter Elizabeth I, queen from 1558 until 1603. During her reign, the English Renaissance reached its apex, both in the flowering of the arts and intellectual enterprises and in overseas expansion. Paradoxically, during these centuries of growing nationalism, intellectuals and artists from all parts of Europe were feeling a growing continuity with one another, in part because the printing press had made ideas so easy to pass along. But the main political thrust of the Renaissance was toward European populations defining themselves more sharply in terms of political boundaries and national identities, becoming more clearly focused on secular issues. As the Papacy played less and less of a role in European politics, events were often seen as being shaped by particularly strong lay personalities.

In the widest scope, almost all of our texts in these two volumes touch upon politics, but none more centrally than the writings of Machiavelli (1469–1527), who with *The Prince* became the first recorded political theorist to take an uncompromisingly realistic view of European questions of power, authority, and administration. Which "prince" wins in the secular arena, and how and why, are his themes, as he defines the rules of the new game of power politics not only for his time, but for our own as well. Prospero's perfidious brother Antonio and the scheming Sebastian of *The Tempest* have read well in Machiavelli's book; Prospero initially loses his dukedom because he has neglected its lessons about doing whatever is necessary to remain in power. *Don Quixote* can be read as a kind of conversation with Machiavelli, as it initially appears to recommend to us a hard-eyed Machiavellian view of the world, and then leaves us, finally, hopelessly in love with the Don and his idealism, his imagination, and his gallant morality. But we see Machiavellian attitudes most chillingly at work, perhaps, in two nonfictional texts here, the selections from Columbus's log and the accounts of the conquest of Mexico.

The Renaissance lies at the beginning of an ongoing era of great scientific advancement, as more and more people dared to rely on observation and experiment instead of received opinion on matters ranging from the movements of the stars to the circulation of blood through the bodies of living creatures. In about 1512, Copernicus published his theory that Pythagoreans of the fifth century B.C.E. had been right in asserting that the sun rather than the earth is at the center of the solar system. By 1632, Galileo's observations with a telescope confirmed that theory, demolishing the comfortable concept of a human earth encircled obediently by lesser spheres, an earth at the center of God's eye as it was thought to be at the center of the cosmic system.

Like Renaissance artists, Renaissance scientists were paying closer attention to the human body. For fifteen hundred years, people concerned with the structure and workings of the body had depended not upon autopsies and dissection of corpses for their knowledge of anatomy and physiology, but rather upon the writings of the Greek physician Galen (c. 130–200) who, because dissection of the human body was forbidden in his day as well, had relied upon his observations of the bodies of pigs and monkeys. Andrew Vesalius (1514–1564) published the first medical diagrams of the systems of the human body that were not mere "zodiac man" charts showing which organs were ruled by which astrological signs, but were instead based upon dissection of human cadavers. William Harvey (1578–1657) disproved Galen's theory that the heart was a sort of furnace dispensing heat to the body. Instead, he demonstrated that the heart was a pump that kept blood recycling through the circulatory system. All these were valuable discoveries, but as healers concentrated more upon anatomical structures and dissection of the dead, the attendance upon people who were ill or in pain began to become more mechanical and dominated by educated men.

Probably the single most influential inventions of the Renaissance lay not in pure science, but in technology. In the 1430s, Johannes Gutenberg devised the movable type that would make possible the wide dissemination of everything from scripture to love poems, travelers' tales, revolutionary political and scientific theories, and circulars advertising exhibitions of two-headed calves, sea serpents, and captive people native to the Western Hemisphere. By 1500, more than nine million books had been printed on the presses of Europe. Gutenberg printed his Bible in 1455, opening God's word to the scrutiny of many individuals; the greater availability of scholarly materials eased the work of Martin Luther and others in translating the Bible from Hebrew and Greek texts into vernacular languages. The printing press played a large part in the spread of humanist studies in general, but its impact on the Protestant reformation in particular was enormous. A person who had a copy of the scriptures available to be examined at leisure was much more likely to dispute received interpretations of texts than if he or she were merely receiving the Bible orally through a priest.

The growing interest in scientific discovery and technological innovation is found in Marlowe's *Doctor Faustus* (1592–1593), whose hero, able to be granted any wish, initially asks Mephistophilis to show him the secrets of the celestial spheres. It is illustrated in the exchange of letters between Kepler and Galileo, mirrored in the imagery of many of the lyric poems, and presented with full panoply in Bacon's *New Atlantis,* where Bacon constructs a utopia centered around a bureaucratically organized and administered research institution complete with its own version of corporate spies.

If the writers and artists of the Renaissance were reaching into a classical past for their aesthetics and subjects, religious reformers such as John Wyclif (1328–1384), Jan Hus (c. 1370–1415), Martin Luther (1483–1546), and John Calvin (1509–1564) believed they were looking back toward the days of the apostles to try to recover a simpler and more immediate Christian faith than the vast, complex, and often corrupt machineries of the Roman Catholic Church. The Protestant sects that emerged during the Renaissance all believed in principles that, in essence, are very much in the spirit of the times, for they

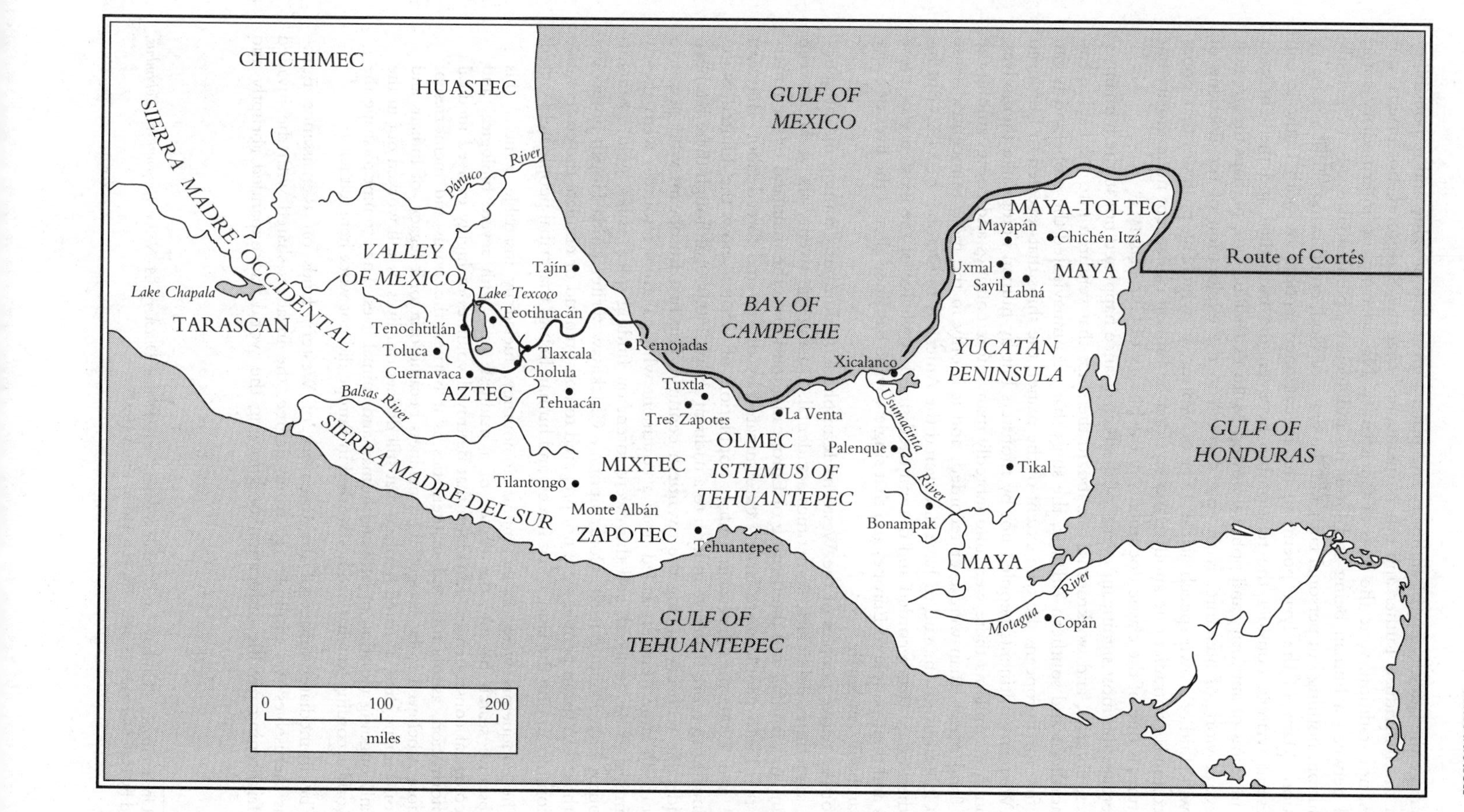

MESOAMERICA IN 1519–1520

encourage the questioning of authority and place a great deal of value and responsibility upon the individual. Luther and others maintained that the Scriptures, not priests, nor popes, nor tradition, were the basis of Christianity. No doctrine, no intermediary could stand between a human being and God; no indulgences, penitential deeds, or priestly absolution, nothing but personal faith and the grace of God, could bring about a person's salvation. Many of the lyric poems in the Renaissance section, by both Catholic and Protestant writers, consider the relationship between the individual and the Christian God in terms of authority and political power. Milton's *Paradise Lost,* perhaps the greatest Protestant work of literature, is an epic devoted to the exploration of the doctrine of free will. Luther's own speech at the Diet of Worms, in which he professes that popes and counsels contradict one another and says that he himself can accept no authority but scripture, is one of the classic documents in the history of Christianity.

Perhaps the most significant events of the Renaissance happened not in the humanists' studies, libraries, and workrooms, but aboard the ships that ventured into the Pacific and the northern and southern Atlantic, the ships that circumnavigated the globe and began to define for Europeans the true extent of the planet, the ships that revealed to European eyes Western continents peopled not by monsters but by human beings like themselves. Throughout millenia there were undoubtedly many more comings and goings among the great land masses than were ever recorded, and it is only in the most Eurocentric sense that Columbus can be said to have discovered the Americas in October of 1492. But his was the voyage that recorded and disseminated sure knowledge of the existence of those lands and their people to Europe, and that single voyage has since altered the lives of every human being on Earth.

For the native peoples of the Western Hemisphere, Columbus's coming meant genocide, sometimes deliberate, sometimes accidental. During the twenty-six years between Columbus's landfall and the turning of European attention to the mainland of the Americas, the Taino people were largely exterminated by disease and forced labor. Between 1492 and 1900, the American Indian population of what is now the United States declined from more than five million to a nadir of about 250,000, although there has been considerable recovery during the twentieth century. The first Europeans who began to colonize in large numbers sailed from a continent whose natural resources were already beginning to be depleted, and they were intent on finding spices, silks, gold, fountains of youth, even Paradise itself. Contemporary Chickasaw writer Linda Hogan points out that those European people were not prepared to comprehend or emulate the cooperative relationship among the land, spirit forces, and human beings that tribal people held sacred:

> The conquerors were on an impossible journey, fueled by insatiable wants . . . this obsessive search became the center of a madness, one with severe biological and ecological consequences, a madness that destroyed volumes of highly evolved medical information, astronomy, and mathematics as it burned the words and memories of those it believed to be savages. This madness became our joint legacy, of Indians and non-Indians alike, a shared heritage that still defines our lives, is still worked out in the daily ongoing violation of land and human and animal lives. The attempt to shape the world according to what had not worked in Europe did not work here, either.[1]

The immediate impact of the discovery of Western lands on Renaissance Europeans themselves was multiple. To some degree, the invaders shared with the invaded the frightening psychic dislocation of knowing the world had expanded abruptly and

[1]Linda Hogan, "Journeys and Other Stories," in *Without Discovery: A Native Response to Columbus,* edited by Ray Gonzales (Seattle: Broken Moon Press, 1992).

wildly in size and possibilities; Europe, Africa, and Asia were no longer the only land masses depicted on maps. Corn and chocolate, precious metals and potatoes, beaver and otter fur, quinine, cotton, and tobacco were among the products that would have an enormous impact on European society. But so would American Indian agricultural technology, wilderness survival techniques, styles of fighting, and modes of governance.

The sudden influx of new products such as coffee, sugarcane, and tobacco and the growing need to cultivate them as cash crops in the Americas altered the European economy and led to a dramatic increase in slave labor of American Indians and African tribal peoples. Europeans had a vast new theater to act upon and theorize about, and little sense of responsibility about how to conduct themselves in that vastness.

At the very beginning of contact between Europe and the Americas, the moral consequences of colonization were not especially troubling to most Europeans; Columbus himself in the *Diarios* speaks easily at one moment of the generosity and gentleness of the Taino people, and then at the next of how their temperament and minimal technology of warfare will make it easy to enslave them. Issues surrounding exploration and colonization and the wielding of power abroad soon became important, and appear in many of our selections. Metaphors of exploration and navigation abound, especially in the love poetry of the Renaissance. European culture, despite the presence of powerful women such as Queen Isabella of Spain and Queen Elizabeth I of England, defined itself as male and the newly discovered world as female. Explorers described American territory in very sexual terms, as "virgin" and "unhusbanded"—that is, not penetrated by European presence or pierced by metal ax or plow. Woman was to man as the colonies were to the Europeans; they believed she was made for him. Hence, Donne's mistress' breasts are "hemispheres" where he is free to roam, and Marvell conducts a leisurely courtship with his reluctant lover that spans the ages and the globe, the area between the Humber and the Ganges at the service of their relationship, suggesting that he will woo her and at last make love to her in wonderfully slow and rich and sensuous time.

Other writers thought of the New World as Eden or used the Americas and other newly found lands as a way to reflect upon European society. Montaigne asks whether the Europeans who invented Inquisitions and elaborate machineries of torture are not indeed more barbarous than the native Brazilians, whom he is told by reliable sources eat flesh only in a ritual context. Sir Francis Bacon imagines North America to be the lost Atlantis, and the American Indians as debased survivors of its flood; other Atlanteans, he tells us, escaped to found an island civilization that received a special and separate revelation of the divinity of Christ, a civilization that has become a monument to scientific research and exploration as the New Atlanteans secretly cruise around the globe, appropriating ideas and inventions from other cultures. From Mexico City, Sor Juana Inés de la Cruz, one of the first Euro-American writers born in the Western Hemisphere and herself a speaker of Spanish, Latin, and Nahuatl, composes an allegorical play about the conversion of the Mexicans that dares suggest that native people's ways and beliefs may be defensible, even beautiful. Almost every question that might be raised about the ethics of colonization and the effects of colonization upon both the rulers and the ruled is implicitly or explicitly contained in Shakespeare's *The Tempest.*

Renaissance Literature

Much of the great literature of the European Renaissance reflects in one way or another the humanistic values characteristic of the age. *Humanism* is an elastic term, but Renaissance humanists generally embraced certain crucial ideas, primarily the idea that human beings are the central and most fascinating components of creation. They considered people to have a great deal of autonomy and the ability to determine their own fate, and had faith in the perfectability of human societies and individual people. Finally, these humanists tended to accept the whole of an entity rather than one part over another. Soul *and* body; ancient *and* modern culture; public *and* private life; the sacred *and* the secular arenas—all were thought important.

These values are reflected in the Renaissance treatment of the most primeval of literary forms, the epic, which traditionally expresses the ethos of the age in which it is written. That genre is represented here by two selections. John Milton's *Paradise Lost* pays constant homage to his classical predecessors and centers upon that favorite topic of humanists, the free will of human beings. It also paints intimate portraits of its protagonists, revealing the individual personalities and capturing the private moments of Adam and Eve and the very human Satan. In Cervantes' *Don Quixote,* the author explores in complex ways the conflict between the idealism of the Don's beloved medieval romances and the modern interest in a more pragmatic and here-and-now world.

Given the age's interest in the individual, it is quite appropriate that the genre we call the essay emerged during the Renaissance. Its inventor, Michel de Montaigne of France, began by preparing lists of quotations from his reading, accompanied by his personal annotations; gradually, the annotations came to outweigh the quotations and developed into the essay. Montaigne speaks familiarly to us as he makes his relaxed, witty observations. He confides particulars about his personal life, tells us anecdotes, and cites the observations of his friends while he circles loosely around a central subject. Although he is often self-deprecating, his Renaissance assumption is clearly that his private life is interesting and significant and that his opinions matter.

Taking into account the Renaissance's interest in recovering classical texts, its preoccupation with strong individuals, and its new delight in the details of social life, it also seems natural that this age should have seen a new flowering of drama, in both tragic and comic modes, for the first time since ancient Greece. Many Greek and Roman playwrights ranging from Aeschylus to Plautus were recovered and restored to the public via the printing press during the Renaissance; the medieval folk drama, with its cosmic scope, rousing comic characters, and the homely personal touches given to the lives of saints and scriptural figures, continued to influence Renaissance drama as well. Two nations in particular, Spain and England, enjoyed golden ages of the stage during the sixteenth and seventeenth centuries. Moreover, during the Renaissance—thanks largely to Italian ingenuity—the mechanics of mounting theatrical productions grew far more sophisticated. Now Faust's complex personality could gradually reveal itself not on a bare stage, but in a credible humanist's study, and Prospero's powers could call up an astonishing variety of special effects. Charismatic male characters claiming great personal power for themselves dominate three of our four Renaissance plays. Faustus and Prospero turn, respectively, to black and white magic to increase their mastery over the world, although Faustus seems not to know what to do with power once he has it and Prospero vows to abandon his once events in his sphere have been set aright. Many modern readers will find Tirso de Molina's account of Don Juan and his misuse of his very human powers a far more frightening play. The chilling story of Tirso's philanderer makes it clear that womanizing and rape are not about love but rather about the urge to dominate and the lust for sheer experience. This Don Juan is aided in his sexual exploits by the patriarchal establishment until his power becomes so threatening that the king and the male nobility, living and dead, must join to halt his excesses. Even so, Don Juan goes to his death reveling in the conquests he has dared to make. In our fourth sample of Renaissance drama, the prelude to Sor Juana's *The Divine Narcissus,* the action is allegorical, and what is represented is one religion and people asserting dominion over another; it is interesting to observe the genders Sor Juana attributes to these allegorical figures. The bloody-minded Zeal is male, and gentle Christian Religion is female; the native population is represented by a couple, the male Occident and the female America, who seem equal in status. Sor Juana may be describing more than issues of colonial power between states in her dramatic prologue.

The great vehicle for the expression of Renaissance individuality, even more than the drama or the essay, is the lyric, and Francis Petrarch's name dominated the genre for nearly three hundred years of Renaissance poetry. Drawing from the courtly love tradition of the medieval troubadours and the poems of Dante's *Vita Nuova,* writing in sonnets and other short lyric forms, Petrarch chronicled intimately his shifting emotions toward life, art, and, above all, love, creating in his Laura a secular saint. The most minute details of their relationship, the smallest alteration in his emotional temperature, all are significant as Petrarch addresses issues of power and powerlessness in the sexual arena. Petrarch set the standard for the Renaissance lyric's typical mixture of sensuality and idealism. Like Petrarch, other poets of the Renaissance often wrote of sexual love in terms of divine adoration and describe religious experience in sexual terms. Inevitably, poets began to critique the idealizing tendency of the Petrarchan tradition in poems such as Shakespeare's sonnet 130, which begins by stating categorically "My mistress' eyes are nothing like the sun."

Many of our Renaissance lyric poets, playwrights, and essayists raise issues of gender and unequal power. The Renaissance, like many periods traditionally considered to have been progressive, was a time when most women were actually more repressed than in the ages preceding and following. Between the thirteenth and the seventeenth century, millions of women were executed as witches; some estimates run as high as nine million. During these centuries, women were being excluded from particular crafts and trades and from the practice of midwifery and healing, occupations they had once been permitted to follow. The feistiness of a Marguerite de Navarre or a Sor Juana are rarely recorded in the Renaissance; when Miranda tries to tell Prospero something and he snaps at her that his "foot" should not presume to be his tutor, that is a typical Renaissance moment between the sexes. In Bacon's *New Atlantis,* the patriarchs are publicly honored for prolific fatherhood while the mothers who bore the children watch the ceremonies from curtained niches; Milton's Adam is to live "for God only" while his wife Eve is to live for "God in him," the divine spark in her earthly lord's being. Few women characters in our Renaissance texts are fully realized. Social historian Margaret King in her book on Renaissance women speaks of "an obdurate substratum of Renaissance thinking about women: their role is to reproduce, their home is their fortress and their prison, their destiny is endless work with needle and spindle." The texts reflect that obdurance. Except for a few extraordinary figures such as Elizabeth I, it seems accurate to say that European women did not get to experience a Renaissance.

Our World Context selections for the Renaissance come from opposite ends of the globe and represent two cultures that were at their height when the European Renaissance was taking place. The peoples of Mexico were vulnerable to exploration, domination, and destruction; the Chinese Empire, on the other hand, was then relatively safe from Western imperialism, and was exploring India and Africa in its own right. Our Aztec materials give a sense of the complexity of the culture of preconquest Mexico, so often typified in European documents only as a culture that practiced human sacrifice. But our texts speak as well of a beautiful city on a lake, of causeways and great temples, of flower-sellers and poets, marketplaces and cornfields. We present both Aztec and European voices describing the terrible realities of Spanish conquest and colonization. Ming Dynasty China, with its elaborate bureaucratic government and its highly developed arts of the novel, drama, architecture, painting, and ceramics, had just begun to be accessible to a few European merchants and Dominican and Franciscan missionaries when Wu Ch'êng-ên wrote. *Monkey,* also known as *The Western Journey,* provides a small glimpse of that civilization.

PETRARCH'S *CANZONIERE* AND "ASCENT OF MT. VENTOUX"; MARLOWE'S *DOCTOR FAUSTUS*

The Renaissance story we focus upon is the story of how people who seek empowerment choose among the different sources of authority available to them. As the secular world becomes more and more attractive to people during the Renaissance, people seek empowerment in many different theaters of action: within the church, at court, in government, within a sexual relationship, in the home, in the act of colonizing foreign lands. Many of these texts concern people who forsake an accepted authority—Aristotelian logic, Pauline thought, or Christian humanism, for example—for a suppressed authority such as feminism, magic, personal experience, or romantic love. In a number of these texts, the central action is people's struggle to reconcile the human dependence upon authority with the equally human urge to overthrow it.

The writer of our first representative text, Petrarch (1304–1374), is also our earliest Renaissance writer. Petrarch was a Renaissance man in the sense we often use that term today, a person of wide-ranging secular interests; besides being a minor cleric, a poet, and a scholarly editor and translator, he played the lute, fished, gardened, and climbed mountains. Our first text is his famous letter to his friend Dionisio Da Borga San Sepolchro describing how he climbed Mount Ventoux with his brother in about 1336. To compare this account of mountain climbing with Dante's ascents of the "little hill" in *The Inferno* or of Mount Purgatory in *The Purgatorio* swiftly suggests the contrast between the Middle Ages and the Renaissance. In the first place, although Petrarch's mountain certainly acquires symbolic overtones in the course of his account, it is above all an actual and quite formidable peak in the French Alps made of real rock.

Second, Petrarch, who has longed to climb that mountain since he was a child, tells us he wants to do so not because it is in his path or because the ascent promises to yield any particular reward, but because of "the wish to see what so great a height had to offer," because it is there and he is curious. This is not only the first recorded Western expression of the desire to climb mountains for the sheer sake of doing so, it is a genuinely fresh way for literate Europeans to think about the physical world and people's place in it. The authority of personal impulse and desire, a very Renaissance sort of authority, moves Petrarch to an act that he is careful to explain will be viewed by others as silly, unusual, and unnecessary.

Third, in true Renaissance style, this adventure is saturated with appeals to classical authorities, not all of them the Christian humanist's "baptized classics," that is, Greek or Latin texts so impeccably moral or spiritual that they could easily pass for Christian. Petrarch is impelled to make the climb he has dreamed of after he reads Livy's description of Philip of Macedon climbing a Balkan peak: once atop Ventoux, the proud Petrarch pulls out his pocket edition of Saint Augustine's *Confessions* and rebukes himself for his vanity.

The contention between secular and sacred, between public authority and private feeling, also marks Petrarch's most famous work, the *Canzoniere* (1330–1374), his poems written in Italian about his "pure" love for Laura, a woman who was probably real and probably married and who Petrarch tells us died in the plague that swept Europe almost twenty-one years to the day after he first laid eyes upon her. Taken together, these poems record his wavering between his sense of his own sinfulness and the siren call of all that is lovely and tragically mortal. Living and dead, Laura's appeal is rather different from that of Dante's Beatrice. Although, like Beatrice, Laura comes to represent excellence, inspiration, and perfection, her earthly beauty is never forgotten, and its power to elate and torment Petrarch persists even in the poems written after her death.

Our other representative text, Christopher Marlowe's *Doctor Faustus,* is also one of our latest Renaissance texts. Here is another story of contending authorities, but nearly three hundred years separate Petrarch from Marlowe. Petrarch chronicled his guilty joy in the triumph he felt at conquering a mountain and his joyous guilt in his forbidden love for Laura. These emotions seem tame in comparison to Faustus' all-out determination to ascend to the heights of the universe and to take for his lover the most beautiful mortal in all human history, to claim power through experience, even if the price be eternal damnation. In the early scenes Faustus, like many Renaissance thinkers, rejects in turn the authority of each of the medieval scholastic disciplines of logic, medicine, law, and theology, mocking their dry limitations. As he sees it, the end of logic is only to dispute well, not the gaining of infinite power. The object of medicine is only to heal the body, and studying it will not yield him the secret of immortality. The law is too "servile and illiberal," designed only to cramp people's style and keep them in their places, and theology appears to Faustus to offer only a grim world view in which people cannot avoid sin and thus are almost certainly damned. So Faustus, like Marlowe and like a good many of his contemporaries, turns to "magick" as the field that best promises to accommodate his apparently boundless human potential and thirst for experience. But even after Faustus has squandered his opportunities and the devil has come to claim his due, Faustus' defiant seeking seems far nobler than the "wise" man the moralizing chorus celebrates, the man who would never dare to try to penetrate the secrets of the universe, and who is content "only . . . to wonder at unlawful things."

For all the differences in degree between Petrarch's version of his own experiences and Marlowe's story of Faustus, both texts celebrate the physical world, assume books and learning as a natural component of any civilized life, and grant authority to the personal and the idiosyncratic desire to explore and test the limits of the universe and the self.

Suggested Readings

Helpful general introductions to the Renaissance include E. M. W. Tilyard's *The Elizabethan World Picture* (1946), J. H. Plumb's *The Renaissance* (1961), and Paul Oscar Kristeller's *Renaissance Thought: The Classic, Scholastic, and Humanist Strains* (1961). Daniel J. Boorstin's *The Discoverers* (1983) is a good survey of Renaissance exploration and scientific discovery for the lay reader. Margaret L. King's *Women of the Renaissance* (1991) synthesizes much of what is known about the status and roles of women in Renaissance Europe. Mary Beth Rose's *Women in the Middle Ages and the Renaissance* (1986) also explores the place of women in the Renaissance.

REPRESENTATIVE TEXTS

FRANCESCO PETRARCH

[1304–1374]

Although only forty years separate Francesco Petrarch from his countryman Dante, Petrarch is often described as the first Renaissance man, partly because of the breadth of his interests. Even more than Dante, he was multitalented: a poet in both his native Italian and in Latin, a classical scholar who recovered and edited manuscripts of Cicero and Livy and wrote the biographies of a number of Roman heroes, an unofficial diplomat who gave advice to the Doge of Venice and the Holy Roman Emperor, a traveler who knew the Rhineland, the Netherlands, and most of France and Italy, a landscape gardener, a fisherman, a lutanist, and a climber of mountains. But more than the multiplicity of his interests, the shape those interests took marks him as a Renaissance figure. Observing at close hand the corruption of the Papal court in Avignon, Petrarch grew concerned with how a person might learn to lead a moral life through guidance and pursuits that lay beyond as well as within the Church, specifically through the study of the pre-Christian writers of Greece and Rome and through one's own practice of arts and letters. Petrarch does not simply make his humanistic studies the handmaidens of Christian doctrine. His work grants this world its own value and does not scorn the pleasures and the beauty it offers. He pays a highly self-conscious attention to the drama of his own personal life as a lover, scholar, and aspiring man of letters.

Life

Petrarch was born on July 20, 1304, "on a Monday, at dawn," as he tells us in his autobiography. His birthplace was Arezzo, a small town in Tuscany. Like Dante's, Petrarch's parents, Pietro Petrarca and Elleta Canigiani, had been exiled from Florence in 1301 for being on the wrong side of one of the many factional disputes that troubled the city, although whether Dante's and Petrarch's families were exiled over the same incident is not known. Although Petrarch was never even to visit Florence for any length of time, that urban center of Renaissance culture always claimed to be his home. In truth, the fact that Petrarch knew no single stable home from very early childhood on may have helped to make him the universally-minded, pan-European figure he became.

While Petrarch was still a child, his lawyer father moved the family first to Incisa and then to Pisa in Italy before settling in southern France in the Provençal city of Avignon in 1312, when Petrarch was eight. In 1309, Pope Clement V, pressured by the increasingly powerful French monarchy to center the Catholic Church in France rather than in Rome, had moved the Papacy to Avignon. The small city was overcrowded because of the presence of the Papal court, and Petrarch was taken to live with his mother and younger brother Gherardo in the little village of Carpentras, fifteen miles to the northeast. There followed four idyllic years when he studied grammar, logic, and rhetoric under a Tuscan schoolmaster, read the Cicero and Virgil he learned early to love, and roamed the beautiful Provençal countryside with Gherardo, to whom he would always remain close.

This childhood that Petrarch remembered as a dreamy time of security and peace, of "freedom in the town and . . . silence in the countryside" came to an end when he turned twelve and his father sent him southeast to Montpellier to begin his studies for the law, the profession his father chose for him. But even in his early teens it was clear that the law was not to be Petrarch's real vocation, and he neglected his studies to read the Latin classics in secret. His father, visiting him at school, discovered his hidden hoard of books and burned them, but the boy's grief made him relent in time to save Virgil and Cicero from the flames. Petrarch also suffered his first profound experience of human loss at Montpellier in 1319 when his mother died; his earliest surviving poem is an elegy to her written in Virgilian hexameters.

At the age of sixteen, in 1320, he was sent to the University of Bologna, then the leading European center for legal studies, where he remained for the next six years. In his autobiographical *Letter to Posterity* (c. 1373), Petrarch tells us that although he revered the law for its power and its roots in Roman antiquity, he thought its practitioners corrupt, and says, "I hated the idea of learning an art which I would not practice dishonestly, and could hardly hope to practice otherwise."

At his father's death in 1326, the twenty-two year old was suddenly free to do as he pleased, and for the next four years he moved in Avignon's faster social circles. He and Gherardo, living the life of young fops, were preoccupied with the latest styles in fancy gowns and shoes and fashionable entertainment; they even hesitated to go outside in windy weather for fear of mussing their modishly curled hair. By 1330, most of their estate had been squandered, and Petrarch took minor orders in the Church, accepting a post as private chaplain to Cardinal Giovanni Colonna, who respected Petrarch's classical learning and allowed him time for study. Petrarch would remain attached to Colonna's household until 1348. This change to a steadier life may well have been precipitated not only by personal finances, but by Petrarch's first glimpse of the woman he calls Laura. He first saw her in the Church of Saint Claire in Avignon on April 6, 1327, and he was anxious to be worthy of her, however unattainable she might be.

Who Laura was, whether she was married, how well she and Petrarch knew one another, what kept them from becoming lovers, even whether she was an actual person rather than an idealized composite woman—these are all questions for which scholars have no definitive answers. We know Laura only from the *Canzoniere* (*The Songbook*, c. 1330–1374), the collection of 366 Italian lyrics that celebrate her in life and in death. Petrarch sometimes dismissed these vernacular poems as "bagatelles," or trifles, but he kept writing and reworking them from the 1330s until his own death in 1374, and it is for these poems rather than for his more ambitious Latin works that Petrarch is best remembered.

From 1330 on, Petrarch continued to hold minor clerical offices that left him time for writing, editing, and scholarship; throughout his life he several times declined higher posts that would interfere with his studies. Despite his love for Laura, Petrarch fathered at least two children by an unknown woman; in time, he had them declared legitimate. In 1337, after his first trip to Rome, he established a residence at Vaucluse, a small town near Avignon where he would reside off and on for the next twenty years, attempting to live a life of disciplined simplicity. About this time Petrarch began what he thought would be his major work, an epic poem on the Roman general Scipio Africanus; he believed that if he were to be the fit heir of Virgil and Dante, he would have to produce an epic poem, for epics were what the greatest poets wrote. Petrarch's *Africa* is seldom read today, but in 1341 that work-in-progress earned him simultaneous bids from both Paris and Rome to crown him as poet laureate. In accord with his devotion to classical ideals he chose Rome, and in the month of April, always a significant season for him, Petrarch was crowned on the Capitoline Hill in a ceremony that seemed to affirm the growing interest of many citizens in newly revering the classical heritage of arts and letters.

In 1343, Petrarch's brother Gherardo became a Carthusian monk; Petrarch was both admiring and somewhat chagrined, for he had never felt similarly able to renounce the world. Five years later, in 1348, while he was traveling in Parma, Petrarch received news of Laura's death on April 6, the anniversary of their meeting. Both of these events affected him deeply, and probably influenced his *Secretum* (*The Secret*) begun in 1342, a work in the form of a dialogue between Petrarch and Saint Augustine. In it, he explores the problems of reconciling his Christianity with his keen appetite for worldly fame and his love for Laura and for literature written by pagan authors.

Petrarch returned to Rome in 1350 for the Papal Jubilee, and on his way he stopped in Florence to meet Boccaccio. In the following year, the Pope begged Petrarch to return to Avignon to work for the Curia, while at the same time Boccaccio entreated him to accept a professorship at the University in Florence, promising to restore the family property that had been seized. Petrarch chose to go to Avignon, but he soon regretted that decision, given the "seething, obscene, terrible" corruption he observed in the "New Babylon" of the French Papacy, corruption he lambasted in a series of writings titled *Letters without a Name*. Between 1353 and 1361 he lived largely in Milan under the patronage of Giovanni Visconti, performing minor diplomatic missions, writing and studying, and producing a number of pleas for peace among the fractious Italian cities and states. In 1361 he moved to Padua to escape a new outbreak of the plague in which his son and a number of close friends died, and for the remainder of his life he used Padua and Venice as his bases for travel and study. His patron in Padua, Francesco de Carrerra, gave him a plot of land south of Padua in the Eugenaean Hills, and there Petrarch built a villa where he retired in 1370. He continued to work on the *Canzoniere* and other pieces up until his death, which came on the night before his seventieth birthday, July 19, 1374.

Work

We present here samples of Petrarch's prose and poetry. His letter to his friend Dionisio Da Borga San Sepolchro, describing his ascent of Mont Ventoux ("Windy Mountain") in about 1336 in company with his brother Gherardo, suggests his Renaissance sensibilities. First, in this letter Petrarch gives us a world that is quite solid and material. To be sure, Petrarch fashions an allegory out of the ascent, contrasting, for example, the climbing styles of himself and his more determined brother: Gherardo climbs as vertically as possible, choosing the steeper but shorter path, while Petrarch makes his circuitous way to the top, ultimately wearying himself more. Petrarch makes the inevitable comparison between climbing the mountain and attaining "the blessed life" through spiritual discipline. But this mountain is a genuine peak in the French Alps, as opposed to Dante's wholly symbolic Mount Purgatory. Mont Ventoux is made of real rock; real shepherds dwell in its foothills, and Petrarch does not let us forget that he is describing with relish an actual physical feat.

Second, Petrarch makes this climb he has dreamed of since childhood not because he thinks any spiritual, military, or scientific purpose will be served, but because of "the wish to see what so great a height had to offer"—in other words, because it is there. Petrarch's is the first recorded Western expression of the desire to climb a mountain for the sheer sake of doing so, and an early example of the Renaissance European's zest for discovery and adventure. Private impulse and personal desire are for Petrarch valid reasons for undertaking a project others might deem silly, reckless, or unnecessary.

Third, even this vigorous outdoor excursion is saturated with and partly determined by appeals to both classical and Christian authority; Petrarch is presenting himself here equally as an alpinist and as a Christian humanist. He makes plans to climb the peak after reading a passage in Livy describing Philip of Macedon ascending Mount Haemus in the Balkans and surveying two seas at once from that summit. In the course of the letter, Petrarch casually alludes to many other classical authors, texts, and historical figures, confident his readers will not have to strain to catch his allusions. Finally, once atop Mont Ventoux, Petrarch pulls his copy of St. Augustine's *Confessions* out of his pocket and reproaches himself for taking such delight and pride in a physical feat; St. Augustine is the voice of conscience that impels him to vow to give up such worldly vanity. But it is very like the moment in the *The Tempest* when Prospero, who has shown us so many rich wonders, vows to drown his book and meditate upon his death. Petrarch has evoked already the thrill of ascending those windy heights; the appeal of the physical world has already been thoroughly set forth, and cannot wholly be called back.

The tug of war in the human heart between contending authorities that is our Renaissance paradigm also marks Petrarch's most famous work, the *Canzoniere*, the Italian lyrics in honor of Laura that occupied him from his twenties until his death. These poems borrow their form and their themes from the earlier medieval poetry of courtly love. Petrarch was not the first to discover the sonnet form, nor the first to write in Italian rather than in Latin, and certainly he was not the first to make an unattainable beloved the central image of a body of poems, but he was the first to show others how supple the sonnet form could be, and how richly suited to poetry the Italian language might be in the hands of a master. In a manner that almost seems to anticipate the romantic writers of centuries to come, Petrarch brings his own personality to the fore, insisting upon writing in his own name, preserving and revising his manuscripts, and keeping a poetic record of the minutely detailed shifts in his emotions and physical sensations and the contrasts between the outer world and his own inner state.

In sonnet 164 of the *Canzoniere*, the night world may lie in halcyon calm, but Petrarch's inner landscape is quite different:

> But I, I wake and brood, rage, weep, my eyes
> Always behold my love, my foe, my pain.
> I *am* a war. Here wrath and sorrow reign,
> Yet solely in her image I find peace.

Petrarch invents paradoxical similes and metaphors to describe the lady who simultaneously hurts and ennobles him:

> It was her healing hand gave me my wound,
> And where the pure and living spring wells forth
> I drink at once sweet water, bitter gall . . .

In 148, she is both the source of the love that turns him into a battered victim stumbling dazed through life, and the green laurel tree that sweetly shelters him, takes on his sorrow, and inspires his poems. There is a piquant element of sin and shame in his love for Laura, and yet it is in part through his celebration of her in his poems that Petrarch envisions himself as gaining salvation. Through his words, the world "may better learn her grace / and love her "(333). If he has written of her truly, Petrarch's prayer will be granted, and her spirit will be the watcher at his own deathbed, accompanying him into Paradise.

Although Dante's Beatrice and Petrarch's Laura are related in the sense that they are both the female ideals of male poets, women whose real personalities and histories are nearly unknown to us, Laura is more clearly a living, earthly woman than Beatrice, both in life and in death. Even though, like Beatrice, she represents beauty, purity, and inspiration, Laura's physical presence is always evident, and its power to elate and torment Petrarch persists even after her death. In 292, more than half the sonnet evokes her living appearance so vividly she scarcely seems gone; in other poems she comes, sits by the poet's bed, and carries on conversations with him.

Petrarch's sonnets often seem stale to modern readers because so many writers of love poems who have come after Petrarch have borrowed his themes and techniques. *Petrarchan* has become a pejorative word among critics because Petrarch did what he did so well that writers are still copying him; we are too accustomed in poems and popular song lyrics to catalogues of the wonders of a beloved woman's lips and eyes and voice and hair, to hyperbole and paradox and pledges of undying love. Moreover, it is difficult for any English translation to suggest Petrarch's intricate music; English has far fewer rhyming words than Italian, and if a translator tries to replicate in English Petrarch's rhyme schemes, the result often sounds jangling and unnatural, more like a snappy Gilbert and Sullivan patter song than a sensuous or anguished love lyric. Our translations abandon the elaborate rhyme scheme in hopes of suggesting in English the pace and texture of Petrarch's Italian.

The real delight of the *Canzoniere* sonnets for modern readers, and their most intensely Renaissance quality, lies in the way they form a kind of private psychic and spiritual journal over Petrarch's lifetime. Taken together, they record his wavering among his sense of his own sinfulness, his longing for peace and salvation, his craving for adventure and honor, his pride in the work that signals him the heir of Dante and Virgil, his impassioned response to the call of all that is lovely and mortal, and, above all, his acceptance of his own vacillation. Throughout the *Canzoniere,* Petrarch refuses to come down on any side of all the varied conflicts his life presents to him; he does not pass any final judgment, but he does create for us with power and tenderness the contradictions of the physical and moral world he knew.

Suggested Readings

Morris Bishop's *Petrarch and His World* (1963) is a good critical biography. Marguerite R. Waller's *Petrarch's Poetics and Literary History* (1980) works extensively with the *Canzoniere*. Kenelm Foster's *Petrarch, Poet and Humanist* is a wide-ranging biographical and critical study.

The Ascent of Mount Ventoux

Translated by Mark Musa

Today I climbed the highest mountain in this region, which is not improperly called Ventosum (Windy). The only motive for my ascent was the wish to see what so great a height had to offer. I had had the project in mind for many years, for, as you know, I have lived in these parts from childhood on, having been cast there by the fate which determines human affairs. And so the mountain, which is visible from a great distance, was always before my eyes, and for a long time I planned on doing what I have finally done today. The impulse to make the climb actually took hold of me while I was reading Livy's History of Rome yesterday, and I happened upon the place where Philip of Macedon, the one who waged the war against the Romans, climbed Mount Haemus in Thessaly. From its summit, it was reported that he was able to see two seas, the Adriatic and the Euxine. Whether this is true or false I do not know, for the mountain is too far away, and there is disagreement among the commentators. Pomponius Mela, the cosmographer—not to mention the many others who have talked about this occurrence—accepts the truth of this statement without hesitation while Livy, on the other hand, thinks it false. I, certainly, would not have left the question long in doubt if that mountain had been as easy to explore as this one. But let us drop the matter and return to my mountain here: I thought it proper for a young man in private life to attempt what no one would criticize in an aged king.

When I thought about looking for a companion for the ascent I realized, strangely enough, that hardly any of my friends were suitable—so rarely does one find, even among those most dear to one, the perfect combination of character and purpose. One was too phlegmatic, another too anxious; one too slow, another too hasty; one too sad, another too happy; one too simple, another more sagacious than I would like. I was frightened by the fact that one never spoke while another talked too much; the heavy deliberation of some repelled me as much as the lean incapacity of others. I rejected some for their cold lack of interest and others for their excessive enthusiasm. Such defects as these, however grave, are tolerable enough at home (for charity suffers all things, and friendship rejects no burden), but it is another matter on a journey, where such weaknesses become more serious. So, with only my own pleasure in mind, with great care I looked about weighing the various characteristics of my friends against one another without committing any breach of friendship and silently condemning any trait which might prove to be disagreeable on my journey. And would you believe it? I finally turned to my own family for help and proposed the ascent to my younger brother, the only one I have, and whom you know well. He was delighted beyond measure and gratified by the thought of acting at the same time as a friend as well as a brother.

On the appointed day we left the house and by evening reached Malaucène which lies at the foot of the mountain on the north side. We rested there a day and finally this morning made the ascent with no one except two servants. And it is a most difficult task indeed, for the mountain is a very steep and almost inaccessible mass of rocky terrain. But, as a poet once put it well: 'Remorseless labour conquers all.' The day was long and the air invigorating, our spirits were high and our agile bodies strong, and everything else necessary for such an undertaking helped us on our way. The only difficulty we had to face was the nature of the place itself. We found an old shepherd among the mountain's ridges who tried at great length to discourage us from the ascent, saying that some fifty years before he had, in the same ardour of youth, climbed to the summit and had got nothing from it except fatigue and repentance and torn clothes and scratches from the rocks and briars. Never, according to what he or his friends knew, had anyone ever tried the ascent before or after him. But his counsels merely increased our eagerness to go on, as a young man's mind is usually suspicious of warnings. So the old man, finding his efforts were useless, went along with us a little way and pointed out a steep path among the rocks, continuing to cry out admonitions even after we had left him behind. Having left him with those garments and anything else we thought might prove burdensome to us, we made ready for the ascent and started to climb at a good pace. But, as often happens, fatigue soon followed upon our strenuous effort, and before long we had to rest on some rock. Then we started on again, but more slowly, I especially taking the rocky path at a more modest pace. My brother chose the steepest course straight up the ridge, while I weakly took an easier one which turned along the slopes. And when he called me back showing me the shorter way, I replied that I hoped to find an easier way up on the other side, and that I did not mind taking a longer course if it were not so steep. But this was merely an excuse for my laziness; and when the others had already reached a considerable height I was still wandering in the hollows, and having failed to find an easier means of ascent, I had only lengthened the journey and increased the difficulty of the ascent. Finally I became disgusted with the tedious way I had chosen, and decided to climb straight up. By the time I reached my brother, who had managed to have a good rest while waiting for me, I was tired and irritated. We walked along together for a while, but hardly had we left that rise when I forgot all about the circuitous route I had just taken and again tended to take a lower one. Thus, once again I found myself taking the easy way, the roundabout path of winding hollows, only to find myself soon back in my old difficulty. I was simply putting off the trouble of climbing; but no man's wit can alter the nature of things, and there is no way to reach the heights by going downward. In short, I tell you that I made this same mistake three or more times within a few hours, much to my brother's amusement and my anger.

After being misled in this way a number of times, I finally sat down in a hollow and my thoughts quickly turned from material things to the spiritual, and I said to myself more or less what follows: 'What you have experienced so often today in the ascent of this mountain, certainly happens to you as it does to many others in their journey toward the blessèd life. But this is not so easily perceived by men, for the movements of the body are out in the open while those of the soul are invisible and hidden. The life we call blessèd is to be sought on a high level, and straight is the way that leads to it. Many, also, are the hills that stand in the way that leads to it, and we must ascend from virtue to virtue up glorious steps. At the summit is both the end of our struggles and the goal of our journey's climb. Everyone wishes to reach this goal, but, as Ovid says: "To wish is not enough; you must yearn with ardent eagerness to gain your end." And you certainly both wish and ardently yearn, unless you are deceiving yourself in this matter, as you so often do. What, then, is holding you back? Nothing, surely, except that you take a path which seems at first sight easier leading through low and worldly pleasures. Nevertheless in the end, after long wanderings, you will either have to climb up the steeper path under the burden of labours long deferred to its blessèd culmination, or lie down in the valley of your sins; and—I shudder to think of it!—if the shadow of death finds you there, you will spend an eternal night in constant torment.' These thoughts stimulated my body and mind to a remarkable degree and made me face up to the difficulties which still remained. Oh, that my soul might follow that other road for which I long day and night, even as today I conquered material obstacles by bodily force! And why should it not be far easier: after all, the agile, immortal soul can reach its goal in the twinkling of an eye without intermediate space, while progress today had to be slow because my feeble body was burdened by its heavy members.

One mountain peak, the highest of all, the country people call Filiolus ('Sonny'); why, I do not know, unless by antiphrasis, as is sometimes the case, for the peak in question seems to be the father of all the surrounding ones. At its top is a little level place, and it was there that we could, at last, rest our weary bodies.

My good father, since you have listened to the troubles mounting in the heart of a man who ascends, listen now to the rest of the story, and devote one hour, I pray you, to reviewing the events of my day. At first, because I was not accustomed to the quality of the air and the effect of the wide expanse of view spread out before me, I stood there like a dazed person. I could see the clouds under our feet, and the tales I had read of Athos and Olympus seemed less incredible as I myself was witnessing the very same things from a less famous mountain. I turned my eyes toward Italy, the place to which my heart was most inclined. The great and snow-capped Alps seemed to rise close by, though they were far away—those same Alps through which that fierce enemy of the Roman name once made his way, splitting the rocks, if we can believe the story, by means of vinegar. I sighed, I must admit, for Italian skies which I beheld more with my thought than with my eyes, and an inexpressible longing came over me to see once more my friend and my country, though at the same time I reproached myself for this double weakness which came from a soul not yet up to manly resistance—and yet there were excuses for both my desires, and several excellent authorities could be cited to support me.

Then a new idea came to me, and I started thinking in terms of time rather than space. I thought: 'Today marks ten years since you completed your youthful studies and left Bologna. Oh, eternal God! Oh, immutable wisdom! Think of all the changes in your character these intervening years have seen! I suppress a great deal, for I have not yet reached a safe harbour where I can calmly recall past storms. The time, perhaps, will come when I can review all the experiences of the past in their order saying with the words of your St Augustine: "I wish to recall my foul past and the carnal corruption of my soul, not that I love them, but that I may the more love you, O my God." Much that is dubious and evil still clings to me, but what I once loved, I love no longer. Come now, what am I saying? I still love it, but more moderately. No, not so, but with more shame, with more heaviness of heart. Now, at last, I have told the truth. The fact is I love, but I love what I long not to love, what I would like to hate. Though I hate to do so, though constrained, though sad and sorrowing, I love none the less, and I feel in my miserable self the meaning of the well-known words: "I will hate if I can; if not, I will love against my will!" Not three years have passed since that perverse and wicked desire which had me in tight hold and held undisputed sway in my heart began to discover a rebellious opponent who was no longer willing to yield in obedience. These two adversaries have joined in close combat for supremacy, and for a long time now a gruelling war, the outcome of which is still doubtful, has been waging in the field of my mind.'

Thus my thoughts turned back over the last ten years, and then with concentrated thought on the future, I asked myself: 'If you should, by chance, prolong this uncertain life of yours for another ten years, advancing toward virtue in proportion to the distance from which you departed from your original infatuation during the past two years since the new longing first encountered the old, could you not face death on reaching forty years of age, if not with complete assurance at least with hopefulness, calmly dismissing from your thoughts the residuum of life that fades into old age?'

Such thoughts as these, father, occurred to me. I rejoiced in my progress, mourned for my weaknesses, and took pity on universal inconstancy of human conduct. I had by this time forgotten where I was and why we had come; then, dismissing my anxieties to a more appropriate occasion, I decided to look about me and see what we had come to see. The sun was sinking and the shadows of the mountain were already lengthening below, warning us that the time for us to go was near at hand. As if suddenly roused from sleep, I turned to gaze at the west. I could not see the tops of the Pyrenees, which form the barrier between France and Spain, not because of any intervening obstacle that I know of but simply because of the inadequacy of mortal vision. But off to the right I could see most clearly the mountains of the region around Lyons and to the left the bay of Marseilles and the sea that beats against the shores of Aigues-Mortes, though all these places were at a distance requiring a journey of several days to reach them. The Rhône was flowing under our very eyes.

While my thoughts were divided thus, now turning my attention to thoughts of some worldly object before me, now uplifting my soul, as I had done my body, to higher planes, it occurred to me to look at Augustine's *Confessions,* a gift of your love that I always keep with me in memory of the author and the giver. I opened the little volume, small in size but infinitely sweet, with the intention of reading whatever came to hand, for what else could I happen upon if not edifying and devout words. Now I happened by chance to open it to the tenth book. My brother stood attentively waiting to hear what St Augustine would say from my lips. As God is my witness and my brother too, the first words my eyes fell upon were: 'And men go about admiring the high mountains and the mighty waves of the sea and the wide sweep of rivers and the sound of the ocean and the movement of the stars, but they themselves they abandon.' I was ashamed, and asking my brother, who was anxious to hear more, not to bother me, I closed the book, angry with myself for continuing to admire the things of this world when I should have learned a long time ago from the pagan philosophers themselves that nothing is admirable but the soul beside whose greatness nothing can be as great. Then, having seen enough of the mountain I turned an inward eye upon myself, and from that moment on not a syllable passed my lips until we reached the bottom. The words I had read had given me enough food for thought and I could not believe that I happened to turn to them by mere chance. I believed that what I had read there was written for me and no one else, and I remembered that St Augustine had once thought the same thing in his own case, as he himself tells us when opening the book of the Apostle, the first words he saw were: 'Not in rioting and drunkenness, not in chambering and wantonness, not in strife and envy, but put ye on the Lord Jesus Christ, and make not provision for the flesh in its concupiscences.' The same thing happened earlier to St Anthony, as he listened to the Gospel where it is written, 'If thou wilt be perfect, go and sell what thou hast, and give to the poor, and thou shalt have treasure in heaven; and come follow me.' He believed this scripture to have been spoken specifically for him, and by means of it he guided himself to the Kingdom of Heaven, as the biographer Athanasius tells us. And as Anthony on hearing these words asked for nothing more, and as Augustine after reading the Apostle's admonition sought no farther, so did I conclude my reading after the few words which I have recorded. I thought in silence of the vanity in us mortals who neglect what is noblest in ourselves in a vain show only because we look around ourselves for what can be found only within us. I wondered at the natural nobility of that human soul which unless degenerate has deserted its original state and turned to dishonour what God has given it for its honour. How many times I turned back that day to look at the mountain top which seemed scarcely more than a cubit high compared with the height of human contemplation, unless it is immersed in the foulness of earth? As I descended I asked myself: 'If we are willing to endure so much sweat and labour in order to raise our bodies a little closer to heaven, how can a soul struggling toward God, up the steeps of human pride and mortal destiny, fear any cross or prison or sting of fortune?' How few, I thought, are they who are not diverted from this path for fear of hardship or the love of ease! And how happy those few, if any such there be! It is they, I feel, the poet had in mind when he wrote:

> Blessèd the man who is skilled to understand
> The hidden cause of things; who beneath his feet
> All fear casts, and death's relentless doom,
> And the howlings of greedy Acheron.[1]

How earnestly should we strive to trample beneath our feet not mountain-tops but the appetites which spring from earthly impulses!

In the middle of the night, unaware of the difficulties of the way back and amid the preoccupations which I have so frankly revealed, we came by the friendly light of a full moon to the little inn which we had left that morning before day-break. Then, while the servants were busy preparing our supper, I spent my time in a secluded part of the house, hurriedly and extemporaneously writing all this down, fearing that if I were to put off the task, my mood would change on leaving the place, and I would lose interest in writing to you.

You see, dearest father, that I wish to conceal nothing of myself from you. I describe to you not only the course of my life but even my individual thoughts. And I ask for your prayers that these vague and wandering thoughts of mine may some day become coherent and, having been so vainly cast in all directions, that they may direct themselves at last to the one, true, certain, and never-ending good.

Canzoniere

Translated by Patricia Clark Smith

1: "Oh you, who in these scattered rhymes may find"

> Oh you, who in these scattered rhymes may find
> echoes of sighs that I once fed my heart
> when I was young, when I was still in part
> this man you see, that boy now left behind;

[1] Virgil, *The Georgics,* II, 490–93.

if you yourself have had one turn to writhe
in love's extremes of harsh delight, soft pain,
balanced between false hope, sweet love-in-vain,
I pray you'll read and pity and forgive.

There's talk of me on every street in town,
and I know why; although I feel that shame, 10
shame's not the deepest reason why I weep,

nor even penitence, but that stark dawn
of understanding how it's all a dream,
all that we love, all that we ache to keep.

3: "It was the very day the sun's own light"

It was the very day the sun's own light
grew dim to mark the passion of Our Lord
when I myself succumbed without a word,
struck down, my lady, simply by your sight.[1]

That one day least auspicious for romance
I walked unwary through the people's sorrow,
through grieving streets, all open to the blow
Love dealt amid that universal penance.

Love found its way to my heart through my eyes;
now my tears pool and gather, overflow 10
outward through those same gates where I was breached.

But you, my love, were never so surprised,
and I ask whether it is fair, or no,
Love laid me low, and left you so untouched?

90: "Sometimes she'd comb her yellow braids out loose"

Sometimes she'd comb her yellow braids out loose
for winds to tease and tangle in bright air,
and all that light caught in her eyes, her hair.
Most things have faded now. But once I used

to see her gauging me with thoughtful eyes:
with pity true or false, it's all the same.
My soul dry kindling, waiting for her flame,
and could I help it I was set ablaze?

[1]The day Petrarch first saw Laura was April 6, 1327, then supposed to be the exact anniversary of the crucifixion, as opposed to the movable feast of Good Friday. He also tells us Laura died of plague on that same date in 1348.

I tell you, she was like a goddess walking,
a pulsing sun to keep a man from cold, 10
radiant, gold, that spirit danced abroad;

when she spoke, I divined the angels talking.
You say she's just a woman growing old?
Her bow's gone slack, her arrow's in my side.

148: "Not Tiber, Tesin, Po, nor Arno, Rhône"

Not Tiber, Tesin, Po, nor Arno, Rhône,
Tigris, Euphrates, Nile, Erme, Indus, Seine,
Alphaeus, Elbe; not breaking sea, nor Rhine,
Ebro, Loire, Garonne, Don, Danube—none

can quench me! What's more, no pine,
spruce, ivy, juniper can shelter
me from sun! And yet there is one river
who shares my grief; one sapling bears my pain.[2]

They succor me through every heavy blow
of Love, who still compels me to bear arms 10
as I go reeling headlong far abroad.

Grow green, dear laurel, by this riverflow;
let me who planted you inscribe true poems
here where sweet water ripples in your shade.

164: "All silent now lie earth and wind and sky"

All silent now lie earth and wind and sky,
And sleep enfolds all animals and birds.
Night turns the wheel of stars. No wave disturbs
The wide unrippled sameness of the sea.

But I, I wake and brood, rage, weep, my eyes
always behold my love, my foe, my pain.

---

[2]The stream that consoles Petrarch as none of the great storied rivers of the world can is the Sorgue, which flows through the town of Vaucluse in southern France, near Avignon, where Petrarch often made his home. The sapling is almost certainly a real laurel tree he planted, for he loved gardening and landscape design. But the laurel tree also puns on the name of Laura, who sustains him even as his love for her wounds him. The tree also symbolizes Petrarch's growing body of poems, for in European tradition the laurel is the tree sacred to poets. Its leaves are like pages, and a laurel wreath is the prize for the poet who has written well.

I *am* a war! Here wrath and sorrow reign,
Yet solely in her image I find peace.

It was her healing hand gave me my wound,
And where the pure and living spring wells forth 10
I drink at once sweet water, bitter gall;

Storm-driven and extreme, remote from land,
A thousand times I suffer birth and death,
Swept far from any salvage of my soul.

292: "Those eyes I raved about in ardent rhyme"

Those eyes I raved about in ardent rhyme,
the arms, the hands, the feet, the loving face
that split my soul in two, and made me pass
my life apart from all the common throng,

the tumbled mane of uncut gold that shone,
that angel smile whose flash made me surmise
the very earth had turned to Paradise,
have come to dust: no life, no sense. Undone.

And I live on, in sorrow and self-scorn
here where the light I steered by gleams no more 10
for my dismasted ship, wracked by the storm.

Let there be no more love songs! The dear spring
of my accustomed art has been drained dry,
my lyre itself dissolved in so much weeping.

310: "West Wind comes leading into warmth and light"

West Wind comes leading into warmth and light
his whole sweet family of flowers and grass,
and Sparrow's chirp, and Nightingale's *alas*,
and Springtime born again in red and white.

The meadows smile, the sky burns blue above,
and Jove beams with delight upon his daughter.
Love animates the air, the earth, the water;
all creatures yield their beings up to Love!

All that returns for me are weary sighs
drawn from the most profound depths of my heart 10
by her who kept its keys to Paradise;

so birdsong, and the softly blooming leas,
and lovely women, generous and wise,
seem only deserts, forests, savage beasts.

333: "Go forth, my elegies, to that hard stone"

Go forth, my elegies, to that hard stone
beneath whose weight my dearest treasure lies.
Call her, and she may answer from the skies,
but here lies only rotting flesh and bone.

Tell her how I grow weary of my life,
of navigating through this dark expanse;
only these scattered pages save my sense,
these stepping-stones to lead me out of grief.

I'll go on telling how she lived and died,
and how she's living now, beyond all death, 10
so that the world may better learn her grace

and love her. Let her linger by my side
at my death, which grows nearer as I breathe,
to beckon me toward her transcendant peace.

CHRISTOPHER MARLOWE

[1564–1593]

Although information about Christopher Marlowe's life is very sketchy, it is clear that he was using his writings and his friendships to raise questions about traditional beliefs and social change, to explore new ideas about personality and power. Tragically killed in a tavern fight at age twenty-nine, after having written four plays, he is nevertheless ranked close to Shakespeare. His powerful poetic dramas explore essential themes of the Renaissance; he is especially adept at showing how the quest for political or intellectual power is inevitably compromised by human limitations.

Faustus, one of Marlowe's most important characters, epitomizes the struggle involved with leaving the medieval world of sin and salvation and entering the humanistic frontiers of the Renaissance. Faustus has a foot in both worlds, in two time periods. The medieval Catholic Church fostered a concern with one's inward state, its relation to a transcendent deity, and the eternal salvation of one's soul. The material world was meaningful as a reflection of the spiritual world. In contrast, the Renaissance artist and thinker rediscovered the tangible contours of this physical existence and seemed to be celebrating it for its own sake. Explorers were as occupied with finding the routes to countries and peoples halfway around the globe as they were with articulating the pathway to heaven.

The consciousness of Europeans was changing, and an inevitable conflict arose between the sacred world view of the past and the secular horizons of the present and future. The dialogues between good and evil, old and new, church and state, spirit and flesh, the collective and the individual, were carried on in the universities and the culture at large, and became the polarized conversations of Marlowe's play *Doctor Faustus*. As long as one's eye was ultimately focused on the salvific rewards of the next world, the dichotomy between heaven and the temptations of earthly life was perhaps bearable; but just as soon as human beings learned to love and care for earthly existence, its beauty and transience, the world view of the Church would inevitably come under scrutiny. Marlowe's Faustus and the progress of his own life provided an early stage in the unraveling of the logic of redemption.

LIFE

The facts about Marlowe's life are few and ambiguous, but enough is known to appreciate his personal rebellion against social mores and his contribution to the evolution of British theater. He was born into a prosperous middle-class family in Canterbury on February 6, 1564. His father was a tanner and shoemaker. He was educated first at the King's School in Canterbury. In 1581 he was given a scholarship to Cambridge, where he received a BA in 1584. Apparently the University intended to withhold his MA, but the Queen's Privy Council, a powerful group, intervened with a letter that commended him for service "in matters touching the benefit of the country" and insisted that Marlowe receive his degree "this next Commencement," in 1587. Marlowe apparently was employed abroad in secret service for the government.

Although his student scholarship pointed toward a vocation as a clergyman, Marlowe moved to London where he made his living as a professional writer—a new cultural phenomenon—and aggravated conventional morality with his liberal opinions and free spirit. His entire career was squeezed into the period between 1587 and 1593. His earliest play was probably *Dido, Queen of Carthage,* but his four major dramas began with the two-part *Tamburlaine the Great* (c. 1587), where with his "mighty line" he established blank verse—unrhymed lines of ten syllables each—as the preferred poetic form for Elizabethan tragedy. Marlowe captures the spirit of the Renaissance with his hero's conquering might and dreams of power, although Tamburlaine's obsession becomes tiring by the end of the second play. In Marlowe's second major play, *The Jew of Malta* (c. 1588), he creates a villain who is greedy and treacherous, a Machiavellian figure wholly devoted to self-advancement. *The Troublesome Raigne and Lamentable Death of Edward the Second* (c. 1592) contributed to the genre of the history play with a portrayal of a character whose weaknesses are, nevertheless, sympathetic. *Doctor Faustus* (1592–1593) is Marlowe's most famous and most important play. Unlike the rather static character of Tamburlaine, Faustus captures the dramatic conflict of a man who steps beyond the accepted boundaries of his day; this play became a model for the great poetic tragedies of the Elizabethan Age.

In addition to a translation of Ovid's *Amores* that was so erotic it was burned by the Archbishop of Canterbury in 1599, Marlowe wrote a long poem, *Hero and Leander;* although incomplete, it is notable for the passionate descriptions of the lovers and their meetings.

In May 1593, there were political rumblings caused by subversive comments about religion. When the playwright Thomas Kyd was arrested, he attributed a paper denying the divinity of Christ to possessions left behind by Christopher Marlowe when they had roomed together two years earlier. A spy, Richard Baines, made a list of heretical ideas associated with one "Christopher Marly." "Marly" was said to have claimed that Jesus had illicit affairs with two women of Samaria and with St. John the Evangelist, and that religion came into being to "keep men in awe." On May 18, the Privy Council issued orders for Marlowe's arrest. On May 30, Marlowe had an argument over the payment of a bill with Ingram Frizer; Marlowe apparently grabbed Frizer's dagger, but as Frizer defended himself the dagger pierced Marlowe's eye, killing him.

Work

Marlowe's greatest play, *Doctor Faustus,* which was first published in 1604 and then again in 1616, is a dramatization of a book published in German in 1587 and translated into English as *The History of the damnable life and deserved death of Dr. John Faustus* in 1592, the earliest version available to Marlowe. Scholars have noted an unknown collaborator and the possibility of additions to the play after Marlowe's death. Nevertheless, the depth of psychological insight with the character of Faustus and the struggles of Marlowe himself with the strictures of his culture continue to provoke relevant issues for a modern, technological age. Three years after Marlowe's death, Thomas Beard, in a book called *The Theatre of God's Judgment,* used Marlowe as an example of how God treats atheists and other transgressors.

The legendary German prototype of Faustus was born in the late fifteenth century. He learned numerous languages such as Persian, Hebrew, Arabic, and Greek in order to study the "infernal arts" of "necromancy, charms, soothsaying, witchcraft, enchantment." This Faustus, who reportedly sold his soul to the devil for twenty-four years of earthly power, wandered through Germany gaining a reputation as a magician and astrologer. After practicing his secret arts for a number of years in Wittenberg, he died from a chemical explosion in 1540 or 1541, and according to legend went to hell. His reputation quickly spread and his biography, the *Historia von D. Iohan Fausten*—the German Faust Book—was published anonymously in Frankfort in 1587. An English translation—called the English Faust Book—contains most of the plot material for Marlowe's play.

Marlowe's play is fully rooted in the complexities of his time. The prologue prepares us for the conflict in Faustus' personality; born of "base stock," reflecting a new middle class, he is educated, especially in theology. But he is discontented and wants to exceed his reach by leaving the earth like Icarus and mounting into the sky, risking life and limb in the face of the sun. We first see Faustus in his study—a symbol of learning and the intellectual aspirations of the Renaissance—where he debates with himself about the state of his own education and decides to risk even his soul in order to break out of the limits of the traditional, humanistic education associated with Greek philosophy, physics, Roman law, and the Vulgate Bible. Faustus wants to gain new understanding through the power and exotic trappings of magic and necromancy—a course consistent with Marlowe's own youthful intellect and imagination. In addition, the "metaphysics of magicians" suggests theatrical spectacle for Elizabethan audiences.

Marlowe next introduces the mechanism of a medieval morality play by including a dialogue between Good Angel and Bad Angel, a device illustrative of Faustus' own inner struggle between piety and profligacy and an indication of the larger dialogue between religion and the rising spirit of secularism. The use of the two Scholars and the two Angels is reminiscent of the chorus in Greek tragedy; they reflect on the course of Faustus' life and discuss options open for him, debating the ongoing question of whether he can be saved. Faustus is not unlike the Greek figure of Prometheus, who discovers that there is a price for challenging authority and cherishing the fire of intellect.

The play gathers intensity as Faustus stabs his arm for the blood necessary for signing a compact with the devil; some part of him, however, resists this ultimate act. He admits, "My blood congeals, and I can write no more." Mephistophilis brings fire—plainly symbolic—to dissolve the blood, and the pact is sealed. What can Faustus possibly request that will compensate for his damnation? He asks for a curious mixture of knowledge, power, and pranks. The answer to his question about the location of hell is surprisingly modern in its implications:

> Hell hath no limits nor is circumscribed
> In one self place, but where we are is hell,
> And where hell is there must we ever be.

When Faustus wants to blame Mephistophilis for being deprived of heaven, his attention, in true Renaissance fashion, is redirected to the earth and the wonder of human beings:

> But think'st thou heaven is such a glorious thing?
> I tell thee, Faustus, it is not half so fair
> As thou or any man that breathe on earth.

Some of the wonder associated with an age of travel and discovery, of explorers and new worlds, is reflected in Faustus' speeches about his travels from Paris to Germany, to "Venice, Padua and the rest," and finally to Rome. There are interludes of comedy and slapstick, tricks that seem inappropriate perhaps for the magnitude of Faustus' soulful compact; he seems to waste his time with trivialities. Rather than complete any grand projects, Faustus abuses his powers with selfish whims. After all, the Helen who evokes Faustus' immortal lines is a ghost and not the real thing. Has Faustus sold his immortal soul for frippery?

The end of the play, with Faustus' struggle with death and damnation, again reaches toward the grandeur of authentic tragedy and is intensified by Marlowe's own poetic powers. The emptiness of Faustus' tricks lends poignancy to the ultimate rejection of his educational training.

> O would I had never seen Wittenberg, never read book! And what wonders I have done all Germany can witness, yea all the world, for which Faustus had lost both Germany and the world, yea heaven itself—heaven the seat of God, the throne of the blessed, the kingdom of joy, and must remain in hell forever.

Morality plays tend to end with the sinner repenting and the promise of salvation, but Faustus is a tragic hero who appears to remain true to his agreement and courageously faces a vision of hell and eternal punishment, as if he were a necessary sacrifice to the old order. The modern witness to Faustus' agonizing spiritual deliberations does not have to literally believe in a fiery pit to appreciate Faustus' sense of despair and estrangement. Is it courage or foolhardiness that allows him to face his own demise?

Regardless of any faults in Marlowe's portrayal of Faustus, there is something very modern and compelling about this Renaissance figure. The Faustus figures of each succeeding age would carry less baggage from the past and extend in ever-widening circles the frontiers of imagination and possibility, as well as the potential for destruction. Later writers such as Goethe and Thomas Mann recreated his questioning, iconoclastic personality for their own periods in history. In the twentieth century, the growing distance between technological marvels and the human capacity to use or integrate them seems to reflect a modern Faustian bargain with the unknown. The devilish figures might wear different masks in today's version, but there is a definite unease—even misgiving—about the complexities of modern knowledge, especially with weapons, chemicals, and medicine, and their capacity to harm us and even destroy the planet.

Suggested Readings

A good biography and general introduction is Frederick S. Boas's *Christopher Marlowe: A Biographical and Critical Study* (1940). Both Wilbur Sanders's *The Dramatist and the Received Idea* (1968) and G. B. Harrison's *Elizabethan Plays & Players* (1956) provide the context of Elizabethan theater. A variety of perspectives is included in Willard Farnham, ed., *Twentieth Century Interpretations of Doctor Faustus* (1969). A unique thematic perspective is Harry Levin's *The Overreacher* (1952). One of the best short commentaries is T. S. Eliot's essay in *The Sacred Wood* (1920).

Doctor Faustus

DRAMATIS PERSONAE:

THE CHORUS
DOCTOR FAUSTUS
WAGNER, *his servant*
VALDES } *friends to* FAUSTUS
CORNELIUS } *friends to* FAUSTUS
THREE SCHOLARS
AN OLD MAN

THE POPE
RAYMOND, *King of Hungary*
BRUNO
TWO CARDINALS
ARCHBISHOP OF RHEIMS
CARDINAL OF LORRAINE
CHARLES, *Emperor of Germany*
MARTINO } *Gentlemen of his Court*
FREDERICK } *Gentlemen of his Court*
BENVOLIO } *Gentlemen of his Court*
A KNIGHT
DUKE OF SAXONY
DUKE OF ANHOLT
DUCHESS OF ANHOLT
BISHOPS, MONKS, FRIARS, SOLDIERS, *and* ATTENDANTS

CLOWN
ROBIN, *an ostler*
DICK
RALPH
A VINTNER
A HORSE-COURSER
A CARTER
HOSTESS

GOOD ANGEL
BAD ANGEL
EVIL ANGEL
MEPHISTOPHILIS
LUCIFER
BELZEBUB
DEVILS
THE SEVEN DEADLY SINS
ALEXANDER THE GREAT } *Spirits*
PARAMOUR OF ALEXANDER } *Spirits*
DARIUS } *Spirits*
HELEN } *Spirits*
TWO CUPIDS } *Spirits*

Act I

Prologue

[*Enter* CHORUS.]

CHORUS:

Not marching in the fields of Thrasimen,
Where Mars did mate the warlike Carthagens;
Nor sporting in the dalliance of love,
In courts of kings, where state[1] is over-turn'd;
Nor in the pomp of proud audacious deeds,
Intends our Muse to vaunt his heavenly verse:
Only this, Gentles—we must now perform
The form of Faustus' fortunes, good or bad:
And now to patient judgments we appeal,
And speak for Faustus in his infancy. 10
Now is he born, of parents base of stock,
In Germany, within a town call'd Rhode:
At riper years, to Wittenberg[2] he went,
Whereas his kinsmen chiefly brought him up.
So much he profits in divinity,
The fruitful plot of scholarism grac'd,

---

[1]Political power.
[2]The famous university attended by Martin Luther.

That shortly he was grac'd with Doctor's name,
Excelling all and sweetly can dispute
In th' heavenly matters of theology;
Till swoln with cunning, of a self-conceit, 20
His waxen wings did mount above his reach,[3]
And, melting, heavens conspir'd his overthrow;
For, falling to a devilish exercise,
And glutted now with learning's golden gifts,
He surfeits upon cursed necromancy;
Nothing so sweet as magic is to him,
Which he prefers before his chiefest bliss:[4]
And this the man that in his study sits.

[*Exit.*]

Scene 1

FAUSTUS *in his Study.*

FAUSTUS:

Settle thy studies, Faustus, and begin
To sound the depth of that thou wilt profess:
Having commenc'd,[5] be a divine in show,
Yet level[6] at the end of every art,
And live and die in Aristotle's works.
Sweet Analytics,[7] 'tis thou hast ravish'd me!
Bene disserere est finis logices.
Is, to dispute well, logic's chiefest end?
Affords this art no greater miracle?
Then read no more; thou hast attain'd that end. 10
A greater subject fitteth Faustus' wit:
Bid ὂν χαὶ μὴ ὂν[8] farewell; and Galen come;
Seeing, *Ubi desinit philosophus ibi incipit medicus,*[9]
Be a physician, Faustus; heap up gold,
And be eternis'd for some wondrous cure!
Summum bonum medicinæ sanitas,[10]
The end of physic is our body's health.
Why, Faustus, hast thou not attain'd that end?
Is not thy common talk sound aphorisms?[11]
Are not thy bills hung up as monuments, 20
Whereby whole cities have escap'd the plague,
And thousand desp'rate maladies been cur'd?
Yet art thou still but Faustus, and a man.
Couldst thou make men to live eternally,

[3]The Greek myth of Icarus and Daedalus.
[4]Eternal salvation.
[5]Graduated.
[6]Aim.
[7]Aristotle's treatise on logic.
[8]"Being and not being."
[9]"Where the philosopher leaves off the physician begins."
[10]"Good health is the object of medicine."
[11]Medical opinions.

Or, being dead, raise them to life again,
Then this profession were to be esteem'd.
Physic, farewell! Where is Justinian? [*Reads.*]
'Si una eademque res legatur duobus
Alter rem, alter valorem rei,' etc.[12]
A petty case of paltry legacies! [*Reads.*] 30
'Exhæreditare filium non potest pater nisi'[13]—
Such is the subject of the Institute,
And universal body of the law.
This study fits a mercenary drudge,
Who aims at nothing but external trash;
Too servile and illiberal for me.
When all is done, divinity is best:
Jeromë's Bible,[14] Faustus; view it well. [*Reads.*]
'Stipendium peccati mors est.' Ha! *'Stipendium,' etc.*
The reward of sin is death: that's hard. [*Reads.*] 40
'Si peccasse negamus, fallimur
Et nulla est in nobis veritas.'[15]
If we say that we have no sin,
We deceive ourselves, and there is no truth in us.
Why, then, belike we must sin,
And so consequently die:
Ay, we must die an everlasting death.
What doctrine call you this, *Che sera, sera:*
What will be, shall be? Divinity, adieu!
These metaphysics of magicians, 50
And necromantic books are heavenly;
Lines, circles, letters, and characters;
Ay, these are those that Faustus most desires.
O, what a world of profit and delight,
Of power, of honour, and omnipotence,
Is promised to the studious artizan!
All things that move between the quiet poles
Shall be at my command: emperors and kings
Are but obey'd in their several provinces,
Nor can they raise the wind, or rend the clouds; 60
But his dominion that exceeds in this,
Stretcheth as far as doth the mind of man;
A sound magician is a demigod:
Here, tire my brain to get a deity!
[*Enter* WAGNER.]
Wagner, commend me to my dearest friends,
The German Valdes and Cornelius;
Request them earnestly to visit me.

WAGNER:
I will, sir.

[*Exit.*]

[12]"If something is bequeathed to two persons, one shall have the thing itself, the other something of equal value."
[13]"A father cannot disinherit his son unless."
[14]St. Jerome's translation of the Bible: the Latin or Vulgate translation (fourth century C.E.).
[15]I John 1:8, translated in the next two lines.

FAUSTUS:
Their conference will be a greater help to me
Than all my labours, plot I ne'er so fast. 70
[*Enter the* GOOD ANGEL *and* BAD ANGEL.]

GOOD ANGEL:
O, Faustus, lay that damned book aside,
And gaze not on it, lest it tempt thy soul,
And heap God's heavy wrath upon thy head!
Read, read the Scriptures:—that is blasphemy.

BAD ANGEL:
Go forward, Faustus, in that famous art
Wherein all Nature's treasure is contain'd:
Be thou on earth as Jove is in the sky,
Lord and commander of these elements.
[*Exeunt* ANGELS.]

FAUSTUS:
How am I glutted with conceit of this!
Shall I make spirits fetch me what I please, 80
Resolve me of all ambiguities,
Perform what desperate enterprise I will?
I'll have them fly to India for gold,
Ransack the ocean for orient pearl,
And search all corners of the new-found world
For pleasant fruits and princely delicates;
I'll have them read me strange philosophy,
And tell the secrets of all foreign kings;
I'll have them wall all Germany with brass,
And make swift Rhine circle fair Wittenberg. 90
I'll have them fill the public schools with silk,
Wherewith the students shall be bravely clad;
I'll levy soldiers with the coin they bring,
And chase the Prince of Parma[16] from our land,
And reign sole king of all the Provinces;
Yea, stranger engines for the brunt of war,
Than was the fiery keel[17] at Antwerp's bridge,
I'll make my servile spirits to invent. [*He calls within.*]
[*Enter* VALDES *and* CORNELIUS.]
Come, German Valdes, and Cornelius,
And make me blest with your sage conference! 100
Valdes, sweet Valdes, and Cornelius,
Know that your words have won me at the last
To practise magic and concealed arts:
Yet not your words only, but mine own fantasy,
That will receive no object,[18] for my head
But ruminates on necromantic skill.
Philosophy is odious and obscure;
Both law and physic are for petty wits;
Divinity is basest of the three,

[16]The Spanish governor of the Low Countries from 1579 to 1592.
[17]A burning ship sent into Antwerp's bridge.
[18]That will entertain no academic objection.

Unpleasant, harsh, contemptible, and vile: 110
'Tis magic, magic, that hath ravish'd me.
Then, gentle friends, aid me in this attempt
And I, that have with subtle syllogisms
Gravell'd[19] the pastors of the German church,
And made the flowering pride of Wittenberg
Swarm to my problems, as the infernal spirits
On sweet Musaeus when he came to hell,
Will be as cunning as Agrippa[20] was,
Whose shadows made all Europe honour him.

VALDES:

Faustus, these books, thy wit, and our experience 120
Shall make all nations to canonize us.
As Indian Moors[21] obey their Spanish lords,
So shall the spirits of every element
Be always serviceable to us three;
Like lions shall they guard us when we please;
Like Almain rutters[22] with their horsemen's staves,
Or Lapland giants, trotting by our sides;
Sometimes like women, or unwedded maids,
Shadowing more beauty in their airy brows
Than has the white breasts of the queen of love; 130
From Venice shall they drag huge argosies,
And from America the golden fleece
That yearly stuffs old Philip's[23] treasury;
If learned Faustus will be resolute.

FAUSTUS:

Valdes, as resolute am I in this
As thou to live: therefore object it not.

CORNELIUS:

The miracles that magic will perform
Will make thee vow to study nothing else.
He that is grounded in astrology,
Enrich'd with tongues, well seen in minerals, 140
Hath all the principles magic doth require:
Then doubt not, Faustus, but to be renown'd,
And more frequented for this mystery
Than heretofore the Delphian oracle.
The spirits tell me they can dry the sea,
And fetch the treasure of all foreign wrecks,
Yea, all the wealth that our forefathers hid
Within the massy entrails of the earth:
Then tell me, Faustus, what shall we three want?

FAUSTUS:

Nothing, Cornelius. O, this cheers my soul! 150
Come, show me some demonstrations magical,

---

19 Confounded.
20 Cornelius Agrippa, a German necromancer.
21 American Indians.
22 German horsemen.
23 Philip II, King of Spain.

That I may conjure in some bushy grove,
And have these joys in full possession.

VALDES:
Then haste thee to some solitary grove,
And bear wise Bacon's and Albertus'[24] works,
The Hebrew Psalter, and New Testament;
And whatsoever else is requisite
We will inform thee ere our conference cease.

CORNELIUS:
Valdes, first let him know the words of art;
And then, all other ceremonies learn'd, 160
Faustus may try his cunning by himself.

VALDES:
First I'll instruct thee in the rudiments,
And then wilt thou be perfecter than I.

FAUSTUS:
Then come and dine with me, and, after meat,
We'll canvass every quiddity thereof;
For, ere I sleep, I'll try what I can do:
This night I'll conjure, though I die therefore.

[*Exeunt omnes.*]

Scene 2

Before FAUSTUS' *house.*

[*Enter* TWO SCHOLARS.]

FIRST SCHOLAR: I wonder what's become of Faustus, that was wont to make our schools ring with *sic probo.*[25]

[*Enter* WAGNER.]

SECOND SCHOLAR: That shall we presently know; here comes his boy.

FIRST SCHOLAR: How now, sirrah! where's thy master?

WAGNER: God in heaven knows.

SECOND SCHOLAR: Why, dost not thou know, then?

WAGNER: Yes, I know; but that follows not.

FIRST SCHOLAR: Go to, sirrah! leave your jesting, and tell us where he is.

WAGNER: That follows not by force of argument, which you, being Licentiates, should stand upon; therefore acknowledge your error, and be attentive. 10

SECOND SCHOLAR: Then you will not tell us?

WAGNER: You are deceiv'd, for I will tell you: yet, if you were not dunces, you would never ask me such a question; for is he not *corpus naturale*? and is not that *mobile*?[26] Then wherefore should you ask me such a question? But that I am by nature phlegmatic, slow to wrath, and prone to lechery (to love, I would say), it were not for you to come within forty foot of the place of execution,[27] although I do not doubt but to see you both hanged the next sessions. Thus having triumph'd over you, I will set my countenance like a precisian,[28] and begin to speak thus:—Truly, my dear brethren, my master is within at dinner, with Valdes and Cornelius, as this wine, if it could speak, would inform your 20

[24] Albertus Magnus, a thirteenth-century magician.
[25] "Thus I prove."
[26] Natural, movable matter: a scholastic definition of the physical world.
[27] Dining room.
[28] Puritan.

worships: and so, the Lord bless you, preserve you, and keep you, my dear brethren.

[*Exit.*]

FIRST SCHOLAR:

O Faustus. Then I fear that which I have long suspected,
That thou are fallen into that damned art
For which they two are infamous through the world.

SECOND SCHOLAR:

Were he a stranger, not allied to me,
The danger of his soul would make me mourn.
But, come, let us go and inform the Rector,
It may be his grave counsel may reclaim him. 30

FIRST SCHOLAR:

I fear me nothing will reclaim him now!

SECOND SCHOLAR:

Yet let us see what we can do.

[*Exeunt.*]

Scene 3

A grove.

[*Enter* FAUSTUS *to conjure.*]

FAUSTUS:

Now that the gloomy shadow of the night,
Longing to view Orion's drizzling look,
Leaps from th' antarctic world unto the sky,
And dims the welkin with her pitchy breath,
Faustus, begin thine incantations,
And try if devils will obey thy hest,
Seeing thou hast pray'd and sacrific'd to them.
Within this circle is Jehovah's name,
Forward and backward anagrammatiz'd;
Th' abbreviated names of holy saints, 10
Figures of every adjunct to the heavens,
And characters of signs and erring stars,
By which the spirits are enforc'd to rise:
Then fear not, Faustus, to be resolute,
And try the utmost magic can perform. [*Thunder.*]
'Sint mihi Dii Acherontis propitii! Valeat numen triplex Jehovæ! Ignis, aeris, aquæ, terrae spiritus, salvete! Orientis princeps, Belzebub, inferni ardentis monarcha, et Demogorgon, propitiamus vos, ut appareat et surgat Mephistophilis. [*Enter* DRAGON *above.*] *Quid tu moraris? per Jehovam, Gehennam, et consecratam aquam quam nunc spargo, signumque crucis quod nunc facio, et per vota nostra, ipse nunc surgat nobis dicatus Mephistophilis!'*[29] 20

[*Enter* MEPHISTOPHILIS.]

I charge thee to return, and change thy shape;
Thou art too ugly to attend on me:

---

[29]"Unto me be the gods of Acheron propitious. May the triple name of Jehovah prevail. Spirits of fire, air, water, and earth, hail! Belzebub, Prince of the East, Sovereign of burning Hell and Demogorgon, we propitiate you, that Mephistophilis may appear and rise. Why do you delay? By Jehovah, Gehenna, and the holy water which now I sprinkle, and the sign of the cross which now I make, and by our prayer, may Mephistophilis, by us summoned, now arise."

Go, and return an old Franciscan friar;
That holy shape becomes a devil best.

[*Exit* MEPHISTOPHILIS.]

I see there's virtue in my heavenly words:
Who would not be proficient in this art?
How pliant is this Mephistophilis,
Full of obedience and humility!
Such is the force of magic and my spells: 30
Now, Faustus, thou art conjuror laureat,
That canst command great Mephistophilis.
Quin redis, Mephistophilis, fratris imagine![30]

[*Re-enter* MEPHISTOPHILIS *like a Franciscan friar.*]

MEPHISTOPHILIS:
Now, Faustus, what would'st thou have me do?

FAUSTUS:
I charge thee wait upon me whilst I live,
To do whatever Faustus shall command,
Be it to make the moon drop from her sphere,
Or the ocean to overwhelm the world.

MEPHISTOPHILIS:
I am a servant to great Lucifer,
And may not follow thee without his leave; 40
No more than he commands must we perform.

FAUSTUS:
Did not he charge thee to appear to me?

MEPHISTOPHILIS:
No, I came now hither of mine own accord.

FAUSTUS:
Did not my conjuring raise thee? speak.

MEPHISTOPHILIS:
That was the cause, but yet *per accidens*;[31]
For, when we hear one rack the name of God,
Abjure the Scriptures and his Saviour Christ,
We fly, in hope to get his glorious soul;
Nor will we come, unless he use such means
Whereby he is in danger to be damn'd. 50
Therefore the shortest cut for conjuring
Is stoutly to abjure the Trinity,
And pray devoutly to the prince of hell.

FAUSTUS:
So Faustus hath
Already done; and holds this principle,
There is no chief but only Belzebub;
To whom Faustus doth dedicate himself.
This word 'damnation' terrifies not me,
For I confound hell in Elysium:
My ghost be with the old philosophers![32] 60
But, leaving these vain trifles of men's souls,
Tell me what is that Lucifer thy lord?

---

[30] "Mephistophilis, return in the likeness of a friar."
[31] By the accidental cause (not the ultimate cause).
[32] Pre-Christian philosophers.

MEPHISTOPHILIS:
Arch-regent and commander of all spirits.
FAUSTUS:
Was not that Lucifer an angel once?
MEPHISTOPHILIS:
Yes, Faustus, and most dearly lov'd of God.
FAUSTUS:
How comes it then that he is prince of devils?
MEPHISTOPHILIS:
O, by aspiring pride and insolence;
For which God threw him from the face of heaven.
FAUSTUS:
And what are you that live with Lucifer?
MEPHISTOPHILIS:
Unhappy spirits that fell with Lucifer, 70
Conspir'd against our God with Lucifer,
And are for ever damn'd with Lucifer.
FAUSTUS:
Where are you damn'd?
MEPHISTOPHILIS:
In hell.
FAUSTUS:
How comes it then that thou art out of hell?
MEPHISTOPHILIS:
Why this is hell, nor am I out of it:
Think'st thou that I, that saw the face of God,
And tasted the eternal joys of Heaven,
Am not tormented with ten thousand hells,
In being depriv'd of everlasting bliss?
O, Faustus, leave these frivolous demands, 80
Which strikes a terror to my fainting soul!
FAUSTUS:
What, is great Mephistophilis so passionate
For being deprived of the joys of heaven?
Learn thou of Faustus manly fortitude,
And scorn those joys thou never shalt possess.
Go bear these tidings to great Lucifer:
Seeing Faustus hath incurr'd eternal death
By desperate thoughts against Jove's deity,
Say, he surrenders up to him his soul,
So he will spare him four-and-twenty years, 90
Letting him live in all voluptuousness;
Having thee ever to attend on me,
To give me whatsoever I shall ask,
To tell me whatsoever I demand,
To slay mine enemies, and to aid my friends,
And always be obedient to my will.
Go, and return to mighty Lucifer,
And meet me in my study at midnight,
And then resolve me of thy master's mind.
MEPHISTOPHILIS:
I will, Faustus. 100
[*Exit.*]

FAUSTUS:
Had I as many souls as there be stars,
I'd give them all for Mephistophilis.
By him I'll be great Emperor of the world,
And make a bridge through the moving air,
To pass the ocean with a band of men;
I'll join the hills that bind the Afric shore,
And make that country continent to Spain,
And both contributory to my crown:
The Emperor shall not live but by my leave,
Nor any potentate of Germany. 110
Now that I have obtain'd what I desir'd,
I'll live in speculation of this art,
Till Mephistophilis return again.

[*Exit.*]

Scene 4

[*Enter* WAGNER *and the* CLOWN.[33]]

WAGNER: Come hither, sirrah boy.

CLOWN: Boy! O disgrace to my person. Zounds, boy in your face! You have seen many boys with beards, I am sure.

WAGNER: Sirrah, hast thou no comings in?[34]

CLOWN: Yes, and goings out too, you may see, sir.

WAGNER: Alas, poor slave! see how poverty jests in his nakedness! I know the villain's out of service, and so hungry, that I know he would give his soul to the devil for a shoulder of mutton, though it were blood-raw.

CLOWN: Not so, neither. I had need to have it well-roasted, and good sauce to it, if I pay so dear, I can tell you. 10

WAGNER: Sirrah, wilt thou be my man and wait on me, and I will make thee go like *Qui mihi discipulus*?[35]

CLOWN: What, in verse?

WAGNER: No slave; in beaten silk and stavesacre.[36]

CLOWN: Stavesacre! that's good to kill vermin. Then, belike, if I serve you, I shall be lousy.

WAGNER: Why, so thou shalt be, whether thou do'st it or no. For, sirrah, if thou do'st not presently bind thyself to me for seven years, I'll turn all the lice about thee into familiars,[37] and make them tear thee in pieces.

CLOWN: Nay, sir, you may save yourself a labour, for they are as familiar with me as if they had paid for their meat and drink, I can tell you. 20

WAGNER: Well, sirrah, leave your jesting and take these guilders.

CLOWN: Yes, marry, sir, and I thank you too.

WAGNER: So, now thou art to be at an hour's warning, whensoever and wheresoever the devil shall fetch thee.

CLOWN: Here, take your guilders again, I'll none of 'em.

WAGNER: Not I, thou art pressed, for I will presently raise up two devils to carry thee away—Banio, Belcher!

---

[33] A rustic or buffoon.
[34] Income.
[35] "One who is my pupil."
[36] A powder used to kill vermin.
[37] Devils.

CLOWN: Belcher! and Belcher come here, I'll belch him. I am not afraid of a devil. 30

[*Enter two* DEVILS.]

WAGNER: How now, sir, will you serve me now?
CLOWN: Ay, good Wagner, take away the devil then.
WAGNER: Spirits, away! Now, sirrah, follow me.

[*Exeunt* DEVILS.]

CLOWN: I will, sir, but hark you, master, will you teach me this conjuring occupation?
WAGNER: Ay, sirrah, I'll teach thee to turn thyself to a dog, or a cat, or a mouse, or a rat, or any thing.
CLOWN: A dog, or a cat, or a mouse, or a rat, O brave Wagner!
WAGNER: Villain, call me Master Wagner, and see that you walk attentively and let your right eye be always diametrally fixed upon my left heel, that thou may'st *quasi vestigias nostras insistere.*[38] 40
CLOWN: Well, sir, I warrant you.

[*Exeunt.*]

ACT II

Scene 1

[*Enter* FAUSTUS *in his study.*]

FAUSTUS:
Now, Faustus, must
Thou needs be damn'd, and canst thou not be sav'd.
What boots[39] it, then, to think on God or heaven?
Away with such vain fancies, and despair;
Despair in God, and trust in Belzebub:
Now go not backward; Faustus, be resolute:
Why waver'st thou? O, something soundeth in mine ear,
'Abjure this magic, turn to God again!'
Ay, and Faustus will turn to God again.
To God? he loves thee not; 10
The God thou serv'st is thine own appetite,
Wherein is fix'd the love of Belzebub:
To him I'll build an altar and a church,
And offer lukewarm blood of newborn babes.

[*Enter the two* ANGELS.]

BAD ANGEL:
Go forward, Faustus, in that famous art.
GOOD ANGEL:
Sweet Faustus, leave that execrable art.
FAUSTUS:
Contrition, prayer, repentance—what of these?
GOOD ANGEL:
O, they are means to bring thee unto heaven!
BAD ANGEL:
Rather illusions, fruits of lunacy,
That make them foolish that do use them most. 20

---

[38] As if to tread my tracks.
[39] Avails.

GOOD ANGEL:
Sweet Faustus, think of heaven and heavenly things.
BAD ANGEL:
No, Faustus; think of honour and of wealth.
[*Exeunt* ANGELS.]
FAUSTUS:
Wealth! Why, the signiory of Emden[40] shall be mine.
When Mephistophilis shall stand by me,
What power can hurt me? Faustus, thou art safe:
Cast no more doubts—Mephistophilis, come!
And bring glad tidings from great Lucifer;—
Is't not midnight?—come, Mephistophilis,
Veni,[41] *veni, Mephistophile!*
[*Enter* MEPHISTOPHILIS.]
Now tell me what saith Lucifer, thy lord? 30
MEPHISTOPHILIS:
That I shall wait on Faustus while he lives,
So he will buy my service with his soul.
FAUSTUS:
Already Faustus hath hazarded that for thee.
MEPHISTOPHILIS:
But now thou must bequeath it solemnly,
And write a deed of gift with thine own blood;
For that security craves Lucifer.
If thou deny it, I must back to hell.
FAUSTUS:
Stay, Mephistophilis, tell me what good
Will my soul do thy lord?
MEPHISTOPHILIS:
Enlarge his kingdom. 40
FAUSTUS:
Is that the reason why he tempts us thus?
MEPHISTOPHILIS:
Solamen miseris socios habuisse doloris.[42]
FAUSTUS:
Why, have you any pain that torture others?
MEPHISTOPHILIS:
As great as have the human souls of men.
But tell me, Faustus, shall I have thy soul?
And I will be thy slave, and wait on thee,
And give thee more than thou hast wit to ask.
FAUSTUS:
Ay, Mephistophilis, I'll give it him.
MEPHISTOPHILIS:
Then, Faustus, stab thy arm courageously,
And bind thy soul, that at some certain day 50
Great Lucifer may claim it as his own;
And then be thou as great as Lucifer.

[40] A wealthy German city.
[41] Come.
[42] Misery loves company.

Faustus[*stabbing his arm*]:
Lo, Mephistophilis, for love of thee,
I cut mine arm, and with my proper blood
Assure my soul to be great Lucifer's,
Chief lord and regent of perpetual night!
View here this blood that trickles from mine arm,
And let it be propitious for my wish.

MEPHISTOPHILIS:
But, Faustus,
Write it in manner of a deed of gift. 60

FAUSTUS:
Ay, so I do. [*Writes.*] But, Mephistophilis,
My blood congeals, and I can write no more.

MEPHISTOPHILIS:
I'll fetch thee fire to dissolve it straight.
[*Exit.*]

FAUSTUS:
Why might the staying of my blood portend?
Is it unwilling I should write this bill?
Why streams it not, that I may write afresh?
Faustus gives to thee his soul: oh, there it stay'd!
Why shouldst thou not? is not thy soul thine own?
Then write again, *Faustus gives to thee his soul.*
[*Re-enter* MEPHISTOPHILIS *with a chafer of fire.*]

MEPHISTOPHILIS:
See, Faustus, here is fire, set it on. 70

FAUSTUS:
So, now the blood begins to clear again;
Now will I make an end immediately. [*Writes.*]

MEPHISTOPHILIS:
What will not I do to obtain his soul? [*Aside.*]

FAUSTUS:
Consummatum est![43] this bill is ended,
And Faustus hath bequeath'd his soul to Lucifer.
But what is this inscription on mine arm?
Homo, fuge![44] Whither should I fly?
If unto God, he'll throw me down to hell.
My senses are deceiv'd; here's nothing writ:—
O yes, I see it plain; even here is writ, 80
Homo, fuge! Yet shall not Faustus fly.

MEPHISTOPHILIS: I'll fetch him somewhat to delight his mind.
[*Aside, and then exit.*]

[*Enter* DEVILS, *giving crowns and rich apparel to* FAUSTUS. *They dance, and then depart.*]
[*Enter Mephistophilis*]

FAUSTUS:
What means this show? Speak, Mephistophilis.

MEPHISTOPHILIS:
Nothing, Faustus, but to delight thy mind,
And let thee see what magic can perform.

---

[43]"It is finished."
[44]"Man, fly!"

FAUSTUS:
But may I raise such spirits when I please?
MEPHISTOPHILIS:
Ay, Faustus, and do greater things than these.
FAUSTUS:
Then there's enough for a thousand souls.
Here, Mephistophilis, receive this scroll,
A deed of gift of body and of soul: 90
But yet conditionally that thou perform
All articles prescrib'd between us both.
MEPHISTOPHILIS:
Faustus, I swear by hell and Lucifer
To effect all promises between us made!
FAUSTUS:
Then hear me read it, Mephistophilis.

On these conditions following.
First, that Faustus may be a spirit in form and substance.
Secondly, that Mephistophilis shall be his servant, and at his command.
Thirdly, that Mephistophilis shall do for him, and bring him whatsoever.
Fourthly, that he shall be in his chamber or house invisible. 100
Lastly, that he shall appear to the said John Faustus at all times, in what form or shape soever he please.
I, John Faustus, of Wittenberg, Doctor, by these presents, do give both body and soul to Lucifer Prince of the East, and his minister Mephistophilis; and furthermore grant unto them that, four and twenty years being expired, and these articles above written being inviolate, full power to fetch or carry the said John Faustus, body and soul, flesh, blood, or goods, into their habitation wheresoever.
By me, John Faustus.

MEPHISTOPHILIS:
Speak, Faustus, do you deliver this as your deed?
FAUSTUS:
Ay, take it, and the devil give thee good of it! 110
MEPHISTOPHILIS:
So, now, Faustus, ask me what thou wilt.
FAUSTUS:
First I will question with thee about hell.
Tell me, where is the place that men call hell?
MEPHISTOPHILIS:
Under the heavens.
FAUSTUS:
Ay, so are all things else, but whereabouts?
MEPHISTOPHILIS:
Within the bowels of these elements,
Where we are tortur'd and remain for ever:
Hell hath no limits, nor is circumscrib'd
In one self place; but where we are is hell,
And where hell is, there must we ever be: 120
And, to be short, when all the world dissolves,
And every creature shall be purified,
All places shall be hell that is not heaven.

FAUSTUS:
I think hell's a fable.
MEPHISTOPHILIS:
Ay, think so, till experience change thy mind.
FAUSTUS:
Why, dost thou think that Faustus shall be damn'd?
MEPHISTOPHILIS:
Ay, of necessity, for here's the scroll
In which thou hast given thy soul to Lucifer.
FAUSTUS:
Ay, and body too: but what of that?
Think'st thou that Faustus is so fond to imagine 130
That, after this life, there is any pain?
No, these are trifles and mere old wives' tales.
MEPHISTOPHILIS:
But I am an instance to prove the contrary;
For I tell thee I am damn'd, and now in hell.
FAUSTUS:
Nay, and this be hell, I'll willingly be damn'd:
What! sleeping, eating, walking, and disputing!
But, leaving off this, let me have a wife,
The fairest maid in Germany, for I
Am wanton and lascivious
And cannot live without a wife. 140
MEPHISTOPHILIS:
I prithee, Faustus, talk not of a wife.
FAUSTUS:
Nay, sweet Mephistophilis, fetch me one, for I will have one.
MEPHISTOPHILIS:
Well, Faustus, thou shalt have a wife.
[*He fetches in a* WOMAN-DEVIL.]
FAUSTUS:
What sight is this?
MEPHISTOPHILIS:
Now, Faustus, wilt thou have a wife?
FAUSTUS:
Here's a hot whore indeed! No, I'll no wife.
MEPHISTOPHILIS:
Marriage is but a ceremonial toy:
And if thou lovest me, think no more of it.
I'll cull thee out the fairest courtesans,
And bring them ev'ry morning to thy bed: 150
She whom thine eye shall like, thy heart shall have,
Were she as chaste as was Penelope,
As wise as Saba,[45] or as beautiful
As was bright Lucifer before his fall.
Here, take this book, and peruse it well:
The iterating of these lines brings gold;
The framing of this circle on the ground

[45] The Queen of Sheba.

Brings thunder, whirlwinds, storm and lightning;
Pronounce this thrice devoutly to thyself,
And men in harness shall appear to thee, 160
Ready to execute what thou command'st.

FAUSTUS:
Thanks, Mephistophilis, for this sweet book.
This will I keep as chary as my life.

[*Exeunt.*]

Scene 2

[*Enter* FAUSTUS *in his study and* MEPHISTOPHILIS.]

FAUSTUS:
When I behold the heavens, then I repent,
And curse thee, wicked Mephistophilis,
Because thou hast depriv'd me of those joys.

MEPHISTOPHILIS:
'Twas thine own seeking, Faustus, thank thyself.
But think'st thou heaven is such a glorious thing?
I tell thee, Faustus, it is not half so fair
As thou, or any man that breathes on earth.

FAUSTUS:
How prov'st thou that?

MEPHISTOPHILIS:
'Twas made for man; then he's more excellent.

FAUSTUS:
If heaven was made for man, 'twas made for me: 10
I will renounce this magic and repent.

[*Enter the two* ANGELS.]

GOOD ANGEL:
Faustus, repent; yet God will pity thee.

BAD ANGEL:
Thou art a spirit; God cannot pity thee.

FAUSTUS:
Who buzzeth in mine ears, I am a spirit?
Be I a devil, yet God may pity me;
Yea, God will pity me, if I repent.

BAD ANGEL:
Ay, but Faustus never shall repent.

[*Exeunt* ANGELS.]

FAUSTUS:
My heart is harden'd, I cannot repent:
Scarce can I name salvation, faith, or heaven,
But fearful echoes thunders in mine ears, 20
'Faustus, thou art damn'd!' Then swords, and knives,
Poison, guns, halters, and envenom'd steel
Are laid before me to despatch myself;
And long ere this I should have done the deed,
Had not sweet pleasure conquer'd deep despair.
Have not I made blind Homer sing to me
Of Alexander's[46] love and Oenon's death?

---

[46] Another name for Paris, Oenon's lover.

And hath not he, that built the walls of Thebes,
With ravishing sound of his melodious harp,
Made music with my Mephistophilis? 30
Why should I die, then, or basely despair?
I am resolv'd; Faustus shall not repent.—
Come, Mephistophilis, let us dispute again,
And reason of divine astrology.
Speak, are there many spheres above the moon?
Are all celestial bodies but one globe,
As is the substance of this centric earth?

MEPHISTOPHILIS:
As are the elements, such are the heavens,
Even from the moon unto the imperial orb,
Mutually folded in each others' spheres, 40
And jointly move upon one axletree,
Whose termine is termed the world's wide pole;
Nor are the names of Saturn, Mars, or Jupiter
Feign'd but are erring stars.

FAUSTUS:
But have they all
One motion, both *situ et tempore*?[47]

MEPHISTOPHILIS: All move from east to west in four and twenty hours upon the poles of the world, but differ in their motions upon the poles of the zodiac.

FAUSTUS:
These slender questions Wagner can decide:
Hath Mephistophilis no greater skill?
Who knows not the double motion of the planets? 50
That the first is finish'd in a natural day;
The second thus: Saturn in thirty years;
Jupiter in twelve; Mars in four; the Sun, Venus, and Mercury in a year; the Moon in twenty-eight days. These are freshmen's questions. But, tell me, hath every sphere a dominion or intelligentia?

MEPHISTOPHILIS: Ay.

FAUSTUS: How many heavens or spheres are there?

MEPHISTOPHILIS: Nine; the seven planets, the firmament, and the imperial heaven.

FAUSTUS: But is there not *coelum igneum, et cristallinum*?[48]

MEPHISTOPHILIS: No, Faustus, they be but fables. 60

FAUSTUS: Resolve me then in this one question: why are not conjunctions, oppositions, aspects, eclipses, all at one time, but in some years we have more, in some less?

MEPHISTOPHILIS: *Per inaequalem motum respectus totius*.[49]

FAUSTUS: Well, I am answer'd. Now tell me who made the world.

MEPHISTOPHILIS: I will not.

FAUSTUS: Sweet Mephistophilis, tell me.

MEPHISTOPHILIS: Move me not, Faustus.

FAUSTUS: Villain, have not I bound thee to tell me any thing?

---

[47] In both the direction and the duration of their revolutions.

[48] The "heaven of fire" and the "crystalline sphere."

[49] "Because of their uneven speeds within the system."

MEPHISTOPHILIS:
Ay, that is not against our kingdom. 70
This is: thou art damn'd; think thou of hell.

FAUSTUS:
Think, Faustus, upon God that made the world.

MEPHISTOPHILIS:
Remember this.

[*Exit.*]

FAUSTUS:
Ay, go, accursed spirit, to ugly hell!
'Tis thou hast damn'd distressed Faustus' soul.
Is't not too late?

[*Enter the two* ANGELS.]

BAD ANGEL:
Too late.

GOOD ANGEL:
Never too late, if Faustus will repent.

BAD ANGEL:
If thou repent, devils will tear thee in pieces.

GOOD ANGEL:
Repent, and they shall never raze thy skin. 80

[*Exeunt* ANGELS.]

FAUSTUS:
O, Christ, my Saviour, my Saviour,
Help to save distressed Faustus' soul!

[*Enter* LUCIFER, BELZEBUB, *and* MEPHISTOPHILIS.]

LUCIFER:
Christ cannot save thy soul, for he is just:
There's none but I have interest in the same.

FAUSTUS:
O, what art thou that look'st so terribly?

LUCIFER:
I am Lucifer,
And this is my companion prince in hell.

FAUSTUS:
O, Faustus, they are come to fetch thy soul!

BELZEBUB:
We are come to tell thee thou dost injure us.

LUCIFER:
Thou call'st on Christ, contrary to thy promise. 90

BELZEBUB:
Thou shouldst not think on God.

LUCIFER:
Think on the devil.

BELZEBUB:
And his dam too.

FAUSTUS:
Nor will I henceforth: pardon me in this,
And Faustus vows never to look to heaven,
Never to name God, or to pray to him,
To burn his Scriptures, slay his ministers,
And make my spirits pull his churches down.

LUCIFER:
So shalt thou show thyself an obedient servant,
And we will highly gratify thee for it. 100

BELZEBUB: Faustus, we are come from hell in person to show thee some pastime: sit down, and thou shalt behold the Seven Deadly Sins appear to thee in their own proper shapes and likeness.

FAUSTUS:
That sight will be as pleasing unto me,
As Paradise was to Adam, the first day
Of his creation.

LUCIFER:
Talk not of Paradise or creation; but mark the show.
Go, Mephistophilis, fetch them in.

[*Enter the* SEVEN DEADLY SINS.]

BELZEBUB: Now, Faustus, question them of their names and dispositions.

FAUSTUS: That shall I soon. What are thou, the first? 110

PRIDE: I am Pride. I disdain to have any parents. I am like Ovid's flea; I can creep into every corner of a wench; sometimes, like a periwig, I sit upon her brow; next, like a necklace I hang about her neck; then, like a fan of feathers, I kiss her lips, and then turning myself to a wrought smock do what I list. But, fie, what a smell is here! I'll not speak another word, unless the ground be perfum'd, and cover'd with cloth of arras.

FAUSTUS: Thou art a proud knave, indeed! What are thou, the second?

COVETOUSNESS: I am Covetousness, begotten of an old churl in a leather bag: and might I now obtain my wish, this house, you and all, should turn to gold, that I might lock you safe into my chest. O my sweet gold! 120

FAUSTUS: And what are thou, the third?

ENVY: I am Envy, begotten of a chimney-sweeper and an oyster-wife. I cannot read, and therefore wish all books burn'd. I am lean with seeing others eat. O, that there would come a famine over all the world, that all might die, and I live alone! then thou should'st see how fat I'd be. But must thou sit, and I stand? come down, with a vengeance!

FAUSTUS: Out, envious wretch!—But what art thou, the fourth?

WRATH: I am Wrath. I had neither father nor mother: I leapt out of a lion's mouth when I was scarce an hour old; and ever since have run up and down the world with these case of rapiers, wounding myself when I could get none to fight 130 withal. I was born in hell; and look to it, for some of you shall be my father.

FAUSTUS: And what are thou, the fifth?

GLUTTONY: I am Gluttony. My parents are all dead, and the devil a penny they have left me, but a small pension, and that buys me thirty meals a day and ten bevers[50]—a small trifle to suffice nature. I come of a royal pedigree! my father was a Gammon of Bacon,[51] and my mother was a Hogshead of Claret wine; my godfathers were these, Peter Pickled-herring and Martin Martlemas-beef. But my godmother, O she was an ancient gentlewoman; her name was Margery March-beer. Now, Faustus, thou hast heard all my progeny; wilt thou bid me to supper? 140

FAUSTUS: Not I.

---

[50]Snacks.

[51]Lower side of bacon.

GLUTTONY: Then the devil choke thee.
FAUSTUS: Choke thyself, glutton!—What art thou, the sixth?
SLOTH: Heigh ho! I am Sloth. I was begotten on a sunny bank, where I have lain ever since; and you have done me great injury to bring me from thence: let me be carried thither again by Gluttony and Lechery. Heigh ho! I'll not speak a word more for a king's ransom.
FAUSTUS: And what are you, Mistress Minx, the seventh and last?
LECHERY: Who, I, sir? I am one that loves an inch of raw mutton[52] better than an ell of fried stockfish, and the first letter of my name begins with Lechery. 150
LUCIFER: Away, to hell, away, on Piper!

[*Exeunt the* SEVEN SINS.]

FAUSTUS: O, how this sight doth delight my soul!
LUCIFER: But, Faustus, in hell is all manner of delight.
FAUSTUS: O, might I see hell, and return again safe, how happy were I then!
LUCIFER:
Faustus, thou shalt. At midnight I will send for thee.
Meanwhile peruse this book and view it thoroughly,
And thou shalt turn thyself into what shape thou wilt.
FAUSTUS:
Thanks, mighty Lucifer!
This will I keep as chary as my life.
LUCIFER:
Now, Faustus, farewell. 160
FAUSTUS:
Farewell, great Lucifer. Come, Mephistophilis.

[*Exeunt omnes several ways.*]

Scene 3

An inn yard.

[*Enter* ROBIN *with a book.*]

ROBIN: What, Dick, look to the horses there, till I come again. I have gotten one of Doctor Faustus' conjuring books, and now we'll have such knavery, as't passes.

[*Enter* DICK.]

DICK: What, Robin, you must come away and walk the horses.
ROBIN: I walk the horses? I scorn't, 'faith, I have other matters in hand, let the horses walk themselves and they will. [*Reads.*] *A per se;*[53] *a, t.h.e. the: o per se; o deny orgon, gorgon.*[54] Keep further from me, O thou illiterate and unlearned hostler.
DICK: 'Snails, what hast thou got there? a book? why, thou canst not tell ne'er a word on't.
ROBIN: That thou shalt see presently. Keep out of the circle, I say, lest I send you into the ostry[55] with a vengeance. 10
DICK: That's like, 'faith: you had best leave your foolery, for an my master come, he'll conjure you, 'faith.

---

[52]Penis.
[53]"A by itself": a beginner's method of reading the alphabet.
[54]A parody of Faustus when he invoked the Demogorgon.
[55]Stable.

ROBIN: My master conjure me? I'll tell thee what, an my master come here, I'll clap as fair a pair of horns on's head as e'er thou sawest in thy life.[56]
DICK: Thou need'st not do that, for my mistress hath done it.
ROBIN: Ay, there be of us here that have waded as deep into matters as other men, if they were disposed to talk.
DICK: A plague take you, I thought you did not sneak up and down after her for nothing. But I prithee, tell me, in good sadness, Robin, is that a conjuring book? 20
ROBIN: Do but speak what thou'lt have me to do, and I'll do't: If thou'lt dance naked, put off thy clothes, and I'll conjure thee about presently: or if thou'lt go but to the tavern with me, I'll give thee white wine, red wine, claret wine, sack, muscadine, malmesey, and whippin-crust,[57] hold belly, hold, and we'll not pay one penny for it.
DICK: O brave, prithee let's to it presently, for I am as dry as a dog.
ROBIN: Come then, let's away.

[*Exeunt.*]

ACT III

Prologue

[*Enter the* CHORUS.]

CHORUS:
Learned Faustus,
To find the secrets of astronomy
Graven in the book of Jove's high firmament,
Did mount him up to scale Olympus' top,
Where sitting in a chariot burning bright,
Drawn by the strength of yoked dragons' necks,
He views the clouds, the planets, and the stars,
The tropic zones, and quarters of the sky,
From the bright circle of the hornèd moon,
E'en to the height of *Primum Mobile:*[58] 10
And whirling round with this circumference,
Within the concave compass of the pole;
From east to west his dragons swiftly glide,
And in eight days did bring him home again.
Not long he stayed within his quiet house,
To rest his bones after his weary toil,
But new exploits do hale him out again,
And mounted then upon a dragon's back,
That with his wings did part the subtle air,
He now is gone to prove cosmography, 20
That measures coasts, and kingdoms of the earth:
And, as I guess, will first arrive at Rome,
To see the Pope and manner of his court,
And take some part of holy Peter's feast,
The which this day is highly solemniz'd.

[*Exit.*]

---

[56] A cuckold's horns.
[57] "Hippocras," a type of wine.
[58] The empyrean.

Scene 1

The Pope's privy chamber.

[*Enter* FAUSTUS *and* MEPHISTOPHILIS.]

FAUSTUS:
Having now, my good Mephistophilis,
Pass'd with delight the stately town of Trier,
Environ'd round with airy mountain tops,
With walls of flint, and deep entrenched lakes,
Not to be won by any conquering prince;
From Paris next, coasting the realm of France,
We saw the river Maine fall into Rhine,
Whose banks are set with groves of fruitful vines;
Then up to Naples, rich Campania,
Whose buildings fair and gorgeous to the eye, 10
The streets straight forth, and paved with finest brick,
Quarters the town in four equivalents;
There saw we learned Maro's[59] golden tomb,
The way he cut, an English mile in length,
Through a rock of stone, in one night's space;
From thence to Venice, Padua, and the East,
In one of which a sumptuous temple stands,
That threats the stars with her aspiring top,
Whose frame is paved with sundry coloured stones,
And roof'd aloft with curious work in gold. 20
Thus hitherto hath Faustus spent his time:
But tell me now, what resting place is this?
Hast thou, as erst I did command,
Conducted me within the walls of Rome?

MEPHISTOPHILIS:
I have, my Faustus, and for proof thereof
This is the goodly Palace of the Pope;
And cause we are no common guests
I choose his privy chamber for our use.

FAUSTUS:
I hope his Holiness will bid us welcome.

MEPHISTOPHILIS:
All's one, for we'll be bold with his venison. 30
But now, my Faustus, that thou may'st perceive
What Rome contains for to delight thine eyes,
Know that this city stands upon seven hills
That underprop the groundwork of the same:
Just through the midst runs flowing Tiber's stream,
With winding banks that cut it in two parts;
Over the which four stately bridges lean,
That make safe passage to each part of Rome:
Upon the bridge called Ponte Angelo

[59] Virgil's.

Erected is a castle passing strong, 40
Where thou shalt see such store of ordinance,
As that the double cannons, forg'd of brass,
Do match the number of the days contain'd
Within the compass of one complete year:
Beside the gates, and high pyramides,[60]
That Julius Caesar brought from Africa.

FAUSTUS:
Now, by the kingdoms of infernal rule,
Of Styx, of Acheron, and the fiery lake
Of ever-burning Phlegethon, I swear
That I do long to see the monuments 50
And situation of bright splendent Rome:
Come, therefore, let's away.

MEPHISTOPHILIS:
Nay, stay, my Faustus; I know you'd see the Pope
And take some part of holy Peter's feast,
The which, in state and high solemnity,
This day is held through Rome and Italy,
In honour of the Pope's triumphant victory.

FAUSTUS:
Sweet Mephistophilis, thou pleasest me,
Whilst I am here on earth, let me be cloy'd
With all things that delight the heart of man. 60
My four-and-twenty years of liberty
I'll spend in pleasure and in dalliance,
That Faustus' name, whilst this bright frame doth stand,
May be admired through the furthest land.

MEPHISTOPHILIS:
'Tis well said, Faustus, come then, stand by me
And thou shalt see them come immediately.

FAUSTUS:
Nay, stay, my gentle Mephistophilis,
And grant me my request, and then I go.
Thou know'st within the compass of eight days
We view'd the face of heaven, of earth and hell. 70
So high our dragons soar'd into the air,
That looking down, the earth appear'd to me
No bigger than my hand in quantity.
There did we view the kingdoms of the world,
And what might please mine eye, I there beheld.
Then in this show let me an actor be,
That this proud Pope may Faustus' cunning see.

MEPHISTOPHILIS:
Let it be so, my Faustus, but, first stay,
And view their triumphs, as they pass this way.
And then devise what best contents thy mind 80
By cunning in thine art to cross the Pope,
Or dash the pride of this solemnity;
To make his monks and abbots stand like apes,

---

[60]Obelisk.

And point like antics at his triple crown:
To beat the beads about the friars' pates,
Or clap huge horns upon the Cardinals' heads;
Or any villainy thou canst devise,
And I'll perform it, Faustus: Hark! they come:
This day shall make thee be admir'd in Rome.

[*Enter the* CARDINALS *and* BISHOPS, *some bearing crosiers, some the pillars,*[61] MONKS *and* FRIARS *singing their procession. Then the* POPE, *and* RAYMOND, *King of Hungary, with* BRUNO[62] *led in chains.*]

POPE:
Cast down our footstool.

RAYMOND:
Saxon Bruno, stoop,
Whilst on thy back his Holiness ascends
Saint Peter's chair and state pontifical.

BRUNO:
Proud Lucifer, that state belongs to me:
But thus I fall to Peter, not to thee.

POPE:
To me and Peter shalt thou grovelling lie,
And crouch before the Papal dignity;
Sound trumpets, then, for thus Saint Peter's heir,
From Bruno's back, ascends Saint Peter's chair.
[*A flourish while he ascends.*]
Thus, as the gods creep on with feet of wool,
Long ere with iron hands they punish men,
So shall our sleeping vengeance now arise,
And smite with death thy hated enterprise.
Lord Cardinals of France and Padua,
Go forthwith to our holy Consistory,
And read amongst the Statutes Decretal,
What, by the holy Council held at Trent,
The sacred synod hath decreed for him
That doth assume the Papal government
Without election, and a true consent:
Away, and bring us word with speed.

FIRST CARDINAL:
We go, my lord.
[*Exeunt* CARDINALS.]

POPE:
Lord Raymond.

FAUSTUS:
Go, haste thee, gentle Mephistophilis,
Follow the Cardinals to the Consistory;
And as they turn their superstitious books,
Strike them with sloth, and drowsy idleness;
And make them sleep so sound, that in their shapes
Thyself and I may parley with this Pope,
This proud confronter of the Emperor:[63]

[61] Objects symbolizing their official ranks.
[62] Fictitious figure; the emperor's nominee for the papacy.
[63] Holy Roman Emperor.

And in despite of all his Holiness
Restore this Bruno to his liberty,
And bear him to the States of Germany.

MEPHISTOPHILIS:
Faustus, I go.

FAUSTUS:
Despatch it soon,
The Pope shall curse that Faustus came to Rome.

[*Exeunt* FAUSTUS *and* MEPHISTOPHILIS.]

BRUNO:
Pope Adrian, let me have right of law,
I was elected by the Emperor.

POPE:
We will depose the Emperor for that deed,
And curse the people that submit to him; 130
Both he and thou shalt stand excommunicate,
And interdict from Church's privilege
And all society of holy men:
He grows too proud in his authority,
Lifting his lofty head above the clouds,
And like a steeple overpeers the Church:
But we'll pull down his haughty insolence.
And as Pope Alexander,[64] our progenitor,
Trod on the neck of German Frederick,
Adding this golden sentence to our praise:— 140
'That Peter's heirs should tread on Emperors,
And walk upon the dreadful adder's back,
Treading the lion and the dragon down,
And fearless spurn the killing basilisk':
So will we quell that haughty schismatic;
And by authority apostolical
Depose him from his regal government.

BRUNO:
Pope Julius swore to princely Sigismond,
For him, and the succeeding Popes of Rome,
To hold the Emperors their lawful lords. 150

POPE:
Pope Julius did abuse the Church's rites,
And therefore none of his decrees can stand.
Is not all power on earth bestowed on us?
And therefore, though we would, we cannot err.
Behold this silver belt, whereto is fix'd
Seven golden keys fast sealed with seven seals
In token of our sevenfold power from Heaven,
To bind or loose, lock fast, condemn, or judge,
Resign, or seal, or whatso pleaseth us.
Then he and thou, and all the world shall stoop, 160
Or be assured of our dreadful curse,
To light as heavy as the pains of hell.

[*Enter* FAUSTUS *and* MEPHISTOPHILIS *like the* CARDINALS.]

[64] Alexander III (1159–1181).

MEPHISTOPHILIS:
Now tell me, Faustus, are we not fitted well?
FAUSTUS:
Yes, Mephistophilis, and two such Cardinals
Ne'er serv'd a holy Pope as we shall do.
But whilst they sleep within the Consistory,
Let us salute his reverend Fatherhood.
RAYMOND:
Behold, my Lord, the Cardinals are return'd.
POPE:
Welcome, grave Fathers, answer presently,
What have our holy Council there decreed, 170
Concerning Bruno and the Emperor,
In quittance of their late conspiracy
Against our state and Papal dignity?
FAUSTUS:
Most sacred Patron of the Church of Rome
By full consent of all the synod
Of priests and prelates, it is thus decreed:
That Bruno and the German Emperor
Be held as Lollards and bold schismatics
And proud disturbers of the Church's peace.
And if that Bruno, by his own assent, 180
Without enforcement of the German peers,
Did seek to wear the triple diadem,
And by your death to climb Saint Peter's chair,
The Statutes Decretal have thus decreed,
He shall be straight condemn'd of heresy,
And on a pile of fagots burnt to death.
POPE:
It is enough: Here, take him to your charge,
and bear him straight to Ponte Angelo,
And in the strongest tower enclose him fast;
Tomorrow, sitting in our Consistory 190
With all our college of grave Cardinals,
We will determine of his life or death.
Here, take his triple crown along with you,
And leave it in the Church's treasury.
Make haste again, my good Lord Cardinals,
And take our blessing apostolical.
MEPHISTOPHILIS:
So, so; was never devil thus blessed before.
FAUSTUS:
Away, sweet Mephistophilis, be gone,
The Cardinals will be plagu'd for this anon.
[*Exeunt* FAUSTUS *and* MEPHISTOPHILIS, *with* BRUNO.]
POPE:
Go presently and bring a banquet forth, 200
That we may solemnize Saint Peter's feast,
And with Lord Raymond, King of Hungary,
Drink to our late and happy victory.
[*Exeunt.*]

Scene 2

A sennet while the banquet is brought in; and then enter FAUSTUS *and* MEPHISTOPHILIS *in their own shapes.*

MEPHISTOPHILIS:
Now, Faustus, come, prepare thyself for mirth:
The sleepy Cardinals are hard at hand
To censure Bruno, that is posted hence,
and on a proud-pac'd steed, as swift as thought,
Flies o'er the Alps to fruitful Germany,
There to salute the woeful Emperor.

FAUSTUS:
The Pope will curse them for their sloth today,
That slept both Bruno and his crown away:
But now, that Faustus may delight his mind,
And by their folly make some merriment, 10
Sweet Mephistophilis, so charm me here,
That I may walk invisible to all,
And do whate'er I please, unseen of any.

MEPHISTOPHILIS:
Faustus, thou shalt, then kneel down presently:

Whilst on thy head I lay my hand,
And charm thee with this magic wand.
First wear this girdle, then appear
Invisible to all are here:
The Planets seven, the gloomy air,
Hell and the Furies' forked hair, 20
Pluto's blue fire, and Hecate's tree,
With magic spells so compass thee,
That no eye may thy body see.

So, Faustus, now for all their holiness,
Do what thou wilt, thou shalt not be discern'd.

FAUSTUS:
Thanks, Mephistophilis; now, friars, take heed,
Lest Faustus make your shaven crowns to bleed.

MEPHISTOPHILIS:
Faustus, no more: see where the Cardinals come.

[*Enter* POPE *and all the* LORDS. *Enter the* CARDINALS *with a book.*]

POPE:
Welcome, Lord Cardinals: come, sit down.
Lord Raymond, take your seat. Friars, attend, 30
And see that all things be in readiness,
As best beseems this solemn festival.

FIRST CARDINAL:
First, may it please your sacred Holiness
To view the sentence of the reverend synod,
Concerning Bruno and the Emperor?

POPE:
What needs this question? Did I not tell you,
Tomorrow we would sit i' th' Consistory,
And there determine of his punishment?
You brought us word even now, it was decreed

That Bruno and the cursed Emperor 40
Were by the holy Council both condemn'd
For loathed Lollards and base schismatics:
Then wherefore would you have me view that book?

FIRST CARDINAL:
Your Grace mistakes, you gave us no such charge.

RAYMOND:
Deny it not, we all are witnesses
That Bruno here was late deliver'd you,
With his rich triple crown to be reserv'd
And put into the Church's treasury.

BOTH CARDINALS:
By holy Paul, we saw them not.

POPE:
By Peter, you shall die, 50
Unless you bring them forth immediately:
Hale them to prison, lade their limbs with gyves:[65]
False prelates, for this hateful treachery,
Curs'd be your souls to hellish misery.

[*Exeunt* ATTENDANTS *with the two* CARDINALS.]

FAUSTUS:
So, they are safe: now, Faustus, to the feast,
The Pope had never such a frolic guest.

POPE:
Lord Archbishop of Reames, sit down with us.

ARCHBISHOP:
I thank your Holiness.

FAUSTUS:
Fall to, the devil choke you an you spare.

POPE:
How now? Who's that which spake?—Friars, look about. 60

FRIAR:
Here's nobody, if it like your Holiness.

POPE:
Lord Raymond, pray fall to. I am beholding
To the Bishop of Milan for this so rare a present.

FAUSTUS:
I thank you, sir. [*Snatches the dish.*]

POPE:
How now? who's that which snatch'd the meat from me?
Villains, why speak you not?—
My good Lord Archbishop, here's a most dainty dish,
Was sent me from a Cardinal in France.

FAUSTUS:
I'll have that too. [*Snatches the dish.*]

POPE:
What Lollards do attend our Holiness, 70
That we receive such great indignity?
Fetch me some wine.

FAUSTUS:
Ay, pray do, for Faustus is adry.

---

[65]Prisoners' shackles.

POPE:
Lord Raymond, I drink unto your grace.
FAUSTUS:
I pledge your grace. [*Snatches the cup.*]
POPE:
My wine gone too?—ye lubbers, look about
And find the man that doth this villainy,
Or by our sanctitude, you all shall die.
I pray, my lords, have patience at this
Troublesome banquet. 80
ARCHBISHOP:
Please it your Holiness, I think it be
Some ghost crept out of Purgatory, and now
Is come unto your Holiness for his pardon.
POPE:
It may be so:
God then command our priests to sing a dirge,
To lay the fury of this same troublesome ghost.
[*Exit an* ATTENDANT.]
Once again, my Lord, fall to. [*The* POPE *crosseth himself.*]
FAUSTUS:
How now?
Must every bit be spicéd with a cross?
Nay then, take that. [*Strikes the* POPE.] 90
POPE:
O I am slain, help me, my lords;
O come and help to bear my body hence:—
Damn'd be his soul for ever for this deed!
[*Exeunt the* POPE *and his train.*]
MEPHISTOPHILIS: Now, Faustus, what will you do now, for I can tell you you'll be curs'd with bell, book, and candle.
FAUSTUS:
Bell, book, and candle,—candle, book, and bell,—
Forward and backward, to curse Faustus to hell!
[*Enter the* FRIARS *with bell, book, and candle for the Dirge.*]
FIRST FRIAR: Come, brethren, let's about our business with good devotion. [*Sing this.*]

Cursed be he that stole his Holiness' meat from the table!
Maledicat Dominus![66] 100
Cursed be he that struck his Holiness a blow on the face!
Maledicat Dominus!
Cursed be he that took Friar Sandelo a blow on the pate!
Maledicat Dominus!
Cursed be he that disturbeth our holy dirge!
Maledicat Dominus!
Cursed be he that took away his Holiness' wine!
Maledicat Dominus!
Et omnes Sancti![67] *Amen!*

[MEPHISTOPHILIS *and* FAUSTUS *beat the* FRIARS, *fling fireworks among them, and exeunt.*]

[66] "May the Lord curse him."
[67] "And all the saints."

Scene 3

A street, near an inn.

[*Enter* ROBIN *and* DICK, *with a cup.*]

DICK: Sirrah Robin, we were best look that your devil can answer the stealing of this same cup, for the vintner's boy follows us at the hard heels.

ROBIN: 'Tis no matter! let him come; and he follow us I'll so conjure him as he was never conjured in his life. I warrant him. Let me see the cup.

[*Enter* VINTNER.]

DICK: Here 't is. Yonder he comes. Now, Robin, now or never show thy cunning.

VINTNER: O are you here? I am glad I have found you, you are a couple of fine companions; pray, where's the cup you stole from the tavern?

ROBIN: How, how? we steal a cup? Take heed what you say; we look not like cup-stealers, I can tell you.

VINTNER: Never deny 't, for I know you have it, and I'll search you. 10

ROBIN: Search me? Ay, and spare not. Hold the cup, Dick [*aside to* DICK]. Come, come, search me, search me! [VINTNER *searches him.*]

VINTNER [*to* DICK]: Come on, sirrah, let me search you now!

DICK: Ay, ay, do! Hold the cup, Robin [*aside to* ROBIN]. I fear not your searching; we scorn to steal your cups, I can tell you. [VINTNER *searches him.*]

VINTNER: Never outface me for the matter, for, sure, the cup is between you two.

ROBIN: Nay, there you lie, 'tis beyond us both.

VINTNER: A plague take you! I thought 't was your knavery to take it away; come, give it me again.

ROBIN: Ay much; when? can you tell? Dick, make me a circle, and stand close at my back, and stir not for thy life. Vintner, you shall have your cup anon. Say nothing, Dick. [*Reads.*] *O per se, o Demogorgon, Belcher and Mephistophilis!* 20

[*Enter* MEPHISTOPHILIS.]

MEPHISTOPHILIS:

You princely legions of infernal rule,
How am I vexed by these villains' charms!
From Constantinople have they brought me now
Only for pleasure of these damned slaves.

[*Exit* VINTNER.]

ROBIN: By Lady, sir, you have had a shrewd journey of it. Will it please you to take a shoulder of mutton to supper, and a tester[68] in your purse, and go back again?

DICK: Aye, aye. I pray you heartily, sir, for we call'd you but in jest, I promise you.

MEPHISTOPHILIS:

To purge the rashness of this cursed deed, 30
First be thou turned to this ugly shape,
For apish deeds transformed to an ape.

ROBIN: O brave! an Ape! I pray, sir, let me have the carrying of him about to show some tricks.

MEPHISTOPHILIS: And so thou shalt: be thou transformed to a dog, And carry him upon thy back. Away, be gone!

ROBIN: A dog! that's excellent; let the maids look well to their porridge-pots, for I'll into the kitchen presently. Come, Dick, come.

[*Exeunt the* TWO CLOWNS.]

---

[68] Sixpence.

MEPHISTOPHILIS:
Now with the flames of ever-burning fire,
I'll wing myself, and forthwith fly amain 40
Unto my Faustus, to the Great Turk's Court.

[*Exit.*]

ACT IV

Prologue

[*Enter* CHORUS.]

CHORUS:
When Faustus had with pleasure ta'en the view
Of rarest things, and royal courts of kings,
He stay'd his course, and so returned home;
Where such as bear his absence but with grief,
I mean his friends and near'st companions,
Did gratulate his safety with kind words,
And in their conference of what befell,
Touching his journey through the world and air,
They put forth questions of astrology,
Which Faustus answer'd with such learned skill 10
As they admir'd and wonder'd at his wit.
Now is his fame spread forth in every land:
Amongst the rest the Emperor is one,
Carolus the Fifth,[69] at whose palace now
Faustus is feasted 'mongst his noblemen.
What there he did, in trial of his art,
I leave untold; your eyes shall see perform'd.

[*Exit.*]

Scene 1

A room in the Emperor's Court at Innsbruck.

[*Enter* MARTINO *and* FREDERICK *at several doors.*]

MARTINO:
What ho, officers, gentlemen,
Hie to the presence to attend the Emperor,
Good Frederick, see the rooms be voided straight,
His majesty is coming to the hall;
Go back, and see the state[70] in readiness.

FREDERICK:
But where is Bruno, our elected Pope,
That on a fury's back came post from Rome?
Will not his Grace consort the Emperor?

MARTINO:
O yes, and with him comes the German conjuror,
The learned Faustus, fame of Wittenberg, 10

---

[69]Charles V (1519–1556).
[70]Throne.

The wonder of the world for magic art;
And he intends to show great Carolus
The race of all his stout progenitors;
And bring in presence of his Majesty
The royal shapes and warlike semblances
Of Alexander and his beauteous paramour.[71]

FREDERICK:
Where is Benvolio?

MARTINO:
Fast asleep, I warrant you,
He took his rouse with stoups of Rhenish wine
So kindly yesternight to Bruno's health, 20
That all this day the sluggard keeps his bed.

FREDERICK:
See, see, his window's ope, we'll call to him.

MARTINO:
What ho, Benvolio!

[*Enter* BENVOLIO *above, at a window, in his nightcap; buttoning.*]

BENVOLIO:
What a devil ail you two?

MARTINO:
Speak softly, sir, lest the devil hear you:
For Faustus at the court is late arriv'd,
And at his heels a thousand furies wait,
To accomplish whatsoever the Doctor please.

BENVOLIO:
What of this?

MARTINO:
Come, leave thy chamber first, and thou shalt see 30
This conjuror perform such rare exploits,
Before the Pope and royal Emperor,
As never yet was seen in Germany.

BENVOLIO:
Has not the Pope enough of conjuring yet?
He was upon the devil's back late enough;
And if he be so far in love with him,
I would he would post with him to Rome again.

FREDERICK:
Speak, wilt thou come and see this sport?

BENVOLIO:
Not I.

MARTINO:
Wilt thou stand in thy window, and see it then? 40

BENVOLIO:
Ay, an I fall not asleep i' th' meantime.

MARTINO:
The Emperor is at hand, who comes to see
What wonders by black spells may compass'd be.

BENVOLIO: Well, go you attend the Emperor: I am content for this once to thrust my head out at a window; for they say if a man be drunk overnight the devil

[71] Alexander the Great and Thais.

cannot hurt him in the morning; if that be true, I have a charm in my head shall control him as well as the conjuror, I warrant you.

[*Exeunt* FREDERICK *and* MARTINO.]

Scene 2

The Presence Chamber in the Court.

[*A sennet. Enter* CHARLES, *the* GERMAN EMPEROR, BRUNO, DUKE OF SAXONY, FAUSTUS, MEPHISTOPHILIS, FREDERICK, MARTINO, *and* ATTENDANTS.]

EMPEROR:
Wonder of men, renown'd magician,
Thrice-learned Faustus, welcome to our Court.
This deed of thine, in setting Bruno free
From his and our professed enemy,
Shall add more excellence unto thine art,
Than if by powerful necromantic spells,
Thou couldst command the world's obedience:
For ever be belov'd of Carolus,
And if this Bruno thou hast late redeem'd,
In peace possess the triple diadem, 10
And sit in Peter's chair, despite of chance,
Thou shalt be famous through all Italy,
And honour'd of the German Emperor.

FAUSTUS:
These gracious words, most royal Carolus,
Shall make poor Faustus, to his utmost power,
Both love and serve the German Emperor,
And lay his life at holy Bruno's feet.
For proof whereof, if so your Grace be pleas'd,
The Doctor stands prepar'd by power of art
To cast his magic charms, that shall pierce through 20
The ebon gates of ever-burning hell,
And hale the stubborn Furies from their caves,
To compass whatsoe'er your Grace commands.

BENVOLIO [*above*]: 'Blood, he speaks terribly: but for all that I do not greatly believe him: he looks as like a conjuror as the Pope to a costermonger.

EMPEROR:
Then, Faustus, as thou late did'st promise us,
We would behold that famous conqueror,
Great Alexander and his paramour
In their true shapes and state majestical,
That we may wonder at their excellence. 30

FAUSTUS:
Your Majesty shall see them presently.
Mephistophilis, away.
And with a solemn noise of trumpets' sound
Present before this royal Emperor,
Great Alexander and his beauteous paramour.

MEPHISTOPHILIS: Faustus, I will.

BENVOLIO: Well, Master Doctor, an your devils come not away quickly, you shall have me asleep presently: zounds, I could eat myself for anger, to think I have been such an ass all this while to stand gaping after the devil's governor, and can see nothing. 40

FAUSTUS:
I'll make you feel something anon, if my art fail me not.—
My lord, I must forewarn your Majesty,
That when my spirits present the royal shapes
Of Alexander and his paramour,
Your Grace demand no questions of the king,
But in dumb silence let them come and go.

EMPEROR:
Be it as Faustus please, we are content.

BENVOLIO: Ay, ay, and I am content too; and thou bring Alexander and his paramour before the Emperor, I'll be Acteon and turn myself to a stag.

FAUSTUS: And I'll play Diana, and send you the horns presently. 50

[*Sennet. Enter at one door the* EMPEROR ALEXANDER, *at the other* DARIUS; *they meet.* DARIUS *is thrown down.* ALEXANDER *kills him; takes off his crown and offering to go out, his paramour meets him, he embraceth her, and sets Darius' crown upon her head; and coming back, both salute the* EMPEROR, *who, leaving his state, offers to embrace them, which,* FAUSTUS *seeing, suddenly stays him. Then trumpets cease, and music sounds.*]

My gracious lord, you do forget yourself,
These are but shadows, not substantial.

EMPEROR:
O pardon me, my thoughts are so ravished
With sight of this renowned Emperor,
That in mine arms I would have compass'd him.
But, Faustus, since I may not speak to them,
To satisfy my longing thoughts at full,
Let me this tell thee: I have heard it said,
That this fair lady whilst she liv'd on earth,
Had on her neck, a little wart, or mole; 60
How may I prove that saying to be true?

FAUSTUS:
Your Majesty may boldly go and see.

EMPEROR:
Faustus, I see it plain,
And in this sight thou better pleasest me,
Than if I gain'd another monarchy.

FAUSTUS: Away, be gone!

[*Exit show.*]

See, see, my gracious lord, what strange beast is yon, that thrusts his head out at window?

EMPEROR:
O wondrous sight: see, Duke of Saxony,
Two spreading horns most strangely fastened
Upon the head of young Benvolio. 70

SAX:
What, is he asleep, or dead?

FAUSTUS:
He sleeps, my lord, but dreams not of his horns.

EMPEROR:
This sport is excellent; we'll call and wake him.
What ho, Benvolio.

BENVOLIO: A plague upon you, let me sleep a while.

EMPEROR: I blame thee not to sleep much, having such a head of thine own.

SAX: Look up, Benvolio, 'tis the Emperor calls.

BENVOLIO: The Emperor? where—O zounds, my head!
EMPEROR: Nay, and thy horns hold, 'tis no matter for thy head, for that's arm'd sufficiently. 80
FAUSTUS: Why, how now, Sir Knight, what, hang'd by the horns? this is most horrible: fie, fie, pull in your head for shame, let not all the world wonder at you.
BENVOLIO: Zounds, Doctor, is this your villainy?
FAUSTUS:
O say not so, sir: the Doctor has no skill,
No art, no cunning, to present these lords,
Or bring before this royal Emperor
The mighty monarch, warlike Alexander.
If Faustus do it, you are straight resolv'd
In bold Acteon's shape to turn a stag. 90
And therefore, my lord, so please your Majesty,
I'll raise a kennel of hounds, shall hunt him so,
As all his footmanship shall scarce prevail
To keep his carcase from their bloody fangs.
Ho, Belimote, Argiron, Asterote.
BENVOLIO:
Hold, hold! Zounds, he'll raise up a kennel of devils,
I think, anon: good, my lord, entreat for me: 'sblood,
I am never able to endure these torments.
EMPEROR:
Then, good Master Doctor,
Let me entreat you to remove his horns, 100
He has done penance now sufficiently.
FAUSTUS: My gracious lord, not so much for injury done to me, as to delight your Majesty with some mirth, hath Faustus justly requited this injurious knight, which being all I desire, I am content to remove his horns. Mephistophilis, transform him [MEPHISTOPHILIS *removes the horns*], and hereafter, sir, look you speak well of scholars.
BENVOLIO: Speak well of ye? 'sblood, and scholars be such cuckold-makers to clap horns of honest men's head o' this order, I'll e'er trust smooth faces and small ruffs more. But an I be not reveng'd for this, would I might be turn'd to a gaping oyster, and drink nothing but salt water. 110
[*Aside, and then exit above.*]
EMPEROR:
Come, Faustus, while the Emperor lives,
In recompense of this thy high desert,
Thou shalt command the state of Germany,
And live belov'd of mighty Carolus.
[*Exeunt omnes.*]

Scene 3

Near a grove, outside Innsbruck.

[*Enter* BENVOLIO, MARTINO, FREDERICK, *and* SOLDIERS.]
MARTINO:
Nay, sweet Benvolio, let us sway thy thoughts
From this attempt against the conjuror.
BENVOLIO:
Away, you love me not, to urge me thus.
Shall I let slip so great an injury,

When every servile groom jests at my wrongs,
And in their rustic gambols proudly say,
'Benvolio's head was graced with horns today'?
O may these eyelids never close again,
Till with my sword I have that conjuror slain.
If you will aid me in this enterprise, 10
Then draw your weapons, and be resolute:
If not, depart: here will Benvolio die,
But Faustus' death shall quit[72] my infamy.

FREDERICK:
Nay, we will stay with thee, betide what may,
And kill that Doctor if he come this way.

BENVOLIO:
Then, gentle Frederick, hie thee to the grove,
And place our servants and our followers
Close in an ambush there behind the trees.
By this (I know) the conjuror is near;
I saw him kneel and kiss the Emperor's hand, 20
And take his leave laden with rich rewards.
Then, soldiers, boldly fight; if Faustus die,
Take you the wealth, leave us the victory.

FREDERICK:
Come, soldiers, follow me unto the grove;
Who kills him shall have gold and endless love.

[*Exit* FREDERICK *with the* SOLDIERS.]

BENVOLIO:
My head is lighter than it was by th' horns,
But yet my heart's more ponderous than my head,
And pants until I see that conjuror dead.

MARTINO:
Where shall we place ourselves, Benvolio?

BENVOLIO:
Here will we stay to bide the first assault. 30
O were that damned hellhound but in place,
Thou soon shouldst see me quit my foul disgrace.

[*Enter* FREDERICK.]

FREDERICK:
Close, close, the conjuror is at hand,
And all alone comes walking in his gown;
Be ready then, and strike the peasant down.

BENVOLIO:
Mine be that honour then: now, sword, strike home,
For horns he gave I'll have his head anon.

[*Enter* FAUSTUS *with the false head.*]

MARTINO:
See, see, he comes.

BENVOLIO:
No words: this blow ends all,
Hell take his soul, his body thus must fall. [*Stabs* FAUSTUS.] 40

FAUSTUS [*falling*]:
Oh!

---

[72] Avenge.

FREDERICK:
Groan you, Master Doctor?
BENVOLIO:
Break may his heart with groans: dear Frederick, see,
Thus will I end his griefs immediately.
MARTINO:
Strike with a willing hand. [BENVOLIO *strikes off* FAUSTUS' *false head.*]
His head is off.
BENVOLIO:
The devil's dead, the Furies now may laugh.
FREDERICK:
Was this that stern aspect, that awful frown,
Made the grim monarch of infernal spirits
Tremble and quake at his commanding charms? 50
MARTINO:
Was this that damned head, whose art conspir'd
Benvolio's shame before the Emperor?
BENVOLIO:
Ay, that's the head, and here the body lies,
Justly rewarded for his villainies.
FREDERICK:
Come, let's devise how we may add more shame
To the black scandal of his hated name.
BENVOLIO:
First, on his head, in quittance of my wrongs,
I'll nail huge forked horns, and let them hang
Within the window where he yok'd me first,
That all the world may see my just revenge. 60
MARTINO: What use shall we put his beard to?
BENVOLIO: We'll sell it to a chimney-sweeper; it will wear out ten birchen brooms. I warrant you.
FREDERICK: What shall his eyes do?
BENVOLIO: We'll put out his eyes, and they shall serve for buttons to his lips, to keep his tongue from catching cold.
MARTINO: An excellent policy: and now, sirs, having divided him, what shall the body do? [*Faustus rises.*]
BENVOLIO: Zounds, the devil's alive again.
FREDRICK:
Give him his head, for God's sake. 70
FAUSTUS:
Nay, keep it: Faustus will have heads and hands,
Ay, all your hearts to recompense this deed.
Knew you not, traitors, I was limited
For four-and-twenty years to breathe on earth?
And had you cut my body with your swords,
Or hew'd this flesh and bones as small as sand,
Yet in a minute had my spirit return'd,
And I had breath'd a man made free from harm.
But wherefore do I dally my revenge?
Asteroth, Belimoth, Mephistophilis, 80
[*Enter* MEPHISTOPHILIS *and other* DEVILS.]
Go, horse these traitors on your fiery backs,
And mount aloft with them as high as heaven,

Thence pitch them headlong to the lowest hell:
Yet, stay, the world shall see their misery,
And hell shall after plague their treachery.
Go, Belimoth, and take this caitiff hence,
And hurl him in some lake of mud and dirt:
Take thou this other, drag him through the woods,
Amongst the pricking thorns, and sharpest briers,
Whilst with my gentle Mephistophilis, 90
This traitor flies unto some steepy rock,
That, rolling down, may break the villain's bones,
As he intended to dismember me.
Fly hence, despatch my charge immediately.

FREDERICK:
Pity us, gentle Faustus, save our lives!

FAUSTUS:
Away!

FREDERICK:
He must needs go that the devil drives.

[*Exeunt* SPIRITS *with the* KNIGHTS.]

[*Enter the ambushed* SOLDIERS.]

FIRST SOLDIER:
Come, sirs, prepare yourselves in readiness,
Make haste to help these noble gentlemen,
I heard them parley with the conjuror. 100

SECOND SOLDIER:
See where he comes, despatch, and kill the slave.

FAUSTUS:
What's here? an ambush to betray my life:
Then, Faustus, try thy skill: base peasants, stand:
For lo! these trees remove at my command,
And stand as bulwarks 'twixt yourselves and me,
To shield me from your hated treachery:
Yet to encounter this your weak attempt,
Behold an army comes incontinent.[73]

[FAUSTUS *strikes the door, and enter a devil playing on a drum, after him another bearing an ensign; and divers with weapons,* MEPHISTOPHILIS *with fireworks; they set upon the* SOLDIERS, *and drive them out. Exit* FAUSTUS.]

Scene 4

[*Enter at several doors* BENVOLIO, FREDERICK, *and* MARTINO, *their heads and faces bloody, and besmear'd with mud and dirt, all having horns on their heads.*]

MARTINO:
What ho, Benvolio!

BENVOLIO:
Here, what, Frederick, ho!

FREDERICK:
O help me, gentle friend; where is Martino?

MARTINO:
Dear Frederick, here,
Half smother'd in a lake of mud and dirt,
Through which the furies dragg'd me by the heels.

[73] Immediately.

FREDERICK:
Martino, see Benvolio's horns again.
MARTINO:
O misery, how now, Benvolio?
BENVOLIO:
Defend me, heaven, shall I be haunted still?
MARTINO:
Nay, fear not, man; we have no power to kill. 10
BENVOLIO:
My friends transformed thus! O hellish spite,
Your heads are all set with horns.
FREDERICK:
You hit it right:
It is your own you mean, feel on your head.
BENVOLIO:
'Zounds, horns again!
MARTINO:
Nay, chafe not, man, we all are sped.[74]
BENVOLIO:
What devil attends this damn'd magician,
That, spite of spite, our wrongs are doubled?
FREDERICK:
What may we do, that we may hide our shames?
BENVOLIO:
If we should follow him to work revenge,
He'd join long asses' ears to these huge horns,
And make us laughingstocks to all the world. 20
MARTINO:
What shall we then do, dear Benvolio?
BENVOLIO:
I have a castle joining near these woods,
And thither we'll repair and live obscure,
Till time shall alter these our brutish shapes:
Sith black disgrace hath thus eclips'd our fame,
We'll rather die with grief than live with shame.
[*Exeunt omnes.*]

Scene 5

At the entrance to the house of FAUSTUS.

[*Enter* FAUSTUS *and the* HORSE-COURSER.[75]]

HORSE-COURSER: I beseech, your worship, accept of these forty dollars.

FAUSTUS: Friend, thou canst not buy so good a horse, for so small a price. I have no great need to sell him, but if thou likest him for ten dollars more take him, because I see thou hast a good mind to him.

HORSE-COURSER: I beseech you, sir, accept of this; I am a very poor man and have lost very much of late by horseflesh, and this bargain will set me up again.

FAUSTUS: Well, I will not stand with thee, give me the money. [HORSE-COURSER *gives* FAUSTUS *the money.*] Now, sirrah, I must tell you that you may ride him o'er

[74] "We are all done for."
[75] Horse trader.

hedge and ditch, and spare him not; but, do you hear? in any case ride him not into the water.

HORSE-COURSER: How, sir, not into the water? Why, will he not drink of all waters? 10

FAUSTUS: Yes, he will drink of all waters, but ride him not into the water; o'er hedge and ditch, or where thou wilt, but not into the water. Go, bid the ostler deliver him unto you, and remember what I say.

HORSE-COURSER: I warrant you, sir. O joyful day, now am I a made man for ever. [*Exit.*]

FAUSTUS:

What art thou, Faustus, but a man condemn'd to die?
Thy fatal time draws to a final end,
Despair doth drive distrust into my thoughts.
Confound these passions with a quiet sleep. 20
Tush! Christ did call the thief upon the Cross;
Then rest thee, Faustus, quiet in conceit. [*He sits to sleep.*]

[*Re-enter the* HORSE-COURSER *wet.*]

HORSE-COURSER: O what a cozening Doctor was this? I was riding my horse into the water, thinking some hidden mystery had been in the horse, I had nothing under me but a little straw, and had much ado to escape drowning. Well, I'll go rouse him, and make him give me my forty dollars again. Ho, sirrah Doctor, you cozening scab! Master Doctor, awake and rise, and give me my money again, for your horse is turned to a bottle[76] of hay, master Doctor. [*He pulls off his leg.*] Alas! I am undone, what shall I do? I have pull'd off his leg.

FAUSTUS: O, help, help, the villain hath murder'd me. 30

HORSE-COURSER: Murder, or not murder, now he has but one leg, I'll outrun him, and cast this leg into some ditch or other.

[*Aside, and then runs out.*]

FAUSTUS: Stop him, stop him, stop him!—ha, ha, ha, Faustus hath his leg again, and the horse-courser a bundle of hay for his forty dollars.

[*Enter* WAGNER.]

How now, Wagner, what news with thee?

WAGNER: If it please you, the Duke of Anholt doth earnestly entreat your company, and hath sent some of his men to attend you with provision fit for your journey.

FAUSTUS: The Duke of Anholt's an honourable gentleman, and one to whom I must be no niggard of my cunning. Come away!

[*Exeunt.*]

Scene 6

An Inn.

[*Enter* ROBIN, DICK, *the* HORSE-COURSER, *and a* CARTER.]

CARTER: Come, my masters, I'll bring you to the best beer in Europe. What ho, hostess!—where be these whores?

[*Enter* HOSTESS.]

HOSTESS: How now, what lack you? What, my old guests, welcome.

ROBIN: Sirra Dick, dost thou know why I stand so mute?

DICK: No, Robin, why is't?

ROBIN: I am eighteenpence on the score,[77] but say nothing, see if she have forgotten me.

---

[76]Bundle. [77]Account.

HOSTESS: Who's this, that stands so solemnly by himself? what, my old guest?
ROBIN: O hostess, how do you? I hope my score stands still.
HOSTESS: Ay, there's no doubt of that, for methinks you make no haste to wipe it out. 10
DICK: Why, hostess, I say, fetch us some beer.
HOSTESS: You shall presently: look up in th' hall there, ho!

[*Exit.*]

DICK: Come, sirs, what shall we do now till mine hostess comes?
CARTER: Marry, sir, I'll tell you the bravest tale how a conjuror served me; you know Doctor Fauster?
HORSE-COURSER: Ay, a plague take him, here's some on's have cause to know him; did he conjure thee too?
CARTER: I'll tell you how he serv'd me: As I was going to Wittenberg t'other day, with a load of hay, he met me, and asked me what he should give me for as much hay as he could eat; now, sir, I thinking that a little would serve his turn, bade him take as much as he would for three farthings; so he presently gave me my money, and fell to eating; and, as I am a cursen man, he never left eating, till he had eat up all my load of hay. 20
ALL: O monstrous, eat a whole load of hay!
ROBIN: Yes, yes, that may be; for I have heard of one that has eat a load of logs.[78]
HORSE-COURSER: Now sirs, you shall hear how villainously he serv'd me: I went to him yesterday to buy a horse of him, and he would by no means sell him under forty dollars; so, sir, because I knew him to be such a horse as would run over hedge and ditch and never tire, I gave him his money. So when I had my horse, Doctor Fauster bade me ride him night and day, and spare him no time; but, quoth he, in any case, ride him not into the water. Now, sir, I thinking the horse had had some rare quality that he would not have me know of, what did I but rid him into a great river, and when I came just in the midst, my horse vanish'd away, and I sat straddling upon a bottle of hay. 30
ALL: O brave Doctor!
HORSE-COURSER: But you shall hear how bravely I serv'd him for it; I went me home to his house, and there I found him asleep; I kept a hallooing and whooping in his ears, but all could not wake him: I seeing that, took him by the leg, and never rested pulling, till I had pull'd me his leg quite off, and now 'tis at home in mine hostry. 40
DICK: And has the Doctor but one leg then? that's excellent, for one of his devils turn'd me into the likeness of an ape's face.
CARTER: Some more drink, hostess.
ROBIN: Hark you, we'll into another room and drink a while, and then we'll go seek out the Doctor.

[*Exeunt omnes.*]

Scene 7

The Court of the DUKE OF ANHOLT.

[*Enter the* DUKE OF ANHOLT, *his* DUCHESS, FAUSTUS, *and* MEPHISTOPHILIS.]

DUKE: Thanks, master Doctor, for these pleasant sights. Nor know I how sufficiently to recompense your great deserts in erecting that enchanted castle in the air, the sight whereof so delighted me,
As nothing in the world could please me more.

[78] Been drunk.

FAUSTUS: I do think myself, my good Lord, highly recompensed in that it pleaseth your Grace to think but well of that which Faustus hath performed. But gracious lady, it may be that you have taken no pleasure in those sights; therefore, I pray you tell me, what is the thing you most desire to have; be it in the world, it shall be yours. I have heard that great-bellied women do long for things are rare and dainty. 10

DUCHESS: True, master Doctor, and since I find you so kind, I will make known unto you what my heart desires to have; and were it now summer, as it is January, a dead time of the winter, I would request no better meat than a dish of ripe grapes.

FAUSTUS: This is but a small matter. Go, Mephistophilis, away!

[*Exit* MEPHISTOPHILIS.]

Madam, I will do more than this for your content.

[*Enter* MEPHISTOPHILIS *again with the grapes.*]

Here now taste ye these, they should be good,
For they come from a far country, I can tell you.

DUKE:
This makes me wonder more than all the rest
That at this time of the year, when every tree 20
Is barren of his fruit, from whence you had
These ripe grapes.

FAUSTUS: Please it your Grace the year is divided into two circles over the whole world, so that when it is winter with us, in the contrary circle it is likewise summer with them, as in India, Saba and such countries that lie far east, where they have fruit twice a year. From whence, by means of a swift spirit that I have, I had these grapes brought, as you see.

DUCHESS: And trust me, they are the sweetest grapes that e'er I tasted.

[*The* CLOWNS *bounce*[79] *at the gate within.*]

DUKE:
What rude disturbers have we at the gate?
Go, pacify their fury, set it ope, 30
And then demand of them what they would have.

[*They knock again, and call out to talk with* FAUSTUS.]

A SERVANT:
Why, how now, masters, what a coil[80] is there?
What is the reason you disturb the Duke?

DICK: We have no reason for it, therefore a fig[81] for him.

SERVANT: Why, saucy varlets, dare you be so bold?

HORSE-COURSER: I hope, sir, we have wit enough to be more bold than welcome.

SERVANT: It appears so, pray be bold elsewhere, and trouble not the Duke.

DUKE: What would they have?

SERVANT: They all cry out to speak with Doctor Faustus.

CARTER: Ay, and we will speak with him. 40

DUKE: Will you, sir? Commit the rascals.

DICK: Commit with us! he were as good commit with his father as commit with us.

FAUSTUS:
I do beseech your Grace let them come in,
They are good subject for a merriment.

DUKE:
Do as thou wilt, Faustus, I give thee leave.

---

[79]Bang. [80]Disturbance. [81]Obscene gesture.

FAUSTUS:
I thank your Grace.
[*Enter* ROBIN, DICK, CARTER, *and* HORSE-COURSER.]
Why, how now, my good friends?
Faith you are too outrageous, but come near,
'I have procur'd your pardons: welcome all. 50
ROBIN: Nay, sir, we will be welcome for our money, and we will pay for what we take. What ho, give's half a dozen of beer here, and be hang'd.
FAUSTUS: Nay, hark you, can you tell me where you are?
CARTER: Ay, marry can I; we are under heaven.
SERVANT: Ay, but, sir sauce-box, know you in what place?
HORSE-COURSER: Ay, ay, the house is good enough to drink in:
Zounds, fill us some beer, or we'll break all the barrels in the house, and dash out all your brains with your bottles.
FAUSTUS:
Be not so furious: come, you shall have beer.
My lord, beseech you give me leave a while, 60
I'll gage my credit 'twill content your Grace.
DUKE:
With all my heart, kind Doctor, please thyself;
Our servants and our Court's at thy command.
FAUSTUS:
I humbly thank your Grace: then fetch some beer.
HORSE-COURSER: Ay, marry, there spake a Doctor indeed, and, 'faith, I'll drink a health to thy wooden leg for that word.
FAUSTUS: My wooden leg! what dost thou mean by that?
CARTER: Ha, ha, ha, dost hear him, Dick? He has forgot his leg.
HORSE-COURSER: Ay, ay, he does not stand much upon that.
FAUSTUS: No, 'faith not much upon a wooden leg. 70
CARTER: Good Lord, that flesh and blood should be so frail with your Worship. Do not you remember a horse-courser you sold a horse to?
FAUSTUS: Yes, I remember I sold one a horse.
CARTER: And do you remember you bid he should not ride him onto the water?
FAUSTUS: Yes, I do very well remember that.
CARTER: And do you remember nothing of your leg?
FAUSTUS: No, in good sooth.
CARTER: Then, I pray, remember your curtsy.
FAUSTUS: I thank you, sir.
CARTER: 'Tis not so much worth; I pray you tell me one thing. 80
FAUSTUS: What's that?
CARTER: Be both your legs bedfellows every night together?
FAUSTUS: Wouldst thou make a Colossus of me, that thou askest me such questions?
CARTER: No, truly, sir: I would make nothing of you, but I would fain know that.
[*Enter* HOSTESS *with drink.*]
FAUSTUS: Then I assure thee certainly they are.
CARTER: I thank you, I am fully satisfied.
FAUSTUS: But wherefore dost thou ask?
CARTER: For nothing, sir: but methinks you should have a wooden bedfellow of one of 'em.
HORSE-COURSER: Why, do you hear, sir, did not I pull off one of your legs when you were asleep? 90
FAUSTUS: But I have it again, now I am awake: look you here, sir.
ALL: O horrible, had the Doctor three legs?

CARTER: Do you remember, sir, how you cozened me and ate up my load of—

[FAUSTUS *charms him dumb.*]

DICK: Do you remember how you made me wear an ape's—

HORSE-COURSER: You whoreson conjuring scab, do you remember how you cozened me with a ho—

ROBIN: Ha' you forgotten me? you think to carry it away with your *hey-pass* and *re-pass,*[82] do you remember the dog's fa— 100

[*Exeunt* CLOWNS.]

HOSTESS: Who pays for the ale? hear you, Master Doctor, now you have sent away my guests, I pray who shall pay me for my a—

[*Exit* HOSTESS.]

LADY:

My Lord,
We are much beholding to this learned man.

DUKE:

So are we, Madam, which we will recompense
With all the love and kindness that we may.
His artful sport drives all sad thoughts away.

[*Exeunt.*]

ACT V

Scene 1

Thunder and lightning.

[*Enter* DEVILS *with cover'd dishes.* MEPHISTOPHILIS *leads them into Faustus' study. Then enter* WAGNER.]

WAGNER:

I think my master means to die shortly,
He has made his will, and given me his wealth,
His house, his goods, and store of golden plate,
Besides two thousand ducats ready coin'd.
I wonder what he means; if death were nigh
He would not frolic thus. He's now at supper
With the scholars, where there's such belly-cheer
As Wagner in his life ne'er saw the like.
And see where they come, belike the feast is done.

[*Exit.*]

[*Enter* FAUSTUS, MEPHISTOPHILIS, *and two or three* SCHOLARS.]

FIRST SCHOLAR: Master Doctor Faustus, since our conference about fair ladies, which was the beautifullest in all the world, we have determined with ourselves that Helen of Greece was the admirablest lady that ever liv'd: therefore, Master Doctor, if you will do us so much favour, as to let us see that peerless dame of Greece, we should think ourselves much beholding unto you. 10

FAUSTUS:

Gentlemen,
For that I know your friendship is unfeign'd,
It is not Faustus' custom to deny
The just request of those that wish him well,
You shall behold that peerless dame of Greece, 20

[82] Expressions used by a conjurer.

No otherwise for pomp or majesty
Than when Sir Paris cross'd the seas with her,
And brought the spoil to rich Dardania.[83]
Be silent, then, for danger is in words.

[*Music sounds,* MEPHISTOPHILIS *brings in* HELEN, *she passeth over the stage.*]

SECOND SCHOLAR:
Was this fair Helen, whose admired worth
Made Greece with ten years' wars afflict poor Troy?
Too simple is my wit to tell her praise,
Whom all the world admires for majesty.

THIRD SCHOLAR:
No marvel though the angry Greeks pursued
With ten years' war the rape of such a queen, 30
Whose heavenly beauty passeth all compare.

FIRST SCHOLAR:
Now we have seen the pride of Nature's work,
And only paragon of excellence,
We'll take our leaves; and for this glorious deed
Happy and blest be Faustus evermore!

FAUSTUS:
Gentlemen, farewell: the same wish I to you.

[*Exeunt* SCHOLARS.]

[*Enter an* OLD MAN.]

OLD MAN:
O gentle Faustus, leave this damned art,
This magic, that will charm thy soul to hell,
And quite bereave[84] thee of salvation.
Though thou hast now offended like a man, 40
Do not persever in it like a devil;
Yet, yet, thou hast an amiable soul,
If sin by custom grow not into nature:
Then, Faustus, will repentance come too late,
Then thou art banish'd from the sight of heaven;
No mortal can express the pains of hell.
It may be this my exhortation
Seems harsh and all unpleasant; let it not,
For, gentle son, I speak it not in wrath,
Or envy of thee, but in tender love, 50
And pity of thy future misery.
And so have hope, that this my kind rebuke,
Checking thy body, may amend thy soul.

FAUSTUS:
Break heart, drop blood, and mingle it with tears,
Tears falling from repentant heaviness
Of thy most vile and loathsome filthiness,
The stench whereof corrupts the inward soul
With such flagitious crimes of heinous sins
As no commiseration may expel,
But mercy, Faustus, of thy Saviour sweet, 60
Whose blood alone must wash away thy guilt—

[83] Troy. [84] Deprive.

Where art thou, Faustus? wretch, what has thou done?
Damn'd art thou, Faustus, damn'd; despair and die!
[MEPHISTOPHILIS *gives him a dagger.*]
Hell claims his right, and with a roaring voice
Says, 'Faustus, come; thine hour is almost come';
And Faustus now will come to do thee right.

OLD MAN:
Oh, stay, good Faustus, stay thy desperate steps!
I see an angel hover o'er thy head,
And, with a vial full of precious grace,
Offers to pour the same into thy soul: 70
Then call for mercy, and avoid despair.

FAUSTUS:
O friend, I feel
Thy words to comfort my distressed soul!
Leave me a while to ponder on my sins.

OLD MAN:
Faustus, I leave thee; but with grief of heart,
Fearing the enemy of thy hapless soul.
[*Exit.*]

FAUSTUS:
Accursed Faustus, where is mercy now?
I do repent; and yet I do despair:
Hell strives with grace for conquest in my breast:
What shall I do to shun the snares of death? 80

MEPHISTOPHILIS:
Thou traitor, Faustus, I arrest thy soul
For disobedience to my sovereign lord:
Revolt, or I'll in piecemeal tear thy flesh.

FAUSTUS:
I do repent I e'er offended him.
Sweet Mephistophilis, entreat thy lord
To pardon my unjust presumption,
And with my blood again I will confirm
The former vow I made to Lucifer.

MEPHISTOPHILIS:
Do it, then, Faustus with unfeigned heart,
Lest greater dangers do attend thy drift. 90
[FAUSTUS *stabs his arm, and writes on a paper with his blood.*]

FAUSTUS:
Torment, sweet friend, that base and aged man
That durst dissuade me from thy Lucifer,
With greatest torments that our hell affords.

MEPHISTOPHILIS:
His faith is great; I cannot touch his soul;
But what I may afflict his body with
I will attempt, which is but little worth.

FAUSTUS:
One thing, good servant, let me crave of thee,
To glut the longing of my heart's desire,—
That I may have unto my paramour
That heavenly Helen which I saw of late, 100

Whose sweet embraces may extinguish clean
Those thoughts that do dissuade me from my vow,
And keep my oath I made to Lucifer.

MEPHISTOPHILIS:
This, or what else, my Faustus shall desire,
Shall be perform'd in twinkling of an eye.
[*Enter* HELEN *again, passing over the stage between two* CUPIDS.]

FAUSTUS:
Was this the face that launch'd a thousand ships,
And burnt the topless towers of Ilium?—
Sweet Helen, make me immortal with a kiss.— [*She kisses him.*]
Her lips suck forth my soul: see where it flies!—
Come, Helen, come, give me my soul again. 110
Here will I dwell, for heaven is in these lips
And all is dross that is not Helena. [*Enter* OLD MAN.]
I will be Paris, and for love of thee,
Instead of Troy, shall Wittenberg be sack'd;
And I will combat with weak Menelaus,
And wear thy colours on my plumed crest:
Yea, I will wound Achilles in the heel,
And then return to Helen for a kiss.
O, thou art fairer than the evening's air
Clad in the beauty of a thousand stars; 120
Brighter art thou than flaming Jupiter
When he appear'd to hapless Semele;
More lovely than the monarch of the sky
In wanton Arethusa's[85] azured arms;
And none but thou shalt be my paramour!
[*Exeunt* FAUSTUS, HELEN, *and* CUPIDS.]

OLD MAN:
Accursed Faustus, miserable man,
That from thy soul exclud'st the grace of Heaven,
And fliest the throne of his tribunal-seat!
[*Enter the* DEVILS.]
Satan begins to sift me with his pride:
As in this furnace God shall try my faith, 130
My faith, vile hell, shall triumph over thee.
Ambitious fiends, see how the heavens smiles
At your repulse, and laughs your state to scorn!
Hence, hell! for hence I fly unto my God.
[*Exeunt.*]

Scene 2

FAUSTUS' *Study. Thunder.*

[*Enter above* LUCIFER, BELZEBUB, *and* MEPHISTOPHILIS.]

LUCIFER:
Thus from infernal Dis do we ascend
To view the subjects of our monarchy,
Those souls which sin seals the black sons of hell,
'Mong which as chief, Faustus, we come to thee,

---

[85] A nymph of a fountain.

Bringing with us lasting damnation
To wait upon thy soul; the time is come
Which makes it forfeit.

MEPHISTOPHILIS:
And this gloomy night,
Here in this room will wretched Faustus be.

BELZEBUB:
And here we'll stay, 10
To mark him how he doth demean himself.

MEPHISTOPHILIS:
How should he, but in desperate lunacy?
Fond worldling, now his heart-blood dries with grief,
His conscience kills it and his labouring brain
Begets a world of idle fantasies,
To overreach the Devil; but all in vain,
His store of pleasures must be sauc'd with pain.
He and his servant, Wagner, are at hand.
Both come from drawing Faustus' latest will.
See where they come! 20

[*Enter* FAUSTUS *and* WAGNER.]

FAUSTUS:
Say, Wagner, thou hast perus'd my will,
How dost thou like it?

WAGNER:
Sir, so wondrous well,
As in all humble duty, I do yield
My life and lasting service for your love.

[*Enter the* SCHOLARS.]

FAUSTUS: Gramercies, Wagner. Welcome, gentlemen.

[*Exit* WAGNER.]

FIRST SCHOLAR: Now, worthy Faustus, methinks your looks are changed.

FAUSTUS: O, gentlemen!

SECOND SCHOLAR: What ails Faustus?

FAUSTUS: Ah, my sweet chamber-fellow, had I liv'd with thee, then had I lived still! but now must die eternally. Look, sirs, comes he not? comes he not? 30

FIRST SCHOLAR: O my dear Faustus, what imports this fear?

SECOND SCHOLAR: Is all our pleasure turn'd to melancholy?

THIRD SCHOLAR: He is not well with being over-solitary.

SECOND SCHOLAR:
If it be so, we'll have physicians
And Faustus shall be cur'd.

THIRD SCHOLAR: 'Tis but a surfeit,[86] sir; fear nothing.

FAUSTUS: A surfeit of deadly sin, that hath damn'd both body and soul.

SECOND SCHOLAR: Yet, Faustus, look up to heaven; remember God's mercies are infinite. 40

FAUSTUS: But Faustus' offence can ne'er be pardoned: the serpent that tempted Eve may be saved, but not Faustus. O, gentlemen, hear me with patience, and tremble not at my speeches! Though my heart pant and quiver to remember that I have been a student here these thirty years, O, would I had never seen Wittenberg, never read book! and what wonders I have done, all Germany can

[86] Indigestion.

witness, yea, all the world; for which Faustus hath lost both Germany and the world; yea, heaven itself, heaven, the seat of God, the throne of the blessed, the kingdom of joy; and must remain in hell for ever—hell, oh, hell for ever! Sweet friends, what shall become of Faustus, being in hell for ever? 50

SECOND SCHOLAR: Yet, Faustus, call on God.

FAUSTUS: On God, whom Faustus hath abjur'd! on God, whom Faustus hath blasphem'd! Oh, my God, I would weep! but the devil draws in my tears. Gush forth blood, instead of tears! yea, life and soul—Oh, he stays my tongue! I would lift up my hands; but see, they hold 'em, they hold 'em!

ALL: Who, Faustus?

FAUSTUS: Why, Lucifer and Mephistophilis. O, gentlemen, I gave them my soul for my cunning!

ALL: Oh, God forbid!

FAUSTUS: God forbade it, indeed; but Faustus hath done it: for the vain pleasure of four and twenty years hath Faustus lost eternal joy and felicity. I writ them a bill with mine own blood: the date is expired; this is the time, and he will fetch me. 60

FIRST SCHOLAR: Why did not Faustus tell us of this before, that divines might have pray'd for thee?

FAUSTUS: Oft have I thought to have done so; but the devil threaten'd to tear me in pieces, if I nam'd God; to fetch me, body and soul, if I once gave ear to divinity: and now 'tis too late. Gentlemen, away, lest you perish with me.

SECOND SCHOLAR: O, what may we do to save Faustus? 70

FAUSTUS: Talk not of me, but save yourselves, and depart.

THIRD SCHOLAR: God will strengthen me; I will stay with Faustus.

FIRST SCHOLAR: Tempt not God, sweet friend; but let us into the next room, and pray for him.

FAUSTUS: Ay, pray for me, pray for me; and what noise soever you hear, come not unto me, for nothing can rescue me.

SECOND SCHOLAR: Pray thou, and we will pray that God may have mercy upon thee.

FAUSTUS: Gentlemen, farewell: if I live till morning, I'll visit you; if not, Faustus is gone to hell. 80

ALL: Faustus, farewell.

[*Exeunt* SCHOLARS.]

MEPHISTOPHILIS [*above*]:

Ay, Faustus, now thou hast no hope of heaven;
Therefore despair, think only upon hell,
For that must be thy mansion, there to dwell.

FAUSTUS:

O thou bewitching fiend, 'twas thy temptation
Hath robb'd me of eternal happiness.

MEPHISTOPHILIS:

I do confess it, Faustus, and rejoice;
'Twas I, that when thou wert i' the way to heaven,
Damm'd up thy passage; when thou took'st the book,
To view the Scriptures, then I turn'd the leaves, 90
And led thine eye.—
What, weep'st thou? 'tis too late, despair, farewell!
Fool that will laugh on earth, must weep in hell.

[*Exeunt* LUCIFER, BELZEBUB, MEPHISTOPHILIS.]

[*Enter the* GOOD ANGEL *and the* BAD ANGEL *at several doors.*]

GOOD ANGEL:
Oh, Faustus, if thou hadst given ear to me,
Innumerable joys had followed thee.
But thou didst love the world.

BAD ANGEL:
Gave ear to me,
And now must taste hell's pains perpetually.

GOOD ANGEL:
O what will all thy riches, pleasures, pomps,
Avail thee now?

BAD ANGEL:
Nothing but vex thee more, 100
To want in hell, that had on earth such store.

[*Music while the throne descends.*]

GOOD ANGEL:
O thou hast lost celestial happiness,
Pleasures unspeakable, bliss without end.
Hadst thou affected sweet divinity,
Hell, or the devil, had had no power on thee.
Hadst thou kept on that way, Faustus, behold,
In what resplendent glory thou hadst sit
In yonder throne, like those bright shining saints,
And triumph'd over hell: that hast thou lost:
And now, poor soul, must thy good angel leave thee,

[*The throne ascends.*]

The jaws of hell are open to receive thee. 110

[*Exit.*]

[*Hell is discovered.*]

BAD ANGEL:
Now, Faustus, let thine eyes with horror stare
Into that vast perpetual torture-house.
There are the Furies tossing damned souls
On burning forks; their bodies boil in lead:
There are live quarters[87] broiling on the coals,
That ne'er can die: this ever-burning chair
Is for o'er-tortured souls to rest them in;
These that are fed with sops of flaming fire,
Were gluttons and lov'd only delicates, 120
And laugh'd to see the poor starve at their gates:
But yet all these are nothing; thou shalt see
Ten thousand tortures that more horrid be.

FAUSTUS:
O, I have seen enough to torture me.

BAD ANGEL:
Nay, thou must feel them, taste the smart of all:
He that loves pleasure, must for pleasure fall:
And so I leave thee, Faustus, till anon;
Then wilt thou tumble in confusion.

[*Exit.*]

[*Hell disappears.*]
[*The clock strikes eleven.*]

---

[87] Bodies.

FAUSTUS:

Ah, Faustus,
Now hast thou but one bare hour to live, 130
And then thou must be damn'd perpetually!
Stand still, you ever moving spheres of heaven,
That time may cease, and midnight never come;
Fair Nature's eye, rise, rise again, and make
Perpetual day; or let this hour be but
A year, a month, a week, a natural day,
That Faustus may repent and save his soul!
O lente, lente currite, noctis equi![88]
The stars move still, time runs, the clock will strike,
The devil will come, and Faustus must be damn'd. 140
O, I'll leap up to my God!—Who pulls me down?—
See, see, where Christ's blood streams in the firmament!
One drop would save my soul, half a drop: ah, my Christ!—
Ah, rend not my heart for naming of my Christ!
Yet will I call on him: O, spare me, Lucifer!—
Where is it now? 'tis gone: and see, where God
Stretcheth out his arm, and bends his ireful brows!
Mountains and hills, come, come, and fall on me,
And hide me from the heavy wrath of God!
No, no! 150
Then will I headlong run into the earth:
Earth, gape! O, no, it will not harbour me!
You stars that reign'd at my nativity,
Whose influence hath allotted death and hell,
Now draw up Faustus, like a foggy mist,
Into the entrails of yon lab'ring cloud
That, when you vomit forth into the air,
My limbs may issue from your smoky mouths,
So that my soul may but ascend into heaven!
[*The clock strikes.*]
Ah, half the hour is past! 'twill all be passed anon. 160
O God,
If thou wilt not have mercy on my soul,
Yet for Christ's sake, whose blood hath ransom'd me,
Impose some end to my incessant pain;
Let Faustus live in hell a thousand years,
A hundred thousand, and at last be sav'd!
O, no end is limited to damned souls!
Why wert thou not a creature wanting soul?
Or why is this immortal that thou hast?
Ah, Pythagoras' *metempsychosis*,[89] were that true, 170
This soul should fly from me, and I be changed
Unto some brutish beast! all beasts are happy,
For, when they die,
Their souls are soon dissolved in elements;
But mine must live still to be plagu'd in hell.

---

[88] "O slowly, slowly run, horses of the night."
[89] Transmigration of souls.

Curs'd be the parents that engender'd me!
No, Faustus, curse thyself, curse Lucifer
That hath depriv'd thee of the joys of heaven.
[*The clock striketh twelve.*]
O, it strikes, it strikes! Now, body, turn to air,
Or Lucifer will bear thee quick[90] to hell! 180
O soul, be changed into little water drops,
And fall into the ocean, ne'er be found!
[*Thunder and enter the* DEVILS.]
My God, my God, look not so fierce on me!
Adders and serpents, let me breathe a while!
Ugly hell, gape not! come not, Lucifer!
I'll burn my books!—Ah, Mephistophilis!
[*Exeunt with him.*]

Scene 3

A room next to FAUSTUS' *study.*

[*Enter the* SCHOLARS.]

FIRST SCHOLAR:
Come, gentlemen, let us go visit Faustus,
For such a dreadful night was never seen,
Since first the world's creation did begin.
Such fearful shrieks and cries were never heard:
Pray heaven the Doctor have escap'd the danger.

SECOND SCHOLAR:
O help us heaven! see, here are Faustus' limbs,
All torn asunder by the hand of death.

THIRD SCHOLAR:
The devils whom Faustus serv'd have torn him thus:
For 'twixt the hours of twelve and one, methought
I heard him shriek and call aloud for help: 10
At which self[91] time the house seem'd all on fire,
With dreadful horror of these damned fiends.

SECOND SCHOLAR:
Well, gentlemen, though Faustus' end be such
As every Christian heart laments to think on,
Yet for he was a scholar, once admired
For wondrous knowledge in our German schools,
We'll give his mangled limbs due burial;
And all the students, clothed in mourning black,
Shall wait upon his heavy funeral.
[*Exeunt.*]

Epilogue

[*Enter* CHORUS.]

CHORUS:
Cut is the branch that might have grown full straight, 20
And burned is Apollo's laurel bough,
That sometime grew within this learned man.

[90] Alive.
[91] Same.

Faustus is gone: regard his hellish fall,
Whose fiendful fortune may exhort the wise,
Only to wonder at unlawful things,
Whose deepness doth entice such forward wits
To practise more than heavenly power permits.

[*Exit.*]

Terminat hora diem; terminat Author opus.

WESTERN TEXTS

CHRISTOPHER COLUMBUS

[C. 1451–1506]

The *Diario*, or log, of Christopher Columbus records the encounter between Europe and the Americas that was to alter radically almost every significant natural and social feature of our planet: its flora, fauna, epidemiology, genetic pools and populations, economics, politics, and arts. The only text that survives is a condensation of the original log made by Bartolomé de las Casas. It was lucky that Columbus kept a journal of his voyage, for daily ship's logs were not common until the sixteenth century, and Columbus seems not to have kept one on subsequent voyages. In its mixture of dogged detail, shrewd observation, self-revelation, delusional idealism, poetry, and real-estate promotion, the *Diario* suggests the shimmer of expectations through which Columbus beheld American lands and peoples; the *Diario* can almost be seen as a working script for the subsequent history of American colonization.

If anyone "discovered" the Americas, it was American Indians, who were present some 16,000 years ago or earlier. Given wind-patterns, currents, the sophisticated seacraft of many ancient peoples, and the human spirit of adventure, it would actually be rather strange if there had not been occasional landfalls, both deliberate and accidental, over the millennia. Old stories suggest Phoenicians, West Africans from Guiana, Chinese, Portuguese, Basques, and others may have preceded Columbus; American Indian stories and archaeological evidence hint of voyages made from west to east, as well. Norse explorers definitely tried to colonize North America by the tenth century C.E., but they were simply too far from European support to survive, and the stories of their discoveries passed into the folk history of the sagas, an oral literature not known to most of Europe.

In contrast, the impact of Columbus's voyage was enormous because news of it traveled fast, and from the moment of his first landfall the Americas were never again empty of Europeans. His voyage took place at a time when Spain, under the joint rule of Ferdinand and Isabella, had newly become a unified and homogeneously Catholic nation, eager to extend its enterprises and to compete with Portugal, France, and England in the business of foreign trade and colonization. Granada, the last Moorish stronghold in Spain, fell in 1492. Also in that year, the monarchs signed a decree expelling all Jews; although a lot of estates had been confiscated, much capital left the country with the exiled Jewish families, leaving Spain gold-poor. Columbus presented his plan to reach the Asian sources of gold and spice at a most opportune time.

LIFE

Christopher Columbus, Cristóbal Colón, as he is called in Spanish, the man whose name means "Christ-bearing dove," was born in the republic of Genoa, Italy, probably in 1451, the son of a weaver. There are many mysteries about his origins. Some evidence suggests he came from a *converso* family of Spanish Jews who had become Christians under the threat of the Inquisition; in such a family, secrecy would have been a survival strategy. In his adult life, the only people he fully trusted were two of his brothers, Bartholomé and Diego, who shared in his voyages.

Columbus probably learned to read and write only as an adult. "At a tender age," as he says, he went to sea for the first time, probably on short voyages along the coastlines. His first long voyage, in 1474, was to the island of Chios, a Genoese colony in the Aegean renowned for its gum mastic, the sap of an evergreen tree used as a painkiller; Columbus later would mistakenly believe he had found a new source for it in the Caribbean. One of the most disputed arguments about Columbus concerns the quality of his seamanship; it may be that the young Columbus sailed not as a seaman, but rather as a clerk representing traders, and had little early experience of navigation, although he traveled to England, Ireland, and perhaps even to Iceland.

In 1476, when a merchant ship Columbus served on was attacked and sunk off the coast of Portugal, he swam ashore and made his way to Lisbon, the European center of navigational study, where he lived in the Genoese community. Sometime between his coming to Lisbon and 1484, when he began his quest to finance an expedition, he became obsessed with the idea that it would be possible to reach the Indies by sailing westward.

The familiar image of a brave Columbus ringed by smug jeering courtiers who are certain the earth is flat derives mainly from the romantic 1829 biography by Washington Irving, the same writer who gave us Rip van Winkle. By Columbus's time, the idea of a spherical earth was fairly widely accepted, and the real difficulty people found with his proposal lay in his estimate of the distance between Europe and the Indies; many thought—rightly—that he underestimated, and that ships of the time could not carry enough provisions to cross the open ocean presumed to lie between Europe and Asia.

Failing to interest Portugal in his plan, Columbus finally convinced the Spanish monarchs Ferdinand and Isabella to finance the expedition. That he was admitted at all into the presence of royalty and permitted to explain his ideas is astonishing, given that he was neither famous nor noble, and says much about his persuasive powers; there are many doubts cast upon Columbus's origins, history, intelligence, integrity, and seamanship, even his sanity, but there can be no doubt of his single-minded intensity of purpose.

The three caravels, the *Pinta*, the *Niña*, and the *Santa María*, with Columbus as captain, left Spain on August 3, 1492, heading for the Canary Islands; from there, the trip was remarkably uneventful except for the growing anxiety and surliness of the crew, whom Columbus tried to calm by falsifying the log, telling them each day that they had sailed fewer miles than he thought was actually the case, assuring them they could not expect to see land. The ships made landfall on the sunny morning of October 12, 1492, at a still-disputed place in the Bahamas, where Taino people came running down the beach and swimming out to greet the ships. On this first voyage Columbus explored the island where he landed and the shores of Hispaniola and Cuba, which he believed to be Japan. The *Santa María* ran aground off Hispaniola on Christmas Day, and a fort called La Navidad was built from its shattered timbers; thirty-nine men stayed behind to run it. The *Pinta* and the *Niña* set sail for home with a number of Indian prisoners, most of whom died on the passage or soon after landing on European soil in the spring of 1493.

Columbus immediately readied a second voyage to establish a colony on Hispaniola. When his seventeen ships arrived on November 3, 1493, in the Lesser Antilles, word had obviously traveled around the Caribbean about the prisoners who had been snatched on the earlier expedition; this time, villages stood empty everywhere they passed. If any hope of goodwill and humanity on the part of the Europeans might be read into the chronicle of the first voyage, it vanishes in the accounts of this second trip. When the fleet of ships did surprise Indian people, the Europeans captured, killed, and raped. No mention was made of making Christians out of the native people, who had clearly become objects of use. The fort erected on Hispaniola lay silent when Columbus fired a cannon to alert the crew who stayed behind; it proved that all were dead. The thirty-nine men had split into rival gangs, roving the island, commandeering what gold the native people could scrape up, and amassing private harems of women and boys. The native leaders had seen enough, and they ambushed and killed all the remaining Spaniards.

Columbus left his brother Diego in charge of a company at a new fort and sailed off to explore Jamaica and the Cuban coastline, which he now decided must be the mainland of Asia. During Columbus's absence his brother Bartholomé came from Europe to join him, and a number of men sailed back to Spain to entreat the Crown to recall Columbus and put someone else in charge, for the colony was in chaos and the treatment of the Indians vicious even by the standards of those times. Columbus himself was anxious, for he knew he had not fulfilled his promise to the Crown about providing unlimited gold. He loaded some ships instead with five hundred slaves, three hundred of whom were still alive when the ships reached Spain. Aware that shipments of debilitated slaves would not be enough to earn the Crown's continued confidence in his enterprise, Columbus and his brothers instituted a rigid system whereby each native person was responsible for bringing to the fort a certain amount of gold dust regularly; if they failed, their hands were cut off. In 1496, when the meager gold supply was clearly exhausted, the brothers instead ordered all Indians to labor on one of the plantations the Spanish apportioned for themselves.

In March of 1496, aware that the crown was looking into the reports of mismanagement, Columbus set sail back to Spain on the *Niña*. African slaves were already being imported as hardier workers than the Taino, who were dying off rapidly; they had also begun to commit mass suicide with cassava poison. They were too enfeebled to attempt a revolt, but an inadvertent sort of revenge was taking place, nonetheless. On this second voyage, it became apparent that a strange new disease was claiming European lives; it was syphilis, which the Spaniards probably contracted from the Taino, who were more immune to it. The Spanish monarchs received Columbus coolly, agreeing to outfit one more small expedition that left for the Caribbean in May of 1498. Columbus, determined to reach China and speak with the great Khan, made landfall at Trinidad and then sailed along the coast of Venezuela; for the first time, he actually discovered the mainland of a continent, but it is not clear whether Columbus ever admitted to himself that he never reached Asia. In a long report to Ferdinand and Isabella, Columbus wrote that the earth was not round after all, but pear-shaped, like a woman's breast; the original Paradise, the biblical Eden, would lie at its mid and highest point, like a nipple positioned at the equator, and he believed that nipple, that well-watered garden, the flowing source of endless succor, would prove to lie in the interior of Venezuela. The world was a woman's breast waiting to be suckled, and he proposed yet another expedition to find this paradise.

Columbus may not have discovered Paradise, but he had certainly presided over a hell. Back on Hispaniola, the death toll of Indians rose, and the syphilitic Spanish colonists, who were not skilled farmers, quarreled viciously among themselves. Those who spoke against Columbus were hanged. For two more years the brothers ruled the colony, until in 1500 the Court sent an emissary to assume control. The three brothers were sent back in chains for trial; never one to forgive, Columbus, even after he was released, kept the chains with him. He was allowed to keep his titles, but he had lost all real credibility. The men who succeeded Columbus as overseers of the colony systematically killed off the remaining Taino. At a peace conference arranged by the cacique Anacoana between the Spanish and the eighty-four native leaders, the Spanish ambushed the assembly and murdered them all.

In 1502, Columbus somehow wrangled one more voyage from the Court, another stab at finding China. His successor on Hispaniola denied him permission to land, and the expedition headed for the Central American coast, skirting Honduras and Panama. Columbus wrote letters back to the court describing gold fields he was sure lay inland, and telling of how God had spoken to him, comparing him to Moses. The fourth voyage is mainly a sad tale of more slaughter and slavery, more wishful guesses about gold. The crew members were stranded on Jamaica for almost a year, too dispirited and divided even to repair their own boats. Columbus arrived back in Spain in 1504, depressed and anticipating death. He lived for two more years in ill health; although he had vowed to pilgrimage to Rome, he stayed in Spain to lay claim to a greater share of the profits that had come from Hispaniola. When he died in May 1506, his body was originally laid in the crypt of the monastery of Valladolid, but it was moved and no one knows where his bones now lie.

Work

These passages from the log of the first voyage, "in that time," as de las Casas puts it, "so new and like to no other," show that one part of Columbus's success is that he sees what he wishes to see, finds what he wants to find. In the early part of the voyage, when he wants to discover land within a certain number of nautical miles, he consciously manipulates reality for his crew by altering the log. But once on the islands, his consciousness of altering reality and his ability to question or examine his own judgments vanishes—this *is* Asia; it is just a question of what part. When he finds a large island like Cuba, he sails only a very short distance along its coast before concluding it is a piece of the mainland and sailing off, as if his desire matters more than the truth. And if this mainland *is* Asia, there must be spices; there must be gold. Columbus proclaims that American plants are identical with valued European or Asian specimens, such as the tree he mistakes for the source of gum mastic. The plants all have their own American identities, their own virtues and uses, but Columbus desperately needs to see them as plants he already knows about. Observing that some Indians wear gold ornaments understandably confirms his hopes, but the accounts of all four voyages are grimly repetitive in the theme of gold hoped-for, gold demanded, native people killed over gold not forthcoming; despite all evidence, there must be gold.

As for the Taino, Columbus is initially struck most of all by the nakedness of the people who greet him, not because he is especially prurient, but because he thinks clothing and civilization go together; these people are naked, he thinks, without any real culture, and utterly devoid of religion. They are not a people in themselves, really, but a sort of pleasant and docile human void waiting to be given shape and purpose. In fact, the Taino, who lived in a marvelously balanced ecosystem, had a religion of earth and animal presences that might have been apparent even to a casual observer; modern archaeology has uncovered stone sculptures of animals on the islands, effigies called *zemi* that helped the people get in touch with the spirit world. Later, when it becomes more convenient for him, Columbus will describe these same Taino as vicious, duplicitous, cruel. Initially, when he knows the least about them, they are a wonderful source of knowledge; long before any significant means of communication could conceivably have been worked out, Columbus is reporting complicated conversations with the Taino and other tribal people, all delivering news he wishes to hear, that he himself has invented; their own words, their names, their emotions, what actually was spoken, is lost.

Suggested Readings

Samuel Eliot Morrison's *Admiral of the Ocean Sea* (1942) is an admiring biography of Columbus written by a man who was both sailor and scholar. Hans Koning's *Columbus: His Enterprise* (1976) is a readable book sharply critical of Columbus. John Noble Wilford's *The Mysterious History of Columbus* (1991) does a good job of putting many of the controversies about the man and his acts in perspective. A good cultural study of Columbus is contained in Tzvetan Todorov's *The Conquest of America* (1985).

FROM

Diario

Translated by Robert H. Fuson

The Outward Voyage
3 August to 10 October 1492

In the Name of Our Lord Jesus Christ

Most Christian, exalted, excellent, and powerful princes, King and Queen of the Spains and of the islands of the sea, our Sovereigns: It was in this year of 1492 that Your Highnesses concluded the war with the Moors who reigned in Europe. On the second day of January, in the great city of Granada, I saw the royal banners of Your Highnesses placed by force of arms on the towers of the Alhambra, which is the fortress of the city. And I saw the Moorish king come to the city gates and kiss the royal hands of Your Highnesses, and those of the Prince, my Lord. Afterwards, in that same month, based on the information that I had given Your Highnesses about the land of India and about a Prince who is called the Great Khan, which in our language means "Kings of Kings," Your Highnesses decided to send me, Christopher Columbus,[1] to the regions of India, to see the Princes there and the peoples and the lands, and to learn of their disposition, and of everything, and the measures which could be taken for their conversion to our Holy Faith.

I informed Your Highnesses how this Great Khan and his predecessors had sent to Rome many times to beg for men learned in our Holy Faith so that his people might be instructed therein, and that the Holy Father had never furnished them, and therefore, many peoples believing in idolatries and receiving among themselves sects of perdition were lost.

Your Highnesses, as Catholic Christians and Princes devoted to the Holy Christian faith and to the spreading of it, and as enemies of the Muslim sect and of all idolatries and heresies, ordered that I should go to the east, but not by land as is customary. I was to go by way of the west, whence until today we do not know with certainty that anyone has gone.

[1] The transcription reads, "*pensarō de embiarme a mi xpoual Colon*" ("You thought of sending me, Cristóval Colón"). Inasmuch as Columbus never signed his name in this conventional form, some believe that the entire Prologue was written by Las Casas. It is more reasonable to assume that Las Casas inserted the name when he made his abstract. [All notes in this selection are translator's notes.]

Therefore, after having banished all the Jews[2] from all your Kingdoms and realms, during this same month of January Your Highnesses ordered me to go with a sufficient fleet to the said regions of India. For that purpose I was granted great favors and ennobled; from then henceforward I might entitle myself *Don* and be High Admiral of the Ocean Sea and Viceroy and perpetual Governor of all the islands and continental land that I might discover and acquire, as well as any other future discoveries in the Ocean Sea. Further, my eldest son shall succeed to the same position, and so on from generation to generation for ever after.

I left Granada on Saturday, the 12th day of the month of May in the same year of 1492 and went to the town of Palos, which is a seaport. There I fitted out three vessels, very suited to such an undertaking. I left the said port well supplied with a large quantity of provisions and with many seamen on the third day of the month of August in the said year, on a Friday, half an hour before sunrise. I set my course for the Canary Islands of Your Highnesses, which are in the Ocean Sea, from there to embark on a voyage that will last until I arrive in the Indies and deliver the letter of Your Highnesses to those Princes, and do all that Your Highnesses have commanded me to do.

To this end I decided to write down everything I might do and see and experience on this voyage, from day to day, and very carefully. Also, Sovereign Princes, besides describing each night what takes place during the day, and during the day the sailings of the night, I propose to make a new chart for navigation, on which I will set down all the sea and lands of the Ocean Sea, in their correct locations and with their correct bearings. Further, I shall compile a book and shall map everything by latitude and longitude. And above all, it is fitting that I forget about sleeping and devote much attention to navigation in order to accomplish this. And these things will be a great task.

. . .

Monday, 1 October 1492

I sailed onward to the west for 75 miles, but reckoned 60. At sunrise a tern flew over the ship, and a pair flew over at 10 o'clock. It rained very hard this morning. The pilot of the *Santa María* calculated that we were 1,734 miles west of Hierro; my corrected figure that I gave him was 1,752 miles. My personal calculation shows that we have come 2,121 miles. I did not reveal this figure to the men because they would become frightened, finding themselves so far from home, or at least thinking they were that far.

. . .

Saturday, 6 October 1492

I maintained my course to the west and made 120 miles between day and night, but told the people 99. This evening Martín Alonso Pinzón told me that he thought it would be wise to steer to the SW by west in order to reach the island of Japan, which is marked on the chart that I had shown him. In my opinion it is better to continue directly west until we reach the mainland. Later we can go to the islands

[2]The General Edict on the expulsion of the Jews from Spain was actually issued on March 31, 1492. This complicated situation, which evolved over the course of many years, is carefully analyzed by Simon Wiesenthal in *The Secret Mission of Christopher Columbus*.

on the return voyage to Spain. My decision has not pleased the men, for they continue to murmur and complain. Despite their grumblings I held fast to the west.

Sunday, 7 October 1492

I sailed to the west and made 9 knots for 2 hours and then 6 knots for 8 1/2 hours. I went about 69 miles up until an hour before sunset, but told the crew 54.

This morning we saw what appeared to be land to the west, but it was not very distinct. Furthermore, no one wished to make a false claim of discovery, for I had ordered that if anyone make such a claim and, after sailing three days, the claim proved to be false, the 10,000 *maravedíes*[3] reward promised by the Catholic Sovereigns would be forfeited, even if afterwards he actually did see it. Being warned of this, no one aboard the *Santa María* or *Pinta* dared call out "Land, land!" However, after we had rendezvoused this morning at sunrise (I had ordered that we assemble at sunrise and sunset because that is when there is the least haze and we can see the farthest) the *Niña,* which is a better sailer, ran ahead and fired a cannon and ran up a flag on her mast to indicate that land had been sighted. Joy turned to dismay as the day progressed, for by evening we had found no land and had to face the reality that it was only an illusion. God did offer us, however, a small token of comfort: many large flocks of birds flew over, coming from the north and flying to the SW. They were more varied in kind than any we had seen before and they were land birds, either going to sleep ashore or fleeing the winter in the lands whence they came. I know that most of the islands discovered by the Portuguese have been found because of birds. For these reasons I have decided to alter course and turn the prow to the WSW. This I did an hour before sunset, and I shall proceed on this course for two days. I added another 15 miles before darkness, making a total of 84 miles by night and by day.

. . .

The Discovery of the Bahamas
11 October to 27 October 1492

Thursday, 11 October 1492

I sailed to the WSW, and we took more water aboard than at any other time on the voyage. I saw several things that were indications of land. At one time a large flock of sea birds flew overhead, and a green reed was found floating near the ship. The crew of the *Pinta* spotted some of the same reeds and some other plants; they also saw what looked like a small board or plank. A stick was recovered that looks manmade, perhaps carved with an iron tool. Those on the *Niña* saw a little stick covered with barnacles. I am certain that many things were overlooked because of the heavy sea, but even these few made the crew breathe easier; in fact, the men have even become cheerful. I sailed 81 miles from sunset yesterday to sunset today. As is our custom, vespers were said in the late afternoon, and a special thanksgiving was offered to God for giving us renewed hope through the many signs of land He has provided.

After sunset I ordered the pilot to return to my original westerly course, and I urged the crew to be ever-vigilant. I took the added precaution of doubling the number of lookouts, and I reminded the men that the first to sight land would

---

[3] 10,000 *maravedíes* equals about $540.

be given a silk doublet as a personal token from me. Further, he would be given an annuity of 10,000 maravedíes from the Sovereigns.

About 10 o'clock at night, while standing on the sterncastle, I thought I saw a light to the west. It looked like a little wax candle bobbing up and down. It had the same appearance as a light or torch belonging to fishermen or travellers who alternately raised and lowered it, or perhaps were going from house to house. I am the first to admit that I was so eager to find land that I did not trust my own senses, so I called for Pedro Gutiérrez, the representative of the King's household, and asked him to watch for the light. After a few moments, he too saw it. I then summoned Rodrigo Sánchez of Segovia, the comptroller of the fleet, and asked him to watch for the light. He saw nothing, nor did any other member of the crew. It was such an uncertain thing that I did not feel it was adequate proof of land.

The moon, in its third quarter, rose in the east shortly before midnight. I estimate that we were making about 9 knots and had gone some 67½ miles between the beginning of night and 2 o'clock in the morning. Then, at two hours after midnight, the *Pinta* fired a cannon, my prearranged signal for the sighting of land.

I now believe that the light I saw earlier was a sign from God and that it was truly the first positive indication of land. When we caught up with the *Pinta,* which was always running ahead because she was a swift sailer, I learned that the first man to sight land was Rodrigo de Triana, a seaman from Lepe.

I hauled in all sails but the mainsail and lay-to till daylight. The land is about six miles to the west.

Friday, 12 October 1492
(Log entry for 12 October is combined with that of 11 October.)

At dawn we saw naked people, and I went ashore in the ship's boat, armed, followed by Martín Alonso Pinzón, captain of the *Pinta,* and his brother, Vincente Yáñez Pinzón, captain of the *Niña.* I unfurled the royal banner and the captains brought the flags which displayed a large green cross with the letters F and Y at the left and right side of the cross. Over each letter was the appropriate crown of that Sovereign. These flags were carried as a standard on all of the ships. After a prayer of thanksgiving I ordered the captains of the *Pinta* and *Niña,* together with Rodrigo de Escobedo (secretary of the fleet), and Rodrigo Sánchez of Segovia (comptroller of the fleet) to bear faith and witness that I was taking possession of this island for the King and Queen. I made all the necessary declarations and had these testimonies carefully written down by the secretary. In addition to those named above, the entire company of the fleet bore witness to this act. To this island I gave the name *San Salvador,*[4] in honor of our Blessed Lord.

No sooner had we concluded the formalities of taking possession of the island than people began to come to the beach, all as naked as their mothers bore them, and the women also, although I did not see more than one very young girl. All those that I saw were young people, none of whom was over 30 years old. They are very well-built people, with handsome bodies and very fine faces, though their appearance is marred somewhat by very broad heads and foreheads, more so than I have ever seen in any other race. Their eyes are large and very pretty, and their skin is the color of Canary Islanders or of sunburned peasants, not at all black, as would be expected because we are on an east–west line with Hierro in the Canaries. These are tall people and their legs, with no exceptions, are quite straight, and none of them has a paunch. They are, in fact, well proportioned. Their hair is not kinky,

---

[4]Samana Cay.

but straight, and coarse like horsehair. They wear it short over the eyebrows, but they have a long hank in the back that they never cut. Many of the natives paint their faces; others paint their whole bodies; some, only the eyes or nose. Some are painted black, some white, some red; others are of different colors.

The people here called this island *Guanahaní* in their language, and their speech is very fluent, although I do not understand any of it. They are friendly and well-dispositioned people who bare no arms except for small spears, and they have no iron. I showed one my sword, and through ignorance he grabbed it by the blade and cut himself. Their spears are made of wood, to which they attach a fish tooth at one end, or some other sharp thing.

I want the natives to develop a friendly attitude toward us because I know that they are a people who can be made free and converted to our Holy Faith more by love than by force. I therefore gave red caps to some and glass beads to others. They hung the beads around their necks, along with some other things of slight value that I gave them. And they took great pleasure in this and became so friendly that it was a marvel. They traded and gave everything they had with good will, but it seems to me that they have very little and are poor in everything. I warned my men to take nothing from the people without giving something in exchange.

This afternoon the people of San Salvador came swimming to our ships and in boats made from one log. They brought us parrots, balls of cotton thread, spears, and many other things, including a kind of dry leaf[5] that they hold in great esteem. For these things we swapped them little glass beads and hawks' bells.

Many of the men I have seen have scars on their bodies, and when I made signs to them to find out how this happened, they indicated that people from other nearby islands come to San Salvador to capture them; they defend themselves the best they can. I believe that people from the mainland come here to take them as slaves. They ought to make good and skilled servants, for they repeat very quickly whatever we say to them. I think they can easily be made Christians, for they seem to have no religion. If it pleases Our Lord, I will take six of them to Your Highnesses when I depart, in order that they may learn our language.

Saturday, 13 October 1492

After sunrise people from San Salvador again began to come to our ships in boats fashioned in one piece from the trunks of trees. These boats are wonderfully made, considering the country we are in, and every bit as fine as those I have seen in Guinea. They come in all sizes. Some can carry 40 or 50 men; some are so small that only one man rides in it. The men move very swiftly over the water, rowing with a blade that looks like a baker's peel. They do not use oarlocks, but dip the peel in the water and push themselves forward. If a boat capsizes they all begin to swim, and they rock the boat until about half of the water is splashed out. Then they bail out the rest of the water with gourds that they carry for that purpose.

The people brought more balls of spun cotton, spears, and parrots. Other than the parrots, I have seen no beast of any kind on this island.

I have been very attentive and have tried very hard to find out if there is any gold here. I have seen a few natives who wear a little piece of gold hanging from a hole made in the nose. By signs, if I interpret them correctly, I have learned that by going to the south, or rounding the island to the south, I can find a king who

[5]The "dry leaves" are not actually mentioned until the October 15 entry. At that time Columbus tells us that these highly prized dry leaves were offered to him on 12 October. It is reasonable, then, that the tobacco was part of "the many other things" cited in the Log entry.

possesses a lot of gold and has great containers of it. I have tried to find some natives who will take me to this great king, but none seems inclined to make the journey.

Tomorrow afternoon I intend to go to the SW. The natives have indicated to me that not only is there land to the south and SW, but also to the NW. I shall go to the SW and look for gold and precious stones. Furthermore, if I understand correctly, it is from the NW that strangers come to fight and capture the people here.

The island is fairly large and very flat. It is green, with many trees and several bodies of water. There is a very large lagoon[6] in the middle of the island and there are no mountains. It is a pleasure to gaze upon this place because it is all so green, and the weather is delightful. In fact, since we left the Canaries, God has not failed to provide one perfect day after the other.

I cannot get over the fact of how docile these people are. They have so little to give but will give it all for whatever we give them, if only broken pieces of glass and crockery. One seaman gave three Portuguese *ceitis* (not even worth a penny!) for about 25 pounds of spun cotton. I probably should have forbidden this exchange, but I wanted to take the cotton to Your Highnesses, and it seems to be in abundance. I think the cotton is grown on San Salvador, but I cannot say for sure because I have not been here that long. Also, the gold they wear hanging from their noses comes from here, but in order not to lose time I want to go to see if I can find the island of Japan.

When night came, all of the people went ashore in their boats.

Sunday, 14 October 1492

At daybreak I ordered the small boats to be made ready, that is, put in tow behind, and I went along the island to the NNE, to see the other part of the east and the villages. Soon I saw two or three of them, and the people came to the beach, shouting and praising God. Some brought us water; others, things to eat. Others, seeing that I did not care to go ashore, jumped into the sea and swam out to us. By the signs they made I think they were asking if we came from Heaven. One old man even climbed into the boat we were towing, and others shouted in loud voices to everyone on the beach, saying, "Come see the men from Heaven; bring them food and drink." Many men and women came, each one with something. They threw themselves on the sand and raised their hands to the sky, shouting for us to come ashore, while giving thanks to God. I kept going this morning despite the pleas of the people to come ashore, for I was alarmed at seeing that the entire island is surrounded by a large reef. Between the reef and the island it remained deep, and this port is large enough to hold all the ships of Christendom. There are a few shoal spots, to be sure, and the sea in it moves no more than water in a well. I found a very narrow entrance, which I entered with the ship's boat.

I kept moving in order to see all of this so that I can give an account of everything to Your Highnesses. Also, I wanted to see if I could find a suitable place to build a fort. I saw a piece of land that looked like an island, even though it is not, with six houses on it. I believe that it could be cut through and made into an island in two days. I do not think this is necessary, however, for these people are very unskilled in

---

[6]The Log states: "*. . . y muchas aguas y una laguna en medio muy grande. . . .*" The word is *laguna* (lagoon), not *lago* (lake). Columbus probably meant that the island had many small lakes and ponds (*muchas aguas*) and a saltwater lagoon in the middle ("halfway," "in between") on the coast he was on. This description fits Samana, not Watlings.

arms. Your Highnesses will see this for yourselves when I bring to you the seven[7] that I have taken. After they learn our language I shall return them, unless Your Highnesses order that the entire population be taken to Castile, or held captive here. With 50 men you could subject everyone and make them do what you wished.

Next to the little peninsula, which looks like an island, there are groves of the most beautiful trees I have ever seen. They are as green and leafy as those of Spain in the months of April and May. And there are many ponds and lakes nearby. Also, I saw what looks like an abandoned quarry, but it is natural.

I inspected the entire harbor before returning to the ship. I made sail and saw so many islands that I could not decide where to go first. The men whom I had captured made signs indicating there were so many islands that they could not be counted, and they named, in their language, more than a hundred. All the islands I saw were level and most of them are inhabited. Finally, I looked for the largest island and decided to go there. It is probably 15 miles from San Salvador, though some of the other islands are nearer, some farther. Since it was getting late, I knew that I could not reach the island before sunset, and decided to lay-to until dawn tomorrow.

Monday, 15 October 1492
(The entries for 15–16 October are confused in the original Log. Both appear to have been written late on the 16th.)

I had lain-to last night for fear of approaching the shore in the dark and because I did not know if the coast were clear of rocks, and at dawn I intended to haul in sail. I discovered that the island was nearer to 21 miles from San Salvador than my first estimate of 15 miles, and the tide detained me. I did not reach the island until noon.

The coast that faces San Salvador lies in a north–south line and extends for 15 miles. The other coast, which I followed, runs east and west, and is more than 30 miles long. Having sighted from this island another larger one to the west, I hauled in the sails, for I had sailed all day until night; otherwise I would not have been able to reach the western cape. To this island I gave the name *Santa María de la Concepción.*[8]

I anchored at sunset near the cape in order to find out if there was any gold there. The men from San Salvador told me that people on this island wear big golden bracelets on their arms and legs. I really did not believe them but think they made up the tale in order to get me to put ashore so that they could escape. Nevertheless, I did stop, for I have no desire to sail strange waters at night. It is not my wish to bypass any island without taking possession, although having taken one you can claim them all.

Tuesday, 16 October 1492

At daybreak I went ashore in the small boat. People met us on the beach. There were many people, and they went naked and in the same condition as those of San Salvador. They let us go anywhere we desired and gave us anything we asked.

I decided not to linger very long at Santa María de la Concepción, for I saw that there was no gold there and the wind freshened to a SE crosswind. I departed

[7]The entry for 12 October said six. Columbus is inconsistent on this point.

[8]Literally, Saint Mary of the Conception. Probably the north coast of Acklins-Crooked, which is the correct length. Morison thinks this is Rum Cay, which is farther from San Salvador than Columbus states and is one-third the size given.

the island for the ship after a two hours' stay. Just as I was preparing to board the ship, a big dugout came alongside the *Niña,* and one of the men from San Salvador jumped overboard and escaped in it. This is the second such incident, for in the middle of last night another man leaped into the sea and escaped by dugout. Some of the men went after the boat last night, but there was no way they could catch up to it, even though they were armed. Those boats go very swiftly.

This morning some men of my company tried to catch the second dugout, but again, it outran them. They found it abandoned on the beach, and the men in it fled like chickens. The sailors brought the boat back to the *Niña,* to which had come still another boat with one man in it. He had come from another cape and wanted to trade a ball of cotton. Some sailors jumped into the sea and seized him because he would not come aboard the caravel. Watching all this from the poopdeck, I sent for him. I gave the man a red cap and some little beads of green glass, which I placed on his arm, and two hawks' bells, which I placed on his ears. I also ordered the men of the *Niña* to return his dugout and sent him ashore. I did not take the ball of cotton, even though he wished to give it to me. I could see that he was surrounded by people when he reached shore, and they held it a great marvel and were convinced that we were good people. I wanted them to think that the men who had fled had done us some harm and that was why we were carrying them along with us. Thus I used him for these reasons and gave him all the aforesaid articles in order that the people might hold us in such esteem that on some other occasion when Your Highnesses send men back here they will be well treated. All that I gave him was not worth two cents.

Not only was there a shifting wind and no gold here, I was also afraid that all the men from San Salvador would escape if I did not move on and get farther away. I wanted to go to another large island that I determined lay to the west.[9]

Judging by the clouds and the signs made by the men from San Salvador, this large island to the west was about 27 miles distant. They said that there is a lot of gold there and that the people wear it on their arms, legs, ears, noses, and necks. I do not know if this is another ruse of theirs or not, for I am beginning to believe that all they want to do is escape and they will tell me anything I want to hear.

I ordered the *Niña* to cast adrift the dugout its sailors had brought from the beach, and I departed at 10 o'clock in the morning, or maybe a little later. The wind was veering SE and south, but the sea was calm. We had been sailing west for three or four hours toward that large island when we came upon a man in a dugout. He, too, was passing from Santa María de la Concepción to that other island. He carried a bit of bread about the size of your fist and a gourd full of water. Also, he had a lump of bright red earth,[10] which was powdered and kneaded, and some of those dry leaves which are much valued by these people, for they brought some to me on San Salvador as a gift. Also, he carried a basket of the style made here, in which he had a string of glass beads and two Spanish coins. These were things that I had given out at San Salvador, so I knew he had come from there and was going to the large island I saw in the west.

He came alongside the ship and I brought him aboard, as he requested. I had his boat hoisted to the deck and ordered his possessions to be guarded, after which I

---

[9]The large island to the west was Long Island, which Columbus named *Fernandina,* for King Ferdinand. Long Island cannot be seen from Crooked Island, but it is usually covered with a bank of cumulus clouds, a certain island-indicator.

[10]The "bright red earth" (*tierra bermeja*) may have been dough made from the sweet potato. *Bermeja* may also be translated as reddish, light brown, or ginger-colored.

gave him some of our bread and honey and drink. I will take him to the very large island that has appeared in the west and to which we are going, and then I will give him back all his things. In this way he will give a good account of us when, please be Our Lord, Your Highnesses send other men here. Those who come will be made welcome and given all that they need.

The sea was very smooth, and I sailed all this day with calms. We arrived at the island just at sunset. It was too dark to see the bottom in order to find a clear place, and it is necessary to be very careful in order not to lose the anchors. The beaches are all clear, without boulders, but there are some rocks underwater near the shore, and you must keep your eyes peeled when you wish to anchor and not anchor too near shore. The water is very clear and you can see the bottom during the daylight hours, but a couple of lombard shots[11] offshore there is so much depth that you cannot find bottom. On this side of the island the coast runs NW–SE. I decided to lay-to until daylight tomorrow, but I allowed the man we had taken in mid-channel to take his dugout and go ashore.

Wednesday, 17 October 1492

At first light I moved the ships closer to shore and anchored at a cape near a small village. It was to this village that the man we brought from mid-channel had gone last night. And he must have given a good account of us, for no sooner had we anchored than dugouts began to come to the ships. They brought us water and all manner of things. As was my custom, I ordered each person to be given something, if only a few beads; 10 or 12 glass ones that cost a penny or two, and some eyelets for lacing shirts and shoes. They found these things to be of great value. I also gave them honey when they came aboard.

At 9 o'clock in the morning I sent the ship's boat ashore for water, and those on the island, with very good will, showed my people where the water was. They even carried the full casks to the boat and took great delight in pleasing us.

I named this island *Fernandina.*[12] It is very big and about 24 miles due west of Santa María de la Concepción. This entire part of the island where I am anchored runs NNW–SSE. It appears that this coast I am on runs for 21 miles or more,[13] and I saw 15 miles of it, but it did not end there. It is very level without any mountains. These islands are very green and fertile and the air is balmy. There are many things that I will probably never know because I cannot stay long enough to see everything. I must move on to discover others and to find gold. Since these people know what gold is, I know that with our Lord's help I cannot fail to find its source.

Fernandina is very large and I have determined to sail around it. Although I know that Japan is to the south or SW, and that I am about to take a detour, I understand that there is a mine of gold either in Fernandina or near it. Now, as I am writing this, I have made sail with the wind from the south, in order to sail around the whole island and work my way to a place the people here call *Samoet*[14] in their

---

[11] A *lombard* (lombarda) was a small cannon with a range of about 300 yards. Two lombard shots equals about 600 yards.

[12] Long Island.

[13] The Log states that the coast of Fernandina extended for more than 28 leagues (84 NM) and that Columbus saw 20 leagues (60 NM) of it. Sighting distances and time allowances make these distances impossible. On 12 known occasions, Las Casas wrote *leagues* in the abstract and then crossed the word out, substituting *miles.* It appears as though Columbus logged miles in the original Log and Las Casas converted these references to leagues. There is a good possibility here that Las Casas did not catch his own error, and that the original read 28 miles and 20 miles.

[14] Fortune Island and (possibly) the SW part of Crooked Island; also called *Saometo* in the Log. The Indians may have been referring to the entire Acklins-Crooked-Fortune group.

tongue. This is either an island or a city where there is gold, as all those on board have told me and as I heard also on the islands of San Salvador and Santa María.

All the people I have seen so far resemble each other. They have the same language and customs, except that these on Fernandina seem to be somewhat more domestic and tractable, and more subtle, because I notice that when they bring cotton and other things to the ship they drive a harder bargain than those of the first islands visited. And also, on Fernandina I saw cotton clothes made like short tunics. The people seem better disposed, and the women wear a small piece of cotton in front of their bodies, though it barely covers their private parts. I do not recognize any religion in the people, and I believe that they would turn Christian quickly, for they seem to understand things quite well.

This is a very green, level, and fertile island, and I have no doubt that the people sow and reap grain, and also many other things, year around. I saw many trees quite different from ours. Many of them have branches of different kinds, all on one trunk;[15] one twig is of one kind and another of another, and so different from each other that it is the greatest wonder of the world. How great is the diversity of one kind from the other. For example, one branch has leaves like cane, another like mastic; thus on one tree five or six kinds, and all so different. Nor are these grafted so that one can say that the graft does it, for these trees are right there in the woods, and the people do not take care of them.

Here the fishes are so unlike ours that it is amazing; there are some like dorados, of the brightest colors in the world—blue, yellow, red, multi-colored, colored in a thousand ways; and the colors are so bright that anyone would marvel and take a great delight at seeing them. Also, there are whales. I have seen no land animals of any sort, except parrots and lizards—although a boy told me that he saw a big snake. I have not seen sheep, goats, or any other beasts, but I have only been here a very short time—half a day—yet if there were any, I could not have failed to have seen some. The circumnavigation of this island I shall write about after I have done it.

I left this village at noon—the place where I was anchored and where I took in water—to sail around this island of Fernandina. The wind was SW and south, and I wanted to follow the coast of this island to the SE because it all runs NNW–SSE, and the Indians[16] whom I had aboard (and another from whom I got instructions) told me that a southerly course leads to the island they call Samoet, where the gold is. Furthermore, Martín Alonso Pinzón, captain of the caravel *Pinta,* on whose ship I had placed three of the San Salvador Indians, came to me and told me that one of them very definitely had led him to believe that Fernandina would be easier to circumnavigate by going NNW. Since the wind was not helping me to take the SE course that I wished, but was good for the other, I set sail to the NNW.

After I had sailed six miles from the island's cape where I had been anchored, I discovered a very wonderful harbor with one entrance,[17] or rather, one may say two entrances, for there is an island in the middle. Both passages are very narrow, but once within, the harbor itself is wide enough for 100 ships. I did not think that either the entrance or the harbor was deep enough, however, nor did I feel that the bottom was clear of rocks. It seemed reasonable to me to look it over well and take soundings, so I anchored outside and went in with the small boats. It was fortunate that I did, for there was no depth at all. I did find what looked like a small river, and

[15]There is no such tree, but Columbus may have seen a complex community of epiphytes and vines amid the trees.

[16]First use of term Indians (*Indios*) for native inhabitants.

[17]Little Harbour, Long Island.

I ordered casks to be broken out to get water. On shore I found eight or 10 men who took us to a nearby village. I waited in the village for some two hours while my men—some armed and some with casks—went for the water.

During this time I walked among the trees, which are the most beautiful I have ever seen. I saw as much greenery, in such density, as I would have seen in Andalucia in May. And all of the trees are so different from ours as day is from night, and so are the fruits, the herbage, the rocks, and everything. It is true that some of the trees are like those in Castile, but most of them are very different. There are so many trees of so many different kinds that no one can say what they are, nor compare them to those of Castile.

The people on Fernandina are the same as the others already mentioned: of the same condition, usually nude, of the same stature, and willing to give what they had for whatever we gave them. Some of the ships' boys traded broken glass and bowls to them for spears. The others that had gone for the water told me that they had been in the houses and found them very simple but clean, with beds and furnishings that were like nets[18] of cotton.

The houses look like Moorish tents, very tall, with good chimneys. But I have not seen a village yet with more than 12 or 15 houses. I also learned that the cotton coverings were worn by married women or women over 18 years of age. Young girls go naked. And I saw dogs: mastiffs and pointers. One man was found who had a piece of gold in his nose, about half the size of a *castellano,*[19] and on which my men say they saw letters. I scolded them because they would not exchange or give what was wanted, for I wished to see what and whose money that was, but they answered me that the man would not barter for it.

After taking on water, I returned to the ship and sailed to the NW until I had explored all that part of the island as far as the coast that runs east–west. The Indians on board began to say that this island was smaller than Samoet, and that it would be a good idea to turn around to get there sooner. The wind went calm, then began to blow from the WNW, which was contrary to the way we had come. I turned and sailed all this night to the ESE, sometimes due east and sometimes to the SE. I had to do this to keep clear of land, for there were heavy clouds and the weather was very threatening. But there was little wind and I was unable to approach land to anchor. Later it rained very hard from midnight to daylight, and it is still cloudy and threatening. We will go to the SE cape of the island, where I hope to anchor until it clears it up. It has rained every day since I have been in these Indies, some times more, some less. Your Highnesses may rest assured that this land is the best and most fertile and temperate and level and good that there is in the world.

Thursday, 18 October 1492

After it cleared up, I followed the wind and sailed around the island as far as I could. When it was too dark to sail, I anchored and did not go ashore.

Friday, 19 October 1492

At daybreak I hauled in the anchors and sent the caravel *Pinta* to the ESE and the caravel *Niña* to the SSE; with my own ship I went to the SE. I gave orders that these courses should be followed until noon, and at that time the *Pinta* and *Niña* should alter courses and join me if land was not sighted. Before we had sailed three hours

[18]Columbus's first reference to hammocks, although he had almost certainly seen them before on San Salvador.

[19]Half of a gold *ducat,* worth about $10.

we saw an island to the east, for which we steered, and before midday all three ships reached a small island at the north point. There is a rocky reef at this island that runs to the north, and between the reef and the large island to the north is another island. The men on board from San Salvador called this large island Samoet, but I gave it the name *Isabela.*[20]

The wind was still blowing from the north, and this small island is east of Fernandina, from which I had departed. To the NE[21] of this small island there is a great bay and many wooded places that are thick and extensive. I wanted to anchor in that bay and go ashore and see such beauty, but the water is shallow and I could not anchor.

The coast trends west for 12 miles from the small island[22] to a cape, and as the wind was favorable for coming to this cape, I have done so. I have named it *Cabo Hermoso,*[23] and beautiful it is. It is round and the water is deep, with no shoals offshore.

As I approached the harbor, I found some rocks and shoals at the entrance, but within, it is a sandy beach like most of this coast. I anchored here this night, Friday.

This island is one of the most beautiful I have ever seen; if the others are beautiful, then this is more so. Of what I have seen so far, the coast is almost all sandy beach. It has many large, beautiful, green trees. The island is a little higher than the others I have seen, and there is a large hill, nothing that can be called a mountain, that adds to the beauty. There are many lakes and ponds in the middle of the island.

I think that this Cabo Hermoso is on an island separate from Isabela, which the natives call Samoet, and there may even be another island between it and Isabela. I do not really care to know such detail, for I could never see it all in fifty years anyhow. I merely want to see and discover as much as possible before returning to Your Highnesses, Our Lord willing, next April. It is true, however, that should I find gold or spices in abundance, I would delay my return to Spain until I have gathered as much as possible. Accordingly, I can do nothing more than press on and try to find these things.

I simply do not know where to go next. I never tire from looking at such luxurious vegetation, which is so different from ours. I believe that there are many plants and trees here that could be worth a lot in Spain for use as dyes, spices, and medicines, but to my great sorrow I do not recognize them. You can even smell the flowers as you approach this coast; it is the most fragrant thing on earth.

Tomorrow before I depart, I am going ashore to explore. There is no village on the coast, but the men from San Salvador tell me there is one further inland where there is a king with a lot of gold. Tomorrow I am going to find that village and talk with that king. According to the signs the Indians make, he is lord of all the neighboring islands, and he wears clothes and many golden adornments. I do not hold much faith in what they tell me, for I have been fooled before. It is possible, however, that there is a lord who wears a little bit of gold, for these Indians are so poor that any gold trinket would seem like a fortune to them.

---

[20]Southern Crooked Island and probably including Fortune Island; named for Queen Isabella.

[21]The Log uses the word *angla,* which is used eight times during the voyage. Four times it means *cape*; four times, *bay*. Columbus was referring to the Bight of Acklins.

[22]The Log reads "12 leagues to the west," but this is impossible. If the coast extended west for 12 leagues (36 miles), Columbus would have seen it on the approach from Fernandina; furthermore, he would have run aground on it when later he sailed SW for Cuba. This is another example of Las Casas transposing leagues and miles. The coast trended for 12 miles, and to the SW, not west.

[23]Beautiful Cape, probably the westernmost cape of Fortune Island.

Saturday, 20 October 1492

Today I weighed anchors at sunrise and departed Cabo Hermoso. I thought that I might sail around the island to the NE and to the east, from the SE and south, where I am told by the men with me that there is a settlement and its king. But the bottom is so shallow that I cannot enter or sail to the village. I saw that if I followed a SW course, it would be a very long way around, so for this reason I decided to return by the way I had come, to the NNE from the west part, and sail around the island from there. The SW cape of the island of Saometo I named *Cabo de la Laguna*.[24]

Because of the wind I could only sail at night, and I did not dare approach the coast in the dark. The *Pinta* and the *Niña* did anchor near the coast, but I stayed clear and lay-to all night, even though they made signals as they were accustomed to do and thought I would anchor, but I did not wish to.

Sunday, 21 October 1492

At 10 o'clock in the morning I arrived at *Cabo del Isleo*[25] and anchored, as did the other two ships. After having eaten, I went ashore and found no settlement except one house. I found no one; the inhabitants must have fled in fear, for all their housewares were left behind. I did not permit my men to touch a thing, and I went with my captains to see the island. If the other islands are very green and beautiful and fertile, this is much more, with great and green groves of trees. There are some large lakes and above and around them is the most wonderful wooded area. The woods and vegetation are as green as in April in Andalucía, and the song of the little birds might make a man wish never to leave here. The flocks of parrots that darken the sun and the large and small birds of so many species are so different from our own that it is a wonder. In addition, there are trees of a thousand kinds, all with fruit according to their kind, and they all give off a marvelous fragrance. I am the saddest man in the world for not knowing what kinds of things these are because I am very sure that they are valuable. I am bringing a sample of everything I can.

While going around one of the lagoons I saw a serpent,[26] which we killed with lances, and I am bringing Your Highnesses the skin. When it saw us, it went into the lagoon, and we followed it in because the water is not very deep. This serpent is about 6 feet long. I think there are many such serpents in these lagoons. The people here eat them and the meat is white and tastes like chicken.

I recognized the aloe[27] here, and tomorrow I am going to have 1,000 pounds of it brought to the ship because they tell me that it is very valuable. Also, while looking for good water, we stumbled onto a settlement about two miles from where we are anchored. When the people sensed our coming, they left their houses and fled, hiding their clothing and other things they had in the woods. I did not allow my men to take anything, not even something the value of one pin. Eventually some of the men came to us, and I gave one of them some hawks' bells and some small glass beads. He left very contented and very happy. And in order that our friendship might grow, and that something be asked of them, I requested water.

---

[24] Cape of the Lagoon, probably at the SE tip of Fortune Island.

[25] "Cape of the Island."

[26] An iguana.

[27] Columbus was probably confusing *Agave americana* (or one of its close relatives) with either *Aloe vera* or with *lignum aloe*. The former is grown as an ornamental indoor plant that serves as a readily accessible burn remedy. It is native to the Mediterranean area and was certainly known to Columbus. *Lignum aloe* is mentioned by Marco Polo. It is a fragrant, resinous wood used as incense. Columbus used the term *lignaloe*, which is a common name for this wood today.

Later, after I returned to the ship, they came to the beach with their gourds filled and were very delighted to give it to us. I ordered that they be given another string of glass beads, and they said they would return in the morning. I wanted to top off all of the ships' water casks while I had the chance.

If the weather permits, I shall depart this Cabo del Isleo and sail around Isabela until I find the king and see if I can get from him the gold which I hear that he wears. Then I shall sail for another great island which I strongly believe should be Japan, according to the signs made by the San Salvador Indians with me. They call that island *Colba,*[28] where they say there are many great ships and navigators. And from that island I intend to go to another that they call *Bohío,*[29] which is also very large. As to any others that lie in between, I shall see them in passing, and according to what gold or spices I find, I will determine what I must do. But I have already decided to go to the mainland and to the city of Quisay,[30] and give Your Highnesses' letters to the Grand Khan and ask for a reply and return with it.

Monday, 22 October 1492

I was here all last night and today waiting to see if the king on this island, or some other persons, would bring gold or something else substantial. And there came many of these people, similar to the others on the other islands, also naked and also painted. Some are painted white, some red, some black; others are in different colors. They brought spears and balls of cotton which they traded with some sailors for pieces of glass, broken cups, and pieces of clay bowls. A few brought pieces of gold hanging from their noses, which, with good will, they gave for a hawk's bell or small glass beads. It is so little that it is nothing. But it is true that they will trade anything they have for what little thing we may give them.

These people hold our arrival with great wonder and believe that we have come from heaven. We have been getting our water from a lake near the Cabo del Isleo, and in that lagoon Martín Alonso Pinzón, captain of the *Pinta,* killed another serpent like the one that was killed yesterday. It was about the same length. I have taken as much of the aloe as I could find.

Tuesday, 23 October 1492

I want to leave today for the island of Cuba,[31] which I believe to be Japan, according to the signs these people give of its magnificence and wealth. I do not want to tarry here any longer or explore this island looking for a settlement, even though I had originally planned to do this. I am not going to waste any more time looking for this king or lord, since I know there is no gold mine here. Furthermore, to sail around these small islands would require winds from many directions, and it does not blow that way; usually the wind is from the east or NE. And since I must go where there might be great commerce, it is foolish to delay. I must move on and discover many lands, until I come across a very profitable one. This island of Isabela may have many valuable spices, but I do not recognize them, and this causes me a great deal of sorrow, for I see a thousand kinds of fruit trees, each of which is as green now as in Spain during the months of May and June; there are also a thousand kinds of plants and herbs, and the same with flowers. And I know nothing except this aloe which I am carrying to Your Highnesses in great quantity.

---

[28]The reference is the first to Cuba, but the name *Cuba* is not used until 23 October.

[29]The Indian name for Hispaniola.

[30]Quinsay; the modern city of Hangzhou, China.

[31]This is the first correct spelling of the Indian name. It is one of the few native place-names that has survived.

I cannot sail today for Cuba because there is no wind; it is dead calm. It has rained a lot today, as yesterday, but it has not gotten cold; rather, the days are hot and the nights moderate, as in May in Spain and Andalucía.

Wednesday, 24 October 1492

At midnight I weighed anchors from the island of Isabela, from Cabo del Isleo which is in the north part, in order to go to the island of Cuba, which the Indians tell me is very large and has much commerce; gold, spices, ships, and merchants. The Indians indicated that I should sail to the SW to get to Cuba, and I believe them because all my globes and world maps seem to indicate that the island of Japan is in this vicinity and I am sure that Cuba and Japan are one and the same.

I sailed all night in the rain to the WSW. At dawn the wind calmed, but the rain continued. There was little wind until past noon, when it began to blow very gently. I set all my sails—mainsail and two bonnets, foresail and spritsail, mizzen and topsail. I even set the sail of the small boat on the poopdeck. Thus I went on course until dusk. And then the green cape of Fernandina,[32] which is on the SW part of that island, bore to the NW 21 miles.

Because the wind blew strongly now, and I did not know how far it might be to Cuba, I did not want to look for it at night. It is very deep off all these islands, there being no bottom at all except at a distance of two cannon shots, and near the land the bottom is dotted with rocks and shoals. One cannot anchor where it is so deep, and one cannot anchor where it is shallow with security, except by sight. I lowered all sails except the foresail and sailed with it. In a little while the wind increased greatly and the ship made great headway on a dubious course. And there was rain and threatening weather. Eventually I had to lower the foresail. I did not make six miles this night.

Thursday, 25 October 1492

After sunrise the weather cleared somewhat, and I sailed WSW. By 9 o'clock in the morning I had gone 15 miles. Then I changed course to the west and went at a speed of 6 knots until 1 o'clock and $4\frac{1}{2}$ knots until 3 o'clock, or a total of 33 miles since 9 this morning. At 3 o'clock I saw land. There were seven or eight islands, all in a line from north to south, about 15 miles distant.

Friday, 26 October 1492

I have been anchored about 15 to 18 miles south of those islands that I call the *Islas de Arena,*[33] and it is all shallow between them and me. The Indians indicated that it is a journey of a day-and-a-half from there to Cuba in their dugouts,[34] little boats made of a single log, with no sail.

Saturday, 27 October 1492

I hauled up the anchor at sunrise and departed for Cuba, which I am told is magnificent, with gold and pearls. I am now certain that Cuba is the Indian name for Japan. I made 6 knots from sunrise until 1 o'clock in the afternoon, to the SSW. I added another 21 miles before nightfall on the same course, for a total of 51 miles. Just before sunset I saw land, but it rained so hard that we had to beat about all this night.

---

[32]South Point, Long Island.

[33]Sand Islands, now called the Ragged Islands.

[34]The Indian word *canoa* appears in the manuscript, but was probably introduced at this point by Las Casas, not Columbus.

NICCOLO MACHIAVELLI

[1469–1527]

Niccolo Machiavelli has been called the "Galileo of politics," a title well suited for the thinker who transformed political writing and is sometimes thought to be the founder of modern political science. Abandoning the examples of Aristotle and Plato, whose political works construct a model of an ideal society, Machiavelli turned directly to the turbulent and corrupt affairs of state in his native fifteenth-century Florence to construct a model of society as it actually was. Drawing upon his own experience as a public official, military analyst, diplomat, and political exile, Machiavelli was in a perfect position to observe the political and historical events that swept through Florence and the other Italian city-states. The picture that he drew of the strategies a prince must exercise in order to maintain power during such times has earned him the reputation of cynic, pessimist, and genius from his own time down to ours. What is certain is that Machiavelli's work continues to be read and to generate debate over questions of power, authority, and the administration of the modern state.

In the fifteenth century, Italy was divided into five major city-states or republics—Venice, Naples, Rome, Milan, and Florence—modeled on the classical city-state of ancient Greece. Self-described democracies answerable to their citizens, these republics were actually controlled by powerful religious or secular interests. Rome, for example, was the center of the Papal States; a small oligarchy of powerful merchants ran Venice; and Florence answered to the Medici family. Under the Treaty of Lodi (1454), which established a balance of power among these states for almost fifty years, the Medicis in Florence, the Sforza in Milan, and the papacy in Rome lavished their considerable wealth upon artists, scholars, and writers to promote what we call the Italian Renaissance—an unprecedented revival of classical learning and a flourishing of the arts and sciences.

Despite the relative stability under the Treaty of Lodi, rivalries existed between the great families of the various states, and eventually Milan invited France to help protect its interests against Florence and Naples. Driven by the desire to expand France's borders and his own glory, Charles VIII answered by invading the peninsula with more than 30,000 troops; after forcing the Medici family to flee Florence, he pushed south to capture Naples. Fearing it might lose Sicily to France, Spain joined with the Papal States, the Holy Roman Empire, Milan, and Venice against France, thereby plunging Italy into a melee of continuing warfare and a succession of changing alliances among the republics from 1499 until 1529.

Eventually Charles V, the Hapsburg ruler of the Holy Roman Empire (consisting primarily of Austria and the Low Countries), returned the Medici family to power in Florence and then restored a kind of captive peace to the Italian states. The march of the "new monarchies" over the Italian city-states marked the demise of the papacy's hegemony over Europe and showed the weakness of lesser principalities when threatened with the collective might and territorial ambitions of absolute monarchs. In this atmosphere of self-glorifying patronage, fierce international competition for power, and the rise of monarchs bent on expanding their borders, what we might call a "realpolitik" for domestic and external affairs emerged. That is, ideal philosophical principles gave way to a system of doing politics based on the realities of power. Niccolo Machiavelli attempted in *The Prince* to set down the practical rules of the new political game.

LIFE

Niccolo Machiavelli was born into a family struggling to gain a secure footing among the Florentine aristocracy to whom the family linked its ancestry. Although his father,

Bernardo di Niccolo di Buoninsegna, received a small inheritance and practiced law in Florence, the family did not enjoy a secure or large fortune, so Machiavelli received only a modest education in Latin, grammar, and mathematics from a series of tutors. Machiavelli gives us a mere glimpse of his early life, about which little has been recorded, when he writes, "I was born poor, and I learned to know want before enjoyment."

From his modest origins, Machiavelli rose to be elected Secretary to the Second Chancery, beginning a fourteen-year career as civil servant, military advisor, and diplomat for the Florentine republic. In this position, which he held from 1498 to 1512, he served as a kind of secretary and emissary, concerned with matters of domestic and foreign policy. During his visits to the various Italian city-states and the courts of other European rulers, such as Louis XII, king of France, and Maximilian, emperor of the Holy Roman Empire, Machiavelli witnessed firsthand the political intrigue that he describes with various emphases in *The Art of War* (1521), *The Discourses* (1531), *The History of Florence* (1532), and, most famously, in *The Prince* (1513; published 1532). When the Medicis returned to power in 1512, they removed Machiavelli from office and forced him to abandon hopes of any political preferment. Unjustly imprisoned and tortured for crimes against the state (his name had appeared on a list of possible conspirators), Machiavelli was ousted from his post and banished from Florence. Experiencing with painful immediacy the manipulations of power he so brilliantly analyzes, Machiavelli retired to his home at Sant'Andrea, only seven miles from Florence, and began writing *The Prince* and *Discourses on the First Decade of Titus Livius*, partly in hopes of regaining the grace of the Medicis. Explaining to his friend Francesco Vettori why he dedicated *The Prince* to Giuliano de' Medici, Machiavelli gives us a sense of his hopes for that work: "If they read this work of mine, they would see that the fifteen years I have spent in the study of politics, I have not wasted or gambled away; and anyone ought to be glad to use a man who has gained a great deal of experience at other people's expense."

Over the next few years Machiavelli turned to more literary pursuits, writing a satirical poem, *The Ass*, a comedy *Mandragola*, and possibly (their date of composition is uncertain) a few short tales including *Belfagor* and *Life of Castruccio Castracani*. In 1520 he completed *On the Art of War*, a study of military tactics characterized by his application of reading in the classics to his observation of contemporary affairs—a typical strategy in his writings overall. After being commissioned to write the history of Florence, Machiavelli attained a partial reconciliation with the Medici family, who in 1526 placed him in charge of a commission overseeing the fortification of Florence, newly threatened by hostilities between France and the Holy Roman Empire. After the sack of Rome in May 1527, Republican factions in Florence drove the Medicis into exile. Although Machiavelli had long sympathized with the Republicans, he had been too closely bound to the Medicis to maintain a place in the new government. Shortly after he was passed by for his old position at the Second Chancery, Machiavelli became ill; he died on June 21, 1527, after telling a story to those gathered at his bedside about a man who preferred going to Hell where he could discuss politics with Plato, Plutarch, Tacitus, and other men of noble minds, than to go to paradise with a beggarly crowd of blessed saints.

WORK

Combined with a fascination for, if not obsession with, the history of ancient Rome, Machiavelli's minute observations of the strategies of warfare, diplomacy, and the intricate workings of power in *The Prince* and other writings set him apart from earlier political thinkers. Aristotle in *The Politics* and Plato in *The Republic* had sought to create a philosophical vision of the ideal republic, to construct politics as they should be. On the other hand, Machiavelli seeks in *The Prince* to create a practical vision of the actual republic as he saw it, to construct politics as they really are. Machiavelli explains his departure from earlier writers on the rules of conduct for a prince when he writes: "It being my intention to write a thing which shall be useful to him who apprehends it, it appears to me more appropriate to follow up the real truth of a matter than the imagination of it; for many have pictured republics and principalities which in fact have never been known or seen, because how one lives is so far distant from how one ought to live, that he who neglects what is done for what ought to be done, sooner effects his ruin than his preservation." For philosophical speculation, Machiavelli substitutes practical observation, and for this shift in focus his work has sometimes been considered—with some qualification—to be the forerunner of political science.

The Prince sets out to enumerate the necessary strategies of a prince who wants to gain power in a state and then to keep it. Indeed, Machiavelli's matter-of-factness and his dismissal of questions about the morality of the actions he describes have earned him the severe criticism of thinkers from his own contemporaries down to the present time. Espousing a doctrine of efficiency as an end in itself, Machiavelli describes how a ruler can successfully secure and maintain power while arousing the least amount of resistance from the ruled. Although a prince should hope for the chance to practice kindness and generosity to his subjects, to govern with honesty and compassion, when pressed the prince must do whatever is necessary to remain in control by keeping a good name even when circumstances force him to resort to vices such as deception, parsimony, and terror. As Machiavelli puts it, "anyone who determines to act in all circumstances the part of a good man must come to ruin among so many who are not good. Hence, if a prince wishes to maintain himself, he must learn how to be not good, and to use that ability or not as is required." This emphasis upon expedience in Machiavelli's treatise suggests, as has often been remarked, that the end—staying in power—justifies whatever means the prince must use, however devious or unscrupulous they may be.

Given the political turbulence of Machiavelli's Florence, one can see why he might be interested above all in presenting a guide to achieve stability in government; yet Machiavelli's basic outlook on human nature—one later followed by Thomas Hobbes and to a lesser degree by Adam Smith—has caused critics to label him a cynic. Insisting that human beings act in the last instance out of self-interest and therefore cannot be trusted, *The Prince* advises would-be rulers to use deceit, cunning, and force, if necessary, to achieve their ultimate objective—to remain in power. Above all, the ruler must keep up the appearance of being in control and acting for the benefit of the governed, when in fact he may be primarily concerned to preserve his own power.

While raising the ire of many readers, Machiavelli has not been without his sympathizers, who include such figures as Francis Bacon, Cardinal Richelieu, Spinoza, and Napoleon Bonaparte. Moreover, whether *The Prince* is amoral or immoral and whether Machiavelli is a realist or a pessimist, the significance of his work as a testament of the Renaissance preoccupation with secular power and conquest cannot be denied. Indeed, his name has been memorialized as a household word, "Machiavellian," signifying an act of sheer expedience without regard for scruples. In those ages (or in those institutions) where power protects its interests through the presentation of spectacle, like that conjured up by Prospero in Shakespeare's *The Tempest*, for example, accusations of Machiavellianism are sure to be heard once the smoke clears and the mirrors are exposed.

SUGGESTED READINGS

Roberto Ridolfi's *The Life of Niccolo Machiavelli* (1954; trans. 1963) remains the standard biography of Machiavelli, whereas J. R. Hale's *Machiavelli and Renaissance Italy* (1961) places the life in the context of the complex history we have only touched upon here. Sebastian De Grazia's *Machiavelli in Hell* (1989), Peter Donaldson's *Machiavelli and Mystery of State* (1988), and Hanna Pitkin's *Fortune Is a Woman: Gender and Politics in the Thought of Niccolo Machiavelli* (1984) focus upon Machiavelli's political writings, including *The Prince.*

The Prince

Translated by Allan H. Gilbert

CHAPTER 2

On Hereditary Principates

I shall omit any discussion of republics, because I have elsewhere dealt with them at length.[1] I shall concern myself only with princely governments, and shall proceed to spin my web about the classes mentioned, and discuss how these princely governments can be managed and maintained.

I say, then, that hereditary states, being accustomed to the family of their prince, are maintained with fewer difficulties than new ones, because it is enough for the hereditary ruler merely not to go beyond the customs of his ancestors, and otherwise to deal with accidents by moving slowly and cautiously. This is so true that if such a prince is of ordinary diligence, he will always maintain himself in his position, unless some extraordinary and excessive force deprives him of it; and even if he is deprived of it, he will get it back whenever the conqueror falls into misfortune.

We have in Italy, for example, the Duke of Ferrara, who sustained the assaults of the Venetians in 1484 and of Pope Julius[2] in 1510 for no other reason than that he had long been established in that dominion. For a hereditary prince has fewer causes for doing injury and less necessity for it than a new one; hence it is normal that he will be more loved, and if extraordinary vices do not make him hated, it is reasonable that he will naturally have the good wishes of his people. Moreover, if his government is old and has long been settled, new measures and their causes have been forgotten; for one change always leaves points of attachment for the building of another.

CHAPTER 3

On Mixed Principates

A new princely government, however, encounters difficulties. And first, if it is not wholly new but a member of a larger unit (so that the whole may be called a mixed principate), changes originate chiefly in a natural difficulty found in all new principalities; namely that men are glad to change their rulers, in the belief that

---

[1] In *Discourses on the First Decade of Titus Livius* (1513–1521).

[2] Under Duke of Ferrara, Machiavelli refers to both Ercole d'Este (1431–1505), defeated by the Venetians in 1484, and Alfonso d'Este (1476–1534), who fell to Pope Julius II in 1510; Giuliano della Rovere (1443–1513), Pope Julius II, reigned from 1503 to 1513.

they will better themselves, and this belief makes them take arms against the prince; but they deceive themselves in it, because afterwards they learn from experience that they are worse off. This depends on another natural and normal necessity, which makes it always necessary for a new ruler to harm those over whom he places himself, because he must employ soldiers and inflict various injuries incident to his new acquisition. Hence as a new prince you make enemies of all those you have damaged in occupying your position as ruler, and are not able to keep as friends those who have placed you there, because you cannot satisfy them in the manner they have been looking forward to, and you cannot use strong medicine against them because you are under obligation to them; it is always true, even when one's armies are very powerful, that one who is to enter a province needs the favor of the inhabitants. For these reasons Louis XII, the king of France, quickly occupied Milan and quickly lost it. The forces of Lodovico[3] himself were enough to take it away from him the first time, because the people who had opened the gates of the city, finding themselves deceived in their opinions and in the benefits they had looked forward to, were not able to endure the annoyances caused by the new prince.

It is indeed quite true that when a country that has rebelled is acquired for the second time, it is less easily lost, because the ruler, taking his opportunity from the rebellion, is less hesitant in making himself solid by punishing those who failed him, getting at the truth about those he suspects, and strengthening his weakest points. So then, the disturbance Duke Lodovico made on the borders was enough to cause the French king to lose Milan the first time, but if the King was to lose the city a second time he had to have all the world against him and his armies had to be destroyed or driven from Italy. This all resulted from the causes mentioned above. Nevertheless, the city was taken from him both the first time and the second.

The general causes of the first loss have been discussed; it now remains to give those of the second, and to see what means of prevention he had, and what one in his condition can do, to enable him to maintain himself in his acquisition better than the king of France did. I say, then, that those states which, when they are gained, are joined to the old dominion of him who gains them, either are of the same region and the same language, or they are not. When they are, it is very easy to hold them, especially when they are not accustomed to independence. In order to have secure possession, it is enough to extirpate the line of the prince who was ruling them, because, when their methods of government are kept up and there is no dissimilarity in customs, men live quietly enough with respect to other things. It can be seen that this has been done in Burgundy, Brittany, Gascony, and Normandy, which have long been under the king of France; and though there is some unlikeness of language, yet the customs are similar, and the peoples can easily tolerate each other. He who acquires such new provinces and wishes to hold them, ought to be attentive to two matters: one is that the race of the old prince be wiped out; the other is that there be no change in laws or taxes, so that in a very short time the new province and the old become one body.

But when states are acquired in a region different in language, customs, and laws, there are many difficulties. He who will retain them needs to have great good fortune and great shrewdness. One of the most important and effective devices is that the person who acquires them should go into them to live. This will make his possession more secure and more durable. The Turk has used this method in Greece; if, in addition to all the other methods practised by him to hold that country, he had

---

[3]Ludovico Sforza, Duke of Milan from 1494 to 1499, lost Milan to Louis XII in September 1499; he recaptured it in the next year, only to lose it again to Pope Julius II and the Holy League in 1502.

not gone there to live, he could not possibly have held it. The reason is that, since he lives there, he can see troubles when they arise and can remedy them quickly; but if he is not there, he learns of them when they are already big and there is no remedy for them. In addition, the province cannot be plundered by his officials, and the subjects are pleased by having easy access to their prince; hence they have good cause to love him if they intend to be good, and to fear him if they intend to be otherwise. Any foreigner who wishes to assail that state is therefore more hesitant about it. Hence a prince who lives in a new province can lose it only with the greatest difficulty.

Another excellent remedy is to send colonies into one or two places, to serve as fetters for that state. It is necessary either to do this or to keep there sufficient men-at-arms and infantry. Not much is spent on colonies; they can be sent out and kept up without any expense, or very little; this method damages only those—and they are a very small part of the new state—whose fields and houses are taken away in order to give them to the new inhabitants; those whom the prince damages, since they are scattered and poor, can do no harm, and all the others are undisturbed and uninjured. For this reason the latter are likely to be quiet, and on the other hand they are afraid of doing something wrong, and fear that the same thing may happen to them as to those who have been plundered. I conclude that such colonies are not expensive, are very faithful, and do little damage; those who are harmed are unable to do injury, since they are poor and dispersed, as has been said. From this it may be concluded that men should be either caressed or exterminated, because they can avenge light injuries, but not severe ones. The damage done to a man should be such that there is no fear of revenge. But if a prince keeps men-at-arms in his new province, instead of sending colonies, he will spend much more, since he will consume all the revenues of his state in guarding it; hence his acquisition will cause him loss; and he does much more damage, because he injures the whole state by shifting the encampments of his army. Everybody feels something of this annoyance, and the enemies he makes by it are able to injure him because, if they are beaten, they remain at home. In every way then, this method of protection is useless, but the colonial method is useful.

He who goes into a region unlike his own, such as has been spoken of, ought also to make himself head and defender of the neighboring minor rulers of the region, endeavor to weaken the powerful ones, and take precautions against any accident that might cause the entrance of a foreigner as powerful as himself. Those in the province who are discontented, either through too great ambition or through fear, will always try to bring in such a foreigner, as was seen long ago when the Etolians[4] brought the Romans into Greece; in fact the natives of every country the Romans occupied brought them into it. And the course of things is such that as soon as a powerful foreigner enters a land, all the less powerful rulers adhere to him, moved by their envy against the one who has been in power over them. This is so true that the foreigner has to take no trouble to win the lesser rulers, because at once and all together they willingly unite in one body with the supporters he has gained there. He has only to see to it that they do not grasp too much power and too much authority; then, with his forces and their favor, he can put down those who are powerful, and remain in every way master of that land. And he who does not attend carefully to this matter will quickly lose what he has acquired; and while he holds his territory he will have countless difficulties and troubles within it.

[4]Inhabitants of Aetolia, a region in ancient Greece; in the second century B.C.E. it allied with Rome to defeat Philip V of Macedonia (207–192 B.C.E.), who was making incursions into Greek provinces.

The Romans fully observed these requirements in the lands they took; they sent colonies, they sheltered the less powerful men without increasing the latter's power, they weakened the more powerful, and did not allow powerful foreigners to obtain prestige. I think the province of Greece alone will be a sufficient example: the Achaeans and the Aetolians were received; the kingdom of Macedonia was weakened; Antiochus was driven out of Greece; the merits of the Achaeans and the Aetolians did not cause Rome to permit their influence to grow; the persuasions of Philip did not ever induce her to be his friend without lessening his importance; the power of Antiochus could not force her to consent to his having any authority in that province.[5] In fact, the Romans did in these matters what all wise princes ought to do, for they are obliged to take thought not merely about immediate rebellions but about future ones, and to use every effort to forestall them, because if they are foreseen they can easily be remedied, but if they are awaited until they are near at hand, medicine cannot be given in time, because the malady has become incurable. The same thing happens in hectic fever: the physicians say that at the beginning the disease is easy to cure and hard to diagnose, but if it is not diagnosed and treated at the beginning, and a long time elapses, it grows easy to diagnose and hard to cure. So it is in matters of state, for if the ills of a policy are recognized early (something that can be done only by a prudent man), they are soon cured; but when, not being diagnosed early, they are allowed to increase in such fashion that everybody recognizes them, no remedy can then be found.

So the Romans, seeing difficulties in advance, always remedied them, and did not let them go on in order to escape a war, because they knew that war could not be avoided but would be deferred to the advantage of others. Hence they determined to make war with Philip and Antiochus in Greece in order not to have to make it with them in Italy, yet at that time they were able to escape both wars; but they did not wish to do so. Nor were they ever satisfied with the saying that is always in the mouths of the wise men of our days, about enjoying the benefit the day brings with it, but preferred what they could derive from their own vigor and prudence, because Time sweeps everything before him, and can bring along good as well as evil, and evil as well as good.

. . .

Chapter 15

On the Things for Which Men, and Especially Princes, Are Praised or Censured

It now remains to see what should be the methods and conduct of a prince in dealing with his subjects and his friends. And because I know that many have written on this topic, I fear that when I too write I shall be thought presumptuous, because, in discussing it, I break away completely from the principles laid down by my predecessors. But since it is my purpose to write something useful to an attentive reader, I think it more effective to go back to the practical truth of the subject than to depend on my fancies about it. And many have imagined republics and principalities that never have been seen or known to exist in reality. For there

[5]Like the Aetolians, the Achaeans, who lived in a region of Greece just south of Aetolia, fought to drive Philip V from their territories; Rome intervened, defeating Philip. When Rome refused to punish Philip, the Aetolians turned against Rome and allied with Antiochus III, "The Great," ruler of Syria from 223 to 187 B.C.E.; Rome defeated this alliance at Thermopylae in 191 B.C.E., thus preventing Syria from gaining a foothold in Greece.

is such a difference between the way men live and the way they ought to live, that anybody who abandons what is for what ought to be will learn something that will ruin rather than preserve him, because anyone who determines to act in all circumstances the part of a good man must come to ruin among so many who are not good. Hence, if a prince wishes to maintain himself, he must learn how to be not good, and to use that ability or not as is required.

Leaving out of account, then, things about an imaginary prince, and considering things that are true, I say that all men, when they are spoken of, and especially princes, because they are set higher, are marked with some of the qualities that bring them either blame or praise. To wit, one man is thought liberal, another stingy (using a Tuscan word, because *avaricious* in our language is still applied to one who desires to get things through violence, but *stingy* we apply to him who refrains too much from using his own property); one is thought open-handed, another grasping; one cruel, the other compassionate; one is a breaker of faith, the other reliable; one is effeminate and cowardly, the other vigorous and spirited; one is philanthropic, the other egotistic; one is lascivious, the other chaste; one is straight-forward, the other crafty; one hard, the other easy to deal with; one is firm, the other unsettled; one is religious, the other unbelieving; and so on.

And I know that everybody will admit that it would be very praiseworthy for a prince to possess all of the above-mentioned qualities that are considered good. But since he is not able to have them or to observe them completely, because human conditions do not allow him to, it is necessary that he be prudent enough to understand how to avoid getting a bad name because he is given to those vices that will deprive him of his position. He should also, if he can, guard himself from those vices that will not take his place away from him, but if he cannot do it, he can with less anxiety let them go. Moreover, he should not be troubled if he gets a bad name because of vices without which it will be difficult for him to preserve his position. I say this because, if everything is considered, it will be seen that some things seem to be virtuous, but if they are put into practice will be ruinous to him; other things seem to be vices, yet if put into practice will bring the prince security and well-being.

Chapter 16

On Liberality and Parsimony

Beginning, then, with the first of the above-mentioned qualities, I assert that it is good to be thought liberal.[6] Yet liberality, practiced in such a way that you get a reputation for it, is damaging to you, for the following reasons: If you use it wisely and as it ought to be used, it will not become known, and you will not escape being censured for the opposite vice. Hence, if you wish to have men call you liberal, it is necessary not to omit any sort of lavishness. A prince who does this will always be obliged to use up all his property in lavish actions; he will then, if he wishes to keep the name of liberal, be forced to lay heavy taxes on his people and exact money from them, and do everything he can to raise money. This will begin to make his subjects hate him, and as he grows poor he will be little esteemed by anybody. So it comes about that because of this liberality of his, with which he has damaged a large number and been of advantage to but a few, he is affected by every petty annoyance and is in peril from every slight danger. If he recognizes this and wishes to draw back, he quickly gets a bad name for stinginess.

[6]Generous.

Since, then, a prince cannot without harming himself practice this virtue of liberality to such an extent that it will be recognized, he will, if he is prudent, not care about being called stingy. As time goes on he will be thought more and more liberal, for the people will see that because of his economy his income is enough for him, that he can defend himself from those who make war against him, and that he can enter upon undertakings without burdening his people. Such a prince is in the end liberal to all those from whom he takes nothing, and they are numerous; he is stingy to those to whom he does not give, and they are few. In our times we have seen big things done only by those who have been looked on as stingy; the others have utterly failed. Pope Julius II,[7] though he made use of a reputation for liberality to attain the papacy, did not then try to maintain it, because he wished to be able to make war. The present King of France[8] has carried on great wars without laying unusually heavy taxes on his people, merely because his long economy has made provision for heavy expenditures. The present King of Spain,[9] if he had continued liberal, would not have carried on or completed so many undertakings.

Therefore a prince ought to care little about getting called stingy, if as a result he does not have to rob his subjects, is able to defend himself, does not become poor and contemptible, and is not obliged to become grasping. For this vice of stinginess is one of those that enables him to rule. Somebody may say: Caesar,[10] by means of his liberality, became emperor, and many others have come to high positions because they have been liberal and have been thought so. I answer: Either you are already a prince, or you are on the way to become one. In the first case liberality is dangerous; in the second it is very necessary to be thought liberal. Caesar was one of those who wished to attain dominion over Rome. But if, when he had attained it, he had lived for a long time and had not moderated his expenses, he would have destroyed his authority. Somebody may answer: Many who have been thought very liberal have been princes and done great things with their armies. I answer: The prince spends either his own property and that of his subjects or that of others. In the first case he ought to be frugal; in the second he ought to abstain from no sort of liberality. When he marches with his army and lives on plunder, loot, and ransom, a prince controls the property of others. To him liberality is essential, for without it his soldiers would not follow him. You can be a free giver of what does not belong to you or your subjects, as were Cyrus, Caesar, and Alexander,[11] because to spend the money of others does not decrease your reputation but adds to it. It is only the spending of your own money that hurts you.

There is nothing that eats itself up as fast as does liberality, for when you practice it you lose the power to practice it, and become poor and contemptible, or else to escape poverty you become rapacious and therefore are hated. And of all the things against which a prince must guard himself, the first is being an object of contempt and hatred. Liberality leads you to both of these. Hence there is more wisdom in keeping a name for stinginess, which produces a bad reputation without hatred, than in striving for the name of liberal, only to be forced to get the name of rapacious, which brings forth both bad reputation and hatred.

---

[7]See note 2.

[8]Louis XII (1462–1515), king of France from 1498 to 1515.

[9]King Ferdinand "the Catholic" (1452–1516) jointly ruled Spain with Isabella I from 1474 to 1504, and was also king of Aragón, Sicily, and Naples.

[10]Julius Caesar (100–44 B.C.E.), powerful member of the First Triumvirate of Rome, was appointed dictator of Rome in 44 B.C.E., the year of his famous assassination on the Ides of March by Marcus Brutus.

[11]Cyrus the Great (d. 529 B.C.E.), King of Persia from 559 B.C.E. and ruler of the Persian empire from 550 to 529 B.C.E.

CHAPTER 17

On Cruelty and Pity, and Whether It Is Better to Be Loved or to Be Feared, and Vice Versa

Coming then to the other qualities already mentioned, I say that every prince should wish to be thought compassionate and not cruel; still, he should be careful not to make a bad use of the pity he feels. Cesare Borgia[12] was considered cruel, yet this cruelty of his pacified the Romagna, united it, and changed its condition to that of peace and loyalty. If the matter is well considered, it will be seen that Cesare was much more compassionate than the people of Florence, for in order to escape the name of cruel they allowed Pistoia[13] to be destroyed. Hence a prince ought not to be troubled by the stigma of cruelty, acquired in keeping his subjects united and faithful. By giving a very few examples of cruelty he can be more truly compassionate than those who through too much compassion allow disturbances to continue, from which arise murders or acts of plunder. Lawless acts are injurious to a large group, but the executions ordered by the prince injure a single person. The new prince, above all other princes, cannot possibly avoid the name of cruel, because new states are full of perils. Dido in Vergil puts it thus: "Hard circumstances and the newness of my realm force me to do such things, and to keep watch and ward over all my lands."[14]

All the same, he should be slow in believing and acting, and should make no one afraid of him, his procedure should be so tempered with prudence and humanity that too much confidence does not make him incautious, and too much suspicion does not make him unbearable.

All this gives rise to a question for debate: Is it better to be loved than to be feared, or the reverse? I answer that a prince should wish for both. But because it is difficult to reconcile them, I hold that it is much more secure to be feared than to be loved, if one of them must be given up. The reason for my answer is that one must say of men generally that they are ungrateful, mutable, pretenders and dissemblers, prone to avoid danger, thirsty for gain. So long as you benefit them they are all yours; as I said above, they offer you their blood, their property, their lives, their children, when the need for such things is remote. But when need comes upon you, they turn around. So if a prince has relied wholly on their words, and is lacking in other preparations, he falls. For friendships that are gained with money, and not with greatness and nobility of spirit, are deserved but not possessed, and in the nick of time one cannot avail himself of them. Men hesitate less to injure a man who makes himself loved than to injure one who makes himself feared, for their love is held by a chain of obligation, which, because of men's wickedness, is broken on every occasion for the sake of selfish profit; but their fear is secured by a dread of punishment which never fails you.

Nevertheless the prince should make himself feared in such a way that, if he does not win love, he escapes hatred. This is possible, for to be feared and not to be hated can easily coexist. In fact it is always possible, if the ruler abstains from the property of his citizens and subjects, and from their women. And if, as sometimes happens, he finds that he must inflict the penalty of death, he should do it when he has proper justification and evident reason. But above all he must refrain from taking property, for men forget the death of a father more quickly than the loss of

---

[12] The son of Pope Alexander VI, Borgia (1476–1507) resigned his cardinalship to lead a treacherous campaign to seize power over the cities of Romagna.

[13] A city under Florentine rule that was plagued with bloody factional rioting while Florentine authorities looked on without taking definitive action against the rival parties.

[14] *Aeneid* I, 563–64.

their patrimony. Further, causes for taking property are never lacking, and he who begins to live on plunder is always finding cause to seize what belongs to others. But on the contrary, reasons for taking life are rarer and fail sooner.

But when a prince is with his army and has a great number of soldiers under his command, then above all he must pay no heed to being called cruel, because if he does not have that name he cannot keep his army united or ready for duty. It should be numbered among the wonderful feats of Hannibal[15] that he led to war in foreign lands a large army, made up of countless types of men, yet never suffered from dissension, either among the soldiers or against the general, in either bad or good fortune. His success resulted from nothing else than his inhuman cruelty, which, when added to his numerous other strong qualities, made him respected and terrible in the sight of his soldiers. Yet without his cruelty his other qualities would not have been adequate. So it seems that those writers have not thought very deeply who on one side admire his accomplishment and on the other condemn the chief cause for it.

The truth that his other qualities alone would not have been adequate may be learned from Scipio,[16] a man of the most unusual powers not only in his own times but in all ages we know of. When he was in Spain his armies mutinied. This resulted from nothing other than his compassion, which had allowed his soldiers more license than befits military discipline. This fault was censured before the Senate by Fabius Maximus,[17] and Scipio was called by him the corruptor of the Roman soldiery. The Locrians[18] were destroyed by a lieutenant of Scipio's, yet he did not avenge them or punish the disobedience of that lieutenant. This all came from his easy nature, which was so well understood that one who wished to excuse him in the Senate said there were many men who knew better how not to err than how to punish errors. This easy nature would in time have overthrown the fame and glory of Scipio if, in spite of his weakness, he had kept on in independent command. But since he was under the orders of the Senate, this bad quality was not merely concealed but was a glory to him.

Returning, then, to the debate on being loved and feared, I conclude that since men love as they please and fear as the prince pleases, a wise prince will evidently rely on what is in his own power and not on what is in the power of another. As I have said, he need only take pains to avoid hatred.

Chapter 18

In What Way Faith Should Be Kept by Princes

Everybody knows how laudable it is in a prince to keep his faith and to be an honest man and not a trickster. Nevertheless, the experience of our times shows that the princes who have done great things are the ones who have taken little account of their promises and who have known how to addle the brains of men with craft. In the end they have conquered those who have put their reliance on good faith.

---

[15]Carthaginian general (247–182 B.C.E.), one of Rome's greatest threats, who led his troops over the Alps from Spain into Italy.

[16]Publius Cornelius Scipio, Africanus Major (236–182 B.C.E.), Roman general who defeated Hannibal and Carthage; the mutiny took place in 206 B.C.E.

[17]Quintus Fabius Maximus Maximus Varrucosus (d. 203 B.C.E.), Roman general called "the Delayer" for his cat-and-mouse tactics against Hannibal.

[18]Citizens of Locri, in Sicily.

You must realize, then, that there are two ways to fight. In one kind the laws are used, in the other, force. The first is suitable to man, the second to animals. But because the first often falls short, one has to turn to the second. Hence a prince must know perfectly how to act like a beast and like a man. This truth was covertly taught to princes by ancient authors, who write that Achilles and many other ancient princes were turned over for their up-bringing to Chiron the centaur,[19] that he might keep them under his tuition. To have as teacher one who is half beast and half man means nothing else than that a prince needs to know how to use the qualities of both creatures. The one without the other will not last long.

Since, then, it is necessary for a prince to understand how to make good use of the conduct of the animals, he should select among them the fox and the lion, because the lion cannot protect himself from traps, and the fox cannot protect himself from the wolves. So the prince needs to be a fox that he may know how to deal with traps, and a lion that he may frighten the wolves. Those who act like the lion alone do not understand their business. A prudent ruler, therefore, cannot and should not observe faith when such observance is to his disadvantage and the causes that made him give his promise have vanished. If men were all good, this advice would not be good, but since men are wicked and do not keep their promises to you, you likewise do not have to keep yours to them. Lawful reasons to excuse his failure to keep them will never be lacking to a prince. It would be possible to give innumerable modern examples of this and to show many treaties and promises that have been made null and void by the faithlessness of princes. And the prince who has best known how to act as a fox has come out best. But one who has this capacity must understand how to keep it covered, and be a skilful pretender and dissembler. Men are so simple and so subject to present needs that he who deceives in this way will always find those who will let themselves be deceived.

I do not wish to keep still about one of the recent instances. Alexander VI[20] did nothing else than deceive men, and had no other intention; yet he always found a subject to work on. There never was a man more effective in swearing that things were true, and the greater the oaths with which he made a promise, the less he observed it. Nonetheless his deceptions always succeeded to his wish, because he thoroughly understood this aspect of the world.

It is not necessary, then, for a prince really to have all the virtues mentioned above, but it is very necessary to seem to have them. I will even venture to say that they damage a prince who possesses them and always observes them, but if he seems to have them they are useful. I mean that he should seem compassionate, trustworthy, humane, honest, and religious, and actually be so; but yet he should have his mind so trained that, when it is necessary not to practice these virtues, he can change to the opposite, and do it skilfully. It is to be understood that a prince, especially a new prince, cannot observe all the things because of which men are considered good, because he is often obliged, if he wishes to maintain his government, to act contrary to faith, contrary to charity, contrary to humanity, contrary to religion. It is therefore necessary that he have a mind capable of turning in whatever direction the winds of Fortune and the variations of affairs require, and, as I said above, that he should not depart from what is morally right, if he can observe it, but should know how to adopt what is bad, when he is obliged to.

---

[19]Mythical half man, half horse; said to be the tutor of legendary heroes Achilles, Theseus, Jason, and Hercules.

[20]Cardinal Rodrigo Borgia, pope from 1492 to 1503 and father of Cesare Borgia.

A prince, then, should be very careful that there does not issue from his mouth anything that is not full of the above-mentioned five qualities. To those who see and hear him he should seem all compassion, all faith, all honesty, all humanity, all religion. There is nothing more necessary to make a show of possessing than this last quality. For men in general judge more by their eyes than by their hands; everybody is fitted to see, few to understand. Everybody sees what you appear to be; few make out what you really are. And these few do not dare to oppose the opinion of the many, who have the majesty of the state to confirm their view. In the actions of all men, and especially those of princes, where there is no court to which to appeal, people think of the outcome. A prince needs only to conquer and to maintain his position. The means he has used will always be judged honorable and will be praised by everybody, because the crowd is always caught by appearance and by the outcome of events, and the crowd is all there is in the world; there is no place for the few when the many have room enough. A certain prince of the present day,[21] whom it is not good to name, preaches nothing else than peace and faith, and is wholly opposed to both of them, and both of them, if he had observed them, would many times have taken from him either his reputation or his throne.

CHAPTER 19

On Avoiding Contempt and Hatred

But because I have spoken of the more important of the qualities above, I wish to cover the others briefly with this generality. To wit, the prince should give his attention, as is in part explained above, to avoiding the things that make him hateful and contemptible. As long as he escapes them, he will have done his duty, and will find no danger in other injuries to his reputation. Hatred, as I have said, comes upon him chiefly from being rapacious and seizing the property and women of his subjects. He ought to abstain from both of these, for the majority of men live in contentment when they are not deprived of property or honor. Hence the prince has to struggle only with the ambition of the few, which can be restrained in many ways and with ease. Contempt is his portion if he is held to be variable, volatile, effeminate, cowardly, or irresolute. From these a prince should guard himself as from a rock in the sea. He should strive in all his actions to give evident signs of greatness, spirit, gravity, and fortitude. Also in the private affairs of his subjects he should make it understood that his opinion is irrevocable. In short he should keep up such a reputation that nobody thinks of trying to deceive him or outwit him.

The prince who makes people hold that opinion has prestige enough. And if a prince has a high reputation, men hesitate to conspire against him and hesitate to attack him, simply because he is supposed to be of high ability and respected by his subjects. For a prince must needs have two kinds of fear: one within his state, because of his subjects; the other without, because of foreign rulers. From these dangers he defends himself with good weapons and good friends. And if his weapons are good, he will always have good friends. Conditions within the state, too, will always remain settled when those without are settled, if they have not already been unsettled by some conspiracy. And when things without are in movement, if he has

[21] Ferdinand II of Spain.

ruled and lived as I have said, and does not fail himself, he will surely repel every attack, as I said Nabis the Spartan did.[22]

But with respect to his subjects, when there is no movement without, he has to fear that they will make a secret conspiracy. From this the prince protects himself adequately if he avoids being hated and despised and keeps the people satisfied with him. The latter necessarily follows the former, as was explained above at length. Indeed one of the most potent remedies the prince can have against conspiracies is not to be hated by the majority of his subjects. The reason for this is that a man who conspires always thinks he will please the people by killing the prince; but when he thinks he will offend them by it, he does not pluck up courage to adopt such a plan, because the difficulties that fall to the portion of conspirators are numerous. Experience shows that there have been many conspiracies and that few have come out well. They fail because the conspirator cannot be alone, and he can get companions only from those who, he thinks, are discontented. But as soon as you have revealed your purpose to a malcontent, you have given him an opportunity to become contented, because he evidently can hope to gain every advantage from his knowledge. Such is his position that, seeing on the one hand certain gain, and on the other gain that is uncertain and full of danger, he must needs be a rare friend, or, at any rate, an obstinate enemy of the prince, if he keeps faith with you. To put the thing briefly, I say that on the part of those who conspire there is nothing but fear, jealousy, and the expectation of punishment, which terrifies them. But on the part of the prince are the majesty of his high office, the laws, the power of his friends and his party that protects him. Evidently when the popular good-will is joined to all these things, it is impossible that anybody can be so foolhardy as to conspire against him. Ordinarily the conspirator must be afraid before the execution of his evil deed, but in this case he also has reason to fear after his transgression, because he will have the people against him and therefore cannot hope for any escape.

On this subject numerous examples might be given. But I have decided to be content with one alone, which happened in the memory of our fathers. Messer Annibale Bentivogli, grandfather of the present Messer Annibale, prince of Bologna,[23] was murdered by the Canneschi, who conspired against him. He left no heir save Messer Giovanni, who was in the cradle. Yet immediately after that murder, the people rose up and killed all the Canneschi. This act was the result of the popular good-will that the house of the Bentivogli had in those days, as is shown by what followed. After the death of Annibale, no member of the family who could rule the state was left in Bologna. The Bolognese, however, got a hint that there was in Florence a scion of the Bentivogli[24] who had been supposed until then to be the son of a smith. They came to Florence after him and gave him control of their city, which he governed from that time until Messer Giovanni reached an age capable of ruling it.

I conclude, therefore, that a prince need not pay much attention to conspiracies when the people are well-disposed to him. But when they are unfriendly and hate him, he must fear everything and everybody. Further, well-organized governments and wise princes have striven with all diligence not to make the upper classes feel

---

[22] A tyrant of Sparta (207–192 B.C.E.), noted for his cruelty.

[23] The Bentivoglis were a powerful ruling family in Bologna. Annibale Sr. died in 1445 at the hands of the Canneschi, a rival family. Giovanni Bentivogli (1447–1508) ruled Bologna from 1462 to 1506, when he was driven out by Julius II.

[24] Santi Bentivoglio of Florence, who ruled Bologna from 1446 to 1462, when Giovanni came of age.

desperate, and to satisfy the populace and keep them contented. In fact this is one of the most important matters a prince has to deal with.

Among the kingdoms well organized and well governed in our times is France. In this country there are numerous good institutions on which depend the liberty and security of the king. The first of these is the parliament and its authority. He who organized this kingdom[25] set up the parliament because he knew the ambition of the nobles and their arrogance, and judged it necessary that the nobility should have a bit in its mouth to restrain it. On the other hand, he knew the hatred, founded on fear, of the generality of men for the nobles, and intended to secure the position of the latter. Yet he did not wish this to be the special concern of the king, because he wished to relieve the king from the hatred he would arouse among the great if he favored the people, and among the people if he favored the nobles. Therefore he set up a third party as judge, to be the one who, without bringing hatred on the king, should restrain the nobles and favor the people. This institution could not be better or more prudent, nor could there be a stronger cause for the security of the king and the realm. From this can be deduced another important idea: to wit, princes should have things that will bring them hatred done by their agents, but should do in person those that will give pleasure. Once more I conclude that a prince should esteem the nobles, but should not make himself hated by the populace.

. . .

Chapter 25

The Power of Fortune in Human Affairs, and to What Extent She Should Be Relied On

It is not unknown to me that many have been and still are of the opinion that the affairs of this world are so under the direction of Fortune and of God that man's prudence cannot control them; in fact, that man has no resource against them. For this reason many think there is no use in sweating much over such matters, but that one might as well let Chance take control. This opinion has been the more accepted in our times, because of the great changes in the state of the world that have been and now are seen every day, beyond all human surmise. And I myself, when thinking on these things, have now and then in some measure inclined to their view. Nevertheless, because the freedom of the will should not be wholly annulled, I think it may be true that Fortune is arbiter of half of our actions, but that she still leaves the control of the other half, or about that, to us.

I liken her to one of those raging streams that, when they go mad, flood the plains, ruin the trees and the buildings, and take away the fields from one bank and put them down on the other. Everybody flees before them; everybody yields to their onrush without being able to resist anywhere. And though this is their nature, it does not cease to be true that, in calm weather, men can make some provision against them with walls and dykes, so that, when the streams swell, their waters will go off through a canal, or their currents will not be so wild and do so much damage. The same is true of Fortune. She shows her power where there is no wise preparation for resisting her, and turns her fury where she knows that no walls and dykes have been made to hold her in. And if you consider Italy—the place where these variations occur and the cause that has set them in motion—you will see that

---

[25]Possibly Louis IX (1214–1270), who promoted the use of Roman law in France and set up the Parlement of Paris.

she is a country without dykes and without any wall of defence. If, like Germany, Spain, and France, she had had a sufficient bulwark of military vigor, this flood would not have made the great changes it has, or would not have come at all.

And this, I think, is all I need to say on opposing oneself to Fortune, in general. But limiting myself more to particulars, I say that a prince may be seen prospering today and falling in ruin tomorrow, though it does not appear that he has changed in his nature or any of his qualities. I believe this comes, in the first place, from the causes that have been discussed at length in preceding chapters. That is, if a prince bases himself entirely on Fortune, he will fall when she varies. I also believe that a ruler will be successful who adapts his mode of procedure to the quality of the times, and likewise that he will be unsuccessful if the times are out of accord with his procedure. Because it may be seen that in things leading to the end each has before him, namely glory and riches, men proceed differently. One acts with caution, another rashly; one with violence, another with skill; one with patience, another with its opposite; yet with these different methods each one attains his end. Still further, two cautious men will be seen, of whom one comes to his goal, the other does not. Likewise you will see two who succeed with two different methods, one of them being cautious and the other rash. These results are caused by nothing else than the nature of the times, which is or is not in harmony with the procedure of men. It also accounts for what I have mentioned, namely, that two persons, working differently, chance to arrive at the same result; and that of two who work in the same way, one attains his end, but the other does not.

On the nature of the times also depends the variability of the best method. If a man conducts himself with caution and patience, times and affairs may come around in such a way that his procedure is good, and he goes on successfully. But if times and circumstances change, he is ruined, because he does not change his method of action. There is no man so prudent as to understand how to fit himself to this condition, either because he is unable to deviate from the course to which nature inclines him, or because, having always prospered by walking in one path, he cannot persuade himself to leave it. So the cautious man, when the time comes to go at a reckless pace, does not know how to do it. Hence he comes to ruin. Yet if he could change his nature with the times and with circumstances, his fortune would not be altered.

Pope Julius II proceeded rashly in all his actions, and found the times and circumstances so harmonious with his mode of procedure that he was always so lucky as to succeed. Consider the first enterprise he engaged in, that of Bologna, while Messer Giovanni Bentivogli was still alive. The Venetians were not pleased with it; the King of Spain felt the same way; the Pope was debating such an enterprise with the King of France. Nevertheless, in his courage and rashness Julius personally undertook that expedition. This movement made the King of Spain and the Venetians stand irresolute and motionless, the latter for fear, and the King because of his wish to recover the entire kingdom of Naples. On the other side, the King of France was dragged behind Julius, because the King, seeing that the Pope had moved and wishing to make him a friend in order to put down the Venetians, judged he could not refuse him soldiers without doing him open injury. Julius, then, with his rash movement, attained what no other pontiff, with the utmost human prudence, would have attained. If he had waited to leave Rome until the agreements were fixed and everything arranged, as any other pontiff would have done, he would never have succeeded, for the King of France would have had a thousand excuses, and the others would have raised a thousand fears. I wish to omit his other acts, which are all of the same sort, and all succeeded perfectly. The brevity of his life did not allow him to know anything different. Yet if times had come in which it was necessary to act with caution, they would have ruined him, for he would never have deviated from the methods to which nature inclined him.

I conclude, then, that since Fortune is variable and men are set in their ways, they are successful when they are in harmony with Fortune and unsuccessful when they disagree with her. Yet I am of the opinion that it is better to be rash than over-cautious, because Fortune is a woman and, if you wish to keep her down, you must beat her and pound her. It is evident that she allows herself to be overcome by men who treat her in that way rather than by those who proceed coldly. For that reason, like a woman, she is always the friend of young men, because they are less cautious, and more courageous, and command her with more boldness.

MARGUERITE DE NAVARRE

[1492–1549]

A member of the French royal family, Marguerite de Navarre was at the center of the political and cultural life of her time. With her brother, Francis I, who ruled France from 1515 to 1547, she participated in bringing the learning and culture of Italy to France and facilitating the French Renaissance. Her best-known literary work, *The Heptameron* (1558), was modeled on Boccaccio's *Decameron.* It explores conflicting ideals of love and male and female codes of sexuality, courtship, and marriage, and contrasts the conventions of the Middle Ages with the emerging individualism of the Renaissance.

LIFE

The daughter of Charles of Orléans, Count of Angoulême, and Louise of Savoy, Marguerite, as the sister of an heir to the throne, received an extraordinary education for a woman of her time. She was especially proficient in languages and studied Latin, Italian, Spanish, German, Greek, and Hebrew. There were unsuccessful negotiations to marry her to Prince Henry of England (Henry VIII) and to Charles of Austria, who would later become the Holy Roman Emperor Charles V, but the king of France at the time of her marriage, Louis XII, insisted that she marry Charles, Duke of Alençon. The two were never particularly compatible and her brother Francis remained a more important figure in her life than her first husband. When Francis was crowned in 1515, Marguerite became one of the most important persons in his court, advising him, carrying out diplomatic missions and treaty negotiations, and meeting the many important visitors who came to the court, including such artists as Leonardo da Vinci and Benvenuto Cellini. Francis and Marguerite were the two central figures in bringing the Italian Renaissance to France, presiding over a court inspired by the art and literature of Italy.

When Francis went to Italy in 1524 to pursue the French war with the Holy Roman Emperor, Charles V of Spain, Marguerite and her mother, the two remaining members of the ruling family "trinity," as it was called, governed France in his absence. After Francis's defeat and capture at the Battle of Pavia in 1525, Marguerite went to Madrid to negotiate the treaty that ended the hostilities and secured her brother's release. In the same year her first husband, Charles, Duke of Alençon, died.

Her second marriage in 1527 to Henri d'Albret, King of Navarre, was also an arranged union, but one that took account of her wishes. Henri, ten years her junior, was a military hero who had made a daring escape from imprisonment in Italy after the Battle of Pavia. Although she married him for love as well as position, he was not her intellectual equal.

Nevertheless, Marguerite was able to establish a courtly salon in Navarre, his kingdom on the Atlantic coast at the western end of the Pyrenees; here intellectuals and religious reformers met and exchanged ideas. As she became increasingly engaged in intellectual and literary pursuits, Marguerite became a supporter and protector of artists and thinkers, particularly of such religious reformers as Clement Marot, Gerard Roussel, and Lefèvre d'Etapes. She corresponded with Erasmus and Calvin; Rabelais dedicated the third volume of *Gargantua and Pantagruel* to her. Although she was particularly interested in the writings of Martin Luther, she did not leave the Church; she remained convinced that reform could take place within it.

Her first published work, *The Mirror of the Sinful Soul* (1531), a devotional poem, was attacked for Protestant "heresy" by the theologians at the Sorbonne, and her brother had to intervene on her behalf. Although she never left the Catholic faith, her acquaintance with Protestant reformers and with intellectuals within the Church made her suspect in the eyes of conservative theologians, especially at a time when the differences between Catholics and Protestants were the basis for continuing civil strife.

During the last decade of her life, strains in her relationships with Francis and especially with Henri II, his successor, led to her attending the French court for only brief periods. She spent most of her time in Navarre and in retreat in a convent at Tusson. The mystical and devotional character of much of her later work, in many of the plays and poems collected in *Marguerites de la Marguerite des Princesses* (*Pearls of the Pearl of Princesses*, 1547), for example, reveals her growing concern for spiritual issues. Her long poem, *Prisons* (c. 1548), describes a mystical journey from the various prisons of this world to ascend to unity with God. She died in Navarre in 1549, two years after Francis, with her husband at her side. Their only surviving child, Jeanne, born in 1527, would become the mother of Henry IV of France.

Work

Boccaccio's *Decameron* was the model for *The Heptameron*. Marguerite had commissioned a French translation of Boccaccio's work from Antoine Le Maçon, one of Francis I's councilors, and a member of her literary coterie. It appeared in 1545, just a few years before her death, and is mentioned in the Prologue to *The Heptameron*. The frame story for Marguerite's work is similar to Boccaccio's. A group of travelers are brought together by traumatic experiences and natural disasters. Assaulted by bandits, chased by bears, and nearly drowned in torrential rivers, five men and five women find themselves gathered for safety in a remote monastery. There they must wait for ten days while a rude bridge is constructed to enable them to escape the floods. They decide to while away the time pleasurably by reenacting *The Decameron:* Each of them will tell a story each day and by the end of their stay they will have made another collection of 100 tales. But unlike Boccaccio's stories, all their tales are to be true. Modern scholarship has confirmed that nearly a third of the tales are based in historical fact.

Even though Marguerite had not completed her original plan for 100 stories and had not organized the manuscript by the time of her death, most contemporary scholars think that she wrote most of the seventy-two tales included in modern editions of the work. Her maid reported that Marguerite found time to write the stories in between her many courtly duties or while she was traveling in her litter, scribbling them on scraps of paper or dictating them to companions. The tales were first published nine years after her death. Since its first edition, the stories have been placed in different orders and varying numbers of tales have been included by different editors. The sexual subject matter and the many tales dealing with the sexual indulgences of monks have seemed to some readers inconsistent with the pietistic and devotional tone of much of Marguerite's other work and have led to speculation that Marguerite did not compose many of the tales. However, one has only to look at *The Decameron, The Canterbury Tales,* or the poetry of John Donne to see how Marguerite's melding of carnal and spiritual themes was characteristic of her time.

Like Boccaccio's stories, Marguerite's address love and sexual relationships; her storytellers, modeled on real people, engage in an ongoing discussion on the relations between men and women. These conversations frame the tales and frequently boil over into a battle between the sexes. The tale we include, for example, is told by Parlamente, the female narrator usually identified as Marguerite's representation of herself, in response to a male challenge to tell a story of a faithful woman. Parlamente does much more than meet the challenge. She turns the conventional "male" love story on its head and redefines faithfulness from a female point of view.

The story of Amadour and Florida also reveals the changes taking place in Marguerite's time. It begins as a medieval romance, like *Amadis of Gaul* or *Launcelot,* the fantastic stories that so distorted Don Quixote's sense of reality. Amadour is described as the perfect knight, handsome, self-possessed, daring, and articulate. But he is left speechless when he first meets Florida, even though she is only twelve years old, and she becomes the object of his knightly intentions. He is too far beneath her socially to hope to marry her, but he plans to serve her, to win her love, and to make her his lady. His goals are altogether consistent with the medieval code of courtly love and his success will be measured by how far he is faithful to his lady and the chivalric ideal she represents.

To fulfill his quest, Amadour undertakes a secret strategy. He marries Florida's best friend, Avanturada, so that he will have access to Florida, and he attaches himself to the man she loves and will probably marry, the son of the Fortunate Infante. Amadour's secret strategems are not apparent to Florida; she accepts him as a pure and courtly servitor. But his machinations warn the reader that he is not all he appears to be and that this courtly romance may have a dark underside. By the time of the crisis in the story, when Avanturada's death threatens to separate Amadour from Florida and he attempts to rape her, the sexuality suppressed by the romantic story comes to the surface. The rest of the story is a proto-novel exploring Florida's psychology as she attempts to reconcile her love for Amadour with his threatening sexuality. The second half of the story looks forward to novels such as *The Princess of Clèves,* where psychological issues predominate.

The conflict in the story is between two ideas of love and two ideas of honor. Florida—and Marguerite de Navarre—affirm Platonic love, love purified of its sexuality, that transforms the earthly into the spiritual. Marguerite described "perfect lovers [as] those who seek some perfection in the object of their love, be it beauty, kindness, or good grace, tending to virtue, and who have such high and honest hearts that they will not even for fear of death do base things that honour and conscience blame." Although Amadour's courtship seems to promise such transforming love, his underlying motives prove to be sensual. He cannot control the love that drives him to attempt to take Florida by force and that prompts him to threaten to kill himself if she does not give herself bodily to him. In this struggle with Amadour, Florida is alone. Avanturada is dead and even her mother seems sympathetic to Amadour's cause. The established chivalric code has turned against her and she has nothing to rely on but her own conscience. Florida is like the Protestant reformer who, betrayed by the corrupt practices of the Church, had only an inner voice to trust.

By the end of the story, a female perspective has replaced the male perspective with which the story began. Instead of Amadour and his quest as its heroic subject matter, Florida and her conscience have become the focus. The discussion in the frame-narrative following the story concentrates on this shift. When Parlamente asks Hircan to confirm her reading that the story shows "a lady . . . tried to the utmost . . . [who] resisted virtuously," he responds by praising Amadour for doing "his duty" by attempting to "master" Florida.

Clearly the tale has not resolved the conflict between these opposing views of male and female honor, but it has brought the powerful struggle between men and women and between tradition and the individual conscience into clear definition.

Suggested Readings

Two useful introductions to Marguerite's life and work are Jules Gelernt's *World of Many Loves: The Heptameron of Marguerite de Navarre* (1966) and Samuel Putnam's *Marguerite of Navarre* (1935). P. A. Chilton's introduction to his translation of *The Heptameron* (1984) is an especially good introduction to the work, its editorial and critical problems, and to the context from which it came. Marcel Tetel's *Marguerite de Navarre's "Heptameron": Themes, Language, and Structure* (1973) offers a sophisticated discussion of some literary aspects of the whole work; Patricia Francis Cholakian, in *Rape and Writing in the Heptaméron of Marguerite de Navarre* (1991) provides a feminist reading of *The Heptameron,* including one chapter on the story of Amadour and Florida.

The Heptameron

Translated by John Smith Chartres

FROM Tale 9

"What think you of that, gentlemen, you who would not believe what I said?[1] Is not this example sufficient to make you confess that perfect love, when concealed and disregarded, may bring folks to the grave? There is not one among you but knows the kinsfolk on the one and the other side, and so you cannot doubt the story, although nobody would be disposed to believe it unless he had some experience in the matter."

When the ladies heard this they all had tears in their eyes, but Hircan said to them—

"He was the greatest fool I ever heard of. By your faith, now, I ask you, is it reasonable that we should die for women who are made only for us, or that we should be afraid to ask them for what God has commanded them to give us? I do not speak for myself nor for any who are married. I myself have all that I want or more; but I say it for such men as are in need. To my thinking, they must be fools to fear those whom they should rather make afraid. Do you not perceive how greatly this poor damsel regretted her folly? Since she embraced the gentleman's dead body—an action repugnant to human nature—she would not have refused

[1]In the frame-narrative that precedes the tale, the participants are discussing the previous story. That tale is of a poor lover who, awed by the purity of the lady he desires and aware of his own unworthiness, is unable to reveal his love. Finally, when he is on his death-bed, he confesses his love to his sweetheart and requests one final embrace. He dies holding her in his arms. The first speaker among the group of storytellers, Dagoucin, who has just finished telling this tale, is a self-effacing man who puts women on a pedestal. The other two young men, Hircan and Saffredent, are cynical and naturalistic misogynists. Geburon, an older man, cautions the women against their masculine aggressiveness. The masculine view is countered by the women who believe that women are more moral than men: Oisille, an older woman, celebrates spirituality, and the younger women, Longarine and Parlamente, the teller of Tale 10, defend an idealized Platonic love.

him while he was alive had he then trusted as much to boldness as he trusted to pity when he lay upon his death-bed."

"Nevertheless," said Oisille, "the gentleman most plainly showed that he bore her an honourable love, and for this he will ever be worthy of all praise. Chastity in a lover's heart is something divine rather than human."

"Madam," said Saffredent, "in support of Hircan's opinion, which is also mine, I pray you believe that Fortune favours the bold, and that there is no man loved by a lady but may at last, in whole or in part, obtain from her what he desires, provided he seek it with wisdom and passion. But ignorance and foolish fear cause men to lose many a good chance; and then they impute their loss to their mistress's virtue, which they have never verified with so much as the tip of the finger. A fortress was never well assailed but it was taken."

"Nay," said Parlamente, "I am amazed that you two should dare to talk in this way. Those whom you have loved owe you but little thanks, or else your courting has been carried on in such evil places that you deem all women to be alike."

"For myself, madam," said Saffredent, "I have been so unfortunate that I am unable to boast; but I impute my bad luck less to the virtue of the ladies than to my own fault, in not conducting my enterprises with sufficient prudence and sagacity. In support of my opinion I will cite no other authority than the old woman in the *Romance of the Rose,* who says—

> 'Of all, fair sirs, it truly may be said,
> Woman for man and man for woman's made.'

Accordingly I shall always believe that if love once enters a woman's heart, her lover will have fair fortune, provided he be not a simpleton."

"Well," said Parlamente, "if I were to name to you a very loving woman who was greatly sought after, beset and importuned, and who, like a virtuous lady, proved victorious over her heart, flesh, love and lover, would you believe this true thing possible?"

"Yes," said he, "I would."

"Then," said Parlamente, "you must all be hard of belief if you do not believe this story."

"Madam," said Dagoucin, "since I have given an example to show how the love of a virtuous gentleman lasted even until death, I pray you, if you know any such story to the honour of a lady, to tell it to us, and so end this day. And be not afraid to speak at length, for there is yet time to relate many a pleasant matter."

"Then, since I am to wind up the day," said Parlamente, "I will make no long preamble, for my story is so beautiful and true that I long to have you know it as well as I do myself. Although I was not an actual witness of the events, they were told to me by one of my best and dearest friends in praise of the man whom of all the world he had loved the most. But he charged me, should I ever chance to relate them, to change the names of the persons. Apart, therefore, from the names of persons and places the story is wholly true."

Tale 10

Florida, after virtuously resisting Amadour, who had assailed her honour almost to the last extremity, repaired, upon her husband's death, to the convent of Jesus, and there took the veil.

In the county of Aranda in Aragon, there lived a lady who, while still very young, was left a widow, with a son and a daughter, by the Count of Aranda, the name of the daughter being Florida. This lady strove to bring up her children in all the virtues and qualities which beseem lords and gentlemen, so that her house was reputed to be one of the most honourable in all the Spains. She often went to Toledo, where the King of Spain dwelt, and when she came to Saragossa, which was not far from her house, she would remain a long while with the Queen and the Court, by whom she was held in as high esteem as any lady could be.

Going one day, according to her custom, to visit the King, then at his castle of La Jasserye, at Saragossa, this lady passed through a village belonging to the Viceroy of Catalonia,[2] who, by reason of the great wars between the kings of France and Spain, had not been wont to stir from the frontier at Perpignan. But for the time being there was peace, so that the Viceroy and all his captains had come to do homage to the King.[3] The Viceroy, learning that the Countess of Aranda was passing through his domain, went to meet her, not only for the sake of the ancient friendship he bore her, but in order to do her honour as a kinswoman of the King's.

Now he had in his train many honourable gentlemen, who, in the long waging of war, had gained such great honour and renown that all who saw them and consorted with them deemed themselves fortunate. Among others there was one named Amadour, who, although but eighteen or nineteen years old, was possessed of such well-assured grace and of such excellent understanding that he would have been chosen from a thousand to hold a public office. It is true that his excellence of understanding was accompanied by such rare and winsome beauty that none could look at him without pleasure. And if his comeliness was of the choicest, it was so hard pressed by his speech that one knew not whether to give the greatest honour to his grace, his beauty, or the excellence of his conversation. What caused him, however, to be still more highly esteemed was his great daring, which was no whit diminished by his youth. He had already shown in many places what he could do, so that not only the Spains, but France and Italy also made great account of his merits. For in all the wars in which he had taken part he had never spared himself, and when his country was at peace he would go in quest of wars in foreign lands, where he was loved and honoured by both friend and foe.

This gentleman, for the love he bore his commander, had come to the domain where the Countess of Aranda had arrived, and remarking the beauty and grace of her daughter Florida, who was then only twelve years old, he thought to himself that she was the fairest maiden he had ever seen, and that if he could win her favour it would give him greater satisfaction than all the wealth and pleasure he might obtain from another. After looking at her for a long time he resolved to love her, although his reason told him that what he desired was impossible by reason of her lineage as well as of her age, which was such that she could not yet understand any amorous discourse. In spite of this, he fortified himself with hope, and reflected that time and patience might bring his efforts to a happy issue. And from that moment the kindly love, which of itself alone had entered Amadour's heart, assured him of all favour and the means of attaining his end.

To overcome the greatest difficulty before him, which consisted in the remoteness of his own home and the few opportunities he would have of seeing Florida again, he resolved to get married. This was contrary to what he had determined whilst with the ladies of Barcelona and Perpignan, in which places he was in such favour that little or nothing was refused him; and, indeed, by reason of the wars, he

---

[2]Henry of Aragon, Duke of Segorbe and Count of Ribagorce, was Viceroy of Catalonia at this time. He was called the Infante of Fortune because his father died before he was born in 1445.

[3]Ferdinand II of Aragon. The tale takes place at the end of the thirteenth century and the beginning of the fourteenth century when Spain, during the rule of Ferdinand and Isabella, was engaged in an ongoing border war with France for control of the Pyrenees.

had dwelt so long on the frontiers that, although he was born near Toledo, he seemed rather a Catalan than a Castilian. He came of a rich and honourable house, but being a younger son, he was without patrimony; and thus it was that Love and Fortune, seeing him neglected by his kin, determined to make him their masterpiece, endowing him with such qualities as might obtain what the laws of the land had refused him. He was of much experience in the art of war, and was so beloved by all lords and princes that he refused their favours more frequently than he had occasion to seek them.

The Countess, of whom I have spoken, arrived then at Saragossa and was well received by the King and all his Court. The Governor of Catalonia often came to visit her, and Amadour failed not to accompany him that he might have the pleasure of merely seeing Florida, for he had no opportunity of speaking with her. In order to establish himself in this goodly company he paid his addresses to the daughter of an old knight, his neighbour. This maiden was named Avanturada, and was so intimate with Florida that she knew all the secrets of her heart. Amadour, as much for the worth which he found in Avanturada as for the three thousand ducats a year which formed her dowry, determined to address her as a suitor, and she willingly gave ear to him. But as he was poor and her father was rich, she feared that the latter would never consent to the marriage except at the instance of the Countess of Aranda. She therefore had recourse to the lady Florida and said to her—

"You have seen, madam, that Castilian gentleman who often talks to me. I believe that all his aim is to have me in marriage. You know, however, what kind of father I have; he will never consent to the match unless he be earnestly entreated by the Countess and you."

Florida, who loved the damsel as herself, assured her that she would lay the matter to heart as though it were for her own benefit; and Avanturada then ventured so far as to present Amadour to her. He was like to swoon for joy on kissing Florida's hand, and although he was accounted the readiest speaker in Spain, yet in her presence he became dumb. At this she was greatly surprised, for, although she was only twelve years old, she had already often heard it said that there was no man in Spain who could speak better or with more grace. So, finding that he said nothing to her, she herself spoke.

"Señor Amadour," she began, "the renown you enjoy throughout all the Spains has made you known to everybody here, and all are desirous of affording you pleasure. If therefore I can in any way do this, you may dispose of me."

Amadour was in such rapture at sight of the lady's beauty that he could scarcely utter his thanks. However, although Florida was astonished to find that he made no further reply, she imputed it rather to some whim than to the power of love; and so she withdrew, without saying anything more.

Amadour, who perceived the qualities which even in earliest youth were beginning to show themselves in Florida, now said to her whom he desired to marry—

"Do not be surprised if I lost the power of utterance in presence of the lady Florida. I was so astonished at finding such qualities and such sensible speech in one so very young that I knew not what to say to her. But I pray you, Avanturada, you who know her secrets, tell me if she does not of necessity possess the hearts of all the gentlemen of the Court. Any who know her and do not love her must be stones or brutes."

Avanturada, who already loved Amadour more than any other man in the world, could conceal nothing from him, but told him that Florida was loved by every one. However, by reason of the custom of the country, few spoke to her, and only two had as yet made any show of love towards her. These were two princes of Spain, and they desired to marry her, one being the son of the Infante of Fortune and the other the young Duke of Cardona.

"I pray you," said Amadour, "tell me which of them you think she loves the most."

"She is so discreet," said Avanturada, "that on no account would she confess to having any wish but her mother's. Nevertheless, as far as can be judged, she likes the son of the Infante of Fortune far more than she likes the young Duke of Cardona. But her mother would rather have her at Cardona, for then she would not be so far away. I hold you for a man of good understanding, and, if you are so minded, you may judge of her choice this very day, for the son of the Infante of Fortune, who is one of the handsomest and most accomplished princes in Christendom, is being brought up at this Court. If we damsels could decide the marriage by our opinions, he would be sure of having the Lady Florida, for they would make the comeliest couple in all Spain. You must know that, although they are both young, she being but twelve and he but fifteen, it is now three years since their love for each other first began; and if you would secure her favour, I advise you to become his friend and follower."

Amadour was well pleased to find that Florida loved something, hoping that in time he might gain the place not of husband but of lover. He had no fear in regard to her virtue, but was rather afraid lest she should be insensible to love. After this conversation he began to consort with the son of the Infante of Fortune, and readily gained his favour, being well skilled in all the pastimes that the young Prince was fond of, especially in the handling of horses, in the practice of all kinds of weapons, and indeed in every diversion and pastime befitting a young man.

However, war broke out again in Languedoc, and it was necessary that Amadour should return thither with the Governor. This he did, but not without great regret, since he could in no wise contrive to return to where he might see Florida. Accordingly, when he was setting forth, he spoke to a brother of his, who was majordomo to the Queen of Spain, and told him of the good match he had found in the Countess of Aranda's house, in the person of Avanturada; entreating him, in his absence, to do all that he could to bring about the marriage, by employing his credit with the King, the Queen, and all his friends. The majordomo, who was attached to his brother, not only by reason of their kinship, but on account of Amadour's excellent qualities, promised to do his best. This he did in such wise that the avaricious old father forgot his own nature to ponder over the qualities of Amadour, as pictured to him by the Countess of Aranda, and especially by the fair Florida, as well as by the young Count of Aranda, who was now beginning to grow up, and to esteem people of merit. When the marriage had been agreed upon by the kinsfolk, the Queen's majordomo sent for his brother, there being at that time a truce between the two kings.

Meanwhile, the King of Spain withdrew to Madrid to avoid the bad air which prevailed in divers places, and, by the advice of his Council, as well as at the request of the Countess of Aranda, he consented to the marriage of the young Count with the heiress Duchess of Medina Celi. He did this no less for their contentment and the union of the two houses than for the affection he bore the Countess of Aranda; and he caused the marriage to be celebrated at the castle of Madrid.

Amadour was present at this wedding, and succeeded so well in furthering his own union, that he married Avanturada, whose affection for him was far greater than his was for her. But this marriage furnished him with a very convenient cloak, and gave him an excuse for resorting to the place where his spirit ever dwelt. After he was married he became very bold and familiar in the Countess of Aranda's household, so that he was no more distrusted than if he had been a woman. And although he was now only twenty-two years of age, he showed such good sense that the Countess of Aranda informed him of all her affairs, and bade her son consult with him and follow his counsel.

Having gained their esteem thus far, Amadour comported himself so prudently and calmly that even the lady he loved was not aware of his affection for her. By reason, however, of the love she bore his wife, to whom she was more attached than to any other woman, she concealed none of her thoughts from him, and was pleased to tell him of all her love for the son of the Infante of Fortune. Although Amadour's sole aim was to win her entirely for himself, he continually spoke to her of the Prince; indeed, he cared not what might be the subject of their converse, provided only that he could talk to her for a long time. However, he had not remained a month in this society after his marriage when he was constrained to return to the war, and he was absent for more than two years without returning to see his wife, who continued to live in the place where she had been brought up.

Meanwhile Amadour often wrote to her, but his letters were for the most part messages to Florida, who on her side never failed to return them, and would with her own hand add some pleasant words to the letters which Avanturada wrote. It was on this account that the husband of the latter wrote to her very frequently; yet of all this Florida knew nothing except that she loved Amadour as if he had been her brother. Several times during the course of five years did Amadour return and go away again; yet so short was his stay that he did not see Florida for two months altogether. Nevertheless, in spite of distance and length of absence, his love continued to increase.

At last it happened that he made a journey to see his wife, and found the Countess far removed from the Court, for the King of Spain was gone into Andalusia, taking with him the young Count of Aranda, who was already beginning to bear arms. Thus the Countess had withdrawn to a country-house belonging to her on the frontiers of Aragon and Navarre. She was well pleased on seeing Amadour, who had now been away for nearly three years. He was made welcome by all, and the Countess commanded that he should be treated like her own son. Whilst he was with her she informed him of all the affairs of her household, leaving most of them to his judgment. And so much credit did he win in her house that wherever he visited all doors were opened to him, and, indeed, people held his prudence in such high esteem that he was trusted in all things as though he had been an angel or a saint.

Florida, by reason of the love she bore his wife and himself, sought him out wherever he went. She had no suspicion of his purpose, and was unrestrained in her manners, for her heart was free from love, save that she felt great contentment whenever she was near Amadour. To more than this she gave not a thought.

Amadour, however, had a hard task to escape the observation of those who knew by experience how to distinguish a lover's looks from another man's; for when Florida, thinking no evil, came and spoke familiarly to him, the fire that was hidden in his heart so consumed him that he could not keep the colour from rising to his face or sparks of flame darting from his eyes. Thus, in order that none might be any the wiser, he began to pay court to a very beautiful lady named Paulina, a woman so famed for beauty in her day that few men who saw her escaped from her toils.

This Paulina had heard how Amadour had made love at Barcelona and Perpignan, insomuch that he had gained the affection of the highest and most beautiful ladies in the land, especially that of a certain Countess of Palamos, who was esteemed the first for beauty among all the ladies of Spain; and she told him that she greatly pitied him, since, after so much good fortune, he had married such an ugly wife. Amadour, who well understood by these words that she had a mind to supply his need, made her the fairest speeches he could devise, seeking to conceal the truth by persuading her of a falsehood. But she, being subtle and experienced in love, was not to be put off with mere words; and feeling sure that his heart was not to be satisfied with such love as she could give him, she suspected he wished to make her serve as a cloak, and so kept close watch upon his eyes. These, however, knew so well how to dissemble, that she had nothing to guide her but the barest suspicion.

Nevertheless, her observation sorely troubled Amadour; for Florida, who was ignorant of all these wiles, often spoke to him before Paulina in such a familiar fashion that he had to make wondrous efforts to compel his eyes to belie his heart. To avoid unpleasant consequences, he one day, while leaning against a window, spoke thus to Florida—

"I pray you, sweetheart, counsel me whether it is better for a man to speak or die?"

Florida forthwith replied—

"I shall always counsel my friends to speak and not to die. There are few words that cannot be mended, but life once lost can never be regained."

"Will you promise me, then," said Amadour, "that you will not be displeased by what I wish to tell you, nor yet alarmed at it, until you have heard me to the end?"

"Say what you will," she replied; "if you alarm me, none can reassure me."

"For two reasons," he then began, "I have hitherto been unwilling to tell you of the great affection that I feel for you. First, I wished to prove it to you by long service, and secondly, I feared that you might deem it presumption in me, who am but a simple gentleman, to address myself to one upon whom it is not fitting that I should look. And even though I were of royal station like your own, your heart, in its loyalty, would suffer none save the son of the Infante of Fortune, who has won it, to speak to you of love. But just as in a great war necessity compels men to devastate their own possessions and to destroy their corn in the blade, that the enemy may derive no profit therefrom, so do I risk anticipating the fruit which I had hoped to gather in season, lest your enemies and mine profit by it to your detriment. Know, then, that from your earliest youth I have devoted myself to your service and have ever striven to win your favour. For this purpose alone I married her whom I thought you loved best, and, being acquainted with the love you bear to the son of the Infante of Fortune, I have striven to serve him and consort with him, as you yourself know. I have sought with all my power for everything that I thought could give you pleasure. You see that I have won the esteem of your mother, the Countess, and of your brother, the Count, and of all you love, so that I am regarded here, not as a dependant, but as one of the family. All my efforts for five years past have had no other end than that I might spend my whole life near you.

"Understand that I am not one of those who would by these means seek to obtain from you any favour or pleasure otherwise than virtuous. I know that I cannot marry you, and even if I could, I would not do so in face of the love you bear him whom I would fain see your husband. And as for loving you with a vicious love like those who hope that long service will bring them a reward to the dishonour of a lady, that is far from my purpose. I would rather see you dead than know that you were less worthy of being loved, or that your virtue had diminished for the sake of any pleasure to me. For the end and reward of my service I ask but one thing, namely, that you will be so faithful a mistress to me, as never to take your favour from me, and that you will suffer me to continue as I now am, trusting in me more than in any other, and accepting from me the assurance that if for your honour's sake, or for aught concerning you, you ever have need of a gentleman's life, I will gladly place mine at your disposal. You may be sure also that whatever

I may do that is honourable and virtuous, will be done solely for love of you. If for the sake of ladies less worthy than you I have ever done anything that has been considered of account, be sure that, for a mistress like yourself, my enterprise will so increase, that things I heretofore found impossible will become very easy to me. If, however, you will not accept me as wholly yours, I am resolved to lay aside my arms and to renounce the valour which has failed to help me in my need. So I pray you grant me my just request, for your honour and conscience cannot refuse it."

The maiden, hearing these unwonted words, began to change colour and to cast down her eyes like a woman in alarm. However, being sensible and discreet, she replied—

"Since you already have what you ask of me, Amadour, why make me such a long harangue? I fear me lest beneath your honourable words there be some hidden guile to deceive my ignorance and youth, and I am sorely perplexed what to reply. Were I to refuse the honourable love you offer, I should do contrary to what I have hitherto done, for I have always trusted you more than any other man in the world. Neither my conscience nor my honour oppose your request, nor yet the love I bear the son of the Infante of Fortune, for that is founded on marriage, to which you do not aspire. I know of nothing that should hinder me from answering you according to your desire, if it be not a fear arising from the small need you have for talking to me in this wise; for if what you ask is already yours, why speak of it so ardently?"

Amadour, who was at no loss for an answer, then said to her—

"Madam, you speak very discreetly, and you honour me so greatly by the trust which you say you have in me, that if I were not satisfied with such good fortune I should be quite unworthy of it. But consider, madam, that he who would build an edifice to last for ever must be careful to have a sure and stable foundation. In the same way I, wishing to continue for ever in your service, must not only take care to have the means of remaining near to you, but also to prevent any one from knowing of the great affection that I bear you. Although it is honourable enough to be everywhere proclaimed, yet those who know nothing of lovers' hearts often judge contrary to the truth, and thence come reports as mischievous as though they were true. I have been prompted to say this, and led to declare my love to you, because Paulina, feeling in her heart that I cannot love her, holds me in suspicion and does nought but watch my face wherever I may be. Hence, when you come and speak to me so familiarly in her presence, I am in great fear lest I should make some sign on which she may ground her judgment, and should so fall into that which I am anxious to avoid. For this reason I am led to entreat you not to come and speak to me so suddenly before her or before others whom you know to be equally malicious, for I would rather die than have any living creature know the truth. Were I not so regardful of your honour, I should not have sought this converse with you, for I hold myself sufficiently happy in the love and trust you bear me, and I ask nothing more save that they may continue."

Florida, who could not have been better pleased, began to be sensible of an unwonted feeling in her heart. She saw how honourable were the reasons which he laid before her; and she told him that virtue and honour replied for her, and that she granted him his request. Amadour's joy at this no true lover can doubt.

Florida, however, gave more heed to his counsel than he desired, for she became timid not only in presence of Paulina but elsewhere, and ceased to seek him out as she had been accustomed to do. While they were thus separated she took Amadour's constant converse with Paulina in bad part, for, seeing that the latter was beautiful, she could not believe that Amadour did not love her. To beguile her sorrow she conversed continually with Avanturada, who was beginning to feel very jealous of her husband and Paulina, and often complained of them to Florida, who comforted her as well as she could, being herself smitten with the same disease. Amadour soon perceived the change in Florida's demeanour, and forthwith thought that she was keeping aloof from him not merely by his own advice, but also on account of some bitter fancies of her own.

One day, when they were coming from vespers at a monastery, he spoke to her, and asked—

"What countenance is this you show me, madam?"

"That which I believe you desire," replied Florida.

Thereupon, suspecting the truth, and desiring to know whether he was right, he said to her—

"I have used my time so well, madam, that Paulina no longer has any suspicion of you."

"You could not do better," she replied, "both for yourself and for me. While giving pleasure to yourself you bring me honour."

Amadour gathered from this speech that she believed he took pleasure in conversing with Paulina, and so great was his despair that he could not refrain from saying angrily to her—

"In truth, madam, you begin betimes to torment your lover and pelt him with hard words. I do not think I ever had a more irksome task than to be obliged to hold converse with a lady I do not love. But since you take what I have done to serve you in bad part, I will never speak to her again, happen what may. And that I may hide my wrath as I have hidden my joy, I will betake me to some place in the neighbourhood, and there wait till your caprice has passed away. I hope, however, I shall there receive tidings from my captain and be called back to the war, where I will remain long enough to show you that nothing but yourself has kept me here."

So saying, he forthwith departed without waiting for her reply.

Florida felt the greatest vexation and sorrow imaginable; and love, meeting with opposition, began to put forth its mighty strength. She perceived that she had been in the wrong, and wrote continually to Amadour entreating him to return, which he did after a few days, when his anger had abated.

I cannot undertake to tell you minutely all that they said to each other in order to destroy this jealousy. But at all events he won the victory, and she promised him that not only would she never believe he loved Paulina, but that she would ever be convinced he found it an intolerable martyrdom to speak either to Paulina or to any one else except to do herself a service.

When love had conquered this first suspicion, and while the two lovers were beginning to take fresh pleasure in conversing together, news came that the King of Spain was sending all his army to Salces.[4] Amadour, accustomed ever to be the first in battle, failed not to seize this opportunity of winning renown; but in truth he set forth with unwonted regret, both on account of the pleasure he was losing and because he feared that he might find a change on his return. He knew that Florida, who was now fifteen or sixteen years old, was sought in marriage by many great princes and lords, and he reflected that if she were married during his absence he might have no further opportunity of seeing her, unless, indeed, the Countess of Aranda gave her his wife, Avanturada, as a companion. However, by skillful management with his friends, he obtained a promise from both mother and daughter that wherever Florida might go after her marriage thither should his wife, Avanturada, accompany her. Although it was proposed to marry Florida in

---

[4]A fortress town in the Corbière Mountains between Spain and France, Salces was a site of frequent battles in the wars between Spain and France. The battle in question here took place in 1503.

Portugal, it was nevertheless resolved that Avanturada should never leave her. With this assurance, yet not without unspeakable regret, Amadour went away and left his wife with the Countess.

When Florida found herself alone after his departure, she set about doing such good and virtuous works as she hoped might win her the reputation that belongs to the most perfect women, and might prove her to be worthy of such a lover as Amadour. He having arrived at Barcelona, was there welcomed by the ladies as of old; but they found a greater change in him than they believed it possible for marriage to effect in any man. He seemed to be vexed by the sight of things he had formerly desired; and even the Countess of Palamos, whom he had loved exceedingly, could not persuade him to visit her.

Amadour remained at Barcelona as short a time as possible, for he was impatient to reach Salces, where he alone was now awaited. When he arrived, there began between the two kings that great and cruel war which I do not purpose to describe. Neither will I recount the noble deeds that were done by Amadour, for then my story would take up an entire day; but you must know that he won renown far above all his comrades. The Duke of Najera having arrived at Perpignan in command of two thousand men, requested Amadour to be his lieutenant, and so well did Amadour fulfil his duty with this band, that in every skirmish the only cry was "Najera!"

Now it came to pass that the King of Tunis, who for a long time had been at war with the Spaniards, heard that the kings of France and Spain were warring with each other on the frontiers of Perpignan and Narbonne, and bethought himself that he could have no better opportunity of vexing the King of Spain. Accordingly, he sent a great number of light galleys and other vessels to plunder and destroy all such badly-guarded places as they could find on the coasts of Spain. The people of Barcelona seeing a great fleet passing in front of their town, sent word of the matter to the Viceroy, who was at Salces, and he forthwith despatched the Duke of Najera to Palamos.[5] When the Moors saw that place so well guarded, they made a feint of passing on; but returning at midnight, they landed a large number of men, and the Duke of Najera, being surprised by the enemy, was taken prisoner.

Amadour, who was on the alert and heard the din, forthwith assembled as many of his men as possible, and defended himself so stoutly that the enemy, in spite of their numbers, were for a long time unable to prevail against him. But at last, hearing that the Duke of Najera was taken, and that the Turks had resolved to set fire to Palamos and burn him in the house which he was holding against them, he thought it better to yield than to cause the destruction of the brave men who were with him. He also hoped that by paying a ransom he might yet see Florida again. Accordingly, he gave himself up to a Turk named Dorlin, a governor of the King of Tunis, who brought him to his master. By the latter he was well received and still better guarded; for the King deemed that in him he held the Achilles of all the Spains.

Thus Amadour continued for two years in the service of the King of Tunis. The news of the captures having reached Spain, the kinsfolk of the Duke of Najera were in great sorrow; but those who held the country's honour dear deemed Amadour the greater loss. The rumour came to the house of the Countess of Aranda, where the hapless Avanturada at that time lay grievously sick. The Countess, who had great misgivings as to the affection which Amadour bore to her daughter, though she suffered it and concealed it for the sake of the merits she perceived in him,

[5]A village on the Mediterranean coast north of Barcelona.

took Florida apart and told her the mournful tidings. Florida, who was well able to dissemble, replied that it was a great loss to the entire household, and that above all she pitied his poor wife, who was herself so ill. Nevertheless, seeing that her mother wept exceedingly, she shed a few tears to bear her company; for she feared that if she dissembled too far the feint might be discovered. From that time the Countess often spoke to her of Amadour, but never could she surprise a look to guide her judgment.

I will pass over the pilgrimages, prayers, supplications, and fasts which Florida regularly performed to ensure the safety of Amadour. As soon as he had arrived at Tunis, he failed not to send tidings of himself to his friends, and by a trusty messenger he apprised Florida that he was in good health, and had hopes of seeing her again. This was the only consolation the poor lady had in her grief, and you may be sure that, since she was permitted to write, she did so with all diligence, so that Amadour had no lack of her letters to comfort him.

The Countess of Aranda was about this time commanded to repair to Saragossa, where the King had arrived; and here she found the young Duke of Cardona, who so pressed the King and Queen that they begged the Countess to give him her daughter in marriage. The Countess consented, for she was unwilling to disobey them in anything, and moreover she considered that her daughter, being so young, could have no will of her own. When all was settled, she told Florida that she had chosen for her the match which seemed most suitable. Florida, knowing that when a thing is once done there is small room for counsel, replied that God was to be praised for all things; and, finding her mother look coldly upon her, she sought rather to obey her than to take pity on herself. It scarcely comforted her in her sorrows to learn that the son of the Infante of Fortune was sick even to death; but never, either in presence of her mother or of any one else, did she show any sign of grief. So strongly did she constrain herself, that her tears, driven perforce back into her heart, caused so great a loss of blood from the nose that her life was endangered; and, that she might be restored to health, she was given in marriage to one whom she would willingly have exchanged for death.

After the marriage Florida departed with her husband to the duchy of Cardona, taking with her Avanturada, whom she privately acquainted with her sorrow, both as regards her mother's harshness and her own regret at having lost the son of the Infante of Fortune; but she never spoke of her regret for Amadour except to console his wife.

This young lady then resolved to keep God and honour before her eyes. So well did she conceal her grief, that none of her friends perceived that her husband was displeasing to her.

In this way she spent a long time, living a life that was worse than death, as she failed not to inform her lover Amadour, who, knowing the virtue and greatness of her heart, as well as the love that she had borne to the son of the Infante of Fortune, thought it impossible that she could live long, and mourned for her as for one that was more than dead. This sorrow was an increase to his former grief, and forgetting his own distress in that which he knew his sweetheart was enduring, he would willingly have continued all his life the slave he was if Florida could thereby have had a husband after her own heart. He learnt from a friend whom he had gained at the Court of Tunis that the King, wishing to keep him if only he could make a good Turk of him, intended to give him his choice between impalement and the renunciation of his faith. Thereupon he so addressed himself to his master, the governor who had taken him prisoner, that he persuaded him to release him on parole. His master named, however, a much higher ransom than he thought could be raised by a man of such little wealth, and then, without speaking to the King, he let him go.

When Amadour reached the Court of the King of Spain, he stayed there but a short time, and then, in order to seek his ransom among his friends, he repaired to Barcelona, whither the young Duke of Cardona, his mother, and Florida had gone on business. As soon as Avanturada heard that her husband was returned, she told the news to Florida, who rejoiced as though for love of her friend. Fearing, however, that her joy at seeing Amadour might make her change her countenance, and that those who did not know her might think wrongly of her, she remained at a window in order to see him coming from afar. As soon as she perceived him she went down by a dark staircase, so that none could see whether she changed colour, and embracing Amadour, led him to her room, and thence to her mother-in-law, who had never seen him. He had not been there for two days before he was loved as much as he had been in the household of the Countess of Aranda.

I leave you to imagine the conversation that he and Florida had together, and how she complained to him of the misfortunes that had come to her in his absence. After shedding many tears of sorrow, both for having been married against her will and also for having lost one she loved so dearly without any hope of seeing him again, she resolved to take consolation from the love and trust she had towards Amadour. Though she durst not declare the truth, he suspected it, and lost neither time nor opportunity to show her how much he loved her.

Just when Florida was all but persuaded to receive him, not as a lover, but as a true and perfect friend, a misfortune came to pass, for the King summoned Amadour to him concerning some important matter.

His wife was so grieved on hearing these tidings that she swooned, and falling down a staircase on which she was standing, was so hurt that she never rose again. Florida having by this death lost all her consolation, mourned like one who felt herself bereft of friends and kin. But Amadour grieved still more; for on the one part he lost one of the best wives that ever lived, and on the other the means of ever seeing Florida again. This caused him such sorrow that he was near coming by a sudden death. The old Duchess of Cardona visited him incessantly, reciting the arguments of philosophers why he should endure his loss with patience. But all was of no avail; for if on the one hand his wife's death afflicted him, on the other his love increased his martyrdom. Having no longer any excuse to stay when his wife was buried, and his master again summoned him, his despair was such that he was like to lose his reason.

Florida, who thinking to comfort him, was herself the cause of his greatest grief, spent a whole afternoon in the most gracious converse with him in order to lessen his sorrow, and assured him that she would find means to see him oftener than he thought. Then, as he was to depart on the following morning, and was so weak that he could scarcely stir from his bed, he prayed her to come and see him in the evening after every one else had left him. This she promised to do, not knowing that love in extremity is void of reason.

Amadour altogether despaired of ever again seeing her whom he had loved so long, and from whom he had received no other treatment than I have described. Racked by secret passion and by despair at losing all means of consorting with her, he resolved to play at double or quits, and either lose her altogether or else wholly win her, and so pay himself in an hour the reward which he thought he had deserved. Accordingly he had his bed curtained in such a manner that those who came into the room could not see him; and he complained so much more than he had done previously that all the people of the house thought he had not twenty-four hours to live.

After every one else had visited him, Florida, at the request of her husband himself, came in the evening, hoping to comfort him by declaring her affection and by telling him that, so far as honour allowed, she was willing to love him. She sat down on a chair beside the head of his bed, and began her consolation by weeping with him. Amadour, seeing her filled with such sorrow, thought that in her distress he might the more readily achieve his purpose, and raised himself up in the bed. Florida, thinking that he was too weak to do this, sought to prevent him, but he threw himself on his knees before her saying, "Must I lose sight of you for ever?" Then he fell into her arms like one exhausted. The hapless Florida embraced him and supported him for a long time, doing all she could to comfort him. But what she offered him to cure his pain only increased it; and while feigning to be half dead, he, without saying a word, strove to obtain that which the honour of ladies forbids.

When Florida perceived his evil purpose, in which she could hardly believe after all his honourable conversation, she asked him what he sought to do. Amadour, fearing her reply, which he knew could not be otherwise than chaste and virtuous, said nothing, but pursued his attempt with all the strength that he could muster. Florida, greatly astonished, suspected rather that he had lost his senses than that he was really bent upon her dishonour, and called out to a gentleman whom she knew to be in the room; whereupon Amadour in extreme despair flung himself back upon his bed so suddenly that the gentleman thought him dead.

Florida, who had risen from her chair, then said to the gentleman—

"Go quickly for some strong vinegar."

This the gentleman did, whereupon Florida said—

"What madness, Amadour, has mounted to your brain? What was it you thought and wished to do?"

Amadour, who had lost all reason in the vehemence of his love, replied—

"Does so long a service merit so cruel a reward?"

"And what of the honour of which you have so often preached to me?" said Florida.

"Ah! madam," said Amadour, "it would be impossible to hold your honour more dear than I have held it. Before you were married, I was able so to subdue my heart that you knew nothing of my desires, but now that you are wedded and your honour may be shielded, do I wrong you in asking for what is mine? By the strength of my love I have won you. He who first possessed your heart had so little desire for your person that he deserved to lose both. He who now owns your person is not worthy to have your heart, and hence even your person does not properly belong to him. But for five or six years I have for your sake borne many pains and woes, which must show you that your body and heart belong to me alone. Think not to defend yourself by speaking of conscience, for when love constrains body and heart sin is never imputed. Those who are driven by frenzy so far as to slay themselves cannot sin, for passion leaves no room for reason; and if the passion of love be more intolerable than any other, and more blinding to the senses, what sin could you fasten upon one who yields to the conduct of such indomitable power? I am going away, and have no hope of ever seeing you again; but if before my departure I could have of you that assurance which the greatness of my love deserves, I should be strengthened sufficiently to endure in patience the sorrows of a long separation. If you will not grant me my request you will ere long learn that your harshness has brought me to a miserable and a cruel death."

Florida was not less grieved than astonished to hear these words from one whom she had never imagined capable of such discourse, and, weeping, she thus replied—

"Alas, Amadour, is this the honourable converse that we used to have together when I was young? Is this the honour or conscience which many a time you counselled me to value more than life? Have you forgotten both the worthy examples you set before me of virtuous ladies who withstood unholy love, and also your own contempt for erring women? I cannot believe you so changed, Amadour, that regard for God, your own conscience, and my honour is wholly dead within you. But if it indeed be as you say, I praise the divine goodness which has prevented the misfortune into which I was about to fall, and has revealed to me by your own words the heart of which I was so ignorant. Having lost the son of the Infante of Fortune, not only by my marriage, but also, as is known to me, by reason of his love for another, and finding myself wedded to a man whom, strive as I may, I cannot love, I resolved to set heart and affection entirely on loving you. This love I built upon that virtue which I had so often perceived in you, and to which by your own assistance I think I have attained—I mean the virtue of loving one's honour and conscience more than life. I came hither thinking to make this rock of virtue a sure foundation of love. But you have in a moment shown me, Amadour, that instead of a pure and cleanly rock, this foundation would have been one of shifting sand or filthy mire; and although a great part of the house in which I hoped always to dwell had already been raised, you have suddenly demolished it. Lay aside, therefore, any hope you had concerning me, and make up your mind not to see me by look or word wherever I may be, or to hope that I shall ever be able or willing to change my resolve. It is with the deepest sorrow that I tell you this, though I had gone so far as to swear eternal love with you, I know that my heart could not have lived through this meeting. Even now I am so confounded to find myself deceived, that I am sure my life will be either short or sad. With these words I bid you farewell, and for ever."

I will not try to describe to you the grief that Amadour felt on hearing this speech. It is impossible not only to describe it, but even to conceive it, except indeed to such as have experienced the like. Seeing that with this cruel conclusion she was about to leave him, he seized her by the arm, knowing full well that, if he did not remove her evil opinion of him, he would lose her for ever. Accordingly he dissembled his looks as well as he could, and said—

"During my whole life, madam, I have desired to love a woman of virtue, and having found so few of them, I minded to put you to proof, and so discover whether you were as well worthy of esteem as of love. Now I know for certain that you are; and therefore I give praise to God, who has inclined my heart to the love of such great perfection. I entreat you to pardon my mad and foolhardy attempt, seeing that the issue of it has turned to your honour and to my great satisfaction."

Florida was beginning to learn through him the deceitfulness of men; and, just as she had formerly found it difficult to believe in evil where it existed, so did she now find it even more difficult to believe in virtue where there was none.

"Would to God you spoke the truth," she said to him; "but I am not so ignorant as not to know by my experience in marriage that the blindness of strong passion led you to act as you did. Had God given me a loose rein I am sure that you would not have drawn bridle. Those who go in quest of virtue are wont to take a different road to yours. But enough; if I have been too hasty in crediting you with some goodness, it is time I learned the truth, by which I am now delivered out of your hands."

So saying, Florida left the room. As long as the night lasted she did nought but weep; for the change that had taken place caused her intense grief, and her heart had much ado to hold out against the sorrowing of love. Although, guided by reason, she had resolved to love no more, yet the heart, which cannot be subdued, would in no wise permit this. Thus she was unable to love him less than before, and knowing that love had been the cause of his offence, she made up her mind to satisfy love by continuing to love him with her whole heart, and to obey honour by never giving any sign of her affection either to him or to anyone else.

In the morning Amadour departed in the distress that I have described. Nevertheless his heart, which was so lofty that there was none like it in the world, suffered him not to despair, but prompted him to new devices for seeing Florida again and winning her favour. So as he proceeded to the King of Spain, who was then at Toledo, he took his way through the county of Aranda, where he arrived very late one evening, and found the Countess in great sadness on account of the absence of her daughter.

When she saw Amadour she kissed and embraced him as though he had been her own son, and this no less for the love she herself bore him as for that which she suspected he had for Florida. She asked minutely for news of her daughter, and he told her what he could, though not the entire truth. However, he confessed the love which existed between them, and which Florida had always concealed; and he begged the Countess to aid him in hearing often of Florida, and to take her as speedily as possible to Aranda.

At daybreak he went on his way, and when he had despatched his business with the King he left for the war. So sad was he and so changed in every way that ladies, captains, and acquaintances alike could scarcely recognise him. He now wore nothing but black, and this of a heavier pile than was needful as mourning for his dead wife; but indeed her death served only as a cloak for the sorrow that was in his heart. Thus Amadour spent three or four years without returning to Court.

The Countess of Aranda hearing that Florida was changed and that it was pitiful to see her, sent for her, hoping that she would return home. The contrary, however, happened. When Florida learned that Amadour had told her mother of their love, and that she, although so discreet and virtuous, had approved of it, she was in extraordinary perplexity. On the one hand she perceived that if her mother, who had such great esteem for Amadour, were told the truth some mischief might befall the latter; and this even to save her life she would not have brought to pass, for she felt strong enough to punish his folly herself without calling on her kinsfolk for assistance. On the other hand she saw that, if she concealed the evil she knew of him, she would be constrained by her mother and all her friends to speak to him and show him favour, and this she feared would only strengthen his evil purpose. However, as he was a long way off, she kept her own counsel, and wrote to him whenever the Countess commanded her. Still her letters were such that he could see they were written more out of obedience than goodwill; and the grief he felt in reading them was as great as his joy had been in reading the earlier ones.

At the end of two or three years, when he had performed so many noble deeds that all the paper in Spain could not contain the records of them, he conceived a very skilful device, not indeed to win Florida's heart, which he looked upon as lost, but to gain the victory over his enemy, since such she had shown herself to be. He put aside all the promptings of reason and even the fear of death, and at the risk of his life resolved to act in the following way. He persuaded the chief Governor[6] to send him on an embassy to the King concerning some secret attempt against Leucate;[7] and he procured a command to take counsel with the Countess of Aranda about the matter before communicating it to the King.

Then he came post haste to the county of Aranda, where he knew Florida to be, and secretly sent a friend to inform the Countess of his coming, praying her to keep it secret, and to grant him audience at nightfall without the knowledge of any one.

[6]The Viceroy of Catalonia.

[7]A fortified town near Salces.

The Countess, who was very pleased at his coming, spoke of it to Florida, and sent her to undress in her husband's room, that she might be ready when sent for after every one was gone to bed. Florida had not yet recovered from her first alarm, but she said nothing of it to her mother, and withdrew to an oratory in order to commend herself to Our Lord. While she was praying that her heart might be preserved from all evil affection, she remembered that Amadour had often praised her beauty, and that in spite of long illness it had not been impaired. Being, therefore, more willing to injure her beauty than suffer it to kindle an evil flame in the heart of an honourable gentleman, she took a stone which lay in the chapel and struck herself a grievous blow on the face so that her mouth, nose, and eyes were quite disfigured. Then, in order that no one might suspect it to be of her own doing, she let herself fall upon her face on leaving the chapel when summoned by the Countess, and cried out loudly. The Countess coming thither found her in this pitiful state, and forthwith caused her face to be dressed and bandaged.

Then the countess led her to her own apartment, and begged her to go to her room and entertain Amadour until she herself had got rid of her company. This Florida did, thinking that there were others with him.

But when she found herself alone with him, and the door closed upon her, she was as greatly troubled as he was pleased. He thought that, by love or violence, he would now have what he desired; so he spoke to her, and finding that she made the same reply as before, and that even to save her life she would not change her resolve, he was beside himself with despair.

"Before God, Florida," he said to her, "your scruples shall not rob me of the fruits of my labour. Since love, patience, and humble entreaty are of no avail, I will spare no strength of mine to gain the boon, upon which all its existence depends."

Florida saw that his eyes and countenance were altered exceedingly, so that his complexion, naturally the fairest in the world, was now as red as fire, and his look, usually so gentle and pleasant, had become as horrible and furious as though fierce flames were blazing in his heart and face. In his frenzy he seized her delicate, weak hands in his own strong, powerful ones; and she, finding herself in such bondage that she could neither defend herself nor fly, thought that her only chance was to try whether he had not retained some traces of his former love, for the sake of which he might forego his cruelty. She therefore said to him—

"If you now look upon me, Amadour, in the light of an enemy, I entreat you, by that pure love which I once thought was in your heart, to hearken to me before you put me to torture."

Seeing that he became attentive, she continued—

"Alas! Amadour, what can prompt you to seek after a thing that can afford you no satisfaction, and thus afflict me with the profoundest grief? You made trial of my inclinations in the days of my youth and earliest beauty, and they perhaps served to excuse your passion; but I am amazed that now, when I am old, and ugly, and sorrow-stricken, you should seek for what you know you can never find. I am sure you do not doubt that my mind is as it used to be, and so by force alone can you obtain what you desire. If you observe the condition of my face, and lay aside the memory of the beauty that once you saw in it, you will have no inclination to draw any nearer; and if you still retain within you any remnants of your past love, it is impossible that pity will not subdue your frenzy. To this pity, which I have often found in you, I appeal with prayers for mercy. Suffer me to live in peace, and in that honour which by your own counsel I have resolved to preserve. But if the love you once bore me is now turned to hate, and you desire, in vengeance rather than in love, to make me the unhappiest woman alive, I protest to you that it shall not be so. You will force me against my will to make your evil purpose known to her who thinks so highly of you; and you may be sure that, when she learns it, your life will not be safe."

But Amadour interrupted her.

"If I must die," he said, "I shall be the sooner rid of my torment. The disfigurement of your face, which I believe is of your own seeking, shall not restrain me from making you mine. Though I could have nothing but your bones, I would yet hold them close to me."

When Florida saw that prayers, reasoning and tears were alike of no avail, and that while he cruelly pursued his evil purpose she lacked the strength to resist him, she summoned the aid which she dreaded as greatly as death, and in a sad and pitious voice called as loudly as she could upon her mother. The Countess, hearing her daughter's cries, had grave misgivings of the truth, and hastened into the room with all possible speed.

Amadour, who was not so ready to die as he affirmed, desisted promptly from his enterprise; and when the lady opened the door she found him close beside it, and Florida some distance from him. "Amadour," said the Countess, "what is the matter? Tell me the truth."

Amadour, who was never at a loss for invention, replied with a pale and daunted face—

"Alas! madam, what change is this in the lady Florida? I was never so astonished before, for, as I have told you, I thought I had a share in her favour; but I now see clearly that I have lost it all. While she was being brought up by you, she was, I think, no less discreet or virtuous than she is at present; however, she had then no qualms of conscience about speaking with any one. But now, when I sought to look at her, she would not suffer me to do so. When I saw this behaviour on her part I thought I must be dreaming, and asked her for her hand to kiss it after the manner of the country. This she utterly refused me. I acknowledge, madam, that then I acted wrongfully, and I entreat your pardon for it; for I took her hand, as it were by force, and kissed it. I asked nothing more of her, but I believe that she intends my death, for she called out to you as you know. Why she did this I cannot tell, unless indeed she feared that I had some other purpose in view. Nevertheless, madam, be this as it may, I confess that I am in the wrong; for although she ought to love all who are devoted to you, fortune wills it that I, who am of all most attached to her, am banished from her good graces. Still, I shall ever continue the same both to you and to her; and I entreat you to continue me in your good favour since, by no fault of my own, I have now lost hers."

The Countess, who partly believed and partly suspected him, went up to her daughter and asked—"Why did you call me so loudly?"

Florida replied that she had felt afraid; and, although the Countess questioned her minutely on many points, she would give no other reply. Finding that she had escaped from her enemy she deemed him sufficiently punished by the failure of his attempt.

After the Countess had had a long conversation with Amadour, she suffered him to speak again in her presence with Florida, to see how he would behave. He said but little, save that he thanked her for not having confessed the truth to her mother, and begged that since she had expelled him from her heart, she would at least allow no other to take his place.

"If my voice had not been my only means of defending myself," she replied, "it would never have been heard; and from me you shall have no worse punishment, if you do not force me to it by troubling me again as you have done. Do not fear that

I can ever love another; since I have not found the good I wished for in a heart that I considered to be the most virtuous in the world, I do not expect to find it in any man. This evil fortune will henceforth free me of all the passion that love can give."

With these words she bade him farewell.

Her mother, who had been watching her face, was unable to form any opinion; though from that time forth she clearly saw that her daughter had lost all affection for Amadour. She imagined her so devoid of reason as to hate everything that she herself loved; and from that hour she warred with her in a strange way, spending seven years without speaking to her except in anger, all which she did at Amadour's request.

Meanwhile, on account of her mother's harsh treatment, Florida's former dread of being with her husband was changed into a desire of never leaving him. Seeing, however, that all her efforts were useless, she resolved to deceive Amadour, and laying aside her coldness for a day or two, she advised him to pay court to a lady who, she said, had been speaking of their love.

This lady lived with the Queen of Spain, and was called Loretta. Amadour believed the story, and, thinking that he might in this way regain Florida's good graces, he made love to Loretta, who was the wife of a captain, one of the viceroys of the King of Spain. She, in her pleasure at having gained such a lover, showed so much elation that the affair was rumoured abroad. Even the Countess of Aranda, who was at Court, had knowledge of it, and thenceforward treated Florida less harshly than before.

One day Florida heard that the captain, Loretta's husband, had grown jealous, and was resolved to kill Amadour in one way or another as best he might. In spite of her altered treatment of Amadour, Florida did not desire that evil should befall him, and so she immediately informed him of what she had heard. He was quite ready to hark back again to his first love, and thereupon told her that, if she would grant him three hours of her conversation every day, he would never again speak to Loretta. But this she would not grant. "Then," said Amadour,"if you will not give me life, why prevent me from dying, unless indeed you hope to make me suffer more pain during life than any death could cause? But though death shun me, I will seek it until I find it; then only shall I have rest."

While they were on this footing, news came that the King of Granada was entering upon a great war against the King of Spain. The latter, therefore, sent the Prince, his son, to the war, and with him the Constable of Castille and the Duke of Alba, two old and prudent lords. The Duke of Cardona and the Count of Aranda were unwilling to remain behind, and prayed the King to give them some command. This he did as befitted their rank, and gave them into the safe keeping of Amadour, who performed such extraordinary deeds during the war, that they seemed to be acts as much of despair as of bravery.

Coming now to the point of my story, I have to relate how his overboldness was proved by his death. The Moors had made a show of offering battle, and finding the Christian army very numerous had feigned a retreat. The Spaniards started in pursuit, but the old Constable and the Duke of Alba, who suspected the trickery of the Moors, restrained the Prince of Spain against his will from crossing the river. The Count of Aranda, however, and the Duke of Cardona crossed, although it was forbidden; and when the Moors saw that they were pursued by only a few men they faced about again. The Duke of Cardona was struck down and killed with a blow of a scimitar, and the Count of Aranda was so grievously wounded that he was left for dead. Thereupon Amadour came up filled with rage and fury, and bursting through the throng, caused the two bodies to be taken up and carried to the camp of the Prince, who mourned for them as for his own brothers. On examining their wounds the Count of Aranda was found to be still alive, and was sent in a litter to his home, where he lay ill for a long time. On the other hand, the Duke's body was sent back to Cardona.

Meanwhile Amadour, having made this effort to rescue the two bodies, had thought so little of his own safety that he found himself surrounded by a large number of Moors. Not desiring his person to be captured any more than he had captured that of his mistress, nor to break his faith with God as he had broken faith with her—for he knew that, if he were taken to the King of Granada, he must either die a cruel death or renounce Christianity—he resolved to withhold from his enemies the glory either of his death or capture. So kissing the cross of his sword and commending his body and soul to God, he dealt himself such a thrust as to be past all help.

Thus died the unhappy Amadour, lamented as deeply as his virtues deserved. The news spread through the whole of Spain; and the rumour of it came to Florida, who was at Barcelona, where her husband had formerly commanded that he should be buried. She gave him an honourable funeral, and then, without saying anything to her mother or mother-in-law, she became a nun in the Convent of Jesus, taking for husband and lover Him who had delivered her from such a violent love as that of Amadour's, and from such great affliction as she had endured in the company of her husband. Thus were all her affections directed to the perfect loving of God; and, after living for a long time as a nun, she yielded up her soul with gladness, like that of the bride when she goes forth to meet the bridegroom.

"I am well aware, ladies, that this long tale may have been wearisome to some among you, but had I told it as it was told to me it would have been longer still. Take example, I beg you, by the virtue of Florida, but be somewhat less cruel; and think not so well of any man that, when you are undeceived, you occasion him a cruel death and yourselves a life of sorrow."

Having had a long and fair hearing Parlamente said to Hircan—

"Do you not think that this lady was pressed to extremities and that she held out virtuously?"

"No," said Hircan; "a woman can make no more feeble resistance than to cry out. If she had been in a place where none could hear her I do not know how she would have fared. And if Amadour had had more love and less fear he would not have desisted from his attempt for so little. So this story will not cause me to change my firm opinion that no man ever perfectly loved a lady, or was loved by her, that he did not prove successful if only he went the right way to work. Nevertheless, I must praise Amadour for having in part done his duty."

"What duty?" asked Oisille. "Do you call it a lover's duty to try and take his mistress by force when he owes her all reverence and submission?"

Here Saffredent took up the discourse.

"Madam," he said, "when our mistresses hold their state in chamber or hall, seated at their ease as though they were our judges, we lead them to the dance in fear; we wait upon them with all diligence and anticipate their commands; and we are so afraid of offending them and so desirous of doing them service that those who see us pity us, and often deem us more witless than brutes. They account us dull and void of understanding, and give praise to the ladies, whose faces are so imperious and their speech so fair that they make themselves feared, loved, and honoured by those who only know them outwardly. But when we are together in private, and love alone can judge our behaviour, we know full well that they are women and we are men. Then is the name 'mistress' changed to 'sweetheart,' and the 'slave' becomes a 'lover.' As the proverb says—'By service true and loyalty, do servants rise to mastery.' They have honour equally with men, who can give it to them and can take it away; and seeing us suffer in patience, they should reward us when they can do so without hurt to their honour."

"You do not speak of that true honour," said Longarine, "which is the greatest happiness this world can give. If every one calls me a virtuous woman, and I myself know the contrary, the praise I receive only increases my shame and puts me in secret to still greater confusion. In the same way, if people condemn me and I know that I am innocent, their condemnation will only make me the better pleased with myself."

"In spite of what you all have said," interposed Geburon, "it seems to me that Amadour was as noble and virtuous a knight as ever lived, and I think I can recognize him under his feigned name. Since Parlamente would not name him, neither will I. But you may rest assured that, if he be the man whom I have in mind, his heart never knew fear, nor was ever void of love and bravery."

"The day has been spent so pleasantly," said Oisille, "that if the others are like it I think our talk will make the time pass quickly by. But see where the sun is, and listen to the abbey bell, which has long been calling us to vespers. I did not mention this to you before, for I was more inclined to hear the end of the story than to go to prayers."

At these words they all rose, and when they reached the abbey they found that the monks had been waiting for them a full hour and more. After vespers they went to supper, and during the whole evening they conversed about the stories they had heard, all of them searching every corner of their memories to try and make the second day as pleasant as the first. And after playing many games in the meadow they went to bed, and so made a glad and happy ending of the first day.

MICHEL EYQUEM DE MONTAIGNE

[1533–1592]

Reading Montaigne, one is immediately struck by the apparent modernity of his views, especially his skepticism about absolute truth, his questioning of the shifting grounds of identity, his acceptance of the limits of human understanding, and his tolerant recognition of cultural differences. Yet, as his biographers and critics have noted, the author of the *Essays* (1580–1588), a collection of desultory and unpretentious reflections on his own life, is rooted firmly in the material and intellectual experience of the Renaissance. Montaigne's renunciation of human claims to knowledge, power, and authority seems to fly in the face of the great celebrations of those qualities in Leonardo da Vinci, Niccolo Machiavelli, and Pico della Mirandola, but his *Essays* combine the nobleman's graceful poise, the humanist's love of the classics, and the explorer's ardent curiosity. Above all, he shares with his age its desire for self-understanding, characterized most notably in an epithet Montaigne had engraved upon a medallion: *"Que scais je?"*—"What do I know?" His *Essays,* composed over the last twenty years of his life and in the midst of relentless political turmoil, represent Montaigne's attempts to answer that question. If the answer he ultimately discovers is that "there is no end to our investigations," Montaigne nonetheless believes, with Socrates, that through self-study a person can gain the wisdom to accept life in all its mutability and diversity.

Life

Montaigne's father, Pierre Eyquem de Montaigne, descended from a trading family who had acquired enough wealth and property to claim status as nobles, ensured that his son would be able to experience diversity. When Michel de Montaigne was born on February 28, 1533, his father brought him up for two years among peasants in order to bond him with people of the lowest class before hiring a German tutor and two attendants to care for his son and to speak to him only in Latin. Montaigne tells us that he was six years old before he understood his native French, and he praises his father for enabling him to acquire a flawless Latin "without the whip and tears" of a grammar school. From age six to twelve Montaigne attended the College de Guyenne in Bordeaux, where he says he learned to love the works of Ovid, Virgil, and Horace, which he read as a kind of confection to sweeten the standard school fare of Cicero. Once he left school, Montaigne probably spent a good deal of time in Paris before beginning his career as a lawyer in the high court of Bordeaux; there he formed a strong friendship with his colleague and erudite classicist Étienne de La Boétie, a bond that lasted until his friend's untimely death in 1563. As a magistrate, Montaigne was necessarily involved in the growing conflict between the Catholics and Protestants in France, which eventually amounted to religious civil war, culminating in the War of the Three Henries. Although he was a Catholic loyalist, Montaigne disagreed with the cruel punishments the government dealt to the Protestant Huguenots, and his outrage at these sufferings are echoed in his appeals for tolerance and moderation in the *Essays*.

Two years after his marriage to Françoise de La Chassaigne in 1565, Montaigne translated Raymond Sebond's *Book of the Creatures, or Natural Theology*, a fifteenth-century defense of Christian faith and Montaigne's first publication. When his father died in 1569, Montaigne inherited the family estate, the Chateau de Montaigne, about thirty miles from Bordeaux; two years later, the thirty-eight-year-old Montaigne retired to his beloved book-lined study in the tower at the Chateau in order to study and to begin his *Essays*, after having completed an edition of La Boétie's works.

Montaigne's retirement, however, was not complete, and he continued to be involved in public and state affairs. He received the Order of Saint Michael in 1571 and was appointed gentleman-in-ordinary of the king's chamber in 1573. He served in the army at the siege of La Fère in Normandy in 1580, and from September 1580 to November 1581 he toured Germany, Switzerland, Austria, and Italy, partly to see Venice and Rome, but partly to seek relief in the baths at Lucca from a painful kidney stone that would torment him for the rest of his life. Called back to Bordeaux to serve as mayor from 1581 to 1585, a time of plague and religious fighting in the city, Montaigne resigned, only to become embroiled in attempts to strengthen the alliance against the Catholic League, whose soldiers had pillaged his land when they attacked Castillon in 1587. Over the next few years Montaigne continued to be involved in the struggles for power among the three Henries. Amid these public responsibilities, Montaigne wrote and revised his essays, the first of which was published in 1580. Montaigne revised and added to his *Essays* until the end of his life, publishing three editions before his death in 1592, after which appeared the complete four-book version we read today.

Work

The *essais,* or "attempts," were unique to the literary world of the Renaissance; indeed, Montaigne is often known as the "father of the essay" for his invention of this casual, exploratory form. In the essay, Montaigne discovered a form with which to set down his thoughts and observations with a subjectivity and gentle irony that leaves his ideas open for further exploration. Montaigne describes his method best in "Of Democritus and Heraclitus" (1580), noting that "I take the first subject that chance offers. They are all equally good for me. And I never plan to develop them completely. For I do not see the whole of anything; nor do those who promise to show it to us." There is something here of the nobleman's *sprezzatura*, a poised casualness and practiced spontaneity; yet he is sincere, more so than Rousseau in *The Confessions*, when he describes in "Of Coaches" (1588) the limits of our knowledge in a phrase that equally characterizes his essay style: "We do not go in a straight line; we rather ramble and turn this way and that. We retrace our steps." Moreover, the *Essays* give us not just a sense of the ostensible subject but, most importantly, the personality and character of the writer. As he explains his intentions, "I want to be seen here in my simple, natural, and ordinary fashion, without straining or artifice; for it is myself that I portray." To this end, Montaigne thinks out loud in a language that is accessible and plain and entertains ideas with a personal and playful openness. Thus, many of the essays show Montaigne fusing an event or idea with personal reflection without making claims to some absolute truth, yet each essay demonstrates the breadth of Montaigne's reading and experience, marking him as a true man of the Renaissance.

Montaigne began writing the *Essays*, for which he is known today, in 1572 at a time when France was racked between warring factions of the Protestant Huguenots and ultra-Catholics led by Henri, the Duke of Guise. Perhaps the folly of such sectarian warfare, which resulted in thousands of deaths between 1562 and 1593, contributed to Montaigne's religious toleration—not only between Catholics and Protestants, but between Christians and non-Christians. Moreover, writing in the wake of the new astronomy of Copernicus and the discovery of new peoples and ways of life in the Americas, Montaigne shows an open-mindedness remarkable not only for his day, but for ours as well.

In contrast to the prevalent deference to the authority of the classics, Montaigne introduces a modest skepticism rooted in both reason and experience—a philosophical idea that anticipates the empiricism of Francis Bacon and the eighteenth-century *philosophes*. As he puts it in "Of the Education of Children" (1580), "Wonderful brilliance may be gained for human judgment by getting to know men. We are all huddled and concentrated within ourselves, and our vision is reduced to the length of our nose." Prescient in his belief in the fallibility and imperfection of human reason, Montaigne anticipates the satirists of the eighteenth century in his critique of the vanity of human wishes, institutions, and values, all of which, in his view, vary according to differences in time and place. As he says in "Of Presumption" (1580), "We are nothing but ceremony; ceremony carries us away, and we leave the substance of things." And even when we do pay attention to them, he might add from "On the Uncertainty of Our Judgement" (1580), unreliable fortune "involves our reason . . . in her uncertainties and confusion" to the degree that our judgment, as Timaeus says in Plato, "'has in it a large element of chance.'"

In both of the essays below, "Of Cannibals" (1580) and "Of Coaches," we see a perhaps cautious, but nonetheless genuine, respect for cultural values and practices of non-European people. Both essays contain Montaigne's version of what we would call cultural relativism. He states the case for cultural relativism clearly throughout his work, as in the "Apology for Raimond Sebond" (1580), where he writes, "Those who return from that New World which was discovered in our fathers' time by the Spaniards can testify to us how much more lawfully and regulatedly these nations live without magistrates and without law than ours, where there are more officers and laws than there are other men and actions."

In "Of Cannibals" Montaigne engages the question of cultural difference evident between the various human communities, especially here along the gradient between what

Claude Lévi-Strauss calls the raw and the cooked, the wild and the tame, or the primitive and the civilized. What Montaigne notices is that human perception of other cultures is relative to the perspective of the beholder, and he wonders characteristically whether it is not the so-called civilized peoples who are the true barbarians. As in "Of Coaches," despite his love of classical learning, Montaigne entertains the possibility that the native peoples of the Americas might be able to teach Europeans something about human relationships, politics, and philosophy. Breaking with the view, sometimes linked to Machiavelli, that Graeco-Roman history and philosophy should serve up the only models for European states, Montaigne sees possible models for statecraft in the new world. As he says in "Of Cannibals," "I am sorry that Lycurgus and Plato did not know [the natives]; for it seems to me that what we actually see in these nations surpasses not only all the pictures in which poets have idealized the golden age and all their inventions in imagining a happy state of man, but also the conceptions and the very desire of philosophy. They could not imagine a naturalness so pure and simple as we see by experience; nor could they believe that our society could be maintained with so little artifice and human solder." This tolerance, inquisitiveness, respect for others, and acceptance of the limits of Montaigne's own position characterize "Of Coaches," where the atrocities and barbarism of the Spanish conquest—the effects of a "civilized" state—cause Montaigne and his readers to pause over the complacency with which they accept their supposed superiority over another culture.

Suggested Readings

The best biography in English is Donald Frame's *Montaigne: A Biography* (1984). All of the critical books on Montaigne focus, of course, primarily upon the *Essays*. Good general introductions to the *Essays* in relation to Montaigne's life and milieu include Donald Frame's *Montaigne's Essais: A Study* (1969) and R. A. Sayce's *The Essays of Montaigne: A Critical Exploration* (1972). More specialized approaches to the *Essays* include Ermanno Bencivenga's *The Discipline of Subjectivity: An Essay on Montaigne* (1990), Richard L. Regosin's *The Matter of My Book: Montaigne's* Essais *as the Book of the Self* (1977), and Jean Starobinski's *Montaigne in Motion* (1982; trans. Arthur Goldhammer 1985).

Essays

Translated by Donald M. Frame

Of Cannibals

When King Pyrrhus[1] passed over into Italy, after he had reconnoitered the formation of the army that the Romans were sending to meet him, he said: "I do not know what barbarians these are" (for so the Greeks called all foreign nations), "but the formation of this army that I see is not at all barbarous." The Greeks said as much of the army that Flaminius brought into their country, and so did Philip, seeing from a knoll the order and distribution of the Roman camp, in his kingdom, under Publius Sulpicius Galba.[2] Thus we should beware of clinging to vulgar opinions, and judge things by reason's way, not by popular say.

[1] King of Epirus (c. 318–272 B.C.E.), who invaded Rome in 280 B.C.E. at a high cost of lives among his soldiers.

[2] Flaminius and Galba were Roman generals who fought against Philip V, King of Macedon (221–179 B.C.E.).

I had with me for a long time a man who had lived for ten or twelve years in that other world which has been discovered in our century, in the place where Villegaignon landed, and which he called Antarctic France.[3] This discovery of a boundless country seems worthy of consideration. I don't know if I can guarantee that some other such discovery will not be made in the future, so many personages greater than ourselves having been mistaken about this one. I am afraid we have eyes bigger than our stomachs, and more curiosity than capacity. We embrace everything, but we clasp only wind.

Plato[4] brings in Solon, telling how he had learned from the priests of the city of Saïs in Egypt that in days of old, before the Flood, there was a great island named Atlantis, right at the mouth of the Strait of Gibraltar, which contained more land than Africa and Asia put together, and that the kings of that country, who not only possessed that island but had stretched out so far on the mainland that they held the breadth of Africa as far as Egypt, and the length of Europe as far as Tuscany, undertook to step over into Asia and subjugate all the nations that border on the Mediterranean, as far as the Black Sea; and for this purpose crossed the Spains, Gaul, Italy, as far as Greece, where the Athenians checked them; but that some time after, both the Athenians and themselves and their island were swallowed up by the Flood.

It is quite likely that the extreme devastation of waters made amazing changes in the habitations of the earth, as people maintain that the sea cut off Sicily from Italy—

> 'Tis said an earthquake once asunder tore
> These lands with dreadful havoc, which before
> Formed but one land, one coast
>
> –VIRGIL

—Cyprus from Syria, the island of Euboea from the mainland of Boeotia; and elsewhere joined lands that were divided, filling the channels between them with sand and mud:

> A sterile marsh, long fit for rowing, now
> Feeds neighbor towns, and feels the heavy plow.
>
> –HORACE

But there is no great likelihood that that island was the new world which we have just discovered; for it almost touched Spain, and it would be an incredible result of a flood to have forced it away as far as it is, more than twelve hundred leagues; besides, the travels of the moderns have already almost revealed that it is not an island, but a mainland connected with the East Indies on one side, and elsewhere with the lands under the two poles; or, if it is separated from them, it is by so narrow a strait and interval that it does not deserve to be called an island on that account.

It seems that there are movements, some natural, others feverish, in these great bodies, just as in our own. When I consider the inroads that my river, the Dordogne, is making in my lifetime into the right bank in its descent, and that in twenty years it has gained so much ground and stolen away the foundations of several buildings, I clearly see that this is an extraordinary disturbance; for if it had always gone at this rate, or was to do so in the future, the face of the world would be turned topsy-turvy. But rivers are subject to changes: now they overflow in one direction, now in another, now they keep to their course. I am not speaking of the sudden

---

[3]Brazil, in 1557. [4]In the *Timaeus.*

inundations whose causes are manifest. In Médoc, along the seashore, my brother, the sieur d'Arsac, can see an estate of his buried under the sands that the sea spews forth; the tops of some buildings are still visible; his farms and domains have changed into very thin pasturage. The inhabitants say that for some time the sea has been pushing toward them so hard that they have lost four leagues of land. These sands are its harbingers; and we see great dunes of moving sand that march half a league ahead of it and keep conquering land.

The other testimony of antiquity with which some would connect this discovery is in Aristotle, at least if that little book *Of Unheard-of Wonders* is by him. He there relates that certain Carthaginians, after setting out upon the Atlantic Ocean from the Strait of Gibraltar and sailing a long time, at last discovered a great fertile island, all clothed in woods and watered by great deep rivers, far remote from any mainland; and that they, and others since, attracted by the goodness and fertility of the soil, went there with their wives and children, and began to settle there. The lords of Carthage, seeing that their country was gradually becoming depopulated, expressly forbade anyone to go there any more, on pain of death, and drove out these new inhabitants, fearing, it is said, that in course of time they might come to multiply so greatly as to supplant their former masters and ruin their state. This story of Aristotle does not fit our new lands any better than the other.

This man I had was a simple, crude fellow—a character fit to bear true witness; for clever people observe more things and more curiously, but they interpret them; and to lend weight and conviction to their interpretation, they cannot help altering history a little. They never show you things as they are, but bend and disguise them according to the way they have seen them; and to give credence to their judgment and attract you to it, they are prone to add something to their matter, to stretch it out and amplify it. We need a man either very honest, or so simple that he has not the stuff to build up false inventions and give them plausibility; and wedded to no theory. Such was my man; and besides this, he at various times brought sailors and merchants, whom he had known on that trip, to see me. So I content myself with his information, without inquiring what the cosmographers say about it.

We ought to have topographers who would give us an exact account of the places where they have been. But because they have over us the advantage of having seen Palestine, they want to enjoy the privilege of telling us news about all the rest of the world. I would like everyone to write what he knows, and as much as he knows, not only in this, but in all other subjects; for a man may have some special knowledge and experience of the nature of a river or a fountain, who in other matters knows only what everybody knows. However, to circulate this little scrap of knowledge, he will undertake to write the whole of physics. From this vice spring many great abuses.

Now, to return to my subject, I think there is nothing barbarous and savage in that nation, from what I have been told, except that each man calls barbarism whatever is not his own practice; for indeed it seems we have no other test of truth and reason than the example and pattern of the opinions and customs of the country we live in. *There* is always the perfect religion, the perfect government, the perfect and accomplished manners in all things. Those people are wild, just as we call wild the fruits that Nature has produced by herself and in her normal course; whereas really it is those that we have changed artificially and led astray from the common order, that we should rather call wild. The former retain alive and vigorous their genuine, their most useful and natural, virtues and properties, which we have debased in the latter in adapting them to gratify our corrupted taste. And yet for all that, the savor and delicacy of some uncultivated fruits of those countries is quite as excellent, even to our taste, as that of our own. It is not reasonable that art should win the place of honor over our great and powerful mother Nature. We have so overloaded the beauty and richness of her works by our inventions that we have quite smothered her. Yet wherever her purity shines forth, she wonderfully puts to shame our vain and frivolous attempts:

> Ivy comes readier without our care;
> In lonely caves the arbutus grows more fair;
> No art with artless bird song can compare.
>
> –PROPERTIUS

All our efforts cannot even succeed in reproducing the nest of the tiniest little bird, its contexture, its beauty and convenience; or even the web of the puny spider. All things, says Plato, are produced by nature, by fortune, or by art; the greatest and most beautiful by one or the other of the first two, the least and most imperfect by the last.

These nations, then, seem to me barbarous in this sense, that they have been fashioned very little by the human mind, and are still very close to their original naturalness. The laws of nature still rule them, very little corrupted by ours; and they are in such a state of purity that I am sometimes vexed that they were unknown earlier, in the days when there were men able to judge them better than we. I am sorry that Lycurgus[5] and Plato did not know of them; for it seems to me that what we actually see in these nations surpasses not only all the pictures in which poets have idealized the golden age and all their inventions in imagining a happy state of man, but also the conceptions and the very desire of philosophy. They could not imagine a naturalness so pure and simple as we see by experience; nor could they believe that our society could be maintained with so little artifice and human solder. This is a nation, I should say to Plato, in which there is no sort of traffic, no knowledge of letters, no science of numbers, no name for a magistrate or for political superiority, no custom of servitude, no riches or poverty, no contracts, no successions, no partitions, no occupations but leisure ones, no care for any but common kinship, no clothes, no agriculture, no metal, no use of wine or wheat. The very words that signify lying, treachery, dissimulation, avarice, envy, belittling, pardon—unheard of.[6] How far from this perfection would he find the republic that he imagined: *Men fresh sprung from the gods* [Seneca].

> These manners nature first ordained.
>
> –VIRGIL

For the rest, they live in a country with a very pleasant and temperate climate, so that according to my witnesses it is rare to see a sick man there; and they have assured me that they never saw one palsied, bleary-eyed, toothless, or bent with age. They are settled along the sea and shut in on the land side by great high mountains, with a stretch about a hundred leagues wide in between. They have a great abundance of fish and flesh which bear no resemblance to ours, and they eat them with no other artifice than cooking. The first man who rode a horse there, though he had had dealings with them on several other trips, so horrified them in this posture that they shot him dead with arrows before they could recognize him.

---

[5]A Spartan lawgiver of the ninth century B.C.E. who wrote about ideal societies.

[6]In Florio's translation, Shakespeare borrowed from this passage for *The Tempest,* Act II, scene 1.

Their buildings are very long, with a capacity of two or three hundred souls; they are covered with the bark of great trees, the strips reaching to the ground at one end and supporting and leaning on one another at the top, in the manner of some of our barns, whose covering hangs down to the ground and acts as a side. They have wood so hard that they cut with it and make of it their swords and grills to cook their food. Their beds are of a cotton weave, hung from the roof like those in our ships, each man having his own; for the wives sleep apart from their husbands.

They get up with the sun, and eat immediately upon rising, to last them through the day; for they take no other meal than that one. Like some other Eastern peoples, of whom Suidas[7] tells us, who drank apart from meals, they do not drink then; but they drink several times a day, and to capacity. Their drink is made of some root, and is of the color of our claret wines. They drink it only lukewarm. This beverage keeps only two or three days; it has a slightly sharp taste, is not at all heady, is good for the stomach, and has a laxative effect upon those who are not used to it; it is a very pleasant drink for anyone who is accustomed to it. In place of bread they use a certain white substance like preserved coriander. I have tried it; it tastes sweet and a little flat.

The whole day is spent in dancing. The younger men go to hunt animals with bows. Some of the women busy themselves meanwhile with warming their drink, which is their chief duty. Some one of the old men, in the morning before they begin to eat, preaches to the whole barnful in common, walking from one end to the other, and repeating one single sentence several times until he has completed the circuit (for the buildings are fully a hundred paces long). He recommends to them only two things: valor against the enemy and love for their wives. And they never fail to point out this obligation, as their refrain, that it is their wives who keep their drink warm and seasoned.

There may be seen in several places, including my own house, specimens of their beds, of their ropes, of their wooden swords and the bracelets with which they cover their wrists in combats, and of the big canes, open at one end, by whose sound they keep time in their dances. They are close shaven all over, and shave themselves much more cleanly than we, with nothing but a wooden or stone razor. They believe that souls are immortal, and that those who have deserved well of the gods are lodged in that part of heaven where the sun rises, and the damned in the west.

They have some sort of priests and prophets, but they rarely appear before the people, having their home in the mountains. On their arrival there is a great feast and solemn assembly of several villages—each barn, as I have described it, makes up a village, and they are about one French league from each other. The prophet speaks to them in public, exhorting them to virtue and their duty; but their whole ethical science contains only these two articles: resoluteness in war and affection for their wives. He prophesies to them things to come and the results they are to expect from their undertakings, and urges them to war or holds them back from it; but this is on the condition that when he fails to prophesy correctly, and if things turn out otherwise than he has predicted, he is cut into a thousand pieces if they catch him, and condemned as a false prophet. For this reason, the prophet who has once been mistaken is never seen again.

---

[7] A Greek lexicographer from the tenth century C.E.

Divination is a gift of God; that is why its abuse should be punished as imposture. Among the Scythians,[8] when the soothsayers failed to hit the mark, they were laid, chained hand and foot, on carts full of heather and drawn by oxen, on which they were burned. Those who handle matters subject to the control of human capacity are excusable if they do the best they can. But these others, who come and trick us with assurances of an extraordinary faculty that is beyond our ken, should they not be punished for not making good their promise, and for the temerity of their imposture?

They have their wars with the nations beyond the mountains, further inland, to which they go quite naked, with no other arms than bows or wooden swords ending in a sharp point, in the manner of the tongues of our boar spears. It is astonishing what firmness they show in their combats, which never end but in slaughter and bloodshed; for as to routs and terror, they know nothing of either.

Each man brings back as his trophy the head of the enemy he has killed, and sets it up at the entrance of his dwelling. After they have treated their prisoners well for a long time with all the hospitality they can think of, each man who has a prisoner calls a great assembly of his acquaintances. He ties a rope to one of the prisoner's arms, by the end of which he holds him, a few steps away, for fear of being hurt, and gives his dearest friend the other arm to hold in the same way; and these two, in the presence of the whole assembly, kill him with their swords. This done, they roast him and eat him in common and send some pieces to their absent friends. This is not, as people think, for nourishment, as of old the Scythians used to do; it is to betoken an extreme revenge. And the proof of this came when they saw the Portuguese, who had joined forces with their adversaries, inflict a different kind of death on them when they took them prisoner, which was to bury them up to the waist, shoot the rest of their body full of arrows, and afterward hang them. They thought that these people from the other world, being men who had sown the knowledge of many vices among their neighbors and were much greater masters than themselves in every sort of wickedness, did not adopt this sort of vengeance without some reason, and that it must be more painful than their own; so they began to give up their old method and follow this one.

I am not sorry that we notice the barbarous horror of such acts, but I am heartily sorry that, judging their faults rightly, we should be so blind to our own. I think there is more barbarity in eating a man alive than in eating him dead; and in tearing by tortures and the rack a body still full of feeling, in roasting a man bit by bit, in having him bitten and mangled by dogs and swine (as we have not only read but seen within fresh memory, not among ancient enemies, but among neighbors and fellow citizens, and what is worse, on the pretext of piety and religion), than in roasting and eating him after he is dead.

Indeed, Chrysippus and Zeno, heads of the Stoic sect, thought there was nothing wrong in using our carcasses for any purpose in case of need, and getting nourishment from them; just as our ancestors, when besieged by Caesar in the city of Alésia, resolved to relieve their famine by eating old men, women, and other people useless for fighting.

> The Gascons once, 'tis said, their life renewed
> By eating of such food.
>
> –JUVENAL

[8]Nomadic people noted for barbarity who occupied southeastern Europe until about 300 B.C.E.

And physicians do not fear to use human flesh in all sorts of ways for our health, applying it either inwardly or outwardly. But there never was any opinion so disordered as to excuse treachery, disloyalty, tyranny, and cruelty, which are our ordinary vices.

So we may well call these people barbarians, in respect to the rules of reason, but not in respect to ourselves, who surpass them in every kind of barbarity.

Their warfare is wholly noble and generous, and as excusable and beautiful as this human disease can be; its only basis among them is their rivalry in valor. They are not fighting for the conquest of new lands, for they still enjoy that natural abundance that provides them without toil and trouble with all necessary things in such profusion that they have no wish to enlarge their boundaries. They are still in that happy state of desiring only as much as their natural needs demand; anything beyond that is superfluous to them.

They generally call those of the same age, brothers; those who are younger, children; and the old men are fathers to all the others. These leave to their heirs in common the full possession of their property, without division or any other title at all than just the one that Nature gives to her creatures in bringing them into the world.

If their neighbors cross the mountains to attack them and win a victory, the gain of the victor is glory, and the advantage of having proved the master in valor and virtue; for apart from this they have no use for the goods of the vanquished, and they return to their own country, where they lack neither anything necessary nor that great thing, the knowledge of how to enjoy their condition happily and be content with it. These men of ours do the same in their turn. They demand of their prisoners no other ransom than that they confess and acknowledge their defeat. But there is not one in a whole century who does not choose to die rather than to relax a single bit, by word or look, from the grandeur of an invincible courage; not one who would not rather be killed and eaten than so much as ask not to be. They treat them very freely, so that life may be all the dearer to them, and usually entertain them with threats of their coming death, of the torments they will have to suffer, the preparations that are being made for that purpose, the cutting up of their limbs, and the feast that will be made at their expense. All this is done for the sole purpose of extorting from their lips some weak or base word, or making them want to flee, so as to gain the advantage of having terrified them and broken down their firmness. For indeed, if you take it the right way, it is in this point alone that true victory lies:

> It is no victory
> Unless the vanquished foe admits your mastery.
> –CLAUDIAN

The Hungarians, very bellicose fighters, did not in olden times pursue their advantage beyond putting the enemy at their mercy. For having wrung a confession from him to this effect, they let him go unharmed and unransomed, except, at most, for exacting his promise never again to take up arms against them.

We win enough advantages over our enemies that are borrowed advantages, not really our own. It is the quality of a porter, not of valor, to have sturdier arms and legs; agility is a dead and corporeal quality; it is a stroke of luck to make our enemy stumble, or dazzle his eyes by the sunlight; it is a trick of art and technique, which may be found in a worthless coward, to be an able fencer. The worth and value of a man is in his heart and his will; there lies his real honor. Valor is the strength, not of legs and arms, but of heart and soul; it consists not in the worth of our horse or our weapons, but in our own. He who falls obstinate in his courage, *if he has fallen, he fights on his knees* [Seneca]. He who relaxes none of his assurance, no matter how great the danger of imminent death; who, giving up his soul, still looks firmly and scornfully at his enemy—he is beaten not by us, but by fortune; he is killed, not conquered.

The most valiant are sometimes the most unfortunate. Thus there are triumphant defeats that rival victories. Nor did those four sister victories, the fairest that the sun ever set eyes on—Salamis, Plataea, Mycale, and Sicily—ever dare match all their combined glory against the glory of the annihilation of King Leonidas and his men at the pass of Thermopylae.[9]

Who ever hastened with more glorious and ambitious desire to win a battle than Captain Ischolas to lose one? Who ever secured his safety more ingeniously and painstakingly than he did his destruction? He was charged to defend a certain pass in the Peloponnesus against the Arcadians. Finding himself wholly incapable of doing this, in view of the nature of the place and the inequality of the forces, he made up his mind that all who confronted the enemy would necessarily have to remain on the field. On the other hand, deeming it unworthy both of his own virtue and magnanimity and of the Lacedaemonian name to fail in his charge, he took a middle course between these two extremes, in this way. The youngest and fittest of his band he preserved for the defense and service of their country, and sent them home; and with those whose loss was less important, he determined to hold this pass, and by their death to make the enemy buy their entry as dearly as he could. And so it turned out. For he was presently surrounded on all sides by the Arcadians, and after slaughtering a large number of them, he and his men were all put to the sword. Is there a trophy dedicated to victors that would not be more due to these vanquished? The role of true victory is in fighting, not in coming off safely; and the honor of valor consists in combating, not in beating.

To return to our story. These prisoners are so far from giving in, in spite of all that is done to them, that on the contrary, during the two or three months that they are kept, they wear a gay expression; they urge their captors to hurry and put them to the test; they defy them, insult them, reproach them with their cowardice and the number of battles they have lost to the prisoners' own people.

I have a song composed by a prisoner which contains this challenge, that they should all come boldly and gather to dine off him, for they will be eating at the same time their own fathers and grandfathers, who have served to feed and nourish his body. "These muscles," he says, "this flesh and these veins are your own, poor fools that you are. You do not recognize that the substance of your ancestors' limbs is still contained in them. Savor them well; you will find in them the taste of your own flesh." An idea that certainly does not smack of barbarity. Those that paint these people dying, and who show the execution, portray the prisoner spitting in the face of his slayers and scowling at them. Indeed, to the last gasp they never stop braving and defying their enemies by word and look. Truly here are real savages by our standards; for either they must be thoroughly so, or we must be; there is an amazing distance between their character and ours.

The men there have several wives, and the higher their reputation for valor the more wives they have. It is a remarkably beautiful thing about their marriages that

---

[9]Sites of famous Greek victories against the Persians and Carthaginians in the fifth century B.C.E.; Leonidas was the Spartan king who led the famous standoff against the Persians at Thermopylae in 480 B.C.E.

the same jealousy our wives have to keep us from the affection and kindness of other women, theirs have to win this for them. Being more concerned for their husbands' honor than for anything else, they strive and scheme to have as many companions as they can, since that is a sign of their husbands' valor.

Our wives will cry "Miracle!" but it is no miracle. It is a properly matrimonial virtue, but one of the highest order. In the Bible, Leah, Rachel, Sarah, and Jacob's wives gave their beautiful handmaids to their husbands; and Livia seconded the appetites of Augustus, to her own disadvantage; and Stratonice, the wife of King Deiotarus,[10] not only lent her husband for his use a very beautiful young chambermaid in her service, but carefully brought up her children, and backed them up to succeed to their father's estates.

And lest it be thought that all this is done through a simple and servile bondage to usage and through the pressure of the authority of their ancient customs, without reasoning or judgment, and because their minds are so stupid that they cannot take any other course, I must cite some examples of their capacity. Besides the warlike song I have just quoted, I have another, a love song, which begins in this vein: "Adder, stay; stay, adder, that from the pattern of your coloring my sister may draw the fashion and the workmanship of a rich girdle that I may give to my love; so may your beauty and your pattern be forever preferred to all other serpents." This first couplet is the refrain of the song. Now I am familiar enough with poetry to be a judge of this: not only is there nothing barbarous in this fancy, but it is altogether Anacreontic. Their language, moreover, is a soft language, with an agreeable sound, somewhat like Greek in its endings.

Three of these men, ignorant of the price they will pay some day, in loss of repose and happiness, for gaining knowledge of the corruptions of this side of the ocean; ignorant also of the fact that of this intercourse will come their ruin (which I suppose is already well advanced: poor wretches, to let themselves be tricked by the desire for new things, and to have left the serenity of their own sky to come and see ours!)—three of these men were at Rouen, at the time the late King Charles IX was there. The king talked to them for a long time; they were shown our ways, our splendor, the aspect of a fine city. After that, someone asked their opinion, and wanted to know what they had found most amazing. They mentioned three things, of which I have forgotten the third, and I am very sorry for it; but I still remember two of them. They said that in the first place they thought it very strange that so many grown men, bearded, strong, and armed, who were around the king (it is likely that they were talking about the Swiss of his guard) should submit to obey a child, and that one of them was not chosen to command instead. Second (they have a way in their language of speaking of men as halves of one another), they had noticed that there were among us men full and gorged with all sorts of good things, and that their other halves were beggars at their doors, emaciated with hunger and poverty; and they thought it strange that these needy halves could endure such an injustice, and did not take the others by the throat, or set fire to their houses.

I had a very long talk with one of them; but I had an interpreter who followed my meaning so badly, and who was so hindered by his stupidity in taking in my ideas, that I could get hardly any satisfaction from the man. When I asked him what profit he gained from his superior position among his people (for he was a captain, and our sailors called him king), he told me that it was to march foremost

[10]Suetonius' *Life of Augustus* tells the story of Livia; Plutarch's *Bravery of Women* tells that of Stratonice and Deiotarus, the Tetrarch of Galatia.

in war. How many men followed him? He pointed to a piece of ground, to signify as many as such a space could hold; it might have been four or five thousand men. Did all his authority expire with the war? He said that this much remained, that when he visited the villages dependent on him, they made paths for him through the underbrush by which he might pass quite comfortably.

All this is not too bad—but what's the use? They don't wear breeches.

Of Coaches

It is very easy to demonstrate that great authors, when they write about causes, adduce not only those they think are true but also those they do not believe in, provided they have some originality and beauty. They speak truly and usefully enough if they speak ingeniously. We cannot make sure of the master cause; we pile up several of them, to see if by chance it will be found among them,

> For one cause will not do;
> We must state many, one of which is true.
> –Lucretius

Do you ask me whence comes this custom of blessing those who sneeze? We produce three sorts of wind. That which issues from below is too foul; that which issues from the mouth carries some reproach of gluttony; the third is sneezing. And because it comes from the head and is blameless, we give it this civil reception. Do not laugh at this piece of subtlety; it is, they say, from Aristotle.

It seems to me I have read in Plutarch[11] (who, of all the authors I know, is the one who best combined art with nature and judgment with knowledge) that he gives the reason for the heaving of the stomach that afflicts those who travel by sea, as fear, having found some reason by which he proves that fear can produce such an effect. I, who am very subject to seasickness, know very well that this cause does not affect me, and I know it, not by reasoning, but by necessary experience. Not to mention what I have been told, that the same thing often happens to animals, and especially to pigs, without any apprehension of danger; and what an acquaintance of mine has told me about himself, that though he was very subject to it, the desire to vomit had left him two or three times when he found himself oppressed with fright in a big storm. And hear this ancient: *I was too sick to think about the danger* [Seneca]. I was never afraid on the water, nor indeed anywhere else (and I have often enough had just occasions, if death is one), at least not to the point of being confused or bewildered.

Fear sometimes arises from want of judgment as well as from want of courage. All the dangers I have seen, I have seen with open eyes, with my sight free, sound, and entire; besides, it takes courage to be afraid. It once served me in good stead, compared with others, so to conduct my flight and keep it orderly, that it was carried out, if not without fear, at all events without terror and without dismay; it was excited, but not dazed or distracted.

Great souls go much further yet and offer us examples of flights not merely composed and healthy, but proud. Let us tell of the one that Alcibiades[12] reports of Socrates, his comrade in arms: "I found him," he says, "after the rout of our

---

[11] Greek biographer and essayist (c. 46–120 C.E.).

[12] The Athenian general (c. 450-404 B.C.E.) who led Athens against Sparta in the Peloponnesian war.

army, him and Laches, among the last of the fugitives; and I observed him at my leisure and in safety, for I was on a good horse and he on foot, and we had fought that way. I noticed first how much presence of mind and resolution he showed compared with Laches; and then the boldness of his walk, no different from his ordinary one, his firm and steady gaze, considering and judging what was going on around him, looking now at one side, now the other, friends and enemies, in a way that encouraged the former and signified to the latter that he was a man to sell his blood and his life very dear to anyone who should try to take them away. And thus they made their escape; for people are not inclined to attack such men; they run after the frightened ones." That is the testimony of the great captain, which teaches us what we experience every day, that there is nothing that throws us so much into dangers as an unthinking eagerness to get clear of them. *Where there is less fear, there is generally less danger* [Livy].

Our common people are wrong to say that such-and-such a man fears death, when they mean to say that he thinks about it and foresees it. Foresight is equally suitable in whatever concerns us, whether for good or ill. To consider and judge the danger is in a way the opposite of being stunned by it.

I do not feel myself strong enough to sustain the impact and impetuosity of this passion of fear, or of any other vehement passion. If I were once conquered and thrown by it, I would never get up again quite intact. If anything made my soul lose its footing, it would never set it back upright in its place; it probes and searches itself too keenly and deeply, and therefore would never let the wound that had pierced it close up and heal. It has been well for me that no illness has yet laid it low. Each attack made on me I meet and fight off in my full armor; thus the first one that swept me off my feet would leave me without resources. I have no secondary defense: no matter where the torrent should break my dike, I would be helpless and be drowned for good.

Epicurus[13] says that the wise man can never pass into a contrary state. I have an opinion about the converse of this saying: that anyone who has once been very foolish will never at any other time be very wise.

God tempers the cold according to the cloak, and gives me passions according to my means of withstanding them. Nature, having uncovered me on one side, has covered me up on the other; having disarmed me of strength, she has armed me with insensibility and a controlled, or dull, apprehensiveness.

Now I cannot long endure (and I could endure them less easily in my youth) either coach, or litter, or boat; and I hate any other transportation than horseback, both in town and in the country. But I can endure a litter less than a coach, and for the same reason I can more easily bear a rough tossing on the water, whereby fear is produced, than the movement felt in calm weather. By that slight jolt given by the oars, stealing the vessel from under us, I somehow feel my head and stomach troubled, as I cannot bear a shaky seat under me. When the sail or the current carries us along evenly or when we are towed, this uniform movement does not bother me at all. It is an interrupted motion that annoys me, and most of all when it is languid. I cannot otherwise describe its nature. The doctors have ordered me to bind and swathe my abdomen with a towel to remedy this trouble; which I have not tried, being accustomed to wrestle with the weaknesses that are in me and overcome them by myself.

[13]Greek philosopher (341–270 B.C.E.) who taught that refined pleasure is the greatest good in life.

If my memory were sufficiently stored with them, I should not begrudge my time to tell here the infinite variety of examples that histories offer us of the use of coaches in the service of war, varying according to the nations and according to the age; of great effect, it seems to me, and very necessary, so that it is a wonder that we have lost all knowledge of them. I will say only this, that quite recently, in our fathers' time, the Hungarians put coaches very usefully to work against the Turks, there being in each one a targeteer and a musketeer and a number of harquebuses lined up, loaded and ready, the whole thing covered with a wall of shields, like a galiot. They formed their battlefront of three thousand such coaches, and after the cannon had played, had them advance and made the enemy swallow this salvo before tasting the rest; which was no slight advantage. Or they launched them into the enemy squadrons to break them and open them up; not to mention the advantage they could derive from them by flanking enemy troops on their march through open country where they were vulnerable, or by covering a camp in haste and fortifying it.

In my time a gentleman on one of our frontiers, who was unwieldy of person and found no horse capable of bearing his weight, having a feud on his hands, went about the country in a coach of this very description, and made out very well. But let us leave these war coaches. The kings of our first dynasty went about the country in a chariot drawn by four oxen.

Mark Antony was the first who had himself drawn in Rome—and a minstrel girl beside him—by lions harnessed to a chariot. Heliogabalus did as much later, calling himself Cybele, the mother of the gods; and also by tigers, imitating the god Bacchus; he also sometimes harnessed two stags to his coach, and another time four dogs, and yet again four naked wenches, having himself, stark naked too, drawn by them in pomp. The Emperor Firmus had his chariot drawn by ostriches of marvelous size, so that it seemed rather to fly than to roll.[14]

The strangeness of these inventions puts into my head this other notion: that it is a sort of pusillanimity in monarchs, and evidence of not sufficiently feeling what they are, to labor at showing off and making a display by excessive expense. It would be excusable in a foreign country; but among his own subjects, where he is all-powerful, he derives from his dignity the highest degree of honor he can attain. Just as, it seems to me, for a gentleman it is superfluous to dress with studied care at home: his house, his retinue, his cuisine, answer for him sufficiently.

The advice that Isocrates[15] gives his king seems to me not without reason: that he be splendid in furniture and plate, since that is a lasting investment which passes on to his successors; and that he avoid all magnificences that flow away immediately out of use and memory.

I liked to adorn myself when I was a youth, for lack of other adornments, and it was becoming to me; there are those on whom fine clothes weep. We have marvelous stories of the frugality of our kings about their own persons and in their gifts—kings great in prestige, in valor, and in fortune. Demosthenes[16] fights tooth and nail against the law of his city that allotted public monies to lavish games

[14]Mark Antony (c. 83–30 B.C.E.) became Consul of Rome, a member of the Second Triumvirate, and after settling in Alexandria where he was Cleopatra's lover, he led a civil war against his former partner Octavian. Heliogabalus, or Marcus Aurelius Antoninus (c. 204–222 C.E.), was Roman emperor from 218 to 222.

[15]Greek orator and teacher (436–338 B.C.E.), a student of Socrates.

[16]The most famous Greek orator (384–322 B.C.E.).

and feasts; he wants the greatness of the city to be manifest in its quantity of well-equipped ships and of good, well-supplied armies.

And Theophrastus[17] is rightly blamed for setting forth a contrary opinion in his book on riches, and maintaining that lavish expenditure was the true fruit of opulence. These are pleasures, says Aristotle, that touch only the lowest of the people, that vanish from memory as soon as people are sated with them, and that no judicious and serious man can esteem. The outlay would seem to me much more royal as well as more useful, just, and durable, if it were spent on ports, harbors, fortifications, and walls, on sumptuous buildings, churches, hospitals, colleges, and the improvement of streets and roads, for which Pope Gregory XIII is gratefully remembered in my time, and in which our Queen Catherine would leave evidence for many years of her natural liberality and munificence, if her means were equal to her wish. Fortune has given me great displeasure by interrupting the construction of the handsome new bridge[18] of our great city, and depriving me of the hope of seeing it in full use before I die.

Besides, it seems to the subjects, spectators of these triumphs, that they are given a display of their own riches, and entertained at their own expense. For peoples are apt to assume about kings, as we do about our servants, that they should take care to prepare for us in abundance all we need, but that they should not touch it at all for their own part. And therefore the Emperor Galba,[19] having taken pleasure in a musician's playing during his supper, sent for his money box and gave into his hand a handful of crowns that he fished out of it, with these words: "This is not the public money, this is my own." At all events, it most often happens that the people are right, and that their eyes are feasted with what should go to feed their bellies.

Liberality itself is not in its proper light in the hands of a sovereign; private people have more right to exercise it. For, to be precise about it, a king has nothing that is properly his own; he owes his very self to others.

The authority to judge is not given for the sake of the judge, but for the sake of the person judged. A superior is never appointed for his own benefit, but for the benefit of the inferior, and a doctor for the sick, not for himself. All authority, like all art, has its end outside of itself: *no art is directed to itself* [Cicero].

Wherefore the tutors of young princes who make it a point to impress on them this virtue of liberality and preach to them not to know how to refuse anything, and to think nothing so well spent as what they give away (a lesson that I have seen in great favor in my time), either look more to their own profit than to their master's, or do not well understand to whom they speak. It is all too easy to impress liberality on a man who has the means to practice it all he wants at the expense of others. And since its value is reckoned not by the measure of the gift, but by the measure of the giver's means, it amounts to nothing in such powerful hands. They find themselves prodigal before they are liberal. Therefore liberality is little to be commended compared with other royal virtues, and it is the only one, as the tyrant Dionysius[20] said, that goes with tyranny itself. I would rather teach him this verse of the ancient farmer: that whoever wants to reap a good crop must sow with the hand, not pour out of the sack; he must scatter the seed, not spill it; and that since he has to give, or, to put it better, pay and restore to so many people according to

---

[17] Greek philosopher (c. 370–285 B.C.E.), a student of Plato and Aristotle.

[18] The Pont Neuf, built in 1604.

[19] Serbius Sulpicius Galba, successor to the infamous Nero as emperor of Rome; his financially troubled reign from 68–69 C.E. lasted less than a year.

[20] Dionysius the Elder (c. 430–367 B.C.E.), known as the Tyrant of Syracuse.

their deserts, he should be a fair and wise distributor. If the liberality of a prince is without discretion and without measure, I would rather he were a miser.

Royal virtue seems to consist most of all in justice; and of all the parts of justice, that one best marks kings which accompanies liberality; for they have particularly reserved it as their function, whereas they are prone to exercise all other justice through the intermediary of others. Immoderate largesse is a feeble means for them to acquire good will; for it alienates more people than it wins over: *The more you have already practiced it on, the fewer you will be able to practice it on. What is more foolish than to take pains so that you can no longer do what you enjoy doing?* [Cicero.] And if it is exercised without regard to merit, it puts to shame him who receives it, and is received ungraciously. Tyrants have been sacrificed to the hatred of the people by the hands of the very ones whom they have unjustly advanced; for such men think to assure their possession of undeserved goods by showing contempt and hatred for the man from whom they received them, and rallying to the judgment and opinion of the people in that respect.

The subjects of a prince who is excessive in gifts become excessive in requests; they adjust themselves not to reason but to example. Surely we often have reason to blush for our impudence; we are overpaid according to justice when the recompense equals our service; for do we owe no service to our prince by natural obligation? If he bears our expenses, he does too much; it is enough that he helps out. The surplus is called benefit, and it cannot be exacted, for the very name of liberality rings of liberty. By our method, it is never done; the receipts are no longer taken into account; people love only the future liberality. Wherefore the more a prince exhausts himself in giving, the poorer he makes himself in friends. How could he assuage desires that grow the more they are fulfilled? He who has his mind on taking, no longer has it on what he has taken. Covetousness has nothing so characteristic about it as ingratitude.

The example of Cyrus will not be amiss here to serve the kings of our time as a touchstone for ascertaining whether their gifts are well or ill bestowed, and to make them see how much more happily that emperor dealt them out than they do. Whereby they are reduced to doing their borrowing from unknown subjects, and rather from those they have wronged than from those they have benefited; and from them they receive no aid that is gratuitous in anything but the name.

Croesus reproached Cyrus[21] for his extravagance and calculated how much his treasure would amount to if he had been more close-fisted. Cyrus, wanting to justify his liberality, sent dispatches in all directions to the grandees of his state whose career he had particularly advanced, and asked each one to help him out with as much money as he could for an urgent need of his, and to send him a declaration of the amount. When all these statements were brought to him, since each of his friends, thinking it was not enough to offer him merely as much as he had received from his munificence, added much that was more properly his own, it turned out that the total amounted to much more than the savings estimated by Croesus. Whereupon Cyrus said to him: "I am no less in love with riches than other princes, and am rather a more careful manager of them. You see at how small a cost I have acquired the inestimable treasure of so many friends, and how much more faithful treasurers they are to me than mercenary men without obligation, without affection, would be; and how much better my wealth is lodged than in coffers, where it would call down upon me the hatred, envy, and contempt of other princes."

---

[21]Cyrus the Great (d. 529 B.C.E.) was king of Persia and conqueror of Lydia, ruled by Croesus (d. c. 544 B.C.E.), its last king.

The emperors derived an excuse for the superfluity of their public games and spectacles from the fact that their authority depended somewhat (at least in appearance) on the will of the Roman people, who from time immemorial had been accustomed to being flattered by that sort of spectacle and extravagance. But it was private citizens who had nourished this custom of gratifying their fellow citizens and companions, chiefly out of their own purse, by such profusion and magnificence; this had an altogether different flavor when it was the masters who came to imitate it. *The transfer of money from its rightful owners to strangers should not be regarded as liberality* [Cicero].

Philip,[22] because his son was trying to win the good will of the Macedonians by presents, scolded him for it in a letter in this manner: "What, do you want your subjects to regard you as their purser, not as their king? Do you want to win them over? Win them over with the benefits of your virtue, not the benefits of your coffers."

It was, however, a fine thing to bring and plant in the amphitheater a great quantity of big trees, all branching and green, representing a great shady forest, arranged in beautiful symmetry, and on the first day to cast into it a thousand ostriches, a thousand stags, a thousand wild boars, and a thousand fallow deer, leaving them to be hunted down by the people; on the next day to have a hundred big lions, a hundred leopards, and three hundred bears slaughtered in their presence; and for the third day, to have three hundred pairs of gladiators fight it out to the death, as the Emperor Probus[23] did.

It was also a fine thing to see those great amphitheaters faced with marble on the outside, wrought with ornaments and statues, the inside sparkling with many rare enrichments—

> Here is the diamond circle, the golden portico
>
> –CALPURNIUS

—all the sides of this vast space filled and surrounded from top to bottom with three or four score tiers of seats, also of marble, covered with cushions—

> "Let him begone," he says,
> "And leave the cushioned seats of knights, seeing he pays
> None of the lawful tax"
>
> –JUVENAL

—where a hundred thousand men could sit at their ease. Also, first of all, to have the place at the bottom, where the games were played, open artificially and split into crevasses representing caverns that vomited forth the beasts destined for the spectacle; and then, second, to flood it with a deep sea, full of sea monsters and laden with armed vessels to represent a naval battle; and third, to level it and dry it off again for the combat of the gladiators; and for the fourth show to strew it with vermilion and storax instead of sand, in order to set up a stately banquet there for all that huge number of people—the final act of a single day:

> How often have we seen
> Part of the sandy floor sink down, wild beasts emerge
> Out of the open chasm, and from its depths upsurge
> Forests of golden growing trees with yellow bark.

---

[22]See note 2.

[23]Marcus Aurelius Probus, emperor of Rome from 276–282 C.E., noted for securing the borders of the empire and securing Gaul from the Germans.

Not only forest monsters were for us to mark,
But I saw sea-calves mingled in with fighting bears,
And hippopotami, the shapeless herd that wears
The name of river-horse.

—CALPURNIUS

Sometimes they created a high mountain there, full of fruit trees and other trees in leaf, spouting a stream of water from its top as from the mouth of a living spring. Sometimes they brought in a great ship which opened and came apart of itself and, after having spewed forth from its belly four or five hundred fighting beasts, closed up again and vanished without assistance. At other times, from the floor of the place, they made spouts and jets of water spring forth which shot upward to an infinite height, then sprinkled and perfumed that infinite multitude. To protect themselves against damage from the weather, they had that immense space hung with awnings, sometimes made of purple worked with the needle, sometimes of silk of one color or another, and they drew them forward or back in a moment, as they had a mind to:

The awnings, though the sun scorches the skin,
Are, when Hermogenes appears, drawn in.

—MARTIAL

The nets, too, which they put in front of the people to protect them from the violence of the loosened beasts, were woven of gold:

Even the woven nets
Glitter with gold.

—CALPURNIUS

If there is anything excusable in such extravagances, it is when the inventiveness and the novelty of them, not the expense, provide amazement.

Even in these vanities we discover how fertile those ages were in minds different from ours. It is with this sort of fertility as with all other productions of Nature. This is not to say that she then put forth her utmost effort. We do not go in a straight line; we rather ramble, and turn this way and that. We retrace our steps. I fear that our knowledge is weak in every direction; we do not see very far ahead or very far behind. It embraces little and has a short life, short in both extent of time and extent of matter:

Ere Agamemnon, heroes were the same;
Many there were, but no one knows their name;
They all are hurried on unwept
Into unending night.

—HORACE

Before the Trojan War, before Troy fell,
Were other bards with other tales to tell.

—LUCRETIUS

And Solon's[24] story of what he had heard from the priests of Egypt about the long life of their state, and their manner of learning and preserving the histories of other countries, does not seem to me a testimony to be rejected in this consideration. *If we could view that expanse of countries and ages, boundless in every direction, into which the mind, plunging and spreading itself, travels so far and wide that it can find no limit where*

[24]Statesman and eventual leader of Athens, Solon (c. 639–559 B.C.E.) instituted major democratic reforms during his rule.

it can stop, there would appear in that immensity an infinite capacity to produce innumerable forms [adapted from Cicero].

Even if all that has come down to us by report from the past should be true and known by someone, it would be less than nothing compared with what is unknown. And of this very image of the world which glides along while we live on it, how puny and limited is the knowledge of even the most curious! Not only of particular events which fortune often renders exemplary and weighty, but of the state of great governments and nations, there escapes us a hundred times more than comes to our knowledge. We exclaim at the miracle of the invention of our artillery, of our printing; other men in another corner of the world, in China, enjoyed these a thousand years earlier. If we saw as much of the world as we do not see, we would perceive, it is likely, a perpetual multiplication and vicissitude of forms.

There is nothing unique and rare as regards nature, but there certainly is as regards our knowledge, which is a miserable foundation for our rules and which is apt to represent to us a very false picture of things. As vainly as we today infer the decline and decrepitude of the world from the arguments we draw from our own weakness and decay—

> This age is broken down, and broken down the earth
>
> –LUCRETIUS

—so vainly did this poet infer the world's birth and youth from the vigor he saw in the minds of his time, abounding in novelties and inventions in various arts:

> The universe, I think, is very new,
> The world is young, its birth not far behind;
> Hence certain arts grow more and more refined
> Even today; the naval art is one.
>
> –LUCRETIUS

Our world has just discovered another world (and who will guarantee us that it is the last of its brothers, since the daemons, the Sibyls, and we ourselves have up to now been ignorant of this one?) no less great, full, and well-limbed than itself, yet so new and so infantile that it is still being taught its A B C; not fifty years ago it knew neither letters, nor weights and measures, nor clothes, nor wheat, nor vines. It was still quite naked at the breast, and lived only on what its nursing mother provided. If we are right to infer the end of our world, and that poet is right about the youth of his own age, this other world will only be coming into the light when ours is leaving it. The universe will fall into paralysis; one member will be crippled, the other in full vigor.

I am much afraid that we shall have very greatly hastened the decline and ruin of this new world by our contagion, and that we will have sold it our opinions and our arts very dear. It was an infant world; yet we have not whipped it and subjected it to our discipline by the advantage of our natural valor and strength, nor won it over by our justice and goodness, nor subjugated it by our magnanimity. Most of the responses of these people and most of our dealings with them show that they were not at all behind us in natural brightness of mind and pertinence.

The awesome magnificence of the cities of Cuzco and Mexico[25] (and, among many similar things, the garden of that king in which all the trees, the fruits, and

---

[25]Cuzco was the capital of the Inca empire, plundered by Spanish conqueror Francisco Pizarro in 1533; Mexico was the capital city of the Aztec empire, captured and plundered by the Spanish conqueror Hernán Cortés in 1521.

all the herbs were excellently fashioned in gold, and of such size and so arranged as they might be in an ordinary garden; and in his curio room were gold replicas of all the living creatures native to his country and its waters), and the beauty of their workmanship in jewelry, feathers, cotton, and painting, show that they were not behind us in industry either. But as for devoutness, observance of the laws, goodness, liberality, loyalty, and frankness, it served us well not to have as much as they: by their advantage in this they lost, sold, and betrayed themselves.

As for boldness and courage, as for firmness, constancy, resoluteness against pains and hunger and death, I would not fear to oppose the examples I could find among them to the most famous ancient examples that we have in the memories of our world on this side of the ocean. For as regards the men who subjugated them, take away the ruses and tricks that they used to deceive them, and the people's natural astonishment at seeing the unexpected arrival of bearded men, different in language, religion, shape, and countenance, from a part of the world so remote, where they had never imagined there was any sort of human habitation, mounted on great unknown monsters, opposed to men who had never seen not only a horse, but any sort of animal trained to carry and endure a man or any other burden; men equipped with a hard and shiny skin and a sharp and glittering weapon, against men who, for the miracle of a mirror or a knife, would exchange a great treasure in gold and pearls, and who had neither the knowledge nor the material by which, even in full leisure, they could pierce our steel; add to this the lightning and thunder of our cannon and harquebuses—capable of disturbing Caesar himself, if he had been surprised by them with as little experience and in his time—against people who were naked (except in some regions where the invention of some cotton fabric had reached them), without other arms at the most than bows, stones, sticks, and wooden bucklers; people taken by surprise, under color of friendship and good faith, by curiosity to see strange and unknown things: eliminate this disparity, I say, and you take from the conquerors the whole basis of so many victories.

When I consider that indomitable ardor with which so many thousands of men, women, and children came forth and hurled themselves so many times into inevitable dangers for the defense of their gods and of their liberty, and that noble, stubborn readiness to suffer all extremities and hardships, even death, rather than submit to the domination of those by whom they had been so shamefully deceived (for some of them when captured chose rather to let themselves perish of hunger and fasting than to accept food from the hands of such basely victorious enemies), I conclude that if anyone had attacked them on equal terms, with equal arms, experience, and numbers, it would have been just as dangerous for him as in any other war we know of, and more so.

Why did not such a noble conquest fall to Alexander[26] or to those ancient Greeks and Romans? Why did not such a great change and alteration of so many empires and peoples fall into hands that would have gently polished and cleared away whatever was barbarous in them, and would have strengthened and fostered the good seeds that nature had produced in them, not only adding to the cultivation of the earth and the adornment of cities the arts of our side of the ocean, in so far as they would have been necessary, but also adding the Greek and Roman virtues to those originally in that region? What an improvement that would have been, and what an amelioration for the entire globe, if the first examples of our conduct that were offered over there had called those peoples to the admiration and

[26] Alexander the Great (356–323 B.C.E.), a student of Aristotle, was king of Macedon and eventually gained control over all of Greece by defeating the Persian Empire of Darius III.

imitation of virtue and had set up between them and us a brotherly fellowship and understanding! How easy it would have been to make good use of souls so fresh, so famished to learn, and having, for the most part, such fine natural beginnings! On the contrary, we took advantage of their ignorance and inexperience to incline them the more easily toward treachery, lewdness, avarice, and every sort of inhumanity and cruelty, after the example and pattern of our ways. Who ever set the utility of commerce and trading at such a price? So many cities razed, so many nations exterminated, so many millions of people put to the sword, and the richest and most beautiful part of the world turned upside down, for the traffic in pearls and pepper! Base and mechanical victories! Never did ambition, never did public enmities, drive men against one another to such horrible hostilities and such miserable calamities.

Coasting the sea in quest of their mines, certain Spaniards landed in a fertile, pleasant, well-populated country, and made their usual declarations to its people: that they were peaceable men, coming from distant voyages, sent on behalf of the king of Castile, the greatest prince of the habitable world, to whom the Pope, representing God on earth, had given the principality of all the Indies; that if these people would be tributaries to him, they would be very kindly treated. They demanded of them food to eat and gold to be used in a certain medicine, and expounded to them the belief in one single God and the truth of our religion, which they advised them to accept, adding a few threats.

The answer was this: As for being peaceable, they did not look like it, if they were. As for their king, since he was begging, he must be indigent and needy; and he who had awarded their country to him must be a man fond of dissension, to go and give another person something that was not his and thus set him at strife with its ancient possessors. As for food, they would supply them. Gold they had little of, and it was a thing they held in no esteem, since it was useless to the service of their life, their sole concern being with passing life happily and pleasantly; however, they might boldly take any they could find, except what was employed in the service of their gods. As for one single God, the account had pleased them, but they did not want to change their religion, having followed it so advantageously for so long, and they were not accustomed to take counsel except of their friends and acquaintances. As for the threats, it was a sign of lack of judgment to threaten people whose nature and means were unknown to them. Thus they should promptly hurry up and vacate their land, for they were not accustomed to take in good part the civilities and declarations of armed strangers; otherwise they would do to them as they had done to these others—showing them the heads of some executed men around their city.

There we have an example of the babbling of this infancy. But at all events, neither in that place nor in several others where the Spaniards did not find the merchandise they were looking for, did they make any stay or any attack, whatever other advantages there might be; witness my Cannibals.

Of the two most powerful monarchs of that world, and perhaps of this as well, kings of so many kings, the last two that they drove out, one, the king of Peru,[27] was taken in a battle and put to so excessive a ransom that it surpasses all belief; and when this had been faithfully paid, and the king in his dealings had given signs of a frank, liberal, and steadfast spirit and a clear and well-ordered understanding, the conquerors, after having extracted from him one million three hundred and twenty-five thousand five hundred ounces of gold, besides silver and other things that amounted to no less, so that their horses thenceforth went shod with solid gold, were seized with the desire to see also, at the price of whatever treachery, what

[27] Atahualpa, leader of the Incas, was executed by Pizarro in 1532.

could be the remainder of this king's treasures, and to enjoy freely what he had reserved. They trumped up against him a false accusation and false evidence that he was planning to rouse his provinces in order to regain his freedom. Whereupon, in a beautiful sentence pronounced by those very men who had set afoot this treachery against him, he was condemned to be publicly hanged and strangled, after being permitted to buy his way out of the torment of being burned alive by submitting to baptism at the moment of the execution. A horrible and unheard-of calamity, which nevertheless he bore without belying himself either by look or word, with a truly royal bearing and gravity. And then, to lull the people, stunned and dazed by such a strange thing, they counterfeited great mourning over his death and ordered a sumptuous funeral for him.

The other one, the king of Mexico,[28] had long defended his besieged city and shown in this siege all that endurance and perseverance can do, if ever prince and people did so, when his bad fortune put him in his enemies' hands alive, on their promise that they would treat him as a king; nor did he in his captivity show anything unworthy of this title. After this victory, his enemies, not finding all the gold they had promised themselves, first ransacked and searched everything, and then set about seeking information by inflicting the cruelest tortures they could think up on the prisoners they held. But having gained nothing by this, and finding their prisoners' courage stronger than their torments, they finally flew into such a rage that, against their word and against all law of nations, they condemned the king himself and one of the principal lords of his court to the torture in each other's presence. This lord, finding himself overcome with the pain, surrounded with burning braziers, in the end turned his gaze piteously toward his master, as if to ask his pardon because he could hold out no longer. The king, fixing his eyes proudly and severely on him in reproach for his cowardice and pusillanimity, said to him only these words, in a stern, firm voice: "And I, am I in a bath? Am I more comfortable than you?" The other immediately after succumbed to the pain and died on the spot. The king, half roasted, was carried away from there, not so much out of pity (for what pity ever touched souls who, for dubious information about some gold vase to pillage, had a man grilled before their eyes, and what is more, a king so great in fortune and merit?), but because his fortitude made their cruelty more and more shameful. They hanged him later for having courageously attempted to deliver himself by arms from such a long captivity and subjection, and he made an end worthy of a great-souled prince.

Another time they burned alive, all at once and in the same fire, four hundred and sixty men, the four hundred being of the common people, the sixty from among the chief lords of a province, all merely prisoners of war.

We have these narrations from themselves, for they not only admit them but boast of them and preach them. Would it be as a testimonial to their justice or their zeal for religion? Truly, those are ways too contrary and hostile to so holy an end. If they had proposed to extend our faith, they would have reflected that faith is not spread by possession of territory but by possession of men, and they would have been more than satisfied with the murders brought about by the necessity of war, without adding to these an indiscriminate butchery, as of wild animals, as universal as fire and sword could make it, after purposely sparing only as many as they wanted to make into miserable slaves for the working and service of their mines: with the result that many of the leaders were punished with death by order of the kings of Castile, who were justly shocked by the horror of their conduct; and almost

[28]Montezuma, ruler of the Aztec empire, was captured by Cortés and eventually killed in 1520.

all were disesteemed and loathed. God deservedly allowed this great plunder to be swallowed up by the sea in transit, or by the intestine wars in which they devoured one another; and most of them were buried on the spot without any profit from their victory.

As for the fact that the revenue from this, even in the hands of a thrifty and prudent prince,[29] corresponds so little to the expectation of it given to his predecessors and to the abundance of riches that was first encountered in these new lands (for although much is being gotten out, we see that it is nothing compared with what was to be expected), the reason is that the use of money was entirely unknown, and that consequently their gold was found all collected together, being of no other use than for show and parade, like a chattel preserved from father to son by many powerful kings who were constantly exhausting their mines to make that great heap of vases and statues for the adornment of their palaces and their temples; whereas our gold is all in circulation and in trade. We cut it up small and change it into a thousand forms; we scatter and disperse it. Imagine it if our kings thus accumulated all the gold they could find for many centuries and kept it idle.

The people of the kingdom of Mexico were somewhat more civilized and skilled in the arts than the other nations over there. Thus they judged, as we do, that the universe was near its end, and they took as a sign of this the desolation that we brought upon them. They believed that the existence of the world was divided into five ages and into the life of five successive suns, of which four had already run their time, and that the one which gave them light was the fifth. The first perished with all other creatures by a universal flood of water. The second, by the heavens falling on us, which suffocated every living thing; to which age they assign the giants, and they showed the Spaniards some of their bones, judging by the size of which these men must have stood twenty hands high. The third, by fire, which burned and consumed everything. The fourth, by a turbulence of air and wind which beat down even many mountains; the men did not die, but they were changed into baboons (to what notions will the laxness of human credulity not submit!). After the death of this fourth sun, the world was twenty-five years in perpetual darkness, in the fifteenth of which a man and a woman were created who remade the human race; ten years later, on a certain day of their calendar, the sun appeared newly created, and since then they reckon their years from that day. The third day after its creation the old gods died; the new ones have been born since little by little. What they think about the manner in which this last sun will perish, my author[30] did not learn. But their calculation of this fourth change coincides with that great conjunction of stars which produced, some eight hundred years ago, according to the reckoning of the astrologers, many great alterations and innovations in the world.

As for pomp and magnificence, whereby I entered upon this subject, neither Greece nor Rome nor Egypt can compare any of its works, whether in utility or difficulty or nobility, with the road which is seen in Peru, laid out by the kings of the country, from the city of Quito as far as Cuzco (a distance of three hundred leagues), straight, even, twenty-five paces wide, paved, lined on both sides with

[29] King Philip II of Spain.

[30] Lopez de Gomara, a contemporary of Montaigne, who read his histories of Cortés and the West Indies.

fine high walls, and along these, on the inside, two ever-flowing streams, bordered by beautiful trees, which they call *molly*. Wherever they encountered mountains and rocks, they cut through and leveled them, and filled the hollows with stone and lime. At the end of each day's journey there are fine palaces furnished with provisions, clothes, and arms, for travelers as well as for the armies that have to pass that way.

In my estimate of this work I have counted the difficulty, which is particularly considerable in that place. They did not build with any stones less than ten feet square; they had no other means of carrying than by strength of arm, dragging their load along; and they had not even the art of scaffolding, knowing no other device than to raise an equal height of earth against their building as it rose, and remove it afterward.

Let us fall back to our coaches. Instead of these or any other form of transport, they had themselves carried by men, and on their shoulders. That last king of Peru, the day that he was taken, was thus carried on shafts of gold, seated in a chair of gold, in the midst of his army. As many of these carriers as they killed to make him fall—for they wanted to take him alive—so many others vied to take the place of the dead ones, so that they never could bring him down, however great a slaughter they made of those people, until a horseman seized him around the body and pulled him to the ground.

MIGUEL DE CERVANTES SAAVEDRA

[1547–1616]

One of the great works of world literature, *Don Quixote* (1605, 1615) has been translated into more languages than any other book except the Bible. It is usually considered the first Western novel. Its story of a wanderer encountering a series of adventures, its use of a hero and a contrasting foil, its challenge to romantic conventions and ideas, and its thematic conflict between illusion and reality have become commonplaces of later novels.

Don Quixote seems to tell a story that will reveal the absurdity of romantic idealism, but by the end it apparently reverses itself. For as foolish and mistaken as Don Quixote is, he nevertheless wins the love and allegiance of those he meets and of the reader. The novel may begin with a Machiavellian intent, to make us more aware of the realities of the world, but by the end we are celebrating idealism and imagination, no matter how impractical they are.

Thus *Don Quixote* is a text that qualifies our Renaissance paradigm, a work that tests the realism and individualism of its time by celebrating an impossible chivalric dream, an idealistic mythology of a Golden Age inherited from the past and kept alive in an age of iron by an absurd and improbable knight. This unlikely hero does not prove himself by seeking new lands to rule, nor does he revel in playing tricks on those in power. True to his inner vision, Don Quixote represents the triumph of the ideal that challenges the worldliness and realism informing many of the texts of the period.

LIFE

The life of Miguel de Cervantes Saavedra reads like an improbable romance played out on the stage of Spain at the height of its Golden Age. The fourth of seven children of a poor doctor, Cervantes spent his childhood fleeing with his family from his father's creditors. After a brief formal education at a Jesuit school in Seville and perhaps at the University of Salamanca, he was convicted of dueling and fled to Italy to avoid his sentence. In Rome he served the Cardinal Nuncio Acquaviva for a time before enlisting in the Spanish army, then engaged in battling the Turks for control of the Mediterranean. At the Battle of Lepanto in 1571, Cervantes got up from his sick bed to fight heroically. He was decorated for his bravery, but battle wounds left him permanently disabled in his left hand. Nevertheless he went on to participate in campaigns at Tunis, Sardinia, Naples, Sicily, and Genoa before returning to Spain. On the return trip in 1575, his ship was captured by pirates and he and his brother Rodrigo were both sold into slavery in Algiers. During five years in slavery, Cervantes made five unsuccessful escape attempts; his daring so impressed the Dey of Algiers, Hassan Pacha, that his life was spared after each attempt. Finally, in 1580, he was ransomed and returned to Spain.

Penniless and desperate, Cervantes turned to the stage to make money, but he was not a successful playwright, even after writing twenty or thirty plays. After he married Catalina Salaza y Vozmediano in 1584, to support his growing family he accepted a civil service job as a commissary collecting food for the Spanish navy. The post of provisioner for the Armada afforded opportunities for creative accounting, and Cervantes spent several stints in jail as a result of disputes with the Treasury Department, which claimed he had illegally appropriated wheat or money for himself.

During his time in jail, as legend has it, Cervantes wrote the first part of *Don Quixote*, which was published in 1605. With this novel he achieved the recognition he had failed to find writing for the theater. In the next decade *Don Quixote* went through ten editions, and prompted an imitator (writing under the pen name Alonzo Fernandez de Avellaneda) to publish a sequel. This pseudo-Quixote was partly responsible for prompting Cervantes to write his own continuation of the story. *Don Quixote*, Part II appeared in 1615, not long before he died, the same day as William Shakespeare's death, April 23, 1616. Besides *Don Quixote*, Cervantes' most notable works are *Persiles and Sigismunda*, a romance published after his death in 1617, and *Exemplary Novels* (1613), a collection of twelve short romantic adventure tales that illustrate various kinds of behavior to avoid.

Work

Don Quixote is ostensibly a work challenging medieval idealism from the point of view of Renaissance realism. The Don—a gentleman farmer, not a nobleman—has read so many chivalric romances, notably *Amadis of Gaul* (1508) and *Launcelot* (early thirteenth century), that he has decided to undertake his own knightly quest. In rusty armor and a makeshift helmet, he sets out to aid damsels in distress and to fight for the glory of his imaginary lady Dulcinea. He has been so imbued with the tales of adventure he has read that everything he sees is transformed in the romantic filter of his mind: Windmills become giants, a herd of sheep becomes an attacking army, country inns are castles. Don Quixote does not look like a hero. Tall and gaunt and leaning on his lance, he is physically unprepossessing. In spite of his armor, he is not a man of power. He is not a prince, nor is he a trickster or magician. When tricks are played in *Don Quixote*, they are usually played on the Don. He is the butt, not the perpetrator. The Duke and Duchess invite him to their castle, for example, so that they can contrive a series of practical jokes to play on him.

Unlike his Renaissance compatriots—whether politicians, scientists, or explorers—Quixote does not seek to master external reality. He is uncomfortable in his time and he does not relish the struggle for power and supremacy. His speech to Sancho in Book I, chapter 11 describes the lost golden age that embodied the chivalric ideals he pursues. In that time, he tells Sancho, "Fraud, deceit, or malice had not yet mingled with truth and sincerity. Justice held her ground, undisturbed and unassailed by the efforts of favor and interest, that now so much impair, pervert, and beset her. Arbitrary law had not yet established itself in the mind of the judge, for then there was no cause to judge and no one to be judged." His mission as knight-errant is to attack the wickedness of his age of iron and remain true to his vision of a past golden age. The symbol of Quixote's idealism is Dulcinea, the lady for whom he undertakes his knightly quest. Although she turns out to be a figment of his imagination or just a peasant girl, Dulcinea is nonetheless real as an ideal for him to believe in. Unlike the Renaissance sonneteers who blamed their lovers for the pains of love, Quixote never blames Dulcinea for the frustrations of his quest. When he loses his vision and realizes that Dulcinea is an illusion, the knight has nothing to live for and he dies.

His squire, the peasant Sancho Panza, recognizes the common reality in Quixote's adventures, but he is unable to make his master see what he sees. So this unlikely duo—the gaunt and doleful idealist and his rotund and realistic squire—become an anomalous pair of chivalric adventurers in a world of con men, government agents, and shrewd innkeepers and shopkeepers; their adventures degenerate into a series of misunderstandings, miscommunications, slapstick encounters, and practical jokes. On more than one occasion Don Quixote makes things worse by his chivalric interference. Yet through it all he retains his belief in himself, his mistress, and his mission.

Sancho Panza goes on the road for more down-to-earth reasons. As a realist—a person of common sense who knows that windmills are windmills—he has a large stock of folk sayings and proverbs that explain any situation, and he is savvy enough to survive a host of dangerous encounters. He accompanies Quixote to better himself. His dream is the Renaissance dream of power: he wants, like Prospero, to rule an island. Near the end of Part II, his dream comes true, if only as part of an elaborate practical joke. There are wonderful parodic echoes of Machiavelli's advice to the prince in Quixote's advice to Sancho as he goes off to govern Baratario. Sancho is a surprisingly successful governor, especially shrewd when faced with impossible judicial decisions. But just as surprisingly, he gives up his kingdom and returns to serve again as Don Quixote's squire. He learns the limitations of power and leaves his "island" to rejoin Quixote and his ideals.

In the end, Sancho's realism is transformed by the Don's idealism, and *Don Quixote* seems to have reversed its original intent. Instead of being a critique of chivalric idealism, it has become a celebration of Quixote's idealistic madness. Even the practical Sancho is won over to the impossible ideals of his master: he believes in the imaginary Dulcinea and is ready to start out on another journey. Don Quixote, no longer mad, is at last aware that Dulcinea was an illusion. He and Sancho have changed places, and the final pages of the novel make us aware of the loss when such divine madness is gone from the world.

We have selected only ten percent or so of the novel to represent all of *Don Quixote*. By tracing the relationship between Quixote and Sancho and following the motif of Sancho's desire to rule the island, we have made the novel seem simpler and more thematically focused than it actually is. In the original, the particular strand of the novel that we present is woven into a complex fabric of stories tracing the progress of Don Quixote's madness, his search for the ideal, his adventures throughout Spain, and the stories of many others he encounters on the road. Interspersed amid these stories are ongoing discussions of literature, imagination, ideals, history, and many other topics. Our selection can follow only a few of the threads in this rich literary tapestry.

Suggested Readings

Melveena McKendrick's *Cervantes* (1980) is a readable and accurate account of Cervantes' life. Some good recent critical introductions to *Don Quixote* are P. E. Russell's *Cervantes* (1985), E. C. Riley's *Don Quixote* (1986), and A. J. Close's *Don Quixote* (1990).

Don Quixote

Translated by John Ormsby

Part I

Chapter 1

Which treats of the character and pursuits of the famous gentleman Don Quixote of La Mancha

In a village of La Mancha, the name of which I have no desire to call to mind, there lived not long since one of those gentlemen that keep a lance in the lance-rack, an old buckler, a lean hack, and a greyhound for coursing. An olla of rather more beef than mutton, a salad on most nights, scraps on Saturdays, lentils on Fridays, and a pigeon or so extra on Sundays, made away with three-quarters of his income. The rest of it went in a doublet of fine cloth and velvet breeches and shoes to match for holidays, while on week-days he made a brave figure in his best homespun. He had in his house a housekeeper past forty, a niece under twenty, and a lad for the field and market-place, who used to saddle the hack as well as handle the bill-hook. The age of this gentleman of ours was bordering on fifty, he was of a hardy habit, spare, gaunt-featured, a very early riser and a great sportsman. They will have it his surname was Quixada or Quesada (for here there is some difference of opinion among the authors who write on the subject), although from reasonable conjectures it seems plain that he was called Quixana. This, however, is of but little importance to our tale; it will be enough not to stray a hair's breadth from the truth in the telling of it.

You must know, then, that the above-named gentleman whenever he was at leisure (which was mostly all the year round) gave himself up to reading books of chivalry with such ardor and avidity that he almost entirely neglected the pursuit of his field-sports, and even the management of his property; and to such a pitch did his eagerness and infatuation go that he sold many an acre of tillage-land to buy books of chivalry to read, and brought home as many of them as he could get. But of all there were none he liked so well as those of the famous Feliciano de Silva's[1] composition, for their lucidity of style and complicated conceits were as pearls in his sight, particularly when in his reading he came upon courtships and cartels, where he often found passages like "*the reason of the unreason with which my reason is afflicted so weakens my reason that with reason I murmur at your beauty*"; or again, "*the high heavens, that of your divinity divinely fortify you with the stars, render you deserving of the desert your greatness deserves.*" Over conceits of this sort the poor gentleman lost his wits, and used to lie awake striving to understand them and worm the meaning out of them; what Aristotle himself could not have made out or extracted had

[1] A writer of romances, best known for the chronicle of *Don Florisel de Niquea* (1532) and *Amadis of Gaul* (1535). The quotation is from *Don Florisel.*

he come to life again for that special purpose. He was not at all easy about the wounds which Don Belianis[2] gave and took, because it seemed to him that, great as were the surgeons who had cured him, he must have had his face and body covered all over with seams and scars. He commended, however, the author's way of ending his book with the promise of that interminable adventure, and many a time was he tempted to take up his pen and finish it properly as is there proposed, which no doubt he would have done, and made a successful piece of work of it too, had not greater and more absorbing thoughts prevented him.

Many an argument did he have with the curate of his village (a learned man, and a graduate of Siguenza[3]) as to which had been the better knight, Palmerin of England or Amadis of Gaul.[4] Master Nicholas, the village barber, however, used to say that neither of them came up to the Knight of Phœbus, and that if there was any that could compare with *him* it was Don Galaor, the brother of Amadis of Gaul, because he had a spirit that was equal to every occasion, and was no finikin knight, nor lachrymose like his brother, while in the matter of valor he was not a whit behind him. In short, he became so absorbed in his books that he spent his nights from sunset to sunrise, and his days from dawn to dark, poring over them; and what with little sleep and much reading his brains got so dry that he lost his wits. His fancy grew full of what he used to read about in his books, enchantments, quarrels, battles, challenges, wounds, wooings, loves, agonies, and all sorts of impossible nonsense; and it so possessed his mind that the whole fabric of invention and fancy he read of was true, that to him no history in the world had more reality in it. He used to say the Cid Ruy Diaz was a very good knight, but that he was not to be compared with the Knight of the Burning Sword who with one back-stroke cut in half two fierce and monstrous giants. He thought more of Bernardo del Carpio because at Roncesvalles he slew Roland in spite of enchantments, availing himself of the artifice of Hercules when he strangled Antæus the son of Terra in his arms. He approved highly of the giant Morgante, because, although of the giant breed which is always arrogant and ill-conditioned, he alone was affable and well-bred. But above all he admired Reinaldos of Montalban, especially when he saw him sallying forth from his castle and robbing every one he met, and when beyond the seas he stole that image of Mahomet which, as his history says, was entirely of gold. And to have a bout of kicking at that traitor of a Ganelon[5] he would have given his housekeeper, and his niece into the bargain.

In short, his wits being quite gone, he hit upon the strangest notion that ever madman in this world hit upon, and that was that he fancied it was right and requisite, as well for the support of his own honor as for the service of his country, that he should make a knight-errant of himself, roaming the world over in full armor and on horseback in quest of adventures, and putting in practice himself all that he had read of as being the usual practices of knights-errant; righting every kind of wrong, and exposing himself to peril and danger from which, in the issue, he was to reap eternal renown and fame. Already the poor man saw himself crowned by the might of his arm Emperor of Trebizond at least; and so, led away by the

---

[2]A character in a romance by Jerónimo Fernández.

[3]A minor university often mocked by the Spanish humorists.

[4]The heroes of two famous romances, as are the Knight of Phoebus, Don Galaor, Cid Ruy Diaz, the Knight of the Burning Sword, Bernardo del Carpio, Morgante, and Reinaldos of Montalbán.

[5]The knight who betrayed Roland.

intense enjoyment he found in these pleasant fancies, he set himself forthwith to put his scheme into execution.

The first thing he did was to clean up some armor that had belonged to his great-grandfather, and had been for ages lying forgotten in a corner eaten with rust and covered with mildew. He scoured and polished it as best he could, but he perceived one great defect in it, that it had no closed helmet, nothing but a simple morion.[6] This deficiency, however, his ingenuity supplied, for he contrived a kind of half-helmet of pasteboard which, fitted on to the morion, looked like a whole one. It is true that, in order to see if it was strong and fit to stand a cut, he drew his sword and gave it a couple of slashes, the first of which undid in an instant what had taken him a week to do. The ease with which he had knocked it to pieces disconcerted him somewhat, and to guard against that danger he set to work again, fixing bars of iron on the inside until he was satisfied with its strength; and then, not caring to try any more experiments with it, he passed it and adopted it as a helmet of the most perfect construction.

He next proceeded to inspect his hack, which, with more quartos than a real[7] and more blemishes than the steed of Gonela, that *tantum pellis et ossa fuit*,[8] surpassed in his eyes the Bucephalus of Alexander or the Babieca of the Cid.[9] Four days were spent in thinking what name to give him, because (as he said to himself) it was not right that a horse belonging to a knight so famous, and one with such merits of his own, should be without some distinctive name, and he strove to adapt it so as to indicate what he had been before belonging to a knight-errant, and what he then was; for it was only reasonable that, his master taking a new character, he should take a new name, and that it should be a distinguished and full-sounding one, befitting the new order and calling he was about to follow. And so, after having composed, struck out, rejected, added to, unmade, and remade a multitude of names out of his memory and fancy, he decided upon calling him Rocinante, a name, to his thinking, lofty, sonorous, and significant of his condition as a hack before he became what he now was, the first and foremost of all the hacks in the world.

Having got a name for his horse so much to his taste, he was anxious to get one for himself, and he was eight days more pondering over this point, till at last he made up his mind to call himself Don Quixote, whence, as has been already said, the authors of this veracious history have inferred that his name must have been beyond a doubt Quixada, and not Quesada as others would have it. Recollecting, however, that the valiant Amadis was not content to call himself curtly Amadis and nothing more, but added the name of his kingdom and country to make it famous, and called himself Amadis of Gaul, he, like a good knight, resolved to add on the name of his, and to style himself Don Quixote of La Mancha, whereby, he considered, he described accurately his origin and country, and did honor to it in taking his surname from it.

So then, his armor being furbished, his morion turned into a helmet, his hack christened, and he himself confirmed, he came to the conclusion that nothing more

---

[6] A helmet, like those worn by the Spanish conquistadores, that covered only the top of the head. The gentleman wants one that also covers his face, like those worn by medieval knights.

[7] A coin worth about five cents. There were eight quartos in a real.

[8] Was "all skin and bones." Pedro Gonela, the clown of the Duke of Ferrara in the fifteenth century, had a horse that was the butt of many jokes.

[9] Babieca, the horse of Ruy Diaz, hero of *The Cid*, a twelfth-century Spanish epic.

was needed now but a look out for a lady to be in love with; for a knight-errant without love was like a tree without leaves or fruit, or a body without a soul. As he said to himself, "If, for my sins, or by my good fortune, I come across some giant hereabouts, a common occurrence with knights-errant, and overthrow him in one onslaught, or cleave him asunder to the waist, or, in short, vanquish and subdue him, will it not be well to have some one I may send him to as a present, that he may come in and fall on his knees before my sweet lady, and in a humble, submissive voice say, 'I am the giant Caraculiambro, lord of the island of Malindrania, vanquished in single combat by the never sufficiently extolled knight Don Quixote of La Mancha, who has commanded me to present myself before your Grace, that your Highness dispose of me at your pleasure?' " Oh, how our good gentleman enjoyed the delivery of this speech, especially when he had thought of some one to call his Lady! There was, so the story goes, in a village near his own a very good-looking farm girl with whom he had been at one time in love, though, so far as is known, she never knew it nor gave a thought to the matter. Her name was Aldonza Lorenzo, and upon her he thought fit to confer the title of Lady of his Thoughts; and after some search for a name which should not be out of harmony with her own, and should suggest and indicate that of a princess and great lady, he decided upon calling her Dulcinea del Toboso—she being of El Toboso—a name, to his mind, musical, uncommon, and significant, like all those he had already bestowed upon himself and the things belonging to him.

Chapter 2

Which treats of the first sally the ingenious Don Quixote made from home

These preliminaries settled, he did not care to put off any longer the execution of his design, urged on to it by the thought of all the world was losing by his delay, seeing what wrongs he intended to right, grievances to redress, injustices to repair, abuses to remove, and duties to discharge. So, without giving notice of his intention to any one, and without anybody seeing him, one morning before the dawning of the day (which was one of the hottest of the month of July) he donned his suit of armor, mounted Rocinante with his patched-up helmet on, braced his buckler, took his lance, and by the back door of the yard sallied forth upon the plain in the highest contentment and satisfaction at seeing with what ease he had made a beginning with his grand purpose. But scarcely did he find himself upon the open plain, when a terrible thought struck him, one all but enough to make him abandon the enterprise at the very outset. It occured to him that he had not been dubbed a knight, and that according to the law of chivalry he neither could nor ought to bear arms against any knight; and that even if he had been, still he ought, as a novice knight, to wear white armor, without a device upon the shield until by his prowess he had earned one. These reflections made him waver in his purpose, but his craze being stronger than any reasoning he made up his mind to have himself dubbed a knight by the first one he came across, following the example of others in the same case, as he had read in the books that brought him to this pass. As for white armor, he resolved, on the first opportunity, to scour his until it was whiter than an ermine; and so comforting himself he pursued his way, taking that which his horse chose, for in this he believed lay the essence of adventures.

Thus setting out, our new-fledged adventurer paced along, talking to himself and saying, "Who knows but that in time to come, when the veracious history of my famous deeds is made known, the sage who writes it, when he has to set forth my first sally in the early morning, will do it after this fashion? 'Scarce had the rubicund Apollo spread o'er the face of the broad spacious earth the golden threads of his bright hair, scarce had the little birds of painted plumage attuned their notes to hail with dulcet and mellifluous harmony the coming of the rosy Dawn, that, deserting the soft couch of her jealous spouse, was appearing to mortals at the gates and balconies of the Manchegan horizon, when the renowned knight Don Quixote of La Mancha, quitting the lazy down, mounted his celebrated steed Rocinante and began to traverse the ancient and famous Campo de Montiel' ";[10] which in fact he was actually traversing. "Happy the age, happy the time," he continued, "in which shall be made known my deeds of fame, worthy to be moulded in brass, carved in marble, limned in pictures, for a memorial forever. And thou, O sage magician, whoever thou art, to whom it shall fall to be the chronicler of this wondrous history, forget not, I entreat thee, my good Rocinante, the constant companion of my ways and wanderings." Presently he broke out again, as if he were love-stricken in earnest, "O Princess Dulcinea, lady of this captive heart, a grievous wrong hast thou done me to drive me forth with scorn, and with inexorable obduracy banish me from the presence of thy beauty. O lady, deign to hold in remembrance this heart, thy vassal, that thus in anguish pines for love of thee."

So he went on stringing together these and other absurdities, all in the style of those his books had taught him, imitating their language as well as he could; and all the while he rode so slowly and the sun mounted so rapidly and with such fervor that it was enough to melt his brains if he had any. Nearly all day he travelled without anything remarkable happening to him, at which he was in despair, for he was anxious to encounter some one at once upon whom to try the might of his strong arm.

Writers there are who say the first adventure he met with was that of Puerto Lápice; others say it was that of the windmills; but what I have ascertained on this point, and what I have found written in the annals of La Mancha, is that he was on the road all day, and towards nightfall his hack and he found themselves dead tired and hungry, when, looking all around to see if he could discover any castle or shepherd's shanty where he might refresh himself and relieve his sore wants, he perceived not far out of his road an inn, which was welcome as a star guiding him to the portals, if not the palaces, of his redemption; and quickening his pace he reached it just as night was setting in. At the door were standing two young women, girls of the district as they call them, on their way to Seville with some carriers who had chanced to halt that night at the inn; and as, happen what might to our adventurer, everything he saw or imagined seemed to him to be and to happen after the fashion of what he had read of, the moment he saw the inn he pictured it to himself as a castle with its four turrets and pinnacles of shining silver, not forgetting the drawbridge and moat and all the belongings usually ascribed to castles of the sort. To this inn, which to him seemed a castle, he advanced, and at a short distance from it he checked Rocinante, hoping that some dwarf would show himself upon the battlements, and by sound of trumpet give notice that a knight was approaching the castle. But seeing that they were slow about it, and that Rocinante was in a hurry to reach the stable, he made for the inn door, and perceived the two gay damsels who were standing there, and who seemed to him to be two fair maidens or lovely ladies taking their ease at the castle gate.

---

[10]Site of a famous battle in 1369.

At this moment it so happened that a swineherd who was going through the stubbles collecting a drove of pigs (for, without any apology, that is what they are called) gave a blast of his horn to bring them together, and forthwith it seemed to Don Quixote to be what he was expecting, the signal of some dwarf announcing his arrival; and so with prodigious satisfaction he rode up to the inn and to the ladies, who, seeing a man of this sort approaching in full armor and with lance and buckler, were turning in dismay into the inn, when Don Quixote, guessing their fear by their flight, raising his pasteboard visor, disclosed his dry, dusty visage, and with courteous bearing and gentle voice addressed them, "Your ladyships need not fly or fear any rudeness, for that it belongs not to the order of knighthood which I profess to offer to any one, much less to high-born maidens as your appearance proclaims you to be." The girls were looking at him and straining their eyes to make out the features which the clumsy visor obscured, but when they heard themselves called maidens, a thing so much out of their line, they could not restrain their laughter, which made Don Quixote wax indignant, and say, "Modesty becomes the fair, and moreover laughter that has little cause is great silliness; this, however, I say not to pain or anger you, for my desire is none other than to serve you."

The incomprehensible language and the unpromising looks of our cavalier only increased the ladies' laughter, and that increased his irritation, and matters might have gone farther if at that moment the landlord had not come out, who, being a very fat man, was a very peaceful one. He, seeing this grotesque figure clad in armor that did not match any more than his saddle, bridle, lance, buckler, or corselet, was not at all indisposed to joint the damsels in their manifestations of amusement; but, in truth, standing in awe of such a complicated armament, he thought it best to speak him fairly, so he said, "Señor Caballero, if your worship wants lodging, bating the bed (for there is not one in the inn) there is plenty of everything else here." Don Quixote, observing the respectful bearing of the Alcaide of the fortress (for so innkeeper and inn seemed in his eyes), made answer, "Sir Castellan, for me anything will suffice, for

My armor is my only wear,
My only rest the fray.

The host fancied he called him Castellan because he took him for a "worthy of Castile,"[11] though he was in fact an Andalusian, and one from the Strand of San Lucar, as crafty a thief as Casus[12] and as full of tricks as a student or a page. "In that case," said he,

Your bed is on the flinty rock,
Your sleep to watch alway;

and if so, you may dismount and safely reckon upon any quantity of sleeplessness under this roof for a twelvemonth, not to say for a single night." So saying, he advanced to hold the stirrup for Don Quixote, who got down with great difficulty and exertion (for he had not broken his fast all day), and then charged the host to take great care of his horse as he was the best bit of flesh that ever ate bread in this world. The landlord eyed him over, but did not find him as good as Don Quixote said, nor even half as good, and putting him up in the stable, he returned to see what might be wanted by his guest, whom the damsels, who had by this time made

[11] *Castellano* and *alcaide* both mean governor of a castle or fortress, but the former also means "a Castilian."

[12] The son of Vulcan who robbed the Italians of their cattle; hence, a thief.

their peace with him, were now relieving of his armor. They had taken off his breastplate and backpiece, but they neither knew nor saw how to open his gorget or remove his make-shift helmet, for he had fastened it with green ribbons, which, as there was no untying the knots, required to be cut. This, however, he would not by any means consent to, so he remained all the evening with his helmet on, the drollest and oddest figure that can be imagined; and while they were removing his armor, taking the baggages who were about it for ladies of high degree belonging to the castle, he said to them with great sprightliness:

Oh, never, surely, was there knight
So served by hand of dame,
As served was he, Don Quixote hight,
When from his town he came;
With maidens waiting on himself,
Princesses on his hack—

—or Rocinante, for that, ladies mine, is my horse's name, and Don Quixote of La Mancha is my own; for though I had no intention of declaring myself until my achievements in your service and honor had made me known, the necessity of adapting that old ballad of Lancelot to the present occasion has given you the knowledge of my name altogether prematurely. A time, however, will come for your ladyships to command and me to obey, and then the might of my arm will show my desire to serve you."

The girls, who were not used to hearing rhetoric of this sort, had nothing to say in reply: they only asked him if he wanted anything to eat. "I would gladly eat a bit of something," said Don Quixote, "for I feel it would come very seasonably." The day happened to be a Friday, and in the whole inn there was nothing but some pieces of the fish they call in Castile *abadejo*, in Andalusia *bacallao*, and in some places *curadillo*, and in others *troutlet*; so they asked him if he thought he could eat troutlet, for there was no other fish to give him. "If there be troutlets enough," said Don Quixote, "they will be the same thing as a trout; for it is all one to me whether I am given eight reals in small change or a piece of eight; moreover, it may be that these troutlets are like veal, which is better than beef, or kid, which is better than goat. But whatever it be let it come quickly, for the burden and pressure of arms cannot be borne without support to the inside." They laid a table for him at the door of the inn for the sake of the air, and the host brought him a portion of ill-soaked and worse cooked stockfish, and a piece of bread as black and mouldy as his own armor; but a laughable sight it was to see him eating, for having his helmet on and the beaver up, he could not with his own hands put anything into his mouth unless some one else placed it there, and this service one of the ladies rendered him. But to give him anything to drink was impossible, or would have been so had not the landlord bored a reed, and putting one end in his mouth poured the wine into him through the other; all which he bore with patience rather than sever the ribbons of his helmet.

While this was going on there came up to the inn a pig-gelder, who, as he approached, sounded his reed pipe four or five times, and thereby completely convinced Don Quixote that he was in some famous castle, and that they were regaling him with music, and that the stockfish was trout, the bread the whitest, the wenches ladies, and the landlord the castellan of the castle; and consequently he held that his enterprise and sally had been to some purpose. But still it distressed him to think he had not been dubbed a knight, for it was plain to him he could not lawfully engage in any adventure without receiving the order of knighthood.

. . .

FROM

Chapter 7

Of the second sally of our worthy knight Don Quixote of La Mancha

. . . Meanwhile Don Quixote worked upon a farm laborer, a neighbor of his, an honest man (if indeed that title can be given to him who is poor), but with very little wit in his pate. In a word, he so talked him over, and with such persuasions and promises, that the poor clown made up his mind to sally forth with him and serve him as esquire. Don Quixote, among other things, told him he ought to be ready to go with him gladly, because any moment an adventure might occur that might win an island in the twinkling of an eye and leave him governor of it. On these and the like promises Sancho Panza (for so the laborer was called) left wife and children, and engaged himself as esquire to his neighbor. Don Quixote next set about getting some money; and selling one thing and pawning another, and making a bad bargain in every case, he got together a fair sum. He provided himself with a buckler, which he begged as a loan from a friend, and, restoring his battered helmet as best he could, he warned his squire Sancho of the day and hour he meant to set out, that he might provide himself with what he thought most needful. Above all, he charged him to take *alforjas*[13] with him. The other said he would, and that he meant to take also a very good ass he had, as he was not much given to going on foot. About the ass, Don Quixote hesitated a little, trying whether he could call to mind any knight-errant taking with him an esquire mounted on ass-back, but no instance occurred to his memory. For all that, however, he determined to take him, intending to furnish him with a more honorable mount when a chance of it presented itself, by appropriating the horse of the first discourteous knight he encountered. Himself he provided with shirts and such other things as he could, according to the advice the host had given him; all which being settled and done, without taking leave, Sancho Panza of his wife and children, or Don Quixote of his housekeeper and niece, they sallied forth unseen by anybody from the village one night, and made such good way in the course of it that by daylight they held themselves safe from discovery, even should search be made for them.

Sancho rode on his ass like a patriarch with his *alforjas* and *bota,*[14] and longing to see himself soon governor of the island his master had promised him. Don Quixote decided upon taking the same route and road he had taken on his first journey, that over the Campo de Montiel, which he travelled with less discomfort than on the last occasion, for, as it was early morning and the rays of the sun fell on them obliquely, the heat did not distress them.

And now said Sancho Panza to his master, "Your worship will take care, Señor Knight-errant, not to forget about the island you have promised me, for be it ever so big I'll be equal to governing it."

To which Don Quixote replied, "Thou must know, friend Sancho Panza, that it was a practice very much in vogue with the knights-errant of old to make their squires governors of the islands or kingdoms they won, and I am determined that there shall be no failure on my part in so liberal a custom; on the contrary, I mean to improve upon it, for they sometimes, and perhaps most frequently, waited until their squires were old, and then when they had had enough of service and hard days and worse nights, they gave them some title or other, of count, or at the most

---

[13]Saddlebags that were often carried slung across the shoulder.

[14]A leather wine-bag.

marquis, of some valley or province more or less; but if thou livest and I live, it may well be that before six days are over, I may have won some kingdom that has others dependent upon it, which will be just the thing to enable thee to be crowned king of one of them. Nor needst thou count this wonderful, for things and chances fall to the lot of such knights in ways so unexampled and unexpected that I might easily give thee even more than I promise thee."

"In that case," said Sancho Panza, "if I should become a king by one of those miracles your worship speaks of, even Juana Gutierrez, my old woman, would come to be queen and my children infantas."

"Well, who doubts it?" said Don Quixote.

"I doubt it," replied Sancho Panza, "because for my part I am persuaded that though God should shower down kingdoms upon earth, not one of them would fit the head of Mari Gutierrez.[15] Let me tell you, señor, she is not worth two maravedís for a queen; countess will fit her better, and that only with God's help."

"Leave it to God, Sancho," returned Don Quixote, "for he will give her what suits her best; but do not undervalue thyself so much as to come to be content with anything less than being governor of a province."

"I will not, señor," answered Sancho, "especially as I have a man of such quality for a master in your worship, who will be able to give me all that will be suitable for me and that I can bear."

FROM
Chapter 8

Of the good fortune which the valiant Don Quixote had in the terrible and undreamt-of adventure of the windmills, with other occurrences worthy to be fitly recorded

At this point they came in sight of thirty or forty windmills that there are on that plain, and as soon as Don Quixote saw them he said to his squire, "Fortune is arranging matters for us better than we could have shaped our desires ourselves, for look there, friend Sancho Panza, where thirty or more monstrous giants present themselves, all of whom I mean to engage in battle and slay, and with whose spoils we shall begin to make our fortunes; for this is righteous warfare, and it is God's good service to sweep so evil a breed from off the face of the earth."

"What giants?" said Sancho Panza.

"Those thou seest there," answered his master, "with the long arms, and some have them nearly two leagues long."

"Look, your worship," said Sancho "what we see there are not giants but windmills, and what seem to be their arms are the sails that turned by the wind make the millstone go."

"It is easy to see," replied Don Quixote, "that thou are not used to this business of adventures; those are giants; and if thou art afraid, away with thee out of this and betake thyself to prayer while I engage them in fierce and unequal combat."

So saying, he gave the spur to his steed Rocinante, heedless of the cries his squire Sancho sent after him, warning him that most certainly they were windmills and not giants he was going to attack. He, however, was so positive they were giants that he neither heard the cries of Sancho, nor perceived, near as he was, what they were, but made at them shouting, "Fly not, cowards and vile beings, for it is a single knight that attacks you."

[15] Gutierrez is the maiden name of Juana (or Mari) Panza. In Part II, Cervantes (apparently forgetting how he named her in Part I) gives her the maiden name of Teresa Cascajo.

A slight breeze at this moment sprang up, and the great sails began to move, seeing which Don Quixote exclaimed, "Though ye flourish more arms than the giant Briareus,[16] ye have to reckon with me."

So saying, and commending himself with all his heart to his lady Dulcinea, imploring her to support him in such a peril, with lance in rest and covered by his buckler, he charged at Rocinante's fullest gallop and fell upon the first mill that stood in front of him; but as he drove his lance-point into the sail the wind whirled it round with such force that it shivered the lance to pieces, sweeping with it horse and rider, who went rolling over on the plain, in a sorry condition. Sancho hastened to his assistance as fast as his ass could go, and when he came up found him unable to move, with such a shock had Rocinante fallen on him.

"God bless me!" said Sancho, "did I not tell your worship to mind what you were about, for they were only windmills? And no one could have made any mistake about it but one who had something of the same kind in his head."

"Hush, friend Sancho," replied Don Quixote, "the fortunes of war more than any other are liable to frequent fluctuations; and moreover I think, and it is the truth, that that same sage Friston who carried off my study and books, has turned these giants into mills in order to rob me of the glory of vanquishing them, such is the enmity he bears me; but in the end his wicked arts will avail but little against my good sword."

"God order it as he may," said Sancho Panza, and helping him to rise got him up again on Rocinante, whose shoulder was half out; and then, discussing the late adventure, they followed the road to Puerto Lápice, for there, said Don Quixote, they could not fail to find adventures in abundance and variety, as it was a great thoroughfare. For all that, he was much grieved at the loss of his lance, and saying so to his squire, he added, "I remember having read how a Spanish knight, Diego Perez de Vargas by name, having broken his sword in battle, tore from an oak a ponderous bough or branch, and with it did such things that day, and pounded so many Moors, that he got the surname of Machuca, and he and his descendants from that day forth were called Vargas y Machuca.[17] I mention this because from the first oak I see I mean to rend such another branch, large and stout like that, with which I am determined and resolved to do such deeds that thou mayest deem thyself very fortunate in being found worthy to come and see them, and be an eye-witness of things that will with difficulty be believed."

"Be that as God will," said Sancho, "I believe it all as your worship says it; but straighten yourself a little, for you seem all on one side, maybe from the shaking of the fall."

"That is the truth," said Don Quixote, "and if I make no complaint of the pain it is because knights-errant are not permitted to complain of any wound, even though their bowels be coming out through it."

"If so," said Sancho, "I have nothing to say; but God knows I would rather your worship complained when anything ailed you. For my part, I confess I must complain however small the ache may be; unless indeed this rule about not complaining extends to the squires of knights-errant also."

Don Quixote could not help laughing at his squire's simplicity, and he assured him he might complain whenever and however he chose, just as he liked, for, so far, he had never read of anything to the contrary in the order of knighthood.

---

[16] In Greek mythology, a giant with a hundred arms.

[17] Machuca, "The Crusher," was the hero of a popular ballad.

Sancho bade him remember it was dinnertime, to which his master answered that he wanted nothing himself just then, but that he might eat when he had a mind. With this permission Sancho settled himself as comfortably as he could on his beast, and taking out of the *alforjas* what he had stowed away in them, he jogged along behind his master munching deliberately, and from time to time taking a pull at the *bota* with a relish that the thirstiest tapster in Malaga might have envied; and while he went on in this way, gulping down draught after draught, he never gave a thought to any of the promises his master had made him, nor did he rate it as hardship but rather as recreation going in quest of adventures, however dangerous they might be. Finally they passed the night among some trees, from one of which Don Quixote plucked a dry branch to serve him after a fashion as a lance, and fixed on it the head he had removed from the broken one. All that night Don Quixote lay awake thinking of his lady Dulcinea, in order to conform to what he had read in his books, how many a night in the forests and deserts knights used to lie sleepless supported by the memory of their mistresses. Not so did Sancho Panza spend it, for having his stomach full of something stronger than chiccory water he made but one sleep of it, and, if his master had not called him, neither the rays of the sun beating on his face nor all the cheery notes of the birds welcoming the approach of day would have had power to waken him. On getting up he tried the *bota* and found it somewhat less full than the night before, which grieved his heart because they did not seem to be on the way to remedy the deficiency readily. Don Quixote did not care to break his fast, for, as has been already said, he confined himself to savory recollections for nourishment.

They returned to the road they had set out with, leading to Puerto Lápice, and at three in the afternoon they came in sight of it. "Here, brother Sancho Panza," said Don Quixote when he saw it, "we may plunge our hands up to the elbows in what they call adventures; but observe, even shouldst thou see me in the greatest danger in the world, thou must not put a hand to thy sword in my defence, unless, indeed, thou perceivest that those who assail me are rabble or base folk; for in that case thou mayest very properly aid me; but if they be knights it is on no account permitted or allowed thee by the laws of knighthood to help me until thou has been dubbed a knight."

"Most certainly, señor," replied Sancho, "your worship shall be fully obeyed in this matter; all the more as of myself I am peaceful and no friend to mixing in strife and quarrels: it is true that as regards the defence of my own person I shall not give much heed to those laws, for laws human and divine allow each one to defend himself against any assailant whatever."

"That I grant," said Don Quixote, "but in this matter of aiding me against knights thou must put a restraint upon thy natural impetuosity."

"I will do so, I promise you," answered Sancho, "and I will keep this precept as carefully as Sunday."

While they were thus talking there appeared on the road two friars of the order of St. Benedict, mounted on two dromedaries, for not less tall were the two mules they rode on. They wore travelling spectacles and carried sunshades; and behind them came a coach attended by four or five persons on horseback and two muleteers on foot. In the coach there was, as afterwards appeared, a Biscay lady on her way to Seville, where her husband was about to take passage for the Indies with an appointment of high honor. The friars, though going the same road, were not in her company; but the moment Don Quixote perceived them he said to his squire, "Either I am mistaken, or this is going to be the most famous adventure that has ever been seen, for those black bodies we see there must be, and doubtless are, magicians who are carrying off some stolen princess in that coach, and with all my might I must undo this wrong."

"This will be worse than the windmills," said Sancho. "Look, señor; those are friars of St. Benedict, and the coach plainly belongs to some travellers: mind, I tell you to mind well what you are about and don't let the devil mislead you."

"I have told thee already, Sancho," replied Don Quixote, "that on the subject of adventures thou knowest little. What I say is the truth, as thou shalt see presently."

So saying, he advanced and posted himself in the middle of the road along which the friars were coming, and as soon as he thought they had come near enough to hear what he said, he cried aloud, "Devilish and unnatural beings, release instantly the high-born princesses whom you are carrying off by force in this coach, else prepare to meet a speedy death as the just punishment of your evil deeds."

The friars drew rein and stood wondering at the appearance of Don Quixote as well as at his words, to which they replied, "Señor Caballero, we are not devilish or unnatural, but two brothers of St. Benedict following our road, nor do we know whether or not there are any captive princesses coming in this coach."

"No soft words with me, for I know you, lying rabble," said Don Quixote, and without waiting for a reply he spurred Rocinante and with levelled lance charged the first friar with such fury and determination that, if the friar had not flung himself off the mule, he would have brought him to the ground against his will, and sore wounded, if not killed outright. The second brother, seeing how his comrade was treated, drove his heels into his castle of a mule and made off across the country faster than the wind.

Sancho Panza, when he saw the friar on the ground, dismounting briskly from his ass, rushed towards him and began to strip off his gown. At that instant the friars' muleteers came up and asked what he was stripping him for. Sancho answered them that this fell to him lawfully as spoil of the battle which his lord Don Quixote had won. The muleteers, who had no idea of a joke and did not understand all this about battles and spoils, seeing that Don Quixote was some distance off talking to the travellers in the coach, fell upon Sancho, knocked him down, and leaving hardly a hair in his beard, belabored him with kicks and left him stretched breathless and senseless on the ground; and without any more delay helped the friar to mount, who, trembling, terrified, and pale, as soon as he found himself in the saddle, spurred after his companion, who was standing at a distance looking on, watching the result of the onslaught; then, not caring to wait for the end of the affair just begun, they pursued their journey making more crosses than if they had the devil after them.

Don Quixote was, as has been said, speaking to the lady in the coach: "Your beauty, lady mine," said he, "may now dispose of your person as may be most in accordance with your pleasure, for the pride of your ravishers lies prostrate on the ground through this strong arm of mine; and lest you should be pining to know the name of your deliverer, know that I am called Don Quixote of La Mancha, knight-errant and adventurer, and captive to the peerless and beautiful lady Dulcinea del Toboso; and in return for the service you have received of me I ask no more than that you should return to El Toboso, and on my behalf present yourself before that lady and tell her what I have done to set you free."

One of the squires in attendance upon the coach, a Biscayan, was listening to all Don Quixote was saying, and, perceiving that he would not allow the coach to go on, but was saying it must return at once to El Toboso, he made at him, and seizing his lance addressed him in bad Castilian and worse Biscayan after this fashion, "Begone, caballero, and ill go with thee; by the God that made me, unless thou quittest coach, slayest thee as art here a Biscayan."

Don Quixote understood him quite well, and answered him very quietly, "If thou wert a knight, as thou art none, I should have already chastised thy folly and rashness, miserable creature." To which the Biscayan returned, "I no gentleman!—I swear to God thou liest as I am Christian: if thou droppest lance and drawest sword, soon shalt thou see thou art carrying water to the cat: Biscayan on land, hidalgo at sea, hidalgo at the devil, and look, if thou sayest otherwise thou liest."

"'You will see presently,' said Agrajes,"[18] replied Don Quixote; and throwing his lance on the ground he drew his sword, braced his buckler on his arm, and attacked the Biscayan, bent upon taking his life.

The Biscayan, when he saw him coming on, though he wished to dismount from his mule, in which, being one of those sorry ones let out for hire, he had no confidence, had no choice but to draw his sword; it was lucky for him, however, that he was near the coach, from which he was able to snatch a cushion that served him for a shield; and then they went at one another as if they had been two mortal enemies. The others strove to make peace between them, but could not, for the Biscayan declared in his disjointed phrase that if they did not let him finish his battle he would kill his mistress and every one that strove to prevent him. The lady in the coach, amazed and terrified at what she saw, ordered the coachman to draw aside a little, and set herself to watch this severe struggle, in the course of which the Biscayan smote Don Quixote a mighty stroke on the shoulder over the top of his buckler, which, given to one without armor, would have cleft him to the waist. Don Quixote, feeling the weight of this prodigious blow, cried aloud, saying: "O lady of my soul, Dulcinea, flower of beauty, come to the aid of this your knight, who, in fulfilling his obligations to your beauty, finds himself in this extreme peril." To say this, to lift his sword, to shelter himself well behind his buckler, and to assail the Biscayan was the work of an instant, determined as he was to venture all upon a single blow. The Biscayan, seeing him come on in this way, was convinced of his courage by his spirited bearing, and resolved to follow his example, so he waited for him keeping well under cover of his cushion, being unable to execute any sort of manœuvre with his mule, which, dead tired and never meant for this kind of game, could not stir a step. . . .

FROM

Chapter 10

Of the pleasant discourse that passed between Don Quixote and his squire Sancho Panza

Now by this time Sancho had risen, rather the worse for the handling of the friars' muleteers, and stood watching the battle of his master, Don Quixote, and praying to God in his heart that it might be his will to grant him the victory, and that he might thereby win some island to make him governor of, as he had promised. Seeing, therefore, that the struggle was now over, and that his master was returning to mount Rocinante, he approached to hold the stirrup for him, and, before he could mount, he went on his knees before him, and taking his hand, kissed it saying, "May it please your worship, Señor Don Quixote, to give me the government of that island which has been won in this hard fight, for be it ever so big I feel myself in sufficient force to be able to govern it as much and as well as any one in the world who has ever governed islands."

[18] Quixote is quoting Agrajes from *Amadis of Gaul*; the challenge has become the conventional opener for a fight.

To which Don Quixote replied, "Thou must take notice, brother Sancho, that this adventure and those like it are not adventures of islands, but of cross-roads, in which nothing is got except a broken head or an ear the less: have patience, for adventures will present themselves from which I may make you not only a governor, but something more."

Sancho gave him many thanks, and again kissing his hand and the skirt of his hauberk, helped him to mount Rocinante, and mounting his ass himself, proceeded to follow his master, who at a brisk pace, without taking leave, or saying anything further to the ladies belonging to the coach, turned into a wood that was hard by. Sancho followed him at his ass's best trot, but Rocinante stepped out so that, seeing himself left behind, he was forced to call to his master to wait for him. Don Quixote did so, reining in Rocinante until his weary squire came up, who on reaching him said, "It seems to me, señor, it would be prudent in us to go and take refuge in some church, for, seeing how mauled he with whom you fought has been left, it will be no wonder if they give information of the affair to the Holy Brotherhood[19] and arrest us, and, faith, if they do, before we come out of gaol we shall have to sweat for it."

"Peace," said Don Quixote; "where hast thou ever seen or heard that a knight-errant has been arraigned before a court of justice, however many homicides he may have committed?"

"I know nothing about omecils,"[20] answered Sancho, "nor in my life have had anything to do with one; I only know that the Holy Brotherhood looks after those who fight in the fields, and in that other matter I do not meddle."

"Then thou needest have no uneasiness, my friend," said Don Quixote, "for I will deliver thee out of the hands of the Chaldeans, much more out of those of the Brotherhood. But tell me, as thou livest, hast thou seen a more valiant knight than I in all the known world; hast thou read in history of any who has or had higher mettle in attack, more spirit in maintaining it, more dexterity in wounding or skill in over-throwing?"

"The truth is," answered Sancho, "that I have never read any history, for I can neither read nor write, but what I will venture to bet is that a more daring master than your worship I have never served in all the days of my life, and God grant that this daring be not paid for where I have said; what I beg of your worship is to dress your wound, for a great deal of blood flows from that ear, and I have here some lint and a little white ointment in the *alforjas*."

"All that might be well dispensed with," said Don Quixote, "if I had remembered to make a vial of the balsam of Fierabras,[21] for time and medicine are saved by one single drop."

"What vial and what balsam is that?" said Sancho Panza.

"It is a balsam," answered Don Quixote, "the receipt[22] of which I have in my memory, with which one need have no fear of death, or dread dying of any wound; and so when I make it and give it to thee thou hast nothing to do when in some battle thou seest they have cut me in half through the middle of the body—as is wont to happen frequently—but neatly and with great nicety, ere the blood congeal, to place that portion of the body which shall have fallen to the ground upon the other half which remains in the saddle, taking care to fit it on evenly and exactly.

---

[19]A tribunal for highway robbers, established by Ferdinand and Isabella at the end of the fifteenth century.

[20]Grudges.

[21]In Roman legend, a giant who stole the liquid with which Jesus was embalmed, which could miraculously heal wounds.

[22]Recipe.

Then thou shalt give me to drink but two drops of the balsam I have mentioned, and thou shalt see me become sounder than an apple."

"If that be so," said Panza, "I renounce henceforth the government of the promised island, and desire nothing more in payment of my many and faithful services than that your worship give me the receipt of this supreme liquor, for I am persuaded it will be worth more than two reals an ounce anywhere, and I want no more to pass the rest of my life in ease and honor; but it remains to be told if it costs much to make it."

"With less than three reals six quarts of it may be made," said Don Quixote.

"Sinner that I am!" said Sancho, "then why does your worship put off making it and teaching it to me."

"Peace, friend," answered Don Quixote; "greater secrets I mean to teach thee and greater favors to bestow upon thee; and for the present let us see to the dressing, for my ear pains me more than I could wish."

Sancho took out some lint and ointment from the *alforjas*; but when Don Quixote came to see his helmet shattered, he was like to lose his senses, and, clapping his hand upon his sword and raising his eyes to heaven, he said, "I swear by the Creator of all things and the four Gospels in their fullest extent, to do as the great Marquis of Mantua did when he swore to avenge the death of his nephew Baldwin (and that was not to eat bread from a table-cloth, nor embrace his wife, and other points which, though I cannot now call them to mind, I here grant as expressed), until I take complete vengeance upon him who has committed such an offence against me."

Hearing this, Sancho said to him, "Your worship should bear in mind, Señor Don Quixote, that if the knight has done what was commanded him in going to present himself before my lady Dulcinea del Toboso, he will have done all that he was bound to do, and does not deserve further punishment unless he commits some new offence."

"Thou hast said well and hit the point," answered Don Quixote; "and so I recall the oath in so far as relates to taking fresh vengeance on him, but I make and confirm it anew to lead the life I have said until such time as I take by force from some knight another helmet such as this and as good; and think not, Sancho, that I am raising smoke with straw in doing so, for I have one to imitate in the matter, since the very same thing to a hair happened in the case of Mambrino's helmet, which cost Sacripante so dear."[23]

"Señor," replied Sancho, "let your worship send all such oaths to the devil, for they are very pernicious to salvation and prejudicial to the conscience; just tell me now, if for several days to come we fall in with no man armed with a helmet, what are we to do? Is the oath to be observed in spite of all the inconvenience and discomfort it will be to sleep in your clothes, and not to sleep in a house, and a thousand other mortifications contained in the oath of that old fool, the Marquis of Mantua, which your worship is now wanting to revive? Let your worship observe that there are no men in armor travelling on any of these roads, nothing but carriers and carters, who not only do not wear helmets, but perhaps never heard tell of them all their lives."

"Thou art wrong there," said Don Quixote, "for we shall not have been two hours among these cross-roads before we see more men in armor than came to Albraca to win the fair Angelica."[24]

---

[23] Mambrino, a Moorish king in the epic poem *Orlando Innamorato (Roland in Love)* by Matteo Maria Boiardo, has his enchanted helmet stolen by Rinaldo.

[24] Also in *Orlando Innamorato*.

"Enough," said Sancho; "so be it then, and God grant us success, and that the time for winning that island which is costing me so dear may soon come, and then let me die."

"I have already told thee, Sancho," said Don Quixote, "not to give thyself any uneasiness on that score; for if an island should fail, there is the kingdom of Denmark, or of Sobradisa, which will fit thee as a ring fits the finger, and all the more that being on *terra firma* thou wilt all the better enjoy thyself. But let us leave that to its own time; see if thou hast anything for us to eat in those *alforjas,* because we must presently go in quest of some castle where we may lodge tonight and make the balsam I told thee of, for I swear to thee by God, this ear is giving me great pain."

"I have here an onion and a little cheese and a few scraps of bread," said Sancho, "but they are not victuals fit for a valiant knight like your worship."

"How little thou knowest about it," answered Don Quixote; "I would have thee know, Sancho, that it is the glory of knights-errant to go without eating for a month, and even when they do eat, that it should be of what comes first to hand; and this would have been clear to thee hadst thou read as many histories as I have, for, though they are very many, among them all I have found no mention made of knights-errant eating, unless by accident or at some sumptuous banquets prepared for them, and the rest of the time they passed in dalliance. And though it is plain they could not do without eating and performing all the other natural functions, because, in fact, they were men like ourselves, it is plain too that, wandering as they did the most part of their lives through woods and wilds and without a cook, their most usual fare would be rustic viands such as those thou dost now offer me; so that, friend Sancho, let not that distress thee which pleases me, and do not seek to make a new world or pervert knight-errantry."

"Pardon me, your worship," said Sancho, "for, as I can not read or write, as I said just now, I neither know nor comprehend the rules of the profession of chivalry: henceforward I will stock the *alforjas* with every kind of dry fruit for your worship, as you are a knight; and for myself, as I am not one, I will furnish them with poultry and other things more substantial."

"I do not say, Sancho," replied Don Quixote, "that it is imperative on knights-errant not to eat anything else but the fruits thou speakest of; only that their more usual diet must be those, and certain herbs they found in the fields which they knew and I know too."

"A good thing it is," answered Sancho, "to know those herbs, for to my thinking it will be needful some day to put that knowledge into practice."

And here taking out what he said he had brought, the pair made their repast peaceably and sociably. But anxious to find quarters for the night, they with all despatch made an end of their poor dry fare, mounted at once, and made haste to reach some habitation before night set in. . . .

Chapter 20

Of the unexampled and unheard-of adventure which was achieved by the valiant Don Quixote of La Mancha with less peril than any ever achieved by any famous knight in the world

"It can not be, señor, but that this grass is a proof that there must be hard by some spring or brook to give it moisture, so it would be well to move a little farther on, that we may find some place where we may quench this terrible thirst that plagues us, which beyond a doubt is more distressing than hunger."

The advice seemed good to Don Quixote, and, he leading Rocinante by the bridle and Sancho the ass by the halter, after he had packed away upon him the remains of the supper, they advanced up the meadow feeling their way, for the darkness of the night made it impossible to see anything; but they had not gone two hundred paces when a loud noise of water, as if falling from great high rocks, struck their ears. The sound cheered them greatly; but halting to make out by listening from what quarter it came they heard unseasonably another noise which spoiled the satisfaction the sound of the water gave them, especially for Sancho, who was by nature timid and faint-hearted; they heard, I say, strokes falling with a measured beat, and a certain rattling of iron and chains that, together with the furious din of the water, would have struck terror into any heart but Don Quixote's. The night was, as has been said, dark, and they had happened to reach a spot in among some tall trees, whose leaves stirred by a gentle breeze made a low ominous sound; so that, what with the solitude, the place, the darkness, the noise of the water, and the rustling of the leaves, everything inspired awe and dread; more especially as they perceived that the strokes did not cease, nor the wind lull, nor morning approach; to all which might be added their ignorance as to where they were.

But Don Quixote, supported by his intrepid heart, leaped on Rocinante, and bracing his buckler on his arm, brought his pike to the slope, and said, "Friend Sancho, know that I by Heaven's will have been born in this our iron age to revive in it the age of gold, or the golden as it is called; I am he for whom perils, mighty achievements, and valiant deeds are reserved; I am, I say again, he who is to revive the Knights of the Round Table, the Twelve of France and the Nine Worthies; and he who is to consign to oblivion the Platirs, the Tablantes, the Olivantes and Tirantes, the Phœbuses and Belianises, with the whole herd of famous knights-errant of days gone by, performing in these in which I live such exploits, marvels, and feats of arms as shall obscure their brightest deeds. Thou dost mark well, faithful and trusty squire, the gloom of this night, its strange silence, the dull confused murmur of these trees, the awful sound of that water in quest of which we came, that seems as though it were precipitating and dashing itself down from the lofty mountains of the moon, and that incessant hammering that wounds and pains our ears; which things all together and each of itself are enough to instil fear, dread, and dismay into the breast of Mars himself, much more into one not used to hazards and adventures of the kind. Well, then, all this that I put before thee is but an incentive and stimulant to my spirit, making my heart burst in my bosom through eagerness to engage in this adventure, arduous as it promises to be; therefore tighten Rocinante's girths a little, and God be with thee; wait for me here three days and no more, and if in that time I come not back, thou canst return to our village, and thence, to do me a favor and a service, thou wilt go to El Toboso, where thou shalt say to my incomparable lady Dulcinea that her captive knight hath died in attempting things that might make him worthy of being called hers."

When Sancho heard his master's words he began to weep in the most pathetic way, saying, "Señor, I know not why your worship wants to attempt this so dreadful adventure; it is night now, no one sees us here, we can easily turn about and take ourselves out of danger, even if we don't drink for three days to come; and as there is no one to see us, all the less will there be any one to set us down as cowards; besides, I have many a time heard the curate of our village, whom your worship knows well, preach that he who seeks danger perishes in it; so it is not right to tempt God by trying so tremendous a feat from which there can be no escape save by a miracle, and Heaven has performed enough of them for your worship in delivering you from being blanketed as I was,[25] and bringing you out victorious and safe

[25]Sancho had been tossed in a blanket at an inn on one of their adventures.

and sound from among all those enemies that were with the dead man; and if all this does not move or soften that hard heart, let this thought and reflection move it, that you will have hardly quitted this spot when from pure fear I shall yield my soul up to any one that will take it. I left home and wife and children to come and serve your worship, trusting to do better and not worse; but, as covetousness bursts the bag, it has rent my hopes asunder, for just as I had them highest about getting that wretched unlucky island your worship has so often promised me, I see that instead and in lieu of it you mean to desert me now in a place so far from human reach; for God's sake, master mine, deal not so unjustly by me, and if your worship will not entirely give up attempting this feat, at least put it off till morning, for by what the lore I learned when I was a shepherd tells me it can not want three hours of dawn now, because the mouth of the Horn is overhead and makes midnight in the line of the left arm."[26]

"How canst thou see, Sancho," said Don Quixote, "where it makes that line, or where the mouth or head is that thou talkest of, when the night is so dark that there is not a star to be seen in the whole heaven?"

"That's true," said Sancho, "but fear has sharp eyes, and sees things underground, much more above in the heavens; besides, there is good reason to show that it now wants but little of day."

"Let it want what it may," replied Don Quixote, "it shall not be said of me now or at any time that tears or entreaties turned me aside from doing what was in accordance with knightly usage; and so I beg of thee, Sancho, to hold thy peace, for God, who has put it into my heart to undertake now this so unexampled and terrible adventure, will take care to watch over my safety and console thy sorrow; what thou hast to do is to tighten Rocinante's girths well, and wait here, for I shall come back shortly, alive or dead."

Sancho perceiving it his master's final resolve, and how little his tears, counsels, and entreaties prevailed with him, determined to have recourse to his own ingenuity and compel him if he could to wait till daylight; and so, while tightening the girths of the horse, he quietly and without being felt, tied both Rocinante's fore-legs, so that when Don Quixote strove to go he was unable as the horse could only move by jumps. Seeing the success of his trick, Sancho Panza said, "See there, señor! Heaven, moved by my tears and prayers, has so ordered it that Rocinante can not stir; and if you will be obstinate, and spur and strike him, you will only provoke fortune, and kick, as they say, against the pricks."

Don Quixote at this grew desperate, but the more he drove his heels into the horse, the less he stirred him; and not having any suspicion of the tying, he was fain to resign himself and wait till daybreak or until Rocinante could move, firmly persuaded that all this came of something other than Sancho's ingenuity. So he said to him, "As it is so, Sancho, and as Rocinante can not move, I am content to wait till dawn smiles upon us, even though I weep while it delays its coming."

"There is no need to weep," answered Sancho, "for I will amuse your worship by telling stories from this till daylight, unless, indeed, you like to dismount and lie down to sleep a little on the green grass after the fashion of knights-errant, so as to be fresher when day comes and the moment arrives for attempting this extraordinary adventure you are looking forward to."

---

[26]The Little Dipper resembles a curved hunting horn. One could tell the hour by facing the horn and extending one's arms horizontally. The time was told by the position of the horn relative to the arms.

"What art thou talking about dismounting or sleeping for?" said Don Quixote. "Am I, thinkest thou, one of those knights that take their rest in the presence of danger? Sleep thou who art born to sleep, or do as thou wilt, for I will act as I think most consistent with my character."

"Be not angry, master mine," replied Sancho, "I did not mean to say that"; and coming close to him he laid one hand on the pommel of the saddle and the other on the cantle, so that he held his master's left thigh in his embrace, not daring to separate a finger's length from him; so much afraid was he of the strokes which still resounded with a regular beat. Don Quixote bade him tell some story to amuse him as he had proposed, to which Sancho replied that he would if his dread of what he heard would let him; "Still," said he, "I will strive to tell a story which, if I can manage to relate it, and it escapes me not, is the best of stories, and let your worship give me your attention, for here I begin. What was, was; and may the good that is to come be for all, and the evil for him who goes to look for it—your worship must know that the beginning the old folk used to put to their tales was not just as each one pleased; it was a maxim of Cato Zonzorino the Roman[27] that says 'the evil for him that goes to look for it,' and it comes as pat to the purpose now as ring to finger, to show that your worship should keep quiet and not go looking for evil in any quarter, and that we should go back by some other road, since nobody forces us to follow this in which so many terrors affright us."

"Go on with thy story, Sancho," said Don Quixote, "and leave the choice of our road to my care."

"I say then," continued Sancho, "that in a village of Estremadura there was a goat-shepherd—that is to say, one who tended goats—which shepherd or goatherd, as my story goes, was called Lope Ruiz, and this Lope Ruiz was in love with a shepherdess called Torralva, which shepherdess called Torralva was the daughter of a rich grazier, and this rich grazier"—

"If that is the way thou tellest thy tale, Sancho," said Don Quixote, "repeating twice all thou hast to say, thou wilt not have done these two days; go straight on with it, and tell it like a reasonable man, or else say nothing."

"Tales are always told in my country in the very way I am telling this," answered Sancho, "and I can not tell it in any other, nor is it right of your worship to ask me to make new customs."

"Tell it as thou wilt," replied Don Quixote; "and as fate will have it that I can not help listening to thee, go on."

"And so, lord of my soul," continued Sancho, "as I have said, this shepherd was in love with Torralva the shepherdess, who was a wild buxom lass with something of the look of a man about her, for she had little mustaches; I fancy I see her now."

"Then you knew her?" said Don Quixote.

"I did not know her," said Sancho, "but he who told me the story said it was so true and certain that when I told it to another I might safely declare and swear I had seen it all myself. And so in course of time, the devil, who never sleeps and puts everything in confusion, contrived that the love the shepherd bore the shepherdess turned into hatred and ill-will, and the reason, according to evil tongues, was some little jealousy she had caused him that crossed the line and trespassed on forbidden ground; and so much did the shepherd hate her from that time forward that, in order to escape from her, he determined to quit the country and go where he

---

[27] Cato Censorino, or Cato the Censor. "Cato Zonzorino" would derive from *zonzo*, Spanish for "stupid."

should never set eyes on her again. Torralva, when she found herself spurned by Lope, was immediately smitten with love for him, though she had never loved him before."

"That is the natural way of women," said Don Quixote, "to scorn the one that loves them, and love the one that hates them: go on, Sancho."

"It came to pass," said Sancho, "that the shepherd carried out his intention, and driving his goats before him took his way across the plains of Estremadura to pass over into the Kingdom of Portugal. Torralva, who knew of it, went after him, and on foot and barefooted followed him at a distance, with a pilgrim's staff in her hand and a scrip round her neck, in which she carried, it is said, a bit of looking-glass, and a piece of a comb and some little pot or other of paint for her face; but let her carry what she did, I am not going to trouble myself to prove it; all I say is, that the shepherd, they say, came with his flock to cross over the river Guadiana, which was at that time swollen and almost overflowing its banks, and at the spot he came to there was neither ferry nor boat nor any one to carry him or his flock to the other side, at which he was much vexed, for he perceived that Torralva was approaching and would give him great annoyance with her tears and entreaties; however, he went looking about so closely that he discovered a fisherman who had alongside of him a boat so small that it could only hold one person and one goat; but for all that he spoke to him and agreed with him to carry himself and his three hundred goats across. The fisherman got into the boat and carried one goat over; he came back and carried another over; he came back again, and again brought over another—let your worship keep count of the goats the fisherman is taking across, for if one escapes the memory there will be an end of the story, and it will be impossible to tell another word of it. To proceed, I must tell you the landing place on the other side was miry and slippery, and the fisherman lost a great deal of time in going and coming; still he returned for another goat, and another, and another."

"Take it for granted he brought them all across," said Don Quixote, "and don't keep going and coming in this way, or thou wilt not make an end of bringing them over this twelve-month."

"How many have gone across so far?" said Sancho.

"How the devil do I know?" replied Don Quixote.

"There it is," said Sancho, "what I told you, that you must keep a good count; well then, by God, there is an end of the story, for there is no going any farther."

"How can that be?" said Don Quixote; "is it so essential to the story to know to a nicety the goats that have crossed over, that if there be a mistake of one in the reckoning, thou canst not go on with it?"

"No, señor, not a bit," replied Sancho; "for when I asked your worship to tell me how many goats had crossed, and you answered you did not know, at that very instant all I had to say passed away out of my memory, and faith, there was much virtue in it, and entertainment."

"So, then," said Don Quixote, "the story has come to an end?"

"As much as my mother has," said Sancho.

"In truth," said Don Quixote, "thou hast told one of the rarest stories, tales, or histories, that any one in the world could have imagined, and such a way of telling it and ending it was never seen nor will be in a lifetime; though I expected nothing else from thy excellent understanding. But I do not wonder, for perhaps those ceaseless strokes may have confused thy wits."

"All that may be," replied Sancho, "but I know that as to my story, all that can be said is that it ends there where the mistake in the count of the passage of the goats begins."

"Let it end where it will, well and good," said Don Quixote, "and let us see if Rocinante can go"; and again he spurred him, and again Rocinante made jumps and remained where he was, so well tied was he.

Just then, whether it was the cold of the morning that was now approaching, or that he had eaten something laxative at supper, or that it was only natural (as is most likely), Sancho felt a desire to do what no one could do for him; but so great was the fear that had penetrated his heart, he dared not separate himself from his master by so much as the black of his nail; to escape doing what he wanted was, however, also impossible; so what he did for peace' sake was to remove his right hand, which held the back of the saddle, and with it to untie gently and silently the running string which alone held up his breeches, so that on loosening it they at once fell down round his feet like fetters; he then raised his shirt as well as he could and bared his hind quarters, no slim ones. But this accomplished, which he fancied was all he had to do to get out of this terrible strait and embarrassment, another still greater difficulty presented itself, for it seemed to him impossible to relieve himself without making some noise, and he ground his teeth and squeezed his shoulders together, holding his breath as much as he could; but in spite of his precautions he was unlucky enough after all to make a little noise, very different from that which was causing him so much fear.

Don Quixote, hearing it, said, "What noise is that, Sancho?"

"I don't know, señor," said he; "it must be something new, for adventures and misadventures never begin with a trifle." Once more he tried his luck, and succeeded so well, that without any further noise or disturbance he found himself relieved of the burden that had given him so much discomfort. But as Don Quixote's sense of smell was as acute as his hearing, and as Sancho was so closely linked with him that the fumes rose almost in a straight line, it could not be but that some should reach his nose, and as soon as they did he came to its relief by compressing it between his fingers, saying in a rather snuffling tone, "Sancho, it strikes me thou art in great fear."

"I am," answered Sancho; "but how does your worship perceive it now more than ever?"

"Because just now thou smellest stronger than ever, and not of ambergris," answered Don Quixote.

"Very likely," said Sancho, "but that's not my fault, but your worship's, for leading me about at unseasonable hours and at such unwonted paces."

"Then go back three or four, my friend," said Don Quixote, all the time with his fingers to his nose; "and for the future pay more attention to thy person and to what thou owest to mine; for it is my great familiarity with thee that has bred this contempt."

"I'll bet," replied Sancho, "that your worship thinks I have done something I ought not with my person."

"It makes it worse to stir it, friend Sancho," returned Don Quixote.

With this and other talk of the same sort master and man passed the night, till Sancho, perceiving that daybreak was coming on apace, very cautiously untied Rocinante and tied up his breeches. As soon as Rocinante found himself free, though by nature he was not at all mettlesome, he seemed to feel lively and began pawing—for as to capering, begging his pardon, he knew not what it meant. Don Quixote, then, observing that Rocinante could move, took it as a good sign and a signal that he should attempt the dread adventure. By this time day had fully broken and everything showed distinctly, and Don Quixote saw that he was among some tall trees, chestnuts, which cast a very deep shade; he perceived likewise that the sound of the strokes did not cease, but could not discover what caused it, and so without any further delay he let Rocinante feel the spur, and once more taking leave of Sancho, he told him to wait for him there three days at most, as he had said before, and if he should not have returned by that time, he might feel sure it had been God's will that he should end his days in that perilous adventure. He again repeated the message and commission with which he was to go on his behalf to his lady Dulcinea, and said he was not to be uneasy as to the payment of his services, for before leaving home he had made his will, in which he would find himself fully recompensed in the matter of wages in due proportion to the time he had served; but if God delivered him safe, sound, and unhurt out of that danger, he might look upon the promised island as much more than certain. Sancho began weeping afresh on again hearing the affecting words of his good master, and resolved to stay with him until the final issue and end of the business. From these tears and this honorable resolve of Sancho Panza's the author of this history infers that he must have been of good birth and at least an old Christian;[28] and the feeling he displayed touched his master somewhat, but not so much as to make him show any weakness; on the contrary, hiding what he felt as well as he could, he began to move towards that quarter whence the sound of the water and of the strokes seemed to come.

Sancho followed him on foot, leading by the halter, as his custom was, his ass, his constant comrade in prosperity or adversity; and advancing some distance through the shady chestnut trees they came up on a little meadow at the foot of some high rocks, down which a mighty rush of water flung itself. At the foot of the rocks were some rudely constructed houses looking more like ruins than houses, from among which came, they perceived, the din and clatter of blows, which still continued without intermission. Rocinante took fright at the noise of the water and of the blows, but quieting him Don Quixote advanced step by step towards the houses, commending himself with all his heart to his lady, imploring her support in that dread pass and enterprise, and on the way commended himself to God, too, not to forget him. Sancho, who never quitted his side, stretched his neck as far as he could and peered between the legs of Rocinante to see if he could now discover what it was that caused him such fear and apprehension. They went it might be a hundred paces farther, when on turning a corner the true cause, beyond the possibility of any mistake, of that dread-sounding and to them awe-inspiring noise that had kept them all the night in such fear and perplexity, appeared plain and obvious; and it was (if, reader, thou art not disgusted and disappointed) six fulling hammers which by their alternate strokes made all the din.[29]

When Don Quixote perceived what it was, he was struck dumb and rigid from head to foot. Sancho glanced at him and saw him with his head bent down upon his breast in manifest mortification; and Don Quixote glanced at Sancho and saw him with his cheeks puffed out and his mouth full of laughter, and evidently ready to explode with it, and in spite of his vexation he could not help laughing at the sight of him; and when Sancho saw his master begin he let go so heartily that he had to hold his sides with both hands to keep himself from bursting with laughter. Four times he stopped, and as many times did his laughter break out afresh with the same violence as at first, whereat Don Quixote grew furious, above all when he heard him say mockingly, "Thou must know, friend Sancho, that of Heaven's will I was born in this our iron age to revive in it the golden or age of gold; I am

[28]One who had no trace of Moorish or Jewish blood in his veins.

[29]The sound came from a wool-finishing mill, where heavy hammers pounded cloth for hours on end.

he for whom are reserved perils, mighty achievements, valiant deeds"; and here he went on repeating all or most of the words that Don Quixote uttered the first time they heard the awful strokes.

Don Quixote, then, seeing that Sancho was turning him into ridicule, was so mortified and vexed that he lifted up his pike and smote him two such blows that if, instead of catching them on his shoulders, he had caught them on his head, there would have been no wages to pay, unless indeed to his heirs. Sancho seeing that he was getting an awkward return in earnest for his jest, and fearing his master might carry it still further, said to him very humbly, "Calm yourself, sir, for by God I am only joking."

"Well, then, if you are joking I am not," replied Don Quixote. "Look here, my lively gentleman, if these, instead of being fulling hammers, had been some perilous adventure, have I not, think you, shown the courage required for the attempt and achievement? Am I, perchance, being, as I am, a gentleman, bound to know and distinguish sounds and tell whether they come from fulling mills or not; and that, when perhaps, as is the case, I have never in my life seen any as you have, low boor as you are, that have been born and bred among them? But turn me these six hammers into six giants, and bring them to beard me, one by one or all together, and if I do not knock them head over heels, then make what mockery you like of me."

"No more of that, señor," returned Sancho; "I own I went a little far with the joke. But tell me, your worship, now that peace is made between us (and may God bring you out of all the adventures that may befall you as safe and sound as He has brought you out of this one), was it not a thing to laugh at, and is it not a good story, the great fear we were in?—at least that I was in; for as to your worship I see now that you neither know nor understand what either fear or dismay is."

"I do not deny," said Don Quixote, "that what happened to us may be worth laughing at, but it is not worth making a story about, for it is not every one that is shrewd enough to hit the right point of a thing."

"At any rate," said Sancho, "your worship knew how to hit the right point with your pike, aiming at my head and hitting me on the shoulders, thanks be to God and my own smartness in dodging it. But let that pass; all will come out in the scouring; for I have heard say 'he loves thee well that makes thee weep'; and moreover that it is the way with great lords after any hard words they give a servant to give him a pair of breeches; though I do not know what they give after blows, unless it be that knights-errant after blows give islands, or kingdoms on the mainland."

"It may be on the dice," said Don Quixote, "that all thou sayest will come true; overlook the past, for thou art shrewd enough to know that our first movements are not in our own control; and one thing for the future bear in mind, that thou curb and restrain thy loquacity in my company; for in all the books of chivalry that I have read, and they are innumerable, I never met with a squire who talked so much to his lord as thou dost to thine; and in fact I feel it to be a great fault of thine and of mine: of thine, that thou hast so little respect for me; of mine, that I do not make myself more respected. There was Gandalin, the squire of Amadis of Gaul, that was Count of the Insula Firme, and we read of him that he always addressed his lord with his cap in his hand, his head bowed down and his body bent double, *more turquesco*.[30] And then, what shall we say of Gasabal, the squire of Galaor, who was so silent that in order to indicate to us

[30]"In Turkish fashion."

the greatness of his marvellous taciturnity his name is only once mentioned in the whole of that history, as long as it is truthful? From all I have said thou wilt gather, Sancho, that there must be a difference between master and man, between lord and lackey, between knight and squire: so that from this day forward in our intercourse we must observe more respect and take less liberties, for in whatever way I may be provoked with you it will be bad for the pitcher. The favors and benefits that I have promised you will come in due time, and if they do not your wages at least will not be lost, as I have already told you."

"All that your worship says is very well," said Sancho, "but I should like to know (in case the time of favors should not come, and it might be necessary to fall back upon wages) how much did the squire of a knight-errant get in those days, and did they agree by the month, or by the day like bricklayers?"

"I do not believe," replied Don Quixote, "that such squires were ever on wages, but were dependent on favor; and if I have now mentioned thine in the sealed will I have left at home, it was with a view to what may happen; for as yet I know not how chivalry will turn out in these wretched times of ours, and I do not wish my soul to suffer for trifles in the other world; for I would have thee know, Sancho, that in this there is no condition more hazardous than that of adventures."

"That is true," said Sancho, "since the mere noise of the hammers of a fulling mill can disturb and disquiet the heart of such a valiant errant adventurer as your worship; but you may be sure I will not open my lips henceforward to make light of anything of your worship's, but only to honor you as my master and natural lord."

"By so doing," replied Don Quixote, "shalt thou live long on the face of the earth; for next to parents, masters are to be respected as though they were parents."

. . .

FROM

Chapter 25

Which treats of the strange things that happened to the stout knight of La Mancha in the Sierra Morena, and of his imitation of the penance of Beltenebros

. . . They reached the foot of a high mountain which stood like an isolated peak among the others that surrounded it. Past its base there flowed a gentle brook, all around it spread a meadow so green and luxuriant that it was a delight to the eyes to look upon it, and forest trees in abundance, and shrubs and flowers, added to the charms of the spot. Upon this place the Knight of the Rueful Countenance fixed his choice for the performance of his penance, and as he beheld it exclaimed in a loud voice as though he were out of his senses, "This is the place, oh, ye heavens, that I select and choose for bewailing the misfortune in which ye yourselves have plunged me: this is the spot where the overflowings of mine eyes shall swell the waters of yon little brook, and my deep and endless sighs shall stir unceasingly the leaves of these mountain trees, in testimony and token of the pain my persecuted heart is suffering. Oh, ye rural deities, whoever ye be that haunt this lone spot, give ear to the complaint of a wretched lover whom long absence and brooding jealousy have driven to bewail his fate among these wilds and complain of the hard heart of that fair and ungrateful one, the end and limit of all human beauty! Oh, ye wood nymphs and dryads, that dwell in the thickets of the forest, so may the nimble wanton satyrs by whom ye are vainly wooed never disturb your sweet repose, help me to lament my hard fate or at least weary not at listening to it! Oh, Dulcinea del Toboso, day of my night, glory of my pain, guide of my path, star of my fortune, so may Heaven grant thee in full all thou seekest of it, bethink thee of the place and condition to which absence from thee has brought me, and make that return in kindness that is due to my fidelity! Oh, lonely trees, that from this day forward shall bear me company in my solitude, give me some sign by the gentle movement of your boughs that my presence is not distasteful to you! Oh, thou, my squire, pleasant companion in my prosperous and adverse fortunes, fix well in thy memory what thou shalt see me do here, so that thou mayest relate and report it to the sole cause of all," and so saying he dismounted from Rocinante, and in an instant relieved him of saddle and bridle, and giving him a slap on the croup, said, "He gives thee freedom who is bereft of it himself, oh steed as excellent in deed as thou art unfortunate in thy lot; begone where thou wilt, for thou bearest written on thy forehead that neither Astolfo's hippogriff, nor the famed Frontino that cost Bradamante so dear, could equal thee in speed."[31]

Seeing this Sancho said, "Good luck to him who has saved us the trouble of stripping the pack-saddle off Dapple! By my faith he would not have gone without a slap on the croup and something said in his praise; though if he were here I would not let any one strip him, for there would be no occasion, as he had nothing of the lover or victim of despair about him, inasmuch as his master, which I was while it was God's pleasure, was nothing of the sort; and indeed, Sir Knight of the Rueful Countenance, if my departure and your worship's madness are to come off in earnest, it will be as well to saddle Rocinante again in order that he may supply the want of Dapple, because it will save me time in going and returning; for if I go on foot I don't know when I shall get there or when I shall get back, as I am, in truth, a bad walker."

"I declare, Sancho," returned Don Quixote, "it shall be as thou wilt, for thy plan does not seem to me a bad one, and three days hence thou wilt depart, for I wish thee to observe in the mean time what I do and say for her sake, that thou mayest be able to tell it." . . .

Don Quixote took out the note-book, and, retiring to one side, very deliberately began to write the letter, and when he had finished it he called to Sancho, saying he wished to read it to him, so that he might commit it to memory, in case of losing it on the road; for with evil fortune like his anything might be apprehended. To which Sancho replied, "Write it two or three times there in the book and give it to me, and I will carry it very carefully, because to expect me to keep it in my memory is all nonsense, for I have such a bad one that I often forget my own name; but for all that repeat it to me, as I shall like to hear it, for surely it will run as if it was in print."

"Listen," said Don Quixote, "this is what it says:

DON QUIXOTE'S LETTER TO DULCINEA DEL TOBOSO

SOVEREIGN AND EXALTED LADY, The pierced by the point of absence, the wounded to the heart's core, sends thee, sweetest Dulcinea del Toboso, the health that he himself enjoys not. If thy beauty despises me, if thy worth is not for me, if thy scorn is my affliction, though I be sufficiently long-suffering, hardly shall I endure this anxiety, which, besides being oppressive, is protracted. My good Squire Sancho will relate to thee in full, fair ingrate, dear enemy, the condition to which I am reduced on thy account; if it be thy pleasure to give me relief, I am thine; if not, do as may be pleasing to thee; for by ending my life I shall satisfy thy cruelty and my desire.

Thine till death,
THE KNIGHT OF THE RUEFUL COUNTENANCE

[31] In Aristo's *Orlando Furioso*, Astolfo's hippogriff was a winged horse; Frontino was the horse of Ruggiero, Bradamante's lover.

"By the life of my father," said Sancho, when he heard the letter, "it is the loftiest thing I ever heard. Body of me! how your worship says everything as you like in it! And how well you fit in 'The Knight of the Rueful Countenance' into the signature. I declare your worship is indeed the very devil, and there is nothing you don't know."

"Everything is needed for the calling I follow," said Don Quixote.

"Now then," said Sancho, "let your worship put the order for the three ass-colts on the other side, and sign it very plainly, that they may recognize it at first sight."

"With all my heart," said Don Quixote, and as soon as he had written it he read it to this effect:

> MISTRESS NIECE, By this first of ass-colts please pay to Sancho Panza, my squire, three of the five I left at home in your charge: said three ass-colts to be paid and delivered for the same number received here in hand, which upon this and upon his receipt shall be duly paid. Done in the heart of the Sierra Morena, the twenty-seventh of August of this present year.

"That will do," said Sancho; "now let your worship sign it."

"There is no need to sign it," said Don Quixote, "but merely to put my flourish, which is the same as a signature, and enough for three asses, or even three hundred."

"I can trust your worship," returned Sancho; "let me go and saddle Rocinante, and be ready to give me your blessing, for I mean to go at once without seeing the fooleries your worship is going to do; I'll say I saw you do so many that she will not want any more." . . .

"Do you know what I am afraid of?" said Sancho upon this; "that I shall not be able to find my way back to this spot where I am leaving you, it is such an out-of-the-way place."

"Observe the landmarks well," said Don Quixote, "for I will try not to go far from this neighborhood, and I will even take care to mount the highest of these rocks to see if I can discover thee returning; however, not to miss me and lose thyself, the best plan will be to cut some branches of the broom that is so abundant about here, and as thou goest to lay them at intervals until thou hast come out upon the plain; these will serve thee, after the fashion of the clew in the labyrinth of Theseus, as marks and signs for finding me on thy return."

"So I will," said Sancho Panza, and having cut some, he asked his master's blessing, and not without many tears on both sides took his leave of him, and mounting Rocinante, of whom Don Quixote charged him earnestly to have as much care as of his own person, he set out for the plain, strewing at intervals the branches of broom as his master had recommended him; and so he went his way, though Don Quixote still entreated him to see him do were it only a couple of mad acts. He had not gone a hundred paces, however, when he returned and said, "I must say, señor, your worship said quite right, that in order to be able to swear without a weight on my conscience that I had seen you do mad things, it would be well for me to see if it were only one; though in your worship's remaining here I have seen a very great one."

"Did I not tell thee so?" said Don Quixote. "Wait, Sancho, and I will do them in the saying of a *credo,*" and pulling off his breeches in all haste he stripped himself to his skin and his shirt, and then, without more ado, he cut a couple of *gambados* in the air, and a couple of somersaults, heels over head, making such a display that, not to see it a second time, Sancho wheeled Rocinante round, and felt easy, and satisfied in his mind that he could swear he had left his master mad; and so we will leave him to follow his road until his return, which was a quick one.

. . .

FROM

Chapter 31

Of the delectable discussion between Don Quixote and Sancho Panza, his squire, together with other incidents

"All that is not unsatisfactory to me," said Don Quixote. "Go on; thou didst reach her; and what was that queen of beauty doing? Surely thou didst find her stringing pearls, or embroidering some device in gold thread for this her enslaved knight."

"I did not," said Sancho, "but I found her winnowing two bushels of wheat in the yard of her house."

"Then depend upon it," said Don Quixote, "the grains of that wheat were pearls when touched by her hands; and didst thou look, friend? was it white wheat or brown?"

"It was neither, but red," said Sancho.

"Then I promise thee," said Don Quixote, "that, winnowed by her hands, beyond a doubt the bread it made was of the whitest; but go on; when thou gavest her my letter, did she kiss it? Did she place it on her head? Did she perform any ceremony befitting such a letter, or what did she do?"

"When I went to give it to her," replied Sancho, "she was hard at it swaying from side to side with a lot of wheat she had in the sieve, and she said to me, 'Lay the letter, friend, on the top of that sack, for I can not read it until I have done sifting all this.' "

"Discreet lady!" said Don Quixote; "that was in order to read it at her leisure and enjoy it; proceed, Sancho; while she was engaged in her occupation what converse did she hold with thee? What did she ask about me, and what answer didst thou give? Make haste; tell me all, and let not an atom be left behind in the ink-bottle."

"She asked me nothing," said Sancho; "but I told her how your worship was left doing penance in her service, naked from the waist up, in among these mountains like a savage, sleeping on the ground, not eating bread off a tablecloth nor combing your beard, weeping and cursing your fortune."

"In saying I cursed my fortune thou saidst wrong," said Don Quixote; "for rather do I bless it and shall bless it all the days of my life for having made me worthy of aspiring to love so lofty a lady as Dulcinea del Toboso."

"And so lofty she is," said Sancho, "that she overtops me by more than a hand's-breadth."

"What! Sancho," said Don Quixote, "didst thou measure with her?"

"I measured in this way," said Sancho; "going to help her to put a sack of wheat on the back of an ass, we came so close together that I could see she stood more than a good palm over me."

"Well!" said Don Quixote, "and doth she not of a truth accompany and adorn this greatness with a thousand million charms of mind! But one thing thou wilt not deny, Sancho; when thou camest close to her didst thou not perceive a Sabæan[32] odor, an aromatic fragrance, a, I know not what, delicious, that I can not find a name for; I mean a redolence, an exhalation, as if thou wert in the shop of some dainty glover?"

"All I can say is," said Sancho, "that I did perceive a little odor, something goaty; it must have been that she was all in a sweat with hard work."

"It could not be that," said Don Quixote, "but thou must have been suffering from cold in the head, or must have smelt thyself; for I know well what would be the scent of that rose among thorns, that lily of the field, that dissolved amber."

[32]From Saba or Sheba, an area known for perfume.

"Maybe so," replied Sancho; "there often comes from myself that same odor which then seemed to me to come from her grace the lady Dulcinea; but that's no wonder, for one devil is like another."

"Well then," continued Don Quixote, "now she has done sifting the corn and sent it to the mill; what did she do when she read the letter?"

"As for the letter," said Sancho, "she did not read it, for she said she could neither read nor write; instead of that she tore it up into small pieces, saying that she did not want to let any one read it lest her secrets should become known in the village, and that what I had told her by word of mouth about the love your worship bore her, and the extraordinary penance you were doing for her sake, was enough; and, to make an end of it, she told me to tell your worship that she kissed your hands, and that she had a greater desire to see you than to write to you; and that therefore she entreated and commanded you, on sight of this present, to come out of these thickets, and to have done with carrying on absurdities, and to set out at once for El Toboso, unless something else of greater importance should happen, for she had a great desire to see your worship. She laughed greatly when I told her how your worship was called the Knight of the Rueful Countenance; I asked her if that Biscayan the other day had been there; and she told me he had, and that he was a very honest fellow; I asked her too about the galley slaves, but she said she had not seen any yet."

"So far all goes well," said Don Quixote; "but tell me what jewel was it that she gave thee on taking thy leave, in return for thy tidings of me? For it is a usual and ancient custom with knights and ladies errant to give the squires, damsels, or dwarfs who bring tidings of their ladies to the knights, or of their knights to the ladies, some rich jewel as a guerdon for good news, and acknowledgment of the message."

"That is likely," said Sancho, "and a good custom it was, to my mind; but that must have been in days gone by, for now it would seem to be the custom only to give a piece of bread and cheese; because that was what my lady Dulcinea gave me over the top of the yard-wall when I took leave of her; and more by token it was sheep's-milk cheese."

"She is generous in the extreme," said Don Quixote, "and if she did not give thee a jewel of gold, no doubt it must have been because she had not one to hand there to give thee, but sleeves are good after Easter; I shall see her and all shall be made right. But knowest thou what amazes me, Sancho? It seems to me thou must have gone and come through the air, for thou has taken but little more than three days to go to El Toboso and return, though it is more than thirty leagues from here to there. From which I am inclined to think that the sage magician who is my friend, and watches over my interests (for of necessity there is and must be one, or else I should not be a right knight-errant), that this same, I say, must have helped thee to travel without thy knowledge; for some of these sages will catch up a knight-errant sleeping in his bed, and without his knowing how or in what way it happened, he wakes up the next day more than a thousand leagues away from the place where he went to sleep. And if it were not for this, knights-errant would not be able to give aid to one another in peril, as they do at every turn. For a knight, maybe, is fighting in the mountains of Armenia with some dragon, or fierce serpent, or another knight, and gets the worst of the battle, and is at the point of death; but when he least looks for it, there appears over against him on a cloud, or chariot of fire, another knight, a friend of his, who just before had been in England, and who takes his part, and delivers him from death; and at night he finds himself in his own quarters supping very much to his satisfaction; and yet from one place to the other will have been two or three thousand leagues. And all this is done by the craft and skill of the sage enchanters who take care of those valiant knights; so that, friend Sancho, I find no difficulty in believing that thou mayest have gone from this place to El Toboso and returned in such a short time, since, as I have said, some friendly sage must have carried thee through the air without thee perceiving it." . . .

FROM

Chapter 50

Of the shrewd controversy which Don Quixote and the Canon held, together with other incidents

"A good joke, that!' returned Don Quixote. "Books that have been printed with the king's license, and with the approbation of those to whom they have been submitted, and read with universal delight, and extolled by great and small, rich and poor, learned and ignorant, gentle and simple, in a word by people of every sort, of whatever rank or condition they may be—that these should be lies! And above all when they carry such an appearance of truth with them; for they tell us the father, mother, country, kindred, age, place, and the achievements, step by step, and day by day, performed by such and such a knight or knights! Hush, sir; utter not such blasphemy; trust me I am advising you now to act as a sensible man should; only read them, and you will see the pleasure you will derive from them. For, come, tell me, can there be anything more delightful than to see, as it were, here now displayed before us a vast lake of bubbling pitch with a host of snakes and serpents and lizards, and ferocious and terrible creatures of all sorts swimming about in it, while from the middle of the lake there comes a plaintive voice saying: 'Knight, whosoever thou art who beholdest this dread lake, if thou wouldst win the prize that lies hidden beneath these dusky waves, prove the valor of thy stout heart and cast thyself into the midst of its dark burning waters, else thou shalt not be worthy to see the mighty wonders contained in the seven castles of the seven Fays that lie beneath this black expanse'; and then the knight, almost ere the awful voice has ceased, without stopping to consider, without pausing to reflect upon the danger to which he is exposing himself, without even relieving himself of the weight of his massive armor, commending himself to God and to his lady, plunges into the mist of the boiling lake, and when he little looks for it, or knows what his fate is to be, he finds himself among flowery meadows, with which the Elysian fields are not to be compared. The sky seems more transparent there, and the sun shines with a strange brilliancy, and a delightful grove of green leafy trees presents itself to the eyes and charms the sight with its verdure, while the ear is soothed by the sweet untutored melody of the countless birds of gay plumage that flit to and fro among the interlacing branches. Here he sees a brook whose limpid waters, like liquid crystal, ripple over fine sands and white pebbles that look like sifted gold and purest pearls. There he perceives a cunningly wrought fountain of many-colored jasper and polished marble; here another of rustic fashion where the little mussel-shells and the spiral white and yellow mansions of the snail disposed in studious disorder, mingled with fragments of glittering crystal and mock emeralds, make up a work of varied aspect, where art, imitating nature, seems to have outdone it. Suddenly there is presented to his sight a strong castle or gorgeous palace with walls of massy gold, turrets of diamond and gates of jacinth; in short, so marvellous is its structure that though the materials of which it is built are nothing less than diamonds, carbuncles, rubies, pearls, gold, and emeralds, the workmanship is still more rare. And after having seen all this, what can be more charming than to see how a bevy of damsels comes forth from the gate of the castle in gay and gorgeous attire, such that, were I to set myself now to depict it as the histories describe it to us, I should never have done; and then how she who seems to be the first among them all takes the bold knight who plunged into the boiling lake by the hand, and without addressing a word to him leads him into the rich palace or castle, and strips him as naked as when his mother bore him, and bathes him in lukewarm water, and anoints him all over with sweet-smelling unguents, and clothes him in a shirt of the softest sendal, all scented and perfumed, while another damsel comes and throws over his shoulders a mantle which is said to be worth at the very least a city, and even more? How charming it is, then, when they tell us how, after all this, they lead him to another chamber where he finds the tables set out in such style that he is filled with amazement and wonder; to see how they pour out water for his hands distilled from amber and sweet-scented flowers; how they seat him on an ivory chair; to see how the damsels wait on him all in profound silence; how they bring him such a variety of dainties so temptingly prepared that the appetite is at a loss which to select; to hear the music that resounds while he is at table, by whom or whence produced he knows not. And then when the repast is over and the tables removed, for the knight to recline in the chair, picking his teeth perhaps as usual, and a damsel, much lovelier than any of the others, to enter unexpectedly by the chamber door, and seat herself by his side, and begin to tell him what the castle is, and how she is held enchanted there, and other things that amaze the knight and astonish the readers who are perusing his history. But I will not expatiate any further upon this, as it may be gathered from it that whatever part of whatever history of a knight-errant one reads, it will fill the reader, whoever he be, with delight and wonder; and take my advice, sir, and, as I said before, read these books and you will see how they will banish any melancholy you may feel and raise your spirits should they be depressed. For myself I can say that since I have been a knight-errant I have become valiant, polite, generous, well-bred, magnanimous, courteous, dauntless, gentle, patient, and have learned to bear hardships, imprisonments, and enchantments; and though it be such a short time since I have seen myself shut up in a cage like a madman, I hope by the might of my arm, if Heaven aid me and fortune thwart me not, to see myself king of some kingdom where I may be able to show the gratitude and generosity that dwell in my heart; for by my faith, señor, the poor man is incapacitated from showing the virtue of generosity to any one, though he may possess it in the highest degree; and gratitude that consists of disposition only is a dead thing, just as faith without works is dead. For this reason I should be glad were fortune soon to offer me some opportunity of making myself an emperor, so as to show my heart in doing good to my friends, particularly to this poor Sancho Panza, my squire, who is the best fellow in the world; and I would gladly give him a county I have promised him this ever so long, only that I am afraid he has not the capacity to govern his realm."

Sancho partly heard these last words of his master, and said to him, "Strive hard you, Señor Don Quixote, to give me that county so often promised by you and so long looked for by me, for I promise you there will be no want of capacity in me to govern it; and even if there is, I have heard say there are men in the world who farm seigniories, paying so much a year, and they themselves taking charge of the government, while the lord, with his legs stretched out, enjoys the revenue they pay him, without troubling himself about anything else. That's what I'll do, and not stand haggling over trifles, but wash my hands at once of the whole business, and enjoy my rents like a duke, and let things go their own way."

"That, brother Sancho," said the canon, "only holds good as far as the enjoyment of the revenue goes; but the lord of the seigniory must attend to the administration of justice, and here capacity and sound judgment come in, and above all a firm determination to find out the truth; for if this be wanting in the beginning, the middle and the end will always go wrong; and God as commonly aids the honest intentions of the simple as he frustrates the evil designs of the crafty."

"I don't understand those philosophies," returned Sancho Panza; "all I know is I would I had the county as soon as I shall know how to govern it; for I have as much soul as another, and as much body as any one, and I shall be as much king of my realm as any other of his; and being so I should do as I liked, and doing as I liked I should please myself, and pleasing myself I should be content, and when one is content he has nothing more to desire, and when one has nothing more to desire there is an end of it; so let the county come, and God be with you, and let us see one another, as one blind man said to the other."

"That is not bad philosophy thou art talking, Sancho," said the canon; "but for all that there is a good deal to be said on this matter of counties."

To which Don Quixote returned, "I know not what more there is to be said; I only guide myself by the example set me by the great Amadis of Gaul, when he made his squire count of the Insula Firme; and so, without any scruples of conscience, I can make a count of Sancho Panza, for he is one of the best squires that ever knight-errant had."

The canon was astonished at the methodical nonsense (if nonsense be capable of method) that Don Quixote uttered, at the way in which he had described the adventure of the knight of the lake, at the impression that the deliberate lies of the books he read had made upon him, and lastly he marvelled at the simplicity of Sancho, who desired so eagerly to obtain the county his master had promised him. . . .

Part II

Chapter 3

Of the laughable conversation that passed between Don Quixote, Sancho Panza, and the Bachelor Samson Carrasco

Don Quixote remained very deep in thought, waiting for the bachelor Carrasco,[33] from whom he was to hear how he himself had been put into a book as Sancho said; and he could not persuade himself that any such history could be in existence, for the blood of the enemies he had slain was not yet dry on the blade of his sword, and now they wanted to make out that his mighty achievements were going about in print. For all that, he fancied some sage, either a friend or an enemy, might, by the aid of magic, have given them to the press; if a friend, in order to magnify and exalt them above the most famous ever achieved by any knight-errant; if an enemy, to bring them to naught and degrade them below the meanest ever recorded of any low squire, though, as he said to himself, the achievements of squires never were recorded. If, however, it were the fact that such a history were in existence, it must necessarily, being the story of a knight-errant, be grandiloquent, lofty, imposing, grand and true. With this he comforted himself somewhat, though it made him uncomfortable to think that the author was a Moor, judging by the title of "Cid";[34] and that no truth was to be looked for from Moors, as they are all impostors, cheats, and schemers. He was afraid he might have dealt with his love affairs in some indecorous fashion, that might tend to the discredit and prejudice of the purity of his lady Dulcinea del Toboso; he would have had him set

[33]A young man from La Mancha who has just earned his bachelor's degree at the University of Salamanca and returned home. He informs the Don that his story has been published in a book.

[34]Carrasco has told Sancho that the author of Don Quixote's adventures is called Cid Hamet Benengele.

forth the fidelity and respect he had always observed towards her, spurning queens, empresses, and damsels of all sorts, and keeping in check the impetuosity of his natural impulses. Absorbed and wrapped up in these and divers other cogitations, he was found by Sancho and Carrasco, whom Don Quixote received with great courtesy.

The bachelor, though he was called Samson, was of no great bodily size, but he was a very great wag; he was of a sallow complexion, but very sharp-witted, somewhere about four-and-twenty years of age, with a round face, flat nose, and a large mouth, all indications of a mischievous disposition and a love of fun and jokes; and of this he gave a sample as soon as he saw Don Quixote, by falling on his knees before him and saying, "Let me kiss your mightiness's hand, Señor Don Quixote of La Mancha, for, by the habit of St. Peter that I wear, though I have no more than the first four orders, your worship is one of the most famous knights-errant that have ever been, or will be, all the world over. A blessing on Cid Hamet Benengeli, who has written the history of your great deeds, and a double blessing on that connoisseur who took the trouble of having it translated out of the Arabic into our Castilian vulgar tongue for the universal entertainment of the people!"

Don Quixote made him rise, and said, "So, then, it is true that there is a history of me, and that it was a Moor and a sage who wrote it?"

"So true is it, señor," said Samson, "that my belief is there are more than twelve thousand volumes of the said history in print this very day. Only ask Portugal, Barcelona, and Valencia, where they have been printed, and moreover there is a report that it is being printed at Antwerp, and I am persuaded there will not be a country or language in which there will not be a translation of it."

"One of the things," here observed Don Quixote, "that ought to give most pleasure to a virtuous and eminent man is to find himself in his lifetime in print and in type, familiar in people's mouths with a good name; I say with a good name, for if it be the opposite, then there is no death to be compared to it."

"If it goes by good name and fame," said the bachelor, "your worship alone bears away the palm from all the knights-errant; for the Moor in his own language, and the Christian in his, have taken care to set before us your gallantry, your high courage in encountering dangers, your fortitude in adversity, your patience under misfortunes as well as wounds, the purity and continence of the platonic loves of your worship and my lady Doña Dulcinea del Toboso"—

"I never heard my lady Dulcinea called Doña," observed Sancho here; "nothing more than the lady Dulcinea del Toboso; so here already the history is wrong."

"That is not an objection of any importance," replied Carrasco.

"Certainly not," said Don Quixote; "but tell me, señor bachelor, what deeds of mine are they that are made most of in this history?"

"On that point," replied the bachelor, "opinions differ, as tastes do; some swear by the adventure of the windmills that your worship took to be Briareuses and giants; others by that of the fulling mills; one cries up the description of the two armies that afterwards took the appearance of two droves of sheep; another that of the dead body on its way to be buried at Segovia; a third says the liberation of the galley slaves is the best of all, and a fourth that nothing comes up to the affair with the Benedictine giants, and the battle with the valiant Biscayan."[35]

"Tell me, señor bachelor," said Sancho at this point, "does the adventure with the Yanguesans come in, when our good Rocinante went hankering after dainties?"

---

[35]These are all episodes from Part I.

"The sage has left nothing in the ink-bottle," replied Samson; "he tells all and sets down everything, even to the capers the worthy Sancho cut in the blanket."

"I cut no capers in the blanket," returned Sancho; "in the air I did, and more of them than I liked."

"There is no human history in the world, I suppose," said Don Quixote, "that has not its ups and downs, but more than others such as deal with chivalry, for they can never be entirely made up of prosperous adventures."

"For all that," replied the bachelor, "there are those who have read the history who say they would have been glad if the author had left out some of the countless cudgellings that were inflicted on Señor Don Quixote in various encounters."

"That's where the truth of the history comes in," said Sancho.

"At the same time they might fairly have passed them over in silence," observed Don Quixote; "for there is no need of recording events which do not change or affect the truth of a history, if they tend to bring the hero of it into contempt. Æneas was not in truth and earnest so pious as Virgil represents him, nor Ulysses so wise as Homer describes him."

"That is true," said Samson; "but it is one thing to write as a poet, another to write as a historian; the poet may describe or sing things, not as they were, but as they ought to have been; but the historian has to write them down, not as they ought to have been, but as they were, without adding anything to the truth or taking anything from it."

"Well then," said Sancho, "if this señor Moor goes in for telling the truth, no doubt among my master's drubbings mine are to be found; for they never took the measure of his worship's shoulders without doing the same for my whole body; but I have no right to wonder at that, for, as my master himself says, the members must share the pain of the head."

"You are a sly dog, Sancho," said Don Quixote; "i' faith, you have no want of memory when you choose to remember."

"If I were to try to forget the thwacks they gave me," said Sancho, "my weals would not let me, for they are still fresh on my ribs."

"Hush, Sancho," said Don Quixote, "and don't interrupt the bachelor, whom I entreat to go on and tell me all that is said about me in this same history."

"And about me," said Sancho, "for they say, too, that I am one of the principal presonages in it."

"Personages, not presonages, friend Sancho," said Samson.

"What! Another word-catcher!" said Sancho; "if that's to be the way we shall not make an end in a lifetime."

"May God shorten mine, Sancho," returned the bachelor, "if you are not the second person in the history, and there are even some who would rather hear you talk than the cleverest in the whole book; though there are some, too, who say you showed yourself over-credulous in believing there was any possibility in the government of that island offered you by Señor Don Quixote here."

"There is still sunshine on the wall," said Don Quixote; "and when Sancho is somewhat more advanced in life, with the experience that years bring, he will be fitter and better qualified for being a governor than he is at present."

"By God, master," said Sancho, "the island that I can not govern with the years I have, I'll not be able to govern with the years of Methuselam; the difficulty is that the said island keeps its distance somewhere, I know not where; and not that there is any want of head in me to govern it."

"Leave it to God, Sancho," said Don Quixote, "for all will be well, and perhaps better than you think; no leaf on the tree stirs but by God's will."

"That is true," said Samson; "and if it be God's will, there will not be any want of a thousand islands, much less one, for Sancho to govern."

"I have seen governors in these parts," said Sancho, "that are not to be compared to my shoesole; and for all that they are called 'your lordship' and served on silver."

"Those are not governors of islands," observed Samson, "but of other governments of an easier kind: those that govern islands must at least know grammar."

"I could manage the gram well enough," said Sancho; "but for the mar I have neither leaning nor liking, for I don't know what it is; but leaving this matter of the government in God's hands, to send me wherever it may be most to his service, I may tell you, señor bachelor Samson Carrasco, it has pleased me beyond measure that the author of this history should have spoken of me in such a way that what is said of me gives no offence; for, on the faith of a true squire, if he had said anything about me that was at all unbecoming an old Christian, such as I am, the deaf would have heard of it."

"That would be working miracles," said Samson.

"Miracles or no miracles," said Sancho, "let every one mind how he speaks or writes about people, and not set down at random the first thing that comes into his head."

"One of the faults they find with this history," said the bachelor, "is that its author inserted in it a novel called *The Ill-advised Curiosity;* not that it is bad or ill-told, but that it is out of place and has nothing to do with the history of his worship Señor Don Quixote."

"I will bet the son of a dog has mixed the cabbages and the baskets," said Sancho.

"Then, I say," said Don Quixote, "the author of my history was no sage, but some ignorant chatterer, who, in a haphazard and heedless way, set about writing it, let it turn out as it might, just as Orbaneja, the painter of Úbeda, used to do, who, when they asked him what he was painting, answered 'What it may turn out.' Sometimes he would paint a cock in such a fashion, and so unlike, that he had to write alongside of it in Gothic letters, 'This is a cock'; and so it will be with my history, which will require a commentary to make it intelligible."

"No fear of that," returned Samson, "for it is so plain that there is nothing in it to puzzle over; the children turn its leaves, the young people read it, the grown men understand it, the old folk praise; in a word, it is so thumbed, and read, and got by heart by people of all sorts, that the instant they see any lean hack, they say, 'There goes Rocinante.' And those that are most given to reading it are the pages, for there is not a lord's ante-chamber where there is not a *Don Quixote* to be found; one takes it up if another lays it down; this one pounces upon it, and that begs for it. In short, the said history is the most delightful and least injurious entertainment that has been hitherto seen, for there is not to be found in the whole of it even the semblance of an immodest word, or a thought that is other than Catholic."

"To write in any other way," said Don Quixote, "would not be to write truth, but falsehood, and historians who have recourse to falsehood, ought to be burned, like those who coin false money; and I know not what could have led the author to have recourse to novels and irrelevant stories, when he had so much to write about in mine; no doubt he must have gone by the proverb 'with straw or with hay, etc.,'[36] for by merely setting forth my thoughts, my sighs, my tears, my lofty purposes, my enterprises, he might have made a volume as large, or larger than all

[36] ". . . fill my belly all the way."

the works of El Tostado[37] would make up. In fact, the conclusion I arrive at, señor bachelor, is, that to write histories, or books of any kind, there is need of great judgment and a ripe understanding. To give expression to humor, and write in a strain of graceful pleasantry, is the gift of great geniuses. The cleverest character in comedy is the clown, for he who would make people take him for a fool, must not be one. History is in a measure a sacred thing, for it should be true, and where the truth is, there God is, so far as truth is concerned; but notwithstanding this, there are some who write and fling books broadcast on the world as if they were fritters."

"There is no book so bad but it has something good in it," said the bachelor.

"No doubt of that," replied Don Quixote; "but it often happens that those who have acquired and attained a well-desired reputation by their writings, lose it entirely, or damage it in some degree, when they give them to the press."

"The reason of that," said Samson, "is, that as printed works are examined leisurely, their faults are easily seen; and the greater the fame of the writer, the more closely are they scrutinized. Men famous for their genius, great poets, illustrious historians, are always, or most commonly, envied by those who take a particular delight and pleasure in criticising the writings of others, without having produced any of their own."

"That is no wonder," said Don Quixote; "for there are many divines who are no good for the pulpit, but excellent in detecting the defects or excesses of those who preach."

"All that is true, Señor Don Quixote," said Carrasco; "but I wish such fault-finders were more lenient and less exacting, and did not pay so much attention to the spots on the bright sun of the work they grumble at; for if *aliquando bonus dormitat Homerus,*[38] they should remember how long he remained awake to shed the light of his work with as little shade as possible; and perhaps it may be that what they find fault with may be moles, that sometimes heighten the beauty of the face that bears them; and so I say very great is the risk to which he who prints a book exposes himself, for of all impossibilities the greatest is to write one that will satisfy and please all readers."

"That which treats of me must have pleased few," said Don Quixote.

"Quite the contrary," said the bachelor; "for, as *stultorum infinitus est numerus,*[39] innumerable are those who have relished the said history; but some have brought a charge against the author's memory, inasmuch as he forgot to say who the thief was who stole Sancho's Dapple; for it is not stated there, but only to be inferred from what is set down, that he was stolen, and a little farther on we see Sancho mounted on the same ass, without any re-appearance of it. They say, too, that he forgot to state what Sancho did with those hundred crowns that he found in the valise in the Sierra Morena, as he never alludes to them again, and there are many who would be glad to know what he did with them, or what he spent them on, for it is one of the serious omissions of the work."

"Señor Samson, I am not in a humor now for going into accounts or explanations," said Sancho; "for there's a sinking of the stomach come over me, and unless I doctor it with a couple of sups of the old stuff it will put me on the thorn of Santa Lucia.[40] I have it at home, and my old woman is waiting for me; after dinner I'll come back, and will answer you and all the world every question you may choose to

[37] An author of many devotional works.
[38] ". . . worthy Homer sometimes nods" (Horace, *Art of Poetry*).
[39] "Infinite is the number of fools." (*Ecclesiastes*, I:15).
[40] Made me weak with hunger.

ask, as well about the loss of the ass as about the spending of the hundred crowns"; and without another word or waiting for a reply he made off home.

Don Quixote begged and entreated the bachelor to stay and do penance with him. The bachelor accepted the invitation and remained, a couple of young pigeons were added to the ordinary fare, at dinner they talked chivalry, Carrasco fell in with his host's humor, the banquet came to an end, they took their afternoon sleep, Sancho returned, and the previous conversation was resumed.

FROM

Chapter 4

In which Sancho Panza gives a satisfactory reply to the doubts and questions of the bachelor Samson Carrasco, together with other matters worth knowing and mentioning

. . . "Does the author promise a second part at all?" said Don Quixote.

"He does promise one," replied Samson; "but he says he has not found it, nor does he know who has got it; and we can not say whether it will appear or not; and so, on that head, as some say that no second part has ever been good, and others that enough has been already written about Don Quixote, it is thought there will be no second part; though some, who are jovial rather than saturnine, say, 'Let us have more Quixotades, let Don Quixote charge and Sancho chatter, and no matter what it may turn out, we shall be satisfied with that.' "

"And what does the author mean to do?" said Don Quixote.

"What?" replied Samson; "why, as soon as he has found the history which he is now searching for with extraordinary diligence, he will at once give it to the press, moved more by the profit that may accrue to him from doing so than by any thought of praise."

Whereat Sancho observed, "The author looks for money and profit, does he? It will be a wonder if he succeeds, for it will be only hurry, hurry, with him, like the tailor on Easter Eve; and works done in a hurry are never finished as perfectly as they ought to be. Let Master Moor, or whatever he is, pay attention to what he is doing, and I and my master will give him as much grouting ready to his hand, in the way of adventures and accidents of all sorts, as would make up not only one second part, but a hundred. The good man fancies, no doubt, that we are fast asleep in the straw here, but let him hold up our feet to be shod and he will see which foot it is we go lame on. All I say is, that if my master would take my advice, we would be now afield, redressing outrages and righting wrongs, as is the use and custom of good knights-errant."

Sancho had hardly uttered these words when the neighing of Rocinante fell upon their ears, which neighing Don Quixote accepted as a happy omen, and he resolved to make another sally in three or four days from that time. Announcing his intention to the bachelor, he asked his advice as to the quarter in which he ought to commence his expedition, and the bachelor replied that in his opinion he ought to go to the kingdom of Aragon, and the city of Saragossa, where there were to be certain solemn joustings at the festival of St. George, at which he might win renown above all the knights of Aragon, which would be winning it above all the knights of the world. He commended his very praiseworthy and gallant resolution, but admonished him to proceed with greater caution in encountering dangers, because his life did not belong to him, but to all those who had need of him to protect and aid them in their misfortunes.

"There's where it is, what I abominate, Señor Samson," said Sancho here; "my master will attack a hundred armed men as a greedy boy would a half dozen melons.

Body of the world, señor bachelor! there is a time to attack and a time to retreat, and it is not to be always 'Santiago, and close Spain!' Moreover, I have heard it said (and I think by my master himself, if I remember rightly) that the mean of valor lies between the extremes of cowardice and rashness; and if that be so, I don't want him to fly without having good reason, or to attack when the odds make it better not. But, above all things, I warn my master that if he is to take me with him it must be on the condition that he is to do all the fighting, and that I am not to be called upon to do anything except what concerns keeping him clean and comfortable; in this I will dance attendance on him readily; but to expect me to draw sword, even against rascally churls of the hatchet and hood, is idle. I don't set up to be a fighting man, Señor Samson, but only the best and most loyal squire that ever served knight-errant; and if my master Don Quixote, in consideration of my many faithful services, is pleased to give me some island of the many his worship says one may stumble on in these parts, I will take it as a great favor; and if he does not give it to me, I was born like every one else, and a man must not live in dependence on any one except God; and what is more, my bread will taste as well, and perhaps even better, without a government than if I were a governor; and how do I know but that in these governments the devil may have prepared some trip for me, to make me lose my footing and fall and knock my grinders out? Sancho I was born and Sancho I mean to die. But for all that, if Heaven were to make me a fair offer of an island or something else of the kind, without much trouble and without much risk, I am not such a fool as to refuse it; for they say, too, 'when they offer thee a heifer, run with a halter'; and 'when good luck comes to thee, take it in.' "

"Brother Sancho," said Carrasco, "you have spoken like a professor; but, for all that, put your trust in God and in Señor Don Quixote, for he will give you a kingdom, not to say an island."

"It is all the same, be it more or be it less," replied Sancho; "though I can tell Señor Carrasco that my master would not throw the kingdom he might give me into a sack all in holes; for I have felt my own pulse and I find myself sound enough to rule kingdoms and govern islands; and I have before now told my master as much."

"Take care, Sancho," said Samson; "honors change manners, and perhaps when you find yourself a governor you won't know the mother that bore you."

"That may hold good of those that are born in the ditches," said Sancho, "not of those who have the fat of an old Christian four fingers deep on their souls, as I have. Nay, only look at my disposition, is that likely to show ingratitude to any one?"

"God grant it," said Don Quixote; "we shall see when the government comes; and I seem to see it already."

He then begged the bachelor, if he were a poet, to do him the favor of composing some verses for him conveying the farewell he meant to take of his lady Dulcinea del Toboso, and to see that a letter of her name was placed at the beginning of each line, so that, at the end of the verses, "Dulcinea del Toboso" might be read by putting together the first letters. The bachelor replied that although he was not one of the famous poets of Spain, who were, they said, only three and a half, he would not fail to compose the required verses; though he saw a great difficulty in the task, as the letters which made up the name were seventeen; so, if he made four ballad stanzas of four lines each, there would be a letter over, and if he made them of five, what they called *decimas* or *redondillas*, there were three letters short; nevertheless he would try to drop a letter as well as he could, so that the name "Dulcinea del Toboso" might be got into four ballad stanzas.

"It must be, by some means or other," said Don Quixote, "for unless the name stands there plain and manifest, no woman would believe the verses were made for her."

They agreed upon this, and that the departure should take place in three days from that time. Don Quixote charged the bachelor to keep it a secret, especially from the curate and Master Nicholas, and from his niece and the housekeeper, lest they should prevent the execution of his praiseworthy and valiant purpose. Carrasco promised all, and then took his leave, charging Don Quixote to inform him of his good or evil fortunes whenever he had an opportunity; and thus they bade each other farewell, and Sancho went away to make the necessary preparations for their expedition.

Chapter 5

Of the shrewd and droll conversation that passed between Sancho Panza and his wife Teresa Panza, and other matters worthy of being duly recorded

The translator of this history, when he comes to write this fifth chapter, says that he considers it apocryphal, because in it Sancho Panza speaks in a style unlike that which might have been expected from his limited intelligence, and says things so subtle that he does not think it possible he could have conceived them; however, desirous of doing what his task imposed upon him, he was unwilling to leave it untranslated, and therefore he went on to say:

Sancho came home in such glee and spirits that his wife noticed his happiness a bowshot off, so much so that it made her ask him, "What have you got, Sancho friend, that you are so glad?"

To which he replied, "Wife, if it were God's will, I should be very glad not to be so well pleased as I show myself."

"I don't understand you, husband," said she, "and I don't know what you mean by saying you would be glad, if it were God's will, not to be well pleased; for, fool as I am, I don't know how one can find pleasure in not having it."

"Hark ye, Teresa," replied Sancho, "I am glad because I have made up my mind to go back to the service of my master Don Quixote, who means to go out a third time to seek for adventures; and I am going with him again, for my necessities will have it so, and also the hope that cheers me with the thought that I may find another hundred crowns like those we have spent; though it makes me sad to have to leave thee and the children; and if God would be pleased to let me have my daily bread, dry-shod and at home, without taking me out into the byways and cross-roads—and he could do it at small cost by merely willing it—it is clear my happiness would be more solid and lasting, for the happiness I have is mingled with sorrow at leaving thee; so that I was right in saying I would be glad, if it were God's will, not to be well pleased."

"Look here, Sancho," said Teresa; "ever since you joined on to a knight-errant you talk in such a roundabout way that there is no understanding you."

"It is enough that God understands me, wife," replied Sancho; "for he is the understander of all things; that will do; but mind, sister, you must look to Dapple carefully for the next three days, so that he may be fit to take arms; double his feed and see to the pack-saddle and other harness, for it is not to a wedding we are bound, but to go round the world, and play at give and take with giants and dragons and monsters, and hear hissings and roarings and bellowings and howlings; and even all this would be lavender, if we had not to reckon with Yanguesans and enchanted Moors."

"I know well enough, husband," said Teresa, "that squires-errant don't eat their bread for nothing, and so I will be always praying to our Lord to deliver you speedily from all that hard fortune."

"I can tell you, wife," said Sancho, "if I did not expect to see myself governor of an island before long, I would drop down dead on the spot."

"Nay, then, husband," said Teresa, "let the hen live, though it be with her pip; live, and let the devil take all the governments in the world; you came out of your mother's womb without a government, you have lived until now without a government, and when it is God's will you will go, or be carried, to your grave without a government. How many there are in the world who live without a government, and continue to live all the same, and are reckoned in the number of the people. The best sauce in the world is hunger, and as the poor are never without that, they always eat with a relish. But mind, Sancho, if by good luck you should find yourself with some government, don't forget me and your children. Remember that Sanchico is now full fifteen, and it is right he should go to school, if his uncle the abbot has a mind to have him trained for the Church. Consider, too, that your daughter Mari-Sancha will not die of grief if we marry her; for I have my suspicions that she is as eager to get a husband as you to get a government; and, after all, a daughter looks better ill-married than well kept."

"By my faith," replied Sancho, "if God brings me to get any sort of a government, I intend, wife, to make such a high match for Mari-Sancha that there will be no approaching her without calling her 'my lady.' "

"Nay, Sancho," returned Teresa, "marry her to her equal, that is the safest plan; for if you put her out of wooden clogs into high-heeled shoes, out of her gray flannel petticoat into hoops and silk gowns, out the plain 'Marica' and 'thou,' into 'Doña So-and-so' and 'my lady,' the girl won't know where she is, and at every turn she will fall into a thousand blunders that will show the thread of her coarse homespun stuff."

"Tut, you fool," said Sancho; "it will be only to practise it for two or three years; and then dignity and decorum will fit her as easily as a glove; and if not, what matter? Let her be 'my lady,' and never mind what happens."

"Keep to your own station, Sancho," replied Teresa; "don't try to raise yourself higher, and bear in mind the proverb that says, 'wipe the nose of your neighbor's son, and take him into your house.' A fine thing it would be, indeed, to marry our Maria to some great count or grand gentleman, who, when the humor took him, would abuse her and call her clown-bred and clodhopper's daughter and spinning wench. I have not been bringing up my daughter for that all this time, I can tell you, husband. Do you bring home money, Sancho, and leave marrying her to my care; there is Lope Tocho, Juan Tocho's son, a stout, sturdy young fellow that we know, and I can see he does not look sour at the girl; and with him, one of our own sort, she will be well married, and we shall have her always under our eyes, and be all one family, parents and children, grandchildren and sons-in-law, and the peace and blessing of God will dwell among us; so don't you go marrying her in those courts and grand palaces where they won't know what to make of her, or she what to make of herself."

"Why, you idiot and wife for Barabbas," said Sancho, "what do you mean by trying, without why or wherefore, to keep me from marrying my daughter to one who will give me grandchildren that will be called 'your lordship?' Look ye, Teresa, I have always heard my elders say that he who does not know how to take advantage of luck when it comes to him, has no right to complain if it gives him the go-by; and now that it is knocking at our door, it will not do to shut it out; let us go with the favoring breeze that blows upon us." (It is this sort of talk, and what Sancho says lower down, that made the translator of the history say he considered this chapter apocryphal.) "Don't you see, you animal," continued Sancho, "that it will be well for me to drop into some profitable government that will lift us out of the mire, and marry Mari-Sancha to whom I like; and you yourself will find yourself called 'Doña Teresa Panza,' and sitting in church on a fine carpet and cushions and draperies, in spite and in defiance of all the born ladies of the town? No, stay as you are, growing neither greater nor less, like a tapestry figure—Let us say no more about it, for Sanchia shall be a countess, say what you will."

"Are you sure of all you say, husband?" replied Teresa. "Well, for all that, I am afraid this rank of countess for my daughter will be her ruin. You do as you like, make a duchess or a princess of her, but I can tell you it will not be with my will and consent. I was always a lover of equality, brother, and I can't bear to see people give themselves airs without any right. They called me Teresa at my baptism, a plain, simple name, without any additions or tags or fringes of Dons or Doñas; Cascajo was my father's name, and as I am your wife, I am called Teresa Panza, though by right I ought to be called Teresa Cascajo; but 'kings go where laws like,' and I am content with this name without having the 'Don' put on top of it to make it so heavy that I can not carry it; and I don't want to make people talk about me when they see me go dressed like a countess or governor's wife; for they will say at once, 'See what airs the slut gives herself! Only yesterday she was always spinning flax, and used to go to Mass with the tail of her petticoat over her head instead of a mantle, and there she goes today in a hooped gown with her brooches and airs, as if we didn't know her!' If God keeps me in my seven senses, or five, or whatever number I have, I am not going to bring myself to such a pass; go you, brother, and be a government or an island man, and swagger as much as you like; for by the soul of my mother, neither my daughter nor I are going to stir a step from our village; a respectable woman should have a broken leg and keep at home; and to be busy at something is a virtuous damsel's holiday; be off to your adventures along with your Don Quixote, and leave us to our misadventures, for God will mend them for us according as we deserve it. I don't know, I'm sure, who fixed the 'Don' to him, what neither his father nor grandfather ever had."

"I declare thou hast a devil of some sort in thy body!" said Sancho. "God help thee, woman, what a lot of things thou hast strung together, one after the other, without head or tail! What have Cascajo, and the brooches and the proverbs and the airs, to do with what I say? Look here, fool and dolt (for so I may call you, when you don't understand my words, and run away from good fortune), if I had said that my daughter was to throw herself down from a tower, or go roaming the world, as the Infanta Doña Urraca[41] wanted to do, you would be right in not giving way to my will; but if in an instant, in less than the twinkling of an eye, I put the 'Don' and 'my lady' on her back, and take her out of the stubble, and place her under the canopy, on a daïs, and on a couch, with more velvet cushions than all the Almohades of Morocco[42] ever had in their family, why won't you consent and fall in with my wishes?"

"Do you know why, husband?" replied Teresa; "because of the proverb that says 'who covers thee, discovers thee.' At the poor man people only throw a hasty glance; on the rich man they fixed their eyes; and if the said rich man was once on a time poor, it is then there is the sneering and the tattle and spite of backbiters; and in the streets here they swarm as thick as bees."

---

[41]When Doña Urraca was left out of her father's will, she threatened to take up a disreputable life on the streets. He then changed his will and left her the city of Zamora.

[42]Sancho confuses the Spanish word for cushion (*almohada*) with an Islamic sect from North Africa, the Almohades.

"Look here, Teresa," said Sancho, "and listen to what I am now going to say to you; maybe you never heard it in all your life; and I do not give my own notions, for what I am about to say are the opinions of his reverence the preacher, who preached in this town last Lent, and who said, if I remember rightly, that all things present that our eyes behold, bring themselves before us, and remain and fix themselves on our memory much better and more forcibly than things past." (These observations which Sancho makes here are the other ones on account of which the translator says he regards this chapter as apocryphal, inasmuch as they are beyond Sancho's capacity.) "Whence it arises," he continued, "that when we see any person well-dressed and making a figure with rich garments and retinue of servants, it seems to lead and impel us perforce to respect him, though memory may at the same moment recall to us some lowly condition in which we have seen him, but which, whether it may have been poverty or low birth, being now a thing of the past, has no existence; while the only thing that has any existence is what we see before us; and if this person whom fortune has raised from his original lowly state (these were the very words the padre used) to his present height of prosperity, be well bred, generous, courteous to all, without seeking to vie with those whose nobility is of ancient date, depend upon it, Teresa, no one will remember what he was, and every one will respect what he is, except indeed the envious, from whom no fair fortune is safe."

"I do not understand you, husband," replied Teresa; "do as you like, and don't break my head with any more speechifying and rhetoric; and if you have revolved to do what you say"—

"Resolved, you should say, woman," said Sancho, "not revolved."

"Don't set yourself to wrangle with me, husband," said Teresa; "I speak as God pleases, and don't deal in out-of-the-way phrases; and I say if you are bent upon having a government, take your son Sancho with you, and teach him from this time on how to hold a government; for sons ought to inherit and learn the trades of their fathers."

"As soon as I have the government," said Sancho, "I will send for him by post, and I will send thee money, of which I shall have no lack, for there is never any want of people to lend it to governors when they have not got it; and do thou dress him so as to hide what he is and make him look what he is to be."

"You send the money," said Teresa, "and I'll dress him up for you as fine as you please."

"Then we are agreed that our daughter is to be a countess," said Sancho.

"The day that I see her a countess," replied Teresa, "it will be the same to me as if I was burying her; but once more I say do as you please, for we women are born to this burden of being obedient to our husbands, though they be blockheads"; and with this she began to weep in downright earnest, as if she already saw Sanchica dead and buried.

Sancho consoled her by saying that though he must make her a countess, he would put it off as long as possible. Here their conversation came to an end, and Sancho went back to see Don Quixote, and make arrangements for their departure.

• • •

FROM

Chapter 22

Wherein is related the grand adventure of the cave of Montesinos in the heart of La Mancha, which the valiant Don Quixote brought to a happy termination

. . . Don Quixote begged the fencing licentiate to find him a guide to show him the way to the cave of Montesinos, as he had a great desire to enter it and see with his own eyes if the wonderful tales that were told of it all over the country were true. The licentiate said he would get him a cousin of his own, a famous scholar, and one very much given to reading books of chivalry, who would have great pleasure in conducting him to the mouth of the very cave, and would show him the lakes of Ruidera, which were likewise famous all over La Mancha, and even all over Spain; and he assured him he would find him entertaining, for he was a youth who could write books good enough to be printed and dedicated to princes. The cousin arrived at last, leading an ass in foal, with a pack-saddle covered with a party-colored carpet or sackcloth; Sancho saddled Rocinante, got Dapple ready, and stocked his *alforjas,* along with which went those of the cousin, likewise well filled; and so, commending themselves to God and bidding farewell to all, they set out, taking the road for the famous cave of Montesinos.

On the way Don Quixote asked the cousin of what sort and character his pursuits, avocations, and studies were, to which he replied that he was by profession a humanist, and that his pursuits and studies were making books for the press, all of great utility and no less entertainment to the nation. One was called *The Book of Liveries,* in which he described seven hundred and three liveries, with their colors, mottoes, and ciphers, from which gentlemen of the court might pick and choose any they fancied for festivals and revels, without having to go a begging for them from any one, or puzzling their brains, as the saying is, to have them appropriate to their objects and purposes; "for," said he, "I give the jealous, the rejected, the forgotten, the absent, what will suit them, and fit them without fail. I have another book, too, which I shall call *Metamorphoses, or the Spanish Ovid,*[43] one of rare and original invention; for, imitating Ovid in burlesque style, I show in it who the Giralda of Seville and the Angel of the Magdalena were, what the sewer of Vecinguerra at Cordova was, what the bulls of Guisando, the Sierra Morena, the Leganitos and Lavapiés fountains at Madrid, not forgetting those of el Piojo, of the Caño Dorado, and of the Priora; and all with their allegories, metaphors, and changes, so that they are amusing, interesting, and instructive, all at once. Another book I have which I call *The Supplement to Polydore Vergil,*[44] which treats of the invention of things, and is a work of great erudition and research, for I establish and elucidate elegantly some things of great importance which Polydore omitted to mention. He forgot to tell us who was the first man in the world that had a cold in his head, and who was the first to try salivation for the French disease, but I give it accurately set forth, and quote more than five-and-twenty authors in proof of it, so your worship may perceive I have labored to good purpose and that the book will be of service to the whole world."

Sancho, who had been very attentive to the cousin's words, said to him, "Tell me, señor,—and God give you luck in printing your books,—can you tell me (for of course you know, as you know everything) who was the first man that scratched his head? For to my thinking it must have been our father Adam."

"So it must," replied the cousin; "for there is no doubt but Adam had a head and hair; and being the first man in the world he would have scratched himself sometimes."

"So I think," said Sancho; "but now tell me, who was the first tumbler in the world?"

"Really, brother," answered the cousin, "I could not at this moment say positively without having investigated it; I will look it up when I go back to where I have my books, and will satisfy you the next time we meet, for this will not be the last time."

---

[43]Ovid's *Metamorphoses* told Greek and Roman legends, many of which explained the origins of place names.

[44]Polydore Vergil (1470–1550) compiled a list of discoveries from classical sources.

"Look here, señor," said Sancho, "don't give yourself any trouble about it, for I have just this minute hit upon what I asked you. The first tumbler in the world, you must know, was Lucifer, when they cast or pitched him out of heaven; for he came tumbling into the bottomless pit."

"You are right, friend," said the cousin; and said Don Quixote, "Sancho, that question and answer are not thine own; thou hast heard them from some one else."

"Hold your peace, señor," said Sancho; "faith, if I take to asking questions and answering, I'll go on from this till tomorrow morning. Nay! to ask foolish things and answer nonsense I needn't go looking for help from my neighbors."

"Thou hast said more than thou art aware of, Sancho," said Don Quixote; "for there are some who weary themselves out in learning and proving things that, after they are known and proved, are not worth a farthing to the understanding or memory."

In this and other pleasant conversation the day went by, and that night they put up at a small hamlet whence it was not more than two leagues to the cave of Montesinos, so the cousin told Don Quixote, adding that if he was bent upon entering it, it would be requisite for him to provide himself with ropes, so that he might be tied and lowered into its depths. Don Quixote said that even if it reached to the bottomless pit he meant to see where it went to; so they bought about a hundred fathoms of rope, and the next day at two in the afternoon they arrived at the cave, the mouth of which is spacious and wide, but full of thorn and wild-fig bushes and brambles and briers, so thick and matted that they completely close it up and cover it over.

On coming within sight of it the cousin, Sancho, and Don Quixote dismounted, and the first two immediately tied the latter very firmly with the ropes, and as they were girding and swathing him Sancho said to him, "Mind what you are about, master mine; don't go burying yourself alive, or putting yourself where you'll be like a bottle put to cool in a well; it's no affair or business of your worship's to become the explorer of this, which must be worse than a Moorish dungeon."

"Tie me and hold thy peace," said Don Quixote, "for an emprise like this, friend Sancho, was reserved for me"; and said the guide, "I beg of you, Señor Don Quixote, to observe carefully and examine with a hundred eyes everything that is within there; perhaps there may be some things for me to put into my book of transformations."

"The drum is in hands that will know how to beat it well enough," said Sancho Panza.

When he had said this and finished the tying (which was not over the armor, but only over the doublet) Don Quixote observed, "It was careless of us not to have provided ourselves with a small cattle-bell to be tied on the rope close to me, the sound of which would show that I was still descending and alive; but as this is out of the question now, in God's hand be it to guide me"; and forthwith he fell on his knees and in a low voice offered up a prayer to Heaven, imploring God to aid him and grant him success in this to all appearance perilous and untried adventure, and then exclaimed aloud, "O mistress of my actions and movements, illustrious and peerless Dulcinea del Toboso, if so be the prayers and supplications of this thy fortunate lover can reach thy ears, by thy incomparable beauty I entreat thee to listen to them, for they but ask thee not to refuse me thy favor and protection now that I stand in such need of them. I am about to precipitate, to sink, to plunge myself into the abyss that is here before me, only to let the world know that while thou dost favor me there is no impossibility I will not attempt and accomplish." With these words he approached the cavern, and perceived that it was impossible to let himself down or effect an entrance except by sheer force or cleaving a passage; so drawing his sword he began to demolish and cut away the brambles at the mouth of the cave, at the noise of which a vast multitude of crows and choughs flew out of it so thick and so fast that they knocked Don Quixote down; and if he had been as much of a believer in augury as he was a Catholic Christian he would have taken it as a bad omen and declined to bury himself in such a place. He got up, however, and as there came no more crows, or nightbirds like the bats that flew out at the same time with the crows, the cousin and Sancho giving him rope, he lowered himself into the depths of the dread cavern; and as he entered it Sancho sent his blessing after him, making a thousand crosses over him and saying, "God, and the Peña de Francia, and the Trinity of Gaeta guide thee,[45] O flower and cream of knights-errant. There thou goest, thou dare-devil of the earth, heart of steel, arm of brass; once more, God guide thee and send thee back safe, and sound, and unhurt to the light of this world thou art leaving to bury thyself in the darkness thou art seeking there"; and the cousin offered up almost the same prayers and supplications.

Don Quixote kept calling to them to give him rope and more rope, and they gave it out little by little, and by the time the calls, which came out of the cave as out of a pipe, ceased to be heard they had let down the hundred fathoms of rope. They were inclined to pull Don Quixote up again, as they could give him no more rope; however, they waited about half an hour, at the end of which time they began to gather in the rope again with great ease and without feeling any weight, which made them fancy Don Quixote was remaining below; and persuaded that it was so, Sancho wept bitterly, and hauled away in great haste in order to settle the question. When, however, they had come to, as it seemed, rather more than eighty fathoms they felt a weight, at which they were greatly delighted; and at last, at ten fathoms more, they saw Don Quixote distinctly, and Sancho called out to him, saying, "Welcome back, señor, for we had begun to think you were going to stop there to found a family." But Don Quixote answered not a word, and drawing him out entirely they perceived he had his eyes shut and every appearance of being fast asleep.

They stretched him on the ground and untied him, but still he did not awake; however, they rolled him back and forwards and shook and pulled him about, so that after some time he came to himself, stretching himself just as if he were waking up from a deep and sound sleep, and looking about him as if scared he said, "God forgive you, friends; ye have taken me away from the sweetest and most delightful existence and spectacle that ever human being enjoyed or beheld. Now indeed do I know that all the pleasures of this life pass away like a shadow and a dream, or fade like the flower of the field. O ill-fated Montesinos! O sore-wounded Durandarte! O unhappy Belerma! O tearful Guadiana, and ye O hapless daughters of Ruidera who show in your waves the tears that flowed from your beauteous eyes!"

The cousin and Sancho Panza listened with deep attention to the words of Don Quixote, who uttered them as though with immense pain he drew them up from his very bowels. They begged of him to explain himself, and tell them what he had seen in that hell down there.

"Hell do you call it?" said Don Quixote; "call it by no such name, for it does not deserve it, as ye shall soon see."

He then begged them to give him something to eat, as he was very hungry. They spread the cousin's sack-cloth on the grass, and put the stores of the *alforjas* into requisition, and all three sitting down lovingly and sociably, they made a luncheon and a supper of it all in one; and when the sackcloth was removed, Don Quixote of La Mancha said, "Let no one rise; and attend to me, my sons, both of you."

[45]La Peña de Francia is a mountain near Ciudad Rodrigo, where an image of the Virgin is said to have appeared in the fifteenth century. The Trinity of Gaeta is a chapel dedicated to the Trinity.

Chapter 23

Of the wonderful things the incomparable Don Quixote said he saw in the profound cave of Montesinos, the impossibility and magnitude of which cause this adventure to be deemed apocryphal

It was about four in the afternoon when the sun, veiled in clouds, with subdued light and tempered beams, enabled Don Quixote to relate, without heat or inconvenience, what he had seen in the cave of Montesinos to his two illustrious hearers, and he began as follows:

"A matter of some twelve or fourteen times a man's height down in this pit, on the left-hand side, there is a recess or space, roomy enough to contain a large cart with its mules. A little light reaches it through some chinks or crevices, communicating with it and open to the surface of the earth. This recess or space I perceived when I was already growing weary and disgusted at finding myself hanging suspended by the rope, travelling downwards into that dark region without any certainty or knowledge of where I was going to, so I resolved to enter it and rest myself for a while. I called out, telling you not to let out more rope until I bade you, but you can not have heard me. I then gathered in the rope you were sending me, and making a coil or pile of it I seated myself upon it, ruminating and considering what I was to do to lower myself to the bottom, having no one to hold me up; and I was thus deep in thought and perplexity, suddenly and without provocation a profound sleep fell upon me, and when I least expected it, I know not how, I awoke and found myself in the midst of the most beautiful, delicious, delightful meadow that nature could produce or the most lively human imagination conceive. I opened my eyes, I rubbed them, and found I was not asleep, but thoroughly awake. Nevertheless, I felt my head and breast to satisfy myself whether it was I myself who was there or some empty delusive phantom; but touch, feeling, the collected thoughts that passed through my mind, all convinced me that I was the same then and there that I am this moment. Next there presented itself to my sight a stately royal palace or castle, with walls that seemed built of clear transparent crystal; and through two great doors that opened wide therein, I saw coming forth and advancing towards me a venerable old man, clad in a long gown of mulberry-colored serge that trailed upon the ground. On his shoulders and breast he had a green satin collegiate hood, and covering his head a black Milanese bonnet, and his snow-white beard fell below his girdle. He carried no arms whatever, nothing but a rosary of beads bigger than fair-sized filberts, each tenth bead being like a moderate ostrich egg; his bearing, his gait, his dignity and imposing presence held me spellbound and wondering. He approached me, and the first thing he did was to embrace me closely, and then he said to me, 'For a long time now, O valiant knight Don Quixote of La Mancha, we who are here enchanted in these solitudes have been hoping to see thee, that thou mayest make known to the world what is shut up and concealed in this deep cave, called the cave of Montesinos, which thou hast entered, an achievement reserved for thy invincible heart and stupendous courage alone to attempt. Come with me, illustrious sir, and I will show thee the marvels hidden within this transparent castle, whereof I am the *alcaide* and perpetual warden; for I am Montesinos himself, from whom the cave takes its name.'[46]

"The instant he told me he was Montesinos, I asked him if the story they told in the world above here was true, that he had taken out the heart of his great friend Durandarte from his breast with a little dagger, and carried it to the lady Belerma,

[46]Montesinos, hero of half a dozen ballads, was a Peer and a grandson of Charlemagne.

as his friend when at the point of death had commanded him. He said in reply that they spoke the truth in every respect except as to the dagger, for it was not a dagger, nor little, but a burnished poniard sharper than an awl."

"That poniard must have been made by Ramon de Hoces the Sevillian," said Sancho.

"I do not know," said Don Quixote; "it could not have been by that poniard maker, however, because Ramon de Hoces was a man of yesterday, and the affair of Roncesvalles, where this mishap occurred, was long ago; but the question is of no great importance, nor does it affect or make any alteration in the truth or substance of the story."

"That is true," said the cousin; "continue, Señor Don Quixote, for I am listening to you with the greatest pleasure in the world."

"And with no less do I tell the tale," said Don Quixote: "and so, to proceed—the venerable Montesinos led me into the palace of crystal, where, in a lower chamber, strangely cool and entirely of alabaster, was an elaborately wrought marble tomb, upon which I beheld, stretched at full length, a knight, not of bronze, or marble, or jasper, as are seen on other tombs, but of actual flesh and bone. His right hand (which seemed to me somewhat hairy and sinewy, a sign of great strength in its owner) lay on the side of his heart; but before I could put any question to Montesinos, he, seeing me gazing at the tomb in amazement, said to me, 'This is my friend Durandarte, flower and mirror of the true lovers and valiant knights of his time. He is held enchanted here, as I myself and many others are, by that French enchanter Merlin, who, they say, was the devil's son; but my belief is, not that he was the devil's son, but that he knew, as the saying is, a point more than the devil. How or why he enchanted us, no one knows, but time will tell, and I suspect that time is not far off. What I marvel at is, that I know it to be as sure as that it is now day, that Durandarte ended his life in my arms, and that, after his death, I took out his heart with my own hands; and indeed it must have weighed more than two pounds, for, according to naturalists, he who has a large heart is more largely endowed with valor than he who has a small one. Then, as this is the case, and as the knight did really die, how comes it that he now moans and sighs from time to time, as if he were still alive?'

"As he said this, the wretched Durandarte cried out in a loud voice:

O cousin Montesinos!
'Twas my last request of thee,
When my soul hath left the body,
And that lying dead I be,
With thy poniard or thy dagger
Cut the heart from out my breast,
And bear it to Belerma.
This was my last request.

On hearing which, the venerable Montesinos fell on his knees before the unhappy knight, and with tearful eyes exclaimed, 'Long since, O Señor Durandarte, my beloved cousin, long since have I done what you bade me on that sad day when I lost you; I took out your heart as well as I could, not leaving an atom of it in your breast, I wiped it with a lace handkerchief, and I took the road to France with it, having first laid you in the bosom of the earth with tears enough to wash and cleanse my hands of the blood that covered them after wandering among your bowels; and more by token, O cousin of my soul, at the first village I came to after leaving Roncesvalles, I sprinkled a little salt upon your heart to keep it sweet, and bring it, if not fresh, at least pickled, into the presence of the lady Belerma, whom, together with you, myself, Guadiana your squire, the duenna Ruidera and her seven daughters and two nieces, and many more of your friends and acquaintances, the sage Merlin has been keeping enchanted here these many years; and although more than five hundred have gone by, not one of us has died; Ruidera and her daughters and nieces alone are missing, and these, because of the tears they shed, Merlin, out of the compassion he seems to have felt for them, changed into so many lakes, which to this day in the world of the living, and in the province of La Mancha, are called the lakes of Ruidera. The seven daughters belong to the kings of Spain, and the two nieces to the knights of a very holy order called the Order of St. John. Guadiana your squire, likewise bewailing your fate, was changed into a river of his own name, but when he came to the surface and beheld the sun of another heaven, so great was his grief at finding he was leaving you, that he plunged into the bowels of the earth; however, as he can not help following his natural course, he from time to time comes forth and shows himself to the sun and the world. The lakes aforesaid send him their waters, and with these, and others that come to him, he makes a grand and imposing entrance into Portugal; but for all that, go where he may, he shows his melancholy and sadness, and takes no pride in breeding dainty choice fish, only coarse and tasteless sorts, very different from those of the golden Tagus. All this that I tell you now, O cousin mine, I have told you many times before, and as you make no answer, I fear that either you believe me not, or do not hear me, whereat I feel God knows what grief. I have now news to give you, which, if it serves not to alleviate your sufferings, will not in any wise increase them. Know that you have here before you (open your eyes and you will see) that great knight of whom the sage Merlin has prophesied such great things; that Don Quixote of La Mancha I mean, who has again, and to better purpose than in past times, revived in these days knight-errantry, long since forgotten, and by whose intervention and aid it may be we shall be disenchanted; for great deeds are reserved for great men.'

" 'And if that may not be,' said the wretched Durandarte in a low and feeble voice, 'if that may not be, then, O my cousin, I say "patience and shuffle" '; and turning over on his side, he relapsed into his former silence without uttering another word.

"And now there was heard a great outcry and lamentation, accompanied by deep sighs and bitter sobs. I looked round and through the crystal wall I saw passing through another chamber a procession of two lines of fair damsels all clad in mourning, and with white turbans of Turkish fashion on their heads. Behind, in the rear of these, there came a lady, for so from her dignity she seemed to be, also clad in black, with a white veil so long and ample that it swept the ground. Her turban was twice as large as the largest of any of the others; her eyebrows met, her nose was rather flat, her mouth was large but with ruddy lips, and her teeth, of which at times she allowed a glimpse, were seen to be sparse and ill-set, though as white as peeled almonds. She carried in her hands a fine cloth, and in it, as well as I could make out, a heart that had been mummied, so parched and dried was it. Montesinos told me that all those forming the procession were the attendants of Durandarte and Belerma, who were enchanted there with their master and mistress, and that the last, she who carried the heart in the cloth, was the lady Belerma, who, with her damsels, four days in the week went in procession singing, or rather weeping, dirges over the body and miserable heart of his cousin; and that if she appeared to me somewhat ill-favored, or not so beautiful as fame reported her, it was because of the bad nights and worse days that she passed in that enchantment, as I could see by the great dark circles round her eyes, and her sickly complexion; 'her sallowness, and the rings round her eyes,' said he, 'are not caused by the periodical ailment usual with women, for it is many months and even years since she has had any, but by the grief her own heart suffers because of that which she holds in her hand perpetually, and which recalls and brings back to her memory the sad fate of her lost lover; were it not for this, hardly would the great Dulcinea del Toboso, so celebrated in all these parts, and even in all the world, come up to her for beauty, grace, and gayety.'

" 'Hold hard!' said I at this, 'tell your story as you ought, Señor Don Montesinos, for you know very well that all comparisons are odious, and there is no occasion to compare one person with another; the peerless Dulcinea del Toboso is what she is, and the lady Doña Belerma is what *she* is and has been, and that's enough.' To which he made answer, 'Forgive me, Señor Don Quixote; I own I was wrong and spoke unadvisedly in saying that the lady Dulcinea could scarcely come up to the lady Belerma; for it were enough for me to have learned, by what means I know not, that you are her knight, to make me bite my tongue out before I compared her to anything save heaven itself.' After this apology which the great Montesinos made me, my heart recovered itself from the shock I had received in hearing my lady compared with Belerma."

"Still I wonder," said Sancho, "that your worship did not get upon the old fellow and bruise every bone of him with kicks, and pluck his beard until you didn't leave a hair in it."

"Nay, Sancho, my friend," said Don Quixote, "it would not have been right in me to do that, for we are all bound to pay respect to the aged, even though they be not knights, but especially those who are, and who are enchanted; I only know I gave him as good as he brought in the many other questions and answers we exchanged."

"I can not understand, Señor Don Quixote," remarked the cousin here, "how it is that your worship, in such a short space of time as you have been below there, could have seen so many things, and said and answered so much."

"How long is it since I went down?" asked Don Quixote.

"Little better than an hour," replied Sancho.

"That can not be," returned Don Quixote, "because night overtook me while I was there, and day came, and it was night again and day again three times; so that, by my reckoning, I have been three days in those remote regions beyond our ken."

"My master must be right," replied Sancho; "for as everything that has happened to him is by enchantment, maybe what seems to us an hour would seem three days and nights there."

"That's it," said Don Quixote.

"And did your worship eat anything all that time, señor?" asked the cousin.

"I never touched a morsel," answered Don Quixote, "nor did I even feel hunger, or think of it."

"And do the enchanted eat?" said the cousin.

"They neither eat," said Don Quixote; "nor are they subject to the greater excrements, though it is thought that their nails, beards, and hair grow."

"And do the enchanted sleep, now, señor?" asked Sancho.

"Certainly not," replied Don Quixote; "at least, during those three days I was with them not one of them closed an eye, nor did I either."

"The proverb, 'Tell me what company thou keepest and I'll tell thee what thou art,' is to the point here," said Sancho; "your worship keeps company with enchanted people that are always fasting and watching; what wonder is it, then, that you neither eat nor sleep while you are with them? But forgive me, señor, if I say that of all this you have told us now, may God take me—I was just going to say the devil—if I believe a single particle."

"What!" said the cousin, "has Señor Don Quixote, then, been lying? Why, even if he wished it he has not had time to imagine and put together such a host of lies."

"I don't believe my master lies," said Sancho.

"If not, what dost thou believe?" asked Don Quixote.

"I believe," replied Sancho, "that this Merlin, or those enchanters who enchanted the whole crew your worship says you saw and discoursed with down there, stuffed your imagination or your mind with all this rigmarole you have been treating us to, and all that is still to come."

"All that might be, Sancho," replied Don Quixote; "but it is not so, for everything that I have told you I saw with my own eyes, and touched with my own hands. But what will you say when I tell you now how, among the countless other marvellous things Montesinos showed me (of which at leisure and at the proper time I will give thee an account in the course of our journey, for they would not be all in place here), he showed me three country girls who went skipping and capering like goats over the pleasant fields there, and the instant I beheld them I knew one to be the peerless Dulcinea del Toboso, and the other two those same country girls that were with her and that we spoke to on the road from El Toboso! I asked Montesinos if he knew them, and he told me he did not, but he thought they must be some enchanted ladies of distinction, for it was only a few days before that they had made their appearance in those meadows; but I was not to be surprised at that, because there were a great many other ladies there of times past and present, enchanted in various strange shapes, and among them he had recognized Queen Guinevere and her dame Quintañona, she who poured out the wine for Lancelot when he came from Britain."

When Sancho Panza heard his master say this he was ready to take leave of his senses, or die with laughter; for, as he knew the real truth about the pretended enchantment of Dulcinea, in which he himself had been the enchanter and concocter of all the evidence, he made up his mind at last that, beyond all doubt, his master was out of his wits and stark mad, so he said to him, "It was an evil hour, a worse season, and a sorrowful day, when your worship, dear master mine, went down to the other world, and an unlucky moment when you met with Señor Montesinos, who has sent you back to us like this. You were well enough here above in your full senses, such as God had given you, delivering maxims and giving advice at every turn, and not as you are now, talking the greatest nonsense that can be imagined."

"As I know thee, Sancho," said Don Quixote, "I heed not thy words."

"Nor I your worship's," said Sancho, "whether you beat me or kill me for those I have spoken, and will speak if you don't correct and mend your own. But tell me, while we are still at peace, how or by what did you recognize the lady our mistress; and if you spoke to her, what did you say, and what did she answer?"

"I recognized her," said Don Quixote, "by her wearing the same garments she wore when thou didst point her out to me. I spoke to her, but she did not utter a word in reply; on the contrary, she turned her back on me and took to flight, at such a pace that a crossbow bolt could not have overtaken her. I wished to follow her, and would have done so had not Montesinos recommended me not to take the trouble as it would be useless, particularly as the time was drawing near when it would be necessary for me to quit the cavern. He told me, moreover, that in course of time he would let me know how he and Belerma, and Durandarte, and all who were there, were to be disenchanted. But of all I saw and observed down there, what gave me most pain was, that while Montesinos was speaking to me, one of the two companions of the hapless Dulcinea approached me on one side, without my having seen her coming and with tears in her eyes said to me, in a low, agitated voice, 'My lady Dulcinea del Toboso kisses your worship's hands and entreats you to do her the favor of letting her know how you are; and, being in great need, she also entreats your worship as earnestly as she can to be so good as to lend her half a dozen reals, or as much as you may have about you, on this new dimity petticoat that I have here; and she promises to repay them very speedily.' I was amazed and taken aback by such a message, and turning to Señor Montesinos I asked him, 'Is it possible, Señor Montesinos, that persons of distinction under enchantment can be in need?' To which he replied, 'Believe me, Señor Don Quixote, that which is called need is to be met with everywhere, and penetrates all quarters and reaches every one, and does not spare even the enchanted; and as the lady Dulcinea del Toboso sends to beg those six reals, and the pledge is to all appearance a good one, there is nothing for it but to give them to her, for no doubt she must be in some great strait.' 'I will take no pledge of her,' I replied, 'nor yet can I give her what she asks, for all I have is four reals'; which I gave (they were those which thou, Sancho, gavest me the other day to bestow in alms upon the poor I met along the road), and I said, 'Tell your mistress, my dear, that I am grieved to the heart because of her distresses, and wish I was a Fucar[47] to remedy them, and that I would have her know that I can not be, and ought not be, in health while deprived of the happiness of seeing her and enjoying her discreet conversation, and that I implore her as earnestly as I can, to allow herself to be seen and addressed by this her captive servant and forlorn knight. Tell her, too, that when she least expects it she will hear it announced that I have made an oath and vow after the fashion of that which the Marquis of Mantua made to avenge his nephew Baldwin, when he found him at the point of death in the heart of the mountains, which was, not to eat bread off a table-cloth, and the other trifling matters which he added, until he had avenged him; and I will make the same to take no rest, and to roam the seven regions of the earth more thoroughly than the Infante Don Pedro of Portugal ever roamed them, until I have disenchanted her.' 'All that, and more, you owe my lady,' was the damsel's answer to me, and taking the four reals, instead of making me a courtesy she cut a caper, springing two full yards into the air."

"O blessed God!" exclaimed Sancho aloud at this, "is it possible that such things can be in the world, and that enchanters and enchantments can have such power in it as to have changed my master's right senses into a craze so full of absurdity! O señor, señor, for God's sake, consider yourself, have a care for your honor, and give no credit to this silly stuff that has left you scant and short of wits."

"Thou talkest in this way because thou lovest me, Sancho," said Don Quixote; "and not being experienced in the things of the world, everything that has some difficulty about it, seems to thee impossible; but time will pass, as I said before, and I will tell thee some of the things I saw down there which will make thee believe what I have related now, the truth of which admits of neither reply nor question."

. . .

FROM

Chapter 28

Of matters that Benengeli says he who reads them will know, if he reads them with attention

. . . "When I worked for Tomé Carrasco, the father of the bachelor Samson Carrasco that your worship knows," replied Sancho, "I used to earn two ducats a month besides my food; I can't tell what I can earn with your worship, though I know a knight-errant's squire has harder times of it than he who works for a

[47] Fucar (or Fugger) was a German banking family of the sixteenth century.

farmer; for after all, we who work for farmers, however much we toil all day, at the worst, at night, we have our olla supper and sleep in a bed, which I have not slept in since I have been in your worship's service, if it wasn't the short time we were in Don Diego de Miranda's house, and the feast I had with the skimmings I took off Camacho's pots, and what I ate, drank, and slept in Basilio's house; all the rest of the time I have been sleeping on the hard ground under the open sky, exposed to what they call the inclemencies of heaven, keeping life in me with scraps of cheese and crusts of bread, and drinking water either from the brooks or from the springs we come to on these by-paths we travel."

"I own, Sancho," said Don Quixote, "that all thou sayest is true; how much, thinkest thou, ought I to give thee over and above what Tomé Carrasco gave thee?"

"I think," said Sancho, "that if your worship was to add on two reals a month I'd consider myself well paid; that is, as far as the wages of my labor go; but to make up to me for your worship's pledge and promise to give me the government of an island, it would be fair to add six reals more, making thirty in all."

"Very good," said Don Quixote; "it is twenty-five days since we left our village, so reckon up, Sancho, according to the wages you have made out for yourself, and see how much I owe you in proportion, and pay yourself, as I said before, out of your own hand."

"O body o' me!" said Sancho, "but your worship is very much out in that reckoning; for when it comes to the promise of the island we must count from the day your worship promised it to me to this present hour we are at now."

"Well, how long is it, Sancho, since I promised it to you?" said Don Quixote.

"If I remember rightly," said Sancho, "it must be over twenty years, three days more or less."

Don Quixote gave himself a great slap on the forehead and began to laugh heartily, and said he, "Why, I have not been wandering, either in the Sierra Morena or in the whole course of our sallies, but barely two months, and thou sayest, Sancho, that it is twenty years since I promised thee the island. I believe now thou wouldst have all the money thou hast of mine go in thy wages. If so, and if that be thy pleasure, I give it to thee now, once and for all, and much good may it do thee, for so long as I see myself rid of such a good-for-nothing squire, I'll be glad to be left a pauper without a rap. But tell me, thou perverter of the squirely rules of knight-errantry, where hast thou ever seen or read that any knight-errant's squire made terms with his lord, 'you must give me so much a month for serving you'? Plunge, O scoundrel, rogue, monster—for such I take thee to be—plunge, I say, into the *mare magnum*[48] of their histories; and if thou shalt find that any squire ever said or thought what thou has said now, I will let thee nail it on my forehead, and give me, over and above, four sound slaps in the face. Turn the rein, or the halter, of thy Dapple, and begone home; for one single step farther thou shalt not make in my company. O bread thanklessly received! O promises ill-bestowed! O man more beast than human being! Now, when I was about to raise thee to such a position, that, in spite of thy wife, they would call thee 'my lord,' thou art leaving me? Thou art going now when I had a firm and fixed intention of making thee lord of the best island in the world? Well, as thou thyself hast said before now, honey is not for the mouth of the ass. Ass thou art, ass thou wilt be, and ass thou wilt end when the course of thy life is run; for I know it will come to its close before thou dost perceive or discern that thou art a beast."

[48] The great sea.

Sancho regarded Don Quixote earnestly while he was giving him his rating, and was so touched by remorse that the tears came to his eyes, and in a piteous and broken voice he said to him, "Master mine, I confess that, to be a complete ass, all I want is a tail; if your worship will only fix one on to me, I'll look on it as rightly placed, and I'll serve you as an ass all the remaining days of my life. Forgive me and have pity on my folly, and remember I know but little, and, if I talk much, it's more from infirmity than malice; but he who sins and mends commends himself to God."

"I should have been surprised, Sancho," said Don Quixote, "if thou hadst not introduced some bit of proverb into thy speech. Well, well, I forgive thee, provided thou dost mend and not show thyself in future so fond of thine own interest, but try to be of good cheer and take heart, and encourage thyself to look forward to the fulfilment of my promises, which, by being delayed, does not become impossible."

Sancho said he would do so, and keep up his heart as best he could. They then entered the grove, and Don Quixote settled himself at the foot of an elm, and Sancho at that of a beech, for trees of this kind and others like them always have feet but no hands. Sancho passed the night in pain, for with the evening dews the blow of the staff made itself felt all the more. Don Quixote passed it in his never-failing meditations; but, for all that, they had some winks of sleep, and with the appearance of daylight they pursued their journey in quest of the banks of the famous Ebro, where that befell them which will be told in the following chapter.

• • •

FROM

Chapter 30

Of Don Quixote's adventure with a fair huntress

. . . It so happened that the next day towards sunset, on coming out of a wood, Don Quixote cast his eyes over a green meadow, and at the far end of it observed some people, and as he drew nearer saw that it was a hawking party. Coming closer, he distinguished among them a lady of graceful mien, on a pure white palfrey or hackney caparisoned with green trappings and a silver-mounted side-saddle. The lady was also in green, and so richly and splendidly dressed that splendor itself seemed personified in her. On her left hand she bore a hawk, a proof to Don Quixote's mind that she must be some great lady and the mistress of the whole hunting party, which was the fact; so he said to Sancho, "Run, Sancho, my son, and say to that lady on the palfrey with the hawk that I, the Knight of the Lions, kiss the hands of her exalted beauty, and if her excellence will grant me leave I will go and kiss them in person and place myself at her service for aught that may be in my power and her highness may command; and mind, Sancho, how thou speakest, and take care not to thrust in any of thy proverbs into thy message."

"You've got a likely one here to thrust any in!" said Sancho; "leave me alone for that! Why, this is not the first time in my life I have carried messages to high and exalted ladies."

"Except that thou didst carry to the lady Dulcinea," said Don Quixote, "I know not that thou hast carried any other, at least in my service."

"That is true," replied Sancho; "but pledges don't distress a good paymaster, and in a house where there's plenty supper is soon cooked; I mean there's no need of telling or warning me about anything; for I'm ready for everything and know a little of everything."

"That I believe, Sancho," said Don Quixote; "go and good luck to thee, and God speed thee."

Sancho went off at top speed, forcing Dapple out of his regular pace, and came to where the fair huntress was standing, and dismounting knelt before her and said, "Fair lady, that knight that you see there, the Knight of the Lions by name, is my master, and I am a squire of his, and at home they call me Sancho Panza. This same Knight of the Lions, who was called not long since the Knight of the Rueful Countenance, sends by me to say may it please your highness to give him leave that, with your permission, approbation, and consent, he may come and carry out his wishes, which are, as he says and I believe, to serve your exalted loftiness and beauty; and if you give it, your ladyship will do a thing which will redound to your honor, and he will receive a most distinguished favor and happiness."

"You have indeed, worthy squire," said the lady, "delivered your message with all the formalities such messages require; rise up, for it is not right that the squire of a knight so great as he of the Rueful Countenance, of whom we have already heard a great deal here, should remain on his knees; rise, my friend, and bid your master welcome to the services of myself and the duke my husband, in a country house we have here."

Sancho got up, charmed as much by the beauty of the good lady as by her high-bred air and her courtesy, but, above all, by what she had said about having heard of his master, the Knight of the Rueful Countenance; for if she did not call him Knight of the Lions it was no doubt because he had so lately taken the name. "Tell me, brother squire," asked the duchess (whose title, however, is not known), "this master of yours, is he not one of whom there is a history extant in print, called *The Ingenious Gentleman, Don Quixote of La Mancha,* who has for the lady of his heart a certain Dulcinea del Toboso?"

"He is the same, señora," replied Sancho; "and that squire of his who figures, or ought to figure, in the said history under the name of Sancho Panza, is myself, unless they have changed me in the cradle, I mean in the press."

"I am rejoiced at this," said the duchess; "go, brother Panza, and tell your master that he is welcome to my estate, and that nothing could happen to me that could give me greater pleasure."

Sancho returned to his master mightily pleased with this gratifying answer, and told him all the great lady had said to him, lauding to the skies, in his rustic phrase, her rare beauty, her graceful gayety, and her courtesy. Don Quixote drew himself up briskly in his saddle, fixed himself in his stirrups, settled his visor, gave Rocinante the spur, and with an easy bearing advanced to kiss the hands of the duchess, who, having sent to summon the duke her husband, told him while Don Quixote was approaching all about the message; and as both of them had read the First Part of this history, and from it were aware of Don Quixote's crazy turn, they awaited him with the greatest delight and anxiety to make his acquaintance, meaning to fall in with his humor and agree with everything he said, and, so long as he stayed with them, to treat him as a knight-errant, with all the ceremonies usual in the books of chivalry they had read, for they themselves were very fond of them.

Don Quixote now came up with his visor raised, and as he seemed about to dismount Sancho made haste to go and hold his stirrup for him; but getting down off Dapple he was so unlucky as to hitch his foot in one of the ropes of the pack-saddle in such a way that he was unable to free it, and was left hanging by it with his face and breast on the ground. Don Quixote, who was not used to dismount without having the stirrup held, fancying that Sancho had by this time come to hold it for him, threw himself off with a lurch and brought Rocinante's saddle after him, which was no doubt badly girthed, and saddle and he both came to the ground; nor without discomfiture to him and abundant curses muttered between his teeth against the unlucky Sancho, who had his foot still in the shackles. The duke ordered his huntsmen to go to the help of knight and squire, and they raised Don Quixote sorely shaken by his fall; and he, limping, advanced as best he could to kneel before the noble pair. This, however, the duke would by no means permit; on the contrary, dismounting from his horse, he went and embraced Don Quixote, saying, "I am grieved, Sir Knight of the Rueful Countenance, that your first experience on my ground should have been such an unfortunate one as we have seen; but the carelessness of squires is often the cause of worse accidents."

"That which has happened me in meeting you, mighty prince," replied Don Quixote, "can not be unfortunate, even if my fall had not stopped short of the depths of the bottomless pit, for the glory of having seen you would have lifted me up and delivered me from it. My squire, God's curse upon him, is better at unloosing his tongue in talking impertinence than in tightening the girths of a saddle to keep it steady; but however I may be, fallen or raised up, on foot or on horseback, I shall always be at your service and that of my lady the duchess, your worthy consort, worthy queen of beauty and paramount princess of courtesy."

"Gently, Señor Don Quixote of La Mancha," said the duke; "where my lady Doña Dulcinea del Toboso is, it is not right that other beauties should be praised."

Sancho, by this time released from his entanglement, was standing by, and before his master could answer he said, "There is no denying, and it must be maintained, that my lady Dulcinea del Toboso is very beautiful; but the hare jumps up where one least expects it; and I have heard say that what we call nature is like a potter that makes vessels of clay, and he who makes one fair vessel can as well make two, or three, or a hundred; I say so because, by my faith, my lady the duchess is in no way behind my mistress the lady Dulcinea del Toboso."

Don Quixote turned to the duchess and said, "Your highness may conceive that never had knight-errant in this world a more talkative or a droller squire than I have, and he will prove the truth of what I say, if your highness is pleased to accept of my services for a few days."

To which the duchess made answer, "That worthy Sancho is droll I consider a very good thing, because it is a sign that he is shrewd; for drollery and sprightliness, Señor Don Quixote, as you very well know, do not take up their abode with dull wits; and as good Sancho is droll and sprightly I here set him down as shrewd."

"And talkative," added Don Quixote.

"So much the better," said the duke, "for many droll things can not be said in few words; but not to lose time in talking, come, great Knight of the Rueful Countenance"—

"Of the Lions, your highness must say," said Sancho, "for there is no Rueful Countenance nor any such character now."

"He of the Lions be it," continued the duke; "I say, let Sir Knight of the Lions come to a castle of mine close by, where he shall be given that reception which is due to so exalted a personage, and which the duchess and I are wont to give to all knights-errant who come there."

By this time Sancho had fixed and girthed Rocinante's saddle, and Don Quixote having got on his back and the duke mounted a fine horse, they placed the duchess in the middle and set out for the castle. The duchess desired Sancho to come to her side, for she found infinite enjoyment in listening to his shrewd remarks. Sancho required no pressing, but pushed himself in between them and made a fourth in the conversation, to the great amusement of the duchess and the duke, who thought it rare good fortune to receive such a knight-errant and such a homely squire in their castle.

. . .

FROM

Chapter 32

Of the reply Don Quixote gave his censurer, with other incidents, grave and droll

. . . The duchess begged Don Quixote, as he seemed to have a retentive memory, to describe and portray to her the beauty and features of the lady Dulcinea del Toboso, for, judging by what fame trumpeted abroad of her beauty, she felt sure she must be the fairest creature in the world, nay in all La Mancha.

Don Quixote sighed on hearing the duchess's request, and said, "If I could pluck out my heart, and lay it on a plate on this table here before your highness's eyes, it would spare my tongue the pain of telling what can hardly be thought of, for in it your excellence would see her portrayed in full. But why should I attempt to depict and describe in detail, and feature by feature, the beauty of the peerless Dulcinea, the burden being one worthy of other shoulders than mine, an enterprise wherein the pencils of Parrhasius, Timantes, and Apelles, and the graver of Lysippus[49] ought to be employed, to paint it in pictures and carve it in marble and bronze, and Ciceronian and Demosthenian eloquence to sound its praises?"

"What does Demosthenian mean, Señor Don Quixote?" said the duchess; "it is a word I never heard in all my life."

"Demosthenian eloquence," said Don Quixote, "means the eloquence of Demosthenes, as Ciceronian means that of Cicero, who were the two most eloquent orators in the world."

"True," said the duke; "you must have lost your wits to ask such a question. Nevertheless, Señor Don Quixote would greatly gratify us if he would depict her to us; for never fear, even in an outline or sketch she will be something to make the fairest envious."

"I would do so certainly," said Don Quixote, "had she not been blurred to my mind's eye by the misfortune that fell upon her a short time since, one of such a nature that I am more ready to weep over it than to describe it. For your highnesses must know that, going a few days back to kiss her hands and receive her benediction, approbation, and permission for this third sally, I found her altogether a different being from the one I sought; I found her enchanted and changed from a princess into a peasant, from fair to foul, from an angel into a devil, from fragrant to pestiferous, from refined to clownish, from a dignified lady into a jumping tomboy, from a light to darkness, and, in a word, from Dulcinea del Toboso into a coarse Sayago wench."

"God bless me!" said the duke aloud at this, "who can have done the world such an injury? Who can have robbed it of the beauty that gladdened it, of the grace and gayety that charmed it, of the modesty that shed a lustre upon it?"

"Who?" replied Don Quixote; "who could it be but some malignant enchanter of the many that persecute me out of envy—that accursed race born into the world to obscure and bring to naught the achievements of the good, and glorify and exalt the deeds of the wicked? Enchanters have persecuted me, enchanters persecute me still, and enchanters will continue to persecute me until they have sunk me and my lofty chivalry in the deep abyss of oblivion; and they injure and wound me where they know I feel it most. For to deprive a knight-errant of his lady is to deprive him of the eyes he sees with, of the sun that gives him light, of the food whereby he lives. Many a time before have I said it, and I say it now once more, a knight-errant without a lady is like a tree without leaves, a building without a foundation, or a shadow without the body that causes it."

---

[49] Ancient Greek artists.

"There is no denying it," said the duchess; "but still, if we are to believe the history of Don Quixote that has come out here lately with general applause, it is to be inferred from it, if I mistake not, that you never saw the lady Dulcinea, and that the said lady is nothing in the world but an imaginary lady, one that you yourself begot and gave birth to in your brain, and adorned with whatever charms and perfections you chose."

"There is a good deal to be said on that point," said Don Quixote; "God knows whether there be any Dulcinea or not in the world, or whether she is imaginary or not imaginary; these are things the proof of which must not be pushed to extreme lengths. I have not begotten nor given birth to my lady, though I behold her as she needs must be, a lady who contains in herself all the qualities to make her famous throughout the world, beautiful without blemish, dignified without haughtiness, tender and yet modest, gracious from courtesy and courteous from good breeding, and lastly of exalted lineage, because beauty shines forth and excels with a higher degree of perfection upon good blood than in the fair of lowly birth."

"That is true," said the duke; "but Señor Don Quixote will give me leave to say what I am constrained to say by the story of his exploits that I have read, from which it is to be inferred that, granting there is a Dulcinea in El Toboso, or out of it, and that she is in the highest degree beautiful as you have described her to us, as regards the loftiness of her lineage she is not on a par with the Orianas, Alastrajareas, Madasimas, or others of that sort, with whom, as you well know, the histories abound."

"To that I may reply," said Don Quixote, "that Dulcinea is the daughter of her own works, and that virtues rectify blood, and that lowly virtue is more to be regarded and esteemed than exalted vice. Dulcinea, besides, has that within her that may raise her to be a crowned and sceptred queen; for the merit of a fair and virtuous woman is capable of performing greater miracles; and virtually, though not formally, she has in herself higher fortunes."

"I protest, Señor Don Quixote," said the duchess, "that in all you say, you go most cautiously and lead in hand, as the saying is; henceforth I will believe myself, and I will take care that every one in my house believes, even my lord the duke if needs be, that there is a Dulcinea in El Toboso, and that she is living to-day, and that she is beautiful and nobly born and deserves to have such a knight as Señor Don Quixote in her service, and that is the highest praise that it is in my power to give her or that I can think of. But I can not help entertaining a doubt, and having a certain grudge against Sancho Panza; the doubt is this, that the aforesaid history declares that the said Sancho Panza, when he carried a letter on your worship's behalf to the said lady Dulcinea, found her sifting a sack of wheat: and more by token it says it was red wheat: a thing which makes me doubt the loftiness of her lineage."

To this Don Quixote made answer, "Señora, your highness must know that everything or almost everything that happens to me transcends the ordinary limits of what happens to other knights-errant; whether it be that it is directed by the inscrutable will of destiny, or by the malice of some jealous enchanter. Now it is an established fact that all or most famous knights-errant have some special gift, one that of being proof against enchantment, another that of being made of such invulnerable flesh that he can not be wounded, as was the famous Roland, one of the twelve peers of France, of whom it is related that he could not be wounded except in the sole of his left foot, and that it must be with the point of a stout pin and not with any other sort of weapon whatever; and so, when Bernardo del Carpio slew him at Roncesvalles, finding that he could not wound him with steel, he lifted him up from the ground in his arms and strangled him, calling to mind seasonably the death which Hercules inflicted on Antæus, the fierce giant that they say was the son of Terra. I would infer from what I have mentioned that perhaps I may have some gift of this kind, not that of being invulnerable, because experience has many times proved to me that I am of tender flesh and not at all impenetrable; nor that of being proof against enchantment, for I have already seen myself thrust into a cage, in which all the world would not have been able to confine me except by force of enchantments. But as I delivered myself from that one, I am inclined to believe that there is no other that can hurt me; and so, these enchanters, seeing that they can not exert their vile craft against my person, revenge themselves on what I love most, and seek to rob me of life by maltreating that of Dulcinea in whom I live; and therefore I am convinced that when my squire carried my message to her, they changed her into a common peasant girl, engaged in such a mean occupation as sifting wheat; I have already said, however, that that wheat was not red wheat, nor wheat at all, but grains of orient pearl. And as a proof of all this, I must tell your highnesses that, coming to El Toboso a short time back, I was altogether unable to discover the palace of Dulcinea; and that the next day, though Sancho, my squire, saw her in her own proper shape, which is the fairest in the world, to me she appeared to be a coarse, ill-favored, farm-wench, and by no means a well-spoken one, she who is propriety itself. And so, as I am not and, so far as one can judge, can not be enchanted, she it is that is enchanted, that is smitten, that is altered, changed, and transformed; in her have my enemies revenged themselves upon me, and for her shall I live in ceaseless tears, until I see her in her pristine state. I have mentioned this lest anybody should mind what Sancho said about Dulcinea's winnowing or sifting; for, as they changed her to me, it is no wonder if they changed her to him. Dulcinea is illustrious and well-born, and of one of the gentle families of El Toboso, which are many, ancient, and good. Therein, most assuredly, not small is the share of the peerless Dulcinea, through whom her town will be famous and celebrated in ages to come, as Troy was through Helen, and Spain through La Cava,[50] though with a better title and tradition. For another thing; I would have your graces understand that Sancho Panza is one of the drollest squires that ever served knight-errant; sometimes there is a simplicity about him so acute that it is an amusement to try and make out whether he is simple or sharp; he has mischievous tricks that stamp him rogue, and blundering ways that prove him a booby; he doubts everything and believes everything; when I fancy he is on the point of coming down headlong from sheer stupidity, he comes out with something shrewd that sends him up to the skies. After all, I would not exchange him for another squire, though I were given a city to boot, and therefore I am in doubt whether it will be well to send him to the government your highness has bestowed upon him; though I perceive in him a certain aptitude for the work of governing, so that, with a little trimming of his understanding, he would manage any government as easily as the king does his taxes; and moreover, we know already by ample experience that it does not require much cleverness or much learning to be a governor, for there are a hundred round about us that scarcely know how to read, and govern like gerfalcons. The main point is that they should have good intentions and be desirous of doing right in all things, for they will never be at a loss for persons to advise and direct them in what they have to do, like those knight-governors who, being no lawyers, pronounce sentences with the aid of an assessor. My advice to him will be to take no bribe and surrender no right, and I have some other little matters in reserve, that shall be produced in due season for Sancho's benefit and the advantage of the island he is to govern." . . .

[50] La Cava, daughter of Count Julian, was seduced by Rodrigo, the last king of the Visigoths.

Chapter 33

Of the delectable discourse which the duchess and her damsels held with Sancho Panza, well worth reading and noting

The history records that Sancho did not sleep that afternoon, but in order to keep his word came, before he had well done dinner, to visit the duchess, who, finding enjoyment in listening to him, made him sit down beside her on a low seat, though Sancho, out of pure good breeding, wanted not to sit down; the duchess, however, told him he was to sit down as governor and talk as squire, as in both respects he was worthy of even the chair of the Cid Ruy Diaz the Campeador. Sancho shrugged his shoulders, obeyed, and sat down, and all the duchess's damsels and duennas gathered round him, waiting in profound silence to hear what he would say. It was the duchess, however, who spoke first, saying, "Now that we are alone, and that there is nobody here to overhear us, I should be glad if the señor governor would relieve me of certain doubts I have, rising out of the history of the great Don Quixote that is now in print. One is: inasmuch as worthy Sancho never saw Dulcinea, I mean the lady Dulcinea del Toboso, nor took Don Quixote's letter to her, for it was left in the memorandum book in the Sierra Morena, how did he dare to invent the answer and all that about finding her sifting wheat, the whole story being a deception and falsehood, and so much to the prejudice of the peerless Dulcinea's good name, a thing that is not at all becoming the character and fidelity of a good squire?"

At these words, Sancho, without uttering one in reply, got up from his chair, and with noiseless steps, with his body bent and his finger on his lips, went all round the room lifting up the hangings; and this was done, he came back to his seat and said, "Now, señora, that I have seen that there is no one except the bystanders listening to us on the sly, I will answer what you have asked me, and all you may ask me, without fear or dread. And the first thing I have got to say is, that for my own part I hold my master Don Quixote to be stark mad, though sometimes he says things that, to my mind, and indeed everybody's that listens to him, are so wise, and run in such a straight furrow, that Satan himself could not have said them better; but for all that, really, and beyond all question, it's my firm belief he is cracked. Well, then, as this is clear to my mind, I can venture to make him believe things that have neither head nor tail, like that affair of the answer to the letter, and that other of six or eight days ago, which is not yet in history, that is to say, the affair of the enchantment of my lady Dulcinea; for I made him believe she is enchanted, though there's no more truth in it than over the hills of Úbeda."[51]

The duchess begged him to tell her about the enchantment or deception, so Sancho told the whole story exactly as it had happened, and his hearers were not a little amused by it; and then resuming, the duchess said, "In consequence of what worthy Sancho has told me, a doubt starts up in my mind, and there comes a kind of whisper to my ear that says, 'If Don Quixote be mad, crazy, and cracked, and Sancho Panza his squire knows it, and, notwithstanding, serves and follows him, and goes trusting to his empty promises, there can be no doubt he must be still madder and sillier than his master; and that being so, it will be cast in your teeth, señora duchess, if you give the said Sancho an island to govern; for how will he who does not know how to govern himself know how to govern others?'"

[51]There are no hills near Úbeda; hence, the story is a fiction.

"By God, señora," said Sancho, "but that doubt comes timely; but your grace may say it out, and speak plainly, or as you like; for I know what you say is true, and if I were wise I should have left my master long ago; but this was my fate, this was my bad luck; I can't help it. I must follow him; we're from the same village, I have eaten his bread, I'm fond of him, I'm grateful, he gave me his ass-colts, and above all I'm faithful; so it's quite impossible for anything to separate us, except the pickaxe and shovel. And if your highness does not like to give me the government you promised, God made me without it, and maybe your not giving it to me will be all the better for my conscience, for fool as I am I know the proverb 'to her hurt the ant got wings,' and it may be that Sancho the squire will get to heaven sooner than Sancho the governer. 'They make as good bread here as in France,' and 'by night all cats are gray,' and 'a hard case enough his, who hasn't broken his fast at two in the afternoon,' and 'there's no stomach a hand's breadth bigger than another,' and the same can be filled 'with straw or hay,' as the saying is, and 'the little birds of the field have God for their purveyor and caterer,' and 'four yards of Cuenca frieze keep one warmer than four of Segovia broadcloth,' and 'when we quit this world and are put underground the prince travels by as narrow a path as the journeyman,' and 'the Pope's body does not take up more feet of earth than the sacristan's,' for all that the one is higher than the other; for when we go to our graves we all pack ourselves up and make ourselves small, or rather they pack us up and make us small in spite of us, and then–good night to us. And I say once more, if your ladyship does not like to give me the island because I'm a fool, like a wise man I will take care to give myself no trouble about it; I have heard say that 'behind the cross there's the devil,' and that 'all that glitters is not gold,' and that from among the oxen, and the ploughs, and the yokes, Wamba the husbandman was taken to be made King of Spain, and from among brocades, and pleasures, and riches, Roderick was taken to be devoured by adders, if the verses of the old ballads don't lie."[52]

"To be sure they don't lie!" exclaimed Doña Rodriguez, the duenna, who was one of the listeners. "Why, there's a ballad that says they put King Rodrigo alive into a tomb full of toads, and adders, and lizards, and that two days afterwards the King, in a plaintive, feeble voice, cried out from within the tomb—

> They gnaw me now, they gnaw me now,
> There where I most did sin.

And according to that the gentleman has good reason to say he would rather be a laboring man than a king, if vermin are to eat him."

The duchess could not help laughing at the simplicity of her duenna, or wondering at the language and proverbs of Sancho, to whom she said, "Worthy Sancho knows very well that when once a knight has made a promise he strives to keep it, though it should cost him his life. My lord and husband the duke, though not one of the errant sort, is none the less a knight for that reason, and will keep his word about the promised island, in spite of the envy and malice of the world. Let Sancho be of good cheer; for when he least expects it he will find himself seated on the throne of his island and seat of dignity, and will take possession of his government that he may discard it for another of three-bordered brocade. The charge I give him is to be careful how he governs his vassals, bearing in mind that they are all loyal and well-born."

"As to governing them well," said Sancho, "there's no need of charging me to do that, for I'm kind-hearted by nature, and full of compassion for the poor; 'there's

[52] A reference to old ballads telling the story of King Rodrigo, last king of the Visigoths.

no stealing the loaf from him who kneads and bakes'; and by my faith it won't do to throw false dice with me; I am an old dog, and I know all about *'tus, tus';* I can be wide awake if need be, and I don't let clouds come before my eyes, for I know where the shoe pinches me; I say so, because with me the good will have support and protection, and the bad neither footing nor access. And it seems to me that, in governments, to make a beginning is everything; and maybe, after having been governor a fortnight, I'll take kindly to the work and know more about it than the field labor I have been brought up to."

"You are right, Sancho," said the duchess, "for no one is born ready taught, and the bishops are made out of men and not out of stones. But to return to the subject we were discussing just now, the enchantment of the lady Dulcinea, I look upon it as certain, and something more than evident, that Sancho's idea of practising a deception upon his master, making him believe that the peasant girl was Dulcinea and that if he did not recognize her it must be because she was enchanted, was all a device of one of the enchanters that persecute Don Quixote. For in truth and earnest, I know from good authority that the coarse country wench who jumped up on the ass was and is Dulcinea del Toboso, and that worthy Sancho, though he fancies himself the deceiver, is the one that is deceived; and that there is no more reason to doubt the truth of this, than of anything else we never saw. Señor Sancho Panza must know that we too have enchanters here that are well disposed to us, and tell us what goes on in the world, plainly and distinctly, without subterfuge or deception; and believe me, Sancho, that agile country lass was and is Dulcinea del Toboso, who is as much enchanted as the mother that bore her; and when we least expect it, we shall see her in her own proper form, and then Sancho will be disabused of the error he is under at present."

"All that's very possible," said Sancho Panza; "and now I'm willing to believe what my master says about what he saw in the cave of Montesinos, where he says he saw the lady Dulcinea del Toboso in the very same dress and apparel that I said I had seen her in when I enchanted her all to please myself. It must be all exactly the other way, as your ladyship says; because it is impossible to suppose that out of my poor wit such a cunning trick could be concocted in a moment, nor do I think my master is so mad that by my weak and feeble persuasion he could be made to believe a thing so out of all reason. But, señora, your excellence must not therefore think me ill-disposed, for a dolt like me is not bound to see into the thoughts and plots of those vile enchanters. I invented all that to escape my master's scolding, and not with any intention of hurting him; and if it has turned out differently, there is a God in heaven who judges our hearts."

"That is true," said the duchess; "but tell me, Sancho, what is this you say about the cave of Montesinos, for I should like to know."

Sancho upon this related to her, word for word, what has been said already touching that adventure, and having heard it the duchess said, "From this occurrence it may be inferred that, as the great Don Quixote says he saw there the same country wench Sancho saw on the way from El Toboso, it is, no doubt, Dulcinea, and that there are some very active and exceedingly busy enchanters about."

"So I say," said Sancho, "and if my lady Dulcinea is enchanted, so much the worse for her, and I'm not going to pick a quarrel with my master's enemies, who seem to be many and spiteful. The truth is that the one I saw was a country wench, and I set her down to be a country wench; and if that was Dulcinea it must not be laid at my door, nor should I be called to answer for it or take the consequences. But they must go nagging at me every step—'Sancho said it, Sancho did it, Sancho here, Sancho there,' as if Sancho was nobody at all, and not that same Sancho Panza that's now going all over the world in books, so Samson Carrasco told me, and he's at any rate one that's a bachelor of Salamanca; and people of that sort can't lie, except when the whim seizes them or they have some very good reason for it. So there's no occasion for anybody to quarrel with me; and then I have a good character, and, as I have heard my master say, 'a good name is better than great riches'; let them only stick me into this government and they'll see wonders, for one who has been a good squire will be a good governor."

"All worthy Sancho's observations," said the duchess, "are Catonian sentences, or at any rate out of the very heart of Michael Verino himself, who *florentibus occidit annis*.[53] In fact, to speak in his own style, 'under a bad cloak there's often a good drinker.'"

"Indeed, señora," said Sancho, "I never yet drank out of wickedness; from thirst I have very likely, for I have nothing of the hypocrite in me; I drink when I'm inclined, or, if I'm not inclined, when they offer it to me, so as not to look either strait-laced or ill-bred; for when a friend drinks one's health what heart can be so hard as not to return it? But if I put on my shoes I don't dirty them; besides, squires to knights-errant mostly drink water, for they are always wandering among woods, forests and meadows, mountains and crags, without a drop of wine to be had if they gave their eyes for it."

"So I believe," said the duchess; "and now let Sancho go and take his sleep, and we will talk by-and-by at greater length, and settle how he may soon go and stick himself into the government, as he says."

Sancho once more kissed the duchess's hand, and entreated her to be so kind as to let good care be taken of his Dapple, for he was the light of his eyes.

"What is Dapple?" said the duchess.

"My ass," said Sancho, "which, not to mention him by that name, I'm accustomed to call Dapple; I begged this lady duenna here to take care of him when I came into the castle, and she got as angry as if I had said she was ugly or old, though it ought to be more natural and proper for duennas to feed asses than to ornament chambers. God bless me! what a spite a gentleman of my village had against these ladies!"

"He must have been some clown," said Doña Rodriguez the duenna; "for if he had been a gentleman and well-born he would have exalted them higher than the horns of the moon."

"That will do," said the duchess; "no more of this; hush, Doña Rodriguez, and let Señor Panza rest easy and leave the treatment of Dapple in my charge, for as he is a treasure of Sancho's, I'll put him on the apple of my eye."

"It will be enough for him to be in the stable," said Sancho, "for neither he nor I are worthy to rest a moment in the apple of your highness's eye, and I'd as soon stab myself as consent to it; for though my master says that in civilities it is better to lose by a card too many than a card too few, when it comes to civilities to asses we must mind what we are about and keep within due bounds."

"Take him to your government, Sancho," said the duchess, "and there you will be able to make as much of him as you like, and even release him from work and pension him off."

"Don't think, señora duchess, that you have said anything absurd," said Sancho; "I have seen more than two asses go to governments, and for me to take mine with me would be nothing new."

[53]"Died in the flower of his youth." Michael Verino was the author of a poem written in the style of Cato.

Sancho's words made the duchess laugh again and gave her fresh amusement, and dismissing him to sleep she went away to tell the duke the conversation she had had with him, and between them they plotted and arranged to play a joke upon Don Quixote that was to be a rare one and entirely in knight-errantry style, and in that same style they practised several upon him, so much in keeping and so clever that they form the best adventures this great history contains.

• • •

FROM

Chapter 42

Of the counsels which Don Quixote gave Sancho Panza before he set out to govern the island, together with other well-considered matters

The duke and duchess . . . having laid their plans and given instructions to their servants and vassals how to behave to Sancho in his government of the promised island, the next day, . . . the duke told Sancho to prepare and get ready to go and be governor, for his islanders were already looking out for him as for the showers of May.

Sancho made him an obeisance, and said, "Ever since I came down from heaven, and from the top of it beheld the earth, and saw how little it is, the great desire I had to be a governor has been partly cooled in me; for what is there grand in being ruler on a grain of mustard seed, or what dignity or authority in governing half a dozen men about as big as hazel nuts; for, so far as I could see, there were no more on the whole earth? If your lordship would be so good as to give me ever so small a bit of heaven, were it no more than half a league, I'd rather have it than the best island in the world."

"Take notice, friend Sancho," said the duke, "I can not give a bit of heaven, no not so much as the breadth of my nail, to any one; rewards and favors of that sort are reserved for God alone. What I can give I give you, and that is a real, genuine island, compact, well-proportioned, and uncommonly fertile and fruitful, where, if you know how to use your opportunities, you may, with the help of the world's riches, gain those of heaven."

"Well then," said Sancho, "let the island come; and I'll try and be such a governor, that in spite of scoundrels I'll go to heaven; and it's not from any craving to quit my own humble condition or better myself, but from the desire I have to try what it tastes like to be a governor."

"If you once make trial of it, Sancho," said the duke, "you'll eat your fingers off after the government, so sweet a thing is it to command and be obeyed. Depend upon it when your master comes to be emperor (as he will beyond a doubt from the course his affairs are taking), it will be no easy matter to wrest the dignity from him, and he will be sore and sorry at heart to have been so long without becoming one."

"Señor," said Sancho, "it is my belief it's a good thing to be in command, if it's only over a drove of cattle."

"May I be buried with you, Sancho," said the duke, "but you know everything; I hope you will make as good a governor as your sagacity promises, and that is all I have to say; and now remember to-morrow is the day you must set out for the government of the island, and this evening they will provide you with the proper attire for you to wear, and all things requisite for your departure."

"Let them dress me as they like," said Sancho; "however I'm dressed I'll be Sancho Panza."

"That's true," said the duke; "but one's dress must be suited to the office or rank one holds; for it would not do for a jurist to dress like a soldier, or a soldier like a priest. You, Sancho, shall go partly as a lawyer, partly as a captain, for, in the island I am giving you, arms are needed as much as letters, and letters as much as arms."

"Of letters I know but little," said Sancho, "for I don't even know the A B C; but it is enough for me to have the Christus[54] in my memory to be a good governor. As for arms, I'll handle those they give me till I drop, and then, God be my help!"

"With so good a memory," said the duke, "Sancho can not go wrong in anything."

Here Don Quixote joined them; and learning what passed, and how soon Sancho was to go to his government, he with the duke's permission took him by the hand, and retired to his room with him for the purpose of giving him advice as to how he was to demean himself in his office. As soon as they had entered the chamber he closed the door after him, and almost by force made Sancho sit down beside him, and in a quiet tone thus addressed him: "I give infinite thanks to Heaven, friend Sancho, that before I have met with any good luck, fortune has come forward to meet thee. I who counted upon my good fortune to discharge the recompense of thy services, find myself still waiting for advancement, while thou, before the time, and contrary to all reasonable expectation, seest thyself blessed in the fulfilment of thy desires. Some will bribe, beg, solicit, rise early, entreat, persist, without attaining the object of their suit; while another comes, and without knowing why or wherefore, finds himself invested with the place or office so many have sued for; and here it is that the common saying, 'There is good luck as well as bad luck in suits,' applies. Thou, who, to my thinking, art beyond all doubt a dullard, without early rising or night watching or taking any trouble, with the mere breath of knight errantry that has breathed upon thee, seest thyself without more ado governor of an island, as though it were a mere matter of course. This I say, Sancho, that thou attribute not the favor thou hast received to thine own merits, but give thanks to Heaven that disposes matters beneficently, and secondly thanks to the great power the profession of knight-errantry contains in itself. With a heart, then, inclined to believe what I have said to thee, attend, my son, to thy Cato here who would counsel thee and be thy pole-star and guide to direct and pilot thee to a safe haven out of this stormy sea wherein thou art about to ingulf thyself; for offices and great trusts are nothing else but a mighty gulf of troubles.

"First of all, my son, thou must fear God, for in the fear of him is wisdom, and being wise thou canst not err in aught.

"Secondly, thou must keep in view what thou art, striving to know thyself, the most difficult thing to know that the mind can imagine. If thou knowest thyself, it will follow thou wilt not puff thyself up like the frog that strove to make himself as large as the ox; if thou dost, the recollection of having kept pigs in thine own country will serve as the ugly feet for the wheel of thy folly."

"That's the truth," said Sancho; "but that was when I was a boy; afterwards when I was something more of a man it was geese I kept, not pigs. But to my thinking that has nothing to do with it; for not all who are governors come of kingly stock."

"True," said Don Quixote, "and for that reason those who are not of noble origin should take care that the dignity of the office they hold be accompanied by a gentle suavity, which wisely managed will save them from the sneers of malice that no station escapes.

---

[54] A cross prefixed to the alphabet in schoolbooks.

"Glory in thy humble birth, Sancho, and be not ashamed of saying thou art peasant-born; for when it is seen thou art not ashamed no one will set himself to put thee to the blush; and pride thyself rather upon being one of lowly virtue than a lofty sinner. Countless are they who, born of mean parentage, have risen to the highest dignities, pontifical and imperial, and of the truth of this I could give thee instances enough to weary thee.

"Remember, Sancho, if thou make virtue thy aim, and take a pride in doing virtuous actions, thou wilt have no cause to envy those who are born princes and lords, for blood is an inheritance, but virtue an acquisition, and virtue has in itself a worth that blood does not possess.

"This being so, if perchance any one of thy kinsfolk should come to see thee when thou art in thine island, thou art not to repel or slight him, but on the contrary to welcome him, entertain him, and make much of him; for in so doing thou wilt be approved of Heaven (which is not pleased that any should despise what it hath made), and wilt comply with the laws of well-ordered nature.

"If thou carriest thy wife with thee (and it is not well for those that administer governments to be long without their wives), teach and instruct her, and strive to smooth down her natural roughness; for all that may be gained by a wise governor may be lost and wasted by a boorish stupid wife.

"If perchance thou art left a widower—a thing which may happen—and in virtue of thy office seekest a consort of higher degree, choose not one to serve thee for a hook, or for a fishing-rod, or for the hood of thy 'won't have it';[55] for verily, I tell thee, for all the judge's wife receives, the husband will be held accountable at the general calling to account; where he will have to repay in death fourfold, items that in life he regarded as naught.

"Never go by arbitrary law, which is so much favored by ignorant men who plume themselves on cleverness.

"Let the tears of the poor man find with thee more compassion, but not more justice, than the pleadings of the rich.

"Strive to lay bare the truth, as well amid the promises and presents of the rich man, as amid the sobs and entreaties of the poor.

"When equity may and should be brought into play, press not the utmost rigor of the law against the guilty; for the reputation of the stern judge stands not higher than that of the compassionate.

"If perchance thou permittest the staff of justice to swerve, let it be not by the weight of a gift, but by that of mercy.

"If it should happen to thee to give judgment in the cause of one who is thine enemy, turn thy thoughts away from thy injury and fix them on the justice of the case.

"Let not thine own passion blind thee in another man's cause; for the errors thou wilt thus commit will be most frequently irremediable; or if not, only to be remedied at the expense of thy good name and fortune.

"If any handsome woman come to seek justice of thee, turn away thine eyes from her tears and thine ears from her lamentations, and consider deliberately the merits of her demand, if thou wouldst not have thy reason swept away by her weeping, and thy rectitude by her sighs.

"Abuse not by word him whom thou hast to punish in deed, for the pain of punishment is enough for the unfortunate without the addition of thine objurgations.

---

[55] An allusion to a popular joke about begging friars, who were said to make a pretense of refusing gifts, while hinting that gifts might be thrown into the hoods of their robes.

"Bear in mind that the culprit who comes under thy jurisdiction is but a miserable man subject to all the propensities of our depraved nature, and so far as may be in thy power show thyself lenient and forbearing; for though the attributes of God are all equal, to our eyes that of mercy is brighter and loftier than that of justice.

"If thou followest these precepts and rules, Sancho, thy days will be long, thy fame eternal, thy reward abundant, thy felicity unutterable; thou wilt marry thy children as thou wouldst; they and thy grandchildren will bear titles; thou wilt live in peace and concord with all men; and, when life draws to a close, death will come to thee in calm and ripe old age, and the light and loving hands of thy great-grandchildren will close thine eyes.

"What I have thus far addressed to thee are instructions for the adornment of thy mind; listen now to those which tend to that of the body."

Chapter 43

Of the second set of counsels Don Quixote gave Sancho Panza

Who, hearing the foregoing discourse of Don Quixote, would not have set him down for a person of great good sense and greater rectitude of purpose? But, as has been frequently observed in the course of this great history, he only talked nonsense when he touched on chivalry, and in discussing all other subjects showed that he had a clear and unbiassed understanding; so that at every turn his acts gave the lie to his intellect, and his intellect to his acts; but in the case of these second counsels that he gave Sancho he showed himself to have a lively turn of humor, and displayed conspicuously his wisdom, and also his folly.

Sancho listened to him with the deepest attention, and endeavored to fix his counsels in his memory, like one who meant to follow them and by their means bring the full promise of his government to a happy issue. Don Quixote, then, went on to say:

"With regard to the mode in which thou shouldst govern thy person and thy house, Sancho, the first charge I have to give thee is to be clean, and to cut thy nails, not letting them grow as some do, whose ignorance makes them fancy that long nails are an ornament to their hands, as if those excrescences they neglect to cut were nails, and not the talons of a lizard-catching kestrel—a filthy and unnatural abuse.

"Go not ungirt and loose, Sancho; for disordered attire is a sign of an unstable mind, unless indeed the slovenliness and slackness is to be set down to craft, as was the common opinion in the case of Julius Cæsar.

"Ascertain cautiously what thy office may be worth; and if it will allow thee to give liveries to thy servants, give them respectable and serviceable, rather than showy and gay ones, and divide them between thy servants and the poor; that is to say, if thou canst clothe six pages, clothe three and three poor men, and thus thou wilt have pages for heaven and pages for earth; the vainglorious never think of this new mode of giving liveries.

"Eat not garlic nor onions, lest they find out thy boorish origin by the smell; walk slowly and speak deliberately, but not in such a way as to make it seem thou art listening to thyself; for all affectation is bad.

"Dine sparingly and sup more sparingly still; for the health of the whole body is forged in the workshop of the stomach.

"Be temperate in drinking, bearing in mind that wine in excess keeps neither secrets nor promises.

"Take care, Sancho, not to chew on both sides, and not to eruct in anybody's presence."

"Eruct!" said Sancho; "I don't know what that means."

"To eruct, Sancho," said Don Quixote, "means to belch, and that is one of the filthiest words in the Spanish language, though a very expressive one; and therefore nice folk have had recourse to the Latin, and instead of belch say eruct, and instead of belches say eructations; and if some do not understand these terms it matters little, for custom will bring them into use in the course of time, so that they will be readily understood; that is the way a language is enriched; custom and the public are all-powerful there."

"In truth, señor," said Sancho, "one of the counsels and cautions I mean to bear in mind shall be this, not to belch, for I'm constantly doing it."

"Eruct, Sancho, not belch," said Don Quixote.

"Eruct, I shall say henceforth, and I swear not to forget it," said Sancho.

"Likewise, Sancho," said Don Quixote, "thou must not mingle such a quantity of proverbs in thy discourse as thou dost; for though proverbs are short maxims, thou dost drag them in so often by the head and shoulders that they savor more of nonsense than of maxims."

"God alone can cure that," said Sancho; "for I have more proverbs in me than a book, and when I speak they come so thick together into my mouth that they fall to fighting among themselves to get out; that's why my tongue lets fly the first that come, though they may not be pat to the purpose. But I'll take care henceforward to use such as befit the dignity of my office; for 'in a house where there's plenty, supper is soon cooked,' and 'he who binds does not wrangle,' and 'the bell-ringer's in a safe berth,' and 'giving and keeping require brains.'"

"That's it, Sancho!" said Don Quixote; "pack, tack, string proverbs together; nobody is hindering thee! 'My mother beats me, and I go on with my tricks.' I am bidding thee avoid proverbs, and here in a second thou hast shot out a whole litany of them, which have as much to do with what we are talking about as 'over the hills of Úbeda.' Mind, Sancho, I do not say that a proverb aptly brought in is objectionable; but to pile up and string together proverbs at random makes conversation dull and vulgar.

"When thou ridest on horseback, do not go lolling with thy body on the back of the saddle, nor carry thy legs stiff or sticking out from the horse's belly, nor yet sit so loosely that one would suppose thou wert on Dapple; for the seat on a horse makes gentlemen of some and grooms of others.

"Be moderate in thy sleep; for he who does not rise early does not get the benefit of the day; and remember, Sancho, diligence is the mother of good fortune, and indolence, its opposite, never yet attained the object of an honest ambition.

"The last counsel I will give thee now, though it does not tend to bodily improvement, I would have thee carry carefully in thy memory, for I believe it will be no less useful to thee than those I have given thee already, and it is this—never engage in a dispute about families, at least in the way of comparing them one with another; for necessarily one of those compared will be better than the other, and thou wilt be hated by the one thou hast disparaged, and get nothing in any shape from the one thou hast exalted.

"Thy attire shall be hose of full length, a long jerkin, and a cloak a trifle longer; loose breeches by no means, for they are becoming neither for gentlemen nor for governors.

"For the present, Sancho, this is all that has occurred to me to advise thee; as time goes by and occasions arise my instructions shall follow, if thou take care to let me know how thou art circumstanced."

"Señor," said Sancho, "I see well enough that all these things your worship has said to me are good, holy, and profitable; but what use will they be to me if I don't remember one of them? To be sure that about not letting my nails grow, and marrying again if I have the chance, will not slip out of my head; but all that other hash, muddle, and jumble—I don't and can't recollect any more of it than of last year's clouds; so it must be given me in writing; for though I can't either read or write, I'll give it to my confessor to drive it into me and remind me of it whenever it is necessary."

"Ah, sinner that I am!" said Don Quixote, "how bad it looks in governors not to know how to read or write; for let me tell thee, Sancho, when a man knows not how to read, or is left-handed, it argues one of two things; either that he was the son of exceedingly mean and lowly parents, or that he himself was so incorrigible and ill-conditioned that neither good company nor good teaching could make any impression on him. It is a great defect that thou laborest under, and therefore I would have thee learn at any rate to sign thy name."

"I can sign my name well enough," said Sancho, "for when I was steward of the brotherhood in my village I learned to make certain letters, like the marks on bales of goods, which they told me made out my name. Besides I can pretend my right hand is disabled and make some one else sign for me, for 'there's a remedy for everything except death'; and as I shall be in command and hold the staff, I can do as I like; moreover, 'he who has the alcalde for his father—,'[56] and I'll be governor, and that's higher than alcalde. Only come and see! Let them make light of me and abuse me; 'they'll come for wool and go back shorn'; 'whom God loves, his house is sweet to him'; 'the silly sayings of the rich pass for saws in the world'; and as I'll be rich, being a governor, and at the same time generous, as I mean to be, no fault will be seen in me. 'Only make yourself honey and the flies will suck you'; 'as much as thou hast so much art thou worth,' as my grandmother used to say; and 'thou canst have no revenge of a man of substance.' "

"Oh, God's curse upon thee, Sancho!" here exclaimed Don Quixote; "sixty thousand devils fly away with thee and thy proverbs! For the last hour thou hast been stringing them together and inflicting the pangs of torture on me with every one of them. Those proverbs will bring thee to the gallows one day, I promise thee; thy subjects will take the government from thee, or there will be revolts among them, all because of them. Tell me, where dost thou pick them up, thou booby? How dost thou apply them, thou blockhead? For with me, to utter one and make it apply properly, I have to sweat and labor as if I were digging."

"By God, master mine," said Sancho, "your worship is making a fuss about very little. Why the devil should you be vexed if I make use of what is my own? And I have got nothing else, nor any other stock in trade except proverbs and more proverbs; and here are four just this instant come into my head, pat to the purpose and like pears in a basket; but I won't repeat them, for 'Sage silence is called Sancho.' "

"That, Sancho, thou art not," said Don Quixote; "for not only art thou not sage silence, but thou art pestilent prate and perversity; still I would like to know what four proverbs have just now come into thy memory, for I have been turning over mine own—and it is a good one—and not one occurs to me."

"What can be better," said Sancho, "than 'never put thy thumbs between two back teeth'; and 'to "*get out of my house*" and "*what do you want with my wife?*" there is no answer'; and 'whether the pitcher hits the stone, or the stone the pitcher, it's a bad business for the pitcher'; all which fit to a hair? For no one should quarrel with his governor, or him in authority over him, because he will come off the worst, as he does who puts his finger between two back teeth, and if they are not

[56]The full proverb is "He who has the alcalde for his father goes into court with an easy mind."

back teeth it makes no difference, so long as they are teeth; and to whatever the governor may say there's no answer, any more than to 'get out of my house' and 'what do you want with my wife?' and then, as for that about the stone and the pitcher, a blind man could see that. So that he who sees the mote in another's eye had need to see the beam in his own, that it be not said of himself, 'the dead woman was frightened at the one with her throat cut'; and your worship knows well that the fool knows more in his own house than the wise man in another's."

"Nay, Sancho," said Don Quixote, "the fool knows nothing, either in his own house or in anybody else's, for no wise structure of any sort can stand on a foundation of folly; but let us say no more about it, Sancho, for if thou governest badly, thine will be the fault and mine the shame; but I comfort myself with having done my duty in advising thee as earnestly and as wisely as I could; and thus I am released from my obligations and my promise. God guide thee, Sancho, and govern thee in thy government, and deliver me from the misgiving I have that thou wilt turn the whole island upside down, a thing I might prevent by explaining to the duke what thou art and telling him that all that fat little person of thine is nothing else but a sack full of proverbs and sauciness."

"Señor," said Sancho, "if your worship thinks I'm not fit for this government, I give it up on the spot; for the mere black of the nail of my soul is dearer to me than my whole body; and I can live just as well, simple Sancho, on bread and onions, as governor, on partridges and capons; and what's more, while we're asleep we're all equal, great and small, rich and poor. But if your worship looks into it, you will see it was your worship alone that put me on to this business of governing; for I know no more about the government of islands than a buzzard; and if there's any reason to think that because of my being a governor the devil will get hold of me, I'd rather go Sancho to heaven than governor to hell."

"By God, Sancho," said Don Quixote, "for those last words thou hast uttered alone, I consider thou deservest to be governor of a thousand islands. Thou hast good natural instincts, without which no knowledge is worth anything; commend thyself to God, and try not to swerve in the pursuit of thy main object; I mean, always make it thy aim and fixed purpose to do right in all matters that come before thee, for Heaven always helps good intentions; and now let us go to dinner, for I think my lord and lady are waiting for us."

• • •

FROM

Chapter 45

Of how the great Sancho Panza took possession of his island, and of how he made a beginning in governing

O perpetual discoverer of the antipodes, torch of the world, eye of heaven, sweet stimulator of the water-coolers! Thymbræus here, Phœbus there, now archer, now physician, father of poetry, inventor of music; thou that always risest and, notwithstanding appearances, never settest! To thee, O Sun, by whose aid man begetteth man, to thee I appeal to help me and lighten the darkness of my wit that I may be able to proceed with scrupulous exactitude in giving an account of the great Sancho Panza's government; for without thee I feel myself weak, feeble, and uncertain.

To come to the point, then—Sancho with all his attendants arrived at a village of some thousand inhabitants, and one of the largest the duke possessed. They informed him that it was called the island of Barataria, either because the name of the village was Baratario, or because of the joke by way of which the government had been conferred upon him.[57] On reaching the gates of the town, which was a walled one, the municipality came forth to meet him, the bells rang out a peal, and the inhabitants showed every sign of general satisfaction; and with great pomp they conducted him to the principal church to give thanks to God, and then with burlesque ceremonies they presented him with the keys of the town, and acknowledged him as perpetual governor of the island of Barataria. The costume, the beard, and the fat squat figure of the new governor astonished all those who were not in the secret, and even all who were, and they were not a few. Finally, leading him out of the church they carried him to the judgment seat and seated him on it, and the duke's majordomo said to him, "It is an ancient custom in this island, señor governor, that he who comes to take possession of this famous island is bound to answer a question which shall be put to him, and which must be a somewhat knotty and difficult one; and by his answer the people take the measure of their new governor's wit, and hail with joy or deplore his arrival accordingly."

While the majordomo was making this speech Sancho was gazing at several large letters inscribed on the wall opposite his seat, and as he could not read he asked what that was painted on the wall. The answer was, "Señor, there is written and recorded the day on which your lordship took possession of this island, and the inscription says, *This day, the so-and-so of such-and-such a month and year, Señor Don Sancho Panza took possession of this island; many years may he enjoy it.*"

"And whom do they call Don Sancho Panza?" asked Sancho.

"Your lordship," replied the majordomo; "for no other Panza but the one who is now seated in that chair has ever entered this island."

"Well then, let me tell you, brother," said Sancho, "I haven't got the 'Don,' nor has any one of my family ever had it; my name is plain Sancho Panza, and Sancho was my father's name, and Sancho was my grandfather's, and they were all Panzas, without any Dons or Doñas tacked on; I suspect that in this island there are more Dons than stones; but never mind; God knows what I mean, and maybe if my government lasts four days I'll weed out these Dons that no doubt are as great a nuisance as the midges, they're so plenty. Let the majordomo go on with his question, and I'll give the best answer I can, whether the people deplore or not."

At this instant there came into court two old men, one carrying a cane by way of a walking-stick, and the one who had no stick said, "Señor, some time ago I lent this good man ten gold-crowns in gold to gratify him and do him a service, on the condition that he was to return them to me whenever I should ask for them. A long time passed before I asked for them, for I would not put him to any greater straits to return them than he was in when I lent them to him; but thinking he was growing careless about payment I asked for them once and several times; and not only will he not give them back, but he denies that he owes them, and says I never lent him any such crowns; or if I did, that he repaid them; and I have no witnesses either of the loan, or of the payment, for he never paid me; I want your worship to put him to his oath, and if he swears he returned them to me I forgive him the debt here and before God."

"What say you to this, good old man, you with the stick?" said Sancho.

To which the old man replied, "I admit, señor, that he lent them to me; but let your worship lower your staff, and as he leaves it to my oath, I'll swear that I gave them back, and paid him really and truly."

The governor lowered the staff, and as he did so the old man who had the stick handed it to the other old man to hold for him while he swore, as if he found it in

[57] *Barato*, in old Spanish, is a trick or practical joke.

his way; and then laid his hand on the cross of the staff, saying that it was true the ten crowns that were demanded of him had been lent him; but that he had with his own hand given them back into the hand of the other, and that he, not recollecting it, was every minute asking for them.

Seeing this the great governor asked the creditor what answer he had to make to what his opponent said. He said that no doubt his debtor had told the truth, for he believed him to be an honest man and a good Christian, and he himself must have forgotten when and how he had given him back the crowns; and that from that time forth he would make no further demand upon him.

The debtor took his stick again, and bowing his head left the court. Observing this, and how, without another word, he made off, and observing too the resignation of the plantiff, Sancho buried his head in his bosom and remained for a short space in deep thought, with the forefinger of his right hand on his brow and nose; then he raised his head and bade them call back the old man with the stick, for he had already taken his departure. They brought him back, and as soon as Sancho saw him he said, "Honest man, give me that stick, for I want it."

"Willingly," said the old man; "here it is, señor," and he put it into his hand.

Sancho took it and handing it to the other old man, said to him, "Go, and God be with you; for now you are paid."

"I, señor!" returned the old man; "why, is this cane worth ten gold-crowns?"

"Yes," said the governor, "or if not I am the greatest dolt in the world; now you will see whether I have got the head-piece to govern a whole kingdom"; and he ordered the cane to be broken in two, there, in the presence of all. It was done, and in the middle of it they found ten gold-crowns. All were filled with amazement, and looked upon their governor as another Solomon. They asked him how he had come to the conclusion that the ten crowns were in the cane; he replied that, observing how the old man who swore gave the stick to his opponent while he was taking the oath, and swore that he had really and truly given him the crowns, and how as soon as he had done swearing he asked for the stick again, it came into his head that the sum demanded must be inside it; and from this he said it might be seen that God sometimes guides those who govern in their judgments, even though they may be fools; besides he had heard the curate himself mention just such another case, and he had so good a memory, that if it was not that he forgot everything he wished to remember, there would not be such a memory in all the island. To conclude, the old men went off, one crestfallen, and the other in high contentment, all who were present were astonished, and he who was recording the words, deeds, and movements of Sancho could not make up his mind whether he was to look upon him and set him down as a fool or as a man of sense.

As soon as this case was disposed of, there came into court a woman holding on with a tight grip to a man dressed like a well-to-do cattle dealer, and she came forward making a great outcry and exclaiming, "Justice, señor governor, justice! and if I don't get it on earth I'll go look for it in heaven. Señor governor of my soul, this wicked man caught me in the middle of the fields here and used my body as if it was an ill-washed rag, and, woe is me! got from me what I had kept these three-and-twenty years and more, defending it against Moors and Christians, natives and strangers; and I always as hard as an oak, and keeping myself as pure as a salamander in the fire, or wool among the brambles, for this good fellow to come now with clean hands to handle me!"

"It remains to be proved whether this gallant has clean hands or not," said Sancho; and turning to the man he asked him what he had to say in answer to the woman's charge.

He all in confusion made answer, "Sirs, I am a poor pig dealer, and this morning I left the village to sell (saving your presence) four pigs, and between dues and cribbings they got out of me little less than the worth of them. As I was returning to my village I fell in on the road with this good dame, and the devil who makes a coil and a mess out of everything, yoked us together. I paid her fairly, but she not contented laid hold of me and never let go until she brought me here; she says I forced her, but she lies by the oath I swear or am ready to swear; and this is the whole truth and every particle of it."

The governor on this asked him if he had any money in silver about him; he said he had about twenty ducats in a leather purse in his bosom. The governor bade him take it out and hand it to the complainant; he obeyed trembling; the woman took it, and making a thousand salaams to all and praying to God for the long life and health of the señor governor who had such regard for distressed orphans and virgins, she hurried out of court with the purse grasped in both her hands, first looking, however, to see if the money it contained was silver.

As soon as she was gone Sancho said to the cattle dealer, whose tears were already starting and whose eyes and heart were following his purse, "Good fellow, go after that woman and take the purse from her, by force even, and come back with it here"; and he did not say it to one who was a fool or deaf, for the man was off at once like a flash of lightning, and ran to do as he was bid.

All the bystanders waited anxiously to see the end of the case, and presently both man and woman came back at even closer grips than before, she with her petticoat up and the purse in the lap of it, and he struggling hard to take it from her, but all to no purpose, so stout was the woman's defence, she all the while crying out,"Justice from God and the world! see here, señor governor, the shamelessness and boldness of this villain, who in the middle of the town, in the middle of the street, wanted to take from me the purse your worship bade him give me."

"And did he take it ?" asked the governor.

"Take it!" said the woman; "I'd let my life be taken from me sooner than the purse. A pretty child I'd be! It's another sort of cat they must throw in my face, and not that poor scurvy knave. Pincers and hammers, mallets and chisels would not get it out of my grip; no, nor lions' claws; the soul from out of my body first!"

"She is right," said the man; "I own myself beaten and powerless; I confess I haven't the strength to take it from her"; and he let go his hold of her.

Upon this the governor said to the woman, "Let me see that purse, my worthy and sturdy friend." She handed it to him at once, and the governor returned it to the man, and said to the unforced mistress of force, "Sister, if you had shown as much, or only half as much, spirit and vigor in defending your body as you have shown in defending that purse, the strength of Hercules could not have forced you. Be off, and God speed you, and bad luck to you, and don't show your face in all this island, or within six leagues of it on any side, under pain of two hundred lashes; be off at once, I say, you shameless, cheating shrew."

The woman was cowed and went off disconsolately, hanging her head; and the governor said to the man, "Honest man, go home with your money, and God speed you; and for the future, if you don't want to lose it, see that you don't take it into your head to yoke with anybody." The man thanked him as clumsily as he could and went his way, and the bystanders were again filled with admiration at their new governor's judgments and sentences.

Next, two men, one apparently a farm-laborer, and the other a tailor, for he had a pair of shears in his hand, presented themselves before him, and the tailor said, "Señor governor, this laborer and I come before your worship by reason of this honest man coming to my shop yesterday (for saving everybody's presence I'm a passed tailor, God be thanked), and putting a piece of cloth into my hands and asking me, 'Señor, will there be enough in this cloth to make me a cap?' Measuring the cloth I said there would. He probably suspected—as I supposed, and I supposed right—that I wanted to steal some of the cloth, led to think so by his own roguery and the bad opinion people have of tailors; and he told me to see if there would be enough for two. I guessed what he would be at, and I said 'yes.' He, still following up his original unworthy notion, went on adding cap after cap, and I 'yes' after 'yes,' until we got as far as five. He has just this moment come for them; and I gave them to him, but he won't pay me for the making; on the contrary, he calls upon me to pay *him,* or else return his cloth."

"Is all this true, brother?" said Sancho.

"Yes, señor," replied the man; "but will your worship make him show the five caps he has made me?"

"With all my heart," said the tailor; and drawing his hand from under his cloak he showed five caps stuck upon the five fingers of it, and said, "there are the five caps this good man asks for; and by God and upon my conscience I haven't a scrap of cloth left, and I'll let the work be examined by the inspectors of the trade."

All present laughed at the number of caps and the novelty of the suit; Sancho set himself to think for a moment, and then said, "It seems to me that in this case it is not necessary to deliver long-winded arguments, but only to give off-hand the judgment of an honest man; and so my decision is that the tailor lose the making and the laborer the cloth, and that the caps go to the prisoners in the jail, and let there be no more about it."

If the previous decision about the cattle dealer's purse excited the admiration of the bystanders, this provoked their laughter; however, the governor's orders were after all executed. All this, having been taken down by his chronicler, was at once despatched to the duke, who was looking out for it with great eagerness. . . .

FROM

Chapter 47

Wherein is continued the account of how Sancho Panza conducted himself in his government

The history says that from the justice court they carried Sancho to a sumptuous palace, where in a spacious chamber there was a table laid out with royal magnificence. The clarions sounded as Sancho entered the room, and four pages came forward to present him with water for his hands, which Sancho received with great dignity. The music ceased, and Sancho seated himself at the head of the table, for there was only that seat placed, and no more than the one cover laid. A personage, who it appeared afterwards was a physician, placed himself standing by his side with a whalebone wand in his hand. They then lifted up a fine white cloth covering fruit and a great variety of dishes of different sorts; one who looked like a student said grace, and a page put a laced bib on Sancho, while another who played the part of head carver placed a dish of fruit before him. But hardly had he tasted a morsel when the man with the wand touched the plate with it, and they took it away from before him with the utmost celerity. The carver, however, brought him another dish, and Sancho proceeded to try it; but before he could get at it, not to say taste it, already the wand had touched it and a page had carried it off with the same promptitude as the fruit. Sancho seeing this was puzzled, and looking from one to another asked if this dinner was to be eaten after the fashion of a jugglery trick.

To this he with the wand replied, "It is not to be eaten, señor governor, except as is usual and customary in other islands where there are governors. I, señor, am a physician, and I am paid a salary in this island to serve its governors as such, and

I have a much greater regard for their health than for my own, studying day and night making myself acquainted with the governor's constitution, in order to be able to cure him when he falls sick. The chief thing I have to do is to attend at his dinners and suppers and allow him to eat what appears to me to be fit for him and keep from him what I think will do him harm and be injurious to his stomach; and therefore I ordered that plate of fruit to be removed as being too moist, and that other dish I ordered to be removed as being too hot and containing many spices that stimulate thirst; for he who drinks much kills and consumes the radical moisture wherein life consists."

"Well then," said Sancho, "that dish of roast partridges there that seems so savory will not do me any harm."

To this the physician replied, "Of those my lord the governor shall not eat so long as I live."

"Why so?" said Sancho.

"Because," replied the doctor, "our master Hippocrates, the polestar and beacon of medicine, says in one of his aphorisms *omnis saturatio mala, perdicis autem pessima*, which means 'all repletion is bad, but that of partridge is the worst of all.'"

"In that case," said Sancho, "let señor doctor see among the dishes that are on the table what will do me most good and least harm, and let me eat it, without tapping it with his stick; for by the life of the governor, and so may God suffer me to enjoy it, but I'm dying of hunger; and in spite of the doctor and all he may say, to deny me food is the way to take my life instead of prolonging it."

"Your worship is right, señor governor," said the physician; "and therefore your worship, I consider, should not eat of those stewed rabbits there, because it is a furry kind of food; if that veal were not roasted and served with pickles, you might try it; but it is out of the question."

"That big dish that is smoking farther off," said Sancho, "seems to me to be an *olla podrida*,[58] and out of the diversity of things in such *ollas*, I can't fail to light upon something tasty and good for me."

"*Absit*," said the doctor; "far from us be any such base thought! There is nothing in the world less nourishing than an *olla podrida*; to canons, or rectors of colleges, or peasants' weddings with your *ollas podridas*, but let us have none of them on the tables of governors, where everything that is present should be delicate and refined; and the reason is, that always, everywhere and by everybody, simple medicines are more esteemed than compound ones, for we cannot go wrong in those that are simple, while in the compound we may, by merely altering the quantity of the things composing them. But what I am of opinion the governor should eat now in order to preserve and fortify his health is a hundred or so of wafer cakes and a few thin slices of conserve of quinces, which will settle his stomach and help his digestion."

Sancho on hearing this threw himself back in his chair and surveyed the doctor steadily, and in a solemn tone asked him what his name was and where he had studied.

He replied, "My name, Señor Governor, is Doctor Pedro Recio de Aguero, I am a native of a place called Tirteafuera which lies between Caracuel and Almodóvar del Campo, on the right-hand side, and I have the degree of doctor from the university of Osuna."

[58] A stew.

To which Sancho, glowing all over with rage, returned, "Then let Doctor Pedro Recio de Mal-aguero, native of Tirteafuera,[59] a place that's on the right-hand side as we go from Caracuel to Almodóvar del Campo, graduate of Osuna, get out of my presence at once; or I swear by the sun I'll take a cudgel, and by dint of blows, beginning with him, I'll not leave a doctor in the whole island; at least of those I know to be ignorant; for as to learned, wise, sensible physicians, them I will reverence and honor as divine persons. Once more I say let Pedro Recio get out of this or I'll take this chair I am sitting on and break it over his head. And if they call me to account for it, I'll clear myself by saying I served God in killing a bad doctor—a general executioner. And now give me something to eat, or else take your government; for a trade that does not feed its master is not worth two beans."

The doctor was dismayed when he saw the governor in such a passion, and he would have made a *Tirteafuera* out of the room but that the same instant a posthorn sounded in the street; and the carver putting his head out of the window turned round and said, "It's a courier from my lord the duke, no doubt with some despatch of importance."

The courier came in all sweating and flurried, and taking a paper from his bosom, placed it in the governor's hands. Sancho handed it to the majordomo and bade him read the superscription, which ran thus:

TO DON SANCHO PANZA, GOVERNOR OF THE ISLAND OF
BARATARIA, INTO HIS OWN HANDS OR THOSE OF HIS SECRETARY.

Sancho when he heard this said, "Which of you is my secretary?" "I am, señor," said one of those present, "for I can read and write, and am a Biscayan." "With that addition," said Sancho, "you might be secretary to the emperor himself; open this paper and see what it says." The new-born secretary obeyed, and having read the contents said the matter was one to be discussed in private. Sancho ordered the chamber to be cleared, the majordomo and the carver only remaining; so the doctor and the others withdrew, and then the secretary read the letter, which was as follows:

It has come to my knowledge, Señor Don Sancho Panza, that certain enemies of mine and of the island are about to make a furious attack upon it some night, I know not when. It behooves you to be on the alert and keep watch, that they surprise you not. I also know by trustworthy spies that four persons have entered the town in disguise in order to take your life, because they stand in dread of your great capacity; keep your eyes open and take heed who approaches you to address you, and eat nothing that is presented to you. I will take care to send you aid if you find yourself in difficulty, but in all things you will act as may be expected of your judgment. From this place, the Sixteenth of August, at four in the morning.

Your friend,
THE DUKE.

Sancho was astonished, and those who stood by made believe to be so too, and turning to the majordomo he said to him, "What we have got to do first, and it must be done at once, is to put Doctor Recio in the lock-up; for if anyone wants to kill me it is he, and by a slow death and the worst of all, which is hunger."

"Likewise," said the carver, "it is my opinion your worship should not eat anything that is on this table, for the whole was a present from some nuns; and as they say, 'behind the cross there's the devil.' "

---

[59] *Recio* means "obstinate"; *mal-aguero* means "evil omen." *Tirteafuera* means, literally, "take thyself off."

"I don't deny it," said Sancho; "so for the present give me a piece of bread and four pound or so of grapes; no poison can come in them; for the fact is I can't go on without eating; and if we are to be prepared for these battles that are threatening us we must be well provisioned; for it is the tripes that carry the heart and not the heart the tripes. And you, secretary, answer my lord the duke and tell him that all his commands shall be obeyed to the letter, as he directs; and say from me to my lady the duchess that I kiss her hands, and that I beg her not to forget to send my letter and bundle to my wife Teresa Panza by a messenger; and I will take it as a great favor and will not fail to serve her in all that may lie within my power; and as you are about it you may enclose a kiss of the hand to my master Don Quixote that he may see I am grateful bread; and as a good secretary and a good Biscayan you may add whatever you like, and whatever will come in best; and now take away this cloth and give me something to eat, and I'll be ready to meet all the spies and assassins and enchanters that may come against me or my island."

At this instant a page entered saying, "Here is a farmer on business, who wants to speak to your lordship on a matter of great importance, he says."

"It's very odd," said Sancho, "the ways of these men on business; is it possible they can be such fools as not to see that an hour like this is no hour for coming on business? We who govern and we who are judges—are we not men of flesh and blood, are we not to be allowed the time required for taking rest, unless they'd have us made of marble? By God and on my conscience, if the government remains in my hands (which I have a notion it won't), I'll bring more than one man on business to order. However, tell this good man to come in; but take care first of all that he is not some spy or one of my assassins."

"No, my lord," said the page, "for he looks like a simple fellow, and either I know very little or he is as good as good bread."

"There is nothing to be afraid of," said the majordomo, "for we are all here."

"Would it be possible, carver," said Sancho, "now that Doctor Pedro Recio is not here, to let me eat something solid and substantial, if it were even a piece of bread and an onion?"

"To-night at supper," said the carver, "the shortcomings of the dinner shall be made good, and your lordship shall be fully satisfied and contented."

"God grant it," said Sancho.

The farmer now came in, a well-favored man that one might see a thousand leagues off was an honest fellow and a good soul. The first thing he said was, "Which is the señor governor here?"

"Which should it be," said the secretary, "but he who is seated in the chair?"

"Then I humble myself before him," said the farmer; and going on his knees he asked for his hand, to kiss it. Sancho refused it, and bade him stand up and say what he wanted. The farmer obeyed, and then said, "I am a farmer, señor, a native of Miguelturra, a village two leagues from Ciudad Real."

"Another Tirteafuera!" said Sancho; "say on, brother; I know Miguelturra very well I can tell you, for it's not very far from my own town."

"The case is this, señor," continued the farmer, "that by God's mercy I am married with the leave and license of the holy Roman Catholic Church; I have two sons, students, and the younger is studying to become bachelor, and the elder to be licentiate; I am a widower, for my wife died, or more properly speaking, a bad doctor killed her on my hands, giving her a purge when she was with child; and if it had pleased God that the child had been born, and was a boy, I would have put him to study for doctor, that he might not envy his brothers the bachelor and the licentiate."

"So that if your wife had not died, or had not been killed, you would not now be a widower," said Sancho.

"No, señor, certainly not," said the farmer.

"We've got that much settled," said Sancho; "get on, brother, for it's more bedtime than business-time."

"Well then," said the farmer, "this son of mine who is going to be a bachelor fell in love in the said town with a damsel called Clara Perlerina, daughter of Andres Perlerino, a very rich farmer, and this name of Perlerines does not come to them by ancestry or descent, but because all the family are paralytics, and for a better name they call them Perlerines though to tell the truth the damsel is as fair as an Oriental pearl, and like a flower of the field, if you look at her on the right side; on the left not so much, for on that side she wants an eye that she lost by smallpox; and though her face is thickly and deeply pitted, those who love her say they are not pits that are there, but the graves where the hearts of her lovers are buried. She is so cleanly that not to soil her face she carries her nose turned up, as they say, so that one would fancy it was running away from her mouth; and with all this she looks extremely well, for she has a wide mouth; and but for wanting ten or a dozen teeth and grinders she might compare and compete with the comeliest. Of her lips I say nothing, for they are so fine and thin that, if lips might be reeled, one might make a skein of them; but being of a different color from ordinary lips they are wonderful, for they are mottled, blue, green, and purple—let my lord the governor pardon me for painting so minutely the charms of her who some time or other will be my daughter; for I love her, and I don't find her amiss."

"Paint what you will," said Sancho; "I enjoy your painting, and if I had dined there could be no dessert more to my taste than your portrait."

"That I have still to furnish," said the farmer; "but a time may come when we may be able if we are not now; and I can tell you, señor, if I could paint her gracefulness and her tall figure, it would astonish you; but that is impossible because she is bent double with her knees up to her mouth; but for all that it is easy to see that if she could stand up she'd knock her head against the ceiling; and she would have given her hand to my bachelor ere this, only that she can't stretch it out, for it's contracted; but still one can see its elegance and fine make by its long furrowed nails."

"That will do, brother," said Sancho; "consider you have painted her from head to foot; what is it you want now? Come to the point without all this beating about the bush, and all these scraps and additions."

"I want your worship, señor," said the farmer, "to do me the favor of giving me a letter of recommendation to the girl's father, begging him to be so good as to let this marriage take place, as we are not ill-matched either in the gifts of fortune or of nature; for to tell the truth, señor governor, my son is possessed of a devil, and there is not a day but the evil spirits torment him three or four times; and from having once fallen into the fire, he has his face puckered up like a piece of parchment, and his eyes watery and always running; but he has the disposition of an angel, and if it was not for belaboring and pummelling himself he'd be a saint."

"Is there anything else you want, good man?" said Sancho.

"There's another thing I'd like," said the farmer, "but I'm afraid to mention it; however, out it must; for after all I can't let it be rotting in my breast, come what may. I mean, señor, that I'd like your worship to give me three hundred or six hundred ducats as a help to my bachelor's portion, to help him in setting up house, I mean; for they must, in short, live by themselves, without being subject to the interferences of their fathers-in-law."

"Just see if there's anything else you'd like?" said Sancho, "and don't hold back from mentioning it out of bashfulness or modesty."

"No, indeed there is not," said the farmer.

The moment he said this the governor started to his feet, and seizing the chair he had been sitting on exclaimed, "By all that's good you ill-bred, boorish Don Bumpkin, if you don't get out of this at once and hide yourself from my sight, I'll lay your head open with this chair. You whoreson rascal, you devil's own painter, and is it at this hour you come to ask me for six hundred ducats! How should I have them, you stinking brute? And why should I give them to you if I had them, you knave and blockhead? What have I to do with Miguelturra or the whole family of the Perlerines? Get out I say, or by the life of my lord the duke I'll do as I said. You're not from Miguelturra, but some knave sent here from hell to tempt me. Why, you villain, I have not yet had the government half a day, and you want me to have six hundred ducats already!"

The carver made signs to the farmer to leave the room, which he did with his head down, and to all appearance in terror lest the governor should carry his threats into effect, for the rogue knew very well how to play his part. . . .

FROM

Chapter 49

Of what happened to Sancho in making the round of his island

. . . Night came, and with the permission of Doctor Pedro Recio, the governor had supper. They then got ready to go the rounds, and he started with the majordomo, the secretary, the head-carver, the chronicler charged with recording his deeds, and *alguacils*[60] and notaries enough to form a fair-sized squadron. In the midst marched Sancho with his staff, as fine a sight as one could wish to see, and but a few streets of the town had been traversed when they heard a noise as of a clashing of swords. They hastened to the spot, and found that the combatants were but two, who seeing the authorities approaching stood still, and one of them exclaimed, "Help, in the name of God and the king! Are men to be allowed to rob in the middle of this town, and rush out and attack people in the very streets?"

"Be calm, my good man," said Sancho, "and tell me what the cause of this quarrel is; for I am the governor."

Said the other combatant, "Señor governor, I will tell you in a very few words. Your worship must know that this gentleman has just now won more than a thousand reals in that gambling house opposite, and God knows how. I was there, and gave more than one doubtful point in his favor, very much against what my conscience told me. He made off with his winnings, and when I made sure he was going to give me a crown or so at least by way of a present, as it is usual and customary to give men of quality of my sort who stand by to see fair or foul play, and back up swindles, and prevent quarrels, he pocketed his money and left the house. Indignant at this I followed him, and speaking him fairly and civilly asked him to give me if it were only eight reals, for he knows I am an honest man and that I have neither profession nor property, for my parents never brought me up to any or left me any; but the rogue, who is a greater thief than Cacus and a greater sharper than Andradilla, would not give me more than four reals; so your worship

[60]Bailiffs.

may see how little shame and conscience he has. But by my faith if you had not come up I'd have made him disgorge his winnings, and he'd have learned what the range of the steelyard was."

"What say you to this?" asked Sancho. The other replied that all his antagonist said was true, and that he did not choose to give him more than four reals because he very often gave him money; and that those who expected presents ought to be civil and take what is given them with a cheerful countenance, and not make any claim against winners unless they know them for certain to be sharpers and their winnings to be unfairly won; and that there could be no better proof that he himself was an honest man than his having refused to give anything; for sharpers always pay tribute to lookers-on who know them.

"This is true," said the majordomo; "let your worship consider what is to be done with these men."

"What is to be done," said Sancho, "is this; you, the winner, be you good, bad, or indifferent, give this assailant of yours a hundred reals at once, and you must disburse thirty more for the poor prisoners; and you who have neither profession nor property, and hang about the island in idleness, take these hundred reals now, and some time of the day tomorrow quit the island under sentence of banishment for ten years, and under pain of completing it in another life if you violate the sentence, for I'll hang you on a gibbet, or at least the hangman will by my orders; not a word from either of you, or I'll make him feel my hand."

The one paid down the money and the other took it, and the latter quitted the island, while the other went home; and then the governor said, "Either I am not good for much, or I'll get rid of these gambling houses, for it strikes me they are very mischievous."

"This one at least," said one of the notaries, "your worship will not be able to get rid of, for a great man owns it, and what he loses every year is beyond all comparison more than what he makes by the cards. On the minor gambling houses your worship may exercise your power, and it is they that do most harm and shelter the most barefaced practices; for in the houses of lords and gentlemen of quality the notorious sharpers dare not attempt to play their tricks; and as the vice of gambling has become common, it is better that men should play in houses of repute than in some tradesman's, where they catch an unlucky fellow in the small hours of the morning and skin him alive."

"I know already, notary, that there is a good deal to be said on that point," said Sancho.

And now a tipstaff came up with a young man in his grasp, and said, "Señor governor, this youth was coming towards us, and as soon as he saw the officers of justice he turned about and ran like a deer, a sure proof that he must be some evil-doer; I ran after him, and had it not been that he stumbled and fell, I should never have caught him."

"What did you run for, fellow?" said Sancho.

To which the young man replied, "Señor, it was to avoid answering all the questions officers of justice put."

"What are you by trade?"

"A weaver."

"And what do you weave?"

"Lance heads, with your worship's good leave."

"You're facetious with me! You plume yourself on being a wag? Very good; and where were you going just now?"

"To take the air, señor."

"And where does one take the air in this island?"

"Where it blows."

"Good! your answers are very much to the point; you are a smart youth; but take notice that I am the air, and that I blow upon you astern, and send you to jail. Ho there! lay hold of him and take him off; I'll make him sleep there tonight without air."

"By God," said the young man, "your worship will make me sleep in jail just as soon as make me king."

"Why shan't I make thee sleep in jail?" said Sancho. "Have I not the power to arrest thee and release thee whenever I like?"

"All the power your worship has," said the young man, "won't be able to make me sleep in jail."

"How? not able!" said Sancho; "take him away at once where he'll see his mistake with his own eyes, even if the jailer is willing to exert his interested generosity on his behalf; for I'll lay a penalty of two thousand ducats on him if he allows him to stir a step from the prison."

"That's ridiculous," said the young man; "the fact is, all the men on earth will not make me sleep in prison."

"Tell me, you devil," said Sancho, "have you got any angel that will deliver you, and take off the irons I am going to order them to put upon you?"

"Now, señor governor," said the young man in a sprightly manner, "let us be reasonable and come to the point. Granted your worship may order me to be taken to prison, and have irons and chains put on me, and to be shut up in a cell, and may lay heavy penalties on the jailer if he lets me out, and that he obeys your orders; still, if I don't choose to sleep, and choose to remain awake all night without closing an eye, will your worship with all your power be able to make me sleep if I don't choose?"

"No, truly," said the secretary, "and the fellow has made his point."

"So then," said Sancho, "it would be entirely of your own choice you would keep from sleeping; not in opposition to my will?"

"No, señor," said the youth, "certainly not."

"Well then, go, and God be with you," said Sancho; "be off home to sleep, and God give you sound sleep, for I don't want to rob you of it; but for the future, let me advise you don't joke with the authorities, because you may come across some one who will bring down the joke on your own skull."

The young man went his way, and the governor continued his round, and shortly afterwards two tipstaffs came up with a man in custody, and said, "Señor governor, this person, who seems to be a man, is not so, but a woman, and not an ill-favored one, in man's clothes." They raised two or three lanterns to her face, and by their light they distinguished the features of a woman to all appearance of the age of sixteen or a little more, with her hair gathered into a gold and green silk net, and fair as a thousand pearls. They scanned her from head to foot, and observed that she had on red silk stockings with garters of white taffety bordered with gold and pearl; her breeches were of green and gold stuff, and under an open jacket or jerkin of the same she wore a doublet of the finest white and gold cloth; her shoes were white and such as men wear; she carried no sword at her belt, but only a richly ornamented dagger, and on her fingers she had several handsome rings. In short, the girl seemed fair to look at in the eyes of all, and none of those who beheld her knew her, the people of the town said they could not imagine who she was, and those who were in the secret of the jokes that were to be practised upon Sancho were the ones who were most surprised, for this incident or discovery had not been arranged by them; and they watched anxiously to see how the affair would end.

Sancho was fascinated by the girl's beauty, and he asked her who she was, where she was going, and what had induced her to dress herself in that garb. She with her eyes fixed on the ground answered in modest confusion, "I cannot tell you, señor, before so many people what it is of such consequence to me to have kept secret; one thing I wish to be known, that I am no thief or evil-doer, but only an unhappy maiden whom the power of jealousy has led to break through the respect that is due to modesty."

Hearing this the majordomo said to Sancho, "Make the people stand back, señor governor, that this lady may say what she wishes with less embarrassment."

Sancho gave the order, and all except the majordomo, the head-carver, and the secretary fell back. Finding herself then in the presence of no more, the damsel went on to say, "I am the daughter, sirs, of Pedro Perez Mazorca, the wool-farmer of this town, who is in the habit of coming very often to my father's house."

"That won't do, señora," said the majordomo; "for I know Pedro Perez very well, and I know he has no child at all, either son or daughter; and besides, though you say he is your father you add then that he comes very often to your father's house."

"I have already noticed that," said Sancho.

"I am confused just now, sirs," said the damsel, "and I don't know what I am saying; but the truth is that I am the daughter of Diego de la Llana, whom you must all know."

"Ay, that will do," said the majordomo; "for I know Diego de la Llana, and know that he is a gentleman of position and a rich man, and that he has a son and a daughter, and that since he was left a widower nobody in all this town can speak to having seen his daughter's face; for he keeps her so closely shut up that he does not give even the sun a chance of seeing her; and for all that report says she is extremely beautiful."

"It is true," said the damsel, "and I am that daughter; whether report lies or not as to my beauty, you, sirs, will have decided by this time, as you have seen me"; and with this she began to weep bitterly.

On seeing this the secretary leant over to the head-carver's ear, and said to him in a low voice, "Something serious has no doubt happened to this poor maiden, that she goes wandering from home in such a dress and at such an hour, and one of her rank too." "There can be no doubt about it," returned the carver, "and moreover her tears confirm your suspicion." Sancho gave her the best comfort he could, and entreated her to tell them without any fear what had happened to her, as they would all earnestly and by every means in their power endeavor to relieve her.

"The fact is, sirs," said she, "that my father has kept me shut up these ten years, for so long is it since the earth received my mother. Mass is said at home in a sumptuous chapel, and all this time I have seen but the sun in the heaven by day, and the moon and the stars by night; nor do I know what streets are like, or plazas, or churches, or even men, except my father and a brother I have, and Pedro Perez the wool-farmer; whom, because he came frequently to our house, I took it into my head to call my father, to avoid naming my own. This seclusion and the restrictions laid upon my going out, were it only to church, have been keeping me unhappy for many a day and month past; I longed to see the world, or at least the town where I was born, and it did not seem to me that this wish was inconsistent with the respect maidens of good quality should have for themselves. When I heard them talking of bull-fights taking place, and of javelin games, and of acting plays, I asked my brother, who is a year younger than myself, to tell me what sort of things these were, and many more that I had never seen; he explained them to me as well as he could, but the only effect was to kindle in me a still stronger desire to see them. At last, to cut short the story of my ruin, I begged and entreated my brother—O that I had never made such an entreaty"—And once more she gave way to a burst of weeping.

"Proceed, señora," said the majordomo, "and finish your story of what has happened to you, for your words and tears are keeping us all in suspense."

"I have but little more to say, though many a tear to shed," said the damsel; "for ill-placed desires can only be paid for in some such way."

The maiden's beauty had made a deep impression on the head-carver's heart, and he again raised his lantern for another look at her, and thought they were not tears she was shedding, but seed-pearl or dew of the meadow, nay, he exalted them still higher, and made Oriental pearls of them, and fervently hoped her misfortune might not be so great a one as her tears and sobs seemed to indicate. The governor was losing patience at the length of time the girl was taking to tell her story, and told her not to keep them waiting any longer; for it was late, and there still remained a good deal of the town to be gone over.

She, with broken sobs and half-suppressed sighs, went on to say, "My misfortune, my misadventure, is simply this, that I entreated my brother to dress me up as a man in a suit of his clothes, and take me some night, when our father was asleep, to see the whole town; he, overcome by my entreaties, consented, and dressing me in this suit and himself in clothes of mine that fitted him as if made for him (for he has not a hair on his chin, and might pass for a very beautiful young girl), to-night, about an hour ago, more or less, we left the house, and guided by our youthful and foolish impulse we made the circuit of the whole town, and then, as we were about to return home, we saw a great troop of people coming, and my brother said to me, 'Sister, this must be the round, stir your feet and put wings to them, and follow me as fast as you can, lest they recognize us, for that would be a bad business for us'; and so saying he turned about and began, I cannot say to run but to fly; in less than six paces I fell from fright, and then the officer of justice came up and carried me before your worships, where I find myself put to shame before all these people as whimsical and vicious."

"So then, señora," said Sancho, "no other mishap has befallen you, nor was it jealousy that made you leave home, as you said at the beginning of your story?"

"Nothing has happened to me," said she, "nor was it jealousy that brought me out, but merely a longing to see the world, which did not go beyond seeing the streets of this town."

The appearance of the tipstaffs with her brother in custody, whom one of them had overtaken as he ran away from his sister, now fully confirmed the truth of what the damsel said. He had nothing on but a rich petticoat and a short blue damask cloak with fine gold lace, and his head was uncovered and adorned only with its own hair, which looked like rings of gold, so bright and curly was it. The governor, the majordomo, and the carver went aside with him, and, unheard by his sister, asked him how he came to be in that dress, and he with no less shame and embarrassment told exactly the same story as his sister, to the great delight of the enamoured carver; the governor, however, said to them, "In truth, young lady and gentleman, this has been a very childish affair, and to explain your folly and rashness there was no necessity for all this delay and all these tears and sighs; for if you had said we are so-and-so, and we escaped from our father's house in this way in order to ramble about, out of mere curiosity and with no other object, there would have been an end of the matter, and none of these little sobs and tears and all the rest of it."

"That is true," said the damsel, "but you see the confusion I was in was so great it did not let me behave as I ought."

"No harm has been done," said Sancho; "come, we will leave you at your father's house; perhaps they will not have missed you; and another time don't be so childish or eager to see the world; for a respectable damsel and a broken leg should keep at home; and the woman and the hen by gadding about are soon lost; and she who is eager to see is also eager to be seen; I say no more."

The youth thanked the governor for his kind offer to take them home, and they directed their steps towards the house, which was not far off. On reaching it the youth threw a pebble up at a grating, and immediately a woman-servant who was waiting for them came down and opened the door to them, and they went in, leaving the party marvelling as much at their grace and beauty as at the fancy they had for seeing the world by night and without quitting the village; which, however, they set down to their youth.

The head-carver was left with a heart pierced through and through, and he made up his mind on the spot to demand the damsel in marriage of her father on the morrow, making sure she would not be refused him as he was a servant of the duke's; and even to Sancho ideas and schemes of marrying the youth to his daughter Sanchica suggested themselves, and he resolved to open the negotiation at the proper season, persuading himself that no husband could be refused to a governor's daughter. And so the night's round came to an end, and a couple of days later the government, whereby all his plans were over-thrown and swept away, as will be seen farther on.

Chapter 50

Wherein is set forth who the enchanters and executioners were who flogged the duenna and pinched Don Quixote, and also what befell the page who carried the letter to Teresa Panza, Sancho Panza's wife

Cid Hamet, the painstaking investigator of the minute points of this veracious history, says that when Doña Rodriguez left her own room to go to Don Quixote's, another duenna who slept with her observed her, and as all duennas are fond of prying, listening, and sniffing, she followed her so silently that the good Rodriguez never perceived it; and as soon as the duenna saw her enter Don Quixote's room, not to fail in a duenna's invariable practice of tattling, she hurried off that instant to report to the duchess how Doña Rodriguez was closeted with Don Quixote. The duchess told the duke, and asked him to let her and Altisidora go and see what the said duenna wanted with Don Quixote. The duke gave them leave, and the pair cautiously and quietly crept to the door of the room and posted themselves so close to it that they could hear all that was said inside. But when the duchess heard how Rodriguez had made public the Aranjuez of her issues she could not restrain herself, nor Altisidora either; and so, filled with rage and thirsting for vengeance, they burst into the room and tormented Don Quixote and flogged the duenna in the manner already described; for indignities offered to their charms and self-esteem mightily provoke the anger of women and make them eager for revenge. The duchess told the duke what had happened, and he was much amused by it; and she, in pursuance of her design of making merry and diverting herself with Don Quixote, despatched the page who had played the part of Dulcinea in the negotiations for her disenchantment (which Sancho Panza in the cares of government had forgotten all about) to Teresa Panza his wife with her husband's letter and another from herself, and also a great string of fine coral beads as a present.

Now the history says this page was very sharp and quick-witted; and eager to serve his lord and lady he set off very willingly for Sancho's village. Before he entered it he observed a number of women washing in a brook, and asked them if they could tell him whether there lived there a woman of the name of Teresa Panza, wife of one Sancho Panza, squire to a knight called Don Quixote of La Mancha. At the question a young girl who was washing stood up and said, "Teresa Panza is my mother, and that Sancho is my father, and that knight is our master."

"Well then, miss," said the page, "come and show me where your mother is, for I bring her a letter and a present from your father."

"That I will with all my heart, señor," said the girl, who seemed to be about fourteen, more or less; and leaving the clothes she was washing to one of her companions, and without putting anything on her head or feet, for she was bare-legged and had her hair hanging about her, away she skipped in front of the page's horse, saying, "Come, your worship, our house is at the entrance of the town, and my mother is there, sorrowful enough at not having had any news of my father this ever so long."

"Well," said the page, "I am bringing her such good news that she will have reason to thank God for it."

And then, skipping, running, and capering, the girl reached the town, but before going into the house she called out at the door, "Come out, mother Teresa, come out, come out; here's a gentleman with letters and other things from my good father." At these words her mother Teresa Panza came out spinning a bundle of flax, in a gray petticoat (so short was it one would have fancied "they to her shame had cut it short"[61]), a gray bodice of the same stuff, and a smock. She was not very old, though plainly past forty, strong, healthy, vigorous, and sun-dried; and seeing her daughter and the page on horseback, she exclaimed, "What's this, child? What gentleman is this?"

"A servant of my lady, Doña Teresa Panza," replied the page; and suiting the action to the word he flung himself off his horse, and with great humility advanced to kneel before the lady Teresa, saying, "Let me kiss your hand, Señora Doña Teresa, as the lawful and only wife of Señor Don Sancho Panza, rightful governor of the island of Barataria."

"Ah, señor, get up, don't do that," said Teresa; "for I'm not a bit of a court lady, but only a poor countrywoman, the daughter of a clod-crusher, and the wife of a squire-errant and not of any governor at all."

"You are," said the page, "the most worthy wife of a most arch-worthy governor; and as a proof of what I say accept this letter and this present"; and at the same time he took out of his pocket a string of coral beads with gold clasps, and placed it on her neck, and said, "This letter is from his lordship the governor, and the other as well as these coral beads from my lady the duchess, who sends me to your worship."

Teresa stood lost in astonishment, and her daughter just as much, and the girl said, "May I die but our master Don Quixote's at the bottom of this; he must have given father the government or country he so often promised him."

"That is the truth," said the page; "for it is through Señor Don Quixote that Señor Sancho is now governor of the island of Barataria, as will be seen by this letter."

"Will your worship read it to me, noble sir?" said Teresa; "for though I can spin I can't read, not a scrap."

"Nor I either," said Sanchica; "but wait a bit, and I'll go and fetch some one who can read it, either the curate himself or the bachelor Samson Carrasco, and they'll come gladly to hear any news of my father."

---

[61]Docking the skirts was a punishment for misconduct.

"There is no need to fetch anybody," said the page; "for though I can't spin I can read, and I'll read it"; and so he read it through, but as it has already been given it is not inserted here; and then he took out the other one from the duchess, which ran as follows:

> FRIEND TERESA, Your husband Sancho's good qualities, of heart as well as of head, induced and compelled me to request my husband the duke to give him the government of one of his many islands. I am told he governs like a gerfalcon, of which I am very glad, and my lord the duke, of course, also; and I am very thankful to Heaven that I have not made a mistake in choosing him for that same government; for I would have Señora Teresa know that a good governor is hard to find in this world, and may God make me as good as Sancho's way of governing. Herewith I send you, my dear, a string of coral beads with gold clasps; I wish they were Oriental pearls; but "he who gives thee a bone does not wish to see thee dead"; a time will come when we shall become acquainted and meet one another, but God knows the future. Commend me to your daughter Sanchica, and tell her from me to hold herself in readiness, for I mean to make a high match for her when she least expects it. They tell me there are big acorns in your village; send me a couple of dozen or so, and I shall value them greatly as coming from your hand; and write to me at length to assure me of your health and well-being; and if there be anything you stand in need of, it is but to open your mouth, and that shall be the measure; and so God keep you.
>
> From this place.
> Your loving friend,
> THE DUCHESS

"Ah, what a good, plain, lowly lady!" said Teresa when she heard the letter; "that I may be buried with ladies of that sort, and not the gentlewomen we have in this town, that fancy because they are gentlewomen the wind must not touch them, and go to church with as much airs as if they were queens, no less, and seem to think they are disgraced if they look at a farmer's wife! And see here how this good lady, for all she's a duchess, calls me 'friend,' and treats me as if I was her equal—and equal may I see her with the tallest church-tower in La Mancha! And as for the acorns, señor, I'll send her ladyship a peck and such big ones that one might come to see them as a show and a wonder. And now, Sanchica, see that the gentleman is comfortable; put up his horse, and get some eggs out of the stable, and cut plenty of bacon, and let's give him his dinner like a prince; for the good news he has brought, and his own bonny face deserve it all; and meanwhile I'll run out and give the neighbors the news of our good luck, and father curate, and Master Nicholas the barber, who are and always have been such friends of thy father's."

"That I will, mother," said Sanchica; "but mind, you must give me half of that string; for I don't think my lady the duchess could have been so stupid as to send it all to you."

"It is all for thee, my child," said Teresa; "but let me wear it round my neck for a few days; for verily it seems to make my heart glad."

"You will be glad, too" said the page, "when you see the bundle there is in this portmanteau, for it is a suit of the finest cloth, that the governor only wore one day out hunting and now sends, all for Señora Sanchica."

"May he live a thousand years," said Sanchica, "and the bearer as many, nay two thousand, if needful."

With this Teresa hurried out of the house with the letters, and with the string of beads round her neck, and went along thrumming the letters as if they were a tambourine, and by chance coming across the curate and Samson Carrasco she began capering and saying, "None of us poor now, faith! We've got a little government! Ay, let the finest fine lady tackle me, and I'll give her a setting down!"

"What's all this, Teresa Panza," said they; "what madness is this, and what papers are those?"

"The madness is only this," said she, "that these are the letters of duchesses and governors, and these I have on my neck are fine coral beads, with ave marias and paternosters of beaten gold, and I am a governess."

"God help us," said the curate, "we don't understand you, Teresa, or know what you are talking about."

"There, you may see it yourselves," said Teresa, and she handed them the letters.

The curate read them out for Samson Carrasco to hear, and Samson and he regarded one another with looks of astonishment at what they had read, and the bachelor asked who had brought the letters. Teresa in reply bade them come with her to her house and they would see the messenger, a most elegant youth, who had brought another present which was worth as much more. The curate took the coral beads from her neck and examined them again and again, and having satisfied himself as to their fineness he fell to wondering afresh, and said, "By the gown I wear I don't know what to say or think of these letters and presents; on the one hand I can see and feel the fineness of these coral beads, and on the other I read how a duchess sends to beg for a couple of dozen acorns."

"Square that if you can," said Carrasco; "well, let's go and see the messenger, and from him we'll learn something about this mystery that has turned up."

They did so, and Teresa returned with them. They found the page sifting a little barley for his horse, and Sanchica cutting a rasher of bacon to be paved with eggs for his dinner. His looks and his handsome apparel pleased them both greatly; and after they had saluted him courteously, and he them, Samson begged him to give them his news, as well of Don Quixote as of Sancho Panza, for, he said, though they had read the letters from Sancho and her ladyship the duchess, they were still puzzled and could not make out what was meant by Sancho's government, and above all of an island, when all or most of those in the Mediterranean belonged to his majesty.

To this the page replied, "As to Señor Sancho Panza's being a governor there is no doubt whatever; but whether it is an island or not that he governs, with that I have nothing to do; suffice it that it is a town of more than a thousand inhabitants; with regard to the acorns I may tell you my lady the duchess is so unpretending and unassuming that, not to speak of sending to beg for acorns from a peasant woman, she has been known to send to ask for the loan of a comb from one of her neighbors; for I would have your worships know that the ladies of Aragon, though they are just as illustrious, are not so punctilious and haughty as the Castilian ladies; they treat people with greater familiarity."

In the middle of this conversation Sanchica came in with her skirt full of eggs, and said she to the page, "Tell me, señor, does my father wear trunk-hose since he has been governor?"

"I have not noticed," said the page; "but no doubt he wears them."

"Ah! my God!" said Sanchica, "what a sight it must be to see my father in tights! Isn't it odd that ever since I was born I have had a longing to see my father in trunk-hose?"

"As things go you will see that if you live," said the page; "by God, he is in the way to take the road with a sunshade if the government only lasts him two months more."

The curate and the bachelor could see plainly enough that the page spoke in a waggish vein; but the fineness of the coral beads, and the hunting suit that Sancho sent (for Teresa had already shown it to them) did away with the impression; and they could not help laughing at Sanchica's wish, and still more when Teresa said,

"Señor curate, look about if there's anybody here going to Madrid or Toledo, to buy me a hooped petticoat, a proper fashionable one of the best quality; for indeed and indeed I must do honor to my husband's government as well as I can; nay, if I am put to it, I'll go to court and set up a coach like all the world; for she who has a governor for her husband may very well have one and keep one."

"And why not, mother!" said Sanchica; "would to God it were to-day instead of to-morrow, even though they were to say when they saw me seated in the coach with my mother, 'See that rubbish, that garlic-stuffed fellow's daughter, how she goes stretched at her ease in a coach as if she was a she-pope!' But let them tramp through the mud, and let me go in my coach with my feet off the ground. Bad luck to backbiters all over the world; 'let me go warm and the people may laugh.' Do I say right, mother?"

"To be sure you do, my child," said Teresa; "and all this good luck, and even more, my good Sancho foretold me; and thou wilt see, my daughter, he won't stop till he has made me a countess; for to make a beginning is everything in luck; and as I have heard thy good father say many a time (for besides being thy father he's the father of proverbs too), 'When they offer thee a heifer, run with a halter; when they offer thee a government, take it; when they would give thee a country, seize it; when they say "Here, here!" to thee with something good, swallow it.' Oh no! go to sleep, and don't answer the strokes of good fortune and the lucky chances that are knocking at the door of your house!"

"And what do I care," added Sanchica, "whether anybody says when he sees me holding my head up, 'The dog saw himself in hempen breeches,' and the rest of it?"

Hearing this the curate said, "I do believe that all this family of the Panzas are born with a sackful of proverbs in their insides, every one of them; I never saw one of them that does not pour them out at all times and on all occasions."

"That is true," said the page, "for Señor Governor Sancho utters them at every turn; and though a great many of them are not to the purpose, still they amuse one, and my lady the duchess and the duke praise them highly."

"Then you still maintain that all this about Sancho's government is true, señor," said the bachelor, "and that there actually is a duchess who sends him presents and writes to him? Because we, although we have handled the presents and read the letters, don't believe it, and suspect it to be something in the line of our fellow-townsman Don Quixote, who fancies that everything is done by enchantment; and for this reason I am almost ready to say that I'd like to touch and feel your worship to see whether you are a mere ambassador of the imagination or a man of flesh and blood."

"All I know, sirs," replied the page, "is that I am a real ambassador, and that Señor Sancho Panza is governor as a matter of fact, and that my lord and lady the duke and duchess can give, and have given him this same government, and that I have heard the said Sancho Panza bears himself very stoutly therein; whether there be any enchantment in all this or not, it is for your worships to settle between you; for that's all I know by the oath I swear, and that is by the life of my parents whom I have still alive, and love dearly."

"It may be so," said the bachelor, "but *dubitat Augustinus.*"[62]

"Doubt who will," said the page; "what I have told you is the truth, and that will always rise above falsehood as oil above water; if not *operibus credite, et non verbis.*[63] Let

[62]"But Augustine doubts it." Carrasco means that he is not convinced.

[63]"Believe in my actions, not my words."

one of you come with me, and he will see with his eyes what he does not believe with his ears."

"It's for me to make that trip," said Sanchica; "take me with you, señor, behind you on your horse; for I'll go with all my heart to see my father."

"Governors' daughters," said the page, "must not travel along the roads alone, but accompanied by coaches and litters and a great number of attendants."

"By God," said Sanchica, "I can go just as well mounted on a she-ass as in a coach; what a dainty lass you must take me for!"

"Hush, girl," said Teresa; "you don't know what you're talking about; the gentleman is quite right, for 'as the time so the behavior'; when it was Sancho it was 'Sancha'; when it is governor it's 'señora'; I don't know if I'm right."

"Señora Teresa says more than she is aware of," said the page; "and now give me something to eat and let me go at once, for I mean to return this evening."

"Come and do penance with me," said the curate at this; "for Señora Teresa has more will than means to serve so worthy a guest."

The page refused, but had to consent at last for his own sake; and the curate took him home with him very gladly, in order to have an opportunity of questioning him at leisure about Don Quixote and his doings. The bachelor offered to write the letters in reply for Teresa; but she did not care to let him mix himself up in her affairs, for she thought him somewhat given to joking; and so she gave a cake and a couple of eggs to a young acolyte who was a penman, and he wrote for her two letters, one for her husband and the other for the duchess, dictated out of her own head, and these are not the worst inserted in this great history, as will be seen farther on.

Chapter 51

Of the progress of Sancho's government, and other such entertaining matters

Day came after the night of the governor's round; a night which the head-carver passed without sleeping, so full were his thoughts of the face and air and beauty of the disguised damsel, while the majordomo spent what was left of it in writing an account to his lord and lady of all Sancho said and did, being as much amazed at his sayings as at his doings, for there was a mixture of shrewdness and simplicity in all his words and deeds. The señor governor got up, and by Doctor Pedro Recio's directions they made him break his fast on a little conserve and four sups of cold water, which Sancho would have readily exchanged for a piece of bread and a bunch of grapes; but seeing there was no help for it, he submitted with no little sorrow of heart and discomfort of stomach; Pedro Recio having persuaded him that light and delicate diet enlivened the wits, and that was what was most essential for persons placed in command and in responsible situations, where they have to employ not only the bodily powers but those of the mind also.

By means of this sophistry Sancho was made to endure hunger, and hunger so keen that in his heart he cursed the government, and even him who had given it to him; however, with his hunger and his conserve he undertook to deliver judgments that day, and the first thing that came before him was a question that was submitted to him by a stranger, in the presence of the majordomo and the other attendants, and it was in these words: "Señor, a large river separated two districts of one and the same lordship—will your worship please to pay attention, for the case is an important and a rather knotty one? Well then, on this river there was a bridge, and at one end of it a gallows, and a sort of tribunal, where four judges commonly sat to administer the law which the lord of the river, the bridge and the lordship had enacted, and which was to this effect, 'If any one crosses by this bridge from one side to the other he shall declare on oath where he is going and with what object; and if he swears truly, he shall be allowed to pass, but if falsely, he shall, without any remission, be put to death for it by hanging on the gallows erected there.' Though the law and its severe penalty were known, many persons crossed, but in their declarations it was easy to see at once they were telling the truth, and the judges let them pass free. It happened, however, that one man, when they came to take his declaration, swore and said that by the oath he took he was going to die upon that gallows that stood there, and nothing else. The judges held a consultation over the oath, and they said, 'If we let this man pass free he has sworn falsely, and by the law he ought to die; but if we hang him, as he swore he was going to die on that gallows, and therefore swore the truth, by the same law he ought to go free.' It is asked of your worship, señor governor, what are the judges to do with this man? For they are still in doubt and perplexity; and having heard of your worship's acute and exalted intellect, they have sent me to entreat your worship on their behalf to give your opinion on this very intricate and puzzling case."

To this Sancho made answer, "Indeed those gentlemen the judges that send you to me might have spared themselves the trouble, for I have more of the obtuse than the acute in me; however, repeat the case over again, so that I may understand it, and then perhaps I may be able to hit the point."

The querist repeated again and again what he had said before, and then Sancho said, "It seems to me I can set the matter right in a moment, and in this way; the man swears that he is going to die upon the gallows; but if he dies upon it, he has sworn the truth, and by the law enacted deserves to go free and pass over the bridge; but if they don't hang him, then he has sworn falsely, and by the same law deserves to be hanged."

"It is as the señor governor says," said the messenger; "and as regards a complete comprehension of the case, there is nothing left to desire or hesitate about."

"Well then I say," said Sancho, "that of this man they should let pass the part that has sworn truly, and hang the part that has lied; and in this way the conditions of the passage will be fully complied with."

"But then, señor governor," replied the querist, "the man will have to be divided into two parts; and if he is divided of course he will die; and so none of the requirements of the law will be carried out, and it is absolutely necessary to comply with it."

"Look here, my good sir," said Sancho; "either I'm a numskull or else there is the same reason for this passenger dying as for his living and passing over the bridge; for if the truth saves him the falsehood equally condemns him; and that being the case it is my opinion you should say to the gentlemen who sent you to me that as the arguments for condemning him and for absolving him are exactly balanced, they should let him pass freely, as it is always more praiseworthy to do good than to do evil; this I would give signed with my name if I knew how to sign; and what I have said in this case is not out of my own head, but one of the many precepts my master Don Quixote gave me the night before I left to become governor of this island, that came into my mind, and it was this, that when there was any doubt about the justice of a case I should lean to mercy; and it is God's will that I should recollect it now, for it fits this case as if it was made for it."

"That is true," said the majordomo; "and I maintain that Lycurgus himself, who gave laws to the Lacædemonians, could not have pronounced a better decision than the great Panza has given; let the morning's audience close with this, and I will see that the señor governor has dinner entirely to his liking."

"That's all I ask for—fair play," said Sancho; "give me my dinner, and then let it rain cases and questions on me, and I'll despatch them in a twinkling."

The majordomo kept his word, for he felt it against his conscience to kill so wise a governor by hunger; particularly as he intended to have done with him that same night, playing off the last joke he was commissioned to practise upon him.

It came to pass, then, that after he had dined that day, in opposition to the rules and aphorisms of Doctor Tirteafuera, as they were taking away the cloth there came a courier with a letter from Don Quixote for the governor. Sancho ordered the secretary to read it to himself, and if there was nothing in it that demanded secrecy to read it aloud. The secretary did so, and after he had skimmed the contents he said, "It may well be read aloud, for what Señor Don Quixote writes to your worship deserves to be printed or written in letters of gold, and it is as follows."

DON QUIXOTE OF LA MANCHA'S LETTER TO SANCHO PANZA, GOVERNOR OF THE ISLAND OF BARATARIA.

When I was expecting to hear of thy stupidities and blunders, friend Sancho, I have received intelligence of thy displays of good sense, for which I give special thanks to Heaven that can raise the poor from the dunghill and of fools to make wise men. They tell me thou dost govern as if thou wert a man, and art a man as if thou wert a beast, so great is the humility wherewith thou dost comport thyself. But I would have thee bear in mind, Sancho, that very often it is fitting and necessary for the authority of office to resist the humility of the heart; for the seemly array of one who is invested with grave duties should be such as they require and not measured by what his own humble tastes may lead him to prefer. Dress well; a stick dressed up does not look like a stick; I do not say thou shouldst wear trinkets or fine raiment, or that being a judge thou shouldst dress like a soldier, but that thou shouldst array thyself in the apparel thy office requires, and that at the same time it be neat and handsome. To win the good-will of the people thou governest there are two things, among others, that thou must do; one is to be civil to all (this, however, I told thee before) and the other to take care that food be abundant, for there is nothing that vexes the heart of the poor more than hunger and high prices. Make not many proclamations; but those thou makest take care that they be good ones, and above all that they be observed and carried out; for proclamations that are not observed are the same as if they did not exist; nay, they encourage the idea that the prince who had the wisdom and authority to make them had not the power to enforce them; and laws that threaten and are not enforced come to be like the log, the king of the frogs, that frightened them at first, but that in time they despised and mounted upon. Be a father to virtue and a step-father to vice. Be not always strict, nor yet always lenient, but observe a mean between these two extremes, for in that is the aim of wisdom. Visit the jails, the slaughter-houses, and the market-places; for the presence of the governor is of great importance in such places; it comforts the prisoners who are in hopes of a speedy release, it is the bugbear of the butchers who have then to give just weight, and it is the terror of the market-women for the same reason. Let it not be seen that thou art (even if perchance thou art, which I do not believe) covetous, a follower of women, or a glutton; for when the people and those that have dealings with thee become aware of thy special weakness they will bring their batteries to bear upon thee in that quarter, till they have brought thee down to the depths of perdition. Consider and reconsider, con and con over again the advice and the instructions I gave thee before thy departure hence to thy government, and thou wilt see that in them, if thou dost follow them, thou hast a help at hand that will lighten for thee the troubles and difficulties that beset governors at every step. Write to thy lord and lady and show thyself grateful to them, for ingratitude is the daughter of pride, and one of the greatest sins we know of; and he who is grateful to those who have been good to him shows that he will be so to God also who has bestowed and still bestows so many blessings upon him.

My lady the duchess sent off a messenger with thy suit and another present to thy wife Teresa Panza; we expect the answer every moment. I have been a little indisposed through a certain cat-scratching I came in for, not very much to the benefit of my nose; but it was nothing; for if there are enchanters who maltreat me, there are also some who defend me. Let me know if the majordomo who is with thee had any share in the Trifaldi performance, as thou didst suspect; and keep me informed of everything that happens to thee, as the distance is so short; all the more as I am thinking of giving over very shortly this idle life I am now leading, for I was not born for it. A thing has occurred to me which I am inclined to think will put me out of favor with the duke and duchess; but though I am sorry for it I do not care, for after all I must obey my calling rather than their pleasure, in accordance with the common saying *amicus Plato, sed magis amica veritas.*[64] I quote this Latin to thee because I conclude that since thou hast been a governor thou wilt have learned it. Adieu; God keep thee from being an object of pity to any one.

Thy friend
DON QUIXOTE OF LA MANCHA

Sancho listened to the letter with great attention, and it was praised and considered wise by all who heard it; he then rose up from table, and calling his secretary shut himself in with him in his own room, and without putting it off any longer set about answering his master Don Quixote at once; and he bade the secretary write down what he told him without adding or suppressing anything, which he did, and the answer was to the following effect.

SANCHO PANZA'S LETTER TO DON QUIXOTE OF LA MANCHA.

The pressure of business is so great upon me that I have no time to scratch my head or even to cut my nails; and I wear them so long—God send a remedy for it. I say this, master of my soul, that you may not be surprised if I have not until now sent you word of how I fare, well or ill, in this government, in which I am suffering more hunger than when we two were wandering through the woods and wastes.

My lord the duke wrote to me the other day to warn me that certain spies had got into this island to kill me; but up to the present I have not found out any except a certain doctor who receives a salary in this town for killing all the governors that come here; he is called Doctor Pedro Recio, and is from Tirteafuera; so you see what a name he has to make me dread dying under his hands. This doctor says of himself that he does not cure diseases when there are any, but prevents them coming, and the medicines he uses are diet and more diet, until he brings one down to bare bones; as if leanness was not worse than fever.

In short he is killing me with hunger, and I am dying myself of vexation; for when I thought I was coming to this government to get my meat hot and my drink cool, and take my ease between holland sheets on feather beds, I find I have come to do penance as if I was a hermit; and as I don't do it willingly I suspect that in the end the devil will carry me off.

So far I have not handled any dues or taken any bribes, and I don't know what to think of it; for here they tell me that the governors that come to this island, before entering it have plenty of money either given to them or lent to them by the people of the town, and that this is the usual custom not only here but with all who enter upon governments.

Last night going the rounds I came upon a fair damsel in man's clothes, and a brother of hers dressed as a woman; my head-carver has fallen in love with the girl, and has in his own mind chosen her for a wife, so he says, and I have chosen the youth for a son-in-law; to-day we are going to explain our intentions to the father of the pair, who is one Diego de la Llana, a gentleman and an old Christian as much as you please.

I have visited the market-places, as your worship advises me, and yesterday I found a stall-keeper selling new hazelnuts and proved her to have mixed a bushel of old empty rotten nuts with a bushel of new; I confiscated the whole for the children of the charity

[64]"Plato is a friend, but Truth is a better friend."

school, who will know how to distinguish them well enough, and I sentenced her not to come into the market-place for a fortnight; they told me I did bravely. I can tell your worship it is commonly said in this town that there are no people worse than the marketwomen, for they are all barefaced, unconscionable, and impudent, and I can well believe it from what I have seen of them in other towns.

I am very glad my lady the duchess has written to my wife Teresa Panza and sent her the present your worship speaks of; and I will strive to show myself grateful when the time comes; kiss her hands for me, and tell her I say she has not thrown it into a sack with a hole in it, as she will see in the end. I should not like your worship to have any difference with my lord and lady; for if you fall out with them it is plain it must do me harm; and as you give me advice to be grateful it will not do for your worship not to be so yourself to those who have shown you such kindness, and by whom you have been treated so hospitably in their castle.

That about the cat-scratching I don't understand; but I suppose it must be one of the ill-turns the wicked enchanters are always doing your worship; when we meet I shall know all about it. I wish I could send your worship something; but I don't know what to send, unless it be some very curious clyster pipes, to work with bladders, that they make in this island; but if the office remains with me I'll find out something to send, one way or another. If my wife Teresa Panza writes to me, pay the postage and send me the letter, for I have a very great desire to hear how my house and wife and children are going on. And so, may God deliver your worship from evil-minded enchanters, and bring me well and peacefully out of this government, which I doubt, for I expect to take leave of it and my life together, from the way Doctor Pedro Recio treats me.

Your worship's servant
SANCHO PANZA THE GOVERNOR

The secretary sealed the letter, and immediately dismissed the courier; and those who were carrying on the joke against Sancho putting their heads together arranged how he was to be dismissed from the government. Sancho spent the afternoon in drawing up certain ordinances relating to the good government of what he fancied the island; and he ordained that there were to be no provision hucksters in the State, and that men might import wine into it from any place they please, provided they declared the quarter it came from, so that a price might be put upon it according to its quality, reputation, and the estimation it was held in; and he that watered his wine, or changed the name, was to forfeit his life for it. He reduced the prices of all manner of shoes, boots, and stockings, but of shoes in particular, as they seemed to him to run extravagantly high. He established a fixed rate for servants' wages, which were becoming recklessly exorbitant. He laid extremely heavy penalties upon those who sang lewd or loose songs either by day or night. He decreed that no blind man should sing of any miracle in verse, unless he could produce authentic evidence that it was true, for it was his opinion that most of those the blind men sing are trumped up, to the detriment of the true ones. He established and created an *alguacil* of the poor, not to harass them, but to examine them and see whether they really were so; for many a sturdy thief or drunkard goes about under cover of a make-believe crippled limb or a sham sore. In a word, he made so many good rules that to this day they are preserved there, and are called *The constitutions of the great governor Sancho Panza.*

FROM

Chapter 52

Wherein is related the adventures of the second distressed or afflicted duenna, otherwise called Doña Rodriguez

Cid Hamet relates that Don Quixote being now cured of his scratches felt that the life he was leading in the castle was entirely inconsistent with the order of chivalry he professed, so he determined to ask the duke and duchess to permit him to take his departure for Saragossa, as the time of the festival was now drawing near, and he hoped to win there the suit of armor which is the prize at festivals of the sort. But one day at table with the duke and duchess, just as he was about to carry his resolution into effect and ask for their permission, . . . the page who had carried the letters and presents to Teresa Panza, the wife of the governor Sancho, entered the hall; and the duke and duchess were very well pleased to see him, being anxious to know the result of his journey; but when they asked him the page said in reply that he could not give it before so many people or in a few words, and begged their excellences to be pleased to let it wait for a private opportunity, and in the meantime amuse themselves with these letters; and taking out the letters he placed them in the duchess's hand. One bore by way of address, *Letter for my lady the Duchess So-and-so, of I don't know where;* and the other, *To my husband Sancho Panza, governor of the island of Barataria, whom God prosper longer than me.* The duchess's bread would not bake, as the saying is, until she had read her letter; and having looked over it herself and seen that it might be read aloud for the duke and all present to hear, she read out as follows.

TERESA PANZA'S LETTER TO THE DUCHESS.

The letter your highness wrote me, my lady, gave me great pleasure, for indeed I found it very welcome. The string of coral beads is very fine, and my husband's hunting suit does not fall short of it. All this village is very much pleased that your ladyship has made a governor of my good man Sancho; though nobody will believe it, particularly the curate, and Master Nicholas the barber, and the bachelor Samson Carrasco; but I don't care for that, for so long as it is true, as it is, they may all say what they like; though, to tell the truth, if the coral beads and the suit had not come I would not have believed it either; for in this village everybody thinks my husband a numskull, and except for governing a flock of goats, they cannot fancy what sort of government he can be fit for. God grant it, and direct him according as he sees his children stand in need of it. I am resolved with your worship's leave, lady of my soul, to make the most of this fair day, and go to Court to stretch myself at ease in a coach, and make all those I have envying me already burst their eyes out; so I beg your excellence to order my husband to send me a small trifle of money, and to let it be something to speak of, because one's expenses are heavy at the Court; for a loaf costs a real, and meat thirty maravedís a pound, which is beyond everything; and if he does not want me to go let him tell me in time, for my feet are on the fidgets to be off; and my friends and neighbors tell me that if my daughter and I make a figure and a brave show at Court, my husband will come to be known far more by me than I by him, for of course plenty of people will ask, "Who are those ladies in that coach?" and some servant of mine will answer, "The wife and daughter of Sancho Panza, governor of the island of Barataria"; and in this way Sancho will become known, and I'll be thought well of, and 'to Rome for everything.' I am as vexed as vexed can be that they have gathered no acorns this year in our village; for all that I send your highness about half a peck that I went to the wood to gather and pick out one by one myself, and I could find no bigger ones; I wish they were as big as ostrich eggs.

Let not your high mightiness forget to write to me; and I will take care to answer, and let you know how I am, and whatever news there may be in this place, where I remain, praying our Lord to have your highness in his keeping and not to forget me.

Sancha, my daughter, and my son, kiss your worship's hands.

She who would rather see your ladyship than write to you,

Your servant,
TERESA PANZA

All were greatly amused by Teresa Panza's letter, but particularly the duke and duchess; and the duchess asked Don Quixote's opinion whether they might open the letter that had come for the governor, which she suspected must be very good. Don Quixote said that to gratify them he would open it, and did so, and found that it ran as follows.

TERESA PANZA'S LETTER TO HER HUSBAND SANCHO PANZA.

I got thy letter, Sancho of my soul, and I promise thee and swear as a Catholic Christian that I was within two fingers' breadth of going mad, I was so happy. I can tell thee, brother, when I came to hear that thou wert a governor I thought I should have dropped dead with pure joy; and thou knowest they say sudden joy kills as well as great sorrow; and as for Sanchica thy daughter, she leaked from sheer happiness. I had before me the suit thou didst send me, and the coral beads my lady the duchess sent me round my neck, and the letters in my hands, and there was the bearer of them standing by, and in spite of all this I verily believed and thought that what I saw and handled was all a dream; for who could have thought that a goat-herd would come to be a governor of islands? Thou knowest, my friend, what my mother used to say, that one must live long to see much; I say it because I expect to see more if I live longer; for I don't expect to stop until I see thee a farmer of taxes or a collector of revenue, which are offices where, though the devil carries off those who make a bad use of them, still they make and handle money. My lady the duchess will tell thee the desire I have to go to the Court; consider the matter and let me know thy pleasure; I will try to do honor to thee by going in a coach.

Neither the curate, nor the barber, nor the bachelor, not even the sacristan, can believe that thou art a governor, and they say the whole thing is a delusion or an enchantment affair, like everything belonging to thy master Don Quixote; and Samson says he must go in search of thee and drive the government out of thy head and the madness out of Don Quixote's skull; I only laugh, and look at my string of beads, and plan out the dress I am going to make for our daughter out of thy suit. I sent some acorns to my lady the duchess; I wish they had been gold. Send me some strings of pearls if they are in fashion in that island. Here is the news of the village; La Berrueca has married her daughter to a good-for-nothing painter, who came here to paint anything that might turn up. The council gave him an order to paint his Majesty's arms over the door of the town hall; he asked two ducats, which they paid him in advance; he worked for eight days, and at the end of them had nothing painted, and then said he had no turn for painting such trifling things; he returned the money, and for all that has married on the pretence of being a good workman; to be sure he has now laid aside his paintbrush and taken a spade in hand, and goes to the field like a gentleman. Pedro Lobo's son has received the first orders and tonsure, with the intention of becoming a priest. Minguilla, Mingo Silvato's granddaughter, found it out, and has gone to law with him on the score of having given her promise of marriage. Evil tongues say she is with child by him, but he denies it stoutly. There are no olives this year, and there is not a drop of vinegar to be had in the whole village. A company of soldiers passed through here; when they left they took away with them three of the girls of the village; I will not tell thee who they are; perhaps they will come back, and they will be sure to find those who will take them for wives with all their blemishes, good or bad. Sanchica is making bonelace; she earns eight maravedís a day clear, which she puts into a money-box as a help towards house furnishing; but now that she is a governor's daughter thou wilt give her a portion without her working for it. The fountain in the plaza has run dry. A flash of lightning struck the gibbet, and I wish they all lit there. I look for an answer to this, and to know thy mind about my going to the Court; and so, God keep thee longer than me, or as long, for I would not leave thee in this world without me.

Thy wife,
TERESA PANZA

The letters were applauded, laughed over, relished, and admired; and then, as if to put the seal to the business, the courier arrived, bringing the one Sancho sent to Don Quixote, and this, too, was read out, and it raised some doubts as to the governor's simplicity. The duchess withdrew to hear from the page about his adventures in Sancho's village, which he narrated at full length without leaving a single circumstance unmentioned. He gave her the acorns, and also a cheese which Teresa had given him as being particularly good and superior to those of Tronchon.

The duchess received it with greatest delight, in which we will leave her, to describe the end of the government of the great Sancho Panza, flower and mirror of all governors of islands.

Chapter 53

Of the troublous end and termination Sancho Panza's government came to

To fancy that in this life anything belonging to it will remain forever in the same state, is an idle fancy; on the contrary, in it everything seems to go in a circle, I mean round and round. The spring succeeds the summer, the summer the fall, the fall the autumn, the autumn the winter, and the winter the spring, and so time rolls with never-ceasing wheel. Man's life alone, swifter than time, speeds onward to its end without any hope of renewal, save it be in that other life which is endless and boundless. Thus saith Cid Hamet the Mahometan philosopher; for there are many that by the light of nature alone, without the light of faith, have a comprehension of the fleeting nature and instability of this present life and the endless duration of that eternal life we hope for; but our author is here speaking of the rapidity with which Sancho's government came to an end, melted away, disappeared, vanished as it were in smoke and shadow. For as he lay in bed on the night of the seventh day of his government, sated, not with bread and wine, but with delivering judgments and giving opinions and making laws and proclamations, just as sleep, in spite of hunger, was beginning to close his eyelids, he heard such a noise of bell-ringing and shouting that one would have fancied the whole island was going to the bottom. He sat up in bed and remained listening intently to try if he could make out what could be the cause of so great an uproar; not only, however, was he unable to discover what it was, but as countless drums and trumpets now helped to swell the din of the bells and shouts, he was more puzzled than ever, and filled with fear and terror; and getting up he put on a pair of slippers because of the dampness of the floor, and without throwing a dressing-gown or anything of the kind over him he rushed out of the door of his room, just in time to see approaching along a corridor a band of more than twenty persons with lighted torches and naked swords in their hands, all shouting out, "To arms, to arms, Señor Governor, to arms! The enemy is in the island in countless numbers, and we are lost unless your skill and valor come to our support."

Keeping up this noise, tumult, and uproar, they came to where Sancho stood dazed and bewildered by what he saw and heard, and as they approached one of them called out to him, "Arm at once, your lordship, if you would not have yourself destroyed and the whole island lost."

"What have I to do with arming?" said Sancho. "What do I know about arms or supports? Better leave all that to my master Don Quixote, who will settle it and make all safe in a trice; for I, sinner that I am, God help me, don't understand these scuffles."

"Ah, Señor Governor," said another, "what slackness of mettle this is! Arm yourself; here are arms for you, offensive and defensive; come out to the plaza and be our leader and captain; it falls upon you by right to be so, for you are our governor."

"Arm me then, in God's name," said Sancho, and they at once produced two large shields they had come provided with, and placed them upon him over his shirt, without letting him put on anything else, one shield in front and the other behind, and passing his arms through openings they had made, they bound him tight with ropes, so that there he was walled and boarded up as straight as a spindle and unable to bend his knees or stir a single step. In his hand they placed a lance, on which he leant to keep himself from falling, and as soon as they had him thus fixed, they bade him march forward and lead them on and give them all courage; for with him for their guide and lamp and morning star, they were sure to bring their business to a successful issue.

"How am I to march, unlucky being that I am?" said Sancho, "when I can't stir my kneecaps, for these boards I have bound so tight to my body won't let me. What you must do is to carry me in your arms, and lay me across or set me upright in some postern, and I'll hold it either with this lance or with my body."

"On, Señor Governor!" cried another, "it is fear more than the boards that keeps you from moving; make haste, stir yourself, for there is no time to lose; the enemy is increasing in numbers, the shouts grow louder, and the danger is pressing."

Urged by these exhortations and reproaches the poor governor made an attempt to advance, but fell to the ground with such a crash that he fancied he had broken himself all to pieces. There he lay like a tortoise enclosed in its shell, or a side of bacon between two kneading-troughs, or a boat bottom up on the beach; nor did the gang of jokers feel any compassion for him when they saw him down; so far from that, extinguishing their torches they began to shout afresh and to renew the calls to arms with such energy, trampling on poor Sancho, and slashing at him over the shield with their swords in such a way that, if he had not gathered himself together and made himself small and drawn in his head between the shields, it would have fared badly with the poor governor, as, squeezed into that narrow compass, he lay, sweating and sweating again, and commending himself with all his heart to God to deliver him from his present peril. Some stumbled over him, others fell upon him, and one there was who took up a position on top of him for some time, and from thence as if from a watch-tower issued orders to the troops, shouting out, "Here, our side! Here the enemy is thickest! Hold the breach there! Shut that gate! Barricade those ladders! Here with your stink-pots of pitch and resin, and kettles of boiling oil! Block the streets with feather beds!" In short, in his ardor he mentioned every little thing, and every implement and engine of war by means of which an assault upon a city is warded off, while the bruised and battered Sancho, who heard and suffered all, was saying to himself,"O if it would only please the Lord to let the island be lost at once, and I could see myself either dead or out of this torture!" Heaven heard his prayer, and when he least expected it he heard voices exclaiming, "Victory, victory! The enemy retreats beaten! Come, Señor Governor, get up, and come and enjoy the victory, and divide the spoils that have been won from the foe by the might of that invincible arm."

"Lift me up," said the wretched Sancho in a woe-begone voice. They helped him to rise, and as soon as he was on his feet he said, "The enemy I have beaten you may nail to my forehead; I don't want to divide the spoils of the foe, I only beg and entreat some friend, if I have one, to give me a sup of wine, for I'm parched with thirst, and wipe me dry, for I'm turning to water."

They rubbed him down, fetched him wine and unbound the shields, and he seated himself upon his bed, and with fear, agitation, and fatigue he fainted away. Those who had been concerned in the joke were now sorry they had pushed it so far; however, the anxiety his fainting away had caused them was relieved by his returning to himself. He asked what o'clock it was; they told him it was just daybreak. He said no more, and in silence began to dress himself, while all watched him, waiting to see what the haste with which he was putting on his clothes meant.

He got himself dressed at last, and then, slowly, for he was sorely bruised and could not go fast, he proceeded to the stable, followed by all who were present, and going up to Dapple embraced him and gave him a loving kiss on the forehead, and said to him, not without tears in his eyes, "Come along, comrade and friend and partner of my toils and sorrows; when I was with you and had no cares to trouble me except mending your harness and feeding your little carcass, happy were my hours, my days, and my years; but since I left you, and mounted the towers of ambition and pride, a thousand miseries, a thousand troubles, and four thousand anxieties have entered into my soul"; and all the while he was speaking in this strain he was fixing the pack-saddle on the ass, without a word from any one. Then having Dapple saddled, he, with great pain and difficulty, got up on him, and addressing himself to the majordomo, the secretary, the head-carver, and Pedro Recio the doctor and several others who stood by, he said, "Make way, gentlemen, and let me go back to my old freedom; let me go look for my past life, and raise myself up from this present death. I was not born to be a governor or protect islands or cities from the enemies that choose to attack them. Ploughing and digging, vine-dressing and pruning, are more in my way than defending provinces or kingdoms. Saint Peter is very well at Rome; I mean each of us is best following the trade he was born to. A reaping-hook fits my hand better than a governor's sceptre; I'd rather have my fill of *gazpacho* than be subject to the misery of a meddling doctor who kills me with hunger, and I'd rather lie in summer under the shade of an oak, and in winter wrap myself in a double sheepskin jacket in freedom, than go to bed between holland sheets and dress in sables under the restraint of a government. God be with your worships, and tell my lord the duke that 'naked I was born, naked I find myself, I neither lose nor gain'; I mean that without a farthing I came into this government, and without a farthing I go out of it, very different from the way governors commonly leave other islands. Stand aside and let me go; I have to plaster myself, for I believe every one of my ribs is crushed, thanks to the enemies that have been trampling over me to-night."

"That is unnecessary, Señor Governor," said Doctor Recio, "for I will give your worship a draught against falls and bruises that will soon make you as sound and strong as ever; and as for your diet I promise your worship to behave better, and let you eat plentifully of whatever you like."

"You spoke late," said Sancho. "I'd as soon turn Turk as stay any longer. Those jokes won't pass a second time. By God I'd as soon remain in this government, or take another, even if it was offered me between two plates, as fly to heaven without wings. I am of the breed of the Panzas, and they are every one of them obstinate, and if they once say 'odds,' odds it must be, no matter if it is evens, in spite of all the world. Here in this stable I leave the ant's wings that lifted me up into the air for the swifts and other birds to eat me, and let's take to level ground and our feet once more; and if they're not shod in pinked shoes of cordovan, they won't want for rough sandals of hemp; 'every ewe to her like,' 'and let no one stretch his leg beyond the length of the sheet'; and now let me pass, for it's growing late with me."

To this the majordomo said, "Señor Governor, we would let your worship go with all our hearts, though it sorely grieves us to lose you, for your wit and Christian conduct naturally make us regret you; but it is well known that every governor, before he leaves the place where he has been governing, is bound first of all to render an account. Let your worship do so for the ten days you have held the government, and then you may go and the peace of God go with you."

"No one can demand it of me," said Sancho, "but he whom my lord the duke shall appoint; I am going to meet him, and to him I will render an exact one; besides, when I go forth naked as I do, there is no other proof needed to show that I have governed like an angel."

"By God the great Sancho is right," said Doctor Recio, "and it is my opinion we should let him go, for the duke will be beyond measure glad to see him."

They all agreed to this, and allowed him to go, first offering to bear him company and furnish him with all he wanted for his own comfort or for the journey. Sancho said he did not want anything more than a little barley for Dapple, and half a cheese and half a loaf for himself; for the distance being so short there was no occasion for any better or bulkier provant. They all embraced him, and he with tears embraced all of them, and left them filled with admiration not only at his remarks but at his firm and sensible resolution.

• • •

FROM

Chapter 55

Of what befell Sancho on the road, and other things that cannot be surpassed

The length of time he delayed . . . prevented Sancho from reaching the duke's castle that day, though he was within half a league of it when night, somewhat dark and cloudy, overtook him. This, however, as it was summer time, did not give him much uneasiness, and he turned aside out of the road intending to wait for morning; but his ill luck and hard fate so willed it that as he was searching about for a place to make himself as comfortable as possible, he and Dapple fell into a deep dark hole that lay among some very old buildings. As he fell he commended himself with all his heart to God, fancying he was not going to stop until he reached the depths of the bottomless pit; but it did not turn out so, for at little more than thrice a man's height Dapple touched bottom, and he found himself sitting on him without having received any hurt or damage whatever. He felt himself all over and held his breath to try whether he was quite sound or had a hole made in him anywhere, and finding himself all right and whole and in perfect health he was profuse in his thanks to God our Lord for the mercy that had been shown him, for he thought surely he had been broken into a thousand pieces. He also felt along the sides of the pit with his hands to see if it were possible to get out of it without help, but he found they were quite smooth and afforded no hold anywhere, at which he was greatly distressed, especially when he heard how pathetically and dolefully Dapple was bemoaning himself, and no wonder he complained, nor was it from ill-temper, for in truth he was not in a very good case.

"Alas," said Sancho, "what unexpected accidents happen at every step to those who live in this miserable world! Who would have said that one who saw himself yesterday sitting on a throne, governor of an island, giving orders to his servants and his vassals, would see himself to-day buried in a pit without a soul to help him, or servant or vassal to come to his relief! Here must we perish with hunger, my ass and myself, if indeed we don't die first, he of his bruises and injuries, and I of grief and sorrow. At any rate I shall not be as lucky as my master Don Quixote of La Mancha, when he went down into the cave of that enchanted Montesinos, where he found people to make more of him than if he had been in his own house; for it seems he came in for a table laid out and a bed ready made. There he saw fair and pleasant visions, but here I shall see, I imagine, toads and adders. Unlucky wretch that I am, what an end my follies and fancies have come to! They'll take up my bones out of this, when it is Heaven's will that I'm found, picked clean, white and polished, and my good Dapple's with them, and by that, perhaps, it will be found out who we are, at least by such as have heard that Sancho Panza never separated from his ass, nor his ass from Sancho Panza. Unlucky wretches, I say again, that our hard fate should not let us die in our own country and among our own people, where if there was no help for our misfortune, at any rate there would be some one to grieve for it and to close our eyes as we passed away! O comrade and friend, how ill have I repaid thy faithful services! Forgive me, and entreat Fortune, as well as thou canst, to deliver us out of this miserable strait we are both in; and I promise to put a crown of laurel on thy head, and make thee look like a poet laureate, and give thee double feeds."

In this strain did Sancho bewail himself, and his ass listened to him, but answered him never a word, such was the distress and anguish the poor beast found himself in. At length, after a night spent in bitter moanings and lamentations, day came, and by its light Sancho perceived that it was wholly impossible to escape out of that pit without help, and he fell to bemoaning his fate and uttering loud shouts to find out if there was any one within hearing; but all his shouting was only crying in the wilderness, for there was not a soul anywhere in the neighborhood to hear him, and then at last he gave himself up for dead. Dapple was lying on his back, and Sancho helped him to his feet, which he was scarcely able to keep; and then taking a piece of bread out of his *alforjas* which had shared their fortunes in the fall, he gave it to the ass, to whom it was not unwelcome, saying to him as if he understood him, "With bread all sorrows are less."

And now he perceived on one side of the pit a hole large enough to admit a person if he stooped and squeezed himself into a small compass. Sancho made for it, and entered it by creeping, and found it wide and spacious on the inside, which he was able to see as a ray of sunlight that penetrated what might be called the roof showed it all plainly. He observed, too, that it opened and widened out into another spacious cavity; seeing which he made his way back to where the ass was, and with a stone began to pick away the clay from the hole until in a short time he had made room for the beast to pass easily, and this accomplished, taking him by the halter, he proceeded to traverse the cavern to see if there was any outlet at the other end. He advanced, sometimes in the dark, sometimes with light, but never without fear; "God Almighty help me!" said he to himself; "this that is a misadventure to me would make a good adventure for my master Don Quixote. He would have been sure to take these depths and dungeons for flowery gardens or the palaces of Galiana,[65] and would have counted upon issuing out of this darkness and imprisonment into some blooming meadow; but I, unlucky that I am, hopeless and spiritless, expect at every step another pit deeper than the first to open under my feet and swallow me up for good; 'welcome evil, if thou comest alone.'"

In this way and with these reflections he seemed to himself to have travelled rather more than half a league, when at last he perceived a dim light that looked like daylight and found its way in on one side, showing that this road, which appeared to him the road to the other world, led to some opening.

Here Cid Hamet leaves him, and returns to Don Quixote, who, . . . as he was putting Rocinante through his paces or pressing him to the charge, he brought his feet so close to a pit that but for reining him in tightly it would have been impossible for him to avoid falling into it. He pulled him up, however, without a fall, and coming a little closer examined the hole without dismounting; but as he was looking at it he heard loud cries proceeding from it, and by listening attentively was able to make out that he who uttered them was saying, "Ho, above there! is there any Christian that hears me, or any charitable gentleman that will take pity on a sinner buried alive, or an unfortunate disgoverned governor?"

It struck Don Quixote that it was the voice of Sancho Panza he heard, whereat he was taken aback and amazed, and raising his own voice as much as he could, he cried out, "Who is below there? Who is that complaining?"

[65] A lengendary Moorish princess.

"Who should be here, or who should complain," was the answer, "but the forlorn Sancho Panza, for his sins and for his ill-luck governor of the island of Barataria, squire that was to the famous knight Don Quixote of La Mancha?"

When Don Quixote heard this his amazement was redoubled and his perturbation grew greater than ever, for it suggested itself to his mind that Sancho must be dead, and that his soul was in torment down there; and carried away by this idea he exclaimed, "I conjure thee by everything that as a Catholic Christian I can conjure thee by, tell me who thou art; and if thou art a soul in torment, tell me what thou wouldst have me do for thee; for as my profession is to give aid and succor to those that need it in this world, it will also extend to aiding and succoring the distressed of the other, who cannot help themselves."

"In that case," answered the voice, "your worship who speaks to me must be my master Don Quixote of La Mancha; nay, from the tone of the voice it is plain it can be nobody else."

"Don Quixote I am," replied Don Quixote, "he whose profession it is to aid and succor the living and the dead in their necessities; wherefore tell me who thou art, for thou art keeping me in suspense; because, if thou art my squire Sancho Panza, and art dead, since the devils have not carried thee off, and thou art by God's mercy in purgatory, our holy mother the Roman Catholic Church has intercessory means sufficient to release thee from the pains thou art in; and I for my part will plead with her to that end, so far as my substance will go; without further delay, therefore, declare thyself, and tell me who thou art."

"By all that's good," was the answer, "and by the birth of whomsoever your worship chooses, I swear, Señor Don Quixote of La Mancha, that I am your squire Sancho Panza, and that I have never died all my life; but that, having given up my government for reasons that would require more time to explain, I fell last night into this pit where I am now, and Dapple is witness and won't let me lie, for more by token he is here with me."

Nor was this all; one would have fancied the ass understood what Sancho said, because that moment he began to bray so loudly that the whole cave rang again.

"Famous testimony!" exclaimed Don Quixote; "I know that bray as well as if I was its mother, and thy voice, too, my Sancho. Wait while I go to the duke's castle, which is close by, and I will bring some one to take thee out of this pit into which thy sins no doubt have brought thee."

"Go, your worship," said Sancho, "and come back quick for God's sake; for I cannot bear being buried alive here any longer, and I'm dying of fear."

Don Quixote left him, and hastened to the castle to tell the duke and duchess what had happened to Sancho, and they were not a little astonished at it, although they could easily understand his having fallen, from the confirmatory circumstance of the cave which had been in existence there from time immemorial; but they could not imagine how he had quitted the government without their receiving any intimation of his coming. To be brief, they fetched ropes and tackle, as the saying is, and by dint of many hands and much labor they drew up Dapple and Sancho Panza out of the darkness into the light of day. A student who saw him remarked, "That's the way all bad governors should come out of their governments, as this sinner comes out of the depths of the pit, dead with hunger, pale, and I suppose without a farthing."

Sancho overheard him and said, "It is eight or ten days, brother growler, since I entered upon the government of the island they gave me, and all that time I never had a bellyfull of victuals, no not for an hour; doctors persecuted me and enemies crushed my bones; nor had I any opportunity of taking bribes or levying taxes; and if that be the case, as it is, I don't deserve, I think, to come out in this fashion, but 'man proposes and God disposes'; and God knows what is best, and what suits each one best; and 'as the occasion, so the behaviour'; and 'let nobody say "I won't drink of this water"'; and 'where one thinks there are flitches, there are no pegs'; God knows my meaning and that's enough; I say no more, though I could."

"Be not angry or annoyed at what thou hearest, Sancho," said Don Quixote, "or there will never be an end of it; keep a safe conscience and let them say what they like; for trying to stop slanderers' tongues is like trying to put gates to the open plain. If a governor comes out of his government rich, they say he has been a thief; and if he comes out poor, that he has been a noodle and a blockhead."

"They'll be pretty sure this time," said Sancho, "to set me down for a fool rather than a thief."

Thus talking, and surrounded by boys and a crowd of people, they reached the castle, where in one of the corridors the duke and duchess stood waiting for them; but Sancho would not go up to see the duke until he had first put up Dapple in the stable, for he said he had passed a very bad night in his last quarters; then he went upstairs to see his lord and lady, and kneeling before them he said, "Because it was your highnesses' pleasure, not because of any desert of my own, I went to govern your island of Barataria, which I entered naked, 'and naked I find myself; I neither lose nor gain.' Whether I have governed well or ill, I have had witnesses who will say what they think fit. I have answered questions, I have decided causes, and always dying of hunger, for Dr. Pedro Recio of Tirteafuera, the islandish and governorish doctor, would have it so. Enemies attacked us by night and put us in a great quandary, but the people of the island say they came off safe and victorious by the might of my arm; and may God give them as much health as there's truth in what they say. In short, during that time I have weighed the cares and responsibilities governing brings with it, and by my reckoning I find my shoulders can't bear them, nor are they a load for my loins or arrows for my quiver; and so, before the government threw me over, I preferred to throw the government over; and yesterday morning I left the island as I found it, with the same streets, houses, and roofs it had when I entered it. I asked no loan of anybody, nor did I try to fill my pocket; and though I meant to make some useful laws, I made hardly any, as I was afraid they would not be kept; for in that case it comes to the same thing to make them or not to make them. I quitted the island, as I said, without any escort except my ass; I fell into a pit, I pushed on through it, until this morning by the light of the sun I saw an outlet, but not so easy a one but that, had not Heaven sent me my master Don Quixote, I'd have stayed there till the end of the world. So now, my lord and lady duke and duchess, here is your governor Sancho Panza, who in the bare ten days he has held the government has come by the knowledge that he would not give anything to be governor, not to say of an island, but of the whole world; and that point being settled, kissing your worships' feet, and imitating the game of the boys when they say 'leap thou, and give me one,' I take a leap out of the government and pass into the service of my master Don Quixote; for after all, though in it I eat my bread in fear and trembling, at any rate I take my fill; and for my part, so long as I'm full, it's all alike to me whether it's with carrots or with partridges."

Here Sancho brought his long speech to an end, Don Quixote having been the whole time in dread of his uttering a host of absurdities; and when he found him leave off with so few, he thanked Heaven in his heart. The duke embraced Sancho and told him he was heartily sorry he had given up the government so soon, but that he would see that he was provided with some other post on his estate less onerous and more profitable. The duchess also embraced him, and gave orders that he should be taken good care of, as it was plain to see he had been badly treated and worse bruised.

. . .

Chapter 73

Of the omens Don Quixote had as he entered his own village, and other incidents that embellish and give a color to this great history

At the entrance of the village, so says Cid Hamet, Don Quixote saw two boys quarrelling on the village threshing-floor, one of whom said to the other, "Take it easy, Periquillo; thou shalt never see it again as long as thou livest."

Don Quixote heard this, and said he to Sancho, "Dost thou not mark, friend, what that boy said, 'Thou shalt never see it again as long as thou livest'?"

"Well," said Sancho, "what does it matter if the boy said so?"

"What!" said Don Quixote, "dost thou not see that, applied to the object of my desires, the words mean that I am never to see Dulcinea more?"

Sancho was about to answer, when his attention was diverted by seeing a hare come flying across the plain pursued by several greyhounds and sportsmen. In its terror it ran to take shelter and hide itself under Dapple. Sancho caught it alive and presented it to Don Quixote, who was saying, "*Malum signum, malum signum!*[66] a hare flies, greyhounds chase it. Dulcinea appears not."

"Your worship's a strange man," said Sancho; "let's take it for granted that this hare is Dulcinea, and these greyhounds chasing it the malignant enchanters who turned her into a country wench; she flies, and I catch her and put her into your worship's hands, and you hold her in your arms and cherish her; what bad sign is that, or what ill omen is there to be found here?"

The two boys who had been quarrelling came over to look at the hare, and Sancho asked one of them what their quarrel was about. He was answered by the one who had said, "Thou shalt never see it again as long as thou livest," that he had taken a cage full of crickets from the other boy, and did not mean to give it back to him as long as he lived. Sancho took out four cuartos from his pocket and gave them to the boy for the cage, which he placed in Don Quixote's hands, saying, "There, señor! there are the omens broken and destroyed, and they have no more to do with our affairs, to my thinking, fool as I am, than with last year's clouds; and if I remember rightly I have heard the curate of our village say that it does not become Christians or sensible people to give any heed to these silly things; and even you yourself said the same to me some time ago, telling me that all Christians who minded omens were fools; but there's no need of making words about it; let us push on and go into our village."

The sportsmen came up and asked for their hare, which Don Quixote gave them. They then went on, and upon the green at the entrance of the town they came upon the curate and the bachelor Samson Carrasco busy with their breviaries. It should be mentioned that Sancho had thrown, by way of a sumpter-cloth, over Dapple and over the bundle of armor, the buckram robe painted with flames which they had put upon him at the duke's castle the night Altisidora came back to life. He had also fixed the mitre on Dapple's head, the oddest transformation and decoration that ever ass in the world underwent. They were at once recognized by both the curate and the bachelor, who came towards them with open arms. Don Quixote dismounted and received them with a close embrace; and the boys, who are lynxes that nothing escapes, spied out the ass's mitre and came running to see it, calling out to one another, "Come here, boys, and see Sancho Panza's ass rigged out finer than Mingo, and Don Quixote's beast leaner than ever."

---

[66] "A bad sign, a bad sign!"

So at length, with the boys capering round them, and accompanied by the curate and the bachelor, they made their entrance into the town, and proceeded to Don Quixote's house, at the door of which they found his housekeeper and niece, whom the news of his arrival had already reached. It had been brought to Teresa Panza, Sancho's wife, as well, and she with her hair all loose and half naked, dragging Sanchica her daughter by the hand, ran out to meet her husband; but seeing him coming in by no means as good case as she thought a governor ought to be, she said to him, "How is it you come this way, husband? It seems to me you come tramping and footsore, and looking more like a disorderly vagabond than a governor."

"Hold your tongue, Teresa," said Sancho; "often where there are pegs there are no flitches; let's go into the house and there you'll hear strange things. I bring money, and that's the main thing, got by my own industry without wronging anybody."

"You bring the money, my good husband," said Teresa, "and no matter whether it was got this way or that; for, however you may have got it, you'll not have brought any new practice into the world."

Sanchica embraced her father and asked him if he brought her anything, for she had been looking out for him as for the showers of May; and she taking hold of him by the girdle on one side, and his wife by the hand, while the daughter led Dapple, they made for their house, leaving Don Quixote in his, in the hands of his niece and housekeeper, and in the company of the curate and the bachelor.

Don Quixote at once, without any regard to time or season, withdrew in private with the bachelor and the curate, and in a few words told them of his defeat, and of the engagement he was under not to quit his village for a year,[67] which he meant to keep to the letter without departing a hair's breadth from it, as became a knight-errant bound by scrupulous good faith and the laws of knight-errantry; and of how he thought of turning shepherd for that year, and taking his diversion in the solitude of the fields, where he could with perfect freedom give range to his thoughts of love while he followed the virtuous pastoral calling; and he besought them, if they had not a great deal to do and were not prevented by more important business, to consent to be his companions, for he would buy sheep enough to qualify them for shepherds; and the most important point of the whole affair, he could tell them, was settled, for he had given them names that would fit them to a T. The curate asked what they were. Don Quixote replied that he himself was to be called the shepherd Quixotiz and the bachelor the shepherd Carrascon, and the curate the shepherd Curiambro, and Sancho Panza the shepherd Pancino.

Both were astounded at Don Quixote's new craze; however, lest he should once more make off out of the village from them in pursuit of chivalry, they, trusting that in the course of the year he might be cured, fell in with his new project, applauded his crazy idea as a bright one, and offered to share the life with him. "And what's more," said Samson Carrasco, "I am, as all the world knows, a very famous poet, and I'll be always making verses, pastoral, or courtly, or as it may come into my head, to pass away our time in those secluded regions where we shall be roaming. But what is most needful, sirs, is that each of us should choose the name of the shepherdess he means to glorify in his verses, and that we should not leave a tree, be it ever so hard, without writing up and carving her name on it, as is the habit and custom of love-smitten shepherds."

---

[67]Before being defeated in a single combat with the White Knight (Samson Carrasco in disguise), Quixote has agreed that if he loses the fight he will return to La Mancha and stay there for a year.

"That's the very thing," said Don Quixote; "though I am relieved from looking for the name of an imaginary shepherdess, for there's the peerless Dulcinea del Toboso, the glory of these brook-sides, the ornament of these meadows, the mainstay of beauty, the cream of all the graces, and, in a word, the being to whom all praise is appropriate, be it ever so hyperbolical."

"Very true," said the curate; "but we the others must look about for accommodating shepherdesses that will answer our purpose one way or another."

"And," added Samson Carrasco, "if they fail us, we can call them by the names of the ones in print that the world is filled with, Filidas, Amarilises, Dianas, Fleridas, Galateas, Belisardas; for as they sell them in the market-places we may fairly buy them and make them our own. If my lady, or I should say my shepherdess, happens to be called Ana, I'll sing her praises under the name of Anarda, and if Francisca, I'll call her Francenia, and if Lucia, Lucinda, for it all comes to the same thing; and Sancho Panza, if he joins this fraternity, may glorify his wife Teresa Panza as Teresaina."

Don Quixote laughed at the adaptation of the name, and the curate bestowed vast praise upon the worthy and honorable resolution he had made, and again offered to bear him company all that he could spare from his imperative duties. And so they took their leave of him, recommending and beseeching him to take care of his health and treat himself to a generous diet.

It so happened his niece and the housekeeper overheard all the three of them said; and as soon as they were gone they both of them came in to Don Quixote, and said the niece, "What's this, uncle? Now that we were thinking you had come back to stay at home and lead a quiet respectable life there, are you going to get into fresh entanglements, and turn 'young shepherd, thou that comest here, young shepherd going there'? Nay! indeed 'the straw is too hard now to make pipes of.' "

"And," added the housekeeper, "will your worship be able to bear, out in the fields, the heats of summer, and the chills of winter, and the howling of the wolves? Not you; for that's a life and a business for hardy men, bred and seasoned to such work almost from the time they were in swaddling-clothes. Why, to make choice of evils, it's better to be a knight-errant than a shepherd! Look here, señor; take my advice—and I'm not giving it to you full of bread and wine, but fasting, and with fifty years upon my head—stay at home, look after your affairs, go often to confession, be good to the poor, and upon my soul be it if any evil comes to you."

"Hold your peace, my daughters," said Don Quixote; "I know very well what my duty is; help me to bed, for I don't feel very well; and rest assured that, knight-errant now or wandering shepherd to be, I shall never fail to have a care for your interests, as you will see in the end." And the good wenches (for that they undoubtedly were), the housekeeper and niece, helped him to bed, where they gave him something to eat and made him as comfortable as possible.

Chapter 74

Of how Don Quixote fell sick, and of the will he made, and how he died

As nothing that is man's can last forever, but all tends ever downwards from its beginning to its end, and above all man's life, and as Don Quixote's enjoyed no special dispensation from Heaven to stay its course, its end and close came when he least looked for it. For—whether it was of the dejection the thought of his defeat produced, or of Heaven's will that so ordered it—a fever settled upon him and kept him in his bed for six days, during which he was often visited by his friends the curate, the bachelor, and the barber, while his good squire Sancho

Panza never quitted his bedside. They, persuaded that it was grief at finding himself vanquished, and the object of his heart, the liberation and disenchantment of Dulcinea, unattained, that kept him in this state, strove by all the means in their power to cheer him up; the bachelor bidding him take heart and get up to begin his pastoral life, for which he himself, he said, had already composed an eclogue that would take the shine out of all Sannazaro had ever written, and had bought with his own money two famous dogs to guard the flock, one called Barcino and the other Butron, which a herdsman of Quintanar had sold him.

But for all this Don Quixote could not shake off his sadness. His friends called in the doctor, who felt his pulse and was not very well satisfied with it, and said that in any case it would be well for him to attend to the health of his soul, as that of his body was in a bad way. Don Quixote heard this calmly; but not so his housekeeper, his niece, and his squire, who fell weeping bitterly, as if they had him lying dead before them. The doctor's opinion was that melancholy and depression were bringing him to his end. Don Quixote begged them to leave him to himself, as he had a wish to sleep a little. They obeyed, and he slept at one stretch, as the saying is, more than six hours, so that the housekeeper and niece thought he was going to sleep forever. But at the end of that time he woke up, and in a loud voice exclaimed, "Blessed be Almighty God, who has shown me such goodness. In truth his mercies are boundless, and the sins of men can neither limit them nor keep them back!"

The niece listened with attention to her uncle's words, and they struck her as more coherent than what usually fell from him, at least during his illness, so she asked, "What are you saying, señor? Has anything strange occurred? What mercies or what sins of men are you talking of?"

"The mercies, niece," said Don Quixote, "are those that God has this moment shown me, and with him, as I said, my sins are no impediment to them. My reason is now free and clear, rid of the dark shadows of ignorance that my unhappy constant study of those detestable books of chivalry cast over it. Now I see through their absurdities and deceptions, and it only grieves me that this destruction of my illusions has come so late that it leaves me no time to make some amends by reading other books that might be a light to my soul. Niece, I feel myself at the point of death, and I would fain meet it in such a way as to show that my life has not been so ill that I should leave behind me the name of a madman; for though I have been one, I would not that the fact should be made plainer at my death. Call in to me, my dear, my good friends the Curate, the Bachelor Samson Carrasco, and Master Nicholas the barber, for I wish to confess and make my will." But his niece was saved the trouble by the entrance of the three. The instant Don Quixote saw them he exclaimed, "Good news for you, good sirs, that I am no longer Don Quixote of La Mancha, but Alonso Quixano, whose way of life won for him the name of Good. Now am I the enemy of Amadis of Gaul and of the whole countless troop of his descendants; odious to me now are all the profane stories of knight-errantry; now I perceive my folly, and the peril into which reading them brought me; now, by God's mercy schooled into my right senses, I loathe them."

When the three heard him speak in this way, they had no doubt whatever that some new craze had taken possession of him; and said Samson, "What? Señor Don Quixote! Now that we have intelligence of the lady Dulcinea being disenchanted, are you taking this line; now, just as we are on the point of becoming shepherds, to pass our lives singing, like princes, are you thinking of turning hermit? Hush for Heaven's sake, be rational, and let's have no more nonsense."

"All that nonsense," said Don Quixote, "that until now has been a reality to my hurt, my death will, with Heaven's help, turn to my good. I feel, sirs, that I am rapidly drawing near death; a truce to jesting; let me have a confessor to confess me, and a notary to make my will; for in extremities like this, man must not trifle with his soul; and while the curate is confessing me let some one, I beg, go for the notary."

They looked at one another, wondering at Don Quixote's words; but, though uncertain, they were inclined to believe him, and one of the signs by which they came to the conclusion he was dying was this so sudden and complete return to his senses after having been mad; for to the words already quoted he added much more, so well expressed, so devout, and so rational, as to banish all doubt and convince them that he was sound of mind. The curate turned them all out, and left alone with him confessed him. The bachelor went for the notary and returned shortly afterwards with him and with Sancho, who, having already learned from the bachelor the condition his master was in, and finding the housekeeper and niece weeping, began to blubber and shed tears.

The confession over, the curate came out saying, "Alonso Quixano the Good is indeed dying, and is indeed in his right mind; we may now go in to him while he makes his will."

This news gave a tremendous impulse to the brimming eyes of the housekeeper, the niece, and Sancho Panza his good squire, making the tears burst from their eyes and a host of sighs from their hearts; for of a truth, as has been said more than once, whether as plain Alonso Quixano the Good, or as Don Quixote of La Mancha, Don Quixote was always of a gentle disposition and kindly in all his ways, and hence he was beloved, not only by those of his own house, but by all who knew him.

The notary came in with the rest, and as soon as the preamble of the will had been set out and Don Quixote had commended his soul to God with all the devout formalities that are usual, coming to the bequests, he said, "Item, it is my will that, touching certain moneys in the hands of Sancho Panza (whom in my madness I made my squire), inasmuch as between him and me there have been certain accounts and debits and credits, no claim be made against him, nor any account demanded of him in respect of them; but that if anything remain over and above, after he has paid himself what I owe him, the balance, which will be but little, shall be his, and much good may it do him; and if, as when I was mad I had a share in giving him the government of an island, so, now that I am in my senses, I could give him that of a kingdom, it should be his, for the simplicity of his character and the fidelity of his conduct deserve it." And then, turning to Sancho, he said, "Forgive me, my friend, that I led thee to seem as mad as myself, making thee fall into the same error I myself fell into, that there were and still are knights-errant in the world."

"Ah!" said Sancho weeping, "don't die, master, but take my advice and live many years; for the foolishest thing a man can do in this life is to let himself die without rhyme or reason, without anybody killing him, or any hands but melancholy's making an end of him. Come, don't be lazy, but get up from your bed and let us take to the fields in shepherd's trim as we agreed. Perhaps behind some bush we shall find the lady Dulcinea disenchanted, as fine as fine can be. If it be that you are dying of vexation at having been vanquished, lay the blame on me, and say you were overthrown because I had girthed Rocinante badly; besides you must have seen in your books of chivalry that it is a common thing for knights to upset one another, and for him who is conquered to-day to be conqueror to-morrow."

"Very true," said Samson, "and good Sancho Panza's view of these cases is quite right."

"Sirs, not so fast," said Don Quixote, "'in last year's nests there are no birds this year.' I was mad, now I am in my senses; I was Don Quixote of La Mancha, I am now, as I said, Alonso Quixano the Good; and may my repentance and sincerity restore me to the esteem you used to have for me; and now let Master Notary proceed.

"Item, I leave all my property absolutely to Antonia Quixana my niece, here present, after all has been deducted from the most available portion of it that may be required to satisfy the bequests I have made. And the first disbursement I desire to be made is the payment of the wages I owe for the time my housekeeper has served me, with twenty ducats, over and above for a gown. The curate and the bachelor Samson Carrasco, now present, I appoint my executors.

"Item, it is my wish that if Antonia Quixana, my niece, desires to marry, she shall marry a man of whom it shall be first of all ascertained by information taken that he does not know what books of chivalry are; and if it should be proved that he does, and if, in spite of this, my niece insists upon marrying him, and does marry him, then that she shall forfeit the whole of what I have left her, which my executors shall devote to works of charity as they please.

"Item, I entreat the aforesaid gentlemen my executors, that if any happy chance should lead them to discover the author who is said to have written a history now going about under the title of *Second Part of the Achievements of Don Quixote of La Mancha,* they beg of him on my behalf as earnestly as they can to forgive me for having been, without intending it, the cause of his writing so many and such monstrous absurdities as he has written in it; for I am leaving the world with a feeling of compunction at having provoked him to write them."

With this he closed his will, and a faintness coming over him he stretched himself out at full length on the bed. All were in a flutter and made haste to relieve him, and during the three days he lived after that on which he made his will he fainted away very often. The house was all in confusion; but still the niece ate and the housekeeper drank and Sancho Panza enjoyed himself; for inheriting property wipes out or softens down in the heir the feeling of grief the dead man might be expected to leave behind him.

At last Don Quixote's end came, after he had received all the sacraments, and had in full and forcible terms expressed his detestation of books of chivalry. The notary was there at the time, and he said that in no book of chivalry had he ever read of any knight-errant dying in his bed so calmly and so like a Christian as Don Quixote, who amid the tears and lamentations of all present yielded up his spirit, that is to say died. On perceiving it the curate begged the notary to bear witness that Alonso Quixano the Good, commonly called Don Quixote of La Mancha, had passed away from his present life, and died naturally; and said he desired this testimony in order to remove the possibility of any other author save Cid Hamet Benengeli bringing him to life again falsely and making interminable stories out of his achievements.

Such was the end of the Ingenious Gentleman of La Mancha, whose village Cid Hamet would not indicate precisely, in order to leave all the towns and villages of La Mancha to contend among themselves for the right to adopt him and claim him as a son, as the seven cities of Greece contended for Homer. The lamentations of Sancho and the niece and housekeeper are omitted here, as well as the new epitaphs upon his tomb; Samson Carrasco, however, put the following:

A doughty gentleman lies here;
A stranger all his life to fear;
Nor in his death could Death prevail,
In that lost hour, to make him quail.

He for the world but little cared;
And at his feats the world was scared;

A crazy man his life he passed,
But in his senses died at last.

And said most sage Cid Hamet to his pen, "Rest here, hung up by this brass wire, upon this shelf, O my pen, whether of skilful make or clumsy cut I know not; here shalt thou remain long ages hence, unless presumptuous or malignant story-tellers take thee down to profane thee. But ere they touch thee warn them, and, as best thou canst, say to them:

Hold off! ye weaklings; hold your hands!
Adventure it let none,
For this emprise, my lord the king,
Was meant for me alone.

For me alone was Don Quixote born, and I for him; it was his to act; mine to write; we two together make but one, notwithstanding and in spite of that pretended Tordesillesque writer who has ventured or would venture with his great, coarse, ill-trimmed ostrich quill to write the achievements of my valiant knight;—no burden for his shoulders, nor subject for his frozen wit: whom, if perchance thou shouldst come to know him, thou shalt warn to leave at rest where they lie the weary mouldering bones of Don Quixote, and not to attempt to carry him off, in opposition to all the privileges of death, to Old Castile, making him rise from the grave where in reality and truth he lies stretched at full length, powerless to make any third expedition or new sally; for the two that he has already made, so much to the enjoyment and approval of everybody to whom they have become known, in this as well as in foreign countries, are quite sufficient for the purpose of turning into ridicule the whole of those made by the whole set of the knights-errant; and so doing shalt thou discharge thy Christian calling, giving good counsel to one that bears ill-will to thee. And I shall remain satisfied, and proud to have been the first who has ever enjoined the fruit of his writings as fully as he could desire; for my desire has been no other than to deliver over to the detestation of mankind the false and foolish tales of the books of chivalry, which, thanks to that of my true Don Quixote, are even now tottering, and doubtless doomed to fall forever. Farewell."

FRANCIS BACON

[1567–1626]

The dates of Francis Bacon's life place him at the end of the Renaissance, but in many ways Bacon's interests and ideas are those of the late seventeenth century and early eighteenth century. Unlike many of his Renaissance contemporaries who associated science with magic, Bacon described science as the careful and controlled observation of nature. Marlowe's Doctor Faustus learns his "science" by studying old books, but the scholars in Salomon's House in Bacon's *New Atlantis* (1621) develop their knowledge through controlled observation and experiment. Although he did little experimentation himself, Bacon's descriptions of the processes by which scientific knowledge is discovered have earned him the reputation of being the father of the scientific method. He set out to free the science of his time from the deductive methods that medieval scholasticism had derived from Aristotle. In *The Advancement of Learning* (1605) and the *Novum Organum* (1620) Bacon challenged the assumptions of his predecessors and attempted to develop a systematic method for the direct observation of nature. In doing so, he turned the Renaissance reverence for ancient texts on its head, asserting that "Books must follow sciences, and not sciences books."

"There are and can be only two ways of searching into and discovering truth," Bacon wrote in the *Novum Organum.* "The one flies from the senses and particulars to the most general axioms. . . . This way is now in fashion. The other derives axioms from the senses and particulars, rising by gradual and unbroken ascent, so that it arrives at the most general axioms last of all. This is the true way, but as yet untried." To break the hold of deductive science and initiate a new way of discovering truth, Bacon argued that we must become aware of the four "idols" of the mind—Idols of the Tribe, the Cave, the Market-Place, and the Theater—that interfered with the direct observation of nature. If we can free ourselves from preconceptions brought on by our human position in relation to the rest of the world, by our personal experiences, our ideological biases, and the conventional ideas of those around us, then we may begin to see the world for what it is and develop appropriate experiments to increase our knowledge.

Bacon was better at identifying the weaknesses of his predecessors than in defining the new method. He suggested that simply by observing nature, we would see general scientific truths. By modern standards he undervalued the importance of hypothesis and exaggerated the role of simple observation, but his descriptions of scientific investigation are closer to our own sense of how such discovery occurs than they are to the magical activities depicted in many earlier works.

Along with his Renaissance contemporaries, Bacon believed that knowledge is power. He was at least as interested in the utilitarian applications of scientific discoveries as he was in the discoveries themselves. Bacon differed from Machiavelli or Cesare Borgia only in his belief that scientific knowledge, rather than politics, was the route to power.

Life

By profession, Bacon was not a scientist. At Cambridge he studied law and he spent his working years as a member of Parliament and as a legal advisor. Under King James I, he attained the highest position in the legal profession when he was named Lord Chancellor of England in 1618. His tenure was brief, however, for after only three years he admitted taking bribes and lost his position and reputation. The last five years of his life were the only time during his maturity that he spent outside the corridors of power. Appropriately, he died as a result of a scientific experiment. Pursuing the questions, "What happens to flesh if it be frozen? Is putrefaction perhaps delayed?" Bacon went into the country in winter and experimentally stuffed the carcass of a fowl with snow. While doing so he was seized with a sudden chill that led to his death.

Work

Lawyer, politician, and philosopher of science, Bacon was also the first practitioner of the essay in English. His only predecessor in the form was France's Michel de Montaigne (1533–1592), whose personal and introspective *essais* are considerably different from Bacon's "trials" in the new form. Rather than probing the self as Montaigne had done, Bacon sought to speak plainly, simply, and directly about common topics. In his *Essays,* first published in 1597 and in revised editions in 1612 and 1625, he considered such subjects as reading, study, marriage, and superstition, treating them in a terse and aphoristic style.

New Atlantis is one of a number of Renaissance works describing ideal communities that began with Sir Thomas More's *Utopia* (1516), the work that introduced the word "utopia" into the language. Such works were particularly fashionable in the early seventeenth century, when Johann Andrese, a German, published *Christianopolis* (1619) and Thomas Campanella, an Italian, published *City of the Sun* (1623). Bacon, writing at the same time, did not concentrate on the ideal government of his society as his contemporaries did, perhaps because his work was not completed, or perhaps because he imagined a new society based on the organization of scientific endeavor.

New Atlantis shows both the Renaissance and Enlightenment sides of Bacon's character. The religion of Bensalem is based in a Renaissance trust in ancient texts, and seems to depart from Bacon's principle that knowledge should be derived from experience rather than books. There are no deists on the island who seek to ground religion in reason rather than tradition. The social order on the island, shown dramatically in the Feast of the Family, is also based on tradition and established authority, not in social experimentation. Had Bacon completed *New Atlantis,* one wonders whether it would also have included a description of the politics and government of the island, topics of nearly obsessive interest to Bacon's Renaissance contemporaries. Would Bacon's account of Bensalem's government have been based in traditional authority or, taking a utopian turn, would he have sought to describe a new social order?

Bacon's island is not altogether defined by tradition. It is, after all, a *new* Atlantis, not the Golden Age ideal described by Plato in the *Timaeus* and the *Critias* dialogues. The Atlantis described by Plato was a utopia inhabited by the children of the gods, a society that gradually declined as later generations lost touch with their divine origins. In the end an earthquake shook the island until it sunk into the sea. The progressive, Enlightenment character of Bacon's *New Atlantis* is most evident in Salomon's House, the scientific research center that is its most important institution. Devoted to the orderly and controlled pursuit of scientific knowledge, the projects at Salomon's House have made this new Atlantis an advanced society. The responsibilities of the various experimenters engaged in the work of the institution suggest a new and different social order from that celebrated in the Feast of the Family, so in its description of Salomon's House, *New Atlantis* becomes a kind of scientific utopia. It presents the brave new world that could result if a whole society were devoted to Bacon's "true way . . . as yet untried."

The two halves of Bacon's vision—the traditional and the experimental—are not reconciled in the story. Bacon does not discuss, for example, how a conflict between revealed religion and experimental science would be resolved. Bensalem's traditional religion and family structure, like the fires of Hell that consume Doctor Faustus or the stone patriarch who defeats Don Juan, embody the authority of established ideas inherited from the past. But *New Atlantis* is also an imaginary journey, a literary form of special interest to such Enlightenment writers as Swift, Voltaire, and Diderot. On these journeys, Enlightenment travelers discovered realms of possibility, societies of the mind that articulated their rational ideals. These ideals were based in hopes for future progress rather than in traditions from the past. The utopia that Bacon's travelers discover in the Pacific is organized around the processes of scientific discovery. The text itself remains unfinished, its incompleteness suggesting the open-endedness of the scientific point of view. If *New Atlantis* does not reconcile its competing perspectives, it does nonetheless open one of the doorways by which the Renaissance entered the Enlightenment.

Suggested Readings

Charles Williams's *Bacon* (1933) and F. H. Anderson's *Francis Bacon: His Career and His Thought* (1962) provide a good introduction to Bacon's life and work. Anthony Quinton's *Francis Bacon* (1980) offers a short and readable account of Bacon's philosophy. Loren Eisley in *The Man Who Saw through Time* (1961, 1973) provides an assessment of Bacon's importance in the history of science. Judah Bierman discusses Bacon's utopia in "New Atlantis Revisited," *Studies in the Literary Imagination* 4 (1971), 121–141.

New Atlantis

We sailed from Peru (where we had continued by the space of one whole year) for China and Japan, by the South Sea, taking with us victuals for twelve months; and had good winds from the east, though soft and weak, for five months' space and more. But then the wind came about, and settled in the west for many days, so as we could make little or no way, and were sometimes in purpose to turn back. But then again there arose strong and great winds from the south, with a point east; which carried us up, for all that we could do, towards the north: by which time our victuals failed us, though we had made good spare[1] of them. So that finding ourselves, in the midst of the greatest wilderness of waters in the world, without victual, we gave ourselves for lost men, and prepared for death. Yet we did lift up our hearts and voices to God above, who "showeth His wonders in the deep"; beseeching Him of His mercy, that as in the beginning He discovered the face of the deep, and brought forth dry land, so He would now discover land to us, that we might not perish.

And it came to pass, that the next day about evening we saw within a kenning[2] before us, towards the north, as it were thick clouds, which did put us in some hope of land; knowing how that part of the South Sea was utterly unknown; and might have islands or continents that hitherto were not come to light. Wherefore we bent our course thither, where we saw the appearance of land, all that night; and in the dawning of the next day, we might plainly discern that it was a land, flat to our sight, and full of boscage, which made it show the more dark. And after an hour and a half's sailing, we entered into a good haven, being the port of a fair city: not great indeed, but well built, and that gave a pleasant view from the sea. And we thinking every minute long till we were on land, came close to the shore and offered to land. But straightways we saw divers of the people, with bastons[3] in their hands, as it were, forbidding us to land: yet without any cries or fierceness, but only as warning us off, by signs that they made. Whereupon being not a little discomforted, we were advising with ourselves what we should do.

During which time there made forth to us a small boat, with about eight persons in it, whereof one of them had in his hand a tipstaff of a yellow cane, tipped at both ends with blue, who came aboard our ship, without any show of distrust at all. And when he saw one of our number present himself somewhat afore the rest, he drew forth a little scroll of parchment (somewhat yellower than our parchment, and shining like the leaves of writing tables,[4] but otherwise soft and flexible), and delivered it to our foremost man. In which scroll were written in ancient Hebrew, and in ancient Greek, and in good Latin of the School, and in Spanish, these words: "Land ye not, none of you, and provide to be gone from this coast within sixteen days, except you have further time given you. Meanwhile, if you want fresh water, or victual, or help for your sick, or that your ship needeth repair, write down your wants, and you shall have that which belongeth to mercy." This scroll was signed with a stamp of cherubin's wings, not spread, but hanging downwards; and by them a cross. This being delivered, the officer returned, and left only a servant with us to receive our answer.

Consulting hereupon amongst ourselves, we were much perplexed. The denial of landing, and hasty warning us away, troubled us much: on the other side, to find that the people had languages, and were so full of humanity, did comfort us not a little. And above all, the sign of the Cross to that instrument, was to us a great rejoicing, and as it were a certain presage of good. Our answer was in the

[1]Been very sparing. [2]In sight.
[3]Staffs or cudgels. [4]Tablets.

Spanish tongue, "That for our ship, it was well; for we had rather met with calms and contrary winds, than any tempests. For our sick, they were many, and in very ill case; so that if they were not permitted to land, they ran in danger of their lives." Our other wants we set down in particular, adding, "That we had some little store of merchandise, which if it pleased them to deal for, it might supply our wants, without being chargeable unto them." We offered some reward in pistolets unto the servant, and a piece of crimson velvet to be presented to the officer: but the servant took them not, nor would scarce look upon them; and so left us, and went back in another little boat which was sent for him.

About three hours after we had dispatched our answer there came towards us a person (as it seemed) of place. He had on him a gown with wide sleeves, of a kind of water chamolet,[5] of an excellent azure colour, far more glossy than ours: his under apparel was green, and so was his hat, being in the form of a turban, daintily made, and not so huge as the Turkish turbans; and the locks of his hair came down below the brims of it. A reverend man was he to behold. He came in a boat, gilt in some parts of it, with four persons more only in that boat; and was followed by another boat, wherein were some twenty. When he was come within a flight-shot[6] of our ship, signs were made to us that we should send forth some to meet him upon the water, which we presently did in our ship-boat, sending the principal man amongst us save one, and four of our number with him.

When we were come within six yards of their boat, they called to us to stay, and not to approach farther, which we did. And thereupon the man, whom I before described, stood up, and with a loud voice, in Spanish, asked, "Are ye Christians?" We answered, we were; fearing the less, because of the Cross we had seen in the subscription. At which answer the said person lift up his right hand towards Heaven, and drew it softly to his mouth (which is the gesture they use, when they thank God), and then said: "If ye will swear, all of you, by the merits of the Saviour, that ye are no pirates, nor have shed blood, lawfully nor unlawfully, within forty days past, you may have license to come on land." We said, we were all ready to take that oath. Whereupon one of those that were with him, being (as it seemed) a notary, made an entry of this act. Which done, another of the attendants of the great person, which was with him in the same boat, after his lord had spoken a little to him, said aloud: "My lord would have you know, that it is not of pride, or greatness, that he cometh not aboard your ship: but for that, in your answer, you declare that you have many sick amongst you, he was warned by the Conservator of Health of the city that he should keep a distance." We bowed ourselves towards him, and answered, we were his humble servants; and accounted for great honour and singular humanity towards us, that which was already done: but hoped well, that the nature of the sickness of our men was not infectious. So he returned; and a while after came the notary to us aboard our ship, holding in his hand a fruit of that country, like an orange, but of colour between orange-tawney and scarlet: which cast a most excellent odour. He used it (as it seemed) for a preservative against infection. He gave us our oath, "By the name of Jesus, and His merits": and after told us, that the next day, by six of the clock in the morning, we should be sent to, and brought to the Strangers' House (so he called it), where we should be accommodated of things, both for our whole and for our sick. So he left us; and when we offered him some pistolets, he smiling, said, he must not be twice paid

[5] A fabric made of goat's hair.

[6] The distance an arrow can be shot, about 200 yards.

for one labour: meaning (as I take it) that he had salary sufficient of the State for his service. For (as I after learned) they call an officer that taketh rewards, twice-paid.

The next morning early, there came to us the same officer that came to us at first with his cane, and told us: "He came to conduct us to the Strangers' House: and that he had prevented[7] the hour, because we might have the whole day before us for our business. For (said he) if you will follow my advice, there shall first go with me some few of you, and see the place, and how it may be made convenient for you; and then you may send for your sick, and the rest of your number, which ye will bring on land." We thanked him, and said, that this care which he took of desolate strangers, God would reward. And so six of us went on land with him; and when we were on land, he went before us, and turned to us, and said, he was but our servant, and our guide. He led us through three fair streets; and all the way we went there were gathered some people on both sides, standing in a row; but in so civil a fashion, as if it had been, not to wonder at us, but to welcome us; and divers of them, as we passed by them, put their arms a little abroad, which is their gesture when they bid any welcome.

The Strangers' House is a fair and spacious house, built of brick, of somewhat a bluer colour than our brick; and with handsome windows, some of glass, some of a kind of cambric oiled. He brought us first into a fair parlour above stairs, and then asked us, what number of persons we were? and how many sick? We answered, we were in all (sick and whole) one and fifty persons, whereof our sick were seventeen. He desired us to have patience a little, and to stay till he came back to us, which was about an hour after; and then he led us to see the chambers which were provided for us, being in number nineteen. They having cast it (as it seemeth) that four of those chambers, which were better than the rest, might receive four of the principal men of our company; and lodge them alone by themselves; and the other fifteen chambers were to lodge us, two and two together. The chambers were handsome and cheerful chambers, and furnished civilly. Then he led us to a long gallery, like a dorture,[8] where he showed us all along the one side (for the other side was but wall and window) seventeen cells, very neat ones, having partitions of cedar wood. Which gallery and cells, being in all forty (many more than we needed), were instituted as an infirmary for sick persons. And he told us withal, that as any of our sick waxed well, he might be removed from his cell to a chamber: for which purpose there were set forth ten spare chambers, besides the number we spake of before. This done, he brought us back to the parlour, and lifting up his cane a little (as they do when they give any charge or command), said to us, "Ye are to know that the custom of the land requireth, that after this day and to-morrow (which we give you for removing your people from your ship), you are to keep within doors for three days. But let it not trouble you, nor do not think yourselves restrained, but rather left to your ease and rest. You shall want nothing, and there are six of our people appointed to attend you for any business you may have abroad." We gave him thanks with all affection and respect, and said, "God surely is manifested in this land." We offered him also twenty pistolets; but he smiled, and only said: "What? twice paid!" And so he left us.

Soon after our dinner was served in; which was right good viands, both for bread and meat: better than any collegiate diet that I have known in Europe. We had also drink of three sorts, all wholesome and good; wine of the grape; a drink

[7]Come earlier than.

[8]Dormitory.

of grain, such as is with us our ale, but more clear; and a kind of cider made of a fruit of that country; a wonderful pleasing and refreshing drink. Besides, there were brought in to us great store of those scarlet oranges for our sick; which (they said) were an assured remedy for sickness taken at sea. There was given us also a box of small grey or whitish pills, which they wished our sick should take, one of the pills every night before sleep; which (they said) would hasten their recovery.

The next day, after that our trouble of carriage and removing of our men and goods out of our ship was somewhat settled and quiet, I thought good to call our company together, and when they were assembled, said unto them, "My dear friends, let us know ourselves, and how it standeth with us. We are men cast on land, as Jonas was out of the whale's belly, when we were as buried in the deep; and now we are on land, we are but between death and life, for we are beyond both the Old World and the New; and whether ever we shall see Europe, God only knoweth. It is a kind of miracle hath brought us hither, and it must be little less that shall bring us hence. Therefore in regard of our deliverance past, and our danger present and to come, let us look up to God, and every man reform his own ways. Besides we are come here amongst a Christian people, full of piety and humanity: let us not bring that confusion of face upon ourselves, as to show our vices or unworthiness before them. Yet there is more, for they have by commandment (though in form of courtesy) cloistered us within these walls for three days: who knoweth whether it be not to take some taste of our manners and conditions? And if they find them bad, to banish us straightways; if good, to give us further time. For these men that they have given us for attendance, may withal have an eye upon us. Therefore, for God's love, and as we love the weal of our souls and bodies, let us so behave ourselves, as we may be at peace with God, and may find grace in the eyes of this people." Our company with one voice thanked me for my good admonition, and promised me to live soberly and civilly, and without giving any the least occasion of offence. So we spent our three days joyfully, and without care, in expectation what would be done with us when they were expired. During which time, we had every hour joy of the amendment of our sick, who thought themselves cast into some divine pool of healing, they mended so kindly and so fast.

The morrow after our three days were past, there came to us a new man, that we had not seen before, clothed in blue as the former was, save that his turban was white with a small red cross on the top. He had also a tippet[9] of fine linen. At his coming in, he did bend to us a little, and put his arms abroad. We of our parts saluted him in a very lowly and submissive manner; as looking that from him we should receive sentence of life or death. He desired to speak with some few of us. Whereupon six of us only stayed, and the rest avoided[10] the room. He said, "I am by office Governor of this House of Strangers, and by vocation I am a Christian priest; and therefore am come to you to offer you my service, both as strangers, and chiefly as Christians. Some things I may tell you, which I think you will not be unwilling to hear. The State hath given you licence to stay on land for the space of six weeks: and let it not trouble you, if your occasions ask further time, for the law in this point is not precise; and I do not doubt but myself shall be able to obtain for you such further time as shall be convenient. Ye shall also understand, that the Strangers' House is at this time rich, and much aforehand; for it hath laid up revenue these thirty-seven years: for so long it is since any stranger arrived in this part: and therefore take ye no care; the State will defray you all the time you stay. Neither

[9]A long hood or cape.
[10]Left.

shall you stay one day the less for that. As for any merchandise ye have brought, ye shall be well used, and have your return, either in merchandise or in gold and silver: for to us it is all one. And if you have any other request to make, hide it not; for ye shall find we will not make your countenance to fall by the answer ye shall receive. Only this I must tell you, that none of you must go above a karan (that is with them a mile and a half) from the walls of the city, without especial leave."

We answered, after we had looked awhile one upon another, admiring this gracious and parent-like usage, that we could not tell what to say, for we wanted words to express our thanks; and his noble free offers left us nothing to ask. It seemed to us, that we had before us a picture of our salvation in Heaven; for we that were a while since in the jaws of death, were now brought into a place where we found nothing but consolations. For the commandment laid upon us, we would not fail to obey it, though it was impossible but our hearts should be inflamed to tread further upon this happy and holy ground. We added, that our tongues should first cleave to the roofs of our mouths, ere we should forget, either his reverend person, or this whole nation, in our prayers. We also most humbly besought him to accept of us as his true servants, by as just a right as ever men on earth were bounden; laying and presenting both our persons and all we had at his feet. He said he was a priest, and looked for a priest's reward; which was our brotherly love, and the good of our souls and bodies. So he went from us, not without tears of tenderness in his eyes, and left us also confused with joy and kindness, saying amongst ourselves that we were come into a land of angels, which did appear to us daily, and present us with comforts, which we thought not of, much less expected.

The next day, about ten of the clock, the Governor came to us again, and after salutations, said familiarly, that he was come to visit us; and called for a chair, and sat him down; and we, being some ten of us (the rest were of the meaner sort, or else gone abroad), sat down with him; and when we were set, he began thus: "We of this island of Bensalem (for so they called it in their language) have this: that by means of our solitary situation, and of the laws of secrecy, which we have for our travellers, and our rare admission of strangers, we know well most part of the habitable world, and are ourselves unknown. Therefore because he that knoweth least is fitted to ask questions, it is more reason, for the entertainment of the time, that ye ask me questions, than that I ask you."

We answered, that we humbly thanked him, that he would give us leave so to do: and that we conceived, by the taste we had already, that there was no worldly thing on earth more worthy to be known than the state of that happy land. But above all (we said) since that we were met from the several ends of the world, and hoped assuredly that we should meet one day in the kingdom of Heaven (for that we were both part Christians), we desired to know (in respect that land was so remote, and so divided by vast and unknown seas from the land where our Saviour walked on earth) who was the apostle of that nation, and how it was converted to the faith? It appeared in his face, that he took great contentment in this our question; he said, "Ye knit my heart to you, by asking this question in the first place: for it showeth that you first seek the kingdom of Heaven: and I shall gladly, and briefly, satisfy your demand.

"About twenty years after the Ascension of our Saviour it came to pass, that there was seen by the people of Renfusa (a city upon the eastern coast of our island), within sight, (the night was cloudy and calm), as it might be some mile in the sea, a great pillar of light; not sharp, but in form of a column, or cylinder, rising from the sea, a great way up towards Heaven; and on the top of it was seen a large cross of light, more bright and resplendent than the body of the pillar. Upon which so strange a spectacle the people of the city gathered apace together upon the sands, to wonder; and so after put themselves into a number of small boats to go nearer to this marvellous sight. But when the boats were come within about sixty yards of the pillar they found themselves all bound, and could go no further, yet so as they might move to go about, but might not approach nearer: so as the boats stood all as in a theatre, beholding this light, as an heavenly sign. It so fell out, that there was in one of the boats one of our wise men, of the Society of Salomon's House; which house or college, my good brethren, is the very eye of this kingdom, who having awhile attentively and devoutly viewed and contemplated this pillar and cross, fell down upon his face; and then raised himself upon his knees, and lifting up his hands to Heaven, made his prayers in this manner:

" 'Lord God of Heaven and Earth; Thou hast vouchsafed of Thy grace, to those of our order, to know Thy works of creation, and the secrets of them; and to discern (as far as appertaineth to the generations of men) between divine miracles, works of Nature, works of art, and impostures and illusions of all sorts. I do here acknowledge and testify before this people, that the thing which we now see before our eyes is Thy finger, and a true miracle. And forasmuch as we learn in our books that Thou never workest miracles, but to a divine and excellent end (for the laws of nature are Thine own laws, and Thou exceedest them not but upon great cause), we most humbly beseech Thee to prosper this great sign, and to give us the interpretation and use of it in mercy; which Thou dost in some part secretly promise, by sending it unto us.'

"When he had made his prayer, he presently found the boat he was in movable and unbound; whereas all the rest remained still fast; and taking that for an assurance of leave to approach, he caused the boat to be softly and with silence rowed towards the pillar. But ere he came near it, the pillar and cross of light broke up, and cast itself abroad, as it were, into a firmament of many stars, which also vanished soon after, and there was nothing left to be seen but a small ark, or chest of cedar, dry, and not wet at all with water, though it swam. And in the fore-end of it, which was towards him, grew a small green branch of palm; and when the wise man had taken it with all reverence into his boat, it opened of itself, and there were found in it a book and a letter, both written in fine parchment, and wrapped in sindons[11] of linen. The book contained all the canonical books of the Old and New Testament, according as you have them (for we know well what the churches with you receive), and the Apocalypse itself; and some other books of the New Testament, which were not at that time written, were nevertheless in the book. And for the letter, it was in these words:

" 'I Bartholomew, a servant of the Highest, and apostle of Jesus Christ, was warned by an angel that appeared to me in a vision of glory, that I should commit this ark to the floods of the sea. Therefore I do testify and declare unto that people where God shall ordain this ark to come to land, that in the same day is come unto them salvation and peace, and goodwill, from the Father, and from the Lord Jesus.'

"There was also in both these writings, as well the book as the letter, wrought a great miracle, conform[12] to that of the apostles, in the original gift of tongues. For there being at that time, in this land, Hebrews, Persians, and Indians, besides the natives, every one read upon the book and letter, as if they had been written in his own language. And thus was this land saved from infidelity (as the remain of the Old World was from water) by an ark, through the apostolical and miraculous evangelism of St. Bartholomew." And here he paused, and a messenger came, and called him forth from us. So this was all that passed in that conference.

---

[11] Pieces. [12] Similar.

The next day, the same Governor came again to us, immediately after dinner, and excused himself, saying, that the day before he was called from us somewhat abruptly, but now he would make us amends, and spend time with us, if we held his company and conference agreeable. We answered, that we held it so agreeable and pleasing to us, as we forgot both dangers past, and fears to come, for the time we heard him speak; and that we thought an hour spent with him was worth years of our former life. He bowed himself a little to us, and after we were set again, he said, "Well, the questions are on your part."

One of our number said, after a little pause, that there was a matter we were no less desirous to know than fearful to ask, lest we might presume too far. But encouraged by his rare humanity towards us (that could scarce think ourselves strangers, being his vowed and professed servants), we would take the hardness to propound it; humbly beseeching him, if he thought it not fit to be answered, that he would pardon it, though he rejected it. We said, we well observed those his words, which he formerly spake, that this happy island, where we now stood, was known to few, and yet knew most of the nations of the world, which we found to be true, considering they had the languages of Europe, and knew much of our state and business; and yet we in Europe (notwithstanding all the remote discoveries and navigations of this last age) never heard any of the least inkling or glimpse of this island. This we found wonderful strange; for that all nations have interknowledge one of another, either by voyage into foreign parts, or by strangers that come to them; and though the traveller into a foreign country doth commonly know more by the eye than he that stayeth at home can by relation of the traveller; yet both ways suffice to make a mutual knowledge, in some degree, on both parts. But for this island, we never heard tell of any ship of theirs that had been seen to arrive upon any shore of Europe; no, nor of either the East or West Indies, nor yet of any ship of any other part of the world, that had made return from them. And yet the marvel rested not in this; for the situation of it (as his lordship said) in the secret conclave of such a vast sea mought cause it. But then, that they should have knowledge of the languages, books, affairs, of those that lie such a distance from them, it was a thing we could not tell what to make of; for that it seemed to us a condition and propriety[13] of divine powers and beings, to be hidden and unseen to others, and yet to have others open, and as in a light to them.

At this speech the Governor gave a gracious smile and said, that we did well to ask pardon for this question we now asked, for that it imported, as if we thought this land a land of magicians, that sent forth spirits of the air into all parts, to bring them news and intelligence of other countries. It was answered by us all, in all possible humbleness, but yet with a countenance taking knowledge,[14] that we knew he spake it but merrily; that we were apt enough to think there was somewhat supernatural in this island, but yet rather as angelical than magical. But to let his lordship know truly what it was that made us tender and doubtful to ask this question, it was not any such conceit, but because we remembered he had given a touch[15] in his former speech that this land had laws of secrecy touching strangers. To this he said, "You remember it aright; and therefore in that I shall say to you, I must reserve some particulars, which it is not lawful for me to reveal, but there will be enough left to give you satisfaction.

"You shall understand (that which perhaps you will scarce think credible) that about three thousand years ago, or somewhat more, the navigation of the world (especially for remote voyages) was greater than at this day. Do not think with

---

[13]Characteristic. [14]Knowing look. [15]Hint.

yourselves, that I know not how much it is increased with you, within these six-score years; I know it well, and yet I say, greater then than now; whether it was, that the example of the Ark, that saved the remnant of men from the universal deluge, gave men confidence to adventure upon the waters, or what it was; but such is the truth. The Phoenicians, and specially the Tyrians, had great fleets; so had the Carthaginians their colony, which is yet further west. Toward the east the shipping of Egypt, and of Palestine, was likewise great. China also, and the great Atlantis (that you call America), which have now but junks and canoes, abounded then in tall ships. This island (as appeareth by faithful registers of those times) had then fifteen hundred strong ships, of great content. Of all this there is with you sparing memory, or none; but we have large knowledge thereof.

"At that time, this land was known and frequented by the ships and vessels of all the nations before named. And (as it cometh to pass) they had many times men of other countries, that were no sailors, that came with them; as Persians, Chaldeans, Arabians, so as almost all nations of might and fame resorted hither; of whom we have some stirps[16] and little tribes with us at this day. And for our own ships, they went sundry voyages, as well to your straits, which you call the Pillars of Hercules, as to other parts in the Atlantic and Mediterranean Seas; as to Paguin (which is the same with Cambaline) and Quinzy, upon the Oriental Seas, as far as to the borders of the East Tartary.[17]

"At the same time, and an age after or more, the inhabitants of the great Atlantis did flourish. For though the narration and description which is made by a great man[18] with you, that the descendants of Neptune planted there, and of the magnificent temple, palace, city, and hill; and the manifold streams of goodly navigable rivers (which as so many chains environed the same site and temple); and the several degrees of ascent, whereby men did climb up to the same, as if it had been a Scala Caeli;[19] be all poetical and fabulous; yet so much is true, that the said country of Atlantis, as well that of Peru, then called Coya, as that of Mexico, then named Tyrambel, were mighty and proud kingdoms, in arms, shipping, and riches: so mighty as at one time (or at least within the space of ten years), they both made two great expeditions; they of Tyrambel through the Atlantic to the Mediterranean Sea; and they of Coya, through the South Sea upon this our island; and for the former of these, which was into Europe, the same author amongst you (as it seemeth) had some relation from the Egyptian priest, whom he citeth. For assuredly such a thing there was. But whether it were the ancient Athenians that had the glory of the repulse and resistance of those forces, I can say nothing; but certain it is there never came back either ship or man from that voyage. Neither had the other voyage of those of Coya upon us had better fortune, if they had not met with enemies of greater clemency. For the king of this island, by name Altabin, a wise man and a great warrior, knowing well both his own strength and that of his enemies, handled the matter so, as he cut off their land forces from their ships, and entoiled both their navy and their camp with a greater power than theirs, both by sea and land, and compelled them to render themselves without striking stroke; and after they were at his mercy, contenting himself only with their oath, that they should no more bear arms against him, dismissed them all in safety.

But the divine revenge overtook not long after those proud enterprises. For within less than the space of one hundred years the Great Atlantis was utterly lost

[16]Families.

[17]Paguin (Cambaline) is Peking or Beijing; Quinzy is Hangchow.

[18]Plato describes Atlantis in the *Critias* and *Timaeus*.

[19]A ladder to heaven.

and destroyed; not by a great earthquake, as your man saith (for that whole tract is little subject to earthquakes), but by a particular deluge or inundation, those countries having at this day far greater rivers and far higher mountains to pour down waters, than any part of the Old World. But it is true that the same inundation was not deep, not past forty foot in most places from the ground, so that although it destroyed man and beast generally, yet some few wild inhabitants of the wood escaped. Birds also were saved by flying to the high trees and woods. For as for men, although they had buildings in many places higher than the depth of the water, yet that inundation, though it were shallow, had a long continuance, whereby they of the vale that were not drowned perished for want of food, and other things necessary.

"So as marvel you not at the thin population of America, nor at the rudeness and ignorance of the people; for you must account your inhabitants of America as a young people, younger a thousand years at the least than the rest of the world, for that there was so much time between the universal flood and their particular inundation. For the poor remnant of human seed which remained in their mountains peopled the country again slowly, by little and little, and being simple and savage people (not like Noah and his sons, which was the chief family of the earth) they were not able to leave letters, arts, and civility to their posterity; and having likewise in their mountainous habitations been used (in respect of the extreme cold of those regions) to clothe themselves with the skins of tigers, bears, and great hairy goats, that they have in those parts; when after they came down into the valley, and found the intolerable heats which are there, and knew no means of lighter apparel, they were forced to begin the custom of going naked, which continueth at this day. Only they take great pride and delight in the feathers of birds, and this also they took from those their ancestors of the mountains, who were invited unto it, by the infinite flight of birds that came up to the high grounds, while the waters stood below. So you see, by this main accident of time, we lost our traffic with the Americans, with whom of all others, in regard they lay nearest to us, we had most commerce.

"As for the other parts of the world, it is most manifest that in the ages following (whether it were in respect of wars, or by a natural revolution of time) navigation did everywhere greatly decay, and specially far voyages (the rather by the use of galleys, and such vessels as could hardly brook the ocean) were altogether left and omitted. So then, that part of intercourse which could be from other nations, to sail to us, you see how it hath long since ceased; except it were by some rare accident, as this of yours. But now of the cessation of that other part of intercourse, which mought be by our sailing to other nations, I must yield you some other cause. For I cannot say, if I shall say truly, but our shipping, for number, strength, mariners, pilots, and all things that appertain to navigation, is as great as ever; and therefore why we should sit at home, I shall now give you an account by itself; and it will draw nearer, to give you satisfaction, to your principal question.

"There reigned in this island about 1,900 years ago, a king, whose memory of all others we most adore; not superstitiously, but as a divine instrument, though a mortal man: his name was Solamona; and we esteem him as the lawgiver of our nation. This king had a large heart, inscrutable for good, and was wholly bent to make his kingdom and people happy. He therefore taking into consideration how sufficient and substantive this land was, to maintain itself without any aid at all of the foreigner; being 5,600 miles in circuit, and of rare fertility of soil, in the greatest part thereof; and finding also the shipping of this country mought be plentifully set on work, both by fishing and by transportations from port to port, and likewise by sailing unto some small islands that are not far from us, and are under the crown and laws of this State; and recalling into his memory the happy and flourishing estate wherein this land then was, so as it mought be a thousand ways altered to the worse, but scarce any one way to the better; though nothing wanted to his noble and heroical intentions, but only (as far as human foresight mought reach) to give perpetuity to that which was in his time so happily established. Therefore amongst his other fundamental laws of this kingdom he did ordain the interdicts and prohibitions which we have touching entrance of strangers; which at that time (though it was after the calamity of America) was frequent; doubting[20] novelties and commixture of manners. It is true, the like law against the admission of strangers without licence is an ancient law in the kingdom of China, and yet continued in use. But there it is a poor thing; and hath made them a curious, ignorant, fearful, foolish nation. But our lawgiver made his law of another temper. For first, he hath preserved all points of humanity, in taking order and making provision for the relief of strangers distressed; whereof you have tasted."

At which speech (as reason was) we all rose up, and bowed ourselves. He went on:

"That king also still desiring to join humanity and policy together; and thinking it against humanity, to detain strangers here against their wills; and against policy, that they should return, and discover their knowledge of this estate, he took this course: he did ordain, that of the strangers that should be permitted to land, as many (at all times) mought depart as would; but as many as would stay, should have very good conditions, and means to live from the State. Wherein he saw so far, that now in so many ages since the prohibition, we have memory not of one ship that ever returned, and but of thirteen persons only, at several times, that chose to return in our bottoms. What those few that returned may have reported abroad I know not. But you must think, whatsoever they have said, could be taken where they came but for a dream. Now for our travelling from hence into parts abroad, our lawgiver thought fit altogether to restrain it. So is it not in China. For the Chinese sail where they will, or can; which showeth, that their law of keeping out strangers is a law of pusillanimity and fear. But this restraint of ours hath one only exception, which is admirable; preserving the good which cometh by communicating with strangers, and avoiding the hurt: and I will now open it to you. And here I shall seem a little to digress, but you will by and by find it pertinent.

"Ye shall understand, my dear friends, that amongst the excellent acts of that king, one above all hath the pre-eminence. It was the erection and institution of an order, or society, which we call Salomon's House; the noblest foundation, as we think, that ever was upon the earth, and the lantern of this kingdom. It is dedicated to the study of the works and creatures of God. Some think it beareth the founder's name a little corrupted, as if it should be Solamona's House. But the records write it as it is spoken. So as I take it to be denominate[21] of the king of the Hebrews, which is famous with you, and no stranger to us; for we have some parts of his works which with you are lost; namely, that Natural History which he wrote of all plants, from the cedar of Libanus to the moss that groweth out of the wall; and of all things that have life and motion. This maketh me think that our king finding himself to symbolize,[22] in many things, with that king of the Hebrews (which lived many years before him) honoured him with the title of this foundation. And I am the rather induced to be of this opinion, for that I find in ancient records, this order or society is sometimes called Salomon's House, and sometimes the College of the Six Day's Works; whereby I am satisfied that our excellent king had learned from the Hebrews that God had created the world, and all that therein is, within six days:

---

[20] Fearing.

[21] Named after. [22] Agree.

and therefore he instituting that house, for the finding out of the true nature of all things (whereby God mought have the more glory in the workmanship of them, and men the more fruit in the use of them), did give it also that second name.

"But now to come to our present purpose. When the king had forbidden to all his people navigation into any part that was not under his crown, he made nevertheless this ordinance: that every twelve years there should be set forth out of this kingdom two ships, appointed to several voyages; that in either of these ships there should be a mission of three of the fellows or brethren of Salomon's House, whose errand was only to give us knowledge of the affairs and state of those countries to which they were designed;[23] and especially of the sciences, arts, manufactures, and inventions of all the world; and withal to bring unto us books, instruments, and patterns in every kind: that the ships, after they had landed the brethren, should return; and that the brethren should stay abroad till the new mission. These ships are not otherwise fraught[24] than with store of victuals, and good quantity of treasure to remain with the brethren, for the buying of such things, and rewarding of such persons, as they should think fit. Now for me to tell you how the vulgar sort of mariners are contained from being discovered at land, and how they that must be put on shore for any time, colour themselves under the names of other nations, and to what places these voyages have been designed, and what places of rendezvous are appointed for the new missions, and the like circumstances of the practice, I may not do it, neither is it much to your desire. But thus you see we maintain a trade, not for gold, silver, or jewels, nor for silks, nor for spices, nor any other commodity of matter; but only for God's first creature, which was light: to have light, I say, of the growth of all parts of the world."

And when he had said this, he was silent, and so were we all; for indeed we were all astonished to hear so strange things so probably told. And he perceiving that we were willing to say somewhat, but had it not ready, in great courtesy took us off, and descended to ask us questions of our voyage and fortunes, and in the end concluded that we mought do well to think with ourselves, what time of stay we would demand of the State, and bade us not to scant ourselves; for he would procure such time as we desired. Whereupon we all rose up and presented ourselves to kiss the skirt of his tippet, but he would not suffer us, and so took his leave. But when it came once amongst our people, that the State used to offer conditions to strangers that would stay, we had work enough to get any of our men to look to our ship, and to keep them from going presently to the Governor, to crave conditions; but with much ado we restrained them, till we mought agree what course to take.

We took ourselves now for free men, seeing there was no danger of our utter perdition, and lived most joyfully, going abroad and seeing what was to be seen in the city and places adjacent, within our tedder;[25] and obtaining acquaintance with many of the city, not of the meanest quality, at whose hands we found such humanity, and such a freedom and desire to take strangers, as it were, into their bosom, as was enough to make us forget all that was dear to us in our own countries; and continually we met with many things, right worthy of observation and relation; as indeed, if there be a mirror in the world, worthy to hold men's eyes, it is that country.

One day there were two of our company bidden to a feast of the family, as they call it; a most natural, pious, and reverend custom it is, showing that nation to be compounded of all goodness. This is the manner of it. It is granted to any man that shall live to see thirty persons descended of his body, alive together, and all

---

[23]Designated to go. [24]Loaded.
[25]Tether or range.

above three years old, to make this feast, which is done at the cost of the State. The father of the family, whom they call the Tirsan, two days before the feast, taketh to him three of such friends as he liketh to choose, and is assisted also by the Governor of the city or place where the feast is celebrated, and all the persons of the family, of both sexes, are summoned to attend him. These two days the Tirsan sitteth in consultation, concerning the good estate of the family. There, if there be any discord or suits between any of the family, they are compounded and appeased. There, if any of the family be distressed or decayed, order is taken for their relief, and competent means to live. There, if any be subject to vice, or take ill courses, they are reproved and censured. So likewise direction is given touching marriages, and the courses of life which any of them should take, with divers other the like orders and advices. The Governor assisteth, to the end to put in execution, by his public authority, the decrees and orders of the Tirsan, if they should be disobeyed though that seldom needeth;[26] such reverence and obedience they give to the order of Nature. The Tirsan doth also then ever choose one man from amongst his sons, to live in house with him; who is called ever after the Son of the Vine. The reason will hereafter appear.

On the feast day, the father or Tirsan cometh forth after divine service into a large room where the feast is celebrated; which room hath an half-pace at the upper end. Against the wall, in the middle of the half-pace, is a chair placed for him, with a table and carpet before it. Over the chair is a state,[27] made round or oval, and it is of ivy; an ivy somewhat whiter than ours, like the leaf of a silver asp, but more shining; for it is green all winter. And the state is curiously wrought with silver and silk of divers colours, broiding[28] or binding in the ivy; and is ever of the work of some of the daughters of the family, and veiled over at the top, with a fine net of silk and silver. But the substance of it is true ivy; whereof, after it is taken down, the friends of the family are desirous to have some leaf or sprig to keep.

The Tirsan cometh forth with all his generation or lineage, the males before him, and the females following him; and if there be a mother from whose body the whole lineage is descended, there is a traverse[29] placed in a loft above, on the right hand of the chair, with a privy door, and a carved window of glass, leaded with gold and blue; where she sitteth, but is not seen. When the Tirsan is come forth, he sitteth down in the chair; and all the lineage place themselves against the wall, both at his back, and upon the return of the half-pace, in order of their years, without difference of sex, and stand upon their feet. When he is set, the room being always full of company, but well kept and without disorder, after some pause there cometh in from the lower end of the room a Taratan (which is as much as an herald), and on either side of him two young lads: whereof one carrieth a scroll of their shining yellow parchment, and the other a cluster of grapes of gold, with a long foot or stalk. The herald and children are clothed with mantles of sea-water green satin; but the herald's mantle is streamed with gold, and hath a train.

Then the herald with three curtsies, or rather inclinations, cometh up as far as the half-pace and there first taketh into his hand the scroll. This scroll is the king's charter, containing gift of revenue, and many privileges, exemptions, and points of honour, granted to the father of the family; and it is ever styled and directed, "To such an one, our well-beloved friend and creditor," which is a title proper only to this case. For they say, the king is debtor to no man, but for propagation of his subjects. The seal set to the king's charter is the king's image, embossed or moulded in gold; and though such charters be expedited of course, and as of right, yet they

[26] Is necessary. [27] Canopy. [28] Braiding. [29] Curtain.

are varied by discretion, according to the number and dignity of the family. This charter the herald readeth aloud; and while it is read, the father or Tirsan standeth up, supported by two of his sons, such as he chooseth. Then the herald mounteth the half-pace, and delivereth the charter into his hand; and with that there is an acclamation, by all that are present, in their language, which is thus much, "Happy are the people of Bensalem."

Then the herald taketh into his hand from the other child the cluster of grapes, which is of gold; both the stalk and the grapes. But the grapes are daintily enamelled; and if the males of the family be the greater number, the grapes are enamelled purple, with a little sun set on the top; if the females, then they are enamelled into a greenish yellow, with a crescent on the top. The grapes are in number as many as there are descendants of the family. This golden cluster the herald delivereth also to the Tirsan; who presently delivereth it over to that son that he had formerly chosen to be in house with him; who beareth it before his father, as an ensign of honour, when he goeth in public ever after; and is thereupon called the Son of the Vine.

After this ceremony ended the father or Tirsan retireth; and after some time cometh forth again to dinner, where he sitteth alone under the state, as before; and none of his descendants sit with him, of what degree or dignity so ever, except he hap to be of Salomon's House. He is served only by his own children, such as are male; who perform unto him all service of the table upon the knee, and the women only stand about him, leaning against the wall. The room below the half-pace hath tables on the sides for the guests that are bidden; who are served with great and comely order; and towards the end of dinner (which in the greatest feasts with them lasteth never above an hour and a half) there is a hymn sung, varied according to the invention of him that composeth it (for they have excellent poesy); but the subject of it is always the praises of Adam, and Noah, and Abraham; whereof the former two peopled the world, and the last was the father of the faithful: concluding ever with a thanksgiving for the nativity of our Saviour, in whose birth the births of all are only blessed.

Dinner being done, the Tirsan retireth again; and having withdrawn himself alone into a place, where he maketh some private prayers, he cometh forth the third time, to give the blessing, with all his descendants, who stand about him as at the first. Then he calleth them forth by one and by one, by name as he pleaseth, though seldom the order of age be inverted. The person that is called (the table being before removed) kneeleth down before the chair, and the father layeth his hand upon his head, or her head, and giveth the blessing in these words: "Son of Bensalem (or daughter of Bensalem), thy father saith it; the man by whom thou hast breath and life speaketh the word; the blessing of the everlasting Father, the Prince of Peace, and the Holy Dove, be upon thee, and make the days of thy pilgrimage good and many." This he saith to every of them; and that done, if there be any of his sons of eminent merit and virtue (so they be not above two), he calleth for them again, and saith, laying his arm over their shoulders, they standing: "Sons, it is well ye are born, give God the praise, and persevere to the end." And withal delivereth to either of them a jewel, made in the figure of an ear of wheat, which they ever after wear in the front of their turban, or hat. This done, they fall to music and dances, and other recreations, after their manner, for the rest of the day. This is the full order of that feast.

By that time six or seven days were spent, I was fallen into straight acquaintance with a merchant of that city, whose name was Joabin. He was a Jew and circumcised; for they have some few stirps of Jews yet remaining amongst them, whom they leave to their own religion. Which they may the better do, because they are of a far differing disposition from the Jews in other parts. For whereas they hate the name of Christ, and have a secret inbred rancour against the people amongst whom they live; these, contrariwise, give unto our Saviour many high attributes, and love the nation of Bensalem extremely. Surely this man of whom I speak would ever acknowledge that Christ was born of a Virgin and that He was more than a man; and he would tell how God made Him ruler of the seraphim, which guard His throne; and they call Him also the Milken Way, and the Eliah of the Messiah, and many other high names, which though they be inferior to His divine majesty, yet they are far from the language of other Jews.

And for the country of Bensalem, this man would make no end of commending it, being desirous by tradition among the Jews there to have it believed that the people thereof were of the generations of Abraham, by another son, whom they call Nachoran; and that Moses by a secret cabala ordained the laws of Bensalem which they now use; and that when the Messiah should come, and sit in His throne at Jerusalem, the King of Bensalem should sit at His feet, whereas other kings should keep a great distance. But yet setting aside these Jewish dreams, the man was a wise man and learned, and of great policy, and excellently seen in the laws and customs of that nation.

Amongst other discourses one day I told him, I was much affected with the relation I had from some of the company of their custom in holding the feast of the family, for that, methought, I had never heard of a solemnity wherein Nature did so much preside. And because propagation of families proceedeth from the nuptial copulation, I desired to know of him what laws and customs they had concerning marriage, and whether they kept marriage well, and whether they were tied to one wife? For that where population is so much affected,[30] and such as with them it seemed to be, there is commonly permission of plurality of wives.

To this he said:

"You have reason for to commend that excellent institution of the feast of the family; and indeed we have experience, that those families that are partakers of the blessings of that feast, do flourish and prosper ever after, in an extraordinary manner. But hear me now, and I will tell you what I know. You shall understand that there is not under the heavens so chaste a nation as this of Bensalem, nor so free from all pollution or foulness. It is the virgin of the world; I remember, I have read in one of your European books, of a holy hermit among you, that desired to see the spirit of fornication, and there appeared to him a little foul ugly Ethiope; but if he had desired to see the spirit of chastity of Bensalem, it would have appeared to him in the likeness of a fair beautiful cherub. For there is nothing, among mortal men, more fair and admirable than the chaste minds of this people.

"Know, therefore, that with them there are no stews, no dissolute houses, no courtesans, nor anything of that kind. Nay, they wonder, with detestation, at you in Europe, which permit such things. They say ye have put marriage out of office; for marriage is ordained a remedy for unlawful concupiscence; and natural concupiscence seemeth as a spur to marriage. But when men have at hand a remedy, more agreeable to their corrupt will, marriage is almost expulsed.[31] And therefore there are with you seen infinite men that marry not, but choose rather a libertine and impure single life, than to be yoked in marriage; and many that do marry, marry late, when the prime and strength of their years are past. And when they do marry, what is marriage to them but a very bargain; wherein is sought alliance, or portion, or reputation, with some desire (almost indifferent) of issue; and not the faithful nuptial union of man and wife, that was first instituted. Neither is it possible

[30]Desired. [31]Expelled.

that those that have cast away so basely so much of their strength, should greatly esteem children (being of the same matter) as chaste men do. So likewise during marriage is the case much amended, as it ought to be if those things were tolerated only for necessity; no, but they remain still as a very affront to marriage.

"The haunting of those dissolute places, or resort to courtesans, are no more punished in married men than in bachelors. And the depraved custom of change, and the delight in meretricious embracements (where sin is turned into art), maketh marriage a dull thing, and a kind of imposition or tax. They hear you defend these things, as done to avoid greater evils; as advoutries,[32] deflowering of virgins, unnatural lust, and the like. But they say this is a preposterous wisdom; and they call it Lot's offer, who to save his guests from abusing, offered his daughters; nay, they say further, that there is little gained in this; for that the same vices and appetites do still remain and abound, unlawful lust being like a furnace, that if you stop the flames altogether it will quench, but if you give it any vent it will rage; as for masculine love, they have no touch of it; and yet there are not so faithful and inviolate friendships in the world again as are there, and to speak generally (as I said before) I have not read of any such chastity in any people as theirs. And their usual saying is that whosoever is unchaste cannot reverence himself; and they say that the reverence of a man's self, is, next religion, the chiefest bridle of all vices."

And when he had said this the good Jew paused a little; whereupon I, far more willing to hear him speak on than to speak myself; yet thinking it decent that upon his pause of speech I should not be altogether silent, said only this; that I would say to him, as the widow of Sarepta said to Elias: "that he was come to bring to memory our sins;" and that I confess the righteousness of Bensalem was greater than the righteousness of Europe. At which speech he bowed his head, and went on this manner:

"They have also many wise and excellent laws, touching marriage. They allow no polygamy. They have ordained that none do intermarry, or contract, until a month be past from their first interview. Marriage without consent of parents they do not make void, but they mulct[33] it in the inheritors; for the children of such marriages are not admitted to inherit above a third part of their parents' inheritance. I have read in a book of one of your men, of a feigned commonwealth, where the married couple are permitted, before they contract, to see one another naked. This they dislike; for they think it a scorn to give a refusal after so familiar knowledge; but because of many hidden defects in men and women's bodies, they have a more civil way; for they have near every town a couple of pools (which they call Adam and Eve's pools), where it is permitted to one of the friends of the man, and another of the friends of the woman, to see them severally bathe naked."

And as we were thus in conference, there came one that seemed to be a messenger, in a rich huke,[34] that spake with the Jew; whereupon he turned to me, and said, "You will pardon me, for I am commanded away in haste." The next morning he came to me again, joyful as it seemed, and said, "There is word come to the Governor of the city, that one of the fathers of Salomon's House will be here this day seven-night; we have seen none of them this dozen years. His coming is in state; but the cause of his coming is secret. I will provide you and your fellows of a good standing to see his entry." I thanked him, and told him I was most glad of the news.

The day being come he made his entry. He was a man of middle stature and age, comely of person, and had an aspect as if he pitied men. He was clothed in

[32]Adulteries. [33]Penalize.

[34]A cape with a hood.

a robe of fine black cloth, with wide sleeves, and a cape: his under garment was of excellent white linen down to the foot, girt with a girdle of the same; and a sindon or tippet of the same about his neck. He had gloves that were curious,[35] and set with stone; and shoes of peach-coloured velvet. His neck was bare to the shoulders. His hat was like a helmet, or Spanish montero;[36] and his locks curled below it decently: they were of colour brown. His beard was cut round and of the same colour with his hair, somewhat lighter. He was carried in a rich chariot, without wheels, litterwise, with two horses at either end, richly trapped in blue velvet embroidered; and two footmen on each side in the like attire. The chariot was all of cedar, gilt, and adorned with crystal; save that the fore-end had panels of sapphire, set in borders of gold, and the hinder-end the like of emeralds of the Peru colour. There was also a sun of gold, radiant upon the top, in the midst; and on the top before, a small cherub of gold, with wings displayed. The chariot was covered with cloth of gold tissued upon blue. He had before him fifty attendants, young men all, in white satin loose coats to the midleg; and stockings of white silk, and shoes of blue velvet; and hats of blue velvet, with fine plumes of divers colours, set round like hat-bands. Next before the chariot went two men, bare-headed, in linen garments down to the foot, girt, and shoes of blue velvet, who carried the one a crosier, the other a pastoral staff like a sheep-hook: neither of them of metal, but the crosier of balm-wood, the pastoral staff of cedar. Horsemen he had none, neither before nor behind his chariot: as it seemeth, to avoid all tumult and trouble. Behind his chariot went all the officers and principals of the companies of the city. He sat alone, upon cushions, of a kind of excellent plush, blue; and under his foot curious carpets of silk of divers colours, like the Persian, but far finer. He held up his bare hand, as he went, as blessing the people, but in silence. The street was wonderfully well kept; so that there was never any army had their men stand in better battle-array than the people stood. The windows likewise were not crowded, but every one stood in them, as if they had been placed.

When the show was passed, the Jew said to me, "I shall not be able to attend you as I would, in regard of some charge the city hath laid upon me for the entertaining of this great person." Three days after the Jew came to me again, and said, "Ye are happy men; for the father of Salomon's House taketh knowledge of your being here, and commanded me to tell you, that he will admit all your company to his presence, and have private conference with one of you, that ye shall choose; and for this hath appointed the next day after to-morrow. And because he meaneth to give you his blessing, he hath appointed it in the forenoon."

We came at our day and hour, and I was chosen by my fellows for the private access. We found him in a fair chamber, richly hanged, and carpeted under foot, without any degrees to the state.[37] He was set upon a low throne richly adorned, and a rich cloth of state over his head, of blue satin embroidered. He was alone, save that he had two pages of honour, on either hand one, finely attired in white. His under garments were the like that we saw him wear in the chariot; but instead of his gown, he had on him a mantle with a cape, of the same fine black, fastened about him. When we came in, as we were taught, we bowed low at our first entrance; and when we were come near his chair, he stood up, holding forth his hand ungloved, and in posture of blessing; and we every one of us stooped down, and kissed the hem of his tippet. That done, the rest departed, and I remained. Then he warned

[35] Carefully made.
[36] A hat with ear flaps.
[37] Without any steps leading up to the throne.

the pages forth of the room, and caused me to sit down beside him, and spake to me thus in the Spanish tongue:

"God bless thee, my son; I will give thee the greatest jewel I have. For I will impart unto thee, for the love of God and men, a relation of the true state of Salomon's House. Son, to make you know the true state of Salomon's House, I will keep this order. First, I will set forth unto you the end of our foundation. Secondly, the preparations and instruments we have for our works. Thirdly, the several employments and functions whereto our fellows are assigned. And fourthly, the ordinances and rites which we observe.

"The end of our foundation is the knowledge of causes, and secret motions of things; and the enlarging of the bounds of human empire, to the effecting of all things possible.

"The preparations and instruments are these. We have large and deep caves of several depths: the deepest are sunk six hundred fathoms; and some of them are digged and made under great hills and mountains; so that if you reckon together the depth of the hill, and the depth of the cave, they are, some of them, above three miles deep. For we find that the depth of a hill, and the depth of a cave from the flat, is the same thing; both remote alike from the sun and heaven's beams, and from the open air. These caves we call the lower region, and we use them for all coagulations, indurations, refrigerations, and conservations of bodies. We use them likewise for the imitation of natural mines, and the producing also of new artificial metals, by compositions and materials which we use, and lay there for many years. We use them also sometimes (which may seem strange) for curing of some diseases, and for prolongation of life, in some hermits that choose to live there, well accommodated of all things necessary, and indeed live very long; by whom also we learn many things.

"We have burials in several earths, where we put divers cements, as the Chinese do their porcelain. But we have them in greater variety, and some of them more fine. We also have great variety of composts and soils, for the making of the earth fruitful.

"We have high towers, the highest about half a mile in height, and some of them likewise set upon high mountains, so that the vantage of the hill, with the tower, is in the highest of them three miles at least. And these places we call the upper region, accounting the air between the high places and the low as a middle region. We use these towers, according to their several heights and situations, for insulation, refrigeration, conservation, and for the view of divers meteors[38]—as winds, rain, snow, hail; and some of the fiery meteors also. And upon them, in some places, are dwellings of hermits, whom we visit sometimes, and instruct what to observe.

"We have great lakes, both salt and fresh, whereof we have use for the fish and fowl. We use them also for burials of some natural bodies, for we find a difference in things buried in earth, or in air below the earth, and things buried in water. We have also pools, of which some do strain fresh water out of salt, and others by art do turn fresh water into salt. We have also some rocks in the midst of the sea, and some bays upon the shore for some works, wherein is required the air and vapour of the sea. We have likewise violent streams and cataracts, which serve us for many motions; and likewise engines for multiplying and enforcing[39] of winds to set also on divers motions.

[38]In the Renaissance, a meteor was anything that fell from the sky.

[39]Reinforcing.

"We have also a number of artificial wells and fountains, made in imitation of the natural sources and baths, as tincted upon vitriol, sulphur, steel, brass, lead, nitre, and other minerals; and again, we have little wells for infusions of many things, where the waters take the virtue quicker and better than in vessels or basins. And amongst them we have a water, which we call Water of Paradise, being by that we do to it made very sovereign for health and prolongation of life.

"We have also great and spacious houses, where we imitate and demonstrate meteors—as snow, hail, rain, some artificial rains of bodies, and not of water, thunders, lightnings; also generations of bodies in air—as frogs, flies, and divers others.

"We have also certain chambers, which we call chambers of health, where we qualify the air as we think good and proper for the cure of divers diseases, and preservation of health.

"We have also fair and large baths, of several mixtures, for the cure of diseases, and the restoring of man's body from arefaction;[40] and others for the confirming of it in strength of sinews, vital parts, and the very juice and substance of the body.

"We have also large and various orchards and gardens, wherein we do not so much respect beauty as variety of ground and soil, proper for divers trees and herbs, and some very spacious, where trees and berries are set, whereof we make divers kinds of drinks, besides the vineyards. In these we practise likewise all conclusions of grafting and inoculating, as well of wild-trees as fruit-trees, which produceth many effects. And we make by art, in the same orchards and gardens, trees and flowers, to come earlier or later than their seasons, and to come up and bear more speedily than by their natural course they do. We make them also by art greater much than their nature; and their fruit greater and sweeter, and of differing taste, smell, colour, and figure, from their nature. And many of them we so order as they become of medicinal use.

"We have also means to make divers plants rise by mixtures of earths without seeds, and likewise to make divers new plants, differing from the vulgar, and to make one tree or plant turn into another.

"We have also parks, and enclosures of all sorts, of beasts and birds; which we use not only for view or rareness, but likewise for dissections and trials, that thereby we may take light what may be wrought upon the body of man. Wherein we find many strange effects: as continuing life in them, though divers parts, which you account vital, be perished and taken forth; resuscitating of some that seem dead in appearance, and the like. We try also all poisons, and other medicines upon them, as well of chirurgery[41] as physic. By art likewise we make them greater or taller than their kind is, and contrariwise dwarf them and stay their growth; we make them more fruitful and bearing than their kind is, and contrariwise barren and not generative. Also we make them differ in colour, shape, activity, many ways. We find means to make commixtures and copulations of divers kinds, which have produced many new kinds, and them not barren, as the general opinion is. We make a number of kinds, of serpents, worms, flies, fishes, of putrefaction, whereof some are advanced (in effect) to be perfect creatures, like beasts or birds, and have sexes, and do propagate. Neither do we this by chance, but we know beforehand of what matter and commixture, what kind of those creatures will arise.

"We have also particular pools where we make trials upon fishes, as we have said before of beasts and birds.

---

[40] Drying up.

[41] Surgery.

"We have also places for breed and generation of those kinds of worms and flies which are of special use; such as are with you your silkworms and bees.

"I will not hold you long with recounting of our brew-houses, bake-houses, and kitchens, where are made divers drinks, breads, and meats, rare and of special effects. Wines we have of grapes, and drinks of other juice, of fruits, of grains, and of roots, and of mixtures with honey, sugar, manna, and fruits dried and decocted;[42] also of the tears or woundings of trees, and of the pulp of canes. And these drinks are of several ages, some to the age or last[43] of forty years. We have drinks also brewed with several herbs, and roots and spices; yea, with several fleshes and white-meats; whereof some of the drinks are such as they are in effect meat and drink both, so that divers, especially in age, do desire to live with them with little or no meat or bread. And above all we strive to have drinks of extreme thin parts, to insinuate into the body, and yet without all biting, sharpness, or fretting; insomuch as some of them, put upon the back of your hand, will with a little stay pass through to the palm, and taste yet mild to the mouth. We have also waters, which we ripen in that fashion, as they become nourishing, so that they are indeed excellent drinks, and many will use no other. Bread we have of several grains, roots, and kernels; yea, and some of flesh, and fish, dried; with divers kinds of leavenings and seasonings; so that some do extremely move appetites, some do nourish so, as divers do live of them, without any other meat, who live very long. So for meats, we have some of them so beaten, and made tender, and mortified,[44] yet without all corrupting, as a weak heat of the stomach will turn them into good chilus,[45] as well as a strong heat would meat otherwise prepared. We have some meats also, and breads, and drinks, which taken by men, enable them to fast long after; and some other, that used make the very flesh of men's bodies sensibly more hard and tough, and their strength far greater than otherwise it would be.

"We have dispensatories or shops of medicines; wherein you may easily think, if we have such variety of plants, and living creatures, more than you have in Europe (for we know what you have), the simples,[46] drugs and ingredients of medicines, must likewise be in so much the greater variety. We have them likewise of divers ages, and long fermentations. And for their preparations, we have not only all manner of exquisite distillations and separations, and especially by gentle heats, and percolations through divers strainers, yea, and substances; but also exact forms of composition, whereby they incorporate almost as they were natural simples.

"We have also divers mechanical arts, which you have not; and stuffs made by them, as papers, linen, silks, tissues, dainty works of feathers of wonderful lustre, excellent dyes, and many others: and shops likewise, as well for such as are not brought into vulgar use amongst us, as for those that are. For you must know, that of the things before recited, many of them are grown into use throughout the kingdom, but yet, if they did flow from our invention, we have of them also for patterns and principles.

"We have also furnaces of great diversities, and that keep great diversity of heats: fierce and quick, strong and constant, soft and mild; blown, quiet, dry, moist, and the like. But above all we have heats, in imitation of the sun's and heavenly bodies' heats, that pass divers inequalities, and (as it were) orbs, progresses, and returns, whereby we produce admirable effects. Besides, we have heats of dungs, and of

[42]Dissolved in water.

[43]Duration. [44]Softened.

[45]Food softened by heat into a digestible form.

[46]Herbs.

bellies and maws of living creatures and of their bloods and bodies, and of hays and herbs laid up moist, of lime unquenched, and such like. Instruments also which generate heat only by motion. And farther, places for strong insulations; and again, places under the earth, which by nature or art yield heat. These divers heats we use as the nature of the operation which we intend requireth.

"We have also perspective houses, where we make demonstrations of all lights and radiations, and of all colours; and out of things uncoloured and transparent, we can represent unto you all several colours, not in rainbows (as it is in gems and prisms), but of themselves single. We represent also all multiplications of light, which we carry to great distance, and make so sharp, as to discern small points and lines. Also all colourations of light; all delusions and deceits of the sight, in figures, magnitudes, motions, colours; all demonstrations of shadows. We find also divers means yet unknown to you, of producing of light, originally from divers bodies. We procure means of seeing objects afar off, as in the heaven and remote places; and represent things near as afar off, and things afar off as near; making feigned distances. We have also helps for the sight, far above spectacles and glasses in use. We have also glasses and means to see small and minute bodies, perfectly and distinctly; as the shapes and colours of small flies and worms, grains, and flaws in gems which cannot otherwise be seen, observations in urine and blood not otherwise to be seen. We make artificial rainbows, halos, and circles about light. We represent also all manner of reflections, refractions, and multiplications of visual beams of objects.

"We have also precious stones of all kinds, many of them of great beauty and to you unknown; crystals likewise, and glasses of divers kinds; and amongst them some of metals vitrificated, and other materials, besides those of which you make glass. Also a number of fossils and imperfect minerals, which you have not. Likewise loadstones of prodigious virtue: and other rare stones, both natural and artificial.

"We have also sound-houses, where we practise and demonstrate all sounds and their generation. We have harmonies which you have not, of quarter-sounds and lesser slides of sounds. Divers instruments of music likewise to you unknown, some sweeter than any you have; together with bells and rings that are dainty and sweet. We represent small sounds as great and deep; likewise great sounds, extenuate and sharp; we make divers tremblings and warblings of sounds, which in their original are entire. We represent and imitate all articulate sounds and letters, and the voices and notes of beasts and birds. We have certain helps, which set to the ear do further the hearing greatly. We have also divers strange and artificial echoes, reflecting the voice many times, and as it were tossing it; and some that give back the voice louder than it came, some shriller and some deeper; yea, some rendering the voice, differing in the letters or articulate sound from that they receive. We have also means to convey sounds in trunks and pipes, in strange lines and distances.

"We have also perfume-houses, wherewith we join also practices of taste. We multiply smells, which may seem strange: we imitate smells, making all smells to breathe out of other mixtures than those that give them. We make divers imitations of taste likewise, so that they will deceive any man's taste. And in this house we contain also a confiture-house, where we make all sweetmeats, dry and moist, and divers pleasant wines, milks, broths, and salads, far in greater variety than you have.

"We have also engine-houses, where are prepared engines and instruments for all sorts of motions. There we imitate and practise to make swifter motions than any you have, either out of your muskets or any engine that you have; and to make them and multiply them more easily and with small force, by wheels and other means, and to make them stronger and more violent than yours are, exceeding your greatest cannons and basilisks.[47] We represent also ordnance and instruments of war and engines of all kinds; and likewise new mixtures and compositions of gunpowder, wild-fires burning in water and unquenchable, also fire-works of all variety, both for pleasure and use. We imitate also flights of birds; we have some degrees of flying in the air. We have ships and boats for going under water and brooking of seas, also swimming-girdles and supporters. We have divers curious clocks, and other like motions of return, and some perpetual motions. We imitate also motions of living creatures by images of men, beasts, birds, fishes, and serpents; we have also a great number of other various motions, strange for equality, fineness, and subtilty.

"We have also a mathematical-house, where are represented all instruments, as well of geometry as astronomy, exquisitely made.

"We have also houses of deceits of the senses, where we represent all manner of feats of juggling, false apparitions, impostures, and illusions, and their fallacies. And surely you will easily believe that we, that have so many things truly natural which induce admiration, could in a world of particulars deceive the senses if we would disguise those things, and labour to make them seem more miraculous. But we do hate all impostures and lies, insomuch as we have severely forbidden it to all our fellows, under pain of ignominy and fines, that they do not show any natural work or thing adorned or swelling, but only pure as it is, and without all affectation of strangeness.

"These are, my son, the riches of Salomon's House.

"For the several employments and offices of our fellows, we have twelve that sail into foreign countries under the names of other nations (for our own we conceal), who bring us the books and abstracts, and patterns of experiments of all other parts. These we call Merchants of Light.

"We have three that collect the experiments which are in all books. These we call Depredators.

"We have three that collect the experiments of all mechanical arts, and also of liberal sciences, and also of practises which are not brought into arts. These we call Mystery-men.

"We have three that try new experiments, such as themselves think good. These we call Pioneers or Miners.

"We have three that draw the experiments of the former four into titles and tables, to give the better light for the drawing of observations and axioms out of them. These we call Compilers.

"We have three that bend themselves, looking into the experiments of their fellows, and cast about how to draw out of them things of use and practice for man's life and knowledge, as well for works as for plain demonstration of causes, means of natural divinations, and the easy and clear discovery of the virtues and parts of bodies. These we call Dowry-men or Benefactors.

"Then after divers meetings and consults of our whole number, to consider of the former labours and collections, we have three that take care out of them to direct new experiments, of a higher light, more penetrating into Nature than the former. These we call Lamps.

"We have three others that do execute the experiments so directed, and report them. These we call Inoculators.

"Lastly, we have three that raise the former discoveries by experiments into greater observations, axioms, and aphorisms. These we call Interpreters of Nature.

[47]Large cannons.

"We have also, as you must think, novices and apprentices, that the succession of the former employed men do not fail; besides a great number of servants and attendants, men and women. And this we do also: we have consultations, which of the inventions and experiences which we have discovered shall be published, and which not: and take all an oath of secrecy for the concealing of those which we think fit to keep secret: though some of those we do reveal sometimes to the State, and some not.

"For our ordinances and rites, we have two very long and fair galleries: in one of these we place patterns and samples of all manner of the more rare and excellent inventions: in the other we place the statues of all principal inventors. There we have the statue of your Columbus, that discovered the West Indies: also the inventor of ships: your Monk that was the inventor of ordnance and of gunpowder: the inventor of music: the inventor of letters: the inventor of printing: the inventor of observations of astronomy: the inventor of works in metal: the inventor of glass: the inventor of silk of the worm: the inventor of wine: the inventor of corn and bread: the inventor of sugars: and all these by more certain tradition than you have. Then we have divers inventors of our own, of excellent works, which since you have not seen, it were too long to make descriptions of them; and besides, in the right understanding of those descriptions you might easily err. For upon every invention of value we erect a statue to the inventor, and give him a liberal and honourable reward. These statues are some of brass, some of marble and touchstone, some of cedar and other special woods gilt and adorned; some of iron, some of silver, some of gold.

"We have certain hymns and services, which we say daily, of laud and thanks to God for His marvellous works. And forms of prayer, imploring His aid and blessing for the illumination of our labours, and the turning of them into good and holy uses.

"Lastly, we have circuits or visits, of divers principal cities of the kingdom; where, as it cometh to pass, we do publish such new profitable inventions as we think good. And we do also declare natural divinations of diseases, plagues, swarms of hurtful creatures, scarcity, tempests, earthquakes, great inundations, comets, temperature of the year, and divers other things; and we give counsel thereupon, what the people shall do for the prevention and remedy of them."

And when he had said this he stood up; and I, as I had been taught, knelt down; and he laid his right hand upon my head, and said, "God bless thee, my son, and God bless this relation which I have made. I give thee leave to publish it, for the good of other nations; for we here are in God's bosom, a land unknown." And so he left me; having assigned a value of about two thousand ducats for a bounty to me and my fellows. For they give great largesses, where they come, upon all occasions.

The rest was not perfected

WILLIAM SHAKESPEARE

[1564–1616]

In the 1623 Folio, the first collected edition of William Shakespeare's works, fellow poet and critic Ben Jonson paid tribute to his great contemporary:

> Triumph, my *Britaine,* thou hast one to showe,
> To whom all scenes of *Europe* homage owe.
> He was not of an age, but for all time!

Jonson's lines do not exaggerate, for from the sixteenth century to the present Shakespeare's tragedies, comedies, histories, and romances throughout the world have been performed on stage, adapted for film, and studied for their dramatic techniques, the complexity of their characters, their history, and their philosophy. From the noble magnanimity of King Lear and the mean vindictiveness of Iago, through the hopeless innocence of Juliet and the sprightly savvy of Beatrice, to the deep vexation of Hamlet, Shakespeare's plays evoke a full range of human passions and experiences. The plays allow us to see the Renaissance mind in all its complexity, as characters vie for love and power in an atmosphere shot through with a tragic sense that forces beyond human reckoning may at any moment thwart the best contrived human efforts. Against the forces of "Devouring Time," as Shakespeare calls it in Sonnet 19, each of us must seize those moments of fulfillment, hope, love, and self-esteem before they vanish; yet in his work Shakespeare, the poet, held one stop against mutability, and his concluding couplet has proved to be self-prophetic: "Yet do thy worst, old Time: despite thy wrong, / My love shall in my verse ever live young."

LIFE

About William Shakespeare's early life little is known, but much has been invented. He was born in Stratford-on-Avon, a market town in Warwickshire, just northwest of London, in April 1564. William's father, John Shakespeare, was a glove maker and leather worker who through his trade and a fortunate marriage to Mary Arden, heiress of a small estate, rose to become a member of the city council and Bailiff at Stratford. As the son in a respectable family, young William most likely received the standard education in Latin grammar, reading, and writing at the Stratford grammar school. Biographers have speculated that Shakespeare must have enjoyed the bustling life of Stratford, with its renowned local fairs, visiting theater companies, and ample countryside in which a young imaginative boy could exercise his fancy. All we know for certain is that on November 27, 1582, the Bishop of Worcester issued a marriage license to William Shakespeare and Anne Hathaway; the parish records show shortly thereafter the birth of a daughter in 1583 and a set of twins, a son and daughter, in 1585. Sometime between 1582 and 1592, Shakespeare began to take an active part in the theater in London, for which Robert Greene in a letter called the young actor and writer "an upstart Crow," a player so bold as to think he could write plays.

When London theaters reopened in 1594 after being closed for two years by an outbreak of the plague, Shakespeare was performing with one of the most prominent acting companies, the Lord Chamberlain's Men, along with the great actors Richard Burbage and William Kemp. During the lull in dramatic activity, Shakespeare had written his two important nondramatic poems, *Venus and Adonis* (1593) and *The Rape of Lucrece* (1594), both dedicated to the Earl of Southampton and showing his debt to, and command of, the classical education he had received as a youth. Proceeds from his theatrical endeavors, Southampton's patronage, and various business transactions were proving remarkably profitable for the young actor and writer, and in 1597 Shakespeare purchased New Place, one of the finest houses in Stratford. Two years later Shakespeare joined Richard Burbage and others to found the Globe Theatre, one of the most important playhouses in London, which was built to the specifications of the actor–proprietors, members of the Chamberlain's Men. After Queen Elizabeth's death in 1603, this troupe, now called the King's Men and fast becoming the preeminent company at Court and in the city, received the sponsorship of James I, who made them Grooms of the Chamber.

By this time, Shakespeare was already celebrated as a writer. In 1598, Francis Mere compared Shakespeare favorably to Plautus and Seneca, noting in his *Palladis Tamia: Wit's Treasury* that whereas these writers are known for comedy and tragedy, respectively, "Shakespeare among the English is the most excellent in both kinds for the stage."

Among the plays written up to this time are many of the histories, including Parts One through Three of *Henry the Sixth, Richard III, King John,* and Parts One and Two of *Henry IV; The Comedy of Errors, A Midsummer Night's Dream,* and *The Taming of the Shrew* among other comedies; and *Titus Andronicus* and *Romeo and Juliet* among the tragedies. Between 1598 and 1609, a period of incredible artistic productivity for the poet–dramatist, Shakespeare completed more than fifteen major plays, including *Hamlet, Othello,* and *King Lear,* among the tragedies; *As You Like It* and *All's Well That Ends Well,* among the comedies; and *Pericles,* a romance. The King's Men now had established a veritable stronghold over London theater, having acquired in 1608 Blackfriar's Theatre. Unlike the Globe, Blackfriar's was an enclosed playhouse, which enabled the players to hold winter performances. Around 1610, Shakespeare retired from London to his home at Stratford, where he wrote his final plays—*Cymbeline, The Winter's Tale, The Tempest,* and *Henry VIII*—and where he died April 23, 1616.

WORK

The vast range of Shakespeare's dramatic production, the diversity of characters, and the variations of dramatic form among the plays do not admit of much generalization. As Ben Jonson's tribute points out, Shakespeare was at home writing both tragedies and comedies, but he was equally adept at writing history plays and what some call romances; most important, however, many of his greatest dramas blur the boundaries among these genres. Like many other Elizabethan dramatists, Shakespeare often disregarded the classical "unities," derived from Aristotle's *Poetics,* refusing to limit the action to a single day and to a single place. English theater during this period did not look to Sophocles, Aristophanes, Terence, or Plautus for its models.

What distinguishes Shakespeare's plays are their intricacy of plot, their brilliant display of language, and their presentation of complex characters that, despite their historical particularity, have fascinated and served the interests of readers throughout the world for almost four hundred years. Prince Hal from *Henry IV,* Hamlet, and Rosalind from *As You Like It* come to us as visitations from a political and social reality constructed entirely differently from ours; yet with their differences as well as their similarities they exert a lively, almost palpable presence even to contemporary readers and spectators. Through his art, Shakespeare transformed stock dramatic types, such as the *miles gloriosus*—the boastful soldier—into the likable character of Falstaff in *Henry IV.*

It is important to keep in mind that the Elizabethan England in which Shakespeare wrote his plays operated on a model of hierarchical stratification—the great chain of being—that was thought to stretch from the lowliest form of inert matter up to God, the purest form of active spirit. Ulysses' often-quoted speech on degree from *Troilus and Cressida* describes the systematic correspondence between heaven and earth, cautioning that any transgression of the vested degrees sends a fault along the entire system: "Take but degree away, untune that string, / And hark what discord follows" (I.iii.109-10). At the center of the universal ladder stood humanity, fraught with the physical limitations of the animal kingdom, yet endowed with the spiritual and intellectual essence of the higher forms of life. In *The Tempest,* Caliban and Ariel symbolize the two sides of this imperfect match in human nature, and Prospero's manipulation of them suggests the balance that humanity can achieve between its physical and spiritual elements. In some plays, such as *Hamlet,* Shakespeare thematizes the consequences of a world untuned and the vexation that such duality can impose upon human beings. Thus, Hamlet complains to Ophelia, "what should such fellows as I do, crawling between earth and heaven?" (III.ii.127–28).

The Globe Theatre itself, for which Shakespeare's plays were written, was a slice of the Elizabethan's stratified society. Built in the shape of a polyhedron around an open courtyard, the theater had galleries on its sides, with the stage extending from one side out into the center of the courtyard. Wealthier spectators occupied the three floors of galleries, and those with less money, the groundlings, stood in the courtyard, or pit, and looked across to the stage that stood five feet above the ground. The stage itself embodied the structure of the religious cosmos. The area under the stage was called Hell (from which ghosts and devils emerged by means of a trap door); the area above the stage, a covered ceiling space from which gods and angels descended, was called the Heavens. At the back of the stage was another enclosed area that could be used in the productions, and behind that the "tiring house," where actors waited for their cues. Just above the back of the stage was a gallery for musicians, when called for in the play, or on which to stage balcony scenes. In the cosmic scheme of its design, the stage obviously represented the world, a point that Shakespeare toys with repeatedly in his drama, perhaps most familiarly in *As You Like It,* where Jacques declares "All the world's a stage, / And all the men and women merely players . . ." (II.vii.139–40). In *The Tempest,* Shakespeare again depends on the audience's awareness that the Globe Theatre could symbolize the world in miniature, when Prospero points to the transience of life and the products of human labor:

> . . . the great globe itself,
> Yea, all which it inherit, shall dissolve,
> And, like this insubstantial pageant faded,
> Leave not a rack behind. (IV.i.153–56)

Thus, the Globe was a microcosm of the ordered universe, reproducing in its design and in its organization of spectators the cosmic and social divisions along a structured gradient of high and low. The mixing of high and low at the Globe and other theaters had important consequences for Elizabethan playwrights, who took care to address all levels of the mixed audience in their plays. As we'll see in *The Tempest,* dramatists offered a blend of subtle and crude humor, refined and coarse language, serious and comic plots and subplots, to engage the variety of spectators.

The final play by Shakespeare's own hand, *The Tempest,* was first performed at Court in 1611. *The Tempest* seems deliberately to elude categorization and has been called a romance, a romantic comedy, a tragicomedy, and a romantic tragicomedy. Its transgressive spirit and deliberate mixing of forms—tragedy, comedy, masque, satire—suggest that *The Tempest* self-consciously addresses the playwright's art and celebrates the artist's power to transcend the social and aesthetic codes and conventions of the time, even as it questions the moral consequences of breaking such boundaries. The play more generally questions the relationship between nature and art, especially as that relationship is negotiated by the playwright, here compared to a magician. Indeed, Prospero becomes a composite figure of the forms of power, assembling in his various guises the prince, the playwright, the magician, and the father, thus blurring the distinctions and highlighting the resemblances among those roles. The comic subplot involving Stephano and Trinculo parodies, as it mirrors, the important questions about the responsibilities of princes, the governance of state, the building of empires, and the treatment (and nature) of the prince's subjects. Although Prospero shapes the events that take place on his island and even exerts dominion over nature, as when he conjures up the storm that sets the plot in motion, unlike Faustus he recognizes and accepts the limitations of his legitimate power. Thus, like Marlowe's *Doctor Faustus, The Tempest* raises questions about knowledge and power—for the artist as well as for the prince.

Although many of Shakespeare's plays are based on earlier plays or popular stories, *The Tempest* may have its origins in the story of the wreck of a ship, the *Sea Adventurer,* off the coast of Bermuda in 1609. En route to Virginia from Plymouth, the *Sea Adventurer's* passengers included the new Governor of Virginia, Sir Thomas Gates. After being stranded for nine months, the entire group of 150 crew and passengers managed to sail back to Jamestown on two smaller boats that they had built. Accounts of these adventures began to appear in 1610, leading to speculation that Shakespeare either had read the accounts or may have been acquainted with one of the authors. What is important, however, is that Shakespeare constructs out of such an adventure a play that engages key questions about the nature of power, politics, art, and humanity.

Taking place on an island that symbolizes the New World, seen through European eyes as a blank space upon which to build new forms of society, the play places these questions of power directly into the context of European colonization. Caliban, who stands in the place of the disinherited native, becomes subject to Prospero's attempts first to civilize him, then to control him. Drawing upon John Florio's translation of Montaigne's "Of Cannibals," the play speculates on the nature of human beings in the New World. Whereas Montaigne's essay suggests that the Brazilian natives display a considerable amount of complexity and rational organization in their customs, this play places Caliban on the chain of being in a position below the power of reason. As a consequence, *The Tempest* has become an important play for the study of European responses to the New World during the Renaissance, and it has been reworked in our time, most notably by Aimé Césaire and George Lamming, from Caliban's point of view.

Suggested Readings

E. K. Chambers's *William Shakespeare: A Study of Facts and Problems* (1930) remains the standard biography. Frank Kermode's edition of *The Tempest* (1954) contains a thorough and helpful introduction to the play and its historical setting; Stephen Orgel's edition of the play (1984) offers a new perspective that students may usefully compare to Kermode's. Works that treat the politics of power in *The Tempest,* Prospero's role as magician, and the colonial aspects of the play include Alvin B. Kernan's *The Playwright as Magician: Shakespeare's Image of the Poet in the English Public Theater* (1979) and Richard Hillman's *Shakespearean Subversions: The Trickster and the Play-Text* (1992). For postcolonial readings of *The Tempest,* see George Lamming's *The Pleasures of Exile* (1987); Aimé Césaire rewrote the play as *Une tempête: d'après La Tempête de Shakespeare* (1969). Leslie Fiedler's *The Stranger in Shakespeare* (1972) studies the way America functions as myth in the play.

The Tempest

The Scene: An uninhabited island.

NAMES OF THE ACTORS

ALONSO, *King of Naples*
SEBASTIAN, *his brother*
PROSPERO, *the right Duke of Milan*
ANTONIO, *his brother, the usurping Duke of Milan*
FERDINAND, *son to the King of Naples*
GONZALO, *an honest old councilor*
ADRIAN *and* FRANCISCO, *lords*
CALIBAN, *a savage and deformed slave*
TRINCULO, *a jester*
STEPHANO, *a drunken butler*
MASTER OF A SHIP
BOATSWAIN
MARINERS
MIRANDA, *daughter to Prospero*
ARIEL, *an airy spirit*
IRIS, CERES, JUNO, NYMPHS, REAPERS — *[presented by] spirits*
[OTHER SPIRITS ATTENDING ON PROSPERO]

ACT I

Scene 1

On a ship at sea.

A tempestuous noise of thunder and lightning heard. Enter a SHIPMASTER *and a* BOATSWAIN.

MASTER: Boatswain!

BOATSWAIN: Here, master. What cheer?

MASTER: Good,[1] speak to th' mariners! Fall to't yarely,[2] or we run ourselves aground. Bestir, bestir! *Exit.*

Enter MARINERS.

BOATSWAIN: Heigh, my hearts! Cheerly, cheerly, my hearts! Yare, yare! Take in the topsail! Tend to th' master's whistle! Blow till thou burst thy wind, if room enough![3]

Enter ALONSO, SEBASTIAN, ANTONIO, FERDINAND, GONZALO, *and others.*

ALONSO: Good boatswain, have care. Where's the master? Play the men.[4] 10

BOATSWAIN: I pray now, keep below.

ANTONIO: Where is the master, bos'n?

BOATSWAIN: Do you not hear him? You mar our labor. Keep your cabins; you do assist the storm.

GONZALO: Nay, good, be patient.

BOATSWAIN: When the sea is. Hence! What cares these roarers for the name of king? To cabin! Silence! Trouble us not!

GONZALO: Good, yet remember whom thou hast aboard. 20

BOATSWAIN: None that I more love than myself. You are a councilor; if you can command these elements to silence and work the peace of the present,[5] we will not hand[6] a rope more. Use your authority. If you cannot, give thanks you have lived so long, and make yourself ready in your cabin for the mischance of the hour, if it so hap. Cheerly, good hearts! Out of our way, I say. *Exit.*

GONZALO: I have great comfort from this fellow. Methinks he hath no drowning mark upon him; his complexion is perfect gallows.[7] Stand fast, good Fate, to his hanging! Make the rope of his destiny our cable, for our own doth little advantage.[8] If he be not born to be hanged, our case is miserable. 30

Exit [with the rest].

Enter BOATSWAIN.

BOATSWAIN: Down with the topmast! Yare! Lower, lower! Bring her to try with main course![9] [*A cry within.*] A plague upon this howling! They are louder than the weather or our office.

Enter SEBASTIAN, ANTONIO, *and* GONZALO.

---

[1] Good fellow. [All notes in this selection are from editor Robert Langbaum.]

[2] Briskly.

[3] The storm can blow and split itself as long as there is open sea without rocks to maneuver in.

[4] Act like men.

[5] Restore the present to peace (since as a councilor his job is to quell disorder).

[6] Handle.

[7] Alluding to the proverb, "He that's born to be hanged need fear no drowning."

[8] Gives us little advantage.

[9] Heave to, under the mainsail.

Yet again? What do you here? Shall we give o'er[10] and drown? Have you a mind to sink? 40

SEBASTIAN: A pox o' your throat, you bawling, blasphemous, incharitable dog!

BOATSWAIN: Work you, then.

ANTONIO: Hang, cur! Hang, you whoreson, insolent noisemaker! We are less afraid to be drowned than thou art.

GONZALO: I'll warrant him for[11] drowning, though the ship were no stronger than a nutshell and as leaky as an unstanched[12] wench.

BOATSWAIN: Lay her ahold, ahold! Set her two courses![13] Off to sea again! Lay her off![14] 50

Enter MARINERS *wet.*

MARINERS:
All lost! To prayers, to prayers! All lost! [*Exeunt.*]

BOATSWAIN:
What, must our mouths be cold?

GONZALO:
The King and Prince at prayers! Let's assist them,
For our case is as theirs.

SEBASTIAN:
I am out of patience.

ANTONIO:
We are merely[15] cheated of our lives by drunkards.
This wide-chopped[16] rascal—would thou mightst lie drowning
The washing of ten tides![17]

GONZALO:
He'll be hanged yet,
Though every drop of water swear against it
And gape at wid'st to glut him.

A confused noise within: "Mercy on us!" 60
"We split, we split!" "Farewell, my wife and children!"
"Farewell, brother!" "We split, we split, we split!"
[*Exit* BOATSWAIN.]

ANTONIO:
Let's all sink wi' th' King.

SEBASTIAN:
Let's take leave of him.
Exit [*with* ANTONIO.]

GONZALO: Now would I give a thousand furlongs of sea for an acre of barren ground—long heath,[18] brown furze, anything. The wills above be done, but I would fain die a dry death. *Exit.*

---

[10] Give up trying to run the ship.

[11] Guarantee him against.

[12] Wide-open.

[13] The ship is still being blown dangerously to shore, so the boatswain orders that the foresail be set in addition to the mainsail; but the ship still moves toward shore.

[14] Away from the shore.

[15] Completely. [16] Big-mouthed.

[17] Pirates were hanged on the shore and left there until three tides had washed over them.

[18] Heather.

Scene 2

The island. In front of PROSPERO*'s cell.*

Enter PROSPERO *and* MIRANDA.

MIRANDA:

If by your art, my dearest father, you have
Put the wild waters in this roar, allay them.
The sky, it seems, would pour down stinking pitch
But that the sea, mounting to th' welkin's cheek,[19]
Dashes the fire out. O, I have suffered
With those that I saw suffer! A brave[20] vessel
(Who had no doubt some noble creature in her)
Dashed all to pieces! O, the cry did knock
Against my very heart! Poor souls, they perished!
Had I been any god of power, I would 10
Have sunk the sea within the earth or ere
It should the good ship so have swallowed and
The fraughting[21] souls within her.

PROSPERO:

Be collected.
No more amazement. Tell your piteous heart
There's no harm done.

MIRANDA:

O, woe the day!

PROSPERO:

No harm.
I have done nothing but in care of thee,
Of thee my dear one, thee my daughter, who
Art ignorant of what thou art, naught knowing
Of whence I am, nor that I am more better
Than Prospero, master of a full poor cell, 20
And thy no greater father.[22]

MIRANDA:

More to know
Did never meddle[23] with my thoughts.

PROSPERO:

'Tis time
I should inform thee farther. Lend thy hand
And pluck my magic garment from me. So.
[*Lays down his robe.*]
Lie there, my art. Wipe thou thine eyes; have comfort.
The direful spectacle of the wrack, which touched
The very virtue of compassion in thee,
I have with such provision[24] in mine art
So safely ordered that there is no soul—

---

[19] Face of the sky.
[20] Fine, gallant (the word often has this meaning in the play).
[21] Forming her freight.
[22] Thy father, no greater than the Prospero just described.
[23] Mingle. [24] Foresight.

No, not so much perdition[25] as an hair 30
Betid[26] to any creature in the vessel
Which thou heard'st cry, which thou saw'st sink. Sit down;
For thou must now know farther.

MIRANDA:
You have often
Begun to tell me what I am; but stopped
And left me to a bootless inquisition,
Concluding, "Stay; not yet."

PROSPERO:
The hour's now come;
The very minute bids thee ope thine ear.
Obey, and be attentive. Canst thou remember
A time before we came unto this cell?
I do not think thou canst, for then thou wast not 40
Out[27] three years old.

MIRANDA:
Certainly, sir, I can.

PROSPERO:
By what? By any other house or person?
Of anything the image tell me that
Hath kept with thy remembrance.

MIRANDA:
'Tis far off,
And rather like a dream than an assurance
That my remembrance warrants.[28] Had I not
Four or five women once that tended me?

PROSPERO:
Thou hadst, and more, Miranda. But how is it
That this lives in thy mind? What seest thou else
In the dark backward and abysm of time? 50
If thou remember'st aught ere thou cam'st here,
How thou cam'st here thou mayst.

MIRANDA:
But that I do not.

PROSPERO:
Twelve year since, Miranda, twelve year since,
Thy father was the Duke of Milan and
A prince of power.

MIRANDA:
Sir, are not you my father?

PROSPERO:
Thy mother was a piece[29] of virtue, and
She said thou wast my daughter; and thy father
Was Duke of Milan; and his only heir
And princess, no worse issued.[30]

[25] Loss. [26] Happened. [27] Fully.
[28] Memory guarantees. [29] Masterpiece.
[30] Of no meaner lineage than he.

MIRANDA:

O the heavens!
What foul play had we that we came from thence? 60
Or blessèd was't we did?

PROSPERO:

Both, both, my girl!
By foul play, as thou say'st, were we heaved thence,
But blessedly holp[31] hither.

MIRANDA:

O, my heart bleeds
To think o' th' teen that I have turned you to,[32]
Which is from my remembrance! Please you, farther.

PROSPERO:

My brother and thy uncle, called Antonio—
I pray thee mark me—that a brother should
Be so perfidious!—he whom next thyself
Of all the world I loved, and to him put
The manage of my state,[33] as at that time 70
Through all the signories[34] it was the first,
And Prospero the prime duke, being so reputed
In dignity, and for the liberal arts
Without a parallel. Those being all my study,
The government I cast upon my brother
And to my state grew stranger, being transported
And rapt in secret studies. Thy false uncle—
Dost thou attend me?

MIRANDA:

Sir, most heedfully.

PROSPERO:

Being once perfected[35] how to grant suits,
How to deny them, who t' advance, and who 80
To trash for overtopping,[36] new-created
The creatures that were mine, I say—or changed 'em,
Or else new-formed 'em[37]—having both the key[38]
Of officer and office, set all hearts i' th' state
To what tune pleased his ear, that now he was
The ivy which had hid my princely trunk
And sucked my verdure out on't. Thou attend'st not?

MIRANDA:

O, good sir, I do.

---

[31] Helped.

[32] Sorrow I have caused you to remember.

[33] Management of my domain.

[34] Lordships (of Italy).

[35] Grown skillful.

[36] (1) Check the speed of (as of hounds); (2) cut down to size (as of overtall trees) the aspirants for political favor who are growing too bold.

[37] He recreated my following—either exchanging my adherents for his own, or else transforming my adherents into different people.

[38] A pun leading to the musical metaphor.

PROSPERO:

I pray thee mark me.
I thus neglecting worldly ends, all dedicated
To closeness[39] and the bettering of my mind— 90
With that which, but by being so retired,
O'erprized all popular rate, in my false brother
Awaked an evil nature,[40] and my trust,
Like a good parent,[41] did beget of him
A falsehood in its contrary as great
As my trust was, which had indeed no limit,
A confidence sans bound. He being thus lorded—
Not only with what my revenue yielded
But what my power might else exact, like one
Who having into truth—by telling of it,[42] 100
Made such a sinner of his memory
To credit his own lie, he did believe
He was indeed the Duke, out o' th' substitution
And executing th' outward face of royalty
With all prerogative.[43] Hence his ambition growing—
Dost thou hear?

MIRANDA:

Your tale, sir, would cure deafness.

PROSPERO:

To have no screen between this part he played
And him he played it for, he needs will be
Absolute Milan.[44] Me (poor man) my library
Was dukedom large enough. Of temporal royalties 110
He thinks me now incapable; confederates
(So dry[45] he was for sway) wi' th' King of Naples
To give him annual tribute, do him homage,
Subject his coronet to his crown, and bend
The dukedom, yet unbowed (alas, poor Milan!),
To most ignoble stooping.

MIRANDA:

O the heavens!

PROSPERO:

Mark his condition,[46] and th' event;[47] then tell me
If this might be a brother.

MIRANDA:

I should sin
To think but nobly of my grandmother.
Good wombs have borne bad sons.

---

[39]Seclusion.

[40]With that dedication to the mind which, were it not that it kept me from exercising the duties of my office, would surpass in value all ordinary estimate, I awakened evil in my brother's nature.

[41]Alluding to the proverb cited by Miranda in line 120.

[42]Like one who really had these things—by repeatedly saying he had them (*into* = unto).

[43]As a result of his acting as my substitute and performing the outward functions of royalty with all its prerogatives.

[44]Duke of Milan in fact.

[45]Thirsty.

[46]Terms of his pact with Naples.

[47]Outcome.

PROSPERO:

Now the condition. 120
This King of Naples, being an enemy
To me inveterate, hearkens my brother's suit;
Which was, that he, in lieu o' th' premises[48]
Of homage and I know not how much tribute,
Should presently extirpate me and mine
Out of the dukedom and confer fair Milan,
With all the honors, on my brother. Whereon,
A treacherous army levied, one midnight
Fated to th' purpose, did Antonio open
The gates of Milan; and, i' th' dead of darkness, 130
The ministers[49] for th' purpose hurried thence
Me and thy crying self.

MIRANDA:

Alack, for pity!
I, not rememb'ring how I cried out then,
Will cry it o'er again; it is a hint[50]
That wrings mine eyes to't.

PROSPERO:

Hear a little further,
And then I'll bring thee to the present business
Which now's upon's; without the which this story
Were most impertinent.

MIRANDA:

Wherefore did they not
That hour destroy us?

PROSPERO:

Well demanded, wench.
My tale provokes that question. Dear, they durst not, 140
So dear the love my people bore me; nor set
A mark so bloody on the business; but,
With colors fairer, painted their foul ends.
In few,[51] they hurried us aboard a bark;
Bore us some leagues to sea, where they prepared
A rotten carcass of a butt,[52] not rigged,
Nor tackle, sail, nor mast; the very rats
Instinctively have quit it. There they hoist us,
To cry to th' sea that roared to us; to sigh
To th' winds, whose pity, sighing back again, 150
Did us but loving wrong.

MIRANDA:

Alack, what trouble
Was I then to you!

PROSPERO:

O, a cherubin
Thou wast that did preserve me! Thou didst smile,
Infusèd with a fortitude from heaven,

[48] In return for the guarantees.
[49] Agents. [50] Occasion. [51] Few words. [52] Tub.

When I have decked[53] the sea with drops full salt,
Under my burden groaned; which[54] raised in me
An undergoing stomach,[55] to bear up
Against what should ensue.

MIRANDA:

How came we ashore?

PROSPERO:

By providence divine.
Some food we had, and some fresh water, that 160
A noble Neapolitan, Gonzalo,
Out of his charity, who being then appointed
Master of this design, did give us, with
Rich garments, linens, stuffs, and necessaries
Which since have steaded[56] much. So, of his gentleness,
Knowing I loved my books, he furnished me
From mine own library with volumes that
I prize above my dukedom.

MIRANDA:

Would I might
But ever see that man!

PROSPERO:

Now I arise.
Sit still, and hear the last of our sea sorrow. 170
Here in this island we arrived; and here
Have I, thy schoolmaster, made thee more profit
Than other princess' can,[57] that have more time
For vainer hours, and tutors not so careful.

MIRANDA:

Heavens thank you for't! And now I pray you, sir—
For still 'tis beating in my mind—your reason
For raising this sea storm?

PROSPERO:

Know thus far forth.
By accident most strange, bountiful Fortune
(Now my dear lady)[58] hath mine enemies
Brought to this shore; and by my prescience 180
I find my zenith[59] doth depend upon
A most auspicious star, whose influence
If now I court not, but omit,[60] my fortunes
Will ever after droop. Here cease more questions.
Thou art inclined to sleep. 'Tis a good dullness,
And give it way. I know thou canst not choose.

[MIRANDA *sleeps*.]

---

[53]Covered (wept salt tears into the sea).
[54]Miranda's smile.
[55]Spirit of endurance.
[56]Been of use.
[57]Princesses can have.
[58]Formerly my foe, now my patroness.
[59]Apex of fortune.
[60]Neglect.

Come away, servant, come! I am ready now.
Approach, my Ariel! Come!

Enter ARIEL.

ARIEL:

All hail, great master! Grave sir, hail! I come
To answer thy best pleasure; be't to fly, 190
To swim, to dive into the fire, to ride
On the curled clouds. To thy strong bidding task[61]
Ariel and all his quality.[62]

PROSPERO:

Hast thou, spirit,
Performed, to point,[63] the tempest that I bade thee?

ARIEL:

To every article.
I boarded the King's ship. Now on the beak,[64]
Now in the waist,[65] the deck,[66] in every cabin,
I flamed amazement.[67] Sometimes I'd divide
And burn in many places; on the topmast,
The yards, and boresprit[68] would I flame distinctly,[69] 200
Then meet and join. Jove's lightnings, the precursors
O' th' dreadful thunderclaps, more momentary
And sight-outrunning were not. The fire and cracks
Of sulfurous roaring the most mighty Neptune
Seem to besiege, and make his bold waves tremble;
Yea, his dread trident shake.

PROSPERO: My brave spirit!

Who was so firm, so constant, that this coil[70]
Would not infect his reason?

ARIEL:

Not a soul
But felt a fever of the mad and played
Some tricks of desperation. All but mariners 210
Plunged in the foaming brine and quit the vessel,
Then all afire with me. The King's son Ferdinand,
With hair up-staring[71] (then like reeds, not hair),
Was the first man that leapt; cried "Hell is empty,
And all the devils are here!"

PROSPERO:

Why, that's my spirit!
But was not this nigh shore?

---

[61] Tax to the utmost.
[62] Cohorts (Ariel is leader of a band of spirits).
[63] In every detail.
[64] Prow.
[65] Amidships.
[66] Poop.
[67] Struck terror by appearing as (St. Elmo's) fire.
[68] Bowsprit.
[69] In different places.
[70] Uproar.
[71] Standing on end.

ARIEL:

Close by, my master.

PROSPERO:

But are they, Ariel, safe?

ARIEL:

Not a hair perished.
On their sustaining[72] garments not a blemish,
But fresher than before; and as thou bad'st me,
In troops I have dispersed them 'bout the isle. 220
The King's son have I landed by himself,
Whom I left cooling of the air with sighs
In an odd angle of the isle, and sitting,
His arms in this sad knot.

[*Illustrates with a gesture.*]

PROSPERO:

Of the King's ship,
The mariners, say how thou hast disposed,
And all the rest o' th' fleet.

ARIEL:

Safely in harbor
Is the King's ship; in the deep nook where once
Thou call'dst me up at midnight to fetch dew
From the still-vexed Bermoothes,[73] there she's hid;
The mariners all under hatches stowed, 230
Who, with a charm joined to their suff'red[74] labor,
I have left alseep. And for the rest o' th' fleet,
Which I dispersed, they all have met again,
And are upon the Mediterranean flote[75]
Bound sadly home for Naples,
Supposing that they saw the King's ship wracked
And his great person perish.

PROSPERO:

Ariel, thy charge
Exactly is performed; but there's more work.
What is the time o' th' day?

ARIEL:

Past the mid season.[76]

PROSPERO:

At least two glasses.[77] The time 'twixt six and now 240
Must by us both be spent most preciously.

ARIEL:

Is there more toil? Since thou dost give me pains,[78]
Let me remember[79] thee what thou hast promised,
Which is not yet performed me.

PROSPERO:

How now? Moody?
What is't thou canst demand?

---

[72]Buoying them up.
[73]Bermudas. [74]Undergone. [75]Sea. [76]Noon.
[77]Two o'clock. [78]Hard tasks. [79]Remind.

ARIEL:

My liberty.

PROSPERO:

Before the time be out? No more!

ARIEL:

I prithee,

Remember I have done thee worthy service,
Told thee no lies, made thee no mistakings, served
Without or grudge or grumblings. Thou did promise
To bate me[80] a full year.

PROSPERO:

Dost thou forget 250

From what a torment I did free thee?

ARIEL:

No.

PROSPERO:

Thou dost; and think'st it much to tread the ooze
Of the salt deep,
To run upon the sharp wind of the North,
To do me business in the veins[81] o' th' earth
When it is baked[82] with frost.

ARIEL:

I do not, sir.

PROSPERO:

Thou liest, malignant thing! Hast thou forgot
The foul witch Sycorax,[83] who with age and envy
Was grown into a hoop? Hast thou forgot her?

ARIEL:

No, sir.

PROSPERO:

Thou hast. Where was she born? Speak! Tell me! 260

ARIEL:

Sir, in Argier.[84]

PROSPERO:

O, was she so? I must

Once in a month recount what thou hast been,
Which thou forget'st. This damned witch Sycorax,
For mischiefs manifold, and sorceries terrible
To enter human hearing, from Argier,
Thou know'st, was banished. For one thing she did
They would not take her life. Is not this true?

ARIEL:

Ay, sir.

PROSPERO:

This blue-eyed[85] hag was hither brought with child
And here was left by th' sailors. Thou, my slave, 270

---

[80]Reduce my term of service.

[81]Streams. [82]Caked.

[83]Name not found elsewhere; probably derived from Greek *sys*, "sow," and *korax*, which means both "raven"—see line 322—and "hook"—hence perhaps "hoop."

[84]Algiers.

[85]Referring to the livid color of the eyelid, a sign of pregnancy.

As thou report'st thyself, wast then her servant.
And, for thou wast a spirit too delicate
To act her earthy and abhorred commands,
Refusing her grand hests,[86] she did confine thee,
By help of her more potent ministers,
And in her most unmitigable rage,
Into a cloven pine; within which rift
Imprisoned thou didst painfully remain
A dozen years; within which space she died
And left thee there, where thou didst vent thy groans 280
As fast as millwheels strike. Then was this island
(Save for the son that she did litter here,
A freckled whelp, hagborn) not honored with
A human shape.

ARIEL:

Yes, Caliban her son.

PROSPERO:

Dull thing, I say so! He, that Caliban
Whom now I keep in service. Thou best know'st
What torment I did find thee in; thy groans
Did make wolves howl and penetrate the breasts
Of ever-angry bears. It was a torment
To lay upon the damned, which Sycorax 290
Could not again undo. It was mine art,
When I arrived and heard thee, that made gape
The pine, and let thee out.

ARIEL:

I thank thee, master.

PROSPERO:

If thou more murmur'st, I will rend an oak
And peg thee in his knotty entrails till
Thou hast howled away twelve winters.

ARIEL:

Pardon, master.

I will be correspondent[87] to command
And do my spriting gently.[88]

PROSPERO:

Do so; and after two days

I will discharge thee.

ARIEL:

That's my noble master!

What shall I do? Say what? What shall I do? 300

PROSPERO:

Go make thyself like a nymph o' th' sea. Be subject
To no sight but thine and mine, invisible
To every eyeball else.[89] Go take this shape

---

[86] Commands.
[87] Obedient.
[88] Render graciously my services as a spirit.
[89] Ariel is invisible to everyone in the play except Prospero; Henslowe's *Diary,* an Elizabethan stage account, lists "a robe for to go invisible."

And hither come in't. Go! Hence with diligence! *Exit* [ARIEL].
Awake, dear heart, awake! Thou hast slept well.
Awake!

MIRANDA:
The strangeness of your story put
Heaviness in me.

PROSPERO:
Shake it off. Come on.
We'll visit Caliban, my slave, who never
Yields us kind answer.

MIRANDA:
'Tis a villain, sir,
I do not love to look on.

PROSPERO:
But as 'tis, 310
We cannot miss[90] him. He does make our fire,
Fetch in our wood, and serves in offices
That profit us. What, ho! Slave! Caliban!
Thou earth, thou! Speak!

CALIBAN [*Within*]:
There's wood enough within.

PROSPERO:
Come forth, I say! There's other business for thee.
Come, thou tortoise! When?[91]

Enter ARIEL *like a water nymph.*

Fine apparition! My quaint[92] Ariel,
Hark in thine ear.

[*Whispers.*]

ARIEL:
My lord, it shall be done. *Exit.*

PROSPERO:
Thou poisonous slave, got by the devil himself
Upon thy wicked dam, come forth! 320

Enter CALIBAN.

CALIBAN:
As wicked dew as e'er my mother brushed
With raven's feather from unwholesome fen
Drop on you both! A southwest blow on ye
And blister you all o'er!

PROSPERO:
For this, be sure, tonight thou shalt have cramps,
Side-stitches that shall pen thy breath up. Urchins[93]
Shall, for that vast of night that they may work,[94]
All exercise on thee; thou shalt be pinched

---

[90]Do without.
[91]Expression of impatience.
[92]Ingenious.
[93]Goblins in the shape of hedgehogs.
[94]The long, empty stretch of night during which malignant spirits are allowed to be active.

As thick as honeycomb, each pinch more stinging
Than bees that made 'em.

CALIBAN:

I must eat my dinner. 330
This island's mine by Sycorax my mother,
Which thou tak'st from me. When thou cam'st first,
Thou strok'st me and made much of me; wouldst give me
Water with berries in't; and teach me how
To name the bigger light, and how the less,
That burn by day and night. And then I loved thee
And showed thee all the qualities o' th' isle,
The fresh springs, brine pits, barren place and fertile.
Cursed be I that did so! All the charms
Of Sycorax—toads, beetles, bats, light on you! 340
For I am all the subjects that you have,
Which first was mine own king; and here you sty me
In this hard rock, whiles you do keep from me
The rest o' th' island.

PROSPERO:

Thou most lying slave,
Whom stripes[95] may move, not kindness! I have used thee
(Filth as thou art) with humane care, and lodged thee
In mine own cell till thou didst seek to violate
The honor of my child.

CALIBAN:

O ho, O ho! Would't had been done!
Thou didst prevent me; I had peopled else 350
This isle with Calibans.

MIRANDA:[96]

Abhorrèd slave,
Which any print of goodness wilt not take,
Being capable of all ill![97] I pitied thee,
Took pains to make thee speak, taught thee each hour
One thing or other. When thou didst not, savage,
Know thine own meaning, but wouldst gabble like
A thing most brutish, I endowed thy purposes
With words that made them known. But thy vile race,
Though thou didst learn, had that in't which good natures
Could not abide to be with. Therefore wast thou 360
Deservedly confined into this rock, who hadst
Deserved more than a prison.

CALIBAN:

You taught me language, and my profit on't
Is, I know how to curse. The red plague rid you
For learning me your language!

---

[95] Lashes.
[96] Many editors transfer this speech to Prospero as inappropriate to Miranda.
[97] Susceptible only to evil impressions.

PROSPERO:

Hagseed, hence!
Fetch us in fuel. And be quick, thou'rt best,[98]
To answer other business. Shrug'st thou, malice?
If thou neglect'st or dost unwillingly
What I command, I'll rack thee with old[99] cramps,
Fill all thy bones with aches, make thee roar 370
That beasts shall tremble at thy din.

CALIBAN:

No, pray thee.
[*Aside*] I must obey. His art is of such pow'r
It would control my dam's god, Setebos,
And make a vassal of him.

PROSPERO:

So, slave; hence! *Exit* CALIBAN.

Enter FERDINAND; *and* ARIEL (*invisible*), *playing and singing.*

Ariel's song.

Come unto these yellow sands,
And then take hands.
Curtsied when you have and kissed
The wild waves whist,[100]
Foot it featly[101] here and there;
And, sweet sprites, the burden bear. 380
Hark, hark!
Burden, dispersedly.[102] Bow, wow!
The watchdogs bark.
[*Burden, dispersedly.*] Bow, wow!
Hark, hark! I hear
The strain of strutting chanticleer
Cry cock-a-diddle-dow.

FERDINAND:

Where should this music be? I' th' air or th' earth?
It sounds no more; and sure it waits upon
Some god o' th' island. Sitting on a bank, 390
Weeping again the King my father's wrack,
This music crept by me upon the waters,
Allaying both their fury and my passion[103]
With its sweet air. Thence I have followed it,
Or it hath drawn me rather; but 'tis gone.
No, it begins again.

---

[98] You'd better.
[99] Plenty of (with an additional suggestion, "such as old people have").
[100] When you have, through the harmony of kissing in the dance, kissed the wild waves into silence (?); when you have kissed in the dance, the wild waves being silenced (?).
[101] Nimbly.
[102] An undersong, coming from all parts of the stage; it imitates the barking of dogs and perhaps in the end the crowing of a cock.
[103] Grief.

Ariel's song.

Full fathom five thy father lies;
Of his bones are coral made;
Those are pearls that were his eyes;
Nothing of him that doth fade 400
But doth suffer a sea change
Into something rich and strange.
Sea nymphs hourly ring his knell:
Burden. Ding-dong.
Hark! Now I hear them—ding-dong bell.

FERDINAND:
The ditty does remember my drowned father.
This is no mortal business, nor no sound
That the earth owes.[104] I hear it now above me.
PROSPERO:
The fringèd curtains of thine eye advance[105]
And say what thou seest yond.
MIRANDA:
What is't? A spirit? 410
Lord, how it looks about! Believe me, sir,
It carries a brave form. But 'tis a spirit.
PROSPERO:
No, wench; it eats, and sleeps, and hath such senses
As we have, such. This gallant which thou seest
Was in the wrack; and, but he's something stained
With grief (that's beauty's canker), thou mightst call him
A goodly person. He hath lost his fellows
And strays about to find 'em.
MIRANDA:
I might call him
A thing divine; for nothing natural
I ever saw so noble.
PROSPERO:
[*Aside*] It goes on, I see, 420
As my soul prompts it. Spirit, fine spirit, I'll free thee
Within two days for this.
FERDINAND:
Most sure, the goddess
On whom these airs attend! Vouchsafe my prayer
May know if you remain[106] upon this island,
And that you will some good instruction give
How I may bear me[107] here. My prime request,
Which do I last pronounce, is (O you wonder!)
If you be maid or no?
MIRANDA:
No wonder, sir,
But certainly a maid.

---

[104]Owns. [105]Raise.
[106]May my prayer induce you to inform me whether you dwell.
[107]Conduct myself.

FERDINAND:

My language? Heavens!
I am the best of them that speak this speech, 430
Were I but where 'tis spoken.

PROSPERO:

How? The best?
What wert thou if the King of Naples heard thee?

FERDINAND:

A single[108] thing, as I am now, that wonders
To hear thee speak of Naples. He does hear me;
And that he does I weep. Myself am Naples,
Who with mine eyes, never since at ebb, beheld
The King my father wracked.

MIRANDA:

Alack, for mercy!

FERDINAND:

Yes, faith, and all his lords, the Duke of Milan
And his brave son[109] being twain.[110]

PROSPERO:

[*Aside*] The Duke of Milan
And his more braver daughter could control[111] thee, 440
If now 'twere fit to do't. At the first sight
They have changed eyes.[112] Delicate Ariel,
I'll set thee free for this. [*To* FERDINAND] A word, good sir.
I fear you have done yourself some wrong.[113] A word!

MIRANDA:

Why speaks my father so ungently? This
Is the third man that e'er I saw; the first
That e'er I sighed for. Pity move my father
To be inclined my way!

FERDINAND:

O, if a virgin,
And your affection not gone forth, I'll make you
The Queen of Naples.

PROSPERO:

Soft, sir! One word more. 450
[*Aside*] They are both in either's pow'rs. But this swift business
I must uneasy make, lest too light winning
Make the prize light. [*To* FERDINAND] One word more! I charge thee
That thou attend me. Thou dost here usurp
The name thou ow'st not, and hast put thyself
Upon this island as a spy, to win it
From me, the lord on't.

FERDINAND:

No, as I am a man!

---

[108] (1) Solitary; (2) helpless.

[109] The only time Antonio's son is mentioned.

[110] Two (of these lords).

[111] Refute.

[112] Fallen in love.

[113] Said what is not so.

MIRANDA:
There's nothing ill can dwell in such a temple.
If the ill spirit have so fair a house,
Good things will strive to dwell with't.
PROSPERO:
Follow me. 460
[*To* MIRANDA] Speak not you for him; he's a traitor. [*To* FERDINAND] Come!
I'll manacle thy neck and feet together;
Sea water shalt thou drink; thy food shall be
The fresh-brook mussels, withered roots, and husks
Wherein the acorn cradled. Follow!
FERDINAND:
No.
I will resist such entertainment till
Mine enemy has more pow'r.
He draws, and is charmed from moving.
MIRANDA:
O dear father,
Make not too rash a trial of him, for
He's gentle and not fearful.[114]
PROSPERO:
What, I say,
My foot my tutor?[115] [*To* FERDINAND] Put thy sword up, traitor— 470
Who mak'st a show but dar'st not strike, thy conscience
Is so possessed with guilt! Come, from thy ward![116]
For I can here disarm thee with this stick[117]
And make thy weapon drop.
MIRANDA:
Beseech you, father!
PROSPERO:
Hence! Hang not on my garments.
MIRANDA:
Sir, have pity.
I'll be his surety.
PROSPERO:
Silence! One word more
Shall make me chide thee, if not hate thee. What,
An advocate for an impostor? Hush!
Thou think'st there is no more such shapes as he,
Having seen but him and Caliban. Foolish wench! 480
To th' most of men this is a Caliban,
And they to him are angels.
MIRANDA:
My affections
Are then most humble. I have no ambition
To see a goodlier man.

---

[114] Of noble birth and no coward.
[115] Am I to be instructed by my inferior?
[116] Fighting posture.
[117] His wand.

PROSPERO:
[*To* FERDINAND] Come on, obey!
Thy nerves[118] are in their infancy again
And have no vigor in them.
FERDINAND:
So they are.
My spirits, as in a dream, are all bound up.
My father's loss, the weakness which I feel,
The wrack of all my friends, nor this man's threats
To whom I am subdued, are but light to me, 490
Might I but through my prison once a day
Behold this maid. All corners else o' th' earth
Let liberty make use of. Space enough
Have I in such a prison.
PROSPERO:
[*Aside*] It works. [*To* FERDINAND] Come on.
[*To* ARIEL] Thou hast done well, fine Ariel! [*To* FERDINAND] Follow me.
[*To* ARIEL] Hark what thou else shalt do me.
MIRANDA:
Be of comfort.
My father's of a better nature, sir,
Than he appears by speech. This is unwonted
Which now came from him.
PROSPERO:
Thou shalt be as free
As mountain winds; but then[119] exactly do 500
All points of my command.
ARIEL:
To th' syllable.
PROSPERO:
[*To* FERDINAND] Come, follow. [*To* MIRANDA] Speak not for him. *Exeunt.*

ACT II

Scene 1

Another part of the island.

Enter ALONSO, SEBASTIAN, ANTONIO, GONZALO, ADRIAN, FRANCISCO, *and others.*
GONZALO:
Beseech you, sir, be merry. You have cause
(So have we all) of joy; for our escape
Is much beyond our loss. Our hint of[120] woe
Is common; every day some sailor's wife,
The master of some merchant,[121] and the merchant,
Have just our theme of woe. But for the miracle,
I mean our preservation, few in millions
Can speak like us. Then wisely, good sir, weigh
Our sorrow with our comfort.

---

[118]Sinews. [119]Until then. [120]Occasion for.
[121]Captain of some merchant ship.

ALONSO:
Prithee, peace.

SEBASTIAN [*Aside to* ANTONIO]: He receives comfort like cold porridge.[122] 10
ANTONIO [*Aside to* SEBASTIAN]: The visitor[123] will not give him o'er so.[124]
SEBASTIAN: Look, he's winding up the watch of his wit; by and by it will strike.
GONZALO: Sir—
SEBASTIAN [*Aside to* ANTONIO]: One. Tell.[125]
GONZALO:
When every grief is entertained, that's[126] offered
Comes to th' entertainer—
SEBASTIAN: A dollar. 20
GONZALO: Dolor comes to him, indeed. You have spoken truer than you purposed.
SEBASTIAN: You have taken it wiselier[127] than I meant you should.
GONZALO: Therefore, my lord—
ANTONIO: Fie, what a spendthrift is he of his tongue!
ALONSO: I prithee, spare.[128]
GONZALO: Well, I have done. But yet—
SEBASTIAN: He will be talking.
ANTONIO: Which, of he or Adrian, for a good wager, first begins to crow? 30
SEBASTIAN: The old cock.[129]
ANTONIO: The cock'rel.[130]
SEBASTIAN: Done! The wager?
ANTONIO: A laughter.[131]
SEBASTIAN: A match!
ADRIAN: Though this island seem to be desert—
ANTONIO: Ha, ha, ha!
SEBASTIAN: So, you're paid.
ADRIAN: Uninhabitable and almost inaccessible— 40
SEBASTIAN: Yet—
ADRIAN: Yet—
ANTONIO: He could not miss't.
ADRIAN: It must needs be of subtle, tender, and delicate temperance.[132]
ANTONIO: Temperance was a delicate wench.
SEBASTIAN: Ay, and a subtle, as he mostly learnedly delivered.
ADRIAN: The air breathes upon us here most sweetly.
SEBASTIAN: As if it had lungs, and rotten ones. 50
ANTONIO: Or as 'twere perfumed by a fen.
GONZALO: Here is everything advantageous to life.
ANTONIO: True; save means to live.
SEBASTIAN: Of that there's none, or little.
GONZALO: How lush and lusty the grass looks! How green!

---

[122]"He" is Alonso; a pun on "peace," since porridge contained peas.
[123]Spiritual comforter.
[124]Release him so easily.
[125]He has struck one; keep count.
[126]That which is.
[127]Understood my pun.
[128]Spare your words.
[129]Gonzalo.
[130]Young cock; Adrian.
[131]The winner will have the laugh on the loser.
[132]Climate (in the next line, a girl's name).

ANTONIO: The ground indeed is tawny.
SEBASTIAN: With an eye[133] of green in't.
ANTONIO: He misses not much.
SEBASTIAN: No; he doth but mistake the truth totally. 60
GONZALO: But the rarity of it is—which is indeed almost beyond credit—
SEBASTIAN: As many vouched rarities are.
GONZALO: That our garments, being, as they were, drenched in the sea, hold, notwithstanding, their freshness and glosses, being rather new-dyed than stained with salt water.
ANTONIO: If but one of his pockets could speak, would it not say he lies?[134]
SEBASTIAN: Ay, or very falsely pocket up his report.[135] 70
GONZALO: Methinks our garments are now as fresh as when we put them on first in Afric, at the marriage of the King's fair daughter Claribel to the King of Tunis.
SEBASTIAN: 'Twas a sweet marriage, and we prosper well in our return.
ADRIAN: Tunis was never graced before with such a paragon to their queen.
GONZALO: Not since widow Dido's time.
ANTONIO: Widow? A pox o' that! How came that "widow" in? Widow Dido! 80
SEBASTIAN: What if he had said "widower Aeneas"[136] too? Good Lord, how you take it!
ADRIAN: "Widow Dido," said you? You make me study of that. She was of Carthage, not of Tunis.
GONZALO: This Tunis, sir, was Carthage.
ADRIAN: Carthage?
GONZALO: I assure you, Carthage.
ANTONIO: His word is more than the miraculous harp.[137] 90
SEBASTIAN: He hath raised the wall and houses too.
ANTONIO: What impossible matter will he make easy next?
SEBASTIAN: I think he will carry this island home in his pocket and give it his son for an apple.
ANTONIO: And, sowing the kernels of it in the sea, bring forth more islands.
GONZALO: Ay!
ANTONIO: Why, in good time.[138]
GONZALO [*To* ALONSO]: Sir, we were talking that our garments seem now as fresh as when we were at Tunis at the marriage of your daughter, who is now Queen. 100
ANTONIO: And the rarest that e'er came there.
SEBASTIAN: Bate,[139] I beseech you, widow Dido.
ANTONIO: O, widow Dido? Ay, widow Dido!
GONZALO: Is not, sir, my doublet as fresh as the first day I wore it? I mean, in a sort.
ANTONIO: That "sort" was well fished for.

---

[133] Spot (also perhaps Gonzalo's eye).

[134] The inside of Gonzalo's pockets are stained.

[135] Unless the pocket were, like a false knave, to receive without resentment the imputation that it is unstained.

[136] The point of the joke is that Dido was a widow, but one doesn't ordinarily think of her that way; and the same with Aeneas.

[137] Of Amphion, which only raised the *walls* of Thebes; whereas Gonzalo has rebuilt the whole ancient city of Carthage by identifying it mistakenly with modern Tunis.

[138] Hearing Gonzalo reaffirm his false statement about Tunis and Carthage, Antonio suggests that Gonzalo will indeed, at the first opportunity, carry this island home in his pocket.

[139] Except.

GONZALO: When I wore it at your daughter's marriage. 110
ALONSO:
You cram these words into mine ears against
The stomach of my sense.[140] Would I had never
Married my daughter there! For, coming thence,
My son is lost; and, in my rate,[141] she too,
Who is so far from Italy removed
I ne'er again shall see her. O thou mine heir
Of Naples and of Milan, what strange fish
Hath made his meal on thee?
FRANCISCO:
Sir, he may live.
I saw him beat the surges under him
And ride upon their backs. He trod the water, 120
Whose enmity he flung aside, and breasted
The surge most swol'n that met him. His bold head
'Bove the contentious waves he kept, and oared
Himself with his good arms in lusty stroke
To th' shore, that o'er his wave-worn basis bowed,[142]
As stooping to relieve him. I not doubt
He came alive to land.
ALONSO:
No, no, he's gone.
SEBASTIAN [*To* ALONSO]:
Sir, you may thank yourself for this great loss,
That would not bless our Europe with your daughter,
But rather loose her to an African, 130
Where she, at least, is banished from your eye
Who hath cause to wet the grief on't.
ALONSO:
Prithee, peace.
SEBASTIAN:
You were kneeled to and importuned otherwise
By all of us; and the fair soul herself
Weighed, between loathness and obedience, at
Which end o' th' beam should bow.[143] We have lost your son,
I fear, forever. Milan and Naples have
Moe widows in them of this business' making
Than we bring men to comfort them.
The fault's your own.
ALONSO:
So is the dear'st o' th' loss. 140
GONZALO:
My Lord Sebastian,
The truth you speak doth lack some gentleness,
And time to speak it in. You rub the sore
When you should bring the plaster.

---

[140] Though my mind (or feelings) have no appetite for them.
[141] Opinion.
[142] The image is of a guardian cliff on the shore.
[143] Claribel's unwillingness to marry was outweighed by her obedience to her father.

SEBASTIAN:

Very well.

ANTONIO:

And most chirurgeonly.[144]

GONZALO [*To* ALONSO]:

It is foul weather in us all, good sir,
When you are cloudy.

SEBASTIAN [*Aside to* ANTONIO]:

Foul weather?

ANTONIO [*Aside to* SEBASTIAN]:

Very foul.

GONZALO:

Had I plantation[145] of this isle, my lord—

ANTONIO:

He'd sow't with nettle seed.

SEBASTIAN:

Or docks, or mallows.

GONZALO:

And were the king on't, what would I do? 150

SEBASTIAN:

Scape being drunk for want of wine.

GONZALO:

I' th' commonwealth I would by contraries[146]
Execute all things. For no kind of traffic[147]
Would I admit; no name of magistrate;
Letters[148] should not be known; riches, poverty,
And use of service,[149] none; contract, succession,[150]
Bourn,[151] bound of land, tilth,[152] vineyard, none;
No use of metal, corn, or wine, or oil;
No occupation; all men idle, all;
And women too, but innocent and pure; 160
No sovereignty.

SEBASTIAN:

Yet he would be king on't.

ANTONIO:

The latter end of his commonwealth forgets the beginning.

GONZALO:

All things in common nature should produce
Without sweat or endeavor. Treason, felony,
Sword, pike, knife, gun, or need of any engine[153]
Would I not have; but nature should bring forth,
Of it own kind, all foison,[154] all abundance,
To feed my innocent people.

SEBASTIAN:

No marrying 'mong his subjects? 170

---

[144]Like a surgeon.
[145]Colonization (Antonio then puns by taking the word in its other sense).
[146]In contrast to the usual customs.
[147]Trade. [148]Learning. [149]Servants. [150]Inheritance.
[151]Boundary. [152]Agriculture. [153]Weapon. [154]Abundance.

ANTONIO:
None, man, all idle—whores and knaves.
GONZALO:
I would with such perfection govern, sir,
T' excel the Golden Age.
SEBASTIAN [*Loudly*]:
Save his Majesty!
ANTONIO [*Loudly*]:
Long live Gonzalo!
GONZALO:
And—do you mark me, sir?
ALONSO:
Prithee, no more. Thou dost talk nothing to me.
GONZALO: I do well believe your Highness; and did it to minister occasion[155] to these gentlemen, who are of such sensible[156] and nimble lungs that they always use to laugh at nothing.
ANTONIO: 'Twas you we laughed at. 180
GONZALO: Who in this kind of merry fooling am nothing to you; so you may continue, and laugh at nothing still.
ANTONIO: What a blow was there given!
SEBASTIAN: And it had not fall'n flatlong.[157]
GONZALO: You are gentlemen of brave mettle; you would lift the moon out of her sphere if she would continue in it five weeks without changing.
Enter ARIEL (*invisible*) *playing solemn music.*
SEBASTIAN: We would so, and then go a-batfowling.[158]
ANTONIO: Nay, good my lord, be not angry. 190
GONZALO: No, I warrant you; I will not adventure my discretion so weakly.[159] Will you laugh me asleep? For I am very heavy.
ANTONIO: Go sleep, and hear us.
[*All sleep except* ALONSO, SEBASTIAN, *and* ANTONIO.]
ALONSO:
What, all so soon asleep? I wish mine eyes
Would, with themselves, shut up my thoughts. I find
They are inclined to do so.
SEBASTIAN:
Please you, sir,
Do not omit the heavy offer of it.
It seldom visits sorrow; when it doth,
It is a comforter.
ANTONIO:
We two, my lord, 200
Will guard your person while you take your rest,
And watch your safety.
ALONSO:
Thank you. Wondrous heavy.
[ALONSO *sleeps. Exit* ARIEL.]

---

[155] Afford opportunity.
[156] Sensitive.
[157] With the flat of the sword.
[158] We would use the moon for a lantern in order to hunt birds at night by attracting them with a light and beating them down with bats; i.e., in order to gull simpletons like you (?).
[159] Risk my reputation for good sense because of your weak wit.

SEBASTIAN:
What a strange drowsiness possesses them!
ANTONIO:
It is the quality o' th' climate.
SEBASTIAN:
Why
Doth it not then our eyelids sink? I find not
Myself disposed to sleep.
ANTONIO:
Nor I: my spirits are nimble.
They fell together all, as by consent.
They dropped as by a thunderstroke. What might,
Worthy Sebastian—O, what might?—No more!
And yet methinks I see it in thy face, 210
What thou shouldst be. Th' occasion speaks thee, and
My strong imagination sees a crown
Dropping upon thy head.
SEBASTIAN:
What? Art thou waking?
ANTONIO:
Do you not hear me speak?
SEBASTIAN:
I do; and surely
It is a sleepy language, and thou speak'st
Out of thy sleep. What is it thou didst say?
This is a strange repose, to be asleep
With eyes wide open; standing, speaking, moving,
And yet so fast asleep.
ANTONIO:
Noble Sebastian,
Thou let'st thy fortune sleep—die, rather; wink'st 220
Whiles thou art waking.
SEBASTIAN:
Thou dost snore distinctly;
There's meaning in thy snores.
ANTONIO:
I am more serious than my custom. You
Must be so too, if heed me; which to do
Trebles thee o'er.[160]
SEBASTIAN:
Well, I am standing water.
ANTONIO:
I'll teach you how to flow.
SEBASTIAN:
Do so. To ebb
Hereditary sloth instructs me.
ANTONIO:
O,
If you but knew how you the purpose cherish
Whiles thus you mock it; how, in stripping it,

---

[160] Makes thee three times what thou now art.

You more invest it![161] Ebbing men, indeed, 230
Most often do so near the bottom run
By their own fear or sloth.

SEBASTIAN:

Prithee, say on.
The setting of thine eye and cheek proclaim
A matter from thee; and a birth, indeed,
Which throes thee much[162] to yield.

ANTONIO:

Thus, sir:
Although this lord of weak remembrance, this
Who shall be of as little memory
When he is earthed, hath here almost persuaded
(For he's a spirit of persuasion, only
Professes to persuade[163]) the King his son's alive, 240
'Tis as impossible that he's undrowned
As he that sleeps here swims.

SEBASTIAN:

I have no hope
That he's undrowned.

ANTONIO:

O, out of that no hope
What great hope have you! No hope that way is
Another way so high a hope that even
Ambition cannot pierce a wink beyond,
But doubt discovery there.[164] Will you grant with me
That Ferdinand is drowned?

SEBASTIAN:

He's gone.

ANTONIO:

Then tell me,
Who's the next heir of Naples?

SEBASTIAN:

Claribel.

ANTONIO:

She that is Queen of Tunis; she that dwells 250
Ten leagues beyond man's life;[165] she that from Naples
Can have no note—unless the sun were post;[166]
The man i' th' moon's too slow—till newborn chins
Be rough and razorable; she that from whom
We all were sea-swallowed,[167] though some cast[168] again,
And, by that destiny, to perform an act

---

[161] In stripping the purpose off you, you clothe yourself with it all the more.

[162] Causes much pain.

[163] His only profession is to persuade.

[164] The eye of ambition can reach no farther, but must even doubt the reality of what it discerns thus far.

[165] It would take a lifetime to get within ten leagues of the place.

[166] Messenger.

[167] She who is separated from Naples by so dangerous a sea that we were ourselves swallowed up by it.

[168] Cast upon the shore (with a suggestion of its theatrical meaning, which leads to the next metaphor).

Whereof what's past is prologue, what to come,
In yours and my discharge.

SEBASTIAN:

What stuff is this? How say you?
'Tis true my brother's daughter's Queen of Tunis;
So is she heir of Naples; 'twixt which regions 260
There is some space.

ANTONIO:

A space whose ev'ry cubit
Seems to cry out "How shall that Claribel
Measure us back to Naples? Keep in Tunis,
And let Sebastian wake!" Say this were death
That now hath seized them, why, they were no worse
Than now they are. There be that can rule Naples
As well as he that sleeps; lords that can prate
As amply and unnecessarily
As this Gonzalo; I myself could make
A chough[169] of as deep chat. O, that you bore 270
The mind that I do! What a sleep were this
For your advancement! Do you understand me?

SEBASTIAN:

Methinks I do.

ANTONIO:

And how does your content
Tender[170] your own good fortune?

SEBASTIAN:

I remember
You did supplant your brother Prospero.

ANTONIO:

True.
And look how well my garments sit upon me,
Much feater[171] than before. My brother's servants
Were then my fellows; now they are my men.

SEBASTIAN:

But, for your conscience—

ANTONIO:

Ay, sir, where lies that? If 'twere a kibe,[172] 280
'Twould put me to my slipper; but I feel not
This deity in my bosom. Twenty consciences
That stand 'twixt me and Milan, candied be they
And melt, ere they molest! Here lies your brother,
No better than the earth he lies upon—
If he were that which now he's like, that's dead—
Whom I with this obedient steel (three inches of it)
Can lay to bed forever; whiles you, doing thus,
To the perpetual wink for aye might put

[169]Jackdaw (a bird that can be taught to speak a few words).
[170]Regard (i.e., do you like your good fortune).
[171]More becomingly.
[172]Chilblain on the heel.

This ancient morsel, this Sir Prudence, who 290
Should not upbraid our course. For all the rest,
They'll take suggestion as a cat laps milk;
They'll tell the clock[173] to any business that
We say befits the hour.

SEBASTIAN:
Thy case, dear friend,
Shall be my precedent. As thou got'st Milan,
I'll come by Naples. Draw thy sword. One stroke
Shall free thee from the tribute which thou payest,
And I the King shall love thee.

ANTONIO:
Draw together;
And when I rear my hand, do you the like,
To fall it on Gonzalo.

[*They draw.*]

SEBASTIAN:
O, but one word! 300

Enter ARIEL (*invisible*) *with music and song.*

ARIEL:
My master through his art foresees the danger
That you, his friend, are in, and sends me forth
(For else his project dies) to keep them living.

Sings in GONZALO*'s ear.*

While you here do snoring lie,
Opened-eye conspiracy
His time doth take.
If of life you keep a care,
Shake off slumber and beware.
Awake, awake!

ANTONIO:
Then let us both be sudden.

GONZALO [*Wakes*]:
Now good angels 310
Preserve the King!

[*The others wake.*]

ALONSO:
Why, how now? Ho, awake! Why are you drawn?
Wherefore this ghastly looking?

GONZALO:
What's the matter?

SEBASTIAN:
Whiles we stood here securing your repose,
Even now, we heard a hollow burst of bellowing
Like bulls, or rather lions. Did't not wake you?
It struck mine ear most terribly.

---

[173] Say yes.

ALONSO:

I heard nothing.

ANTONIO:

O, 'twas a din to fright a monster's ear,
To make an earthquake! Sure it was the roar
Of a whole herd of lions.

ALONSO:

Heard you this, Gonzalo? 320

GONZALO:

Upon mine honor, sir, I heard a humming,
And that a strange one too, which did awake me.
I shaked you, sir, and cried. As mine eyes opened,
I saw their weapons drawn. There was a noise,
That's verily.[174] 'Tis best we stand upon our guard,
Or that we quit this place. Let's draw our weapons.

ALONSO:

Lead off this ground, and let's make further search
For my poor son.

GONZALO:

Heavens keep him from these beasts!
For he is, sure, i' th' island.

ALONSO:

Lead away.

ARIEL:

Prospero my lord shall know what I have done. 330
So, King, go safely on to seek thy son. *Exeunt.*

Scene 2

Another part of the island.

Enter CALIBAN *with a burden of wood. A noise of thunder heard.*

CALIBAN:

All the infections that the sun sucks up
From bogs, fens, flats, on Prosper fall, and make him
By inchmeal[175] a disease! His spirits hear me,
And yet I needs must curse. But they'll nor pinch,
Fright me with urchin shows,[176] pitch me i' th' mire,
Nor lead me, like a firebrand,[177] in the dark
Out of my way, unless he bid 'em. But
For every trifle are they set upon me;
Sometime like apes that mow[178] and chatter at me,
And after bite me; then like hedgehogs which 10
Lie tumbling in my barefoot way and mount

[174]The truth.
[175]Inch by inch.
[176]Impish apparitions.
[177]In the form of a will-o'-the-wisp.
[178]Make faces.

Their pricks at my footfall; sometime am I
All wound with adders, who with cloven tongues
Do hiss me into madness.

Enter TRINCULO.

Lo, now, lo!
Here comes a spirit of his, and to torment me
For bringing wood in slowly. I'll fall flat.
Perchance he will not mind me.

[*Lies down.*]

TRINCULO: Here's neither bush nor shrub to bear off[179] any weather at all, and another storm brewing; I hear it sing i' th' wind. Yond same black cloud, yond huge one, looks like a foul bombard[180] that would shed his liquor. If it should thunder as it did before, I know not where to hide my head. Yond same cloud cannot choose but fall by pailfuls. What have we here? A man or a fish? Dead or alive? A fish! He smells like a fish; a very ancient and fishlike smell; a kind of not of the newest Poor John.[181] A strange fish! Were I in England now, as once I was, and had but this fish painted,[182] not a holiday fool there but would give a piece of silver. There would this monster make a man;[183] any strange beast there makes a man. When they will not give a doit[184] to relieve a lame beggar, they will lay out ten to see a dead Indian. Legged like a man! And his fins like arms! Warm, o' my troth! I do now let loose my opinion, hold it no longer. This is no fish, but an islander, that hath lately suffered by a thunderbolt. [*Thunder.*] Alas, the storm is come again! My best way is to creep under his gaberdine; there is no other shelter hereabout. Misery acquaints a man with strange bedfellows. I will here shroud till the dregs of the storm be past.

[*Creeps under* CALIBAN*'s garment.*]

Enter STEPHANO *singing, a bottle in his hand.*

STEPHANO:

I shall no more to sea, to sea;
Here shall I die ashore.

This is a very scurvy tune to sing at a man's funeral. Well, here's my comfort. *Drinks.*

The master, the swabber, the boatswain, and I,
The gunner, and his mate,
Loved Mall, Meg, and Marian, and Margery,
But none of us cared for Kate.
For she had a tongue with a tang,
Would cry to a sailor "Go hang!"
She loved not the savor of tar nor of pitch;
Yet a tailor might scratch her where'er she did itch.
Then to sea, boys, and let her go hang!

This is a scurvy tune too; but here's my comfort. *Drinks.*

---

[179] Ward off.
[180] Large leather jug.
[181] Dried hake.
[182] As a sign hung outside a booth at a fair.
[183] Pun: make a man's fortune.
[184] Smallest coin.

CALIBAN: Do not torment me! O!

STEPHANO: What's the matter? Have we devils here? Do you put tricks upon 's with savages and men of Inde, ha? I have not scaped drowning to be afeared now of your four legs. For it hath been said, "As proper a man as ever went on four legs cannot make him give ground"; and it shall be said so again, while Stephano breathes at' nostrils. 60

CALIBAN: The spirit torments me. O!

STEPHANO: This is some monster of the isle, with four legs, who hath got, as I take it, an ague. Where the devil should he learn our language? I will give him some relief, if it be but for that. If I can recover him, and keep him tame, and get to Naples with him, he's a present for any emperor that ever trod on neat's leather.[185] 70

CALIBAN: Do not torment me, prithee; I'll bring my wood home faster.

STEPHANO: He's in his fit now and does not talk after the wisest. He shall taste of my bottle; if he have never drunk wine afore, it will go near to remove his fit. If I can recover him and keep him tame, I will not take too much[186] for him. He shall pay for him that hath him, and that soundly. 80

CALIBAN: Thou dost me yet but little hurt. Thou wilt anon; I know it by thy trembling.[187] Now Prosper works upon thee.

STEPHANO: Come on your ways, open your mouth; here is that which will give language to you, cat.[188] Open your mouth. This will shake your shaking, I can tell you, and that soundly. [*Gives* CALIBAN *drink.*] You cannot tell who's your friend. Open your chaps[189] again.

TRINCULO: I should know that voice. It should be—but he is drowned; and these are devils. O, defend me! 90

STEPHANO: Four legs and two voices—a most delicate monster! His forward voice now is to speak well of his friend; his backward voice is to utter foul speeches and to detract. If all the wine in my bottle will recover him, I will help his ague. Come! [*Gives drink.*] Amen! I will pour some in thy other mouth.

TRINCULO: Stephano! 100

STEPHANO: Doth thy other mouth call me? Mercy, mercy! This is a devil, and no monster. I will leave him; I have no long spoon.[190]

TRINCULO: Stephano! If thou beest Stephano, touch me and speak to me; for I am Trinculo—be not afeared—thy good friend Trinculo.

STEPHANO: If thou beest Trinculo, come forth. I'll pull thee by the lesser legs. If any be Trinculo's legs, these are they. [*Draws him out from under* CALIBAN*'s garment.*] Thou art very Trinculo indeed! How cam'st thou to be the siege[191] of this mooncalf?[192] Can he vent Trinculos? 110

TRINCULO: I took him to be killed with a thunderstroke. But art thou not drowned, Stephano? I hope now thou art not drowned. Is the storm overblown? I hid me under the dead mooncalf's gaberdine for fear of the storm. And art thou living, Stephano? O Stephano, two Neapolitans scaped!

STEPHANO: Prithee do not turn me about; my stomach is not constant. 120

---

[185] Cowhide.

[186] Too much will not be enough.

[187] Trinculo is shaking with fear.

[188] Alluding to the proverb "Liquor will make a cat talk."

[189] Jaws.

[190] Alluding to the proverb "He who sups with (i.e., from the same dish as) the devil must have a long spoon."

[191] Excrement.

[192] Monstrosity.

CALIBAN:
[*Aside*] These be fine things, and if they be not sprites.
That's a brave god and bears celestial liquor.
I will kneel to him.

STEPHANO: How didst thou scape? How cam'st thou hither? Swear by this bottle how thou cam'st hither. I escaped upon a butt of sack which the sailors heaved o'erboard—by this bottle which I made of the bark of a tree with mine own hands since I was cast ashore.

CALIBAN: I'll swear upon that bottle to be thy true subject, for the liquor is not earthly. 130

STEPHANO: Here! Swear then how thou escap'dst.

TRINCULO: Swum ashore, man, like a duck. I can swim like a duck, I'll be sworn.

STEPHANO: Here, kiss the book. [*Gives him drink.*] Though thou canst swim like a duck, thou art made like a goose.

TRINCULO: O Stephano, hast any more of this?

STEPHANO: The whole butt, man. My cellar is in a rock by th' seaside, where my wine is hid. How now, mooncalf? How does thine ague? 140

CALIBAN: Hast thou not dropped from heaven?

STEPHANO: Out o' th' moon, I do assure thee. I was the Man i' th' Moon when time was.

CALIBAN: I have seen thee in her, and I do adore thee. My mistress showed me thee, and thy dog, and thy bush.[193]

STEPHANO: Come, swear to that; kiss the book. [*Gives him drink.*] I will furnish it anon with new contents. Swear. [CALIBAN *drinks.*] 150

TRINCULO: By this good light, this is a very shallow monster! I afeard of him? A very weak monster! The Man i' th' Moon? A most poor credulous monster! Well drawn,[194] monster, in good sooth!

CALIBAN: I'll show thee every fertile inch o' th' island; and I will kiss thy foot. I prithee, be my god.

TRINCULO: By this light, a most perfidious and drunken monster! When's god's asleep, he'll rob his bottle.

CALIBAN: I'll kiss thy foot. I'll swear myself thy subject. 160

STEPHANO: Come on then. Down, and swear!

TRINCULO: I shall laugh myself to death at this puppy-headed monster. A most scurvy monster! I could find in my heart to beat him—

STEPHANO: Come, kiss.

TRINCULO: But that the poor monster's in drink. An abominable monster!

CALIBAN:
I'll show thee the best springs; I'll pluck thee berries;
I'll fish for thee, and get thee wood enough.
A plague upon the tyrant that I serve! 170
I'll bear him no more sticks, but follow thee,
Thou wondrous man.

TRINCULO: A most ridiculous monster, to make a wonder of a poor drunkard!

CALIBAN:
I prithee let me bring thee where crabs[195] grow;
And I with my long nails will dig thee pignuts,[196]

[193]The Man in the Moon was banished there, according to legend, for gathering brushwood with his dog on Sunday.

[194]A good pull at the bottle.

[195]Crab apples.

[196]Earthnuts.

Show thee a jay's nest, and instruct thee how
To snare the nimble marmoset. I'll bring thee
To clust'ring filberts, and sometimes I'll get thee
Young scamels[197] from the rock. Wilt thou go with me? 180

STEPHANO: I prithee now, lead the way without any more talking. Trinculo, the King and all our company else being drowned, we will inherit here. Here, bear my bottle. Fellow Trinculo, we'll fill him by and by again.

CALIBAN *sings drunkenly.*

CALIBAN: Farewell, master; farewell, farewell!

TRINCULO: A howling monster! A drunken monster!

CALIBAN:

No more dams I'll make for fish,
Nor fetch in firing
At requiring, 190
Nor scrape trenchering,[198] nor wash dish.
'Ban, 'Ban, Ca—Caliban
Has a new master. Get a new man!

Freedom, high day! High day, freedom! Freedom, high day, freedom!

STEPHANO: O brave monster! Lead the way. *Exeunt.*

Act III

Scene 1

In front of PROSPERO*'s cell.*

Enter FERDINAND, *bearing a log.*

FERDINAND:

There be some sports are painful, and their labor
Delight in them sets off;[199] some kinds of baseness
Are nobly undergone, and most poor matters
Point to rich ends. This my mean task
Would be as heavy to me as odious, but
The mistress which I serve quickens what's dead
And makes my labors pleasures. O, she is
Ten times more gentle than her father's crabbed;
And he's composed of harshness. I must remove
Some thousands of these logs and pile them up, 10
Upon a sore injunction. My sweet mistress
Weeps when she sees me work, and says such baseness
Had never like executor. I forget;[200]
But these sweet thoughts do even refresh my labors,
Most busiest when I do it.[201]

Enter MIRANDA; *and* PROSPERO *(behind, unseen).*

---

[197] Perhaps a misprint for "seamels" or "seamews," a kind of sea bird.

[198] Trenchers, wooden plates.

[199] Cancels.

[200] My task.

[201] My thoughts are busiest when I am (the Folio's *busie lest* has been variously emended; *it* may refer to "task," line 4, the understood object in line 13).

MIRANDA:

Alas, now pray you,
Work not so hard! I would the lightning had
Burnt up those logs that you are enjoined to pile!
Pray set it down and rest you. When this burns,
'Twill weep for having wearied you. My father
Is hard at study; pray now rest yourself; 20
He's safe for these three hours.

FERDINAND:

O most dear mistress,
The sun will set before I shall discharge
What I must strive to do.

MIRANDA:

If you'll sit down,
I'll bear your logs the while. Pray give me that;
I'll carry it to the pile.

FERDINAND:

No, precious creature,
I had rather crack my sinews, break my back,
Than you should such dishonor undergo
While I sit lazy by.

MIRANDA:

It would become me
As well as it does you; and I should do it
With much more ease; for my good will is to it, 30
And yours it is against.

PROSPERO [*Aside*]:

Poor worm, thou art infected!
This visitation[202] shows it.

MIRANDA:

You look wearily.

FERDINAND:

No, noble mistress, 'tis fresh morning with me
When you are by at night. I do beseech you,
Chiefly that I might set it in my prayers,
What is your name?

MIRANDA:

Miranda. O my father,
I have broke your hest to say so!

FERDINAND:

Admired Miranda![203]
Indeed the top of admiration, worth
What's dearest to the world! Full many a lady
I have eyed with best regard, and many a time 40
Th' harmony of their tongues hath into bondage
Brought my too diligent ear. For several virtues
Have I liked several women; never any
With so full soul but some defect in her

[202] (1) Visit; (2) attack of plague (referring to metaphor of "infected").
[203] "Admired" means "to be wondered at"; the Latin "Miranda" means "wonderful."

Did quarrel with the noblest grace she owed,
And put it to the foil.[204] But you, O you,
So perfect and so peerless, are created
Of every creature's best.

MIRANDA:

I do not know
One of my sex; no woman's face remember,
Save, from my glass, mine own. Nor have I seen 50
More that I may call men than you, good friend,
And my dear father. How features are abroad
I am skilless of; but, by my modesty
(The jewel in my dower), I would not wish
Any companion in the world but you;
Nor can imagination form a shape,
Besides yourself, to like of. But I prattle
Something too wildly, and my father's precepts
I therein do forget.

FERDINAND:

I am, in my condition,
A prince, Miranda; I do think, a king
(I would not so), and would no more endure
This wooden slavery than to suffer
The fleshfly blow my mouth. Hear my soul speak!
The very instant that I saw you, did
My heart fly to your service; there resides,
To make me slave to it; and for your sake
Am I this patient log-man.

MIRANDA:

Do you love me?

FERDINAND:

O heaven, O earth, bear witness to this sound,
And crown what I profess with kind event
If I speak true! If hollowly, invert
What best is boded me[205] to mischief! I,
Beyond all limit of what else i' th' world,
Do love, prize, honor you.

MIRANDA:

I am a fool
To weep at what I am glad of.

PROSPERO:

[*Aside*] Fair encounter
Of two most rare affections! Heavens rain grace
On that which breeds between 'em!

FERDINAND:

Wherefore weep you?

MIRANDA:

At mine unworthiness, that dare not offer
What I desire to give, and much less take

---

[204] Defeated it.

[205] Whatever good fortune fate has in store for me.

What I shall die to want. But this is trifling;[206]
And all the more it seeks to hide itself, 80
The bigger bulk it shows. Hence, bashful cunning,
And prompt me, plain and holy innocence!
I am your wife, if you will marry me;
If not, I'll die your maid. To be your fellow
You may deny me; but I'll be your servant,
Whether you will or no.

FERDINAND:
My mistress, dearest,
And I thus humble ever.

MIRANDA:
My husband then?

FERDINAND:
Ay, with a heart as willing
As bondage e'er of freedom.[207] Here's my hand.

MIRANDA:
And mine, with my heart in't; and now farewell 90
Till half an hour hence.

FERDINAND:
A thousand thousand!

Exeunt FERDINAND *and* MIRANDA *in different directions.*

PROSPERO:
So glad of this as they I cannot be,
Who are surprised withal; but my rejoicing
At nothing can be more. I'll to my book;
For yet ere suppertime must I perform
Much business appertaining. *Exit.*

Scene 2

Another part of the island.

Enter CALIBAN, STEPHANO, *and* TRINCULO.

STEPHANO: Tell not me! When the butt is out, we will drink water; not a drop before. Therefore bear up and board 'em![208] Servant monster, drink to me.

TRINCULO: Servant monster? The folly of this island! They say there's but five upon this isle; we are three of them. If th' other two be brained like us, the state totters.

STEPHANO: Drink, servant monster, when I bid thee; thy eyes are almost set in thy head.

TRINCULO: Where should they be set else? He were a brave monster indeed if they were set in his tail. 10

STEPHANO: My man-monster hath drowned his tongue in sack. For my part, the sea cannot drown me. I swam, ere I could recover the shore, five-and-thirty leagues off and on, by this light. Thou shalt be my lieutenant, monster, or my standard.[209]

[206] To speak in riddles like this.
[207] To win freedom.
[208] Drink up.
[209] Standard-bearer, ensign (pun since Caliban is so drunk he cannot stand).

TRINCULO: Your lieutenant, if you list;[210] he's no standard.
STEPHANO: We'll not run, Monsieur Monster.
TRINCULO: Nor go[211] neither; but you'll lie like dogs, and yet say nothing neither. 20
STEPHANO: Mooncalf, speak once in thy life, if thou beest a good mooncalf.
CALIBAN: How does thy honor? Let me lick thy shoe. I'll not serve him; he is not valiant.
TRINCULO: Thou liest, most ignorant monster; I am in case[212] to justle[213] a constable. Why, thou deboshed[214] fish thou, was there ever man a coward that hath drunk so much sack as I today? Wilt thou tell a monstrous lie, being but half a fish and half a monster? 30
CALIBAN: Lo, how he mocks me! Wilt thou let him, my lord?
TRINCULO: "Lord" quoth he? That a monster should be such a natural![215]
CALIBAN: Lo, lo, again! Bite him to death, I prithee.
STEPHANO: Trinculo, keep a good tongue in your head. If you prove a mutineer—the next tree![216] The poor monster's my subject, and he shall not suffer indignity. 40
CALIBAN: I thank my noble lord. Wilt thou be pleased to hearken once again to the suit I made to thee?
STEPHANO: Marry,[217] will I. Kneel and repeat it; I will stand, and so shall Trinculo.

Enter ARIEL, *invisible.*

CALIBAN:
As I told thee before, I am subject to a tyrant,
A sorcerer, that by his cunning hath
Cheated me of the island.
ARIEL:
Thou liest.
CALIBAN:
Thou liest, thou jesting monkey thou!
I would my valiant master would destroy thee.
I do not lie. 50
STEPHANO: Trinculo, if you trouble him any more in's tale, by this hand, I will supplant some of your teeth.
TRINCULO: Why, I said nothing.
STEPHANO: Mum then, and no more. Proceed.
CALIBAN:
I say by sorcery he got this isle;
From me he got it. If thy greatness will
Revenge it on him—for I know thou dar'st,
But this thing[218] dare not—
STEPHANO:
That's most certain. 60
CALIBAN:
Thou shalt be lord of it, and I'll serve thee.
STEPHANO:
How now shall this be compassed?
Canst thou bring me to the party?

[210] If it please you (with pun on "list" as pertaining to a ship that leans over to one side).
[211] Walk. [212] Fit condition. [213] Jostle. [214] Debauched.
[215] Idiot.
[216] You will be hanged.
[217] An expletive, from "By the Virgin Mary."
[218] Trinculo.

CALIBAN:
Yea, yea, my lord! I'll yield him thee asleep,
Where thou mayst knock a nail into his head.
ARIEL:
Thou liest; thou canst not.
CALIBAN:
What a pied[219] ninny's this! Thou scurvy patch![220]
I do beseech thy greatness, give him blows
And take his bottle from him. When that's gone,
He shall drink naught but brine, for I'll not show him 70
Where the quick freshes[221] are.
STEPHANO: Trinculo, run into no further danger! Interrupt the monster one word further and, by this hand, I'll turn my mercy out o' doors and make a stockfish[222] of thee.
TRINCULO: Why, what did I? I did nothing. I'll go farther off.
STEPHANO: Didst thou not say he lied?
ARIEL: Thou liest.
STEPHANO: Do I so? Take thou that! [*Strikes* TRINCULO.] As you like this, give me the lie another time. 80
TRINCULO: I did not give the lie. Out o' your wits, and hearing too? A pox o' your bottle! This can sack and drinking do. A murrain[223] on your monster, and the devil take your fingers!
CALIBAN: Ha, ha, ha!
STEPHANO: Now forward with your tale. [*To* TRINCULO] Prithee, stand further off.
CALIBAN:
Beat him enough. After a little time
I'll beat him too.
STEPHANO:
Stand farther. Come, proceed. 90
CALIBAN:
Why, as I told thee, 'tis a custom with him
I' th' afternoon to sleep. There thou mayst brain him,
Having first seized his books, or with a log
Batter his skull, or paunch[224] him with a stake,
Or cut his wezand[225] with thy knife. Remember
First to possess his books; for without them
He's but a sot, as I am, nor hath not
One spirit to command. They all do hate him
As rootedly as I. Burn but his books.
He has brave utensils[226] (for so he calls them) 100
Which, when he has a house, he'll deck withal.
And that most deeply to consider is
The beauty of his daughter. He himself
Calls her a nonpareil. I never saw a woman
But only Sycorax my dam and she;

---

[219]Referring to Trinculo's parti-colored jester's costume.
[220]Clown.
[221]Living springs of fresh water.
[222]Dried cod, softened by beating.
[223]Plague (that infects cattle).
[224]Stab in the belly.
[225]Windpipe.
[226]Fine furnishings.

But she as far surpasseth Sycorax
As great'st does least.

STEPHANO:
Is it so brave a lass?

CALIBAN:
Ay, lord. She will become thy bed, I warrant,
And bring thee forth brave brood.

STEPHANO: Monster, I will kill this man. His daughter and I will be King and Queen—save our Graces!—and Trinculo and thyself shall be viceroys. Dost thou like the plot, Trinculo? 110

TRINCULO: Excellent.

STEPHANO: Give me thy hand. I am sorry I beat thee; but while thou liv'st, keep a good tongue in thy head.

CALIBAN:
Within this half hour will he be asleep.
Wilt thou destroy him then?

STEPHANO:
Ay, on mine honor.

ARIEL:
This will I tell my master. 120

CALIBAN:
Thou mak'st me merry; I am full of pleasure.
Let us be jocund. Will you troll the catch[227]
You taught me but whilere?[228]

STEPHANO: At thy request, monster, I will do reason, any reason.[229] Come on, Trinculo, let us sing. *Sings.*

Flout 'em and scout[230] 'em
And scout 'em and flout 'em!
Thought is free.

CALIBAN: That's not the tune.

ARIEL *plays the tune on a tabor*[231] *and pipe.*

STEPHANO: What is this same? 130

TRINCULO: This is the tune of our catch, played by the picture of Nobody.[232]

STEPHANO: If thou beest a man, show thyself in thy likeness. If thou beest a devil, take't as thou list.

TRINCULO: O, forgive me my sins!

STEPHANO: He that dies pays all debts. I defy thee. Mercy upon us!

CALIBAN: Art thou afeard?

STEPHANO: No, monster, not I.

CALIBAN:
Be not afeard; the isle is full of noises, 140
Sounds and sweet airs that give delight and hurt not.

---

[227] Sing the round.
[228] Just now.
[229] Anything within reason.
[230] Jeer at.
[231] Small drum worn at the side.
[232] Alluding to the picture of No-body—a man all head, legs, and arms, but without trunk—on the title page of the anonymous comedy *No-body and Some-body.*

Sometimes a thousand twangling instruments
Will hum about mine ears; and sometime voices
That, if I then had waked after long sleep,
Will make me sleep again; and then, in dreaming,
The clouds methought would open and show riches
Ready to drop upon me, that, when I waked,
I cried to dream again.

STEPHANO: This will prove a brave kingdom to me, where I shall have my music for nothing. 150

CALIBAN: When Prospero is destroyed.

STEPHANO: That shall be by and by; I remember the story.

TRINCULO: The sound is going away; let's follow it, and after do our work.

STEPHANO: Lead, monster; we'll follow. I would I could see this taborer; he lays it on.

TRINCULO [*To* CALIBAN]: Wilt come?[233] I'll follow Stephano. *Exeunt.*

Scene 3

Another part of the island.

Enter ALONSO, SEBASTIAN, ANTONIO, GONZALO, ADRIAN, FRANCISCO, *etc.*

GONZALO:
By'r Lakin,[234] I can go no further, sir;
My old bones ache. Here's a maze trod indeed
Through forthrights and meanders.[235] By your patience,
I needs must rest me.

ALONSO:
Old lord, I cannot blame thee,
Who am myself attached[236] with weariness
To th' dulling of my spirits. Sit down and rest.
Even here I will put off my hope, and keep it
No longer for my flatterer. He is drowned
Whom thus we stray to find; and the sea mocks
Our frustrate search on land. Well, let him go. 10

ANTONIO:
[*Aside to* SEBASTIAN] I am right glad that he's so out of hope.
Do not for one repulse forgo the purpose
That you resolved t' effect.

SEBASTIAN:
[*Aside to* ANTONIO] The next advantage
Will we take throughly.

ANTONIO:
[*Aside to* SEBASTIAN] Let it be tonight;
For, now they are oppressed with travel, they
Will not nor cannot use such vigilance
As when they are fresh.

---

[233] Caliban lingers because the other two are being distracted from his purpose by the music.
[234] By our Lady.
[235] Straight and winding paths.
[236] Seized.

SEBASTIAN:
[*Aside to* ANTONIO] I say tonight. No more.
Solemn and strange music; and PROSPERO *on the top*[237] *(invisible).*
Enter several strange Shapes, bringing in a banquet; and dance about it with gentle actions of salutations; and, inviting the King etc. to eat, they depart.

ALONSO:
What harmony is this? My good friends, hark!

GONZALO:
Marvelous sweet music!

ALONSO:
Give us kind keepers,[238] heavens! What were these? 20

SEBASTIAN:
A living drollery.[239] Now I will believe
That there are unicorns; that in Arabia
There is one tree, the phoenix' throne; one phoenix
At this hour reigning there.

ANTONIO:
I'll believe both;
And what does else want credit, come to me,
And I'll be sworn 'tis true. Travelers ne'er did lie,
Though fools at home condemn 'em.

GONZALO:
If in Naples
I should report this now, would they believe me
If I should say I saw such islanders?
(For certes these are people of the island) 30
Who, though they are of monstrous shape, yet note,
Their manners are more gentle, kind, than of
Our human generation you shall find
Many—nay, almost any.

PROSPERO:
[*Aside*] Honest lord,
Thou hast said well; for some of you there present
Are worse than devils.

ALONSO:
I cannot too much muse
Such shapes, such gesture, and such sound, expressing
(Although they want the use of tongue) a kind
Of excellent dumb discourse.

PROSPERO:
[*Aside*] Praise in departing.[240]

FRANCISCO:
They vanished strangely.

SEBASTIAN:
No matter, since 40
They have left their viands behind; for we have stomachs.
Will't please you taste of what is here?

---

[237] Upper stage (or perhaps a playing area above it).
[238] Guardian angels.
[239] Puppet show.
[240] Save your praise for the end.

ALONSO:

Not I.

GONZALO:

Faith, sir, you need not fear. When we were boys,
Who would believe that there were mountaineers
Dewlapped[241] like bulls, whose throats had hanging at 'em
Wallets of flesh? Or that there were such men
Whose heads stood in their breasts? Which now we find
Each putter-out of five for one[242] will bring us
Good warrant of.

ALONSO:

I will stand to, and feed;
Although my last, no matter, since I feel 50
The best is past. Brother, my lord the Duke,
Stand to, and do as we.

Thunder and lightning. Enter ARIEL, *like a harpy; claps his wings upon the table; and with a quaint device the banquet vanishes.*

ARIEL:

You are three men of sin, whom destiny—
That hath to instrument this lower world
And what is in't—the never-surfeited sea
Hath caused to belch up you and on this island,
Where man doth not inhabit, you 'mongst men
Being most unfit to live. I have made you mad;
And even with suchlike valor[243] men hang and drown
Their proper selves.

[ALONSO, SEBASTIAN, *etc. draw their swords.*]

You fools! I and my fellows 60
Are ministers of Fate. The elements,
Of whom your swords are tempered, may as well
Wound the loud winds, or with bemocked-at stabs
Kill the still-closing[244] waters, as diminish
One dowle[245] that's in my plume. My fellow ministers
Are like invulnerable. If you could hurt,[246]
Your swords are now too massy for your strengths
And will not be uplifted. But remember
(For that's my business to you) that you three
From Milan did supplant good Prospero; 70
Exposed unto the sea, which hath requit it,[247]
Him and his innocent child; for which foul deed
The pow'rs, delaying, not forgetting, have
Incensed the seas and shores, yea, all the creatures,
Against your peace. Thee of thy son, Alonso,
They have bereft; and do pronounce by me
Ling'ring perdition (worse than any death

[241] With skin hanging from the neck (like mountaineers with goiter).
[242] Traveler who insures himself by depositing a sum of money to be repaid fivefold if he returns safely.
[243] The courage that comes of madness.
[244] Ever closing again (as soon as wounded).
[245] Bit of down.
[246] Even if you could hurt us.
[247] Avenged that crime.

Can be at once) shall step by step attend
You and your ways; whose wraths to guard you from,
Which here, in this most desolate isle, else falls 80
Upon your heads, is nothing but heart's sorrow[248]
And a clear life ensuing.

He vanishes in thunder; then, to soft music, enter the Shapes again, and dance with mocks and mows,[249] and carrying out the table.

PROSPERO:
Bravely the figure of this harpy hast thou
Performed, my Ariel; a grace it had, devouring.[250]
Of my instruction hast thou nothing bated
In what thou hadst to say. So, with good life[251]
And observation strange,[252] my meaner ministers[253]
Their several kinds have done.[254] My high charms work,
And these, mine enemies, are all knit up
In their distractions. They now are in my pow'r; 90
And in these fits I leave them, while I visit
Young Ferdinand, whom they suppose is drowned,
And his and mine loved darling. [*Exit above.*]

GONZALO:
I' th' name of something holy, sir, why stand you
In this strange stare?

ALONSO:
O, it is monstrous, monstrous!
Methought the billows spoke and told me of it;
The winds did sing it to me; and the thunder,
That deep and dreadful organ pipe, pronounced
The name of Prosper; it did bass my trespass.[255]
Therefore my son i' th' ooze is bedded; and 100
I'll seek him deeper than e'er plummet sounded
And with him there lie mudded. *Exit.*

SEBASTIAN:
But one fiend at a time,
I'll fight their legions o'er![256]

ANTONIO:
I'll be thy second.
Exeunt [SEBASTIAN *and* ANTONIO].

GONZALO:
All three of them are desperate; their great guilt,
Like poison given to work a great time after,
Now 'gins to bite the spirits. I do beseech you,
That are of suppler joints, follow them swiftly

---

[248] Only repentance (will protect you from the wrath of these powers).
[249] Mocking gestures and grimaces.
[250] In making the banquet disappear.
[251] Good lifelike acting.
[252] Remarkable attention to my wishes.
[253] Inferior to Ariel.
[254] Have acted the parts their natures suited them for.
[255] Made me understand my trespass by turning it into music for which the thunder provided the bass part.
[256] One after another to the last.

And hinder them from what this ecstasy[257]
May now provoke them to.

ADRIAN:

Follow, I pray you.

Exeunt omnes.

Act IV

Scene 1

In front of PROSPERO*'s cell.*

Enter PROSPERO, FERDINAND, *and* MIRANDA.

PROSPERO:

If I have too austerely punished you,
Your compensation makes amends; for I
Have given you here a third of mine own life,
Or that for which I live; who once again
I tender to thy hand. All thy vexations
Were but my trials of thy love, and thou
Hast strangely[258] stood the test. Here, afore heaven,
I ratify this my rich gift. O Ferdinand,
Do not smile at me that I boast her off,[259]
For thou shalt find she will outstrip all praise 10
And make it halt[260] behind her.

FERDINAND:

I do believe it
Against an oracle.[261]

PROSPERO:

Then, as my gift, and thine own acquisition
Worthily purchased, take my daughter. But
If thou dost break her virgin-knot before
All sanctimonious ceremonies may
With full and holy rite be minist'red,
No sweet aspersion[262] shall the heavens let fall
To make this contract grow; but barren hate,
Sour-eyed disdain, and discord shall bestrew 20
The union of your bed with weeds so loathly
That you shall hate it both. Therefore take heed,
As Hymen's lamps shall light you.[263]

FERDINAND:

As I hope
For quiet days, fair issue, and long life,
With such love as 'tis now, the murkiest den,
The most opportune place, the strong'st suggestion

---

[257] Madness. [258] Wonderfully.
[259] Includes perhaps the idea of showing her off.
[260] Limp.
[261] Though an oracle should declare otherwise.
[262] Blessing (like rain on crops).
[263] As earnestly as you pray that the torch of the god of marriage shall burn without smoke (a good omen for wedded happiness).

Our worser genius can,[264] shall never melt
Mine honor into lust, to take away
The edge[265] of that day's celebration
When I shall think or Phoebus' steeds are foundered[266] 30
Or Night kept chained below.[267]

PROSPERO:

Fairly spoke.
Sit then and talk with her; she is thine own.
What, Ariel! My industrious servant, Ariel!

Enter ARIEL.

ARIEL:

What would my potent master? Here I am.

PROSPERO:

Thou and thy meaner fellows your last service
Did worthily perform; and I must use you
In such another trick. Go bring the rabble,[268]
O'er whom I give thee pow'r, here to this place.
Incite them to quick motion; for I must
Bestow upon the eyes of this young couple 40
Some vanity of[269] mine art. It is my promise,
And they expect it from me.

ARIEL:

Presently?

PROSPERO:

Ay, with a twink.

ARIEL:

Before you can say "Come" and "Go,"
And breathe twice and cry, "So, so,"
Each one, tripping on his toe,
Will be here with mop and mow.
Do you love me, master? No?

PROSPERO:

Dearly, my delicate Ariel. Do not approach
Till thou dost hear me call.

ARIEL:

Well; I conceive.[270] *Exit.* 50

PROSPERO:

Look thou be true.[271] Do not give dalliance
Too much the rein; the strongest oaths are straw
To th' fire i' th' blood. Be more abstemious,
Or else good night your vow!

FERDINAND:

I warrant you, sir.
The white cold virgin snow upon my heart[272]
Abates the ardor of my liver.[273]

---

[264]Our evil spirit can offer.
[265]Keen enjoyment. [266]Lamed.
[267]That either day will never end or night will never come.
[268]"Thy meaner fellows."
[269]Illusion conjured up by. [270]Understand.
[271]Prospero appears to have caught the lovers in an embrace.
[272]Her pure white breast on mine (?).
[273]Supposed seat of sexual passion.

PROSPERO:

Well.

Now come, my Ariel; bring a corollary[274]
Rather than want a spirit. Appear, and pertly!
No tongue! All eyes! Be silent. *Soft music.*

Enter IRIS.[275]

IRIS:

Ceres, most bounteous lady, thy rich leas 60
Of wheat, rye, barley, fetches,[276] oats, and peas;
Thy turfy mountains, where live nibbling sheep,
And flat meads thatched with stover,[277] them to keep;
Thy banks with pionèd and twillèd brims,[278]
Which spongy April at thy hest betrims
To make cold nymphs chaste crowns; and thy broom groves,
Whose shadow the dismissèd bachelor loves,
Being lasslorn; thy pole-clipt vineyard;[279]
And thy sea-marge, sterile and rocky-hard,
Where thou thyself dost air[280]—the queen o' th' sky,[281] 70
Whose wat'ry arch and messenger am I,
Bids thee leave these, and with her sovereign grace,

JUNO *descends.*[282]

Here on this grass plot, in this very place,
To come and sport; her peacocks fly amain.[283]
Approach, rich Ceres, her to entertain.

Enter CERES.

CERES:

Hail, many-colored messenger, that ne'er
Dost disobey the wife of Jupiter,
Who, with thy saffron wings, upon my flow'rs
Diffusest honey drops, refreshing show'rs,
And with each end of thy blue bow dost crown 80
My bosky[284] acres and my unshrubbed down,
Rich scarf to my proud earth. Why hath thy queen
Summoned me hither to this short-grassed green?

IRIS:

A contract of true love to celebrate
And some donation freely to estate[285]
On the blessed lovers.

---

[274]Surplus (of spirits).

[275]Goddess of the rainbow and Juno's messenger.

[276]Vetch (a kind of forage).

[277]Meadows covered with a kind of grass used for winter fodder.

[278]Obscure; may refer to the trenched and ridged edges of banks that have been repaired after the erosions of winter.

[279]Vineyard whose vines grow neatly around (embrace) poles (though possibly the word is "poll-clipped," i.e, pruned).

[280]Take the air.

[281]Juno.

[282]This direction seems to come too soon, but the machine may have lowered her very slowly.

[283]Swiftly (peacocks, sacred to Juno, drew her chariot).

[284]Shrubbed.

[285]Bestow.

CERES:

Tell me, heavenly bow,
If Venus or her son, as thou dost know,
Do now attend the Queen? Since they did plot
The means that dusky Dis my daughter got,[286]
Her and her blind boy's scandaled company 90
I have forsworn.

IRIS:

Of her society
Be not afraid; I met her Deity
Cutting the clouds towards Paphos,[287] and her son
Dove-drawn with her. Here thought they to have done
Some wanton charm upon this man and maid,
Whose vows are, that no bed-right shall be paid
Till Hymen's torch be lighted. But in vain;
Mars's hot minion is returned again;[288]
Her waspish-headed son[289] has broke his arrows,
Swears he will shoot no more, but play with sparrows 100
And be a boy right out.[290]

[JUNO *alights.*]

CERES:

Highest queen of state,
Great Juno, comes; I know her by her gait.

JUNO:

How does my bounteous sister? Go with me
To bless this twain, that they may prosperous be
And honored in their issue.

They sing.

JUNO:

Honor, riches, marriage blessing,
Long continuance, and increasing,
Hourly joys be still upon you!
Juno sings her blessings on you.

[CERES:]

Earth's increase, foison plenty, 110
Barns and garners never empty,
Vines with clust'ring bunches growing,
Plants with goodly burden bowing;
Spring come to you at the farthest
In the very end of harvest.[291]
Scarcity and want shall shun you,
Ceres' blessing so is on you.

---

[286] Alluding to the abduction of Proserpine by Pluto (Dis), god of the underworld.
[287] In Cyprus, center of Venus' cult.
[288] Mars's lustful mistress (Venus) is on her way back to Paphos.
[289] Cupid is irritable and stings with his arrows.
[290] An ordinary boy.
[291] May there be no winter in your lives.

FERDINAND:
This is a most majestic vision, and
Harmonious charmingly. May I be bold
To think these spirits?

PROSPERO:
Spirits, which by mine art 120
I have from their confines called to enact
My present fancies.

FERDINAND:
Let me live here ever!
So rare a wond'red[292] father and a wise
Makes this place Paradise.

JUNO and CERES whisper, and send IRIS on employment.

PROSPERO:
Sweet now, silence!
Juno and Ceres whisper seriously.
There's something else to do. Hush and be mute,
Or else our spell is marred.

IRIS:
You nymphs, called Naiades, of the windring[293] brooks,
With your sedged crowns and ever-harmless looks,
Leave your crisp[294] channels, and on this green land 130
Answer your summons; Juno does command.
Come, temperate nymphs, and help to celebrate
A contract of true love; be not too late.

Enter certain NYMPHS.

You sunburned sicklemen, of August weary,
Come hither from the furrow and be merry.
Make holiday; your rye-straw hats put on,
And these fresh nymphs encounter everyone
In country footing.[295]

Enter certain REAPERS, properly habited. They join with the NYMPHS in a graceful dance; towards the end whereof PROSPERO starts suddenly and speaks;[296] after which, to a strange, hollow, and confused noise, they heavily[297] vanish.

PROSPERO:
[*Aside*] I had forgot that foul conspiracy
Of the beast Caliban and his confederates 140
Against my life. The minute of their plot
Is almost come. [*To the* SPIRITS] Well done!
Avoid![298] No more!

FERDINAND:
This is strange. Your father's in some passion
That works him strongly.

MIRANDA:
Never till this day
Saw I him touched with anger so distempered.

---

[292]Possessed of wonders; i.e., both wonderful and wonder-working, and therefore to be wondered at.
[293]Winding and wandering (?).
[294]Rippling. [295]Dance.
[296]Breaking the spell, which depends on silence.
[297]Reluctantly. [298]Begone.

PROSPERO:
You do look, my son, in a movèd sort,[299]
As if you were dismayed; be cheerful, sir.
Our revels now are ended. These our actors,
As I foretold you, were all spirits and
Are melted into air, into thin air; 150
And, like the baseless fabric of this vision,
The cloud-capped towers, the gorgeous palaces,
The solemn temples, the great globe itself,
Yea, all which it inherit, shall dissolve,
And, like this insubstantial pageant faded,
Leave not a rack[300] behind. We are such stuff
As dreams are made on, and our little life
Is rounded with a sleep. Sir, I am vexed.
Bear with my weakness; my old brain is troubled.
Be not disturbed with my infirmity. 160
If you be pleased, retire into my cell
And there repose. A turn or two I'll walk
To still my beating mind.

FERDINAND, MIRANDA:
We wish your peace.
Exit [FERDINAND *with* MIRANDA].

PROSPERO:
Come with a thought! I thank thee, Ariel.[301] Come.
Enter ARIEL.

ARIEL:
Thy thoughts I cleave to. What's thy pleasure?

PROSPERO:
Spirit,
We must prepare to meet with Caliban.

ARIEL:
Ay, my commander. When I presented[302] Ceres,
I thought to have told thee of it, but I feared
Lest I might anger thee.

PROSPERO:
Say again, where didst thou leave these varlets?[303] 170

ARIEL:
I told you, sir, they were red-hot with drinking;
So full of valor that they smote the air
For breathing in their faces, beat the ground
For kissing of their feet; yet always bending
Towards their project. Then I beat my tabor;
At which like unbacked[304] colts they pricked their ears,
Advanced[305] their eyelids, lifted up their noses
As they smelt music. So I charmed their ears
That calflike they my lowing followed through

[299] Troubled state.
[300] Wisp of cloud.
[301] For the masque (?).
[302] Acted the part of (?); introduced (?).
[303] Ruffians. [304] Unbroken. [305] Lifted up.

Toothed briers, sharp furzes, pricking goss,[306] and thorns, 180
Which ent'red their frail shins. At last I left them
I' th' filthy mantled[307] pool beyond your cell,
There dancing up to th' chins, that the foul lake
O'erstunk their feet.

PROSPERO:
This was well done, my bird.
Thy shape invisible retain thou still.
The trumpery[308] in my house, go bring it hither
For stale[309] to catch these thieves.

ARIEL:
I go, I go. *Exit.*

PROSPERO:
A devil, a born devil, on whose nature
Nurture can never stick; on whom my pains,
Humanely taken, all, all lost, quite lost! 190
And as with age his body uglier grows,
So his mind cankers. I will plague them all,
Even to roaring. *Enter* ARIEL, *loaden with glistering apparel, etc.*
Come, hang them on this line.[310]

[PROSPERO *and* ARIEL *remain, invisible.*] *Enter* CALIBAN, STEPHANO, *and* TRINCULO, *all wet.*

CALIBAN:
Pray you tread softly, that the blind mole may not
Hear a foot fall. We now are near his cell.

STEPHANO: Monster, your fairy, which you say is a harmless fairy, has done little better than played the Jack[311] with us.

TRINCULO: Monster, I do smell all horse piss, at which my nose is in great indignation. 200

STEPHANO: So is mine. Do you hear, monster? If I should take a displeasure against you, look you—

TRINCULO: Thou wert but a lost monster.

CALIBAN:
Good my lord, give me thy favor still.
Be patient, for the prize I'll bring thee to
Shall hoodwink[312] this mischance. Therefore speak softly.
All's hushed as midnight yet.

TRINCULO: Ay, but to lose our bottles in the pool—

STEPHANO: There is not only disgrace and dishonor in that, monster, but an infinite loss. 210

TRINCULO: That's more to me than my wetting. Yet this is your harmless fairy, monster.

STEPHANO: I will fetch off my bottle, though I be o'er ears[313] for my labor.

306 Gorse.
307 Covered with filthy scum.
308 The "glistering apparel" mentioned in the next stage direction.
309 Decoy.
310 Lime tree (linden).
311 (1) Knave; (2) jack-o'-lantern, will-o'-the-wisp.
312 Put out of sight.
313 Over my ears in water.

CALIBAN:
Prithee, my king, be quiet. Seest thou here?
This is the mouth o' th' cell. No noise, and enter.
Do that good mischief which may make this island
Thine own forever, and I, thy Caliban,
For aye thy footlicker.

STEPHANO: Give me thy hand. I do begin to have bloody thoughts. 220

TRINCULO: O King Stephano! O peer![314] O worthy Stephano, look what a wardrobe here is for thee!

CALIBAN: Let it alone, thou fool! It is but trash.

TRINCULO: O, ho, monster! We know what belongs to a frippery.[315] O King Stephano!

STEPHANO: Put off that gown, Trinculo! By this hand, I'll have that gown!

TRINCULO: Thy Grace shall have it.

CALIBAN:
The dropsy drown this fool! What do you mean 230
To dote thus on such luggage?[316] Let't alone,
And do the murder first. If he awake,
From toe to crown he'll fill our skins with pinches,
Make us strange stuff.

STEPHANO: Be you quiet, monster. Mistress line, is not this my jerkin?[317] [*Takes it down.*] Now is the jerkin under the line.[318] Now, jerkin, you are like to lose your hair and prove a bald jerkin.[319]

TRINCULO: Do, do! We steal by line and level,[320] and't like[321] your Grace. 240

STEPHANO: I thank thee for that jest. Here's a garment for't. Wit shall not go unrewarded while I am king of this country. "Steal by line and level" is an excellent pass of pate.[322] There's another garment for't.

TRINCULO: Monster, come put some lime[323] upon your fingers, and away with the rest.

CALIBAN:
I will have none on't. We shall lose our time
And all be turned to barnacles,[324] or to apes
With foreheads villainous low.

STEPHANO: Monster, lay-to your fingers; help to bear this away where my hogshead 250 of wine is, or I'll turn you out of my kingdom. Go to, carry this.

TRINCULO: And this.

STEPHANO: Ay, and this.

A noise of hunters heard. Enter divers SPIRITS *in shape of dogs and hounds, hunting them about;* PROSPERO *and* ARIEL *setting them on.*

PROSPERO: Hey, Mountain, hey!

ARIEL: Silver! There it goes, Silver!

---

[314] Alluding to the song "King Stephen was and a worthy peer; / His breeches cost him but a crown," quoted in *Othello* II, iii.
[315] Old-clothes shop; i.e., we are good judges of castoff clothes.
[316] Useless encumbrances.
[317] Kind of jacket.
[318] Pun: (1) under the lime tree; (2) under the equator.
[319] Sailors proverbially lost their hair from fevers contracted while crossing the equator.
[320] By plumb line and carpenter's level; i.e., according to rule (with pun on "line").
[321] If it please.
[322] Sally of wit.
[323] Birdlime (which is sticky; thieves have sticky fingers).
[324] Kind of geese supposed to have developed from shellfish.

PROSPERO:
Fury, Fury! There, Tyrant, there! Hark, hark!
[CALIBAN, STEPHANO, *and* TRINCULO *are driven out.*]
Go, charge my goblins that they grind their joints
With dry convulsions,[325] shorten up their sinews
With agèd cramps, and more pinch-spotted make them 260
Than pard or cat o' mountain.[326]

ARIEL:
Hark, they roar!

PROSPERO: Let them be hunted soundly. At this hour
Lies at my mercy all mine enemies.
Shortly shall all my labors end, and thou
Shalt have the air at freedom. For a little,
Follow, and do me service. *Exeunt.*

ACT V

Scene 1

In front of PROSPERO*'s cell.*

Enter PROSPERO *in his magic robes, and* ARIEL.

PROSPERO:
Now does my project gather to a head.
My charms crack not, my spirits obey, and time
Goes upright with his carriage.[327] How's the day?

ARIEL:
On the sixth hour, at which time, my lord,
You said our work should cease.

PROSPERO:
I did say so
When first I raised the tempest. Say, my spirit,
How fares the King and 's followers?

ARIEL:
Confined together
In the same fashion as you gave in charge,
Just as you left them—all prisoners, sir,
In the line grove which weather-fends[328] your cell. 10
They cannot budge till your release. The King,
His brother, and yours abide all three distracted,
And the remainder mourning over them,
Brimful of sorrow and dismay; but chiefly
Him that you termed, sir, the good old Lord Gonzalo.
His tears runs down his beard like winter's drops
From eaves of reeds.[329] Your charm so strongly works 'em,

---

[325] Such as come when the joints are dry from old age.
[326] Leopard or catamount.
[327] Time does not stoop under his burden (because there is so little left to do).
[328] Protects from the weather.
[329] A thatched roof.

That if you now beheld them, your affections
Would become tender.

PROSPERO:

Dost thou think so, spirit?

ARIEL:

Mine would, sir, were I human.

PROSPERO:

And mine shall. 20
Hast thou, which art but air, a touch, a feeling
Of their afflictions, and shall not myself,
One of their kind, that relish all as sharply,
Passion as they, be kindlier moved than thou art?
Though with their high wrongs I am struck to th' quick,
Yet with my nobler reason 'gainst my fury
Do I take part. The rarer action is
In virtue than in vengeance. They being penitent,
The sole drift of my purpose doth extend
Not a frown further. Go, release them, Ariel. 30
My charms I'll break, their senses I'll restore,
And they shall be themselves.

ARIEL:

I'll fetch them, sir. *Exit.*

PROSPERO:

Ye elves of hills, brooks, standing lakes, and groves,
And ye that on the sands with printless foot
Do chase the ebbing Neptune, and do fly him[330]
When he comes back; you demi-puppets that
By moonshine do the green sour ringlets[331] make,
Whereof the ewe not bites; and you whose pastime
Is to make midnight mushrumps,[332] that rejoice
To hear the solemn curfew; by whose aid 40
(Weak masters[333] though ye be) I have bedimmed
The noontide sun, called forth the mutinous winds,
And 'twixt the green sea and the azured vault
Set roaring war; to the dread rattling thunder
Have I given fire and rifted Jove's stout oak
With his own bolt; the strong-based promontory
Have I made shake and by the spurs[334] plucked up
The pine and cedar; graves at my command
Have waked their sleepers, oped, and let 'em forth
By my so potent art. But this rough magic 50
I here abjure; and when I have required
Some heavenly music (which even now I do)
To work mine end upon their senses that
This airy charm is for, I'll break my staff,
Bury it certain fathoms in the earth,

---

[330]Fly with him.
[331]"Fairy rings," little circles of rank grass supposed to be formed by the dancing of fairies.
[332]Mushrooms.
[333]Masters of supernatural power.
[334]Roots.

And deeper than did ever plummet sound
I'll drown my book.

[*Solemn music.*]

Here enters ARIEL *before; then* ALONSO, *with a frantic gesture, attended by* GONZALO; SEBASTIAN *and* ANTONIO *in like manner, attended by* ADRIAN *and* FRANCISCO. *They all enter the circle which* PROSPERO *had made, and there stand charmed; which* PROSPERO *observing, speaks.*

A solemn air, and the best comforter
To an unsettled fancy, cure thy brains,
Now useless, boiled within thy skull! There stand, 60
For you are spell-stopped.
Holy Gonzalo, honorable man,
Mine eyes, ev'n sociable to the show of thine,
Fall fellowly drops.[335] The charm dissolves apace;
And as the morning steals upon the night,
Melting the darkness, so their rising senses
Begin to chase the ignorant fumes that mantle
Their clearer reason. O good Gonzalo,
My true preserver, and a loyal sir
To him thou follow'st, I will pay thy graces 70
Home[336] both in word and deed. Most cruelly
Didst thou, Alonso, use me and my daughter.
Thy brother was a furtherer in the act.
Thou art pinched for't now, Sebastian. Flesh and blood,
You, brother mine, that entertained ambition,
Expelled remorse and nature;[337] whom, with Sebastian
(Whose inward pinches therefore are most strong),
Would here have killed your king, I do forgive thee,
Unnatural though thou art. Their understanding
Begins to swell, and the approaching tide 80
Will shortly fill the reasonable shore,
That now lies foul and muddy. Not one of them
That yet looks on me or would know me. Ariel,
Fetch me the hat and rapier in my cell.
I will discase me,[338] and myself present
As I was sometime Milan. Quickly, spirit!
Thou shalt ere long be free.

[*Exit* ARIEL *and returns immediately.*]

ARIEL *sings and helps to attire him.*

Where the bee sucks, there suck I;
In a cowslip's bell I lie;
There I couch when owls do cry. 90
On the bat's back I do fly
After summer merrily.
Merrily, merrily shall I live now
Under the blossom that hangs on the bough.

---

[335] Associating themselves with the (tearful) appearance of your eyes, shed tears in sympathy.
[336] Repay thy favors thoroughly.
[337] Natural feeling.
[338] Disrobe.

PROSPERO:
Why, that's my dainty Ariel! I shall miss thee,
But yet thou shalt have freedom; so, so, so.
To the King's ship, invisible as thou art!
There shalt thou find the mariners asleep
Under the hatches. The master and the boatswain
Being awake, enforce them to this place, 100
And presently, I prithee.

ARIEL:
I drink the air before me, and return
Or ere your pulse twice beat. *Exit.*

GONZALO:
All torment, trouble, wonder, and amazement
Inhabits here. Some heavenly power guide us
Out of this fearful country!

PROSPERO:
Behold, sir King,
The wrongèd Duke of Milan, Prospero.
For more assurance that a living prince
Does now speak to thee, I embrace thy body,
And to thee and thy company I bid 110
A hearty welcome.

ALONSO:
Whe'r thou be'st he or no,
Or some enchanted trifle[339] to abuse me,
As late I have been, I not know. Thy pulse
Beats, as of flesh and blood; and, since I saw thee,
Th' affliction of my mind amends, with which,
I fear, a madness held me. This must crave[340]
(And if this be at all) a most strange story.
Thy dukedom I resign and do entreat
Thou pardon me my wrongs. But how should Prospero
Be living and be here?

PROSPERO:
First, noble friend, 120
Let me embrace thine age, whose honor cannot
Be measured or confined.

GONZALO:
Whether this be
Or be not, I'll not swear.

PROSPERO:
You do yet taste
Some subtleties[341] o' th' isle, that will not let you
Believe things certain. Welcome, my friends all.
[*Aside to* SEBASTIAN *and* ANTONIO] But you, my brace of lords, were I so minded,
I here could pluck his Highness' frown upon you,

---

[339] Apparition.
[340] Require (to account for it).
[341] Deceptions (referring to pastries made to look like something else, e.g., castles made out of sugar).

And justify[342] you traitors. At this time
I will tell no tales.

SEBASTIAN:

[*Aside*] The devil speaks in him.

PROSPERO:

No.

For you, most wicked sir, whom to call brother 130
Would even infect my mouth, I do forgive
Thy rankest fault—all of them; and require
My dukedom of thee, which perforce I know
Thou must restore.

ALONSO:

If thou beest Prospero,
Give us particulars of thy preservation;
How thou hast met us here, whom three hours since
Were wracked upon this shore; where I have lost
(How sharp the point of this remembrance is!)
My dear son Ferdinand.

PROSPERO:

I am woe for't, sir.

ALONSO:

Irreparable is the loss, and patience 140
Says it is past her cure.

PROSPERO:

I rather think
You have not sought her help, of whose soft grace
For the like loss I have her sovereign aid
And rest myself content.

ALONSO:

You the like loss?

PROSPERO:

As great to me, as late,[343] and supportable
To make the dear loss, have I means much weaker
Than you may call to comfort you; for I
Have lost my daughter.

ALONSO:

A daughter?
O heavens, that they were living both in Naples,
The King and Queen there! That they were, I wish 150
Myself were mudded in that oozy bed
Where my son lies. When did you lose your daughter?

PROSPERO:

In this last tempest. I perceive these lords
At this encounter do so much admire[344]
That they devour their reason, and scarce think
Their eyes do offices[345] of truth, their words
Are natural breath. But, howsoev'r you have
Been justled from your senses, know for certain
That I am Prospero, and that very duke

[342] Prove.
[343] As great to me as your loss, and as recent.
[344] Wonder. [345] Perform services.

Which was thrust forth of Milan, who most strangely 160
Upon this shore, where you were wracked, was landed
To be the lord on't. No more yet of this;
For 'tis a chronicle of day by day,
Not a relation for a breakfast, nor
Befitting this first meeting. Welcome, sir;
This cell's my court. Here have I few attendants,
And subjects none abroad.[346] Pray you look in.
My dukedom since you have given me again,
I will requite you with as good a thing,
At least bring forth a wonder to content ye 170
As much as me my dukedom.

Here PROSPERO *discovers*[347] FERDINAND *and* MIRANDA *playing at chess.*

MIRANDA:
Sweet lord, you play me false.

FERDINAND:
No, my dearest love,
I would not for the world.

MIRANDA:
Yes, for a score of kingdoms you should wrangle,
And I would call it fair play.[348]

ALONSO:
If this prove
A vision of the island, one dear son
Shall I twice lose.

SEBASTIAN:
A most high miracle!

FERDINAND:
Though the seas threaten, they are merciful.
I have cursed them without cause.
[*Kneels.*]

ALONSO:
Now all the blessings
Of a glad father compass thee about! 180
Arise, and say how thou cam'st here.

MIRANDA:
O, wonder!
How many goodly creatures are there here!
How beauteous mankind is! O brave new world
That has such people in't!

PROSPERO:
'Tis new to thee.

ALONSO:
What is this maid with whom thou wast at play?
Your eld'st acquaintance cannot be three hours.
Is she the goddess that hath severed us
And brought us thus together?

---

[346]On the island.

[347]Reveals (by opening a curtain at the back of the stage).

[348]If we were playing for stakes just short of the world, you would protest as now; but then, the issue being important, I would call it fair play so much do I love you (?).

FERDINAND:

Sir, she is mortal;
But by immortal providence she's mine.
I chose her when I could not ask my father 190
For his advice, nor thought I had one. She
Is daughter to this famous Duke of Milan,
Of whom so often I have heard renown
But never saw before; of whom I have
Received a second life; and second father
This lady makes him to me.

ALONSO:

I am hers.
But, O, how oddly will it sound that I
Must ask my child forgiveness!

PROSPERO:

There, sir, stop.
Let us not burden our remembrance with
A heaviness that's gone.

GONZALO:

I have inly wept, 200
Or should have spoke ere this. Look down, you gods,
And on this couple drop a blessèd crown!
For it is you that have chalked forth the way
Which brought us hither.

ALONSO:

I say amen, Gonzalo.

GONZALO:

Was Milan thrust from Milan that his issue
Should become kings of Naples? O, rejoice
Beyond a common joy, and set it down
With gold on lasting pillars. In one voyage
Did Claribel her husband find at Tunis,
And Ferdinand her brother found a wife 210
Where he himself was lost; Prospero his dukedom
In a poor isle; and all of us ourselves
When no man was his own.

ALONSO:

[*To* FERDINAND *and* MIRANDA] Give me your hands.
Let grief and sorrow still embrace his heart
That doth not wish you joy.

GONZALO:

Be it so! Amen!

Enter ARIEL, *with the* MASTER *and* BOATSWAIN *amazedly following.*

O, look, sir; look, sir! Here is more of us!
I prophesied if a gallows were on land,
This fellow could not drown. Now, blasphemy,
That swear'st grace o'erboard,[349] not an oath on shore?
Hast thou no mouth by land? What is the news? 220

BOATSWAIN:

The best news is that we have safely found
Our king and company; the next, our ship,

[349] That (at sea) swearest enough to cause grace to be withdrawn from the ship.

Which, but three glasses since, we gave out split,
Is tight and yare[350] and bravely rigged as when
We first put out to sea.

ARIEL:
[*Aside to* PROSPERO] Sir, all this service
Have I done since I went.

PROSPERO:
[*Aside to* ARIEL] My tricksy spirit!

ALONSO:
These are not natural events; they strengthen
From strange to stranger. Say, how came you hither?

BOATSWAIN:
If I did think, sir, I were well awake,
I'd strive to tell you. We were dead of sleep 230
And (how we know not) all clapped under hatches;
Where, but even now, with strange and several noises
Of roaring, shrieking, howling, jingling chains,
And moe diversity of sounds, all horrible,
We were awaked; straightway at liberty;
Where we, in all our trim, freshly beheld
Our royal, good, and gallant ship, our master
Cap'ring to eye[351] her. On a trice, so please you,
Even in a dream, were we divided from them
And were brought moping[352] hither.

ARIEL:
[*Aside to* PROSPERO] Was't well done? 240

PROSPERO:
[*Aside to* ARIEL] Bravely, my diligence. Thou shalt be free.

ALONSO:
This is as strange a maze as e'er men trod,
And there is in this business more than nature
Was ever conduct[353] of. Some oracle
Must rectify our knowledge.

PROSPERO:
Sir, my liege,
Do not infest your mind with beating on
The strangeness of this business. At picked leisure,
Which shall be shortly, single I'll resolve you
(Which to you shall seem probable) of every
These happened accidents;[354] till when, be cheerful 250
And think of each thing well. [*Aside to* ARIEL] Come hither, spirit.
Set Caliban and his companions free.
Untie the spell. [*Exit* ARIEL.] How fares my gracious sir?
There are yet missing of your company
Some few odd lads that you remember not.

Enter ARIEL, *driving in* CALIBAN, STEPHANO, *and* TRINCULO, *in their stolen apparel.*

---

[350] Shipshape.
[351] Dancing to see.
[352] In a daze.
[353] Conductor.
[354] I myself will solve the problems (and my story will make sense to you) concerning each and every incident that has happened.

STEPHANO: Every man shift for all the rest, and let no man take care for himself; for all is but fortune. *Coragio,*[355] bully-monster, *coragio!*

TRINCULO: If these be true spies which I wear in my head, here's a goodly sight. 260

CALIBAN:
O Setebos,[356] there be brave spirits indeed!
How fine my master is! I am afraid
He will chastise me.

SEBASTIAN:
Ha, ha!
What things are these, my Lord Antonio?
Will money buy 'em?

ANTONIO:
Very like. One of them
Is a plain fish and no doubt marketable.

PROSPERO:
Mark but the badges[357] of these men, my lords,
Then say if they be true. This misshapen knave,
His mother was a witch, and one so strong
That could control the moon, make flows and ebbs, 270
And deal in her command without her power.[358]
These three have robbed me, and this demi-devil
(For he's a bastard one) had plotted with them
To take my life. Two of these fellows you
Must know and own; this thing of darkness I
Acknowledge mine.

CALIBAN:
I shall be pinched to death.

ALONSO:
Is not this Stephano, my drunken butler?

SEBASTIAN:
He is drunk now. Where had he wine?

ALONSO:
And Trinculo is reeling ripe. Where should they
Find this grand liquor that hath gilded 'em? 280
How cam'st thou in this pickle?

TRINCULO: I have been in such a pickle, since I saw you last, that I fear me will never out of my bones. I shall not fear flyblowing.[359]

SEBASTIAN: Why, how now, Stephano?

STEPHANO: O, touch me not! I am not Stephano, but a cramp.

PROSPERO: You'd be king o' the isle, sirrah?

STEPHANO: I should have been a sore[360] one then.

ALONSO: This is a strange thing as e'er I looked on. 290

PROSPERO:
He is as disproportioned in his manners
As in his shape. Go, sirrah, to my cell;

---

[355] Courage (Italian).

[356] The god of Caliban's mother.

[357] Worn by servants to indicate to whose service they belong; in this case, the stolen clothes are badges of their rascality.

[358] Dabble in the moon's realm without the moon's legitimate authority.

[359] Pickling preserves meat from flies.

[360] (1) Tyrannical; (2) aching.

Take with you your companions. As you look
To have my pardon, trim it handsomely.

CALIBAN:
Ay, that I will; and I'll be wise hereafter,
And seek for grace. What a thrice-double ass
Was I to take this drunkard for a god
And worship this dull fool!

PROSPERO:
Go to! Away!

ALONSO:
Hence, and bestow your luggage where you found it.

SEBASTIAN:
Or stole it rather. 300

[*Exeunt* CALIBAN, STEPHANO, *and* TRINCULO.]

PROSPERO:
Sir, I invite your Highness and your train
To my poor cell, where you shall take your rest
For this one night; which, part of it, I'll waste
With such discourse as, I not doubt, shall make it
Go quick away—the story of my life,
And the particular accidents gone by
Since I came to this isle. And in the morn
I'll bring you to your ship, and so to Naples,
Where I have hope to see the nuptial
Of these our dear-beloved solemnizèd; 310
And thence retire me to my Milan, where
Every third thought shall be my grave.

ALONSO:
I long
To hear the story of your life, which must
Take[361] the ear strangely.

PROSPERO:
I'll deliver[362] all;
And promise you calm seas, auspicious gales,
And sail so expeditious that shall catch
Your royal fleet far off. [*Aside to* ARIEL] My Ariel, chick,
That is thy charge. Then to the elements
Be free, and fare thou well! [*To the others*] Please you, draw near.

Exeunt omnes.

EPILOGUE

Spoken by PROSPERO.

Now my charms are all o'erthrown,
And what strength I have's mine own,
Which is most faint. Now 'tis true
I must be here confined by you,

[361] Captivate. [362] Tell.

Or sent to Naples. Let me not,
Since I have my dukedom got
And pardoned the deceiver, dwell
In this bare island by your spell;
But release me from my bands[363]
With the help of your good hands.[364] 10
Gentle breath[365] of yours my sails
Must fill, or else my project fails,
Which was to please. Now I want[366]
Spirits to enforce, art to enchant;
And my ending is despair
Unless I be relieved by prayer,[367]
Which pierces so that it assaults
Mercy itself and frees all faults.
As you from crimes would pardoned be,
Let your indulgence set me free. *Exit.* 20

TIRSO DE MOLINA

[C. 1580–1648]

If Tirso de Molina's play *The Love-Rogue of Seville* were to be judged by its influence on later drama, it would probably be considered the most important play of the Golden Age of Spanish drama. The Don Juan story that it introduced into Western literature has been retold numerous times, most notably in plays by Molière and George Bernard Shaw, in Byron's satiric epic *Don Juan,* and in Mozart's opera *Don Giovanni.* Tirso's play, written during the second or third decade of the seventeenth century, presents a Don Juan unfamiliar to those of us who remember the intellectual cleverness of Shaw's figure or who associate the type with a seductive lover. Tirso's protagonist plays out his life against a background that pits the secular individualism of the Renaissance against the theological world view of the Middle Ages. Like Doctor Faustus, Don Juan challenges the medieval constraints on individual expression, but in the end he too discovers that he has overreached himself and challenged institutions that are more powerful than he is.

Tirso de Molina, the pen name of Father Gabriel Téllez, was one of the three great playwrights of the Spanish Golden Age. The other two were Lope de Vega and Pedro Calderón de la Barca. During the century between 1580 and 1680, and especially between 1610 and 1640, these three playwrights transformed the Spanish drama from religious morality plays and saints' lives to a vital and prolific secular literature. Lope de Vega alone is reputed to have written more than 2,000 plays, and Tirso himself claimed that he wrote over 400 plays in his twenty years as an active playwright.

---

[363]Bonds.
[364]Applause to break the spell.
[365]Favorable comment.
[366]Lack.
[367]This petition.

Life

Although some scholars speculate that Tirso was the illegitimate son of an aristocratic family, his origins remain obscure. His birth has been set anywhere between 1570 and 1584, although recent scholarship suggests that he was probably born in 1580 or 1581. We do know that he became a monk of the Mercedarian Order in 1600 and that he had a religious career that continued throughout his life alongside his theatrical career. He eventually became the chronicler of his order and wrote in 1639 the *History of the Mercedarian Order*.

Tirso's career as a dramatist seems to have begun after he completed his theological studies in 1610 or 1611. During the following decade he wrote a great many plays, even though he spent two years away from Spain on a missionary assignment in Hispaniola (now the Dominican Republic). The frivolous comedies, often developing sexual themes, may seem surprising work for a monk, but Tirso also wrote on religious themes and dramatized the lives of various saints. In this mixture of secular and traditional religious drama, Tirso's work reflects the theater of his time, as an emerging secular drama displaced the religious plays of the Middle Ages.

Tirso entered a second prolific period of play writing in the 1620s, when his order transferred him to Madrid, the center of the Spanish theater at the time. But in 1625, Tirso drew the displeasure of the authorities, probably for political satire in some of his plays. He was sent away from Madrid and his theatrical activities were discouraged. By 1630, his dramatic career was essentially over, although some collections of his plays appeared during the decade that followed. He died in 1648.

Work

Although Tirso claimed to have written over 400 plays, only 54 survive that modern scholars can definitely identify as his work. Another 23 of questionable authorship are also extant. *El Burlador de Seville,* or *The Love-Rogue of Seville,* is among the latter, although scholars agree that most of the surviving play is clearly Tirso's work.

Tirso's play has been dated as early as 1616 and as late as 1630, but in any case it is the work that introduced the Don Juan into Western literature, although, like the Faustus story, the Don Juan story is based on folk tales that circulated before it was published. The "burlador" in Tirso's title has been variously translated as "playboy," "trickster," "libertine," and "love-rogue," and Tirso's Don Juan is clearly quite different from the lover or seducer with which his name has become associated. His *burlas,* or tricks, involve the seductions of a series of women, but he pursues them not so much for the sex involved as for the excitement of the conquest and the triumph over his competitors. Nearly all of the women in the play are identified as signs or tokens in male power struggles. Tenorio is much more excited by power than he is by love. As he taunts his victims, he is an exultant individualist who has no respect for established institutions or beliefs.

Don Juan's exploits take place against a background of a corrupt social system that tolerates or even encourages his perversity. Although he is chided for the seduction of Isabela that opens the play, his uncle colludes in his escape, and the King, who will later condemn the young renegade, is tolerant of his first transgressions. After all, Don Juan is a gentleman, the son of one of the King's close advisors, and his delinquent behavior is tolerated, even expected, in a young, aristocratic male. Indeed, Don Juan aims his tricks at his male peers as much as, if not more than, at the women he seduces. The men he tricks or triumphs over are little better than he is. De la Mota, for example, has been his companion at whoring, and Gaseno is anxious to barter for his daughter's social advancement. The society that Don Juan takes advantage of is composed of those whose greed and desire for power make them willing dupes to his machinations.

It is also a society where the religious condemnation of such excesses calls up thoughts of the fiery punishments of Hell, for the medieval world view had not been altogether displaced by puissant Renaissance individualism. Don Juan is frequently reminded that his deeds, almost always carried out under the cover of night and darkness, will ultimately be brought into the light, if only the firelight of his final punishment. Although he is frequently reminded that his quest for power will be judged in his salvation or damnation, Don Juan dismisses such reminders as irrelevant or as far in the future.

Like Doctor Faustus, Don Juan lives to challenge authority. But when he offends the patriarchy by killing one of its representatives, Don Gonzalo de Ulloa, the social forces ally with religious tradition to ensure Don Juan's punishment. In the end, a terrified Don Juan learns that his *burlas* are not clever enough to defeat the established powers and to prevent his eternal punishment.

The Love-Rogue raises numerous issues about the character of Don Juan, both in the play and in the story that has embedded itself in our culture. In what ways is he an admirable or heroic figure? What motivates his career of seduction? Is he driven by aspects of his personality or by social norms? Certainly his exploits are encouraged by the code of honor that he and others in his society subscribe to. His seductions of Isabela and Doña Ana differ from those of Tisbea and Aminta. How are the sexual politics of his story related to class politics? What is Don Juan's relationship to Catalinón? The Don Juan story can be seen as part of the secularization of life in the Renaissance, a myth that makes sex the key to a secular mysticism that undermined the traditional authority of religion. To what degree does the story of Don Juan still have currency in our culture? Have we changed the story or the character of Don Juan to reflect changed attitudes toward relationships between the sexes?

Suggested Readings

Two good introductions to Tirso in English are Margaret Wilson's *Tirso de Molina* (1977), which introduces Tirso and his work, and Ion Tudor Agheana's *The Situational Drama of Tirso de Molina* (1972), which discusses Tirso's plays. Gerald E. Wade focuses specifically on Tirso's version of the Don Juan figure in "The Character of Don Juan of *El Burlador de Sevilla*," *Hispanic Studies in Honor of Nicholson B. Adams,* ed. J. E. Keller and K. Selig (1966), pp. 167–78. James Mandrell's recent *Don Juan and the Point of Honor* (1992) discusses the Don Juan figure in many literary works. Otto Rank's classic essay, *The Don Juan Legend* (1924; English translation 1975), develops a psychoanalytic interpretation of the Don Juan figure.

The Love-Rogue of Seville

Translated by Harry Kemp

PEOPLE IN THE PLAY (IN ORDER OF APPEARANCE)

DON JUAN TENORIO, *the Love-Rogue*
THE DUCHESS ISABELA, *betrothed to Duke Octavio*
THE KING OF NAPLES
DON PEDRO TENORIO, *Don Juan's uncle, and ambassador plenipotentiary from Spain to Naples*
THE DUKE OCTAVIO
RIPIO, *his valet*
TISBEA, *a fisher maiden*
CATALINÓN, *Don Juan's valet*
CORIDON, *a fisherman*
ANFRISO, *a fisherman*
ALONZO, *King of Spain*

DON GONZALO DE ULLOA, *the Knight Commander of Calatrava*
LUCINDA, *fisher maiden*
ATANDRA, *fisher maiden*
BELISA, *fisher maiden*
DON DIEGO TENORIO, *Don Juan's father*
THE MARQUIS DE LA MOTA, *Don Juan's crony, in love with Doña Ana*
DOÑA ANA
BATRICIO, *a country laborer*
AMINTA, *a country girl, his betrothed*
GASENO, *her father*
BELISA, *a country girl*
FABIO, *a laborer attending Isabela*
THE STONE IMAGE OF DON GONZALO DE ULLOA
Guards, Servants, Fishermen, Musicians, Soldiers, Peasants.
Black-draped figures that serve at the graveyard banquet.

ACT I

Scene 1

Court of the KING OF NAPLES—*inner room of the palace. It is dark. Enter* DON JUAN *and the* DUCHESS ISABELA.

ISABELA:
Since I have given all a woman can
I hope you'll prove as generous a man:
Only your faith fulfilled can keep me pure . . . [*showing door*]
Octavio, here's the way that's most secure!

DON JUAN [*Kissing* ISABELA *good-bye*]:
Don't doubt me, I will keep my promise, dear.

ISABELA:
I should have been a trifle more severe . . . [*turning*]
Wait till I bring a light!

DON JUAN [*Impatiently*]:
A light! . . . what for?

ISABELA [*Pausing—gently*]:
Humour my fond mood for a little space;
I would look deeper, dear, into your face. 10

DON JUAN [*With sudden wantonness, as he goes*]:
I have put out the only light you bore.

ISABELA [*Stepping toward him, frightened*]:
"The only light I bore"! . . . what man are you?

DON JUAN:
A man without a name . . .

ISABELA:
Not the Duke!

DON JUAN [*With great brutality*]:
No!

ISABELA [*Desperately getting between him and the door*]:
You mean that you—are not—Octavio? . . .
I'll rouse the King and all his serving men!

DON JUAN [*Cajoling*]:
Wait, Duchess! let me have your hand again,—
Keep silence, if but for your honour's sake!

ISABELA [*Crying out, with great distraction*]:
Don't touch me, villain! Everybody, wake,— 20
King! courtiers! . . .

Scene 2

Enter, rapidly, the KING OF NAPLES, *with a candle.*

KING OF NAPLES:
What's wrong?

ISABELA:
I am undone!

KING OF NAPLES:
Who is it? Tell me, woman, who's the one
That dares?

DON JUAN [*Putting in nonchalantly*]:
Why take the trouble to enquire?
It's nothing but a man and woman, sire!

KING [*Apart*]:
The rogue's adroit. . . . [*Aloud*] Ho, guards, arrest this man!

ISABELA:
I've given to him all a woman can,
I've lost my honour, and I am undone. 30

[ISABELA *goes out*]

Scene 3

Enter, DON PEDRO, *with guard.*

DON PEDRO [*To the* KING]:
In your apartments I heard voices, sire,
That cried for help,
Breaking the sacred silence of the night. . . .
I come to seek the cause.

KING:
Don Pedro Tenorio,
I render up this man into your charge:
Be brief: move quickly . . . find out who they were,
These two; and hold enquiry secretly,
For that which I suspect I must not see,
Lest I must needs delve deeper into it 40
And to an ill deed, equal judgment fit.

[*The* KING *goes out*]

Scene 4

DON PEDRO [*To the guards*]:
Take him!

DON JUAN [*Drawing sword*]:
Let the man who dares
Come on and try,—a life the more or less
Is nothing to me, and I must confess
If any would take mine, they'll have to lay
A dearer price to it than they might care to pay.

DON PEDRO [*Vehemently*]:
Then slay him and have done.

DON JUAN [*Advancing his sword*]:
Don't play with death!

I am resolved to fight to the last breath; 50
Then you can take my corpse when I am slain—
Because I am a Spanish nobleman
Attending the Ambassador from Spain! [*To* DON PEDRO]
So, sir, I would explain to you alone.

DON PEDRO [*To the guards*]:
Go where the woman went.... [*They go*] [*To* DON JUAN] We'll walk apart....

Scene 5

DON PEDRO [*Alone with* DON JUAN. *Vehemently, whipping out his sword*]:
Now we're but two, alone,—show if your heart
Is equal to your boasting.

DON JUAN [*Impudently*]:
Uncle, do
Put up your sword...why should I fight with you?

DON PEDRO [*Stepping back, astounded*]:
Why, who are you? 60

DON JUAN:
I've said it.... I'm your nephew.

DON PEDRO [*Apart*]:
Good God! what fresh betrayal must I fear? [*To* DON JUAN]
Tell me, my nephew, yet my enemy,
Quickly, what evil thing has taken place,
What unheard outrage, or what new disgrace
Born of this madness burning in your brain?...
Come, speak, what have you done?
[*As* DON JUAN *stands silent, smiling*]

DON JUAN:
My uncle and my elder,
I was a boy and I am still a boy:
In making love, you know, I find most joy.... 70
Let making love, then, be my sole defence....
Descending from romance to common sense,
And pleading but my passion and my youth,
Listen, and I will tell the brief, sweet truth:
While all the palace slept, I have employed
An hour to happier purpose; I've enjoyed
The Duchess Isabela, deceiving her—

DON PEDRO [*Interrupting quickly*]:
Hold your mouth! Keep a still tongue in your head!
[*Continuing, with the sly, lascivious curiosity of an old man*]
So...you deceived her...was that what...you said?...
Tell me just how you did it, quietly, so.... 80

DON JUAN [*Coming up close... mischievously*]:
Pretending I was Duke Octavio—

DON PEDRO [*Stepping back, startled, and breaking in*]:
Stop! Say no more! If the King hears of this
You are a dead man... all my wit and strength
I'll have to strain for such a dangerous business.
It was for a like crime, my precious nephew,
Your father sent you hither from Castille
And gave you to these bright Italian shores;

And you return its hospitality
And stab sharp to its very heart of honour
By cozening a woman of its first — 90
Nobility—but, come, while we stand talking
Each minute darkens danger over you. . . .
Tell me, my boy, what you propose to do?

DON JUAN [*With mock humility*]:
The thing I've done is ugly to the sight;
I do not seek to paint its blackness white;
Uncle, shed all my blood to cleanse my guilt: [*kneels and presents sword*]
Here, take my sword and plunge it to the hilt!
I kneel down, I surrender at your feet.

DON PEDRO [*Mollified*]:
Your humbleness plays on my heart; arise,
And show again as great a bravery— 100
Dare you leap over from this balcony,
Far down below, where yon green garden lies?

DON JUAN:
To win once more your favour that I lack
I would grow angel's wings upon my back.

DON PEDRO:
I'll help you . . . that's the way to talk . . . leap down . . .
Make all speed to Sicilia or Milan,
And hide yourself away a little while,
Till this blows over.

DON JUAN:
I will go straightway.

DON PEDRO:
From day to day 110
I'll send you letters and keep you informed
Of this sad case.

DON JUAN [*Apart*]:
To me so great a pleasure
That still my heart flows on with quicker measure . . . [*to his uncle with playful hypocrisy*]
Alas, sir, I confess my sinfulness.

DON PEDRO [*Smug and sententious*]:
We've all beguiled our women, more or less,
And youth's a time of snares, and hours misspent. . . .
Leap down . . . the garden mould is soft with rain. . . .

DON JUAN [*Apart*]:
In just this way I had to flee from Spain,
Rejoicing in my cause of banishment. [*He leaps*] 120

Scene 6

The KING *re-enters.*

THE KING:
Has he been brought to death?

DON PEDRO:
He has escaped,

Has broken through the guards' sharp, circling points
That ringed him round.

THE KING:

How was that possible?

DON PEDRO [*Lying to save* DON JUAN]:

Sire, you had barely given your command
To take him when, with keen, drawn blade in hand,—
Over his shoulder he flung back his cape
And fought an open way for his escape....
With bravery and swift magnificence 130
He pushed your soldiers to their own defence
And then burst through, and leapt the balcony,
Flinging himself beneath... through the first door
Your soldiers swarmed to take him... on the ground
They found him, like a wounded snake coiled round
In agony—but up he leapt again,
His face all streaked with blood, and fought your men,
Inviting them to death, and with such might
That he broke forth, and they were pushed to flight.
The woman who's the base of all this pother— 140
The Duchess Isabela and no other—
(I see you start and draw your brow with doom)
I've got her prisoned safely in that room—
She says it was the Duke Octavio
That cozened her with tricks and cunning so!

KING [*Agitated*]:

What's that?

DON PEDRO:

I tell what she herself confessed.

KING:

Oh, you poor thing called honour,—at the best
How fading is the lamp you lift in man—
Can we expect you to burn steadier 150
Within a woman's soft, luxurious breast? [*Calling*]
Holla! within there!

Scene 7

Enter, a SERVANT.

SERVANT [*Making an obeisance*]:

Great sire?

KING:

Bring the woman here!

DON PEDRO:

The guard comes with her now.

[*Enter, the guard, with* ISABELA.]

ISABELA [*Apart*]:

With what eyes shall I meet the King's stern face?

KING [*To guard*]:

Go, keep the doors that lead into this place. [*To* ISABELA]
Now, tell me, woman,—

Under the influence of what insane star
Did you walk, when you dared, 160
With pride of beauty and high vanity,
Profane the sacred precincts of my palace?

ISABELA [*Beginning*]:
Great Sire!—

KING [*Interrupting*]:
Be silent! to your tongue give halt!
It cannot gild the baseness of your fault
That lives to my continual offence . . . [*a pause*]
Was it the Duke Octavio?

ISABELA [*Beginning again*]:
Sire—

KING [*Again interrupting*]:
My guards, my servants, and these solid walls,
My battlemented merlons, know no strength 170
Against a nude boy of a cubit's length,
This god of love, who, heedless of all shame,
Breaks through all things, and makes the world his game. . . .
[*Turning to* DON PEDRO]
In brief, Don Pedro, let the Duke be sought,
Wherever he is, and have this word conveyed,
That he must lead this lady to the priest
And keep the promises he doubtless made.

ISABELA [*Wringing her hands in hopelessness*]:
Sire, turn but once and let me see your face.
[*Apart, in a low voice of indignation*]
They say that women fight for the last word,
But men will never let their case be heard. 180

KING:
Behind my back you wrought me this disgrace:
So, if I keep my shoulders turned to you,
Reason and right proclaim it but your due.
[*The* KING *goes out*]

DON PEDRO [*Motioning*]:
Come, Duchess!

ISABELA:
Nothing but dire revenge can cleanse my sin
Or lift me from the pit I've fallen in—
But still it won't be such a great miscarriage
If Duke Octavio takes my hand in marriage!

Scene 8

OCTAVIO*'s bed-chamber. The* DUKE *lies abed and calls for his servant,* RIPIO.

OCTAVIO:
Ripio! Ripio!

RIPIO [*Coming in*]:
Why is it that you wake so early, sir? 190

OCTAVIO:
Where is the doctor that can minister
To still this raging fire in my breast

That love has kindled? nothing gives me rest.
I've lost my appetite for my soft bed
With delicate Holland sheets; I toss all night
Though I am covered with the ermine's white.
I lie down (childish, it must be confessed)
But wake up before dawn and know no rest. . . .
And yet I am so easily beguiled
With trifles, that I must play like a child. . . . 200
And dreams of Isabela live with me
When I'm alone, keeping me company;
And, as the soul within the body lives,
So, every hour, every moment gives,
Absent or present, hopes I place upon her
That watch before the castle of her honour.

RIPIO:
It seems to me the love you represent . . .
Is, begging pardon, damned impertinent!

OCTAVIO [*Startled, then amused*]:
What are you saying, donkey?

RIPIO:
I only say 210
It's impudent to love in such a way . . .
Shall I go on?

OCTAVIO [*Now thoroughly amused*]:
Go on!

RIPIO:
Does Isabela love you?

OCTAVIO:
Fool, have you any doubt that it is true?

RIPIO:
No, but I only ask—do you love her?

OCTAVIO:
Of course!

RIPIO:
Then, if you'll promise not to stir
A hand against me, nor cause me be sent
Back to the country's hated banishment, 220
Stripping me of my easy valet's task—
I have a further question that I'd ask:
Why do I love a woman, and she, me? . . .
If she don't love you, it's your place to tender
Presents and worship till you win surrender;
But, if you both love with an equal flame,
Why make a difficulty of the same?
Surely this is of all men's tasks the least;
In God's name, is it hard to find a priest?

OCTAVIO:
Lackeys and laundry women marry so . . . 230
Don't be an ass!

RIPIO:
Well, then, I'd like to know
What is the difference between mine and yours?—
The serving women and laundry women that toil,

That wash and rub and moil,
That bake your bread and serve it hot and white,—
And your fine ladies, that, from dawn to night,
Do nothing only think of their delight—
Give them some trifling present and they're glad:
It is the lack of small things makes them sad; 240
Pursue them, woo them . . . that's the way to gain
Your Isabela . . . all fish to the seine—

[*A* SERVANT *enters, interrupting* RIPIO'S *further discourse*]

SERVANT [*Bowing low*]:
My master,—the Ambassador from Spain
Is at our door; his fiery violence
Cries out for an immediate audience;
To seize upon your person seems his will;
Let us pray God he means no further ill.

OCTAVIO:
Tell the Ambassador from Spain to enter!

[*Enter,* DON PEDRO. . . . *He pretends irony over* OCTAVIO*'s wakefulness, as if the latter had just popped into bed to cover his tracks.*]

DON PEDRO [*Sarcastically*]:
The man who can sleep with such indolence
Must bear an easy conscience. 250

OCTAVIO:
When Your Excellence
Comes so, to honour and to favour me,
It is not fitting I should lie asleep;
Then all my life should keep watch in your honor. . . .
But why am I so visited?

DON PEDRO:
The King has sent me here.

OCTAVIO [*With a gentle demeanour*]:
Then if the King has had me in his mind
At this hour, this occasion, let him find
My life laid at his feet to my last breath.
Tell me, what happiness or what kind fate, 260
Or what good star shines over my estate
That our great King should turn his mind to me?

DON PEDRO [*Beginning severely*]:
It's a black star that sits above you, for
I come to you, the King's Ambassador,—

[*Halts, moved, in spite of himself, by the enormity of what he is about to perpetrate on a guiltless man*]

OCTAVIO [*Mildly*]:
Marquis, speak on. . . . I wait your further word. . . .

DON PEDRO:
The King has sent me
To seize upon your person!

[*Halts again, affected still more by* OCTAVIO*'s innocent behaviour*]

OCTAVIO [*With continued simplicity*]:
To seize upon me? Now my heart stands still.
And yet I know I've done no deed of ill.
What am I charged with? 270

DON PEDRO:
You know better than I.
If I deceive myself, then undeceive me:
I'll tell you now why the King sent me here. . . .
When the gigantic shadows of the night,
Crowding each other down the gathering dark,
Struck the pavilions of the fading light—
The fittest time for statesmen to embark
On schemes of vast design—the King, with me,
Walked, pondering affairs of state and polity:
When, all at once, we heard a woman crying 280
For help,—her voice gave birth to echoes dying
Down the night's dusk, unpeopled corridors. . . .
The King himself trod over the long floors
To rescue. . . .

OCTAVIO:
—The woman?—

DON PEDRO:
—Duke—was—Isabela!
Struggling against the embrace of a man
Who was so great
His head and shoulders went up in the sky!
The King called for his guards to seize on him; 290
He proved so strong it almost seemed a demon
Had found in him the flesh and form of Man.
He soared the balcony at one swift bound
And flew, rather than vaulted, to the ground,
Alighting at the base of those two elms
With whose green tops the palace roofs are crowned. . . .
And, further, when the King commanded of
The Duchess, who it was who had so used her,
She hung her head before the gathered court
And answered "my betrothed, Duke Octavio!" 300

OCTAVIO [*Overwhelmed with astonishment*]:
What is it that you say?

DON PEDRO:
—That which you know, as well as all the world does,
That Isabela, by a thousand slights—

OCTAVIO [*In anguish, interrupting*]:
Leave off, I beg of you, Don Pedro,
Nor charge me with so monstrous a betrayal. [*Pause of emotion, resumes*]
Oh, could it be true that her love for me
Dwelt in so frail an earthly habitation!—[*A long pause*]
Could it be true that she forgot herself
Unto the pitch of filling me with death? . . .
How sweet has been my sleep in trusting her, 310
How ill my waking, in the dread you wake! [*Another long pause of emotion*]
Sir Marquis, could it really come to pass
A woman white and fair
As Isabela was,
Could turn, as with one goatish caper, rank,
And make love, that's a god, a mountebank? . . . [*Crying out*]

O woman! O Isabela!...
Oh, frightful use
Of honour, making all the devils glad...
This night? 320
In the palace
A man—
With Isabela?...
Swear it's a jest, or I— [*He leaps violently out of bed*]
Oh, I am going mad!

DON PEDRO:
Birds soar in the great air, fish throng the sea;
Often one finds in friends deep loyalty;
There is betrayal in an enemy;
The heart of man gets pride in finding glory;
There's light in day, in night, security— 330
So I have only put truth in my story!

OCTAVIO [*In his dressing gown, that by this time* RIPIO *has helped him into*]:
Well, Marquis, after all,
Though you will scarce believe me,
None of this wakes amazement in my heart...
Not now... not in the least:
For the most constant woman is—a woman!
You need no longer ply me to believe,
For this is sure, that I have cause to grieve,
And that my injury is most manifest.

DON PEDRO [*Significantly*]:
I'm sure your wisdom will embrace the best, 340
And point a middle course that waits for you.

OCTAVIO:
Then only show me what is best to do—

DON PEDRO [*Pointing first one way, then the other*]:
This way unto the prison we proceed,—
And there's the garden gate to serve your need.

OCTAVIO [*As* RIPIO *brings his clothes forward to him*]:
I'll get into a boat and go to Spain
And cleanse my ill with wind and sun and rain...
Ah, whirling weather-cock, ah, feeble reed!
Shame falls on me like judgment in the night;
To stranger, unknown shores I shape my flight,
Condemned for taking what another had... 350
My fatherland, good-bye!... [*Distracted and overwhelmed again*]
A man!—[*Drops in chair and takes his head in his hands, then lifts it after a pause*]
In the palace—
With Isabela!...
God pity me, Don Pedro, I am running mad!

Scene 9

The coast of Tarragon, Spain. TISBEA, *the fisher maiden, alone.*

TISBEA [*Solus*]:
Wreathed as with flowers, foam-chapleted,
In and out the billows tread

On feet of jasmine, rose, and gold,—
Each dallying long enough to give
Its lapsing kiss, that, fugitive, 360
Falls back before another's motion—
Till all the shore has kissed the ocean.
From sky to sky the land and sea
Lie close on one another's breast
And, resting, never are at rest,—
While I, in lone felicity,
Queen of my heart's tranquillity,
Live here, a fishermaid, content
With the wide sky's imprisonment
That keeps a world of men from me. 370
In this sweet, unfrequented spot
I share the simple fisher's lot;
I watch the sun caress the wave
Asleep with little sapphire dreams
Till purple shadows tread their gleams—
Then into golden spray they break
By the sun's passion touched awake!
I hear the sea birds give quick cries
Of querulous matings, hear the waves
Wrestling in languid love-strife where 380
The rocks lie, gleaming jet, half bare,
Washed up and back by the heave and fall....
Here, with my slender, bending reed,
I make my line shine through the air:
The little fish wake silver trouble
And bend my lissome fish rod double;
Or I draw my corded net
The larger fish to get
That lie couched deep in sand and shells
Where ever a green twilight dwells.... 390
Free as the unseen wind I go,
A child, yet wise enough to know
That girls who yield to lovers, clasp,
More like than not, a stinging asp.
My friends go in their evening boats
Combing the forehead of the sea;
They sing of unrequited love;
I laugh at them; they envy me....
Dear God of Love, you have a world to feed on,
A thousand other roads of happiness 400
To tread, than down the little path that leads
To my poor fisher hut that's built of straw!
I dwell there in sequestered
Maiden happiness.
I beg you, Love, to leave me as I am;
The birds build in my eaves it is so still,
And sit and sing upon my window sill,—
Not love-crazed turtle doves, but gentle things
With shining eyes and happy, folded wings.
I know I'm like the fruit that we conserve 410

Shut into glass that the least blow will break—
Spare me, if only for that frailty's sake!...
Of all our fisher boys whose fire of valour
Bursts forth when pirates drop to prey upon
The silver-winding shores of Tarragon,
There is not one
That shakes my pulse a moment, but they dwell
Whether I will or not, beneath my spell
Though I'm an unmoved tyrant to their prayers,
And their sighs are so many idle airs 420
That beat about my hard, unheeding ears,
And I'm rock to their promises... now there's
Anfriso!—poor Anfriso!
The capable hands of God have given him
All gifts of manhood... he's as great of soul
As body; there is honey in his words;
His hands are full of services for me;
He is enduring under my disdain;
His anguish never finds a voice for chiding!
And when the silver moon is out 430
Washing the world as white as snow
From dark to dawn he walks about
My hut, voicing his lover's woe.
And all night long till the last star
Empties its bright urn into day
He blows upon his melting flute
Or sets his soft guitar a-play.
Though still the tyrant I abide
Of love's dominions set apart,
He draws sweet from its bitterness 440
And glories in his broken heart.
While all the other fishermaids
Hunger for his strong arms in vain
He turns to me, I turn away
And wield the death of my disdain:
For this the sad estate of love
Whose flying moments never wait:
Men yield their hearts plucked from the roots
And gain a recompense of hate....
And so I pass my happy days, 450
My youth's first flower, in liberty,
Safe from love's lies, his hot pursuits,
His endless nets of flattery....
But, come, I waste my time with words
On that which has no weight with me—
I am too long neglectful of
My little fish that swim the sea....

[*Pausing, she puts her hands over her eyes, shading them, and looks out over the ocean, where something draws her attention*]

What's that? a boat that rides upon a reef,
And two men cast out in the rolling surf!
The onrush of the waves goes over it, 460

And now its crumpled sails fall, flat outspread,
Bright like a peacock's tail with painted eyes...
And now the sea has utterly drawn it down...
Its crew all lost!... where are the men I saw?...
No, not all lost!... there are the two again...
Two bobbing heads move onward toward the shore
Struggling for land and life....
There! one of them goes under... no, there he is
Again!

[*Cry within of* "Help, help, I drown!"]

TISBEA [*Continuing*]:
Sweet gallantry! 470
The other
Saves him... he has found foot,
At last, in shallow water... he bears his comrade
Across his shoulders... so Æneas would
Have borne Anchises, if Troy had been the ocean....
Ah!
He's stepped off into a deep place again...
Two waves go over his head...
He's up again... he swims beneath the other,
Untiring in his courage. Up and down 480
The shore I look and see no one at hand
To bring aid to them. I'll cry out for some one!
Tirso! Anfriso! Alfredo!... Help, help, help!
Pray God they hear me, or else—[*a pause*] ah!
Miraculously they have reached the shore—
The one who swam is close to his last breath
And he who weighed his back is still as death!

[CATALINÓN *enters from the sea; he bears his master,* DON JUAN, *on his back; he lays him gently on the sand*]

Scene 10

CATALINÓN:
Keep me from further harm, dear Cana's daughter
For whom Christ reddened into wine that water!
Saints, but the sea's salt!... [*Disgorges water*] 490
If I must drown again, let God perform
Anew, that miracle of His power divine,
But, this time, change the ocean into wine.
Salt water, pah! a sweet predicament
For one who doesn't fish!
To perish in fresh water's bad enough—
One drowns twice, swallowing this nasty stuff! [*Spews out more water*]
I'll gladly drink the cheapest vintage now;
If once I get this ocean from my guts
Water shall never wet my throat again; 500
I've still enough down here to last a lifetime.

[*Stooping and touching* DON JUAN*'s face*]

Ah, master, you are cold! [*Talking into his ear*]
Answer me, are you dead?
My wits are running wild... accursed be he

Whose hands first built a ship to sail the sea
And taught some strips of timber, joined together,
How to maintain their course through wind and weather;
His work was father to this vile disaster—[*feeling* DON JUAN*'s pulse*]
Alas, he's dead, and I'm without a master. . . .
Poor Catalinón, what is there left to do! 510

TISBEA:
Fellow, what brought you both to such an ill?

CATALINÓN:
Sweet fisher girl,
Much evil, and an equal lack of good.
Look for me; see if he is breathing still.
It seems to me he's dead.

TISBEA [*Putting her hand on* DON JUAN*'s breast*]:
He breathes, but scarcely breathes.

CATALINÓN:
He breathes? through what place? where?

TISBEA:
Why do you ask "what place"?

CATALINÓN:
—Since I can breathe through each end!—

TISBEA [*Severely*]:
You're a fool! 520

CATALINÓN:
I kiss your hand, contrite!

TISBEA:
Go, call the fishermen
That live here . . . who is the man?

CATALINÓN:
The son
Of the King's Chamberlain.

TISBEA:
What is his name?

CATALINÓN:
Don Juan Tenorio.

TISBEA:
—Go, call my people.

CATALINÓN:
I go!

[*He goes out*]

Scene 11

TISBEA [*Taking the still unconscious form of* DON JUAN *in her arms, resting his head in her lap. . . . Solus*]:
He's quite a seemly bachelor at that: 530
Each part of him speaks the aristocrat.
[*To* DON JUAN]
Gentleman! look at me!

DON JUAN [*Slowly opening his eyes and taking in, even half-drowned, as if by instinct, the situation*]:
Where am I?

TISBEA [*Sportively*]:
Why, can't you see?—
That you are in a woman's arms
It is as plain as plain can be!
DON JUAN [*With a sigh of content*]:
I live in you, as in the sea I died:
My fear goes out with the receding tide
That fought to suck me down to its black hell—
Whence I have leaped high into the blue heaven 540
Of your delicious arms . . . so may God bless
My wreck and loss in the waves' wilderness,
Those multitudinous, boiling waves that beat
My ship to boards—but cast me at your feet.
If the receding ocean leave one pearl
It has not rolled in vain, my lovely girl—[*Pauses*]
TISBEA [*Apart*]:
I've never in my life heard such conceit!
DON JUAN [*Gathering strength and continuing*]:
—In the divine and single pearl of you
My life and love has found itself anew!
TISBEA [*Apart, with a shiver of delight*]:
The darling! [*Starts to give him an impulsive hug, before she knows what she is doing*] 550
No, I must be more discreet!
[*To* DON JUAN]
Whom the sea takes it holds with iron grip,
But in you there is something like a ship;
You have but now slid from the jaws of death
Yet you breathe braveries with every breath,
And every word that you address to me
Has somewhat of the largeness of the sea—
Pray God that you mean more than gallantry!
Like the Greek horse that brought Troy flame and slaughter
You come as if you got shape from the water, 560
And yet you bear a burning fire in you—
Pray God you'll do the things you'll promise to—
If, drowned and drenched, you prove so bold a lover,
What madness won't you dare when you recover?
DON JUAN [*Striving to overcome a faintness*]:
O, shepherdess, had I foreseen this case
I'd have begged God, still in the sea's embrace,
To let me perish, with my whole mind, there,
Rather than die, half mad from love's despair,
Here, under your disdain. . . . Ocean, between
Its infinite, silver shores, with many waters 570
Might drown me deep: it could not burn me up
As you do. You are like the sun above,
So hot its gold shines almost white, sweet love!
My snowy woman! [*Faints in her arms*]
TISBEA [*Chafing his hands*]:
The colder that you grow
The more the fire within you seems to glow! [*Weeps with gentle emotion*]
[CATALINÓN *enters, with* CORIDON, ANFRISO, *and other fishermen*]

Scene 12

CATALINÓN [*To the fishermen*]:
This way, all!
TISBEA [*Eagerly, to* CATALINÓN]:
Your master is alive!
DON JUAN [*Coming to again, to* TISBEA]:
It was you gave me new breath to survive.
CORIDON [*Glancing menacingly at* DON JUAN, *to* TISBEA]:
Tisbea, what is it you command of us? 580
TISBEA [*Already smitten with love . . . reaches out her hands spontaneously toward the fishermen . . . then halts with confusion*]:
Coridon! Anfriso! [*A pause*] O my friends! [*Halts again*]
CORIDON [*With rude vigour*]:
It is our happy fate
To be, each one of us, at your command
To the uttermost you ask. [*With a sullen glance at* DON JUAN]
You need but tell us what you'd have us do,
With those sweet lips that shame the rose's hue.
There's not a one of us but loves you so
That he would gladly go
Without a breath's pause over hill or plain
Treading down living fire with all disdain, 590
Wading whole seas, forbidding the wind's flow—
[*Stops, overcome with emotion*]
TISBEA [*Apart*]:
Yesterday I hated this as flattery—
To-day I know it as plain-speaking homage,
Rude words from honest lips that hate the lie.
[*To the fishermen*]
As I stood fishing on this jutting rock
I saw a ship that broke upon a reef
And fell apart beneath the waves; I saw
These two men, ocean-whelmed; I called for help,
But there was no one anywhere to hear. . . .
Borne under and under by the tumbling surf 600
He [*indicates* CATALINÓN] brought this gentleman landward on his back
And laid him without life along the sand.
And, while I stayed to take care of the master
(He touched so close on death), I sent the servant
To fetch you here.
ANFRISO [*With a rapid look of distrust and suspicion from* TISBEA *to* DON JUAN *and back*]:
Well, here we're all arrived, and here we stand
Waiting, as Coridon said, on your command!
TISBEA [*Stepping apart from* DON JUAN]:
Then take him up as gently as you can . . .
My father is an honest, pious man:
He'll gladly give him shelter, clothes and food. 610
CATALINÓN [*Apart*]:
Good hospitality, though somewhat rude!
DON JUAN [*Aside, to* CATALINÓN]:
Pst! [CATALINÓN *comes over to him*] listen to me!

CATALINÓN [*Aside, to* DON JUAN]:
I am all ear, my master!
DON JUAN [*Aside, to* CATALINÓN]:
If they ask who I am, you're not to know.
CATALINÓN [*Panic-stricken because he has already told* TISBEA; *apart*]:
Alas, half drowned, yet courting fresh disaster!
[*To* DON JUAN]
Pray tell me now which way the wind's to blow?
DON JUAN [*With a groan of genuine feeling*]:
I perish for this lovely fisher girl:
Yes, I shall die, unless, this very night,
I gain possession of my full delight—
I must, if it's the last day I fulfil. 620
CATALINÓN [*Frightened*]:
Master, dear Christ!—
DON JUAN [*Reaching up from a half-recumbent position and pushing* CATALINÓN *away*]:
Go quickly and be still!
CORIDON [*To* ANFRISO]:
Anfriso, at the twilight of this day
The fishers meet to sing and dance and play.
ANFRISO:
That's fine: but first we must do what we can
To bring to his full health this gentleman.
DON JUAN [*Aside, to* TISBEA]:
I die!
TISBEA [*With simplicity, aside to* DON JUAN]:
Alas, and aren't you any better?
DON JUAN [*Meaningfully, aside to* TISBEA]:
Tisbea, can't you see the pain I suffer? [*lower*]
For you, my Tisbea, my snowy woman? 630
TISBEA [*Aside, rebukingly, to* DON JUAN]:
You talk too much!
DON JUAN:
—And mean more than I say!

Scene 13

Palace of the KING OF SPAIN, *at Seville.* DON GONZALO DE ULLOA *and the* KING ALONZO, *discovered.*

KING:
How have you got on with your embassage,
My good Lord Chamberlain?
DON GONZALO:
I found the King of Portugal
With thirty galleys held in readiness.
KING:
And whither aimed?
DON GONZALO:
He said for Goa, but I think
He means an expedition to Tangier,
Or Ceuta, in the following summer's season. 640

KING:
God give him aid! May heaven increase his glory!...
What cities serve him?

DON GONZALO:
Serpa and Mora, Olivencia, Toro,
Villaverde, and Mertota, and Hererra
That sits between Castille and Portugal.

KING:
I'm glad in fine to see such harmony...
But tell me of your journey... did you arrive
Wearied?

DON GONZALO [*Bowing deeply*]:
Sire, in your service,—no!

KING:
Long have I meditated 650
Your better fortune, Don Gonzalo;
You have a daughter—

DON GONZALO:
I have, great Sire—
A bright and beautiful maiden, in whose face
Nature outshines herself.

KING:
You wish her marriage,
Given from my royal hand?

DON GONZALO:
I had never hoped so high... but who is to be
The bridegroom?

KING:
Though he is not in Castille at present, 660
He is Don Juan Tenorio of Seville.

DON GONZALO:
I'll straight convey the news to Doña Ana.

KING:
Go, then, Gonzalo, and bring her acceptance.

Scene 14

The coast of Tarragon, as before. DON JUAN *and* CATALINÓN *come in.*

DON JUAN:
Get the two mares; have them ready to gallop away.

CATALINÓN:
Yes, as I'm Catalinón and a true man,
I'll see to it that there's exactly two
So that they shan't fall on *me* with their clubs
And pay me doubly for the lack of you.

DON JUAN [*Gaily*]:
While the fishers dance and play
Take two mares whose flying feet 670
Will whisk us off at break of day
And add the sauce to my deceit.

CATALINÓN [*With another faltering attempt at dissuasion*]:
And so you hold your purpose still
To cozen Tisbea to your will?
DON JUAN [*Impatiently*]:
To turn this trick with women has become
A habit of my very blood—you know
My nature, then why ask me foolish questions?
CATALINÓN [*Shaking his head sadly*]:
Yes, yes, I know by now
You are a scourge for women.
DON JUAN [*Hungrily*]:
Ah, I die 680
For Tisbea . . . she'll make a dainty morsel.
CATALINÓN:
Fine payment for their hospitality,
I must say.
DON JUAN [*With a sly smile*]:
You ninny, I've a classic precedent
In what Æneas did to royal Dido.
CATALINÓN [*Sighing*]:
Some day you'll find your death in fooling women.
DON JUAN:
You're generous, I must say,
In your prognostications, and, thereby,
You live up to your name
Of Catalinón, "the cautious one." 690
CATALINÓN:
Unless you twist that edge of irony
Against yourself, and also grow more cautious
At your grand game of cozening and deceit,
You'll surely pay with some most monstrous ill.
DON JUAN:
You've talked enough . . . go, get the two mares ready. [*Laughs*]
CATALINÓN [*Going, apart*]:
Poor little woman, you'll be well rewarded!
[*He goes out.* TISBEA *enters*]

Scene 15

TISBEA [*To* DON JUAN]:
When I am not with you time is a sick thing.
DON JUAN:
Don't speak that way—because—I don't believe you.
TISBEA [*Hurt*]:
You don't—believe me?—
DON JUAN:
If it is true you love me 700
You'd fill my empty heart with more than words.
TISBEA [*Distressed*]:
I am all yours. What more can you require?
DON JUAN:
Then why withhold the love we both desire?

TISBEA [*Wringing her hands*]:
Because that same love tears my life apart!
DON JUAN [*Impetuously*]:
Accept the full devotion of my heart....
I lay my life in service at your feet.... [*Takes her slowly in his arms*]
Now give me all, and make your gift complete. [*A pause*]
Then—we'll get married!
TISBEA [*Struggling gently*]:
No, my place in life
Is low, as yours is high... that could not be! 710
DON JUAN [*Holding her close*]:
Rank clad in silk and beauty clad in wool
Are equal in love's kingdom... beautiful
Are you! [*He tries to kiss her. She pulls her face back, looking at him in fascinated fear.*]
TISBEA [*Half to herself*]:
I almost make myself believe
That what you say is true—yet—[*struggling anew*]—men deceive!
DON JUAN [*Letting go his embrace and bringing her face close to his, with both hands*]:
Oh, can't you see I love as I declare....
Look deep into my eyes... my soul waits there
That you could trammel with a single hair....
TISBEA [*Taking his hands away in hers, and holding them*]:
Give me your solemn word, your hand, that you
Will wed me, then, as you—you promise to! 720
DON JUAN:
I swear by your sweet eyes that madden me
Marriage shall seal our stolen ecstasy.
TISBEA:
Remember, if you lie, there's God and Death.
DON JUAN:
I swear again that while God gives me breath
I'll be the servant of your least command;
Here is my solemn word, and here's my hand.
You can put your utmost faith in me.
TISBEA [*Coming slowly, of her own will, into his embrace... looking at him gravely*]:
Then take me; do with me as you desire.
DON JUAN [*Madly*]:
Only the uttermost can quench this fire.
TISBEA [*Responding*]:
Come then, my little fisher hut will be 730
Our bridal bower... stay hidden in these reeds
Until the hour of opportunity.
DON JUAN [*Avidly*]:
What way shall I get in?
TISBEA:
I'll come and show you.
DON JUAN [*Kissing her again and again*]:
You have laid bare heaven's brightness for me.
TISBEA:
The very way I give myself should bind you:
If it does not, then God revenge your crime.

DON JUAN:
I'll keep my faith until the end of time.

[*They go out*]

Scene 16

Enter, CORIDON, ANFRISO, BELISA, *and musicians.*

CORIDON:
Call the other boys and girls . . . call Tisbea;
Our stranger guest has taken her apart 740
And with his honeyed speech attempts her heart
I fear.
ANFRISO [*Calling—with fear in his voice*]:
Tisbea! Lucinda! Atandra!

Scene 17

Enter, LUCINDA *and* ATANDRA.

LUCINDA [*Joyously*]:
We're ready for the twilight dance!
ATANDRA [*Eagerly*]:
We have our castanets . . . but where is Tisbea?
ANFRISO:
Oh, I have never seen a case more cruel!
Our love burns all about her,
But she is like that fabled beast that dwells
In fire, and thrives on it . . . [*with determination*] before we dance
We must find Tisbea, and bring her with us. 750
BELISA:
Come on . . . we'll go and get her.
CORIDON [*To* ANFRISO, *who mopes*]:
Come, Anfriso!
BELISA:
She is in
Her cabin. . . .
CORIDON:
Can't you see
That she is busied with this ill-starred stranger
Who wakes a thousand envies by his favour?
ANFRISO [*Sullenly*]:
Tisbea is always envied for her favours—
Given to all, except to those who love her!
CORIDON [*Putting his hand affectionately on* ANFRISO*'s shoulder*]:
That is the virgin's way, till love wakes in her, 760
And then, and only then, she gives herself!
BELISA:
The sun is setting . . . as we go along
To join the dance, let us strike up a song.

SONG

The Fisher maid, she casts her net
Again and yet again
But in the place of struggling fish
She snares the souls of men!

[*They go out as they sing*]

Scene 18

TISBEA *comes in.*

TISBEA [*Solus*]:
Fire! Fire! my world is overturning,
My little hut of straw is burning
Of a flame that never ends! 770
Ring all the bells! help, help, my friends!
The Fire that once I pleased to flout
All my tears cannot put out;
The sudden, climbing flames destroy
My cottage, like another Troy.
How could I hope that love's great power
That beats down citadels, would spare
My virgin frailty an hour
Beyond the time he found it fair?
Help, help, my friends! the flames roar past control: 780
Have mercy, love, you burn my very soul!
My little cottage built of straw,
How sweet you were till you became
A vile, abandoned cave of thieves
That bound and made me slave to shame!
Poor, silly girl! . . . the burning stars
Of passion shot their streams of fire
And caught those tresses that you combed
In vanity and light desire!
False guest! you came up from the waves 790
And swooped upon me like a cloud
Heavy with night and falling fire
And black woes raining in a crowd,—
To leave, when it had served your mood,
My frail, dishonoured womanhood!
Help, help, my friends! the flames roar past control!
Have mercy, love, you burn my very soul!
Alas, I've made a jest of men
And I am served right fittingly
If, ravaging my virgin pride, 800
A man should make a jest of me. [*Crying hysterically, in a loud voice*]
The gentleman, beneath his word of honour
And his sworn faith, has reaped my flower of honour.
Promising me that he would marry me
He has defiled my honesty and bed,
And I'm deceived, deceived! . . . and worse, alas,
I alone gave his cruelty wings to fly

In my two mares that my own hands have reared—
For he pretended we should fly on them,
But with them he has mocked me and escaped. . . 810
[*A pause of exhaustion . . . resuming, with a great voice of anguish*]
Pursue him, every one! . . . [*Lower, moaning*]
But it does not matter
Which way he goes, for I'll go to the King
And on my naked knees with cries and tears
Implore his sacred Majesty for vengeance! . . .
Help, help, my friends, the flames roar past control!
Have mercy, love! you burn my very soul!

[TISBEA *goes out*]

Scene 19

Enter, running, CORIDON, ANFRISO.

CORIDON:
Follow the vile fellow!

ANFRISO:
How hard the lot
Of him who has to suffer and keep silence. . . . 820
O God in heaven, look on me this hour,
Deliver this vile ingrate to my power! [*Halts*]
No, rather let us seek out Tisbea,—
Heart-heavy with dishonour, she might still
Attempt to cure it with a greater ill!

CORIDON:
So high a pride must always come to grief:
Her frenzy is as great as her belief
And blind conceit. . . .

TISBEA [*Without*]:
Oh, the fire that burns in me!

ANFRISO:
Quick, or she'll cast herself into the sea! 830

CORIDON:
Wait, Tisbea, we are friends, and bring relief!

TISBEA [*Without, wailing*]:
Help, help, my friends, the flames roar past control! . . .
Have mercy, love, you burn my very soul!

[END OF FIRST ACT]

ACT II

Scene 1

In the Palace of ALONZO, KING OF SPAIN, *at Seville. The* KING *and* DON JUAN'*s father,* DON DIEGO TENORIO.

KING [*Shocked*]:
—What is it that you tell me?

DON DIEGO:
—I hold a letter here from your ambassador,
My brother, which makes plain how he was taken
Together with a lady of the court,
In dereliction.
KING:
Does it say what her rank is?
DON DIEGO:
It says she is the Duchess Isabela.
KING [*Starting angrily*]:
Isabela?
DON DIEGO [*Bowing submissively*]:
She, and none other.
KING:
What headlong madness! . . . [*A pause*] Where is Don Juan now? 10
DON DIEGO [*After a moment's hesitation*]:
Great Sire, from your high majesty
No truth can long bide hidden. On this night
He reaches Seville, with his single servant.
KING [*Not unkindly*]:
Tenorio, I would have you understand
In what esteem I hold you for informing
Your King straightway of this sad accident—
The ruin of the Duchess Isabela
And Duke Octavio's heartbreak; wherefore I
Must send your erring son to banishment.
DON DIEGO [*Unhappily*]:
Sire, whither would you send him? 20
KING:
It will appease my anger for the present
If he depart from Seville. Let him hasten
To Lebrija this very night, and thank
His father's merit for his neck's salvation.
But what shall I say now to Don Gonzalo
To avoid his offense?—
He has already spoken with his daughter
Concerning her espousals to Don Juan. . . .
Look where I will, I find no remedy.
DON DIEGO:
Trust in me, Sire, to find an honest way 30
With which to suit the honour of a lady
Honoured with such a father.
KING:
Yours be the task, then.
[*Enter, a* SERVANT]

Scene 2

SERVANT:
There is a gentleman who waits outside
Hot from the highway, and he says he is
The Duke Octavio.
KING [*Repeating, in amazement*]:
The Duke Octavio?

SERVANT:
Such were his words, great Sire.

KING:
No doubt he comes to fall upon his knees
And beg permission to avenge his wrong
In mortal combat... 'tis a quick return
For Juan's folly. [*Nods for* SERVANT *to show* DUKE *in*]

DON DIEGO:
Great and august Sire,
In your heroic hands you hold my life,
Holding my son's life, in whose life I live,
Though he be graceless. But let me assure you
That though he's but a lad, he goes so headlong
In bold, out-braving daring, that his fellows
Have nicknamed him "The Hector of Seville";
For always he leaps first before he looks
And trusts that God will drop him on his feet....
A word of reason used in time is golden:
If it be possible, prevent this challenge.

KING:
Enough, Tenorio, I understand
The honour of a father—here's the Duke!
[*Enter* DUKE OCTAVIO]

Scene 3

OCTAVIO [*Casting himself at the* KING'*s feet*]:
A miserable, banished wayfarer,
I cast myself down in your royal presence:
Humbly I press my lips against your feet;
Your granted audience turns my way's rough hardships
To pleasantness.

KING [*Kindly*]:
Aye, Duke Octavio!

OCTAVIO:
Made heart-sick by a woman's cruel folly
And by the outrage of some nobleman
Whose boldness caused that folly—I have come
To pray for retribution.

KING:
Duke Octavio, arise!
Your innocence is known to us already
And we shall write your king, urging upon him
Your restoration to your former state,
For you are an abused and honest man,
Though ill your absence be interpreted....
And, also, I'll arrange a marriage for you—
[*Aside, to* DON DIEGO]
This will assuage the honour of Gonzalo—
With a woman here in Seville;—one of such beauty
That if your Isabela were an angel
She'd seem deformed and black in her comparison...
Others are unto her as are the stars

Before the dawn, that dims their points of light.
Gonzalo de Ulloa, the Knight Commander
Of Calatrava, is a warrior 80
And nobleman, before whom the swart Moor
In flattering cowardice bows . . . he has a daughter
Who equally for purity as for beauty
Is famous. I myself will ask her hand
For you.

OCTAVIO:
I hold my journey fortunate
If only that it brought me to your favour.

KING [*To* SERVANT]:
Give the Duke lodging in the palace—see
That he lacks nothing for his entertainment.

OCTAVIO [*Bowing deeply*]:
I note that kingly is your least behest . . . 90
The Eleventh Alonzo, still you're first and best!

[*The* KING *goes out with* DON DIEGO *and* SERVANT]

Scene 4

RIPIO *comes in.*

RIPIO [*To* OCTAVIO]:
Well, how have things succeeded with you, master?

OCTAVIO:
As well as I could wish, and better, Ripio.
I've spoken with the King, and he has looked
On me with honour, as Cæsar treats with Cæsar;
For I have come, and urged my cause, and conquered,
And he has sworn not only to effect
Reversal of our king's decree against me
But with his own hand to advance my marriage.

RIPIO:
It is not without cause they call him "generous"— 100
But did you say he's marrying you to—some one?

OCTAVIO:
Yes, friend—unto a woman of Seville.
For in Seville you'll find as many women
Beautiful, as there are gallant gentlemen:
Where can you find the cloak close-drawn to cover
The amorous design more frequently
Than here? My promised happiness already
Has drawn the sting of sorrow from my heart.

Scene 5

DON JUAN *and* CATALINÓN *come in.*

CATALINÓN [*Plucking* DON JUAN*'s sleeve . . . aside*]:
Master, take care! here's Sagitarius,
The innocent archer, who aimed at Isabela 110

And, missing her, passed into Capricorn
Because you taught his brows to wear the horn.

DON JUAN [*Aside, to* CATALINÓN]:
Pst! don't let on!

CATALINÓN [*Aside, to* DON JUAN]:
Look out, he'll fawn on you while he betrays!

DON JUAN [*To* DUKE OCTAVIO]:
I flew from Naples down the dusty ways
Spurred by an instant summons from the King
Whose slightest wish becomes immediate law,—
And so, my friend, you see the reason why
I didn't have the time to say good-bye.

OCTAVIO:
I cannot look upon an act as ill 120
That joins us in new friendship in Seville.

DON JUAN [*With hidden irony*]:
Who would have thought that I'd have found you here
Where I perhaps may be of service to you
According to your high desert . . . I see
You, too, have left Naples, that lovely city,
Which none could leave, but for Seville alone.

OCTAVIO:
Friend, if it were in Naples that you spoke
I'd think that you were making me a joke.
Yes, Seville is a pretty place to dwell in . . .
But who comes here? 130

DON JUAN [*Seeking to get rid of* OCTAVIO, *that he might speak with his old crony alone, and thinking that* OCTAVIO*'s simpleness of nature spells cowardice in him*]:
It is the Marquis de la Mota. . . .
He comes in violent and haughty pride.

OCTAVIO [*With sturdy sincerity*]:
Well, if you stand in need of help at all
My blade and good right arm are on your side.

CATALINÓN [*Apart*]:
—And, if it comes his way—untouched by shame,
He'll fool another woman in your name,
You valiant ass!

OCTAVIO [*Continuing warmly to* DON JUAN]:
I'm proud to take your side!

[DON JUAN *makes an easy gesture to* OCTAVIO *that everything is all right*]

CATALINÓN [*Making an elaborate bow*]:
Gentlemen, if you've any further need
Of Catalinón, you can always get him 140
For further service at—

RIPIO [*Scenting a drink*]:
What place?

CATALINÓN [*Winking across to* DON JUAN]:
The Inn
Of Little Birds, where they draw most divine
And excellent draughts of care-forgetting wine.

[CATALINÓN *still lingers, however. He only said he was going because he sees that his master wants to be alone with* MOTA. . . . OCTAVIO *and* RIPIO *slowly go out. The* MARQUIS DE LA MOTA *enters.*]

Scene 6

MOTA [*To* DON JUAN]:
All day long I've looked for you
But couldn't find you anywhere.
Don Juan, how could you be
In Seville, and yet not send
A single notice to your friend 150
Who suffered from your lack?

DON JUAN [*Fervently*]:
By heaven! Dear friend, I thank you for your welcome!
How can I repay your friendship? [*Wrings* MOTA*'s hand warmly.*]

CATALINÓN [*Apart*]:
Just put a woman in his way,
Or half her like, and he'll repay!
You'll find he won't betray your trust
As long as you don't thwart his lust
Or fall a-foul some amorous plan—
In short, he's just a nobleman!...

DON JUAN [*To* MOTA]:
How goes it in Seville these days? 160

MOTA:
Great changes, friend, have taken place
In a short time.

DON JUAN:
—The women?

MOTA:
They
Are—[*with a shrug*]—well, what can a fellow say?

DON JUAN:
Inez?

MOTA:
She's gone to Vejel.

DON JUAN:
—A rare
Abiding place, if she be there.

MOTA:
Time has retired her to that town. 170

DON JUAN:
—Time, that must bring all beauty down....
Constanza?

MOTA:
Ay! but it is sad
To see the eyebrows she once had
Grown bald now as her thinning hair;
They call her "the old Portuguese trull"
But still she thinks she's beautiful!

DON JUAN:
—And the two sisters?—

MOTA:
Sweet Tolú, Celestina's daughter,
Observes as constantly as ever 180
The lessons that her mother taught her.

DON JUAN:
And Bercebú,
Has she grown any better than before?
MOTA:
Better, and worse, in hell's despite:
She has a saint for every fast.
DON JUAN [*Laughing*]:
She keeps her vigils, too, each night?
MOTA [*Laughing*]:
—A holy woman till the last!
DON JUAN:
And how about the other one?
MOTA:
—As universal as the sun
That favours all it shines upon. 190
DON JUAN:
And don't you know some jolly lark
To send us laughing down the dark?
MOTA:
To-night Don Pedro de Esquivél
And I, have turned one jest quite well,
And I know two more yet to do
Before the dawn.
DON JUAN:
I'll go with you:
Perhaps the nest you have in view
Might yield a soft squab for me, too.
On earth or under, let's begin! 200
MOTA [*With a sudden turn toward seriousness*]:
I lead you to no goatish sin
In this, nor pitch of roaring mirth... [*sadly*]
Through it I'm almost brought under the earth.
DON JUAN [*Putting an arm around* MOTA*'s shoulder*]:
Is any woman so hard to obtain?
MOTA [*Shaking his head sadly*]:
I fear that all that I can do is vain.
DON JUAN:
You mean, when you advance she draws apart?
MOTA:
Oh, no! she meets me halfway with her heart.
DON JUAN [*Growing curious*]:
Who is she?
MOTA:
My cousin, Doña Ana;
She just arrived the other day at Seville. 210
DON JUAN:
And where was she before?
MOTA:
She was at Lisbon
Accompanying her father on his embassage.
DON JUAN [*Quickly*]:
And—is she—beautiful?

MOTA:

Past all conception,

For in her, nature outsoars nature's self.

DON JUAN:

If she's as wonderful as you report

[*Hungrily*] God keep life in me till I see her face!

MOTA [*In a revery*]:

And when you do you will behold a beauty

Greater than any that the sun shines on. 220

DON JUAN [*Probing*]:

Marry her, then, if she's so glorious!

MOTA [*In deep melancholy*]:

The King already has her match in hand

But I don't know to whom he means to give her.

DON JUAN:

But she—she favours you?

MOTA [*Proudly*]:

She writes and writes me.

CATALINÓN [*Apart*]:

Take care! The greatest rogue of love in Spain

Will have his jest with you in his old vein.

DON JUAN [*With great passion*]:

Are you a man, and can you walk apart

With such a love that waits you? God's great heart,

If I were you I'd dare the worst misfortune, 230

Assured of love like that, I would importune

The utmost; haunt her window day and night—

And when I couldn't speak to her, I'd write!

Or at her portals wake impetuous thunder

Until the world caught flame and burst asunder!

MOTA [*Catching the contagion of* DON JUAN*'s fire*]:

I'll be as desperate as your persuasion.

DON JUAN [*Slyly*]:

Don't waste the hour that houses the occasion.

MOTA:

I'll put the issue to immediate test.

[*The* MARQUIS *and his servant hasten out*]

CATALINÓN [*Apart*]:

Aha! my master shapes another jest!

DON JUAN [*To* CATALINÓN]:

The Marquis goes to the palace . . . follow him. 240

[CATALINÓN *goes out*]

Scene 7

A WOMAN *shows her face at the grating.*

WOMAN [*Softly, to* DON JUAN]:

Who is that I speak to?

DON JUAN [*Coming forward . . . cautiously*]:

Who is it that you want?

WOMAN:

Since you are courteous and circumspect

I'll give this letter, sir, into your keeping. . . .

See that it comes into the Marquis' hands
Straightway, because a maiden's happiness
Depends upon it.

DON JUAN [*With satisfaction*]:
I'll take it to him straightway.... [*As the* WOMAN *hesitates*] You can trust me....
I am a gentleman and his tried friend... [*As she still hesitates*] 250
You have a pretty face!

WOMAN [*Flattered*]:
Although you are a stranger to me, sir,
Yet you seem trustworthy.... God shield you, sir!
[*She hands him the letter and disappears*]

Scene 8

DON JUAN [*Solus*]:
The hunt is on: the bugles call
To chase the greatest game of all,
Woman!... in devious pursuit
I track her course from place to place,
Then trap her like a frightened brute
And snatch the trophies of the chase. [*Turning the letter about*]
This letter comes as from nowhere, 260
A daughter of the unseen wind
Dropping like magic out of air.... [*Meditatively*]
Yes, she's the girl, without a doubt,
My friend the Marquis brags about.
He dared his fate in telling me
About his white divinity.
All Seville calls me Love's buffoon;
Has he forgot my tricks so soon?
He thinks, perhaps, a friend's immune!
Doesn't he know that I employ 270
My days and nights for one great joy,
One only, fooling womenkind,
Ruining, and leaving them behind!...
Come, then, I'll open this and read... [*Tears open letter*]
It makes me smile as I proceed:
Its freshness brings me life again:
To him who dares the way is plain.
The scent is close: I sight the game...
It's signed with Doña Ana's name—
"My faithless father has arranged my marriage 280
In secret, with another—being weak
And feminine, it is beyond my strength
To overcome his will; I cannot live:
For he will not relent, and I shall die
Before another takes me mouth to mouth....
Oh, if my love gives any sweetness to you,
And the love you protest be kin to truth,
The time and opportunity is here
For you to show it... and, that you may know
In what regard and confidence I hold you, 290
Come to my garden gate this very star-time:

You'll find it open at the eleventh hour,
And I will yield myself into your power,
When you, my love, may reap your utmost wish
And round the consummation of your hope.
Wear a red mantle as a sign by which
Leonorilla and my other women
May know you and admit you, my heart's glory!—
Your most ill-fated sweetheart,

DOÑA ANA."

[*Laughing*]

And so I'm offered the same cup to quaff 300
Brimmed with the same good wine... I've got to laugh!...
With the same turn of craft and the same gust
In Naples Isabela served my lust.

[*Destroys letter.* CATALINÓN *comes in again*]

Scene 9

CATALINÓN [*To* DON JUAN]:
The Marquis comes.
DON JUAN:
That's good and right—
We have a game afoot to-night.
CATALINÓN:
You've still a new deceit to play?
DON JUAN:
A jollier jest than words can say.
CATALINÓN [*With great seriousness*]:
Master, I can't approve of this,
For things are sure to run amiss 310
Some day; a first or second time
Fate may seem to forget your crime,
But, know, her judgments never rest
Until the jester pays his jest.
DON JUAN:
I didn't hire you for a preacher;
You are my valet, not my teacher.
CATALINÓN [*Persisting*]:
The brave man always stops to think.
DON JUAN:
The coward, to hesitate and shrink!...
The man who goes in service must,
With the first bread he eats, entrust 320
His whole will to another's whim
Nor ask the "how" or "why" of him—
It's his to listen and obey,
To wait, to do, and not to say....
Suppose you served some praying master
Who snuffed each wind for far disaster—
You too would have to kneel and pray
And bear a visage long and sad:
With me, your task is to be gay...
So you should thank God, and be glad! 330

CATALINÓN [*Hedging*]:
I do. I vow I'll stop protesting
And join in all your pranks and jesting.
DON JUAN [*Smiling mischievously*]:
Servants that speak their masters' will
Are seldom bidden to be still.
I always lend a ready ear
To the advice I want to hear.
CATALINÓN:
I swear, from now on, that I'll do
Whatever you require me to—
Like a mad elephant or tiger
I'll go with you through every prank; 340
Only just drop a guiding word
And any hour of day or night
I'll hold my tongue, or I will fight.
DON JUAN:
Be quiet now . . . we will be heard.
Our friend the Marquis comes in sight!
[*The* MARQUIS DE LA MOTA *comes in*]

Scene 10

DON JUAN [*To* MOTA]:
A woman whom I could not see
('Twas only by her voice I knew her sex)
Whispered this good news through the grating to me,
For you . . . that you should come . . . at the twelfth hour . . .
In secret, to her garden gate, which would 350
Be open at eleven, where she'd wait.
And yield her soul and body in your power,
Giving you full and free control thereof
That you might reap the utmost fruits of love. . . .
Furthermore, she required
That you should wear a red cape, by which sign
Leonorilla and her other women
Might know you, who you were, and let you in.
MOTA [*Overjoyed*]:
What do you tell me!
DON JUAN [*A curious smile playing over his features*]:
I repeat 360
That which was whispered through the grating to me,
By whom—I do not know.
MOTA:
The message you've conveyed, my good, true friend,
Heaps up the measure of my happiness
Till it bursts over . . . I fall down at your feet
And press them with my lips!
DON JUAN [*Amused, preventing him*]:
I'm not your cousin, though one would think I were:
Kissing my feet is not enjoying her.
MOTA:
I do so from excess of happiness
And because you have saved my life for me. 370

DON JUAN:
He's a sad friend that will not help a lover.
MOTA:
O sun, amend your footsteps toward the west!
DON JUAN:
He verges downward to his setting now.
MOTA:
Come, let us go and make our preparation
For the ensuing night, my worthy friend!
Oh, I am going mad for very joy!
DON JUAN [*Apart*]:
I do not doubt that you are mad: but wait
Till the twelfth hour tolls at the midnight gate,
When such a madness you will entertain
As heaven only grants to the insane! 380
MOTA:
My cousin! sweet kinswoman of my soul,
To-night love's dart will find a double goal!
CATALINÓN [*Apart*]:
Christ's God! I think love's shaft will miss its mark
And strike another target, in the dark.
[*The* MARQUIS *goes out.* DON DIEGO, DON JUAN*'s father, comes in.*]

Scene 11

DON DIEGO [*To* DON JUAN]:
Juan!
CATALINÓN [*To* DON JUAN]:
Your father speaks to you.
DON JUAN:
What do you wish, my honoured sir?
DON DIEGO:
—To see you more discreet, my son,
And with a better fame than you have won;
For, as it is, with every breath, 390
You hasten on your father's death!
DON JUAN:
Father, what brings you to such sadness?
DON DIEGO:
Your evil deeds and headlong madness . . .
The King, in his just anger at you,
And your still uncorrected badness
Has told me that you must be sent
Forth from Seville, in banishment;
For he already knows your deed—
An action of such infamy,
He cannot think how to proceed 400
In its correction . . . in the royal palace
A dark betrayal of a noble friend! . . . [*As* DON JUAN *smiles*]
Traitor, I'll leave you in the hands of God,
He alone knows what punishment to send.

Remember, no ill thing can long be hidden
From Him, nor any act that is forbidden;
There is no soul that knows a turn so fleet
As to out-pace His dreadful, following feet—
And when you step beyond your utmost breath
You'll learn, too late, He is your Judge, in death. 410

DON JUAN [*Unable to keep from a certain savage playfulness*]:
—In death? . . .
That leaves me a wide scope to fill;
From now to death is a great journey still.

DON DIEGO [*Severely*]:
The longest life, the widest span of days
Lends all too little time to mend your ways.

DON JUAN [*Stretching*]:
Well, tell me, father, when I'm to begin
This life-long purging of a native sin . . .
How heavy is the wage I'll have to pay?

DON DIEGO:
At Lebrija you are to make your stay
Until your banishment strikes recompense 420
Unto Octavio's undeserved offence,
And till in every way you've paid the shot
Of Isabela's sad, unhappy lot—
Straightway the King commands this banishment:
For your offence a gentle punishment.

CATALINÓN [*Apart*]:
Ah, if the good old man suspected
That prank my master practised when
He fooled the little fisher girl,
His honour would be so affected
That he would fret and fume again! 430

DON DIEGO:
Since nothing I can do or say
Can move your heart in any way,
Since you're too old to taste the rod [*with a burst of wrath*]
I'll leave you to the whips of God!

[DON DIEGO *goes out, tears streaming down his cheeks*]

Scene 12

CATALINÓN [*To* DON JUAN]:
The poor old man was moved to tears!

DON JUAN [*Easily*]:
That's a condition of his years. . . .
But come, the dark is settling slow,
Let's find the Marquis.

CATALINÓN:
Yes, let's go.
Where you'll beguile another dame. 440

DON JUAN [*With a shrug of the shoulders*]:
They say that's how I'm known to fame.

CATALINÓN:
May we get out as we get in!

DON JUAN [*Contemptuously*]:
You mean "may luck save Catalinón's skin"!
CATALINÓN [*Placatively*]:
Ah, master, as the locusts fall
On sweet, green fields and blacken all
The landscape, leaving dearth behind—
So you behave with womenkind! [*Following the humour of his fancy*]
Through every city in all Spain
The town-crier should ring his bell
To bid each maiden be on guard 450
Against your bold and sudden spell:
"All wives, beware!
All maids, take care,
If ever you held virtue dear!—
The great love-rogue of Spain is here!"
DON JUAN [*In a ringing voice*]:
You've given me a noble name
And I take pride in such a fame!
[*It is now dusky-dark. The* MARQUIS *comes in, with musicians.*
The MARQUIS *goes across the stage. The musicians follow, singing.*]

Scene 13

MUSICIANS' SONG

He who would suck all love's sweetness
From its flower so white and fair
Must not hope for unmixed honey 460
Where hope's self is half despair,
Where hope's self is half despair!

MOTA:
O star-vast night, so cool and sweet,
Hasten your stars to still midnight
When I shall compass my delight—
But then delay their silver feet,
In halted millions let them burn
And never let the day return.
DON JUAN:
What's this that comes?
CATALINÓN:
Music and song! 470
MOTA [*To* DON JUAN, *exaltedly*]:
In this great night with stars a-throng
What poet is it speaks with me?
DON JUAN:
A friend!
MOTA:
Don Juan?
DON JUAN:
It is he . . .
Are you the Marquis?

MOTA:

Faithfully.

But what would I be without you?

DON JUAN:

As your red cape came into view

I knew you. . . . 480

MOTA:

Let's move further on. . . .

[*To the musicians, that they might be busied during his conference with* DON JUAN]

Sing, while I talk with Don Juan.

MUSICIANS' SONG (*continued*)

He who would suck all love's sweetness
From its flower so white and fair
Must not hope for unmixed honey
Where hope's self is half despair. . . .

He who would suck all love's sweetness
From its flower so white and fair
Must be quick as woman's fancy
Or his lips will drink despair— 490
Or his lips will drink despair.

DON JUAN:

Whose dwelling is it that we're aiming at?

MOTA:

The house of Don Gonzalo de Ulloa.

Scene 14

Before the house of DON GONZALO DE ULLOA.

MOTA [*To* DON JUAN]:

This is the place where the brave venture waits me!

[*A clock in a tower strikes eleven*]

DON JUAN [*To* MOTA]:

It's just eleven. You've an hour's wait yet . . .

Perhaps some deadly ambush has been set

For you, my friend, so lend your cape to me

That, while you wait here, I may go and see . . .

Within this archway for the moment loiter:

I'll take a turn or two, and reconnoitre. 500

MOTA:

You advise rightly: take my cape and go.

DON JUAN [*With scarcely concealed eagerness*]:

Show me which place it is!

MOTA:

Take on my mien and manner of speech also . . .

Look where I point—you see that grating yonder?

DON JUAN [*Intensely, yet imitating* MOTA*'s manner of speech so that he makes the latter laugh*]:

I see it!

MOTA:
Press your lips close and whisper "Beatriz!"
And she will let you in.
DON JUAN [*Catching a new scent*]:
What sort of woman
Is she?
MOTA:
You mean Beatriz, Ana's serving maid? [*Misled, teasing*] 510
Pretty as a white rose, and yet as cold
As is a mountain brook, to men.
CATALINÓN [*Apart; thinking, with* MOTA, *for the moment, that* DON JUAN *has his mind set on a side-divertisement with the maid*]:
Here's one, it seems,
Will give a chill dash to my master's hot
Desire!
MOTA [*Grinning—to* DON JUAN]:
I catch your drift now . . . danger, indeed!
While I'm a-trot you'll also ride your steed . . .
Always trust Don Juan to serve his need. . . .
DON JUAN:
You're clever, Marquis—adios! [*Going*]
MOTA:
Adios!
CATALINÓN [*Back on the right scent, remembering his master's deed in Naples . . . aside to him, as he passes by*]:
Master, is it the white or the red rose? 520
DON JUAN [*Aside, to* CATALINÓN]:
Be silent, donkey, you're the one who knows,
If any ought to, above all the rest—
I go to practise my unceasing jest.
CATALINÓN [*Aside, to* DON JUAN]:
But when she finds the lie beneath the cape
He [*looking fearfully toward* MOTA] will be here, and you cannot escape!
DON JUAN [*Aside, to* CATALINÓN]:
It's dangerous, but too keen a jest to lose.
CATALINÓN [*Aside, to* DON JUAN]:
You thrust your neck into a dangling noose . . .
You wave a red cape for a mad bull's charge.
DON JUAN [*Aside, to* CATALINÓN, *grimly*]:
No, I am the mad bull that runs at large.
[DON JUAN *goes up to the grating, and is admitted within*]
MOTA [*Laughing, as at a great joke*]:
—And Beatriz will think that it is I! 530
A MUSICIAN [*To* MOTA]:
Your jolly friend will soon show how she's wrong.
MOTA:
Through two deceits I come to Ana's side.
A MUSICIAN:
The whole world has gone blind, with none to guide.
MOTA [*To* MUSICIANS]:
Now make it seem some harmless lover's song
Sung innocently in some garden-side.

MUSICIANS' SONG

He who would suck all love's sweetness
From its flower so white and fair
Must not hope for unmixed honey
Where hope's self is half despair...

He who would suck all love's sweetness 540
From its flower so white and fair
Must be quick as woman's fancy
Or his lips will drink despair...

He who would suck all love's sweetness
From its flower so white and fair
Must mix passion with discreetness,
Must of sudden traps beware!—
Must of sudden traps beware!

[*They go into another part of the garden, as they sing*]

DOÑA ANA [*Crying within*]:
You have deceived me! you are not the Marquis!

DON JUAN [*Making an effort to quiet her, speaking within*]:
I am the Marquis... hush, you'll rouse your father! 550

ANA [*Beside herself with grief, within*]:
You are an enemy,—you have betrayed me!

[DON GONZALO *appears, rushing in, sword in hand*]

Scene 15

DON GONZALO:
I know that voice... my daughter calls for help.

ANA [*Within*]:
Is there no manhood near to kill this traitor,
This mad assassin of my maiden honour?

DON GONZALO:
Does any one walk with such monstrous boldness
As to have done a deed like this, my daughter?
I think your tongue is also a betrayer,—
Why, like a courtesan, has it lain silent
Till the transgression's fact grew manifest?
It should have shattered midnight like a clarion. 560

ANA [*Within*]:
Kill him!

[DON GONZALO *starts in, sword in hand, when the gate is wrenched open and* DON JUAN *comes out, with* CATALINÓN, *both having drawn swords in hand.*]

DON JUAN [*Facing* DON GONZALO *with steady assurance*]:
What man are you?

DON GONZALO:
Traitor, you have sent crashing from its base
The goodly house of honour that I govern.

DON JUAN [*Insolently*]:
Let me go by!

DON GONZALO [*With fury*]:
—Go by! yes, through my sword's point.

DON JUAN:
You are a dead man if you hinder me.

DON GONZALO:
To die is life now.
DON JUAN:
I see that I must slay you.
DON GONZALO [*Attacking with great fury*]:
Seducer, die! 570
DON JUAN:
This is the way I die!
[*With a sudden thrust he runs* DON GONZALO *through*]
CATALINÓN [*Apart*]:
If we escape, uncaught, from this fine shambles,
I go no more upon my master's gambols.
DON GONZALO [*Falling*]:
Ai! you have given me my death!
DON JUAN:
You took
Your life itself in setting so on me,—
I warned you.
DON GONZALO [*With a deep groan*]:
I had nothing then to live for!
DON JUAN:
I, everything!
[DON JUAN *and* CATALINÓN *go out*]
DON GONZALO:
I am dying: there was no one near to aid me... 580
My murderer, may my hatred follow you
And pluck you down from that life's pride you boast.
You're a seducer and a coward, too,
For all your daring: only cowards betray
A woman's honour, and then run away! [*Dies*]

Scene 16

Another part of the garden. The MARQUIS DE LA MOTA *and musicians.*

MOTA:
It will soon be twelve o'clock
And still Don Juan stays within....
Waiting is a heavy task.
[DON JUAN *and* CATALINÓN *come in*]
DON JUAN:
Is this the Marquis?
MOTA:
Are you Don Juan? 590
DON JUAN:
Here, take your mantle back.
MOTA:
You have had your jest?
DON JUAN [*With a shrug of the shoulders*]:
Yes, all in all, I think I've done my best.
MOTA:
You played your game quite through?

DON JUAN:

I have essayed

A gambol for which some one's dearly paid.

MOTA [*Flinging the red mantle, returned, over his own shoulders*]:

I'll take the mistress as you took the maid:

And if the latter has a plaint to make

I'll smoothe it over for our friendship's sake.

DON JUAN [*With a slight tinge of irony*]:

Marquis, farewell! 600

CATALINÓN [*Aside, to* DON JUAN]:

My mad and fortunate master,

So far we ride the crest of all disaster.

DON JUAN [*Aside, to* CATALINÓN]:

I think that Mota will not like the joke

When he is seized, wearing his tell-tale cloak.

Come, let us fly!

CATALINÓN [*Aside, to* DON JUAN]:

Master, I'm with you there.

I'll go so fast my feet will singe the air.

[*They hurry out*]

MOTA [*To the musicians*]:

You may turn home now... I would be alone.

A MUSICIAN [*Yawning sleepily*]:

That God made nights for sleep is widely known.

[*The musicians go out. The* MARQUIS DE LA MOTA *goes up to the grating*]

MOTA [*Whispering*]:

Beatriz!... 610

[*Just as he is about to give the password a second time, a great outcry wakes within*]

VOICE WITHIN:

O, monstrous ill that cannot find a name!

The greater evil crowns the unheard shame!

[*More voices heard... and people moving about. Torches are seen in motion*]

MOTA [*Solus*]:

I hear the voices of the Guard approaching,

What could bring them here this time of night?

A chill strikes through my marrow. They deploy

With torches that pour flames like burning Troy...

They move in groups. They wind this way and that.

I'll join with them and find out what they're at.

[DON DIEGO *and guards come in, carrying torches*]

DON DIEGO [*To* MOTA, *holding the torch up, for closer scrutiny, in the latter's face*]:

Who are you?

MOTA [*With innocent boldness*]:

One who would like to learn 620

The reason for this clamour and disturbance.

DON DIEGO [*Abruptly, turning to the guards*]:

Arrest this man!

MOTA [*Whipping out his sword*]:

—Arrest me?

DON DIEGO:

Put up your sword,—

The greater bravery goes weaponless.

MOTA [*Keeping them off with his sword's point*]:
Who chides the Marquis de la Mota?
DON DIEGO:
Render up your sword in the King's name, Marquis!
MOTA [*Instantly handing over his sword to* DON DIEGO—*as an obedient subject*]:
Now God protect me!
[*Enter, the* KING *with retinue*]

Scene 17

KING:
—The like of this has not been heard in Spain—
Nor, if one went to Italy, could its like 630
Be hit on there.
DON DIEGO:
Sire, here is the Marquis!
MOTA:
Could it be true your Highness gives command
For my arrest?
KING [*Ignoring the* MARQUIS. *To* DON DIEGO]:
Have his head struck off. Let it be caught up
On iron hooks where all may see the monster!
[*Turning sharply on* MOTA]
Dare you defend your outrage in my presence?
MOTA [*In despair*]:
Love is a tyrant even in his joys,
Pleasant and soft are they for their brief moment
Like melting honey dripping on the tongue: 640
But, afterward, dead-heavy life drags on
In slow, monotonous, unescaping pain
Day on interminable, weary day,
Until the day of doom, which quickly comes,
Thank God, for me—the wise man well has said:
"Between the mouth and the brim-tilted flagon
Peril can step and spill the thwarted wine" . . .
Yet the King's sudden wrath bewilders me—
Am I condemned because I breathe the air?
DON DIEGO:
There's no one better knows the cause than you do! 650
MOTA [*Staggered*]:
Than I?—
DON DIEGO [*Taking him roughly by the arm*]:
Come!
MOTA:
I feel as if the sky had fallen on me.
KING:
Wing the proceedings with the lightning's speed.
His head must leave his shoulders by to-morrow.
As for Gonzalo, my slain general,
His funeral shall have all the pomp and grandeur
Enjoyed by emperors when they depart
Their day of life. In bronze and valued stone

I shall cause men to lift his sepulchre, 660
And set his noble semblance, as in life,
Upon it. Underneath shall be inscribed
In work Mosaic and great Gothic letters
A vow of vengeance on the slayer's soul...

[*To* DON DIEGO]

Where has Doña Ana gone?

DON DIEGO:

Her Majesty, the Queen, gives her asylum.

KING:

All Castille knows and bewails its loss
In Don Gonzalo de Ulloa
The famous Captain of Calatrava.

[*All go out*]

Scene 18

A rustic scene of flowers and meadows. BATRICIO *comes in. He is a young countryman, about to be married to the country girl,* AMINTA, *who accompanies him. And there is* GASENO, *an old man, and* AMINTA*'s father, and* BELISA, *and shepherds who know music and can sing and play.*

SONG

Once again the holy sun 670
Rises on its April duty
Of kindling colours in the flowers
And worshipping Aminta's beauty.

BATRICIO:

No kinglier carpet ever spread
Than these long, marching fields of white and red;
The lusty sun walks overhead
Attending us with gentle strength
Through the sweet day's rejoicing length
To our love-watched marriage bed.

AMINTA [*To the shepherd-musicians*]:

Shepherds, sing again that song 680
As we stroll along.

THE SHEPHERDS [*Drolly varying the song, to* AMINTA*'s further praise*]:

Everywhere the April sun
Warms some maiden's peeping breast;
But we know Aminta's whiteness
He esteems the prettiest.

[*The birds begin to sing, as if moved to melody by the* SHEPHERDS*' song*]

GASENO:

Friends, so sweetly do you sing
That music wakes in everything.

BATRICIO [*To* AMINTA]:

The sun enjoys his morning hours
Because he takes your lips for flowers.

AMINTA [*To* BATRICIO]:
Batricio, such sweet speech you know 690
I fear you draw the flatterer's bow;
But feed me with your man's clear light
And I will be your subject moon
That, walking up the azure night,
Thinks only of the sun's delight
And to a silver use does turn
The fire he pours her from his urn.

[*They all go out, singing*]

SONG

Once again the holy sun
Rises on its April duty
Of kindling colours in the flowers 700
And worshipping Aminta's beauty.

Everywhere the April sun
Warms some maiden's peeping breast,
But we know Aminta's whiteness
He esteems the prettiest.

AMINTA:
I am so happy that I could die now!

[CATALINÓN *comes in from the highway*]

Scene 19

CATALINÓN:
Gentlemen, I come to claim
Your hospitality, in my master's name.

GASENO:
It is a world-wide custom to afford
Feasting and good cheer at the wedding board 710
To all who come—who is your master?

CATALINÓN:
Don Juan Tenorio.

GASENO:
The elder?

CATALINÓN:
Just Don Juan.

BELISA [*Explaining to the others*]:
It must be the Court Chamberlain's gallant son.

BATRICIO:
Whoever he be
I take it as an evil augury—
For every time these lads of noble birth
Come to wake jealousy and spoil our mirth . . .
Who gave him notice of my marriage day? 720

CATALINÓN:
He heard of it while he was on the way
To Lebrija, and thought he'd turn aside
And pay his passing tribute to the bride.

BATRICIO:
I think it was the Devil brought him here,
Whispering invitation in his ear.
Why must he come to harry me? Let all
The noblemen of all the wide world call
At my sweet marriage feast... but one, alone,
With dark foreboding makes my spirit groan.

GASENO [*Rollicking hugely, till, toward the end of his chant, all swing and rollic with him*]:
Let the Colossus come, 730
The Pope, and Prester John;
Let Don Alonzo the Eleventh
With all his court draw on,—
They'll find Gaseno's heart
Will never slack a beat:
He'll pour them Guadalquivers of wine,
Heap mountains of bread to eat;
Sierras of potted cheese,
Piled Babylons of bacon
We'll merely serve as sauce 740
To make true hunger waken:
Whole armies of frightened birds
We'll pluck and turn and toast,—
We'll interlard the mighty feast
With pullet and pigeon roast;
Let them all come: we've wine
To quench the Devil's thirst,
And food enough to stuff their guts
Until their bellies burst!

[*They all clap their hands and laugh*]

BELISA [*Musing to herself*]:
He is the son of the King's Chamberlain. 750

BATRICIO [*Apart*]:
Although they'll laugh at me if I complain,—
As sure as evil storm-clouds multiply
While growing thunder growls from sky to sky,
Now here, now there, till, in one drumming roar,
Heap upon heap the smoking waters pour,—
I hear the voice of far calamity—
What is the ill that fate destines for me?
For it's the custom of the countryside
To seat the guest of honour by the bride....
The bridegroom takes the right, the guest takes the left side.... 760
My joy dissolves... but it seems heaven's will,
So I must love, and suffer, and be still.

[DON JUAN *comes in*]

Scene 20

DON JUAN [*Looking around, with easy impudence*]:
I learned by chance, while passing by,
Of your festivities, so I

Have come to help you celebrate;
I think myself quite fortunate. [*Looking across at* AMINTA]

GASENO [*Making a rustic curtsey*]:
Your coming greatens us with honour, sir!

BATRICIO [*Bursting forth rudely, oppressed with premonitory despair*]:
No, I, who am the master of this feast,
Proclaim this hour as dark and sinister
That finds our company by you increased! 770

GASENO [*Shocked by* BATRICIO'*s outburst and lack of hospitable behaviour*]:
What? You won't make the gentleman a place?

DON JUAN [*Airily*]:
This seat will serve the purpose, by your grace!

[*He seats himself nonchalantly on the right of the bride—as they, of course, wait for him, as chief guest and nobleman, to be seated first*]

BATRICIO [*Uneasily, to* DON JUAN]:
Pardon me, but you've got the bridegroom's place.

DON JUAN [*Glancing with bold admiration towards* AMINTA]:
I think there are worse things a man might take.

GASENO [*Trying to explain to* DON JUAN, *who pretends not to understand*]:
You've put the bridegroom in an awkward case.

DON JUAN:
Pardon the ignorance of my mistake!

[*But still he does not make a move to give up the bridegroom's seat to* BATRICIO, *to whom it rightfully belongs. An uneasy titter runs about the board. The peasants are disquieted by* DON JUAN'*s boldness, yet cannot help laughing at* BATRICIO'*s surly discomfiture, in the face of* DON JUAN'*s easiness.*]

[*Aside, to* CATALINÓN—*who stands behind him*]

The bumpkin is abashed.

CATALINÓN [*Aside, to* DON JUAN]:
A rustic fool,—
Yet, fronted by the horns of a mad bull,
Who would not be abashed? 780
I would not give, with you pressed close upon her,
A penny for his woman and his honour.
Unfortunate man, whichever way you stir
You're caught close in the paws of Lucifer!

DON JUAN [*To* AMINTA, *aside*]:
Lady, I never thought that time would wait
Upon me with a day so fortunate—
There is one fact alone that makes me sigh,
The bridegroom is more fortunate than I.

AMINTA [*Aside, to* DON JUAN—*shy but flirtatious*]:
You're stroking me with hands of flattery.

BATRICIO [*Apart*]:
My heart forebodes some black calamity. 790

GASENO [*Uneasily, to* DON JUAN, *interrupting his tête-à-tête with* AMINTA]:
Your Lordship lets your cut of beef get cold,
Your ale grows flat, if I may be so bold!

DON JUAN [*Aside again to* AMINTA, *not heeding* GASENO—*possessing the hand of* AMINTA *under the table edge*]:
Why do you hide a hand that's so divine,
Milk-coloured, satin-soft!

AMINTA [*Aside, to* DON JUAN—*timidly*]:
It is no longer mine!
[*Nevertheless, she leaves it in his*]
GASENO [*Perturbed, he starts to rise—in order to break up* DON JUAN'*s impudent attentions to* AMINTA.]:
Come, let us go!
BELISA:
Come, let us sing and play!
DON JUAN [*Aside, to* CATALINÓN]:
Let's follow out the jest, what do you say?
CATALINÓN [*Aside, to* DON JUAN]:
I say that I fear for this simple folk
And the vile death you'll deal them for a joke. 800
DON JUAN [*Tenaciously, aside to* AMINTA]:
Sweet eyes, soft hands, you kindle my desire,
And burn my being up with climbing fire.
CATALINÓN [*Apart*]:
He'll brand you now and mark you of his fold,
Then cast you forth to perish in the cold!
DON JUAN [*As he rises, to go out with the company,—aside, to* AMINTA, *who is still seated in confusion—in a last audacity—with insinuating intimacy*]:
Come, they observe us!
BATRICIO [*Muttering, apart*]:
To have nobility
At my poor board bodes ill, I fear, for me!
GASENO [*Frantically*]:
Sing!
[*The tune of "Once again the holy sun" is struck up and they try to sing*]
BATRICIO [*Sadly*]:
Death is on me like a falcon's sweep.

END OF ACT TWO

ACT III

Scene 1

*Later on in day—same place—*BATRICIO *discovered alone.*

BATRICIO [*Solus*]:
Jealousy, the slow-crawling clock, and care
Have dragged out every hour a separate day,
Have given me to madness as a prey
And heaped me with confusion and despair.
O jealousy, you live in other's scorn;
Your votaries are by suspicions torn
Of that, which, true or false, they never know:
Your slavery wields its whip on high and low.
But torture me no more, for, in my case,
The evidence is plain of my disgrace; 10
Put back your dreadful arrows in their sheath:
Love's arrows give me life, yours give me death.

I was not wrong when I foresaw my woe;
Why, noble sir, must you torment me so?
Perhaps you think it is a clever trick
To eat by my own woman's side, and stick
Your fingers in the plate where mine should go! . . .
Yet my own comrades whispered "'Tricio"
When I protested mildly on that head—
"Don't make the gentleman think we're ill-bred." 20
And when I tried to lead a friend apart
And show how indignation gnawed my heart,
He'd answer, with a laugh that cut me short,—
"Don't worry, it's the custom held at court."
The custom! yes, a last and worst abuse:
Sodom itself would not accept its use—
Another man to surfeit with the bride
While the unhappy bridegroom fasts beside . . .
Then, outrage put to outrage, they would say:
"Why don't you come and eat?" and I'd reply: 30
"No," because first I'd have to eat my pride . . .
After a little while I slunk away
And posed this riddle to set wits at strife—
"Is a man married when he has no wife?" [*A pause*]
I could not stay and eat with Christian folk
Where those two sat and shared the bread they broke . . .
And then, when bedtime comes, to cap the jest,
We must afford his lordship a night's rest,
And, I suppose, when I seek my wife's bed,
They'll say—"the gentleman! . . . don't be ill-bred!" 40
[*With a sob*]
Oh, I am sick with shame, and, come what may,
I only seek a place to hide away
And at least keep my sight by distance blind
To what I see already in my mind.

Scene 2

DON JUAN *comes in.*

DON JUAN:
Batricio!
[BATRICIO *lifts up his head sullenly*]
BATRICIO:
What does your lordship want?
DON JUAN:
To tell you—something—
BATRICIO [*Apart*]:
Has he come to taunt
My patience with new insults?
DON JUAN [*Boldly*]:
For many days I have given my soul and heart, 50
Batricio, to Aminta, and have had
Her soul and heart in turn!

BATRICIO [*Gasping with surprise at the unexpected declaration, but, with puzzled, rustic honesty, accepting it*]:

You have, sir?

DON JUAN [*Steadfastly*]:

I have.

BATRICIO [*Bitterly*]:

I do not doubt the clear and manifest
Witness of what my eyes have seen already,
For I am sure Aminta never would
Have stabbed me so with open suffering
Unless she loved you—though it's somewhat strange,
This unknown bond between you, gentleman! 60
Why is it that I never knew of it?

DON JUAN:

It was a secret that we kept between us;
But, briefly, this is what has brought me here:
Aminta, growing jealous of my absence
Or perhaps desperate because she thought
I had forgotten her, even on the eve
Of her indenture to an alien master
In marriage, posthaste sent this letter to me.

[*He shows a letter to* BATRICIO, *who awkwardly and self-consciously turns it about in all directions, not being able to read. He scratches his head, nods in affected comprehension, hands it back*]

DON JUAN [*Proceeding*]:

As you have seen, the general drift of it
Is frank avowal of her love for me. 70
I am the man she loves, not you; your honour
Demands it, then, that you should aid us both
And open us an avenue of flight,
Which given or not, if any should impede,
Over his corpse my purpose shall proceed.

BATRICIO:

You've served me up a most unsavory dish
But I shall do the unheard thing you wish . . .
Honour? Its high exactions prove in vain
When to dishonour one is honour-bound;
Women? they always lose more than they gain 80
Because they judge the bell but by its sound:
And woman's reason flies away on wings
When the cracked bell of love and passion rings;
With her, man's "right" and "wrong" 's a game to play,
A tossed-up coin that tumbles either way;
Her being "good" or "bad" is only chance,
For as the music plays her feet must dance.
Take her, your lordship, for a thousand years,
And I will be the last that interferes
Since I cannot enjoy her when alive, 90
And I have heard that dead men never wive!

[BATRICIO *mopes forth disconsolate*]

Scene 3

DON JUAN [*Solus*]:

And so the mere use of a word called "honour"
Has conquered him: country folk always carry
Their honour open in their honest hands
Where they can hold it up and gaze upon it—
And have it snatched away by the quick wit.
And it is well that this "word" has come down
From city court and town
To take its habitation in the fields:
For now I reap the harvest that it yields; 100
A hint plied here and there, and I have won
By lies and craft what armies had not done.
Before I brush the morning dew from her,
This yokel's promised bride,
I'll gain the artless sanction of her father
With a few words to mould him to my use:
From now on, Honour, I will keep a taper
Burning before your shrine continually.
I go to seek the old man out; night strides
Down the road like a traveller, and the sky 110
Falls dark . . . O stars of heaven, light me on
To safe enjoyment of my new desire,—
But if death this time prove my labour's hire,
Your friendly office still administer
And let me perish while embracing her.

[DON JUAN *goes out*]

Scene 4

AMINTA *and* BELISA *come in.*

BELISA:

Go to your cabin, Aminta, and get ready;
The stars are waiting for your bridal now:
Batricio, your bridegroom, will come soon,
Breathing impatience, hungry for your arms
As one who starves craves meat that's set before him 120
To his repletion.

AMINTA [*Groaning*]:

Oh, my unhappy 'spousals! [*With a little sigh*]
Belisa, what makes men
So unforgiving, for a little play?
Why, all the while, Batricio gloomed apart
Bathed in a black cloud of melancholy,
Confused and jealous! Oh, what dark disaster!
Tell me, who was that handsome nobleman
Who stepped between me and my honest man?
Are impudence and noble blood the same, 130
Or is the passionate Spanish sun to blame?
Oh, how ashamed I am to have been so witless!

Hell's night fall on this easy cavalier
Who moved me here and there with soft persuasions
And laid hands on my silly womanhood,
Robbing my heart's peace.

BELISA [*Putting her finger to her lips*]:
Be still!
[*They both listen*]
Aminta, I think the bridegroom comes
With a man's tread of lusty confidence. [*Going*]

AMINTA [*Clinging to her friend frantically*]:
Oh, my sweetest, sweetest Belisa, 140
Do not go just yet . . . stay—stay—a while—yet!

BELISA [*Stroking* AMINTA*'s hair*]:
You silly little child, don't be afraid!
Why must this panic take a woman's heart
With her first lover? . . . dearest Aminta,
One would think you were going to your death,
Your heart makes such a tumult in your body.
Just stop his mouth with kisses if he chides;
Appease his anger in enfolding arms,
And make your haughty man a playful boy.
[*She goes out*]

AMINTA [*Folding her hands and lifting them heavenward in prayer*]:
From tears and kisses and repentant sighs 150
May new-born love and confidence arise!
[*She goes out*]

Scene 5

Enter GASENO, DON JUAN, CATALINÓN.

DON JUAN [*Walking fast, to overtake* GASENO]:
Gaseno, for God's pity just stay a moment!

GASENO [*Halting*]:
I want to go ahead and offer felicitations
To my daughter, on the luck that has come her way.

DON JUAN [*Looking across merrily to* CATALINÓN, *as he responds*]:
Won't there be time enough to-morrow?

GASENO [*Pausing and stupidly scratching his head*]:
You're right . . . there will be . . . [*Heartily*]
Dear sir, I give my whole soul in the bargain
Along with my little girl. . . .

DON JUAN [*Taking the old man's hand*]:
You should say "your wife" now, not "my little girl"!
[GASENO *goes out*]

Scene 6

DON JUAN [*Wheeling with great energy, to* CATALINÓN]:
At the first grey rift of dawn 160
We must be riding hard a-breast
Or death, not we, might turn the jest.

CATALINÓN:
It's just as well to have your sport.
A marriage of another sort
Waits you at Lebrija—a life
Perhaps, of exile, for a wife,—
If this diversion by the way
Comes to the King's ears, he'll unsay
All clemency!

DON JUAN:
What e'er befall, 170
Till dawn I'll play the best of all
My jests.

CATALINÓN:
And once again I'll shape
My lips in prayer for our escape.

DON JUAN:
At court my father holds possession
Of the King's confidential ear:
He'll plead my crime, youth's indiscretion,
Then what on earth have you to fear?

CATALINÓN:
Nothing . . . on earth . . . but God remands
The judgment from the judge's hands 180
When earthly justice turns corrupt:
Within His Great Hand, squirming, cupped,
The judge and those he spared will lie
And lack the blue, protecting sky
While in its stead will stand His Face—
Then Hell will seem a kinder place! . . .
Master, I've often wondered why
God doesn't end our souls' disgrace
With one aimed bolt from heaven thrust
To sift our bodies back to dust. 190

DON JUAN:
Again I ask you to be still:
You go and get the horses ready,
And, if you keep your courage steady,
We'll rest, to-morrow, in Seville!

CATALINÓN [*Dropping his jaw in frightened astonishment*]:
To-morrow? . . . in Seville?

DON JUAN [*Crisply*]:
You heard!

CATALINÓN:
Sweet master, grant me but a word:
I marvel at what you have done
Already,—now I marvel more
At the black seas you're steering for, 200
Filling your sails with life's sweet breath
To make the port of early death.
Although you've broken every law,
Why sail into destruction's maw?

DON JUAN [*Wildly*]:
Suppose I'm punished? I'll but pay
A little, for a little play.
I've sprung my bag of tricks on life—
Why should I shun the headsman's knife?
CATALINÓN [*Trembling, and kneeling to* DON JUAN]:
Master, loved master! [*Puts up his hands in supplication*]
DON JUAN [*Half-drawing his sword*]:
Shut up or I'll lop off your ears, 210
Why must you always pester me
With your extraordinary fears?
CATALINÓN [*Apart*]:
More furious than a Scythian
Or Garamant, with one eye in his chest,
Or Japanese that wears a dragon vest,
Or the fierce Troglydyte who finds both grave
And home, alike, within his gloomy cave,—
My master draws his scarlet threads of sin
Across the amber cloth of death and shame,
His eyes delighted with the pretty game,— 220
Absorbed just like the small, white maiden in
The Song, who never leaves her tabour-frame!

[CATALINÓN *goes out*]

Scene 7

DON JUAN [*Solus*]:
The night in great black silence bends
Over me, and the pole extends
Above the wheeling Pleiades;
Orion wades through breaking seas
Of stars as thick and white as foam.
O infinite, tremendous dome,
O gulfs of space, I go to do
What all your stars impel me to! 230
Love guides me like a sun in flight;
No man can overcome his might.
By his unceasing madness led
I go to find Aminta's bed. . . .
Aminta!

Scene 8

AMINTA *comes in.*

AMINTA [*Answering* DON JUAN *with a soft, lute-like call of mating in her voice*]:
Who calls Aminta?—my Batricio?
DON JUAN:
No, I'm not your Batricio!

AMINTA [*With fright in her voice*]:
Who, then, are you?
DON JUAN [*Amorously*]:
Wonder a space who I could be, Aminta!
AMINTA [*Now recognising him*]:
Alas, you play me false, coming at these 240
Late hours, to my chamber.
DON JUAN:
Late or not,
They are sweet hours, being mine and yours together.
AMINTA [*Shrinking back*]:
Turn and depart the way you came, or I
Will cry out on the night for help. Do not
Exceed that courtesy you owe Batricio.
Think of the slaying swords that found out Tarquin!
DON JUAN:
Listen to but two words from me, and you
Will send that maiden colour from your cheeks
—Richer and far more precious than the dye 250
Yielded up by the Tyrian shell for kings—
Back to your heart; pale wonder will usurp
Its place, a starry moment.
AMINTA:
Stop, before
My husband comes.
DON JUAN:
I am your husband.
AMINTA [*Mocking*]:
When
Were our espousals made?
DON JUAN:
They are made now.
AMINTA:
Who wrote the marriage contract? 260
DON JUAN:
My happy fortune.
AMINTA [*With a playful laugh*]:
And who pronounced the bans?
DON JUAN:
Your eyes.
AMINTA:
How could
My eyes do that?
DON JUAN [*Taking her hand*]:
With their sweet looks, beloved.
AMINTA [*With a shy, downward glance*]:
And—does Batricio know of this?
DON JUAN:
Yes, and he sulks. . . .
He walks apart and swears he has forgot you.
AMINTA [*Pouting*]:
—Forgot me!— 270

DON JUAN [*Pressing her hand to his face*]:
Yes, forgot, as I adore you.
AMINTA:
How?
DON JUAN [*Making to embrace her*]:
With my arms.
AMINTA [*Struggling back from him. Putting the back of her hand to her forehead in a gesture of bewilderment*]:
Now go... leave off your silken phrases, sir.
You make me dizzy with your words...
[*As he comes close to her again*]
Please go!
DON JUAN:
Aminta, listen, if you'd seek
To be assured that what I speak
Is very truth... for women are
The friends of Truth... the Shepherds' Star 280
Shone for a Woman, who gave birth
To the One God of Truth on earth...
I am a nobleman: my house began
In the far days when my forefather warriors
Won Seville from the Moors... next to the King
My father shines in men's regard and worth
While in the court his lips speak life and death... [*Pause*]
As chance would have it, I was riding this way
When love, in one of his most golden moods,
Brought you across my passage; I saw, adored, 290
And burned, as, in one flash of golden lightning,
The earth, the sky, the sea, are hurled together...
So swift the action of love's lightning fell...
And love for you breathed through my life so largely
That I must marry you, or cease to live!
Let the realm's wrath sing in my ears for this,
I will brush off their buzzing,—let the King
Bid "no," I'll breast his storm to harbour safely;
Let, let my father brandish all his angers
Over my head! I'll marry you, despite 300
The realm,—I'll marry you despite the King,—
Despite my father's wrath I'll marry you:
I'll marry you in hell's, earth's, heaven's despite...
Oh, answer yes, or let me die to-night!
AMINTA [*Frightened, yet exalted by the sweep of* DON JUAN*'s fire*]:
I do not know what I should say or do!
You waken realms in me I never knew,
Kingdoms of womanhood... and yet I'm weak!
Tell me, is it the truth, or lies, you speak? [*Clinging to him wildly*]
Your lofty words, surely they are no trick
Of the court's fashionable rhetoric!... 310
But words are vain. It is impossible
Even for the passing of a dream to dwell
In the sweet heaven you'd build... Batricio
Is my betrothed: he will not let me go.

DON JUAN [*Pressing the instant*]:
But see, whether in malice, jest, or hate
Your bridegroom does not come to consummate
The marriage rites—

AMINTA:
Piqued for the hour's span,
He mopes apart,—an honest, simple man!

DON JUAN:
You forgive easily. Give me your hand 320
And you will have a noble at command,
No country bumpkin, absent for a look.

AMINTA [*In a last instinctive effort for escape*]:
How delicately, sir, you bait your hook!

DON JUAN:
I am the one that's caught. You are the snare.
[*He draws her to himself. He kisses her again and again, in the dusk*]

AMINTA [*Slowly yielding*]:
O God, what man is this?—Oh, will you swear
To follow out each promise to its goal?

DON JUAN:
I swear with all my body, heart, and soul!
I swear by your strange, burning body of snow!

AMINTA [*Passionately*]:
May God destroy you if you do not so!

DON JUAN [*Maddened by her passionate response*]:
Oh, if by any chance my word or faith 330
Fail you, may God send me a second death
Flaming for all eternity in hell,
Thin jets of fire from every pore descried,
If perfidy or treason in me dwell!

AMINTA:
Then with these great oaths I become your bride.

DON JUAN:
You make my soul grow white like God, inside
Your heaven of gathering arms!

AMINTA [*Crying out and sobbing*]:
My life's life, my soul's soul!

DON JUAN [*Naïvely now, like a boy*]:
Aye, my Aminta, white feast of all my eyes!
Like a small, opened gate of paradise 340
To-morrow the court's life will shine on you.
On each white, little foot a silver shoe
Will sit to soft perfection; nails of gold
And clasps of diamond shall the insteps hold;
Your throat shall be a prisoner to pearls;
You'll be a star above a thousand girls;
And living rings of every kind of stone
Will weigh your ten, soft, delicate fingers down.

AMINTA [*Swooning*]:
My body that was mine, my chaste-kept soul
Be now your body's body, your soul's soul! 350
My only heaven be, to do your will!
[*She faints in his arms*]

DON JUAN [*With a curious guttural sound of passion in his voice*]:
Mine now, a handled puppet to control!
How ill you know the love-rogue of Seville!
[*He carries her out in his arms*]

Scene 9

Highway on the coast of Tarragon. ISABELA *and* FABIO *come in.*

ISABELA:
Soft sleep has poured life back into my body
And knit my broken ends of weariness
Into new vigour,—sleep I sought so long;
That priceless jewel to him who has it not,
Refuge from the harsh fact of day-to-day,
The tabernacle of a thousand dreams
That lend enfranchisement to life's chained slaves... 360
Day-veiling night, you draw your sable curtain
With kindly hands, across an evil world,
And usher in the 'spousals of the heart
To happiest, fancied dreams!

FABIO:
What does this sadness,
Filling your soul, and shadowing your eyes,
Avail you, Isabela! Love is the only
King who thrives on treachery and treason;
Unhappiness is meat and drink to him:
He stabs the broken heart with further outrage; 370
And when you laugh for joy of him, beware,—
In a brief space your grief will be as great.
But look, a storm is blowing up at sea;
The galleys put in with their purple sails;
Bubbling the ocean from their prows; they make for
The inlet over which that tower stands
Crowning the countryside.

ISABELA:
Where are we now?

FABIO:
In Tarragon.
But a short passage hence 380
Will bring us to Valencia,
A beautiful city which is
The very palace of the sun.
There you may rest yourself a day or two
Before we set out for Seville,
The eighth wonder of the world...
Where, if you've lost Octavio, you'll find
Don Juan, a man more gallant, and of a house
Of ancient fame... so why are you unhappy?
The King himself will expedite your marriage 390

To him—whose father holds the foremost
Power in the palace.

ISABELA [*Disconsolately*]:
I am not sad because I may become
The wife of Don Juan, for all the world
Knows he's of gentle birth,—but I shall weep
As long as I am living, for the voice
Of shame that's sown abroad concerning me,
And for my lost repute!

FABIO [*Gently*]:
Here comes a fisher girl; in gentle passion
Breathing forth laments and sighs, and weeping 400
As gently; she intends this way; her eyes
Swim toward you; while I go and find the dwellers
On this sea coast, I'll leave you two alone
To be-weep, with tender women's tears,
Perhaps a common sorrow.

[FABIO *goes out.* TISBEA *comes in*]

Scene 10

TISBEA:
Man-giving sea of Spain,
You swept in waves of fire
Over that little Troy,
My hut, and made a pyre
Of it, to burn from me 410
My cool virginity.
I curse the ship that brought
Across my bitter ways
The flame from which I caught
My life into a blaze.
I curse the ship that came . . .
I curse your waves of flame!

ISABELA [*To* TISBEA]:
Tell me, my lovely fisher girl, why do you
Call down curses on the sea, with a voice
So sweet it makes each curse a benediction? 420

TISBEA:
I'd like to heap a thousand maledictions
Upon your waves, accursed Spanish sea:
As I was fishing, guileless, by your shores,
You brought the ruin of my life to me!

ISABELA:
Leave off your quarrel with the ocean, girl,
And tell me where you came from.

TISBEA:
Do you see that cluster of straw-sloping cabins
Battered by ocean wind and weather? whose walls
Stand full of clefts and fissures where the birds
Seem to find space to build a thousand nests?— 430

In one of those I passed my virgin days;
My strength of chastity was clear and strong
As any valued diamond, till the ocean
Thrust up an arrogant monster-birth upon me
Whose impudent and yet soft-stroking words
Flattered me from my virgin surety
As the sun's fierce and fire-abundant rays
Softens the firmest wax—
[*whimsically,—dashing her hand across her eyes and smiling through her tears*]
Are you Europa,
The lovely one?—and does the Bull bear you, too, 440
To Seville?

ISABELA:
I am on my way there to be married—[*Sadly*]
Beyond any will of mine.

TISBEA:
Oh, if the stain that has been laid against
My whiteness no more virgin, move your pity,
And if the shame the sea has cast up on me
Have place within your heart, give me, then, place
In your companionship; take me with you
And I will wait upon you as your slave
Until the sorrow of this cruel affront 450
Stops up my life... let me accompany you
And fling myself at the King's feet for judgment
Against the malice of the sea's deceit...
May all the waters of the sky descend
And whelm him under; may the ocean heave
In one great wave, to claim its spawn again,
And sweep entirely from the living earth
This Don Juan Tenorio who betrayed me...
For I gave meat and shelter to the bad
Notorious traveller, and the vile guest 460
Struck like a viper hidden in the grass.
With words of sweet espousal he persuaded
My honour from me,—with solemn promises
Of holy union that he turned to play—
And then he and his servant rode away.
The woman who puts trust in men, sews stitches
In rotten cloth... he used me, cast me by...
Is it not just that I should cry for judgment?

ISABELA [*With a sudden outburst*]:
Hold your tongue, you ill-speaking woman!
Go from me, you have given me my death! [*subsiding—more gently*] 470
No, no, your sorrow troubles you so deeply
I will not blame you. Will you swear to me
That you have told the truth?

TISBEA:
It is as true as that heaven bends above me.

ISABELA:
Alas, for her who puts her trust in men...
Have you companions for your journey?

TISBEA:
A fisherman,
Anfriso,—and my father,—go with me
To witness to the wrong I have endured.

ISABELA:
There is no vengeance now that can be great 480
Enough to counterpoise my injury . . .
Yes, you and yours may join me, if you will!

TISBEA:
The maid who trusts in men thrives always ill!

[*They go out*]

Scene 11

Near the sepulchre of DON GONZALO DE ULLOA, *outskirts of the city of Seville.* CATALINÓN *and* DON JUAN.

CATALINÓN:
Master, we've raised the world about our ears.

DON JUAN:
—Still harping on imaginary fears?

CATALINÓN:
I wish
They were . . . but Octavio will soon have found
What pirate brought his ship of love a-ground
In Naples,—Mota, 'scaping by a breath
The headsman's axe and the red block of death, 490
Will tell how you deceived him as a friend,
(God cannot let him go so horribly)
Will tell about his cape you wore to gain
The full fruition of a dastard end—
Will tell the story to the King of Spain
Of how, pretending you were he, you won
To Doña Ana's side, and left undone,
Despoiled, her womanhood—

DON JUAN [*Breaking in angrily*]:
You donkey, you!
Another word, my sword shall spit you through! [*Draws sword*] 500

CATALINÓN [*Backing away fearsomely*]:
From now on I will keep my tongue as still
As if a millstone struck me in the mouth.

DON JUAN [*Now playfully*]:
Who fed you such a heap of jumbled nonsense?

CATALINÓN [*Gasping*]:
Nonsense, Master? You know that it is true!

DON JUAN:
Whether it is or not, I do not care.
If Mota or Octavio seek me out
To kill me, does that mean that I'm already
Dead? . . . not while I have sword-hand left to fight with.
[*A pause*]
Where have you got me lodging?

CATALINÓN:
In a side street 510
Hidden away and secret.
DON JUAN:
Good!
CATALINÓN [*Looking fearfully about*]:
Master, we
Are near earth that is sacred; there, before us,
Stands a church; yonder, in the gathering dusk,
White tombstones glimmer.
DON JUAN:
Why need I give a thought
To graveyards yet? That day's a long way off
When I'll lie dead in such a place...
Have you seen 520
The Bridegroom in the play of "The Two Sisters"?
CATALINÓN:
I saw how he was always full of care
And sorrowful.
DON JUAN [*Gaily*]:
I am the enemy
Of bridegrooms... [*a pause*]
For two weeks Aminta has
Been the butt of my rare jest.
CATALINÓN:
Yes, she was handsomely befooled,—
They call her "Your ladyship, Doña Aminta" now.
DON JUAN:
It was a delicate trick. 530
CATALINÓN:
It was,—for people say
She never ceases weeping, night or day.
DON JUAN [*Observing for the first time the sepulchre and monument of* DON GONZALO DE ULLOA]:
Whose sepulchre is this?
CATALINÓN [*Starting*]:
Here Don Gonzalo
Lies buried.
DON JUAN:
It was I who made him a dead man.
What a stately monument they've reared him!
CATALINÓN:
They reared it up, stone upon weighty stone,
At the King's order—what have they lettered on it?
DON JUAN [*Reading*]:
It says— 540
"Here lies a nobleman, who, foully murdered,
Waits to be revenged upon the traitor
Who slew him." This inscription shakes me deep
With laughter... [*laughing—to the Statue*]
Grey lad, though you have a beard
All stone, I'll pluck it to your further insult.
[*Seizing the Statue's beard*]

CATALINÓN [*Trembling*]:
Don't pluck it, sir,—there is an ancient proverb
That says there's power and danger in plucked beards.
DON JUAN [*Continuing to address the Statue—flamboyantly*]:
Old bully, listen to my invitation—
If you have hearing in those ears of stone; 550
Come to my inn to-night and dine with me.
I hurl defiance in your marble visage;
If vengeance seem so sweet, come take it then;
Although I think you'll have a harder task
Than ever, fighting with a sword of stone.
CATALINÓN [*Quaking with superstitious fear*]:
Master, it's getting darker every instant;
Let's go . . . this place is not much to my liking.
DON JUAN [*Madly, still to the Statue*]:
The vengeance you would execute on me,
Old dotard, stretches to eternity,
And I shall draw full many a jolly breath 560
Before we meet, the other side of death.
There is no man, alive, on earth, I dread,—
And I have yet to fear a man that's dead.
So, if you care to come to-night and dine,
I'll serve you with cold meat and boiling wine,
As I have heard men wine and dine in hell!
CATALINÓN [*Shivering with an ague of fear*]:
Master, you speak as if you wove a spell.

[*They go out*]

Scene 12

Room in an Inn. Two servants setting table for a banquet.

1ST SERVANT:
Who is it comes to dine with Don Juan?
2ND SERVANT:
God knows . . . at least we've set the table right.
1ST SERVANT:
If I obeyed my feet, I'd take to flight. 570
2ND SERVANT:
I feel the same as you. The icy meat
Is cold as carrion that grave-things eat,
And the wine bubbles with infernal heat . . .
Who ordered this disordered banquet so
For Don Juan?
1ST SERVANT:
Have patience . . . soon we'll know.
[DON JUAN *and* CATALINÓN *come in*]

Scene 13

DON JUAN [*To* CATALINÓN]:
Have you barred and bolted every door?
They say the Dead can walk through wood and stone,
And we shall try his power. . . .

CATALINÓN:
I have obeyed you, sir, as heretofore. 580
DON JUAN [*To servants*]:
Ho, there, bring on the banquet!
2ND SERVANT [*Bringing in viands, followed by* 1ST SERVANT]:
Here it is, sir!
DON JUAN:
Catalinón, sit down!
CATALINÓN [*All a-tremble—placatively*]:
I'll—I'll drink a round with you.
[*Takes up goblet, sees wine bubbling strangely in it. Sets goblet down in horrified, slow fascination*]
DON JUAN [*Laughing, but in a stern voice*]:
Sit down, I say!
[*A tremendous knock is heard without*]
CATALINÓN [*Crossing himself*]:
There's some one . . . knocking . . .
DON JUAN [*Grimly*]:
I can imagine who it is that knocks!
[*To* 1ST SERVANT]
But go and see!
1ST SERVANT:
I'll go and see, sir.
[*He goes*]
CATALINÓN [*His knees jostling together*]:
What if it be—the Statue, come for vengeance? 590
DON JUAN:
Then let it be. *You* have no cause for fear.
[*The* 1ST SERVANT *reappears. He flies as if from some feared, invisible pursuit. To servant*]
Who is it? . . . why do you stand there quaking?
[1ST SERVANT *tries several times to speak, but each time his voice fails him*]
CATALINÓN:
His silence witnesses some monstrous evil.
DON JUAN [*Half-rising from his seat—violently*]:
He'll find my anger worse than the worst devil.
[*To* 1ST SERVANT]
Speak . . . answer me . . . what have you seen, you fool?
Has some flame-eyed inhabitant of hell
Visited you to dumbness?
[*After a long pause, during which the servant tries to speak, but cannot. To* CATALINÓN, *as another tremendous knock is heard*]
You go and see who's knocking at the door.
Come on, don't stand there gaping,—go and see!
CATALINÓN [*Stupified with fright*]:
Who? . . . me? . . . 600
DON JUAN [*Contemptuously*]:
Yes, you! [*ironically*]
Lift up one foot and place it
Before the other, till you reach the door.
CATALINÓN:
I felt the fear of death rise in my throat,
Bunched in a choking knot, at that first knock.

It sounded to me like a dreadful summons
To call my soul forth to eternal torment...
That knock, it is the last thing I would hear.
[*The knock comes for the third time*]

DON JUAN [*Inexorably, to* CATALINÓN]:
Why do you halt? How dare you disobey me?
[DON JUAN *whips out his sword*]

CATALINÓN [*Moving fearfully and slowly toward the door*]:
Catalinón must do what Catalinón 610
Must!... [*Coming to a terrified halt*] But suppose the monstrous being
Has come to wreak God's wrath on both of us?
[DON JUAN *menaces him again.* CATALINÓN *scurries toward the door and disappears. There is a moment of silence. Then a scuffling is heard without*]

DON JUAN [*Calling to* CATALINÓN]:
What's there?

CATALINÓN [*In a far, weak voice*]:
God have mercy and protect me,—
They are slaying me... they hold me fast...

DON JUAN:
Who holds you fast? who slays you?
[*Starts to go to his valet's rescue, when the latter staggers in, falls, gets up again*]
What have you seen there?

CATALINÓN [*Hysterically*]:
Something seized on me, something held me close
Yet never touched me with a mortal hand....
I looked... and blindness fell, black, over me... 620
I swear to God that what I say is true...
I spoke as in the dark, "Who are you, sir?"
And IT replied... [*he stumbles in speech*]... and I replied... thereto...
And IT struck hard against me... and I saw...

DON JUAN: [*His voice fails*]
Who was it that you saw?

CATALINÓN [*In renewed terror*]:
I do not know!

DON JUAN [*Scornfully*]:
The wine has mixed your wits up... give me the candle...
[*He takes the candle out of* CATALINÓN*'s hand*]
You're always like a cackling hen... I'll go
And see what manner of man—or thing—it is!

[DON JUAN *goes toward the door with the candle in his left hand, his drawn sword in his right. He encounters the Stone Image of* DON GONZALO, *just as it was on the sepulchre. He presents the point of his sword to the solemnly, slowly advancing Image. He retreats backward, step by step,—the Statue following him to the centre of the stage.*]

Scene 14

DON JUAN [*As he and the Statue halt—perturbed, for the first time*]:
Who comes here? 630

DON GONZALO'S STATUE [*In a hollow, sepulchral voice*]:
It is I.

DON JUAN:
"I"! Who are you?

DON GONZALO'S STATUE:
I am the honourable gentleman
That you invited here to dine with you.
DON JUAN [*With all his old self-possession, putting up his sword*]:
The table is already set for two,
But if you bring more of your graveyard cronies
Let them come in: we'll find a seat for each one.
Be seated, sir!
[DON GONZALO'S STATUE *seats itself*]
CATALINÓN [*Crossing himself repeatedly*]:
Now God be near, and guard me!
Protect me, Saints Panencio and Antón! 640
When the Dead banquet it is death they feed on!
DON JUAN [*With mock politeness*]:
Be seated, Catalinón. Join our company!
CATALINÓN:
No, thank you, sir...
[*Looking fearfully at the* STATUE,*—continuing, not to offend the latter*]
I have already dined.
DON JUAN [*Laughing, to* STATUE]:
Pardon my servant; he's a trifle bashful!
CATALINÓN [*Aside, to* DON JUAN]:
I do not relish eating with the Dead,—
You dine with your invited guest, instead.
DON JUAN [*Aside, to* CATALINÓN]:
Sit down. You'll know no harm while I am here.
CATALINÓN [*Shivering—aside, to* DON JUAN]:
It makes me think I'm dead—with dead men near.
[*As the two servants set the food before the* STATUE
and DON JUAN, *they tremble so that the dishes rattle*]
DON JUAN [*To the servants*]:
—And you, too, all a-sweat! 650
CATALINÓN [*Resuming, aside to* DON JUAN]:
I never dine
With aught save honest countrymen of mine;
Strange-looking gentlemen I leave alone—
Much more a solemn gentleman of stone.
DON JUAN:
It is a fool's conceit that makes you shake;
Or flesh or stone, what are the odds at stake?
CATALINÓN [*Whispering, but rather loudly*]:
His wounds show, sir!
DON JUAN:
Speak with more courtesy.
CATALINÓN [*To the* STATUE, *plucking up a little courage*]:
Sir, does the other country suit you well?
Is it a good land where you dead folk dwell? 660
Do they have rhyme and song among the dead?
[*The* STATUE *nods yes*]
1ST SERVANT:
See, he assents: he nods "yes" with his head.

CATALINÓN [*Growing more bold*]:
—And, tell me, have they lots of wine shops there?
If so, does not old Noah sit in one of them,
Drinking and drinking of the grape's good blood,
Trying to drown the memory of the Flood?
DON JUAN [*Heartily, liking* CATALINÓN*'s witticisms—to servants*]:
Come, bring us more food to eat, more drink!
CATALINÓN [*Continuing, with a sly glance toward his master . . . he sees he is pleasing the latter*]:
—And can't you sometimes cool your wine with snow,
Although I've heard you drink it hot, below?
[*The* STATUE *nods yes*]
It's a good country, then. 670
DON JUAN [*To the* STATUE]:
If you would like
To hear a song,—I'll have the servants strike
A tune up.
[STATUE *nods his head in assent*]
2ND SERVANT [*Now at his full ease at last*]:
He nods "yes."
CATALINÓN:
The nobleman,
Though dead, knows what is good.
1ST SERVANT:
He is a friend
To pleasure, and that proves his noble blood.

SONG

[*Sung without*]

Kiss me, sweetheart, while you may,—
Kiss me, love, with every breath: 680
Lose no moment of our day;
Don't believe men when they say
They'll be faithful unto death!

DON JUAN [*Making a motion, for the last time, for* CATALINÓN *to sit down, which the latter finally does*]
CATALINÓN [*Apart*]:
The old dead lad seems rather weak:
He doesn't eat; he doesn't speak.
My courage comes a little late,
Yet, trembling still, I'll clean my plate.
[*He devours food with avidity—looks around carefully—sees nothing unusual has ensued*]
Don Juan and he seem loth
To drink . . . I'll make up for them both.
[*He lifts up an immense goblet, with both hands. But he stops, thunder-struck, as he does so, for, with a simultaneous motion, the* STATUE *does the same, with his goblet,—only he lifts it with one hand, like a gentleman*]
CATALINÓN [*Finally resuming his drinking, though still warily observing the* STATUE *over the rim of his goblet*]:
I fear no more. He drinks like other men. 690
[*Lustily, to the servants, with* DON JUAN*'s approval*]
Come, fellows, [*pounds table*] fill my goblet full again!

SONG
[*Continued*]

Put a joy off till the morrow,
Over-night it may be sorrow:
Snatch at love that passes soon—
If the place be opportune!...

Kiss me, sweetheart, while you may,—
Kiss me, dear, with every breath:
Lose no moment of our day:
Don't believe men when they say
They'll be faithful unto death! 700

CATALINÓN:
Master, how many women have you softened
To yielding, with that song?

DON JUAN:
It makes me laugh to count them, Catalinón,
They are so many—
Not counting those before my father sent me
To Italy... now, there was Isabela—
That time we were at Naples—

CATALINÓN [*Impudently*]:
We cannot speak of her as being cheated
Because I've heard she is to marry you
Soon—but that fisher girl, you paid her well 710
With hard coin, for her hospitality
And harbourage—and—you cheated Doña Ana—

DON JUAN [*Gripping* CATALINÓN*'s wrist so hard the latter winces. Aside*]:
Always you prate! The old boy yonder
Is here perhaps for just that reason—to have
Revenge,—don't put the thought into his mind.
There's no use meeting danger till it comes.

CATALINÓN [*Aside*]:
Master, your courage is like life itself,
But you are made of flesh, and he is stone...
The proverb says, "Let well enough alone."
[*The* STATUE *makes signs that it is leaving the banquet, and that they should follow*]

DON JUAN [*Aside, to* CATALINÓN]:
Come, let us leave the table,—the old boy 720
Gives a dumb sign of invitation to us
To follow him.

CATALINÓN [*Rising—fear sweeping over him again—backing away and hastily crossing himself*]:
God heap his heaviest malediction on me
Before I follow that huge, upraised paw
Of stone, that with one sweep could flail the soul
Out of my body.

DON JUAN [*Flamboyantly*]:
Follow him, all!
[CATALINÓN *and the two servants stand huddled in a group of fear. To* STATUE]
I'll go with you, my bully boy, *I'll* show you
That Don Juan is always Don Juan.

[*Now the* STATUE, *as if changing his purpose,—perhaps out of contempt for the fear the others show—makes a motion with his hand that they may leave. Which they do with a laughably concerted rush of alacrity, leaving* DON JUAN *alone with the* STATUE]

Scene 15

DON JUAN:
Phantastic vision from another world, 730
Ghost, dead man,—what quest was it brought you here?
If, under torment of enduring fire,
You seek your soul's cure, and my help avails,—
Say, and I'll follow out your least injunction!
Tell me through what sad fate you merit this?—
Speak, sir . . . I wait your word.
DON GONZALO [*With a voice as from another world*]:
Will you fulfil your word as nobles should?
DON JUAN:
That's the one point of honour that I hold:
The rest is but a cloak for coward's use
That honour's seeming may escape dishonour. 740
I'll tip the balance of each word I give
With bolder action, like a man of blood.
DON GONZALO:
Then give me your hand on that: and do not fear.
DON JUAN [*Resenting the imputation of fear*]:
What is that thing you utter? Fear, and I?
I have chased fear around the world and back again
Till fear himself's afraid of Don Juan.
If you caught all the realms of hell together
In your one person, I would take your hand.
DON GONZALO:
Give me your hand and word, then,—
To-morrow, at the tenth hour, I will set 750
My banquet for you, so be sure to come.
DON JUAN:
There's no power in the three worlds that can stay me,
In this earth, heaven, or hell; I'll be your guest
To-morrow, if I must come in the ghost,
As you have come to me . . . where shall I come?
DON GONZALO:
To my mortuary chapel.
DON JUAN:
—Alone?
DON GONZALO:
No, both of you.
Fulfil your word as I did mine!
DON JUAN [*Violently*]:
I'll keep my word, as I'm Tenorio, 760
Don Juan Tenorio!
DON GONZALO [*Proudly*]:
—And I, as I'm Ulloa,
Don Gonzalo de Ulloa!

DON JUAN [*Scornfully*]:
I'll come with as firm pace as if I used
Your feet of stone.
DON GONZALO [*His eyes burning*]:
I put all faith in you.
[*Going toward door*]
DON JUAN [*Changing his mood on the instant to one of light grace*]:
Wait, till I light your way!
[*He takes up candle*]
DON GONZALO:
You need not, sir,—
I thank you!
[*Step by step, as he entered, the* STATUE OF DON GONZALO *goes out backward, with* DON JUAN *following him, face to face*]

Scene 16

And now, alone, in spite of himself, DON JUAN *begins to shake all over with a fear which he cannot stay.*

DON JUAN [*Solus—trembling violently, as if with ague*]:
I do not fear, yet Fear has found me out: 770
But I will grapple with him till I slay him.
[*Striking himself on the chest*]
Base thing, vile, mortal frame that I inherit,
Remember you are the body of Don Juan,
And not some coward soul's,—remember, too,
As long as I am in you, I'll be master.
Good arm, what would you do now, if an enemy
Of ours, set on us?—you who used the sword so well.
God help me!—why, I even call on God! . . .
I'm glad this came after the Statue went
Else he could publish through the walks of hell 780
How he had made me tremble: rillets of sweat
Run over all my body: a winter frost
Clutching my guts, contracts my shivering courage.
When his stone fingers closed about my hand
I knew the world of shadows crowding close
Ready to burst in hideous ranks about me.
He breathed the breath of that dark, other world
So cold and yet so charnel-hot, the frigid,
Yet fiery air of hell; his voice spoke *in* me:
It was my soul that listened, not my ears . . . 790
Pah, these are rank growths of imagination:
Fear, in its very character, is vile,
But it's more villainous to fear the dead;
I am dwelling in a body
Whose veins and arteries run noble blood,—
I have pride, and strength of reason, and a soul—
Then shall I fear a body without life,
Or soul, or strength of reason! . . . Don Juan,
Shame on you, that this gave you pause of thought.
To-morrow I'll go to the Dead Man's chapel 800

And eat his food, and drink his wine of hell
As deep and well as he . . . and all Seville
Will stand a-gape, and marvel at my daring!
[*Vigorously, and once more entirely himself,* DON JUAN *goes out*]

Scene 17

Palace of the KING, *Seville. The* KING *and* DON DIEGO.

THE KING:
Has Isabela reached Seville?
DON DIEGO:
Yes, and she is much distressed of heart.
KING:
Does she not know of the marriage
Arranged for her, in all points advantageous?
DON DIEGO:
She mourns because her name grows infamous.
KING:
She should bewail her loss of chastity
More than her loss of name . . . where have you lodged her? 810
DON DIEGO:
Sire, in the Convent of de Las Descalzas.
KING:
Let her come from the Convent to the Palace;
For the time being she shall wait in tendance
Upon the Queen.
DON DIEGO:
Since she has been betrothed to Don Juan
She asks an audience with your majesty.
KING [*Impatiently*]:
I know, I know . . . the lady craves an audience
To learn *exactly* what terms of redress
I mean to grant her for her injured name . . .
So go, inform this honour-hungry dame 820
I will translate her husband's banishment
Into a term of honour,—he shall be
The Earl of Lebrija from now, forever:
She lost a Duke, to win an earldom's name—
I hope this will restore the lady's fame . . .
Your rascal son bristles with business—
He sends the world to me to ask redress.
If he were as active in the works of God
As at his Devil's play, he would be Pope!
DON DIEGO:
Your Royal Goodness almost equals God's— 830
I kiss your feet for the honour you have done me
In the person of my son, who knows no honour.
KING:
Diego, your deserts still run ahead
Of any favour I can ever show you.
The services that you have rendered me

Still in excess thrust up the balanced beam.
We will recall your erring boy from exile
And send him back to govern Lebrija
To which he went under my banishment.
And, at the time he marries Isabela, 840
We'll hold the spousal rites of Doña Ana—

DON DIEGO:
With—De la Mota—or Octavio?

KING:
It is not just that Duke Octavio,
Wronged once himself,
Should be redresser of another's wrong.

DON DIEGO:
But De la Mota slew her father?

KING:
Doña Ana,
With the Queen kneeling in a like petition,
Has begged that I should grant the Marquis' pardon.
She has confessed she sent for him herself 850
On that midnight of murder, fearing that
Her father meant to wed her to another,
And not to De la Mota, whom she loved.
Her father set on Mota in the dark—
He did not know it was her father he fought,
Till, driven to his own extreme defence,
He slew him.

DON DIEGO:
But why must Ana raise that first out-cry
That brought her hapless father to her rescue?

KING:
She said she thought for the moment that it was not 860
De la Mota, and so she cried for help
Under the abuse of phantasy.

DON DIEGO [*Perturbed, pondering gravely*]:
There is something strange in this,
A deeper thing than we have yet come at,—
For De la Mota, moping in the dungeon,
Maintains a sullen silence, except to beg,
With both hands clasped, and anguish in his face,
One day of freedom, for revenge on—some one!
Some one he will not name—but men will know—
And he'll be willing to return and die. 870

KING:
Go, and release him from his prisonment:
Take one or two with you; effect it quietly.
Tell him we pardon him his first offence;
But let him look to it he meditate
No other, or we'll leave off clemency.

DON DIEGO:
I think, despite his strangeness, he will obey you.

KING:
And now I will amend my first resolve:
We will not wait for Don Juan's return;

Ana shall lie in Mota's arms to-night,
And he'll forget his strangeness in her love... 880
It's good that old men live to guide and govern.

DON DIEGO:
Their counsels keep the world from running mad...
The Marquis will be easily assuaged,
And Doña Ana likewise will be glad.

KING:
But still Octavio's case remains to settle.
The Duke is one of those good, stupid men
Destined to sure unhappiness with women.
They tell me that his heart boils up with wrath
At Don Juan.

DON DIEGO:
And with good reason it does. 890
I do not wonder that his soul flames high
Since he has found out that it was my son
Who brought all this black evil on his head...
But, by the wounds of God, behold, he comes!

Scene 18

DUKE OCTAVIO [*Rushing in, and flinging himself down at the* KING*'s feet*]:
Unconquered King, the most insulted man
In all the world hurls himself at your feet.

KING:
Rise up again, good Duke, and cover your head.
What would you of me? [*Looking uneasily at* DON DIEGO]

OCTAVIO:
Thus I prostrate myself before you, Sire,
Begging a boon of you, 900
Which the just God in heaven grants already—
You need but set your seal to it on earth.

KING:
Duke, if it be a just boon, it is granted
Already—ask, and I will deal you justice.

OCTAVIO [*Insanely*]:
O King, you know already, through the letters
Of your Ambassador—as all the world knows
Through all the tongues of shame that wag abroad—
You know how Don Juan Tenorio
With Spanish arrogance and cruel pride
Upon a night at Naples, upon a night 910
That will live black in me forever,—under
The cloak of my good name that thought no evil,—
Defiled the whiteness of a woman's honour—

KING [*Deeply moved by the suffering of the* DUKE]:
My poor, good man, I pray you dwell no more
On that occasion... what is your petition?

OCTAVIO:
—Permission to meet him in open field
Defying him because he is a traitor!

DON DIEGO [*Angrily—beside himself*]:
He is no traitor! His blood is clean and honoured...
KING [*Swiftly*]:
Don Diego!
DON DIEGO [*Restraining himself with difficulty*]:
Your Majesty! 920
OCTAVIO [*Flashing back*]:
Who is it dares to give the lie to truth,
Yes, even in the presence of the King,
Tell me, who is it dares?...
DON DIEGO [*Haughtily*]:
A man who does not answer
Because the King commands him not to answer,
Who, if the King but gave him leave to answer,
Would still say naught, but answer with his sword!
OCTAVIO [*Marvelling*]:
You are an old man!
DON DIEGO [*Vigorously*]:
I was in Italy when I was young—
A time when swords were readier than the tongue; 930
We met each other always man to man:
They knew my sword in Naples and Milan.
OCTAVIO [*In angry scorn*]:
Your blood is frosty now, and thick with age—
Not "what I was" avails, but "what I am."
DON DIEGO [*Whipping out his rapier*]:
Then WHAT I WAS I AM STILL, now I'll prove it!
[*They start at each other. The* KING *steps between the points of their swords,—and, lowering them a little, they fall back on either hand*]
KING [*With stern command*]:
Hold, put your rapiers back, put them back, I say! [*Reluctantly they obey*]
Good! [*To* DON DIEGO]
Don Diego, I forbid one word,
As you have any reverence or respect
Left, as it seems you have not, for your Sovereign. [*To the* DUKE] 940
As for you, my Duke,
After we have arranged your new espousals
We'll give you easier opportunity
To discuss this matter more at leisure...
But, for the present, I would have you know
That Don Juan is a gentleman of my court,
A branch that grows from me—[*a pause, haughtily*]
I marvel, sir,
At your presumption!
OCTAVIO:
Your Majesty knows I yield to your commandments— 950
Even beyond my flesh and blood I yield.
Yes, I am most contrite as I'm most injured.
KING [*Peremptorily*]:
Come with me, Don Diego.
DON DIEGO [*Apart*]:
Oh, my own son, my little, wicked son,
How ill you pay me for the love I bear you!

KING [*Peremptorily, to the* DUKE]:
Duke!
OCTAVIO:
Your Majesty?
KING:
To-morrow
We will arrange your marriage.
OCTAVIO [*Confused*]:
My marriage? ah, yes! arrange it as you will, Sire! 960
[*The* KING *and* DON DIEGO *go out.* GASENO *and* AMINTA *come in*]

Scene 19

GASENO [*Aside, to* AMINTA]:
Perhaps this gentleman can tell us where
Don Juan Tenorio lives—[*To* OCTAVIO] Sir, pardon, sir! [*scraping*]
But is there anywhere about here, sir,
That well-known nobleman named Don Juan?
OCTAVIO [*Crisply*]:
Don Juan Tenorio, I presume?
AMINTA [*Naïvely*]:
Yes, sir, that is the Don Juan we mean, sir!
OCTAVIO [*With growing curiosity*]:
Why do you come to find his whereabouts?
AMINTA:
Briefly, sir, the gentleman is my husband.
OCTAVIO [*With a start*]:
What?
AMINTA [*With simplicity*]:
Could you be of the court, and not know that? 970
OCTAVIO [*With grim humor*]:
Don Juan said nothing to me about it.
GASENO [*Incredulous*]:
Could it be possible you do not know?
OCTAVIO [*Moved by the man's simplicity*]:
I swear to God, old man, I do not know.
GASENO:
Then I will tell you, in a few, plain words;
Doña—[*hestitates*] Aminta, here, has won great honour...
Because the two of them—Don Juan and she—
Are getting married... yes, she marries Don Juan,—
(I do not wonder at your amazement—I myself
Can scarce believe, at times)—and breaks off with
Batricio! 980
OCTAVIO [*Apart*]:
Here is another jest
Of Don Juan's. But these simple people come
To help my vengeance. [*To them*] State your petition!
I am a courtier at court.
GASENO [*Uneasily*]:
We would either have this marriage take place shortly
Or lay our case before the King himself.

OCTAVIO:
I say you have a cause that is all justice.
GASENO:
There is no doubt that judgment sits with us.
OCTAVIO [*Apart*]:
'Tis the occasion of a thousand years
Hitting upon the ripeness of the hour... [*To them*] 990
Yes—we will hold the marriage here at court.
AMINTA [*Dubiously*]:
I hope you mean my marriage, not another's?
OCTAVIO:
If you will help me with my stratagem
We will make sure of that, my hapless girl,—
Come, I will have you dressed in courtly fashion,
Then we will go and see the King together.
AMINTA:
And you'll procure me Don Juan in marriage?
OCTAVIO:
By a few strokes of craft it can be done.
GASENO:
Well, I can be as shifty as the next one.
OCTAVIO [*Apart*]:
These simple people will afford me vengeance 1000
On that vile, traitorous love-rogue, Don Juan!

[*They go out*]

Scene 20

DON JUAN *and* CATALINÓN.

CATALINÓN:
How did the King receive you?
DON JUAN [*Grinning*]:
With more love than my father.
CATALINÓN:
Have you seen Isabela?
DON JUAN [*Nonchalantly*]:
Oh, yes, I've seen her.
CATALINÓN:
How is she?
DON JUAN:
Like the Angel of the Evangel
She has no imperfections but perfection.
CATALINÓN:
Did she receive you well?
DON JUAN:
Yes, she forgave me... 1010
If you would win a woman's love, just give her
Something she can forgive you for, she'll love you!...
She shone upon me like the evening star
With soft and tender feminine forgiveness;
Her face was like a white rose fresh with dew—
Touched not with red, but with the shadow of red.

CATALINÓN [*With a pleased grin of relief*]:
In short, you'll marry her to-morrow?
DON JUAN:
It will be something new I've never done;
Long have I wooed and won, but never married.
CATALINÓN:
If you had only done so in the first place 1020
You would not have deceived so many women...
For when you once get married, sir, you'll find
Your ship is laden with so great a cargo
You cannot tack and veer with every wind,
You'll steer straight to the port, not lag behind.
DON JUAN:
God, you begin to be a fool again
Just when I think you've made a start at sense.
CATALINÓN:
I tell you, master, it is well for you
That you will be a married man to-morrow,
Because to-day is an unlucky day. 1030
DON JUAN:
Indeed, what day is it?
CATALINÓN:
Tuesday,—and the old proverb says
"Tuesday is a day for bad beginnings."
DON JUAN:
The common people have a crazy brain
And the fool's wisdom of their proverbs shows it—
I only call that day an evil day,
Unfortunate, and most detestable,
On which I have an empty pocketbook.
Give me a good foundation laid with gold:
The rest is a man's own to make or mar... 1040
For after that the gentleman begins.
CATALINÓN:
To-morrow is the wedding, but to-night,
The feast of the betrothal: you would best
Let me lay your fine dress out.
DON JUAN:
Yes, lay my silken best out, but, before that,
I have another business at hand.
CATALINÓN:
Concerning what?
DON JUAN:
My dinner with the Dead.
CATALINÓN [*Persuasively*]:
You must attend the feast of your betrothal.
DON JUAN:
Must I not go where I have placed my word? 1050
CATALINÓN:
Suppose you break it, will it hurt or hinder?
What can you gain or lose by keeping faith
With a man made of jasper or of stone?

DON JUAN:
Even the Dead would call me despicable.
A man must keep to every word he gives
Except to women,—there False matches False.

CATALINÓN:
What do you care for a Dead Man's opinion? . . .
Come, master, let us get away from here,
[*perceiving that they stand near the mortuary chapel of* GONZALO]
For, anyhow, the chapel gate is locked,—
This is the same place we were at before . . . 1060
[*a bell begins monotonously*]
I hear a sleepy bell far off that drones
As from beneath the ground . . . I am afraid.

DON JUAN:
Ay, Catalinón, he is always afraid.
Knock at the gate!
[*The gate swings open of itself*]

CATALINÓN:
As soon as you say "knock" it answers you.
Any moment *something* might walk out.

DON JUAN:
—An honest invitation to come in.

CATALINÓN:
I'll go in if a friar goes before me
Wearing his robes and sprinkling holy water.

DON JUAN [*Impatiently*]:
Follow me and hold your clacking tongue! 1070

CATALINÓN [*Shivering with fear*]:
But talking, master, keeps my courage up,
And thinking makes it fail.

DON JUAN [*Testily*]:
By God, be still!

CATALINÓN [*Praying*]:
God, bring me safely through this dreadful venture
And I will leave my master's mad-man service
And give my days to You—if You require them!
[*They enter at one gate, and are seen passing on through another*]
O master, stay by me!
I think that something plucked me by the cape.
[*The* STATUE OF DON GONZALO *comes out, as before, and meets with* DON JUAN]

Scene 21

DON JUAN:
Who comes?

DON GONZALO:
It is I! 1080

CATALINÓN [*Quaking violently*]:
Oh, I am dead already—here comes our Dead Man!

DON GONZALO:
Yes, I am dead. It is my natural state now;
No man could live with such a wound as this.
[*Shows wound.* CATALINÓN *shrinks behind his master*]

I hardly thought that you would keep your word
Since your one pleasure is deception, sir!

DON JUAN:
Surely you did not think I am a coward?

DON GONZALO:
I did . . . because you ran away that night
On which you put my age to death.

DON JUAN:
I fled to escape being known
And not for any fear: to-night you'll find me 1090
Ready for any danger . . . tell me swiftly
Your will.

DON GONZALO:
Merely that I've invited you to dine.

CATALINÓN [*Weakly, from behind*]:
Excuse us from your table, sir, to-night.
Your food is cold, and I observe no kitchen
To heat it in.

DON JUAN [*To* CATALINÓN]:
Be quiet! [*To* DON GONZALO] Then let us dine!

DON GONZALO:
To dine, we'll have to lift this burial slab.

DON JUAN:
I'll tear the tombstones up for seats, if need be.
[DON JUAN *and* DON GONZALO *lift the burial slab and place it across two tombstones for table. The slab miraculously turns golden*]

DON GONZALO:
You are no coward; you are brave indeed! 1100

DON JUAN:
It is not that I'm more than other men,
But that I rule my flesh with resolution.

CATALINÓN [*Losing his fear for the moment in his cupidity*]:
Pst! master, see, the table's made of gold!

DON GONZALO:
Be seated, guests!

DON JUAN:
I find no chairs to sit on.

CATALINÓN [*In renewed terror*]:
Here come his two black footmen, bearing chairs.
[*Two black-shrouded figures, bearing chairs, come in*]

DON GONZALO [*Severely, to* CATALINÓN]:
Sit down!

CATALINÓN:
I, sir—I lunched quite late, sir.

DON GONZALO:
Don't answer back!

CATALINÓN:
Yes, I won't answer back, sir. [*He sinks into a seat. Apart*] 1110
Now may God bring me from this place alive;
I see it isn't pleasant, being dead. [*Surveying gingerly the plate that one of the black mutes sets before him*]
What dish is this, sir?

DON GONZALO:
A dish of scorpions.
CATALINÓN [*Placatively*]:
What a dainty dish!
DON GONZALO [*To* DON JUAN]:
This is the favourite food we dead men eat—
Why don't you eat?
DON JUAN [*Bestirring himself*]:
I'll eat your food
If you serve all the asps that hell contains.
DON GONZALO [*To* DON JUAN]:
And now I'll have them sing a song for you. 1120
CATALINÓN [*Surreptitiously pouring out his plate of hellish food on the ground*]:
What kind of wine do dead men drink?
DON GONZALO:
Taste and see.
CATALINÓN [*Tasting and spitting*]:
—A bitter drink of gall and vinegar.
DON GONZALO:
It is the only wine our presses give.

SONG
[*Without*]

Behold the souls whom God has judged
Beyond the crimes of men:
They'll see no rest until they've paid
Again and yet again.

CATALINÓN [*Aside, to* DON JUAN]:
I find an evil meaning in that song,
It's sung at us. 1130
DON JUAN [*Gasping angrily*]:
A living fire from hell
Clutches my breast.

SONG
[*Continued*]

Though Man walk big about the earth
It is not fitting he should say
"I have a long time yet to live,"
Because the living die each day.

DON JUAN:
Now that we've dined, let's put the burial slab
Back where we found it.
DON GONZALO [*Rising, with* DON JUAN *and* CATALINÓN—*in a hollow, fearful monotone*]:
Give—me—your—hand—you—do—not—fear—to—give—me—
Your—hand? 1140
DON JUAN [*Disdainfully*]:
Why must you always ask me if I fear?
[*Gives his hand—with a suppressed cry*]
You burn me! do not burn me with your fire!

DON GONZALO:
This—is—a—foretaste—of—the—fire—you'll—know—
The—miracles—of—God—are—manifest—
And—are—past—finding—out—as—they—are—many—
Witness—it—that—you—pay—now—for—your—crimes—
At—a—slain—man's—hands—the—man—you—murdered—
The—Living—Dead—that—pays—you—in—this—fashion—
Beyond—the—knowledge—of—recorded—time—
There—is—no—stranger—thing—than—God's—revenge— 1150
For—your—strange—sins—you—pay—in—a—strange—way!

DON JUAN [*Groaning and swaying. Striving in vain to get free of the Statue's crushing grasp*]:
Alas, a searing fire flows through my body.
From you—your hand crushes my aching fingers
Until the blood streams from their bursting ends.
[*Striking suddenly with a dagger in his left hand*]
You monstrous hell-thing,
Take this in the wound I gave you!
[*He strikes again and again, but the dagger seems only to pierce through emptiness*]
It only wounds the unwounded air with blows.
[DON JUAN *casts the dagger down—struggles again to wrest free, but in vain—with an awful, heartrending cry*]
No more, good God! no more! [*in a long cry*]
I swear I did not touch your daughter, sir—
You came—before—I played the game—quite through! 1160

DON GONZALO:
That—will—not—save—you—in—your—soul—you—did.

DON JUAN [*In bitter, extreme agony, yet forcing his voice lower*]:
Let me go but a little while . . .
I will come back . . . my word, you know, is good . . .
I am Don Juan Tenorio . . .
A gentleman of the King's court . . .
I will come back . . .
As you're a Christian, let me die confessed.

DON GONZALO:
Upon—the—threshold—of—eternity—
It—is—too—late—now—for—a—good—resolve.

DON JUAN [*Suppressing a scream of agony*]:
God, how I burn! God, how the flames melt through me! 1170
They pour like water, yet they spread like fire!
I . . . die . . .

[*The* STATUE OF DON GONZALO *lets go.* DON JUAN *sinks prone at his feet; then, dying, slowly he reaches again for the dagger. He half rises to his feet . . . tottering, he makes a last bold thrust at the monster*]

DON JUAN:
I am myself again!
I die: but before God and hell and earth,
With my last breath I perish Don Juan!
[*He falls in a heap, dead*]

CATALINÓN [*Crouching on all fours, gibbering madly*]:
There is no way
For me

To flee.
Death reaches hands of fire
At me. 1180
I see
That I must take the last disaster
And perish by my brave and wicked master!
[*But, for all his fear,* CATALINÓN *creeps toward* DON JUAN*'s body, with instinctive fidelity, like a dog*]

DON GONZALO:
God's—judgments—never—fall—asleep—
As—you—sow—so—shall—you—reap—
God's—judgments—never—go—a-stray—
As—you—do—so—shall—you—pay!

[*With a great succession of thunder-claps the mortuary chapel tilts and sinks, as if dissolving into earth, with* DON JUAN *lying prone,* DON GONZALO'S STATUE *looming huge and upright, the eyes flaming. For the moment* CATALINÓN *seems to have gone under with the chapel. But presently he creeps forth as if from a hole in the ground, trailing himself along like a wounded animal. But he is only hurt by fright*]

CATALINÓN:
God save me, what does all this mean?
What have I done, where been, what seen?
Each hair stands hard upon my head; 1190
I have been dining with the Dead....
Yet here I'm whole... hands, feet, and head.
I'll crawl, and feel my way about...
I'll seek my master's father out
And tell him of this monstrous case...
How shall I get out of this place?
Saint George and dear Saint Lamb of God,
Kindly guide my hands and feet,
Protect me till I find the street.

Scene 22

At court—the KING *and* DON DIEGO.

DON DIEGO:
I have released the Marquis from his prison,— 1200
He craves an instant audience with you.

KING:
The Injured and the Injurer, all shall gather
Here at my court, and I'll compound a peace
Between them... go now, and rebuke your son,
The new-made earl, because he has not heeded
My summons yet.
[BATRICIO *and* GASENO *come in*]

Scene 23

BATRICIO [*Emboldened by anguish. Kneeling to the* KING]:
Why, Royal Sire, if I may speak out boldly,
Do you permit the servants of your court
To play such impudent tricks on humbler subjects?

KING:
What impudent tricks? you must expand more widely 1210
The drift of your complaint.

BATRICIO:
I have my witnesses who wait outside . . .
Don Juan Tenorio came to us
The night of my betrothal feast; he took
Advantage of our hospitality
And used the woman who would have been my wife
Most vilely.

Scene 24

Enter TISBEA, ISABELA, *and company.*

TISBEA [*Kneeling*]:
Sire, if your Royal Highness will not level
Your bolt of justice at Don Juan's head,
From men to God, from God to men I'll cry 1220
My many woes, until the day I die . . .
Half dead from whelming seas, the ocean
Cast him up at my feet; I pitied him
And gave him life and hospitable care,
And, in return, he cast a net of lies
About me, and deceived me in the name
Of promised marriage.

KING:
What do you say, my girl?

TISBEA [*Glancing toward entrance*]:
Just half the truth:
For here come more, I think, who'll tell the rest. 1230
[DUKE OCTAVIO *and* AMINTA *come in*]

Scene 25

AMINTA [*Looking tearfully about*]:
Where is my husband?

KING [*Regarding her steadfastly*]:
And who may *your* husband be?

AMINTA[*Naïvely*]:
Sire, is it possible you do not know?
He is Don Juan Tenorio.
I came to court to consummate our spousals.
In honour he has bound himself to me;
For he is noble and will not deny
His plighted faith . . . so . . . I demand my marriage!
[*The* MARQUIS DE LA MOTA *comes in, wildly*]

Scene 26

MOTA [*Throwing himself at the* KING*'s feet*]:
Great Sire, the day of truth has dawned at last,
The light that succours truth and innocence 1240

Has dawned upon us, ushering in the day...
Know, Sire, the crime I have been charged with, was
Committed by Don Juan Tenorio,
My friend, who caught me in a cruel deceit—
Who went, wearing my cape, to Doña Ana,
Then ran her father through when he was thwarted—
I have two witnesses outside, to add
Weight to my words, with truthful testimony
To this effect!

KING:
Each insolent deed of his 1250
Piles on new, impudent outrage never known before.
Seize on him straightway; have him put to death!
This time, despite his broken, aged father,
Who stands by me in bowed and speechless sorrow,
Despite his patent of nobility,
Despite the earldom I've conferred upon him,
I will delay the hand of God no longer!

DON DIEGO [*In great sorrow*]:
O King of Kings, accept my most assistance
In taking him. Let him pay to the hilt
For his unfilial hate, his monstrous guilt. 1260
I'll plead no more for him, lest heaven, instead,
Empty its angers on my guiltless head....
He has become so black with nameless crimes
That he's my child no longer.

KING:
Let the court guards search the fellow out
And bring him here!

[*At this point* CATALINÓN *drags himself in, ghost-pale and wearied. They all stop still at the extraordinary sight of his appearance, as if an apparition had stepped in among them*]

Scene 27

CATALINÓN:
Most royal, just, and mighty King of Spain—
Gentlemen, listen to me while I tell
A story such as since creation's day
A world of marvels never knew before; 1270
Then, after you have heard me, let me die,
Or live,—it does not matter which it be—
Already I have smelt the grave and touched
Upon the edges of eternity....
Don Juan, nobleman, a courtier of
The King's... my former master!... [*Halts, then resumes*]
After a day of revelry and madness,
Deceit in love and graceless cozening,—
Don Juan and I
Brought up by accident beside Gonzalo's Statue,— 1280
By accident, if God knows accident,
And all be not ordained...
My master, in a mad, extravagant mood,
Plucked, insolent, the Statue's stony beard

And urged him, in all hell's despite, to come
That night, and wine and dine with him—which (not
To weary you with a narration that
I can resume at greater length) the Thing,
Somehow got motion in its limbs and did.
And if God could put motion in these hands, 1290
These limbs of feeble flesh, why might not hell
Infuse infernal life in firmer stone! . . .
And now the Statue strode with measured strides
That rumbled like the thunder in the sky,
Looking ahead with eyes like lifeless moons . . .
He dines with us . . . we are invited to
Dine with him, in return, the night to come. . . .
Which was last night . . . thank Christ to-day's to-day! . . .
Filled with a thousand fears I dared not name,
I begged my master to give up the game . . . 1300
He said he only held one virtue
That he regarded . . . he must keep his word
With men—excepting women; it was there
False, with the False, he swore. . . .
But—I forget! . . .
We stood before the mortuary chapel . . .
A far bell droned as if deep under ground
(Perhaps they held a black mass down in hell
And some fiend lifted an infernal host).
My master walked in boldly. . . . 1310
(That he was brave
All hell will now rise up and testify). . . .
We dined . . . a hideous banquet . . . on a slab
Torn from a tomb. . . .
Then, as we rose to go,
The Dead Man reached his hand forth in farewell. . . .
Don Juan, scorning fear, gave him his hand. . . .
Then flames grew up from earth . . . the Statue kept
My master's hand within his monstrous clasp
And would not let him go. . . . 1320
And so
He perished . . . [*After a pause, rather proudly*]
Don Juan to the end, though!

KING:
What tale is this that you pour in our ears?

CATALINÓN:
A tale as true, God help me,
As it is passing strange and wonderful.

KING:
Did Don Juan say nothing as he died?

CATALINÓN [*Nodding his head assentingly*]:
—That Doña Ana is a maiden still,
Because she cried for help before he quite
Encompassed her deceit. 1330

MOTA [*Breaking in happily*]:
I'll weigh you out a thousand crowns for this!

KING:

Behold the equal punishment of Heaven,—
For a strange life of crime meting an ending
As strange, or stranger!
Even the headsman's axe
Had glanced from this man, since he was devoted
To Heaven's vengeance only, not to Man's.
No earthly punishment
Could weigh against his evil. . . .
And now we will
Arrange the weddings that he disarranged—
Since he is dead who was, alive, the life
Of all these grievous mishaps and disasters.

OCTAVIO:

I ask the hand of widowed Isabela.

MOTA:

And I, my cousin Doña Ana's hand.

BATRICIO [*To* AMINTA]:

Aminta, will you take me back again?

AMINTA:

I think it was the Devil took me from you.

TISBEA:

I'll go back to the Tarragonian sea
And learn to practise kindness toward Anfriso
Who loves me still as he has always loved me. [*Takes* ANFRISO*'s hand*]

KING [*From his throne, whither he has proceeded*]:

We will commemorate the monstrous end
Of Don Juan Tenorio—

DON DIEGO [*Interrupting*]:

Tenorio no more, just Don Juan!
No more a son of mine, but of the Devil's!

KING [*Resuming*]:

—By carrying the Statue of Ulloa
Where all the world can see it, to Madrid.
There it shall gloom in everlasting stone
As a memorial most marvellous
Of Don Juan and his just punishment.

JOHN MILTON
[1608–1674]

John Milton, an English Puritan and a courageous defender of political liberty, defied both pope and king and was therefore in many respects a prophetic voice of the European opposition to established authority in the late Renaissance. His service to the Puritan cause during the English Civil War, including the writing of pamphlets containing strongly held views on public matters, made him a compelling figure in English society. His great poetry, most of it written in his later years while he was totally blind, left the world its ineradicable Renaissance version of tragedy, defined as the freedom to seek our own destiny coupled with the prospect of failure should we overreach ourselves in defiance of God.

Life

Milton's early training was primarily classical. As a schoolboy at Eton and later as a student at Cambridge, he excelled in Hebrew, Greek, and Latin. After graduating with an MA from Christ College, Cambridge, in 1632, he traveled to Europe, visiting Hugo Grotius, the famed doctor of jurisprudence, and Galileo, perhaps the greatest figure in Western science, then under the watchful eye of the Vatican for his views on astronomy. By 1637, having returned to England, Milton had established himself as a poet: His elegy *Lycidas,* on the death of a friend, promised more to come. But in his active political years during the Cromwell rebellion (1640–1649), he devoted himself to prose treatises, the most famous of which are *Areopagitica* (1644), on freedom of the press and individual liberty, and *The Tenure of Kings and Magistrates* (1649), on the right of the people to overthrow their sovereign authority. The appearance of this document in the year of the beheading of Charles I put Milton's own life temporarily in jeopardy more than a decade later. Milton went totally blind in 1651 and was relieved of his political duties shortly thereafter; he wrote *Paradise Lost,* his masterpiece, by dictation from the middle 1650s until its publication in 1667. He followed this work with *Paradise Regained* and *Samson Agonistes* in 1671, three years before his death from gout.

Work

Paradise Lost is the epic of the Fall of Man conceived in Christian terms. Following Virgil's *Aeneid,* it is a heroic legend that is, in Milton's words, "doctrinal and exemplary to a nation." Milton's hero, Adam, represents a complex truth about individual freedom: Although God ordains everything that happens in the world, man has been given free will to choose; man chooses to do good or evil and hence seals his own fate. In other words, God's omnipotence and omniscience do not cancel out man's responsibility for his choice. Thus Milton sees the Christian epic as the new version of the classical struggle of the soul against pride. Never inclined to modesty, Milton in *Paradise Lost* asks his muse to help his poem excel all previous epics in this respect:

> . . . What in me is dark
> Illumine, what is low raise and support,
> That to the height of this great argument
> I may assert eternal providence,
> And justify the ways of God to man. (1, 22–26)

Enlarging the structure and meaning of *Paradise Lost* is the theme of Satan's fall from Heaven. Unlike Adam, whose fall from bliss is due in part to pride, in part to weakness, and in part to Satan's guile, Satan falls from Heaven along with his retinue of co-conspirators after openly proclaiming rebellion against God. Satan, however, is not a wholly unattractive figure. His intelligence, rhetorical skill, and courage are evident in the opening books of *Paradise Lost*. Indeed, Milton tantalized future generations by putting in Satan's mouth the same arguments for individual liberty that he himself had used in other contexts, especially *Areopagitica*. Viewing the simultaneously attractive and repulsive figure of Satan, the English romantic poet William Blake went so far as to contend that Milton was of "the Devil's party without knowing it."

Book 1 of *Paradise Lost* shows Satan and his followers newly arrived in Hell, chained to the fiery lake at its pit. We see Satan's pride even as he rises to survey his ruined kingdom:

> . . . What though the field be lost?
> All is not lost; th' unconquerable will
> And study of revenge, immortal hate,
> And courage never to submit or yield . . . (1, 105–8)

To his lieutenant, Beelzebub, he reconfirms his dedication to evil ("ever to do ill our sole delight," 1, 160). Rousing the host of devils from their supine positions, he assembles them in council and conducts a debate on whether to begin open warfare with God. After the recently defeated princes mull over the perils of this action and the unlikelihood of their success, Beelzebub adroitly redirects their attention to "some easier enterprise" (2, 345), namely the corruption of Eden, where Adam and Eve dwell. When the devils approve his plan, he asks, "Whom shall we send / In search of this new world?" (2, 402–3). Only Satan volunteers, and he is chosen.

In Book 4, Satan arrives in Paradise, which is compared to the unspoiled landscapes of classical antiquity (4, 268–87). Here the poet describes Adam and Eve, "Godlike erect" (4, 289), with the beasts of the earth playing around them. Satan, though struck by their beauty, grimly prophesies their destruction at his hands:

> . . . Hell shall unfold
> To entertain you two her widest gates
> And send forth all her kings; there will be room,
> Not like these narrow limits, to receive
> Your numerous offspring. (4, 381–85)

Adam warns Eve of the Tree of Knowledge, which is also the Tree of Death, cautioning her against eating its fruit. Vowing revenge, Satan leaves them "emparadis'd in one another's arms" (4, 506).

The temptation and fall of Adam and Eve lie at the dramatic center of *Paradise Lost,* in Book 9 of the epic. Milton signals his intent: "I now must change / These notes to tragic" (9, 5–6). Satan returns to Eden, taking the shape of a serpent. Eve tells Adam that she ought to be allowed to leave his side and tend the garden, and he reluctantly agrees. The serpent, beautiful and seductive, addresses Eve. Appealing first to her vanity and curiosity, then to her pride, he convinces her to eat the forbidden fruit. All of nature is damaged by her act:

> Earth felt the wound, and nature from her seat
> Sighing through all her works gave signs of woe
> That all was lost. (9, 782–84)

Eve, sensing her new difference from Adam, tempts him to repeat her act. Although he recognizes its consequences for all humanity, he obeys her, because "to lose thee were to lose myself" (9, 959). The couple at first relish the pleasures of their newly acquired knowledge, but soon turn to mutual recrimination.

At the end of the poem, when the archangel Michael comes to lead the pair from Eden, they look back to the eastern side and see it "With dreadful faces throng'd and fiery arms" (12, 644). Then they make their way into the world, conscious that their union will last only until death and that their new life must be lived on different terms, "with wandering steps and slow" (12, 648), "solitary" in the sense of being separated from God (12, 649). Their tragedy will become that of their descendants as well; and because it thus accounts for all of human history, Milton can claim that his epic encompasses all of humanity, surpassing classical epics before it.

How do we place Milton in European intellectual history? His sense of humanity's seeking to know God's law suggests a line of descent from St. Augustine's *Confessions,* but his emphasis on individual liberty anticipates the Protestant ethic of modern times.

His pamphlet *Areopagitica* influenced the seventeenth-century philosopher John Locke and, later, the Declaration of Independence of the United States. Almost unique among English poets, Milton was an active revolutionary; his middle-class revolution substituted the rights of the individual (enforced by a citizen Protector) for the sovereign authority of church and state. Even today we have not seen the end of Milton. His radicalism may seem conservative to modern readers, but it is still a force to be reckoned with in Western society.

Paradise Lost is one of the greatest poems in English; its astonishing sound effects and stately metrical quality convey a unique richness. It is difficult for the modern reader because of the word order and poetic diction. Like Latin, Milton's English does not rely on word order but on inflection. Also, many words have archaic meanings: "study" means "pursuit," "sentence" means "opinion," and so on. We have paraphrased some of Milton's more difficult sentences; when in doubt about a word, consult a good etymological dictionary.

Suggested Readings

The best text of Milton is Merritt Hughes, ed., *Complete Poems and Major Prose of John Milton* (1957). An abridged edition by Tony Davies, *John Milton: Selected Longer Poems and Prose* (1992), includes a good introduction and commentary. A good contemporary biography is *The Life of John Milton* by A. N. Wilson (1983). Collections of essays include Frank Kermode, ed., *The Living Milton* (1960); Arthur E. Barker, ed., *Milton: Modern Essays in Criticism* (1965); and Alan Rudrum, ed., *Milton: Modern Judgments* (1968). Catherine Belsey, in *Milton: Language, Gender, Power* (1988), reassesses Milton's work from more recent perspectives in scholarship.

Paradise Lost

FROM

Book 1

Of man's first disobedience,[1] and the fruit
Of that forbidden tree whose mortal taste
Brought death into the world, and all our woe,
With loss of Eden, till one greater man[2]
Restore us and regain that blissful seat,
Sing, heavenly Muse, that on the secret top
Of Oreb or of Sinai didst inspire
That shepherd who first taught the chosen seed[3]
In the beginning how the heavens and earth
Rose out of chaos; or if Sion hill[4] 10
Delight thee more, and Siloa's brook that flow'd

[1] This famous opening begins with a prepositional phrase followed by an imperative verb ("Sing") governing the rest of the sentence.

[2] Christ, greater than Adam.

[3] The people of Israel, chosen by God.

[4] Sion hill is the site of the holy temple in Jerusalem. He contrasts it to Mount Helicon, site of the classical Muses. Milton's verse will fly with "no middle flight," that is, even higher than classical epic.

Fast by the oracle of God, I thence
Invoke thy aid to my advent'rous song,
That with no middle flight intends to soar
Above th'Aonian mount while it pursues
Things unattempted yet in prose or rhyme.
And chiefly thou, O Spirit,[5] that dost prefer
Before all temples the upright heart and pure,
Instruct me, for thou know'st; thou from the first[6]
Wast present, and with mighty wings outspread 20
Dove-like sat'st brooding on the vast abyss
And mad'st it pregnant. What in me is dark
Illumine, what is low raise and support,
That to the height of this great argument
I may assert eternal providence,
And justify the ways of God to men.
Say first,[7] for heaven hides nothing from thy view
Nor the deep tract of hell, say first what cause
Mov'd our grand parents in that happy state,
Favour'd of heaven so highly, to fall off 30
From their creator, and transgress his will
For one restraint, lords of the world besides?[8]
Who first seduc'd them to that foul revolt?
Th' infernal serpent;[9] he it was whose guile
Stirr'd up with envy and revenge deceiv'd
The mother of mankind, what time his pride
Had cast him out from heaven with all his host
Of rebel angels, by whose aid aspiring
To set himself in glory above his peers
He trusted to have equall'd the most high 40
If he oppos'd, and with ambitious aim
Against the throne and monarchy of God
Rais'd impious war in heaven and battle proud
With vain attempt. Him the almighty power[10]
Hurl'd headlong flaming from th'etherial sky
With hideous ruin and combustion down
To bottomless perdition, there to dwell
In adamantine chains and penal fire
Who durst defy th'omnipotent to arms.
Nine times the space that measures day and night 50
To mortal men he with his horrid crew
Lay vanquish'd, rolling in the fiery gulf,

---

[5]The Holy Spirit, contrasted to the classical muse.

[6]Cf. "And the spirit of God moved upon the face of the Waters" (Genesis 1:2). Milton links the creative force of his poem with the source of the original creation in God.

[7]Milton begins by invoking the story of the Fall.

[8]The whole phrase modifies "parents."

[9]It was Satan the serpent's guile that first corrupted Eve, after his pride had cast him out of Heaven, where he had tried to oppose God accompanied by his angels. Milton puts the onus for all these acts squarely on Satan.

[10]God hurled him down to Hell and cast him and the other fallen angels in chains. Cf. "How art thou fallen from Heaven, O Lucifer, son of the morning!" (Isaiah 14:12).

Confounded though immortal; but his doom
Reserv'd him to more wrath, for now the thought
Both of lost happiness and lasting pain
Torments him. Round he throws his baleful eyes
That witness'd huge affliction and dismay
Mix'd with obdurate pride and steadfast hate.
At once as far as angels ken[11] he views
The dismal situation waste and wild: 60
A dungeon horrible on all sides round
As one great furnace flam'd, yet from those flames
No light but rather darkness visible
Serv'd only to discover sights of woe,
Regions of sorrow, doleful shades, where peace
And rest can never dwell, hope never comes[12]
That comes to all, but torture without end
Still urges, and a fiery deluge fed
With ever-burning sulphur unconsum'd.
Such place eternal justice had prepar'd 70
For these rebellious, here their prison ordain'd
In utter darkness, and their portion set
As far remov'd from God and light of heaven
As from the centre thrice to th'utmost pole.
O how unlike the place from whence they fell!
There the companions of his fall o'erwhelm'd[13]
With floods and whirlwinds of tempestuous fire
He soon discerns, and weltering by his side
One next himself in power and next in crime,
Long after known in Palestine and nam'd 80
Beelzebub; to whom th'arch-enemy,
And thence in heaven call'd Satan, with bold words
Breaking the horrid silence thus began.
If thou beest he[14]—but O how fall'n! how chang'd
From him who in the happy realms of light
Cloth'd with transparent brightness didst outshine
Myriads though bright; if he whom mutual league,
United thoughts and counsels, equal hope
And hazard in the glorious enterprise
Join'd with me once, now misery hath join'd 90
In equal ruin; into what pit thou seest
From what height fall'n, so much the stronger prov'd
He with his thunder; and till then who knew
The force of those dire arms? Yet not for those,[15]
Nor what the potent victor in his rage
Can else inflict, do I repent or change,
Though chang'd in outward lustre, that fix'd mind

---

[11] "As far as angels ken": either "As far as angels know" or "As far as angels' knowledge."

[12] Cf. "Abandon hope, all ye who enter here" in Dante's *Inferno* 3:9.

[13] Satan sees his companions, including Beelzebub, to whom he begins to speak.

[14] Satan, taken aback by Hell, says "If you are really my old companion, see what has been done to us; but how could we have known God's power?"

[15] Satan vows never to change his intentions, despite the bitter defeat he and his followers have suffered.

And high disdain from sense of injur'd merit
That with the mightiest rais'd me to contend,
And to the fierce contention brought along 100
Innumerable force of spirits arm'd
That durst dislike his reign and, me preferring,
His utmost power with adverse power oppos'd
In dubious battle on the plains of heaven
And shook his throne. What though the field be lost?
All is not lost: th' unconquerable will
And study[16] of revenge, immortal hate,
And courage never to submit or yield,
And what is else not to be overcome.
That glory never shall his wrath or might 110
Extort from me. To bow and sue for grace
With suppliant knee, and deify his power
Who from the terror of this arm so late
Doubted his empire, that were low indeed;
That were an ignominy and shame beneath
This downfall. Since by fate the strength of gods
And this empyreal substance cannot fail,
Since through experience of this great event
In arms not worse, in foresight much advanc'd,
We may with more successful hope resolve 120
To wage by force or guile eternal war
Irreconcilable to our grand foe,
Who now triumphs and in th'excess of joy
Sole reigning holds the tyranny of heaven.

So spake th'apostate angel, though in pain,
Vaunting aloud, but rack'd with deep despair;
And him thus answer'd soon his bold compeer.

O Prince, O chief of many throned powers
That led th'embattl'd seraphim to war
Under thy conduct, and in dreadful deeds 130
Fearless endanger'd heaven's perpetual king
And put to proof his high supremacy,
Whether upheld by strength or chance or fate,
Too well I see and rue the dire event
That with sad overthrow and foul defeat
Hath lost us heaven, and all this mighty host
In horrible destruction laid thus low,
As far as gods and heavenly essences
Can perish;[17] for the mind and spirit remains
Invincible, and vigour soon returns, 140
Though all our glory extinct and happy state
Here swallow'd up in endless misery.
But what if he our conqueror (whom I now
Of force believe almighty,[18] since no less
Than such could have o'erpower'd such force as ours)

---

[16]Pursuit.

[17]God will not utterly destroy Satan and the fallen angels, although he may severely wound them.

[18]Beelzebub will eventually propose a course of action other than renewed warfare in Heaven.

Have left us this our spirit and strength entire
Strongly to suffer and support our pains,
That we may so suffice his vengeful ire,
Or do him mightier service as his thralls
By right of war, whate'er his business be 150
Here in the heart of hell, to work in fire
Or do his errands in the gloomy deep?
What can it then avail though yet we feel
Strength undiminish'd, or eternal being
To undergo eternal punishment?
Whereto with speedy words the fiend repli'd.
Fall'n cherub, to be weak is miserable,
Doing or suffering;[19] but of this be sure,
To do aught good never will be our task,
But ever to do ill our sole delight, 160
As being the contrary to his high will
Whom we resist. If then his providence
Out of our evil seek to bring forth good,
Our labour must be to pervert that end
And out of good still to find means of evil;
Which oft-times may succeed, so as perhaps
To grieve him, if I fail not, and disturb
His inmost counsels from their destin'd aim.
But see, the angry victor hath recall'd
His ministers of vengeance and pursuit 170
Back to the gates of heaven. The sulphurous hail
Shot after us in storm o'erblown hath laid
The fiery surge that from the precipice
Of heaven receiv'd us falling, and the thunder,
Wing'd with red lightning and impetuous rage,
Perhaps hath spent his shafts, and ceases now
To bellow through the vast and boundless deep.
Let us not slip th'occasion, whether scorn
Or satiate fury yield it from our foe.
Seest thou yon dreary plain forlorn and wild, 180
The seat of desolation, void of light
Save what the glimmering of these livid flames
Casts pale and dreadful? Thither let us tend
From off the tossing of these fiery waves,
There rest, if any rest can harbour there,
And reassembling our afflicted powers[20]
Consult how we may henceforth most offend
Our enemy, our own loss how repair,
How overcome this dire calamity,
What reinforcement we may gain from hope, 190
If not what resolution from despair.
Thus Satan, talking to his dearest mate
With head uplift above the wave and eyes
That sparkling blaz'd; his other parts besides

[19] Whether one is active or passive.
[20] Calling together the fallen angels.

Prone on the flood extended long and large
Lay floating many a rood,[21] in bulk as huge
As whom the fables name of monstrous size,
Titanian or Earth-born, that warr'd on Jove:
Briareus or Typhon, whom the den
By ancient Tarsus held, or that sea-beast 200
Leviathan, which God of all his works
Created hugest that swim the ocean stream.
Him haply slumb'ring on the Norway foam
The pilot of some small night-founder'd skiff
Deeming some island oft, as seamen tell,
With fixed anchor in his scaly rind
Moors by his side under the lee, while night
Invests the sea and wished morn delays.
So stretch'd out huge in length the arch-fiend lay
Chain'd on the burning lake, nor ever thence 210
Had ris'n or heav'd his head[22] but that the will
And high permission of all-ruling heaven
Left him at large to his own dark designs,
That with reiterated crimes he might
Heap on himself damnation while he sought
Evil to others, and enrag'd might see
How all his malice serv'd but to bring forth
Infinite goodness, grace and mercy shown
On man by him seduc'd, but on himself
Treble confusion, wrath and vengeance pour'd. 220
Forthwith upright he rears from off the pool
His mighty stature. On each hand the flames
Driv'n backward slope their pointing spires, and roll'd
In billows leave i'the midst a horrid vale.
Then with expanded wings he steers his flight
Aloft, incumbent on the dusky air
That felt unusual weight, till on dry land
He lights, if it were land that ever burn'd
With solid as the lake with liquid fire,
And such appear'd in hue as when the force 230
Of subterranean wind transports a hill
Torn from Pelorus or the shatter'd side
Of thundering Etna, whose combustible
And fuell'd entrails, thence conceiving fire,
Sublim'd with mineral fury aid the winds
And leave a singed bottom, all involv'd
With stench and smoke: such resting found the sole
Of unbless'd feet. Him follow'd his next mate,
Both glorying to have scap'd the Stygian flood
As gods, and by their own recover'd strength, 240
Not by the sufferance of supernal power.

---

[21]Rood: quarter of an acre. The comparison to mythological giants is half-satirical; Satan is far more important than these fabulous creatures. Leviathan the whale is from Job 41.

[22]Satan could never have risen from his chains except through the will of God. This passage tells us something of God's plan to show Satan to disadvantage whatever he may attempt, whereas God will show his grace to best advantage to humanity.

Is this the region, this the soil, the clime,
Said then the lost archangel, this the seat
That we must change for heaven, this mournful gloom
For that celestial light? Be it so, since he
Who now is sovereign can dispose and bid
What shall be right. Furthest from him is best[23]
Whom reason hath equall'd, force hath made supreme
Above his equals. Farewell, happy fields
Where joy for ever dwells; hail horrors, hail 250
Infernal world, and thou, profoundest hell,
Receive thy new possessor, one who brings
A mind not to be chang'd by place or time.
The mind is its own place, and in itself
Can make a heaven of hell, a hell of heaven.
What matter where, if I be still the same
And what I should be, all but less than he
Whom thunder hath made greater? Here at least
We shall be free. Th'almighty hath not built
Here for his envy, will not drive us hence. 260
Here we may reign secure, and in my choice
To reign is worth ambition though in hell:
Better to reign in hell than serve in heaven.
But wherefore let we then our faithful friends,
Th' associates and copartners of our loss,
Lie thus astonish'd on th'oblivious pool,
And call them not to share with us their part
In this unhappy mansion, or once more
With rallied arms to try what may be yet
Regain'd in heaven, or what more lost in hell? 270
So Satan spake, and him Beelzebub
Thus answer'd. Leader of those armies bright
Which but th'omnipotent none could have foil'd,
If once they hear that voice, their liveliest pledge
Of hope in fears and dangers, heard so oft
In worst extremes and on the perilous edge
Of battle when it rag'd, in all assaults
Their surest signal, they will soon resume
New courage and revive,[24] though now they lie
Grovelling and prostrate on yon lake of fire, 280
As we erewhile, astounded and amaz'd;
No wonder, fall'n such a pernicious height. . . .

FROM
BOOK 2

High on a throne of royal state which far
Outshone the wealth of Ormus and of Ind,
Or where the gorgeous East with richest hand

[23]Satan settles for Hell because it is farthest from God.

[24]Beelzebub assures Satan that once the fallen angels recognize his voice, they will rise from their chains and follow him.

Showers on her kings barbaric pearl and gold,
Satan exalted sat, by merit rais'd
To that bad eminence; and from despair
Thus high uplifted beyond hope aspires
Beyond thus high, insatiate to pursue
Vain war with heaven, and by success untaught
His proud imaginations thus display'd. 10
  Powers and dominions, deities of heaven,
For since no deep within her gulf can hold
Immortal vigour, though oppress'd and fallen,
I give not heaven for lost. From this descent
Celestial virtues rising will appear
More glorious and more dread than from no fall,
And trust themselves to fear no second fate.
Me though just right and the fix'd laws of heaven
Did first create your leader, next free choice,
With what besides in counsel or in fight 20
Hath been achiev'd of merit, yet this loss,
Thus far at least recover'd, hath much more
Establish'd in a safe unenvi'd throne
Yielded with full consent.[25] The happier state
In heaven which follows dignity might draw
Envy from each inferior; but who here
Will envy whom the highest place exposes
Foremost to stand against the thunderer's aim
Your bulwark, and condemns to greatest share
Of endless pain? Where there is then no good 30
For which to strive, no strife can grow up there
From faction; for none sure will claim in hell
Precedence, none whose portion is so small
Of present pain with that ambitious mind
Will covet more. With this advantage then
To union, and firm faith and firm accord
More than can be in heaven, we now return
To claim our just inheritance of old,
Surer to prosper than prosperity
Could have assur'd us; and by what best way, 40
Whether of open war or covert guile,[26]
We now debate. Who can advise may speak.
  He ceas'd, and next him Moloch, sceptr'd king,
Stood up, the strongest and the fiercest spirit
That fought in heaven, now fiercer by despair.
His trust was with th'eternal to be deem'd
Equal in strength, and rather than be less
Car'd not to be at all. With that care lost
Went all his fear: of God or hell or worse
He reck'd not, and these words thereafter spake. 50

---

[25] Satan points out that their recent loss of Heaven has yielded them a safe throne with the full consent of God.

[26] Satan frames the debate around the question of *how* the fallen angels will regain Heaven. The fallen angels, however, will gravitate to other ideas, particularly how to subvert God's plans without risking a direct encounter.

My sentence is for open war. Of wiles
More unexpert I boast not; them let those
Contrive who need, or when they need, not now.
For while they sit contriving, shall the rest,
Millions that stand in arms and longing wait
The signal to ascend, sit lingering here
Heaven's fugitives, and for their dwelling place
Accept this dark opprobrious den of shame,
The prison of his tyranny who reigns
By our delay? No, let us rather choose 60
Arm'd with hell flames and fury all at once
O'er heaven's high towers to force resistless way,
Turning our tortures into horrid arms
Against the torturer, when to meet the noise
Of his almighty engine he shall hear
Infernal thunder, and for lightning see
Black fire and horror shot with equal rage
Among his angels, and his throne itself
Mix'd with Tartarean sulphur and strange fire,
His own invented torments. But perhaps 70
The way seems difficult and steep to scale
With upright wing against a higher foe?
Let such bethink them, if the sleepy drench
Of that forgetful lake benumb not still,
That in our proper motion we ascend
Up to our native seat: descent and fall
To us is adverse. Who but felt of late,
When the fierce foe hung on our broken rear
Insulting and pursu'd us through the deep,
With what compulsion and laborious flight 80
We sunk thus low? The ascent is easy, then;
The event is fear'd: should we again provoke
Our stronger, some worse way his wrath may find
To our destruction, if there be in hell
Fear to be worse destroy'd. What can be worse
Than to dwell here, driv'n out from bliss, condemn'd
In this abhorred deep to utter woe,
Where pain of unextinguishable fire
Must exercise us without hope of end,
The vassals of his anger, when the scourge 90
Inexorably and the torturing hour
Call us to penance? More destroy'd than thus
We should be quite abolish'd and expire.
What fear we then? What doubt we to incense
His utmost ire, which to the height enrag'd
Will either quite consume us and reduce
To nothing this essential, happier far
Than miserable to have eternal being,
Or if our substance be indeed divine
And cannot cease to be, we are at worst 100
On this side nothing? And by proof we feel
Our power sufficient to disturb his heaven,

And with perpetual inroads to alarm,
Though inaccessible, his fatal throne;
Which, if not victory, is yet revenge.
He ended, frowning, and his look denounc'd[27]
Desperate revenge and battle dangerous
To less than gods. On th' other side up rose
Belial, in act more graceful and humane.
A fairer person lost not heaven; he seem'd 110
For dignity compos'd and high exploit.
But all was false and hollow, though his tongue
Dropp'd manna and could make the worse appear
The better reason, to perplex and dash
Maturest counsels, for his thoughts were low,
To vice industrious but to nobler deeds
Timorous and slothful. Yet he pleas'd the ear,
And with persuasive accent thus began.
I should be much for open war, O peers,
As not behind in hate, if what was urg'd 120
Main reason to persuade immediate war
Did not dissuade me most, and seem to cast
Ominous conjecture on the whole success,
When he who most excels in fact of arms,
In what he counsels and in what excels
Mistrustful, grounds his courage on despair
And utter dissolution as the scope
Of all his aim, after some dire revenge.
First, what revenge? The towers of heaven are fill'd
With armed watch that render all access 130
Impregnable; oft on the bordering deep
Encamp their legions, or with obscure wing
Scout far and wide into the realm of night,
Scorning surprise. Or could we break our way
By force, and at our heels all hell should rise
With blackest insurrection to confound
Heaven's purest light, yet our great enemy
All incorruptible would on his throne
Sit unpolluted and th'ethereal mould,
Incapable of stain, would soon expel 140
Her mischief and purge off the baser fire
Victorious. Thus repuls'd, our final hope
Is flat despair: we must exasperate
Th'almighty victor to spend all his rage,
And that must end us, that must be our cure,
To be no more. Sad cure, for who would lose
Though full of pain this intellectual being,
Those thoughts that wander through eternity,
To perish rather, swallow'd up and lost
In the wide womb of uncreated night, 150
Devoid of sense and motion. And who knows,

[27]Proclaimed.

Let this be good, whether our angry foe
Can give it, or will ever? How he can
Is doubtful; that he never will is sure.
Will he, so wise let loose at once his ire,
Belike through impotence or unware,
To give his enemies their wish and end
Then in his anger, whom his anger saves
To punish endless? Wherefore cease we then?
Say they who counsel war, we are decreed, 160
Reserv'd and destin'd to eternal woe;
Whatever doing, what can we suffer more,
What can we suffer worse? Is this then worst,
Thus sitting, thus consulting, thus in arms?
What when we fled amain, pursu'd and struck
With heaven's afflicting thunder, and besought
The deep to shelter us? This hell then seem'd
A refuge from those wounds. Or when we lay
Chain'd on the burning lake? That sure was worse.
What if the breath that kindled those grim fires 170
Awak'd should blow them into sevenfold rage
And plunge us in the flames? Or from above
Should intermitted vengeance arm again
His red right hand to plague us? What if all
Her stores were open'd, and this firmament
Of hell should spout her cataracts of fire,
Impendent horrors, threatening hideous fall
One day upon our heads, while we, perhaps
Designing or exhorting glorious war,
Caught in a fiery tempest shall be hurl'd, 180
Each on his rock transfix'd, the sport and prey
Of racking whirlwinds, or for ever sunk
Under yon boiling ocean, wrapp'd in chains,
There to converse with everlasting groans
Unrespited, unpitied, unrepriev'd
Ages of hopeless end? This would be worse.
War therefore open or conceal'd alike
My voice dissuades; for what can force or guile
With him, or who deceive his mind, whose eye
Views all things at one view? He from heaven's height 190
All these our motions vain sees and derides,
Not more almighty to resist our might
Than wise to frustrate all our plots and wiles.
Shall we then live thus vile, the race of heaven
Thus trampl'd, thus expell'd to suffer here
Chains and these torments? Better these than worse
By my advice, since fate inevitable
Subdues us and omnipotent decree,
The victor's will. To suffer, as to do,
Our strength is equal, nor the law unjust 200
That so ordains; this was at first resolv'd
If we were wise, against so great a foe
Contending, and so doubtful what might fall.

I laugh when those who at the spear are bold
And vent'rous, if that fail them, shrink and fear
What yet they know must follow, to endure
Exile or ignominy or bonds or pain,
The sentence of their conqueror. This is now
Our doom, which if we can sustain and bear,
Our supreme foe in time may much remit 210
His anger and perhaps, thus far remov'd,
Not mind us not offending, satisfi'd
With what is punish'd; whence these raging fires
Will slacken, if his breath stir not their flames.
Our purer essence then will overcome
Their noxious vapour, or inur'd not feel,
Or chang'd at length and to the place conform'd
In temper and in nature will receive
Familiar the fierce heat and void of pain.
This horror will grow mild, this darkness light; 220
Besides what hope the never-ending flight
Of future days may bring, what chance, what change
Worth waiting, since our present lot appears
For happy though but ill, for ill not worst
If we procure not to ourselves more woe.
Thus Belial with words cloth'd in reason's garb
Counsell'd ignoble ease and peaceful sloth,
Not peace; and after him thus Mammon spake.
Either to disenthrone the king of heaven
We war, if war be best, or to regain 230
Our own right lost. Him to unthrone we then
May hope when everlasting fate shall yield
To fickle chance, and Chaos judge the strife.
The former vain to hope argues as vain
The latter, for what place can be for us
Within heaven's bound unless heaven's lord supreme
We overpower? Suppose he should relent
And publish grace to all on promise made
Of new subjection? With what eyes could we
Stand in his presence humble and receive 240
Strict laws impos'd, to celebrate his throne
With warbled hymns and to his godhead sing
Forc'd hallelujahs, while he lordly sits
Our envied sovereign and his altar breathes
Ambrosial odours and ambrosial flowers,
Our servile offerings? This must be our task
In heaven, this our delight; how wearisome
Eternity so spent in worship paid
To whom we hate. Let us not then pursue
By force impossible, by leave obtain'd 250
Unacceptable though in heaven, our state
Of splendid vassalage, but rather seek
Our own good from ourselves and from our own
Live to ourselves, though in this vast recess,
Free and to none accountable, preferring

Hard liberty before the easy yoke
Of servile pomp. Our greatness will appear
Then most conspicuous when great things of small,
Useful of hurtful, prosperous of adverse
We can create, and in what place soe'er 260
Thrive under evil and work ease out of pain
Through labour and endurance. This deep world
Of darkness do we dread? How oft amidst
Thick clouds and dark doth heaven's all-ruling sire
Choose to reside, his glory unobscur'd,
And with the majesty of darkness round
Covers his throne, from whence deep thunders roar
Mustering their rage, and heaven resembles hell?
As he our darkness, cannot we his light
Imitate when we please? This desert soil 270
Wants not her hidden lustre, gems and gold;
Nor want we skill and art from whence to raise
Magnificence; and what can heaven show more?
Our torments also may in length of time
Become our elements, these piercing fires
As soft as now severe, our temper chang'd
Into their temper, which must needs remove
The sensible of pain. All things invite
To peaceful counsels and the settl'd state
Of order, how in safety best we may 280
Compose our present evils, with regard
Of what we are and where, dismissing quite
All thoughts of war. Ye have what I advise.
He scarce had finish'd when such murmur fill'd
Th'assembly as when hollow rocks retain
The sound of blust'ring winds which all night long
Had rous'd the sea, now with hoarse cadence lull
Seafaring men o'erwatch'd, whose bark by chance
Or pinnace anchors in a craggy bay
After the tempest; such applause was heard 290
As Mammon ended, and his sentence pleas'd,
Advising peace. For such another field
They dreaded worse than hell, so much the fear
Of thunder and the sword of Michaël
Wrought still within them, and no less desire
To found this nether empire, which might rise
By policy and long process of time
In emulation opposite to heaven.[28]
Which when Beelzebub perceiv'd, than whom,
Satan except, none higher sat, with grave 300
Aspect he rose, and in his rising seem'd
A pillar of state. Deep on his front engraven
Deliberation sat and public care,
And princely counsel in his face yet shone,

[28] Milton sums up the attitude of the fallen angels at this point: They dread the thought of further battle and harbor hopes of making Hell comparable to heaven.

Majestic though in ruin. Sage he stood
With Atlantean shoulders fit to bear
The weight of mightiest monarchies. His look
Drew audience and attention still as night
Or summer's noontide air while thus he spake.
  Thrones and imperial powers, offspring of heaven, 310
Ethereal virtues—or these titles now
Must we renounce, and changing style be call'd
Princes of hell? For so the popular vote
Inclines, here to continue and build up here
A growing empire, doubtless; while we dream,
And know not that the king of heaven hath doom'd
This place our dungeon, not our safe retreat
Beyond his potent arm, to live exempt
From heaven's high jurisdiction, in new league
Banded against his throne, but to remain 320
In strictest bondage though thus far remov'd,
Under th'inevitable curb reserv'd
His captive multitude. For he, be sure,
In height or depth still first and last will reign
Sole king, and of his kingdom lose no part
By our revolt, but over hell extend
His empire and with iron sceptre rule
Us here as with his golden those in heaven.
What sit we then projecting peace and war?
War hath determin'd us and foil'd with loss 330
Irreparable, terms of peace yet none
Vouchsaf'd or sought; for what peace will be given
To us enslav'd, but custody severe
And stripes and arbitrary punishment
Inflicted? And what peace can we return,
But to our power hostility and hate,
Untam'd reluctance, and revenge though slow
Yet ever plotting how the conqueror least
May reap his conquest and may least rejoice
In doing what we most in suffering feel? 340
Nor will occasion want, nor shall we need
With dangerous expedition to invade
Heav'n, whose high walls fear no assault or siege
Or ambush from the deep. What if we find
Some easier enterprise?[29] There is a place
(If ancient and prophetic fame in heaven
Err not), another world, the happy seat
Of some new race call'd Man, about this time
To be created like to us, though less
In power and excellence, but favour'd more 350
Of him who rules above: so was his will
Pronounc'd among the gods, and by an oath
That shook heaven's whole circumference confirm'd.
Thither let us bend all our thoughts, to learn

[29]Here the focus shifts to Earth, and Beelzebub introduces the main line of the poem's action.

What creatures there inhabit, of what mould
Or substance, how endu'd, and what their power,
And where their weakness, how attempted best,
By force or subtlety. Though heaven be shut
And heaven's high arbitrator sit secure
In his own strength, this place may lie expos'd 360
The utmost border of his kingdom, left
To their defence who hold it. Here perhaps
Some advantageous act may be achiev'd
By sudden onset, either with hell fire
To waste his whole creation or possess
All as our own, and drive as we were driven
The puny habitants; or if not drive,
Seduce them to our party, that their God
May prove their foe and with repenting hand
Abolish his own works. This would surpass 370
Common revenge, and interrupt his joy
In our confusion and our joy upraise
In his disturbance, when his darling sons,
Hurl'd headlong to partake with us, shall curse
Their frail original and faded bliss,
Faded so soon. Advise if this be worth
Attempting, or to sit in darkness here
Hatching vain empires. Thus Beelzebub
Pleaded his devilish counsel, first devis'd
By Satan and in part propos'd; for whence 380
But from the author of all ill could spring
So deep a malice, to confound the race
Of mankind in one root and earth with hell
To mingle and involve, done all to spite
The great creator? But their spite still serves
His glory to augment. The bold design
Pleas'd highly those infernal states, and joy
Sparkled in all their eyes. With full assent
They vote, whereat his speech he thus renews.
Well have ye judg'd, well ended long debate, 390
Synod of gods, and like to what ye are,
Great things resolv'd, which from the lowest deep
Will once more lift us up in spite of fate
Nearer our ancient seat, perhaps in view
Of those bright confines, whence with neighbouring arms
And opportune excursion we may chance
Re-enter heav'n, or else in some mild zone
Dwell not unvisited of heaven's fair light
Secure, and at the brightening orient beam
Purge off this gloom; the soft delicious air 400
To heal the scar of these corrosive fires
Shall breathe her balm. But first, whom shall we send
In search of this new world, whom shall we find
Sufficient?[30] Who shall tempt with wand'ring feet

[30]Beelzebub's question is perhaps rhetorical, because only Satan will respond.

The dark unbottom'd infinite abyss,
And through the palpable obscure find out
His uncouth way, or spread his airy flight
Upborne with indefatigable wings
Over the vast abrupt ere he arrive
The happy isle? What strength, what art can then 410
Suffice, or what evasion bear him safe
Through the strict senteries and stations thick
Of angels watching round? Here he had need
All circumspection, and we now no less
Choice in our suffrage; for on whom we send
The weight of all and our last hope relies.
This said, he sat, and expectation held
His look suspense, awaiting who appear'd
To second or oppose, or undertake
The perilous attempt; but all sat mute, 420
Pond'ring the danger with deep thoughts, and each
In other's count'nance read his own dismay
Astonish'd. None among the choice and prime
Of those heaven-warring champions could be found
So hardy as to proffer or accept
Alone the dreadful voyage; till at last
Satan, whom now transcendent glory rais'd
Above his fellows, with monarchal pride
Conscious of highest worth unmov'd thus spake.[31]
O progeny of heaven, empyreal thrones, 430
With reason hath deep silence and demur
Seiz'd us, though undismay'd. Long is the way
And hard that out of hell leads up to light.
Our prison strong, this huge convex of fire
Outrageous to devour, immures us round
Ninefold, and gates of burning adamant
Barr'd over us prohibit all egress.
These pass'd, if any pass, the void profound
Of unessential night receives him next
Wide gaping and with utter loss of being 440
Threatens him, plung'd in that abortive gulf.
If thence he scape into whatever world
Or unknown region, what remains him less
Than unknown dangers and as hard escape?
But I should ill become this throne, O peers,
And this imperial sovereignty adorn'd
With splendour, arm'd with power, if aught propos'd
And judg'd of public moment in the shape
Of difficulty or danger could deter
Me from attempting. Wherefore do I assume 450
These royalties and not refuse to reign,
Refusing to accept as great a share
Of hazard as of honour, due alike
To him who reigns, and so much to him due

[31] Satan literally rises to the occasion. He gains in radiance as he does so.

Of hazard more as he above the rest
High honour'd sits? Go therefore, mighty powers,
Terror of heaven though fall'n; intend at home,
While here shall be our home, what best may ease
The present misery and render hell
More tolerable, if there be cure or charm 460
To respite or deceive or slack the pain
Of this ill mansion. Intermit no watch
Against a wakeful foe, while I abroad
Through all the coasts of dark destruction seek
Deliverance for us all. This enterprise
None shall partake with me. Thus saying rose
The monarch, and prevented all reply;
Prudent, lest from his resolution rais'd
Others among the chief might offer now
(Certain to be refus'd) what erst they fear'd, 470
And so refus'd might in opinion stand
His rivals, winning cheap the high repute
Which he through hazard huge must earn. But they
Dreaded not more th'adventure than his voice
Forbidding, and at once with him they rose.
Their rising all at once was as the sound
Of thunder heard remote. Towards him they bend
With awful reverence prone, and as a god
Extol him equal to the highest in heaven.
Nor fail'd they to express how much they prais'd 480
That for the general safety he despis'd
His own; for neither do the spirits damn'd
Lose all their virtue, lest bad men should boast
Their specious deeds on earth, which glory excites
Or close ambition varnish'd o'er with zeal.
Thus they their doubtful consultations dark
Ended rejoicing in their matchless chief;
As when from mountain-tops the dusky clouds
Ascending, while the north wind sleeps, o'erspread
Heaven's cheerful face, the louring element 490
Scowls o'er the darken'd landscape snow or shower,
If chance the radiant sun with farewell sweet
Extend his evening beam, the fields revive,
The birds their notes renew, and bleating herds
Attest their joy that hill and valley rings. . . .

FROM
BOOK 4

. . . Now to th' ascent of that steep savage hill
Satan had journey'd on, pensive and slow,[32]
But further way found none, so thick entwin'd
As one continu'd brake the undergrowth

[32] As Milton introduces the scene, Satan "journeys to Paradise, whose outward prospect and situation is described."

Of shrubs and tangling bushes had perplex'd
All path of man or beast that pass'd that way.
One gate there only was, and that look'd east
On th'other side, which when th' arch-felon saw
Due entrance he disdain'd and in contempt 180
At one slight bound high over-leap'd all bound
Of hill or highest wall, and sheer within
Lights on his feet. As when a prowling wolf
Whom hunger drives to seek new haunt for prey,
Watching where shepherds pen their flocks at eve
In hurdl'd cotes amid the field secure,
Leaps o'er the fence with ease into the fold,
Or as a thief, bent to unhoard the cash
Of some rich burgher whose substantial doors,
Cross-barr'd and bolted fast, fear no assault, 190
In at the window climbs or o'er the tiles,
So clomb this first grand thief into God's fold;
So since into his church lewd hirelings climb.[33]
Thence up he flew, and on the tree of life,
The middle tree and highest there that grew,
Sat like a cormorant;[34] yet not true life
Thereby regain'd, but sat devising death
To them who liv'd, nor on the virtue thought
Of that life-giving plant, but only us'd
For prospect what well us'd had been the pledge 200
Of immortality. So little knows
Any but God alone to value right
The good before him, but perverts best things
To worst abuse, or to their meanest use.
Beneath him with new wonder now he views
To all delight of human sense expos'd
In narrow room nature's whole wealth, yea more,
A heaven on earth, for blissful Paradise
Of God the garden was, by him in th'east
Of Eden planted. Eden stretch'd her line 210
From Auran eastward to the royal towers
Of great Seleucia, built by Grecian kings,
Or where the sons of Eden long before
Dwelt in Telassar. In this pleasant soil
His far more pleasant garden God ordain'd;
Out of the fertile ground he caus'd to grow
All trees of noblest kind for sight, smell, taste,
And all amid them stood the tree of life
High eminent, blooming ambrosial fruit
Of vegetable gold; and next to life 220
Our death, the tree of knowledge, grew fast by,
Knowledge of good bought dear by knowing ill.
Southward through Eden went a river large,

[33]At the end of this extended simile comparing Satan to a burglar and a wolf among sheep, Milton adds that many today behave similarly when they threaten the Church.

[34]Milton appears to mean that Satan actually takes the shape of the bird, as he will the serpent later on.

Nor chang'd his course, but through the shaggy hill
Pass'd underneath engulf'd, for God had thrown
That mountain as his garden mould high-rais'd
Upon the rapid current, which through veins
Of porous earth with kindly thirst up drawn
Rose a fresh fountain and with many a rill
Water'd the garden, thence united fell 230
Down the steep glade, and met the nether flood
Which from his darksome passage now appears,
And now divided into four main streams
Runs diverse, wand'ring many a famous realm
And country whereof here needs no account;
But rather to tell how, if art could tell,
How from that sapphire fount the crisped brooks
Rolling on orient pearl and sands of gold
With mazy error under pendant shades
Ran nectar, visiting each plant, and fed 240
Flowers worthy of Paradise, which not nice art
In beds and curious knots but nature boon
Pour'd forth profuse on hill and dale and plain,
Both where the morning sun first warmly smote
The open field and where the unpierced shade
Embrown'd the noontide bowers. Thus was this place,[35]
A happy rural seat of various view:
Groves whose rich trees wept odorous gums and balm;
Others whose fruit burnish'd with golden rind
Hung amiable, Hesperian fables true, 250
If true, here only, and of delicious taste;
Betwixt them lawns or level downs and flocks
Grazing the tender herb were interpos'd,
Or palmy hillock or the flowery lap
Of some irriguous valley spread her store,
Flowers of all hue and without thorn the rose;
Another side umbrageous grots and caves
Of cool recess, o'er which the mantling vine
Lays forth her purple grape and gently creeps
Luxuriant; meanwhile murmuring waters fall 260
Down the slope hills dispers'd, or in a lake,
That to the fringed bank with myrtle crown'd
Her crystal mirror holds, unite their streams;
The birds their choir apply; airs, vernal airs
Breathing the smell of field and grove attune
The trembling leaves, while universal Pan
Knit with the Graces and the Hours in dance
Led on th'eternal spring. Not that fair field
Of Enna, where Proserpine gathering flowers
Herself a fairer flower by gloomy Dis 270

[35]The long nature description that follows is an interesting example of baroque poetry, discussed more fully elsewhere in this volume. The long list of classical allusions beginning with line 266 is another aspect of baroque.

Was gather'd, which cost Ceres all that pain
To seek her through the world, nor that sweet grove
Of Daphne, by Orontes and th'inspir'd
Castalian spring, might with this Paradise
Of Eden strive, nor that Nyseian isle
Girt with the river Triton where old Cham,
Whom Gentiles Ammon call and Libyan Jove,
Hid Amalthea and her florid son
Young Bacchus from his stepdame Rhea's eye;
Nor where Abassin kings their issue guard, 280
Mount Amara, though this by some suppos'd
True Paradise, under the Ethiop line
By Nilus' head, enclos'd with shining rock
A whole day's journey high; but wide remote
From this Assyrian garden, where the fiend
Saw undelighted all delight, all kind
Of living creatures new to sight and strange.
Two of far nobler shape,[36] erect and tall,
Godlike erect, with naked honour clad
In naked majesty seem'd lords of all, 290
And worthy seem'd, for in their looks divine
The image of their glorious maker shone,
Truth, wisdom, sanctitude severe and pure,
Severe but in true filial freedom plac'd,
Whence true authority in men;[37] though both
Not equal, as their sex not equal seem'd:
For contemplation he and valour form'd,
For softness she and sweet attractive grace,
He is for God only, she for God in him.
His fair large front and eye sublime declar'd 300
Absolute rule, and hyacinthine locks
Round from his parted forelock manly hung
Clustering, but not beneath his shoulders broad;
She as a veil down to the slender waist
Her unadorned golden tresses wore
Dishevell'd, but in wanton ringlets wav'd
As the vine curls her tendrils, which impli'd
Subjection, but requir'd with gentle sway
And by her yielded, by him best receiv'd
Yielded with coy submission, modest pride 310
And sweet reluctant amorous delay.
Nor those mysterious parts were then conceal'd,
Then was not guilty shame; dishonest shame
Of nature's works, honour dishonourable,
Sin-bred, how have ye troubl'd all mankind
With shows instead, mere shows of seeming pure,

[36]Adam and Eve are introduced along with the lesser creatures, which Satan saw "undelighted." Uncorrupted at this point, they bear the pure image of God.

[37]The lines that follow are a classic example of the patriarchal ideal, giving man the authority over woman.

And banish'd from man's life his happiest life,
Simplicity and spotless innocence.
So pass'd they naked on, nor shunn'd the sight
Of God or angel, for they thought no ill; 320
So hand in hand they pass'd, the loveliest pair
That ever since in love's embraces met,
Adam the goodliest man of men since born
His sons, the fairest of her daughters Eve.
Under a tuft of shade that on a green
Stood whispering soft by a fresh fountain side
They sat them down, and after no more toil
Of their sweet gardening labour than suffic'd
To recommend cool zephyr and made ease
More easy, wholesome thirst and appetite 330
More grateful, to their supper fruits they fell,
Nectarine fruits which the compliant boughs
Yielded them, sidelong as they sat recline
On the soft downy bank damask'd with flowers.
The savoury pulp they chew, and in the rind
Still as they thirsted scoop the brimming stream;
Nor gentle purpose nor endearing smiles
Wanted, nor youthful dalliance, as beseems
Fair couple link'd in happy nuptial league
Alone as they. About them frisking play'd 340
All beasts of th'earth, since wild and of all chase
In wood or wilderness, forest or den.
Sporting the lion ramp'd, and in his paw
Dandl'd the kid; bears, tigers, ounces, pards
Gamboll'd before them; th' unwieldly elephant
To make them mirth us'd all his might, and wreath'd
His lithe proboscis; close the serpent sly
Insinuating wove with Gordian twine
His braided train, and of his fatal guile
Gave proof unheeded. Others on the grass 350
Couch'd, and now fill'd with pasture gazing sat
Or bedward ruminating; for the sun
Declin'd was hasting now with prone career
To th'Ocean isles, and in th'ascending scale
Of heaven the stars that usher evening rose,
When Satan still in gaze, as first he stood,
Scarce thus at length fail'd speech recover'd sad.
O hell![38] What do mine eyes with grief behold?
Into our room of bliss thus high advanc'd
Creatures of other mould, earth-born perhaps, 360
Not spirits, yet to heavenly spirits bright
Little inferior, whom my thoughts pursue
With wonder, and could love, so lively shines
In them divine resemblance and such grace
The hand that form'd them on their shape hath pour'd.

[38]Satan's disturbance on seeing Adam and Eve is an indication that there are traces of nobility in his corrupted nature. Momentarily he is struck by their goodness and beauty.

Ah gentle pair, ye little think how nigh
Your change approaches, when all these delights
Will vanish and deliver ye to woe,
More woe, the more your taste is now of joy;
Happy, but for so happy ill-secur'd 370
Long to continue, and this high seat your heaven
Ill-fenc'd for heaven to keep out such a foe
As now is enter'd; yet no purpos'd foe
To you, whom I could pity thus forlorn,
Though I unpiti'd. League with you I seek
And mutual amity so strait, so close
That I with you must dwell or you with me
Henceforth. My dwelling haply may not please
Like this fair Paradise your sense, yet such
Accept your maker's work; he gave it me, 380
Which I as freely give. Hell shall unfold
To entertain you two her widest gates
And send forth all her kings; there will be room,
Not like these narrow limits, to receive
Your numerous offspring. If no better place,
Thank him who puts me loth to this revenge
On you who wrong'd me not for him who wrong'd;
And should I at your harmless innocence
Melt, as I do, yet public reason just,
Honour, and empire with revenge enlarg'd 390
With conquering this new world compels me now
To do what else though damn'd I should abhor.
So spake the fiend, and with necessity,
The tyrant's plea, excus'd his devilish deeds.[39]
Then from his lofty stand on that high tree
Down he alights among the sportful herd
Of those four-footed kinds, himself now one,
Now other, as their shape serv'd best his end
Nearer to view his prey and unespi'd
To mark what of their state he more might learn 400
By word or action mark'd. About them round
A lion now he stalks with fiery glare,
Then as a tiger, who by chance hath spi'd
In some purlieu two gentle fawns at play,
Straight couches close, then rising changes oft
His couchant watch, as one who chose his ground
Whence rushing he might surest seize them both
Grip'd in each paw; when Adam first of men
To first of women Eve thus moving speech
Turn'd him all ear to hear new utterance flow. 410
Sole partner and sole part of all these joys,
Dearer thyself than all, needs must the power
That made us, and for us this ample world,

[39] "Necessity, the tyrant's plea," is a double reference. God ordains free will, so that one must choose to do evil; Satan says he believes that one is fated to do as he does. Also, by "tyrant" Milton is certainly referring to the British kingship, which he opposed.

Be infinitely good, and of his good
As liberal and free as infinite,
That rais'd us from the dust and plac'd us here
In all this happiness who at his hand
Have nothing merited nor can perform
Aught whereof he hath need, he who requires
From us no other service than to keep 420
This one, this easy charge, of all the trees
In Paradise that bear delicious fruit
So various, not to taste that only tree
Of knowledge, planted by the tree of life.
So near grows death to life, what e'er death is;
Some dreadful thing, no doubt, for well thou know'st
God hath pronounc'd it death to taste that tree,
The only sign of our obedience left
Among so many signs of power and rule
Conferr'd upon us and dominion given 430
Over all other creatures that possess
Earth, air and sea. Then let us not think hard
One easy prohibition, who enjoy
Free leave so large to all things else, and choice
Unlimited of manifold delights,
But let us ever praise him and extol
His bounty, following our delightful task
To prune these growing plants and tend these flowers,
Which were it toilsome, yet with thee were sweet.
To whom thus Eve repli'd. O thou for whom 440
And from whom I was form'd flesh of thy flesh
And without whom am to no end, my guide
And head, what thou hast said is just and right,
For we to him indeed all praises owe
And daily thanks, I chiefly who enjoy
So far the happier lot, enjoying thee
Pre-eminent by so much odds, while thou
Like consort to thyself canst nowhere find.
That day I oft remember, when from sleep
I first awak'd and found myself repos'd 450
Under a shade of flowers, much wondering where
And what I was, whence thither brought and how.
Not distant far from thence a murmuring sound
Of waters issu'd from a cave and spread
Into a liquid plain, then stood unmov'd
Pure as th'expanse of heaven; I thither went
With unexperienc'd thought, and laid me down
On the green bank to look into the clear
Smooth lake that to me seem'd another sky.
As I bent down to look, just opposite 460
A shape within the watery gleam appear'd
Bending to look on me; I started back,
It started back, but pleas'd I soon return'd,
Pleas'd it return'd as soon with answering looks
Of sympathy and love. There I had fix'd
Mine eyes till now and pin'd with vain desire,

Had not a voice thus warn'd me, What thou seest,
What there thou seest, fair creature, is thyself,
With thee it came and goes; but follow me
And I will bring thee where no shadow stays 470
Thy coming and thy soft embraces. He
Whose image thou art, him thou shalt enjoy
Inseparably thine, to him shalt bear
Multitudes like thyself, and thence be call'd
Mother of human race. What could I do
But follow straight, invisibly thus led?
Till I espi'd thee, fair indeed and tall,
Under a platan, yet methought less fair,
Less winning soft, less amiably mild
Than that smooth watery image. Back I turn'd, 480
Thou following cri'dst aloud, Return, fair Eve,
Whom fly'st thou? Whom thou fly'st, of him thou art,
His flesh, his bone. To give thee being I lent
Out of my side to thee nearest my heart
Substantial life, to have thee by my side
Henceforth an individual solace dear.
Part of my soul I seek thee, and thee claim
My other half. With that thy gentle hand
Seiz'd mine, I yielded, and from that time see
How beauty is excell'd by manly grace 490
And wisdom, which alone is truly fair.
So spake our general mother, and with eyes
Of conjugal attraction unreprov'd
And meek surrender half-embracing lean'd
On our first father; half her swelling breast
Naked met his under the flowing gold
Of her loose tresses hid. He in delight
Both of her beauty and submissive charms
Smil'd with superior love, as Jupiter
On Juno smiles when he impregns the clouds 500
That shed May flowers, and press'd her matron lip
With kisses pure. Aside the devil turn'd
For envy, yet with jealous leer malign
Ey'd them askance, and to himself thus plain'd.
Sight hateful, sight tormenting! Thus these two
Imparadis'd in one another's arms,
The happier Eden, shall enjoy their fill
Of bliss on bliss while I to hell am thrust,
Where neither joy nor love but fierce desire,
Among our other torments not the least, 510
Still unfulfill'd with pain of longing pines.
Yet let me not forget what I have gain'd
From their own mouths. All is not theirs, it seems.
One fatal tree there stands, of knowledge call'd,
Forbidden them to taste. Knowledge forbidden?[40]

[40]Satan, seizing on the existence of the Tree of Knowledge, uses false reasoning to support his effort to corrupt Adam and Eve.

Suspicious, reasonless. Why should their lord
Envy them that? Can it be sin to know?
Can it be death? And do they only stand
By ignorance, is that their happy state,
The proof of their obedience and their faith? 520
O fair foundation laid whereon to build
Their ruin! Hence I will excite their minds
With more desire to know, and to reject
Envious commands, invented with design
To keep them low whom knowledge might exalt
Equal with gods. Aspiring to be such,
They taste and die; what likelier can ensue?
But first with narrow search I must walk round
This garden, and no corner leave unspi'd;
A chance, but chance may lead where I may meet 530
Some wand'ring spirit of heaven, by fountain side
Or in thick shade retir'd, from him to draw
What further would be learn'd. Live while ye may,
Yet happy pair; enjoy till I return
Short pleasures, for long woes are to succeed.
So saying, his proud step he scornful turn'd,
But with sly circumspection, and began
Through wood, through waste, o'er hill, o'er dale his roam....

Book 9

No more of talk where God or angel guest
With man, as with his friend, familiar us'd
To sit indulgent and with him partake
Rural repast, permitting him the while
Venial discourse unblam'd;[41] I now must change
These notes to tragic: foul distrust and breach
Disloyal on the part of man, revolt
And disobedience, on the part of heaven
Now alienated, distance and distaste,
Anger and just rebuke and judgement giv'n 10
That brought into this world a world of woe,
Sin and her shadow Death, and misery,
Death's harbinger;[42] sad task, yet argument
Not less but more heroic than the wrath
Of stern Achilles on his foe pursu'd
Thrice fugitive about Troy wall, or rage
Of Turnus for Lavinia disespous'd,
Or Neptune's ire or Juno's, that so long
Perplex'd the Greek and Cytherea's son,
If answerable style I can obtain 20
Of my celestial patroness, who deigns

---

[41]Here Milton refers to Books 5–8, in which Adam and the angel Raphael have held an extended discussion.

[42]This long clause describes the remainder of the action in the epic.

Her nightly visitation unimplor'd,
And dictates to me slumbering, or inspires
Easy my unpremeditated verse,
Since first this subject for heroic song
Pleas'd me, long choosing and beginning late;[43]
Not sedulous by nature to indite
Wars, hitherto the only argument
Heroic deem'd, chief mastery to dissect
With long and tedious havoc fabled knights 30
In battles feign'd, the better fortitude
Of patience and heroic martyrdom
Unsung, or to describe races and games,
Or tilting furniture, emblazon'd shields,
Impreses quaint, caparisons and steeds,
Bases and tinsel trappings, gorgeous knights
At joust and tournament; then marshall'd feast
Serv'd up in hall with sewers and seneschals;
The skill of artifice or office mean,
Not that which justly gives heroic name 40
To person or to poem.[44] Me of these
Not skill'd nor studious higher argument
Remains, sufficient of itself to raise
That name, unless an age too late, or cold
Climate, or years damp my intended wing
Depress'd; and much they may, if all be mine,
Not hers who brings it nightly to my ear.
   The sun was sunk, and after him the star
Of Hesperus whose office is to bring
Twilight upon the earth, short arbiter 50
Twixt day and night, and now from end to end
Night's hemisphere had veil'd th' horizon round,
When Satan, who late fled before the threats
Of Gabriel out of Eden, now improv'd
In meditated fraud and malice bent
On man's destruction, maugre what might hap
Of heavier on himself, fearless return'd.
By night he fled, and at midnight return'd
From compassing the earth, cautious of day
Since Uriel regent of the sun descri'd 60
His entrance and forewarn'd the cherubim
That kept their watch. Thence full of anguish driven
The space of seven continu'd nights he rode
With darkness; thrice the equinoctial line
He circled, four times cross'd the car of night
From pole to pole, traversing each colure,
On th'eighth return'd, and on the coast averse
From entrance or cherubic watch by stealth
Found unsuspected way. There was a place,

---

[43]In this passage, Milton tells why he chose the story of the Fall of Man as his epic theme, and suggests that his Muse, the Holy Spirit, dictates the poem to him in "answerable style," appropriate poetry.

[44]Milton separates himself from, and in part derides, past epics and romances. Particular reference is made to Homer's *Iliad* and Virgil's *Aeneid.*

Now not, though sin not time first wrought the change, 70
Where Tigris at the foot of Paradise
Into a gulf shot under ground, till part
Rose up a fountain by the tree of life;
In with the river sunk and with it rose
Satan involv'd in rising mist, then sought
Where to lie hid. Sea he had search'd and land
From Eden over Pontus and the pool
Maeotis, up beyond the river Ob,
Downward as far as antarctic, and in length
West from Orontes to the ocean barr'd 80
At Darien, thence to the land where flows
Ganges and Indus; thus the orb he roam'd
With narrow search, and with inspection deep
Consider'd every creature, which of all
Most opportune might serve his wiles, and found
The serpent, subtlest beast of all the field.
Him after long debate, irresolute
Of thoughts revolv'd, his final sentence chose
Fit vessel, fittest imp of fraud, in whom
To enter and his dark suggestions hide 90
From sharpest sight; for in the wily snake
Whatever sleights none would suspicious mark,
As from his wit and native subtlety
Proceeding, which in other beasts observ'd
Doubt might beget of diabolic power
Active within, beyond the sense of brute.[45]
Thus he resolv'd, but first from inward grief
His bursting passion into plaints thus pour'd.
O earth, how like to heaven, if not preferr'd
More justly, seat worthier of gods, as built 100
With second thoughts, reforming what was old!
For what god after better worse would build?
Terrestrial heaven, danc'd round by other heavens
That shine, yet bear their bright officious lamps,
Light above light, for thee alone, as seems,
In thee concentring all their precious beams
Of sacred influence. As God in heaven
Is centre yet extends to all, so thou
Centring receiv'st from all those orbs; in thee,
Not in themselves, all their known virtue appears 110
Productive in herb, plant and nobler birth
Of creatures animate with gradual life
Of growth, sense, reason, all summ'd up in man.
With what delight could I have walk'd thee round,
If I could joy in aught, sweet interchange
Of hill and valley, rivers, woods and plains,
Now land, now sea, and shores with forest crown'd,

---

[45]Because the serpent is noted for guile and treachery, Satan chooses to take his form in order to best avoid detection.

Rocks, dens and caves. But I in none of these
Find place or refuge, and the more I see
Pleasures about me, so much more I feel 120
Torment within me, as from the hateful siege
Of contraries; all good to me becomes
Bane, and in heaven much worse would be my state.[46]
But neither here seek I, no, nor in heaven
To dwell, unless by mast'ring heaven's supreme,
Nor hope to be myself less miserable
By what I seek, but others to make such
As I, though thereby worse to me redound;
For only in destroying I find ease
To my relentless thoughts, and him destroy'd 130
Or won to what may work his utter loss
For whom all this was made, all this will soon
Follow, as to him link'd in weal or woe.
In woe, then, that destruction wide may range;
To me shall be the glory sole among
Th'infernal powers, in one day to have marr'd
What he almighty styl'd six nights and days
Continu'd making, and who knows how long
Before had been contriving, though perhaps
Not longer than since I in one night freed 140
From servitude inglorious well-nigh half
Th'angelic name, and thinner left the throng
Of his adorers. He to be aveng'd
And to repair his numbers thus impair'd,
Whether such virtue spent of old now fail'd
More angels to create, if they at least
Are his created, or to spite us more,
Determin'd to advance into our room
A creature form'd of earth and him endow,
Exalted from so base original, 150
With heavenly spoils, our spoils. What he decreed
He effected; man he made, and for him built
Magnificent this world, and earth his seat,
Him lord pronounc'd and, O indignity!
Subjected to his service angel wings
And flaming ministers to watch and tend
Their earthly charge. Of these the vigilance
I dread, and to elude thus wrapp'd in mist
Of midnight vapour glide obscure, and pry
In every bush and brake where hap may find 160
The serpent sleeping, in whose mazy folds
To hide me and the dark intent I bring.
O foul descent! that I who erst contended
With gods to sit the highest am now constrain'd
Into a beast and mix'd with bestial slime,
This essence to incarnate and imbrute

[46]Satan is tortured by the appearance of Paradise because its goodness runs opposite to his very nature.

That to the height of deity aspir'd.[47]
But what will not ambition and revenge
Descend to? Who aspires must down as low
As high he soar'd, obnoxious first or last 170
To basest things. Revenge, at first though sweet,
Bitter ere long back on itself recoils.
Let it; I reck not, so it light well aim'd,
Since higher I fall short, on him who next
Provokes my envy, this new favourite
Of heaven, this man of clay, son of despite,
Whom us the more to spite his maker rais'd
From dust. Spite then with spite is best repaid.
So saying, through each thicket dank or dry
Like a black mist low creeping he held on 180
His midnight search, where soonest he might find
The serpent. Him fast sleeping soon he found
In labyrinth of many a round self-roll'd,
His head the midst, well stor'd with subtle wiles;
Not yet in horrid shade or dismal den,
Nor nocent yet, but on the grassy herb
Fearless unfear'd he slept. In at his mouth
The devil enter'd, and his brutal sense
In heart or head possessing soon inspir'd
With act intelligential, but his sleep 190
Disturb'd not, waiting close th' approach of morn.
Now whenas sacred light began to dawn
In Eden on the humid flowers that breath'd
Their morning incense, when all things that breathe
From th' earth's great altar send up silent praise
To the creator and his nostrils fill
With grateful smell, forth came the human pair
And join'd their vocal worship to the choir
Of creatures wanting voice; that done, partake
The season, prime for sweetest scents and airs; 200
Then commune how that day they best may ply
Their growing work, for much their work outgrew
The hands' dispatch of two, gardening so wide,
And Eve first to her husband thus began.
Adam, well may we labour still to dress
This garden, still to tend plant, herb and flower,
Our pleasant task enjoin'd, but till more hands
Aid us the work under our labour grows,
Luxurious by restraint; what we by day
Lop overgrown or prune or prop or bind 210
One night or two with wanton growth derides
Tending to wild. Thou therefore now advise
Or hear what to my mind first thoughts present.
Let us divide our labours, thou where choice

[47] Although he has chosen the form of the serpent, Satan recognizes his own debasement, which the use of this form signifies.

Leads thee, or where most needs, whether to wind
The woodbine round this arbour or direct
The clasping ivy where to climb, while I
In yonder spring of roses intermix'd
With myrtle find what to redress till noon;
For while so near each other thus all day 220
Our task we choose, what wonder if so near
Looks intervene and smiles, or object new
Casual discourse draw on, which intermits
Our day's work brought to little, though begun
Early, and th' hour of supper comes unearn'd.
To whom mild answer Adam thus return'd.
Sole Eve, associate sole, to me beyond
Compare above all living creatures dear,
Well hast thou motion'd, well thy thoughts employ'd
How we might best fulfil the work which here 230
God hath assign'd us, nor of me shalt pass
Unprais'd; for nothing lovelier can be found
In woman than to study household good
And good works in her husband to promote.
Yet not so strictly hath our lord impos'd
Labour as to debar us when we need
Refreshment, whether food or talk between,
Food of the mind, or this sweet intercourse
Of looks and smiles, for smiles from reason flow
To brute deni'd, and are of love the food, 240
Love not the lowest end of human life;
For not to irksome toil but to delight
He made us, and delight to reason join'd.
These paths and bowers doubt not but our joint hands
Will keep from wilderness with ease as wide
As we need walk, till younger hands ere long
Assist us. But if much converse perhaps
Thee satiate, to short absence I could yield;
For solitude sometimes is best society,
And short retirement urges sweet return. 250
But other doubt possesses me, lest harm
Befall thee sever'd from me, for thou know'st
What hath been warn'd us, what malicious foe
Envying our happiness and of his own
Despairing seeks to work us woe and shame
By sly assault, and somewhere nigh at hand
Watches no doubt with greedy hope to find
His wish and best advantage, us asunder,
Hopeless to circumvent us join'd, where each
To other speedy aid might lend at need; 260
Whether his first design be to withdraw
Our fealty from God or to disturb
Conjugal love, than which perhaps no bliss
Enjoy'd by us excites his envy more.
Or this or worse, leave not the faithful side
That gave thee being, still shades thee and protects.
The wife, where danger or dishonour lurks,

Safest and seemliest by her husband stays,
Who guards her, or with her the worst endures.
  To whom the virgin majesty of Eve, 270
As one who loves and some unkindness meets,
With sweet austere composure thus repli'd.
  Offspring of heaven and earth and all earth's lord,
That such an enemy we have, who seeks
Our ruin, both by thee inform'd I learn
And from the parting angel overheard
As in a shady nook I stood behind,
Just then return'd at shut of ev'ning flowers.
But that thou should'st my firmness therefore doubt
To God or thee because we have a foe 280
May tempt it, I expected not to hear.
His violence thou fear'st not, being such
As we, not capable of death or pain,
Can either not receive or can repel.
His fraud is then thy fear, which plain infers
Thy equal fear that my firm faith and love
Can by his fraud be shaken or seduc'd;
Thoughts which how found they harbour in thy breast,
Adam, misthought of her to thee so dear?
  To whom with healing words Adam repli'd. 290
Daughter of God and man, immortal Eve,
For such thou art, from sin and blame entire,
Not diffident of thee do I dissuade
Thy absence from my sight, but to avoid
Th' attempt itself intended by our foe.
For he who tempts, though in vain, at least asperses
The tempted with dishonour foul, suppos'd
Not incorruptible of faith, not proof
Against temptation. Thou thyself with scorn
And anger would'st resent the offer'd wrong, 300
Though ineffectual found. Misdeem not then
If such affront I labour to avert
From thee alone, which on us both at once
The enemy though bold will hardly dare,
Or daring, first on me th'assault shall light.
Nor thou his malice and false guile contemn;
Subtle he needs must be who could seduce
Angels. Nor think superfluous others' aid;
I from the influence of thy looks receive
Access in every virtue, in thy sight 310
More wise, more watchful, stronger, if need were
Of outward strength, while shame, thou looking on,
Shame to be overcome or overreach'd
Would utmost vigour raise, and rais'd unite.
Why should'st not thou like sense within thee feel
When I am present, and thy trial choose
With me, best witness of thy virtue tri'd?
  So spake domestic Adam in his care
And matrimonial love; but Eve, who thought

Less attributed to her faith sincere, 320
Thus her reply with accent sweet renew'd.
If this be our condition, thus to dwell
In narrow circuit straiten'd by a foe
Subtle or violent, we not endu'd
Single with like defence wherever met,
How are we happy, still in fear of harm?
But harm precedes not sin. Only our foe
Tempting affronts us with his foul esteem
Of our integrity; his foul esteem
Sticks no dishonour on our front, but turns 330
Foul on himself. Then wherefore shunn'd or fear'd
By us? who rather double honour gain
From his surmise prov'd false, find peace within,
Favour from heaven our witness from the event.
And what is faith, love, virtue, unassay'd
Alone, without exterior help sustain'd?[48]
Let us not then suspect our happy state
Left so imperfect by the maker wise
As not secure to single or combined.
Frail is our happiness if this be so, 340
And Eden were no Eden thus expos'd.
To whom thus Adam fervently repli'd.
O woman, best are all things as the will
Of God ordain'd them; his creating hand
Nothing imperfect or deficient left
Of all that he created, much less man
Or aught that might his happy state secure,
Secure from outward force; within himself
The danger lies, yet lies within his power,
Against his will he can receive no harm. 350
But God left free the will, for what obeys
Reason is free, and reason he made right,
But bid her well beware and still erect
Lest by some fair appearing good surpris'd
She dictate false, and misinform the will
To do what God expressly hath forbid.
Not then mistrust but tender love enjoins
That I should mind thee oft, and mind thou me.
Firm we subsist, yet possible to swerve,
Since reason not impossibly may meet 360
Some specious object by the foe suborn'd,
And fall into deception unaware,
Not keeping strictest watch as she was warn'd.
Seek not temptation then, which to avoid
Were better, and most likely if from me
Thou sever not; trial will come unsought.[49]

---

[48]Eve repeats a crucial argument for free will from Milton's *Areopagitica:* True virtue requires knowledge of good and evil. Milton says in that work: "I cannot praise a fugitive and cloistered virtue."

[49]Adam's advice to Eve is sensible: When in doubt, stay out of harm's way. Her curiosity overcomes his sense of restraint.

Would'st thou approve thy constancy, approve
First thy obedience; th' other who can know
Not seeing thee attempted, who attest?
But if thou think trial unsought may find 370
Us both securer than thus warn'd thou seem'st,
Go; for thy stay, not free, absents thee more.
Go in thy native innocence, rely
On what thou hast of virtue, summon all;
For God towards thee hath done his part; do thine.
So spake the patriarch of mankind, but Eve
Persisted, yet submiss though last repli'd.
With thy permission then and thus forewarn'd
Chiefly by what thy own last reasoning words
Touch'd only, that our trial when least sought 380
May find us both perhaps far less prepar'd,
The willinger I go, nor much expect
A foe so proud will first the weaker seek;
So bent, the more shall shame him his repulse.
Thus saying from her husband's hand her hand
Soft she withdrew, and like a wood-nymph light,
Oread or dryad, or of Delia's train,
Betook her to the groves; but Delia's self
In gait surpass'd and goddess-like deport,
Though not as she with bow and quiver arm'd 390
But with such gardening tools as art yet rude
Guiltless of fire had form'd, or angels brought.
To Pales or Pomona thus adorn'd
Likeliest she seem'd, Pomona when she fled
Vertumnus, or to Ceres in her prime,
Yet virgin of Proserpina from Jove.
Her long with ardent look his eye pursu'd
Delighted, but desiring more her stay.
Oft he to her his charge of quick return
Repeated, she to him as oft engag'd 400
To be return'd by noon amid the bower,
And all things in best order to invite
Noontide repast or afternoon's repose.
O much deceiv'd, much failing, hapless Eve,
Of thy presum'd return! Event perverse![50]
Thou never from that hour in Paradise
Found'st either sweet repast or sound repose,
Such ambush hid among sweet flowers and shades
Waited with hellish rancour imminent
To intercept thy way, or send thee back 410
Despoil'd of innocence, of faith, of bliss.
For now and since first break of dawn the fiend,
Mere serpent in appearance, forth was come
And on his quest where likeliest he might find
The only two of mankind, but in them

[50]In this short admonition, Milton the poet bemoans the outcome of Eve's departure alone into the Garden.

The whole included race, his purpos'd prey.
In bower and field he sought, where any tuft
Of grove or garden-plot more pleasant lay,
Their tendance or plantation for delight;
By fountain or by shady rivulet 420
He sought them both, but wish'd his hap might find
Eve separate; he wish'd, but not with hope
Of what so seldom chanc'd, when to his wish,
Beyond his hope, Eve separate he spies,
Veil'd in a cloud of fragrance where she stood,
Half-spi'd, so thick the roses bushing round
About her glow'd, oft stooping to support
Each flower of slender stalk whose head though gay
Carnation, purple, azure or speck'd with gold
Hung drooping unsustain'd; them she upstays 430
Gently with myrtle band, mindless the while
Her self, though fairest unsupported flower,
From her best prop so far, and storm so nigh.
Nearer he drew, and many a walk travers'd
Of stateliest covert, cedar, pine or palm,
Then voluble and bold, now hid, now seen
Among thick-woven arborets and flowers
Emborder'd on each bank, the hand of Eve;
Spot more delicious than those gardens feign'd
Or of reviv'd Adonis or renown'd 440
Alcinous, host of old Laertes' son,
Or that not mystic where the sapient king
Held dalliance with his fair Egyptian spouse.
Much he the place admir'd, the person more,
As one who long in populous city pent,
Where houses thick and sewers annoy the air,
Forth issuing on a summer's morn to breathe
Among the pleasant villages and farms
Adjoin'd, from each thing met conceives delight,
The smell of grain, or tedded grass, or kine, 450
Or dairy, each rural sight, each rural sound,
If chance with nymph-like step fair virgin pass,
What pleasing seem'd, for her now pleases more,
She most, and in her look sums all delight;
Such pleasure took the serpent to behold
This flowery plat, the sweet recess of Eve
Thus early, thus alone. Her heavenly form
Angelic, but more soft and feminine,
Her graceful innocence, her every air
Of gesture or least action overaw'd 460
His malice and with rapine sweet bereav'd
His fierceness of the fierce intent it brought.
That space the evil one abstracted stood
From his own evil, and for the time remain'd
Stupidly good, of enmity disarm'd,
Of guile, of hate, of envy, of revenge.
But the hot hell that always in him burns,
Though in mid-heaven, soon ended his delight,

And tortures him now more the more he sees
Of pleasure not for him ordain'd; then soon 470
Fierce hate he recollects, and all his thoughts
Of mischief gratulating thus excites.
Thoughts, whither have ye led me? With what sweet
Compulsion thus transported, to forget
What hither brought us, hate, not love, nor hope
Of Paradise for hell; hope here to taste
Of pleasure, but all pleasure to destroy,
Save what is in destroying, other joy
To me is lost.[51] Then let me not let pass
Occasion which now smiles. Behold alone 480
The woman, opportune to all attempts,
Her husband, for I view far round, not nigh,
Whose higher intellectual more I shun
And strength, of courage haughty and of limb
Heroic built, though of terrestrial mould,
Foe not informidable, exempt from wound,
I not; so much hath hell debas'd and pain
Enfeebled me to what I was in heaven;
She fair, divinely fair, fit love for gods,
Not terrible, though terror be in love 490
And beauty not approach'd by stronger hate,
Hate stronger under show of love well feign'd,
The way which to her ruin now I tend.
So spake the enemy of mankind, enclos'd
In serpent, inmate bad, and toward Eve
Address'd his way, not with indented wave
Prone on the ground, as since, but on his rear,
Circular base of rising folds that tower'd
Fold above fold a surging maze, his head
Crested aloft and carbuncle his eyes, 500
With burnish'd neck of verdant gold erect
Amidst his circling spires that on the grass
Floated redundant. Pleasing was his shape
And lovely, never since of serpent kind
Lovelier; not those that in Illyria chang'd
Hermione and Cadmus, or the god
In Epidaurus; nor to which transform'd
Ammonian Jove or Capitoline was seen,
He with Olympias, this with her who bore
Scipio, the height of Rome. With tract oblique 510
At first, as one who sought access but fear'd
To interrupt, sidelong he works his way;
As when a ship by skilful steersman wrought
Nigh river's mouth or foreland, where the wind
Veers oft, as oft so steers and shifts her sail,
So varied he, and of his tortuous train
Curl'd many a wanton wreath in sight of Eve

[51] Although struck by a vision of Eve's beauty and goodness, Satan reconfirms his intentions, aware that evil has deformed his personality and limited his capacities.

To lure her eye. She busi'd heard the sound
Of rustling leaves, but minded not, as us'd
To such disport before her through the field 520
From every beast, more duteous at her call
Than at Circean call the herd disguis'd.
He bolder now uncall'd before her stood,
But as in gaze admiring; oft he bow'd
His turret crest and sleek enamel neck,
Fawning, and lick'd the ground whereon she trod.
His gentle dumb expression turn'd at length
The eye of Eve to mark his play. He, glad
Of her attention gain'd, with serpent tongue
Organic or impulse of vocal air 530
His fraudulent temptation thus began.
  Wonder not, sovereign mistress, if perhaps
Thou canst who art sole wonder, much less arm
Thy looks, the heaven of mildness, with disdain,
Displeas'd that I approach thee thus and gaze
Insatiate, I thus single, nor have fear'd
Thy awful brow, more awful thus retir'd.
Fairest resemblance of thy maker fair,
Thee all things living gaze on, all things thine
By gift, and thy celestial beauty adore 540
With ravishment beheld, there best beheld
Where universally admir'd, but here
In this enclosure wild, these beasts among,
Beholders rude and shallow to discern
Half what in thee is fair, one man except,
Who sees thee? and what is one? who should'st be seen
A goddess among gods, ador'd and serv'd
By angels numberless thy daily train.
  So gloz'd the tempter, and his proem tun'd.[52]
Into the heart of Eve his words made way, 550
Though at the voice much marvelling; at length
Not unamaz'd she thus in answer spake.
  What may this mean? Language of man pronounc'd
By tongue of brute, and human sense express'd?
The first at least of these I thought deni'd
To beasts, whom God on their creation day
Created mute to all articulate sound;
The latter I demur, for in their looks
Much reason and in their actions oft appears.
Thee, serpent, subtlest beast of all the field 560
I knew, but not with human voice endu'd.
Redouble then this miracle, and say
How cam'st thou speakable of mute, and how
To me so friendly grown above the rest
Of brutal kind that daily are in sight?
Say, for such wonder claims attention due.

---

[52]"He smoothed over his real intent and refined his approach." Satan's temptation of Eve is fraudulent in the sense that he offers her nothing real, only her own destruction.

To whom the guileful tempter thus repli'd.
Empress of this fair world, resplendent Eve,
Easy to me it is to tell thee all
What thou command'st, and right thou should'st be obey'd. 570
I was at first as other beasts that graze
The trodden herb, of abject thoughts and low
As was my food, nor aught but food discern'd
Or sex, and apprehended nothing high,
Till on a day roving the field I chanc'd
A goodly tree far distant to behold
Loaden with fruit of fairest colours mix'd,
Ruddy and gold. I nearer drew to gaze,
When from the boughs a savoury odour blown
Grateful to appetite more pleas'd my sense 580
Than smell of sweetest fennel or the teats
Of ewe or goat dropping with milk at even,
Unsuck'd of lamb or kid that tend their play.
To satisfy the sharp desire I had
Of tasting those fair apples I resolv'd
Not to defer; hunger and thirst at once,
Powerful persuaders, quicken'd at the scent
Of that alluring fruit, urg'd me so keen.
About the mossy trunk I wound me soon,
For high from ground the branches would require 590
Thy utmost reach or Adam's; round the tree
All other beasts that saw with like desire
Longing and envying stood, but could not reach.
Amid the tree now got, where plenty hung
Tempting so nigh, to pluck and eat my fill
I spar'd not, for such pleasure till that hour
At feed or fountain never had I found.
Sated at length, ere long I might perceive
Strange alteration in me, to degree
Of reason in my inward powers, and speech 600
Wanted not long, though to this shape retain'd.
Thenceforth to speculations high or deep
I turn'd my thoughts and with capacious mind
Consider'd all things visible in heaven
Or earth or middle, all things fair and good;
But all that fair and good in thy divine
Semblance and in thy beauty's heavenly ray
United I beheld, no fair to thine
Equivalent or second, which compell'd
Me thus, though importune perhaps, to come 610
And gaze, and worship thee of right declar'd
Sovereign of creatures, universal dame.
So talk'd the spirited sly snake; and Eve
Yet more amaz'd unwary thus repli'd.
Serpent, thy overpraising leaves in doubt
The virtue of that fruit, in thee first prov'd.
But say, where grows the tree, from hence how far?
For many are the trees of God that grow
In Paradise and various, yet unknown

To us; in such abundance lies our choice 620
As leaves a greater store of fruit untouch'd,
Still hanging incorruptible till men
Grow up to their provision and more hands
Help to disburden nature of her birth.
To whom the wily adder, blithe and glad,
Empress, the way is ready and not long,
Beyond a row of myrtles, on a flat
Fast by a fountain, one small thicket past
Of blowing myrrh and balm. If thou accept
My conduct, I can bring thee thither soon. 630
Lead then, said Eve. He leading swiftly roll'd
In tangles and made intricate seem straight,
To mischief swift. Hope elevates and joy
Brightens his crest, as when a wandering fire,
Compact of unctuous vapour which the night
Condenses and the cold environs round,
Kindled through agitation to a flame
Which oft, they say, some evil spirit attends
Hovering and blazing with delusive light,
Misleads th'amaz'd night-wanderer from his way 640
To bogs and mires, and oft through pond or pool,
There swallow'd up and lost, from succour far.
So glister'd the dire snake, and into fraud
Led Eve our credulous mother to the tree
Of prohibition, root of all our woe;
Which when she saw, thus to her guide she spake.
Serpent, we might have spar'd our coming hither,
Fruitless to me, though fruit be here to excess,
The credit of whose virtue rest with thee,
Wondrous indeed if cause of such effects. 650
But of this tree we may not taste or touch;
God so commanded, and left that command
Sole daughter of his voice; the rest, we live
Law to our selves, our reason is our law.
To whom the tempter guilefully repli'd.
Indeed? Hath God then said that of the fruit
Of all these garden trees ye shall not eat,
Yet lords declar'd of all in earth or air?[53]
To whom thus Eve yet sinless, Of the fruit
Of each tree in the garden we may eat, 660
But of the fruit of this fair tree amidst
The garden God hath said, Ye shall not eat
Thereof, nor shall ye touch it, lest ye die.
She scarce had said, though brief, when now more bold
The tempter, but with show of zeal and love
To man and indignation at his wrong,
New part puts on, and as to passion mov'd

[53]This passage shows Satan in his best argumentative style. Emphasizing his envy of God and flattering Eve at the same time, he convinces her to taste the fruit. He begins with a logical assault on God, who gives humans free will but then tries to restrict their choices.

Fluctuates disturb'd, yet comely and in act
Rais'd, as of some great matter to begin,
As when of old some orator renown'd 670
In Athens or free Rome, where eloquence
Flourish'd, since mute, to some great cause address'd,
Stood in himself collected while each part,
Motion, each act won audience ere the tongue,
Sometimes in height began, as no delay
Of preface brooking through his zeal of right;
So standing, moving or to height upgrown
The tempter all impassion'd thus began.
 O sacred, wise and wisdom-giving plant,
Mother of science, now I feel thy power 680
Within me clear, not only to discern
Things in their causes but to trace the ways
Of highest agents, deem'd however wise.
Queen of this universe, do not believe
Those rigid threats of death: ye shall not die.
How should ye? By the fruit? It gives you life
To knowledge. By the threatener? Look on me,
Me who have touch'd and tasted, yet both live
And life more perfect have attain'd than fate
Meant me, by venturing higher than my lot. 690
Shall that be shut to man which to the beast
Is open? Or will God incense his ire
For such a petty trespass, and not praise
Rather your dauntless virtue whom the pain
Of death denounc'd, whatever thing death be,
Deterr'd not from achieving what might lead
To happier life, knowledge of good and evil;
Of good, how just? Of evil, if what is evil
Be real, why not known, since easier shunn'd?
God therefore cannot hurt ye and be just; 700
Not just, not God; not fear'd then, nor obey'd;
Your fear itself of death removes the fear.
Why then was this forbid? Why but to awe,
Why but to keep ye low and ignorant,
His worshippers? He knows that in the day
Ye eat thereof your eyes, that seem so clear
Yet are but dim, shall perfectly be then
Open'd and clear'd, and ye shall be as gods,
Knowing both good and evil as they know.
That ye should be as gods since I as man, 710
Internal man, is but proportion meet:
I of brute human, ye of human gods.
So ye shall die perhaps, by putting off
Human to put on gods; death to be wish'd,
Though threaten'd, which no worse than this can bring.
And what are gods that man may not become
As they, participating godlike food?
The gods are first, and that advantage use
On our belief that all from them proceeds.
I question it, for this fair earth I see, 720

Warm'd by the sun, producing every kind,
Them nothing; if they all things, who enclos'd
Knowledge of good and evil in this tree,
That whoso eats thereof forthwith attains
Wisdom without their leave? And wherein lies
Th'offence that man should thus attain to know?
What can your knowledge hurt him, or this tree
Impart against his will, if all be his?
Or is it envy, and can envy dwell
In heavenly breasts? These, these and many more 730
Causes import your need of this fair fruit.
Goddess humane, reach then and freely taste.
  He ended, and his words, replete with guile,
Into her heart too easy entrance won.
Fix'd on the fruit she gaz'd, which to behold
Might tempt alone, and in her ears the sound
Yet rung of his persuasive words impregn'd
With reason, to her seeming, and with truth.
Meanwhile the hour of noon drew on, and wak'd
An eager appetite, rais'd by the smell 740
So savoury of that fruit, which with desire
Inclinable now grown to touch or taste
Solicited her longing eye; yet first
Pausing a while thus to herself she mus'd.
  Great are thy virtues, doubtless, best of fruits,
Though kept from man, and worthy to be admir'd,
Whose taste too long forborne at first assay
Gave elocution to the mute and taught
The tongue not made for speech to speak thy praise.
Thy praise he also who forbids thy use 750
Conceals not from us, naming thee the tree
Of knowledge, knowledge both of good and evil;
Forbids us then to taste, but his forbidding
Commends thee more while it infers the good
By thee communicated, and our want;
For good unknown sure is not had, or had
And yet unknown is as not had at all.
In plain, then, what forbids he but to know,
Forbids us good, forbids us to be wise?
Such prohibitions bind not; but if death 760
Bind us with after-bands, what profits then
Our inward freedom? In the day we eat
Of this fair fruit, our doom is, we shall die.
How dies the serpent? He hath eaten, and lives,
And knows, and speaks, and reasons, and discerns,
Irrational till then. For us alone
Was death invented? Or to us deni'd
This intellectual food, for beasts reserv'd?
For beasts it seems; yet that one beast which first
Hath tasted envies not, but brings with joy 770
The good befall'n him, author unsuspect,
Friendly to man, far from deceit or guile.
What fear I then, rather what know to fear

Under this ignorance of good and evil,
Of God or death, of law or penalty?
Here grows the cure of all, this fruit divine,
Fair to the eye, inviting to the taste,
Of virtue to make wise. What hinders then
To reach and feed at once both body and mind?
  So saying, her rash hand in evil hour 780
Forth reaching to the fruit she pluck'd, she ate.
Earth felt the wound, and nature from her seat
Sighing through all her works gave signs of woe
That all was lost.[54] Back to the thicket slunk
The guilty serpent, and well might, for Eve,
Intent now wholly on her taste, naught else
Regarded; such delight till then, as seem'd,
In fruit she never tasted, whether true
Or fanci'd so through expectation high
Of knowledge, nor was godhead from her thought. 790
Greedily she engorg'd without restraint,
And knew not eating death. Satiate at length,
And heighten'd as with wine, jocund and boon,
Thus to herself she pleasingly began.
  O sovereign, virtuous, precious of all trees
In Paradise, of operation bless'd
To sapience hitherto obscur'd, infam'd,
And thy fair fruit let hang as to no end
Created; but henceforth my early care
Not without song each morning and due praise 800
Shall tend thee and the fertile burden ease
Of thy full branches offer'd free to all,
Till dieted by thee I grow mature
In knowledge as the gods, who all things know,
Though others envy what they cannot give,
For had the gift been theirs, it had not here
Thus grown. Experience, next to thee I owe,
Best guide; not following thee, I had remain'd
In ignorance; thou open'st wisdom's way
And giv'st access, though secret she retire. 810
And I perhaps am secret; heaven is high,
High and remote to see from thence distinct
Each thing on earth, and other care perhaps
May have diverted from continual watch
Our great forbidder, safe with all his spies
About him. But to Adam in what sort
Shall I appear?[55] Shall I to him make known
As yet my change and give him to partake
Full happiness with me, or rather not,
But keep the odds of knowledge in my power 820

[54]The Fall is the ruination not only of humanity, but of nature. Compare Matthew 27:51, where the earth trembles at the crucifixion of Christ.

[55]Eve has learned guile, so now she premeditates how she shall appear to Adam. Her reasoning is unbecoming and selfish, and her speech to Adam is full of blandishments and lies.

Without co-partner, so to add what wants
In female sex, the more to draw his love
And render me more equal, and perhaps,
A thing not undesirable, sometime
Superior? For inferior who is free?
This may be well; but what if God hath seen
And death ensue? Then I shall be no more,
And Adam wedded to another Eve
Shall live with her enjoying, I extinct,
A death to think. Confirm'd then I resolve, 830
Adam shall share with me in bliss or woe.
So dear I love him that with him all deaths
I could endure, without him live no life.
    So saying from the tree her step she turn'd,
But first low reverence done, as to the power
That dwelt within, whose presence had infus'd
Into the plant sciential sap deriv'd
From nectar, drink of gods. Adam the while
Waiting desirous her return had wove
Of choicest flowers a garland to adorn 840
Her tresses and her rural labours crown,
As reapers oft are wont their harvest queen.
Great joy he promis'd to his thoughts, and new
Solace in her return so long delay'd;
Yet oft his heart, divine of something ill,
Misgave him, he the falt'ring measure felt,
And forth to meet her went the way she took
That morn when first they parted. By the tree
Of knowledge he must pass; there he her met
Scarce from the tree returning, in her hand 850
A bough of fairest fruit that downy smil'd
New-gather'd and ambrosial smell diffus'd.
To him she hasted; in her face excuse
Came prologue and apology to prompt,
Which with bland words at will she thus address'd.
    Hast thou not wonder'd, Adam, at my stay?
Thee I have miss'd, and thought it long, depriv'd
Thy presence, agony of love till now
Not felt, nor shall be twice, for never more
Mean I to try what rash untri'd I sought, 860
The pain of absence from thy sight. But strange
Hath been the cause and wonderful to hear.
This tree is not as we were told, a tree
Of danger tasted, nor to evil unknown
Op'ning the way, but of divine effect
To open eyes and make them gods who taste,
And hath been tasted such: the serpent wise,
Or not restrain'd as we or nor obeying,
Hath eaten of the fruit, and is become
Not dead, as we are threaten'd, but thenceforth 870
Endu'd with human voice and human sense,
Reasoning to admiration, and with me
Persuasively hath so prevail'd that I

Have also tasted and have also found
Th' effects to correspond, opener mine eyes
Dim erst, dilated spirits, ampler heart,
And growing up to godhead, which for thee
Chiefly I sought, without thee can despise;
For bliss, as thou hast part, to me is bliss,
Tedious unshar'd with thee, and odious soon. 880
Thou therefore also taste, that equal lot
May join us, equal joy as equal love,
Lest thou not tasting, different degree
Disjoin us, and I then too late renounce
Deity for thee when fate will not permit.
  Thus Eve with count'nance blithe her story told,
But in her cheek distemper blushing glow'd.
On th'other side Adam, soon as he heard
The fatal trespass done by Eve, amaz'd,
Astoni'd stood and blank, while horror chill 890
Ran through his veins and all his joints relax'd.
From his slack hand the garland wreath'd for Eve
Down dropp'd and all the faded roses shed.
Speechless he stood and pale, till thus at length
First to himself he inward silence broke.
  O fairest of creation, last and best
Of all God's works, creature in whom excell'd
Whatever can to sight or thought be form'd
Holy, divine, good, amiable or sweet!
How art thou lost, how on a sudden lost, 900
Defac'd, deflower'd and now to death devote?
Rather how hast thou yielded to transgress
The strict forbiddance, how to violate
The sacred fruit forbidden? Some cursed fraud
Of enemy hath beguil'd thee, yet unknown,
And me with thee hath ruin'd, for with thee
Certain my resolution is to die;
How can I live without thee? How forgo
Thy sweet converse and love so dearly join'd
To live again in these wild woods forlorn? 910
Should God create another Eve, and I
Another rib afford, yet loss of thee
Would never from my heart; no, no, I feel
The link of nature draw me, flesh of flesh,
Bone of my bone thou art, and from thy state
Mine never shall be parted, bliss or woe.
  So having said, as one from sad dismay
Recomforted, and after thoughts disturb'd
Submitting to what seem'd remediless,
Thus in calm mood his words to Eve he turn'd. 920
  Bold deed thou hast presum'd, advent'rous Eve,
And peril great provok'd, who thus hast dar'd
Had it been only coveting to eye
That sacred fruit, sacred to abstinence,
Much more to taste it under ban to touch.

But past who can recall or done undo?[56]
Not God omnipotent, nor fate; yet so
Perhaps thou shalt not die, perhaps the fact
Is not so heinous now, foretasted fruit,
Profan'd first by the serpent, by him first 930
Made common and unhallow'd ere our taste,
Nor yet on him found deadly; he yet lives,
Lives, as thou saidst, and gains to live as man
Higher degree of life, inducement strong
To us as likely tasting to attain
Proportional ascent, which cannot be
But to be gods, or angels, demi-gods.
Nor can I think that God, creator wise,
Though threat'ning, will in earnest so destroy
Us his prime creatures, dignifi'd so high, 940
Set over all his works, which in our fall
For us created needs with us must fail,
Dependent made; so God shall uncreate,
Be frustrate, do, undo and labour loose,
Not well conceiv'd of God, who though his power
Creation could repeat yet would be loth
Us to abolish, lest the adversary
Triumph and say, Fickle their state whom God
Most favours; who can please him long? Me first
He ruin'd, now mankind. Whom will he next? 950
Matter of scorn, not to be giv'n the foe.
However I with thee have fix'd my lot,
Certain to undergo like doom; if death
Consort with thee, death is to me as life,
So forcible within my heart I feel
The bond of nature draw me to my own,
My own in thee, for what thou art is mine.[57]
Our state cannot be sever'd, we are one,
One flesh; to lose thee were to lose myself.
So Adam; and thus Eve to him repli'd. 960
O glorious trial of exceeding love,
Illustrious evidence, example high,
Engaging me to emulate, but short
Of thy perfection how shall I attain,
Adam, from whose dear side I boast me sprung
And gladly of our union hear thee speak,
One heart, one soul in both, whereof good proof
This day affords, declaring thee resolv'd,
Rather than death or aught than death more dread
Shall separate us link'd in love so dear, 970

---

[56] While correctly perceiving Eve's fault, Adam acquiesces to it and joins her. Her sin is eating the fruit, his is following her.

[57] Adam's aquiescence to fate (and Eve) is his tragic flaw, comparable to that of various Greek heroes of epic and drama. *Nature* in this passage is a difficult word to define: It is more like *species* or *kind* than nature considered as a whole.

To undergo with me one guilt, one crime,
If any be of tasting this fair fruit
Whose virtue, for of good still good proceeds,
Direct or by occasion hath presented
This happy trial of thy love, which else
So eminently never had been known.
Were it I thought death menac'd would ensue
This my attempt, I would sustain alone
The worst and not persuade thee, rather die
Deserted than oblige thee with a fact 980
Pernicious to thy peace, chiefly assur'd
Remarkably so late of thy so true,
So faithful love unequall'd; but I feel
Far otherwise th' event, not death but life
Augmented, open'd eyes, new hopes, new joys,
Taste so divine that what of sweet before
Hath touch'd my sense flat seems to this and harsh.
On my experience, Adam, freely taste,
And fear of death deliver to the winds.
So saying she embrac'd him and for joy 990
Tenderly wept, much won that he his love
Had so ennobled as of choice to incur
Divine displeasure for her sake and death.
In recompense (for such compliance bad
Such recompense best merits) from the bough
She gave him of that fair enticing fruit
With liberal hand; he scrupl'd not to eat
Against his better knowledge, not deceiv'd
But fondly overcome with female charm.
Earth trembl'd from her entrails as again 1000
In pangs, and nature gave a second groan,
Sky lour'd and muttering thunder some sad drops
Wept at completing of the mortal sin
Original, while Adam took no thought,
Eating his fill, nor Eve to iterate
Her former trespass fear'd, the more to soothe
Him with her lov'd society, that now
As with new wine intoxicated both
They swim in mirth and fancy that they feel
Divinity within them breeding wings 1010
Wherewith to scorn the earth. But that false fruit
Far other operation first display'd,
Carnal desire inflaming; he on Eve
Began to cast lascivious eyes, she him
As wantonly repaid. In lust they burn,
Till Adam thus gan Eve to dalliance move.[58]
Eve, now I see thou art exact of taste
And elegant, of sapience no small part,

[58] It is only after Adam's fall that sex becomes a sin. Milton follows the Christian tradition that sex is designed for the propagation of the race, not personal enjoyment.

Since to each meaning savour we apply
And palate call judicious. I the praise 1020
Yield thee, so well this day thou hast purvey'd.
Much pleasure we have lost while we abstain'd
From this delightful fruit, nor known till now
True relish, tasting. If such pleasure be
In things to us forbidden, it might be wish'd
For this one tree had been forbidden ten.
But come, so well refresh'd now let us play,
As meet is after such delicious fare,
For never did thy beauty since the day
I saw thee first and wedded thee, adorn'd 1030
With all perfections, so inflame my sense
With ardour to enjoy thee, fairer now
Than ever, bounty of this virtuous tree.
So said he, and forbore not glance or toy
Of amorous intent, well understood
Of Eve, whose eye darted contagious fire.
Her hand he seiz'd and to a shady bank
Thick overhead with verdant roof embower'd
He led her nothing loth. Flowers were the couch,
Pansies and violets and asphodel 1040
And hyacinth, earth's freshest softest lap.
There they their fill of love and love's disport
Took largely, of their mutual guilt the seal,
The solace of their sin, till dewy sleep
Oppress'd them, weari'd with their amorous play.
Soon as the force of that fallacious fruit
That with exhilarating vapour bland
About their spirits had play'd and inmost powers
Made err was now exhal'd, and grosser sleep
Bred of unkindly fumes, with conscious dreams 1050
Encumber'd, now had left them, up they rose
As from unrest, and each the other viewing
Soon found their eyes how open'd, and their minds
How darken'd. Innocence, that as a veil
Had shadow'd them from knowing ill, was gone,
Just confidence and native righteousness
And honour from about them; naked left
To guilty shame he cover'd, but his robe
Uncover'd more. So rose the Danite strong,
Herculean Samson, from the harlot lap 1060
Of Philistean Dalilah, and wak'd
Shorn of his strength, they destitute and bare
Of all their virtue.[59] Silent and in face
Confounded long they sat, as strucken mute,
Till Adam, though not less than Eve abash'd,
At length gave utterance to these words constrain'd.

[59]No longer innocent, Adam and Eve feel shame over their bodies and clothe themselves. Milton compares Adam to Samson, shorn of his hair and consequently his power.

O Eve, in evil hour thou didst give ear
To that false worm, of whomsoever taught
To counterfeit man's voice, true in our fall,
False in our promis'd rising, since our eyes 1070
Open'd we find indeed, and find we know
Both good and evil, good lost and evil got,
Bad fruit of knowledge if this be to know
Which leaves us naked thus, of honour void,
Of innocence, of faith, of purity,
Our wonted ornaments now soil'd and stain'd,
And in our faces evident the signs
Of foul concupiscence, whence evil store,
Even shame, the last of evils; of the first
Be sure then. How shall I behold the face 1080
Henceforth of God or angel, erst with joy
And rapture so oft beheld? Those heavenly shapes
Will dazzle now this earthly with their blaze
Insufferably bright. O might I here
In solitude live savage, in some glade
Obscur'd, where highest woods impenetrable
To star or sunlight spread their umbrage broad
And brown as evening; cover me ye pines,
Ye cedars, with innumerable boughs
Hide me where I may never see them more. 1090
But let us now, as in bad plight, devise
What best may for the present serve to hide
The parts of each from other that seem most
To shame obnoxious and unseemliest seen,
Some tree whose broad smooth leaves together sew'd
And girded on our loins may cover round
Those middle parts, that this newcomer, shame,
There sit not and reproach us as unclean.
So counsell'd he, and both together went
Into the thickest wood; there soon they chose 1100
The fig-tree, not that kind for fruit renown'd,
But such as at this day to Indians known
In Malabar or Deccan spreads her arms
Branching so broad and long that in the ground
The bended twigs take root and daughters grow
About the mother tree, a pillar'd shade
High overarch'd, and echoing walks between;
There oft the Indian herdsman shunning heat
Shelters in cool, and tends his pasturing herds
At loopholes cut through thickest shade. Those leaves 1110
They gather'd, broad as Amazonian targe,
And with what skill they had together sew'd
To gird their waist, vain covering if to hide
Their guilt and dreaded shame; O how unlike
To that first naked glory. Such of late
Columbus found th' American so girt
With feather'd cincture, naked else and wild
Among the trees on isles and woody shores.

Thus fenc'd and, as they thought, their shame in part
Cover'd, but not at rest or ease of mind, 1120
They sat them down to weep, nor only tears
Rain'd at their eyes, but high winds worse within
Began to rise, high passions, anger, hate,
Mistrust, suspicion, discord, and shook sore
Their inward state of mind, calm region once
And full of peace, now toss'd and turbulent;
For understanding rul'd not and the will
Heard not her lore, both in subjection now
To sensual appetite who from beneath
Usurping over sovereign reason claim'd 1130
Superior sway. From thus distemper'd breast
Adam, estrang'd in look and alter'd style,
Speech intermitted thus to Eve renew'd.
Would thou hadst hearken'd to my words, and stay'd
With me as I besought thee, when that strange
Desire of wand'ring this unhappy morn
I know not whence possess'd thee; we had then
Remain'd still happy, not as now despoil'd
Of all our good, sham'd, naked, miserable.[60]
Let none henceforth seek needless cause to approve 1140
The faith they owe; when earnestly they seek
Such proof, conclude, they then begin to fall.
To whom soon mov'd with touch of blame thus Eve.
What words have pass'd thy lips, Adam severe?
Imput'st thou that to my default or will
Of wand'ring, as thou call'st it, which who knows
But might as ill have happen'd thou being by,
Or to thyself perhaps? Hadst thou been there,
Or here th'attempt, thou could'st not have discern'd
Fraud in the serpent, speaking as he spake. 1150
No ground of enmity between us known,
Why should he mean me ill or seek to harm?
Was I t' have never parted from thy side?
As good have grown there still a lifeless rib.
Being as I am, why didst not thou the head
Command me absolutely not to go,
Coming into such danger as thou said'st?
Too facile then thou didst not much gainsay,
Nay, didst permit, approve and fair dismiss.
Hadst thou been firm and fix'd in thy dissent, 1160
Neither had I transgress'd nor thou with me.
To whom then first incens'd Adam repli'd.
Is this thy love, is this the recompense
Of mine to thee, ingrateful Eve, express'd
Immutable when thou wert lost, not I,
Who might have liv'd and joy'd immortal bliss,

[60] Adam blames Eve for the Fall. In the next speech he will be "incens'd," and she will blame him as well. Milton is showing how after the Fall marriage will consist in part of "vain contest."

Yet willingly chose rather death with thee?
And am I now upbraided as the cause
Of thy transgressing? Not enough severe,
It seems, in thy restraint; what could I more? 1170
I warn'd thee, I admonish'd thee, foretold
The danger and the lurking enemy
That lay in wait; beyond this had been force,
And force upon free will hath here no place.
But confidence then bore thee on secure
Either to meet no danger or to find
Matter of glorious trial; and perhaps
I also err'd in overmuch admiring
What seem'd in thee so perfect that I thought
No evil durst attempt thee, but I rue 1180
That error now, which is become my crime,
And thou th' accuser. Thus it shall befall
Him who to worth in women overtrusting
Lets her will rule; restraint she will not brook,
And left to herself, if evil thence ensue,
She first his weak indulgence will accuse.
  Thus they in mutual accusation spent
The fruitless hours, but neither self-condemning,
And of their vain contest appear'd no end.

FROM
Book 12

  . . . He ended, and they both descend the hill.[61]
Descended, Adam to the bower where Eve
Lay sleeping ran before, but found her wak'd;
And thus with words not sad she him receiv'd.
  Whence thou return'st and whither went'st I know, 610
For God is also in sleep, and dreams advise,
Which he hath sent propitious, some great good
Presaging, since with sorrow and heart's distress
Weari'd I fell asleep. But now lead on;
In me is no delay. With thee to go
Is to stay here, without thee here to stay
Is to go hence unwilling; thou to me
Art all things under heaven, all places thou,
Who for my wilful crime art banish'd hence.
This further consolation yet secure 620
I carry hence: though all by me is lost,
Such favour I unworthy am vouchsaf'd,
By me the promis'd seed shall all restore.
  So spake our mother Eve, and Adam heard
Well pleas'd but answer'd not; for now too nigh

[61] In Book 11, God sends the angel Michael to Adam to reveal to him "future things" and announce the expulsion from Eden. In Book 12, Adam "descends the hill with Michael" and "wakens Eve, who all the while had slept"; Michael "in either hand leads them out of Paradise, the fiery sword waving behind them, and the cherubim taking their stations to guard the place."

Th' archangel stood, and from the other hill
To their fix'd station all in bright array
The cherubim descended, on the ground
Gliding meteorous, as evening mist
Ris'n from a river o'er the marish glides 630
And gathers ground fast at the labourer's heel
Homeward returning. High in front advanc'd
The brandish'd sword of God before them blaz'd
Fierce as a comet, which with torrid heat
And vapour as the Lybian air adust
Began to parch that temperate clime; whereat
In either hand the hast'ning angel caught
Our lingering parents and to th' eastern gate
Led them direct, and down the cliff as fast
To the subjected plain, then disappear'd. 640
They looking back all th' eastern side beheld
Of Paradise, so late their happy seat,
Wav'd over by that flaming sword, the gate
With dreadful faces throng'd and fiery arms.
Some natural tears they dropp'd, but wip'd them soon;
The world was all before them, where to choose
Their place of rest, and providence their guide.
They hand in hand with wand'ring steps and slow
Through Eden took their solitary way.

SOR JUANA INÉS DE LA CRUZ

[C. 1648–1695]

Latin American writers honor as their forerunner a seventeenth-century woman who became a poet despite her unpromising circumstances. Sor Juana Inés de la Cruz was born out of wedlock into a rural Mexican family. At twenty, she became a nun. Within her convent she wrote plays, poems, and comic verse, as well as theological and philosophical discourses on such unorthodox topics as the dignity and equality of women or the validity of the religious beliefs of Mexican Indian peoples. As an independent-minded, visionary, and witty woman whose work called attention to her and to her views, she was always in danger of being censured; indeed, she spent the last four of her forty-six years in a silence imposed by Roman Catholic authorities who found it necessary to repress her because she wrote about what biographer Octavio Paz has called "the unutterable." Her writings fell from notice after her death, but in the twentieth century, when writers in many Latin American countries have faced the ultimate censorship of death for voicing their ideas, she and her work have become talismanic.

LIFE

Ironically, Sor Juana's voluminous correspondence and many other documents that might have told more about this gentle radical were destroyed in the flames of the Mexican Revolution. Sor Juana herself claimed she was born in 1651, but evidence from church records suggests that the actual date was 1648. Possibly she wished to alter the date in order to mask her illegitimacy. Her mother, Isabel Ramírez, was a *criolla,* the Mexican-born daughter of an intellectual Andalusian father who held land on two haciendas southeast of Mexico City. Juana Inés Ramírez was born on the family estate in San Miguel de Nepentla, among the foothills of the great volcanic mountain Popocatapetl; until she was eight or nine, she lived mainly on her grandfather's lands in the nearby farming community of Panoayán. Juana Inés' father was Pedro Manuel de Asbaje, a Spanish captain who seems to have played little part in his daughter's life. Isabel Ramírez had two other children by Asbaje, and three more by a later lover whom she also did not marry. Although illegitimacy seems to have been an embarrassment for Juana Inés in her later life, her mother's decision not to marry either of the fathers of her children was not uncommon among women in her small-landholder class of seventeenth-century Mexican society, where religious orthodoxy was considered far more important than strict chastity. By remaining single, Doña Isabel made sure of inheriting for herself her father's lands and workforce and being able to administer the estates as she saw fit, a complex responsibility she undertook from her father's death in 1656 until her own in 1688, when the management passed into the hands of one of Sor Juana's sisters.

From her birth, Juana Inés Ramírez was beautiful, precocious, and passionate to learn. She tells us in the *Respuesta* (1691), her rebuttal to Church forces wishing to censure her, that as a little girl she refused to eat cheese even though it was one of her favorite foods because she had heard it dulled the wits. She attended for a while a small primary school in Nepentla and learned to read early, racing through the books in her grandfather's library at the hacienda. Her curiosity was scientific as well as literary; watching two little girls spinning tops one day, she became obsessed with the toys' motion, and "began . . . to meditate on the effortless *motus* of the spherical form, and how the impulse persisted even when free and independent of its cause." Upon hearing there was such a thing as a university at Mexico City, she begged her mother to dress her as a boy and send her there to study. Her mother did not take that request seriously, and yet when Juana Inés was somewhere between eight and ten, Isabel did send her daughter to live in Mexico City with María Ramírez, Isabel's sister, now the wife of a wealthy man with connections in the viceregal court. Perhaps Isabel decided to send Juana Inés away mainly for practical reasons, but it also may be that this independent woman appreciated her oldest daughter's gifts, and understood that the hard physical work on the hacienda would not suit the intensely intellectual Juana Inés.

Even in Mexico City, there was little provision for the education of girls, but Juana Inés managed to learn Latin in twenty lessons soon after her arrival there, and her beauty and brilliance attracted a good deal of notice in the capital. A new viceroy, Antonio Sebastián de Toledo, Marquis de Mancera, and his vicereine, Leonor Carreto, took power in 1664; they were interested in the arts and learning, and Leonor arranged for the sixteen-year-old prodigy from the countryside to become one of her maids-in-waiting. The Marquis, impressed by the depth of Juana Inés' knowledge, invited forty learned men in many different fields to pose her questions, and she is said to have met the challenge with ease.

Juana Inés lived at court until she was nineteen, renowned for her beauty, her wit, and her diplomacy. She wrote occasional verse marking birthdays, gifts, deaths, and anniversaries; lyrics to be sung to popular melodies; satires on court life; and poems following the conventions of courtly love. She remarks in poems that no man attracted her, though she was popular; in the *Respuesta,* she says she felt a "total antipathy" toward marriage. The center of her emotional life was her patroness the Vicereine Leonor Carreto, whom she addressed as "Laura" in Petrarchan poems of passionate devotion.

At nineteen, Juana Inés abruptly withdrew from the court and entered a Carmelite convent as a novice. She lived there for three months, then returned to the court for an interval, perhaps because of illness, or because she found the strictness of the Carmelite order unbearable. A year and a half later, in 1669, she entered the convent of San Jerónimo, whose rule was milder, and remained in that order as Sor Juana Inés de la Cruz for the rest of her life. There has been much romantic speculation about a tragic love affair with a man or a woman that might have driven a despairing Juana Inés to put aside the glittering world of the court and take the veil, but no evidence exists of such an episode. The convent was a common choice for women who did not feel drawn to marriage or who were not especially eligible; Juana Inés Ramírez, with an illegitimate birth, no dowry, a distaste for marriage, and a passion for intellectual pursuits, would seem to fit both categories although, as she remarks in the *Respuesta,* there were "superficial" aspects of joining a religious order—the discipline and the lack of freedom and privacy—that she realized from the first she would find "repugnant to my nature."

There is not a great deal of documentation about Sor Juana's twenty-six years of convent life. Although her friend Leonor Carreto died in 1674, Sor Juana kept up her contacts with the viceregal court through a series of viceroys and their consorts; she was especially close to the Vicereine María Luisa, whose husband, Tomás Antonio de la Cerda, ruled Mexico from 1680 to 1688. Sor Juana organized and presided at *tertulias,* or conversational salons, within the convent, which many people attended. Her writings, almost all published late in her life or posthumously, suggest a real ongoing connection with the vigorous multicultural ambience of Mexico City. They range from the long poem most consider her masterwork, *El Primero Sueño* (*The First Dream,* c. 1685), a surrealistic intellectual apologia describing the ascent of the soul toward God, to ribald parodies of Petrarchan sonnets; from philosophical treatises to *villancicos,* short verses in a peasant tradition depicting in Creole Spanish dialect Guinean slave women in the marketplace; from stately and complex allegorical dramas to *tocotins,* poems written in Nahuatl, set to a Mexican Indian dance form. Her mind and her ear were uncloistered, and the playfulness and intellectual energy of her work are remarkable.

It was almost inevitable that Sor Juana would arouse spite, envy, and fear in those less gifted and more closed-minded. Throughout her life in the convent, she was often shielded from retribution by powerful authority figures in the church and court who admired her. But Sor Juana eventually came up against a church hierarchy that would not be deterred; in 1691, in response to admonishments from a misogynist archbishop and his minions, she wrote her *Respuesta,* a controlled, closely reasoned response to the church's criticisms, arguing for the right of women to study, to teach, and to write. She claims that her passion for intellectual activity was divinely given, "the natural impulse that God placed in me; the Lord God knows why, and for what purpose." She recalls how, even when under orders from an abbess not to study, she could not stop her inquiring brain from observing, forming hypotheses, drawing conclusions, even as she went about the household chores designed to humble her: "And what shall I tell you . . . of the secrets of nature I have discovered while cooking?" Intelligence and the love of learning are natural gifts given to women as well as men, and should be nourished, not suppressed.

The *Respuesta* is a brilliant defense of women in general and of Sor Juana's own particular case. Nonetheless, after writing it, Sor Juana acceded to the Church's wishes. In her own blood she wrote renewals of her vows; she turned her library and her musical and scientific instruments over to the archbishop; she cut off all connection with the viceregal court and began to observe almost total silence. She died four years later on April 17, 1695, while nursing her sisters through an epidemic that ravaged the convent.

Work

The play *The Divine Narcissus* and the *loa,* or short theatrical prologue-piece that precedes it, probably date from sometime between 1686 and 1688. The play was first printed in Mexico in 1690, and the front matter of that edition mentions that Sor Juana's friend the Vicereine María Luisa arranged for the play to be staged before the Spanish court at Madrid soon after her return to Spain; the play seems never to have been performed in Mexico, possibly because by the time it was written, Sor Juana was coming more and more into disfavor with the Archbishop of Mexico, who was particularly opposed to theatrical productions associated with the Church. The complex pageantry of the allegorical main play reconciles classical and Christian myth as it depicts Christ, "The Divine Narcissus," and his relationship with sinful humanity. Looking into the sealed fountain fed by the lifegiving waters that flow from Eden, the Divine Narcissus falls in love not with himself, as in the Greek myth, but with Human Nature, which he sees reflected in his own countenance, and he binds himself to suffer for humankind. The play ends with his resurrection and a triumphant eucharistic hymn.

In the *loa* to the play, Sor Juana makes use of the idea put forth by many Christian humanists that pagan peoples were occasionally capable of experiencing partial, nonbiblical revelations of divine truth. It is one thing to point, as Petrarch and Erasmus do, to the pure moral vision of Cicero, or to suggest as Sor Juana does in *The Divine Narcissus* that a Greek myth may imperfectly mirror a Christian truth; it is quite another to maintain, as she does in this *loa,* that the Indians of the Americas have the beginnings of real spiritual discernment, human sacrifice and all. Sor Juana draws from an account of Torquemada, the early historian of Mexico, who described an Aztec rite called *teocualo,* "God is eaten." In this rite, once celebrated each December third, seeds and grain and the blood of sacrificed children were kneaded together and shaped into a great edible effigy of Huitzilopochtli, the principal protector-god of Mexico; the priests then shattered the figure with arrows and shared the pieces among the celebrants. Sor Juana takes note of the resemblance of the rite, however bloody, to the Christian sacrament of the Eucharist. The female figure of Christian Religion argues with the military-minded male Zeal, urging that the Indians can be won over gently, through persuasion, because they are already receptive to certain elements of Christianity. Indeed, when she patiently points out to the native couple, Occident and America, the similarities of their own religion to Christianity, they are joyously converted.

Sor Juana was a woman of her time, and the native peoples here are evoked, decidedly from the outside, only to be finally integrated into the European and Christian vision. But Sor Juana, who grew up in the countryside, who spoke Nahuatl with evident pleasure, and who seems to have had Indian servant women to whom she was close, gives the allegorical Indian couple more dignity, courage, and presence than any other European writer had yet or would for many years to come. The *loa* seems to take on the passion of personal history; America's eloquent and indignant rebuke of Zeal when he bursts in on their New-World Eden might voice some of Sor Juana's own anger toward the repressive Church authorities who were attempting, even as she wrote, to crush her spirit:

> Oh mad, blind, barbaric man
> disturbing our serenity,
> you bring confusing arguments
> to counter our tranquillity;
> you must immediately cease
> unless it is your wish to find
> all here assembled turned to ash
> with no trace even on the wind!

Suggested Readings

The best single book on Sor Juana is Octavio Paz's monumental critical biography, *Sor Juana, or, The Traps of Faith* (1988).

Loa for The Divine Narcissus

Translated by Margaret Peden

CAST OF CHARACTERS:

OCCIDENT
AMERICA
ZEAL
RELIGION
MUSICIANS
SOLDIERS

SCENE 1

Enter OCCIDENT, *a stately Indian wearing a crown, and* AMERICA *beside him, a noble Indian woman, in the* mantas *and* huipiles *worn when singing a* tocotín. *They sit in two chairs; several Indian men and women dance holding feathers and rattles in their hands, as is traditional during this celebration; as they dance,* MUSIC *sings:*

MUSIC:
Most noble Mexicans,
whose ancient origin
is found in the brilliant rays
cast like arrows by the Sun,
mark well the time of year,
this day is given to laud
and honor in our way
the highest of our gods.
Come clad in ornaments
of your station the sign, 10
and to your piety
let happiness be joined:
with festive pageantry
worship the all-powerful God of Seeds!

MUSIC:
The riches of our lands
in copious plenteousness
are owing to the one
who makes them bounteous.
So bring your fervent thanks,
and at the harvest time, 20
give unto Him his due,
the first fruit of the vine.
Let flow the purest blood,
give from your own veins,
to blend with many bloods
and thus His cult sustain.
With festive pageantry
worship the all-powerful God of Seeds!

[OCCIDENT *and* AMERICA *sit, as* MUSIC *ceases.*]

OCCIDENT:
So great in number are the Gods
that our religion sanctifies, 30
so many in this place alone
the many rites we solemnize,

that this our Royal City is
the scene of cruelest sacrifice:
two thousand gods are satisfied,
but human blood must be the price;
now see the entrails that still throb,
now see hearts that redly beat,
and though the gods are myriad,
our gods so many (I repeat), 40
the greatest God among them all
is our Great God, the God of Seeds!

AMERICA:
And rightly so, for He alone
has long sustained our monarchy,
for all the riches of the field
we owe to Him our fealty,
and as the greatest benefice,
in which all others are contained,
is that abundance of the land,
our life and breath by it maintained, 50
we name Him greatest of the Gods.
What matters all the glittering gold
in which America abounds,
what value precious ores untold,
if their excrescences befoul
and sterilize a fertile earth,
if no fruits ripen, no maize grows,
and no tender buds spring forth?
But the protection of this God
is broader than continuance, 60
with the provision of our food,
of our daily sustenance,
He makes a paste of His own flesh,
and we partake with veneration
(though first the paste is purified
of bodily contamination),
and so our Soul he purifies
of all its blemishes and stains.
And thus in homage to His cult,
may everyone with me proclaim: 70

ALL *and* MUSIC:
In festive pageantry,
worship the all-powerful God of Seeds!

SCENE 2

[*They exit, dancing, and then enter* CHRISTIAN RELIGION, *as a Spanish Lady, and* ZEAL, *as a Captain General, armed; behind them, Spanish* SOLDIERS.]

RELIGION:
How is it, then, as you are Zeal,
your Christian wrath can tolerate
that here with blind conformity

they bow before Idolatry,
and, superstitious, elevate
an Idol, with effrontery,
above our Christianity?

ZEAL:

Religion, do not be dismayed:
my compassion you upbraid,
my tolerance you disavow,
but see, I stand before you now
with arm upraised, unsheathed my blade,
which I address to your revenge.
And now, retire, your cares allayed,
as their transgressions I avenge.

[*Enter, dancing,* OCCIDENT *and* AMERICA, *and from the other side,* MUSIC, *with accompaniment*]

MUSIC:

And with festive pageantry,
worship the all-powerful God of Seeds!

ZEAL:

They are here. I will approach.

RELIGION:

And I as well, with all compassion,
for I would go with tones of peace
(before unleashing your aggression)
to urge them to accept my word,
and in the faith be sanctified.

ZEAL:

Then let us go, for even now
they practice their revolting rite.

MUSIC:

And with festive pageantry,
worship the great God of Seeds!

[ZEAL *and* RELIGION *approach*]

RELIGION:

Hear me, mighty Occident,
America, so beautiful,
your lives are led in misery
though your land is bountiful.
Abandon this unholy cult
which the Devil doth incite.
Open your eyes. Accept my word
and follow in the Path of Light,
fully persuaded by my love.

OCCIDENT:

These unknown persons, who are they
who now before my presence stand?
Oh gods, who ventures thus to stay
the festive moment's rightful course?

AMERICA:

What Nations these, which none has seen?
Do they come here to interfere,
my ancient power contravene?

OCCIDENT:
Oh, Lovely Beauty, who are you,
fair Pilgrim from another nation?
I ask you now, why have you come
to interrupt my celebration?
RELIGION:
Christian Religion is my name, 120
and I propose that all will bend
before the power of my word.
OCCIDENT:
A great endeavor you intend!
AMERICA:
A great madness you display!
OCCIDENT:
The inconceivable you scheme!
AMERICA:
She must be mad, ignore her now,
let them continue with our theme!
ALL *and* MUSIC:
With festive pageantry,
worship the all-powerful God of Seeds!
ZEAL:
How, barbaric Occident, 130
and you, oh blind Idolatry,
Can you presume to scorn my Wife,
beloved Christianity?
For brimming to the vessel's lip
we see your sinful degradation;
the Lord our God will not allow
That you continue in transgression,
and He sends me to punish you.
OCCIDENT:
And who are you, who terrorize
all those who gaze upon your face? 140
ZEAL:
I am Zeal. Whence your surprise?
For when Religion you would scorn
with practices of vile excess,
then Zeal must enter on the scene
to castigate your wickedness.
I am a Minister from God
Who, witnessing your tyranny,
the error of these many years
of lives lived in barbarity,
has reached the limits of His grace 150
and sends His punishment through me.
And thus these armed and mighty Hosts
whose gleaming blades of steel you see
are His ministers of wrath,
the instruments of Holy rage.
OCCIDENT:
What god, what error, what offense,
what punishment do you presage?

I do not understand your words,
nor does your argument persuade;
I know you not, who, brazenly, 160
would thus our rituals invade
and with such zeal that you prevent
that in just worship people say:

MUSIC:
With festive pageantry,
worship the great God of Seeds!

AMERICA:
Oh mad, blind, barbaric man,
disturbing our serenity,
you bring confusing arguments
to counter our tranquillity;
you must immediately cease, 170
unless it is your wish to find
all here assembled turned to ash
with no trace even on the wind!
And you, Husband, and your vassals,

[*to* OCCIDENT]

you must close your ears and eyes,
do not heed their fantasies,
do not listen to their lies;
proceed, continue with your rites!
Our rituals shall not be banned
by these Nations, still unknown, 180
so newly come unto our land.

MUSIC:
And with festive pageantry,
worship the great God of Seeds!

ZEAL:
As our first offering of peace
you have so haughtily disdained,
accept the second, that of war,
from war we will not be restrained!
War! War! To arms! To arms!

[*Sound of drums and trumpets*]

OCCIDENT:
What is this wrath the gods devise?
What are the weapons here displayed 190
that so confound my awestruck eyes?
Ho, my Soldiers, ho there, Guards!
Those arrows that you hold prepared
now send against the enemy!

AMERICA:
Why have the gods their lightning bared
to strike me down? What are these spheres
that fall like fiery leaden hail?
What are these Centaurs, man and horse,
that now my followers assail?

[*Off*]

To arms! To arms! We are at war! 200

[*Drums and trumpets*]

Long live Spain! Her King we hail!

[*The battle is struck:* INDIANS *enter and flee across the stage, pursued by the* SPANISH; OCCIDENT *and* AMERICA *begin to retreat before* RELIGION *and* ZEAL]

SCENE 3

RELIGION:
Surrender, haughty Occident!

OCCIDENT:
Your declarations I defy
and only to your power yield.

ZEAL:
Now bold America must die!

RELIGION:
Hold, Zeal, do not strike them dead,
keep America alive!

ZEAL:
What, you defend America
When she has your faith reviled?

RELIGION:
There is no doubt that her defeat 210
is owing to your bravery,
but now allowing her to live
is witness to my clemency;
it was your duty, with your force,
to conquer her; but now with reason
I, too, work to vanquish her,
but I shall win with soft persuasion.

ZEAL:
But their perversion you have seen,
how they abhor and scorn your Word;
they are blind, is it not better 220
that they die?

RELIGION:
Put up your sword.
Forebear, Zeal, do not attack,
it is my nature to forgive,
I do not want their immolation,
but conversion, let them live.

AMERICA:
If in petitioning for my life,
and in exhibiting compassion,
it is your hope that I will yield,
that you will thus divert my passion,
employing arguments of words 230
as once before you employed arms,
then you will find yourself deceived,
for though my person come to harm,
and though I weep for liberty,

my liberty of will, will grow,
and I shall still adore my Gods!

OCCIDENT:
I have told you, and all know,
that I have bowed before your might,
but this caution you must heed,
that there is no strength or might — 240
that ever can my will impede
from its just course, free of control;
though captive I may moan in pain,
your will can never conquer mine,
and in my heart I will proclaim:
I worship the great God of Seeds!

SCENE 4

RELIGION:
But wait, for what we offer here
is not might, but gentleness.
What God is this that you adore?

OCCIDENT:
The Great Lord of fruitfulness. — 250
He makes fertile all the fields,
all the heavens bow to Him,
it is He the rain obeys,
and finally, of all our sin
He cleanses us, then of His being
makes a feast to nurture us.
Tell me whether there can be,
in a God so bounteous,
any greater benefice
than I give in this summary? — 260

RELIGION [*Aside*]:
May God have mercy! What reflection
do I see, what counterfeit,
thus patterned in their evil lies,
to mock our holy sacred Truths?
Oh, wily Serpent, sly Reptile,
oh, venom from the Viper's tooth!
Oh, Hydra, seven-headed beast
whose seven mouths spew, lethally,
rivers of poison on our heads,
how far, and how maliciously, — 270
can you continue in this way
God's sacred Miracles to mime?
Now if God will grace my tongue,
this same deceit I shall refine
and use your arguments to win.

AMERICA:
What mischief do you fabricate?
Do you not see there is no God,

none other, who corroborates
in benefices all His works?

RELIGION:

Then I shall be like Paul, and speak 280
from holy doctrine; for when he
had come to preach among the Greeks,
he found in Athens the strict law
that he who sought to introduce
an unfamiliar god, would die,
but as he knew they had the use
of faithful worship in a place
devoted to THE UNKNOWN GOD,
he said: this God I give to you
is not unknown, but One you laud, 290
you ignorantly worship Him,
now Him declare I unto you.
And thus do I. . . . Hear, Occident,
Idolatry, attend me, too,
for if you listen to my words
you will find salvation there.

Those many wonders you recount,
the miracles to which you swear,
the shimmering light, the flashing gleam
you glimpsed through Superstition's veil, 300
the prodigies, the prophecies,
the portents we heard you detail,
attributing their consequence
to your mendacious deities,
are but the work of One True God,
His wisdom and His sovereignty.
For if the flowering meadows bloom
and gardens yield their rich supply,
if the fields are fertilized,
and if their fruits do multiply, 310
if the plants from seedlings grow,
and if the clouds their rain distill,
all must come from His right hand,
and never will the arm that tills,
nor the rains that feed the earth,
nor the warmth that wakes the seeds,
have the power to make plants live
if Providence has not decreed
that they have life: all nature's green,
her verdant soul, is His design. 320

AMERICA:

And if all this is as you say,
is He, tell me, so benign,
this God of yours, your Deity,
so kind that he will tolerate
that I touch Him with my hands,
like the Idol I create
from many seeds and from the blood

of innocents, blood that is shed
for this alone, this one intent?

RELIGION:

Although in Essence the Godhead
is both invisible and vast,
as that Essence is combined
And with our Being bound so fast,
thus He is like to Humankind,
and His benevolence allows
that undeserving though they be,
He may be touched by hands of Priests.

AMERICA:

In this much, then, we are agreed.
For of my God the same is true,
and none may touch our Deity
except for those who as His priests
to serve Him have authority;
not only may He not be touched,
but neither may they enter in
His Chapel who are not ordained.

ZEAL:

What reverence, whose origin
were better found in Our True God!

OCCIDENT:

Then tell me, though much more you swear:
is this God formed of elements
that are as exquisite, as rare,
as that of blood shed valiantly
and offered up as sacrifice,
as well as seeds, our sustenance?

RELIGION:

His Majesty, I say this twice
is infinite and without form,
but His divine Humanity,
found in the Sacrament of Mass,
with mercy, not with cruelty,
assuming the white innocence
which in the seeds of wheat resides,
becomes incarnate in these seeds,
in Flesh and Blood is deified;
here in this Chalice is His Blood,
the Blood He sacrificed for us,
which on the Altar of the Cross,
unsullied, pure, in righteousness,
was the Redemption of the World.

AMERICA:

I stand in awe of all you say,
and hearing, I want to believe;
but could this God that you portray
be so loving that as food
He would give Himself to me,
like the God that I adore?

RELIGION:
Yes, for in His Wisdom, He
came down with only this in view,
to lie on earth among mankind.
AMERICA:
So, may I not see this God,
that true persuasion I may find?
OCCIDENT:
And I as well, thus will it be
that my obsession be forgot? 380
RELIGION:
Oh, you will see, once you are washed
in the crystalline, holy font
of Baptism.
OCCIDENT:
Yes, this I know,
before aspiring to come near
the fruitful table, I must bathe;
that ancient rite is practiced here.
ZEAL:
That bathing for your rituals
will not cleanse you of your stains.
OCCIDENT:
What bathing will?
RELIGION:
The Sacrament,
which in pure waters like the rains 390
will cleanse you of your every sin.
AMERICA:
The magnitude of this you bring
as notices, as yet I cannot
comprehend, of everything
I would know more, and in detail,
for I am moved by powers divine,
inspired to know all you can tell.
OCCIDENT:
An even greater thirst is mine,
I would know of the Life and Death
of this great God found in the Bread. 400
RELIGION:
That we shall do. I shall give you
a metaphor, an idea clad
in rhetoric of many colors
and fully visible to view,
this shall I show you, now I know
that you are given to imbue
with meaning what is visible;
it is now clear you value less
what Faith conveys unto your ears,
thus it is better you assess 410
what you can see, and with your eyes
accept the lessons She conveys.

OCCIDENT:
Yes, it is so, for I would see,
and not rely on what you say.

Scene 5

RELIGION:
Let us begin.
ZEAL:
Religion, speak,
to represent the Mysteries,
what form do you plan to employ?
RELIGION:
An allegory it will be,
the better to instruct the two,
an *Auto* that will clearly show 420
America and Occident
all that they now beg to know.
ZEAL:
This Allegory as *Auto,*
what title for it do you plan?
RELIGION:
Divine Narcissus, for although
America, unhappy land,
adored an Idol symbolized
by signs of such complexity
that through that Idol Satan tried
to feign the highest Mystery, 430
that of the Sacred Eucharist,
there was, as well, intelligence
among the Gentiles of this land
of other marvelous events.
ZEAL:
And where will they enact your play?
RELIGION:
In Madrid, the Royal Town,
the Center of our Holy Faith,
the Jewel in the Royal Crown,
the Seat of Catholic Kings and Queens
through whom the Indies have been sent 440
the blessing of Evangel Light
that shines throughout the Occident.
ZEAL:
But does it not seem ill-advised
that what you write in Mexico
be represented in Madrid?
RELIGION:
Oh, tell me, did you never know
an object fashioned in one place
and subsequently used elsewhere?

As for the act of writing it,
you find no whim or fancy there, 450
but only due obedience
attempting the impossible.
Therefore this work, though it may be
inelegant, its lustre dull,
is owing to obedience,
and not born of effrontery.

ZEAL:
Religion, tell me, as the play
is your responsibility,
how do you counter the complaint
that in the Indies was begun 460
what you would carry to Madrid?

RELIGION:
The drama's purpose is but one,
to celebrate the Mystery,
as to the persons introduced,
they are but an abstraction,
symbolic figures who educe
the implication of the work,
and no part need be qualified
though it be taken to Madrid;
for men of reason realize 470
there is no distance that deters,
nor seas that interchange efface.

ZEAL:
Prostrate, at the Royal Feet
that regally Two Worlds embrace,
we seek permission to proceed,

RELIGION:
and of the Queen, our Sovereign,

AMERICA:
at whose feet the Indies kneel
to pledge obeisance once again,

ZEAL:
and of her Supreme Councillers,

RELIGION:
and Ladies, who illuminate 480
the Hemisphere;

AMERICA:
and the Erudite
whom I most humbly supplicate
to pardon the poor lack of wit
in wishing with these clumsy lines
to treat so great a Mystery.

OCCIDENT:
My agony is exquisite,
come, show me how in bread and wine
this God gives of Himself to me.

[AMERICA, OCCIDENT, *and* ZEAL *sing*]

Now are the Indies
all agreed,
there is but One
True God of Seeds!
  With tender tears
by joy distilled,
raise voices high
with gladness filled:

ALL:

Blessed the day
I came to know the great God of the Seeds! 490

[*All exit, dancing and singing*]

LYRIC SAMPLER

[LATE 15TH CENTURY–EARLY 18TH CENTURY]

The poetry of Europe in the sixteenth century brought together the influences of the earlier Renaissance. The writing of poetry was considered a manifestation of character and breeding, to be carefully cultivated. According to Castiglione in *The Courtier,* the gentleman at court (and sometimes the lady as well) was supposed to be able to compose poetry for both the enjoyment and the favor it might bring. The great model was Petrarch, whose sonnets were widely translated and imitated in all the vernacular languages of Europe. Also favored were simple dance songs, where the music carried most of the artist's message, and narrative or argumentive poems directly expressing the feelings of the speaker. Throughout the later Renaissance, these models became more complicated.

The poetry of the late sixteenth and early seventeenth centuries is quite varied, although some critics see it as a unity. Recently, the larger part of it has been designated baroque, using the term from art history. The term *baroque* emphasizes certain concerns supposedly found in the work: its extravagance of theme, language, and form; its concern with appearance and reality; and its reflection of current interests in religion and science. At its farther limit is the idea that the feelings, superior logic, and inspiration of the artist are the only true sources of knowledge. Baroque poetry can take either a secular or religious form or sometimes both, as the work of the English poet John Donne shows. Some of the most effective poetry of the period is the product of two religious mystics otherwise known to history for their piety, St. Teresa de Avila and San Juan de la Cruz.

Metaphysical poetry, usually appearing in the seventeenth century, is often seen as one strain of baroque, emphasizing the artist's use of wit to produce dramatic images of logical and emotional incongruity. Here the stress is on the inventiveness of the artist, whether the poem is in a secular or religious vein. The language of the new sciences is often used in this poetry; in religious works, we often see the juxtaposition of sacred and profane images. Generally speaking, metaphysical poems are either arguments for the beloved's favor or for evocations of mystical communion with God. The best known metaphysical poets were Anglo-Catholics in England, but there are also many European poems, including mystical poems by Catholic and Protestant writers alike, with metaphysical features.

The particular extravagance of baroque and metaphysical poetry rests partly on its use of metaphor and partly on its handling of certain themes such as sex, mystical communion, and death. Sometimes these themes are joined together, as in John Donne's image of rape as a metaphor of the religious vision in "Batter my heart, three-personed God." This forcing of language, called *conceit,* generally praised at the time, was later held to be excessive by writers oriented to the classical tradition.

If baroque poetry represented the main current in poetry of the late sixteenth and seventeenth centuries, some other work was more conservative formally. Sonnets by the English Puritan poet John Milton illustrate the continuity of the classical tradition toward the end of the seventeenth century. Other poetry not in the baroque tradition included the song-dance and narrative forms mentioned before, along with satiric diatribes against the state or against dominant mores of society. This poetry flourished anywhere it was not repressed by the Church or civil authorities.

English Poetry

A leading English Renaissance poet, Sir Thomas Wyatt (1503–1542), a diplomat in the court of Henry VIII, translated and imitated the great Italians, especially Petrarch. His reworking of Petrarch's Song 157, *Una candida cerva sopra l'erba* (*Whoso List to Hunt*), equals or excels the original. Wyatt refashions some elements of Petrarch's poem to conform to the rather dangerous life of the English court: In this version, the "hind" or deer was Anne Boleyn, the young lady of the court under the watchful eye of Henry VIII and therefore not to be approached by anyone ("*Noli me tangere,* for Caesar's I am"). Another Wyatt poem, *They Flee from Me,* is an English dance-song that shows at its best the author's somewhat cynical attitude combined with his graceful method of composition.

William Shakespeare (1564–1616) was the son of an alderman in Stratford-on-Avon who received a good secondary school education and soon moved to London. By 1592, he was jealously regarded by his fellow London playwrights: Robert Greene referred to him as "an upstart crow, beautified with our feathers." In 1597, already financially successful, he was able to buy a house in Stratford and call himself a gentleman. By 1598 he had written a dozen plays, mostly histories and comedies, with his greatest dramas to come in the next decade. Shakespeare privately circulated a collection of his sonnets for many years; he finally published them in 1609. The publisher's dedication to "the only begetter of these ensuing sonnets, Master W. H.," and some of their themes have given rise to a great deal of biographical speculation. There is also the difficulty of some of the poems themselves, since they are often highly mysterious in their references. One might want to read them as codes leading to richer understanding of some aspect of human existence that the poet feels the need to call to our attention, but many of the sonnets are actually very personal poetry written to note a particular occasion.

The artfully compressed Sonnet 73, "That time of year thou mayst in me behold," presents in each of its three quatrains of four-line stanzas a different image of decay, leading to the argument in the final two lines of the poem that the person being addressed should love the poet more in whatever time he has left. Sonnet 94, "They that have power to hurt and will do none," contrasts the powerful restraint of the person described in the first eight lines with the diseased beauty of the "flower" of the last six. Sonnet 129, "Th' expense of spirit in a waste of shame," focuses on the moment of passion, seeing fierce expectation beforehand and bitter woe as its consequence. The word "expense" may have multiple meanings, suggesting masturbation or sexual climax, but also revenge and physical violence. This dark sonnet is often thought to present a riddle of human existence. Sonnet 130, "My mistress' eyes are nothing like the sun," is a much lighter spoof of the Petrarchan sonnet, with its habit of praising the parts of a lady in a poetic catalogue, and is a call for honest feeling. Sonnet 144, "Two loves I have of comfort and despair," portrays conflicting emotions with a premonition that the darker side will win.

Thomas Nashe (1567–1601) was a university wit and London writer, irreverent and blasphemous, who seemed always involved in controversy. His slanderous pamphlets against another writer were banned by ecclesiastical authorities in 1599. His fictional narrative *The Unfortunate Traveler, or the Life of Jack Wilton* (1598) anticipated the picaresque novel of the next century. Like many of his drinking companions and fellow authors, Nashe died young. His narrative poem *A Litany in Time of Plague* captures in unaffected language the fear of early death that had been a constant theme of popular poetry since the Middle Ages.

John Donne (1572–1631) once remarked that he had lived two lives: first as the roguish Jack Donne, a seducer of women and universal cynic, and then as the dignified Doctor Donne, an Anglican priest who became Dean of St. Paul's Cathedral in London. Actually there was a little bit of both the rogue and the God-haunted man of the cloth in Donne all his life, coexisting with difficulty in the same body. Born a Catholic during the worst years of anti-Catholic prejudice in England, Donne would eventually renounce his faith in order to seek preferment. He attended Oxford and Cambridge as well as the law school at Lincoln's Inn, but never finished a degree. He spent his father's small inheritance, traveled abroad when he could, and joined several private expeditions of Sir Walter Raleigh and others from the nobility. After he finally won a court appointment in 1598, Donne compromised his chances of success by secretly marrying the niece of his benefactor. Briefly imprisoned as a result, he relied on his occasional writings for whatever patronage he could find. He even published anti-Catholic treatises in 1610 and 1611. Finally he entered the Anglican ministry, giving in to the combined pleading and threats of King James in 1615. He became a famous preacher and was made Dean of St. Paul's in 1621. Obsessed by death, he preached his own funeral sermon just before his death in 1631 and posed for a final portrait wrapped in a shroud.

Donne's poetry borrows from the Petrarchan and Shakespearean traditions but goes farther in developing a highly concentrated, multiple set of images in longer lyric poetry. The conceits of his early love poems are designed to shock and arouse the reader. Later he employs the same mixture of language—formal and colloquial, sacred and profane—in his religious poetry. At the same time, Donne compresses English syntax to the breaking point. Donne's great contemporary, Ben Jonson, faulted him for the roughness of his verse, but also called him "the first poet in the world in some things."

Donne's love poems are by and large poems of argument. In *The Good Morrow,* he compares the pleasure of the lovers in the small room they now share to the innocence of babyhood in the crib. He also contrasts the lovers with worldly explorers, saying that they find whole "hemispheres" in each others' eyes. In *The Sun Rising,* he addresses the sun coming in the bedroom window as "Busy old fool" and tells it to go away. He contrasts the journey of the sun as it warms the earth each day with the "world" the lovers share together in their room. In *The Canonization,* Donne chides those who criticize him and his lover in a series of high-strung, volatile arguments. He sees the pair as candles that burn themselves up and twin phoenixes that consume each other and rise from their own ashes. He says that the poems he has written to celebrate their love will become their epitaphs and then their "hymns," leading to their canonization as saints of love. This swelling imagery of self-praise is one of Donne's most famous single poetic achievements.

The bravado of these poems is matched by the more carnal appeal of *To His Mistress Going to Bed,* in which Donne fantasizes his lady undressing and presenting herself to him. He addresses her as "O my America! my new-found land," a line frequently used to suggest how close fantasies of sexual conquest were to the waking thoughts of the first European explorers of this continent. On the other hand, in *Holy Sonnet 14,* Donne progresses from the carnal to the holy with remarkably little alteration in imagery: God's assault on the soul is depicted as a form of rape. Finally, *Good Friday, 1613. Riding Westward,* a long, loosely composed meditation on travel, compares the physical to the spiritual world as the poet "turns" in his mind from West to East, to the image of Christ on the Cross, and hence to his own salvation.

Donne's genius is repeated with less strife in the carefully crafted verse of George Herbert (1593–1633), the brilliant but humble country priest who only served his parish three years before dying of consumption. *Redemption* is an ironic but devout account of searching for Christ in the mansions of the wealthy but finding him headed for Calvary, mocked and doomed. *The Collar* pictures the poet grumbling to himself as he plans to leave his responsibilities and Christian duties behind, only to be brought up short by a single admonitory word of the Lord: "Child!" In both of these poems, the center of the Christian message is the unfathomability and absoluteness of God's grace.

John Milton (1608–1674), the author of the elegy *Lycidas* in 1637, took up the cause of the Protestant revolution soon after. From 1640 to 1652, he devoted most of his energies to serving the parliamentary government. Due to increasing blindness, he was finally forced to retire from service and began writing poetry again. "When I consider how my light is spent" is an attempt to console himself for his inability to serve God as he had wished. "Methought I saw my late espousèd saint" depicts a dream in which the blind poet "sees" his second wife, who died in childbirth, return to him. Its measured, dignified tone stands within the classical tradition, far from the excesses of baroque poetry earlier in the century.

Andrew Marvell (1621–1678) lived most of his life in the shadows of the Civil War. A tutor to the daughter of a ranking member of the parliamentary forces, then secretary to John Milton and eventually an intercessor on the old poet's behalf after the Puritan defeat, Marvell wrote his own verses quietly and late in life, dying three years before their publication by his housekeeper in 1681. *To His Coy Mistress,* a love poem cast in the form of argument popularized by Donne, is now one of the most popular poetic works in the English language. *The Garden,* a poem of contemplation, celebrates retirement from a world of strife such as Marvell himself experienced.

French Poetry

Maurice Scève (1510–1564) was part of a poetic circle based in Lyons that sought to infuse French poetry with a new, personal spirit. A follower of Petrarch, he adopted the French form called the *dizain*—a ten-line, ten-syllable poem with an intricate rhyme scheme. His major work, a sequence of 450 *dizains* titled *Délie,* was probably inspired by his infatuation with real-life disciple Pernette du Guillet. The compression of thought and syntax in Scève's poetry is reminiscent of the metaphysical poetry of Donne. The poem "The day we passed together for a while" is characteristic of the *Délie* sequence in expressing the unrequited longing of the poet for his departed lover.

Perhaps the greatest poet of the French Renaissance was Pierre de Ronsard (1524–1585). As a young man in Paris, Ronsard became the leader of the literary circle known as the Pléiade. Though deaf, he published many volumes in different poetic forms derived from Greek and Latin. His *Epitaph on Rabelais* celebrates the life of the bawdy author of *Gargantua* and *Pantagruel,* citing some of the characters of those works and glorying in Rabelais' contribution to French letters. Too much a classicist to be called a baroque poet, Ronsard nonetheless contributed to the enrichment of the national literature by his rediscovery of its Greek and Latin tradition.

Louise Labé (1525–1566), also of the Lyons circle, was a celebrated intellectual, a prodigious beauty, an extraordinary horsewoman and archer, and a champion of free love. She is said to have dressed as a man and fought in military campaigns against Spain. Eventually she married a well-to-do ropemaker, earning herself the nickname *la belle cordière.* Most of her poems, published in 1555 but written earlier, celebrate unrequited love. Although she writes in the form of the Petrarchan sonnet, she presents the emotions directly and with very little artifice. Her Sonnet 18, "Kiss me again," is an unblinking celebration of love despite its consequences for the health of the spirit.

Marc-Antoine de St.-Amant (1594–1661) was an outspoken poet with an interest in common speech rhythms. His libertine behavior in Paris situated many of his poems outside the pale of popular society in the period. The poem included here, "Go in the Whorehouse," is reminiscent of Donne's *To His Mistress Going to Bed.*

Germany and the Low Countries

The Dutch poet Jacobus Revius (1586–1658) was a theologian and teacher at Leiden University, a Calvinist who remained out of the poetic mainstream. His homegrown vision is close to that of Herbert in its immediacy, quietness of voice, and association with the doctrine of grace. *He Bore Our Griefs* is an effective testament to the power of Christian doctrine.

Paul Fleming (1609–1640), a Lutheran, was a disciple of German scholar and poet Martin Opitz at Leipzig University. He went on to study medicine at Leiden before his early death from the plague. Though a follower of Petrarch, he wrote direct, personal love poetry before turning to religious verse full of paradoxes and passionate utterances. *To My Redeemer* bears resemblance to the work of Fleming's contemporary in England, John Donne.

Christian Hofmann von Hofmannswaldau (1617–1679) was, like Fleming, a follower of Martin Opitz. Although he tended to write in a rather overblown, bombastic style, his fusion of themes of love and religious piety was typical of the period. His use of the theme of *memento mori* (remember death) in *The Transience of Beauty* presents old material in a strikingly dramatic way.

Spanish Poetry

Saint Teresa de Avila (1515–1588) joined a Carmelite convent at the age of sixteen and rose to a high administrative position in the Catholic Church. An intense mystic, she was eventually asked by her superiors to write her autobiography and other works on her spiritual development. For the most part, her poetry describes the ecstasy of self-annihilation in a mystical union with God. "See, His blood He's shedding" presents an unorthodox vision of the Christ child expiating the sins of humanity. The time shift between the child and the adult Jesus is typical of Spanish baroque mystical poetry.

San Juan de la Cruz (1542–1591) also entered a Carmelite religious house while young and became a leader of the order. He too was encouraged to write and, following Saint Teresa's example, wrote both autobiographical prose and poetry describing his mystical visions. Influenced by the *Song of Songs,* he mixed images of religious and physical passion. *The Dark Night of the Soul* is his most famous work; it is nearly untranslatable.

Luis de Góngora (1561–1627) abandoned an academic career to become a professional poet. He obtained a sinecure in 1590 and was ordained as a priest in 1605, although he never took his religious offices very seriously. His poetry became more bold after he settled into a life of relative security. After 1609, he adopted the kind of experimentation later known as Góngorism—a deliberately difficult style featuring linguistic innovation and the elaborate use of metaphors. *Allegory of the Brevity of Things Human* presents a familiar theme with lyrical intensity and bright, memorable images.

Francisco de Quevedo (1580–1645) railed at the decadence of poets such as Góngora, blaming it in part for the destruction of the old culture. A pessimist with a stubborn streak, Quevedo was no friend of the declining Spanish court, and suffered various indignities as a result. His *Sonnet: Death Warnings* sounds a characteristic note of gloom.

The Mexican poet Sor Juana Inés de la Cruz (c. 1648–1695) was a brilliant child who served in the royal court. Entering a convent at the age of nineteen, she wrote poetry on the failure of a passionate relationship. As an intellectual she surpassed the wisest men of Mexico and devoted herself to learning throughout her life despite the occasional censure of the authorities. *The Rhetoric of Tears* and *To Her Portrait* reflect the concerns of her early love poems.

Italian Poetry

A sometimes neglected poet of the Renaissance is the great sculptor and painter Michelangelo Buonarroti (1475–1564). Writing nearly two hundred years after Petrarch and one hundred before Donne, he broke with tradition to create poetry not unlike his sculptures—difficult, convoluted, and passionate, revealing its message partly through tensions in its form. *On the Painting of the Sistine Chapel* describes the problems of the painter in the world. The poem beginning "You have a face that's sweeter than grape mash" satirizes the cataloguing of female beauty in the Petrarchan sonnet. *To Luigi del Riccio* is a tender eulogy of a young man composed to comfort his former lover. *Dante* provides a convincing portrait of the Florentine exile who was equally a Christian and a keen observer of men and women.

Slavic Poetry

The Czech poet Adam Michna of Otradovic (1600–1662) set many of his compositions to music. *Disdain for This Transitory World* restates the familiar theme of earthly decay with vivid images and a folk quality to the composition.

The work of Mikhail Vasilevich Lomonosov (1711–1765) may seem too late for this collection, but this first great Russian poet was truly a figure of the Renaissance, which arrived late on Russian soil. Sent abroad by Peter the Great, Lomonosov developed a poetic form suitable to the Russian language; in such works as *Evening Meditation on the Majesty of God on the Occasion of the Great Northern Lights,* he showed himself capable of exploring images and complex metaphors in a typically baroque fashion.

Suggested Readings

Frank J. Warnke in *European Metaphysical Poetry* (1961) discusses the English metaphysical tradition and includes translations from French, German, Dutch, Spanish, and Italian poetry to argue for similarities in the other European languages. Howard Martin Priest's *Renaissance and Baroque Lyrics* (1962) contains a good introduction and another generous selection of poems from Italian, French, and Spanish. Harold B. Segel's *The Baroque Poem* (1974) broadens the comparative approach by including English, American, Dutch, German, French, Italian, Spanish, Mexican, Portuguese, Polish, Modern Latin, Czech, Croatian, and Russian poetry. English metaphysical poetry is available in many collections; one is Helen Gardner's *The Metaphysical Poets* (1966). Some poems of this period still hard to find elsewhere may be located in Aliki and Willis Barnstone, eds., *Women Poets from Antiquity to Now* (1992).

THOMAS WYATT

[1503–1542]

Whoso List to Hunt[1]

Whoso list[2] to hunt, I know where is an hind,
But as for me, alas, I may no more;
The vain travail hath wearied me so sore,
I am of them that furthest come behind.
Yet may I by no means my wearied mind
Draw from the deer, but as she fleeth afore
Fainting I follow; I leave off therefore,
Since in a net I seek to hold the wind.
Who list her hunt, I put him out of doubt,
As well as I, may spend his time in vain. 10
And graven with diamonds in letters plain,
There is written her fair neck round about,
"*Noli me tangere*,[3] for Caesar's I am,
And wild for to hold, though I seem tame."

They Flee from Me

They flee from me, that sometime did me seek,
With naked foot stalking in my chamber.
I have seen them, gentle, tame, and meek,
That now are wild, and do not remember
That sometime they put themselves in danger
To take bread at my hand; and now they range,
Busily seeking with a continual change.

Thanked be Fortune it hath been otherwise,
Twenty times better; but once in special,
In thin array, after a pleasant guise, 10
When her loose gown from her shoulders did fall,
And she caught me in her arms long and small,[1]
And therewith all sweetly did me kiss
And softly said, "Dear heart, how like you this?"

WHOSO LIST TO HUNT

[1]Adapted from Petrarch, Rime 90.

[2]Wishes.

[3]"Touch me not." Caesar's hinds were said to be fitted with collars so inscribed, to keep them safe from poachers. Wyatt is thought to be referring to the young Anne Boleyn, whom Henry VIII had marked for his future bride.

THEY FLEE FROM ME

[1]Slender.

It was no dream, I lay broad waking.
But all is turned, through my gentleness,
Into a strange fashion of forsaking;
And I have leave to go, of her goodness,
And she also to use newfangleness.[2]
But since that I so kindely am served, 20
I fain would know what she hath deserved.

WILLIAM SHAKESPEARE

[1564–1616]

Sonnet 73: "That time of year thou mayst in me behold"

That time of year thou mayst in me behold
When yellow leaves, or none, or few, do hang
Upon those boughs which shake against the cold,
Bare ruined choirs, where late the sweet birds sang.
In me thou see'st the twilight of such day
As after sunset fadeth in the west;
Which by and by black night doth take away,
Death's second self, that seals up all in rest.
In me thou see'st the glowing of such fire,
That on the ashes of his youth doth lie, 10
As the deathbed whereon it must expire,
Consumed with that which it was nourished by.
This thou perceiv'st, which makes thy love more strong,
To love that well which thou must leave ere long.

Sonnet 94: "They that have power to hurt and will do none"

They that have power to hurt and will do none,
That do not do the thing they most do show,[1]
Who, moving others, are themselves as stone,
Unmovéd, cold, and to temptation slow;
They rightly do inherit heaven's graces
And husband nature's riches from expense;[2]
They are the lords and owners of their faces,
Others but stewards of their excellence.
The summer's flower is to the summer sweet,
Though to itself it only live and die, 10

---

[2]Fickleness; infidelity.

SONNET 94

[1]Appear to do.

[2]They make prudent use of natural gifts.

But if that flower with base infection meet,
The basest weed outbraves his dignity:
For sweetest things turn sourest by their deeds;
Lilies that fester smell far worse than weeds.

Sonnet 129: "Th' expense of spirit in a waste of shame"

Th' expense of spirit in a waste of shame
Is lust in action;[1] and till action, lust
Is perjured, murderous, bloody, full of blame,
Savage, extreme, rude, cruel, not to trust;
Enjoyed no sooner but despisèd straight:
Past reason hunted; and no sooner had,
Past reason hated, as a swallowed bait,
On purpose laid to make the taker mad:
Mad in pursuit, and in possession so;
Had, having, and in quest to have, extreme; 10
A bliss in proof,[2] and proved, a very woe;
Before, a joy proposed; behind, a dream.
All this the world well knows; yet none knows well
To shun the heaven that leads men to this hell.

Sonnet 130: "My mistress' eyes are nothing like the sun"[1]

My mistress' eyes are nothing like the sun;
Coral is far more red than her lips' red;
If snow be white, why then her breasts are dun;
If hairs be wires, black wires grow on her head.
I have seen roses damasked, red and white,
But no such roses see I in her cheeks;
And in some perfumes is there more delight
Than in the breath that from my mistress reeks.
I love to hear her speak, yet well I know
That music hath a far more pleasing sound; 10
I grant I never saw a goddess go;
My mistress, when she walks, treads on the ground.
And yet, by heaven, I think my love as rare
As any she belied with false compare.

SONNET 129

[1]The first one and one-half lines might be paraphrased, "Lust, when acted upon, wastes the spirit (life, soul, vital force) in a waste (a desert, as well as a squandering) of shame."

[2]Blissful at the moment it is experienced.

SONNET 130

[1]An anti-Petrarchan sonnet that mocks the conventional comparisons in praise of the beloved's beauty.

Sonnet 144: "Two loves I have of comfort and despair"

Two loves I have of comfort and despair,
Which like two spirits do suggest me still:[1]
The better angel is a man right fair,
The worser spirit a woman colour'd ill.[2]
To win me soon to hell, my female evil
Tempteth my better angel from my side,
And would corrupt my saint to be a devil,
Wooing his purity with her foul pride.
And whether that my angel be turn'd fiend
Suspect I may, yet not directly tell; 10
But being both from me,[3] both to each friend,[4]
I guess one angel in another's hell.
Yet this shall I ne'er know, but live in doubt,
Till my bad angel fire my good one out.[5]

THOMAS NASHE

[1567–1601]

A Litany in Time of Plague

Adieu, farewell, earth's bliss;
This world uncertain is;
Fond[1] are life's lustful joys;
Death proves them all but toys;
None from his darts can fly;
I am sick, I must die.
Lord, have mercy on us!

Rich men, trust not in wealth,
Gold cannot buy you health;
Physic himself must fade. 10
All things to end are made,
The plague full swift goes by;
I am sick, I must die.
Lord, have mercy on us!

SONNET 144

[1]Continually tempt me.

[2]Dark.

[3]Away from me.

[4]Each other; the two angels are friends when they are together in the speaker's absence.

[5]Drive away by means of fire.

A LITANY IN TIME OF PLAGUE

[1]Foolish.

Beauty is but a flower
Which wrinkles will devour;
Brightness falls from the air;
Queens have died young and fair;
Dust hath closed Helen's eye.
I am sick, I must die. 20
  Lord, have mercy on us.

Strength stoops unto the grave,
Worms feed on Hector brave;
Swords may not fight with fate,
Earth still holds ope her gate.
"Come, come!" the bells do cry.
I am sick, I must die.
  Lord, have mercy on us!

Wit with his wantonness
Tasteth death's bitterness; 30
Hell's executioner
Hath no ears for to hear
What vain art can reply.
I am sick, I must die.
  Lord, have mercy on us.

Haste, therefore, each degree,[2]
To welcome destiny;
Heaven is our heritage,
Earth but a player's stage;
Mount we unto the sky. 40
I am sick, I must die.
  Lord, have mercy on us.

JOHN DONNE

[1572–1631]

The Good Morrow

I wonder, by my troth, what thou and I
Did till we loved? were we not weaned till then,
But sucked on country pleasures, childishly?
Or snorted we in the Seven Sleepers' den?[1]

---

[2]People in every social class.

THE GOOD MORROW

[1]Early Christian folklore tells of seven young Christian men of Ephesus who hid in a cave from the persecutions of the emperor Decius; after a miraculous sleep of 187 years, they awoke to find Europe had become Christianized.

'Twas so; but this, all pleasures fancies be.
If ever any beauty I did see
Which I desired, and got, 'twas but a dream of thee.

And now good morrow to our waking souls,
Which watch not one another out of fear;
For love all love of other sights controls, 10
And makes one little room an everywhere.
Let sea-discoverers to new worlds have gone;
Let maps to other, worlds on worlds have shown;
Let us possess one world; each hath one, and is one.

My face in thine eye, thine in mine appears,
And true, plain hearts do in the faces rest;
Where can we find two better hemispheres
Without sharp north, without declining west?
Whatever dies, was not mixed equally;[2]
If our two loves be one, or thou and I 20
Love so alike that none do slacken, none can die.

The Sun Rising

Busy old fool, unruly sun,
Why dost thou thus,
Through windows and through curtains call on us?
Must to thy motions lovers' seasons run?
Saucy pedantic wretch, go chide
Late school boys and sour prentices,
Go tell court huntsmen that the king will ride,[1]
Call country ants to harvest offices;
Love, all alike, no season knows nor clime,
Nor hours, days, months, which are the rags of time. 10

Thy beams, so reverend and strong
Why shouldst thou think?
I could eclipse and cloud them with a wink,
But that I would not lose her sight so long;
If her eyes have not blinded thine,
Look, and tomorrow late tell me,
Whether both th' Indias of spice and mine[2]
Be where thou leftst them, or lie here with me.
Ask for those kings whom thou saw'st yesterday,
And thou shalt hear, All here in one bed lay. 20

---

[2]Alchemy taught that matter in which the elements were not perfectly mixed was subject to change, decay, and death.

THE SUN RISING

[1]King James was notorious for rising early to hunt. The "country ants" are farm workers.

[2]The East Indies were fabled for their spices, the West Indies for their gold.

She's all states, and all princes, I,
Nothing else is.
Princes do but play us; compared to this,
All honor's mimic,[3] all wealth alchemy.
Thou, sun, art half as happy as we,
In that the world's contracted thus;
Thine age asks ease, and since thy duties be
To warm the world, that's done in warming us.
Shine here to us, and thou art everywhere;
This bed thy center is, these walls, thy sphere. 30

The Canonization

For God's sake hold your tongue, and let me love,
Or chide my palsy, or my gout,
My five gray hairs, or ruined fortune, flout,
With wealth your state, your mind with arts improve,
Take you a course, get you a place,
Observe His Honor, or His Grace,[1]
Or the King's real, or his stampéd face[2]
Contémplate; what you will, approve,[3]
So you will let me love.

Alas, alas, who's injured by my love? 10
What merchant's ships have my sighs drowned?
Who says my tears have overflowed his ground?
When did my colds a forward spring remove?[4]
When did the heats which my veins fill
Add one more to the plaguy bill?[5]
Soldiers find wars, and lawyers find out still
Litigious men, which quarrels move,
Though she and I do love.

Call us what you will, we're made such by love;
Call her one, me another fly, 20
We're tapers too, and at our own cost die,[6]

---

[3]A worthless sham.

THE CANONIZATION

[1]Settle on some career, get an appointed position, look to model yourself on a judge or an archbishop.

[2]The king's likeness stamped on coins.

[3]Put to the test.

[4]Donne is mocking Petrarchan lovers' claims that they burned with passion, froze when the beloved ignored them, and drowned in their own piteous tears. A "forward spring" could be either an early springtime or a gushing fountainhead.

[5]The list published weekly of plague victims.

[6]We are both like moths drawn to the candle's flame, and like the candles themselves, destroying ourselves with the heat we generate. In Donne's time "to die" was common slang for "to have an orgasm," and it was commonly believed that each orgasm somewhat shortened one's life expectancy.

And we in us find th' eagle and the dove.[7]
The phoenix[8] riddle hath more wit
By us: we two being one, are it.
So, to one neutral thing both sexes fit.
We die and rise the same, and prove
Mysterious by this love.

We can die by it, if not live by love,
And if unfit for tombs and hearse
Our legend be, it will be fit for verse; 30
And if no piece of chronicle we prove,
We'll build in sonnets pretty rooms;
As well a well-wrought urn becomes
The greatest ashes, as half-acre tombs;
And by these hymns, all shall approve
Us canonized for love:

And thus invoke us: You whom reverend love
Made one another's hermitage;
You, to whom love was peace, that now is rage;
Who did the whole world's soul contract, and drove 40
Into the glasses of your eyes
(So made such mirrors, and such spies,
That they did all to you epitomize)
Countries, towns, courts: Beg from above
A pattern of your love!

To His Mistress Going to Bed

Come, Madam, come, all rest my powers defy,
Until I labor, I in labor lie.[1]
The foe oft-times having the foe in sight,
Is tired with standing, though he never fight.
Off with that girdle, like heaven's zone[2] glittering,
But a far fairer world encompassing.
Unpin that spangled breastplate which you wear,
That th' eyes of busy fools may be stopped there.

---

[7]Eagle and dove are emblematic of power and pity, or of strength and gentleness.

[8]The phoenix was a legendary Arabian bird, only one of which ever existed at any one time. It did not reproduce in the usual way. Instead, it lived for 500 years, and then set fire to its own nest of fragrant spices, arising from its own ashes reborn. It was often used as an emblem of Christ. The lovers make the story of the mythical bird more credible because they combine both sexes in a single entity and rise from the heat of their lovemaking mystically renewed.

TO HIS MISTRESS GOING TO BED

[1]Until I can get to work at making love, I'm in pain.

[2]The zodiac.

Unlace yourself, for that harmonious chime,
Tells me from you that now it is bed time. 10
Off with that happy busk,[3] which I envy,
That still can be, and still can stand so nigh.
Your gown going off, such beauteous state reveals,
As when from flowery meads th'hills shadow steals.
Off with that wiry coronet and show
The hairy diadem which on you doth grow:
Now off with those shoes, and then safely tread
In this love's hallowed temple, this soft bed.
In such white robes, heaven's angels used to be
Received by men; Thou, Angel, bringst with thee 20
A heaven like Mahomet's Paradise;[4] and though
Ill spirits walk in white, we easily know,
By this these angels from an evil sprite,
Those set our hairs, but these our flesh upright.
  Licence my roving hands, and let them go,
Before, behind, between, above, below.
O my America! my new-found-land,
My kingdom, safeliest when with one man manned,
My mine of precious stones, my empery,
How blest am I in this discovering thee! 30
To enter in these bonds, is to be free;
Then where my hand is set, my seal shall be.[5]
  Full nakedness! All joys are due to thee,
As souls unbodied, bodies unclothed must be,
To taste whole joys. Gems which you women use
Are like Atlanta's balls,[6] cast in men's views,
That when a fool's eye lighteth on a gem,
His earthly soul may covet theirs, not them.
Like pictures, or like books' gay coverings made
For lay-men, are all women thus arrayed; 40
Themselves are mystic books, which only we
(Whom their imputed grace will dignify)
Must see revealed. Then since that I may know;[7]
As liberally as to a midwife, show
Thyself: cast all, yea, this white linen hence,
There is no penance due to innocence.
  To teach thee, I am naked first; why then
What needst thou have more covering than a man?

[3]Bodice or corset.

[4]The Islamic paradise contains beautiful female spirits who reward the faithful.

[5]The physical impression of him, and the sign of his ownership.

[6]The swift-footed Atlanta was reluctant to marry Hippomenes, but she agreed to do so if he could outrun her. Hippomenes scattered golden apples in her path and distracted her from their race.

[7]"Know" here means both to learn and to know sexually.

Holy Sonnet 14: "Batter my heart, three-personed God"

Batter my heart, three-personed God; for You
As yet but knock, breathe, shine, and seek to mend;
That I may rise, and stand, o'erthrow me, and bend
Your force, to break, blow, burn and make me new.
I, like an usurped town, to another due,
Labor to admit You, but O, to no end,
Reason Your viceroy in me, me should defend,
But is captived and proves weak or untrue,
Yet dearly I love You, and would be loved fain,
But am betrothed unto Your enemy, 10
Divorce me, untie, or break that knot again,
Take me to You, imprison me, for I,
Except You enthrall me, never shall be free,
Nor ever chaste, except You ravish me.

Good Friday, 1613. Riding Westward

Let man's soul be a sphere, and then, in this,
The intelligence that moves, devotion is,[1]
And as the other spheres, by being grown
Subject to foreign motions, lose their own,
And being by others hurried every day,
Scarce in a year their natural form[2] obey:
Pleasure or business, so, our souls admit
For their first mover, and are whirled by it.[3]
Hence is't, that I am carried towards the West
This day, when my soul's form bends toward the East. 10
There I should see a Sun, by rising set,
And by that setting endless day beget;
But that Christ on this cross, did rise and fall,
Sin had eternally benighted all.
Yet dare I'almost be glad, I do not see
That spectacle of too much weight for me.
Who sees God's face, that is self-life, must die;[4]
What a death were it then to see God die?
It made his own Lieutenant Nature shrink,
It made his footstool crack, and the sun wink. 20
Could I behold those hands which span the Poles,
And tune all spheres at once, pierced with those holes?

---

[1]Just as angelic spirits guide the motions of celestial bodies, so devotion to God guides people's lives.
[2]The principle that ought to guide their actions.
[3]The heavenly bodies can be deflected from their right courses by outside influences, and people can be similarly distracted by pleasure or business.
[4]The God of the Old Testament is not to be looked upon by mortals.

Could I behold that endless height which is
Zenith to us, and to our Antipodes,[5]
Humbled below us? or that blood which is
The seat of all our souls, if not of his,
Make dirt of dust, or that flesh which was worn
By God, for his apparel, ragged, and torn?
If on these things I durst not look, durst I
Upon his miserable mother cast mine eye, 30
Who was God's partner here, and furnish'd thus
Half of that sacrifice, which ransom'd us?
Though these things, as I ride, be from mine eye,
They're present yet unto my memory,
For that looks towards them; and Thou look'st towards me,
O Saviour, as Thou hang'st upon the tree;
I turn my back to Thee, but to receive
Corrections, till Thy mercies bid Thee leave.[6]
O think me worth Thine anger, punish me,
Burn off my rusts, and my deformity, 40
Restore Thine Image, so much, by Thy grace,
That Thou may'st know me, and I'll turn my face.

GEORGE HERBERT

[1593–1633]

Redemption[1]

Having been tenant long to a rich lord,
Not thriving, I resolved to be bold,
And make a suit unto him, to afford
A new small-rented lease, and cancel the old.[2]

In heaven at his manor I him sought;
They told me there that he was lately gone
About some land, which he had dearly bought
Long since on earth, to take possession.

I straight returned, and knowing his great birth,
Sought him accordingly in great resorts; 10
In cities, theaters, gardens, parks, and courts;

[5] The opposite side of the earth from where one is standing.

[6] Leave off, cease.

REDEMPTION

[1] The title word means literally "buying back," and Herbert accordingly uses real estate metaphors throughout.

[2] He will ask the landlord to issue a new lease at a lower rent, and to cancel his old lease.

At length I heard a ragged noise and mirth
Of thieves and murderers; there I him espied,
Who straight, *Your suit is granted*, said, and died.

The Collar[1]

I struck the board[2] and cried, "No more;
I will abroad!
What? shall I ever sigh and pine?
My lines and life are free, free as the road,
Loose as the wind, as large as store.
Shall I be still in suit?[3]
Have I no harvest but a thorn
To let me blood, and not restore
What I have lost with cordial[4] fruit?
Sure there was wine 10
Before my sighs did dry it; there was corn
Before my tears did drown it.
Is the year only lost to me?
Have I no bays to crown it,
No flowers, no garlands gay? All blasted?
All wasted?
Not so, my heart; but there is fruit,
And thou hast hands.
Recover all thy sigh-blown age
On double pleasures: leave thy cold dispute 20
Of what is fit and not. Forsake thy cage,
Thy rope of sands,
Which petty thoughts have made, and made to thee
Good cable, to enforce and draw,
And be thy law,
While thou didst wink and wouldst not see.
Away! take heed;
I will abroad.
Call in thy death's-head there; tie up thy fears.
He that forbears 30
To suit and serve his need,
Deserves his load."
But as I raved and grew more fierce and wild
At every word,
Methought I heard one calling, *Child!*
And I replied, *My Lord.*

[1]The title probably puns on "choler," or anger.
[2]Table.
[3]Waiting for someone to grant a favor.
[4]Heart-restoring.

JOHN MILTON

[1608–1674]

"When I consider how my light is spent"[1]

When I consider how my light is spent
Ere half my days, in this dark world and wide,
And that one talent[2] which is death to hide
Lodged with me useless, though my soul more bent
To serve therewith my Maker, and present
My true account, lest he returning chide;
"Doth God exact day-labor, light denied?"
I fondly[3] ask; but Patience to prevent
That murmur, soon replies, "God doth not need
Either man's work or his own gifts; who best 10
Bear his mild yoke, they serve him best. His state
Is kingly. Thousands at his bidding speed
And post o'er land and ocean without rest:
They also serve who only stand and wait."

"Methought I saw my late espouséd saint"

Methought I saw my late espouséd saint
Brought to me like Alcestis[1] from the grave,
Whom Jove's great son to her glad husband gave,
Rescued from Death by force, though pale and faint.
Mine, as whom washed from spot of child-bed taint
Purification in the Old Law did save,[2]
And such, as yet once more I trust to have
Full sight of her in heaven without restraint,
Came vested all in white, pure as her mind.
Her face was veiled; yet to my fancied sight 10
Love, sweetness, goodness, in her person shined
So clear as in no face with more delight.
But O, as to embrace me she inclined,
I waked, she fled, and day brought back my night.

WHEN I CONSIDER HOW MY LIGHT IS SPENT

[1]Milton had become blind shortly before writing this sonnet.

[2]Milton alludes to the parable of the talents—coins—told in Matthew 25; when servants are given their master's money to tend in his absence, some put it out to earn interest, and one merely keeps it safe and returns exactly the amount he was given. The servants who lent out the money are called good and faithful, while the hoarder who wasted his talents is cast out.

[3]Foolishly.

METHOUGHT I SAW MY LATE ESPOUSÉD SAINT

[1]Alcestis died and was rescued from Hades by Hercules.

[2]Leviticus 12 stipulates the period that a woman shall be deemed unclean after childbirth in Mosaic law. Milton's second wife died from complications of childbirth.

ANDREW MARVELL

[1621–1678]

To His Coy Mistress

Had we but world enough, and time,
This coyness, lady, were no crime.
We would sit down, and think which way
To walk, and pass our long love's day.
Thou by the Indian Ganges' side
Shouldst rubies find; I by the tide
Of Humber would complain. I would
Love you ten years before the flood,
And you should, if you please, refuse
Till the conversion of the Jews.[1] 10
My vegetable[2] love should grow
Vaster than empires and more slow;
An hundred years should go to praise
Thine eyes, and on thy forehead gaze;
Two hundred to adore each breast,
But thirty thousand to the rest;
An age at least to every part,
And the last age should show your heart.
For, lady, you deserve this state,
Nor would I love at lower rate. 20
But at my back I always hear
Time's wingéd chariot hurrying near;
And yonder all before us lie
Deserts of vast eternity.
Thy beauty shall no more be found;
Nor, in thy marble vault, shall sound
My echoing song; then worms shall try
That long-preserved virginity,
And your quaint honor turn to dust,
And into ashes all my lust: 30
The grave's a fine and private place,
But none, I think, do there embrace.
Now therefore, while the youthful hue
Sits on thy skin like morning glow,
And while thy willing soul transpires
At every pore with instant fires,
Now let us sport us while we may,
And now, like amorous birds of prey,
Rather at once our time devour
Than languish in his slow-chapped[3] power. 40

[1] The Jews, it was popularly believed, would be converted just before the Last Judgment.
[2] Slow-moving.
[3] Slow-jawed.

Let us roll all our strength and all
Our sweetness up into one ball,
And tear our pleasures with rough strife
Thorough the iron gates of life:
Thus, though we cannot make our sun
Stand still, yet we will make him run.

The Garden

How vainly men themselves amaze[1]
To win the palm, the oak, or bays,[2]
And their incessant labors see
Crowned from some single herb, or tree,
Whose short and narrow-vergéd shade
Does prudently their toils upbraid;
While all flowers and all trees do close[3]
To weave the garlands of repose!

Fair Quiet, have I found thee here,
And Innocence, thy sister dear? 10
Mistaken long, I sought you then
In busy companies of men.
Your sacred plants, if here below,
Only among the plants will grow;
Society is all but rude
To this delicious solitude.

No white nor red was ever seen
So amorous as this lovely green.[4]
Fond lovers, cruel as their flame,
Cut in these trees their mistress' name: 20
Little, alas, they know or heed
How far these beauties hers exceed!
Fair trees, wheresoe'er your barks I wound,
No name shall but your own be found.

When we have run our passion's heat,
Love hither makes his best retreat.
The gods, that mortal beauty chase,
Still in a tree did end their race:
Apollo hunted Daphne so,
Only that she might laurel grow; 30

[1]Confound.
[2]Emblems of victory in military, civic, and poetic contests.
[3]Come together or agree.
[4]Red and white signified the feminine complexion; the green garden is lovelier than any woman.

And Pan did after Syrinx speed,
Not as a nymph, but for a reed.[5]

What wondrous life is this I lead!
Ripe apples drop about my head;
The luscious clusters of the vine
Upon my mouth do crush their wine;
The nectarine and curious[6] peach
Into my hands themselves do reach;
Stumbling on melons, as I pass,
Insnared with flowers, I fall on grass. 40

Meanwhile the mind, from pleasure less,
Withdraws into its happiness;
The mind, that ocean where each kind
Does straight its own resemblance find;[7]
Yet it creates, transcending these,
Far other worlds and other seas,
Annihilating all that's made
To a green thought in a green shade.

Here at the fountain's sliding foot,
Or at some fruit tree's mossy root, 50
Casting the body's vest aside,
My soul into the boughs does glide:
There, like a bird, it sits and sings,
Then whets and combs its silver wings,
And, till prepared for longer flight,
Waves in its plumes the various light.

Such was that happy garden-state,
While man there walked without a mate:
After a place so pure and sweet,
What other help could yet be meet! 60
But 'twas beyond a mortal's share
To wander solitary there:
Two paradises 'twere in one
To live in paradise alone.

How well the skillful gardener drew
Of flowers and herbs this dial[8] new,
Where, from above, the milder sun
Does through a fragrant zodiac run;

[5]When Apollo pursued the nymph Daphne, she was changed into a laurel to preserve her chastity; the nymph Syrinx, fleeing Pan, similarly was transformed into reeds, which Pan fashioned into pan-pipes.

[6]Rare, choice.

[7]During the Renaissance, it was believed that the ocean contained the marine version of every creature found on land; Marvell says the ocean of the mind contains the images of all created things.

[8]Herbs and flowers planted so as to form a sundial.

And as it works, th' industrious bee
Computes its time as well as we! 70
How could such sweet and wholesome hours
Be reckoned but with herbs and flowers?

MAURICE SCÈVE

[1510–1564]

"The day we passed together for a while"

Translated from the French by Patricia Clark Smith

The day we passed together for a while
Seemed a bright fire on a winter's night,
And showed me how your absence is the dark,
A shadow more oppressive to my soul
Than life is to my frame, that weary weight
Of life, which even now seeks to depart.
For ever since that time you went away
I've been a rabbit burrowed in the wood;
I cock my ear, strain at each distant cry,
All lost within some deep Egyptian shade. 10

PIERRE DE RONSARD

[1524–1585]

Epitaph on Rabelais[1]

Translated from the French by R. N. Currey

If it's true that Nature can
Raise new life from a dead man,
And if generation
Springs out of corruption,
Then a vine should issue forth
From the stomach and huge girth
Of our Rabelais who contrived

[1]François Rabelais (c. 1490–1553) published his exuberant books about a family of robust and learned giants between 1532 and 1556. *Gargantua and Pantagruel* encompasses hilarious farce, telling satire, celebrations of the body and all its appetites, and philosophical debates on almost every subject that interested sixteenth-century French people. Gargantua, Panurge, the Papimanes, Friar John, and Episteme are all characters from these sagas.

To keep on drinking while he lived,
Who, with his mighty throat sucked down
Far more wine, all on his own, 10
Through nose and mouth, in a bulp or two
Than a porker drinking milk can do,
Than Iris from the rivers, or
From the waves of the African shore.

Nobody in morning sun
Ever saw him sober; none
From sunset until late at night
Saw him anything but tight;
Without pause our Rabelais
Kept on drinking night and day. 20
When the fiery dog-days brought
Round the season of the drought,
Half-dressed, with his sleeves rolled up,
He'd lie down flat beside his cup
Among the glasses on the rushes
Among the richly-loaded dishes,
Sprawling there quite shamelessly
Floundering as messily
As a frog does in the mud;
Then, when drunk, he'd sing aloud 30
The praises of his good friend Bacchus,
How he came to be victorious
Over the Thebans, how his mother
With such warmth received his father,
That, instead of making love,
He just burned her up alive![2]

Sing of Gargantua and his mare
And the huge staff he used to bear;
Splendid Panurge; and the domains
Of those gaping Papimanes, 40
Their houses, customs, and strange laws;
Of Friar John of Antoumeures;
And the battles of Episteme;
But Death, who never drinks, took him,
The drinker, to the world below,
Where no other waters flow
Than the turbid streams that run
Down into wide Acheron.
Whoever happen to pass this way
Empty here a glass, I pray; 50
Pour out flagons, scatter cheese,

[2]Bacchus (Dionysus), the god of wine and ecstasy, was conceived when Zeus, disguised as a lightning bolt, struck the Theban Princess Semele, impregnating her as he killed her. The fetus came to term in an incision in Zeus' thigh. Euripides' *The Bacchae* tells of how Bacchus returned to Thebes as a grown god to take revenge on members of his mother's family who denied his godhood.

Legs of ham and sausages;
For if any feeling now
Animates that soul below,
These to lilies would be preferred
However freshly they were gathered!

LOUISE LABÉ
[1525–1566]

Sonnet 18: "Kiss me again"

Translated from the French by Willis Barnstone

Kiss me again, rekiss me, kiss me more,
give me your most consuming, tasty one,
give me your sensual kiss, a savory one,
I'll give you back four burning at the core.
Are you up in arms? Well, I'll give you ten
erotic kisses for your appetite
and we will mingle kisses and excite
our bodies with an easy joy again.
Then we will live a double life, and each
of us will be alone and yet will blend 10
our love. Love, please allow a little madness:
I'm always hurt and live with temperate speech,
veiling these days in which I find no gladness
if I can't leave myself and find my friend.

Sonnet 19: "After having slain very many beasts"

Translated from the French by Willis Barnstone

After having slain very many beasts
Diana went into the thickest wood
and in the coolness, near her nymphs, she stood
a while as I was walking in a feast
of mindless reverie. Then suddenly:
"O worried nymph," I heard a voice call out,
"What are you doing here, wandering about
far from Diana?" And she looked at me
without my bow or quiver. Then she cried,
"Who took your bow and arrows?" But I sighed: 10
"I shot my arrows at a stranger, and
hurled the bow too, trying to reach his heart.
He gazed at me and took them in his hand,
shot a hundred times, tearing me apart."

MARC-ANTOINE DE SAINT-AMANT

[1594–1661]

Go in the Whorehouse

Translated from the French by Frank J. Warnke

Go in the whorehouse with a solemn pace
Like a cock preparing to display his spur;
Call Jenny, Margaret, or some other her,
Or the new city girl with the pretty face.

Explore each hole to the bottom of the cave,
Meet there Perrette and stew a haunch of pig,
And to the flute's sound dance the double jig,
Make on a turnip-bunch a banquet brave;

A rebus find in any picture's stead,
Or an almanac which its abuses spread 10
When Pantagruel destroyed the sausage-men;[1]
For furniture, a mattress old, then spot
A pile of spindles and a chamber-pot
—Behold the sports of Venus' veteran!

JACOBUS REVIUS

[1586–1658]

He Bore Our Griefs

Translated from the Dutch by Henrietta Ten Harmsel

No, it was not the Jews who crucified,
Nor who betrayed you in the judgment place,
Nor who, Lord Jesus, spat into your face,
Nor who with buffets struck you as you died.
No, it was not the soldiers fisted bold
Who lifted up the hammer and the nail,
Or raised the cursed cross on Calvary's hill,
Or, gambling, tossed the dice to win your robe.
I am the one, O Lord, who brought you there,
I am the heavy cross you had to bear, 10

[1]Pantagruel is Rabelais' giant, larger than life not only in size but also in his appetites and adventures. He is involved in a war between cooks and fierce sausages in Book IV of *Gargantua and Pantagruel*.

I am the rope that bound you to the tree,
The whip, the nail, the hammer, and the spear,
The blood-stained crown of thorns you had to wear:
It was my sin, alas, it was for me.

PAUL FLEMING
[1609–1640]

To My Redeemer

Translated from the German by Frank J. Warnke

Hear my cry, thou hearer of all cries,
Help, help of all the world, help also me;
I cannot help myself; only in thee
I comfort find and counsel. Worthy prize

Of all thy teachers, only faith-restorer
Empty of faith I am. O fill me here
With thee and with belief, with spirit's cheer;
Only thy spirit frees from doubt and error.

Sick for thee, Doctor, Fount of Israel,
Whose water slakes the thirsty tired soul, 10
Thy blood, Lamb of Easter, marks my door with red;[1]
Supporter of hearts, I rest myself on thee,
My fortress, rock. My life, live thou in me.
Thy death, death's death, hath struck my own death dead.

CHRISTIAN HOFMANN VON HOFMANNSWALDAU
[1617–1679]

The Transience of Beauty

Translated from the German by Frank J. Warnke

One day pale death shall come with icy hand
And stroke at last, my dearest one, your breasts,
The coral of your lips fade at his tests,
The warm snow of your shoulders turn cold sand.

[1]An allusion to the institution of the Passover, described in Exodus 12; God ordered the Jews enslaved in Egypt to mark their doors with the blood of ritually slaughtered lambs so that he would know to spare those houses from the slaughter of the first-born he visited upon the Egyptians.

Your eyes' sweet lightning and your fingers' force,
On which it falls, shall fall into decay;
Your hair which rivals gold with shining ray
The days and years shall quench without remorse.

Your shapely foot, your gracious movements sweet,
One fall to dust, the others turn to nought; 10
Then none shall worship more your Godhead's pride.
These beauties, yes, and more shall perish'd be,
Only your heart will last eternally:
Of diamond made, it ever must abide.

SAINT TERESA DE AVILA

[1515–1588]

"See, His blood He's shedding"[1]

Translated from the Spanish by E. Allison Peers

See, His blood He's shedding:
Dominguillo, why?
I have no reply.

Why is it, I ask you,
Why in justice' name?
For the child is guiltless,
Free from sin and shame.

Wherefore does He love me?
I have no reply.
Yet He yearns to save me: 10
Dominguillo, why?

Must His cruel torments
At His earth begin?
Yes, for He is dying
To remove our sin.
What a mighty Shepherd
Have we, by my fay!
Dominguillo, eh!

---

[1]The poem is in the form of a dialogue between two shepherds, the speaker and Dominguillo; Brasil and Llorent are two other shepherds. They are apparently witnessing a mystic and time-transcending vision of the infant Jesus shedding blood for their sake, seeing the crucifixion, perhaps, even as they worship at the manger.

You have not yet seen Him:
Such an innocent? 20
"No but I've been told by
Brasil and Llorent."
We must surely love Him
From this very day,
Dominguillo, eh?

SAN JUAN DE LA CRUZ

[1542–1591]

FROM

The Dark Night of the Soul[1]

Translated from the Spanish by Patricia Clark Smith

(Songs of the soul enraptured at attaining the highest state of perfection, its union with God, by the path of spiritual negation)

1

One dark night,
An anguished love aflame within my breast,
(Oh, delicious flight!)
I stole from sight
While all my house lay silently at rest.

Masked by night
Up a dark secret stair I swiftly fled
(Oh, delicious flight!)
Safe-hid from sight,
While all my house lay slumbering abed. 10

My whole being
Safe that happy night from others' eyes,
Myself unseeing,
With no guiding rays,
Save for the fire within my heart ablaze.

Brighter than noon,
How surely you, dear darkness, guided me

[1]There is a tradition that San Juan de la Cruz wrote this poem after escaping from prison. It uses the conventional Christian mystic imagery of a female soul yielding to a male divinity.

Toward that one
Whom I knew certainly,
Waiting there where no other one could be. 20

Dear night, my guide!
O night more wonderful than any morn!
Before dawn
You joined us, groom and bride,
Lover in loved one gloriously reborn.

Pillowed on flowers,
My breasts no one but he may ever share
He drowsed for hours;
While I held him near
Wind in the cedars fanned the balmy air. 30

Fresh off the tower
A gentle breeze toyed with his silky hair.
Then with calm power
My neck all bare
He wounded, and my senses fled me there.

Forgetful, amazed,
I lay my head upon my lover's breast.
Ambition gone, dazed,
Cares put to rest,
I wander here, amid the lilies lost. 40

LUIS DE GÓNGORA
[1561–1627]

Allegory of the Brevity of Things Human

Translated from the Spanish by Roy Campbell

Learn, flowers, from me, what parts we play
from dawn to dusk. Last noon the boast
and marvel of the fields, today
I am not even my own ghost.

The fresh aurora was my cot,
the night my coffin and my shroud;
I perished with no light, save what
the moon could lend me from a cloud.
And thus, all flowers must die—of whom
not one of you can cheat the doom. 10

Learn, flowers, from me, what parts we play
from dawn to dusk. Last noon the boast
and marvel of the fields, today
I am not even my own ghost.

What most consoles me from my fleetness
is the carnation fresh with dew,
since that which gave me one day's sweetness
to her conceded scarcely two:
Ephemerids in briefness vie
my scarlet and her crimson die. 20

Learn, flowers, from me, what parts we play
from dawn to dusk. Last noon the boast
and marvel of the fields, today
I am not even my own ghost.

The jasmine, fairest of the flowers,
is least in size as in longevity.
She forms a star, yet lives less hours
than it has rays. Her soul is brevity.
If amber could a flower be grown
it would be she, and she alone! 30

Learn, flowers, from me, what parts we play
from dawn to dusk. Last noon the boast
and marvel of the fields, today
I am not even my own ghost.

The gillyflower, though plain and coarse,
enjoys on earth a longer stay.
And sees more suns complete their course
—as many as there shine in May.
Yet better far a marvel die
than live a gillyflower, say I! 40

Learn, flowers, from me, what parts we play
from dawn to dusk. Last noon the boast
and marvel of the fields, today
I am not even my own ghost.

To no flower blooming in our sphere did
the daystar grant a longer pardon
than to the Sunflower, golden-bearded
Methusaleh of every garden.
Eying him through as many days
as he shoots petals forth like rays. 50

Yet learn from me, what parts we play
from dawn to dusk. Last noon the boast
and marvel of the fields, today
I am not even my own ghost.

FRANCISCO DE QUEVEDO

[1580–1645]

Sonnet: Death Warnings

Translated from the Spanish by John Masefield

I saw the ramparts of my native land,
One time so strong, now dropping in decay,
Their strength destroyed by this new age's way
That has worn out and rotted what was grand.
I went into the fields; there I could see
The sun drink up the waters newly thawed;
And on the hills the moaning cattle pawed,
Their miseries robbed the light of day for me.
I went into my house; I saw how spotted,
Decaying things made that old home their prize; 10
My withered walking-staff had come to bend.
I felt the age had won; my sword was rotted;
And there was nothing on which to set my eyes
That was not a reminder of the end.

SOR JUANA INÉS DE LA CRUZ

[C. 1648–1695]

The Rhetoric of Tears

Translated from the Spanish by Frank J. Warnke

Tonight, my dearest, when I spoke to thee,
I noted in thy bearing and thy face
That words of mine could not thy doubts erase,
Or prove I wanted thee my heart to see;

Then love, which my avowals came to prop,
Conquer'd, and the impossible occurr'd:
I fell to weeping tears which sorrow pour'd,
Which my melting heart distill'd in copious drop.

No more reproaches, ah my love, forbear;
Let doubt not hold thee in tormenting bonds, 10
Nor let vile jealousy thy peace impair
With foolish shades, with vain and useless wounds,
Since thou hast seen and touch'd a liquid rare—
My molten heart caught up between thy hands.

To Her Portrait

Translated from the Spanish by Patricia Clark Smith

This which you see, this colored counterfeit,
with all its fine technique and gaudy feint
and erring premises set forth in paint
is but a cunning trickery of sight.

Such flattery that smoothly would assuage
the horror multiplying year by year,
and triumph over time, and all we fear,
denying pain, oblivion, old age,

is just a hollow artifice, a thing,
a fragile flower open to high winds, 10
a useless shield against what fate must bring,

futile defense raised in a cause long-lost,
a senile zeal, or, at the very most,
a corpse, a meager shadow, nothing, dust.

MICHELANGELO BUONARROTI

[1475–1564]

On the Painting of the Sistine Chapel

Translated from the Italian by John Addington Symonds

I've grown a goitre by dwelling in this den—
as cats from stagnant streams in Lombardy,
or in what other land they hap to be—
which drives the belly close beneath the chin:
my beard turns up to heaven; my nape falls in,
fixed on my spine: my breast-bone visibly
grows like a harp: a rich embroidery
bedews my face from brush-drops thick and thin.
My loins into my paunch like levers grind:
my buttock like a crupper bears my weight; 10
my feet unguided wander to and fro;
in front my skin grows loose and long; behind,
by bending it becomes more taut and strait;
crosswise I strain me like a Syrian bow:
whence false and quaint, I know,
must be the fruit of squinting brain and eye;
for ill can aim the gun that bends awry.
Come then, Giovanni, try
to succour my dead pictures and my fame;
since foul I fare and painting is my shame. 20

"You have a face that's sweeter than grape mash"

Translated from the Italian by Harold M. Priest

You have a face that's sweeter than grape mash,
that shines as though 'twere tracked o'er by a snail,
more beauteous than a turnip; teeth that flash
as white, I swear, as is a parsnip pale;
you might entice the pope to conduct rash;
your eyes a treacle color, clear and hale;
your hairs more blond, or white, than any leek:
before I die, oh grant the boon I seek.

Your beauty strikes me as more beautiful
than a man's face depicted in a shrine; 10
to me your mouth is like a wallet full
of beans; that's much the same as mine;
your brows, like sooty fryingpan, are dull,
more bent than Syrian bow their arching line;
when sifting meal, your cheeks are white and red,
resembling poppies by fresh cheese or bread.

And when I gaze upon your breasts, the pair
resembles two nice melons in a sack,
whence I am kindled, quick as tow to flare,
even though I'm fagged or have been cudgeled black. 20
I think: if you still had that goblet fair,
I'd follow only you, like hound on track:
wherefore, if I could have a monstrous block,
a wonder I'd create from the bare rock.

To Luigi del Riccio

Translated from the Italian by John Addington Symonds

Scarce had I seen for the first time his eyes
which to your living eyes were life and light,
when closed at last in death's injurious night
he opened them on God in Paradise.

I know it and I weep, too late made wise:
Yet was the fault not mine; for death's fell spite
robbed my desire of that supreme delight,
which in your better memory never dies.

Therefore, Luigi, if the task be mine
to make unique Cecchino smile in stone 10
for ever, now that earth hath made him dim,

if the beloved within the lover shine,
since art without him cannot work alone,
you must I carve to tell the world of him.

Dante[1]

Translated from the Italian by Henry Wadsworth Longfellow

What should be said of him cannot be said;
by too great splendor is his name attended;
to blame is easier those who him offended,
than reach the faintest glory round him shed.
This man descended to the doomed and dead
for our instruction; then to God ascended;
Heaven opened wide to him its portals splendid,
who from his country's, closed against him, fled.
Ungrateful land! To its own prejudice
nurse of his fortunes; and this showeth well 10
that the most perfect most of grief shall see.
Among a thousand proofs let one suffice,
that as his exile hath no parallel,
Ne'er walked the earth a greater man than he.

ADAM MICHNA OF OTRADOVIC

[1600–1662]

Disdain for This Transitory World

Translated from the Czech by E. Osers

What avail is worldly glory?
Flesh like grass is transitory.
Smoke we are, by rough winds carried,
Here to stay, tomorrow buried.

What are royal throne and power,
Princely castle, knightly tower?
All must come to dust and ashes:
Death's last dance will end all passion.

What avail are youth and vigor,
Angel's face on fairest figure? 10
E'en the rose must wilt and wither
Grave rots bone and skin together.

Be your eyes of crystal lightness,
Be your lips of coral brightness,

[1]Both Dante and Michelangelo were Florentines, and both knew ill-treatment from the citizens of that state.

Be your hair like red gold burning:
Soon to clay it will be turning.

Rustling silk or golden treasure,
All which to the eye gives pleasure:
  Gold is sand, like sand you spend it;
  Vain the price that humans lend it. 20

What are crimson robe and ermine?
Merely blood and slime and vermin.
  Pride and riches will be humbled,
  Greatness mercilessly tumbled.

Ye who walk in velvet breeches:
Poverty the Master teaches!
  Silk is but the worm's extrusion,
  Worldly pride is but illusion.

What the silkworm has excreted,
Worthless, horrible and fetid, 30
  Man counts precious and entrancing:
  Silk he wears for feast and dancing.

So adieu, world of the senses,
Tempting me with vain pretenses,
  Brief as smoke and flower vernal:
  I elect the joys eternal.

How the world behaves I care not,
In its vanity I share not:
  I am eager for salvation,
  Turn to pious meditation. 40

MIKHAIL VASILEVICH LOMONOSOV

[1711–1765]

Evening Meditation on the Majesty of God on the Occasion of the Great Northern Lights

Translated from the Russian by Harold B. Segel

The day conceals its countenance,
Dark night has covered over fields;
Black shade has climbed the mountains' heights;
The sun's rays have inclined from us;
A star-filled vault has opened up;

No number is there to the stars,
No bottom is there to the vault.

A grain of sand in waves of sea,
A small spark in eternal ice,
A light dust in a roaring wind, 10
A feather in a raging fire
Am I, engulfed in this abyss,
As worn by thought, I lose my way.

The mouth of sages do proclaim
A multitude of worlds are there;
Innumerable suns burn bright;
And people live and die as we;
And to God's glory ever more,
There nature has an equal force.

But where, O Nature, is your law? 20
The dawn comes up from northern lands!
Does not the sun set there its throne?
Do icy seas not stir the fire?
We have been cloaked by a cold flame!
At night, day came upon the earth!

O You, whose swift gaze penetrates
The volume of eternal laws,
To whom the small sign of a thing
Reveals a principle of life:
To you the planets' course is known. 30
What is it so disturbs us, tell?

At night, what vibrates lucid rays?
What subtle flame cuts firmament?
And without stormy thunderclouds,
Wherefrom does lightning rush to earth?
How can it be that frozen steam
In midst of winter brings forth fire?

Dense fog and water quarrel there;
Or brightly glitter rays of sun,
Inclining to us through thick air. 40
Or tops of fertile mountains burn;
Or zephyrs cease to blow the sea,
And tranquil waves the ether beat.

Your answer is replete with doubts
About the places nearest man.
Pray tell us, how vast is the world?
What lies beyond the smallest stars?
Is creatures' end unknown to You?
Pray tell, how great is God Himself?

THE WORLD CONTEXT

THE ANCIENT MEXICANS

[16TH CENTURY]

In a remarkable book, *The Conquest of New Spain,* Bernal Díaz, one of Hernán Cortés's soldiers, describes the arrival of the Spanish conquistadors on the Mexican coast in 1519, the long march to the highland plateau of Mexico, and their impressions of seeing for the first time the magnificent capital of the Aztecs, Tenochtitlán, situated on an island in the middle of a large lake. Díaz exclaims, "We did not know what to say, or if this was real that we saw before our eyes." He was looking at one of the most beautiful cities in the world. With about 350,000 inhabitants, about five times larger than London, Tenochtitlán was intersected by canals, much like Venice. It contained magnificent buildings, schools, temples, and a huge central marketplace filled with embroidered goods, foods, animals, precious metals and stones, pottery, furniture, flowers, paper, tobacco, and much more. The rich and complex culture of ancient Mexico centered on its ornate ceremonial cities, where scholar–priests made elaborate picture books of omens and heavenly visions, where artists created beautiful murals and jewelry. Poets told amazing stories about gods and goddesses such as Huitzilopochtli and Quetzalcoatl (the Plumed Serpent).

The well-documented encounter between the Spanish and the Aztecs provides important information about the historic meeting of two different cultures—Europe and indigenous America. The eventual destruction of the Aztec empire by the Spanish completely changed the face of Mesoamerica, affecting all the peoples who have since lived on this continent.

HISTORY

The foundation of Mesoamerican civilization began in about 1500 B.C.E. with the Olmec culture on the Gulf Coast, which was responsible for the first urban, ceremonial centers in North America. Urban culture spread quickly throughout the Yucatán and Guatemala with the remarkable Maya, whose classic period was from 300-900 C.E. Their highly developed skills in mathematics, astronomy, hieroglyphic writing, ceramics, architecture, and warfare made possible the creation of an extensive network of over fifty cities. At the same time, civilization was also taking root on the Mexican highlands: Zapotec Indians created the beautiful Monte Albán near present-day Oaxaca, while another group built Teotihuacán, the "City of the Gods," northeast of Mexico City. At the height of its power, from the third to the seventh century, Teotihuacán was a city of an estimated 200,000 people, occupying fifteen square miles, with broad economic and political influence over the entire region.

After the demise of Teotihuacán in about 700 C.E., there was a gradual downfall of ceremonial centers throughout Mesoamerica. Fierce barbarians from the northern plains, called Chichimecs, wandered southward in the ninth century, altering Mexico's history. The Toltecs, who were the descendants of Nahuatl-speaking Chichimecs, inherited the culture of Teotihuacán after its decline and dominated central Mexico until the twelfth century. The name *Toltec* means both a master craftsman and an inhabitant of Tollan. Following the custom of sixteenth-century Spaniards, we call the people who built the next great empire in the Valley of Mexico Aztecs, after their mythical home somewhere up north in Aztlán, the Land of Herons.

Calling themselves *Mexicas* and speaking Nahuatl, the original Aztecs followed a fiercely warlike deity, Huitzilopochtli (Blue Hummingbird) southward in the twelfth century. This deity promised the Aztecs a great destiny and instructed them to build a city where they found an eagle sitting on a cactus with a snake in its mouth. That place was Lake Texcoco, today's Mexico City. Having arrived in the region about 1160 C.E., the Aztecs found other tribes settled in the choice areas around the lake, so they settled on a swampy, rocky island in the middle of the lake, where they began to build Tenochtitlán (Prickly Pear on a Rock) in 1325. Through a series of alliances, intrigues, and conquests, the Aztecs gained ascendancy in the region in 1432 under the leadership of Itzcoatl, and then built an empire that stretched from the Pacific to the Gulf Coast and southward almost to the border of Guatemala, controlling more than a million and a half people in Central Mexico and about eleven million throughout the subjugated area.

The Aztecs are remembered for militarism and human sacrifice. Believing that their destiny was to sustain the life of the sun with blood, they willingly gave their lives for their city and their patron god, Huitzilopochtli. The Aztecs were not particularly good administrators of their empire, having alienated surrounding tribes, and they were strangely vulnerable to the incursion of Europeans with their different values and mindset. In addition to being fierce fighters, the Aztecs were fine poets, having unusually high ideals for the artist and the sage. They revered the Toltecs, who had preceded them on the Mexican Plateau, and adopted Toltec mythology and industry. Long after they had disappeared, the Toltecs served as spiritual models for the Aztecs and were celebrated in their poetry: "The Toltecs were truly wise; / they conversed with their own hearts."

Myth and Literature

Although the peoples of Mesoamerica valued art and education, producing thousands of books, Spanish friars immediately following the Conquest attempted to eradicate the native, "pagan" religion by destroying the written books or codices of the Aztecs and Mayas. Only sixteen of these documents still exist: Three of them are Mayan and the rest are from the Oaxaca region and central Mexico. Ironically, Spanish priests such as Fray Bernardino de Sahagún also became the primary collectors of whatever native materials survived. The priest–ethnographers enlisted native wise men who apparently had access to extant pre-Conquest books and who used the Latin alphabet to record in Nahuatl the ancient myths, sagas, prayers, chronicles, songs, and speeches. It is from these materials that we take our selections.

Myths of Creation

First, we include a sampling of creation myths, which provide a kind of blueprint of the cosmos: the beginnings of the world and the origins of human beings, food, fire, suffering, death, and religious rites—all that is essential for material and spiritual survival. A similar function is provided by the book of Genesis and by the writings of Hesiod and Homer in Greece. The principle of opposition, which produced the Aztec cosmos, originated in the androgynous, supreme god of duality Ometeotl (*Ome* = two; *teotl* = god), who in turn produced four sons who, as the four quarters of space, were transformed into the four ages that preceded this one. The ancient Mexicans, like the Native Americans of the Southwest and analogous to the Hindus of India, believed that there had been different worlds or Suns before this one, roughly corresponding to the four basic elements of the cosmos: earth, air, fire, and water.

Each age was sustained by a delicate balance between opposing forces, dramatized in the myths as a titanic struggle between the gods Quetzalcoatl and Tezcatlipoca. It was not, however, a struggle between good and evil, such as we might find in a Zoroastrian or a Christian version of history, but a question of harmonizing or balancing the antithetical powers of day and night, sky and earth, spirit and matter, as in the Oriental conception of *yin* and *yang*. Disharmony brought destruction and the end of an age. The ancient Mexicans were concerned with time, perhaps obsessed with it. The inevitable destruction of the present age, the Fifth Sun, by earthquakes is reflected in the profound fatalism of Aztec and other Nahuatl-speaking poets. Nevertheless, the end could be postponed if, with sacrifice and penance, the Sun were kept alive and healthy in its passage through the sky. This belief provided a divine mission for the Aztecs as "Warriors of the Sun."

We begin with the myth *The Creation of the Earth,* which tells how Quetzalcoatl and Tezcatlipoca created the heavens and the earth by tearing in two a monstrous earth goddess. Afterwards, feeling badly about the harm they had brought her, they gave her gifts and created the mountains, caves, trees, and flowers from parts of her body. The origin of light is related in the myth *How the Sun and Moon Were Created.* After the gods gather at the ancient site of Teotihuacán, one of them must sacrifice himself to produce the births of the sun and moon; two gods finally are chosen, but their sacrifice is not sufficient to get the sun and the moon to move in their orbits. The central motif of sacrifice becomes a lesson for later mortals. Next, Quetzalcoatl must descend into the underworld to retrieve the necessary bones for creating human beings. Like the descent myths in ancient Greece and Babylonia, his archetypal journey into the earth suggests the analogy of human life to the vegetation cycle, pointing to the primordial idea that the source of both life and death is in the underworld—a place not to be confused with the Christian hell. Quetzalcoatl provided food for humans by changing into a black ant and raiding Tonacatepetl, Food Mountain. In the last creation myth, *The Origin of Ceremony,* Tezcatlipoca reveals the divine source of music and ritual, prime ingredients ever after in Mexican society.

The Myth of Quetzalcoatl

The stories and traditions surrounding Quetzalcoatl, the Plumed Serpent, form one of the most important spiritual legacies of ancient Mexico. At one time, his influence stretched from what is now Guatemala to northern Mexico. The *quetzal* referred to in the first half of his name is a rare and precious bird with long tail feathers used for ceremonial dress, symbolic of the powers of the sky and the aspirations of the spirit. *Coatl* means "snake" or "serpent" and is tied to the energies of the earth, the mysteries behind fertility and cyclic renewal. Thus in *quetzalcoatl,* the "plumed serpent," ancient Mexicans had discovered a deity that combined spirit and matter, or mediated between them, reconciling the two realms of heaven and earth. The winged serpent can be also found in European folklore, but its closest kin are found in the Orient: the Chinese dragon and the genie of rain and fertility.

A merging of mythology with history occurred in the tenth century when the cult of Quetzalcoatl became associated with a Toltec ruler and priest, Ce Acatl (One Reed) Topiltzin, who is perhaps Mexico's first historical figure of record. *The Myth of Quetzalcoatl* begins with the birth of Ce Acatl, whose father was Mixcoatl, the legendary leader of the Toltec-Chichimec tribe. Very little is known about Topiltzin's childhood except that he trains as a warrior and defeats his uncles, who had earlier killed his father. Ultimately Topiltzin becomes a priest of Quetzalcoatl and is made ruler and spiritual model of the Toltecs, respected for his penitential life of self-discipline and piety. He sacrifices snakes, birds, and butterflies, a practice that later draws the anger of those who favor human sacrifice. As a legendary culture-bringer, Topiltzin-Quetzalcoatl, like the Greek Prometheus, invents all the arts necessary for a prosperous life. But the dramatic core of this myth involves Topiltzin's fall from power, his pilgrimage to the sea, and his death and resurrection.

At the height of Toltec fame and prosperity, Topiltzin-Quetzalcoatl withdraws from society into the privacy of his temple. Led by Tezcatlipoca, Quetzalcoatl's mythic adversary, militaristic sorcerers lure Topiltzin out of seclusion and force him to break his ascetic vows by getting him drunk so that he sleeps with his sister, Quetzalpetlatl. Disgraced, Topiltzin-Quetzalcoatl goes into exile, traveling to Tlillan Tlapallan, the "land of black and red" at the eastern horizon, where the morning star announces the rebirth of the sun. Symbolically, it is the place of spiritual fulfillment and enlightenment. There are two different conclusions to this story. Sahagún tells one version that is related to Quetzalcoatl's messianic promise: Quetzalcoatl flies off on a raft of serpents, promising to return one day from over the water. The second version, which is included here, describes Quetzalcoatl's phoenixlike death and resurrection as the morning star, reflecting in its periodic cycles Quetzalcoatl's own death, resurrection, and promise to return. In addition to his reconciling role between heaven and earth, between matter and spirit, the transformation of his spiritual pilgrimage from despair into beauty mark Topiltzin-Quetzalcoatl as a special hero.

The Poetry of Nezahualcoyotl

Nezahualcoyotl (1402–1472 C.E.), who lived a generation before the arrival of the Conquistadors, was the ruler of Texcoco for more than forty years and a remarkable poet–philosopher and sage with numerous talents. When Nezahualcoyotl was a boy, his father was murdered; nevertheless, he received an excellent education and with the assistance of the Aztecs was able to defeat his father's enemies and gain the throne of Texcoco. Nezahualcoyotl, whose name means hungry coyote, then created a golden age for his followers by codifying laws and assembling what was probably the first library in the Americas. As an engineer, he assisted the Aztecs in building their aqueduct and the dikes that separated brackish from sweet water on Lake Texcoco. He worshipped a god called Tloque Nahuaque, the Lord of Everywhere, an invisible deity not to be identified with images or statues—a Mesoamerican version of monotheism.

In his poems, of which over thirty still exist, Nezahualcoyotl addresses issues of mortality, political power, and the mystery of death. The first two poems describe the fragility of human life and affirm that permanence resides only with Tloque Nahuaque, translated as Giver of Life. The next poems pick up themes common to Nahuatl poetry; the Nahuas believed that flowers and songs were meeting grounds between gods and humans. The gods speak through the natural world and they speak through art. The books that contain poems and songs on earth are mirrored by the Giver of Life, who uses the book of paintings to direct life on earth. The last poems are speculations about life after death.

The Conquest of the Aztecs

Because of Bernardino de Sahagún, a Franciscan who arrived in New Spain in 1529, we have an account of the Conquest from the point of view of the Aztecs. Considered to be the originator of Mexican ethnography, Sahagún assembled native informants who wrote and illustrated materials, which Sahagún collected into twelve volumes covering a broad spectrum of Aztec life: religion, history, customs, medicine, and literature. The Nahuatl and Spanish version is called *Historia General de las Cosas de la Nueva España (General History of the Things of New Spain).* The historical account we include was excerpted from the *Codex Florentino,* a copy of the *Historia* sent by Sahagún to Europe in 1580. The excerpts follow generally the chronology of the Conquest, but include important observations and reflections on the events. Some background on the Conquest is helpful.

In 1519, Hernán Cortés, a thirty-four-year-old adventurer from a poor region in Spain, led a trading expedition to the Aztecs of Mexico. Cortés, who helped with the conquest of Cuba, dreamed about the gold he might acquire on his own expedition. With 11 ships, 553 men, and 16 horses, Cortés sailed for Mexico, searching for gold and glory. He was assisted by an extremely intelligent Indian woman, Malinche, whose name was changed to Marina when she converted to Christianity. Marina became Cortés's interpreter and mistress, providing him with essential information about Indian culture, including the all-important fact that the Aztec empire of some eleven million people was vulnerable due to internal dissension. With 1,500 Totonac warriors who had defected from the empire, Cortés began his march to the highland capital of the Aztecs, Tenochtitlán, gathering support from the Tlaxcala army and putting down a rebellion in Cholula.

Moctezuma II, the Aztec ruler, was extremely apprehensive about the arrival of the Spanish. Several years before Cortés's actual arrival, the Aztecs had witnessed bad omens in the sky and on earth. The myth of the god Quetzalcoatl was also revived; he had promised to return in the year *Ce-Acatl* of the Aztec calendar, which happened to coincide with the year 1519. Such was the power of the omens and the myth that the Aztec rulers believed initially that the Spanish were Quetzalcoatl and his retinue returning to claim the throne. Cortés's ships were reported to Moctezuma II as floating mountains or perhaps Quetzalcoatl's four mythic temples, which had been built for penance and symbolized the four directions. This mistake probably contributed to Moctezuma's strange passivity and his indecision about defending the Aztec capital against the outsiders.

On November 8, 1519, Cortés and his band of conquistadors arrived at the magnificent Tenochtitlán, where the first meeting between Cortés and Moctezuma, an unusual, historical confrontation, produced confusion and wonderment on both sides. Certainly as human beings, Spaniard and Aztec were similar; but in their attitudes and values, they represented two radically different world views, two kinds of consciousness. The Spaniards carried with them the Renaissance idea that individuals could make and shape history. As Christians, they lived with a linear concept of time and history, guided by a god whose dominion extended to the entire earth; this god granted them a mandate to conquer and exploit "pagan" lands and peoples, who were, in their view, imprisoned by superstition and ignorance. Tenochtitlán was a stepping stone to larger plans. For Moctezuma and his followers, however, the encounter was initially and fundamentally a religious or mythological event. Their lives were shaped by the precarious, reciprocal relationship between human, natural, and divine worlds. Each day was clothed with references to divine favor or disfavor. Nothing—no tree or bird—was simply itself; everything vibrated within a web of sacred meaning and divine implication. As a result, there was no easy or quick way to untangle the Spaniards from the myth of Quetzalcoatl if omens and signs—plus the exotic physical appearance of the Spaniards—had initially intertwined them.

After being received as guests by Moctezuma, the Spaniards took him prisoner in his own city and held him hostage. Despite the overwhelming odds, Moctezuma put up very little resistance, as if he were bowing to destiny. While Cortés made a trip to the coast, Pedro de Alvarado, the Spanish officer left in charge in Tenochtitlán, gave the command to kill 600 Aztec nobles for their gold. This caused the Aztecs to revolt. Moctezuma was killed trying to pacify his followers. The Spaniards, weighed down into the canals and lake mud by their armor and Aztec gold, suffered terrible losses attempting to escape from Tenochtitlán during the night—the famous *Noche Triste.* Then disaster struck; a smallpox epidemic wiped out hundreds of thousands of Aztecs, including their valiant leader Cuitlahua. In December 1520, Cortés returned with 600 well-equipped Spanish soldiers, 100,000 Indian recruits, and 13 dismantled brigantines to topple the empire. Led by

Cuauhtémoc, a nephew of Moctezuma, the Aztecs put up a courageous fight, despite weakness due to hunger and disease. The Spaniards cut off their water supply and destroyed their food sources. After incredible suffering, the end of the battle came on August 13, 1521, when Cuauhtémoc was caught trying to escape across the lake.

There was little gold left to divide among Cortés's army; according to Bernal Díaz in *The Conquest of New Spain,* many men owed more on their accounts for their weapons and medical bills than they received from the spoils. The native population was searched, enslaved, and struck down by disease. Indian rulers and priests were tortured and hanged, and a few were fed to dogs. Altogether, the Spanish Conquest decimated the indigenous population, reducing it to two and a half million by the year 1600.

A Defense of Aztec Religion

In 1524, three years after the destruction of the Aztec Empire, Pope Adrian VI and the Emperor Carlos V of Spain sent twelve Franciscan friars to convert the Indians of Mexico. After the friars had become briefly acquainted with the native culture, they called a conference with native leaders to explain the basic tenets of Christianity and why the Indians should convert. Many ordinary people converted; one Franciscan friar claimed that he baptized 14,000 Indians in one day, and another friar baptized 400,000 over a lifetime. A few native religious leaders or sages, however, nobly resisted the efforts at conversion. They were allowed to reply to the friars in defense of their beliefs. Their defense, translated below, is an eloquent statement revealing the strength of their character, their refinement as human beings, and the depth of their religious faith.

Conclusion

The debate has continued to the present time about what appear to be contradictions in the Aztec way of life, between the light and the dark side, the humanism and the barbarism. In his letters, Cortés described the Aztecs as an advanced civilization, equal to Europeans in intelligence and creativity. Other scholars concluded that the Aztecs were simply primitive despots. The reputation of Quetzalcoatl continued to grow over the next centuries. Although his religious influence diminished in the nineteenth century, the figure of Quetzalcoatl remains an exemplary hero from ancient Mexico, a model of all that is admirable in Nahua culture, in contrast to the sometimes oppressive picture of Aztec society found in the statistics of human sacrifice.

The sense of tragedy that pervades the demise of both the Aztecs and the Maya continues to intrigue artists, philosophers, novelists, and poets. The rise and fall of these indigenous peoples reflects the fate of native peoples throughout the Americas, and is intertwined with the destiny of the peoples who came later and must negotiate a future that recognizes both the sufferings and accomplishments of the past.

Suggested Readings

Cortés's expedition is vividly described by a soldier who served Cortés, Bernal Díaz, in *The Conquest of New Spain* (1963). Nigel Davies provides a general history in *The Ancient Kingdoms of Mexico* (1982); a more specific history is his *The Aztecs: A History* (1973). A fine biography and introduction to Aztec culture is C. A. Burland's *Montezuma: Lord of the Aztecs* (1973). A bilingual Nahuatl and English edition of Sahagún's history is Arthur J. O. Anderson and Charles E. Dibble's *Florentine Codex: General History of the Things of New Spain* (1950–1969). Excellent introductions to the life and thought of the Aztecs are provided by Miguel León-Portilla's *Aztec Thought and Culture* (1963) and G. C. Vaillant's *Aztecs of Mexico* (1950). The greatness of the Quetzalcoatl myth is explored in Laurette Séjourné's *Burning Water: Thought and Religion in Ancient Mexico* (1956). A classic account of the influence of the Aztecs is Benjamin Keen's *The Aztec Image in Western Thought* (1971). Additional sources of myths are Angel Maria Garibay K.'s *Epica Náhuatl* (1945), Primo F. Velázquez's edition of *Códice Chimalpopoca* (1945), Fray Juan de Torquemada's *Monarquia Indiana* (1943), and Fray Bernardino de Sahagún's *Colloguies y Doctrina Christiana* (1944).

Myths of Creation

Translated by David M. Johnson

The Creation of the Earth

The great gods, Tezcatlipoca[1] and Quetzalcoatl, brought the Earth Goddess down from the heavens. She was an enormous monster full of eyes and mouths. Each of the joints in her body contained a mouth, and these innumerable mouths bit like wild beasts. The world was already full of water, although no one knows its origin.

When the gods saw the huge Earth Monster moving back and forth across the water, they said to each other: "We must create the earth." So they transformed themselves into two large serpents. One of them gripped the goddess from her right hand down to her left foot, while the other took her left hand and right foot. Holding on to her, they turned and twisted with such force that she finally tore in two. They lifted her lower half and made the sky. From the upper part they formed the earth. The rest of the gods looked on and felt ashamed that they had not made anything comparable to this.

Then, in order to make amends for the immense damage inflicted on the Earth Goddess, the other gods came down to console her and give her gifts. As a compensation they declared that out of her body would come all that humans need to sustain themselves and live on the earth. From her hair they made wild grasses, trees and flowers. Her skin was changed into delicate greens and ornamental plants. Her eyes were transformed into small hollows, wells and fountains, her mouth into large caves, her nose into mountains and valleys.

This is the same goddess who sometimes weeps in the night, longing to eat human hearts. She refuses to be silent if she is denied them, and she won't produce fruit unless she is watered with human blood.

How the Sun and Moon Were Created

It is said that before there was day in the world, when all was in darkness, the gods gathered together in Teotihuacán. They counseled together and said: "O gods, who will accept the burden of lighting the world? Who will be the sun and the moon?"

[1] A glossary of Nahuatl names and terms is provided at the end.

Then a god named Tecuciztecatl responded to these words and said: "I will take on the burden of lighting the world."

The gods spoke once again and said: "Who will be the other?" So they looked at each other and discussed who would be the other. None of them dared to offer himself for that task. All of them were afraid and made excuses.

One of the gods, Nanahuatzin, who was covered with sores, went unnoticed. He did not speak, but listened to what the other gods were saying. And the other gods spoke to him and said: "O Nanahuatzin, you be the one who gives light." Willingly he consented to their commands, and replied: "Gratefully, I accept what you have asked of me. So be it!"

Then the two of them began to do penance lasting four days. A fire was lit in a hearth which was built on a precipice—a place now called *Teotexcalli*.

The god Tecuciztecatl's offerings—all of them—were expensive. Instead of branches he offered precious feathers called *quetzalli,* and instead of balls of hay, he offered balls of gold. And instead of maguey spines, he offered spines made from precious stones. In place of spines stained with blood, he offered spines made from red coral. And the copal incense which he offered was excellent.

Instead of branches, the god of pustules, Nanahuatzin, offered green reeds, which were tied in bundles of three, with a total of nine. He offered balls of hay and maguey spines stained with his own blood. And for incense, instead of copal, he offered scabs from his sores.

For each of these gods a tower was erected, like a mountain. On these same mountains they did penance for four nights. Today these mountains are called *tzaqualli* and are the Pyramids of the Sun and the Moon at Teotihuacán.

After they finished the four nights of their penance, they threw away the branches and everything else that they used in the performance of the penance.

This was done at the conclusion of their penance, since on the following night they began to perform the rites of office. Just before midnight the other gods gave their adornments to the one called Tecuciztecatl; they gave him a feather headdress and a linen jacket. As for Nanahuatzin, they covered his head with a paper headdress and dressed him in a paper stole and a paper loincloth. With the approach of midnight, all the gods took their places around the hearth called *Teotexcalli,* where the fire had burned for four days.

The gods arranged themselves in two rows, some on one side of the fire and some on the other. And then the two, Tecuciztecatl and Nanahuatzin, took their places in front of the fire, facing the hearth, in between the two rows of gods.

All of them were standing when the gods spoke and said to Tecuciztecatl: "Now then, Tecuciztecatl! Cast yourself into the fire!" And he readied himself to leap into the fire. But the flames were so fierce that when he felt the unbearable heat he became terrified, and was afraid to throw himself into the fire. So he turned back.

Again he turned to cast himself into the flames which leaped even higher, but he stopped, not daring to cast himself into the fire. Four times he tried, but each time he lost his nerve. It was tradition that no one could try more than four times.

Since Tecuciztecatl had tried four times the gods then spoke to Nanahuatzin and said to him: "Now then, Nanahuatzin! You try!" When the gods had spoken to him, he gathered his courage and, closing his eyes, rushed forth and cast himself into the fire, where he began to crackle and sizzle like someone being roasted. When Tecuciztecatl saw that he had leaped into the flames, he gathered his nerve, rushed forward and threw himself into the fire.

They say that an eagle then flew into the fire and also burned; for this reason it has dark or blackish feathers. Finally a jaguar entered. He wasn't burned, but only singed; and for this reason he continued to be stained black and white. From this came the custom of calling men who are skilled in war *cuauhtlocelotl: cuauhtli* is said first because the eagle entered the fire first; *ocelotl* is said last because the jaguar entered the fire after the eagle.

After these two gods had flung themselves into the fire, and after both had burned, the remaining gods seated themselves, waiting to see from which direction Nanahuatzin would begin to rise. After they had waited a long time, the sky began to redden, and the light of dawn appeared all around them. And they say that after this the gods knelt down, waiting to see where on the horizon the Sun Nanahuatzin would rise.

As they looked in each direction they turned in a circle, but not one could guess or say the place where he would appear. They could not make up their minds about a single thing. Some thought he would appear in the north, and they fixed their attention there. Others fixed on the south. Some suspected that he would emerge in all directions at once, because the radiance of dawn was everywhere. Others got in a position to look east and said: "Here, in this direction, the sun is to rise." The word of these gods was true.

They say that those who looked east were Quetzalcoatl, who is also called Ehecatl; and another called Totec, and by another name Anahuatlitecu, and by another name Tlatlahuic Tezcatlipoca. And others called Mimixcoa, who are innumerable. And four women: one named Tiacapan, the other Teicu, the third Tlacoyehua, the fourth Xocoyotl.

When the sun began to rise, he looked very red and appeared to sway from side to side. No one could look directly at him because his powerful light would blind them. His rays streamed out in a magnificent way and were scattered in all directions.

Afterwards the moon appeared in the east, in the same direction as the sun. First the sun arose, and afterwards the moon. The order that they entered the fire was the order in which they appeared, and were made sun and moon.

And the storytellers say that the light coming from them was of equal intensity. And when the gods saw that they shone equally they discussed it among themselves again and said: "O gods, what shall come of this? Will it actually work if both are alike and move together? Will it be good that they shine with the same intensity?"

The gods made a judgement and said: "Let it be this way, let it thus be done." Then one of them ran up and threw a rabbit into the face of Tecuciztecatl, darkening his face and obscuring the light. And his face remained as it is today.

After both had risen over the earth, the sun and moon stayed in one place without moving. And the gods once more spoke and said: "How are we going to live when the sun doesn't move? Are we to live among the peons? Let us all die and give him vitality with our deaths."

And immediately Ehecatl, the Wind, took charge of slaying all the gods, and he killed them. It is said that one named Xolotl refused to die and said to the gods: "O gods, don't kill me!" He wept so intensely that his eyes swelled from crying.

When the executioner arrived, he ran away and hid in the maize fields, and changed himself into the base of the maize plant with two stalks, which field hands call *xolotl.* He was discovered among the bottoms of the maize plant. Again he ran away and hid among the maguey, turning into a maguey with two bodies, which is called *mexolotl.* Again he was spotted. He ran away and hid in the water, changing himself into a fish, which is named *axolotl.* There they took him and killed him.

And they say that even though the gods were dead, the sun still did not move. And then Ehecatl, the Wind, began to blow. Blowing like a monsoon, he caused him to move and get on his way. After the sun began to travel, the moon remained in the place where he was.

After the sun had set, the moon began to move. In this manner they have their separate ways, coming forth at different times. The sun carries on during the day, and the moon works or illuminates the night. And from this comes the saying: that Tecuciztecatl would have been the sun if he had been the first to leap into the fire, because he was named first and he offered precious things in his penance.

The Creation of Man and Woman

The gods consulted with each other and said: "Who will live here, now that the sky has been dammed up and the earth is secure? Who will live here, O gods?" The ones who were negotiating in this manner were Citlallinicue, Citlallatonac, Apantecuhtli, Tepanquizqui, Tlallamanqui, Huictlollinqui, Quetzalcoatl and Titlacahuan.

Then Quetzalcoatl went down to Mictlan, the land of the Dead. He approached the rulers, Mictlantecuhtli and Mictlancihuatl, and said: "I have come for the precious bones which are under your protection." They asked him: "What are you going to make, Quetzalcoatl?" He answered them by saying: "The gods have discussed using the bones to create the new inhabitants for earth."

Once more the Lord of the Dead spoke: "Very well. Blow my conch shell and circle four times around my throne of jade." But his conch shell had no holes in it, so Quetzalcoatl called for worms who made holes in it. Then large bees and hornets went inside and made it hum with sound. Mictlantecuhtli heard the noise and said: "Very well. Take the bones."

Mictlantecuhtli, however, said to his servants, the Mictecas: "Go after Quetzalcoatl and tell him he must not take them." Quetzalcoatl, planning to carry them away, nevertheless told his *nahual:* "Go and report that I won't be taking them." His *nahual* went and shouted: "I won't be taking them."

Then Quetzalcoatl gathered up the precious bones and quickly began to ascend with them. Gathered together on one side were the man bones, and on the other were the woman bones. Thus he made two bundles and carried them away.

Again Mictlantecuhtli spoke, saying to his servants: "O gods, can it be true that Quetzalcoatl is escaping with the precious bones? Go and dig a deep pit." They went and dug it, and Quetzalcoatl, frightened by some quail, tripped and fell into the pit. He fell like someone who was dead, and at the bottom the precious bones were scattered. Then the quail bit into the bones and chewed on them.

After a time Quetzalcoatl revived. Weeping, he said to his *nahual:* "What will become of this?" His *nahual* replied: "What has come of this? It appears that the negotiations went against us, but all is not lost." Quetzalcoatl again gathered the bones together and made a bundle which he promptly carried to Tamoanchan.

After he arrived with them, the one called Quilaztli (who is also Cihuacoatl) ground them into powder and placed them in a large jade bowl. Unto this powder Quetzalcoatl bled his penis. And immediately all of the gods did penance–Apantecuhtli, Huictlollinqui, Tepanquizqui, Tlallamanac, Tzontemoc, and the sixth, Quetzalcoatl.

Afterwards they made the announcement: "Human beings, servants of the gods, have been born!" Thus it was that for all of us humans the gods did penance.

The Origin of Food

Again the gods consulted with each other and said: "O gods, what will these humans eat? Already all of them are looking for food."

Then the ant came by who had gathered kernels of maize in the center of Tonacatepetl (Food Mountain). Quetzalcoatl confronted the ant, and said to her: "Tell me where you found it!" Several times he asked her, but she didn't want to tell him. Finally she said: "Over there!" pointing to the place. She showed him the way.

Quetzalcoatl changed himself into a black ant in order to follow her. They entered together, and Quetzalcoatl accompanied the red ant into the interior granary. He gathered together the maize and immediately carried it to Tamoanchan.

The gods chewed it and put in in our mouths so that we might be strong and healthy. Then they said: "What shall we do with Tonacatepetl?" It was Quetzalcoatl who singlehandedly tied it up with cords and tried to carry it on his back, but he couldn't lift it.

Then Oxomoco, the first man, divined the maize by throwing it. Cipactonal, the wife of Oxomoco, did the same—because Cipactonal is first woman. Then Oxomoco and Cipactonal said: "Only Nanahuatl can break into the granary in Tonacatepetl." This was according to their divination.

At once they became aware of the many rain gods: the blue ones and the white ones, the yellow ones and the red ones. Then Nanahuatl broke into the granary, and the rain gods carried off the food: white, black, yellow and red maize; beans, amaranth, sage and prickly poppy. All the food was stolen from the mountain.

The Origin of Ceremony

The disciples of those gods who had sacrificed themselves for the Sun walked about sadly, withdrawn in thought. They were wrapped in the shawls left to them by the gods in remembrance. Each with his shawl was searching, looking, wanting to catch sight of their gods, wondering if they might appear.

They say that a disciple of Tezcatlipoca, carrying out his devotion, arrived at the seashore where the god appeared to him in three different forms. The god called to him and said: "Come here my good man! Because you are my friend, I want you to go to the House of the Sun and return with singers and instruments for my fiestas. You should ask the whale, the Siren, and the turtle to help you build a bridge for your passage."

After the bridge was built, the god gave his disciple a song for the road. The Sun, however, overheard it and understood what could happen. So he warned his followers not to listen, for whoever listened would have to return to earth. But some of his followers listened, and thought the song flowed with honey. They listened to the sounds of the three-legged drum and the beating voice of the hollow log.

It is said that they returned to earth and began to create fiestas and dances for their gods. And the songs which were sung in those ceremonies were like prayers, chanted in unison to the same tune and steps, without getting off key or missing a beat. This was carried out with devotion and seriousness. And this same ceremony is still performed today.

The Myth of Quetzalcoatl

Translated by David M. Johnson

The Birth of Ce Acatl

The great warrior, Mixcoatl, marched over the earth conquering towns in the North, the East, and the West. Then Mixcoatl went south to conquer the town of Huitznahuac.

As he approached the battle, the woman Chimalman came out to meet him. He put down his shield on the ground before him, he put down his spear-thrower and his spears. She stood naked before him, without skirt or blouse.

Seeing her, Mixcoatl shot at her with his arrows. The first arrow that he shot at her went above her and she barely had to duck her head. The second one passed by her side, and she twisted away from it. The third one she caught in her hand. And the fourth one that he shot went right between her thighs.

After having shot at her four times, Mixcoatl turned and went away. The woman immediately ran off to hide in the cave of a large canyon.

Once again, Mixcoatl equipped himself, he replenished his arrows, and once more he went looking for the woman, but he saw no one. So he abused the other women of Huitznahuac, and they said, "Let us go look for her!"

They went to bring her back, saying to her, "Because of you, he is violating your younger sisters." They were determined to bring Chimalman back, so she returned to Huitznahuac.

Again Mixcoatl went to her, and she came out to meet him. As before, she stood in front of him with nothing covering her crotch. As before, he put his shield and spears on the ground. Again he shot arrows at her and the same thing happened: one went above her, one went by her side, she caught one in her hand, and one went between her thighs.

After all this happened, he took her. He lay with the woman of Huitznahuac, who was Chimalman. And afterwards she was pregnant.

The birth of Ce Acatl took four days and during this time his mother suffered a great deal. And just when he was born, his mother died.

The year was 1-Reed. Thus it is said that in this year Quetzalcoatl was born, he who was called Topiltzin Priest Ce Acatl Quetzalcoatl. It is said that his mother had the name Chimalman. And some say that she became pregnant when she swallowed a piece of jade.

Ce Acatl Avenges His Father's Murder

Ce Acatl was raised by Quilaztli, who was also called Cihuacoatl.

The years passed; 2-Flint, 3-House, 4-Rabbit, 5-Reed, 6-Flint, 7-House, 8-Rabbit.

9-Reed. When Ce Acatl was a young man he accompanied his father on military expeditions. He learned about being a warrior in a place called Xiuhuacan, where he took several captives.

In that place were Ce Acatl's uncles, the four hundred Mixcoa who hated his father and eventually killed him. After they killed him, they went and buried him in the sand.

In the Year 9-Reed, Ce Acatl looked for his father and asked about him, "What has become of my father? I want to know my father, I want to see his face." Hearing him, a vulture answered and said, "They killed your father. He lies over there where they buried him."

Without any delay, Ce Acatl went there to dig in the earth, he searched for the bones of his father. After he had gathered up the bones, he took them and buried them in his temple, Mixcoatepetl.

Three of the uncles who had killed his father were named Apanecatl, Zolton, and Cuilton. And Ce Acatl asked them, "What should I sacrifice in order to dedicate this temple? Perhaps only a rabbit, or simply a snake."

And they answered him, "Indeed, that would make us very angry. It is better to use a jaguar, an eagle, and a wolf." Ce Acatl replied to them, "Very well—that's what it will be!"

He called a jaguar, an eagle, and a wolf, and said to them, "Come here my uncles. They say I should use you three to dedicate my temple, but you will not die. Instead, you shall devour my father's brothers when I consecrate my temple." For the sake of deception, he tied the animals' necks together.

Then Ce Acatl called to the moles and he told them, "Come, my uncles, dig a tunnel into our temple." Immediately, the moles began to dig, and soon they had made a tunnel. And that is how Ce Acatl got inside and climbed to the summit of his temple where he emerged.

The brother uncles had said, "We will light the fire on the summit." Happily they watched the howling of the jaguar, eagle and wolf, who pretended to be in pain. And while they were thus distracted, Ce Acatl was already lighting the fire.

His uncles were furious and they prepared to fight. Apanecatl went ahead and hurriedly climbed upward. But Ce Acatl stood tall and hit him in the head with a shiny pot, causing him to fall to the base of the temple.

Next he took hold of Zolton and Cuilton and, as the animals blew on the fire, he put them to death in this manner: he spread chili over them and cut off pieces of their flesh. After he had tortured them, he cut open their chests.

Once again Ce Acatl set out to make further conquests.

Becoming a Priest and Ruler of the Toltecs

The years passed: 10-Flint, 11-House, 12-Rabbit, 13-Reed, 1-Flint, 2-House, 3-Rabbit, 4-Reed, 5-Flint, 6-House, 7-Rabbit, 8-Reed, 9-Flint.

10-House. In this year Huactli died, who had been the ruler of Cuauchtitlan for sixty-two years. This was the ruler who did not know how to cultivate edible corn, and whose followers did not know how to weave blankets. So they dressed only in skins. Their food was nothing more than birds, small snakes, rabbits, and deer. Furthermore, they had no houses, since they wandered from place to place.

The year was 11-Rabbit. In this year the Lady Xiuhtlacuilolxochitzin took the throne. Her thatched house, which is still there today, was at the edge of the plaza, beside a rocky ledge. It is said that they gave her the city because she was Huactli's wife, and she could invoke the demon Itzpapalotl.

The years passed: 12-Reed, 13-Flint, 1-House.

2-Rabbit. It was in this year that Quetzalcoatl arrived in Tollantzinco, where he stayed four years. He built his house of penance, which was supported by cross beams made of turquoise. From there he went to Cuextlan. In that place he crossed the river and there he built a sturdy bridge. They say it still exists today.

The years passed: 3-Reed, 4-Flint.

5-House. In this year the Toltecs went to find Quetzalcoatl in order to make him the ruler in Tollan. He was also their priest. This is part of the written record, and can be found elsewhere.

The years passed: 6-Rabbit.

7-Reed. During this year Lady Xiuhtlacuilolxochitzin died. She had ruled in Cuauhtitlan for twelve years.

8-Flint. In this year Ayauhcoyotzin was enthroned as ruler of Cuauhtitlan, in a place called Tecpancuauhtla (Palace of the Woods).

The years passed: 9-House, 10-Rabbit, 11-Reed, 12-Flint, 13-House, 1-Rabbit.

2-Reed. In the annals of Tezcoco, this was the year Topiltzin Quetzalcoatl of Tollan and Colhuacan died. In the year 2-Reed Ce Acatl-Topiltzin Quetzalcoatl built his house of penance, a place for fasting and prayer.

He built his house with four chambers: one with turquoise beams, one with coral, one with white shell, one with quetzal feathers. There he performed his penance, he prayed there and he fasted.

Close to midnight he went down to the stream, to a place called Atecpanamochco (Palace of Water). He inflicted himself with spines on the heights of Xicocotl, on Huitzcoc, on Tzincoc, and also on Mount Nonoalco.

He made his spines from precious stones, and he made laurel boughs from quetzal feathers. With the smoke of incense he sanctified the turquoise, jade, and coral. And for his sacrifices he offered snakes, birds, and butterflies.

And it is said that he reverently sent up his prayers to the center of the heavens. He prayed to Ometeotl, god and goddess in one:

She, Skirt-of-Stars and He, Maker-of-Daylight
Lady-of-Our-Flesh and Lord-of-Our-Flesh
Wrapped-in-Blackness and Wrapped-in-Red
Supports-the-Earth and Moves-Clouds-in-the-Sky

It was known that he cried out to Omeyocan (Place of Duality), which exists above the nine levels of heaven. Thus it was known that he prayed to those who lived there, and he made petitions to them. And he practiced a life of piety and wisdom, becoming a model for other priests. They followed the example of Quetzalcoatl in the city of Tollan.

Furthermore, in his time, he discovered great treasures of jade, fine turquoise, gold, silver, coral, and shells. And the feathers of beautiful birds: the quetzal, the lovely cotinga, the roseate spoonbill, the trogan, and the blue heron. He also discovered various colors of cocoa and several colors of cotton.

It is said that the Toltecs were very wealthy, and that they had all they needed for eating and drinking. The squash were huge, two meters in circumference. And the ears of maize were so big that a single pair of arms could not stretch around them. The amaranth plants were so tall and thick that people could climb them like trees.

He was a very great artist in all his works. Pieces of earthenware for eating and drinking were painted blue, green, yellow, and red. He taught the Toltecs how to work with jade and gold and feathers.

There was a mountain called Tzatzitepetl (Mountain for Shouting), and that is its name today. From the top of it a public crier shouted announcements, and his messages spread over Anahuac. He was heard and the laws were communicated. People came to learn and listen to what Quetzalcoatl had commanded.

During the period of his rule Quetzalcoatl began to build his temple. He put up columns in the shape of serpents, but he did not finish the entire project.

While he lived there he did not show himself in public. He stayed inside a very dark, well protected chamber. His personal servants protected him on all sides. His own chamber was the most remote; in each of the others were his servants. In the rooms were mats of precious stones, quetzal plumes, and gold.

Thus it was said that he erected his fourfold house of penance.

The Temptation and Fall of Quetzalcoatl

They say that during Quetzalcoatl's lifetime sorcerers repeatedly tried to trick him into making human sacrifices, into killing human beings. But he never wanted this, nor did he give in to this, because he deeply loved his followers, who were the Toltecs.

It can be said that always he used only small snakes, birds, and butterflies for his sacrifices.

They say that because of this the sorcerers were angry. When they made demands they would use ridicule and insults in order to dishonor him, and drive him away.

And so it happened.

The years passed: 3-Flint, 4-House, 5-Rabbit, 6-Reed, 7-Flint, 8-House, 9-Rabbit, 10-Reed, 11-Flint, 12-House, 13-Rabbit.

1-Reed. In this year Quetzalcoatl died. They say that he went to Tlillan Tlapallan to die there. In succession, Matlacxochitl took the throne and ruled in Tollan.

This is what is said about why Quetzalcoatl went away.

When he disobeyed the sorcerers and refused to make human sacrifices, they consulted with each other. Their names were Tezcatlipoca, Ihuimecatl, and Toltecatl. They said, "It is necessary that he leave his city, here where we have to live."

They went on to say, "Let us make pulque. We will get him to drink some. And then he will lose his judgement and give up his life of penance."

Tezcatlipoca then spoke, "I say that we should present him with his body, let him really see it." They schemed together in order to accomplish this.

Tezcatlipoca went first. He took a two-sided mirror, about the size of a person's hand, and wrapped it up. When he arrived at the place where Quetzalcoatl was living, he said to the servants who personally cared for him, "Give this message to the priest: 'Lord, a commoner has arrived to present you with your body, to show it to you.' "

The servants went inside to report to Quetzalcoatl, who replied to them: "What is this, grandfather servant? What kind of thing is my *body*? First, you inspect what he has brought, and then he may enter."

Tezcatlipoca did not want it to be seen, however, and told them, "Go tell the priest that I must personally show it to him."

So they went and said to him, "Lord, he won't give in. He insists that he must show it to you." Quetzalcoatl said, "Then let him come in, grandfather."

They went to call Tezcatlipoca, who entered and greeted him, saying: "My son, Priest Ce Acatl-Quetzalcoatl. I salute you, my Lord, and have come to let you see your body."

Quetzalcoatl replied, "You are welcome here, grandfather. Where did you come from? What is this concerning my body? Let me see it!"

And the sorcerer answered, "My son, priest, I am your servant, who has come from the foothills of Mount Nonoalco. My Lord, may you look at your body."

Then he gave him the mirror and said, "Look at yourself and know yourself, my son. See how you appear in the mirror."

At once, Quetzalcoatl saw himself and was filled with fear. He said, "If my subjects were to see me they would probably run away." For his eyelids were puffy, his eye sockets were deeply sunk in a face which was swollen and deformed all over.

After looking into the mirror he said, "Never shall my subjects see me, because I shall remain here, in this place."

Dismissing himself, Tezcatlipoca left. In order to ridicule Quetzalcoatl and make fun of him, he consulted with Ihuimecatl, who said, "Coyotlinahual, the feather artist, must now be the one to go."

They contacted Coyotlinahual, the feather artist, and told him that he was to go, and he said: "So be it! I will go to see Quetzalcoatl."

So he went and said to Quetzalcoatl, "My son, I say that you should come out of hiding so that your subjects can see you. I will prepare you so that they may see you."

Quetzalcoatl replied, "Let's see it! Go ahead, grandfather."

Coyotlinahual, the feather artist, began at once. First, he made Quetzalcoatl's plumed headdress. Then he made a turquoise mask for him. With red coloring he brightened the lips, with yellow he colored the forehead. He made a set of fangs for him. From the feathers of the cotinga and spoonbill, he made his beard which was swept back.

After he had dressed and adorned Quetzalcoatl in this manner, he gave him the mirror. When Quetzalcoatl saw himself he was very pleased, and immediately left the place where he was hiding.

Then the artist Coyotlinahual went to tell Ihuimecatl, "I have forced Quetzalcoatl into the open. Now you go!"

He replied, "All right." And he made friends with Toltecatl, an expert with pulque.

Together they set out and journeyed to Xonacapacoyan (the place where onions are washed). They stayed with the farmer Maxtli, who was guardian of Toltec Mountain.

They began to make a savory stew from herbs, tomatoes, chili, green corn, and string beans. This was made in a few days.

In this area there were also maguey plants, and they asked Maxtli for some. In only four days they made pulque. They harvested the raw pulque, which was then brewed. Discovering some jugs of honey, they added this to the pulque.

Afterwards they went to Tollan, to the house of Quetzalcoatl. And they carried everything: the stew of herbs, chili, and other things. And the pulque.

They arrived for the showdown, but those who guarded Quetzalcoatl did not permit them to enter. Two or three times they returned without being received. Finally, they were asked where they came from. They answered, "From Priests' Mountain, Toltec Mountain." When Quetzalcoatl heard that, he said, "Let them enter."

They entered and greeted him. And at last they gave him the savory stew. After he ate, they pleaded with him again, trying to give him the pulque. But he told them "No, I will not drink it, because I am fasting. It might be intoxicating or deadly."

They said to him, "Try it with your little finger, because this brew is angry, it has power!"

Quetzalcoatl tried it with his finger and liked it. He said, "Grandfather, I am going to have three drinks more." He did this because the sorcerers had told him: "You have to drink at least four."

When they gave him a fifth drink, they said to him, "This is your *libation.*"

After he had his drinks, they served all his personal servants, five rounds of drinks to each of them. They drank them and became thoroughly drunk.

Again the sorcerers spoke to Quetzalcoatl: "My son, sing. Here is the song you are to sing." And Ihuimecatl sang:

> My green house of quetzal plumes
> My yellow house of oriole plumes
> My red house of coral
> I am leaving you *an ya.*

Feeling now so joyful, Quetzalcoatl said, "Go! Bring me my older sister, Quetzalpetlatl, that we might get drunk together."

His servants went to Mount Nonoalco, where she was doing penance, and said to her, "Lady, my daughter, the fasting Quetzalpetlatl, we have come to deliver you. The Priest Quetzalcoatl waits for you. Go and be with him!"

She replied, "Very well. Let us go, grandfather-servant."

When she arrived, she was seated next to Quetzalcoatl. Then they gave her four drinks of pulque, and one more, her *libation*—the fifth.

Having gotten them drunk, Ihuimecatl and Toltecatl performed a musical piece for Quetzalcoatl's older sister. They sang:

Oh Quetzalpetlatl
My sister
Where now do you dwell?
Here, where we drink too much.
Ayn ya ynya ynne an!

After getting intoxicated they no longer said, "But we are still penitents." No more did they go down to the stream. No more did they pierce themselves with spines. No more did they celebrate the dawn.

When they woke up they were filled with remorse, their hearts were broken.

Then Quetzalcoatl said, "My life is ruined!" And he sang the melancholy song which he had composed for his departure.

It is all over
A hard life begins in strange lands
No one wants to stay here now.
If only we could return to the old ways
If only I had the strength for a new kingdom
Never will I be afraid again.

And he sang the second verse of his song:

No more
Shall my mother support me *anya*!
She-of-the-Serpent-Skirt *an*!
A priestess *y yoa*
And her child *yyaa*!
I weep *yya yean*!

While Quetzalcoatl sang, all of his servants were filled with sadness and wept. In turn, they also sang:

In this fallen house
No more will my lords be rich
Quetzalcoatl, no more
With the crown of precious jewels
The beams have been stripped
We are miserable
We weep.

The Journey to the Black and Red Land

After his servants had finished singing, Quetzalcoatl said to them, "Grandfather-servants, that's enough! I am leaving the city. I am leaving. Order a coffin of stone for me."

Quickly a stone coffin was made. And when it was finished, they laid Quetzalcoatl in it.

For a period of four days he lay in the stone coffin. When he no longer felt well, he said to his servants: "That's enough, grandfather-servants! Let us go. Close off everything and hide the riches, the delightful things we discovered—all the beautiful things."

His servants obeyed his wishes. They hid the things where Quetzalcoatl bathed, the place called Atecpanamochco (Palace of Water). Other works were buried in mountains or in canyons.

It is said that Quetzalcoatl ordered that his houses be burned—his house of gold, his house of coral. He changed the cocoa trees into mesquites.

He ordered the birds with the beautiful feathers—the quetzal, the blue cotinga, the roseate spoonbill—to go ahead of him. And they departed for Anahuac.

And then Quetzalcoatl departed. He went on foot. He called all his servants together and wept with them. Then they departed for Tlillan Tlapallan (the Black and Red Land), the burning land.

Quetzalcoatl went down the road and arrived at a place called Cuauhtitlan. A very large tree grew there, broad and tall. He stood close to the tree, and asked his servants for a mirror. Looking at his face in the mirror, he said: "Truly I am old!" So named the place Huehuecuauhtitlan (Beside the Tree of Old Men).

Then he picked up stones and threw them at the tree. All the stones that Quetzalcoatl threw stuck in the tree. For a long time people could see them there. Everyone could see them, from the base of the tree to the top.

So Quetzalcoatl traveled down the road with flute players playing in front of him.

He arrived at another place where he rested placing his hands on a big rock; he then sat down on his hands. Looking back he saw Tollan in the distance, and began to weep with great sadness. The tears which he shed fell to the rock on which he was resting and made holes in it.

As he sat on his hands placed on the rock, he left imprints of his palms, as if they had been placed in mud. He also left the impression of his buttocks on the rock. These marks can be clearly seen today. So he named this place Temacpalco (Rock with Handprints).

Standing up, he then went on further, and arrived at a place called Tepanoayan (Stone Bridge), where a big, wide river flows by. Quetzalcoatl ordered a stone bridge, and it was built across the river. Quetzalcoatl then walked over the bridge, and so the place was called Tepanoayan.

Quetzalcoatl continued on his way and arrived at a place called Coaapan (Serpent's Water). Sorcerers met him there and tried to turn him back, to keep him from going further. They said, "Where are you going? Why did you leave your city? Who is your successor? Who is going to do penance?"

Quetzalcoatl replied to the sorcerers, "You cannot prevent me from going. I must go on."

So the sorcerers asked Quetzalcoatl, "Where are you going?" And Quetzalcoatl replied, "I am going to Tlapallan."

And they asked, "What will you do there?" And Quetzalcoatl answered, "I am called there, the sun has called me."

Thus they said to him, "Very well. Go then. But you must leave behind all the arts and crafts, the creations of the Toltecs." So he left behind all the arts: the casting of gold, the cutting of fine stones, the carving of wood, the painting of books, and the art of feather working.

The sorcerers took everything away from him, and Quetzalcoatl began to throw all of the lovely jewels that he had with him into a spring. And so he named this spring Cozcaapan (Jewels in the Water), the place that is now called Coaapan.

Then he continued on his way down the road. He arrived at a place called Cochtocan (Lying Down to Sleep). A sorcerer came out to meet him and said, "Where are you going?" And he answered, "I am going to Tlapallan."

So the sorcerer said, "Very well. Drink this wine which I brought for you." And Quetzalcoatl said, "No, I cannot drink it, not even a very small taste of it."

But the sorcerer demanded, "You must drink, or at least taste it. No one passes through here without drinking, and getting drunk. So, come! Drink it!"

Quetzalcoatl took the wine and drank it through a reed. Having finished it, he was drunk and fell asleep in the road. His snoring could be heard far and wide.

When he awoke he looked from one side to the other, and arranged his hair with his hand. After that he named this place Cochtocan.

Quetzalcoatl continued on his way, climbing up to a pass between two mountains, Popocatepetl and Iztactepetl. His servants, which were dwarfs and hunchbacks, accompanied him. It snowed, and they died from the cold. Quetzalcoatl felt very sad about the loss of his servants. He wept for them and sang a song of mourning and sighing.

In the distance he saw another white mountain named Poyauhtecatl. Then he visited many places and villages. They say that he left behind many signs of his passing, on the ground and along the roads.

They say that he played on a mountain, sliding down it from the top to the bottom. Maguey grows there now. He ordered a ball court, to be made from square stones. Through the middle of the court he made a line which opened deep into the earth.

At another place he used a silk-cotton tree as an arrow, and he shot it through another silk-cotton tree. In this manner he made a cross. They say he built underground houses at a place called Mictlan.

And furthermore, he erected a large phallic rock, which could be moved with the little finger. But it is said that when several men wanted to move and tilt the rock, they couldn't budge it, even though they were several.

There were many other famous things that Quetzalcoatl did in many villages. He gave names to all the mountains and to all the other places.

Quetzalcoatl's Death and Resurrection

He went seeking and exploring here and there, but no place really suited him. And yet, he arrived at the place for which he was searching. Again he was filled with sorrow, and there he wept.

They say that in the year 1-Reed, having arrived at the sacred shores of the holy sea, he stopped and wept. Then he gathered up his vestments and dressed himself for a ceremony, putting on his robes of quetzal feathers and his turquoise mask.

When he was finished dressing, he immediately set himself on fire, and was consumed by the flames. For this reason the place where Quetzalcoatl was burned is called Tlatlayan (Burning Place).

And it is said that as he burned, his ashes rose, and all the precious birds appeared, rising and circling in the sky: the scarlet guacamaya, the blue jay, the lovely thrush, the shining white bird, the parrots with their yellow feathers, and all the other precious birds.

When the ashes were gone, at that moment, the heart of Quetzalcoatl rose upward. They knew he had risen into the sky and entered the heavens.

The old ones say that he became the star that appears at dawn. They say that it appeared when Quetzalcoatl died, and because of this they named him Lord of the Dawn.

And they say that when he died he was not seen for four days. Thus he went to dwell among the dead in Mictlan. For four days he equipped himself with arrows. And that is why in eight days he appeared as the great star whose name is Quetzalcoatl.

And so it was that he then ascended his heavenly throne and became Lord.

The Poetry of Nezahualcoyotl

Translated by Miguel León-Portilla

"I, Nezahualcoyotl, ask this"

I, Nezahualcoyotl, ask this:
Is it true one really lives on the earth?
Not forever on earth,
only a little while here.
Though it be jade it falls apart,
though it be gold it wears away,
though it be quetzal plumage it is torn asunder.
Not forever on earth,
only a little while here.

"Are You real, are You rooted?"

Are You real, are You rooted?
Only You dominate all things,
the Giver of Life.
Is this true?
Perhaps, as they say, it is not true?

May our hearts
be not tormented;
All that is real
all that is rooted,
they say that it is not real,
that it is not rooted.
The Giver of Life
only appears absolute.

May our hearts
be not tormented,
because He is the Giver of Life.

"With flowers You write"

With flowers You write,
O Giver of Life;
With songs You give color,
with songs You shade
those who must live on the earth.
Later You will destroy eagles and ocelots;
we live only in Your book of paintings,
here, on the earth.

With black ink You will blot out
all that was friendship,
brotherhood, nobility.

You give shading
to those who must live on the earth.
We live only in Your book of paintings,
here on the earth.

"I COMPREHEND THE SECRET, THE HIDDEN"

I comprehend the secret, the hidden:
O my lords!

Thus we are,
we are mortal,
men through and through,
we all will have to go away,
we all will have to die on earth.
Like a painting,
we will be erased.
Like a flower,
we will dry up
here on earth.
Like plumed vestments of the precious bird,
that precious bird with the agile neck,
we will come to an end...
Think on this, my lords,
eagles and ocelots,
though you be of jade,
though you be of gold
you also will go there,
to the place of the fleshless.
We will have to disappear,
no one can remain.

"I AM INTOXICATED, I WEEP, I GRIEVE"

I am intoxicated, I weep, I grieve,
I think, I speak,
within myself I discover this:
indeed, I shall never die,
indeed, I shall never disappear.
There where there is no death,
there where death is overcome,
let me go there.
Indeed I shall never die,
indeed, I shall never disappear.

"There, alone, in the interior of heaven"

There, alone, in the interior of heaven
You invent Your word,
Giver of Life!
What will You decide?

Do You disdain us here?
Do You conceal Your fame
and Your glory on the earth?
What will You decide?
No one can be intimate
with the Giver of Life...
Then, where shall we go?
Direct yourselves,
We all go to the place of mystery.

The Conquest of Mexico[1]

Translated by Angel Maria Garibay K., Lysander Kemp, and David M. Johnson
Edited by Miguel León-Portilla

The Omens as Described by Sahagún's Informants

The first bad omen: Ten years before the Spaniards first came here, a bad omen appeared in the sky. It was like a flaming ear of corn, or a fiery signal, or the blaze of daybreak; it seemed to bleed fire, drop by drop, like a wound in the sky. It was wide at the base and narrow at the peak, and it shone in the very heart of the heavens.

This is how it appeared: it shone in the eastern sky in the middle of the night. It appeared at midnight and burned till the break of day, but it vanished at the rising of the sun. The time during which it appeared to us was a full year, beginning in the year 12-House.

When it first appeared, there was great outcry and confusion. The people clapped their hands against their mouths; they were amazed and frightened, and asked themselves what it could mean.

The second bad omen: The temple of Huitzilopochtli burst into flames. It is thought that no one set it afire, that it burned down of its own accord. The name of its divine site was Tlacateccan [House of Authority].

And now it is burning, the wooden columns are burning! The flames, the tongues of fire shoot out, the bursts of fire shoot up into the sky!

[1] Translated from Nahuatl into Spanish by Angel Maria Garibay K.; translated into English by Lysander Kemp. Our selection includes two chapters from Sahagún's *Historia General* that are not included in *The Broken Spears*; they are translated by David M. Johnson.

The flames swiftly destroyed all the woodwork of the temple. When the fire was first seen, the people shouted: "Mexicanos, come running! We can put it out! Bring your water jars . . . !" But when they threw water on the blaze it only flamed higher. They could not put it out, and the temple burned to the ground.

The third bad omen: A temple was damaged by a lightning-bolt. This was the temple of Xiuhtecuhtli, which was built of straw, in the place known as Tzonmolco. It was raining that day, but it was only a light rain or a drizzle, and no thunder was heard. Therefore the lightning-bolt was taken as an omen. The people said: "The temple was struck by a blow from the sun."

The fourth bad omen: Fire streamed through the sky while the sun was still shining. It was divided into three parts. It flashed out from where the sun sets and raced straight to where the sun rises, giving off a shower of sparks like a red-hot coal. When the people saw its long train streaming through the heavens, there was a great outcry and confusion, as if they were shaking a thousand little bells.

The fifth bad omen: The wind lashed the water until it boiled. It was as if it were boiling with rage, as if it were shattering itself in its frenzy. It began from far off, rose high in the air and dashed against the walls of the houses. The flooded houses collapsed into the water. This was in the lake that is next to us.

The sixth bad omen: The people heard a weeping woman night after night. She passed by in the middle of the night, wailing and crying out in a loud voice: "My children, we must flee far away from this city!" At other times she cried: "My children, where shall I take you?"[2]

The seventh bad omen: A strange creature was captured in the nets. The men who fish the lakes caught a bird the color of ashes, a bird resembling a crane. They brought it to Motecuhzoma in the Black House.

This bird wore a strange mirror in the crown of its head. The mirror was pierced in the center like a spindle whorl, and the night sky could be seen in its face. The hour was noon, but the stars and the *mamalhuaztli* could be seen in the face of that mirror. Motecuhzoma took it as a great and bad omen when he saw the stars and the *mamalhuaztli*.

But when he looked at the mirror a second time, he saw a distant plain. People were moving across it, spread out in ranks and coming forward in great haste. They made war against each other and rode on the backs of animals resembling deer.

Motecuhzoma called for his magicians and wise men and asked them: "Can you explain what I have seen? Creatures like human beings, running and fighting . . . !" But when they looked into the mirror to answer him, all had vanished away, and they saw nothing.

The eighth bad omen: Monstrous beings appeared in the streets of the city: deformed men with two heads but only one body. They were taken to the Black House and shown to Motecuhzoma; but the moment he saw them, they all vanished away.

Motecuhzoma Instructs His Messengers

Motecuhzoma then gave orders to Pinotl of Cuetlaxtlan and to other officials. He said to them: "Give out this order: a watch is to be kept along all the shores at Nauhtla, Tuztlan, Mictlancuauhtla, wherever the strangers appear." The officials left at once and gave orders for the watch to be kept.

---

[2]Perhaps a reference to Cihuacoatl, an earth goddess.

Motecuhzoma now called his chiefs together: Tlilpotonque, the serpent woman, Cuappiatzin, the chief of the house of arrows, Quetzalaztatzin, the keeper of the chalk, and Hecateupatiltzin, the chief of the refugees from the south. He told them the news that had been brought to him and showed them the objects he had ordered made. He said: "We all admire these blue turquoises, and they must be guarded well. The whole treasure must be guarded well. If anything is lost, your houses will be destroyed and your children killed, even those who are still in the womb."

The year 13-Rabbit now approached its end. And when it was about to end, they appeared, they were seen again. The report of their coming was brought to Motecuhzoma, who immediately sent out messengers. It was as if he thought the new arrival was our prince Quetzalcoatl.

This is what he felt in his heart: *He has appeared! He has come back! He will come here, to the place of his throne and canopy, for that is what he promised when he departed!*

Motecuhzoma sent five messengers to greet the strangers and to bring them gifts. They were led by the priest in charge of the sanctuary of Yohualichan. The second was from Tepoztlan; the third, from Tizatlan; the fourth, from Huehuetlan; and the fifth, from Mictlan the Great. He said to them: "Come forward, my Jaguar Knights, come forward. It is said that our lord has returned to this land. Go to meet him. Go to hear him. Listen well to what he tells you; listen and remember."

The Gifts Sent to the New Arrivals

Motecuhzoma also said to the messengers: "Here is what you are to bring our lord. This is the treasure of Quetzalcoatl." This treasure was the god's finery: a serpent mask inlaid with turquoise, a decoration for the breast made of quetzal feathers, a collar woven in the petatillo style[3] with a gold disk in the center, and a shield decorated with gold and mother-of-pearl and bordered with quetzal feathers with a pendant of the same feathers.

There was also a mirror like those which the ritual dancers wore on their buttocks. The reverse of this mirror was a turquoise mosaic: it was encrusted and adorned with turquoises. And there was a spear-thrower inlaid with turquoise, a bracelet of *chalchihuites*[4] hung with little gold bells and a pair of sandals as black as obsidian.

Motecuhzoma also gave them the finery of Tezcatlipoca. This finery was: a helmet in the shape of a cone, yellow with gold and set with many stars, a number of earrings adorned with little gold bells, a fringed and painted vest with feathers as delicate as foam and a blue cloak known as "the ringing bell," which reached to the ears and was fastened with a knot.

There was also a collar of fine shells to cover the breast. This collar was adorned with the finest snail shells, which seemed to escape from the edges. And there was a mirror to be hung in back, a set of little gold bells and a pair of white sandals.

Then Motecuhzoma gave them the finery of Tlaloc. This finery was: a headdress made of quetzal feathers, as green as if it were growing, with an ornament of gold and mother-of-pearl, earrings in the form of serpents, made of *chalchihuites,* a vest adorned with *chalchihuites* and a collar also of *chalchihuites,* woven in the petatillo style, with a disk of gold.

---

[3]Like a rush mat, but a finer weave.

[4]Green stones like jade and emerald.

There was also a serpent wand inlaid with turquoise, a mirror to be hung in back, with little bells, and a cloak bordered with red rings.

Then Motecuhzoma gave them the finery of Quetzalcoatl. This finery was: a diadem made of jaguar skin and pheasant feathers and adorned with a large green stone, round turquoise earrings with curved pendants of shell and gold, a collar of *chalchihuites* in the petatillo style with a disk of gold in the center, a cloak with red borders, and little gold bells for the feet.

There was also a golden shield, pierced in the middle, with quetzal feathers around the rim and a pendant of the same feathers, the crooked staff of Ehecatl with a cluster of white stones at the crook, and his sandals of fine soft rubber.

These were the many kinds of adornments that were known as "divine adornments." They were placed in the possession of the messengers to be taken as gifts of welcome along with many other objects, such as a golden snail shell and a golden diadem. All these objects were packed into great baskets; they were loaded into panniers for the long journey.

Then Motecuhzoma gave the messengers his final orders. He said to them: "Go now, without delay. Do reverence to our lord the god. Say to him: 'Your deputy, Motecuhzoma, has sent us to you. Here are the presents with which he welcomes you home to Mexico.' "

The Messengers Contact the Spaniards

When they arrived at the shore of the sea, they were taken in canoes to Xicalanco. They placed the baskets in the same canoes in which they rode, in order to keep them under their personal vigilance. From Xicalanco they followed the coast until they sighted the ships of the strangers.

When they came up to the ships, the strangers asked them: "Who are you? Where are you from?"

"We have come from the City of Mexico."[5]

The strangers said: "You may have come from there, or you may not have. Perhaps you are only inventing it. Perhaps you are mocking us." But their hearts were convinced; they were satisfied in their hearts. They lowered a hook from the bow of the ship, and then a ladder, and the messengers came aboard.

One by one they did reverence to Cortés by touching the ground before him with their lips. They said to him: "If the god will deign to hear us, your deputy Motecuhzoma has sent us to render you homage. He has the City of Mexico in his care. He says: 'The god is weary.' "

Then they arrayed the Captain in the finery they had brought him as presents. With great care they fastened the turquoise mask in place, the mask of the god with its crossband of quetzal feathers. A golden earring hung down on either side of this mask. They dressed him in the decorated vest and the collar woven in the petatillo style—the collar of *chalchihuites,* with a disk of gold in the center.

Next they fastened the mirror to his hips, dressed him in the cloak known as "the ringing bell" and adorned his feet with the greaves used by the Huastecas,

[5]The Spaniards and messengers could communicate because of La Malinche (called Doña Marina by the Spanish), an Indian from the Gulf Coast who spoke Mayan and Nahuatl, and Jerónimo de Aguilar, who spoke Mayan and Spanish.

which were set with *chalchihuites* and hung with little gold bells. In his hand they placed the shield with its fringe and pendant of quetzal feathers, its ornaments of gold and mother-of-pearl. Finally they set before him the pair of black sandals. As for the other objects of divine finery, they only laid them out for him to see.

The Captain then asked them: "And is this all? Is this your gift of welcome? Is this how you greet people?"

They replied: "This is all, our lord. This is what we have brought you."

Cortés Frightens the Messengers

Then the Captain gave orders, and the messengers were chained by the feet and by the neck. When this had been done, the great cannon was fired off. The messengers lost their senses and fainted away. They fell down side by side and lay where they had fallen. But the Spaniards quickly revived them: they lifted them up, gave them wine to drink and then offered them food.

The Captain said to them: "I have heard that the Mexicans are very great warriors, very brave and terrible. If a Mexican is fighting alone, he knows how to retreat, turn back, rush forward and conquer, even if his opponents are ten or even twenty. But my heart is not convinced. I want to see it for myself. I want to find out if you are truly that strong and brave."

Then he gave them swords, spears and leather shields. He said: "It will take place very early, at daybreak. We are going to fight each other in pairs, and in this way we will learn the truth. We will see who falls to the ground!"

They said to the Captain: "Our lord, we were not sent here for this by your deputy Motecuhzoma! We have come on an exclusive mission, to offer you rest and repose and to bring you presents. What the lord desires is not within our warrant. If we were to do this, it might anger Motecuhzoma, and he would surely put us to death."

The Captain replied: "No, it must take place. I want to see for myself, because even in Castile they say you are famous as brave warriors. Therefore, eat an early meal. I will eat too. Good cheer!"

With these words he sent them away from the ship. They were scarcely into their canoes when they began to paddle furiously. Some of them even paddled with their hands, so fierce was the anxiety burning in their souls. They said to each other: "My captains, paddle with all your might! Faster, faster! Nothing must happen to us here! Nothing must happen . . . !"

They arrived in great haste at Xicalanco, took a hurried meal there, and then pressed on until they came to Tecpantlayacac. From there they rushed ahead and arrived in Cuetlaxtlan. As on the previous journey, they stopped there to rest. When they were about to depart, the village official said to them: "Rest for at least a day! At least catch your breath!"

They said: "No, we must keep on! We must report to our king, Motecuhzoma. We will tell him what we have seen, and it is a terrifying thing. Nothing like it has ever been seen before!" Then they left in great haste and continued to the City of Mexico. They entered the city at night, in the middle of the night.

Motecuhzoma Awaits Word from the Messengers

While the messengers were away, Motecuhzoma could neither sleep nor eat, and no one could speak with him. He thought that everything he did was in vain, and he sighed almost every moment. He was lost in despair, in the deepest gloom and sorrow. Nothing could comfort him, nothing could calm him, nothing could give him any pleasure.

He said: "What will happen to us? Who will outlive it? Ah, in other times I was contented, but now I have death in my heart! My heart burns and suffers, as if it were drowned in spices . . . ! But will our lord come here?"

Then he gave orders to the watchmen, to the men who guarded the palace: "Tell me, even if I am sleeping: 'The messengers have come back from the sea.'" But when they went to tell him, he immediately said: "They are not to report to me here. I will receive them in the House of the Serpent. Tell them to go there." And he gave this order: "Two captives are to be painted with chalk."

The messengers went to the House of the Serpent, and Motecuhzoma arrived. The two captives were then sacrificed before his eyes: their breasts were torn open, and the messengers were sprinkled with their blood. This was done because the messengers had completed a difficult mission: they had seen the gods, their eyes had looked on their faces. They had even conversed with the gods!

The Messengers' Report

When the sacrifice was finished, the messengers reported to the king. They told him how they had made the journey, and what they had seen, and what food the strangers ate. Motecuhzoma was astonished and terrified by their report, and the description of the strangers' food astonished him above all else.

He was also terrified to learn how the cannon roared, how its noise resounded, how it caused one to faint and grow deaf. The messengers told him: "A thing like a ball of stone comes out of its entrails: it comes out shooting sparks and raining fire. The smoke that comes out with it has a pestilent odor, like that of rotten mud. This odor penetrates even to the brain and causes the greatest discomfort. If the cannon is aimed against a mountain, the mountain splits and cracks open. If the cannon is aimed against a tree, it shatters the tree into splinters. This is a most unnatural sight, as if the tree had exploded from within."

The messengers also said: "Their trappings and arms are all made of iron. They dress in iron and wear iron casques on their heads. Their swords are iron; their bows are iron; their shields are iron; their spears are iron. Their deer carry them on their backs wherever they wish to go. These deer, our lord, are as tall as the roof of a house.

"The strangers' bodies are completely covered, so that only their faces can be seen. Their skin is white, as if it were made of lime. They have yellow hair, though some of them have black. Their beards are long and yellow, and their moustaches are also yellow. Their hair is curly, with very fine strands.

"As for their food, it is like human food. It is large and white, and not heavy. It is something like straw, but with the taste of a cornstalk, of the pith of a cornstalk. It is a little sweet, as if it were flavored with honey; it tastes of honey, it is sweet-tasting food.

"Their dogs are enormous, with flat ears and long, dangling tongues. The color of their eyes is a burning yellow; their eyes flash fire and shoot off sparks. Their bellies are hollow, their flanks long and narrow. They are tireless and very powerful. They bound here and there, panting, with their tongues hanging out. And they are spotted like an ocelot."

When Motecuhzoma heard this report, he was filled with terror. It was as if his heart had fainted, as if it had shriveled. It was as if he were conquered by despair.[6]

The Spaniards March Inland

At last they came. At last they began to march toward us.

A man from Cempoala, who was known as the Tlacochcalcatl [Chief of the House of Arrows], was the first official to welcome them as they entered our lands and cities. This man spoke Nahuatl. He showed them the best routes and the shortest ways; he guided and advised them, traveling at the head of the party.

When they came to Tecoac, in the land of the Tlaxcaltecas, they found it was inhabited by Otomies. The Otomies came out to meet them in battle array; they greeted the strangers with their shields.

But the strangers conquered the Otomies of Tecoac; they utterly destroyed them. They divided their ranks, fired the cannons at them, attacked them with their swords and shot them with their crossbows. Not just a few, but all of them, perished in the battle.

And when Tecoac had been defeated, the Tlaxcaltecas soon heard the news; they learned what had taken place there. They felt premonitions of death: terror overwhelmed them, and they were filled with foreboding.

Therefore the chiefs assembled; the captains met together in a council. They talked about what had happened, and said: "What shall we do? Shall we go out to meet them? The Otomi is a brave warrior, but he was helpless against them: they scorned him as a mere nothing! They destroyed the poor *macehual* with a look, with a glance of their eyes! We should go over to their side: we should make friends with them and be their allies. If not, they will destroy us too. . . ."

The Arrival at Tlaxcala

Therefore the lords of Tlaxcala went out to meet them, bringing many things to eat: hens and hens' eggs and the finest tortillas. They said to the strangers: "Our lords, you are weary."

The strangers replied: "Where do you live? Where are you from?"

They said: "We are from Tlaxcala. You have come here, you have entered our land. We are from Tlaxcala; our city is the City of the Eagle, Tlaxcala." (For in ancient times it was called Texcala, and its people were known as Texcaltecas.)

Then they guided them to the city; they brought them there and invited them to enter. They paid them great honors, attended to their every want, joined with them as allies and even gave them their daughters.

The Spaniards asked: "Where is the City of Mexico? Is it far from here?"

They said: "No, it is not far, it is only a three-day march. And it is a great city. The Aztecs are very brave. They are great warriors and conquerors and have defeated their neighbors on every side."

---

[6]Motecuhzoma sent out wizards and magicians to stop the advance of the Spaniards, but they failed. The Spaniards continued their march.

Intrigues against Cholula

At this time the Tlaxcaltecas were enemies of Cholula. They feared the Cholultecas; they envied and cursed them; their souls burned with hatred for the people of Cholula. This is why they brought certain rumors to Cortés, so that he would destroy them. They said to him: "Cholula is our enemy. It is an evil city. The people are as brave as the Aztecs and they are the Aztecs' friends."

When the Spaniards heard this, they marched against Cholula. They were guided and accompanied by the Tlaxcaltecas and the chiefs from Cempoala, and they all marched in battle array.

The Massacre at Cholula

When they arrived, the Tlaxcaltecas and the men of Cholula called to each other and shouted greetings. An assembly was held in the courtyard of the god, but when they had all gathered together, the entrances were closed, so that there was no way of escaping.

Then the sudden slaughter began: knife strokes, and sword strokes, and death. The people of Cholula had not foreseen it, had not suspected it. They faced the Spaniards without weapons, without their swords or their shields. The cause of the slaughter was treachery. They died blindly, without knowing why, because of the lies of the Tlaxcaltecas.

And when this had taken place, word of it was brought to Motecuhzoma. The messengers came and departed, journeying back and forth between Tenochtitlán and Cholula. The common people were terrified by the news; they could do nothing but tremble with fright. It was as if the earth trembled beneath them, or as if the world were spinning before their eyes, as it spins during a fit of vertigo. . . .

When the massacre at Cholula was complete, the strangers set out again toward the City of Mexico. They came in battle array, as conquerors, and the dust rose in whirlwinds on the roads. Their spears glinted in the sun, and their pennons fluttered like bats. They made a loud clamour as they marched, for their coats of mail and their weapons clashed and rattled. Some of them were dressed in glistening iron from head to foot; they terrified everyone who saw them.

Their dogs came with them, running ahead of the column. They raised their muzzles high; they lifted their muzzles to the wind. They raced on before with saliva dripping from their jaws.

The Spaniards See the Objects of Gold

Then Motecuhzoma dispatched various chiefs. Tzihuacpopocatzin was at their head, and he took with him a great many of his representatives. They went out to meet the Spaniards in the vicinity of Popocatepetl and Iztactepetl, there in the Eagle Pass.

They gave the "gods" ensigns of gold, and ensigns of quetzal feathers, and golden necklaces. And when they were given these presents, the Spaniards burst into smiles; their eyes shone with pleasure; they were delighted by them. They picked up the gold and fingered it like monkeys; they seemed to be transported by joy, as if their hearts were illumined and made new.

The truth is that they longed and lusted for gold. Their bodies swelled with greed, and their hunger was ravenous; they hungered like pigs for that gold. They snatched at the golden ensigns, waved them from side to side and examined every inch of them. They were like one who speaks a barbarous tongue: everything they said was in a barbarous tongue.

TZIHUACPOPOCATZIN PRETENDS TO BE MOTECUHZOMA

When they saw Tzihuacpopocatzin, they asked: "Is this Motecuhzoma, by any chance?" They asked this of their allies, the liars from Tlaxcala and Cempoala, their shrewd and deceitful confederates.

They replied: "He is not Motecuhzoma, our lords. He is his envoy Tzihuacpopocatzin."

The Spaniards asked him: "Are you Motecuhzoma, by any chance?"

"Yes," he said, "I am your servant. I am Motecuhzoma."

But the allies said: "You fool! Why try to deceive us? Who do you think we are?" And they said:

> "You cannot deceive us; you cannot make fools of us.
> You cannot frighten us; you cannot blind our eyes.
> You cannot stare us down; we will not look away.
> You cannot bewitch our eyes or turn them aside.
> You cannot dim our eyes or make them swoon.
> You cannot fill them with dust or shut them with slime.
>
> "You are not Motecuhzoma: he is there in his city.
> He cannot hide from us. Where can he go?
> Can he fly away like a bird? Can he tunnel the earth?
> Can he burrow into a mountain, to hide inside it?
> We are coming to see him, to meet him face to face.
> We are coming to hear his words from his own lips."

They taunted and threatened the envoys in this fashion, and the gifts of welcome and the greetings were another failure. Therefore the envoys hastened back to the city.

THE APPARITION OF TEZCATLIPOCA

But then there was another series of envoys: magicians, wizards and priests. They also left the city and went out to meet the strangers, but they were completely helpless: they could not blind their eyes or overcome them in any way.

They even failed to meet and speak with the "gods," because a certain drunkard blundered across their path. He used gestures that are used by the people of Chalco, and he was dressed like a Chalca, with eight cords of couch-grass across his breast. He seemed to be very drunk; he feigned drunkenness; he pretended to be a drunkard.

He came up to them while they were about to meet the Spaniards. He rushed up to the Mexicanos and cried: "Why have you come here? For what purpose? What is it you want? What is Motecuhzoma trying to do? Has he still not recovered his wits? Does he still tremble and beg? He has committed many errors and destroyed a multitude of people. Some have been beaten and others wrapped in shrouds; some have been betrayed and others mocked and derided."

When the magicians heard these words, they tried in vain to approach him. They wanted to ask his help, and they hurriedly built him a small temple and altar and a seat made of couch-grass. But for a while they could not see him.

They labored in vain, they prepared his temple in vain, for he spoke to them only in oracles. He terrified them with his harsh reproofs and spoke to them as if from a great distance: "Why have you come here? It is useless. Mexico will be destroyed! Mexico will be left in ruins!" He said: "Go back, go back! Turn your eyes toward the city. What was fated to happen has already taken place!"

They looked in the direction of Tenochtitlán. The temples were in flames, and so were the communal halls, the religious schools and all the houses. It was as if a great battle were raging in the city.

When the magicians saw this, they lost heart. They could not speak clearly, but talked as if they were drunk: "It was not proper for us to have seen this vision. Motecuhzoma himself should have beheld it! This was not a mere mortal. This was the young Tezcatlipoca!"

Suddenly the god disappeared, and they saw him no longer. The envoys did not go forward to meet the Spaniards; they did not speak with them. The priests and magicians turned and went back to report to Motecuhzoma.

Motecuhzoma's Despair

When the envoys arrived in the city, they told Motecuhzoma what had happened and what they had seen. Motecuhzoma listened to their report and then bowed his head without speaking a word. For a long time he remained thus, with his head bent down. And when he spoke at last, it was only to say: "What help is there now, my friends? Is there a mountain for us to climb? Should we run away? We are Mexicanos: would this bring any glory to the Mexican nation?

"Pity the old men, and the old women, and the innocent little children. How can they save themselves? But there is no help. What can we do? Is there nothing left us?

"We will be judged and punished. And however it may be, and whenever it may be, we can do nothing but wait."

Motecuhzoma Commands That the Road Be Closed[7]

Motecuhzoma in vain commanded that the road be closed off. They planted the one to Mexico with a wall of maguey plants. The Spaniards saw through this plan of blocking the road. They tore up the maguey plants and threw them away.

They slept at Amaquemecan. The next day they left there and traveled to Cuitlauac and spent the night.

They assembled the rulers who were responsible for the people of the floating gardens—Xochimilco, Cuitlauac, Mizquic. They spoke to them in the same way that they had spoken to the Chalcan rulers. And these rulers of the people of the floating gardens at once also submitted to them.

When the Spaniards were satisfied, they moved on, resting at Itztapalapan. They summoned the local rulers who were known as the Four Lords: of Itztapalapan, of Mexicatzinco, of Colhuacan, of Uitzilopochco. In the same manner as they had spoken to others, they spoke to these rulers, who peacefully submitted to the Spaniards.

[7]The next two sections were translated by David M. Johnson.

Motecuhzoma did not command that war should be made against them. No one was to fight them. He commanded only that they not be ignored.

When this happened, it was as if Mexico lay silent. No one went outside. Mothers kept their children in. The roads were empty, wide open as in early morning. People stayed in their houses with their fears. They spoke to each other: "Let happen what will happen. We are ready to die. The time comes when we will be destroyed. Here we await our death."

The Spaniards Travel from Itztapalapan to Mexico

On the last stage of the journey to Mexico, the Spaniards put on their battle dress. They arranged their horses into neat and orderly rows.

Four horsemen went in front as the vanguard. And as they went they continually turned around facing the people, looking here and there. They looked at all the houses, they looked up at the roof terraces. They also had their dogs in the procession, which panted and sniffed at things.

A lone standard bearer marched along holding the standard on his shoulders and shaking it from side to side in the breeze. Bobbing up and down it looked like a warrior.

Following him came the bearers of iron swords, which flashed in the sun. They carried their wooden and leather shields on their shoulders.

In a second group came the soldiers on horses wearing their cotton breast protectors. They carried leather shields, iron swords and lances hanging at the horses' necks. Each horse had bells which loudly rang. The horses which were thought to be deer, neighed and sweat. They sweat so much it looked as if water flowed from them. Flecks of foam bubbled from their mouths like soapsuds. Their hooves beat on the ground with the sound of pounding stones. Each hoof left its mark in the ground, both the forelegs and the hind legs.

In the third group came the men with the iron crossbows, which were carried in their arms. Some pointed the crossbows here and there, while others rested them on their shoulders. Their quivers hung at their sides filled with iron tipped arrows. Their dense, close-woven cotton armor reached to their knees. Their heads were covered in the same way with cotton armor, which had precious feathers sticking out on top.

The fourth group had horsemen dressed like the second.

The fifth group carried arquebuses on their shoulders. Some had them pointed upwards and fired them when they entered the great palace, the residence of the rulers. The shots were like explosions of thunder with large clouds of smoke spreading around. It smelled awful and some people fainted.

At the very rear came the commander, who was the same as the *tlacateccatl,* the battle chief. Surrounding him were his personal attendants and his insignia bearers, who were like the brave Otomi warriors attending the Mexica rulers.

Following behind were warriors from distant cities—the Tlaxcallan, the Tliliuhquitepecan, the Huexotzincan. They were dressed for war, each in his cotton armor, each with his shield, each with his bow. Each one's quiver was filled with feathered arrows, some with barbed points, some blunted, some obsidian-pointed. They walked in a crouch, yelling and striking their mouths with their hands. They sang the Tocuillan song while whistling and shaking their heads. Some carried supplies on their backs with a tump line around their foreheads or a band around their chests. Some used frames or deep baskets for their loads. Other men dragged the great lombard guns which rested on wooden wheels. They sang as they moved them along.

Motecuhzoma Goes Out to Meet Cortés

The Spaniards arrived in Xoloco, near the entrance to Tenochtitlán. That was the end of the march, for they had reached their goal.

Motecuhzoma now arrayed himself in his finery, preparing to go out to meet them. The other great princes also adorned their persons, as did the nobles and their chieftains and knights. They all went out together to meet the strangers.

They brought trays heaped with the finest flowers—the flower that resembles a shield; the flower shaped like a heart; in the center, the flower with the sweetest aroma; and the fragrant yellow flower, the most precious of all. They also brought garlands of flowers, and ornaments for the breast, and necklaces of gold, necklaces hung with rich stones, necklaces fashioned in the petatillo style.

Thus Motecuhzoma went out to meet them, there in Huitzillan. He presented many gifts to the Captain and his commanders, those who had come to make war. He showered gifts upon them and hung flowers around their necks; he gave them necklaces of flowers and bands of flowers to adorn their breasts; he set garlands of flowers upon their heads. Then he hung the gold necklaces around their necks and gave them presents of every sort as gifts of welcome.

Speeches of Motecuhzoma and Cortés

When Motecuhzoma had given necklaces to each one, Cortés asked him: "Are you Motecuhzoma? Are you the king? Is it true that you are the king Motecuhzoma?"

And the king said: "Yes, I am Motecuhzoma." Then he stood up to welcome Cortés; he came forward, bowed his head low and addressed him in these words: "Our lord, you are weary. The journey has tired you, but now you have arrived on the earth. You have come to your city, Mexico. You have come here to sit on your throne, to sit under its canopy.

"The kings who have gone before, your representatives, guarded it and preserved it for your coming. The kings Itzcoatl, Motecuhzoma the Elder, Axayacatl, Tizoc and Ahuitzol ruled for you in the City of Mexico. The people were protected by their swords and sheltered by their shields.

"Do the kings know the destiny of those they left behind, their posterity? If only they are watching! If only they can see what I see!

"No, it is not a dream. I am not walking in my sleep. I am not seeing you in my dreams. . . . I have seen you at last! I have met you face to face! I was in agony for five days, for ten days, with my eyes fixed on the Region of the Mystery. And now you have come out of the clouds and mists to sit on your throne again.

"This was foretold by the kings who governed your city, and now it has taken place. You have come back to us; you have come down from the sky. Rest now, and take possession of your royal houses. Welcome to your land, my lords!"

When Motecuhzoma had finished, La Malinche translated his address into Spanish so that the Captain could understand it. Cortés replied in his strange and savage tongue, speaking first to La Malinche: "Tell Motecuhzoma that we are his friends. There is nothing to fear. We have wanted to see him for a long time, and now we have seen his face and heard his words. Tell him that we love him well and that our hearts are contented."

Then he said to Motecuhzoma: "We have come to your house in Mexico as friends. There is nothing to fear."

La Malinche translated this speech and the Spaniards grasped Motecuhzoma's hands and patted his back to show their affection for him.

Attitudes of the Spaniards and the Native Lords

The Spaniards examined everything they saw. They dismounted from their horses, and mounted them again, and dismounted again, so as not to miss anything of interest.

The chiefs who accompanied Motecuhzoma were: Cacama, king of Tezcoco; Tetlepanquetzaltzin, king of Tlacopan; Itzcuauhtzin the Tlacochcalcatl, lord of Tlatelolco; and Topantemoc, Motecuhzoma's treasurer in Tlatelolco. These four chiefs were standing in a file.

The other princes were: Atlixcatzin [chief who has taken captives]; Tepeoatzin, The Tlacochcalcatl; Quetzalaztatzin, the keeper of the chalk; Totomotzin; Hecateupatiltzin; and Cuappiatzin.

When Motechuzoma was imprisoned, they all went into hiding. They ran away to hide and treacherously abandoned him!

The Spaniards Take Possession of the City

When the Spaniards entered the Royal House, they placed Motecuhzoma under guard and kept him under their vigilance. They also placed a guard over Itzcuauhtzin, but the other lords were permitted to depart.

Then the Spaniards fired one of their cannons, and this caused great confusion in the city. The people scattered in every direction; they fled without rhyme or reason; they ran off as if they were being pursued. It was as if they had eaten the mushrooms that confuse the mind, or had seen some dreadful apparition. They were all overcome by terror, as if their hearts had fainted. And when night fell, the panic spread through the city and their fears would not let them sleep.

In the morning the Spaniards told Motecuhzoma what they needed in the way of supplies: tortillas, fried chickens, hens' eggs, pure water, firewood and charcoal. Also: large, clean cooking pots, water jars, pitchers, dishes and other pottery. Motecuhzoma ordered that it be sent to them. The chiefs who received this order were angry with the king and no longer revered or respected him. But they furnished the Spaniards with all the provisions they needed—food, beverages and water, and fodder for the horses.

The Spaniards Reveal Their Greed

When the Spaniards were installed in the palace, they asked Motecuhzoma about the city's resources and reserves and about the warriors' ensigns and shields. They questioned him closely and then demanded gold.

Motecuhzoma guided them to it. They surrounded him and crowded close with their weapons. He walked in the center, while they formed a circle around him.

When they arrived at the treasure house called Teucalco, the riches of gold and feathers were brought out to them: ornaments made of quetzal feathers, richly worked shields, disks of gold, the necklaces of the idols, gold nose plugs, gold greaves and bracelets and crowns.

The Spaniards immediately stripped the feathers from the gold shields and ensigns. They gathered all the gold into a great mound and set fire to everything else, regardless of its value. Then they melted down the gold into ingots. As for the precious green stones, they took only the best of them; the rest were snatched up by the Tlaxcaltecas. The Spaniards searched through the whole treasure house, questioning and quarreling, and seized every object they thought was beautiful.

The Seizure of Motecuhzoma's Treasures

Next they went to Motecuhzoma's storehouse, in the place called Totocalco [Place of the Palace of the Birds], where his personal treasures were kept. The Spaniards grinned like little beasts and patted each other with delight.

When they entered the hall of treasures, it was as if they had arrived in Paradise. They searched everywhere and coveted everything; they were slaves to their own greed. All of Motecuhzoma's possessions were brought out: fine bracelets, necklaces with large stones, ankle rings with little gold bells, the royal crowns and all the royal finery—everything that belonged to the king and was reserved to him only. They seized these treasures as if they were their own, as if this plunder were merely a stroke of good luck. And when they had taken all the gold, they heaped up everything else in the middle of the patio.

La Malinche called the nobles together. She climbed up to the palace roof and cried: "Mexicanos, come forward! The Spaniards need your help! Bring them food and pure water. They are tired and hungry; they are almost fainting from exhaustion! Why do you not come forward? Are you angry with them?"

The Mexicans were too frightened to approach. They were crushed by terror and would not risk coming forward. They shied away as if the Spaniards were wild beasts, as if the hour were midnight on the blackest night of the year. Yet they did not abandon the Spaniards to hunger and thirst. They brought them whatever they needed, but shook with fear as they did so. They delivered the supplies to the Spaniards with trembling hands, then turned and hurried away.

The Preparations for the Fiesta

The Aztecs begged permission of their king to hold the fiesta of Huitzilopochtli. The Spaniards wanted to see this fiesta to learn how it was celebrated. A delegation of the celebrants came to the palace where Motecuhzoma was a prisoner, and when their spokesman asked his permission, he granted it to them.

As soon as the delegation returned, the women began to grind seeds of the chicalote. These women had fasted for a whole year. They ground the seeds in the patio of the temple.

The Spaniards came out of the palace together, dressed in armor and carrying their weapons with them. They stalked among the women and looked at them one by one; they stared into the faces of the women who were grinding seeds. After this cold inspection, they went back into the palace. It is said that they planned to kill the celebrants if the men entered the patio.

The Statue of Huitzilopochtli

On the evening before the fiesta of Toxcatl, the celebrants began to model a statue of Huitzilopochtli. They gave it such a human appearance that it seemed the body of a living man. Yet they made the statue with nothing but a paste made of the ground seeds of the chicalote, which they shaped over an armature of sticks.

When the statue was finished, they dressed it in rich feathers, and they painted crosses over and under its eyes. They also clipped on its earrings of turquoise mosaic; these were in the shape of serpents, with gold rings hanging from them. Its nose plug, in the shape of an arrow, was made of gold and was inlaid with fine stones.

They placed the magic headdress of hummingbird feathers on its head. They also adorned it with an *anecuyotl,* which was a belt made of feathers, with a cone at the back. Then they hung around its neck an ornament of yellow parrot feathers, fringed like the locks of a young boy. Over this they put its nettle-leaf cape, which was painted black and decorated with five clusters of eagle feathers.

Next they wrapped it in its cloak, which was painted with skulls and bones, and over this they fastened its vest. The vest was painted with dismembered human parts: skulls, ears, hearts, intestines, torsos, breasts, hands and feet. They also put on its *maxtlatl,* or loincloth, which was decorated with images of dissevered limbs and fringed with amate paper. This *maxlatl* was painted with vertical stripes of bright blue.

They fastened a red paper flag at its shoulder and placed on its head what looked like a sacrificial flint knife. This too was made of red paper; it seemed to have been steeped in blood.

The statue carried a *tehuehuelli,* a bamboo shield decorated with four clusters of fine eagle feathers. The pendant of this shield was blood-red, like the knife and the shoulder flag. The statue also carried four arrows.

Finally, they put the wristbands on its arms. These bands, made of coyote skin, were fringed with paper cut into little strips.

The Beginning of the Fiesta

Early the next morning, the statue's face was uncovered by those who had been chosen for that ceremony. They gathered in front of the idol in single file and offered it gifts of food, such as round seedcakes or perhaps human flesh. But they did not carry it up to its temple on top of the pyramid.

All the young warriors were eager for the fiesta to begin. They had sworn to dance and sing with all their hearts, so that the Spaniards would marvel at the beauty of the rituals.

The procession began, and the celebrants filed into the temple patio to dance the Dance of the Serpent. When they were all together in the patio, the songs and the dance began. Those who had fasted for twenty days and those who had fasted for a year were in command of the others; they kept the dancers in file with their pine wands. (If anyone wished to urinate, he did not stop dancing, but simply opened his clothing at the hips and separated his clusters of heron feathers.)

If anyone disobeyed the leaders or was not in his proper place they struck him on the hips and shoulders. Then they drove him out of the patio, beating him and shoving him from behind. They pushed him so hard that he sprawled to the ground, and they dragged him outside by the ears. No one dared to say a word about this punishment, for those who had fasted during the year were feared and venerated; they had earned the exclusive title "Brothers of Huitzilopochtli."

The great captains, the bravest warriors, danced at the head of the files to guide the others. The youths followed at a slight distance. Some of the youths wore their hair gathered into large locks, a sign that they had never taken any captives. Others carried their headdresses on their shoulders; they had taken captives, but only with help.

Then came the recruits, who were called "the young warriors." They had each captured an enemy or two. The others called to them: "Come, comrades, show us how brave you are! Dance with all your hearts! "

The Spaniards Attack the Celebrants

At this moment in the fiesta, when the dance was loveliest and when song was linked to song, the Spaniards were seized with an urge to kill the celebrants. They all ran forward, armed as if for battle. They closed the entrances and passageways, all the gates of the patio: the Eagle Gate in the lesser palace, the Gate of the Canestalk and the Gate of the Serpent of Mirrors. They posted guards so that no one could escape, and then rushed into the Sacred Patio to slaughter the celebrants. They came on foot, carrying their swords and their wooden or metal shields.

They ran in among the dancers, forcing their way to the place where the drums were played. They attacked the man who was drumming and cut off his arms. Then they cut off his head, and it rolled across the floor.

They attacked all the celebrants, stabbing them, spearing them, striking them with their swords. They attacked some of them from behind, and these fell instantly to the ground with their entrails hanging out. Others they beheaded: they cut off their heads, or split their heads to pieces.

They struck others in the shoulders, and their arms were torn from their bodies. They wounded some in the thigh and some in the calf. They slashed others in the abdomen, and their entrails all spilled to the ground. Some attempted to run away, but their intestines dragged as they ran; they seemed to tangle their feet in their own entrails. No matter how they tried to save themselves, they could find no escape.

Some attempted to force their way out, but the Spaniards murdered them at the gates. Others climbed the walls, but they could not save themselves. Those who ran into the communal houses were safe there for a while; so were those who lay down among the victims and pretended to be dead. But if they stood up again, the Spaniards saw them and killed them.

The blood of the warriors flowed like water and gathered into pools. The pools widened, and the stench of blood and entrails filled the air. The Spaniards ran into the communal houses to kill those who were hiding. They ran everywhere and searched everywhere; they invaded every room, hunting and killing.

The Aztecs Retaliate

When the news of this massacre was heard outside the Sacred Patio, a great cry went up: "Mexicanos, come running! Bring your spears and shields! The strangers have murdered our warriors!"

This cry was answered with a roar of grief and anger: the people shouted and wailed and beat their palms against their mouths. The captains assembled at once, as if the hour had been determined in advance. They all carried their spears and shields.

Then the battle began. The Aztecs attacked with javelins and arrows, even with the light spears that are used for hunting birds. They hurled their javelins with all their strength, and the cloud of missiles spread out over the Spaniards like a yellow cloak.

The Spaniards immediately took refuge in the palace. They began to shoot at the Mexicans with their iron arrows and to fire their cannons and arquebuses. And they shackled Motecuhzoma in chains.

The Lament for the Dead

The Mexicans who had died in the massacre were taken out of the patio one by one and inquiries were made to discover their names. The fathers and mothers of the dead wept and lamented.

Each victim was taken first to his own home and then to the Sacred Patio, where all the dead were brought together. Some of the bodies were later burned in the place called the Eagle Urn, and others in the House of the Young Men.

Motecuhzoma's Message

At sunset, Itzcuauhtzin climbed onto the roof of the palace and shouted this proclamation: "Mexicanos! Tlatelolcas! Your king, the lord Motecuhzoma, has sent me to speak for him. Mexicanos, hear me, for these are his words to you: 'We must not fight them. We are not their equals in battle. Put down your shields and arrows.'

"He tells you this because it is the aged who will suffer most, and they deserve your pity. The humblest classes will also suffer, and so will the innocent children who still crawl on all fours, who still sleep in their cradles.

"Therefore your king says: 'We are not strong enough to defeat them. Stop fighting, and return to your homes.' Mexicanos, they have put your king in chains; his feet are bound with chains."

When Itzcuauhtzin had finished speaking, there was a great uproar among the people. They shouted insults at him in their fury, and cried: "Who is Motecuhzoma to give us orders? We are no longer his slaves!" They shouted war cries and fired arrows at the rooftop. The Spaniards quickly hid Motecuhzoma and Itzcuauhtzin behind their shields so that the arrows would not find them.

The Mexicans were enraged because the attack on the captains had been so treacherous: their warriors had been killed without the slightest warning. Now they refused to go away or to put down their arms.

The Spaniards Are Besieged

The royal palace was placed under siege. The Mexicans kept a close watch to prevent anyone from stealing in with food for the Spaniards. They also stopped delivering supplies: they brought them absolutely nothing, and waited for them to die of hunger.

A few people attempted to communicate with the Spaniards. They hoped to win their favor by giving them advice and information or by secretly bringing them food. But the guards found them and killed them on the spot: they broke their necks or stoned them to death.

Once a group of porters was discovered bringing rabbit skins into the city. They let slip the fact that other persons had been hiding in their midst. Therefore strict orders were issued to maintain a watch over all the roads and causeways leading to the city. The porters themselves had been sent by the chiefs of Ayotzintepec and Chinantlan. They were only performing their duties, but the guards seized them and put them to death for no reason. They would shout: "Here is another one!" and then kill him. And if they happened to see one of Motecuhzoma's servants with his glass lip plug, they slaughtered him at once, claiming: "He was bringing food to Motecuhzoma."

They seized anyone who was dressed like a porter or any other servant. "Here is another traitor," they would say. "He is bringing news to Motecuhzoma." The prisoner would try to save his life by pleading with them: "What are you doing, Mexicanos? I am not a traitor!" But they would answer: "Yes, you are. We know you are one of his servants." And they would immediately put him to death.

They stopped and examined everyone in the same way, studying each man's face and questioning him about his work. No one could walk out of doors without being arrested and accused. They sentenced a great many people for imaginary crimes; the victims were executed for acts they had never committed. The other servants, therefore, went home and hid themselves. They were afraid to be seen in public: they knew what would happen to them if they fell into the hands of the guards or other warriors.

After they had trapped the Spaniards in the palace, the Mexicans kept them under attack for seven days, and for twenty-three days they foiled all their attempts to break out. During this time all the causeways were closed off. The Mexicans tore up the bridges, opened great gaps in the pavement and built a whole series of barricades; they did everything they could to make the causeways impassable. They also closed off the roads by building walls and roadblocks; they obstructed all the roads and streets of the city.

The Spaniards Abandon the City

At midnight the Spaniards and Tlaxcaltecas came out in closed ranks, the Spaniards going first and the Tlaxcaltecas following. The allies kept very close behind, as if they were crowding up against a wall. The sky was overcast and rain fell all night in the darkness, but it was gentle rain, more like drizzle or a heavy dew.

The Spaniards carried portable wooden bridges to cross the canals. They set them in place, crossed over and raised them again. They were able to pass the first three canals—the Tecpantzinco, the Tzapotlan and the Atenchicalco–without being seen. But when they reached the fourth, the Mixcoatechialtitlan, their retreat was discovered.

The Battle Begins

The first alarm was raised by a woman who was drawing water at the edge of the canal. She cried: "Mexicanos, come running! They are crossing the canal! Our enemies are escaping!"

Then a priest of Huitzilopochtli shouted the call to arms from the temple pyramid. His voice rang out over the city: "Captains, warriors, Mexicanos! Our enemies are escaping! Follow them in your boats. Cut them off, and destroy them!"

When they heard this cry, the warriors leaped into the boats and set out in pursuit. These boats were from the garrisons of Tenochtitlán and Tlatelolco, and were protected by the warriors' shields. The boatmen paddled with all their might; they lashed the water of the lake until it boiled.

Other warriors set out on foot, racing to Nonohualco and then to Tlacopan to cut off the retreat.

The boats converged on the Spaniards from both sides of the causeway, and the warriors loosed a storm of arrows at the fleeing army. But the Spaniards also turned to shoot at the Aztecs; they fired their crossbows and their arquebuses. The Spaniards and Tlaxcaltecas suffered many casualties, but many of the Aztec warriors were also killed or wounded.

The Massacre at the Canal of the Toltecs

When the Spaniards reached the Canal of the Toltecs, in Tlaltecayohuacan, they hurled themselves headlong into the water, as if they were leaping from a cliff. The Tlaxcaltecas, the allies from Tliliuhquitepec, the Spanish foot soldiers and horsemen, the few women who accompanied the army—all came to the brink and plunged over it.

The canal was soon choked with the bodies of men and horses; they filled the gap in the causeway with their own drowned bodies. Those who followed crossed to the other side by walking on the corpses.

When they reached Petlalco, where there was another canal, they crossed over on their portable bridge without being attacked by the Aztecs. They stopped and rested there for a short while, and began to feel more like men again. Then they marched on to Popotla.

Dawn was breaking as they entered the village. Their hearts were cheered by the brightening light of this new day: they thought the horrors of the retreat by night were all behind them. But suddenly they heard war cries and the Aztecs swarmed through the streets and surrounded them. They had come to capture Tlaxcaltecas for their sacrifices. They also wanted to complete their revenge against the Spaniards.

The Aztecs harried the army all the way to Tlacopan. Chimalpopoca, the son of Motecuhzoma, was killed in the action at Tlilyuhcan by an arrow from the crossbows. Tlaltecatzin, the Tepanec prince, was wounded in the same action and died shortly after. He had served the Spaniards as a guide and advisor, pointing out the best roads and short cuts.

The Spaniards Take Refuge in Teocalhueyacan

Then the Spaniards forded a small river called the Tepzolatl. Next they crossed two rivers, the Tepzolac and the Acueco, and stopped in Otoncalpulco, where the temple patio was surrounded by a wooden wall. They rested there in safety, catching their breath and recovering their strength.

While they were resting, the lord of Teocalhueyacan paid them a visit. He was known as The Otomi, a title reserved for the nobility. He greeted them and offered them the gifts of food his servants had brought: tortillas, eggs, roast chickens, a few live hens and various kinds of fruit. He placed these offerings in front of the Captain and said: "My lords, you are weary. You have suffered many heartaches. We beg the gods to rest now and enjoy these gifts."

La Malinche said: "My lord, the Captain wishes to know where you are from."

He answered: "Tell our lord that we are from Teocalhueyacan. Tell him that we hope he will visit us."

La Malinche said: "The Captain thanks you. We shall arrive tomorrow or the day after."

The Aztecs Recover the Spoils

As soon as it was daylight, the Aztecs cleared the dead Spaniards and Tlaxcaltecas out of the canals and stripped them of everything they wore. They loaded the bodies of the Tlaxcaltecas into canoes and took them out to where the rushes grow; they threw them among the rushes without burying them, without giving them another glance.

They also threw out the corpses of the women who had been killed in the retreat. The naked bodies of these women were the color of ripe corn, for they had painted themselves with yellow paint.

But they laid out the corpses of the Spaniards apart from the others; they lined them up in rows in a separate place. Their bodies were as white as the new buds of the canestalk, as white as the buds of the maguey. They also removed the dead "stags" that had carried the "gods" on their shoulders.

Then they gathered up everything the Spaniards had abandoned in their terror. When a man saw something he wanted, he took it, and it became his property; he hefted it onto his shoulders and carried it home. They also collected all the weapons that had been left behind or had fallen into the canal—the cannons, arquebuses, swords, spears, bows and arrows—along with all the steel helmets, coats of mail and breastplates, and the shields of metal, wood and hide. They recovered the gold ingots, the gold disks, the tubes of gold dust and the *chalchihuite* collars with their gold pendants.

They gathered up everything they could find and searched the waters of the canal with the greatest care. Some of them groped with their hands and others felt about with their feet. Those who went first were able to keep their balance but those who came along behind them all fell into the water.

Tenochtitlán after the Departure of Cortés

When the Spaniards left Tenochtitlán, the Aztecs thought they had departed for good and would never return. Therefore they repaired and decorated the temple of their god, sweeping it clean and throwing out all the dirt and wreckage.

Then the eighth month arrived, and the Aztecs celebrated it as always. They adorned the impersonators of the gods, all those who played the part of gods in the ceremonies, decking them with necklaces and turquoise masks and dressing them in the sacred clothing. This clothing was made of quetzal feathers, eagle feathers and yellow parrot feathers. The finery of the gods was in the care of the great princes.

The Plague Ravages the City

While the Spaniards were in Tlaxcala, a great plague broke out here in Tenochtitlán. It began to spread during the thirteenth month and lasted for seventy days, striking everywhere in the city and killing a vast number of our people. Sores erupted on our faces, our breasts, our bellies; we were covered with agonizing sores from head to foot.

The illness was so dreadful that no one could walk or move. The sick were so utterly helpless that they could only lie on their beds like corpses, unable to move their limbs or even their heads. They could not lie face down or roll from one side to the other. If they did move their bodies, they screamed with pain.

A great many died from this plague, and many others died of hunger. They could not get up to search for food, and everyone else was too sick to care for them, so they starved to death in their beds.

Some people came down with a milder form of the disease; they suffered less than the others and made a good recovery. But they could not escape entirely. Their looks were ravaged, for wherever a sore broke out, it gouged an ugly pockmark in the skin. And a few of the survivors were left completely blind.

The first cases were reported in Cuatlan. By the time the danger was recognized, the plague was so well established that nothing could halt it, and eventually it spread all the way to Chalco. Then its virulence diminished considerably, though there were isolated cases for many months after. The first victims were stricken during the fiesta of Teotlecco, and the faces of our warriors were not clean and free of sores until the fiesta of Panquetzaliztli.

The Spaniards Return

And now the Spaniards came back again. They marched here by way of Tezcoco, set up headquarters in Tlacopan and then divided their forces. Pedro de Alvarado was assigned the road to the Tlatelolco quarter as his personal responsibility, while Cortés himself took charge of the Coyoacan area and the road from Acachinanco to Tenochtitlán proper. Cortés knew that the captain of Tenochtitlán was extremely brave.

The first battle began outside Tlatelolco, either at the ash pits or at the place called the Point of the Alders, and then shifted to Nonohualco. Our warriors put the enemy to flight and not a single Aztec was killed. The Spaniards tried a second advance but our warriors attacked them from their boats, loosing such a storm of arrows that the Spaniards were forced to retreat again.

Cortés, however, set out for Acachinanco and reached his goal. He moved his headquarters there, just outside the city. Heavy fighting ensued, but the Aztecs could not dislodge him.

The Spaniards Launch Their Brigantines

Finally the ships, a dozen in all, came from Tezcoco and anchored near Acachinanco. Cortés went out to inspect the canals that traversed the causeways, to discover the best passages for his fleet. He wanted to know which were the nearest, the shortest, the deepest, the straightest, so that none of his ships would run aground or be trapped inside. One of the canals across the Xoloco thoroughfare was so twisted and narrow that only two of the smaller ships were able to pass through it.

The Spaniards now decided to attack Tenochtitlán and destroy its people. The cannons were mounted in the ships, the sails were raised and the fleet moved out onto the lake. The flagship led the way, flying a great linen standard with Cortés's coat of arms. The soldiers beat their drums and blew their trumpets; they played their flutes and chirimias[8] and whistles.

When the ships approached the Zoquiapan quarter,[9] the common people were terrified at the sight. They gathered their children into the canoes and fled helter-skelter across the lake, moaning with fear and paddling as swiftly as they could. They left all their possessions behind them and abandoned their little farms without looking back.

Our enemies seized all our possessions. They gathered up everything they could find and loaded it into the ships in great bundles. They stole our cloaks and blankets, our battle dress, our tabors and drums, and carried them all away. The Tlatelolcas

[8]Similar to shepherd's pipes.

[9]Southwestern Tenochtitlán.

followed and attacked the Spaniards from their boats but could not save any of the plunder.

When the Spaniards reached Xoloco, near the entrance to Tenochtitlán, they found that the Indians had built a wall across the road to block their progress. They destroyed it with four shots from the largest cannon. The first shot did little harm, but the second split it and the third opened a great hole. With the fourth shot, the wall lay in ruins on the ground.

Two of the brigantines, both with cannons mounted in their bows, attacked a flotilla of our shielded canoes. The cannons were fired into the thick of the flotilla, wherever the canoes were crowded closest together. Many of our warriors were killed outright; others drowned because they were too crippled by their wounds to swim away. The water was red with the blood of the dead and dying. Those who were hit by the steel arrows were also doomed; they died instantly and sank to the bottom of the lake.

Defensive Tactics of the Aztecs

When the Aztecs discovered that the shots from the arquebuses and cannons always flew in a straight line, they no longer ran away in the line of fire. They ran to the right or left or in zigzags, not in front of the guns. If they saw that a cannon was about to be fired and they could not escape by running, they threw themselves to the ground and lay flat until the shot had passed over them. The warriors also took cover among the houses, darting into the spaces between them. The road was suddenly as empty as if it passed through a desert.

Then the Spaniards arrived in Huitzillan, where they found another wall blocking the road. A great crowd of our warriors was hiding behind it to escape the gunfire.

The Spaniards Debark

The brigantines came up and anchored nearby. They had been pursuing our war canoes in the open lake, but when they had almost run them down, they suddenly turned and sailed toward the causeway. Now they anchored a short distance from the houses. As soon as the cannons in their bows were loaded again, the soldiers aimed and fired them at the new wall.

The first shot cracked it in a dozen places, but it remained standing. They fired again: this time it cracked from one end to the other and crumpled to the ground. A moment later the road was completely empty. The warriors had all fled when they saw the wall collapsing; they ran blindly, this way and that, howling with fear.

Then the Spaniards debarked and filled in the canal. Working hurriedly, they threw in the stones from the shattered wall, the roof beams and adobe bricks from the nearest houses, anything they could find, until the surface of the fill was level with the causeway. Then a squad of about ten horsemen crossed over it. They galloped to and fro, scouting both sides of the road; they raced and wheeled and clattered back and forth. Soon they were joined by another squad that rode up to support them.

A number of Tlatelolcas had rushed into the palace where Motecuhzoma lived before he was slain. When they came out again, they unexpectedly met the Spanish cavalry. The lead horseman stabbed one of the Tlatelolcas, but the wounded man was able to clutch the lance and cling to it. His friends ran to his aid and twisted it from the Spaniard's hands. They knocked the horseman from his saddle, beat and kicked him as he lay on his back on the ground, and then cut off his head.

The Spaniards now joined all their forces into one unit and marched together as far as the Eagle Gate, where they set up the cannons they had brought with them. It was called the Eagle Gate because it was decorated with an enormous eagle carved of stone. The eagle was flanked on one side by a stone jaguar; on the other side there was a large honey bear, also of carved stone.

Two rows of tall columns led into the city from this gate. Some of the Aztecs hid behind the columns when they saw the Spaniards and their guns; others climbed onto the roofs of the communal houses. None of the warriors dared to show his face openly.

The Spaniards wasted no time as they loaded and fired the cannons. The smoke belched out in black clouds that darkened the sky, as if night were falling. The warriors hidden behind the columns broke from cover and fled; those on the rooftops climbed down and ran after them. When the smoke cleared away, the Spaniards could not see a single Aztec.

The Spaniards Advance to the Heart of the City

Then the Spaniards brought forward the largest cannon and set it up on the sacrificial stone. The priests of Huitzilopochtli immediately began to beat their great ritual drums from the top of the pyramid. The deep throbbing of the drums resounded over the city, calling the warriors to defend the shrine of their god. But two of the Spanish soldiers climbed the stairway to the temple platform, cut the priests down with their swords and pitched them headlong over the brink.

The great captains and warriors who had been fighting from their canoes now returned and landed. The canoes were paddled by the younger warriors and the recruits. As soon as the warriors landed, they ran through the streets, hunting the enemy and shouting: "Mexicanos, come find them!"

The Spaniards, seeing that an attack was imminent, tightened their ranks and clenched the hilts of their swords. The next moment, all was noise and confusion. The Aztecs charged into the plaza from every direction, and the air was black with arrows and gunsmoke.

The battle was so furious that both sides had to pull back. The Aztecs withdrew to Xoloco to catch their breath and dress their wounds, while the Spaniards retreated to their camp in Acachinanco, abandoning the cannon they had set up on the sacrificial stone. Later the warriors dragged this cannon to the edge of the canal and toppled it in. It sank at a place called the Stone Toad.

The Aztecs Take Refuge

During this time the Aztecs took refuge in the Tlatelolco quarter. They deserted the Tenochtitlán quarters all in one day, weeping and lamenting like women. Husbands searched for their wives, and fathers carried their small children on their shoulders. Tears of grief and despair streamed down their cheeks.

The Tlatelolcas, however, refused to give up. They raced into Tenochtitlán to continue the fight and the Spaniards soon learned how brave they were. Pedro de Alvarado launched an attack against the Point of the Alders, in the direction of Nonohualco, but his troops were shattered as if he had sent them against a stone cliff. The battle was fought both on dry land and on the water, where the Indians shot at the Spaniards from their shielded canoes. Alvarado was routed and had to draw back to Tlacopan.

On the following day, two brigantines came up loaded with troops, and the Spaniards united all their forces on the outskirts of Nonohualco. The soldiers in the brigantines came ashore and the whole army marched into the very heart of Tenochtitlán. Wherever they went, they found the streets empty, with no Indians anywhere in sight.

THE LAST STAND

Then the great captain Tzilacatzin arrived, bringing with him three large, round stones of the kind used for building walls. He carried one of them in his hand; the other two hung from his shield. When he hurled these stones at the Spaniards, they turned and fled the city.

Tzilacatzin's military rank was that of Otomi, and he clipped his hair in the style of the Otomies. He scorned his enemies, Spaniards as well as Indians; they all shook with terror at the mere sight of him.

When the Spaniards found out how dangerous he was, they tried desperately to kill him. They attacked him with their swords and spears, fired at him with their crossbows and arquebuses, and tried every other means they could think of to kill or cripple him. Therefore he wore various disguises to prevent them from recognizing him.

Sometimes he wore his lip plug, his gold earrings and all the rest of his full regalia, but left his head uncovered to show that he was an Otomi. At other times he wore only his cotton armor, with a thin kerchief wrapped around his head. At still other times, he put on the finery of the priests who cast the victims into the fire: a plumed headdress with the eagle symbol on its crest, and gleaming gold bracelets on both arms, and circular bands of gleaming gold on both ankles.

The Spaniards came back again the next day. They brought their ships to a point just off Nonohualco, close to the place called the House of Mist. Their other troops arrived on foot, along with the Tlaxcaltecas. As soon as they had formed ranks, they charged the Aztec warriors.

The heaviest fighting began when they entered Nonohualco. None of our enemies and none of our own warriors escaped harm. Everyone was wounded, and the toll of the dead was grievous on both sides. The struggle continued all day and all night.

Only three captains never retreated. They were contemptuous of their enemies and gave no thought whatever to their own safety. The first of these heroes was Tzoyectzin; the second, Temoctzin; and the third, the great Tzilacatazin.

At last the Spaniards were too exhausted to keep on fighting. After one final attempt to break the Aztec ranks, they withdrew to their camp to rest and recover, with their allies trailing behind.

FIFTEEN SPANIARDS ARE CAPTURED AND SACRIFICED

The warriors advanced to the sound of flutes. They shouted their war cries and beat their shields like drums. They pursued the Spaniards, harried and terrified them, and at last took fifteen of them prisoners. The rest of the Spaniards retreated to their ships and sailed out into the middle of the lake.

The prisoners were sacrificed in the place called Tlacochcalco [House of the Arsenal]. Their captors quickly plundered them, seizing their weapons, their cotton armor and everything else, until they stood naked. Then they were sacrificed to the god, while their comrades on the lake watched them being put to death.

Two of the barkentines sailed to Xocotitlan again. They anchored there, and the Spaniards began attacking the houses along the shore. But when Tzilacatzin and other warriors saw what was happening, they ran to the defense and drove the invaders into the water.

On another occasion, the barkentines approached Coyonacazco to attack the houses. As the ships closed in, a few Spaniards jumped out, ready for battle. They were led by Castaneda and by Xicotencatl, who was wearing his headdress of quetzal feathers.

Then Castaneda shot the catapult. It struck one of the Aztecs in the forehead and he fell dead where he was standing. The warriors charged the Spaniards, driving them into the water, and then loosed a hail of stones from their slings. Castaneda would have been killed in this action if a barkentine had not taken him aboard and sailed away toward Xocotitlan.

Another barkentine was anchored near the turn in the wall, and still another near Teotlecco, where the road runs straight to Tepetzinco. They were stationed as guards in order to control the lake. They sailed away that night, but after a few days they came back again to their stations.

The Spaniards advanced from the direction of Cuahuecatitlan. Their allies from Tlaxcala, Acolhuacan and Chalco filled up the canal so that the army could pass. They threw in adobe bricks and all the woodwork of the nearby houses: the lintels, the doorjambs, the beams and pillars. They even threw canestalks and rushes into the water.

The Spaniards Attack Again

When the canal had been filled up, the Spaniards marched over it. They advanced cautiously, with their standard-bearer in the lead, and they beat their drums and played their chirimias as they came. The Tlaxcaltecas and the other allies followed close behind. The Tlaxcaltecas held their heads high and pounded their breasts with their hands, hoping to frighten us with their arrogance and courage. They sang songs as they marched, but the Aztecs were also singing. It was as if both sides were challenging each other with their songs. They sang whatever they happened to remember and the music strengthened their hearts.

The Aztec warriors hid when the enemy reached solid ground. They crouched down to make themselves as small as possible and waited for the signal, the shout that told them it was the moment to stand up and attack. Suddenly they heard it: "Mexicanos, now is the time!"

The captain Hecatzin leaped up and raced toward the Spaniards, shouting: "Warriors of Tlatelolco, now is the time! Who are these barbarians? Let them come ahead!" He attacked one of the Spaniards and knocked him to the ground, but the Spaniard also managed to knock Hecatzin down. The captain got up and clubbed the Spaniard again, and other warriors rushed forward to drag him away.

Then all the Aztecs sprang up and charged into battle. The Spaniards were so astonished that they blundered here and there like drunkards; they ran through the streets with the warriors in pursuit. This was when the taking of captains began. A great many of the allies from Tlaxcala, Acolhuacan, Chalco and Xochimilco were overpowered by the Aztecs, and there was a great harvesting of prisoners, a great reaping of victims to be sacrificed.

The Spaniards and their allies waded into the lake because the road had become too slippery for them. The mud was so slick that they sprawled and floundered and could not stand up to fight. The Aztecs seized them as captives and dragged them across the mud.

The Spanish standard was taken and carried off during this encounter. The warriors from Tlatelolco captured it in the place known today as San Martin, but they were scornful of their prize and considered it of little importance.

Some of the Spaniards were able to escape with their lives. They retreated in the direction of Culhuacan, on the edge of the canal, and gathered there to recover their strength.

Fifty-three Spaniards Are Sacrificed

The Aztecs took their prisoners to Yacacolco, hurrying them along the road under the strictest guard. Some of the captives were weeping, some were keening, and others were beating their palms against their mouths.

When they arrived in Yacacolco, they were lined up in long rows. One by one they were forced to climb to the temple platform, where they were sacrificed by the priests. The Spaniards went first, then their allies, and all were put to death.

As soon as the sacrifices were finished, the Aztecs ranged the Spaniards' heads in rows on pikes. They also lined up their horses' heads. They placed the horses' heads at the bottom and the heads of the Spaniards above, and arranged them all so that the faces were toward the sun. However, they did not display any of the allies' heads. All told, fifty-three Spaniards and four horses were sacrificed there in Yacacolco.

The fighting continued in many different places. At one point, the allies from Xochimilco surrounded us in their canoes, and the toll of the dead and captured was heavy on both sides.

The Sufferings of the Inhabitants

The Spanish blockade caused great anguish in the city. The people were tormented by hunger, and many starved to death. There was no fresh water to drink, only stagnant water and the brine of the lake, and many people died of dysentery.

The only food was lizards, swallows, corncobs and the salt grasses of the lake. The people also ate water lilies and the seeds of the colorin, and chewed on deerhides and pieces of leather. They roasted and seared and scorched whatever they could find and then ate it. They ate the bitterest weeds and even dirt.

Nothing can compare with the horrors of that siege and the agonies of the starving. We were so weakened by hunger that, little by little, the enemy forced us to retreat. Little by little they forced us to the wall.

The Battle in the Market Place

On one occasion, four Spanish cavalrymen entered the market place. They rode through it in a great circle, stabbing and killing many of our warriors and trampling everything under their horses' hooves. This was the first time the Spaniards had entered the market place, and our warriors were taken by surprise. But when the horsemen withdrew, the warriors recovered their wits and ran in pursuit.

It was at this same time that the Spaniards set fire to the temple and burned it to the ground. The flames and smoke leaped high into the air with a terrible roar. The people wept when they saw their temple on fire; they wept and cried out, fearing that afterward it would be plundered.

The battle lasted for many hours and extended to almost every corner of the market place. There was no action along the wall where the vendors sold lime, but the fighting raged among the flower stalls, and the stalls offering snails, and all the passageways between them.

Some of our warriors stationed themselves on the rooftops of the Quecholan district, which is near the entrance to the market place, and from there they hurled stones and fired arrows at the enemy. Others broke holes in the rear walls of all the houses of Quecholan, holes just big enough for a man's body to pass through. When the cavalry attacked and were about to spear our warriors, or trample them, or cut off their retreat, they slipped through the holes and the mounted men could not follow.

Other Battles

On another occasion the Spaniards entered Atliyacapan. They ransacked the houses and captured a number of prisoners, but when the warriors saw what was happening, they loosed their arrows and rushed forward to attack. The leader of this attack, a valiant chief named Axoquentzin, pressed the enemy so hard that they were forced to release their prisoners and drop all their spoils. But this great chief died when a Spanish sword entered his breast and found his heart.

There were other battles in Yacacolco, where the enemy killed many of the Aztecs with their crossbows. The warriors drew back and tried to waylay the rear guard, but a few of the allies saw them and climbed to the rooftops. They cried: "Warriors of Tlaxcala, come here! Your enemies are here!" The Tlaxcaltecas shot so many arrows at the men in ambush that they had to break and run.

Later in the day, the Aztecs put up a much stronger resistance, and the Spaniards and their allies could not break their ranks. The Tlatelolcas took up positions on the opposite side of the canal, hurling stones and shooting arrows across it. The enemy could not advance or capture any of the bridges.

The Catapult Is Set Up in the Market Place

During this time, the Spaniards mounted a wooden catapult on the temple platform to fling stones at the Indians. While it was being set up, the Indians who had gathered in Amaxac came out to stare at it. They pointed at the machine and asked each other what it could be. When the Spaniards had finished their preparations and were ready to shoot it at the crowd, they wound it up until the wooden beams stood erect. Then they released it like a great sling.

But the stone did not fall among the Indians. It flew over their heads and crashed into a corner of the market place. This seemed a cause for argument among the Spaniards: they gestured toward the Indians and shouted at each other. But still they could not aim the machine correctly. It threw out its stones in every direction.

Finally the Indians were able to see how it worked: it had a sling inside it, worked by a heavy rope. The Indians named it "the wooden sling."

The Spaniards and Tlaxcaltecas retreated again, marching back to Yacacolco and Tecpancaltitlan in closed ranks. Their leader was directing the campaign against us from his headquarters in Acocolecan.

The Aztec Defense

Our warriors rallied to defend the city. Their spirits and courage were high; not one of them showed any fear or behaved like a woman. They cried: "Mexicanos, come here and join us! Who are these savages? A mere rabble from the south!" They did not move in a direct line; they moved in a zigzag course, never in a straight line.

The Spanish soldiers often disguised themselves so that they would not be recognized. They wore cloaks like those of the Aztecs and put on the same battle dress and adornments, hoping to deceive our warriors into thinking they were not Spaniards.

Whenever the Aztecs saw the enemy notching their arrows, they either dispersed or flattened themselves on the ground. The warriors of Tlatelolco were very alert; they were very cautious and vigilant, and watched intently to see where the shots were coming from.

But step by step the Spaniards gained more ground and captured more houses. They forced us backward along the Amaxac road with their spears and shields.

The Quetzal-Owl

Cuauhtemoc consulted with a group of his captains and then called in a great captain named Opochtzin, who was a dyer by trade. They dressed him in the finery of the Quetzal-Owl, which had belonged to King Ahuitzotl. Then Cuauhtemoc said to him: "This regalia belonged to my father, the great warrior Ahuitzotl. Terrify our enemies with it. Annihilate our enemies with it. Let them behold it and tremble."

The king ordered four captains to go with Opochtzin as a rear guard. He placed in the captain's hands the magic object that was the most important part of the regalia. This was an arrow with a long shaft and an obsidian tip.

The captain Tlacotzin said: "Mexicanos, the power of Huitzilopochtli resides in this finery. Loose the sacred arrow at our enemies, for it is the Serpent of Fire, the Arrow that Pierces the Fire. Loose it at the invaders; drive them away with the power of Huitzilopochtli. But shoot it straight and well, for it must not fall to earth. And if it should wound one or two of our foes, then we shall still have a little time left and a chance to conquer them. Now, let us see what the god's will may be!"

The Quetzal-Owl departed with the four captains, and the quetzal feathers seemed to open out, making him appear even greater and more terrifying. When our enemies saw him approach, they quaked as if they thought a mountain were about to fall on them. They trembled with dread, as if they knew the finery could work magic.

The Quetzal-Owl climbed up onto a rooftop. When our enemies saw him, they came forward and prepared to attack him, but he succeeded in driving them away. Then he came down from the rooftop with his quetzal feathers and his gold ornaments. He was not killed in this action and our enemies could not capture the feathers or the gold. Three of the enemy soldiers were taken prisoner.

Suddenly the battle ended. Neither side moved against the other; the night was calm and silent, with no incidents of any kind. On the following day, absolutely nothing took place, and neither the Spaniards nor the Indians spoke a word. The Indians waited in their defense works, and the Spaniards waited in their positions. Each side watched the other closely but made no plans for launching an attack. Both sides passed the whole day in this fashion, merely watching and waiting.

The Final Omen

At nightfall it began to rain, but it was more like a heavy dew than a rain. Suddenly the omen appeared, blazing like a great bonfire in the sky. It wheeled in enormous spirals like a whirlwind and gave off a shower of sparks and red-hot coals, some great and some little. It also made loud noises, rumbling and hissing like a metal tube placed over a fire. It circled the wall nearest the lakeshore and then hovered for a while above Coyonacazco. From there it moved out into the middle of the lake, where it suddenly disappeared. No one cried out when this omen came into view: the people knew what it meant and they watched it in silence.

Nothing whatever occurred on the following day. Our warriors and the Spanish soldiers merely waited in their positions. Cortés kept a constant watch, standing under a many-colored canopy on the roof of the lord Aztautzin's house, which is near Amaxac. His officers stood around him, talking among themselves.

Cuauhtemoc's Surrender

The Aztec leaders gathered in Tolmayecan to discuss what they should do. Cuauhtemoc and the other nobles tried to determine how much tribute they would have to pay and how best to surrender to the strangers. Then the nobles put Cuauhtemoc into a war canoe, with only three men to accompany him: a captain named Teputztitloloc, a servant named Iaztachimal and a boatman named Cenyautl. When the people saw their chief departing, they wept and cried out: "Our youngest prince is leaving us! He is going to surrender to the Spaniards! He is going to surrender to the 'gods'!"

The Spaniards came out to meet him. They took him by the hand, led him up to the rooftop and brought him into the presence of Cortés. The Captain stared at him for a moment and then patted him on the head. Then he gestured toward a chair and the two leaders sat down side by side.

The Spaniards began to shoot off their cannons, but they were not trying to hit anyone. They merely loaded and fired, and the cannonballs flew over the Indians' heads. Later they put one of the cannons into a boat and took it to the house of Coyohuehuetzin, where they hoisted it to the rooftop.

The Flight from the City

Once again the Spaniards started killing and a great many Indians died. The flight from the city began and with this the war came to an end. The people cried: "We have suffered enough! Let us leave the city! Let us go live on weeds!" Some fled across the lake, others along the causeways, and even then there were many killings. The Spaniards were angry because our warriors still carried their shields and *macanas*.[10]

Those who lived in the center of the city went straight toward Amaxac, to the fork in the road. From there they fled in various directions, some toward Tepeyacac, others toward Xoxohuiltitlan and Nonohualco; but no one went toward Xoloco or Mazatzintamalco. Those who lived in boats or on the wooden rafts anchored in the lake fled by water, as did the inhabitants of Tolmayecan. Some of them waded

[10] Flattened clubs.

in water up to their chests and even up to their necks. Others drowned when they reached water above their heads.

The grownups carried their young children on their shoulders. Many of the children were weeping with terror, but a few of them laughed and smiled, thinking it was great sport to be carried like that along the road.

Some of the people who owned canoes departed in the daytime, but the others, the majority, left by night. They almost crashed into each other in their haste as they paddled away from the city.

The Spaniards Humiliate the Refugees

The Spanish soldiers were stationed along the roads to search the fleeing inhabitants. They were looking only for gold and paid no attention to jade, turquoise or quetzal feathers. The women carried their gold under their skirts and the men carried it in their mouths or under their loincloths. Some of the women, knowing they would be searched if they looked prosperous, covered their faces with mud and dressed themselves in rags. They put on rags for skirts and rags for blouses; everything they wore was in tatters. But the Spaniards searched all the women without exception: those with light skins, those with dark skins, those with dark bodies.

A few of the men were separated from the others. These men were the bravest and strongest warriors, the warriors with manly hearts. The youths who served them were also told to stand apart. The Spaniards immediately branded them with hot irons, either on the cheek or the lips.

The day on which we laid down our shields and admitted defeat was the day 1-Serpent in the year 3-House.[11] . . .

A Defense of Aztec Religion

Translated by David M. Johnson and Armando Jimarez

Our Lords, esteemed Lords.

We welcome you to our lands and cities. We who are so unworthy are reluctant to look on the faces of such valiant persons.

You brought a lord, our Prince, to govern us. We are ignorant about where you came from, where your gods and lords live, because you came by sea, between clouds and fog. A road we do not know.

Via your ears, eyes and mouth, your god was sent among us. That which is invisible and spiritual was made visible. With our ears we heard the words about living and being which you brought us. With admiration we have heard the words of the Lord of the World whose love brought you to us, and brought also the book of heavenly words.

And now, what can we say about ourselves? What words can we lift to your ears that would be worthy of your status? We are nothing, common people of low status. By the rule of iron your king forced us into the corners of his dais.

Nevertheless, with two or three reasons, we will contradict the words of the giver of life, the Lord of the World.

[11] August 13, 1521.

Perhaps we will provoke his anger against us, and cause our downfall, cause our ultimate ruin. Perhaps we are already doomed. What can we do, we who are ordinary people, and mortal besides?

If we die, we die. Leave us then to perish. The truth is, gods also die.

Do not be sad of heart, dear lords, because with delicacy and care we want to examine the divine secrets, like a thief who opens a coffer of riches to see what is inside.

You have told us that we don't know the Lord and Giver of Life, the Lord of sky and earth. You have said that the ones we worship are not true gods.

This way of talking is new to us and very disturbing. We are troubled with statements like these, because our forefathers, those who begot us and ruled over us, didn't tell us these things.

Long ago they left us the customs that we have for worshipping our gods. They believed in them and worshipped them all the time that they lived on the earth. They taught us the way that we should honor them: we kneel on the earth for ritual meals; we do penance by bleeding ourselves; we keep our words; we burn incense; and we offer sacrifices.

They told us that because of the gods' sacrifices we have life. We deserved life because we belonged to them and served them. And this was customary during the time before the sun began to shine.

They said that these gods whom we worship gave us all the things necessary for our physical life: maize, beans, sage and amaranth. To them we pray for rain, so things on this earth can grow.

These our gods are very rich. All delights and riches are theirs. They live in a wonderful place, where there are always flowers and vegetables. A refreshing place not seen or known by mortals, called Tlalocan. A place where there is never hunger, poverty or sickness.

These gods give us the honors, our capacity to fight and to rule, gold and silver, precious feathers and precious stones.

There is no record of when our gods were first honored, invoked and adored. Fortunately, for several centuries, there have been places where they were celebrated, places where sacred events occurred and answers given. Places like Tula, Huapalcalco, Xuchatlapan, Tlamohuanchan, Yohuallichan, Teotihuacán.

The inhabitants of these places took possession of the earth and governed our world. They give us order, fame, glory and majesty.

It would be foolish of us to destroy the ancient laws and customs left to us by the Chichimecs, the Toltecs, the Acolhuas, the Tepanecs. Into the service of our gods we were born and we were raised. We have it imprinted on our hearts.

Oh Lords. Listen to us.

Do not disturb and harm our people. How could poor old men and old women leave a way of life which they have believed in for their whole lives?

Do not make us invite the anger of our gods. Do not make the people rebel against us by having us tell them that the gods they believed in are not gods at all.

It has been necessary, dear lords, to look into this matter with patience and unity. We are not satisfied nor are we persuaded by what you have said. We do not agree with what you have said about our gods.

It saddens us, lords and priests, to speak in this way. In attendance are the lords who have the responsibility to rule the kingdoms of this world. But we all feel the same way about this.

It is enough for us to have lost, to have the power and rule taken from us. When it comes to our gods, first we will die rather than leave their worship and service.

This is our determination. Do with us what you want. Our answer to you is sufficient. We have nothing more to say.

Glossary of Nahuatl Names and Terms

AMATE PAPER Native paper made from the flattened bark of wild fig trees.

ANAHUAC A Nahuatl word meaning "at the edge of the water"; it was used to refer to the Valley of Mexico, the Gulf and Pacific Coasts, and the earth itself, which the Nahuas believed was a disk surrounded by water.

APANECATL, ZOLTON, CUILTON Three leaders of the Mimixcoa, Mixcoatl's brothers. Apanecatl was part of the divine retinue following Huitzilopochtli, the god of war who led the Aztecs from their origins in Aztlán to the Valley of Mexico.

APANTECUHTLI, TEPANQUIZQUI, TLALLAMANQUI, HUICTLOLLINQUI, TZŒNTEMOC Sky gods associated with the creation of man and woman; probably aspects of the primary dual-god, Ometeotl.

AZTEC Aztec refers to the seven Nahuatl-speaking tribes (Acolhua, Chalca, Mexica, Tepaneca, Tlalhuica, Tlaxcalteca, and Xochimilca) who left their mythic home in the north, the legendary Chicomoztoc (Seven Caves) or Aztlán (The Place of Herons), migrated south in the twelfth century C.E., and settled in the Valley of Mexico. By 1428, the Mexicas emerged at the top of the other tribes, and building on the earlier Toltecs, created what is called the Aztec empire, which stretched from the Gulf of Mexico to the Pacific Ocean, and southeast to Chiapas. See *Nahua/Nahuatl* below.

CE ACATL In Nahuatl, it means one reed, and refers to the calendar day (1-Reed) on which Ce Acatl-Topiltzin was born, the hero who came to be known as Quetzalcoatl. The year 1-Reed defined Quetzalcoatl's reign in Tollan (from 1-Reed to 1-Reed) and his promised return after being driven out.

CHALCHIHUITES Green stones: jade.

CHICALOTE *Argemone mexicana,* an edible plant.

CHIMALMAN The earth-goddess mother of Quetzalcoatl. Her name comes from the Nahuatl *chimalli,* meaning Shield, and is probably related to the incident when she lay down her shield before Mixcoatl.

CIHUACOATL An earth-goddess whose name means Serpent Woman and who is associated with pregnancy and childbirth.

CIPACTONAL See OXOMOCO AND CIPACTONAL.

CITLALLINICUE AND CITLALLATONAC Goddess and god of the heavens, sometimes translated as Skirt-of-the-Stars and Light-of-Day; manifestations of the primary dual god, Ometeotl.

COYOTLINAHUAL A sorcerer, whose name is formed from *coyotl,* meaning coyote, and *nahual,* meaning cunning or deceitful. Used alone, *nahual* means animal double or alter ego.

CUAUHTEMOC A nephew of Moctezuma; a valiant warrior and the last Aztec ruler. His name means Descending Eagle—the sunset. He was tortured and executed by Cortés in Honduras.

CUAUHTITLÁN A city located on the northwestern shore of Lake Texcoco, the lake forming the center of numerous settlements in the Valley of Mexico. The *Anales de Cuauhtitlán* relate its history. *Cuauhtitlán* is Nahuatl for Tree Side.

CUAUHTLOCELOTL *Cuauhtli* means eagle; *ocelotl* means jaguar. Eagle and jaguar symbolize the eternal struggle between sky forces and earth forces in the creation and destruction of worlds. Two classes of Aztec warriors were Eagle-Knights and Jaguar-Knights.

EHECATL/ECATL God of wind; a manifestation of Quetzalcoatl.

HUASTECAS Indians of eastern Mexico.

HUITZILOPOCHTLI Exclusively an Aztec god of sun and war, who was brought with the Aztecs on their migration from the north. Fed by the sacrificial energy of blood in his aspect as the sun, he begins each day battling the moon and stars for dominance. His name means Left Hand Like a Hummingbird.

HUITZNAHUAC A place called Land of the Thorns—that is, the south; from the Nahuatl *huitz,* thorn, and *nahuac,* place or vicinity.

MAMALHUAZTLI Three stars in the constellation Taurus.

MICTLAN The underground, as well as the land of the dead, the underworld. Similar to the Greek Hades.

MICTLANTECUHTLI AND MICTLANCIHUATL Lord and Lady of the Underworld, corresponding to Hades and Persephone in Greek mythology.

MIMIXCOA The plural form of Mixcoatl (Cloud Serpents), referring to the numerous star brothers of Mixcoatl; Centzonmimixcoa means 400 or numberless cloud serpents, and indicates the stars of the northern constellation or Milky Way.

MIXCOATL Leader of a chichimec tribe that migrated into the Valley of Mexico and settled in Colhuacan. His history becomes legendary when he is elevated to a deity. Father of Ce Acatl-Topiltzin, his name means Cloud Serpent, referring to a tornado or perhaps to the Milky Way.

MIXCOATEPETL *Tepetl* is Nahuatl for "mountain," so Mixcoatepetl means Mixcoatl's Mountain, his pyramid or temple.

MOCTEZUMA/MONTEZUMA/MOTECUHZOMA Different spellings for the ninth Aztec ruler (1502-1520 C.E.), the second Aztec ruler with that name.

NAHUA/NAHUATL The name Nahua is used generically for several groups who spoke Nahuatl and shared a common cultural heritage in the Valley of Mexico.

NAHUAL Sometimes spelled *nagual;* an alter ego or double. Also a person's soul residing outside the body in an animal or bird.

NANAHUATZIN/NANAHUATL God of syphilis, leprosy, or sores. Linked to Quetzalcoatl.

OMETEOTL The primordial dual-god of the Mexicas, from the Nahuatl *ome,* meaning two, and *teotl,* meaning god.

OTOMIES A tribe in the Valley of Mexico.

OXOMOCO AND CIPACTONAL First man and first woman, Adam and Eve for the Nahuas. They founded the art of divination by using kernels of corn.

QUETZALCOATL The most famous and important god of Mesoamerica, whose name means Plumed Serpent or Precious Twin. (*Quetzal* refers to the prized bird by that name; *coatl* means serpent or snake.) As a god, he was instrumental in creating the four previous worlds. As hero-ruler of Tollan (Ce Acatl-Topiltzin), he assumed the mantle of the priesthood of Quetzalcoatl, fell from grace, and delivered a messianic promise to return.

QUETZALPETLATL The sister or wife of Quetzalcoatl. Her name combines *quetzal,* quetzal feathers or precious, and *petlatl,* mat, perhaps referring to a mat of quetzal feathers used for religious or ceremonial purposes.

QUILAZTLI An earth goddess associated with childbirth. An aspect of Chihuacoatl.

TAMOANCHAN The mythic place of origins, similar to Eden; *tamoanchan* means Land of the Bird-Snake, an association with Quetzalcoatl.

TECUCIZTECATL God of the Moon; his name means Person from Tecuciztlán. (Tecuciztlán means Near Conch Shells.) Linked to Tezcatlipoca.

TEOCALLI Literally, god's house; a pyramid or temple.

TEOTEXCALLI *Texcalli* is an oven or an outcropping of volcanic rocks and *teo* means god; thus the word means god's oven or god's hearth.

TEOTIHUACÁN The name means Place of the Gods. Historically, an important cultural center, and now a popular archeological site northwest of Mexico City. Famed for its magnificent Pyramids of the Sun and Moon and the Pyramid of Quetzalcoatl.

TEPANECAS A tribe that was dominant in the Valley of Mexico before the arrival of the Mexicas or Aztecs.

TEZCATLIPOCA, IHUIMECATL, AND TOLTECATL Tezcatlipoca was a powerful deity associated with disease and war. A sometime brother of Quetzalcoatl, he was always his adversary and antithesis. His name means Smoking Mirror. Ihuimecatl's name means Cord of

Feathers, which connects him to Huitzilopochtli, the patron god of the Aztecs who promoted war and human sacrifice. Toltecatl, whose name indicates his origin in Tollan, was a god of drunkenness.

TIACAPAN, TEICU, TLACOYEHUA, AND XOCOYOTL Four goddesses who complement the four gods of the four directions in the creation of the Fifth Sun. Probably aspects of the earth goddess Tlazolteotl.

TITLACAHUAN Another name for Tezcatlipoca.

TLALOC God of rain.

TLATELOLCO A section of Tenochtitlán.

TLILLAN TLAPALLAN The mythic and mystical destination of Quetzalcoatl after leaving Tula. The two names in Nahuatl mean The Black and Red Land or Land of Black and Red Ink. Metaphorically, the inks indicate a place of writing (painting books), and therefore Tlillan Tlapallan is the place of wisdom, learning, and enlightenment. From there Quetzalcoatl announced that he would return in the year Ce Acatl (1-Reed).

TOLLAN A place meaning literally Near the Rushes, it was the legendary capital of the Toltecs; under the leadership of Topiltzin, Tollan was located at Tula, north of Mexico City.

TONACATEPETL The mountain of agricultural produce or sustenance; the mythic source of all food.

TOPILTZIN-QUETZALCOATL In about the tenth century, a leader arose among the Toltecs who was a priest of Quetzalcoatl and was called Ce Acatl Topiltzin (Prince One-Reed). He moved the Toltec capital to Tula, developed its culture, and favored a life of piety while opposing human sacrifice.

TOTEC, ANAHUATLITECU, TLATLAHUIC-TEZCATLIPOCA Gods representing the various directions, with matching goddesses; see TIACAPAN *et al.*

TULANZINGO A very old cultural site associated with Quetzalcoatl, and an important stop-over on the migration route of the Toltecs before they reached Tollan.

TZAQUALLI/TZACUALLI A Nahuatl word meaning pyramid.

TZONMOLCO Part of the main temple at Tenochtitlán.

VULTURE The word for *vulture* in Nahuatl is *cozcacuauhtli,* meaning Eagle with a Reddish Necklace, or King Vulture. It is common for the mythic hero to receive aid from the animal world.

XIUHTECUHTLI A fire god.

XIUHUACAN The name means Place of the Turquoise; according to Edward Seler, it is located on the Pacific Coast beyond Michoacán.

XOLOTL God of the planet Venus as evening star; twin brother of Quetzalcoatl. A clever sorcerer.

WU CH'ÊNG-ÊN

[c. 1506–1582]

Monkey, or, by its Chinese title, *Hsi Yu Chi,* is one of the great Chinese novels of the sixteenth century. For Western readers it includes an unusual mixture of mythology, legend, religious allegory, and satire. Linking comic satire with serious religious themes may seem sacrilegious to Westerners, but similar mixing occurs in Western literature, especially in such medieval works as Chaucer's *Canterbury Tales*. An allegorical story of a religious pilgrimage, *Monkey* is like some medieval literature of the West, but its unusual hero, a fabulous stone monkey, is more reminiscent of the power-seeking tricksters of the Renaissance.

LIFE

Little is known of Wu Ch'êng-ên. A native of Huaian in Kiangsu province, about one hundred miles north of Nanking, Wu seems to have taken up writing after retiring from a career as a District Magistrate. Some of his poems survive in anthologies of verse from the Ming period (1368–1644). He also wrote stories that, like the poems, were in the accepted neoclassical style of his time, imitating the work of the T'ang writers (618–906 C.E.). Wu's one great work was *Hsi Yu Chi,* in which he broke with neoclassical conventions to write in the vernacular. It was one of three great Chinese novels of the sixteenth century. The other two were Lo Mao-teng's *Hsi Yang Chi* (*Adventures to the Western Ocean*), a tale about a fifteenth-century explorer; and *Chin P'ing Mei,* an anonymous novel of contemporary life. All three of these novels broke with the neoclassical conventions that dominated the literature of the period to explore fresh subjects in a vernacular language. Wu's novel, published anonymously, drew on folk materials, popular legends, and oral history. It has remained one of the most popular works of Chinese literature down to the present time.

WORK

The central story of the novel, the pilgrimage of the monk Hsüan Tsang (also San-tsang and Tripitaka), is grounded in historical fact. The actual journey from China to India to bring back the Buddhist scriptures took seventeen years, from 629 to 645. In Hsüan Tsang's own account of his travels, the monk described his difficulties starting his journey, when he was forbidden to leave China; his years in India, where he learned Sanskrit and became a Buddhist scholar; and his triumphant return with the scriptures to become a favorite of the Chinese emperor. In the popular culture, his story was expanded with folk tales, animal fables, and myths, and many literary works drawing on these materials and describing his journey have been written, both before and after *Hsi Yu Chi.*

Historically, the story reflects the growing Chinese interest in the territories to the west during the T'ang period. The important trade routes to India began at Chang'an, the capital of the dynasty and the largest city in the world at the time. Hsüan Tsang's journey also represents an important period in Chinese Buddhism. After he returned to China, the T'ang emperor T'ai-tsung, who traced his ancestry back to Lao Tzu, became a proponent of Buddhism.

Hsüan Tsang is often called Tripitaka in the novel, a name that derives from the scriptures he brought back from India to China. Although he is the hero of the pilgrimage story, his disciple, Monkey, has the dominant role in Wu's vernacular novel. Monkey's story opens the novel, and he is the one who overcomes the obstacles to make the pilgrimage successful. Arthur Waley, whose translation we reprint here, acknowledges this changed emphasis in the Hsüan Tsang story by titling his abridged translation *Monkey* rather than the more literal *Record of a Journey to the West.* In the original novel, the first seven chapters describe Monkey's origins, how he achieves his power, and how he misbehaves and ends up imprisoned in a mountain. The next five chapters introduce Hsüan Tsang, giving a mythological account of his birth and childhood, not unlike the story of Moses in certain details, and describing how he comes by his mission to secure the scriptures from India. The rest of the novel's one hundred chapters describe the eighty-one tests Tripitaka undergoes on the journey and his final success in obtaining the scriptures.

Nearly all of the tests involve overcoming monsters or dragons, and Monkey, with his quick wits and magical needle, is a match for even the most powerful dragons.

This combination of animal fable, physical comedy, superhero romance, political and religious satire, and spiritual journey gives rich variety in incident and mood to the story. But *Monkey* is also fairly repetitive. After the first four or five encounters with dragons, all dragons may begin to look alike to a Western reader. To the Chinese reader, however, each of the eighty-one obstacles Tripitaka and Monkey must overcome adds a new allegorical dimension to the spiritual achievement that is unfolding. Although it is hard for a Western reader to distinguish between the dragons, the basic allegory is clear. Tripitaka, mythical hero and potential saint (bodhisattva), is a kind of everyman. Naive, even simple-minded, he trusts nearly everyone he meets, and this trust gets him into trouble. He needs the help of his disciples, especially Monkey—a figure related to Hanuman, the Indian monkey-god—who represents human genius in this allegory. Monkey's cleverness is essential for getting the pilgrims out of one scrape after another. But it occasionally gets them into trouble, for Monkey is proud and impetuous. He is a kind of comic Prometheus who will take on anyone, even the gods. Only when his intelligence is disciplined, reined in by the cap given to Tripitaka by the bodhisattva Kuan-yin, does Monkey become a useful servant to the monk. The other two disciples, Pigsy, who represents the gross physical appetites, and Sandy, whose allegorical significance is unclear, make up the unusual group of pilgrims who together manage to secure the scriptures from India.

In its melding of the spiritual and the worldly, *Monkey* has some of the flavor of medieval romances where fabulous adventures take on spiritual significance. But the realm of the gods in *Monkey* is more like an Olympian bureaucracy; they are forever setting down rules and enforcing trivial decrees. Spiritual enlightenment does not seem to be a result of becoming familiar with this divine bureaucracy or learning their rules. It is rather a product of the journey itself. Tripitaka and his disciples all grow spiritually as they help each other to overcome the obstacles in their path. It is the journey itself, not the goal, that constitutes their process of enlightenment.

Monkey, a trickster who challenges all who oppose him, is related to figures such as Coyote in Native American folklore and Prometheus in classical myth. He is not cowed by arbitrary power. He seeks out challenges, for he is, as he boastfully reminds others, "The Great Sage, Equal of Heaven." In his arrogance and self-confidence, he is a soul-brother to such overreaching tricksters of the Renaissance as Don Juan and Faustus. Like them, he enjoys challenges, confrontations, and combats, for in such tests of strength, he can prove his intelligence and his power. But his exploits do not end in damnation. Constrained by the cap given to Tripitaka by Kuan-yin, Monkey's exploits serve his master and in the end he is rewarded with sainthood.

Suggested Readings

Arthur Waley's translation of *Hsi Yu Chi,* titled *Monkey* (1942), abridges the novel to about a third of its original length by reducing the number of tests that Tripitaka must overcome. Anthony Yu has prepared a complete English translation of the *Journey to the West* (1983). Arthur Waley has also written a historical account of Tripitaka's actual journey and added a chapter to his translation of *Monkey* in *The Real Tripitaka and Other Pieces* (1952). Some useful discussions of the novel can be found in C. T. Hsia's "Monstrous Appetite: Comedy and Myth in the *Hsi yu chi,*" in *Wen-lin,* ed. Chow Tse-Tsung (1968); in Glen Dudbridge's *The "Hsi-yu chi": A Study of Antecedents to the Sixteenth-Century Chinese Novel* (1970); and in Andrew H. Plaks's "Allegory in *Hsi-yu chi,*" *Chinese Narrative: Critical and Theoretical Essays,* ed. A. H. Plaks (1977).

Monkey

Translated by Arthur Waley

Chapter 8

One day when Buddha had been preaching to the Bodhisattvas and Arhats, he said at the end of his sermon, "I have been noticing that there is a lot of difference in the inhabitants of the Four Continents of the universe. Those in the Eastern Continent are respectful, peaceable and cheerful; those of the Northern are somewhat prone to take life, but they are so dumb, lethargic and stupid that they don't do much harm. In our Western Continent, there is no greed or slaughter; we nurture our humours and hide our magic, and although we have no supreme illuminates everyone is safe against the assaults of age. But in Jumbudvīpa, the Southern Continent, they are greedy, lustful, murderous, and quarrelsome. I wonder whether a knowledge of the True Scriptures would not cause some improvement in them?"

"Do you yourself possess those scriptures?" asked the Bodhisattvas.

"Yes, three baskets of them," said Buddha. "One contains the Vinaya, which speaks of heaven, one contains the Saastras, which tell of Earth, one contains the Sutras, which save the damned. The whole is divided into thirty-five divisions written on 15,144 rolls. These are the path to perfection, the only gate to virtue. I would send it straight to the people of the common world; but they are so stupid that they would only jeer at the truth, misunderstand the meaning of my Law, and scorn the true sect of Yoga. I wish I knew of a holy one who would go to the eastern land and find a believer who could be sent over hill and dale, all the way from China to this place. I would give him the scriptures to take back to China, and he would explain them to the people and change their hearts. That would be an untold blessing. Is any of you willing to go?"

Kuan-yin came up to the lotus platform, bowed three times to the Buddha, and said, "I don't know if I can make a success of it, but I should like to go to the eastern land and find someone to fetch the scriptures."

"You're just the person," said Buddha. "A venerable Bodhisattva with great sanctity and magic powers—we couldn't do better."

"Have you any particular instructions?" asked Kuan-yin.

"I want you," said Buddha, "to make a thorough study of the air at a fairly low altitude, not up among the stars. Keep an eye on the mountains and rivers, and make careful note of the distances and travelling-stages, so that you may assist the scripture-seeker. But it is going to be a very difficult journey for him, and I have five talismans which I should like you to give him." An embroidered cassock and a priest's staff with nine rings were then fetched, and he said to Kuan-yin, "When he feels his courage failing him on the road, let him put on this cassock. If he carries this staff, he will never meet with poison or violence. And here," Buddha continued, "I have three fillets. They are all alike, but their use is different; each has its separate spell. If on his journey the pilgrim meets with any ogre of superlative powers, you must attempt to convert this ogre and make him the scripture-seeker's disciple. If he resists, the pilgrim is to put one of these fillets on his head, reciting the spell that belongs to it. Whereupon the ogre's eyes will swell and his head ache so excruciatingly that he will feel as if his brains were bursting, and he will be only too glad to embrace our Faith."

Kuan-yin bowed and called upon her disciple Hui-yen to follow her. He carried a great iron cudgel, weighing a thousand pounds, and hovered round the Bodhisattva, acting as her bodyguard. Kuan-yin made the cassock into a bundle and put it on his back. She took the fillets herself and held the nine-ringed staff in her hand. When they came to the Weak Waters, which form the boundary of the River of Sand, Kuan-yin said, "My disciple, this place is very difficult going. The scripture-seeker will be a man of common mortal birth. How will he get across?"

"Tell me first," said Hui-yen, "how wide is the River of Sands?"

The Bodhisattva was examining the river, when suddenly there was a great splash, and out jumped the most hideous monster imaginable. Holding a staff in its hand this creature made straight for the Bodhisattva.

"Halt!" cried Hui-yen, fending off the monster with his iron cudgel; and there on the shore of the River of Sands a fearful combat began. Up and down the shore the battle moved, and they had fought twenty or thirty bouts without reaching a decision, when the monster halted with his iron cudgel held up in front of him and said, "What priest are you, and where do you come from, that you dare resist me?"

"I am Prince Moksha, second son of Vaiśravana, now called Hui-yen.[1] I am now defending my superior on the journey to China, where we hope to find one who will come and fetch scriptures. What creature are you who dare to bar our path?"

"Ah," said the monster, suddenly remembering, "didn't I use to see you in Kuan-yin's bamboo-grove, practising austerities? What have you done with the Bodhisattva?"

"You didn't realize then that it was she on the bank?" said Hui-yen.

The creature was aghast; he lowered his weapon and allowed himself to be brought to Kuan-yin. "Bodhisattva, forgive my crime," he cried, bowing profoundly. "I am not the monster that I seem, but was a marshal of the hosts of Heaven, charged to wait upon the Jade Emperor when he rode in his Phoenix Chariot. But at a heavenly banquet I had the misfortune to break a crystal dish. By the Emperor's orders I received 800 lashes, and was banished to the world below, transformed into my present hideous shape. He sends flying swords that stab my breast and sides one day in every seven. I get nothing to eat, and every few days hunger drives me to come out and look for some traveller, on whose flesh I feed. Little did I think today that the traveller whom I was blindly attacking was none other than the Bodhisattva."

"It was for sinning in Heaven," said Kuan-yin, "that you were banished. Yet here you are adding sin to sin, slaying living creatures. I am on my way to China to look for a scripture-seeker. Why don't you join our sect, reform your ways, become a disciple of the scripture-seeker, and go with him to India to fetch the scriptures? I'll see to it that the flying swords stop piercing you. If the expedition is a success, you will have expiated your crime and be allowed to go back to your old employment in Heaven. Doesn't that idea please you?"

"I would gladly embrace the Faith," said the creature, "but there is something I must first confess. I have since I came here devoured countless human beings. Pilgrims have come this way several times, and I ate them all. The heads I threw into the River of Flowing Sands, and they sank to the bottom (such is the nature of this river that not even a goosefeather will float upon it). But there were nine skulls that remained floating on the water and would not sink. Seeing that these skulls behaved so strangely, I moored them with a rope, and in leisure moments drew

[1] The guardian spirit of the north; his name means "he who has heard everything."

them in and sported with them. If this is known, it seems likely that future pilgrims will not care to come this way, and my chances of salvation are lost."

"Not come this way! Nonsense!" said the Bodhisattva. "You can take the skulls and hang them round your neck. When the scripture-seeker arrives, a good use will be found for them." The monster accordingly took his vows and was received into the Faith, receiving the name of Sandy Priest. Having escorted Kuan-yin across the river, he went back and devoted himself to penances and purifications, never again taking life, but watching all the while for the pilgrim who was destined to come.

So the Bodhisattva parted with him and went on with Hui-yen towards China. After a while they came to a high mountain, from which there came an extremely bad smell. They had just decided to ride high over it on their clouds when there came a mad blast of wind, and there suddenly appeared before them a monster of hideous appearance. His lips curled and drooped like withered lotus leaves, his ears flapped like rush-work fans. He had tusks sharp as awls and a snout like the nozzle of a bellows. He rushed straight at Kuan-yin, striking at her with a muck-rake. Hui-yen warded off the blow, crying, "Foul fiend, mend your manners, and look out for my cudgel."

"This priest," cried the monster, "little knows what he is up against. Look out for my rake!"

And at the foot of the mountain the two of them had a great fight. Just when it was at its best, Kuan-yin who was watching in the sky above threw down some lotus flowers which fell just between the cudgel and the rake.

"What sort of a priest are you?" the monster cried, "that you dare play upon me the trick of the 'flower in the eye.'"

"Grovelling, low-born monster," said Hui-yen, "I am a disciple of the Bodhisattva Kuan-yin, and it was she who threw down these flowers. Didn't you recognize her?"

"You don't mean it!" said he. "The great Bodhisattva, the one that saves us from the three calamities and eight disasters?"

"Whom else should I mean?" said Hui-yen.

The monster dropped his rake and bowed low. "Old chap," he said, "where is the Bodhisattva? I wish you'd introduce me."

Hui-yen looked up and pointed. "There she is all right," he said.

The monster kowtowed skyward, crying in a loud voice, "Forgive me, Bodhisattva, forgive me."

Kuan-yin lowered her cloud and came up to him, saying, "How dare a filthy old pig-spirit like you attempt to bar my path?"

"I am not really a pig at all," he said. "I was a marshal of the hosts of Heaven, but one day I got a bit drunk and misbehaved with the Goddess of the Moon. For this the Jade Emperor had me soundly thrashed and banished me to the world below. When the time came for my next incarnation, I lost my way and got by mistake into the belly of an old mother pig, which accounts for what I look like now. I spend my time eating people, that I own. But I never noticed it was you I had run into. Save me, save me!"

"There is a proverb," said the Bodhisattva, "which runs: 'Works of damnation cannot lead to salvation.' Having been banished from Heaven because you broke its laws, you have not repented, but live on human flesh. Are you not inviting a double punishment for both your crimes?"

"Salvation indeed!" cried the monster. "If I followed your advice, what should I live on? On the wind, I suppose. There's another proverb which says, 'If the

Government gets hold of you they'll flog you to death; if the Buddhists get hold of you they'll starve you to death.' Go away! I see I shall get on much better by catching a family of travellers now and then, and eating their daughter if she's buxom and tasty, no matter whether that's two crimes, three crimes, or a thousand crimes."

"There is a saying," the Bodhisattva replied, " 'Heaven helps those who mean well.' If you give up your evil ways, you may be sure you won't lack nourishment. There are five crops in the world; so there is no need to starve. Why should you feed on human flesh?"

The monster was like one who wakes from a dream. "I should like to reform," he said, "but 'Him no prayer can help who has sinned against Heaven.' "

"Here's a chance for you," said Kuan-yin. "We are on our way to China to look for a seeker of scriptures. If you were to become his disciple and go with him to India, you would wipe out all your old sin."

"I will, I will," blurted out the creature. All that remained now was to tonsure him and administer the vows, and it was agreed that he should be known in religion as Pigsy. He was told to fast, do penance, and keep all the while on the watch for the destined pilgrim.

Proceeding on their way Kuan-yin and Hui-yen were presently accosted by a dragon. "What dragon are you?" asked the Bodhisattva, "and what have you done that you should be cast adrift here?"

"I am a son of the Dragon King of the Western Ocean," the dragon said. "I inadvertently set fire to his palace and some of his Pearls of Wisdom were burnt. My father insisted that I had done it on purpose and accused me in the Courts of Heaven of attempted rebellion. The Jade Emperor hung me up here in the sky, had me given 300 cuts of the lash, and in a few days I am to be executed. Can you do anything to help me?"

Kuan-yin promptly went up to Heaven, secured an interview with the Jade Emperor, and begged that the dragon might be forgiven, on condition that he allowed himself to be ridden upon by the pilgrim who was going to India to bring back the true scriptures. The request was granted, and the Bodhisattva ordered the little dragon to go down into a deep canyon and await the arrival of the pilgrim. It was then to change into a white horse and carry him to India.

Kuan-yin and Hui-yen had not gone far on their way to China when they suddenly saw great shafts of golden light and many wreaths of magic vapour.

"That is the Mountain of the Five Elements," said Hui-yen. "I can see the imprint of Buddha's seal upon it."

"Is not that the mountain," said Kuan-yin, "under which is imprisoned the Sage Equal of Heaven, who upset the Peach Banquet and ran amok in the halls of Heaven?"

"Very true," said Hui-yen.

They alighted on the mountain and examined the seal, which was the six-syllable spell OM MANI PADME HUM. Kuan-yin sighed a deep sigh, and recited the following poem:

> "Long ago performed in vain prodigies of valour.
> In his blackness of heart he upset the Heavenly Peach Banquet;
> In mad rashness he dared to rob the Patriarch of Tao.
> A hundred thousand heavenly troops could not overcome him;
> He terrorized the realm of Heaven throughout its nine spheres.
> At last in Buddha Tathagata Monkey met his match.
> Will he ever again be set at large and win back his renown?"

"Who is it," a voice came from inside the mountain, "who recites verses that tell of my misdoings?"

Kuan-yin came down towards the place from which the voice seemed to come, and at the foot of a cliff found the guardian deities of the place, who after welcoming the Bodhisattva, led her to where Monkey was imprisoned. He was pent in a kind of stone box, and though he could speak he could not move hand or foot.

"Monkey," cried the Bodhisattva, "do you know me or not?"

He peered through a chink with his steely, fiery eyes and cried aloud, "How should I not know you? You are she of Potalaka, the Saviour Kuan-yin. To what do I owe this pleasure? Here where days and years are one to me, no friend or acquaintance has ever come to seek me out. Where, pray, do you come from?"

"Buddha sent me," said she, "to China, to look for one who will come to India and fetch the scriptures, and as this place is on the way, I took the opportunity of calling upon you."

"Buddha tricked me," said Monkey, "and imprisoned me under this mountain five hundred years ago, and here I have been ever since. I entreat you to use your powers to rescue me."

"Your sins were very great," she said, "and I am by no means confident that if you get out you would not at once get into trouble again."

"No," said Monkey, "I have repented, and now want only to embrace the Faith and devote myself to good works."

"Very well, then," said the Bodhisattva, delighted. "Wait while I go to the land of T'ang and find my scripture-seeker. He shall deliver you. You shall be his disciple and embrace our Faith."

"With all my heart," said Monkey.

"In that case," said Kuan-yin, "you will have to have a name in religion."

"I've got one," said Monkey. "I am called Aware-of-Vacuity."

"In that case," said Kuan-yin, "there is nothing more I need tell you at present. I must be going."

They left Monkey and went on eastwards. In a few days they reached the land of T'ang, and soon came to the city of Ch'ang-an,[2] where they changed themselves into shabby wandering priests, and coming to the shrine of a local deity in one of the main streets, they went straight in. The deity and his attendant demons recognized Kuan-yin at once, despite her disguise, and welcomed her with a great flurry of bowings and scrapings. Then he sent word to the god of the Municipal Shrine, and all the temples in Ch'ang-an, informing the gods that the Bodhisattva had arrived. Presently they all came tramping along, begging to be excused for not having come to meet her. "This must not get out," she said. "I am here completely incognito. I have come by Buddha's orders to look for someone to bring the scriptures from India. I should like to put up for a day or two in one of your temples, and as soon as I have found my pilgrim I shall leave."

The gods then all retired to their temples, Kuan-yin and Hui-yen putting up for the time being in the shrine of the Municipal God, where they passed for a couple of ordinary priests.

If you do not know whom they found to fetch scriptures, you must listen to what is told in the next chapter. . . .

[2]Ancient city at the site of the present-day Xi'an in Shaanxi province. At the time of the T'ang dynasty (618–907), it was the cultural capital of East Asia and the largest city in the world.

FROM
Chapter 12

. . . Meanwhile the Bodhisattva Kuan-yin had been looking everywhere in Ch'ang-an for a priest to fetch the scriptures from India. Hearing that the Emperor T'ai Tsung[3] was celebrating a great Mass, and that the ceremony was being directed by that River Float with whose birth she had herself been connected, "Who," she asked herself, "could be better fitted for that mission than he?" And she set out into the streets, taking with her Moksha, and the treasures that Buddha had given to her. "What were these treasures?" you ask. They were a magic brocaded cassock, and a priest's staff with nine rings. Apart from these, there were the three magic fillets which she left in safe keeping for future use, only taking with her the cassock and staff. Wandering about the streets of Ch'ang-an was a stupid priest who had failed to be chosen to take part in the Mass. Seeing the Bodhisattva, disguised as a shabby priest, barefoot and in rags, holding up his shining cassock as though for sale, he remembered that he still had a few strings of cash upon him, and coming forward he said, "What would you take for the cassock?"

"The cassock," said Kuan-yin, "is worth five thousand pounds; the staff, two thousand."

"Seven thousand pounds for a couple of coarse, low-class articles like that! You must be mad," he said. "Why, if it were guaranteed that the user of them would be immortal, or that he would become a living Buddha, they wouldn't fetch that price. Be off with you! I don't want them."

The Bodhisattva said not a word more, but signing to Moksha went on her way. They had not gone far before they reached the Eastern Flower Gate, where whom should they meet but the minister Hsiao Yü, just returning from Court. His outriders were clearing the streets, but Kuan-yin, so far from removing herself, stood right in the minister's path, holding up the cassock. He reined in his horse, and seeing this dazzling object held up in front of him, he told a servant to ask the price.

"Five thousand pounds for the cassock and two thousand for the staff," said Kuan-yin.

"What makes them so expensive?" asked Hsiao.

"The cassock," said Kuan-yin, "would be valuable to some people and quite the reverse to others; it would cost some people a lot of money, and others none at all."

"What does that mean?" asked Hsiao.

"The wearer of my cassock," said Kuan-yin, "will not be drowned or poisoned or meet wild beasts upon his way. But that is only if he is a good man; if it gets on to the back of a gluttonous, lustful priest, or one who does not keep his vows, or of a layman who destroys scriptures and speaks evil of Buddha, he will rue the day that he saw this cassock."

"And what do you mean," asked Hsiao, "by saying that it would cost some people a lot of money and others none at all?"

"To a purchaser who does not reverence Buddha's Law and Three Treasures, the price of the cassock and staff together would be seven thousand pounds," said Kuan-yin. "But a pious and reverent man, devoted to our Buddha, could have them both for the asking."

Hearing this, Hsiao dismounted, and bowing respectfully, "Reverend Sir," he said, "the Emperor of this great land is himself a most devout man, and all

[3] Second emperor of the T'ang dynasty, who ruled from 626 to 649.

his ministers vie with one another in carrying out his behests. At present he is celebrating a Great Mass, and this cassock might well be worn by the high priest Hsüan Tsang, who is in charge of the whole ceremony. Let us go to the palace and speak to the Emperor about this."

The Emperor was delighted at this proposal, and at once told Hsüan Tsang to put on the cassock and hold the staff in his hand. Then he appointed a retinue to accompany him, and had him led through the city in triumph, for all the world like a successful candidate at the examinations. In the great city of Ch'ang-an travelling merchants and tradesmen, princes and nobles, writers and scholars, grown men and young girls all fought with one another for good places from which to view the procession. "A noble priest! A Lohan[4] come to earth, a living Bodhisattva!" they cried in admiration when they saw Hsüan Tsang pass. And the priests in his temple when he returned, seeing him thus accoutred, could scarcely believe that it was not the Bodhisattva Kshitigarbha[5] himself who had come to visit them.

Time passed, and now at last came the final ceremonies of the forty-ninth day, at which Hsüan Tsang was to deliver the closing sermon. "The Great Mass closes today," said Kuan-yin to Moksha. "Let us mingle in the throng, so that we may see how the ceremonies are conducted and what blessing there is in our gift, and hear what school of Buddhism he preaches." The great Hsüan Tsang, mounted on a high dais, first read the Sutra on the Salvation of the Dead, then discussed the Collect upon the Security of kingdoms, and finally expounded the Exhortation to Pious Works. At this point Kuan-yin approached the dais, and cried in a loud voice, "Why can't you give us some Big Vehicle Scriptures?"

So far from being put out by this interruption, Hsüan Tsang was delighted to hear of other scriptures, and scrambling down from the dais he saluted his interrupter and said, "Reverend Sir, forgive me for not knowing that I had one so learned as you in my audience. It is true that we have none of us any knowledge of the Big Vehicle, and have only expounded the Little Vehicle."

"Your Little Vehicle," said Kuan-yin, "cannot save the souls of the dead, and only leads to general misapprehension and confusion. I have three sections of Great Vehicle teaching, called the Tripitaka or Three Baskets. These can carry the souls of the dead to Heaven, can save all those that are in trouble, can add immeasurably to life's span, and can deliver those that trust in it from the comings and goings of Incarnation."

At this point one of the ushers rushed to the Emperor and announced that two shabby priests had interrupted the Master, pulled him down from the dais, and started some nonsensical argument with him. The Emperor ordered them to be seized and brought to him. On appearing before the Emperor they did not prostrate themselves or even salute him, but merely asked what he wanted of them.

"Are you not the priest who gave me the cassock the other day?" said the Emperor. "I am," said Kuan-yin.

"You had a perfect right," said the Emperor, "to come here and listen to the preaching, eat with the other priests, and go away quietly. But you have no business to interrupt the preaching and disturb the whole proceedings."

"Your preacher," Kuan-yin said, "knows only about the Little Vehicle, which cannot save souls. We possess the Tripitaka of the Big Vehicle, which saves the souls of the dead and succours those that are in peril."

The Emperor was delighted at this news, and asked at once where it was.

---

[4]A Buddhist saint or martyr.

[5]The savior who delivers souls from the underworld.

"It is in India," said Kuan-yin, "at the temple of the Great Thunder Clap, where the Buddha Tathagata dwells."

"Do you know these teachings by heart?" asked the Emperor.

"I do," said the Bodhisattva.

"Then Hsüan Tsang shall retire," said the Emperor, "and you shall mount the dais and expound them to us." But instead of doing so Kuan-yin floated up into the sky and revealed herself in all the glory of her true form, holding the willow-spray and the sacred vase, while Moksha stood at her left side, holding his staff.

The Emperor hastened to prostrate himself, and all his ministers knelt down and burned incense, while the audience, priests, nuns, officers, craftsmen and merchants, bowed down, crying, "The Bodhisattva, the Bodhisattva!"

The Emperor's joy was so great that he forgot his rivers and hills, his ministers in their excitement broke every rule of etiquette, and all the multitude murmured again and again "Glory be to the Great Bodhisattva Kuan-yin." His Majesty decided to have a picture of the Bodhisattva painted by a skilful artist, in full colours. His choice fell upon Wu Tao-tzu, that genius of the brush, that prodigy of portraiture, that fabulous embodiment of vision and inspiration. It was this painter who afterwards made the portraits of the heroes of the dynasty in the Tower of Rising Smoke. He now wielded his magic brush and rendered every detail of these sacred forms. Presently the figures began to recede farther and farther into the sky, and finally their golden effulgence could be seen no more.

At this point the Emperor dismissed the assembly, and declared that the next thing to do was to find a traveller who would go to India and fetch the Scriptures. An inquiry was made in the temple, and Hsüan Tsang immediately came forward and bowing low said, "I am a humble cleric, devoid of any capacity; but I am ready to undertake the quest of these Scriptures, be the fatigues and difficulties what they may, if by doing so I may promote the security of your Majesty's streams and hills." The Emperor was delighted, and raising him from his knees with his royal hand, "Reverend Sir," he said, "if indeed you are willing to do me this loyal service, undeterred by the length of the journey and all the mountains and rivers that you will have to cross, I will make you my bond-brother." And true to his word, in front of the Buddha image in that temple, he bowed four times to Hsüan Tsang and addressed him as "Holy Priest, my brother." Hsüan Tsang on his side, burning incense before the Buddha, swore to do all that lay in his power to reach India. "And if I do not reach India and do not bring back the Scriptures, may I fall into the nethermost pit of Hell, rather than return empty-handed to China."

When Hsüan Tsang rejoined the other priests, they pressed round him, asking whether it was indeed true that he had sworn to go to India. "For I have heard," one of them said, "that it is a very long way and that on the road there are many tigers, panthers and evil spirits. I fear you will not come back to us alive." "I have taken my oath," said Hsüan Tsang, "and I must faithfully fulfil it. I know well enough that the hazards of such a journey are great." And presently he said, "My disciples, I may be away for two or three years, or five, or seven. If you see the branches of the pine-tree at the gate turning eastward, you will know I am coming back. If not, it will mean that I shall never return."

Early next day, in the presence of all his ministers, the Emperor signed a rescript authorizing Hsüan Tsang's quest, and stamped it with the seal of free passage. The astrologers announced that the posture of the heavens made the day particularly favourable for the start of a long journey. At this point, Hsüan Tsang himself was announced. "Brother," said the Emperor, "I am told that this would be a lucky day for you to start. Here are your travelling papers, and here is a golden bowl for you to collect alms in during your journey. I have chosen two followers to go with you, and a horse for you to ride. It only remains for you to start." Hsüan Tsang was ready enough, and taking the Emperor's present set out towards the gates of the city, accompanied by the Emperor and a host of officials. When they reached the gates, they found that the priests of the Hung-fu temple were waiting there with a provision of winter and summer clothing. When it had been added to the luggage, the Emperor told a servant to bring wine, and raising the cup he asked Hsüan Tsang if he had a by-name.

"Being a priest," said Hsüan Tsang, "I have not thought it proper to assume a by-name."

"The Bodhisattva mentioned," said the Emperor, "that the Scriptures in India are called the Tripitaka. How would it be if you took 'Tripitaka' as your by-name?"

Hsüan Tsang accepted with thanks, but when he was offered the wine-cup, he declined, saying that abstinence from wine was the first rule of priesthood, and that he never took it. "This is an exceptional occasion," said the Emperor, "and the wine is not at all strong; just drink one cup to speed you on your journey." Tripitaka dared not refuse; but just as he was going to drink, the Emperor stooped down and with his royal fingers scooped up a handful of dust and threw it into the cup. At first Tripitaka could not make out why he had done this, but the Emperor said laughing, "Tell me, brother, how long do you expect to be away?"

"I hope," said Tripitaka, "to be back in three years."

"That's a long time," said the Emperor, "and you have a long way to go. You would do well to drink this cup, for are we not told that a handful of one's country's soil is worth more than ten thousand pounds of foreign gold?"

Then Tripitaka understood why the Emperor had thrown the dust into the cup, drank it down to the last dregs, and set out upon his way. And if you do not know how he fared upon that way, listen to what is told in the next chapter.

FROM
CHAPTER 13

. . . Tripitaka . . . travelled over difficult country for half a day, without seeing any sign of human habitation. He was now very hungry, and the road was extremely precipitous. He was at the height of his difficulties when he heard two tigers roaring just ahead of him and saw behind him several huge serpents twisting and twining. To make matters worse, on his left was some species of deadly scorpion, and on his right a wild beast of unknown species. To cope single-handed with such a situation was clearly impossible, and there was nothing for it but to resign himself to his fate. Soon his horse sank quivering on to its knees and refused to budge. Suddenly a medley of tigers and wolves, with other wild and fearful creatures, set upon him all together. He would have been utterly lost, had there not at this very moment appeared a man with a three-pronged spear in his hand and bow and arrows at his waist. "Save me, save me!" cried Tripitaka. The man rushed forward and throwing aside his spear, raised Tripitaka from his knees. "Do not be afraid," he said, "I am a hunter, and I came out to find a couple of mountain creatures to eat for my supper. You must forgive me for intruding upon you so unceremoniously." Tripitaka thanked the hunter, and explained what brought him to this place. "I live near here," said the hunter, "and spend all my time in dealing with tigers and serpents and the like, so that such creatures are afraid of the sight of me and run away. If you indeed come from the Court of T'ang we are fellow-countrymen, for the frontier of the empire is a little way beyond here."

. . .

Mountain scenery of indescribable beauty stretched out before them. Towards noon they came to a gigantic mountain, up which Tripitaka began to clamber with great pains, while the hunter sprang up it as though he had been walking on flat ground. Halfway up the hunter halted, and turning to Tripitaka, he said, "I fear at this point we must part."

"I entreat you to take me just one stage farther," begged Tripitaka.

"Sir," said the hunter, "you do not know. This mountain is called the Mountain of the Two Frontiers. Its east side belongs to our land of T'ang; on the west side lies the land of the Tartars. The wolves and tigers on the far side I have not subjected, moreover I have not the right to cross the frontier. You must go on alone."

Tripitaka wrung his hands in despair, clutched at the hunter's sleeve and wept copiously. At this point there came from under the mountain a stentorian voice, crying repeatedly, "The Master has come." Both Tripitaka and the hunter started, in great surprise. If you do not know whose voice it was they heard, listen to what is told in the next chapter.

CHAPTER 14

The hunter and Tripitaka were still wondering who had spoken, when again they heard the voice saying, "The Master has come."

The hunter's servants said, "That is the voice of the old monkey who is shut up in the stone casket of the mountain side."

"Why, to be sure it is!" said the hunter.

"What old monkey is that?" asked Tripitaka.

"This mountain," said the hunter, "was once called the Mountain of the Five Elements. But after our great T'ang Dynasty had carried out its campaigns to the West, its name was changed to Mountain of the Two Frontiers. Years ago a very old man told me that at the time when Wang Mang overthrew the First Han Dynasty, Heaven dropped this mountain in order to imprison a magic monkey under it. He has local spirits as his gaolers, who, when he is hungry, give him iron pills to eat, and when he is thirsty give him copper-juice to drink, so that despite cold and short commons he is still alive. That cry certainly comes from him. You need not be uneasy. We'll go down and have a look."

After going downhill for some way they came to the stone box, in which there was really a monkey. Only his head was visible, and one paw, which he waved violently through the opening, saying, "Welcome, Master! Welcome! Get me out of here, and I will protect you on your journey to the West."

The hunter stepped boldly up, and removing the grasses from Monkey's hair and brushing away the grit from under his chin, "What have you got to say for yourself?" he asked.

"To you, nothing," said Monkey. "But I have something to ask of that priest. Tell him to come here."

"What do you want to ask me?" said Tripitaka.

"Were you sent by the Emperor of T'ang to look for Scriptures in India?" asked Monkey.

"I was," said Tripitaka. "And what of that?"

"I am the Great Sage Equal of Heaven," said Monkey. "Five hundred years ago I made trouble in the Halls of Heaven, and Buddha clamped me down in this place. Not long ago the Bodhisattva Kuan-yin, whom Buddha had ordered to look around for someone to fetch Scriptures from India, came here and promised me that if I would amend my ways and faithfully protect the pilgrim on his way, I was to be released, and afterwards would find salvation. Ever since then I have been waiting impatiently night and day for you to come and let me out. I will protect you while you are going to get Scriptures and follow you as your disciple."

Tripitaka was delighted. "The only trouble is," he said, "that I have no axe or chisel, so how am I to get you out?"

"There is no need for axe or chisel," said Monkey. "You have only to want me to be out, and I shall be out."

"How can that be?" asked Tripitaka.

"On the top of the mountain," said Monkey, "is a seal stamped with golden letters by Buddha himself. Take it away, and I shall be out."

Tripitaka was for doing so at once, but the hunter took him aside and said there was no telling whether one could believe the monkey or not. "It's true, it's true!" screamed Monkey from inside the casket. At last the hunter was prevailed upon to come with him and, scrambling back again to the very top, they did indeed see innumerable beams of golden light streaming from a great square slab of rock, on which was imprinted in golden letters the inscription OM MANI PADME HUM.

Tripitaka knelt down and did reverence to the inscription, saying, "If this monkey is indeed worthy to be a disciple, may this imprint be removed and may the monkey be released and accompany me to the seat of Buddha. But if he is not fit to be a disciple, but an unruly monster who would discredit my undertaking, may the imprint of this seal remain where it is." At once there came a gust of fragrant wind that carried the six letters of the inscription up into the air, and a voice was heard saying, "I am the Great Sage's gaoler. Today the time of his penance is ended and I am going to ask Buddha to let him loose." Having bowed reverently in the direction from which the voice came, Tripitaka and the hunter went back to the stone casket and said to Monkey, "The inscription is removed. You can come out."

"You must go to a little distance," said Monkey. "I don't want to frighten you."

They withdrew a little way, but heard Monkey calling to them "Farther, farther!" They did as they were bid, and presently heard a tremendous crushing and rending. They were all in great consternation, expecting the mountain to come hurtling on top of them, when suddenly the noise subsided, and Monkey appeared, kneeling in front of Tripitaka's horse, crying, "Master, I am out!" Then he sprang up and called to the hunter, "Brother, I'll trouble you to dust the grass-wisps from my cheek." Then he put together the packs and hoisted them on to the horse, which on seeing him became at once completely obedient. For Monkey had been a groom in Heaven, and it was natural that an ordinary horse should hold him in great awe.

Tripitaka, seeing that he knew how to make himself useful and looked as though he would make a pretty tolerable śramana,[6] said to him, "Disciple, we must give you a name in religion."

"No need for that," said Monkey, "I have one already. My name in religion is 'Aware-of-Vacuity.' "

"Excellent!" said Tripitaka. "That fits in very well with the names of my other disciples. You shall be Monkey Aware-of-Vacuity."

The hunter, seeing that Monkey had got everything ready, said to Tripitaka, "I am very glad you have been fortunate enough to pick up this excellent disciple. As you are so well provided for, I will bid you good-bye and turn back."

---

[6] A monk.

"I have brought you a long way from home," said Tripitaka, "and cannot thank you enough. Please also apologize to your mother and wife for all the trouble I gave, and tell them I will thank them in person on my return."

Tripitaka had not been long on the road with Monkey and had only just got clear of the Mountain of the Two Frontiers, when a tiger suddenly appeared, roaring savagely and lashing its tail. Tripitaka was terrified, but Monkey seemed delighted. "Don't be frightened, Master," he said. "He has only come to supply me with an apron." So saying, he took a needle from behind his ear and, turning his face to the wind, made a few magic passes, and instantly it became a huge iron cudgel. "It is five hundred years since I last used this precious thing," he said, "and today it is going to furnish me with a little much-needed clothing."

Look at him! He strides forward, crying, "Cursed creature, stand your ground!" The tiger crouched in the dust and dared not budge. Down came the cudgel on its head. The earth was spattered with its blood. Tripitaka rolled off his horse as best he could, crying with an awe-struck voice, "Heavens! When the hunter killed that stripy tiger yesterday, he struggled with it for hours on end. But this disciple of mine walked straight up to the tiger and struck it dead. True indeed is the saying 'Strong though he be, there is always a stronger.' "

"Sit down a while," said Monkey, "and wait while I undress him; then when I am dressed, we'll go on."

"How can you undress him?" said Tripitaka. "He hasn't got any clothes."

"Don't worry about me," said Monkey. "I know what I am about."

Dear Monkey! He took a hair from his tail, blew on it with magic breath, and it became a sharp little knife, with which he slit the tiger's skin straight down and ripped it off in one piece. Then he cut off the paws and head, and trimmed the skin into one big square. Holding it out, he measured it with his eye, and said, "A bit too wide. I must divide it in two." He cut it in half, put one half aside and the other round his waist, making it fast with some rattan that he pulled up from the roadside. "Now we can go," he said, "and when we get to the next house, I'll borrow a needle and thread and sew it up properly."

"What has become of your cudgel?" asked Tripitaka, when they were on their way again.

"I must explain to you," said Monkey. "This cudgel is a piece of magic iron that I got in the Dragon King's palace, and it was with it that I made havoc in Heaven. I can make it as large or as small as I please. Just now I made it the size of an embroidery needle and put it away behind my ear, where it is always at hand in case I need it."

"And why," asked Tripitaka, "did that tiger, as soon as it saw you, crouch down motionless and allow you to strike it just as you chose?"

"The fact is," said Monkey, "that not only tigers but dragons too dare not do anything against me. But that is not all. I have such arts as can make rivers turn back in their course, and can raise tempests on the sea. Small wonder, then, that I can filch a tiger's skin. When we get into real difficulties you will see what I am really capable of."

"Master," said Monkey presently, "it is getting late. Over there is a clump of trees, and I think there must be a house. We had better see if we can spend the night there." Tripitaka whipped his horse, and soon they did indeed come to a farm, outside the gates of which he dismounted. Monkey cried "Open the door!" and presently there appeared a very old man, leaning on a staff. Muttering to himself, he began to push open the door, but when he saw Monkey, looking (with the tiger skin at his waist) for all the world like a thunder demon, he was terrified out of his wits and could only murmur "There's a devil at the door, sure enough there's a devil!" Tripitaka came up to him just in time to prevent him hobbling away. "Old patron," he said, "you need not be afraid. This is not a devil; it is my disciple." Seeing that Tripitaka at any rate was a clean-built, comely man, he took comfort a little and said, "I don't know what temple you come from, but you have no right to bring such an evil-looking fellow to my house."

"I come from the Court of T'ang," said Tripitaka, "and I am going to India to get Scriptures. As my way brought me near your house, I have come here in the hope that you would consent to give me a night's lodging. I shall be starting off again tomorrow before daybreak."

"You may be a man of T'ang," said the old man, "but I'll warrant that villainous fellow is no man of T'ang!"

"Have you no eyes in your head," shouted Monkey. "The man of T'ang is my master. I am his disciple, and no man of T'ang or sugar-man[7] or honey-man either. I am the Great Sage Equal of Heaven. You people here know me well enough, and I have seen you before."

"Where have you seen me?" he asked. "Didn't you when you were small cut the brushwood from in front of my face and gather the herbs that grew on my cheek?"

"The stone monkey in the stone casket!" gasped the old man. "I see that you are a little like him. But how did you get out?"

Monkey told the whole story, and the old man at once bowed before him, and asked them both to step inside.

"Great Sage, how old are you?" the old man asked, when they were seated.

"Let us first hear your age," said Monkey.

"A hundred and thirty," said the old man.

"Then you are young enough to be my great-great-grandson at least," said Monkey. "I have no idea when I was born. But I was under that mountain for five hundred years."

"True enough," said the old man. "I remember my grandfather telling me that this mountain was dropped from Heaven in order to trap a monkey divinity, and you say that you have only just got out. When I used to see you in my childhood, there was grass growing out of your head and mud on your cheeks. I was not at all afraid of you then. Now there is no mud on your cheeks and no grass on your head. You look thinner, and with that tiger-skin at your waist, who would know that you weren't a devil?"

"I don't want to give you all a lot of trouble," said Monkey presently, "but it is five hundred years since I last washed. Could you let us have a little hot water? I am sure my Master would be glad to wash too."

When they had both washed, they sat down in front of the lamp. "One more request," said Monkey. "Could you lend me a needle and thread?"

"By all means, by all means," said the old man, and he told his old wife to bring them. Just then Monkey caught sight of a white shirt that Tripitaka had taken off when he washed and not put on again. He snatched it up and put it on. Then he wriggled out of the tiger-skin, sewed it up in one piece, made a "horse-face fold"[8] and put it round his waist again, fastening the rattan belt. Presenting himself to Tripitaka he said, "How do you like me in this garb? Is it an improvement?"

"Splendid!" said Tripitaka. "Now you really do look like a pilgrim."

"Disciple," added Tripitaka, "if you don't mind accepting an off-cast, you can have that shirt for your own."

[7]"Sugar" in Chinese is *T'ang*.

[8]Meaning uncertain. The modern edition substitutes "sewed it into a skirt."

They rose early next day, and the old man brought them washing-water and breakfast. Then they set out again on their way, lodging late and starting early for many days. One morning they suddenly heard a cry and six men rushed out at them from the roadside, all armed with pikes and swords. "Halt, priest!" they cried. "We want your horse and your packs, and quickly too, or you will not escape with your life."

Tripitaka, in great alarm, slid down from his horse and stood there speechless.

"Don't worry," said Monkey. "This only means more clothes and travelling-money for us."

"Monkey, are you deaf?" said Tripitaka. "They ordered us to surrender the horse and luggage, and you talk of getting clothes and money from them!"

"You keep an eye on the packs and the horse," said Monkey, "while I settle matters with them! You'll soon see what I mean."

"They are very strong men and there are six of them," said Tripitaka. "How can a little fellow like you hope to stand up against them single-handed?"

Monkey did not stop to argue, but strode forward and, folding his arms across his chest, bowed to the robbers and said, "Sirs, for what reason do you stop poor priests from going on their way?"

"We are robber kings," they said, "mountain lords among the Benevolent.[9] Everyone knows us. How comes it that you are so ignorant? Hand over your things at once, and we will let you pass. But if half the word 'no' leaves your lips, we shall hack you to pieces and grind your bones to powder."

"I, too," said Monkey, "am a great hereditary king, and lord of a mountain for hundreds of years; yet I have never heard your names."

"In that case, let us tell you," they said. "The first of us is called Eye that Sees and Delights; the second, Ear that Hears and is Angry; the third, Nose that Smells and Covets; the fourth, Tongue that Tastes and Desires; the fifth, Mind that Conceives and Lusts; the sixth, Body that Supports and Suffers."

"You're nothing but six hairy ruffians," said Monkey, laughing. "We priests, I would have you know, are your lords and masters, yet you dare block our path. Bring out all the stolen goods you have about you and divide them into seven parts. Then, if you leave me one part, I will spare your lives."

The robbers were so taken aback that they did not know whether to be angry or amused. "You must be mad," they said. "You've just lost all you possess, and you talk of sharing our booty with us!" Brandishing their spears and flourishing their swords they all rushed forward and began to rain blows upon Monkey's head. But he stood stock still and betrayed not the slightest concern.

"Priest, your head must be very hard!" they cried.

"That's all right," said Monkey, "I'm not in a hurry. But when your arms are tired, I'll take out my needle and do my turn."

"What does he mean?" they said. "Perhaps he's a doctor turned priest. But we are none of us ill, so why should he talk about using the needle?"

Monkey took his needle from behind his ear, recited a spell which changed it into a huge cudgel, and cried, "Hold your ground and let old Monkey try his hand upon you!" The robbers fled in confusion, but in an instant he was among them and striking right and left he slew them all, stripped off their clothing and seized their baggage. Then he came back to Tripitaka and said laughing, "Master, we can start now; I have killed them all."

---

[9] "Benevolent" was thieves' slang for "bandit."

"I am very sorry to hear it," said Tripitaka. "One has no right to kill robbers, however violent and wicked they may be. The most one may do is to bring them before a magistrate. It would have been quite enough in this case if you had driven them away. Why kill them? You have behaved with a cruelty that ill becomes one of your sacred calling."

"If I had not killed them," said Monkey, "they would have killed you."

"A priest," said Tripitaka, "should be ready to die rather than commit acts of violence."

"I don't mind telling you," said Monkey, "that five hundred years ago, when I was a king, I killed a pretty fair number of people, and if I had held your view I should certainly never have become the Great Sage Equal of Heaven."

"It was because of your unfortunate performances in Heaven," said Tripitaka, "that you had to do penance for five hundred years. If now that you have repented and become a priest you go on behaving as in old days, you can't come with me to India. You've made a very bad start."

The one thing Monkey had never been able to bear was to be scolded, and when Tripitaka began to lecture him like this, he flared up at once and cried, "All right! I'll give up being a priest, and won't go with you to India. You needn't go on at me any more. I'm off!"

Tripitaka did not answer. His silence enraged Monkey even further. He shook himself and with a last "I'm off!" he bounded away. When Tripitaka looked up, he had completely disappeared. "It's no use trying to teach people like that," said Tripitaka to himself gloomily. "I only said a word or two, and off he goes. Very well then. Evidently it is not my fate to have a disciple; so I must get on as best I can without one."

He collected the luggage, hoisted it on to the horse's back and set out on foot, leading the horse with one hand and carrying his priest's staff with the other, in very low spirits. He had not gone far, when he saw an old woman carrying a brocaded coat and embroidered cap. As she came near, Tripitaka drew his horse to the side of the road to let her pass.

"Where are you off to all alone?" she asked.

"The Emperor of China has sent me to India to fetch Scriptures," said Tripitaka.

"The Temple of the Great Thunder Clap where Buddha lives," said she, "is a hundred and one thousand leagues away. You surely don't expect to get there with only one horse and no disciple to wait upon you?"

"I picked up a disciple a few days ago," said Tripitaka, "but he behaved badly and I was obliged to speak rather severely to him; whereupon he went off in a huff, and I have not seen him since."

"I've got a brocade coat and a cap with a metal band," said the old woman. "They belonged to my son. He entered a monastery, but when he had been a monk for three days, he died. I went and fetched them from the monastery to keep in memory of him. If you had a disciple, I should be very glad to let you have them."

"That is very kind of you," said Tripitaka, "but my disciple has run away, so I cannot accept them."

"Which way did he go?" asked the old woman.

"The last time I heard his voice, it came from the east," said Tripitaka.

"That's the way that my house lies," said the old woman. "I expect he'll turn up there. I've got a spell here which I'll let you learn, if you promise not to teach it to anybody. I'll go and look for him and send him back to you. Make him wear this cap and coat. If he disobeys you, say the spell, and he'll give no more trouble and never dare to leave you."

Suddenly the old woman changed into a shaft of golden light, which disappeared towards the east. Tripitaka at once guessed that she was the Bodhisattva Kuan-yin in disguise. He bowed and burned incense towards the east. Then having stored away the cap and coat he sat at the roadside, practising the spell.

After Monkey left the Master, he somersaulted through the clouds and landed right in the palace of the Dragon King of the Eastern Ocean.

"I heard recently that your penance was over," said the dragon, "and made sure you would have gone back to be king in your fairy cave."

"That's what I am doing," said Monkey. "But to start with I became a priest."

"A priest?" said the dragon. "How did that happen?"

"Kuan-yin persuaded me to accompany a priest of T'ang," said Monkey, "who is going to India to get Scriptures; so I was admitted to the Order."

"That's certainly a step in the right direction," said the dragon. "I am sure I congratulate you. But in that case, what are you doing here in the east?"

"It comes of my master being so unpractical," said Monkey. "We met some brigands, and naturally I killed them. Then he started scolding me. You may imagine I wasn't going to stand that. So I left him at once, and am going back to my kingdom. But I thought I would look you up on the way, and see if you could give me a cup of tea."

When he had been given his cup of tea, he looked round the room, and saw on the wall a picture of Chang Liang[10] offering the slipper. Monkey asked what it was about. "You were in Heaven at the time," said the dragon, "and naturally would not know about it. The immortal in the picture is Huang Shih Kung, and the other figure is Chang Liang. Once when Shih Kung was sitting on a bridge, his shoe came off and fell under the bridge. He called to Chang Liang to pick it up and bring it to him. Chang Liang did so, whereupon the Immortal at once let it fall again, and Chang Liang again fetched it. This happened three times, without Chang Liang showing the slightest sign of impatience. Huang Shih Kung then gave him a magic treatise, by means of which he defeated all the enemies of the House of Han, and became the greatest hero the Han dynasty. In his old age he became a disciple of the Immortal Red Pine Seed and achieved Tao. Great Sage, you must learn to have a little more patience, if you hope to accompany the pilgrim to India and gain the Fruits of Illumination." Monkey looked thoughtful. "Great Sage," said the dragon, "you must learn to control yourself and submit to the will of others, if you are not to spoil all your chances."

"Not another word!" said Monkey, "I'll go back at once."

On the way he met the Bodhisattva Kuan-yin. "What are you doing here?" she asked.

"The seal was removed and I got out," said Monkey, "and became Tripitaka's disciple. But he said I didn't know how to behave, and I gave him the slip. But now I am going back to look after him."

"Go as fast as you can," said the Bodhisattva, "and try to do better this time."

"Master," said Monkey, when he came back and found Tripitaka sitting dejectedly by the roadside, "what are you doing still sitting here?"

"And where have you been?" asked Tripitaka. "I hadn't the heart to go on, and was just sitting here waiting for you."

"I only went to the Dragon of the Eastern Ocean," said Monkey, "to drink a cup of tea."

[10] A warrior who died in 189 B.C.E., famous for his part in assisting the Han dynasty against the Ch'in.

"Now Monkey," said Tripitaka, "priests must always be careful to tell the truth. You know quite well that the Dragon King lives far away in the east, and you have only been gone an hour."

"That's easily explained," said Monkey. "I have the art of somersaulting through the clouds. One bound takes me a hundred and eight thousand leagues."

"It seemed to me that you went off in a huff," said Tripitaka, "because I had to speak rather sharply to you. It's all very well for you to go off and get tea like that, if you are able to. But I think you might remember that I can't go with you. Doesn't it occur to you that I may be thirsty and hungry too?"

"If you are," said Monkey, "I'll take a bowl and go and beg for you."

"There isn't any need to do that," said Tripitaka. "There are some dried provisions in the pack."

When Monkey opened the pack, his eye was caught by something bright. "Did you bring this coat and cap with you from the east?" he asked.

"I used to wear them when I was young," replied Tripitaka, saying the first thing that came into his head. "Anyone who wears this cap can recite scriptures without having to learn them. Anyone who wears this coat can perform ceremonies without having practised them."

"Dear Master," said Monkey, "let me put them on."

"By all means," said Tripitaka.

Monkey put on the coat and cap, and Tripitaka, pretending to be eating the dried provisions, silently mumbled the spell. "My head is hurting!" screamed Monkey. Tripitaka went on reciting, and Monkey rolled over on the ground, frantically trying to break the metal fillet of the cap. Fearing that he would succeed, Tripitaka stopped for a moment. Instantly the pain stopped. Monkey felt his head. The cap seemed to have taken root upon it. He took out his needle and tried to lever it up; but all in vain. Fearing once more that he would break the band, Tripitaka began to recite again. Monkey was soon writhing and turning somersaults. He grew purple in the face and his eyes bulged out of his head. Tripitaka, unable to bear the sight of such agony, stopped reciting, and at once Monkey's head stopped hurting.

"You've been putting a spell upon me," he said.

"Nothing of the kind," said Tripitaka. "I've only been reciting the Scripture of the Tight Fillet."

"Start reciting again," said Monkey. When he did so, the pain began at once.

"Stop, stop!" screamed Monkey. "Directly you begin, the pain starts; you can't pretend it's not you that are causing it."

"In future, will you attend to what I say?" asked Tripitaka.

"Indeed I will," said Monkey.

"And never be troublesome again?" said Tripitaka.

"I shouldn't dare," said Monkey. So he said, but in his heart there was still lurking a very evil intent. He took out his cudgel and rushed at Tripitaka, fully intending to strike. Much alarmed, the Master began to recite again, and Monkey fell writhing upon the ground; the cudgel dropped from his hand.

"I give in, I give in!" he cried.

"Is it possible," said Tripitaka, "that you were going to be so wicked as to strike me?"

"I shouldn't dare, I shouldn't dare," groaned Monkey. "Master, how did you come by this spell?"

"It was taught me by an old woman whom I met just now," said Tripitaka.

"Not another word!" said Monkey. "I know well enough who she was. It was the Bodhisattva Kuan-yin. How dare she plot against me like that? Just wait a minute while I go to the Southern Ocean and give her a taste of my stick."

"As it was she who taught me the spell," said Tripitaka, "she can presumably use it herself. What will become of you then?"

Monkey saw the logic of this, and kneeling down he said contritely, "Master, this spell is too much for me. Let me go with you to India. You won't need to be always saying this spell. I will protect you faithfully to the end."

"Very well then," said Tripitaka. "Help me on to my horse."

Very crestfallen, Monkey put the luggage together, and they started off again towards the west.

If you do not know how the story goes on, you must listen to what is told in the next chapter.

. . .

CHAPTER 16

They had been travelling for several days through very wild country when at last, very late in the evening, they saw a group of houses in the far distance.

"Monkey," said Tripitaka, "I think that is a farm over there. Wouldn't it be a good plan to see if we can't sleep there tonight?"

"Let me go and have a look at it," said Monkey, "to see whether it looks lucky or unlucky, and we can then act accordingly."

"You can proceed," Monkey reported presently. "I am certain that good people live there."

Tripitaka urged on the white horse and soon came to a gate leading into a lane down which came a lad with a cotton wrap round his head, wearing a blue jacket, umbrella in hand and a bundle on his back. He was striding along, with a defiant air. "Where are you off to?" said Monkey stopping him. "There's something I want to ask you. What place is this?"

The man tried to brush him aside, muttering, "Is there no one else on the farm, that you must needs pester me with questions?"

"Now don't be cross," said Monkey laughing. "What harm can it do you to tell me the name of a place? If you're obliging to us, maybe we can do something to oblige you."

Finding he could not get past, for Monkey was holding on to him tightly, he began to dance about in a great rage. "It's enough to put anyone out," he cried. "I've just been insulted by the master of the house, and then I run straight into this wretched bald-pate, and have to swallow his impudence!"

"Unless you're clever enough to shake me off, which I very much doubt," said Monkey, "here you'll stay." The man wriggled this way and that, but all to no purpose. He was caught as though by iron pincers. In the struggle he dropped his bundle, dropped his umbrella, and began to rain blows on Monkey with both fists. Monkey kept one hand free to catch on to the luggage, and with the other held the lad fast.

"Monkey," said Tripitaka, "I think there's someone coming over there. Wouldn't it do just as well if you asked him, and let this lad go?"

"Master," said Monkey, "you don't know what you're talking about. There's no point in asking anyone else. This is the only fellow out of whom we can get what we want."

At last, seeing that he would never get free, the lad said, "This is called old Mr Kao's farm. Most of the people that live and work here have the surname Kao, so the whole place is called Kao Farm. Now let me go!"

"You look as if you were going on a journey," said Monkey. "Tell me where you are going, and on what business, and I will let you go."

"My name," he said, "is Kao Ts'ai. Old Mr Kao has a daughter about twenty years old and unmarried. Three years ago she was carried off by a monster, who since has kept her as his wife, and lived with her here on the farm. Old Mr Kao was not pleased. 'To have a monster as a son-in-law in the house,' he says, 'doesn't work very well. It's definitely discreditable to the house, and unpleasant not to be able to look forward to comings and goings between the two families.' He did everything in his power to drive away the monster, but it was no good; and in the end the creature took the girl and locked her away in that back building, where she has been for six months and no one in the family has seen her.

"Old Mr Kao gave me two or three pieces of silver and told me to go and find an exorcist, and I spent a long time chasing round all over the countryside. I succeeded at last in getting the names of three or four practitioners, but they all turned out to be unfrocked priests or mouldy Taoists, quite incapable of dealing with such a monster. Mr Kao only just now gave me a great scolding and accused me of bungling the business. Then he gave me five pieces of silver to pay for my travelling expenses and told me to go on looking till I found a really good exorcist, and I should be looking for one now if I hadn't run into this little scamp who won't let me pass. There! You have forced me to tell you how things are, and now you can let me go."

"You've thrown a lucky number," said Monkey. "This is just my job. You needn't go a step farther or spend an ounce of your silver. I'm no unfrocked priest or mouldy Taoist, I really do know how to catch monsters. You've 'got your stye cured on the way to the doctor's.' I'll trouble you to go to the master of the house, and tell him that a priest and his disciple have come, who are on their way to get scriptures in India, and that they can deal with any monster."

"I hope you're telling me the truth," said the lad. "You'll get me into great trouble if you fail."

"I'll positively guarantee," said Monkey, "that I'm not deceiving you. Make haste and lead us in."

The lad saw nothing for it but to pick up his bundle and go back to the house. "You half-wit," roared old Mr Kao, "what have you come back for?" But as soon as he had heard the lad's story, he quickly changed into his best clothes and came out to greet the guests, smiling affably. Tripitaka returned his greeting, but Monkey did not bow or say a word. The old man looked him up and down, and not knowing quite what to make of him did not ask him how he did.

"And how about me? Don't you want to know how I am?" said Monkey.

"Isn't it enough to have a monster in the house as son-in-law," grumbled the old man, "without your bringing in this frightful creature to molest me?"

"In all the years you've lived," said Monkey, "you've evidently learnt very little wisdom. If you judge people by their appearances, you'll always be going wrong. I'm not much to look at, I grant; but I have great powers, and if you are having any trouble with bogeys or monsters in the house, that's just where I come in. I'm going to get you back your daughter, so you had better stop grumbling about my appearance."

Mr Kao, trembling with fear, managed at last to pull himself together sufficiently to invite them both in. Monkey, without so much as by-your-leave, led the horse into the courtyard and tied it to a pillar. Then he drew up an old weather-beaten stool, asked Tripitaka to be seated, and taking another stool for himself calmly sat down at Tripitaka's side.

"The little priest knows how to make himself at home," said Mr Kao.

"This is nothing," said Monkey. "Keep me here a few months and you'll see me really making myself at home!"

"I don't quite understand," said the old man, "whether you've come for a night's lodging or to drive out the monster."

"We've come for a night's lodging," said Monkey, "but if there are any monsters about I don't mind dealing with them, just to pass the time. But first, I should like to know how many of them there are?"

"Heavens!" cried the old man, "isn't one monster enough to afflict the household, living here as my son-in-law?"

"Just tell me about it from the beginning," said Monkey. "If I know what he's good for, I can deal with him."

"We'd never had any trouble with ghosts or goblins or monsters on this farm before," said the old man. "Unfortunately I have no son, but only three daughters. The eldest is called Fragrant Orchid, the second Jade Orchid, and the third Blue Orchid. The first two were betrothed from childhood into neighbouring families. Our plan for the youngest was to marry her to someone who would come and live with her here and help look after us in our old age. About three years ago a very nice-looking young fellow turned up, saying that he came from Fu-ling, and that his surname was Hog. He said he had no parents or brothers and sisters, and was looking for a family where he would be taken as son-in-law, in return for the work that he did about the place. He sounded just the sort we wanted, and I accepted him. I must say he worked very hard. He pushed the plough himself and never asked to use a bull; he managed to do all his reaping without knife or staff. For some time we were perfectly satisfied, except for one thing—his appearance began to change in a very odd way."

"In what way?" asked Monkey.

"When he first came," said the old man, "he was just a dark, stoutish fellow. But afterwards his nose began to turn into a regular snout, his ears became larger and larger, and great bristles began to grow at the back of his neck. In fact, he began to look more and more like a hog. His appetite is enormous. He eats four or five pounds of rice at each meal, and as a light collation in the morning I've known him to get through over a hundred pasties. He's not at all averse to fruit and vegetables either, and what with this and all the wine he drinks, in the course of the last six months he's pretty well eaten and drunk us out of house and home."

"No doubt," said Tripitaka, "anyone who works so hard as he does needs a lot of nourishment."

"If it were only this business of food," said the old man, "it wouldn't be so bad. But he frightens everybody round by raising magic winds, suddenly vanishing and appearing again, making stones fly through the air and such like tricks. Worst of all, he has locked up Blue Orchid in the back outhouse, and it is six months since we set eyes on her. We don't even know if she is dead or alive. It is evident that he's an ogre of some kind, and that is why we were trying to get hold of an exorcist."

"Don't you worry," said Monkey. "This very night I'll catch him and make him sign a Deed of Relinquishment and give you back your daughter."

"The main thing is to catch him," said Mr Kao. "It doesn't so much matter about documents."

"Perfectly easy," said Monkey. "Tonight as soon as it is dark, you'll see the whole thing settled."

"What weapons do you need, and how many men to help you?" asked Mr Kao. "We must get on with the preparations."

"I'm armed already," said Monkey.

"So far as I can see, all you've got between you is a priest's staff," said the old man. "That wouldn't be much use against such a fiend as this."

Monkey took his embroidery needle from behind his ear and once more changed it into a great iron cudgel. "Does this satisfy you?" he asked. "I doubt if your house could provide anything tougher."

"How about followers?" said the old man.

"I need no followers," said Monkey. "All I ask for is some decent elderly person to sit with my master and keep him company."

Several respectable friends and relatives were fetched, and having looked them up and down Monkey said to Tripitaka, "Sit here quietly and don't worry. I'm off to do this job."

"Take me to the back building," he said to Mr Kao, grasping his cudgel. "I'd like to have a look at the monster's lodging-place."

"Give me the key," he said, when they came to the door.

"Think what you're saying," said the old man. "Do you suppose that if a key was all that was wanted, we should be troubling you?"

"What's the use of living so long in the world if you haven't learnt even to recognize a joke when you hear one?" said Monkey laughing. Then he went up to the door and with a terrific blow of his cudgel smashed it down. Within, it was pitch dark. "Call to your daughter and see if she is there," said Monkey. The old man summoned up his courage and cried, "Miss Three!" Recognizing her father's voice, she answered with a faint "Papa, I am here." Monkey peered into the darkness with his steely eyes, and it was a pitiable sight that he saw. Unwashed cheeks, matted hair, bloodless lips, weak and trembling. She tottered towards her father, flung her arms round him and burst into tears. "Don't make that noise," said Monkey, "but tell us where your monster is."

"I don't know," she said. "Nowadays he goes out at dawn and comes back at dusk, I can't keep track of him at all. He knows that you're trying to find someone to exorcise him; that's why he keeps away all day."

"Not a word more!" said Monkey. "Old man, take your darling back to the house and calm her down. I'll wait here for the monster. If he doesn't come, it is not my fault, and if he comes I'll pluck up your trouble by the roots."

Left alone, Monkey used his magic arts to change himself into the exact image of Blue Orchid, and sat waiting for the monster to return. Presently there was a great gust of wind; stones and gravel hurtled through the air. When the wind subsided there appeared a monster of truly terrible appearance. He had short bristles on his swarthy cheeks, a long snout, and huge ears. He wore a cotton jacket that was green but not green, blue but not blue, and had a spotted handkerchief tied round his head. "That's the article," laughed Monkey to himself.

Dear Monkey! He did not go to meet the monster or ask him how he did, but lay on the bed groaning, as though he were ill. The monster, quite taken in, came up to the bed and grabbing at Monkey tried to kiss him. "None of your lewd tricks on old Monkey!" laughed Monkey to himself, and giving the monster a great clout on the nose sent him reeling.

"Dear sister," said the monster, picking himself up, "why are you cross with me today? Is it because I am so late?"

"I'm not cross," said Monkey.

"If you're not cross," said the monster, "why do you push me away?"

"You've got such a clumsy way of kissing," said Monkey. "You might have known that I'm not feeling well today, when you saw I did not come to the door to meet you. Take off your clothes and get into bed." Still suspecting nothing the monster began to undress. Monkey meanwhile jumped up and sat on the commode. When the monster got into bed he felt everywhere but could not find his bride.

"Sister," he called, "what has become of you? Take off your clothes and get into bed."

"You go to sleep first," said Monkey. "I'll follow when I've done my duties." Monkey suddenly began to sigh, murmuring "Was there ever such an unhappy girl as I?"

"What are you grumbling about?" said the monster. "Since I came here, I've cost you something in food and drink, that I own. But I've more than earned what I have got. Haven't I cleaned the ground and drained ditches, carried bricks and tiles, built walls, ploughed fields, planted grain, and improved the farm out of all knowing? You've good clothes to wear and all the food you need. What's all this childish nonsense about being unhappy?"

"That's not it at all," said Monkey. "Today my parents came and made a fearful scene through the partition wall."

"What did they make a scene about?" said the monster.

"They don't like having you here as their son-in-law," said Monkey. "They say you've got an ugly face, and they don't know who your father is and haven't seen any of your relations. They say you come and go no one knows when or where, and it's bad for the credit of the house that we don't know your name or anything at all about you. That's what they said, and it has made me miserable."

"What do looks matter?" said the monster. "It's a strong man they need about the place, and they can't say anything against me on that score. And if they think so ill of me, why did they accept me here at all? As for who I am, there's no mystery about it. I come from the Cloud-Ladder Cave at Fu-ling, and because I look a bit like a pig they call me Pigsy—Pigsy Bristles; next time they ask just tell them that."

"Confiding monster!" thought Monkey. "It needs no tortures to get a confession from him. Now we know where he comes from and who he is. It only remains to catch him."

"They are looking for an exorcist to drive you away," he said to the monster.

"Go to sleep," said Pigsy, "and don't worry about them any more. Am not I strong enough, with my nine-pronged muck-rake, to frighten off any exorcist or priest or what-not? Even if your old man's prayers could bring down the master of all devils from the Ninth Heaven, as a matter of fact he's an old friend of mine and wouldn't do anything against me."

"He's done more than that," said Monkey. "He has called in the Great Sage, who five hundred years ago made turmoil in Heaven."

"If that's so," said Pigsy, "I'm off! There'll be no more kissing tonight!"

"Why are you going?" asked Monkey.

"You don't know," said Pigsy. "That chap is terribly powerful, and I don't know that I could deal with him. I'm frightened of losing my reputation." He dressed hastily, opened the door, and went out. But Monkey caught hold of him and making a magic pass changed himself back into his true form. "Monster, look round," he cried, "and you will see that I am he."

When Pigsy turned and saw Monkey with his sharp little teeth and grinning mouth, his fiery, steely eyes, his flat head and hairy cheeks, for all the world like a veritable thunder-demon, he was so startled that his hands fell limp beside him and his legs gave way. With a scream he tore himself free, leaving part of his coat in Monkey's hand, and was gone like a whirlwind. Monkey struck out with his cudgel; but Pigsy had already begun to make for the cave he came from. Soon Monkey was after him, crying, "Where are you off to? If you go up to Heaven I will follow you to the summit of the Pole Star, and if you go down into the earth I will follow you to the deepest pit of hell."

If you do not know how far he chased him or which of them won the fight, you must listen to what is told in the next chapter.

CHAPTER 17

The monster fled with Monkey at his heels, till they came at last to a high mountain, and here the monster disappeared into a cave, and a moment later came back brandishing a nine-pronged muck-rake. They set to at once and battled all night long, from the second watch till dawn began to whiten in the sky. At last the monster could hold his ground no longer, and retreating into the cave bolted the door behind him. Standing outside the cave-door, Monkey saw that on a slab of rock was the inscription "Cloud-ladder Cave." As the monster showed no sign of coming out again and it was now broad daylight, Monkey thought to himself, "The Master will be wondering what has happened to me. I had better go and see him and then come back and catch the monster." So tripping from cloud to cloud he made his way back to the farm.

Tripitaka was still sitting with the old man, talking of this and that. He had not slept all night. He was just wondering why Monkey did not return when Monkey alighted in the courtyard, and suddenly stood before them. "Master, here I am," he said. The old men all bowed down before him, and supposing that he had accomplished his task thanked him for all his trouble.

"You must have had a long way to go, to catch the creature," said Tripitaka.

"Master," said Monkey, "the monster is not a common incubus or elf. I have recognized him as a former inhabitant of Heaven, where he was in command of all the watery hosts. He was expelled to earth after an escapade with the daughter of the Moon Goddess, and though he was here re-incarnated with a pig-like form, he retains all his magic powers. I chased him to his mountain-cave, where he fetched out a nine-pronged muck-rake, and we fought together all night. Just at dawn he gave up the fight, and locked himself up in his cave. I would have beaten down the door and forced him to fight to a decision, but I was afraid the Master might be getting anxious, so I thought I had better come back first and report."

"Reverend Sir," said old Mr Kao to Monkey, "I am afraid this hasn't helped matters much. True, you have driven him away; but after you have gone he's certain to come back again, and where shall we be then? We shall have to trouble you to catch him for us. That is the only way to pluck out our trouble by the root. I'll see to it that you have no cause to regret the trouble you take. You shall have half of all that is ours, both land and goods. If you like, my friends and relations shall sign a document to this effect. It will be well worth their while, if only we can remove this shame from our home."

"I think you make too much of the whole affair," said Monkey. "The monster himself admits that his appetite is large; but he has done quite a lot of useful work. All the recent improvements in the estate are his work. He claims to be well worth what he costs in keep, and does not see why you should be so anxious to get rid of him. He is a divinity from Heaven, although condemned to live on earth, he helps to keep things going, and so far as I can see he hasn't done any harm to your daughter."

"It may be true," said old Mr Kao, "that he's had no influence upon her. But I stick to it that it's very bad for our reputation. Wherever I go I hear people saying 'Mr Kao has taken a monster as his son-in-law.' What is one to say to that?"

"Now, Monkey," said Tripitaka, "don't you think you had better go and have one more fight with him and see if you can't settle the business once and for all?"

"As a matter of fact," said Monkey, "I was only having a little game with him, to see how things would go. This time I shall certainly catch him and bring him back for you to see. Don't you worry! Look after my master," he cried to Mr Kao, "I'm off!"

So saying, he disappeared into the clouds and soon arrived at the cave. With one blow of his cudgel he beat the doors to bits, and standing at the entrance he cried, "You noisome lout, come out and fight with Old Monkey." Pigsy lay fast asleep within, snoring heavily. But when he heard the door being beaten down and heard himself called a noisome lout, he was so much enraged that he snatched up his rake, pulled himself together, and rushed out, crying, "You wretched stableman, if ever there was a rogue, you're he! What have I to do with you, that you should come and knock down my door? Go and look at the Statute Book. You'll find that 'obtaining entry to premises by forcing a main door' is a Miscellaneous Capital Offence."

"You fool," said Monkey. "Haven't I a perfectly good justification at law for forcing your door? Remember that you laid violent hands on a respectable girl, and lived with her without matchmaker or testimony, tea, scarlet, wine, or any other ceremony. Are you aware that heads are cut off for less than that?"

"Stop that nonsense, and look at Old Pig's rake," cried Pigsy.

He struck out, but Monkey warded off the blow, crying, "I suppose that's the rake you used when you worked on the farm. Why should you expect me to be frightened of it?"

"You are very much mistaken," said Pigsy. "This rake was given to me by the Jade Emperor himself."

"A lie!" cried Monkey. "Here's my head. Hit as hard as you please, and we'll see!"

Pigsy raised the rake and brought it down with such force on Monkey's head that the sparks flew. But there was not a bruise or scratch. Pigsy was so much taken aback, that his hands fell limp at his side. "What a head!" he exclaimed.

"You've still something to learn about me," said Monkey. "After I made havoc in Heaven and was caught by Erh-lang,[11] all the deities of Heaven hacked me with their axes, hammered me with their mallets, slashed me with their swords, set fire to me, hurled thunderbolts at me, but not a hair of my body was hurt. Lao Tzu[12] put me in his alchemic stove and cooked me with holy fire. But all that happened was that my eyes became fiery, my head and shoulders hard as steel. If you don't believe it, try again, and see whether you can hurt me or not."

"I remember," said Pigsy, "that before you made havoc in Heaven, you lived in the Cave of the Water Curtain. Lately nothing has been heard of you. How did you get here? Perhaps my father-in-law asked you to come and deal with me."

"Not at all," said Monkey, "I have been converted and am now a priest, and am going with a Chinese pilgrim called Tripitaka, who has been sent by the Emperor to fetch scriptures from India. On our way we happened to come past Mr Kao's farm, and we asked for a night's lodging. In the course of conversation Mr Kao asked for help about his daughter. That's why I'm after you, you noisome lout!"

No sooner did Pigsy hear these words than the rake fell from his hand. "Where is that pilgrim?" he gasped. "Take me to him."

"What do you want to see him for?" asked Monkey.

"I've been converted," said Pigsy. "Didn't you know? The Bodhisattva Kuan-yin converted me and put me here to prepare myself by fasting and abstention for going to India with a pilgrim to fetch scriptures; after which, I am to receive illumination. That all happened some years ago, and since then I have had no news of this pilgrim. If you are his disciple, what on earth possessed you not to mention this

[11] A legendary figure in Chinese mythology, famous for slaying dragons and quelling floods.

[12] The founder of Taoism was a popular figure in Chinese legends by the time of *Monkey*. He is described as having the powers of a sage, healer, and magician.

scripture-seeking business? Why did you prefer to pick a quarrel and knock me about in front of my own door?"

"I suspect," said Monkey, "that you are just making all this up, in order to get away. If it's really true that you want to escort my Master to India, you must make a solemn vow to Heaven that you're telling the truth. Then I'll take you to him." Pigsy flung himself upon his knees and, kow-towing at the void, up and down like a pestle in the mortar, he cried, "I swear before the Buddha Amitabha,[13] praised be his name, that I am telling the truth; and if I am not, may I be condemned once more by the tribunals of Heaven and sliced into ten thousand pieces."

When Monkey heard him make this solemn vow, "Very well then," he said. "First take a torch and burn down your lair, and then I will take you with me." Pigsy took some reeds and brambles, lit a fire and soon reduced the cave to the state of a burnt-out kiln.

"You've nothing against me now," he said. "Take me along with you."

"You'd better give your rake to me," said Monkey. When Pigsy had handed over the rake, Monkey took a hair, blew on it with magic breath, and changed it into a three-ply hemp cord. Pigsy put his hands behind his back and let himself be bound. Then Monkey caught hold of his ear and dragged him along, crying, "Hurry up! Hurry up!"

"Don't be so rough," begged Pigsy. "You're hurting my ear."

"Rough indeed!" said Monkey. "I shouldn't get far by being gentle with you. The proverb says, 'The better the pig, the harder to hold.' Wait till you have seen the Master and shown that you are in earnest. Then we'll let you go."

When they reached the farm, Monkey twitched Pigsy's ear, saying, "You see that old fellow sitting so solemnly up there? That's my Master." Mr Kao and the other old men, seeing Monkey leading the monster by the ear, were delighted beyond measure, and came out into the courtyard to meet him. "Reverend Sir," they cried, "that's the creature, sure enough, that married our master's daughter." Pigsy fell upon his knees and with his hands still tied behind his back, kow-towed to Tripitaka, crying, "Master, forgive me for failing to give you a proper reception. If I had known that it was you who were staying with my father-in-law I would have come to pay my respects, and all these unpleasantnesses would never have happened."

"Monkey," said Tripitaka, "how did you manage to bring him to this state of mind?" Monkey let go his ear, and giving him a knock with the handle of the rake, shouted, "Speak, fool!" Pigsy then told how he had been commissioned by Kuan-yin. "Mr Kao," said Tripitaka, when he heard the story, "this is the occasion for a little incense." Mr Kao then brought out the incense tray, and Tripitaka washed his hands, and burning incense he turned towards the south and said, "I am much beholden, Bodhisattva!" Then he went up into the hall and resumed his seat, bidding Monkey release Pigsy from his bonds. Monkey shook himself; the rope became a hair again and returned to his body. Pigsy was free. He again did obeisance, and vowed that he would follow Tripitaka to the west. Then he bowed to Monkey, whom as the senior disciple he addressed as "Elder Brother and Teacher."

"Where's my wife?" said Pigsy to Mr Kao. "I should like her to pay her respects to my Father and Brother in the Law." "Wife indeed!" laughed Monkey. "You haven't got a wife now. There are some sorts of Taoists that are family men; but who ever heard of a Buddhist priest calmly talking about his 'wife'? Sit down and eat your supper, and early tomorrow we'll all start out for India."

---

[13] The Buddha of the Pure Land School of Buddhism, which envisioned an extremely material Paradise.

After supper Mr Kao brought out a red lacquer bowl full of broken pieces of silver and gold, and offered the contents to the three priests, as a contribution towards their travelling expenses. He also offered them three pieces of fine silk to make clothes. Tripitaka said, "Travelling priests must beg their way as they go. We cannot accept money or silk." But Monkey came up and plunging his hand into the dish took out a handful of gold and silver, and called to the lad Kao Ts'ai, "You were kind enough yesterday to introduce my Master into the house and we owe it to you that we have found a new disciple. I have no other way of showing my thanks but giving you these broken pieces of gold and silver, which I hope you will use to buy yourself a pair of shoes. If you come across any more monsters, please bespeak them for me, and I shall be even further obliged to you."

"Reverend Sirs," said Mr Kao, "if I can't persuade you to accept silver or gold, I hope that you will at least let me show my gratitude by giving you these few pieces of coarse stuff, to make into cassocks."

"A priest who accepts so much as a thread of silk," said Tripitaka, "must do penance for a thousand aeons to expiate his crime. All I ask is a few scraps left over from the household meal, to take with us as dry provisions."

"Wait a minute," cried Pigsy. "If I get my due for all I've done on this estate since I married into the family, I should carry away several tons of provisions. That's by the way. But I think my father-in-law might in decency give me a new jacket. My old one was torn by Brother Monkey in the fight last night. And my shoes are all in pieces; I should be glad of a new pair."

Mr Kao acceded to his request, and Pigsy, delighted by his new finery, strutted up and down in front of the company, calling to Mr Kao, "Be so kind as to inform my mother-in-law, my sisters-in-law, and all my kinsmen by marriage that I have become a priest and must ask their pardon for going off without saying good-bye to them in person. And father-in-law, I'll trouble you to take good care of my bride. For if we don't bring off this scripture business, I shall turn layman again and live with you as your son-in-law."

"Lout!" cried Monkey. "Don't talk rubbish."

"It's not rubbish," said Pigsy. "Things may go wrong, and then I shall be in a pretty pass! No salvation, and no wife either."

"Kindly stop this silly argument," said Tripitaka. "It is high time we started." So they put together the luggage, which Pigsy was told to carry, and when the white horse was saddled Tripitaka was set astride. Monkey, with his cudgel over his shoulder, led the way. And so, parting from Mr Kao and all his relations, the three of them set out for the West. And if you do not know what befell them, you must listen to what is told in the next chapter.

CHAPTER 18

So the three of them travelled on towards the west, and came at last to a great plain. Summer had passed and autumn come. They heard "the cicada singing in the rotten willow," saw "the Fire-Star rolling to the west." At last they came to a huge and turbulent river, racing along with gigantic waves. "That's a very broad river," cried Tripitaka from on horseback. "There does not seem to be a ferry anywhere about. How are we to get across?"

"A boat wouldn't be much use in waters as rough as that," said Pigsy.

Monkey leapt into the air, and shading his eyes with his hand gazed at the waters. "Master," he cried, "this is going to be no easy matter. For me, yes. I should only have to shake my hips, and I should be across at one bound. But for you it's not going to be such easy work."

"I can't even see the other side," said Tripitaka. "How far is it, do you suppose?"

"About eight hundred leagues," said Monkey.

"How do you come to that reckoning?" asked Pigsy.

"I'll tell you frankly," said Monkey. "My sight is so good that I can see everything, lucky or unlucky, a thousand leagues away, and when I looked down on this river from above I could see well enough that it must be a good eight hundred leagues across." Tripitaka was very much depressed, and was just turning his horse when he saw a slab of stone on which was the inscription "River of Flowing Sand." Underneath in small letters was the verse:

> In the Floating Sands, eight hundred wide,
> In the Dead Waters, three thousand deep,
> A goose-feather will not keep afloat,
> A rush-flower sinks straight to the bottom.

They were looking at this inscription when suddenly a monster of horrifying aspect came surging through the mountainous waves. His hair was flaming red, his eyes were like two lanterns; at his neck were strung nine skulls, and he carried a huge priest's staff. Like a whirlwind he rushed straight at the pilgrims. Monkey seized Tripitaka and hurried him up the bank to a safe distance. Pigsy dropped his load and rushed at the monster with his rake. The monster fended off the blow with his priest's staff. The fight that followed was a good one, each displaying his powers on the shores of the River of Flowing Sands. They fought twenty bouts without reaching a decision. Monkey, seeing the grand fight that was in progress, itched to go and join in it. At last he said to Tripitaka, "You sit here and don't worry. I am going off to have a bit of fun with the creature." Tripitaka did his best to dissuade him. But Monkey with a wild whoop leapt into the fray. At this moment the two of them were locked in combat, and it was hard to get between them. But Monkey managed to put in a tremendous blow of the cudgel right on the monster's head. At once the monster broke away, and rushing madly back to the water's edge leapt in and disappeared. Pigsy was furious.

"Heigh, brother," he cried. "Who asked you to interfere? The monster was just beginning to tire. After another three or four rounds he would not have been able to fend off my rake, and I should have had him at my mercy. But as soon as he saw your ugly face he took to his heels. You've spoilt everything!"

"I'll just tell you how it happened," said Monkey. "It's months since I had a chance to use my cudgel, and when I saw you having such a rare time with him my feet itched with longing not to miss the fun, and I couldn't hold myself back. How was I to know that the monster wouldn't play?" So hand in hand, laughing and talking, the two of them went back to Tripitaka.

"Have you caught the monster?" he asked.

"He gave up the fight," said Monkey, "and went back again into the water."

"It wouldn't be a bad thing," said Tripitaka, "if we could persuade him to show us how to get across. He's lived here a long time and must know this river inside out. Otherwise I don't see how we are to get across an enormous river like this without a boat."

"There is something in that," said Monkey. "Does not the proverb say 'You cannot live near cinnabar without becoming red, or near ink without becoming black.' If we succeed in catching him we certainly ought not to kill him, but make him take the Master across this river and then dispose of him."

"You shall have your chance this time," said Pigsy to Monkey. "I'll stay here and look after the Master."

"That's all very well," said Monkey, "but this job is not at all in my line. I'm not at my best in the water. To get along here, I have to change myself into some water creature, such as a fish or crab. If it were a matter of going up into the clouds, I have tricks enough to deal with the ugliest situation. But in the water I confess I am at a disadvantage."

"I used, of course," said Pigsy, "to be Marshal of the River of Heaven, and had the command of eighty thousand watery fellows, so that I certainly ought to know something about that element. My only fear is that if whole broods of water-creatures were to come to the monster's help, I might get myself into a bit of a fix."

"What you must do," said Monkey, "is to lure the monster out, and not get yourself involved in more of a scrap than you can help. Once he is out, I'll come to your assistance."

"That's the best plan," said Pigsy, "I'll go at once."

So saying, he stripped off his blue embroidered jacket and shoes, and brandishing his rake plunged into the river. He found that he had forgotten none of his old water-magic, and lashing through the waves soon reached the bed of the stream and made his way straight ahead. After retiring from the fight, the monster lay down and had a nap. Soon however he was woken by the sound of someone coming through the water, and starting up he saw Pigsy pushing through the waves, rake in hand. Seizing his staff, he came towards him shouting, "Now then, shaven pate, just look where you're going or you'll get a nasty knock with this staff!"

Pigsy struck the staff aside with his rake, crying, "What monster are you, that you dare to bar my path?"

"I'm surprised that you don't recognize me," said the monster. "I am not an ordinary spook, but a divinity with name and surname."

"If that is so," said Pigsy, "what are you doing here, taking human lives? Tell me who you are, and I'll spare you!"

"So great was my skill in alchemic arts," said the monster, "that I was summoned to Heaven by the Jade Emperor and became a Marshal of the Hosts of Heaven. One day, at a celestial banquet, my hand slipped and I broke a crystal cup. The Jade Emperor was furious, and I was hurried away to the execution ground. Fortunately for me the Red-legged Immortal begged for my release, and my sentence was changed to one of banishment to the River of Flowing Sands. When I am hungry I go ashore and eat whatever living thing comes my way. Many are the woodmen and fishermen who have fallen to me as my prey, and I don't mind telling you I am very hungry at this moment. Don't imagine that your flesh would be too coarse for me to eat. Chopped up fine and well sauced, you'll suit me nicely!"

"Coarse indeed!" said Pigsy. "I'm a dainty enough morsel to make any mouth water. Mind your manners, and swallow your grandfather's rake!"

The monster ducked and avoided the blow. Then both of them came up to the surface of the water, and treading the waves fought stubbornly for two hours without reaching a decision. It was a case of "the copper bowl meeting the iron broom, the jade gong confronted by the metal bell."

After some thirty rounds Pigsy pretended to give in, and dragging his rake after him made for the shore, with the monster hard on his heels. "Come on!" cried Pigsy. "With firm ground under our feet we'll have a better fight than before."

"I know what you're up to," cried the monster. "You've lured me up here, so that your partner may come and help you. We'll go back into the water and finish the fight there."

The monster was too wily to come any farther up the bank and they soon were fighting again, this time at the very edge of the water. This was too much for

Monkey, who was watching them from a distance. "Wait here," he said to Tripitaka, "while I try the trick called 'The ravening eagle pouncing on its prey.' " So saying, he catapulted into the air and swooped down on the monster, who swiftly turning his head and seeing Monkey pouncing down upon him from the clouds, leapt straight into the water and was seen no more.

"He's given us the slip," said Monkey. "He's not likely to come out on the bank again. What are we going to do?"

"It's a tough job," said Pigsy, "I doubt if I can beat him. Even if I sweat till I burst I can't get beyond quits."

"Let's go and see the Master," said Monkey.

They climbed the bank, and finding Tripitaka they told him of their predicament. Tripitaka burst into tears.

"We shall never get across," he sobbed.

"Don't you worry," said Monkey. "It is true that with that creature lying in wait for us, we can't get across. But Pigsy, you stay here by the Master and don't attempt to do any more fighting. I am going off to the Southern Ocean."

"And what are you going to do there?" asked Pigsy.

"This scripture-seeking business," said Monkey, "is an invention of the Bodhisattva, and it was she who converted us. It is surely for her to find some way of getting us over this river. I'll go and ask her. It's a better idea than fighting with the monster."

"Brother," said Pigsy, "when you're there you might say a word to her for me; tell her I'm very much obliged indeed for having been put on the right way."

"If you are going," said Tripitaka, "you had better start at once and get back as soon as you can."

Monkey somersaulted into the clouds, and in less than half an hour he had reached the Southern Ocean and saw Mount Potalaka rise before him. After landing, he went straight to the Purple Bamboo Grove, where he was met by the Spirits of the Twenty-Four Ways.

"Great Sage, what brings you here?" they said.

"My Master is in difficulties," said Monkey, "and I wish to have an interview with the Bodhisattva."

"Sit down," they said, "and we will announce you."

The Bodhisattva was leaning against the parapet of the Lotus Pool, looking at the flowers, with the Dragon King's daughter, bearer of the Magic Pearl, at her side. "Why aren't you looking after your Master?" she said to Monkey, when he was brought in.

"When we came to the River of Flowing Sands," said Monkey, "we found it guarded by a monster formidable in the arts of war. My fellow-disciple Pigsy, whom we picked up on the way, did his best to subdue the creature, but was not successful. That is why I have ventured to come and ask you to take pity on us, and rescue my Master from this predicament."

"You obstinate ape," said the Bodhisattva, "this is the same thing all over again. Why didn't you say that you were in charge of the priest of T'ang?"

"We were both far too busy trying to catch him and make him take the Master across," said Monkey.

"I put him there on purpose to help scripture-seekers," said Kuan-yin. "If only you had mentioned the fact that you had come from China to look for scriptures, you would have found him very helpful."

"At present," said Monkey, "he is skulking at the bottom of the river. How are we to get him to come out and make himself useful? And how is Tripitaka going to get across the river?"

The Bodhisattva summoned her disciple Hui-yen, and taking a red gourd from her sleeve she said to him, "Take this gourd, go with Monkey to the river and shout 'Sandy!' He will come out at once, and you must then bring him to the Master to make his submission. Next string together the nine skulls that he wears at his neck according to the disposition of the Magic Square, with the gourd in the middle, and you will find you have a holy ship that will carry Tripitaka across the River of Flowing Sands."

Soon Hui-yen and Monkey alighted on the river-bank. Seeing who Monkey had brought with him, Pigsy led forward the Master to meet them. After salutations had been exchanged, Hui-yen went to the edge of the water and called, "Sandy, Sandy! The scripture-seekers have been here a long time. Why do you not come out and pay your respects to them?"

The monster Sandy, knowing that this must be a messenger from Kuan-yin, hastened to the surface, and as soon as his head was above water he saw Hui-yen and Monkey. He put on a polite smile and came towards them bowing and saying to Hui-yen, "Forgive me for not coming to meet you. Where is the Bodhisattva?"

"She has not come," said Hui-yen. "She sent me to tell you to put yourself at Tripitaka's disposal and become his disciple. She also told me to take the skulls that you wear at your neck and this gourd that I have brought, and make a holy ship to carry the Master across."

"Where are the pilgrims?" asked Sandy.

"Sitting there on the eastern bank," said Hui-yen.

"Well," said Sandy, looking at Pigsy, "that filthy creature never said a word about scriptures, though I fought with him for two days." Then seeing Monkey, "What, is that fellow there too?" he cried. "He's the other's partner. I'm not going near them."

"The first is Pigsy," said Hui-yen, "and the second is Monkey. They are both Tripitaka's disciples and both were converted by the Bodhisattva. You have nothing to fear from them. I myself will introduce you to the Master."

Sandy put away his staff, tidied himself and scrambled up the bank. When they reached Tripitaka, Sandy knelt before him, exclaiming, "How can I have been so blind as not to recognize you? Forgive me for all my rudeness!"

"You brazen creature," said Pigsy, "why did you insist on having a row with us, instead of joining our party from the start?"

"Brother," laughed Monkey, "don't scold him. It is we who are to blame, for never having told him that we were going to get scriptures."

"Is it indeed your earnest desire to dedicate yourself to our religion?" asked Tripitaka.

Sandy bowed his assent, and Tripitaka told Monkey to take a knife and shave his head. He then once more did homage to Tripitaka, and in a less degree to Monkey and Pigsy. Tripitaka thought that Sandy shaped very well as a priest, and was thoroughly satisfied with him.

"You had better be quick and get on with your boat-building," said Hui-yen.

Sandy obediently took the skulls from his neck, and tying them in the pattern of the Magic Square he put the Bodhisattva's gourd in the middle, and called to Tripitaka to come down to the water. Tripitaka then ascended the holy ship, which he found as secure as any light craft. Pigsy supported him on the left, Sandy on the right, while Monkey in the stern held the halter of the white horse, which followed as best it could. Hui-yen floated just above them. They soon arrived in perfect safety at the other side.

And if you do not know how long it was before they got Illumination you must listen to what is told in the next chapter.

Chapter 19

Tripitaka sat in the Zen Hall of the Treasure Wood Temple, under the lamp; he recited the Water Litany of the Liang Emperor and read through the True Scripture of the Peacock. It was now the third watch (12 p.m.), and he put his books back into their bag, and was just going to get up and go to bed when he heard a great banging outside the gate and felt a dank blast of ghostly wind. Fearing the lamp would be blown out, he hastened to screen it with his sleeve. But the lamp continued to flicker in the strangest way, and Tripitaka began to tremble. He was, however, very tired, and presently he lay down across the reading-desk and dozed. Although his eyes were closed, he still knew what was going on about him, and in his ears still sounded the dank wind that moaned outside the window. And when the wind had passed by, he heard a voice outside the Zen Hall whispering: "Master!"

Tripitaka raised his head, and in his dream he saw a man standing there, dripping from head to foot, with tears in his eyes, and continually murmuring, "Master, Master." Tripitaka sat up and said, "What can you be but a hobgoblin, evil spirit, monster or foul bogey, that you should come to this place and molest me in the middle of the night? But I must tell you that I am no common scrambler in the greedy world of man. I am a great and illustrious priest who at the bidding of the Emperor of T'ang am going to the west to worship the Buddha and seek scriptures. And I have three disciples, each of whom is adept in quelling dragons and subduing tigers, removing monsters and making away with bogeys. If these disciples were to see you, they would grind you to powder. I tell you this for your own good, in kindness and compassion. You had best hide at once, and not set foot in this place of Meditation."

But the man drew nearer to the room and said, "Master, I am no hobgoblin, evil spirit, monster, nor foul bogey either."

"If you are none of these things," said Tripitaka, "what are you doing here at depth of night?"

"Master," said the man, "rest your eyes upon me and look at me well."

Then Tripitaka looked at him with a fixed gaze and saw that there was a crown upon his head and a sceptre at his waist, and that he was dressed and shod as only a king can be.

When Tripitaka saw this he was much startled and amazed. At once he bowed down and cried out with a loud voice: "Of what court is your majesty the king? I beg of you, be seated." But the hand he stretched to help the king to his seat plunged through empty space. Yet when he was back in his seat and looked up, the man was still there.

"Tell me, your majesty," he cried, "of what are you emperor, of where are you king? Doubtless there were troubles in your land, wicked ministers rebelled against you and at midnight you fled for your life. What is your tale? Tell it for me to hear."

"Master," he said, "my home is due west of here, only forty leagues away. At that place, there is a city moated and walled, and this city is where my kingdom was founded."

"And what is its name?" asked Tripitaka.

"I will not deceive you," he said. "When my dynasty was set up there, a new name was given to it, and it was called Crow-cock."

"But tell me," said Tripitaka, "what brings you here in such consternation?"

"Master," he said, "five years ago there was a great drought. The grass did not grow and my people were all dying of hunger. It was pitiful indeed!"

Tripitaka nodded. "Your majesty," he said, "there is an ancient saying, 'Heaven favours, where virtue rules.' I fear you have no compassion for your people; for now that they are in trouble, you leave your city. Go back and open your store-houses, sustain your people, repent your misdeeds, and do present good twofold to make recompense. Release from captivity any whom you have unjustly condemned, and Heaven will see to it that rain comes and the winds are tempered."

"All the granaries in my kingdom were empty," he said, "I had neither cash nor grain. My officers civil and military were unpaid, and even at my own board no relish could be served. I have shared sweet and bitter with my people no less than Yü the Great[14] when he quelled the floods; I have bathed and done penance; morning and night I have burnt incense and prayed. For three years it was like this, till the rivers were all empty, the wells dry.

"Suddenly, when things were at their worst, there came a magician from the Chung-nan mountains who could call the winds and summon the rain, and make stones into gold. First he obtained audience with my many officers, civil and military, and then with me. At once I begged him to mount the altar and pray for rain. He did so, and was answered; no sooner did his magic tablet resound than floods of rain fell. I told him three feet would be ample. But he said after so long a drought, it took a lot to soak the ground, and he brought down another two inches. And I, seeing him to be of such great powers, prostrated myself before him and treated him henceforth as my elder brother."

"This was a great piece of luck," said Tripitaka.

"Whence should my luck come?" asked he.

"Why," said Tripitaka, "if your magician could make rain when you wanted it, and gold whenever you needed it, what did you lack that you must needs leave your kingdom and come to me here?"

"For two years," he said, "he was my fellow at board and bed. Then at spring time when all the fruit trees were in blossom and young men and girls from every house, gallants from every quarter, went out to enjoy the sights of spring, there came a time when my officers had all returned to their desks and the ladies of the court to their bowers. I with that magician went slowly stepping hand in hand, till we came to the flower-garden and to the eight-cornered crystal well. Here he threw down something, I do not know what, and at once there was a great golden light. He led me to the well-side, wondering what treasure was in the well. Then he conceived an evil intent, and with a great shove pushed me into the well; then took a paving-stone and covered the well-top and sealed it with clay, and planted a banana-plant on top of it... Pity me! I have been dead three years; I am the phantom unavenged of one that perished at the bottom of a well."

When the man said that he was a ghost, Tripitaka was terrified; his legs grew flabby beneath him, and his hair stood on end. Controlling himself at last, he asked him saying "Your Majesty's story is hard to reconcile with reason. You say you have been dead for three years. How is it that in all this time none of your officers civil and military, nor of your queens and concubines and chamberlains ever came to look for you?"

"I have told you already," the man said, "of the magician's powers. There can be few others like him in all the world. He had but to give himself a shake, and there and then, in the flower-garden, he changed himself into the exact image of me. And now he holds my rivers and hills, and has stolen away my kingdom. All of my officers, the four hundred gentlemen of my court, my queens and concubines—all, all are his."

[14]An emperor who ruled from 2205 to 2197 B.C.E., legendary for draining the great floods with nine years of incessant labor.

"Your Majesty is easily daunted," said Tripitaka.

"Easily daunted?" he asked.

"Yes," said Tripitaka, "that magician may have strange powers, turn himself into your image, steal your lands, your officers knowing nothing, and your ladies unaware. But you that were dead at least knew that you were dead. Why did you not go to Yama, King of Death,[15] and put in a complaint?"

"The magician's power," he said, "is very great, and he is on close terms with the clerks and officers of Death. The Spirit of Wall and Moat is forever drinking with him; all the Dragon Kings of the Sea are his kinsmen. The God of the Eastern Peak is his good friend; the ten kings of Judgement are his cousins. I should be barred in every effort to lay my plaint before the King of Death."

"If your Majesty," said Tripitaka, "is unable to lay your case before the Courts of the Dead, what makes you come to the world of the living with any hope of redress?"

"Master," he said, "how should a wronged ghost dare approach your door? The Spirit that Wanders at Night caught me in a gust of magic wind and blew me along. He said my three years' water-misery was ended and that I was to present myself before you; for at your service, he said, there was a great disciple, the Monkey Sage, most able to conquer demons and subdue impostors. I beg of you to come to my kingdom, lay hands on the magician and make clear the false from the true. Then, Master, I would repay you with all that will be mine to give."

"So then," said Tripitaka, "you have come to ask that my disciple should drive out the false magician?"

"Indeed, indeed," he said.

"My disciple," said Tripitaka, "in other ways is not all that he should be. But subduing monsters and evil spirits just suits his powers. I fear however that the circumstances make it hard for him to deal with this evil power."

"Why so?" asked the king.

"Because," said Tripitaka, "the magician has used his magic powers to change himself into the image of you. All the officers of your court have gone over to him, and all your ladies have accepted him. My disciple could no doubt deal with them; but he would hesitate to do violence to them. For should he do so, would not he and I be held guilty of conspiring to destroy your kingdom? And what would this be but to paint the tiger and carve the swan?"[16]

"There is still someone of mine at Court," he said.

"Excellent, excellent," said Tripitaka. "No doubt it is some personal attendant, who is guarding some fastness for you."

"Not at all," he said. "It is my own heir apparent."

"But surely," said Tripitaka, "the false magician has driven him away."

"Not at all," he said. "He is in the Palace of Golden Bells, in the Tower of the Five Phoenixes, studying with his tutor, or on the steps of the magician's throne. But all these three years he has forbidden the prince to go into the inner chambers of the Palace, and he can never see his mother."

"Why is that?" asked Tripitaka.

"It is the magician's scheme," he said. "He fears that if they were to meet, the queen might in the course of conversation let drop some word that would arouse the prince's suspicions. So these two never meet, and he all this long time has lived secure."

---

[15]Ruler of the underworld.

[16]I.e., an enterprise that, if successful, does more harm than inaction.

"The disaster that has befallen you, no doubt at Heaven's behest, is much like my own misfortune. My own father was killed by brigands, who seized my mother and after three months she gave birth to me. I at length escaped from their hands and by good chance met with kindness from a priest of the Golden Mountain Temple, who brought me up. Remembering my own unhappy state, without father or mother, I can sympathize with your prince, who has lost both his parents. But tell me, granted that this prince is still at Court, how can I manage to see him?"

"What difficulty in that?" he said.

"Because he is kept under strict control," said Tripitaka, "and is not even allowed to see the mother who bore him. How will a stray monk get to him?"

"Tomorrow," the king said, "he leaves the Court at daybreak."

"For what purpose?"

"Tomorrow, early in the morning, with three thousand followers and falcons and dogs, he will go hunting outside the city, and it will certainly be easy for you to see him. You must then tell him what I have told you, and he cannot fail to believe you."

"He is only a common mortal," said Tripitaka, "utterly deceived by the false magician in the palace, and at every turn calling him father and king. Why should he believe what I tell him?"

"If that is what worries you," the king said, "I will give you a token to show to him."

"And what can you give me?"

In his hand the king carried a tablet of white jade, bordered with gold. This he laid before Tripitaka saying, "Here is my token."

"What thing is this?" asked Tripitaka.

"When the magician disguised himself as me," said the king, "this treasure was the one thing he forgot about. When the queen asked what had become of it, he said that the wonder-worker who came to make rain took it away with him. If my prince sees it, his heart will be stirred towards me and he will avenge me."

"That will do," said Tripitaka. "Wait for me a little, while I tell my disciple to arrange this matter for you. Where shall I find you?"

"I dare not wait," he said. "I must ask the Spirit that wanders at Night to blow me to the inner chambers of the palace, where I will appear to the queen in a dream and tell her how to work with her son, and to conspire with you and your disciple."

Tripitaka nodded and agreed, saying, "Go, if you will."

Then the wronged ghost beat its head on the floor and turned as though to depart. Somehow it stumbled, and went sprawling with a loud noise that woke Tripitaka up. He knew that it had all been a dream, and finding himself sitting with the dying lamp in front of him, he hurriedly cried: "Disciple, disciple!"

"Hey, what's that?" cried Pigsy, waking up and coming across to him. "In the old days when I was a decent chap and had my whack of human flesh whenever I wanted, and all the stinking victuals I needed, that was a happy life indeed. A very different matter from coddling an old cleric on his journey! I thought I was to be an acolyte, but this is more like being a slave. By day I hoist the luggage and lead the horse; by night I run my legs off bringing you your pot. No sleep early or late! What's the matter this time?"

"Disciple," said Tripitaka, "I was dozing just now at my desk, and had a strange dream."

At this point Monkey sat up, coming across to Tripitaka said, "Master, dreams come from waking thoughts. Each time we come to a hill before we have even begun to climb it, you are in a panic about ogres and demons. And you are always brooding about what a long way it is to India, and wondering if we shall ever get there; and thinking about Ch'ang-an, and wondering if you will ever see it again. All this brooding makes dreams. You should be like me. I think only about seeing Buddha in the west, and not a dream comes near me."

"Disciple," said Tripitaka, "this was not a dream of home-sickness. No sooner had I closed my eyes than there came a wild gust of wind, and there at the door stood an Emperor, who said he was the King of Crow-cock. He was dripping from head to foot, and his eyes were full of tears." Then he told Monkey the whole story.

"You need say no more," said Monkey. "It is clear enough that this dream came to you in order to bring a little business my way. No doubt at all that this magician is an ogre who has usurped the throne. Just let me put him to the test. I don't doubt my stick will make short work of him."

"Disciple," said Tripitaka, "he said the magician was terribly powerful."

"What do I care how powerful he is?" said Monkey. "If he had any inkling that Monkey might arrive on the scene, he would have cleared out long ago."

"Now I come to think of it," said Tripitaka, "he left a token."

Pigsy laughed. "Now, Master," he said, "you must pull yourself together. A dream's a dream. Now it is time to talk sense again."

But Sandy broke in, " 'He who does not believe that straight is straight must guard against the wickedness of good.' Let us light torches, open the gate, and see for ourselves whether the token has been left or not."

Monkey did indeed open the gate, and there, in the light of the stars and moon, with no need for torches, they saw lying on the ramp of the steps a tablet of white jade with gold edges. Pigsy stepped forward and picked it up, saying, "Brother, what's this thing?"

"This," said Monkey, "is the treasure that the king carried in his hand. It is called a jade tablet. Master, now that we have found this thing, there is no more doubt about the matter. Tomorrow it will be my job to catch this fiend."

Dear Monkey! He plucked a hair from his tail, blew on it with magic breath, cried out "Change!," and it became a casket lacquered in red and gold; he laid the tablet in it, and said, "Master, take this in your hand, and when day comes put on your embroidered cassock, and sit reading the scriptures in the great hall. Meanwhile I will inspect that walled city. If I find that an ogre is indeed ruling there, I will slay him, and do a deed by which I shall be remembered here. But if it is not an ogre, we must beware of meddling in the business at all."

"You are right," said Tripitaka.

"If," said Monkey, "the prince does not go out hunting, then there is nothing to be done. But if the dream comes true, I will bring him here to see you."

"And if he comes here, how am I to receive him?"

"When I let you know that he is coming, open the casket and wait while I change myself into a little priest two inches long, and put me in the casket. When the prince comes here, he will go and bow to the Buddha. Don't you take any notice of the prince or kneel down before him. When he sees that you, a commoner, do not bow down to him, he will order his followers to seize you. You will, of course, let yourself be seized, and beaten too, if they choose to beat you, and bound if they choose to bind you. Let them kill you, indeed, if they want to."

"They will be well armed," said Tripitaka. "They might very well kill me. That is not a good idea at all."

"It would not matter," said Monkey. "I could deal with that. I will see to it that nothing really serious happens. If he questions you, say that you were sent by the Emperor of China to worship Buddha and get scriptures, and that you have brought treasures with you. When he asks what treasures, show him your cassock and say it is the least of the three treasures, and that there are two others. Then show him the casket and tell him that there is a treasure within that knows what happened five hundred years ago, and what will happen in five hundred years long hence, and five hundred years between. One thousand five hundred years in all, of things past and present. Then let me out of the casket and I will tell the prince what was revealed in the dream. If he believes, I will go and seize the magician and the prince will be avenged upon his father's murderer and we shall win renown. But if he does not believe, I will show him the jade tablet. Only I fear he is too young, and will not recognize it."

Tripitaka was delighted. "An excellent plan," he said. "But what shall we call the third treasure? The first is the embroidered cassock, the second the white jade tablet. What is your transformation to be called?"

"Call it," said Monkey, "the Baggage that makes Kings." Tripitaka agreed, and committed the name to memory.

Neither disciple nor teacher could sleep. How gladly would they have been able, by a nod, to call up the sun from the Mulberry Tree where it rests, and by a puff of breath blow away the stars that filled the sky!

However, at last it began to grow white in the east, and Monkey got up and gave his orders to Pigsy and Sandy. "Do not," he said, "upset the other priests in the temple by coming out of your cell and rollicking about. Wait till I have done my work, and then we will go on again together."

As soon as he had left them he turned a somersault and leapt into the air. Looking due west with his fiery eyes he soon saw a walled and moated city. You may ask how it was that he could see it. Well, it was only forty leagues away from the temple, and being so high in the air he could see as far as that.

Going on a little way and looking closely, he saw that baleful clouds hung round the city and fumes of discontent surrounded it, and suspended in mid-air Monkey recited:

> "Were he a true king seated on the throne,
> Then there would be a lucky gleam and fire-coloured clouds.
> But as it is, a false fiend has seized the Dragon Seat,
> And coiling wreaths of black fume tarnish the Golden Gate."

While he was gazing at this sad sight, Monkey suddenly heard a great clanging, and looking down he saw the eastern gate of the city open, and from it a great throng of men and horses come out; truly a host of huntsmen. Indeed, a brave show; look at them:

> At dawn they left the east of the Forbidden City;
> They parted and rounded up in the field of low grass,
> Their bright banners opened and caught the sun,
> Their white palfreys charged abreast the wind.
> Their skin drums clatter with a loud roll;
> The hurled spears fly each to its mark.

The hunters left the city and proceeded eastwards for twenty leagues towards a high plain. Now Monkey could see that in the midst of them was a little, little general in helmet and breast-plate, in his hand a jewelled sword, riding a bay charger, his bow at his waist. "Don't tell me!" said Monkey in the air, "that is the prince. Let me go and play a trick on him."

Dear Monkey! He lowered himself on his cloud, made his way through the ranks of the huntsmen and, when he came to the prince, changed himself into a white hare and ran in front of the prince's horse. The prince was delighted, took an arrow from his quiver, strung it and shot at the hare, which he hit. But Monkey had willed the arrow to find its aim, and with a swift grab, just as it was about to touch him, he caught hold of it and ran on.

The prince, seeing that he had hit his mark, broke away from his companions and set out in pursuit. When the horse galloped fast, Monkey ran like the wind; when it slowed down, Monkey slowed down. The distance between them remained always the same, and so bit by bit he enticed the prince to the gates of the Treasure Wood Temple. The hare had vanished, for Monkey went back to his own form. But in the door-post an arrow was stuck.

"Here we are, Master," said Monkey, and at once changed again into a two-inch priest and hid in the casket.

Now when the prince came to the temple-gate and found no hare, but only his own arrow sticking in the gate-post, "Very strange!" said the prince, "I am certain I hit the hare. How is it that the hare has disappeared, but the arrow is here? I think it was not a common hare, but one that had lived too long and changed at last into a sprite."

He pulled out the arrow, and looking up saw that above the gate of the temple was an inscription which said "Treasure Wood Temple, erected by Royal Command." "Why, of course!" said the prince. "I remember years ago my father the king ordered an officer to take gold and precious stuffs to the priests of this temple, so that they might repair the chapel and images. I little thought that I would come here one day like this! A couplet says:

"Chance brought me to a priest's cell
and I listened to his holy talk;
From the life of the troubled world I got
Half a day's rest.

I will go in."

The prince leapt from his horse's back and was just going in when three thousand officers who were in attendance upon him came galloping up in a great throng, and were soon pouring into the courtyard. The priests of the temple, much astonished, came out to do homage to the prince, and escort him into the Buddha Hall, to worship the Buddha. The prince was admiring the cloisters, when suddenly he came upon a priest who sat there and did not budge when he came past. "Has this priest no manners?" the prince cried in a rage. "As no warning was given that I was visiting this place, I could not expect to be met at a distance. But so soon as you saw men-at-arms approaching the gate, you ought to have stood up. How comes it that you are still sitting here without budging? Seize him!"

No sooner had he uttered the command than soldiers rushed from the sides, dragged Tripitaka off with them and made ready to bind him hand and foot. But Monkey in the casket soundlessly invoked the guardian spirits, Devas that protect the Law, and Lu Ting and Lu Chia: "I am now on an errand to subdue an evil spirit. But this prince, in his ignorance, has bade his servants bind my master, and you must come at once to his aid. If he is indeed bound, you will be held responsible!"

Thus secretly addressed by Monkey, how could they venture to disobey? They set a magic ring about Tripitaka, so that each time any one tried to lay hands on him, he could not be reached, any more than if he had been hedged in with a stout wall. "Where do you come from," the prince asked at last, "that you can cheat us like this, making yourself unapproachable?"

Tripitaka now came forward and bowed. "I have no such art," he said. "I am only a priest from China, going to the west to worship Buddha and get scriptures."

"China?" said the prince. "Although it is called The Middle Land, it is a most destitute place. Tell me, for example, if you have anything of value upon you."

"There is the cassock on my back," said Tripitaka. "It is only a third-class treasure. But I have treasures of the first and second class, which are far superior."

"A coat like yours," said the prince, "that leaves half the body bare! It seems a queer thing to call that a treasure."

"This cassock," said Tripitaka, "although it covers only half my body, is described in a poem:

> 'Buddha's coat left one side bare,
> But it hid the Absolute from the world's dust.
> Its ten thousand threads and thousand stitches fulfilled the fruits of Meditation.
> Is it a wonder that when I saw you come I did not rise to greet you?
> You who call yourself a man, yet have failed to avenge a father's death!' "

"What wild nonsense this priest is talking!" said the prince in a great rage. "That half-coat, if it has done nothing else for you, has given you the courage to babble ridiculous fustian. How can my father's death be unavenged, since he is not dead? Just tell me that!"

Tripitaka came out one step forward, pressed the palms of his hands together and said: "Your Majesty, to how many things does man, born into the world, owe gratitude?"

"To four things," said the prince.

"To what four things?"

"He is grateful," said the prince, "to Heaven and Earth for covering and supporting him, to the sun and moon for shining upon him, to the king for lending him water and earth, and to his father and mother for rearing him."

Tripitaka laughed. "To the other three he owes gratitude indeed," he said. "But what need has he of a father and mother to rear him?"

"That's all very well for you," said the prince, "who are a shaven-headed, disloyal, food-cadging wanderer. But if a man had no father or mother, how could he come into the world?"

"Your Majesty," said Tripitaka, "I do not know. But in this casket there is a treasure called 'The baggage that makes kings.' It knows everything that happened during the five hundred years long ago, the five hundred years between, and the five hundred years to come, one thousand five hundred years in all. If he can quote a case where there was no gratitude to father and mother, then let me be detained captive here."

"Show him to me," said the prince. Tripitaka took off the cover and out jumped Monkey, and began to skip about this way and that. "A little fellow like that can't know much," said the prince. Hearing himself described as too small, Monkey used his magic power and stretched himself till he was three feet four inches high. The huntsmen were astonished, and said, "If he goes on growing like this, in a few days he will be bumping his head against the sky." But when he reached his usual height, Monkey stopped growing. At this point the prince said to him, "Baggage who makes Kings, the old priest says you know all things good and ill, in past and present. Do you divine by the tortoise or by the milfoil? Or do you decide men's fates by sentences from books?"

"Not a bit of it," said Monkey; "all I rely on is my three inches of tongue, that tells about everything."

"This fellow talks great nonsense," said the prince. "It has always been by the *Book of Changes*[17] that mysteries have been elucidated and the prospects of the world

[17]The *Book of Changes*, or the *I Ching*, a Chinese classic from the twelfth century B.C.E., interprets sixty-four hexagrams for their moral, political, and spiritual significance.

decided, so that people might know what to pursue and what to avoid. Is it not said: 'The tortoise for divination, the milfoil for prognostication'? But so far as I can make out you go on no principle at all. You talk at random about fate and the future exciting and misleading people to no purpose."

"Now don't be in a hurry, Your Highness," said Monkey, "but listen to me. You are the Crown Prince of Crow-cock. Five years ago there was a famine in your land. The king and his ministers prayed and fasted, but they could not get a speck of rain. Then there came a wizard from the Chung-nan mountains who could call the winds, fetch rain, and turn stone into gold. The king was deceived by his wiles and hailed him as elder brother. Is this true?"

"Yes, yes, yes," said the prince. "Go on!"

"For the last three years the magician has not been seen," said Monkey. "Who is it that has been on the throne?"

"It is true about the wizard," said the prince. "My father did make this wizard his brother, and ate with him and slept with him. But three years ago, when they were walking in the flower garden and admiring the view, a gust of magic wind that the magician sent blew the jade tablet that the king carried out of his hand, and the magician went off with it straight to the Chung-nan mountains. My father still misses him and has no heart to walk in the flower garden without him. Indeed, for three years it has been locked up and no one has set foot in it. If the king is not my father, who is he?"

At this Monkey began to laugh, and did not stop laughing when the prince asked him what was the matter, till the prince lost his temper.

"Why don't you say something?" he said, "instead of standing there laughing."

"I have quite a lot to say," said Monkey, "but I cannot say it in front of all these people."

The prince thought this reasonable, and motioned to the huntsmen to retire. The leader gave his orders, and soon the three thousand men and horses were all stationed outside the gates. None of the priests of the temple were about. Monkey stopped laughing and said, "Your Highness, he who vanished was the father that begot you; he who sits on the throne is the magician that brought rain."

"Nonsense," cried the prince. "Since the magician left us, the winds have been favouring, the people have been at peace. But according to you it is not my father who is on the throne. It is all very well to say such things to me who am young and let it pass; but if my father were to hear you uttering this subversive talk, he would have you seized and torn into ten thousand pieces." He began railing at Monkey, who turned to Tripitaka and said, "What is to be done? I have told him and he does not believe me. Let's get to work. Show him your treasure, and then get your papers seen to, and go off to India." Tripitaka handed the lacquer-box to Monkey, and Monkey taking it gave himself a shake, and the box became invisible. For it was in reality one of Monkey's hairs, which he had changed into a box, but now put back again as a hair on his body. But the white jade tablet he presented to the prince.

"A fine sort of priest," the prince exclaimed. "You it was who came five years ago disguised as a magician, and stole the family treasure, and now, disguised as a priest, are offering it back again! Seize him!" This command startled Tripitaka out of his wits and pointing at Monkey, "It's you," he cried, "you wretched horse-groom, who have brought this trouble on us for no reason at all." Monkey rushed forward and checked him. "Hold your tongue," he said, "and don't let out my secrets. I am not called 'the Baggage that makes Kings.' My real name is quite different."

"I shall be glad to know your real name," said the prince, "that I may send you to the magistrate to be dealt with as you deserve."

"My name then," said Monkey, "is the Great Monkey Sage, and I am this old man's chief disciple. I was going with my Master to India to get scriptures, and last night we came to this temple and asked for shelter. My Master was reading scriptures by night, and at the third watch he had a dream. He dreamt that your father came to him and said he had been attacked by that magician, who in the flower garden pushed him into the eight-cornered crystal well. Then the wizard changed himself into your father's likeness. The court and all the officers were completely deceived; you yourself were too young to know. You were forbidden to enter the inner apartments of the Palace and the flower garden was shut up, lest the secret should get out. Tonight your father came and asked me to subdue the false magician. I was not sure that he was an evil spirit, but when I looked down from the sky I was quite certain of it. I was just going to seize him, when I met you and your huntsmen. The white hare you shot was me. It was I who led you here and brought you to my Master. This is the truth, every word of it. You have recognized the white tablet, and all that remains is for you to repay your father's care and revenge yourself on his enemy."

This upset the prince very much. "If I do not believe this story," he said to himself, "it must in any case have an unpleasant amount of truth in it. But if I believe it, how can I any longer look upon the present king as my father?" He was in great perplexity.

"If you are in doubt," said Monkey, "ride home and ask your mother a question that will decide it. Ask whether she and the king, as man and wife, are on changed terms, these last three years."

"That is a good idea," said the prince. "Just wait while I go and ask my mother." He snatched up the jade tablet and was about to make off, when Monkey stopped him, saying, "If all your gentlemen follow you back to the palace, suspicions will be aroused, and how can I succeed in my task? You must go back all alone and attract no attention. Do not go in at the main gate but by the back gate. And when you get to the inner apartments and see your mother, do not speak loudly or clearly, but in a low whisper; for if the magician should hear you, so great is his power that your life and your mother's would be in danger."

The prince did as he was told, and as he left the temple he told his followers to remain there on guard and not to move. "I have some business," he said. "Wait till I have got to the city and then come on yourselves!" Look at him!

> He gives his orders to the men-at-arms,
> Flies on horseback home to the citadel.

If you do not know whether on this occasion he succeeded in seeing his mother, and if so what passed between them, you must listen to the next chapter.

Chapter 20

The Prince was soon back at the city of Crow-cock, and as instructed he made no attempt to go in by the main gate, but without announcing himself went to the back gate, where several eunuchs were on guard. They did not dare to stop him, and (dear prince!) he rode in all alone, and soon reached the Arbour of Brocade Perfume, where he found his mother surrounded by her women, who were fanning her, while she leant weeping over a carven balustrade. Why, you will ask, was she weeping? At the fourth watch she had had a dream, half of which she could remember and half of which had faded; and she was thinking hard. Leaping from his horse, the prince knelt down before her and cried "Mother!" She forced herself to put on a happier countenance, and exclaimed, "Child, this is a joy indeed! For years past you have been so busy in the men's quarters at the Palace, studying with your father, that I have never seen you, which has been a great sorrow to me. How have you managed to find time today? It is an unspeakable pleasure! My child, why is your voice so mournful? Your father is growing old. Soon the time will come when the 'dragon returns to the pearl-grey sea, the phoenix to the pink mists'; you will then become king. Why should you be dispirited?"

The prince struck the floor with his forehead. "Mother, I ask you," he said, "who is it that sits upon the throne?"

"He has gone mad," said the queen. "The ruler is your father and king. Why should you ask?"

"Mother," the prince said, "if you will promise me forgiveness I will speak. But if not, I dare not speak."

"How can there be questions of guilt and pardon between mother and son? Of course, you are free to speak. Be quick and begin."

"Mother," said the prince, "if you compare your life with my father these last three years with your life with him before, should you say that his affection was as great?"

Hearing this question the queen altogether lost her presence of mind, and leaping to her feet ran down from the arbour and flung herself into his arms, saying, "Child, why, when I have not seen you for so long, should you suddenly come and ask me such a question?"

"Mother," said the prince hotly, "do not evade this question. For much hangs upon the answer to it."

Then the queen sent away all the Court ladies, and with tears in her eyes said in a low voice, "Had you not asked me, I would have gone down to the Nine Springs of Death without ever breathing a word about this matter. But since you have asked, hear what I have to say:

> 'What three years ago was warm and bland,
> These last three years has been cold as ice.
> When at the pillow's side I questioned him,
> He told me age had impaired his strength
> and that things did not work.' "

When he heard this, the prince shook himself free, gripped the saddle, and mounted his horse. His mother tried to hold him back, saying, "Child, what is it that makes you rush off before our talk is done?"

The prince returned and knelt in front of her. "Mother," he said, "I dare not speak. Today at dawn I received a command to go hunting outside the city with falcon and dog. By chance I met a priest sent by the Emperor of China to fetch scriptures. He has a chief disciple named Monkey, who is very good at subduing evil spirits. According to him my father the king was drowned in the crystal well in the flower garden, and a wizard impersonated him and seized his throne. Last night at the third watch my father appeared in a dream to this priest and asked him to come to the city and seize the impostor. I did not believe all this, and so came to question you. But what you have just told me makes me certain that it is an evil spirit."

"My child," said the queen, "why should you believe strangers, of whom you have no knowledge?"

"I should not," said the prince, "have dared to accept the story as true, had not the king my father left behind a token in the hands of these people." The queen asked what it was, and the prince took out from his sleeve the white jade tablet bordered with gold, and handed it to his mother. When she saw that it was indeed a treasure that had been the king's in old days, she could not stop her tears gushing out like a waterspring. "My lord and master," she cried, "why have you been dead three years and never come to me, but went first to a priest and afterwards to the prince?"

"Mother," said the prince, "what do these words mean?"

"My child," she said, "at the fourth watch I too had a dream. I dreamt I saw your father stand in front of me, all dripping wet, saying that he was dead, and that his soul had visited a priest of T'ang and asked him to defeat the false king and rescue his own body from where it had been thrown. That is all I can remember, and it is only half. The other half I cannot get clear, and I was puzzling about it when you came. It is strange that you should just at this moment come with this tale, and bring this tablet with you. I will put it away, and you must go and ask that priest to come at once and do what he promises. If he can drive away the impostor and distinguish the false from the true, you will have repaid the king your father for the pains he bestowed upon your upbringing."

The prince was soon back at the gates of the Treasure Wood Temple, where he was joined by his followers. The sun's red disc was now falling. He told his followers to stay quietly where they were, went into the temple alone, arranged his hat and clothes, and paid his respects to Monkey, who came hopping and skipping from the main hall. The prince knelt down, saying, "Here I am again, Father."

Monkey raised him from his knees. "Did you ask anyone anything when you were in the city?" he said.

"I questioned my mother," said the prince; and he told the whole story.

Monkey smiled. "If it is as cold as that," he said, "he is probably a transformation of some chilly creature. No matter! Just wait while I mop him up for you. But today it is growing late, and I cannot very well start doing anything. You go back now, and I will come early tomorrow."

"Master," said the prince, kneeling before him, "let me wait here till the morning, and then go along with you."

"That will not do," said Monkey. "If I were to come into the city at the same time as you, the suspicions of the impostor would be aroused. He would not believe that I forced myself upon you, but would be sure you had invited me. And in this way the blame would fall on you."

"I shall get into trouble anyhow," said the prince, "if I go into the city now."

"What about?" asked Monkey.

"I was sent out hunting," said the prince, "and I have not got a single piece of game. How dare I face the king? If he accuses me of incompetence and casts me into prison, who will you have to look after you when you arrive tomorrow? There is not one of the officers who knows you."

"What matter?" said Monkey. "You have only to mention that you need some game, and I will procure it for you." Dear Monkey! Watch him while he displays his arts before the prince. He gives himself a shake, jumps up on to the fringe of a cloud, performs a magic pass and murmurs a spell which compels the spirits of the mountain and the local deities to come before him and do obeisance.

"Great Sage," they said, "what orders have you for us little divinities?"

"I guarded a priest of T'ang on his way here," said Monkey. "I want to seize an evil spirit, but this prince here has nothing to show for his hunting, and does not dare return to Court. I have sent for you divinities to ask you to do me a favour. Find some musk deer, wild boar, hares and so on—any wild beasts or birds you can discover, and bring them here."

The divinities dared not disobey. "How many do you require of each?" they asked.

"It does not matter exactly how many," said Monkey. "Just bring some along; that is all."

Then these divinities, using the secret instruments that appertained to them, made a magic wind that drew together wild beasts. Soon there were hundreds and thousands of wild fowl, deer, foxes, hares, tigers, panthers, and wolves collected in front of Monkey. "It is not I who want them!" he cried. "You must get them on the move again, and string them out on each side of the road for forty leagues. The hunters will be able to take them home without use of falcon or dog. That is all that is required of you."

The divinities obeyed, and spread out the game on each side of the road. Monkey then lowered his cloud and said to the prince, "Your Highness may now go back. There is game all along the road; you have only to collect it."

When the prince saw him floating about in the air and exercising magic powers, he was deeply impressed, and bent his head on the ground in prostration before Monkey, from whom he humbly took his leave. He then went out in front of the temple and gave orders to the huntsmen to return to Court. They were astonished to find endless wild game on each side of the road, which they took without use of falcon or dog, merely by laying hands upon it. They all believed that this blessing had been vouchsafed to the prince, and had no idea that it was Monkey's doing. Listen to the songs of triumph that they sing as they throng back to the city!

When the priests of the temple saw on what terms Tripitaka and the rest were with the prince, they began to treat them with a new deference. They invited them to refreshments, and again put the Zen Hall at Tripitaka's disposal. It was near the first watch; but Monkey had something on his mind and could not get to sleep at once. Presently he crept across to Tripitaka's bed and called, "Master!" Tripitaka was not asleep either; but knowing that Monkey liked giving people a start, he pretended to be asleep. Monkey rubbed his tonsure and shaking him violently, he said, "Master, why are you sleeping?"

"The rogue!" cried Tripitaka crossly. "Why can't you go to sleep, instead of pestering me like this?"

"Master," said Monkey, "there is something you must give me your advice about."

"What is that?" said Tripitaka.

"I talked very big to the prince," said Monkey, "giving him to understand that my powers were high as the hills and deep as the sea, and that I could catch the false wizard as easily as one takes things out of a bag—I had only to stretch out my hand and carry him off. But I cannot get to sleep, for it has occurred to me that it may not be so easy."

"If you think it's too difficult, why do it?" said Tripitaka.

"It's not that there's any difficulty about catching him," said Monkey. "The only question is whether it is legal."

"What nonsense this monkey talks," said Tripitaka. "How can it be illegal to arrest a monster that has seized a monarch's throne?"

"You only know how to read scriptures, worship Buddha, and practise Zen, and have never studied the Code of Hsiao Ho. But you must at least know the proverb 'Take robber, take loot.' The magician has been king for three years and not the slightest suspicion has been felt by anyone. All the late king's ladies sleep with him, and the ministers civil and military disport themselves with him. Even if I succeed in catching him, how am I to convince anyone of his guilt?"

"What is the difficulty?" asked Tripitaka. "Even if he were as dumb as a calabash, he would be able to talk one down. He would say boldly, 'I am the king of Crow-cock. What crime have I committed against Heaven that you should arrest me?' How would one argue with him then?"

"And you," said Tripitaka, "what plan have you got?"

"My plan is already made," said Monkey smiling. "The only obstacle is that you have a partiality."

"A partiality for whom?" said Tripitaka.

"Pigsy," said Monkey; "you have a preference for him because he is so strong."

"What makes you think that?" asked Tripitaka.

"If it were not so," said Monkey, "you would pull yourself together and have the courage to stay here with Sandy to look after you, while I and Pigsy go off to the city of Crow-cock, find the flower garden, uncover the well, and bring up the Emperor's body, which we will wrap in our wrapper, and next day bring to Court. There we will get our papers put in order, confront the Magician, and I will fell him with my cudgel. If he tries to exonerate himself, I will show him the body and say, 'Here is the man you drowned.' And I will make the prince come forward and wail over his father, the queen come out and recognize her husband, the officers civil and military look upon their lord, and then I and my brother will get to work. In this way the whole thing will be on a proper footing."

Tripitaka thought this was a splendid plan, but he was not sure that Pigsy would consent. "Why not?" said Monkey. "Didn't I say you were partial to him and did not want him to go? You think he would refuse to go because you know that when I call you it is often half an hour before you take any notice. You'll see when I start, that I shall only need a turn or two of my three-inch tongue, and no matter if he is Pigsy or Wigsy I am quite capable of making him follow me."

"Very well," said Tripitaka, "call him when you go."

"Pigsy, Pigsy," cried Monkey at Pigsy's bedside. That fool did most of the hard work when they were on the road, and no sooner did his head touch the pillow than he was snoring, and it took a great deal more than a shout to wake him.

Monkey pulled his ears, tweaked his bristles, and dragged him from the pillow, shouting "Pigsy!" That fool pushed him away. Monkey shouted again.

"Go to sleep and don't be so stupid," Pigsy said. "Tomorrow we have got to be on the road again."

"I am not being stupid," said Monkey, "there is a bit of business I want your help in."

"What business?" asked Pigsy.

"You heard what the prince said?" said Monkey.

"No," said Pigsy, "I did not set eyes on him, or hear anything he said."

"He told me," said Monkey, "that the magician has a treasure worth more than any army of ten thousand men. When we go to the city tomorrow, we are sure to fall foul of him, he will use it to overthrow us. Wouldn't it be much better if we got in first and stole the treasure?"

"Brother," said Pigsy, "are you asking me to commit robbery? If so, that's a business I have experience of and can really be of some help. But there is one thing we must get clear. If I steal a treasure or subdue a magician I expect more than a petty, skunking share. The treasure must be mine."

"What do you want it for?" asked Monkey. "I am not so clever as you are at talking people into giving me alms. I am strong, but I have a very common way of talking, and I don't know how to recite the scriptures. When we get into a tight place, wouldn't this treasure be good to exchange for something to eat and drink?"

"I only care for fame," said Monkey. "I don't want any treasures. You may have it all to yourself."

That fool, when he heard that it was all to be his, was in high glee. He rolled out of bed, hustled into his clothes, and set out with Monkey.

> Clear wine brings a blush to the cheeks;
> Yellow gold moves even a philosophic heart.

The two of them opened the temple gate very quietly and, leaving Tripitaka, mounted a wreath of cloud and soon reached the city, where they lowered their cloud, just as the second watch was being sounded on the tower.

"Brother! it's the second watch," said Monkey.

"Couldn't be better," said Pigsy. "Everyone will just be deep in their first sleep."

They did not go to the main gate, but to the back gate, where they heard the sound of the watchman's clappers and bells.

"Brother," said Monkey, "they are on the alert at all the gates. How shall we get in?"

"When did thieves ever go in by a gate?" said Pigsy. "We must scramble over the wall." Monkey did so, and at a bound was over the rampart and wall. Pigsy followed, and the two stealthily made their way in, soon rejoining the road from the gate. They followed this till they came to the flower garden.

In front of them was a gate-tower with three thatched white gables, and high up was an inscription in shining letters, catching the light of the moon and stars. It said "Imperial Flower Garden." When Monkey came close, he saw that the locks were sealed up several layers deep, and he told Pigsy to get to work. That fool wielded his iron rake, which he brought crashing down upon the gate and smashed it to bits. Monkey stepped over the fragments, and once inside could not stop himself jumping and shouting for joy. "Brother," said Pigsy, "you'll be the ruin of us. Who ever heard of a thief making all that noise? You'll wake everyone up, we shall be arrested and taken before the judge, and if we are not condemned to death we shall certainly be sent back to where we came from and drafted into the army."

"Why try to make me nervous?" said Monkey. "Look!

> 'The painted and carven balustrades are scattered and strewn;
> The jewel-studded arbours and trees are toppling down.
> The sedgy islands and knot-weed banks are buried in dust;
> The white peonies and yellow glove-flowers, all dust-destroyed.
> Jasmine and rose perfume the night;
> The red peony and tiger-lily bloom in vain,
> The hibiscus and Syrian mallow are choked with weeds;
> Strange plant and rare flower are crushed and die.' "

"And what does it matter if they do?" said Pigsy. "Let's get on with our business."

Monkey, although deeply affected by the scene, called to mind Tripitaka's dream, in which he was told that the well was underneath a banana-plant, and when they had gone a little further they did indeed discover a most singular banana-plant, which grew very thick and high.

"Now Pigsy," said Monkey. "Are you ready? The treasure is buried under this tree." That fool lifted his rake in both hands, beat down the banana-tree and began to nuzzle with his snout till he had made a hole three or four feet deep. At last he came to a slab of stone. "Brother," he cried, "here's luck. We've found the treasure. It's bound to be under this slab. If it's not in a coffer it will be in a jar."

"Hoist it up and see," said Monkey.

Pigsy went to work again with his snout and raised the slab till they could see underneath. Something sparkled and flashed. "Didn't I say we were in luck," said Pigsy. "That is the treasure glittering." But when they looked closer, it was the light of the stars and moon reflected in a well.

"Brother," said Pigsy, "you should not think so much of the trunk that you forget the root."

"Now, what does that mean?" asked Monkey.

"This is a well," said Pigsy. "If you had told me before we started that the treasure was in a well, I should have brought with me the two ropes we tie up our bundles with, and you could have contrived to let me down. As it is, how are we to get at anything down there and bring it up again?"

"You intend to go down?" said Monkey.

"That's what I should do," said Pigsy, "if I had any rope."

"Take off your clothes," said Monkey, "and I'll manage it for you."

"I don't go in for much in the way of clothes," said Pigsy. "But I'll take off my jerkin, if that's any good."

Dear Monkey! He took out his metal-clasped cudgel, called to it "Stretch!," and when it was some thirty feet long he said to Pigsy, "You catch hold of one end, and I'll let you down."

"Brother," said Pigsy, "let me down as far as you like, so long as you stop when I come to the water."

"Just so," said Monkey.

Pigsy caught hold of one end of the staff, and was very gently raised and let down into the well by Monkey. He soon reached the water. "I'm at the water," he called up. Monkey, hearing this, let him down just a little further. That fool Pigsy, when he felt the water touch him, began to beat out with his trotters, let go of the staff and flopped right into the water. "The rascal!" he cried, spluttering and blowing. "I told him to stop when I came to the water, and instead he let me down further."

Monkey only laughed, and withdrew the staff. "Brother," he said, "have you found the treasure?"

"Treasure indeed!" said Pigsy. "There's nothing but well-water."

"The treasure is under the water," said Monkey. "Just have a look."

Pigsy, it so happened, was thoroughly at home in the water. He took a great plunge straight down into the well. But, oh what a long way it was to the bottom! He dived again with all his might, and suddenly opening his eyes saw in front of him an entrance, above which was written "The Crystal Palace." This astonished him very much. "That finishes it," he cried. "I've come the wrong way and got into the sea! There is a Crystal Palace in the sea; but I never heard of one down a well." For he did not know that the Dragon King of the Well also has a Crystal Palace.

Pigsy was thus debating with himself when a yaksha,[18] on patrol-duty in the waters, opened the door, saw the intruder, and immediately withdrew to the interior, announcing: "Great King, a calamity! A long-snouted, long-eared priest has dropped down into our well, all naked and dripping. He is still alive, and speaks to himself rationally."

The Dragon King of the Well was, however, not at all surprised. "If I am not mistaken," he said, "this is General Pigsy. Last night the Spirit that Wanders by Night received orders to come here and fetch the soul of the king of Crow-cock

[18]A species of demon or genie living in the earth or waters.

and bring it to the priest of T'ang to ask the Monkey Sage to subdue the wicked magician. I imagine that Monkey has come, as well as General Pigsy. They must be treated with great consideration. Go at once and ask the General to come in." The Dragon King then tidied his clothes, adjusted his hat, and bringing with him all his watery kinsmen he came to the gate and cried in a loud voice: "General Pigsy, pray come inside and be seated!"

Pigsy was delighted. "Fancy meeting with an old friend!" he said. And without thinking what he was in for, that fool went into the Crystal Palace. Caring nothing for good manners, all dripping as he was, he sat down in the seat of honour.

"General," said the Dragon King, "I heard lately that your life was spared to you on condition you should embrace the faith of Sakyamuni[19] and protect Tripitaka on his journey to India. What then are you doing down here?"

"It's just in that connexion that I come," said Pigsy. "My brother Monkey presents his best compliments and sends me to fetch some treasure or other."

"I am sorry," said the Dragon King, "but what should I be doing with any treasure? You're mixing me up with the dragons of the Yangtze, the Yellow River, the Huai and the Chi, who soar about the sky and assume many shapes. They no doubt have treasures. But I stay down here all the time in this wretched hole never catching a glimpse of the sky above. Where should I get a treasure from?"

"Don't make excuses," said Pigsy. "I know you have got it; so bring it out at once."

"The one treasure I have," said the Dragon King, "can't be brought out. I suggest you should go and look at it for yourself."

"Excellent," said Pigsy. "I'll come and have a look."

The Dragon King led him through the Crystal Palace till they came to a cloister in which lay a body six feet long. Pointing at it the Dragon King said, "General, there is your treasure." Pigsy went up to it, and oh! what did he see before him? It was a dead Emperor, on his head a tall crown, dressed in a red gown, on his feet upturned shoes, girded with a belt of jades, who lay stretched full length upon the floor. Pigsy laughed. "You won't kid me like that," he said. "Since when did this count as a treasure? Why, when I was an ogre in the mountains I made my supper on them every day. When one has not only seen a thing time after time, but also eaten it again and again, can one be expected to regard it as a treasure?"

"General," said the Dragon King, "you do not understand. This is the body of the King of Crow-cock. When he fell into the well I preserved him with a magic pearl, and he suffered no decay. If you care to take him up with you, show him to Monkey and succeed in bringing him back to his senses, you need worry no more about 'treasures,' you'll be able to get anything out of him that you choose to ask for."

"Very well then," said Pigsy, "I'll remove him for you, if you'll let me know how much I shall get as my undertaker's fee."

"I haven't got any money," said the Dragon King.

"So you expect to get jobs done for nothing?" said Pigsy. "If you haven't got any money I won't remove him."

"If you won't," said the Dragon King, "I must ask you to go away."

Pigsy at once retired. The Dragon King ordered two powerful yakshas to carry the body to the gate of the Crystal Palace and leave it just outside. They removed from the gate its water-fending pearls, and at once there was a sound of rushing waters! Pigsy looked round. The gate had vanished, and while he was poking about

[19] A title sometimes given to Gautama, the Buddha.

for it, his hand touched the dead king's body, which gave him such a start that his legs gave way under him. He scrambled to the surface of the water, and squeezing against the well-wall, he cried, "Brother, let down your staff and get me out of this."

"Did you find the treasure?" asked Monkey.

"How should I?" said Pigsy. "All I found was a Dragon King at the bottom of the water, who wanted me to remove a corpse. I refused, and he had me put out at the door. Then his palace vanished, and I found myself touching the corpse. It gave me such a turn that I feel quite weak. Brother, you must get me out of this."

"That was your treasure," said Monkey. "Why didn't you bring it up with you?"

"I knew he had been dead a long time," said Pigsy. "What was the sense of bringing him?"

"You'd better," said Monkey, "or I shall go away."

"Go?" said Pigsy. "Where to?"

"I shall go back to the temple," said Monkey, "and go to sleep like Tripitaka."

"And I shall be left down here?" said Pigsy.

"If you can climb out," said Monkey, "there is no reason why you should stay here; but if you can't there's an end of it."

Pigsy was thoroughly frightened; he knew he could not possibly climb out. "Just think," he said, "even a city wall is difficult to get up. But this well-shaft has a big belly and a small mouth. Its walls slope in, and as no water has been drawn from it for several years they have become all covered with slime. It's far too slippery to climb. Brother, just to keep up a nice spirit between friends, I'll carry it up."

"That's right," said Monkey. "And be quick about it, so that we can both of us go home to bed."

That fool Pigsy dived down again, found the corpse, hoisted it on to his back, clambered up to the surface of the water, and propped himself and the body against the wall. "Brother," he called. "I've brought it." Monkey peered down, and seeing that Pigsy had indeed a burden on his back, he lowered his staff into the well.

That fool was a creature of much determination. He opened his mouth wide, bit hard on the staff, and Monkey pulled him gently up. Putting down the corpse, Pigsy pulled himself into his clothes. The Emperor, Monkey found on examining him, was indeed in the most perfect preservation. "Brother," he asked, "how comes it that a man who has been dead for three years can look so fresh?"

"According to the Dragon King of the Well," said Pigsy, "he used a magic pearl which prevented the body from decaying."

"That was a bit of luck," said Monkey. "But it still remains to take vengeance upon his enemy and win glory for ourselves. Make haste and carry him off."

"Where to?" asked Pigsy.

"To the temple," said Monkey, "to show him to Tripitaka."

"What an idea!" grumbled Pigsy to himself. "A fellow was having a nice, sound sleep, and along comes this baboon with a wonderful yarn about a job that must be done, and in the end it turns out to be nothing but this silly game of carting about a corpse. Carry that stinking thing! It will dribble filthy water all over me and dirty my clothes; there's no one to wash them for me. There are patches in several places, and if the water gets through I have nothing to change into."

"Don't worry about your clothes," said Monkey. "Get the body to the temple, and I will give you a change of clothes."

"Impudence!" cried Pigsy. "You've none of your own. How can you give me any to change into?"

"Does that twaddle mean that you won't carry it?" asked Monkey.

"I'm not going to carry it," said Pigsy.

"Then hold out your paw and take twenty," said Monkey.

"Brother," said Pigsy, much alarmed, "that cudgel is very heavy; after twenty strokes of it there would not be much to choose between me and this Emperor."

"If you don't want to be beaten," said Monkey, "make haste and carry it off.'

Pigsy did indeed fear the cudgel, and sorely against his will he hoisted the corpse on to his back and began to drag himself along towards the garden gate. Dear Monkey! He performed a magic pass, recited a spell, traced a magic square on the ground, and going to it blew a breath that turned into a great gust of wind which blew Pigsy clean out of the palace grounds and clear of the city moat. The wind stopped, and alighting they set out slowly on their way. Pigsy was feeling very ill-used and thought of a plan to revenge himself. "This monkey," he said to himself "has played a dirty trick on me, but I'll get even with him all right when we get back to the temple, I will tell Tripitaka that Monkey can bring the dead to life. If he says he can't, I shall persuade Tripitaka to recite the spell that makes this monkey's head ache, and I shan't be satisfied till his brains are bursting out of his head." But thinking about it as he went along, he said to himself, "That's no good! If he is asked to bring the king to life, he won't have any difficulty; he will go straight to Yama, King of Death, ask for the soul, and so bring the king to life. I must make it clear that he is not to go to the Dark Realm, but must do his cure here in the World of Light. That's the thing to do."

They were now at the temple gate, went straight in, and put down the corpse at the door of the Zen Hall, saying, "Master, get up and look!" Tripitaka was not asleep, but was discussing with Sandy why the others were away so long. Suddenly he heard them calling, and jumping up he said, "Disciples, what is this I see?"

"Monkey's father-in-law," said Pigsy; "he made me carry him."

"You rotten fool," said Monkey, "where have I any father-in-law?"

"Brother, if he isn't your father-in-law," said Pigsy, "why did you make me carry him? It has been tiring work for me, I can tell you that!"

When Tripitaka and Sandy examined the body, and saw that the Emperor looked just like a live man, Tripitaka suddenly burst into lamentation. "Alas, poor Emperor," he cried, "in some forgotten existence you doubtless did great wrong to one that in this incarnation has now confounded you, and brought you to destruction. You were torn from wife and child; none of your generals or counsellors knew, none of your officers were aware. Alas, for the blindness of your queen and prince that offered no incense, no tea to your soul!" Here he broke down, and his tears fell like rain.

"Master," said Pigsy, "what does it matter to you that he is dead? He is not your father or grandfather, why should you wail over him?"

"Disciple," said Tripitaka, "for us who are followers of Buddha compassion is the root, indulgence the gate. Why is your heart so hard?"

"It isn't that my heart is hard," said Pigsy. "But Brother Monkey tells me he can bring him to life. If he fails I am certainly not going to cart him about any more."

Now Tripitaka, being by nature pliable as water, was easily moved by that fool's story. "'Monkey," he said, "if you can indeed bring this Emperor back to life, you will be doing what matters more than that we should reach the Holy Mountain and worship the Buddha. They say 'To save one life is better than to build a seven-storeyed pagoda.' "

"Master," said Monkey, "do you really believe this fool's wild talk? When a man is dead, in three times seven, five times seven, or at the end of seven hundred days, when he has done penance for his sins in the World of Light, his turn comes to be born again. This king has been dead for three years. How can he possibly be saved?"

"I expect we had better give up the idea," said Tripitaka, when he heard this.

But Pigsy was not to be cheated of his revenge. "Don't let him put you off," he said to Tripitaka. "Remember, his head is very susceptible. You have only to recite that stuff of yours, and I guarantee that he'll turn the king into a live man."

Tripitaka accordingly did recite the headache spell, and it gripped so tight that Monkey's eyes started out of his head, and he suffered frightful pain.

If you do not know whether in the end this king was brought to life, you must listen to what is unfolded in the next chapter.

Chapter 21

The pain in that great Monkey Sage's head was so severe that at last he could bear it no longer and cried piteously, "Master, stop praying, stop praying! I'll doctor him."

"How will you do it?" asked Tripitaka.

"The only way is to visit Yama, King of Death, in the Land of Darkness, and get him to let me have the king's soul," said Monkey.

"Don't believe him, Master," said Pigsy. "He told me there was no need to go to the Land of Darkness. He said he knew how to cure him here and now, in the World of Light."

Tripitaka believed this wicked lie, and began praying again; and Monkey was so harassed that he soon gave in. "All right, all right," he cried. "I'll cure him in the World of Light."

"Don't stop," said Pigsy. "Go on praying as hard as you can."

"You ill-begotten idiot," cursed Monkey, "I'll pay you out for making the Master put a spell upon me."

Pigsy laughed till he fell over. "Ho, ho, brother," he cried, "you thought it was only on me that tricks could be played. You didn't think that I could play a trick on you."

"Master, stop praying," said Monkey, "and let me cure him in the World of Light."

"How can that be done?" asked Tripitaka.

"I will rise on my cloud trapeze," said Monkey, "and force my way into the southern gate of Heaven. I shall not go to the Palace of the Pole and Ox, nor to the Hall of Holy Mists, but go straight up to the thirty-third heaven, and in the Trayaśimstra Courtyard of the heavenly palace of Quit Grief I shall visit Lao Tzu and ask for a grain of his Nine Times Sublimated Life Restoring Elixir, and with it I shall bring the king back to life."

This suggestion pleased Tripitaka very much. "Lose no time about it," he said.

"It is only the third watch," said Monkey. "I shall be back before it is light. But it would look all wrong if the rest of you went quietly to sleep. It is only decent that someone should watch by the corpse and mourn."

"You need say no more," said Pigsy. "I can see that you expect me to act as mourner."

"I should like to see you refuse!" said Monkey. "If you don't act as mourner, I certainly shan't bring him to life."

"Be off, Brother," said Pigsy, "and I'll do the mourning."

"There are more ways than one of mourning," said Monkey. "Mere bellowing with dry eyes is no good. Nor is it any better just to squeeze out a few tears. What counts is a good hearty howling, with tears as well. That's what is wanted for a real, miserable mourning."

"I'll give you a specimen," said Pigsy. He then from somewhere or other produced a piece of paper which he twisted into a paper-spill and thrust up his nostrils. This soon set him snivelling and his eyes running, and when he began to howl he kept up such a din that anyone would have thought he had indeed lost his dearest relative. The effect was so mournful that Tripitaka too soon began to weep bitterly.

"That's what you've got to keep up the whole time I'm away," said Monkey laughing. "What I am frightened of is that this fool, the moment my back is turned, will stop wailing. I shall creep back and listen, and if he shows any sign of leaving off he will get twenty on the paw."

"Be off with you," laughed Pigsy. "I could easily keep this up for two days on end."

Sandy, seeing that Pigsy had settled down to his job, went off to look for some sticks of incense to burn as an offering. "Excellent!" laughed Monkey. "The whole family is engaged in works of piety! Now's the time for Old Monkey to get to business."

Dear Monkey! Just at midnight he left his teacher and fellow-disciples, mounted his cloud trapeze and flew in at the southern gate of Heaven. He did not indeed call at the Precious Hall of Holy Mists or go on to the Palace of the Pole and Ox, but only along a path of cloudy light went straight to the thirty-third heaven, to the Trayaśimstra Courtyard of the heavenly palace of Quit Grief. Just inside the gate he saw Lao Tzu in his alchemical studio, with a number of fairy boys holding banana-leaf fans, and fanning the fire in which the cinnabar was sublimating.

As soon as Lao Tzu saw him coming, he called to the boys, "Be careful, all of you. Here's the thief who stole the elixir come back again."

Monkey bowed, and said laughing, "Reverend Sir, there is no need to be in such a fret. You need take no precautions against me. I have come on quite different business."

"Monkey," said Lao Tzu, "five hundred years ago you made great trouble in the Palace of Heaven, and stole a great quantity of my holy elixir; for which crime you were arrested and placed in my crucible, where you were smelted for forty-nine days, at the cost of I know not how much charcoal. Now you have been lucky enough to obtain forgiveness, enter the service of Buddha, and go with Tripitaka, the priest of T'ang, to get scriptures in India. Some while ago you quelled a demon in the Flat Topped Mountain and tricked disaster, but did not give me my share in the treasure. What brings you here today?"

"In those old days," said Monkey, "I lost no time in returning to you those five treasures of yours. You have no reason to be suspicious of me."

"But what are you doing here?" asked Lao Tzu, "creeping into my palace instead of getting on with your journey?"

"On our way to the west," said Monkey, "we came to a country called Crow-cock. The king of the country employed a wizard, who had disguised himself as a Taoist, to bring rain. This wizard secretly did away with the king, whose form he assumed, and now he is ensconced in the Hall of Golden Bells. My Master was reading the scriptures in the Treasure Wood Temple, when the soul of the king came to him and earnestly requested that I might be sent to subdue the wizard, and expose his imposture. I felt that I had no proof of the crime, and went with my fellow-disciple Pigsy. We broke into the flower garden by night, and looked for the crystal well into which the king had been thrown. We fished him up, and found him still sound and fresh. When we got back to the temple and saw Tripitaka, his compassion was aroused and he ordered me to bring the king to life. But I was not to go to the World of Darkness to recover his soul; I must cure him here in the World of Light. I could think of no way but to ask for your help. Would you be so kind as to lend me a thousand of your nine times sublimated life-restoring pills? Then I shall be able to set him right."

"A thousand pills indeed!" exclaimed Lao Tzu. "Why not two thousand? Is he to have them at every meal instead of rice? Do you think one has only to stoop and pick them up like dirt from the ground? Shoo! Be off with you! I've nothing for you."

"I'd take a hundred," said Monkey laughing.

"I dare say," said Lao Tzu. "But I haven't any."

"I'd take ten," said Monkey.

"A curse on this Monkey!" said Lao Tzu, very angry. "Will he never stop haggling? Be off with you immediately."

"If you really haven't got any," said Monkey, "I shall have to find some other way of bringing him to life."

"Go, go, go!" screamed Lao Tzu.

Very reluctantly Monkey turned away. But suddenly Lao Tzu thought to himself: "This monkey is very crafty. If he really went away and stayed away, it would be all right. But I am afraid he will slip back again and steal some." So he sent a fairy boy to bring Monkey back, and said to him, "If you are really so anxious to have some, I'll spare you just one pill."

"Sir," said Monkey, "if you had an inkling of what I can do if I choose, you would think yourself lucky to go shares in it with me. If you hadn't given in, I should have come with my dredge and fished up the whole lot."

Lao Tzu took a gourd-shaped pot and, tilting it up, emptied one grain of elixir and passed it across to Monkey, saying, "That's all you'll get, so be off with it. And if with this one grain you can bring the king back to life, you are welcome to the credit of it."

"Not so fast," said Monkey. "I must taste it first. I don't want to be put off with a sham." So saying, he tossed it into his mouth. Lao Tzu rushed forward to stop him, and pressing his fists against his skull-cap he cried in despair, "If you swallow it, I shall kill you on the spot!"

"Revolting meanness," said Monkey. "Keep calm; no one is eating anything of yours. And how much is it worth, anyhow? It's pretty wretched stuff, and come to that, I haven't swallowed it; it's here."

For the fact is that monkeys have a pouch under the gullet, and Monkey had stored the grain of elixir in his pouch. Lao Tzu pinched him and said, "Be off with you, be off with you, and don't let me find you hanging round here any more." So Monkey took leave of him, and quitted the Trayaśimstra Heaven. In a moment he had left by the Southern Gate, and turning eastward he saw the great globe of the sun just mounting. Lowering his cloud-seat, he soon reached the Treasure Wood Temple, where even before he entered the gate he could hear Pigsy still howling. He stepped briskly forward and cried "Master."

"Is that Monkey?" said Tripitaka delightedly. "Have you got your elixir?"

"Certainly," said Monkey.

"What's the use of asking?" said Pigsy. "You can count on a sneak like that to bring back some trifle that doesn't belong to him."

"Brother," laughed Monkey, "you can retire. We don't need you any more. Wipe your eyes, and if you want to do more howling do it elsewhere. And you, Sandy, bring me a little water." Sandy hurried out to the well behind the temple, where there was a bucket of water ready drawn. He dipped his bowl into it and brought half a bowlful of water. Monkey filled his mouth with water, and then spat out the elixir into the Emperor's lips. Next he forced open his jaws, and pouring in some clean water, he floated the elixir down into his belly. In a few moments there was a gurgling sound inside; but the body still did not move. "Master," said Monkey, "what will become of me if my elixir fails? Shall I be beaten to death?"

"I don't see how it can fail," said Tripitaka. "It's already a miracle that a corpse that has been dead so long can swallow water. After the elixir entered his belly, we heard the guts ring. When the guts ring, the veins move in harmony. It only remains to get the breath into circulation. But even a piece of iron gets a bit rusty when it has been under water for three years; it is only natural that something of the same kind should happen to a man. All that's wrong with him is that he needs a supply of breath. If someone puts a mouthful of good breath into him, he would be quite himself again."

Pigsy at once offered himself for this service, but Tripitaka held him back. "You're no use for that," he cried. "Let Monkey do it." Tripitaka knew what he was talking about. For Pigsy had in his early days eaten living things, and even monstrously devoured human flesh, so that all his stock of breath was defiled. Whereas Monkey had always lived on pine-seeds, cypress cones, peaches, and the like, and his breath was pure.

So Monkey stepped forward, and putting his wide mouth against the Emperor's lips he blew hard into his throat. The breath went down to the Two-Storeyed Tower, round the Hall of Light, on to the Cinnabar Field, and from the Jetting Spring went back again into the Mud Wall Palace. Whereupon there was a deep panting sound. The king's humours concentrated, his spirits returned. He rolled over, brandished his fist, and bent his legs. Then with a cry "Master!" he knelt down in the dust and said, "Little did I think, when my soul visited you last night, that today at dawn I should again belong to the World of Light!" Tripitaka quickly raised him from his knees and said, "Your Majesty, this is no doing of mine. You must thank my disciple."

"What talk is that?" said Monkey laughing. "The proverb says 'A household cannot have two masters.' There is no harm in letting him pay his respects to you."

Tripitaka, still feeling somewhat embarrassed, raised the Emperor to his feet and brought him to the Hall of Meditation, where he and his disciples again prostrated themselves, and set him on a seat. The priests of the temple had got ready their breakfast, and invited Tripitaka and his party to join them. Imagine their astonishment when they saw an Emperor, his clothes still dripping. "Don't be surprised," said Monkey, coming forward. "This is the King of Crow-cock, your rightful lord. Three years ago he was robbed of his life by a fiend, and tonight I brought him back to life. Now we must take him to the city and expose the impostor. If you have anything for us to eat, serve it now, and we will start as soon as we have breakfasted."

The priests brought the Emperor hot water to wash in, and helped him out of his clothes. The almoner brought him a cloth jacket, and instead of his jade belt tied a silk sash round his waist; took off his upturned shoes, and gave him a pair of old priest's sandals. Then they all had breakfast, and saddled the horse.

"Pigsy, is your luggage very heavy?" asked Monkey.

"Brother, I've carried it so many days on end that I don't know whether it's heavy or not."

"Divide the pack into two," said Monkey, "take one half yourself, and give the other to this Emperor to carry. In that way we shall get quicker to the city and dispose of our business."

"That's a bit of luck," said Pigsy. "It was a nuisance getting him here. But now that he's been made alive, he is coming in useful as a partner."

Pigsy then divided the luggage after his own methods. Borrowing a hod from the priests of the temple he put everything light into his own load, and everything heavy into the king's. "I hope your Majesty has no objection," said Monkey laughing, "to being dressed up like this, and carrying the luggage, and following us on foot."

"Master," said the Emperor, instantly flinging himself upon his knees, "I can only regard you as my second progenitor, and let alone carrying luggage for you, my heartfelt desire is to go with you all the way to India, even if I were only to serve you as the lowest menial, running beside you whip in hand as you ride."

"There's no need for you to go to India," said Monkey. "That's our special concern. All you have to do is to carry the luggage forty leagues to the city and then let us seize the fiend. After which you can go on being Emperor again, and we can go on looking for scriptures."

"That's all very well," said Pigsy. "But in that case he gets off with forty leagues, while I shall be on the job all the time."

"Brother," said Monkey, "don't talk nonsense, but be quick and lead the way out." Pigsy and the Emperor accordingly led the way, while Sandy supported Tripitaka on his horse and Monkey followed behind. They were accompanied to the gates by five hundred priests in gorgeous procession, blowing conches as they walked. "Don't come with us any further," said Monkey. "If some official were to notice, our plans might get out, and everything would go wrong. Go back at once, and have the Emperor's clothes well cleaned, and send them to the city tonight or early tomorrow. I will see to it that you are well paid for your pains."

They had not travelled for half a day when the walls and moat of the city of Crow-cock came into view. "Monkey," said Tripitaka, "I think this place in front of us must be the city of Crow-cock."

"It certainly is," said Monkey. "Let us hurry on and do our business."

When they reached the city they found the streets and markets thronging with people, and everywhere a great stir and bustle. Soon they saw rising before them towers and gables of great magnificence. "Disciples," said Tripitaka, "let us go at once to Court and get our papers put in order. Then we shall have no more trouble hanging about in government offices."

"That is a good idea," said Monkey. "We will all come with you; the more the tellers, the better the story."

"Well, if you all come," said Tripitaka, "you must behave nicely, and not say anything till you have done homage as humble subjects of the throne."

"But that means bowing down," said Monkey.

"To be sure," said Tripitaka. "You have to bow down five times and strike your forehead on the ground three times."

"Master," said Monkey, "that's not a good idea. To pay homage to a thing like that is really too silly. Let me go in first, and I will decide what we are to do. If he addresses us, let me answer him. If you see me bow, then you must bow too; if I squat, then you must squat."

Look at him, that Monkey King, maker of many troubles, how he goes straight up to the door and says to the high officer in charge: "We were sent by the Emperor of China to worship Buddha in India, and fetch scriptures. We want to have our papers put in order here, and would trouble you to announce our arrival. By doing so, you will not fail to gain religious merit." The eunuch went in and knelt on the steps of the throne, announcing the visitors and their request. "I did not think it right to let them straight in," he said. "They await your orders outside the door."

The false king then summoned them in. Tripitaka entered, accompanied by the true king, who as he went could not stop the tears that coursed down his cheeks.

"Alas," he sighed to himself, "for my dragon-guarded rivers and hills, my iron-girt shrines! Who would have guessed that a creature of darkness would possess you all?"

"Emperor," said Monkey, "you must control your emotion, or we shall be discovered. I can feel the truncheon behind my ear twitching, and I am certain that I shall be successful. Leave it to me to slay the monster and when things are cleaned up, those rivers and hills will soon be yours again."

The true king dared not demur. He wiped away his tears, and followed as best he could. At last they reached the Hall of Golden Bells, where they saw the two rows of officials civil and military, and the four hundred Court officers, all of imposing stature and magnificently apparelled. Monkey led forward Tripitaka to the white jade steps, where they both stood motionless and erect. The officials were in consternation. "Are these priests so utterly bereft of decency and reason?" they exclaimed. "How comes it that, seeing our king, they do not bow down or greet him with any word of blessing? Not even a cry of salutation escaped their lips. Never have we seen such impudent lack of manners!"

"Where do they come from?" interrupted the false king.

"We were sent from the eastern land of T'ang in Southern Jambudvīpa," said Monkey haughtily, "by royal command, to go to India that is in the Western Region, and there to worship the Living Buddha in the Temple of the Great Thunder Clap, and obtain true scriptures. Having arrived here we dare not proceed without coming first to you to have our passports put in order."

The false king was very angry. "What is this eastern land of yours?" he said. "Do I pay tribute to it, that you should appear before me in this rude fashion, without bowing down? I have never had any dealings with your country."

"Our eastern land," said Monkey, "long ago set up a Heavenly Court and became a Great Power. Whereas yours is a Minor Power, a mere frontier land. There is an old saying, 'The king of a Great Country is father and lord; the king of a lesser country is vassal and son.' You admit that you have had no dealings with our country. How dare you contend that we ought to bow down?"

"Remove that uncivil priest," the king called to his officers of war. At this all the officers sprang forward. But Monkey made a magic pass and cried "Halt!" The magic of the pass was such that these officers all suddenly remained rooted to the spot and could not stir. Well might it be said:

> The captains standing round the steps became like figures of wood,
> The generals on the Royal Dais were like figures of clay.

Seeing that Monkey had brought his officers civil and military to a standstill, the false king leapt from his Dragon Couch and made as though to seize him. "Good," said Monkey to himself. "That is just what I wanted. Even if his hand is made of iron, this cudgel of mine will make some pretty dents in it!"

But just at this moment a star of rescue arrived. "Who can this have been?" you ask. It was no other than the prince of Crow-cock, who hastened forward and clutched at the false king's sleeve, and kneeling before him cried, "Father and king, stay your anger."

"Little son," asked the king, "why should you say this?"

"I must inform my father and king," said the prince. "Three years ago I heard someone say that a priest had been sent from T'ang to get scriptures in India, and it is he who has now unexpectedly arrived in our country. If my father and king, yielding to the ferocity of his noble nature, now arrests and beheads this priest, I fear that the news will one day reach the Emperor of T'ang, who will be furiously angry. You must know that after Li Shih-min[20] had established this great dynasty of T'ang and united the whole land, his heart was still not content, and he has now begun to conquer far-away lands. If he hears that you have done harm to his favourite priest, he will raise his hosts and come to make war upon you. Our troops are few and our generals feeble. You will, when it is too late, be sorry indeed that you provoked him. If you were to follow your small son's advice, you would question these four priests, and only punish such of them as are proved not to travel at the King of China's bidding."

This was a stratagem of the prince's. For he feared that harm might come to Tripitaka, and therefore tried to check the king, not knowing that Monkey was ready to strike.

The false king believed him, and standing in front of the Dragon Couch, he cried in a loud voice: "Priest, how long ago did you leave China, and why were you sent to get scriptures?"

"My Master," said Monkey haughtily, "is called Tripitaka, and is treated by the Emperor of China as his younger brother. The Emperor in a vision went to the Realms of Death, and on his return he ordered a great Mass for all souls in torment. On this occasion my Master recited so well and showed such compassionate piety that the Goddess Kuan-yin chose him to go on a mission to the west. My Master vowed that he would faithfully perform this task in return for his sovereign's bounties, and he was furnished by the Emperor with credentials for the journey. He started in the thirteenth year of the Emperor's reign, in the ninth month, three days before the full moon. After leaving China, he came first to the Land of the Two Frontiers, where he picked up me, and made me his chief disciple. In the hamlet of the Kao family, on the borders of the country of Wu-ssu, he picked up a second disciple, called Pigsy; and at the river of Flowing Sands he picked up a third, whom we call Sandy. Finally a few days ago, at the Temple of the Treasure Wood, he found another recruit—the servant who is carrying the luggage."

The false king thought it unwise to ask any more questions about Tripitaka; but he turned savagely upon Monkey and addressed to him a crafty question. "I can accept," he said, "that one priest set out from China, and picked up three priests on the way. But your story about the fourth member of your party I altogether disbelieve. This servant is certainly someone whom you have kidnapped. What is his name? Has he a passport, or has he none? Bring him before me to make his deposition!"

The true king shook with fright. "Master," he whispered, "what am I to depose?"

"That's all right," said Monkey. "I'll make your deposition for you."

Dear Monkey! He stepped boldly forward and cried to the magician in a loud, clear voice: "Your Majesty, this old man is dumb and rather hard of hearing. But it so happens that when he was young, he travelled in India, and knows the way there. I know all about his career and origins and with your Majesty's permission I will make a deposition on his behalf."

"Make haste," said the false king, "and furnish a true deposition or you will get into trouble."

[20]Another name for T'ai-tsung, second emperor of the T'ang dynasty.

Monkey then recited as follows:

"The subject of this deposition is far advanced in years; he is deaf and dumb, and has fallen on evil days. His family for generations has lived in these parts; but five years ago disaster overtook his house. Heaven sent no rain; the people perished of drought, the lord king and all his subjects fasted and did penance. They burned incense, purified themselves and called upon the Lord of Heaven; but in all the sky not a wisp of cloud appeared. The hungry peasants dropped by the roadside, when suddenly there came a Taoist magician from the Chung-nan Mountains, a monster in human form. He called to the winds and summoned the rain, displaying godlike power; but soon after secretly destroyed this wretched man's life. In the flower-garden he pushed him down into the crystal well; then set himself on the Dragon Throne, none knowing it was he. Luckily I came and achieved a great success; I raised him from the dead and restored him to life without hurt or harm. He earnestly begged to be admitted to our faith, and act as carrier on the road, to join with us in our quest and journey to the Western Land. The false king who sits on the throne is that foul magician; he that now carries our load is Crow-cock's rightful king!"

When the false king in the Palace of Golden Bells heard these words, he was so startled that his heart fluttered like the heart of a small deer. Then clouds of shame suffused his face, and leaping to his feet he was about to flee, when he remembered that he was unarmed. Looking round he saw a captain of the Guard with a dagger at his waist, standing there dumb and foolish as a result of Monkey's spell. The false king rushed at him and snatched the dagger; then leapt upon a cloud and disappeared into space.

Sandy burst into an exclamation of rage, and Pigsy loudly abused Monkey for his slowness. "It's a pity you didn't look sharp and stop him," he said. "Now he has sailed off on a cloud, and we shall never be able to find him."

"Don't shout at me, brothers!" said Monkey laughing. "Let us call to the prince to come and do reverence to his true father, and the queen to her husband.' Then undoing by a magic pass the spell that he had put upon the officers, he told them to wake up and do homage to their lord, acknowledging him as their true king. "Give me a few facts to go upon," he said, "and as soon as I have got things clear, I will go and look for him."

Dear Monkey! He instructed Pigsy and Sandy to take good care of the prince, king, ministers, queen, and Tripitaka; but while he was speaking he suddenly vanished from sight. He had already jumped up into the empyrean, and was peering round on every side, looking for the wizard. Presently he saw that monster flying for his life towards the north-east. Monkey caught him up and shouted, "Monster, where are you off to? Monkey has come." The wizard turned swiftly, drew his dagger, and cried, "Monkey, you scamp, what has it got to do with you whether I usurp someone else's throne? Why should you come calling me to account and letting out my secrets?"

"Ho, ho," laughed Monkey. "You impudent rascal! Do you think I am going to allow you to play the emperor? Knowing who I am you would have done well to keep out of my way. Why did you bully my master, demanding depositions and what not? You must admit now that the deposition was not far from the truth. Stand your ground and take old Monkey's cudgel like a man!"

The wizard dodged and parried with a thrust of his dagger at Monkey's face. It was a fine fight! After several bouts the magician could no longer stand up against Monkey, and suddenly turning he fled back the way he had come, leapt into the city, and slipped in among the officers who were assembled before the steps of the throne. Then giving himself a shake, he changed into an absolute counterpart of Tripitaka and stood beside him in front of the steps. Monkey rushed up and was about to strike what he supposed to be the wizard, when this Tripitaka said,

"Disciple, do not strike! It is I!" It was impossible to distinguish between them. "If I kill Tripitaka, who is a transformation of the wizard, then I shall have achieved a glorious success; but supposing, on the other hand, it turns out that I have killed the real Tripitaka, that would not be so good..." There was nothing for it but to stay his hand, and calling to Pigsy and Sandy he asked, "Which really is the wizard, and which is our master? Just point for me, and I will strike the one you point at."

"We were watching you going for one another up in the air," said Pigsy, "when suddenly we looked round and saw that there were two Tripitakas. We have no idea which is the real one."

When Monkey heard this, he made a single pass and recited a spell to summon the *devas* that protect the Law, the local deities and the spirits of the neighbouring hills, and told them of his predicament. The wizard thought it time to mount the clouds again, and began to make towards the door. Thinking that Tripitaka was clearing the ground for him, Monkey raised his cudgel, and had it not been for the deities he had summoned he would have struck such a big blow at his master as would have made mince-meat of twenty Tripitakas. But in the nick of time the guardian deities stopped him, saying, "Great Sage, the wizard is just going to mount the clouds again." Monkey rushed after him, and was just about to cut off his retreat, when the wizard turned round, slipped back again into the crowd, and was once more indistinguishable from the real Tripitaka.

Much to Monkey's annoyance, Pigsy stood by, laughing at his discomfiture. "You've nothing to laugh at, you hulking brute," he said. "This means you've got two masters to order you about. It's not going to do you much good."

"Brother," said Pigsy, "you call me a fool, but you're a worse fool than I. You can't recognize your own Master, and it's a waste of effort to go on trying. But you would at least recognize your own headache, and if you ask our Master to recite his spell, Sandy and I will stand by and listen. The one who doesn't know the spell will certainly be the wizard. Then all will be easy."

"Brother," said Monkey, "I am much obliged to you. There are only three people who know that spell. It sprouted from the heart of the Lord Buddha himself; it was handed down to the Bodhisattva Kuan-yin, and was then taught to our master by the Bodhisattva herself. No one else knows it. Good, then! Master, recite!"

The real Tripitaka at once began to recite the spell; while the wizard could do nothing but mumble senseless sounds. "That's the wizard," cried Pigsy. "He's only mumbling." And at the same time he raised his rake and was about to strike when the wizard sprang into the air and ran up along the clouds. Dear Pigsy! With a loud cry he set off in pursuit, and Sandy, leaving Tripitaka, hastened to the attack with his priest's staff. Tripitaka stopped reciting, and Monkey, released from his headache, seized his iron cudgel and sped through the air. Heigh, what a fight! Three wild priests beleaguered one foul fiend. With rake and staff Pigsy and Sandy assailed him from right and left. "If I join in," said Monkey, "and attack him in front, I fear he is so frightened of me that he will run away again. Let me get into position above him and give him a real garlic-pounding blow that will finish him off for good and all." He sprang up into the empyrean, and was about to deliver a tremendous blow when, from a many-coloured cloud in the north-east, there came a voice which said, "Monkey, stay your hand!" Monkey looked round and saw it was the Bodhisattva Manjuśrī.[21] He withdrew his cudgel, and coming forward did obeisance, saying "Bodhisattva, where are you going to?"

[21] The primary figure in one cult of Tantric Buddhism, centered at Wu-T'ai-Shan (Mountain of the Five Terraces) in India.

"I came to take this monster off your hands," said Manjuśrī.

"I am sorry you should have the trouble," said Monkey.

The Bodhisattva then drew from his sleeve a magic mirror that showed demons in their true form. Monkey called to the other two to come and look, and in the mirror they saw the wizard in his true shape. He was Manjuśrī's lion! "Bodhisattva," said Monkey, "this is the blue-maned lion that you sit upon. How comes it that it ran away and turned into an evil spirit? Can't you keep it under control?"

"It did not run away," said Manjuśrī. "It acted under orders from Buddha himself."

"You mean to tell me," said Monkey, "that it was Buddha who told this creature to turn into an evil spirit and seize the Emperor's throne? In that case all the troubles I meet with while escorting Tripitaka are very likely ordered by His Holiness. A nice thought!"

"Monkey," said Manjuśrī, "you don't understand. In the beginning this king of Crow-cock was devoted to good works and the entertaining of priests. Buddha was so pleased that he sent me to fetch him away to the Western Paradise, where he was to assume a golden body and become an Arhat.[22] As it was not proper for me to show myself in my true form I came disguised as a priest and begged for alms. Something I said gave him offence, and not knowing that I was anyone in particular he had me bound and cast into the river, where I remained under water for three nights and three days, till at last a guardian spirit rescued me and brought me back to Paradise. I complained to Buddha, who sent this creature to throw the king into the well, and let him remain there three years as a retaliation for the three days that I was in the river. You know the saying: 'Not a sip, not a sup . . .'[23] But now you have arrived on the scene, the episode is successfully closed."

"That is all very well," said Monkey. "All these 'sips and sups' may have enabled you to get even with your enemy. But what about all the unfortunate people whom this fiend has ruined?"

"He hasn't ruined any one," said Manjuśrī. "During the three years that he was on the throne, rain has fallen, the crops have been good, and the people at perfect peace. How can you speak of his ruining people?"

"That may be," said Monkey. "But how about all the ladies of the Court who have been sleeping with him and unwittingly been led into a heinous and unnatural offence? They would hardly subscribe to the view that he had done no harm."

"He isn't in a position to defile anyone," said Manjuśrī. "He's a gelded lion!"

At this Pigsy came up to the wizard and felt him. "Quite true," he announced, laughing. "This is a 'blotchy nose that never sniffed wine'; 'a bad name and nothing to show for it.'"

"Very well then," said Monkey. "Take him away. If you had not come just in time, he'd have been dead by now."

Manjuśrī then recited a spell and said, "Creature, back to your true shape and look sharp about it!" The wizard at once changed into his real lion form, and Manjuśrī, putting down the lotus that he carried in his hand, harnessed the lion, mounted him, and rode away over the clouds.

If you do not know how Tripitaka and his disciples left the city you must listen while it is explained to you in the next chapter.

---

[22] One who has reached the end of the fourfold way and attained Nirvana.

[23] Everything that happens depends on *karma*.

FROM
CHAPTER 22

Monkey and the other two disciples lowered the clouds on which they rode and returned to Court, where they received the humble thanks of the king, his ministers, heir and consort, and all the officers. Monkey told them how Manjuśrī had reclaimed the fiend, at which they prostrated themselves with extreme awe and reverence. In the midst of these congratulations and rejoicings a eunuch suddenly arrived, saying, "My lord and master, four more priests have arrived."

"Brother," said Pigsy, in consternation, "what if it should turn out that the fiend, having disguised himself as Manjuśrī and taken us all in, has now turned himself into a priest, in the hope of confounding us?"

"Impossible!" said Monkey, and he ordered them to be shown in. The officers of the Court sent word that they were to be admitted, and when they appeared Monkey saw at once that they were priests from the Treasure Wood Temple, bringing the crown, belt, cloak and upturned shoes of the king. "Just at the right moment!" said Monkey, delighted. He then called to the "porter" to come forward, took off his head-wrap and put on the crown, took off his cloth coat and put on the royal robe, undid the sash and girded him with the belt of jades, slipped off his priest's sandals and put on the upturned shoes. Then he told the prince to bring out the white jade tablet, and put it in the king's hand, bidding him mount the dais and proclaim his sovereignty, in accordance with the old saying "A court must not, even for a day, be without a sovereign."

But the king was very loth to sit upon the throne, and weeping bitterly he knelt on the centre of the steps, saying, "I was dead for three years, and having now by your doing been brought back to life, how can I dare proclaim myself your sovereign? It would be better that one of you priests should be king, and that I should take my wife and child and live like a commoner outside the walls of the city."

Tripitaka of course would not accept, as his heart was set upon going to worship the Buddha and get scriptures. The king then asked Monkey. "Gentlemen," said Monkey laughing, "I will not deceive you. If I had wanted to be an Emperor, I could have had the throne in any of the ten thousand lands and nine continents under heaven. But I have got used to being a priest and leading a lazy, comfortable existence. An Emperor has to wear his hair long; at nightfall he may not doze, at the fifth drum he must be awake. Each time there is news from the frontier his heart jumps; when there are calamities and disasters he is plunged in sorrow and despair; I should never get used to it. You go back to your job as Emperor, and let me go back to mine as priest, doing my deeds and going upon my way."

Seeing that it was useless to refuse, the king at last mounted the dais, turned towards his subjects and proclaimed his sovereignty, announcing a great amnesty throughout his realm. He loaded the priests from the Treasure Wood Temple with presents and sent them home. Then he opened the eastern upper room and held a banquet for Tripitaka. He also sent for a painter to make portraits of the blessed countenances of Tripitaka and his disciples, which were to be hung in the Palace of Golden Bells, and reverenced as objects of worship.

Having put the king upon his throne, Tripitaka and his disciples were anxious to start out again as soon as possible. The king, his ladies, the prince, and all the ministers pressed upon them all the heirlooms of the kingdom, and gold, silver, silks, and satins, to show their deep gratitude. But Tripitaka would not accept so much as a split hair, and when their passports had been put in order, he urged Monkey and the rest to get the horse saddled, so that they might start at once. The king, very loth to part with them, ordered his State Coach to be got ready and made Tripitaka ride in it. He was drawn by officers civil and military, while the prince and ladies of the Court pushed at the sides, till they were beyond the walls of the town. Here Tripitaka alighted, and took leave of them all. . . .

FROM
CHAPTER 28

They travelled westward for many months, and at last began to be aware that the country through which they were now passing was different from any that they had seen. Everywhere they came across gem-like flowers and magical grasses, with many ancient cypresses and hoary pines. In the villages through which they passed every family seemed to devote itself to the entertainment of priests and other pious works. On every hill were hermits practising austerities, in every wood pilgrims chanting holy writ. Finding hospitality each night and starting again at dawn, they journeyed for many days, till they came at last within sudden sight of a cluster of high eaves and towers.

"Monkey, that's a fine place," said Tripitaka, pointing to it with his whip.

"Considering," said Monkey, "how often you have insisted upon prostrating yourself at the sight of false magicians' palaces and arch impostors' lairs, it is strange that when at last you see before you Buddha's true citadel, you should not even dismount from your horse."

At this Tripitaka in great excitement sprang from his saddle, and walking beside the horse was soon at the gates of the high building. A young Taoist came out to meet them. "Aren't you the people who have come from the east to fetch scriptures?" he asked. Tripitaka hastily tidied his clothes and looking up saw that the boy was clad in gorgeous brocades and carried a bowl of jade dust in his hand. Monkey knew him at once.

"This," he said to Tripitaka, "is the Golden Crested Great Immortal of the Jade Truth Temple at the foot of the Holy Mountain."

Tripitaka at once advanced bowing. "Well, here you are at last!" said the Immortal. "The Bodhisattva misinformed me. Ten years ago she was told by Buddha to go to China and find someone who would fetch scriptures from India. She told me she had found someone who would arrive here in two or three years. Year after year I waited, but never a sign! This meeting is indeed a surprise."

"I cannot thank you enough, Great Immortal, for your patience," said Tripitaka.

Then they all went into the temple and were shown round by the Immortal; tea and refreshments were served, and perfumed hot water was brought for Tripitaka to wash in. Soon they all turned in for the night. Early next day Tripitaka changed into his brocaded cassock and jewelled cap, and staff in hand presented himself to the Immortal in the hall of the temple, to take his leave. "That's better!" said the Immortal. "Yesterday you were looking a bit shabby; but now you look a true child of Buddha!"

Tripitaka was just going when the Immortal stopped him, saying, "You must let me see you off."

"It's really not necessary," said Tripitaka. "Monkey knows the way."

"He only knows the way by air," said the Immortal. "You have got to go on the ground."

"That's true enough," said Monkey. "We will trouble you just to set us on the right way. My Master is pining to get into the presence of the Buddha, and it would be a pity if there were any delay."

Taking Tripitaka by the hand he led him right through the temple and out at the back. For the road did not go from the front gate, but traversed the courtyards and led on to the hill behind.

"You see that highest point, wreathed in magic rainbow mists," said the Immortal, pointing to the mountain. "That is the Vulture Peak, the sacred precinct of the Buddha."

Tripitaka at once began kow-towing. "Master," said Monkey, "you had better keep that for later on. If you are going to kow-tow all the way up to the top, there won't be much left of your head by the time we get there. It's still a long way off."

"You stand already on Blessed Ground," said the Immortal. "The Holy Mountain is before you. I shall now turn back."

Monkey led them up the hill at a leisurely pace. They had not gone more than five or six leagues when they came to a great water about eight leagues wide. It was exceedingly swift and rough. No one was to be seen in any direction.

"I don't think this can be the right way," said Tripitaka. "Do you think the Immortal can possibly have been mistaken? This water is so wide and so rough that we cannot possibly get across."

"This is the way all right," said Monkey. "Look! Just over there is a bridge. That's the right way to Salvation."

Presently Tripitaka came to a notice-board on which was written Cloud Reach Bridge. But it proved, when they came up to it, that the bridge consisted simply of slim tree trunks laid end on end, and was hardly wider than the palm of a man's hand.

"Monkey," protested Tripitaka in great alarm, "it's not humanly possible to balance on such a bridge as that. We must find some other way to get across."

"This is the right way," said Monkey, grinning.

"It may be the right way," said Pigsy, "but it's so narrow and slippery that no one would ever dare set foot on it. And think how far there is to go, and what it's like underneath."

"All wait where you are, and watch while I show you how," cried Monkey. Dear Monkey! He strode up to the bridge, leapt lightly on to it, and had soon slipped across. "I'm over!" he shouted, waving from the other side. Tripitaka showed no sign of following him, and Pigsy and Sandy bit their fingers murmuring, "Can't be done! Can't be done!" Monkey sprang back again and pulled at Pigsy, saying, "Fool, follow me across."

But Pigsy lay on the ground and would not budge. "It's much too slippery," he said. "Let me off. Why can't I have a wind to carry me?"

"What would be the good of that?" said Monkey. "Unless you go by the bridge you won't turn into a Buddha."

"Buddha or no Buddha," said Pigsy, "I'm not going on to that bridge."

The quarrel was at its height, when Sandy ran between them and at last succeeded in making peace. Suddenly Tripitaka saw someone punting a boat towards the shore and crying, "Ferry, ferry!"

"Stop your quarrelling, disciples," said Tripitaka. "A boat is coming."

They all gazed with one accord at the spot to which he pointed. A boat was coming indeed; but when it was a little nearer they saw to their consternation that it had no bottom. Monkey with his sharp eyes had already recognized the ferryman as the Conductor of Souls, also called Light of the Banner. But he did not tell the others, merely crying "Ahoy, ferry, ahoy!" When the boat was along shore, the ferryman again cried "Ferry, ferry!"

"Your boat is broken and bottomless," said Tripitaka, much perturbed. "How can you take people across?"

"You may well think," said the ferryman, "that in a bottomless boat such a river as this could never be crossed. But since the beginning of time I have carried countless souls to their Salvation."

"Get on board, Master," said Monkey. "You will find that this boat, although it has no bottom, is remarkably steady, however rough the waters may be."

Seeing Tripitaka still hesitate, Monkey took him by the scruff of the neck and pushed him on board. There was nothing for Tripitaka's feet to rest on, and he went straight into the water. The ferryman caught at him and dragged him up to the side of the boat. Sitting miserably there, he wrung out his clothes, shook out his shoes, and grumbled at Monkey for having got him into this scrape. But Monkey, taking no notice, put Pigsy and Sandy, horse and baggage, all on board, ensconcing them as best he could in the gunwale. The ferryman punted them dexterously out from shore. Suddenly they saw a body in the water, drifting rapidly down stream. Tripitaka stared at it in consternation. Monkey laughed.

"Don't be frightened, Master," he said. "That's you."

And Pigsy said, "It's you, it's you."

Sandy clapped his hands. "It's you, it's you," he cried.

The ferryman too joined in the chorus. "There *you* go!" he cried. "My best congratulations." He went on punting, and in a very short while they were all safe and sound at the other side. Tripitaka stepped lightly ashore. He had discarded his earthly body; he was cleansed from the corruption of the senses, from the fleshly inheritance of those bygone years. His was now the transcendent wisdom that leads to the Further Shore, the mastery that knows no bounds.

When they were at the top of the bank, they turned round and found to their astonishment that boat and ferryman had both vanished. Only then did Monkey tell them who the ferryman was. Tripitaka began thanking his disciples for all they had done for him. "Every one of us," said Monkey, "is equally indebted to the other. If the Master had not received our vows and accepted us as his disciples we should not have had the chance to do good works and win salvation. If we had not protected the Master and mounted guard over him, he would never have got rid of his mortal body. Look, Master, at this realm of flowers and happy creatures—of phoenixes, cranes, and deer. Is it not a better place indeed than the haunted deserts through which you and I have passed?" Tripitaka still murmured his thanks, and with a strange feeling of lightness and exhilaration they all set off up the Holy Mountain and were soon in sight of the Temple of the Thunder Clap, with its mighty towers brushing the firmament, its giant foundations rooted in the seams of the Hill of Life.

Near the top of the hill they came upon a party of Upasakas filing through the green pinewoods, and under a clump of emerald cedars they saw bands of the Blessed. Tripitaka hastened to bow down to them. Worshippers male and female, monks and nuns pressed together the palms of their hands, crying. "Holy priest, it is not to us that your homage should be addressed. Wait till you have seen Sakyamuni, and afterwards come and greet us each according to his rank."

"He's always in too much of a hurry," laughed Monkey. "Come along at once and let us pay our respects to the people at the top."

Twitching with excitement Tripitaka followed Monkey to the gates of the Temple. Here they were met by the Vajrapani[24] of the Four Elements.

[24] "The thunderbolt-handed," a personification of force.

"So your Reverence has at last arrived!" he exclaimed.

"Your disciple Hsüan Tsang has indeed arrived," said Tripitaka, bowing.

"I must trouble you to wait here a moment, till your arrival has been announced," said the Vajrapani.

He then gave instructions to the porter at the outer gate to tell the porter at the second gate that the Vajrapani wished to report that the priest from China had arrived. The porter at the second gate sent word to the porter at the third gate. At this gate were holy priests with direct access to the Powers Above. They hurried to the Great Hall and informed the Tathagata,[25] the Most Honoured One, even Sakyamuni Buddha himself that the priest from the Court of China had arrived at the Mountain to fetch scriptures.

Father Buddha was delighted. He ordered the Bodhisattva, Vajrapanis, Arhats, Protectors, Planets, and Temple Guardians to form up in two lines. Then he gave orders that the priest of T'ang was to be shown in. Again the word was passed along from gate to gate: "The priest of T'ang is to be shown in." Tripitaka, Monkey, Pigsy, and Sandy, carefully following the rules of etiquette prescribed to them, all went forward, horse and baggage following. When they reached the Great Hall they first prostrated themselves before the Tathagata and then bowed to right and left. This they repeated three times, and then knelt before the Buddha and presented their passports. He looked through them one by one and handed them back to Tripitaka, who bent his head in acknowledgement, saying, "The disciple Hsüan Tsang has come by order of the Emperor of the great land of T'ang, all the way to this Holy Mountain, to fetch the true scriptures which are to be the salvation of all mankind. May the Lord Buddha accord this favour and grant me a quick return to my native land."

Hereupon the Tathagata opened the mouth of compassion and gave vent to the mercy of his heart: "In all the vast and populous bounds of your Eastern Land, greed, slaughter, lust, and lying have long prevailed. There is no respect for Buddha's teaching, no striving towards good works. So full and abundant is the measure of the people's sins that they go down forever into the darkness of Hell, where some are pounded in mortars, some take on animal form, furry and horned. In which guise they are done by as they did on earth, their flesh becoming men's food. Confucius stood by their side teaching them all the virtues, king after king in vain corrected them with fresh penalties and pains. No law could curb their reckless debauches, no ray of wisdom penetrate their blindness.

"But I have three Baskets of Scripture that can save mankind from its torments and afflictions. One contains the Law, which tells of Heaven, one contains the Discourses, which speak of Earth, one contains the Scriptures, which save the dead. They are divided into thirty-five sections and are written upon fifteen thousand one hundred and forty-four scrolls. They are the path to Perfection, the gate that leads to True Good. In them may be learnt all the motions of the stars and divisions of earth, all that appertains to man, bird, beast, flower, tree and implement of use; in short, all that concerns mankind is found therein. In consideration of the fact that you have come so far, I would give you them all to take back. But the people of China are foolish and boisterous; they would mock at my mysteries and would not understand the hidden meaning of our Order . . . Ānanda, Kaśyapa,"[26] he cried, "take these four to the room under the tower, and when they have refreshed

[25] The Buddha.

[26] Ānanda: one of the foremost disciples of the Buddha, his name means "joy." Kaśyapa: a Buddhist sage and writer of hymns.

themselves, open the doors of the Treasury, and select from each of the thirty-five sections a few scrolls for these priests to take back to the east, to be a boon there forever."

In the lower room they saw countless rarities and treasures, and were still gazing upon them in wonder when spirits ministrant began to spread the feast. The foods were all fairy fruits and dainties unknown in the common world. Master and disciples bowed acknowledgement of Buddha's favour and set to with a good will. This time it was Pigsy who was in luck and Sandy who scored; for Buddha had provided for their fare such viands as confer long life and health and magically transform the substance of common flesh and bone. When Ānanda and Kaśyapa had seen to it that the four had all they wanted, they went into the Treasury. The moment the door was opened, beams of magic light shot forth, filling the whole air far around. On chests and jewelled boxes were stuck red labels, on which were written the names of the holy books. The two disciples of Buddha led Tripitaka up to the place where the scriptures lay, and inviting him to study the titles said, "Having come here from China you have no doubt brought a few little gifts for us. If you will kindly hand them over, you shall have your scriptures at once."

"During all my long journey," said Tripitaka, "I have never once found it necessary to lay in anything of the kind."

"Splendid," said the disciples. "So we're to spend our days handing over scriptures gratis! Not a very bright outlook for our heirs!"

Thinking by their sarcastic tone that they had no intention of parting with the scriptures, Monkey could not refrain from shouting angrily, "Come along, Master! We'll tell Buddha about this and make him come and give us the scriptures himself."

"Don't shout," said Ānanda. "There's nothing in the situation that demands all this bullying and blustering. Come here and fetch your scriptures."

Pigsy and Sandy, mastering their rage and managing to restrain Monkey, came across to take the books. Scroll by scroll was packed away into the bundle, which was hoisted on to the horse's back. Then the two luggage packs were tied up and given to Pigsy and Sandy to carry. They first went and kow-towed their thanks to Buddha.

. . .

"These books," said Ānanda, "written on five thousand and forty-eight scrolls, have all been given to the priests of China to keep forever in their land. They are all now securely packed on their horse's back or in parcels to be carried by hand, and the pilgrims are here to thank you."

Tripitaka and the disciples tethered the horse, put down the burdens and bowed with the palms of their hands pressed together. "The efficacy of these scriptures is boundless," said Buddha. "They are not only the mirror of our Faith, but also the source and origin of all three religions. When you return to the world and show them to common mortals, they must not be lightly handled. No scroll must be opened save by one who has fasted and bathed. Treasure them, value them! For in them is secreted the mystic lore of Immortality, in them is revealed the wondrous receipt for ten thousand transformations."

Tripitaka kow-towed his thanks, doing leal homage, and prostrating himself three times, as he had done before. When they reached the outer gates, they paid their respects to the bands of the faithful, and went on their way.

After dismissing the pilgrims, Buddha broke up the assembly. Presently the Bodhisattva Kuan-yin appeared before the throne, saying, "Long ago I was instructed by you to find someone in China who would come here to fetch scriptures. He has now achieved this task, which has taken him five thousand and forty days. The number of the scrolls delivered to him is five thousand and forty-eight. I suggest that it would be appropriate if he were given eight days in which to complete his mission, so that the two figures may concord."

"A very good idea," said Buddha. "You may have that put into effect."

He then sent for the eight Vajrapanis and said to them, "You are to exert your magic powers and carry back Tripitaka to the east. When he has deposited the scriptures, you are to bring him back here. All this must be done in eight days, that the number of days taken by the journey may concord with the number of scrolls allotted to him." The Vajrapanis at once went after Tripitaka, caught him up and said to him, "Scripture-taker, follow us." A sudden lightness and agility possessed the pilgrims and they were borne aloft upon a magic cloud.

BACKGROUND TEXTS

GIOVANNI PICO DELLA MIRANDOLA

[1463–1494]

The reawakened interest in Greek and Latin writers during the Renaissance provided scholars such as Giovanni Pico della Mirandola with classical ideas of human dignity and human capability. Such Greeks as Plato and Aristotle contributed to the foundation of Renaissance humanism with their faith that the intellect can understand this world and how to live in it, that humans are capable of working out their destinies. Pico della Mirandola described himself as an *explorator,* and the depth of his learning led him to value not only human potential but the wisdom of all ages and cultures. He believed that beneath the symbolic surfaces of differing philosophical and religious traditions was a unitary thread binding them together. At the very center of this intellectual complex were his ideas about the dignity of human beings, ideas that became the standard for Renaissance humanism. In a brief passage in *On the Dignity of Man,* where the Creator is speaking to Adam, Pico defines the essential core of humanism:

> In conformity with thy free judgment, in whose hands I have placed thee, thou art confined by no bounds; and thou wilt fix limits of nature for thyself. I have placed thee at the center of the world, that from there thou mayest more conveniently look around and see whatsoever is in the world. . . . Thou, like a judge appointed for being honorable, art the molder and maker of thyself; thou mayest sculpt thyself into whatever shape thou dost prefer.

Giovanni Pico, a child prodigy, was the youngest son of the ruler of Mirandola, a principality in northern Italy. At the age of sixteen he studied at the University of Ferrara, then moved on to the universities at Padua and Paris, absorbing Greek and Latin classics, the Hebrew Cabala and Talmud, Arabic philosophy, and Christian theology. For such a young mind, he was a prodigious synthesizer and planned treatises that would exhibit the compatibility of various philosophies and the basic unity of truth. When he was just twenty-three, he took a first step in this direction; he published 900 theses as a kind of compendium of philosophical assertions to be debated in Rome by the best intellects of Europe. He intended the oration *On the Dignity of Man* (1486)—an excerpt of which is included below—as an introduction to the debate. The Roman Church, however, under Pope Innocent VIII found thirteen of Pico's ideas heretical and prevented the debate.

Like the figure of Faustus in Marlowe's play, Pico took the world's learning as his domain, but he found there was a price to pay for challenging the establishment. Pico retired from public view and wrote an *Apology* (1488) to defend his religious ideas. While in retirement at Fiesole, he wrote *Heptaplus* (1489), commentaries on the Psalms, *On Being and the One* (1491), and *Disputations against Astrology* (1494). Pico submitted to the authority of the Roman Church, and shortly before his death of a fever on November 17, 1494, in Bologna, Pope Alexander VI removed the ban on his writings.

FROM

On the Dignity of Man

Translated by Charles Glenn Wallis

Most venerable fathers, I have read in the records of the Arabians that Abdul the Saracen,[1] on being asked what thing on, so to speak, the world's stage, he viewed as most greatly worthy of wonder, answered that he viewed nothing more wonderful than man. And Mercury's, "a great wonder, Asclepius,[2] is man!" agrees with that opinion. On thinking over the reason for these sayings, I was not satisfied by the many assertions made by many men concerning the outstandingness of human nature: that man is the messenger between creatures, familiar with the upper and king of the lower; by the sharpsightedness of the senses, by the hunting-power of reason, and by the light of intelligence, the interpreter of nature; the part in between the standstill of eternity and the flow of time; and, as the Persians say, the bond tying the world together, nay, the nuptial bond; and, according to David, "a little lower than the angels." These reasons are great but not the chief ones, that is, they are not reasons for a lawful claim to the highest wonder as to a prerogative. Why should we not wonder more at the angels themselves and at the very blessed heavenly choirs?

Finally, it seemed to me that I understood why man is the animal that is most happy, and is therefore worthy of all wonder; and lastly, what the state is that is allotted to man in the succession of things,[3] and that is capable of arousing envy not only in the brutes but also in the stars and even in minds beyond the world. It is wonderful and beyond belief. For this is the reason why man is rightly said and thought to be a great marvel and the animal really worthy of wonder. Now hear what it is, fathers; and with kindly ears and for the sake of your humanity, give me your close attention:

Now the highest Father, God the master-builder, had, by the laws of His secret wisdom, fabricated this house, this world which we see, a very superb temple of divinity. He had adorned the super-celestial region with minds. He had animated the celestial globes with eternal souls; He had filled with a diverse throng of animals the cast-off and residual parts of the lower world. But, with the work finished, the Artisan desired that there be someone to reckon up the reason of such a big work, to love its beauty, and to wonder at its greatness. Accordingly, now that all things

---

[1] Probably Abd Allah, Muhammad's cousin (c. seventh century C.E.).

[2] Asclepius is one of the speakers in Mercury's (that is, Hermes Trismegistus's) dialogues.

[3] That is, the great chain of being, or hierarchical pattern from God down to the smallest organism.

had been completed, as Moses and Timaeus[4] testify, He lastly considered creating man. But there was nothing in the archetypes from which He could mold a new sprout, nor anything in His storehouses which He could bestow as a heritage upon a new son, nor was there an empty judiciary seat where this contemplator of the universe could sit. Everything was filled up; all things had been laid out in the highest, the lowest, and the middle orders. But it did not belong to the paternal power to have failed in the final parturition, as though exhausted by childbearing; it did not belong to wisdom, in a case of necessity, to have been tossed back and forth through want of a plan; it did not belong to the loving-kindness which was going to praise divine liberality in others to be forced to condemn itself. Finally, the best of workmen decided that that to which nothing of its very own could be given should be, in composite fashion, whatsoever had belonged individually to each and every thing. Therefore He took up man, a work of indeterminate form; and, placing him at the midpoint of the world, He spoke to him as follows:

"We have given to thee, Adam, no fixed seat, no form of thy very own, no gift peculiarly thine, that thou mayest feel as thine own, have as thine own, possess as thine own the seat, the form, the gifts which thou thyself shalt desire. A limited nature in other creatures is confined within the laws written down by Us. In conformity with thy free judgment, in whose hands I have placed thee, thou art confined by no bounds; and thou wilt fix limits of nature for thyself. I have placed thee at the center of the world, that from there thou mayest more conveniently look around and see whatsoever is in the world. Neither heavenly nor earthly, neither mortal nor immortal have We made thee. Thou, like a judge appointed for being honorable, art the molder and maker of thyself; thou mayest sculpt thyself into whatever shape thou dost prefer. Thou canst grow downward into the lower natures which are brutes. Thou canst again grow upward from thy soul's reason into the higher natures which are divine."

O great liberality of God the Father! O great and wonderful happiness of man! It is given him to have that which he chooses and to be that which he wills. As soon as brutes are born, they bring with them, "from their dam's bag," as Lucilius[5] says, what they are going to possess. Highest spirits have been, either from the beginning or soon after, that which they are going to be throughout everlasting eternity. At man's birth the Father placed in him every sort of seed and sprouts of every kind of life. The seeds that each man cultivates will grow and bear their fruit in him. If he cultivates vegetable seeds, he will become a plant. If the seeds of sensation, he will grow into brute. If rational, he will come out a heavenly animal. If intellectual, he will be an angel, and a son of God. And if he is not contented with the lot of any creature but takes himself up into the center of his own unity, then, made one spirit with God and settled in the solitary darkness of the Father, who is above all things, he will stand ahead of all things. Who does not wonder at this chameleon which we are? Or who at all feels more wonder at anything else whatsoever? It was not unfittingly that Asclepius the Athenian said that man was symbolized by Prometheus in the secret rites, by reason of our nature sloughing its skin and transforming itself; hence metamorphoses were popular among the Jews and the Pythagoreans. For the more secret Hebrew theology at one time reshapes holy Enoch into an angel of divinity, whom they call *malach hashechina,* and at other times reshapes other men into other divinities. According to the Pythagoreans, wicked men are deformed into brutes and, if you believe Empedocles, into plants too. And copying them, Maumeth [Mohammed] often had it on his lips that he who draws back from divine law becomes

[4]A speaker in one of Plato's dialogues.

[5]A Roman satirical poet (second century B.C.E.).

a brute. And his saying so was reasonable: for it is not the rind which makes the plant, but a dull and non-sentient nature; not the hide which makes a beast of burden, but a brutal and sensual soul; not the spherical body which makes the heavens, but right reason; and not a separateness from the body but a spiritual intelligence which makes an angel. For example, if you see a man given over to his belly and crawling upon the ground, it is a bush not a man that you see. If you see anyone blinded by the illusions of his empty and Calypso-like[6] imagination, seized by the desire of scratching, and delivered over to the senses, it is a brute not a man that you see. If you come upon a philosopher winnowing out all things by right reason, he is a heavenly not an earthly animal. If you come upon a pure contemplator, ignorant of the body, banished to the innermost places of the mind, he is not an earthly, not a heavenly animal; he more superbly is a divinity clothed with human flesh.

Who is there that does not wonder at man? And it is not unreasonable that in the Mosaic and Christian holy writ man is sometimes denoted by the name "all flesh" and at other times by that of "every creature"; and man fashions, fabricates, transforms himself into the shape of all flesh, into the character of every creature. Accordingly, where Evantes the Persian tells of the Chaldaean theology, he writes that man is not any inborn image of himself, but many images coming in from the outside: hence that saying of the Chaldaeans: *enosh hu shinuy vekamah tevaoth baal chayim,* that is, man is an animal of diverse, multiform, and destructible nature.

But why all this? In order for us to understand that, after having been born in this state so that we may be what we will to be, then, since we are held in honor, we ought to take particular care that no one may say against us that we do not know that we are made similar to brutes and mindless beasts of burden. But rather, as Asaph the prophet says: "Ye are all gods, and sons of the most high," unless by abusing the very indulgent liberality of the Father, we make the free choice, which he gave to us, harmful to ourselves instead of helpful toward salvation. Let a certain holy ambition invade the mind, so that we may not be content with mean things but may aspire to the highest things and strive with all our forces to attain them: for if we will to, we can. Let us spurn earthly things; let us struggle toward the heavenly. Let us put in last place whatever is of the world; and let us fly beyond the chambers of the world to the chamber nearest the most lofty divinity. There, as the sacred mysteries reveal, the seraphim, cherubim, and thrones[7] occupy the first places. Ignorant of how to yield to them and unable to endure the second places, let us compete with the angels in dignity and glory. When we have willed it, we shall be not at all below them.

MARTIN LUTHER

[1483–1546]

There had been religious dissidents prior to the sixteenth century who had cried out against the abuses of the Roman Church and the immorality of its clergy, but the dramatic inauguration of the Reformation took place when a German monk named Martin Luther wrote ninety-five theses about the corrupt practice of selling indulgences for saving souls and, according to tradition, nailed these theses on the church door in Wittenberg on October 31, 1517.

[6]Pico is perhaps confusing Calypso with Circe from *The Odyssey*.

[7]In the medieval Christian hierarchy, seraphim, cherubim, and thrones constitute the highest order of angels.

Under the guidance of Luther, one of the most fascinating, complex, and contradictory figures of the Renaissance, the Protestant Reformation was more a revolution than what its name implies, for the so-called reformation created a major break from the medieval authority of the Catholic Church and affirmed the Renaissance ideals of individual responsibility and questioning authority.

Luther's roots were in the Middle Ages. Son of a peasant miner, he grew up in a religious household. Intending to study law at the University of Erfurt, he had a conversion experience in 1505 and instead of attending Erfurt entered an Augustinian monastery. During his assignment to the new University of Wittenberg, where he taught theology courses, Luther discovered in Paul's letter to the Romans the foundation of his theology: the doctrine that humans are justified by faith alone—not by works, not by priestly mediation, not by sacraments, not by church membership. Faith was the answer, Luther believed, to the uncompromising judgments of a terrifying Father-God. He focused on the individual's direct relationship with God, as guided by the authority of God's word in the Bible.

In 1510, on a mission to Rome, Luther was shocked by the secular excesses of the Church hierarchy, and he began to formulate plans for reforming the Church. He was supported by humanists such as Erasmus, who also searched for ways to curb the excesses of indulgences, relic worship, and the proliferation of saints. Luther's Ninety-five Theses, his defiance of the pope and the Church, led inevitably to open confrontations with the Catholic hierarchy. The first hearing on his writings and ideas was held at Augsburg in 1518 before Cardinal Cajetan; Luther refused to recant. When the Church issued a papal bull of condemnation to Luther in 1520, he publicly burned it. Excommunication did not immediately follow because Frederick the Wise of Saxony, Luther's own prince, enabled Luther to have a hearing before the Diet of Worms and Charles of Hapsburg.

One can only imagine the drama surrounding this meeting. Luther, a simple monk armed with biblical theology, stood before the extraordinary wealth and power of Charles of Hapsburg, newly elected Holy Roman Emperor, Lord of Austria, Burgundy, the Low Countries, Spain, and Naples. Luther was asked whether he defended his writings or rejected them—of special concern was *The Babylonian Captivity,* in which Luther had recommended two rather than seven sacraments. Surprisingly, Luther asked for time to think, and the hearing was postponed. The next day, Luther defended his writings to a crowded hall, giving the famous answers documented in the piece included here. Following the direction of Charles, four of six electors declared Luther a heretic.

The Diet of Worms failed to heal the breach, which continued to widen as Luther's movement gained support from laity as well as princes. Luther married, had children, and spent the rest of his life writing and formulating the direction for the new Lutheran church. Luther introduced hymn singing and church services in German. He reformed the liturgy. His greatest literary and religious contribution to the Reformation, however, was his translation of the Bible into a vernacular German, making it accessible to ordinary people.

Speech at the Diet of Worms

Translated by Roger A. Hornsby

[Here I Stand]

"Most serene emperor, most illustrious princes, most clement lords, obedient to the time set for me yesterday evening, I appear before you, beseeching you, by the mercy of God, that your most serene majesty and your most illustrious lordships may deign to listen graciously to this my cause—which is, as I hope, a cause of justice and of truth. If through my inexperience I have either not given the proper titles to some, or have offended in some manner against court customs and etiquette, I beseech you to kindly pardon me, as a man accustomed not to courts but to the cells of monks. I can bear no other witness about myself but that I have taught and written up to this time with simplicity of heart, as I had in view only the glory of God and the sound instruction of Christ's faithful.

"Most serene emperor, most illustrious princes, concerning those questions proposed to me yesterday on behalf of your serene majesty, whether I acknowledged as mine the books enumerated and published in my name and whether I wished to persevere in their defense or to retract them, I have given to the first question my full and complete answer, in which I still persist and shall persist forever. These books are mine and they have been published in my name by me, unless in the meantime, either through the craft or the mistaken wisdom of my emulators, something in them has been changed or wrongly cut out. For plainly I cannot acknowledge anything except what is mine alone and what has been written by me alone, to the exclusion of all interpretations of anyone at all.

"In replying to the second question, I ask that your most serene majesty and your lordships may deign to note that my books are not all of the same kind.

"For there are some in which I have discussed religious faith and morals simply and evangelically, so that even my enemies themselves are compelled to admit that these are useful, harmless, and clearly worthy to be read by Christians. Even the bull, although harsh and cruel, admits that some of my books are inoffensive, and yet allows these also to be condemned with a judgment which is utterly monstrous. Thus, if I should begin to disavow them, I ask you, what would I be doing? Would not I, alone of all men, be condemning the very truth upon which friends and enemies equally agree, striving alone against the harmonious confession of all?

"Another group of my books attacks the papacy and the affairs of the papists as those who both by their doctrines and very wicked examples have laid waste the Christian world with evil that affects the spirit and the body. For no one can deny or conceal this fact, when the experience of all and the complaints of everyone witness that through the decrees of the pope and the doctrines of men the consciences of the faithful have been most miserably entangled, tortured, and torn to pieces. Also, property and possessions, especially in this illustrious nation of Germany, have been devoured by an unbelievable tyranny and are being devoured to this time without letup and by unworthy means. [Yet the papists] by their own decrees (as in dist. 9 and 25; ques. 1 and 2) warn that the papal laws and doctrines which are contrary to the gospel or the opinions of the fathers are to be regarded as erroneous and reprehensible. If, therefore, I should have retracted these writings, I should have done nothing other than to have added strength to this [papal] tyranny and I should have opened not only windows but doors to such great godlessness. It would rage farther and more freely than ever it has dared up to this time. Yes, from the proof of such a revocation on my part, their wholly lawless and unrestrained kingdom of wickedness would become still more intolerable for the already wretched people; and their rule would be further strengthened and established, especially if it should be reported that this evil deed had been done by me by virtue of the authority of your most serene majesty and of the whole Roman Empire. Good God! What a cover for wickedness and tyranny I should have then become.

"I have written a third sort of book against some private and (as they say) distinguished individuals—those, namely, who strive to preserve the Roman tyranny and to destroy the godliness taught by me. Against these I confess I have been more violent than my religion or profession demands. But then, I do not set myself up as a saint; neither am I disputing about my life, but about the teaching of Christ. It is not proper for me to retract these works, because by this retraction it would again happen that tyranny and godlessness would, with my patronage, rule and rage among the people of God more violently than ever before.

"However, because I am a man and not God, I am not able to shield my books with any other protection than that which my Lord Jesus Christ himself offered for his teaching. When questioned before Annas about his teaching and struck by a servant, he said: 'If I have spoken wrongly, bear witness to the wrong' [John 18:19-23]. If the Lord himself, who knew that he could not err, did not refuse to hear testimony against his teaching, even from the lowliest servant, how much more ought I, who am the lowest scum and able to do nothing except err, desire and expect that somebody should want to offer testimony against my teaching! Therefore, I ask by the mercy of God, may your most serene majesty, most illustrious lordships, or anyone at all who is able, either high or low, bear witness, expose my errors, overthrowing them by the writings of the prophets and the evangelists. Once I have been taught I shall be quite ready to renounce every error, and I shall be the first to cast my books into the fire.

"From these remarks I think it is clear that I have sufficiently considered and weighed the hazards and dangers, as well as the excitement and dissensions aroused in the world as a result of my teachings, things about which I was gravely and forcefully warned yesterday. To see excitement and dissension arise because of the Word of God is to me clearly the most joyful aspect of all in these matters. For this is the way, the opportunity, and the result of the Word of God, just as He [Christ] said, 'I have not come to bring peace, but a sword. For I have come to set a man against his father,' etc. [Matt. 10:34-35]. Therefore, we ought to think how marvelous and terrible is our God in his counsels, lest by chance what is attempted for settling strife grows rather into an intolerable deluge of evils, if we begin by condemning the Word of God. And concern must be shown lest the reign of this most noble youth, Prince Charles (in whom after God is our great hope), become unhappy and inauspicious. I could illustrate this with abundant examples from Scripture—like Pharaoh, the king of Babylon, and the kings of Israel who, when they endeavored to pacify and strengthen their kingdoms by the wisest counsels, most surely destroyed themselves. For it is He who takes the wise in their own craftiness [Job 5:13] and overturns mountains before they know it [Job 9:5]. Therefore we must fear God. I do not say these things because there is a need of either my teachings or my warnings for such leaders as you, but because I must not withhold the allegiance which I owe my Germany. With these words I commend myself to your most serene majesty and to your lordships, humbly asking that I not be allowed through the agitation of my enemies, without cause, to be made hateful to you. I have finished."

When I had finished, the speaker for the emperor said, as if in reproach, that I had not answered the question, that I ought not call into question those things which had been condemned and defined in councils; therefore what was sought from me was not a horned response, but a simple one, whether or not I wished to retract.

Here I answered:

"Since then your serene majesty and your lordships seek a simple answer, I will give it in this manner, neither horned nor toothed: Unless I am convinced by the testimony of the Scriptures or by clear reason (for I do not trust either in the pope or in councils alone, since it is well known that they have often erred and contradicted themselves), I am bound by the Scriptures I have quoted and my conscience is captive to the Word of God. I cannot and I will not retract anything, since it is neither safe nor right to go against conscience.

"I cannot do otherwise, here I stand, may God help me, Amen."[1]

BENVENUTO CELLINI

[1500–1571]

Born in Florence into an artistic family, Benvenuto Cellini abandoned his father's hopes for him to become a musician and instead achieved distinction as one of the great Renaissance goldsmiths and sculptors. At age fifteen, he left home to study his craft with goldsmith Antonio di Sandro in Florence, and by his early twenties Cellini was living in Rome, where he witnessed the sack of that city in 1527 by forces of the Holy Roman Empire. In his famous *Autobiography,* he claims to have shot the arrow that killed the leader of the invading forces on that fateful day. In Rome, Cellini designed a vase for the Bishop of Salamanca, which brought him to the attention of Pope Clement VII. Though imprisoned in 1538 for purportedly stealing the jewels of the pontifical tiara, Cellini won release through the influence of the Cardinal d'Este of Ferrara, one of his patrons. For the next seven years, he lived in France and practiced his art; his superior skill and inventiveness can be seen in a gold salt-cellar designed for Francis I in 1543. In 1545, Cellini returned to his native Florence, where he won the patronage of Cosimo de' Medici and eventually was granted title in 1554.

In 1558, Cellini began his *Autobiography,* a remarkable and lively account of his travails as an artist seeking mastery and patronage in a web of political intrigue and intense rivalry with other artists. The *Autobiography* opens a window onto the rich and complex world of Renaissance Florence, as Cellini entices his readers' interest (and sometimes taxes their credulity) with the self-aggrandizing and inflated account of his many lovers, bitter rivalries with other artists, involvement in murder, and fluctuating fortunes under various patrons. The narrative is dotted with extravagant tales, such as Cellini raising up devils in the Colosseum after a lover's rebuff or seeing a halo appear around his head after his imprisonment in Rome. Nonetheless, the *Autobiography,* completed in 1562, remains one of the important documents of Renaissance life in Italy.

Known in his own time as a master goldsmith who struck medallions for Pope Clement and Alessandro de' Medici, among others, he is most remembered today for his writing and his sculpture. The passage we include below describes Cellini's making of his most famous work, the bronze sculpture of *Perseus with the Head of Medusa,* completed in 1554. The *Perseus,* in the Piazza della Signoria in Florence, shows Perseus standing on the headless body of the Gorgon, Medusa. His right arm holds his sword at waist length, while in triumph he extends his left arm, holding up the head of Medusa. The *Perseus,* as the *Autobiography* makes clear, was to be the statue that would push Florentine sculpture into the highest rank of international fame. In addition to the *Perseus,* Cellini created many other statues in bronze and in marble on classical themes: the Ganymede, Apollo and Hyacinth, and the Narcissus, among others. The tense pose of his figures typifies what art

[1]These particular words are in German in the Latin text from which the translation is taken.

historians call the mannerist style of the late Renaissance; in both writing and sculpture, Cellini embodies the intensive labor, passion, imagination, sheer will, and even arrogance that the artist required to survive in the competitive political and cultural atmosphere of sixteenth-century Florence. His writing, as well, captivates readers with rich detail and a charming, personable style.

The Autobiography of Benvenuto Cellini

Translated by John Addington Symonds

[The Casting of Perseus]

53

The Duke of Florence at this time, which was the month of August 1545, had retired to Poggio a Cajano, ten miles distant from Florence.[1] Thither then I went to pay him my respects, with the sole object of acting as duty required, first because I was a Florentine, and next because my forefathers had always been adherents of the Medicean party, and I yielded to none of them in affection for this Duke Cosimo. As I have said, then, I rode to Poggio with the sole object of paying my respects, and with no intention of accepting service under him, as God, who does all things well, did then appoint for me.

When I was introduced, the Duke received me very kindly; then he and the Duchess put questions concerning the works which I had executed for the King.[2] I answered willingly and in detail. After listening to my story, he answered that he had heard as much, and that I spoke the truth. Then he assumed a tone of sympathy, and added: "How small a recompense for such great and noble masterpieces! Friend Benvenuto, if you feel inclined to execute something for me too, I am ready to pay you far better than that King of yours has done, for whom your excellent nature prompts you to speak so gratefully." When I understood his drift, I described the deep obligations under which I lay to his Majesty, who first obtained my liberation from that iniquitous prison, and afterwards supplied me with the means of carrying out more admirable works than any artist of my quality had ever had the chance to do. While I was thus speaking, my lord the Duke writhed on his chair, and seemed as though he could not bear to hear me to the end. Then, when I had concluded, he rejoined: "If you are disposed to work for me, I will treat you in a way that will astonish you, provided the fruits of your labours give me satisfaction, of which I have no doubt." I, poor unhappy mortal, burning with desire to show the noble school[3] of Florence that, after leaving her in youth, I had practised other branches of the art than she imagined, gave answer to the Duke that I would willingly erect for him in marble or in bronze a mighty statue on his fine piazza. He replied that, for a first essay, he should like me to produce a Perseus; he had long set his heart on having such a monument, and he begged me to begin a model for the same.[4] I very gladly set myself to the task, and in a few weeks I finished my model, which

---

[1]Cosimo I de' Medici; Poggio a Cajano is the Medici villa just outside of Florence.

[2]The king is Francis I, of France; the duchess is Eleanora di Toledo, daughter of the Viceroy of Naples.

[3]The Collegio dei Maestri di Belle Arti in Florence.

[4]In Greek mythology, Perseus, the son of Zeus and Danaë, brought King Polydectes the head of the Gorgon Medusa, whose gaze would turn a person to stone.

was about a cubit high, in yellow wax and very delicately finished in all its details. I had made it with the most thorough study and art. . . .

54

Being now inflamed with a great desire to begin working, I told his Excellency that I had need of a house where I could install myself and erect furnaces, in order to commence operations in clay and bronze, and also, according to their separate requirements, in gold and silver. I knew that he was well aware how thoroughly I could serve him in those several branches, and I required some dwelling fitted for my business. In order that his Excellency might perceive how earnestly I wished to work for him, I had already chosen a convenient house, in a quarter much to my liking. As I did not want to trench upon his Excellency for money or anything of that sort, I had brought with me from France two jewels, with which I begged him to purchase me the house, and to keep them until I earned it with my labour. These jewels were excellently executed by my workmen, after my own designs. When he had inspected them with minute attention, he uttered these spirited words, which clothed my soul with a false hope: "Take back your jewels, Benvenuto! I want you, and not them; you shall have your house free of charges." After this, he signed a rescript underneath the petition I had drawn up, and which I have always preserved among my papers. The rescript ran as follows: *"Let the house be seen to, and who is the vendor, and at what price; for we wish to comply with Benvenuto's request."* I naturally thought that this would secure me in possession of the house; being over and above convinced that my performances must far exceed what I promised.

His Excellency committed the execution of these orders to his majordomo, who was named Ser Pier Francesco Riccio. The man came from Prato, and had been the Duke's pedagogue. I talked, then, to this donkey, and described my requirements, for there was a garden adjoining the house, on which I wanted to erect a workshop. He handed the matter over to a paymaster, dry and meagre, who bore the name of Lattanzio Gorini. This flimsy little fellow, with his tiny spider's hands and small gnat's voice, moved about the business at a snail's pace; yet in an evil hour he sent me stones, sand, and lime enough to build perhaps a pigeonhouse with careful management. When I saw how coldly things were going forward, I began to feel dismayed; however, I said to myself: "Little beginnings sometimes have great endings;" and I fostered hope in my heart by noticing how many thousand ducats had recently been squandered upon ugly pieces of bad sculpture turned out by that beast of a Buaccio Bandinello.[5] So I rallied my spirits and kept prodding at Lattanzio Gorini, to make him go a little faster. It was like shouting to a pack of lame donkeys with a blind dwarf for their driver. Under these difficulties, and by the use of my own money, I had soon marked out the foundations of the workshop and cleared the ground of trees and vines, labouring on, according to my wont, with fire, and perhaps a trifle of impatience.

On the other side, I was in the hands of Tasso the carpenter, a great friend of mine, who had received my instructions for making a wooden framework to set up the Perseus. This Tasso was a most excellent craftsman, the best, I believe, who ever lived in his own branch of art. Personally, he was gay and merry by temperament; and whenever I went to see him, he met me laughing, with some little song in falsetto on his lips. Half in despair as I then was, news coming that

[5]Cellini refers to his great rival Bernardo (Baccio) Bandinello; Buaccio, which means "great ox" in Italian, is a mischievous corruption of the spelling.

my affairs in France were going wrong, and these in Florence promising but ill through the luke-warmness of my patron, I could never stop listening till half the song was finished; and so in the end I used to cheer up a little with my friend, and drove away, as well as I was able, some few of the gloomy thoughts which weighed upon me.

. . .

57

While the workshop for executing my Perseus was in building, I used to work in a ground-floor room. Here I modelled the statue in plaster, giving it the same dimensions as the bronze was meant to have, and intending to cast it from this mould. But finding that it would take rather long to carry it out in this way, I resolved upon another expedient especially as now a wretched little studio had been erected, brick on brick, so miserably built that the mere recollection of it gives me pain. So then I began the figure of Medusa, and constructed the skeleton in iron. Afterwards I put on the clay, and when that was modelled, baked it.

I had no assistants except some little shopboys, among whom was one of great beauty; he was the son of a prostitute called La Gambetta. I made use of the lad as a model, for the only books which teach this art are the natural human body. Meanwhile, as I could not do everything alone, I looked about for workmen in order to put the business quickly through; but I was unable to find any. There were indeed some in Florence who would willingly have come, but Bandinello prevented them, and after keeping me in want of aid awhile, told the Duke that I was trying to entice his workpeople because I was quite incapable of setting up so great a statue by myself. I complained to the Duke of the annoyance which the brute gave me, and begged him to allow me some of the labourers from the Opera. My request inclined him to lend ear to Bandinello's calumnies; and when I noticed that, I set about to do my utmost by myself alone. The labour was enormous: I had to strain every muscle night and day; and just then the husband of my sister sickened, and died after a few days' illness. He left my sister, still young, with six girls of all ages, on my hands. This was the first great trial I endured in Florence, to be made the father and guardian of such a distressed family.

. . .

61

Meanwhile I was advancing with my great statue of Medusa. I had covered the iron skeleton with clay, which I modelled like an anatomical subject, and about half an inch thinner than the bronze would be. This I baked well, and then began to spread on the wax surface, in order to complete the figure to my liking. The Duke, who often came to inspect it, was so anxious lest I should not succeed with the bronze, that he wanted me to call in some master to cast it for me. . . .

62

. . . At last [the Duke] bade me apply myself to business, and complete his Perseus. So I returned home glad and light-hearted, and comforted my family, that is to say, my sister and her six daughters. Then I resumed my work, and pushed it forward as briskly as I could.

63

The first piece I cast in bronze was that great bust, the portrait of his Excellency, which I had modelled in the goldsmith's workroom while suffering from those pains in my back. It gave much pleasure when it was completed, though my sole object in making it was to obtain experience of clays suitable for bronze-casting. I was of course aware that the admirable sculptor Donatello had cast his bronzes with the clay of Florence; yet it seemed to me that he had met with enormous difficulties in their execution. As I thought that this was due to some fault in the earth, I wanted to make these first experiments before I undertook my Perseus. From them I learned that the clay was good enough, but had not been well understood by Donatello, inasmuch as I could see that his pieces had been cast with the very greatest trouble. Accordingly, as I have described above, I prepared the earth by artificial methods, and found it serve me well, and with it I cast the bust; but since I had not yet constructed my own furnace, I employed that of Maestro Zanobi di Pagno, a bellfounder.

When I saw that this bust came out sharp and clean, I set at once to construct a little furnace in the workshop erected for me by the Duke, after my own plans and design, in the house which the Duke had given me. No sooner was the furnace ready than I went to work with all diligence upon the casting of Medusa, that is, the woman twisted in a heap beneath the feet of Perseus. It was an extremely difficult task, and I was anxious to observe all the niceties of art which I had learned, so as not to lapse into some error. The first cast I took in my furnace succeeded in the superlative degree, and was so clean that my friends thought I should not need to retouch it. It is true that certain Germans and Frenchmen, who vaunt the possession of marvellous secrets, pretend that they can cast bronzes without retouching them; but this is really nonsense, because the bronze, when it has first been cast, ought to be worked over and beaten in with hammers and chisels, according to the manner of the ancients and also to that of the moderns—I mean such moderns as have known how to work in bronze.

The result of this casting greatly pleased his Excellency, who often came to my house to inspect it, encouraging me by the interest he showed to do my best. The furious envy of Bandinello, however, who kept always whispering in the Duke's ears, had such effect that he made him believe my first successes with a single figure or two proved nothing; I should never be able to put the whole large piece together, since I was new to the craft, and his Excellency ought to take good heed he did not throw his money away. These insinuations operated so efficiently upon the Duke's illustrious ears, that part of my allowance for workpeople was withdrawn. I felt compelled to complain pretty sharply to his Excellency; and having gone to wait on him one morning in the Via de' Servi, I spoke as follows: "My lord, I do not now receive the monies necessary for my task, which makes me fear that your Excellency has lost confidence in me. Once more then I tell you that I feel quite able to execute this statue three times better than the model, as I have before engaged my word."

. . .

65

. . . One day his most illustrious Excellency handed me several pounds weight of silver, and said: "This is some of the silver from my mines; take it, and make a fine vase." Now I did not choose to neglect my Perseus, and at the same time I wished to serve the Duke, so I entrusted the metal, together with my designs and models in wax, to a rascal called Piero di Martino, a goldsmith by trade. He set the work up badly, and moreover ceased to labour at it, so that I lost more time than if I had taken it in hand myself. After several months were wasted, and Piero would neither work nor put men to work upon the piece, I made him give it back. I moved heaven and earth to get back the body of the vase, which he had begun badly, as I have already said, together with the remainder of the silver. The Duke, hearing something of these disputes, sent for the vase and the models, and never told me why or wherefore. Suffice it to say, that he placed some of my designs in the hands of divers persons at Venice and elsewhere, and was very ill served by them.

66

I now stayed at home, and went rarely to the palace, labouring with great diligence to complete my statue. I had to pay the workmen out of my own pocket; for the Duke, after giving Lattanzio Gorini orders to discharge their wages, at the end of about eighteen months, grew tired, and withdrew this subsidy. I asked Lattanzio why he did not pay me as usual. The man replied, gesticulating with those spidery hands of his, in a shrill gnat's voice: "Why do not you finish your work? One thinks that you will never get it done." In a rage I up and answered: "May the plague catch you and all who dare to think I shall not finish it!"

So I went home with despair at heart to my unlucky Perseus, not without weeping, when I remembered the prosperity I had abandoned in Paris under the patronage of that marvellous King Francis, where I had abundance of all kinds, and here had everything to want for. Many a time I had it in my soul to cast myself away for lost. . . .

[Cellini has received a block of marble from Bandinello, after the Duke has settled a dispute between the two sculptors.]

72

I had it brought at once into my studio, and began to chisel it. While I was rough-hewing the block, I made a model. But my eagerness to work in marble was so strong, that I had not patience to finish the model as correctly as this art demands. I soon noticed that the stone rang false beneath my strokes, which made me oftentimes repent commencing on it. Yet I got what I could out of the piece—that is, the Apollo and Hyacinth, which may still be seen unfinished in my workshop. While I was thus engaged, the Duke came to my house, and often said to me: "Leave your bronze awhile, and let me watch you working on the marble." Then I took chisel and mallet, and went at it blithely. He asked about the model I had made for my statue; to which I answered: "Duke, this marble is all cracked, but I shall carve something from it in spite of that; therefore I have not been able to settle the model, but shall go on doing the best I can."

His Excellency sent to Rome post-haste for a block of Greek marble, in order that I might restore his antique Ganymede, which was the cause of that dispute with Bandinello. When it arrived, I thought it a sin to cut it up for the head and arms and other bits wanting in the Ganymede; so I provided myself with another piece of stone, and reserved the Greek marble for a Narcissus which I modelled on a small scale in wax. I found that the block had two holes, penetrating to the depth of a quarter of a cubit, and two good inches wide. This led me to choose the attitude which may be noticed in my statue, avoiding the holes and keeping my figure free from them. But rain had fallen scores of years upon the stone, filtering so deeply from the holes into its substance that the marble was decayed. Of this I had full proof at the time of a great inundation of the Arno, when the river rose to the height of more than a cubit and a half in my workshop.[6] Now the Narcissus stood

[6]The flood occurred in 1547.

upon a square of wood, and the water overturned it, causing the statue to break in two above the breasts. I had to join the pieces; and in order that the line of breakage might not be observed, I wreathed that garland of flowers round it which may still be seen upon the bosom. I went on working at the surface, employing some hours before sunrise, or now and then on feast-days, so as not to lose the time I needed for my Perseus.

It so happened on one of those mornings, while I was getting some little chisels into trim to work on the Narcissus, that a very fine splinter of steel flew into my right eye, and embedded itself so deeply in the pupil that it could not be extracted. I thought for certain I must lose the sight of that eye. After some days I sent for Maestro Raffaello dé Pilli, the surgeon, who obtained a couple of live pigeons, and placing me upon my back across a table, took the birds and opened a large vein they have beneath the wing, so that the blood gushed out into my eye. I felt immediately relieved, and in the space of two days the splinter came away, and I remained with eyesight greatly improved. Against the feast of S. Lucia, which came round in three days, I made a golden eye out of a French crown, and had it presented at her shrine by one of my six nieces, daughters of my sister Liperata; the girl was ten years of age, and in her company I returned thanks to God and S. Lucia. For some while afterwards I did not work at the Narcissus, but pushed my Perseus forward under all the difficulties I have described. It was my purpose to finish it, and then to bid farewell to Florence.

73

Having succeeded so well with the cast of the Medusa, I had great hope of bringing my Perseus through; for I had laid the wax on, and felt confident that it would come out in bronze as perfectly as the Medusa. The waxen model produced so fine an effect, that when the Duke saw it and was struck with its beauty—whether somebody had persuaded him it could not be carried out with the same finish in metal, or whether he thought so for himself—he came to visit me more frequently than usual, and on one occasion said: "Benvenuto, this figure cannot succeed in bronze; the laws of art do not admit of it." These words of his Excellency stung me so sharply that I answered: "My lord, I know how very little confidence you have in me; and I believe the reason of this is that your most illustrious Excellency lends too ready an ear to my calumniators, or else indeed that you do not understand my art." He hardly let me close the sentence when he broke in: "I profess myself a connoisseur, and understand it very well indeed." I replied: "Yes, like a prince, not like an artist; for if your Excellency understood my trade as well as you imagine, you would trust me on the proofs I have already given. These are, first, the colossal bronze bust of your Excellency, which is now in Elba; secondly, the restoration of the Ganymede in marble, which offered so many difficulties and cost me so much trouble, that I would rather have made the whole statue new from the beginning; thirdly, the Medusa, cast by me in bronze, here now before your Excellency's eyes, the execution of which was a greater triumph of strength and skill than any of my predecessors in this fiendish art have yet achieved. Look you, my lord! I constructed that furnace anew on principles quite different from those of other founders; in addition to many technical improvements and ingenious devices, I supplied it with two issues for the metal, because this difficult and twisted figure could not otherwise have come out perfect. It is only owing to my intelligent insight into means and appliances that the statue turned out as it did; a triumph judged impossible by all the practitioners of this art. I should like you furthermore to be aware, my lord, for certain, that the sole reason why I succeeded with all those great arduous works in France under his most admirable Majesty King Francis, was the high courage which that good monarch put into my heart by the liberal allowances he made me, and the multitude of workpeople he left at my disposal. I could have as many as I asked for, and employed at times above forty, all chosen by myself. These were the causes of my having there produced so many masterpieces in so short a space of time. Now then, my lord, put trust in me; supply me with the aid I need. I am confident of being able to complete a work which will delight your soul. But if your Excellency goes on disheartening me, and does not advance me the assistance which is absolutely required, neither I nor any man alive upon this earth can hope to achieve the slightest thing of value."

74

It was as much as the Duke could do to stand by and listen to my pleadings. He kept turning first this way and then that; while I, in despair, poor wretched I, was calling up remembrance of the noble state I held in France, to the great sorrow of my soul. All at once he cried: "Come, tell me, Benvenuto, how is it possible that yonder splendid head of Medusa, so high up there in the grasp of Perseus, should ever come out perfect?" I replied upon the instant: "Look you now, my lord! If your Excellency possessed that knowledge of the craft which you affirm you have, you would not fear one moment for the splendid head you speak of. There is good reason, on the other hand, to feel uneasy about this right foot, so far below and at a distance from the rest." When he heard these words, the Duke turned, half in anger, to some gentlemen in waiting, and exclaimed: "I verily believe that this Benvenuto prides himself on contradicting everything one says." Then he faced round to me with a touch of mockery, upon which his attendants did the like, and began to speak as follows: "I will listen patiently to any argument you can possibly produce in explanation of your statement, which may convince me of its probability." I said in answer: "I will adduce so sound an argument that your Excellency shall perceive the full force of it." So I began: "You must know, my lord, that the nature of fire is to ascend, and therefore I promise you that Medusa's head will come out famously; but since it is not in the nature of fire to descend, and I must force it downwards six cubits by artificial means, I assure your Excellency upon this most convincing ground of proof that the foot cannot possibly come out. It will, however, be quite easy for me to restore it." "Why, then," said the Duke "did you not devise it so that the foot should come out as well as you affirm the head will?" I answered: "I must have made a much larger furnace, with a conduit as thick as my leg; and so I might have forced the molten metal by its own weight to descend so far. Now, my pipe, which runs six cubits to the statue's foot, as I have said, is not thicker than two fingers. However, it was not worth the trouble and expense to make a larger; for I shall easily be able to mend what is lacking. But when my mould is more than half full, as I expect, from this middle point upwards, the fire ascending by its natural property, then the heads of Perseus and Medusa will come out admirably; you may be quite sure of it." After I had thus expounded these convincing arguments, together with many more of the same kind, which it would be tedious to set down here, the Duke shook his head and departed without further ceremony.

75

Abandoned thus to my own resources, I took new courage, and banished the sad thoughts which kept recurring to my mind, making me often weep bitter tears of repentance for having left France; for though I did so only to revisit Florence, my sweet birthplace, in order that I might charitably succour my six nieces, this good action, as I well perceived, had been the beginning of my great misfortune. Nevertheless, I felt convinced that when my Perseus was accomplished, all these trials would be turned to high felicity and glorious well-being.

Accordingly I strengthened my heart, and with all the forces of my body and my purse, employing what little money still remained to me, I set to work. First I provided myself with several loads of pinewood from the forests of Serristori, in the neighbourhood of Montelupo. While these were on their way, I clothed my Perseus with the clay which I had prepared many months beforehand, in order that it might be duly seasoned. After making its clay tunic (for that is the term used in this art) and properly arming it and fencing it with iron girders, I began to draw the wax out by means of a slow fire. This melted and issued through numerous air-vents I had made; for the more there are of these, the better will the mould fill. When I had finished drawing off the wax, I constructed a funnel-shaped furnace all round the model of my Perseus. It was built of bricks, so interlaced, the one above the other, that numerous apertures were left for the fire to exhale at. Then I began to lay on wood by degrees, and kept it burning two whole days and nights. At length, when all the wax was gone, and the mould was well baked, I set to work at digging the pit in which to sink it. This I performed with scrupulous regard to all the rules of art. When I had finished that part of my work, I raised the mould by windlasses and stout ropes to a perpendicular position, and suspending it with the greatest care one cubit above the level of the furnace, so that it hung exactly above the middle of the pit, I next lowered it gently down into the very bottom of the furnace, and had it firmly placed with every possible precaution for its safety. When this delicate operation was accomplished, I began to bank it up with the earth I had excavated; and, ever as the earth grew higher, I introduced its proper air-vents, which were little tubes of earthenware, such as folk use for drains and such-like purposes. At length, I felt sure that it was admirably fixed, and that the filling-in of the pit and the placing of the air-vents had been properly performed. I also could see that my workpeople understood my method, which differed very considerably from that of all the other masters in the trade. Feeling confident, then, that I could rely upon them, I next turned to my furnace, which I had filled with numerous pigs of copper and other bronze stuff. The pieces were piled according to the laws of art, that is to say, so resting one upon the other that the flames could play freely through them, in order that the metal might heat and liquefy the sooner. At last I called out heartily to set the furnace going. The logs of pine were heaped in, and, what with the unctuous resin of the wood and the good draught I had given, my furnace worked so well that I was obliged to rush from side to side to keep it going. The labour was more than I could stand; yet I forced myself to strain every nerve and muscle. To increase my anxieties, the workshop took fire, and we were afraid lest the roof should fall upon our heads; while, from the garden, such a storm of wind and rain kept blowing in, that it perceptibly cooled the furnace.

Battling thus with all these untoward circumstances for several hours, and exerting myself beyond even the measure of my powerful constitution, I could at last bear up no longer, and a sudden fever, of the utmost possible intensity, attacked me. I felt absolutely obliged to go and fling myself upon my bed. Sorely against my will having to drag myself away from the spot, I turned to my assistants, about ten or more in all, what with master-founders, hand-workers, country-fellows, and my own special journeymen, among whom was Bernardino Mannellini of Mugello, my apprentice through several years. To him in particular I spoke: "Look, my dear

Bernardino, that you observe the rules which I have taught you; do your best with all despatch, for the metal will soon be fused. You cannot go wrong; these honest men will get the channels ready; you will easily be able to drive back the two plugs with this pair of iron crooks; and I am sure that my mould will fill miraculously. I feel more ill than I ever did in all my life, and verily believe that it will kill me before a few hours are over." Thus, with despair at heart, I left them, and betook myself to bed.

76

No sooner had I got to bed, than I ordered my serving-maids to carry food and wine for all the men into the workshop; at the same time I cried: "I shall not be alive tomorrow." They tried to encourage me, arguing that my illness would pass over, since it came from excessive fatigue. In this way I spent two hours battling with the fever, which steadily increased, and calling out continually: "I feel that I am dying." My housekeeper, who was named Mona Fiore da Castel del Rio, a very notable manager and no less warmhearted, kept chiding me for my discouragement; but, on the other hand, she paid me every kind attention which was possible. However, the sight of my physical pain and moral dejection so affected her, that, in spite of that brave heart of hers, she could not refrain from shedding tears; and yet, so far as she was able, she took good care I should not see them. While I was thus terribly afflicted, I beheld the figure of a man enter my chamber, twisted in his body into the form of a capital S. He raised a lamentable, doleful voice, like one who announces their last hour to men condemned to die upon the scaffold, and spoke these words: "O Benvenuto! your statue is spoiled, and there is no hope whatever of saving it." No sooner had I heard the shriek of that wretch than I gave a howl which might have been heard from the sphere of flame. Jumping from my bed, I seized my clothes and began to dress. The maids, and my lads, and every one who came around to help me, got kicks or blows of the fist, while I kept crying out in lamentation: "Ah! traitors! enviers! This is an act of treason, done by malice prepense! But I swear by God that I will sift it to the bottom, and before I die will leave such witness to the world of what I can do as shall make a score of mortals marvel."

When I had got my clothes on, I strode with soul bent on mischief toward the workshop; there I beheld the men, whom I had left erewhile in such high spirits, standing stupefied and downcast. I began at once and spoke: "Up with you! Attend to me! Since you have not been able or willing to obey the directions I gave you, obey me now that I am with you to conduct my work in person. Let no one contradict me, for in cases like this we need the aid of hand and hearing, not of advice." When I had uttered these words, a certain Maestro Alessandro Lastricati broke silence and said: "Look you, Benvenuto, you are going to attempt an enterprise which the laws of art do not sanction, and which cannot succeed." I turned upon him with such fury and so full of mischief, that he and all the rest of them exclaimed with one voice: "On then! Give orders! We will obey your least commands, so long as life is left in us." I believe they spoke thus feelingly because they thought I must fall shortly dead upon the ground. I went immediately to inspect the furnace, and found that the metal was all curdled; an accident which we express by "being caked." I told two of the hands to cross the road, and fetch from the house of the butcher Capretta a load of young oak-wood, which had lain dry for above a year; this wood had been previously offered me by Madame Ginevra, wife of the said Capretta. So soon as the first armfuls arrived, I began to fill the grate beneath the furnace. Now oak-wood of that kind heats more powerfully than any other sort of tree; and for this reason, where a slow fire is wanted, as in the case of gun-foundry, alder or pine is preferred. Accordingly, when the logs took fire, oh! how the cake began to stir beneath that awful heat, to glow and sparkle in a blaze! At the same time I kept stirring up the channels, and sent men upon the roof to stop the conflagration, which had gathered force from the increased combustion in the furnace; also I caused boards, carpets, and other hangings to be set up against the garden, in order to protect us from the violence of the rain.

77

When I had thus provided against these several disasters, I roared out first to one man and then to another: "Bring this thing here! Take that thing there!" At this crisis, when the whole gang saw the cake was on the point of melting, they did my bidding, each fellow working with the strength of three. I then ordered half a pig of pewter to be brought, which weighed about sixty pounds, and flung it into the middle of the cake inside the furnace. By this means, and by piling on wood and stirring now with pokers and now with iron rods, the curdled mass rapidly began to liquefy. Then, knowing I had brought the dead to life again, against the firm opinion of those ignoramuses, I felt such vigour fill my veins, that all those pains of fever, all those fears of death, were quite forgotten.

All of a sudden an explosion took place, attended by a tremendous flash of flame, as though a thunderbolt had formed and been discharged amongst us. Unwonted and appalling terror astonished every one, and me more even than the rest. When the din was over and the dazzling light extinguished, we began to look each other in the face. Then I discovered that the cap of the furnace had blown up, and the bronze was bubbling over from its source beneath. So I had the mouths of my mould immediately opened, and at the same time drove in the two plugs which kept back the molten metal. But I noticed that it did not flow as rapidly as usual, the reason being probably that the fierce heat of the fire we kindled had consumed its base alloy. Accordingly I sent for all my pewter platters, porringers, and dishes, to the number of some two hundred pieces, and had a portion of them cast, one by one, into the channels, the rest into the furnace. This expedient succeeded, and every one could now perceive that my bronze was in most perfect liquefaction, and my mould was filling; whereupon they all with heartiness and happy cheer assisted and obeyed my bidding, while I, now here, now there, gave orders, helped with my own hands, and cried aloud: "O God! Thou that by Thy immeasurable power didst rise from the dead, and in Thy glory didst ascend to heaven!". . . . even thus in a moment my mould was filled; and seeing my work finished, I fell upon my knees, and with all my heart gave thanks to God.

After all was over, I turned to a plate of salad on a bench there, and ate with hearty appetite, and drank together with the whole crew. Afterwards I retired to bed, healthy and happy, for it was now two hours before morning, and slept as sweetly as though I had never felt a touch of illness. My good housekeeper, without my giving any orders, had prepared a fat capon for my repast. So that, when I rose, about the hour for breaking fast, she presented herself with a smiling countenance, and said: "Oh! is that the man who felt that he was dying? Upon my word, I think the blows and kicks you dealt us last night, when you were so enraged, and had that demon in your body as it seemed, must have frightened away your mortal fever! The fever feared that it might catch it too, as we did!" All my poor household, relieved in like measure from anxiety and overwhelming labour, went at once to buy earthen vessels in order to replace the pewter I had cast away. Then we dined together joyfully; nay, I cannot remember a day in my whole life when I dined with greater gladness or a better appetite.

After our meal I received visits from the several men who had assisted me. They exchanged congratulations, and thanked God for our success, saying they had learned and seen things done which other masters judged impossible. I too grew somewhat glorious; and deeming I had shown myself a man of talent, indulged a boastful humour. So I thrust my hand into my purse, and paid them all to their full satisfaction.

That evil fellow, my mortal foe, Messer Pier Francesco Ricci, majordomo of the Duke, took great pains to find out how the affair had gone. In answer to his questions, the two men whom I suspected of having caked my metal for me, said I was no man, but of a certainty some powerful devil, since I had accomplished what no craft of the art could do; indeed they did not believe a mere ordinary fiend could work such miracles as I in other ways had shown. They exaggerated the whole affair so much, possibly in order to excuse their own part in it, that the majordomo wrote an account to the Duke, who was then in Pisa, far more marvellous and full of thrilling incidents than what they had narrated.

78

After I had let my statue cool for two whole days, I began to uncover it by slow degrees. The first thing I found was that the head of Medusa had come out most admirably, thanks to the air-vents; for, as I had told the Duke, it is the nature of fire to ascend. Upon advancing farther, I discovered that the other head, that, namely, of Perseus, had succeeded no less admirably; and this astonished me far more, because it is at a considerably lower level than that of the Medusa. Now the mouths of the mould were placed above the head of Perseus and behind his shoulders; and I found that all the bronze my furnace contained had been exhausted in the head of this figure. It was a miracle to observe that not one fragment remained in the orifice of the channel, and that nothing was wanting to the statue. In my great astonishment I seemed to see in this the hand of God arranging and controlling all.

I went on uncovering the statue with success, and ascertained that everything had come out in perfect order, until I reached the foot of the right leg on which the statue rests. There the heel itself was formed, and going farther, I found the foot apparently complete. This gave me great joy on the one side, but was half unwelcome to me on the other, merely because I had told the Duke that it could not come out. However, when I reached the end, it appeared that the toes and a little piece above them were unfinished, so that about half the foot was wanting. Although I knew that this would add a trifle to my labour, I was very well pleased, because I could now prove to the Duke how well I understood my business. It is true that far more of the foot than I expected had been perfectly formed; the reason of this was that, from causes I have recently described, the bronze was hotter than our rules of art prescribe; also that I had been obliged to supplement the alloy with my pewter cups and platters, which no one else, I think, had ever done before.

Having now ascertained how successfully my work had been accomplished, I lost no time in hurrying to Pisa, where I found the Duke. He gave me a most gracious reception, as did also the Duchess; and although the majordomo had informed them of the whole proceedings, their Excellencies deemed my performance far more stupendous and astonishing when they heard the tale from my own mouth. When I arrived at the foot of Perseus, and said it had not come out perfect, just as I previously warned his Excellency, I saw an expression of wonder pass over his face, while he related to the Duchess how I had predicted this beforehand. Observing the princes to be so well disposed towards me, I begged leave from the Duke to go to Rome. He granted it in most obliging terms, and bade me return as soon as possible to complete his Perseus; giving me letters of recommendation meanwhile to his ambassador, Averardo Serristori. We were then in the first years of Pope Giulio de Monti.[7]

GALILEO GALILEI
[1564–1642]

AND

JOHANNES KEPLER
[1571–1630]

Late in his life, Einstein remarked in an interview, "It has always pained me that Galilei did not acknowledge the work of Kepler . . . that, alas, is vanity. You find it in so many scientists." Whether or not Einstein's generalization is correct, it is certainly true that these two pioneering astronomers, both eager to prove that Copernicus was correct in saying that the earth revolved around the sun, were desperately different men, and Galileo's stubborn refusal to acknowledge the work of his German colleague or to aid Kepler in his research is a sour footnote in the history of science. In Galileo's insistence on individual glory and personal authority, we glimpse a quintessentially Renaissance personality; the self-effacing Kepler may have been the more pleasant man, and in some ways the better scientist of the two. Each of them, however—the proud man and the humble one alike—exemplifies the Renaissance passion for discovery.

The deep and mystical love Johannes Kepler felt for the stars was given to him by his eccentric mother, later accused of witchcraft, who carried her little son outside to view the comet of 1577. The adult Kepler was poor, a sloppy dresser, a rather bumbling, gentle soul who mainly made his living by casting horoscopes. He was also a man on fire to understand the secret motions of the universe he found so beautiful. He made plenty of mistakes, but he was an acute observer who, with the help of painstaking measurements recorded by the Danish astronomer Tycho Brahe, formulated three mathematical statements about planetary motion known as Kepler's Laws, which he published in two books, *Astronomia Nova* (1609) and *Harmonici Mundi* (1619). Among other things, these laws postulated that each planet's orbit is an ellipse with the sun at one focus, and that planets move more rapidly when their orbits bring them close to the sun, and more slowly when distant from it. Later in the century, Sir Isaac Newton would provide the physical explanations for Kepler's correct observations. Kepler died at age forty-eight, his family and his affairs scattered in the Thirty Years' War and the plagues that accompanied it; on his deathbed, it is said that he kept pointing first to his own head, then upward at the stars.

Galileo—urbane, vain, close to court figures, and good at promoting himself and his ideas—was a brilliant scientist. At age nineteen, using his pulse for a timer, he observed that a pendulum accomplished each swing in the same amount of time, whether its arc was wide or narrow. He did not invent the telescope, as he liked to say he had, but he

---

[7]Elected pope in February 1550.

was the first to point one heavenward. He found that the moon looked like an orb of rugged rocky terrain instead of a glowing disc, discovered the four largest satellites of Jupiter, and observed that Venus has phases like the moon.

Despite the initial promise of their first exchange of letters, reprinted here, Galileo responded almost not at all to Kepler's pleas for help in making astronomical observations, nor to his later request to be sent a telescope or even a lens, "so that at last I too can enjoy, like yourself, the spectacle of the skies." Galileo had a good many of the instruments at his disposal, and was in the habit of giving them away to friends at court, but sent none to Kepler. These two men, both of whom possessed partial answers to the mysteries of gravitation, inertia, and planetary movement, might have indeed become "comrades in the pursuit of truth" had they been able to cooperate. As it is, it is Galileo's name that has come to be more familiar to us, thanks in part to his forced recantation, at the hands of the Inquisition, of the Copernican theory set forth in his *Dialogue Concerning the Two Chief World Systems* (1632). In his last years, spent under house arrest in his Florentine villa, he was visited by the English poet John Milton; it is fascinating to think that some of Galileo's ideas may have influenced not only the scientists who came after him, but also Milton, in his grand visions of the cosmos "revolv'd on heaven's great axle."

[Galileo–Kepler Correspondence]

Translated by Mary Martin McLaughlin

Galileo to Kepler

Padua, August 4, 1597

I received your book, most learned sir, which you sent me by Paulus Amberger, not some days since, but only a few hours ago. And as this Paulus has notified me of his return to Germany, I would consider myself ungrateful if I did not now send you my thanks in the present letter. I thank you, therefore, and most especially because you have judged me worthy of such a token of your friendship. So far I have read only the introduction of your work, but I have to some extent gathered your plan from it, and I congratulate myself on the exceptional good fortune of having such a man as a comrade in the pursuit of truth. For it is too bad that there are so few who seek the truth and so few who do not follow a mistaken method in philosophy. This is not, however, the place to lament the misery of our century, but to rejoice with you over such beautiful ideas for proving the truth. So I add only, and I promise, that I shall read your book at leisure; for I am certain that I shall find the noblest things in it. And this I shall do the more gladly, because I accepted the view of Copernicus many years ago, and from this standpoint I have discovered from their origins many natural phenomena, which doubtless cannot be explained on the basis of the more commonly accepted hypothesis. I have written many direct and indirect arguments for the Copernican view, but until now I have not dared to publish them, alarmed by the fate of Copernicus himself, our master. He has won for himself undying fame in the eyes of a few, but he has been mocked and hooted at by an infinite multitude (for so large is the number of fools). I would dare to come forward publicly with my ideas if there were more people of your way of thinking. As this is not the case, I shall refrain. The shortness of time and my eager desire to read your book compel me to close, but I assure you of my sympathy, and I shall always gladly be at your service. Farewell and do not neglect to send me further good news of yourself.

Kepler to Galileo

Graz, October 13, 1597

I received your letter of August 4 on September 1. It gave me a twofold pleasure, first, because it sealed my friendship with you, the Italian, and second, because of the agreement in our opinions concerning Copernican cosmography. Since at the end of your letter you invite me in friendly fashion to carry on a correspondence with you, and I myself am impelled to do so, I will not overlook the opportunity of sending you a letter by the present young nobleman. Meanwhile, if your time has permitted, I hope that you have come to study my little book more thoroughly. So a great desire has seized me to hear your judgment of it. For it is my way to urge all those to whom I write to give me their true opinion; believe me, I much prefer the sharpest criticism of a single intelligent man to the thoughtless approval of the great masses.

I could only have wished that you, who have so profound an insight, would choose another way. You advise us, by your personal example, and in discreetly veiled fashion, to retreat before the general ignorance and not to expose ourselves or heedlessly to oppose the violent attacks of the mob of scholars (and in this you follow Plato and Pythagoras, our true preceptors). But after a tremendous task has been begun in our time, first by Copernicus and then by many very learned mathematicians, and when the assertion that the earth moves can no longer be considered something new, would it not be much better to pull the wagon to its goal by our joint efforts, now that we have got it under way, and gradually, with powerful voices, to shout down the common herd, which really does not weigh the arguments very carefully? Thus perhaps by cleverness we may bring it to a knowledge of the truth. With your arguments you would at the same time help your comrades who endure so many unjust judgments, for they would obtain either comfort from your agreement or protection from your influential position. It is not only your Italians who cannot believe that they move if they do not feel it, but we in Germany also do not by any means endear ourselves with this idea. Yet there are ways by which we protect ourselves against these difficulties. . . .

Be of good cheer, Galileo, and come out publicly. If I judge correctly, there are only a few of the distinguished mathematicians of Europe who would part company with us, so great is the power of truth. If Italy seems less a favourable place for your publication, and if you look for difficulties there, perhaps Germany will allow us this freedom. But enough of this. Let me know privately at least, if you do not want to do so publicly, what you have discovered in support of Copernicus.

Now I should like to ask you for an observation; since I possess no instruments, I must appeal to others. Do you own a quadrant on which minutes and quarter-minutes can be read? If so, please observe, around the time of December 19, the greatest and smallest altitude, in the same night, of the middle star of the handle of the Great Dipper. Also, observe about December 26 both altitudes of the polar star. Also, watch the first star around March 19, 1598, in its height at midnight, the second about September 28, also around midnight. If, as I wish, there could be shown a difference between the two observations, of one or another minute, or even of 10 to 15 minutes, this would be proof of something of great importance for all of astronomy. If no difference is shown, however, we shall still earn together the fame of exploring a very significant problem not hitherto examined by anyone [the fixed-star parallax]. This is enough for those who are enlightened! . . . Farewell, and answer me with a very long letter.

(continued from copyright page)

Homer, "The Odyssey" from THE ODYSSEY, translated by Allen Mandelbaum. Copyright© 1990 by Allen Mandelbaum. Reprinted with the permission of Bantam Books, a division of Bantam Doubleday Dell Publishing Group, Inc.

Sappho, selections from SAPPHO: A New Translation by Mary Barnard. Copyright© 1958 by The Regents of the University of California, © renewed 1984 by Mary Barnard. Reprinted with the permission of the University of California Press.

Aeschylus, "Agamemnon" and "The Eumenides" from THE ORESTEIAN TRILOGY, revised edition, translated by Philip Vellacott. Copyright© 1956, 1959 by Philip Vellacott. Reprinted with the permission of Penguin Books Ltd.

Sophocles, "Antigone" from SOPHOCLES, THE OEDIPUS CYCLE: An English Version by Robert Fitzgerald and Dudley Fitts, copyright 1939 by Harcourt Brace & Company and renewed 1967 by Dudley Fitts and Robert Fitzgerald, reprinted by permission of the publisher. CAUTION: All rights, including professional, amateur, motion picture, recitation, lecturing, performance, public reading, radio broadcasting, and television are strictly reserved. Inquiries on all rights should be addressed to Harcourt Brace & Company, Permissions Department, Orlando, FL 32887-6777.

Euripides, "Medea" from MEDEA AND OTHER PLAYS, translated by Philip Vellacott. Copyright© 1963 by Philip Vellacott. Reprinted with the permission of Penguin Books Ltd.

Aristophanes, "Lysistrata," translated by Charles T. Murphy from GREEK LITERATURE IN TRANSLATION by Whitney Jennings Oates and Charles T. Murphy. Copyright© 1944 by Longman Publishing Group. Reprinted with the permission of Longman Publishing Group.

Aristotle, "Metaphysics" and "Nicomachean Ethics" from THE WAY OF PHILOSOPHY, translated by Philip Ellis Wheelwright. Copyright© 1960 by Macmillan Publishing Company. Reprinted with the permission of Macmillan Publishing Company.

Catullus poems, from THE POEMS OF CATULLUS, translated by Horace Gregory. Copyright© 1956 by Horace Gregory. Reprinted with the permission of Grove Press, Inc.

Virgil, "The Aeneid" from THE AENEID, translated by Frank O. Copley and Brooks Otis (Indianapolis: Bobbs-Merrill, 1965). Copyright© 1965 by Macmillan Publishing Company. Reprinted with the permission of Macmillan Publishing Company.

Ovid, "Metamorphoses" from METAMORPHOSES, translated by Rolfe Humphries. Copyright© 1955 by Rolfe Humphries. Reprinted with the permission of Indiana University Press.

"The Descent of Inanna," translated by Samuel Noah Kramer, from SUMERIAN MYTHOLOGY: A Study of Spiritual and Literary Achievement in the Third Millennium B.C. (Philadelphia, PA: The University of Pennsylvania Press, 1972). Reprinted with the permission of The University of Pennsylvania Press and Mrs. Samuel N. Kramer.

"The Epic of Gilgamesh," translated by N. K. Sandars from THE EPIC OF GILGAMESH, Second Revised Edition. Copyright© 1960, 1964, 1972 by N. K. Sandars. Reprinted with the permission of Penguin Books Ltd.

Lao Tzu poems from THE WAY OF LIFE ACCORDING TO LAO TZU, translated by Witter Bynner. Copyright 1944 by Witter Bynner, renewed © 1972 by Dorothy Chauvenet and Paul Horgan. Reprinted with the permission of HarperCollins Publishers, Inc.

Chuang Tzu, from CHUANG TZU: Basic Writings, translated by Burton Watson. Copyright© 1963 by Columbia University Press. Reprinted with the permission of the publisher.

Confucius, "The Analects" from THE ANALECTS OF CONFUCIUS, translated by Arthur Waley. Copyright© 1955 by George Allen & Unwin, Ltd. Reprinted with the permission of Macmillan Publishing Company and George Allen & Unwin, now Unwin Hyman, an imprint of HarperCollins Publishers Limited.

"Dead Sea Scrolls" from THE DEAD SEA SCROLLS IN ENGLISH, Third Edition translated by G. Vermes. Copyright© 1962, 1965, 1968, 1975, 1987 by G. Vermes. Reprinted with the permission of Penguin Books Ltd.

"The Gospel of Mary" translated by George W. MacRae and R. McL. Wilson; edited by Douglas M. Parrot, from THE NAG HAMMADI LIBRARY, edited by James M. Robinson. Copyright© 1978 by E. J. Brill, Leiden, The Netherlands. Reprinted with the permission of HarperCollins Publishers, Inc.

St. Augustine, "The Confessions" from THE CONFESSIONS OF ST. AUGUSTINE, by John K. Ryan. Copyright© 1960 by Doubleday, a division of Bantam Doubleday Dell Publishing Group, Inc. Reprinted with the permission of the publisher.

Dante Alighieri, "The Divine Comedy," translated by John Ciardi. Copyright© 1961, 1965, 1967, 1970, 1977 by John Ciardi. Reprinted with the permission of W. W. Norton & Company, Inc.

"Exile of the Sons of Uisliu" from THE TAIN (London: Oxford University Press, 1970), translated by Thomas Kinsella. Copyright 1969 by Thomas Kinsella. Reprinted with the permission of the translator.

Taliesin, "The Battle of Argoed Llwyfain" and "Death Song for Owain ab Urien," translated by Anthony Conran. Copyright© 1967, 1986 by Anthony Conran. Reprinted with the permission of Poetry Wales Press.

Aneirin, "The Gododdin" from THE EARLIEST WELSH POETRY (London: Macmillan/ New York: St. Martin's Press, 1970), translated by Joseph P. Clancy. Reprinted with the permission of the translator.

"Widsith, the Minstrel," "Cotton MS. Maxims," "The Wanderer," "The Ruin," "The Wife's Lament," and "The Husband's Message" from AN ANTHOLOGY OF OLD ENGLISH POETRY, translated by Charles W. Kennedy. Copyright© 1960 by Oxford University Press, Inc., renewed 1988 by Elizabeth D. Kennedy. Reprinted with the permission of the publisher.

"Beowulf" from BEOWULF: The Oldest English Epic, translated by Charles W. Kennedy. Copyright 1940 by Oxford University Press, Inc., renewed © 1968 by Charles W. Kennedy. Reprinted with the permission of the publisher.

"The Song of Roland" excerpts from THE SONG OF ROLAND, translated by Frederick Goldin. Copyright© 1978 by W. W. Norton & Company, Inc. Reprinted with the permission of the publishers.

"Lament for the Cuckoo," "Lament for Alcuin," "The Wandering Scholar," "Of Gardening," "Easter Sunday," "He Complains to Bishop Hartgar of Thirst," "Come, sweetheart, come," "Softly the west wind blows," and "Confession," from MEDIEVAL LATIN LYRICS, translated by Helen Waddell. Reprinted with the permission of Constable Publishers Limited.

Provençal Poetry from THE LYRICS OF THE TROUBADOUR, TROUVERES, translated by Frederick Goldin. Copyright© 1973 by Frederick Goldin. Reprinted with the permission of Doubleday, a division of Bantam Doubleday Dell Publishing Group, Inc. Countess of Dia, "I've lately been in great distress" and "Of things I'd rather keep in silence, I must sing" from THE WOMAN TROUBADOURS, translated by Magda Bogin (London: Paddington, 1976).

Marie de France, "The Lay of Chevrefoil" from THE LAIS OF MARIE DE FRANCE (Durham, NC: Labyrinth Press, 1983), edited and translated by Robert Hanning and Joan Ferrante. Reprinted with the permission of The Labyrinth Press.

Giovanni Boccaccio, excerpts from "The Decameron" from THE DECAMERON (New York: Garden City, 1930), translated by Richard Aldington. Copyright 1957, 1985 by Richard Aldington. Reprinted with the permission of Rosica Colin Ltd.

John Mandeville, "The Travels of Sir John Mandeville" from THE TRAVELS OF SIR JOHN MANDEVILLE (New York: Dover, 1964). Reprinted with the permission of Dover Publications, Inc.

Geoffrey Chaucer, excerpts from "The Canterbury Tales" from THE PORTABLE CHAUCER, by Theodore Morrison. Copyright 1949, renewed © 1977 by Theodore Morrison. Reprinted with the permission of Viking Penguin, a division of Penguin Books USA Inc.

Christine de Pizan, selections from THE BOOK OF THE CITY OF LADIES, translated by Earl Jeffrey Richards. Copyright© 1982 by Persea Books. Reprinted with the permission of the publisher.

Margery Kempe, excerpts from THE BOOK OF MARGERY KEMPE, translated by W. Butler-Bowden. Copyright 1944 by Devin-Adair, Publishers, Inc., Old Greenwich, CT, 06870. Reprinted with the permission of the publishers.

Ibn Hazm, "The Dove's Necklace" from THE RING AND THE DOVE, translated by A. J. Arberry (London: Luzac & Co., Ltd., 1953).

Usamah Ibn Munqidh, "The Book of Reflections" from A MUSLIM VIEW OF THE CRUSADERS, translated by Philip K. Hitti.

Li Po, "Sent to My Two Little Children in the East of Lu," "Bring the Wine!," and "Summer Day in the Mountains" from THE COLUMBIA BOOK OF CHINESE POETRY: From Early Times to the Thirteenth-Century, translated by Burton Watson. Copyright© 1984 by Columbia University Press. Reprinted with the permission of the publisher.

Li Po, "The Road to Shu is Hard" and "Sitting Alone in Ching-t'ing Mountain," translated by Irving Y. Lo; "T'ien-mu Mountain Ascended in a Dream," translated by Wu-chi Liu; "Calling on a Taoist Priest in Tai-t'ien Mountain," translated by Joseph J. Lee; from SUNFLOWER SPLENDOR: THREE THOUSAND YEARS OF CHINESE POETRY, edited by Wu-chi Liu and Irving Yucheng Lo

(Bloomington, IN: Indiana University Press, 1975). Reprinted with the permission of the translators.

"Drinking with a Friend, Among the Mountains," "Searching for Master Yung," "Seeing Off a Friend," "Drinking Alone under the Moon," and "Ballad of Ch'ang-kan," translated by Jerome P. Seaton, from CHINESE POETIC WRITING WITH AN ANTHOLOGY OF T'ANG POETRY, edited by François Cheng, translated from the French by Donald A. Riggs and Jerome P. Seaton. Copyright© 1977 by Editions de Seuil. English translation copyright© 1982 by Indiana University Press. Reprinted with the permission of Indiana University Press.

Murasaki Shikibu, Lady Murasaki, excerpts from THE TALE OF GENJI, translated by Edward G. Seidensticker. Copyright© 1976 by Edward G. Seidensticker. Reprinted with the permission of Alfred A. Knopf, Inc.

Bede, "Ecclesiastical History of the English People" from ECCLESIASTICAL HISTORY OF THE ENGLISH PEOPLE by Bede, Revised Edition, translated by Leo Sherley-Price. Translation copyright© 1955, 1968 by Leo Sherley-Price. Reprinted with the permission of Penguin Books Ltd.

Anonymous, "History of the First Crusade," translated by James B. Ross, from THE PORTABLE MEDIEVAL READER by James Bruce Ross and Mary Martin McLaughlin. Copyright 1949 by Viking Penguin, Inc., renewed © 1976 by James Bruce Ross and Mary Martin McLaughlin. Reprinted with the permission of Viking Penguin, a division of Penguin Books USA Inc.

Andreas Capellanus, excerpts from "The Art of Courtly Love," translated by John J. Parry, from THE ART OF COURTLY LOVE, edited and abridged by Frederick W. Locke. Copyright© 1957, 1985 by Frederick Ungar Publishing Company. Reprinted with the permission of The Continuum Publishing Company.

St. Francis of Assisi, "The Canticle of Brother Sun" and Anonymous, excerpts from "The Little Flowers of Saint Francis" from THE LITTLE FLOWERS OF ST. FRANCIS OF ASSISI, translated by Raphael Brown. Copyright© 1958 by Beverly Brown. Reprinted with the permission of Doubleday, a division of Bantam Doubleday Dell Publishing Group, Inc.

Francesco Petrarch, "The Ascent of Mount Ventoux" from PETRARCH: Selections from the Canzoniere and Other Works translated by Mark Musa. Copyright© 1985 by Mark Musa. Reprinted with the permission of Oxford University Press. Selections from the *Canzoniere* are translated by Patricia Clark Smith and are reprinted with the permission of the translator.

Christopher Columbus, "Diario" selections, from THE LOG OF CHRISTOPHER COLUMBUS by Robert H. Fuson. Copyright© 1987 by Robert H. Fuson. Reprinted with the permission of International Marine Publishing, an imprint of TAB Books, a Division of McGraw-Hill, Inc., Blue Ridge Summit, PA 17294-0850 (1-800-233-1128).

Niccolo Machiavelli, excerpts from "The Prince" from MACHIAVELLI: The Prince and Other Works, translated by Allan H. Gilbert (Putney, VT: Hendricks House, Inc. Publishers, 1964). Reprinted with the permission of the publisher.

Michel Eyquem de Montaigne, "Of Cannibals" and "Of Coaches" from THE COMPLETE ESSAYS OF MONTAIGNE, translated by Donald M. Frame. Copyright© 1958 by the Board of Trustees of the Leland Stanford Junior University, renewed 1986 by Donald M. Frame. Reprinted with the permission of the publishers, Stanford University Press.

William Shakespeare, "The Tempest," edited by Robert Langbaum. Copyright© 1964, 1987 by Robert Langbaum for Introduction, Annotations and Compilation. Reprinted with the permission of New American Library, a division of Penguin Books USA Inc.

Sor Juana Inés de la Cruz, *Loa* for "The Divine Narcissus" from SOR JUANA INÉS DE LA CRUZ POEMS: A Bilingual Anthology, translated by Margaret Sayers Peden. Copyright© 1985. Reprinted with the permission of Bilingual Press/Editorial Bilingüe, Arizona State University, Tempe, AZ 85287-2702.

Maurice Scève, "The day we passed together for a while," translated by Patricia Clark Smith. Reprinted with the permission of the translator.

Pierre de Ronsard, "Epitaph on Rabelais" from FORMAL SPRING: French Renaissance Poems, translated by R. N. Currey (London: Oxford University Press, 1950). Reprinted with the permission of the translator.

Louise Labé, Sonnet 18 and Sonnet 19, translated by Willis Barnstone, from BOOK OF WOMEN POETS FROM ANTIQUITY TO NOW by Willis and Aliki Barnstone. Copyright© 1980 by Schocken Books, Inc. Reprinted by permission of Schocken Books, published by Pantheon Books, a division of Random House, Inc.

Marc-Antoine de St.-Amant, "Go in the Whorehouse" from EUROPEAN METAPHYSICAL POETRY, translated by Frank J. Warnke. Copyright© 1961 by Yale University Press. Reprinted with the permission of the publisher.

Jacobus Revius, "He Bore Our Griefs," translated by Henrietta Ten Harmsel. Reprinted with the permission of Wayne State University Press.

Paul Fleming, "To My Redeemer" from EUROPEAN METAPHYSICAL POETRY, translated by Frank J. Warnke. Copyright© 1961 by Yale University Press. Reprinted with the permission of the publisher.

Christian Hoffman von Hofmannswaldau, "The Transience of Beauty" from EUROPEAN METAPHYSICAL POETRY, translated by Frank J. Warnke. Copyright© 1961 by Yale University Press. Reprinted with the permission of the publisher.

Saint Teresa de Avila, "See, His blood He's shedding" from THE COMPLETE WORKS OF STE. TERESA, translated by E. Allison Peers (New York: Sheed & Ward, Inc., 1962). Reprinted with the permission of the publisher.

San Juan de la Cruz, "The Dark Night of the Soul," translated by Patricia Clark Smith. Reprinted with the permission of the translator.

Luis de Góngora, "Allegory of the Brevity of Things Human," translated by Roy Campbell, from AN ANTHOLOGY OF SPANISH POETRY FROM GARCILASO TO GARCÍA LORCA IN ENGLISH, edited by Angel Flores (Garden City, NJ: Doubleday/Anchor, 1961). Reprinted with the permission of the Estate of Angel Flores.

Sor Juana Inés de la Cruz, "The Rhetoric of Tears" from EUROPEAN METAPHYSICAL POETRY, translated by Frank J. Warnke. Copyright© 1961 by Yale University Press. Reprinted with the permission of the publisher.

Sor Juana Inés de la Cruz, "To Her Portrait," translated by Patricia Clark Smith. Reprinted with the permission of the translator.

Michelangelo Buonarroti, "You have a face that's sweeter than grape mash," translated by Harold M. Priest, from RENAISSANCE AND BAROQUE LYRICS: An Anthology of Translations from the Italian, French, and Spanish (Evanston, IL: Northwestern University Press, 1962). Reprinted with the permission of the publisher.

Adam Michna of Otradovic, "Disdain for this Transitory World," translated by Ewald Osers, from CZECH POETRY: A Bilingual Anthology, Volume 1, edited by Alfred French. Reprinted with the permission of Michigan Slavic Publications, Department of Slavic Languages and Literatures, University of Michigan.

Mikhail Vasilevich Lomonosov, "Evening Meditation on the Majesty of God on the Occasion of the Great Northern Lights" from THE LITERATURE OF EIGHTEENTH-CENTURY RUSSIA, Volume I, translated and edited by Harold B. Segel. Translation copyright ©1967 by Harold B. Segel. Reprinted with the permission of Dutton, an imprint of New American Library, a division of Penguin Books USA Inc.

The Ancient Mexicans, "Myths of Creation" and "The Myth of Quetzalcoatl" from Sahagún's HISTORIA GENERAL, translated by David M. Johnson, and *A Defense of Aztec Religion,* translated by David M. Johnson and Armondo Jimarez, reprinted with the permission of David M. Johnson. "The Poetry of Nezahualcoyotl," translated by Miguel León-Portilla, from NATIVE MESOAMERICAN SPIRITUALITY, edited by Miguel León-Portilla. Copyright© 1980 by The Missionary Society of St. Paul the Apostle in the State of New York. Reprinted with the permission of Paulist Press. *The Conquest of Mexico,* translated by Angel Maria Garibay K., Lysander Kemp, and David M. Johnson, from THE BROKEN SPEARS: THE AZTEC ACCOUNT OF THE CONQUEST OF MEXICO, edited by Miguel León-Portilla. Copyright© 1962 by Beacon Press. Reprinted with the permission of the publisher.

Wu Ch'êng-ên, excerpts from MONKEY, translated by Arthur Waley (London: George Allen & Unwin, Ltd., 1942).

Giovanni Pico della Mirandola, "On the Dignity of Man" from PICO DELLA MIRANDOLA ON THE DIGNITY OF MAN, translated by Charles Glenn Wallis (Indianapolis, IN: Bobbs-Merrill/Library of Liberal Arts, 1965). Copyright 1940 by Charles Glenn Wallis. Reprinted with the permission of Eleanor Van Trump Glenn.

Martin Luther, "Speech at the Diet of Worms," translated by Roger A. Hornsby, from LUTHER'S WORKS: Career of the Reformer, volume 32, copyright© 1958 by Fortress Press. Reprinted with the permission of Augsburg Fortress.

Galileo Galilei and Johannes Kepler correspondence, translated by Mary Martin McLaughlin, from THE PORTABLE RENAISSANCE READER, edited by James B. Ross and Mary Martin McLaughlin. Copyright 1953, renewed © 1981 by Viking Penguin Inc. Reprinted with the permission of Viking Penguin, a division of Penguin Books USA Inc.

INDEX

A

B

C

D

E

I

J

M

N

O

S

T

U

V

W

Y

A NOTE ON THE TYPE

The type used in this book is Bembo. Created by Monotype in 1929, the font has its origins in Renaissance Venice, modeled after a roman typeface that Francesco Griffo created in 1495. The italic is based on a type designed by Giovanni Tagliente in the 1520s. Although Bembo is quieter than a true Renaissance type, it retains the elegance and structure of its roots and translates well to the digital format of modern computerized typesetting.